A TEXTBOOK OF

FLUID MECHANICS
AND
HYDRAULIC MACHINES

in

SI UNITS

MULTICOLOUR EDITION

A TEXTBOOK OF

FLUID MECHANICS AND HYDRAULIC MACHINES

in

SI UNITS

Er. R.K. Rajput

M.E. (Hons.) Gold Medallist; Grad.-Mech. Engg. & Elect. Engg.; MIE (India); MSESI; MISTE; CE (India)

Recipient of :

"Best Teacher (Academic) Award"

"Distinguished Author Award"

"Jawahar Lal Nehru Memorial Gold Medal" for an Outstanding Research Paper (Institution of Engineers—India)

***Principal** (Formerly)*

- *Thapar Polytechnic College;*
- *Punjab College of Information Technology;*

PATIALA

S. CHAND
PUBLISHING
empowering minds

S Chand And Company Limited

(ISO 9001 Certified Company)

RAM NAGAR, NEW DELHI - 110 055

S Chand And Company Limited

(ISO 9001 Certified Company)

S. CHAND PUBLISHING
empowering minds

Head Office: 7361, RAM NAGAR, QUTAB ROAD, NEW DELHI - 110 055
Phone: 23672080-81-82, 66672000 Fax: 91-11-23677446
www.**schandpublishing.com**; e-mail: **info@schandpublishing.com**

Branches:

Ahmedabad	:	Ph: 27541965, 27542369, ahmedabad@schandpublishing.com
Bengaluru	:	Ph: 22268048, 22354008, bangalore@schandpublishing.com
Bhopal	:	Ph: 4209587, bhopal@schandpublishing.com
Chandigarh	:	Ph: 2625356, 2625546, 4025418, chandigarh@schandpublishing.com
Chennai	:	Ph: 28410027, 28410058, chennai@schandpublishing.com
Coimbatore	:	Ph: 2323620, 4217136, coimbatore@schandpublishing.com (Marketing Office)
Cuttack	:	Ph: 2332580, 2332581, cuttack@schandpublishing.com
Dehradun	:	Ph: 2711101, 2710861, dehradun@schandpublishing.com
Guwahati	:	Ph: 2738811, 2735640, guwahati@schandpublishing.com
Hyderabad	:	Ph: 27550194, 27550195, hyderabad@schandpublishing.com
Jaipur	:	Ph: 2219175, 2219176, jaipur@schandpublishing.com
Jalandhar	:	Ph: 2401630, jalandhar@schandpublishing.com
Kochi	:	Ph: 2809208, 2808207, cochin@schandpublishing.com
Kolkata	:	Ph: 23353914, 23357458, kolkata@schandpublishing.com
Lucknow	:	Ph: 4065646, lucknow@schandpublishing.com
Mumbai	:	Ph: 22690881, 22610885, 22610886, mumbai@schandpublishing.com
Nagpur	:	Ph: 2720523, 2777666, nagpur@schandpublishing.com
Patna	:	Ph: 2300489, 2260011, patna@schandpublishing.com
Pune	:	Ph: 64017298, pune@schandpublishing.com
Raipur	:	Ph: 2443142, raipur@schandpublishing.com (Marketing Office)
Ranchi	:	Ph: 2361178, ranchi@schandpublishing.com
Sahibabad	:	Ph: 2771235, 2771238, delhibr-sahibabad@schandpublishing.com

First Edition, 1998
Subsequent Editions and Reprints 2002, 2005, 2006, 2007, 2008 (Twice), 2009 (Twice), 2010 (Twice), 2011, 2013, 2014; Sixth Edition 2015, 2016 (Twice), 2017
Reprint 2018 (Twice)

ISBN : 978-93-854-0137-4 **Code :** 1010B 185

PRINTED IN INDIA

By Vikas Publishing House Pvt. Ltd., Plot 20/4, Site-IV, Industrial Area Sahibabad, Ghaziabad-201010 and Published by S Chand And Company Limited, 7361, Ram Nagar, New Delhi-110 055.

To my wife

Ramesh Rajput

PREFACE TO THE SIXTH EDITION

I am pleased to present the **Sixth Edition** (Multicolour) of this book. The warm reception, which the previous editions and reprints of this book have enjoyed all over India and abroad has been a matter of satisfaction to me.

In this edition, two new chapters numbered **18** in **"Fluid Mechanics" (Part-I)** and **9** in **"Hydraulic Machines" (Part-II)** with the following common title and contents have been added :

Chapters 18, 9 : ***GATE and UPSC EXAMINATIONS' QUESTIONS with ANSWERS/ SOLUTIONS (Latest-Selected)*** :

A. ***Conventional Questions with Answers/Solutions.***

B. ***Multiple-Choice Questions with Answers and 'Explanations'.***

I'm thankful to the Management Team and the Editorial Department of S. Chand & Company Pvt. Ltd. for all help and support in the publication of this book.

Any constructive suggestions for the improvement of this book are most welcome.

Er. R.K. Rajput
(Author)

PREFACE TO THE FIRST EDITION

The main object of writing this book on the subject of Fluid Mechanics and Hydraulic Machines is to present to the student community, a book which should contain comprehensive treatment of the subject matter in simple, lucid and direct language and envelope a large number of solved problems properly graded, including typical examples, from examination point of view.

The book comprises 22 chapters and is divided into two parts: Part I deals with '*Fluid Mechanics*' while Part II deals with '*Hydraulic Machines*' (Fluid Power Engineering). All chapters of the book are saturated with much needed text supported by simple and self-explanatory figures and large number of *Worked Examples* including *Typical Examples* (for competitive examinations). At the end of each chapter *Highlights, Objective Type Questions, Theoretical Questions* and *Unsolved Examples* have been added to make the book a comprehensive and a complete unit in all respects.

The book will prove to be a boon to the students preparing for engineering undergraduate, AMIE Section B (India) and competitive examinations.

The author's thanks are due to his wife Ramesh Rajput for extending all cooperation during preparation of the manuscript.

In the end the author wishes to express his gratitude to Shri Ravindra Kumar Gupta, Director, S. Chand & Company Ltd., New Delhi, for taking a lot of pains in bringing out the book, with extremely good presentation, in a short span of time.

Although every care has been taken to make the book free of errors both in the text as well as solved examples, yet the author shall feel obliged if errors present are brought to his notice. Constructive criticism of the book will be warmly received.

Er. R.K. Rajput
(Author)

NOMENCLATURE

a	Acceleration
A	Area
A_s	Area of suction pipe, surge tank
A_d	Area of delivery pipe
B	Width of wheel (turbine)
b	Width, bed width of rectangular or trapezoidal channel
c_p	Specific heat at constant pressure
CP	Centipoise
C_v	Specific heat at constant volume
C	Chezy's discharge coefficient
C	Celerity of a pressure wave
C_c	Coefficient of contraction
C_d	Discharge coefficient of weirs, orifice plates
C_D	Drag coefficient
C_D	Local drag coefficient
C_v	Coefficient of velocity
d	Diameter of orifice plate, pipe, particle
D	Diameter of pipe, wheel
d_d	Diameter of delivery pipe
d_s	Diameter of suction pipe
e	Linear strain
E	Young's modulus of elasticity of material
f	Darcy Weisbach friction coefficient, frequency
F	Force
F_B	Force exerted by boundary on the fluid
F_D	Drag force on the body
F_L	Lift force
F_r	Froude number
g	Gravitational acceleration
h	Piezometric head, specific enthalpy
h_d	Delivery head
h_f	Frictional loss of head
h_s	Suction head
H_g	Gross head
H	Total energy head, net head
h_{ad}	Acceleration head for delivery pipe
h_{as}	Acceleration head for suction pipe
I	Moment of inertia (of area), moment of inertia (of mass)
l_d	Length of delivery pipe
l_s	Length of suction pipe
l_d'	Length of delivery pipe between cylinder to air vessel
l_s'	Length of suction pipe between cylinder and air vessel

k	Roughness height
K	Conveyance
K	Head loss coefficient, bulk modulus of elasticity, blade friction coefficient
K_t	Vane thickness factor
K_u	Speed ratio
K_f	Flow ratio
m	Mass
M	Momentum, Mach number
n	ratio B/D
N	Manning's roughness coefficient, revolutions per minute
N_s	Specific speed
p, p_s	Pressure, stagnation pressure
P	Power, shaft power (turbine), Poise, force
q	Discharge per unit width, discharge per jet
Q	Discharge, heat
r	Distance from the centre
R	Radius of pipe, hydraulic radius, radius of pipe bend
R_o	Universal gas constant
Re	Reynolds number
S	Specific gravity, bed slope of channel
t	Thickness, time
T	Absolute temperature in Kelvins
T	Torque, water surface width
u	Instantaneous velocity at a point in X-direction
u_f	Shear friction velocity
U	Free stream velocity
V_d	Velocity of flow in delivery pipe
V	Velocity of flow in the cylinder
V_s	Velocity of flow in suction pipe
v	Instantaneous velocity at a point in Y-direction
v	Specific volume
v_c	Critical velocity
V_a	Velocity of approach
v	Time averaged velocity at a point in Y-direction
V_r	Relative velocity
V_f	Velocity of flow (in turbines and pumps)
V_w	Velocity of swirl (in turbines and pumps)
V	Volume
w	Weight density, Instantaneous velocity at a point in Z-direction
W	Weight of fluid, workdone
x	Distance in X-direction
y	Distance in Y-direction, depth of flow
y_c	Critical depth
x	Depth of centroid of area below water surface
Z	Number of buckets/vanes
z	elevation

Greek Notations

α	Energy correction factor, Mach angle, angle
β	Momentum correction factor, angle
γ	Ratio of specific heats
δ	Boundary layer thickness
δ'	Laminar sub-layer thickness
δ	Displacement thickness of boundary layer
*Δs	Change in entropy
η	Efficiency, dimensionless distance (y/δ)
θ	Angle, momentum thickness of boundary layer
μ	Coefficient of dynamic viscosity
ν	Kinematic viscosity
ρ	Mass density of fluid
σ	Coefficient of surface tension, cavitation number (Thoma number)
τ	Shear stress
τ_0	Bottom shear stress
ϕ	Angle, velocity potential
ψ	Stream function
ω	Angular velocity
Γ	Circulation
Ω	Vorticity

Subscript 0	refer to any quantity at reference section
Subscripts 1, 2	refer to any quantity at section 1 or 2
Subscripts x, y, z	refer to any quantity in x, y, z direction
Subscripts m, p	refer to any quantity in model and prototype
Subscript r	refer to the ratio of any quantity in model to that in prototype.

CONTENTS

PART – I
FLUID MECHANICS

PART – II
HYDRAULIC MACHINES

PART - I

FLUID MECHANICS

Chapter 1

PROPERTIES OF FLUIDS

1.1. INTRODUCTION

Hydraulics:

Hydraulics (this word has been derived from a Greek work 'Hudour' which means water) may be defined as follows :

"It is that branch of Engineering-science, which deals with water (at rest or in motion)."

or

"It is that branch of Engineering-science which is based on experimental observation of water flow."

Fluid Mechanics:

Fluid mechanics may be defined as *that branch of Engineering-science which deals with the behaviour of fluid under the conditions of rest and motion.*

The fluid mechanics may be divided into three parts: *Statics*, *kinematics* and *dynamics*.

Statics. The study of incompressible fluids under static conditions is called *hydrostatics* and that dealing with the compressible static gases is termed as *aerostatics*.

Kinematics. It deals with the velocities, accelerations and the patterns of flow only. Forces or energy causing velocity and acceleration are *not* dealt under this heading.

Dynamics. It deals with the relations between velocities, accelerations of fluid *with the forces or energy causing them.*

Properties of Fluids–General Aspects:

The matter can be classified on the basis of the *spacing between the molecules* of the matter as follows:

1. Solid state, and
2. Fluid state,
   (*i*) Liquid state, and (*ii*) Gaseous state.

In *solids*, the molecules are very closely spaced whereas in *liquids* the spacing between the different molecules is relatively large and in *gases* the spacing between the molecules is still large. It means that inter-molecular cohesive forces are *large* in solids, *smaller* in liquids and *extremely small* in gases, and on account of this fact, solids possess compact and rigid form, liquid molecules can move freely within the liquid mass and the molecules of gases have greater freedom of movement so that the gases fill the container completely in which they are placed.

A *solid* can resist tensile, compressive and shear stresses upto a certain limit whereas a fluid has no tensile strength or very little of it and it can resist the compressive forces only when it is kept in a container. When a fluid is subjected to a shearing force it deforms continuously as long as the force is applied. The amount of shear stress in a fluid depends on the magnitude of the rate of deformation of the fluid element.

Liquids and *gases* exhibit different characteristics. The liquids under ordinary conditions are quite difficult to compress (and therefore they may for most purposes be regarded as incompressible) whereas gases can be compressed much readily under the action of external pressure (and when the external pressure is removed the gases tend to expand indefinitely).

1.2. FLUID

A fluid may be defined as follows:

"A fluid is a substance which is capable of flowing."

or

"A fluid is a substance which deforms continuously when subjected to external shearing force."

A fluid has the following *characteristics*:

1. It has no definite shape of its own, but conforms to the shape of the containing vessel.
2. Even a small amount of shear force exerted on a liquid/fluid will cause it to undergo a deformation which continues as long as the force continues to be applied.

A fluid may be *classified* as follows:

A. (*i*) *Liquid*, (*ii*) *Gas*, (*iii*) *Vapour*.

B. (*i*) *Ideal fluids* (*ii*) *Real fluids*.

Liquid

- A liquid is a fluid which possesses a *definite volume* (which varies only slightly with temperature and pressure).
- Liquids have bulk elastic modulus when under compression and will store up energy in the same manner as a solid. As the contraction of volume of a liquid under compression is extremely small, it is usually ignored and the *liquid is assumed to be incompressible*. A liquid will withstand a slight amount of tension due to molecular attraction between the particles which will cause an apparent shear resistance, between two adjacent layers. This phenomenon is known as **viscosity**.
- All known liquids vaporise at narrow pressures above zero, depending on the temperature.

Gas. It possesses *no definite volume* and is *compressible*.

Vapour. It is a gas whose temperature and pressure are such that it is very near the liquid state (*e.g.*, steam).

Ideal fluids. An ideal fluid is one which has *no viscosity* and *surface tension* and is *incompressible*. In true sense no such fluid exists in nature. However fluids which have low viscosities such as water and air can be treated as ideal fluids under certain conditions. The assumption of ideal fluids helps in simplifying the mathematical analysis.

Real fluids. *A real practical fluid is one which has viscosity, surface tension and compressibility in addition to the density.* The real fluids are actually available in nature.

Continuum. *A continuous and homogeneous medium is called* ***continuum.*** From the *continuum view point, the overall properties and behaviour of fluids can be studied without regard for its atomic and molecular structure.*

1.3. LIQUIDS AND THEIR PROPERTIES

- Liquid can be easily distinguished from a solid or a gas.
- Solid has a definite shape.
- A liquid takes the shape of vessel into which it is poured.
- A gas completely fills the vessel which contains it.

The properties of water are of much importance because the subject of hydraulics is mainly concerned with it. Some important properties of water which will be considered are:

(*i*) Density,	(*ii*) Specific gravity,	(*iii*) Viscosity,
(*iv*) Vapour pressure,	(*v*) Cohesion,	(*vi*) Adhesion,
(*vii*) Surface tension,	(*viii*) Capillarity, and	(*ix*) Compressibility.

1.4. DENSITY

1.4.1 Mass Density

The *density* (also known as *mass density or specific mass*) of a liquid may be defined as *the mass per unit volume* $\left(\frac{m}{V}\right)$ *at a standard temperature and pressure*. It is usually denoted by ρ (rho).

Its units are kg/m^3, *i.e.*,

$$\rho = \frac{m}{V} \qquad \text{...(1.1)}$$

1.4.2 Weight Density

The weight density (also known as specific weight) is defined as the *weight per unit volume at the standard temperature and pressure*. It is usually denoted by *w*.

$$w = g \qquad \text{...(1.2)}$$

For the purposes of all calculations, relating to Hydraulics and hydraulic machines, the specific weight of water is taken as follows:

In S.I. Units: $w = 9.81$ kN/m^3 (or 9.81×10^{-6} N/mm^3)

In M.K.S. Units: $w = 1000$ kg$_f$/m^3

1.4.3 Specific volume

It is defined as *volume per unit mass of fluid*. It is denoted by *v*.

Mathematically,

$$v = \frac{V}{m} = \frac{1}{\rho} \qquad \text{...(1.3)}$$

1.5. SPECIFIC GRAVITY

Specific gravity is the ratio of the specific weight of the liquid to the specific weight of a standard fluid. It is dimensionless and has no units. It is represented by *S*.

For liquids, the standard fluid is pure water at 4°C.

$$\therefore \quad \text{Specific gravity} = \frac{\text{Specific weight of liquid}}{\text{Specific weight of pure water}} = \frac{w_{liquid}}{w_{water}}$$

Example 1.1. *Calculate the specific weight, specific mass, specific volume and specific gravity of a liquid having a volume of 6 m³ and weight of 44 kN.*

Solution: Volume of the liquid = 6 m³

Weight of the liquid = 44 kN

Specific weight, *w* :

$$w = \frac{\text{Weight of liquid}}{\text{Volume of liquid}} = \frac{44}{6} = \mathbf{7.333\ kN/m^3\ (Ans.)}$$

Specific mass or mass density, ρ :

$$\rho = \frac{w}{g} = \frac{7.333 \times 1000}{9.81} = \mathbf{747.5\ kg/m^3\ (Ans.)}$$

$$\text{Specific volume,} \quad v = \frac{1}{\rho} = \frac{1}{747.5} = \mathbf{0.00134\ m^3/kg\ (Ans.)}$$

Specific gravity, *S* :

$$S = \frac{w_{liquid}}{w_{water}} = \frac{7.333}{9.81} = \mathbf{0.747\ (Ans.)}$$

1.6. VISCOSITY

Viscosity may be defined as the *property of a fluid which determines its resistance to shearing stresses*. It is a measure of the internal fluid friction which causes resistance to flow. It is primarily *due to cohesion and molecular momentum exchange between fluid layers*, and as flow occurs, these effects appear as shearing stresses between the moving layers of fluid.

An *ideal fluid has no viscosity*. There is no fluid which can be classified as a perfectly ideal fluid. However, the fluids with very little viscosity are sometimes considered as ideal fluids.

Viscosity of fluids is due to *cohesion and interaction between particles*.

Refer to Fig 1.1. When two layers of fluid, at a distance '*dy*' apart, move one over the other at different velocities, say u and $u + du$, the viscosity together with relative velocity causes a shear stress acting between the fluid layers. The top layer causes a shear stress on the adjacent lower layer while the lower layer causes a shear stress on the adjacent top layer. This shear stress is proportional to the rate of change of velocity with respect to y. It is denoted by τ (called Tau).

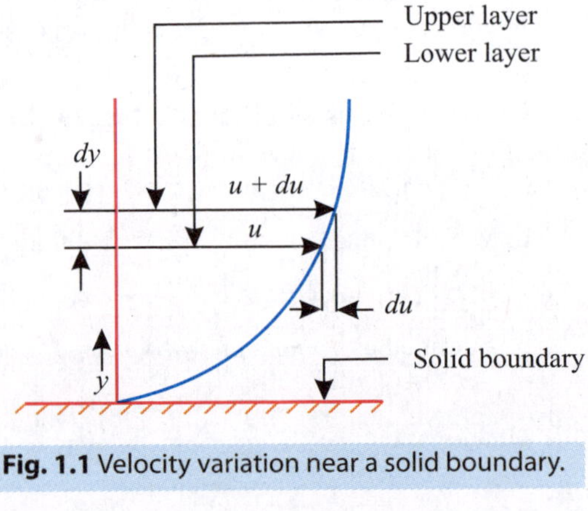

Fig. 1.1 Velocity variation near a solid boundary.

$$\text{Mathematically} \qquad \tau \propto \frac{du}{dy}$$

$$\text{or} \qquad \tau = \mu.\frac{du}{dy} \qquad \text{...(1.4)}$$

where, μ = Constant of proportionality and is known as *co-efficient of* ***dynamic viscosity*** or *only viscosity.*

$\frac{du}{dy}$ = Rate of shear stress or rate of shear deformation or velocity gradient.

From Fig. 1.1, we have $$\mu = \frac{\tau}{\left[\frac{du}{dy}\right]} \qquad ...(1.5)$$

Thus viscosity may also be defined as the *shear stress required to produce unit rate of shear strain.*

Units of Viscosity:

In *S.I. Units*: $N.s/m^2$

In *M.K.S. Units:* $kg_f.sec/m^2$

$$\left[\because \ \mu = \frac{\text{force/area}}{(\text{length/time}) \times \frac{1}{\text{length}}} = \frac{\text{force/length}^2}{\frac{1}{\text{length}}} = \frac{\text{force} \times \text{time}}{(\text{length})^2}\right]$$

The unit of viscosity in C.G.S. is also called *poise* = $\frac{\text{dyne} - \text{sec}}{\text{cm}^2}$. One poise = $\frac{1}{10}$ $N.s/m^2$

Note. The viscosity of water at 20°C is $\frac{1}{100}$ poise or one centipoise.

Kinematic Viscosity :

Kinematic viscosity is defined as the *ratio between the dynamic viscosity and density of fluid.* It is denoted by ν (called nu).

$$\text{Mathematically,} \quad \nu = \frac{\text{Viscosity}}{\text{Density}} = \frac{\mu}{\rho} \qquad ...(1.6)$$

Units of kinematic viscosity:

In SI units: m^2/s

In M.K.S. units: $m^2/sec.$

In C.G.S. units the kinematic viscosity is also known as stoke (= $cm^2/sec.$)

One stoke = 10^{-4} m^2/s

Note: *Centistoke* means $\frac{1}{100}$ stoke.

1.6.1. Newton's Law of Viscosity

This law states that the *shear stress* (τ) *on a fluid element layer is directly proportional to the rate of shear strain.* The constant of proportionality is called the *co-efficient of viscosity.*

$$\text{Mathematically,} \quad \tau = \mu \frac{du}{dy} \qquad ...(1.7)$$

The fluids which follow this law are known as *Newtonian fluids.*

1.6.2. Types of Fluids

The fluids may be of the following types:

Refer to Fig.1.2.

1. Newtonian fluids. These fluids follow Newton's viscosity equation (*i.e.* eqn. 1.7). For such fluids μ *does not change with rate of deformation.*

Examples. Water, kerosene, air etc.

2. Non-Newtonian fluids. Fluids which *do not* follow the linear relationship between shear stress and rate of deformation (given by eqn. 1.7) are termed as *Non-Newtonian fluids*. Such fluids are relatively uncommon.

Examples. *Solutions or suspensions (slurries), mud flows, polymer solutions, blood* etc. These fluids are generally complex mixtures and are studied under *rheology*, a science of deformation and flow.

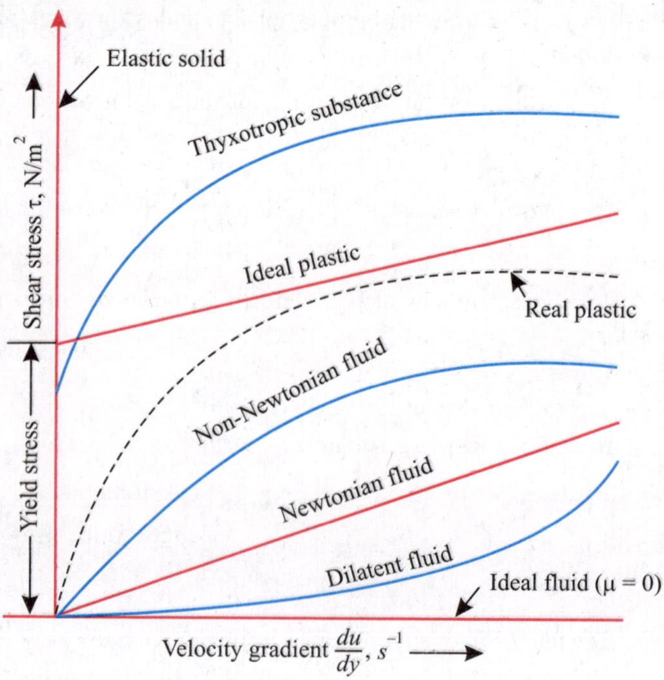

Fig. 1.2. Variation of shear stess with velocity gradient.

3. Plastic fluids. In the case of a plastic substance which is non-Newtonian fluid an initial yield stress is to be exceeded to cause a continuous deformation. These substances are represented by straight line intersecting the vertical axis at the "*yield stress*" (Refer to Fig. 1.2).

An ideal plastic (or Binigham plastic) has a definite yield stress and a constant linear relation between shear stress and the rate of angular deformation. Examples: *Sewage sludge, drilling muds etc.*

A *thyxotropic substance*, which is non-Newtonian fluid, has a non-linear relationship between the shear stress and the rate of angular deformation, beyond an initial yield stress. The *printer's ink* is an example of thyxotropic substance.

4. Ideal fluid. An ideal fluid is one which is incompressible and has zero viscosity (or in other words shear stress is always zero regardless of the motion of the fluid). Thus an ideal fluid is represented by the horizontal axis ($\tau = 0$).

A *true elastic solid* may be represented by the vertical axis of the diagram.

Summary of relations between shear stress (τ) *and rate of angular deformation for various types of fluids*:

(*i*) *Ideal fluids*: $\tau = 0$, (*ii*) *Newtonian fluids*: $\tau = \mu \cdot \dfrac{du}{dy}$,

(*iii*) *Ideal plastics*: $\tau = const. + \mu \cdot \dfrac{du}{dy}$, (*iv*) *Thyxotropic fluids*: $\tau = const. + \mu . \left(\dfrac{du}{dy}\right)^n$, *and*

(*v*) *Non-Newtonian fluids*: $\tau = \left(\dfrac{du}{dy}\right)^n$.

In case of non-Newtonian fluids, if n is *less* than unity then are called **pseudo-plastics** (*e.g., paper pulp, rubber suspension paints*) while fluids in which n is *greater* than unity are known as **dilatents.** (*e.g., Butter, printing ink*).

Ostwald-de-Waele Equation. It is an empirical solution to express steaty-state shear stress as a function of velocity gradient, and is given as

$$\tau_{yx} = \alpha \left|\frac{du}{dy}\right|^{n-1} \frac{du}{dy}$$

If $n = 1$, this reduces to Newton's law of viscosity, with $\alpha = \mu$

Example 1.2. **(*a*)** *What are the characteristics of an ideal fluid ?*

(*b*) *The general relation between shear stress and velocity gradient of a fluid can be written as*

$$\tau = A\left(\frac{du}{dy}\right)^n + B$$

where A, B and n are constants that depend upon the type of fluid and conditions imposed on the flow. Comment on the value of these constants so that the fluid may behave as:

(*i*) *an ideal fluid,*

(*ii*) *a Newtonian fluid* and

(*iii*) *A non-Newtonian fluid.*

(c) *Indicate whether the fluid with the following characteristics is a Newtonian or non-Newtonian.*

(*i*) $\tau = Ay + B$ and $u = C_1 + C_2 y + C_3 y^2$

(*ii*) $\tau = Ay^{n(n-1)}$ and $u = Cy^n$

Solution. **(*a*)** An ideal fluid has the following *characteristics*:

- No viscosity (*i.e.*, $\mu = 0$)
- No surface tension.
- Incompressible (*i.e.*, ρ = constant)

An ideal fluid can slip near a solid boundary and cannot sustain any shear force however small it may be.

(*b*) $\tau = A\left(\frac{du}{dy}\right)^n + B$

(*i*) *An ideal fluid*:

Since an ideal fluid has zero viscosity (*i.e.*, shear stress is always zero regardless of the motion of the fluid), therefore.

$$A = B = 0$$

(*ii*) *A Newtonian fluid*:

Since a Newtonian fluid follows Newton's law of viscosity;

$$\tau = \mu\frac{du}{dy}, \text{ therefore:}$$

- $n = 1$ and $B = 0$
- The constant A takes the value of dynamic viscosity μ for the fluid.

Air, water, kerosene etc. behave as Newtonian fluids under normal working conditions.

(*iii*) *A non-Newtonian fluid*:

Depending on the value of power index n, the non-Newtonian fluids are classified as:

- If $n > 1$ and $B = 0$ ... **Dilatant fluids.**

Examples: *Sugar solution, aqueous suspension* and *printing ink.*

- If $n < 1$ and $B = 0$ .. ***Pseudo plastic fluids.***

Examples : *Blood, milk, liquid cement and clay.*

- If $n = 1$ and $B = \tau_0$ .... **Bingham fluid or ideal plastic.**

An ideal plastic fluid has a definite yield stress and a constant-linear relation between shear stress developed and rate of deformation:

i.e.
$$\tau = \tau_0 + \mu \frac{du}{dy}$$

Examples: *Sewage sludge, water suspension of clay and flyash, etc.*

(c) **(*i*)** $\tau = Ay + B$ and $u = C_1 + C_2 y + C_3 y^2$

Now,
$$\frac{du}{dy} = \frac{d}{dy}(C_1 + C_2 y + C_3 y_2) = C_2 + 2C_3 y$$

For Newtonian fluid,
$$\tau = \mu \frac{du}{dy}$$

$\therefore$
$$\tau = \mu(C_2 + 2C_3 y) = 2\mu C_3 y + \mu C_2$$

which can be rewritten as

$$\tau = Ay + B \text{ where } A = 2\mu C_3 \text{ and } B = \mu C_2$$

Since this has the same form as the given shear stress, therefore the fluid characteristics correspond to that of an *ideal fluid*.

(*ii*) $\tau = Ay^{n(n-1)}$ and $u = Cy^n$

Now,
$$\frac{du}{dy} = \frac{d}{dy}(Cy^n) = Cn(y)^{n-1}$$

For a Newtonian fluid
$$\tau = \mu \frac{du}{dy} = \mu Cn(y)^{n-1}$$

This expression does not conform to the value of shear stress and as such the fluid is *non-Newtonian* in character.

1.6.3. Effect of Temperature on Viscosity

Viscosity is effected by temperature. The viscosity of *liquids decreases* but that of *gases* increases with *increase in temperature*. This is due to the reason that in *liquids* the shear stress is due to the inter-molecular cohesion which *decreases* with increase of temperature. In gases the inter-molecular cohesion is negligible and the shear stress is due to exchange of momentum of the molecules, normal to the direction of motion. The molecular activity increases with rise in temperature and so does the viscosity of gas.

For liquids:
$$\mu_T = Ae^{\beta/T} \quad \text{...(1.8)}$$

For gases:
$$\mu T = \frac{bT^{1/2}}{1 + a/T} \quad \text{...(1.9)}$$

where,
μ_T = Dynamic viscosity at absolute temperature T,
A, β = Constants (for a given liquid), and
a, b = Constants (for a given gas).

1.6.4. Effect of Pressure on Viscosity

The viscosity under ordinary conditions is not appreciably affected by the changes in pressure. However, the viscosity of some oils has been found to increase with increase in pressure.

Example 1.3. *A plate 0.05 mm distant from a fixed plate moves at 1.2 m/s and requires a force of 2.2 N/m² to maintain this speed. Find the viscosity of the fluid between the plates.*

Solution: Velocity of the moving plate, $u = 1.2$ m/s

Distance between the plates, $dy = 0.05$ mm $= 0.05 \times 10^{-3}$ m

Force on the moving plate, $F = 2.2$ N/m^2

Viscosity of the fluid, μ:

We know, $\tau = \mu . \dfrac{du}{dy}$

where τ = shear stress or force per unit area = 2.2 N/m^2,

du = change of velocity = $u - 0 = 1.2$ m/s and

dy = change of distance = 0.05×10^{-3}m.

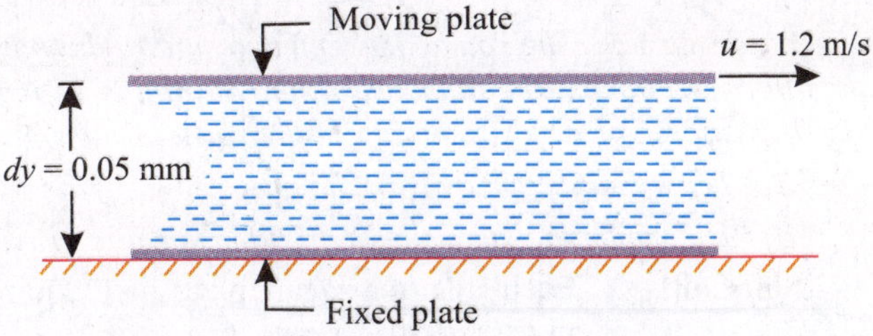

Fig. 1.3

$$\therefore \quad 2.2 = \mu \times \frac{1.2}{0.05 \times 10^{-3}}$$

or, $$\mu = \frac{2.2 \times 0.05 \times 10^{-3}}{1.2} = 9.16 \times 10^{-5} \text{N.s/m}^2 \qquad \left[\because 1 \text{ poise} = \frac{1}{10}\frac{\text{N.s}}{\text{m}^2}\right]$$

$= \mathbf{9.16 \times 10^{-4}}$ **poise (Ans.)**

Example 1.4. *A plate having an area of 0.6 m^2 is sliding down the inclined plane at 30° to the horizontal with a velocity of 0.36 m/s. There is a cushion of fluid 1.8 mm thick between the plane and the plate. Find the viscosity of the fluid if the weight of the plate is 280 N.*

Solution: Area of plate, $A = 0.6$ m^2

Weight of plate, $W = 280$ N

Velocity of plate, $u = 0.36$ m/s

Thickness of film, $t = dy = 1.8$ mm $= 1.8 \times 10^{-3}$ m

Viscosity of the fluid, μ:

Component of W along the plate $= W \sin \theta = 280 \sin 30° = 140$ N

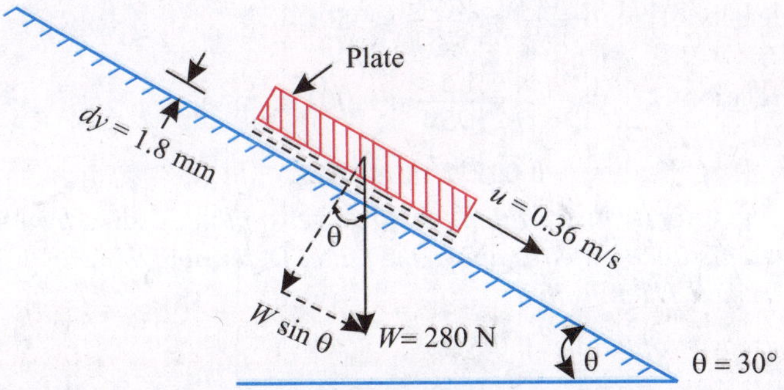

Fig. 1.4

∴ Shear force on the bottom surface of the plate, $F = 140$ N and shear stress,

$$\tau = \frac{F}{A} = \frac{140}{0.6} = 233.33 \text{N/m}^2$$

We know, $$\tau = \mu . \frac{du}{dy}$$

Where, du = change of velocity $= u - 0 = 0.36$ m/s

$$dy = t = 1.8 \times 10^{-3} \text{ m}$$

$$\therefore \quad 233.33 = \mu \times \frac{0.36}{1.8 \times 10^{-3}}$$

or,
$$\mu = \frac{233.33 \times 1.8 \times 10^{-3}}{0.36} = 1.166 \text{ N.s/m}^2 = \mathbf{11.66 \text{ poise}} \text{ (Ans.)}$$

Example 1.5. *The space between two square flat parallel plates is filled with oil. Each side of the plate is 720 mm. The thickness of the oil film is 15 mm. The upper plate, which moves at 3 m/s requires a force of 120 N to maintain the speed. Determine:*

(i) The dynamic viscosity of the oil;

(ii) The kinematic viscosity of oil if the specific gravity of oil is 0.95.

Solution. Each side of a square plate = 720 mm = 0.72 m

The thickness of the oil, dy = 15 mm = 0.015 m

Velocity of the upper plate = 3 m/s

∴ Change of velocity between plates, du = 3 – 0 = 3 m/s

Force required on upper plate, F = 120 N

$$\therefore \quad \text{Shear stress, } \tau = \frac{\text{force}}{\text{area}} = \frac{120}{0.72 \times 0.72} = 231.5 \text{ N/m}^2$$

(i) Dynamic viscosity, μ:

We know that,

$$\tau = \mu \cdot \frac{du}{dy}$$

$$231.5 = \mu \cdot \frac{3}{0.015}$$

$$\therefore \quad \mu = \frac{231.5 \times 0.015}{3} = \mathbf{1.16 \text{ N.s/m}^2} \text{ (Ans.)}$$

(ii) Kinematic viscosity, ν:

Weight density of oil, $w = 0.95 \times 9.81 \text{ kN/m}^2 = 9.32 \text{ kN/m}^2$ = or 9320 N/m^3

Mass density of oil, $\rho = \frac{w}{g} = \frac{9320}{9.81} = 950$

Using the relation: $\nu = \frac{\mu}{\rho} = \frac{1.16}{950} = 0.00122 \text{ m}^2/\text{s}$

Hence $\nu = \mathbf{0.00122 \text{ m}^2/\text{s}}$ **(Ans.)**

Example 1.6. *The velocity distribution for flow over a plate is gives by $u = 2y - y^2$ where u is the velocity in m/s at a distance y metres above the plate. Determine the velocity gradient and shear stress at the boundary and 1.5 m from it.*

Take dynamic viscosity of fluid as 0.9 N.s/m².

Soluton. $u = 2y - y^2$ ...(given) $\quad \therefore \frac{du}{dy} = 2 - 2y$

(i) Velocity gradient, $\frac{du}{dy}$:

At the boundary : At $y = 0$, $\left(\frac{du}{dy}\right)_{y=0} = \mathbf{2 \text{ s}^{-1}}$ **(Ans.)**

At 0.15 m from the boundary:

At $y = 0.15$ m, $\left(\frac{du}{dy}\right)_{y=0.15} = 2 - 2 \times 0.15 = \mathbf{1.7 \text{ s}^{-1}}$ **(Ans.)**

(ii) Shear stress, τ:

$$(\tau)_{y=0} = \mu \cdot \left(\frac{du}{dy}\right)_{y=0} = 0.9 \times 2 = \mathbf{1.8\ N/m^2}\ \textbf{(Ans.)}$$

and,

$$(\tau)_{y=0.15} = \mu \left(\frac{du}{dy}\right)_{y=0.15} = 0.9 \times 1.7 = \mathbf{1.53\ N/m^2}\ \textbf{(Ans.)}$$

[Where $\mu = 0.9$ N.s/m^2 ... (given)]

Example 1.7. *A lubricating oil of viscosity μ undergoes steady shear between a fixed lower plate and an upper plate moving at speed V. The clearance between the plates is t. Show that a linear velocity profile results if the fluid does not slip at either plate.*

Solution. For the given geometry and motion, the shear stress τ is constant throughout. From Newton's law of viscosity, we have

$$\frac{du}{dy} = \frac{\tau}{\mu} = \text{constant}$$

or $u = ly + m$

The constantS l and m are evaluated from the no slip conditions at the upper and lower plates.

At $y = 0, \mu = 0 \quad \therefore m = 0$

At $y = t, u = V$

$\therefore \quad V = lt + 0$ or $l = \frac{V}{t}$

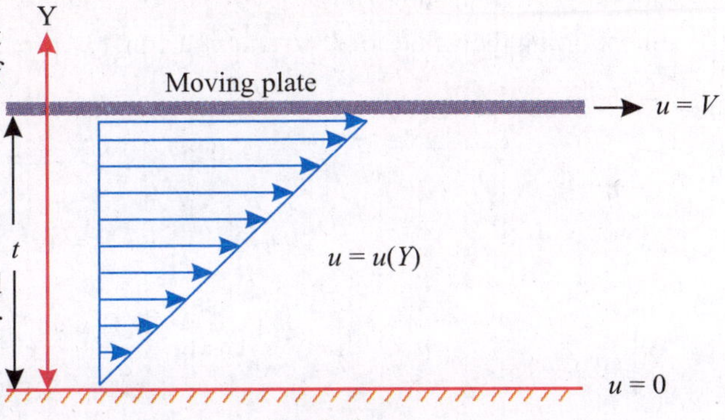

Fig. 1.5

∴ The velocity profile between plates is then given by:

$u = \frac{Vy}{t}$ and is *linear* as indicated in Fig 1.5 **(Ans.)**

Example 1.8. *The velocity distribution of flow over a plate is parabolic with vertex 30 cm from the plate, where the velocity is 180 cm/s. If the viscosity of the fluid is 0.9 N.s/m^2 find the velocity gradients and shear stresses at distances of 0, 15 cm and 30 cm from the plate.*

Solution. Distance of the vertex from the plate = 30 cm.

Velocity at vertex, $u = 180$ cm/s

Viscosity of the fluid = 0.9 N.s/m^2

The equation of velocity profile, which is parabolic, is given by

$$u = ly^2 + my + n \qquad ...(1)$$

where l, m and n are constants. The values of these constants are found from the following boundary conditions:

(i) At $y = 0, u = 0$,

(ii) At $y = 30$ cm,

$u = 180$ cm/s and

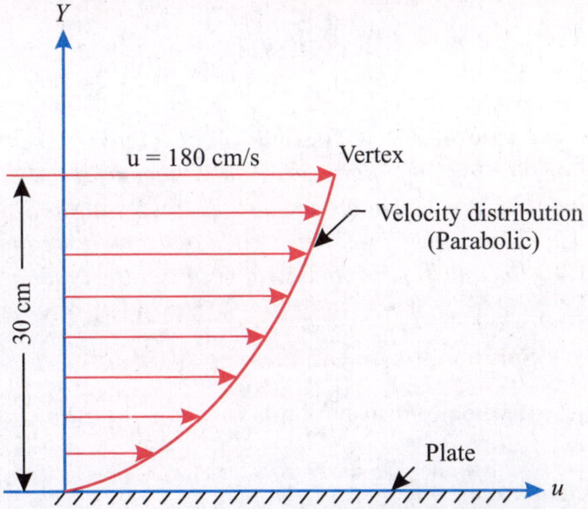

Fig. 1.6

(*iii*) At $y = 30$ cm, $\frac{du}{dy} = 0$.

Substituting boundary conditions (*i*) in eqn. (1), we get

$$0 = 0 + 0 + n \quad \therefore n = 0$$

Substituting boundary conditions (*ii*) in eqn. (1), we get

$$180 = l \times (30)^2 + m \times 30 \quad \text{or} \quad 180 = 900\,l + 30\,m \qquad ...(2)$$

Substituting boundary conditions (*iii*) in eqn. (1), we get

$$\frac{du}{dy} = 2ly + m \quad \therefore \quad 0 = 2l \times 30 + m \quad \text{or} \quad 0 = 60l + m \qquad ...(3)$$

Solving eqns. (2) and (3), we have $l = -0.2$ and $m = 12$.

Substituting the values of l, m and n in eqn. (1), we get $u = -0.2\,y^2 + 12y$

Velocity gradients, $\frac{du}{dy}$:

$$\frac{du}{dy} = -0.2 \times 2y + 12 = -0.4y + 12$$

At $y = 0$, $\left(\frac{du}{dy}\right)_{y=0}$ = **12/s (Ans.)**

At $y = 15$ cm, $\left(\frac{du}{dy}\right)_{y=15} = -0.4 \times 15 + 12 =$ **6/s (Ans.)**

At $y = 30$ cm, $\left(\frac{du}{dy}\right)_{y=30} = -0.4 \times 30 + 12 =$ **0 (Ans.)**

Shear stresses, τ:

We know, $\tau = \mu \frac{du}{dy}$

At $y = 0$, $(\tau)_{y=0} = \mu.\left(\frac{du}{dy}\right)_{y=0} = 0.9 \times 12 =$ **10.8 N/m² (Ans.)**

At $y = 15$, $(\tau)_{y=15} = \mu.\left(\frac{du}{dy}\right)_{y=15} = 0.9 \times 6 =$ **5.4 N/m² (Ans.)**

At $y = 30$, $(\tau)_{y=30} = \mu.\left(\frac{du}{dy}\right)_{y=30} = 0.9 \times 0 =$ **0 (Ans.)**

Example 1.9. *A fluid has an absolute viscosity of 0.048 Pa-s and a specific gravity of 0.913. For flow of such a fluid over a solid flat surface, the velocity at a point 75 mm away from the surface is 1.125 m/s. Calculate the shear stresses at the solid boundary and also at points 25 mm, 50 mm and 75 mm away from the surface in normal direction, if the velocity distribution across the surface is (i) linear, (ii) parabolic with vertex at the point 75 mm away from the surface.*

(UPTU)

Solution. (*i*) Linear velocity distribution:

If velocity distribution is *linear*, $\frac{du}{dy}$ *is same at every point within the boundary layer and is equal to* $\frac{du}{dy} = \frac{1.125}{0.075}$ per s.

Shear stress for all the locations,

$$\tau = \mu \frac{du}{dy} = 0.048 \times \frac{1.125}{0.075} = \mathbf{0.72\ N/m\ (Ans.)}$$

(*ii*) Parabolic velocity distribution:

For parabolic velocity distribution, let the velocity profile be $u = ly^2 + my + n$ where the constants, l, m, and n are found from the boundary conditions.

At $y = 0,\ u = 0$, giving $n = 0$

At $y = 0.075$ m, $u = 1.125$ m/s, giving

$$1.125 = (0.075)^2 l + 0.075\ \text{m} \qquad ...(i)$$

or $$1.125 = 5.625 \times 10^{-3}\ l + 0.075\ \text{m}$$

At $$y = 0.075\ \text{m},\ \frac{du}{dy} = 0 = 2ly + \text{m}$$

or $$0 = 2l \times 0.075 + \text{m} \quad \text{or} \quad \text{m} = -0.15\ l \qquad ...(ii)$$

Substituting (*ii*) in (*i*), we get

$$1.125 = 5.625 \times 10^{-3} l - 0.075 \times 0.15\ l$$
$$= l\,(5.625 \times 10^{-3} - 0.075 \times 0.15) = -0.005625\ l$$

$$\therefore \qquad l = -\frac{1.125}{0.005625} = -200$$

and from (*ii*), we have $m = 30$.

Hence the velocity distribution becomes $u = -200y^2 + 30y$, and $\frac{du}{dy} = 30 - 400\,y$

Hence the shear stresses at the required locations, y, are determined in the table below:

$y\ (m)$	0	0.025	0.05	0.075
$\frac{du}{dy}$ (per second)	30	20	10	0
Shere stress = $\mu \frac{du}{dy}$ N/m^2	1.44	0.96	0.48	0

(Ans.)

Example 1.10. *A 400 mm diameter shaft is rotating at 200 r.p.m. in a bearing of length 120 mm. If the thickness of oil film is 1.5 mm and the dynamic viscosity of the oil is 0.7 N.s/m², determine:*

(*i*) *Torque required to overcome friction in bearing;*

(*ii*) *Power utilised in overcoming viscous resistance.*

Assume a linear velocity profile.

Solution. Diameter of the shaft, $d = 400$ mm $= 0.4$ m

Speed of the shaft, $N = 200$ r.p.m.

Thickness of the oil film, $t = 1.5$ mm $= 1.5 \times 10^{-3}$ m

Length of the bearing, $l = 120$ mm $= 0.12$ m

Viscosity, $\mu = 0.7$ N.s/m^2

Tangential velocity of the shaft, $u = \frac{\pi d N}{60} = \frac{\pi \times 0.4 \times 200}{60} = 4.19$ m/s

(i) Torque required to overcome friction, *T* :

We know, $\tau = \mu.\frac{du}{dy}$

where du = change of velocity = $u - 0 = 4.19$ m/s

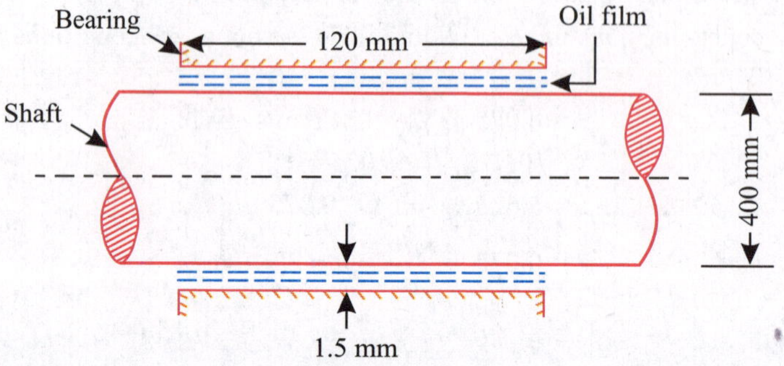

Fig. 1.7

$$dy = t = 1.5 \times 10^{-3} \text{ m}$$

$$\therefore \quad \tau = 0.7 \times \frac{4.19}{1.5 \times 10^{-3}}$$

$$= 1955.3 \text{ N/m}^2.$$

$\therefore$ Shear force, F = shear stress × area

$$= \tau \cdot \pi dl$$

$$= 1955.3 \times \pi \times 0.4 \times 0.12$$

$$= 294.85 \text{ N}$$

Hence, viscous torque = $F \times d/2 = 294.85 \times \frac{0.4}{2}$

= **58.97 Nm (Ans.)**

(ii) Power utilised, *P*:

$$P = T \times \frac{2\pi N}{60} \text{ watts, where } T \text{ is in Nm}$$

$$P = 58.97 \times \frac{2\pi \times 200}{60} = 1235 \text{ W}$$ or **1.235 kW (Ans.)**

Example 1.11. *A 150 mm diameter shaft rotates at 1500 r.p.m. in a 200 mm long journal bearing with 150.5 mm internal diameter. The uniform annular space between the shaft and the bearing is filled with oil of dynamic viscosity 0.8 poise. Calculate the power dissipated as heat.*

(Anna University)

Solution. *Given*: d_{shaft} = 150 mm; $d_{bearing}$ = 150.5 mm; l = 200 mm = 0.2 m
N = 1500 r.p.m.; μ = 0.8 poise = 0.8 × 0.1 = 0.08 Ns/m^2

Power dissipated as heat:

Radial thickness of the oil, $dy = \frac{(150.5 - 150)/2}{1000} \text{ m} = 0.00025 \text{ m}$

Tangential velocity of the shaft, $u = \frac{\pi dN}{60} = \frac{\pi \times (150 \times 10^{-3}) \times 1500}{60} = 11.78 \text{ m/s}$

∴ Change of velocity, $du = u - 0 = 11.78$ m/s

Tangential stress in the oil layer,

$$\tau = \mu.\frac{du}{dy}$$

∴ $$\tau = 0.08 \times \frac{11.78}{0.00025} = 3769.6 \text{ N/m}^2$$

Power dissipated as heat = shear force × tangential velocity of this shaft

$= [\tau \times (\pi\, dl)] \times u$

$= 769.6 \times \pi \times (150 \times 10^{-3}) \times 0.2 \times 11.78$

= 4185 W or **4.185 kW (Ans.)**

Example 1.12. *A vertical cylinder of diameter 180 mm rotates concentrically inside another cylinder of diameter 181.2 mm. Both the cylinders are 300 mm high. The space between the cylinders is filled with a liquid whose viscosity is unknown. Determine the viscosity of the fluid if a torque of 20 Nm is required to rotate the inner cylinder at 120 r.p.m.*

Solution. *Given*: Diameter of inner cylinder, d = 180 mm = 0.18 m

Diameter of outer cylinder, D = 181.2 mm = 0.1812 m

Length of each cylinder, l = 300 mm = 0.3 m

Speed of the inner cylinder, N = 120 r.p.m.

Torque, T = 20 Nm.

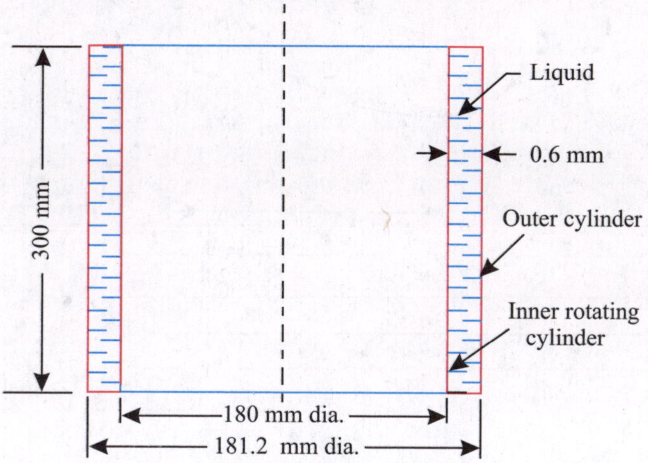

Fig. 1.8

Viscosity of the liquid, μ:

Tangential velocity of the inner cylinder

$$u = \frac{\pi d N}{60} = \frac{\pi \times 0.18 \times 120}{60} = 1.13 \text{ m/s}$$

Surface area of the inner cylinder,

$$A = \pi dl = \pi \times 0.18 \times 0.3$$
$$= 0.1696 \text{ m}^2$$

Using the relation:

$$\tau = \mu.\frac{du}{dy}$$

where, $du = u - 0 = 1.13 - 0$

$= 1.13$ m/s

and $dy = \dfrac{0.1812 - 0.180}{2} = 0.0006$ m

$\tau = \mu \times \dfrac{1.13}{0.0006} = 1883.33\mu$

$\therefore$ Shear force, $F = \tau \times A = 1883.33\ \mu \times 0.1696$ N

$\therefore$ Torque, $T = F \times F \times \dfrac{d}{2}$

$= 1883.33\ \mu \times 0.1696 \times \dfrac{0.18}{2}$

or $20 = 1883.33\ \mu \times 0.1696 \times 0.09$

or $\mu = \dfrac{20}{1883.33 \times 0.1696 \times 0.09} = 0.696\ \text{Ns/m}^2$

i.e., $\mu =$ **6.96 poise (Ans.)**

Example 1.13. *A circular disc of diameter D is slowly rotated in a liquid of large viscosity* (μ) *at a small distance* (*h*) *from a fixed surface. Derive an expression of torque* (*T*) *necessary to maintain an angular velocity* (ω). **(M.U.)**

Solution. The arrangement is shown in Fig. 1.9.

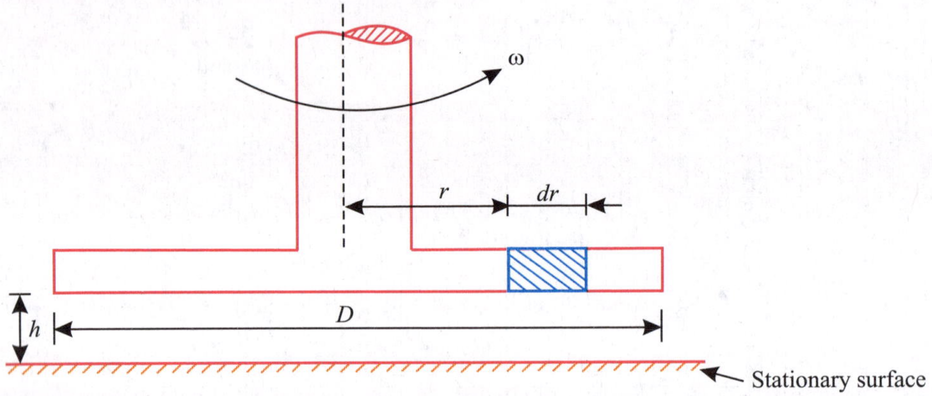

Fig. 1.9

Consider an elementary ring of disc at radius *r* and having a width *dr*. Linear velocity at this radius is ω*r*.

Shear stress, $\tau = \mu \dfrac{du}{dy}$

Torque = shear stress × area × *r*

$= \tau \times 2\pi r\, dr \times r$

$= \mu \dfrac{du}{dy} \times 2\pi r^2 \times dr$

Assuming the gap *h* to be *small so that the velocity distribution may be assumed linear.*

$$\frac{du}{dy} = \frac{\omega r}{h}$$

∴ Torque on the element

$$dT = \mu\frac{\omega r}{h} \times 2\pi r^2 \times dr = \frac{2\pi\mu\omega}{h}r^3 \times dr$$

∴ Total torque, $T = \int_0^{\pi/2} \frac{2\pi\mu\omega}{h}r^3 \times dr$

or $$T = \frac{2\pi\mu\omega}{h}\left[\frac{r^4}{4}\right]_0^{D/2} = \frac{2\pi\mu\omega}{h}\cdot\frac{1}{4}\left(\frac{D}{2}\right)^4$$

or $T = \dfrac{\pi\mu\omega D^4}{32h}$, which is the *required expression.* **(Ans.)**

Example 1.14. *A 120 mm disc rotates on a table separated by an oil film of 1.8 mm thickness. Find the viscosity of oil if the torque required to rotate the disc at 60 r.p.m is 3.6 × 10^{-4} Nm. Assume the velocity gradient in the oil film to be linear.*

Solution. *Given*: Diameter of the disc, D = 120 mm = 0.12 m

Thickness of oil film, t = 1.8 mm = 1.8 × 10^{-3} m

Torque, T = 3.6 × 10^{-4} Nm

Speed of the disc, N = 60 r.p.m.

∴ Angular speed of the disc, $\omega = \frac{2\pi N}{60} = \frac{2\pi \times 60}{60} = 2\pi$ rad/s

Viscosity, μ:

We know that when the velocity gradient is linear,

$$\frac{du}{dy} = \frac{u}{t}$$

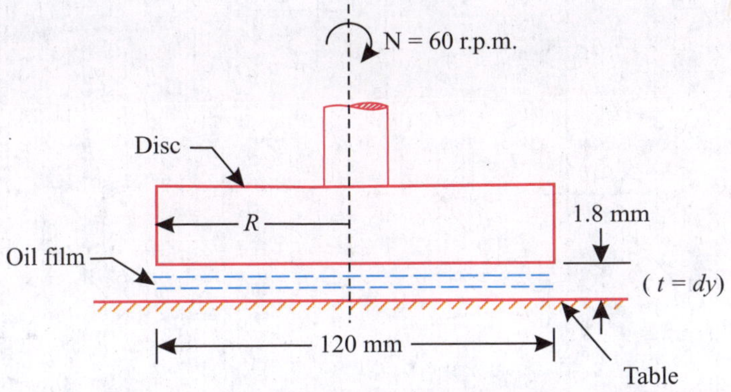

Fig. 1.10

Shearing stress, $\tau = \mu.\frac{u}{t}$.

Shearing force = Shearing stress × Area

$= \mu.\frac{u}{t}.2\pi r\,dr$ (considering an element at radius r and thickness dr)

$= \mu.\frac{\omega r}{t}.2\pi r\,dr = \frac{2\pi\mu\omega r^2.dr}{t}$ (where $u = \omega r$, ω being the angular velocity)

$\therefore$ Viscous torque = Shearing force × r

$$= \frac{2\pi\mu\omega r^2 . dr}{t} . r = \frac{2\pi\mu\omega r^3 . dr}{t}$$

$\therefore$ Total viscous torque,

$$T = \int_0^R \frac{2\pi\mu\omega r^3 dr}{t} = \frac{2\pi\mu\omega}{t}\int_0^R r^3 dr = \frac{\pi\mu\omega R^4}{2t}$$

i.e., $$T = \frac{\pi\mu\omega R^4}{2t}$$

Substituting the values, we get:

$$3.6 \times 10^{-4} = \frac{\pi \times \mu \times 2\pi \times (0.12/2)^4}{2 \times 1.8 \times 10^{-3}}$$

or $$\mu = \frac{3.6 \times 10^{-4} \times 2 \times 1.8 \times 10^{-3}}{\pi \times 2\pi \times (0.06)^4} = 0.00506 \text{ N.s/m}^2 = 0.0506 \text{ poise.}$$

Hence, μ = **0.0506 poise (Ans.)**

Example 1.15. *A solid cone of maximum radius R and vertex angle 2θ is to rotate at angular velocity ω. An oil of viscosity μ and thickness t fills the gap between the cone and the housing. Derive an expression for the torque required and the rate of heat dissipation in the bearing.*

Solution. *Given*: Maximum radius of the cone = R

Vertex angle = 2θ

Viscosity the oil = μ

Thickness of oil = t

Refer Fig. to 1.11.

Consider an elementary area dA at radius r of the cone.

$$dA = 2\pi r \text{ ds} \times \frac{dr}{\sin\theta}$$

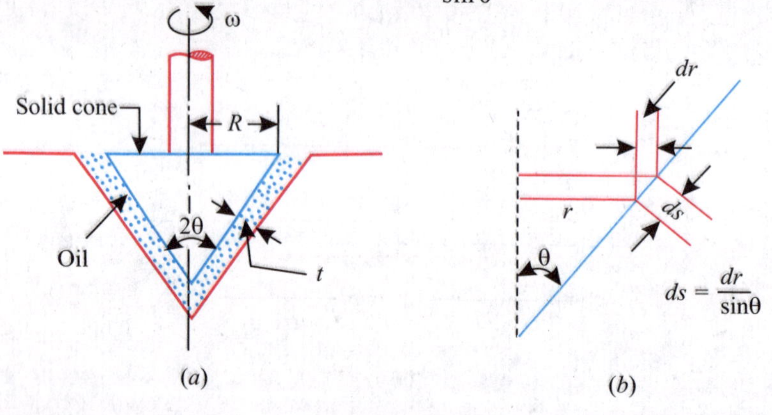

Fig. 1.11

$$\text{Shear stress } \tau = \mu\frac{du}{dy} = \mu\frac{u}{t}$$

Shear force = shear stress × area of the element

$$= \mu\frac{u}{t}\left(2\pi r \times \frac{dr}{\sin\theta}\right)$$

Viscous torque on the element, $$dT = \mu\frac{u}{t}\left(2\pi r \times \frac{dr}{\sin\theta}\right) \times r$$

Since the cone rotates with angular velocity ω rad/sec., the tangential velocity, $u = \omega r$

or, $$dT = \mu\frac{\omega r}{t}\left(2\pi r \times \frac{dr}{\sin\theta}\right) \times r = \frac{2\pi\mu\omega}{t\sin\theta} r^3\, dr$$

∴ *Total torque,* $$T = \frac{2\pi\mu\omega}{t\sin\theta}\int_0^R r^3\, dr$$

i.e., $$\boldsymbol{T} = \frac{2\pi\mu\omega}{t\sin\theta} \times \frac{R^4}{4} = \frac{\boldsymbol{\pi\mu\omega}}{\boldsymbol{2t\sin\theta}}\boldsymbol{R^4} \quad \textbf{(Ans.)}$$

Power utilised in overcoming the resistance (or rate of heat dissipation in the bearing),

$$\boldsymbol{P} = T\omega = \left(\frac{\boldsymbol{\pi\mu\omega^2}}{\boldsymbol{2t\sin\theta}}\boldsymbol{R^4}\right) \quad \textbf{(Ans.)}$$

Example 1.16. *Two large fixed parallel planes are 12 mm apart. The space between the surfaces is filled with oil of viscosity 0.972 N.s/m². A flat thin plate 0.25 m² area moves through the oil at a velocity of 0.3 m/s. Calculate the drag force:*

(i) When the plate is equidistant from both the planes, and

(ii) When the thin plate is at a distance of 4 mm from one of the plane surfaces.

Solution. Given: Distance between the fixed parallel planes = 12 mm = 0.012 m

Area of *thin* plate, $A = 0.25\ m^2$

Velocity of plate, $u = 0.3$ m/s

Viscosity of oil = 0.972 N.s/m²

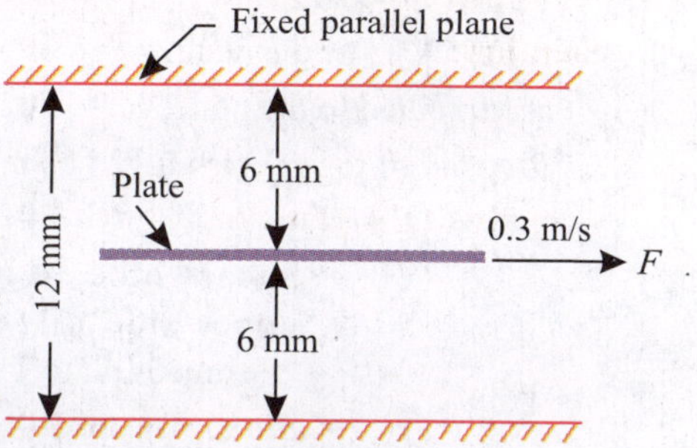

Fig. 1.12

Drag force, *F*:

(i) When the plate is equidistant from both the planes:

Let, F_1 = Shear force on the upper side of the thin plate,

F_2 = Shear force on the lower side of the thin plate,

F = Total force required to drag the plate $(= F_1 + F_2)$.

The shear τ_1, on the upper side of the thin plate is given by:

$$t_1 = \mu\,.\left(\frac{du}{dy}\right)_1$$

where, $du = 0.3$ m/s (relative velocity between upper fixed plane and the plate), and dy = 6 mm = 0.006 m (distance between the upper fixed plane and the plate)

(Thickness of the plate neglected).

∴ $$\tau_1 = 0.972 \times \frac{0.3}{0.006} = 48.6\,\text{N/m}^2$$

∴ Shear force, $F_1 = \tau_1 A = 48.6 \times 0.25 = 12.15$ N

Similarly shear stress (τ_2) on the lower side of the thin plate is given by

$$\tau_2 = u\,.\left(\frac{du}{dy}\right)_2 = 0.972 \times \frac{0.3}{0.06} = 48.6\ \text{N/m}^2$$

and $F_2 = \tau_2\,.A = 48.6 \times 0.25 = 12.15$ N

∴ $F = F_1 + F_2 = 12.15 + 12.15 =$ **24.30 N (Ans.)**

(ii) When the thin plate is at a distance of 40 *mm from one of the plane surfaces*: Refer to Fig. 1.13.

The shear force on the upper side of the thin plate,

$$F_1 = \tau_1 \cdot A = \mu \cdot \left(\frac{du}{dy}\right)_1 \times A$$

$$= 0.972 \times \frac{0.3}{0.008} \times 0.25 = 9.11 \text{N}$$

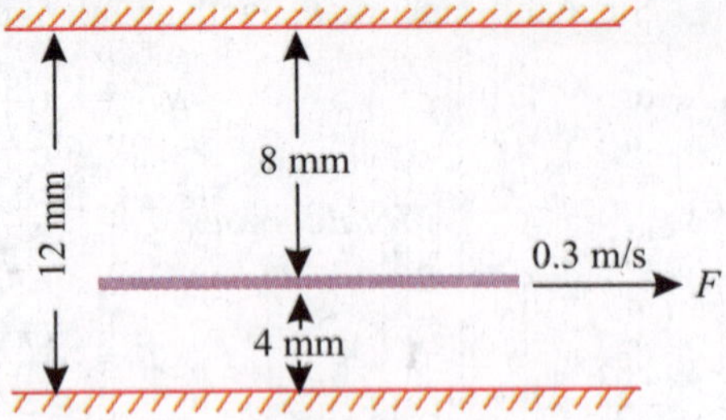

Fig. 1.13

The shear force on the lower side of the thin plate,

$$F_2 = \tau_2 \times A = \mu \cdot \left(\frac{du}{dy}\right)_2 \times A$$

$$= 0.972 \times \left(\frac{0.3}{0.004}\right) \times 0.25 = 18.22 \text{N}$$

$\therefore$ Total force $F = F_1 + F_2 = 9.11 + 18.22 =$ **27.33 N (Ans.)**

Example 1.17. *In the Fig. 1.14 is shown a central plate of area 6 m² being pulled with a force of 160 N. If the dynamic viscosities of the two oils are in the ratio of 1:3 and the viscosity of top oil is 0.12 N.s/m² determine the velocity at which the central plate will move.*

Solution: Area of the plate, $A = 6 \text{ m}^2$

Force applied to the plate, $F = 160$ N

Viscosity of top oil, $\mu = 0.12 \text{ N.s/m}^2$

Velocity of the plate, *u*:

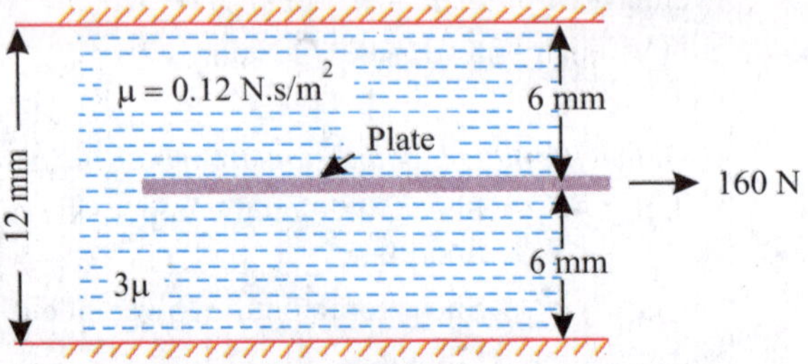

Fig. 1.14

Let F_1 = Shear force in the upper side of *thin* (assumed) plate,

F_2 = Shear force on the lower side of the thin plate, and

F = Total force required to drag the plate $(= F_1 + F_2)$

Then, $F = F_1 + F_2 = \tau_1 \times A + \tau_2 \times A$

$$= \mu\left(\frac{\partial u}{\partial y}\right)_1 \times A + 3\mu\left(\frac{du}{dy}\right)_2 \times A$$

(where τ_1 and τ_2 are the shear stresses on the two sides of the plate)

$$160 = 0.12 \times \frac{u}{6 \times 10^{-3}} \times 6 + 3 \times 0.12 \times \frac{u}{6 \times 10^{-3}} \times 6$$

or $160 = 120u + 360u = 480u$ or $u = \frac{160}{480} =$ **0.333 m/s (Ans.)**

Example 1.18. *A metal plate 1.25 m × 1.25 m × 6 mm thick and weighing 90 N is placed midway in the 24 mm gap between the two vertical plane surfaces as shown in the Fig. 1.15. The gap is filled with an oil of specific gravity 0.85 and dynamic viscosity 3.0 N.s/m². Determine the force required to lift the plate with a constant velocity of 0.15 m/s.*

Solution. *Given*: Dimensions of the plate = 1.25 m × 1.25 m × 6 mm

$\therefore$ Area of the plate, $A = 1.25 \times 1.25 = 1.5625 \text{ m}^2$

Thickness of the plate = 6 mm

$$\therefore \quad t_1 = t_2 = \frac{24 - 6}{2} = 9 \text{ mm}$$

(Since the plate is situated midway in the gap)

Specific gravity of oil = 0.85

Dynamic viscosity of oil = 3 N.s/m^2

Velocity of the plate = 0.15 m/s

Weight of the plate = 90 N

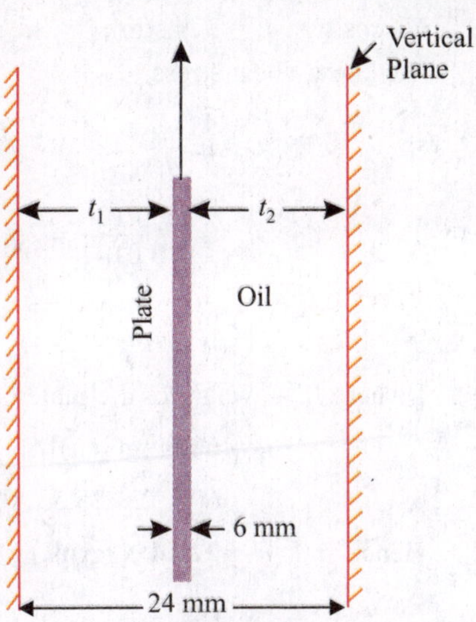

Fig. 1.15

Force required to lift the plate:

Drag force (or viscous resistance) against the motion of the plate,

$$F = \tau_1 \cdot A + \tau_2 \cdot A$$

(where τ_1 and τ_2 are the shear stresses on two sides of the plate)

$$= \mu \cdot \left(\frac{du}{dy}\right)_1 \times A + \mu\left(\frac{du}{dy}\right)_2 \times A$$

$$= \mu \cdot \frac{u}{t_1} \times A + \mu \cdot \frac{u}{t_2} \times A$$

$$= \mu A u \cdot \left(\frac{1}{t_1} + \frac{1}{t_2}\right)$$

or $$F = 3 \times 1.5625 \times 0.15 \left(\frac{1}{9 \times 10^{-3}} + \frac{1}{9 \times 10^{-3}}\right)$$

$$= 3 \times 1.5625 \times 0.15 \times \frac{2}{9 \times 10^{-3}} = 156.25 \text{ N}$$

Upward thrust or buoyant force on the plate = specific weight × volume of oil displaced

$$= 0.85 \times 9810 \times (1.25 \times 1.25 \times 0.006) = 78.17 \text{ N}$$

Effective weight of the plate = 90 – 78.17 = 11.83 N

∴ Total force required to lift the plate at velocity of 0.15 m/s = F + effective weight of the plate

= 156.25 + 11.83 = **168.08 N (Ans.)**

Example 1.19. *A square metal plate 1.8 m side and 1.8 mm thick weighing 60 N is to be lifted through a vertical gap of 30 mm of infinite extent. The oil in the gap has a specific gravity of 0.95 and viscosity of 3 N.s/m^2. If the metal plate is to be lifted at a constant speed of 0.12 m/s, find the force and power required.*

Solution. Area of metal plate, A = 1.8 × 1.8 = 3.24 m^2

Thickness of the oil film, $t = dy = \frac{30 - 1.8}{2 \times 1000} = 0.0141$

Speed of the metal plate, u = 0.12 m/s.

Change of speed,

$$du = 0.12 - 0 = 0.12 \text{ m/s}$$

Viscosity, $\mu = 3\ N.s/m^2$

We know, shear stress,

$$\tau = \mu.\frac{du}{dy}$$

$$\therefore \quad \tau = 3 \times \frac{0.12}{0.0141} = 25.53\ N/m^2$$

Force required, *F*:

$$F = W + 2\,(\tau\,.A)$$

[where W = weight of the plate
= 60 N (given)]

$$= 60 + 2 \times 25.53 \times 3.24 = 225.4\ N$$

Hence F = **225.4 N (Ans.)**

Power required, *P*:

$$P = F \times u = 225.4 \times 0.12 = 27.05\ W$$

Hence P = **27.05 (Ans.)**

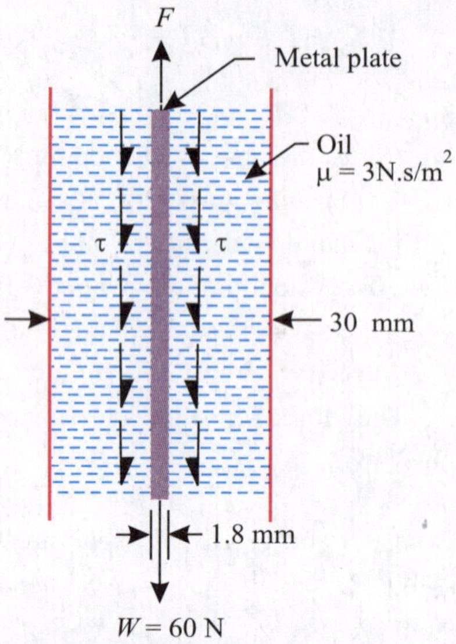

Fig. 1.16

Example 1.20. *A thin plate of very large area is placed in a gap of height h with oils of viscosities μ' and μ'' on the two sides of the plate. The plate is pulled at a constant velocity V. Calculate the position of plate so that :*

(i) *The shear force on the two sides of the plate is equal*

(ii) *The force required to drag the plate is minimum.*

Assume viscous flow and neglect all end effects.

Solution. *Given* : Height of the gap = h

Viscosities of oils = u' *and* u''

Velocity of the plate = V

Position of the plate, *y*:

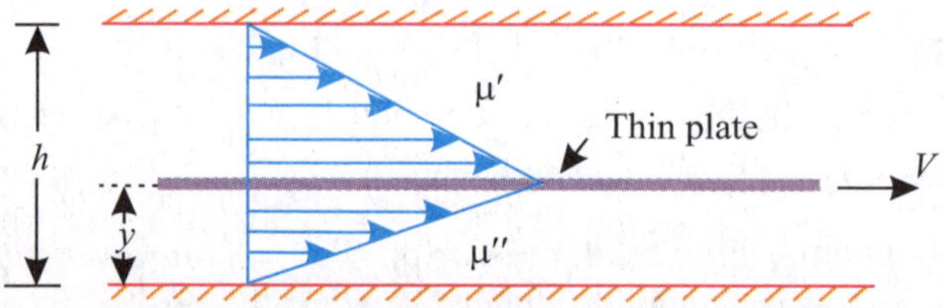

Fig. 1.17

Let y = The distance of the thin plate from one of the surfaces of the gap.

Force on the upper side of the plate,

$$F_{upper} = \mu\frac{du}{dy} = \mu' \times \frac{V}{(h-y)}A$$

Force on the lower side of the plate, $F_{lower} = \mu'' \times \frac{V}{y}A$

(i) Since the forces on the two sides of the plate are equal (given) we have,

i.e., $F_{upper} = F_{lower}$

$$\therefore \quad \mu' \times \frac{V}{(h-y)} A = \mu'' \times \frac{V}{y} A$$

or,
$$\frac{\mu'}{h-y} = \frac{\mu''}{y} \quad \text{or} \quad \mu' y = \mu'' h - \mu'' y$$

$$\therefore \quad y = \frac{\mu'' h}{\mu' + \mu''} \quad \textbf{(Ans.)}$$

(ii) Total drag force = sum of the forces on the upper and lower surfaces of the plate.

i.e.,
$$F = F_{upper} + F_{lower}$$

or,
$$F = \mu' \times \frac{V}{h-y} \times A + \mu'' \times \frac{V}{y} A$$

For the drag force to be *minimum* $\frac{dF}{dy} = 0$

i.e.,
$$\frac{d}{dy}\left[\mu' \times \frac{V}{h-y} \times A + \mu'' \times \frac{V}{y} A\right] = 0$$

or,
$$\frac{\mu' VA}{(h-y)^2} - \frac{\mu'' VA}{y^2} = 0$$

or,
$$\frac{\mu'}{\mu''} = \frac{(h-y)^2}{y^2} = \frac{h^2 + y^2 - 2hy}{y^2} = \frac{h^2}{y^2} + 1 - \frac{2h}{y}$$

$$\therefore \quad = \frac{h^2}{y^2} - \frac{2h}{y} + \left(1 + \frac{\mu'}{\mu''}\right)$$

or,
$$\frac{h}{y} = \frac{2 \pm \sqrt{4 - 4(1 - \mu'/\mu'')}}{2} = 1 \pm \sqrt{(\mu'/\mu'')}$$

Since, $\frac{h}{y}$ cannot be less than unity, therefore

$$\frac{h}{y} = 1 + \sqrt{\mu'/\mu''} \quad \text{or} \quad \boldsymbol{y = \frac{h}{1 + \sqrt{\mu'/\mu''}}} \quad \textbf{(Ans.)}$$

1.7. THERMODYNAMIC PROPERTIES

The thermodynamic properties need to be considered when a fluid is influenced by change of temperature. The following equation, known as the *characteristic equation of a state of a perfect gas,* is used for this purpose.

$$pV = mRT \qquad ...(1.10)$$

where, p = Absolute pressure, m = Mass of gas,
V = Volume of m kg of gas, R = Characteristic gas constant, and
T = Absolute temperature.

The characteristic equation in *another form,* can be derived by using *kilogram-mole as a unit.* The *kilogram-mole* is defined as a quantity of a gas equivalent to M kg of the gas, where M is the molecular weight of the gas (*i.e.,* since the molecular weight of oxygen is 32, then 1 kg mole of oxygen is equivalent to 32 kg of oxygen).

As per definition of the kilogram-mole, for m kg of a gas, we have:

$$m = nM \qquad ...(1.11)$$

where, n = No. of moles.

Note. Since the standard of mass is the kg, kilogram-mole will be written simply as mole.

Substituting for m from eqn. 1.11 in Eqn. 1.10 gives:

$$pV = nMRT \quad \text{or} \quad MR = \frac{pV}{nT}$$

According to Avogadro's hypothesis the volume of 1 mole of any gas is the same as the volume of 1 mole of any other gas, when the gases are at same temperature and pressure. Therefore, $\frac{V}{n}$ is the same for all gases at the same value of p and T. That is the quantity $\frac{pV}{nT}$ is a constant for all gases. This constant is called '*universal gas constant*', and is given the symbol, R_0,

i.e.,
$$MR = R_0 = \frac{pV}{nT} \quad \text{or} \quad pV = nR_0T \qquad \text{...(1.12)}$$

Since,
$$MR = R_0, \text{ then } R = \frac{R_0}{M} \qquad \text{...(1.13)}$$

It has been found experimentally that the volume of 1 mole of any perfect gas at 1 bar and 0°C is approximately 22.71 m^3. Therefore from eqn. 1.12,

$$R_0 = \frac{pV}{nT} = \frac{1 \times 10^5 \times 22.71}{1 \times 273.15} = 8314.3 \text{ Nm/mole K}$$

Using eqn. 1.13, the gas constant for any gas can be found when the molecular weight is known.

Example. *For oxygen which has a molecular weight of 32, the gas constant*

$$R = \frac{R_0}{M} = \frac{8314}{32} = 259.8 \text{ Nm/kg K.}$$

If the value of R is known, the specific weight of any gas can be computed at any temperature. The density can be changed by changing temperature or pressure.

(*i*) When the change in the state of the fluid system is affected at *constant pressure* the process is known as **isobaric** or **constant pressure process.**

Here $\frac{V}{T}$ = constant; (Charle's law) or $\frac{\text{v}}{T}$ = constant or $\frac{\text{v}}{T} = \frac{1}{\rho T}$ = constant ...(1.14)

(*ii*) When the change in the state of the fluid system is affected at *constant temperature* the process is known as **isothermal process.**

Here $p\text{v}^\gamma$ = constant; (Boyle's Law) or $p\text{v} = \frac{p}{\rho}$ = constant ...(1.15)

(*iii*) *When no heat is transferred* to or from the fluid during the change in the state of fluid system, the process is called **adiabatic process.**

Here, $p\text{v}^\gamma$ = constant or $p\text{v}^\gamma = \frac{p}{\rho^\gamma}$ = constant ...(1.16)

where
$$\gamma = \frac{c_p}{c_v},$$

c_p = Specific heat of gas at constant pressure, and

c_v = Specific heat of gas at constant volume.

γ depends upon the molecular structure of the gas.

Note. For details regarding compression and expansion of gases please refer to chapter on "*Compressible flow.*"

Example 1.21. *The pressure and temperature of carbon-dioxide in a vessel are 600 kN/m² abs. and 30°C respectively. Find its mass density, specific weight and specific volume.*

Solution. *Given*: Pressure of CO_2 = 600 kN/m² abs.

Temperature of $CO_2 = 30 + 273 = 303$ K

Molecular weight of $CO_2 = 12 + 2 \times 16 = 44$

Universal gas constant, $R_0 = 8314.3$ Nm/mole K

$$\therefore \text{ Characteristic gas constant, } R = \frac{R_0}{M} = \frac{8314.3}{44} = 189 \text{ Nm/kg K}$$

(*i*) Mass density, ρ:

We know, $pV = mRT \qquad \therefore \quad \frac{m}{V} = \frac{p}{RT}$

or, $$\rho = \frac{p}{RT} = \frac{600 \times 10^3}{189 \times 313} = 10.14 \text{ kg/m}^3$$

i.e., ρ = **10.14 kg/m³ (Ans.)**

(*ii*) Specific weight, *w*:

$$w = \rho g = 10.14 \times 9.81 = \mathbf{99.47 \text{ N/m}^3} \textbf{ (Ans.)}$$

(*iii*) Specific volume *v*:

$$v = \frac{1}{\rho} = \frac{1}{10.14} = \mathbf{0.0986 \text{ m}^3\text{/kg}} \textbf{ (Ans.)}$$

1.8. SURFACE TENSION AND CAPILLARITY

1.8.1. Surface Tension

Cohesion. Cohesion means intermolecular attraction between *molecules of the same liquid.* It enables a liquid to resist small amount of tensile stresses. Cohesion is a tendency of the liquid to remain as one *assemblage of particles. "Surface tension" is due to cohesion between particles at the free surface.*

Adhesion. *Adhesion* means *attraction between the molecules of a liquid and the molecules of a solid boundary surface in contact with the liquid.* This property enables a liquid to stick to *another body.*

Capillary action is due to both *cohesion* and *adhesion.*

Surface tension is caused by the *force of cohesion at the free surface.* A liquid molecule in the interior of the liquid mass is surrounded by other molecules all around and is in equilibrium. At the free surface of the liquid, there are no liquid molecules above the surface to balance the force of the molecules below it. Consequently, as shown in Fig. 1.18, there is a net inward force on the molecule. The force is normal to the liquid surface. At the free surface a thin layer of molecules is formed. This is because of this *film that a thin small needle can float on the free surface* (the layer acts as a *membrane*).

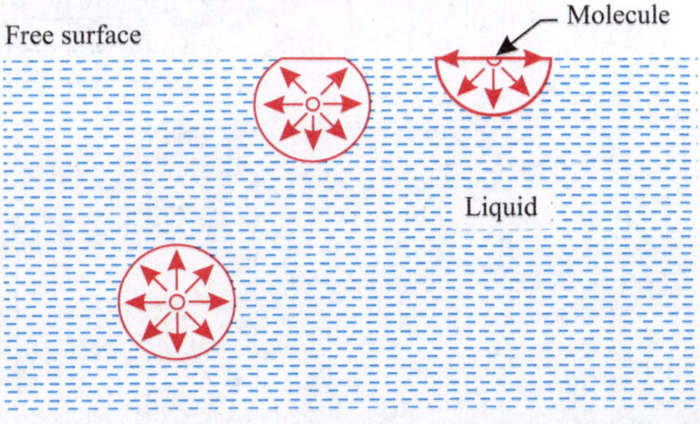

Fig. 1.18

Some *important examples of phenomenon of surface tension* are as follows:

(*i*) Rain drops (A falling rain drop becomes spherical due to cohesion and surface tension).
(*ii*) Rise of sap in a tree.
(*iii*) Bird can drink water from ponds.
(*iv*) Capillary rise and capillary siphoning.
(*v*) Collection of dust particles on water surface.
(*vi*) Break up of liquid jets.

Dimensional formula for surface tension:

The dimensional formula for surface tension is given by:

$$\left[\frac{E}{L}\right] \text{ or } \left[\frac{M}{T^2}\right]$$

It is usually expressed in N/m. The value of surface tension depends upon the following *factors*:

(*i*) Nature of the liquid,
(*ii*) Nature of the surrounding matter (*e.g.*, solid, liquid or gas), and
(*iii*) Kinetic energy (and hence the temperature of the liquid molecules).

Note. As compared to pressure and gravitational forces surface tension forces are generally negligible but *become quite significant when there is a free surface and the boundary conditions are small as in the case of small scale models of hydraulic engineering structures.*

Surface tension of water and mercury when in contact with air:

Water-air ... 0.073 N/m at 20°C; Water-air ... 0.058 N/m at 100°C;
Mercury-air ... 0.1 N/m length.

1.8.1.1. Pressure Inside a Water Droplet, Soap Bubble and a Liquid Jet

Case I. Water droplet:

Let, p = Pressure inside the droplet above outside pressure (*i.e.*, $\Delta p = p - 0 = p$ above atmospheric pressure)

d = Diameter of the droplet and

σ = Surface tension of the liquid.

From free body diagram (Fig. 1.19 *d*), we have:

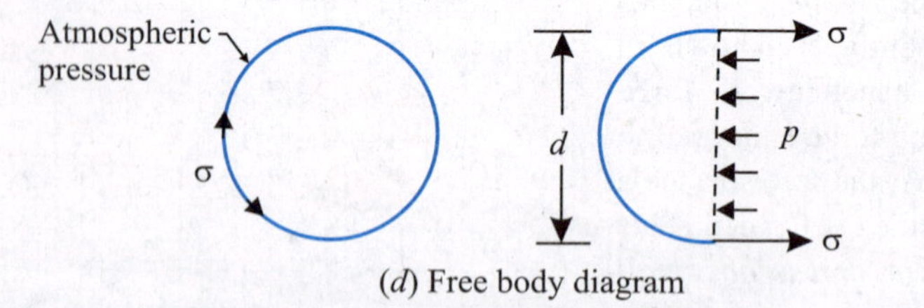

Fig. 1.19. Pressure inside a water droplet.

(*i*) Pressure force = $p \times \frac{\pi}{4} d^2$, and

(*ii*) Surface tension force acting around the circumference = $\sigma \times \pi d$.

Under equilibrium conditions these two forces will be equal and opposite,

i.e., $$\overleftarrow{p \times \frac{\pi}{4} d^2} = \overrightarrow{\sigma \times \pi d}$$

$$\therefore \quad p = \frac{\sigma \times \pi d}{\frac{\pi}{4} d^2} = \frac{4\sigma}{d} \qquad ...(1.17)$$

Eqn. 1.17 shows that *with an increase in size of the droplet the pressure intensity decreases.*

Case II. Soap (or hollow) bubble:

Soap bubbles have two surfaces on which surface tension σ acts.

From the free body diagram (Fig. 1.20), we have

$$\overleftarrow{p \times \frac{\pi}{4} d^2} = 2 \times (\overrightarrow{\sigma \times \pi d})$$

$$\therefore \quad p = \frac{2\sigma \times \pi d}{\frac{\pi}{4} d^2} = \frac{8\sigma}{d} \qquad ...(1.18)$$

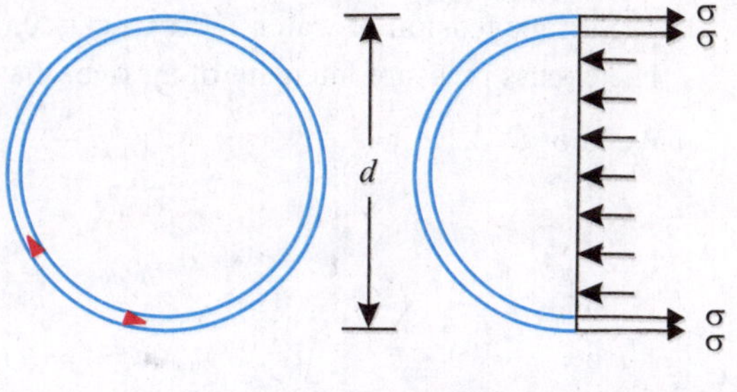

Fig. 1.20. Pressure inside a soap bubble.

Since the soap solution has a high value of surface tension σ, even with small pressure of blowing a soap bubble will tend to grow larger in diameter (hence formation of large soap bubbles).

Case III. A Liquid jet:

Let us consider a cylindrical liquid jet of diameter *d* and length *l*. Fig. 1.21 shows a semi-jet.

Pressure force $= p \times l \times d$

Surface tension force $= \sigma \times 2l$

Equating the two forces, we have:

$$p \times l \times d = \sigma \times 2l$$

$$\therefore \quad p = \frac{\sigma \times 2l}{l \times d} = \frac{2\sigma}{d} \qquad ...(1.19)$$

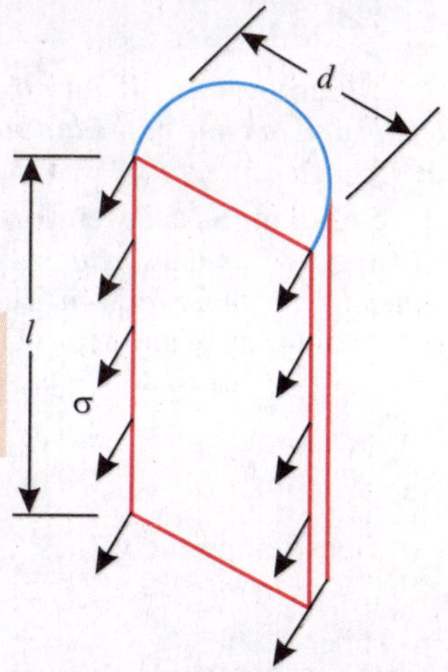

Fig. 1.21. Forces on liquid jet.

Example 1.22. *If the surface tension at air-water interface is 0.069 N/m, what is the pressure difference between inside and outside of an air bubble of diameter 0.009 mm?*

Solution. *Given*: σ = 0.069 N/m; *d* = 0.009 mm

An air bubble has only one surface. Hence,

$$p = \frac{4\sigma}{d}$$

$$= \frac{4 \times 0.069}{0.009 \times 10^{-3}} = 30667 \text{ N/m}^2$$

$$= \mathbf{30.667 \text{ kN/m}^2 \text{ or kPa (Ans.)}}$$

Example 1.23. *If the surface tension at the soap-air interface is 0.09 N/m, calculate the internal pressure in a soap bubble of 28 mm diameter.*

Solution. *Given*: σ = 0.09 N/m; *d* = 28 mm.

In a soap bubble there are two interfaces. Hence,

$$p = \frac{8\sigma}{d} = \frac{8 \times 0.09}{28 \times 10^{-3}}$$

$$= \mathbf{25.71\ N/m^2\ (above\ atmospheric\ pressure)\ (Ans.)}$$

Example 1.24. *In order to form a stream of bubbles, air is introduced through a nozzle into a tank of water at 20°C. If the process requires 3.0 mm diameter bubbles to be formed, by how much the air pressure at the nozzle must exceed that of the surrounding water?*

What would be the absolute pressure inside the bubble if the surrounding water is at 100.3 kN/m²?

Take surface tension of water at 20°C = 0.0735 N/m.

Solution. Diameter of a bubble, $d = 3.0\ \text{mm} = 3 \times 10^{-3}\ \text{m}$

Surface tension of water at 20°C, $\sigma = 0.0735$ N/m

The excess pressure intensity of air over that of surrounding water, $\Delta p = p$.

We know,

$$p = \frac{4\sigma}{d} = \frac{4 \times 0.0735}{3 \times 10^{-3}} = \mathbf{98\ N/m^2\ (Ans.)}$$

Absolute pressure inside the bubble, p_{abs}:

$$p_{abs} = p + p_{atm}$$

$$= 98 \times 10^{-3} + 100.3$$

$$= 0.098 + 100.3 = \mathbf{100.398\ kN/m^2\ (Ans.)}$$

Example 1.25. *A soap bubble 62.5 mm diameter has an internal pressure in excess of the outside pressure of 20 N/m². What is tension in the soap film?*

Solution. *Given*: Diameter of the bubble, $d = 62.5\ \text{mm} = 62.5 \times 10^{-3}$ m;

Internal pressure in excess of the outside pressure, $p = 20\ \text{N/m}^2$.

Surface tension, σ:

Using the relation,

$$p = \frac{8\sigma}{d}$$

i.e.,

$$20 = \frac{8\sigma}{62.5 \times 10^{-3}} \quad \therefore \quad \sigma = 20 \times \frac{62.5 \times 10^{-3}}{8} = \mathbf{0.156\ N/m\ (Ans.)}$$

Example 1.26. *What do you mean by surface tension? If the pressure difference between the inside and outside of the air bubble of diameter 0.01 mm is 29.2 kPa, what will be the surface tension at air-water interface?* **(N.U.)**

Solution. Surface tension is defined *as the tensile force acting on the surface of a liquid in contact with a gas or on the surface between two immiscible liquids such that the contact surface behaves like a membrane under tension.* The magnitude of this force per unit length of the free surface will have the same value as the surface energy per unit area. It is denoted by the letter σ and is expressed as N/m.

$$p \times \frac{\pi}{4} d^2 = \sigma (\pi d)$$

or

$$\sigma = p \times \frac{d}{4}$$

Substituting the values; $d = 0.01 \times 10^{-3}$ m; $p = 29.2 \times 10^3$ Pa (or N/m²), we get

$$\sigma = 29.2 \times 10^3 \times \frac{0.01 \times 10^{-3}}{4} = \mathbf{0.073\ N/m\ (Ans.)}$$

1.8.2. Capillarity

***Capillarity** is a phenomenon by which a liquid (depending upon its specific gravity) rises into a thin glass tube above or below its general level.* This phenomenon is due to the *combined effect of cohesion and adhesion of liquid particles.*

Fig. 1.22 shows the phenomenon of rising water in the tube of *smaller* diameters.

Let, d = Diameter of the capillary tube,

θ = Angle of contact of the water surface,

σ = Surface tension force for unit length, and

w = Weight density (ρg).

Now, upward surface tension force (lifting force) = weight of the water column in the tube (*gravity force*)

$$\pi d.\sigma \cos\theta = \frac{\pi}{4} d^2 \times h \times w$$

$$\therefore \quad h = \frac{4\sigma \cos\theta}{wd} \quad \text{...(1.20)}$$

For water and glass: $\theta \simeq 0$.

Hence the capillary rise of water in the glass tube,

$$h = \frac{4\sigma}{wd} \quad \text{...(1.21)}$$

In case of mercury there is a capillary depression as shown in Fig. 1.23, and the angle of depression is $\theta \simeq 140°$. (It may be noted that here $\cos\theta = \cos 140° = \cos(180 - 40°) = -\cos 40°$, therefore, h is *negative* indicating capillary depression).

Following points are worth noting:

(*i*) Smaller the diameter of the capillary tube, greater is the capillary rise or depression.

(*ii*) The measurement of liquid level in laboratory capillary (glass) tubes should not be smaller than 8 mm.

(*iii*) Capillary effects are negligible for tubes longer than 12 mm.

(*iv*) For *wetting liquid* (water): $\theta < \pi/2$. For water: $\theta = 0$ when pure water is in contact with clean glass. But θ becomes as high as 25° when water is slightly contaminated.

For *non-wetting* liquid (mercury): $\theta > \pi/2$.

(For mercury: θ varies between 130° to 150°)

Refer Fig. 1.24 which illustrates the liquid gas interface with a solid surface.

(*v*) The effects of surface tension are *negligible* in many flow problems *except those involving*:

— capillary rise;

— formation of drops and bubbles;

— the break up of liquid jets, and

— hydraulic model studies where the model or flow depth is small.

Capillary inversion. Due to surface tension the liquid passing out of an elliptical orifice tends to assume a circular or minimum perimeter cross-section. Here transformation of surface energy into

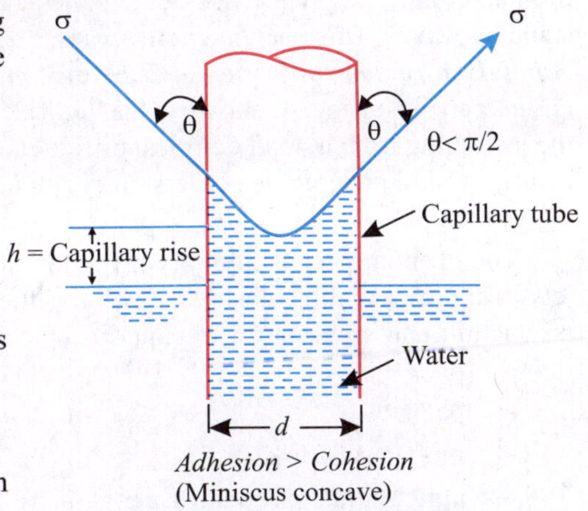

Fig. 1.22. Effect of capillarity.

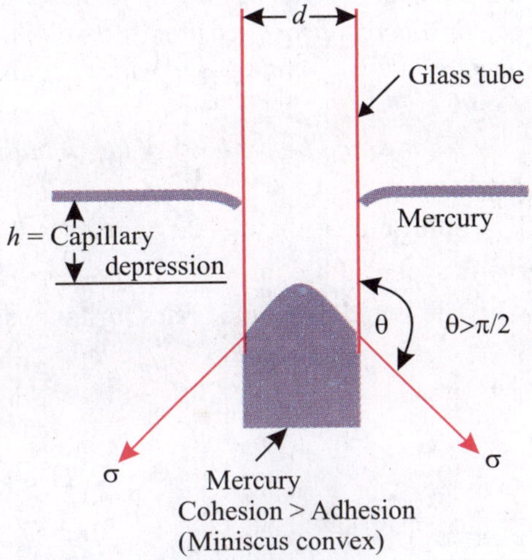

Fig. 1.23

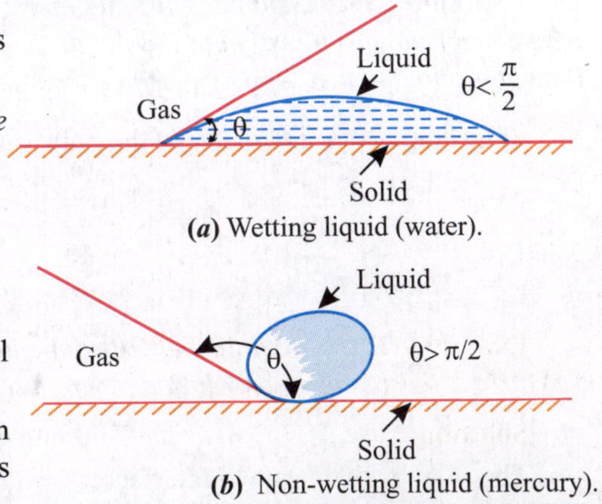

Fig. 1.24

kinetic energy takes place; the flow pattern varies as the Weber number changes and the motion continues giving rise to a series of standing waves. This phenomenon is known as *capillary inversion* of jet for orifices of *non-circular* cross-section. As shown in the Fig. 1.25 the jet issuing from a small elliptical orifice can be observed to undergo two inversion cycles in a given length.

The phenomenon of capillary inversion of jets is significant for industries involving the production and size control of liquid droplets like:

— paint,
— molten shot, and
— agricultural insecticides, *etc.*

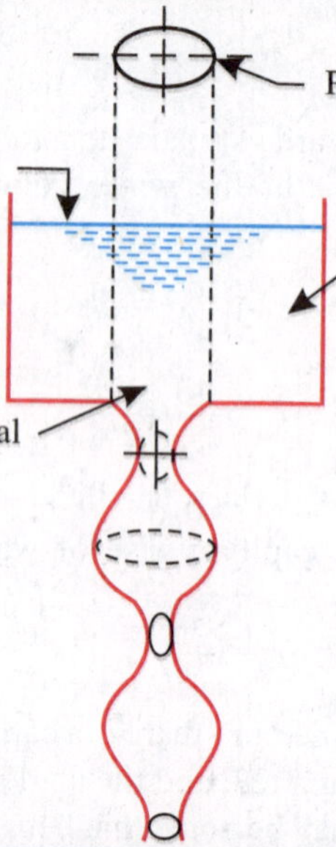

Fig. 1.25. Capillary inversion of a liquid jet.

Example 1.27. *A clean tube of diameter 2.5 mm is immersed in a liquid with a coefficient of surface tension = 0.4 N/m. The angle of contact of the liquid with the glass can be assumed to be 135°. The density of the liquid = 13600 kg/m³.*

What would be the level of the liquid in the tube relative to the free surface of the liquid inside the tube.

Solution. *Given:* $d = 2.5$ mm ; $\sigma = 4$ N/m, $\theta = 135°$; $\rho = 13600$ kg/m^3

Level of the liquid in the tube, *h*:

The liquid in the tube rises (or falls) due to capillarity. The capillary rise (or fall),

$$h = \frac{4\sigma \cos\theta}{wd} \qquad \text{...[Eqn. (1.20)]}$$

$$= \frac{4 \times 0.4 \times \cos 135°}{(9.81 \times 13600) \times 2.5 \times 10^{-3}} \qquad (\because w = \rho g)$$

$$= -3.39 \times 10^{-3} \text{m or} -3.39 \text{ mm}$$

Negative sign indicates that there is a capillary **depression (fall) of 3.39 mm. (Ans.)**

Example 1.28. *Assuming that the interstices in a clay are of size equal to one tenth the mean diameter of the grain, estimate the height to which water will rise in a clay soil of average grain diameter of 0.048 mm. Assume surface tension at air-water interface as 0.074 N/m.*

Solution. *Given:* Diameter of the pores, $d = \frac{1}{10} \times 0.048 = 0.0048$ mm; $\sigma = 0.074$ N/m

Assuming $\theta = 0°$

$$h = \frac{4\sigma}{wd} = \frac{4 \times 0.074}{(9.81 \times 1000) \times 0.0048 \times 10^{-3}} = \mathbf{6.286\ m\ (Ans.)}$$

Example 1.29. *Calculate the work done in blowing a soap bubble of diameter 100 mm. Assume the surface tension of soap solution = 0.038 N/m.*

Solution. *Given:* $d = 100$ mm or 0.1 m; $\sigma = 0.038$ N/m.

The soap bubble has two interfaces.

∴ Work done = Surface tension × total surface area

$$= 0.038 \times 4\pi \times \left(\frac{0.1}{2}\right)^2 \times 2$$

$$= \mathbf{0.002388\ Nm}$$ **(Ans.)**

Example 1.30. *Determine the minimum size of glass tubing that can be used to measure water level, if the capillary rise in the tube is not to exceed 0.3 mm. Take surface tension of water in contact with air as 0.0735 N/m.*

Solution. *Given* :Capillary rise, $h = 0.3 \text{ mm} = 0.3 \times 10^{-3}$ m

Surface tension, $\sigma = 0.0735$ N/m

Specific weight of water, $w = 9810 \text{ N/m}^3$.

Size of glass tubing, *d*:

$$\text{Capillary rise, } h = \frac{4\sigma\cos\theta}{wd} = \frac{4\sigma}{wd}$$

(Assuming $\theta = 0$ for water)

$$0.3 \times 10^{-3} = \frac{4 \times 0.0735}{9810 \times d}$$

$$\therefore \quad d = \frac{4 \times 0.0735}{0.3 \times 10^{-3} \times 9810} = 0.1 \text{ m} = \mathbf{100\ mm}$$ **(Ans.)**

Example 1.31. *A U-tube is made up of two capillaries of bores 1.2 m and 2.4 mm respectively. The tube is held vertical and partially filled with liquid of surface tension 0.06 N/m and zero contact angle. If the estimated difference in the level of two menisci is 15 mm, determine the mass density of the liquid.*

Solution. *Given*: Bores of the capillaries:

$$d_1 = 1.2 \text{ mm} = 0.0012 \text{ m}$$

$$d_2 = 2.4 \text{ mm} = 0.0024 \text{ m}$$

Difference of level, $h_1 - h_2 = 15 \text{ mm} = 0.015$ m; Angle of contact, $\theta = 0$

Mass density of the liquid, ρ:

$$h_1 = \frac{4\sigma\cos\theta}{wd_1}, \quad \text{and} \quad h_2 = \frac{4\sigma\cos\theta}{wd_2}$$

[where w (= ρg) = weight density of the liquid)]

$$\therefore \quad h_1 - h_2 = \frac{4\sigma}{w}\left[\frac{1}{d_1} - \frac{1}{d_2}\right] \qquad (\because \theta = 0)$$

$$0.015 = \frac{4 \times 0.06}{\rho \times 9.81}\left[\frac{1}{0.0012} - \frac{1}{0.0024}\right] = \frac{0.02446}{\rho} \times 416.67$$

$$\therefore \quad \rho = \frac{0.02446 \times 416.67}{0.015} = \mathbf{679.45\ kg/m^3}$$ **(Ans.)**

Example 1.32. *Derive an expression for the capillary rise at a liquid having surface tension σ and contact angle θ between two vertical parallel plates at a distance W apart. If the plates are of glass, what will be the capillary rise of water having σ = 0.073 N/m, θ = 0°?. Take W = 1 mm.*

(Anna University)

Solution. Refer to Fig. 1.26. Consider two vertical parallel plates immersed in a liquid whose weight density is w.

Given : σ = Surface tension;

θ = Contact angle.

Let, h = Height of liquid between plates above general liquid surface.

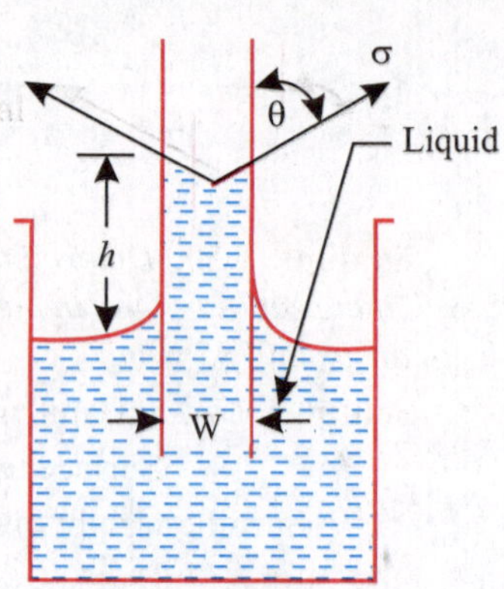

Fig. 1.26

Under a state of equilibrium, the weight of liquid of height h is balanced by the force at the surface of liquid between the plates.

Then weight of liquid of height h is balanced by the force between the plates

= volume of liquid of height h between the plates × w

$= W \times L \times h \times w$ ...(1)

where, L = length of plate, and w = weight density of the liquid.

Vertical component of surface tensile force

$= (\sigma \times \text{circumference}) \times \cos\theta$

$= \sigma \times 2L \times \cos\theta$ ...(2)

For equilibrium, eqns. (1) and (2) must balance.

∴ $W \times L \times h \times w = \sigma \times 2L \times \cos\theta$ ...(3)

or, $$h = \frac{2\sigma\cos\theta}{W \times w}$$

Eqn. (3) is the *expression for capillary rise.* **(Ans.)**

When plates are of glass,

$\theta = 0°$, $\sigma = 0.073$ N/m

$W = 1$ mm $= 0.001$ m, $w = 9810$ N/m^3

Capillary rise of water, $$h = \frac{2\sigma\cos\theta}{W \times w}$$

$$= \frac{2 \times 0.073 \times \cos 0°}{0.001 \times 9810} = 0.0149 \text{ m or } 14.9 \text{ mm}$$

Hence, capillary rise = **14.9 mm (Ans.)**

Example 1.33. *A single column U-tube manometer, made of glass tubing having a nominal inside diameter of 2.4 mm, has been used to measure pressure in a pipe or vessel containing air. If the limb opened to atmosphere is 10 percent oversize, find the error in mm of mercury in the measurement of air pressure due to surface tension effects. It is stated that mercury is the manometric fluid for which surface tension σ = 0.52* N/m *and angle of contact α = 140°*

Solution. *Given:* $d_1 = 2.4$ mm; $d_2 = 2.4 \times 1.1 = 2.64$ mm; $\sigma = 0.52$ N/m; $\alpha = 140°$.

Error in measurement due to surface tension effects:

The surface tension manifests the phenomenon of capillary action due to which rise or depression of manometric liquid in a tube is given by

$$h = \frac{4\sigma\cos\theta}{wd_1}$$

Now, $$h_1 = \frac{4 \times 0.52 \times \cos 140°}{(13.6 \times 9810) \times (2.4 \times 10^{-3})} = 4.97 \times 10^{-3} \text{ m}$$

(Negative sign indicates capillary depression)

$$h_2 = \frac{4 \times 0.52 \times \cos 140°}{(13.6 \times 9810) \times (2.64 \times 10^{-3})} = -4.52 \times 10^{-3} \text{ m}$$

Hence, error in measurement due to surface tension effects

$= (4.97 - 4.52) \times 10^{-3} = 0.45 \times 10^{-3}$ m = **0.45 mm (Ans.)**

Example 1.34. *Calculate the capillary effect in millimetres in a glass tube of 4 mm diameter, when immersed in (i) water and (ii) mercury. The temperature of the liquid is 20°C and the values of surface tension of water and mercury at 20°C in contact with air are 0.0735 N/m and 0.51 N/m respectively. The contact angle for water θ = 0° and for mercury θ = 130°. Take specific weight of water at 20°C as equal to 9790 N/m³.* **[Engg. Services]**

Solution. *Given:* Diameter of glass tube, $d = 4$ mm = 0.004 m

Surface tension at 20°C, σ:

$$\sigma_{water} = 0.0735 \text{ N/m}, \qquad \sigma_{mercury} = 0.051 \text{ N/m}$$

Specific weight of water at 20°C = 9790 N/m³

The rise or depression h of a liquid in a capillary tube is given by

$$h = \frac{4\sigma \cos\theta}{wd}$$

where, σ = surface tension, θ = angle of contact, and w = specific weight.

(*i*) Capillary effect for water:

$$h = \frac{4 \times 0.0735 \times \cos 0^\circ}{9790 \times 0.004} \qquad (\because \theta_{water} = 0^\circ \text{ ...given})$$

$$= 7.51 \times 10^{-3} \text{ m} = \mathbf{7.51 \text{ mm (rise) (Ans.)}}$$

(*ii*) Capillary effect for mercury

$$h = \frac{4 \times 0.051 \times \cos 130^\circ}{(13.6 \times 9790) \times 0.004} \qquad (\because \theta_{mercury} = 130^\circ \text{ ... given})$$

or, $= -2.46 \times 10^{-3} \text{ m} = -2.46 \text{ mm}$

i.e., $h =$ **2.46 mm (depression) (Ans.)**

Example 1.35. *In measuring the unit energy of a mineral oil (specific gravity = 0.85) by the bubble method, a tube having an internal diameter of 1.5 mm is immersed to depth of 12.5 mm in oil. Air is forced through the tube forming a bubble at the lower end. What magnitude of the unit surface energy will be indicated by a maximum bubble pressure intensity of 150 N/m².* **[Engg. Services]**

Solution. Sp. gravity of oil = 0.85

Internal diameter of the tube,

$d = 1.5$ mm = 0.0015 m

Depth, $h = 12.5$ mm = 0.0125 m

Gauge pressure *inside* the bubble

$p_i = 150$ N/m²

Unit surface energy, σ:

Gauge pressure *outside* the bubble,

$p_0 = wh = (0.85 \times 9810) \times 0.0125 = 104.23$ N/m²

∴ Net pressure attributable to surface tension

$p = p_i - p_0 = 150 - 104.23 = 45.77$ N/m²

Also, $p_i - p_0 = \dfrac{4\sigma}{d}$

Assuming diameter of bubble equal to that of the tube,

$$45.77 = \frac{4\sigma}{0.0015}$$

$$\therefore \quad \sigma = \frac{45.77 \times 0.0015}{4} = \mathbf{0.0172 \text{ N/m (Ans.)}}$$

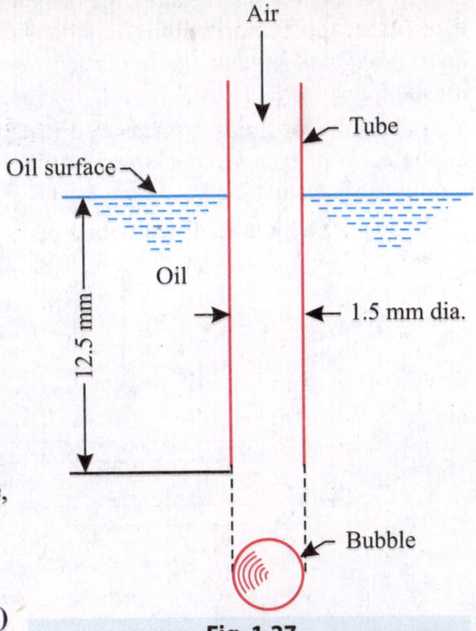

Fig. 1.27

Example 1.36. *Two coaxial glass tubes forming an annulus with small gap are immersed in water in a trough. The inner and outer radii of the annulus are r_i and r_0 respectively. What is the capillary rise if σ is the surface tension of water in contact with air?* **(PTU)**

Solution. Refer to Fig. 1.28. If the angle of contact between the liquid and the curved tube surface is θ, the water in the annulus will continue to rise until the vertical component of the surface tension force which acts over the wetted length (outer curve of the inner tube and inner curve of the outer tube) equals the height of the water column, or

$T \cos\theta = \pi (r_0^2 - r_i^2) h\rho g$, where $T = \sigma \pi (r_0 + r_i)$; substituting for T, we get

$$\sigma\pi (r_0 + r_i) \cos\theta = \pi (r_0^2 - r_i^2) h\rho g$$

or,
$$h = \text{capillary rise} = \frac{\sigma \cos\theta}{(r_0 - r_i)\rho g}$$

For pure water and clean glass $\theta \simeq 0$ and $h = \dfrac{\sigma}{(r_0 - r_i)\rho g}$

Under *actual conditions,* neither water is pure, nor glass is clean.

Gibson has obtained the value of θ **as 25° 32′.**

Thus,
$$h = \frac{\sigma \cos 25°32'}{(r_0 - r_i)\rho g} = \frac{0.902\sigma}{(r_0 - r_i)\rho g} \quad \textbf{(Ans.)}$$

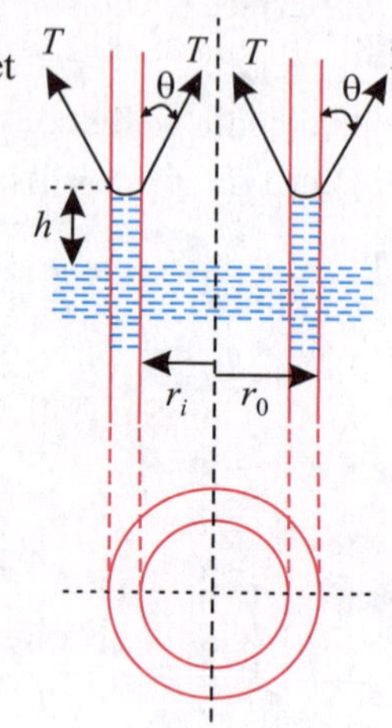

Fig. 1.28

1.9. COMPRESSIBILITY AND BULK MODULUS

The property by virtue of which fluids undergo a change in volume under the action of external pressure is known as ***compressibility.*** It decreases with the increases in pressure of fluid as the volume modulus increases with the increase of pressure.

The variation in volume of water, with variation of pressure, is so small that for all practical purposes it is neglected. Thus, the water is considered to be an incompressible liquid. However in case of water flowing through pipes when sudden or large changes in pressure (*e.g.* water hammer) take place, the compressibility cannot be neglected. The *compressibility* in Fluid Mechanics is *considered mainly when the velocity of flow is high enough reaching 20 percent of speed of sound in the medium.*

Elasticity of fluids is measured in terms of ***bulk modulus of elasticity*** (K) which is defined as the *ratio of compressive stress to volumetric strain.* Compressibility is the reciprocal of bulk modulus of elasticity.

Consider a cylinder fitted with a piston as shown in Fig. 1.29.

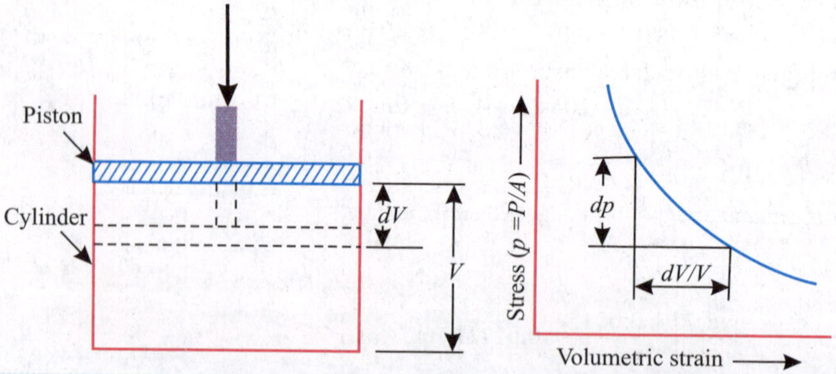

Fig. 1.29

Let, V = Volume of gas enclosed in the cylinder, and

p = Pressure of gas when volume is V

$= \frac{P}{A}$, where A is the area of cross-section of the cylinder.

Let the pressure is increased to $p + dp$, the volume of gas decreases from V to $V - dV$.
Then increase in pressure = dp; Decrease in volume = dV

$$\therefore \quad \text{Volumetric strain} = -\frac{dV}{V}$$

(Negative sign indicates *decrease in volume with increase of pressure*)

$$\therefore \quad \text{Bulk modulus, } K = \frac{dp\,(\text{increase of pressure})}{-dV/V\,(\text{volumetric strain})}$$

i.e.,
$$K = \frac{dp}{-dV/V}$$

$$\left(\text{Compressibility} = \frac{1}{K}\right) \quad \text{...(1.22)}$$

Steepening of the curve (Fig. 1.29) with increasing pressure shows that as fluids are compressed it becomes increasingly difficult to compress them further. In other words, the *value of K increases with increase of pressure.*

The following points are worth noting:

1. The bulk modulus of elasticity (K) of a fluid is not constant, but it increases with increase in pressure. This is so because when a fluid mass is compressed its molecules become close together and its resistance to further compression increases *i.e.,* K increases. (*e.g.* the value of K roughly doubles as the pressure is raised from 1 atmosphere to 3500 atmosphere).

2. The bulk modulus of elasticity (K) of the fluid is affected by the temperature of the fluid. In the case of *liquids* there is a *decrease* of K with *increase of temperature.* However, for gases since pressure and temperature are inter-related and as temperature increases, pressure also increases, an *increase in temperature* results in an *increase* in the value of K.

3. At NTP (normal temperature and pressure):

$K_{water} = 2.07 \times 10^6$ kN/m², $\qquad K_{air} = 101.3$ kN/m²

Example 1.37. *When the pressure of liquid is increased from 3.5 MN/m² to MN/m² its volume is found to decrease by 0.08 percent. What is the bulk modulus of elasticity of the liquid?*

Solution. Initial pressure = 3.5 MN/m²

Final pressure = 6.5 MN/m²

$\therefore$ Increase in pressure, dp = 6.5 – 3.5 = 3.0 MN/m²

Decrease in volume = 0.08 percent $\therefore -\frac{dV}{V} = \frac{0.08}{100}$

Bulk modulus (K) is given by:

$$K = \frac{dp}{-\frac{dV}{V}} = \frac{3 \times 10^6}{\frac{0.08}{100}} = 3.75 \times 10^9 \text{ N/m}^2 \text{ or } 3.75 \text{ GN/m}^2$$

Hence, K = **3.75 GN/m² (Ans.)**

Example 1.38. *When a pressure of 20.7 MN/m² is applied to 100 litres of a liquid its volume decreases by 1 litre. Find the bulk modulus of the liquid and identify this liquid.*

Solution. Net pressure applied, dp = 20.7 MN/m²

Decrease in volume, $dV = 1$ litre

Initial volume, $V = 100$ litres $\therefore \quad -\frac{dV}{V} = \frac{1}{100}$

Bulk modulus K:

$$K = -\frac{dp}{-dV/V} = \frac{20.7 \times 10^6}{1/100} = 20.7 \times 10^8 \text{ N/m}^2 = 2.07 \text{ GN/m}^2$$

i.e., $K = $ **2.07 GN/m² (Ans.)**

Evidently the liquid is **water (Ans.).**

Example 1.39. *Define compressibility of a fluid. Gas A at 125 kPa (abs.) is compressed isothermally and gas B at 100 kPa (abs.) is compressed isentropically ($\gamma = 1.4$). Which gas is more compressible?* **(N.U.)**

Solution. Compressibility is *the measure of relative change of volume (For density) when the fluid is subjected to a pressure change.* It is the *reciprocal* of the bulks modulus of elasticity (K).

It is expressed mathetically as:

$$Z = \frac{1}{K} = \frac{-(dV/V)}{dp}$$

For an ideal gas, if the compression is isothermal, $Z = \frac{1}{p}$, and if the compression is isentropic, $Z = \frac{1}{\gamma p}$.

For the given **gas *A*,** $Z_A = \frac{1}{p} = \frac{1}{125} = 0.008 \text{ m}^2/\text{kN}$

For the **gas *B*,** $Z_B = \frac{1}{\gamma p} = \frac{1}{1.4 \times 100} = 0.007143 \text{ m}^2/\text{kN}$

Hence **gas *A* more compressible. (Ans.).**

Example 1.40. *Find an expression for isothermal bulk modulus of elasticity for a gas which obeys Van der Waals' law of state according to the equation:*

$$p = pRT\left[\frac{1}{1 - b\rho} - \frac{a\rho}{RT}\right]$$

where a, b are constants and p, ρ, R and T have their usual meanings. **(P.E.C.)**

Solution. Bulk modulus of elasticity,

$$K = -\frac{dp}{\left(\frac{dV}{V}\right)} = -V\frac{dp}{dV},$$

where, V is volume $= -\text{v}\frac{dp}{d\text{v}}$, v is specific volume.

Since, $\text{v} = \frac{1}{\rho}$ or $\rho\text{v} = 1$, $\frac{d\text{v}}{\text{v}} = -\frac{d\rho}{\rho}$

$\therefore \quad K = \rho\frac{dp}{d\rho}$; $p = \rho RT\left[\frac{1}{1 - b\rho} - \frac{a\rho}{RT}\right]$ ...*(Given)*

$$\therefore \quad \frac{dp}{d\rho} = RT\left[\frac{1}{1 - b\rho} - \frac{a\rho}{RT}\right] + \rho RT\left[\frac{b}{(1 - b\rho)^2} - \frac{a}{RT}\right] = \frac{RT}{1 - b\rho} - a\rho + \frac{b\rho RT}{(1 - b\rho)^2} - a\rho$$

$$= \frac{RT}{1-b\rho}\left[1+\frac{b\rho}{1-b\rho}\right] - 2a\rho = \frac{RT}{(1-b\rho)^2} - 2a\rho$$

and, $$K = \rho\frac{dp}{d\rho} = \frac{\rho RT}{(1-b\rho)^2} - 2a\rho^2$$ ... **Required expression (Ans.).**

1.10. VAPOUR PRESSURE

All liquids have a tendency to evaporate or vaporize (*i.e.*, to change from the liquid to the gaseous state). Molecules are continuously projected from the free surface to the atmosphere. These ejected molecules are in a gaseous state and exert their own partial vapour pressure on the liquid surface. This pressure is known as the vapour pressure of the liquid (p_v). If the surface above the liquid is confined, the partial vapour pressure exerted by the molecules increases till the rate at which the molecules re-enter the liquid is equal to the rate at which they leave the surface. When the equilibrium condition is reached, the vapour pressure is called saturation vapour pressure (p_{vs}).

The following points are worth noting:

1. If the pressure on the liquid surface is *lower than or equal to the saturation vapour pressure, boiling takes place.*

2. *Vapour pressure increases with the rise in temperature.*

3. Mercury has a *very low vapour pressure and hence,* it is an excellent fluid to be used in a *barometer.*

Table 1.1. Summary of Fluid Characteristics

Sr. No.	Characteristics	Symbol	Definition	Dimensions	Units
1.	*Mass density*	ρ	Mass per unit volume, $\frac{m}{V}$	ML^{-3}	kg/m^3
2.	*Weight density* (or *specific weight*)	w	Weight per unit volume, $\frac{W}{V}$	FL^{-3}	N/m^3
3.	*Specific volume*	v	Volume per unit mass $\frac{V}{m} = \frac{1}{\rho}$	L^3M^{-1}	m^3/kg
4.	*Specific gravity*	S	$\frac{\text{Specific weight of liquid}}{\text{Specific weight of pure water}} = \frac{w_{liquid}}{w_{water}}$		
5.	*Dynamic viscosity*	μ	Newton's law: $\tau = \mu.\frac{du}{dy}$	FTL^{-2}	N.s/m^2 poise, centipoise
6.	*Kinematic viscosity*	v	$v = \frac{\mu}{\rho}$	L^2T^{-1}	m^2/s stoke, centistoke
7.	*Bulk modulus*	K	$K = -\frac{\Delta p}{dV/V}$	FL^{-2}	N/m^2
8.	*Surface tension*	σ	Force per unit length	FL^{-1}	N/m
9.	*Vapour pressure*	p	$p_v = \frac{F}{A}$	FL^{-2}	N/m^2

Table 1.2. Properties of Some Common Fluids at 20°C and Atmospheric Pressure

Fluid	Mass density ρ(kN/m^3)	Specific weight w(kN/m^3)	Dynamic viscosity μ		Kinematic viscosity ν		Modulus of elasticity E(N/m^2)	Surface tension in contact with air, σ (N/m)	Vapour pressure (N/m^2)
			Poise	kg/ms	Stoke	m^2/s			
Air	1.208	0.01185	1.85×10^{-4}	1.85×10^{-5}	1.53×10^{-1}	1.53×10^{-5}	–	–	–
Benzene	860	8.434	0.007	7.00×1^{-4}	8.14×10^{-3}	8.14×10^{-7}	1.0356×10^{9}	0.0255	1.000×10^{4}
Castor oil	960	9.414	9.800	9.80×10^{-1}	1.00×10^{1}	1.00×10^{3}	1.441×10^{9}	0.0392	–
Carbon tetrachloride	1594	15.632	0.010	1.00×10^{-3}	6.04×10^{-3}	6.04×10^{-7}	1.104×10^{9}	0.0265	1.275×10^{4}
Ethyl alcohol	789	7.737	0.012	1.20×10^{-3}	1.52×10^{-2}	1.52×10^{-6}	1.118×10^{9}	0.0216	5.786×10^{3}
Glycerine	1260	12.356	8.350	8.35×10^{-1}	6.63	6.63×10^{-4}	4.354×10^{9}	0.0637	1.373×10^{-2}
Kerosene	800	7.845	0.020	2.00×10^{-3}	2.50×10^{-2}	2.50×10^{-6}	–	0.0235	–
Mercury	13550	132.880	0.016	1.60×10^{-3}	1.18×10^{-3}	1.18×10^{-7}	2.431×10^{10}	0.510	1.726×10^{-1}

HIGHLIGHTS

1. *Hydraulics* is that branch of Engineering science, which deals with water at rest or in motion.
2. *Fluid mechanics* may be defined as that branch of Engineering science which deals with the behaviour of fluid under the conditions of rest and motion.
3. A *fluid* is substance which is capable of flowing.
4. *Mass density* is the mass per unit volume whereas weight density (or specific weight) is the weight per unit volume at the standard temperature and pressure.
5. *Specific gravity* is the ratio of the specific weight of the liquid to the specific weight of a standard fluid. It is dimensionless and has no units.
6. *Viscosity* is the property of a fluid which determines its resistance to shearing stresses.

   Newton's law of viscosity states that the shear stress (τ) on a fluid element layer is directly proportional to the rate of shear strain. The constant of proportionality is called the co-efficient of viscosity.

   Mathematically, $$\tau = \mu \cdot \frac{du}{dy},$$

   where μ = co-efficient of dynamic viscosity, and $\frac{du}{dy}$ = rate of shear deformation or velocity gradient.

   Kinematic viscosity is the ratio between the dynamic viscosity and density of fluid. It is denoted by ν (nu).

   i.e., $$\nu = \frac{\mu}{\rho}$$
7. *Cohesion and adhesion:*

   Cohesion means intermolecular attraction between molecules of the same liquid.

   Adhesion means attraction between molecules of a liquid and the molecules of a solid boundary surface in contact with the liquid.
8. *Surface tension* (ρ) is caused by the force of cohesion at the free surface. It is usually expressed in N/m.

   Pressure inside:

   (*a*) Water droplet: $p = \frac{4\sigma}{d}$, (*b*) Soap bubble : $p = \frac{8\sigma}{d}$, and

   (c) Liquid jet: $p = \frac{2\sigma}{d}$ (where *d* stands for diameter).
9. *Capillarity* is a phenomenon by which a liquid (depending upon its specific gravity) rises into a thin glass tube or below its general level.

   $$h = \frac{4\sigma\cos\theta}{wd}$$

   where, h = Height of capillary rise,
   d = Diameter of the capillary tube,
   θ = Angle of contact of the water surface,
   σ = Surface tension per unit length, and
   w = Weight density (ρg).

10. *Compressibility* is the property by virtue of which fluid undergoes a change in volume under the action of external pressure. It is the *reciprocal* of bulk modulus of elasticity (K).

$$K = dp \text{ (increase of pressure)} / -\frac{dV}{V} \text{ (volumetric strain)}$$

$$\left(\text{compressibility} = \frac{1}{K}\right)$$

OBJECTIVE TYPE QUESTIONS

Choose the Correct Answer:

1. The branch of Engineering-science, which deals with water at rest or in motion is called
(*a*) hydraulics (*b*) fluid mechanic s
(*c*) applied mechanics (*d*) kinematics.

2. A solid can resist which of the following stresses?
(*a*) Tensile (*b*) Compressive
(*c*) Shear (*d*) All of the above.

3. .... possesses no definite volume and is compressible.
(*a*) Solid (*b*) Liquid
(*c*) Gas (*d*) Vapour.

4. A real practical fluid possesses which of the following?
(*a*) Viscosity (b) Surface tension
(c) Compressibility (d) density.

5. The ratio of the specific weight of the liquid to the specific weight of a standard fluid is known as
(*a*) specific volume (*b*) weight density
(*c*) specific gravity (*d*) viscosity.

6. The property of a fluid which determines its resistance to shearing stress is called
(*a*) viscosity (*b*) surface tension
(*c*) compressibility (*d*) none of the above.

7. Newton's law of viscosity is given by the relation:
(*a*) $\tau = \mu^2 \frac{du}{dy}$ (*b*) $\tau = \sqrt{\mu} \frac{du}{dy}$
(*c*) $\tau = \mu . \frac{du}{dy}$ (*d*) $\tau = (\mu)^{3/2} \frac{du}{dy}$

8. Fluids which do not follow the linear relationship between shear stress and rate of deformation are termed as .... fluids.
(*a*) Newtonian (*b*) Non-Newtonian
(*c*) dilatent (*d*) ideal

9. The printer's ink is an example of
(*a*) Newtonian fluid
(*b*) Non-Newtonian
(*c*) Thyxotropic substance
(*d*) Elastic solid.

10. The viscosity of liquids ..... with increase in temperature.
(*a*) decreases
(*b*) increases
(*c*) first decreases and then increases
(*d*) first increases and then decreases.

11. Surface tension is caused by the force of ..... at the free surface.
(*a*) cohesion (*b*) adhesion
(*c*) both (*a*) and (*b*) (*d*) none of the above.

12. Which of the following is an example of phenomenon of surface tension?
(*a*) Rain drops
(*b*) Rise of sap in a tree
(*c*) Break up of liquid jets
(*d*) All of the above.

13. Surface tension is expressed in
(*a*) N/m (*b*) N/m^2
(*c*) N^2/m (*d*) N/m^3.

14. Pressure inside a water droplet is given by the relation
(*a*) $p = \frac{4\sigma}{d}$ (*b*) $p = \frac{3\sigma}{d}$
(*c*) $p = \frac{8\sigma}{d}$ (*d*) $p = \frac{16\sigma}{d}$

15. ...... is a phenomenon by which a liquid rises into a thin glass tube above or below its general level.
(*a*) Surface tension (*b*) Capillarity
(*c*) Cohesion (*d*) Adhesion.

16. The capillary rise of water in the glass tube is given by
(*a*) $h = \frac{2\sigma}{wd}$ (*b*) $h = \frac{3\sigma}{wd}$
(*c*) $h = \frac{4\sigma}{wd}$ (*d*) $h = \frac{6\sigma}{wd}$

17. Elasticity of fluids is measured in terms of
(*a*) Young's modulus of elasticity
(*b*) shear modulus of elasticity
(*c*) bulk modulus of elasticity
(*d*) none of the above.

18. Compressibility is the reciprocal of
(*a*) bulk modulus of elasticity
(b) shear modulus of elasticity
(*c*) Young's modulus of elasticity
(*d*) any of the above.

19. Bulk modulus of elasticity is the ratio of
(*a*) tensile stress to tensilestrain
(*b*) compressive stress to compressive strain
(*c*) compressive stress to volumetric strain
(*d*) none of the above.

20. The value of bulk modulus of elasticity .... with increase of pressure.
(*a*) increases (*b*) decreases
(*c*) either of the above
(*d*) none of the above.

ANSWERS

1. (*a*)	**2.** (*d*)	**3.** (*c*)	**4.** (*e*)	**5.** (*c*)	**6.** (*a*)
7. (*c*)	**8.** (*b*)	**9.** (*c*)	**10.** (*a*)	**11.** (*a*)	**12.** (*d*)
13. (*a*)	**14.** (*a*)	**15.** (*b*)	**16.** (*c*)	**17.** (*c*)	**18.** (*a*)
19. (*c*)	**20.** (*a*)				

THEORETICAL QUESTIONS

1. Define the following:
(*i*) Hydraulics (*ii*) Fluid mechanics
(*iii*) Fluid (*iv*) Aerostatics.

2. What is a fluid? How are fluids classified?

3. What is the difference between an ideal and a real fluid?

4. Name some important properties of liquids.

5. Explain briefly the following terms:
(*i*) Mass density (*ii*) Weight density
(*iii*) Specific volume (*iv*) Specific gravity.

6. What do you mean by the term 'Viscosity'?

7. State and explain the Newton's law of viscosity.

8. What is dynamic viscosity? What are its units?

9. What is kinematic viscosity? What are its units?

10. What is a Newtonian fluid?

11. Define the term vapour pressure. How does it vary with temperature?

12. What is the difference between cohesion and adhesion?

13. Explain briefly the following:
(*i*) Surface tension, and
(*ii*) Compressibility.

14. What is capillarity? Derive expression for height of capillary rise.

UNSOLVED EXAMPLES

1. Determine the mass density, specific volume and specific weight of a liquid whose specific gravity is 0.85.
[**Ans.** 850 kg/m^3, 0.00118 m^3/kg, 8350 N/m^3]

2. A liquid has a specific gravity of 1.9 and kinematic viscosity of 6 stokes. What is its dynamic viscosity? [**Ans.** 11.38 poise]

3. The space between two parallel plates 5 mm apart is filled with crude oil. A force of 2 N is required to drag the upper plate at a constant velocity of 0.8 m/s. The lower plate is stationary. The area of the upper plate is 0.09 m^2. Determine: (*i*) The dynamic viscosity, and (*ii*) the kinematic viscosity of the oil in stokes if the specific gravity of oil is 0.9. [**Ans.** (*i*) 1.39 poise, (*ii*) 1.52 stokes]

4. A plate has an area of 1 m^2. It slides down an inclined plane, having angle of inclination 45° to the horizontal, with a velocity of 0.5 m/s. The thickness of oil film between the plane and the plate is 1 mm. Find the viscosity of the fluid if the weight of the plate is 70.72 N.
[**Ans.** 1 poise]

5. The velocity distribution over a plate is given by

$$u = \frac{3}{2}y - \frac{1}{2}y^2$$

where, u = velocity, m/s, and
y = distance from the plate boundary, m.
If the viscosity of the fluid is 8 poise find the

shear stress at the plate boundary and at $y = 0.15$ m from the plate. **[Ans.** 1.20 N/m^2, 1.08 N/m^2**]**

6. A flat plate weighing 0.45 kN has a surface area of 0.1 m^2. It slides down an inclined plane at 30° to the horizontal, at a constant speed of 3 m/s. If the inclined plane is lubricated with an oil of viscosity 0.1 N.s/m^2, find the thickness of the oil film. **[Ans. 0.133 mm]**

7. A flat thin plate is dragged at a constant velocity of 4 m/s on the top of a 5 mm deep liquid layer of viscosity 20 centipoise. If the area of the plate is 1 m^2 find the drag force.

   Assume variation of velocity in the liquid to be linear. **[Ans.** 16 N**]**

8. A square metal plate 1.5 m side and 1.5 mm thick weighing 50 N is to be lifted through a vertical gap of 25 mm of infinite extent. The oil in the air gap has a specific gravity of 0.95 and viscosity of 2.5 N.s/m^2. If the metal plate is to be lifted at a constant speed of 0.1 m/s find the force and power required. **[Ans. 145.7 N, 14.57 W]**

9. Inside a 60 mm diameter cylinder a piston of 59 mm diameter rotates concentrically. Both the cylinder and piston are 80 mm long. If the space between the cylinder and piston is filled with oil of viscosity of 0.3 N.s/m^2 and a torque of 1.5 Nm is applied, find:

   (*i*) The r.p.m. of the piston, and

   (*ii*) The power required.

   [Ans. (*i*) 1850 r.p.m. (*ii*) 290.5 W]

10. Two large fixed parallel planes are 240 mm apart. The space between the surfaces is filled with oil of viscosity 0.81 N.s/m^2. A flat thin plate 0.5 m^2 area moves through the oil at a velocity of 0.6 m/s. Calculate the drag force (*i*) when the plate is equidistant from both the planes, and (*ii*) when the thin plate is at a distance of 80 mm from one of the plane surfaces.

    [Ans. (*i*) 40.5 N (*ii*) 45.54 N]

11. A cylinder of 100 mm diameter and 300 mm length rotates about a vertical axis inside a fixed cylindrical tube of 105 mm diameter and 300 mm length. If the space between the tube and the cylinder is filled with liquid of dynamic viscosity of 0.125 N.s/m^2, determine the speed of rotation of the cylinder which will be obtained if an external torque of 1 Nm is applied to it.

    [Ans. 81.03 r.p.m.]

12. Determine the mass density, specific weight, and specific volume of CO_2 contained in a vessel at a pressure of 800 kN/m^2 and temperature 25°C.

    [Ans. 14.2 kg/m^3, 139.4 N/m^3, 0.0703 m^3/kg]

13. A soap bubble 50 mm diameter has an internal pressure in excess of the outside pressure of 25 N/m^2. Calculate tension in the soap film.

    [Ans. 0.156 N/m]

14. Air is introduced through a nozzle into a tank of water (at 20°C) to form a stream of bubbles. If the process requires 2.5 mm diameter bubbles to be formed, by how much the air pressure at the nozzle must exceed that of surrounding water.

    Take surface tension of water at 20°C = 0.0735 N/m. **[Ans. 117.4 N/m^2]**

15. Determine the minimum size of glass tubing that can be used to measure water level, if the capillary rise in the tube is not to exceed 0.25 mm. Take surface tension of water in contact with air as 0.0735 N/m. **[Ans. 120 mm]**

16. A U-tube is made up of two capillaries of bore 1 mm and 2 mm respectively. The tube is held vertically and is partially filled with liquid of surface tension 0.05 N/m and zero contact angle. Calculate the mass density of the liquid if the estimated difference in the level of two menisci is 12.5 mm. **[Ans. 816 kg/m^3]**

17. Determine the bulk modulus of elasticity of a liquid, if the pressure of the liquid is increased from 7 MN/m^2 to 13 MN/m^2. The volume of liquid decreases by 0.15%. **[Ans. 4 GN/m^2]**

18. A 20 mm wide gap between two vertical plane surfaces is filled with an oil of specific gravity 0.85 and dynamic viscosity 2.5 N.s/m^2. A metal plate 1.25 m × 1.25 m × 2 mm thick and weighing 30 N is placed midway in the gap. Determine the force required to lift the plate with a constant velocity of 0.18 m/s. **[Ans. 160.2 N]**

Chapter 2

PRESSURE MEASUREMENT

2.1. PRESSURE OF A LIQUID

When a fluid is contained in a vessel, it exerts force at all points on the sides and bottom and top of the container. The *force per unit area is called* **pressure.**

If, P = The force, and

A = Area on which the force acts; then

intensity of pressure, $p = \dfrac{P}{A}$ ...(2.1)

The pressure of a fluid on a surface will *always act normal to the surface*.

2.2. PRESSURE HEAD OF A LIQUID

A liquid is subjected to pressure due to its own weight, this pressure increases as the depth of the liquid increases.

Consider a vessel containing liquid, as shown in Fig. 2.1. The liquid will exert pressure on all sides and bottom of the vessel. Now, let cylinder be made to stand in the liquid, as shown in the figure.

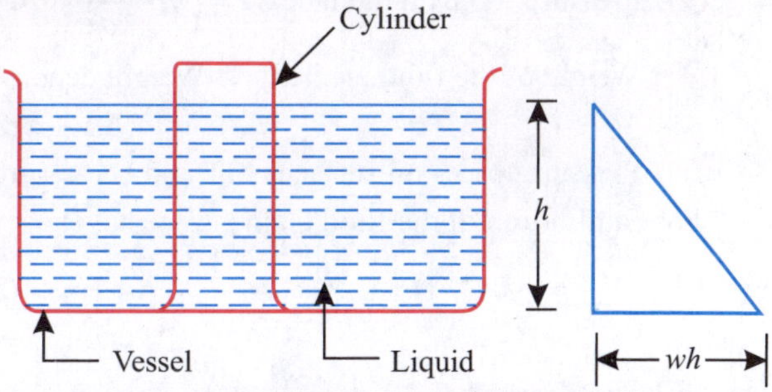

Fig. 2.1. Pressure head.

Let, h = Height of liquid in the cylinder,

A = Area of the cylinder base,

w = Specific weight of the liquid,

and, p = Intensity of pressure.

Now, Total pressure on the base of the cylinder = Weight of liquid in the cylinder

i.e., $$p.\,A. = wAh$$

$$p = \frac{wAh}{A} = wh \qquad i.e.,\ p = wh \qquad ...(2.2)$$

As $p = wh$, *the intensity of pressure in a liquid due to its depth will vary directly with depth.*

As the pressure at any point in a liquid depends on height of the free surface above that point, it is sometimes convenient to express a liquid pressure by the *height of the free surface* which would cause the pressure, *i.e.*,

$$h = \frac{p}{w} \qquad \text{[from eqn. (2.2)]}$$

The height of the free surface above any point is known as the *static head* at that point. In this case, static head is h.

Hence, the intensity of pressure of a liquid may be expressed in the following two ways:

1. As a force per unit area (*i.e.*, N/mm^2, N/m^2), and
2. As an equivalent static head (*i.e.*, metres, mm or cm of liquid).

Alternatively:

Pressure variation in fluid at rest:

In order to determine the pressure at any point in a fluid at rest "*hydrostatic law*" is used; the law states as follows:

"The rate of increase of pressure in a vertically downward direction must be equal to the specific weight of the fluid at that point."

The proof of the law is as follows.

Refer to Fig. 2.2

Let, p = Intensity of pressure on face LM,

ΔA = Cross-sectional area of the element,

Z = Distance of the fluid element from free surface, and

ΔZ = Height of the fluid element.

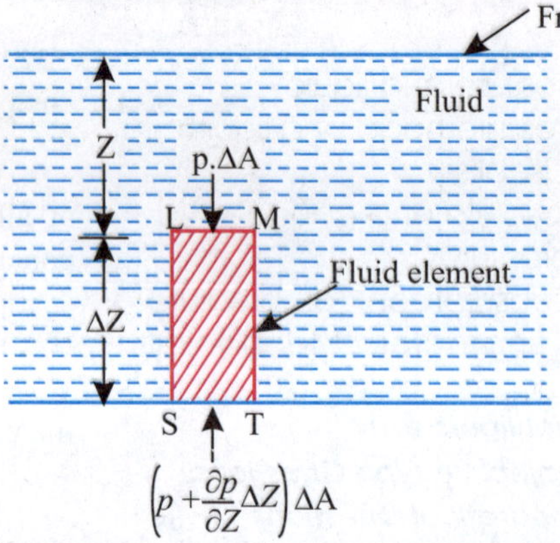

Fig. 2.2. Forces acting on a fluid element.

The forces acting on the element are:

(*i*) Pressure force on the face $LM = p \times \Delta A$ ...(acting downward)

(*ii*) Pressure force on the face $ST = \left(p + \frac{\partial p}{\partial Z} \times \Delta Z\right) \times \Delta A$ ... (acting upward)

(*iii*) Weight of the fluid element $=$ Weight density $\times$ volume $= w \times (\Delta A \times \Delta Z)$

(*iv*) Pressure forces on surfaces MT and LS ..... are equal and opposite.

For equilibrium of the fluid element, we have:

$$p \times \Delta A - \left[p + \frac{\partial p}{\partial Z} \times \Delta Z\right] \times \Delta A + w \times (\Delta A \times \Delta Z) = 0$$

or, $$p \times \Delta A - p \times \Delta A - \frac{\partial p}{\partial Z} \times \Delta Z \times \Delta A + w \times \Delta A \times \Delta Z = 0$$

or, $$\frac{\partial p}{\partial Z}\Delta Z \times \Delta A + w \times \Delta A \times \Delta Z = 0$$

or, $$\frac{\partial p}{\partial Z} = w \text{ (cancelling } \Delta Z \times \Delta A \text{ from both the sides)}$$

or, $$\frac{\partial p}{\partial Z} = \rho \times g \qquad (\because w = \rho \times g) \qquad ...(2.3)$$

Eqn. (2.3.) states *that rate of increase of pressure in a vertical direction is equal to weight density of the fluid at that point*. This is "**hydrostatic law**".

On integrating the eqn. (2.3), we get:

$$\int dp = \int \rho g . dZ$$

or, $$p = \rho g. \quad Z(= wZ) \quad ...(2.4)$$

where, p is the pressure above atmospheric pressure.

From eqn. (2.4), we have:

$$Z = \frac{p}{\rho.g}\left(= \frac{p}{w}\right) \quad ... (2.5)$$

Here Z is known as *pressure head*.

Example 2.1. *Find the pressure at a depth of 15 m below the free surface of water in a reservoir.*

Solution. Depth of water, $h = 15$ m

Specific weight of water, $w = 9.81$ kN/m^3

Pressure p:

We know that, $p = wh = 9.81 \times 15 = 147.15$ kN/m^2

i.e., $p = 147.15$ kN/m^2 = **147.15 kPa (Ans.)**

Example 2.2. *Find the height of water column corresponding to a pressure of 54 kN/m^2.*

Solution. Intensity of pressure, $p = 54$ kN/m^2

Specific weight of water, $w = 9.81$ kN/m^3

Height of water column, h:

Using the relation: $p = wh;\ h = \frac{p}{w} = \frac{54}{9.81} =$ **5.5 m (Ans.)**

2.3. PASCAL'S LAW

The **Pascal's law** states as follows :

"The intensity of pressure at any point in a liquid at rest, is the same in all directions".

Proof. Let us consider a very small wedge shaped element LMN of a liquid, as shown in Fig. 2.3.

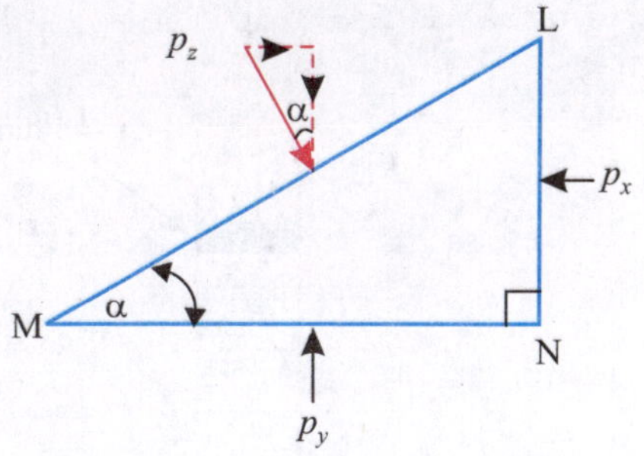

Fig. 2.3. Pressure on a fluid element at rest.

Let, p_x = Intensity of horizontal pressure on the element of liquid,

p_y = Intensity of vertical pressure on the element of liquid,

p_z = Intensity of pressure on the diagonal of the right angled triangular element,

α = Angle of the element of the liquid,

P_x = Total pressure on the vertical side LN of the liquid,

P_y = Total pressure on the horizontal side MN of the liquid, and

P_z = Total pressure on the diagonal LM of the liquid.

Now, $$P_x = p_x \times LN \quad ...(i)$$

and, $$P_y = p_y \times MN \quad ...(ii)$$

and, $$P_z = p_z \times LM \quad ...(iii)$$

As the element of the liquid is at rest, therefore the *sum of horizontal and vertical components of the liquid pressures must be equal to zero.*

Resolving the forces *horizontally*:

$$P_z \sin \alpha = P_x$$

$$p_z \, . \, LM. \sin\alpha = p_x \, . \, LN \qquad (\because P_z = p_z . LM)$$

But, $\quad LM \, . \sin\alpha = LN$ ... From Fig 2.3

$\therefore \quad p_z = p_x$ ...(*iv*)

Resolving the forces *vertically*:

$$P_z .\cos\alpha = P_y - W$$

(where, W = weight of the liquid element)

Since the element is very small, neglecting its weight, we have:

$$P_z \cos\alpha = P_y \quad \text{or} \quad p_z \, . \, LM \cos\alpha = p_y \, .MN$$

But, $\quad LM \cos\alpha = MN$ ...From Fig 2.3

$\therefore \quad p_z = p_y$ ...(*v*)

From (*iv*) and (*v*), we get: $p_x = p_y = p_z$,

which is independent of α.

Hence, at *any point in a fluid at rest the intensity of pressure is exerted equally in all directions, which is called* **Pascal's law.**

Example 2.3. *The diameters of ram and plunger of an hydraulic press are 200 mm and 30 mm respectively. Find the weight lifted by the hydraulic press when the force applied at the plunger is 400 N.*

Solution. Diameter of the ram, D = 200 mm = 0.2 m

Diameter of the plunger, d = 30 mm = 0.03 m

Force on the plunger, F = 400 N

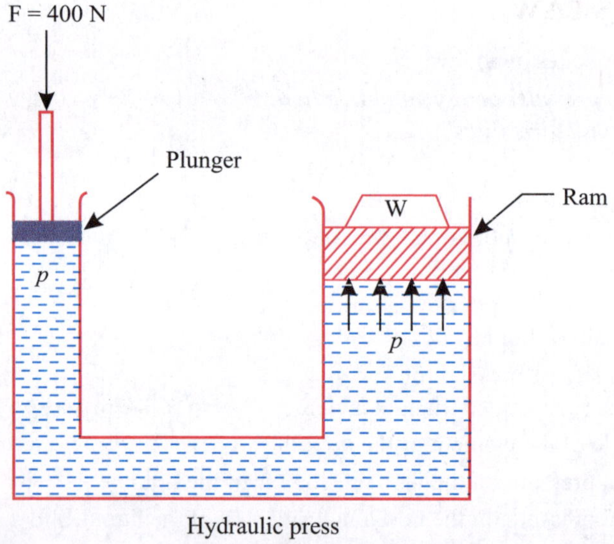

Fig. 2.4

Load lifted, W:

$$\text{Area of ram, } A = \frac{\pi}{4} D^2 = \frac{\pi}{4} \times 0.2^2 = 0.0314 \text{ m}^2$$

$$\text{Area of plunger, } a = \frac{\pi}{4} d^2 = \frac{\pi}{4} \times 0.03^2 = 7.068 \times 10^{-4} \text{ m}^2$$

Intensity of pressure due to plunger,

$$p = \frac{F}{a} = \frac{400}{7.068 \times 10^{-4}} = 5.66 \times 10^5 \text{ N/m}^2$$

Since the intensity of pressure will be equally transmitted (due to Pascal's law), therefore the intensity of pressure at the ram is also

$$= p = 5.66 \times 10^5 \text{ N/m}^2$$

But intensity of pressure at the ram $= \dfrac{\text{Weight}}{\text{Area of ram}} = \dfrac{W}{A} = \dfrac{W}{0.0314} \text{ N/m}^2$

$\therefore \quad \dfrac{W}{0.0314} = 5.66 \times 10^5$ or $W = 0.0314 \times 5.66 \times 10^5$ N $= 17.77 \times 10^3$ N or **17.77 kN (Ans.)**

Example 2.4. *For the hydraulic jack shown in Fig. 2.5 find the load lifted by the large piston when a force of 400 N is applied on the small piston. Assume the specific weight of the liquid in the jack is 9810 N/m³.*

Solution. Diameter of small piston, $d = 30$ mm $= 0.03$ m

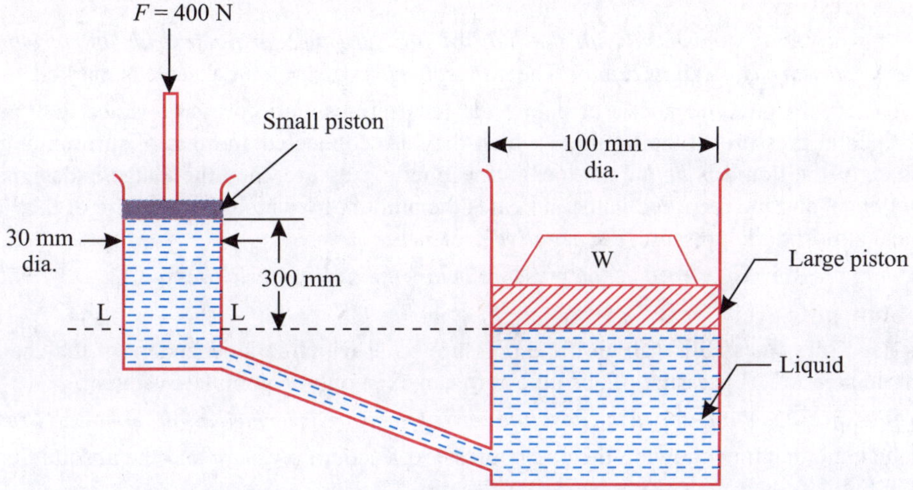

Fig. 2.5

Area of small piston, $a = \dfrac{\pi}{4} d^2 = \dfrac{\pi}{4} \times 0.03^2 = 7.068 \times 10^{-4} \text{ m}^2$

Diameter of the large piston, $D = 100$ mm $= 0.1$ m

Area of large piston, $A = \dfrac{\pi}{4} D^2 = \dfrac{\pi}{4} \times 0.1^2 = 7.854 \times 10^{-3} \text{ m}^2$

Force on small piston, $F = 400$ N

Load lifted, *W*:

Pressure intensity on small piston, $p = \dfrac{F}{a} = \dfrac{400}{7.068 \times 10^{-4}} = 5.66 \times 105 \text{ N/m}^2$

Pressure intensity at section *LL*,

$$p_{LL} = \frac{F}{a} + \text{Pressure intensity due to height of 300 mm of liquid}$$

$$= \frac{F}{a} + wh = 5.66 \times 10^5 + 9810 \times \frac{300}{1000}$$

$$= 5.66 \times 10^5 + 2943 = 5.689 \times 10^5 \text{ N/m}^2$$

Pressure intensity transmitted to the large piston = 5.689×10^5 N/m^2

$$\text{Force on the large piston} = \text{Pressure intensity} \times \text{area of large piston}$$
$$= 5.689 \times 10^5 \times 7.854 \times 10^{-3} = 4468 \text{ N}$$

Hence, *load lifted by the large piston* = **4468 N (Ans.)**

2.4. ABSOLUTE AND GAUGE PRESSURES

Atmospheric pressure:

The atmospheric air exerts a normal pressure upon all surfaces with which it is in contact, and it is known as *atmospheric pressure*. The atmospheric pressure is also known as *'Barometric pressure'*.

The atmospheric pressure at sea level (above absolute zero) is called *'Standard atmospheric pressure'*.

Note. The local atmospheric pressure may be a little lower than these values if the place under question is higher than sea level, and higher values if the place is lower than sea level, due to the corresponding decrease or increase of the column of air standing, respectively.

Gauge pressure:

It is the pressure, measured with the help of pressure measuring instrument, in which the atmospheric pressure is taken as datum. The *atmospheric pressure* on the scale is marked as *zero.*

Gauges record pressure above or below the local atmospheric pressure, since they measure the difference in pressure of the liquid to which they are connected and that of surrounding air. If the pressure of the liquid is *below* the local atmospheric pressure, then the gauge is designated as '*vacuum gauge*' and the recorded value indicates the amount by which the pressure of the liquid is *below* local atmospheric pressure, i.e. *negative pressure.*

(*Vacuum pressure* is defined as the pressure *below the atmospheric pressure*).

Absolute pressure:

It is necessary to establish an absolute pressure scale which is independent of the changes in atmospheric pressure. A pressure of absolute zero can exist only in complete vacuum.

Any pressure measured above the absolute zero of pressure is termed as an '**absolute pressure**'.

A schematic diagram showing the gauge pressure, vacuum pressure and the absolute pressure is given in Fig. 2.6.

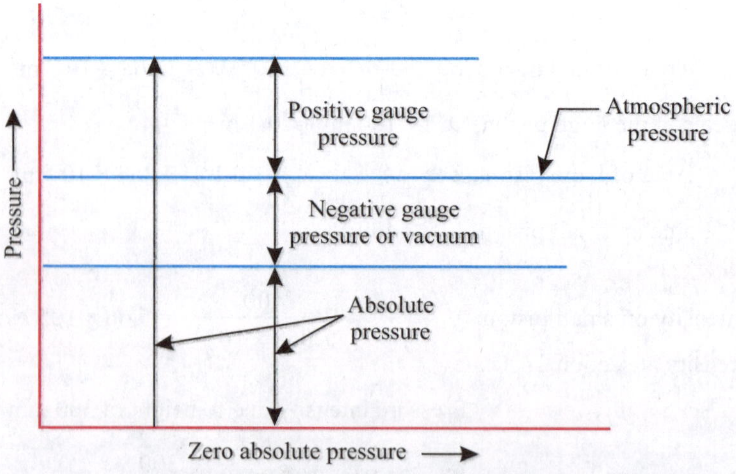

Fig. 2.6. Relationship between pressures.

Mathematically:

1. *Absolute pressure* = Atmospheric pressure + gauge pressure

   i.e., $p_{abs} = p_{atm} + p_{gauge}$

2. *Vacuum pressure* = Atmospheric pressure – absolute pressure

Units for pressure:

The fundamental S.I. unit of pressure is newton per square metre (N/m^2). This is also known as *Pascal.*

Low pressures are often expressed in terms of mm of water or mm of mercury. This is an abbreviated way of saying that the pressure is such that will support a liquid column of stated height.

Note. When the local atmospheric pressure is not given in a problem, it is taken as 100 kN/m^2 or 10 m of water for simplicity of calculations.

Standard atmospheric pressure has the following equivalent values:

101.3 kN/m^2 or 101.3 kPa; 10.3 m of water; 760 mm of mercury; 1013 mb (millibar) ≃ 1 bar ≃100 kPa = 10^5 N/m^2.

Example 2.5. *Given that:*

Barometer reading = 740 mm of mercury;

Specific gravity of mercury = 13.6; Intensity of pressure = 40 kPa.

Express the intensity of pressure in S.I. units, both gauge and absolute.

Solution. Intensity of pressure, p = 40 kPa

Gauge pressure:

(*i*) $p = 40 \text{ kPa} = 40 \text{ kN/m}^2 = 0.4 \times 10^5 \text{ N/m}^2 =$ **0.4 bar (Ans.)**

(1 bar = 10^5 N/m^2)

(*ii*) $h = \dfrac{p}{w} = \dfrac{0.4 \times 10^5}{9.81 \times 10^3}$ = **4.077 m of water (Ans.)**

(*iii*) $h = \dfrac{p}{w} = \dfrac{0.4 \times 10^5}{9.81 \times 10^3 \times 13.6}$ = **0.299 m of mercury (Ans.)**

$$\left[\begin{array}{l}\text{Where, } w = \text{specific weight;}\\ \text{For water : } w = 9.81 \text{ kN/m}^3\\ \text{For mercury : } w = 9.81 \times 13.6 \text{kN/m}^3\end{array}\right]$$

Absolute pressure:

Barometer reading (atmospheric pressure)

$$= 740 \text{ mm of mercury} = 740 \times 13.6 \text{ mm of water}$$

$$= \frac{740 \times 13.6}{1000} = 10.6 \text{ m of water}$$

Absolute pressure ($p_{abs.}$) = Atmospheric pressure ($p_{atm.}$) + gauge pressure (p_{gauge}).

$\therefore \quad p_{abs}$ = 10.06 + 4.077 = **14.137 m of water (Ans.)**

= 14.137 × (9.81 × 10^3) = **1.38 × 10^5 N/m^2 (Ans.)** ($p = wh$)

= **1.38 bar (Ans.)** (1 bar = 10^5 N/m^2)

$= \dfrac{14.137}{13.6}$ = **1.039 m of mercury. (Ans.)**

Example 2.6. *Calculate the pressure at a point 5 m below the free water surface in a liquid that has a variable density given by relation:*

$$\rho = (350 + Ay)\ kg/m^3$$

where, $A = 8\ kg/m^4$ and y is the distance in metres measured from the free surface.

Solution. As per hydrostatic equation

$$dp = \rho.g.dy = g\,(350 + Ay)dy$$

Integrating both sides, we get:

$$\int dp = \int_0^5 g(350 + Ay)\,dy = g\int_0^5 (350 + 8y)\,dy$$

$$p = g\left|350y + 8 \times \frac{y^2}{2}\right|_0^5$$

$$= 9.81\left(350 \times 5 + 8 \times \frac{5^2}{2}\right) = 18148\ N/m^2 \simeq \mathbf{18.15\ kN/m^2}$$

(Ans.)

Example 2.7. *On the suction side of a pump a gauge shows a negative pressure of 0.35 bar. Express this pressure in terms of:*

(i) Intensity of pressure, kPa,
(ii) N/m^2 absolute,
(iii) Metres of water gauge,
(iv) Metres of oil (specific gravity 0.82) absolute, and
(v) Centimetres of mercury gauge,

Take atmospheric pressure as 76 cm of Hg and relative density of mercury as 13.6.

Solution. *Given*: Reading of the *vacuum* gauge = 0.35 bar

(*i*) Intensity of pressure, kPa:

$$\text{Gauge reading} = 0.35\ \text{bar} = 0.35 \times 10^5\ N/m^2$$
$$= 0.35 \times 10^5\ Pa = \mathbf{35\ kPa}\ \textbf{(Ans.)}$$

(*ii*) N/m^2 absolute:

$$\text{Atmospheric pressure, } p_{atm.} = 76\ \text{cm of Hg}$$
$$= (13.6 \times 9810) \times \frac{76}{100} = 101396\ N/m^2$$

$$\text{Absolute pressure} = \text{Atmospheric pressure} - \textit{Vacuum}\ \text{pressure}$$
$$p_{abs.} = p_{atm} - p_{vac.}$$
$$= 101396 - 35000 = \mathbf{66396\ N/m^2\ absolute}\ \textbf{(Ans.)}$$

(*iii*) Metres of water gauge:

$$p = \rho g h = wh$$

$$\therefore \quad h_{water}\,(\text{gauge}) = \frac{p}{w} = \frac{0.35 \times 10^5}{9810} = \mathbf{3.567\,m}\ (\textit{gauge})\ \textbf{(Ans.)}$$

(*iv*) Metres of oil (sp. gr. = 0.82) absolute:

$$h_{oil}\,(\text{absolute}) = \frac{66396}{0.82 \times 9810} = \mathbf{8.254\ m\ of\ water}\ (\textit{absolute})\ \textbf{(Ans.)}$$

(*v*) Centimetres of mercury gauge:

$$h_{mercury}(\text{gauge}) = \frac{0.35 \times 10^5}{13.6 \times 9810} = 0.2623\ \text{m of mercury}$$

$$= \mathbf{26.236\ cm\ of\ mercury}\ \textbf{(Ans.)}$$

Example 2.8. *The inlet to pump is 10.5 m above the bottom of sump from which it draws water through a suction pipe. If the pressure at the pump inlet is not to fall below 28 kN/m² absolute, work out the minimum depth of water in the tank.*

Assume atmospheric pressure as 100 kPa.

Solution. *Given*: $p_{atm.} = 100$ kPa $= 100$ kN/m²; $p_{abs.} = 28$ kN/m².

Minimum depth of water in the tank:

Let, $p_{vac.}$ = The vacuum (suction) pressure at the pump inlet.

Then,
$$p_{vac.} = p_{atm.} - p_{abs.}$$
$$= (100 - 28) = 72 \text{ kN/m}^2 \quad \text{or} \quad 72000 \text{ N/m}^2$$

Further, let h be the distance between the pump inlet and free water surface in the sump. Invoking hydrostatic equation, we have:

$$p = wh$$
$$72000 = 9810 \times h$$

or,
$$h = \frac{72000}{9810} = 7.339 \text{ m}$$

∴ Minimum depth of water in the tank

$$= 10.5 - 7.339 = \mathbf{3.161 \text{ m}} \text{ (Ans.)}$$

Example 2.9. *A cylindrical tank of cross-sectional area 600 mm² and 2.6 m height is filled with water upto a height of 1.5 m and remaining with oil of specific gravity 0.78. The vessel is open to atmospheric pressure. Calculate:*

(i) Intensity of pressure at the interface.

(ii) Absolute and gauge pressures on the base of the tank in terms of water head, oil head and N/m².

(iii) The net force experienced by the base of the tank.

Assume atmospheric pressure as 1.0132 bar.

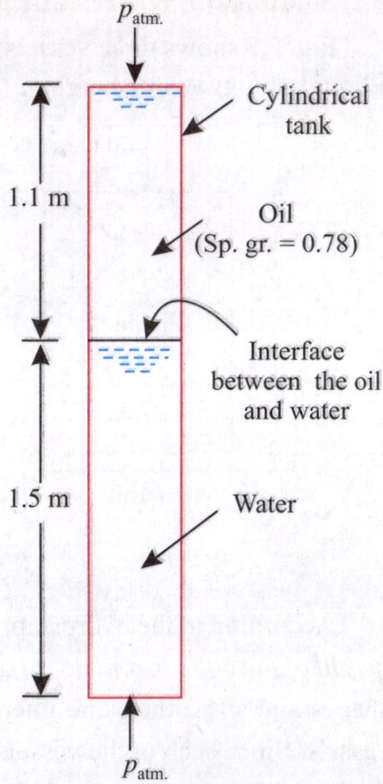

Fig. 2.7

Solution. *Given:* Area of cross-section of the tank, $A = 600$ mm² $= 600 \times 10^{-6}$; Sp.gr. of oil $= 0.78$; $p_{atm.} = 1.0132$ bar.

***(i)* Intensity of pressure at the interface:**

The pressure intensity at the interface between the oil and water is due to 1.1 m of oil and is given by:

$$p_{interface} = wh$$
$$= (0.78 \times 9810) \times 1.1$$
$$= \mathbf{8417 \text{ N/m}^2} \text{ (Ans.)}$$

***(ii)* Absolute and gauge pressures on the base of the tank:**

Pressure at the base of the tank

= Pressure at the interface (due to 1.1 m of oil) + pressure due to 1.5 m of water,

i.e.,
$$p_{base\,(gauge)} = 8417 + (9810 \times 1.5)$$
$$= \mathbf{23132 \text{ N/m}^2 \text{ (gauge)}} \text{ (Ans.)}$$
$$= \frac{23132}{9810} = \mathbf{2.358 \text{ m of water (gauge)}} \text{ (Ans.)}$$
$$= \frac{23132}{0.78 \times 9810} = \mathbf{3.023 \text{ m of oil (gauge)}} \text{ (Ans.)}$$

$$\text{Atmospheric pressure, } p_{atm.} = 1.0132 \text{ bar}$$
$$= 1.0132 \times 10^5 \text{ N/m}^2$$
$$= \frac{1.0132 \times 10^5}{9810} = 10.328 \text{ m of water}$$
$$= \frac{1.0132 \times 10^5}{0.78 \times 9810} = 13.241 \text{ m of oil}$$

Absolute pressure = Atmospheric pressure + gauge pressure

p_{base} (absolute) = 10.328 + 2.358 = **12.686 m of water (Ans.)**

= 13.241 + 3.023 = **16.264 m of oil (Ans.)**

= 101320 + 23132 = **124452 N/m² (Ans.)**

(*iii*) The net force experienced by the base of the tank:

$F (= P) = p_{base}$(gauge) × cross-sectional area

= $23132 \times 600 \times 10^{-6}$ = **13.879 N (Ans.)**

Example 2.10. (*a*) *What is hydrostatic paradox?*

(*b*) *A cylinder of 0.25 m diameter and 1.2 m height is fixed centrally on the top of a large cylinder of 0.9 m diameter and 0.8 m height. Both the cylinders are filled with water. Calculate:*

(*i*) *Total pressure at the bottom of the bigger cylinder, and*

(*ii*) *Weight of total volume of water.*

What is hydrostatic paradox between the two results and how this difference can be reconciled?

Solution. (*a*) Hydrostatic paradox:

Fig. 2.8 shows three vessels 1, 2 and 3 having the same area *A* at the bottom and each filled with a liquid upto the same height *h*.

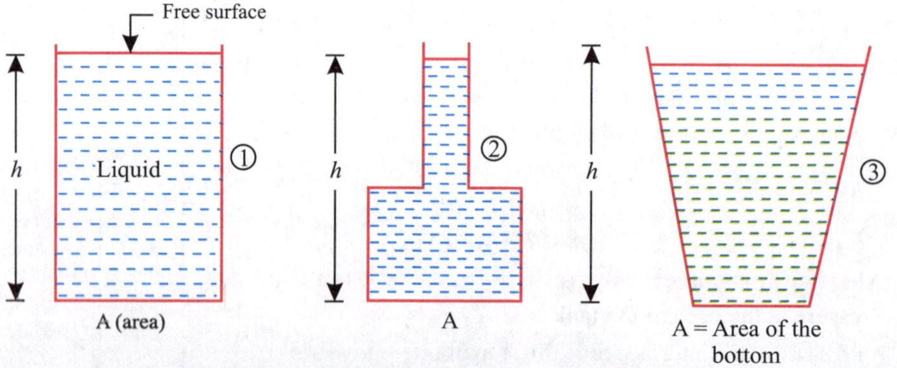

Fig. 2.8. Hydrostatic paradox.

According to the hydrostatic equation, $p = wh$; the intensity of pressure (p) *depends only on the height of the column and not at all upon the size of the column.* Thus, in all these vessels of different shapes and sizes, the same intensity of pressure would be exerted on the bottom of each of these vessels. Since each of the vessels has the same area *A* at the bottom, the pressure force $P = p \times A$ on the base of each vessel would be same. This is independent of the fact that the weight of liquid in each vessel is different. *This situation is referred to as* **hydrostatic paradox.**

(b) Area at the bottom:

$$A = \frac{\pi}{4} \times (0.9)^2 = 0.6362 \text{ m}^2$$

Intensity of pressure at the bottom

$$p = wh = 9810 \times (1.2 + 0.8)$$
$$= 19620 \text{ N/m}^2$$

Total pressure force at the bottom

$$P = p \times A = 19620 \times 0.6362 = 12482 \text{ N}$$

Weight of total volume of water contained in the cylinders,

$$W = w \times \text{volume of water}$$
$$= 9810 \left[\frac{\pi}{4} \times 0.9^2 \times 0.8 + \frac{\pi}{4} \times 0.25^2 \times 1.2\right]$$
$$= 5571 \text{ N}$$

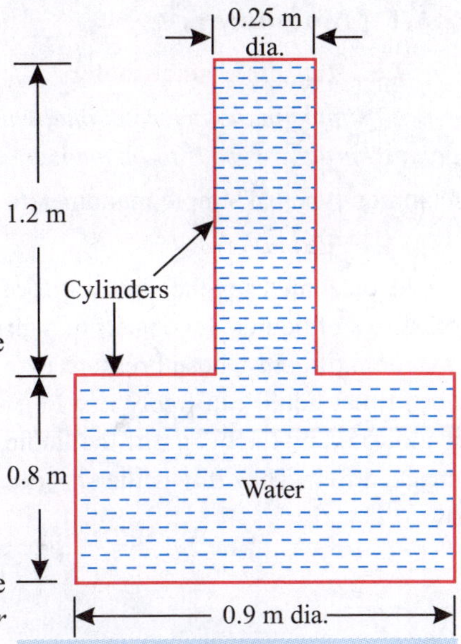

Fig. 2.9

From the above calculations it may be observed that the *total pressure force at the bottom of the cylinder is greater than the weight of total volume of water (W) contained in the cylinders. This is* **hydrostatic paradox.**

The following is the *explanation of the hydrostatic paradox*: Refer to Fig. 2.9.

Total pressure force on the bottom of bigger tank = 12482 N (downward). A reaction at the roof of the lower tank is caused by the upward force which equals,

$$wAh = 9810 \times \frac{\pi}{4}(0.9^2 - 0.25^2) \times 1.2 = 6911 \text{ N (upward)}$$

The distance h corresponding to depth of water in the cylinder fixed centrally on the top of larger cylinder.

Net downward force exerted by water = 12482 – 6911 = 5571 N and it equals the weight of water in the two cylinder.

2.5. MEASUREMENT OF PRESSURE

The pressure of a fluid may be measured by the following devices:

1. Manometers:

Manometers *are defined as the devices used for measuring the pressure at a point in a fluid by balancing the column of fluid by the same or another column of liquid.* These are classified as follows:

(*a*) Simple manometers:

(*i*) Piezometer, (*ii*) U-tube manometer, and (*iii*) Single column manometer.

(*b*) Differential manometers.

2. Mechanical gauges:

These are the devices in which the pressure is measured by balancing the fluid column by spring (elastic element) or dead weight. Generally these gauges are used for measuring *high pressure* and where *high precision is not required.* Some commonly used mechanical gauges are:

(*i*) Bourdon tube pressure gauge, (*ii*) Diaphragm pressure gauge,

(*iii*) Bellow pressure gauge, and (*iv*) Dead-weight pressure gauge.

2.5.1 Manometers

2.5.1.1. Simple manometers

A "simple manometer" is one which consists of a glass tube whose one end is connected to a point where pressure is to be measured and the other end remains open to atmosphere.

Common types of simple manometers are discussed below:

1. Piezometer:

A piezometer is the simplest form of manometer which can be used for measuring *moderate pressures* of liquids. It consists of a glass tube (Fig 2.10) inserted in the wall of a vessel or of a pipe, containing liquid whose pressure is to be measured. The tube extends vertically upward to such a height that liquid can freely rise in it without overflowing. The pressure at any point in the liquid is indicated by the height of the liquid in the tube above that point, which can be read on the scale attached to it. Thus if w is the specific weight of the liquid, then the pressure at point $A(p)$ is given by:

$$p = wh$$

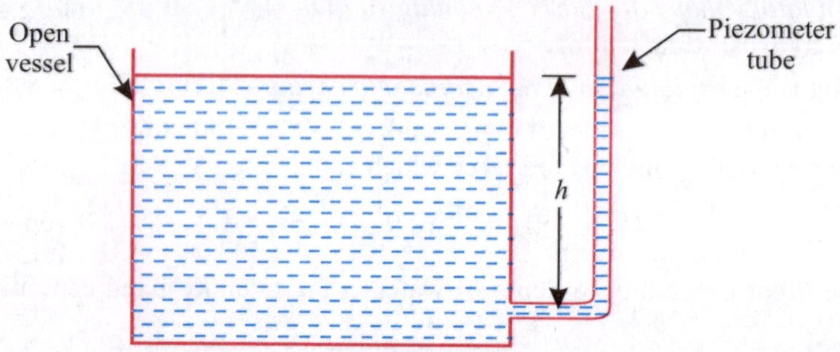

Fig. 2.10. (*a*) Piezometer tube fitted to open vessel.

Piezometers measure *gauge pressure only* (at the surface of the liquid), since the surface of the liquid in the tube is subjected to atmospheric pressure. A piezometer tube is *not suitable* for measuring *negative pressure*; as in such a case the air will enter in pipe through the tube.

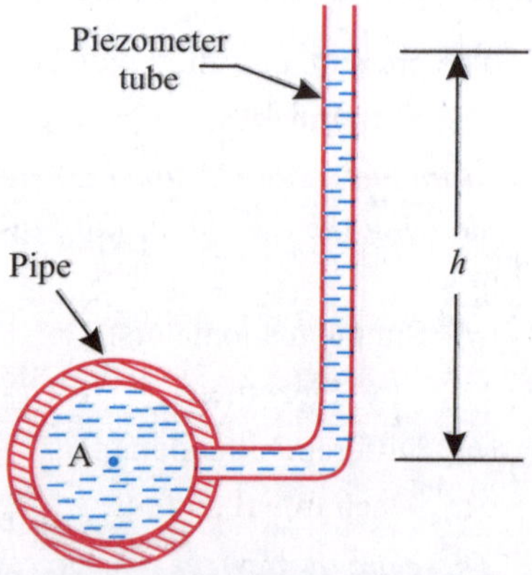

Fig. 2.10. (*b*) Piezometer tube fitted to a closed pipe.

2. U-tube manometer:

Piezometers cannot be employed when large pressures in the *lighter liquids* are to be measured, since this would require *very long tubes*, which cannot be handled conveniently. Furthermore gas pressures cannot be measured by the piezometers because a *gas forms no free atmospheric surface*. These limitations can be overcome by the use of U-tube manometers.

A U-tube manometer consists of a glass tube bent in U-shape, one end of which is connected to a point at which pressure is to be measured and other end remains open to the atmosphere as shown in Fig. 2.11.

(i) For positive pressure:

Refer to Fig. 2.11 (*a*).

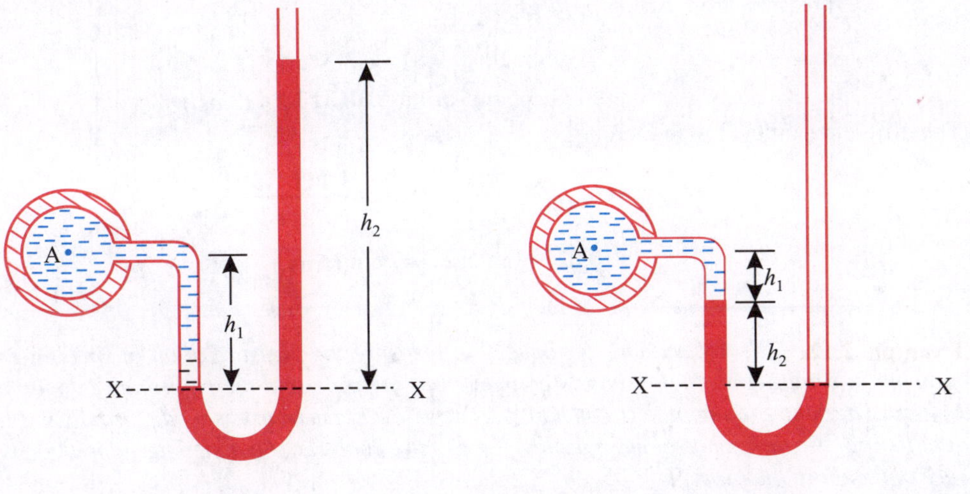

Fig. 2.11. U-tube manometer.

Let, *A* be the point at which pressure is to be measured. *X–X* is the datum line as shown in Fig. 2.11 (*a*).

Let, h_1 = Height of the light liquid in the left limb above the datum line,

h_2 = Height of the heavy liquid in the right limb above the datum line,

h = Pressure in pipe, expressed in terms of head,

S_1 = Specific gravity of the light liquid, and

S_2 = Specific gravity of the heavy liquid.

The pressures in the left limb and right limb above the datum line *X–X* are equal (*as the pressures at two points at the same level in a continuous homogeneous liquid are equal*).

Pressure head above *X–X* in the *left limb* = $h + h_1 S_1$

Pressure head above *X–X* in the *right limb* = $h_2 S_2$

Equating these two pressures, we get:

$$h + h_1 S_1 = h_2 S_2 \quad \text{or} \quad h = h_2 S_2 - h_1 S_1 \qquad ...(2.6)$$

(ii) For negative pressure:

Refer to Fig. 2.11 (*b*).

Pressure head above *X–X* in the *left limb* = $h + h_1 S_1 + h_2 S_2$

Pressure head above *X–X* in the *right limb* = 0.

Equating these two pressures, we get:

$$h + h_1 S_1 + h_2 S_2 = 0 \quad \text{or} \quad h = -(h_1 S_1 + h_2 S_2) \qquad ...(2.7)$$

Example 2.11. *In a pipeline water is flowing. A manometer is used to measure the pressure drop for flow through the pipe. The difference in level was found to be 20 cm. If the manometric fluid is CCl_4, find the pressure drop in S.I units (density of CCl_4 = 1.596 g/cm^3). If the manometric fluid is changed to mercury (ρ = 13.6gm/cm^3) what will be the difference in level?*

(UPTU)

Solution. *Given:* h_{CCl_4} = 20 cm = 0.2 m; ρ_{CCl_4} = 1.596 g/cm^3

$= 1.596 \times 10^3$ kg/m^3

$\rho_{Hg} = 13.6 \times 10^3$ kg/m^3

Pressure drop, $\Delta p = \rho_{CCl_4} g h_{CCl_4}$

$= 1.596 \times 10^3 \times 9.81 \times 0.2$ N/m^2

$= 3131.3$ N/m^2 or Pa = **3.131 kPa (Ans.)**

The difference in level with mercury,

$$h_{Hg} = h_{CCl_4} \times \frac{\rho_{CCl_4}}{\rho_{Hg}} = 0.20 \times \frac{1.596 \times 10^3}{13.6 \times 10^3}$$

$= 0.02347$ m or **2.347 cm (Ans.)**

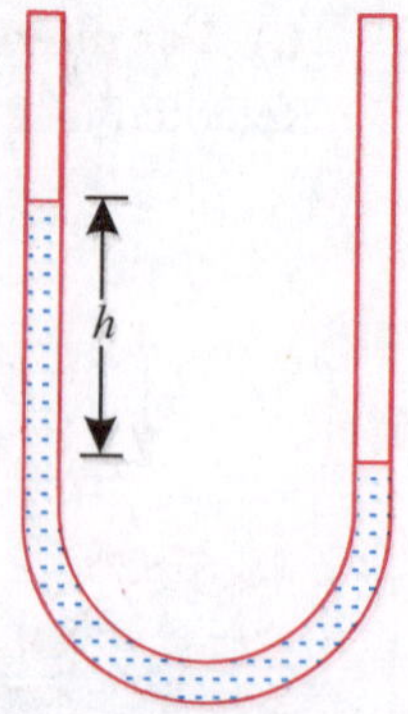

Fig. 2.12

Example 2.12. *A U-tube manometer is used to measure the pressure of oil of specific gravity 0.85 flowing in a pipe line. Its left end is connected to the pipe and the right-limb is open to the atmosphere. The centre of the pipe is 100 mm below the level of mercury (specific gravity = 13.6) in the right limb. If the difference of mercury level in the two limbs is 160 mm, determine the absolute pressure of the oil in the pipe.*

Solution. Specific gravity of oil, $S_1 = 0.85$

Specific gravity of mercury, $S_2 = 13.6$

Height of the oil in the left limb,

$h_1 = 160 - 100 = 60$ mm $= 0.06$ m

Difference of mercury level,

$h_2 = 160$ mm $= 0.16$ m.

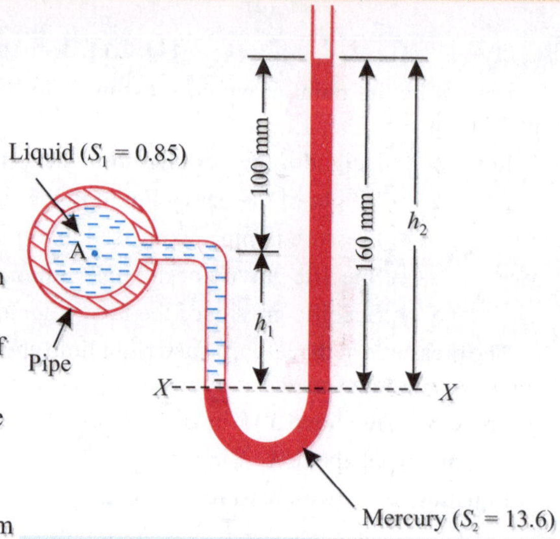

Fig. 2.13

Absolute pressure of oil:

Let, h_1 = Gauge pressure in the pipe in terms of head of water, and

p = Gauge pressure in terms of kN/m^2.

Equating the pressure heads above the datum line X–X, we get:

$$h + h_1 S_1 = h_2 S_2$$

or, $h + 0.06 \times 0.85 = 0.16 \times 13.6 = 2.125$ m

The pressure p is given by:

$$p = wh$$

$= 9.81 \times 2.125$ kN/m^2

$= 20.84$ kPa $\quad (\because w = 9.81$ kN/m^3 in S.I. units)

Absolute pressure of oil in the tube,

$$p_{abs.} = p_{atm.} + p_{gauge}$$

$= 100 + 20.84 =$ **120.84 kPa (Ans.)**

Example 2.13. *U-tube manometer containing mercury was used to find the negative pressure in the pipe, containing water. The right limb was open to the atmosphere. Find the vacuum pressure in the pipe, if the difference of mercury level in the two limbs was 100 mm and height of water in the left limb from the centre of the pipe was found to be 40 mm below.*

Solution. Specific gravity of water, $S_1 = 1$

Specific gravity of mercury, $S_2 = 13.6$

Height of water in the left limb,

$$h_1 = 40 \text{ mm} = 0.04 \text{ m}$$

Height of mercury in the left limb,

$$h_2 = 100 \text{ mm} = 0.1 \text{ m}$$

Let, h = Pressure in the pipe in terms of head of water (*below* the atmosphere).

Equating the pressure heads above the datum line X–X, we get:

$$h + h_1S_1 + h_2S_2 = 0$$

or,

$$\begin{aligned} h &= -(h_1S_1 + h_2S_2) \\ &= -(0.04 \times 1 + 0.1 \times 13.6) \\ &= -1.4 \text{ m of water} \end{aligned}$$

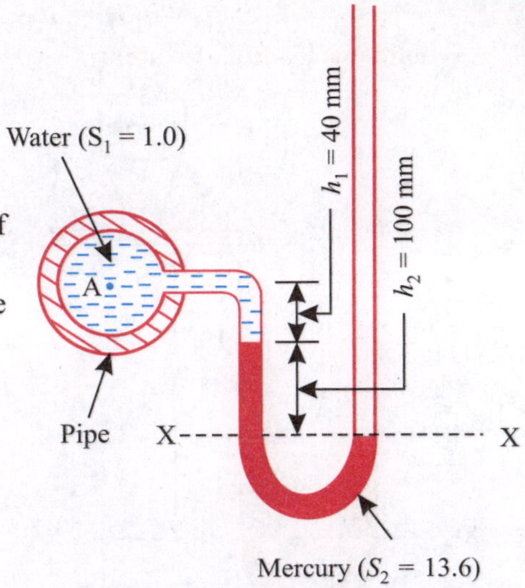

Fig. 2.14

Pressure p is given by:

$$\begin{aligned} p &= wh \\ &= 9.81 \times (-1.4) \text{ kN/m}^2 \\ &= -13.73 \text{ kPa} \end{aligned}$$

$$= \mathbf{13.73 \text{ kPa (vacuum)}} \textbf{ (Ans.)}$$

Example 2.14. *A simple U-tube manometer is installed across an orificemeter. The manometer is filled with mercury (sp. gravity = 13.6) and the liquid above the mercury is carbon tetrachloride (sp. gravity = 1.6). The manometer reads 200 mm. What is the pressure difference over the manometer in newtons per square metre.*

Solution. Specific gravity of heavier liquid, $S_{hl} = 13.6$

Specific gravity of lighter liquid, $S_{ll} = 1.6$

Reading of the manometer, $y = 200$ mm

Pressure difference over the manometer : p

Differential head,

$$h = y\left[\frac{S_{hl}}{S_{ll}} - 1\right]$$

$$200\left[\frac{13.6}{1.6} - 1\right] = 1500 \text{ mm of carbon tetrachloride}$$

Pressure difference over manometer,

$$p = wh = (1.6 \times 9810) \times \left(\frac{1500}{1000}\right)$$

or

$$p = \mathbf{23544 \text{ N/m}^2} \textbf{ (Ans.)}$$

Example 2.15. *In Fig. 2.15 is shown a conical vessel having its outlet at L to which U-tube manometer is connected. The reading of the manometer given in figure shows when the vessel is empty. Find the reading of the manometer when the vessel is completely filled with water.*

Solution. When vessel is empty: (Refer to Fig. 2.15)

Let, h_1 = Height of water above X–X

Specific gravity of water, $S_1 = 1.0$

Specific gravity of mercury, $S_2 = 13.6$

Equating the pressure heads about the datum line X–X, we get:

$$h_1 S_1 = h_2 S_2 \quad \text{or} \quad h_1 \times 1.0 = 150 \times 13.6 \quad \text{or} \quad h_1 = 2040 \text{ mm}$$

When vessel is full of water:

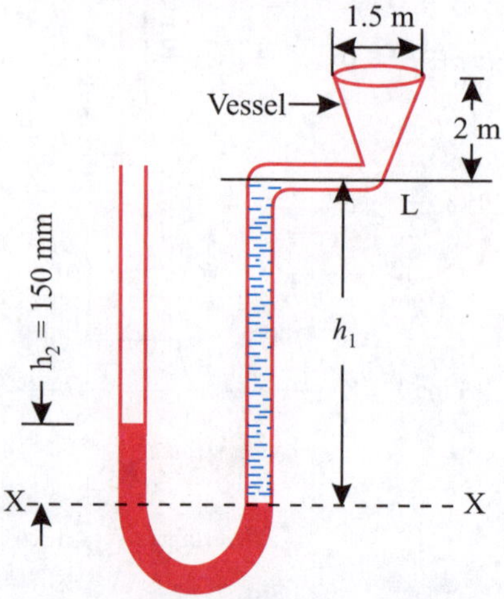

Fig. 2.15. Vessel is empty.

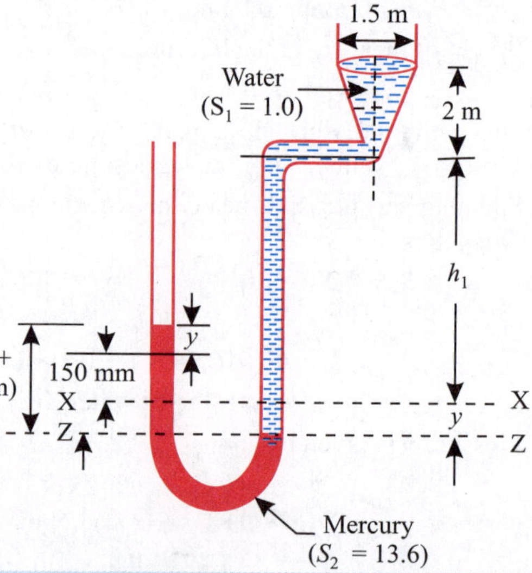

Fig. 2.16. Vessel is full of water.

Refer to Fig. 2.16. Consider the vessel to be completely filled with water. As a result of this let the mercury level go down by y mm in the right limb, and the mercury level go up by the same amount in the left limb. Now the datum line is *Z–Z*.

Equating the pressure heads above the datum line Z–Z, we get:

$$(150 + 2y) \times 13.6 = (h_1 + y + 2000) \times 1$$

or, $$150 \times 13.6 + 2y \times 13.6 = 2040 + y + 2000 \quad [\because h_1 = 2040 \text{ mm, calculated earlier}]$$

or, $$2040 + 27.2y = 4040 + y = 76.3 \text{ mm}$$

Thus the reading of the manometer when the vessel is completely filled with water

$$= (150 + 2y) = 150 + 2 \times 76.3 = 302.6 \text{ mm}$$

Hence, *reading of the manometer* 302.6 mm or **0.3026 m (Ans.)**

Example. 2.16. *Fig. 2.17 shows a pressure gauge with the following particulars:*

Cross-sectional area of each of the bulbs L and M = *1200* mm^2*;*

Cross-sectional area of each vertical limb = *30* mm^2*;*

Specific gravity of the liquid filled in bulb M = *0.9;*

If the surface of separation is in the limb attached to M find the displacement of surface of separation when the pressure on the surface in M is greater than that in L by an amount equal to 20 mm of head of water.

Solution.

Cross-sectional area of each vertical limb, $a = 30 \text{ m}^2$

Specific gravity of water, $S_1 = 1.0$

Specific gravity of the liquid, $S_2 = 0.9$.

Let, *X–X* = Initial level of separation,

h_L = Height of water above *X–X*, and

h_M = Height of liquid ($S_2 = 0.9$) above *X–X*.

Pressure head above *X–X* in the left limb = h_L

Pressure head above *X–X* in the right limb = $S_2 h_M = 0.9\, h_M$

Equating the pressure heads above $X–X$, we get:

$$h_L = 0.9\, h_M \qquad ...(i)$$

When the pressure on the surface in bulb M is increased by 20 mm of water, let the separation level fall by an amount equal to y. Then Z–Z is the *new separation level*.

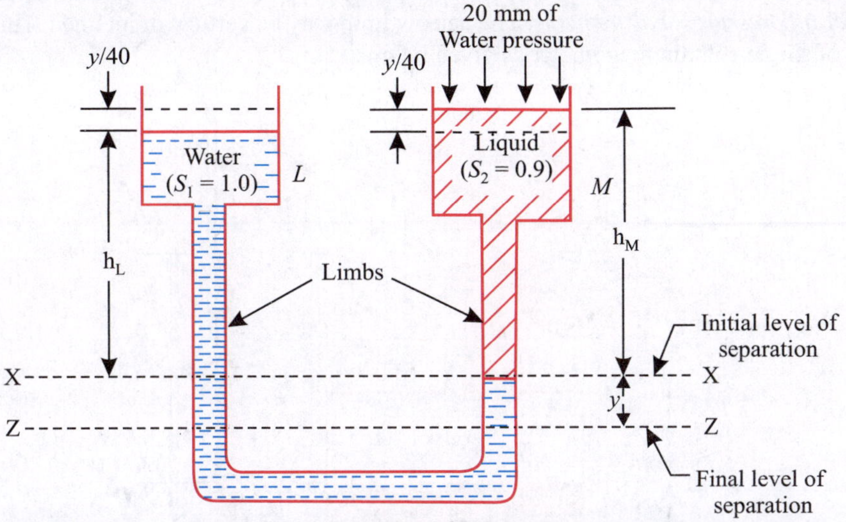

Fig. 2.17

Now, A × fall in separation level in bulb $M = a$ × fall in separation level in the limb (y).

$$\text{Fall in separation level in bulb } M = \frac{a \times y}{A} = \frac{30 \times y}{1200} = \frac{y}{40}$$

Also, fall in separation level in bulb M = Rise in surface level of $L = \dfrac{y}{40}$

Considering pressure heads above $Z–Z$, we have:

$$\text{Pressure head in the left limb} = \left[\frac{y}{40} + h_L + y\right]$$

$$\text{Pressure head in the right limb} = \left(h_M + y - \frac{y}{40}\right) \times 0.9 + 20$$

Equating the pressure heads, we get:

$$\left[\frac{y}{40} + h_L + y\right] = \left[h_M + y - \frac{y}{40}\right] \times 0.9 + 20$$

or, $$\frac{y}{40} + 0.9\, h_M + y = 0.9\, h_M + \frac{39y}{40} \times 0.9 + 20 \qquad (\because h_L = 0.9\, h_M)$$

or, $$\frac{41y}{40} = \frac{39y}{40} \times 0.9 + 20 \quad \text{or} \quad \frac{41y}{40} - \frac{39y}{40} \times 0.9 = 20$$

or, $$1.025y - 0.877y = 20 \quad \text{or} \quad y = 135.1 \text{ mm}$$

Hence, *displacement of the surface of separation* = **135.1 mm (Ans.)**

3. Single column manometer (micro-manometer):

The U-tube manometer described above usually requires reading of fluid levels at two or more points since a change in pressure causes a rise of liquid in one limb of the manometer and a drop in the other. This difficulty is however overcome by using single column manometers. A single column manometer is a modified form of a U-tube manometer in which a shallow reservoir having a large cross-sectional area (about 100 times) as compared to the area of the tube is connected to one limb of the manometer, as shown in Fig. 2.18. *For any variation in pressure, the change in the liquid level in the reservoir will be so small that it may be neglected, and the pressure is indicated by the height of the liquid in the other limb*. As such only *one reading in the narrow limb of the manometer need be taken for all pressure measurements*. The narrow limb may be vertical or inclined. Thus there are two types of single column manometer as given below:

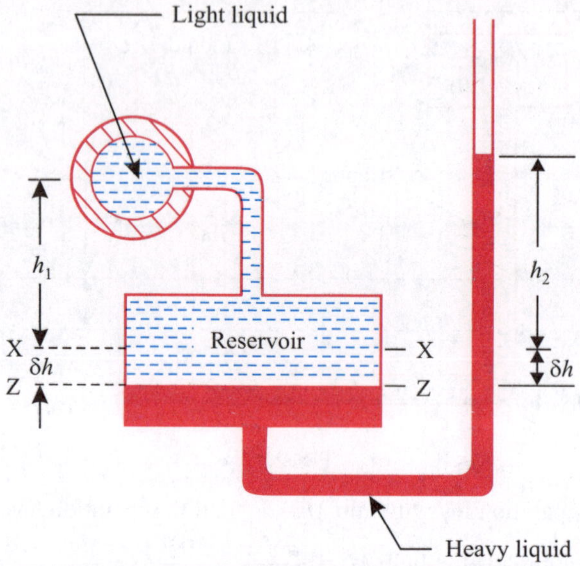

Fig. 2.18. Vertical single column manometer.

(*a*) Vertical single column manometer, and

(*b*) Inclined single column manometer.

(*a*) Vertical single column manometer:

Refer to Fig. 2.18

Let *X–X* be the datum line in the reservoir when the single column manometer is not connected to the pipe. Now consider that the manometer is connected to a pipe containing light liquid under a very high pressure. The pressure in the pipe will force the light liquid to push the heavy liquid in the reservoir downwards. As the area of the reservoir is very large, the fall of the heavy liquid level will be very small. This downward movement of the heavy liquid, in the reservoir, will cause a considerable rise of the heavy liquid in the right limb.

Let, h_1 = Height of the centre of the pipe above X–X,

h_2 = Rise of heavy liquid (after experiment) in the right limb,

δh = Fall of heavy liquid level in the reservoir,

h = Pressure in the pipe, expressed in terms of head of water,

A = Cross-sectional area of the reservoir,

a = Cross-sectional area of the tube (right limb),

S_1 = Specific gravity of light liquid in pipe, and

S_2 = Specific gravity of the heavy liquid.

We know that fall of heavy liquid in reservoir will cause a rise of heavy liquid level in the right limb.

Thus, $A \times \delta h = a \times h_2$ or $\delta h = \dfrac{a \times h_2}{A}$ ...(*i*)

Let us now consider pressure heads above the datum line *Z–Z* as shown in Fig. 2.18.

Pressure head in the left limb $= h + (h_1 + \delta h)S_1$

Pressure head in the right limb $= (h_2 + \delta h)S_2$

Equating the pressure heads, we get:

$$h + (h_1 + \delta h)S_1 = (h_2 + \delta h)S_2 \quad \text{or} \quad h = (h_2 + \delta h)\, S_2 - (h_1 + \delta h)\, S_1$$
$$= \delta h\,(S_2 - S_1) + h_2 S_2 - h_1 S_1$$

But, $\delta h = \dfrac{a \times h_2}{A}$ ...[Eqn. (*i*)]

$$h = \frac{a \times h_2}{A}(S_2 - S_1) + h_2 S_2 - h_1 S_1 \qquad ...(2.8)$$

When the area A is very large as compared to *a*, then the ratio $\dfrac{a}{A}$ becomes very small, and thus is neglected. Then the above equation becomes

$$h = h_2 S_2 - h_1 S_1 \qquad ...(2.9)$$

(*b*) Inclined single column manometer:

This type of manometer is useful for the measurement of *small pressures and is more sensitive than the vertical tube type*. Due to inclination the distance moved by the heavy liquid in the right limb is *more*.

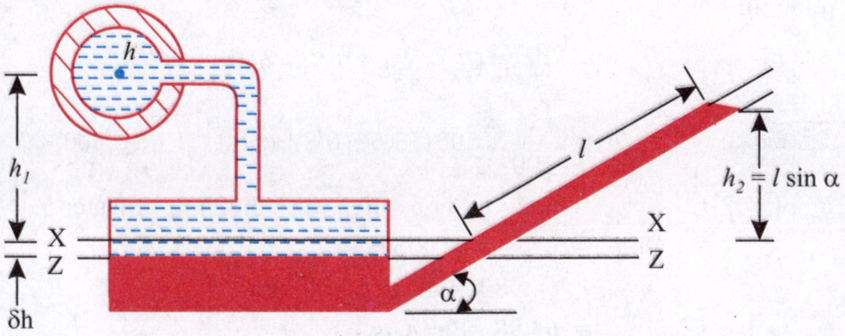

Fig. 2.19. Inclined single column manometer.

Let, l = Length of the heavy liquid moved in right limb,

α = Inclination of right limb horizontal, and

h_2 = Vertical rise of liquid in right limb from *X–X* $= l \sin \alpha$.

Putting the value of h_2 in eqn. 2.9, we get:

$$h = l \sin \alpha \times S_2 - h_1\, S_1 \qquad ...(2.10)$$

Example. 2.17. *Fig. 2.20 shows a single column manometer connected to a pipe containing liquid of specific gravity 0.8. The ratio of area of the reservoir to that of the limb is 100. Find the pressure in the pipe.*

Take specific gravity of mercury as 13.6.

Solution. Specific gravity of liquid in the pipe, $S_1 = 0.8$.

Specific gravity of mercury, $S_2 = 13.6$

$$\frac{\text{Area of reservoir}}{\text{Area of right limb}} = \frac{A}{a} = 100$$

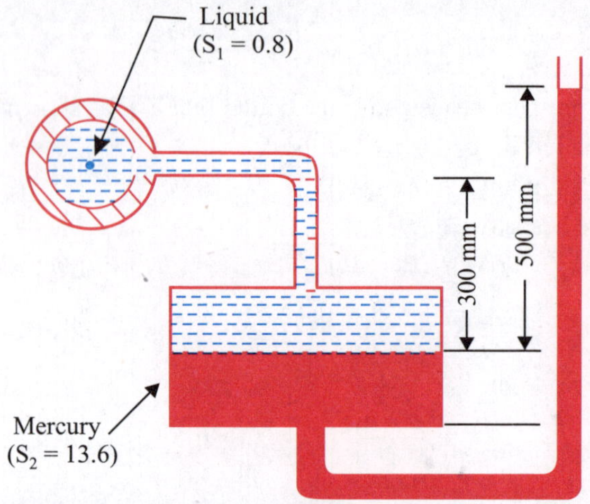

Fig. 2.20

Height of the liquid in the left limb,

$$h_1 = 300 \text{ mm}$$

Height of mercury in the right limb,

$$h_2 = 500 \text{ mm}$$

Let, h = Pressure head in the pipe.

Using the relation:

$$h = \frac{a}{A} h_2 (S_2 - S_1) + h_2 S_2 - h_1 S_1$$

or,

$$h = \frac{1}{100} \times 500(13.6 - 0.8) + 500 \times 13.6 - 300 \times 0.8 \text{ mm of water}$$

$$= 6624 \text{ mm of water} \quad \text{or} \quad 6.624 \text{ m of water}$$

Pressure,

$$p = wh = 9.81 \times 6.624$$

$$= 64.98 \text{ kN/m}^2 \text{ or } 64.98 \text{ kPa}$$

i.e., $\boldsymbol{p = 64.98}$ **kPa (Ans.)**

Example 2.18. *A manometer consists of an inclined glass tube which communicates with a metal cylinder standing upright; liquid fills the apparatus to a fixed zero mark on the tube when both the cylinder and the tube are open to atmosphere. The upper end of the cylinder is then connected to a gas supply at a pressure p and manometric liquid rises through a distance l in the tube. Establish the relation:*

$$h = Sl\left[\sin\alpha + \left(\frac{d}{D}\right)^2\right]$$

for the pressure head h of water column in terms of inclination α of the tube, specific gravity S of the liquid, and ratio of diameter d of the tube to the diameter D of the cylinder.

Also determine the value of $\left(\frac{D}{d}\right)$ *so that the error due to disregarding the change in level in the cylinder will not exceed 0.1 percent when α = 25°.*

Solution. Vertical rise in the tube $= l \sin\alpha$

Fall of liquid level in the cylinder $= l \times \frac{a}{A} = l \times \left(\frac{d}{D}\right)^2$

∴ Net change in level of manometric liquid due to the applied pressure

$$= l \sin\alpha + l \times \left(\frac{d}{D}\right)^2 = l\left[\sin\alpha + \left(\frac{d}{D}\right)^2\right]$$

Now the increase in pressure,

p = Specific weight of manometric liquid × net change in the level of manometric head

$$= w_m\, l\left[\sin\alpha + \left(\frac{d}{D}\right)^2\right]$$

or, in terms of water column,

$$\frac{p}{w} = \frac{w_m}{w} \times l\left[\sin\alpha + \left(\frac{d}{D}\right)^2\right]$$

or, $$h = S \times l\left[\sin\alpha + \left(\frac{d}{D}\right)^2\right]$$ **...Proved**

Change in the liquid level when variation of liquid in the cylinder is *considered*

$$= l\left[\sin\alpha + \left(\frac{d}{D}\right)^2\right]$$

Change in the liquid level when variation of liquid in the cylinder is *disregarded* $= l \sin\alpha$

$$\therefore \quad \frac{S\,l\left[\sin\alpha + \left(\frac{d}{D}\right)^2\right] - S\,l \sin\alpha}{S\,l\left[\sin\alpha + \left(\frac{d}{D}\right)^2\right]} = 0.001$$ ...(*Given*)

or, $$1 - \frac{\sin\alpha}{\sin\alpha + \left(\frac{d}{D}\right)^2} = 0.001$$

or, $$1 - \frac{\sin 25°}{\sin 25° + \left(\frac{d}{D}\right)^2} = 0.001$$

or, $$1 - \frac{0.4226}{0.4226 + \left(\frac{d}{D}\right)^2} = 0.001$$

or, $$\frac{0.4226}{0.4226 + \left(\frac{d}{D}\right)^2} = 0.999$$

or, $$\left(\frac{d}{D}\right)^2 = \frac{0.4226}{0.999} - 0.4226 = 0.000423$$

or, $$\frac{d}{D} = 0.02057$$

or, $$\frac{D}{d} = 48.61 \textbf{ (Ans.)}$$

2.5.1.2. Differential Manometers

A **differential manometer** *is used to measure the difference in pressures between two points in a pipe, or in two different pipes.* In its simplest form a differential manometer consists of a

U-tube, containing a heavy liquid, whose two ends are connected to the points, whose difference of pressures is required to be found out. Following are the most commonly used types of differential manometers:

1. U-tube differential manometer.
2. Inverted U-tube differential manometer.

1. U-tube differential manometer:

A U-tube differential manometer is shown in Fig. 2.21.

Case I. Fig. 2.21 (*a*) shows a differential manometer whose two ends are connected with two different points A and B at the same level and containing same liquid.

Let, h = Difference of mercury levels (heavy liquid) in the U-tube,

h_1 = Distance of the centre of A from the mercury level in the right limb,

$S_1\ (= S_2)$ = Specific gravity of liquid at the two points A and B

S = Specific gravity of heavy liquid or mercury in the U-tube,

h_A = Pressure head at A, and

h_B = Pressure head at B.

We know that the pressures in the left limb and right limb, above the datum line, are equal.

Pressure head in the *left limb*

$$= h_A + (h_1 + h)\, S_1$$

Pressure head in the *right limb*

$$= h_B + h_1 \times S_1 + h \times S$$

$$h_A + (h_1 + h)S_1 = h_B + h_1S_1 + hS$$

or,
$$h_A - h_B = h_1S_1 + hS - (h_1 + h)\, S_1$$
$$= h_1\, S_1 + hS - h_1S_1 + hS_1 = h\,(S - S_1)$$

i.e., Difference of pressure head,

$$h_A - h_B = h\,(S - S_1) \qquad \text{...(2.11)}$$

Case II. Fig. 2.21 (*b*) shows a differential manometer whose two ends are connected to two different points A and B at different levels and containing different liquids.

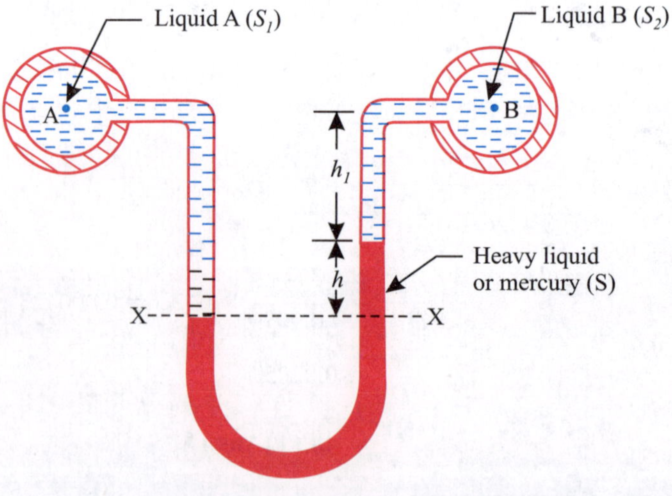

Fig. 2.21. (*a*) Two pipes at same level.

Let, h = Difference of mercury levels (heavy liquid) in the U-tube,

h_1 = Distance of the centre of A, from the mercury level in the left limb,

h_2 = Distance of the centre of B, from the mercury level in the right limb,

S_1 = Specific gravity of liquid in pipe A,

S_2 = Specific gravity of liquid in pipe B,

S = Specific gravity of heavy liquid or mercury,

h_A = Pressure head at A, and

h_B = Pressure head at B.

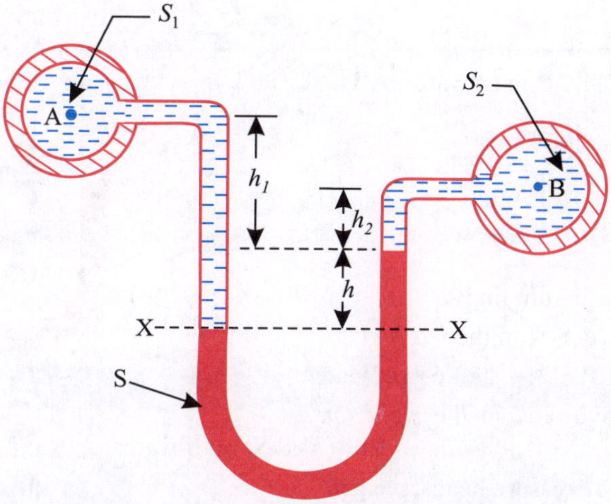

Fig. 2.21. (b) U-tube differential manometers.

Considering the pressure heads above the datum line $X–X$, we get:

Pressure head in the *left limb* $= h_A + (h_1 + h)\,S_1$

Pressure head in the *right limb* $= h_B + h_2 \times S_2 + h \times S$

Equating the above pressure heads, we get:

$$h_A + (h_1 + h)\,S_1 = h_B + h_2 \times S_2 + h \times S$$

$$(h_A - h_B) = h_2 \times S_2 + h \times S - (h_1 + h)\,S_1$$

$$= h_2 \times S_2 + h \times S - h_1S_1 - hS_1 = h\,(S - S_1) + h_2S_2 - h_1S_1$$

i.e., Difference of pressure heads at A and B,

$$h_A - h_B = h\,(S - S_1) + h_2S_2 - h_1S_1 \qquad ...(2.12)$$

Example 2.19. *A differential manometer connected at the two points A and B in a pipe containing an oil of specific gravity of 0.9 shows a difference in mercury levels as 150 mm. Find the difference in pressures at the two points.*

Solution. Specific gravity of oil, $S_1 = 0.9$

Specific gravity of mercury, $S = 13.6$

Difference of mercury levels, $h = 150$ mm

Let, $h_A - h_B$ = Difference of pressures between A and B, in terms of head of water, and

$p_A - p_B$ = Difference of pressures between A and B.

Using the relation: $h_A - h_B = h\,(S - S_1)$ [Eqn. (2.11)]

$= 150\,(13.6 - 0.9) = 1905$ mm $=$ **1.905 m of water (Ans.)**

Now, using the relation,

$p_A - p_B = wh$, we have, $p_A - p_B = 9.81 \times 1.905 = 18.68$ kN/m^2 = **18.68 kPa (Ans.)**

Example 2.20. *Fig 2.22 shows a U-tube differential manometer connecting two pressure pipes at A and B. The pipe A contains a liquid of specific gravity 1.6 under a pressure of 110 kN/m^2. The pipe B contains oil of specific gravity 0.8 under a pressure of 200 kN/m^2. Find the difference of pressure measured by mercury as fluid filling U-tube.*

Solution. Specific gravity of liquid at *A*, $S_1 = 1.6$

Specific gravity of liquid at *B*, $S_2 = 0.8$

Pressure at *A*, $p_A = 110$ kN/m^2

Pressure head at *A*,

$$h_A = \frac{p_A}{w} = \frac{110}{9.81} = 11.21 \text{ m of water}$$

Pressure at *B*, $p_B = 200$ kN/m^2

Pressure head at *B*,

$$h_B = \frac{p_B}{w} = \frac{200}{9.81} = 20.38 \text{ m of water}$$

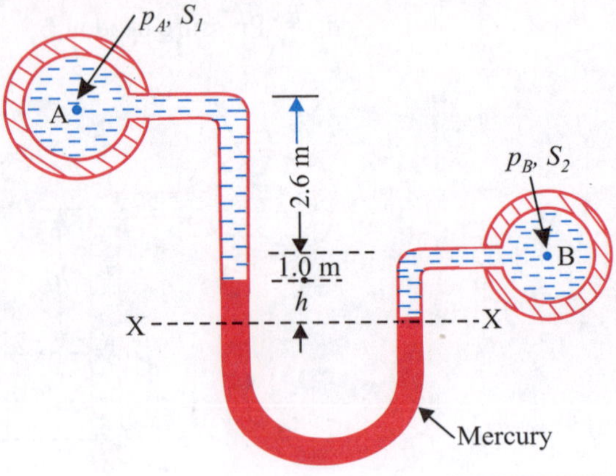

Fig. 2.22

Taking $X - X$ as the datum line:

Pressure head above *X–X* in the *left limb*

$= h_A + (2.6 + 1.0) S_1 + h \times 13.6$ m of water

Pressure head above *X–X* in the *right limb*

$= h_B + (1.0 + h) \times S_2$ m of water

Equating the above pressure heads, we get:

$$h_A + (2.6 + 1.0) S_1 + h \times 13.6 = h_B + (1.0 + h) S_2$$

$$11.21 + 5.76 + 13.6\,h = 20.38 + (1.0 + h) \times 0.8$$

or, $16.97 + 13.6\,h = 20.38 + 0.8 + 0.8\,h$ or $12.8h = 4.21$

or, $h = 0.329$ m or **329 mm (Ans.)**

Example 2.21. *Fig. 2.23. shows a differential manometer connected at two points A and B. At A air pressure is 100 kN/m^2. Find the absolute pressure at B.*

Solution. Pressure of air at A,

$$p_A = 100 \text{ kN/m}^2$$

Pressure head at A,

$$h_A = \frac{100}{9.81} = 10.2 \text{m}$$

Let the pressure at *B* is p_B.

Then, pressure head at $B = \dfrac{p_B}{w}$

Considering pressure heads above the atum line *X–X*, we have:

Pressure head in the *left limb*

$$= \frac{650}{1000} + h_A = 0.65 + 10.2 = 10.85 \text{ m}$$

Pressure head in the *right limb*

$$= h_B + \frac{250}{1000} \times 0.85 + \frac{150}{1000} \times 13.6$$

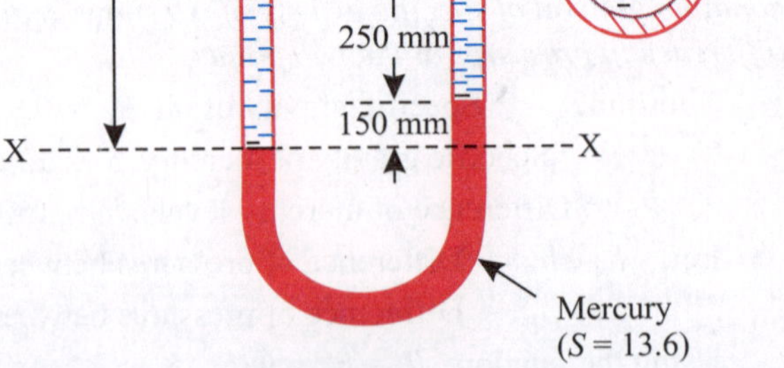

Fig. 2.23

$$= h_B + 0.212 + 2.04 = h_B + 2.25$$

Equating the above pressure heads, we get:

$$10.85 = h_B + 2.25 \quad \text{or} \quad h_B = 8.6 \text{ m}$$

But, $$h_B = \frac{P_B}{w}$$

$$p_B = wh_B = 9.81 \times 8.6 = 84.36 \text{ kN/m}^2$$

or, $$p_B = \mathbf{84.36\ kPa}\ \textbf{(Ans.)}$$

2. Inverted U-tube differential manometer:

This type of manometer is used for measuring difference of two pressures where *accuracy is the major consideration.*

Refer to Fig. 2.24. It consists of an inverted U-tube, containing *light liquid,* whose two ends are connected to the points, (*A* and *B*) whose difference of pressures is to be found out. Let the pressure at *A* is more than the pressure at *B*.

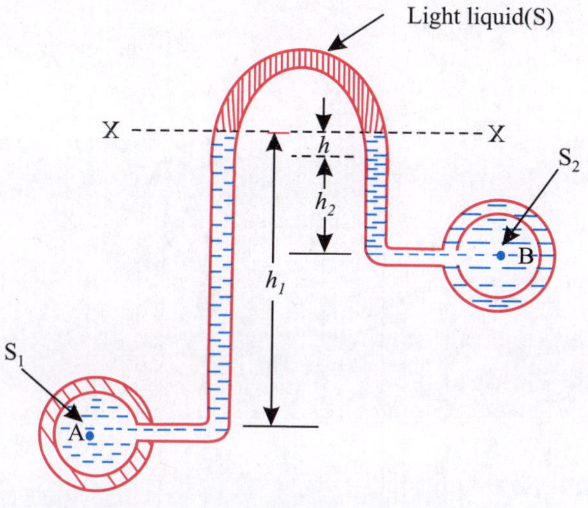

Fig. 2.24. Inverted differential manometer.

Let, h_1 = Height of liquid in the left limb below the datum line *X–X*,

h_2 = Height of liquid in the right limb below the datum line,

h = Difference of levels of the light liquid in the right and left limbs (also known as manometer reading),

S_1 = Specific gravity of the liquid in the left limb,

S_2 = Specific gravity of the liquid in the right limb,

S = Specific gravity of the light liquid,

h_A = Pressure head at *A*, and

h_B = Pressure head at *B*.

We know that pressure heads in the left limb and the right limb below the datum line *X–X* are *equal.*

Pressure head in the *left limb* below $X–X = h_A - h_1 \times S_1$

Pressure head in the *right limb* below $X–X = h_B - h_2 \times S_2 - h \times S$

Equating the above heads, we get:

$$h_A - h_1 \times S_1 = h_B - h_2 \times S_2 - h \times S$$

$$h_A - h_B = h_1 \times S_1 - h_2 \times S_2 - h \times S$$

i.e.,

$$h_A - h_B = h_1S_1 - h_2S_2 - hS \quad \text{...(2.13)}$$

Example 2.22. *Fig. 2.25 shows an inverted differential manometer having an oil of specific gravity 0.8 connected to two different pipes carrying water under pressure. Determine the pressure in the pipe B. The pressure in pipe A is 2.0 metres of water.*

Solution. Height of water in the left limb,

$$h_1 = 300 \text{ mm}$$

Height of water in the right limb,

$$h_2 = 100 \text{ mm}$$

Height of light liquid in right limb,

$$h = 150 \text{ mm}$$

Pressure in pipe A, $h_A = 2.0$ m of water

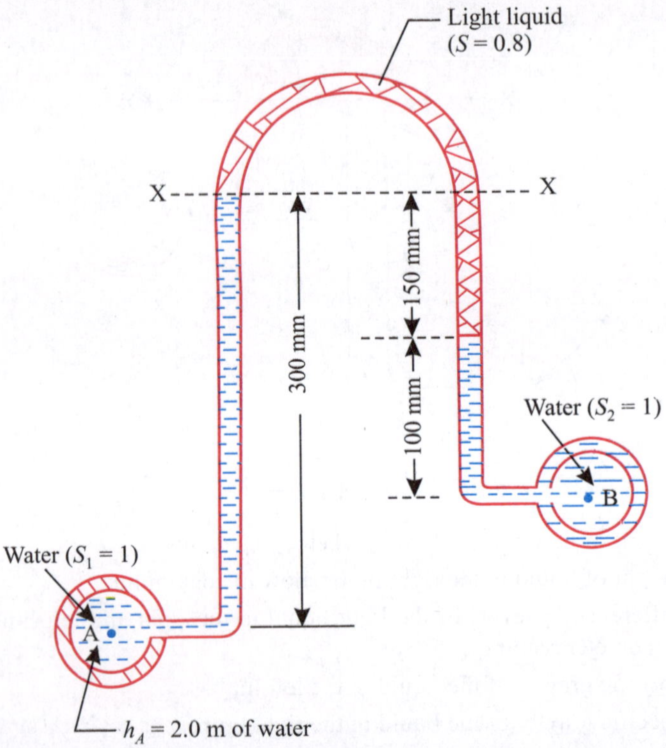

Fig. 2.25

Let, $S_1, S_2 = 1$ (sp. gr. of water)

We know that pressure heads in the left and right limbs below the datum line $X–X$ are *equal*.

Pressure head in the *left limb* below $X–X$

$$= h_A - h_1S_1$$

$$= 2.0 - \frac{300}{1000} \times 1 = 1.7 \text{ m}$$

Pressure head in the right limb below $X–X$

$$= h_B - h_2S_2 - hS$$

$$= h_B - \frac{100}{1000} \times 1 - \frac{150}{1000} \times 0.8$$

$$= h_B - 0.1 - 0.12 = h_B - 0.22$$

Equating the two pressure heads, we get: $1.7 = h_B - 0.22$

or, h_B = **1.92 m (Ans.)**

Also, $p_B = wh_B = 9.81 \times 1.92 = 18.8 \text{ kN/m}^2$

= **18.8 kPa (Ans.)**

Example 2.23. *An inverted differential manometer is connected to two pipes A and B carrying water under pressure as shown in Fig. 2.26. The fluid in the manometer is oil of specific gravity 0.75. Determine the pressure difference between A and B.*

Solution. Specific gravity of oil, $S = 0.75$

Specific gravity of water, $S_1, S_2 = 1$

Difference of oil in the two limbs = (450 + 200) – 450 = 200 mm

We know that pressure heads on the left and right limbs below the datum line *X–X* are *equal.*

Pressure head in the left limb below *X–X*

$$= h_A - \frac{450}{1000} \times 1 = h_A - 0.45$$

Pressure head in the right limb below *X–X*

$$= h_B - \frac{450}{1000} \times 1 - \frac{200}{1000} \times 0.75$$

$$= h_B - 0.45 - 0.15 = h_B - 0.6$$

Equating the two pressure heads, we get:

$$h_A - 0.45 = h_B - 0.6$$

$$h_B - h_A = \mathbf{0.15 \text{ m (Ans.)}}$$

or, $\frac{p_B}{w} - \frac{p_A}{w} = 0.15$ or $p_B - p_A$

$= w \times 0.15 = 9.81 \times 0.15 = 1.47 \text{ kN/m}^2 =$ **1.47 kPa (Ans.)**

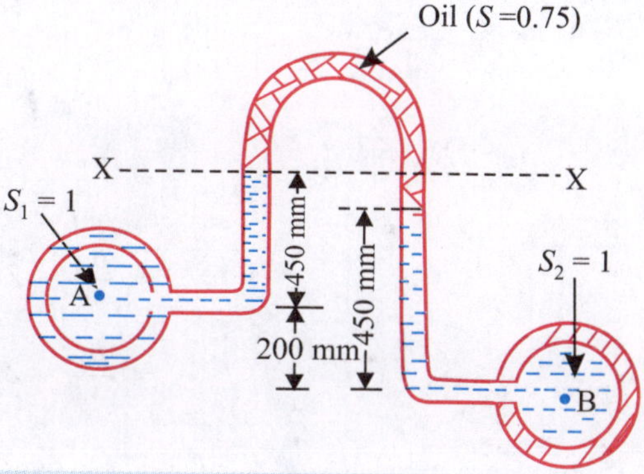

Fig. 2.26

Example 2.24. *Describe, giving a sketch, a micromanometer. Explain how it could be used for measuring small pressure difference.* **(N.U.)**

Solution: ***Micromanometer.*** It is shown in the Fig. 2.27 and is *used for measuring small pressure differences.* It utilizes two manometer liquids which are *immiscible with each other and also with the fluid whose pressure difference is to be measured.* The heavier liquid fills the lower part of the U-tube upto 0-0 and then the lighter liquid is added on both sides filling the tanks C and D upto the level *X–X*. The fluid (liquid or a gas) whose pressure difference is to be measured fills the space above *X–X*. When the pressure p_A is slightly greater than p_B, the liquid levels will be as shown in the figure. The volume of the liquid displaced in each tank is equal to the volume of liquid displaced in the U-tube. If *a* is the cross-sectional area of the U-tube, and *A* that of the tank, then

$$A \, \Delta Z = \frac{h}{2} a \qquad \text{...(i)}$$

Let S_1 be the specific gravity of heavier manometric liquid, and S_2 be that of the lighter manometric liquid. An expression relating p_A and p_B may be obtained by equating pressures along *L–L* in the U-tube. If *w* is specific weight of water, then:

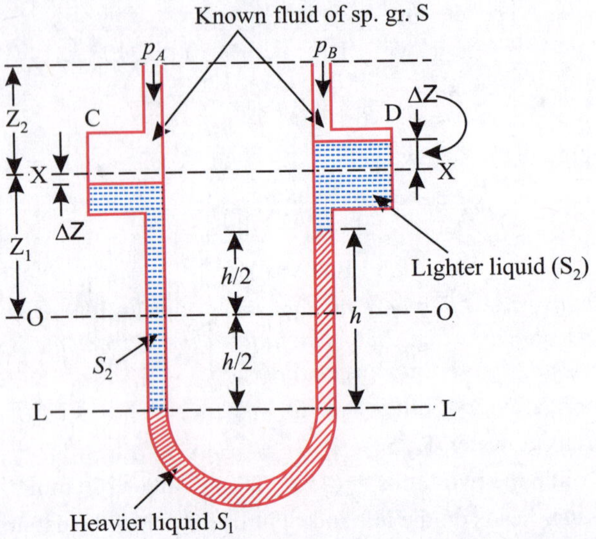

Fig. 2.27

$$\frac{p_A}{w} + (Z_2 + \Delta Z)S + \left(Z_1 - \Delta Z + \frac{h}{2}S_2\right)$$

$$= \frac{p_B}{w} + (Z_2 + \Delta Z)\, S + \left(Z_1 + \Delta Z - \frac{h}{2}\right) S_2 + hS_1$$

or,
$$= \frac{p_A}{w} + Z_2 S + \Delta Z\, S + Z_1 S_2 - \Delta Z\, S_2 + \frac{h}{2} S_2$$

$$= \frac{p_B}{w} + Z_2 S - \Delta Z\, S + Z_1 S_2 + \Delta Z\, S_2 - \frac{h}{2} S_2 + hS_1$$

$\therefore$ Pressure difference, $\dfrac{p_A - p_B}{w} = \Delta Z\,(S_2 - S + S_2 - S) + h\left(S_1 - \dfrac{S_2}{2} - \dfrac{S_2}{2}\right)$

Substituting for $\Delta Z = \dfrac{ha}{2A}$ from (*i*) and simplifying, we get:

or,
$$\frac{p_A - p_B}{w} = \frac{ha}{2A}[(2S_2 - 2S)] + h[S_1 - S_2]$$

$$= h\left[\frac{a}{A}(S_2 - S) + (S_1 - S_2)\right] = hK \textbf{ (Ans.)}$$

The quantity K within the bracket is a *constant* for a given manometer and given manometric liquids of specific gravities S_1, S_2 and known fluid of specific gravity S.

Example 2.25. *Fig. 2.28. shows a fuel gauge, for a gasoline tank in car, which reads proportional to the bottom gauge. The tank is 30 cm deep and accidently contains 1.8 cm of water in addition to the gasoline. Determine the height of air remaining at the top when the gauge erroneously reads full.*

Take: $w_{gasoline} = 6.65 \text{ kN/m}^3$, and

$w_{air} = 0.0118 \text{ kN/m}^3$. **(Punjab University)**

Solution. When the tank is full of gasoline,

$$p_{gauge} = wh = 6.65 \times \frac{30}{100} = 1.995 \text{ kN/m}^2$$

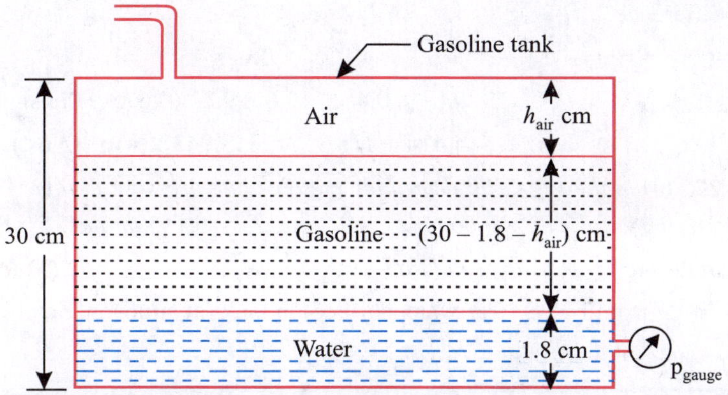

Fig. 2.28

The gauge would erroneously read 1.995 kN/m^2 even when h cm of air remains at the top; evidently when water is also accidently present.

∴ Pressure due to h cm height of air + pressure due to $[30 - 1.8 - h_{air}]$ cm height of gasoline + pressure due to 1.8 cm of water = 1.995

or, $$0.0118 \times \frac{h_{air}}{100} + 6.65 \times \frac{(30 - 1.8 - h_{air})}{100} + 9.81 \times \frac{1.8}{100} = 1.995$$

or, $$0.0118\, h + 187.53 - 6.65\, h_{air} + 17.658 = 199.5$$

or, $$h_{air} = \frac{187.53 + 17.658 - 199.5}{6.638} = \mathbf{0.857\ cm}$$ **(Ans.)**

Example 2.26. *For the Fig. 2.29 determine the pressure difference between pipes A and B. Take $Z_1 = 0.45$ m, $Z_2 = 0.225$ m, $Z_3 = 0.675$ m and $Z_4 = 0.3$ m.*

Neglect pressure due to pressure of air column in the inclined tube.

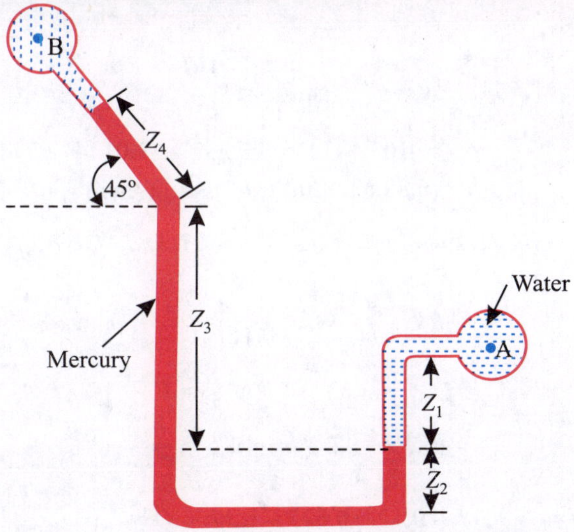

Fig. 2.29

Solution. Starting from point A, the governing manometric equation is:

$$p_A + w_w Z_1 - w_m (Z_3 + Z_4 \sin 45°) = p_B$$

∴ Pressure difference,

$$p_A - p_B = -w_m Z_1 + w_m (Z_3 + Z_4 \sin 45°)$$
$$= -9.81 \times 0.45 + 13.6 \times 9.81\,(0.675 + 0.3 \sin 45°)$$
$$= -4.414 + 118.357 = \mathbf{113.943\ kN/m^2}\ \textbf{(Ans.)}$$

Example 2.27. *From the Fig. 2.30 determine the absolute pressure in pipe A that contains oil of specific gravity = 0.88. Take $Z_1 = 0.66$ m, $Z_2 = 0.33$ m, $Z_3 = 0.165$ m and $Z_4 = 0.11$ m. Assume an atmospheric pressure 105 kPa.* **(Madras University)**

Solution. Starting from F.W.S (free water surface) in tank (at atmospheric pressure), we get

$$p_{atm} + w_w Z_1 - w_w Z_2 - w_m Z_3 + w_0\,(Z_3 + Z_4) = p_A$$

$$105 + 9.81 \times 0.66 - 9.81 \times 0.33 - 13.6 \times 9.81 \times 0.165 + 0.88 \times 9.81 \times (0.165 + 0.11) = p_A$$

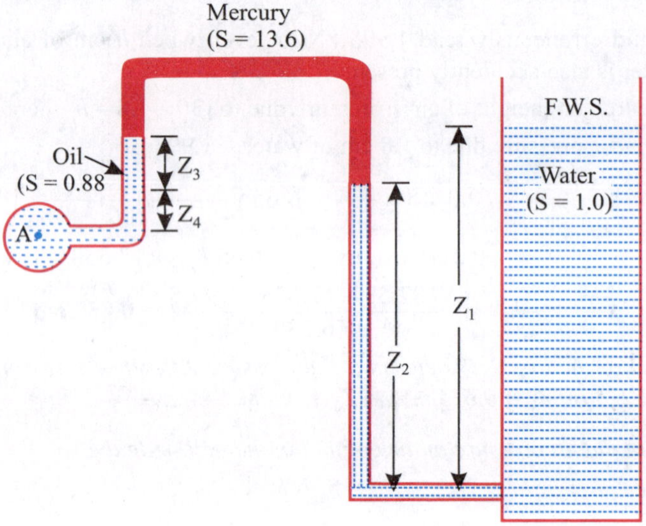

Fig. 2.30

or,
$$p_A = 105 + 6.475 - 3.237 - 22.014 + 2.374$$
$$= \mathbf{88.6\ kN/m^2}\ (\textit{absolute})\ \textbf{(Ans.)}$$

Example 2.28. *Find the pressure difference between L and M in Fig. 2.31.*

Solution. $p_L - p_M$:

$$\frac{p_L}{w} + h \times 1.5 - 0.15 \times 0.8$$

(at *L*) (at *N*) (at *U* = *V*)

$$+ (0.15 + 0.2 - h) \times 1.5 = \frac{p_M}{w}$$

$$\frac{p_L}{w} + 1.5\,h - 0.12 + 0.525 - 1.5\,h = \frac{p_M}{w}$$

or,
$$\frac{p_L - p_M}{w} = -0.405 \text{ m}$$

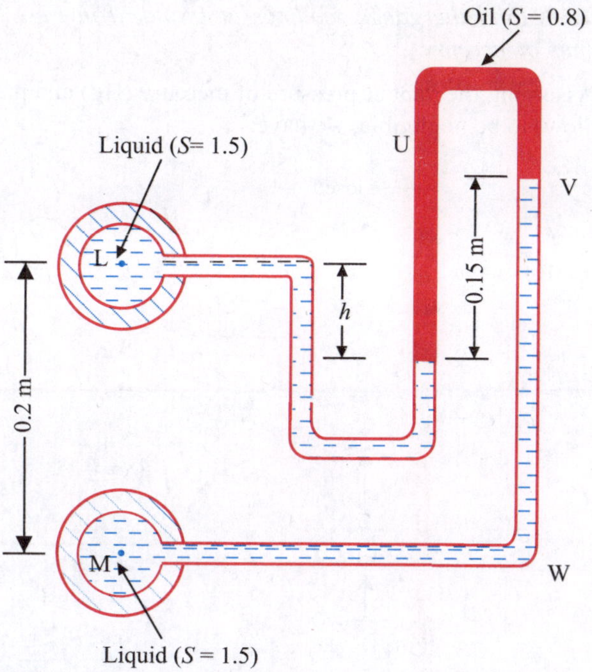

Fig. 2.31

Negative sign indicates $p_M > p_L$

i.e., $p_M - p_L = 0.405 \times 9.81$

$= \mathbf{3.97\ kN/m^2}$ **(Ans.)**

Example 2.29. *In the Fig. 2.32, if the local atmospheric pressure is 755 mm of mercury (sp. gravity = 13.6), calculate:*

(i) Absolute pressure of air in the tank;

(ii) Pressure gauge reading at L.

Solution. ***(i)*** **Absolute pressure of air,** $(p_{abs})_{air}$:

Starting from the open end, we have:

$0 - (13.6 \times w) \times 0.6 = p_{air}$ (pressure of air)

i.e., $p_{air} = -13.6 \times 9.81 \times 0.6 = -80\ \text{kN/m}^2$

$p_{atm.}$ = (atmospheric pressure)

$= \dfrac{755}{1000} \times 13.6 \times 9.81 = 100.73\ \text{kN/m}^2$

$(p_{abs.})_{air} = p_{air} + p_{atm.} = -80 + 100.73 = 20.73\ \text{kN/m}^2$

Hence, $(p_{abs.})_{air} = \mathbf{20.73\ kN/m^2}$ **(Ans.)**

(ii) **Pressure gauge reading at L:**

Pressure at $L = p_{abs.}$ (air) + wh

$p_L = 20.73 + 9.81 \times 2 = 40.35\ \text{kN/m}^2$ *abs.*

Now, $40.35 = p_{gauge} + p_{atm.}$

$p_{gauge(L)} = 40.35 - p_{atm.} = 40.35 - 100.73$

$= -60.38\ \text{kN/m}^2$

i.e., Vacuum pressure = $60.38\ \text{kN/m}^2$

Hence, *pressure gauge reading at L* = $\mathbf{60.38\ kN/m^2}$ **(vacuum) (Ans.)**

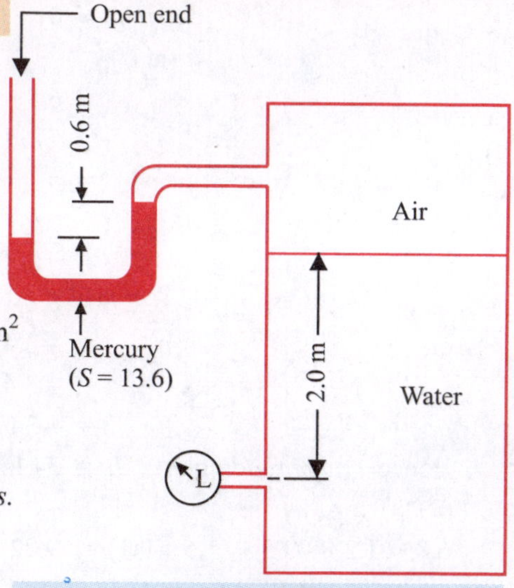

Fig. 2.32

Example 2.30. *Find the gauge readings at L and M in Fig. 2.33 if the local atmospheric pressure is 755 mm of mercury.*

Solution. Assuming the vapour pressure of mercury (Hg) and pressure due to short column of air (w_{air} is very low) to be negligible, we have:

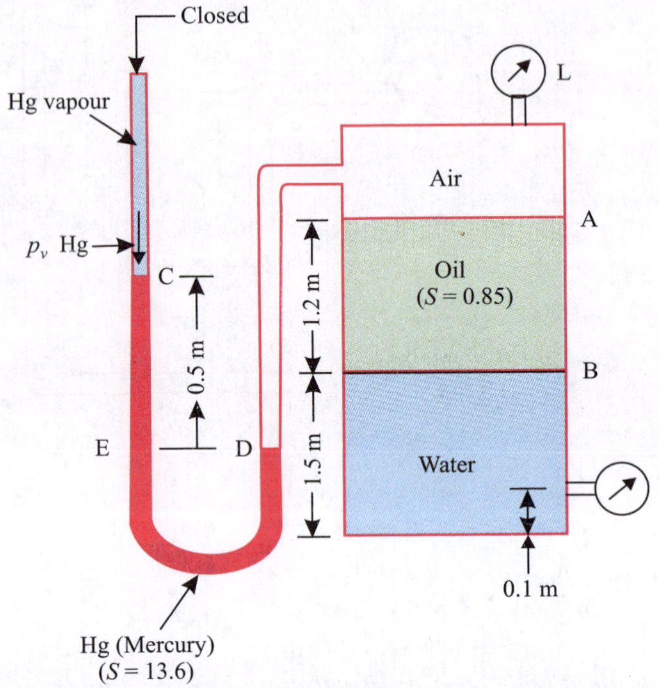

Fig. 2.33

(i) $(p_{gauge})_L$**:**

$$\underset{(\text{at } C)}{(p_v Hg \approx 0)} + \underset{(\text{at } D = E = A)}{0.5 \times 13.6} = \underset{(\text{at } A)}{6.8 \text{ m of water } abs.}$$

$$p_{gauge} + p_{atm.} = p_{abs.}$$

But, $$p_{atm.} = \frac{755}{1000} \times 13.6 = 10.27 \text{ m of water}$$

$\therefore$ $$p_{gauge} + 10.27 = 6.8$$

or, $$p_{gauge} = -3.47 \text{ m of water}$$
$$= -3.47 \times 9.81$$
$$= -34 \text{ kN/m}^2$$

Hence, *gauge reading at* L = **34 kN/m²** *(vacuum)* **(Ans.)**

(ii) $(p_{gauge})_M$**:**

$$\underset{(\text{at } A)}{6.8} + \underset{(\text{at } B)}{1.2 \times 0.85} + \underset{(\text{at } M)}{(1.5 - 0.1)} = 9.22 \text{ m of water } abs.$$

$$p_{gauge} + p_{atm.} = p_{abs.}$$
$$p_{gauge} + 10.27 = 9.22$$

or, $\quad p_{gauge} = -1.05$ m of water

$= -1.05 \times 9.81 = -10.3$ kN/m^2

Hence, *gauge reading at* $\quad M = \mathbf{10.3\ kN/m^2}$ (*vacuum*) **(Ans.)**

Example 2.31. *For the Fig 2.34 determine specific gravity of gauge liquid B if the gauge pressure at A is – 18 kN/m^2.*

Solution. Sp. gravity of liquid B:

Pressure at L = pressure at M

i.e., $-18 + (1.5 \times 9.81 \times 0.6) = p_M$

or, $\quad p_M = -9.17$ kN/m^2

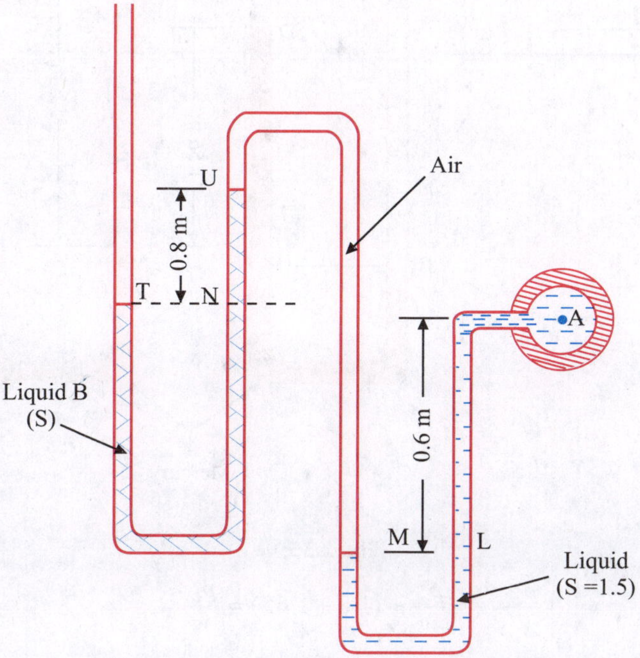

Fig. 2.34

Between points M and U, since there is an air column which can be neglected, therefore,

$$p_M = p_U\ (= -9.17 \text{ kN/m}^2)$$

Also, $\quad$ pressure at N = pressure at T.

But point T being at atmospheric pressure,

$$p_T = 0 = p_N$$

Thus, $\quad p_N = p_U + S \times 9.81 \times 0.8 = 0$

or, $\quad 0 = -9.17 + 7.848\ S$

$$\mathbf{S = 1.17}\ \textbf{(Ans.)}$$

Example 2.32. **(*Compound manometer*).** *In the Fig. 2.35 is shown a compound manometer. Find the gauge pressure at A if the manometric fluid is mercury and the fluid in the pipe and in the tubing which connects the two U-tubes is water.*

Solution. Gauge pressure at A, p_A:

Pressure at B = Pressure at C

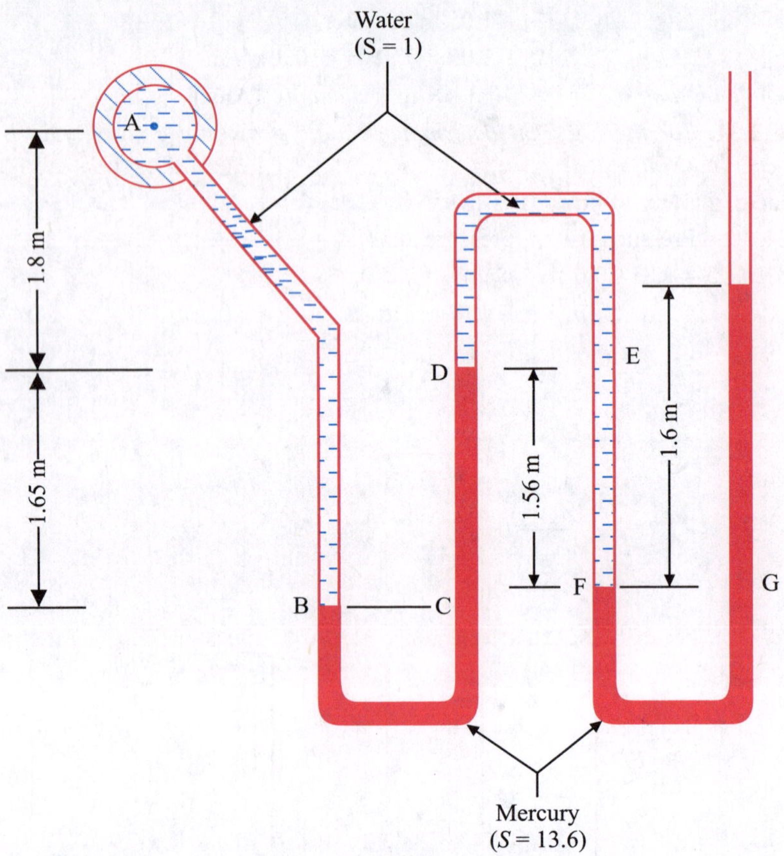

Fig. 2.35

$$\therefore \quad \frac{p_B}{w} = \frac{p_A}{w} + (1.8 + 1.65) = \frac{p_C}{w}$$

Further,

Pressure at D,

$$\frac{p_D}{w} = \frac{p_C}{w} - 1.65 \times 13.6$$

$$= \frac{p_A}{w} + (1.8 + 1.65) - 1.65 \times 13.6$$

$$= \frac{p_A}{w} + 3.45 - 22.44$$

or, $$\frac{p_D}{w} = \frac{p_A}{w} - 18.99 \quad ...(1)$$

Also, $$p_D = p_E \text{ and } p_F = p_G$$

But, $$\frac{p_F}{w} = \frac{p_E}{w} + 1.56$$

and, $$\frac{p_G}{w} = 1.6 \times 13.6 = 21.76$$

i.e., $$\frac{p_E}{w} + 1.56 = 21.76 \quad (\because p_F = p_G)$$

or, $\frac{p_E}{w} = 20.2$ or $\frac{p_D}{w} = 20.2$ $(\because p_D = p_E)$

Substituting the value of $\frac{p_D}{w}$ in eqn. (1), we get: $20.2 = \frac{p_A}{w} - 18.99$

or, $\frac{p_A}{w} = 20.2 + 18.99 = 39.19$ m of water.

i.e., $p_A = 9.81 \times 39.19 = \mathbf{384.4\ kN/m^2}$ **(Ans.)**

Example 2.33. (Compound manometer). *In the Fig. 2.36 is shown a compound manometer. Calculate pressure difference between the points A and B. Take $w_w = 10\ kN/m^3$ for water, $w_m = 136\ kN/m^3$ for mercury and $w_0 = 8.5\ kN/m^3$ for oil.* **(Punjab University)**

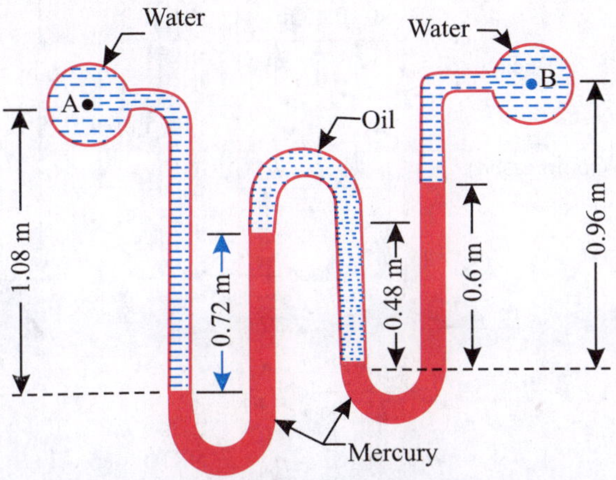

Fig. 2.36

Solution. *Given:* $w_w = 10\ kN/m^3$; $w_m = 136\ kN/m^3$; $w_0 = 8.5\ kN/m^3$

$p_A - p_B$:

Starting from point A, the governing manometric equation is:

$$p_A + w_w \times 1.08 - w_m \times 0.72 + w_0 \times 0.48 - w_m \times 0.6 - w_w (0.96 - 0.6) = p_B$$

or, $p_A = 10 \times 1.08 - 136 \times 0.72 + 8.5 \times 0.48 - 136 \times 0.6 - 10 (0.96 - 0.6) = p_B$

or, $p_A + 10.8 - 97.92 + 4.08 - 81.6 - 3.6 = p_B$

or, $\mathbf{p_A - p_B = 168.24\ kN/m^2}$ **(Ans.)**

Example 2.34. *A cylindrical bucket (empty) 450 mm in diameter and 750 mm long is forced with its open end first into water until its lower edge is 6 m below the surface. Determine the force required to maintain position, assuming the trapped air remains at constant temperature during the whole operation. Atmospheric pressure = 1.01 bar.*

The wall thickness and weight of the bucket may be considered as negligible.

Solution. Diameter of the bucket, d = 450 mm = 0.45 m

Length of the bucket, l = 750 mm = 0.75 m

Atmospheric pressure, p_{atm} = 1.01 bar.

Force required to maintain position, F: Refer to Fig 2.37.

Let, p_{air} = Absolute pressure of compressed air trapped in the cylindrical bucket, and

y = Depth of water raised in the bucket.

Then, since the temperature of air remains constant, therefore, as per isothermal condition, we have:

$$p_{atm.} \times \frac{\pi}{4} \times 0.45^2 \times 0.75 = p_{air} \times \frac{\pi}{4} \times 0.45^2 \times (0.75 - y)$$

($\because p_1 V_1 = p_2 V_2$ ..... for isothermal process)

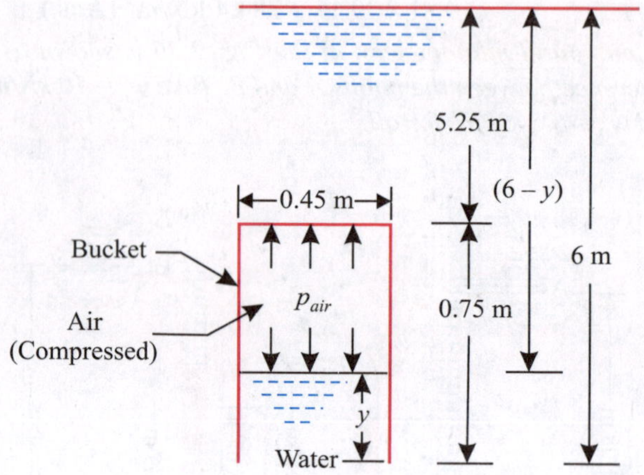

Fig. 2.37

or, $$P_{air} = \left(\frac{0.75}{0.75 - y}\right) p_{atm.} \quad ...(i)$$

Also, $$p_{air} = p_{atm.} + wh = p_{atm.} + 9810 \times (6 - y) \quad ...(ii)$$

($\because w = 9810$ N/m^3)

From eqn. (*i*) and (*ii*), we have:

$$\left(\frac{0.75}{0.75 - y}\right) p_{atm.} = P_{atm.} + 9810\,(6 - y)$$

or, $$\left(\frac{0.75}{0.75 - y}\right) \times 1.01 \times 10^5 = 1.01 \times 10^5 + 9810\,(6 - y)$$

or, $$1.01 \times 10^5 \left(\frac{0.75}{0.75 - y} - 1\right) = 9810\,(6 - y)$$

or, $$\frac{1.01 \times 10^5}{9810}\left(\frac{0.75 - 0.75 + y}{0.75 - y}\right) = 6 - y$$

or, $$10.29 \times \left(\frac{y}{0.75 - y}\right) = 6 - y \quad \text{or} \quad \frac{10.29\,y}{0.75 - y} + y = 6$$

or, $$10.29\,y + y\,(0.75 - y) = 6\,(0.75 - y)$$

or, $$10.29y + 0.75y - y^2 = 4.5 - 6y \quad \text{or} \quad y^2 - 17.04y + 4.5 = 0$$

or, $$y = \frac{17.04 \pm \sqrt{17.04^2 - 4 \times 4.5}}{2} = \frac{17.04 \pm 16.5}{2} = 0.27 \text{ m}$$

(ignoring + ve sign, being not possible)

Substituting the value of *y* in (*i*), we get:

$$p_{air} = \left(\frac{0.75}{0.75 - 0.27}\right) \times 1.01 = 1.578 \text{ bar}$$

The force tending to move the bucket in *upward direction,*

$$P_1 = p_{air} \times \frac{\pi}{4} \times 0.45^2$$

$$= (1.578 \times 10^5) \times \frac{\pi}{4} \times 0.45^2 \times 10^{-3} \text{ kN} = 25.097 \text{ kN}$$

The force acting on the bucket in the *downward direction,*

$$P_2 = (1.01 \times 10^5 + 9810 \times 5.25) \times \frac{\pi}{4} \times 0.45^2 \times 10^{-3} \text{ kN} = 24.254 \text{ kN}$$

∴ The force required to maintain the bucket in position,

$$F = P_1 - P_2 = 25.097 - 24.254 = \mathbf{0.843\ kN}\ \textbf{(Ans.)}$$

Example 2.35. *A glass tube of uniform bore is bent into the form of a square of sides l and filled with equal amounts of three invisible liquids of densities ρ_1, ρ_2 and ρ_3. It is known that $\rho_1 < \rho_2 < \rho_3$. If the tube arrangement is placed in a vertical plane (i.e. two sides vertical) and if one of the vertical sides is completely filled with the liquid of density ρ_2:*

(i) Show that $\frac{1}{3}(2\rho_3 + \rho_1) > \rho_2 > \frac{1}{3}(\rho_3 + 2\rho_1)$

(ii) If the relative densities of the first and third liquids are 1.0 and 1.22 respectively, find the range of the relative densities of the second liquid which makes the above arrangement possible.

Solution. Refer to Fig 2.38.

(*i*) **To prove,** $\frac{1}{3}(2\rho_3 + \rho_1) > \rho_2 > \frac{1}{3}(\rho_3 + 2\rho_1)$:

Let *E, F* and *G* be the interfaces, and

$$EA = x$$

Then, $DE = l - x$

Total length of the glass tube = $4l$

∴ Length of each liquid = $\frac{4}{3}l$

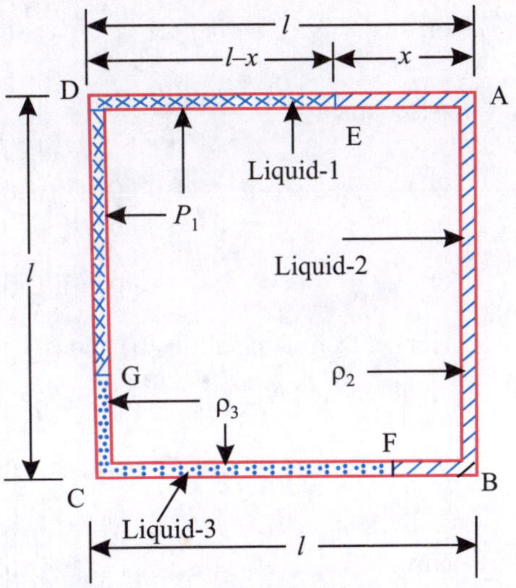

Fig. 2.38

For liquid-1:

$$EG = \frac{4}{3}l$$

$$DG = \frac{4}{3}l - (l - x) = \frac{1}{3}l + x$$

For liquid-3:

$$GC = l - \left(\frac{1}{3}l + x\right) = \frac{2}{3}l - x$$

$$FB = l - \left(\frac{2}{3}l + x\right) = \frac{1}{3}l - x$$

$$\left(\because FC = \frac{4l}{3} - GC = \frac{4l}{3} - \left(\frac{2}{3}l - x\right) = \frac{2}{3}l + x\right)$$

[Check: $FB + BA + AE = (\frac{1}{3}l - x) + l + x = \frac{4}{3}l$]

The pressure balance at the interface F is given by:
Pressure of (column DG + column GC) = pressure of column AB

$$\rho_1 g\left(\frac{1}{3}l + x\right) + \rho_3 g\left(\frac{2}{3}l - x\right) = \rho_2 g l$$

or,
$$\rho_1\left(\frac{1}{3}l + x\right) + \rho_3\left(\frac{2}{3}l - x\right) = \rho_2 l$$

$$x(\rho_1 - \rho_3) = \frac{1}{3}l\,(-\rho_1 + 3\rho_2 - 2\rho_3)$$

or,
$$x = \frac{\frac{1}{3}l\,(-\rho_1 + 3\rho_2 - 2\rho_3)}{(\rho_1 - \rho_3)} = \frac{\frac{1}{3}l(2\rho_3 - 3\rho_2 + \rho_1)}{(\rho_3 - \rho_1)}$$

It is known that $x > 0$ and also $x < \frac{1}{3}l$

Hence,
$$0 < x < \frac{l}{3}$$

$\therefore$
$$0 < \frac{(2\rho_3 - 3\rho_2 + \rho_1)}{(\rho_3 - \rho_1)} < 1$$

Also, since $\rho_1 < \rho_2 < \rho_3$ the denominator $(\rho_3 - \rho_1)$ is positive.
Hence, numerator is:

$$0 < (2\rho_3 - 3\rho_2 + \rho_1) < 1$$

or,
$$\rho_1 + 2\rho_3 > 3\rho_2$$

or,
$$\rho_2 < \frac{1}{3}(2\rho_3 + \rho_1) \qquad \text{...}(i)$$

Also, since
$$\frac{2\rho_3 - 3\rho_2 + \rho_1}{\rho_3 - \rho_1} < 1$$

or,
$$2\rho_3 - 3\rho_2 + \rho_1 < (\rho_3 - \rho_1)$$

or,
$$3\rho_2 > \rho_3 + 2\rho_1$$

or,
$$\rho_2 > \frac{1}{3}(\rho_3 + 2\rho_1) \qquad \text{...}(ii)$$

Hence, from inequalities (*i*) and (*ii*), we have:

$$\frac{1}{3}(2\rho_3 + \rho_1) > \rho_2 > \frac{1}{3}(\rho_3 + 2\rho_1)$$

(*ii*) Range of relative densities of the second liquid:

Given:
$$\rho_1 = 1.0; \quad \rho_3 = 1.22$$

Now,
$$\rho_2 > \frac{1}{3}(\rho_3 + 2\rho_1)$$

$$> \frac{1}{3}(1.22 + 2 \times 1.0) > 1.0733$$

Also,
$$\rho_2 > \frac{1}{3}(2\rho_3 + \rho_1)$$

$$> \frac{1}{3}(2 \times 1.22 + 1.0) > 1.1467$$

Hence,
$$\mathbf{1.0733 < \rho_2 < 1.1467}\ \textbf{(Ans.)}$$

2.5.1.3. Advantages and Limitations of Manometers

Advantages:

1. Easy to fabricate and relatively inexpensive.
2. Good accuracy.
3. High sensitivity.
4. Require little maintenance.
5. Not affected by vibration.
6. Specially suitable for low pressure and low differential pressures.
7. It is easy to change the sensitivity by affecting a change in the quantity of manometic liquid in the manometer.

Limitations:

1. Usually bulky and large in size.
2. Being fragile, get broken easily.
3. Readings of the manometers are affected by changes in temperature, altitude and gravity.
4. A capillary effect is created due to surface tension of manometric fluid.
5. For better accuracy meniscus has to be measured by accurate means.

2.5.2. Mechanical Gauges

The manometers (discussed earlier) are suitable for *comparatively low pressures*. For high pressures they become unnecessarily larger even when they are filled with heavy liquids. Therefore, for measuring medium and high pressures we make use of *elastic pressure gauges*. They employ different forms of elastic systems such as tubes, diaphragms or bellows etc. to measure the pressure. The elastic deformation of these elements is used to show the effect of pressure. Since these elements are deformed within the elastic limit only, therefore these gauges are sometimes called *elastic gauges*. Sometimes they are also called *secondary instruments, which implies that they must be calibrated by comparison with primary instruments such as manometers etc.*

Some of the important types of these gauges are enumerated and discussed below:

1. Bourdon tube pressure gauge,
2. Diaphragm gauge, and
3. Vacuum gauge.

1. Bourdon tube pressure gauge:

Bourdon tube pressure gauge is used for measuring high as well as low pressures. A simple form of this gauge is shown in Fig. 2.39. In this case, the pressure element consists of a metal tube of approximately elliptical cross-section. This tube is bent in the form of a segment of a circle and responds to pressure changes. When one end of the tube which is attached to the gauge case, is connected to the source of pressure, the internal pressure causes the tube to expand, whereby circumferential stress *i.e.*, hoop tension is set up. The free end of the tube moves and is in turn connected by suitable levers to a rack, which engages with a small pinion mounted on the same spindle as the pointer. Thus the pressure applied to the tube causes the rack and pinion to move. The pressure is indicated by the pointer over a dial which can be graduated in a suitable scale.

The Bourdon tubes are generally made of *bronze or nickel steel.* The *former* is generally used for *low pressures* and the *latter for high pressures.*

Depending upon the purpose for which they are required Bourdon tube gauges are made in different forms, some of them are:

(*i*) *Compound Bourdon tube*–used for measuring pressures both *above and below atmospheric pressure.*

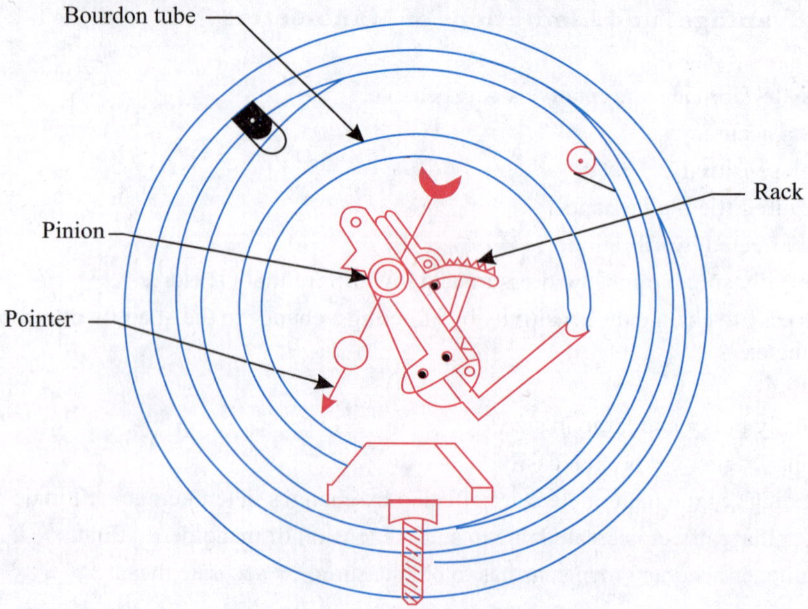

Fig. 2.39. Bourdon tube pressure gauge.

(*ii*) *Double Bourdon tube*–used where *vibrations are encountered.*

2. Diaphragm gauge:

This type of gauge employs a metallic disc or diaphragm instead of a bent tube. This disc or diaphragm is used for *actuating* the indicating device.

Refer to Fig. 2.40. When pressure is applied on the lower side of the diaphragm it is deflected upward. This movement of the diaphragm is transmitted to a rack and pinion. The latter is attached to the spindle of needle moving on a graduated dial. The dial can again be graduated in a suitable scale.

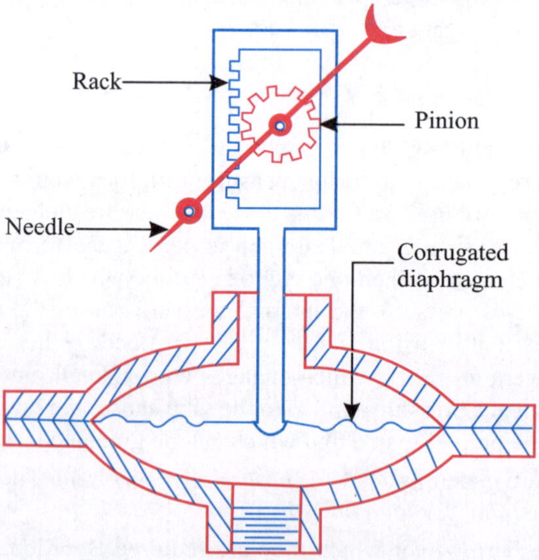

Fig. 2.40. Diaphragm gauge.

3. Vacuum gauge:

Bourdon gauges discussed earlier can be used to measure vacuum instead of pressure. Slight changes in the design are required in this purpose. Thus, in this case, the tube be *bent inward instead of outward* as in pressure gauges. *Vacuum gauges* are graduated in millimetres of mercury below atmospheric pressure. In such cases, therefore, absolute pressure in millimetres of mercury is the difference between barometer reading and vacuum gauge reading.

Vacuum gauges are used to measure the vacuum in the condensers, etc. If there is leakage, the vacuum will drop.

The pressure gauge installation requires the following considerations:

1. Flexible copper tubing and compression fittings are recommended for most installations.

2. The installation of a gauge cock and tee in the line close to the gauge is recommended because it permits the gauge to be removed for testing or replacement without having to shut down the system.

3. Pulsating pressures in the gauge line are not required.

4. The gauge and its connecting line is filled with an inert liquid and as such liquid seals are provided. Trapped air at any point of gauge lines may cause serious errors in pressure reading.

2.6. PRESSURE AT A POINT IN COMPRESSIBLE FLUID

In case of compressible fluids, the density (ρ) changes with the change of pressure and temperature. In the fields of meteorology, oceanography and aeronautics, we come across with problems involving atmospheric air where density, pressure and temperature change with the elevation. Therefore, for fluids having variable density eqn. (2.4) cannot be intergrated unless relation between ρ and p is known.

The 'equation of state' for gases is given as:

$$p = \rho RT \qquad ...(2.13)$$

or,

$$\rho = \frac{p}{RT}$$

We know that,

$$\frac{dp}{dZ} = w = \rho \times g \qquad \text{(Eqn.2.4)}$$

$$= \frac{p}{RT} \times g$$

$$\therefore \quad \frac{dp}{p} = \frac{g}{RT} \times dZ \qquad ...(2.14)$$

When Z is measured *vertically upward*, the above equation reduces to:

$$\frac{dp}{p} = \frac{-g}{RT} \times dZ \qquad ...(2.15)$$

Isothermal process:

In an isothermal process, temperature T remains constant, therefore, integrating eqn. (2.15) we get:

$$\int_{p_0}^{p} \frac{dp}{p} = -\int_{Z_0}^{Z} -\frac{g}{RT}\, dZ = -\frac{g}{RT}\int_{Z_0}^{Z} dZ$$

or,

$$ln\left(\frac{p}{p_0}\right) = \frac{g}{RT}(Z - Z_0)$$

where, p_0 is the pressure, and Z_0 is the height.

If the datum line is taken at Z_0, then Z_0 becomes zero and p_0 becomes the pressure at datum line.

$$ln\left(\frac{p}{p_0}\right) = -\frac{g}{RT}.Z$$

or,
$$\frac{p}{p_0} = e^{(-gZ/RT)}$$

or, Pressure at a height Z is given by: ...(2.16)

$$p = p_0 e^{(-gZ/RT)}$$

Adiabatic process:

When the process follows an adiabatic law, the relation between pressure and density is given by:

$$\frac{p}{\rho^\gamma} = \text{constant} = C \quad ...(i)$$

where, γ is the ratio of specific heats.

$$\therefore \quad \rho^\gamma = \frac{p}{C}$$

or,
$$\rho = \left(\frac{p}{C}\right)^{1/\gamma} \quad ...(ii)$$

Now eqn. (2.4) becomes:

$$\frac{dp}{dZ} = -\rho g = -\left(\frac{p}{C}\right)^{1/\gamma}.g \quad \text{.... } Z \text{ measured vertically up}$$

or,
$$\frac{dp}{\left(\frac{p}{C}\right)^{1/\gamma}} = -g.\,dZ \quad \text{or} \quad C^{1/\gamma} \times \frac{dp}{(p)^{1/\gamma}} = -g.dZ$$

Integrating the above equation, we get:

$$C^{1/\gamma}\left[\frac{p^{\left(-\frac{1}{\gamma}+1\right)}}{-\frac{1}{\gamma}+1}\right]_{p_0}^{p} = -g[Z]_{Z_0}^{Z}$$

or,
$$\left[\frac{C^{1/\gamma} p^{\left(-\frac{1}{\gamma}+1\right)}}{-\frac{1}{\gamma}+1}\right]_{p_0}^{p} = -g[Z]_{Z_0}^{Z}$$

From eqn. (*i*), we have, $C^{1/\gamma} = \left[\frac{p}{\rho^\gamma}\right]^{1/\gamma} = \frac{p^{1/\gamma}}{\rho}$ (C being constant, can be taken inside)

Substituting this value of $C^{1/\gamma}$ in the above equation, we get:

$$\left[\frac{p^{1/\gamma} p^{\left(-\frac{1}{\gamma}+1\right)}}{\rho\left(\frac{\gamma-1}{\gamma}\right)}\right]_{p_0}^{p} = -g\,[Z-Z_0]$$

or, $$\frac{\gamma}{\gamma-1}\left[\frac{p}{\rho}\right]_{p_0}^{p} = -g\,(Z - Z_0)$$

$$= \frac{\gamma}{\gamma-1}\left[\frac{p}{\rho} - \frac{p_0}{\rho_0}\right] = -g\,(Z - Z_0)$$

If datum line is taken at Z_0 (where pressure, temperature and density are p_0, T_0, ρ_0), then $Z_0 = 0$.

$$\therefore \quad \frac{\gamma}{\gamma-1}\left[\frac{p}{\rho} - \frac{p_0}{\rho_0}\right] = -g\,Z$$

or, $$\left(\frac{p}{\rho} - \frac{p_0}{\rho_0}\right) = -gZ\left(\frac{\gamma-1}{\gamma}\right)$$

or, $$\frac{p}{\rho} = \frac{p_0}{\rho_0} - gZ\left(\frac{\gamma-1}{\gamma}\right) = \frac{p_0}{\rho_0}\left[1 - \frac{\gamma-1}{\gamma}gZ \times \frac{\rho_0}{p_0}\right]$$

or, $$\frac{p}{\rho} \times \frac{\rho_0}{p_0} = \left[1 - \frac{\gamma-1}{\gamma}gZ \times \frac{\rho_0}{p_0}\right] \qquad ...(iii)$$

But from eqn. (*i*), $$\frac{p}{\rho^{\gamma}} = \frac{p_0}{\rho_0^{\gamma}} \quad \text{or} \quad \left(\frac{\rho_0}{\rho}\right)^{\gamma} = \frac{p_0}{p} \quad \text{or} \quad \frac{\rho_0}{\rho} = \left(\frac{p_0}{p}\right)^{1/\gamma}$$

Substituting the value of $\frac{\rho_0}{\rho}$ in eqn. (*iii*), we get:

$$\frac{p}{p_0} \times \left(\frac{p_0}{p}\right)^{1/\gamma} = \left[1 - \frac{\gamma-1}{\gamma}gZ \times \frac{\rho_0}{p_0}\right]$$

or, $$\frac{p}{p_0} \times \left(\frac{p}{p_0}\right)^{-1/\gamma} = \left[1 - \frac{\gamma-1}{\gamma}gZ \times \frac{\rho_0}{p_0}\right]$$

or, $$\left(\frac{p}{p_0}\right)^{1-\frac{1}{\gamma}} = \left[1 - \frac{\gamma-1}{\gamma}gZ \times \frac{\rho_0}{p_0}\right]$$

or, $$\left(\frac{p}{p_0}\right)^{\frac{\gamma-1}{\gamma}} = \left[1 - \frac{\gamma-1}{\gamma}gZ \times \frac{\rho_0}{p_0}\right]$$

or, $$\frac{p}{p_0} = \left[1 - \frac{\gamma-1}{\gamma}gZ \times \frac{\rho_0}{p_0}\right]^{\frac{\gamma}{\gamma-1}}$$

$\therefore$ Pressure (p) at a height Z from the ground level is given by:

$$p = p_0\left[1 - \frac{\gamma-1}{\gamma}gZ \times \frac{\rho_0}{p_0}\right]^{\frac{\gamma}{\gamma-1}} \qquad ...(2.17)$$

where, p_0 = Pressure at ground level (when $Z_0 = 0$), and

ρ_0 = Density of air at ground level.

Also, equation of state is:

$$\frac{p_0}{\rho_0} = RT_0 \quad \text{or} \quad \frac{\rho_0}{p_0} = \frac{1}{RT_0}$$

Substituting the value of $\frac{\rho_0}{p_0}$ is eqn. (2.17), we get:

$$p = p_0 \left[1 - \frac{\gamma - 1}{\gamma} \times \frac{gZ}{RT_0}\right]^{\frac{\gamma}{\gamma - 1}} \quad ...(2.18)$$

- *Temperature at any point in compressible fluid in an adiabatic process is calculated as follows:*

Equation of state at ground level and at a height Z from the ground level is written as:

$$\frac{p_0}{\rho_0} = RT_0, \quad \text{and} \quad \frac{p}{\rho} = RT$$

Dividing these equations, we have:

$$\frac{p_0}{\rho_0} \times \frac{\rho}{p} = \frac{RT_0}{RT}$$

or,

$$\frac{T}{T_0} = \frac{p}{p_0} \times \frac{\rho_0}{\rho} \quad ...(iv)$$

But from eqn. (2.18), $\frac{p}{p_0}$ is given by:

$$\frac{p}{p_0} = \left[1 - \frac{\gamma - 1}{\gamma} \times \frac{gZ}{RT_0}\right]^{\frac{\gamma}{\gamma - 1}}$$

Also for *adiabatic process* $\frac{p}{\rho^\gamma} = \frac{p_0}{\rho_0^\gamma}$ or $\left(\frac{\rho_0}{\rho}\right)^\gamma = \frac{p_0}{p}$

or,

$$\frac{\rho_0}{\rho} = \left(\frac{p_0}{p}\right)^{1/\gamma} = \left(\frac{p}{p_0}\right)^{-1/\gamma}$$

or,

$$\frac{\rho_0}{\rho} = \left[1 - \frac{\gamma - 1}{\gamma} \times \frac{gZ}{RT_0}\right]^{\left(\frac{\gamma}{\gamma - 1}\right) \times \left(-\frac{1}{\gamma}\right)}$$

or,

$$\frac{\rho_0}{\rho} = \left[1 - \frac{\gamma - 1}{\gamma} \times \frac{gZ}{RT_0}\right]^{-\frac{1}{\gamma - 1}}$$

Substituting the values of $\frac{p}{p_0}$ and $\frac{\rho_0}{\rho}$ in eqn. (*iv*), we get:

$$\frac{T}{T_0} = \left[1 - \frac{\gamma - 1}{\gamma} \times \frac{gZ}{RT_0}\right]^{\frac{\gamma}{\gamma - 1}} \times \left[1 - \frac{\gamma - 1}{\gamma} \times \frac{gZ}{RT_0}\right]^{-\frac{1}{\gamma - 1}}$$

$$= \left[1 - \frac{\gamma - 1}{\gamma} \times \frac{gZ}{RT_0}\right]^{\frac{\gamma}{\gamma - 1} - \frac{1}{\gamma - 1}} = \left[1 - \frac{\gamma - 1}{\gamma} \times \frac{gZ}{RT_0}\right]$$

∴

$$T = T_0 \left[1 - \frac{\gamma - 1}{\gamma} \times \frac{gZ}{RT_0}\right] \quad ...(2.19)$$

Temperature lapse rate (L):

It is defined as the *rate at which the temperature changes with elevation.* It can be obtained by differentiating the eqn. w.r.t. *Z* as follows:

$$\frac{dT}{dZ} = \frac{d}{dZ}\left[T_0\left\{1 - \frac{\gamma - 1}{\gamma}\right\} \times \frac{gZ}{RT_0}\right]$$

where, T_0, γ, g and R are constant.

$$\therefore \quad \frac{dT}{dZ} = T_0\left\{-\frac{\gamma - 1}{\gamma} \times \frac{g}{RT_0}\right\} = -\frac{g}{R}\left(\frac{\gamma - 1}{\gamma}\right)$$

Hence, temperature lapse–rate, $L = \frac{dT}{dZ} = -\frac{g}{R}\left(\frac{\gamma - 1}{\gamma}\right)$ ...(2.20)

— In this eqn., if $\gamma = 1$ the process in an isothermal one which means $\frac{dT}{dZ} = 0$; it indicates that temperature does not *change* with height.

— If $\gamma > 1$, lapse-rate is negative which means that *temperature decreases with increase of height.*

Following points are worth noting:

— The value of γ in atmosphere varies with height.

— Upto an elevation of 11km, above sea level, the temperature of air *decreases* at the rate of 0.0065° C/m. From 11 km to 32 km, the temperature remains constant but *rises* above 32 km of height.

Example 2.36. *Derive an expression for the pressure ratio in the troposphere if the absolute temperature is assumed to vary according to the law $T = T_0 - \alpha(Z - Z_0)$, where, T_0 is the absolute temperature at sea level and α is the temperature gradient.* **(Nagpur University)**

Solution. The variation in altitude is given by:

$$dp = -\rho\, gdZ = -wdZ$$

where, ρ = Density of air, kg/m^3, and

w = Specific weight, N/m^3.

Since, $\rho = \frac{p}{RT}$, substituting in above relation, we get $dp = \left(-\frac{p}{RT}\right)gdZ$

or, $$\frac{dp}{p} = -\frac{g}{RT}dZ \quad ...(i)$$

Since, $$T = T_0 - \alpha(Z - Z_0) \quad ...(Given)$$

$$\therefore \quad dT = -\alpha\, dZ$$

Substituting for dZ in (*i*), we have:

$$\frac{dp}{p} = \frac{g}{\alpha R}\frac{dT}{T}$$

Integrating between (p_0, p) to (Z_0, Z), where suffix 0 denotes sea level conditions, we get:

$$ln\left(\frac{p}{p_0}\right) = \frac{g}{\alpha R}ln\left(\frac{T}{T_0}\right) = \frac{g}{\alpha R}ln\left[\frac{T_0 - \alpha(Z - Z_0)}{T_0}\right]$$

or, $$\frac{p}{p_0} = \left[1 - \frac{\alpha(Z - Z_0)}{T_0}\right]$$ **.....Required expression (Ans.)**

Example 2.37. *The temperature of the earth's atmosphere drops about 5°C for every 1000 m of elevation above the earth's surface. If the air temperature at the ground level is 15°C and the pressure is 760 mm Hg, at what elevation is the pressure 380 mm Hg? Assume that air behaves as an ideal gas.* **(Roorkee University)**

Solution: *Given:* T_0 = 15 + 273 = 288 K; p_0 = 760 mm Hg; p = 380 mm Hg;

$$\frac{dT}{dZ} = -\frac{5}{1000} \,°C/m$$

Elevation Z:

Temperature lapse-rate, $$L = \frac{dT}{dZ} = -\frac{g}{R}\left(\frac{\gamma - 1}{\gamma}\right)$$

$\therefore$ $$L = -\frac{5}{1000} = -\frac{g}{R}\left(\frac{\gamma - 1}{\gamma}\right)$$

or, $$\frac{5}{1000} = \frac{9.81}{287}\left(\frac{\gamma - 1}{\gamma}\right)$$

$\therefore$ $$\frac{\gamma - 1}{\gamma} = 0.1463$$

Using the relation: $$p = p_0\left[1 - \frac{\gamma - 1}{\gamma} \cdot \frac{gZ}{RT_0}\right]^{\frac{\gamma}{\gamma - 1}}$$

or, $$380 = 760\left[1 - 0.1463 \times \frac{9.81 \times Z}{287 \times 288}\right]^{\frac{1}{0.1463}}$$

or, $$\left(\frac{380}{760}\right)^{0.1463} = 1 - 0.1463 \times \frac{9.81\, Z}{287 \times 288} = 1 - 1.736 \times 10^{-5}\, Z$$

or, $$1.736 \times 10^{-5}\, Z = 1 - \left(\frac{380}{760}\right)^{0.1463} = 0.0964$$

or, $$Z = \frac{0.0964}{1.736 \times 10^{-5}} = \mathbf{5553\ m\ (Ans)}$$

Example 2.38. *The barometric pressure at sea level is 760 mm of mercury while that on a mountain top is 735 mm. If the density of air is assumed constant at 1.2 kg/m³, what is the elevation of the mountain top?* **(Punjab University)**

Solution. *Given*: Pressure at sea level, $p_0 = 760$ mm of Hg

$$= \frac{760}{1000} \times (13.6 \times 1000) \times 9.81 = 101396 \text{ N/m}^2$$

Pressure at mountain, p = 735 mm of Hg

$$= \frac{735}{1000} \times (13.6\ 5\ 1000) \times 9.81 = 98060 \text{ N/m}^2$$

Density of air, ρ = 1.2 kg/m³

Height of the mountain top from sea-level, h:

It is a known fact that as the elevation above the sea-level increases, the atmospheric pressure decreases. As the density is constant (given), hence the pressure at any height '*h*' above the sea-level is given by the equation,

$p = p_0 - \rho g h$ or $$h = \frac{p_0 - p}{\rho g} = \frac{(101396 - 98060)}{1.2 \times 9.81} = \mathbf{283.4\ m\ (Ans.)}$$

Example 2.39. *Determine the pressure at a height of 800 m above sea level if the atmospheric pressure is 10.139 × 10⁴ N/m² and temperature is 15°C at sea level assuming:*

(i) Air is incompressible;

(ii) Pressure variation follows isothermal law;

(iii) Pressure variation follows adiabatic law.

Take: Density of air at sea level = 1.285 kg/m³

Neglect variation of g with altitude. **(PTU)**

Solution. *Given*: Height above sea-level, $Z = 8000$ m

Pressure at sea-level, $p_0 = 10.139 \times 10^4$ N/m²

Temperature at sea level, $t_0 = 15°C \quad \therefore \; T_0 = 15 + 273 = 288$ K

Density of air, $\rho = \rho_0 = 1.285$ kg/m³.

Pressure *p*:

(i) When air is incompressible:

We know that, $\dfrac{dp}{dz} = -\rho g \; ; \qquad \therefore \int_{p_0}^{p} dp = -\int_{Z_0}^{Z} \rho g \, dz$

or, $p - p_0 = -\rho g (Z - Z_0)$

or, $p = p_0 - \rho g Z \qquad (\because Z_0 = \text{datum line} = 0)$

$= 10.139 \times 10^4 - 1.285 \times 9.81 \times 8000 = \mathbf{543.2\ N/m^2}$ **(Ans.)**

(ii) When pressure variation follows isothermal law :

We know that, $p = p_0 \, e^{(-gZ/RT)}$ ...(Eqn. 2.16)

$$= p_0 \, e^{(-gZ\rho_0/p_0)} \left[\because \frac{p_0}{\rho_0} = RT \text{ or } \frac{\rho_0}{p_0} = \frac{1}{RT} \right]$$

$$= 10.139 \times 10^4 \times e^{(-9.81 \times 8000 \times 1.285/101390)}$$

$$= 10.139 \times 10^4 \times e^{-0.9946} = 10.139 \times 10^4 \times 0.3699$$

$= 37504$ N/m² or **3.75 N/cm² (Ans.)**

(iii) When pressure variation follows adiabatic law ($\gamma = 1.4$):

Using the equation: $p = p_0 \left[1 - \dfrac{\gamma - 1}{\gamma} gZ \dfrac{\rho_0}{p_0} \right]^{\gamma/\gamma - 1}$ ...[Eqn.2.17]

Substituting the values, we get:

$$p = 10.139 \times 10^4 \left[1 - \frac{1.4 - 1.0}{1.4} \times 9.81 \times 8000 \times \frac{1.285}{10.139 \times 10^4} \right]^{\left(\frac{1.4}{1.4-1}\right)}$$

$$= 101390 \, (1 - 0.2842)^{(1.4/0.4)} = 101390 \times (0.7158)^{3.5}$$

$= 31460$ N/m² or **3.146 N/cm² (Ans)**

Example 40. *Determine the pressure and density of air at a height of 4500 m from sea-level where pressure and temperature of the air are 101400 N/m² and 15°C respectively. Density of air at sea-level is equal to 1.285 kg/m³ and the temperature lapse-rate is 0.0065°K/m.*

Solution. *Given*: Height, $Z = 4500$ m

Pressure at sea-level; $p_0 = 101400$ N/m²

Temperature at sea-level, $T_0 = t + 273 = 15 + 273 = 288$ K

Temperature lapse–rate, $L = \dfrac{dT}{dZ} - 0.0065°$ C/m

Density of air at sea level, $\rho_0 = 1.285$ kg/m³

We know that, $$L = \frac{dT}{dZ} = -\frac{g}{R}\left(\frac{\gamma-1}{\gamma}\right) \qquad \text{...[Eqn. (2.20)]}$$

where, $$R = \frac{p_0}{\rho_0 T_0} = \frac{101400}{1.285 \times 288} = 274$$

Substituting the values in the above equation, we get:

$$-0.0065 = -\frac{9.81}{274}\left(\frac{\gamma-1}{\gamma}\right)$$

$$\therefore \quad \frac{\gamma-1}{\gamma} = \frac{0.0065 \times 274}{9.81} = 0.1815$$

$$\therefore \quad \gamma(1-0.1815) = 1 \quad \text{or} \quad \gamma = \frac{1}{1-0.1815} = 1.22$$

Pressure (p) and density (ρ) of air at a height of 4500 m:

We know that, $$p = p_0\left[1 - \frac{\gamma-1}{\gamma} gZ \frac{\rho_0}{p_0}\right]^{(\gamma/\gamma-1)} \qquad \text{...[Eqn. (2.17)]}$$

Substituting the values, we get:

$$p = 101400\left[1 - \frac{1.22-1}{1.22} \times 9.81 \times 4500 \times \frac{1.285}{101400}\right]^{\frac{1.22}{0.22}}$$

$$= 101400\,(1-0.1)^{5.545} = 56534 \text{ N/m}^2 \text{ or } \mathbf{5.6534\ N/cm^2} \text{ (Ans.)}$$

Also, $$\frac{p}{\rho} = RT$$

where, p, ρ and T are pressure, density and temperature respectively at a height of 4500 m.

Now the value of T is calculated from temperature lapse-rate as follows :

$$t \text{ at } 4500 \text{ m} = t_0 + \frac{dT}{dZ} \times 4500 = 15 - 0.0065 \times 4500 = -14.25° \text{ C}$$

$$\therefore \quad T = 273 + (-14.25) = 258.75 \text{ K}$$

$\therefore$ Density of air at a height of 4500 m; $\rho = \frac{p}{RT} = \frac{56534}{274 \times 258.75} = \mathbf{0.797\ kg/m^3}$ **(Ans.)**

Example 2.41. *Calculate the pressure round an aeroplane which is flying at an altitude of 4200 m. The temperature lapse-rate is 0.0065 K/m. The pressure, temperature and density of air at ground level are 101400 N/m², 15°C and 1.285 kg/m³ respectively.*

Variation of g with altitude may be neglected.

Solution. *Given:* Height, Z = 4200 m; Lapse-rate, $L = \frac{dT}{dZ} = -0.0065$ K/m;

$$p_0 = 101400 \text{ N/m}^2;\ T_0 = 15 + 273 = 288 \text{ K};\ \rho_0 = 1.285 \text{ kg/m}^3$$

Pressure round the aeroplane, p;

Let us first calculate the value of power index γ as follows:

We know that, $$L = \frac{dT}{dZ} = -\frac{g}{R}\left(\frac{\gamma-1}{\gamma}\right) \qquad \text{...[Eqn. (2.20)]}$$

where, $$R = \frac{p_0}{\rho_0 T_0} = \frac{101400}{1.285 \times 288} = 274$$

Substituting the value, we have:

$$-0.0065 = -\frac{9.81}{274}\left(\frac{\gamma-1}{\gamma}\right)$$

or, $\frac{\gamma - 1}{\gamma} = \frac{0.0065 \times 274}{9.81} = 0.1815$ or $\gamma = 1.22$

Pressure round the aeroplane is given as: $p = p_0 \left[1 - \frac{\gamma - 1}{\gamma} gZ \frac{\rho_0}{p_0}\right]^{\frac{\gamma}{\gamma - 1}}$ ...[Eqn. (2.17)]

$$= 101400\left[1 - \frac{1.22 - 1}{1.22} \times 9.81 \times 4200 \times \frac{1.285}{101400}\right]^{\frac{1.22}{0.22}}$$

$$= 101400\,[1 - 0.094]^{5.545} = 58656 \text{ N/m}^2 = \mathbf{5.8656 \text{ N/cm}^2} \text{ (Ans.)}$$

HIGHLIGHTS

1. The force (P) per unit area (A) is called pressure (p); mathematically, $p = \frac{P}{A}$
2. Pressure head of a liquid, $h = \frac{p}{w}$ $(\because p = wh)$

   where, w is the specific weight of the liquid.
3. *Pascal's law* states as follows:

   "The intensity of pressure at any point in a liquid at rest, is the same in all directions".
4. The atmospheric pressure at sea level (above absolute zero) is called standard atmospheric pressure.

   (*i*) Absolute pressure = atmospheric pressure + gauge pressure

   $$p_{abs.} = p_{atm.} + p_{gauge}$$

   (*ii*) Vacuum pressure = Atmospheric pressure – absolute pressure (Vacuum pressure is defined as the pressure below the atmospheric pressure)
5. *Manometers* are defined as the devices used for measuring the pressure at a point in fluid by balancing the column of fluid by the same or another column of liquid.
6. *Mechanical gauges* are the devices in which the pressure is measured by balancing the fluid column by spring (elastic element) or dead weight. Some commonly used mechanical gauges are:

   (*i*) Bourdon tube pressure gauge, (*ii*) Diaphragm pressure gauge,

   (*iii*) Bellow pressure gauge, and (*iv*) Dead-weight pressure gauge.
7. The pressure at a height Z in a static compressible fluid (gas) undergoing isothermal compression $\left(\frac{p}{\rho} = \text{const.}\right)$,

   $$p = p_0 e^{(-gZ/RT)}$$

   where, p_0 = Absolute pressure at sea-level or at ground level,

   Z = Height from sea or ground level,

   R = Gas constant, and

   T = Absolute temperature.
8. The pressure and temperature at a height Z in a static compressible fluid (gas) undergoing adiabatic compression (p/ρ^{γ} = const.):

   $$p = p_0 \left[1 - \frac{\gamma - 1}{\gamma} gZ \frac{\rho_0}{p_0}\right]^{\frac{\gamma}{\gamma - 1}} = p_0 \left[1 - \frac{\gamma - 1}{\gamma} \frac{gZ}{RT_0}\right]^{\frac{\gamma}{\gamma - 1}}$$

and, temperature, $T = T_0\left[1 - \frac{\gamma - 1}{\gamma}\frac{gZ}{RT_0}\right]$

where, p_0, T_0 are pressure and temperature at sea-level; $\gamma = 1.4$ for air.

9. The rate at which the temperature changes with elevation is known as *Temperature Lapse-Rate*. It is given by,

$$L = \frac{-g}{R}\left(\frac{\gamma - 1}{\gamma}\right)$$

If (*i*) $\gamma = 1$, temperature is zero; (*ii*) $\gamma > 1$, temperature decreases with the increase of height.

OBJECTIVE TYPE QUESTIONS

Choose the Correct Answer:

1. The force per unit area is called
(*a*) pressure (*b*) strain
(*c*) surface tension (*d*) none of the above.

2. The pressure of a liquid on a surface will always act ...... to the surface.
(*a*) parallel (*b*) normal
(*c*) 45° (*d*) 60°.

3. The pressure .... as the depth of the liquid increases.
(*a*) increases
(*b*) decreases
(*c*) remain unchanged
(*d*) none of the above.

4. The intensity of pressure in a liquid due to its depth will vary .... with depth.
(*a*) directly
(*b*) indirectly
(*c*) either of the above
(*d*) none of the above.

5. The height of the free surface above any point is known as
(*a*) static head
(*b*) intensity of pressure
(*c*) either of the above
(*d*) none of the above.

6. "The intensity of pressure at any point in a liquid at rest is the same in all directions."
The above statement is known as
(*a*) Kirchhoff's law (*b*) Pascal's law
(*c*) either of the above (*d*) none of the above.

7. Any pressure measured above the absolute zero of pressure is termed as
(*a*) atmospheric pressure
(*b*) gauge pressure
(*c*) either of the above
(*d*) none of the above.

8. The fundamental S.I. unit of pressure is N/m^2; this is also known as ......
(*a*) Pascal (*b*) Stoke
(*c*) Poise (*d*) none of the above.

9. The devices used for measuring the pressure at a point in a fluid by balancing the column fluid by the same or another column of liquid are known as
(*a*) mechanical gauges
(*b*) manometers
(*c*) either of the above
(*d*) none of the above.

10. The simplest form of manometer which can be used for measuring moderate pressures of liquid is
(*a*) piezometer
(*b*) differential manometer
(*c*) U-tube manometer
(*d*) none of the above

11. Piezometers measure ..... pressure only.
(*a*) absolute (*b*) gauge
(*c*) atmospheric (*d*) any of the above.

12. A piezometer tube is not suitable for measuring .... pressure.
(*a*) positive (*b*) negative
(*c*) atmospheric (*d*) none of the above.

13. Inclined single column manometer is useful for the measurement of ..... pressures.
(*a*) small (*b*) medium
(*c*) high (*d*) negative.

14. Which of the following is used to measure the difference in pressures between two points in a pipe, or in two different pipes?
(*a*) Piezometer
(*b*) Single column manometer
(*c*) Differential manometer
(*a*) None of the above.

15. The manometers are suitable for comparatively ..... pressures.
(*a*) low (*b*) high
(*c*) very high (*d*) none of the above.

16. A Bourdon tube pressure gauge is used for measuring .... pressures.
(*a*) low (*b*) high
(*c*) high as well as low (*d*) none of the above.

17. The Bourdon tubes are generally made of
(*a*) copper (*b*) tin
(*c*) mild steel
(*a*) bronze or nickel steel.

18. Which of the following is a mechanical gauge?
(*a*) Diaphragm gauge
(*b*) Dead weight pressure gauge
(*c*) Bourdon tube pressure gauge
(*d*) All of the above.

19. Which of the following is an advantage of manometers?
(*a*) Good accuracy (*b*) High sensitivity
(*c*) Little maintenance (*d*) All of the above.

20. Which of the following is limitation of manometers?
(*a*) Fragile
(*b*) Bulky and large in size
(*c*) Capillary effect is created due to surface tension of manometric fluid
(*d*) All of the above.

ANSWERS

1. (*a*)	**2.** (*b*)	**3.** (*a*)	**4.** (*a*)	**5.** (*a*)	**6.** (*b*)
7. (*c*)	**8.** (*a*)	**9.** (*b*)	**10.** (*a*)	**11.** (*b*)	**12.** (*b*)
13. (*a*)	**14.** (*c*)	**15.** (*a*)	**16.** (*c*)	**17.** (*d*)	**18.** (*d*)
19. (*d*)	**20.** (*d*).				

THEORETICAL QUESTIONS

1. Define the term 'pressure'.
2. State and prove 'Pascal's Law'.
3. Define the following:
(*i*) Atmospheric pressure,
(*ii*) Gauge pressure,
(*iii*) Vacuum pressure, and
(*iv*) Absolute pressure.
4. How is pressure measured?
5. What are manometers?
6. How are manometers classified?
7. Explain briefly the following:
(*i*) Piezometer
(*ii*) U-tube manometer.
8. What are differential manometers?
9. What are mechanical gauges? Name three important mechanical gauges.
10. Explain briefly the following mechanical gauges:
(*i*) Bourdon tube pressure gauge, and
(*ii*) Diaphragm gauge.
11. Derive an expressiton for the pressure at a height Z from sea-level for a static air when the compression of the air is assumed isothermal. The pressure and temperature at sea-level are p_0 and T_0 respectively.
12. Prove that the pressure and temperature for an adiabatic process at a height Z from sea-level for static air are:

$$p = p_0\left[1 - \frac{\gamma - 1}{\gamma}\frac{gZ}{RT_0}\right]^{\gamma/\gamma - 1}, \text{ and}$$

$$T = T_0\left[1 - \frac{\gamma - 1}{\gamma}.\frac{gZ}{RT_0}\right]$$ where p_0 and T_0 are the pressure and temperature at sea-level.

13. What do you understand by the term 'Temperature lapse-Rate'? Obtain an expression for the Temperature Lapse-Rate.

UNSOLVED EXAMPLES

1. If a mercury barometer reads 700 mm and a Bourdon gauge at a point in a flow system reads 500 kN/m^2, what is the absolute pressure at the point? **[Ans.** 595 kN/m^2 abs.]

2. Find the depth of a point below water surface in sea where the pressure intensity is 100.55 kN/m^2. Specific gravity of sea water is 1.025. **[Ans.** 10 m]

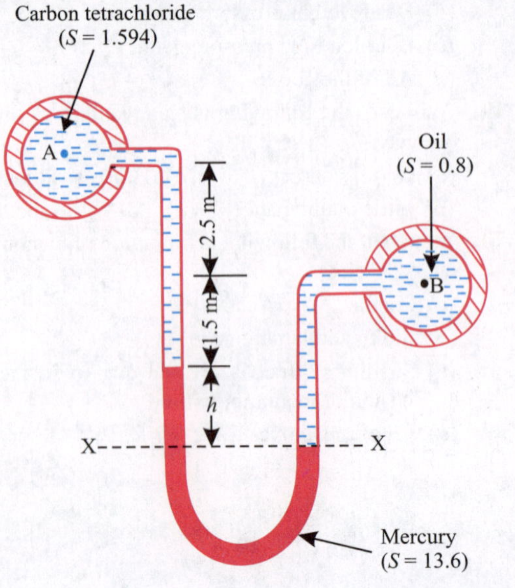

Fig. 2.41

3. Convert a pressure head of 100 m of water to
   (*i*) kerosene of specific gravity 0.81, and
   (*ii*) carbon tetrachloride of specific gravity 1.6.

   [**Ans.** (*i*) 123.4 m, (*ii*) 62.5 m]

   [**Hint.** $h_1S_1 = h_2S_2$]

4. As shown in Fig. 2.41, pipe A contains carbon tetrachloride of specific gravity 1.594 under a pressure of 103 kN/m^2 and pipe B contains oil of specific gravity 0.8. If the pressure in the pipe B is 171.6 kN/m^2 and the manometric fluid is mercury, find the difference *h* between the levels of mercury. [**Ans.** 142 mm]

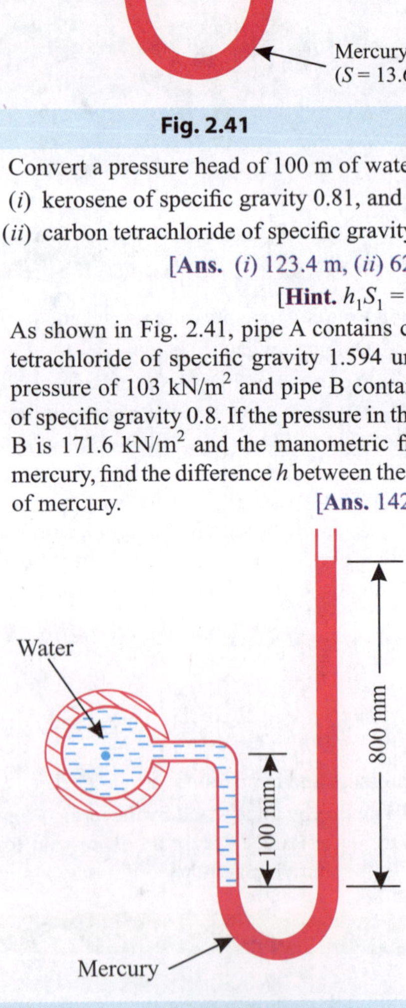

Fig. 2.42

5. The pressure of water in a pipeline was measured by means of a simple manometer containing mercury. The reading of the manometer is shown in Fig. 2.42. Calculate the pressure of the oil, if the difference of mercury level be 0.5 m.

   [**Ans.** 2.0 m; 19.62 kPa]

6. A U-tube containing mercury is used to measure the pressure of an oil of specific gravity 0.8 as shown in Fig. 2.43. Calculate the pressure of the oil, if the difference of mercury level be 0.5 m.

   [**Ans.** 14 m]

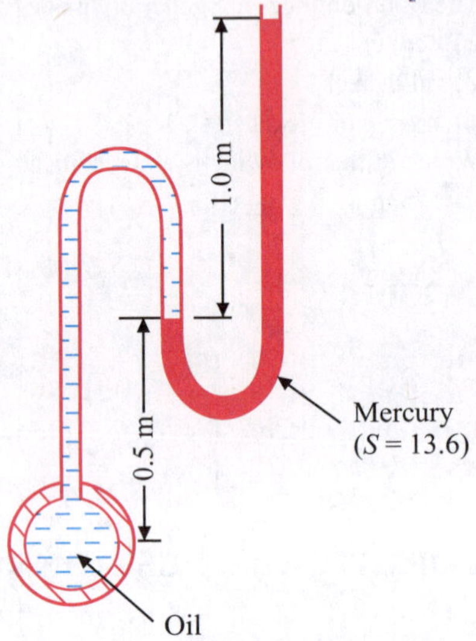

Fig. 2.43

7. A simple manometer (U-tube) containing mercury is connected to a pipe in which an oil of specific gravity 0.8 is flowing. The pressure in the pipe is vacuum. The other end of the manometer is open to atmosphere. Find the vacuum pressure in pipe, if the difference of mercury level in the two limbs is 200 mm and height of oil in the left-limb from the centre of the pipe is 150 mm below. [**Ans.** – 278.6 kPa]

8. Fig. 2.44 shows a differential manometer connected at two points A and B. If at A air pressure is 78.5 kN/m^2, find the absolute pressure at B.

   [**Ans.** 69.1 kN/m^2]

9. A single column vertical manometer is connected to a pipe containing oil of specific gravity 0.9. The area of the reservoir is 80 times the area of the manometer tube. The reservoir contains mercury of specific gravity 13.6. The level of mercury in the reservoir is at a height of 300 mm below the centre of the pipe and difference of mercury levels in the reservoir and right limb is 500 mm. Find the pressure in the pipe.

   [**Ans.** 64.7 kN/m^2]

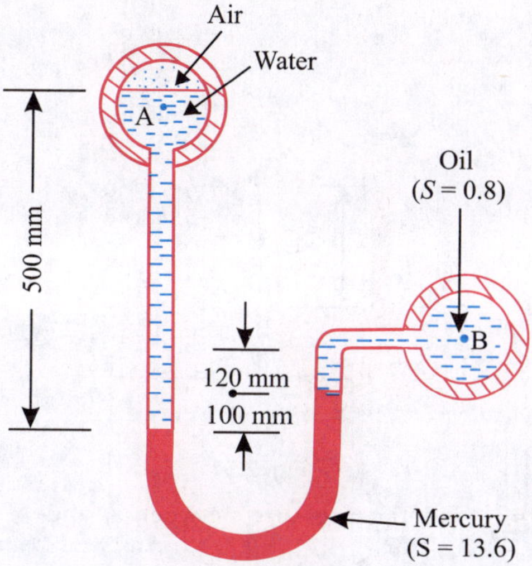

Fig. 2.44

10. A micrometer, having a ratio of reservoir to limb areas as 40, was used to determine the pressure in a pipe containing water. Determine the pressure in the pipe for manometer reading shown in Fig. 2.45. **[Ans.** 688.8 mm]

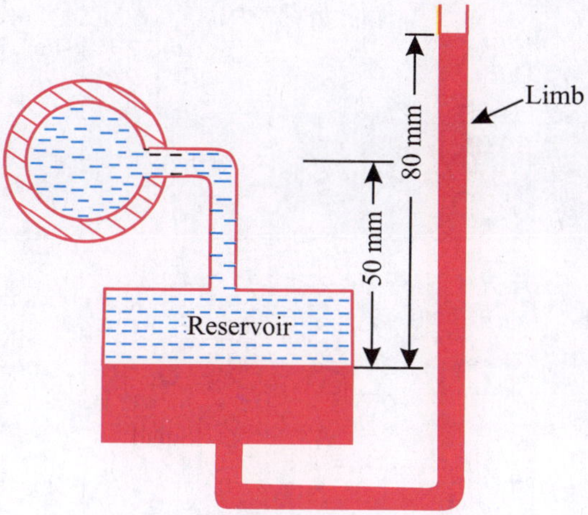

Fig. 2.45

11. A U-tube mercury differential manometer is used to measure the difference of pressure between inlet throat of a venturimeter placed with its axis horizontal in a pipeline. Calculate the difference in pressure between inlet and throat when the manometer reading is 250 mm and water flows through the pipeline. **[Ans.** 3.15 m of water]

12. Calculate the pressure difference between two points A and B in Fig. 2.46.

[Ans. 13.83 kN/m^2]

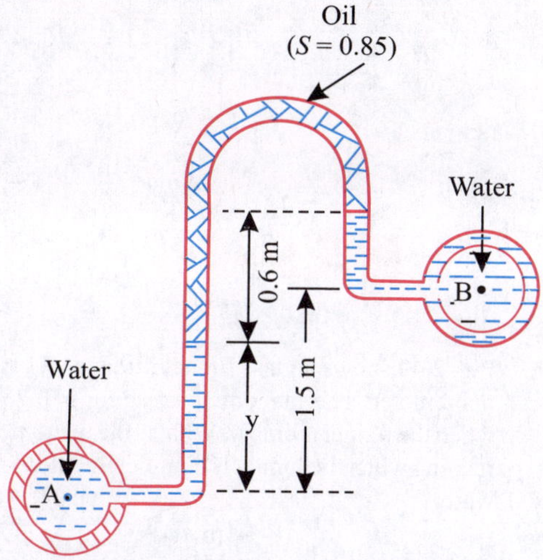

Fig. 2.46

13. Find the difference in pressures between points A and B in Fig. 2.47. Neglect weight of air.

[Ans. $p_B - p_A$ = 17.66 kN/m^2]

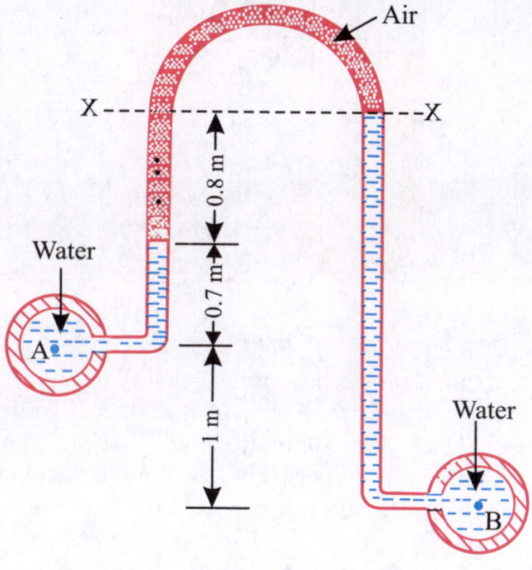

Fig. 2.47

14. An inverted differential manometer containing an oil of sp. gravity 0.9 is connected to find the difference of pressures at two points of a pipe containing water. If the manometer reading is 400 mm, find the difference of pressures.

[Ans. 40 mm of water]

15. Fig. 2.48 shows a mercury manometer fitted to a venturimeter in which water is flowing. Determine the difference of pressures between the points A and B. **[Ans.** – 18.94 kN/m^2]

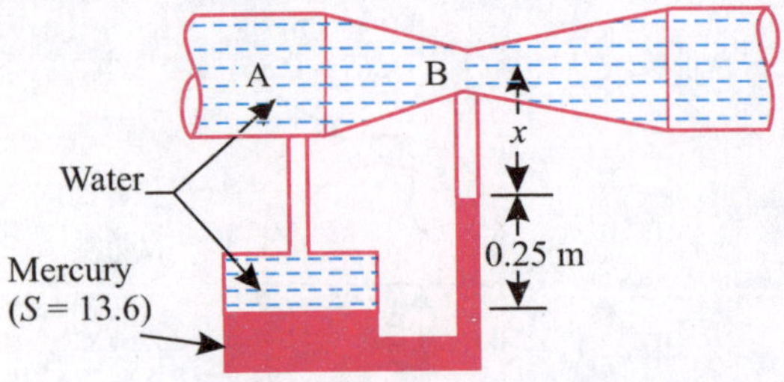

Fig. 2.48

16. Fig. 2.49 shows a glass funnel fitted to a U-type manometer. The manometer reading is 0.25 m when the funnel is empty. What is the manometer reading when the funnel is completely filled with water? **[Ans.** 0.4 m]

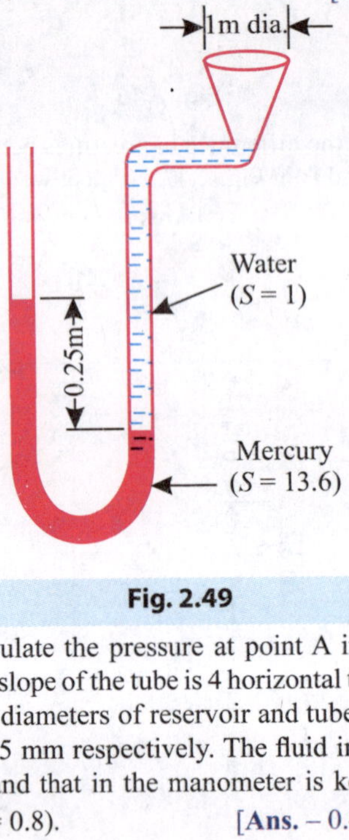

Fig. 2.49

17. Calculate the pressure at point A in Fig. 2.50. The slope of the tube is 4 horizontal to 1 vertical. The diameters of reservoir and tube are 50 mm and 5 mm respectively. The fluid in the pipe is air and that in the manometer is kerosene (sp. gr. = 0.8). **[Ans.** – 0.494 kN/m^2]

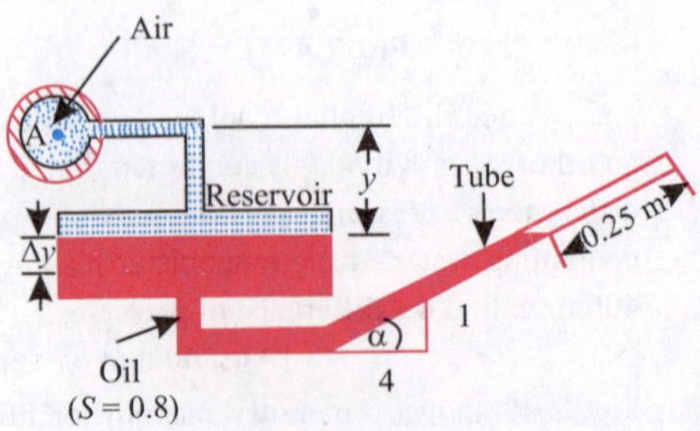

Fig. 2.50

18. Find the gauge readings at A and B in Fig. 2.51. **[Ans.** 17.39 kN/m^2 (vacuum), 12.61 kN/m^2]

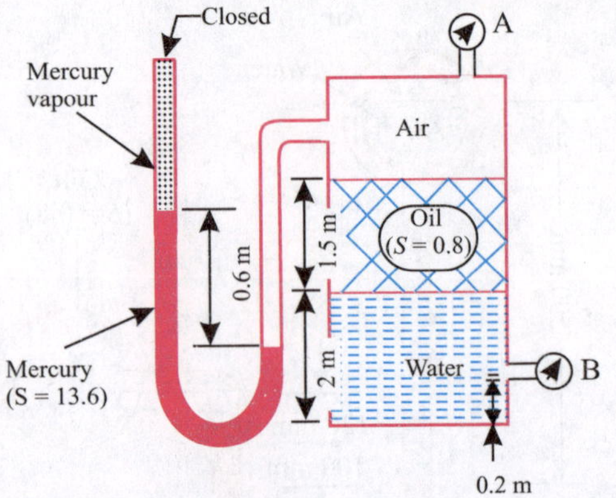

Fig. 2.51

19. Find the pressure between L and M in Fig. 2.52. **[Ans.** 8.32 kN/m^2]

20. Calculate the pressure at a height of 8000 m above sea-level if the atmospheric pressure is 101.3 kN/m^2 and temperature is 15°C at the sea-level assuming (*i*) air is incompressible, (*ii*) pressure variation follows adiabatic law, and (*iii*) pressure variation follows isothermal law. Take the density of air at the sea-level equal to 1.285 kg/m^3. Neglect variation of g with altitude. **[Ans.** (*i*) 607.5 N/m^2, (*ii*) 31.5 kN/m^2 (*iii*) 37.45 kN/m^2]

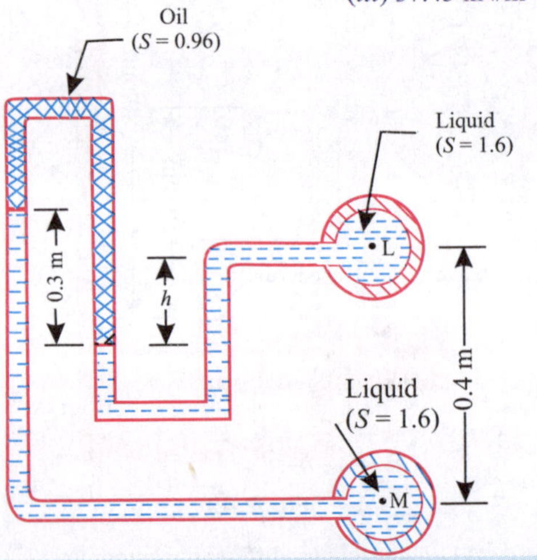

Fig. 2.52

21. The atmospheric pressure at the sea-level is 101.3 kN/m^2 and the temperature is 15°C. Calculate the pressure 8000 m above sea-level, assuming (*i*) air is in compressible, (*ii*) isothermal variation of pressure and density, and (*iii*) adiabatic variation of pressure and density. Assume density of air at sea-level as 1.285 kg/m^3. Neglect variation of 'g' with altitude. **[Ans.** (*i*) 501.3 N/m^2, (*ii*) 37.45 kN/m^2 (*iii*) 31.5 kN/m^2]

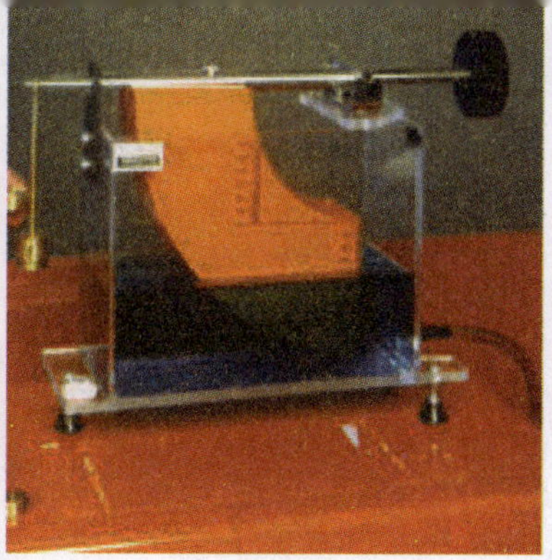

Chapter 3

HYDROSTATIC FORCES ON SURFACES

3.1. INTRODUCTION

In chapter 2, we have studied that a liquid, at rest, exerts some pressure on all sides of the container. The intensity of pressure (p) was related to specific weight w of the liquid and vertical depth h of the point by eqn. $p = wh$. In this chapter, we shall discuss the total pressure on a surface and its position. The term '*hydrostatics*' means the study of pressure, exerted by a liquid *at rest*. The direction of such a pressure is *always perpendicular to the surface, on which it acts.*

3.2. TOTAL PRESSURE AND CENTRE OF PRESSURE

Total pressure. It is defined as the *force exerted by static fluid on a surface (either plane or curved) when the fluid comes in contact with the surface. This force is always at right angle (or normal) to the surface.*

Centre of pressure. It is defined as the *point of application of the total pressure on the surface.*

Now we shall discuss the total pressure exerted by a liquid on the immersed surface. The immersed surfaces may be:

1. Horizontal plane surface;
2. Vertical plane surface;
3. Inclined plane surface;
4. Curved surface.

3.3. HORIZONTALLY IMMERSED SURFACE

Total Pressure (P):

Refer to Fig. 3.1. Consider a plane horizontal surface immersed in a liquid.

Let, A = Area of the immersed surface,

$\bar{x}$ = Depth of horizontal surface from the liquid, and

w = Specific weight of the liquid.

The total pressure on the surface,

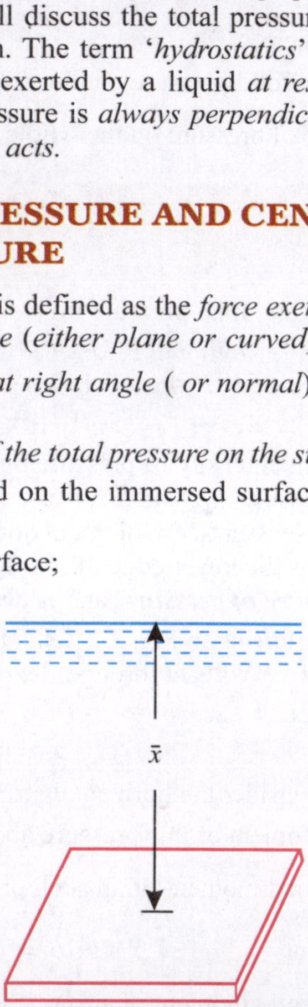

Fig. 3.1. Horizontally immersed surface.

P = Weight of the liquid above the immersed surface

= Specific weight of liquid × volume of liquid

= Specific weight of liquid × area of surface × depth of liquid

$= wA\bar{x}$

3.4. VERTICALLY IMMERSED SURFACE

Consider a plane vertical surface of arbitrary shape immersed in a liquid as shown in Fig. 3.2.

Let, A = Total area of the surface,

G = Centre of the area of the surface,

$\bar{x}$ = Depth of centre of area,

OO = Free surface of liquid, and

$\bar{h}$ = Distance of centre of pressure from free surface of liquid.

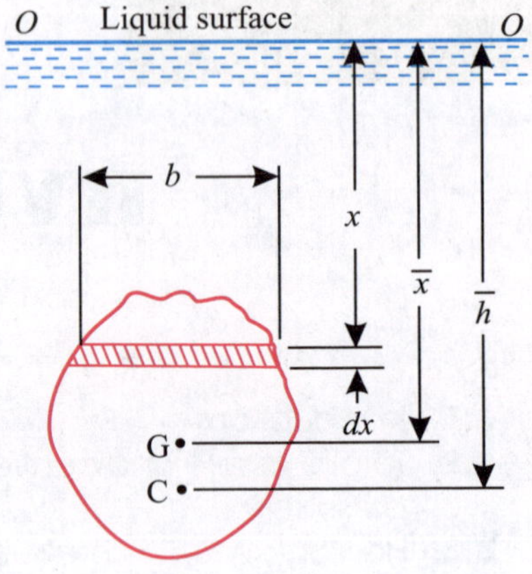

Fig. 3.2. Vertically immersed surface.

(*a*) Total pressure (P):

Consider a thin horizontal strip of the surface of thickness dx and breadth b. Let the depth of the strip be x. Let the intensity of pressure on strip be p; this may be taken as uniform as the strip is extremely small. Then,

$$p = wx$$

where, w = specific weight of the liquid.

Total pressure on the strip $= p.b.dx. = wx\,.\,bdx$

Total pressure on the whole area, $P = \int wx\,.\,bdx = w\int bdx\,.\,x$

But, $\int bdx\,.\,x$ = Moment of the surface area about the liquid level $= A\bar{x}$

$\therefore \qquad P = w.A\bar{x}$ ...[same as in Art. 3.3]

or, the total pressure on a surface is equal to the *area multiplied by the intensity of pressure at the centre of area of the figure.*

The eqn., $P = wA\bar{x}$ holds good for all surfaces whether flat or curved.

(*b*) Centre of pressure ($\bar{h}$):

The intensity of pressure on an immersed surface is not uniform, but *increases with depth.* As the pressure is greater over the lower portion of the figure, therefore the resultant pressure, on any immersed surface will act at some point, below the centre of gravity of the immersed surface and towards the lower edge of the figure. *The point through which this resultant pressure acts is known as* '***centre of pressure***' and is always expressed in terms of *depth* from the liquid surface.

Referring to Fig. 3.2, let C be the centre of pressure of the immersed figure. Then the resultant pressure P will act through the point.

Let, $\bar{h}$ = Depth of centre of pressure below free liquid surface, and

I_0 = Moment of inertia of the surface about OO.

Consider the horizontal strip of thickness dx. Total pressure on strip $= w.x.b.dx$

Moment of this pressure about free surface $OO = (w.x.\,b.dx)\,x = w.x^2.b.dx$

Total moment of all such pressures for whole area, $M = \int w.x^2.b.dx. = w\int x^2.b.dx$

But, $\int x^2.b.dx = I_0$ = Moment of inertia of the surface about the free surface OO (or second moment of area)

$$M = wI_0 \quad ...(i)$$

The sum of the moments of the pressure is also equal to $P \times \bar{h}$ ...(*ii*)

Now equating eqns. (*i*) and (*ii*), we get:

$$P \times \bar{h} = wI_0.$$

$$wA\bar{x} \times \bar{h} = wI_0 \quad (\because P = wA\bar{x})$$

$$\bar{h} = \frac{I_0}{A\bar{x}} \quad ...(iii)$$

Also, $I = I_G + Ah^2$ (Theorem of parallel axis)

where, I_G = Moment of inertia of the figure about horizontal axis through its centre of gravity, and

h = Distance between the free liquid surface and the centre of gravity of the figure ($\bar{x}$ in this case)

Thus rearranging equation (*iii*), we have

Table 3.1. The Centre of Gravity (G) and Moment of Inertia (I) of Some Important Geometrical Figures:

S.No.	Name of figure	C.G. from the base	Area	I about an axis passing through C.G. and parallel to the base	I about base
1.	Triangle Fig. 3.3	$x = \frac{h}{3}$	$\frac{bh}{2}$	$\frac{bh^3}{36}$	$\frac{bh^3}{12}$
2.	Rectangle Fig. 3.4	$x = \frac{d}{2}$	bd	$\frac{bd^3}{12}$	$\frac{bd^3}{3}$
3.	Circle Fig. 3.5	$x = \frac{d}{2}$	$\frac{\pi d^2}{4}$	$\frac{\pi d^4}{64}$	—
4.	Trapezium Fig. 3.6	$x = \left[\frac{2a+b}{a+b}\right]\frac{h}{3}$	$\left(\frac{a+b}{2}\right)h$	$\left(\frac{a^2+4ab+b^2}{3b(a+b)}\right) \times h^2$	—

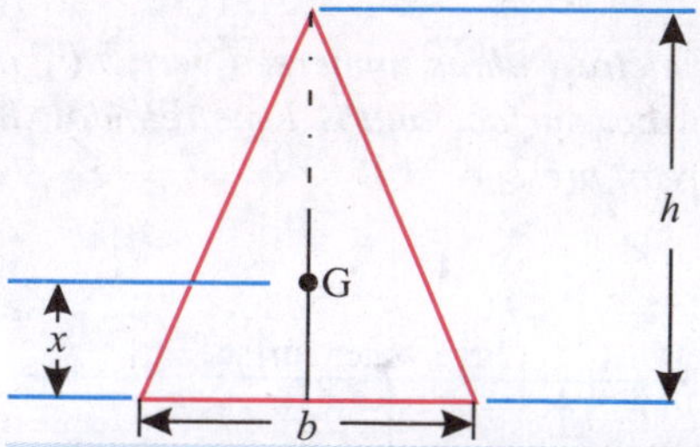

Fig. 3.3

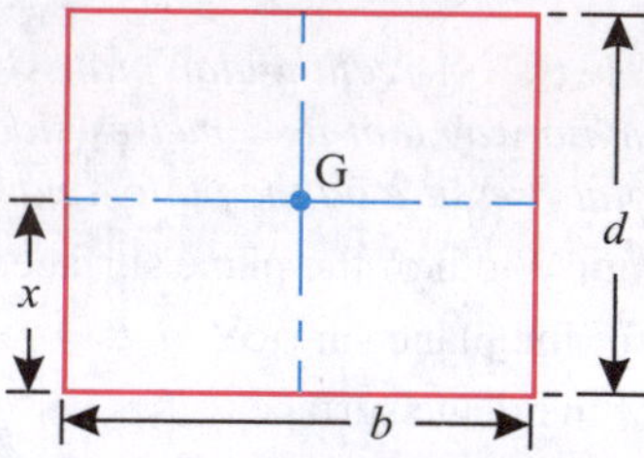

Fig. 3.4

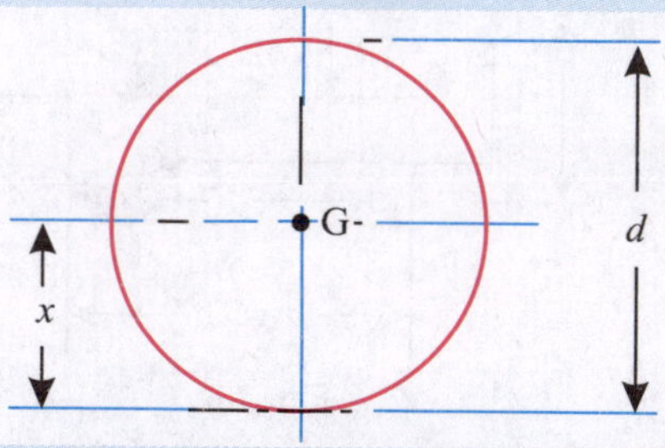

Fig. 3.5

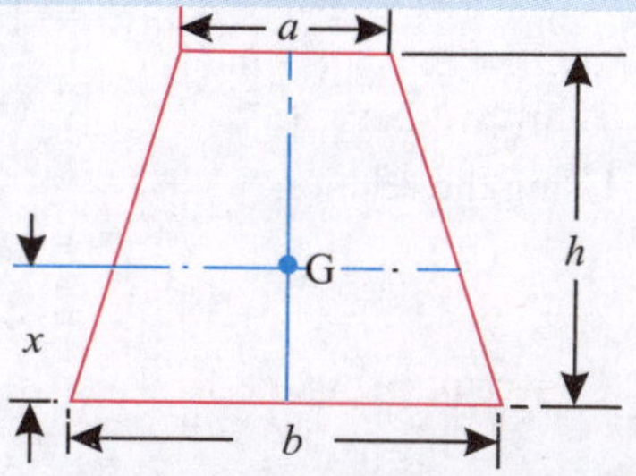

Fig. 3.6

$$\bar{h} = \frac{I_G + A\bar{x}^2}{A\bar{x}} = \frac{I_G}{A\bar{x}} + \bar{x}$$

Hence, *centre of pressure,*

$$\bar{h} = \frac{I_G}{A\bar{x}} + \bar{x} \qquad ...(3.2)$$

Example 3.1. *Fig. 3.7 shows a circular plate of diameter 1.2 m placed vertically in water in such a way that the centre of the place is 2.5 m below the free surface of water. Determine: (i) Total pressure on the plate. (ii) Position of centre of pressure.*

Solution. Diameter of the plate, $d = 1.2$ m

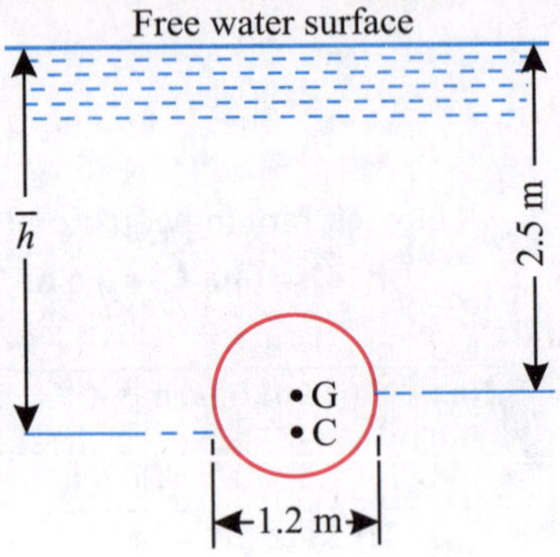

Fig. 3.7

Area,

$$A = \frac{\pi}{4} d^2 = \frac{\pi}{4} \times 1.2^2 = 1.13 \text{ m}^2$$

$$\bar{x} = 2.5 \text{ m}$$

***(i)* Total pressure, P:**

Using the relation:

$$P = wA\bar{x} = 9.81 \times 1.13 \times 2.5$$

$$= \textbf{27.7 kN (Ans.)}$$

***(ii)* Position of centre of pressure, $\bar{h}$:**

Using the relation:

$$\bar{h} = \frac{I_G}{A\bar{x}} + \bar{x}$$

where,

$$I_G = \frac{\pi}{64} d^4 = \frac{\pi}{64} \times 1.2^4 = 0.1018 \text{ m}^4$$

$$\bar{h} = \frac{0.1018}{1.13 \times 2.5} + 2.5 = 2.536 \text{ m}$$

i.e. $\bar{h} = \textbf{2.536 m (Ans.)}$

Example 3.2. *A rectangular plate 3 metres long and 1 metre wide is immersed vertically in water in such a way that its 3 metres side is parallel to the water surface and is 1 metre below it. Find: **(i)** Total pressure on the plate, and **(ii)** Position of centre of pressure.*

Solution. Width of the plane surface, $b = 3$ m

Depth of the plane surface, $d = 1$ m

Area of the plane surface,

$$A = b \times d = 3 \times 1 = 3 \text{ m}^2$$

$$\bar{x} = 1 + \frac{1}{2} = 1.5 \text{ m}$$

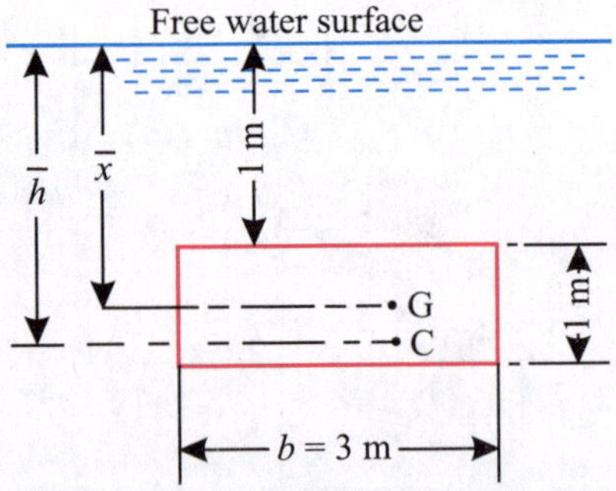

Fig. 3.8

***(i)* Total pressure P:**

Using the relation:

$$P = wA\bar{x} = 9.81 \times 3 \times 1.5$$

$$= \textbf{44.14 kN (Ans.)}$$

***(ii)* Centre of pressure, $\bar{h}$:**

Using the relation: $\bar{h} = \dfrac{I_G}{A\bar{x}} + \bar{x}$

But, $I_G = \dfrac{bd^3}{12} = \dfrac{3 \times 1^3}{12} = 0.25\text{m}^4$

$\therefore$ $\bar{h} = \dfrac{0.25}{3 \times 1.5} + 1.5 = 1.556 \text{ m}$

i.e. $\bar{h} =$ **1.556 m (Ans.)**

Example 3.3. *An isosceles triangular plate of base 3 m and altitude 3 m is immersed vertically in an oil of specific gravity 0.8. The base of the plate coincides with the free surface of oil. Determine:*

(i) Total pressure on the plate; *(ii) Centre of pressure.*

Solution. Base of the plate, $b = 3$ m

Height of the plate, $h = 3$ m

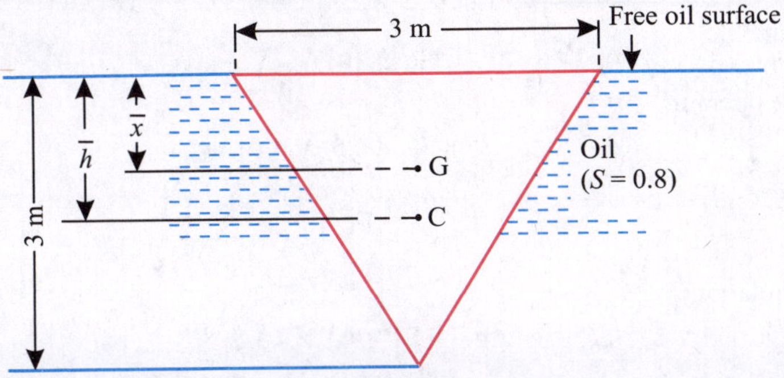

Fig. 3.9

Area, $A = \dfrac{b \times h}{2} = \dfrac{3 \times 3}{2} = 4.5 \text{ m}^2$

Specific gravity of oil, $S = 0.8$

The distance of C.G. from the free surface of oil,

$$\bar{x} = \frac{1}{3}h = \frac{1}{3} \times 3 = 1 \text{ m}$$

(i) Total pressure on the plate, *P*:

We know that, $P = wA\bar{x}$

$= (0.8 \times 9.81) \times 4.5 \times 1$

$P =$ **35.3 kN (Ans.)**

(ii) Centre of pressure, $\bar{h}$:

Centre of pressure is given by the relation:

$$\bar{h} = \frac{I_G}{A\bar{x}} + \bar{x} = \frac{(bh^3/36)}{A\bar{x}} + \bar{x}$$

$$= \frac{(3 \times 3^3/36)}{4.5 \times 1} + 1$$

$\bar{h} =$ **1.5 m (Ans.)**

Example 3.4. *A circular opening, 2.5 m diameter, in a vertical side of tank is closed by a disc of 2.5 m diameter which can rotate about a horizontal diameter. Determine:*

(i) The force on the disc;

(ii) The torque required to maintain the disc in equilibrium in vertical position when the head of water above horizontal diameter is 3.5 m.

Solution. Diameter of the opening, $d = 2.5$ m

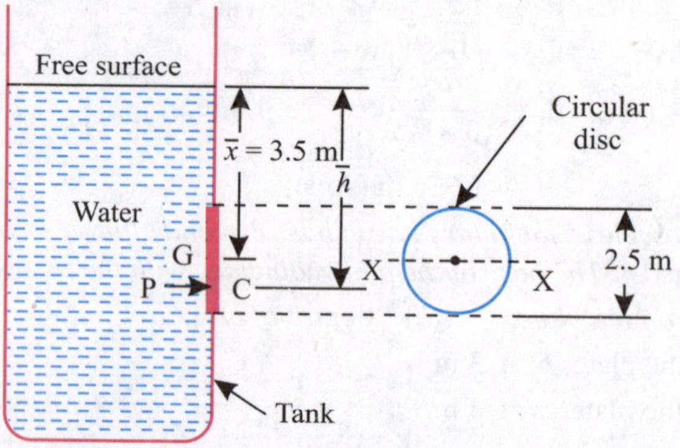

Fig. 3.10

∴ Area of the opening,

$$A = \frac{\pi}{4} d^2 = \frac{\pi}{4} \times 2.5^2 = 4.91 \text{ m}^2$$

Depth of C.G., $\bar{x} = 3.5$ m

(i) Force on the disc, P:

Using the relation:

$$P = wA\bar{x} = 9.81 \times 4.91 \times 3.5$$
$$= \mathbf{168.6\ kN}\ \textbf{(Ans.)}$$

(ii) Torque required, T:

In order to determine the torque (T) required to maintain the disc in equilibrium, let us first calculate the point of application of force acting on the disc, *i.e.* centre of pressure of the force P. The depth of centre of pressure ($\bar{h}$) is given by the relation:

$$\bar{h} = \frac{I_G}{A\bar{x}} + \bar{x} = \frac{(\pi/64 \times d^4)}{(\pi/4 \times d^2)\bar{x}} + \bar{x} \qquad \left[\because I_G = \frac{\pi}{64} \times d^4\right]$$

$$= \frac{(\pi/64 \times 2.5^4)}{(\pi/4 \times 2.5^2) \times 3.5} + 3.5 = 3.61 \text{ m}$$

i.e., the force P is acting at a distance of 3.61 m from the free surface. Moment of this force about horizontal diameter $X - X$

$$= P(\bar{h} - \bar{x}) = 168.6\,(3.61 - 3.5)$$
$$= 18.55 \text{ kNm.} \qquad \textit{(anticlockwise)}$$

Hence a torque (T) of **18.55 kNm** must be applied on the disc in the **clockwise direction** to maintain the disc in equilibrium position. **(Ans.)**

Example 3.5. *A square aperture in the vertical side of a tank has one diagonal vertical and is completely covered by a plane plate hinged along one of the upper sides of the aperture. The diagonals of the aperture are 2.4 m long and the tank contains a liquid of specific gravity 1.2. The centre of aperture is 1.8 m below the free surface. Calculate:*

(i) The thrust exerted on the plate by the liquid;

(ii) The position of its centre of pressure. **(Anna University)**

Solution. Refer to Fig. 3.11

Diagonal of aperture, $PR = QS = 2.4$ m

Area of square aperture, A = area of $\Delta\, PQR$ + area of ΔPSR.

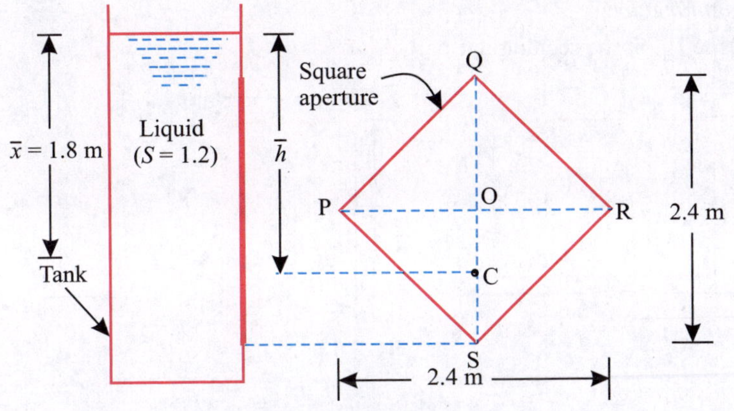

Fig. 3.11

$$= \frac{1}{2} PR \times OQ + \frac{1}{2} PR \times OS$$

$$= \frac{1}{2} \times 2.4 \times \left(\frac{2.4}{2}\right) + \frac{1}{2} \times 2.4 \times \left(\frac{2.4}{2}\right) = 2.88 \text{ m}^2$$

Depth of centre of aperture plate from free liquid surface, $\bar{x} = 1.8$m

(*i*) Thrust exerted on the plate *P*:

Pressure force or thrust on the plate,

$$P = wA\bar{x} = (1.2 \times 9.81) \times 2.88 \times 1.8 = \mathbf{61.026\ kN}$$ **(Ans.)**

(*ii*) The position of its centre of pressure, $\bar{h}$:

Centre of pressure is given by the relation:

$$\bar{h} = \frac{I_G}{A\bar{x}} + \bar{x}$$

where, I_G = M. O. I of *PQRS* about diagonal *PR*.

= M.O.I. of Δ *PQR* + M.O.I of *PSR* ...about PR

$$= \frac{2.4 \times (1.2)^3}{12} + \frac{2.4 \times (1.2)^3}{12} = 0.6912 \text{ m}^4 \qquad (\because OQ = OS)$$

[∵ The M.O.I. of a triangle about its base equals $\frac{\text{base} \times (\text{height})^3}{12}$]

$$\therefore \quad \bar{h} = \frac{0.6912}{2.88 \times 1.8} + 1.8 = \mathbf{1.933\ m}$$ **(Ans.)**

Example 3.6. *A trapezoidal plate of parallel sides l and 2l and height h immersed vertically in water with its side of length l horizontal and topmost. The top edge is at a depth h below the water surface. Determine:*

(*i*) *The total force on one side of the plate.*

(*ii*) *The location of the centre of pressure.*

Solution. Refer to Fig. 3.12, the trapezium can be considered to be made of:

(*i*) A rectangle: *l* (width) × *h* (height)

(*ii*) A triangle: *l (base)* × *h* (height)

(*i*) Total force on one side of the plate *P*:

Refer to Fig. 3.13.

For Rectangular part:

Pressure force P_1 on the rectangular part,

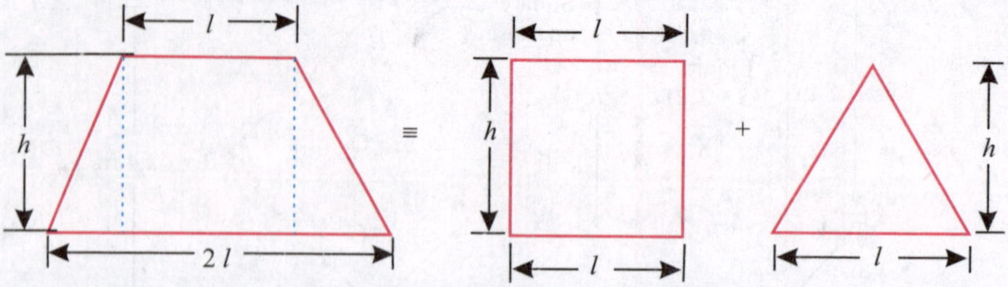

Fig. 3.12

$$P_1 = w(l \times h)\left(h + \frac{h}{2}\right) = \frac{3}{2}\,wlh^2$$

Centre of pressure of force P_1,

$$\bar{h}_1 = \frac{I_G}{A\bar{x}} + \bar{x} = \frac{(l \times h^3/12)}{(l \times h) \times \left(h + \frac{h}{2}\right)} + \left(h + \frac{h}{2}\right)$$

$$= \frac{h}{18} + \frac{3h}{2} = \frac{14}{9}h$$

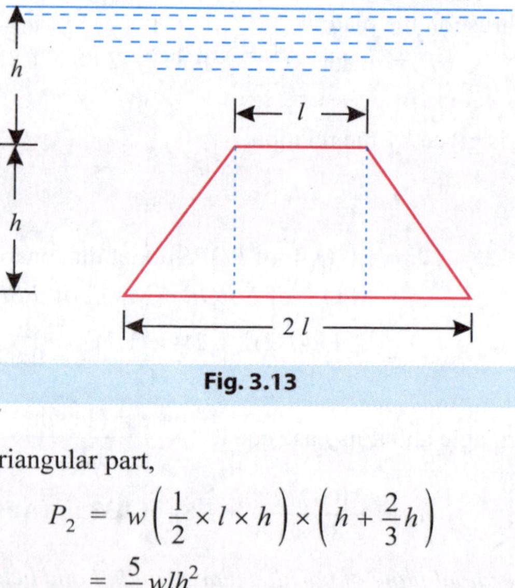

Fig. 3.13

For Triangular part:

Pressure force on the triangular part,

$$P_2 = w\left(\frac{1}{2} \times l \times h\right) \times \left(h + \frac{2}{3}h\right)$$

$$= \frac{5}{6}\,wlh^2$$

Centre of pressure of force P_2,

$$\bar{h}_2 = \frac{I_G}{A\bar{x}} + \bar{x} = \frac{(lh^3/36)}{\left(\frac{1}{2}l \times h\right) \times \left(h + \frac{2}{3}h\right)} + \left(h + \frac{2}{3}h\right)$$

$$= \frac{h}{30} + \frac{5h}{3} = \frac{51}{30}h$$

$\therefore$ Total force/thrust, $P = P_1 + P_2$

$$= \frac{3}{2}\,wlh^2 + \frac{5}{6}\,wlh^2 = \frac{7}{3}\,\boldsymbol{wlh^2} \quad \textbf{(Ans.)}$$

(*ii*) The location of the centre of pressure, $\bar{h}$:

Centre of pressure of total force,

$$\bar{h} = \frac{P_1\bar{h}_1 + P_2\bar{h}_2}{P}$$

$$= \frac{\frac{3}{2}wlh^2 \times \frac{14}{8}h + \frac{5}{6}wlh^2 \times \frac{51}{30}h}{\frac{7}{3}wlh^2} = \frac{45}{28}h$$

i.e. $\bar{h} = \frac{45}{28}$**h (Ans.)**

Example 3.7. *A trapezoidal 2 m wide at the bottom and 1 m deep has side slopes 1: 1. Determine:*

(i) Total pressure;

(ii) Centre of pressure on the vertical gate closing the channel when it is full of water.

Solution. Refer to Fig. 3.14

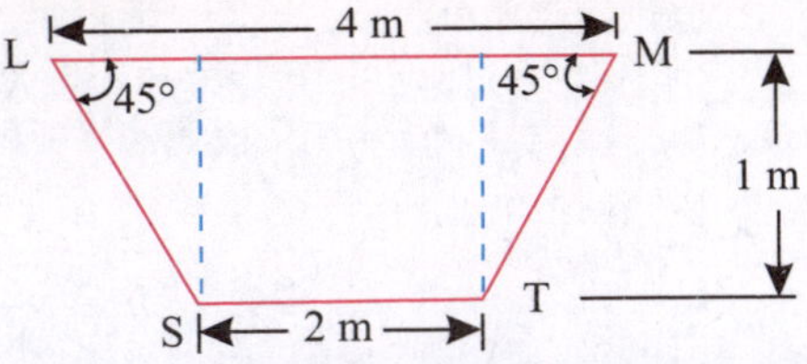

Fig. 3.14

(*i*) Total Pressure, P :

For rectangle:

Area, $A_1 = 2 \times 1 = 2\text{m}^2$

$\bar{x} = \frac{1}{2} = 0.5\text{m}$

$P_1 = wA\bar{x} = 9.81 \times 2 \times 0.5 = 9.81$ kN

This acts at a depth $\bar{h}_1$.

But, $\bar{h}_1 = \frac{I_G}{A\bar{x}} + \bar{x} = \frac{(2 \times 1^3/12)}{2 \times 0.5} + 0.5 = 0.6$ m ... from the top

For triangles:

Area, $A_2 = 2 \times \frac{1}{2} \times 1 \times 1 = 1\ \text{m}^2$ (there are two triangles); $\bar{x} = \frac{1}{3}$ m

$P_2 = wA\bar{x} = 9.81 \times 1 \times \frac{1}{3} = 3.27$ kN

This acts at a depth of $\bar{h}_2$.

But, $\bar{h}_2 = \frac{I_G}{A\bar{x}} + \bar{x} = \frac{(2 \times 1^3/36)}{1 \times 1/3} + \frac{1}{3} = 0.5$ m ...from the top.

i.e. $\bar{h}_2 = 0.5$ m

Total pressure,

$P = P_1 + P_2 = 9.81 + 3.27 =$ **13.08 kN (Ans.)**

(*ii*) Centre of pressure , $\bar{h}$:

Taking moments about the top, we get: $P \times \bar{h} = P_1 \times \bar{h}_1 + P_2 \times \bar{h}_2$

or, $\bar{h} = \frac{P_1\bar{h}_1 + P_2\bar{h}_2}{P} = \frac{9.81 \times 0.66 + 3.27 \times 0.5}{13.08} =$ **0.62 m (Ans.)**

Example 3.8. *An isosceles triangle of base 3 metres and altitude 6 metres is immersed vertically in water, with its axis of symmetry horizontal, as shown in Fig. 3.15. If the head of water on it is 9 metres, determine:*

(i) Total pressure on the plate, and (ii) The position of the centre of pressure.

Solution. Area of the triangle,

$$A = \frac{1}{2} \times 3 \times 6 = 9\text{m}^2$$

Depth of C.G. of the plate from the water surface,

$$\bar{x} = 9\text{m}$$

(*i*) Total pressure, *P*:

We know that, $$P = wA\bar{x} = 9.81 \times 9 \times 9$$
$$= \mathbf{794.6\ kN\ (Ans.)}$$

(*ii*) Centre of pressure, $\bar{h}$:

Using the relation: $$\bar{h} = \frac{I_G}{A\bar{x}} + \bar{x}$$

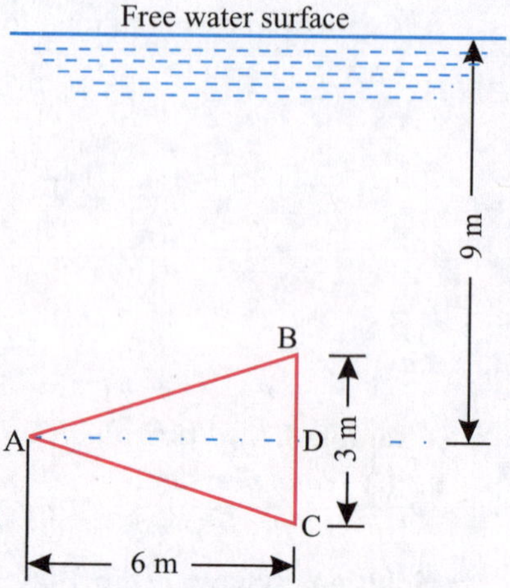

Fig. 3.15

But, I_G= moment of inertia of ΔABD about AD + moment of inertia of $\Delta\ ACD$ about AD

$$= \frac{6 \times 1.5^3}{12} + \frac{6 \times 1.5^3}{12}$$

$$= 3.375\ \text{m}^4$$

$$\bar{h} = \frac{3.375}{9 \times 9} + 9 = \mathbf{9.04\ m\ (Ans.)}$$

Example 3.9. *A circular lamina of radius R is kept immersed in a liquid such that its top most point A is on the free surface. Determine the depth and width of the horizontal chord BC so that the total thrust due to hydrostatic pressure on the triangle ABC is maximum.* **(UPTU)**

Solution. Refer to Fig. 3.16.

The total thrust/pressure on the submerged triangle *ABC* is,

$$F = P = wA\,\bar{x} = w \times \left(\frac{1}{2} \times b \times h\right) \times \frac{2h}{3} = \frac{1}{3} wbh^2$$

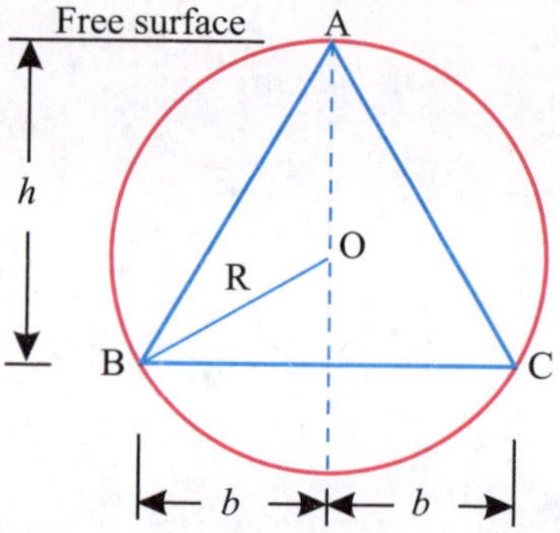

Fig. 3.16

But, $h = R + \sqrt{R^2 - b^2}$ (*O* is the centre of the circle)

$$\therefore \quad F = \frac{1}{3} wb\left[R + \sqrt{R^2 - b^2}\ \right]^2$$

For F to be maximum, $\frac{dF}{db} = 0$

i.e. $$\frac{d}{db}\left[b(R + \sqrt{R^2 - b^2})^2\ \right] = 0$$

$$b \times 2\left(R + \sqrt{R^2 - b^2}\right) \times \frac{1}{2}(R^2 - b^2)^{-1/2}(-2b) + \left(R + \sqrt{R^2 - b^2}\right)^2 = 0$$

$$\frac{-2b^2}{\sqrt{R^2 - b^2}} + R + \sqrt{R^2 - b^2} = 0$$

or, $$-2b^2 + R\sqrt{(R^2 - b^2)} + R^2 - b^2 = 0$$

or, $$R\sqrt{(R^2 - b^2)} + R^2 - 3b^2 = 0$$

or, $$R\sqrt{(R^2 - b^2)} = 3b^2 - R^2$$

Squaring both sides, we get:

$$R^2 (R^2 - b^2) = 9b^4 + R^4 - 6R^2b^2$$

$$R^4 - R^2b^2 = 9b^4 + R^4 - 6R^2b^2$$

$$9b^4 = 5R^2b^2$$

or
$$9b^2 = 5R^2$$

or
$$b = \sqrt{\frac{5}{9}}\,R = \frac{\sqrt{5}}{3}R$$

and
$$h = R + \sqrt{R^2 - \frac{5}{9}R^2} = \frac{5}{3}R$$

Hence, for maximum thrust, the depth and width of the chord are:

Depth, $\boldsymbol{h = \frac{5}{3}R}$, and

width, $\boldsymbol{2b = \frac{2}{3}\sqrt{5}\,R}$ **(Ans.)**

Example 3.10. *Determine the total force and location of centre of pressure for plate LMSUT immersed vertically as shown in Fig.* 3.17.

Solution. Area *LMST*, $A_1 = 2 \times 2 = 4\text{m}^2$

Area *TSU*, $A_2 = \frac{1}{2} \times 2 \times 2 = 2\text{ m}^2$

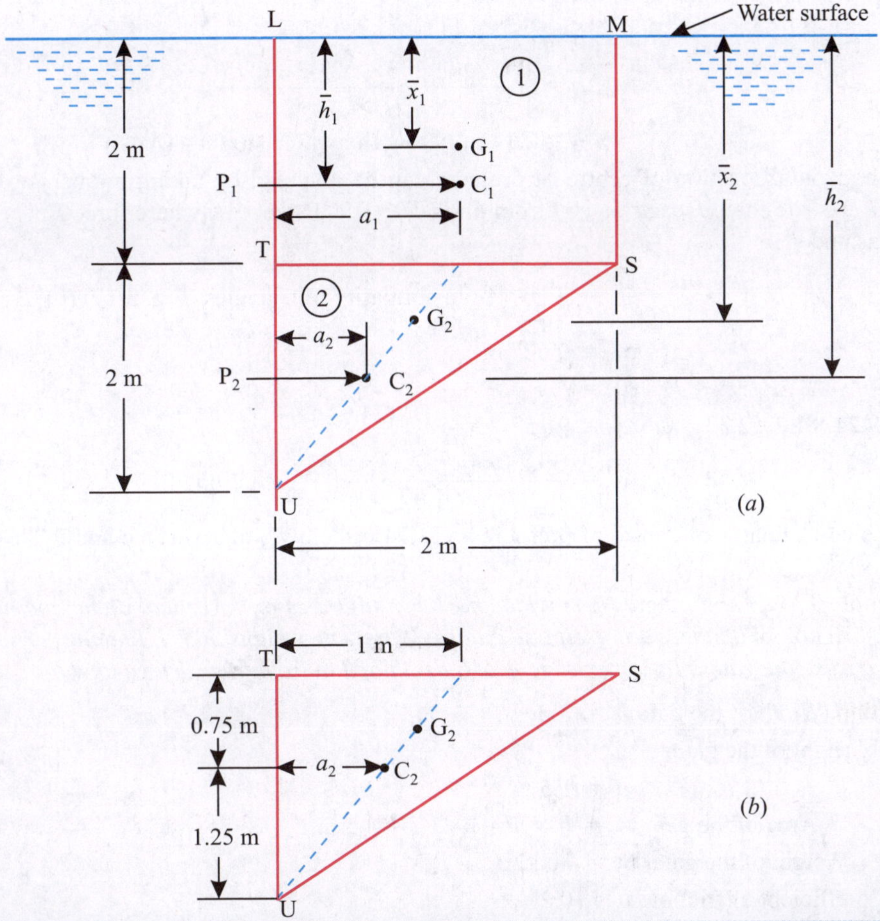

Fig. 3.17

Distance of centroid G_1 from water surface, $\bar{x}_1 = \frac{2}{2} = 1$ m

Distance of centroid G_2 from water surface, $\bar{x}_2 = 2 + \frac{2}{3} = 2.667$ m

$$\text{Total pressure on area } LMST,\ P_1 = wA_1\bar{x}_1 = 9.81 \times 4 \times 1 = 39.24 \text{ kN}$$
$$\text{Total pressure on area } TSU,\ P_2 = wA_2\bar{x}_2 = 9.81 \times 2 \times 2.667 = 52.33 \text{ kN}$$
$$\text{Total pressure, } P = P_1 + P_2 = 39.24 + 52.33 = 91.57 \text{ kN}$$

Distance of centre of pressure (C_1) of area *LMST* from free water surface,

$$\bar{h}_1 = \frac{I_{G_1}}{A_1\bar{x}_1} + \bar{x}_1 = \frac{\frac{2 \times 2^3}{12}}{2 \times 2 \times 1} + 1 = 1.333 \text{ m}$$

Distance of centre of pressure (C_2) of area *TSU* from the free water surface,

$$\bar{h}_2 = \frac{I_{G_2}}{A_2\bar{x}_2} + \bar{x}_2 = \frac{\frac{2 \times 2^3}{36}}{2 \times 2.667} + 2.667 = 2.75 \text{ m}$$

The depth ($\bar{h}$) at which the resultant force will act can be determined by taking moments of forces P_1 and P_2 about water surface.

i.e. $$P_1 \times \bar{h}_1 + P_2 \times \bar{h}_2 = P \times \bar{h}$$
$$39.24 \times 1.333 + 52.33 \times 2.75 = 91.57 \times \bar{h}$$
$$\therefore \quad \bar{h} = \frac{39.24 \times 1.333 + 52.33 \times 2.75}{91.57}$$

= **2.14 m below the water surface (Ans.)**

The horizontal location of centre of pressure can be obtained by taking moments of P_1 and P_2 about *LTU*. The force P_1 acts at 1 m from line *LTU*. The distance a_2 where force P_2 acts can be obtained as under:

$$\frac{1}{2} = \frac{a_2}{1.25} \quad \text{[from similarity of triangles (Fig. 3.17) (b)]}$$

or, $$a_2 = 0.625 \text{ m}$$
$$\therefore \quad P_1 \,.\, a_1 + P_2 \,.\, a_2 = P.\bar{a}$$
$$39.24 \times 1 + 52.33 \times 0.625 = 91.57 \times \bar{a}$$
$$\therefore \quad \bar{a} = \frac{39.24 \times 1 + 52.33 \times 0.625}{91.57} = 0.786 \text{ m}$$

Hence co-ordinates of centre of pressure are 2.14 m below water surface and 0.786 m from *LTU*. **(Ans.)**

Example 3.11. *A sliding gate 3 m wide and 1.5 m high lies on a vertical plane and has a co-efficient of friction of 0.2 between itself and guides. If the gate weighs 30 kN, find the vertical force required to raise the gate if its upper edge is at a depth of 9 m from free surface of water.*

Solution. Width of the gate, $b = 3$ m

Depth/height of the gate,

$$d = 1.5 \text{ m}$$
$$\text{Area of the gate, } A = b \times d = 3 \times 1.5 = 4.5 \text{ m}^2$$
$$\text{Weight of the gate, } W = 30 \text{ kN}$$
$$\text{Co-efficient of friction, } \mu = 0.2$$

Vertical force required to raise the gate:

Depth of *c.g.* of the gate from water surface,

$$\bar{x} = 9 + \frac{1.5}{2} = 9.75 \text{ m}$$

Pressure force on the gate,

$$P = wA\bar{x} = 9.81 \times 4.5 \times 9.75 = 430.4 \text{ kN}$$

Force required to raise the gate

$$= \text{Frictional force} + \text{weight of the gate}$$

$$= \mu P + W$$

$$= 0.2 \times 430.4 + 30$$

$$= \mathbf{116.08 \text{ kN}} \text{ (Ans.)}$$

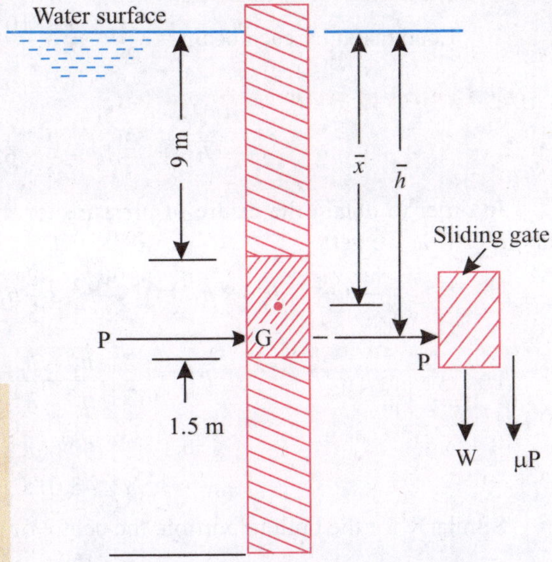

Fig. 3.18

Example 3.12. *The hydrostatic water pressure acts only on one side and to a depth of 12 m from the top of a dock gate which is reinforced with three horizontal beams.*

(i) Calculate the load taken by each beam.

(ii) Locate the positions of beams in order that each carries an equal load.

Solution. Refer to Fig. 3.19. Consider an elementary strip of thickness *dh* at a depth *h*. Then for a unit width of the gate, we have:

Pressure/force on the element,

$$dP = w \times (dh \times 1) \times h = wh\,dh$$

Pressure on section 1,

$$P_1 = \int_0^{h_1} wh\,dh = \frac{w}{2} h_1^2$$

Pressure on section 2,

$$P_2 = \int_{h_1}^{h_2} wh\,dh = \frac{w}{2}\left(h_1^2 - h_2^2\right)$$

Pressure on section 3,

$$P_3 = \int_{h_2}^{h_3} wh\,dh = \frac{w}{2}\left(h_3^2 - h_2^2\right)$$

Total pressure on the gate,

$$\int_0^{h_3} wh\,dh = \frac{w}{2} h_3^2$$

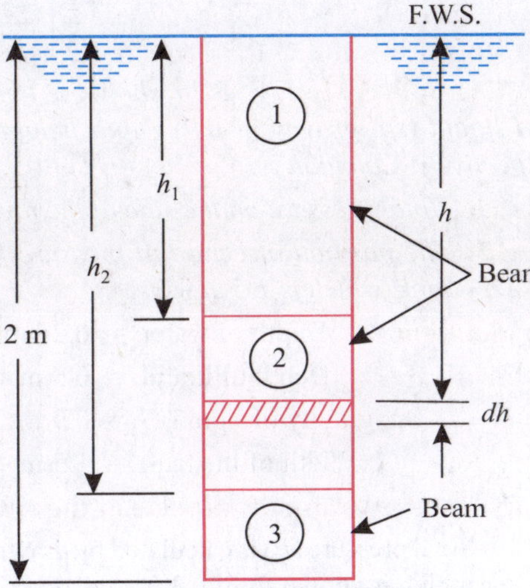

Fig. 3.19

Load carried by each section is same and it equals $\frac{1}{3}$ *rd* of total pressure/force on the gate.

Thus,
$$\frac{w}{2} h_1^2 = \frac{w}{2}(h_2^2 - h_1^2) = \frac{w}{2}(h_3^2 - h_2^2) = \frac{1}{3} \times \frac{w}{2} h_3^2$$

$$\therefore \quad h_1^2 = h_2^2 - h_1^2 = 144 - h_2^2 = \frac{144}{3} = 48$$

Solving the above equations, we get:

$$h_1 = 6.93 \text{ m}; h_2 = 9.8 \text{ m}$$

(i) Load taken by each beam:

$$\text{Load taken by each beam} = \frac{w}{2}h_1^2 = \frac{9810}{2} \times 6.93^2 = \mathbf{235562}\ \textbf{(Ans.)}$$

(ii) Centres of pressure, $\bar{h}_1, \bar{h}_2, \bar{h}_3$:

$$\bar{h}_1 = \frac{2}{3}h_1 = \frac{2}{3} \times 6.93 = \mathbf{4.62\ m}\ \textbf{(Ans.)}$$

In order to obtain the centre of pressure for the section 2, taking moments of relevant forces about F.W.S., we get:

$$\frac{w}{2}(h_2^2 - h_1^2) \times \bar{h}_2 = \left(\frac{w}{2}h_2^2 \times \frac{2}{3}h_2\right) - \left(\frac{w}{2}h_1^2 \times \frac{2}{3}h_1\right)$$

or,

$$\bar{h}_2 = \frac{2}{3}\left[\frac{h_2^3 - h_1^3}{h_2^2 - h_1^2}\right] = \frac{2}{3}\left[\frac{(9.8)^3 - (6.93)^3}{(9.8)^2 - (6.93)^2}\right]$$

$$= \frac{2}{3}\left[\frac{608.38}{48.015}\right] = \mathbf{8.45}\ \textbf{(Ans.)}$$

Similarly for the bottom portion, the centre of pressure from the F.W.S.,

$$\bar{h}_3 = \frac{2}{3}\left[\frac{h_3^3 - h_2^3}{h_3^2 - h_2^2}\right] = \frac{2}{3}\left[\frac{(12)^3 - (9.8)^3}{(12)^2 - (9.8)^2}\right]$$

$$= \frac{2}{3}\left[\frac{786.81}{47.96}\right] = \mathbf{10.94\ m}\ \textbf{(Ans.)}$$

Example 3.13. *Fig. 3.20 shows a tank containing water and liquid (sp. gravity = 0.9) upto height 0.25 m and 0.5 m respectively. Calculate:*

(i) *Total pressure on the side of the tank;*

(ii) *The position of centre of pressure from one side of the tank, which is 1.5 m wide.* **(U.P.S.C.)**

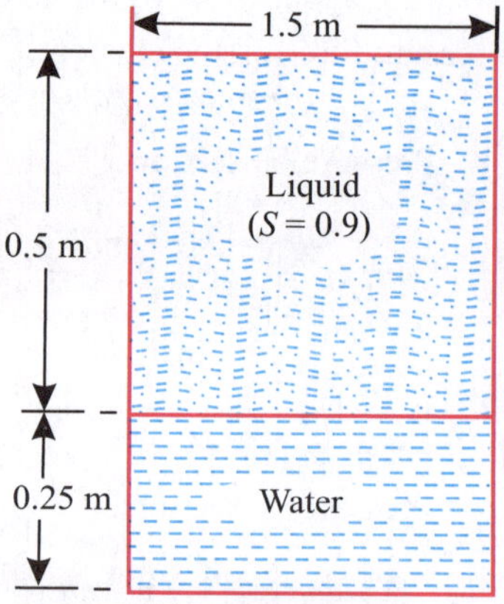

Fig. 3.20

Solution. Depth of water = 0.25 m

Depth of liquid = 0.5 m

Sp. gravity of liquid, S = 0.9

Width of the tank = 1.5 m

(i) Total pressure on one side of the tank, *P*:

Total pressure (P) is calculated by drawing pressure diagram, which is shown in Fig. 3.21.

Intensity of pressure on top, $p_L = 0$

Intensity of pressure on T (or TS),

$$p_T = w_1 h_1 = (0.9 \times 9.81) \times 0.5 = 4.41\ \text{kN/m}^2$$

Intensity of pressure on the base (or MN),

$$p_M = w_1 h_1 + w_2 h_2 = 4.41 + 9.81 \times 0.25$$

$$= 4.41 + 2.45 = 6.86\ \text{kN/m}^2$$

Now, force P_1 = area of the ΔLTS × width of the tank

$$= \frac{1}{2} \times LT \times TS \times 1.5$$

$$= \frac{1}{2} \times 0.5 \times 4.41 \times 1.5 = 1.65\ \text{kN}$$

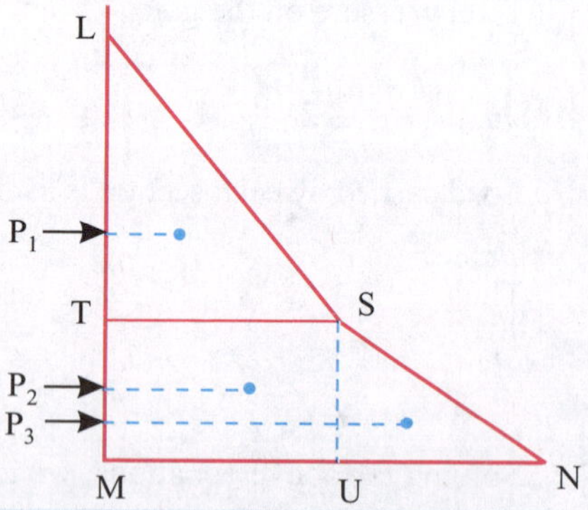

Fig. 3.21. Pressure diagram.

Force, P_2 = area of rectangle $MTSU$ × width of the tank = $MT \times TS \times 1.5$

$= 0.25 \times 4.41 \times 1.5 = 1.65$ kN

P_3 = area of $\Delta\, SUN$ × width of the tank

$$= \frac{1}{2} \times SU \times UN \times 1.5 = \frac{1}{2} = \times 0.25 \times 2.45 \times 1.5 = 0.46 \text{ kN}$$

Total pressure, $P = P_1 + P_2 + P_3 = 1.65 + 1.65 + 0.46 = \mathbf{3.76\ kN}$ **(Ans.)**

(*ii*) Centre of pressure, $\bar{h}$:

Taking moments of all the forces about L, we get:

$$P \times \bar{h} = P_1 \times \frac{2}{3} LT + P_2 \times \left(LT + \frac{1}{2} TM \right) + P_3 \times \left(LT + \frac{2}{3} MT \right)$$

$$3.76 \times \bar{h} = 1.65 \times \frac{2}{3} \times 0.5 + 1.65 \left(0.5 + \frac{1}{2} \times 0.25 \right) + 0.46 \left(0.5 + \frac{2}{3} \times 0.25 \right)$$

$$= 0.55 + 1.03 + 0.306$$

$$\bar{h} = \mathbf{0.5016\ m\ from\ the\ top}\ \textbf{(Ans.)}$$

Example 3.14. *An opening in a dam is covered by the use of a vertical sluice gate. The opening is 2 m wide and 1.2 m high. On the upstream of the gate the liquid of specific gravity 1.45 lies upto a height of 1.5 m above the top of the gate, whereas on the downstream side the water is available upto a height touching the top of the gate. Find:*

(*i*) *The resultant force acting on the gate and position of centre of pressure;*

(*ii*) *The force acting horizontally at the top of the gate which is capable of opening it.*

Assume that the gate is hinged at the bottom.

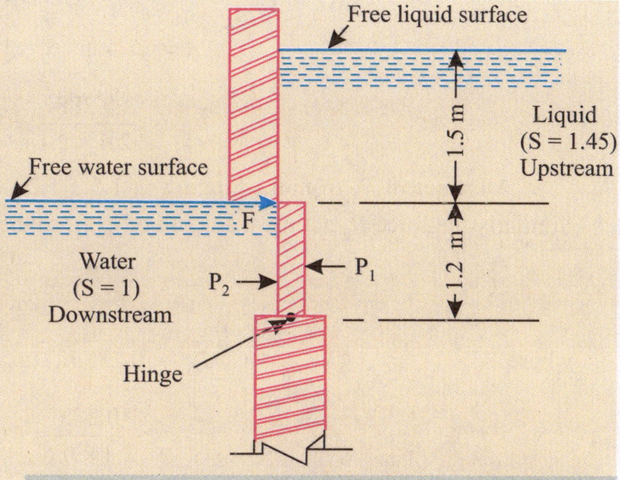

Fig. 3.22

(Rajasthan University

Solution. Width of the gate, $b = 2$ m

Depth of the gate, $d = 1.2$ m

Area, $A = b \times d = 2 \times 1.2 = 2.4\ \text{m}^2$

Specific gravity of liquid = 1.45

Let, P_1 = Force exerted by the liquid of sp. gravity 1.45 on the gate, and

P_2 = Force exerted by water on the gate.

(*i*) Resultant force, P:

Position of centre of pressure of resultant force:

We know that, $P_1 = wA\bar{x}_1$

where, $w = 9.81 \times 1.45 = 14.22\ \text{kN/m}^3$,

$A = 2 \times 1.2 = 2.4\ \text{m}^2$

$$\bar{x}_1 = 1.5 + \frac{1.2}{2} = 2.1 \text{ m}$$

$$P_1 = 14.22 \times 2.4 \times 2.1 = 71.67 \text{ kN.}$$

Similarly, $P_2 = wA\bar{x}_2$

where, $w = 9.81 \text{ kN/m}^3.$

$$A = 2.4 \text{ m}^2,$$

$$\bar{x}_2 = \frac{1.2}{2} = 0.6 \text{ m}$$

$$P_2 = 9.81 \times 2.4 \times 0.6 = 14.13 \text{ kN.}$$

Resultant force, $P = P_1 - P_2 = 71.67 - 14.13$

$= \mathbf{57.54 \text{ kN}}$ **(Ans.)**

The force P_1 acts at a depth of $\bar{h}_1$ from free liquid surface, which is given by:

$$\bar{h}_1 = \frac{I_G}{A\bar{x}_1} + \bar{x}_1$$

where, $I_G = \frac{bd^3}{12} = \frac{2 \times 1.2^3}{12} = 0.288 \text{ m}^4$

$$A = 2.4 \text{ m}^2, \bar{x} = 1.5 + \frac{1.2}{2} = 2.1 \text{ m}$$

$$\bar{h}_1 = \frac{0.288}{2.4 \times 2.1} + 2.1 = 2.157 \text{ m}$$

$\therefore$ Distance of P_1 from the hinge $= (1.5 + 1.2) - \bar{h}_1 = 2.7 - 2.157 = 0.543$ m

Similarly the force P_2 acting at a depth of $\bar{h}_2$ from the liquid surface is given by:

$$\bar{h}_2 = \frac{I_G}{A\bar{x}_2} + \bar{x}_2$$

where, $I_G = 0.288 \text{ m}^4$ (as above); $\bar{x}_2 = \frac{1.2}{2} = 0.6$ m; $A = 2.4 \text{ m}^2$

$\therefore$ $$\bar{h}_2 = \frac{0.288}{2.4 \times 0.6} + 0.6 = 0.8 \text{ m}$$

$\therefore$ Distance of P_2 from the hinge $= 1.2 - 0.8 = 0.4$ m

Now the resultant force will act at a distance given by:

$$\frac{71.67 \times 0.543 - 14.13 \times 0.4}{57.54} = \mathbf{0.578 \text{ m above the hinge}}$$ **(Ans.)**

(*ii*) Force required to open the gate, *F*:

Taking moments of P_1, P_2 and F about the hinge, we get:

$$F \times 1.2 + P_2 \times 0.4 = P_1 \times 0.543$$

or, $$F \times 1.2 + 14.13 \times 0.4 = 71.67 \times 0.543$$

or, $$F = \frac{71.67 \times 0.543 - 14.13 \times 0.4}{1.2} = \mathbf{27.72 \text{ kN}}$$ **(Ans.)**

Example 3.15. *For the system shown in Fig. 3.23 calculate the height H of the oil at which the rectangular hinged gate will just begin to rotate anticlockwise.*

Solution.

Refer to Fig. 3.23.

Height H of the oil:

- *Force due to oil,* $P_1 = w_0 A\bar{x}$

$$= (0.8 \times 9.81) \times (0.6 \times 1.5) \times \left[(H - 1.5) + \frac{1.5}{2} \right]$$

$$= 7.063\,(H - 0.75) = 7.063\,H - 5.297$$

Centre of pressure of force P_1,

$$\bar{h}_1 = \frac{I_G}{A\bar{x}} + \bar{x} = \frac{0.6 \times (1.5)^3/12}{(0.6 \times 1.5) \times (H - 0.75)} + (H - 0.75)$$

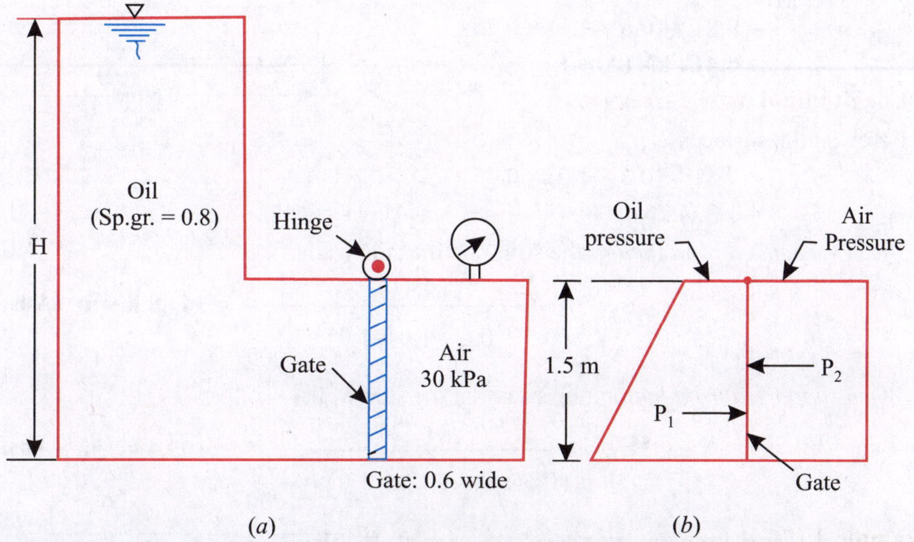

Fig. 3.23

$$= \frac{0.1875}{(H - 0.75)} + (H - 0.75)$$

- *Force due to air pressure,* $P_2 = p.A$

$$= 30 \times (0.6 \times 1.5) = 27\text{kN}$$

Centre of pressure of this force (below the oil surface),

$$\bar{h}_2 = (H - 0.75)$$

Taking moment about the hinge, we get:

$$P_1 \times [\bar{h}_2 - (H - 1.5)] = P_2 \times [\bar{h}_2 - (H - 1.5)]$$

$$(7.063\,H - 5.297)\left\{\frac{0.1875}{(H - 0.75)} + (H - 0.75) - (H - 1.5)\right\}$$

$$= 27 \times \{(H - 0.75) - (H - 1.5)\}$$

$$(7.063\,H - 5.297)\left\{\frac{0.1875}{(H - 0.75)} + 0.75\right\} = 27 \times 0.75$$

On solving by trial and error, we get:

H = **4.324 m (Ans.)**

Example 3.16. *A tank of 1m length and of cross-section shown in fig. 3.24 contains water. The tank is made of 4 mm steel plates.*

(*i*) *What is the force on the bottom due to water?*

(*ii*) *What are the longitudinal tensile stresses in the side walls AB if (a) the tank is suspended from the top and (b) it is supported at the bottom?*

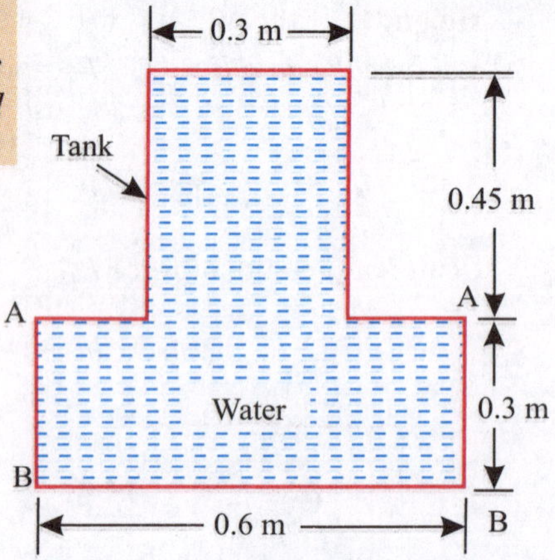

Fig. 3.24

Solution.

Refer to Fig. 3.24

(*i*) Force on the bottom:

Force on the bottom due to water,

$$P_{bottom} = wA\bar{x}$$
$$= 9.81 \times (0.6 \times 1.0) \times 0.75$$
$$= \textbf{4.414 kN}$$ **(Ans.)**

(*ii*) Longitudinal tensile stresses:

Force on the surface *AA*,

$$P_{AA} = 9.81 \times (0.3 \times 1.0) \times 0.45$$
$$= 1.324 \text{ kN}$$

(*a*) *When suspended from the top* the stress on the side walls,

$$\sigma = \frac{4.414}{(0.6 + 0.6 + 1.0 + 1.0) \times \dfrac{4}{1000}} = \textbf{344.8 kN/m}^2$$ **(Ans.)**

(*b*) *When supported from bottom* the stress on the side walls,

$$\sigma = \frac{1.324}{(0.6 + 0.6 + 1.0 + 1.0) \times \dfrac{4}{1000}} = \textbf{103.4 kN/m}^2$$ **(Ans.)**

Example 3.17. *A vertical square 1.2 m × 1.2 m is submerged in the water with upper edge 0.6 m below the water surface. Locate the horizontal line on the surface of the square such that the force on the upper portion equals the force on the lower portion.*

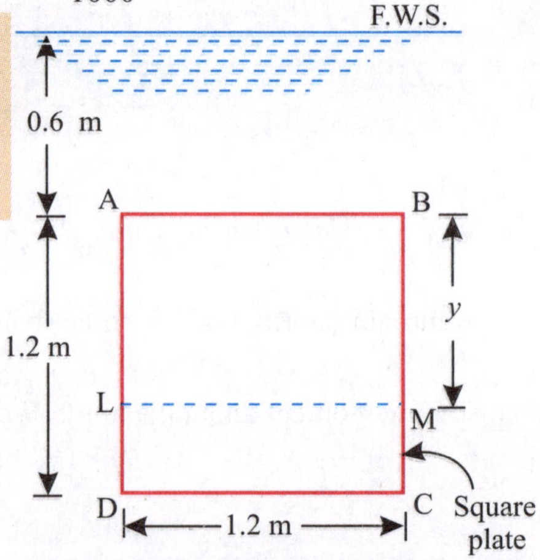

Fig. 3.25

Solution. Refer to Fig. 3.25. *ABCD* is the square plate submerged vertically in water with upper edge *AB* at a depth of 0.6 m below the free water surface (*F. W. S.*)

Let *LM* be the line such that force on *ALMB* equals the force on *LDCM,* and evidently the force on each portion equals half the total force on the entire plate *ABCD*.

Total pressure on the plate *ABCD*

$$= wA\bar{x}$$
$$= w \times (1.2 \times 1.2) \times \left(0.6 + \frac{1.2}{2}\right)$$
$$= 1.728\, w$$

Total pressure on the position *ALMB*

$$= w \times (1.2 \times y) \times \left(0.6 + \frac{y}{2}\right) = 1.2\, wy\left(0.6 + \frac{y}{2}\right)$$

Now, pressure force on *ALMB* $= \dfrac{1}{2} \times$ pressure force on *ABCD*

$$1.2\,wy\left(0.6+\frac{y}{2}\right) = \frac{1}{2}\times 1.728\,w$$

or, $$0.6y+\frac{y^2}{2} = 0.72$$

or, $$y^2+1.2y-1.44 = 0$$

or, $$y = \frac{-1.2\pm\sqrt{(1.2)^2+4\times 1.44}}{2} = \frac{-1.2\pm 2.683}{2}$$

$$= 0.7415 \text{ m or } -1.9415 \text{ m.}$$

i.e., y = **0.7415 m (Ans.)**

Example 3.18. *A rectangular vertical door, 2.4 m (height) × 1.2 m (wide), is fastened by two hinges situated 18 cm below the top and 18 cm above the bottom on one vertical edge, and by one clamp at the centre of other vertical edge. The door is subjected to water pressure on one side and the depth of water above the top of door is 1.2 m. Calculate the reactions at the hinges and at the clamp.*

Solution. Refer to Fig. 3.26.

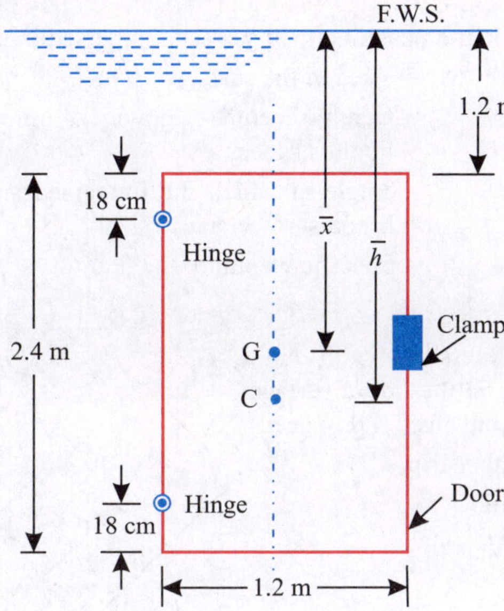

Fig. 3.26

Depth of centroid of the door, $\bar{x} = 1.2+\frac{2.4}{2} = 2.4$ m

Area of the door, $A = 2.4\times 1.2 = 2.88 \text{ m}^2$

Total pressure on the door,

$$P = wA\bar{x} = 9.81\times 2.88\times 2.4 = 67.8 \text{ kN}$$

Depth of centre of pressure,

$$\bar{h} = \frac{I_G}{A\bar{x}}+\bar{x}$$

$$\frac{(1.2\times 2.4^3/12)}{2.88\times 2.4}+2.4 = 2.6 \text{ m}$$

i.e., $(2.4 + 1.2) - 2.6 = 1$ m from the base

Let, R_{th} = Reaction at the top hinge,

R_{bh} = Reaction at the bottom hinge, and

R_{cl} = Reaction at the clamp.

The symmetry of the arrangement suggests that half of the total pressure force is taken by the two hinges and the other half by the clamp.

∴ *Reaction at the clamp.* $\mathbf{R_{cl}} = \frac{67.8}{2} = \mathbf{33.9\ kN}$ **(Ans.)**

Taking moments of all forces about the horizontal axis through the bottom hinge, we get:

$$P \times (1 - 0.18) = R_{cl} \times \left(\frac{2.4}{2} - 0.18\right) + R_{th} \times (2.4 - 0.18 - 0.18)$$

$$67.8 \times 0.82 = 33.9 \times 1.02 + R_{th} \times 2.04$$

or, $\mathbf{R_{th} = 10.3\ kN}$ **(Ans.)**

∴ Reaction at the bottom hinge, $\mathbf{R_{bh}} = 33.9 - R_{th} = 33.9 - 10.3 = \mathbf{23.6\ kN}$ **(Ans.)**

3.5. INCLINED IMMERSED SURFACE

Refer to Fig. 3.27. Consider a plane inclined surface, immersed in a liquid.

Let, A = Area of the surface,

$\bar{x}$ = Depth of centre of gravity of immersed surface from the free liquid surface,

θ = Angle at which the immersed surface is inclined with the liquid surface, and

w = Specific weight of the liquid.

(*a*) Total pressure (*P*):

Consider a strip of thickness dx, width b at a distance l from O (A point, on the liquid surface, where the immersed surface will meet, if produced).

The intensity of pressure on the strip

$= wl \sin\theta$

Area of the strip $= b.dx$

Pressure on the strip

= Intensity of pressure × *area*

$= wl \sin\theta \,.\, b.\, dx$

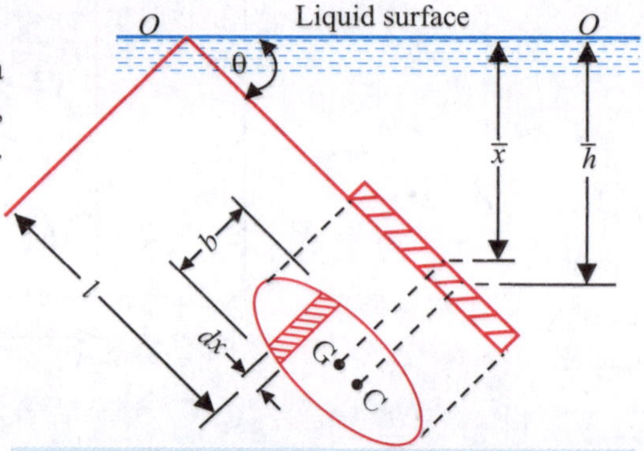

Fig. 3.27. Inclined immersed surface.

Now total pressure on the surface,

$$P = \int wl \sin\theta \,.\, b \,.\, dx = w \sin\theta \int l \,.\, b \,.\, dx$$

But, $\int l \,.\, b \,.\, dx$ = moment of surface area about 00

$$= \frac{A\bar{x}}{\sin\theta},$$

$$\therefore \quad P = w \sin\theta \,.\, \frac{A\bar{x}}{\sin\theta} = wA\bar{x} \text{ (same as in Arts. 3.3 and 3.4)}$$

(b) Centre of pressure ($\bar{h}$):

Referring to Fig 3.27, let C be the centre of pressure of the inclined surface.

Let, $\bar{h}$ = Depth of centre of pressure below free liquid surface,

I_G = Moment of inertia of the immersed surface about OO,

$\bar{x}$ = Depth of centre of gravity of the surface from the liquid surface,

θ = Angle at which the immersed surface is inclined with the liquid surface, and

A = Area of the surface.

Consider a strip of thickness of dx, width b and at distance l from OO.

The intensity of pressure on the strip = $wl\sin\theta$

Area of strip = $b \,.\, dx$

$\therefore$ Pressure on the strip = Intensity of pressure × area = $wl \sin\theta \, b \,.\, dx$

Moment of the pressure about OO = $(wl \sin\theta \,.\, b.dx)\, l = wl^2 \sin\theta \,.\, b \,.\, dx$

Now sum of moments of all such pressures about O,

$$M = \int wl^2 \sin\theta \,.\, b\, dx = w \sin\theta \int l^2 \,.\, b \,.\, dx$$

But, $\int l^2 \,.\, b \,.\, dx = I_0$ = moment of inertia of the surface about the point 0 (or the second moment of area)

$$M = w \sin\theta \,.\, I_0 \qquad ...(i)$$

The sum of moments of all such pressures about O is also equal to $\dfrac{P\bar{h}}{\sin\theta}$ ...(*ii*)

where, P is the total pressure on the surface.

Equating eqns. (*i*) and (*ii*), we get:

$$\frac{P\bar{h}}{\sin\theta} = w \sin\theta \,.\, I_0$$

$$\frac{wA\bar{x}\bar{h}}{\sin\theta} = w \sin\theta \,.\, I_0 \qquad (\because P = wA\bar{x})$$

or,

$$\bar{h} = \frac{I_0 \sin^2\theta}{A\bar{x}} \qquad ...(iii)$$

Also, $I_0 = I_G + Ah^2$ ...Theorem of parallel axes.

where, I_G = Moment of inertia of figure about horizontal axis through its centre of gravity, and

h = Distance between 0 and the centre of gravity of the figure $= l\left(=\dfrac{\bar{x}}{\sin\theta}\right)$ in this case.

Rearranging equation (*iii*), we have:

$$\bar{h} = \frac{\sin^2\theta}{A\bar{x}}(I_G + Al^2)$$

$$= \frac{\sin^2\theta}{A\bar{x}}\left[I_G + A\left(\frac{\bar{x}}{\sin\theta}\right)^2\right] = \frac{I_G \sin^2\theta}{A\bar{x}} + \bar{x}$$

Hence, *centre of pressure*

$$\bar{h} = \frac{I_G \sin^2\theta}{A\bar{x}} + \bar{x} \qquad ...(3.3)$$

It will be noticed that if $\theta = 90°$ eqn (3.3) becomes the same as equation (3.2).

Example 3.19. *A 1m wide and 1.5 m deep rectangular plane surface lies in water in such a way that its plane makes an angle of 30° with the free water surface. Determine the total pressure and position of centre of pressure when the upper edge is 0.75 m below the free water surface.*

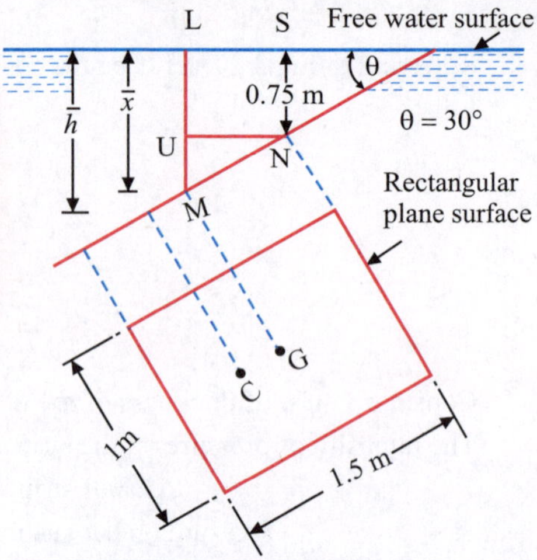

Fig. 3.28

Solution. Width of the plane surface = 1m

Depth of the plane surface = 1.5 m

Inclination, $\theta = 30°$

Distance of upper edge from free water surface = 0.75 m

(i) Total pressure, P:

Using the relation, $P = wA\bar{x}$

where, $w = 9.81$ kN/m^3,

Area, $A = 1.5 \times 1 = 1.5$ m^2,

$$\bar{x} = LU + UM = 0.75 + MN \sin 30°$$

$$= 0.75 + \frac{1.5}{2} \times 0.5 = 1.125 \text{ m}$$

$$P = 9.81 \times 1.5 \times 1.125 \text{ m}$$

$$= \textbf{16.55 kN (Ans.)}$$

(ii) Centre of pressure, $\bar{h}$:

Using the relation, $\bar{h} = \dfrac{I_G \sin^2 \theta}{A\bar{x}} + \bar{x}$

where, $I_G = \dfrac{1 \times 1.5^3}{12} = 0.281$ m^4

i.e.,

$$\bar{h} = \frac{0.281 \times (0.5)^2}{1.5 \times 1.125} + 1.125 = \textbf{1.166 m (Ans.)}$$

Example 3.20. *A circular plate 1.5 m diameter is submerged in water, with its greatest and least depths below the surface being 2 m and 0.75 m respectively. Determine:*

(i) The total pressure on one face of the plate, and

(ii) The position of the centre of pressure.

Solution. Diameter of the plate, = 1.5 m

Area of the plate,

$$A = \frac{\pi}{4} . d^2 = \frac{\pi}{4} \times 1.52 = 1.767 \text{ m}^2$$

Refer to Fig. 3.29

Distance, $SN = 0.75$ m, $UM = 2$m

Distance of *c.g.* from free surface,

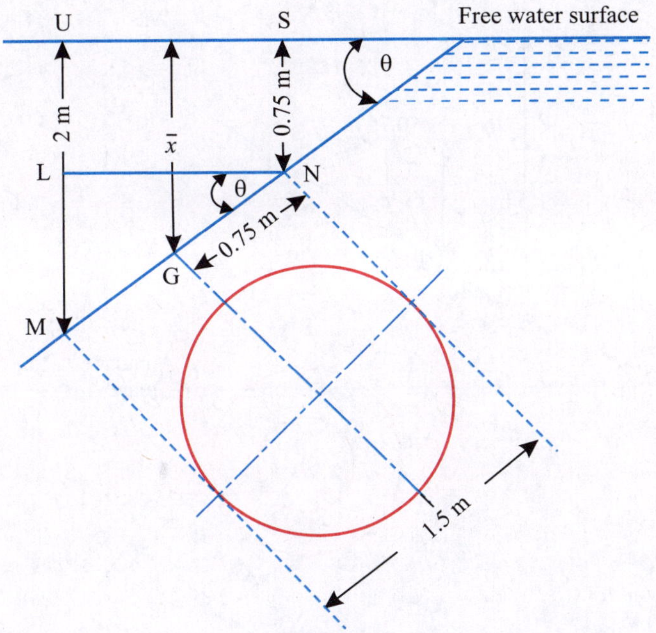

Fig. 3.29

$$\bar{x} = SN + GN \sin\theta$$

$$= 0.75 + 0.75 \sin\theta$$

But, $$\sin\theta = \frac{LM}{MN} = \frac{UM - UL}{MN}$$

$$= \frac{2 - 0.75}{1.5} = 0.8333$$

∴ $$\bar{x} = 0.75 + 0.75 \times 0.8333 = 1.375 \text{ m}$$

(*i*) Total pressure, *P*:

We know that,

$$P = wA\bar{x} = 9.81 \times 1.767 \times 1.375$$

$$= \mathbf{23.83 \text{ kN (Ans.)}}$$

(*ii*) Centre of pressure, $\bar{h}$:

Using the relation,

$$\bar{h} = \frac{I_G \sin^2\theta}{A\bar{x}} + \bar{x}$$

$$= \frac{\pi/64 \times 1.5^4 \times (0.8333)^2}{1.767 \times 1.375} + 1.375 = 1.446$$

i.e., $$\bar{h} = \mathbf{1.446 \text{ m (Ans.)}}$$

Example 3.21. *An annular plate 2m external diameter and 1m internal diameter with its greatest and least depths below the surface being 1.5 m and 0.75 m respectively. Calculate the magnitude, direction and location of the force acting upon one side of the plate due to water pressure.*

Solution. Refer to Fig. 3.30. From the geometry of the figure, we have:

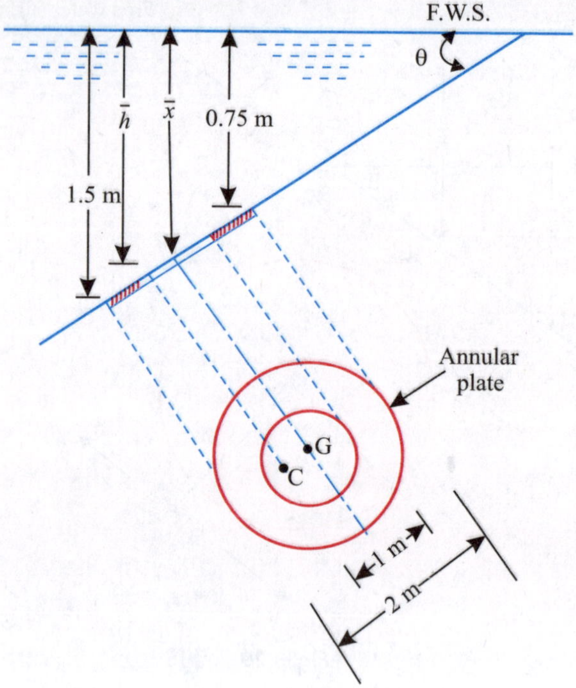

Fig. 3.30

$$\sin\theta = \frac{1.5 - 0.75}{2} = 0.375$$

$$\therefore \quad \theta = \sin^{-1}(0.375) = 22°$$

$$\text{Area of the plate, } A = \frac{\pi}{4}(2^2 - 1^2) = 2.356 \text{ m}^2$$

$$\text{Depth of centroid, } \bar{x} = \frac{1.5 + 0.75}{2} = 1.125 \text{ m}$$

Total pressure force,

$$P = wA\bar{x} = 9.81 \times 2.356 \times 1.125 = \mathbf{26\ kN}\ \textbf{(Ans.)}$$

This force acts perpendicular to the plate so it is acting in a direction which is 90° – 22° = **68° to the vertical (Ans.)**

Depth of centre of pressure,

$$\bar{h} = \frac{I_G \sin^2\theta}{A\bar{x}} + \bar{x}$$

$$= \frac{\frac{\pi}{64}(2^4 - 1^4) \times (\sin 22°)^2}{\frac{\pi}{4}(2^2 - 1^2) \times 1.125} + 1.125$$

$$= \frac{0.1033}{2.651} + 1.125 = \mathbf{1.164\ m}\ \textbf{(Ans.)}$$

Example 3.22. *A triangular plate of 1 metre base and 1.5 metre altitude is immersed in water. The plane of the plate is inclined at 30° with free water surface and the base is parallel to and at a depth of 2 metres from water surface. Find the total pressure on the plate and the position of centre of pressure.*

Solution. Refer to Fig. 3.31.

Area of the plate,

$$A = \frac{1}{2} \times 1 \times 1.5 = 0.75 \text{ m}^2$$

Inclination of the plate, $\theta = 30°$

Total pressure on the plate, *P*:

The depth of *c.g.* of the plate from water surface,

$$\bar{x} = 2 + \frac{1.5}{3} \sin 30°$$

$$= 2 + 0.5 \times 0.5 = 2.25 \text{ m}$$

Using the relation,

$$P = wA\bar{x} = 9.81 \times 0.75 \times 2.25$$

$$= \mathbf{16.55 \text{ kN}} \textbf{ (Ans.)}$$

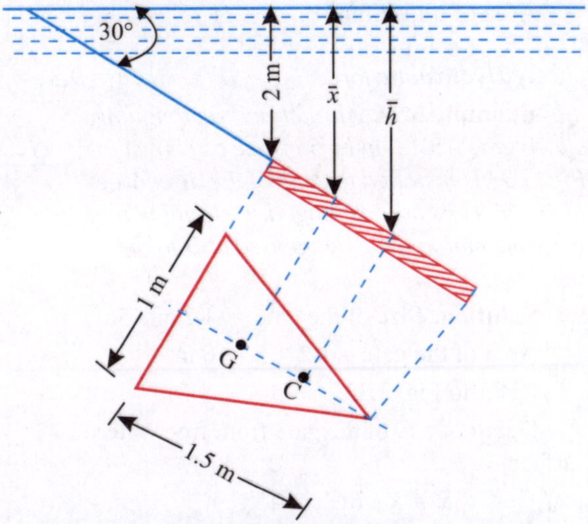

Fig. 3.31

Depth of centre of pressure, $\bar{h}$:

Moment of inertia of a triangular section about its *c.g.*,

$$I_G = \frac{1 \times 1.5^3}{36} = 0.09375 \text{ m}^4$$

Using the relation,

$$\bar{h} = \frac{I_G \sin^2 \theta}{A\bar{x}} + \bar{x} = \frac{0.09375 \sin^2 30°}{0.75 \times 2.25} + 2.25$$

$$= \mathbf{2.264 \text{ m}} \textbf{ (Ans.)}$$

Example 3.23. *A trapezoidal plate measuring 1 m at the top edge and 1.5 m at the bottom edge is immersed in water with the plan making an angle of 30° to the free surface of water. The top and the bottom edges lie at 0.5 m and 1 m respectively from the surface. Determine the hydrostatic force on the plate.*

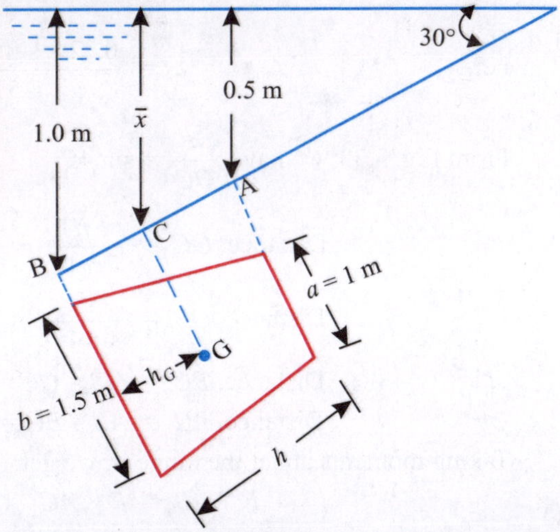

Fig. 3.32

Solution.

Refer to Fig. 3.32, *Given*:

$$a = 1 \text{ m}; b = 1.5 \text{ m};$$

$$h = AB = \frac{1.0 - 0.5}{\sin 30°} = 1 \text{m}$$

Distance of centroid of a trapezium plate from its base,

$$h_G = \frac{h}{3}\left(\frac{2a + b}{a + b}\right)$$

$$= \frac{1}{3}\left(\frac{2 \times 1 + 1.5}{1 + 1.5}\right) = 0.467 \text{ m}$$

Depth of centroid from the free water, surface,

$$\bar{x} = 1.0 - BC \sin 30° = 1.0 - 0.467 \times \sin 30° = 0.7665 \text{ m}$$

Area of trapezium, $A = \left(\frac{a+b}{2}\right)h = \left(\frac{1+1.5}{2}\right) \times 1 = 1.25 \text{ m}^2$

∴ *Hydrostatic force* $P = wA\bar{x} = 9.81 \times 1.25 \times 0.7665 = \mathbf{9.399 \text{ kN}}$ **(Ans.)**

Example 3.24. *An inclined rectangular sluice gate AB 1.2 m by 5 m size as shown in Fig. 3.33 is installed to control the discharge of water. The end A is hinged. Determine the force normal to the gate applied at B to open it.*

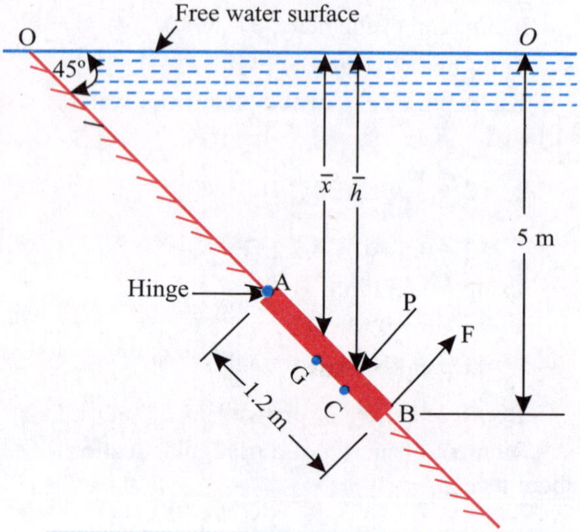

Fig. 3.33

Solution. Size of the gate = 1.2 m × 5m

Area of the gate = 1.2 × 5 = 6 m²

Refer to Fig. 3.33.

Depth of c.g. of the gate from free water surface,

$$\bar{x} = 5 - BG \sin 45°$$
$$= 5 - 0.6 \times 0.707 = 4.576 \text{ m}$$

The total pressure force (P) acting on the gate,

$$P = wA\bar{x}$$
$$= 9.81 \times 6 \times 4.576 = 269.3 \text{ kN}$$

This force acts at a depth h, given by the relation:

$$\bar{h} = \frac{I_G \sin^2 \theta}{A\bar{x}} + \bar{x}$$

where, $I_G = M.O.I. \text{ of gate} = \frac{bd^3}{12} = \frac{5 \times 1.2^3}{12} = 0.72 \text{ m}^4, \theta = 45°$

i.e., $\bar{h} = \frac{0.72 \times \sin^2 45°}{6 \times 4.576} + 4.576 = 4.589 \text{ m}$

From Fig. 3.33, we have $\frac{\bar{h}}{OC} = \sin 45°$

Distance, $OC = \frac{\bar{h}}{\sin 45°} = \frac{4.589}{0.707} = 6.49 \text{ m};$

Distance, $OB = \frac{5}{\sin 45°} = 7.072 \text{ m}$

∴ Distance, $BC = OB - OC = 7.072 - 6.49 = 0.582 \text{ m}$

Distance, $AC = AB - BC = 1.2 - 0.582 = 0.618 \text{ m}$

Taking moments about the hinge A, we get:

$$F \times AB = P \times AC$$

or, $F = \frac{P \times AC}{AB} = \frac{269.3 \times 0.618}{1.2} = \mathbf{138.69 \text{ kN}}$ **(Ans.)**

Example 3.25. *A 6 m × 2 m rectangular gate is hinged at the base and is inclined at an angle of 60° with the horizontal. The upper end of the gate is kept in position by a weight of 60 kN acting at angle of 90° as shown in Fig. 3.34. Neglecting the weight of the gate, find the level of water when the gate begins to fall.*

Solution. Length of the gate, $l = 6$ m

Width of the gate, $b = 2$ m

Inclination, $\theta = 60°$

Weight, $W = 60$ kN

Level of water when the gate begins to fall:

Refer to Fig. 3.34

Let, h = Height of free water surface from the bottom when the gate just begins to fall.

Then, length of gate in the shape of plate, submerged in water,

$$AD = \frac{AC}{\sin\theta} = \frac{h}{\sin 60°} = \frac{h}{0.866}$$

$$= 1.1547\, h$$

∴ Area of the gate immersed in water,

$$A = AD \times \text{width}$$

$$= 1.1547\, h \times 2 = 2.309\, h \text{ m}^2$$

Also depth of *c.g.* of the immersed area,

$$\bar{x} = \frac{h}{2} = 0.5\, h$$

Total pressure on the gate,

$$P = wA\bar{x} = 9.81 \times 2.309\, h \times 0.5\, h$$

$$= 11.326\, h^2 \text{ kN}$$

The centre of pressure of the immersed surface ($\bar{h}$) is given by:

$$\bar{h} = \frac{I_G \sin^2\theta}{A\bar{x}} + \bar{x}$$

where, I_G = moment of inertia of the *immersed area*

$$= \frac{b \times AD^3}{12} = \frac{2}{12}(1.1547\, h)^3$$

$$= 0.2566\, h^3$$

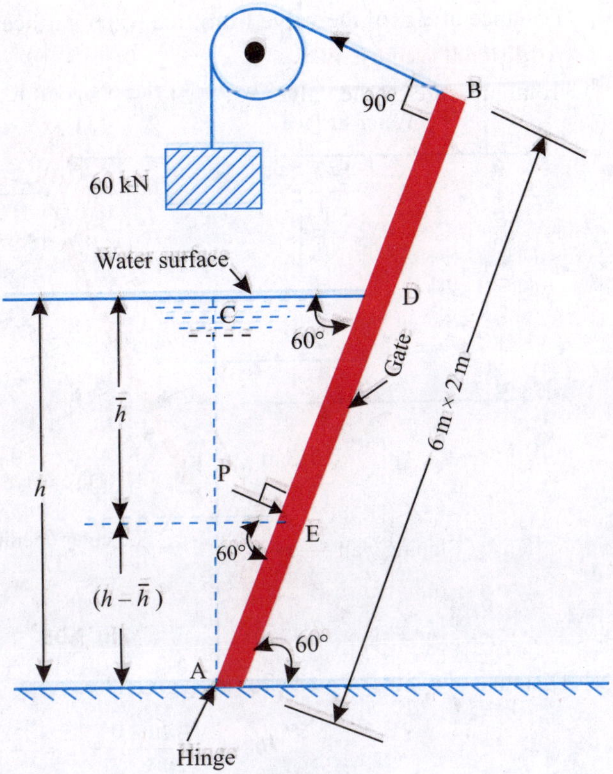

Fig. 3.34

$$\bar{h} = \frac{0.2566 h^3 \times (\sin 60°)^2}{2.309 h \times 0.5 h} + 0.5\, h = 0.667\, h \text{ metres.}$$

Distance of centre of pressure from the hinge (or pivot) along the length of the gate,

$$AE = \frac{h - \bar{h}}{\sin 60°} = \frac{h - 0.667\, h}{0.866} = 0.384\, h$$

Taking moments about the hinge, we get:

$$P \times AE = 60 \times AB$$

$$11.326\, h^2 \times 0.384\, h = 60 \times 6$$

or $$h^3 = \frac{60 \times 6}{11.326 \times 0.384} = 82.774$$

or $$h = \mathbf{4.36\ m}$$ **(Ans.)**

Example 3.26. *Fig. 3.35 shows a circular opening in the sloping wall of the reservoir closed by disc valve 0.9 m diameter. The disc is hinged at H and a balance weight W is just sufficient to hold the valve closed when the reservoir is empty. How much additional weight should be placed on the arm, 1.2 m from the hinge, in order that the valve shall remain closed until the water level is 0.72 m above the centre of the valve.*

Solution. Dia. of the valve, $d = 0.9$ m

$$\text{Area of the valve, } A = \frac{\pi}{4}d^2 = \frac{\pi}{4} \times 0.9^2 = 0.636 \text{ m}^2$$

$$\text{Inclination, } \theta = 60°$$

Distance of *c.g.* of the valve from free water surface, $\bar{x} = 0.72$ m

Additional weight, W′:

Total pressure on the valve, $P = wA\bar{x} = 9.81 \times 0.636 \times 0.72 = 4.49$ kN

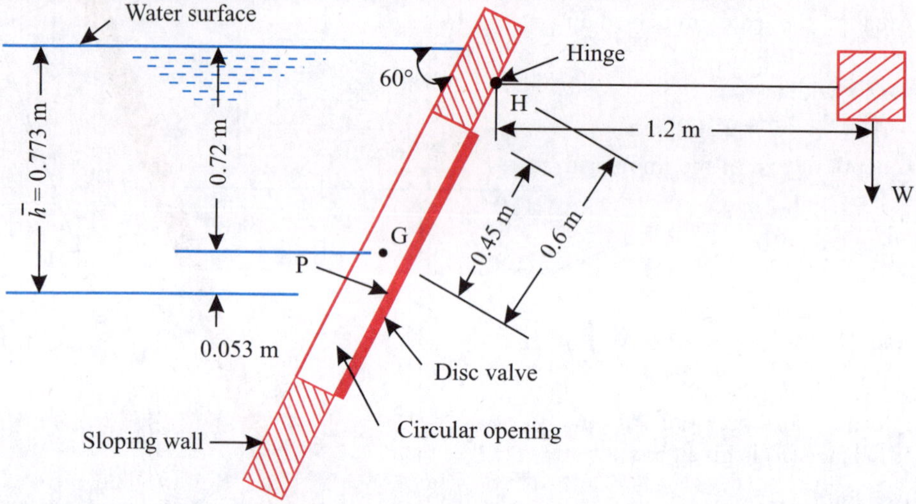

Fig. 3.35

Distance of centre of pressure ($\bar{h}$) is given by:

$$\bar{h} = \frac{I_G \sin^2\theta}{A\bar{x}} + \bar{x} = \frac{\pi/64 \times 0.9^4 \times (\sin 60°)^2}{0.636 \times 0.72} + 0.72$$

$$= 0.773 \text{ m (from free water surface)}$$

$$= 0.053 \text{ m below the centroid } G.$$

Taking moments of all the forces about the hinge, we have:

$$P\left(\frac{0.053}{\sin 60°} + 0.6\right) = W' \times 1.2$$

or, $\quad 4.49\,(0.0612 + 0.6) = W' \times 1.2$ or W'

$$= \mathbf{2.47\ kN\ (Ans.)}$$

Example 3.27. *Fig. 3.36 shows a gate supporting water. Taking the width of the gate as unity find:* ***(i)*** *Depth of water (h) so that the gate tips about the hinge;*

(ii) *Reaction at the hinge.*

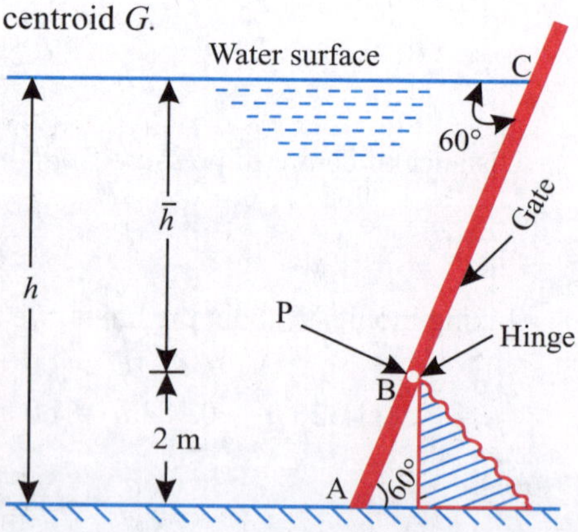

Fig. 3.36

Solution. Inclination of the gate, $\theta = 60°$

(*i*) Depth of water, *h*:

As the depth of water increases, the total pressure P on the gate moves upwards, and just before tipping, P acts at the hinge.

∴ Depth of centre of pressure

$$\bar{h} = (h - 2) \text{ m}$$

But $\bar{h}$ is also given by:

$$\bar{h} = \frac{I_G \sin^2 \theta}{A\bar{x}} + \bar{x}$$

Taking width of gate unity, we have:

$$\text{Area, } A = AC \times 1 = \frac{h}{\sin 60°} \times 1$$

$$= 1.1547\, h \qquad \left(\because AC = \frac{h}{\sin 60°}\right)$$

Distance of *c.g.* from water surface, $\bar{x} = \frac{h}{2} = 0.5\, h.$

Moment of inertia, $$I_G = \frac{1 \times AC^3}{12} = \frac{1}{12} \times (h / \sin 60°)^3 = 0.1283\, h^3$$

$$\therefore \quad \bar{h} = \frac{0.1283 h^3 \times (\sin 60°)^2}{1.1547 h \times 0.5 h} + 0.5\, h = 0.667\, h$$

Equating the two values of h, we get: $h - 2 = 0.667\, h$ or $0.333\, h = 2$

or, h = **6 m (Ans.)**

Example 3.28. *A gate supporting water takes the form of an inclined shield which swings around a hinged axis O (Fig. 3.37).*

Determine: **(*i*)** *The position x of the hinge at which a water level of h = 5.1 m on the left would cause the gate to tip over the hinge;*

(*ii*) *The magnitude of hydrostatic free on the gate just before it opens (tips about the hinge) automatically. Neglect frictional effects.*

Solution. Refer to Fig. 3.37.

(*i*) The position *x* of the hinge:

The gate would tip about the hinge point O when the line of action of the resultant pressure force lies from O to B anywhere on the gate; the limiting condition being the situation when the resultant force passes through the hinged point O. The resultant also passes through the centroid of the pressure diagram, and the centroid lies at a distance $\frac{1}{3} \times AB$ from the bottom point A.

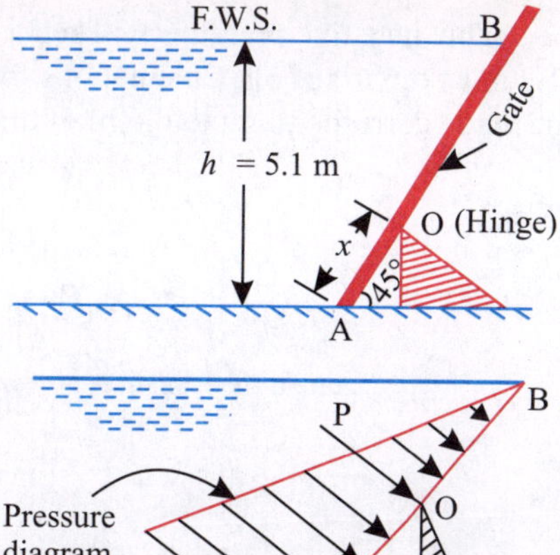

Fig. 3.37

$$\therefore \quad x = \frac{1}{3} \times AB$$

or, AB (length of the gate) $= 3x$

Depth of water, $h = 3x \times \sin 45°$

i.e. $5.1 = 3x \times \sin 45°$

$$\therefore \quad x = \frac{5.1}{3 \times \sin 45°}$$

$$= \textbf{2.4 m (Ans.)}$$

(i) The magnitude of hydrostatic force *P*:

$$P = \text{Area of pressure diagram} \times \text{width of gate}$$

$$= \left(\frac{1}{2} \times AB \times wh\right) \times 1 \quad \text{... considering unit width}$$

$$= \left[\frac{1}{2} \times (3 \times 2.4) \times 9.81 \times 5.1\right] \times 1 \quad (\because AB = 3x)$$

$$= \mathbf{180.11\ kN\ (Ans.)}$$

Example 3.29. *A 3.6 m square gate provided in an oil tank is hinged at its top edge (Fig. 3.38). The tank contains gasoline (sp. gr = 0.7) upto a height of 1.8 m above the top edge of the plate. The space above the oil is subjected to a negative pressure of 8250 N/m². Determine the necessary vertical pull to be applied at the lower edge to open the gate.* **(GATE)**

Solution. Refer to Fig. 3.38.

Head of oil equivalent to negative pressure 8250 N/m²,

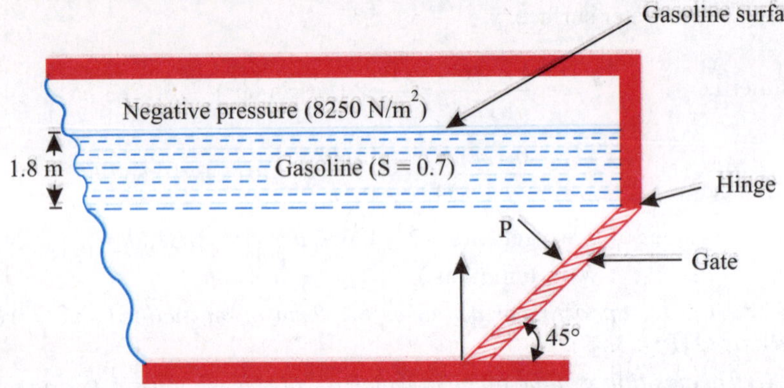

Fig. 3.38

$$h = \frac{p}{w} = \frac{8250}{0.7 \times 9810} = 1.2 \text{ m}$$

This negative pressure will reduce the oil head above the top edge of the gate from 1.8 m to 1.2 m (= 0.6 m) of oil. Calculations for the magnitude and location of the pressure force are thus to be made corresponding to 0.6 m of oil.

Now, $$\bar{x} = 0.6 + \frac{3.6}{2} \sin 45° = 1.873 \text{ m}$$

$$\text{Area, } A = 3.6 \times 3.6 = 12.96 \text{ m}^2$$

$$\text{Pressure, } P = wA\bar{x} = 0.7 \times 9810 \times 12.96 \times 1.873 = 166690 \text{ N}$$

$$\text{Centre of pressure, } \bar{h} = \frac{I_G \sin^2\theta}{A\bar{x}} + \bar{x}$$

$$= \frac{\frac{1}{12} \times 3.6 \times (3.6)^3 \times (\sin 45°)^2}{12.96 \times 1.873} + 1.873 = 2.16 \text{ m}$$

$\therefore$ Vertical distance of centre of pressure below top edge of the gate

$$= 2.16 - 0.6 = 1.56 \text{ m}$$

Taking moments about the hinge, we get:

$$F \sin 45° \times 3.6 = P \times \frac{1.56}{\sin 45°}$$

Hence, vertical force, $F = \frac{P \times 1.56}{3.6 \times (\sin 45°)^2} = \frac{166690 \times 1.56}{3.6 \times (\sin 45°)^2} = \mathbf{144465\ N}$ **(Ans.)**

Example 3.30. *There is an opening in a container shown in Fig. 3.39. Find the force F and the reaction at the hinge.*

Solution. Gauge pressure $= 23.5\ \text{kN/m}^2$

$$= \frac{23.5}{9.81 \times 0.8} \simeq 3 \text{ m of oil} \qquad \left(\because h = \frac{p}{w}\right)$$

The free liquid surface may be considered as 3 m above the hinge A (Fig. 3.40)

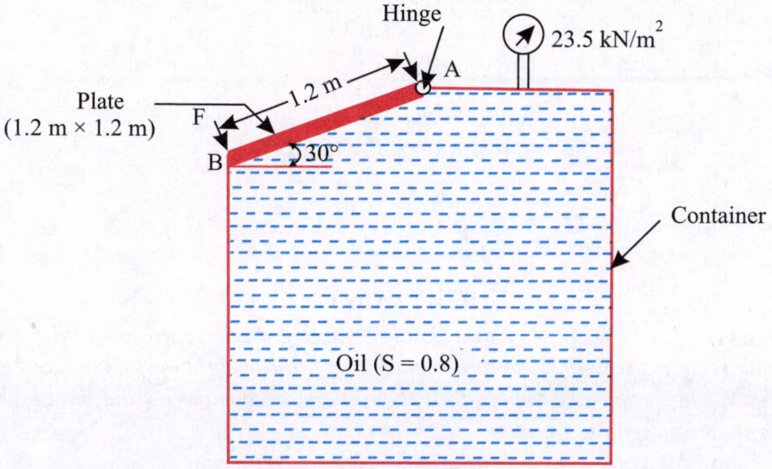

Fig. 3.39

Now, distance of centroid G of the plate from the oil surface,

$$\bar{x} = 3 + 0.6 \sin 30° = 3.3 \text{ m}$$

Total pressure on the plate,

$$P = wA\bar{x}$$
$$= (9.81 \times 0.8) \times (1.2 \times 1.2) \times 3.3$$
$$= 37.29 \text{ kN}$$

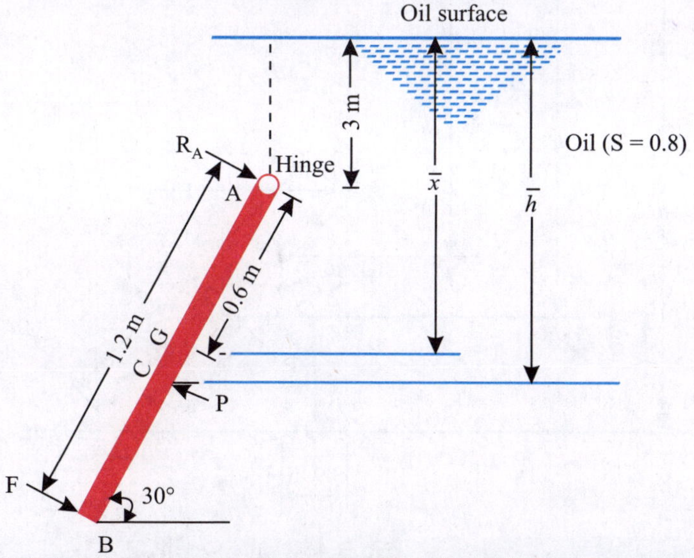

Fig. 3.40. Free body diagram.

Distance of centre of pressure ($\bar{h}$) is given by:

$$\bar{h} = \frac{I_G \sin^2\theta}{A\bar{x}} + \bar{x} = \frac{\frac{1.2 \times 1.2^3}{12} \times (\sin 30°)^2}{(1.2 \times 1.2) \times 3.3} + 3.3 = 3.309 \text{ m}$$

Taking moments about the hinge A, we get:

$$F \times 1.2 = P \times CA = P \times \left[\frac{(\bar{h} - 3)}{\sin 30°}\right]$$

or, $$F \times 1.2 = 37.29 \times \frac{(3.309 - 3)}{\sin 30°}$$

$$= 23.045$$

or, $$F = 19.2 \text{ kN}$$

Let, R_A = Reaction at the hinge,

Then, $$R_A + F = P$$

or, $$R_A = P - F$$

$$= 37.29 - 19.2$$

$$= \textbf{18.09 kN}$$ **(Ans.)**

Example 3.31. *Fig. 3.41. shows a rectangular sluice gate AB, 3 m wide and 4.5 m long hinged at A. It is kept closed by a weight fixed to the gate. The total weight of the gate and weight fixed to the gate is 515 kN. The centre of gravity of the weight and gate is at G. Find the height of the water h which will first cause the gate to open.*

Solution. Width of gate, b = 3 m, Length of gate; l = 4.5 m

Area, $A = 3 \times 4.5 = 13.5 \text{ m}^2$

Weight of gate, W = 515 kN; angle of inclination, $\theta = 45°$

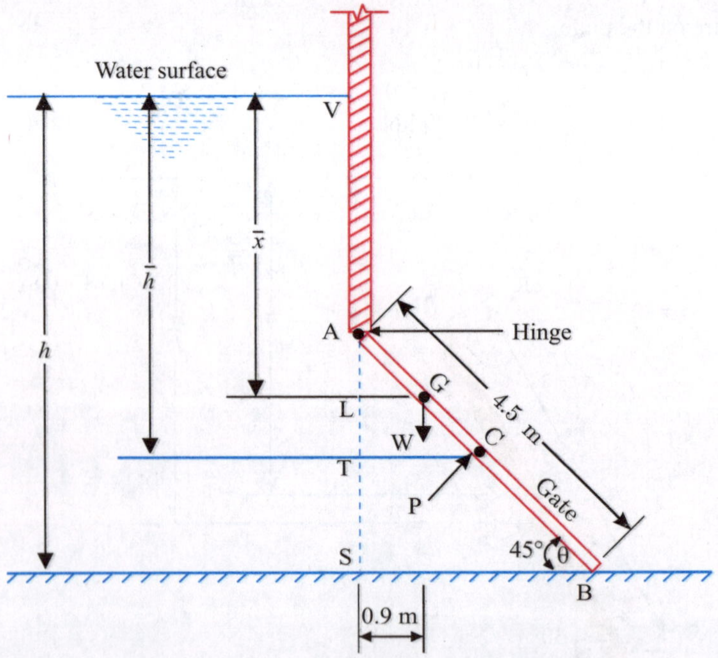

Fig. 3.41

Height of water, *h*:

$$\bar{x} = h - LS = h - (AS - AL) = h - (AB \sin\theta - LG \tan\theta)$$
$$= h - (4.5 \sin 45° - 0.9 \tan 45°)$$
$$= h - (3.18 - 0.9) = (h - 2.28) \text{ m}$$

The total pressure (P) is given by:

$$P = wA\bar{x} = 9.81 \times 13.5 \times (h - 2.28) = 132.43\,(h - 2.28)$$

The total pressure is acting at centre of pressure at C as shown in the Fig. 3.41. The depth of C from the free surface is given by:

$$\bar{h} = \frac{I_G \sin^2\theta}{A\bar{x}} + \bar{x} = \frac{\dfrac{3 \times 4.5^3}{12} \times (\sin 45°)^2}{13.5 \times (h - 2.28)} + (h - 2.28)$$

or,
$$\bar{h} = \frac{0.843}{(h - 2.28)} + (h - 2.28)$$

Now taking moments about hinge A, we get:

$$515 \times LG = P \times AC$$

or,
$$515 \times 0.9 = 132.43\,(h - 2.28) \times \frac{AT}{\sin 45°}$$

$\therefore$
$$AT = \frac{515 \times 0.9 \times \sin 45°}{132.43(h - 2.28)} = \frac{2.47}{(h - 2.28)} \quad ...(i)$$

But,
$$AT = \bar{h} - VA$$

or,
$$AT = \frac{0.843}{(h - 2.28)} + (h - 2.28) - VA \quad ...(ii)$$

But,
$$VA = VS - AS = h - 4.5 \sin 45°$$
$$= h - 3.18$$

Substituting this value in (*ii*), we get:

$$AT = \frac{0.843}{(h - 2.28)} + (h - 2.28) - (h - 3.18)$$
$$= \frac{0.843}{(h - 2.28)} + 3.18 - 2.28$$

or,
$$AT = \frac{0.843}{h - 2.28} + 0.9 \quad ...(iii)$$

Equating the values of AT from (*i*) and (*iii*), we get:

$$\frac{2.47}{h - 2.28} = \frac{0.843}{h - 2.28} + 0.9$$

$$2.47 = 0.843 + 0.9\,(h - 2.28) = 0.843 + 0.9\,h - 2.052$$

or,
$$0.9\,h = 2.47 - 0.843 + 2.052 = 3.679$$

$$h = \frac{3.679}{0.9} = \mathbf{4.08\ m}\ \textbf{(Ans.)}$$

3.6. CURVED IMMERSED SURFACE

Consider a curved surface LM submerged in a static fluid as shown in Fig. 3.42. At any point on the curved surface, the pressure acts normal to the surface. Thus if dA is the area of a small element of the curved surface lying at a vertical depth of h from surface of the liquid, then the total pressure on the elemental area is,

$$dp = p \times dA = (wh) \times dA \quad ...(3.4)$$

This force dP acts normal to the surface. Further integration of eqn. (3.4) would provide the total pressure on the curved surface and hence,

$$P = \int whdA \qquad ...(3.5)$$

But, is case of curved surface the direction of the total pressures on the elementary areas are not in the same direction, but varies from point to point. Thus the integration of eqn. (3.5) for curved surface is impossible. The problem, however, can be solved by resolving the force P into horizontal and vertical components P_H and P_V. Then total force on the curved surface is,

$$P = \sqrt{P_H^2 + P_V^2} \qquad ...(3.6)$$

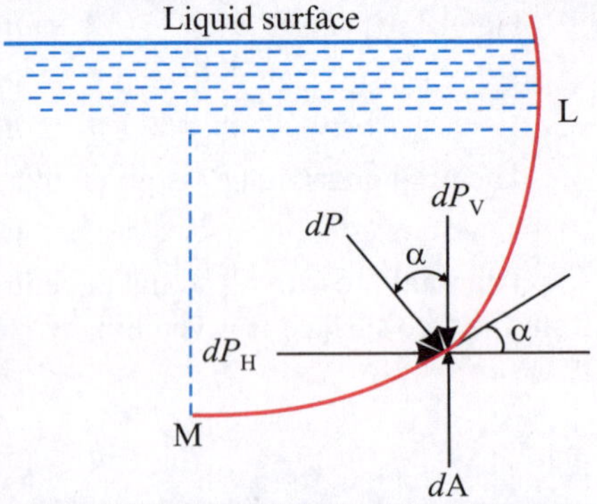

Fig. 3.42

The direction of the resultant force P with the horizontal is given by: $\tan\theta = \dfrac{P_V}{P_H}$

or, $$\theta = \tan^{-1}\left(\frac{P_V}{P_H}\right) \qquad ...(3.7)$$

Here, P_H = Total pressure force on the projected area of the curved surface on vertical plane, and

P_V = Weight of the liquid supported by the curved surface upto free surface of liquid.

Example 3.32. *The profile of a vessel is quadrant of a circle of radius R. Determine the horizontal and vertical components of the total pressure force, from the first principles.*

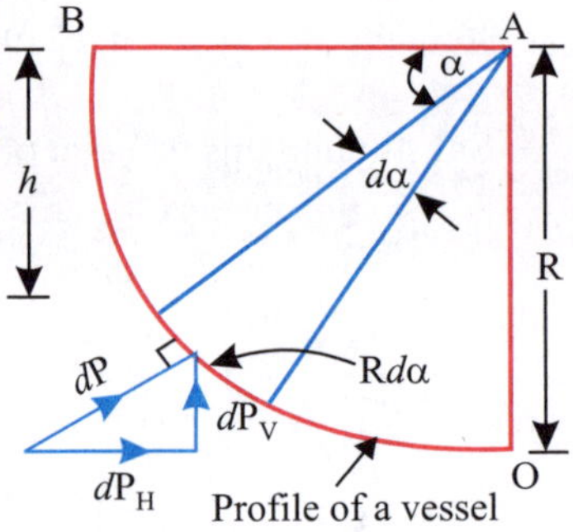

Fig. 3.43

Solution. Consider an elementary strip of radius R at depth h and subtending an angle as shown in Fig. 3.43.

Let the vessel has a unit depth perpendicular to the plane of paper. Then Area of the element,

$$dA = Rd\alpha \times \text{unit depth} = Rd\alpha$$

$$\text{Depth, } h = R\sin\alpha$$

$$\text{Intensity of pressure, } p = wh = wR\sin\alpha$$

$$\text{Pressure force, } dp = p \times dA = wR\sin\alpha \times Rd\alpha$$

$$= wR^2 \sin\alpha\, d\alpha$$

Vertical component of dP,

$$dP_V = wR^2 \sin\alpha\, d\alpha \times \sin\alpha = wR^2 \sin^2\alpha\, d\alpha$$

Horizontal component of dP,

$$dP_H = wR^2 \sin\alpha\, d\alpha \times \cos\alpha = wR^2 \sin\alpha \cos\alpha\, d\alpha$$

∴ Total vertical pressure force,

$$P_V = \int_0^{\pi/2} wR^2 \sin^2\alpha\, d\alpha$$

$$= \frac{wR^2}{2}\left[\int_0^{\pi/2}\left(\frac{1-\cos 2\alpha}{2}\right)d\alpha\right]$$

$$= \frac{wR^2}{2}\left[|\alpha|_0^{\pi/2} - \left|\frac{\sin 2\alpha}{2}\right|_0^{\pi/2}\right] = \frac{wR^2\pi}{4}$$

$$= w\left(\frac{\pi R^2}{4} \times \text{unit length}\right)$$

= specific weight × (volume of liquid contained in curved surface).

- Thus the *vertical component of pressure force on a curved surface equals the weight of the volume liquid extending vertically from the curved surface to the free surface of liquid.*

(Ans.)

Total *horizontal* pressure force,

$$P_H = \int_0^{\pi/2} wR^2 \sin\alpha \cos\alpha \, d\alpha$$

$$= \frac{wR^2}{2}\int_0^{\pi/2} 2\sin\alpha \cos\alpha \, d\alpha$$

$$= \frac{wR^2}{2}\int_0^{\pi/2} \sin 2\alpha \, d\alpha = \frac{wR^2}{2}\left[-\frac{\cos 2\alpha}{2}\right]_0^{\pi/2} = \frac{wR^2}{2}$$

$$= w\,(R \times \text{unit length}) \times \frac{R}{2} \equiv wA\bar{x}$$

- *Thus the horizontal component of pressure force on a curved surface equals the force on projected area of curved surface on a vertical plane.*

Example 3.33. *A hemisphere projection of diameter 0.6 m exists on one of the vertical sides of a tank. If the tank contains water to an elevation of 1.5 m above the centre of the hemisphere, calculate the vertical and horizontal forces acting on the projection.*

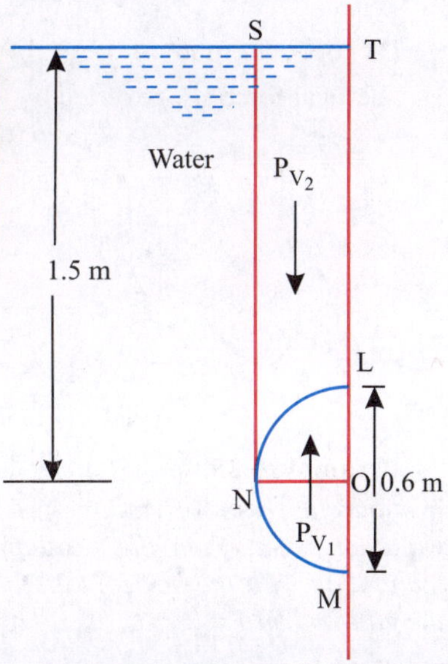

Fig. 3.44

Solution. Refer to Fig. 3.44.

Vertical force, $P_V = P_{V_1} - P_{V_2}$

= Weight volume of water MNST – weight of volume of water LNST

= Weight of water contained by the hemisphere LNM

$$= w \times \frac{1}{2}\left(\frac{4}{3}\pi R^3\right)$$

$$= 9.81 \times \frac{1}{2} \times \frac{4}{3} \times \pi \times (0.3)^3$$

= **0.555 kN (Ans.)**

Horizontal force, $P_H = wA\bar{x}$

$= 9.81 \times \pi \times (0.3)^2 \times 1.5 =$ **4.16 kN (Ans.)**

Example 3.34. *Fig. 3.45. shows a curved surface LM, which is in the form of a quadrant of a circle of radius 3 m, immersed in the water. If the width of the gate is unity, calculate the horizontal and vertical components of the total force acting on the curved surface.*

Solution. Radius of the gate = 3 m

Width of the gate = 1m

Refer to Fig. 3.45.

Distance $LO = OM = 3$ m

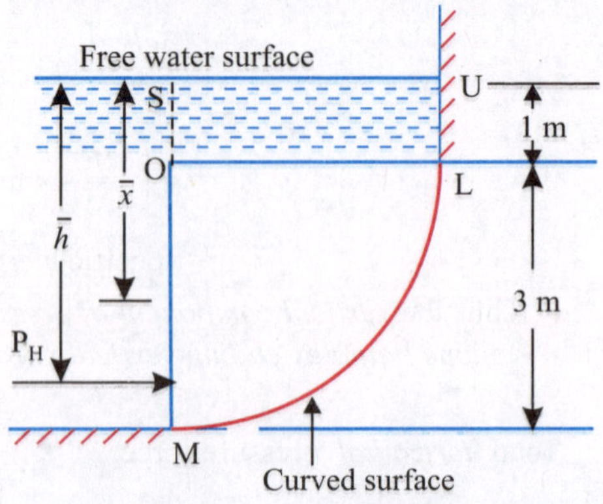

Fig. 3.45. Curved surface (gate).

Horizontal component of total force, P_H:

Horizontal force (P_H) exerted by water on gate is given by,

P_H = Total pressure force on the projected area of curved surface LM on vertical plane

= Total pressure force on OM

(projected area of curved surface on vertical plane

$= OM \times 1) = wA\bar{x}$

But, $A = OM \times 1 = 3 \times 1 = 3\text{m}^2$ and $\bar{x} = 1 + \frac{3}{2} = 2.5$ m

$P_H = 9.81 \times (3 \times 1) \times 2.5 =$ **73.57 kN (Ans.)**

The point of application of P_H is given by:

$$\bar{h} = \frac{I_G}{A\bar{x}} + \bar{x}$$

where, I_G = M.O.I. of OM about its c.g. $= \frac{bd^3}{12} = \frac{1 \times 3^3}{12} = 2.25\ \text{m}^4$

$\therefore$ $\bar{h} = \frac{2.25}{(3 \times 1) \times 2.5} + 2.5 =$ **2.8 m from water surface (Ans.)**

Vertical component of total force, P_V:

Vertical force (P_V) exerted by water is given by:

P_V = Weight of water supported by LM upto free surface

= weight of portion $ULMOS$

= weight of $ULOS$ + weight of water in LOM

= w (volume of $ULOS$ + volume of LOM)

$$= 9.81\left[UL \times LO + \frac{\pi \times (LO)^2}{4} \times 1\right] = 9.81\left[1 \times 3 + \frac{\pi \times 3^2}{4} \times 1\right]$$

$= 9.81\ (3 + 7.068)\ \text{kN} =$ **98.77 kN (Ans.)**

Example 3.35. *Fig. 3.46 shows a gate having a quadrant shape of radius of 1 m subjected to water pressure. Find the resultant force and its inclination with the horizontal. Take the length of the gate as 2 m.*

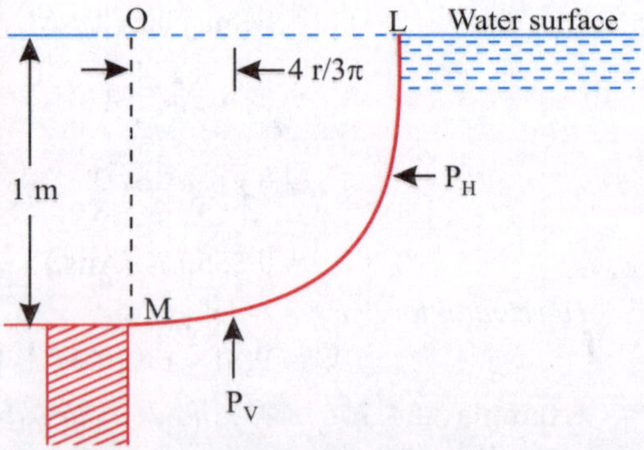

Fig. 3.46

Solution.

Radius of the gate, r = 1m

Length of the gate = 2 m

Horizontal force, P_H:

P_H = Force on the projected area of the curved surface on vertical plane

$$= \text{force on } MO = wA\bar{x}$$

where, $w = 9.81 \text{ kN/m}^3$,

$$A = \text{Area of } MO \text{ (projected area)} = 1 \times 2 = 2 \text{ m}^2$$

$$\bar{x} = \frac{1}{2} = 0.5 \text{ m}$$

$$P_H = 9.81 \times 2 \times 0.5 = 9.81 \text{ kN}$$

Vertical force, P_V:

$$P_V = \text{Weight of water (imagined) supported by } LM$$

$$= w \times \text{area of } LOM \times 2.0 = w \times \frac{\pi \times r^2}{4} \times 2$$

$$= 9.81 \times \frac{\pi}{4} \times 1^2 \times 2 = 15.4 \text{ kN}$$

(*i*) Resultant force *P*:

$$P = \sqrt{P_H^2 + P_V^2} = \sqrt{9.81^2 + 15.4^2} = 18.26 \text{ kN (Ans.)}$$

(*ii*) The angle made by the resultant force with the horizontal, θ:

We know that,

$$\tan\theta = \frac{P_V}{P_H} = \frac{15.4}{9.81} = 1.569 \quad \text{or} \quad \theta = \mathbf{57.48°} \text{ (Ans.)}$$

Example 3.36. *A liquid of specific gravity 0.9 is filled in a container, shown in Fig. 3.47, upto a depth of 2.4 m. Determine the magnitude and direction of hydrostatic pressure force per unit length of container exerted on its vertical face MN and curved corner NQ.*

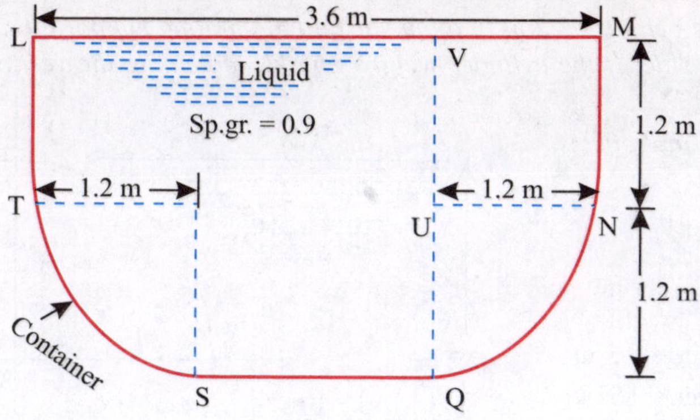

Fig. 3.47

Solution. Refer to Fig 3.47.

Vertical face MN:

$$P = wA\bar{x} = w \times (MN \times \text{unit length}) \times \frac{MN}{2}$$

$$= (9.81 \times 0.9) \times (1.2 \times 1) \times \frac{1.2}{2} = \mathbf{6.357 \text{ kN (Ans.)}}$$

This force acts horizontally towards right and its point of application is given by:

$$\bar{h} = \frac{I_G}{A\bar{x}} + \bar{x} = \frac{1 \times \frac{1.2^3}{12}}{(1.2 \times 1) \times \frac{1.2}{2}} + \frac{1.2}{2} = \mathbf{0.8 \text{ m (Ans.)}}$$

Curved surface NQ:

Horizontal component of hydrostatic pressure force on the curved corner *NQ*,

P_H = Specific weight × vertical projected area × depth of centre of vertical projection

$$= w \times (QU \times \text{unit length}) \times \left(VU + \frac{UQ}{2}\right)$$

$$= (9.81 \times 0.9) \times (1.2 \times 1) \times \left(1.2 + \frac{1.2}{2}\right) = 19.07 \text{ kN}$$

Vertical component of hydrostatic pressure force on the curved corner,

P_V = Weight of liquid contained in portion *MNQUV*

= Specific weight [Volume of liquid in portion *MNUV* + volume of liquid in portion *NQU*]

$$= w\left[MN \times NU \times \text{unit length} + \frac{1}{4}\pi \times (NU)^2 \times \text{unit length}\right]$$

$$= (9.81 \times 0.9)\left[1.2 \times 1.2 \times 1 + \frac{1}{4} \times \pi \times (1.2)^2 \times 1\right] = 22.7 \text{ kN}$$

Resultant pressure force, $P = \sqrt{P_H^2 + P_V^2} = \sqrt{(19.07)^2 + (22.7)^2}$ = **29.65 kN (Ans.)**

The angle made by the resultant with the horizontal,

$$\theta = \tan^{-1}\left(\frac{P_V}{P_H}\right) = \tan^{-1}\left(\frac{22.7}{19.07}\right) = \mathbf{49.97° \text{ (Ans.)}}$$

Example 3.37. *A cylinder 2.2 m in diameter and 3.3 m long supported as shown in Fig. 3.48 retains water on one side. If the cylinder weighs 165 kN, calculate the vertical reaction at L and horizontal reaction at M.*

Neglect the frictional effects.

Solution.

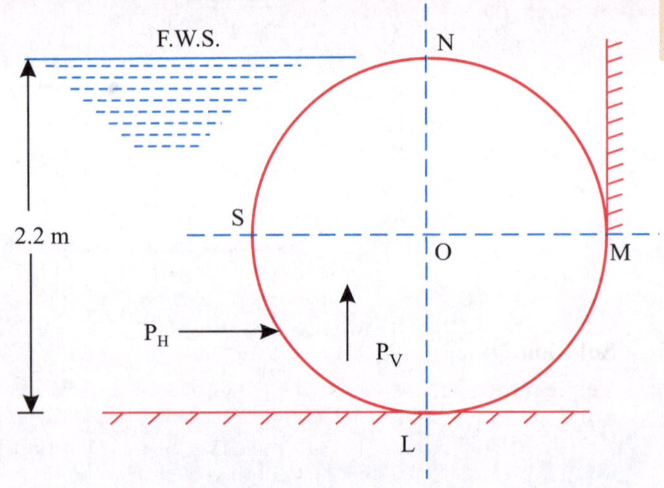

Fig. 3.48

Radius of cylinder

$$= \frac{2.2}{2} = 1.1 \text{ m}$$

Length of cylinder = 3.3 m

Weight of cylinder = 165 kN

- The horizontal component of the resultant hydrostatic force acting on the gate is the horizontal force on the projected area of the curved surface on a vertical plane.

  i.e. P_H = Hydrostatic pressure force on the curved area *LSN* projected on the vertical plane *LON*,

$$= wA\bar{x}$$

$$= 9.81 \times (2.2 \times 3.3) \times \frac{2.2}{2} = 78.34 \text{ kN}$$

∴ *Horizontal reaction at M* = **78.34 kN (Ans.)**

- The *vertical component* of the resultant hydrostatic force is the weight of water supported by the curved surface LSN which represents a semicircle.

$$\therefore \quad P_V = w \times \text{volume of surface LSN}$$

$$= w \times \left(\frac{\pi}{2} \times (\text{radius})^2 \times \text{length}\right)$$

$$= 9.81 \times \left[\frac{\pi}{2} \times (1.1)^2 \times 3.3\right] = 61.53 \text{ kN}$$

P_V is acting in the *upward direction,*

∴ For equilibrium of cylinder,

$$\textit{Vertical reaction at L} = \text{Weight of cylinder} - P_V$$

$$= 165 - 61.53 = \mathbf{103.47\ kN\ (Ans.)}$$

Example 3.38. *Fig. 3.49 shows a radial gate. If it is 3 m long, find the magnitude and direction of the resultant force acting on it.*

Solution. Length of radial gate = 3 m

Refer to Fig. 3.49.

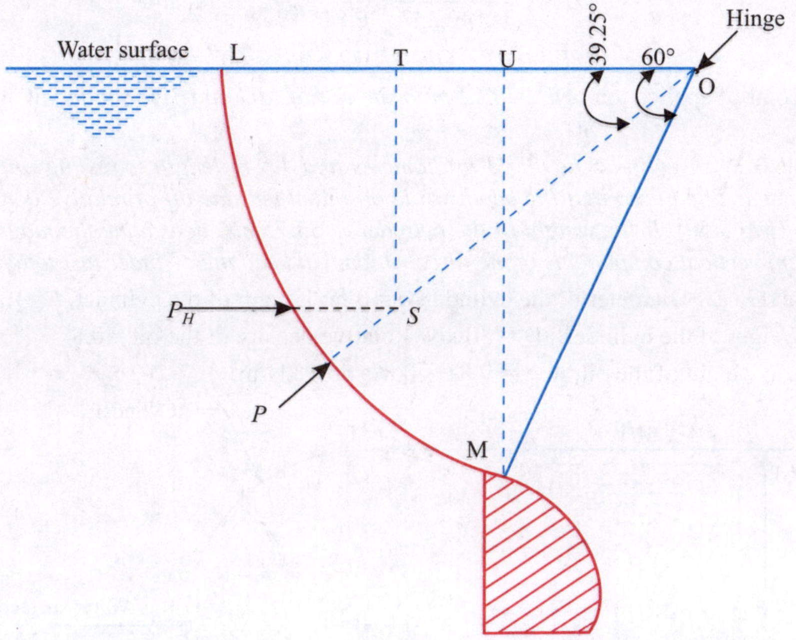

Fig. 3.49

$$MU = 3 \sin 60° = 2.6 \text{ m}$$

Horizontal force on the curved surface,

$$P_H = wA\bar{x}$$

$$= 9.81 \times (2.6 \times 3) \times \frac{2.6}{2}$$

$$= 99.47 \text{ kN}$$

It will act at $\frac{2.6}{3}$ or 0.867 m above *M.*

$$\text{Vertical force, } P_V = \text{Weight of water displaced}$$

$= \text{weight of volume equal to } LMU \times 3.$

Now, Area $LMU = \text{area } LOM - \text{area } MUO$

$$= \pi R^2 \times \frac{60^0}{360^0} - \frac{1}{2} \times 2.6 \times 3 \cos 60°$$

$$= \pi \times 3^2 \times 1/6 - \frac{1}{2} \times 2.6 \times 3 \times 0.5 = 4.712 - 1.95 = 2.762 \text{ m}^2$$

$$P_V = 2.762 \times 3 \times 9.81 = 81.28 \text{ kN};$$

$$P = \sqrt{P_H^2 + P_V^2} = \sqrt{99.47^2 + 81.28^2} = 128.45 \text{ kN}$$

Hence magnitude of resultant force = **128.45 kN (Ans.)**

Let, θ = Inclination of P with horizontal.

Then, $\tan\theta = \frac{P_V}{P_H} = \frac{81.28}{99.47} = 0.817$ or $\theta =$ **39.25° (Ans.)**

and *P must pass through O.*

As P_H acts at $(2.6 - 0.867)$ = 1.733 m below water surface,

$$OT = \frac{ST}{\tan 39.25°} = \frac{1.733}{0.817} = 2.12 \text{ m, and}$$

$$UT = OT - OU = 2.12 - 3 \cos 60° = 0.62 \text{ m}$$

Hence point of application of P is *0.62 m to the left of MU and 1.733 m below water surface.* **(Ans.)**

Example 3.39. *A cylinder having 3 m diameter and 1.5 m length is resting on the floor. On one side, water is filled upto half the depth while on the other side oil of relative density 0.8 filled upto the top (Fig 3.50). If the weight of the cylinder is 33.75 kN, determine the magnitudes of the horizontal and vertical components of the force which will keep the cylinder just touching the floor.*

Solution. *Given:* Diameter of the cylinder, $d = 3$ m; Length of the cylinder, $l = 1.5$ m

Weight of the cylinder, W = 30 kN; Relative density of the oil = 0.8

Specific weight of the oil, $w_{oil} = 9.81 \times 0.8 = 7.85 \text{ kN/m}^3$

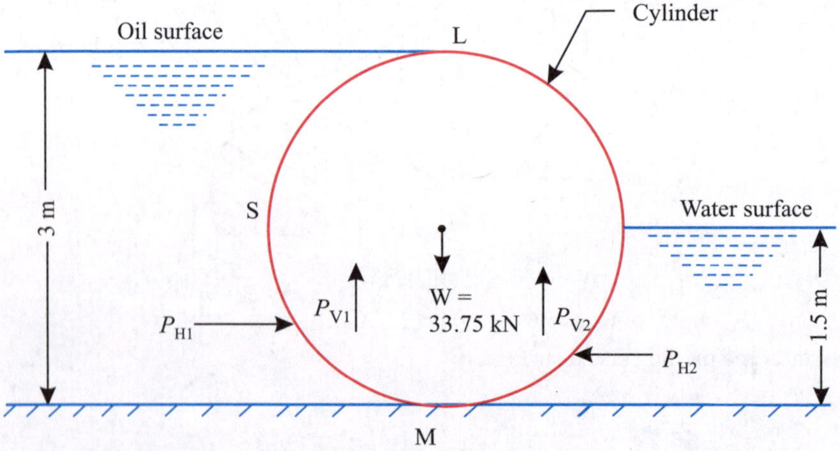

Fig. 3.50

Horizontal components:

Horizontal force, $P_{H1} = 7.85 \times (3 \times 1.5) \times \frac{3}{2} = 52.98 \text{ kN}$

This will act at $\frac{3}{3}$ or 1 m from bed.

$$\text{Horizontal force, } P_{H2} = 9.81 \times (1.5 \times 1.5) \times \frac{1.5}{2} = 16.55 \text{ kN}$$

This will act at $\frac{1.5}{3}$ or 0.5 m from bottom.

Hence, $(52.98 - 16.55) =$ **36.43 kN** *force acting towards right is required to hold the cylinder stationary.* **(Ans.)**

If it acts at a distance y, then taking moments about the bed, we get:

$$P_{H1} \times 1 - P_{H2} \times 0.5 = (P_{H1} - P_{H2}) \times y$$

$$52.98 - 16.55 \times 0.5 = (52.98 - 16.55) \times h_1$$

$$\therefore \quad y = \frac{52.98 - 16.55 \times 0.5}{52.98 - 16.55} = \frac{44.7}{36.43} = \mathbf{1.227\ m\ (Ans.)}$$

Vertical components:

$$P_{V_1} = 7.85 \times \frac{\pi \times 1.5^2}{2} \times 1.5 = 41.61 \text{ kN}$$

It will act at $\frac{4 \times 1.5}{3\pi} = 0.636$ m to left of *LM*;

$$P_{V_2} = 9.81 \times \frac{\pi \times 1.5^2}{4} \times 1.5 = 26 \text{ kN}$$

It will act at 0.636 m right of *LM*.

Since vertical forces must balance, therefore,

External force required $= 41.61 + 26 - 33.75 =$ **33.86 kN (Ans.)**

This external force is required in *vertically downward* direction. To find out its line of action, taking moments about the vertical line along which P_{V2} acts, we get:

$$W \times 0.636 + 33.86 \times x = P_{V1} \times (0.636 + 0.636)$$

$$33.75 \times 0.636 + 33.86\, x = 41.61 \times 1.272$$

$$x = \mathbf{0.929\ m\ (Ans.)}$$

Example 3.40. *A tank is filled with water under pressure and the pressure gauge fitted at the top indicates a pressure of 18 kPa. The tank measures 3 m perpendicular to the plane of the paper, and the curved surface LM of the top is quarter of a circular cylinder of radius 2.4 m. Determine:*

(i) Horizontal and vertical components of water pressure on the curved surface LM, and

(ii) Magnitude and direction of the resultant force.

Solution. Refer to Fig. 3.51.

Pressure indicated by pressure gauge, $p = 18 \text{ kPa} = 18 \times 10^3 \text{ N/m}^2$

$\therefore$ The water head equivalent,

$$h = \frac{p}{w} = \frac{18 \times 10^3}{9810} = 1.835 \text{ m}$$

Hence the free water surface can be imagined to be 1.835 m above the top of the tank.

P_H ***(Horizontal component)*** = Hydrostatic pressure force on vertical projection MN or the curved surface LM

$$= wA\bar{x}$$

$$= 9.81 \times (2.4 \times 3) \times \left(1.835 + \frac{2.4}{2}\right)$$

$$= \mathbf{214.37\ kN} \rightarrow \textbf{(Ans.)}$$

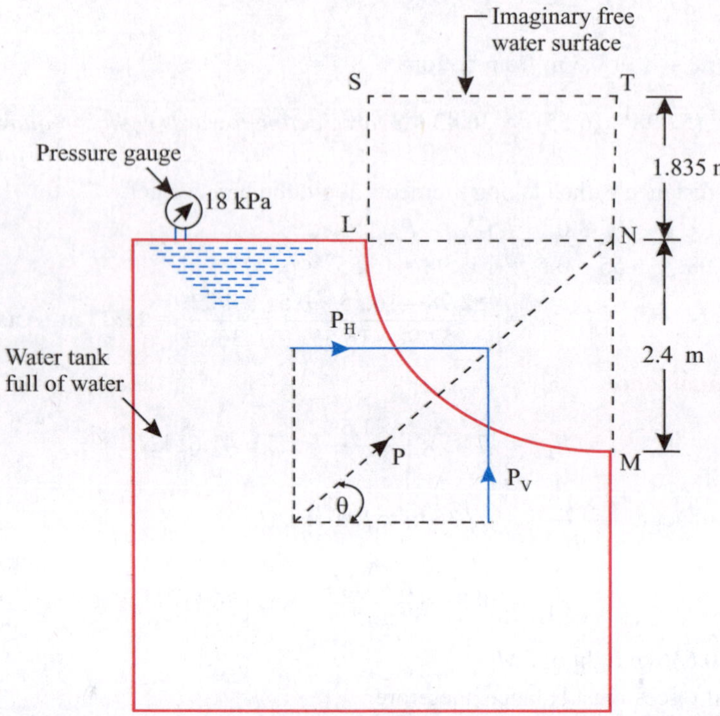

Fig. 3.51

***P_V* (*Vertical component*)** = Weight of volume of water above *LM* upto imaginary water surface *i.e., of volume* SLMNT

$$= \left\{1.835 \times 2.4 + \frac{1}{4} \times \pi \times 2.4^2\right\} \times 3 \times 9.81 = \mathbf{262.75 kN} \uparrow \textbf{(Ans.)}$$

The resultant force, $P = \sqrt{(P_H)^2 + (P_V)^2} = \sqrt{(214.37)^2 + (262.75)^2}$

$$= \mathbf{339.1\ kN\ (Ans.)}$$

The inclination of *P* with the horizontal,

$$\theta = \tan^{-1}\left(\frac{P_V}{P_H}\right) = \tan^{-1}\left(\frac{262.75}{214.37}\right) = \mathbf{50.8° \ (Ans.)}$$

Example 3.41. *In the Fig. 3.52. is shown the cross-section of the tank full of water under pressure. The length of the tank is 3 m. An empty cylinder lies along the length of the tank on one of its corners as shown. Find the horizontal and vertical components of the force acting on the curved surface LMN of the cylinder.*

Solution. Length of the tank = 3 m

Radius, r = 1.5 m

Pressure, p = 30 kN/m²

Pressure head, $hp = \frac{p}{w} = \frac{30}{9.81} \simeq 3\text{m}$

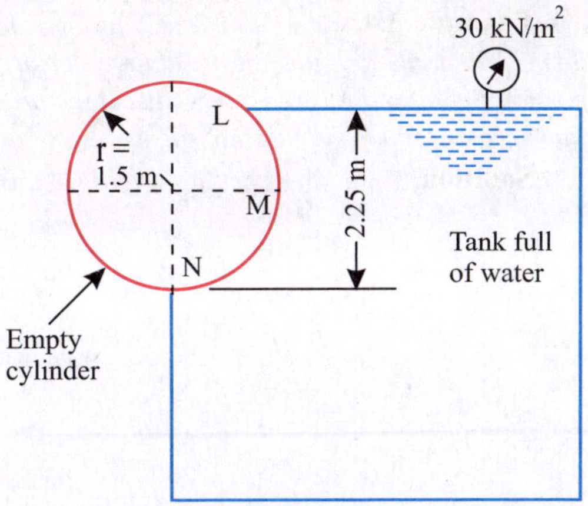

Fig. 3.52

Free water surface will be at a height of 3 from the top of the tank; equivalent free water surface is shown in Fig. 3.53.

(*i*) Horizontal component of force, P_H:

$P_H = wA\bar{x}$

where, w = Specific weight of water ($= 9.81\ kN/m^2$)

A = Area projected on vertical plane $= 2.25 \times 3 = 6.75\ m^2$

$$\bar{x} = 3 + \frac{2.25}{2} = 4.125\ m$$

$P_H = 9.81 \times 6.75 \times 4.125$

$= \mathbf{273.15\ kN}$ **(Ans.)**

(*ii*) Vertical component of force, P_V:

P_V = Weight of water enclosed or supported actually or imaginary by curved surface *LMN*

= Weight of water in the portion *NOTULMN*

= Weight of water in *NOTZMN* – weight of water in *LUZM*.

But, weight of water in *NOTZMN* = weight of water in NOM + weight of water in *OMZTO*

$$= w\left(\frac{\pi r^2}{4} + OM \times MZ\right) \times 3$$

$$= 9.81\left(\frac{\pi \times 1.5^2}{4} + 1.5 \times 3.75\right) \times 3$$

$= 217.5$ kN

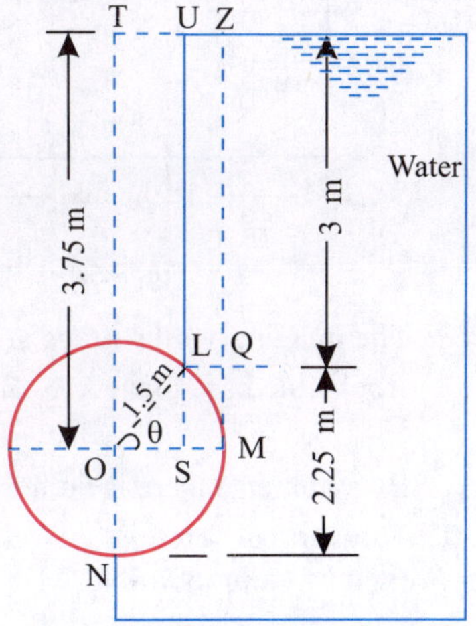

Fig. 3.53

Weight of water in *LUZM* = w (area of *LUZM*) × 3

= 9.81 [area of *LUZQ* + *LQMS* – *LSM*] × 3

In ΔLSO, $\sin\theta = \dfrac{LS}{OL} = \dfrac{0.75}{1.5} = 0.5, \quad \therefore \theta = 30°$

$MS = MO - SO = 1.5 - OL\cos\theta$

$= 1.5 - 1.5 \times \cos 30° = 0.2$ m

Area $LSM = LMO - LSO$

$$= \pi r^2 \times \frac{30°}{360°} - \frac{1}{2} \times OS \times LS$$

$$= \pi \times 1.5^2 \times \frac{1}{12} - \frac{1}{2} \times (1.5 \times \cos 30°) \times (1.5 \sin 30°)$$

$= 0.589 - 0.487 = 0.102$ m

∴ Weight of water in *LUZM*

$= 9.81[\,LQ \times ZQ + LQ \times QM - 0.102] \times 3$

$= 9.81[\,0.2 \times 3 + 0.2 \times 1.5 \sin 30° - 0.102\,] \times 3 \quad (\because LQ = MS)$

$= 9.81\,(0.6 + 0.15 - 0.102) \times 3$

$= 19.07$ kN

$P_V = 217.5 - 19.07 = \mathbf{198.43\ kN}$ **(Ans.)**

Example 3.42. *A cylindrical tank of 1.5 m diameter and height 0.75 m has a hemispherical dome. The tank contains oil of relative density 0.84 [Fig. 3.54]. The dome is joined to the cylinder portion by four equally spaced bolts. If the pressure gauge at a point M, 0.3 m, above the base of the tanks, reads 50 kPa determine the force on each bolt.*

Solution. Equivalent of pressure p_L in terms of oil column,

$$p_L = w_0 \, h_L$$

$$50 = (0.84 \times 9.81) h_L$$

$$\therefore \quad h_L = \frac{50}{0.84 \times 9.81} = 6.07 \text{ m of oil}$$

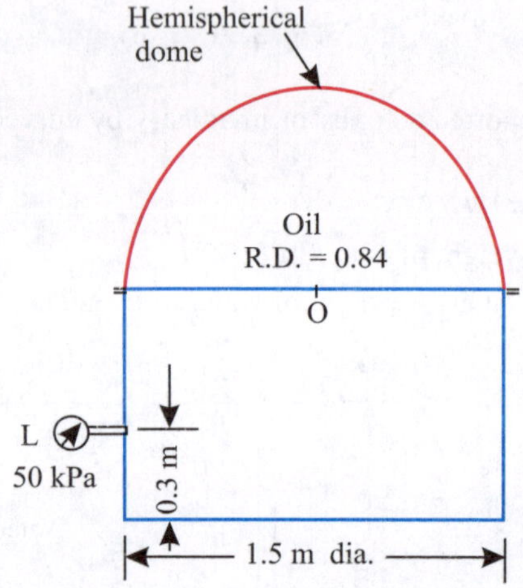

Fig. 3.54

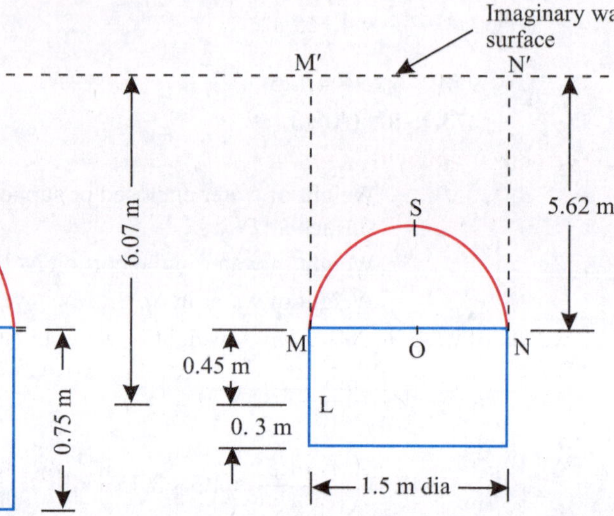

Fig. 3.55

The imaginary oil surface at an elevation of h_L = 6.07 m is now considered (Fig. 3.55).

Above the base plane MN of the dome the elevation of the imaginary oil surface is

$$= 6.07 - 0.45 = 5.62 \text{ m}$$

By symmetry there is no horizontal force on the done.

The vertical force P_V = Weight of oil above the dome surface upto the imaginary oil surface = Weight of volume MSNN′M′

$$= 0.84 \times 9.81 \left[\left\{ \frac{\pi \times (1.5)^2}{4} \times 5.62 \right\} - \left\{ \frac{1}{2} \times \frac{4}{3} \pi \, (0.75)^3 \right\} \right]$$

$$= 8.24 \, (9.931 - 0.884) = 74.55 \text{ kN}$$

This force is shared by four bolts.

$$\therefore \quad \text{Tensile force on each bolt} = \frac{74.55}{4} = \textbf{18.64 kN} \text{ (Ans.)}$$

3.7. DAMS

A **dam** *is a massive structure, built up mostly with R.C.C. or stone or earth, across a river or a stream for the purpose of impounding or storing water.* Its cross-section may be triangular, rectangular or trapezoidal. That side of the dam to which the water from the river or the stream approaches is known *upstream* and the other, *downstream.* A dam which resists the water pressure by its own weight only, is termed as a *gravity dam* (viz Bhakra dam).

Fig 3.56 shows the trapezoidal cross-section of the dam with a vertical face and a straight slope or batter for the back.

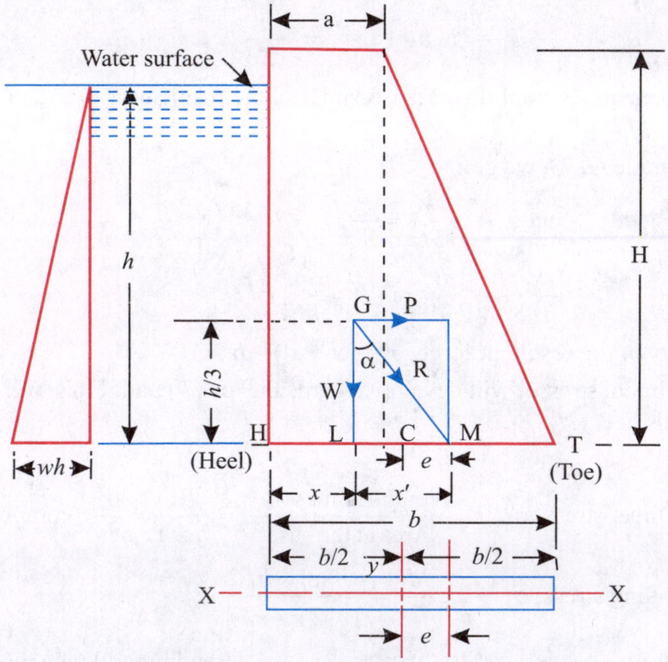

Fig. 3.56

Let,

a = Top width of the dam,

b = Base width of the dam,

H = Height of the dam, and

h = Height of water column.

Consider 1 m length of the dam.

Weight of masonry = Area × length × density of masonry

$$\therefore \quad W = \left(\frac{a+b}{2}\right) \times H \times 1 \times \text{density of masonry} \quad ...(3.8)$$

Let the *c.g.* of the section be at a distance *x* from the vertical face. Now dividing the trapezium into a rectangle and a triangle and taking moments about the vertical face, we get:

$$a \times h \times \frac{a}{2} + \frac{1}{2}(b-a) \times h\left[a + \left(\frac{b-a}{3}\right)\right]$$

$$= \left[a \times h + \left(\frac{b-a}{2}\right) \times h\right]\bar{x}$$

$$\therefore \quad \bar{x} = \frac{a \times h \times \frac{a}{2} + \frac{1}{2}(b-a) \times h\left[a + \frac{b-a}{3}\right]}{a \times h + \left(\frac{b-a}{2}\right) \times h}$$

or, $$\bar{x} = \frac{a^2 + ab + b^2}{3(a+b)} \quad \text{...(3.9)}$$

Total water pressure (P) = Area × average pressure

$$\therefore \quad P = (l \times h) \times \frac{wh}{2} = \frac{wh^2}{2}$$

This pressure acts at $h/3$ from the base of dam. Let the resultant R of P and W cuts the base of the dam at the point M.

Then, from triangle GLM, we get:

$$\tan \alpha = \frac{LM}{GL} = \frac{P}{W}$$

i.e., $$\frac{x'}{h/3} = \frac{P}{W} \text{ or } x' = \frac{P}{W} . h/3 \quad \text{...(3.10)}$$

The *eccentricity* of the resultant force, $e = (x + x') - b/2$ ...(3.11)

If e is +ve maximum stresses will develop towards the toe (T) and if it is –ve, maximum stresses will develop towards heel (H)

Stresses at the base:

$$\text{Direct stress, } \sigma_d = \frac{\text{Weight of masonry}}{\text{Area at the base}} = \frac{W}{b \times 1} = \frac{W}{b} \text{ (compressive)} \quad \text{...(3.12)}$$

$$\text{Bending stress, } \sigma_b = \pm \frac{My}{I} = \frac{(W.e) \times b/2}{1/12 \times l \times b^3}$$

[Bending will take place about Y–Y axis]

$$= \pm \frac{6\,W.e}{b^2} \text{ (–}ve\text{ sign stands for tensile stress here)} \quad \text{...(3.13)}$$

Maximum intensity of stress,

$$\sigma_{max} = \sigma_d + \sigma_b$$

$$= +\frac{W}{b} + \frac{6We}{b^2} = +\frac{W}{b}\left(1 + \frac{6e}{b}\right) \text{ (Compressive)} \quad \text{...(3.14)}$$

Minimum intensity of stress,

$$\sigma_{min} = \sigma_d + (-\sigma_b) = \frac{W}{b} - \frac{6We}{b^2} = \frac{W}{b}\left(1 - \frac{6We}{b}\right) \text{ (Compressive)} \quad \text{...(3.15)}$$

It may be noted that σ_{min} may be tensile or compressive.

3.8. POSSIBILITIES OF DAM FAILURE

The following are the *possibilities of dam failure*:

(*i*) Failure due to sliding along its base.

(*ii*) Failure due to tension or compression.

(*iii*) Failure due to shear at the weakest section.

(*iv*) Failure due to overturning.

(*i*) Failure due to sliding along its base:

The sliding of the dam is caused by the horizontal water pressure, P. The foundation offers frictional resistance which resists sliding. *The dam will be stable against sliding if the frictional resistance is more than the sliding (or driving) force P.*

Now, frictional force, $F = \mu W$

where, μ is the co-efficient of friction between two adjacent surfaces along which sliding is likely to take place.

$$\text{Sliding or driving force} = P$$

$$\text{Factor of safety against sliding} = \frac{\mu W}{P} \quad \text{(This value } \textit{must be greater than unity}\text{).}$$

(*ii*) Failure due to tension or compression:

The dam will be stable if no tensile stress across the cross-section is produced. It means σ_d should be more than or equal to σ_b. In certain cases where tension cannot be avoided it should not increase more than 0.4 N/mm^2.

i.e.,
$$\sigma_d \geq \sigma_b$$

$$\frac{W}{b} \geq \frac{6W.e}{b^2} \quad \text{or} \quad 1 \geq \frac{6 \times e}{b} \quad \text{or} \quad e \leq \frac{b}{6} \qquad ...(3.16)$$

Now, when
$$e = \frac{b}{6}$$

$$HM = x + x' = \frac{b}{2} + e = \frac{b}{2} + \frac{b}{6} = \frac{2b}{3} \qquad ...(3.17)$$

Therefore the resultant must always be in the *middle third* of the base.

(*iii*) Failure due to shear at the weakest section:

If, A' = The least cross-sectional area of the dam at any section, and

$\sigma_{s(max)}$ = Maximum safe shear stress of the dam material,

Then, resistance against shear $= \sigma_{s(max)} \times A'$

$$\text{Factor of safety against shear} = \frac{\sigma_{s(max)} \times A'}{P'} \qquad \text{(It must be } \textit{greater than unity}\text{)}$$

where, P' = Total liquid pressure due to water column *above the section.*

(*iv*) Failure due to overturning:

Referring to Fig. 3.56 we find that water pressure tends to overturn the wall about the toe T whereas W tends to counteract the turning effect.

Taking moments of P and W about toe T, we get overturning moment $= P \times h/3$.

and resisting moment $= W(b - x)$

$$\text{Factor of safety against overturning} = \frac{W(b-x)}{P \times (h/3)}$$

$$= \frac{3W(b-x)}{Ph} \qquad \text{(It must be } \textit{greater than unity}\text{)}$$

Example 3.43. *A concrete dam of trapezoidal section having water on vertical face is 12 m high. The base of the dam is 8 metres wide and top 2 metres wide. Find the resultant thrust on the base per metre length of dam, and the point where it intersects the base. Take the specific weight of masonry as 240 kN/m^3 and water level coinciding with the top of the dam.*

Solution. Refer to Fig. 3.57.

Top width = 2 m, base width = 8 m, height = 12 m

Consider 1 m length of dam.

Weight of masonry,

$$W = \left(\frac{8+2}{2}\right) \times 12 \times 1 \times 24 = 1440 \text{ kN}$$

Water pressure,

$$P = \frac{wh^2}{2} = \frac{9.81 \times 12^2}{2} = 706 \text{ kN}$$

Resultant thrust, $R = \sqrt{P^2 + W^2}$

$$= \sqrt{(706)^2 + (1440)^2} = \mathbf{1604\ kN\ (Ans.)}$$

The point, where the resultant thrust cuts the base:

Let x metres be the distance of *c.g.* from the vertical face. Dividing the trapezium into rectangle and triangle and taking moments about the vertical face, we have:

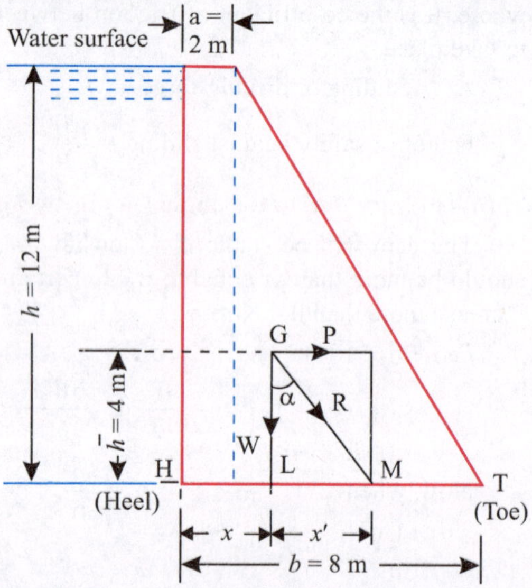

Fig. 3.57

$$12 \times 2 \times \frac{2}{2} + \frac{1}{2} \times 12 \times 6\left(2 + \frac{6}{3}\right)$$

$$= (12 \times 2 + \frac{1}{2} \times 12 \times 6) \times x$$

$$= 24 + 36 \times 4 = 60\,x$$

or, $$x = \frac{24 + 36 \times 4}{60} = 2.8 \text{ m}$$

The value of 'x' can also be found by using the relation:

$$x = \frac{a^2 + ab + b^2}{3(a+b)} = \frac{2^2 + 2 \times 8 + 8^2}{3(2+8)} = 2.8 \text{ m}$$

From Fig. 3.57, $$\tan\alpha = \frac{P}{W} = \frac{706}{1440}$$

Also, $$\tan\alpha = \frac{x'}{4} = \frac{706}{1440} \text{ or } x' = \frac{706 \times 4}{1440} = 1.96 \text{ m}$$

Now, the point where the resultant thrust cuts the base

$$= x + x' = 2.8 + 1.96 = \mathbf{4.76\ m\ from\ H\ (heel)\ (Ans.)}$$

Example 3.44. *A masonry dam trapezoidal in cross-section is 4 m wide at the top, 8 m wide at the base and 10 m high. It retains water level with top against a vertical face. Obtain stress distribution at the base if specific gravity of masonry is 2.5.*

Solution. Refer to Fig. 3.58.

Top width = 4 *m*; base width = 8 *m*; height = 10 *m*

Density of masonry = $2.5 \times 9.81 = 24.5$ kN/m^3

Consider 1 *m* length of the dam.

Weight of masonry acting through *c.g.*,

$$W = \left(\frac{8+4}{2}\right) \times 10 \times 1 \times 24.5 = 1470 \text{ kN}$$

$$\text{Water pressure, } P = \frac{wh^2}{2} = \frac{9.81 \times 10^2}{2} = 490.5 \text{ kN}$$

Let x metres be the distance of *c.g.* from the vertical face. Dividing the trapezium into a rectangle and a triangle and taking moments about the vertical face, we have:

$$10 \times 4 \times \frac{4}{2} + \frac{1}{2} \times 10 \times 4 \left(4 + \frac{4}{3}\right)$$

$$= \left(10 \times 4 + \frac{1}{2} \times 10 \times 4\right) \times x$$

or, $80 + 20 \times 5.333 = 60x$

$$x = \frac{80 + 20 \times 5.33}{60} = 3.11 \text{ m}$$

From Fig. 3.58.,

$$\tan \alpha = \frac{P}{W} = \frac{490.5}{1470}$$

Also, $\tan \alpha = \dfrac{x'}{10/3}$

$$\therefore \quad \frac{x'}{10/3} = \frac{490.5}{1470} = \frac{1}{3}$$

or, $x' = \dfrac{1}{3} \times \dfrac{10}{3} = \dfrac{10}{9} = 1.11$ m

Now, $x + x' = 3.11 + 1.11 = 4.22\ m$ which is well *within two third base width.*

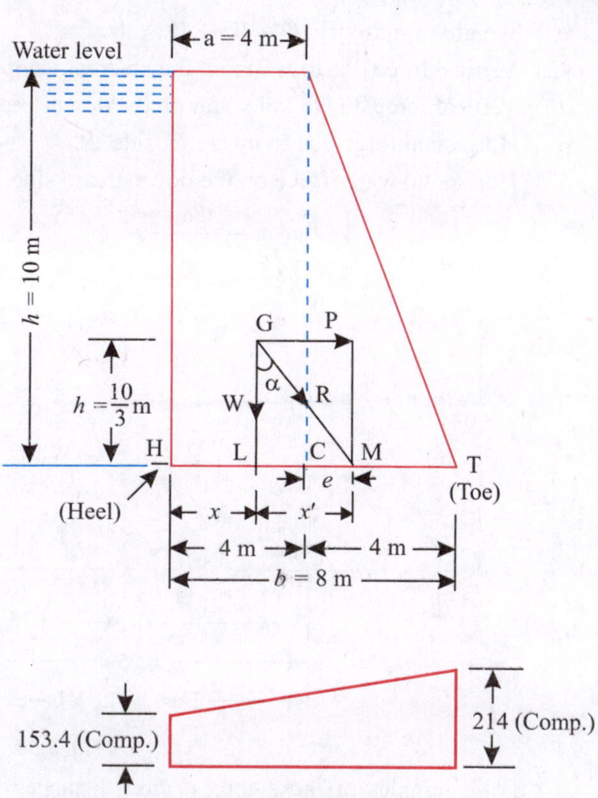

Fig. 3.58

Eccentricity of resultant thrust,

$e = (x + x') - 4 = 4.22 - 4 = 0.22$ m

Bending stress,

$$\sigma_b = \frac{M}{I} y = \frac{(W.e).y}{I}$$

$$= \frac{1470 \times 0.22 \times 8/2}{\frac{1 \times 8^3}{12}} = \frac{1470 \times 0.22 \times 4 \times 12}{8^3} = \pm 30.3 \text{ kN/m}^2$$

Direct stress,

$$\sigma_d = \frac{\text{Weight of masonry}}{\text{Area of base}} = \frac{1470}{8 \times 1} = 183.7 \text{ kN/m}^2$$

$\sigma_{max} = \sigma_d + \sigma_b = 183.7 + 30.3 =$ **214 kN/m² (comp.) (Ans.)**

$\sigma_{min} = \sigma_d - \sigma_b = 183.7 - 30.3 =$ **153.4 kN/m² (comp.) (Ans.)**

Example 3.45. *A masonry weir is of trapezoidal cross-section with a top width of 2m and of height 5m with upstream slope of 1 vertical in 0.1 horizontal and a downstream slope of 1 vertical in 0.75 horizontal. If the weir has water stored upto its crest on the upstream side and has a tail water of 2 m depth on the downstream, calculate, per unit length of weir:*

(i) The resultant force on the base of the weir.

(ii) The minimum and maximum stresses on the base of the weir.

Assume specific weight of masonry as 22 kN/m³ and neglect uplift forces.

Solution. Refer to Fig. 3.59.

Consider 1 m length of the weir.

(i) Resultant force on the base:

The forces acting on the weir are:

(*i*) Weight of masonry, $W = W_1 + W_2 + W_3$

(*ii*) Vertical force due to water on the upstream slope, P_{V1}

(*iii*) Vertical force due to tail water on the downstream slope, P_{V2}

(*iv*) Horizontal force due to upstream side, P_{H1}

(*v*) Horizontal water force on the downstream side, P_{H2}

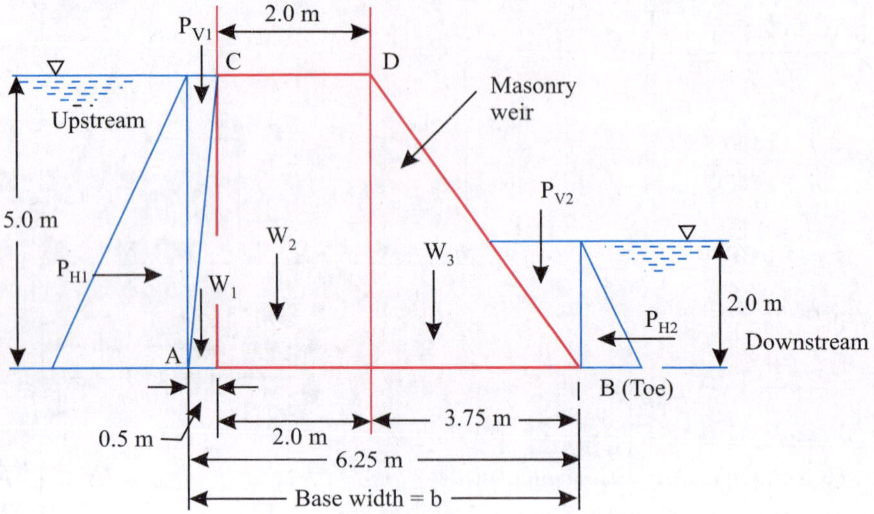

Fig. 3.59

The magnitudes of these forces, their distances from the toe of the weir (edge B) and the moments of these forces about B are tabulated in the table below:

Force	Description Magnitude, kN	Horiz. force	Magnitude, kN Vert. force	Lever arm about B (m)	Moment (Clockwise)	Moment (Anticlockwise)
W_1	$(0.5 \times 5) \times \frac{1}{2} \times 1 \times 22$		27.5	5.917		162.7
W_2	$(2.0 \times 5.0) \times 10 \times 22$		220.0	4.75		1045.0
W_3	$(3.75 \times 5) \times \frac{1}{2} \times 1 \times 22$		206.25	2.50		515.6
P_{V1}	$(0.5 \times 5) \times \frac{1}{2} \times 1 \times 9.81$		12.26	6.083		74.6
P_{V2}	$(1.5 \times 2.0) \times \frac{1}{2} \times 1 \times 9.81$		14.71	0.50		7.36
P_{H1}	$(5 \times 1) \times \frac{5}{2} \times 9.81$	122.62		1.667	204.4	
P_{H2}	$(2 \times 1) \times \frac{2}{2} \times 9.81$	−19.62		0.667		13.08
Sum		**103**	**480.72**		**204.4**	**1818.34**

Sum of vertical forces, $\Sigma V = 480.72$ kN

Sum of horizontal forces, $\Sigma H = 103$ kN

$$\text{Resultant, } R = \sqrt{(\Sigma V)^2 + (\Sigma H)^2}$$

$$= \sqrt{(480.72)^2 + (103)^2} = \mathbf{491.63\ kN\ (Ans.)}$$

If θ is the *inclination* of the resultant to horizontal, then:

$$\tan\theta = \frac{\Sigma V}{\Sigma H} = \frac{480.72}{103} = 4.667$$

or, $\theta = \tan^{-1}(4.667) = \mathbf{77.9°}$ **(Ans.)**

(*ii*) The minimum and maximum stresses; σ_1, σ_2:

$$\Sigma M = 1818.34 - 204.4 = 1613.94 \text{ kNm}$$

x = Distance of point of action of the resultant from B

$$= \frac{\Sigma M}{\Sigma V} = \frac{1613.94}{480.72} = 3.357 \text{ m}$$

As b = base width = 6.25 m, the

$$\text{Eccentricity, } e = x - \frac{b}{2} = 3.357 - \frac{6.25}{2} = 0.232 \text{m}$$

Maximum and minimum stresses,

$$\sigma_{1,2} = \frac{\Sigma V}{b}\left(1 \pm \frac{6e}{b}\right)$$

$$= \frac{480.72}{6.25}\left(1 \pm \frac{6 \times 0.232}{6.25}\right)$$

∴ $\sigma_1 = \mathbf{94.04\ kN/m^2}$ **(Ans.)**

$\sigma_2 = \mathbf{59.78\ kN/m^2}$ **(Ans.)**

Example 3.46. *The curved face of a dam is shaped according to the relation* $y = \frac{x^2}{12.25}$ *as shown in the Fig. 3.60. If the width of the dam is unity and height of water retained by the dam is 12 m, determine the magnitude and direction of the resultant water pressure acting on the curved face of the dam.*

Solution. Profile of the curved face of the dam:

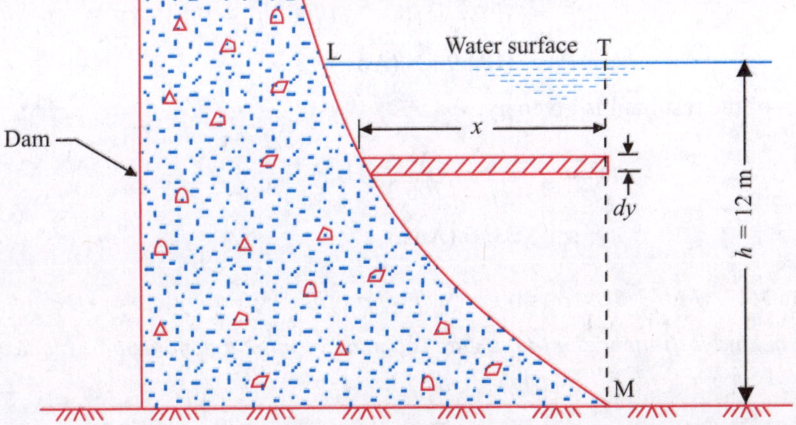

Fig. 3.60

$$y = \frac{x^2}{12.25}$$

or, $$x^2 = 12.25\, y$$

or, $$x = 3.5\sqrt{y}$$

Height of water,

$$h = 12 \text{ m}$$

Width, $$b = 1\text{m}$$

Magnitude and direction of resultant water pressure:

Horizontal component, P_H = Pressure due to water on curved area projected on vertical plane

= Pressure on area $MT = wA\bar{x}$

where, $$A = MT \times 1 = 12 \times 1 = 12 \text{ m}^2$$

$$x = 12/2 = 6 \text{ m}$$

$$\therefore \quad P_H = 9.81 \times 12 \times 6 = 706.3 \text{ kN}$$

Vertical component, P_V = Weight of water supported by the curve LM

= weight of water in portion LMT

$$= w \times (\text{Area of } LMT) \times \text{width of dam} = w\left[\int_0^{12} x\,.\,dy\right] \times 1.0$$

where, $x\,.\,dy$ = area of strip

$$= 9.81 \int_0^{12} 3.5\sqrt{y}\,dy \qquad (\because x = 3.5\sqrt{y})$$

$$= 9.81 \times 3.5 \left[\frac{y^{3/2}}{3/2}\right]_0^{2} = 34.33 \times 2/3\,[(12)^{3/2}] = 951.4 \text{ kN}$$

Resultant water pressure on the dam,

$$P = \sqrt{P_H^2 + P_V^2} = \sqrt{(706.3)^2 + (951.4)^2}$$

or, P = **1184.9 kN (Ans.)**

Direction of the resultant is given by:

$$\tan\alpha = \frac{P_V}{P_H} = \frac{951.4}{706.3} = 1.347$$

$\therefore$ α = **53.4° (Ans.)**

Example 3.47. *Fig. 3.61 shows a gate whose profile is given by $x = \sqrt{y}$. It holds water to a depth of 1 m behind it. If the width of the gate is 5 m, determine the moment M required to hold the gate in place.*

Solution. Profile of the gate: $x = \sqrt{y}$

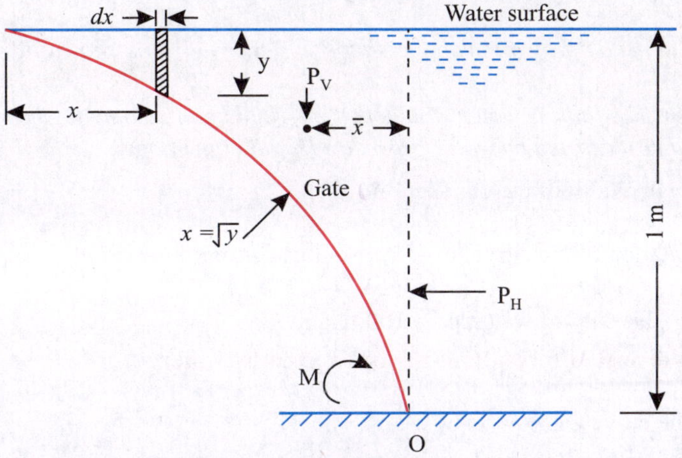

Fig. 3.61

$$\text{Horizontal force, } P_H = wA\bar{x} = 9.81 \times (1 \times 5) \times \frac{1}{2} = 24.25 \text{ kN}$$

It will act at $\frac{1}{3}$ m or 0.333 m from the bottom.

$$P_V = \text{Weight of liquid above the gate}$$

$$= 5 \times w \int y\, dx$$

$$= 5w \int_0^1 x^2\, dx \quad \left[\because x = \sqrt{y} \text{ or } y = x^2\right]$$

$$= 5 \times 9.81 \left| \frac{x^3}{3} \right|_0^1$$

$$= 5 \times 9.81 \times \frac{1}{3} = 16.35 \text{ kN}$$

The vertical line along which P_V will act is obtained by taking moments of elementary force 5 $wy.dx$ about Y-axis and equating it to $P_V \times \bar{x}$.

i.e. $$P_V \times \bar{x} = \int_0^1 5\, wy\,(1 - x)dx = \int_0^1 5wx^2(1 - x)dx$$

$$= 5w \left| \frac{x^3}{3} - \frac{x^4}{4} \right|_0^1 = 5w\left(\frac{1}{3} - \frac{1}{4}\right) = \frac{5w}{12}$$

$\therefore$ $$\bar{x} = \frac{5w}{12 \times P_V} = \frac{5 \times 9.81}{12 \times 16.35} = 0.25 \text{m}$$

Moment M:

Moment (M) of P_H and P_V about Z- axis passing through 0 is given by:

$$M = P_H \times 0.333 + P_V \times 0.25$$

$$= 24.52 \times 0.333 + 16.35 \times 0.25 = 12.25 \text{ kNm}$$

i.e. M = **12.25 kNm (Ans.)**

Example 3.48. *A dam has a parabolic shape* $y = y_0\left(\frac{x}{x_0}\right)^2$ *as shown in Fig 3.62 having* x_0 *= 6 m and* y_0 *= 9 m. The fluid is water with density = 1000 kg/m³. Compute the horizontal, vertical and the resultant thrust exerted by water per metre length of the dam.*

Solution. *Given*: Width of the dam = 1 m;

Equation of the curve, $y = y_0\left(\frac{x}{x_0}\right)^2$; x_0 = 6m; y_0 = 9m;

Density of water, ρ = 1000 kg/m³

Horizontal, vertical and resultant thrust exerted by water:

Equation of the curve OL: $y = y_0\left(\frac{x}{x_0}\right)^2$

$$= 9\left(\frac{x}{6}\right)^2 = 9 \times \frac{x^2}{36} = \frac{x^2}{4}$$

or, $x^2 = 4y$ or $x = 2\sqrt{y}$

Horizontal thrust:

Horizontal thrust exerted by water,

F_x = Force exerted by water on vertical surface OM; the surface obtained by projecting the curved surface on vertical plane.

$$= \rho g A \bar{h}$$

$$= 1000 \times 9.81 \times (9 \times 1) \times \frac{9}{2} = 397305 \text{ N}$$

or, **397.3 kN (Ans.)**

Vertical thrust:

Vertical thrust exerted by water,

F_y = weight of water supported by curved surface OL upto free water surface

= weight of water in portion OLM × width of dam ρg × area of OLM × width of dam

$$= 1000 \times 9.81 \times \left[\int_0^9 x \times dy\right] \times 1.0$$

$$= 1000 \times 9.81 \times \left[\int_0^9 2\sqrt{y} \times dy\right] \times 1.0$$

$$= 19620 \times \left[\frac{y^{3/2}}{3/2}\right]_0^9 = 19620 \times \frac{2}{3} \times (9)^{3/2}$$

= 353160 N or **353.16 kN (Ans.)**

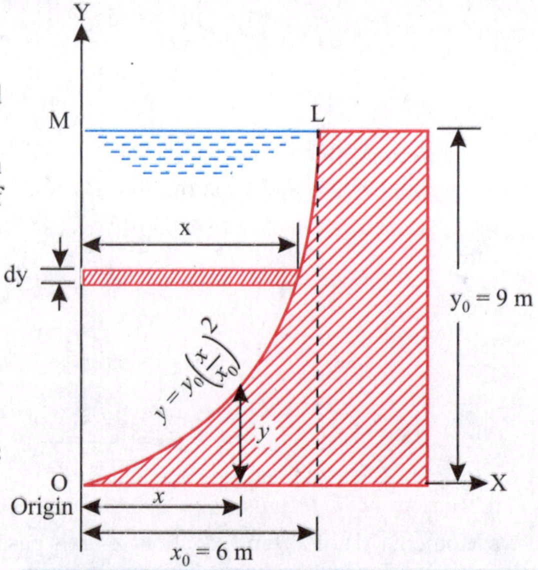

Fig. 3.62

Resultant thrust:

Resultant thrust exerted by water,

$$F = \sqrt{F_x^2 + F_y^2} = \sqrt{(397.3)^2 + (353.16)^2} = \textbf{531.57 kN (Ans.)}$$

Direction of the resultant is given by,

$$\tan\theta = \frac{F_y}{F_x} = \frac{353.16}{397.3} = 0.889$$

$$\therefore \quad \theta = \tan^{-1}(0.889) = \mathbf{41.63° \ (Ans.)}$$

3.9. LOCK GATES

Lock gates *are provided in navigation chambers to change the water level in a canal or river for navigation*. There are two sets of gates G_1 and G_2, one set on either side of the chamber. The working of the gates (Fig.3.63) is as follows:

Suppose the ship is at position 1 (on the left hand side of the chamber) and it is to be transferred to position 2 (on the right hand side). To do so the following *procedure* is adopted:

(*i*) Open the sluice S_1 on the upstream gate G_1 and fill the chamber upto level *L–L*.

(*ii*) Open the lock gate G_1 on the upstream and permit the ship to enter the chamber.

(*iii*) Close the gate G_1.

(*iv*) Open the sluice S_2 and allow the water to fall to level *MM*.

(*v*) Open the downstream gate G_2 and permit the ship to leave the chamber.

(*vi*) Reverse the procedure in case the ship is to be transferred from position 2 to position 1.

Total pressure on the gates and reactions at top and bottom hinges:

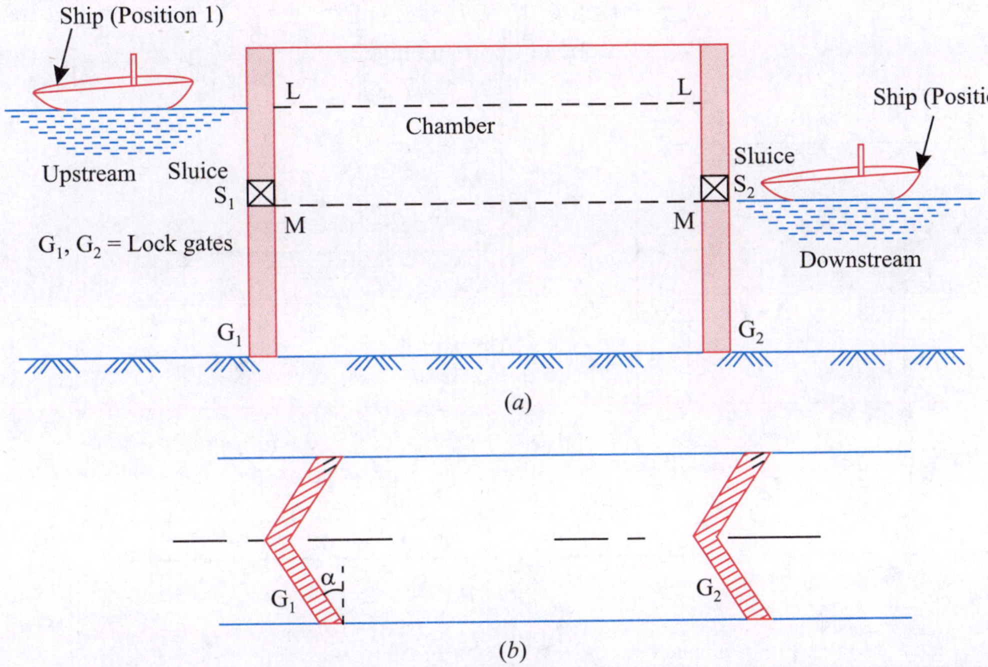

Fig. 3.63

Fig. 3.64 shows plan and elevation of a pair of lock gates. Let *AB* and *BC* be two lock gates, each carried on two hinges fixed on their top and bottom at both *A* and *C*. Due to action of water, the gates are tightly closed to one another at *B*.

Consider the gate AB:

Let, P = Resultant force due to water acting at right angle to the gate,

N = Reaction force supplied by gate *BC* to gate *AB* and acting perpendicular to the contact surfaces,

R = Resultant reaction of the top and bottom hinges (assumed to lie in the same horizontal plane in which P and N lie), and

α = Angle of inclination of gate to normal side of lock.

As the gate is in equilibrium under the forces, P, N and R, they will all intersect at one point. Let P and N intersect at D; then R must pass through this point. Then triangle ABD will be isosceles, as $\angle DBA$ and $\angle DAB$ equal α.

Resolving the forces in a direction parallel to gate (AB),

$$R \cos \alpha = N \cos \alpha \quad \therefore R = N \qquad ...(3.18)$$

Resolving normal to the gate (AB), $P = R \sin \alpha + N \sin \alpha = (R + N) \sin \alpha = 2R \sin \alpha$

$$\therefore \quad R = \frac{P}{2 \sin \alpha} \qquad ...(3.19)$$

(Also, inclination of R to centre line of gate = α)

Consider water pressure on the gate.

Let, H_1 = Height of water to left of gate (*i.e.* upstream side),

H_2 = Height of water to right of gate (*i.e.* downstream side),

H = Height of top hinge from the bottom of gate,

P_1 = Total pressure of water to left of gate,

P_2 = Total pressure of water to right of gate,

R_t = Reaction of top hinge, and

R_b = Reaction of bottom hinge.

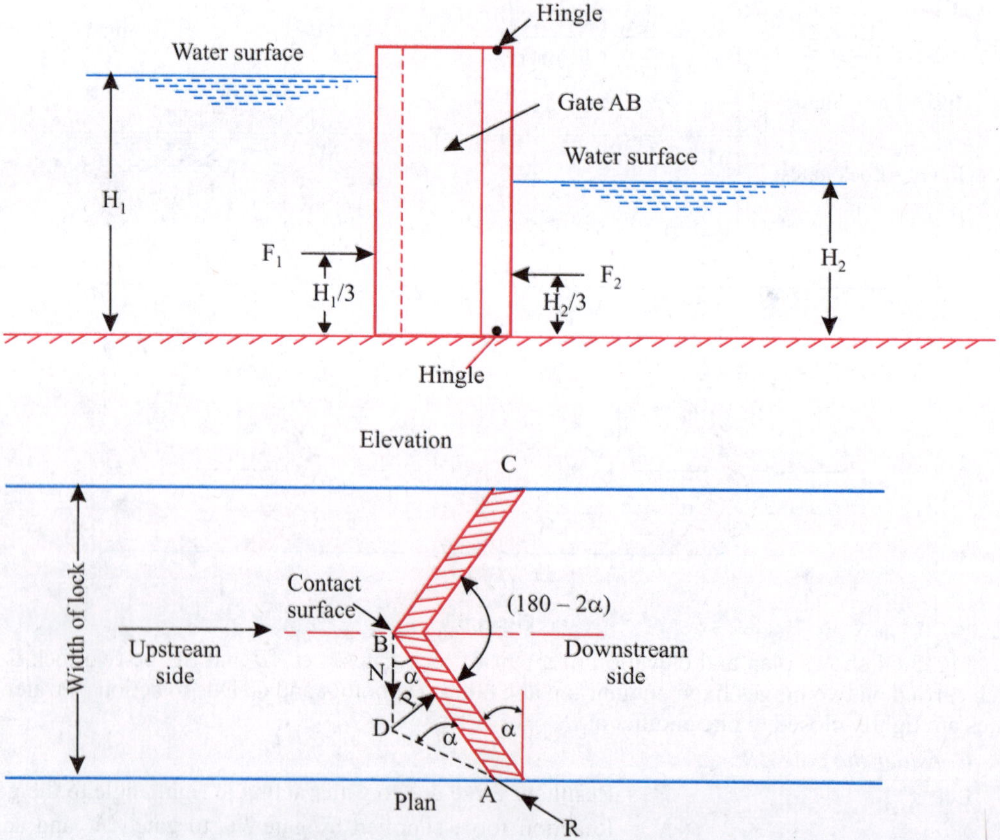

Fig. 3.64. Resultant pressure on lock gates.

Then, $R_t + R_b = R$

Also, $P_1 = \frac{wH_1}{2}$ × wetted area of the gate (It will act at the centre of pressure which is $\frac{H_1}{3}$ from the bottom).

and, $P_2 = \frac{wH_2}{2}$ × wetted area of the gate (It will act at $\frac{H_2}{3}$ from the bottom).

Then, $P = P_1 - P_2$

It may be noted that only half the water pressure may be taken as acting on the hinge edge of the gate; the remaining half will be taken by the reaction of the gate *BC*.

Taking moments about the lower hinge, we have:

$$R_1 \sin\alpha \times H = \left(\frac{P_1}{2} \times \frac{H_1}{3}\right) - \left(\frac{P_2}{2} \times \frac{H_2}{3}\right) \quad ...(i)$$

Resolving the forces *horizontally*, we get:

$$R_t \sin\alpha + R_b \sin\alpha = \frac{P_1}{2} - \frac{P_2}{2} \quad ...(ii)$$

Then, form eqns. (*i*) and (*ii*), R_t and R_b may be found.

Example 3.49. *Each gate of a lock is 6 m high and 5 m wide, supported on one side by two hinges, each 0.5m from the top and from bottom. The angle between the gates in closed position is 120°. If the water levels are 5m and 1.25 m on the upstream and downstream sides respectively, find:*

(*i*) *The magnitude and position of the resultant water pressure on each gate,*

(*ii*) *The magnitude of reaction between the gates, and*

(*iii*) *The magnitudes of the reactions at the hinges.*

Assume the reaction between the gates to be in the same horizontal plane as that of the resultant water pressure. **[Jadavpur University]**

Solution. Height of each gate = 6 m; width of each gate = 5 m

Height of water on upstream side, H_1 = 5 m

Height of water on downstream side, H_2 = 1.25 m

Angle between the gates = 120°, $\therefore \alpha = \frac{180 - 120}{2} = 30°$

(*i*) The magnitude and position of the resultant pressure:

Upstream side: Wetted area of gate, $A_1 = 5 \times 5 = 25 \text{ m}^2$

Total pressure on each gate, $P_1 = wA_1\bar{x}_1 = 9.81 \times 25 \times \frac{5}{2} = 613.12$ kN

Position of centre of pressure $\bar{h}_1 = \frac{H_1}{3}$ from the bottom $= \frac{5}{3}$ m or 1.667m from the bottom

Downstream side: Wetted area of gate, $A_2 = 5 \times 1.25 = 6.25 \text{ m}^2$

Total pressure on each gate, $P_2 = wA_2\bar{x}_2 = 9.81 \times 6.25 \times \frac{1.25}{2} = 38.32$ kN

Position of centre of pressure $\bar{h}_2 = \frac{1.25}{3} = 0.417$ m from the bottom.

Now, resultant water pressure on each gate,

$\mathbf{P} = P_1 - P_2 = 613.12 - 38.32 =$ **574.8 kN (Ans.)**

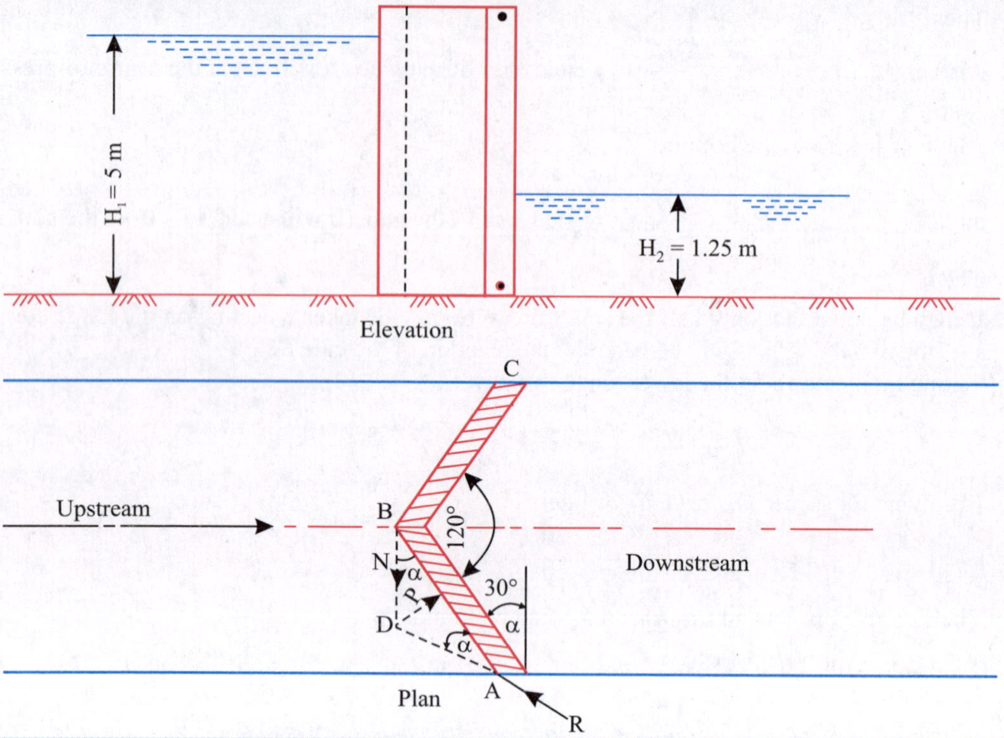

Fig. 3.65 (*a*). Elevation and plan of lock gates.

Let $\bar{h}$ is height of P from the bottom, then taking moments of P_1, P_2 and P about the bottom, we get:

$$P \times \bar{h} = P_1 \times \bar{h}_1 - P_2 \times \bar{h}_2$$

or, $$574.8 \times \bar{h} = 613.12 \times 1.667 - 38.32 \times 0.417 = 1006.09$$

∴ $$\bar{h} = \textbf{1.75 m from the bottom (Ans.)}$$

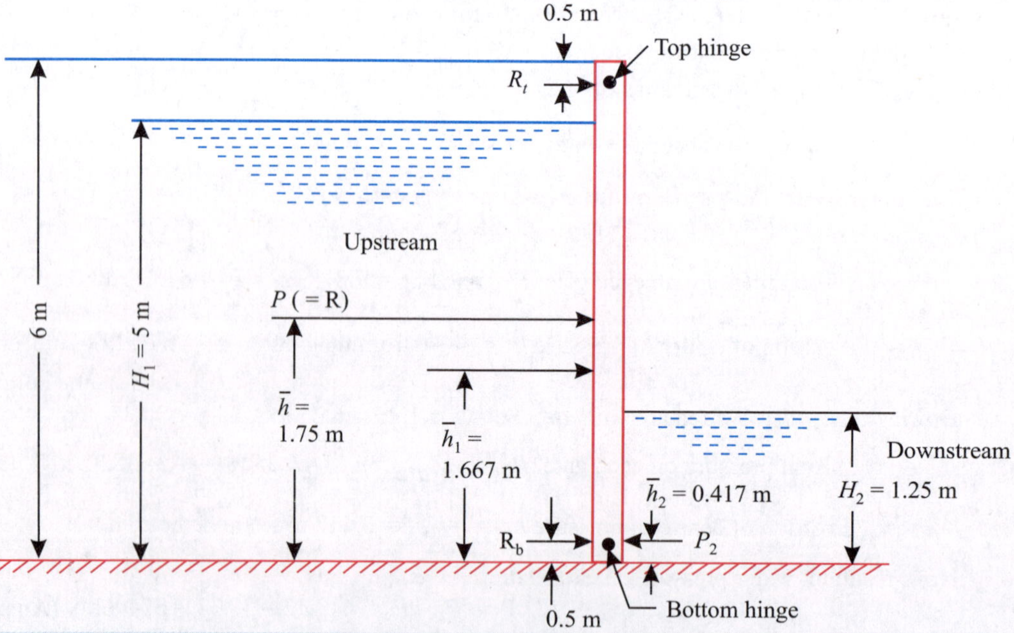

Fig. 3.65 (*b*). Resultant pressure and reactions at hinges of lock gates.

(ii) The magnitude of reaction between the gates, N:

Refer to Fig. 3.65 (*a*).

Resolving the forces at D in a direction parallel to gate (*i.e.* along AB), we have:

$$N \cos \alpha = R \cos \alpha \quad \text{or} \quad N = R$$

Resolving normally to gate (*i.e.* normal to AB), we have:

$$P = R \sin \alpha + N \sin \alpha = (R + N) \sin \alpha = 2N \sin \alpha$$

$$\therefore \quad N (= R) = \frac{P}{2 \sin \alpha} = \frac{574.8}{2 \sin 30°}$$

$$= 574.8 \text{ kN} \textbf{ (Ans.)}$$

(iii) The magnitudes of the reactions at the hinges:

Refer to Fig. 3.65 (*b*).

Let, R_t = Reaction at the top hinge, and

R_b = Reaction at the bottom hinge.

Then, $R_t + R_b = R = 574.8$ kN

Taking moments of hinge reactions R_t, R_b and $P(= R)$ about the bottom hinge, we have:

$$R_t (6 - 1) + R_b \times 0 = R \times (1.75 - 0.5)$$

$$5R_t = 574.8 \times (1.75 - 0.5)$$

$$\therefore \quad \boldsymbol{R_t = 143.7} \textbf{ kN (Ans.)}$$

and, $\boldsymbol{R_b} = 574.8 - 143.7 = \textbf{431.1 kN (Ans.)}$

HIGHLIGHTS

1. The term hydrostatics means the study of pressure, exerted by a fluid at rest.
2. Total pressure (P) is the force exerted by a fluid on a surface (either plane or curved) when the fluid comes in contact with the surface.

   For vertically immersed surface, $P = wA\bar{x}$

   For inclined immersed surface, $P = wA\bar{x}$

   where A = area of immersed surface, and $\bar{x}$ = depth of centre of gravity of immersed surface from the free liquid surface.
3. *Centre of pressure* ($\bar{h}$) is the point through which the resultant pressure acts and is always expressed in terms of depth from the liquid surface.

   For vertically immersed surface, $\bar{h} = \dfrac{I_G}{A\bar{x}} + \bar{x}$

   For inclined immersed surface, $\bar{h} = \dfrac{I_G \sin^2 \theta}{A\bar{x}} + \bar{x}$

   where I_G stands for moment of inertia of figure about horizontal axis through its centre of gravity.
4. The total force on a curved surface is given by:

   $$P = \sqrt{P_H^2 + P_V^2}$$

   where, P_H = Horizontal force on curved surface

   = Total pressure force on the projected area of the curved surface on the vertical plane = $wA\bar{x}$, and

P_V = Vertical force on submerged curved surface
= Weight of liquid actually or imaginary supported by curved surface.

The direction of the resultant force P with the horizontal is given by:

$$\tan\theta = \frac{P_V}{P_H} \quad \text{or} \quad \theta = \tan^{-1}\frac{P_V}{P_H}$$

5. Resultant force on a sluice gate $P = P_1 - P_2$

where, P_1 = Pressure force on the upstream side of the sluice gate, and
P_2 = Pressure force on the downstream side of the sluice gate.

6. For a lock gate, the reaction between two gates is equal to the reaction at the hinge,

i.e., $N = R$

Also reaction between the two gates, $N = \dfrac{P}{2\sin\alpha}$

where, P = Resultant water pressure on the lock gate = $P_1 - P_2$, and
α = Inclination of the gate to normal side of lock.

OBJECTIVE TYPE QUESTION

Choose the correct Answer:

1. The intensity of pressure p is related to specific weight w of the liquid and vertical depth h of the point by the equation

(*a*) $p = wh$ (*b*) $h = pw$
(*c*) $p = wh^2$ (*d*) $p = wh^3$.

2. The point of application of the total pressure on the surface is

(*a*) centroid of the surface
(*b*) centre of pressure
(*c*) either of the above
(*d*) none of the above.

3. If A is the area of the immersed surface, w is the specific weight of the liquid and $\bar{x}$ is the depth of horizontal surface from the liquid surface, then the total pressure P on the surface is given by

(*a*) $p = wA^2\bar{x}$ (*b*) $p = w^2A\bar{x}$
(*c*) $p = wA\bar{x}$ (*d*) $p = wA\bar{x}^2$

4. Centre of pressure $(\bar{h})$ in case of an inclined immersed surface is given by

(*a*) $\bar{h} = \dfrac{I_G\sin\theta}{A\bar{x}} + \bar{x}$ (*b*) $\bar{h} = \dfrac{I_G\sin\theta}{A^2\bar{x}} + \bar{x}$

(*c*) $\bar{h} = \dfrac{I_G^2\sin\theta}{A\bar{x}} + \bar{x}$ (*d*) $\bar{h} = \dfrac{I_G\sin^2\theta}{A\bar{x}} + \bar{x}$

5. The side of the dam to which the water from the river or the stream approaches is known as

(*a*) downstream (*b*) upstream
(*c*) either of the above (*d*) none of the above.

6. Which of the following is a possibility of dam failure?

(*a*) Failure due to sliding along its base
(*b*) Failure due to tension or compression
(*c*) Failure due to shear at the weakest section
(*d*) Failure due to overturning
(*e*) All of the above.

7. Lock gates are provided to

(*a*) change the water level in a canal or river for irrigation
(*b*) store water for irrigation purpose
(*c*) either of the above
(*d*) none of the above.

8. Total force on a curved surface is given by

(*a*) $P = (P_H^2 + P_V^2)^{3/2}$ (*b*) $P = \sqrt{P_H^2 + P_V^2}$

(*c*) $P = \left(P_H^2 + P_V^2\right)^{5/2}$ (*d*) $P = P_H + P_V$

9. Resultant pressure on a sluice gate is given by

(*a*) $P = P_1 - P_2$ (*b*) $P = P_1 + P_2$

(*c*) $P = \sqrt{P_1^2 + P_2^2}$ (*d*) $P = (P_1^2 + P_2^2)^{3/2}$.

10. The term........ means the study of pressure exerted by a fluid at rest.

(*a*) hydrostatics (*b*) fluid mechanics
(*c*) continuum (*d*) kinetics.

ANSWERS

1. (*a*) 2. (*b*) 3. (*c*) 4. (*d*) 5. (*b*) 6. (*e*)
7. (*a*) 8. (*b*) 9. (*a*) 10. (*a*)

THEORETICAL QUESTIONS

1. Define the following terms:
   (*i*) Total pressure, and
   (*ii*) Centre of pressure.
2. Derive expressions for total pressure and centre of pressure for a vertically immersed surface.
3. Derive an expression for the depth of centre of pressure from free surface of liquid of an inclined plane surface submerged in the liquid.
4. Derive an expression for the reaction between the gates as:

$$R = \frac{P}{2\sin\alpha}$$

where, P = Resultant force due to water acting at right angles to the gate, and

α = Angle of inclination of gate to normal side of lock.

UNSOLVED EXAMPLES

1. A rectangular plate 2m × 4m is vertically immersed in water is such a way that 2 metres side is parallel to the water surface and 2.5 metres below it. Find the total pressure on the rectangular plate. Take $w = 9.81$ kN/m^3.
[Ans. 353.16 kN]
2. A circular door of 0.5 m diameter closes on an opening in the vertical side of a bulk head, which retains water. The centre of the opening is at a depth of 2m from the water level. Determine the total pressure on the door. Take specific gravity of sea water as 1.03. **[Ans.** 3.968 kN]
3. A circular plate of diameter 1.5 m is placed vertically in water in such a away that the centre of the plate is 3 m below the free surface of water. Determine:
   (*i*) Total pressure on the plate, and
   (*ii*) Position of the centre of pressure
[Ans. (*i*) 52 kN, (*ii*) 3.0468 m]
4. A rectangular sluice gate is situated on the vertical wall of a lock. The vertical side of the sluice is '*d*' metres in length and depth of centroid of the area is '*p*' metres below the water surface. Prove that the depth of pressure is equal to $\left(p + \frac{d^2}{12p}\right)$.
5. A circular opening, 3 m diameter, in a vertical side of a tank is closed by a disc of 3 m diameter which can rotate about a horizontal diameter. Calculate:
   (*i*) The force on the disc, and
   (*ii*) The torque required to maintain the disc in equilibrium in the vertical position when the head of water above the horizontal diameter is 6 m.
[Ans. 416 kN (*ii*) 39 kNm]
6. An isosceles triangular plate of base 5 m and altitude 5 m is immersed vertically in an oil of specific gravity 0.8. The base of the plate is 1 m below the free water surface, determine:
   (*i*) The total pressure, and
   (*ii*) The centre of pressure.
[Ans. (*i*) 261.93 kN (*ii*) 3.19 m]
7. Determine the total pressure and centre of pressure on an isosceles triangular plate of base 4 m and altitude 4 m when it is immersed vertically in an oil of specific gravity 0.9. The base of the plate coincides with the free oil surface.
[Ans. 94.15 kN, 1.99 m]
8. A tank contains water upto a height of 0.5 m above the base. An immiscible liquid of specific gravity 0.8 is filled on the top of water upto 1 m height. Calculate: (*i*) Total pressure on one side of the tank; (*ii*) The position of centre of pressure for one side of the tank, which is 2m wide.
[Ans. 18.15 kN, 1.009 m from the top]

9. A circular plate of 1 m diameter is immersed in water in such a way that its plane makes an angle of 30° with the horizontal and its top edge is 1.25 m below the water surface. Find the total pressure on the plate and the point, where it acts.

[**Ans.** 11.56 kN, 1.51 m]

10. A triangular plate of 1 m base and 1.5 m altitude is immersed in water. The plane of the plate is inclined at 30° with water surface while the base is parallel to and at a depth of 2 m from the water surface. Calculate:

(*i*) The total pressure on the plate, and

(*ii*) The position of the centre of pressure

[**Ans.** 16.54 kN, (*ii*) 2.264 m]

11. A circular plate 3 metres in diameter is submerged in water in such a way that the greatest and least depths of the surface (below water surface) are 2 m and 1 m respectively, calculate:

(*i*) The total pressure on front face of the plate;

(*ii*) The position of centre of pressure.

[**Ans.** (*i*) 104 kN, (*ii*) 1.54 m]

12. A rectangular plane surface 1 m wide and 3 m deep lies in water in such a way that its plane makes an angle of 30° with the free water surface. Determine the total pressure and position of centre of pressure when the upper edge is 2 m below the free surface.

[**Ans.** 228.69 kN, 3.427 m from free surface]

13. Fig 3.66 shows a gate having a quadrant shape of radius of 3 m. Find the resultant force due to water per metre length of the gate. Also find the angle at which this resultant force will act.

[**Ans.** 82.2 kN, 57°31′]

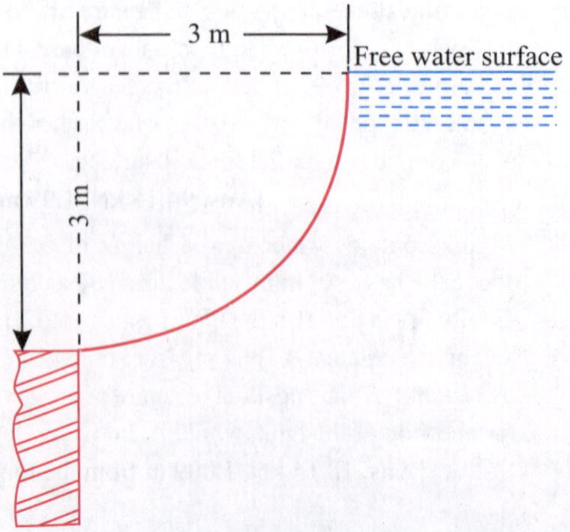

Fig. 3.66

14. A masonry dam 7 m high has a top width of 1.5 m and bottom width of 5 m. Maximum water level in the dam is 1.0 m below the top of the dam. Determine the maximum and minimum pressure intensities at the base when the dam is full. Take weight of water = 9.81 kN/m^3 and weight of masonry = 21.6 kN/m^3.

[**Ans.** 117.5 kN/m^2, 78.8 kN/m^2 both compressive]

15. The masonry dam of trapezoidal section has its upstream face vertical. The height is 10 m and top is 3 m wide. Find the minimum width of base if there is no tension at the base and water reaches the top of the dam. Take weight of water = 9.81 kN/m^3 and weight of masonry = 22 kN/m^3. What is then maximum compressive stress at the base? [**Ans.** b = 6 m, 330 kN/m^2]

16. Each gate of a lock is 6 m high and is supported by two hinges placed at the top and bottom of the gate. When the gates are closed, they make an angle of 120°. The width of lock is 5 m. If the water levels are 4 m and 2 m on upstream and downstream sides respectively, find:

(*i*) Resultant water pressure on each gate, and

(*ii*) Reaction at the hinges.

[**Ans.** (*i*) 169.9 kN (*ii*) R_t = 43.9 kN, R_b = 126 kN]

$$\left[\textbf{Hint}: \text{Width of each lock gate} = \frac{2.5}{\cos 30°}\right]$$

17. A gate which is 2 m wide and 1.2 m high lies in vertical plane and is hinged at the bottom. There is a liquid on upstream side of the gate which extends 1.5 m above the top of the gate and has a specific gravity of 1.45. On the downstream side of the gate there is water upto the top of the gate. Find:

(*i*) The resultant force acting on the gate,

(*ii*) The position of the centre of pressure, and

(*iii*) The least force acting horizontally on the top of the gate which is capable of opening it. **[IIT Kharagpur]**

[**Ans.** (*i*) 57.48 kN, (*ii*) 2.123 m below the free surface of upstream, (*iii*) 27.66 kN]

18. Fig. 3.67 shows a flash board. Find the depth of water h and the compressive force in the strut per metre of the crest at the instant when the water is just ready to tip the flash board.

[IIT Kharagpur]

[**Ans.** 2.6 m, 38.26 kN]

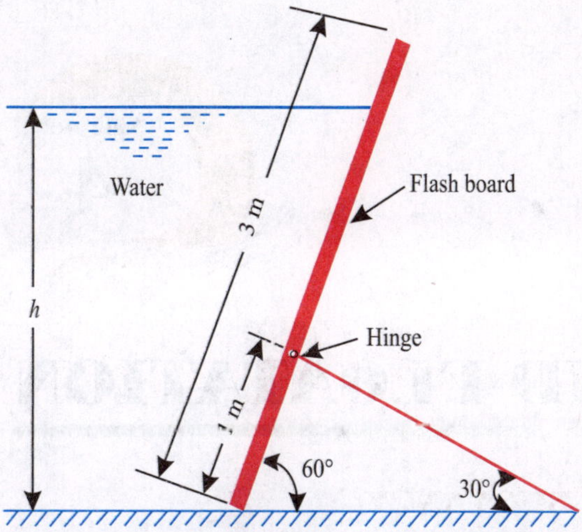

Fig. 3.67

19. A rectangular door covering an opening 3m × 1.75 high in a vertical wall, is hinged about its vertical edge by two points placed symmetrically 0.4 m from either end. The door is locked by clamp placed at the centre of other vertical edge. Determine the reactions at the two hinges and the clamp, when the height of water is 1m above the top edge of the opening.

[Ans. 48.28 kN; 37.96 kN, 10.137 kN]

20. Determine the magnitude and direction of the resultant force acting on the radial gate shown in Fig. 3.68, if its length is 4 m.

[Ans. 303.63 kN, $\alpha = 39.32°$]

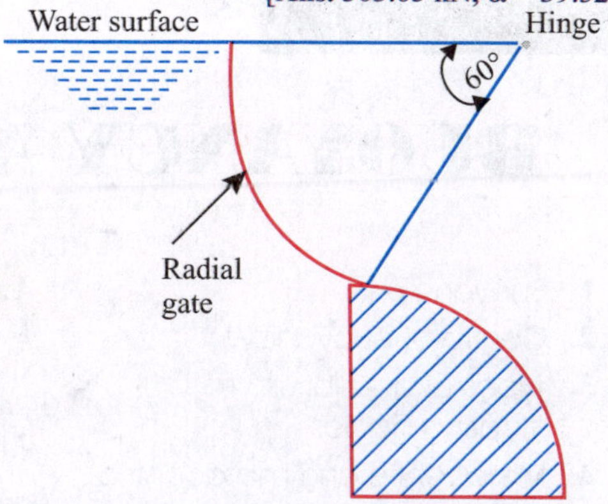

Fig. 3.68

BUOYANCY AND FLOATATION

4.1. BUOYANCY

Whenever a body is immersed wholly or partially in a fluid it is subjected to an upward force which tends to lift (or buoy) it up. This *tendency for an immersed body to be lifted up in the fluid, due to an upward force opposite to action of gravity is known as* **buoyancy.** The force tending to lift up the body under such conditions is known as *buoyant force* or *force of buoyancy* or *upthrust.* The magnitude of the buoyant force can be determined by ***Archimedes' principle*** which states as follows:

"When a body is immersed in a fluid either wholly or partially, it is buoyed or lifted up by a force, which is equal to the weight of fluid displaced by the body."

4.2. CENTRE OF BUOYANCY

The point of application of the force of buoyancy on the body is known as the **centre of buoyancy.** It is *always the centre of gravity of the volume of fluid displaced.*

Example 4.1. *A wooden block of width 1.25* m, *depth 0.75 m and length 3.0 m is floating in water. Specific weight of the wood is 6.4 kN/m³. Find:*

(*i*) *Volume of water displaced, and*

(*ii*) *Position of centre of buoyancy.*

Solution. Width of the wooden block = 1.25 m

Depth of the wooden block = 0.75 m

Length of the wooden block = 3.0 m

Volume of the block = $1.25 \times 0.75 \times 3 = 2.812 \text{ m}^3$

Specific weight of wood, $w = 6.4 \text{ kN/m}^3$

Weight of the block = $6.4 \times 2.812 = 18$ kN

(*i*) Volume of water displaced:

For equilibrium the weight of water displaced

= Weight of wooden block = 18 N

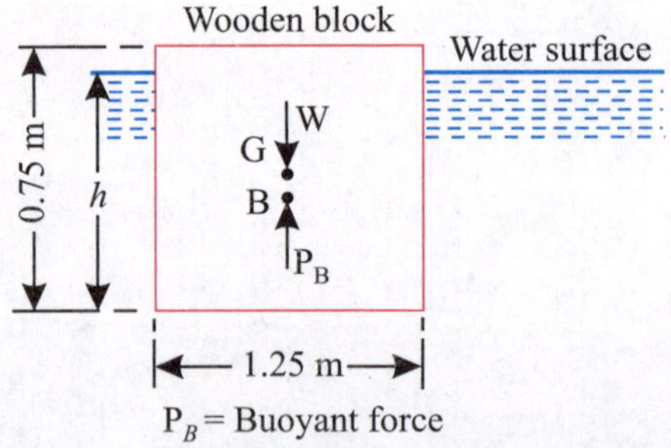

Fig. 4.1

Volume of water displaced

$$= \frac{\text{Weight of water displaced}}{\text{Weight density of water}}$$

$$= \frac{18}{9.81} = \mathbf{1.835\ m^3\ (Ans)} \quad (\because \text{Weight density of water} = 9.81\ \text{kN/m}^3)$$

(*ii*) Position of centre of buoyancy:

We know that,

Volume of wooden block in water = Volume of water displaced.

or, $1.25 \times h \times 3.0 = 1.835$

(where, h = depth of wooden block in water)

$$\therefore \quad h = \frac{1.835}{1.25 \times 3.0} = 0.489\ \text{m}$$

$$\text{Hence centre of buoyancy} = \frac{0.489}{2} = \mathbf{0.244\ from\ the\ base\ (Ans.)}$$

Example 4.2. *A wooden block of specific gravity 0.7 and having a size of 2 m × 0.5m × 0.25 m is floating in water. Determine the volume of concrete of specific weight 25 kN/m^3, that may be placed which will immerse (i) the block completely in water, and (ii) the block and concrete completely in water.*

Solution. Size of the block = 2 m × 0.5 m × 0.25 m

∴ Volume of the block = 0.25 m^3

Specific gravity of the block = 0.7

Specific weight of the block = $0.7 \times 9.81 = 6.867\ \text{kN/m}^3$

Weight of the block = $6.867 \times 0.25 = 1.716$ kN

(∵ Specific weight of water = 9.81 kN/m^3)

Let, W_c = Weight of concrete required to be placed on the block, and

V_c = Volume of concrete required to be placed on the block.

Total weight of the block = $W_c + 1.716$ kN ...(*i*)

(*i*) Immersion of the block only:

When the block is completely immersed, the volume of water displaced = 0.25 m^3

∴ Upward thrust at the time of complete immersion

$= 0.25 \times 9.81 = 2.45$ kN ...(*ii*)

Now equating (*i*) and (*ii*), we get:

$$W_c + 1.716 = 2.45$$

or $$W_c = 0.734\ \text{kN}$$

$$\text{Volume of concrete, } V_c = \frac{\text{Weight}}{\text{Sp. weight}} = \frac{0.734}{25} = \mathbf{0.0294\ m^4\ (Ans.)}$$

(*ii*) Immersion of block and concrete:

Total weight of the block = $25\ V_c + 1.716$ ...(*i*)

Upward thrust = $(V_c + 0.25) \times 9.81$ ...(*ii*)

Equating (*i*) and (*ii*), we get:

$$25V_c + 1.716 = (V_c + 0.25) \times 9.81$$

or, $25\ V_c + 1.716 = 9.81V_c + 2.45$ or $15.19\ V_c = 0.734$

or, $V_c = \mathbf{0.0483\ m^3}$ **(Ans.)**

Example 4.3. *Find the density of a metallic body which floats at the interface of mercury of specific gravity 13.6 and water such that 35 percent of its volume is submerged in mercury and 65 percent in water.*

Solution. Let, V = Volume of the body, m^3.

Then, volume of body submerged in mercury

$$= \frac{35}{100} \times V = 0.35\ V\ m^3$$

Volume of body submerged in water

$$= \frac{65}{100} \times V = 0.65\ V\ m^3$$

The body will be in equilibrium when,

Total buoyant (upward) force = weight of the body

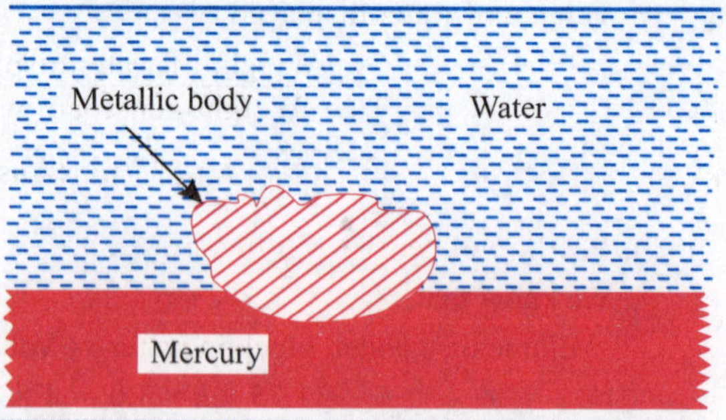

Fig. 4.2

But, Total buoyant force = Force of buoyancy due to water + force of buoyancy due to mercury
= weight of water displaced by the body + weight of mercury displaced by the body
= (weight density of water × volume of water displaced) + (weight density of mercury × volume of mercury displaced)
= $9.81 \times 0.65\ V$ (kN) + $13.6 \times 9.81 \times 0.35\ V$ (kN)

and, Weight of the body = weight density × volume of the body

$$= w_{body} \times V$$

(where, w_{body} = weight density of the metallic body)

For equilibrium, we have:

$$9.81 \times 0.65\ V + 13.6 \times 9.81 \times 0.35\ V = w_{body} \times V$$

$$\therefore \quad w_{body} = \mathbf{53.07\ kN/m^3}$$ **(Ans.)**

Example 4.4. *A metallic cube 30 cm side and weighing 450 N is lowered into a tank containing a two-fluid layer of water and mercury. Determine the position of block at mercury-water interface when it has reached equilibrium.*

(Anna University)

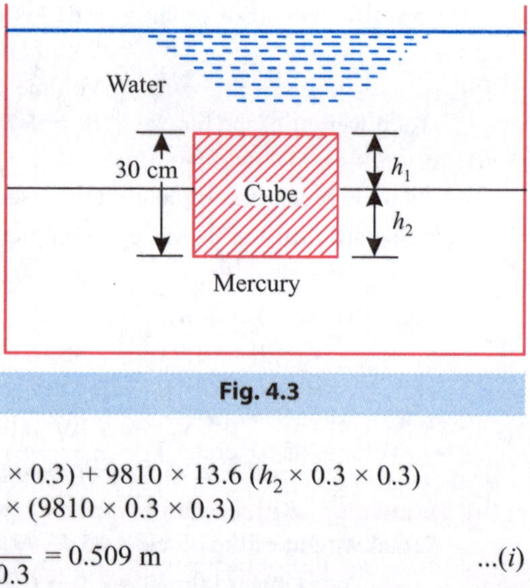

Fig. 4.3

Solution. Refer to Fig. 4.3. The metallic cube sinks beneath the water surface and comes to rest at the water-mercury interface.

As per principle of floatation, we have weight of cubical block = buoyant force

= weight of water and mercury displaced by the block.

Thus, $450 = 9810\,(h_1 \times 0.3 \times 0.3) + 9810 \times 13.6\,(h_2 \times 0.3 \times 0.3)$

$= (h_1 + 13.6\,h_2) \times (9810 \times 0.3 \times 0.3)$

or, $$(h_1 + 13.6\,h_2) = \frac{450}{9810 \times 0.3 \times 0.3} = 0.509 \text{ m} \qquad ...(i)$$

Also, $$h_1 + h_2 = 0.3 \text{ m} \qquad ...(ii)$$

From (*i*) and (*ii*), we have the depth of cube below the water-mercury interface,

$$h_2 = \frac{(0.509 - 0.3)}{12.6} = \mathbf{0.01658\ m\ or\ 16.58\ mm}$$ **(Ans.)**

Example 4.5. *A 8 cm side cube weighing 4 N is immersed in a liquid of relative density 0.8 contained in a rectangular tank of cross-sectional area 12 cm × 12 cm. If the tank contained liquid to a height of 6.4 cm before the immersion, determine the levels of the bottom of the cube and the liquid surface.*

Solution. Refer to Fig. 4.4.

Let, h_1 = Depth to which the bottom of the cube falls below original liquid surface (cm),

h_2 = Height of rise of liquid above the original liquid surface (cm), and

$(h_1 + h_2)$ = Depth and submergence of the cube (cm).

Now, Volume L = Volume M

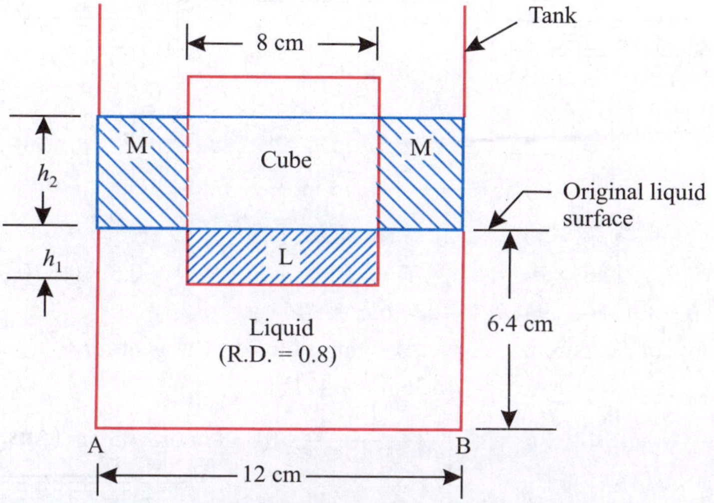

Fig. 4.4

$$8 \times 8 \times h_1 = (12^2 - 8^2) \times h_2$$

or, $h_1 = 1.25\, h_2$

Weight of the cube, W = 4N ...(Given)

$$W = \text{Buoyant force} = \frac{(8 \times 8) \times (h_1 + h_2) \times 0.8 \times 9810}{10^6}$$

or, $4 = 0.5023\,(h_1 + h_2)$

or, $4 = 0.5023\,(1.25\,h_2 + h_2) = 1.13\,h_2$

$\therefore$ $h_2 = 3.54$ cm

and, $h_1 = 1.25 \times 3.54 = 4.425$ cm

Level of bottom of cube above plane AB = $6.4 - h_1 = 6.4 - 4.425 =$ **1.975 cm (Ans.)**

Level of the liquid surface above plane AB = $6.4 + h_2 = 6.4 + 3.54 =$ **9.94 cm (Ans.)**

Example 4.6. *A cube 50 cm side is inserted in a two-layer fluid with specific gravity 1.2 and 0.9 respectively. The upper and lower halves of the cube are composed of materials with specific gravity 0.6 and 1.4 respectively. What is the distance of the top of cube above interface?* **(UPSC)**

Solution. Refer to Fig. 4.5.

Weight of cube = $[S_1\,(= 0.6) \times 9.81 \times 0.5 \times 0.5 \times 0.25)] + [S_2\,(= 1.4) \times 9.81 \times 0.5 \times 0.5 \times 0.25]$

= 1.226 kN

Let, h = Height of top of the cube above the interface.

Then, Buoyant force = Weight of lighter and heavier liquids displaced by the block

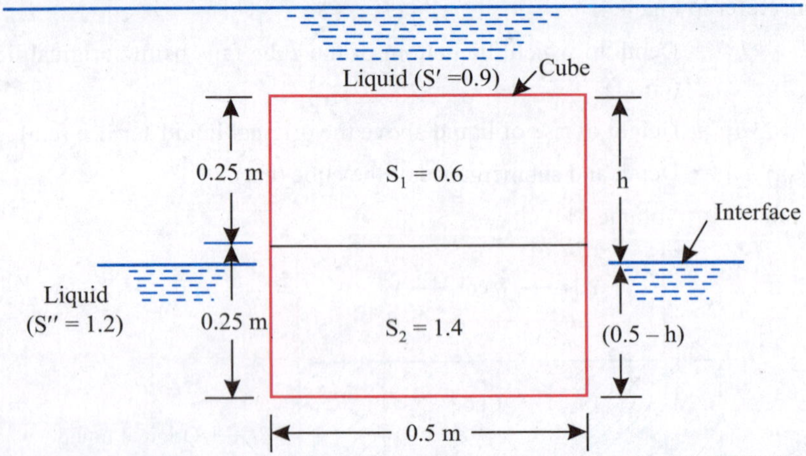

Fig. 4.5

$$= [S' (= 0.91) \times 9.81 \times 0.5 \times 0.5 \times h] + [S'' (= 1.2) \times 9.81 \times 0.5 \times 0.5\,(0.5 - h)]$$

$$= 2.207\,h + 1.471 - 2.943\,h = -0.736\,h = 1.471$$

As per principle of floatation, we have: Weight of block = Buoyant force

i.e. $$1.226 = -0.736\,h + 1.471$$

$$\therefore \quad h = \frac{(1.471 - 1.226)}{0.736} = 0.333 \text{ m or } 33.3 \text{ cm}$$ **(Ans.)**

Example 4.7. *A spherical object of 1.45 m diameter is completely immersed in a water reservoir and chained to the bottom. If the chain has a tension of 5.20 kN, find the weight of the object when it is taken out of the reservoir into the air.*

Solution. *Given:* $d = 1.45$ m; $T = 5.20$ kN.

Weight of the object, *W*:

Buoyant force, $P_B = W$ (weight of the object) + T (tension in the chain)

$$\therefore \quad W = P_B - T$$

$$= \frac{4}{3}\pi \times \left(\frac{1.45}{2}\right)^3 \times 9.81 - 5.20$$

$$= 10.46 \text{ kN}$$ **(Ans.)**

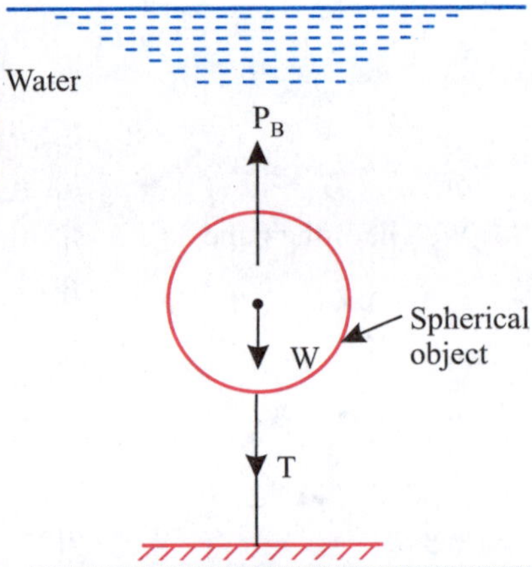

Fig. 4.6

Example 4.8. *A cylinder of mass 10 kg and area of cross-section 0.1 m² is tied down with string in a vessel containing two liquids as shown in figure 4.7. Calculate gauge pressure on the the cylinder bottom and the tension in the string. Density of water = 1000 kg/m³. Specific gravity of A = 0.8. Specific gravity of B (water) = 1.0* **(GATE)**

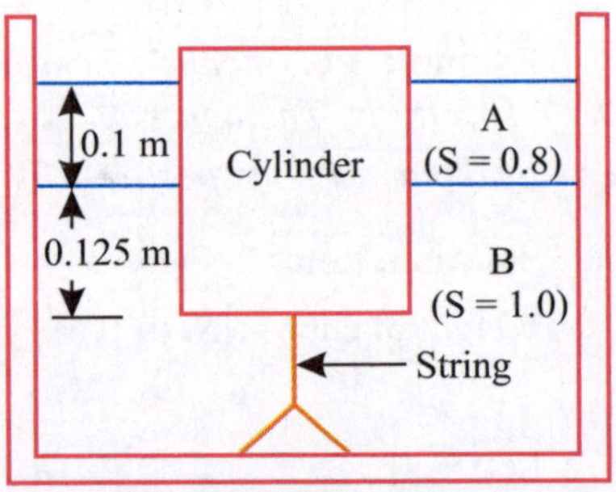

Fig. 4.7

Solution. *Given*: Mass of cylinder, m = 10 kg

Area of cross-section = 0.1 m^2

Density of water (liquid B) = 1000 kg/m^3

Density of liquid $A = 0.8 \times 1000 = 800 \text{ kg/m}^3$

Tension in string, *T*:

Volume of liquid A displaced $= 0.1 \times 0.1$

$= 0.01 \text{ m}^3$

∴ Mass of liquid A displaced, $m_A = 0.01 \times 800 = 8$ kg

∴ Volume of liquid B displaced $= 0.1 \times 0.125 = 0.0125$ m^3

∴ Mass of liquid B displaced, $m_B = 0.0125 \times 1000 = 12.5$ kg

Total mass of liquid displaced $= m_A + m_B = 8 + 12.5 = 20.5$ kg

Upward thrust $= 20.5 \times 9.81 = 201.1$ N

Weight of cylinder $=$ mg $= 10 \times 9.81 = 98.1$ N

Net upward thrust $= 201.1 - 98.1 = 103$ N

∴ Tension in the string, **T = 103 N (Ans.)**

Pressure (gauge) on the cylinder bottom, *p*:

$$p = \frac{\text{Net upward thrust}}{\text{Area of cross-section}} = \frac{103}{0.1} = 1030 \text{ N/m}^2 \textbf{ (Ans.)}$$

4.2. TYPES OF EQUILIBRIUM OF FLOATING BODIES

The equilibrium of floating bodies is of the following types:

1. Stable equilibrium, 2. Unstable equilibrium, and 3. Neutral equilibrium.

4.3.1. Stable Equilibrium

When a body is given a small angular displacement (i.e. tilted slightly), by some external force, and then it returns back to its original position due to the internal forces (the weight and the upthrust), such an equilibrium is called **stable equilibrium**.

4.3.2. Unstable Equilibrium

If the body does not return to its original position from the slightly displaced angular position and heels farther away, when given a small angular displacement, such an equilibrium is called an **unstable equilibrium.**

4.3.3. Neutral Equilibrium

If a body, when given a small angular displacement, occupies a new position and remains at rest in this new position, it is said to possess a **neutral equilibrium.**

4.4. METACENTRE AND METACENTRIC HEIGHT

Metacentre :

Fig. 4.8 (*a*) shows body floating in a liquid in a state of equilibrium. When it is given a small angular displacement [see Fig. 4.8 (*b*)] it starts oscillating about some point (*M*). This point, *about which the body starts oscillating*, is called **metacentre.**

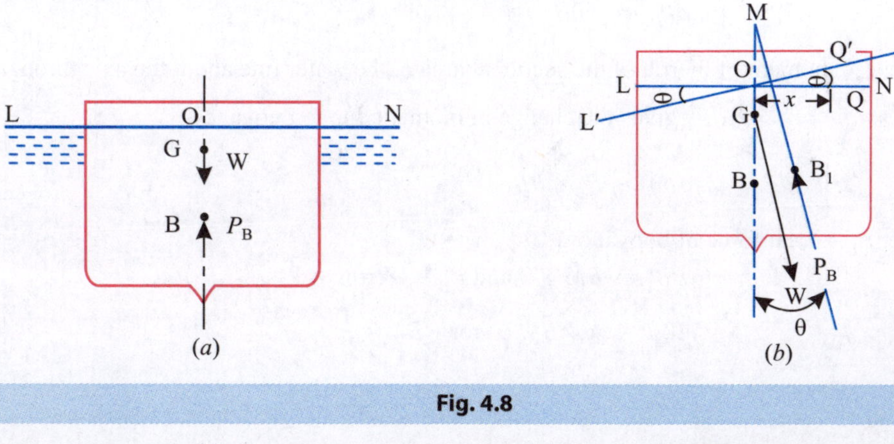

Fig. 4.8

The **metacentre** may also be defined as *a point of intersection of the axis of body passing through c.g.(G) and, original centre of buoyancy (B) and a vertical line passing through the centre of buoyancy (B_1) of the tilted position of the body.*

The position of metacentre, M remains practically constant for the small angle of tilt θ.

Metacentric height:

The distance between the centre of gravity of a floating body and the metacentre (*i.e.* distance GM as shown in Fig.4.8 (*b*) is called **metacentric height.**

- *For stable equilibrium,* the position of metacentre M remains *higher* than *c.g.* of the body, G.
- *For unstable equilibrium,* the position of metacentre *M* remains *lower* than G.
- *For neutral equilibrium,* the position of metacentre *M coincides* with G.

4.5 DETERMINATION OF METACENTRIC HEIGHT

The metacentric height may be determined by the following two methods:

1. Analytical method.
2. Experimental method.

4.5.1 Analytical Method

Refer to Fig. 4.8 (*b*). It shows the tilted position of the floating body, the line L′ON′ represents the water surface. The portion N′ON of the body is submerged and the portion L′OL is lifted because of tilting. As a result of this, the centre of buoyancy changes it position from B to B_1. The intersection of axis of the body and the vertical line through B_1 locates the metacentre, M of the body.

To find the metacentric height GM consider an elementary cylindrical prism QQ' of portion N′ON at a distance 'x' from O. Let the area of this elementary prism be δA. The height of this elementary prism is given by $x.\theta$. The volume of this elementary prism is given by:

$$\delta V = x.\theta.\delta A. \qquad ...(i)$$

The upward force or buoyancy force acting at this prism (δP_B) is given by:

$$\delta P_B = w.\delta V = w.\, x.\theta.\delta A \qquad ...(ii)$$

(where, w = unit weight of liquid)

The moment of this buoyancy force about O

$$x.\delta P = w.\theta.x^2.\delta A \qquad ...(iii)$$

For the total portion N′ON, this moment is given by:

$$\int x.\, dP_B = \int w.\theta.\, x^2.dA = w\theta \int x^2 \, dA \qquad ...(iv)$$

or,

$$\int x.dP_B = w\theta.I$$

(where, I = moment of inertia of the sectional area at the water line about the axis through O)

$\int x.dP_B$ gives the change in moment due to buoyancy.

Now, $$\int x.dP_B \,(= w\theta.I) = P_B \times BB_1$$

(where, P_B = total force of buoyancy)

But, $$BB_1 = BM \times \theta \text{ and } P_B = W = w \times V$$

$$\therefore \quad w.\theta.I = w.V.BM.\theta \quad \text{or} \quad BM = \frac{1}{V} \qquad ...(4.1)$$

Now metacentric height, $GM = BM \pm BG$

+ ve sign : when G is *lower* than B

– ve sign : when G is *higher* than B

4.5.2. Experimental Method

Refer to Fig. 4.9.

In this method, a known weight W_1 is shifted by a distance z across the axis of tilt. The change in moment due to this shift is $W_1\ z$. Let the angle of tilt be θ. This angle of tilt may be measured experimentally by using a plumb bob. The change in moment due to this tilt is equal to $W.GG_1$ or $W.GM \tan\theta$.

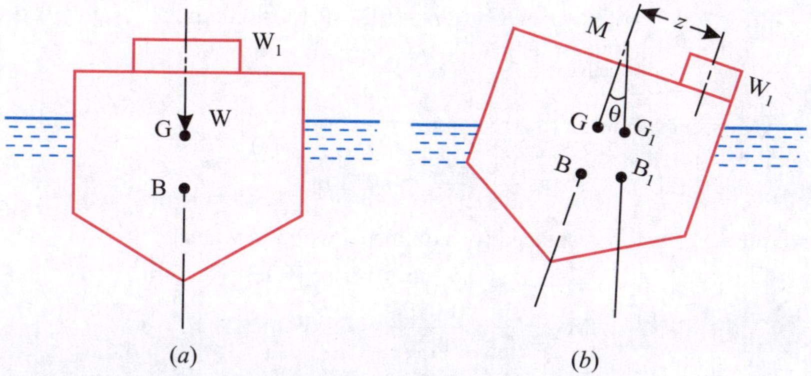

Fig. 4.9. Experimental method for determination of metacentric height.

$$\therefore \quad W_1.z = W.Gm.\tan\theta \quad \text{or} \quad GM = \frac{W_1.z}{W.\tan\theta} \qquad ...(4.2)$$

If, l = Length of plumb bob, and

d = Displacement of the plumb bob,

Then, $\tan\theta = \dfrac{d}{l}$

and, metacentric height is given by:

$$GM = \frac{W_1.z.l}{W.d} \qquad ...(4.3)$$

Example 4.9. *A wooden block of specific gravity 0.75 floats in water. If the size of the block is 1 m × 0.5 m × 0.4 m, find its metacentric height.*

Solution. Size (or dimensions) of the block = 1*m* × 0.5 *m* × 0.4 *m*

Specifice gravity of wood = 0.75

Specific weight $w = 0.75 \times 9.81 = 7.36\ kN/m^3$

Weight of wooden block = specific weight × volume

= 7.36 × 1× 0.5 × 0.4 = 1.472 kN

Let depth of immersion = h metres.

Weight of water displaced

= Specific weight of water × volume of the wood submerged in water

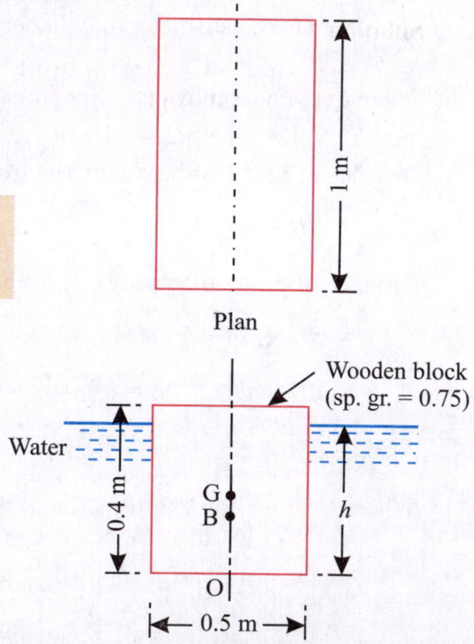

Fig. 4.10

$= 9.81 \times 1 \times 0.5 \times h = 4.9\,h$ kN

Now, for equilibrium:

Weight of wooden block = Weight of water displaced *i.e.,* $1.472 = 4.9\,h$

or, $$h = \frac{1.472}{4.9} = 0.3 \text{ m}$$

∴ Distance of centre of buoyancy from bottom *i.e.,*

$$OB = \frac{h}{2} = \frac{0.3}{2} = 0.15 \text{ m}$$

and, $$OG = \frac{0.4}{2} = 0.2 \text{ m}$$

∴ $$BG = OG - OB = 0.2 - 0.15 = 0.05 \text{ m}$$

Also, $$BM = \frac{I}{V}$$

Where, I = Moment of inertia of a rectangular section

$$= \frac{1 \times 0.5^3}{12} = 0.014 \text{ m}^4$$

and, V = Volume of water displaced (or volume of wood in water)

$$= 1 \times 0.5 \times h = 1 \times 0.5 \times 0.3 = 0.15 \text{ m}^3$$

$$BM = \frac{I}{V} = \frac{0.0104}{0.15} = 0.069 \text{ m}$$

We know that the metacentric height,

$$GM = BM - BG \qquad (\because G \text{ is above } B)$$

$$= 0.069 - 0.05 = \mathbf{0.019 \text{ m}} \textbf{ (Ans.)}$$

Example 4.10. *A solid cylinder 2 m in diameter and 2m high is floating in water with its axis vertical. If the specific gravity of the material of cylinder is 0.65 find its metacentric height. State also whether the equilibrium is stable or unstable.*

Solution. *Given:* Diameter of cylinder, $d = 2$ *m*; Height of cylinder, $h = 2m$; Specific gravity = 0.65

Depth of cylinder in water = Sp. gravity × h

$= 0.65 \times 2.0 = 1.3$ *m*

Distance of centre of buoyancy (B) from O,

$$OB = \frac{1.3}{2} = 0.65 \text{ m}$$

Distance of centre of gravity (G) from O,

$$OG = \frac{2.0}{2} = 1.0 \text{ m}$$

$$BG = OG - OB = 1.0 - 0.65 = 0.35 \text{ m}$$

Also, $$BM = \frac{I}{V}$$

Where, I = Moment of inertia of the plan of the body about Y–Y

$$= \frac{\pi}{64} d^4 = \frac{\pi}{64} \times 2^4 = 0.785 \text{ m}^4$$

and, V = Volume of cylinder of water

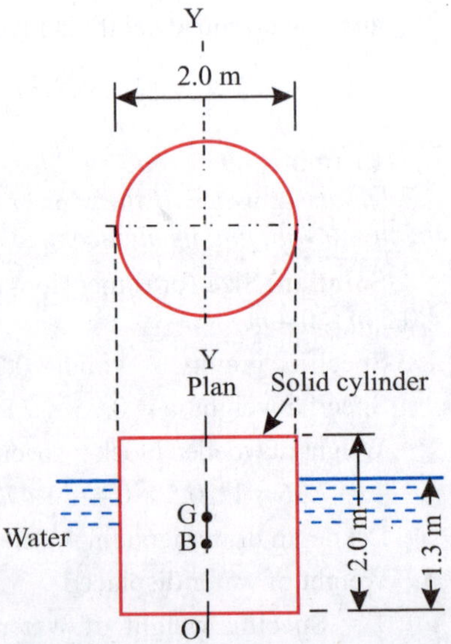

Fig. 4.11

$$= \frac{\pi}{4} d^2 \times \text{depth of cylinder in water}$$

$$= \frac{\pi}{4} \times 2^2 \times 1.3 = 4.084 \text{ m}^3$$

$$\therefore \quad BM = \frac{I}{V} = \frac{0.785}{4.084} = 0.192 \text{ m}$$

We know that the metacentric height,

$$GM = BM - BG = 0.192 - 0.35$$

$$= \mathbf{-0.158 \text{ m (Ans.)}}$$

–ve sign means that the metacentric (M) is *below* the centre of gravity (G). Thus the cylinder is in **unstable equilibrium. (Ans.)**

Example 4.11. *A weight of 100 kN is moved through a distance of 8 metres across the deck of a pontoon of 7500 kN displacement floating in water. This makes a pendulum 2.5 metres long to move through 120 mm horizontally. Calculate the metacentric height of the pontoon.*

Solution. Weight of the movable load, W_1 = 100 kN

Distance through which load is moved, z = 8 m

Weight of pontoon, W = 7500 kN

Length of the plumb bob, l = 2.5 m

Displacement of the plumb bob, d = 120 mm = 0.12 m

Let, GM = metacentric height of the pontoon.

Using the relation:

$$GM = \frac{W_1 . z . l}{W . d} = \frac{100 \times 8 \times 2.5}{7500 \times 0.12} = \mathbf{2.22 \text{ m (Ans.)}}$$

Example 4.12. *A body has the cylindrical upper portion of 4m diameter and 2.4 m deep. The lower portion, which is curved, displaces a volume of 800 litres of water and its centre of buoyancy is situated 2.6 m below the top of the cylinder. The centre of gravity of the whole body is 1.6 m below the top of the cylinder and the total displacement of water is 52 kN. Find the metacentric height of the body.*

Solution. *Given:* Diameter of body, d = 4 m

Depth of cylindrical portion = 2.4 m

Volume of curved portion = 800 litres = 0.8 m^3

Distance between centre of buoyancy of curved portion and top of body,

$$OB_1 = 2.6 \text{ m}$$

Distance between centre of gravity of the whole body and top of the cylinder, OG = 1.6 m

Total volume of water displaced, $V = \frac{52}{9.81} = 5.3 \text{ m}^3$

Volume of water displaced by the cylindrical portion

$= 5.3 - 0.8 = 4.5 \text{ m}^3$

If y is the distance between the water surface and the top of the body, then:

$$4.5 = \frac{\pi}{4} \times 4^2 \times (2.4 - y)$$

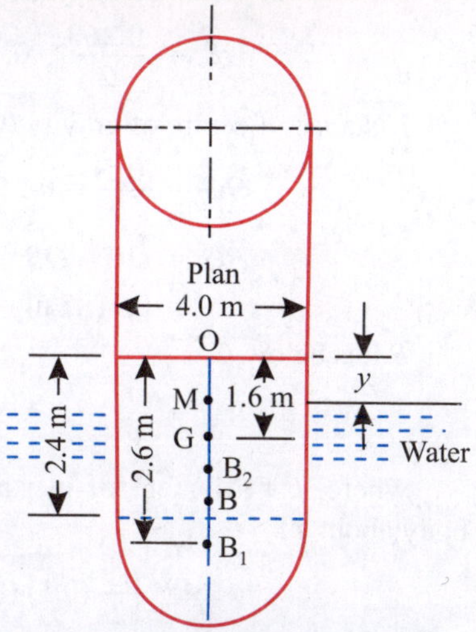

Fig. 4.12

$$y = 2.4 - \frac{4.5 \times 4}{\pi \times 4^2} = 2.04 \text{ m}$$

Distance of the centre of buoyancy of the cylindrical portion from the top of the body,

$$OB_2 = y + \left(\frac{2.4 - y}{2}\right) = 2.04 + \frac{2.4 - 2.04}{2} = 2.22 \text{ m}$$

If B be the centre of buoyancy of the whole body, then:

$$OB = \frac{(0.8 \times 2.6) + (4.5 \times 2.22)}{0.8 + 4.5} = 2.227 \text{ m}$$

Now, $BG = OB - OG = 2.277 - 1.6 = 0.677$ m

Now, $BM = \frac{I}{V}$

where, I = Moment of inertia of the cylindrical portion (top portion) about its *c.g.*

$$= \frac{\pi}{64} \times 4^4 \text{ m}^4 = 12.566 \text{ m}^4$$

and, $V = 5.3 \text{ m}^3$ (already calculated earlier)

$$BM = \frac{12.566}{5.3} = 2.37$$

Metacentric height, $GM = BM - BG = 2.37 - 0.677 =$ **1.693 m (Ans.)**

Example 4.13. *A solid cube of sides 0.5 m each is made of a material of relative density 0.5. The cube floats in a liquid of relative density 0.95 with two of its faces horizontal. Examine its stability.* **(MDU, Haryana)**

Solution. *Given*: Side of the cube = 0.5 m; Specific gravity of cube material = 0.5, Relative density of liquid = 0.95.

Depth of cube in liquid,

$$h = \frac{0.5 \times 0.5}{0.95} \; 0.263 \text{ m}$$

Distance of centre of buoyancy (B) from O,

$$OB = \frac{0.263}{2} = 0.1315 \text{ m}$$

Distance of centre of gravity (G) from O,

$$OG = \frac{0.5}{2} = 0.25 \text{ m}$$

$$BG = OG - OB = 0.25 - 0.1315$$
$$= 0.1185 \text{ m}$$

B lies below *G*.

$$BM = \frac{I}{V}$$

where, I = Moment of inertia of the plane of the body about YY

$$= \frac{1}{12} (0.5)(0.5)^3 = 0.005208 \text{ m}^4$$

V = Volume of liquid displaced

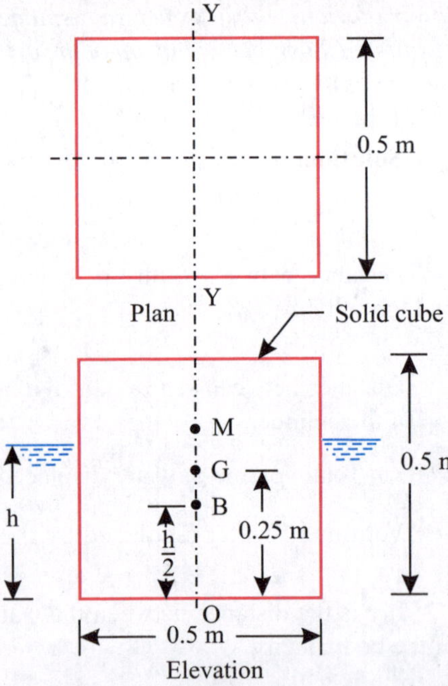

Fig. 4.13

$$= 0.5 \times 0.5 \times 0.263 = 0.06575 \text{ m}^3$$

$$\therefore \quad BM = \frac{I}{V} = \frac{0.005208}{0.06575} = 0.0792 \text{ m}$$

Metacentric height, $GM = BM - BG = 0.0792 - 0.1185 = -0.0393$ m

–ve sign means that the metacentre (M) is *below* the centre of gravity (G). Thus the cube will be **unstable.**

Example 4.14. *A hollow cylinder closed at both ends has an outside diameter of 1.25 m, length 3.5 m and specific weight 75 kN/m³. If cylinder is to float just in stable equilibrium in sea water (specific weight 10 kN/m³), find its minimum permissible thickness.*

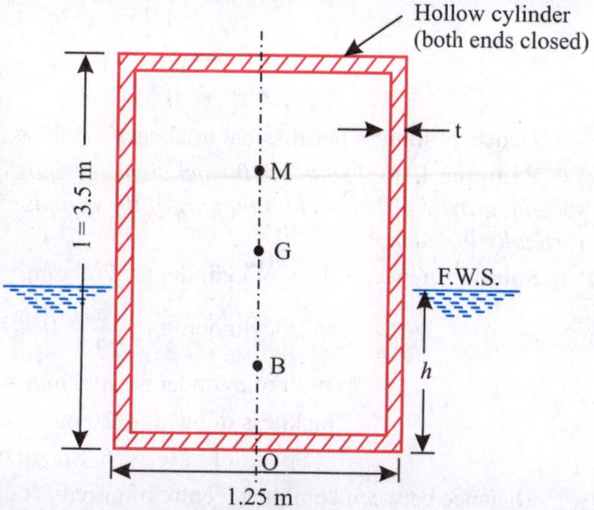

Fig. 4.14

Solution. *Given*: $d = 1.25$ m, $l = 3.5$ m, $w_c = 75$ kN/m³; $w_w = 10$ kN/m³

Minimum permissible thickness, *t*:

Let, h = Depth of immersion, *m*.

Weight of sea water displaced

$$= \frac{\pi}{4} d^2 h \times w_w$$

$$= \frac{\pi}{4} \times 1.25^2 \times h \times 10 = 12.27\, h \text{ kN}$$

Weight of cylinder = Volume of cylinder × Specific weight.

= (Volume of two end sections + volume of circular portion) × specific weight

$$= \left[2 \times \frac{\pi}{4} d^2 \times t + \frac{\pi}{4} \left\{ d^2 - (d - 2t)^2 \right\} l \right] \times w_c$$

$$= \left[2 \times \frac{\pi}{4} d^2 t + \pi d t l \right] \times w_c \qquad \text{(assuming } t << l\text{)}$$

(Ignoring term involving t^2)

$$\left[2 \times \frac{\pi}{4} \times 1.25^2 \times t + \pi \times 1.25 \times t \times 3.5 \right] \times 75$$

$$= 1215\, t \text{ kN}$$

Under equilibrium conditions:

Weight of cylinder = Weight of sea water displaced.

i.e., $12.27\, h = 1215\, t$ or $h = 99\, t$

Volume of cylinder under water or volume of sea water displaced,

$$V = \frac{1215t}{10} = 121.5t$$

If M is the metacentre, then:

$$BM = \frac{I}{V} = \frac{\frac{\pi}{64} \times 1.25^4}{121.5t} = \frac{0.00099}{t}$$

$$OB = \frac{h}{2} = \frac{99t}{2} = 49.5t$$

$$OG = \frac{3.5}{2} = 1.75 \text{ m}$$

$$BG = OG - OB = 1.75 - 49.5\,t$$

For the cylinder to float just in stable equilibrium:

$$BG = BM \quad \text{i.e.,} \quad 1.75 - 49.5\,t = \frac{0.00099}{t}$$

or, $49.5\,t^2 - 1.75\,t + 0.00099 = 0$

or,
$$t = \frac{1.75 \pm \sqrt{(1.75)^2 - 4 \times 49.5 \times 0.00099}}{2 \times 49.5} = \frac{1.75 \pm 1.69}{99}$$

$$= 0.0347 \text{ m} \quad \text{or} \quad 6.06 \times 10^{-4} \text{ m}$$

Hence, minimum permissible thickness = 6.06×10^{-4} m or **0.606 mm (Ans.)**

Example 4.15. *A solid of 200 mm diameter and 800 mm length has its base 20 mm thick and of specific gravity 6. The remaining part of the cylinder is of specific gravity 0.6. State, if it can float vertically in water.*

Solution. *Given:* Dia. of cylinder = 200 mm = 0.2 m

Area of cylinder, $A = \frac{\pi}{4} \times 0.2^2 = 0.0314 \text{ m}^2$

Length of cylinder = 800 mm = 0.8 m

Thickness of base = 20 mm = 0.02 m

Sp. gr. of base = 6, Sp. gr. of remaining portion = 0.6

Distance between combined centre of gravity (G) and the bottom of the cylinder (O),

$$OG = \frac{\left[A \times 0.78 \times 0.6\left(\frac{0.78}{2} + 0.02\right)\right] + \left[A \times 0.02 \times 6 \times \frac{0.02}{2}\right]}{(A \times 0.78 \times 0.6) + (A \times 0.02 \times 6)}$$

(where, A = area of cylinder)

$$= \frac{0.1919 + 0.0012}{0.468 + 0.12} = 0.3284 \text{ m (or 328.4 mm)}$$

Combined sp. gr. of the cylinder

$$= \frac{(0.78 \times 0.6) + (0.02 \times 6)}{0.78 + 0.02} = 0.735$$

Depth of immersion of the cylinder

$$= 0.8 \times 0.735 = 0.588 \text{ m}$$

Distance of centre of buoyancy from the bottom of the cylinder,

$$OB = \frac{0.588}{2} = 0.294 \text{ (or 29.4 mm)}$$

$$BG = OG - OB = 0.3284 - 0.294$$
$$= 0.0344 \text{ m (or 34.4 mm)}$$

Now, $BM = \frac{I}{V}$

where, I = Moment of inertia of circular section

$$= \frac{\pi}{64} \times 0.2^4 = 2.5 \times 10^{-5}\,\pi \text{ m}^4$$

and, V = volume of water displaced

$$= \frac{\pi}{4} \times 0.2^2 \times 0.588 = 0.00588\,\pi$$

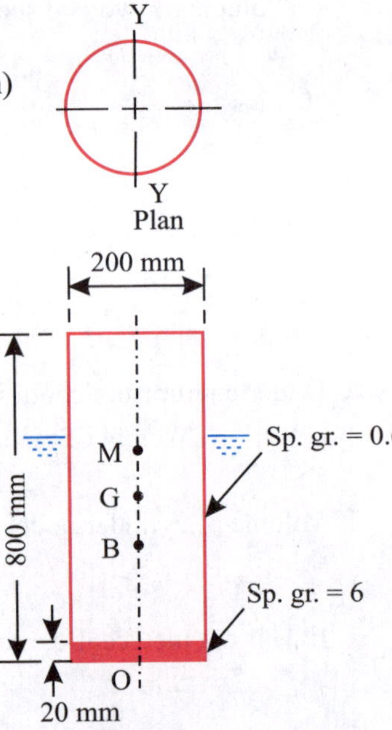

Fig. 4.15

$$\therefore \qquad BM = \frac{2.5 \times 10^{-5}\pi}{0.00588\pi}$$

$$= 0.00425 \text{ m or } 4.25 \text{ mm}$$

Now metacentric height,

$$GM = BM - BG = 4.25 - 34.4 \text{ mm} = -30.15 \text{ mm}$$

Negative sign means that the metacentre (*M*) is *below* the centre of gravity (*G*). Thus the cylinder is in *unstable equilibrium and it* ***cannot float*** *vertically in water.* **(Ans.)**

Example 4.16. *An 80 mm diameter composite solid cylinder consists of an 80 mm diameter, 20 mm thick metallic plate having specific gravity 4.0 attached at the lower end of an 80 mm diameter wooden cylinder of specific gravity 0.8. Find the limits of the length of the wooden portion so that the composite cylinder can float in stable equilibrium in water (specific gravity 1.0) with its axis vertical.* **(MGU Kerala)**

Solution. Refer to Fig. 4.16. *Given*: $d = 80$ mm; $a = 20$ mm; $S_1 = 4$; $S_2 = 0.8$

Limits of the length of the wooden portion:

The cylinder will float vertically in water if its metacentric height GM is +ve. To find the metacentric height, the locations of centre of gravity G and centre of buoyancy B of the combined cylinder is to be found.

The distance of the centre of gravity of the solid cylinder from O is given by:

$$OG = \frac{\left[\frac{\pi}{4}d^2 \times a \times S_1\right] \times \frac{a}{2} + \left[\frac{\pi}{4}d^2 \times b \times S_2\right] \times \left[a + \frac{b}{2}\right]}{\left[\frac{\pi}{4}d^2 \times a \times S_1 + \frac{\pi}{4}d^2 \times b \times S_2\right]}$$

$$= \frac{\left(a \times S_1 \times \frac{a}{2}\right) + b \times S_2\left(a + \frac{b}{2}\right)}{a \times S_1 + b \times S_2}$$

$$= \frac{\left(20 \times 4 \times \frac{20}{2}\right) + b \times 0.8\left(20 + \frac{b}{2}\right)}{20 \times 4 + b \times 0.8}$$

$$= \left[\frac{800 + 0.8b\left(20 + \frac{b}{2}\right)}{80 + 0.8b}\right] = \left[\frac{1000 + 20b + \frac{b^2}{2}}{100 + b}\right] \qquad ...(i)$$

(Dividing numerator and denominator by 0.8 and simplifying)

Let, height of immersion of cylinder = $(h + a)$

Also, Weight of cylinder = Weight of water displaced

$$\text{or,} \quad \frac{\pi}{4}d^2 \times a \times S_1 + \frac{\pi}{4}d^2 \times b \times S_2 = \frac{\pi}{4}d^2(h + a) \times S_{water}$$

$$a \times S_1 + b \times S_2 = (h + a) \qquad (\because S_{water} = 1)$$

$$\text{or, } 20 \times 4 + b \times 0.8 = (h + a)$$

$$\text{i.e.} \qquad h + a = 80 + 0.8\,b \qquad ...(ii)$$

$$\text{Now,} \quad OB = \frac{h + a}{2} = \frac{80 + 0.8b}{2} = 40 + 0.4b \quad ...(iii)$$

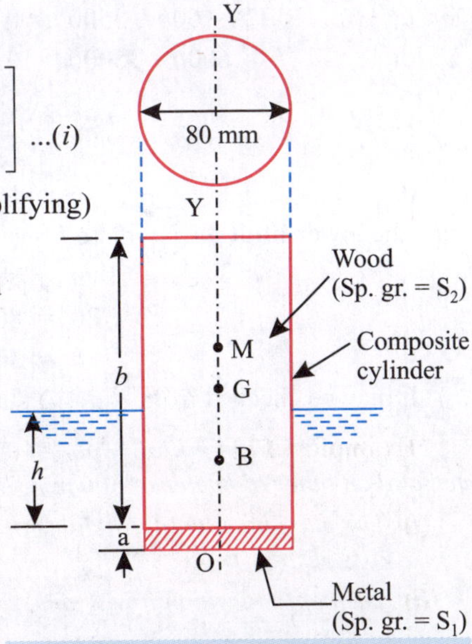

Fig. 4.16

$$BG = OG - OB = \left[\frac{1000 + 20b + \frac{b^2}{2}}{100 + b}\right]$$

$$- (40 + 0.4b) \qquad \text{[From } (i) \text{ and } (iii)]$$

$$= \frac{1}{(100 + b)}\left[\left(1000 + 20b + \frac{b^2}{2}\right) - (4000 + 80b + 0.4b^2)\right]$$

$$= \frac{1}{(100 + b)}[0.1b^2 - 60b - 3000] \qquad ...(iv)$$

$$I = \text{Second moment of area of the section about } Y\text{–}Y = \frac{\pi d^4}{64}$$

$$V = \text{Volume of water displaced} = \frac{\pi}{4} d^2 (h + a)$$

$$BM = \frac{I}{V} = \frac{\pi d^4 / 64}{\frac{\pi}{4} d^2 (h + a)} = \frac{\pi d^4}{64} \times \frac{4}{\pi d^2 (h + a)} = \frac{d^2}{16(h + a)}$$

$$= \frac{(80)^2}{16(80 + 0.8b)} \qquad \text{using } (ii) \text{ for } (h + a)$$

$$= \frac{400}{80 + 0.8b} = \frac{500}{100 + b} \qquad ...(v)$$

$$GM = BM - BG = \frac{500}{(100 + b)} - \frac{1}{(100 + b)}$$

$$[0.1b^2 - 60b - 3000] \quad [\text{using } (iv)] \text{ and } (v)]$$

or,
$$GM = \frac{3500 + 60b - 0.1b^2}{(100 + b)} \qquad ...(vi)$$

It should be +ve and in the limit = 0

i.e. $0.1b^2 - 60b - 3500 = 0$

or, $b^2 - 600b - 35000 = 0$

or,
$$b = \frac{600 + \sqrt{(600)^2 + 4 \times 35000}}{2} \qquad \text{(taking +ve value of } b)$$

or, $b = 653.55$ mm. *This is the* **upper limit** *for b.* **(Ans.)**

The **lower limit** *for b* will be $b = h$, and from eqn. (*ii*), we have:

$$h + a = 80 + 0.8\,b$$

$$b + 20 = 80 + 0.8\,b$$

$$b = \mathbf{300\ mm\ (Ans.)}$$

It may be checked from eqn. (*ii*) that it gives a + ve value of GM.

Example 4.17. *A hollow wooden cylinder of specific gravity 0.6 has an outer diameter of 600 mm and an inner diameter of 300 mm. It is required to float in oil of specific gravity 0.9. Calculate:*

(*i*) *The maximum length (height) of the cylinder so that it shall be stable when floating with it axis vertical;*

(*ii*) *The depth to which it will sink.*

Solution. Outer diameter of cylinder, $D = 600$ mm $= 0.6$ m

Inner diameter of cylinder, d = 300 mm = 0.3 m

Specific weight = $0.6 \times 9.81 = 5.886$ kN/m^3

$\therefore$ Weight of cylinder = volume of cylinder × specific weight

$$= \pi/4\,(D^2 - d^2) \times l \times 5.886 = \frac{\pi}{4}\,(0.6^2 - 0.3^2) \times l \times 5.886$$

$$= 1.248\, l \text{ kN}$$

(where, l = length/height of the cylinder)

This also represents the weight of oil displaced.

$$\therefore \text{ Volume of oil displaced, } V = \frac{1.248 l}{0.9 \times 9.81} = 0.1413\, l$$

i.e. Volume of cylinder immersed in oil, $V = 0.1413 l$

$$\text{Depth of immersion, } h = \frac{\text{volume of cylinder under oil}}{\text{cross-section area of cylinder}}$$

$$= \frac{0.1413 l}{\frac{\pi}{4}(0.6^2 - 0.3^2)} = 0.666\, l$$

Height of centre of buoyancy (B) from O,

$$i.e. \quad OB = \frac{h}{2} = \frac{0.666 l}{2} = 0.333\, l$$

If M is the metacentre, then

$$BM = \frac{I}{V} = \frac{\frac{\pi}{64}(0.6^4 - 0.3^4)}{0.1413\, l} = \frac{0.0422}{l}$$

$$OM = OB + BM = 0.333\, l + \frac{0.0422}{l}$$

Distance of centre of gravity (G) from the point O,

$$OG = \frac{l}{2} = 0.5\, l$$

For stable equilibrium, M should be at a level greater than G, *i.e.* $OM > OG$

$$\text{or,} \quad \left(0.333\, l + \frac{0.0422}{l}\right) > 0.5\, l$$

$$\text{or,} \quad \frac{0.0422}{l} > 0.167\, l \quad \text{or} \quad 0.0422 > 0.167\, l^2$$

$$\text{or,} \quad 0.167\, l^2 < 0.0422 \quad \text{or} \quad l < \left(\frac{0.0422}{0.167}\right)^{1/2} < 0.503 \text{ m}$$

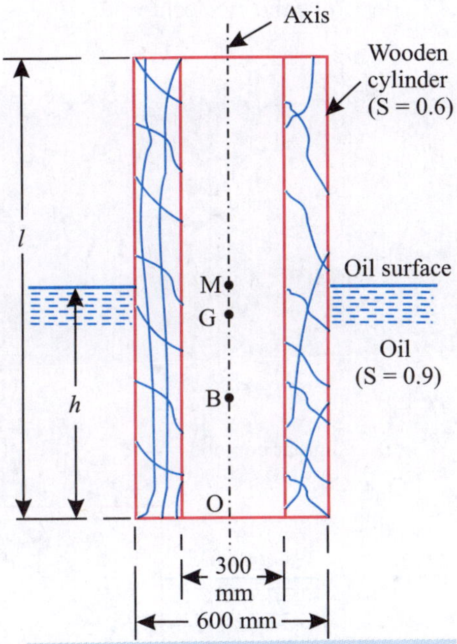

Fig. 4.17

$\therefore$ l_{max} = **0.503 m (Ans.)**

and, $h = 0.666\, l = 0.666 \times 0.503 =$ **0.335 m (Ans.)**

Example 4.18. *A rectangular pontoon 12 m long, 9 m wide and 3 m deep weighs 1380 kN and floats in sea water. The pontoon carries on its upper deck a boiler 6 m diameter and weighing 864 kN. The centre of gravity of each unit coincides with geometrical centre of the arrangement and lies in the same vertical line.*

(i) What is the metacentric height?

(ii) *Is the arrangement stable?*

Take specific weight of sea water = 10 kN/m³

Solution. Total weight of the arrangement, $W = 1380 + 864 = 2244$ kN

This also represent the weight of water displaced.

Volume of sea water displaced,

$$\therefore \quad V = \frac{\text{Weight of water displaced}}{\text{Specific weight of water}} = \frac{2244}{10} = 224.4 \text{ m}^3$$

i.e. Volume of the arrangement under water, $V = 224.4$ m³

Depth of immersion,

$$h = \frac{\text{Volume of the arrangement under water}}{\text{Cross-sectional area of the pontoon}}$$

$$= \frac{224.4}{9 \times 12} = 2.077 \text{ m}$$

Distance of centre of buoyancy (B) from the base point O, $OB = \frac{2.077}{2} = 1.0385$ m

Let, M be the metacentre.

Then, $$BM = \frac{I}{V} = \frac{\frac{1}{12} \times 12 \times 9^3}{224.4} - 3.248 \text{ m}$$

$$OM = OB + BM = 1.0385 + 3.248 = 4.286 \text{ m}$$

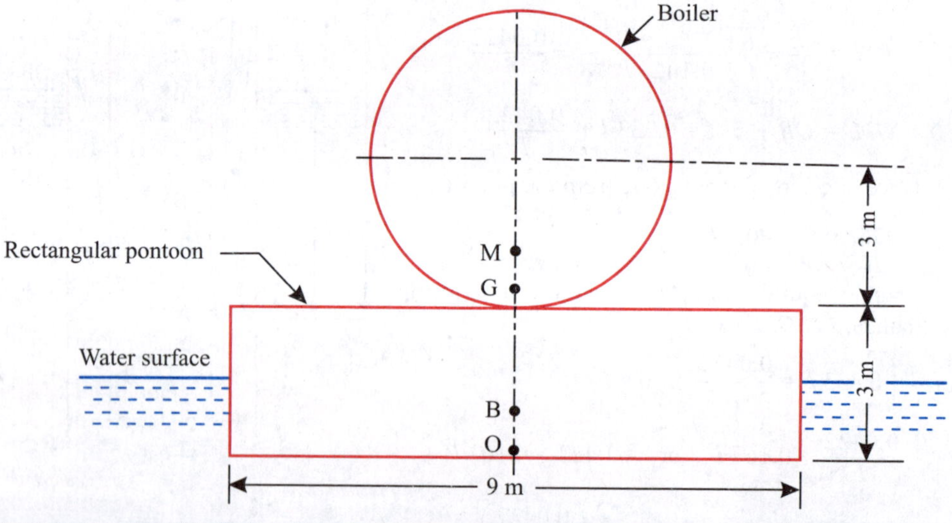

Fig. 4.18

To find the position of combined centre of gravity above the base point O, taking moments about O, we get:

$$1380 \times 1.5 + 864 \times 6 = 2244 \times OG$$

$$\therefore \quad OG = \frac{1380 \times 1.5 + 864 \times 6}{2244} = 3.232 \text{ m}$$

***(i)* Metacentric height, GM:** $GM = OM - OG = 4.286 - 3.232 =$ **1.054 m (Ans.)**

***(ii)* Stability of the arrangement:**

Since $OM > OG$, M is at a higher level than G.

Hence the arrangement is **stable (Ans.)**

Example 4.19. *A buoy having a diameter of 2.4 m and length 1.95 m is floating with its axis vertical in sea water (specific weight = 10 kN/m³). Its weight is 16.5 kN and a load of 1.65 kN is placed centrally at its top. If the buoy is to remain in stable equilibrium, find the maximum permissible height of the centre of gravity of the load above the top of the buoy.*

Solution. *Given:* Diameter of the buoy, $d = 2.4$ m; Length of the buoy, $l = 1.95$ m

Weight of the buoy, $W_{buoy} = 16.5$ kN

Weight placed at the top of the buoy, $W = 1.65$ kN

Specific weight of sea water $= 10$ kN/m³

Total weight of the arrangement $W_t = W_{buoy} + W$
$= 16.5 + 1.65 = 18.15$ kN

This is also the weight of water displaced by the arrangement.

Volume of water displaced,

$$V = \frac{W_t}{\text{Sp. weight of water}}$$

$$= \frac{18.15}{10} = 1.815 \text{ m}^3$$

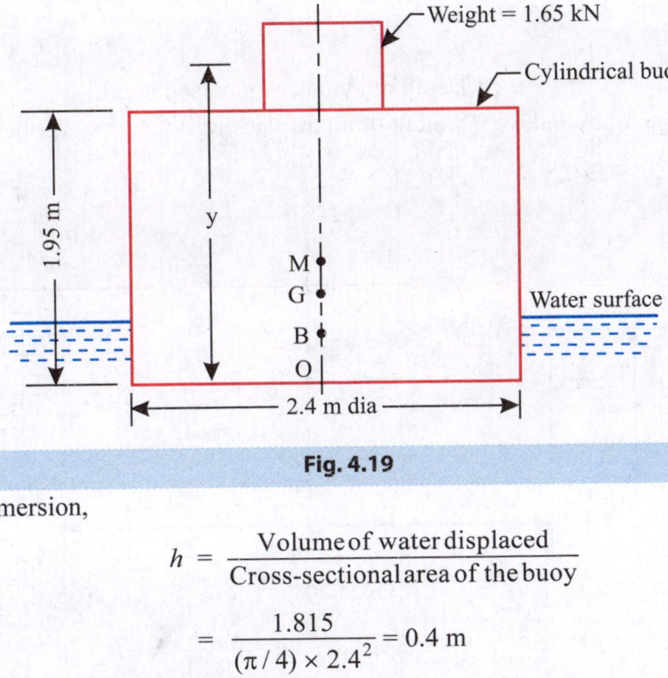

Fig. 4.19

Depth of immersion,

$$h = \frac{\text{Volume of water displaced}}{\text{Cross-sectional area of the buoy}}$$

$$= \frac{1.815}{(\pi/4) \times 2.4^2} = 0.4 \text{ m}$$

Height of centre of buoyancy (B) above base point O,

$$OB = \frac{h}{2} = \frac{0.4}{2} = 0.2 \text{ m}$$

If M is the metacentre, then:

$$BM = \frac{I}{V} = \frac{(\pi/64) \times 2.4^4}{1.815}$$

$$OM = OB + BM = 0.2 + 0.897 = 1.097 \text{ m}$$

Let, y = Height of centre of gravity of the load above the base O.

To find the position of combined centre of gravity above the base point O, taking moments about O, we get:

$$16.5 \times \frac{1.95}{2} + 1.65 \times y = 18.15 \times OG$$

or, $$16.087 + 1.65\,y = 18.15 \times OG$$

or, $$OG = \frac{16.087 + 1.65\,y}{18.15} = 0.886 + 0.091y$$

The equilibrium will be stable when $OM > OG$ *i.e.* $1.097 > (0.886 + 0.091y)$

or, $0.211 > 0.091y$ or $0.091y < 0.211$ or $y < 2.318$ m

But the height of buoy = 1.95 m

∴ The height of centre of gravity of the load above the buoy should *not be greater than* (2.318 – 1.95) or **0.368 m (Ans.)**

Example 4.20. *A wooden cylinder (sp. gravity = 0.54) of diameter d and length l is required to float in oil (sp. gravity = 0.81). Find the l/d ratio for the cylinder to float with its longitudinal axis vertical in oil.*

Solution. *Given:* Diameter of the cylinder = d; Length of the cylinder = l;

Sp. gravity, $S_1 = 0.54$; sp. gravity of oil, $S_2 = 0.81$.

$\frac{l}{d}$ ratio:

Let, h = Depth of cylinder immersed in oil.

Now, Weight of cylinder = Weight of oil displaced ...(principle of buoyancy)

or, $$\frac{\pi}{4} d^2 l \times S_1 = \frac{\pi}{4} d^2 h \times S_2$$

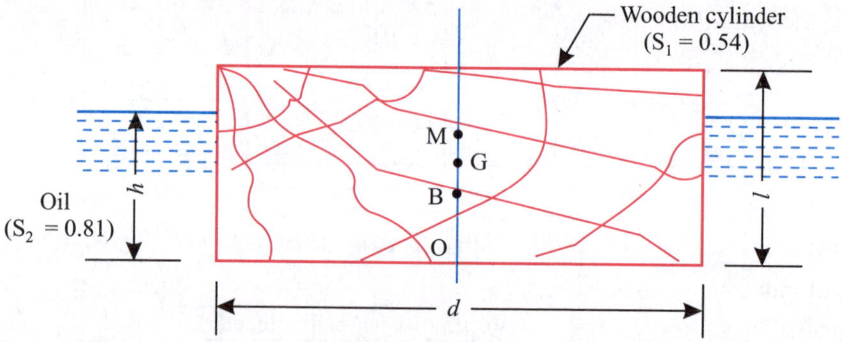

Fig. 4.20

$$l \times 0.54 = h \times 0.81 \quad \text{i.e.,} \quad h = \frac{0.54\,l}{0.81} = \frac{2}{3}l$$

∴ The distance of centre of buoyancy B from O, $OB = \frac{h}{2} = \frac{1}{3}l$

The distance of centre of gravity G from base point O, $OG = l/2$

∴ If M is the metacentre, then:

$$BM = \frac{I}{V} = \frac{\frac{\pi}{64}d^4}{\frac{\pi}{4}d^2 h} = \frac{d^2}{16h} = \frac{d^2}{16 \times \frac{2}{3}l} = \frac{3d^2}{32l}$$

$\therefore \quad OM = OB + BM = \frac{1}{3}l + \frac{3d^2}{32l}$

For stable equilibrium: $OM > OG$ or $\left(\frac{1}{3}l + \frac{3d^2}{32l}\right) > \frac{l}{2}$

or, $\frac{3d^2}{32l} > \left(\frac{l}{2} - \frac{l}{3}\right)$ or $\frac{3d^2}{32l} > \frac{l}{6}$

or, $\frac{3d^2}{32l^2} > \frac{1}{6}$ or $\frac{18}{32} > \frac{l^2}{d^2}$

or, $\frac{l^2}{d^2} < \frac{18}{32}$ or $\frac{l}{d} < \left(\frac{18}{32}\right)^{1/2}$ or $(9/16)^{1/2}$ or 3/4

$\therefore \quad \frac{l}{d} <$ **3/4 (Ans.)**

Example 4.21. *A log of wood 0.9 m in diameter and 7.5 m long is floating in river water. If the specific gravity of log is 0.7, what is the depth of the wooden log in water?*

Solution. *Given:* Diameter of the wooden log, $d = 0.9$ m;

Length of the log, $l = 7.5$ m

Specific gravity, $S = 0.7$

Weight of the log $= (0.7 \times 9.81) \times \frac{\pi}{4} d^2 l$

$= 0.7 \times 9.81 \times \frac{\pi}{4} \times 0.9^2 \times 7.5 = 32.76$ kN

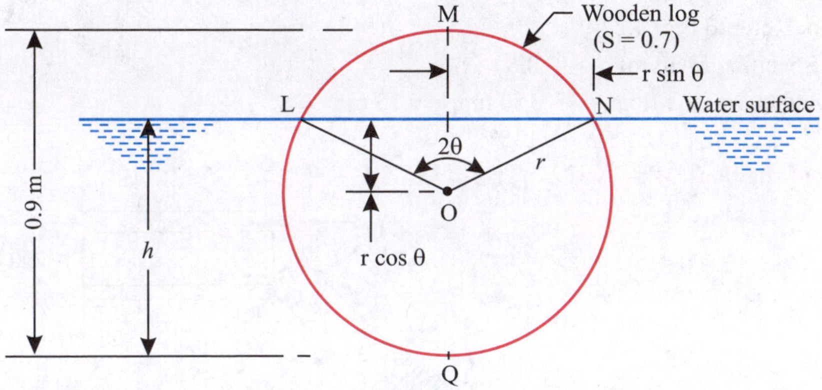

Fig. 4.21

This also represents the weight of water displaced.

Volume of water displaced $= \frac{32.76}{9.81} = 3.34 \text{ m}^3$

Let, h = Depth of immersion.

$\therefore$ Volume of log inside water = Volume of water displaced = 3.34 m^3

$3.34 = \text{Area } LQNL \times 7.5$

Area, $LQNL = \frac{3.34}{7.5} = 0.4453 \text{ m}^2$

Also, Area, $LQNL$ = Area $LQNOL$ + area LON

$$= \pi r^2 \left[\frac{360 - 2\theta}{360}\right] + \frac{1}{2} \times 2r\sin\theta \times r\cos\theta$$

$$= \pi r^2 \left(1 - \frac{\theta}{180}\right) + r^2 \sin\theta \cos\theta$$

$\therefore$ $$0.4453 = \pi \times 0.45^2 \left(1 - \frac{\theta}{180}\right) + 0.45^2 \sin\theta \cos\theta$$

or, $$0.4453 = 0.6362 - 0.003534\,\theta + 0.2025 \sin\theta \cos\theta$$

or, $$0.003534\,\theta - 0.2025 \sin\theta \cos\theta = 0.6362 - 0.4453 = 0.1909$$

or, $$\theta - \frac{0.2025}{0.003534} \sin\theta \cos\theta = \frac{0.1909}{0.003534}$$

or, $$\theta - 57.3 \sin\theta \cos\theta = 54.02$$

or, $$\theta - 57.3 \sin\theta \cos\theta - 54.02 = 0$$

By hit and trial, we get, $\theta \simeq 71.5°$

$\therefore$ Depth of wooden log in water, $h \simeq r + r\cos\theta$

$$\simeq 0.45 + 0.45 \cos 71.5° \text{ or } h = \mathbf{0.593\ m}$$ **(Ans.)**

Example 4.22. *A float valve regulates the flow of oil of specific gravity* 0.8 *in a cistern. The spherical float is 150 mm in diameter. AOB is a weightless link carrying the float at one end, and a valve at the other end which closes the pipe through which oil flows into the cistern. The link is mounted in a frictionless hinge at 0 and angle AOB is 135°. The length of OA is 200 mm, and the distance between the centre of the float and hinge is 500 mm. When the flow is stopped AO will be vertical. The valve is to be pressed on to the seat with a force of 10 N to completely stop the flow of oil into the cistern. It was observed that the flow of oil is stopped when the free surface of oil in the cistern is 350* mm *below the hinge. Determine the weight of the float.* **[UPSC Engg. Services]**

Solution. Refer to Fig. 4.22.

Specific gravity of oil = 0.8

Diameter of the float, d = 150 mm = 0.15 m

$\angle AOB$ = 135°

Weight of the float, *W*:

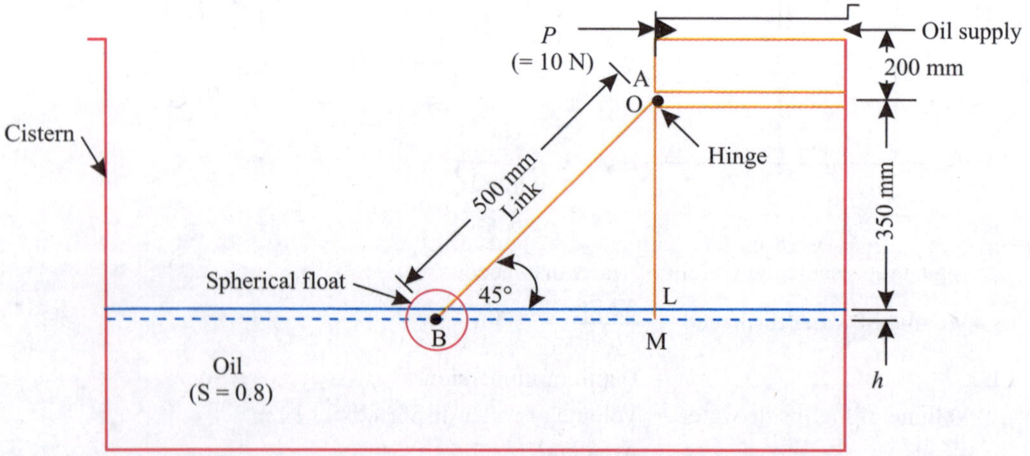

Fig. 4.22

When the oil flow is stopped, the level of oil is as shown in Fig. 4.22; the centre of float is below the level of oil by a depth h.

In ΔOBM: $\sin 45° = \dfrac{OM}{OB} = \dfrac{OL + LM}{OB} = \dfrac{0.35 + h}{0.5}$

$$0.5 \sin 45° = 0.35 + h \quad \text{or} \quad h = 0.00355 \text{ m}$$

$$\text{Volume of oil displaced} = \frac{2}{3}\pi r^3 + \pi r^3 \times h$$

$$= \frac{2}{3} \times \pi\left(\frac{0.15}{2}\right)^3 + \pi + \left(\frac{0.15}{2}\right)^2 \times 0.00355 = 0.000946 \text{ m}^3$$

Buoyant force = Weight of oil displaced

= Volume of oil displaced × sp. gravity of oil

= 0.000946 × (0.8 × 9.81) = 0.007424 kN or 7.42 N

Since the buoyant force and the weight of the float passes through the same vertical line, therefore,

Net force on float = Buoyant force – Weight of float = 7.42 – W

Taking moments about the hinge O, we get:

$$P \times 0.2 = (7.42 - W) \times BM$$

or, $$10 \times 0.2 = (7.42 - W) \times 0.5 \cos 45°$$

$\therefore$ $$W = 7.42 - \frac{10 \times 0.2}{0.5 \cos 45°} = 1.76 \text{ N}$$ *i.e.* W= **1.76 N (Ans.)**

Example 4.23. *A cylindrical buoy is 2 m in diameter and 2.5m long and weighs 22 kN. The specific weight of sea water is 10.25 kN/m³. Show that the buoy does not float with its axis vertical? What minimum pull should be applied to a chain attached to the centre of the base to keep the buoy vertical?* **[UPSC]**

Solution. *Given:* Diameter of the buoy, d = 2 m;

Length of the buoy, l = 2.5 m;

Weight of the buoy, W = 22 kN;

Specific weight of sea water = 10.25 kN/m³.

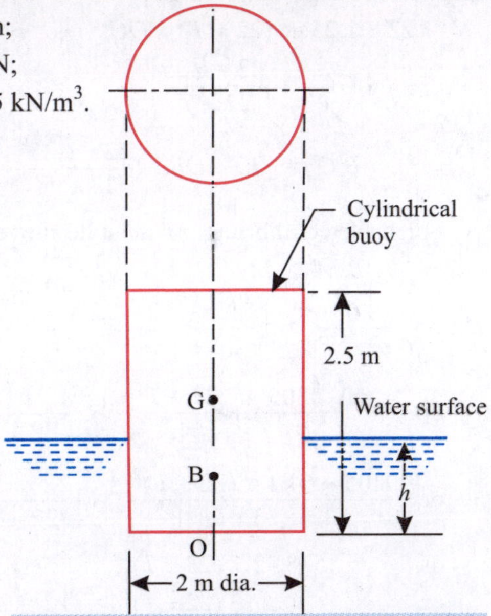

Fig. 6.23

Part I: ***To show that the buoy does not float with its axis vertical:***

$$V = \frac{\text{Weight of water displaced}}{\text{Specific weight of water}}$$

(Weight of the buoy = Weight of water displaced)

$$= \frac{22}{10.25} = 2.146 \text{ m}^2$$

i.e., Volume of buoy immersed in water

$$= 2.146 \text{ m}^3$$

Let, h = Depth of immersion.

Then, $$h = \frac{\text{Volume of buoy immersed in water}}{\text{Cross-sectional area of the buoy}}$$

$$= \frac{2.146}{(\pi/4) \times 2^2} = 0.683 \text{ m}$$

Distance of centre of buoyance (B) from the base point O,

$$OB = \frac{h}{2} = \frac{0.683}{2} \simeq 0.342 \text{ m}$$

Let, M be the metacentre.

Then: $$BM = \frac{I}{V} = \frac{(\pi/64) \times 2^4}{2.146} = 0.366 \text{ m}$$

$$OM = OB + BM = 0.342 + 0.366 = 0.708 \text{ m}$$

Distance of centre of gravity (G) from the base point O, $OG = \frac{2.5}{2} = 1.25$ m

Since $OM < OG$, therefore, the buoy is **unstable** when floating with axis vertical. **(Ans.)**

Part II: ***Minimum pull required to keep the buoy vertical*:**

Let, T = Minimum pull (kN) which should be applied to chain attached to the centre of the base to keep the buoy vertical.

$$\text{Total downward force} = W + T = (22 + T)$$

$$\text{Displaced volume of water} = \left(\frac{22+T}{10.25}\right) \text{m}^3$$

$$\text{New depth of immersion, } h' = \frac{22+T}{10.25 \times (\pi/4) \times 2^2} = \frac{22+T}{32.2} \text{ m}$$

$$\therefore \quad OB' = \frac{h'}{2} = \frac{22+T}{2 \times 32.2} = \frac{22+T}{64.4} \text{ m}$$

$$B'M' = \frac{I}{V} = \frac{(\pi/64) \times 2^4}{\frac{22+T}{10.25}} = \frac{8.05}{22+T}$$

To find new centre of gravity G' due to self weight acting at G and tension T in the chain, taking moments about point O, we get:

$$22 \times 1.25 = (22 + T) \times OG'$$

$$\therefore \quad OG' = \frac{22 \times 1.25}{22+T}$$

$$B'G' = OG' - OB' = \frac{22 \times 1.25}{22+T} - \frac{22+T}{64.4}$$

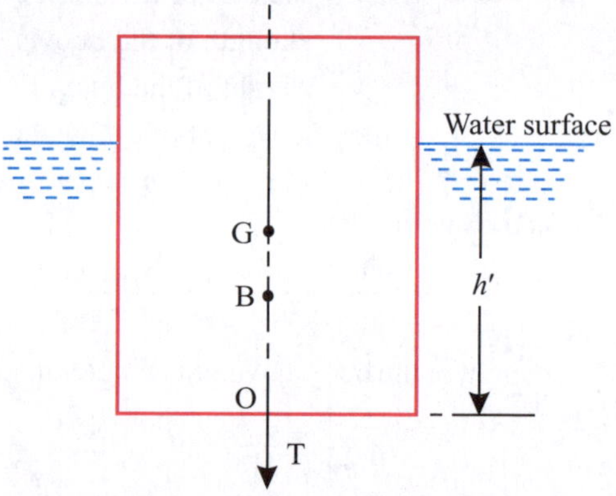

Fig. 4.24

For stable equilibrium, M' must lie above G', *i.e.*

$$B'M' > B'G'$$

$$\therefore \quad \frac{8.05}{22+T} > \left[\frac{22 \times 1.25}{22+T} - \frac{22+T}{64.4}\right]$$

$$\text{or,} \quad \left[\frac{8.05}{22+T} + \frac{22+T}{64.4}\right] > \frac{22 \times 1.25}{22+T}$$

$$\text{or,} \quad \frac{8.05 \times 64.4 + (22+T)^2}{(22+T) \times 64.4} > \frac{22 \times 1.25}{22+T}$$

$$\text{or,} \quad 518.42 + (22+T)^2 > 22 \times 1.25 \times 64.4$$

$$\text{or,} \quad (22+T)^2 > [22 \times 1.25 \times 64.4 - 518.42] \text{ or } > 1252.58$$

$$\text{or,} \quad 22 + T > 35.39 \text{ or } T > 13.39 \text{ kN}$$

Hence, *minimum pull in the chain required to keep the buoy vertical* = **13.39 kN (Ans.)**

Example 4.24. *A solid cone floats in a liquid with its apex downwards. The specific gravity of the material of the cone and the liquid are* 0.7 *and* 0.95 *respectively. Determine the least apex angle of cone for stable equilibrium.*

Solution. Specific weight of cone = $0.7 \times 9.81 = 6.87\ kN/m^2$

Specific weight of liquid = $0.95 \times 9.81 = 9.32\ kN/m^2$

Let, H = Height of the cone,

h = Height of cone immersed in liquid, and

2α = Apex angle of the cone.

Weight of the cone = Volume × sp. weight

$$= \frac{1}{3}\pi R^2 H \times 6.87 = \frac{1}{3}\pi H^3 \tan^2\alpha \times 6.87 \text{ kN}$$

$$\left[\because \tan\alpha = \frac{R}{H} \text{ i.e. } R = H\tan\alpha \quad \text{and} \quad r = h\tan\alpha\right]$$

$$\text{Weight of liquid displaced} = \frac{1}{3}\pi r^2 h \times 9.32 = \frac{1}{3}\pi h^3 \tan^2\alpha \times 9.32 \text{ kN}$$

Now, Weight of cone = Weight of liquid displaced (since the cone is floating)

i.e.,
$$\frac{1}{3}\pi H^3 \tan^2 a \times 6.87 = \frac{1}{3}\pi h^3 \tan^2\alpha \times 9.32 \text{ kN}$$

$$\therefore \quad h = H\left[\frac{6.87}{9.32}\right]^{1/3} = 0.9\,H$$

Distance of centre of buoyancy from the apex, $OB = \frac{3}{4}h = \frac{3}{4} \times 0.9H = 0.675H$

Distance of centre of gravity G from the apex, $OG = \frac{3}{4}H = 0.75\,H$

For stable equilibrium, the metacentre (M) should be *above* G or may *coincide* with G.

i.e. $\quad BG \le BM$ or $OG - OB \le BM \quad$ ...(*i*)

Now, $BM = \dfrac{I}{V}$

where, I = Moment of inertia of the circular section about the liquid level

$$= \frac{\pi r^4}{4} = \frac{\pi \times h^4 \tan^4\alpha}{4}$$

and, V = Volume of liquid displaced

$$= \frac{1}{3}\pi h^3 \tan^2\alpha$$

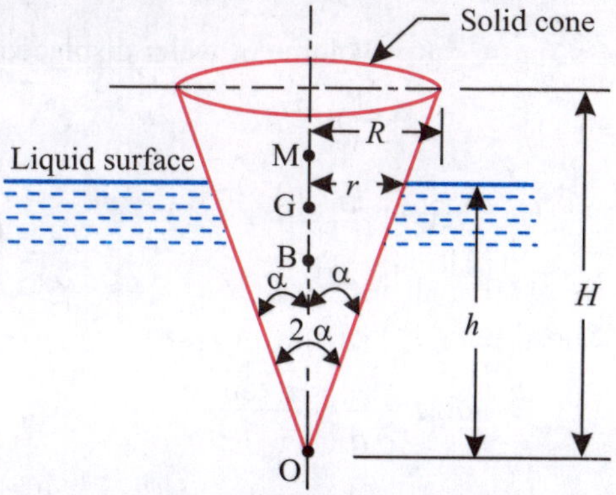

Fig. 4.25

Substituting various values in (*i*), we get:

$$0.75\,H - 0.675\,H \le \frac{\left(\dfrac{\pi h^4 \tan^4\alpha}{4}\right)}{\left(\dfrac{1}{3}\pi h^3 \tan^2\alpha\right)} \quad \text{or} \quad 0.75\,H \le \frac{h^4\tan^4\alpha}{4} \times \frac{3}{\pi h^3 \tan^2\alpha}$$

or, $\quad 0.075\,H \le 0.75\,h\tan^2\alpha$

or, $\quad 0.075\,H \le 0.75 \times (0.9\,H)\tan^2\alpha \quad (\because\ h = 0.9\,H)$

or $\tan^2 \alpha \geq \dfrac{0.75}{0.75 \times 0.9} \geq 0.111$

or $\tan \alpha \geq 0.333$ or $\alpha \geq 18° 24'$

∴ Least apex angle, 2α = **36° 48′ (Ans.)**

Example 4.25. *A cone of specific gravity S, is floating in water with its apex downwards. It has a radius R and vertical height H. Show that for stable equilibrium of cone,*

(i) $Sec^2 \alpha \dfrac{H}{h}$ *(ii)* $H < \left[\dfrac{R^2 S^{1/3}}{1 - S^{1/3}}\right]^{1/2}$

where, h is the depth of immersion and α is the half apex angle.

Solution. Radius of the cone = R; Height of the cone = H;

Sp. gravity of the cone = S

Let, h = Depth of immersion, 2α = apex angle,

r = Radius of cone at the water surface, O = apex of the cone,

G = Centre of gravity of the cone,

B = Centre of buoyancy, and

M = Position of metacentre.

Then, $OG = 3/4\, H$; $OB = 3/4\, h$

(i) $Sec^2 \alpha \dfrac{H}{h}$:

Now, $BM = \dfrac{I}{V}$

where, I = Moment of inertia

$= \dfrac{\pi r^4}{4}$, and

V = Volume of water displaced

$= \dfrac{1}{3} \pi r^2 h$

$$BM = \frac{\pi r^4 / 4}{\frac{1}{3}\pi r^2 h} = \frac{3}{4} \times \frac{r^2}{h}$$

Substituting $r = h \tan \alpha$, we get:

$$BM = \frac{3}{4} \times \frac{h^2 \tan^2 \alpha}{h}$$

$$= \frac{3}{4} h \tan^2 \alpha \quad \left(\because \frac{r}{h} = \tan \alpha\right)$$

$$OM = OB + BM = \frac{3}{4} h + \frac{3}{4} h \tan^2 \alpha$$

$$= \frac{3}{4} h (1 + \tan^2 \alpha) = \frac{3}{4} h \sec^2 \alpha$$

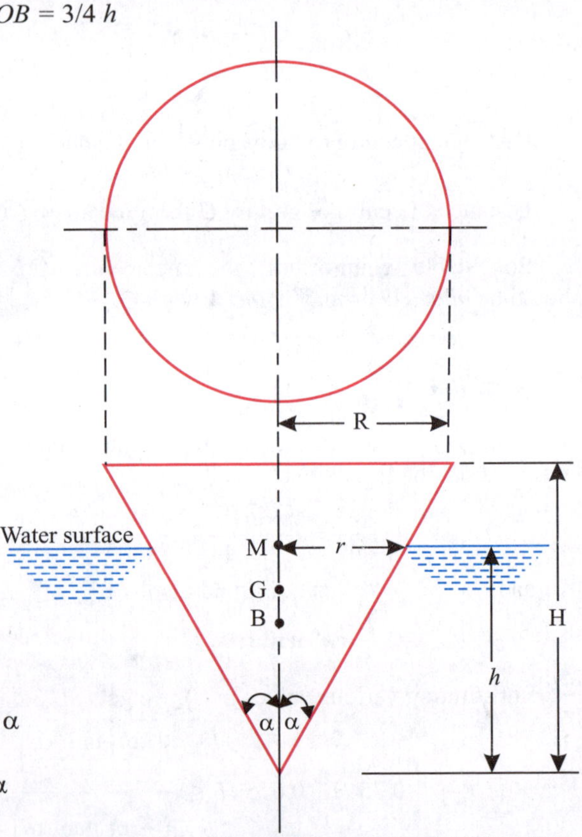

Fig. 4.26

For stable equilibrium:

$BM > BG$ or $OM > OG$

$= \dfrac{3}{4} h \sec^2 \alpha > \dfrac{3}{4} H$ or $Sec^2 \alpha > \dfrac{H}{h}$ ...**Proved (Ans.)**

(ii) $\mathbf{H < \left(\frac{R^2 S^{1/3}}{1 - S^{1/3}}\right)^{1/2}}$ **:**

As per principle of floatation:

$$\text{Weight of cone} = \text{weight of water displaced}$$

or, $$\frac{1}{3}\pi R^2 H \times w_c = \frac{1}{3}\pi r^2 h \times w$$

(where w_c and w are the specific weights of cone material and water respectively).

Substituting, $R = H \tan\alpha$, and $r = h \tan\alpha$, we get:

$$\frac{1}{3}\pi H^2 \tan^2\alpha \times H \times w_c = \frac{1}{3}\pi h^2 \tan^2\alpha \times h \times w$$

$$H^3 \tan^2\alpha \times S = h^3 \tan^2\alpha \qquad \left(\because \frac{w_c}{w} = S\right)$$

or, $$h^3 = H^3 S \text{ or } h = H.S^{1/3}$$

(where, S is the sp. gravity of cone material).

From the relations $\text{Sec}^2\alpha > \frac{H}{h}$ and $h = H.S^{1/3}$ (derived above), we have $\text{Sec}^2\alpha > \frac{1}{S^{1/3}}$

or, $$(1 + \tan^2\alpha) > \frac{1}{S^{1/3}} \quad \text{or} \quad \tan^2\alpha > \frac{1}{S^{1/3}} - 1 \quad \text{or} \quad \tan^2\alpha > \frac{1 - S^{1/3}}{S^{1/3}}$$

Substituting, $\tan\alpha = \frac{R}{H}$, we get $\frac{R^2}{H^2} > \frac{1 - S^{1/3}}{S^{1/3}}$

or, $$\frac{H^2}{R^2} < \frac{S^{1/3}}{1 - S^{1/3}} \quad \text{or} \quad H^2 < \frac{R^2 S^{1/3}}{1 - S^{1/3}}$$

or, $$H < \left(\frac{R^2 S^{1/3}}{1 - S^{1/3}}\right)^{1/2}$$ ...**Proved (Ans.)**

Example 4.26. *A solid cone (S = 0.8) diameter 36 cm and height 30 cm floats with its vertex downwards in water as shown is fig. 4.27. Is this cone in stable equilibrium?*

Solution. *Given:* $D = 36$ cm, $H = 30$ cm; $S = 0.8$

Let, θ = Semivertex angle,

Then, $\tan\theta = \frac{18}{30} = 0.6$

or, $\theta = \tan^{-1}(0.6) = 30.96°$

Diameter of the cone at water surface,

$$d = 2y \tan\theta \quad \left(\because \frac{d/2}{h} = \tan\theta\right)$$

Weight of cone = Weight of water displaced

$$\frac{1}{3} \times \pi \left(\frac{D}{2}\right)^2 \times H \times (w \times S) = \frac{1}{3}\pi \left(\frac{d}{2}\right)^2 \times h \times w$$

$$\therefore \quad D^2 HS = d^2 y$$

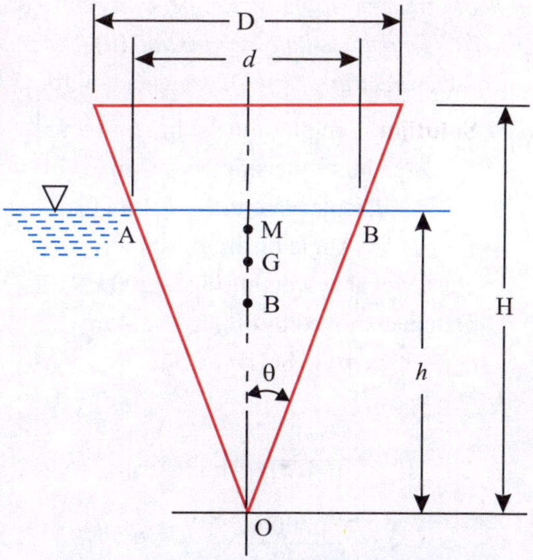

Fig. 4.27

$$= (2h \tan \theta)^2 \times h = 4h^3 \tan^2 \theta$$

$$= 4h^3 \left(\frac{D}{2H}\right)^2 \qquad \left(\because \frac{D/2}{H} = \tan\theta\right)$$

or, $$h^3 = H^3 S$$

or, $$h = HS^{1/3}$$

$$= 30 \times (0.8)^{1/3} = 27.85 \text{ cm}$$

If B is the centre of buoyancy,

$$OB = \frac{3}{4}h = \frac{3}{4} \times 27.85 = 20.89 \text{ cm}$$

$$OG = \frac{3}{4}H = \frac{3}{4} \times 30 = 22.5 \text{ cm}$$

Now, $$d = 2h \tan \theta = 2\times 27.85 \times 0.6 = 33.42 \text{ cm}$$

$$BM = \frac{I}{V} = \frac{(\pi d^4)/64}{\frac{1}{3}\pi\left(\frac{d}{2}\right)^2 \times h} = \frac{3}{16}\left(\frac{d^2}{h}\right)$$

$$= \frac{3}{16} \times \frac{(33.42)^2}{27.85} = 7.52 \text{ cm}$$

$$OM = OB + BM$$

$$= 20.89 + 7.52 = 28.41 \text{ cm}$$

$$OG = 22.5 \text{ cm}$$

$$MG = OM - OG = 28.41 - 22.5 = 5.91 \text{ cm}$$

i.e., M is above G by 5.91 cm

Hence the cone is under **stable equilibrium. (Ans.)**

Example 4.27. *A ship 63 m long and 9 m broad has a displacement of 16000 kN. When a weight of 200 kN is moved across the deck through a distance of 5.4 m, the ship is tilted through 5°. The second moment of area of the water line section about its fore–and–oft axis is 75 per cent of that of circumscribing rectangle, and centre of buoyancy is 2.1m below the water line. Determine.*

(i) The metacentric height, and (ii) The position of centre of gravity of ship.

Take specific weight of sea water = 10.25 kN/m³

Solution. Length of the ship, $l = 63$ m

Breadth of the ship, $b = 9$ m

Displacement, $W = 16000$ kN

Angle of tilt, $\theta = 5°$

Movable weight, $W_1 = 200$ kN

Distance moved by W_1, $z = 5.4$ m

***(i)* Metacentric height, GM:**

We know,

$$GM = \frac{W_1 z}{W \tan\theta} \quad \text{(Eqn. 4.2)}$$

$$= \frac{200 \times 5.4}{16000 \times \tan 5°} = 0.77 \text{ m}$$

i.e. $GM =$ **0.77 m (Ans.)**

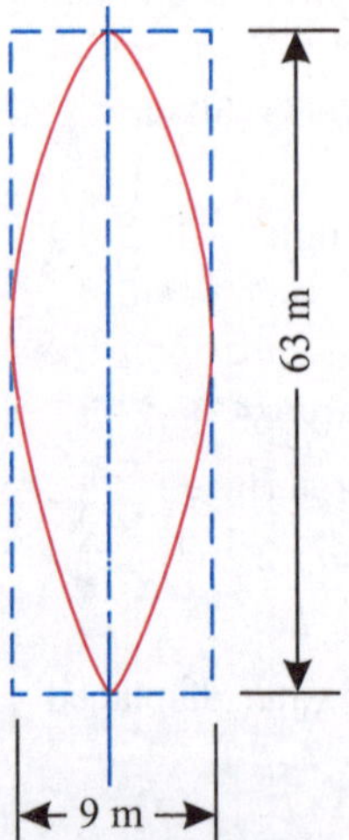

Fig. 4.28

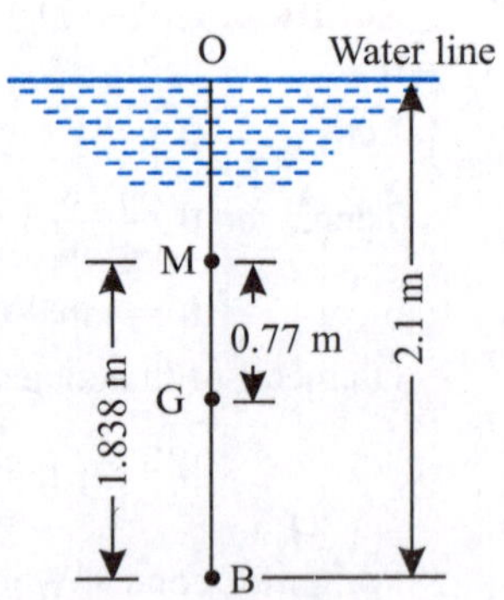

Fig. 4.29

(*ii*) The position of centre of gravity of the ship:

Distance between the metacentre M and the centre of buoyancy is given by: $BM = \frac{I}{V}$

where, I = Second moment of area of the water line section

$$= 0.75 \times \left(\frac{63 \times 9^3}{12}\right) = 2870\ m^4$$

and, V = Volume of water displaced by the vessel

$$= \frac{\text{Weight of the vessel}}{\text{Specific weight of vessel}} = \frac{16000}{10.25} = 1561\ \text{m}^3$$

$$\therefore \quad BM = \frac{2870}{1561} = 1.838\ \text{m}$$

Now, $OG = OM + MG = (OB - MB) + MG$

$= (2.1 - 1.838) + 0.77 = 1.032$ m

i.e. OG = **1.032 m** (below the water line) **(Ans.)**

4.6. OSCILLATION (ROLLING OF A FLOATING BODY

It has been observed that whenever a body floating in a liquid is given a small angular displacement, it starts oscillating about its metacentre M (see Fig. 4.30) in the same manner as a pendulum oscillates about its point of suspension.

Let, W = Weight of floating body,

θ = Angle (in radians) through which the body is depressed,

α = Angular acceleration of the body in rad/s^2,

T = Time of rolling (*i.e.* one complete oscillation) in seconds,

k = Radius of gyration about G, and

I = Moment of inertia of the body about its centre of gravity G

$= \frac{W}{g} k^2$

GM = Metacentric height of the body.

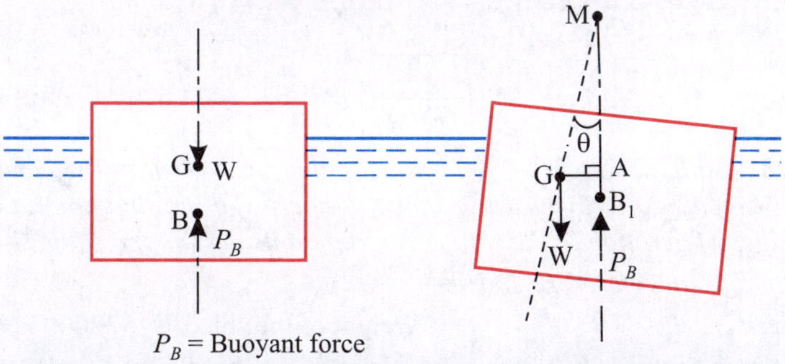

Fig. 4.30

When the force which has caused angular displacement is removed the only force acting on the body is due to the restoring couple due to the weight W of the body and the force of buoyancy P_B.

$\therefore$ *Restoring couple* $= W \times GA$

$= W \times GM \tan\theta$ ...(*i*)

$= W \,.\, GM \,.\, \theta$

[assuming θ to be small (tan θ = θ)]

Angular acceleration of the body, $\alpha = -\dfrac{d^2\theta}{dt^2}$

– ve sign indicates that the force is acting in such a way that it tends to *decrease* the angle θ.

Also, Inertia torque = Moment of inertia × Angular acceleration

$$= I.\alpha = -\frac{W}{g}k^2 \times \frac{d^2\theta}{dt^2} \quad ...(ii)$$

Equating (*i*) and (*ii*), we get:

$$W.\,GM.\theta = -\frac{W}{g}k^2 \times \frac{d^2\theta}{dt^2} \quad \text{or} \quad \frac{W}{g}k^2\frac{d^2\theta}{dt^2} + W.GM.\theta = 0$$

Dividing both sides by *W*, we get:

$$\frac{k^2}{g} \times \frac{d^2\theta}{dt^2} + GM.\theta = 0$$

Again, dividing both sides by $\dfrac{k^2}{g}$, we get:

$$\frac{d^2\theta}{dt^2} + \frac{GM.g\theta}{k^2} = 0$$

The above equation is a differential equation of second degree, whose solution is:

$$Q = C_1 \sin\left[\sqrt{\frac{GM.g}{k^2}} \times t\right] + C_2 \cos\left[\sqrt{\frac{GM.g}{k^2}} \times t\right] \quad ...(iii)$$

where, C_1 and C_2 are constants of integration.

The values of C_1 and C_2 are obtained from the following boundary conditions:

1. At $t = 0, \theta = 0$

   $C_2 = 0$ [By substitution of $t = 0, \theta = 0$ in (*iii*)]

2. At $t = \dfrac{T}{2}, \theta = 0$

   $$\therefore\ 0 = C_1 \sin\left[\sqrt{\frac{GM.g}{k^2}} \times \frac{T}{2}\right]$$

Since C_1 cannot be equal to zero, therefore:

$$\sin\left[\sqrt{\frac{GM.g}{k^2}} \times \frac{T}{2}\right] = 0 \quad \text{or} \quad \sqrt{\frac{GM.g}{k^2}} \times \frac{T}{2} = \pi \quad (\because \sin\pi = 0)$$

or,

$$T = 2\pi\sqrt{\frac{k^2}{GM.g}} \quad ...(4.4)$$

Example 4.28. *A ship of weight 32000 kN is floating in sea water. The centre of buoyancy is 1.6 meters below its centre of gravity. The moment of inertia of the ship area at the water level is 8320 m⁴. If the radius of gyration of the ship is 3.2 m, find its period of rolling.*

Take sp. weight of sea water = 10.1 kN/m³

Solution. *Given:*

Weight of the ship, $W = 32000$ kN

Distance between centre of buoyancy and centre of gravity, $BG = 1.6$ m

Moment of inertia, $I = 8320\ \text{m}^4$

Radius of gyration, $k = 3.2$ m

Period of rolling of the ship, *T*:

Volume of sea water displaced,

$$V = \frac{\text{Weight}}{\text{Specific weight of sea water}} = \frac{32000}{10.1} = 3168.3\,\text{m}^3$$

Using the relation, $BM = \frac{I}{V} = \frac{8320}{3168.3} = 2.626\,\text{m}$

Also, the metacentric height, $GM = BM - BG = 2.626 - 1.6 = 1.026$ m

Now using the relation, $T = 2\pi\sqrt{\frac{k^2}{GM.g}} = 2\pi\sqrt{\frac{3.2^2}{1.028 \times 9.81}}$ = **6.33 s (Ans.)**

HIGHLIGHTS

1. The tendency for an immersed body to be lifted up in the fluid due to an upward force opposite to action of gravity is known as *buoyancy.*
2. The floating bodies may have the following types of equilibrium:
   (*i*) Stable equilibrium,
   (*ii*) Unstable equilibrium, and
   (*iii*) Neutral equilibrium.
3. The *metacentre* is defined as a point of intersection of the axis of body passing through *c.g.* (*G*) and original centre of buoyancy (*B*), and a vertical line passing through the centre of buoyancy (B_1) of the titled position of the body.
4. The distance between the centre of gravity (*G*) of a floating body and the metacentre (*M*) is called *metacentric height.*
5. The metacentric height (*GM*) by experimental method is given by:

$$GM = \frac{W_1.z.l}{W.d}\left(= \frac{W_1.z}{W \tan\theta}\right)$$

where, W_1 = Known weight,

z = Distance through which W_1 is shifted across the axis of the tilt,

l = Displacement of the plumb bob, and

θ = Angle of tilt $\left(\tan\theta = \frac{d}{l}\right)$.

6. Time of rolling, $T = 2\pi\sqrt{\frac{k^2}{GM.g}}$

where, k = Radius of gyration about *c.g.* (*G*), and

GM = Metacentric height of the body.

OBJECTIVE TYPE QUESTIONS

Choose the Correct Answer.

1. The tendency for an immersed body to be lifted up in the fluid, due to an upward force opposite to the action of gravity is known as
   (*a*) buoyancy
   (*b*) centre of buoyancy
   (*c*) buoyant force
   (*d*) none of the above.
2. The magnitude of the buoyant force can be determined by
   (*a*) Newton's second law of motion
   (*b*) Archimedes' principle
   (*c*) Principle of moments
   (*d*) none of the above.
3. When a body is immersed in a fluid, partially or completely, the force of buoyancy is equal to

(a) the weight of the body
(b) the weight of the fluid displaced by the body
(c) the weight of the volume of the fluid equal to the volume of body
(d) none of the above.

4. The point of application of the force of buoyancy on the body is known as
(a) centre of gravity
(b) centre of buoyancy
(c) metacentre
(d) none of the above.

5. "When a body is immersed in a fluid either wholly or partially, it is buoyed or lifted up by a force which is equal to the weight of fluid displaced by the body".
This principle was enunciated by
(a) Archimedes (b) Newton
(c) Pascal (d) Kirchhoff.

6. A floating body is in stable equilibrium when
(a) the metacentre is below its centre of gravity
(b) the metacentre is above its centre of gravity
(c) the metacentric height is zero.
(d) its centre of gravity is below the centre of buoyancy.

7. An ice-cube is floating in glass of water. As the cube melts the water level
(a) remain constant (b) falls
(c) rises (d) none of the above.

8. If the position of metacentre M remains lower than c.g. of the body, G, the body will remain in a state of
(a) stable equilibrium
(b) unstable equilibrium
(c) neutral equilibrium
(a) any of the above.

9. Metacentric height can be determined by
(a) only analytical method
(b) only experimental method
(c) both (a) and (b)
(d) none of the above.

10. If a body does not return to its original position from the slightly displaced angular position and heels farther away, when given a small angular displacement; such an equilibrium is called
(a) stable equilibrium
(b) unstable equilibrium
(c) neutral equilibrium
(d) any of the above.

ANSWERS

1. (a)	**2.** (b)	**3.** (b)	**4.** (b)	**5.** (a)	**6.** (b)
7. (b)	**8.** (b)	**9.** (c)	**10.** (b).		

THEORETICAL QUESTIONS

1. What is buoyancy?
2. What is centre of buoyancy?
3. Explain briefly the following types of equilibrium of floating bodies:
(i) Stable equilibrium,
(ii) Unstable equilibrium, and
(iii) Neutral equilibrium.
4. Define and explain the following terms:
(i) Metacentre, and
(ii) Metacentric height.
5. Derive an expression for calculating time of rolling of a floating body.

UNSOLVED EXAMPLES

1. A wooden block of width 2.5 m, depth 1.5 m and length 6 m is floating horizontally in water. If the specific gravity of block is 0.65 find:
(i) The volume of water displaced, and
(ii) Position of centre of buoyancy.
[Ans. (i) 14.625 m^3; (ii) 0.4875 m from base]

2. A wooden block 4 m × 1 m × 0.5 m is floating in water. Its specific gravity is 0.76. Find the volume of concrete, of sp. gravity 2.5, that may be placed on the block which will immerse (i) the block completely in water, and (ii) the block and concrete completely in water.
[Ans. (i) 0.2 m^3; (ii) 0.33 m^3]

3. The following data relate to a pontoon floating in sea water:
Length = 5 m, width 3 m, height = 1.2 m
The depth of immersion = 0.8 m
Centre of gravity above the bottom of pontoon = 0.6 m

Sp. gravity of sea water = 1.025

Determine the metacentric height.

[Ans. 0.7375 m]

4. A wooden block 1 m × 0.4 m × 0.3 m is floating in water. If its specific gravity is 0.8 determine the metacentric height for tilt about its longitudinal axis. **[Ans. 0.0255 m]**

5. The following data relate to a body (consisting of cylindrical upper portion and curved lower portion) floating in water:

Diameter of cylindrical upper portion = 2 m

Depth of upper portion = 1.2 m

Volume of water displaced by the curved lower portion = 0.4 m^3

Centre of buoyancy of the lower portion below the top of the cylinder = 1.3 m

Centre of bouyancy of whole body below the top of cylinder = 0.8 m

Total displacement of water = 25.5 kN. Determine the metacentric height of the body.

[Ans. GM = 0.182 m]

6. A wooden block of size 2 m × 1 m × 0.8 m is floating in water. If its specific gravity is 0.7 find its metacentric height. **[Ans. 0.0288 m]**

7. A wooden cylinder of sp. gravity 0.6 and diameter 0.4 m is required to float in an oil of sp. gravity 0.8. Find the maximum length of the cylinder in order that it may float vertically in water. **[Ans. 0.326 m]**

8. A solid cylinder 4 m in diameter and 4 m high is floating in water with its axis vertical. If its specific gravity is 0.6, find the metacentric height. Also state whether the equilibrium is stable or unstable. **[Ans. *GM* = – 0.3833 m, unstable]**

9. A weight 100 kN is moved through a distance of 9 metres across the deck of pontoon of 7500 kN displacement, floating in water. This makes a pendulum 2.7 metres long, move through 0.13 m horizontally. Calculate the metacentric height of the pontoon. **[Ans. 2.5 m]**

10. The following data correspond to a ship floating in a sea water:

Weight of the ship = 4000 tonnes

Centre of buoyancy below its *c.g.* (*G*) = 2 m

Moment of inertia of the ship area at the water level = 10400 m^4

Radius of gyration of the ship = 4 m

Sp. gravity of sea water = 1.03

Find the period of rolling of the ship.

[Ans. 9.73 s]

11. Find the density of a metallic body which floats at the interface of mercury of specific gravity 13.6 and water such that 40 per cent of its volumes is submerged in mercury and 60 per cent in water. **[Ans. 59.25 kN/m^3]**

12. A hollow wooden cylinder of specific gravity 0.56 has an outer diameter of 600 mm and an inner diameter of 300 mm. It is required to float in oil of specific gravity 0.85. Calculate:

(*i*) The maximum length/height of the cylinder so that it shall be stable when floating with its axis vertical.

(*ii*) The depth to which it will sink.

[Ans. (*i*) 0.5 m (*ii*) 0.3295 m]

13. A pontoon measuring 10 m (length) × 7.5 m (width) × 2.5 m (depth) weighing 800 kN floats in sea water. On its upper deck it carries a boiler 5 m in diameter and weighing 500 kN. The centre of gravity of each unit coincides with geometrical centre of the arrangement and lies in the same vertical line.

Calculate the metacentric height.

Take the specific weight of sea water = 10 kN/m^3 **[Ans. 0.875 m]**

14. A log of wood 0.6 m in diameter and 5 m long is floating in river water. If the specific gravity of log is 0.7 what is depth of the wooden log in water ? **[Ans. 0.395 m]**

15. A wooden cylinder (specific gravity = 0.6) of circular cross-section is required to float in oil of specific gravity 0.8. If l and d are the length and diameter of the cylinder respectively, find the $\frac{l}{d}$ ratio for the cylinder to float with its longitudinal axis vertical in oil.

[Ans. $\frac{l}{d} < 0.816$]

16. A solid cone (sp. gravity of material = 0.7) floats in water with its apex downward. Determine the least apex angle of cone for equilibrium.

[Ans. 39°7′]

17. A cylindrical buoy weighing 20 kN is floating in ocean. The buoy has a diameter of 2 m and height 2.5 m. Can the buoy float with its axis vertical? If now, a chain may be tied at the bottom of the buoy and anchored, what is the tension required in the anchor chain to make the buoy stable? Take sp. gravity of sea water = 1.025.

[Ans. 12.9 kN]

18. A vessel has a length of 60 m, width 12 m and a displacement of 19620 kN. When a weight of 294.3 kN is rolled off transversely across the deck through a distance of 6.5 m, the vessel tilts through 5°. The second moment of area of the water line section about its fore-and-oft axis is 75 per cent of that of the circumscribing rectangle. The centre of buoyancy is 2.75 m below the water line. Find:

(*i*) The metacentric height;

(*ii*) The position of centre of gravity of the vessel.

Take specific weight of sea water = 10.104 kN/m^3

[Ans. (*i*) 1.1145 m (*ii*) 0.53 m below water surface]

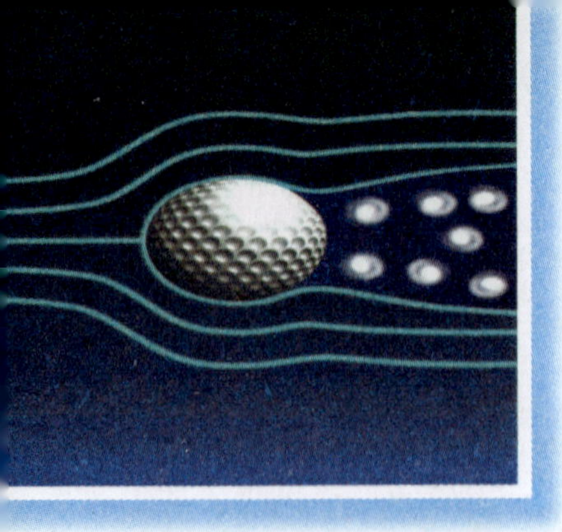

Chapter 5

FLUID KINEMATICS

5.1. INTRODUCTION

Fluid kinematics may be defined as follows:

Fluid kinematics *is a branch of 'Fluid mechanics' which deals with the study of velocity and acceleration of the particles of fluids in motion and their distribution in space without considering any force or energy involved.* The motion of fluid can be described fully by an expression describing the location of a fluid particle in space at different times thus enabling determination of the magnitude and direction of velocity and acceleration in the flow field at any instant of time.

In the chapter we shall deal with the conception of fluid flow in general.

5.2. DESCRIPTION OF FLUID MOTION

The motion of fluid particles may be described by the following methods:

1. Langrangian method.
2. Eulerian method.

5.2.1. Langrangian Method

In this method, the observer *concentrates on the movement of a single particle*. The path taken by the particle and the changes in its velocity and acceleration are studied.

In the Cartesian system, the position of the fluid particle in space (x, y, z) at any time t from its position (a, b, c) at time $t = 0$ shall be given as:

$$x = f_1 (a, b, c, t)$$
$$y = f_2 (a, b, c, t)$$
$$z = f_3 (a, b, c, t) \quad ...(5.1)$$

The velocity and acceleration components (obtained by taking derivatives with respect to time) are given by:

Velocity components:

$$\left.\begin{aligned} u &= \frac{\partial x}{\partial t} \\ v &= \frac{\partial y}{\partial t} \\ w &= \frac{\partial z}{\partial t} \end{aligned}\right\} \quad \text{...(5.2)}$$

Acceleration components :

$$\left.\begin{aligned} a_x &= \frac{\partial^2 x}{\partial t^2} \\ a_y &= \frac{\partial^2 y}{\partial t^2} \\ a_z &= \frac{\partial^2 z}{\partial t^2} \end{aligned}\right\} \quad \text{...(5.3)}$$

At any point, the resultant velocity or acceleration shall be the *resultant* of three components of the respective quantity at that point.

$\therefore$ Resultant velocity, $V = \sqrt{u^2 + v^2 + w^2}$ ...(5.4)

Acceleration, $a = \sqrt{a_x^2 + a_y^2 + a_z^2}$ ...(5.5)

Similarly, other quantities like pressure, density, etc. can be found.

This method entails the following *shortcomings:*

1. Cumbersome and complex.
2. The equations of motion are very difficult to solve and the motion is hard to understand.

5.2.2. Eulerian Method

In Eulerian method, the observer *concentrates on a point in the fluid system*. Velocity, acceleration and other characteristics of the fluid at that particular point are studied.

This method is almost *exclusively used* in fluid mechanics, especially because of its *mathematical simplicity*. In fluid mechanics, we are not concerned with the motion of each particle, but we study the general state of motion at various points in the fluid system.

The velocities at any point (x, y, z) can be written as:

$$\left.\begin{aligned} u &= f_1(x, y, z, t) \\ v &= f_2(x, y, z, t) \\ w &= f_3(x, y, z, t) \end{aligned}\right\} \quad \text{...(5.6)}$$

The components of acceleration of the fluid particle can be worked out by partial differentiation as follows:

$$du = \frac{\partial u}{\partial x}.dx + \frac{\partial u}{\partial y}.dy + \frac{\partial u}{\partial z}.dz + \frac{\partial u}{\partial t}.dt$$

$$a_x = \frac{\partial u}{dt} = \left(\frac{\partial u}{\partial x}.\frac{dx}{dt} + \frac{\partial u}{\partial y}.\frac{dy}{dt} + \frac{\partial u}{dz}.\frac{dz}{dt}\right) + \frac{\partial u}{\partial t}.\frac{dt}{dt}$$

But, $\dfrac{dx}{dt} = u, \dfrac{dy}{dt} = v, \dfrac{dz}{dt} = w$

$$\therefore \quad \left.\begin{aligned} a_x = \frac{du}{dt} &= \left(u\frac{\partial u}{\partial x} + v\frac{\partial u}{\partial y} + w\frac{\partial u}{\partial z}\right) + \frac{\partial u}{\partial t} \\ \text{Similarly,} \quad a_y = \frac{dv}{dt} &= \left(u\frac{\partial v}{\partial x} + v\frac{\partial v}{\partial y} + w\frac{\partial v}{\partial z}\right) + \frac{\partial v}{\partial t} \\ a_z = \frac{dw}{dt} &= \left(u\frac{\partial w}{\partial x} + v\frac{\partial w}{\partial y} + w\frac{\partial w}{\partial z}\right) + \frac{\partial w}{\partial t} \end{aligned}\right\} \quad ...(5.7)$$

Now, resultant velocity: $V = \sqrt{u^2 + v^2 + w^2}$ ...(5.8)

Resultant acceleration, $a = \sqrt{a_x^2 + a_y^2 + a_z^2}$ ...(5.9)

In *vector notation*:

Velocity vector: $V = ui + vj + wk$ ...(5.10)

Acceleration vector: $a = \frac{dV}{dt} = \left(u\frac{\partial V}{\partial x} + v\frac{\partial V}{\partial y} + w\frac{\partial V}{\partial z}\right) + \frac{\partial V}{\partial t}$ ...(5.11)

$a = a_x i + a_y j + a_z k$ ...(5.12)

and, $|V| = \sqrt{u^2 + v^2 + w^2}$ ...(5.13)

$|a| = \sqrt{a_x^2 + a_y^2 + a_z^2}$ ...(5.14)

Vectorially,

$$a = (V.\nabla)\,V + \frac{\partial V}{\partial t} \quad ...(5.15)$$

The velocity, in general, is a function of space(s) and time (t) *i.e.*

$V = f(x, y, z, t)$

or, $V = f(s, t)$

and, The acceleration,

$$a = \frac{dV}{dt} = \frac{\partial V}{\partial s}\cdot\frac{ds}{dt} + \frac{\partial V}{\partial t}$$

$$\therefore \quad a = V\frac{\partial V}{\partial s} + \frac{\partial V}{\partial t} \quad ...(5.16)$$

Thus the acceleration consists of the two parts:

(*i*) $V\frac{\partial V}{\partial s}$: This part is due to change in position or movement and is called **convective acceleration.**

$\therefore$ Convective acceleration $= V\frac{\partial V}{\partial s} = \frac{1}{2}\frac{\partial (V)^2}{\partial s}$ ...(5.17)

= terms in the parenthesis of Eqn. (5.7)

(*ii*) $\frac{\partial V}{\partial t}$: This part is with respect to time at a given location and is called **local** (or *temporal*) **acceleration**.

$\therefore$ Local acceleration $= \frac{\partial V}{\partial t}$ ...(5.18)

$$= \frac{\partial u}{\partial t}, \frac{\partial v}{\partial t}, \frac{\partial w}{\partial t} \text{ in Eqn. (5.7)}$$

Tangential and normal acceleration: Refer to Fig. 5.1.

When the motion is curvilinear eqn. 5.16 gives the *tangential acceleration*. A particle moving in a curved path will always have a normal acceleration $a_n = \frac{V^2}{r}$ towards the centre of the curved path (r being the radius of the path), though its tangential acceleration (a_s) may be zero as in the case of uniform circular motion.

For motion along a curved path, in general,

$$a = a_s + a_n$$

$$= \left(V\frac{\partial V}{\partial s} + \frac{\partial V}{\partial t} + \frac{V^2}{r} \right) \quad ...(5.19)$$

5.3. TYPES OF FLUID FLOW

Fluids may be *classified* as follows:

1. Steady and unsteady flows
2. Uniform and non-uniform flows
3. One, two and three dimensional flows
4. Rotational and irrotational flows
5. Laminar and turbulent flows
6. Compressible and incompressible flows.

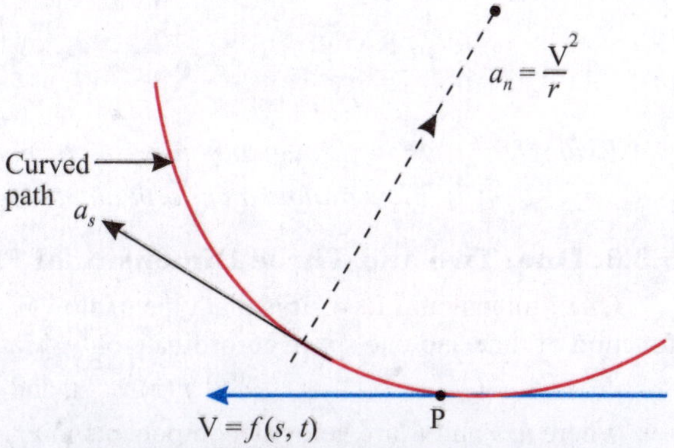

Fig. 5.1. Tangential and normal acceleration.

5.3.1. Steady and Unsteady Flows

Steady flow. The type of flow in which the fluid characteristics like velocity, pressure, density, etc. at a point *do not change* with time is called *steady flow*. Mathematically, we have:

$$\left(\frac{\partial u}{\partial t}\right)_{x_0, y_0, z_0} = 0; \left(\frac{\partial v}{\partial t}\right)_{x_0, y_0, z_0} = 0; \left(\frac{\partial w}{\partial t}\right)_{x_0, y_0, z_0} = 0$$

$$\left(\frac{\partial p}{\partial t}\right)_{x_0, y_0, z_0} = 0; \left(\frac{\partial \rho}{\partial t}\right)_{x_0, y_0, z_0} = 0; \text{ and so on}$$

where (x_0, y_0, z_0) is a fixed point in a fluid field where these variables are being measured *w.r.t.* time.

Example. *Flow through a prismatic or non-prismatic conduit at a constant flow rate Q* m^3/s *is steady.*

(A prismatic conduit has a constant size shape and has a velocity equation in the form $u = ax^2 + bx + c$, which is independent of time t).

Unsteady flow. It is that type of flow in which the velocity, pressure or density at a point *change* w.r.t. time. Mathematically, we have:

$$\left(\frac{\partial u}{\partial t}\right)_{x_0, y_0, z_0} \neq 0; \left(\frac{\partial v}{\partial t}\right)_{x_0, y_0, z_0} \neq 0; \left(\frac{\partial w}{\partial t}\right)_{x_0, y_0, z_0} \neq 0$$

$$\left(\frac{\partial p}{\partial t}\right)_{x_0, y_0, z_0} \neq 0; \left(\frac{\partial \rho}{\partial t}\right)_{x_0, y_0, z_0} \neq 0; \text{ and so on}$$

Example. *The flow in a pipe whose valve is being opened or closed gradually (velocity equation is in the form* $u = ax^2 + bxt$ *).*

5.3.2. Uniform and Non-uniform Flows

Uniform flow. The type of flow, in which the velocity at any given time *does not change* with respect to space is called *uniform flow*. Mathematically, we have:

$$\left(\frac{\partial V}{\partial s}\right)_{t\,=\,\text{constant}} = 0$$

where, ∂V = Change in velocity, and

∂s = Displacement in any direction.

Example. *Flow through a straight prismatic conduit (i.e. flow through a straight pipe of constant diameter).*

Non-uniform flow. It is that type of flow in which the velocity at any given time *changes* with respect to space. Mathematically,

$$\left(\frac{\partial V}{\partial s}\right)_{t\,=\,\text{constant}} \neq 0$$

Example. (*i*) *Flow through a non-prismatic conduit.*

(*ii*) *Flow around a uniform diameter pipe-bend or a canal bend.*

5.3.3. One, Two and Three Dimensional Flows

One dimensional flow. It is that type of flow in which the flow parameter such as velocity is a function of time and one space co-ordinate only. Mathematically:

$$u = f(x), v = 0 \text{ and } w = 0$$

where u, v and w are velocity components in x, y and z directions respectively.

Example. *Flow in a pipe where average flow parameters are considered for analysis.*

Two dimensional flow. The flow in which the velocity is a function of time and two rectangular space coordinates is called *two dimensional flow*. Mathematically:

$$u = f_1(x, y)$$
$$v = f_2(x, y)$$
$$w = 0$$

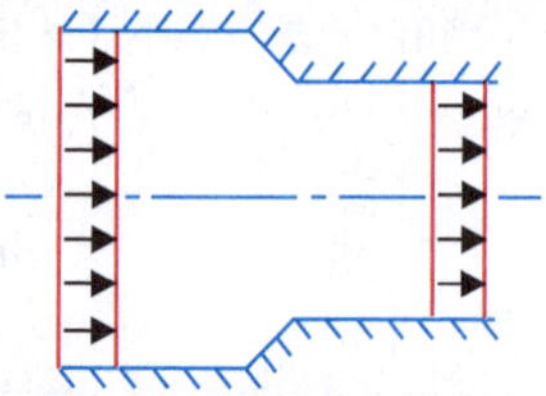

Fig. 5.2. One dimensional flow.

Examples. (*i*) *Flow between parallel plates of infinite extent.*

(*ii*) *Flow in the main stream of a wide river.*

Three dimensional flow. It is that type of flow in which the velocity is a function of time and three mutually perpendicular directions. Mathematically:

$$u = f_1(x, y, z)$$
$$v = f_2(x, y, z)$$
$$w = f_3(x, y, z)$$

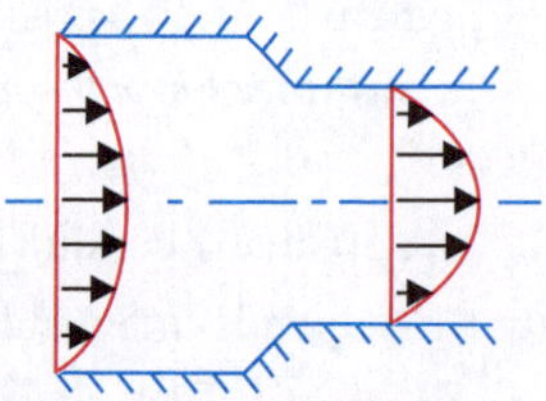

Fig. 5.3. Two dimensional flow.

Examples. (*i*) *Flow in a converging or diverging pipe or channel.*

(*ii*) *Flow in a prismatic open channel in which the width and the water depth are of the same order of magnitude.*

5.3.4. Rotational and Irrotational Flows

Rotational flow. A flow is said to be *rotational* if the fluid particles while moving in the direction of flow *rotate* about their mass centres. *Flow near the solid boundaries is rotational.*

Example. *Motion of liquid in a rotating tank.*

Irrotational flow. A flow is said to be *irrotational* if the fluid particles while moving in the direction of flow *do not rotate* about their mass centres. Flow outside the boundary layer is generally considered irrotational.

Example. *Flow above a drain hole of a stationary tank or a wash basin.*

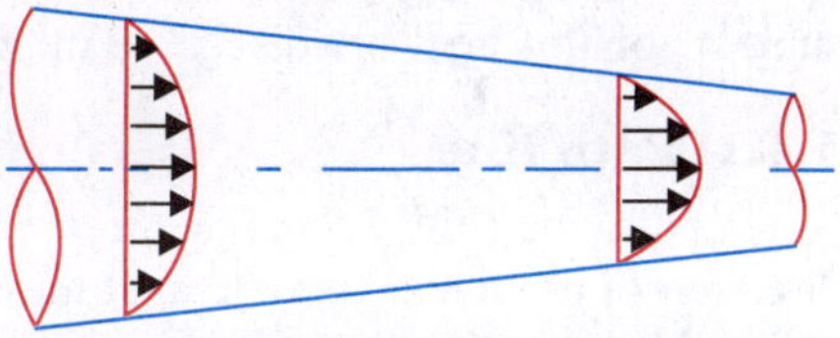

Fig. 5.4. Thee dimensional flow.

Note. If the flow is irrotational as well as steady, it is known as ***Potential flow***.

5.3.5. Laminar and Turbulent Flows

Laminar flow. A laminar flow is one in which *paths taken by the individual particles do not cross one another and move along well defined paths* (Fig. 5.5), This type of flow is also called *stream-line flow or viscous flow.*

Examples. (*i*) *Flow through a capillary tube.*

(*ii*) *Flow of blood in veins and arteries.*

(*iii*) *Ground water flow.*

Turbulent flow. A turbulent flow is that flow in which fluid *particles move in a zig zag way* (Fig. 5.6).

Example. *High velocity flow in a conduit of large size. Nearly all fluid flow problems encountered in engineering practice have a turbulent character.*

Fig. 5.5. Laminar flow.

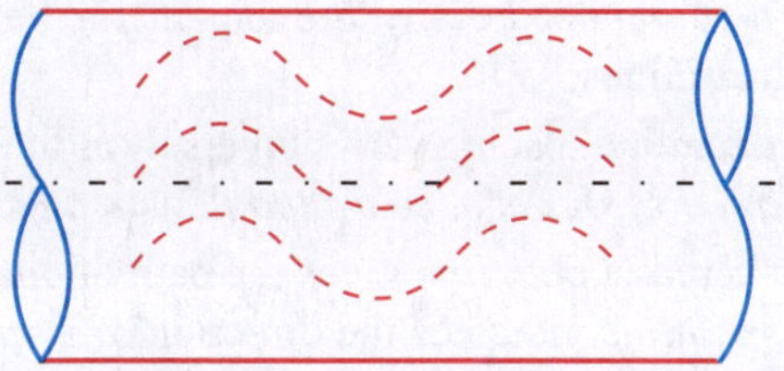

Fig. 5.6. Turbulent flow.

Laminar and turbulent flows are characterised on the basis of Reynolds number (refer to chapter 10).

For Reynolds number (Re) < 2000 ... flow in pipes is *laminar*.

For Reynolds number (Re) > 4000 ... flow in pipes is *turbulent*

For Re between 2000 and 4000 ... flow in pipes *may be laminar or turbulent*.

5.3.6. Compressible and Incompressible Flows

Compressible flow. It is that type of flow in which the *density* (ρ) *of the fluid changes* from point to point (or in other words *density is not constant for this flow*).

Mathematically: $\rho \neq$ constant.

Example. *Flow of gases through orifices, nozzles, gas turbines, etc.*

Incompressible flow. *It is that type of flow in which density is constant for the fluid flow. Liquids are generally considered flowing incompressibly.*

Mathematically: $\rho =$ constant.

Example. *Subsonic aerodynamics.*

5.4. TYPES OF FLOW LINES

Whenever a fluid is in motion, its innumerable particles move along certain lines depending upon the conditions of flow. Although flow lines are of several types, yet some important from subject point of view are discussed in the following subarticles.

5.4.1. Path line

A path line (Fig. 5.7) is the *path followed by a fluid particle in motion*. A path line shows the direction of particular particle as it moves ahead. In general, this is the curve in three-dimensional space. However, if the conditions are such that the flow is two-dimensional the curve becomes two-dimensional.

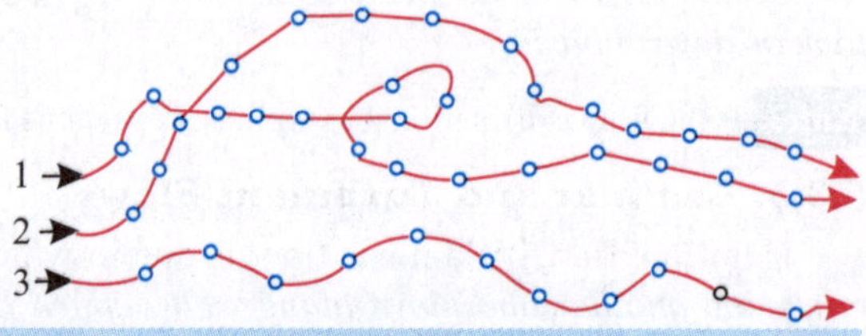

Fig. 5.7. Path lines.

5.4.2. Stream line

A ***stream line*** way be defined as *an imaginary line within the flow so that the tangent at any point on it indicates the velocity at that point.*

Equation of a stream line in a three-dimensional flow is given as:

$$\frac{dx}{u} = \frac{dy}{v} = \frac{dz}{w} \quad ...(5.20)$$

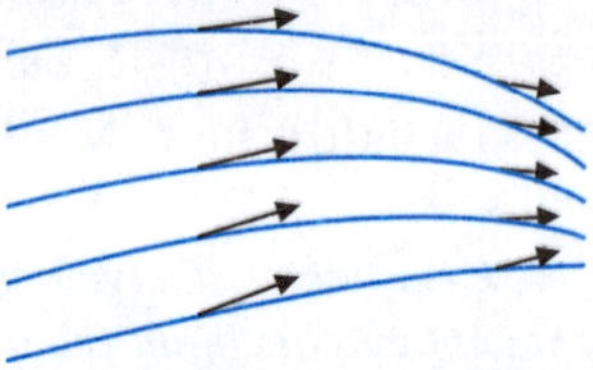

Fig. 5.8. Stream line.

Following *points* about streamlines are *worth noting*:

1. A streamline cannot intersect itself, nor two streamlines can cross.
2. There cannot be any movement of the fluid mass across the streamlines.
3. Streamline spacing varies inversely as the velocity; *converging of streamlines in any particular direction shows accelerated flow in that direction.*
4. Whereas a *path line* gives the path of *one particular particle* at successive instants of time, *a streamline* indicates the direction of a *number of particles* at the same instant.
5. The series of streamlines represent the flow pattern at an instant.

- In *steady flow*, the pattern of streamlines remains invariant with time. The path lines and streamlines will then be identical.
- In *unsteady flow*, the pattern of streamlines may or may not remain the same at the next instant.

5.4.3. Stream Tube

A ***stream tube*** is a *fluid mass bounded by a group of streamlines*. The contents of a stream tube are known as '*current filament*'.

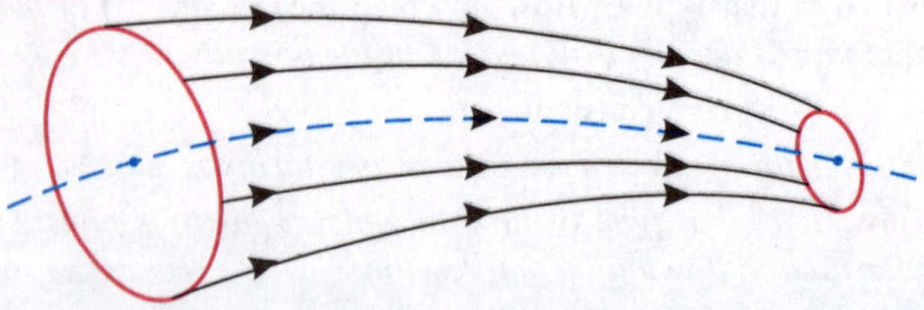

Fig. 5.9. Stream tube.

Examples of stream tube: *Pipes* and *nozzles*.

Following *points* about stream tube are *worth noting*:

1. The stream tube has finite dimensions.
2. As there is no flow perpendicular to stream lines, therefore, there is no flow across the surface (called *stream surface*) of the stream tube. The stream surface functions as if it were a solid wall.
3. The shape of a stream tube changes from one instant to another because of change in the position of streamlines.

5.4.4. Streak Line

The ***streak line*** *is a curve which gives an instantaneous picture of the location of the fluid particles, which have passed through a given point.*

Examples. (*i*) *The path taken by smoke coming out of chimney* (Fig. 5.10).

(*ii*) *In an experimental work to trace the motion of fluid particles, a coloured dye may be injected into the flowing fluid and the resulting coloured filament lines at a given location give the streak lines* (Fig 5.11).

Note. In case of a *steady flow* there is no geometrical distinction between the streamlines, path lines and streak lines; they are coincident if they originate at the same point. For an *unsteady flow* (*e.g.* a person giving out whiff of smoke from a cigarette), the path, streak and stream lines are all different.

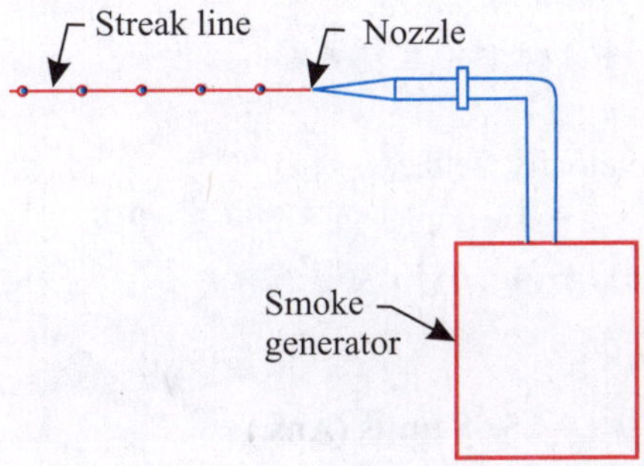

Fig. 5.10. Streak line of smoke issuing from a nozzle.

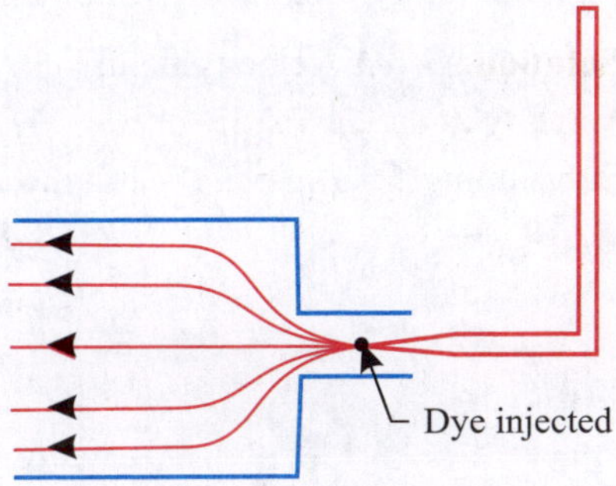

Fig. 5.11. Streak lines at $t = t_1$.

Example 5.1. *In a fluid, the velocity field is given by*

$$V = (3x + 2y)\,i + (2z + 3x^2)\,j + (2t - 3z)\,k$$

Determine:

(*i*) *The velocity components u, v, w at any point in the flow field;*

(*ii*) *The speed at point* (*1, 1, 1*);

(*iii*) *The speed at time t* = 2s *at point* (*0, 0, 2*).

Also classify the velocity field as steady, or unsteady, uniform or non-uniform and one, two or three dimensional.

Solution. *Given*: Velocity field, $V = (3x + 2y)\,i + (2z + 3x^2)\,j + (2t - 3z)\,k$

(*i*) Velocity components:

The velocity components are:

$$\mathbf{u = 3x + 2y,\ v = (2z + 3x^2),\ w = (2t - 3z)} \quad \textbf{(Ans.)}$$

(*ii*) Speed at point (1, 1, 1), $V_{(1,1,1)}$:

Substituting $x = 1, y = 1, z = 1$ in the expressions for u, v and w, we have:

$$u = (3 + 2) = 5,\ v = (2 + 3) = 5,\ w = (2t - 3)$$

$$\therefore \quad V^2 = u^2 + v^2 + w^2$$

$$= 5^2 + 5^2 + (2t - 3)^2$$
$$= 25 + 25 + 4t^2 - 12t + 9$$
$$= 4t^2 - 12t + 59$$

$$\therefore \quad \mathbf{V}_{(1,1,1)} = \sqrt{4t^2 - 12t + 59} \ \textbf{(Ans.)}$$

(*iii*) Speed at $t = 2s$ at point (0, 0, 2):

Substituting $t = 2, x = 0, y = 0, z = 2$ in the expressions for u, v and w, we get:

$$u = 0,\ v = (2 \times 2 + 0) = 4,\ w = (2 \times 2 - 3 \times 2) = -2$$

$$\therefore \quad V^2 = u^2 + v^2 + w^2 = 0 + 4^2 + (-2)^2 = 20$$

or, $$\mathbf{V}_{(0,0,2)} = \sqrt{20} = \mathbf{4.472\ units\ (Ans.)}$$

Velocity field, type:

(*i*) Since V at given (x, y, z) *depends on* t it is **unsteady flow, (Ans.)**

(*ii*) Since at given t velocity changes in the X direction it is **non-uniform flow. (Ans.)**

(*iii*) Since V depends on x, y, z it is three **dimensional flow. (Ans.)**

Example 5.2 *Velocity for a two dimensional flow field is given by*

$$V = (3 + 2xy + 4t^2)\, i + (xy^2 + 3t)\, j$$

Find the velocity and acceleration at a point (1,2) *after 2 sec.*

Solution. *Given*: Velocity field: $V = (3 + 2xy + 4t^2)\, i + (xy^2 + 3t)\, j$

Velocity at (1, 2), $\mathbf{V}_{(1,2)}$:

Substituting $x = 1, y = 2, t = 2$ in the expression of velocity field, we get:

$$V = (3 + 2 \times 1 \times 2 + 4 \times 2^2)\, i + (1 \times 2^2 + 3 \times 2)\, j$$
$$= (3 + 4 + 16)\, i + (4 + 6)\, j$$
$$= 23i + 10j$$

$$\therefore \quad V_{(1,2)} = \sqrt{23^2 + 10^2} = \mathbf{25.08\ units\ (Ans.)}$$

Acceleration at point (1, 2), $\mathbf{a}_{(1,2)}$:

We know that: $$a = \frac{dV}{dt} = \left(u\frac{\partial V}{\partial x} + v\frac{\partial V}{\partial y}\right) + \frac{\partial V}{\partial t}$$

Also, $$V = (3 + 2xy + 4t^2)i + (xy^2 + 3t)\, j \quad ...(Given)$$

$$\therefore \quad \frac{\partial V}{\partial x} = 2yi + y^2 j,$$

$$\frac{\partial V}{\partial y} = 2xi + 2xyj, \text{ and}$$

$$\frac{\partial V}{\partial t} = 8\, ti + 3\, j$$

$$\therefore \quad a = (3 + 2xy + 4t^2)(2yi + y^2 j) + (xy^2 + 3t)(2xi + 2xyj) + (8ti + 3j)$$
$$(\because u = 3 + 2xy + 4t^2 \text{ and } v = xy^2 + 3t)$$

Substituting the values, we get:

$$a = (3 + 2 \times 1 \times 2 + 4 \times 2^2)(2 \times 2i + 2^2 j) + (1 \times 2^2 + 3 \times 2)$$
$$(2 \times 1i + 2 \times 1 \times 2j) + (8 \times 2 \times i + 3\, j)$$
$$= (3 + 4 + 16)(4i + 4j) + (4 + 6)(2i + 4j) + (16i + 3j)$$

$$= 23(4i + 4j) + 10\,(2i + 4j) + (16i + 3j)$$
$$= 92i + 92j + 20i + 40j + 16i + 3j$$
$$= 128\,i + 135\,j$$
$$\therefore \quad a_{(1,2)} = \sqrt{128^2 + 135^2} = \textbf{186.03 units (Ans.)}$$

Example 5.3. *Find the velocity and acceleration at a point (1, 2, 3) after 1 sec. for a three-dimensional flow given by u = yz + t, v = xz – t, w = xy m/s.*

Solution. *Given*: Three-dimensional flow field is given as:

$$u = yz + t,\ v = xz - t,\ w = xy \text{ m/s}$$

Velocity at a point 1, 2, 3 $V_{(1, 2, 3)}$:

Velocity at a point (1, 2, 3) after 1s is calculated as follows:

$$u = yz + t = 2 \times 3 + 1 = 7 \text{ m/s},\ v = xz - t = 1 \times 3 - 1 = 2 \text{ m/s and}$$
$$w = xy = 1 \times 2 = 2 \text{ m/s.}$$
$$\therefore \quad V_{(1,2,3)} = 7i + 2j + 2k$$
$$= \sqrt{7^2 + 2^2 + 2^2} = 7.55 \text{ m/s}$$

Hence, $V_{(1, 2, 3)} = \textbf{7.55 m/s (Ans.)}$

Acceleration, $a_{(1,2,3)}$:

Now, $V = (yz + t)i + (xz - t)\,j + xy\,k$ m/s

Acceleration, $$a = \frac{dV}{dt} = \left(u\frac{\partial V}{\partial x} + v\frac{\partial V}{\partial y} + w\frac{\partial V}{\partial z}\right) + \frac{\partial V}{\partial t}$$

$$a = (yz + t)\,(zi + yk) + (xz - t)\,(zi + xk) + xy\,(yi + xj) + (1i - 1j)$$
$$\therefore \quad a_{(1, 2, 3)} = 7(3j + 2k) + 2(3i + 1k) + 2\,(2i + 1j) + (1i - 1j)$$
$$= (21j + 14k) + (6i + 2k) + (4i + 2j) + (1i - 1j)$$
$$= (10i + 23j + 16k) + (1i - 1j)$$

The *convective acceleration components are*: (10, 23, 16) m/s^2

The *local acceleration components are*: (1, –1) m/s^2 along *x* and *y* directions.

The total acceleration of fluid particles at the points (1, 2, 3) is given by:

$$a_{(1, 2, 3)} = \sqrt{(10 + 1)^2 + [23 + (-1)]^2 + 16^2}$$
$$= \sqrt{11^2 + 22^2 + 16^2} = 29.34 \text{ m/s}^2$$

Hence, $a_{(1, 2, 3)} = \textbf{29.34 m/s}^2$ **(Ans.)**

Example 5.4. *The velocity along the centreline of a nozzle of length l is given by*

$$V = 2t\left(1 - \frac{x}{2l}\right)^2$$

where V = velocity in m/s, t = time in seconds from commencement of flow, x = distance from inlet to nozzle. Calculate the local acceleration, convective acceleration and the total acceleration when t = 6s, x = 1m and l = 1.6 m.

Solution. The velocity along the centreline of a nozzle, $V = 2t\left(1 - \frac{x}{2l}\right)^2$ ...(*Given*)

Local acceleration:

$$\text{Local acceleration} = \frac{\partial V}{\partial t} = 2\left(1 - \frac{x}{2l}\right)^2$$

At $t = 6\,s$ and $x = 1m$,

$$\frac{\partial V}{\partial t} = 2\left(1 - \frac{1}{2 \times 1.6}\right)^2 = \mathbf{0.945\ m/s^2\ (Ans.)}$$

Convective acceleration:

$$\text{Convective acceleration} = V\frac{\partial V}{\partial x}$$

$$= 2t\left(1 - \frac{x}{2l}\right)^2 \times 2t \times 2\left(1 - \frac{x}{2l}\right)\left(-\frac{1}{2l}\right)$$

$$= -\frac{4t^2}{l}\left(1 - \frac{x}{2l}\right)^3$$

At $t = 6s$ and $x = 1$ m,

$$\text{Convective acceleration} = -\frac{4 \times 6^2}{1.6}\left(1 - \frac{1}{2 \times 1.6}\right)^3$$

$$= \mathbf{-29.24\ m/s^2\ (Ans.)}$$

Total acceleration:

$$\text{Total acceleration} = \text{Local acceleration} + \text{convective acceleration}$$

$$= 0.945 + (-29.24) = \mathbf{-28.295\ m/s^2\ (Ans.)}$$

Example 5.5. *A conical pipe diverges uniformly from 100 mm to 200 m diameter over a length of 1 m. Determine the local and convective acceleration at the mid-section assuming*

(i) *Rate of flow is 0.12 m^3/s and it remains constant;*

(ii) *Rate of flow varies uniformly from 0.12 m^3/s to 0.24 m^3/s in 5 sec., at t = 2 sec.*

Solution. *Given:*

Diameter at the inlet, $D_1 = 0.1m.$

Diameter at the outlet, $D_2 = 0.2\ m$

Length, $l = 1\ m$

Diameter at any distance x metres from the inlet,

$$D = D_1 + \left(\frac{D_2 - D_1}{l}\right) \times x$$

$$= 0.1 + \left(\frac{0.2 - 0.1}{1}\right) \times x$$

$$= 0.1 + 0.1x = 0.1\,(1 + x)$$

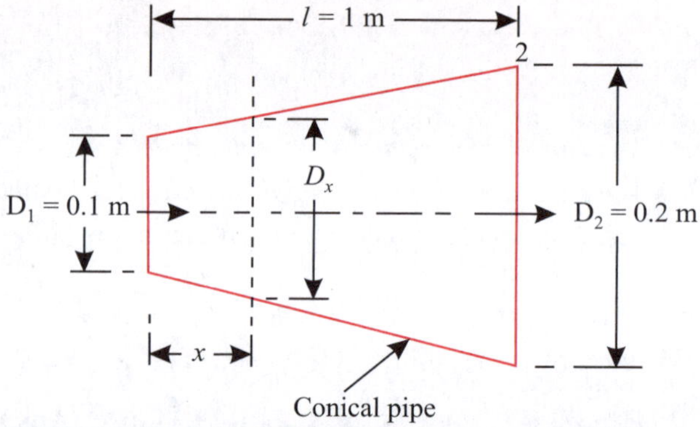

Fig. 5.12

$\therefore$ Cross-sectional area,

$$A_x = \frac{\pi}{4} \times D_x^2 = \frac{\pi}{4}\{0.1(1 + x)\}^2$$

$$= 0.00785\,(1 + x)^2$$

$$\text{Velocity of flow, } u_x\,(= u) = \frac{Q}{A_x} = \frac{Q}{0.00785(1 + x)^2}$$

$$\text{Velocity gradient, } \frac{\partial u}{\partial x} = \frac{\partial}{\partial x}\left[\frac{Q}{0.00785\,(1 + x)^2}\right] = \frac{-2Q}{0.00785(1 + x)^3}$$

(*i*) Discharge Q = 0.12 m^3/s = constant (at any section)

$$\text{Acceleration} = \frac{\partial u}{\partial t} + u\frac{\partial u}{\partial x}$$

(a) The local acceleration:

The local acceleration at *mid-section*

$$= \frac{\partial u}{\partial t} = 0, \text{ since the flow is } \textit{steady} \textbf{ (Ans.)}$$

(b) The convective acceleration:

The convective acceleration,

$$a_x = u\frac{\partial u}{\partial x} = \frac{Q}{0.00785\,(1+x)^2} \times \frac{-2Q}{0.00785\,(1+x)^3}$$

$$= \frac{-2Q^2}{(0.00785)^2\,(1+x)^5}$$

∴ The convective acceleration at *mid-section*,

$$(a_x)_{x=0.5\text{m}} = \frac{-2 \times (0.12)^2}{(0.00785)^2\;(1+0.5)^5}$$

$$= \mathbf{-61{\cdot}5\ m/s^2\ (Ans.)}$$

The –*ve* sign indicates *decrease in velocity* along the direction of flow (this is so as the cross-sectional area is increasing)

(ii) Discharge Q varies w.r.t. time:

The discharge Q varies from 0.12 m^3/s to 0.24 m^3/s in 5 s.

At t = 2 s, the discharge is,

$$Q = 0.12 + \frac{0.24 - 0.12}{5} \times 2 = 0.168\ \text{m}^3/\text{s}$$

(a) The local acceleration:

The local acceleration at *mid-section*,

$$= \frac{\partial u}{\partial t} = \frac{\partial}{\partial t}\left[\frac{Q}{0.00785\,(1+x)^2}\right] = \frac{1}{0.00785\,(1+x)^2} \times \frac{\partial Q}{\partial t}$$

$$= \frac{1}{0.00785(1+0.5)^2} \times \left(\frac{0.168 - 0.12}{2}\right)$$

[since discharge changes 0.12 m^3/s to 0.168 m^3/s in 2*s*]

$$= \mathbf{1.36\ m/s^2\ (Ans.)}$$

(b) The convective acceleration:

The convective acceleration at *mid-section*,

$$(a_x)_{x=0.5} = \frac{-2Q^2}{(0.00785)^2\,(1+x)^5} = \frac{-2 \times 0.168^2}{(0.00785)^2\;(1+0.5)^5}$$

$$= \mathbf{-120{\cdot}6\ m/s^2\ (Ans.)}$$

Total acceleration along the main flow is,

$$(a)_{\text{total}} = (a)_{\text{local}} + (a)_{\text{conv.}}$$

$$= 1.36 - 120.6 = \mathbf{-119.24\ m/s^2\ (Ans.)}$$

Example 5.6. *At entry to the pump intake the velocity is found to vary inversely as the square of radial distance from inlet to suction pipe. The velocity was found to be 0.6 m/s at a radial distance of 1.5 m. Calculate the acceleration of flow at radial distances of 0.5 m, 1.0 m and 1.5 m from the inlet. Consider the streamlines to be radial.*

Solution. The distribution of velocity is given by the relation:

$$v = \frac{C}{r^2} \quad ...(1)$$

(where, r = radial distance from the intake)

Since the streamlines are *radial,* normal acceleration is *zero.*

$$\text{Acceleration, } a = \frac{\partial v}{\partial t} + v\frac{\partial v}{\partial s}$$

But $\frac{\partial v}{\partial t}$ = 0... the flow being steady (as the velocity is dependent only on the radial distance from intake).

$$\therefore \quad a = v.\frac{\partial v}{\partial s}$$

Also, $v = \frac{C}{r^2}$ and $\frac{\partial v}{\partial s} = \frac{\partial v}{\partial r}$

(since, r is measured along the streamline)

and, $\frac{\partial v}{\partial r} = -\frac{2C}{r^3}$

$$\therefore \quad a = v\frac{\partial v}{\partial s} = \frac{C}{r^2}\left(-\frac{2C}{r^3}\right) = -\frac{2C^2}{r^5} \quad ...(2)$$

At r = 1.5 m, v = 0.6 m/s

Substituting these values in eqn. (1), we get:

$$0.6 = \frac{C}{1.5^2} \quad \text{or} \quad C = 1.35 \text{ m}^3\text{/s}$$

Substituting, now, C = 1.35 in eqn. (2), we have:

$$a = -\frac{2 \times 1.35^2}{r^5} = -\frac{3.645}{r^5}$$

(*i*) Acceleration of flow at r = 0.5 m = $-\frac{3.645}{(0.5)^5}$ = **–116.64 m/s² (Ans.)**

(*ii*) Acceleration of flow at r = 1.0 m = $-\frac{3.645}{(1.0)^5}$ **– 3.645 m/s² (Ans.)**

(*iii*) Acceleration of flow at r = 1.5 m = $-\frac{3.645}{(1.5)^5}$ = **– 0.48 m/s² (Ans.)**

Example 5.7. *For a three-dimensional flow the velocity distribution is given by $u = -x$, $v = 3 - y$ and $w = 3 - z$. What is the equation of a streamline passing through (1,2,2)?*

Solution. *Given:* $u = -x$, $v = 3 - y$, $w = 3 - z$ ...(velocity distribution)

Equation of a streamline passing through (1, 2, 2):

The streamlines are defined by:

$$\frac{dx}{u} = \frac{dy}{v} = \frac{dz}{w}$$

Substituting for u, v and w, we get:

$$\frac{dx}{-x} = \frac{dy}{3-y} = \frac{dz}{3-z}$$
$$(i) \qquad (ii) \qquad (iii)$$

Considering the expressions (i) and (ii) and integrating, we get:

$$\int \frac{dx}{-x} = \int \frac{dz}{(3-y)}$$

$$= -\log_e x = -\log_e (3-y) + C_1$$

(where, C_1 = constant of integration).

Since the streamline passes through $x = 1, y = 2$ $\quad \therefore C_1 = 0$

$\therefore \qquad (x)^{-1} = (3-y)^{-1} \quad$ or $\quad x = (3-y) \qquad$ ...(1)

Considering the expressions (i) and (iii), and integrating, we get:

$$\int \frac{dx}{-x} = \int \frac{dy}{3-z}$$

or, $\qquad -\log_e x = -\log (3-z) + C_2$

(where C_2 = constant of integration)

Since the streamline passes through $x = 1, z = 2$ $\quad \therefore C_2 = 0$

$\therefore \qquad x^{-1} = (3-z)^{-1}$

or, $\qquad x = (3-z) \qquad$ ...(2)

From (1) and (2), the equation of the streamline passing through (1, 2, 2) is given as:

$$\mathbf{x = (3-y) = (3-z)} \text{ (Ans.)}$$

Example 5.8. *Obtain the equation to the streamlines for the velocity field given as:*

$$V = 2x^3 i - 6x^2 yj$$

Solution. *Given*: Velocity field, $V = 2x^3 i - 6x^2 yj$

Here, $\qquad u = 2x^3, v = 6x^2 y$

The streamlines in two dimensions are defined by:

$$\frac{dx}{u} = \frac{dy}{v}$$

or, $\qquad \dfrac{dy}{dx} = \dfrac{v}{u} = \dfrac{-6x^2 y}{2x^3} = \dfrac{-3y}{x}$

Separating the variables, we have:

$$\frac{dy}{y} = \frac{-3dx}{x}$$

Integrating, we get:

$$ln(y) = -3ln(x) + C_1$$

or, $\qquad ln(y) + 3\,ln(x) = C_1$

or, $\qquad yx^3 = \mathbf{C}$ **(Ans.)**

Note. The streamlines in the first quadrant can be sketched by giving different values for the constant $C\left(y = \dfrac{C}{x^3}\right)$.

Example 5.9. *For the following flows find the equation of the streamline passing through* (2,2):

(*i*) $V = 3xi - 3yj$

(*ii*) $V = -y^2 i - 6xj$

Solution. Equation of the streamline passing through (2, 2):

(*i*)
$$V = 3xi - 3yj$$
$$u = 3x \text{ and } v = -3y$$

The equation of a streamline in two-dimensional flow is given as:

$$\frac{dx}{u} = \frac{dy}{v}$$

or,
$$\frac{dx}{3x} = -\frac{dy}{3y}$$

Integrating both sides, we get:

$$\int \frac{dy}{3x} = -\int \frac{dy}{3y}$$

$$\frac{1}{3} ln(x) = -\frac{1}{3} ln(y) + \frac{1}{3} ln(C)$$

where, C is constant.

or,
$$ln\,(xy) = ln\,(C) \quad \text{or} \quad xy = C$$

For the streamline passing through (2, 2),

$$C = 2 \times 2 = 4$$

Hence, the required streamline equation is: $\boldsymbol{xy = 4}$ **(Ans.)**

(*ii*)
$$V = -y^2 i - 6xj$$
$$u = -y^2 \text{ and } v = -6x$$

$$-\frac{dx}{y^2} = -\frac{dy}{6x} \quad \text{or} \quad 6x\,dx = y^2 dy$$

$$\int 6x\,dx = \int y^2\,dy$$

or,
$$\frac{6x^2}{2} = \frac{y^3}{3} + C$$

or,
$$3x^2 - \frac{y^3}{3} = C$$

Putting, $x = 2$, $y = 2$, we get:

$$3 \times (2)^2 - \frac{(2)^3}{3} = C \quad \text{or} \quad C = \frac{28}{3}$$

Hence the equations of the required streamline is:

$$3x^2 - \frac{y^3}{3} = \frac{28}{3}$$

$$\boldsymbol{9x^2 - y^3 = 28} \textbf{ (Ans.)}$$

Example 5.10. *The velocity vector in a flow is given by:*

$$V = 3xi + 4yj - 7zk$$

Determine the equation passing through a point L(1, 2, 3).

Solution. The equation of a streamline is given as:

$$\frac{dx}{u} = \frac{dy}{v} = \frac{dz}{w}$$

Here, $u = 3x, v = 4y,$ and $w = -7z$

$$\therefore \quad \frac{dx}{3x} = \frac{dy}{4y} = -\frac{dz}{7z}$$

Considering equations involving x and y, on integration we get:

$$\frac{1}{3} ln(x) = \frac{1}{4} ln(y) + ln(C_1') \text{ where } C'_1 = \text{a constant}$$

or, $$y = C_1 x^{4/3} \quad ...(i)$$

where, C_1 is another constant:

Similarly, by considering equations with x and z and on integration, we have:

$$\frac{1}{3} ln(x) = -\frac{1}{7} ln(z) + ln(C_2'), \text{ where } C_2' = \text{ a constant}$$

or, $$z = \frac{C_2}{x^{7/3}} \quad ...(ii)$$

where, C_2 is another constant.

Inserting the coordinates of the point L(1, 2, 3), we get:

From eqn. (*i*) $$C_1 = \frac{y}{(x)^{4/3}} = \frac{2}{(1)^{4/3}} = 2$$

From eqn. (*ii*) $$C_2 = zx^{7/3} = 3 \times (1)^{7/3} = 3$$

Hence, the streamline passing through L is given by:

$$\boldsymbol{y = 2x^{4/3} \text{ and } z = \frac{3}{x^{7/3}}} \textbf{ (Ans.)}$$

5.5. RATE OF FLOW OR DISCHARGE

Rate of flow (or **discharge**) *is defined as* the *quantity of a liquid flowing per second through a section of pipe or a channel.* It is generally denoted by Q. Let us consider a liquid flowing through a pipe.

Let, A = Area of cross-section of the pipe, and

V = Average velocity of the liquid.

$\therefore$ Discharge, Q = Area × average velocity *i.e.,* $Q = A.V$ ...(5.21)

If area is in m^2 and velocity is in m/s, then the discharge,

$$Q = m^2 \times m/s = m^3/s = \text{cumecs.}$$

5.6. CONTINUITY EQUATION

The **continuity equation** *is based on the principle of conservation of mass.* It states as follows:

"If no fluid is added or removed from the pipe in any length then the mass passing across different sections shall be same."

Consider two cross-sections of a pipe as shown in Fig 5.13

Let, A_1 = Area of the pipe at section 1–1,

V_1 = Velocity of the fluid at section 1–1,

ρ_1 = Density of the fluid at section 1–1,

and A_2, V_2, ρ_2 are corresponding values at sections 2–2.

The total quantity of fluid passing through section 1–1= $\rho_1 A_1 V_1$

and, the total quantity of fluid passing through section 2–2 = $\rho_2 A_2 V_2$

From the law of conservation of mass (theorem of continuity), we have:

$$\rho_1 A_1 V_1 = \rho_2 A_2 V_2 \qquad \text{...(5.22)}$$

Eqn. (5.22) is applicable to the compressible as well as incompressible fluids and is called ***Continuity Equation.*** In case of *incompressible fluids,* $\rho_1 = \rho_2$ and the continuity eqn. (5.21) reduces to:

$$A_1 V_1 = A_2 V_2 \qquad \text{...(5.23)}$$

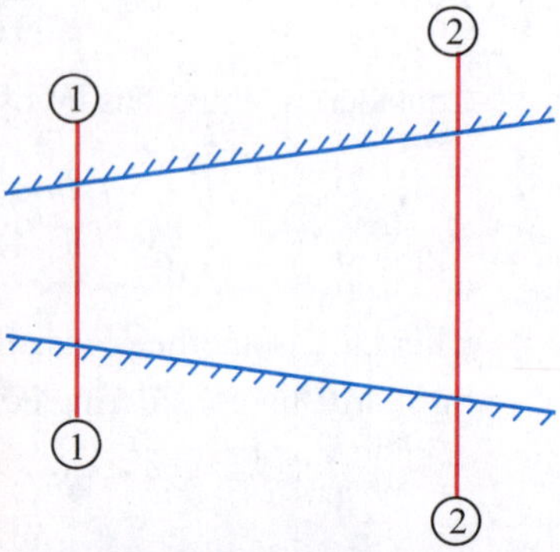

Fig. 5.13. Fluid flow through a pipe.

Example 5.11. *The diameters of a pipe at the sections 1-1and 2-2 are 200 mm and 300 mm respectively. If the velocity of water flowing through the pipe at section 1-1 is 4m/s, find:*

(i) Discharge through the pipe, and

(ii) Velocity of water at section 2-2

Solution. Diameter of the pipe at *section* 1-1,

$$D_1 = 200 \text{ mm} = 0.2 \text{ m}$$

$$\therefore \quad \text{Area, } A_1 = \frac{\pi}{4} D_1^2 = \frac{\pi}{4} \times 0.2^2 = 0.0314 \text{ m}^2$$

$$\text{Velocity, } V_1 = 4 \text{ m/s}$$

Diameter of the pipe at *section* 2-2,

$$D_2 = 300 \text{ mm}$$

$$\therefore \quad \text{Area, } A_2 = \frac{\pi}{4} D_2^2 = \frac{\pi}{4} \times 0.3^2 = 0.0707 \text{ m}^2$$

(*i*) Discharge through the pipe, Q:

Using the relation,

$Q = A_1 V_1$, we have:

$Q = 0.0314 \times 4 = \mathbf{0.1256\ m^3/s}$ **(Ans.)**

(*ii*) Velocity of water at section 2-2, V_2:

Using the relation,

$A_1 V_1 = A_2 V_2$, we have:

$$V_2 = \frac{A_1 V_1}{A_2} = \frac{0.0314 \times 4}{0.0707}$$

$= \mathbf{1.77\ m/s}$ **(Ans.)**

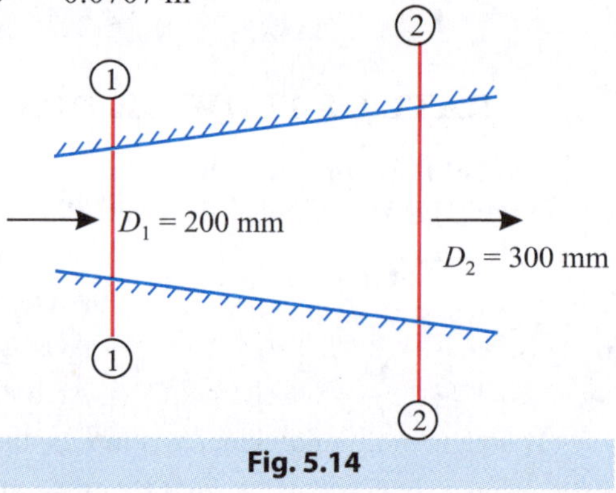

Fig. 5.14

Example 5.12. *A pipe (1) 450 mm in diameter branches into two pipes (2 and 3) of diameters 300 mm and 200 mm respectively as shown in Fig. 5.15. If the average velocity in 450 mm diameter pipe is 3 m/s find:*

(i) Discharge through 450 mm diameter pipe;

(ii) Velocity in 200 mm diameter pipe if the average velocity in 300 mm pipe is 2.5 m/s.

Solution. Diameter, $D_1 = 450 \text{ mm} = 0.45 \text{ m}$

$$\therefore \quad \text{Area, } A_1 = \frac{\pi}{4} \times 0.45^2 = 0.159 \text{ m}^2$$

Velocity, $V_1 = 3$ m/s

Diameter, $D_2 = 300$ mm $= 0.3$ m

$\therefore$ Area, $A_2 = \frac{\pi}{4} \times 0.3^2 = 0.0707$ m^2

Velocity, $V_2 = 2.5$ m/s

Diameter, $D_3 = 200$ mm $= 0.2$ m

Area, $A_3 = \frac{\pi}{4} \times 0.2^2 = 0.0314$ m^2

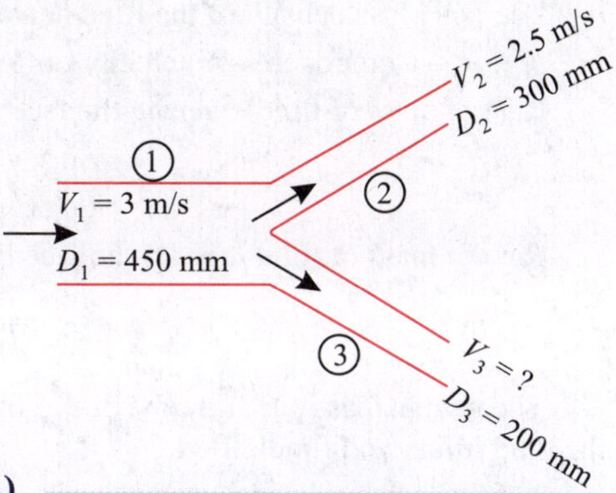

Fig. 5.15

(*i*) Discharge through pipe (1) Q_1:

Using the relation, $Q_1 = A_1V_1 = 0.159 \times 3$

$= \mathbf{0.477}$ **m^3/s (Ans.)**

(*ii*) Velocity in pipe of diameter 200 mm i.e. V_3:

Let Q_1, Q_2 and Q_3 be the discharge in pipes 1, 2 and 3 respectively.

Then, according to continuity equation:

$$Q_1 = Q_2 + Q_3 \quad ...(i)$$

where, $Q_1 = 0.477$ m^3/s (calculated earlier)

and, $Q_2 = A_2V_2 = 0.0707 \times 2.5 = 0.1767$ m^3/s

$\therefore$ $0.477 = 0.1767 + Q_2$ [from eq. (*i*)]

or, $Q_3 = 0.477 - 0.1767 \simeq 0.3$ m^3/s

But, $Q_3 = A_3V_3$

$$\therefore \quad V_3 = \frac{Q_3}{A_3} = \frac{0.3}{0.0314} = 9.55 \text{ m/s}$$

i.e. $V_3 =$ **9.55 m/s (Ans.)**

5.7. CONTINUITY EQUATION IN CARTESIAN CO-ORDINATES

Consider a fluid element (control volume) – parallelopiped with sides *dx*, *dy* and *dz* as shown in Fig. 5.16.

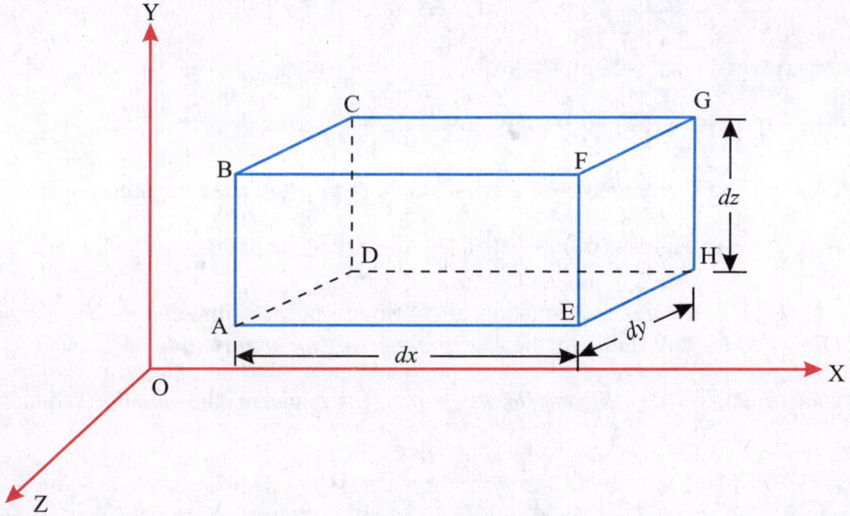

Fig. 5.16. Fluid element in three-dimensional flow.

Let, ρ = Mass density of the fluid at a particular instant;

u, v, w = Components of velocity of flow entering the three faces of the parallelopiped.

Rate of mass of fluid *entering* the face ABCD (*i.e.* fluid *influx*).

$$= \rho \times \text{velocity in } X\text{-direction} \times \text{area of ABCD}$$

$$= \rho\, u dy\, dz \qquad ...(i)$$

Rate of mass of fluid *leaving* the face EFGH (*i.e.* fluid *efflux*).

$$= \rho\, u\, dy\, dz + \frac{\partial}{\partial x}(\rho u\, dy\, dz)\, dx \qquad ...(ii)$$

The gain in mass per unit time due to flow in the X-direction is given by the difference between the fluid influx and fluid efflux.

$\therefore$ Mass accumulated per unit time due to flow in X-direction

$$= \rho u\, dy\, dz - \left[\rho u + \frac{\partial}{\partial x}(\rho u)\, dx\right] dy\, dz$$

$$= -\frac{\partial}{\partial x}(\rho u)\, dx\, dy\, dz \qquad ...(iii)$$

Similarly, the gain in fluid mass per unit time in the parallelopiped due to flow in Y and Z-directions

$$= -\frac{\partial}{\partial y}(\rho v)\, dx\, dy\, dz \ \text{(in Y-direction)} \qquad ...(iv)$$

$$= -\frac{\partial}{\partial z}(\rho w)\, dx\, dy\, dz \ \text{(in Z-direction)} \qquad ...(v)$$

The total (or net) gain in fluid mass per unit for fluid along three co-ordinate axes

$$= -\left[\frac{\partial}{\partial x}(\rho u) + \frac{\partial}{\partial y}(\rho v) + \frac{\partial}{\partial z}(\rho w)\right] dx\, dy\, dz \qquad ...(vi)$$

Rate of change of mass of the parallelopiped (control volume)

$$= \frac{\partial}{\partial t}(\rho\, dx\, dy\, dz) \qquad ...(vii)$$

Equations (*vi*) and (*vii*), we get:

$$-\left[\frac{\partial}{\partial x}(\rho u) + \frac{\partial}{\partial y}(\rho v) + \frac{\partial}{\partial z}(\rho w)\right] dx\, dy\, dz = \frac{\partial}{\partial t}(\rho\, dx\, dy\, dz)$$

Simplification and rearrangement of terms would reduce the above expression to:

$$\frac{\partial}{\partial x}(\rho u) + \frac{\partial}{\partial y}(\rho v) + \frac{\partial}{\partial z}(\rho w) + \frac{\partial \rho}{\partial t} = 0 \qquad ...(5.24)$$

This eqn. (5.24) is the general equation of continuity in three-dimensions and is applicable to *any type of flow* and for any fluid whether *compressible or incompressible*.

For *steady flow* $\left(\frac{\partial \rho}{dt} = 0\right)$ *incompressible fluids* (ρ = constant) the equation reduces to:

$$\frac{\partial u}{\partial x} + \frac{\partial v}{\partial y} + \frac{\partial w}{\partial y} = 0 \qquad ...(5.25)$$

For *two dimensional flow*, eqn. (5.25) reduces to:

$$\frac{\partial u}{\partial x} + \frac{\partial v}{\partial y} = 0 \qquad (\because w = 0)$$

For *one dimensional flow*, say in *X*-direction, eqn. (5.25) takes the form:

$$\frac{\partial u}{\partial x} = 0 \qquad (\because v = 0, w = 0)$$

Integrating with respect to *x*, we get:

$$u = \text{constant} \qquad \text{...(5.26)}$$

If the area of flow is *a* then the rate of flow is

$$Q = a.u = \text{constant for } \textit{steady flow}$$

which is the same eqn. (5.23) and states that if area of flow *a* is constant the velocity of flow *u* will also be constant.

5.8. EQUATION OF CONTINUITY IN POLAR COORDINATES

Consider a fluid element LMST as shown in Fig. 5.17. The sides of the element has the following dimensions.

$$LT = MS = dr;\ LM = rd\theta \text{ and } ST = (r + dr)d\theta$$

Let, V_r = Component of the velocity in the radial direction, and

V_θ = Component of the velocity in the tangential direction.

Further, let thickness of the element perpendicular to the plane of paper be *unity.* As the fluid flows through the element, changes will place in its velocity as well as in the density.

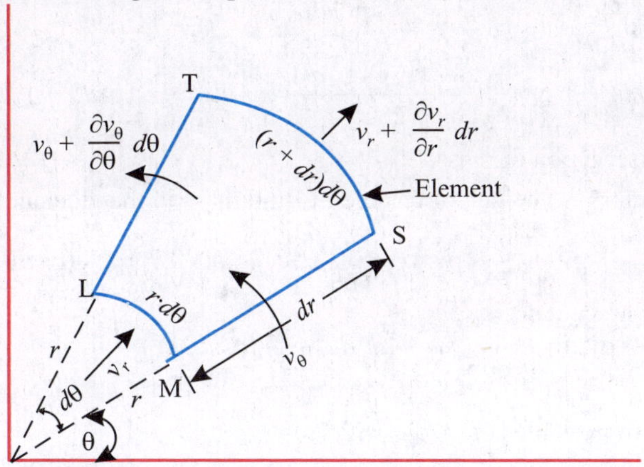

Fig. 5.17. Control volume for equation of continuity in polar coordinates.

Flow in radial direction:

Mass of fluid *entering the face LM* during time *dt* is given by:

$$\text{Fluid } \textit{influx} = \text{Density} \times (\text{velocity} \times \text{area}) \times \text{time}$$

$$= \rho \times (v_r \times rd\theta) \times dt$$

Mass of fluid *leaving the face ST* during the same time *dt* is given by:

$$\text{Fluid } \textit{efflux} = \left[\rho v_r + \frac{\partial}{\partial r}(\rho v_r)\, dr\right](r + dr)\, d\theta.dt$$

Mass accumulated in the element because of flow in radial direction

= Fluid inffux – fluid efflux

$$= \rho \times (v_r \times r d\theta) \times dt - \left[\rho v_r + \frac{\partial}{\partial r} (\rho v_r) dr \right] (r + dr)\, d\theta\, dt$$

$$= -\left[\rho v_r\, dr\, d\theta + \frac{\partial}{\partial r} (\rho v_r) dr \cdot d\theta \right] dt$$

[Neglecting terms containing $(dr)^2$]

Flow in tangential direction:

The mass accumulated due to flow in the tangential direction (by a similar treatment as discussed earlier).

$$= \left[\rho v_\theta\, dr - \left\{ \rho v_\theta + \frac{\partial}{\partial \theta} (\rho v_\theta) d\theta \right\} dr \right] dt = -\frac{\partial}{\partial \theta} (\rho v_\theta)\, dr\, d\theta\, dt$$

∴ Total gain in fluid mass

$$= -\left[\rho v_r\, dr\, d\theta + \frac{\partial}{\partial r} (\rho v_r) dr\; r d\theta + \frac{\partial}{\partial \theta} (\rho v_\theta) dr\, d\theta \right] dt$$

$$= -\left[\rho v_r + \frac{\partial}{\partial r} (\rho v_r) r + \frac{\partial}{\partial \theta} (\rho v_\theta) \right] dr\, d\theta\, dt \qquad ...(i)$$

Also, the rate of change of fluid mass in the element LMST

$$= \frac{\partial}{\partial t} (\text{Density} \times \text{Volume})\, dt$$

$$= \frac{\partial}{\partial t} \left[\rho \times \frac{r d\theta + (r + dr) d\theta}{2} dr \right] dt = \frac{\partial}{\partial t} (\rho r d\theta\, dr)\, dt \qquad ...(ii)$$

As per law of conservation of mass:

The total gain in mass = The rate of change of fluid mass in the element LMST

$$\therefore \qquad -\left[\rho v_r + \frac{\partial}{\partial r} (\rho v_r) r + \frac{\partial}{\partial \theta} (\rho v_\theta) \right] dr\, d\theta\, dt = \frac{\partial}{\partial t} (\rho r\, d\theta\, dr\, dt)$$

or, $$\left[\rho v_r + \frac{\partial}{\partial r} (\rho v_r) r + \frac{\partial}{\partial \theta} (\rho v_\theta) \right] dr\, d\theta + \frac{\partial}{\partial t} (\rho r\, d\theta\, dr) = 0$$

For steady and compressible flow, $\frac{\partial}{\partial t} \rho r d\theta dr = 0$

$$\therefore \qquad \left[\rho v_r + \frac{\partial}{\partial r} (\rho v_r) r + \frac{\partial}{\partial \theta} (\rho v_\theta) \right] dr\, d\theta = 0 \qquad ...(5.27)$$

Further, for *incompressible flow*, ρ = constant.

$$\therefore \qquad v_r + \frac{\partial}{\partial r} (v_r) r + \frac{\partial}{\partial \theta} (v_\theta)$$

or, $$\frac{v_r}{r} + \frac{\partial v_r}{\partial r} + \frac{\partial v_\theta}{r \partial \theta} = 0 \qquad ...(5.28)$$

Example 5.13. *Determine which of the velocity component sets given below satisfy the equation of continuity:*

(*i*) $u = A \sin xy$

$v = -A \sin xy$

(ii) $u = x + y$

$v = x - y$

(iii) $u = 2x^2 + 3y$

$v = -2xy + 3y^3 + 3zy$

$w = -\frac{3}{2} z^2 - 2xz - 6yz$

Solution. (i) $u = A \sin xy;\ v = -A\sin xy$

$$\frac{\partial u}{\partial x} = Ay \cos xy\ ;\ \frac{\partial v}{\partial y} = -Ax \cos xy$$

$$\frac{\partial u}{\partial x} + \frac{\partial v}{\partial y} = Ay \cos xy - Ax \cos xy \neq 0$$

i.e. Continuity equation is **not satisfied. (Ans.)**

(ii) $u = x + y;\ v = x - y$

$$\frac{\partial u}{\partial x} = 1;\ \frac{\partial v}{\partial y} = 1$$

$$\frac{\partial u}{\partial x} + \frac{\partial v}{\partial y} = 1 - 1 = 0$$

i.e. Continuity equation is **satisfied (Ans.)**

(iii) $u = 2x^2 + 3y;\ v = -2xy + 3y^3 + 3zy;\ w = -\frac{3}{2} z^2 - 2xz - 6yz$

$$\frac{\partial u}{\partial x} = 4x;\ \frac{\partial v}{\partial y} = -2x + 9y^2 + 3z\ ;\ \frac{\partial w}{\partial z} = -3z - 2x - 6y$$

Hence, $$\frac{\partial u}{\partial x} + \frac{\partial v}{\partial y} + \frac{\partial w}{\partial z} = 4x - 2x + 9y^2 + 3z - 3z - 2x - 6y \neq 0$$

i.e. Continuity equation is **not satisfied (Ans.)**

Example 5.14. *Calculate the unknown velocity component in the following, so that the equation of continuity is satisfied.*

(i) $u = Ae^x$ **(ii)** $u = Aln\left(\frac{x}{l}\right)$ **(iii)** $u = ?$

$v = ?$ $v = ?$ $v = Axy$

Solution.

(i) $u = Ae^x;\ v = ?$

$$\frac{\partial u}{\partial x} = Ae^x = -\frac{\partial v}{\partial y}$$

$$v = \int -Ae^x\, dy = -Ae^x y + f(x)$$ **(Ans.)**

(ii) $u = -Aln\left(\frac{x}{l}\right)\ ;\ v = ?$

$$\frac{\partial u}{\partial x} = -\frac{A}{(x/l)} \times \frac{1}{l} = -\frac{A}{x} = -\frac{\partial v}{\partial y}$$

$$v = \int \frac{A}{x}\, dy = \frac{Ay}{x} + f(x) \textbf{ (Ans.)}$$

(*iii*) $u = ?;\ v = Axy$

$$\frac{\partial v}{\partial y} = Ax = -\frac{\partial u}{\partial x}$$

$$u = \int -Ax\, dx = -\frac{Ax^2}{2} + f(y) \textbf{ (Ans.)}$$

Example 5.15. *In three-dimensional incompressible third flow, the velocity components in x and y-directions are:*

$$u = x^2 + y^2z^3;\quad v = -(xy + yz + zx)$$

Use continuity equation to evaluate an expression for the velocity component w in the z-direction.

(Banglore University)

Solution. The continuity equation for a steady, three-dimensional incompressible fluid flow is

$$\frac{\partial u}{\partial x} + \frac{\partial v}{\partial y} + \frac{\partial w}{\partial z} = 0 \quad ...(i)$$

$$u = x^2 + y^2z^3;\ v = -(xy + yz + zx)$$

$$\frac{\partial u}{\partial x} = 2x\ ;\ \frac{\partial v}{\partial y} = -(x + z)$$

Substituting these values in eqn. (*i*), we get:

$$2x - (x + z) + \frac{\partial w}{\partial z} = 0$$

or,
$$\frac{\partial w}{\partial z} = -x + z$$

Integrating *w.r.t.z* we have:

$$w = -xz + \frac{z^2}{2} + C$$

where C is a constant of integration which should be independent of z but may be function of x and/or y *i.e.* $C = f(x, y)$

$$\therefore \quad w = -x + \frac{z^2}{2} + f(x, y) \textbf{ (Ans.)}$$

Example 5.16. *Given* $u = ln\,(y^2 + z^2)$ *and* $w = ln\,(x^2 + y^2)$. *What is the most general form of v so that the flow is possible for a steady three-dimensional incompressible flow?*

Solution. $u = ln\,(y^2 + z^2);\ w = ln\,(x^2 + y^2)$

$$\frac{\partial u}{\partial x} = 0;\ \frac{\partial w}{\partial z} = 0$$

Substituting these values in continuity equation, we get:

$$\frac{\partial u}{\partial x} + \frac{\partial v}{\partial y} + \frac{\partial w}{\partial z} = 0$$

$$\frac{\partial v}{\partial y} = 0$$

Upon integration *w.r.t. z.*, we get:

$$v = f(x, z)$$

By symmetry, one of the values of velocity component could be

$$v = \boldsymbol{ln\,(x^2 + z^2)}\ \textbf{(Ans.)}$$

Example 5.17. *For an incompressible fluid the velocity components are:* $u = x^3 - y^3 - z^2 x$, $v = y^3 - z^3$, $w = -3x^2z - 3y^2z + \frac{z^3}{3}$. *Determine whether the continuity equation is satisfied.*

Solution. *Given*: $u = x^3 - y^3 - z^3 x$, $v = y^3 - z^3$, $w = -3x^2z - 3y^2z + \frac{z^3}{3}$ ... velocity components

Now,

$$\frac{\partial u}{\partial x} = 3x^2 - z^2$$

$$\frac{\partial v}{\partial y} = 3y^2$$

$$\frac{\partial w}{\partial z} = -3x^2 - 3y^2 + z^2$$

$$\therefore \quad \frac{\partial u}{\partial x} + \frac{\partial v}{\partial y} + \frac{\partial w}{\partial z} = (3x^2 - z^2) + 3y^2 + (-3x^2 - 3y^2 + z^2) = 0$$

Hence, the **continuity equation is satisfied. (Ans.)**

Example 5.18. *In a three-dimensional incompressible flow, the velocity components in y and z directions are* $v = ax^3 - by^2 + cz^2$; $w = bx^3 - cy^2 + az^2x$. *Determine the missing component of velocity distribution such that continuity equation is satisfied.*

Solution. *Given*:

$$v = ax^3 - by^2 + cz^2, \text{ and}$$

$$w = bx^3 - cy^2 + az^2x$$

Missing component, *u*:

The continuity equation for an incompressible fluid flow is given as:

$$\frac{\partial u}{\partial x} + \frac{\partial v}{\partial y} + \frac{\partial w}{\partial z} = 0 \quad ...(i)$$

From the given velocity components:

$$\frac{\partial v}{\partial y} = -2by\ ; \quad \frac{\partial w}{\partial z} = 2az\,x$$

Substituting these values in eqn. (*i*), we get:

$$\frac{\partial u}{\partial x} - 2by + 2az\,x = 0$$

or,

$$\frac{\partial u}{\partial x} = 2by - 2az\,x$$

Integrating w.r.t. x, we get:

$$u = \mathbf{2byx - 2az\frac{x^2}{2} + C}\ \textbf{(Ans.)}$$

[where $C = f(y, z)$, the exact value will be known if the boundary conditions are known].

The constant of integration C is either a numerical constant or a function which is independent of x. If this constant is *omitted,* the velocity component may be expressed as:

$$u = \mathbf{2byx - azx^2}\ \textbf{(Ans.)}$$

Example 5.19. *The velocity components in x and y directions are given as* $u = 2xy^3/3 - x^2y$ *and* $v = xy^2 - 2yx^3/3$. *Indicate whether the given velocity distribution is:*

(i) A possible field of flow;

(ii) Not a possible field of flow. **[UPSC Exam.]**

Solution. *Given.* $u = 2xy^3/3 - x^2y,\ v = xy^2 - 2yx^3/3$ ...Velocity components

A possible flow field (two-dimensional) must satisfy the continuity equation.

$$\therefore \quad \frac{\partial u}{\partial x} + \frac{\partial v}{\partial y} = 0 \quad ...(i)$$

Now,

$$\frac{\partial u}{\partial x} = \frac{2}{3}y^3 - 2xy,\ \frac{\partial v}{\partial y} = 2xy - \frac{2}{3}x^3$$

Substituting these values in eqn. (*i*), we get:

$$\left(\frac{2}{3}y^3 - 2xy\right) + \left(2xy - \frac{2}{3}x^3\right) = \frac{2}{3}(y^3 - x^3)$$

Since the continuity equation is *not* satisfied, the given velocity components, therefore, **do not represent a possible flow field. (Ans.)**

Example 5.20. *In an incompressible flow, the velocity vector is given by:*

$$V = (6xt + yz^2)i + (3t + xy^2)j + (xy - 2xyz - 6\,tz)\,k$$

(i) Verify whether the continuity equation is satisfied.

(ii) Determine the acceleration vector at point L (2, 2, 2) at t = 2.0.

Solution. (*i*)

$$V = (6xt + yz^2)\,i + (3t + xy^2)\,j + (xy - 2xyz - 6tz)\,k \quad ...(Given)$$

$$= ui + vj + wk$$

$$u = 6xt + yz^2,\ \frac{\partial u}{\partial x} = 6t$$

$$v = 3t + xy^2,\ \frac{\partial v}{\partial y} = 2xy$$

$$w = xy - 2xyz - 6tz, = \frac{\partial w}{\partial z} - 2xy - 6t$$

$$\frac{\partial u}{\partial x} + \frac{\partial v}{\partial y} + \frac{\partial w}{\partial z} = 6t + 2xy - 2xy - 6t = 0$$

Hence, the **continuity equation is satisfied (Ans.)**

(*ii*) Acceleration, $a = a_x i + a_y j + a_z k$

$$a_x = \frac{\partial u}{\partial t} + u\frac{\partial u}{\partial x} + v\frac{\partial u}{\partial y} + w\frac{\partial u}{\partial z}$$

$$= 6x + (6xt + yz^2)(6t) + (3t + xy^2)(z^2) + (xy - 2xyz - 6tz)(2yz)$$

At point L (2,2,2) and at $t = 2$,

$$a_x = 6 \times 2 + (6 \times 2 \times 2 + 2 \times 2^2)(6 \times 2) + (3 \times 2 + 2 \times 2^2)(2^2)$$

$$+ (2 \times 2 - 2 \times 2 \times 2 \times 2 - 6 \times 2 \times 2)(2 \times 2 \times 2)$$

$$= 12 + (32)(12) + (14)(4) + (-36)(8) = 164 \text{ units}$$

$$a_y = \frac{\partial v}{\partial t} + u\frac{\partial v}{\partial x} + v\frac{\partial v}{\partial y} + w\frac{\partial v}{\partial z}$$

$$= 3 + (6xt + yz^2)(y^2) + (3t + xy^2)(2xy) + (xy - 2xyz - 6tz)(0)$$

At point $L(2, 2, 2)$ and at $t = 2$

$$a_y = 3 + (6 \times 2 \times 2 + 2 \times 2^2)(2^2) + (3 \times 2 + 2 \times 2^2)(2 \times 2 \times 2) + (2 \times 2 - 2 \times 2 \times 2 - 6 \times 2 \times 2)(0)$$

$$= 3 + (32)(4) + (14)(8) = 243 \text{ units.}$$

Similarly,
$$a_z = \frac{\partial w}{\partial t} + u\frac{\partial w}{\partial x} + v\frac{\partial w}{\partial y} + w\frac{\partial w}{\partial z}$$

$$= -6z + (6xt + yz^2)(y - 2yz) + (3t + xy^2)(x - 2xz) + (xy - 2xyz - 6tz)(-2xy - 6t)$$

At point L (2, 2, 2) and at $t = 2$,

$$a_z = -6 \times 2 + (6 \times 2 \times 2 + 2 \times 2^2)(2 - 2 \times 2 \times 2) + (3 \times 2 + 2 \times 2^2)(2 - 2 \times 2 \times 2) + (2 \times 2 - 2 \times 2 \times 2 \times 2 - 6 \times 2 \times 2)(-2 \times 2 \times 2 - 6 \times 2)$$

$$= -12 + (32)(-6) + (14)(-6) + (-36)(-20) = 432 \text{ units.}$$

Hence at L (2, 2, 2) and at $t = 2$,

$$a = a_x i + a_y j + a_z k$$

or, $$\boldsymbol{a = 164\, i + 243 j + 432 k} \textbf{ (Ans.)}$$

Example 5.21. *A two-dimensional incompressible flow in cylindrical polar coordinates is given by:*

$$v_r = 2r \sin\theta \cos\theta;\ v_\theta = -2r \sin^2\theta$$

Determine whether these velocity components represent a physically possible flow field.

Solution. The continuity equation for a steady, two-dimensional incompressible flow is

$$\frac{v_r}{r} + \frac{\partial v_r}{\partial r} + \frac{\partial v_\theta}{r\partial\theta} = 0 \quad \text{...[Eqn. (5.28)]}$$

From the given velocity components, we have:

$$\frac{\partial v_r}{\partial r} = \frac{\partial}{\partial r}(2r \sin\theta \cos\theta) = 2 \sin\theta \cos\theta$$

$$\frac{\partial v_\theta}{\partial\theta} = \frac{\partial}{\partial\theta}(-2r\sin^2\theta) = -4r \sin\theta \cos\theta$$

Inserting these values in the above equation, we get:

$$\frac{2r\sin\theta\cos\theta}{r} + 2\sin\theta\cos\theta - \frac{4r\sin\theta\cos\theta}{r} = 0$$

or
$$2\sin\theta \cos\theta + 2 \sin\theta \cos\theta - 4 \sin\theta \cos\theta = 0$$

i.e., *L. H. S.* = 0

Thus the continuity equation is satisfied and hence the **flow is physically possible. (Ans.)**

Example 5.22. *The tangential component of velocity in a two-dimensional flow of incompressible fluid is*

$$v_\theta = -\frac{C\sin\theta}{r^2}$$

where C is a constant.

(i) Using continuity equation, determine the expression for radial velocity v.

(ii) Find the magnitude and direction of resultant velocity.

Solution. *Given:*
$$v_\theta = -\frac{C\sin\theta}{r^2}$$

(i) Expression for v_r:

The continuity equation for a two-dimensional, steady incompressible flow is

$$\frac{v_r}{r} + \frac{\partial v_r}{\partial r} + \frac{\partial v_\theta}{r\partial \theta} = 0 \qquad \text{[Eqn. (5.28)]}$$

or $$\frac{\partial}{\partial r}(rv_r) + \frac{\partial}{\partial \theta}(v_\theta) = 0 \qquad ...(i)$$

For the given velocity component:

$$\frac{\partial v_\theta}{\partial \theta} = \frac{\partial}{\partial \theta}\left(-\frac{C\sin\theta}{r^2}\right) = -\frac{C}{r^2}\cos\theta \qquad ...(ii)$$

From eqn. (i) and (ii), we have:

$$\frac{\partial}{\partial r}(rv_r) = \frac{C}{r^2}\cos\theta$$

Integrating both sides w.r.t. r we have:

$$rv_r = \int_0^r \frac{C}{r^2}\cos\theta\, dr = -\frac{C\cos\theta}{r}$$

$\therefore$ Radial component; $\quad \boldsymbol{v_r = \frac{C\cos\theta}{r^2}}$ **(Ans.)**

(ii) Resultant velocity:

$$\text{Resultant velocity} = \sqrt{v_r^2 + v_\theta^2}$$

$$= \sqrt{\left(-\frac{C\cos\theta}{r^2}\right)^2 + \left(-\frac{C\sin\theta}{r^2}\right)^2}$$

$$= \frac{C}{r^2}\sqrt{(\cos^2\theta + \sin^2\theta)} = \boldsymbol{\frac{C}{r^2}} \text{ (Ans.)}$$

5.9. CIRCULATION AND VORTICITY

Let us consider a closed curve in a two-dimensional flow field shown in Fig. 5.18; the curve being cut by the stream lines. Let P be the point of intersection of the curve with one stream line, θ be the angle which the stream line makes with the curve. The component of velocity along the closed curve at the point of intersection is equal to $V\cos\theta$. **Circulation Γ** *is defined mathematically as the line integral of the tangential velocity about a closed path (contour).*

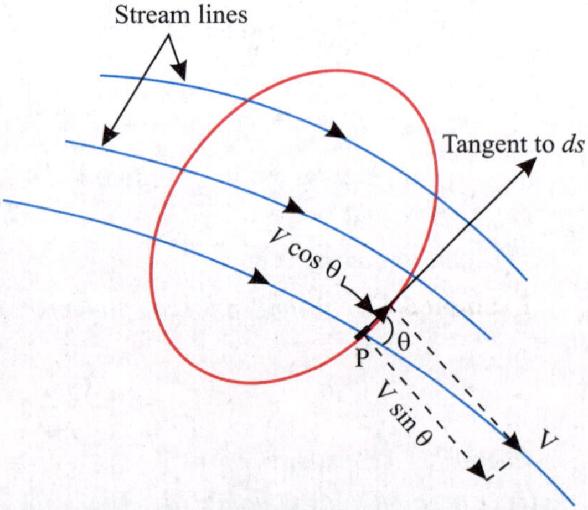

Fig. 5.18. Circulation in a two-dimensional flow.

Thus,

$$\Gamma = \oint V\cos\theta . ds$$

where, V = Velocity in the flow field at the element ds, and

θ = Angle between V and tangent to the path (in the positive anticlockwise direction along the path) at that point.

Circulation around regular curves can be obtained by integration. Let us consider the circulation around an elementary box (fluid element ABCD) shown in Fig. 5.19.

Starting from A and proceeding anticlockwise, we have:

$$d\Gamma = u\Delta x + \left(v + \frac{\partial v}{\partial x}\Delta x\right)\Delta y - \left(u + \frac{\partial u}{\partial y}\Delta y\right)\Delta x - v\Delta y$$

$$= \left(\frac{\partial v}{\partial x} - \frac{\partial u}{\partial y}\right)\Delta x . \Delta y$$

The **vorticity** (Ω) is defined as the *circulation per unit of enclosed area,*

$$\Omega = \frac{\Gamma}{A}. \text{ Thus,}$$

$$\Omega = \frac{d\Gamma}{\Delta x . \Delta y} = \frac{\partial v}{\partial x} - \frac{\partial u}{\partial y} \quad ...(5.29)$$

If *a flow possesses vorticity, it is rotational.* **Rotation** ω *(omega) is defined as one-half of the vorticity*, or

$$\omega = \frac{1}{2}\left[\frac{\partial v}{\partial x} - \frac{\partial u}{\partial y}\right]$$

The flow is irrotational if rotation ω *is zero.*

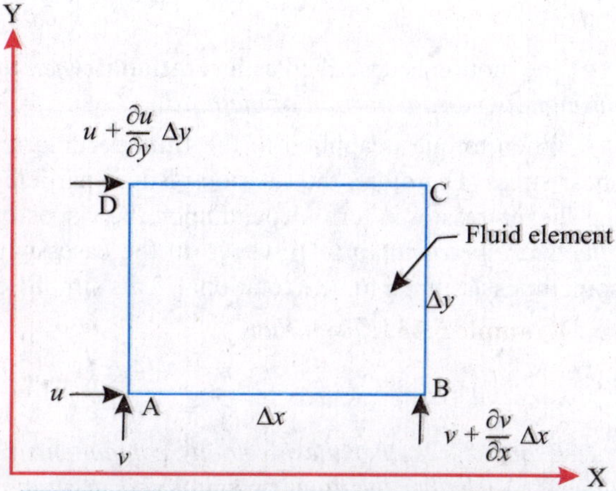

Fig. 5.19. Irrotational flow condition.

For a three-dimensional flow the rotation is possible about three axes. The expressions for rotation ω_z, ω_x *and* ω_y can be obtained in like manner:

$$\left.\begin{aligned} \omega_z &= \frac{1}{2}\left(\frac{\partial v}{\partial x} - \frac{\partial u}{\partial y}\right) \\ \omega_x &= \frac{1}{2}\left(\frac{\partial w}{\partial y} - \frac{\partial v}{\partial z}\right) \\ \omega_y &= \frac{1}{2}\left(\frac{\partial u}{\partial z} - \frac{\partial w}{\partial x}\right) \end{aligned}\right\} \quad ...(5.30)$$

In the vector notation, the above equation can be rewritten as:

$$\omega = \frac{1}{2}[\omega_x i + \omega_y j + \omega_z k]$$

$$= \frac{1}{2}(\Delta \times V) \quad ...(5.31)$$

The vector $(\Delta \times V)$ is the ***curl*** of velocity vector.

Vorticity in a fluid motion is taken numerically equal to *twice the value of rotation.*

$$\text{Vorticity, } \Omega = \text{curl } V = (\Delta \times V) \quad ...(5.32)$$

Which may be expressed as:

$$\Omega = (\nabla \times V) \begin{vmatrix} i & j & k \\ \frac{\partial}{\partial x} & \frac{\partial}{\partial y} & \frac{\partial}{\partial z} \\ u & v & w \end{vmatrix}$$

$$= \Omega_x i + \Omega_y j + \Omega_z k \quad ...(5.33)$$

The vorticity components are separately given by:

$$\Omega_x = 2\omega_x = \left(\frac{\partial w}{\partial y} - \frac{\partial v}{\partial z}\right)$$

$$\Omega_y = 2\omega_y = \left(\frac{\partial u}{\partial z} - \frac{\partial w}{\partial x}\right)$$

$$\Omega_z = 2\omega_z = \left(\frac{\partial v}{\partial x} - \frac{\partial u}{\partial y}\right) \quad ...(5.34)$$

The motion is described as **irrotational** *when the components of rotation or vorticity are 'zero' throughout certain portion of the fluid.*

When torque is applied to the fluid particle it will give rise to *rotation*; the torque is due to shear stress. Therefore, the rotation of fluid particle will always be associated with shear stress. As the shear stresses, in turn, depend upon the viscosity, the *rotational flow occurs where the viscosity effects are predominant.* However, in the cases where the viscosity effects are small, the flow is sometimes assumed to be irrotational. This simplifies analysis of problems of fluid flow.

Example 5.23. *Given that*

$$u = -4ax(x^2 - 3y^2)$$
$$v = 4ay(3x^2 - y^2)$$

Examine whether these velocity components represent a physically possible two-dimensional flow; if so whether the flow is rotational or irrotational?

Solution. *Given*:

$$u = -4ax(x^2 - 3y^2)$$
$$v = 4ay(3x^2 - y^2) \quad \text{...Velocity components}$$

A two-dimensional flow will be *continuous* if $\frac{\partial u}{\partial x} + \frac{\partial v}{\partial y} = 0$

Now,
$$\frac{\partial u}{\partial x} = \frac{\partial}{\partial x}[-4ax(x^2 - 3y^2)] = \frac{\partial}{\partial x}(-4ax^3 + 12axy^2) = -12ax^2 + 12ay^2$$

and,
$$\frac{\partial v}{\partial y} = \frac{\partial}{\partial y}[4ay(3x^2 - y^2)] = \frac{\partial}{\partial y}[12ayx^2 - 4ay^3] = 12ax^2 - 12ay^2$$

$$\therefore \quad \frac{\partial u}{\partial x} + \frac{\partial v}{\partial y} = (-12ax^2 + 12ay^2) + (12ax^2 - 12ay^2) = 0$$

Hence the given velocity components **represent a physically possible two-dimensional flow. (Ans.)**

The flow will be *irrotational* if,

$$\frac{\partial u}{\partial y} = \frac{\partial v}{\partial x}$$

Now,
$$\frac{\partial u}{\partial y} = \frac{\partial}{\partial y}[-4ax(x^2 - 3y^2)] = \frac{\partial}{\partial y}(-4ax^3 + 12axy^2) = 24axy$$

$$\frac{\partial v}{\partial x} = \frac{\partial}{\partial x}[4ay(3x^2 - y^2)] = \frac{\partial}{\partial x}[12ayx^2 - 4ay^3] = 24ayx$$

$\therefore \quad \frac{\partial u}{\partial y} = \frac{\partial v}{\partial x}$, hence the flow is **irrotational. (Ans.)**

Example 5.24. *Given that $u = xy$, $v = 2yz$. Examine whether these velocity components represent two or three-dimensional incompressible flow; if three-dimensional, determine the third component.*

Solution. *Given:* $u = xy, v = 2yz$ ...Velocity components

A *two dimensional flow* should satisfy the continuity equation,

$$\frac{\partial u}{\partial x} + \frac{\partial v}{\partial y} = 0$$

But, $$\frac{\partial u}{\partial x} = \frac{\partial}{\partial x}(xy) = y$$

and, $$\frac{\partial v}{\partial y} = \frac{\partial}{\partial y}(2yz) = 2z$$

$\therefore$ $$y + 2z \neq 0$$

Hence, the flow is **not two-dimensional.**

For the flow to be *three-dimensional*, it should satisfy the continuity equation,

$$\frac{\partial u}{\partial x} + \frac{\partial v}{\partial y} + \frac{\partial w}{\partial z} = 0$$

or, $$y + 2z + \frac{\partial w}{\partial z} = 0$$

or, $$\frac{\partial w}{\partial z} = -(y + 2z)$$

or, $$w = [-(y + 2z)]\, dz + f(x, y, t)$$

$$= -\left(yz + 2.\frac{z^2}{2}\right) + f(x,y,t)$$

$$= -yz + z^2 + f(x, y, t)$$

Hence, the third component,

$$\mathbf{w = -yz + z^2 + f(x, y, t)} \textbf{ (Ans.)}$$

Example 5.25. *For a two-dimensional flow, the velocity components are $u = x/(x^2 + y^2)$, $v = y/(x^2 + y^2)$. Determine:* **(i)** *The acceleration components a_x and a_y;* **(ii)** *The rotation of w_z.*

Solution. *Given:* $a = x/(x^2+ y^2)$, $v = y/ (x^2 + y^2)$ ... Velocity components

(i) The acceleration components, a_x and a_y:

We know that:

$$a_x = u\frac{\partial u}{\partial x} + v\frac{\partial u}{\partial y} \quad ...(i)$$

$$a_y = u\frac{\partial v}{\partial x} + v\frac{\partial v}{\partial y} \quad ...(ii)$$

$$\frac{\partial u}{\partial x} = \frac{\partial}{\partial x}\left(\frac{x}{x^2 + y^2}\right) = \frac{(x^2 + y^2) \times 1 - x(2x)}{(x^2 + y^2)^2} = \frac{y^2 - x^2}{(x^2 + y^2)^2}$$

$$\frac{\partial u}{\partial y} = \frac{\partial}{\partial y}\left(\frac{x}{x^2 + y^2}\right) = \frac{\partial}{\partial y}\,[x(x^2 + y^2)^{-1}] = x \times [-(x^2 + y^2)^{-2} \times 2y] = -\frac{2xy}{(x^2 + y^2)^2}$$

$$\frac{\partial v}{\partial x} = \frac{\partial}{\partial x}\left(\frac{y}{x^2 + y^2}\right) = \frac{\partial}{\partial x}[y(x^2 + y^2)^{-1}] = y \times -(x^2 + y^2)^{-2} \times 2x = -\frac{2xy}{(x^2 + y^2)^2}$$

$$\frac{\partial v}{\partial y} = \frac{\partial}{\partial y}\left(\frac{y}{x^2 + y^2}\right) = \frac{(x^2 + y^2) \times 1 - y\,(2y)}{(x^2 + y^2)^2} = \frac{x^2 - y^2}{(x^2 + y^2)^2}$$

Substituting these values in eqns. (*i*) and (*ii*), we get:

$$a_x = \frac{x}{(x^2 + y^2)} \times \frac{(y^2 - x^2)}{(x^2 + y^2)^2} - \frac{y}{x^2 + y^2} \times \frac{2xy}{(x^2 + y^2)^2}$$

$$= \frac{xy^2 - x^3}{(x^2 + y^2)^3} - \frac{2xy^2}{(x^2 + y^2)^3} = \frac{-x^3 - xy^2}{(x^2 + y^2)^3} = \frac{x(x^2 + y^2)}{(x^2 + y^2)^3} = -\frac{x}{(x^2 + y^2)^2}$$

Hence, $a_x = -\dfrac{\mathbf{x}}{(\mathbf{x}^2 + \mathbf{y}^2)^2}$ **(Ans.)**

$$a_y = \left(\frac{x}{x^2 + y^2}\right) \times \left[-\frac{2xy}{(x^2 + y^2)^2}\right] + \frac{y}{(x^2 + y^2)} \times \left(\frac{(x^2 - y^2)}{(x^2 + y^2)^2}\right)$$

$$= -\frac{2x^2 y}{(x^2 + y^2)^3} + \frac{y(x^2 - y^2)}{(x^2 + y^2)^3} = \frac{-2x^2 y + x^2 y - y^3}{(x^2 + y^2)^3}$$

$$= \frac{-y(x^2 + y^2)}{(x^2 + y^2)^3} = -\frac{y}{(x^2 + y^2)^2}$$

Hence, $a_y = -\dfrac{\mathbf{y}}{(\mathbf{x}^2 + \mathbf{y}^2)^2}$ **(Ans.)**

(*ii*) The rotation of ω_z:

We know that:

$$\omega_z = \frac{1}{2}\left(\frac{\partial v}{\partial x} - \frac{\partial u}{\partial y}\right)$$

$$= \frac{1}{2}\left[-\frac{2xy}{(x^2 + y^2)^2} + \frac{2xy}{(x^2 + y^2)^2}\right] = 0$$

Hence the **flow is irrotational. (Ans.)**

Example 5.26. *If the velocity field is given by* $u = (16y - 8x)$, $v = (8y - 7x)$ *find the circulation around the closed curve defined by* $x = 4$, $y = 2$, $x = 8$, $y = 8$.

Solution. *Given:*

$u = (16\,y - 8x)$, $v = (8y - 7x)$ ...Velocity field

Refer to Fig 5.20.

$$\Gamma_{ABCD} = \int_{ABCD} (udx + vdy)$$

$$= \int_{AB} (udx + vdy) + \int_{BC} (udx + vdy) + \int_{CD} (udx + vdy) + \int_{DA} (udx + vdy)$$

$$= \int_4^8 (16\,y - 8x)\,dx + \int_2^8 (8\,y - 7x)\,dy + \int_8^4 (16\,y - 8x)\,dx + \int_8^2 (8\,y - 7x)\,dy$$

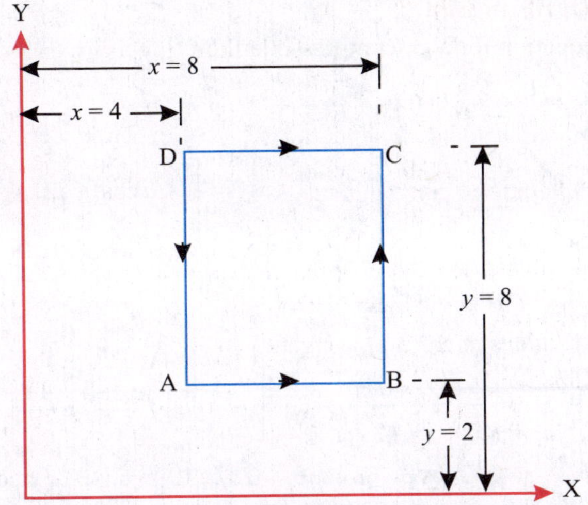

Fig. 5.20

$$= \left[16yx - 4x^2\right]_4^8 + \left[4y^2 - 7xy\right]_2^8 + \left[16yx - 4y^2\right]_8^4 + \left[4y^2 - 7xy\right]_8^2$$

(*i*) (*ii*) (*iii*) (*iv*)

In integral (*i*): $y = 2$
In integral (*ii*): $x = 8$
In integral (*iii*): $y = 8$
In integral (*iv*): $x = 4$

Substituting these values, we have:

$$\begin{aligned}\Gamma_{ABCD} &= [16 \times 2 \times 8 - 4 \times 8 \times 8 - 16 \times 2 \times 4 + 4 \times 4^2] \\ &\quad + [4 \times 8^2 - 2 \times 8 \times 8 - 4 \times 2^2 + 7 \times 8 \times 2] \\ &\quad + [16 \times 8 \times 4 - 4 \times 4^2 - 16 \times 8 \times 8 + 4 \times 8^2] \\ &\quad + [4 \times 2^2 - 7 \times 4 \times 2 - 4 \times 8^2 + 7 \times 4 \times 8] \\ &= [256 - 256 - 128 + 64] + [256 - 448 - 16 + 112] \\ &\quad + [512 - 64 - 1024 + 256] + [16 - 56 - 256 + 224] \\ &= -64 - 96 - 320 - 72 = -552\end{aligned}$$

Area of the curve $ABCD = (8 - 4) \times (8 - 2) = 24$

$\therefore$ Circulation per unit area $= -\dfrac{552}{24} = -$ **23 (Ans.)**

Example 5.27. *A fluid flow is given by*

$$v_r = \left(1 - \frac{a}{r^2}\right)\cos\theta,\ v_t = -\left(1 + \frac{a}{r^2}\right)\sin\theta$$

(*i*) *Show that it represents a physically possible flow.*

(*ii*) *Determine whether the flow is rotational or irrotational.*

Solution. *Given:* $v_r = \left(1 - \dfrac{a}{r^2}\right)\cos\theta,\ v_\theta = -\left(1 + \dfrac{a}{r^2}\right)\sin\theta$ ...Velocity components

(i) Is the flow physically possible?

The continuity equation for an incompressible fluid flow is given by:

$$\frac{v_r}{r} + \frac{\partial v_r}{\partial r} + \frac{1}{r}\frac{\partial v_\theta}{\partial \theta} = 0 \qquad ...(1)$$

Now, $$\frac{\partial}{\partial r} v_r = \frac{\partial}{\partial r}\left(1 - \frac{a}{r^2}\right)\cos\theta = \left[-a\cos\theta[-2].\frac{1}{r^3}\right]$$

and, $$\frac{\partial}{\partial \theta} v_\theta = \frac{\partial}{\partial \theta}\left[-\left(1 + \frac{a}{r^2}\right)\sin\theta\right] = \left[-\left(1 + \frac{a}{r^2}\right)\cos\theta\right]$$

Substituting these values in eqn. (1), we get:

$$\frac{1}{r}\left(1 - \frac{a}{r^2}\right)\cos\theta + \left[-a\cos\theta + (-2).\frac{1}{r^2}\right] + \frac{1}{r}\left[-\left(1 + \frac{a}{r^2}\right)\cos\theta\right]$$

$$= \frac{\cos\theta}{r} - \frac{a\cos\theta}{r^3} + \frac{2a\cos\theta}{r^2} - \frac{\cos\theta}{r} - \frac{a\cos\theta}{r^3} = 0$$

Since the continuity equation is satisfied, therefore, **the flow is physically possible. (Ans.)**

(ii) Flow–rotational or irrotational?

Let us check for rotationality.

Vorticity is given by:

$$\Omega = \frac{\partial v_\theta}{\partial r} + \frac{v_\theta}{r} - \frac{1}{r}\frac{\partial v_r}{\partial \theta} \qquad ...(2)$$

Now, $$\frac{\partial v_\theta}{\partial r} = \frac{\partial}{\partial r}(v_\theta) = \frac{\partial}{\partial r}\left[-\left(1 + \frac{a}{r^2}\right)\sin\theta\right] = \left[-a\sin\theta(-2)\frac{1}{r^3}\right]$$

and, $$\frac{\partial v_r}{\partial \theta} = \frac{\partial}{\partial \theta}(v_r) = \frac{\partial}{\partial \theta}\left(1 - \frac{a}{r^2}\right)\cos\theta = \left[\left(1 - \frac{a}{r^2}\right) \times (-\sin\theta)\right]$$

Substituting these values in eqn. (2), we get:

$$\Omega = \left[-a\sin\theta(-2).\frac{1}{r^3}\right] + \frac{1}{r}\left[-\left(1 + \frac{a}{r^2}\right)\sin\theta\right]$$

$$-\frac{1}{r}\left[\left(1 - \frac{a}{r^2}\right) \times (-\sin\theta)\right]$$

$$= \frac{2a\sin\theta}{r^3} - \frac{\sin\theta}{r} - \frac{a\sin\theta}{r^3} + \frac{\sin\theta}{r} - \frac{a\sin\theta}{r^3} = 0$$

Hence the **flow is irrotational. (Ans.)**

Example 5.28. *The velocity components for a fluid flow are:* $u = a + by - cz$, $v = d - bx - ez$, $w = f + cx - ey$ *where a, b, c, d, e and f are arbitrary constants.*

(i) Show that it is a possible case of fluid flow.

(ii) Is the fluid flow irrotational? If not, determine the vorticity and rotation.

[RGVP Bhopal]

Solution. *Given:* $u = a + by - cz$, $v = d - bx - ez$, $w = f + cx - ey$ ...Velocity components.

(i) Possible case of fluid flow?

Continuity equation is given as:

$$\frac{\partial u}{\partial x} + \frac{\partial v}{\partial y} + \frac{\partial w}{\partial z} = 0$$

Now, $$\frac{\partial u}{\partial x} = \frac{\partial}{\partial x}(a + by - cz) = 0,$$

$$\frac{\partial v}{\partial y} = \frac{\partial}{\partial y}(d - bx - ez) = 0, \text{ and } \frac{\partial w}{\partial z} = \frac{\partial}{\partial z}(f + cx - ey) = 0$$

Since the equation of continuity is satisfied, therefore, the field is **possible case of fluid flow. (Ans.)**

(*ii*) Is the flow field irrotational?

For the flow to be irrotational, curl $V = O$ i.e. $(\Delta \times V) = 0$

Now, $$(\nabla \times V) = \begin{vmatrix} i & j & k \\ \frac{\partial}{\partial x} & \frac{\partial}{\partial y} & \frac{\partial}{\partial z} \\ u & v & w \end{vmatrix}$$

Substituting velocity components, we have:

$$(\nabla \times V) = \begin{vmatrix} i & j & k \\ \frac{\partial}{\partial x} & \frac{\partial}{\partial y} & \frac{\partial}{\partial z} \\ (a + by - cz) & (d - bx - ez) & (f + cx - ey) \end{vmatrix}$$

or, $$(\nabla \times V) = i\left[\frac{\partial}{\partial y}(f + cx - ey) - \frac{\partial}{\partial z}(d - bx - ez)\right]$$

$$+ j\left[\frac{\partial}{\partial z}(a + by - cz) - \frac{\partial}{\partial x}(f + cx - ey)\right]$$

$$+ k\left[\frac{\partial}{\partial x}(d - bx - ez) - \frac{\partial}{\partial y}(a + by - cz)\right]$$

$$= i(-e + e) + j(-c - c) + k(-b - b)$$

Since $(\nabla \times V) \neq 0$. the *flow is* **not irrotational (Ans.)**

Vorticity Ω:

Vorticity, $$\Omega = (\nabla \times V) = -2(cj + bk)$$

$$= 2\sqrt{c^2 + b^2}$$

Hence, $$\boldsymbol{\Omega = 2\sqrt{c^2 + b^2}} \text{ (Ans.)}$$

Rotation, ω

We know, $$\omega = \frac{\Omega}{2}$$

$$= \frac{1}{2}[2\sqrt{c^2 + b^2}] = \sqrt{c^2 + b^2}$$

Hence, Rotation, $$\omega = \boldsymbol{\sqrt{c^2 + b^2}} \text{ (Ans.)}$$

Example 5.29. *Determine the components of rotation for the following velocity field pertaining to the flow of an incompressible fluid:*

$$u = Cyz;\ v = Czx;\ w = Cxy, \text{ where } C = \text{constant}.$$

State whether the flow is rotational or irrotational.

Solution. *Given:* $u = Cyz;\ v = Czx;\ w = Cxy$ ... Velocity field

The components of rotation are:

$$\omega_x = \frac{1}{2}\left(\frac{\partial w}{\partial y} - \frac{\partial v}{\partial z}\right) = \frac{1}{2}(Cx - Cx) = 0$$

$$\omega_y = \frac{1}{2}\left(\frac{\partial u}{\partial z} - \frac{\partial w}{\partial x}\right) = \frac{1}{2}(Cy - Cy) = 0$$

$$\omega_z = \frac{1}{2}\left(\frac{\partial v}{\partial x} - \frac{\partial u}{\partial y}\right) = \frac{1}{2}(Cz - Cz) = 0$$

Since each of the rotation components is zero, the given flow field represents **irrotational flow. (Ans.)**

Example 5.30. *Determine the components of rotation about the various axes for the following flows:*

(*i*) $u = y^2,\ v = -3x$

(*ii*) $u = 3xy,\ v = \frac{3}{2}x^2 - \frac{3}{2}y^2$

(*iii*) $u = xy^3z,\ v = -y^2z^2,\ w = yz^2 - \frac{y^3z^2}{2}$

Solution. The components of rotation about the various axes are:

$$\omega_z = \frac{1}{2}\left(\frac{\partial v}{\partial x} - \frac{\partial u}{\partial y}\right)$$

$$\omega_x = \frac{1}{2}\left(\frac{\partial w}{\partial y} - \frac{\partial v}{\partial z}\right)$$

$$\omega_y = \frac{1}{2}\left(\frac{\partial u}{\partial z} - \frac{\partial w}{\partial x}\right)$$

(*i*) $u = y^2;\ v = -3x$

$$\omega_z = \frac{1}{2}\left(\frac{\partial v}{\partial x} - \frac{\partial u}{\partial y}\right) = \frac{1}{2}(-3 - 2y) \quad \textbf{(Ans.)}$$

As the flow is two-dimensional in x–y plane, $\omega_x = \omega_y = 0$ **(Ans.)**

(*ii*) $u = 3xy;\ v = \frac{3}{2}x^2 - \frac{3}{2}y^2$

$$\omega_z = \frac{1}{2}\left(\frac{\partial v}{\partial x} - \frac{\partial u}{\partial y}\right) = \frac{1}{2}(3x - 3x) = 0 \quad \textbf{(Ans.)}$$

As the flow is two-dimensional in the $x - y$ plane, $\omega_x = \omega_y = 0$ **(Ans.)**

(*iii*) $u = xy^3z;\ v = -y^2z^2;\ w = yz^2 - \frac{y^3z^2}{2}$

$$\omega_z = \frac{1}{2}\left(\frac{\partial v}{\partial x} - \frac{\partial u}{\partial y}\right) = \frac{1}{2}\,(0 - 3xy^2z) = -\frac{3}{2}\,xy^2z \;\textbf{(Ans.)}$$

$$\omega_x = \frac{1}{2}\left(\frac{\partial w}{\partial y} - \frac{\partial v}{\partial z}\right) = \frac{1}{2}\left(z^2 - \frac{3y^2z^2}{2} + 2y^2z\right) \;\textbf{(Ans.)}$$

$$\omega_y = \frac{1}{2}\left(\frac{\partial u}{\partial z} - \frac{\partial w}{\partial x}\right) = \frac{1}{2}\,(xy^3 - 0) = \frac{1}{2}\,xy^3 \;\textbf{(Ans.)}$$

5.10. VELOCITY POTENTIAL AND STREAM FUNCTION

5.10.1. Velocity Potential

The **velocity potential** *is defined as a scalar function of space and time such that its negative derivative with respect to any direction gives the fluid velocity in that direction.* It is denoted by ϕ (phi). Thus mathematically the velocity potential is defined as:

$$\phi = f(x, y, z, t) \qquad \text{...for } \textit{unsteady} \text{ flow,}$$

and,

$$\phi = f(x, y, z) \qquad \text{...for } \textit{steady} \text{ flow;}$$

such that:

$$\left.\begin{aligned} u &= -\frac{\partial \phi}{\partial x} \\ v &= -\frac{\partial \phi}{\partial y} \\ w &= -\frac{\partial \phi}{\partial z} \end{aligned}\right\} \qquad \text{...(5.35)}$$

where, u, v and w are the components of velocity in the x, y and z directions respectively.

The *negative sign* signifies that ϕ *decreases with an increase in the values of x, y and z.* In other words it indicates that the *flow is always in the direction of decreasing* ϕ.

For *an incompressible steady flow* the continuity equation is given by:

$$\frac{\partial u}{\partial x} + \frac{\partial v}{\partial y} + \frac{\partial w}{\partial z} = 0$$

By substituting the values of u, v and w in terms of ϕ from eqn. 5.35, we get:

$$\frac{\partial}{\partial x}\left(-\frac{\partial \phi}{\partial x}\right) + \frac{\partial}{\partial y}\left(-\frac{\partial \phi}{\partial y}\right) + \frac{\partial}{\partial z}\left(-\frac{\partial \phi}{\partial z}\right) = 0$$

$$\frac{d^2\phi}{\partial x^2} + \frac{\partial^2\phi}{\partial y^2} + \frac{\partial^2\phi}{\partial z^2} = 0 \qquad \text{...(5.36)}$$

This equation is known as **Laplace equation.**

Thus *any function* ϕ *that satisfies the Laplace equation will correspond to some case of fluid flow.*

The *rotational components* are given by [eqn. (5.30)]:

$$\omega_x = \frac{1}{2}\left(\frac{\partial w}{\partial y} - \frac{\partial v}{\partial z}\right)$$

$$\omega_y = \frac{1}{2}\left(\frac{\partial u}{\partial z} - \frac{\partial w}{\partial x}\right)$$

$$\omega_z = \frac{1}{2}\left(\frac{\partial v}{\partial x} - \frac{\partial u}{\partial y}\right)$$

By substituting the values of u, v and w in term of ϕ from eqn. (5.35), we get:

$$\omega_x = \frac{1}{2}\left[\frac{\partial}{\partial y}\left(-\frac{\partial \phi}{\partial z}\right) - \frac{\partial}{\partial z}\left(-\frac{\partial \phi}{\partial y}\right)\right]$$

$$= \frac{1}{2}\left[-\frac{\partial^2 \phi}{\partial y\, \partial z} + \frac{\partial^2 \phi}{\partial z\, \partial y}\right]$$

$$\omega_y = \frac{1}{2}\left[\frac{\partial}{\partial z}\left(-\frac{\partial \phi}{\partial x}\right) - \frac{\partial}{\partial x}\left(-\frac{\partial \phi}{\partial z}\right)\right]$$

$$= \frac{1}{2}\left[-\frac{\partial^2 \phi}{\partial z\, \partial x} + \frac{\partial^2 \phi}{\partial x\, \partial z}\right]$$

$$\omega_z = \frac{1}{2}\left[\frac{\partial}{\partial x}\left(-\frac{\partial \phi}{\partial y}\right) - \frac{\partial}{\partial y}\left(-\frac{\partial \phi}{\partial x}\right)\right] = \frac{1}{2}\left[-\frac{\partial^2 \phi}{\partial x\, \partial y} + \frac{\partial^2 \phi}{\partial y\, \partial x}\right]$$

However, if ϕ is a continuous function then,

$$\frac{\partial^2 \phi}{\partial y\, \partial z} = \frac{\partial^2 \phi}{\partial z\, \partial y};\ \frac{\partial^2 \phi}{\partial z\, \partial x} = \frac{\partial^2 \phi}{\partial x\, \partial z};\ \text{and}\ \frac{\partial^2 \phi}{\partial x\, \partial y} = \frac{\partial^2 \phi}{\partial y\, \partial x}$$

$\therefore$ $\omega_x = \omega_y = \omega_z = 0$ i.e. the flow is *irrotational.*

Thus if *velocity potential* (ϕ) *satisfies the Laplace equation, it represents the possible steady, incompressible, irrotational flow.* Often an *irrotational flow is known as* ***potential flow.***

Equipotential line:

An ***equipotential line*** *is one along which velocity potential* ϕ *is constant.*

i.e. For equipotential line, ϕ = constant.

$\therefore$ $d\phi = 0$

But, $\phi = f(x, y)$ for steady flow.

$$\therefore \quad d\phi = \frac{\partial \phi}{\partial x} dx + \frac{\partial \phi}{\partial y} dy$$

But, $\dfrac{\partial \phi}{\partial x} = -u$ and $\dfrac{\partial \phi}{\partial y} = -v$

$\therefore$ $d\phi = -u dx - v dy = -(u dx + v dy)$

For equipotential line, $d\phi = 0$

or, $-(u dx + v dy) = 0$

or, $(u dx + v dy) = 0$

or, $$\frac{dy}{dx} = -\frac{u}{v} \qquad ...(5.37)$$

where, $\dfrac{dy}{dx}$ = slope of equipotential line.

5.10.2. Stream Function

The **stream function** is *defined as a function of space and time, such that its partial derivative with respect to any direction gives the velocity component at right angles to this direction.* It is denoted by ψ (psi).

In case of two-dimensional flow, the stream function may be defined mathematically as

$$\psi = f(x, y, t) \quad \text{...for } \textit{unsteady} \text{ flow, and}$$

$$\psi = f(x, y) \quad \text{... for } \textit{steady} \text{ flow,}$$

such that:

$$\left.\begin{aligned} u &= \frac{\partial \psi}{\partial y} \\ v &= -\frac{\partial \psi}{\partial x} \end{aligned}\right\} \quad \text{...(5.38)}$$

For two-dimensional flow the continuity equation is

$$\frac{\partial u}{\partial x} + \frac{\partial v}{\partial y} = 0$$

Substituting the values of u and v from eqn. (5.38), we get:

$$\frac{\partial}{\partial x}\left(\frac{\partial \psi}{\partial y}\right) + \frac{\partial}{\partial y}\left(-\frac{\partial \psi}{\partial x}\right) = 0$$

$$\frac{\partial^2 \psi}{\partial x \partial y} - \frac{\partial^2 \psi}{\partial x \partial y} = 0$$

Hence, **existence of ψ means a possible case of fluid flow.**

— The flow may be **'rotational'** or **'irrotational'**.

The rotational component ω_z is given by:

$$\omega_z = \frac{1}{2}\left(\frac{\partial v}{\partial x} - \frac{\partial u}{\partial y}\right)$$

Substituting the values of u and v from eqn. (5.38), we get:

$$\omega_z = \frac{1}{2}\left[\frac{\partial}{\partial x}\left(-\frac{\partial \psi}{\partial x}\right) - \frac{\partial}{\partial y}\left(\frac{\partial \psi}{\partial y}\right)\right]$$

or,

$$\omega_z = -\frac{1}{2}\left[\frac{\partial^2 \psi}{\partial x^2} + \frac{\partial^2 \psi}{\partial y^2}\right] \quad \text{...(5.39)}$$

This equation is known as **Poisson's equation.** For an *irrotational flow*, since $\omega_z = 0$, eqn.(5.39) becomes:

$$\frac{\partial^2 \psi}{\partial x^2} + \frac{\partial^2 \psi}{\partial y^2} = 0 \quad \textit{i.e.,} \quad \Delta^2 \psi = 0$$

which is the ***Laplace equation in*** ψ.

In the *polar co-ordinates*:

$$v_r = \frac{1}{r}\frac{\partial \psi}{\partial \theta}, \; v_\theta = \frac{\partial \psi}{\partial r}$$

— Let $\psi(x, y)$ represent the stream line L (See Fig. 5.21). The $(\psi + d\psi)$ represents the adjacent stream line M. The velocity vector V perpendicular to the line AB has components u and v in the direction of X-axis and Y-axis respectively. From continuity consideration, we have:

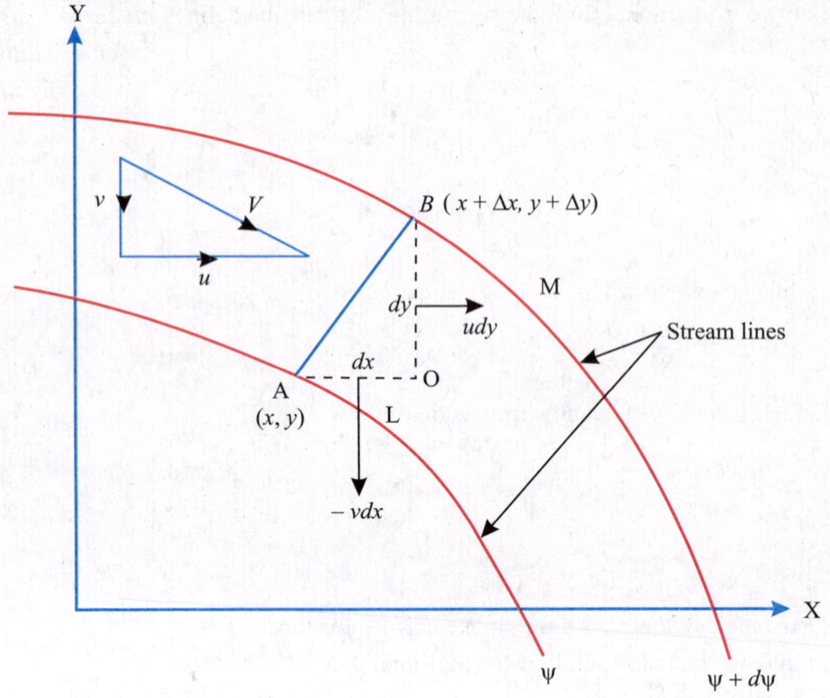

Fig. 5.21. Flow between two points and its relation to stream function.

$$\text{Flow across, } AB = \text{Flow across } AO + \text{flow across } OB$$

$$Vds = -vdx + udy$$

(The minus sign indicates that the velocity v is acting in the *downward direction*).

$$Vds = \frac{\partial \psi}{\partial x}dx + \frac{\partial \psi}{\partial y}dy = d\psi \quad ...(5.40)$$

i.e.

$$dq = d\psi \quad ...(5.41)$$

Obviously, the *stream function* can also be defined as the *flux or flow rate between two stream lines*. The units of ψ are m^3/s discharge per unit thickness of flow.

Properties of stream function

The properties of stream function are:

1. On any stream line, ψ is constant everywhere.

$$\begin{bmatrix} \psi = \text{constant, represents the family of stream lines.} \\ \psi = \text{constant, is a stream line equation.} \end{bmatrix}$$

2. If the flow is *continuous*, the flow around any path in the fluid is *zero*.
3. The rate of change of ψ with distance in arbitrary direction is proportional to the component of velocity normal to that direction.
4. The algebraic sum of stream function for two incompressible flow patterns is the stream function for the flow resulting from the superimposition of these patterns.

i.e.

$$\frac{\partial \psi_1}{\partial s} + \frac{\partial \psi_2}{\partial s} = \frac{\partial (\psi_1 + \psi_2)}{\partial s} \quad ...(5.42)$$

Cauchy Riemann equations:

From the above discussion of velocity potential function and stream function we arrive at the following conclusions:

- *Potential function (ϕ) exists only for irrotational flow.*
- *Stream function (ψ) applies to both the rotational and irrotational flows* (which are steady and incompressible).
- In case of *irrotational flow, both the stream function and velocity function satisfy Laplace equation and as such they are interchangeable.*

For *irrotational incompressible* flow, the following relationship between ϕ and ψ holds good:

$$\left.\begin{aligned} u &= -\frac{\partial \phi}{\partial x} = \frac{\partial \psi}{\partial y} \\ v &= -\frac{\partial \phi}{\partial y} = -\frac{\partial \psi}{\partial x} \end{aligned}\right\} \quad ...(5.43)$$

These equations, in hydrodynamics, are sometimes called "*Cauchy Riemann equations*".

5.10.3. Relation between Stream Function and Velocity Potential

One of the properties of a stream function is that the *difference of its values at two points represent the flow across any line joining the points.* Thus if two lie on the same stream line, then, there being no flow across a stream line, the difference between the stream functions ψ_1 and $\psi_2 = 0$; this means the streamline is given by:

$$\psi = \text{constant.}$$

Similarly, ϕ = constant, represents a case for which the velocity potential is same at every point, and hence it represents an *equipotential line.*

Let, two curves ϕ = constant and ψ = constant intersect each other at any point. At the point of intersection the slopes are:

For the curve ϕ = constant: Slope $= \frac{\partial y}{\partial x} = \frac{\left(\frac{\partial \phi}{\partial x}\right)}{\left(\frac{\partial \phi}{\partial y}\right)} = \frac{-u}{-v} = \frac{u}{v}$

For the curve ψ = constant: Slope $= \frac{\partial y}{\partial x} = \frac{\left(\frac{\partial \psi}{\partial x}\right)}{\left(\frac{\partial \psi}{\partial y}\right)} = \frac{-v}{+u} = -\frac{v}{u}$

Now, product of the slopes of these curves

$$= \frac{u}{v} \times -\frac{v}{u} = -1$$

It shows that these two sets of curves, viz *stream lines* and *equipotential lines intersect each other* **orthogonally** *at all points of intersection.*

5.11. FLOW NETS

A grid obtained by drawing a series of stream lines and equipotential lines is known as a **flow net**. The flow net provides a simple graphical technique for studying two-dimensional irrotational flows especially in the cases where mathematical relations for stream function and velocity function are either not available or are rather difficult and cumbersome to solve.

5.11.1. Methods of Drawing Flow Nets

The following *methods* are used for drawing flow nets:

1. Analytical method (or Mathematical analysis):

— Here, the equations corresponding to the curves ϕ and ψ are first obtained and the same are plotted to give the flow net pattern for the flow of fluid between the given boundary shape.

— This method can be applied to problems with simple and ideal boundary conditions.

2. Graphical method:

— A graphical method consists of drawing stream lines and equipotential lines such that they cut orthogonally and form curvilinear squares.

— This method consumes lot of time and requires lot of erasing to get the proper shape of a flow net.

3. Electrical analogy method:

— This method is a practical method of drawing a flow net for a particular set of boundaries.

— It is based on the fact that the flow of fluids and flow of electricity through a conductor are analogous. These two systems are similar in the respect that electric potential is analogous to the velocity potential, the electric current is analogous to the velocity of flow, and the homogeneous conductor is analogous to the homogeneous fluid.

4. Hydraulic models:

—Stream lines can be traced by injecting a dye in a seepage model or Heleshaw apparatus.

—Then, by drawing equipotential lines the flow net is completed.

Fig 5.22. shows some typical flow nets.

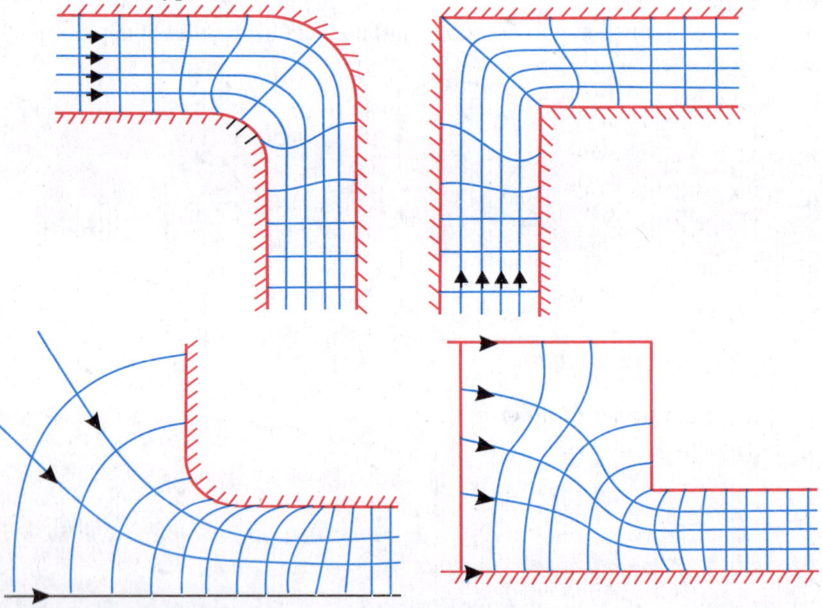

Fig. 5.22. Typical flow nets.

5.11.2. Uses and Limitations of Flow Nets

Use of flow nets:

The following are the *uses* of flow-net analysis:

1. To determine the stream lines and equipotential lines.
2. To determine quantity of seepage and upward lift pressure below hydraulic structure.

3. To determine the velocity and pressure distribution, for given boundaries of flow (provided the velocity distribution and pressure at any reference section are known).
4. To determine the design of the outlets for their streamlining.

Limitations of flow nets:

The following are the *limitations* of flow net:

1. The flow net analysis cannot be applied in the region close to the boundary where the effects of viscosity are predominant.
2. In case of a flow of a fluid past a solid body, while the flow net gives a fairly accurate picture of the flow pattern for the upstream part of the solid body, it can give little information concerning the flow conditions at the rear because of separation and eddies.

Example 5.31. *Verify whether the following functions are valid potential functions*:

(*i*) $\phi = A(x^2 - y^2)$ (*ii*) $\phi = A \cos x$

Solution. (*i*) $\phi = A(x^2 - y^2)$:

$$\frac{\partial \phi}{\partial x} = 2Ax \; ; \quad \frac{\partial \phi}{\partial y} = -2Ay$$

$$\frac{\partial^2 \phi}{\partial x^2} = 2A \; ; \quad \frac{\partial^2 \phi}{\partial y^2} = -2A$$

$$\frac{\partial^2 \phi}{\partial x^2} + \frac{\partial^2 \phi}{\partial y^2} = 2A + (-2A) = 0$$

Hence, $\phi = A(x^2 - y^2)$ is a **valid potential function (Ans.)**

(*ii*) $\phi = A \cos x$:

$$\frac{\partial \phi}{\partial x} = -A \sin x \; ; \quad \frac{\partial \phi}{\partial y} = 0$$

$$\frac{\partial^2 \phi}{\partial x^2} = -A \cos x \; ; \quad \frac{\partial^2 \phi}{\partial y^2} = 0$$

$$\frac{\partial^2 \phi}{\partial x^2} + \frac{\partial^2 \phi}{\partial y^2} = -A \cos x \neq 0$$

Hence, $\phi = A \cos x$ is **not a valid function (Ans.)**

Example 5.32. *Which of the following functions represent possible irrotational flow.?*

(*i*) $\psi = A(x^2 - y^2)$ (*ii*) $\psi = xy$

(*iii*) $\phi = \left(r - \frac{2}{r}\right)\sin\theta$ (*iv*) $\phi = Ur\cos\theta + \frac{U}{r}\cos\theta$

Solution. *For an irrotational fluid flow phenomenon* ϕ *as well* ψ *satisfy Laplace equation.*

(*i*) $\psi = A(x^2 - y^2)$:

$$\frac{\partial \psi}{\partial x} = 2Ax \; ; \quad \frac{\partial \psi}{\partial y} = -2Ay$$

$$\frac{\partial^2 \psi}{\partial x^2} = 2A \; ; \quad \frac{\partial^2 \psi}{\partial y^2} = -2A$$

$$\frac{\partial^2\psi}{\partial x^2} + \frac{\partial^2\psi}{\partial y^2} = 2A - 2A = 0$$

Hence, $\psi = A(x^2 - y^2)$ represents a **possible irrotational flow (Ans.)**

(*ii*) $\psi = xy$:

$$\frac{\partial\psi}{\partial x} = y\,; \quad \frac{\partial\psi}{\partial y} = -x$$

$$\frac{\partial^2\psi}{\partial x^2} = 0; \quad \frac{\partial\psi}{\partial y} = 0$$

$$\therefore \quad \frac{\partial^2\psi}{\partial x^2} + \frac{\partial^2\psi}{\partial y^2} = 0$$

Hence, $\psi = xy$ represents a **possible irrotational flow. (Ans.)**

(*iii*) $\phi = \left(r - \dfrac{2}{r}\right)\sin\theta$:

Laplace equation in radial coordinates (r, θ) is given as:

$$\frac{1}{r}\frac{\partial\phi}{\partial r} + \frac{\partial^2\phi}{\partial r^2} + \frac{1}{r^2}\frac{\partial^2\phi}{\partial\theta^2} = 0$$

$$\frac{\partial\phi}{\partial r} = \left(1 + \frac{2}{r^2}\right)\sin\theta$$

$$\frac{\partial^2\phi}{\partial r^2} = -\frac{2}{r^3}\sin\theta$$

$$\frac{\partial\phi}{\partial\theta} = \left(r - \frac{2}{r}\right)\cos\theta$$

$$\frac{\partial^2\phi}{\partial\theta^2} = -\left(r - \frac{2}{r}\right)\sin\theta = \left(\frac{2}{r} - r\right)\sin\theta$$

L.H.S. of Laplace equation is:

$$\frac{1}{r} \times \left(1 + \frac{2}{r^2}\right)\sin\theta - \frac{2}{r^3}\sin\theta + \frac{1}{r^2}\left(\frac{2}{r} - r\right)\sin\theta$$

$$= \sin\theta\left(\frac{1}{r} + \frac{2}{r^3} - \frac{2}{r^3} + \frac{2}{r^3} - \frac{1}{r}\right)$$

$$= \sin\theta\left(\frac{2}{r^3}\right) \neq 0$$

Hence, the given function **doesnot represent any possible irrotational flow. (Ans.)**

(*iv*) $\phi = Ur\cos\theta + \dfrac{U}{r}\cos\theta$:

$$\frac{\partial\phi}{\partial r} = U\cos\theta - \frac{U}{r^2}\cos\theta$$

$$\frac{\partial^2\phi}{\partial r^2} = \frac{2U}{r^3}\cos\theta$$

$$\frac{\partial \phi}{\partial \theta} = -Ur\sin\theta - \frac{U}{r}\sin\theta$$

$$\frac{\partial^2 \phi}{\partial \theta^2} = -Ur\cos\theta - \frac{U}{r}\cos\theta$$

The Laplace equation, in radial coordinates (r, θ), is given by:

$$\frac{1}{r}\frac{\partial \phi}{\partial r} + \frac{\partial^2 \phi}{\partial r^2} + \frac{1}{r^2}\frac{\partial^2 \phi}{\partial \theta^2} = 0$$

Substituting for L.H.S. terms, we get:

$$= \frac{1}{r}\left(U\cos\theta - \frac{U}{r^2}\cos\theta\right) + \frac{2U}{r^3}\cos\theta + \frac{1}{r^2}\left(-Ur\cos\theta - \frac{U}{r}\cos\theta\right)$$

$$U\cos\theta\left(\frac{1}{r} - \frac{1}{r^3} + \frac{2}{r^3} - \frac{1}{r} - \frac{1}{r^3}\right) = 0$$

The Laplace equation is satisfied and hence the given function ϕ **represents a possible irrotational flow. (Ans.)**

Example 5.33. *The velocity components in a fluid flow are given by:*

$$u = 2xy;\ v = a^2 + x^2 - y^2$$

(i) Show that the flow is possible.

(ii) Derive the relative stream function.

Solution. *Given*: $u = 2xy;\ v = a^2 + x^2 - y^2$ ...Velocity components

(*i*)
$$\frac{\partial u}{\partial x} = 2y\ ;\quad \frac{\partial v}{\partial y} = -2y$$

$$\frac{\partial u}{\partial x} + \frac{\partial v}{\partial y} = 2y + (-2y) = 0$$

The *continuity equation for steady, incompressible flow is satisfied.*

Hence, **flow is possible. (Ans.)**

(*ii*) The stream function ψ is related to u and v as:

$$u = \frac{\partial \psi}{\partial y} = 2xy$$

or,
$$\psi = \int 2xy\, dy = xy^2 + f(x) \qquad ...(i)$$

$$-\frac{\partial \psi}{\partial x} = -y^2 - f'(x) = v = a^2 + x^2 - y^2$$

Hence,
$$f'(x) = -(a^2 + x^2)$$

or,
$$f(x) = -a^2x - \frac{x^3}{3} + \text{constant}$$

Inserting for $f(x)$ in eqn. (*i*) we get:

$$\psi = xy^2 - ax^2 - \frac{x^3}{3} + \text{constant}$$

Thus, the relative ψ = $\boldsymbol{xy^2 - a^2x - \frac{x^3}{3}}$ **+ constant (Ans.)**

Example 5.34. *A stream function is given by:*

$$\psi = 3x^2y + (3 + t)y^2$$

Find the flow rates across the faces of the triangular prism having a thickness of 2.5 m in the Z- direction at the time instant t = 3 seconds.

Solution. Refer to Fig. 5.23.

$$\psi = 3x^2y + (3 + t)\,y^2 \quad \text{...Given}$$

The coordinates of point M are: (0,1)

$\therefore \quad \psi_M = 0 + (3 + 3) \times 1^2 = 6$

The coordinates of point L are: (1.5, 0)

$\therefore \quad \psi_L = 3 \times 1.5^2 \times 0 + (3 + 3) \times 0 = 0$

The coordinates of point L are: (0,0)

$\therefore$ *Flow rate across face* MO = $2.5\,(\psi_M - \psi_O)$

$= 2.5\,(6 - 0) =$ **15 m³/s (Ans.)**

Flow rate across face LO = $2.5\,(\psi_L - \psi_O)$

$= 2.5\,(0 - 0) = 0$

$\therefore$ *Flow rate across face* LM = $2.5\,(\psi_M - \psi_L)$

$= 2.5\,(6 - 0) =$ **15 m³/s (Ans.)**

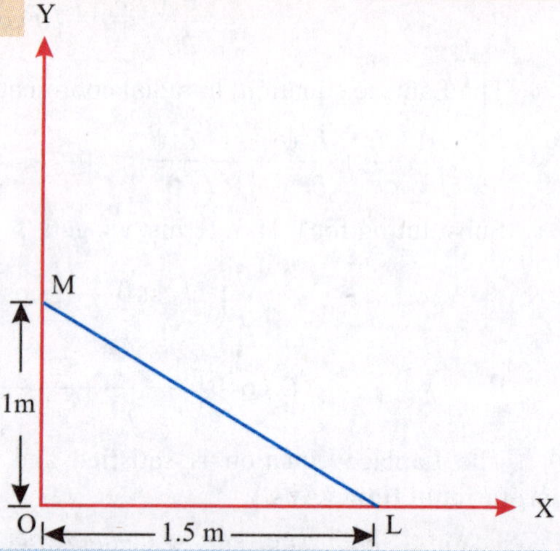

Fig. 5.23

Example 5.35. *A flow is described by the stream function* $\psi = 4xy$ *. Locate the point at which the velocity vector has a magnitude 7 units and makes an angle of 150° with X-axis.*

Solution. Stream function, $\psi = 4xy$ ...Given

The velocity components for the given flow field are:

$$u = \frac{\partial \psi}{\partial y} = \frac{\partial}{\partial y}(4xy) = 4x$$

$$v = -\frac{\partial \psi}{\partial x} = -\frac{\partial}{\partial x}(4xy) = -4y$$

$$V = \sqrt{u^2 + v^2} \quad \text{or} \quad 7 = \sqrt{(4x)^2 + (-4y)^2} = 4\sqrt{x^2 + y^2} \quad \text{...}(i)$$

Also, $\tan\theta = \frac{v}{u}$ or $\tan 150° = \frac{-4y}{4x} = -\frac{y}{x}$

or, $-0.577 = -\frac{y}{x}$ or $y = 0.577\,x$

Substituting for y in eqn. (i), we get:

$$7 = 4\sqrt{x^2 + (0.577\,x)^2} = 4.62\,x$$

$\therefore \quad x = \frac{7}{4.62} =$ **1.515 (Ans.)**

Example. 5.36. *Find a relevant stream function to each of the following sets of velocity components of steady, incompressible flow:*

(i) $u = 2cx;\ v = -2cy$

(ii) $u = -cx/y;\ v = c\ ln\,(xy)$

(iii) $u = x + y\,;\ v = x - y$

Solution. (i) $u = 2cx;\ v = -2cy$:

$$\frac{\partial u}{\partial x} = 2c; \quad \frac{\partial v}{\partial x} = -2c$$

$$\frac{\partial v}{\partial x} + \frac{\partial v}{\partial y} = 2i + (-2c) = 0.$$ Hence the *flow is possible and* ψ *exists.*

$$u = \frac{\partial \psi}{\partial y} = 2cx$$

$$\psi = 2cxy + f(x)$$

$$-\frac{\partial \psi}{\partial x} = -2cy - f'(x) = v = -2cy$$

Hence, $f'(x) = 0$ and $f(x) = c_1 = a$ constant

$\therefore$ $\psi =$ **$2cxy + c_1$ (Ans.)**

(*ii*) $u = -cx/y;\ v = c\ ln\,(xy)$:

$$\frac{\partial u}{\partial x} = -c/y; \quad \frac{\partial v}{\partial y} = c/y$$

$$\frac{\partial u}{\partial x} + \frac{\partial v}{\partial y} = -c/y + c/y = 0$$

Hence, the *flow is possible and* ψ *exists.*

$$u = \frac{\partial \psi}{\partial y} = -cx/y$$

$$\psi = -cx\ ln\,(y) + f(x)$$

$$-\frac{\partial \psi}{\partial x} = c\ ln\,(y) - f'(x) = v = c\ ln\,(xy) = c\ ln\,(x) + c\ ln\,(y)$$

or, $f'(x) = -c\ ln\,(x)$

$$f(x) = -\int c\,ln(x).dx = -c(x\,ln\,(x) - x) + c_2$$

where, c_2 = a constant.

Hence, the stream function representing this flow is:

$\therefore$ $\psi = -cx\ ln\,(y) - c\,(x\ ln\,(x) - x) + c_2$

$= -cx\ ln\,(y) - cx\ ln\,(x) + cx + c_2$

or, **$\psi = -cx\ ln\,(xy) + cx + c_2$ (Ans.)**

(*iii*) $u = x + y;\ v = x - y$:

$$\frac{\partial u}{\partial x} = 1; \quad \frac{\partial v}{\partial y} = -1$$

$$\frac{\partial u}{\partial x} + \frac{\partial v}{\partial y} = 1 + (-1) = 0.$$ Hence the *flow is possible and* ψ *exists.*

$$u = \frac{\partial \psi}{\partial y} = x + y$$

$$\psi = xy + \frac{y^2}{2} + f(x)$$

$$-\frac{\partial \psi}{\partial x} = -y - f'(x) = v = x - y$$

or, $$f'(x) = -x$$

and, $$f(x) = \int -x\,dx = -\frac{x^2}{2} + c \text{. where } c = \text{constant}$$

$\therefore$ $$\psi = xy + \frac{y^2}{2} - \frac{x^2}{2} + c$$

or, $$\psi = \frac{1}{2}(y^2 - x^2) + xy + c \quad \textbf{(Ans.)}$$

Example 5.37. *For the following stream functions calculate velocity at a point (1, 2):*
(i) *$\psi = 3\,xy$* ***(ii)*** *$y = 3x^2y - y^3$*

Solution. (*i*) $\psi = 3xy$: ...(Given)

$$u = \frac{\partial \psi}{\partial y} = 3x$$

$$v = -\frac{\partial \psi}{\partial x} = -3y$$

At (1,2): $u = 3 \times 1 = 3$

$$v = -3 \times 2 = -6$$

$\therefore$ $$\mathbf{V} = \sqrt{u^2 + v^2} = \sqrt{(3)^2 + (-6)^2} = \sqrt{45} \text{ units. } \textbf{(Ans.)}$$

(*ii*) $\psi = 3x^2y - y^3$: ...(Given)

$$u = \frac{\partial \psi}{\partial y} = 3x^2 - 3y^2$$

$$v = -\frac{\partial \psi}{\partial x} = -6xy$$

At (1,2): $u = 3 \times (1)^2 - 3 \times (2)^2 = -9$

$$v = -6 \times 1 \times 2 = -12$$

$$\mathbf{V} = \sqrt{u^2 + v^2} = \sqrt{(-9)^2 + (-12)^2} = \mathbf{15} \textbf{ (Ans.)}$$

Example 5.38. *What is the irrotational velocity field associated with the potential $\phi = 3x^2 - 3x + 3y^2 + 16\,t^2 + 12zt$. Does the flow field satisfy the incompressible continuity equation?* **[UPSC]**

Solution. *Given:* $\phi = 3x^2 - 3x + 3y^2 + 16t^2 + 12\,zt$

The velocity field is represented by:

$$u = -\frac{\partial \phi}{\partial x}, \quad v = -\frac{\partial \phi}{\partial y}$$

$\therefore$ $$u = -\frac{\partial}{\partial x}(3x^2 - 3x + 3y^2 + 16t^2 + 12zt) = -6x + 3$$

and, $$v = -\frac{\partial}{\partial y}(3x^2 - 3x + 3y^2 + 16t^2 + 12zt) = -6y$$

Also, $$\frac{\partial u}{\partial x} = \frac{\partial}{dx}(-6x + 3) = -6$$

and, $$\frac{\partial v}{\partial y} = \frac{\partial}{dy}(-6y) = -6$$

The continuity equation for an incompressible fluid is:

$$\frac{\partial u}{\partial x} + \frac{\partial v}{dy} = 0$$

Substituting the values, we get:

$$\frac{\partial u}{\partial x} + \frac{\partial v}{dy} = -6 - 6 = -12$$

This shows that the given velocity field **does not satisfy the continuity equation. (Ans.)**

Example 5.39. *The velocity potential function for a two-dimensional flow is* $\phi = x(2y - 1)$. *At a point P (4, 5) determine:*

(i) The velocity, and

(ii) The value of stream function. **[UPTU]**

Solution. *Given*: $\phi = x(2y - 1)$...Velocity potential function.

(*i*) The velocity at a point P(4, 5):

The velocity components in x and y directions are:

$$u = -\frac{\partial \phi}{\partial x} = -\frac{\partial}{dx}[x(2y - 1)] = -2y + 1$$

$$v = -\frac{\partial \phi}{\partial y} = -\frac{\partial}{\partial y}[x(2y - 1)] = -2x$$

∴ Resultant velocity,

$$V = \sqrt{u^2 + v^2} = \sqrt{(-2y + 1)^2 + (-2x)^2}$$

∴ At the point $P(4, 5)$ when $x = 4$ and $y = 5$, we have:

$$V = \sqrt{(-2 \times 5 + 1)^2 + (-2 \times 4)^2} = \sqrt{9^2 + 8^2} = \mathbf{12.04 \text{ units}}$$ **(Ans.)**

(*ii*) The value of stream function at the point (4, 5):

For stream function,

$$d\psi = \frac{\partial \psi}{\partial x}dx + \frac{\partial \psi}{\partial y}dy$$

or, $$d\psi = -vdx + udy$$

or, $$d\psi = +2xdx + (-2y + 1)\,dy$$

Integrating both sides, we get:

$$\psi = +2 \times \frac{x^2}{2} + \left(-2 \times \frac{y^2}{2} + y\right) + C$$

(where C = constant of integration)

For $\psi = 0$ at the origin, the constant $C = 0$

$\therefore \quad \psi = +x^2 - y^2 + y$

At the point $P(4,5)$,

$\psi = +(4)^2 - (5)^2 + 5 = -$ **4 units (Ans.)**

Example 5.40. *For a two-dimensional flow the velocity function is given by the expression,* $\phi = x^2 - y^2$.

(i) *Determine velocity components in x and y directions.*

(ii) *Show that the velocity components satisfy the conditions of flow continuity and irrotationality.*

(iii) *Determine stream function and the flow rate between the stream lines (2, 0) and (2, 2).*

(iv) *Show that the streamlines and potential lines intersect orthogonally at the point (2, 2).*

Solution. *Given*: $\phi = x^2 - y^2$ ...Velocity function.

(i) Velocity components in x and y directions:

The velocity components in x and y directions are:

$$u = -\frac{\partial \phi}{\partial x} = -\frac{\partial}{\partial x}(x^2 - y^2) = -2x \text{ (Ans.)}$$

$$v = -\frac{\partial \phi}{\partial y} = -\frac{\partial}{\partial y}(x^2 - y^2) = +2y \text{ (Ans.)}$$

(ii) Continuity, irrotationality = ?

From the velocity components, we have:

$$\frac{\partial u}{\partial x} = -2, \frac{\partial v}{\partial y} = +2$$

Conditions of flow continuity will be satisfied if:

$$\frac{\partial u}{\partial x} + \frac{\partial v}{\partial y} = 0$$

Substituting the values, we get $-2 + 2 = 0$

Hence, the **velocity components satisfy the flow continuity conditions (Ans.)**

Now,
$$\nabla \times V = \begin{vmatrix} i & j & k \\ \frac{\partial}{\partial x} & \frac{\partial}{\partial y} & \frac{\partial}{\partial z} \\ -2x & +2y & 0 \end{vmatrix}$$

$$= i\left[\frac{\partial}{\partial y}(0) - \frac{\partial}{\partial z}(+2y)\right] + j\left[\frac{\partial}{\partial z}(-2x) - \frac{\partial}{\partial x}(0)\right]$$

$$+ \left[\frac{\partial}{\partial x}(+2y) - \frac{\partial}{\partial y}(-2x)\right]$$

Since curl V is zero, hence the flow is **irrotational.** **...(Proved)**

(iii) Stream function and flow rate:

The differential $d\psi$ for the stream function is (eqn. 5.40):

$$d\psi = \frac{\partial \psi}{\partial x}dx + \frac{\partial \psi}{\partial y}dy = -vdx + udy$$

$$= -(+2y)\,dx + (-2x)\,dy = -2d\,(xy)$$

Integrating, we get:

$$\psi = -2xy + C \quad \textbf{(Ans.)}$$

(where, C = constant of integration)

Now, $\psi(2, 0) = 2 \times 2 \times 0 = 0$

and, $\psi(2, 2) = 2 \times 2 \times 2 = 8$

Hence, flow between the streamlines through (2, 0) and (2, 2)

$$= 8 - 0 = \mathbf{8\ m^3/s} \ \textbf{(Ans.)}$$

(*iv*) Intersection of stream lines and potential lines orthogonally at point (2, 2) = ?

Slope of stream line,

$$\left(\frac{\partial y}{\partial x}\right)_{\psi = \text{const.}} = -\frac{v}{u} = -\frac{+2y}{-2x} = 1 \text{ at } (2, 2)$$

Slope of potential line,

$$\left(\frac{\partial y}{\partial x}\right)_{\phi = \text{const.}} = \frac{u}{v} = \left(\frac{-2x}{+2y}\right) = -1 \text{ at } (2, 2)$$

Thus, $$\left(\frac{\partial y}{\partial x}\right)_{\psi = \text{const.}} \times \left(\frac{\partial y}{\partial x}\right)_{\phi = \text{cosnt.}} = 1 \times (-1) = -1$$

which shows that the **stream lines and the potential lines intersect orthogonally.** .....**(Proved)**

Example 5.41. *A two-dimensional flow field is given by* $\phi = 3xy$, *determine:*

(*i*) *The stream function.*

(*ii*) *The velocity at L(2, 6) and M (6,6) and the pressure difference between the points L and M.*

(*iii*) *The discharge between the stream lines passing through the points L and M.*

Solution. *Given.* $\phi = 3xy$ ...Flow field

(*i*) The stream function ψ:

We know that: $$u = -\frac{\partial \phi}{\partial x} = -\frac{\partial}{\partial x}(3xy) = -3y$$

$$v = -\frac{\partial \phi}{\partial y} = -\frac{\partial}{\partial y}(3xy) = -3x$$

Also, $$u = \frac{\partial \psi}{\partial y} = -3y, \text{ and } \quad v = -\frac{\partial \psi}{\partial x} = -3x$$

Again, $$d\psi = \frac{\partial \psi}{\partial x}dx + \frac{\partial \psi}{\partial y}dy \quad \text{or} \quad \partial\psi = 3x dx + (-3y)\, dy$$

Integrating both sides, we get:

$$\psi = \int 3x\, dx + \int (-3y)\, dy$$

$$= 3 \times \frac{x^2}{2} - 3 \times \frac{y^2}{2} + C = \frac{3}{2}(x^2 - y^2) + C$$

(where, C = constant of integration.)

For $\psi = 0$ at the origin, the constant $C = 0$

$$\therefore \quad \psi = \frac{3}{2}(x^2 - y^2) \quad \textbf{(Ans.)}$$

(*ii*) Velocities at L and M:

At $L(2, 6)$: $u = -3 \times 6 = -18$, $v = -3 \times 2 = -6$

$$\therefore \quad \mathbf{V_L} = \sqrt{u^2 + v^2} = \sqrt{(-18)^2 + (-6)^2} = \mathbf{18.97\ units\ (Ans.)}$$

At M(6, 6): $u = -3 \times 6 = -18$, $v = -3 \times 6 = -18$

$$\therefore \quad \mathbf{V_M} = \sqrt{u^2 + v^2} = \sqrt{(-18)^2 + (-18)^2} = \mathbf{25.45\ units\ (Ans.)}$$

Pressure difference between *L* and *M*:

For two-dimensional plane flow:

$$\frac{p_L}{w} + \frac{V_L^2}{2g} = \frac{p_M}{w} + \frac{V_M^2}{2g}$$

$$\therefore \quad \frac{p_L - p_M}{w} = \frac{1}{2g}(V_M^2 - V_L^2) = \frac{648 - 360}{2 \times 9.81} = \mathbf{14.68\ units\ (Ans.)}$$

(*iii*) The discharge between the streamlines, *q*:

$$\psi = \frac{3}{2}(x^2 - y^2)$$

$$\psi_{L(2,6)} = \frac{3}{2}(2^2 - 6^2) = -48 \text{ units.}$$

$$\psi_{M(2,6)} = \frac{3}{2}(6^2 - 6^2) = 0$$

$$\therefore \quad q = \psi_M - \psi_L = 0 - (-48) = \mathbf{48\ units\ (Ans.)}$$

Example 5.42. *If $\phi = 3xy$, find x and y components of velocity at (1, 3) and (3, 3). Determine the discharge passing between stream lines passing through these points.* **[Roorkee University]**

Solution. *Given*: $\phi = 3xy$ ...Velocity potential function.

The velocity components in terms of ϕ are given by:

$$u = -\frac{\partial \phi}{\partial x}, \quad v = -\frac{\partial \phi}{\partial y}$$

But,
$$\frac{\partial \phi}{\partial x} = \frac{\partial}{\partial x}(3xy) = 3y, \text{ and}$$

$$\frac{\partial \phi}{\partial y} = \frac{\partial}{\partial y}(3xy) = 3x$$

$$\therefore \quad u = -3y \text{ and } v = -3x$$

Hence, the velocity components at (1, 3) and (3, 3) are:

At (1, 3) :
$$\left.\begin{aligned} u &= -3 \times 3 = -9 \\ v &= -3 \times 1 = -3 \end{aligned}\right\} \textbf{(Ans)}$$

At (3, 3) :
$$\left.\begin{aligned} u &= -3 \times 3 = -9 \\ v &= -3 \times 3 = -9 \end{aligned}\right\} \textbf{(Ans)}$$

Discharge between the streamlines:

The total derivative ψ may be written as:

$$d\psi = \frac{\partial \psi}{\partial x}dx + \frac{\partial \psi}{\partial y}dy$$

But, $u = \frac{\partial \psi}{\partial y}$ and $v = -\frac{\partial \psi}{\partial x}$

$\therefore$ $\partial \psi = -vdx + udy$

or, $\partial \psi = 3xdx - 3ydy$

Integrating, we get: $\psi = \frac{3}{2}x^2 - \frac{3}{2}y^2 + C$

(where, C = constant of integration)

Discharge between the streamlines passing through (1, 3) and (3, 3)

$$= \psi_{(1,3)} - \psi_{(3,3)} = \frac{3}{2}(1 - 9) - \frac{3}{2}(9 - 9) = -\ 12 \text{ units}$$ **(Ans.)**

Example 5.43. *The streamlines are represented by:*

(*a*) $\psi = x^2 - y^2$ **(*b*)** $\psi = x^2 + y^2$

(*i*) *Determine the velocity and its direction at* (2, 2).

(*ii*) *Sketch the streamlines and show the direction of flow in each case.*

Solution. In a two-dimensional steady flow the velocity components in terms of ψ are given as:

$$u = \frac{\partial \psi}{\partial y} \text{ and } v = -\frac{\partial \psi}{\partial x}$$

Case (*a*) $\psi = x^2 - y^2$:

(*i*) Velocity and its direction at (2, 2):

$$\psi = x^2 - y^2 \quad ...(1)$$

$\therefore$ $\frac{\partial \psi}{\partial y} = -2y$ and $\frac{\partial \psi}{\partial x} = 2x$

$\therefore$ $u = -2y$ and $v = -2x$

$$\therefore \quad V = \sqrt{u^2 + v^2} = \sqrt{(-2y)^2 + (-2x)^2} = 2\sqrt{x^2 + y^2} \quad ...(2)$$

i.e. $V = 2\sqrt{x^2 + y^2}$

$\therefore$ Velocity at (2, 2) $= 2\sqrt{2^2 + 2^2} = \mathbf{4\sqrt{2}}$ **units (Ans.)**

Its direction has a slope, $\frac{\partial y}{\partial x} = -\frac{v}{u} = -\frac{-2x}{-2y} = +1 \quad ...(3)$

$\therefore$ Velocity vector is inclined at **45° to *x*-axis (Ans.)**

(*ii*) Stream lines-sketch:

The streamlines are lines of constant ψ, and for constant ψ, eqn. (1) represents hyperbola, which may be plotted for different values of ψ as shown in the table given below:

$$\left[\frac{\psi = x^2 - y^2}{x = \pm\sqrt{y^2 + \psi}}\right]$$

	y	0	1	2	3
$\psi = 1$	$x = \pm\sqrt{y^2 + \psi}$	± 1	$\pm\sqrt{2}$	$\pm\sqrt{5}$	$\pm\sqrt{10}$
$\psi = 2$	$x = \pm\sqrt{y^2 + \psi}$	$\pm\sqrt{2}$	$\pm\sqrt{3}$	$\pm\sqrt{6}$	$\pm\sqrt{11}$
$\psi = 3$	$x = \pm\sqrt{y^2 + \psi}$	$\pm\sqrt{3}$	$\pm\sqrt{4}$	$\pm\sqrt{7}$	$\pm\sqrt{12}$

Fig. 5.24 shows the pattern of stream lines.

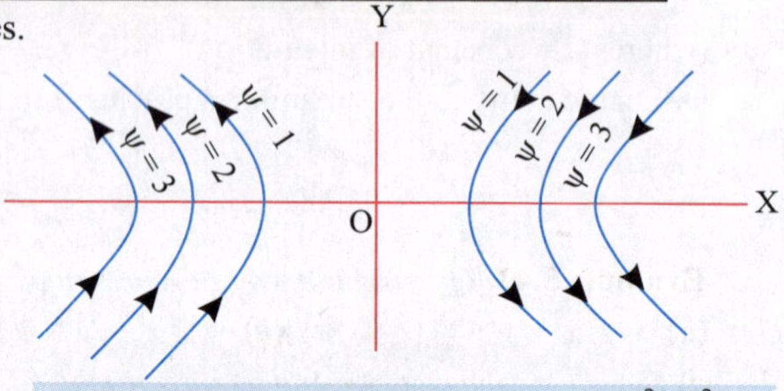

Fig. 5.24. Pattern of streamlines of $\psi = x^2 - y^2$.

Case (b) $\psi = x^2 + y^2$:

(*i*) Velocity and its direction at (2, 2)

$$\psi = x^2 + y^2 \qquad ...(4)$$

Now, $\dfrac{\partial \psi}{\partial y} = 2y$ and $\dfrac{\partial \psi}{\partial x} = 2x$

Hence, $u = 2y$ and $v = -2x$

The resultant velocity,

$$V = \sqrt{u^2 + v^2} = \sqrt{(2y)^2 + (-2x)^2}$$

$$= 2\sqrt{x^2 + y^2}$$

$\therefore$ Velocity at (2, 2) $= 2\sqrt{2^2 + 2^2} = \mathbf{4\sqrt{2}}$ **units (Ans.)**

Its direction has a slope,

$$\frac{\partial y}{\partial x} = -\frac{v}{u} = -\frac{-2x}{2y} = \frac{x}{y} = \frac{2}{2} = 1$$

i.e., velocity makes an angle θ with the axis shown in Fig. 5.25, given by:

tan θ = 1 or θ = **45° (Ans.)**

***(ii)* Stream lines-sketch:**

For a streamlines ψ = constant, and for non-zero value of ψ, eqn. (4) represents *concentric circles* with centre at the origin (0, 0) and radius $\sqrt{\psi}$. In the 1st (i.e. positive) quadrant. (x, y both positive), $u = 2y$ and $v = -2x$ is negative. Therefore, streamlines have clockwise direction as shown in Fig 5.26.

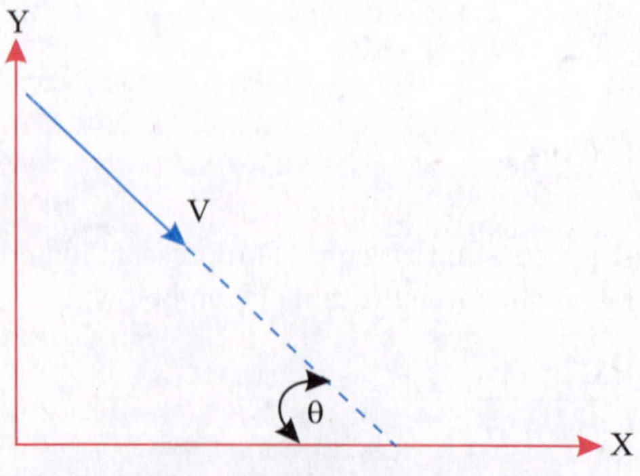

Fig. 5.25

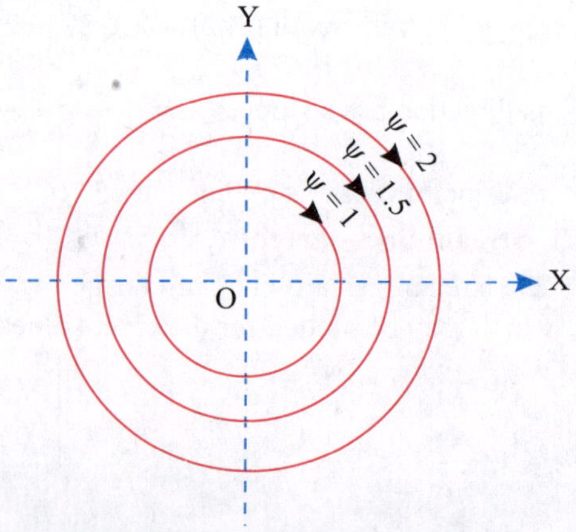

Fig. 5.26. Pattern of streamlines $\psi = x^2 + y^2$.

Example 5.44. *If the expression for stream function is described by* $\psi = x^3 - 3xy^2$, *determine whether flow is rotational or irrotational. If the flow is irrotational, then indicate the correct value of the velocity potential.*

(*a*) $\phi = y^3 - 3xy^2$ (*b*) $\phi = -3x^2y$ **[UPSC]**

Solution. *Given*: $\psi = x^3 - 3xy^2$ ...Stream function

A two-dimensional flow in $x - y$ plane will be irrotational if the vorticity vector in the z-direction is zero.

i.e., $$\Omega_z = \frac{\partial v}{\partial x} - \frac{\partial u}{\partial y} = 0 \quad ...(1)$$

We know, $$u = \frac{\partial \psi}{\partial y} = \frac{\partial}{\partial y}\left(x^3 - 3xy^2\right) = -6xy \text{, and}$$

$$v = -\frac{\partial \psi}{\partial x} = -\frac{\partial}{\partial x}\left(x^3 - 3xy^2\right) = -\left(3x^2 - 3y^2\right) = -3(x^2 - y^2)$$

$$\therefore \quad \frac{\partial u}{\partial y} = -6\text{, and } \frac{\partial v}{\partial x} = -6\text{x}$$

Substituting these value in eqn. (1), we get:

$$\Omega_z = -6x - (-6x) = 0$$

Hence, the **flow is irrotational. (Ans.)**

For an irrotational flow Laplace equation in ϕ must be satisfied.

i.e. $$\frac{\partial^2 \phi}{\partial x^2} + \frac{\partial^2 \phi}{\partial y^2} = 0$$

Let us check the validity for each expression for ϕ:

(*a*) $\phi = y^3 - 3xy^2$

$$\frac{\partial^2 \phi}{\partial x^2} = -6y \quad \text{and} \quad \frac{\partial^2 \phi}{\partial y^2} = 6y$$

$$\therefore \quad \frac{\partial^2 \phi}{\partial x^2} + \frac{\partial^2 \phi}{\partial y^2} = -6y + 6y = 0$$

(*b*) $\phi = -3x^2y$

$$\frac{\partial^2 \phi}{\partial x^2} = -6y \quad \text{and} \quad \frac{\partial^2 \phi}{\partial y^2} = 0$$

$$\therefore \quad \frac{\partial^2 \phi}{\partial x^2} + \frac{\partial^2 \phi}{\partial y} \neq 0$$

Hence, the correct value of ϕ = $\boldsymbol{y^3 - 3xy^2}$ **(Ans.)**

Example 5.45. *In a two-dimensional incompressible flow, the fluid velocity components are given by* $u = x - 4y$ and $v = -y - 4x$. *Show that velocity potential exists and determine its form as well as stream function.* **[PTU]**

Solution. *Given:* $u = x - 4y$ and $v = -y - 4x$ ...Velocity components.

The velocity potential will exist if flow is *irrotational.* Therefore, the *vorticity component in the Z-direction must be zero.*

Now, $\Omega_z = \frac{\partial v}{\partial x} - \frac{\partial u}{\partial y}$

Here, $\frac{\partial v}{\partial x} = \frac{\partial}{\partial x}(-y - 4x) = -4$,

and, $\frac{\partial u}{\partial y} = \frac{\partial}{\partial y}(x - 4y) = -4$

$\therefore$ $\frac{\partial v}{\partial x} - \frac{\partial u}{\partial y} = -4 - (-4) = 0$

Since the *vorticity is zero,* the *flow is irrotational*; hence the **velocity potential exists. (Ans.)**
Total change in velocity potential,

$$d\phi = \frac{\partial \phi}{\partial x}dx + \frac{\partial \phi}{\partial y}dy$$

$$= -udx - vdy = -(x - 4y)dx - (-y - 4x)dy$$

or $d\phi = -xdx + 4ydx + ydy + 4xdy$

Integrating, we get:

$$\phi = -\frac{x^2}{2} + 4xy + \frac{y^2}{2} + 4xy + C$$

$$= \frac{1}{2}(y^2 - x^2) + 8xy + C$$

(where, C = constant of integration).
For $\phi = 0$ at the origin, the constant $C = 0$

$\therefore$ $\boldsymbol{\phi = \frac{1}{2}(y^2 - x^2) + 8xy}$ **(Ans.)**

For *stream function,*

$$d\psi = \frac{\partial \psi}{\partial x}dx + \frac{\partial \psi}{\partial y}dy$$

We know, $u = \frac{\partial \psi}{\partial y}$ and $v = -\frac{\partial \psi}{\partial x}$

$\therefore$ $d\psi = -vdx + udy = [-(-y - 4x)]dx + (x - 4y)dy$

or $d\psi = (y + 4x)dx + (x - 4y)dy$

Integrating, we get:

$$\psi = xy + 4 \times \frac{x^2}{2} + xy - 4 \times \frac{y^2}{2} + C_1$$

$$= xy + 2x^2 + xy - 2y^2 + C_1$$

$$= 2(x^2 - y^2) + 2xy + C_1$$

(where C_1 = constant of integration)
For $\phi = 0$ at the origin, the constant $C_1 = 0$

$\therefore$ $\boldsymbol{\psi = 2(x^2 - y^2) + 2xy}$ **(Ans.)**

Example 5.46. *In the two-dimensional incompressible flow field the velocity components are expressed as:*

$$u = 2x - x^2y + \frac{y^3}{3} \; ; v = xy^2 - 2y - \frac{x^3}{3}$$

(*i*) *Determine the velocity, and acceleration at point* L (x = 1 m, y = 3 m).

(*ii*) *Is the flow possible? If so, obtain an expression for the stream function.*

(*iii*) *What is the discharge between streamlines passing through* (1, 3) *and* (2, 3)?

(*iv*) *Is the flow irrotational? If so, determine the corresponding velocity potential.*

(*v*) *Show that each of the stream, and potential functions satisfy Laplace equation.*

[MDU Haryana]

Solution. *Given*: $u = 2x - x^2y + \frac{y^3}{3}$; $v = xy^2 - 2y - \frac{x^3}{3}$ ...Velocity components

(*i*) Velocity and acceleration at point L(x = 1 m, y = 3 m):

$$u = 2x - x^2y + \frac{y^3}{3} = 2 \times 1 - 1^2 \times 3 + \frac{3^3}{3} = 8 \text{ m/s}$$

$$v = xy^2 - 2y - \frac{x^3}{3} = 1 \times 3^2 - 2 \times 3 - \frac{1^3}{3} = 2.67 \text{ m/s}$$

Resultant velocity, $V = \sqrt{u^2 + v^2} = \sqrt{(8)^2 + (2.67)^2}$ = **8.43 m/s (Ans.)**

If the velocity is at an angle θ with X-axis, then:

$$\tan\theta = \frac{v}{u} = \frac{2.67}{8} = 0.3337 \quad \text{or } \theta = 18.45°$$

For a steady flow,

$$a_x = u\frac{\partial u}{\partial x} + v\frac{\partial u}{\partial y}$$

$$= \left(2x - xy^2 + \frac{y^3}{3}\right)(2 - 2xy) + \left(xy^2 - xy - \frac{x^3}{3}\right)(y^2 - x^2)$$

∴ Acceleration in the X-direction at x = 1and y = 3,

$$a_x = 8\,(2 - 2 \times 1 \times 3) + 2.67\,(3^2 - 1^2) = -\,10.64 \text{ m/s}^2$$

Further, $$a_y = u\,\frac{\partial v}{\partial x} + v\frac{\partial v}{\partial y}$$

$$= \left(2x - xy^2 + \frac{y^3}{3}\right)(y^2 - x^2) + \left(xy^2 - xy - \frac{x^3}{3}\right)(2xy - 2)$$

$$= 8\,(3^2 - 1^2) + 2.67\,(2 \times 1 \times 3 - 2) = 74.68 \text{ m/s}^2$$

Resultant acceleration, $a = \sqrt{a_x^2 + a_y^2} = \sqrt{(-\,10.64)^2 + (74.68)^2}$ = **75.43 m/s² (Ans.)**

(*ii*) Is the flow physically possible:

$$\frac{\partial u}{\partial x} + \frac{\partial v}{\partial y} = (2 - 2xy) + (2xy - 2) = 0$$

As the continuity equation is satisfied, hence the **flow is physically possible. (Ans.)**

Expression for stream function:

The differential $d\psi$ for stream function is,

$$d\psi = \frac{\partial \psi}{\partial x} dx + \frac{\partial \psi}{\partial y} dy$$

$$= -vdx + udy$$

$$= -\left(xy^2 - 2y - \frac{x^3}{3}\right) dx + \left(2x - x^2 y + \frac{y^3}{3}\right) dy$$

$$= \left(-xy^2 + 2y + \frac{x^3}{3}\right) dx + \left(2x - x^2 y + \frac{y^3}{3}\right) dy$$

or, $$d\psi = \frac{x^3}{3} dx + \frac{y^3}{3} dy + 2d(xy) - d\left(\frac{x^2 y^2}{2}\right)$$

On integration, we get:

$$\psi = \mathbf{\frac{x^4}{12} + \frac{y^4}{12} + 2xy - \frac{x^2 y^2}{2}} \quad \textbf{(Ans.)}$$

(*iii*) Discharge between stream lines passing through (1, 3) and (2, 3):

$$\psi_{(1,3)} = \frac{1^4}{12} + \frac{3^4}{12} + 2 \times 1 \times 3 - \frac{1^2 \times 3^2}{2} = 8.33 \text{ m}^3/\text{s}$$

$$\psi_{(2,3)} = \frac{2^4}{12} + \frac{3^4}{12} + 2 \times 2 \times 3 - \frac{2^2 \times 3^2}{2} = 2.08 \text{ m}^3/\text{s}$$

Hence, discharge between the stream lines

$$\psi_{(1,3)} - \psi_{(2,3)} = 8.33 - 2.08 = \mathbf{6.25 \text{ m}^3/\text{s}} \quad \textbf{(Ans.)}$$

(*iv*) Is the flow irrotational?

Rotation (angular velocity), $$\omega_x = \frac{1}{2}\left(\frac{\partial v}{\partial x} - \frac{\partial u}{\partial y}\right)$$

$$= \frac{1}{2}\left[\left(y^2 - x^2\right) - \left(y^2 - x^2\right)\right] = 0$$

As the rotation is zero, the **flow is irrotational** *and the potential function does exist.* **(Ans.)**

Velocity potential:

$$d\phi = \frac{\partial \phi}{\partial x} dx + \frac{\partial \phi}{\partial y} dy = udx + vdy$$

$$= \left(2x - x^2 y + \frac{y^3}{3}\right) dx + \left(xy^2 - 2y - \frac{x^3}{3}\right) dy$$

$$= 2xdx - 2y\,dy + \left(\frac{y^3}{3} dx + xy^2 dy\right) - \left(\frac{x^3}{3} dy + x^2 y dx\right)$$

or, $$d\phi = 2x\,dx - 2ydy + \frac{1}{3} d\,(xy^3) - \frac{1}{3} d(x^3 y)$$

On integration, we get:

$$\phi = \mathbf{x^2 - y^2 + \frac{xy^3}{3} - \frac{x^3 y}{3}} \quad \textbf{(Ans.)}$$

(v) Check for Laplace equation:

We known that, $$\psi = \frac{x^4}{12} + \frac{y^4}{12} + 2xy - \frac{x^2 y^2}{2}$$

$$\frac{\partial \psi}{\partial x} = \frac{x^3}{3} + 2y - xy^2 \; ; \; \frac{\partial^2 \psi}{\partial x^2} = x^2 - y^2$$

$$\frac{\partial \psi}{\partial y} = \frac{y^3}{3} + 2x - yx^2 \; ; \; \frac{\partial^2 \psi}{\partial y^2} = y^2 - x^2$$

$$\therefore \quad \frac{\partial^2 \psi}{\partial x^2} + \frac{\partial^2 \psi}{\partial y^2} = (x^2 - y^2) + (y^2 - x^2) = 0$$

Hence, *stream function* (ψ) **satisfies** *Laplace equation.* **(Ans.)**

Also, $$\phi = x^2 - y^2 + \frac{xy^3}{3} - \frac{x^3 y}{3}$$

$$\frac{\partial \phi}{\partial x} = 2x + \frac{y^3}{3} - x^2 y \; ; \; \frac{\partial^2 \phi}{\partial x^2} = 2 - 2xy$$

$$\frac{\partial \phi}{\partial y} = -2y + xy^2 - \frac{x^3}{3} ; \; \frac{\partial^2 \phi}{\partial y^2} = -2 + 2xy$$

$$\therefore \quad \frac{\partial^2 \phi}{\partial x^2} + \frac{\partial^2 \phi}{\partial y^2} = (2 - 2xy) + (-2 + 2xy) = 0$$

Hence, *potential function* **satisfies** *Laplace equation.* **(Ans.)**

Example 5.47. *In a two-dimensional flow the velocity components are $u = Cy$; $v = 0$ (where C is constant). Find the circulation about the circle $x^2 + y^2 - 2ay = 0$ situated in the flow (a is the radius of the circle).*

Solution. *Given*: $u = Cy$; $v = 0$ ...Velocity components

Equation of the circle: $x^2 + y^2 - 2ay = 0$ (where, a = radius of the circle)

Circulation about the circle, Γ:

First method:

We know, $\Gamma = \Omega A$

where, Ω = Vorticity, and

A = Area.

Here, $\Omega = \frac{\partial v}{\partial x} - \frac{\partial u}{\partial y} = 0 - \frac{\partial}{\partial y}(Cy) = -C$

Now, $A = \pi a^2$

$\therefore \quad \Gamma = -C \times \pi a^2 = -\boldsymbol{C \pi a^2}$ **m²/s (Ans.)**

Second method:

Refer to Fig. 5.27.

We know, $\Gamma = \oint V_\theta . ds$

(where, V_θ is the tangential velocity)

$$= \oint u . dx = \oint C . y \, dx$$

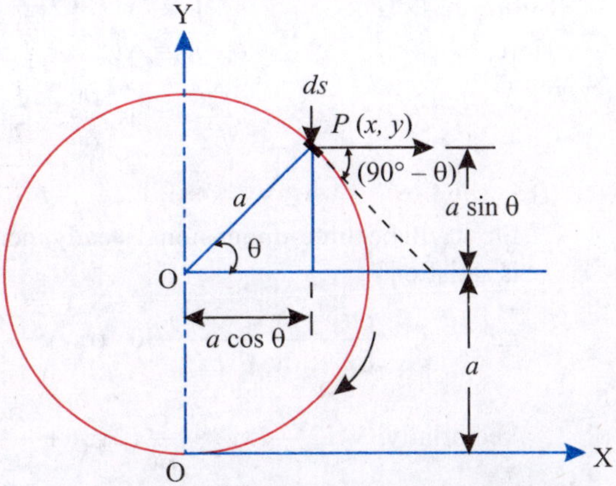

Fig. 5.27. Circulation about a circle.

From Fig. 5.27,

$$x = a\cos\theta;\ y = a + a\sin\theta = a(1+\sin\theta)$$

$$\therefore \quad dx = -a\sin\theta\, d\theta$$

$$\therefore \quad \Gamma = \int_0^{2\pi} Ca(1+\sin\theta).(-a\sin\theta d\theta)$$

$$= -Ca^2\int_0^{2\pi}(\sin\theta + \sin^2\theta)\,d\theta$$

$$= -Ca^2\int_0^{2\pi}\left(\sin\theta + \frac{1-\cos 2\theta}{2}\right)d\theta$$

$$= -\frac{Ca^2}{2}\int_0^{2\pi}(2\sin\theta + 1 - \cos 2\theta)\,d\theta$$

$$= -\frac{Ca^2}{2}\left[-2\cos\theta + \theta - \frac{\sin 2\theta}{2}\right]_0^{2\pi}$$

$$= -\frac{Ca^2}{2}[(-2+2\pi-0)-(-2+0-0)]$$

$$= -\frac{Ca^2}{2}\times 2\pi = -C\pi a^2 \text{ m}^2/\text{s}$$

i.e. $\boldsymbol{\Gamma = -C\pi a^2}$ **m²/s (Ans.)**

Example 5.48. *The flow field of a fluid is given by* $V = xyi + 2yzj - (yz + z^2)k$

(i) Show that it represent a possible three-dimensional steady incompressible continuous flow.

(ii) Is this flow rotational or irrotational?

If rotational, determine at point A (2, 4, 6):

(a) Angular velocity,

(b) Vorticity,

(c) Shear strains, and

(d) Dilatency.

Solution. *Given:* $V = xyi + 2yzj - (yz + z^2)\,k$ ... Fluid flow field

Here, $u = xy,,\ v = 2yz,\ w = -(yz + z^2)$

$$\frac{\partial u}{\partial x} = y,\ \frac{\partial v}{\partial y} = 2z,\ \frac{\partial w}{\partial z} = -(y+2z)$$

(i) Is the flow physically possible?

Flow will be three-dimensional steady incompressible continuous flow, if continuity equation is satisfied,

i.e. $$\frac{\partial u}{\partial x} + \frac{\partial v}{\partial y} + \frac{\partial w}{\partial z} = 0 \text{ or } y + 2z - (y+2z) = 0$$

Vectorially, $\nabla.V \dfrac{\partial}{\partial x}(xy) + \dfrac{\partial}{\partial y}(2yz) + \dfrac{\partial}{\partial z}[-(yz+z^2)] = y + 2z - (y+2z) = 0$

Hence, the **given flow is a three-dimensional steady incompressible flow. (Ans.)**

(ii) Flow-rotational or irrotational?

Now, $$\frac{\partial u}{\partial y} = x, \quad \frac{\partial v}{\partial x} = 0$$

Since, $$\frac{\partial u}{\partial y} \neq \frac{\partial v}{\partial x},$$

therefore, the *flow is* **rotational. (Ans.)**

(a) Angular velocity, ω:

We know, $$\omega = \frac{1}{2}(\Delta \times V)\begin{pmatrix} i & j & k \\ \frac{\partial}{\partial x} & \frac{\partial}{\partial y} & \frac{\partial}{\partial z} \\ xy & 2yz & -(yz+z^2) \end{pmatrix}$$

$$= \frac{1}{2}\left[i\left\{\frac{\partial}{\partial y}(-yz - z^2) - \frac{\partial}{\partial z}(2yz)\right\} + j\left\{\frac{\partial}{\partial z}(xy) - \frac{\partial}{\partial x}\{-(yz+z^2)\}\right\}\right.$$
$$\left. + k\left\{\frac{\partial}{\partial x}(2yz) - \frac{\partial}{\partial y}(xy)\right\}\right]$$

$$= \frac{1}{2}[i(-z-2y) - j(0-0) + k(0-x)]$$

At A (2, 4, 6), $$\omega = -\frac{1}{2}(14i + 2k) \quad \textbf{(Ans.)}$$

(b) Vorticity, Ω:

$$\Omega = 2\omega = -(14i + 2k) \quad \textbf{(Ans.)}$$

(c) Shear strains:

$$\gamma_{xy} = \frac{1}{2}\left(\frac{\partial v}{\partial x} + \frac{\partial u}{\partial y}\right) = \frac{1}{2}(0 + x) = \frac{1}{2}(0+2) = \mathbf{1} \quad \textbf{(Ans.)}$$

$$\gamma_{yz} = \frac{1}{2}\left(\frac{\partial v}{\partial z} + \frac{\partial w}{\partial y}\right) = \frac{1}{2}(2y - z) = \frac{1}{2}(2 \times 4 - 6) = \mathbf{1} \quad \textbf{(Ans.)}$$

$$\gamma_{xz} = \frac{1}{2}\left(\frac{\partial u}{\partial z} + \frac{\partial w}{\partial x}\right) = \frac{1}{2}(0 + 0) = \mathbf{0} \quad \textbf{(Ans.)}$$

(d) Dilatency (linear strains):

$$e_x = \frac{\partial u}{\partial x} = y = \mathbf{4} \quad \textbf{(Ans.)}$$

$$e_y = \frac{\partial v}{\partial y} = 2z = 2 \times 6 = \mathbf{12} \quad \textbf{(Ans.)}$$

$$e_z = \frac{\partial w}{\partial z} = (y + 2z) = -(4 + 2 \times 6) = -\mathbf{16} \quad \textbf{(Ans.)}$$

Example 5.49. *The stream function* ψ = 4*xy, in which* ψ *is in* cm^2*/second and x and y are in metres, describe the incompressible flow between the boundaries shown below (Fig. 5.28). Calculate:*

(*i*) *Velocity at B,*

(ii) Convective acceleration at B, and

(iii) Flow rate per unit width across AB. **[UPSC]**

Solution. *Given:* $\psi = 4xy$... Stream function (where ψ is in cm^2/s and x and y in metres)

Co-ordinates of A are: (3, 0)

Co-ordinates of B are:

$$x = 3 \text{ m}, y = \frac{3}{x} = \frac{3}{3} = 1 \text{ m}$$

$$\left(\because xy = 3, \therefore y = \frac{3}{x} \right)$$

Hence, co-ordinates of B are: (3, 1)

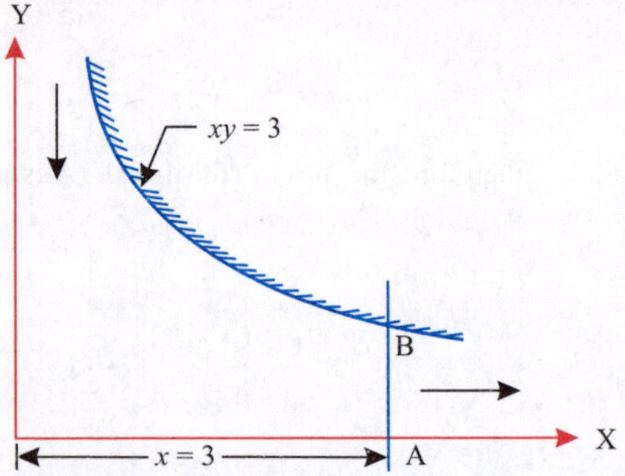

Fig. 5.28

(i) Velocity at B:

Velocity components are given by:

$$u = \frac{\partial \psi}{\partial y} = \frac{\partial}{\partial y}(4xy) = 4x \text{ , and}$$

$$v = -\frac{\partial \psi}{\partial x} = -\frac{\partial}{\partial x}(4xy) = -4y$$

At point B: $u = 4 \times 3 = 12$ cm/s, and

$v = -4 \times 1 = -4$ cm/s

$\therefore$ Velocity at B, $V_B = \sqrt{u^2 + v^2} = \sqrt{12^2 + (-4)^2}$ = **12.65 cm/s (Ans.)**

(ii) Convective acceleration at B, a_B:

Convective acceleration, $a = \sqrt{a_x^2 + a_y^2}$

$$a_x = u\frac{\partial u}{\partial x} + v\frac{\partial u}{\partial y}, \text{ and } a_y = u\frac{\partial v}{\partial x} + v\frac{\partial v}{\partial y}$$

But, $u = 4x$ and $v = -4y$

$$\therefore \quad \frac{\partial u}{\partial x} = 4, \frac{\partial u}{\partial y} = 0; \frac{\partial v}{\partial x} = 0, \frac{\partial v}{\partial y} = -4$$

$\therefore$ $a_x = (4x)(4) + (-4y)(0) = 16x$, and

$a_y = (4x)(0) + (-4y)(-4) = 16y$

Also, $a = \sqrt{a_x^2 + a_y^2} = \sqrt{(16x)^2 + (16y)^2}$

$\therefore$ Convective acceleration at B (3,1) is,

$$a_B = \sqrt{(16 \times 3)^2 + (16 \times 1)^2} = 16\sqrt{3^2 + 1} = \mathbf{50.6 \text{ cm/s}^2} \textbf{ (Ans.)}$$

(iii) Flow rate per unit width across AB, q_{AB}:

$$q_{AB} = \psi_B - \psi_A = \psi_{(3,\,1)} - \psi_{(3,\,0)}$$

$$= 4 \times 3 \times 1 - 4 \times 3 \times 0 = 12 \text{ cm}^3/\text{s/cm}$$

i.e. $\mathbf{q_{AB}}$ **= 12 cm³/s/cm (Ans.)**

HIGHLIGHTS

1. *Fluid kinematics* is a branch of fluid mechanics which deals with the study of velocity and acceleration of the particles of fluids in motion and their distribution in space without considering any forces or energy involved.
2. The motion of fluid particles may be described by the following methods:
   (*i*) *Langrangian method.* In this method, the observer concentrates on the movement of a single particle. The path taken by the particle and the changes in its velocity and acceleration are studied.
   (*ii*) *Eulerian method.* In Eulerian method, the observer concentrates on a point in the fluid system. Velocity, acceleration and other characteristics of the fluid at that particular point are studied.
   The components of acceleration of the fluid particle are given by:

$$a_x = \left(u\frac{\partial u}{\partial x} + v\frac{\partial u}{\partial y} + w\frac{\partial u}{\partial z}\right) + \frac{\partial u}{\partial t}$$

$$a_y = \left(u\frac{\partial v}{\partial x} + v\frac{\partial v}{\partial y} + w\frac{\partial v}{\partial z}\right) + \frac{\partial v}{\partial t}$$

$$a_z = \left(u\frac{\partial w}{\partial x} + v\frac{\partial w}{\partial y} + w\frac{\partial w}{\partial z}\right) + \frac{\partial w}{\partial t}$$

Resultant velocity, $V = \sqrt{u^2 + v^2 + w^2}$

$V = ui + vj + wk$ ... in vector notation.

Resultant acceleration, $a = \sqrt{a_x^2 + a_y^2 + a_z^2}$

$a = a_x i + a_y j + a_z k$ ... in vector notation.

Also, $a = V\dfrac{\partial V}{\partial s} + \dfrac{\partial V}{\partial t}$

where, $\dfrac{V \partial V}{\partial s}$ ...is called *convective acceleration,*

and, $\dfrac{\partial V}{\partial t}$ ... is called *local acceleration.*

3. *Types of fluid flow*:
   (*i*) Steady and unsteady flows
   (*ii*) Uniform and non-uniform flows
   (*iii*) One, two and three-dimensional flows
   (*iv*) Rotational and irrotational flows
   (*v*) Laminar and turbulent flows
   (*vi*) Compressible and incompressible flows.
4. *Types of flow lines*:
   (*i*) *Path line.* It is the path followed by a fluid particle in motion.
   (*ii*) *Stream line.* It is an imaginary line within the flow so that the tangent at any point on it indicates the velocity at that point.

(*iii*) *Stream tube.* It is a fluid mass bounded by a group of stream lines.

(*iv*) *Streak line.* It is a curve which gives an instantaneous picture of the location of the fluid particles which have passed through a given point.

5. The *continuity equation* based on the principle of conservation of mass is stated as follows: "If no fluid is added or removed from the pipe in any length then the mass passing across different sections shall be same".

$$\rho_1 A_1 V_1 = \rho_2 A_2 V_2 \quad \text{...in case of compressible fluids}$$

$$A_1 V_1 = A_2 V_2 \quad \text{...in case of incompressible fluids.}$$

The continuity equation in three dimensions in *cartesian co-ordinates* is given as:

$$\frac{\partial u}{\partial x} + \frac{\partial v}{\partial y} + \frac{\partial w}{\partial z} = 0 \quad \text{...for steady flow of incompressible fluid } (\rho = \text{constant})$$

The continuity equation in *polar co-ordinates* is given as:

$$\frac{1}{r}(\rho v_r) + \frac{\partial}{\partial r}(\rho v_r) + \frac{\partial}{r\partial\theta}(\rho v_\theta) = 0 \quad \text{... for compressible flow}$$

$$\frac{v_r}{r} + \frac{\partial v_r}{\partial r} + \frac{\partial v_\theta}{r\partial\theta} = 0 \quad \text{...for incompressible flow}$$

where, v_r = Velocity component in radial direction, and

v_θ = Velocity component in tangential direction.

6. *Circulation* (Γ) is defined mathematically as the line integral of the tangential velocity about a closed path (contour).

$$\Gamma = \oint V \cos\theta . ds$$

where, V = Velocity in the flow field, and

θ = Angle between V and the tangent to the path (in the positive anticlockwise direction along the path) at that point.

Vorticity (Ω) is defined as the circulation per unit of enclosed area $\left(i.e.\ \Omega = \frac{\Gamma}{A} \right)$.

If *a flow possesses vorticity, it is rotational.* The flow is irrotational if rotation (ω) is zero. The expression for rotation are:

$$w_z = \frac{1}{2}\left(\frac{\partial v}{\partial x} - \frac{\partial u}{\partial y}\right); \quad w_x = \frac{1}{2}\left(\frac{\partial w}{\partial y} - \frac{\partial v}{\partial z}\right); \quad w_y = \frac{1}{2}\left(\frac{\partial u}{\partial z} - \frac{\partial w}{\partial x}\right)$$

7. *Velocity potential* (ϕ) is defined as a scalar function of space and time such that its negative derivative with respect to any direction gives the fluid velocity in that direction.

$$u = -\frac{\partial \phi}{\partial x}, \; v = -\frac{\partial \phi}{\partial y}, \; w = -\frac{\partial \phi}{\partial z}$$

Stream function (ψ) is defined as a scalar function of space and time, such that its partial derivative with respect to any direction gives the velocity components at right angles (in the counterclockwise direction) to this direction.

$$u = \frac{\partial \psi}{\partial y}, \quad v = -\frac{\partial \psi}{\partial x}$$

Existence of ψ means a possible case of flow.

$$\left.\begin{aligned} u &= -\frac{\partial \phi}{\partial x} = \frac{\partial \psi}{\partial y} \\ v &= -\frac{\partial \phi}{\partial y} = -\frac{\partial \psi}{\partial x} \end{aligned}\right\} \text{... are known as Cauchy-Reimann equations.}$$

8. *Flow net.* A grid obtained by drawing a series of stream lines and equipotential lines is known as a flow net.

OBJECTIVE TYPE QUESTIONS

Choose the Correct Answer

1. The motion of fluid particles may be described by which of the following methods?
(*a*) Langrangian method
(*b*) Eulerain method
(*c*) Both (*a*) and (*b*)
(*d*) None of the above.

2. In which of the following methods, the observer concentrates on a point in the fluid system?
(*a*) Langrangian method
(*b*) Eulerian method
(*c*) Any of the above
(*d*) None of the above.

3. Normal acceleration in fluid-flow situation exists only when
(*a*) the flow is unsteady
(*b*) the flow is two-dimensional
(*c*) the streamlines are straight and parallel
(*d*) the streamlines are curved.

4. In a steady flow the velocity
(*a*) does not change from place to place
(*b*) at a given point does not change with time
(*c*) may change its direction but the magnitude remains unchanged
(*d*) none of the above.

5. The flow in a pipe whose valve is being opened or closed gradually is an example of
(*a*) steady flow (*b*) unsteady flow
(*c*) rotational flow
(*d*) compressible flow.

6. The type of flow in which the velocity at any given time does not change with respect to space is called
(*a*) steady flow
(*b*) compressible flow
(*c*) uniform flow (*d*) rotational flow.

7. Flow in a pipe where average flow parameters are considered for analysis is an example of
(*a*) incompressible flow
(*b*) one-dimensional flow
(*c*) two-dimensional flow
(*d*) three-dimensional flow.

8. The flow in a river during the period of heavy rainfall is
(*a*) steady, non-uniform and three-dimensional
(*b*) steady, uniform, two-dimensional
(*c*) unsteady, uniform, three-dimensional
(*d*) unsteady, non-uniform and three-dimensional.

9. Flow between parallel plates of infinite extent is an example of
(*a*) one-dimensional flow
(*b*) two-dimensional flow
(*c*) three-dimensional flow
(*d*) compressible flow.

10. If the flow is irrotational as well as steady it is known as
(*a*) non-uniform flow
(*b*) one-dimensional flow
(*c*) potential flow
(*d*) none of the above.

11. High velocity flow in a conduit of large size is known as
(*a*) laminar flow
(*b*) turbulent flow
(*c*) either of the above
(*d*) none of the above.

12. If the Reynolds number is less than 2000, the flow in a pipe is
(*a*) laminar flow (*b*) turbulent flow
(*c*) transition flow (*d*) none of the above.

13. The path followed by fluid particle in motion is called a
(*a*) streamline (*b*) path line
(*c*) streak line (*d*) none of the above.

14. A....is an imaginary line within the flow so that the tangent at any point on it indicates the velocity at that point.
(*a*) streak line (*b*) stream line

(*c*) path line (*d*) none of the above.

15. A stream line is one

(*a*) in which stream function does not change

(*b*) in which the flow cannot cross the bounding surface

(*c*) which has a constant area throughout its length so that the velocity remains constant.

(*d*) none of the above.

16. ...... is a curve which gives an instantaneous picture of the location of the fluid particles which have passed through a given point.

(*a*) Path line (*b*) Stream line

(*c*) Streak line (*d*) None of the above.

17. In fluid mechanics, the continuity equation is a mathematical statement embodying the principle of

(*a*) conservation of momentum

(*b*) conservation of mass

(*c*) conservation of energy

(*d*) none of the above.

18. An irrotational flow is one in which

(*a*) the stream lines of flow are curved and closely spaced

(*b*) the fluid does not rotate as it moves along

(*c*) the net rotation of fluid particles about their mass centres remains zero

(*d*) none of the above.

19. In a fluid-flow the stream lines are lines

(*a*) along which the vorticity is zero

(*b*) along which the stream function ψ = constant

(*c*) which are parallel to the equipotential lines

(*d*) which exist in irrotational flow only.

20. .... is defined mathematically as the line integral of the tangential velocity about a closed path (contour).

(*a*) circulation (*b*) vorticity

(*c*) either of the above (*d*) none of the above.

21. The concept of stream function which is based on the principle of continuity is applicable to

(*a*) irrotational flow only

(*b*) two-dimensional flow only

(*c*) three-dimensional flow

(*d*) uniform flow only.

22. The motion is described as ......when the components of rotation or vorticity are zero throughout certain point of the fluid.

(*a*) rotational (*b*) irrotational

(*c*) either of the above (*d*) none of the above.

23. .... is defined as a scalar function of space and time such that its negative derivative with respect to any direction gives the fluid velocity in that direction.

(*a*) Velocity potential function

(*b*) Stream function

(*c*) Circulation

(*d*) Vorticity.

24. If velocity potential (ϕ) satisfies the Laplace equation, it represents the possible..... flow.

(*a*) unsteady, compressible, rotational

(*b*) steady, compressible, irrotational

(*c*) unsteady, incompressible, rotational

(*d*) steady, incompressible, irrotational.

25. A flownet is a graphical representation of stream lines and equipotential lines such that these lines

(*a*) intersect each other orthogonally forming curvilinear squares

(*b*) intersect each other at various different angles forming irregular-shaped nets

(*c*) indicate the direction and magnitude of vector

(*d*) none of the above.

26. The flow-net analysis can be used to determine

(*a*) the stream lines and equipotential lines

(*b*) quantity of seepage and upward lift pressure below hydraulic structures

(*c*) the efficient boundary shapes, for which the flow does not separate.

(*d*) the velocity and pressure distribution for given boundaries of flow (provided the velocity distribution and pressure at any reference section are known).

(*e*) all of the above.

ANSWER

1. (*c*)	**2.** (*d*)	**3.** (*b*)	**4.** (*b*)	**5.** (*b*)	**6.** (*c*)
7. (*b*)	**8.** (*d*)	**9.** (*b*)	**10.** (*c*)	**11.** (*b*)	**12.** (*a*)
13. (*b*)	**14.** (*b*)	**15.** (*b*)	**16.** (*c*)	**17.** (*b*)	**18.** (*c*)
19. (*b*)	**20.** (*a*)	**21.** (*b*)	**22.** (*b*)	**23.** (*a*)	**24.** (*d*)
25. (*a*)	**26.** (*e*).				

THEORETICAL QUESTIONS

1. Differentiate between the Eulerian and Lagrangian methods of representing fluid flow.
2. Distinguish between pathlines, stream lines and streak lines.
3. Define convective and local accelerations.
4. Define tangential and normal accelerations.
5. How are fluid flows classified?
6. Define steady, non-steady, uniform and non-uniform flows.
7. Differentiate between the rotational and irrotational flows.
8. Sketch the velocity distribution for uniform irrotational flow.
9. How is the continuity equation based on the principle of conservation of mass stated?
10. Derive the continuity equation in cartesian coordianates.
11. How is 'circulation' defined?
12. What do you understand by vorticity?
13. Define and explain briefly the following: (*i*) Velocity potential; (*ii*) Stream function.
14. In the analysis of two-dimensional irrotational flow what use can the velocity potential and stream function be put to?
15. To what type of flow is the concept of velocity potential and stream function applicable?
16. If stream function exists in a flow problem, does it imply that velocity potential also exists?
17. From the consideration of vorticity and rotation show that in case of ideal fluids the flow is irrotational.
18. Show that the stream lines and equipotential lines form a net of mutually perpendicular lines.
19. What is a 'flow-net'? Enumerate the methods of drawing flow nets.
20. Is the flow-net analysis applicable to rotational flow? If not, why?

UNSOLVED EXAMPLES

1. Given the velocity field:
$V = (6 + 2xy + t^2)i - (xy^2 + 10t)j + 25k.$
What is the acceleration of a particle at (3, 0, 2) at time $t = 1$? **[IIT Bombay]**
[Ans. + 58.35 units]
2. The velocity along a stream line passing through the origin is given by:
$V = 2\sqrt{x^2 + y^2}$.
What is the velocity and acceleration at (4, 3)?
[Ans. 10 m/s, 20 m/s^2]
3. The velocity components in a steady flow are: $u = 2kx$; $v = 2ky$; $w = -4kz$.
What is the equation of a stream line passing through the point (1, 0, 1)?
$$\left[\textbf{Ans. } y = 0,\ z = \frac{1}{x^2}\right]$$
4. Determine whether the continuity equation is satisfied by the following velocity components for an incompressible fluid:
$u = x^2y,\ v = 2xy - xy^2,\ w = x^2 - z^2$
[Ans. Yes, the continuity equation is satisfied]
5. A conical pipe diverges uniformly from 0.1 m to 0.2 m diameter over a length of 1m. Determine the local and convective accelerations at the mid-section assuming (*i*) rate of flow is 0.1m^3/s and it remains constant, and (*ii*) rate of flow varies uniformly from 0.1 to 0.2 m^3/s in 5 sec., at $t = 2$ sec.
[Ans. (*i*) zero, – 42.76 m/s^2
(*ii*) 1.132 m/s^2, – 83.81 m/s^2]
6. Determine the missing component of velocity distribution such that they satisfy continuity equation $u = 2x^2 + 2xy,\ v = 2yz^2 + 3z^2,\ w = ?$
$$\left[\textbf{Ans. } w = -4xz - 2yz - \frac{2}{3}z^3 + f(x, y, t)\right]$$
7. The velocity components in a three-dimensional fluid flow are:
$u = x^2 + y^2 z^3,\ v = -(xy + yz + zx)$
Determine the missing component of velocity distribution such that continuity equation is satisfied.
$$\left[\textbf{Ans. } w = -xz + \frac{z^2}{2} + f(x, y, t)\right]$$
8. The velocity components of fluid flow (incompressible) are:
$u = x^2y,\ v = 2yz - xy^2,\ w = x^2 - z^2$
Show that this flow is kinematically possible.
9. In a three-dimensional incompressible fluid flow, the velocity components are:

$u = x^2 + z^2 + 5, v = y^2 + z^2 - 3$

(*i*) Determine the third component of velocity.

(*ii*) Is the fluid flow irrotational?

[Ans. (*i*) $w = -2(x+y)z + f(x, y, t)$ (*ii*) No.]

10. The velocity potential function (ϕ) is given by:

$$\phi = -\frac{xy^3}{3} - x^2 + \frac{x^3 y}{3} + y^2$$

Determine the velocity components in x and y directions and show that ϕ represents a possible case of flow.

$$\left[\textbf{Ans. } u = \frac{y^3}{3} + 2x - x^2 y, \; v = xy^2 - \frac{x^3}{3} - 2y\right]$$

11. If $\phi = 2xy$ determine ψ.

[Ans. $\psi = (y^2 - x^2) + C$]

12. Does the velocity potential exist for two-dimensional incompressible flow prescribed by $u = x - 4y; v = -(y + 4x)$?

If so determine its form as well as that of stream function.

$$\left[\begin{array}{l}\textbf{Ans. } \phi = \dfrac{x^2}{2} - \dfrac{y^2}{2} - 4xy + \text{constant} \\ \psi = 2x^2 - 2y^2 + xy + \text{constant}\end{array}\right]$$

13. A two-dimensional flow is described by the velocity components:

$u = 5x^3$ and $v = -15x^2y$

Determine the stream function, velocity and acceleration at $P(x = 1\text{m}, y = 2\text{ m})$.

[Ans. 10 m^3/s, 30.41 m/s, 167.70 m/s^2]

14. If $u = ax$ and $v = ay$ and $w = -2az$ are the velocity components for a fluid flow in a particular case, check whether they satisfy the continuity equation. If they do, is the flow rotational or irrotational? Also obtain equation of stream line passing through the point (2, 2, 4)

[Ans. Yes, irrotational, $x = y, xz^{1/2} = 4$]

15. If the velocity field is given by $u = x^2 + 2xy$ and $v = (y^2 + 2xy)$, determine the circulation around a closed curve defined by:

$x = 1, x = 3, y = 1, y = 4.$ **[Ans.** – 86]

16. If the velocity field is given by $u = x^2 - y^2 + x$ and $v = -(2xy + y)$, determine ϕ and ψ.

$$\left[\begin{array}{l}\textbf{Ans. } \phi = \dfrac{y^2}{2} - (2x - 1) - \dfrac{x^3}{3} + C, \\ \psi = -(2x + y) + C\end{array}\right]$$

17. In a two-dimensional flow field for an incompressible fluid the velocity components are:

$$u = \frac{y^3}{3} + 2x - x^2 y$$

$$v = xy^2 - 2y - \frac{x^3}{3}$$

Find an expression for the stream function ψ.

$$\left[\textbf{Ans. } \psi = \frac{x^2y^2}{2} - 2xy - \frac{x^4}{12} - \frac{y^4}{12}\right]$$

18. From the law of conservation of mass, show that whether the flow field represented by

$$u = -3x + y^2 - \frac{1}{x} \text{ and } v = x^2 + 3y + y \log x$$

is a possible velocity field for two-dimensional incompressible fluid flow. **[IIT Delhi]**

[Ans. Not possible]

19. If for two-dimensional flow the stream function is given by $\psi = 2xy$, calculate the velocity at the point (3, 6). Show that velocity potential ϕ exists for this case and deduce it. Draw the stream lines corresponding to $\psi = 100$ amd $\psi = 300$; also equipotential lines corresponding to $\phi = 100$ and $\phi = 300$. About six points on each line to represent its trend would suffice.

[UPSC]

[Ans. $2\sqrt{45}, \phi = y^2 + x^2$].

Chapter 6

FLUID DYNAMICS

6.1. INTRODUCTION

When the fluids are at rest, the only fluid property of significance is the specific weight of the fluids. On the other hand, when a fluid is in motion various other fluid properties become significant, as such the nature of flow of a real fluid is complex. *The science which deals with the geometry of motion of fluids without reference to the forces causing the motion is known as* **"hydrokinematics"** (or simply *kinematics*). Thus, kinematics involves merely the description of the motion of fluids in terms of space-time relationship. *The science which deals with the action of the forces in producing or changing motion of fluids is known as* **"hydrokinetics"** (or simply *kinetics*). Thus, the study of fluids in motion involves the consideration of both the kinematics and kinetics. The dynamic equation of fluid motion is obtained by applying Newton's second law of motion to a fluid element considered as a free body. *The fluid is assumed to be incompressible and non-viscous.*

In fluid mechanics the basic equations are: (*i*) *Continuity equation,* (*ii*) *Energy equation,* and (*iii*) *Impulse-momentum equation.* In this chapter energy equation and impulse-momentum equations will be discussed (Continuity equation has already been discussed in Chapter 5).

6.2. DIFFERENT TYPES OF HEADS (OR ENERGIES) OF A LIQUID IN MOTION

There are three types of energies or heads of flowing liquids:

1. Potential head or potential energy:

This is due to configuration or position above some suitable datum line. It is denoted by z.

2. **Velocity head or kinetic energy:**

This is due to velocity of flowing liquid and is measured as $\frac{V^2}{2g}$ where, V is the velocity of flow and 'g' is the acceleration due to gravity ($g = 9.81$)

3. **Pressure head or pressure energy:**

This is due to the pressure of liquid and reckoned as $\frac{p}{w}$ where, p is the pressure, and w is the weight density of the liquid.

Total head/energy:

Total head of a liquid particle in motion is the sum of its potential head, kinetic head and pressure head. Mathematically,

$$\text{Total head, } H = z + \frac{V^2}{2g} + \frac{p}{w} \text{ m of liquid} \quad \text{...[6.1 (a)]}$$

$$\text{Total energy, } E = z + \frac{V^2}{2g} + \frac{p}{w} \text{ Nm/kg of liquid} \quad \text{...[6.1 (b)]}$$

Example 6.1. *In a pipe of 90 mm diameter water is flowing with a mean velocity of 2 m/s and at a gauge pressure of 350 kN/m². Determine the total head, if the pipe is 8 metres above the datum line. Neglect friction.*

Solution. Diameter of the pipe = 90 mm

Pressure, p = 350 kN/m^2

Velocity of water, V = 2 m/s

Datum head, z = 8 m

Specific weight of water, w = 9.81 kN/m^3

Total head of water, H:

$$H = z + \frac{V^2}{2g} + \frac{p}{w}$$

$$= 8 + \frac{2^2}{2 \times 9.81} + \frac{350}{9.81} = 43.88 \text{ m}$$

H = **43.88 m (Ans.)**

6.3. BERNOULLI'S EQUATION

Bernoulli's equation states as follows:

"In an ideal incompressible fluid when the flow is steady and continuous, the sum of pressure energy, kinetic energy and potential (or datum) energy is constant along a stream line."

Mathematically,

$$\frac{p}{w} + \frac{V^2}{2g} + z = \text{constant}$$

where, $\frac{p}{w}$ = Pressure energy,

$\frac{V^2}{2g}$ = Kinetic energy, and

z = Datum (or elevation) energy.

Proof:

Consider an ideal incompressible liquid through a non-uniform pipe as shown in Fig 6.1. Let us consider two sections LL and MM and assume that the pipe is running full and there is continuity of flow between the two sections;

Let, p_1 = Pressure at LL,

V_1 = Velocity of liquid at LL,

z_1 = Height of LL above the datum,

A_1 = Area of pipe at LL, and

p_2, V_2, z_2, A_2 = Corresponding values at MM.

Let the liquid between the two sections LL and MM move to $L'L'$ and $M'M'$ through very small lengths dl_1 and dl_2 as shown in Fig. 6.1. This movement of liquid between LL and MM is equivalent to the movement of the liquid between LL and $L'L'$ and MM and $M'M'$, the remaining liquid between $L'L'$ and MM being unaffected.

Let, W = Weight of liquid between LL and $L'L'$.

As the flow is continuous,

$$\therefore \quad W = wA_1 \, . \, dl_1 = wA_2 \, . \, dl_2$$

$$\text{or,} \quad A_1 . dl_1 = \frac{W}{w} \quad \text{...(i)}$$

$$\text{Similarly,} \quad A_2 . dl_2 = \frac{W}{w} \quad \text{...(ii)}$$

$$\therefore \quad A_1 \, . \, dl_1 = A_2 . dl_2$$

Work done by pressure at LL, in moving the liquid to $L'L'$

$$= \text{Force} \times \text{distance} = p_1 \, . \, A_1 \, . \, dl_1$$

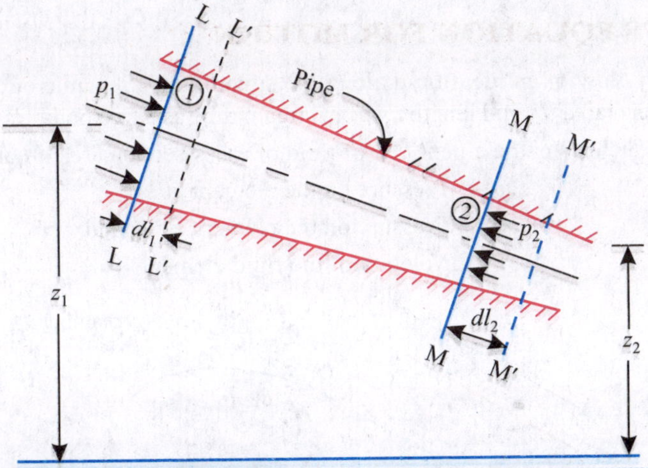

Fig. 6.1. Bernoulli's equation.

Similarly, work done by the pressure at MM in moving the liquid to $M'M' = -p_2.A_2 \, . \, dl_2$

(– ve sign indicates that direction of p_2 is *opposite* to that of p_1)

$\therefore$ Total work done by the pressure

$$= p_1 \, . \, A_1 \, dl_1 - p_2 \, A_2 \, dl_2$$

$$= p_1 \, . \, A_1 \, dl_1 - p_2 \, A_1 \, dl_1 \qquad (\because A_1 dl_1 = A_2 dl_2)$$

$$= A_1 \, . \, dl_1 \, (p_1 - p_2)$$

$$= \frac{W}{w}(p_1 - p_2) \qquad \left(\because A_1 . dl_1 = \frac{W}{w}\right)$$

$$\text{Loss of potential energy} = W(z_1 - z_2)$$

$$\text{Gain in kinetic energy} = W\left(\frac{V_2^2}{2g} - \frac{V_1^2}{2g}\right) = \frac{W}{2g}(V_2^2 - V_1^2)$$

Also, Loss of potential energy + work done by pressure = Gain in kinetic energy

$$\therefore W(z_1 - z_2) + \frac{W}{w}(p_1 - p_2) = \frac{W}{2g}(V_2^2 - V_1^2)$$

$$\text{or,} \quad (z_1 - z_2) + \left(\frac{p_1}{w} - \frac{p_2}{w}\right) = \left(\frac{V_2^2}{2g} - \frac{V_1^2}{2g}\right)$$

$$\text{or,} \quad \frac{p_1}{w} + \frac{V_1^2}{2g} + z_1 = \frac{p_2}{w} + \frac{V_2^2}{2g} + z_2 \qquad ...(6.2)$$

which proves *Bernoulli's equation.*

Assumptions:

It may be mentioned that the following *assumptions* are made in the derivation of Bernoulli's equation:

1. The liquid is ideal and incompressible.
2. The flow is steady and continuous.
3. The flow is along the stream line, *i.e.,* it is one-dimensional.
4. The velocity is uniform over the section and is equal to the mean velocity.
5. The only forces acting on the fluid are the *gravity forces* and the *pressure forces.*

6.4. EULER'S EQUATION FOR MOTION

Consider steady flow of an ideal fluid along the stream tube. Separate out a small element of fluid of cross-sectional area dA and length ds from stream tube as a free body from the moving fluid.

Fig. 6.2 shows such a small element LM of fluid of cross-section area dA and length ds.

Let, p = Pressure on the element at L,

$p + dp$ = Pressure on the element at M, and

V = Velocity of the fluid element.

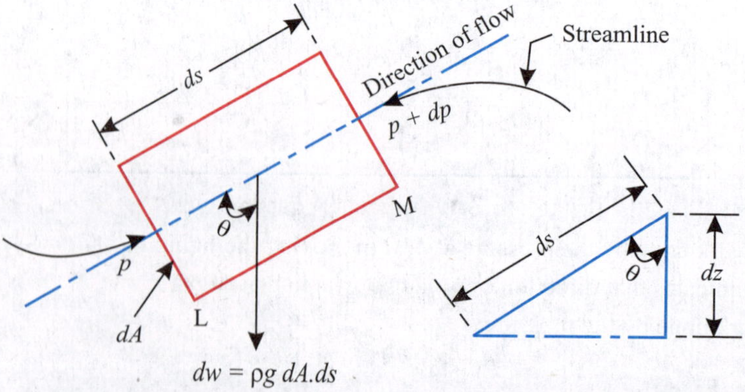

Fig. 6.2. Forces on a fluid element (Euler's equation).

The external forces tending to accelerate the fluid element in the direction of stream line are as follows:

1. Net pressure force in the direction of flow is,

$$p.dA - (p + dp)\, dA = -\, dp\, .\, dA \qquad ...(i)$$

2. Component of the weight of the fluid element in the direction of flow is

$$= -\, \rho.g.dA.ds.\ \cos\theta$$

$$= -\, \rho g.dA.ds \left(\frac{dz}{ds}\right) \qquad \left(\because \cos\theta = \frac{dz}{ds}\right)$$

$$= -\, \rho.g.dA.dz \qquad ...(ii)$$

Mass of the fluid element $= \rho.dA.ds$ ...(iii)

The acceleration of the fluid element

$$a = \frac{dV}{dt} = \frac{dV}{ds} \times \frac{ds}{dt} = V.\frac{dV}{ds} \qquad ...(iv)$$

Now, according to Newton's second law of motion, Force = Mass × acceleration

$$\therefore \qquad -\, dp.dA - \rho.g.dA.\ dz = p.dA.\ ds \times V.\ \frac{dV}{ds}$$

Dividing both sides by $\rho.dA$, we get:

$$\frac{-dp}{\rho} - g.dz = V.\ dV$$

or,

$$\frac{dp}{\rho} + V.dV + g.dz = 0 \qquad ...(6.3)$$

This is the required **Euler's equation** for motion, and is in the form of *differential equation.*

Integrating the above eqn., we get:

$$\frac{1}{\rho}\int dp + \int V.dV + \int g.dz = \text{constant}$$

$$\frac{p}{\rho} + \frac{V^2}{2} + gz = \text{constant}$$

Dividing by g, we get:

$$\frac{p}{\rho g} + \frac{V^2}{2g} + z = \text{constant}$$

or,

$$\frac{p}{w} + \frac{V^2}{2g} + z = \text{constant}$$

or, in other words,

$$\frac{p_1}{w} + \frac{V_1^2}{2g} + z_1 = \frac{p_2}{w} + \frac{V_2^2}{2g} + z_2$$

which proves *Bernoulli's equation.*

Euler's equation in Cartesian coordinates:

Consider an infinitely small mass of fluid enclosed in an elementary parallelopiped of sides dx, dy and dz as shown in Fig. 6.3. The motion of the fluid element is influenced by the following forces:

(*i*) Normal forces due to pressure:

The intensities of hydrostatic pressure acting normal to each face of the parallelepiped are shown in Fig. 6.3.

The net pressure force in the X-direction

$$= p \, . \, dy \, . \, dz - \left(p + \frac{\partial p}{\partial x} dx \right) dy \, dz$$

$$= -\frac{\partial p}{\partial x} dx . dy . dz$$

(*ii*) Gravity or body force:

Let B be the body force *per unit mass of fluid* having components B_x, B_y and B_z in the X, Y and Z directions respectively.

Then, the body force acting on the parallelopiped in the direction of X-coordinate is $= B_x . \rho . dx . dy . dz$.

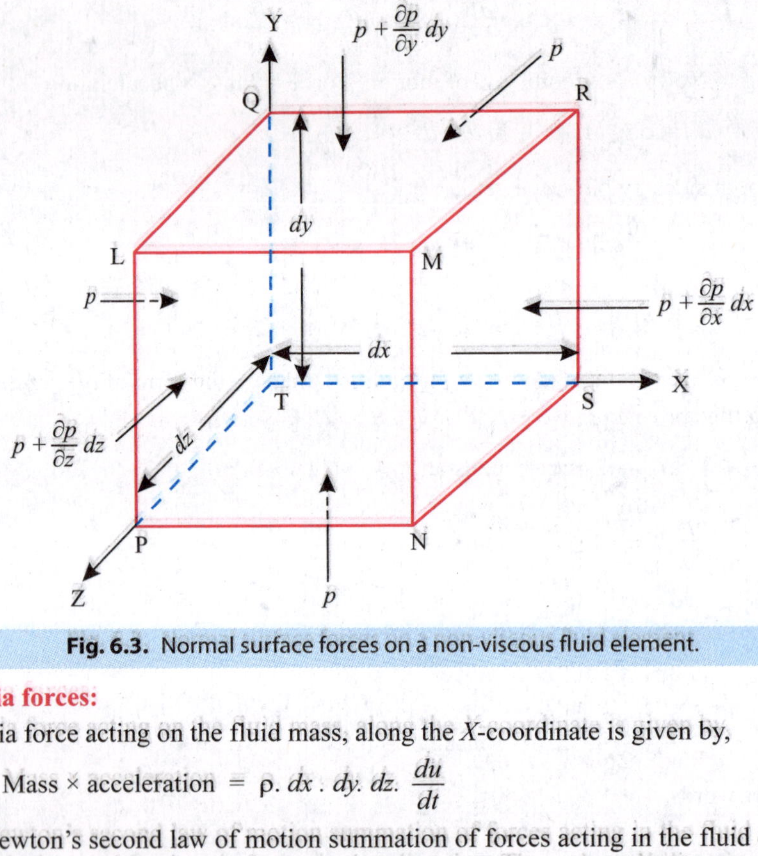

Fig. 6.3. Normal surface forces on a non-viscous fluid element.

(*iii*) Inertia forces:

The inertia force acting on the fluid mass, along the X-coordinate is given by,

$$\text{Mass} \times \text{acceleration} = \rho . \, dx \, . \, dy . \, dz . \, \frac{du}{dt}$$

As per Newton's second law of motion summation of forces acting in the fluid element in any direction equals the resulting inertia forces in that direction. Thus, along X-direction:

$$B_x . \rho . \, dx.dy.dz - \frac{\partial p}{\partial x} dx.dy.dz. = \rho.dx.dy.dz. \frac{du}{dt}$$

Dividing both sides by $\rho.dx.dy.dz$, we have:

$$B_x - \frac{1}{\rho}\frac{\partial p}{\partial x} = \frac{du}{dt} \qquad ...(i)$$

In this equation each term has dimensions of force per unit mass or acceleration. Obviously the total acceleration in a given direction is prescribed by the algebraic sum of the body force and the pressure gradient in that direction since the velocity components are functions of position and time, *i.e.*, $u = f(x, y, z, t)$, therefore, the total derivative of velocity u in the X-direction can be written as:

$$du = \frac{\partial u}{\partial t}dt + \frac{\partial u}{\partial x}dx + \frac{\partial u}{\partial y}dy + \frac{\partial u}{\partial z}dz$$

or,

$$\frac{du}{dt} = \frac{\partial u}{\partial t} + \frac{\partial u}{\partial x}\cdot\frac{dx}{dt} + \frac{\partial u}{\partial y}\cdot\frac{dy}{dt} + \frac{\partial u}{\partial z}\cdot\frac{dz}{dt}$$

Substituting, $\frac{dx}{dt} = u, \frac{dy}{dt} = v$ and $\frac{dz}{dt} = w$; we have:

$$\frac{du}{dt} = \frac{\partial u}{\partial t} + u\frac{\partial u}{\partial x} + v\frac{\partial u}{\partial y} + w\frac{\partial u}{\partial z} \quad ...(ii)$$

Combining eqns. (*i*) and (*ii*), we get the force components as:

$$B_x - \frac{1}{\rho}\frac{\partial p}{\partial x} = \frac{\partial u}{\partial t} + u\frac{\partial u}{\partial x} + v\frac{\partial u}{\partial y} + w\frac{\partial u}{\partial z} \quad ...(iii)$$

Similarly,

$$B_y - \frac{1}{\rho}\frac{\partial p}{\partial y} = \frac{\partial v}{\partial t} + u\frac{\partial v}{\partial x} + v\frac{\partial v}{\partial y} + w\frac{\partial v}{\partial z} \quad ...(iv)$$

and,

$$B_z - \frac{1}{\rho}\frac{\partial p}{\partial z} = \frac{\partial w}{\partial t} + u\frac{\partial w}{\partial x} + v\frac{\partial w}{\partial y} + w\frac{\partial w}{\partial z} \quad ...(v)$$

For steady flow: $\frac{\partial u}{\partial t} = \frac{\partial v}{\partial t} = \frac{\partial w}{\partial t} = 0$

Thus, the Euler's equation for a steady three-dimensional flow can be written as:

$$B_x - \frac{1}{\rho}\frac{\partial p}{\partial x} = u\frac{\partial u}{\partial x} + v\frac{\partial u}{\partial y} + w\frac{\partial u}{\partial z} \quad ...(vi)$$

$$B_y - \frac{1}{\rho}\frac{\partial p}{\partial y} = u\frac{\partial v}{\partial x} + v\frac{\partial v}{\partial y} + w\frac{\partial v}{\partial z} \quad ...(vii)$$

$$B_z - \frac{1}{\rho}\frac{\partial p}{\partial z} = u\frac{\partial w}{\partial x} + v\frac{\partial w}{\partial y} + w\frac{\partial w}{\partial z} \quad ...(viii)$$

In Euler's equation each term represents force per unit mass. Thus, if each equation is multiplied by the respective projections of the elementary displacement, the resulting equation would represent energy. Thus, in order to get total energy in the three-dimensional-steady-incompressible flow, the energy terms can be combined as follows:

$$B_x\,dx - \frac{1}{\rho}\frac{\partial p}{\partial x}dx = u\frac{\partial u}{\partial x}dx + v\frac{\partial u}{\partial y}dx + w\frac{\partial u}{\partial z}dx \quad ...(ix)$$

$$B_y\,dy - \frac{1}{\rho}\frac{\partial p}{\partial y}dy = u\frac{\partial v}{\partial x}dy + v\frac{\partial v}{\partial y}dy + w\frac{\partial v}{\partial z}dy \quad ...(x)$$

$$B_z dz - \frac{1}{\rho}\frac{\partial p}{\partial y}dz = u\frac{\partial w}{\partial x}dz + v\frac{\partial w}{\partial y}dz + w\frac{\partial w}{\partial z}dz \quad ...(xi)$$

From the equation of a stream line in a three-dimensional flow, we have:

$$\frac{dx}{u} = \frac{dy}{v} = \frac{dz}{w}$$

$$udy = vdx;\ vdz = wdy;\ udz = wdx$$

Substituting these values in eqns. (*ix*), (*x*) and (*xi*), we get:

$$B_x dx - \frac{1}{\rho}\frac{\partial p}{\partial x}dx = u\frac{\partial u}{\partial x}dx + u\frac{\partial u}{\partial y}dy + u\frac{\partial u}{\partial z}dz \quad ...(xii)$$

$$B_y dy - \frac{1}{\rho}\frac{\partial p}{\partial y}dy = v\frac{\partial v}{\partial x}dx + v\frac{\partial v}{\partial y}dy + v\frac{\partial v}{\partial z}dz \quad ...(xiii)$$

$$B_z dz - \frac{1}{\rho}\frac{\partial p}{\partial z}dz = w\frac{\partial w}{\partial x}dx + w\frac{\partial w}{\partial y}dy + w\frac{\partial w}{\partial z}dz \quad ...(xiv)$$

Acceleration terms are of form $u\frac{\partial u}{\partial x}$ which can be replaced by $\frac{1}{2}\frac{\partial(u^2)}{\partial x}$. Thus,

$$B_x dx - \frac{1}{\rho}\frac{\partial p}{\partial x}dx = \frac{1}{2}\left[\frac{\partial}{\partial x}(u^2)dx + \frac{\partial}{\partial y}(u^2)\,dy + \frac{\partial}{\partial z}(z^2)dz\right] = \frac{1}{2}d(u^2) \quad ...(xv)$$

Similarly, $$B_y\,dy - \frac{1}{\rho}\frac{\partial p}{\partial y}dy = \frac{1}{2}\,d(v^2) \quad ...(xvi)$$

and, $$B_z\,dz - \frac{1}{\rho}\frac{\partial p}{\partial y}\,dz = \frac{1}{2}\,d(w^2) \quad ...(xvii)$$

Adding eqns. (*xv*), (*xvi*) and (*xvii*), we get:

$$B_x dx + B_y dy + B_z dz - \frac{1}{\rho}\left(\frac{\partial p}{\partial x}dx + \frac{\partial p}{\partial y}dy + \frac{\partial p}{\partial z}dz\right)$$

$$= \frac{1}{2}[d(u^2) + d(v^2) + d(w^2)]$$

or, $$B_x dx + B_y dy + B_z dz - \frac{1}{\rho}dp = \frac{1}{2}\,d(V^2) \quad ...(xviii)$$

where, V = Total velocity vector.

When gravity is the only body force acting on the third element, then:

$$B_x = 0,\ B_z = 0 \text{ and } B_y = -g$$

$B_y = -g$ since the *gravitational force* acts in the *downward* direction which is negative 'with' respect to Y, which is positive upward. Inserting these values in (*xviii*), we get:

$$-g - \frac{1}{\rho}dp = \frac{1}{2}\,d(V^2)$$

or, $$-g - \frac{1}{\rho}dp = VdV$$

or, $$\frac{dp}{\rho} + VdV + g = 0$$ which is the same as Euler's equation (6.3).

Hydrostatic equation from Euler's equation:

If the fluid is at rest then the velocity terms in Euler's eqns, (*vi*), (*vii*) and (*viii*), vanish and we have:

$$B_x - \frac{1}{\rho}\frac{\partial p}{\partial x} = 0;\quad B_y - \frac{1}{\rho}\frac{\partial p}{\partial y} = 0;\quad B_z - \frac{1}{\rho}\frac{\partial p}{\partial z} = 0$$

Further, if gravity is the only body force, then:

$$B_x = 0;\quad B_y = -g;\quad B_z = 0$$

$$\therefore \quad \frac{1}{\rho}\frac{\partial p}{\partial x} = 0;\quad \frac{1}{\rho}\frac{\partial p}{\partial z} = 0 \quad ...(xix)$$

and, $$-g - \frac{1}{\rho}\frac{\partial p}{\partial y} = 0 \quad ...(xx)$$

Eqn. (*xix*) signifies that fluid pressure p is independent of x and z. In that case $\frac{\partial p}{\partial y} = \frac{dp}{dy}$ and

$$-g - \frac{1}{\rho}\frac{dp}{dy} = 0$$

or, $$dp = -\rho g dy \quad \text{or} \quad dp = -w dy$$

Integrating both sides, we get:

$$\int_1^2 dp = -w \int_1^2 dy$$

or, $$(p_2 - p_1) = -w(y_2 - y_1)$$

or, $$dp = w dy$$

which represents the hydrostatic equation. Thus, hydrostatic equation is merely a *corollary of Euler's equation.*

Example 6.2. *A discharge through a 24 cm diameter horizontal pipe increases linearly from 30 to 120 litres/sec. of water in 4 seconds.*

(i) What pressure gradient must exist to produce this acceleration?

(ii) What is the difference in pressure intensity that exists between two sections that lie 9 m apart?

Solution. The Euler's equation for one-dimensional flow along the pipe axis may be written as:

$$B_x - \frac{1}{\rho}\frac{\partial p}{\partial x} = \frac{\partial u}{\partial t} + u\frac{\partial u}{\partial x} \quad ...(i)$$

As the pipe is of uniform cross-sectional area, the velocity remains constant along the flow direction and therefore,

$$\frac{\partial u}{\partial x} = 0$$

Further, since the pipe has been laid horizontally, therefore, the body forces per unit volume in the direction X = 0

Thus, the eqn. (*i*) reduces to:

$$-\frac{1}{\rho}\frac{\partial p}{\partial x} = \frac{\partial u}{\partial t}$$

The change in velocity when the flow changes from 30 to 120 litres/sec

$$\partial u = (u_2 - u_1) = \frac{120 \times 10^{-3}}{\frac{\pi}{4} \times (0.24)^2} - \frac{30 \times 10^{-3}}{\frac{\pi}{4} \times (0.24)^2} = 1.989 \text{ m/s}$$

This change takes place in 4 sec,

$$\therefore \quad \frac{\partial u}{\partial t} = \frac{1.989}{4} = 0.497 \text{ m/s}^2$$

(*i*) Pressure gradient, $\frac{\partial p}{\partial x}$:

$$\frac{\partial p}{\partial x} = -\rho\frac{\partial u}{\partial t} = -1000 \times 0.497 = -\mathbf{497\ N/m^2/m}\ \textbf{(Ans.)}$$

(*ii*) Difference in pressure intensity between the sections:

Difference in pressure intensity between two sections that lie 9 m apart

$$= \frac{\partial p}{\partial x} \times 9 = -497 \times 9 = -\mathbf{4473\ N/m^2}\ \textbf{(Ans.)}$$

Example 6.3. *Brine of specific gravity 1.15 is draining from the bottom of a large open tank through an 80 mm pipe. The drain pipe ends at a point 10 m below the surface of the brine in the tank. Considering a stream line starting at the surface of the brine in the tank and passing through the centre of the drain line to the point of discharge and assuming the friction is negligible, calculate the velocity of flow along the stream line at the point of discharge from the pipe.* **(UPTU)**

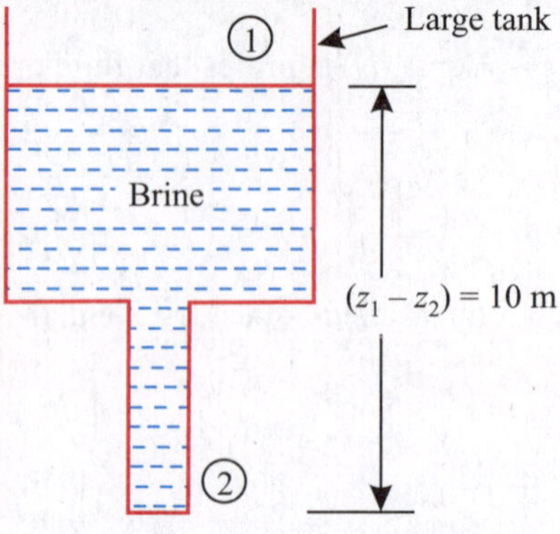

Fig. 6.4

Solution. Refer to Fig. 6.4.

Section 1– The surface of brine in the tank

Section 2 – The point of discharge.

Applying Bernoulli's equation between point 1 and 2, we get:

$$\frac{p_1}{w} + \frac{V_1^2}{2g} + z_1 = \frac{p_2}{w} + \frac{V_2^2}{2g} + z_2$$

Here, $p_1 = p_2 = p_{atm.}$ (atmospheric pressure),

$V_1 = 0$ and $(z_1 - z_2) = 10$ m

$\therefore$ $V_2^2 = 2g\,(z_1 - z_2) = 2g \times 10 = 2 \times 9.81 \times 10 = 196.2$

or, $V_2 \simeq$ **14 m/s (Ans.)**

Example 6.4. *A pipeline (Fig. 6.5) is 15 cm in diameter and it is at an elevation of 100 m at section A. At section B it is at an elevation of 107 m and has diameter of 30 cm. When a discharge of 50 litre/sec of water is passed through this pipeline, pressure at A is 35 kPa. The energy loss in pipe is 2m of water. Calculate pressure at B if flow is from A to B.* **(Anna University)**

Solution. *Given:* $D_A = 15$ cm $= 0.15$ m; $D_B = 30$ cm $= 0.3$ m;

$p_A = 35$ kPa; $Q = 50$ litre/sec $= 0.05\ m^3/s$;

$h_f = 2$ m of water; Direction of flow: from A to B

Fig. 6.5

Pressure at B, p_B:

$$V_A = \frac{Q}{\frac{\pi}{4} \times D_A^2} = \frac{0.05}{\frac{\pi}{4} \times 0.15^2} = 2.829\ \text{m/s}$$

$$V_B = \frac{Q}{\frac{\pi}{4} \times D_B^2} = \frac{0.05}{\frac{\pi}{4} \times (0.3)^2} = 0.707 \text{ m/s}$$

Applying Bernoulli's equation between sections A and B, we get:

$$\frac{P_A}{w} + \frac{V_A^2}{2g} + z_A = \frac{P_B}{w} + \frac{V_B^2}{2g} + z_B + h_f$$

or,
$$\frac{P_B}{w} = \frac{p_A}{w} + \left(\frac{V_A^2 - V_B^2}{2g}\right) + (z_A - z_B) - h_f$$

or,
$$p_B = p_A + w\left[\left(\frac{V_A^2 - V_B^2}{2g}\right) + (z_A - z_B) - h_f\right]$$

$$= 35 + \frac{(1000 \times 9.81)}{1000}\left[\left(\frac{2.829^2 - 0.707^2}{2 \times 9.81}\right) + (100 - 107) - 2\right]$$

$$35 + 9.81\,(0.3824 - 7 - 2) = -49.54 \text{ kPa.}$$

i.e., p_B **= – 49.54 kPa.** This shows that the given pressure at A, 35 kPa is *gauge pressure* and hence there is *vacuum at point B.* **(Ans.)**

Example 6.5. *An open circuit wind tunnel draws in air from the atmosphere through a well contoured nozzle. In the test section, where the flow is straight and nearly uniform, a static pressure tap is drilled into the tunnel wall. A manometer connected to the tap shows that the static pressure within the tunnel is 45 mm of water below atmosphere. Assume that air is incompressible and at 25°C, pressure is 100 kPa (absolute). Calculate the velocity in the wind tunnel section (Refer to Fig. 6.6). Density of water is 999 kg/m³ and characteristic gas constant for air is 287 J/kg K.* **(GATE)**

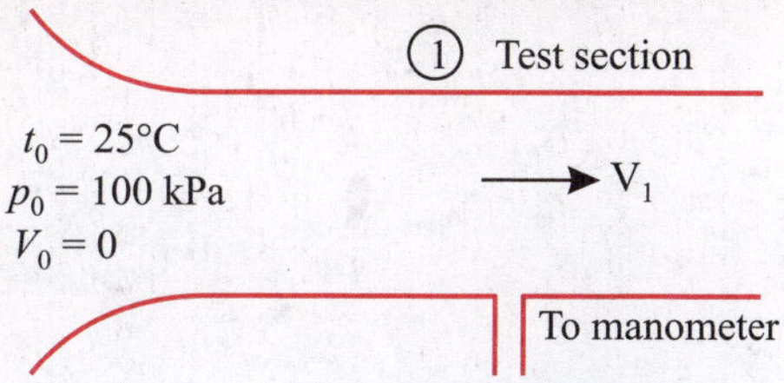

Fig. 6.6

Solution. *Given*: $T_0 = 25 + 273 = 298$ K;

$p_0 = 100$ kPa (abs.); $V_0 = 0$;

Velocity in the wind tunnel section V_1:

As per the problem, air is assumed as incompressible (*i.e.*, $\rho_0 = \rho_1 = \rho$). Velocity at test section can be found by using the equation:

$$\frac{p_0}{w} + \frac{V_0^2}{2g} + z_0 = \frac{p_1}{w} + \frac{V_1^2}{2g} + z_1$$

where,
$$z_0 = z_1;\ V_0 = 0,\ p_0 = 100 \text{ kPa (abs.)}$$

$$p_1 = 45 \text{ mm of water below atmosphere}$$

$$= 999 \times 9.81\ \frac{45}{1000} \text{ Pa}$$

$$= 999 \times 9.81 \times \frac{45}{1000} \times 10^{-3} \text{ kPa} = 0.44 \text{ kPa}$$

$$= 999 \times 9.81\ \frac{45}{1000} \times 10^{-3} \text{ kPa} = 0.44 \text{ kPa below atmosphere}$$

∴
$$p_1(\text{absolute}) = P_{atm.} \text{ (in kPa)} - 0.44 \text{ kPa}$$

$$= 100 - 0.44 = 99.56 \text{ kPa}$$

Also,
$$pV = mRT = \rho RT \qquad (\text{ where, } \rho = \frac{m}{V})$$

or, $$\rho = \frac{p}{RT} = \frac{100 \times 10^3}{287 \times 298} = 1.169 \text{ kg/m}^3$$

$\therefore$ $$w = \rho g = 1.169 \times 9.81 = 11.468 \text{ N/m}^3$$

Substituting these values in (*i*), we get:

$$\frac{100 \times 10^3}{11.468} = \frac{99.56 \times 10^3}{11.468} + \frac{V_1^2}{2 \times 9.81}$$

$$8719.9 = 8681.5 + \frac{V_1^2}{2 \times 9.81}$$

$\therefore$ $$V_1 = \sqrt{(8719.9 - 8681.5) \times 2 \times 9.81} = \mathbf{27.45 \text{ m/s}} \text{ (Ans.)}$$

Example 6.6. *Water flows in a circular pipe. At one section the diameter is 0.3 m, the static pressure is 260 kPa gauge, the velocity is 3 m/s and the elevation is 10 m above ground level. The elevation at a section downstream is 0 m, and the pipe diameter is 0.15 m. Find out the gauge pressure at the downstream section.*

Frictional effects may be neglected. Assume density of water to be 999 kg/m³.

(RGPV, Bhopal)

Solution. Refer to Fig. 6.7. $D_1 = 0.3$ m; $D_2 = 0.15$ m; $z_1 = 0$; $z_2 = 10$ m; $p_1 = 260$ kPa, $V_1 = 3$ m/s; $\rho = 999$ kg/m³.

From continuity equation, $A_1 V_1 = A_2 V_2$,

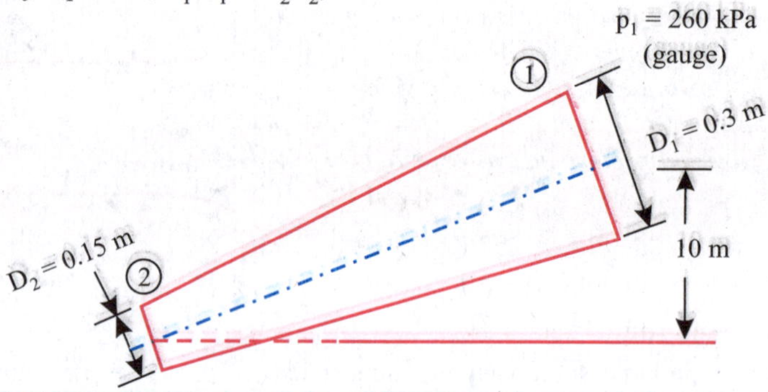

Fig. 6.7

$$V_2 = \frac{A_1}{A_2} \times V_1 = \left(\frac{\frac{\pi}{4} D_1^2}{\frac{\pi}{4} D_2^2}\right) \times V_1$$

$$= \left(\frac{D_1}{D_2}\right)^2 \times V_1 = \left(\frac{0.3}{0.15}\right)^2 \times 3 = 12 \text{ m/s}$$

Weight density of water, $w = \rho g = 999 \times 9.81 = 9800.19 \text{ N/m}^3$

From Bernoulli's equation between sections 1 and 2 (neglecting friction effects as given), we have:

$$\frac{p_1}{w} + \frac{V_1^2}{2g} + z_1 = \frac{p_2}{w} + \frac{V_2^2}{2g} + z_2$$

$$\frac{260 \times 1000}{9800.19} + \frac{(3)^2}{2 \times 9.81} + 10$$

$$= \frac{p_2}{9800.19} + \frac{(12)^2}{2 \times 9.81} + 0$$

$$26.53 + 0.459 + 10 = \frac{p_2}{9800.19} + 7.34$$

or, $p_2 = 290566 \text{ N/m}^2 = \mathbf{290.56 \text{ kPa (Ans.)}}$

Example 6.7. *The water is flowing through a tapering pipe having diameters 300 mm and 150 mm at sections 1 and 2 respectively. The discharge through the pipe is 40 litres/sec. The section 1 is 10 m above datum and section 2 is 6 m above datum. Find the intensity of pressure at section 2 if that at section 1 is 400 kN/m².*

Solution. At Section 1:

Diameter, $D_1 = 300 \text{ mm} = 0.3 \text{ m}$

$\therefore$ Area, $A_1 = \frac{\pi}{4} \times 0.3^2 = 0.0707 \text{ m}^2$

Pressure, $p_1 = 400 \text{ kN/m}^2$

Height of upper end above the datum, $z_1 = 10$ m

At Section 2:

Diameter, $D_2 = 150 \text{ mm} = 0.15 \text{ m}$

$\therefore$ Area, $A_2 = \frac{\pi}{4} \times 0.15^2 = 0.01767 \text{ m}^2$

Height of lower end above the datum, $z_2 = 6$ m

Rate of flow (*i.e.*, discharge),

$$Q = 40 \text{ litres/sec} = \frac{40 \times 10^3}{10^6}$$

$$= 0.04 \text{ m}^3/\text{s}$$

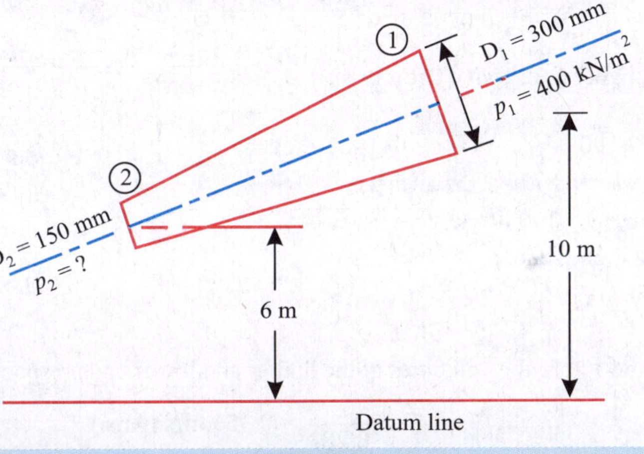

Fig. 6.8

Intensity of pressure at section 2, p_2:

Now, $Q = A_1 V_1 = A_2 V_2$

$$\therefore \quad V_1 = \frac{Q}{A_1} = \frac{0.04}{0.0707} = 0.566 \text{ m/s}$$

and, $$V_2 = \frac{Q}{A_2} = \frac{0.04}{0.01767} = 2.264 \text{ m/s}$$

Applying Bernoulli's equation at sections 1 and 2, we get:

$$\frac{p_1}{w} + \frac{V_1^2}{2g} + z_1 = \frac{p_2}{w} + \frac{V_2^2}{2g} + z_2$$

and, $$\frac{p_2}{w} = \frac{p_1}{w} + \left(\frac{V_1^2}{2g} - \frac{V_2^2}{2g}\right) + (z_1 - z_2)$$

$$= \frac{400}{9.81} + \frac{1}{2 \times 9.81}(0.566^2 - 2.264^2) + (10 - 6)$$

$(\because w = 9.81 \text{ kN/m}^3)$

$$= 40.77 - 0.245 + 4 = 44.525 \text{ m}$$

$\therefore$ $p_2 = 44.525 \times w = 44.525 \times 9.81 =$ **436.8 kN/m²** **(Ans.)**

Example 6.8. *A pipe 200 m long slopes down at 1 in 100 and tapers from 600 mm diameter at the higher end to 300 mm diameter at the lower end, and carries 100 litres/sec of oil (sp. gravity 0.8). If the pressure gauge at the higher end reads 60 kN/m², determine:*

(i) Velocities at the two ends;

(ii) Pressure at the lower end.

Neglect all losses.

Solution. Length of the pipe, l = 200 m; diameter of the pipe at the higher end, D_1 = 600 mm = 0.6 m,

$\therefore$ Area, $A_1 = \frac{\pi}{4} \times 0.6^2 = 0.283 \text{ m}^2$

Diameter of the pipe at the lower end,

D_2 = 300 mm = 0.3 m

$\therefore$ Area, $A_2 = \frac{\pi}{4} \times 0.3^2 = 0.0707 \text{ m}^2$

Height of the higher end, above datum,

$z_1 = \frac{1}{100} \times 200 = 2$ m

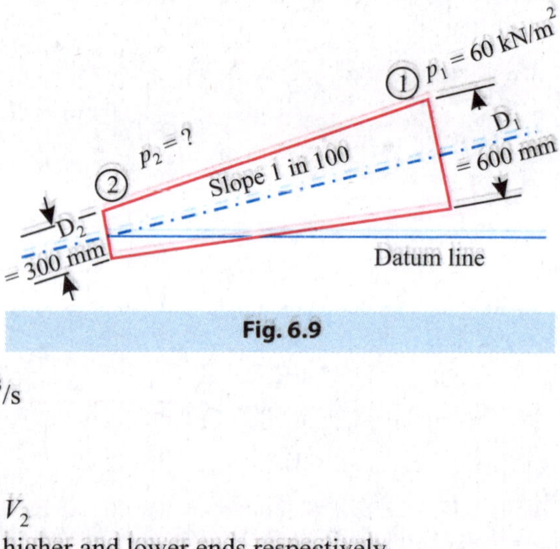

Fig. 6.9

Height of the lower end, above datum $z_2 = 0$

Rate of oil flow, Q = 100 litres/sec = 0.1 m³/s

Pressure at the higher end, p_1 = 60 kN/m²

(i) Velocities, V_1, V_2:

Now, $Q = A_1 V_1 = A_2 V_2$

where, V_1 and V_2 are the velocities at the higher and lower ends respectively.

$\therefore$ $V_1 = \frac{Q}{A_1} = \frac{0.1}{0.283} =$ **0.353 m/s (Ans.)**

and $V_2 = \frac{Q}{A_2} = \frac{0.1}{0.0707} =$ **1.414 m/s (Ans.)**

(ii) Pressure at the lower end p_2:

Using Bernoulli's equation for both ends of pipe, we have:

$$\frac{p_1}{w} + \frac{V_1^2}{2g} + z_1 = \frac{p_2}{w} + \frac{V_2^2}{2g} + z_2$$

$$\frac{60}{0.8 \times 9.81} + \frac{0.353^2}{2 \times 9.81} + 2 = \frac{p_2}{0.8 \times 9.81} + \frac{1.414^2}{2 \times 9.81} + 0$$

$$7.64 + 0.00635 + 2 = \frac{p_2}{0.8 \times 9.81} + 0.102$$

$$\therefore \quad \frac{p_2}{0.8 \times 9.81} = 9.54 \text{ m}$$

or, $$p_2 = \mathbf{74.8 \text{ kN/m}^2} \textbf{ (Ans.)}$$

Example 6.9. *A 6m long pipe is inclined at an angle of 20° with the horizontal. The smaller section of the pipe which is at lower level is of 100 mm diameter and the larger section of the pipe is of 300 mm diameter as shown in Fig. 6.10. If the pipe is uniformly tapering and the velocity of water at the smaller section is 1.8 m/s, determine the difference of pressures between the two sections.*

Solution. Length of the pipe, $l = 6$ m

Angle of inclination, $\theta = 20°$

At Section 1:

Diameter, $D_1 = 100 \text{ mm} = 0.1 \text{ m}$

$\therefore$ Area, $A_1 = \frac{\pi}{4} \times 0.1^2 = 0.00785 \text{ m}^2$

Velocity, $V_1 = 1.8 \text{ m/s}$

Datum, $z_1 = 0$

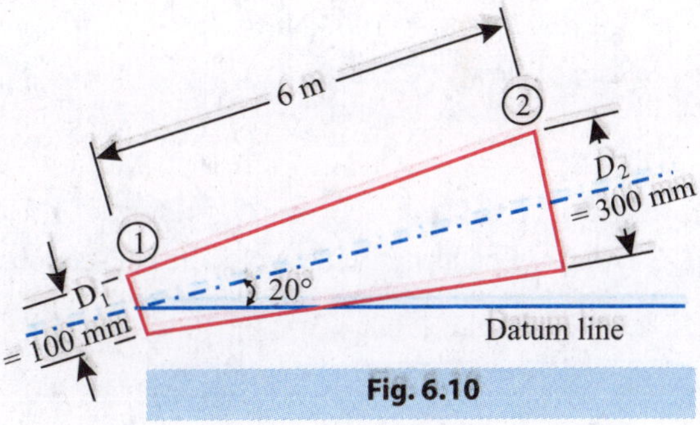

Fig. 6.10

At Section 2:

Diameter, $D_2 = 300 \text{ mm} = 0.3 \text{ m}$

$\therefore$ Area, $A_2 = \frac{\pi}{4} \times 0.3^2 = 0.0707 \text{ m}^2$

Datum, $z_2 = 0 + 6 \sin\theta = 6 \sin 20° = 6 \times 0.342 = 2.05$ m

Let, p_1 = Pressure at section 1 in kN/m^2, and

p_2 = Pressure at section 2 in kN/m^2.

Difference of pressures, $(p_1 - p_2)$:

From the equation of continuity, we know that:

$$A_1V_1 = A_2V_2$$

$$\therefore \quad V_2 = \frac{A_1V_1}{A_2} = \frac{0.00785 \times 1.8}{0.0707} = 0.2 \text{ m/s.}$$

Applying Bernoulli's equation to both sections of the pipe, we get:

$$\frac{p_1}{w} + \frac{V_1^2}{2g} + z_1 = \frac{p_2}{w} + \frac{V_2^2}{2g} + z_2$$

or, $$\left(\frac{p_1}{w} - \frac{p_2}{w}\right) = \left(\frac{V_2^2}{2g} - \frac{V_1^2}{2g}\right) + (z_2 - z_1)$$

$$= \frac{1}{2g}(V_2^2 - V_1^2) + (z_2 - z_1)$$

$$= \frac{1}{2 \times 9.81}(0.2^2 - 1.8^2) + (2.05 - 0) = 1.88$$

$$\therefore \quad (p_1 - p_2) = w \times 1.88 = 9.81 \times 1.88 = \mathbf{18.44\ kN/m^2\ (Ans.)}$$

[$\because$ w (for water) = 9.81 kN/m^3]

Example 6.10. *Water is flowing through a pipe having diameters 600 mm and 400 mm at the bottom and upper end respectively. The intensity of pressure at the bottom end is 350 kN/m² and the pressure at the upper end is 100 kN/m². Determine the difference in datum head if the rate of flow through the pipe is 60 litres/sec.*

Solution. At Section 1:

Diameter, $D_1 = 600\text{ mm} = 0.6\text{ m}$

$\therefore$ Area, $A_1 = \frac{\pi}{4} \times 0.6^2 = 0.283\text{ m}^2$

Pressure, $p_1 = 350\text{ kN/m}^2$

At Section 2:

Diameter, $D_2 = 400\text{ mm} = 0.4\text{ m}$

Area, $A_2 = \frac{\pi}{4} \times 0.4^2 = 0.1257\text{ m}^2$

Pressure, $p_2 = 100\text{ kN/m}^2$

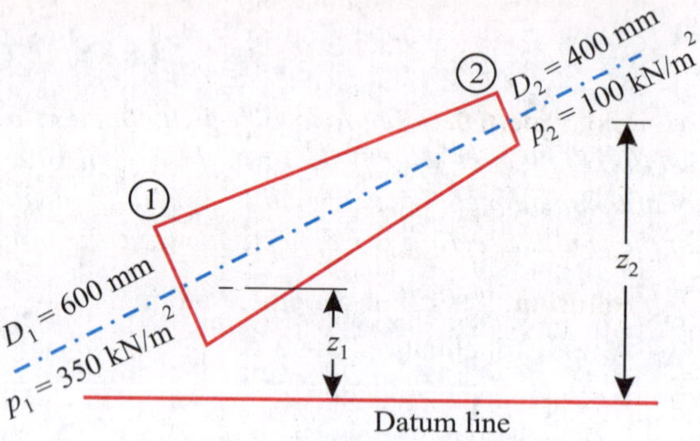

Fig. 6.11

Rate of flow,

$$Q = 60\text{ litres/sec} = \frac{60}{1000} = 0.06\text{ m}^3/\text{sec.}$$

Now, $Q = A_1V_1 = A_2V_2$

[where, V_1 and V_2 are the velocities at sections 1 and 2 respectively.]

$$\therefore \quad V_1 = \frac{Q}{A_1} = \frac{0.06}{0.283} = 0.212\text{ m/s}$$

and,

$$V_2 = \frac{Q}{A_2} = \frac{0.06}{0.1257} = 0.477\text{ m/s}$$

Applying Bernoulli's equation at sections 1 and 2, we get:

$$\frac{p_1}{w} + \frac{V_1^2}{2g} + z_1 = \frac{p_2}{w} + \frac{V_2^2}{2g} + z_2$$

$$\frac{350}{9.81} + \frac{0.212^2}{2 \times 9.81} + z_1 = \frac{100}{9.81} + \frac{0.477^2}{2 \times 9.81} + z_2$$

$$35.67 + 0.0023 + z_1 = 10.19 + 0.0116 + z_2$$

$$z_2 - z_1 = \mathbf{25.47\ m\ (Ans.)}$$

Example 6.11. *Gasoline (sp. gr. 0.8) is flowing upwards a vertical pipeline which tapers from 300 mm to 150 mm diameter. A gasoline mercury differential manometer is connected between 300 mm and 150 mm pipe section to measure the rate of flow. The distance between the manometer tappings is 1 metre and gauge reading is 500 mm of mercury. Find:*

(i) *Differential gauge reading in terms of gasoline head;*

(ii) *Rate of flow.*

Neglect friction and other losses between tappings. **[MGU, Kerala]**

Solution. Sp. gravity of gasoline = 0.8

At Inlet:

$$\text{Diameter, } D_1 = 300 \text{ mm} = 0.3 \text{ m}$$

$$\therefore \quad \text{Area, } A_1 = \frac{\pi}{4} \times 0.3^2 = 0.0707 \text{ m}^2$$

At Outlet:

$$\text{Diameter, } D_2 = 150 \text{ mm} = 0.15 \text{ m}$$

$$\therefore \quad \text{Area, } A_2 = \frac{\pi}{4} \times 0.15^2 = 0.01767 \text{ m}^2$$

Length of the pipe = 1m

Let datum of the pipe at inlet, $z_1 = 0$

$\therefore$ Datum of the pipe at outlet, $z_2 = 0 + 1 = 1$ m

Gauge reading, $h = 500$ mm of mercury = 0.5 m of mercury.

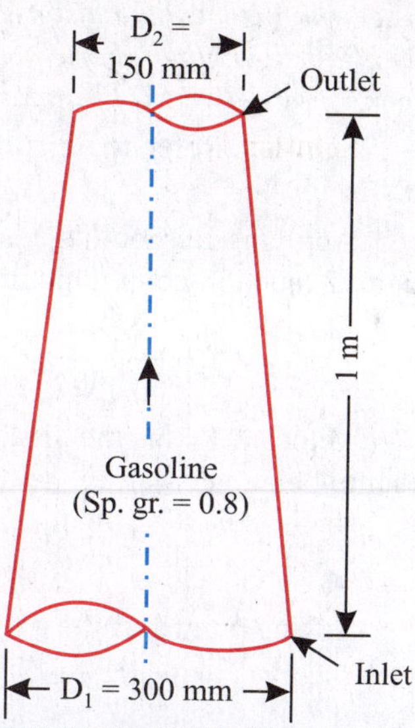

Fig. 6.12

(*i*) Differential gauge reading in terms of gasoline head:

The gauge reading = 0.5 m of mercury

$$= \frac{13.6 - 0.8}{0.8} \times 0.5 \text{ of gasoline}$$

$$= \textbf{8 m of gasoline (Ans.)}$$

(*ii*) Rate of flow, Q:

Let, V_1 = Velocity of gasoline at the inlet, and

V_2 = Velocity of gasoline at the outlet.

We know that, as per equation of continuity:

$$A_1V_1 = A_2V_2$$

$$\therefore \quad V_2 = \frac{A_1V_1}{A_2} = \frac{0.0707 \times V_1}{0.01767} = 4V_1$$

Now, using Bernoulli's equation for the inlet and outlet of the pipe, we get:

$$\frac{p_1}{w} + \frac{V_1^2}{2g} + z_1 = \frac{p_2}{w} + \frac{V_2^2}{2g} + z_2$$

$$\left\{\frac{p_1}{w} - \frac{p_2}{w}\right\} + \left\{\frac{V_1^2}{2g} - \frac{V_2^2}{2g}\right\} + (z_1 - z_2) = 0$$

$$8 + \left[\frac{V_1^2}{2g} - \frac{(4V_1)^2}{2g}\right] + [0 - 1] = 0$$

or,
$$8 - \frac{15V_1^2}{2g} - 1 = 0$$

or,
$$\frac{15V_1^2}{2g} = 7$$

$$\therefore \quad V_1 = \left[\frac{7 \times 2 \times 9.81}{15}\right]^{1/2} = 3.026 \text{ m/s.}$$

$\therefore$ Rate of flow, $Q = A_1V_1 = 0.0707 \times 3.026 =$ **0.2139 m³/s (Ans.)**

Example 6.12. *The suction pipe of a pump rises at a slope of 3 vertical in 4 along the pipe which is 12 cm in diameter. The pipe is 7.2 m long; its lower end being just below the water surface in the* *reservoir. For design reasons, it is desirable that pressure at inlet to the pump shall fall to more than 75 kPa below atmospheric pressure. Neglecting friction, determine the maximum discharge that the pump may deliver. Take atmospheric pressure as 101.32 kPa.* **(Bangalore University)**

Solution. Refer to Fig. 6.13. *Given:* $d = 12$ cm $= 0.12$ m; $l = 7.2$ m; $p_{atm.} = 101.32$ kPa $= 101.32$ kN/m^2.

Applying Bernoulli's equation at point 1 (F.W.S.) and point 2 (suction point to pump), we get:

$$\frac{p_1}{w} + \frac{V_1^2}{2g} + z_1 = \frac{p_2}{w} + \frac{V_2^2}{2g} + z_2 \quad ...(i)$$

Velocity V_1 on the free water surface (F.W.S.) = 0 (sump being very large)

$$p_1 = p_{atm.} = 101.32 \text{ kN/m}^2,$$

$$p_2 = 101{\cdot}32 - 75 = 26.32 \text{ kN/m}^2$$

Taking point 1 as the datum head, we have:

$$z_1 = 0; \; z_2 = 7.2 \times \frac{3}{4} = 5.4 \text{ m}$$

Inserting the various values in eqn (*i*), we have:

$$\frac{101.32}{9.81} + 0 + 0 = \frac{26.32}{9.81} + \frac{V_2^2}{2g} + 5.4$$

or, $$V_2 = 6.64 \text{ m/s}$$

∴ Discharge that the pump may deliver,

$$Q = A_2 \times V_2 = \frac{\pi}{4} \times (0.12)^2 \times 6.64 = \mathbf{0.075 \text{ m}^3/\text{s}} \text{ (Ans.)}$$

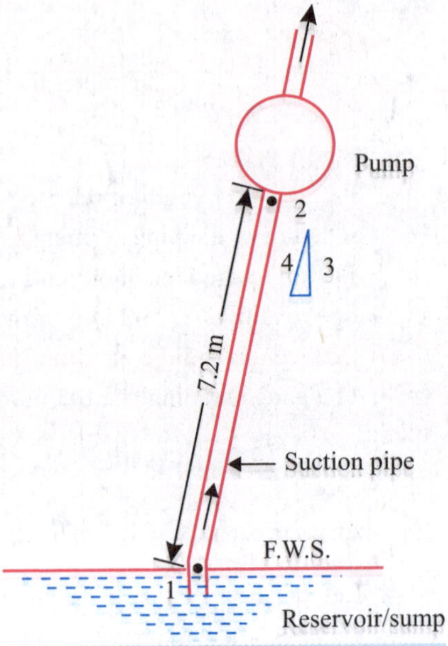

Fig. 6.13

6.5. BERNOULLI'S EQUATION FOR REAL FLUID

Bernoulli's equation earlier derived was based on the assumption that fluid is non-viscous and therefore frictionless. Practically, all fluids are real (and not ideal) and therefore are viscous as such there are always some losses in fluid flows. These losses have, therefore, to be taken into consideration in the application of Bernoulli's equation which gets modified (between sections 1 and 2) for *real fluids* as follows:

$$\frac{p_1}{w} + \frac{V_1^2}{2g} + z_1 = \frac{p_2}{w} + \frac{V_2^2}{2g} + z_2 + h_L \quad ...(6.4)$$

where, h_L = Loss of energy between sections 1and 2.

Example 6.13. *The following data relate to a conical tube of length 3.0 m fixed vertically with its smaller end upwards and carrying fluid in the downward direction.*

The velocity of flow at the smaller end = 10 m/s.

The velocity of flow at the larger end = 4 m/s.

The loss of head in the tube $= \dfrac{0.4\,(V_1 - V_2)^2}{2g}$

where, V_1 and V_2 are velocities at the smaller and larger ends respectively.

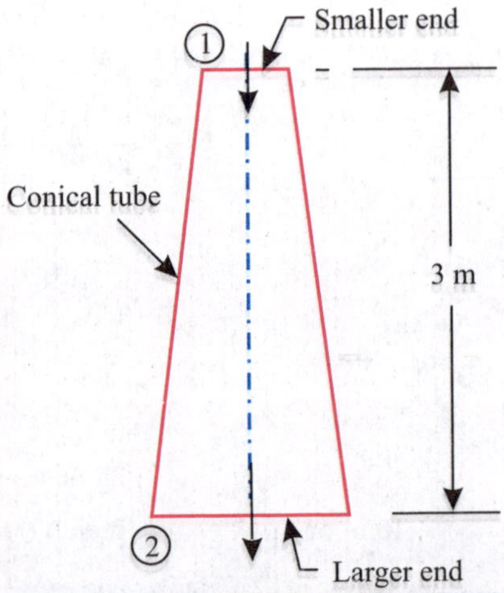

Fig. 6.14

Pressure head at the smaller end = 4 m of liquid.

Determine the pressure head at the larger end.

Solution. Length of tube, $l = 3.0$ m

$$\text{Velocity, } V_1 = 10 \text{ m/s.}$$

$$\text{Pressure head, } \frac{p_1}{w} = 4 \text{ m of liquid.}$$

$$\text{Velocity, } V_2 = 4 \text{ m/s.}$$

$$\text{Loss of head, } h_L = \frac{0.4(V_1 - V_2)^2}{2g} = \frac{0.4(10-4)^2}{2 \times 9.81} = 0.73 \text{ m}$$

Pressure head at the larger end, $\frac{p_2}{w}$:

Applying Bernoulli's equation at sections (1) and (2), we get:

$$\frac{p_1}{w} + \frac{V_1^2}{2g} + z_1 = \frac{p_2}{w} + \frac{V_2^2}{2g} + z_2 + h_L$$

Let the datum line passes through section (2).

Then, $z_2 = 0, z_1 = 3.0$ m

$$\therefore \quad 4 + \frac{10^2}{2g} + 3.0 = \frac{p_2}{2} + \frac{4^2}{2g} + 0 + 0.73$$

$$\text{or,} \quad (4 + 5.09 + 3.0) = \frac{p_2}{w} + 0.815 + 0.73$$

$$\text{or,} \quad 12.09 = \frac{p_2}{w} + 1.54$$

$$\therefore \quad \frac{p_2}{w} = \mathbf{10.55 \text{ m of liquid}} \text{ (Ans.)}$$

Example 6.14. *In a smooth inclined pipe of uniform diameter 250 mm, a pressure of 50 kPa was observed at section 1 which was at elevation 10 m. At another section 2 at elevation 12 m, the pressure was 20 kPa and the velocity was 1.25 m/s. Determine the direction of flow and the head loss between these two sections. The fluid in the pipe is water. The density of water at 20°C and 760 mm Hg is 998 kg/m³.* **(PTU)**

Solution. *Given*:

D = 250 mm = 0.25 m,

p_1 = 50 kPa = 50×10^3 N/m²;

z_1 = 10 m; z_2 = 12 m;

p_2 = 20 kPa = 20×10^3 N/m²,

$V_1 = V_2 = 1.25$ m/s, $\rho = 998$ kg/m³.

Refer to Fig. 6.15.

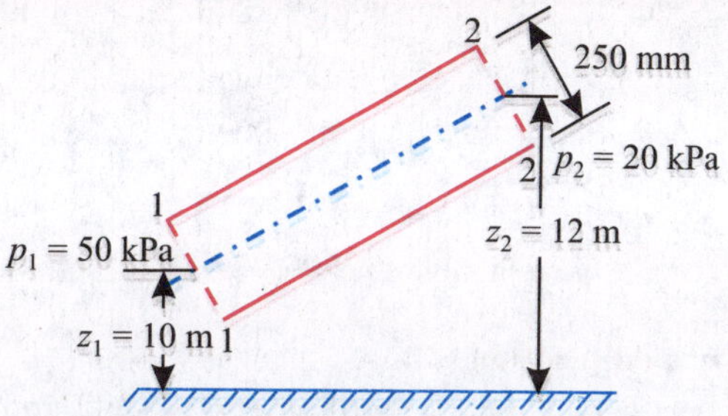

Fig. 6.15

Loss of head h_L:

Total energy at *section 1–1*,

$$E_1 = \frac{p_1}{w} + \frac{V_1^2}{2g} + z_1 = \frac{50 \times 10^3}{998 \times 9.81} + \frac{1.25^2}{2 \times 9.81} + 10 = 15.187 \text{ m}$$

Total energy of *section 2–2*,

$$E_2 = \frac{p_2}{w} + \frac{V_2^2}{2g} + z_2 = \frac{20 \times 10^3}{998 \times 9.81} + \frac{1.25^2}{2 \times 9.81} + 12 = 14.122 \text{ m}$$

∴ Loss of head, $h_L = E_1 - E_2 = 15.187 - 14.122 = \mathbf{1.065\ m}$ **(Ans.)**

Direction of flow:

Since $E_1 > E_2$ *direction of flow is from* **section 1-1 to section 2-2. (Ans.)**

Example 6.15. *A pipe line carrying oil (sp. gr. 0.8) changes in diameter from 300 mm at position 1 to 600 mm diameter at position 2 which is 5 metres at a higher level. If the pressures at positions 1and 2 are 100 kN/m² and 60 kN/m² respectively and the discharge is 300 litres/sec., determine:*

(i) Loss of head, and

(ii) Direction of flow.

Solution. Discharge, $Q = 300$ litres/sec

$$= \frac{300}{1000} = 0.3\ \text{m}^3/\text{s}.$$

Sp. gr. of oil $= 0.8$

∴ Weight of oil, $w = 0.8 \times 9.81 = 7.85\ \text{kN/m}^3$

At position '1':

Diameter of pipe, $D_1 = 300\ \text{mm} = 0.3\ \text{m}$

∴ Area of pipe, $A_1 = \frac{\pi}{4} \times 0.3^2 = 0.0707\ \text{m}^2$

Pressure, $p_1 = 100\ \text{kN/m}^2$

If the datum line passes through section 1 (Fig. 6.16) then datum, $z_1 = 0$

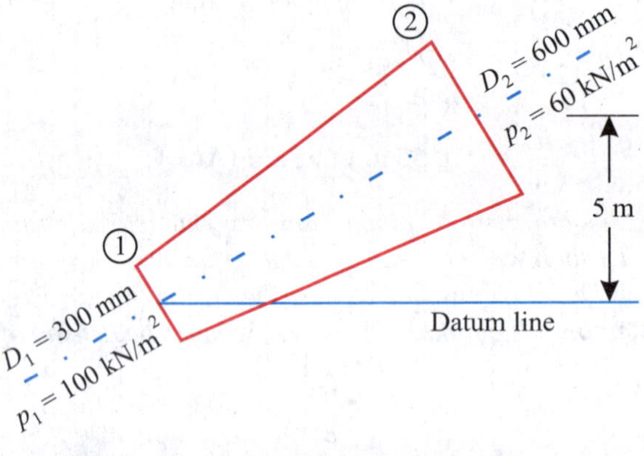

Fig. 6.16

Velocity, $V_1 = \frac{Q}{A_1} = \frac{0.3}{0.0707} = 4.24\ \text{m/s}$

At position '2':

Diameter of pipe, $D_2 = 600\ \text{mm} = 0.6\ \text{m}$

∴ Area of pipe, $A_2 = \frac{\pi}{4} \times 0.6^2 = 0.2888\ \text{m}^2$

Pressure, $p_2 = 60\ \text{kN/m}^2$

Datum, $z_2 = 5\text{m}$

Velocity, $V_2 = \frac{Q}{A_2} = \frac{0.3}{0.2828} = 1.06\ \text{m/s}.$

(i) Loss of head, h_L:

Total energy at *position 1*,

$$E_1 = \frac{p_1}{w} + \frac{V_1^2}{2g} + z_1$$

$$= \frac{100}{7.85} + \frac{(4.24)^2}{2 \times 9.81} + 0 = 12.74 + 0.92 = 13.66 \text{ m}$$

Total energy at *position 2*,

$$E_2 = \frac{p_2}{w} + \frac{V_2^2}{2g} + z_2$$

$$= \frac{60}{7.85} + \frac{(1.06)^2}{2 \times 9.81} + 5 = 7.64 + 0.06 = 7.7 \text{ m}$$

$\therefore$ Loss of head, $h_L = E_1 - E_2$

$= 13.66 - 7.7 = 5.96$ m

i.e., h_L = **5.96 m (Ans.)**

(ii) Direction of Flow:

Since $E_1 > E_2$ therefore flow takes place **from 1 to 2. (Ans.)**

Example 6.16. *A conical tube is fixed vertically with its smaller end upwards and it forms a part of pipeline. The velocity at the smaller end is 4.5 m/s and at the large end 1.5 m/s. Length of conical tube is 1.5 m. The pressure at the upper end is equivalent to a head of 10 m of water.*

(i) Neglecting friction, determine the pressure at the lower end of the tube.

(ii) If head loss in the tube is $\frac{0.3 (V_1 - V_2)^2}{2g}$, *where* V_1 *is the velocity at the smaller end and* V_2 *is the velocity at the larger end, determine the pressure at the lower end (larger cross-section).* **(MDU, Haryana)**

Solution. *Given*: $V_1 = 4.5$ m/s; $V_2 = 1.5$ m/s; $L = z_1 - z_2 = 1.5$ m;

$$\frac{p_1}{w} = 10 \text{ m of water}; \; h_f = \frac{0.3(V_1 - V_2)^2}{2g}$$

Pressure at the lower end, p_2:

(i) ***Neglecting friction*:**

Applying Bernoulli's equation between points 1 and 2, we get:

$$\frac{p_1}{w} + \frac{V_1^2}{2g} + z_1 = \frac{p_2}{w} + \frac{V_2^2}{2g} + z_2$$

or,

$$\frac{p_2}{w} = \frac{p_1}{w} + \frac{1}{2g}(V_1^2 - V_2^2) + (z_1 - z_2)$$

$$= 10 + \frac{1}{2 \times 9.81}(4.5^2 - 1.5^2) + 1.5$$

$$= 10 + 0.917 + 1.5 \simeq 12.42 \text{ m of water}$$

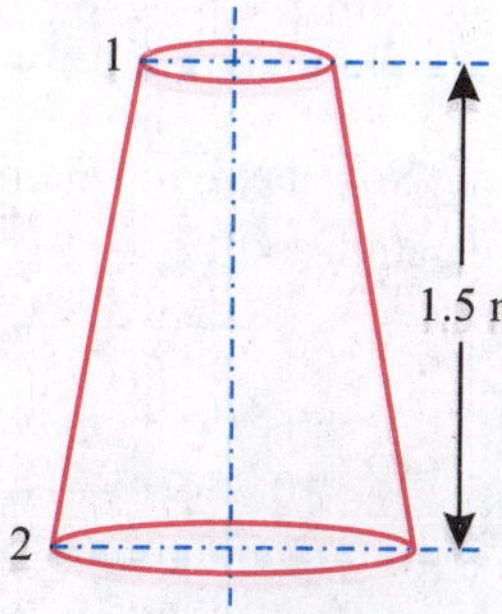

Fig. 6.17

or, $p_2 = 12.42 \times 9810 \text{ N/m}^2 = 12.42 \times 9810 \times 10^{-5}$ bar

= **1.218 bar (Ans.)**

(ii) Considering loss of head (h_f) in the tube :

$$h_f = \frac{0.3(V_1 - V_2)^2}{2g}$$

Applying Bernoulli's equation between points 1 and 2, we have:

$$\frac{p_1}{w} + \frac{V_1^2}{2g} + z_1 = \frac{p_2}{w} + \frac{V_2^2}{2g} + z_2 + h_f$$

or,
$$\frac{p_2}{w} = \frac{p_1}{w} + \frac{1}{2g}(V_1^2 - V_2^2) + (z_1 - z_2) - h_f$$

$$= 10 + \frac{4.5^2 - 1.5^2}{2 \times 9.81} + 1.5 - \frac{0.3(4.5 - 1.5)^2}{2 \times 9.81}$$

$$= 10 + 0.917 + 1.5 - 0.138 = 12.279 \text{ m of water}$$

or,
$$p_2 = 12.279 \times 9810 \times 10^{-5} \text{ bar} = \mathbf{1.204\ bar\ (Ans.)}$$

Example 6.17. *A drainage pump has tapered suction pipe. The pipe is running full of water. The pipe diameters at the inlet and at the upper end are 1 m and 0.5 m respectively. The free water surface is 2 m above the centre of the inlet and centre of upper end is 3 m above the top of free water surface. The pressure at the tip end of the pipe is 25 cm of mercury and it is known that loss of head by friction between top and the bottom section is one-tenth of the velocity head at the top section. Compute the discharge in litre/sec. Neglect loss of head at the entrance of the tapered pipe.*

(UPTU)

Solution. *Given:* D_1 = 1m; D_2 = 1.5 m;

$$p_1 = 76 \text{ cm of Hg} = \frac{76}{100} \times 13.6 = 10.336 \text{ of water;}$$

$$p_2 = 25 \text{ cm of Hg} = \frac{25}{100} \times 13.6 = 3.4 \text{ m of water; } h_f = \frac{1}{10}\frac{V_2^2}{2g}.$$

Discharge, Q:

Refer to Fig. 6.18. Applying continuity equation for the flow through pipe, we get:

$$A_1V_1 = A_2V_2$$

$$\frac{\pi}{4}D_1^2V_1 = \frac{\pi}{4}D_2^2V_2$$

or,
$$D_1^2V_1 = D_2^2V_2$$

or,
$$1^2 \times V_1 = (0.5)^2\ V_2$$

or,
$$V_2 = 4V_1$$

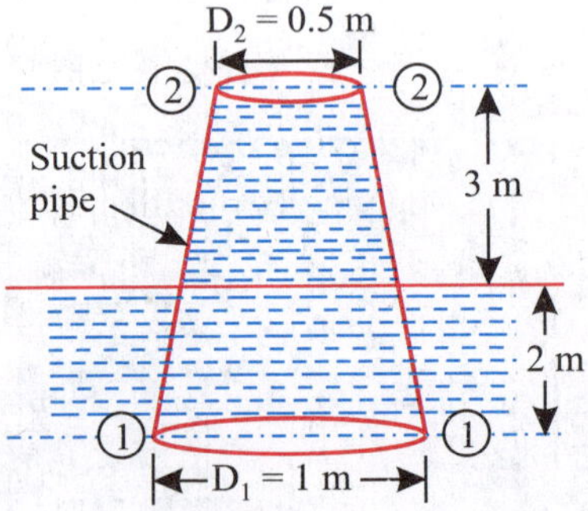

Fig. 6.18

Now, applying Bernoulli's equation at 1-1 and 2-2, we get:

$$\frac{p_1}{w} + \frac{V_1^2}{2g} + z_1 = \frac{p_2}{w} + \frac{V_2^2}{2g} + z_2 + h_f$$

$$10.336 + \frac{V_1^2}{g} + 0 = 3.4 + \frac{16V_1^2}{2g} + 5 + \frac{1}{10} \times \frac{16V_1^2}{2g}$$

$$\frac{16V_1^2}{2g} + \frac{1.6V_1^2}{2g} - \frac{V_1^2}{2g} = 10.336 - 3.4 - 5 = 1.936$$

or,
$$16.6\ V_1^2 = 2 \times 9.81 \times 1.936 = 37.98$$

$\therefore$
$$V_1 = 1.513 \text{ m/s}$$

Discharge $Q = A_1 V_1 = \frac{\pi}{4} \times 1^2 \times 1.513 = 1.188 \text{ m}^3/\text{s}$ = **1188 litres/sec. (Ans.)**

Example 6.18. *The closed tank of a fire engine is partly filled with water, the air space above being under pressure. A 6 cm bore connected to the tank discharges on the roof of a building 2.5 m above the level of water in the tank. The friction losses are 45 cm of water.*

Determine the air pressure which must be maintained in the tank to deliver 20 litres/sec. on the roof. **(Madras University)**

Solution. Refer to Fig. 6.19 *Given*: Diameter of hose pipe $d = 6$ cm = 0.06 m; Friction, $h_f = 45$ cm or 0.45 m of water.

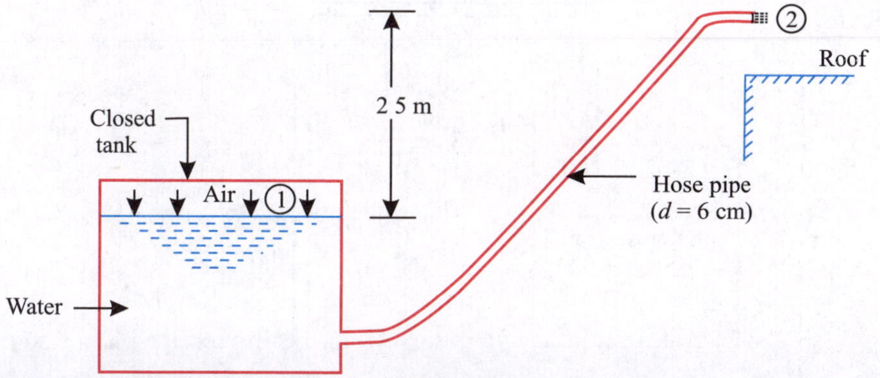

Fig. 6.19

Discharge, Q = 20 *litres/sec.* or 0.02 m^3/s.

Velocity of water in the pipe, $V = \frac{Q}{A} = \frac{0.02}{\frac{\pi}{4} \times (0.06)^2} = 7.07$ m/s.

Applying Bernoulli's theorem at points 1 and 2 respectively, we get:

$$\frac{p_1}{w} + \frac{V_1^2}{2g} + z_1 = \frac{p_2}{w} + \frac{V_2^2}{2g} + z_2 + h_f$$

Here, $V_1 = 0;\ z_1 = 0;\ p_2 = 0;\ V_2 = 7.07 \text{ m/s};\ z_2 = 2.5 \text{ m};\ h_f = 0.45 \text{ m}$

Inserting the various values in the above equation, we get:

$$\frac{p_1}{w} + 0 + 0 = 0 + \frac{(7.07)^2}{2g} + 2.5 + 0.45$$

or,
$$\frac{p_1}{9.81} = \frac{(7.07)^2}{2 \times 9.81} + 2.5 + 0.45$$

$$= 5.497 \text{ m of water (where } p_1 \text{ is in kN/m}^2\text{)}$$

$\therefore$ $p_1 = 9.81 \times 5.497 =$ **53.93 kN/m² (gauge) (Ans.)**

Example 6.19. *A siphon consisting of a pipe of 12cm diameter is used to empty kerosene oil (Sp. gr. = 0.8) from the tank A. The siphon discharges to the atmosphere at an elevation of 1.2 m. The oil surface in the tank is at an elevation of 4.2 m. The centre line of the siphon pipe at its highest point C is at an elevation of 5.7 m. Determine:*

(i) The discharge in the pipe.

(ii) The pressure at point C.

The losses in the pipe may be assumed to be 0.45 m up to summit and 1.25 m from the summit to the outlet.

Solution. Consider points 1 and 2 at the surface of the oil in the tank *A* and at the outlet as shown in Fig. 6.20. The velocity V_1 can be assumed to be zero. Applying Bernoulli's equation at points 1 and 2, we get:

$$\frac{p_1}{w} + \frac{V_1^2}{2g} + z_1 = \frac{p_2}{w} + \frac{V_2^2}{2g} + z_1 + h_{f_{(1-2)}} \text{ (losses)}$$

$$0 + 0 + 4.2 = 0 + \frac{V_2^2}{2g} + 1.2 + (0.45 + 1.25)$$

or, $$V_2 = 5.05 \text{ m/s}$$

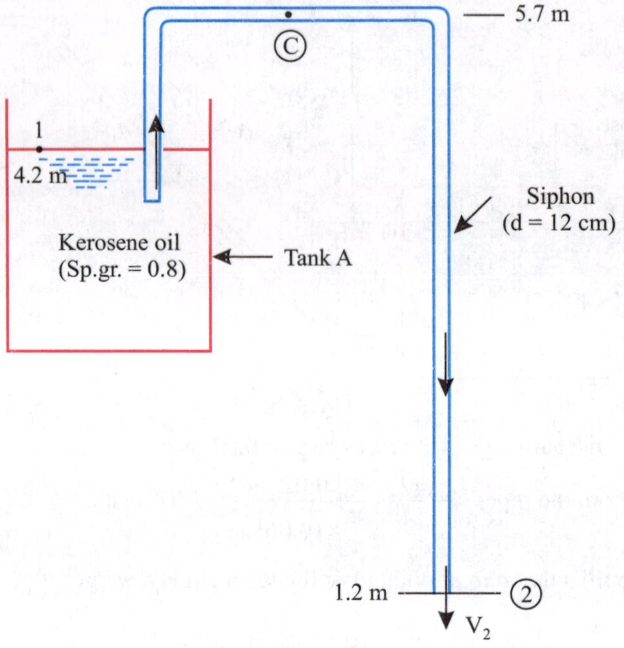

Fig. 6.20

***(i)* The discharge in the pipe, Q:**

$$Q = A_2V_2 = \frac{\pi}{4} \times (0.12)^2 \times 5.05 = \mathbf{0.057\ m^3/s} \textbf{ (Ans.)}$$

***(ii)* The pressure at point C:**

Applying Bernoulli's equation at points 1 and *C*, we get:

$$\frac{p_1}{w} + \frac{V_1^2}{2g} + z_1 = \frac{p_C}{w} + \frac{V_C^2}{2g} + z_C + h_{f_{(1-C)}}$$

$$0 + 0 + 4.2 = \frac{p_C}{w} + \frac{(5.05)^2}{2 \times 9.81} + 5.7 + 0.45$$

or, $$\frac{p_C}{w} = -3.25 \text{ m}$$

or, $$p_C = (0.8 \times 9.81) \times (-3.25)$$
$$= -25.5 \text{ kN/m}^2 \text{ or } -\mathbf{25.5\ kPa\ (gauge)} \textbf{ (Ans.)}$$

Example 6.20. *The outlet at the bottom of a tank is so formed that velocity of water at point A (see Fig. 6.21) is 2.2 times the mean velocity within the outlet pipe. What is the greatest length of* *pipe l which may be used without producing cavitation? Neglect all other losses.*

Take atmospheric pressure = 96.24 kPa (abs.) and vapour pressure = 3.9 kPa (abs.)

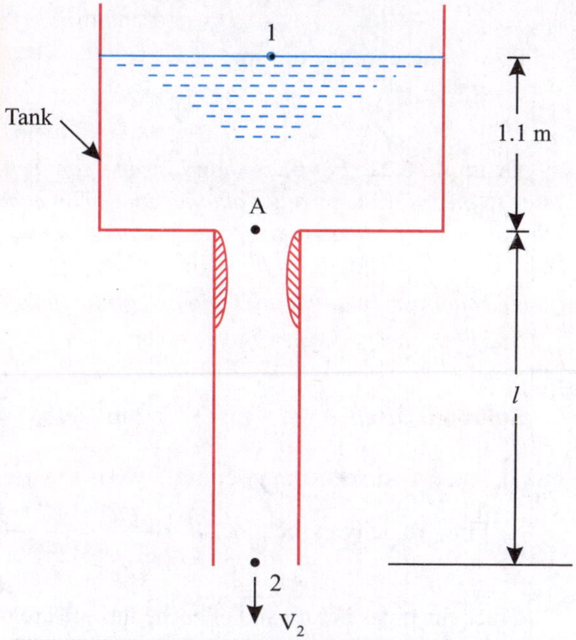

Fig. 6.21

Solution. *Given*: $V_A = 2.2\ V_2$; $p_1 = p_2 = p_{atm.} = 96.24$ kPa $= 96.24$ kN/m^2

Vapour pressure, $p_A = 3.9$ kPa $= 3.9$ kN/m^2 (abs.)

Applying Bernoulli's equation to points 1 and A, we get:

$$\frac{p_1}{w} + \frac{V_1^2}{2g} + z_1 = \frac{p_A}{w} + \frac{V_A^2}{2g} + z_A$$

$$\frac{96.24}{9.81} + 0 + 1.7 = \frac{3.9}{9.81} + \frac{V_A^2}{2 \times 9.81} + 0$$

$$\therefore \quad V_A = 14.76 \text{ m/s}$$

$$V_2 = \frac{V_A}{2.2} = \frac{14.76}{2.2} = 6.71 \text{ m/s}$$

Applying Bernoulli's equations to point 1 and 2, we get:

$$\frac{p_1}{w} + \frac{V_1^2}{2g} + z_1 = \frac{p_2}{w} + \frac{V_2^2}{2g} + z_2$$

$$\frac{96.24}{9.81} + 0 + (l + 1.1) = \frac{96.24}{9.81} + \frac{6.71^2}{2 \times 9.81} + 0$$

$$\therefore \quad l = \mathbf{1.195 \text{ m}} \text{ (Ans.)}$$

Example 6.21. *A turbine has a supply line of diameter 45 cm and a tapering draft tube as shown in Fig. 6.22. When the flow in the pipe is 0.6 m^3/s the pressure head at point L upstream of the turbine is 35 m and at a point M in the draft tube, where the diameter is 65 cm, the pressure head is – 4.1 m. Point M is 2.2 m below the point L. Determine the power output of the turbine by assuming 92% efficiency.*

Solution. $V_L = \dfrac{Q}{A_L} = \dfrac{0.6}{\frac{\pi}{4} \times (0.45)^2} = 3.77$ m/s

$$V_M = \frac{Q}{A_M} = \frac{0.6}{\frac{\pi}{4} \times (0.65)^2} = 1.81 \text{ m/s}$$

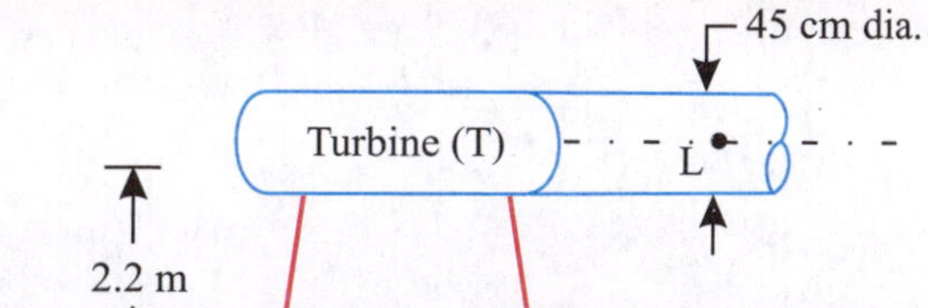

Fig. 6.22

Applying Bernoulli's equation to points L and M:

$$\frac{P_L}{w} + \frac{V_L^2}{2g} + z_L = \frac{P_M}{w} + \frac{V_M^2}{2g} + z_M + H_T$$

$$35 + \frac{(3.77)^2}{2 \times 9.81} + 2.2 = -4.1 + \frac{(1.81)^2}{2 \times 9.81} + 0 + H_T$$

$\therefore \qquad H_T = 41.86$ m

Power output of the turbine,

$$P = wQH_T \times \eta$$
$$= 9.81 \times 0.6 \times 41.86 \times 0.92 = \mathbf{226.68\ kW\ (Ans.)}$$

Example 6.22. *Fig 6.23 shows a pipe connecting a reservoir to a turbine which discharges water to the tail race through another pipe. The head loss between the reservoir and the turbine is 8 times the kinetic head in the pipe and that from the turbine to the tail race is 0.4 times the kinetic head in the pipe. The rate of flow is 1.2 m³/s and the pipe diameter in both cases is 1.1 m. Determine:*

(i) The pressure at the inlet and exit of the turbine.

(ii) The power generated by the turbine.

Solution. *Given*: $d = 1.1$ m; $Q = 1.2\ m^3/s$, $h_{f(1-2)} = 8 \times \frac{V^2}{2g}$; $h_{f(3-4)} = 0.4 \times \frac{V^2}{2g}$

(i) The pressure at the inlet and exit of the turbine; p_2, p_3:

Flow velocity in the pipe, $V = \frac{Q}{\frac{\pi}{4}d^2} = \frac{1.2}{\frac{\pi}{4} \times (1.1)^2} = 1.263$ m/s

Since the pipes before and after the turbine are of equal diameter, therefore,

$$V_2 = V_3 = 1.263 \text{ m/s}$$

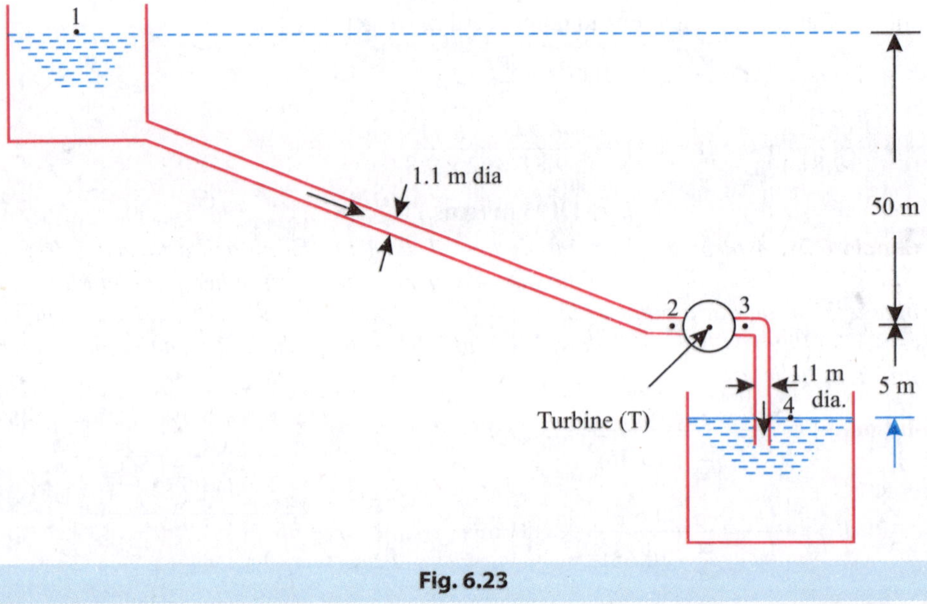

Fig. 6.23

Further, $\qquad V_1 = V_4 = 0; p_1 = p_4 = 0 \qquad$ (atmospheric pressure)

Applying Bernoulli's equation between point 1 and 2, we get:

$$\frac{p_1}{w} + \frac{V_1^2}{2g} + z_1 = \frac{p_2}{w} + \frac{V_2^2}{2g} + z_2 + 8 \times \frac{V_2^2}{2g}$$

$$0 + 0 + 50 = \frac{p_2}{w} + \frac{(1.263)^2}{2 \times 9.81} + 0 + 8 \times \frac{(1.263)^2}{2 \times 9.81}$$

or, $\qquad \frac{p_2}{w} = \mathbf{49.27\ m\ of\ water = 483.34\ kN/m^2\ or\ kPa\ (Ans.)}$

Applying Bernoulli's equation between points 3 and 4, we have:

$$\frac{p_3}{w}+\frac{V_3^2}{2g}+z_3 = \frac{p_4}{w}+\frac{V_4^2}{2g}+z_4+0.4\times\frac{V_3^2}{2g}$$

$$\frac{p_3}{w}+\frac{(1.263)^2}{2\times 9.81}+5 = 0+0+0+0.4\times\frac{(1.263)^2}{2\times 9.81}$$

or, $$\frac{p_3}{w} = -\,\mathbf{5.049\ m\ of\ water} = -\,\mathbf{49.53\ kN/m^2\ or\ kPa}\ \textbf{(Ans.)}$$

(*ii*) The power generated by the turbine, P:

Applying Bernoulli's equation between points 2 and 3, we get:

$$\frac{p_2}{w}+\frac{V_2^2}{2g}+z_2 = \frac{p_3}{w}+\frac{V_3^2}{w}+z_3+H_T$$

where, H_T = Energy developed by the turbine per unit weight of liquid = Nm/N or m of liquid

$$49.27 = -5.049 + H_T \qquad (\because V_2 = V_3 \text{ and } z_2 = z_3)$$

$$\therefore \quad H_T = 54.32 \text{ m of water.}$$

Hence, power generated by the turbine,

$$P = wQH_T = 9.81\times 1.2\times 54.32 = \mathbf{639.46\ kW}\ \textbf{(Ans.)}$$

Example 6.23. *In Fig. 6.24 is shown a turbine with inlet pipe and a draft tube. If the efficiency of turbine is 80 per cent and discharge is 1000 litres/s, find:*

(*i*) *The power developed by the turbine, and*

(*ii*) *The reading of the gauge G.* **(Panjabi University)**

Solution. Efficiency of the turbine, $\eta = 80\%$

Discharge through the turbine Q = 1000 litres/sec. = $1\text{m}^3/\text{s}$

Diameter of the inlet pipe = 0.4 m

$\therefore$ Area of the inlet pipe,

$$A = (\pi/4)\times 0.4^2 = 0.1257 \text{ m}^2$$

$\therefore$ Velocity of water through the pipe,

$$V = \frac{Q}{A} = \frac{1}{0.1257} = 7.96 \text{ m/s}$$

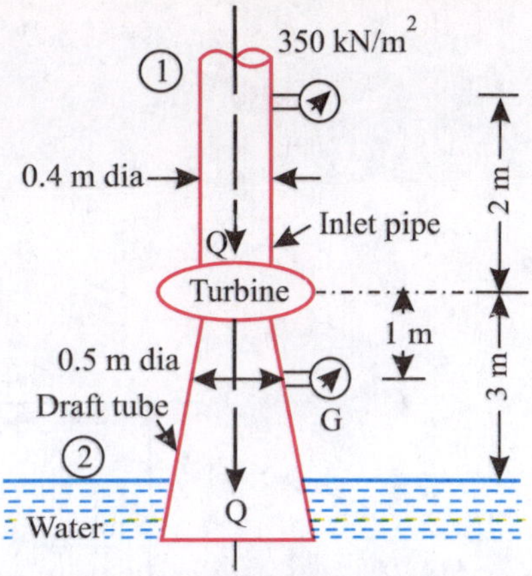

Fig. 6.24

(*i*) Power developed by the turbine, P:

Applying Bernoulli's equation at 1 and 2, we get:

$$\frac{p_1}{w}+\frac{V_1^2}{2g}+z_1 = \frac{p_2}{w}+\frac{V_2^2}{2g}+z_2+\text{losses}+H_T$$

where, H_T = Energy developed by the turbine per unit weight of liquid = Nm/N or m of liquid

$$\frac{350}{9.81}+\frac{7.96^2}{2\times 9.81}+5 = 0+0+0+H_T \quad (\because V = V_1 = 7.96 \text{ m/s}) \quad \text{(neglecting losses)}$$

$$\therefore \quad H_T = 35.68+3.23+5 = 43.91 \text{ m} \quad (\text{where, } w = 9.81 \text{ kN/m}^3)$$

$$\text{Power developed, } P = wQH_T\times\eta\ kW \quad (\text{where, } w = 9.81 \text{ kN/m}^3)$$

$$= 9.81\times 1\times 43.91\times 0.8 = 344.6 \text{ kW}$$

i.e., $$P = \mathbf{344.6\ kW}\ \textbf{(Ans.)}$$

(ii) Reading of the gauge G, p_G:

Applying Bernoulli's equation at 1 and G, we get:

$$\frac{p_1}{w} + \frac{V_1^2}{2g} + z_1 = \frac{p_G}{w} + \frac{V_G^2}{2g} + z_G + H_T$$

$$\frac{350}{9.81} + \frac{7.96^2}{2 \times 9.81} + 3 = \frac{p_G}{w} + \frac{V_G^2}{2g} + 0 + 43.91 \qquad ...(i)$$

But, $$V_G = \frac{Q}{A_G} = \frac{1}{(\pi/4) \times 0.5^2} = 5.09 \text{ m/s}$$

Substituting the value of V_G in (i) and rearranging, we get:

$$\frac{p_G}{w} = \frac{350}{9.81} + \frac{7.96^2}{2 \times 9.81} + 3 - \frac{5.09^2}{2 \times 9.81} - 43.91$$

$$= 35.68 + 3.23 + 3 - 1.32 - 43.91 = -3.32 \text{ m of water}$$

∴ $p_G = 9.81 \times (-3.32) =$ **– 32.57 kN/m² (Ans.)**

Example 6.24. *Fig. 6.25 shows a pump P pumping 72 litres/sec. of water from a tank.*

(i) What will be the pressures at points L and M when the pump delivers 12 kW of power to the flow? Assume the losses in the system to be negligible.

(ii) What will be the pressure at M when the loss in the inlet up to the pump is negligible and between the pump and the point M, a loss equal to 1.8 times the velocity head at B takes place.

Solution. *Given:* Q = 72 litres/sec.
= 0.072 m³/s;

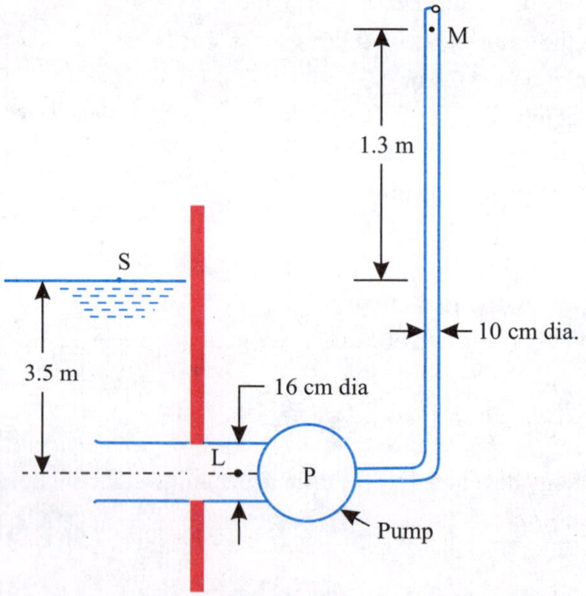

Fig. 6.25

Power delivered by the pump = 12 kW;

Also, $Q = 0.072 = A_L V_L = A_M V_M$

$$V_L = \frac{0.072}{A_L} = \frac{0.072}{\frac{\pi}{4} \times (0.16)^2} = 3.581 \text{ m/s}$$

$$V_M = \frac{0.072}{A_M} = \frac{0.072}{\frac{\pi}{4} \times (0.1)^2} = 9.167 \text{ m/s}$$

Power delivered by the pump P

$$= wQH_P = 12 \text{ kW}$$

or, $9.81 \times 0.072 \times H_P = 12$

$\therefore$ $H_P = 16.99$ m = Head delivered by the pump.

(*i*) Pressures at point L and M:

Applying Bernoulli's equation to points S and L, we have:

$$\frac{p_S}{w} + \frac{V_S^2}{2g} + z_S = \frac{p_L}{w} + \frac{V_L^2}{2g} + z_L$$

$$0 + 0 + 3.5 = \frac{p_L}{w} + \frac{(3.581)^2}{2 \times 9.81} + 0$$

or, $\frac{p_L}{w} = 2.846$ m or $\mathbf{p_L} = 9.81 \times 2.846 = 27.92$ kN/m^2 or **27.92 kPa (Ans.)**

By applying Bernoulli's equation between S and L with level at L as datum, we get:

$$\frac{p_S}{w} + \frac{V_S^2}{2g} + z_S + H_P = \frac{p_M}{w} + \frac{V_M^2}{2g} + z_M$$

$$0 + 0 + 3.5 + 16.99 = \frac{p_M}{w} + \frac{(9.167)^2}{2 \times 9.81} + (3.5 + 1.3)$$

or, $\frac{p_M}{w} = 11.407$ m or $\mathbf{p_M} = 9.81 \times 11.407 =$ **111.9 kN/m^2 or kPa (Ans.)**

(*ii*) Pressure at M when losses are considered:

By applying Bernoulli's equation between S and M with level at L as datum, *considering losses,* we have:

$$\frac{p_S}{w} + \frac{V_S^2}{2g} + z_S + H_P = \frac{p_M}{w} + \frac{V_M^2}{2g} + z_M + \text{losses}\left(i.e.\ 1.8 \times \frac{V_M^2}{2g}\right)$$

or, $$0 + 0 + 3.5 + 16.99 = \frac{p_M}{w} + \frac{(9{\cdot}167)^2}{2 \times 9.81} + (3.5 + 1.3) + 1{\cdot}8 \times \frac{(9{\cdot}167)^2}{2 \times 9{\cdot}81}$$

or, $$3.5 + 16.99 = \frac{p_M}{w} + 16.79$$

or, $\frac{p_M}{w} = 3.7$ m or $p_M = 9.81 \times 3.7 =$ **36.3 kN/m^2 or kPa (Ans.)**

Example 6.25. *Fig. 6.26 shows a pump drawing a solution (specific gravity =1.8) from a storage tank through an 8 cm steel pipe in which the flow velocity is 0.9 m/s. The pump discharges through a 6 cm steel pipe to an overhead tank, the end of discharge is 12 m above the level of the solution in the feed tank. If the friction losses in the entire piping system are 5.5 m and pump efficiency is 65 per cent, determine:*

(*i*) *Power rating of the pump.*

(*ii*) *Pressure developed by the pump.*

Solution. *Given*: $d_2 = 8$ cm or 0.08 m; $d_3 = 6$ cm or 0.06 m; $V_2 = 0.9$ m/s, $\eta_{pump} = 65\%$

(*i*) Power rating of the pump:

From continuity equation, we have:

$$A_2V_2 = A_3V_3$$

or,
$$V_3 (=V_4) = \frac{A_2V_2}{A_3} = \frac{\frac{\pi}{4} \times (0.08)^2 \times 0.9}{\frac{\pi}{4} \times (0.06)^2} = 1.6 \text{ m/s}$$

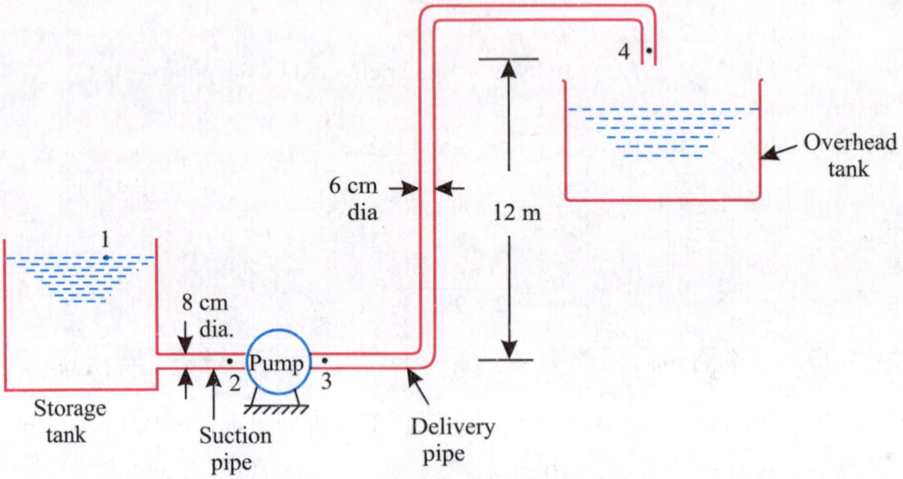

Fig. 6.26

Applying Bernoulli's equation between points 1 and 4, we get:

$$\frac{p_1}{w} + \frac{V_1^2}{2g} + z_1 + H_P = \frac{p_4}{w} + \frac{V_4^2}{2g} + z_4 + \text{Losses}$$

(where, H_P = Energy added by the pump per unit weight of liquid in Nm/N or m of the liquid pumped)

$$0 + 0 + 0 + H_P = 0 + \frac{(1.6)^2}{2 \times 9.81} + 12 + 5.5$$

or,
$$H_P = 17.63 \text{ m of liquid}$$

$$\therefore \text{ Power rating of the pump} = \frac{wQH_P}{\eta_{pump}} = \frac{(9.81 \times 1.8) \times \left(\frac{\pi}{4} \times 0.08^2 \times 0.9\right) \times 17.63}{0.65}$$

$$= \mathbf{2.167 \text{ kW}} \textbf{ (Ans.)}$$

(*ii*) Pressure developed by the pump, ($p_3 - p_2$):

Applying Bernoulli's equation between points 2 and 3, we have:

$$\frac{p_2}{w} + \frac{V_2^2}{2g} + z_2 + H_P = \frac{p_3}{w} + \frac{V_3^2}{2g} + z_3$$

$$\left(\frac{p_3 - p_2}{w}\right) = \left(\frac{V_2^2 - V_3^2}{2g}\right) + H_P \quad \text{...}(\because z_2 = z_3)$$

$$= \frac{(0.9)^2 - (1.6)^2}{2 \times 9.81} + 17.63 = 17.54 \text{ m}$$

or,
$$p_3 - p_2 = 17.54 \times (9.81 \times 1.8) = \mathbf{309.72 \text{ kN/m}^2 \text{ or kPa}} \textbf{ (Ans.)}$$

Example 6.26. *A pump is 2.2 m above the water level in the sump and has a pressure of –20 cm of mercury at the suction side. The suction pipe is of 20 cm diameter and the delivery pipe is short 25 cm diameter pipe ending in a nozzle of 8 cm diameter. If the nozzle is directed vertically upwards at an elevation of 4.2 m above the water sump level, determine:*

(i) The discharge.

(ii) The power input into the flow by the pump.

(iii) The elevation, above the water sump level, to which the jet would reach.

Neglect all losses.

Solution. ***(i)* The discharge, *Q*:**

Applying Bernoulli's equation to points 1 and 2 (Fig 6.27), we get

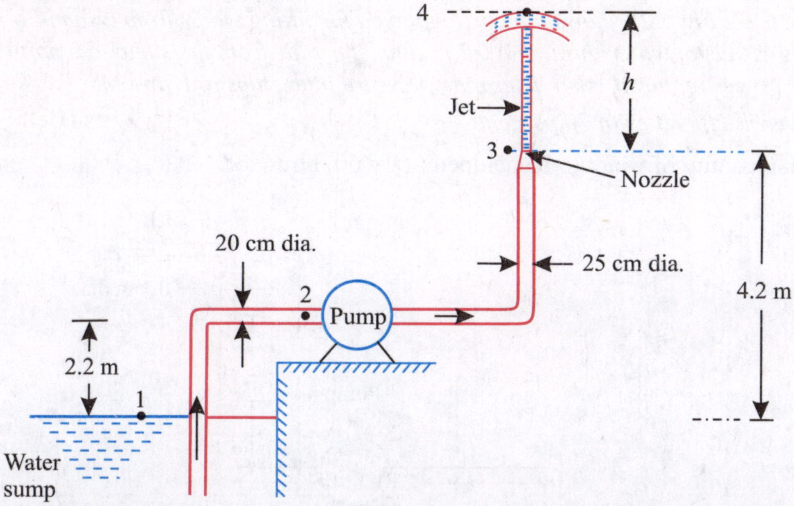

Fig. 6.27

$$\frac{p_1}{w} + \frac{V_1^2}{2g} + z_1 = \frac{p_2}{w} + \frac{V_2^2}{2g} + z_2$$

$$0 + 0 + 0 = (-0.2 \times 13.6) + \frac{V_2^2}{2g} + 2.2$$

or, $$V_2 = 3.194 \text{ m/s}$$

$$\text{Discharge, } Q = \frac{\pi}{4} \times 0.21^2 \times 3.194 = \mathbf{0.1\ m^3/s}\ \textbf{(Ans.)}$$

***(ii)* The elevation, to which the jet will reach, *h*:**

Also, $$Q = A_2 V_2 = A_3 V_3$$

$$\therefore \quad \frac{\pi}{4} \times (0.2)^2 \times 3.194 = \frac{\pi}{4} \times (0.08)^2 \times V_3$$

or, $$V_3 = 19.962 \text{ m/s}$$

or, $$\frac{V_3^2}{2g} = \frac{(19.962)^2}{2 \times 9.81} = 20.31 \text{ m}$$

Hence, the height to which the jet will reach, h = **20.31 m (Ans.)**

(iii) The power input to the flow by the pump, P:

The elevation of point 4, the summit of the jet, is

$$= 4.2 + 20.31 = 24.51 \text{ m}$$

Applying Bernoulli's equation to points 1 and 3, we get:

$$\frac{p_1}{w} + \frac{V_1^2}{2g} + z_1 + H_P = \frac{p_3}{w} + \frac{V_3^2}{2g} + z_3$$

$$0 + 0 + 0 + H_p = 0 + 20.31 + 4.2$$

or, $$H_P = 24.51\text{m}$$

Power delivered by the pump, $p = wQH_p$

$$= 9.81 \times 0.1 \times 24.51 = \mathbf{24.04\ kW\ (Ans.)}$$

Example 6.27. *Fig 6.28 shows a pump employed for lifting water from a sump. If it is required to pump 60 litres/sec. of water through a 0.1 m diameter pipe from the sump to a point 10 m above, determine the power required. Also determine pressure intensities at L and M. Assume an overall efficiency of 70 percent.* **(Delhi University)**

Solution. Quantity of water to be pumped , $Q = 60$ litres/sec.

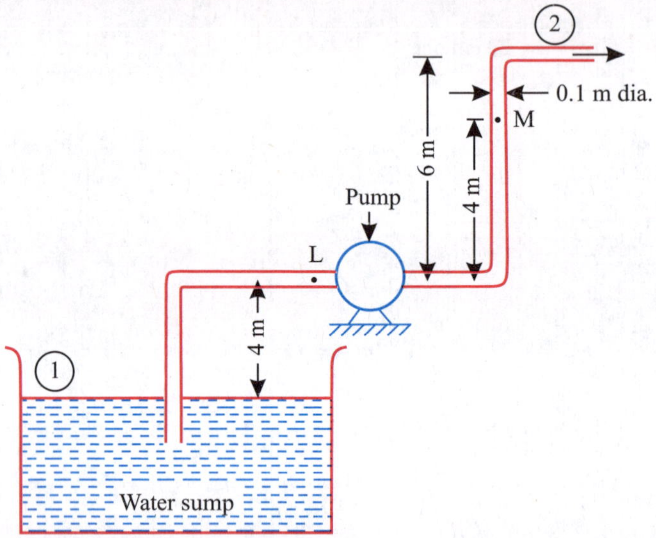

Fig. 6.28

$$= \frac{60}{1000} = 0.06 \text{ m}^3\text{/s}$$

Dia of the pipe, $d = 0.1$ m

∴ Area of the pipe, $A = (\pi/4) \times 0.1^2 = 0.00785 \text{ m}^2$

Overall efficiency, $\eta_0 = 70\%$

Power required, P:

As per continuity equation, $Q = AV$

[where, V = velocity of water in the pipe]

∴ $$0.06 = 0.00785\ V$$

or, $$V = \frac{0.06}{0.00785} = 7.64 \text{ m/s}$$

Applying Bernoulli's equation at 1 and 2 points, we get:

$$\frac{p_1}{w} + \frac{V_1^2}{2g} + z_1 + H_p = \frac{p_2}{w} + \frac{V_2^2}{2g} + z_2$$

(where, H_p = Energy added by the pump per unit weight of liquid in Nm/N or m of the liquid pumped)

$$0 + 0 + 0 + H_p = 0 + \frac{(7.64)^2}{2 \times 9.81} + 10 \qquad (\because V = V_2 = 7.64 \text{ m/s})$$

$$\therefore \quad H_p = 12.97 \text{ m of water}$$

∴ Power required to run the pump,

$$P = \frac{wQH_P}{\eta_0} = \frac{9.81 \times 0.06 \times 12.97}{0.7} \text{kW} \qquad (\because w = 9.81 \text{ kN/m}^3)$$

i.e., P = **10.9 kW (Ans.)**

Pressure intensities at *L* and *M*:

Applying Bernoulli's equation at 1 and *L*, we get:

$$\frac{p_1}{w} + \frac{V_1^2}{2g} + z_1 = \frac{p_L}{w} + \frac{V_2^2}{2g} + z_2$$

$$0 + 0 + 0 = \frac{p_L}{w} + \frac{7.64^2}{2 \times 9.81} + 4$$

$$\therefore \quad \frac{p_L}{w} = -\frac{7.64^2}{2 \times 9.81} - 14 = -6.97 \text{ m} \qquad (\because V_L = V_2 = 7.64 \text{ m/s})$$

or, $P_L = 9.81 \times (-6.97) =$ **– 68.4 kN/m² (Ans.)**

Applying Bernoulli's equation at *l* and *M*, we get:

$$\frac{p_1}{w} + \frac{V_1^2}{2g} + z_1 + H_P = \frac{p_M}{w} + \frac{V_M^2}{2g} + z_M$$

$$0 + 0 + 0 + 12.97 = \frac{p_M}{w} + \frac{7.64^2}{2 \times 9.81} + 8$$

$$\therefore \quad \frac{p_M}{w} = 12.97 - \frac{7.64^2}{2 \times 9.81} - 8 = 12.97 - 2.97 - 8 = 2 \text{ m}$$

or, $p_M = 9.81 \times 2 =$ **19.62 kN/m² (Ans.)**

6.6. PRACTICAL APPLICATIONS OF BERNOULLI'S EQUATION

Although Bernoulli's equation is applicable in all problems of incompressible flow where there is involvement of energy considerations but here we shall discuss its applications in the following *measuring devices*:

1. Venturimeter
2. Orificemeter
3. Rotameter and elbow meter
4. Pitot tube.

6.6.1. Venturimeter

A venturimeter is one of the most important practical applications of Bernoulli's theorem. *It is an instrument used to measure the rate of discharge in a pipeline and is often fixed permanently at different sections of the pipeline to know the discharges there.*

A venturimeter has been named after the 18th century Italian engineer *Venturi.*

Types of venturimeters:

Venturimeters may be *classified* as follows:

1. Horizontal venturimeters.
2. Vertical venturimeters.
3. Inclined venturimeters.

6.6.1.1. Horizontal venturimeters

A venturimeter consists of the following *three* parts:

(*i*) A short converging part,

(*ii*) Throat, and

(*iii*) Diverging part.

Expression for rate of flow:

Fig 6.29 shows a venturimeter fitted in horizontal pipe through which a fluid is flowing.

Let, D_1 = Diameter at inlet or at section 1,

A_1 = Area at inlet $\left(= \frac{\pi}{4} D_1^2\right)$

p_1 = Pressure at section 1,

V_1 = Velocity of fluid at section 1,

and D_2, A_2, p_2, and V_2 are the corresponding values at section 2.

Applying Bernoulli's equation at sections 1 and 2, we get:

$$\frac{p_1}{w} + \frac{V_1^2}{2g} + z_1 = \frac{p_2}{w} + \frac{V_2^2}{2g} + z_2 \qquad ...(i)$$

Here, $z_1 = z_2$ ... since the pipe is horizontal.

$$\therefore \quad \frac{p_1}{w} + \frac{V_1^2}{2g} = \frac{p_2}{w} + \frac{V_2^2}{2g}$$

or,

$$\frac{p_1 - p_2}{w} = \frac{V_2^2}{2g} - \frac{V_1^2}{2g} \qquad ...(ii)$$

But, $\frac{p_1 - p_2}{w}$ = Difference of pressure heads at sections 1 and 2 and is equal to h.

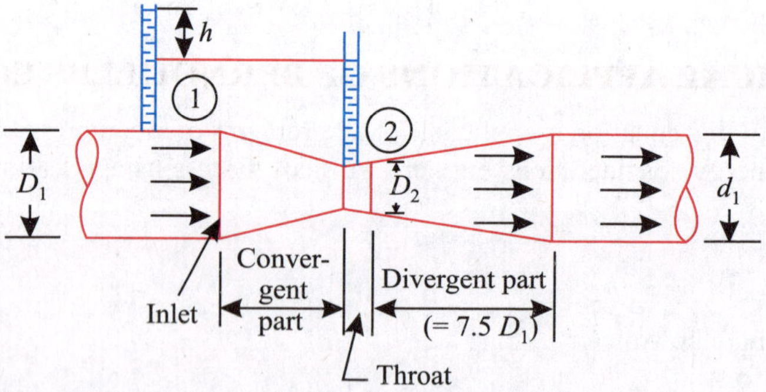

$\left(\text{Throat ratio } \frac{D_2}{D_1} \text{ varies } \frac{1}{4} \text{ to } \frac{3}{4}\right)$

Fig. 6.29. Venturimeter.

i.e., $$\frac{p_1 - p_2}{w} = h$$

Substituting this value of $\frac{p_1 - p_2}{w}$ in eqn. (*ii*), we get:

$$h = \frac{V_2^2}{2g} - \frac{V_1^2}{2g} \quad \text{...(iii)}$$

Applying continuity equation at sections 1 and 2, we have:

$$A_1V_1 = A_2V_2 \quad \text{or} \quad V_1 = \frac{A_2V_2}{A_1}$$

Substituting the value of V_1 in eqn. (*iii*), we get:

$$h = \frac{V_2^2}{2g} - \frac{\left(\frac{A_2V_2}{A_1}\right)^2}{2g} = \frac{V_2^2}{2g}\left(1 - \frac{A_2^2}{A_1^2}\right)$$

or, $$h = \frac{V_2^2}{2g}\left(\frac{A_1^2 - A_2^2}{A_1^2}\right) \quad \text{or} \quad V_2^2 = 2gh\left(\frac{A_1^2}{A_1^2 - A_2^2}\right)$$

or, $$V_2 = \sqrt{2gh\left(\frac{A_1^2}{A_1^2 - A_2^2}\right)} = \frac{A_1}{\sqrt{A_1^2 - A_2^2}}\sqrt{2gh}$$

∴ Discharge, $$Q = A_2V_2 = A_2\frac{A_1}{\sqrt{A_1^2 - A_2^2}} \times \sqrt{2gh}$$

or, $$Q = \frac{A_1A_2}{\sqrt{A_1^2 - A_2^2}} \times \sqrt{2gh} \quad \text{...(6.5)}$$

or, $$Q = C\sqrt{h}$$

where, C = constant of venturimeter

$$= \frac{A_1A_2}{\sqrt{A_1^2 - A_2^2}}\sqrt{2g}$$

Eqn. (6.5) gives the discharge under ideal conditions and is called *theoretical discharge.* Actual discharger (Q_{act}) which is less than the theoretical discharge ($Q_{th.}$) is given by:

$$Q_{act} = C_d \times \frac{A_1A_2}{\sqrt{A_1^2 - A_2^2}} \times \sqrt{2gh} \quad \text{...(6.6)}$$

where, C_d = *Co-efficient of venturimeter* (or co-efficient of discharge) and its value is *less than unity* (varies between 0.96 and 0.98)

- *Due to variation of C_d venturimeters are not suitable for very low velocities.*

Value of '*h*' by differential U-tube manometer:

Case. I. *Differential manometer containing a liquid heavier than the liquid flowing through the pipe.*

Let, S_{hl} = Sp. gravity of heavier liquid,

S_p = Sp. gravity of liquid flowing through pipe, and

y = Difference of the heavier liquid column in *U*-tube.

Then $$h = y\left[\frac{S_{hl}}{S_p} - 1\right] \quad ...(6.7)$$

Case. II. *Differential manometer containing a liquid lighter than the liquid flowing through the pipe.*

Let, S_{ll} = Sp. gravity of lighter liquid,

S_p = Sp. gravity of liquid flowing through pipe, and

y = Difference of lighter liquid column in U-tube.

Then, $$h = y\left[1 - \frac{S_{ll}}{S_p}\right] \quad ...(6.8)$$

Example 6.28. *A horizontal venturimeter with inlet diameter 200 mm and throat diameter 100 mm is used to measure the flow of water. The pressure at inlet is 0.18 N/mm² and the vacuum pressure at the throat is 280 mm of mercury. Find the rate of flow. The value of C_d may be taken as 0.98.*

Solution. Inlet diameter of venturimeter, D_1 = 200 mm = 0.2 m

$\therefore$ Area of inlet, $A_1 = \frac{\pi}{4} \times 0.2^2 = 0.0314 \text{ m}^2$

Throat diameter, D_2 = 100 mm = 0.1 m

$\therefore$ Area of throat, $A_2 = \frac{\pi}{4} \times 0.1^2 = 0.00785 \text{ m}^2$

Pressure at inlet, $p_1 = 0.18 \text{ N/mm}^2 = 180 \text{ kN/m}^2$

$\therefore$ $\frac{p_1}{w} = \frac{180}{9.81} = 18.3$ m

Vacuum pressure at the throat,

$$\frac{p_2}{w} = -280 \text{ mm of mercury}$$

$$= -0.28 \text{ m of mercury} = -0.28 \times 13.6 = -3.8 \text{ m of water}$$

Co-efficient of discharge, C_d = 0.98

$\therefore$ Differential head, $h = \frac{p_1}{w} - \frac{p_2}{w} = 18.3 - (-3.8) = 22.1$ m

Rate of flow, Q:

Using the relation,

$$Q = C_d \times \frac{A_1 A_2}{\sqrt{A_1^2 - A_2^2}} \times \sqrt{2gh}, \text{ we have:}$$

$$= 0.98 \times \frac{0.0314 \times 0.00785}{\sqrt{(0.0314)^2 - (0.00785)^2}} \times \sqrt{2 \times 9.81 \times 22.1}$$

$$= \frac{0.000241}{0.0304} \times 20.82$$

or Q = **0.165 m³/s (Ans.)**

Example 6.29. *A horizontal venturimeter with inlet diameter 200 mm and throat diameter 100 mm is employed to measure the flow of water. The reading of the differential manometer connected to the inlet is 180 mm of mercury. If the co-efficient of discharge is 0.98, determine the rate of flow.*

Solution. Inlet diameter of venturimeter, $D_1 = 200 \text{ mm} = 0.2 \text{ m}$

$\therefore$ Area at inlet, $A_1 = \frac{\pi}{4} \times 0.2^2 = 0.0314 \text{ m}^2$

Throat diameter, $D_2 = 100 \text{ mm} = 0.1 \text{ m}$

$\therefore$ Area of throat, $A_2 = \frac{\pi}{4} \times 0.1^2 = 0.00785 \text{ m}^2$

Reading of differential manometer, $y = 180 \text{ mm } (= 0.18 \text{ m})$ of mercury

Co-efficient of discharge, $C_d = 0.98$

Rate of flow, Q:

To find difference of pressure head (h) using the relation,

$$h = \left[\frac{S_{hl}}{S_p} - 1\right], \text{ we have:}$$

where, S_{hl} = Sp.gr. of mercury (heavy liquid) = 13.6, and

S_p = Sp. gr. of liquid through the pipe *i.e.*, water = 1

$$h = 0.18\left[\frac{13.6}{1} - 1\right] = 2.268 \text{ m}$$

To find Q, using the relation,

$$Q = C_d \frac{A_1 A_2}{\sqrt{A_1^2 - A_2^2}} \times \sqrt{2gh}, \text{ we get:}$$

$$Q = 0.98 \times \frac{0.0314 \times 0.00785}{\sqrt{(0.0314)^2 - (0.00785)^2}} \times \sqrt{2 \times 9.81 \times 2.268}$$

or $$Q = \frac{0.000241}{0.0304} \times 6.67 = \mathbf{0.0528 \text{ m}^3/\text{s}} \text{ (Ans.)}$$

Example 6.30. *A horizontal venturimeter with inlet and throat diameters 300 mm and 100 mm respectively is used to measure the flow of water. The pressure intensity at inlet is 130 kN/m² while the vacuum pressure head at the throat is 350 mm of mercury. Assuming that 3 per cent of head is lost in between the inlet and throat, find:*

(i) The value of C_d (co-efficient of discharge) for the venturimeter, and

(ii) Rate of flow.

Solution. Inlet diameter of the venturimeter, $D_1 = 300 \text{ mm} = 0.3 \text{ m}$

$\therefore$ Area at inlet, $A_1 = \frac{\pi}{4} \times 0.3^2 = 0.07 \text{ m}^2$

Throat diameter, $D_2 = 100 \text{ mm} = 0.1 \text{ m}$

$\therefore$ Area of throat, $A_2 = \frac{\pi}{4} \times 0.1^2 = 0.00785 \text{ m}^2$

Pressure at inlet, $p_1 = 130 \text{ kN/m}^2$

$\therefore$ Pressure head, $\frac{p_1}{w} = \frac{130}{9.81} = 13.25 \text{ m}$

Similarly, pressure head at throat,

$$\frac{p_2}{w} = -350 \text{ mm of mercury} = -0.35 \times 13.6 \text{ m of water} = -4.76 \text{ m}$$

(*i*) Co-efficient of discharge, C_d:

Differential head, $h = \frac{p_1}{w} - \frac{p_2}{w} = 13.25 - (-4.76) = 18.01 \text{ m}$

Head lost, $h_f = 3\%$ of $h = \frac{3}{100} \times 18.01 = 0.54$ m

$$\therefore \quad C_d = \sqrt{\frac{h - h_f}{h}} = \sqrt{\frac{18.01 - 0.54}{18.01}} = 0.985$$

***(ii)* Rate of flow, Q:**

Using the relation,

$$Q = C_d \times \frac{A_1 A_2}{\sqrt{A_1^2 - A_2^2}} \times \sqrt{2gh}, \text{ we have:}$$

$$Q = 0.985 \times \frac{0.07 \times 0.00785}{\sqrt{0.07^2 - 0.00785^2}} \times \sqrt{2 \times 9.81 \times 18.01}$$

$$= \frac{0.000541}{0.0956} \times 18.79 = \mathbf{0.146\ m^3/s\ (Ans.)}$$

Example 6.31. *A venturimeter (throat diameter* = 10.5 *cm) is fitted to a water pipeline (internal diameter* = 21.0 *cm) in order to monitor flow rate. To improve accuracy of measurement, pressure difference across the venturimeter is measured with the help of an inclined tube manometer, the angle of inclination being* 30° *(Fig. 6.30). For a manometer reading of* 9.5 *cm of mercury, find the flow rate. Discharge co-efficient of venturimeter is* 0.984. **(GATE)**

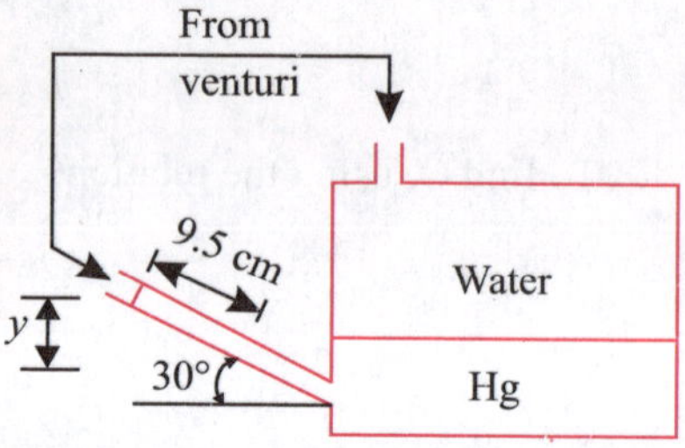

Fig. 6.30

Solution. Internal dia., $D_1 = 21.0$ cm = 0.21 m;

Area of inlet, $A_1 = \frac{\pi}{4} D_1^2 = \frac{\pi}{4} \times (0.21)^2 = 0.0346\ m^2$

Throat dia., $D_2 = 10.5$ cm = 0.105 m

$\therefore$ Area at throat, $A_2 = \frac{\pi}{4} \times D_2^2 = \frac{\pi}{4} \times (0.105)^2 = 0.00866\ m^2$

Discharge co-efficient of venturimeter, $C_d = 0.984$

$$\text{Pressure head, } h = y\left[\frac{S_{Hg}}{S_{water}} - 1\right] = (9.5 \sin 30°)\left[\frac{13.6}{1} - 1\right]$$

$$= 59.85 \text{ cm} = 0.5985 \text{ m}$$

Discharge (Q) through a venturimeter is given by:

$$Q = C_d \frac{A_1 A_2}{\sqrt{A_1^2 - A_2^2}} \times \sqrt{2gh}$$

$$= 0.984 \times \frac{0.0346 \times 0.00866}{\sqrt{(0.0346)^2 - (0.00866)^2}} \times \sqrt{2 \times 9.81 \times 0.5985}$$

$$= 0.984 \times 0.008945 \times 3.427 = \mathbf{0.0302\ m^3/s\ (Ans.)}$$

Example 6.32. *Water at the rate of* 30 *litres/sec. is flowing through a* 0.2 *m. I.D. pipe. A venturimeter of throat diameter* 0.1 *m is fitted in the pipeline. A differential manometer in the pipeline has an indicator liquid M and the manometer reading is* 1.16 *m. What is the relative density of the manometer liquid M? Venturi co-efficient* = 0.96; *Density of water* = 998 *kg/m*^{3}.

(Anna University)

Solution. *Given*: Q = 30 litres/sec. = 30×10^{-3} m^3/s = 0.03 m^3/s = D_1 = 0.2 m; D_2 = 0.1 m; C_d = 0.96; ρ_w = 998 kg/m^3; y = 1.16 m

Assume venturimeter to be *horizontal*. The flow rate is given by,

$$Q = C_d \times \frac{A_1 A_2}{\sqrt{A_1^2 - A_2^2}} \times \sqrt{2gh} \quad ...(i)$$

Here,
$$A_1 = \frac{\pi}{4} \times D_1^2 = \frac{\pi}{4} \times 0.2^2 = 0.03141 \text{ m}^2, \text{ and}$$

$$A_2 = \frac{\pi}{4} \times D_2^2 = \frac{\pi}{4} \times 0.1^2 = 0.007854 \text{ m}^2$$

Substituting the various values in (*i*), we get:

$$0.03 = 0.96 \times \frac{0.03141 \times 0.007854}{\sqrt{0.03141^2 - 0.007854^2}} \times \sqrt{2 \times 9.81} \times \sqrt{h}$$

or,
$$0.03 = 0.96 \times 0.008112 \times 4.43 \times \sqrt{h}$$

or,
$$h = \left(\frac{0.03}{0.96 \times 0.008112 \times 4.43}\right)^2 = 0.756 \text{ m}$$

Also,
$$h = y\left(\frac{S_{hl}}{S_{ll}} - 1\right) \quad \text{[Eqn. (6.7)]}$$

$$0.756 = 1.16\left(\frac{S_{hl}}{0.998} - 1\right)$$

$$\therefore \quad S_{hl} = \left(\frac{0.756}{1.16} + 1\right) \times 0.998 = 1.648$$

Hence specific gravity/relative density of the manometer fluid M = **1.648 (Ans.)**

Example 6.33. *A venturimeter is installed in a pipeline carrying water and is 30 cm in diameter. The throat diameter is 12.5 cm. The pressure in pipeline is 140 kN/m^2, and the vacuum in the throat is 37.5 cm of mercury. Four percent of the differential head is lost between the gauges. Working from first principles find the flow rate in the pipeline in l/s assuming the venturimeter to be horizontal.* **(PTU)**

Solution. Refer to Fig. 6.29. *Given*: D_1 = 30 cm = 0.3 m; D_2 = 12. 5 cm; = 0.125 m; p_1 = 140 kN/m^2, p_2 = – 37.5 cm of mercury

$$= -\frac{37.5 \times 13.6}{100} = -5.1 \text{ m of water;}$$

$$h_f = 4\% \text{ of differential head.}$$

Flow rate in pipeline, Q:

$$\frac{p_1}{w} = \frac{140 \times 10^3}{9810} = 14.27 \text{ m of water}$$

$$\frac{p_2}{w} = -5.1 \text{ m of water (Calculated above)}$$

$$h_f = 4\% \text{ of differential head}$$

$$= \frac{4}{100}\left(\frac{p_1}{w} - \frac{p_2}{w}\right) = \frac{4}{100}[(14.27 - (-5.1)] = 0.775 \text{ m of water.}$$

Applying Bernoulli's equation to the entrance (1) and throat (2) of the venturimeter, we get:

$$\frac{p_1}{w} + \frac{V_1^2}{2g} + z_1 = \frac{p_2}{w} + \frac{V_2^2}{2g} + z_2 + h_f$$

or, $$\frac{V_1^2 - V_2^2}{2g} = \left(\frac{p_2}{w} - \frac{p_1}{w}\right) + h_f \qquad (\because z_1 = z_2)$$

or, $$\frac{V_1^2 - V_2^2}{2g} = -5.1 - 14.27 + 0.775 = -18.59$$

$$\frac{V_1^2}{2g}\left[1 - \left(\frac{V_2}{V_1}\right)^2\right] = -18.59$$

Also, $$A_1V_1 = A_2V_2$$

or, $$\frac{V_2}{V_1} = \frac{A_1}{A_2} = \left(\frac{\frac{\pi}{4}D_1^2}{\frac{\pi}{4}D_2^2}\right) = \left(\frac{D_1}{D_2}\right)^2 = \left(\frac{0.3}{0.125}\right)^2 = 5.76$$

or, $$\frac{V_1^2}{2}\ [1 - (5.76)^2] = -18.59$$

or, $$\frac{V_1^2}{2} \times (-32.18) = 2 \times 9.81 \times (-18.59)$$

or, $$V_1 = \left(\frac{2 \times 9.81 \times 18.59}{32.18}\right)^{1/2} = 3.367 \text{ m/s}$$

Hence, $$\text{Discharge, } Q = A_1V_1 = \frac{\pi}{4} \times (0.3)^2 \times 3.367 \times 10^3 \ l/s$$

$$= \mathbf{238\ l/s\ (Ans.)}$$

6.6.1.2. Vertical and inclined venturimeters

Vertical or inclined venturimeters are employed for measuring discharge on pipelines which are *not horizontal.* The same formula for discharge as used for horizontal venturimeter holds good in these cases as well.

Here, $$h = \left(\frac{p_1}{w} - \frac{p_2}{w}\right) + (z_1 - z_2)$$

[In horizontal venturimeters $z_1 - z_2 = 0$ as $z_1 = z_2$]

Vertical Venturimeters

Example 6.34. *A 200 mm × 100 mm venturimeter is provided in a vertical pipe carrying water, flowing in the upward direction. A differential mercury manometer connected to the inlet and throat gives a reading of 220 mm. Find the rate of flow. Assume $C_d = 0.98$.*

Solution. Diameter at the inlet, $D_1 = 200 \text{ mm} = 0.2 \text{ m}$

∴ Area of inlet, $A_1 = \frac{\pi}{4} \times 0.2^2 = 0.0314 \text{ m}^2$

Diameter at the throat, $D_2 = 100 \text{ mm} = 0.1 \text{ m}$

∴ Area at the throat, $A_2 = \frac{\pi}{4} \times 0.1^2 = 0.00785 \text{ m}^2$

Sp. gravity of heavy liquid (in the manometer), $S_{hl} = 13.6$

Sp. gravity of liquid flowing through pipe, $S_p = 1.0$

Co-efficient of discharge, $C_d = 0.98$

Reading of the differential manometer, $y = 220 \text{ mm} = 0.22 \text{ m}$

Rate of flow, Q:

Differential head,

$$h = \left(\frac{p_1}{w} + z_1\right) - \left(\frac{p_2}{w} + z_2\right) = y\left|\frac{S_{hl}}{S_p} - 1\right|$$

$$= 0.22\left(\frac{13.6}{1.0} - 1.0\right) = 2.77 \text{ m}$$

Using the relation, $Q = C_d \cdot \frac{A_1 A_2}{\sqrt{A_1^2 - A_2^2}} \sqrt{2gh}$, we have

$$Q = 0.98 \times \frac{0.0314 \times 0.00785}{\sqrt{0.0314^2 - 0.00785^2}} \times \sqrt{2 \times 9.81 \times 2.77}$$

$$= \frac{0.000241}{0.0304} \times 7.34 = \mathbf{0.0584\ m^3/s}\ \textbf{(Ans.)}$$

Example 6.35. *A 300 mm × 150 mm venturimeter is provided in a vertical pipeline carrying oil of specific gravity 0.9, flow being upward. The difference in elevation of the throat section and entrance section of the venturimeter is 300 mm. The differential U-tube mercury manometer shows a gauge deflection of 250 mm. Calculate:*

(i) The discharge of oil, and

(ii) The pressure difference between the entrance section and the throat section.

Take the co-efficient of meter as 0.98 and specific gravity of mercury as 13.6. **[UPTU]**

Solution. Diameter at inlet, $D_1 = 300 \text{ mm} = 0.3 \text{ m}$

∴ Area of inlet, $A_1 = \frac{\pi}{4} \times 0.3^2 = 0.07 \text{ m}^2$

Diameter at throat, $D_2 = 150 \text{ mm} = 0.15 \text{ m}$

∴ Area at throat, $A_2 = \frac{\pi}{4} \times 0.15^2 = 0.01767 \text{ m}^2$

Specific gravity of heavy liquid (mercury) in U-tube manometer, $S_{hl} = 13.6$

Specific gravity of liquid (oil) flowing through pipe, $S_p = 0.9$

Reading of differential manometer, $y = 250 \text{ mm} = 0.25 \text{ m}$

The differential 'h' is given by:

$$h = \left(\frac{p_1}{w} + z_1\right) - \left(\frac{p_2}{w} + z_2\right)$$

$$= y\left[\frac{S_{hl}}{S_p} - 1\right] = 0.25\left[\frac{13.6}{0.9} - 1\right]$$

$$= 3.53 \text{ m of oil}$$

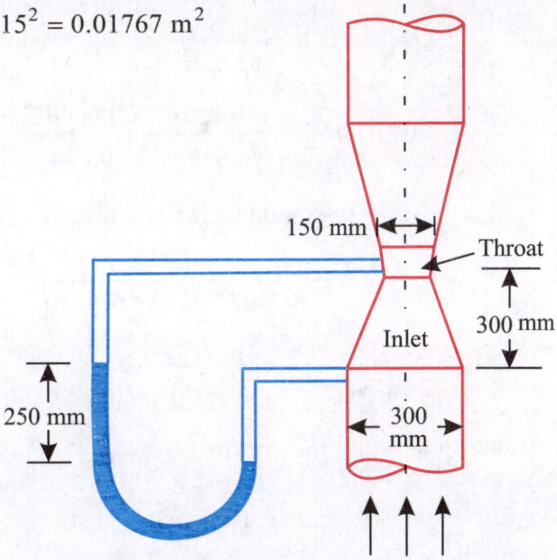

Fig. 6.31

(i) Discharge of oil, Q:

Using the relation,

$$Q = C_d \times \frac{A_1 A_2}{\sqrt{A_1^2 - A_2^2}} \times \sqrt{2gh}, \text{ we have:}$$

$$Q = 0.98 \times \frac{0.07 \times 0.01767}{\sqrt{0.07^2 - 0.01767^2}} \times \sqrt{2 \times 9.81 \times 3.53}$$

$$= \frac{0.001212}{0.0677} \times 8.32 = \mathbf{0.1489\ m^3/s.\ (Ans.)}$$

(*ii*) Pressure difference between entrance and throat sections, $p_1 - p_2$:

We know that, $h = \left(\frac{p_1}{w} + z_1\right) - \left(\frac{p_2}{w} + z_2\right) = 3.53$

or, $\left(\frac{p_1}{w} - \frac{p_2}{w}\right) + (z_1 - z_2) = 3.53$

But, $z_2 - z_1 = 300$ mm or 0.3 m ... (*Given*)

$\therefore$ $\left(\frac{p_1}{w} - \frac{p_2}{w}\right) - 0.3 = 3.53$ or $\frac{p_1 - p_2}{w} = 3.83$

or, $p_1 - p_2 = (9.81 \times 0.9) \times 3.83 = \mathbf{33.8\ kN/m^2}$ **(Ans.)**

Example 6.36. *A vertical venturimeter carries a liquid of relative density 0.8 and has inlet and throat diameters of 150 mm and 75 mm respectively. The pressure connection at the throat is 150 mm above that at the inlet. If the actual rate of flow is 40 litres/sec and the C_d = 0.96, calculate the pressure difference between inlet and throat in N/m^2.* **(Anna University)**

Solution. *Given*: Sp. gravity = 0.8, D_1 = 150 mm = 0.15 m; D_2 = 75 mm = 0.075 m; $z_2 - z_1$ = 150 mm = 0.15 m, Q_{act} = 40 litres/sec. = 0.04 m^3/s, C_d = 0.96.

Pressure difference $(p_1 - p_2)$:

$$A_1 = \frac{\pi}{4} D_1^2 = \frac{\pi}{4} \times 0.15^2 = 0.01767 \text{ m}^2$$

$$A_2 = \frac{\pi}{4} D_2^2 = \frac{\pi}{4} \times (0.075)^2 = 0.00442 \text{ m}^2$$

$$Q_{act} = C_d \times \frac{A_1 A_2}{\sqrt{A_1^2 - A_2^2}} \times \sqrt{2gh}, \text{ we get:}$$

$$0.04 = 0.96 \times \frac{0.01767 \times 0.00442}{\sqrt{0.01767^2 - 0.00442^2}} \times \sqrt{2 \times 9.81} \times \sqrt{h}$$

or, $0.04 = 0.96 \times 0.004565 \times 4.429\sqrt{h}$

$$\therefore \quad h = \left(\frac{0.04}{0.96 \times 0.004565 \times 4.429}\right)^2 = 4.247 \text{ m}$$

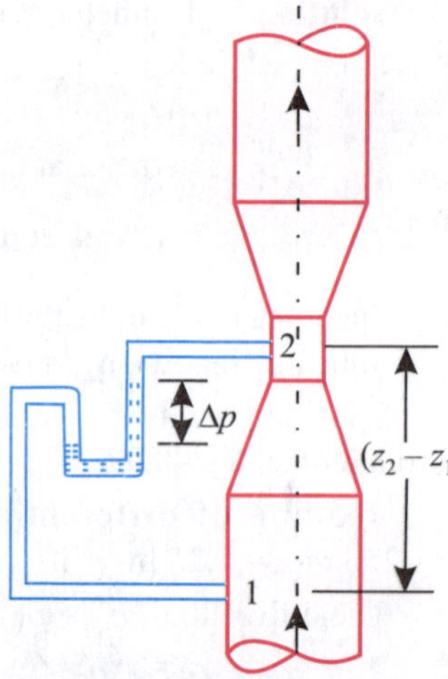

Fig. 6.32. Vertical venturimeter.

Also, $h = \left(\frac{p_1}{w} + z_1\right) - \left(\frac{p_2}{w} + z_2\right)$

or, $4.247 = \left(\frac{p_1}{w} - \frac{p_2}{w}\right) + (z_1 - z_2)$

$= \left(\frac{p_1 - p_2}{\rho g}\right) - 0.15$ $(\because z_2 - z_1 = 0.15 \text{ m})$

or, $(p_1 - p_2) = \rho g\,(4.247 + 0.15)$

$= (0.8 \times 1000 \times 9.81)(4.247 + 0.15)$ N/m^2

$= \mathbf{34.51\ kN/m^2}$ **(Ans.)**

Inclined Venturimeters

Example 6.37. *Determine the rate of flow of water through a pipe of 300 mm diameter placed in an inclined position where a venturimeter is inserted, having a throat diameter of 150 mm. The difference of pressure between the main and throat is measured by a liquid of sp. gravity 0.7 in an inverted U- tube which gives a reading of 260 mm. The loss of head between the main and throat is 0.3 times the kinetic head of the pipe.*

Solution. Diameter at inlet,

$$D_1 = 300 \text{ mm} = 0.3 \text{ m}$$

∴ Area of inlet,

$$A_1 = \frac{\pi}{4} \times 0.3^2 = 0.07 \text{ m}^2$$

Throat diameter,

$$D_2 = 150 \text{ mm} = 0.15 \text{ m}$$

∴ Area at throat,

$$A_2 = \frac{\pi}{4} \times 0.15^2 = 0.01767 \text{ m}^2$$

Specific gravity of lighter liquid (U-tube), $S_{ll} = 0.7$

Specific gravity of liquid (water) flowing through pipe, $S_p = 1.0$

Reading of differential manometer,

$$y = 260 \text{ mm} = 0.26 \text{ m}$$

Difference of pressure head, h is given by:

$$\left(\frac{p_1}{w} + z_1\right) - \left(\frac{p_2}{w} + z_2\right) = h$$

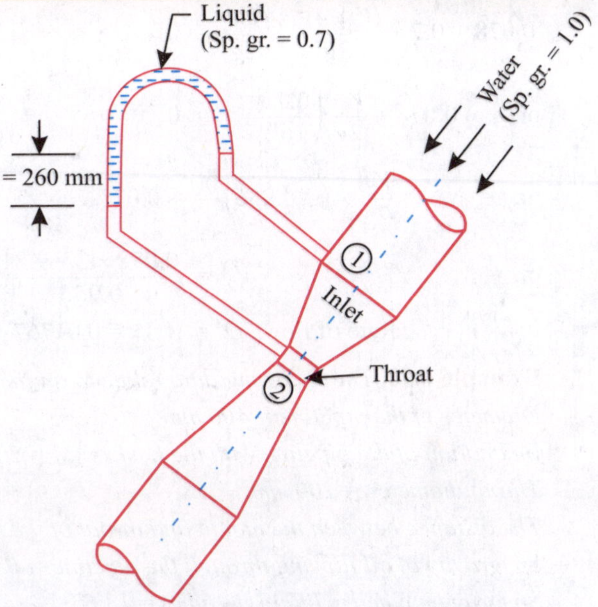

Fig. 6.33

Also,
$$h = y\left(1 - \frac{S_{ll}}{S_p}\right) = 0.26\left(1 - \frac{0.7}{1.0}\right) = 0.078 \text{ m of water}$$

Loss of head, h_L = 0.3 × kinetic head of pipe ...(*Given*)

Now, applying Bernoulli's equation at sections '1' and '2', we get

$$\frac{p_1}{w} + z_1 + \frac{V_1^2}{2g} = \frac{p_2}{w} + z_2 + \frac{V_2^2}{2g} + h_L$$

$$\left(\frac{p_1}{w} + z_1\right) - \left(\frac{p_2}{w} + z_2\right) + \frac{V_1^2}{2g} - \frac{V_2^2}{2g} = h_L$$

But, $\left(\frac{p_1}{w} + z_1\right) - \left(\frac{p_2}{w} + z_2\right) = 0.078$ m of water ... (as above)

and, $h_L = 0.3 \times \frac{V_1^2}{2g}$ ...(*Given*)

$$\therefore \quad 0.078 + \frac{V_1^2}{2g} - \frac{V_2^2}{2g} = 0.3 \times \frac{V_1^2}{2g}$$

or, $0.078 + 0.7\frac{V_1^2}{2g} - \frac{V_2^2}{2g} = 0$ ...(*i*)

Applying continuity equation at sections '1' and '2', we get:

$$A_1V_1 = A_2V_2$$

$$\therefore \quad V_1 = \frac{A_2V_2}{A_1} = \frac{\pi/4 \times 0.15^2}{\pi/4 \times 0.30^2} \times V_2 = \frac{V_2}{4}$$

Substituting this value of V_1 in eqn. (*i*), we get:

$$0.078 + 0.7 \times \frac{(V_2/4)^2}{2g} - \frac{V_2^2}{2g} = 0$$

$$\text{or,} \quad 0.078 + \frac{V_2^2}{2g}\left(\frac{0.7}{16} - 1\right) = 0$$

$$\text{or,} \quad \frac{V_2^2}{2g} \times (-0.956) = -0.078$$

$$\text{or,} \quad V_2^2 = \frac{0.078 \times 2 \times 9.81}{0.956} = 1.6 \text{ m}^2 \text{ or } V_2 = 1.26 \text{ m/s}$$

$\therefore$ Rate of flow, $Q = A_2V_2 = 0.01767 \times 1.26 =$ **0.0222 m³/s. (Ans.)**

Example 6.38. *The following data relate to an inclined venturimeter:*
Diameter of the pipeline = 400 mm
Inclination of the pipeline with the horizontal = 30°
Throat diameter = 200 mm
The distance between the mouth and throat of the meter = 600 mm
Sp. gravity of oil flowing through the pipeline = 0.7
Sp. gravity of heavy liquid (U-tube) = 13.6
Reading of the differential manometer = 50 mm
The co-efficient of the meter = 0.98
Determine the rate of flow in the pipeline. **(Delhi University)**

Solution. Diameter at inlet, $D_1 = 400 \text{ mm} = 0.4 \text{ m}$

$\therefore$ Area of inlet, $A_1 = \frac{\pi}{4} \times 0.4^2 = 0.1257 \text{ m}^2$

Throat diameter, $D_2 = 200 \text{ mm} = 0.2 \text{ m}$

$\therefore$ Area at throat, $A_2 = \frac{\pi}{4} \times 0.02^2 = 0.0314 \text{ m}^2$

Reading of the differential manometer (U-tube), $y = 50 \text{ mm} = 0.05 \text{ m}$

Difference of pressure head h is given by:

$$h = y\left[\frac{S_{hl}}{S_p} - 1\right]$$

where, S_{hl} = Sp. gravity of heavy liquid (*i.e.*, mercury) in U-tube = 13.6, and

S_p = Sp. gravity of liquid (*i.e.*, oil) flowing through the pipe = 0.7

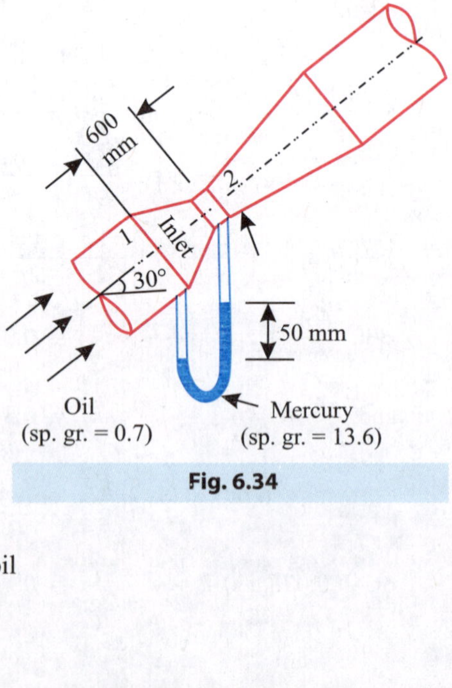

Fig. 6.34

$$\therefore \quad h = 0.05\left(\frac{13.6}{0.7} - 1\right) = 0.92 \text{ m of oil}$$

Now, applying Bernoulli's equation at sections '1' and '2', we get:

$$\frac{p_1}{w} + z_1 + \frac{V_1^2}{2g} = \frac{p_2}{w} + z_2 + \frac{V_2^2}{2g} \quad ...(i)$$

or, $$\left(\frac{p_1}{w} + z_1\right) - \left(\frac{p_2}{w} + z_2\right) + \frac{V_1^2}{2g} - \frac{V_2^2}{2g} = 0$$

But, $$\left(\frac{p_1}{w} + z_1\right) - \left(\frac{p_2}{w} + z_2\right) = h$$

or, $$\left(\frac{p_1}{w} - \frac{p_2}{w}\right) + (z_1 - z_2) = h$$

It may be noted that *differential gauge reading will include in itself the difference of pressure head and the difference of datum head.*

Thus, eqn. (*i*) reduces to:

$$h + \frac{V_1^2}{2g} - \frac{V_2^2}{2g} = 0 \quad ...(ii)$$

Applying continuity equation at sections '1' and '2' we get:

$$A_1 V_1 = A_2 V_2$$

or, $$V_1 = \frac{A_2 V_2}{A_1} = \frac{(\pi/4) \times 0.2^2}{(\pi/4) \times 0.4^2} \times V_2 = \frac{V_2}{4}$$

Substituting the value of V_1 and h in eqn. (*ii*), we get:

$$0.92 + \frac{V_2^2}{16 \times 2g} - \frac{V_2^2}{2g} = 0$$

or, $$\frac{V_2^2}{2g}\left(1 - \frac{1}{16}\right) = 0.92 \quad \text{or} \quad V_2^2 \times \frac{15}{16} = 0.92$$

or, $$V_2^2 = \frac{0.92 \times 2 \times 9.81 \times 16}{15} = 19.25 \quad \text{or} \quad V_2 = 4.38 \text{ m/s}$$

Rate of flow of oil, $Q = A_2 V_2 = 0.0314 \times 4.38 =$ **0.1375 m³/s (Ans.)**

6.6.2. Orificemeter

Orificemeter or orifice plate is *a device* (*cheaper* than a venturimeter) *employed for measuring the discharge of fluid through a pipe.* It also *works on the same principle of a venturimeter.*

It consists of a flat circular plate having a circular sharp edged hole (called orifice) concentric with the pipe. The diameter of the orifice may vary from 0.4 to 0.8 times the diameter of the pipe but its value is generally chosen as 0.5. A differential manometer is connected at section (1) which is at a distance of 1.5 to 2 times the pipe diameter upstream from the orifice plate, and at section (2) which is at a distance of about half the diameter of the orifice from the orifice plate on the downstream side.

Let, A_1 = Area of pipe at section (1),

V_1 = Velocity at section (1),

p_1 = Pressure at section (1), and

A_2, V_2 and p_2 are corresponding values at section (2).

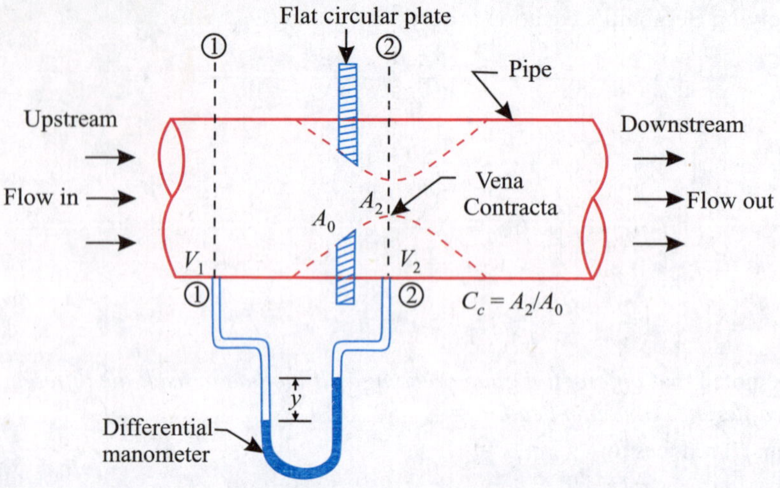

Fig. 6.35. Orificemeter

Applying Bernoulli's equation at sections (1) and (2), we get:

$$\frac{p_1}{w} + \frac{V_1^2}{2g} + z_1 = \frac{p_2}{w} + \frac{V_2^2}{2g} + z_2$$

or, $$\left(\frac{p_1}{w} + z_1\right) - \left(\frac{p_2}{w} + z_2\right) = \frac{V_2^2}{2g} - \frac{V_1^2}{2g}$$

or, $$h = \frac{V_2^2}{2g} - \frac{V_1^2}{2g}$$

$$\left[\because h = \left(\frac{p_1}{w} + z_1\right) - \left(\frac{p_2}{w} + z_2\right) = \text{differential head}\right]$$

or, $$\frac{V_2^2}{2g} = h + \frac{V_1^2}{2g} \qquad ...(i)$$

or, $$V_2 = \sqrt{2g\left(h + \frac{V_1^2}{2g}\right)} = \sqrt{2gh + V_1^2}$$

Now, section (2) is at *vena contracta* and A_2 represents the area at vena contracta. If A_0 is the area of orifice, then we have:

$$C_c = \frac{A_2}{A_0}$$

(where, C_c = co-efficient of contraction)

$$\therefore \quad A_2 = A_0\, C_c \qquad ...(ii)$$

Using continuity equation, we get:

$$A_1 V_1 = A_2 V_2 \quad \text{or} \quad V_1 = \frac{A_2 V_2}{A_1}$$

or, $$V_1 = \frac{A_0 C_c V_2}{A_1} \qquad ...(iii)$$

Substituting the value of V_1 in eqn. (*i*), we get:

$$V_2 = \sqrt{2gh + \frac{A_0^2 . C_c^2 . V_2^2}{A_1^2}}$$

or, $$V_2^2 = 2gh + \left(\frac{A_0}{A_1}\right)^2 \cdot C_2^2 \cdot V_2^2$$

or, $$V_2^2\left[1-\left(\frac{A_0}{A_1}\right)^2 C_2^2\right] = 2gh$$

∴ $$V_2 = \frac{\sqrt{2gh}}{\sqrt{1-(A_0/A_1)^2 C_c^2}}$$

∴ The discharge, $Q = A_2V_2 = A_0.C_c.V_2$

[∵ $A_2 = A_0 \,.\, C_c$... as above {eqn. (*ii*)}]

$$= A_0C_c\frac{\sqrt{2gh}}{\sqrt{1-(A_0/A_1)^2 C_c^2}} \quad ...(iv)$$

The above expression is simplified by using,

$$C_d = C_c\frac{\sqrt{1-(A_0/A_1)^2}}{\sqrt{1-(A_0/A_1)^2 C_c^2}}$$

(where, C_d = co-efficient of discharge)

$$C_c = C_d\frac{\sqrt{1-(A_0/A_1)^2 C_c^2}}{\sqrt{1-(A_0/A_1)^2}}$$

Substituting this value of C_c in eqn. (*iv*), we get:

$$Q = A_0 \cdot C_d\frac{\sqrt{1-(A_0/A_1)^2 C_c^2}}{\sqrt{1-(A_0/A_1)^2}} \times \frac{\sqrt{2gh}}{\sqrt{1-(A_0/A_1)^2 C_c^2}}$$

$$= \frac{C_d \cdot A_0\sqrt{2gh}}{\sqrt{1-(A_0/A_1)^2}} = \frac{C_d \cdot A_0 \cdot A_1\sqrt{2gh}}{\sqrt{A_1^2 - A_0^2}}$$

i.e., $$Q = C_d\frac{A_0 \cdot A_1\sqrt{2gh}}{\sqrt{A_1^2 - A_0^2}} \quad ...(6.9)$$

It may be noted that C_d (co-efficient of discharge) of an orifice is *much smaller than that of a venturimeter.*

Difference between a venturimeter and an orificemeter:

A **venturimeter** is *a device which is inserted into pipeline to measure incompressible fluid flow rates*. It consists of a convergent section which reduces the diameter to between one-half to one-fourth of the pipe diameters. This is followed by a divergent section. The pressure difference between the position just before the venturi and at the throat of the venturi is measured by a differential manometer. The *working of the venturi is based on the Bernoulli's principle,* that is, *when the velocity head increases in an accelerated flow, there is a corresponding reduction in the piezometric head.*

The **orificemeter** *is opening, usually round, located in the side wall of the tank or reservoir, for measuring the flow of a liquid.* The main feature of the orificemeter is that *most of the potential energy of the liquid is converted into kinetic energy of the free jet issuing through the orifice.*

The main points of *difference* between a venturimeter and orificemeter are:

1. The venturimeter can be used for *measuring the flow rates of all incompressible flows.* (gases with low pressure variations, as well as liquids), whereas orificemeters are generally used for measuring the *flow rates of liquids.*
2. Venturimeter is installed *in pipeline only,* and the accelerated flow through the apparatus, is subsequently decelerated to the original velocity at the outlet of the venturimeter. The flow continues through the pipeline. In the orificemeter the entire potential energy of the fluid is converted to kinetic energy, and the jet *discharges freely into the open atmosphere.*
3. In venturimeter, the flow velocity is *measured by noting the pressure difference between the inlet and the throat of the venturimeter,* whereas in the orificemeter the discharge velocity is measured by using *Pitot tube* or by *trajectory method.*

Example 6.39. *The following data relate to an orificemeter:*
Diameter of the pipe = 240 mm
Diameter of the orifice = 120 mm
Sp. gravity of oil = 0.88
Reading of differential manometer = 400 mm of mercury
Co-efficient of discharge of the meter = 0.65.
Determine the rate of flow of oil.

Solution. Diameter of the pipe $D_1 = 240 \text{ mm} = 0.24 \text{ m}$

∴ Area of the pipe, $A_1 = \frac{\pi}{4} \times 0.24^2 = 0.0452 \text{ m}^2$

Diameter of the orifice, $D_0 = 120 \text{ mm} = 0.12 \text{ m}$

∴ Area of the orifice, $A_0 = \frac{\pi}{4} \times 0.12^2 = 0.0113 \text{ m}^2$

Co-efficient of discharge, $C_d = 0.65$

Sp. gravity of oil, $S_0 = 0.88$

Reading of differential manometer, $y = 400$ mm of mercury = 0.4 m of mercury

∴ Differential head, $h = y\left[\frac{S_{hl}}{S_o} - 1\right]$

[where, S_{hl} = sp. gravity of heavier liquid = 13.6 (for mercury)]

$$= 0.4\left[\frac{13.6}{0.88} - 1\right] = 5.78 \text{ m of oil}$$

Discharge Q:

Using the relation, $Q = C_d \dfrac{A_0 . A_1 . \sqrt{2gh}}{\sqrt{A_1^2 - A_0^2}}$, we have:

$$Q = 0.65 \times \frac{0.0113 \times 0.0452 \times \sqrt{2 \times 9.81 \times 5.78}}{\sqrt{(0.0452)^2 - (0.0113)^2}}$$

$$= \frac{0.000353}{0.0437} = \mathbf{0.08 \text{ m}^3/\text{s}} \text{ (Ans.)}$$

Example 6.40. *Water flows at the rate of 0.015 m³/s through a 100 mm diameter orifice used in a 200 mm pipe. What is the difference of pressure head between the upstream section and the vena contracta section? Take co-efficient of contraction $C_c = 0.60$ and $C_v = 1.0$.* **(Delhi University)**

Solution. *Given*: $Q = 0.015\ m^3/s$; $D_0 = 100$ mm = 0.1 m; $D_1 = 200$ mm = 0.2 m; $C_c = 0.60$; $C_v = 1.0$

Difference in pressure head *h*: Refer to Fig. 6.35.

$$A_1 = \frac{\pi}{4} D_1^2 = \frac{\pi}{4} \times 0.2^2 = 0.03142 \text{ m}^2$$

$$A_0 = \frac{\pi}{4} D_0^2 = \frac{\pi}{4} \times 0.1^2 = 0.007854 \text{ m}^2$$

$$C_d = C_c \times C_v = 0.60 \times 1.0 = 0.6$$

Using the relation:

$$Q = C_d \frac{A_0 A_1 \sqrt{2gh}}{\sqrt{A_1^2 - A_0^2}}$$

or,

$$0.015 = 0.6 \times \frac{0.007854 \times 0.03142 \sqrt{2 \times 9.81 \times h}}{\sqrt{(0.03142)^2 - (0.007854)^2}} \quad \text{...[Eqn. (6.9)]}$$

or,

$$0.015 = 0.6 \times \frac{0.001093\sqrt{h}}{0.03042}$$

or,

$$h = \left(\frac{0.015 \times 0.03042}{0.6 \times 0.001093}\right)^2 = \textbf{0.484 m of water (Ans.)}$$

Example 6.41. **(*a*)** *Derive an expression for the volumetric flow rate of a fluid flowing through an orificemeter. Write down the advantages and disadvantages of using orificemeter over a venturimeter.*

(*b*) *Water is flowing through a pipeline of 50 cm ID at 30°C. An orifice is placed in the pipeline to measure the flow rate. Orifice diameter is 20 cm. If the manometer reads 30 cm of Hg, calculate the water flow rate and velocity of the fluid through the pipe.*

$$\rho_{water} \text{ at } 30°C = 987 \text{ kg/m}^3$$

$$\rho_{Hg} = 13600 \text{ kg/m}^3$$

Orifice co-efficient. = 0.6

Sol. (*a*) Refer to Article 6.6.2.

Advantage of orificemeter over venturimeter is that its *length is short and hence it can be used in a wide variety of application. Venturimeter has excessive length.*

The **disadvantage** of orificemeter is that a *sizeable pressure loss is increased because of the flow separation downstream of the plate. In a venturimeter the expanding section keeps boundary layer separation to a minimum, resulting in good pressure recovery across the meter.*

(*b*) *Given*: $D_1 = 50$ cm = 0.5 m; $D_0 = 20$ cm = 0.2; $y = 30$ cm of Hg = 0.3 m of Hg

$$\rho_{water} \text{ at } 30°C = 981 \text{ kg/m}^3, \rho_{Hg} = 13600 \text{ kg/m}^3;$$

$$C_0 = 0.6.$$

Water flow rate, Q:

$$A_1 = \frac{\pi}{4} D_1^2 = \frac{\pi}{4} \times 0.5^2 = 0.1963 \text{ m}^2$$

$$A_0 = \frac{\pi}{4} D_0^2 = \frac{\pi}{4} \times 0.2^2 = 0.0314 \text{ m}^2$$

$$h = y\left(\frac{\rho_{Hg}}{\rho_{H_2O}} - 1\right) = 0.3\left(\frac{13600}{987} - 1\right) = 3.834 \text{ m}$$

Using the relation; $Q = C_d \dfrac{A_0 A_1 \sqrt{2gh}}{\sqrt{A_1^2 - A_0^2}}$, we get:

$$Q = 0.6 \times \frac{0.0314 \times 0.1963 \times \sqrt{2 \times 9.81 \times 3.834}}{\sqrt{(0.1963)^2 - (0.0314)^2}}$$

$$= 0.6 \times \frac{0.05346}{0.1938} = \mathbf{0.1655\ m^3/s}\ \textbf{(Ans.)}$$

Velocity of water through pipe,

$$V_1 = \frac{Q}{A_1} = \frac{0.1655}{0.1963} = \mathbf{0.843\ m/s}\ \textbf{(Ans.)}$$

6.6.3. Rotameter and Elbow meter

6.6.3.1. Rotameter. Refer to Fig. 6.36.

Construction: It consists of a tapered metering glass tube, inside of which is located a rotor or active element (float) of the meter. The tube is provided with inlet and outlet connections. The specific gravity of the float or bob material is higher than that of the fluid to be metered. On a part of the float spherical slots are cut which cause it (float) to rotate slowly about the axis of the tube and keep it centred. Owing to this spinning, accumulation of any sediment on the top or sides of float is checked. However, the stability of the bob may also be ensured by using a guide along which the float would slide.

Working : When the rate of flow increases the float rises in the tube and consequently there is an increase in the annular area between the float and the tube. Thus, the float rides higher or lower depending on the rate of flow.

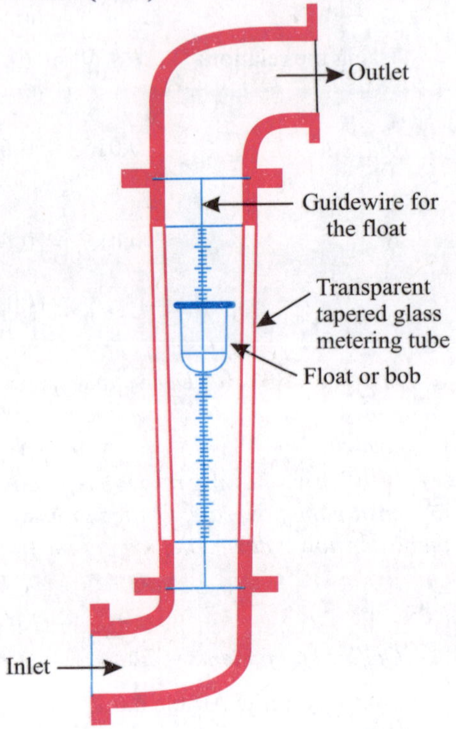

Fig. 6.36. Rotameter.

The discharge through a rotameter is given by:

$$Q = C_d A_{ann} \cdot [2gV_{fl}(\rho_{fl} - \rho_f)/A_f\rho_f]^{1/2} \quad \text{... (6.10)}$$

where,
Q = Volume flow rate,
C_d = Co-efficient of discharge,
$A_{ann.}$ = Annular area between float and tube,
V_{fl} = Volume of float,
ρ_{fl} = Density of float material,
ρ_f = Density of fluid, and
A_f = Maximum cross-sectional area of the fluid.

As the flow area $A_{ann.}$ is a function of height of float in the tube, the flow rate scale can be engraved on the tube corresponding to a particular float.

Advantages :

1. Simpler in operation.
2. Handling and installation easy.
3. Wide variety of corrosive fluids can be handled.
4. Low cost, relatively.

Limitations :

1. Mounted vertically, limited to small pipe sizes and capacities.
2. Less accurate, compared to venturimeter and orificemeter.

6.6.3.2. Elbow meter

When liquid flows around a pipe bend, there is an increase in pressure with radius, *i.e.* the *pressure at the outer wall of the bend is more than that at the inner wall.* This difference of pressure which exists between the outside and inside of the bend is used for the measurement of discharge in a pipeline.

As shown in Fig. 6.37. the pipe bend is provided with two pressure tappings, one each at the inner and outer walls of the bend. These tappings are connected to the limbs of U-tube manometer.

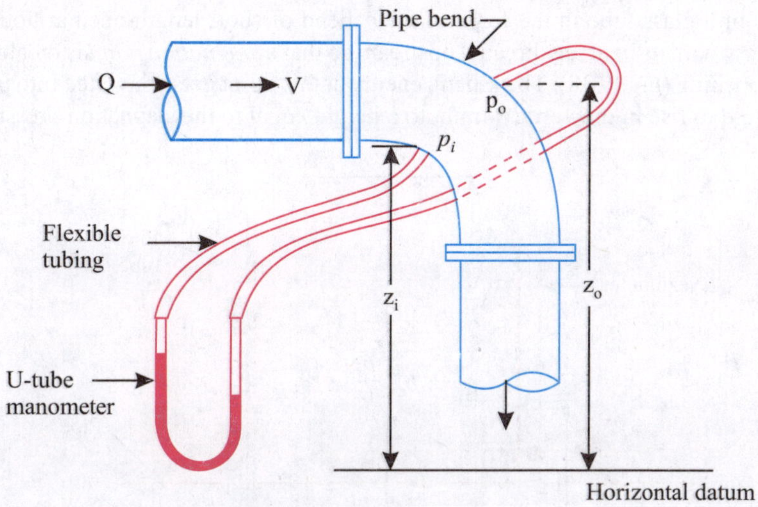

Fig. 6.37. Elbow meter.

As per literature, the following relation between velocity and pressure difference is available:

$$K\frac{V^2}{2g} = \left(\frac{p_0}{w} + z_0\right) - \left(\frac{p_i}{w} + z_i\right) \quad \text{...(6.11)}$$

where, K = Constant (depends upon the shape and size of the bend), *ranges from* 1.3 *to* 3.2, and

V = Velocity of flow.

Suffices 0 and i represent the conditions at the outer and inner walls of the pipe bend.

or,

$$V = \frac{1}{\sqrt{K}}\sqrt{2g}\sqrt{\left(\frac{p_0}{w} + z_0\right) - \left(\frac{p_i}{w} + z_i\right)} \quad \text{...[6.11 (a)]}$$

$\therefore$

$$\text{Discharge, } Q = AV = C_d A \sqrt{2g}\sqrt{\left(\frac{p_0}{w} + z_0\right) - \left(\frac{p_i}{w} + z_i\right)} \quad \text{...(6.12)}$$

where, $C_d = \frac{1}{\sqrt{k}}$ = Co-efficent of discharge, and

A = Cross-sectional area of the pipe.

(C_d varies between 0.56 and 0.88)

The following empirical relation has been suggested:

$$C_d = \sqrt{\frac{R_b}{D}},$$

where, R_b = Radius of pipe bend, and

D = Diameter of the pipe.

- An elbowmeter can be conveniently used for the measurement of discharge in pipes which are fitted with elbows and bends.
- Its accuracy, with proper calibration, approaches that of a venturimeter or nozzle.

6.6.4. Pitot Tube

Pitot tube *is one of the most accurate devices for velocity measurement.* It works on the *principle that if the velocity of flow at a point becomes zero, the pressure there is increased due to conversion of kinetic energy into pressure.*

It consists of a glass tube in the form of a 90° bend of short length open at both its ends. It is placed in the flow with its bent leg directed upstream so that a *stagnation point* is created immediately in front of the opening (Fig. 6.38). The kinetic energy at this point gets converted into pressure energy causing the liquid to rise in the vertical limb, to a height equal to the stagnation pressure.

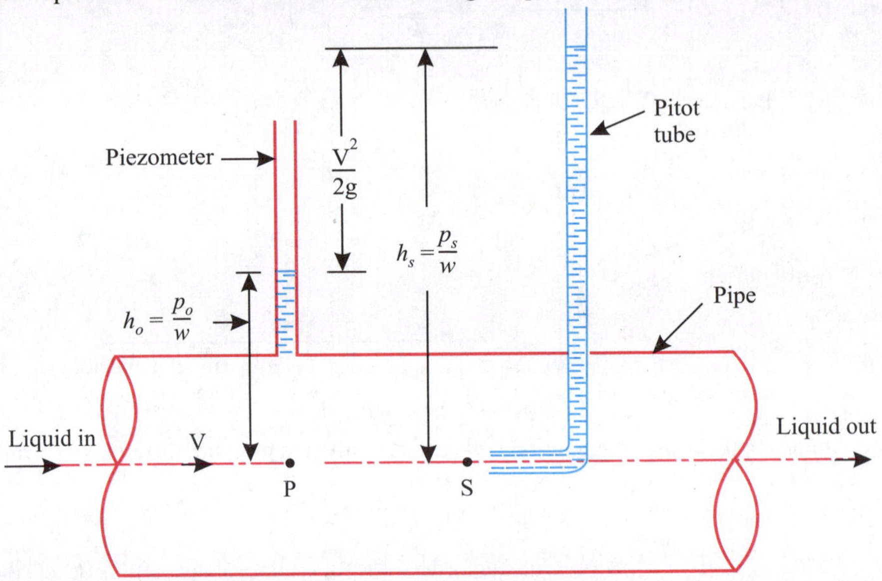

Fig. 6.38. Pitot tube.

Applying Bernoulli's equation between stagnation point (S) and point (P) in the undisturbed flow at the same horizontal plane, we get:

$$\frac{p_0}{w} + \frac{V^2}{2g} = \frac{p_s}{w} \quad \text{or} \quad h_0 + \frac{V^2}{2g} = h_s$$

or, $$V = \sqrt{2g\,(h_s - h_0)} \quad \text{or} \quad \sqrt{2g\,\Delta h} \qquad ...(1)$$

where, p_0 = Pressure at point 'P', *i.e.* static pressure,

V = Velocity at point 'P', *i.e.* free flow velocity,

p_s = Stagnation pressure at point 'S', and

Δh = Dynamic pressure

= Difference between stagnation pressure head (h_s) and static pressure head (h_0).

The height of liquid rise in the Pitot tube indicates the stagnation head. The static pressure head may be measured separately with a piezometer (Fig. 6.38).

Both the static pressure as well as stagnation pressure can be measured in a device known as **Pitot static tube.** (Fig. 6.39).

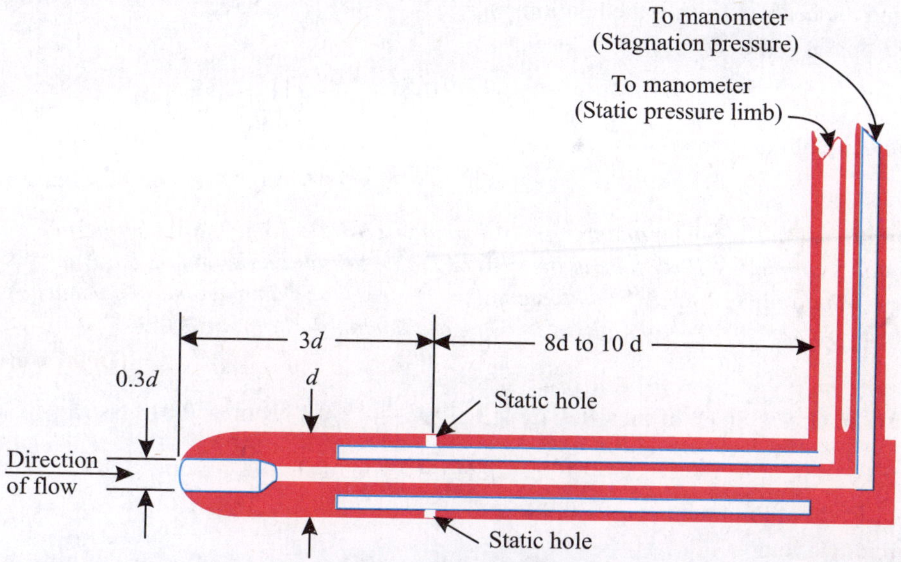

Fig. 6.39. Pitot static tube.

It consists of two concentric Pitot tubes with an annular space in between as shown in the figure. The outer tube has additional two or more holes drilled perpendicular to the direction of flow and thus the liquid level in it gives the static head, while the inner tube works as a normal Pitot tube. If a differential manometer is connected to the tubes of a Pitot static tube it will measure the dynamic pressure head.

If y is the manometric difference, then

$$\Delta h = y\left(\frac{S_m}{S} - 1\right)$$

where, S_m = Specific gravity of manometric liquid, and

S = Specific gravity of the liquid flowing through the pipe.

When a Pitot tube is placed in the fluid-stream the flow along its outer surface gets accelerated and causes the static pressure to decrease. Also the stem, which is perpendicular to the flow direction, tends to produce an excess pressure head. In order to take these effects into account eqn. (1) is modified to give the actual velocities as:

$$V = C\sqrt{2g\Delta h} \qquad \text{...(2)}$$

where, C = A connective coefficient which takes into account the effect of stem and bent leg.

The most commonly used form of Pitot static tube known as the Prandle-Pitot-tube is so designed that the effect of stem and bent leg cancel each other, *i.e.*, $C = 1$.

Example 6.42. *A submarine fitted with a Pitot tube moves horizontally in sea. Its axis is 12 m below the surface of water. The Pitot tube fixed in front of the submarine and along its axis is connected to the two limbs of a U-tube containing mercury, the reading of which is found to be 200 mm. Find the speed of the submarine.*

Take the specific gravity of sea water = 1.025 times fresh water.

Solution. Reading of the manometer, $y = 200$ mm $= 0.2$ m of mercury

Sp. gravity of mercury, $S_{hl} = 13.6$

Sp. gravity of sea water, $S_l = 1.025$

To find the head, (h), using the relation: $h = y\left(\frac{S_{hl}}{S_l} - 1\right)$, we have:

$$h = 0.2\left(\frac{13.6}{1.025} - 1\right) = 2.45$$

$\therefore$ Velocity of the submarine

$$V = \sqrt{2gh} = \sqrt{2 \times 9.81 \times 2.45} = \mathbf{6.93\ m/s\ or\ 24.9\ km/h\ (Ans.)}$$

Example 6.43. *Petroleum oil (sp. gr. = 0.9 and viscosity = 13 cP) flows isothermally through a horizontal 5 cm pipe. A Pitot tube is inserted at the centre of a pipe and its leads are filled with the same oil and attached to a U-tube containing water. The reading on the manometer is 10 cm. Calculate the volumetric flow of oil in m^3/s. The co-efficient of Pitot tube is 0.98.*

(Delhi University)

Solution. *Given*: Sp gr. of oil = 0.9; $\mu = 13$ cP $= \frac{13}{100} \times 0.1$ Ns/m^2 $= 0.013$ Ns/m^2;

$y = 10$ cm of Hg $= 0.1$ m of Hg., $D = 5$ cm $= 0.05$ m;

Co-efficient of Pitot tube, $C_v = 0.98$

Volumetric flow of oil:

$$\text{Differential head, } h = y\left(\frac{S_{Hg}}{S_{Oil}} - 1\right) = 0.1\left(\frac{13.6}{0.9} - 1\right) = 1.411$$

$$\therefore \text{ Actual velocity of flow, } V = C_v\sqrt{2gh} = 0.98\sqrt{2 \times 9.81 \times 1.411} = \mathbf{5.156\ m/s}$$

$$\text{Volumetric flow of oil} = A \times V = \frac{\pi}{4} \times 0.05^2 \times 5.156 = \mathbf{0.01\ m^3/s\ (Ans.)}$$

Example 6.44. *For the flow situation shown in Fig. 6.40 determine the ratio $\frac{h_1}{h_2}$ if the area ratio $\frac{A_1}{A_2} = 1.8$.*

Neglect loses due to friction.

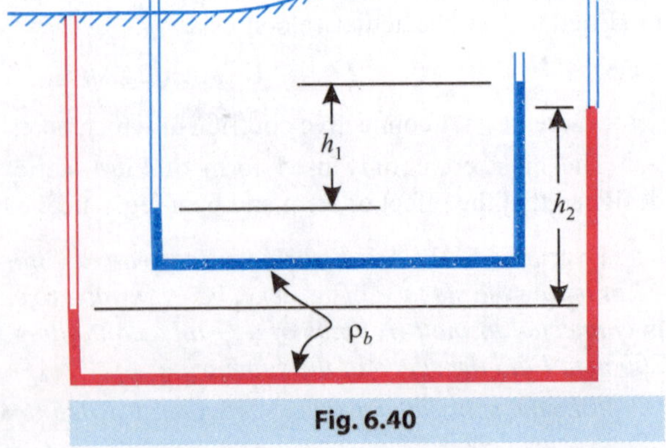

Fig. 6.40

Solution. Refer to Fig. 6.40.

For Pitot tube :

$$p_s + \rho_a g h_1 = p_2 + \rho_b g h_1 \quad \text{...(i)}$$

For piezometric tubes:

$$p_1 + \rho_a g h_2 = p_2 + \rho_b g h_2 \quad \text{...(ii)}$$

Subtracting (*ii*) from (*i*), we get:

$$(p_s - p_1) + \rho_a g(h_1 - h_2) = \rho_b g(h_1 - h_2)$$

$$(p_s - p_1) = (h_1 - h_2)(\rho_b - \rho_a)g$$

$$\frac{p_s - p_1}{\rho_a g} = (h_1 - h_2)\left(\frac{\rho_b}{\rho_a} - 1\right) \quad \text{...(iii)}$$

.....Dividing by $\rho_a g$.

From piezometric tappings,

$$(p_1 - p_2) = h_2 g(\rho_b - \rho_a)$$

$$\frac{p_1 - p_2}{\rho_a g} = h_2\left(\frac{\rho_b}{\rho_a} - 1\right) \quad \text{... (iv)}$$

...Dividing by $\rho_a g$

By Bernoulli's equation:

$$\frac{p_1}{\rho_a g} + \frac{V_1^2}{2g} = \frac{p_2}{\rho_a g} + \frac{V_2^2}{2g} \quad \text{...}(z_1 = z_2)$$

$$\frac{p_1 - p_2}{\rho_a g} = \frac{V_2^2 - V_1^2}{2g}$$

or,
$$\frac{p_1 - p_2}{\rho_a g} = \frac{V_1^2}{2g}\left[\left(\frac{V_2}{V_1}\right)^2 - 1\right] = \frac{V_1^2}{2g}\left[\left(\frac{A_1}{A_2}\right)^2 - 1\right] \quad \text{...(v)}$$

From (*iii*), (*iv*) and (*v*), we have:

$$\therefore \quad h_2\left(\frac{\rho_b}{\rho_a} - 1\right) = (h_1 - h_2)\left(\frac{\rho_b}{\rho_a} - 1\right)\left[(1.8)^2 - 1\right]$$

or,
$$\left(\frac{h_1}{h_2} - 1\right) \times 2.24 = 1 \qquad \left[\because \Delta h = \frac{p_s - p_1}{\rho_a g} = \frac{V_1^2}{2g}\right]$$

or,
$$\frac{h_1}{h_2} = \mathbf{1.446 \ (Ans.)}$$

6.7. FREE LIQUID JET

Refer to Fig. 6.41. A jet of liquid issuing from the nozzle in atmosphere is called a *free liquid jet.* The parabolic path traversed by the liquid jet under the action of gravity is known as *trajectory.* Let the jet A make an angle θ with the horizontal direction. If U is the velocity of the water jet, then $U \cos \theta$ and and $U \sin \theta$ are the horizontal and vertical components of this velocity respectively. Consider another point $P(x, y)$ on the centre line of the jet.

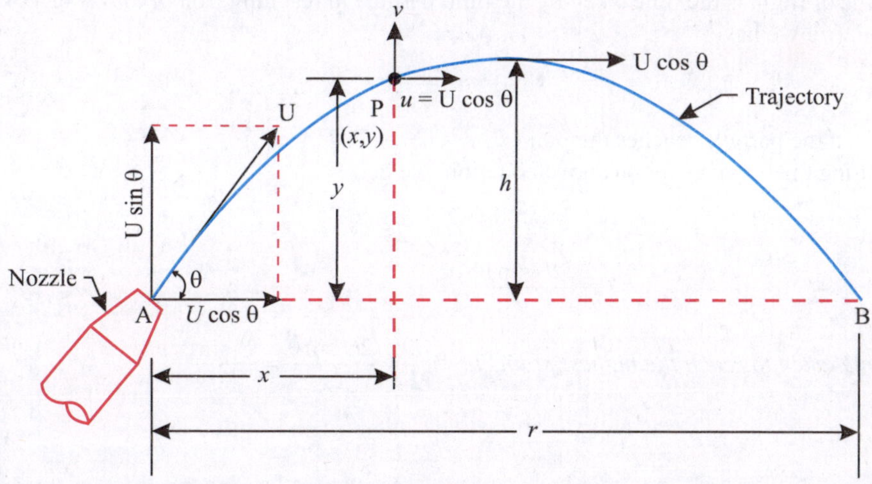

Fig. 6.41

Let, u = Velocity of the jet at point P in X- direction,

v = Velocity of the jet at point P in Y-direction, and

$$t = \text{Time taken by a liquid particle to reach from } A \text{ to } P.$$

Then, $x = u \times t = U\cos\theta \times t$ (where, $u = U\cos\theta$) ...(*i*)

$$y = U\sin\theta \times t - \frac{1}{2}gt^2 \quad ...(ii)$$

(It may be noted that horizontal component of velocity U is $U\cos\theta$ which *remains constant* whereas the vertical component $U\sin\theta$ is *affected by gravity.*)

From eqn. (*i*) we have, $t = \dfrac{x}{U\cos\theta}$

Substituting the value of t in eqn. (*ii*), we get:

$$y = U\sin\theta \times \frac{x}{U\cos\theta} - \frac{1}{2}g \times \frac{x^2}{U^2\cos^2\theta}$$

$$= x\tan\theta - \frac{gx^2}{2U^2\cos^2\theta}$$

$$y = x\tan\theta - \frac{gx^2\sec^2\theta}{2U^2} \quad \left(\because \frac{1}{\cos^2\theta} = \sec^2\theta\right) \quad ...(6.13)$$

This is the equation of *a parabola.*

(*i*) Maximum height attained by the jet, h:

Using the relation:

$V_2^2 - V_1^2 = -2gh$ (– *ve* sign is used as the particle is moving *upward*)

where, V_1 = Initial vertical component = U sin θ, and

V_2 = 0 at the highest point.

$\therefore \quad 0 - (U\sin\theta)^2 = -2gh$

or
$$h = \frac{U^2\sin^2\theta}{2g} \quad ...(6.14)$$

(*ii*) Time of flight, T:

Time of flight is the time taken by the fluid particle in reaching from A to B (Fig. 6.41). From eqn. (*ii*), we have:

$$y = U\sin\theta \times t - \frac{1}{2}gt^2$$

When the particle reaches the point B, $y = 0$, $t = T$

Putting these values in the above equation, we get:

$$0 = U\sin\theta \times T - \frac{1}{2}g \times T^2$$

or,
$$T = \frac{2U\sin\theta}{g} \quad ...(6.15)$$

Time taken to reach the highest point, $T' = \dfrac{T}{2} = \dfrac{2U\sin\theta}{2g} = \dfrac{U\sin\theta}{g}$

i.e.,
$$T' = \frac{U\sin\theta}{g} \quad ...(6.16)$$

(*iii*) Horizontal range of the jet, *r*:

The range (r) of the jet is the total *horizontal distance travelled by the fluid particle.*

Then r, (*i.e.,* distance AB) = Velocity component in direction × time taken by the particle to reach from A to B

$$= U\cos\theta \times T = U\cos\theta \times \frac{2U\sin\theta}{g}$$

$$= \frac{U^2 \times 2\sin\theta \times \cos\theta}{g} = \frac{U^2 \sin 2\theta}{g}$$

i.e., $$r = \frac{U^2 \sin 2\theta}{g} \quad \text{...(6.17)}$$

The range will be maximum, when $\sin 2\theta = 1$

i.e., $$2\theta = 90° \text{ or } \theta = 45°$$

Then maximum range, $$r_{max} = \frac{U^2 \sin(2 \times 45°)}{g} = \frac{U^2}{g}$$

i.e., $$r_{max} = \frac{U^2}{g}$$

Example 6.45. *A nozzle is situated at a distance of 1.2 m above the ground level and is inclined at 60° to the horizontal. The diameter of the nozzle is 40 mm and the jet of water from the nozzle strikes the ground at a horizontal distance of 5 m. Find the flow rate.*

Solution. Distance of nozzle above the ground = 1.2 m

Angle of inclination, $\theta = 60°$

Diameter of the nozzle,

$d = 40 \text{ mm} = 0.04 \text{ m}$

∴ Area of nozzle,

$A = \frac{\pi}{4} \times 0.04^2 = 0.001256 \text{ m}^2$

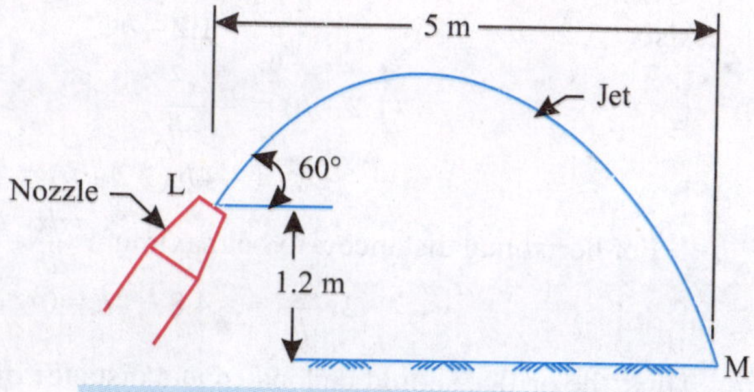

Fig. 6.42

The horizontal distance, $x = 5$ m

The co-ordinates of the point M, which on the centre line of the jet of water and is situated on the ground, with respect to L (origin) are: $x = 5$ m, $y = -1.2$ m (∵ Point M is vertically down by 1.2 m)

The equation of the jet is given by :

$$y = x\tan\theta - \frac{gx^2}{2U^2\cos^2\theta} \quad \text{...}(i)$$

where, U = Velocity of the jet.

Flow rate, Q:

The eqn. (*i*) can be written as:

$$y = x\tan\theta - \frac{gx^2}{2U^2}\sec^2\theta$$

$$-1.2 = 5\tan 60° - \frac{9.81 \times 5^2}{2U^2}(1 + \tan^2 60°) \quad (\because \sec^2\theta = 1 + \tan^2\theta)$$

$$-1.2 = 5 \times 1.732 - \frac{122.62}{U^2}(1 + 3)$$

$$-1.2 = 8.66 - \frac{498.48}{U^2}$$

or, $$U^2 = \frac{498.48}{(8.66 + 1.2)} = 49.74 \quad \text{or} \quad U = 7.05 \text{ m/s}$$

Hence, flow rate, $Q = A \times U = 0.001256 \times 7.05 = \mathbf{0.00885\ m^3/s}$ **(Ans.)**

Example 6.46. *It is required to place an orifice in the side of a tank at such an elevation that the jet will attain a maximum horizontal distance from the tank at the level of its base. What is the proper distance from the orifice to the free surface when the depth of liquid in the tank is maintained at 1.2 m?*

Solution. Depth of liquid in the tank = 1.2 m

$$x = \sqrt{2gh} \times t \quad ...(i)$$

and, $$y = -\frac{1}{2} gt^2 \quad ...(ii)$$

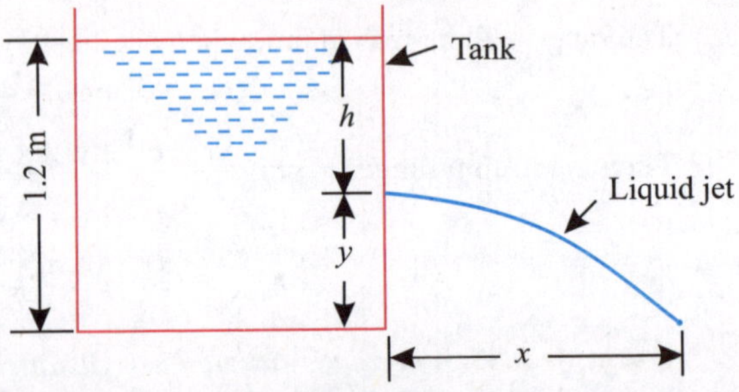

Fig. 6.43

Eliminating t, we get:

$$y = -\frac{1}{2} g \times \left(\frac{x}{\sqrt{2gh}}\right)^2$$

$$= -\frac{1}{2} \times g \times \frac{x^2}{2gh}$$

or, $$y = -\frac{x^2}{4h}$$

Also, $1.2 = h + y$ or $y = 1.2 - h$

$$\therefore \quad (1.2 - h) = -\frac{x^2}{4h}$$

or, $$x^2 = -4h(1.2 - h) = -4.8h + 4h^2$$

For horizontal distance x to be maximum $\frac{dx}{dh} = 0$

$$\therefore \quad 2x\frac{dx}{dh} = -4.8 + 8h = 0 \quad \text{or} \quad h = 0.6 \text{ m}$$

Thus, the orifice should be located at a distance of **0.6 m below the free surface. (Ans.)**

Example 6.47. *Ten nozzles each 25 mm in diameter, all inclined at an angle of 45° with the horizontal are used in an ornamental fountain. The jet issuing from the nozzle falls into a basin at a point 1.5 m vertically beneath the nozzle and 4.5 m horizontally from it. The velocity co-efficient of nozzle is 0.97. Determine:*

(i) Pressure head at the nozzle, and

(ii) Total discharge from the nozzles.

Solution. Diameter of each nozzle,

$$d = 25 \text{ mm} = 0.025 \text{ m}$$

Angle of inclination, $\theta = 45°$

Velocity co-efficient of nozzle,

$$C_v = .97$$

***(i)* Pressure head at the nozzle, H:**

Refer to Fig. 6.44.

Horizontal distance traversed,

$$x = 4.5 \text{ m}$$

Vertical distance traversed,

$$y = -1.5 \text{ m}$$

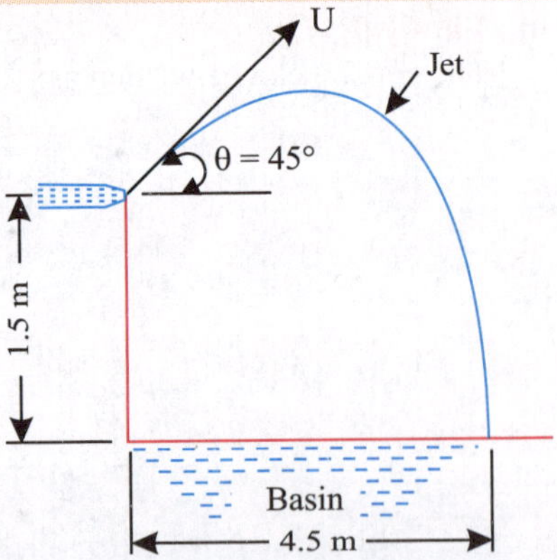

Fig. 6.44

For horizontal motion:

$$x = U \cos \theta \times t$$

or, $$4.5 = U \cos 45° \times t = 0.707\ Ut \qquad ...(i)$$

For vertical motion:

$$y = U \sin \theta . t - \frac{1}{2} gt^2$$

or, $$-1.5 = 0.707\ Ut - \frac{1}{2} gt^2 \qquad ...(ii)$$

From (*i*) and (*ii*), we get:

$$-1.5 = 4.5 - \frac{1}{2} \times 9.81 \times t^2 \quad \text{or} \quad 4.905\ t^2 = 6$$

or, $$t = \left(\frac{6}{4.905}\right)^{1/2} = 1.106\text{s}$$

From eqn. (*i*), we have:

$$U = \frac{4.5}{0.707 \times 1.106} = 5.75 \text{ m/s}$$

Also, $$U = C_v \times \sqrt{2gh} \quad \text{or} \quad 5.75 = 0.97 \times \sqrt{2 \times 9.81 \times H}$$

or, $$5.93 = \sqrt{2 \times 9.81 \times H} \quad \text{or} \quad H = \frac{5.93^2}{2 \times 9.81} = 1.79 \text{ m}$$

i.e., Pressure head at the nozzle **= 1.79 m (Ans.)**

(*ii*) Total discharge from the nozzles:

Total discharge, $Q = (\pi/4 \times d^2 \times U) \times$ number of nozzles

$$= \pi/4 \times 0.025^2 \times 5.75 \times 10 = 0.0282 \text{ m}^3\text{/s}$$

i.e., Total discharge through nozzles = **0.0282 m³/s. (Ans.)**

Example 6.48. *A fireman must reach a window 40 m above the ground with a water jet, issued from a nozzle 30 mm in diameter and discharging 30 kg/s. Assuming the nozzle height to be 2 m above the ground, determine the greatest horizontal distance from the building where the fireman can stand and still reach the jet into the window.* **(MDU, Haryana)**

Solution *Given*: D = 30 mm = 0.03 m; m = 30 kg/s

Refer to Fig. 6.45.

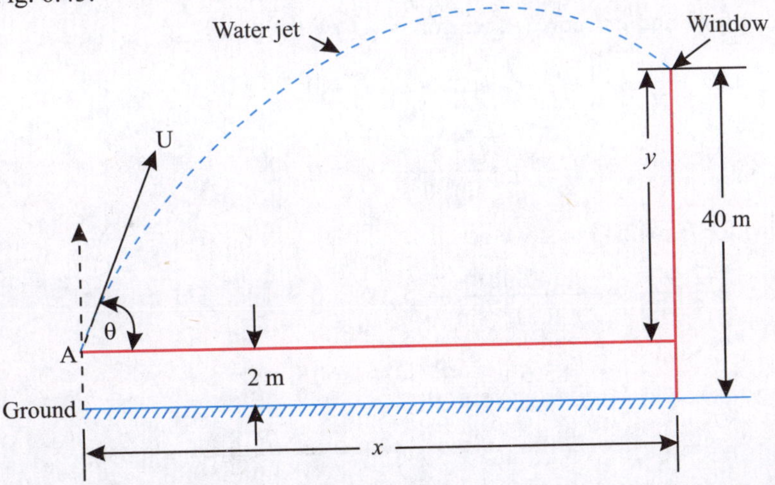

Fig. 6.45

Greatest horizontal distance, x:

Now, $m = \rho A U$ (where, U = velocity of water jet)

$$\therefore \quad U = \frac{m}{\rho A} = \frac{30}{1000 \times \frac{\pi}{4} \times (0.03)^2} = 42.44 \text{ m/s}$$

Let, θ = Angle of inclination of the nozzle.

Then, $x = U \cos\theta \times t$ or $t = \dfrac{x}{U \cos\theta}$

$$y = U \sin\theta \times t - \frac{1}{2} g t^2$$

$$= U \sin\theta \times \frac{x}{U\cos\theta} - \frac{1}{2} g \left(\frac{x}{U\cos\theta}\right)^2$$

$$= x\tan\theta - \frac{1}{2} g \frac{x^2}{U^2 \cos^2\theta} = x\tan\theta - \frac{gx^2}{2U^2}\sec^2\theta$$

or,
$$x\tan\theta - \frac{gx^2}{2U^2}\sec^2\theta - y = 0 \qquad ...(i)$$

The maximum value of x is obtained by differentiating (i) w.r.t. θ, and putting $\dfrac{dx}{d\theta} = 0$

$$\therefore \left[x\sec^2\theta + \tan\theta \times \frac{dx}{dt}\right] - \frac{g}{2U^2}\left[x^2 \times 2\sec\theta \times \sec\theta \tan\theta + \sec^2\theta \times 2x \times \frac{dx}{d\theta}\right] = 0$$

Putting $\dfrac{dx}{d\theta} = 0$, we get:

$$x\sec^2\theta - \frac{g}{2U^2}(2x^2\sec^2\theta . \tan\theta) = 0$$

or,
$$x\sec^2\theta = \frac{g}{2U^2} \times 2x^2 \sec^2\theta . \tan\theta$$

or,
$$x = \frac{U^2}{g\tan\theta}$$

Also,
$$y = 40 - 2 = 38 \text{ m}$$

Substituting for x and y in eqn. (i), we get:

$$\frac{U^2}{g\tan\theta} \times \tan\theta - \frac{g}{2U^2} \times \left(\frac{U^2}{g\tan\theta}\right)\sec^2\theta - 38 = 0$$

$$\frac{U^2}{g} - \frac{U^2}{2g\sin^2\theta} - 38 = 0$$

Substituting for U = 42.44 m/s, we get:

$$\frac{(42.44)^2}{9.81} - \frac{(42.44)^2}{2 \times 9.81 \times \sin^2\theta} - 38 = 0$$

$$183.6 - \frac{91.8}{\sin^2\theta} - 38 = 0$$

$$\sin^2\theta = \frac{91.8}{(183.6 - 38)} = 0.6305$$

or, $\sin\theta = 0.794$ or $\theta = \sin^{-1}(0.794) = 52.56°$

Hence, $x = \dfrac{U^2}{g\tan\theta} = \dfrac{(42.44)^2}{9.81 \times \tan(52.56°)}$ = **140.58 m (Ans.)**

Example 6.49. *The nozzle shown in Fig 6.46. has a jet diameter of 25 mm. The pressures on the water surface on the two sides of the arrangement are $p_1 = 170$ kN/m² (gauge) and $p_2 = 300$ mm of Hg. Determine:*

(i) The discharge through the nozzle;

(ii) The maximum height of the free jet above the nozzle. **[IIT Delhi]**

Solution. Diameter of the jet = 25 mm = 0.025 m

Pressure, p_1 = 170 kN/m²

Pressure, p_2 = 300 mm or 0.3 m of Hg

= 0.3 × 13.6 = 4.08 m of water.

(i) Discharge through the nozzle, Q:

Applying Bernoulli's equation to 1 (water surface) and 2 (the jet as it emerges from the nozzle), we get:

$$\frac{p_1}{w} + \frac{V_1^2}{2g} + z_1 = \frac{p_2}{w} + \frac{V_2^2}{2g} + z_2$$

$$\frac{170}{9.81} + 0 + 3 = 4.08 + \frac{V_2^2}{2g} + 0$$

$$17.33 + 3 = 4.08 + \frac{V_2^2}{2g}$$

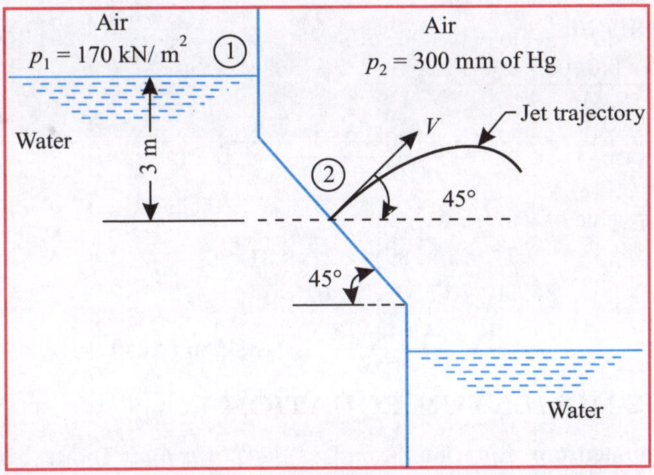

Fig. 6.46

or, $V_2^2 = [(17.33 + 3) - 4.08] \times 2g = 16.25 \times 2 \times 9.81$

∴ $V_2 = 17.85$ m/s $(V_2 = V)$

Hence, $Q = A \times V_2$

$= (\pi/4) \times 0.025^2 \times 17.85 = 0.00876$ m³/s or **8.76 litres/sec. (Ans.)**

(ii) Maximum height of the free jet above the nozzle:

Vertical component of the jet velocity = $V\sin 45° = 17.85 \sin 45° = 12.62$ m/s

∴ Maximum height to which jet will rise,

$$h = \frac{12.62^2}{2 \times 9.81} = \mathbf{8.12\ m\ (Ans.)}$$

Example 6.50. *A vertical jet of water 75 mm in diameter leaving the nozzle with a 9.2 m/s velocity strikes a horizontal and movable disc weighing 170 N (Fig.6.47). The jet is then deflected horizontally. Determine the vertical distance y above the nozzle tip at which the disc will be held in equilibrium.* **[Roorkee University]**

Solution. Diameter of the jet, $d = 75\ \text{mm} = 0.075\ \text{m}$

Velocity of the jet at nozzle exit; $V = 9.2\ \text{m/s}$

Weight of the disc, $W = 170\ \text{N}$

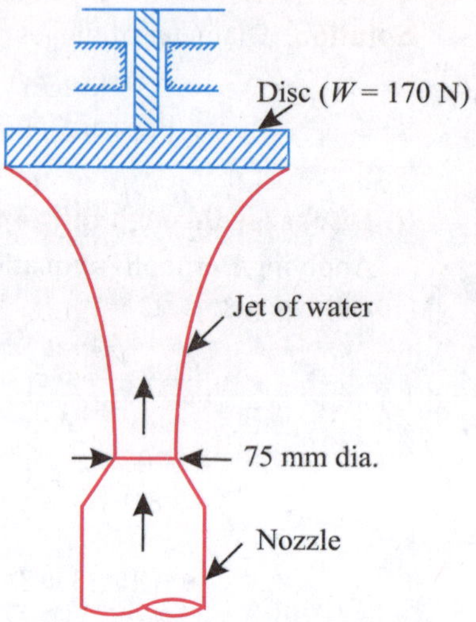

Fig. 6.47

Vertical Distance, y:

Let, v = Jet velocity at an elevation y.

Applying Bernoulli's theorem between the jet at nozzle exit and the jet at an elevation y, we get:

$$\frac{V^2}{2g} = \frac{v^2}{2g} + y$$

or, $$V^2 = v^2 + 2gy \quad ...(i)$$

Also the momentum equation is written as

$$\frac{wQ}{g}.v = 170$$

where, $Q = (\pi/4) \times d^2 \times V = (\pi/4) \times 0.075^2 \times 9.2$

$= 0.0406\ \text{m}^3/\text{s}$, and

$w = 9810\ \text{N/m}^3$

$$\therefore \quad \frac{9810 \times 0.0406 \times v}{9.81} = 170$$

or, $$v = \frac{170 \times 9.81}{9810 \times 0.0406} = 4.187\ \text{m/s}$$

Substituting this value of v in (i), we get:

$$9.2^2 = (4.187)^2 + 2 \times 9.81 \times y$$

or, $$84.64 = 17.53 + 19.62\,y$$

or, $$y = \frac{84.64 - 17.53}{19.62} = \mathbf{3.43\ m\ (Ans.)}$$

6.8. IMPULSE-MOMENTUM EQUATION

The **impulse-momentum equation** is *one of the basic tools* (other being continuity and Bernoulli's equations) *for the solution of flow problems.* Its application leads to the solution of problems in fluid mechanics which *cannot* be solved by energy principles alone. Sometimes it is used in conjunction with the energy equation to obtain complete solution of engineering problems.

The momentum equation is based on the *law of conservation of momentum* or *momentum principle* which states as follows:

"The net force acting on a mass of fluid is equal to change in momentum of flow per unit time in that direction".

As per Newton's second law of motion,

$$F = ma$$

where, m = Mass of fluid,

F = Force acting on the fluid, and

a = Acceleration (acting in the same direction as F).

But acceleration, $$a = \frac{dv}{dt}$$

$$\therefore \quad F = m.\frac{dv}{dt} = \frac{d(mv)}{dt} \quad ...(6.18)$$

('m' is taken inside the differential, being constant)

This equation is known as **momentum principle.** It can also be written as:

$$F.dt = d\,(mv) \quad ...(6.19)$$

This equation is known as **Impulse-momentum equation.** It may be stated as follows:

"The impulse of a force F acting on a fluid mass 'm' in a short interval of time dt is equal to the change of momentum d(mv) in direction of force".

The impulse-momentum equations are often called simply *momentum equations*.

Applications of impulse-momentum equation:

The impulse-momentum equation is used in the following types of problems:

1. *To determine the resultant force acting on the boundary of flow passage by a stream of fluid as the stream changes its direction, magnitude or both.* Problems of this type are:
   (*i*) Pipe bends, (*ii*) Reducers, (*iii*) Moving vanes, (*iv*) Jet propulsion, etc.
2. *To determine the characteristic of flow when there is an abrupt change of flow section.* Problems of this type are:
   (*i*) Sudden enlargement in a pipe, (*ii*) Hydraulic jump in a channel, etc.

Steady flow momentum equation:

The entire flow space may be considered to be made up of innumerable stream tubes. Let us consider one such stream tube lying in the X-Y plane (Fig 6.48) and having steady flow of fluid. Flow can be assumed to be uniform and normal to the inlet and outlet areas.

Let, V_1, ρ_1 = Average velocity and density (of fluid mass) respectively at the entrance, and

V_2, ρ_2 = Average velocity and density respectively at the exit.

Further let the mass of fluid in the region 1 2 3 4 shifts to new position 1′ 2′ 3′ 4′ due to the effect of external forces on the stream after a short interval. Due to gradual increase in the flow area in the direction of flow, velocity of fluid mass and hence the momentum is gradually reduced. Since the area 1′ 2′ 3 4 is common to both the regions 1 2 3 4 and 1′ 2′ 3′ 4′, therefore, it will not experience any change in momentum. Obviously, then the changes in momentum of the fluid masses in the sections 1 2 2′ 1′ and 4 3 3′ 4′ will have to be considered.

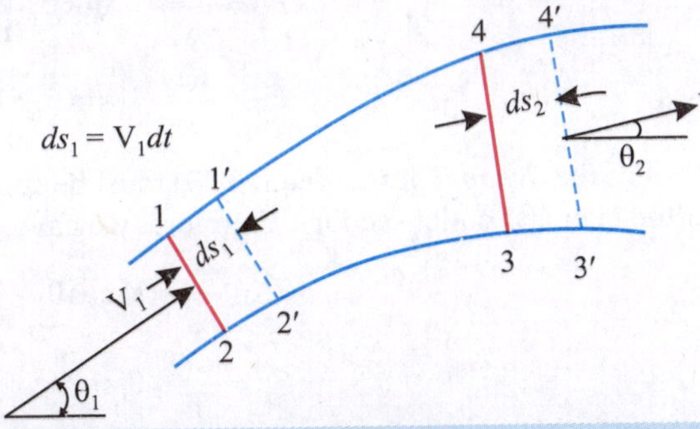

Fig. 6.48

According to the *principle of mass conservation*,

Fluid mass with the region 1 2 2′ 1′ = Fluid mass within the region 4 3 3′ 4′

$$\rho_1 A_1\, ds_1 = \rho_2 A_2 ds_2 \quad ...(6.20)$$

∴ Momentum of fluid mass contained in the region 1 2 2′ 1′

$$= (\rho_1 A_1\, ds_1)\, V_1 = (\rho_1 A_1\, V_1 .\, dt)\, V_1$$

Momentum of fluid mass contained in the region 4 3 3′ 4′

$$= (\rho_2 A_2\, ds_2)\, V_2 = (\rho_2 A_2\, V_2 .\, dt)\, V_2$$

∴ Change in momentum $= (\rho_2 A_2\, V_2 .dt)\, V_2 - (\rho_1 A_1\, V_1 .\, dt)\, V_1$

But, $\rho_1 = \rho_2 = \rho$ ...for steady incompressible flow

and, $A_1 V_1 = A_2 V_2 = Q$ ...from continuity considerations

∴ Change in momentum $= \rho Q (V_2 - V_1)\, dt$

Using impulse-momentum principle, we have:

$$F dt = \rho Q\, (V_2 - V_1) dt \qquad ...(6.21)$$

or,

$$F = \frac{wQ}{g}(V_2 - V_1) \qquad ...(6.22)$$

The quantity $\frac{wQ}{g} = \rho Q$ is the mass flow per second and is called **mass flux.**

Resolving V_1 and V_2 along X-axis and Y-axis, we get:

Components along *X-axis*: $V_1 \cos\theta_1$ and $V_2 \cos\theta_2$

Components along *Y*- axis : $V_1 \sin\theta_1$ and $V_2 \sin\theta_2$

(where, θ_1 and θ_2 are the inclinations with the horizontal of the centre line of the pipe at 1-2 and 3-4).

∴ Components of force F along X-axis and Y-axis are:

$$F_x = \frac{wQ}{g}(V_2 \cos\theta_2 - V_1 \cos\theta_1)$$

$$F_y = \frac{WQ}{g}(V_2 \sin\theta_2 - V_1 \sin\theta_1) \qquad ...(6.23)$$

Eqn. (6.23) represents the components of the force exerted by the *pipe bend on the fluid mass.* Usually, we are interested in the forces by the fluid on the pipe bend. Since action and reaction are equal and opposite (Newton's third law of motion), the fluid mass would exert the same force on the pipe bend but in *opposite direction* and as such the force components exerted by the fluid on the pipe bend are given as follows:

$$\left.\begin{aligned} F_x &= \frac{wQ}{g}(V_1 \cos\theta_1 - V_2 \cos\theta_2) \\ F_y &= \frac{wQ}{g}(V_1 \sin\theta_1 - V_2 \sin\theta_2) \end{aligned}\right\} \qquad ...(6.24)$$

Since the *dynamic* forces (eqn. 6.23) must be supplemented by the *static pressure forces* acting over the inlet and outlet sections, therefore, we have:

$$\left.\begin{aligned} F_x &= \frac{wQ}{g}(V_1 \cos\theta_1 - V_2 \cos\theta_2) + p_1 A_1 \cos\theta_1 - p_2 A_2 \cos\theta_2 \\ F_y &= \frac{wQ}{g}(V_1 \sin\theta_1 - V_2 \sin\theta_2) + p_1 A_1 \sin\theta_1 - p_2 A_2 \sin\theta_2 \end{aligned}\right\} \qquad ...(6.25)$$

The magnitude of the resultant force acting on the pipe bend,

$$F_R = \sqrt{F_x^2 + F_y^2} \qquad ...(6.26)$$

and, the direction of the resultant force with X-axis,

$$\theta = \tan^{-1}\left(\frac{F_y}{F_x}\right) \qquad ...[6.26\ (a)]$$

Example 6.51. *In a 45° bend a rectangular air duct of 1 m^2 cross-sectional area is gradually reduced to 0.5 m^2 area. Find the magnitude and direction of force required to hold the duct in position if the velocity of flow at 1 m^2 section is 10 m/s, and pressure is 30 kN/m^2.*

Take the specific weight of air as 0.0116 *kN/m^3*. **[Anna University]**

Solution. Refer to Fig. 6.49

$$\text{Area at section, '1'} = 1\text{ m}^2;\ \text{Area at section '2'} = 0.5\text{ m}^2$$

$$\text{Velocity at section '1', } V_1 = 10\text{ m/s}$$

$$\text{Pressure at section '1', } p_1 = 30\text{ kN/m}^2$$

$$\text{Sp. weight of air, } w = 0.0116\text{ kN/m}^3$$

As per continuity equation,

$$A_1V_1 = A_2V_2$$

$$\therefore \quad V_2 = \frac{A_1V_1}{A_2} = \frac{1 \times 10}{0.5} = 20\text{ m/s}$$

$$\text{Discharge, } Q = A_1V_1 = 1 \times 10 = 10\text{ m}^3\text{/s}$$

Applying Bernoulli's equation at sections '1' and '2', we get:

$$\frac{p_1}{w} + \frac{V_1^2}{2g} + z_1 = \frac{p_2}{w} + \frac{V_2^2}{2g} + z_2$$

But, $$z_1 = z_2$$

$$\therefore \quad \frac{p_1}{w} + \frac{V_1^2}{2g} = \frac{p_2}{w} + \frac{V_2^2}{2g}$$

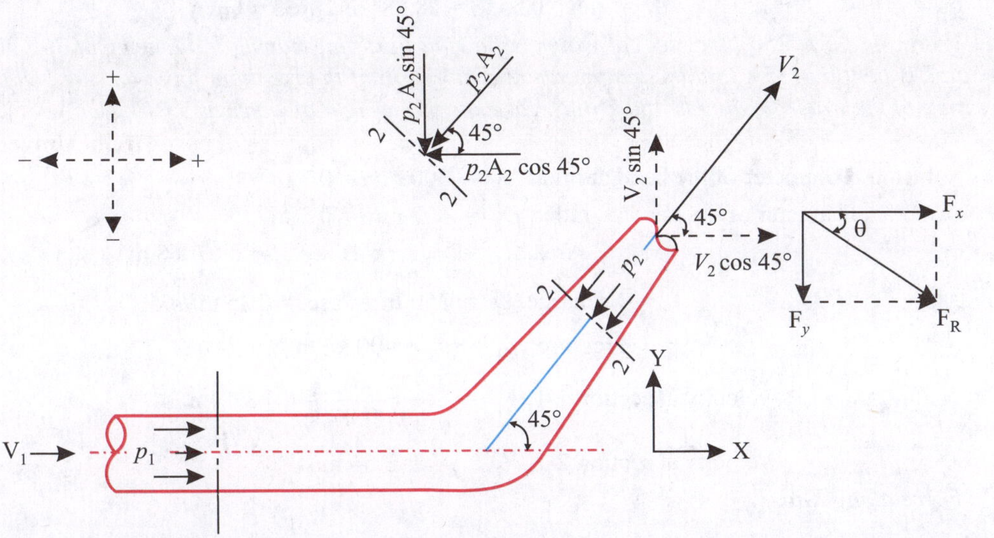

Fig. 6.49

$$\frac{30}{0.0116} + \frac{10^2}{2 \times 9.81} = \frac{p_2}{w} + \frac{20^2}{2 \times 9.81}$$

or, $$2586 + 5.1 = \frac{p_2}{w} + 20.4$$

or, $$\frac{p_2}{w} = 2586 + 5.1 - 20.4 = 2570.7$$

or, $p_2 = 2570.7 \times 0.0116 = 29.82 \text{ kN/m}^2$

Magnitude and direction of force (resultant) F_R:

Force along X-axis:

$$F_x = \frac{wQ}{g}(V_{1x} - V_{2x}) + (p_1A_1)_x + (p_2A_2)_x$$

where, $V_{1x} = 10 \text{ m/s}; V_{2x} = V_2 \cos 45° = 20 \times 0.707 = 14.14 \text{ m/s}$

$(p_1A_1)_x = p_1A_1 = 30 \times 1 = 30 \text{ kN}; (p_2A_2)_x = -p_2A_2 \cos 45° = -29.82 \times 0.5 \times 0.707 = -10.54 \text{ kN}$

$$\therefore \quad F_x = \frac{0.0116}{9.81} \times 10\,(10 - 14.14) + 30 - 10.54 = 19.41 \text{ kN } (\rightarrow)$$

Force along Y-axis:

$$F_y = \frac{wQ}{g}(V_{1y} - V_{2y}) + (p_1A_1)_y + (p_2A_2)_y$$

where, $V_{1y} = 0; V_{2y} = V_2 \sin 45° = 20 \times 0.707 = 14.14 \text{ m/s}$

$(p_1 A_1)_y = 0; (p_2 A_2)_y = -p_2A_2 \sin 45° = -29.82 \times 0.5 \times 0.707 = -10.54 \text{ kN}$

$$\therefore \quad F_y = \frac{0.0116 \times 10}{9.81}(0 - 14.14) + 0 - 10.54 = -10.71 \text{ kN } (\downarrow)$$

$\therefore$ Resultant force, $F_R = \sqrt{F_x^2 + F_y^2} = \sqrt{(19.41)^2 + (10.71)^2} = $ **22.17 kN (Ans.)**

The direction of F_R with X-axis is given as:

$$\tan \theta = \frac{F_y}{F_x} = \frac{10.71}{19.41} = 0.5518$$

or, $\theta = \tan^{-1} 0.5518 = 28.88°$ or **28°53′ (Ans.)**

Example 6.52. 250 *litres/sec. of water is flowing in a pipe having a diameter of 300 mm. If the pipe is bent by 135°, find the magnitude and direction of the resultant force on the bend. The pressure of the water flowing is 400 kN/m². Take specific weight of water as 9.81 kN/m³.*

[Delhi University]

Solution. Diameter of the bend at inlet, $D_1 = 300 \text{ mm} = 0.3 \text{ m}$

Diameter of the bend at outlet, $D_2 = 300 \text{ mm} = 0.3 \text{ m}$

$\therefore$ Area, $A_1 = A_2 = (\pi/4) \times 0.3^2 = 0.07068 \text{ m}^2$

Discharge, $Q = 250 \text{ litres/sec.} = 0.25 \text{ m}^3\text{/s.}$

Pressure, $p_1 = p_2 = 400 \text{ kN/m}^2$

Velocity at section 1-1, $V_1 = \frac{Q}{A_1} = \frac{0.25}{0.07068} = 3.54 \text{ m/s}$

Velocity at section 2-2, $V_2 = V_1 = 3.54 \text{ m/s}$ $(\because A_1 = A_2)$

Force along X-axis:

$$F_x = \frac{wQ}{g}[V_1 - (-V_2 \cos 45°)] + p_1 A_1 + p_2A_2 \cos 45°$$

$$= \frac{9.81 \times 0.25}{9.81}[3.54 - (-3.54 \times 0.707)]$$

$$+ (400 \times 0.07068) + (400 \times 0.07068 \times 0.707)$$

$$= 0.25 \times (3.54 + 3.54 \times 0.707) + 28.27 + 19.98$$

$$= 49.76 \text{ kN } (\rightarrow)$$

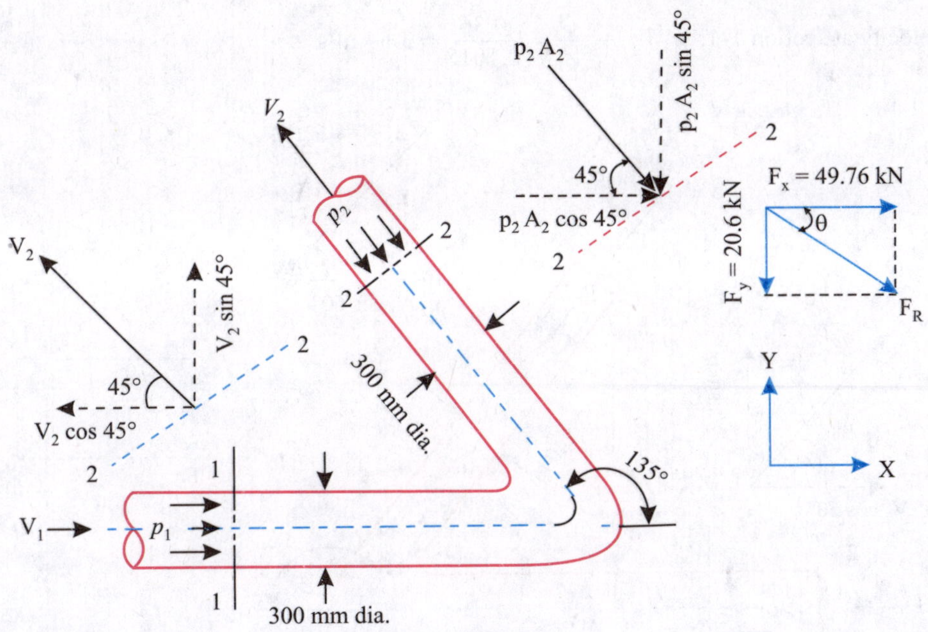

Fig. 6.50

Force along Y-axis:

$$F_y = \frac{wQ}{g}\,[\,0 - V_2 \sin 45°] - p_2\,A_2 \sin 45°$$

$$= \frac{9.81 \times 0.25}{9.81}(0 - 3.54 \times 0.707) - 400 \times 0.07068 \times 0.707$$

$$= -0.625 - 19.98 = -20.6 \text{ kN}(\downarrow)$$

The *magnitude of the resultant force*,

$$F_R = \sqrt{F_x^2 + F_y^2} = \sqrt{49.76^2 + 20.6^2} = \mathbf{53.85\ kN} \quad \textbf{(Ans.)}$$

The *direction of* F_R with *X*- axis is given as:

$$\tan\theta = \frac{F_y}{F_x} = \frac{20.6}{49.76} = 0.414$$

$$\therefore \quad \theta = \tan^{-1} 0.414 = \mathbf{22.5°} \quad \textbf{(Ans.)}$$

Example 6.53. *360 litres per second of water is flowing in a pipe. The pipe is bent by 120°. The pipe bend measures 360 mm × 240 mm and volume of the bend is 0.14 m³. The pressure at the entrance is 73 kN/m² and the exit is 2.4 m above the entrance section.*

Find the force exerted on the bend.

Solution. Discharge through the pipe, Q = 360 litres/sec. = 0.36 m^3/s

Volume of bend = 0.14 m^3

Diameter of the bend at 1-1, D_1 = 360 mm = 0.36 m

$\therefore$ Area, $A_1 = \frac{\pi}{4} \times 0.36^2 = 0.1018\ m^2$

Diameter of the bend at 2-2, D_2 = 240 mm = 0.24 m

$\therefore$ Area, $A_2 = \frac{\pi}{4} \times 0.24^2 = 0.04524\ m^2$

Velocity at section 1-1, $V_1 = \frac{Q}{A_1} = \frac{0.36}{0.1018} = 3.54$ m/s

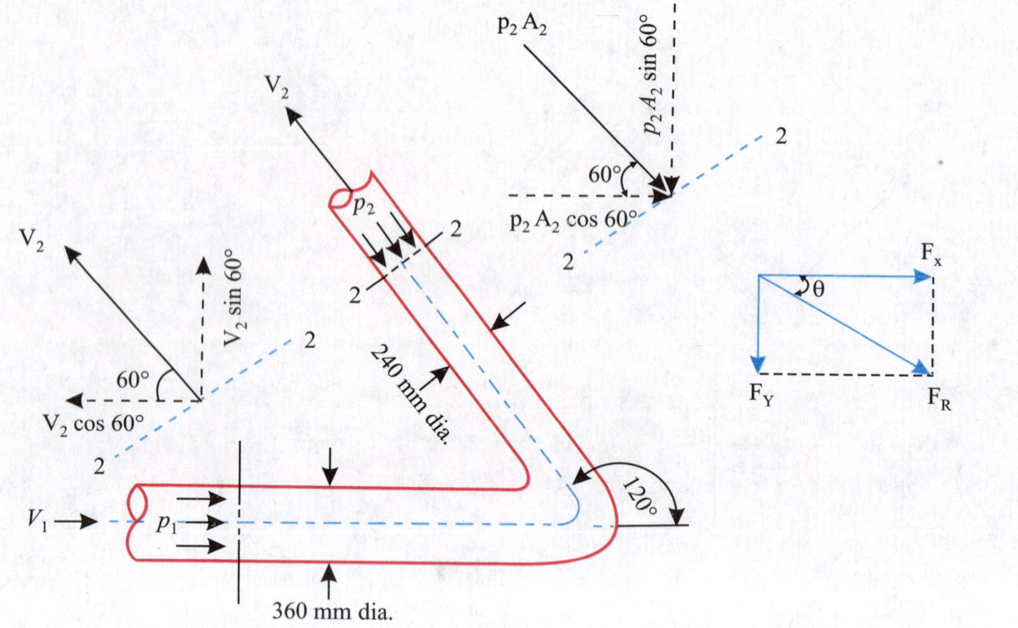

Fig. 6.51

Velocity at section 2-2, $V_2 = \frac{Q}{A_2} = \frac{0.36}{0.04524} = 7.96$ m/s

Considering a horizontal line through the section 1-1 as datum for elevation head and applying Bernoulli's equation to the sections 1-1 and 2-2, we get:

$$\frac{p_1}{w} + \frac{V_1^2}{2g} + z_1 = \frac{p_2}{w} + \frac{V_2^2}{2g} + z_2$$

$$\frac{72}{9.81} + \frac{3.54^2}{2 \times 9.81} + 0 = \frac{p_2}{w} + \frac{7.96^2}{2 \times 9.81} + 2.4 \qquad (\because p_1 = 72 \text{ kN/m}^2 \text{ ... } Given)$$

$$7.34 + 0.64 = \frac{p_2}{w} + 3.23 + 2.4$$

$$\therefore \qquad \frac{p_2}{w} = 2.35 \text{ or } p_2 = 2.35 \times 9.81 = 23.05 \text{ kN/m}^2$$

Force along the X-axis:

$$F_x = \frac{wQ}{g}[V_1 - (-V_2 \cos 60°)] + p_1 A_1 + p_2 A_2 \cos 60°$$

$$= \frac{9.81 \times 0.36}{9.81}[3.54 - (-7.96 \times 0.5)] + 72 \times 0.1018 + 23.05 \times 0.04524 \times 0.5$$

$$= 0.36\,(3.54 + 3.98) + 7.33 + 0.52 = 10.55 \text{ kN } (\rightarrow)$$

Force along Y-axis:

$$F_y = \frac{wQ}{g}[0 - V_2 \sin 60°] - p_2 A_2 \sin 60° - \text{weight of water in the bend}$$

$$= \frac{9.81 \times 0.36}{9.81}(0 - 7.96 \times 0.866) - 23.05 \times 0.04524 \times 0.866 - 0.14 \times 9.81$$

$$= 0.36\,(-6.89) - 0.9 - 1.37 = -4.75 \text{ kN } (\downarrow)$$

Magnitude of the resultant force acting on the bend,

$$F_R = \sqrt{F_x^2 + F_y^2} = \sqrt{10.55^2 + 4.75^2} = \mathbf{11.57\ kN}\ \textbf{(Ans.)}$$

Direction of the resultant force with the X-axis,

$$\tan\theta = \frac{F_y}{F_x} = \frac{4.75}{10.55} = 0.4502 \text{ or } \theta = \mathbf{24.24°}\ \textbf{(Ans.)}$$

Example 6.54. *Fig. 6.52 shows a 90° reducer-bend through which water flows. The pressure at the inlet is 210 kN/m^2 (gauge) where the cross-sectional area is 0.01 m^2. At the exit section, the area is 0.0025 m^2 and the velocity is 16 m/s. The pressure at the exit is atmospheric. Determine the magnitude and direction of the resultant force on the bend.*

Solution. Area at section 1-1, $A_1 = 0.01 \text{ m}^2$

Area at section 2-2, $A_2 = 0.0025 \text{ m}^2$

Velocity at the exit, $V_2 = 16$ m/s.

Discharge, $Q = A_2 V_2 = 0.0025 \times 16 = 0.04 \text{ m}^3/\text{s}$.

$$\therefore \quad V_1 = \frac{Q}{A_1} = \frac{0.04}{0.01} = 4 \text{ m/s}$$

Assume the bend is horizontal and in *XY* plane.

Force along X-axis:

$$F_x = \frac{wQ}{g}(V_1 - 0) + p_1 A_1$$

$$= \frac{9.81 \times 0.04}{9.81}(4 - 0) + 210 \times 0.01 = 0.16 + 2.1 = 2.26 \text{ kN } (\rightarrow)$$

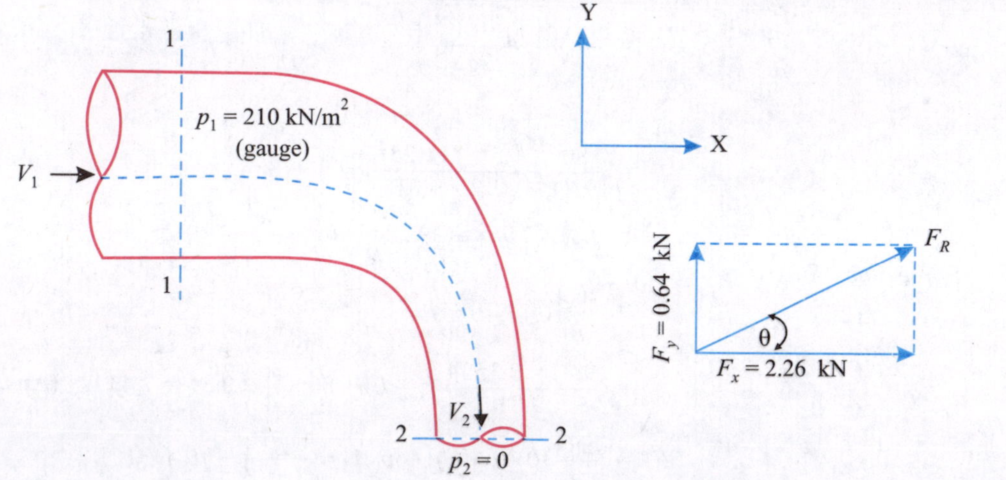

Fig. 6.52

Force along Y-axis:

$$F_y = \frac{wQ}{g}[0 - (-V_2)] + p_2 A_2$$

$$= \frac{9.81 \times 0.04}{9.81}(0 + 16) + 0 = 0.64 \text{ kN } (\uparrow)$$

Magnitude of the resultant force acting on the bend,

$$F_R = \sqrt{F_x^2 + F_y^2} = \sqrt{2.26^2 + 0.64^2} = \mathbf{2.35 \text{ kN (Ans.)}}$$

Direction of the resultant force with the X-axis,

$$\tan\theta = \frac{F_y}{F_x} = \frac{0.64}{2.26} = 0.2832 \quad \therefore \theta = \tan^{-1} 0.2832 = 15.8°$$

$\therefore \qquad \theta = \mathbf{15.8° \text{ (Ans.)}}$

Example 6.55. *Water enters a reducing pipe horizontally and comes out vertically in the downward direction. If the inlet velocity is 5 m/s and pressure is 80 kPa (gauge) and the diameters at the entrance and exit sections are 30 cm and 20 cm respectively, calculate the components of the reaction acting on the pipe.* **(RGPV, Bhopal)**

Solution. *Given*: $D_1 = 30$ cm $= 0.3$ m; $D_2 = 20$ cm $= 0.2$ m; $V_1 = 5$ m/s; $p_1 = 80$ kPa $= 80$ kN/m^2.

Components of the reaction acting on the pipe: Refer to Fig. 6.53.

From continuity equation, we have:

$$Q = A_1V_1 = (\pi/4) \times 0.3^2 \times 5 = 0.3534 \text{ m}^3/\text{s}$$

$$A_1V_1 = A_2V_2 \text{ or } \frac{\pi}{4} \times 0.3^2 \times 5 = \frac{\pi}{4} \times 0.2^2 \times V_2$$

$\therefore \qquad V_2 = 11.25$ m/s

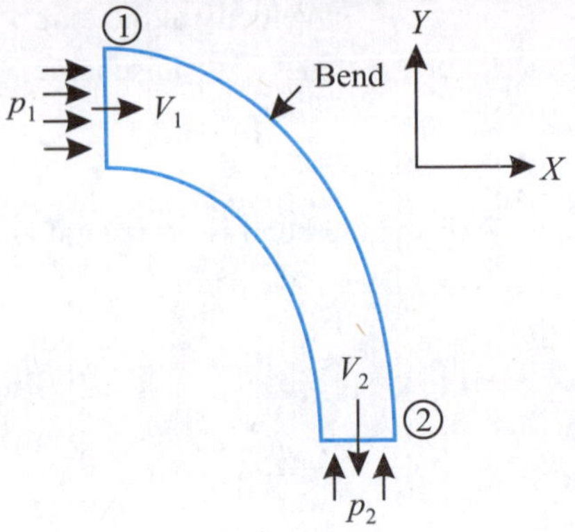

Fig. 6.53

Assume the bend is horizontal and in *XY* plane.

Applying Bernoulli's equation between sections (1) and (2), we have:

$$\frac{p_1}{w} + \frac{V_1^2}{2g} + z_1 = \frac{p_2}{w} + \frac{V_2^2}{2g} + z_2$$

or,
$$\frac{p_2}{w} = \frac{p_1}{w} + \left(\frac{V_1^2 - V_2^2}{2g}\right)$$

$$(\because z_1 = z_2)$$

$$= \frac{80}{9.81} + \left(\frac{5^2 - 11.25^2}{2 \times 9.81}\right) = 2.978 \text{ m}$$

or, $\qquad p_2 = 9.81 \times 2.978 = 29.22$ kN/m^2

Force along X-axis:

$$F_x = \frac{wQ}{g}(V_1 - 0) + p_1A_1$$

$$= \frac{9.81 \times 0.3534}{9.81}(5 - 0) + 80 \times \frac{\pi}{4} \times 0.3^2 = \mathbf{7.42 \text{ kN (Ans.)}}$$

$$F_y = \frac{wQ}{g}[0 - (-V_2)] + p_2A_2 = \frac{wQV_2}{g} + p_2A_2$$

$$= \frac{9.81 \times 0.3534 \times 11.25}{9.81} + 29.22 \times \frac{\pi}{4} \times 0.2^2 = \mathbf{4.89 \text{ kN (Ans.)}}$$

Example 6.56. *The angle of a reducing bend is 60° (that is deviation from initial direction to final direction). Its initial diameter is 300 mm and final diameter 150 mm and is fitted in a pipeline,* *carrying a discharge of 360 litres/sec. The pressure at the commencement of the bend is 2.943 bar. The friction loss in the pipe bend may be assumed as 10 per cent of kinetic energy at exit of the bend. Determine the force exerted by the reducing bend.* **[UPSC Exams.]**

Solution. Diameter at the inlet, $D_1 = 300$ mm $= 0.3$ m

$\therefore$ Area, $A_1 = (\pi/4) \times 0.3^2 = 0.07068$ m^2

Diameter at the outlet, $D_2 = 150$ mm $= 0.15$ m

$\therefore$ Area, $A_2 = (\pi/4) \times 0.15^2 = 0.01767$ m^2

Discharge through the bend, $Q = 3600$ litres/sec. $= 0.36$ m^3/s

Pressure at the inlet, $p_1 = 2.943$ bar $= 294.3$ kN/m^2

[$\because$ 1 bar $= 10^5$ N/m^2 $= 10^2$ kN/m^2]

$$\text{Velocity at the inlet, } V_1 = \frac{Q}{A_1} = \frac{0.36}{0.07068} = 5.09 \text{ m/s}$$

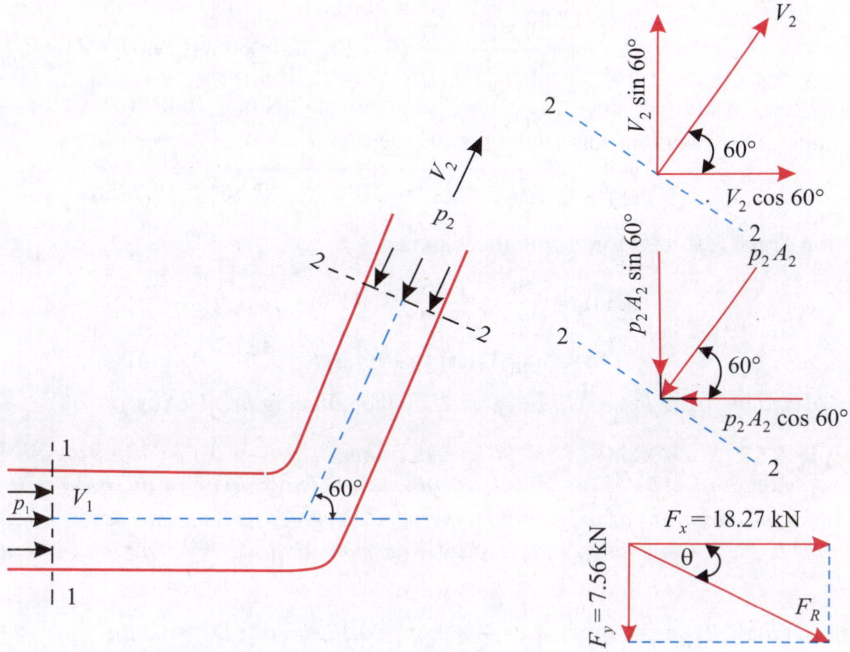

Fig. 6.54

$$\text{Velocity at the outlet, } V_2 = \frac{Q}{A_2} = \frac{0.36}{0.01767} = 20.37 \text{ m/s}$$

$$\text{Friction loss in the pipe} = 0.1 \times \frac{V_2^2}{2g} \qquad \text{...(Given)}$$

Applying Bernoulli's equation at sections 1-1 and 2-2, we get:

$$\frac{p_1}{w} + \frac{V_1^2}{2g} + z_1 = \frac{p_2}{w} + \frac{V_2^2}{2g} + z_2 + 0.1 \times \frac{V_2^2}{2g}$$

($\therefore z_1 = z_2$ since the bend lies in the horizontal plane)

$$\frac{294.3}{9.81} + \frac{5.09^2}{2 \times 9.81} = \frac{p_2}{w} + \frac{20.37^2}{2 \times 9.81} + 0.1 \times \frac{20.37^2}{2 \times 9.81}$$

$$30 + 1.32 = \frac{p_2}{w} + 21.15 + 2.11$$

$$\therefore \quad \frac{p_2}{w} = 8.06 \quad \text{or} \quad p_2 = 9.81 \times 8.06 = 79.07 \text{ kN/m}^2$$

Force along X-axis:

$$F_x = \frac{wQ}{g}[V_1 - V_2 \cos 60°] + p_1 A_1 - p_2 A_2 \cos 60°$$

$$= \frac{9.81 \times 0.36}{9.81}(5.09 - 20.37 \times 0.5) + 294.3 \times 0.07068$$

$$- 79.07 \times 0.01767 \times 0.5$$

$$= -1.8342 + 20.8 - 0.698 = 18.27 \text{ kN } (\rightarrow)$$

Force along the Y-axis:

$$F_y = \frac{wQ}{g}(0 - V_2 \sin 60°) - p_2 A_2 \sin 60°$$

$$= \frac{9.81 \times 0.36}{9.81}(0 - 20.37 \sin 60°) - 79.07 \times 0.01767 \times \sin 60°$$

$$= -6.35 - 1.21 = -7.56 \text{ kN or } 7.56 \text{ kN } (\downarrow)$$

Magnitude of the resultant force acting on the bend,

$$F_R = \sqrt{F_x^2 + F_y^2} = \sqrt{18.27^2 + 7.56^2} = \mathbf{19.77 \text{ kN}}$$

Direction of the resultant force with the X-axis,

$$\tan \theta = \frac{F_y}{F_x} = \frac{7.56}{18{\cdot}27} = 0.4138$$

$$\theta = \tan^{-1} 0.4138 = \mathbf{22.48°}$$

An equal and opposite force will be exerted by the reducing bend. **(Ans.)**

Example 6.57. *A 0.4 m × 0.3 m, 90° vertical bend carries 0.5 m³/s oil of specific gravity 0.85 with a pressure of 118 kN/m² at inlet to the bend. The volume of the bend is 0.1 m³. Find the magnitude and direction of the force on the bend. Neglect friction and assume both inlet and outlet sections to be at same horizontal level. Also assume that water enters the bend at 45° to the horizontal.* **(PTU)**

Solution. *Given*: $D_1 = 0.4$ m, $\therefore A_1 = \frac{\pi}{4} \times 0.4^2 = 0.12566$ m²; $D_2 = 0.3$ m;

$\therefore A_2 = \frac{\pi}{4} \times 0.3^2 = 0.07068$ m²; $Q = 0.5$ m³/s; $S_{oil} = 0.85$; $p_1 = 118$ kN/m²; Volume of bend = 0.1 m³

Refer to Fig. 6.55.

$$V_1 = \frac{Q}{A_1} = \frac{0.5}{0.12566} = 3.98 \text{ m/s}$$

$$V_2 = \frac{Q}{A_2} = \frac{0.5}{0.07068} = 7.074 \text{ m/s}$$

Applying Bernoulli's equation between sections (1) and (2), we get:

$$\frac{p_1}{w} + \frac{V_1^2}{2g} + z_1 = \frac{p_2}{w} + \frac{V_2^2}{2g} + z_2 + \text{losses}$$

Since, $z_1 = z_2$ and losses are negligible (Given),

$$\therefore \quad \frac{p_1}{w} + \frac{V_1^2}{2g} = \frac{p_2}{w} + \frac{V_2^2}{2g}$$

Substituting the values, we get:

$$\frac{118 \times 10^3}{(1000 \times 0.85 \times 9.81)} + \frac{(3.98)^2}{2 \times 9.81} = \frac{p_2}{(1000 \times 0.85 \times 9.81)} + \frac{(7.074)^2}{2 \times 9.81}$$

or, $$\frac{118 \times 10^3}{850} + \frac{(3.98)^2}{2} = \frac{p_2}{850} + \frac{(7.074)^2}{2}$$

or, $$p_2 = 850\left[\frac{118 \times 10^3}{850} + \frac{(3.98)^2 - (7.074)^2}{2}\right] = 103464 \text{ N/m}^2$$

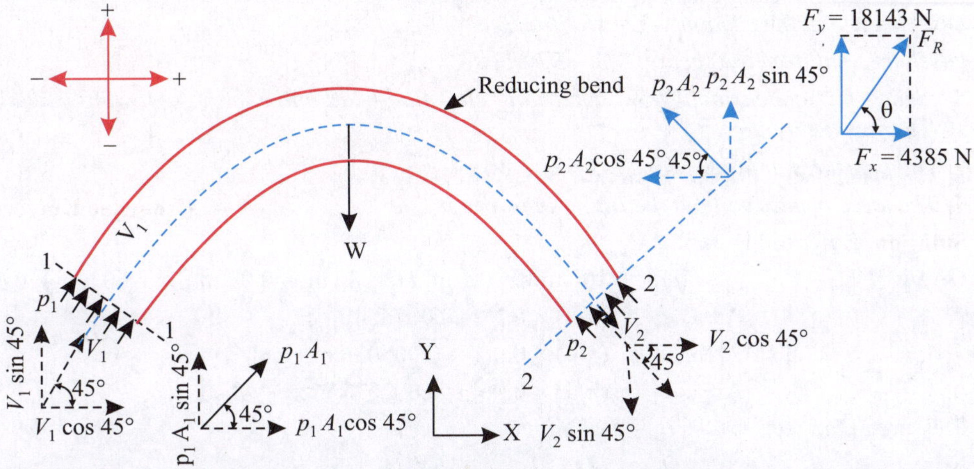

Fig. 6.55

Magnitude and direction of the force (resultant), F_R:

Force along X-axis:

$$F_x = \frac{wQ}{g}[V_{1x} - V_{2x}] + (p_1 A_1)_x + (p_2 A_2)_x$$

where, $V_{1x} = V_1 \cos 45° = 3.98 \cos 45° = 2.814$ m/s,

$V_{2x} \cos 45° = 7.074 \times \cos 45° = 5.0$ m/s

$(p_1A_1)_x = p_1A_1 \cos 45° = 118 \times 10^3 \times 0.12566 \cos 45° = 10484.89$ N,

$(p_2A_2)_x = -p_2A_2 \cos 45° = -103464 \times 0.07068 \cos 45° = -5170.96$ N

$$\therefore F_x = \frac{(1000 \times 0.85 \times 9.81)0.5}{9.81}[2.814 - 5.0] + 10484.89 + (-5170.96) \simeq 4385 \text{ N } (\rightarrow)$$

Force along Y-axis:

$$F_y = \frac{wQ}{g}[V_{1y} - V_{2y}] + (p_1 A_1)_y + (p_2 A_2)_y - W$$

$V_{1y} = V_1 \sin 45° = 3.98 \sin 45° = 2.814$ m/s, $V_{2y} = -V_2 \sin 45°$

$= -7.074 \times \sin 45° = -5.0$ m/s

$(p_1 A_1)_y = p_1 A_1 \sin 45° = 118 \times 10^3 \times 0.12566 \sin 45° = 10484.89$ N

$(p_2A_2)_y = p_2A_2 \sin 45° = 103464 \times 0.07068 \times \sin 45° = 5170.96$ N

$W = 0.1(0.85 \times 1000) \times 9.81 = 833.85$ N

$$\therefore F_y = \frac{(1000 \times 0.85 \times 9.81)0.5}{9.81}[2.814 - (-5.0)] + 10484.89 + 5170.96 - 833.85 = 18143 \text{ N} (\uparrow)$$

∴ Resultant force on the bend,

$$F_R = \sqrt{F_x^2 + F_y^2} = \sqrt{(4385)^2 + (18143)^2} = \mathbf{18665} \textbf{ (Ans.)}$$

Inclination of F_x to the X-direction is,

$$\theta = \tan^{-1}\left(\frac{F_y}{F_x}\right) = \tan^{-1}\left(\frac{18143}{4385}\right) = \mathbf{76.4°} \textbf{ (Ans.)}$$

Example 6.58. *The following data refer to the Y-fitting shown in Fig.* 6.56.

Reading of the pressure gauge at section 1-1 = 30 kN/m^2.

Discharge in at the section 1-1 = 15 *litres/sec.*

Discharge out from the section 3-3 = 5 *litres/sec.*

Assuming one-dimensional flow, neglecting elevation head and energy loss while making the energy balance, determine:

(i) The pressures at the sections 2-2 *and* 3-3;

(ii) The force needed to hold the fitting in position. **(Roorkee University)**

Solution. Refer to Fig. 6.56.

Given: $D_1 = 100$ mm = 0.1 m. $D_2 = 80$ m, = 0.08 m; $D_3 = 60$ mm = 0.06 m

∴ Area, $A_1 = (\pi/4) \times 0.1^2 = 0.007854$ m^2,

Area, $A_2 = (\pi/4) \times 0.08^2 = 0.005026$ m^2, and

Area, $A_3 = (\pi/4) \times 0.06^2 = 0.002827$ m^2

Pressure at the section 1-1, $p_1 = 30$ kN/m^2

Now, $Q_1 = Q_2 + Q_3$ or $15 = Q_2 + 5$

∴ $Q_2 = 10$ litres/sec.

Velocity at the section 1-1, $V_1 = \dfrac{Q_1}{A_1} = \dfrac{15 \times 10^{-3}}{0.007854} = 1.91$ m/s

Velocity at the section 2-2, $V_2 = \dfrac{Q_2}{A_2} = \dfrac{10 \times 10^{-3}}{0.005026} = 1.99$ m/s

Velocity at the section 3-3, $V_3 = \dfrac{Q_3}{A_3} = \dfrac{5 \times 10^{-3}}{0.002827} = 1.77$ m/s

***(i)* Pressures at sections 2-2 and 3-3; p_2, p_3:**

Applying Bernoulli's equation between sections 1-1 and 2-2, we get:

$$\frac{p_1}{w} + \frac{V_1^2}{2g} + z_1 = \frac{p_2}{w} + \frac{V_2^2}{2g} + z_2$$

$$\frac{p_2}{w} - \frac{p_1}{w} = \frac{V_1^2}{2g} - \frac{V_2^2}{2g} \quad \text{(Neglecting elevation datum)}$$

or, $$\frac{p_2 - p_1}{w} = \frac{V_1^2 - V_2^2}{2g}$$

$$= \frac{1.91^2 - 1.99^2}{2 \times 9.81} = -0.0159$$

or, $$p_2 - p_1 = -w \times 0.0159 = -9.81 \times 0.0159 = -0.156 \text{ kN/m}^2$$

($\because$ $w = 9.81$ kN/m^3 for water)

or, $\quad$ $\boldsymbol{p_2} = -0.156 + p_1 = -0.156 + 30 =$ **29.84 kN/m^2 (Ans.)**

Similarly, for sections 1-1 and 3-3; we get:

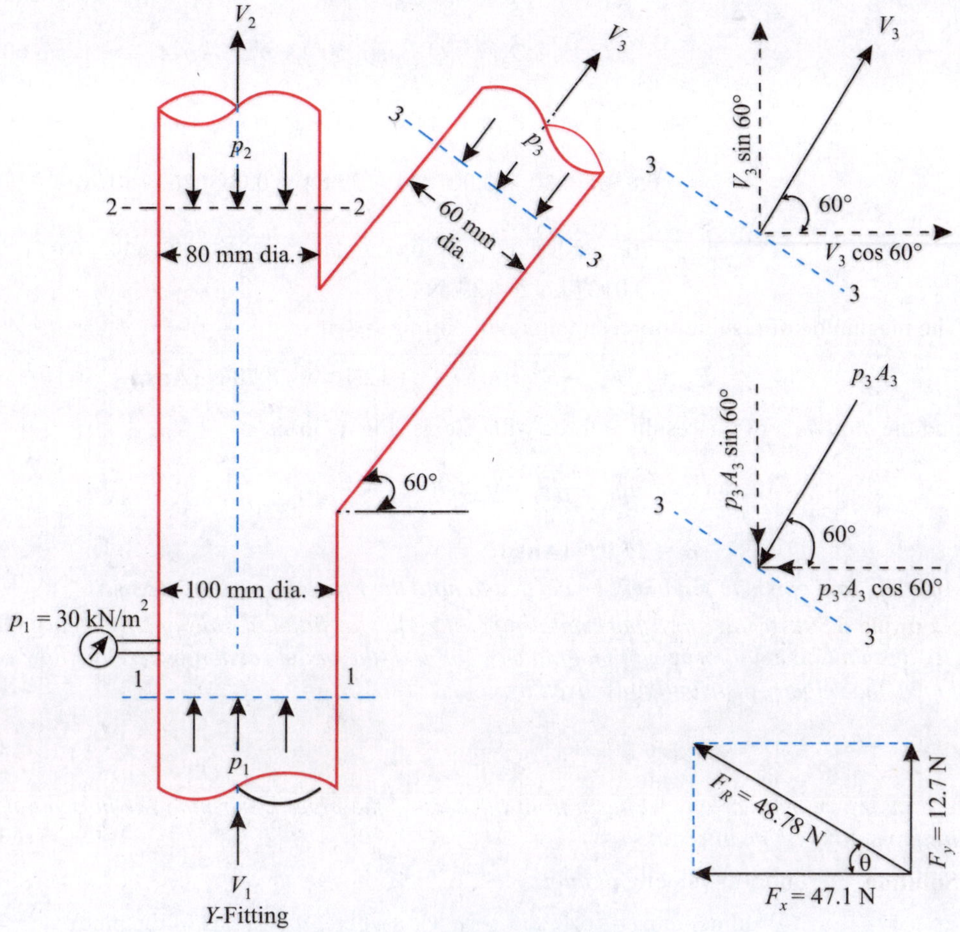

Fig. 6.56

$$\frac{p_3 - p_1}{w} = \frac{V_1^2 - V_3^2}{2g} = \frac{1.91^2 - 1.77^2}{2 \times 9.81} = 0.02626$$

or, $\quad$ $p_3 - p_1 = 9.81 \times 0.2626 = 0.26$

$\therefore$ $\quad$ $\boldsymbol{p_3} = 0.26 + p_1 = 0.26 + 30 =$ **30.26 kN/m^2 (Ans.)**

(*ii*) Force needed to hold the fitting in position :

Force along X-axis:

$$F_x = \frac{wQ_3}{g}(0 - V_3 \cos 60°) - p_3 A_3 \cos 60°$$

(The velocities V_1 and V_2 and pressure p_1 and p_2 have no components in X-direction)

$$= \frac{9.81 \times 5 \times 10^{-3}}{9.81}(0 - 1.77 \times 0.5) - 30{\cdot}26 \times 0.002827 \times 0.5$$

$$= -0.004425 - 0.0427 = -0.00471 \text{ kN or } -47.1 \text{ N}$$

or, $F_x = 47.1$ N (←)

Force along Y-axis:

$$F_y = \frac{wQ_1}{g}V_1 - \frac{wQ_2}{g}V_2 - \frac{wQ_3}{g}V_3 \sin 60° + p_1A_1 - p_2A_2 - p_3A_3 \sin 60°$$

$$= \frac{w}{g}(Q_1V_1 - Q_2V_2 - Q_3V_3 \sin 60°) + p_1A_1 - p_2A_2 - p_3A_3 \sin 60°$$

$$= \frac{9.81}{9.81}(15 \times 10^{-3} \times 1.91 - 10 \times 10^{-3} \times 1.99 - 5 \times 10^{-3} \times 1.77$$

$$\times 0.866) + 30 \times 0.007854 - 29.84 \times 0.005026 - 30.26 \times 0.002827 \times 0.866$$

$$= (0.02865 - 0.0199 - 0.007664) + 0.2356 - 0.1499 - 0.0741$$

$$= 0.0127 \text{ kN or } 12.7 \text{ N } (\uparrow)$$

The magnitude of resultant force acting on the fitting is

$$\boldsymbol{F_R} = \sqrt{F_x^2 + F_y^2} = \sqrt{47.1^2 + 12.7^2} = \mathbf{48.78\ N\ (Ans.)}$$

and the *direction* of the resultant force with *X*-axis (Fig. 6.56) is

$$\tan\theta = \frac{F_y}{F_x} = \frac{12.7}{47.1} = 0.2696$$

$\therefore$ θ = **15.09° (Ans.)**

An equal and opposite force will be needed to hold the fitting in position. **(Ans.)**

Example 6.59. *At inlet to a horizontal pipe of radius a, fitted at side of a vertical tank, the velocity distribution is uniform with magnitude V_0. But at the outlet section, where the flow is fully developed, the velocity distribution is given by,*

$$u = 2V_0\left(1 - \frac{r^2}{a^2}\right)$$

where, u is the velocity at any radius r from the axis of the pipe. Determine the horizontal force required to hold the pipe in position. **(UPSC)**

Solution. For uniform velocity *at inlet,*

$$\text{Momentum} = \rho A V_0^2 = \rho\pi a^2 V_0^2 \quad (\text{where, } a = \text{radius of the pipe})$$

At outlet, momentum $= \int \rho u^2\, dA$

$$= \rho\int_0^a \left\{2V_0\left(1 - \frac{r^2}{a^2}\right)\right\}^2 2\pi r\,.\,dr$$

$$= 8\pi\rho\frac{V_0^2}{a^4}\int_0^a (a^2 - r^2)^2\, r\,.\,dr$$

$$= 8\pi\rho\frac{V_0^2}{a^4}\int_0^a (a^4 r - 2a^2 r^3 + r^5)\,dr$$

$$= 8\pi\rho\frac{V_0^2}{a^4}\left[a^4 \times \frac{r^2}{2} - 2a^2 \times \frac{r^4}{4} + \frac{r^6}{6}\right]_0^a$$

$$= 8\pi\rho\frac{V_0^2}{a^4}\left(\frac{a^6}{2} - \frac{a^6}{2} + \frac{a^6}{6}\right)$$

$$= \frac{4}{3}\pi\rho V_0^2 a^2$$

- Assuming that the *pressures at inlet and outlet are same,* the force required is equal to change in momentum, or

$$\textbf{Force, } F = \text{Momentum at outlet} - \text{Momentum at inlet}$$

$$= \frac{4}{3}\pi\rho V_0^2 a^2 - \rho\pi a^2 V_0^2 = \pi\rho a^2 V_0^2\left(\frac{4}{3}-1\right)$$

$$= \frac{1}{3}\pi\rho a^2 V_0^2 \quad \textbf{(Ans.)}$$

- If the pressures at inlet and outlet are different $(p_1 - p_0) = \Delta p \neq 0$, then the force required,

$$F = \frac{1}{3}\pi\rho a^2 V_0^2 + \Delta p \times \pi a^2 \quad \textbf{(Ans.)}$$

Example 6.60. *Fig. 6.57 shows a rocket of circular cross-section with 2 m as its maximum diameter. The rocket is moving at 200 m/s and the jet of gases leaves at 1000 m/s relative to the rocket. The outside air pressure is 98.1 kN/m² and that of the jet is 93.1 kN/m². The density of outside air is 11.76 N/m³. The rocket breathes in air at the rate of 100 m³/s. Neglecting compressibility effects and assuming that the mass rate of flow of exhaust gases equals the mass flow rate of air breathed in, calculate:*

(*i*) *Thrust developed by the rocket.*

(*ii*) *Energy supplied by the rocket to the air stream per unit weight of air flowing through the rocket.*

(*iii*) *Energy supplied per second by the rocket to the air stream.*

(*iv*) *Power developed by the rocket.* **[IIT Delhi]**

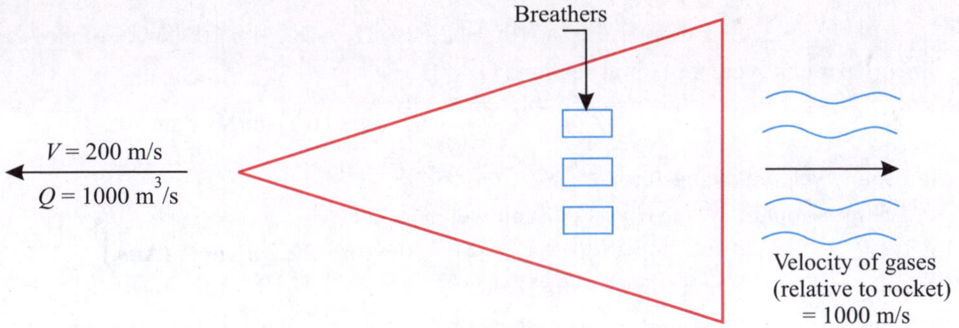

Fig. 6.57

Solution. *Given*: Maximum diameter of the rocket, $D = 2$ m

Speed of the rocket, $V_1 = 200$ m/s

Velocity of gases (relative to rocket), $V_2 = 1000$ m/s

Outside air pressure, $p_1 = 98.1$ kN/m^2

Jet pressure, $p_2 = 93.1$ kN/m^2

Density of outside air, $w = 11.76$ N/m^3

Rate of air breathed in by the rocket, $Q = 100$ m^3/s

(*i*) Thrust developed by the rocket:

Applying momentum equation to the control volume, we get:

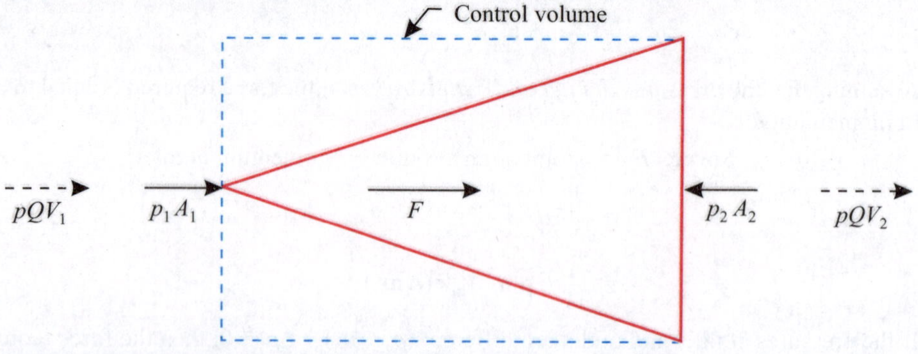

Fig. 6.58

$$F + p_1A_1 - p_2A_2 = \rho Q(V_2 - V_1)$$

or, $$F = \rho Q(V_2 - V_1) + (p_2 - p_1)\, A_2$$

($\because A_1 = A_2$ and pressure p_1 is everywhere the same except in the jet)

or, $$F = \frac{11.76}{9.81} \times 100\,(1000 - 200) + (93.1 - 98.1)\, 10^3 \times \frac{\pi}{4} \times 2^2 \text{ N}$$

or, $$F = 80.2 \times 10^3 \text{ N} = 80.2 \text{ kN}$$

Thrust on the rocket is equal and opposite to F = **80.2 kN. (Ans.)**

(*ii*) Energy supplied by the rocket:

Absolute velocity of the jet = 1000 – 200 = 800 m/s

Energy per unit weight of air at section (2)

$$= \frac{p}{w} + \frac{V^2}{2g} = \frac{93.1 \times 10^3}{11.76} + \frac{800^2}{2 \times 9.81}$$

$$= 7.92 \times 10^3 + 32.62 \times 10^3 = 40.54 \times 10^3 \text{ Nm/N of air}$$

Energy per unit weight of air at section (1)

$$= \frac{p}{w} = \frac{98.1 \times 10^3}{11.76} = 8.34 \times 10^3 \text{ Nm/N of air}$$

(Absolute velocity being zero)

∴ Energy supplied by the rocket per unit weight of air

$= (40.54 - 8.34) \times 10^3$ Nm = **32.2 kNm/N (Ans.)**

(*iii*) Energy supplied per second by the rocket:

Energy supplied per second by the rocket

$= wQ \times 32.2 \times 10^3 = 11.76 \times 100 \times 32.2 \times 10^3$

= **37.86 × 10⁶ Nm (Ans.)**

(*iv*) Power developed by the rocket:

Power developed by the rocket = Energy supplied per second

$= 37.86 \times 10^6$ Nm/s = **37.86×10^3 kW (Ans.)**

6.9. KINETIC ENERGY AND MOMENTUM CORRECTION FACTORS (CORIOLIS CO-EFFICIENTS)

While deriving Bernoulli's equation, it is assumed that the velocity distribution across a single stream tube is uniform. But if there is an appreciable variation in the velocity distribution (on account of viscous and boundary resistance) correction factors α and β have to be applied to obtain the exact amount of kinetic energy or momentum available at a given cross-section.

Kinetic energy correction factor (α):

'Kinetic energy correction factor' is defined as the ratio of the kinetic energy of flow per second based on actual velocity across a section to the kinetic energy of flow per second based on average velocity across the same section. It is denoted by α.

Mathematically, $$\alpha = \frac{\text{Kinetic energy per second based on actual velocity}}{\text{Kinetic energy per second based on average velocity}} \quad ...(6.27)$$

Refer to Fig. 6.59.

Let, $\bar{u}$ = Average velocity at the section LL,

u = Local or point or actual velocity,

dA = Elementary area, and

A = Area of cross-section.

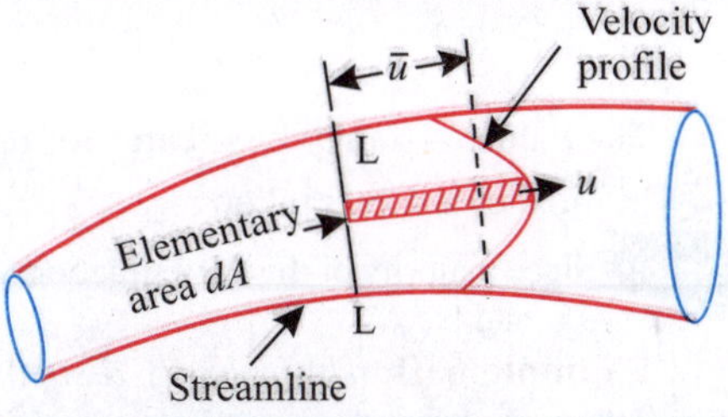

Fig. 6.59

For the velocity variation across the section LL of the stream tube the total K.E. for the entire section is given as:

$$K.E. = \frac{1}{2} m\bar{u}^2 = \frac{1}{2}(\rho A\bar{u})\bar{u}^2 = \frac{1}{2}\rho A\bar{u}^3 \quad ...(i)$$

True K.E. for the entire cross-section

$$= \int \frac{1}{2} dm.u^2 = \int \frac{1}{2}(\rho.dA.u)u^2 = \frac{\rho}{2}\int_A u^3\, dA \quad ...(ii)$$

$$\alpha = \frac{\frac{\rho}{2}\int_A u^3\, dA}{\frac{\rho}{2} A\bar{u}^3} = \frac{1}{A}\int \left(\frac{u}{\bar{u}}\right)^3 dA \quad ...(6.28)$$

$\alpha = 1$ *for uniform velocity distribution and tends to become greater than* 1 *as the distribution of velocity becomes less and less uniform.*

α = 1.02 to 1.15 for *turbulent flows.*

α = 2 for *laminar flow.*

It may be noted that in most of the fluid mechanics computations, α is taken as 1 without introducing much error, since the *velocity is a small percentage of the total head.*

Momentum correction factor (β):

'Momentum correction factor' is defined as the ratio of momentum of the flow per second based on actual velocity to the momentum of the flow per second based on average velocity across a section. **It is denoted by β.**

Mathematically, $$\beta = \frac{\text{Momentum per second based on actual velocity}}{\text{Momentum per second based on average velocity}} \quad ...(6.29)$$

Refer to Fig. 6.59.

The momentum of fluid mass m is

$$= m\bar{u} = (\rho A\bar{u})\bar{u} = \rho A\bar{u}^2 \quad ...(iii)$$

The true momentum at the section LL is given as:

$$\int_{LL} dm.u = \int_{LL} (\rho dA.u)u = \int_A \rho u^2 dA \quad ...(iv)$$

$$\beta = \frac{\int_A \rho u^2 dA}{\rho A \bar{u}^2} = \frac{1}{A}\int_A \left(\frac{u}{\bar{u}}\right)^2 dA \qquad ...(6.30)$$

β = 1 for *uniform flow,*

β = 1.01 to 1.07 for *turbulent flow in pipes,* and

$\beta = \frac{4}{3} = 1.33$ for *laminar flow in pipes.*

The value of β may be greater for open channel flow.

In most cases, β is taken as 1.

Note: Since majority of the flow situations are turbulent in character, the usual practice is to assign *unit value to* α and β.

Example 6.61. *The velocity distribution for turbulent flow in pipe is given approximately by Prandtl's one-seventh power law.*

$$u = U_m\left(\frac{y}{r_0}\right)^{1/7}$$

where u is the local velocity of flow at a distance y from the pipe wall, U_m is the maximum velocity at the centre line of the pipe and r_0 is the pipe radius. Find the following:

(i) *Average velocity,*

(ii) *Kinetic energy correction factor, and*

(iii) *Momentum correction factor.* **[Delhi University]**

Solution. (*i*) Average velocity:

Refer to Fig. 6.60. Consider an elementary area *dA* in the form of a ring at a radius $(r_0 - y)$ and of thickness *dy,* then,

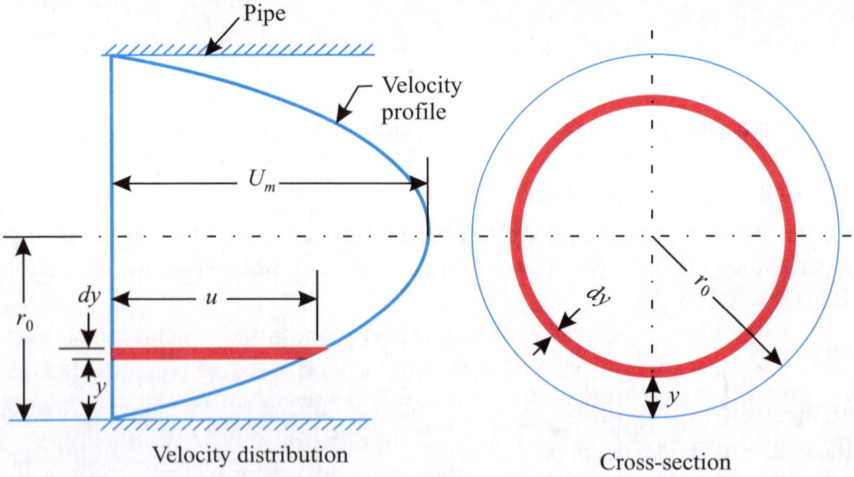

Fig. 6.60. Velocity distribution and cross-section of a circular pipe.

$$dA = 2\pi(r_0 - y)\, dy$$

Rate of fluid flowing through the *ring*

$$= dQ = \text{Area of ring element} \times \text{local velocity}$$

$$= 2\pi(r_0 - y)\, dy\, u$$

$\therefore$ Total flow, $Q = \int_0^{r_0} 2\pi u (r_0 - y) dy$

$$= \int_0^{r_0} 2\pi U_m \left(\frac{y}{r_0}\right)^{1/7} (r_0 - y) dy$$

$$= \frac{2\pi U_m}{(r_0)^{1/7}} \int_0^{r_0} (y)^{1/7} (r_0 - y) dy$$

$$= \frac{2\pi U_m}{(r_0)^{1/7}} \int_0^{r_0} (r_0 y^{1/7} - y^{8/7}) dy$$

$$= \frac{2\pi U_m}{(r_0)^{1/7}} \left[\frac{7}{8} r_0 . y^{8/7} - \frac{7}{15} y^{15/7}\right]_0^{r_0}$$

$$= \frac{2\pi U_m}{(r_0)^{1/7}} \left[\frac{7}{8} r_0 .(r_0)^{8/7} - \frac{7}{15} (r_0)^{15/7}\right]$$

$$= \frac{2\pi U_m}{(r_0)^{1/7}} \left[\frac{7}{8} (r_0)^{15/7} - \frac{7}{15} (r_0)^{15/7}\right]$$

$$= \frac{2\pi U_m}{(r_0)^{1/7}} \times (r_0)^{15/7} \left[\frac{7}{8} - \frac{7}{15}\right]$$

$$= 2\pi U_m \left(\frac{49}{120} r_0^2\right) \quad ...(i)$$

If $\bar{u}$ is the average velocity, then $Q = A\bar{u} = \pi r_0^2 \bar{u}$ ...(*ii*)

From (*i*) and (*ii*), we get:

$$\pi r_0^2 \bar{u} = 2\pi U_m \left(\frac{49}{120} r_0^2\right)$$

$$\therefore \quad \bar{u} = \frac{2\pi U_m \left(\frac{49}{120} r_0^2\right)}{\pi r_0^2} = \frac{49}{60} U_m$$

i.e., $\bar{u} = \frac{49}{60} U_m$ **(Ans.)**

(*ii*) Kinetic energy correction factor, α:

$$\alpha = \frac{1}{A\bar{u}^3} \int_0^{r_0} u^3 dA \quad \text{[Eqn. (6.28)]}$$

$$= \frac{1}{A\bar{u}^3} \int_0^{r_0} U_m^3 \left(\frac{y}{r_0}\right)^{3/7} 2\pi (r_0 - y) dy$$

$$= \frac{2\pi U_m^3}{A\bar{u}^3 (r_0)^{3/7}} \int_0^{r_0} y^{3/7} (r_0 - y) dy$$

$$= \frac{2\pi U_m^3}{A\bar{u}^3 (r_0)^{3/7}} \int_0^{r_0} (r_0 y^{3/7} - y^{10/7})\, dy$$

$$= \frac{2\pi U_m^3}{A\bar{u}^3 (r_0)^{3/7}} \left[r_0 \times \frac{7}{10} y^{10/7} - \frac{7}{17} y^{17/7} \right]_0^{r_0}$$

$$= \frac{2\pi U_m^3}{A\bar{u}^3 (r_0)^{3/7}} \left[\frac{7}{10} (r_0)^{17/7} - \frac{7}{17} (r_0)^{17/7} \right]$$

$$= \frac{2\pi U_m^3}{A\bar{u}^3 (r_0)^{3/7}} \left[\frac{49}{170} (r_0)^{17/7} \right]$$

Substituting the values, $A = \pi r_0^2$ and $\bar{u} = \frac{49}{60} U_m$, we get:

$$\alpha = \frac{2\pi U_m^3}{\pi r_0^2 \left(\frac{49}{60} U_m\right)^3 (r_0)^{3/7}} \left[\frac{49}{170} (r_0)^{17/7} \right] = \mathbf{1.06\ (Ans.)}$$

(*iii*) Momentum correction factor, β:

$$\beta = \frac{1}{A\bar{u}^2} \int u^2\, dA \qquad \text{[Eqn. (6. 29)]}$$

$$= \frac{1}{A\bar{u}^2} \int_0^{r_0} U_m^2 \left(\frac{y}{r_0}\right)^{2/y} 2\pi (r_0 - y)\, dy$$

$$= \frac{2\pi U_m^2}{A\bar{u}^2 (r_0)^{2/7}} \int_0^{r_0} y^{2/7} (r_0 - y)\, dy$$

$$= \frac{2\pi U_m^2}{A\bar{u}^2 (r_0)^{2/7}} \int_0^{r_0} (r_0 y^{2/7} - y^{9/7})\, dy$$

$$= \frac{2\pi U_m^2}{A\bar{u}^2 (r_0)^{2/7}} \left[r_0 \times \frac{7}{9} y^{9/7} - \frac{7}{16} y^{16/7} \right]_0^{r_0}$$

$$= \frac{2\pi U_m^2}{A\bar{u}^2 (r_0)^{2/7}} \left[\frac{7}{9} (r_0)^{16/7} - \frac{7}{16} (r_0)^{16/7} \right]$$

$$= \frac{2\pi U_m^2}{A\bar{u}^2 (r_0)^{2/7}} \left[\frac{49}{144} (r_0)^{16/7} \right]$$

Substituting the values, $A = \pi r_0^2$ and $\bar{u} = \frac{49}{60} U_m$, we get:

$$\beta = \frac{2\pi U_m^2}{\pi r_0^2 \left(\frac{49}{60} U_m\right)^2 (r_0)^{2/7}} \left[\frac{49}{144} (r_0)^{16/7} \right] = \mathbf{1.02\ (Ans.)}$$

Example 6.62. *In a circular pipe the velocity profile is given as*

$$u = U_m \left[1 - \left(\frac{r}{R}\right)^2 \right]$$

where u is the velocity at any radius r, U_m is the velocity at the pipe axis, and R is the radius of the pipe. Find:

(i) Average velocity,

(ii) Energy correction factor, and

(iii) Momentum correction factor. **[Anna University]**

Solution. Refer to Fig. 6.61. Consider an elementary area dA in the form of a ring at a radius r and of thickness dr, then $dA = 2\pi\, r.dr$

Flow rate through the ring = dQ = Elemental area × local velocity = $2\pi r.dr.u$

$$\therefore \quad \text{Total flow } Q = \int_0^R 2\pi r.u.dr$$

$$= \int_0^R 2\pi\, U_m\left(1-\frac{r^2}{R^2}\right) r\, dr$$

$$= 2\pi U_m \int_0^R \left(r - \frac{r^3}{R^2}\right) dr = 2\pi U_m \left[\frac{r^2}{2} - \frac{r^4}{4R^2}\right]_0^R$$

$$= 2\pi U_m\left(\frac{R^2}{2} - \frac{R^2}{4}\right) = 2\pi U_m\left(\frac{R^2}{4}\right)$$

i.e.,
$$Q = 2\pi U_m\left(\frac{R^2}{4}\right) \qquad ...(i)$$

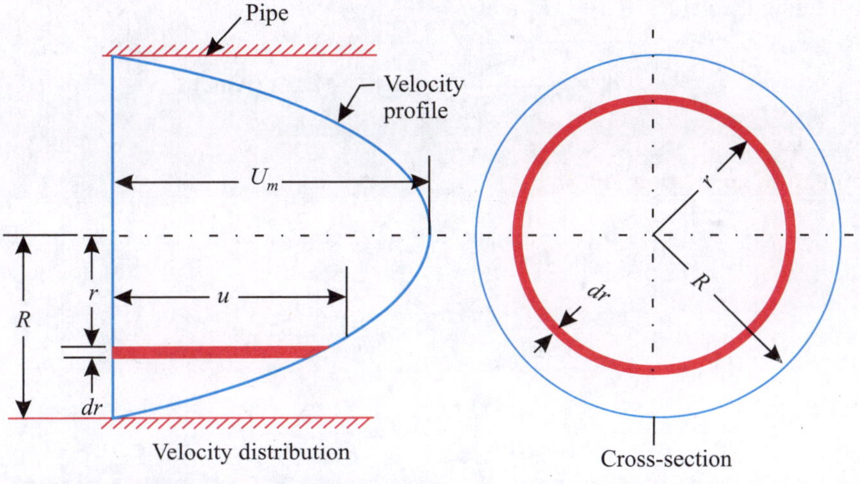

Fig. 6.61. Velocity distribution and cross-section of a pipe.

(ii) Average velocity, $\bar{u}$:

If $\bar{u}$ is the average flow velocity, then:

$$Q = A\bar{u} = \pi R^2 \bar{u} \qquad ...(ii)$$

From (*i*) and (*ii*), we get:

$$\pi R^2 \bar{u} = 2\pi U_m\left(\frac{R^2}{4}\right)$$

$$\therefore \quad \bar{u} = \frac{2\pi U_m\left(\frac{R^2}{4}\right)}{\pi R^2} = \frac{U_m}{2} \quad \textbf{(Ans.)}$$

(iii) Kinetic energy correction factor, α:

$$\alpha = \frac{1}{A\bar{u}^3}\int_0^R u^3\,dA \qquad \text{...[Eqn. 6.28]}$$

$$= \frac{1}{A\bar{u}^3}\int_0^R U_m^3\left[1-\left(\frac{r}{R}\right)^2\right]^3 2\pi\, r dr$$

$$= \frac{2\pi U_m^3}{A\bar{u}^3}\int_0^R\left(1-\frac{3r^2}{R^2}+\frac{3r^4}{R^4}-\frac{r^6}{R^6}\right)r\,dr$$

$$= \frac{2\pi U_m^3}{A\bar{u}^3}\int_0^R\left(r-\frac{3r^3}{R^2}+\frac{3r^5}{R^4}-\frac{r^7}{R^6}\right)dr$$

$$= \frac{2\pi U_m^3}{A\bar{u}^3}\left[\frac{r^2}{2}-\frac{3r^4}{4R^2}+\frac{3r^6}{6R^4}-\frac{r^8}{8R^6}\right]_0^R$$

$$= \frac{2\pi U_m^3}{A\bar{u}^3}\left[\frac{R^2}{2}-\frac{3}{4}R^2+\frac{R^2}{2}-\frac{R^2}{8}\right]$$

$$= \frac{2\pi U_m^3}{A\bar{u}^3}\left(\frac{R^2}{8}\right)$$

Substituting the values $A = \pi R^2$ and $\bar{u} = \frac{U_m}{2}$, we get:

$$\alpha = \frac{2\pi U_m^3}{\pi R^2 \times \left(\frac{U_m}{2}\right)^3}\times\left(\frac{R^2}{8}\right) = \mathbf{2\ (Ans.)}$$

(iv) Momentum correction factor, β:

$$\beta = \frac{1}{A\bar{u}^2}\int u^2\,dA \qquad \text{...[Eqn. 6.29]}$$

$$= \frac{1}{A\bar{u}^2}\int_0^R U_m^2\left[1-\left(\frac{r}{R}\right)^2\right]^2 2\pi r\,dr$$

$$= \frac{2\pi U_m^2}{A\bar{u}^2}\int_0^R\left(1-2\times\frac{r^2}{R^2}+\frac{r^4}{R^4}\right)r\,dr$$

$$= \frac{2\pi U_m^2}{A\bar{u}^2}\int_0^R\left(r-2\times\frac{r^3}{R^2}+\frac{r^5}{R^4}\right)dr$$

$$= \frac{2\pi U_m^2}{A\bar{u}^2}\left[\frac{r^2}{2}-2\times\frac{r^4}{4R^2}+\frac{1}{6}\times\frac{r^6}{R^4}\right]_0^R$$

$$= \frac{2\pi U_m^2}{A\bar{u}^2}\left[\frac{R^2}{2}-\frac{R^2}{2}+\frac{R^2}{6}\right]$$

$$= \frac{2\pi U_m^2}{A\bar{u}^2}\left(\frac{R^2}{6}\right)$$

Substituting the values $A = \pi R^2$ and $\bar{u} = \frac{U_m}{2}$, we get:

$$\beta = \frac{2\pi U_m^2}{\pi R^2 \times \left(\frac{U_m}{2}\right)^2}\left(\frac{R^2}{6}\right) = \mathbf{1.33\ (Ans.)}$$

6.10. MOMENT OF MOMENTUM EQUATION

Moment of momentum equation is derived from *moment of momentum principle* which states as follows:

"The resulting torque acting on a rotating fluid is equal to the rate of change of moment of momentum".

When the moment of momentum of flow leaving a control volume is different from that entering it, the result is a torque acting over the control volume.

Let, Q = Steady rate of flow of fluid,

ρ = Density of fluid,

V_1 = Velocity of fluid at section 1,

r_1 = Radius of curvature at section 1, and

V_2 and r_2 = Velocity and radius of curvature at section 2.

Momentum of fluid at section 1= Mass × velocity = $\rho Q \times V_1$

∴ Moment of momentum per second of fluid at section 1 = $\rho Q \times V_1 \times r_1$

Similarly, moment of momentum per second of fluid at section 2 = $\rho Q \times V_2 \times r_2$

∴ Rate of change of moment of momentum = $\rho Q\, V_2 r_2 - \rho Q V_1 r_1 = \rho Q(V_2 r_2 - V_1 r_1)$

According to the moment of momentum principle,

Resultant torque = Rate of change of moment of momentum

$$T = \rho Q\,(V_2 r_2 - V_1 r_1) \quad \text{...(6.31)}$$

Eqn. (6.31) is known as *moment of momentum equation.* This equation is used:

(*i*) To find torque exerted by water on sprinkler, and

(*ii*) To analyse flow problems in turbines and centrifugal pumps.

Example 6.63. *Fig. 6.62 shows an unsymmetrical sprinkler. It has a frictionless shaft and equal flow through each nozzle with a velocity of 8 m/s relative to the nozzle. Find the speed of rotation in r.p.m.*

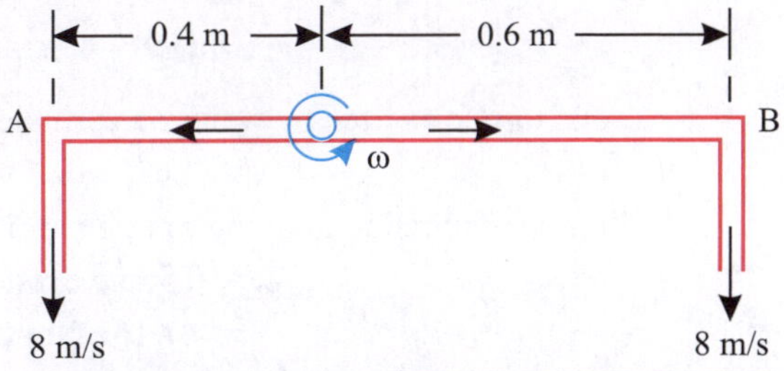

Fig. 6.62

Solution. Refer to Fig. 6.62.

$r_A = 0.4$ m, $r_B = 0.6$ m

Velocity relative to the nozzle

$V_A (= V_B) = 8$ m/s

Let, ω = Angular velocity of the sprinkler.

Absolute velocity, $V_1 = V_A + \omega\, r_A = 8 + \omega \times 0.4 = 8 + 0.4\,\omega$

Absolute velocity, $V_2 = V_B - \omega r_B = 8 - \omega \times 0.6 = 8 - 0.6\,\omega$

Speed of rotaiton, N (r.p.m.):

The moment of momentum of the fluid entering sprinkler is given zero and also there is no external torque applied on the sprinkler. Hence resultant torque is zero, *i.e.*

$$T = 0$$

$$\therefore \quad \rho Q (V_2 r_2 - V_1 r_1) = 0$$

$$\text{or,} \quad V_2 r_2 - V_1 r_1 = 0 \qquad (\because \rho Q \neq 0)$$

$$\text{or,} \quad (8 - 0.6\,\omega) \times 0.6 = (8 + 0.4\,\omega) \times 0.4$$

$$\text{or,} \quad 4.8 - 0.36\,\omega = 3.2 + 0.16\,\omega$$

$$\text{or,} \quad 0.52\,\omega = 1.6$$

$$\text{or,} \quad \omega = 3.077 \text{ rad/s}$$

$$\text{But,} \quad \omega = \frac{2\pi N}{60}$$

$$\therefore \quad N = \frac{60 \times \omega}{2\pi} = \frac{60 \times 3.077}{2\pi} = \mathbf{29.4 \text{ r.p.m.}} \textbf{ (Ans.)}$$

Example 6.64. *A lawn sprinkler shown in Fig 6.63 has 12 mm diameter nozzle at the end of a rotating arm and discharges water with a velocity of 15 m/s. Determine:*

(i) *Torque required to hold the rotating arm stationary, and*

(ii) *Constant speed of rotation of the arm, if free to rotate.*

Solution. Diameter of each nozzle = 12 mm = 0.012 m

∴ Area of each nozzle

$$= \frac{\pi}{4} \times 0.012^2 = 0.000113 \text{m}^2$$

Velocity of flow, $V_A (= V_B) = 15$ m/s

∴ Discharge through each nozzle,

$$Q = \text{Area} \times \text{velocity}$$

$$= 0.000113 \times 15 = 0.001695 \text{ m}^3/\text{s}$$

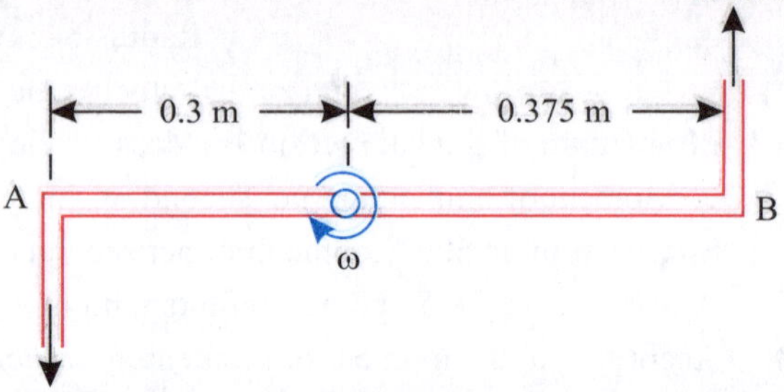

Fig. 6.63

(i) Torque required to hold the rotating arm stationary:

Torque exerted by water coming thorugh nozzle A on the sprinkler

$$= \rho Q V_A \times r_A = \frac{9810}{9.81} \times 0.001695 \times 15 \times 0.3 = 7.627 \text{ Nm}$$

Torque exerted by water coming through nozzle B on the sprinkler

$$= \rho Q V_B \times r_B = \frac{9810}{9.81} \times 0.001695 \times 15 \times 0.375 = 9.534 \text{ Nm}$$

∴ Total torque exerted by water on sprinkler

$$= 7.627 + 9.534 = 17.161 \text{ Nm}$$

∴ Torque required to hold the rotating arm stationary

= Torque exerted by water on sprinkler

= **17.161 Nm (Ans.)**

(ii) Constant speed of rotation of the arm, if free to rotate, N (r.p.m.):

Let, ω = Angular speed of rotation of the sprinkler.

Then, absolute velocities of flow of water at the nozzles A and B are,

$$V_1 = 15 - 0.3\,\omega$$

and

$$V_2 = 15 - 0.375\,\omega$$

Torque exerted by water coming out at A, on sprinkler

$$= \rho Q V_1 \times r_A = \frac{9810}{9.81} \times 0.001695 \times (15 - 0.3\,\omega) \times 0.3$$

$$= 0.5085\,(15 - 0.3\,\omega)$$

Torque exerted by water, coming out at B, on sprinkler

$$= PQV_2 \times r_B = \frac{9810}{9.81} \times 0.001695 \times (15 - 0.375\ \omega) \times 0.375$$

$$= 0.6356\ (15 - 0.375\ \omega)$$

∴ Total torque exerted by water

$$= 0.5085\ (15 - 0.3\ \omega) + 0.6356\ (15 - 0.375\ \omega)$$

Since moment of momentum of the flow entering is zero and no external torque is applied on sprinkler, so the resultant torque on the sprinkler must be zero.

$$\therefore\quad 0.5085\ (15 - 0.3\ \omega) + 0.6356\ (15 - 0.375\ \omega) = 0$$

$$7.627 - 0.1526\ \omega + 9.534 - 0.238\ \omega = 0$$

$$17.161 - 0.3906\ \omega = 0$$

or,
$$\omega = \frac{17.161}{0.3906} = 43.93 \text{ rad/s}$$

Also,
$$\omega = \frac{2\pi N}{60} = 43.93$$

$$\therefore\quad N = \frac{60 \times 43.93}{2\pi} = \mathbf{419.5\ r.p.m.}\ \textbf{(Ans.)}$$

6.11. VORTEX MOTION

Vortex motion *is defined as a motion in which the whole fluid mass rotates about an axis.* A mass of fluid in rotation about a fixed axis is called ***vortex.***

A vortex motion is characterised by a flow pattern wherein the stream lines are curved. When fluid flows between curved stream lines, centrifugal forces are set up and these are counter-balanced by the pressure force acting in the radial direction.

The vortex flow is of the following types:

1. Forced vortex flow, and
2. Free vortex flow.

6.11.1 Forced Vortex Flow

Forced vortex flow *is one in which the fluid mass is made to rotate by means of some external agency.* The external agency is generally the mechanical power which imparts a constant torque on the fluid mass. Then, in such a flow there is always expenditure of energy. The forced vortex motion is also called *flywheel vortex* or *rotational vortex.*

In this type of flow, the fluid mass rotates at a constant angular velocity ω. The tangential velocity of any fluid particle is given by:

$$v = \omega r \quad ...(6.32)$$

(where, r = radius of the fluid particle from the axis of rotation)

∴ Angular velocity. $\omega = \dfrac{v}{r}$ = constant ...[6.32 (*a*)]

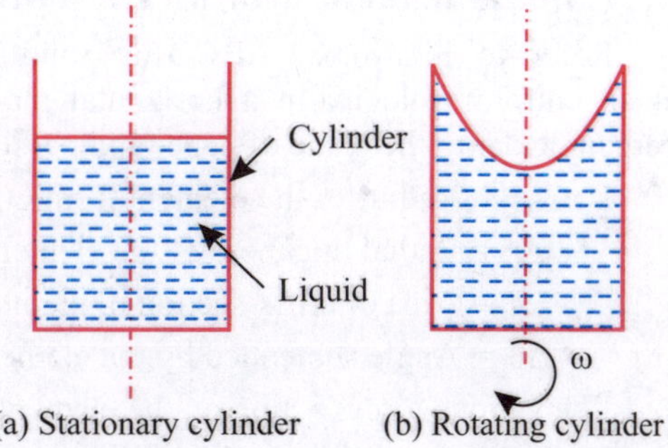

Fig. 6.64. Forced vortex flow.

Example:

1. Rotation of water through the runner of a turbine.
2. Rotation of liquid inside the impeller of a centrifugal pump.
3. Rotation of liquid in a vertical cylinder (Fig. 6.64).

6.11.2 Free Vortex Flow

Free vortex flow *is one in which the fluid mass rotates without any external impressed contact force.* The whole fluid mass rotates either due to fluid pressure itself or the gravity or due to rotation previously imparted. The free vortex motion is also called *potential vortex* or *irrotational vortex.*

Example:

1. Flow around a circular bend.
2. A whirlpool in a river.
3. Flow of liquid in a centrifugal pump casing after it has left the impeller.
4. Flow of water in a turbine casing before it enters the guide vanes.
5. Flow of liquid through a hole/outlet provided at the bottom of a shallow vessel (*e.g.,* wash basin, bath tub, etc.)

In free vortex the relation between velocity and radius is obtained by putting the value of external torque equal to zero, or, the time rate change of angular momentum (*i.e.,* moment of momentum) must be *zero*.

Let us consider a particle of mass m at a radius distance r from the axis of rotation, having a tangential velocity, v. Then:

$$\text{Moment of momentum} = (m \times v) \times r = mvr$$

$\therefore$ Time rate of change of momentum

$$= \frac{\partial}{\partial t}(mvr)$$

But for the vortex, $= \dfrac{\partial}{\partial t}(mvr) = 0$

Integrating, we get: $mvr = \text{constant}$

Since m is constant, $vr = \text{constant} = C$ ...(6.33)

where C is a constant and is known as *strength of vortex.*

$$\therefore \quad v = \frac{C}{r} \quad \text{...(6.34)}$$

$$\text{or,} \quad v \; \alpha \; \frac{1}{r} \quad \text{...(6.34 } a\text{)}$$

i.e. tangentital velocity is *inversely proportional to distance r.*

6.11.3. Equation of Motion for Vortex Flow.

Refer to Fig. 6.65. ABCD is fluid element rotating at a uniform velocity in a horizontal plane about an axis perpendicular to the plane of paper and passing through 0.

Let, r = Radius of the element from O,

Δr = Radial thickness of the element,

ΔA = Area of cross-section of element, and

$\Delta\theta$ = Angle subtended by the element at O.

The various forces acting on the element are:

1. Centrifugal force, $\dfrac{mv^2}{r}$ acting away from the centre, O,
2. Pressure force $p\Delta A$ on the face AB, and

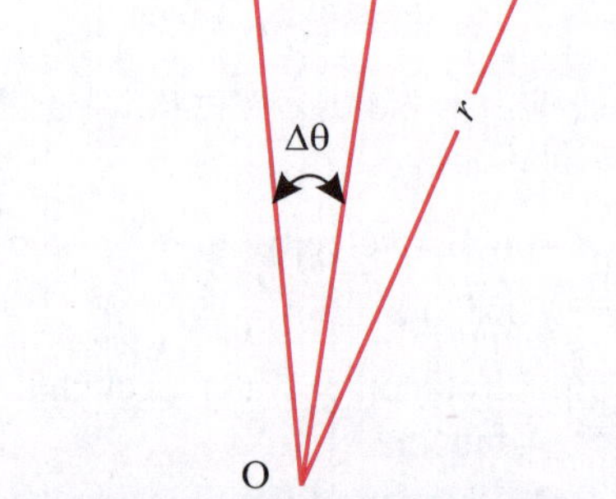

Fig. 6.65. Flow in a circular path.

3. Pressure force $\left(p + \frac{\partial p}{\partial r}\Delta r\right)\Delta A$ on the face *CD*.

Equating the forces in the radial direction, we get:

$$\left(p + \frac{\partial p}{\partial r}.\Delta r\right)\Delta A - p\Delta A = \frac{mv^2}{r}$$

But, m = mass density × volume = $\rho \times \Delta A \times \Delta r$

$$\therefore \quad \left(p + \frac{\partial p}{\partial r}\Delta r\right)\Delta A - p\Delta A = \rho\Delta A\,\Delta r\frac{v^2}{r}$$

$$\text{or,} \quad \rho\Delta A + \frac{\partial p}{\partial r}\Delta r\,\Delta A - p\Delta A = \rho\Delta A\Delta r\frac{v^2}{r}$$

$$\text{or,} \quad \frac{\partial p}{\partial r}\Delta r\,\Delta A = \rho\Delta A\Delta r\frac{v^2}{r}$$

$$\text{or,} \quad \frac{\partial p}{\partial r} = \frac{\rho v^2}{r} \qquad \text{...(6.35)}$$

The expression $\frac{\partial p}{\partial r}$ is called *pressure gradient* in the radial direction.

$\left(\text{Since } \frac{\partial p}{\partial r} \text{ is } +ve, \text{ therefore, pressure increases with the increase of radius } r.\right)$

In the vertical plane, the variation of pressure is given by the hydrostatic law, *i.e.,*

$$\frac{\partial p}{\partial z} = -\rho g \qquad \text{...(6.36)}$$

As the pressure is a function of r and z, therefore total derivative of p,

$$\partial p = \frac{\partial p}{\partial r}dr + \frac{\partial p}{\partial z}dz$$

Substituting the values of $\frac{\partial p}{\partial r}$ and $\frac{\partial p}{\partial z}$ from eqns. (6.35) and (6.36) respectively, we get:

$$dp = \frac{\rho v^2}{r}dr - \rho g\,dz \qquad \text{...(6.37)}$$

Eqn. (6.37) gives the *variation of pressure of a rotating fluid in any plane.*

6.11.4. Equation of Forced Vortex Flow

In case of forced vortex flow,

$$v = \omega r \qquad \text{...[Eqn. 6.32]}$$

(where, ω = constant angular velocity)

Putting the value of v in eqn. (6.37), we get:

$$dp = \frac{\rho\omega^2 r^2}{r}dr - \rho g\,dz$$

$$\text{or,} \quad dp = p\omega^2 r dr - \rho g dz$$

Considering points 1 and 2 in the fluid having forced vortex flow (Fig. 6.66) and integrating the above eqn. for these points, we get:

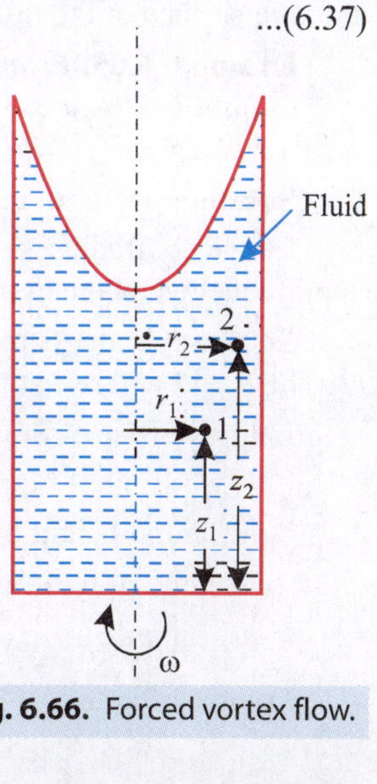

Fig. 6.66. Forced vortex flow.

$$\int_1^2 dp = \int_1^2 \rho\omega^2 r\, dr - \int_1^2 \rho g\, dz$$

or,
$$[p]_1^2 = \rho\omega^2\left[\frac{r^2}{2}\right]_1^2 - \rho g[z]_1^2$$

or,
$$(p_2 - p_1) = \frac{\rho\omega^2}{2}(r_2^2 - r_1^2) - \rho g(z_2 - z_1)$$

$$= \frac{\rho}{2}(\omega^2 r_2^2 - \omega^2 r_1^2) - \rho g(z_2 - z_1)$$

$$= \frac{\rho}{2}(v_2^2 - v_1^2) - \rho g(z_2 - z_1) \qquad [\because v_1 = \omega_1 r_1 \text{ and } v_2 = \omega_2 r_2]$$

— When the points 1 and 2 lie *on the free surface of the liquid*, then $p_1 = p_2$ and the above equation becomes:

$$0 = \frac{\rho}{2}(v_2^2 - v_1^2) - \rho g(z_2 - z_1)$$

or,
$$g(z_2 - z_1) = \left(\frac{v_2^2 - v_1^2}{2}\right)$$

or,
$$z_2 - z_1 = \frac{v_2^2 - v_1^2}{2g}$$

— When the point 1 lies *on the axis of rotation*, then:

$$v_1 = \omega r_1 = \omega \times 0 = 0; \text{ the above eqn. reduces to:}$$

$$z_2 - z_1 = \frac{v_2^2}{2g}$$

If,
$$z_2 - z_1 = z \quad \text{(say), then we have:}$$

$$z = \frac{v_2^2}{2g} = \frac{\omega^2 r_2^2}{2g} \qquad ...(6.38)$$

Thus, z varies with square of r. Hence eqn. (6.38) is an equation of *parabola* which means that the free surface of the liquid is a paraboloid.

Example 6.65. *Prove that in case of force vortex, the rise of liquid level at the ends is equal to the fall of liquid level at the axis of rotation.*

Solution. Refer to Fig. 6.67.

Let, R = Radius of the cylinder, and OO = Initial liquid level when the cylinder is stationary.

Let the cylinder is rotated at constant angular velocity ω. The liquid will rise at the ends and will fall at the centre.

Let, y_r = Rise of liquid at the ends (from OO), and

y_f = Fall of liquid at the centre (from OO)

Now, initial height of liquid = $(h + y_f)$

$\therefore$ Volume of liquid in cylinder

$$= \pi R^2(h + y_f) \qquad ...(i)$$

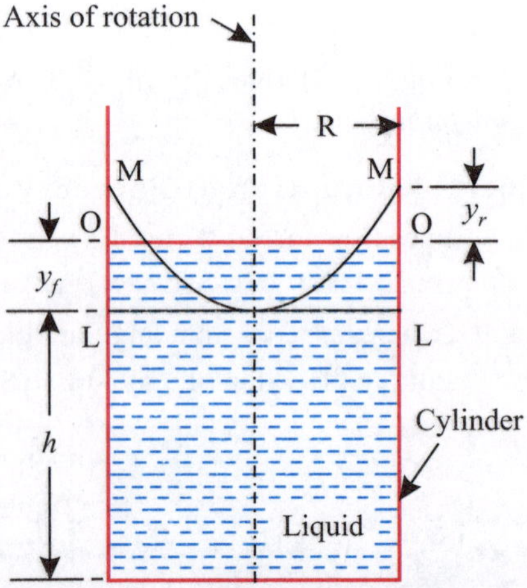

Fig. 6.67

Volume of liquid = [Volume of cylinder up to level MM]

$$- \text{[volume of paraboloid]}$$

$$= (\pi R^2 \times \text{liquid height up to level } MM)$$

$$- \left(\frac{1}{2} \times \pi R^2 \times \text{height of paraboloid}\right)$$

$$= \pi R^2 \times (h + y_f + y_r) - \frac{\pi R^2}{2}(y_f + y_r)$$

$$= \pi R^2 h + \pi R^2 (y_f + y_r) - \frac{\pi R^2}{2}(y_f + y_r)$$

$$= \pi R^2 h + \frac{\pi R^2}{2}(y_f + y_r) \quad ...(ii)$$

Equating (*i*) and (*ii*), we get:

$$\pi R^2 (h + h_f) = \pi R^2 h + \frac{\pi R^2}{2}(y_f + y_r)$$

$$\pi R^2 h + \pi R^2 y_f = \pi R^2 h + \frac{\pi R^2}{2} y_f + \frac{\pi R^2}{2} y_r$$

or, $$\pi R^2 y_f - \frac{\pi R^2}{2} y_f = \frac{\pi R^2}{2} y_r$$

or, $$\frac{\pi R^2}{2} y_f = \frac{\pi R^2}{2} y_r$$

or, $$y_f = y_r$$

i.e., Fall of liquid at centre = Rise of liquid at the ends .....**Proved.**

Example 6.66. *A cylindrical tank 0.9 m in diameter and 2 m high open at top is filled with water to a depth of 1.5 m. It is rotated about its vertical axis at N. r.p.m. Determine the value of N which will raise water level even with the brim.* **(GATE)**

Solution. Refer to Fig. 6.68. *Given*: Radius, $R = \frac{0.9}{2} = 0.45$ m ; Length, = 2m; Initial height of water = 1.5 m.

Speed which will raise water level even with brim, N:

When the vessel is rotated, parboloid is formed.

Volume of air before rotation = Volume of air after rotation

$$\pi R^2 \times 2 - \pi R^2 \times 1.5 = \frac{1}{2} \pi R^2 z$$

or, $z = 1.0$ m

Using the relation:

$$z = \frac{\omega^2 r^2}{2g}, \text{ we get:}$$

$$1.0 = \frac{\omega^2 R^2}{2 \times 9.81} \quad \text{(Here, } r = R\text{)}$$

$$\omega = \sqrt{\frac{1.0 \times 2 \times 9.81}{(0.45)^2}} = 9.843$$

But, $$\omega = \frac{2\pi N}{60}$$

$$\therefore \quad N = \frac{9.843 \times 60}{2\pi} = \mathbf{93.99\ r.p.m.\ (Ans.)}$$

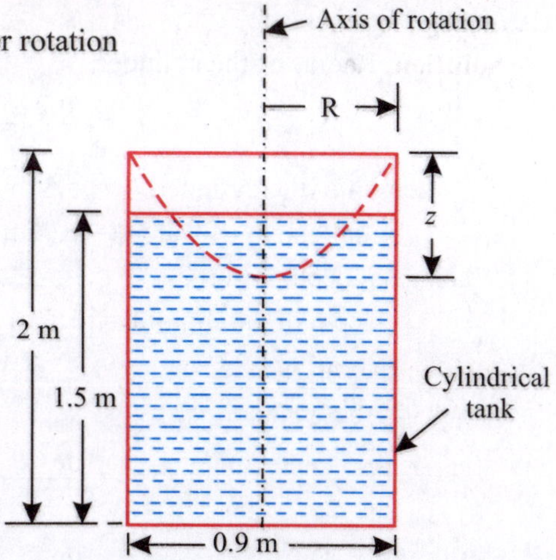

Fig. 6.68

Example. 6.67. *Find the maximum speed of an open circular cylinder, having 180 mm diameter, 1200 mm length and containing water up to a height of 960 mm, at which it should be rotated about its vertical axis so that no water spills.* **(MU)**

Solution. *Given:* Radius of the cylinder, $R = \frac{180}{2} = 90 \text{ mm} = 0.09 \text{ m}$

Length of the cylinder, $l = 1200 \text{ mm} = 1.2 \text{ m}$

Initial height of water, $h = 960 \text{ mm} = 0.96 \text{ m}$

Maximum speed of rotation, *N*:

Let, ω = Angular velocity of the cylinder when the water is about to spin.

We know, Rise of liquid at the ends = Fall of liquid at centre

But, Rise of liquid at the ends = Length of cylinder – initial height

$= 1.2 - 0.96 = 0.24 \text{ m}$

$\therefore$ Fall of liquid at centre $= 0.24$ m

$\therefore$ Height of parabola $= 0.24 + 0.24 = 0.48$ m

$\therefore$ $z = 0.48$ m

Using the relation:

$$z = \frac{\omega^2 R^2}{2g}, \text{ we get}$$

$$0.48 = \frac{\omega^2 \times (0.09)^2}{2 \times 9.81}$$

or, $$\omega^2 = \frac{0.48 \times 2 \times 9.81}{(0.09)^2} = 1162.67 \quad \text{or} \quad \omega = 34.09 \text{ rad/s}$$

But, $$\omega = \frac{2\pi N}{60} \quad \therefore \quad 34.09 = \frac{2\pi N}{60}$$

or, $$N = \frac{34.09 \times 60}{2\pi} = \mathbf{325.5 \text{ r.p.m (Ans.)}}$$

Example 6.68. *A* 0.225*m diameter cylinder is* 1.5 *m long and contains water up to a height of* 1.05 *m. Estimate the speed at which the cylinder may be rotated about its vertical axis so that the axial depth becomes zero.*

Solution. Radius of the cylinder,

$$r = \frac{0.225}{2} = 0.1125 \text{ m}$$

Length of the cylinder, $l = 1.5$ m

Initial height of water $= 1.05$ m

When axial depth is zero,

depth of paraboloid $= 1.5$ m

Speed of rotation N:

Using the relation:

$$z = \frac{\omega^2 R^2}{2g}, \text{ we get:}$$

$$1.5 = \frac{\omega^2 \times 0.1125^2}{2 \times 9.81}$$

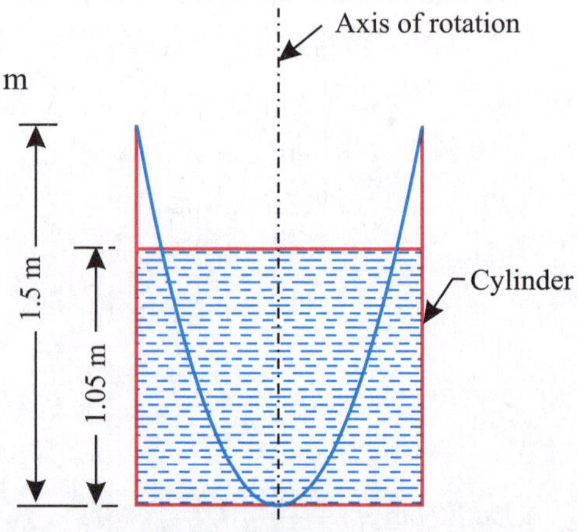

Fig. 6.69

or, $\omega^2 = \dfrac{1.5 \times 2 \times 9.81}{0.1125^2} = 2325.33$

or, $\omega = 48.22$ rad/s

But, $\omega = \dfrac{2\pi N}{60}$

$\therefore \quad 48.22 = \dfrac{2\pi N}{60}$

or, $N = \dfrac{48.22 \times 60}{2\pi}$ = **460.46 r.p.m (Ans.)**

Example 6.69. *For example 6.68 find the difference in total pressure force due to rotation:*

(i) *At the bottom of cylinder, and*

(ii) *On the sides of the cylinder.*

Solution. *Given*: Same as in example 6.68.

(*i*) Difference in total pressure force at the bottom of the cylinder:

Total pressure force at the bottom **before rotation,**

$$F_{\text{before rot.}} = wA\bar{h}$$

where, $w = 9810$ N/m^3,

A = Area of bottom = $\pi R^2 = \pi \times 0{\cdot}1125^2 = 0.03976$ m^2

$\bar{h}$ = 1.05 m.

$\therefore \quad F_{\text{before rot.}} = 9810 \times 0.03976 \times 1.05 = 409.55$ N

After rotation, the depth of water at the bottom is not constant and hence the pressure force due to the height of water *will not be constant.*

Consider an elementary ring of radius r and width dr as shown in Fig. 6.70. Let $z\left(=\dfrac{\omega^2 r^2}{2g}\right)$ be the height of water from the bottom of the tank up to free suface of water at a radius r.

Hydrostatic force on the ring at the bottom,

$$dF = w \times \text{area of ring} \times z$$

$$= 9810 \times 2\pi r\, dr \times \frac{\omega^2 r^2}{2g}$$

$$= 9810 \times 2\pi r \times \frac{\omega^2}{2g} \times r^3 dr$$

$$= 3141.6\, \omega^2 r^3 dr$$

Total pressure force at the bottom,

$$F_{\text{after rot.}} = \int dF = \int_0^{0.1125} 3141.6\omega^2 r^3 dr$$

$$= 3141.6\omega^2 \left| \frac{r^4}{4} \right|_0^{0.1125}$$

[$\because \omega = 48.22$ rad/s, example 6.68]

$$= 3141.6 \times 48.22^2 \times \frac{01125^4}{4}$$

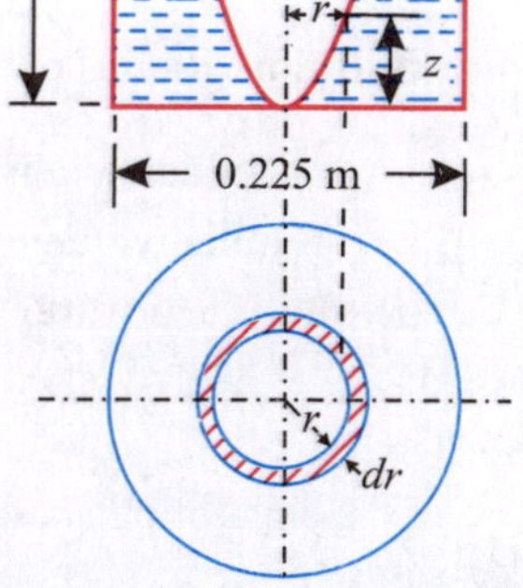

Fig. 6.70

$= 292.52$ N

$\therefore$ Difference in pressure force at the bottom

$$= F_{\text{before rot.}} - F_{\text{after rot.}}$$
$$= 409.55 - 292.52 = \mathbf{117.03\ N\ (Ans.)}$$

(*ii*) Difference in total pressure force on the sides of the cylinder:

Total pressure force on the sides of the cylinder **before rotation,**

$$F_{\text{before rot.}} = wA\bar{h}$$

where, $\omega = 9810$ N/m^3,

A = Surface area of the sides of the cylinder up to height of water

$= \pi D \times$ height of water

$= \pi \times 0.225 \times 1.05 = 0{\cdot}7422$ m^2, and

$\bar{h}$ = *c.g.* of the wetted area of the sides

$$= \frac{1}{2} \times 1.05 = 0.525\,\text{m}.$$

$\therefore$ $F_{\text{before rot.}} = 9810 \times 0.7422 \times 0.525 = 3822.5$ N

After rotation, the water is up to the top of the cylinder and force on the sides,

$$F_{\text{after rot.}} = w \times A \times \bar{h}$$

where, $w = 9810$ N/m^3

A = Wetted area of sides

$= \pi D \times$ height of water $= \pi \times 0.225 \times 1.5 = 1.06$ m^2, and

$$\bar{h} = \frac{1}{2} \times \text{height of water} = \frac{1}{2} \times 1.5 = 0.75 \text{ m}.$$

$\therefore$ $F_{\text{after rot.}} = 9810 \times 1.06 \times 0.75 = 7798.95$ N

$\therefore$ Difference in pressure force on the sides

$$= F_{\text{after rot,}} - F_{\text{before rot.}}$$
$$= 7798.95 - 3822.5 = \mathbf{3976{\cdot}45\ N\ (Ans.)}$$

Example 6.70. *An open cylindrical vessel* 180 *mm in diameter and* 450 *mm deep is filled with water up to the top. Estimate the volume of water left in the vessel when it is rotated about its vertical axis*:

(*i*) *With a speed of 200 r.p.m., and*

(*ii*) *With a speed of 400 r.p.m.*

Solution. Radius of the vessel, $R = \dfrac{180}{2} = 90$ mm $= 0.09$ m

Initial height of water $= 450$ mm $= 0.45$ m

$\therefore$ Initial volume of water $= \pi \times 0.09^2 \times 0.45 = 0.01145$ m^2

(*i*) Volume of water left at a speed of 200 r.p.m.:

$$\text{Angular speed, } \omega = \frac{2\pi N}{60} = \frac{2\pi \times 200}{60} = 20.94 \text{ rad./s}$$

Height of parabola is given by:

$$z = \frac{\omega^2 R^2}{2g} = \frac{(20.94)^2 \times 0.09^2}{2 \times 9.81} = 0.181 \text{ m}$$

Since the vessel is initially full of water, water will be spilled when it is rotated.

Volume of water spilled = Volume of paraboloid.

But, volume of paraboloid, $= \frac{1}{2}$ (Area of cross-section × height of parabola)

$$= \frac{1}{2} \times \pi R^2 \times z = \frac{1}{2} \times \pi \times 0.09^2 \times 0.181 = 0.002303 \text{ m}^3$$

∴ Volume of water left = Initial volume – volume of water spilled

$= 0.01145 - 0.00203 = \mathbf{0.009147\ m^3}$ **(Ans.)**

(*ii*) Volume of water left at a speed of 400 r.p.m.:

$$\text{Angular speed, } \omega = \frac{2\pi N}{60} = \frac{2\pi \times 400}{60} = 41.88 \text{ rad/s}$$

$$\text{Height of the parabola, } z = \frac{\omega^2 R^2}{2g} = \frac{(41.88)^2 \times 0.09^2}{2 \times 9.81} = 0.724 \text{ m}$$

Since the height of parabola is more than the height of the cylinder, therefore, the shape of the imaginary parabola will be as shown in Fig. 6.71

Let, r = Radius of the parabola at the bottom of the vessel

$= 0.724 - 0.45 = 0.274$ m

Volume of water left in the vessel

= Volume of water in the portions *LMN* and *PQS*

= Initial volume of water–volume of paraboloid *LOS* + volume of paraboloid *NOP*

Now, volume of paraboloid *LOS*

$$= \frac{1}{2} (\pi R^2 \times \text{height of parabola})$$

$$= \frac{1}{2} \times \pi \times 0.092 \times 0.724 = 0.00921 \text{ m}^2$$

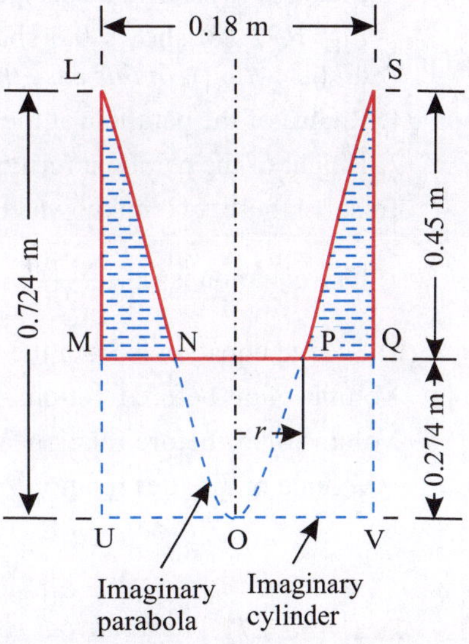

Fig. 6.71

For the imaginary parabola (*NOP*),

ω = 41.88 r.p.m.

z = 0.274 m

r = Radius at the bottom of the vessel

Using the relation,

$$z = \frac{\omega^2 r^2}{2g}, \text{ we get:}$$

$$0.274 = \frac{41.88^2 \times r^2}{2 \times 9.81}$$

$$\text{or, } r^2 = \frac{0.274 \times 2 \times 9.81}{41.88^2} = 0.003065 \text{ m}^2$$

$$\therefore \quad r = 0.0554 \text{ m}$$

∴ Volume of paraboloid *NOP*

$$= \frac{1}{2}(\text{area at the top of the imaginary parabola} \times \text{height of parabola})$$

$$= \frac{1}{2} \times \pi r^2 \times 0.274$$

$$= \frac{1}{2} \times \pi \times 0.0554^2 \times 0.274 = 0.00132 \text{ m}^3$$

∴ Volume of water left

$$= 0.01145 - 0.00921 + 0.00132$$

$$= \mathbf{0.00356\ m^3}\ \textbf{(Ans.)}$$

6.11.5. Rotation of Liquid in a Closed Cylindrical Vessel

When a cylindrical vessel sealed at the top and filled with some liquid is rotated about its vertical geometrical axis, the shape of paraboloid formed due to rotation of the vessel will be as shown in Fig 6.72 for different speeds of rotation.

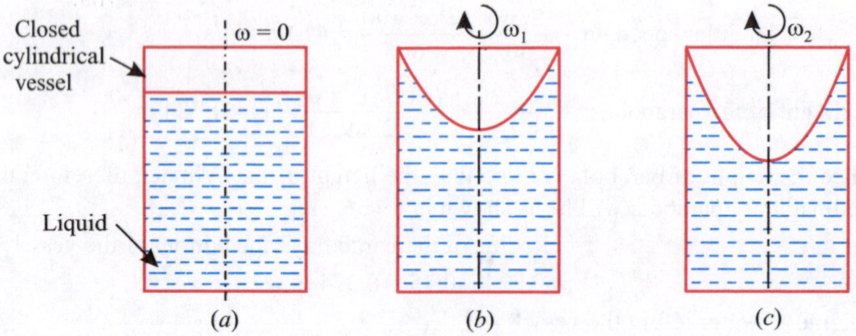

Fig. 6.72. Rotation of liquid in a closed cylindrical vessel.

— Fig. 6.72 (*a*) shows the cylindrical vessel when it is *stationary* (*i.e.,* it is not rotated, $\omega = 0$)

— Fig. 6.72 (*b*) shows the shape of the paraboloid formed when the *speed of rotation is* ω_1.

— Fig. 6.72 (*c*) shows the shape of the paraboloid formed when the *speed of rotation is* $\omega_2 (\omega_2 > \omega_1)$. *In this case the following are unknown*:

1. Radius of the parabola at the top of the vessel, and
2. Height of the parabola formed corresponding to the angular speed, ω_2.

To solve these, two unknown equations are required:

(*i*) One equation is: $z = \dfrac{\omega^2 r^2}{2g}$ ...(*i*)

(*ii*) Second equation is from the fact that for closed Vessel:

Volume of air before rotation = Volume of air after rotation

Volume of air before rotation = Volume of closed vessel – volume of liquid in the vessel

Volume of air after rotation = Volume of paraboloid formed

$$= \frac{1}{2}\pi r^2 \times z.$$

Example 6.71. *A cylindrical vessel closed at the top and bottom is 0.24 m in diameter, 1.44 m long and contains water up to height of 0.96 m.*

(*i*) *Find the height of paraboloid formed, if it is rotated at 480 r.p.m about its vertical axis.*

(*ii*) *Find the speed of rotation of the vessel, when axial depth of water is zero.*

Solution. Radius of the vessel,

$$R = \frac{0.24}{2} = 0.12\text{ m}$$

Length of the vessel, L = 1.44 m

Initial height of water = 0.96 m

(*i*) Height of the paraboloid, *z*:

Speed, $N = 480$ r.p.m.

$$\therefore \quad \omega = \frac{2\pi N}{60} = \frac{2\pi \times 480}{60} = 50.26 \text{ rad/s}$$

When the vessel is rotated, paraboloid is formed (Fig. 6.73)

Let, r = Radius of paraboloid at the top of the vessel, and

z = Height of the paraboloid.

As the vessel is closed one, therefore,

Volume of air before rotation = Volume of air after rotation

or, $$\pi R^2 L - \pi R^2 \times 0.96 = \frac{1}{2}\pi r^2 z$$

or, $$\pi R^2 (1.44 - 0.96) = \frac{1}{2}\pi r^2 z$$

or, $r^2 z = 2 \times 0.12^2 (1.44 - 0.96) = 0.0138$ ...(*i*)

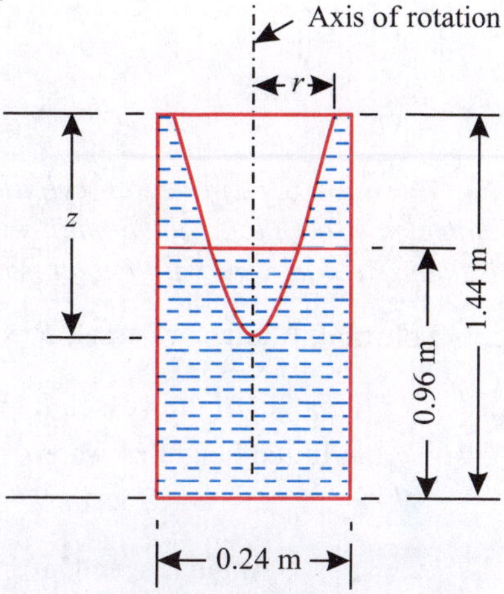

Fig. 6.73

Using the relation,

$$z = \frac{\omega^2 r^2}{2g}, \text{ we get:}$$

$$z = \frac{50.26^2 \times r^2}{2 \times 9.81} = 128.75 r^2$$

$$\therefore \quad r^2 = \frac{z}{128.75}$$

Substituting this value of r^2 in (*i*), we get:

$$= \frac{z}{128.75} \times z = 0.0138$$

$$\therefore \quad z^2 = 0.0138 \times 128.75 = 1.777$$

or, z = **1.333 m (Ans.)**

(*ii*) Speed of rotation, N:

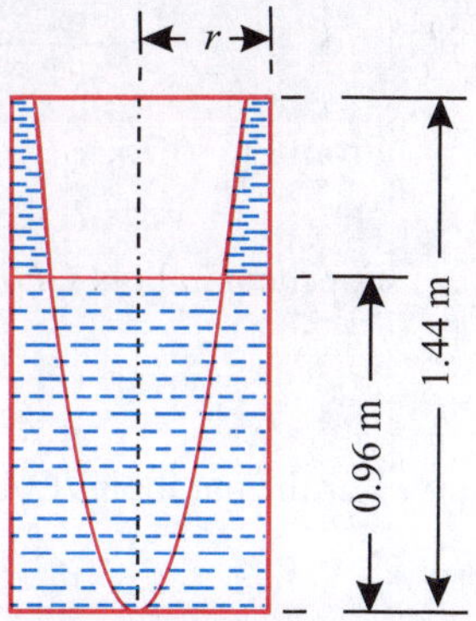

Fig. 6.74

Let ω is the angular velocity, when axial depth is zero.

When axial depth is zero:

The height of paraboloid at the top = r

Using the relation,

$$z = \frac{\omega^2 r^2}{2g}, \text{ we get:}$$

$$1.44 = \frac{\omega^2 r^2}{2 \times 9.81}$$

$$\therefore \quad \omega^2 r^2 = 1.44 \times 2 \times 9.81 = 28.25 \quad ...(i)$$

Volume of air before rotation = Volume of air after rotation

$$\therefore \quad \pi R^2 (1.44 - 0.96) = \text{Volume of paraboloid}$$

$$= \frac{1}{2}\pi r^2 z = \frac{\pi r^2}{2} \times 1.44$$

or, $$\pi \times 0.12^2 \times 0.48 = 0.72\, \pi r^2$$

$$\therefore \quad r^2 = \frac{0.12^2 \times 0.48}{0.72} = 0.0096$$

Substituting the value r^2 in (*i*), we get:

$$\omega^2 \times 0.0096 = 28.25$$

$$\therefore \quad \omega = \left(\frac{28.25}{0.0096}\right)^{1/2} = 54.25 \text{ rad/s}$$

But, $\omega = \frac{2\pi N}{60} \quad \therefore \quad 54.25 = \frac{2\pi N}{60}$

or, $N = \frac{54.25 \times 60}{2\pi} =$ **518 r.p.m. (Ans.)**

Example 6.72. *A vessel, cylindrical in shape and closed at the top and bottom, is* 0.24 *m in diameter,* 1.44 *m long and contains water up to a height of* 0.96 *m. If it is rotated at* 700 *r.p.m. what is the area uncovered at the bottom of the tank?*

Solution. Radius of vessel, $R = \frac{0.24}{2} = 0.12$ m

Length of the vessel, L = 1.44 m

Initial height of water = 0.96 m

Speed, N = 700 r.p.m.

$$\therefore \quad \text{Angular speed, } \omega = \frac{2\pi N}{60} = \frac{2\pi \times 700}{40} = 73.3 \text{ rad/s}$$

Area uncovered at the bottom of the tank:

If the tank is not closed at the top and also is very long, then the height of parabola corresponding to ω = 73.3 rad/s will be

$$= \frac{\omega^2 R^2}{2g} = \frac{73.3^2 \times 0.12^2}{2 \times 9.81} = 3.943 \text{ m}$$

From Fig. 6.75, $y_1 + 1.44 + y_2 = 3.943$

or, $y_1 + y_2 = 2.503$ m ...(*i*)

For the parabola *GOH,* we have:

$$(1.44 + y_1) = \frac{\omega^2 r_1^2}{2g} = \frac{73.3^2 \times r_1^2}{2 \times 9.81} = 273.85\, r_1^2 \quad ...(ii)$$

For the parabola *IOJ,* we have:

$$y_1 = \frac{\omega^2 r_2^2}{2g} = \frac{73.3^2 \times r_2^2}{2 \times 9.81} = 273.85\, r_2^2 \quad ...(iii)$$

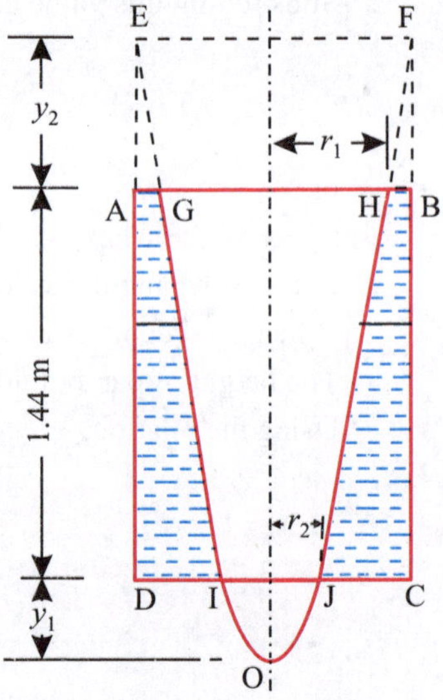

Fig. 6.75

Now, Volume of air before rotation

= Volume of air after rotation

Volume of air before rotation

$$= \pi R^2 (1.44 - 0.96) = \pi \times 0.12^2 \times 0.48$$

$$= 0.0217 \text{ m}^3 \quad ...(iv)$$

Volume of air after rotation = Volume of paraboloid *GOH* – volume of paraboloid *IOJ*.

$$= \frac{1}{2} \times \pi r_1^2 \times (1.44 + y_1) - \frac{1}{2} \pi r_2^2 \times y_1 \quad ...(v)$$

Equating (*iv*) and (*v*), we get:

$$0.0217 = \frac{\pi}{2}[r_1^2 (1.44 + y_1) - r_2^2 y_1] \quad ...(vi)$$

But from (*ii*), we have: $r_1^2 = \left(\frac{1.44 + y_1}{273.85}\right)$

Substituting this value of r_1^2 in (*vi*), we get:

$$0.0217 = \frac{\pi}{2}\left[\left(\frac{1.44 + y_1}{273.85}\right)(1.44 + y_1) - r_2^2 y_1\right]$$

Now, substituting the value of y_1 from (*iii*) in the above eqn., we get:

$$0.0217 = \frac{\pi}{2}\left[\left(\frac{1.44 + 273.85\, r_2^2}{273.85}\right)(1.44 + 273.85 r_2^2) - r_2^2 \times 273.85 r_2^2\right]$$

or, $$\frac{0.0217 \times 2 \times 273.85}{\pi} = (1.44 + 273.85\, r_2^2)^2 - (273.85)^2\, r_2^4$$

$$\left[\text{Multiplying both sides by } 273.85 \times \frac{2}{\pi}\right]$$

or, $$3.783 = (2.074 + 788.69\, r_2^2 + 74994\, r_2^4) - 74994\, r_2^4$$

or, $$788.69 r_2^2 = 1.709$$

or, $$r_2^2 = 0.002167 \text{ m}^2$$

∴ Area uncovered at the base

$$= \pi\, r_2^2 = \pi \times 0.002167 = \mathbf{0.0068\ m^2}\ \textbf{(Ans.)}$$

Example 6.73. *A vessel, cylindrical in shape and closed at the top and bottom, is 0.45 m in diameter and 1.5 m long. It contains water up to a depth of 1.2 m. The air above the water surface is at a pressure of 90 kN/m². If the vessel is rotated at a speed of 300 r.p.m. about its vertical axis find the pressure head at the bottom of the vessel:*

(i) At the centre, and *(ii) At the edge.*

Solution. Radius of the vessel,

$$R = \frac{0.45}{2} = 0.225 \text{ m}$$

Length of the vessel, $L = 1.5$ m

Initial height of water $= 1.2$ m

Pressure of air above water, $p = 90$ kN/m²

Head due to pressure, $h = \frac{p}{w} = \frac{90}{9.81} = 9.17$ m

(∵ w for water = 9.81 kN/m³)

Speed of the vessel, $N = 300$ r.p.m.

∴ Angular velocity,

$$\omega = \frac{2\pi N}{60} = \frac{2\pi \times 300}{60} = 31.41 \text{ rad/s}$$

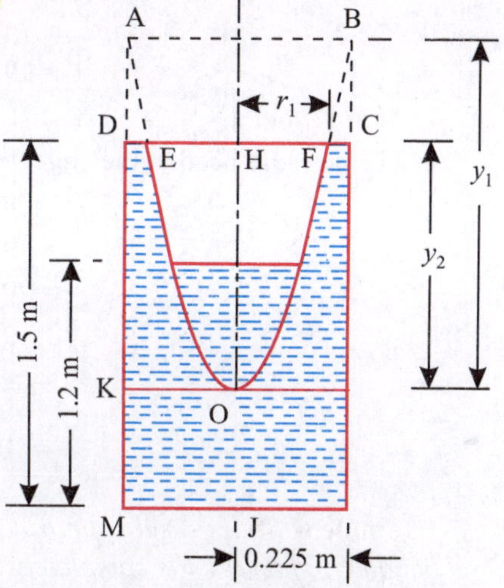

Fig. 6.76

Let, y_1 = Height of paraboloid formed (assuming vessel to be very long and open at the top).

Then, $$y_1 = \frac{\omega^2 R^2}{2g} = \frac{31.41^2 \times 0.225^2}{2 \times 9.81} = 2.545 \text{ m} \quad ...(i)$$

Let, r_1 = Radius of actual parabola of height y_2.

Then, $$y_2 = \frac{\omega^2 r_1^2}{2g} = \frac{31.41^2 \times r_1^2}{2 \times 9.81} = 50.28\, r_1^2 \qquad ...(ii)$$

The volume of air before rotation

$$= \pi R^2 (1.5 - 1.2) = \pi \times 0.225^2 \times 0.3 = 0.0477 \text{ m}^3$$

Volume of air after rotation

$$= \frac{1}{2} \pi r_1^2 \times y_2$$

But, Volume of air before rotation = Volume of air after rotation

$$\therefore \quad 0.0477 = \frac{1}{2} \pi r_1^2 y_2$$

But from (*ii*), $$y_2 = 50.28\, r_1^2$$

$$\therefore \quad 0.0477 = \frac{1}{2} \pi r_1^2 \times 50.28 r_1^2$$

or, $$r_1^4 = \frac{0.0477 \times 2}{\pi \times 50.28} = 6.039 \times 10^{-4} \text{ m}^4$$

or, $$r_1 = (6.039 \times 10^{-4})^{1/4} = 0.156 \text{ m}$$

Substituting the value of r_1 in (*ii*), we get:

$$y_2 = 50.28\, r_1^2 = 50.28 \times (0.156)^2 = 1.224 \text{ m}$$

Pressure head at bottom of the vessel:

***(i) At the centre*:**

The pressure head at the centre *i.e.,* at J.

$$= \text{Pressure head due to air} + OJ$$

$$= 9.17 + (HJ - HO) \qquad (\because OJ = HJ - HO)$$

$$= 9.17 + (1.5 - 1.224) \qquad \left\{ \begin{array}{l} HJ = 1.5 \text{ m} \\ HO = y_2 = 1.224 \text{ m} \end{array} \right\}$$

$$= \textbf{9.446 m of water (Ans.)}$$

***(ii) At the edge*:**

The pressure head at the edge *M*

$$= \text{Pressure head due to air} + \text{height of water above } M$$

$$= 9.17 + AM$$

$$= 9.17 + (AK + KM) = 9.17 + (y_1 + KM)$$

$$= 9.17 + (y_1 + OJ)$$

$$= 9.17 + 2.545 + 0.276 \qquad (\because y_1 = 2.545 \text{ m})$$

$$= \textbf{11.99 m of water (Ans.)} \qquad \left[\begin{array}{l} OJ = HJ - HO \\ \quad = 1.5 - 1.224 = 0.276 \text{ m} \end{array} \right]$$

Example 6.74. *A vessel cylindrical in shape and closed at the top and bottom is of radius R and height H. The vessel is completely filled with water. If it is rotated about its vertical axis with a speed ω radians/sec., what is the total pressure force exerted by water on the top and bottom of the vessel ?*

Solution. Radius of the vessel = R

Height of the vessel = H

Angular speed = ω

As the vessel is closed and completely filled with water, and when it is rotated, the water will exert force on the complete top and bottom of the vessel.

Total pressure force exerted on the top of the vessel, F_{top}:

As the top of the vessel is in contact with water and is in horizontal plane, the pressure variation at any radius in horizontal plane is given as:

$$\frac{\partial p}{\partial r} = \frac{\rho v^2}{r} \qquad \text{[Eqn. (6.35)]}$$

$$= \frac{\rho\omega^2 r^2}{r} = \rho\omega^2 r \qquad [\because v = \omega r)$$

Integrating both sides, we get:

$$\int dp = \int \rho\omega^2 r dr$$

or, $$p = \frac{\rho}{2}\omega^2 r^2$$

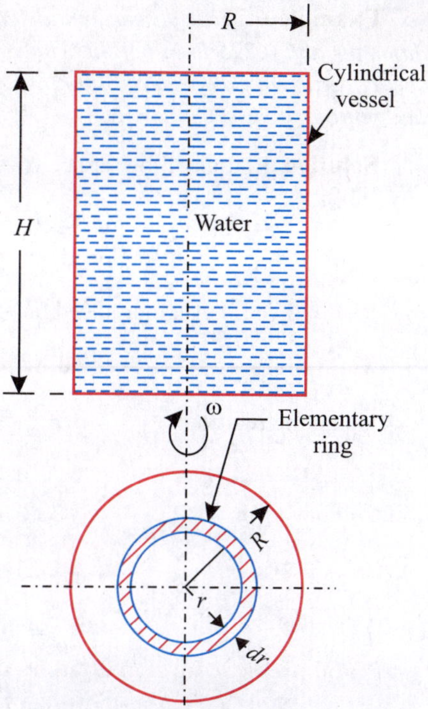

Fig. 6.77

Refer to Fig. 6.77. Consider an elementary ring of radius r and width dr on the top of the vessel.

Area of the elementary ring = $2\pi r dr$

Force on the elementary ring = Intensity of pressure × area of ring

$$= p \times 2\pi r\, dr$$

$$= \frac{\rho}{2}\omega^2 r^2 \times 2\pi r . dr \qquad \left(\because p = \frac{\rho}{2}\omega^2 r^2\right)$$

∴ Total force on the top of the vessel,

$$F_{top} = \int_0^R \frac{\rho}{2}\omega^2 r^2 \times 2\pi r\, dr$$

$$= \frac{\rho}{2}\omega^2 \times 2\pi \int_0^R r^3 dr$$

$$= \frac{\rho}{2}\omega^2 \times 2\pi \left[\frac{r^4}{4}\right]_0^R = \frac{\rho}{2}\omega^2 \times 2\pi \times \frac{R^4}{4}$$

$$= \frac{\rho}{4}\omega^2 \times \pi R^4$$

i.e., $$F_{top} = \frac{\rho}{4}\omega^2 \pi R^4 \qquad \text{...(6.39)}$$

Total pressure force exerted on the bottom of the vessel, F_{bottom}:

F_{bottom} = Total force on the top of the vessel + Weight of water in cylinder

$$= \frac{\rho}{4}\omega^2 \pi R^4 + \omega \times \pi R^2 \times H$$

i.e., $$F_{bottom} = \frac{\rho}{4}\omega\pi R^4 + \omega\pi R^2 H \qquad \text{...(6.40)}$$

Example 6.75. *A vessel cylindrical in shape and closed at the top and bottom is 0.3 m in diameter and 0.225 m in height. The vessel is completely filled with water. If it is rotated about its vertical axis with a speed of 300 r.p.m., what is the total pressure force exerted by water on the top and bottom of vessel ?*

Solution. Radius of the vessel, $R = \frac{0.3}{2} = 0.15\,\text{m}$

Height of the vessel, $H = 0.225$ m.

Speed, $N = 300$ r.p.m.

$\therefore$ Angular speed, $\omega = \frac{2\pi N}{60} = \frac{2\pi \times 300}{60} = 31.41$ rad/sec

Total pressure force exerted by water on the top of the vessel, F_{top}:

Using the relation: $F_{top} = \frac{\rho}{4} \times \omega^2 \times \pi R^4$ [Eqn. (6.39)]

$$= \frac{w}{g \times 4} \omega^2 \pi R^4 \qquad \left[\because \rho = \frac{w}{g},\ w = 9.81\ \text{kN/m}^3\right]$$

$$= \frac{9.81}{9.81 \times 4} \times (31.41)^2 \times \pi \times (0.15)^4 = 0.392\ \text{kN}$$

i.e., F_{top} **= 0.392 kN (Ans.)**

Total pressure force exerted by water on the bottom of the vessel, F_{bottom}:

$$F_{\text{bottom}} = F_{\text{top}} + w \times \pi R^2 \times H$$

$$= 0.392 + 9.81 \times \pi \times 0.15^2 \times 0.225 = 0.548\ \text{kN}$$

$\therefore$ F_{bottom} **= 0.548 kN (Ans.)**

Example 6.76. *A closed vertical cylinder 0.4 m in diameter and 0.4 m in height is completely filled with oil of specific gravity 0.80. If the cylinder is rotated about its vertical axis at 200 rpm, calculate the thrust of oil on top and bottom covers of the cylinder.* **(UPTU)**

Solution. *Given:* $R = \frac{0.4}{2} = 0.2\,\text{m};\ H = 0.4\ \text{m};\ S = 0.8;\ N = 200$ r.p.m.

F_{top}:

Using the relation: $F_{top} = \frac{\rho}{4} \omega^2 \times \pi R^4$ [Eqn. (6.39)]

$$= \frac{0.8 \times 1000}{4} \times \left(\frac{2\pi \times 200}{60}\right)^2 \times \pi \times (0.2)^4 = \mathbf{440.98\ N}\ \textbf{(Ans.)}$$

Again, using the relation: $F_{\text{bottom}} = F_{top} + w \times \pi R^2 \times H$

$$= 440.98 + (0.8 \times 1000 \times 9.81) \times \pi \times 0.2^2 \times 0.4$$

$$= \mathbf{835.46\ N}\ \textbf{(Ans.)}$$

Example 6.77. *A hollow sphere of radius R, completely filled with the liquid, is rotated about its vertical axis at an angular speed ω. Locate the circular line maximum pressure with respect to the centre of the sphere.* **(Delhi University)**

Solution. The circular line of maximum pressure will be a horizontal circle on the internal surface of the circle *aa*. Let its location be at a distance *h* below the centre of the sphere. All points on the circle *aa* will be subjected to a centrifugal pressure $\frac{1}{2}\rho\omega^2 r^2$, and a hydrostatic pressure $\rho g (R + h)$.

The total pressure on any point,

$$p = \frac{1}{2}\rho\omega^2 r^2 + \rho g(R+h)$$

$$= \frac{1}{2}\rho\omega^2 r^2 + \rho g\left\{R + \sqrt{R^2 - r^2}\right\} \quad (\because h = \sqrt{R^2 - r^2})$$

For p to be maximum:

$$\frac{dp}{dr} = 0 = \frac{1}{2}\rho\omega^2 \times 2r + \rho g\left\{\frac{1}{2}(R - r^2)^{-1/2} \times (-2r)\right\}$$

or, $\frac{\omega^2}{g} = \frac{1}{\sqrt{R^2 - r^2}}$ or $(R^2 - r^2) = \left(\frac{g}{\omega^2}\right)^2$

or, $h^2 = R^2 - r^2 = \left(\frac{g}{\omega^2}\right)^2$ or $h = \frac{g}{\omega^2}$

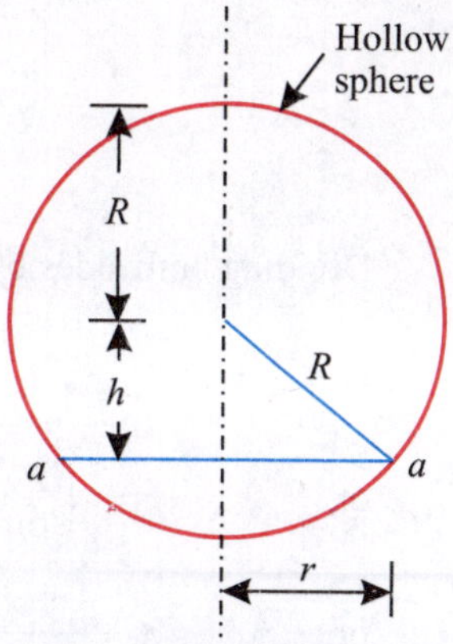

Fig. 6.78

Thus the circular line of maximum pressure is a horizontal circle, at a distance $h = \frac{g}{\omega^2}$ below the centre of the sphere. **(Ans.)**

6.11.6. Equation of Free Vortex Flow

In the case of free vortex flow, from eqn. (6.34), we have:

$$v = \frac{C}{r}$$

Substituting the value of v in eqn. (6.37), we get:

$$dp = \frac{\rho v^2}{r} dr - \rho g\, dz$$

$$= \rho \times \frac{C^2}{r^2 \times r} dr - \rho g dz$$

$$= \frac{\rho C^2}{r^3} dr - \rho g\, dz$$

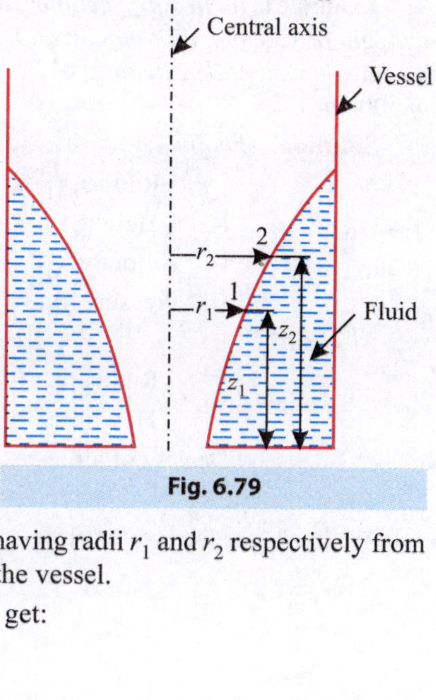

Fig. 6.79

Refer to Fig. 6.79. Consider two points 1and 2 in the fluid having radii r_1 and r_2 respectively from the central axis, their heights being z_1 and z_2 from bottom of the vessel.

Integrating the above equation for the points 1 and 2, we get:

$$\int_1^2 dp = \int_1^2 \frac{\rho C^2}{r^3} dr - \int_1^2 \rho g\, dz$$

or, $$p_2 - p_1 = \rho C^2 \int_1^2 \frac{dr}{r^3} - \rho g \int_1^2 dz$$

$$= \rho C^2 \left[\frac{r^{-3+1}}{-3+1}\right]_1^2 - \rho g(z_2 - z_1)$$

$$= \rho C^2 \left[-\frac{1}{2r^2}\right]_1^2 - \rho g(z_2 - z_1)$$

$$= -\frac{\rho C^2}{2}\left[\frac{1}{r_2^2} - \frac{1}{r_1^2}\right] - \rho g(z_2 - z_1)$$

$$= -\frac{\rho}{2}[v_2^2 - v_1^2] - \rho g(z_2 - z_1) \qquad \left(\because v_2 = \frac{C}{r_2}, v_1 = \frac{C}{r_1}\right)$$

$$= \frac{\rho}{2}(v_1^2 - v_2^2) - \rho g(z_2 - z_1)$$

Dividing both sides by ρg, we get:

$$\frac{p_2 - p_1}{\rho g} = \frac{v_1^2 - v_2^2}{2g} - (z_2 - z_1)$$

or,
$$\left(\frac{p_2}{\rho g} - \frac{p_1}{\rho g}\right) = \left(\frac{v_1^2}{2g} - \frac{v_2^2}{2g}\right) + (z_1 - z_2)$$

or,
$$\frac{p_1}{\rho g} + \frac{v_1^2}{2g} + z_1 = \frac{p_2}{\rho g} + \frac{v_2^2}{2g} + z_2 \qquad ...(6.41)$$

Eqn. (6.41) is the Bernoulli's equation. Hence *Bernoulli's equation is applicable in the case of free vortex flow.*

Example 6.78. *In a free cylindrical vortex flow, at a point in the fluid at a radius of* 300 *mm and a height of* 150 *mm, the velocity and pressure are* 15 *m/s and* 120 *kN/m²* *respectively. If the fluid is air having weight density of* 0.012 *kN/m³, find the pressure at a radius of* 600 *mm and at a height of* 300 *mm.*

Solution. *At point* 1:

Radius, r_1 = 300 mm = 0.3 m
Height, z_1 = 150 mm = 0.15 m
Velocity, v_1 = 15 m/s
Pressure, p_1 = 120 kN/m²

At point 2:

Radius, r_2 = 600 mm = 0.6 m
Height, z_2 = 300 mm = 0.3 m
Density of air, w = 0.012 kN/m²

Pressure, p_2:

We know, for free vortex flow:

$$v \times r = \text{constant} \qquad \text{[Eqn. (6.33)]}$$

$$\therefore \quad v_1 r_1 = v_2 r_2$$

or,
$$v_2 = \frac{v_1 r_1}{r_2} = \frac{15 \times 0.3}{0.6} = 7.5 \text{ m/s}$$

Using the equation:

$$\frac{p_1}{w} + \frac{v_1^2}{2g} + z_1 = \frac{p_2}{w} + \frac{v_2^2}{2g} + z_2$$

or,
$$\frac{120}{0.012} + \frac{15^2}{2 \times 9.81} + 0.15 = \frac{p_2}{w} + \frac{7.5^2}{2 \times 9.81} + 0.3$$

or,
$$10000 + 11.47 + 0.15 = \frac{p_2}{w} + 2.86 + 0.3$$

or,
$$10011.62 = \frac{p_2}{w} + 3.16$$

or, $\frac{p_2}{w} = 10008.46$

or, $p_2 = 0.012 \times 10008.46 = $ **120.1 kN/m² (Ans.)**

Example 6.79. *Two statonary, horizontal flat plates with an external diameter of 400 mm are placed 10 mm apart. A vertical pipe 50 mm in diameter delivers 0.005 m³/s of water to the centre of the plates. The water is discharged to the periphery of the plates at atmospheric pressure of 98 kN/m². Assuming radial flow and neglecting losses, determine the absolute pressure at the entrance of the flow.* **[UPSC Exams.]**

Solution. Diameter of annular space, d_i = 50 mm = 0.05 m

External diameter of the plate, d_0 = 400 mm = 0.4 m

Distance between the plates, t = 10 mm = 0.01 m

Atmospheric pressure, p_0 = 98 kN/m²

Discharge, Q = 0.005 m³/s

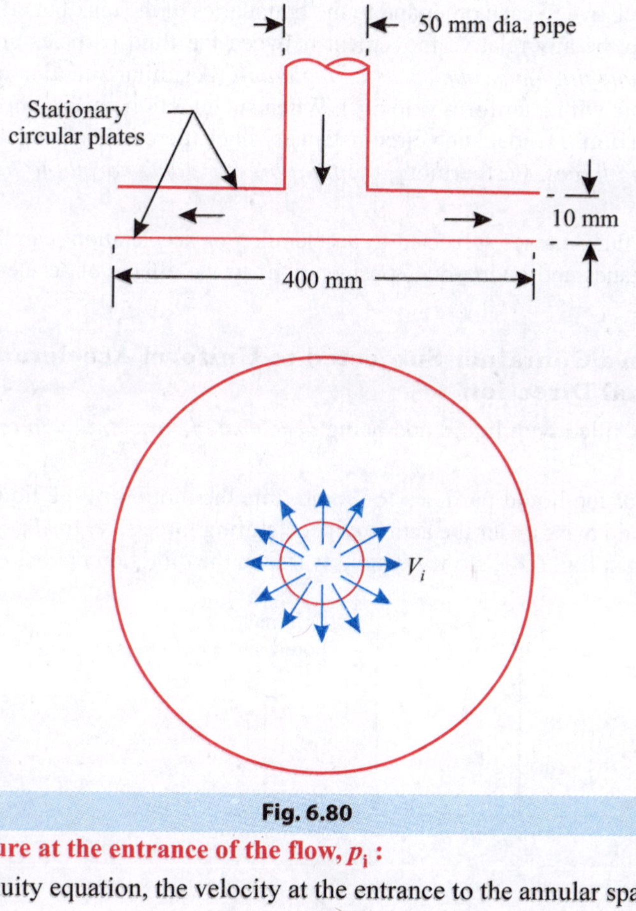

Fig. 6.80

Absolute pressure at the entrance of the flow, p_i :

Using the continuity equation, the velocity at the entrance to the annular space,

$$V_i = \frac{Q}{\pi d_i t} = \frac{0.005}{\pi \times 0.05 \times 0.01} = 3.18 \text{ m/s}$$

Velocity at the periphery of plates,

$$V_0 = \frac{Q}{\pi d_0 t} = \frac{0.005}{\pi \times 0.4 \times 0.01} = 0.398 \text{ m/s}$$

Applying the Bernoulli's equation between the inlet to and exit from plates, we get:

$$\frac{p_i}{w} + \frac{V_i^2}{2g} + z_i = \frac{p_0}{w} + \frac{V_0^2}{2g} + z_0$$

$$\frac{p_i}{w} + \frac{3.18^2}{2 \times 9.81} = \frac{98 \times 10^3}{9810} + \frac{0.398^2}{2 \times 9.81} \qquad (\because z_i = z_0)$$

or, $$\frac{p_i}{w} + 0.515 = 9.989 + 0.00807$$

or, $$\frac{p_i}{w} = 9.482 \quad \text{or} \quad p_i = 9810 \times 9.482 = 93018 \text{ N/m}^2 \text{ or } 93 \text{ kN/m}^2$$

Hence, $$p_i = \mathbf{93 \text{ kN/m}^2} \text{ (Ans.)}$$

6.12. LIQUIDS IN RELATIVE EQUILIBRIUM

When a tank filled with a liquid is made to move with a constant acceleration, initially the fluid particles will move relative to each other and to the boundaries of the tank but, after a certain duration of time there will not be any relative movement between the fluid particles and boundaries of the container and the *whole fluid mass moves as a single unit* (A similar situation arises when the fluid mass is made to rotate with a uniform velocity). When such motion occurs, the fluids are said to be in **"relative equilibrium"**. Under such circumstances, since there is relative motion, the fluid is *not subjected to shearing forces*. Furthermore, the *fluid pressure acts normal to the surface in contact with it.*

Analysis of the fluid masses subjected to acceleration or deceleration can be made by using the principles of hydrostatics and giving due considerations to the effects of accelerating or decelerating forces.

6.12.1. Liquid in a Container Subjected to Uniform Acceleration in the Horizontal Direction

Consider a tank filled with liquid and being *accelerated horizontally to the right with uniform acceleration* a_x.

After slashing of the liquid particles for some time the motion of the liquid stabilizes and the liquid moves as a solid mass under the action of accelerating force. The final position of the liquid in the tank is as shown in Fig. 6.81, slope being upwards in the direction opposite to that of horizontal acceleration.

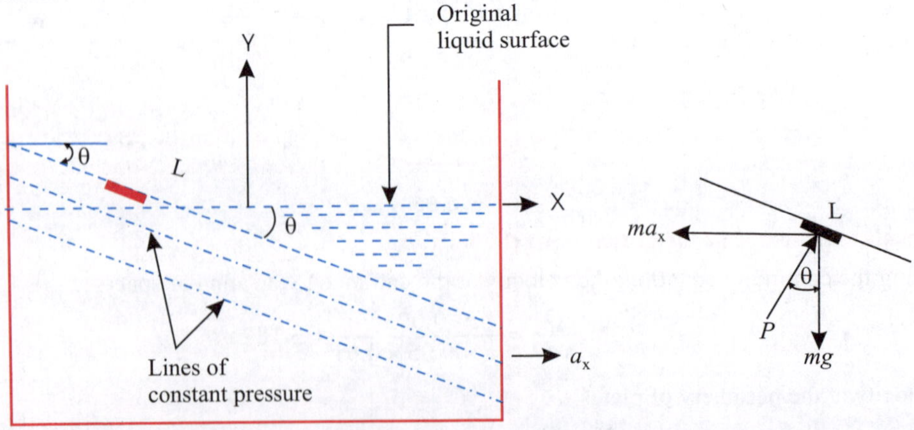

Fig. 6.81. Liquid under constant linear acceleration in horizontal direction.

Now, let us consider the equilibrium of a fluid particle L lying on the free surface. The pressure force P exerted by the surrounding fluid on particle L is normal to the free surface. The particle is subjected to the following forces:

(*i*) Normal pressure force P,

(*ii*) Weight mg acting vertically downwards, and

(*iii*) The accelerating force ma_x acting in horizontal direction.

Resolving horizontally and vertically respectively, we have:

$$P \sin \theta = ma_x \quad \text{...}(i)$$

$$P \cos \theta = mg \quad \text{...}(ii)$$

Dividing (*i*) by (*ii*), we get:

$$\tan \theta = \frac{a_x}{g} \quad \text{...(6.42)}$$

Since the term $\frac{a_x}{g}$ is constant at all points on the free liquid surface, hence $\tan \theta$ is constant and consequently the free surface is a straight plane inclined at θ (downward) along the direction of acceleration (See Fig. 6.81).

Considering the equilibrium of a fluid element at depth h from the free surface we have:

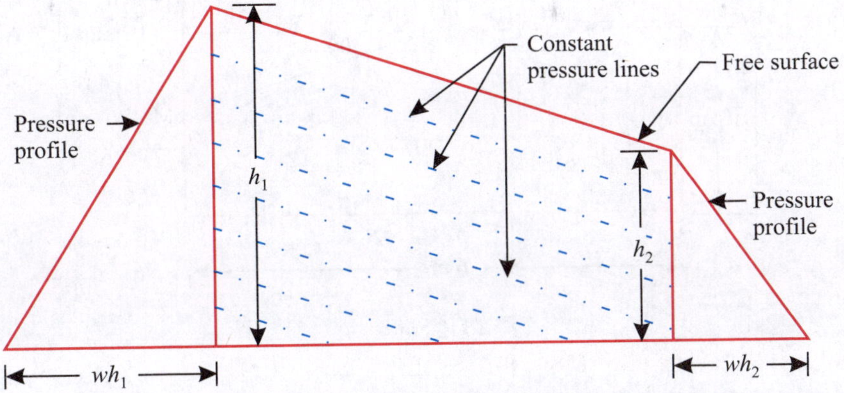

Fig. 6.82. Pressure distribution for horizontally accelerated fluid.

$$pdA = p_{atm.}dA + whdA$$

where,
p_{atm} = Atmospheric pressure, and
dA = Cross-sectional area of an elementary prism.

or,
$$p = p_{atm} + wh; \; p = wh \text{ (gauge)} \quad \text{... (6.43)}$$

This means that *pressure at any point in a liquid subjected to constant horizontal acceleration equals the head above that point.* Thus, *lines of constant pressure will be parallel to the free liquid surface*. Fig. 6.82 shows the constant pressure lines and the variation in liquid pressure on near and front of the tank. With the decrease in depth in the direction of acceleration, the pressure along the bottom of the tank also decreases.

- If the tank is completely filled with liquid and is closed at the top, the pressure builds up at the rear and is greater than that at the point (there being no preliminary adjustment in the surface elevation). The slope of the constant pressure lines is, however, still governed by the relation: $\tan \theta = \frac{a_x}{g}$.
- It may be noted that *so long as the container provides a continuous connection in the liquid mass, its shape does not matter.*

Note. The fuel tank of an aeroplane during take-off is *an example of liquid in a container subjected to uniform acceleration in the horizontal direction.*

Example 6.80. *An open tank 6 m long, 2.4 m deep and 3.6 m wide contains oil of specific gravity* 0.85 *to a depth of* 1.2 *m. If the tank is accelerated along its length on a horizontal track at a constant acceleration* 3.2 *m/s*^{2}, *determine*:

(*i*) *The new position of the oil surface.*

(*ii*) *Pressures at the bottom of the tank at the front and rear edges.*

(*iii*) *The amount of spill if the tank is given a horizontal acceleration of* 4.8 *m/s*^{2} *instead of* 3.2 *m/s*^{2}.

Solution. *Given*: Tank dimensions: 6 m (length) × 3.6 m (width) × 2.4 m (depth),

Sp. gr. of oil = 0.85; a_x = 3.2 m/s^2.

Refer to Fig. 6.83.

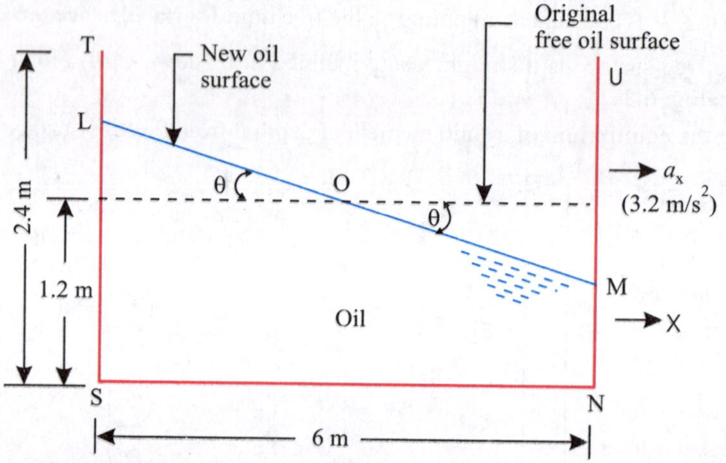

Fig. 6.83

(*i*) New position of the oil surface, θ:

Inclination of the new oil surface (θ) is given by:

$$\tan\theta = \frac{a_x}{g} = \frac{3.2}{9.81} = 0.3262$$

$$\therefore \qquad \theta = \tan^{-1}(0.3262) = \mathbf{18.07° \ (Ans.)}$$

(*ii*) Pressures at the bottom of the tank at the front and rear edges:

The depth of oil at the front edge N,

$$h_N = 1.2 - \frac{6}{2} \times \tan\theta$$

$$= 1.2 - 3 \times 0.3262 = 0.221 \text{ m}$$

The depth of oil at the rear edges,

$$h_S = 1.2 + \frac{6}{2} \times \tan\theta$$

$$= 1.2 + 3 \times 0.3262 = 2.179 \text{ m}$$

∴ Pressure at N, $p_N = wh_N$ = (9.81 × 0.85) × 0.221 = **1.843 kN/m^2 (Ans.)**

and, Pressure at S, $p_S = wh_S$ = (9.81 × 0.85) × 2.179 = **18.169 kN/m^2 (Ans.)**

(*iii*) The amount of spill with an acceleration of 4.8 m/s^2:

Refer to Fig. [6.84 (*i*)].

Inclination of the oil surface,

$$\tan\theta' = \frac{a_x}{g} = \frac{4.8}{9.81} = 0.4893$$

$$(\theta' = \tan^{-1}(0.4893) = 26.07°)$$

If there were no spill, the oil surface would swing about an axis at O. Piezometric head at N,

$$h'_S = 1.2 + \frac{6}{2}\tan\theta' = 1.2 + 3 \times 0.4893 = 2.668\,\text{m}$$

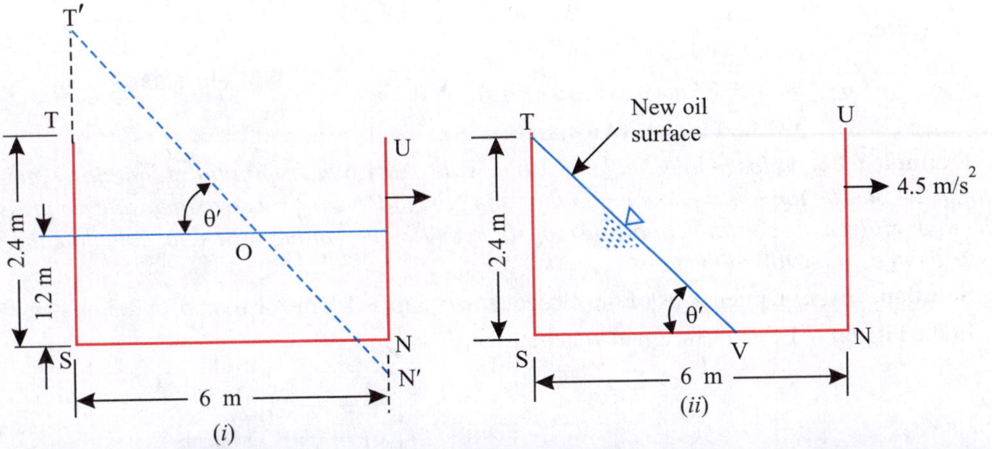

Fig. 6.84

Since this is larger than the depth of the tank there will be a spill of the oil. The new oil surface will have a depth of h_S = depth of tank = 2.4 m at S and a slope of θ′.

X-intercept of the surface at the bottom (SV) can be found from ΔTSV as follows.

$$\frac{TS}{SV} = \tan\theta'$$

or, $$SV = \frac{TS}{\tan\theta'} = \frac{2.4}{0.4893} = 4.9\,\text{m}$$

TV is the new oil surface [Fig. 6.84 (*ii*)].

$$\text{Volume of oil} = \Delta TSV \times \text{width of tank}$$

$$= \left(\frac{1}{2} \times 2.4 \times 4.9\right) \times 3.6 = 21.17\ \text{m}^3$$

$$\text{Original volume of oil} = 6 \times 3.6 \times 1.2 = 25.92\ \text{m}^3$$

∴ *Spill of oil* = 25.92 – 21.17 = **4.75 m³ (Ans.)**

Example 6.81. *A spherical tank of raidus 1.5 m radius is half-filled with oil of specific gravity 0.9. If the tank is given a horizontal acceleration of 11 m/s², calculate:*

(i) *The inclination of the oil surface to the horizontal.*

(ii) *Maximum pressure on the tank.*

Solution. *Given:* Radius of the tank, r = 1.5 m; Sp. gr. of oil = 0.9; a_x = 11 m/s².

***(i)* The inclination of the oil surface to the horizontal θ:**

Refer to Fig. 6.85: $$\tan\theta = \frac{a_x}{g} = \frac{11}{9.81} = 1.1213$$

∴ $$\theta = \tan^{-1}(1.1213) = \mathbf{48.3°}\ \textbf{(Ans.)}$$

(LM is the original oil surface and RS is the new oil surface. The surface tilts around 0).

***(ii)* Maximum pressure on the tank:**

The maximum pressure acts on the boundary point where the *depth* (*measured normal to the free surface*) *is maximum.*

In this case maximum depth is OT = r = 1.5 m

Hence, $\left(\frac{p}{w}\right)_{max} = 1.5$

or, $p_{max} = w \times 1.5 = (9.81 \times 0.9) \times 1.5$

$= \mathbf{13.24\ kN/m^2}$ **(Ans.)**

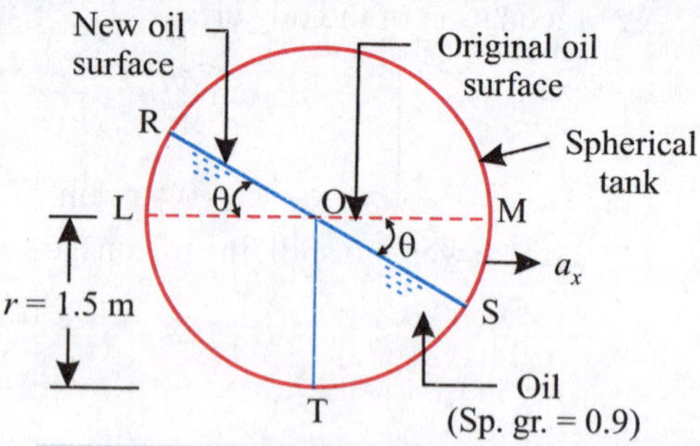

Fig. 6.85

Example 6.82. *A closed tank 5m long, 1.8 m wide and 1.6 m deep initially contains water to a depth of 1.1 m. The top has an opening in the front part to have air space at atmospheric pressure. If the tank is given acceleration at a constant value of 2.5 m/s² along its length, calculate the total pressure force on the top of the tank.*

Solution. *Given:* Dimensions of the closed tank = 5 m × 1.8 m × 1.6 m; $a_x = 2.5\ m/s^2$

In the Fig. 6.86. EF is the original water surface.

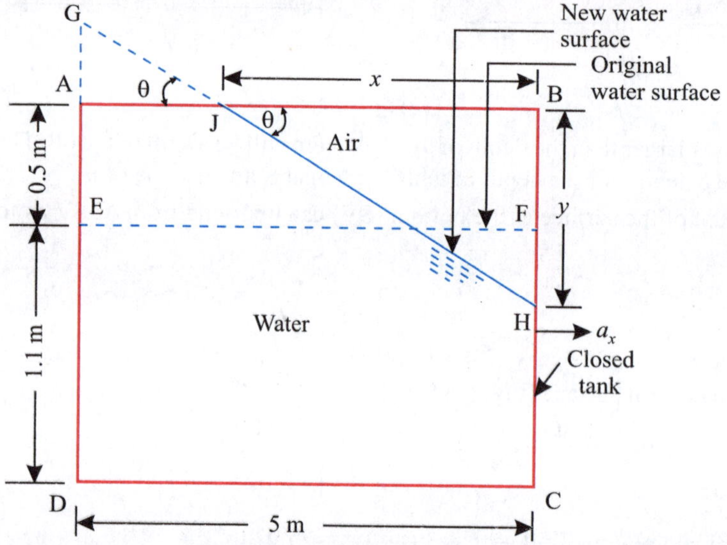

Fig. 6.86

After the acceleration of $a_x = 2.5\ m/s^2$, the water surface slope is

$$\tan\theta = \frac{a_x}{g} = \frac{2.5}{9.81} = 0.2548$$

or, $\theta = \tan^{-1}(0.2548) = 14.29°$

Since there is no spill of water, the air space will remain same as at start.

Air space volume, $V_{air} = 0.5 \times 5 \times 1.8 = 4.5\ m^3$

Let JH be the new water surface at an inclination of θ to the horizontal.

If, JB = x and BH = y, b = breadth of the tank, then:

$$y = x\tan\theta$$

and, $V_{air} = \frac{1}{2} \times x \times y \times b = \frac{1}{2} \times x \times \tan\theta \times b = \frac{1}{2} x^2 b \tan\theta$

or, $$4.5 = \frac{1}{2}x^2 \times 1.8 \times 0.2548$$

$\therefore$ $$x = 4.43 \text{ m, and } y = 4.43 \times 0.2548 = 1.13 \text{ m}$$

Hence CH = Depth of water in the front = 1.6 – 1.13 = 0.47 m

$$AJ = 5 - x = 5 - 4.43 = 0.57 \text{ m}$$

$$AG = AJ \tan \theta = 0.57 \times 0.2548 = 0.145 \text{ m}$$

The pressure profile on the top is represented by the ΔAGJ extending over the width. Pressure force on the top,

$$P_{top} = \left(\frac{1}{2} \times AG \times AJ \times \text{breadth}\right) \times w$$

$$= \frac{1}{2} \times 0.145 \times 0.57 \times 1.8 \times 9.81 = \mathbf{0.73\ kN}\ \textbf{(Ans.)}$$

The force acts vertically upwards at $\frac{AJ}{3} = \frac{0.57}{3} = 0.19$ m *from A at the mid-width section.*

Note: In this case free surface does not tilt at the mid-length. As there is no spill the volume of *water and air volume are conserved.*

Example 6.83. *A closed tank 12 m long, 3.6 m high and 2.4 m wide contains oil of specific gravity 0.85 and is given a horizontal acceleration of 0.28 g to the right in the direction of 12 m side.*

(i) Calculate: *The pressure difference between (a) a point on the top rear edge and a point on the front edge, and (b) a point on the bottom front edge and a point on the top front edge.*

(ii) *Sketch the lines of equal pressure.*

Solution. *Given*: Dimensions of the closed tank = 12 m × 2.4 m × 3.6 m;

Specific gravity of oil = 0.85; Horizontal acceleration, a_x = 0.28 g

Refer to Fig. 6.87. At an acceleration of a_x let UV be the hydraulic gradient line. Its inclination is given by,

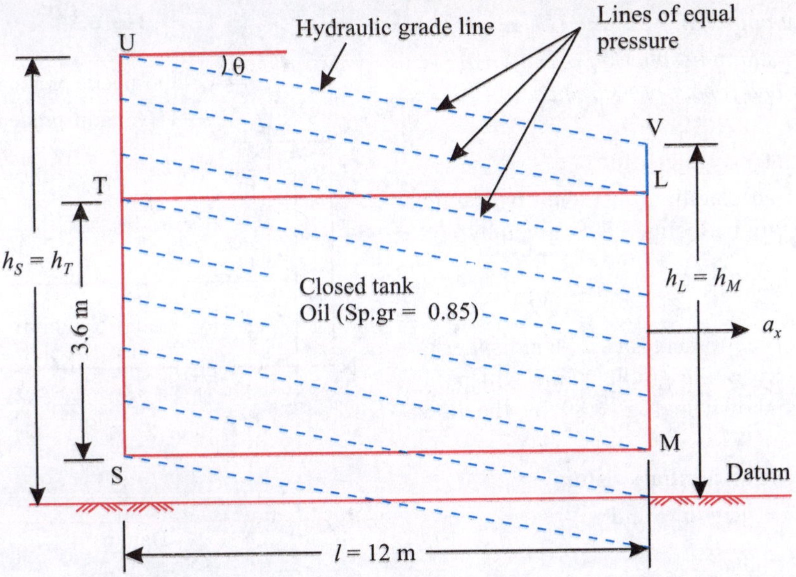

Fig. 6.87

$$\tan \theta = \frac{h_T - h_L}{l} = \frac{a_x}{g} = \frac{0.28\,g}{g} = 0.28$$

or, $\theta = \tan^{-1}(0.2) = 15.64°$

(a) $p_L - p_T$:

$$h_T - h_L = l \times \tan\theta = 12 \times 0.28 = 3.36 \text{ m}$$

But, $$h_T - h_L = \left(\frac{p_T}{w} + z_T\right) - \left(\frac{p_L}{w} + z_L\right)$$

Here, $$z_T = z_L$$

$\therefore$ $$p_T - p_L = w \times 3.36 = (9.81 \times 0.85) \times 3.36 = \mathbf{28.02\ kN/m^2\ (Ans.)}$$

(b) $p_M - p_L$:

Along ML the hydraulic gradient line is constant.

Hence, $$h_M = h_L$$

$$\left(\frac{p_M}{w} + z_M\right) - \left(\frac{p_L}{w} + z_L\right) = 0$$

or, $$p_M - p_L = w(z_L - z_M)$$
$$= (9.81 \times 0.85) \times 3.6 = \mathbf{30.02\ kN/m^2\ (Ans.)}$$

(*ii*) Since the pressure distribution is hydrostatic in any vertical direction and the hydraulic gradient line is inclined at θ to horiznotal (line UV) the lines of equal pressure will be parallel to UV, as shown in Fig. 6.87.

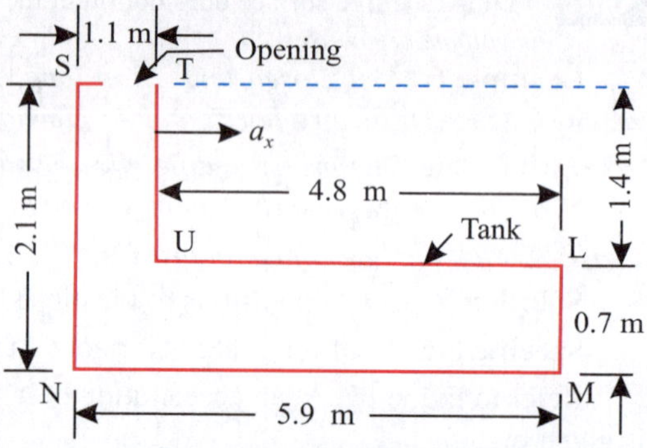

Fig. 6.88

Example 6.84. *A tank LMNSTU shown in Fig. 6.88. is filled with water. A small opening at T keeps the pressure at T atmospheric.*

(*i*) *Calculate the acceleration a_x required to cause onset of cavitation at L.*

(*ii*) *What will be the pressure at that acceleration at points M, N, S and U?*

Assume local atmospheric pressure head = 10 m of water and vapour pressure head = 0.48 m (abs.) of water.

Solution. (*i*) **Acceleration a_x:**

At the acceleration a_x the hydraulic gradient line will be inclined at θ, given by

$$\tan\theta = \frac{a_x}{g}$$

Since p_T = pressure at T = atmspheric pressure, the hydraulic gradient line will pass through T as shown in Fig. 6.89 by the line VTW.

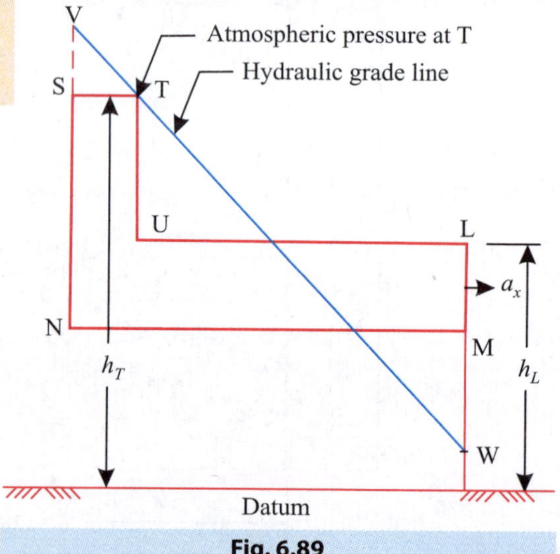

Fig. 6.89

Then above an arbitrary datum:

$$h_T = h_U, \text{ and}$$
$$h_L = h_M$$

Also, $h_T - h_L = LU \tan\theta = 4.8 \tan\theta$

At the onset of cavitation at L,

$$p_L = p_v = \text{Vapour pressure.}$$

Considering the absolute pressures,

$$h_T - h_L = \left(\frac{p_T}{w} + z_T\right) - \left(\frac{p_L}{w} + z_L\right)$$

$$= \left(\frac{p_T}{w} - \frac{p_L}{w}\right) + (z_T - z_L)$$

$$= (10 - 0.48) + (1.4) = 10.92 \text{ m}$$

But, $h_T - h_L = 4.8 \tan\theta$

Hence, $\tan\theta = \frac{a_x}{g} = \frac{h_T - h_L}{4.8} = \frac{10.92}{4.8} = 2.275$

or $a_x = 9.81 \times 2.275 =$ **22.32 m/s² (Ans.)**

(*ii*) Pressures at point M, N, S and U:

Pressure at M, p_M:

$$h_M - h_L = \left(\frac{p_M}{w} + z_M\right) - \left(\frac{p_L}{w} + z_L\right) = 0$$

$$\frac{p_M}{w} = \frac{p_T}{w} + (z_L - z_m) = 0.48 + 0.7 = 1.18 \text{ m}$$

∴ $p_M = 9.81 \times 1.18 =$ **11.576 kN/m² (abs.) (Ans.)**

Pressure at U, p_U:

$$h_T - h_U = \left(\frac{p_S}{w} + z_T\right) - \left(\frac{p_U}{w} + z_u\right) = 0$$

$$\frac{p_U}{w} = \frac{p_T}{w} + (z_T - z_u) = 10 + 1.4 = 1.4 \text{ m}$$

∴ $p_U = 9.81 \times 11.4 =$ **111.834 kN/m² (abs.) (Ans.)**

Pressure at S, p_S:

$$h_S - h_T = 1.1 \tan\theta = 1.1 \times 2.275 = 2.5 \text{ m}$$

Also, $h_S - h_T = \left(\frac{p_S}{w} + z_S\right) - \left(\frac{p_T}{w} + z_T\right) = 0$

$$\frac{p_S}{w} = \frac{p_T}{w} + (z_T - z_S) + 2.5$$

$$= 10 + 0 + 2.5 = 12.5 \text{ m}$$

∴ $p_S = 9.81 \times 12.5 =$ **122.625 kN/m² (Ans.)**

Pressure at N, p_N:

$$h_S - h_N = \left(\frac{p_S}{w} + z_S\right) - \left(\frac{p_N}{w} + z_N\right) = 0$$

$$\frac{p_N}{w} = \frac{p_S}{w} + (z_S - z_N)$$

$$= 12.5 + 2.1 = 14.6 \text{ m}$$

∴ $p_N = 9.81 \times 14.6 =$ **143.226 kN/m² (abs.) (Ans.)**

Example 6.85. *A closed oil tanker 3.5 m long, 1.8 m wide and 2 m deep contains 1.6 m depth of oil of specific gravity 0.8.* Calculate:

(*i*) *The acceleration which may be imparted to the tank in the direction of its length so that bottom front end of the tank is just exposed.*

(ii) The net horizontal force acting on the tanker side and show that this equals the force necessary to accelerate the liquid mass in the tanker.

Take specific weight of water = 9.81 kN/m³ **(Roorkee University)**

Solution. *Given*: Dimensions of the tank: 3.5 m (length) × 1.8 m (width) × 2 m (depth); Depth of oil = 1.6 m; Sp. gr. of oil = 0.8

(*i*) Acceleration a_x:

The following points are worth noting :

- Since the tank is closed, therefore, the liquid cannot spill from it under any acceleration imparted to it. The *quantity of oil inside the tank remains the same.*
- The oil surface which was initially horizontal (indicated by TU) assumes the profile MVS when the front bottom end M is just exposed.

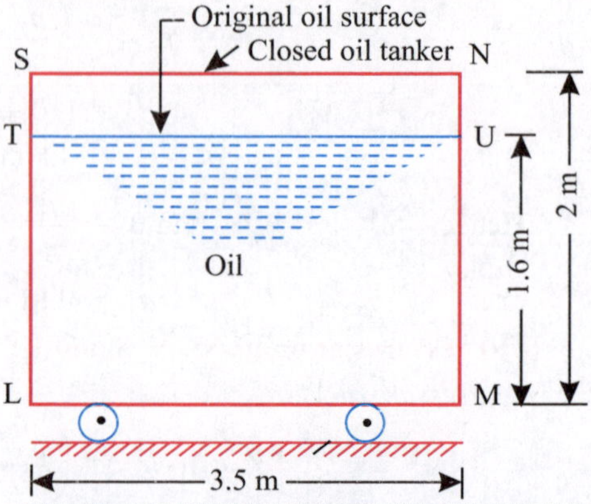

Fig. 6.90

Equating volumes of oil before and after the motion, we have:

Volume of rectangle LMUT = Volume of trapezium LMVS

$$3.5 \times 1.6 \times 1.8 = \frac{3.5 + (3.5 - x)}{2} \times 2 \times 1.8$$

$$\therefore \quad x = 1.4 \text{ m}$$

$$\tan\theta = \frac{MN}{NV} = \frac{2}{1.4} = 1.428$$

Also, $\tan\theta = \frac{a_x}{g} = 1.428$

$$\therefore \quad a_x = 9.81 \times 1.428 = \mathbf{14.01\ m/s^2}\ \textbf{(Ans.)}$$

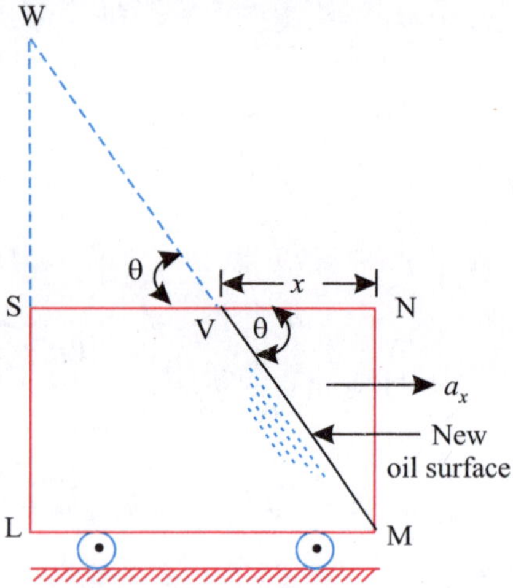

Fig. 6.91

When the free surface MV is extended, it meets LS produced at W.

$$\frac{SW}{SV} = \tan\theta = 1.428$$

$$\therefore \quad SW = (3.5 - 1.4) \times 1.428 = 3 \text{ m}$$

This represents an imaginary column of oil above S.

Now, $p_S = w \times SW = (9.81 \times 0.8) \times 3 = 23.544 \text{ kN/m}^2$

and, $p_L = w \times LW = (9.81 \times 0.8) \times (3 + 2) = 39.24 \text{ kN/m}^2$

∴ Pressure force on the trailing/rear face *LS*,

$$P_{LS} = p_{avg.} \times \text{area}$$

$$= \left(\frac{23.544 + 39.24}{2}\right) \times (2 \times 1.8) = \mathbf{113\ kN}$$

$$\left[\text{Alternatively: } P_{LS} = wA\bar{x} = (9.81 \times 0.8) \times (2 \times 1.8) \times \left(3 + \frac{2}{2}\right) = 113 \text{ kN}\right]$$

The force needed to accelerate the liquid mass in the tank,

$$F = \text{Mass of oil} \times \text{uniform linear acceleration}$$

$$= (0.8 \times 1000) \times 3.5 \times 1.6 \times 1.8 \times 14.01 \times 10^{-3} \text{ kN} \simeq \mathbf{113\ kN}\ \textbf{(Ans.)}$$

Obviously the difference between the force on the two ends of the tanker is *equal to* the force necessary to accelerate the liquid mass in the tanker.

6.12.2. Liquid in a Container Subjected to Uniform Acceleration in the Vertical Direction

Consider a tank containing liquid and moving vertically *upwards* with uniform acceleration a_y (Fig 6.92). The liquid in the tank will have a free horizontal surface *but pressure intensity at any point in the liquid will be different* from what it would be when in a state of absolute rest:

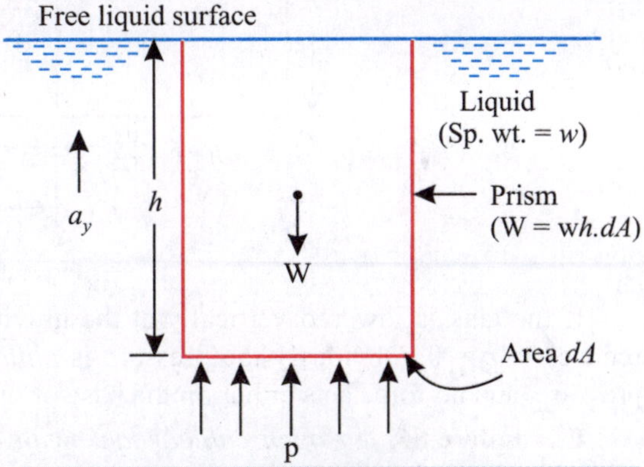

Fig. 6.92

Applying Newton's second law of motion, we have:

$$\Sigma F_y = m \times a_y$$

The force ΣF_y = Pressure force acting upwards – weight of prism acting downwards

$= [p \text{ (intensity of pressure)} \times dA \text{ (area)}] - (w \times \text{volume of prism})$

$= p \times dA - w \times h \times dA$

Also, $m = \dfrac{w}{g} \times$ volume of elementary prism

$= \dfrac{w}{g} \times (h \times dA)$

$$\therefore \quad p \times dA - w \times h \times dA = \frac{w}{g}(h \times dA) \times a_y$$

or,
$$p = wh\left(1 + \frac{a_y}{g}\right) \quad ...(6.44)$$

This equation (6.44) reveals the following:

- The free liquid surface remains *horizontal.*
- The pressure variation in the vertical direction is *linear.*
- The pressure intensity at any point is *more* than the static pressure *wh* by an amount $wh\left(\dfrac{a_y}{g}\right)$ as shown in Fig. 6.93 (*a*).

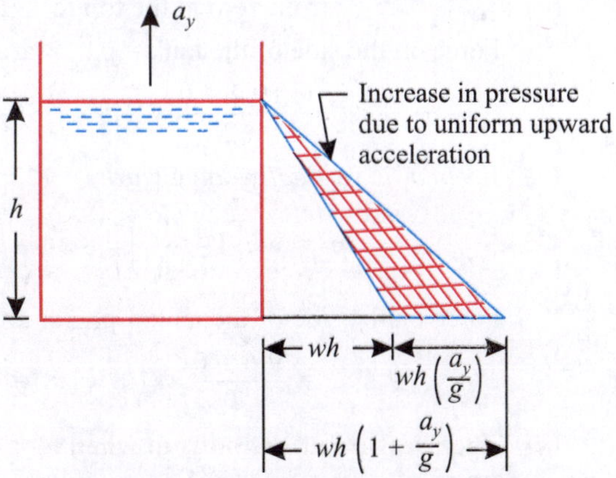

Fig. 6.93. (*a*)

If the liquid mass is uniformly accelerated vertically *downward* direction, a_y shall be negative and then eqn. (6.43) reduces to

$$p = wh\left(1 - \frac{a_y}{g}\right) \quad ...(6.44)$$

i.e., Intensity of pressure at any point is *less* than static pressure *wh* by an amount $wh\left(\dfrac{a_y}{g}\right)$, as shown in (Fig. 6.93 (*b*)).

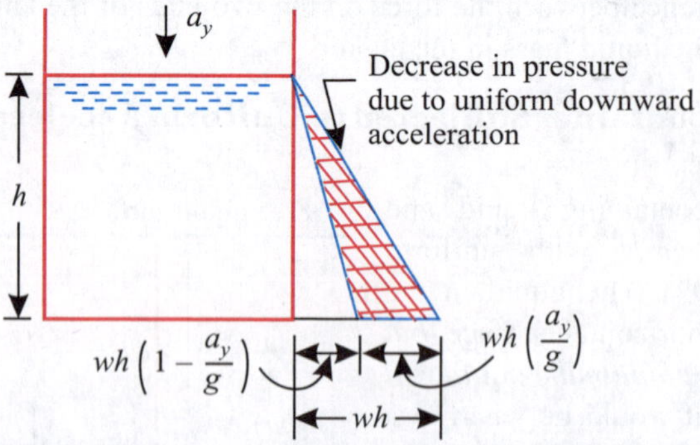

Fig. 6.93. (*b*)

If the tank is lowered vertically at the gravitational acceleation, then $a_y = g$ and eqn. (6.44) reduces to $p = 0$. Obviously the pressure is *uniform and equivalent to surrounding* atmospheric pressure, and no force acts either on the base or on the tank walls.

Example 6.86. *An open cubical tank with each side* 1.8 *m contains oil of specific weight* 8 *kN/m*^{3} *up to a depth of* 1.8 *m.*

Calculate:

(i) The force acting on side of the tank when it is being moved with an acceleration of $\frac{g}{3} m/s^2$ *in vertically upward and downward directions.*

(ii) The pressure at the bottom of the tank when acceleration rate is g m/s^2 *vertically downwards.*

Solution: *Given*: Each side of cubical tank = 1.8 m; Sp. wt of oil, $w = 8$ kN/m^3; a_y (upward and downward) = $\frac{g}{3}$ m/s^2; a_y (downward) = g m/s^2.

(*i*) The force acting on the side of the tank:

(*a*) *When* a_y *is vertically upward*:

$$p = wh\left(1+\frac{a_y}{g}\right) = 8\times 1.8\left(1+\frac{g/3}{g}\right) = 8\times 1.8\left(1+\frac{1}{3}\right) = 19.2 \text{ kN/m}^2$$

On a vertical side, the intensity of pressure varies linearly

from zero at the top to 19.2 kN/m^2 at the bottom.

Force on the side of the tank = $p_{avg} \times$ area

$$= \frac{19.2+0}{2}\times(1.8\times 1.8) = \mathbf{31.1\ kN}$$ **(Ans.)**

(*b*) *When* a_y *is vertically downward*:

$$p = wh\left(1-\frac{a_y}{g}\right) = 8\times 1.8\left(1-\frac{1}{3}\right) = 9.6 \text{ kN/m}^2$$

Force on the side of the tank = $p_{avg.} \times$ area

$$= \frac{9.6+0}{2}\times(1.8\times 1.8) = \mathbf{15.55\ kN}$$ **(Ans.)**

(*ii*) The pressure at the bottom when $a_y = g$:

When the tank is lowered vertically at an acceleration, then:

$$p = wh\left(1-\frac{a_y}{g}\right) = wh\left(1-\frac{g}{g}\right) = 0$$

i.e., the liquid remains at the atmospheric pressure throughout and there is no force on the base or on the tank walls. **(Ans.)**

6.12.3. Liquid in Container Subjected to Uniform Acceleation Along Inclined Plane.

Fig. 6.94 shows a tank filled with a liquid being accelerated *up an inclined plane* with uniform acceleration *a*.

Horizontal component of acceleration, $a_x = a \cos \alpha$

Vertical component of acceleration, $a_y = a \sin \alpha$

A particle *L* of mass *m* lying on the liquid surface is *in equilibrium under the action of following forces:*

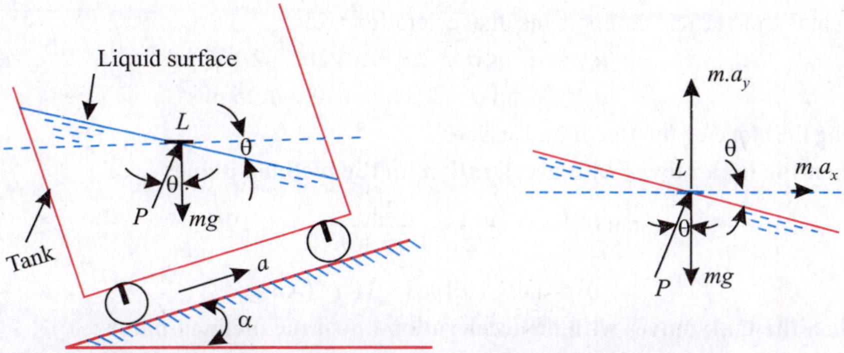

Fig. 6.94. Acceleration of fluid mass along an upward slope.

(*i*) Weight *mg* acting vertically downward,

(*ii*) Pressure force *P* acting *normal* to the surface of the fluid element, and

(*iii*) Accelerating force, (*m.a*) having component $m.a_x$ in the horizontal direction and a component $m.a_y$ in the vertical direction.

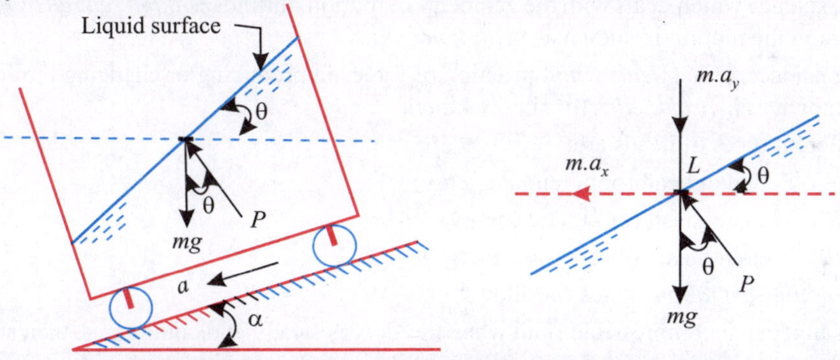

Fig. 6.95. Acceleration of fluid mass along a downward slope.

Resolving *horizontally* and *vertically* respectively, we get:

$$P \sin \theta = m.a_x \quad ...(i)$$

$$P \cos \theta = m.a_y + mg \quad ...(ii)$$

Dividing (*i*) by (*ii*), we get:

$$\tan \theta = \frac{a_x}{a_y + g} \quad ...(6.45)$$

When the fluid mass is subjected to acceleration *down the slope,* we have:

$$P \sin \theta = m \,.\, a_x \quad ...(iii)$$

$$P \cos\theta = mg - m.a_y \quad \text{...(iv)}$$

Dividing (*iii*) by (*iv*), we get:

$$\tan\theta = \frac{a_x}{g - a_y} \quad \text{...(6.46)}$$

Example 6.87. *An open rectangular tank 6 m long and 2.4 m wide is filled with water to a depth of 1.8 m. Find the slope of water surface when the tank moves with an acceleration of 2.5 m/s^2*

(i) *up a 30° inclined plane, and* ***(ii)*** *down a 30° inclined plane.*

Solution. *Given*: Dimensions of the tank: 6 *m* (length) × 2.4 m (width);

Acceleration, $a = 2.5$ m/s^2; Inclination, $\alpha = 30°$.

Horizontal and vertical components of acceleration are:

$$a_x = a\cos\alpha = 2.5 \times \cos 30° = 2.165 \text{ m/s}^2$$

$$a_y = a\sin\alpha = 2.5 \times \sin 30° = 1.25 \text{ m/s}^2$$

Let, θ be the slope of the free liquid surface.

(*i*) When the tank moves with acceleration up the inclined plane:

$$\tan\theta = \frac{a_x}{a_y + g} = \frac{2.165}{1.25 + 9.81} = 0.196$$

$$\theta = \tan^{-1}(0.196) = \mathbf{11.1°} \textbf{ (Ans.)}$$

(*ii*) When the tank moves with an acceleration down the inclined plane :

$$\tan\theta = \frac{a_x}{g - a_y} = \frac{2.165}{9.81 - 1.25} = 0.253$$

$$\theta = \tan^{-1}(0.253) = \mathbf{14.2°} \textbf{ (Ans.)}$$

HIGHLIGHTS

1. The science which deals with the geometry of motion of fluids *without reference* to the forces causing the motion is known as *hydrokinematics*.
2. The science which *deals with* the action of forces in producing or changing motion of fluids is known as *hydrokinetics* (or simply kinetics).
3. Different types of heads are:
   (*i*) Potential head (or potential energy)
   (*ii*) Velocity head (or kinetic energy)
   (*iii*) Pressure head (or pressure energy).
4. *Bernoulli's equation* states as follows:

   "In an ideal, incompressible fluid when the flow is steady and continuous, then sum of pressure energy, potential (or datum) energy and kinetic energy is constant along a streamline." Mathematically,

$$\frac{p}{w} + \frac{V^2}{2g} + z = \text{constant}$$

where $\frac{p}{w}$ = Pressure energy or head,

$\frac{V^2}{2g}$ = Kinetic energy or head, and

z = Datum (or elevation) energy or head.

5. *Euler's equation* for motion is given as:

$$\frac{dp}{\rho} + v.dv + g.dz = 0 \quad \text{...differential form}$$

6. *Bernoulli's equation for real fluid* is given as:

$$\frac{p_1}{w} + \frac{V_1^2}{2g} + z_1 = \frac{p_2}{w} + \frac{V_2^2}{2g} + z_2 + h_L$$

where, h_L = loss of energy between sections 1 and 2.

7. *Practical applications of Bernoulli's equation* are:

(*i*) Venturimeter; (*ii*) Orificemeter;

(*iii*) Rotometer and elbow meter; (*iv*) Pitot tube.

In case of a *venturimeter,* the actual discharge (Q_{act}) is given as:

$$Q_{act.} = C_d \times \frac{A_1 A_2}{\sqrt{A_1^2 - A_2^2}} \times \sqrt{2gh}$$

where, C_d = Co-efficient of discharge (varies between 0.96 and 0.98),

A_1 = Area at inlet,

A_2 = Area at outlet, and

h = Difference of pressure head at sections 1 and 2.

8. *Free liquid jet*:

A jet of liquid from the nozzle in atmosphere is called a *free liquid jet.* The parabolic path traversed by the liquid jet under the action of gravity is known as *trajectory.*

(*i*) Equation of the jet:

$$y = x \tan\theta - \frac{gx^2 \sec^2\theta}{2U^2}$$

where, x, y = Co-ordinates of any point on jet with respect to the nozzle,

U = Velocity of the jet of water issuing from the nozzle, and

θ = Inclination of the jet issuing from nozzle with horizontal.

(*ii*) Maximum height attained by the jet $= \dfrac{U^2 \sin^2\theta}{2g}$

(*iii*) Time of flight, $T = \dfrac{2U\sin\theta}{g}$

(*iv*) Time taken to reach the highest point; $T' = \dfrac{U\sin\theta}{g}$

(*v*) Horizontal range of the jet, $r = \dfrac{U^2 \sin 2\theta}{g}$

(*vi*) Maximum range, $r_{max} = \dfrac{U^2}{2g}$

(The range will be maximum when $\theta = 45°$)

9. *Momentum principle* states as follows:

"The net force acting on a mass of fluid is equal to the change in momentum of flow per unit time in that direction".

10. *Impulse-momentum equation F.dt* = $d(mv)$ may be stated as follows:

"The impulse of a force F acting on a fluid mass m in a short interval of time dt is equal to the change of momentum $d(mv)$ in the direction of force."

11. *Kinetic energy correction factor* (α).

$$\alpha = \frac{\text{Kinetic energy per second based on actual velocity}}{\text{Kinetic energy per second based on average velocity}}$$

Momentum correction factor (β).

$$\beta = \frac{\text{Momentum per second based or actual velocity}}{\text{Momentum per second based on average velocity}}$$

The values of α and β may be calculated by using the following equations:

$$\alpha = \frac{1}{A}\int_A \left(\frac{u}{\bar{u}}\right)^2 dA \text{ and } \beta = \frac{1}{A}\int_A \left(\frac{u}{\bar{u}}\right)^2 dA$$

where,
A = Area of cross-section,
u = Local velocity,
$\bar{u}$ = Average velocity, and
dA = Elementary area.

12. *Moment of momentum equation.* This equation is derived from moment of momentum principle which states that the resulting torque acting on a rotating fluid is equal to the rate of change of momentum.

Mathematically, it is written as:

$$T = \rho Q\,(V_2 r_2 - V_1 r_1)$$

Vortex motion:

The pressure variation along the radial direction for vortex flow along a horizontal plane,

$$\frac{\partial p}{\partial r} = \frac{\rho v^2}{r}$$

and, pressure variation in the vertical plane,

$$\frac{\partial p}{\partial r} = -\rho g$$

Forced vortex flow:

Forced vortex flow is one in which the fluid mass is made to rotate by means of some external agency.

$$v = \omega \times r$$

$$z = \frac{v^2}{2g} = \frac{\omega^2 r^2}{2g} = \frac{\omega^2 R^2}{2g}$$

where,
z = Height of the paraboloid formed, and
ω = Angular velocity.

- For a forced vortex flow in an *open tank*:

  Fall of liquid level at centre = Rise of liquid level at the ends
- In case of a *closed cylinder*:

Volume of air before rotation = volume of air after rotation.

— If a closed cylindrical vessel completely filled with water is rotated about its vertical axis, the total pressure force acting on the top and bottom are:

$$F_{top} = \frac{\rho}{4}\omega^2 \pi R^4$$

and, $$F_{bottom} = F_{top} + \text{weight of water in cylinder}$$
$$= F_{top} + w \times \pi R^2 \times H$$

where, ω = Angular velocity,

R = Radius of the vessel,

H = Height of the vessel, and

ρ = Density of fluid $\left(= \frac{w}{g}\right)$.

Free vortex flow:

When no external torque is required to rotate the fluid mass, type of flow is called free vortex flow. In case of free vortex flow:

$$v \times r = \text{constant} \quad ...(i)$$

$$\frac{p_1}{\rho_g} + \frac{v_1^2}{2g} + z_1 = \frac{p_2}{\rho g} + \frac{v_2^2}{2g} + z_2 \quad ...(ii)$$

OBJECTIVE TYPE QUESTIONS

Choose the Correct Answer:

1. Velocity head is given by

(*a*) $\frac{V}{g}$ (*b*) $\frac{V^2}{2g}$

(*c*) $\frac{V^3}{2g}$ (*d*) $\frac{V^2}{2g^2}$.

2. Bernoulli's equation, mathematically is written as

(*a*) $\frac{p}{w} + \frac{V}{2g} + z = \text{constant}$

(*b*) $\frac{p}{w^2} + \frac{V^2}{2g} + z = \text{constant}$

(*c*) $\frac{p}{w} + \frac{V^2}{2g} + z = \text{constant}$

(*d*) $\frac{p^2}{w} + \frac{V^2}{2g} + z = \text{constant}$.

3. Which of the following assumptions is made in the derivation of Bernoulli's equation?

(*a*) The liquid is ideal and incompressible

(*b*) The flow is steady and continuous

(*c*) The flow is one-dimensional

(*d*) The velocity is uniform over the section and is equal to mean velocity

(*e*) All of the above.

4. Euler's equation (in differential form) is written as:

(*a*) $\frac{dp}{\rho} + v^2.dv + g.dz = 0$

(*b*) $\frac{dp}{\rho} + v.dv + g.dz = 0$

(*c*) $\frac{dp}{\rho} + v.dv + g^2.dz = 0$

(*d*) $\frac{dp}{\rho^2} + v.dv + g.dz = 0$.

5. In which of the following measuring devices Bernoulli's equation is used:

(*a*) Venturimeter (*b*) Orificemeter

(*c*) Pitot tube (*d*) All the above.

6. The co-efficient of discharge of an orificemeter is ......that of a venturimeter.

(*a*) equal to (*b*) much smaller than

(*c*) much more than (*d*) any of these.

7. Which of the following equations is known as momentum principle:

(*a*) $F = \frac{d(m^2v)}{dt}$ (*b*) $F = \frac{dv}{dt}$

(*c*) $F = \frac{d(mv)}{dt}$ (*d*) $F = \frac{d(mv)}{dt^2}$.

8. The piezometric head is the summation of :
(*a*) velocity head and pressure head
(*b*) pressure head and elevation head
(*c*) velocity head and elevation head
(*d*) none of the above.

9. The total energy-line is always higher than the hydraulic gradient line, the vertical distance between the two representing:
(*a*) the pressure head
(*b*) the piezometric head
(*c*) the velocity head
(*d*) none of the above.

10. The total-energy-line in pipe flow is a graphical representation of the Bernoulli's equation and represents the sum of velocity head, pressure head and the elevation head above:
(*a*) the top of the pipeline
(*b*) the arbitrary horizontal datum
(*c*) the centre line of pipe
(*d*) the bottom of the pipe.

11. The total energy represented by the Bernoulli's equation $\left(\frac{p}{w} + \frac{V^2}{2g} + z\right)$ has the units:
(*a*) Nm/s (*b*) Ns/m
(*c*) Nm/m (*d*) Nm/N.

12. The Bernoulli's equation written in the conventional form $\frac{p}{w} + \frac{V^2}{2g} + z =$ constant represents total energy per unit of certain quantity. Identify this quantity from the choices given below:
(*a*) energy per unit mass
(*b*) energy per unit weight
(*c*) energy per unit volume
(*d*) energy per unit specific weight.

13. A venturimeter is used for measuring:
(*a*) pressure (*b*) flow rate
(*c*) total energy (*d*) piezometric head.

14. The co-efficient of discharge (C_d) of venturimeter lies within the limits:
(*a*) 0.95 to 0.99 (*b*) 0.8 to 0.85
(*c*) 0.7 to 0.8 (*d*) 0.6 to 0.7

15. A Pitot-tube is used for measuring:
(*a*) velocity of flow (*b*) pressure of flow
(*c*) flow rate (*d*) total energy.

16. When a Pitot-tube is put to use it must be ensured that its alignment is such that:
(*a*) the horizontal leg should be inclined at 45° in plan
(*b*) its horizontal leg is at right angles to the flow direction
(*c*) its opening faces upstream and the horizontal leg is perfectly aligned with the direction of flow
(*d*) none of the above.

17. The hydraulic gradient-line indicates the variation of which of the following:
(*a*) Velocity head in flow direction
(*b*) Piezometric head in the direction of flow
(*c*) Total energy of flow in the direction of flow
(*d*) None of the above.

18. The kinetic energy correction factor is expressed by:
(*a*) $\frac{1}{A}\int_A \left(\frac{u}{\bar{u}}\right) dA$ (*b*) $\frac{1}{A}\int_A \left(\frac{u}{\bar{u}}\right)^2 dA$
(*c*) $\frac{1}{A}\int_A \left(\frac{u}{\bar{u}}\right)^3 dA$ (*d*) $\frac{1}{A}\int_A \left(\frac{\bar{u}}{u}\right)^3 dA$

19. The momentum correction factor β is used to account for:
(*a*) change in direction of flow
(*b*) change in total energy
(*c*) non-uniform distribution of velocities at inlet and outlet sections
(*d*) change in mass rate of flow.

20. The change in moment of momentum of fluid due to flow along a curved path results in:
(*a*) a change in pressure
(*b*) torque
(*c*) a change in the total energy
(*d*) none of the above.

21. Which of the following is an example of free vortex flow?
(*a*) A whirlpool in a river
(*b*) Flow of liquid through a hole provided at the bottom of a container
(*c*) Flow of liquid around a circular bend in a pipe.
(*d*) All of the above.

22. In case of forced vortex, the rise of liquid level at the ends is .... the fall of liquid level at the axis of rotation.
(*a*) less than (*b*) more than
(*c*) equal to (*d*) none of the above.

23. In case of a closed cylindrical vessel sealed at the top and the bottom the volume of air before rotation is ...... the volume of air after:

(*a*) more than (*b*) less than
(*c*) equal to (*d*) none of the above.

24. If a closed cylindrical vessel completely filled with water is rotated about its vertical axis, the total pressure force acting on the top is equal to:

(*a*) $\frac{\rho}{4}\omega^2 \pi R$ (*b*) $\frac{\rho^2}{4}\omega \pi R^2$

(*c*) $\frac{\rho}{4}\omega^2 \pi R^3$ (*d*) $\frac{\rho}{4}\omega^2 \pi R^4$.

25. For a free vortex flow the equation is:

(*a*) $\frac{p_1}{\rho g} + \frac{V_1}{2g} + z_1 = \frac{p_2}{\rho g} + \frac{V_2}{2g} + z_2$

(*b*) $\frac{p_1}{\rho g} + \frac{V_1^2}{2g} + z_1 = \frac{p_2}{\rho g} + \frac{V_2^2}{2g} + z_2$

(*c*) $\frac{p_1^2}{\rho g} + \frac{V_1^2}{g} + z_1 = \frac{p_2^2}{\rho g} + \frac{V_2^2}{g} + z_2$

(*d*) $\frac{p_1}{\rho g} + \frac{V_1^3}{2g} + z_1 = \frac{p_2}{\rho g} + \frac{V_2^3}{2g} + z_2$.

ANSWERS

1. (*b*)	**2.** (*c*)	**3.** (*e*)	**4.** (*b*)	**5.** (*d*)	**6.** (*b*)
7. (*c*)	**8.** (*b*)	**9.** (*c*)	**10.** (*b*)	**11.** (*d*)	**12.** (*b*)
13. (*b*)	**14.** (*a*)	**15.** (*a*)	**16.** (*c*)	**17.** (*b*)	**18.** (*c*)
19. (*c*)	**20.** (*b*)	**21.** (*d*)	**22.** (*c*)	**23.** (*c*)	**24.** (*d*)
25. (*b*).					

THEORETICAL QUESTIONS

1. Explain briefly the following heads:
(*i*) Potential head
(*ii*) Velocity head
(*iii*) Datum head.

2. State and prove Bernoulli's equation.

3. List the assumptions which are made while deriving Bernoulli's equation.

4. Derive Euler's equation of motion.

5. What are the limitations of the Bernoulli's equation?

6. Describe an orificemeter and find an expression for measuring discharge of fluid through a pipe with this device.

7. Why is co-efficient of discharge of an orifice-meter much smaller than that of venturimeter?

8. What is a pitot tube? How is it used to measure velocity of flow at any point in a pipe or channel?

9. What is a free jet of liquid? Derive an expression for the path travelled by free jet issuing from a nozzle?

10. Prove that the equation of the free jet of liquid is given by the expression

$$y = x\tan\theta - \frac{gx^2}{2U^2}\sec^2\theta$$

where x, y = co-ordinates of a point on the jet,
U = velocity of the jet, and
θ = inclination of the jet with horizontal.

11. What is an impulse-momentum equation?

12. What is the moment of momentum equation?

13. Define the terms: (*i*) Vortex flow, (*ii*) Forced vortex flow, and (*iii*) Free vortex flow.

14. Differentiate between forced vortex flow and free vortex flow.

15. Derive an expression for the depth of paraboloid formed by the surface of a liquid contained in a cylindrical tank which is rotated at a constant angular velocity ω about its vertical axis.

16. Derive an expression for difference of pressure between two points in a free vortex flow.

UNSOLVED EXAMPLES

1. The diameters of a tapering pipe at the sections 1-1 and 2-2 are 100 mm and 150 mm respectively. If the velocity of water flowing through the pipe at section 1-1 is 5 m/s, find:

(*i*) Discharge through the pipe, and

(*ii*) Velocity of water at section 2-2.

[Ans. (*i*) 0.039 m^3/s, (*ii*) 2.22 m/s]

2. A pipe (1) 400 mm in diameter, conveying water, branches into two pipes (2 and 3 of diameters 300 mm and 200 mm respectively.

(*i*) Find the discharge in pipe (1) if the average velocity of water in this pipe is 3 m/s.

(*ii*) Determine the velocity of water in 200 mm pipe if the average velocity in 300 mm diameter pipe is 2 m/s.

[Ans. (*i*) 0.377 m^3/s, (*ii*) 7.5 m/s]

3. The water is flowing through a pipe having diameters 200 mm and 100 mm at sections 1 and 2 respectively. The rate of flow through the pipe is 35 litres/s. The section 1 is 6 m above datum and section 2 is 4 m above datum. If the pressure at section 1 is 400 kN/m^2, find the intensity of pressure at section 2. **[Ans.** 410.5 kN/m^2]

4. A pipe 300 metres long has a slope of 1 in 100 and tapers from 1.0 m diameter at the higher end to 0.5 m at the lower end. Quantity of water flowing is 90 litre/s. If the pressure at higher end is 70 kN/m^2, find the pressure at the lower end.

[Ans. 100 kN/m^2]

5. A pipe 5 m long is inclined at an angle of 15° with the horizontal. The diameters of pipe at smaller section (at lower level) and larger section are 80 mm and 240 mm respectively.

If the pipe is uniformly tapering and the velocity of water at the smaller section is 1 m/s, find the difference of pressures between the two sections. **[Ans.** 12.2 kN/m^2]

6. Water is flowing at the rate of 40 litres/s through a tapering pipe. The diameters at the bottom and upper ends are 300 mm and 200 mm respectively. If the intensities of pressure at the bottom and upper ends are 250 kN/m^2 and 100 kN/m^2 respectively, find the difference in datum head.

[Ans. 13.7 m]

7. A 2 m long conical tube is fixed vertically with its smaller end upwards. It carries liquid in downward direction. The flow velocities at the smaller and larger ends are 5 m/s and 2 m/s respectively. The pressure head at the smaller end is 2.5 m of liquid. If the loss of head in the tube is $\dfrac{0.35(V_1 - V_2)^2}{2g}$ (V_1 and V_2 being the velocities at the smaller and larger ends respectively) determine the pressure head at the larger end.

[Ans. 5.4 m of liquid]

8. A pipeline carrying oil (sp. gr. = 0.87) changes in diameter from 200 mm diameter at position '1' to 500 mm diameter at position '2' which is 4 metres at a higher level. If the pressures at 1 and 2 are 100 kN/m^2 and 60 kN/m^2 respcetively and the discharge is 0.2 m^3/s, determine:

(*i*) Loss of head, and

(*ii*) Direction of flow.

[Ans. (*i*) 2.6 m (*ii*) from 1 to 2]

9. The following data relate to an orificemeter:

Diameter of the pipe = 300 mm

Diameter of the orifice = 150 mm

Reading of the differential manometer = 500 mm of mercury

Sp. gravity of oil = 0.9

Co-effiecient of discharge of meter = 0.64

Determine the rate of flow. **[Ans.** 0.137 m^3/s]

10. A venturimeter with 150 mm diameter at inlet and 100 mm at throat is laid with its axis horizontal and is used for measuring the flow of oil of sp. gr. 0.9. The oil mercury differential manometer shows a gauge difference of 200 mm. Calculate the discharge. Assume the co-efficient of meter as 0.98. **[Ans.** 0.06393 m^3/s]

11. A horizontal venturimeter with inlet and throat diameters 160 mm and 60 mm respectively is used to measure the flow of an oil of specific gravity 0.8. If the discharge of the oil is 0.05 m^3/s, find the deflection of oil mercury gauge. Take venturimeter constant = 1.

[Ans. 296 mm]

12. A horizontal venturimeter 300 mm × 150 mm is used to measure the flow of oil of sp. gravity 0.8. The discharge of oil through venturimeter is 0.5 m^3/s. Find the reading of oil-mercury differntial manometer. Take venturimeter constant = 0.98. **[Ans.** 248. 9 mm]

13. A venturimeter with inlet and throat diameters 300 mm and 150 mm respectively is attached in a vertical pipe in which flow occurs from bottom to top. The distance between the point of entrance

and to the point of throat of the venturimeter is 750 mm. If the difference of mercury levels in the two limbs of differential gauge is 220 mm, find the discharge passing through the vertical pipe. Take co-efficient of discharge, $C_d = 0.98$.
[Ans. 0.146 m^3/s]

14. A venturimeter has its axis vertical, the inlet and throat diameters being 150 mm and 75 mm respectively. The throat is 225 mm above inlet and venturimeter constant = 0.96. Petrol of sp. gravity 0.78 flows up through the meter at a rate of 0.029 m^3/s. Find the pressure difference between inlet and throat. **[Ans.** 18.9 kN/m^2]

15. A venturimeter is used for measuring the flow of petrol in a pipeline inclined at 35° to horizontal. The sp. gravity of the petrol is 0.81 and throat area ratio is 4. If the difference in mercury levels in the gauge is 50 mm, calculate the flow in m^3/s if the pipe diameter is 300 mm. Take venturimeter constant = 0.975. **[Ans.** 0.07 m^3/s]

16. The following data relate to venturimeter fitted to an inclined pipe in which water is flowing.
Diameter of the pipe = 300 mm
Throat diameter = 150 mm
Sp. gravity of liquid used in U-tube manometer = 0.8
Reading of manometer = 400 mm
Loss of head between the inlet and throat = 0.3 × kinetic head of the pipe.
Find the discharge. **[Ans.** 0.0226 m^3/s]

17. A vertical venturimeter of d/D ratio equal to 0.6 is fitted in a 100 mm diameter pipe. The throat is 200 mm above the inlet. The venturimeter constant = 0.92. Determine:
(*i*) Pressure difference as recorded by two gauges fitted at the inlet and throat.
(*ii*) Difference on a vertical differential mercury manometer (sp. gravity = 13.6) when a liquid of sp. gravity 0.8 flows through the meter at the rate of 0.05 m^3/s.
[Ans. (*i*) 130.47 kN/m^2 (*ii*) 1.026 m]

18. A 300 mm diameter 150° bend discharges 0.35 m^3/s of water in the atmosphere. If the pressure of water entering the bend is 150 kN/m^2 (gauge), determine the force required to hold the bend in place. Assume the bend to be in horizontal plane.
[Ans. 10.86 kN, 4.57° with negative X-axis]

19. A 45° reducing bend is connected in pipeline, the diameters at the inlet and outlet of the bend being 400 mm and 200 mm respectively. Find the force exerted by water on the bend if the intensity of pressure at inlet of the bend is 215.8 kN/m^2. The rate of flow of water is 0.5 m^3/s.
[Ans. 22.7 kN: 20°3.5′]

20. A 300 mm diameter pipe carries water under a head of 20 metres with a velocity of 3.5 m/s. If the axis of the pipe turns through 45°, find the magnitude and direction of the resultant force at the bend. **[Ans.** 11.27 kN, 67°28′]

21. A pipeline of 600 mm diameter, carrying oil (sp. gravity = 0.85) at the flow rate of 1800 litres/sec. has a 90° bend in the horizontal plane. The pressure at the entrance to the bend 1.471 bar and the loss of head in the bend is 2 m of oil. Find the magnitude and direction of the force exerted by the oil on the bend and show the direction of the force on a sketch of the bend.
[UPSC Exams.]
[Ans. 69.357 kN, 42.3°]

22. A jet of water is coming out from a nozzle with a velocity of 20 m/s. The nozzle is situated at a distance of 20 m from a vertical wall 8 m high. Find the angle of projection of the nozzle to the horizontal so that the jet of water just clears the top of the wall. **[Ans.** 73° 0.8′or 38°47′]

23. A nozzle inclined at an angle of 45° to the horizontal is situated at a distance of 1 m above the ground level. If the diameter of the nozzle is 50 mm and the jet of water from the nozzle strikes the gound at a horizontal distance of 4 m, find the rate of flow of water. **[Ans.** 0.011 m^3/s]

24. A jet issuing from a 30 mm nozzle held at 0.6 m above the ground level at an angle of 30° to the horizontal strikes the ground 4 m away. Determine:
(*i*) The maximum height reached,
(*ii*) The range of the jet, and
(*iii*) The discharge.
[Ans. (*i*) 0.458 m above the nozzle tip
(*ii*) 3.18 m, 0.00425 m^3/s]

25. A 30 mm fire nozzle held at 1.5 m above ground discharging 10 lps has to reach a window in a wall 15 m away and 10 m above ground. At what angle or angles of the inclination to the horizontal, the nozzle is to be held? Neglect air resistance. **[Ans.** 32°]

26. In Fig 6.96 what is the power developed by the turbine assuming efficiency of 80%?
[Ans. 54 kW]

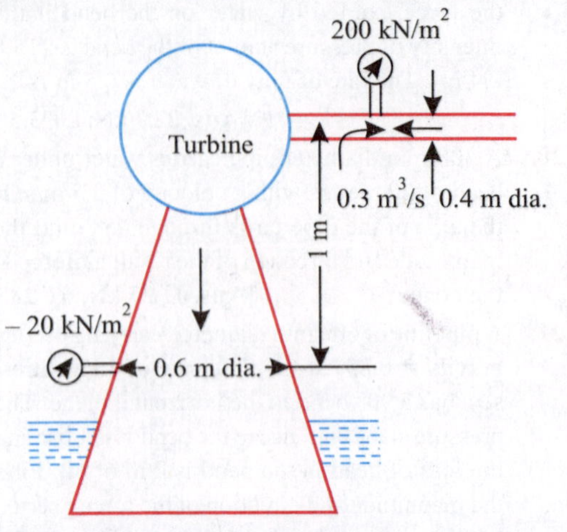

Fig. 6.96

27. The sprinkler shown in Fig 6.97 has nozzles of 5 mm diameter and carries a total discharge of 0.20 litres/sec. Determine:

(*i*) The angular speed of rotation of the sprinkler, and

(*ii*) The torque required to hold the sprinkler stationary.

Assume no friction at the pivot.

[**Ans.** (*i*) 10.192 rad./s (*ii*) 0.05086 Nm]

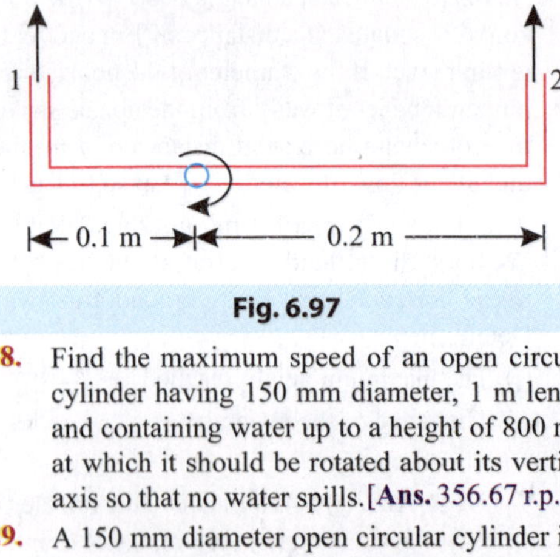

Fig. 6.97

28. Find the maximum speed of an open circular cylinder having 150 mm diameter, 1 m length and containing water up to a height of 800 mm at which it should be rotated about its vertical axis so that no water spills. [**Ans.** 356.67 r.p.m.]

29. A 150 mm diameter open circular cylinder is 1 m long and contains water up to a height of 0.7 m. Estimate the speed at which the cylinder may be rotated about its vertical axis so that the axial depth becomes zero. [**Ans.** 563.88 r.p.m.]

30. For the unsolved example 29, find the difference in total pressure force due to rotation:

(*i*) At the bottom of the cylinder, and

(*ii*) On the sides of the cylinder.

[**Ans.** (*i*) 34.72 N (*ii*) 1178.4 N]

31. An open cylindrical vessel 120 mm in diameter and 300 mm deep is filled with water up to the top. Estimate the volume of water left in the vessel when it is rotated about its vertical axis:

(*i*) With a speed of 300 r.p.m. and

(*ii*) With a speed of 600 r.p.m.

[**Ans.** (*i*) 2369.37 cm^3 (*ii*) 702. 67 cm^3]

32. A cylindrical vessel closed at the top is 0.2 m in diameter, 1.2 m long and contains water up to a height of 0.8 m.

(*i*) Find the height of the paraboloid formed, if it is rotated at 400 r.p.m. about its vertical axis.

(*ii*) Find the speed of rotation of the vessel when axial depth is zero.

[**Ans.** (*i*) 0.845 m (*ii*) 567.2 r.p.m.]

33. A vessel cylindrical in shape and closed at the top and bottom is 300 mm in diameter, 1 m long and contains water up to a depth of 0.8 m. The air above the water surface is at a pressure of 60 kN/m^2. If the vessel is rotated at a speed of 250 r.p.m. about its vertical axis find the pressure head at the bottom of the vessel

(*i*) At the centre, and

(*ii*) At the edge.

[**Ans.** (*i*) 6.439 m of water, (*ii*) 7.225 m of water.]

34. A vessel cylindrical in shape and closed at the top and bottom is 200 mm in diameter and 0.15 m in height. The vessel is completely filled with water. If it is rotated about its vertical axis with a speed of 200 r.p.m., what is the total pressure force exerted by water on the top and bottom of the vessel? [**Ans.** 0.0344 kN, 0.0806 kN]

35. An open tank 5m long, 2m deep and 3 m wide contains oil of relative density 0.9 to a depth of 0.9 m. If the tank is accelerated along its length on a horizontal track at a constant value of 3 m/s^2, determine:

(*i*) The new positon of the oil surface.

(*ii*) The pressures at the bottom of the tank at the front and rear edges.

(*iii*) The amount of spill if the tank is given a horizontal acceleration of 4.5 m/s^2 instead of 3 m/s^2.

[**Ans.** (*i*) $\theta = 17°$; (*ii*) 1.189 kN/m^2, 14.67 kN/m^2; (*iii*) 0.42 m^3]

36. A spherical tank of 1.2 m radius is half-filled with oil of relative density 0.8. If the tank is given a horizontal acceleration of 10 m/s^2, calculate:

(*i*) The inclination of the oil surface to horizontal.

(*ii*) The maximum pressure on the tank.

[**Ans.** (*i*) 45.55°; (*ii*) 9.4 kN/m^2]

37. A closed tank 6 m long, 2 m wide and 1.8 m deep initially contains water to a depth of 1.2 m. The top has an opening in the front part to have air space at atmospheric pressure. If the tank is given a horizontal acceleration at a constant value of 2.4 m/s^2 along its length, calculate the total pressure force on the top of the tank.

[Ans. 0.792 kN**]**

38. An open cubical tank with each side 1.5 m contains oil of the specific weight 7.5 kN/m^3. Calculate:

(*i*) The force acting on side of the tank when it is being moved with an acceleration of $\frac{g}{2}$ m/s^2 in vertically upward and downward directions.

(*ii*) The pressure at bottom of the tank when the acceleration rate is g m/s^2 vertically downwards.

[Ans (*i*) 18.984 kN; 6.328 kN (*ii*) zero**]**

39. An open rectangular tank 5 m long × 2 m wide is filled with water to a depth of 1.5 m. Find the slope of water surface when tank moves with an acceleration of 3m/s^2

(*i*) up a 30° inclined plane, and

(*ii*) down a 30° inclined plane.

[Ans. (*i*) 12.89°; (*ii*) 17.37°**]**

Chapter 7

DIMENSIONAL AND MODEL ANALYSIS

DIMENSIONAL ANALYSIS

7.1. DIMENSIONAL ANALYSIS—INTRODUCTION

Dimensional analysis *is a mathematical technique which makes use of the study of the dimensions for solving several engineering problems.* Each physical phenomenon can be expressed by an equation giving relationship between different quantities, such quantities are dimensional and non-dimensional. Dimensional analysis helps in determining a systematic arrangement of the variables in the physical relationship, combining dimensional variables to form non-dimensional parameters. It is based on the *principle of dimensional homogeneity* and uses the dimensions of relevant variables affecting the phenomenon.

Dimensional analysis has become an important tool for analysing fluid flow problems. It is *specially useful in presenting experimental results in a concise form.*

Uses of dimensional analysis:

The uses of dimensional analysis may be summarised as follows:

1. To test the dimensional homogeneity of any equation of fluid motion.
2. To derive rational formulae for a flow phenomenon.
3. To derive equations expressed in terms of non-dimensional parameters to show the relative significance of each parameter.
4. To plan model tests and present experimental results in a systematic manner, thus making it possible to analyse the complex fluid flow phenomenon.

Advantages of dimensional analysis:

Dimensional analysis entails the following *advantages*:

1. It expresses the functional relationship between the variables in dimensionless terms.
2. In hydraulic model studies it reduces the number of variables involved in a physical phenomenon, generally by *three.*
3. By the proper selection of variables, the dimensionless parameters can be used to make certain logical deductions about the problem.
4. Design curves, by the use of dimensional analysis, can be developed from experimental data or direct solution of the problem.
5. It enables getting up a theoretical equation in a simplified dimensional form.
6. Dimensional analysis provides partial solutions to the problems that are too complex to be dealt with mathematically.
7. The conversion of units of quantities from one system to another is facilitated.

7.2. DIMENSIONS

The various physical quantities used in fluid phenomenon can be expressed in terms of **fundamental quantities** or *primary quantities*. The fundamental quantities are *mass, length, time* and *temperature,* designated by the letters, *M, L, T,* θ respectively. Temperature is specially useful in *compressible flow.* The *quantities which are expressed in terms of the fundamental or primary quantities are called* **derived or secondary quantities,** (*e.g.*, velocity, area, acceleration etc.). *The expression for a derived quantity in terms of the primary quantities is called the* **dimension** *of the physical quantity.*

A quantity may either be expressed dimensionally in *M-L-T* or *F-L-T* system (some engineers prefer to use force instead of mass as fundamental quantity because the force is easy to measure). Table 7.1 gives the dimensions of various quantities used in both the systems.

Example. 7.1. *Determine the dimensions of the following quantities*:

(*i*) *Discharge,* **(*ii*)** *Kinematic viscosity,*

(*ii*) *Force, and* **(*iv*)** *Specific weight.*

Solution. (*i*) *Discharge* = Area × velocity

$$= L^2 \times \frac{L}{T} = \frac{L^3}{T} = \mathbf{L^3T^{-1}} \textbf{ (Ans.)}$$

(*ii*) *Kinematic viscosity* $(\nu) = \frac{\mu}{\rho}$

where μ is given by: $\tau = \mu \frac{du}{dy}$

$$\therefore \quad \mu = \frac{\tau}{\frac{du}{dy}} = \frac{\text{Shear stress}}{\frac{L}{T} \times \frac{I}{L}} = \frac{\text{Force/area}}{1/T}$$

$$= \frac{\text{Mass} \times \text{acceleration}}{\text{Area} \times 1/T} = \frac{M \times \frac{L}{T^2}}{L^2 \times \frac{1}{T}} = \frac{ML}{L^2T^2 \times \frac{1}{T}}$$

$$= \frac{M}{LT} = ML^{-1}T^{-1} \text{ and } \rho = \frac{\text{Mass}}{\text{Volume}} = \frac{M}{L^3} = ML^{-3}$$

$\therefore$ Kinematic viscosity (v) $= \dfrac{\mu}{\rho} = \dfrac{ML^{-1}T^{-1}}{ML^{-3}} = \mathbf{L^2T^{-1}}$ **(Ans.)**

(*iii*) *Force* = mass × acceleration

$$= M \times \frac{\text{length}}{\text{time}^2} = \frac{ML}{T^2} = \mathbf{MLT^{-2}} \text{ (Ans.)}$$

(*iv*) *Specific weight* $= \dfrac{\text{Weight}}{\text{Volume}} = \dfrac{\text{Force}}{\text{Volume}} = \dfrac{MLT^{-2}}{L^3} = \mathbf{ML^{-2}T^{-2}}$ **(Ans.)**

Table 7.1. Quantities used in Fluid Mechanics and Heat Transfer and their Dimensions

S.No.	Quantity	Dimensions	
		M-L-T System	**F-L-T System**
	(*a*) Fundamental Quantities		
1.	Mass, M	M	$FL^{-1}T^2$
2.	Length, L	L	L
3.	Time, T	T	T
	(*b*) Geometric Quantities		
4.	Area, A	L^2	L^2
5.	Volume, $\forall$	L^3	L^3
6.	Moment of inertia	L^4	L^4
	(*c*) Kinematic Quantities		
7.	Linear velocity, u, V, U	LT^{-1}	LT^{-1}
8.	Angular velocity, ω; rotational speed, N	T^{-1}	T^{-1}
9.	Acceleration, a	LT^{-2}	LT^{-2}
10.	Angular acceleration, α	T^{-2}	T^{-2}
11.	Discharge, Q	L^3T^{-1}	L^3T^{-1}
12.	Gravity, g	LT^{-2}	LT^{-2}
13.	Kinematic viscosity, v	L^2T^{-1}	L^2T^{-1}
14.	Stream function, ψ, circulation, Γ	L^2T^{-1}	L^2T^{-1}
15.	Vorticity, Ω	T^{-1}	T^{-1}
	(*d*) Dynamic Quantities		
16.	Force, F	MLT^{-2}	F
17.	Density, ρ	ML^{-3}	$FL^{-4}T^2$
18.	Specific weight, w	$ML^{-2}T^{-2}$	FL^{-3}
19.	Dynamic viscosity, μ	$ML^{-1}T^{-1}$	$FL^{-2}T$
20.	Pressure, p; shear stress, τ	$ML^{-1}T^{-2}$	FL^{-2}
21.	Modulus of elasticity, E, K	$ML^{-1}T^{-2}$	FL^{-2}
22.	Momentum	MLT^{-1}	FT
23.	Angular momentum or moment of momentum	ML^2T^{-1}	FLT
24.	Work, W; energy, E	ML^2T^{-2}	FL
25.	Torque, T	ML^2T^{-2}	FL
26.	Power, P	ML^2T^{-3}	FLT^{-1}
	(*e*) Thermodynamic Quantities		
27.	Temperature	θ	θ
28.	Thermal conductivity	$MLT^{-3}\theta^{-1}$	$FT^{-1}\theta^{-1}$
29.	Enthalpy per unit mass	L^2T^{-2}	L^2T^{-2}

S.No.	Quantity	Dimensions	
		M-L-T System	F-L-T System
30.	Gas constant	$L^2T^{-2}\theta^{-1}$	$L^2T^{-2}\theta^{-1}$
31.	Entropy	$ML^2T^{-2}\theta^{-1}$	$FL\theta^{-1}$
32.	Internal energy per unit mass	L^2T^{-2}	L^2T^{-2}
33.	Heat transfer	ML^2T^{-3}	FLT^{-1}

7.3. DIMENSIONAL HOMOGENEITY

A physical equation is the relationship between two or more physical quantities. Any *correct equation* expressing a physical relationship between quantities *must be dimensionally homogeneous* (*according to Fourier's principle of dimensional homogeneity*) and *numerically equivalent. Dimensional homogeneity* states that *every term in an equation when reduced to fundamental dimensions must contain identical powers of each dimension.* A dimensionally homogeneous equation is applicable to all systems of units. In a dimensionally homogeneous equation, only quantities having the same dimensions can be added, subtracted or equated. Let us consider the equation:

$$p = wh$$

Dimensions of L.H.S. $= ML^{-1}T^{-2}$

Dimensions of R.H.S. $= ML^{-2}\, T^{-2} \times L = ML^{-1}T^{-2}$

Dimensions of L.H.S. = Dimensions of R.H.S.

$\therefore$ Equation $p = wh$ is dimensionally homogeneous; so it can be used in any system of units.

Applications of Dimensional Homogeneity:

The *principle of homogeneity* proves useful in the following ways:

1. It facilitates to determine the dimensions of a physical quantity.
2. It helps to check whether an equation of any physical phenomenon is dimensionally homogeneous or not.
3. It facilitates conversion of units from one system to another.
4. It provides a step towards dimensional analysis which is fruitfully employed to plan experiments and to present the results meaningfully.

Example 7.2. *Determine the dimensions of E in the dimensionally homogeneous Einstein's equation*

$$E = mc^2\left[\frac{1}{\sqrt{1-\left(\frac{v}{c}\right)^2}} - 1\right]$$

where v is the velocity and m is the mass.

Solution. Since the expression is dimensionally homogeneous, the term

$$\frac{1}{\sqrt{1-\left(\frac{v}{c}\right)^2}} \text{ should be dimensionless}$$

i.e., $[c] = [v] = \dfrac{L}{T}$

$$\therefore \quad [E] = m[c]^2 = M\left[\frac{L^2}{T^2}\right] = ML^2T^{-2}$$

i.e. E has the dimensions of **energy. (Ans.)**

7.4. METHODS OF DIMENSIONAL ANALYSIS

With the help of dimensional analysis the equation of a physical phenomenon can be developed in terms of dimensionless groups or parameters and thus reducing the number of variables. *The methods of dimensional analysis are based on the Fourier's principle of homogeneity.* The methods of dimensional analysis are:

1. Rayleigh's method
2. Buckingham's π-method
3. Bridgman's method
4. Matrix-tensor method
5. By visual inspection of the variables involved
6. Rearrangement of differential equations.

Here only first two methods will be dealt with.

7.4.1. Rayleigh's Method

This method gives a special form of relationship among the dimensionless groups, and has the *inherent drawback* that it *does not provide any information regarding the number of dimensionless groups to be obtained as a result of dimensional analysis.* Due to this reason this method has become *obsolete and is not favoured for use.*

Rayleigh's method is used for determining the expression for a variable which depends upon *maximum three or four variables only.* In case the number of independent variables becomes more than four, then it is very difficult to find the expression for the dependent variable.

In this method a functional relationship of some variables is expressed in the form of an exponential equation which must be dimensionally homogeneous. Thus if X is a variable which depends on $X_1, X_2, X_3, ...X_n$; the functional equation can be written as:

$$X = f(X_1, X_2, X_3, ... X_n) \quad ...(7.1)$$

In the above equation X is a *dependent variable,* while $X_1, X_2, X_3, ...X_n$ are *independent variables. A dependent variable is the one about which information is required while independent variables are those which govern the variation of dependent variable.*

Eqn. (7.1) can also be written as:

$$X = C\left(X_1^a, X_2^b, X_3^c, ...X_n^n\right) \quad ...(7.2)$$

where, C is a constant and $a, b, c,...$ are the arbitrary powers. The values of $a, b, c,... n$ are obtained by comparing the powers of the fundamental dimensions on both sides. Thus the expression is obtained for dependent variable.

Example 7.3. *Find an expression for the drag force on smooth sphere of diameter D, moving with a uniform velocity V in a fluid density ρ and dynamic viscosity μ.* **(PTU)**

Solution. The force drag F is a function of

(*i*) Diameter D, (*ii*) Velocity V,
(*iii*) Fluid density ρ, and (*iv*) Dynamic viscosity μ.

Mathematically, $F = f(D, V, \rho, \mu)$ or $F = C\,(D^a \cdot V^b \cdot \rho^c \cdot \mu^d)$ ...(1)

where, C is a non-dimensional constant.

Using *M-L-T* system the corresponding equation for dimensions is:

$$MLT^{-2} = [CL^a . (LT^{-1})^b . (ML^{-3})^c . (ML^{-1}T^{-1})^d]$$

For dimensional homogeneity the exponents of each dimension on both sides of the equation must be identical. Thus:

For M: $1 = c + d$ ...(*i*)

For L: $1 = a + b - 3c - d$ ...(*ii*)

For T: $-2 = -b - d$ ...(*iii*)

There are *four unknowns* (*a, b, c, d*) but *equations are three* in number. Therefore, it is not possible to find the values of *a, b, c* and *d.* However, *three of them can be expressed in terms of fourth variable which is most important*. Here the role of viscosity is vital one and hence a, *b, c* are expressed in terms of *d* (*i.e.* power to viscosity)

$\therefore$ $c = 1 - d$ ... from (*i*)

$b = 2 - d$ ... from (*iii*)

Putting these values in (*i*), we get:

$$a = 1 - b + 3c + d = 1 - 2 + d + 3\,(1 - d) + d$$
$$= 1 - 2 + d + 3 - 3d + d = 2 - d$$

Substituting these values of exponents in eqn. (1), we get:

$$F = C[D^{2-d} . V^{2-d} . \rho^{1-d} . \mu^d]$$
$$= C[D^2 V^2 \rho(D^{-d} . V^{-d} . \rho^{-d} . \mu^d)] = C\left[\rho D^2 V^2 \left(\frac{\mu}{\rho VD}\right)^d\right]$$
$$= \rho D^2 V^2 \phi\left(\frac{\mu}{\rho VD}\right) \textbf{ (Ans.)}$$

Example 7.4. *The efficiency η of a fan depends on the density ρ, the dynamic viscosity μ of the fluid, the angular velocity ω, diameter D of the rotor and the discharge Q. Express η in terms of dimensionless parameters.* **[UPSC]**

Solution. The efficiency η of a fan is a function of:

(*i*) Density ρ, (*ii*) Viscosity μ,

(*iii*) Angular velocity ω, (*iv*) Diameter *D*, and

(*v*) Discharge *Q*.

Mathematically, $\eta = f(\rho, \mu, \omega, D, Q)$

or, $\eta = C(\rho^a, \mu^b, \omega^c, D^d, Q^e)$ ...(1)

where *C* is a non-dimensional constant.

Using M-L-T system, the corresponding equation for dimensions is:

$$M^\circ L^\circ T^\circ = C[(ML^{-3})^a (ML^{-1}T^{-1})^b (T^{-1})^c (L)^d (L^3 T^{-1})^e]$$

For dimensional homogeneity the exponents of each dimension on both sides of the equation must be identical. Thus:

For M: $0 = a + b$

For L: $0 = -3a - b + d + 3e$

For T: $0 = -b - c - e$

There are *five variables* and we have only *three equations*. Experience has shown that recognized dimensionless groups appear if the exponents of *D*, ω and ρ are evaluated in terms of *b* and *e* (exponents of viscosity and discharge which are *more important*)

$\therefore$ $a = -b;\ c = (b + e);$

$$d = 3a + b - 3e = 3(-b) + b - 3e = -2b - 3e = -(2b + 3e)$$

Substituting these values of exponents in eqn. (1), we get:

$$\eta = C(\rho^{-b} . \mu^{b} . \omega^{-(b+e)} . D^{-(2b+3e)} . Q^{e})$$

$$= C(\rho^{-b} . \mu^{b} . \omega^{-b} . \omega^{-e} D^{-2b} . D^{-3e} . Q^{e})$$

$$= C\left[\left(\frac{\mu}{\rho \omega D^2}\right)^b \left(\frac{Q}{\omega D^3}\right)^e\right]$$

$$= \phi\left[\left(\frac{\mu}{\rho \omega D^2}\right), \left(\frac{Q}{\omega D^3}\right)\right] \textbf{ (Ans.)}$$

Example 7.5. *The resistance force R of a supersonic plane during flight can be considered as dependent upon the length of the aircraft l, velocity V, air viscosity μ, air density ρ and bulk modulus of air K. Express the functional relationship between these variables and the resisting force.*

[Anna University]

Solution. The resistance force R is a function of:

(*i*) Length l, (*ii*) Velocity V,
(*iii*) Air viscosity μ, (*iv*) Air density ρ, and
(*v*) Bulk modulus K.

Mathematically, $R = f(l, V, \mu, \rho, K)$

or, $R = C(l^a . V^b . \mu^c . \rho^d . K^e)$ ...(1)

where, C is a non-dimensional constant.

Using M-L-T system, the corresponding equation for dimensions is:

$$MLT^{-2} = C[L^a . (LT^{-1})^b . (ML^{-1}T^{-1})^c . (ML^{-3})^d . (ML^{-1}T^{-2})^e]$$

For dimensional homogeneity the exponents of each dimension on both sides of the equation must be identical. Thus:

For M: $1 = c + d + e$

For L: $1 = a + b - c - 3d - e$

For T: $-2 = -b - c - 2e$

There are *five variables* and we have only *three equations.* Expressing the three unknowns (a, b, d) in terms of c and e (exponents of viscosity and bulk modulus which are *more important*).

$\therefore$

$$d = 1 - c - e$$

$$b = 2 - c - 2e$$

$$a = 1 - b + c + 3d + e$$

$$= 1 - (2 - c - 2e) + c + 3(1 - c - e) + e$$

$$= 1 - 2 + c + 2e + c + 3 - 3c - 3e + e = 2 - c$$

Substituting these values of exponents in eqn. (1), we get:

$$R = C(l^{2-c} . V^{2-c-2e} . \mu^{c} . \rho^{1-c-e} . K^{e})$$

$$= C l^2 . V^2 . \rho(l^{-c} . V^{-c} . \mu^{c} . \rho^{-c}) . V^{-2e} . \rho^{-e} . K^{e}$$

$$= C l^2 V^2 \rho \left(\frac{\mu}{lV\rho}\right)^c . \left(\frac{K}{V^2\rho}\right)^e$$

$$= l^2 V^2 \rho \phi\left[\left(\frac{\mu}{lV\rho}\right), \left(\frac{K}{V^2\rho}\right)\right] \textbf{ (Ans.)}$$

Example 7.6. *A partially submerged body is towed in water. The resistance R to its motion depends on the density ρ, the viscosity μ of water, length l of the body, velocity V of the body and acceleration due to gravity. Show that the resistance to motion can be expressed in the form*

$$R = \rho L^2 V^2 \phi\left[\left(\frac{\mu}{\rho L V}\right), \left(\frac{lg}{V^2}\right)\right]$$

Solution. The resistance R is a function of:

(*i*) Density ρ, (*ii*) Viscosity μ,
(*iii*) Length l, (*iv*) Velocity V, and
(*v*) Acceleration due to gravity g.

Mathematically, $R = f(\rho, \mu, l, V, g)$

or, $R = C(\rho^a . \mu^b . l^c . V^d . g^e)$ ...(1)

where, C is a non-dimensional constant.

Using M-L-T system, the corresponding equation for dimensions is:

$$MLT^{-2} = C[(ML^{-3})^a . (ML^{-1}T^{-1})^b . (L)^c . (LT^{-1})^d . (LT^{-2})^e]$$

For dimensional homogeneity the exponents of each dimension on both sides of the equation must be identical. Thus:

For M: $1 = a + b$

For L: $1 = -3a - b + c + d + e$

For T: $-2 = -b - d - 2e$

There are *five variables* and we have only *three equations.* To get the required result, we shall evaluate exponents of ρ, l, V (*i.e. a, c, d*) in terms of other unknowns (*i.e. b, e*)

$\therefore$ $a = 1 - b$

$d = 2 - b - 2e$

$c = 1 + 3a + b - d - e = 1 + 3(1 - b) + b - (2 - b - 2e) - e$

$= 1 + 3 - 3b + b - 2 + b + 2e - e = 2 - b + e$

Substituting these values of components in eqn. (1), we get:

$$R = C[\rho^{1-b} . \mu^b . l^{2-b+e} . V^{2-b-2e} . g^e]$$

$$= C[\rho l^2 V^2 (\rho^{-b} . \mu^b . l^{-b} . V^{-b})(l^e . V^{-2e} . g^e)]$$

$$= C\left[\rho l^2 V^2 \left(\frac{\mu}{\rho l V}\right)^b . \left(\frac{lg}{V^2}\right)^e\right]$$

$$= \rho l^2 V^2 \phi\left[\left(\frac{\mu}{\rho l V}\right), \left(\frac{lg}{V^2}\right)\right]$$ ...(Proved.)

Example 7.7. *The pressure drop Δp in a pipe of diameter D and length l depends on the density ρ and viscosity μ of fluid flowing, mean velocity V of flow and average height of protuderance t. Show that the pressure drop can be expressed in the form:*

$$\Delta p = \rho V^2 \phi\left(\frac{l}{D}, \frac{\mu}{VD\rho}, \frac{t}{D}\right)$$ **[RGPV, Bhopal]**

Solution. The pressure drop Δp, is a function of : D, l, ρ, μ, V and t

Mathematically, $\Delta p = f(D, l, \rho, \mu, V, t)$

or, $\Delta p = C(D^a . l^b . \rho^c . \mu^d . V^e . t^f)$ ...(1)

where, C is a non-dimensional constant.

Using M-L-T system, the corresponding equation for dimensions is:

$$ML^{-1}T^{-2} = C\,[L^a \,.\, L^b \,.\, (ML^{-3})^c \,.\, (ML^{-1}T^{-1})^d \,.\, (LT^{-1})^e \,.\, (L)^f\,]$$

For dimensional homogeneity the exponents of each dimension on both sides of the equation must be identical. Thus,

For M: $\quad 1 = c + d$

For L: $\quad -1 = a + b - 3c - d + e + f$

For T: $\quad -2 = -d - e$

There are *six variables* and we have only *three equations.* To get the required result, we shall evaluate exponents of *D*, ρ and *V* (*i.e. a, c* and *e*) in terms of the unknowns (*i.e. b, d, f*).

$$\therefore \quad c = 1 - d;\ e = 2 - d$$

$$\begin{aligned} a &= -1 - b + 3c + d - e - f \\ &= -1 - b + 3\,(1 - d) + d - (2 - d) - f \\ &= -1 - b + 3 - 3d + d - 2 + d - f \\ &= -(b + d + f) \end{aligned}$$

Substituting these values of exponents in eqn. (1), we get:

$$\begin{aligned} \Delta p &= C\,(D^{-(b+d+f)} \,.\, l^b \,.\, \rho^{2-d} \,.\, \mu^d \,.\, V^{2-d} \,.\, t^f) \\ &= C[\rho V^2\,(D^{-b} \,.\, l^b)\,(D^{-d}) \,.\, \rho^{-d} \,.\, \mu^d V^{-d})\,(D^{-f} \,.\, t^f) \\ &= C\left[\rho V^2 \left(\frac{l}{D}\right)^b \left(\frac{\mu}{VD\rho}\right)^d \left(\frac{t}{D}\right)^f\right] \\ &= \boldsymbol{\rho V^2\, \phi\left(\frac{l}{D}, \frac{\mu}{VD\rho}, \frac{t}{D}\right)} \end{aligned}$$

...Proved

From experiments it has been observed that Δp is a linear function of $\frac{t}{D}$.

$$\therefore \quad \Delta p = \rho V^2 \frac{l}{D} \phi\left(\frac{\mu}{VD\rho}, \frac{t}{D}\right)$$

or,

$$\frac{\Delta p}{w} = \frac{V^2}{g}\frac{l}{D}\phi\left(\frac{\mu}{VD\rho}, \frac{t}{D}\right) \qquad \left(\because \rho = \frac{w}{g}\right)$$

This is usually written in the form,

$$h_f = \frac{4\,flV^2}{2gD} \qquad \text{(Darcy-Weisbach formula)}$$

where, *f* is the co-efficient of friction which depends upon the Reynolds number $\left(\frac{VD\rho}{\mu}\right)$ and the surface finish of the pipe $\left(\frac{t}{D}\right)$.

7.4.2. Buckingham's π-Method/Theorem

When a large number of physical variables are involved Rayleigh's method of dimensional analysis becomes *increasingly* laborious and *cumbersome.* Buckingham's method is an *improvement* over Rayleigh's method. Buckingham designated the dimensionless group by the Greek capital letter π(Pi). It is therefore often called *Buckingham π-method.* The *advantage of this method over Rayleigh's method is that it lets us know, in advance, of the analysis, as to how many dimensionless groups are to be expected.*

Buckingham's π-theorem states as follows:

"If there are n variables (dependent and independent variables) in a dimensionally homogeneous equation and if these variables contain m fundamental dimensions (such as M, L, T, etc.) then the variables are arranged into (n-m) dimensionless terms. These dimensionless terms are called π-terms."

Mathematically, if any variable X_1, depends on independent variables, $X_2, X_3, X_4, ...X_n$; the functional equation may be written as:

$$X_1 = f(X_2, X_3, X_4, ...X_n) \quad ...(7.3)$$

Eqn. (7.3) can also be written as:

$$f_1(X_1, X_2, X_3, ...X_n) = 0 \quad ...(7.4)$$

It is a dimensionally homogeneous equation and contains *n* variables. If there are *m* fundamental dimensions, then according to Buckingham's π-theorem, it [eqn. (7.4)] can be written in terms of number of π-terms (dimensionless groups) in which number of π-terms is equal to (*n-m*). Hence, eqn. (7.4) becomes as:

$$f_1(\pi_1, \pi_2, \pi_3 ...\pi_{n-m}) = 0 \quad ...(7.5)$$

Each dimensionless π-term is formed by combining *m* variables out of the total *n* variables with *one of the remaining (n-m) variables* i.e. each π-term contains (*m* + 1) variables. These *m* variables which appear repeatedly in each of π-terms are consequently called ***repeating variables*** and are chosen from among the variables such that they together *involve all the fundamental dimensions* and *they themselves do not form a dimensionless parameter.* Let in the above case X_2, X_3 and X_4 are the repeating variables if the fundamental dimensions *m* (*M, L, T*) = 3, then each term is written as:

$$\left.\begin{aligned} \pi_1 &= X_2^{a_1}.X_3^{b_1}.X_4^{c_1}.X_1 \\ \pi_2 &= \left(X_2^{a_2}.X_3^{b_2}.X_4^{c_2}.X_5\right) \\ &\vdots \\ &\vdots \\ \pi_{n-m} &= \left(X_2^{a_{n-m}}.X_3^{b_{n-m}}.X_4^{c_{n-m}}.X_n\right) \end{aligned}\right\} \quad ...(7.6)$$

where $a_1, b_1, c_1; a_2, b_2, c_2$ etc. are the constants, which are determined by considering dimensional homogeneity. These values are substituted in eqn. (7.6) and values of $\pi_1, \pi_2, \pi_3 ....\pi_{n-m}$ are obtained. These values of π's are substituted in eqn. (7.5). The final general equation for the phenomenon may then be obtained by expressing anyone of the π-terms as a function of the other as

$$\left.\begin{aligned} \pi_1 &= \phi(\pi_2, \pi_3, \pi_4,.....\pi_{n-m}) \\ \pi_2 &= \phi(\pi_1, \pi_3, \pi_4,.....\pi_{n-m}) \end{aligned}\right\} \quad ...(7.7)$$

Selection of repeating variables:

The following points should be kept in view while selecting *m* repeating variables:

1. *m* repeating variables must contain *jointly* all the fundamental dimensions involved in the phenomenon. Usually the fundamental dimensions are *M, L* and *T.* However, if only two dimensions are involved, there will be 2 repeating variables and they must contain *together* the two dimensions involved.
2. The repeating variables *must not* form the non-dimensional parameters among themselves.
3. As far as possible, the dependent variable *should not* be selected as repeating variable.
4. *No two repeating variables should have the same dimensions.*
5. The repeating variables should be chosen in such a way that one variable contains **geometric property** (*e.g. length, l; diameter, d; height, H* etc.), other variable contains **flow property**

(*e.g. velocity, V; acceleration, a* etc.) and third variable contains **fluid property** (*e.g. mass density,* ρ; *weight density, w dynamic viscosity,* μ etc.).

The choice of repeating variables, in most of fluid mechanics problems, may be:

(*i*) l, V, ρ (*ii*) d, V, ρ (*iii*) l, V, μ (*iv*) d, V, μ.

The procedure for solving problems by Buckingham's π-theorem in the Example 7.8 below:

Example 7.8. *The resistance R experienced by a partially submerged body depends upon the velocity V, length of the body l, viscosity of the fluid μ, density of the fluid ρ and gravitational acceleration g. Obtain a dimensionless expression for R.* **[UPTU]**

Solution. Step 1. The resistance R is a function of:

(*i*) Velocity V, (*ii*) Length l, (*iii*) Viscosity μ,

(*iv*) Density ρ, and (*v*) Gravitational acceleration g.

Mathematically, $$R = f(V, l, \mu, \rho, g) \quad ...(i)$$

or, $$f_1(R, V, l, \mu, \rho, g) = 0 \quad ...(ii)$$

∴ Total number of variables, $n = 6$

m is obtained by writing dimensions of each variable as: $R = MLT^{-2}$, $V = LT^{-1}$, $\mu = ML^{-1}T^{-1}$, $\rho = ML^{-3}$, $g = LT^{-2}$. Thus the fundamental dimensions in the problem are M, L, T and hence $m = 3$

Number of dimensionless π-terms $= n - m = 6 - 3 = 3$

Thus three π–terms say π_1, π_2, and π_3 are formed.

The eqn. (*ii*) may be written as:

$$f_1(\pi_1, \pi_2, \pi_3) = 0 \quad ...(iii)$$

Step 2. Selection of repeating variables: Out of six variables R, V, l, μ, ρ, g three variables (as $m = 3$) are to be selected as *repeating variables*. R is a dependent variable and should *not* be selected as a repeating variable. Out of the remaining five variables one variable should have *geometric property,* second should have *flow property* and third one should have *fluid property*; these requirements are met by selecting l, V and ρ *as repeating variables.* The repeating variables themselves should not form a dimensionless term and must contain *jointly all fundamental dimensions equal to m i.e.* 3 here. Dimensions of l, V and ρ are L, LT^{-1}, ML^{-3} and hence the three fundamental dimensions exist in l, V and ρ and also *no dimensionless group is formed by them.*

Step 3. Each π-term (= $m + 1$ variables) is written as given in eqn. (7.6), *i.e.,*

$$\left.\begin{aligned} \pi_1 &= l^{a_1}.V^{b_1}.\rho^{c_1}.R \\ \pi_2 &= l^{a_2}.V^{b_2}.\rho^{c_3}.\mu \\ \pi_3 &= l^{a_3}.V^{b_3}.\rho^{c_3}.g \end{aligned}\right\} \quad ...(iv)$$

Step 4. Each π-term is solved by the *principle of dimensional homogeneity, as* follows:

π_1-term:

$$\pi_1 = l^{a_1}.V^{b_1}.\rho^{c_1}.R$$
$$M^0L^0T^0 = L^{a_1}.(LT^{-1})^{b_1}.(ML^{-3})^{c_1}.(MLT^{-2})$$

Equating the exponents of M, L and T respectively, we get:

For M: $0 = c_1 + 1$

For L: $0 = a_1 + b_1 - 3c_1 + 1$

For T: $0 = -b_1 - 2$

$\therefore \quad c_1 = -1;\ b_1 = -2$

and, $\quad a_1 = -b_1 + 3c_1 - 1 = 2 - 3 - 1 = -2$

Substituting the values of a_1, b_1, and c_1 in π_1, we get:

$$\therefore \quad \pi_1 = l^{-2} \cdot V^{-2} \cdot \rho^{-1} \cdot R = \frac{R}{l^2 V^2 \rho} \qquad ...(v)$$

π_2–term:

$$\pi_2 = l^{a_2} \cdot V^{b_2} \cdot \rho^{c_2} \cdot \mu$$

$$M^0L^0T^0 = L^{a_2} \cdot (LT^{-1})^{b_2} \cdot (ML^{-3})^{c_2} \cdot (ML^{-1}T^{-1})$$

Equating the exponents of *M, L* and *T* respectively, we get:

For M: $\quad 0 = c_2 + 1$

For L: $\quad 0 = a_2 + b_2 - 3c_2 - 1$

For T: $\quad 0 = -b_2 - 1$

$\therefore \quad c_2 = -1;\ b_2 = -1$

and, $\quad a_2 = -b_2 + 3c_2 + 1 = 1 - 3 + 1 = -1$

Substituting the values of a_2, b_2, and c_2 in π_2, we get:

$$\therefore \quad \pi_2 = l^{-1} \cdot V^{-1} \cdot \rho^{-1} \cdot \mu = \frac{\mu}{lV\rho}$$

π_3-term:

$$\pi_3 = l^{a_3} \cdot V^{b_3} \cdot \rho^{c_3} \cdot g$$

$$M^0L^0T^0 = L^{a_3} \cdot (LT^{-1})^{b_3} \cdot (ML^{-3})^{c_3} \cdot (LT^{-2})$$

Equating the exponents of *M, L* and *T* respectively, we get:

For M: $\quad 0 = c_3$

For L: $\quad 0 = a_3 + b_3 - 3c_3 + 1$

For T: $\quad 0 = -b_3 - 2$

$\therefore \quad c_3 = 0;\ b_3 = -2$

and, $\quad a_3 = -b_3 + 3c_3 - 1 = 2 + 0 - 1 = 1$

Substituting the values of a_3, b_3, and c_3 in π_3, we get:

$$\therefore \quad \pi_3 = l^1 \cdot V^{-2} \cdot \rho^0 \cdot g = \frac{lg}{V^2}$$

Step 5. Substitute the values of π_1, π_2, π_3 in eqn. (*iii*). The functional relationship becomes:

$$f_1\left(\frac{R}{l^2V^2\rho}, \frac{\mu}{lV\rho}, \frac{lg}{V^2}\right) = 0$$

or,

$$\frac{R}{l^2V^2\rho} = \phi\left(\frac{\mu}{lV\rho}, \frac{lg}{V^2}\right)$$

$$= \phi\left(\frac{\rho Vl}{\mu}, \frac{V}{\sqrt{lg}}\right)$$

The above step has been made on the postulate that *reciprocal of pi-term and its square root is non-dimensional.*

$$R = l^2V^2\rho\, \phi\left(\frac{\rho Vl}{\mu}, \frac{V}{\sqrt{lg}}\right) \quad \textbf{(Ans.)}$$

The resistance R is thus a function of Reynolds number $\left(\frac{\rho Vl}{\mu}\right)$ and Froude's number $\left(\frac{V}{\sqrt{lg}}\right)$.

Example 7.9. *Using Buckingham's π-theorem, show that the velocity through a circular orifice is given by*

$$V = \sqrt{2gH}\,\phi\left[\frac{D}{H}, \frac{\mu}{\rho VH}\right]$$

where, H = *Head causing flow,*
D = *Diameter of the orifice,*
μ = *Co-efficient of viscosity,*
ρ = *Mass density, and*
g = *Acceleration due to gravity.* **[GATE]**

Solution. V is a function of: H, D, μ, ρ and g

Mathematically, $V = f(H, D, \mu, \rho, g)$ ...(*i*)

or, $f_1(V, H, D, \mu, \rho, g) = 0$ ...(*ii*)

∴ Total number of variables, $n = 6$

Writing dimensions of each variable, we have:

$$V = LT^{-1}, H = L, D = L, \mu = ML^{-1}T^{-1}, \rho = ML^{-3}, g = LT^{-2}$$

Thus, number of fundamental dimensions, $m = 3$

∴ Number of π-terms $= n - m = 6 - 3 = 3$

Eqn. (*ii*) can be written as:

$$f_1(\pi_1, \pi_2, \pi_3) = 0 \quad ...(iii)$$

Each π-term contains $(m + 1)$ variables, where $m = 3$ and is also equal to repeating variables. Choosing H, g, ρ as *repeating variables* (V being a dependent variable should not be chosen as repeating variable), we get three π-terms as:

$$\pi_1 = H^{a_1} . g^{b_1} \rho^{c_3} . V$$
$$\pi_2 = H^{a_2} . g^{b_2} \rho^{c_2} . D$$
$$\pi_3 = H^{a_3} . g^{b_3} \rho^{c_3} . \mu$$

π_1-term:

$$\pi_1 = H^{a_1} . g^{b_1} \rho^{c_1} . V$$
$$M^0L^0T^0 = L^{a_1} . (LT^{-2})^{b_1} . (ML^{-3})^{c_1} . (LT^{-1})$$

Equating the exponents of M, L and T respectively, we get:

For M: $0 = c_1$

For L: $0 = a_1 + b_1 - 3c_1 + 1$

For T: $0 = -2b_1 - 1$

∴ $c_1 = 0;\ b_1 = -\frac{1}{2}$

and, $a_1 = -b_1 + 3c_1 - 1 = \frac{1}{2} + 0 - 1 = -\frac{1}{2}$

Substituting the values of a_1, b_1 and c_1 in π_1, we get:

∴ $$\pi_1 = H^{-1/2} . g^{-\frac{1}{2}} \cdot \rho^0 \cdot V = \frac{V}{\sqrt{gh}}$$

π_2-term:

$$\pi_2 = H^{a_2} . g^{b_2} . \rho^{c_2} . D$$
$$M^0L^0T^0 = L^{a_2} . (LT^{-2})^{b_2} . (ML^{-3})^{c_2} . L$$

Equating the exponents of *M, L* and *T* respectively, we get:

For M: $0 = c_2$

For L: $0 = a_2 + b_2 - 3c_2 + 1$

For T: $0 = -2b_2$

$\therefore$ $c_2 = 0; b_2 = 0$

and, $a_2 = -b_2 + 3c_2 - 1 = -1$

Substituting the values of a_2, b_2, and c_2 in π_2, we get:

$$\pi_2 = H^{-1} . g^0 . \rho^0 . D = \frac{D}{H}$$

π_3-term:

$$\pi_3 = H^{a_3} . g^{b_3} . \rho^{c_3} . \mu$$
$$M^0L^0T^0 = L^{a_3} . (LT^{-2})^{b_3} . (ML^{-3})^{c_3} . ML^{-1}T^{-1}$$

Equating the exponents of *M, L* and *T* respectively, we get:

For M: $0 = c_3 + 1$

For L: $0 = a_3 + b_3 - 3c_3 - 1$

For T: $0 = -2b_3 - 1$

$\therefore$ $c_3 = -1; b_3 = -\frac{1}{2}$

and, $a_3 = -b_3 + 3c_3 + 1 = \frac{1}{2} - 3 + 1 = -\frac{3}{2}$

Substituting the values of a_3, b_3, and c_3 in π_3, we get:

$$\pi_3 = H^{-3/2} . g^{-\frac{1}{2}} . \rho^{-1} . \mu = \frac{\mu}{H^{3/2}\rho\sqrt{g}}$$

$$= \frac{\mu}{H\rho\sqrt{gH}} = \frac{\mu V}{H\rho V\sqrt{gH}}$$ (Multiply and divide by V)

$$= \frac{\mu}{H\rho V} \cdot \pi_1$$ $\left(\because \frac{V}{\sqrt{gH}} = \pi_1\right)$

Substituting the values of π_1, π_2 and π_3 in eqn. (*iii*), we get:

$$f_1\left(\frac{V}{\sqrt{gH}}, \frac{D}{H}, \frac{\mu}{HlV} . \pi_1\right) = 0$$

or, $$\frac{V}{\sqrt{gH}} = \phi\left[\frac{D}{H}, \frac{\mu}{H\rho V} . \pi_1\right]$$

or, $$V = \sqrt{2gH}\,\phi\left[\frac{D}{H}, \frac{\mu}{\rho VH}\right]$$ **...Proved.**

(*Multiplying or dividing by any constant does not change the character of π-terms*).

Example 7.10. *Show that the lift F_L on airfoil can be expressed as*

$$F_L = \rho V^2 d^2 \phi\left(\frac{\rho V d}{\mu}, \alpha\right)$$

where, ρ = *Mass density,* V = *Velocity of flow,*
d = *A characteristic depth,* α = *Angle of incidence, and*
μ = *Co-efficient of viscosity.*

Solution. Lift F_L is a function of: ρ, V, d, μ, α

Mathematically, $F_L = f(\rho, V, d, \mu, \alpha)$ ...(*i*)

or, $f_1(F_L, \rho, V, d, \mu, \alpha)$ ...(*ii*)

∴ Total number of variables, $n = 6$

Writing dimensions of each variable, we have:

$$F_L = MLT^{-2}, \rho = ML^{-3}, V = LT^{-1}, d = L, \mu = ML^{-1}T^{-1}, \alpha = M^0L^0T^0$$

Thus, number of fundamental dimensions, $m = 3$

∴ Number of π-terms $= n - m = 6 - 3 = 3$

Eqn. (*ii*) can be written as: $f_1(\pi_1, \pi_2, \pi_3) = 0$ ...(*iii*)

Each π-term contains $(m + 1)$ variables, where $m = 3$ and is also equal to repeating variables. Choosing d, V and ρ as repeating variables, we get these π-terms as:

$$\pi_1 = d^{a_1} . V^{b_1} . \rho^{c_1} . F_L$$
$$\pi_2 = d^{a_2} . V^{b_2} . \rho^{c_2} . \alpha$$
$$\pi_3 = d^{a_3} . V^{b_3} . \rho^{c_3} . \mu$$

π_1-term:

$$\pi_1 = d^{a_1} . V^{b_1} . \rho^{c_1} . F_L$$
$$M^0L^0T^0 = L^{a_1} . (LT^{-1})^{b_1} . (ML^{-3})^{c_1} . (MLT^{-2})$$

Equating the exponents of *M, L* and *T* respectively, we get:

For M: $0 = c_1 + 1$

For L: $0 = a_1 + b_1 - 3c_1 + 1$

For T: $0 = -b_1 - 2$

∴ $c_1 = -1; b_1 = -2$

∴ $a_1 = -b_1 + 3c_1 - 1 = 2 - 3 - 1 = -2$

Substituting the values of a_1, b_1 and c_1 in π_1, we get:

$$\pi_1 = d^{-2} . V^{-2} . \rho^{-1} . F_L = \frac{F_L}{\rho V^2 d^2}$$

π_2-term:

$$\pi_2 = d^{a_2} . V^{b_2} . \rho^{c_2} . \mu$$
$$M^0L^0T^0 = L^{a_2} . (LT^{-1})^{b_2} . (ML^{-3})^{c_2} . (ML^{-1}T^{-1})$$

Equating the exponents of *M, L* and *T* respectively, we get:

For M: $0 = c_2 + 1$

For L: $0 = a_2 + b_2 - 3c_2 - 1$

For T: $0 = -b_2 - 1$

∴ $c_2 = -1; b_2 = -1$

and, $a_2 = -b_2 + 3c_2 + 1 = 1 - 3 + 1 = -1$

Substituting the values of a_2, b_2 and c_2 in π_2, we get:

$$\pi_2 = d^{-1} . V^{-1} . \rho^{-1} . \mu = \frac{\mu}{\rho V d}$$

or, $$\pi_2 = \frac{\rho V d}{\mu}$$

π_3-term:

$$\pi_3 = d^{a_3} . V^{b_3} \rho^{c_3} . \alpha$$

$$M^0L^0T^0 = L^{a_3} . (LT^{-1})^{b_3} . (ML^{-3})^{c_3} . (M^0L^0T^0)$$

Equating the exponents of M, L and T respectively, we get:

For M: $0 = c_3 + 0$

For L: $0 = a_3 + b_3 - 3c_3 + 0$

For T: $0 = - b_3 + 0$

$\therefore$ $c_3 = 0; b_3 = 0$

and, $a_3 = - b_3 + 3c_3 = 0$

Substituting the values of a_3, b_3 and c_3 in π_3, we get:

$$\pi_3 = d^0 . V^0 . \rho^0 . \alpha = \alpha$$

Substituting the values of π_1, π_2 and π_3 in eqn. (*iii*), we get:

$$f_1\left(\frac{F_L}{\rho V^2 d^2}, \frac{\rho V d}{\mu}, \alpha\right)$$

$$\frac{F_L}{\rho V^2 d^2} = \phi\left(\frac{\rho V d}{\mu}, \alpha\right)$$

or, $$F_L = \boldsymbol{\rho V^2 d^2 \phi\left(\frac{\rho V d}{\mu}, \alpha\right)}$$ **...Proved.**

Example 7.11. *The pressure difference Δp in a pipe of diameter D and length l due to turbulent flow depends on the velocity V, viscosity μ, density ρ and roughness k. Using Buckingham's π-theorem, obtain an expression for Δp.* **[Delhi University]**

Solution. The pressure difference Δp is a function of : D, l, V, μ, ρ, k

Mathematically, $\Delta p = f(D, l, V, \mu, \rho, k)$ ...(*i*)

or, $f_1 (\Delta p, D, l, V, \mu, \rho, k) = 0$ ...(*ii*)

$\therefore$ Total number of variables, $n = 7$

Writing dimensions of each variable, we have:

Δp (dimensions of pressure) $= ML^{-1}T^{-2}, D = L, l = L, V = LT^{-1},$

$\mu = ML^{-1}T^{-1}, \rho = ML^{-3}, k = L$

Thus, number of fundamental dimensions, $m = 3$

$\therefore$ Number of π-terms $= n - m = 7 - 3 = 4$

Eqn. (*ii*) can be written as:

$$f_1(\pi_1, \pi_2, \pi_3, \pi_4) = 0 \qquad ...(iii)$$

Each π-term contains $(m + 1)$ variables, where $m = 3$ and is also equal to repeating variables. Choosing D, V and ρ as repeating variables, we get four π-terms as:

$$\pi_1 = D^{a_1} . V^{b_1}.\rho^{c_1} . \Delta_p$$

$$\pi_1 = D^{a_2} . V^{b_2}.\rho^{c_3} . l$$

$$\pi_3 = D^{a_3} . V^{b_3}.\rho^{c_3} . \mu$$

$$\pi_4 = D^{a_4} . V^{b_4}.\rho^{c_4} . k$$

π_1-term:

$$\pi_1 = D^{a_1} . V^{b_1}.\rho^{c_1} . \Delta p$$

$$M^0L^0T^0 = L^{a_1} . (LT^{-1})^{b_1} . (ML^{-3})^{c_1} . (ML^{-3}T^{-2})$$

Equating the exponents of M, L and T respectively, we get:

For M: $0 = c_1 + 1$

For L: $0 = a_1 + b_1 - 3c_1 - 1$

For T: $0 = -b_1 - 2$

$\therefore$ $c_1 = -1; b_1 = -2$

and, $a_1 = -b_1 + 3c_1 + 1 = 2 - 3 + 1 = 0$

Substituting the values of a_1, b_1 and c_1 in π_1, we get:

$$\pi_1 = D^0 . V^{-2} . \rho^{-1} . \Delta p = \frac{\Delta p}{\rho V^2}$$

π_2-term:

$$\pi_2 = D^{a_2} . V^{b_2} . \rho^{c_2} . l$$

$$M^0L^0T^0 = L^{a_2} . (LT^{-1})^{b_2} . (ML^{-3})^{c_2} . L$$

Equating the exponents of M, L and T respectively, we get:

For M: $0 = c_2$

For L: $0 = a_2 + b_2 - 3c_2 + 1$

For T: $0 = -b_2$

$\therefore$ $c_2 = 0; b_2 = 0$

and, $a_2 = -b_2 + 3c_2 - 1 = -1$

Substituting the values of a_2, b_2 and c_2 in π_2, we get:

$$\pi_2 = D^{-1} . V^0 . \rho^0 . l = \frac{l}{D}$$

π_3-term:

$$\pi_3 = D^{a_3} . V^{b_3} . \rho^{c_3} . \mu$$

$$M^0L^0T^0 = L^{a_3} . (LT^{-1})^{b_3} . (LT^{-3})^{c_3} . (ML^{-1} T^{-1})$$

Equating the exponents of M, L and T respectively, we get:

For M: $0 = c_3 + 1$

For L: $0 = a_3 + b_3 - 3c_3 - 1$

For T: $0 = -b_3 - 1$

$\therefore$ $c_3 = -1; b_3 = -1$

and, $a_3 = -b_3 + 3c_3 + 1 = 1 - 3 + 1 = -1$

Substituting the values of a_3, b_3 and c_3 in π_3, we get:

$$\pi_3 = D^{-1} . V^{-1} . \rho^{-1} . \mu = \frac{\mu}{DV\rho}$$

π_4-term:

$$\pi_4 = D^{a_4} . V^{b_4} . \rho^{c_4} . k$$

$$M^0L^0T^0 = L^{a_4} . (LT^{-1})^{b_4} . (ML^{-3})^{c_4} . L$$

(Dimension of $k = L$)

Equating the exponents of M, L and T respectively, we get:

For M: $0 = c_4$

For L: $0 = a_4 + b_4 - 3c_4 + 1$

For T: $0 = -b_4$

$\therefore$ $c_4 = 0; b_4 = 0$

and, $$a_4 = -b_4 + 3c_4 - 1 = 0 + 0 - 1 = -1$$

Substituting the values of a_4, b_4 and c_4 in π_4, we get:

$$\pi_3 = D^{-1} . V^0 . \rho^0 . k = \frac{k}{D}$$

Substituting the values of π_1, π_2, π_3 and π_4 in eqn. (*iii*), we get:

$$f_1\left(\frac{\Delta p}{\rho V^2}, \frac{l}{D}, \frac{\mu}{DV\rho}, \frac{k}{D}\right) = 0$$

or, $$\frac{\Delta p}{\rho V^2} = \phi\left[\frac{l}{D}, \frac{\mu}{DV\rho}, \frac{k}{D}\right]$$

- **Expression for difference of pressure head (h_f):**

As observed from experiments, Δp is a linear function of $\frac{l}{D}$; therefore taking this out of function, we have:

$$\frac{\Delta p}{\rho V^2} = \frac{l}{D}\phi\left[\frac{\mu}{DV\rho}, \frac{k}{D}\right]$$

or, $$\frac{\Delta p}{\rho} = V^2 . \frac{l}{D}\phi\left[\frac{\mu}{DV\rho}, \frac{k}{D}\right]$$

Dividing both sides by g, we get:

$$\frac{\Delta p}{\rho g} = \frac{V^2}{g} . \frac{l}{D}\phi\left[\frac{\mu}{DV\rho}, \frac{k}{D}\right]$$

Now $\phi\left[\frac{\mu}{DV\rho}, \frac{k}{D}\right]$ consists of following two terms:

(*i*) $\frac{\mu}{DV\rho}$ which is $\frac{1}{\text{Reynold number}}$ or $\frac{1}{Re}$

(*ii*) $\frac{k}{D}$ ...called roughness factor

$\therefore$ $\phi\left[\frac{1}{Re}, \frac{k}{D}\right]$ is put equal to f

where, f = Co-efficient of friction (function of Reynold number and roughness factor)

$\therefore$ $$\frac{\Delta p}{\rho g} = \frac{4f}{2} . \frac{V^2 l}{gD} \qquad \left[\because f = \phi\left(\frac{\mu}{DV\rho}, \frac{k}{D}\right)\right]$$

(Multiplying or dividing by any constant does not change the character of π-terms)

$\therefore$ $$\frac{\Delta p}{\rho g} = h_f = \frac{4flV^2}{D \times 2g} \quad \textbf{(Ans.)}$$

Example 7.12. *The discharge Q of a centrifugal pump depends upon the mass density of fluid (ρ), the speed of the pump (N), the diameter of the impeller (D), the manometric head (H_m) and the viscosity of fluid (μ). Show that*

$$Q = ND^3 \phi\left(\frac{gH}{N^2D^2}, \frac{\mu}{\rho ND^2}\right)$$

Solution. The discharge Q is a function of: N, D, g, H, μ, ρ.

Mathematically, $Q = f(N, D, g, H, \mu, \rho)$ ...(*i*)

or, $f_1(Q, N, D, g, H, \mu, \rho) = 0$ ...(*ii*)

Total number of variables, $n = 7$

Writing dimensions of each variable, we have:

$$Q = L^3T^{-1}, N = T^{-1}, D = L, g = LT^{-2},$$
$$H = L, \ \mu = ML^{-1}T^{-1}, \rho = ML^{-3}$$

Thus, number of fundamental dimensions, $m = 3$

$\therefore$ Number of π-terms $= n - m = 7 - 3 = 4$

Eqn. (*ii*) can be written as:

$$f_1(\pi_1, \pi_2, \pi_3, \pi_4) = 0 \quad ...(iii)$$

Each π-term contains $(m + 1)$ variables, where $m = 3$ and is also equal to repeating variables.

Choosing D, N, ρ as *repeating variables,* we get four π-terms as:

$$\pi_1 = D^{a_1} . N^{b_1} . \rho^{c_1} . Q$$
$$\pi_2 = D^{a_2} . N^{b_2} . \rho^{c_2} . g$$
$$\pi_3 = D^{a_3} . N^{b_3} . \rho^{c_3} . H$$
$$\pi_4 = D^{a_4} . N^{b_4} . \rho^{c_4} . \mu$$

π_1-term:

$$\pi_1 = D^{a_1} . N^{b_1} . \rho^{c_1} . Q$$
$$M^0L^0T^0 = L^{a_1} . (T^{-1})^{b_1} . (ML^{-3})^{c_1} (L^3T^{-1})$$

Equating the exponents of M, L and T respectively, we get:

For M: $0 = c_1$

For L: $0 = a_1 - 3c_1 + 3$

For T: $0 = -b_1 - 1$

$\therefore$ $c_1 = 0; b_1 = -1$

and, $a_1 = 3c_1 - 3 = 0 - 3 = -3$

Substituting the values of a_1, b_1 and c_1 in π_1, we get:

$$\pi_1 = D^{-3} . N^{-1} . \rho^0 . Q = \frac{Q}{ND^3}$$

π_2-term:

$$\pi_2 = D^{a_2} . N^{b_2} . \rho^{c_2} . g$$
$$M^0L^0T^0 = L^{a_2} . (T^{-1})^{b_2} . (ML^{-3})^{c_2} . (LT^{-2})$$

Equating the exponents of M, L and T respectively, we get:

For M: $0 = c_2$

For L: $0 = a_2 - 3c_2 + 1$

For T: $0 = -b_1 - 2$

$\therefore$ $c_2 = 0; b_1 = -2$

and, $a_2 = 3c_2 - 1 = 0 - 1 = -1$

Substituting the values of a_2, b_2 and c_2 in π_2, we get:

$$\pi_2 = D^{-1} . N^{-2} . \rho^0 . g = \frac{g}{N^2D}$$

π_3-term:

$$\pi_3 = D^{a_3} . N^{b_3} . \rho^{c_3} . H$$
$$M^0L^0T^0 = L^{a_3} . (T^{-1})^{b_3} . (ML^{-3})^{c_3} . L$$

Equating the exponents of *M, L* and *T* respectively, we get:

For M: $0 = c_3$

For L: $0 = a_3 - 3c_3 + 1$

For T: $0 = -b_3$

$\therefore$ $c_3 = 0; b_3 = 0$

and, $a_3 = 3c_3 - 1 = 0 - 1 = -1$

Substituting the values of a_3, b_3 and c_3 in π_3, we get:

$$\pi_3 = D^{-1} . N^0 . \rho^0 . H = \frac{H}{D}$$

π_4-term:

$$\pi_4 = D^{a_4} . N^{b_4} . \rho^{c_4} . \mu$$
$$M^0L^0T^0 = L^{a_4} . (T^{-1})^{b_4} . (ML^{-3})^{c_4} . ML^{-1}T^{-1}$$

Equating the exponents of *M, L* and *T* respectively, we get:

For M: $0 = c_4 + 1$

For L: $0 = a_4 - 3c_4 - 1$

For T: $0 = -b_4 - 1$

$\therefore$ $c_4 = -1; b_4 = -1$

and, $a_4 = 3c_4 + 1 = 3 \times (-1) + 1 = -2$

Substituting the values of a_4, b_4 and c_4 in π_4, we get:

$$\pi_4 = D^{-2} . N^{-1} . \rho^{-1} . \mu = \frac{\mu}{\rho N D^2}$$

Substituting the values of π_1, π_2, π_3 and π_4 in eqn. (*iii*), we get:

$$f_1\left(\frac{Q}{ND^3}, \frac{g}{N^2D}, \frac{H}{D}, \frac{\mu}{\rho ND^2}\right) = 0$$

As the product of two π-terms is also dimensionless, the terms π_2 and π_3 can be replaced by $\frac{gH}{N^2D^2}$. Thus:

$$f_1\left(\frac{Q}{ND^3}, \frac{gH}{N^2D^2}, \frac{\mu}{\rho ND^2}\right) = 0$$

or, $$\frac{Q}{ND^3} = \phi\left(\frac{gH}{N^2D^2}, \frac{\mu}{\rho ND^2}\right)$$

or, $$Q = ND^3\phi\left(\frac{gH}{N^2D^2}, \frac{\mu}{\rho ND^2}\right)$$ **...Proved.**

Example 7.13. *Derive on the basis of dimensional analysis suitable parameters to present the thrust developed by a propeller. Assume that the thrust P depends upon the angular velocity ω, speed of advance V, diameter D, dynamic viscosity μ, mass density ρ, elasticity of the fluid medium which can be denoted by the speed of sound in the medium C.* **[MDU, Haryana]**

Solution. Thrust P is a function of : $\omega, V, D, \mu, \rho, C$

Mathematically, $P = f(\omega, V, D, \mu, \rho, C)$ ...(*i*)

or, $f_1(P, \omega, V, D, \mu, \rho, C) = 0$ ...(*ii*)

Total number of variables, $n = 7$

Writing dimensions of each variable, we get:

$$P = MLT^{-2}, \omega = T^{-1}, V = LT^{-1}, D = L,$$

$$\mu = ML^{-1}T^{-1}, \rho = ML^{-3}, C = LT^{-1}$$

Thus, number of fundamental dimensions, $m = 3$

$\therefore$ Number of π-terms $= n - m = 7 - 3 = 4$

Eqn. (*ii*) can be written as:

$$f_1(\pi_1, \pi_2, \pi_3, \pi_4) = 0 \quad ...(iii)$$

Each π-term contains $(m + 1)$ variables, where $m = 3$ and also equal to repeating variables. Choosing D, V and ρ as repeating variables, we get four π-terms as:

$$\pi_1 = D^{a_1}.V^{b_1}.\rho^{c_1}.P$$

$$\pi_2 = D^{a_2}.V^{b_2}.\rho^{c_2}.\omega$$

$$\pi_3 = D^{a_3}.V^{b_3}.\rho^{c_3}.\mu$$

$$\pi_4 = D^{a_4}.V^{b_4}.\rho^{c_4}.C$$

π_1-term:

$$\pi_1 = D^{a_1}.V^{b_1}.\rho^{c_1}.P$$

$$M^0L^0T^0 = L^{a_1}.(LT^{-1})^{b_1}.(ML^{-3})^{c_1}.MLT^{-2}$$

Equating the exponents of M, L and T respectively, we get:

For M: $0 = c_1 + 1$

For L: $0 = a_1 + b_1 - 3c_1 + 1$

For T: $0 = -b_1 - 2$

$\therefore$ $c_1 = -1; b_1 = -2$

and $a_1 = -b_1 + 3c_1 - 1 = 2 - 3 - 1 = -2$

Substituting the values of a_1, b_1 and c_1 in π_1, we get:

$$\pi_1 = D^{-2}.V^{-2}.\rho^{-1}.P = \frac{P}{D^2V^2\rho}$$

π_2-term:

$$\pi_2 = D^{a_2}.V^{b_2}.\rho^{c_2}.\omega$$

$$M^0L^0T^0 = L^{a_2}.(LT^{-1})^{b_2}.(ML^{-3})^{c_2}.T^{-1}$$

Equating the exponents of M, L and T respectively, we get:

For M: $0 = c_2$

For L: $0 = a_2 + b_2 - 3c_2$

For T: $0 = -b_2 - 1$

$\therefore$ $c_2 = 0; b_2 = -1$

and, $a_2 = -b_2 + 3c_2 = 1 + 0 = 1$

Substituting the values of a_2, b_2 and c_2 in π_2, we get:

$$\pi_2 = D^1 \cdot V^{-1} \cdot \rho^0 \cdot \omega = \frac{D\omega}{V}$$

π_3-term:

$$\pi_3 = D^{a_3} \cdot V^{b_3} \cdot \rho^{c_3} \cdot \mu$$

$$M^0L^0T^0 = L^{a_3} \cdot (LT^{-1})^{b_3} \cdot (ML^{-3})^{c_3} \cdot ML^{-1}T^{-1}$$

Equating the exponents of M, L and T respectively, we get:

For M: $0 = c_3 + 1$

For L: $0 = a_3 + b_3 - 3c_3 - 1$

For T: $0 = -b_3 - 1$

$\therefore$ $c_3 = -1;\ b_3 = -1$

and, $a_3 = -b_3 + 3c_3 + 1 = 1 - 3 + 1 = -1$

Substituting the values of a_3, b_3 and c_3 in π_3, we get:

$$\pi_3 = D^{-1} \cdot V^{-1} \cdot \rho^{-1} \cdot \mu = \frac{\mu}{DV\rho}$$

π_4-term:

$$\pi_4 = D^{a_4} \cdot V^{b_4} \cdot \rho^{c_4} \cdot C$$

$$M^0L^0T^0 = L^{a_4} \cdot (LT^{-1})^{b_4} \cdot (ML^{-3})^{c_4} \cdot (LT^{-1})$$

Equating the exponents of M, L and T respectively, we get:

For M: $0 = c_4$

For L: $0 = a_4 + b_4 - 3c_4 + 1$

For T: $0 = -b_4 - 1$

$\therefore$ $c_4 = 0;\ b_4 = -1$

and, $a_4 = -b_4 + 3c_4 - 1 = 1 + 0 - 1 = 0$

Substituting the values of a_4, b_4 and c_4 in π_4, we get:

$$\pi_4 = D^0 \cdot V^{-1} \cdot \rho^0 \cdot C = \frac{C}{V}$$

Substituting the values of π_1, π_2, π_3 and π_4 in eqn. (*iii*), we get:

$$f_1\left(\frac{P}{D^2V^2\rho}, \frac{D\omega}{V}, \frac{\mu}{DV\rho}, \frac{C}{V}\right) = 0$$

or, $$\frac{P}{D^2V^2\rho} = \phi\left(\frac{D\omega}{V}, \frac{\mu}{DV\rho}, \frac{C}{V}\right)$$

or, $$P = \boldsymbol{D^2V^2\rho\phi\left(\frac{D\omega}{V}, \frac{\mu}{DV\rho}, \frac{C}{V}\right)} \quad \textbf{(Ans.)}$$

Example 7.14. *Using the method of dimensional analysis obtain an expression for the discharge Q over a rectangular weir. The discharge depends on the head H over the weir, acceleration due to gravity g, length of weir crest L, height of the weir crest over the channel bottom Z and the kinematic viscosity v of the liquid.*

Solution. The discharge Q over the weir is a function of : H, g, L, Z, v

Mathematically, $Q = f(H, g, L, Z, v)$ ...(*i*)

or, $f_1(Q, H, g, L, Z, v)$ ...(*ii*)

Total number of variables, $n = 6$

Writing dimensions of each variable, we get:

$$Q = L^3T^{-1}, H = L, g = LT^{-2}, L = L, Z = L, v = L^2T^{-1}$$

Thus, number of fundamental dimensions, $m = 2$

$\therefore$ Number of π-terms $= n - m = 6 - 2 = 4$

Eqn. (*ii*) can be written as:

$$f_1(\pi_1, \pi_2, \pi_3, \pi_4) = 0 \quad ...(iii)$$

Each π-term contains $(m + 1)$ variables, where $m = 2$ and *also equal to repeating variables*. The head over the weir is the most important independent variable, and the other variable which affect the flow in open channel is the acceleration due to gravity g. These two variables H and g satisfy the requirement of repeating variables. Choosing H and g as repeating variables, we get four π-terms as:

$$\pi_1 = H^{a_1}.g^{b_1}.Q$$

$$\pi_2 = H^{a_2}.g^{b_2}.L$$

$$\pi_3 = H^{a_3}.g^{b_3}.Z$$

$$\pi_4 = H^{a_4}.g^{b_4}.v$$

π_1-term:

$$\pi_1 = H^{a_1}.g^{b_1}.Q$$

$$M^0L^0T^0 = L^{a_1}.(LT^{-2})^{b_1}.(L^3T^{-1})$$

Equating exponents of *M, L* and *T* respectively, we get:

For M: $0 = 0$

For L: $0 = a_1 + b_1 + 3$

For T: $0 = -2b_1 - 1$

$\therefore$ $b_1 = -\frac{1}{2}$

and, $a_1 = -b_1 - 3 = \frac{1}{2} - 3 = -5/2$

Substituting the values of a_1 and b_1 in π_1, we get:

$$\pi_1 = H^{-5/2}\cdot g^{-1/2}\cdot Q = \frac{Q}{g^{1/2}(H)^{5/2}}$$

π_2-term:

$$\pi_2 = H^{a_2}\cdot g^{b_2}\cdot L$$

$$M^0L^0T^0 = L^{a_2}\cdot(LT^{-2})^{b_2}\cdot L$$

Equating exponents of *M, L* and *T* respectively, we get:

For M: $0 = 0$

For L: $0 = a_2 + b_2 + 1$

For T: $0 = -2b_2$

$\therefore$ $b_2 = 0$

and, $a_2 = -b_2 - 1 = -1$

Substituting the values of a_2 and b_2 in π_2, we get:

$$\pi_2 = H^{-1}.g^0.L = \frac{L}{H}$$

π_3-term:

$$\pi_3 = H^{a_3}.g^{b_3}.Z$$

$$M^0L^0T^0 = L^{a_3}.(LT^{-2})^{b_3}.L$$

Equating the exponents of *M, L* and *T* respectively, we get:

For M: $0 = 0$

For L: $0 = a_3 + b_3 + 1$

For T: $0 = -2b_3$

$\therefore$ $b_3 = 0$

and, $a_3 = -b_3 - 1 = -1$

Substituting the values of a_3 and b_3 in π_3, we get

$$\pi_3 = H^{-1}.g^0.Z = \frac{Z}{H}$$

π_4-term:

$$\pi_4 = H^{a_4}.g^{b_4}.v$$

$$M^0L^0T^0 = L^{a_4}.(LT^{-2})^{b_4}.(L^2T^{-1})$$

Equating the exponents of *M, L* and *T* respectively, we get:

For M: $0 = 0$

For L: $0 = a_4 + b_4 + 2$

For D; $0 = -2b_4 - 1$

$b_4 = -1/2$ and $a_4 = -b_4 - 2 = +1/2 - 2 = -3/2$

Substituting the values of a_4 and b_4 in π_4, we get:

$$\pi_4 = H^{-3/2}.g^{-1/2}.\nu = \frac{v}{g^{1/2}H^{3/2}}$$

Substituting the values of π_1, π_2, π_3 and π_4 in eqn. (*iii*), we get:

$$f_1\left(\frac{Q}{g^{1/2}H^{5/2}}, \frac{L}{H}, \frac{Z}{H}, \frac{v}{g^{1/2}H^{3/2}}\right) = 0$$

or,
$$\frac{Q}{g^{1/2}H^{5/2}} = \phi\left(\frac{v}{g^{1/2}H^{3/2}}, \frac{L}{H}, \frac{Z}{H}\right) \quad ...(iv)$$

From the equation of continuity $Q = AV$ and, therefore, $\frac{Q}{AV}$ is dimensionless. In case of a rectangular weir, we may write:

$A \propto LH$ and $V \propto g^{1/2}H^{1/2}$,

Hence, $\frac{Q}{LH\,g^{1/2}H^{1/2}} = \frac{Q}{Lg^{1/2}H^{3/2}}$ is dimensionless quantity.

Thus the left hand side of eqn. (*iv*) may be transformed and written as $\frac{Q}{Lg^{1/2}H^{3/2}}$ and eqn. (*iv*) may be expressed as:

$$\frac{Q}{Lg^{1/2}H^{3/2}} = \phi_1\left(\frac{v}{g^{1/2}H^{3/2}}, \frac{L}{H}, \frac{Z}{H}\right) \quad ...(v)$$

In eqn. (v), $\dfrac{\nu}{g^{1/2}\,H^{3/2}} = \dfrac{\nu}{H\sqrt{gH}}$ is the inverse of Reynolds number. Eqn. (v) may be written as:

$$Q = C\sqrt{g}\,LH^{3/2} \qquad ...(vi)$$

where,
$$C = \phi_2\left(\frac{H\sqrt{gH}}{\nu}, \frac{H}{L}, \frac{H}{Z}\right)$$

and, since g is constant for a place, eqn. (vi) can be expressed as

$$Q = \boldsymbol{KLH^{3/2}} \text{ (Ans.)}$$

Example 7.15. *The resisting force F of a plane during flight can be considered as dependent upon the length of aircraft l, velocity υ, air viscosity μ, air density ρ, and bulk modulus of air K. Express the functional relationship between these variables and the resisting force using dimensional analysis. Explain the physical meaning of the dimensionless groups.*

[UPSC]

Solution. The resisting force F is a function of : l, υ, μ, ρ, K

Mathematically, $F = f(l, \upsilon, \mu, \rho, K)$ ...(i)

or, $f_1(F, l, \upsilon, \mu, \rho, K) = 0$ ...(ii)

Total number of variables, $n = 6$

Writing dimensions of each variable, we get:

$$F = MLT^{-2},\ l = L,\ \upsilon = LT^{-1},\ \mu = ML^{-1}T^{-1},\ \rho = ML^{-3},\ K = ML^{-1}T^{-2}$$

Thus, number of fundamental dimensions, $m = 3$

∴ Number of π-terms $= n - m = 6 - 3 = 3$

Eqn. (ii) can be written as:

$$f_1(\pi_1, \pi_2, \pi_3) = 0 \qquad ...(iii)$$

Each π-term contains $(m + 1)$ variables, where $m = 3$ and also equal to repeating variables.

Choosing l, υ and ρ as repeating variables, we get three terms as:

$$\pi_1 = l^{a_1} \cdot \upsilon^{b_1} \cdot \rho^{c_1} \cdot F$$

$$\pi_2 = l^{a_2} \cdot \upsilon^{b_2} \cdot \rho^{c_2} \cdot \mu$$

$$\pi_3 = l^{a_3} \cdot \upsilon^{b_3} \cdot \rho^{c_3} \cdot K$$

π_1-term:

$$\pi_1 = l^{a_1} \cdot \upsilon^{b_1} \cdot \rho^{c_1} \cdot F$$

$$M^0L^0T^0 = L^{a_1} \cdot (LT^{-1})^{b_1} \cdot (ML^{-3})^{c_1} \cdot MLT^{-2}$$

Equating exponents of M, L and T respectively, we get:

For M: $0 = c_1 + 1$

For L: $0 = a_1 + b_1 - 3c_1 + 1$

For T: $0 = -b_1 - 2$

∴ $c_1 = -1,\ b_1 = -2$

and, $a_1 = -b_1 + 3c_1 - 1 = 2 - 3 - 1 = -2$

Substituting the values of a_1, b_1 and c_1, in π_1, we get:

$$\pi_1 = l^{-2} \,.\, \upsilon^{-2} \,.\, \rho^{-1} \,.\, F = \frac{F}{l^2\,\upsilon^2\,\rho}$$

π_2-term:

$$\pi_2 = l^{a_2} . \upsilon^{b_2} . \rho^{c_2} . \mu$$

$$M^0L^0T^0 = L^{a_2} . (LT^{-1})^{b_2} . (ML^{-3})^{c_2} . ML^{-1}T^{-1}$$

Equating exponents of M, L and T respectively, we get:

For M: $0 = c_2 + 1$

For L: $0 = a_2 + b_2 - 3c_2 - 1$

For T: $0 = -b_2 - 1$

$\therefore$ $c_2 = -1; b_2 = -1$

and, $a_2 = -b_2 + 3c_2 + 1 = 1 - 3 + 1 = -1$

Substituting the values of a_2, b_2 and c_2 in π_2, we get:

$$\pi_2 = l^{-1} . \upsilon^{-1} . \rho^{-1} . \mu = \frac{\mu}{l\upsilon\rho}$$

π_3-term:

$$\pi_3 = l^{a_3} . \upsilon^{b_3} . \rho^{c_3} . K$$

$$M^0L^0T^0 = L^{a_3} . (LT^{-1})^{b_3} . (ML^{-3})^{c_3} . ML^{-1}T^{-2}$$

Equating exponents of M, L and T respectively, we get:

For M: $0 = c_3 + 1$

For L: $0 = a_3 + b_3 - 3c_3 - 1$

For T: $0 = -b_3 - 2$

$\therefore$ $c_3 = -1; b_3 = -2$

and, $a_3 = -b_3 + 3c_3 + 1 = 2 - 3 + 1 = 0$

Substituting the values of a_3, b_3, and c_3 in π_3, we get:

$$\pi_3 = l^0 . \upsilon^{-2} . \rho^{-1} . K = \frac{K}{\upsilon^2\rho}$$

Substituting the values of π_1, π_2 and π_3 in eqn. (*iii*), we get the functional relationship as:

$$f_1\left(\frac{F}{l^2\upsilon^2\rho}, \frac{\mu}{l\upsilon\rho}, \frac{K}{\upsilon^2\rho}\right) = 0$$

or,
$$\frac{F}{l^2\upsilon^2\rho} = \phi\left(\frac{\mu}{l\upsilon\rho}, \frac{K}{\upsilon^2\rho}\right)$$

or,
$$F = l^2\upsilon^2\rho\phi\left(\frac{\mu}{l\upsilon\rho}, \frac{K}{\upsilon^2\rho}\right) \quad \textbf{(Ans.)}$$

Physical meaning of dimensionless groups (π_1, π_2, π_3):

(*i*) $\pi_1 = \frac{F}{l^2\upsilon^2\rho}$: It is the ratio of F and dynamic force $l^2\upsilon^2\rho$. It indicates that the resisting force experienced by an aircraft is dependent on the length and velocity. For any given aircraft, the resistance force will be proportional to the square of velocity.

(*ii*) $\pi_2 = \frac{\mu}{l\upsilon\rho}$: This dimensionless group is the reciprocal of Reynolds number and represents the role of viscous action on the resistance.

(*iii*) $\pi_3 = \dfrac{K}{\rho \upsilon^2}$: It takes into account the role of compressibility in influencing fluid resistance which an aircraft experiences.

Example 7.16. *Show that the power P developed in a water turbine can be expressed as:*

$$P = \rho N^3 D^5 \phi\left(\frac{D}{B}, \frac{\rho D^2 N}{\mu}, \frac{ND}{\sqrt{gH}}\right)$$

where, ρ = *Mass density of the liquid,*

N = *Speed in r.p.m.,*

D = *Diameter of the runner,*

B = *Width of the number, and*

μ = *Co-efficient of dynamic viscosity.*

Under what conditions it can be used to determine the characteristic of a similar machine?

[UPTU]

Solution. The power P developed in a water turbine is a function of : ρ, N, D, B, μ, H, g

Mathematically, $P = f(\rho, N, D, B, \mu, H, g)$ ...(*i*)

or, $f_1(P, \rho, N, D, B, \mu, H, g) = 0$ ...(*ii*)

Total number of variables, $n = 8$

Writing dimensions of each variable, we get:

$$P = ML^2T^{-3}, \rho = ML^{-3}, N = T^{-1}, D = L, B = L, \mu = ML^{-1}T^{-1},$$

$$H = L, \; g = LT^{-2}$$

Thus, the number of fundamental dimensions, $m = 3$

$\therefore$ Number of π-terms $= n - m = 8 - 3 = 5$

Eqn. (*ii*) can be written as:

$$f_1(\pi_1, \pi_2, \pi_3, \pi_4, \pi_5) = 0 \quad ...(iii)$$

Each π-term contains $(m + 1)$ variables, where $m = 3$ and also equal to repeating variables. Choosing D, N and ρ as repeating variables, we get five π-terms as:

$$\pi_1 = D^{a_1} . N^{b_1} . \rho^{c_1} . P$$

$$\pi_2 = D^{a_2} . N^{b_2} . \rho^{c_2} . B$$

$$\pi_3 = D^{a_3} . N^{b_3} . \rho^{c_3} . \mu$$

$$\pi_4 = D^{a_4} . N^{b_4} . \rho^{c_4} . H$$

$$\pi_5 = D^{a_5} . N^{b_5} . \rho^{c_5} . g$$

π_1-term:

$$\pi_1 = D^{a_1} . N^{b_1} . \rho^{c_1} . P$$

$$M^0L^0T^0 = L^{a_1} . (T^{-1})^{b_1} . (ML^{-3})^{c_1} . ML^2T^{-3}$$

Equating the exponents of M, L and T respectively, we get:

For M: $0 = c_1 + 1$

For L: $0 = a_1 - 3c_1 + 2$

For T: $0 = -b_1 - 3$

$\therefore$ $c_1 = -1, b_1 = -3$

and, $a_1 = 3c_1 - 2 = -3 - 2 = -5$

Substituting the values of a_1, b_1 and c_1 in π_1, we get:

$$\pi_1 = D_1^{-5} . N^{-3} . \rho^{-1} . P = \frac{P}{\rho N^3 D^5}$$

π_2-term:

$$\pi_2 = D^{a_2} . N^{b_2} . \rho^{c_2} . B$$

$$M^0L^0T^0 = L^{a_2} . (T^{-1})^{b_2} . (ML^{-3})^{c_2} . L$$

Equating the exponents of M, L and T respectively, we get:

For M: $0 = c_2$

For L: $0 = a_2 - 3c_2 + 1$

For T: $0 = -b_2$

$\therefore$ $c_2 = 0;\ b_2 = 0$

and, $a_2 = 3c_2 - 1 = -1$

Substituting the values of a_2, b_2 and c_2 in π_2, we get:

$$\pi_2 = D^{-1} . N^0 . \rho^0 . B = \frac{B}{D}$$

π_3-term:

$$\pi_3 = D^{a_3} . N^{b_3} . \rho^{c_3} . \mu$$

$$M^0L^0T^0 = L^{a_3} . (T^{-1})^{b_3} . (ML^{-3})^{c_3} . (ML^{-1}T^{-1})$$

Equating the exponents of M, L and T respectively, we get:

For M: $0 = c_3 + 1$

For L: $0 = a_3 - 3c_3 - 1$

For T: $0 = -b_3 - 1$

$\therefore$ $c_3 = -1;\ b_3 = -1$

and, $a_3 = 3c_3 + 1 = -3 + 1 = -2$

Substituting the values of a_3, b_3 and c_3 in π_3, we get:

$$\pi_3 = D^{-2} . N^{-1} . \rho^{-1} . \mu = \frac{\mu}{\rho D^2 N}$$

π_4-term:

$$\pi_4 = D^{a_4} . N^{b_4} . \rho^{c_4} . H$$

$$M^0L^0T^0 = L^{a_4} .(T^{-1})^{b_4} . (ML^{-3})^{c_4} . L$$

Equating the exponents of M, L and T respectively, we get:

For M: $0 = c_4$

For L: $0 = a_4 - 3c_4 + 1$

For T: $0 = -b_4$

$\therefore$ $c_4 = 0;\ b_4 = 0$

and, $a_4 = 3c_4 - 1 = 0 - 1 = -1$

Substituting the values of a_4, b_4 and c_4 in π_4 we get:

$$\pi_4 = D^{-1} . N^0 . \rho^0 . H = \frac{H}{D}$$

π_5-term:

$$\pi_5 = D^{a_5} . N^{b_5} . \rho^{c_5} . g$$

$$M^0L^0T^0 = L^{a_5} .(T^{-1})^{b_5} . (ML^{-3})^{c_5} . (LT^{-2})$$

Equating the exponents of *M, L* and *T* respectively, we get:

For M: $0 = c_5$

For L: $0 = a_5 - 3c_5 + 1$

For T: $0 = -b_5 - 2$

$\therefore$ $c_5 = 0;\ b_5 = -2$

and, $a_5 = 3c_5 - 1 = 0 - 1 = -1$

Substituting the values of a_5, b_5 and c_5 in π_5 we get:

$$\pi_5 = D^{-1} . N^{-2} . \rho^0 . g = \frac{g}{DN^2}$$

Substituting the values of π_1, π_2, π_3, π_4 and π_5 in eqn. (*iii*), we get:

$$f_1\left(\frac{P}{\rho N^3 D^5}, \frac{B}{D}, \frac{\mu}{\rho D^2 N}, \frac{H}{D}, \frac{g}{DN^2}\right) = 0$$

or, $$f_1\left(\frac{P}{\rho N^3 D^5}, \frac{B}{D}, \frac{\mu}{\rho D^2 N}, \frac{gH}{D^2 N^2}\right) = 0$$

$$\left[\because \pi_4 \times \pi_5 \text{ (product of two terms)} = \frac{H}{D} \times \frac{g}{DN^2} = \frac{gH}{D^2N^2} \text{ (non-dimensional)}\right]$$

or, $$f_1\left(\frac{P}{\rho N^3 D^5}, \frac{B}{D}, \frac{\mu}{\rho D^2 N}, \frac{\sqrt{gH}}{ND}\right) = 0$$

$$\left(\because \text{Square root of } \frac{gH}{D^2N^2} \text{ is also dimensionless}\right)$$

or, $$f_1\left(\frac{P}{\rho N^3 D^5}, \frac{D}{B}, \frac{\rho D^2 N}{\mu}, \frac{ND}{\sqrt{gH}}\right) = 0$$

($\because$ Reciprocal of a π-term is non-dimensional)

or, $$\frac{P}{\rho N^3 D^5} = \phi\left(\frac{D}{B}, \frac{\rho D^2 N}{\mu}, \frac{ND}{\sqrt{gH}}\right)$$

or, $$P = \boldsymbol{\rho N^3 D^5 \phi\left(\frac{D}{B}, \frac{\rho D^2 N}{\mu}, \frac{ND}{\sqrt{gH}}\right)} \quad \textbf{(Ans.)}$$

If *the two water turbines are dynamically similar,* then, *all the dimensionless parameters must be the same in both the machines.* In turbines, the viscous forces are less important as compared to gravity forces and, therefore, the parameter $\frac{\rho D^2 N}{\mu}$ has little significance, thus for complete similarity between model and prototype of water turbines following *conditions* need to be satisfied:

(*i*) *For geometric similarity*:

$$\left(\frac{H}{D}\right)_p = \left(\frac{H}{D}\right)_m \text{ and } \left(\frac{D}{B}\right)_p = \left(\frac{D}{B}\right)_m$$

(*ii*) *For kinematic similarity*:

$$\left(\frac{ND}{\sqrt{gH}}\right)_p = \left(\frac{ND}{\sqrt{gH}}\right)_m$$

(*iii*) *For dynamic similarity*:

$$\left(\frac{P}{\rho N^3 D^5}\right)_p = \left(\frac{P}{\rho N^3 D^5}\right)_m$$

The subscripts *p* and *m* refer to the prototype and model respectively. **(Ans.)**

7.4.3. Limitations of Dimensional Analysis

Following are the *limitations* of dimensional analysis:

1. Dimensional analysis does not give any clue regarding the selection of variables. If the variables are wrongly taken, the resulting functional relationship is erroneous. It provides the information about the grouping of variables. In order to decide whether selected variables are pertinent or superfluous experiments have to be performed.
2. The complete information is not provided by dimensional analysis; it only indicates that there is some relationship between parameters. It does not give the values of co-efficients in the functional relationship. The values of co-efficients and hence the nature of functions can be obtained only from experiments or from mathematical analysis.

MODEL ANALYSIS

7.5. MODEL ANALYSIS—INTRODUCTION

In order to know about the performance of the hydraulic structures (*e.g.* dams, spillways etc.) or hydraulic machines (*e.g.* turbines, pumps etc.) before actually constructing or manufacturing them, their models are made and tested to get the required information. The **model** is the *small scale replica of the actual structure or machine.* The *actual structure or machine is* called **Prototype.** The models are not always smaller than the prototype, in some cases a model may be even larger or of the same size as prototype depending upon the need and purpose (*e.g.* the working of a wrist watch or a carburettor can be studied in a large scale model).

Advantages of model testing:

The following are the *advantages* of model analysis:

1. The model tests are quite *economical* and *convenient* (because the design, construction and operation of a model may be changed several times if necessary, without increasing much expenditure, till most suitable design is obtained).
2. With the use of models the performance of hydraulic structures/hydraulic machines can be predicted in advance.
3. While designing a particular portion of the structure if clear cut analytical and reliable method is not available then in such cases it becomes absolutely necessary to know about the safety and reliability of such parts which is possible by means of model testing.
4. Model testing can be used to detect and rectify the defects of an existing structure which is not functioning properly.

Applications of the model testing:

Following are the important fields where applications of the model testing is of great use:

1. Civil engineering structures such as *dams, spillways, weirs, canals* etc.

2. *Flood control, investigation of silting, and scour in rivers, irrigation channels.*
3. *Turbines, pumps and compressors.*
4. Design of *harbours, ships* and *submarines.*
5. *Aeroplanes, rockets* and *missiles.*
6. *Tall buildings* (to predict the wind loads on buildings, the stability characteristics of the buildings and airflow patterns in their vicinity).

7.6. SIMILITUDE

To find solutions to numerous complicated problems in hydraulic engineering and fluid mechanics model studies are usually conducted. In order that results obtained in the model studies represent the behaviour of prototype, the following *three similarities must be ensured* between the model and the prototype.

1. Geometric similarity,
2. Kinematic similarity, and
3. Dynamic similarity.

1. Geometric similarity:

For geometric similarity to exist between the model and the prototype, the ratios of corresponding lengths in the model and in the prototype must be same and the included angles between two corresponding sides must be the same. Models which are not geometrically similar are known as *geometrically distorted models.*

Let, L_m = Length of model,
H_m = Height of model,
D_m = Diameter of model,
A_m = Area of model,
V_m = Volume of model,
and, L_p, B_p, H_p, D_p, A_p and V_p = Corresponding values of the prototype.

Then, for *geometric similarity,* we must have the relation:

$$\frac{L_m}{L_p} = \frac{B_m}{B_p} = \frac{H_m}{H_p} = \frac{D_m}{D_p} = L_r \quad ...(7.8)$$

where L_r is called the *scale ratio* or the *scale factor.*

Similarly, $$A_r = \text{Area ratio} = \frac{A_m}{A_p} = L_r^2 \quad ...(7.9)$$

and, $$V_r = \text{Volume ratio} = \frac{V_m}{V_p} = L_r^3 \quad ...(7.10)$$

2. Kinematic similarity:

Kinematic similarity is the *similarity of motion.* If at the corresponding points in the model and in the prototype, the velocity or acceleration ratios are same and velocity or acceleration vectors point in the *same direction,* the two flows are said to be *kinematically similar.*

Let, $(V_1)_m$ = Velocity of fluid at point 1 in the model,
$(V_2)_m$ = Velocity of fluid at point 2 in the model,
$(a_1)_m$ = Acceleration of fluid at point 1 in the model,
$(a_2)_m$ = Acceleration of fluid at point 2 in the model,

and $(V_1)_p$, $(V_2)_p$, $(a_1)_p$, $(a_2)_p$ = Corresponding values at the corresponding points of fluid velocity and acceleration in the prototype.

Then, for kinematic similarity, we must have:

$$\frac{(V_1)_m}{(V_1)_p} = \frac{(V_2)_m}{(V_2)_p} = V_r \text{ velocity ratio} \quad ...(7.11)$$

Similarly

$$\frac{(a_1)_m}{(a_1)_p} = \frac{(a_2)_m}{(a_2)_p} = a_r \text{ acceleration ratio} \quad ...(7.12)$$

- The *directions* of the velocities in the model and prototype *should be same.*
- The *geometric similarity is a prerequisite for kinematic similarity.*

3. Dynamic similarity:

Dynamic similarity is the *similarity of forces.* The flows in the model and in prototype are dynamically similar if at all the corresponding points, identical types of forces are parallel and bear the same ratio. In dynamic similarity, the force polygons of the two flows can be superimposed by change in force scale.

Let, $(F_i)_m$ = Inertia force at a point in the model,

$(F_v)_m$ = Viscous force at the point in the model,

$(F_g)_m$ = Gravity force at the point in the model,

and, $(F_i)_p$, $(F_v)_p$, $(F_g)_p$ = Corresponding values of forces at the corresponding points in prototype.

Then for *dynamic similarity,* we have:

$$\frac{(F_i)_m}{(F_i)_p} = \frac{(F_v)_m}{(F_v)_p} = \frac{(F_g)_m}{(F_g)_p} \text{ ......} = F_r \text{ (force ratio)} \quad ...(7.13)$$

The directions of the corresponding forces at the corresponding points in the model and prototype should also be same.

7.7. FORCES INFLUENCING HYDRAULIC PHENOMENA

The forces which may affect/influence the flow characteristics of a problem are:

1. Inertia force (F_i):

- It always exists in the fluid flow problem (and hence it is customary to find out the force ratios with respect to inertia force).
- It is equal to the *product of mass and acceleration* of the flowing fluid and acts in the direction *opposite to the direction of acceleration.*

2. Viscous force (F_v):

- It is present in fluid flow problems where viscosity is to play an important role.
- It is equal to the *product of shear stress* (τ) *due to viscosity and surface area of the flow.*

3. Gravity force (F_g):

- It is present in case of open surface flow.
- It is equal to the *product of mass and acceleration due to gravity.*

4. Pressure force (F_p):

- This type of force is present in case of pipe flow.
- It is equal to the *product of pressure intensity and cross-sectional area of the flowing fluid.*

5. Surface tension force (F_s):

- It is equal to the *product of surface tension and length of surface of the flowing fluid.*

6. Elastic force (F_e):

It is equal to the *product of elastic stress and area of the flowing fluid.*

7.8. DIMENSIONLESS NUMBERS AND THEIR SIGNIFICANCE

The *dimensionless numbers* (also called non-dimensional parameters) are obtained by dividing the *inertia force* (which always exists when any mass in motion) by viscous force or gravity force or pressure force or surface tension force or elastic force. The important dimensionless numbers are :

1. Reynolds number
2. Froude's number
3. Euler's number
4. Weber's number
5. Mach's number.

7.8.1. Reynolds Number (*Re*)

It is defined as the *ratio of the inertia force to the viscous force.*

$$\text{Inertia force } (F_i) = \text{Mass} \times \text{acceleration}$$

$$= \rho \times \text{volume} \times \frac{\text{velocity}}{\text{time}}$$

$$= \rho \times \frac{\text{volume}}{\text{time}} \times \text{velocity}$$

$$= \rho \times AV \times V \qquad \left[\because \text{Volume per second} = \text{area} \times \text{velocity} = AV\right]$$

$$= \rho AV^2 \qquad \ldots(7.14)$$

$$\text{Viscous force } (F_v) = \text{Shear stress} \times \text{area} = \tau \times A$$

$$= \left(\mu \frac{du}{dy}\right) \times A$$

$$= \mu \frac{V}{L} \times A \qquad \left(\because \frac{du}{dy} = \frac{V}{L}\right)$$

$\therefore$ Reynolds number,

$$Re = \frac{F_i}{F_v} = \frac{\rho AV^2}{\mu \times \frac{V}{L} \times A} = \frac{\rho VL}{\mu}$$

i.e.

$$Re = \frac{\rho VL}{\mu} = \frac{VL}{\mu/\rho} = \frac{VL}{\nu} \qquad \left(\because \nu = \frac{\mu}{\rho}\right)$$

For pipe flow (where the linear dimension is taken as diameter *d*),

$$Re = \frac{Vd}{\nu} \qquad \ldots(7.15)$$

- Reynolds number *signifies* the relative predominance of the inertia to the viscous forces occurring in the flow systems.
- This number is taken as the criterion of dynamic similarity in the flow situations where the viscous forces predominate; ***examples*** being: (*i*) *Motion of submarine completely under water,* (*ii*) *Low velocity motion around automobiles and aeroplanes,* (*iii*) *Incompressible flow through pipes of smaller sizes, and* (*iv*) *Flow through low speed turbomachines.*

7.8.2. Froude's number (*Fr*)

It is defined as the *square root of the ratio of the inertia force and the gravity force.*

Mathematically, $$Fr = \sqrt{\frac{F_i}{F_g}}$$

where, $F_i = \rho A V^2$ (Eqn. 7.14)

and, F_g = Mass × acceleration due to gravity

$= \rho \times \text{volume} \times g$

$= \rho L^3 g = \rho L^2 . L . g$

$= \rho ALg$ ($\because L^2 = A$ = area)

$$\therefore \quad Fr = \sqrt{\frac{\rho A V^2}{\rho A L g}} = \frac{V}{\sqrt{Lg}} \qquad ...(7.16)$$

- Froude's number governs the dynamic similarity of the flow situations; where *gravitational force is most significant* and all other forces are comparatively negligible, ***examples*** being: (*i*) *Flow over notches and weirs,* (*ii*) *Flow over the spillway of a dam,* (*iii*) *Flow through open channels, considering waves and jumps, and* (*iv*) *Motion of ship in rough and turbulent sea.*

7.8.3. Euler's Number (*Eu*)

It is defined as the *square root of the ratio of the inertia force to the pressure force.*

Mathematically, $$Eu = \sqrt{\frac{F_i}{F_p}}$$

where, $F_i = \rho A V^2$ (Eqn. 7.14)

and, F_p = Intensity of pressure × area = $p \times A$

$$\therefore \quad Eu = \sqrt{\frac{\rho A V^2}{p \times A}} = \sqrt{\frac{V^2}{p/\rho}} = \frac{V}{\sqrt{p/\rho}} \qquad ...(7.17)$$

- The Euler number is important in the flow problems/situations in which a *pressure gradient exists*: ***examples*** being: (*i*) *Discharge through orifices, mouthpieces and sluices,* (*ii*) *Pressure rise due to sudden closure of valves,* (*iii*) *Flow through pipes, and* (*iv*) *Water hammer created in penstocks.*

7.8.4. Weber Number (*We*)

It is defined as the *square root of the ratio of the inertia force to the surface tension force.*

Mathematically, $$We = \sqrt{\frac{F_i}{F_s}}$$

where, $F_i = \rho A V^2$ [Eqn. 7.14]

and, F_s = Surface tension force = surface tension × length

$$\therefore \quad We = \sqrt{\frac{\rho A V^2}{\sigma L}} = \sqrt{\frac{\rho \times L^2 \times V^2}{\sigma L}} \qquad (\because A = L^2)$$

$$= \sqrt{\frac{\rho L \times V^2}{\sigma}} = \frac{V}{\sqrt{\sigma / \rho L}} \qquad ...(7.18)$$

- This number assumes importance in the following flow situations: (*i*) *Capillary movement of water in soils,* (*ii*) *Flow of blood in veins and arteries,* and (*iii*) *Liquid atomisation.*

7.8.5. Mach Number (M)

It is defined as the *square root of the ratio of the inertia force to the elastic force.*

Mathematically, $$M = \sqrt{\frac{F_i}{F_e}}$$

where, $F_i = \rho A V^2$ (Eqn. 7.14)

and, F_e = Elastic force

= Elastic stress × area

$= K \times A = K \times L^2$ (where, K = elastic stress)

$$\therefore \quad M = \sqrt{\frac{\rho A V^2}{K L^2}} = \sqrt{\frac{\rho L^2 V^2}{K L^2}} = \frac{V}{\sqrt{K/\rho}}$$

But, $\sqrt{K/\rho} = C$ = Velocity of sound in the fluid

$$\therefore \quad M = \frac{V}{C} \quad ...(7.19)$$

- The Mach number is important in *compressible flow problems at high velocities, such as high velocity flow in pipes or motion of high-speed projectiles and missiles.*

7.9. MODEL (OR SIMILARITY) LAWS

To ensure *dynamic similarity* between the model and prototype it is necessary that the ratio of the corresponding forces acting at the corresponding points in the model and prototype be made equal. It implies that dimensionless numbers should be same for the model as well as the prototype; this condition is difficult to be satisfied for all the dimensionless numbers. Hence models are *designed on the basis of the force which is dominating in the flow situation. The laws on which the models are designed for dynamic similarity are called* **model or similarity laws;** these are:

1. Reynolds model law,
2. Froude model law,
3. Euler model law,
4. Weber model law, and
5. Mach model law.

7.10. REYNOLDS MODEL LAW

In flow situations where in addition to inertia, viscous force is the other predominant force, the similarity of flow in the model and its prototype can be established if *Reynolds number is same for both the systems.* This is known as Reynolds law and according to this law

$$(Re)_{\text{model}} = (Re)_{\text{prototype}}$$

$$\frac{\rho_m V_m L_m}{\mu_m} = \frac{\rho_p V_p L_p}{\mu_p} \quad ...(7.20)$$

where, ρ_m = Density of fluid in model,

V_m = Velocity of fluid in model,

L_m = Length or linear dimension of the model,

μ_m = Viscosity of fluid in model,

and ρ_p, V_p, L_p and μ_p are the corresponding values of density, velocity, linear dimension and viscosity of fluid in prototype.

or, $$\frac{\rho_p}{\rho_m} \times \frac{V_p}{V_m} \times \frac{L_p}{L_m} \times \frac{1}{(\mu_p / \mu_m)} = 1$$

or, $$\frac{\rho_r V_r L_r}{\mu_r} = 1 \qquad ...(7.21)$$

$$\left[\rho_r = \frac{\rho_p}{\rho_m}, V_r = \frac{V_p}{V_m}, L_r = \frac{L_p}{L_m}\right]$$

where, the various quantities with subscript r represent the corresponding *scale ratios.*

Also, *Time scale ratio,* $T_r = \frac{L_r}{V_r}$ $\left(\because V = \frac{L}{T} \text{ and } T = \frac{L}{V}\right)$

Acceleration scale ratio, $a_r = \frac{V_r}{T_r}$

Force scale ratio, $F_r = (\text{mass} \times \text{acc.})_r$

$= m_r \times a_r$

$= \rho_r A_r V_r \times a_r = \rho_r L_r^2 V_r \times a_r$

Discharge scale ratio, $Q_r = (\rho A V)_r$

$= \rho_r A_r V_r = \rho_r L_r^2 V_r$

- Following are some of the phenomena for which Reynolds model law can be a sufficient criterion for similarity of flow in the model and the prototype:
  (*i*) Motion of air planes,
  (*ii*) Flow of incompressible fluid in closed pipes,
  (*iii*) Motion of submarines completely under water, and
  (*iv*) Flow around structures and other bodies immersed completely under moving fluids.

Example 7.17. *An oil of specific gravity 0.92 and viscosity 0.03 poise is to be transported at the rate of 2500 litres/sec. through a 1.2 m diameter pipe. Tests were conducted on a 12 cm diameter pipe using water at 20°C. If the viscosity water at 20° C is 0.01 poise, find:*

(i) Velocity of flow in the model;

(ii) Rate of flow in the model.

Solution. Sp. gr. of oil, $S_p = 0.92$

Viscosity of oil, $\mu_p = 0.03 \text{ poise} = 0.03 \times \frac{1}{10} \text{ Ns/m}^2 = 0.003 \text{ Ns/m}^2$

Rate of oil flow, $Q = 2500 \text{ litres/s} = 2.5 \text{ m}^3\text{/s}$

Diameter of prototype, $D_p = 1.2$ m

Diameter of the model, $D_m = 12 \text{ cm} = 0.12$ m

Viscosity of water at 20°*C*, $\mu_m = 0.01 \text{ poise} = 0.01 \times \frac{1}{10} = 0.001 \text{ Ns/m}^2$

(*i*) Velocity of flow in the model, V_m:

The dynamic similarity for pipe flow will be obtained if Reynolds number is *same* for both the model and prototype.

$$\therefore \quad \frac{\rho_m V_m D_m}{\mu_m} = \frac{\rho_p V_p D_p}{\mu_p} \qquad ...(\text{Eqn. } 7.20)$$

(For pipe linear dimension is *D*)

or, $$\frac{V_m}{V_p} = \frac{\rho_p}{\rho_m} \cdot \frac{D_p}{D_m} \cdot \frac{\mu_m}{\mu_p}$$

$$= \frac{(9.81 \times 0.92/9.81)}{(9.81/9.81)} \times \frac{1.2}{0.12} \times \frac{0.001}{0.003} = 3.067$$

$$\left[\because \rho_p = \frac{w \times S_p}{g} = \frac{9.81 \times 0.92}{9.81} \text{ and } \rho_m = \frac{w}{g} = \frac{9.81}{9.81}\right]$$

But, $$V_p = \frac{Q_p}{A_p} = \frac{2.5}{\frac{\pi}{4} \times 1.2^2} = 2.21 \text{ m/s}$$

$\therefore$ $V_m = 3.067 \times V_p = 3.067 \times 2.21 =$ **6.78 m/s (Ans.)**

(*ii*) Rate of flow in the model, Q_m:

$$Q_m = A_m \times V_m = (\pi/4) \times D_m^2 \times V_m$$
$$= (\pi/4) \times 0.12^2 \times 6.78 = 0.07668 \text{ m}^3\text{/s or } \mathbf{76.68 \text{ litres/s (Ans.)}}$$

Example 7.18. *A geometrically similar model of an air duct is built to $\frac{1}{25}$ scale and tested with water which is 50 times more viscous and 800 times denser than air. When tested under dynamically similar conditions, the pressure drop is 2 bar in the model. Find the corresponding pressure drop in the full scale prototype.* **[Nagpur University]**

Solution.

Given: Scale ratio, $\frac{L_m}{L_p} = \frac{1}{25}$

$$\frac{\mu_p}{\mu_m} = \frac{1}{50}; \frac{\rho_p}{\rho_m} = \frac{1}{800}$$

Pressure drop in the model = 2 bar

Pressure drop in the prototype:

For dynamic similarity between the prototype and its model, the Reynolds number for both of them should be equal.

$\therefore$ $$\frac{\rho_p V_p L_p}{\mu_p} = \frac{\rho_m V_m L_m}{\mu_m}$$

or, $$\frac{V_p}{V_m} = \frac{\mu_p}{\mu_m} \times \frac{\rho_m}{\rho_p} \times \frac{L_m}{L_p}$$

Substituting the values, we get:

$$\frac{V_p}{V_m} = \frac{1}{50} \times 800 \times \frac{1}{50} = \frac{16}{25}$$

The pressure, $$p = \frac{F}{A} = \frac{\rho L^2 V^2}{L^2} = \rho V^2$$

$$\left[\because F = m \times a = \rho L^3 \times \frac{V}{T} = \rho L^2 \times \frac{L}{T} \times V = \rho L^2 V^2\right]$$

$$\therefore \quad \frac{\text{Pressure drop in prototype}}{\text{Pressure drop in model}} = \frac{\rho_p}{\rho_m} \times \frac{V_p^2}{V_m^2} = \frac{1}{800} \times \left(\frac{16}{25}\right)^2 = 5.12 \times 10^{-4}$$

$$\therefore \text{ Pressure drop in prototype} = \text{Pressure drop in model} \times 5.12 \times 10^{-4}$$
$$= 2 \times 5.12 \times 10^{-4} = 1.024 \times 10^{-3} \text{ bar}$$
$$= 1.024 \times 10^{-3} \times 10^5 \text{ N/m}^2 = 102.4 \text{ N/m}^2$$
$$= \frac{102.4}{9810} \times 1000 \text{ mm} = \mathbf{10.44 \text{ mm}} \text{ (Ans.)}$$

Example 7.19. (*a*) *The thrust T of a screw propeller is dependent upon the diameter D, speed of advance V, revolutions per second N, fluid density ρ and the co-efficient of viscosity μ. Experiments were performed with various models of propellers. What are the dimensionless groups to which the data should be plotted?*

(*b*) *The characteristics of a propeller of 4.8 m diameter and rotational speed 120 r.p.m. are examined by means of a geometrically similar model of 600 mm diameter. When the model is run at 480 r.p.m. by a torque of 30 Nm the thrust developed is 300 N and the speed of advance is 3 m/s. Determine the following for the full scale propeller:*

(i) Speed of advance, (ii) Thrust, and (iii) Torque.

Solution. (*a*) By means of dimensional analysis, it can be shown that the appropriate non-dimensional parameters are:

$$\frac{T}{\rho D^2 V^2} = \phi\left(\frac{VD\rho}{\mu}, \frac{DN}{V}\right)$$

[Please solve this part (*a*) by using Rayleigh's method or Buckingham's π-theorem to obtain the above result.]

The propeller thrust is thus governed by Reynolds number $\left(\frac{VD\rho}{\mu}\right)$ and the factor $\left(\frac{DN}{V}\right)$.

However, both the conditions *cannot be satisfied at the same time.* Usually the *effect of viscosity is neglected* and the factor $\left(\frac{DN}{V}\right)$ is *arranged to be the same* for the dynamic similarity between the model and prototype.

(*b*) *Given*: Diameter of propeller, (prototype) $D_p = 4.8$ m

Speed, $N_p = 120$ r.p.m.

Diameter of the model, $D_m = 600$ mm $= 0.6$ m

Rotational speed, $N_m = 480$ r.p.m.

Torque of the model = 30 Nm

Thrust developed, $T_m = 300$ N

Speed of advance, $V_m = 3$ m/s.

(*i*) Speed of advance for the propeller, V_p:

$$\left(\frac{DN}{V}\right)_m = \left(\frac{DN}{V}\right)_p$$

i.e.,
$$\frac{D_m N_m}{V_m} = \frac{D_p N_p}{V_p}$$

or,
$$V_p = V_m \times \frac{D_p}{D_m} \times \frac{N_p}{N_m}$$

$$= 3 \times \frac{4.8}{0.6} \times \frac{120}{480} = \mathbf{6\,m/s\ (Ans.)}$$

(*ii*) Thrust of the propeller, T_p:

$$\left(\frac{T}{\rho D^2 V^2}\right)_m = \left(\frac{T}{\rho D^2 V^2}\right)_p$$

i.e.

$$\frac{T_m}{\rho_m D_m^2 V_m^2} = \frac{T_p}{\rho_p D_p^2 V_p^2}$$

or,

$$T_p = T_m \times \frac{\rho_p}{\rho_m} \times \left(\frac{V_p}{V_m}\right)^2 \times \left(\frac{D_p}{D_m}\right)^2$$

$$= 300 \times 1 \times \left(\frac{6}{3}\right)^2 \times \left(\frac{4.8}{0.6}\right)^2 \quad \left[\because \rho_p = \rho_m, \text{ the fluid medium being same}\right]$$

$$= \mathbf{76800\ N\ (Ans.)}$$

(*iii*) Torque of the propeller:

Efficiency of the *model propeller*

$$= \frac{\text{Output}}{\text{Input}} = \frac{\text{Thrust} \times \text{speed of advance}}{\text{Torque} \times \text{angular speed}}$$

$$= \frac{300 \times 3}{30 \times \left(\frac{2\pi \times 480}{60}\right)} = 0.597 \text{ or } 59.7\%$$

Assuming that the prototype has the same efficiency as the model we have for the prototype,

$$0.597 = \frac{76800 \times 6}{\text{Torque} \times \left(\frac{2\pi \times 120}{60}\right)}$$

$\therefore$ Torque of the propeller

$$= \frac{76800 \times 6 \times 60}{0.597 \times 2\pi \times 120}$$

$$= \mathbf{61422\ Nm\ (Ans.)}$$

Example 7.20. *Resistance R to the motion of a completely submerged body is given by $R = \rho V^2 L^2 \phi\left(\frac{VL}{\nu}\right)$, where ρ and ν are density and kinematic viscosity of the fluid while L is the length of the body and V is the velocity of flow. If the resistance of a one-eighth scale airship model when tested in water at 12 m/s is 220 N, what will be the resistance in air of the airship at the corresponding speed? Kinematic viscosity of air is 13 times that of water and density of water is 810 times of air.* **[Delhi University]**

Solution. *Given*: Scale ratio $= \frac{L_m}{L_p} = \frac{1}{8}$

Velocity of model, $V_m = 12$ m/s

Resistance of model, $R_m = 220$ N

The fluids for model and the prototype are *water* and *air* respectively.

$\therefore$ Kinematic viscosity of air = 13 × kinematic viscosity of water

or, $\nu_p = 13\nu_m$

$$\text{Density of water} = 810 \times \text{density of air}$$

or, $$\rho_m = 810\,\rho_p$$

Resistance of the airship in air, R_p:

The resistance, R, is given by:

$$R = \rho V^2 L^2 \phi\left(\frac{VL}{\nu}\right)$$

From the above equation, it is obvious that flow in the model will be dynamically similar if the Reynolds numbers are equal in both the systems. Thus, if

$$\left(\frac{VL}{\nu}\right)_m = \left(\frac{VL}{\nu}\right)_p \quad \text{...(i)}$$

then, $$\left(\frac{R}{\rho V^2 L^2}\right)_m = \left(\frac{R}{\rho V^2 L^2}\right)_p \quad \text{...(ii)}$$

From eqn. (*i*), we have:

$$\frac{V_m L_m}{\nu_m} = \frac{V_p L_p}{\nu_p}$$

or, $$V_p = V_m \cdot \frac{L_m}{L_p} \cdot \frac{\nu_p}{\nu_m} = 12 \times \frac{1}{8} \times 13 = 19.5 \text{ m/s}$$

At this prototype velocity, the resistance of the airship is obtained from eqn. (*ii*) as follows:

$$\frac{R_m}{\rho_m V_m^2 L_m^2} = \frac{R_p}{\rho_p V_p^2 L_p^2}$$

or, $$\mathbf{R_p} = R_m \cdot \frac{L_p^2}{L_m^2} \cdot \frac{V_p^2}{V_m^2} \cdot \frac{\rho_p}{\rho_m} = 220 \times 8^2 \times \left(\frac{19.5}{12}\right)^2 \times \frac{1}{810}$$

$$= \mathbf{45.9\ N\ (Ans.)}$$

Example 7.21. (*a*) *What are the various dimensionless groups in fluid mechanics? Under what circumstances is each of these groups important?*

(*b*) *The drag of a small submarine hull is desired when it is moving far below the free surface of water. A $\frac{1}{10}$ scale model is to be tested. What dimensionless group should be duplicated between the model and prototype and why? If the drag of the prototype at 1 knot is desired, at what speed should model be moved to give the drag to be expected by the prototype? Would this result still be true if the prototype were to be moved close to the surface? Explain.* **[Engg. Services]**

Solution.

(*a*) The various dimensionless groups which oftenly appear in fluid mechanics are given in the table (refer to page 426) along with their significance and fields of application.

(*b*) Scale ratio, $$L_r = \frac{L_m}{L_p} = \frac{1}{10} \quad \text{...(Given)}$$

When a submarine is moving far below the free water surface it corresponds to the flow situation where the body is *entirely submerged in an infinite mass of fluid at rest*; *the dynamic* similarity criterion is then prescribed by **Reynolds number** which must be duplicated for model and prototype. For dynamic similarity, equating the Reynolds number, we have:

$$\frac{\rho_m V_m L_m}{\mu_m} = \frac{\rho_p V_p l_p}{\mu_p}$$

or,
$$V_m = \frac{\rho_p}{\rho_m} \times \frac{\mu_m}{\mu_p} \times \frac{L_p}{L_m} \times V_p$$

But, $\rho_m = \rho_p$ and $\mu_m = \mu_p$ since water is the fluid both for model and prototype.

$\therefore$ $V_m = 1 \times 1 \times 10 \times 1 =$ **10 knots (Ans.)**

To evaluate the drag experienced by the prototype let us duplicate the drag co-efficient $F/\rho L^2 V^2$ for the model and the prototype as under:

$$F_p = \frac{\rho_p}{\rho_m} \times \left(\frac{L_p}{L_m}\right)^2 \times \left(\frac{V_p}{V_m}\right)^2 \times F_m$$

$$= 1 \times 10^2 \times \left(\frac{1}{10}\right)^2 \times F_m = F_m$$

Table: Dimensionless Groups/Numbers

Sl. No.	Dimensionless number	Aspects			
		Symbol	**Group of variables**	**Significance**	**Field of application**
1.	*Reynolds number*	*Re*	$\frac{\rho VL}{\mu}$	$\frac{\text{Inertia force}}{\text{Viscous force}}$	Laminar viscous flow in confined passages (where *viscous effects are significant*)
2.	*Froude's number*	*Fr*	$\frac{V}{\sqrt{Lg}}$	$\sqrt{\frac{\text{Inertia force}}{\text{Gravity force}}}$	Free surface flows (where *gravity effects are important*)
3.	*Euler's number*	*Eu*	$\frac{V}{\sqrt{p/\rho}}$	$\sqrt{\frac{\text{Inertia force}}{\text{Pressure force}}}$	Conduit flow (where *pressure variations are significant*)
4.	*Weber's number*	*We*	$\frac{V}{\sqrt{\sigma/\rho L}}$	$\sqrt{\frac{\text{Inertia force}}{\text{Surface tension}}}$	Small surface waves, capillary and sheet flow (where *surface tension is important*)
5.	*Mach's number*	*M*	$\sqrt{\frac{V}{K/\rho}}$	$\sqrt{\frac{\text{Inertia force}}{\text{Elastic Force}}}$	High speed flow (where *compressibility effects are significant*).

Hence when a $\frac{1}{10}$ model moves at a speed of 10 knots, the drag experienced by it will be the same as that experienced by the prototype moving at a speed of 1 knot.

- When the submarine moves close to the surface, the *waves offer additional resistance,* therefore, the gravity effect must also be considered. The above result would therefore, *not be valid* then.

Example 7.22. *A model of submarine is scaled down 1/20 of the prototype and is to be tested in a wind tunnel. The speed of the prototype at which we are to estimate the drag is 8 m/s. What should be the free-stream velocity of the air? What will be ratio of the drag between the model and the prototype? Explain why there would be no dynamic similarity if the submarine prototype is moved near the free surface.*

$$\nu_{sea\ water} = 1.21 \times 10^{-2}\ cm^2/s$$

$$\nu_{air} = 1.64 \times 10^{-1}\ cm^2/s$$

$$\rho_{sea\ water} = 1027\ kg/m^3.$$

$$\rho_{air} = 1.34\ kg/m^3.$$

[IIT Delhi]

Solution. *Given*: Scale ratio = 1/20

Speed of the prototype, V_p = 8 m/s

Free-stream velocity, V_m:

As the submarine is to overcome the *viscous resistance,* the similarity of *Reynolds number* is essential for dynamic similarity between the model and the prototype.

$$\left(\frac{VL}{\nu}\right)_p = \left(\frac{VL}{\nu}\right)_m$$

$$\therefore \quad V_m = V_p \times \frac{L_p}{L_m} \times \frac{\nu_m}{\nu_p} = 8 \times 20 \times \frac{1.64 \times 10^{-1}}{1.21 \times 10^{-2}}$$

$$= \mathbf{2168.6\ m/s.\ (Ans.)}$$

Ratio of drag force:

Also drag force, F = Mass × acceleration

$$= \rho \times L^3 \times \frac{V}{T} = \rho L^2 \times \frac{L}{T} \times V = \rho L^2 V^2$$

∴ The ratio of drag force,

$$\frac{F_p}{F_m} = \frac{\rho_p}{\rho_m} \times \left(\frac{L_p}{L_m}\right)^2 \times \left(\frac{V_p}{V_m}\right)^2$$

$$= \frac{1027}{1.34} \times (20)^2 \times \left(\frac{8}{2168.6}\right)^2 = \mathbf{4.17\ (Ans.)}$$

- When the prototype moves closer to the surface, *gravity force will generate the surface waves and that too will contribute to the surface resistance* and hence there would be no dynamic similarity. The model, therefore, will have to be tested with the similarity of Reynolds and Froude's numbers.

Example 7.23. *An orifice meter to carry water is calibrated with air in a geometrically similar model at 1/5 prototype scale. Dynamically similar flow will be obtained when the discharge ratio (air to water) is*

(i) 0.4 *(ii)* 2.5 *(iii)* 62.5.

Assume the ratio of kinematic viscosity of air to water as 12.5.

[UPSC Exams; Fluid Mechanics]

Solution.

Given: Scale ratio, $\frac{L_m}{L_p} = \frac{1}{5}$

$$\frac{\nu_{air}}{\nu_{water}} = \frac{\nu_m}{\nu_p} = 12.5$$

Discharge ratio:

In case of an orifice which is to carry water and is calibrated with air, the dynamically similar flow will be obtained when the Reynolds numbers in model and prototype are equal, thus:

$$\frac{V_m L_m}{\nu_m} = \frac{V_p L_p}{\nu_p}$$

or, $$\frac{V_m}{V_p} = \frac{\nu_m}{\nu_p} \times \frac{L_p}{L_m} = 12.5 \times 5 = 62.5$$

∴ Discharge ratio (air to water),

$$\frac{Q_m}{Q_p} = \frac{L_m^2}{L_p^2}\frac{V_m}{V_p} = \left(\frac{1}{5}\right)^2 \times 62.5 = \mathbf{2.5} \textbf{ (Ans.)}$$

Example 7.24. *A test was made on a pipe model 15 mm in diameter and 3 m long with water flowing through it at the corresponding speed for frictional resistance. The head loss was found by measurement to be 7 m of water. The prototype pipe is 300 mm in diameter and 240 m long through which air is flowing at 3.6 m/s. Density of water and air are 1000 kg/m³ and 1.22 kg/m³ respectively and co-efficients of viscosity of water and air are 0.01 and 1.8 × 10⁻⁴ poise respectively. Find:*

(i) The corresponding speed of water in the model pipe for dynamic similarity;

(ii) Pressure drop in prototype pipe.

Neglect change of density of the air.

Solution. *For model*:

Diameter of pipe, D_m = 15 mm = 0.015 m

Density of water, ρ_m = 1000 kg/m^3

Dynamic viscosity of water, $\mu_m = 0.01 \text{ poise} = \frac{0.01}{10} = 0.001 \frac{\text{N.s}}{\text{m}^2}$

Length, L_m = 3m

For prototype:

Diameter of pipe, D_p = 300 mm = 0.3 m

Density of air, ρ_p = 1.22 kg/m^3

Dynamic viscosity of air, $\mu_p = 1.8 \times 10^{-4} \text{ poise} = \frac{1.8 \times 10^{-4}}{10} = 1.8 \times 10^{-5} \frac{\text{N.s}}{\text{m}^2}$

Length, L_p = 240 m

Velocity of air, V_p = 3.6 m/s

Head lost in model = 7 m

∴ Pressure drop in model, $(\Delta_p)_m = 7 \times 9.81 = 68.67$ kN/m^2.

(i) Speed of water in the model pipe, V_m:

For dynamic similarity in the case of frictional resistance, the Reynolds number in the model and prototype must be same *i.e.*

$$\left(\frac{\rho V D}{\mu}\right)_m = \left(\frac{\rho V D}{\mu}\right)_p$$

i.e. $$\frac{\rho_m V_m D_m}{\mu_m} = \frac{\rho_p V_p D_p}{\mu_p}$$

or, $$V_m = V_p \times \frac{\rho_p}{\rho_m} \times \frac{D_p}{D_m} \times \frac{\mu_m}{\mu_p}$$

$$= 3.6 \times \frac{1.22}{1000} \times \frac{0.3}{0.015} \times \frac{0.001}{1.8 \times 10^{-5}}$$

$$= \mathbf{4.88\ m/s}\ \textbf{(Ans.)}$$

(ii) Pressure drop in prototype pipe, $(\Delta p)_p$:

We know that for frictional resistance,

$$\frac{R}{\rho L^2 V^2} = \phi\ \text{(Reynolds number)}$$

where, R is the resistance and L^2 represents the characteristic area. In the case of pipe flow the characteristic area may be taken as the wetted area *i.e.*, $\pi\, DL$ where L is the length of pipe under consideration.

As the Reynolds number is the same in model and prototype, the above equation becomes:

$$\left(\frac{R}{\rho \pi D L V^2}\right)_m = \left(\frac{R}{\rho \pi D L V^2}\right)_p$$

Also,
$$R = \Delta p \times \frac{\pi D^2}{4}$$

where, Δp is the pressure drop.

$$\therefore \quad \left(\frac{\Delta p \,.\, D}{\rho L V^2}\right)_m = \left(\frac{\Delta p \,.\, D}{\rho L V^2}\right)_p$$

or,
$$\frac{(\Delta p)_m \,.\, D_m}{\rho_m \,.\, L_m \,.\, V_m^2} = \frac{(\Delta p)_p \,.\, D_p}{\rho_p \,.\, L_p \,.\, V_p^2}$$

or,
$$(\Delta_p)_p = (\Delta p)_m \,.\, \frac{\rho_p}{\rho_m} \,.\, \frac{D_m}{D_p} \,.\, \frac{V_p^2}{V_m^2} \,.\, \frac{L_p}{L_m}$$

$$= 68.67 \times \frac{1.22}{1000} \times \frac{0.015}{0.3} \times \frac{3.6^2}{4.88^2} \times \frac{240}{3}$$

$$= \mathbf{0.182\ kN/m^2}\ \textbf{(Ans.)}$$

Example 7.25. *Water having a coefficient of kinematic viscosity of 1.12×10^{-6} m²/s and a mass density of 1 Mg/m³ flows at a mean speed of 1.75 m/s through a 75 mm diameter pipeline. What corresponding volumetric rate (measured at atmospheric pressure) of air flow through this pipeline would give rise to essentially similar dynamical flow conditions and why would this be so? Air may be assumed to have a coefficient of kinematic viscosity of 14.7×10^{-6} m²/s and a mass density of 1.23 kg/m³. Determine for each fluid, the pressure drop which would occur in* 10 *m length of this pipeline. Take $f_1 = 0.010$ (Darcy's friction factor) for both fluids.* **(MU)**

Solution. *Given*:

Water	*Air*
$\nu = 1.12 \times 10^{-6}\ m^2/s$	$\gamma = 14.7 \times 10^{-6}\ m^2/s$
$\rho = 1\ Mg/m^3 = 1000\ kg/m^3$	$\rho = 1.23\ kg/m^3$
$V = 1.75$ m/s	$V = ?$
$D = 75$ mm $= 0.075$ m	$D = 75$ mm $= 0.075$ m
$L = 10$ m	$L = 10$ m
$f_1 = 0.010$	$f_1 = 0.010$

For similar dynamical flow conditions, the ratio of corresponding forces acting at corresponding points in the model and prototype should be equal. The ratio of forces are dimensionless numbers. It means for dynamic similarity between model and prototype, dimensionless numbers should be same for model and prototype.

In the above question, we are dealing with the flow through pipe for which *Reynolds model law should hold good, which states that Reynolds number for the model must be equal to the Reynolds number for the prototype.*

$$(Re)_{water} = (Re)_{air}$$

$$\left(\frac{\rho VD}{\mu}\right)_{water} = \left(\frac{\rho VD}{\mu}\right)_{air}$$

or,

$$\left(\frac{VD}{\nu}\right)_{water} = \left(\frac{VD}{\nu}\right)_{air}$$

$$V_{air} = V_{water} \times \frac{D_{water}}{D_{air}} \times \frac{\nu_{air}}{\nu_{water}}$$

$$= 1.75 \times \frac{0.075}{0.075} \times \frac{14.7 \times 10^{-6}}{1.12 \times 10^{-6}} = 22.97 \text{ m/s}$$

Volumetric flow rate of air = Area × velocity

$$= \frac{\pi}{4} D_{air}^2 \times V_{air} = \frac{\pi}{4} \times (0.075)^2 \times 22.97$$

$$= \mathbf{0.1015\ m^3/s}$$ **(Ans.)**

For water:

$$Re = \frac{VD}{\nu} = \frac{1.75 \times 0.075}{1.12 \times 10^{-6}} = 117187.5$$

Since Reynolds number is greater than 4000, hence flow is *turbulent,* for which loss is given by:

$$h_f = \frac{4 fLV^2}{D \times 2g}, \text{ where } f = \text{co-efficient of friction.}$$

$$= \frac{f_1 LV^2}{D \times 2g}, \text{ where } f_1 = \text{friction factor}$$

$$= \frac{0.010 \times 10 \times 1.75^2}{0.075 \times 2 \times 9.81} = 0.2081 \text{ m}$$

Pressure drop = 0.2081 *m* water column

$$= 0.2081 \times 1000 \times 9.81 \text{ N/m}^2 = 2041.46 \text{ Pa} \simeq \mathbf{2.04\ kPa}$$ **(Ans.)**

For air:

$$Re = \frac{VD}{\nu} = \frac{22.97 \times 0.075}{14.7 \times 10^{-6}} = 117193.8$$

Since Reynolds number is greater than 4000, hence flow is turbulent for which loss of head is given by:

$$h_f = \frac{f_1 LV^2}{D \times 2g} = \frac{0.010 \times 10 \times (22.97)^2}{0.075 \times 2 \times 9.81} = 35.86 \text{ m}$$

Pressure drop = 35.86 m of air column

$$= 35.86 \times 1.23 \times 9.81 \text{ N/m}^2 = 432.7 \text{ Pa} \simeq \mathbf{0.433\ kPa}$$ **(Ans.)**

Example 7.26. *A model of submarine is scaled down to $\frac{1}{20}$ of the prototype and is to be tested in a wind tunnel where free stream pressure is 2.0 MPa absolute and temperature is 50°C. The speed of the prototype is 7.72 m/s. Determine the free stream velocity of air and the ratio of the drags between model and prototype. Assume kinematic viscosity of sea water as 1.4 × 10^{-6} m²/s and viscosity of air as 0.0184 cP.* **(UPTU)**

Solution. *Given*:

$$L_r = \frac{L_m}{L_p} = \frac{1}{20};\ p = 2.0 \text{ MPa} = 2 \times 10^6 \text{ N/m}^2;\ t = 50°C$$

$$V_p = 7.72 \text{ m/s};\ \nu_p = 1.4 \times 10^{-6} \text{ m}^2\text{/s};\ \mu_{air} = 0.0184 \times 10^{-3} \text{ Ns/m}^2.$$

$$\boldsymbol{V_m;\ \frac{(F_D)_m}{(F_D)_p}}:$$

$$\rho_{air} = \frac{p}{RT} = \frac{2 \times 10^6}{287 \times (50 + 273)} = 21.57 \text{ kg/m}^3$$

$$\nu_m = \frac{\mu_{air}}{\rho_{air}} = \frac{0.0184 \times 10^{-3}}{21.57} = 8.53 \times 10^{-7} \text{ m}^2\text{/s}$$

Since the submarine has to overcome the viscous resistance, there has to be dynamic similarity between the model and the prototype; which implies equality of Reynolds number.

i.e. $$(Re)_p = (Re)_m$$

or, $$\frac{V_p L_p}{\nu_p} = \frac{V_m L_m}{\nu_m}$$

or, $$V_m = \frac{V_p L_p \nu_m}{\nu_p L_m} = \frac{7.72 \times 20 \times 8.53 \times 10^{-7}}{1.4 \times 10^{-6}} = 94.07 \text{ m/s}$$

Hence, *free stream velocity of air* = **94.07 m/s (Ans.)**

Now, $$\frac{(F_D)_m}{(F_D)_p} = \frac{\rho_m}{\rho_p} \times \left(\frac{L_m}{L_p}\right)^2 \times \left(\frac{V_m}{V_p}\right)^2 = \frac{\rho_m}{\rho_p} \times \left(\frac{L_m}{L_p}\frac{V_m}{V_p}\right)^2$$

Assuming density of sea water as 1025 kg/m³,

Ratio of drag forces,

$$\frac{(F_D)_m}{(F_D)_p} = \frac{21.57}{1025}\left[\frac{1}{20} \times \frac{94.07}{7.72}\right]^2 = \mathbf{0.00781} \text{ (Ans.)}$$

Example 7.27. *A torpedo shaped object, 900 mm diameter is to move in air at 60 m/s and its drag is to be estimated from tests in water on a half scale model. Determine the necessary speed of the model and the drag of the full scale object if that of the model is 1140 N. Given properties: air viscosity = 1.86 × 10^{-5} Ns/m², water viscosity = 1.01 × 10^{-3} Ns/m², air density = 1.2 kg/m³, water density = 1000 kg/m³.* **(Anna University)**

Solution. *Given*: Torpedo shaped object (*Prototype*): $V_p = 60$ m/s

$$\mu_p = \mu_{air} = 1.86 \times 10^{-5} \text{ Ns/m}^2;$$

$$\rho_p = \rho_{air} = 1.2 \text{ kg/m}^3$$

Model half size tested in water: $$\mu_m = \mu_{water} = 1.01 \times 10^{-3} \text{ Ns/m}^2;$$

$$\rho_m = \rho_{water} = 1000 \text{ kg/m}^3;\ (F_D)_m = 1140 \text{ N}$$

Also, $$\frac{L_p}{L_m} = \frac{1}{(1/2)} = 2.$$

Speed of the model, V_m:

Now, $$(Re)_{model} = (Re)_{prototype}$$

$$\frac{\rho_m V_m L_m}{\mu_m} = \frac{\rho_p V_p L_p}{\mu_p}$$

$$\therefore \quad V_m = \frac{\mu_m \rho_m V_p L_p}{\mu_p \rho_m L_m} = \frac{1.01 \times 10^{-3} \times 1.2 \times 60}{1.86 \times 10^{-5} \times 1000} \times 2 = \mathbf{7.819\ m/s}\ \textbf{(Ans.)}$$

Drag of the full scale object, $(F_D)_p$:

$$(C_D)_p = (C_D)_m;$$

$$\frac{A_p}{A_m} = \left(\frac{L_p}{L_m}\right)^2$$

$$\frac{(F_D)_p}{(F_D)_m} = \frac{(C_D)_p \times \frac{1}{2} \rho_p A_p V_p^2}{(C_D)_m \times \frac{1}{2} \rho_m A_m V_m^2} = \frac{(\rho_p L_p^2 V_p^2)}{(\rho_m L_m^2 V_m^2)}$$

$$(F_D)_p = (F_D)_m \times \left[\frac{\rho_p . L_p^2 V_p^2}{\rho_m L_m^2 V_m^2}\right]$$

$$= 1140 \times \frac{1.2}{1000} \times (2)^2 \times \frac{(60)^2}{(7.819)^2}$$

$$= \mathbf{322.2\ N}\ \textbf{(Ans.)}$$

Example 7.28. *A geometrically similar model of an air duct is built to $\frac{1}{25}$ scale and tested with water which is 50 times more viscous and 800 times denser than air. When tested under dynamically similar conditions, the pressure drop is 2 bar in model. Find corresponding pressure drop in prototype and express in water column.* **(MGU, Kerala)**

Solution. *Given*: $$\frac{L_p}{L_m} = 25; \frac{\mu_p}{\mu_m} = \frac{1}{50}; \frac{\rho_p}{\rho_m} = \frac{1}{800}; (\Delta p)_m = 2\text{ bar}$$

$(\Delta p)_p$:

For dynamic similarity, the Reynolds number must be equal in model and prototype.

$$\therefore \quad \frac{\rho_m V_m L_m}{\mu_m} = \frac{\rho_p V_p L_p}{\mu_p}$$

or, $$\frac{V_p}{V_m} = \frac{\mu_p}{\mu_m} \times \frac{\rho_m}{\rho_p} \times \frac{L_m}{L_p}$$

$$= \frac{1}{50} \times 800 \times \frac{1}{25} = \frac{16}{25}$$

$$\text{Pressure} = \frac{F}{A} = \frac{\rho L^2 V^2}{L^2} = \rho V^2$$

$$\frac{(\Delta p)_p}{(\Delta p)_m} = \frac{\rho_p}{\rho_m}\left(\frac{V_p}{V_m}\right)^2$$

$$= \frac{1}{800} \times \left(\frac{16}{25}\right)^2 = 0.000512$$

$\therefore$ $$(\Delta)_p = 2 \times 0.000512 \text{ bar}$$

$$= 2 \times 0.000512 \times 10^5 \text{ N/m}^2 = \rho_w g \frac{h_w}{1000}$$

(where, h_w = pressure drop in mm of water column)

$\therefore$ $$h_w = \frac{2 \times 0.000512 \times 10^5 \times 1000}{1000 \times 9.81} = \mathbf{10.438\,mm} \text{ (Ans.)}$$

$(\because \rho_w = 1000 \text{ kg/m}^3)$

Example 7.29. *A ship 300 m long moves in sea-water, whose density is 1030 kg/m^3. A 1 : 100 model of this ship is to be tested in a wind tunnel. The velocity of air in the wind tunnel around the model is 30 m/s and the resistance of the model is 60 N. Determine the velocity of ship in sea-water and also the resistance of the ship in sea-water. The density of air is given as 1.24 kg/m^3. Take the kinematic viscosity of sea-water and air as 0.012 stokes and 0.018 stokes respectively.*

(Delhi University, 2000)

Solution. *Given*:

Prototype	*Model*
$L_p = 300$ m	$L_m = \frac{1}{100} \times 300 = 3$ m
$\rho_p = 1030$ kg/m^3	$\rho_m = 1.24$ kg/m^3
$\nu_p = 0.012 \times 10^{-4}$ m^2/s	$\nu_m = 0.018 \times 10^{-4}$ m^2/s $(\because 1 \text{ stoke} = 10^{-4} \text{ m}^2\text{/s})$
	$V_m = 30$ m/s
	$R_m = 60$ N.

***V_p, R_p*:**

For dynamic similarity between the prototype and its model, the Reynolds number for both of them should be equal.

$\therefore$ $$\frac{V_p \times L_p}{\nu_p} = \frac{V_m \times L_m}{\nu_m}$$

or, $$V_p = \frac{\nu_p}{\nu_m} \times \frac{L_m}{L_p} \times V_m$$

$$= \frac{0.012 \times 10^{-4}}{0.018 \times 10^{-4}} \times \frac{3}{300} \times 30 = 0.2 \text{ m/s}$$

Resistance = Mass × acceleration

$$= \rho L^3 \times \frac{V}{t} = \rho L^2 \times \frac{V}{1} \times \frac{L}{t} = \rho L^2 V^2$$

Then, $$\frac{R_p}{R_m} = \frac{F_p}{F_m} = \frac{(\rho L^2 V^2)_p}{(\rho L^2 V^2)_m}$$

$$= \frac{\rho_p}{\rho_m} \times \left(\frac{L_p}{L_m}\right)^2 \times \left(\frac{V_p}{V_m}\right)^2$$

$$= \frac{1030}{1.24} \times \left(\frac{300}{3}\right)^2 \times \left(\frac{0.2}{30}\right)^2 = 369.17$$

$\therefore$ $R_p = R_m \times 369.17 = 60 \times 369.17 =$ **22150.2 N (Ans.)**

7.11. FROUDE MODEL LAW

When the gravitational force can be considered to be the only predominant force which controls the motion in addition to the inertia force, the similarity of the flow in any two such systems can be established if the Froude's number for both the systems is the same. This is known as ***Froude Model Law.*** Some of the phenomena for which the Froude model law can be sufficient criterion for dynamic similarity to be established in the model and the prototype are:

(*i*) Free surface flows such as flow over spillways, sluices etc.;

(*ii*) Flow of jet from an orifice or nozzle;

(*iii*) Where waves are likely to be formed on the surface;

(*iv*) Where fluids of different mass densities flow over one another.

Let, V_m = Velocity of fluid in model,

L_m = Length (or linear dimension) of the model,

g_m = Acceleration due to gravity (at a place where model is tested),

and V_p, L_p and g_p are the corresponding values of the velocity, length and acceleration due to gravity for the prototype.

Then according to Froude model law:

$$(Fr)_m = (Fr)_p$$

or,
$$\frac{V_m}{\sqrt{g_m L_m}} = \frac{V_p}{\sqrt{g_p L_p}} \quad ...(7.22)$$

As the value of g at the site of model testing will be practically the same as at the site of the proposed prototype, therefore, $g_m = g_p$ and the eqn. (7.22) becomes:

$$\frac{V_m}{\sqrt{L_m}} = \frac{V_p}{\sqrt{L_p}} \quad ...(7.23)$$

or,
$$\frac{V_p}{V_m} = \sqrt{\frac{L_p}{L_m}} = \sqrt{L_r} \qquad \left(\because \frac{L_p}{L_m} = L_r\right)$$

where L_r = Scale ratio for length.

$$\frac{V_p}{V_m} = V_r = \text{Scale ratio for velocity}$$

$\therefore$
$$\frac{V_p}{V_m} = V_r = \sqrt{L_r} \quad ...(7.24)$$

(*i*) *Time scale ratio, T_r*:

We know, $T_m = \frac{L_m}{V_m}$ and $T_p = \frac{L_p}{V_p}$

$$\therefore \qquad T_r = \frac{T_p}{T_m} = \frac{L_p / V_p}{L_m / V_m} = \frac{L_p}{L_m} \times \frac{V_m}{V_p}$$

$$= L_r \times \frac{1}{\sqrt{L_r}} = \sqrt{L_r}$$

i.e.
$$T_r = \sqrt{L_r} \qquad ...(7.25)$$

(*ii*) *Acceleration scale ratio, a_r:*

We know,
$$a = \frac{V}{t}$$

$$\therefore \qquad a_r = \frac{a_p}{a_m} = \frac{V_p / T_p}{V_m / T_m} = \frac{V_p}{V_m} \times \frac{T_m}{T_p} = \sqrt{L_r} \times \frac{1}{\sqrt{L_r}} = 1$$

i.e.
$$a_r = 1 \qquad ...(7.26)$$

(*iii*) *Discharge scale ratio, Q_r:*

The discharge, $Q = A.V = L^2 \times \frac{L}{T} = \frac{L^3}{T}$

$$\therefore \qquad \text{Discharge ratio, } Q_r = \frac{Q_p}{Q_m} = \frac{(L^3 / T)_p}{(L^3 / T)_m} = \left(\frac{L_p}{L_m}\right)^3 \times \left(\frac{T_m}{T_p}\right)$$

$$= L_r^3 \times \frac{1}{\sqrt{L_r}} = L_r^{2.5} \qquad ...(7.27)$$

(*iv*) *Force scale ratio, F_r:*

The force may be expressed from the Newton's second law,

$$F = ma = \rho L^3 \times \frac{V}{T} = \rho L^2 \times \frac{L}{T} \times V = \rho L^2 V^2$$

$$\therefore \qquad \text{Force ratio, } F_r = \frac{F_p}{F_m} = \frac{\rho_p L_p^2 V_p^2}{\rho_m L_m^2 V_m^2} = \rho_r L_r^2 V_r^2$$

If the same fluid is used in the model, then $\rho_r \left(= \frac{\rho_p}{\rho_m} \right) = 1$

$$\therefore \qquad F_r = L_r^2 \times (\sqrt{L_r})^2 = L_r^3 \qquad ...(7.28)$$

$$\left(\because V_r = \sqrt{L_r}\right)$$

(*v*) *Pressure intensity scale ratio, p_r:*

We know,
$$p = \frac{F}{A} = \frac{\rho L^2 V^2}{L^2} = \rho V^2$$

$$\therefore \qquad \text{Pressure ratio, } p_r = \frac{p_p}{p_m} = \frac{\rho_p V_p^2}{\rho_m V_m^2}$$

For the same fluid $\rho_p = \rho_m$

$$\therefore \qquad p_r = \frac{V_p^2}{V_m^2} = (\sqrt{L_r})^2 = L_r \qquad ...(7.29)$$

(*vi*) *Energy or work done scale ratio* E_r:

$$\text{Energy} = \text{Force} \times \text{distance}$$

$$\therefore \quad E = F \times L$$

and, the energy ratio, $E_r = \dfrac{E_p}{E_m} = \dfrac{F_p}{F_m} \times \dfrac{L_p}{L_m} = F_r \,.\, L_r$

or, $E_r = L_r^3 \,.\, L_r = L_r^4$ ...(7.30)

(*vii*) *The momentum or impulse scale ratio* M_r:

The momentum or impulse

$$= mV = \rho L^3 V$$

and, the momentum ratio $= \dfrac{M_p}{M_m} = \dfrac{\rho_p L_p^3 V_p}{\rho_m L_m^3 V_m} = \rho_r \,.\, Lr_r^3 \,.\, V_r$

$$= L_r^3 \sqrt{L_r} = L_r^{7/2} \quad ...(7.31)$$

$(\because \rho_r = 1)$

(*viii*) *Torque scale ratio*, T_r^*:

The torque is given by the product of force and its perpendicular distance from the centre of rotation,

$$T^* = F \,.\, L$$

and the torque ratio, $T_r^* = \dfrac{T_p^*}{T_m^*} = \dfrac{F_p}{F_m} \times \dfrac{L_p}{L_m} = F_r \,.\, L_r$

$$= L_r^3 \,.\, L_r = L_r^4 \quad ...(7.32)$$

(*ix*) *Power scale ratio*, P_r:

The power being the time rate of doing work, is given by: $P = \dfrac{F \times L}{T}$

and, the power ratio, $P_r = \dfrac{P_p}{P_m} = \dfrac{(F_p \times L_p)/T_p}{(F_m \times L_m)/T_m} = \dfrac{F_p}{F_m} \times \dfrac{L_p}{L_m} \times \dfrac{T_m}{T_p}$

$$= F_r \,.\, L_r \,.\, \frac{1}{T_r} = L_r^3 \,.\, L_r \,.\, \frac{1}{\sqrt{L_r}} = L_r^{3.5}$$

i.e. $P_r = L_r^{3.5}$ ...(7.33)

Example 7.30. (*a*) *With Froude's number as the criterion of dynamic similarity for a certain flow situation, work out the scale factors for velocity, time, discharge, acceleration, force, work and power in terms of the scale factor for length.*

(*b*) *A geometrically similar model of spillway is to be laid to a scale of 1 in 50. Calculate the velocity ratio, discharge ratio and acceleration ratio.* **[MDU, Haryana]**

Solution. (*a*) Refer to Article 7.11.

(*b*) Scale ratio, $L_r = \dfrac{L_p}{L_m} = 50$

Velocity ratio [Eqn. (7.24)], $V_r = \dfrac{V_p}{V_m} = \sqrt{L_r} = \sqrt{50} =$ **7.07 (Ans.)**

Discharge ratio [Eqn. (7.27)], $Q_r = \dfrac{Q_p}{Q_m} = (L_r)^{2.5} = (50)^{2.5}$ = **17677.6 (Ans.)**

Acceleration ratio, $a_r = \dfrac{a_p}{a_m}$ = **1 (Ans.)**

Example 7.31. *In the model test of a spillway the discharge and velocity of flow over the model were 2.5 m³/s and 1.5 m/s respectively. Calculate the velocity and discharge over the prototype which is 36 times the model size.* **[PTU]**

Solution. Discharge over the model, Q_m = 2.5 m³/s

Velocity of flow over the model, V_m = 1.5 m/s

Scale ratio (linear), L_r = 36

Velocity over the prototype, V_p:

Using Froude model law [Eqn. (7.24)], we have

$$\frac{V_p}{V_m} = \sqrt{L_r} = \sqrt{36} = 6$$

$\therefore$ $V_p = 1.5 \times 6 =$ **9 m/s (Ans.)**

Discharge over the prototype, Q_p:

Again, using Froude model law [Eqn. (7.27)], we have

$$\frac{Q_p}{Q_m} = (L_r)^{2.5} = (36)^{2.5} = 7776$$

$\therefore$ $Q_p = 2.5 \times 7776 =$ **19440 m³/s (Ans.)**

Example 7.32. *In a geometrically similar model of spillway the discharge per metre length is 0.2 m³/s. If the scale of the model is $\frac{1}{36}$, find the discharge per metre run of the prototype.*

Solution. Discharge per metre length for model = 0.2 m³/s

Scale ratio (linear), L_r = 36

Discharge per metre run for the prototype, Q_p:

According to Froude law:

$$\frac{Q_p}{Q_m} = L_r^{2.5} \qquad \text{[Eqn. (7.27)]}$$

Discharge ratio per metre length is given as:

$$\frac{q_p}{q_m} = \frac{Q_p/L_p}{Q_m/L_m} = \frac{Q_p}{Q_m} \times \frac{L_m}{L_p}$$

$$= L_r^{2.5} \times \frac{1}{L_r} = L_r^{1.5}$$

$\therefore$ $$\frac{q_p}{q_m} = (36)^{1.5} = 216$$

and, $q_p = 0.2 \times 216 =$ **43.2 m³/s (Ans.)**

Example 7.33. *The force required to tow a 1: 30 scale model of a motor boat in a lake at a speed of 2 m/s is 0.5 N. Assuming that the viscous resistance due to water and air is negligible in comparison with the wave resistance, calculate the corresponding speed of the prototype for* *dynamically similar conditions. What would be the force required to propel the prototype at that velocity in the same lake?* **[GATE Exam.]**

Solution. Linear scale ratio, $L_r = \dfrac{L_p}{L_m} = 30$

Speed of the model, $V_m = 2$ m/s

Force required to tow the model, $F_m = 0.5$ N

Speed of the prototype, V_p:

Since the *wave resistance is the dominant force in comparison with the viscous resistance*, therefore, the *dynamic similarity will be attained when the Froude numbers in model and prototype are equal.*

$$\therefore \quad \left(\frac{V}{\sqrt{Lg}}\right)_m = \left(\frac{V}{\sqrt{Lg}}\right)_p$$

$$\text{or,} \quad \frac{V_m}{\sqrt{L_m g_m}} = \frac{V_p}{\sqrt{L_p g_p}}$$

$$\text{or,} \quad \frac{V_p}{V_m} = \sqrt{\frac{L_p}{L_m}} = \sqrt{30} \qquad (\because g_m = g_p)$$

$$\therefore \quad V_p = 2 \times \sqrt{30} = \mathbf{10.95\ m/s\ (Ans.)}$$

Force required to propel the prototype, F_p:

We know,
$$F_r = \frac{F_p}{F_m} = \frac{\rho_p L_p^2 V_p^2}{\rho_m L_m^2 V_m^2} \qquad (\because F = \rho L^2 V^2)$$

$$\text{or,} \quad \frac{F_p}{F_m} = \left(\frac{L_p}{L_m}\right)^2 \times \left(\frac{V_p}{V_m}\right)^2 \qquad [\because \rho_m = \rho_p, \text{ fluid being same}]$$

$$= (30)^2 \times (\sqrt{30})^2 = 30^3$$

$$\therefore \quad F_p = F_m \times 30^3 = 0.5 \times 30^3 = \mathbf{13500\ N\ (Ans.)}$$

Example 7.34. *A spillway model is to be built to a geometrically similar scale of $\frac{1}{50}$ across a flume of 600 mm width. The prototype is 15 metres high and the maximum head on it is expected to be 1.5 metres.*

(i) *What height of model and what head on model should be used?*

(ii) *If flow over the model for a particular head is 12 litres/ second, what flow per metre length of prototype is expected?*

(iii) *If the negative pressure in the model is 200 mm, what is the negative pressure in prototype? Is it practicable?* **[PTU]**

Solution. Linear scale ratio, $L_r = \dfrac{L_p}{L_m} = 50$

Width of model, B_m = 600 mm = 0.6 m

Flow over model, Q_m = 12 litres/sec.

Pressure in model, h_m = – 200 mm of water = – 0.2 m of water

Height of prototype, H_p = 15 m

Head on prototype, h_p = 1.5 m

(i) Height of model, H_m:

Head on model, h_m:

$$\text{Linear scale ratio, } L_r = \frac{H_p}{H_m} = \frac{h_p}{h_m} = 50$$

$$\therefore \quad \text{Height of model, } H_m = \frac{H_p}{50} = \frac{15}{50} = \mathbf{0.3\ m}\ \textbf{(Ans.)}$$

$$\text{Head on model, } h_m = \frac{h_p}{50} = \frac{1.5}{50} = \mathbf{0.03\ m}\ \textbf{(Ans.)}$$

(ii) Discharge per metre length of prototype, q_p:

Width of prototype, $B_p = B_m \times L_r = 0.6 \times 50 = 30$ m

Now, discharge ratio [Eqn. 7.27], $\frac{Q_p}{Q_m} = L_r^{2.5} = (50)^{2.5} = 17677.66$

$$\therefore \quad Q_p = Q_m \times 17677.66 = 12 \times 17677.66 = 212132 \text{ litres/sec.}$$

Discharge per metre length of prototype

$$= \frac{Q_p}{L_p} = \frac{Q_p}{B_p} = \frac{212132}{30} = \mathbf{7071\ litres/sec.}\ \textbf{(Ans.)}$$

(iii) Negative pressure head in prototype:

Negative pressure head in prototype,

$$h_p = h_m \times L_r = -0.2 \times 50 = \mathbf{-10\ m}\ \textbf{(Ans.)}$$

Since the cavitation limits the maximum negative pressure head to 7.5 m, therefore, a negative head of 10 m is **not practicable. (Ans.)**

Example 7.35. *The performance of a spillway of an irrigation project is to be studied by means of a model constructed to a scale of 1 : 9, neglecting the viscous and surface tension effects, determine:*

(i) Rate of flow in model for a prototype discharge of 1200 m^3/s;

(ii) The dissipation of energy in the prototype hydraulic jump, if the jump in the model dissipates 0.25 kW.

Solution. Linear scale ratio, $L_r = \frac{L_p}{L_m} = 9$

Rate of flow in the prototype, $Q_p = 1200\ m^3/s$

Dissipation of energy in the model, $P_m = 0.250$ kW

(i) Rate of flow in the model, Q_m:

For dynamic similarity between the model and its prototype the Froude's numbers must be equal.

$$\therefore \quad \left(\frac{V}{\sqrt{Lg}}\right)_p = \left(\frac{V}{\sqrt{Lg}}\right)_m$$

$$\therefore \quad \frac{V_p}{V_m} = \sqrt{\frac{L_p}{L_m}} \qquad (\because g_p = g_m)$$

$$\text{The discharge ratio, } \quad Q_r = \frac{Q_p}{Q_m} = \frac{L_p^2 \times V_p}{L_m^2 \times V_m} = \left(\frac{L_p}{L_m}\right)^2 \times \frac{V_p}{V_m}$$

$$= (L_r)^2 \times \sqrt{L_r} = (L_r)^{5/2}$$

$$\therefore \quad Q_m = \frac{Q_p}{(L_r)^{5/2}} = \frac{1200}{(9)^{5/2}} = \mathbf{4.938\ m^3/s}\ \textbf{(Ans.)}$$

(*ii*) The dissipation of energy in the prototype hydraulic jump, P_p:

Power = $w\,QH$ (where, H = head of fluid)

$$\therefore \quad \text{Power ratio, } P_r = \frac{P_p}{P_m} = \frac{w_p Q_p H_p}{w_m Q_m H_m} = (L_r)^{5/2} \times L_r = (L_r)^{7/2} \qquad (\because w_p = w_m)$$

$\therefore$ Power dissipated in the prototype,

$$P_p = P_m \times (L_r)^{7/2} = 0.25 \times (9)^{7/2} = \mathbf{546.75\ kW}\ \textbf{(Ans.)}$$

Example 7.36. *The characteristics of the spillway are to be studied by means of a geometrically similar model constructed to the scale ratio of 1 : 10.*

(*i*) *If the maximum rate of flow in the prototype is 28.3 cusecs, what will be the corresponding flow in model?*

(*ii*) *If the measured velocity in the model at a point on the spillway is 2.4 m/s, what will be the corresponding velocity in prototype?*

(*iii*) *If the hydraulic jump at the foot of the model is 50 mm high, what will be the height of jump in prototype?*

(*iv*) *If the energy dissipated per second in the model is 3.5 Nm, what energy is dissipated per second in the prototype?* **(Anna University)**

Solution. *Given*: Scale ratio, $\frac{L_p}{L_m} = 10$; $Q_p = 28.3\ m^3/s$; $V_m = 2.4$ m/s;

$H_m = 50$ mm; $E_m = 3.5$ Nm.

(*i*) Flow in the model, Q_m:

$$\frac{Q_p}{Q_m} = (L_r)^{2.5} = (10)^{2.5} = 316.22$$

$$\therefore \quad Q_m = \frac{Q_p}{316.22} = \frac{28.3}{316.22} = \mathbf{0.0895\ m^3/s}\ \textbf{(Ans.)}$$

(*ii*) Velocity of flow in prototype, V_p:

$$\frac{V_p}{V_m} = \sqrt{L_r} = \sqrt{10} = 3.162$$

$$\therefore \quad V_p = V_m \times 3.162 = 2.4 \times 3.162 = \mathbf{7.589\ m/s}\ \textbf{(Ans.)}$$

(*iii*) Height of jump in prototype, H_p:

$$\frac{H_p}{H_m} = L_r = 10$$

$$\therefore \quad H_p = H_m \times 10 = 50 \times 10 = \mathbf{500\ mm}\ \textbf{(Ans.)}$$

(*iv*) Energy dissipated per second in the prototype, E_p:

$$\frac{E_p}{E_m} = (L_r)^{3.5} = (10)^{3.5} = 3162.28$$

$$\therefore \quad E_p = E_m \times 3162.28 = 3.5 \times 3162.28 = \mathbf{11067.98\ Nm}\ \textbf{(Ans.)}$$

Example 7.37. *A 1 : 64 model is constructed of an open channel in concrete which has Manning's N = 0.014. Find the value of N for the model.* **(Delhi University)**

Solution. *Given*: $L_r = 64; N_p = 0.014.$

Value of N of the model, N_m:

The Manning's formula is given by :

$$V = \frac{1}{N}(R)^{2/3}\,(S)^{1/2}$$

where, R = Hydraulic radius (or hydraulic mean depth) in metres;

S = Slope of the bed of the channel.

Now for the model, the Manning's formula becomes:

$$V_m = \frac{1}{N_m}(R_m)^{2/3}\,(S_m)^{1/2} \quad ...(i)$$

and, for the prototype, the Manning's formula is written as:

$$V_p = \frac{1}{N_p}(R_p)^{2/3}\,(S_p)^{1/2} \quad ...(ii)$$

Dividing (*ii*) by (*i*), we get:

$$\frac{V_p}{V_m} = \frac{\frac{1}{N_p}(R_p)^{2/3}\,(S_p)^{1/2}}{\frac{1}{N_m}(R_m)^{2/3}\,(S_m)^{1/2}} = \frac{N_m}{N_p} \times \left(\frac{R_p}{R_m}\right)^{2/3}\left(\frac{S_p}{S_m}\right)^{1/2} \quad ...(iii)$$

For dynamic similarity, Froude model law is used.

We know that: $$\frac{V_p}{V_m} = \sqrt{L_r} \quad ...[\text{Eqn. } (17.24)]$$

or, $$\frac{V_p}{V_m} = \sqrt{64} = 8$$

Also, $$\frac{R_p}{R_m} = L_r, \text{ and } \frac{S_p}{S_m} = 1 \text{ as } S_p \text{ and } S_m \text{ are dimensionless.}$$

Substituting the values in (*iii*), we get:

$$8 = \frac{N_m}{N_p} \times (L_r)^{2/3} \times 1 = \frac{N_m}{0.014} \times (64)^{2/3}$$

$$\therefore \quad N_m = \frac{8 \times 0.014}{(64)^{2/3}} = \mathbf{0.007} \text{ (Ans.)}$$

Example 7.38. *A 7.2 m high and 15 m long spillway discharges 94 m³/s discharge under a head of 2.03. If 1: 9 scale model of this spillway is to be constructed, determine model dimensions, head over spillway model and the model discharge. If model experiences a force of 7500 N, determine force on the prototype.* **(Panjab University)**

Solution. *Given*: Height, $h_p = 7.2$ m; $L_p = 15$ m; $Q_p = 94$ m^3/s, head $H_p = 2.0$ m;

$L_r = 9$; $F_m = 7500$ *N*

(*i*) Model dimensions (h_m, L_m):

$$\frac{h_p}{h_m} = \frac{L_p}{L_m} = L_r = 9$$

$$\therefore \quad h_m = \frac{h_p}{9} = \frac{7.2}{9} = \mathbf{0.8\ m} \text{ (Ans.)}$$

and, $$L_m = \frac{L_p}{9} = \frac{15}{9} = \mathbf{1.67\ m}\ \textbf{(Ans.)}$$

(ii) Head over the model, H_m:

$$\frac{H_p}{H_m} = L_r = 9$$

$$\therefore \quad H_m = \frac{H_p}{9} = \frac{2.0}{9} = \mathbf{0.222\,m}\ \textbf{(Ans.)}$$

(iii) Discharge through the model, Q_m:

$$\frac{Q_p}{Q_m} = (L_r)^{2.5} = (9)^{2.5} = 243$$

$$\therefore \quad Q_m = \frac{Q_p}{243} = \frac{94}{243} = \mathbf{0.387\ m^3/s}\ \textbf{(Ans.)}$$

(iv) Force on the prototype F_p:

$$F_r = \frac{F_p}{F_m} = (L_r)^3 = (9)^3 = 729$$

$$\therefore \quad F_p = F_m \times 729 = 7500 \times 729 = \mathbf{5467500\ N}\ \textbf{(Ans.)}$$

Example 7.39. *A model of rectangular pier 1.5 m wide and 4.5 m long in the river is built to a scale of 1: 25. The average depth of water in the river is 3 m. The model was tested in a laboratory, where the velocity of flow was maintained constant at 0.6 m/s. It was observed that the force acting on the model was 3.6 N and the height of the standing wave was 30 mm. Determine the following for the prototype:*

(i) *The corresponding speed,*

(ii) *The force acting,*

(iii) *The height of the standing wave at nose,* and

(iv) *The co-efficient of drag resistance.* **[Roorkee University]**

Solution. Linear scale ratio, $L_r = \frac{L_p}{L_m} = 25$

Velocity of flow in the model, $V_m = 0.6$ m/s

Force acting on the model, $F_m = 3.6$ N

Height of standing wave in the model, $H_m = 30$ mm

(i) The corresponding speed in the prototype V_p:

As the flow in a river is a *free surface flow affected by gravity,* the dynamic similarity between the model and its prototype will be achieved by equating the Froude's number.

$$\therefore \quad \frac{V_p}{\sqrt{L_p g_p}} = \frac{V_m}{\sqrt{L_m g_m}}$$

or, $$\frac{V_p}{V_m} = \sqrt{\frac{L_p}{L_m}} = \sqrt{25} = 5 \qquad (\because g_p = g_m)$$

$$\therefore \quad V_p = V_m \times 5 = 0.6 \times 5 = \mathbf{3\ m/s}\ \textbf{(Ans.)}$$

(ii) The force acting on the prototype, F_p:

$$\text{Force} = \text{Mass} \times \text{acceleration} = \rho L^3 \times \frac{V}{T} = \rho L^3 \times \frac{V}{(L/V)} \qquad \left[\because V = \frac{L}{T} \text{ or } T = \frac{L}{V}\right]$$

$$= \rho L^3 \times \frac{V^2}{L} = \rho L^2 V^2$$

$$\text{Force ratio, } F_r = \frac{F_p}{F_m} = \frac{\rho_p}{\rho_m} \times \frac{L_p^2}{L_m^2} \times \frac{V_p^2}{V_m^2} = \rho_r . L_r^2 . V_r^2$$

$$= L_r^2 \times (\sqrt{L_r})^2 = L_r^3$$

$\therefore$
$$F_p = F_m \times L_r^3 = 3.6 \times (25)^3 = \textbf{56250 N (Ans.)}$$

[$\because \rho_r = 1$, fluid being same in model and prototype]

(iii) The height of the standing wave in the prototype, H_p:

$$\frac{H_p}{H_m} = L_r = 25$$

$\therefore$
$$H_p = H_m \times 25 = 30 \times 25 = \textbf{750 mm (Ans.)}$$

(iv) The co-efficeint of drag resistance:

The co-efficient of drag resistance is defined by:

$$F = C_D . \rho A \frac{V^2}{2}$$

$\therefore$
$$C_D = \frac{F}{\frac{1}{2} \times \rho A V^2}$$

or,
$$(C_D)_p = \frac{F_p}{\frac{1}{2} \times \rho_p A_p V_p^2}$$

where, F_p = Force acting on the prototype (= 56250 N),

ρ_p = Density of water (= 1000 kg/m^3),

A_p = Width of the pier × depth of water in the river = 1.5 × 3 = 4.5 m^2, and

V_p = Velocity of flow in the prototype (= 3 m/s).

$\therefore$
$$(C_D)_p = \frac{56250}{\frac{1}{2} \times 1000 \times 4.5 \times 3^2} = \textbf{2.777 (Ans.)}$$

The drag co-efficient will be *same* for model and prototype.

Example 7.40. *A 1 : 40 model of an ocean tanker is dragged through fresh water at 2 m/s with a total measured drag of 117. 7 N. The skin (frictional) drag co-efficeint 'f' for model and prototype are 0.3 and 0.02 respectively in the equation $R_f = f\,AV^2$. The wetted surface area of the model is 25 m^2. Taking the densities for the prototype and the model as 1030 kg/m^3 and 1000 kgN/m^3 respectively, determine:*

(i) *The total drag on the prototype;*

(ii) *Power required to drive the prototype.*

Solution. *Given*:

$$\text{Linear scale ratio, } L_r = 40$$
$$\text{Velocity of model, } V_m = 2 \text{ m/s}$$
$$\text{Total drag of model, } R_m = 117.7 \text{ N}$$
$$\text{Wetted area of model, } A_m = 25 \text{ m}^2$$
$$\text{Co-efficient of friction for model, } f_m = 0.3$$
$$\text{Co-efficient of friction for prototype, } f_p = 0.02$$

(*i*) Total drag on the prototype, R_p:

$$\text{Frictional drag on model, } (R_f)_m = f_m A_m V_m^2 = 0.3 \times 25 \times 2^2 = 30 \text{ N}$$
$$\therefore \text{ Wave drag on model, } (R_w)_m = R_m - (R_f)_m = 117.7 - 30 = 87.7 \text{ N}$$

The wave drag for the prototype can be evaluated by satisfying the following condition for dynamic similarity:

$$\left(\frac{R_w}{\rho L^2 V^2}\right)_p = \left(\frac{R_w}{\rho L^2 V^2}\right)_m$$

$$\therefore \quad (R_w)_p = \frac{\rho_p}{\rho_m} \times \left(\frac{L_p}{L_m}\right)^2 \times \frac{V_p^2}{V_m^2} \times (R_w)_m$$

But,
$$\left(\frac{V_p}{V_m}\right)^2 = \frac{L_p}{L_m}$$

$$\left[\because \frac{V_p}{\sqrt{L_p g_p}} = \frac{V_m}{\sqrt{L_m g_m}} \quad \text{...Froude's number} \right.$$
$$\left. \text{or } \frac{V_p}{V_m} = \sqrt{\frac{L_p}{L_m}} \text{ or } \left(\frac{V_p}{V_m}\right)^2 = \frac{L_p}{L_m} \quad (\because g_p = g_p)\right]$$

$$\therefore \quad (R_w)_p = \frac{\rho_p}{\rho_m} \times \left(\frac{L_p}{L_m}\right)^3 \times (R_w)_m$$

$$= \frac{1030}{1000} \times (40)^3 \times 87.7 \qquad \left[\because \frac{L_p}{L_m} = L_r = 40\right]$$

$$= 5781184 \text{ N}$$

The frictional drag on the prototype is given by:

$$(R_f)_p = f_p A_p V_p^2 \qquad \text{...}(i)$$

where, V_p is velocity of prototype and is obtained from Froude model law as given below:

$$\frac{V_m}{\sqrt{L_m g_m}} = \frac{V_p}{\sqrt{L_p g_p}} \text{ or } \frac{V_m}{\sqrt{L_m}} = \frac{V_p}{\sqrt{L_p}} \qquad (\because g_m = g_p)$$

$$\therefore \quad V_p = V_m \times \sqrt{\frac{L_p}{L_m}} = 2 \times \sqrt{40} = 12.65 \text{ m/s}$$

Also,
$$\frac{A_p}{A_m} = L_r^2 = 40^2 = 1600$$

$$\therefore \quad A_p = A_m \times 1600 = 25 \times 1600 = 40000 \text{ m}^2$$

Substituting these values in (*i*), we get:

$$(R_f)_p = 0.02 \times 40000 \times (12.65)^2 = 128018 \text{ N}$$

Total drag on the prototype,

$$R_p = (R_w)_m + (R_f)_p = 5781184 + 128018$$
$$= 5909202 \text{ N or } \mathbf{5909.2 \text{ kN}} \text{ (Ans.)}$$

(*ii*) Power required to drive the prototype, P:

Power required = Total drag on prototype × velocity of prototype

i.e.
$$P = (R_f)_p \times V_p$$
$$= 5909.2 \times 12.65 \text{ kW}$$
$$= \mathbf{74751.4 \text{ kW}} \text{ (Ans.)}$$

7.12. EULER MODEL LAW

In a fluid system where *pressure forces alone are the controlling forces in addition to the inertia force,* the dynamic similarity is obtained by equating the Euler number for both the model and its prototype. This is known as **Euler model law.** According to this law:

$$(Eu)_{\text{model}} = (Eu)_{\text{prototype}} \quad \text{...(7.34)}$$

If, V_m = Velocity of fluid in model,

p_m = Pressure of fluid in model,

ρ_m = Density of fluid in model,

and V_p, p_p, ρ_p are the corresponding values in prototype, then by substituting these values in eqn. (7.34), we get:

$$\frac{V_m}{\sqrt{p_m/\rho_m}} = \frac{V_p}{\sqrt{p_p/\rho_p}} \quad \text{...(7.35)}$$

when, $\rho_m = \rho_p$ (*i.e.* same fluid in model and prototype) the above equation becomes:

$$\frac{V_m}{\sqrt{p_m}} = \frac{V_p}{\sqrt{p_p}} \quad \text{...(7.36)}$$

This law is applied in the following flow problems:

(*i*) Enclosed fluid system where the turbulence is fully developed so that viscous forces are negligible and also the forces of gravity and surface tension are entirely absent;

(*ii*) Where the phenomenon of cavitation occurs.

Example 7.41. *In an aeroplane model of size $\frac{1}{10}$ of its prototype the pressure drop is 7.5 kN/m^2. The model is tested in water. Find the corresponding pressure drop in the prototype.*
Take: Density of air = 1.24 kg/m^3; Density of water = 1000 kg/m^3;
Viscosity of air = 0.00018 poise; Viscosity of water = 0.01 poise.

Solution. Linear scale ratio, $L_r = 40$; Pressure drop in model, $(\Delta p)_m = 7.5$ kN/m^2;
Density of water, $\rho_m = 1000$ kg/m^3; Viscosity of water, $\mu_m = 0.01$ poise;
Density of air, $\rho_p = 1.24$ kg/m^3; Viscosity of air, $\mu_p = 0.00018$ poise.

Pressure drop in the prototype $(\Delta P)_p$:

Since in the problem pressure and viscous forces are involved, therefore, for dynamic similarity between the model and prototype, Euler's number and Reynolds number should be considered.

Making Reynolds number equal, we get:

$$\left(\frac{\rho VL}{\mu}\right)_m = \left(\frac{\rho VL}{\mu}\right)_p$$

or,
$$\frac{\rho_m V_m L_m}{\mu_m} = \frac{\rho_p V_p L_p}{\mu_p}$$

or,
$$\frac{V_m}{V_p} = \frac{\rho_p}{\rho_m} \times \frac{L_p}{L_m} \times \frac{\mu_m}{\mu_p}$$

Substituting the values, we have:

$$\frac{V_m}{V_p} = \frac{1.24}{1000} \times 40 \times \frac{0.01}{0.00018} = 2.755$$

Now making Euler's number equal, we get:

$$\left(\frac{V}{\sqrt{p/\rho}}\right)_m = \left(\frac{V}{\sqrt{p/\rho}}\right)_p$$

or,
$$\frac{V_m}{\sqrt{(\Delta p)_m / \rho_m}} = \frac{V_p}{\sqrt{(\Delta p)_p / \rho_p}}$$

or,
$$\frac{V_m}{V_p} = \frac{\sqrt{(\Delta p)_m / \rho_m}}{\sqrt{(\Delta p)_p / \rho_p}} = \sqrt{\frac{(\Delta p)_m}{(\Delta p)_p}} \times \sqrt{\frac{\rho_p}{\rho_m}}$$

or,
$$\sqrt{\frac{(\Delta p)_m}{(\Delta p)_p}} = \frac{V_m}{V_p} \times \sqrt{\frac{\rho_m}{\rho_p}} = 2.755 \times \sqrt{\frac{1000}{1.24}} = 78.24$$

∴
$$\frac{(\Delta p)_m}{(\Delta p)_p} = (78.24)^2 = 6121.5$$

or,
$$(\Delta p)_p = \frac{(\Delta p)_m}{6121.5} = \frac{7.5 \times 1000}{6121.5} \text{ N/m}^2 = 1.225 \text{ N/m}^2$$

Hence, pressure drop in the prototype = **1.225 N/m²** **(Ans.)**

7.13. WEBER MODEL LAW

In a fluid system where *surface tension effects predominate in addition to inertia force,* the dynamic similarity is obtained by equating the Weber number for the model and its prototype, which is known as **Weber model law.** According to this law:

$$(We)_{\text{model}} = (We)_{\text{prototype}}$$

where, We (*i.e.* Weber number) $= \dfrac{V}{\sqrt{\sigma / \rho L}}$

If, V_m = Velocity of fluid in model,

σ_m = Surface tension force in model,

ρ_m = Density of fluid in model,

L_m = Length of surface in model,

and V_p, σ_p, ρ_p, L_p are the corresponding values of fluid in the prototype, then according to Weber model law, we have:

$$\frac{V_m}{\sqrt{\sigma_m / \rho_m L_m}} = \frac{V_p}{\sqrt{\sigma_p / \rho_p L_p}} \quad ...(7.37)$$

Weber model law is applied in the following flow situations:

(*i*) Flow over weirs involving very low heads;

(*ii*) Very thin sheet of liquid flowing over a surface;

(*iii*) Capillary waves in channels;

(*iv*) Capillary rise in narrow passages;

(*v*) Capillary movement of water in soil.

7.14. MACH MODEL LAW

When in any fluid system *only the forces resulting from elastic compression are significant in addition to inertial force,* then the dynamic similarity between the model and its prototype may be achieved by equating the Mach numbers, which is known as **Mach model law.** According to this law:

$$(M)_{\text{model}} = (M)_{\text{prototype}}$$

where, M = Mach number = $\dfrac{V}{\sqrt{K / \rho}}$

or,
$$\frac{V_m}{\sqrt{K_m / \rho_m}} = \frac{V_p}{\sqrt{K_p / \rho_p}} \quad ...(7.38)$$

where, V_m = Velocity of fluid in model,

K_m = Elastic stress for model,

ρ_m = Density of fluid in model,

and V_p, K_p, ρ_p are the corresponding values for prototype.

The similitude based on Mach model law finds application in the following:

(*i*) Aerodynamic testing;

(*ii*) Phenomena involving velocities exceeding the speed of sound;

(*iii*) Hydraulic model testing for the cases of unsteady flow, especially water hammer problems; and

(*iv*) Under-water testing of torpedoes.

Example 7.42. (Model testing of ships). *A 1: 20 model of a naval ship having a submerged area of 5 m² and length 8 metres has a total drag of 20 N when towed through water at a velocity of 1.5 m/s. Calculate the total drag on the prototype when moving at the corresponding speed. Use the relation* $F_f = \frac{1}{2} C_f \rho A V^2$ *for calculating the skin resistance. The value of* C_f *is given by,* $C_f = 0.0735/(Re)^{1.5}$.

Take kinematic viscosity of water (or sea water) as 0.01 stoke and the specific weight of water (or sea water) as 9810 N/m³.

Solution. Linear scale ratio, L_r = 20

Submerged area of the model, A_m = 5 m²

Length of the model, L_m = 8 m

Total drag of model, R_m = 20 N

Velocity of model, V_m = 1.5 m/s

Let A_p, L_p, R_p, V_p be the corresponding values for the prototype.

Kinematic viscosity of sea water,

$$\nu_m = \nu_p = 0.01 \text{ stoke} = 0.01 \text{ cm}^2/\text{s} = 0.01 \times 10^{-4} \text{ m}^2/\text{s}$$

Total drag on the prototype:

***(i) Analysis of model*:**

$$\text{Reynolds number, } Re = \left(\frac{VL}{\nu}\right)_m = \frac{V_m L_m}{\nu_m}$$

$$= \frac{1.5 \times 8}{0.01 \times 10^{-4}} = 12 \times 10^6$$

Also, $$C_f = \frac{0.0735}{(Re)^{1/5}} \quad \text{...(Given)}$$

$$\therefore \quad C_{fm} = \frac{0.0735}{(12 \times 10^6)^{1/5}} = 0.00282$$

Frictional or skin resistance of the model is given by:

$$F_f = \frac{1}{2} C_f \rho A V^2 \quad \text{...(Given)}$$

$$\therefore \quad (F_f)_m = (R_f)_m = \frac{1}{2} C_{fm} \rho_m A_m V_m^2 = \frac{1}{2} \times 0.00282 \times \left(\frac{9810}{9.81}\right) \times 5 \times 1.5^2$$

$$= 15.86 \text{ N}$$

Also, $$R_m = (R_w)_m + (R_f)_m$$

$$\left[\begin{array}{l} \text{where, } (R_w)_m = \text{Wave resistance experienced by the model, and} \\ (R_f)_m = \text{Frictional or skin resistance experienced by the model} \end{array}\right]$$

$$\therefore \quad 20 = (R_w)_m + 15.86$$

or $$(R_w)_m = 20 - 15.86 = 4.14 \text{ N}$$

***(ii) Analysis of prototype*:**

Since resistance to wave formation exists, condition will be dynamically similar if the *Froude's number are equal.*

i.e., $$\frac{V_p}{\sqrt{L_p g_p}} = \frac{V_m}{\sqrt{L_m g_m}}$$

or, $$V_p = V_m \times \sqrt{\frac{L_p}{L_m}} = 1.5 \times \sqrt{20} = 6.708 \text{ m/s} \quad (\because g_p = g_m)$$

$$\text{Reynolds number, } Re = \left(\frac{VL}{\nu}\right)_p = \frac{V_p L_p}{\nu_p}$$

$$= \frac{6.708 \times 160}{0.01 \times 10^{-4}} = 10.73 \times 10^8 \quad \left[\begin{array}{l} \because \dfrac{L_p}{L_m} = 20 \\ \therefore L_p = 8 \times 20 = 160 \text{ m} \end{array}\right]$$

$$\therefore \quad C_{fp} = \frac{0.0735}{(10.73 \times 10^8)^{1/5}} = 0.001148$$

∴ Frictional or skin resistance of the prototype is given by:

$$(F_f)_p = (R_f)_p = \frac{1}{2} C_{fp}\, \rho_p\, A_p\, V_p^2 = \frac{1}{2} \times 0.001148 \times \frac{9810}{9.81} \times 2000 \times 6.708^2$$

$$= 51657 \text{ N} \qquad \left[\because A_p = A_m \times L_r^2 = 5 \times 20^2 = 2000\,\text{m}^2\right]$$

Wave resistance R_w for the prototype can be evaluated by satisfying the following condition for dynamic similarity:

$$\left(\frac{R_w}{\rho L^2 V^2}\right)_p = \left(\frac{R_w}{\rho L^2 V^2}\right)_m$$

$$\therefore \quad (R_w)_p = \frac{\rho_p}{\rho_m} \times \left(\frac{L_p}{L_m}\right)^2 \times \frac{V_p^2}{V_m^2} \times (R_w)_m$$

But, $\rho_p = \rho_m$ ...*(Given)*

and, $\left(\frac{V_p}{V_m}\right)^2 = \frac{L_p}{L_m}$ ...[From the equivalent of Froude's number]

$$\therefore \quad (R_w)_p = 1 \times \left(\frac{L_p}{L_m}\right)^3 \times (R_w)_m = (20)^3 \times 4.14 = 33120 \text{ N}$$

Hence, total drag on the prototype,

$$R_p = (R_w)_p + (R_f)_p = 33120 + 51657 = \mathbf{84777\ N\ (Ans.)}$$

7.15. TYPES OF MODELS

The hydraulic models, in general, are *classified* into the following two broad categories:

1. Undistorted models;
2. Distorted models.

7.15.1. Undistorted models

*An **undistorted model** is one which is geometrically similar to its prototype.* The conditions of similitude are *completely satisfied for such models,* hence the results obtained from the model tests are easily used to predict the performance of prototype body. In such models the design and construction of the model and the interpretation of the model results are *simpler.*

7.15.2. Distorted models

*A **distorted model** is one which is not geometrically similar to its prototype.* In such a model *different scale ratios* for the linear dimensions are adopted. For example in case of a wide and shallow *river* it is not possible to obtain the same horizontal and vertical scale ratios, however, if these ratios are taken to be same then because of the small depth of flow the vertical dimensions of the model will become too less in comparison to its horizontal length. Thus in distorted models the *plan form is geometrically similar to that of prototype but the cross-section is distorted.*

A distorted model may have the following *distortions*:

(*i*) *Geometrical distortion.* The geometric distortion can be either of dimensions or that of *configuration.*

— The *distortion of dimensions* results due to adoption of different scales for vertical and horizontal dimensions. This type of distortion is frequently adopted in *river models where a different scale ratio for depth is adopted.*

— When the general configuration of the model does not bear a resemblance with it prototype, it becomes a *distortion* of *configuration.*

(*ii*) *Material distortion.* It involves the use of different materials for the model and prototype.

(*iii*) *Distortion of hydraulic quantities.* This type of distortion occurs due to certain uncontrollable hydraulic quantities such as velocity, discharge etc.

Typical examples for which distorted models are required to be prepared are:

(*i*) Rivers,

(*ii*) Dams across very wide rivers,

(*iii*) Harbours etc.

Reasons for adopting distorted models:

The distorted models are adopted for:

- Maintaining accuracy in vertical dimensions;
- Maintaining turbulent flow;
- Accommodating the available facilities (such as money, water supply, space etc.);
- Obtaining suitable roughness condition;
- Obtaining suitable bed material and its adequate movement.

Merits and Demerits of Distorted Models:

Merits:

1. Due to increase in the depth of fluid or height of waves accurate measurements are made possible.
2. The surface tension can be reduced to minimum.
3. Model size can be sufficiently reduced, thereby *its operation* is *simplified* and also the *cost is lowered considerably.*
4. Sufficient tractive force can be developed to move the bed material of the model.
5. The Reynolds number of flow in a model can be increased that will yield better results.

Demerits:

1. The pressure and velocity distributions are not truly reproduced.
2. A model wave may differ in type and possibly in action from that of the prototype.
3. Slopes of river beds, earth cuts and dikes cannot be truly reproduced.
4. It is difficult to extrapolate and interpolate results obtained from distorted models.
5. The observer experiences an unfavourable psychological effect.

Note. Although the distorted models entail a number of demerits, yet by incorporating judicious allowances in the interpretation of the results obtained from such models, useful information can be obtained (which is otherwise not possible).

7.16. SCALE EFFECT IN MODELS

By model testing it is *not possible* to predict the *exact behaviour of the prototype.* The behaviour of the prototype as predicted by two models with different scale ratios is generally *not the same.* Such *a discrepancy or difference in the prediction of behaviour of the prototype is termed as* **"scale *effect*"**. The magnitude of the scale effect is affected by the type of the problem and the scale ratio used for the performance of experiments on models. The scale effect can be *positive* and *negative* and when applied to the results accordingly, the corrected results then hold good for prototype.

Since it is impossible to have complete similitude satisfying all the requirements, therefore, the discrepancy due to scale effect creeps in. During investigation of models only two or three forces which are *predominant are considered* and the effect of the rest of the forces which are not significant is *neglected. These forces which are not so important cause small but varying effect on the model depending upon the scale of the model,* due to which scale effect creeps in. Sometimes the *imperfect simulation* in different models causes the discrepancy due to scale effect.

In ship models both viscous and gravity forces have to be considered, however it is *not possible* to satisfy Reynolds and Froude's numbers *simultaneously.* Usually the models are tested satisfying only Froude's law, then the results so obtained are corrected by applying the scale effect due to viscosity.

In the models of weirs and orifices with very small scale ratio the scale effect is due to surface tension forces. The surface tension forces which are insignificant in prototype become quite important in small scale models with head less than 15 mm.

Scale effect *can be known by testing a number of models using different scale ratios, and the exact behaviour of the prototype can then be predicted.*

7.17. LIMITATIONS OF HYDRAULIC SIMILITUDE

Model investigation, although very important and valuable, may not provide ready solution to all problems. It has the following **limitations:**

1. The model results, in general, are qualitative but not quantitative.
2. As compared to the cost of analytical work, models are usually expensive.
3. Transferring results to the prototype requires some judgment (the scale effect should be allowed for).
4. The selection of size of a model is a matter of experience.

HIGHLIGHTS

1. *Dimensional analysis* is a mathematical technique which makes use of the study of the dimensions for solving several engineering problems.
2. *Dimensional homogeneity* states that every term in an equation when reduced to fundamental dimensions must contain identical powers of each dimension.
3. Dimensional analysis is generally performed by two methods namely Rayleigh's method and Buckingham's π-theorem.
4. *Rayleigh's method* of dimensional analysis is useful when the number of variables is small. In this method, the equations are expressed in exponential forms. The dimensionless parameters are obtained by first evaluating the exponents so that equation is dimensionally homogeneous, and then by grouping together the variables with like powers to form dimensionless parameters.
5. *Buckingham's π-theorem* states as follows:

   "If there are n variables (dependent and independent variables) in a dimensionally homogeneous equation and if these variables contain m fundamental dimensions (such as M, L, T etc.), the variables are arranged into $(n - m)$ dimensionless terms. These dimensionless terms are called π-terms".
6. *Model analysis* is an experimental method of finding solutions of complex flow problems.

7. A model is a small scale replica of the actual machine or structure. For the model to yield useful information about the characteristics of the prototype, the model must have *geometric, kinematic,* and *dynamic similarities* with the prototype.

   For *geometric similarity,* the ratio of all linear dimensions of the model and of the prototype should be equal.

   Kinematic similarity means the similarity of motion between model and prototype.

   Dynamic similarity means the similarity of forces between the model and prototype.

8. *Reynolds number* is defined as the ratio of inertia force and viscous force of a flowing fluid. It is given by

$$Re = \frac{\rho V L}{\mu} = \frac{V L}{\nu} = \frac{V \times d}{\nu} \text{ for pipe flow}$$

where, V = velocity of flow,
d = diameter of the pipe, and
ν = kinematic viscosity of the fluid.

9. *Froude number* is the ratio of the square root-of inertia and gravity force and is given by,

$$Fe = \sqrt{\frac{F_i}{F_g}} = \frac{V}{\sqrt{Lg}}$$

10. *Euler number* is the ratio of the square root of inertia force and pressure force and is given by,

$$Eu = \sqrt{\frac{F_i}{F_p}} = \frac{V}{\sqrt{p/\rho}}$$

11. *Weber number* is the ratio of the square root of inertia force to the surface tension force and is given by,

$$We = \sqrt{\frac{F_i}{F_s}} = \sqrt{\frac{V}{\sigma/\rho L}}$$

12. *Mach number* is the ratio of the square root of inertia force and elastic force and is given by,

$$M = \sqrt{\frac{F_i}{F_e}} = \frac{V}{\sqrt{K/\rho}} = \frac{V}{C}$$

13. The laws on which the models are designed for dynamic similarity are called *model* or *similarity laws.* The model laws are:

   (*i*) Reynolds model law, (*ii*) Froude model law,
   (*iii*) Euler model law, (*iv*) Weber model law, and
   (*v*) Mach model law.

14. The drag experienced by a ship model (a partially submerged body) is obtained by *Froude's method.*

15. The hydraulic models are classified as:

   (*i*) Undistorted models, and (*ii*) Distorted models.

OBJECTIVE TYPE QUESTIONS

Choose the Correct Answer:

1. Dimensional analysis is used to
(*a*) test the dimensional homogeneity of any equation of fluid motion
(*b*) derive rational formulae for a flow phenomenon
(*c*) derive equations expressed in terms of non–dimensional parameters
(*d*) all of the above.

2. Which of the following is an advantage of dimensional analysis?
(*a*) It expresses the functional relationship between the variables in dimensionless terms
(*b*) In hydraulic model studies it reduces the number of variables involved in a physical phenomenon, generally by three
(*c*) By the use of dimensional analysis design curves can be developed from experimental data or direct solution of the problem
(*d*) all of the above.

3. A dimensionally homogeneous equation is applicable to
(*a*) C.G.S. system only
(*b*) F.P.S. system only
(*c*) M.K.S. and SI systems
(*d*) all systems of units.

4. In which of the following methods of dimensional analysis, a functional relationship of some variables is expressed in the form of an exponential equation, which must be dimensionally homogeneous?
(*a*) Buckingham's π-method
(*b*) Rayleigh's method
(*c*) Bridgman's method
(*d*) Matrix–tensor method.

5. In dimensional analysis the Buckingham's π–theorem is widely used and expresses the resulting equation in terms of
(*a*) the repeating variables
(*b*) geometric, kinematic and dynamic variables
(*c*) $(n - m)$ dimensionless parameters
(*d*) n dimensionless parameters.

6. To apply Buckingham's π–theorem, m repeating variables are selected from amongst the n variables influencing the phenomenon. The repeating variables are selected such that they
(*a*) belong to kinematic and dynamic category of variables
(*b*) must always contain the dependent variables
(*c*) in combination contain each of the m fundamental dimensions involved in the problem.
(*d*) none of the above.

7. In order that results obtained in model studies correctly represent the behaviour of the prototype, which of the following similarities must be ensured between the model and the prototype?
(*a*) Geometric similarity
(*b*) Kinematic similarity
(*c*) Dynamic similarity
(*d*) All of the above.

8. Dynamic similarity between the model and prototype is the
(*a*) similarity of motion
(*b*) similarity of lengths
(*c*) similarity of forces
(*d*) None of the above.

9. ...... is equal to the product of shear stress due to viscosity and surface area of flow.
(*a*) Viscous force (*b*) Inertia force
(*c*) Pressure force (*d*) Gravity force.

10. Kinematic similarity between model and prototype is the
(*a*) similarity of discharge
(*b*) similarity of shape
(*c*) similarity of streamline pattern
(*d*) none of the above.

11. .... is the ratio of the inertia force to the viscous force.
(*a*) Froude's number
(*b*) Weber's number
(*c*) Reynolds number
(*d*) Mach's number.

12. .... is the square root of the ratio of the inertia force to the pressure force.
(*a*) Reynolds number
(*b*) Mach's number
(*c*) Euler's number
(*d*) Froude's number.

13. Euler number is important in which of the following flow situations?
(*a*) Discharge through orifices, mouthpieces and sluices
(*b*) Pressure rise due to sudden closure of valves
(*c*) Flow through pipes
(*d*) All of the above.

14. Mach's number is defined as the square root of the ratio of the
(a) inertia force to the pressure force
(b) inertia force to the surface tension force
(c) inertia force to the elastic force
(d) none of the above.

15. ...... is important in compressible fluid flow problems at high velocities, such as high velocity flow in pipes or motion of high-speed projectiles and missiles.
(a) Euler's number
(b) Mach's number
(c) Reynolds number
(d) Froude's number.

16. Distorted models are required to be prepared for which of the following?
(a) Rivers
(b) Dams across very wide rivers
(c) Harbours
(d) All of the above.

17. The scale effect in models can be
(a) positive only
(b) negative only
(c) both positive and negative
(d) none of the above.

ANSWERS

1. (d)	2. (d)	3. (d)	4. (b)	5. (c)	6. (c)
7. (d)	8. (c)	9. (a)	10. (c)	11. (c)	12. (c)
13. (d)	14. (c)	15. (b)	16. (d)	17. (c).	

THEORETICAL QUESTIONS

1. What is dimensional analysis?
2. What are the uses of dimensional analysis?
3. What do you mean by fundamental units and derived units? Give examples.
4. Explain the term dimensional homogeneity.
5. Enumerate the applications of dimensional homogeneity.
6. What are the various methods of dimensional analysis to obtain a functional relationship between various parameters influencing a physical phenomenon.
7. Describe Rayleigh's method for dimensional analysis.
8. Describe Buckingham's method or π–theorem to formulate a dimensionally homogeneous equation between the various physical quantities effecting a certain phenomenon.
9. What are repeating variables? How are these selected by dimensional analysis?
10. What is model analysis?
11. What are the advantages of model testing?
12. What are applications of model testing?
13. What is meant by geometric, kinematic and dynamic similarities? Are these similarities truly attainable? It not why?
14. What are dimensionless numbers?
15. Define the following dimensionless numbers and state their significance for fluid flow problems.
(i) Reynolds number,
(ii) Froude's number, and
(iii) Mach's number.
16. Enumerate different laws on which models are designed for dynamic similarity. Where are they used?
17. How are hydraulic models classified?
18. What are distorted models? What are the reasons of constructing such models for rivers?
19. What are the merits and demerits of distorted models?
20. Explain scale effect in model testing. How is it found?
21. What are the limitations of hydraulic similitude?

UNSOLVED EXAMPLES

1. Show that the resistance R to the motion of a sphere of diameter D moving with a uniform velocity V through a real fluid of density ρ and viscosity μ is given by:

$$F = \rho D^2 V^2 f\left(\frac{\mu}{VD\rho}\right)$$ **[BHU]**

2. By dimensional analysis, show that the power P developed by a hydraulic turbine is given by:

$$P = \rho N^3 D^5 f\left(\frac{N^2 D^2}{gH}\right)$$

where, ρ = Mass density of liquid,
N = Rotational speed,
D = Diameter of runner,
H = Working head, and
g = Acceleration due to gravity.

3. The resistance R, to the motion of a completely submerged body depends upon the length of the body L, velocity of flow V, mass density of fluid ρ and kinematic viscosity of fluid ν. By dimensional analysis prove that

$$R = \rho V^2 L^2 \phi\left(\frac{VL}{\nu}\right)$$

4. Prove that velocity through an orifice can be expressed as

$$V = \sqrt{2gH}\,\phi\left[\frac{D}{H}, \frac{\mu}{\rho VH}, \frac{\sigma}{\rho V^2 H}\right]$$

where, H = Head causing flow,
D = Diameter of orifice,
μ = Co-efficient of viscosity,
ρ = Mass density, and
σ = Surface tension.

5. Prove that the shear stress (τ) in a fluid flowing through a pipe can be expressed by the equation:

$$\tau = \rho V^2 \phi\left[\frac{\mu}{\rho DV}, \frac{k}{D}\right]$$

where, D = Diameter of pipe,
ρ = Mass density,
V = Velocity,
μ = Viscosity, and
k = Height of roughness projection.

6. The pressure difference Δp in a pipe of diameter D and length L due to viscous flow depends on the velocity V, viscosity μ and density ρ. Using Buckingham's theorem, obtain an expression for Δp.

[Hint: Choose D, V and μ as repeating variables, μ has been chosen repeating variable (instead of ρ) since the flow is *viscous*.]

$$\left[\textbf{Ans. } \Delta p = \frac{\mu V}{D} \times \frac{L}{D}\phi\left(\frac{\rho DV}{\mu}\right)\right]$$

7. The frictional torque T of a disc of diameter D rotating at speed N in a fluid of viscosity μ and density ρ in a turbulent flow is given by:

$$T = D^5 N^2 \rho \phi\left(\frac{\mu}{D^2 N \rho}\right)$$

Prove this by the method of dimensions. **[UPSC]**

8. An oil of sp. gr. 0.9 and viscosity 0.03 poise is to be transported at the rate of 3000 litres/sec. through a 1.5 m diameter pipe. Tests were conducted on a 15 cm diameter pipe using water at 20°C. If the viscosity of water at 20°C is 0.01 poise, find:

(*i*) Velocity of flow in the model;
(*ii*) Rate of flow in the model.

[Ans. (*i*) 5.09 m/s, (*ii*) 80.9 litres/s].

9. A model of a submarine of scale 1/40 is tested in a wind tunnel. Find the speed of air in wind tunnel if the speed of submarine in sea water is 15 m/s. Also find the ratio of the resistance between the model and its prototype. Take the values of kinematic viscosities for sea water and air as 0.012 stokes and 0.016 stokes respectively. The weight densities of sea water and air are given as 10.1 kN/m^3 and 0.0122 kN/m^3 respectively. **[Ans.** 800 m/s, $\frac{F_m}{F_p} = 0.0021$]

10. In 1 : 30 model of a spillway, the velocity and discharge are 1.5 m/sec. and 2.0 m^3/sec. Find the corresponding velocity and discharge in the prototype. **[Ans.** 8.2 m/s, 9859 m^3/s]

11. A 120 m long surface vessel is to be tested by a 3 m long model. If the vessel travels at 10 m/s, at what speed must model be towed for dynamic similarity between model and prototype? If the drag of the model is 9.37 N, what prototype drag is to be expected?

[Ans. 1.58 m/s, 596.4 kN]

12. In an open channel water is flowing at a depth of 1.5 m with a velocity of 7.5 m/s. At a particular location, a hydraulic jump is formed and the depth increases to 2.2 m. Another channel is built where a similar jump is formed. If the flow depth in the new dynamically similar channel is 6 m, estimate the flow velocity and the height of jump. **[GATE]**

[Ans. 15 m/s, 0.8 m]

13. In order to predict the pressure drop in a large air duct a model is constructed with linear dimension $\frac{1}{10}$th that of the prototype, and water is used as the test fluid. If water is 1000 times denser than air and has 100 times the viscosity of air, determine the pressure drop in the prototype for the conditions corresponding to a pressure drop of 70 kPa in the model.

[Ans. 0.07 kPa]

14. If model prototype ratio is 1:75, show that the ratio of discharges per unit width of spillway is given by $\left(\frac{1}{75}\right)^{3/2}$. **[AMIE]**

15. In an aeroplane model of size $\frac{1}{50}$ of its prototype the pressure drop is 4 bar. The model is tested in water. Find the corresponding pressure drop in the prototype. Take specific height of air = 0.0124 kN/m^3. The viscosity of water is 0.01 poise while the viscosity of air is 0.00018 poise. **[Ans.** 0.00042 bar]

16. An air duct is to be modelled to a scale of 1:20 and tested with water which is 50 times viscous and 800 times more dense than air. When tested under dynamically similar conditions, the pressure drop between two sections in the model is 235 kPa. What is the corresponding pressure drop in the prototype? **[Ans.** 189.3 Pa]

17. Explain what is meant by dynamic similarity between a flow system and its model. If the dynamic behaviour of the flow system for an overflow spillway is governed by the Froude law of similarity, what would be the discharge Q_r, when the (model) scale ratio is L_r? Show that the same result would be obtained if the weir formula is used instead and it is assumed that the prototype and the model spillways have the same co-efficient of discharge.

[UPSC Civil Services (IAS) Exam.]

18. A model of rectangular pier 1.2 m wide and 4 m long in the river is built to a scale of 1:20. The average depth of water in the river is 3 m. The model was tested in a laboratory, where the velocity of flow was maintained constant at 0.6 m/s. It was observed that the force acting on the model was 4 N and the height of the standing wave was 35 mm. Make calculations of speed, force, height of standing wave and the co-efficient of drag resistance for the prototype. Assume that the flow in the model and prototype are insensitive to changes in Reynolds number.

[Ans. 2.68 m/s, 32 kN, 700 mm, 2.428]

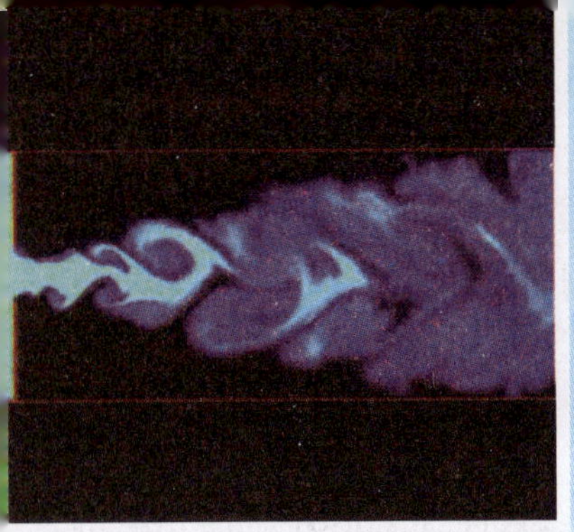

Chapter 8

FLOW THROUGH ORIFICES AND MOUTHPIECES

8.1. INTRODUCTION

An **orifice** *is an opening in the wall or base of a vessel through which the fluid flows*. The *top edge* of the orifice is always below *the free surface* (If the free surface is below the top edge of the orifice, becomes a *weir*)

A **mouthpiece** *is an attachmnent in the form of a small tube or pipe fixed to the orifice (the length of pipe extension is usually 2 to 3 times the orifice diameter) and is used to increase the amount of dischrge.*

- Orifices as well as mouthpieces are used to *measure the discharge.*

8.2. CLASSIFICATION OF ORIFICES

The orifices are *classified* as follows

1. According to size:

(*i*) Small orifice (*ii*) Large orifice.

An orifice is termed *small* when its dimensions are small compared to the head causing flow. The velocity does not vary appreciably from top to the bottom edge of the orifice and is assumed to be uniform.

The orifice is *large* if the dimensions are comparable with the head causing flow. The variation in the velocity from the top to the bottom edge is considerable.

2. According to shape

(*i*) Circular orifice (*ii*) Rectangular orifice

(*iii*) Square orifice (*iv*) Triangular orifice.

3. Shape of upstream edge

(*i*) Sharp-edged orifice

(*ii*) Bell-mouthed orifice.

4. According to discharge conditions

(*i*) Free discharge orifices

(*ii*) Drowned or submerged orifices

(*a*) Fully submereged

(*b*) Partially submerged.

Note. An orifice or a mouthpiece is said to be discharging *free* when it discharges into *atmosphere.* It is said to be *submerged* when it discharges into *another liquid.*

8.3. FLOW THROUGH AN ORIFICE

Fig. 8.1 shows a small circular orifice with sharp edge in the side wall of a tank discharging free into the atmosphere. Let the orifice be at a depth H below the free surface. As the fluid flows through the orifice, it contracts and attains a parallel form (*i.e.,* stream lines bocome parallel) at a distance $\frac{d}{2}$ from the plane of the orifice. *The point at which the stream lines first become parallel is termed as* **vena-contracta** (the cross-sectional area of the jet at the vena contracta is *less* than that of orifice). Beyond this section, the jet *diverges* and is attracted in the downward direction by gravity.

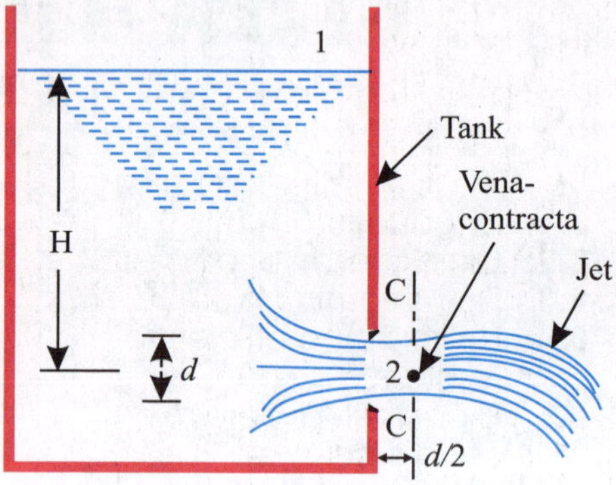

Fig. 8.1. Orifice discharging free.

Considering points 1 and 2 as shown in Fig. 8.1 and applying Bernoulli's theorem, we have:

$$\frac{p_1}{w} + \frac{V_1^2}{2g} + z_1 = \frac{p_2}{w} + \frac{V_2^2}{2g} + z_2$$

But, $p_1 = p_2 = p_a$ (p_a = atmospheric pressure)

$$z_1 = z_2 + H$$

Further, if the cross-sectional area of the tank is very large, the liquid at point 1 is practically standstill and hence $V_1 = 0$

Thus, $$\frac{V_2^2}{2g} = H$$

or, $$V_2 = \sqrt{2gH} \quad \text{... (8.1)}$$

Equation (8.1) is know as **Torricelli's theorem.**

Note. In the problems of orifices it is covenient to work in terms of *gauge pressures*.

8.4. HYDRAULIC CO-EFFICIENTS

The hydraulic co-efficients (or orifice co-efficients) are enumerated and discussed below :

1. Co-efficient of contraction, C_c
2. Co-efficient of velocity, C_v
3. Co-efficient of discharge, C_d
4. Co-efficient of resistance, C_r

8.4.1. Co-efficient of Contraction (C_c)

The ratio of the area of the jet at vena-contracta to the area of the orifice is known as **Co-efficient of contraction.** It is denoted by C_c.

Let, a_c = Area of jet at vena contracta, and

a = Area of orifice.

Then, $$C_c = \frac{a_c}{a} \qquad \text{... (8.2)}$$

The value of C_c varies slightly with the available head of the liquid, size and shape of the orifice; in practice it varies from 0.613 to 0.69 but the average value is taken as 0.64.

8.4.2. Co-efficient of Velocity (C_v)

The ratio of actual velocity (V) of the jet at vena-contracta to the theoretical velocity (V_{th}) is known as **Co-efficient of velocity.** It is denoted by C_v and mathematically, C_v is given as:

$$C_v = \frac{\text{Actual velocity of jet at vena contracta } (V)}{\text{Theoretical velocity } (V_{th})}$$

i.e., $$C_v = \frac{V}{\sqrt{2gH}} \qquad \text{... (8.3)}$$

$$\left[\begin{array}{l}\text{where, } V = \text{Actual velocity, and} \\ \qquad H = \text{Head under which the fluid flows out of the orifice}\end{array}\right]$$

The value of C_v varies from 0.95 to 0.99,depending upon the shape of orifice and the head of liquid under which the flow takes place. For sharp-edged orifices the value of C_v is taken as 0.98.

8.4.3. Co-efficient of Discharge

The ratio of actual discharge (Q) through an arifice to the theorerical discharge,(Q_{th}) is known as **Co-efficient of discharge.** It is dinoted by C_d.

Mathematically, $$C_d = \frac{\text{Actual discharge } (Q)}{\text{Theoretical discharge } (Q_{th.})}$$

$$= \frac{\text{Actual area} \times \text{actual velocity}}{\text{Theoretical area} \times \text{theoretical velocity}}$$

$$= \frac{\text{Actual area}}{\text{Theoretical area}} \times \frac{\text{actual velocity}}{\text{theoretical velocity}}$$

$$\therefore \quad C_d = C_c \times C_v \qquad \text{... (8.4)}$$

The value of C_d varies from 0.62 to 0.65 depending upon size and the shape of the orifice and the head of liquid under which the flow takes place.

8.4.4. Co-efficient of Resistance (C_r)

The ratio of loss of head (or loss of kinetic energy) in the orifice to the head of water (actual kinetic energy) available at the exit of the orifice is known as **Co-efficient of resistance.** It is denoted by C_r.

Mathematically, $$C_r = \frac{\text{Loss of head in the orifice}}{\text{Head of water}}$$

The loss of head in the orifice takes place, because the walls of the orifice offer some resistance to the liquid, as it comes out. While solving numerical problems C_r is *generally neglected.*

Example 8.1. *An orifice 50mm in diameter is discharging water under a head of 10 metres. If $C_d = 0.6$ and $C_v = 0.97$, find :*

(i) Actual discharge, and

(ii) Actual velocity of the jet at vena contracta.

Solution. Diameter of the orifice, $d = 50$ mm $= 0.05$ m

$$\therefore \quad \text{Area of the orifice, } a = \frac{\pi}{4} d^2 = \frac{\pi}{4} \times (0.05)^2 = 0.001963 \text{ m}^2$$

Head, $H = 10$m; $C_d = 0.6$; $C_v = 0.97$

(*i*) Actual discharge

$$C_d = \frac{\text{Actual discharge}}{\text{Theoretical discharge}} = 0.6 \quad \text{...(Given)}$$

But theoretical discharge = Area of orifice × theoretical velocity.

$$= a \times \sqrt{2gH}$$

$$= = 0.001963 \times \sqrt{2 \times 9.81 \times 10}$$

$$= 0.02749 \text{ m}^3/\text{s}$$

$\therefore$ Actual discharge $= 0.6 \times 0.02749 =$ **0.01649 m³/s (Ans.)**

(*ii*) Actual velocity

We know that , $$C_v = \frac{\text{actual velocity}}{\text{theoretical velocity}}$$

$\therefore$ Actual velocity $= C_v \times$ theoretical velocity

$$= 0.97 \times \sqrt{2gH} = 0.97 \times \sqrt{2 \times 9.81 \times 10} = \mathbf{13.58 \text{ m/s}} \textbf{ (Ans.)}$$

Example 8.2. *The head of water over the centre of an orifice of diameter 30 mm is 1.5m. The actual discharge through the orifice is 2.55 litres/sec. Find the co-efficient of discharge.*

Solution. Diameter of the orifice, $d = 30$ mm $= 0.03$m

$$\therefore \quad \text{Area, } a = \frac{\pi}{4} \times 0.03^2 = 0.0007068 \text{ m}^2$$

Head, $H = 1.5$ m

Co-efficient of discharge, C_d

Actual discharge through the orifice, $Q = 2.55$ litres/sec.$= 0.00255$ m³/s

Theoretical discharge, Q_{th} = Area of orifice × theoretical velocity.

But theoretical velocity, $V_{th} = \sqrt{2gH} = \sqrt{2 \times 9.81 \times 1.5} = 5.425$ m/s

$$\therefore \quad Q_{th} = a \times V_{th}$$

$$= 0.0007068 \times 5.425 = 0.004166 \text{m}^3/\text{s}$$

Hence, $$C_d = \frac{Q}{Q_{th}} = \frac{0.00255}{0.004166} = \mathbf{0.612} \textbf{ (Ans.)}$$

8.4. EXPERIMENTAL DETERMINATION OF HYDRAULIC CO-EFFICIENTS

8.5.1. Determination of Co-efficient of Velocity (C_v).

Fig. 8.2 shows a tank containing water at a constant level, maintained by a costant supply. Let the water flow out of the tank through an orifice, fitted in one side of the tank. Let the section *C–C* represents the point of vena contracta. Consider a particle of water in the jet at *P*.

Let, x = Horizontal distance travelled by the particle in time '*t*',

y = Vertical distance between *C-C* and *P*,

V = Actual velocity of the jet at vena-contracta, and

$$H = \text{Constant water head.}$$

Then, horizontal distance, $x = V \times t$ ...(*i*)

and, vertical distance, $y = \frac{1}{2} gt^2$ ...(*ii*)

From eqn. (*i*), $t = \frac{x}{V}$

Substituting this value of '*t*' in eqn. (*ii*), we get:

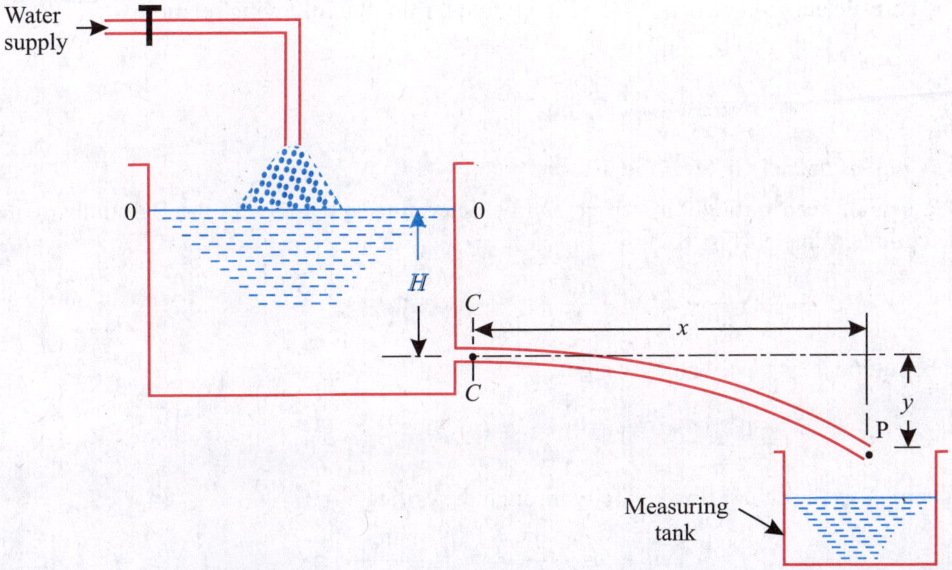

Fig. 8.2. Experiment for hydraulic co-efficients.

$$y = \frac{1}{2} g \times \left(\frac{x}{V}\right)^2 = \frac{gx^2}{2V^2}$$

$$\therefore \quad V^2 = \frac{gx^2}{2y} \text{ or } V = \sqrt{\frac{gx^2}{2y}}$$

But, theoretical velocity, $V_{th} = \sqrt{2gH}$

∴ Co-efficient of velocity,

$$C_v = \frac{V}{V_{th}} = \frac{\sqrt{\frac{gx^2}{2y}}}{\sqrt{2gH}} = \sqrt{\frac{x^2}{4yH}}$$

i.e. $$C_v = \frac{x}{\sqrt{4yH}} \quad ...(8.5)$$

8.5.2. Determination of Co-efficient of Discharge (C_d)

The water flowing through the orifice under the constant head *H* is collected in a measuring tank for a known time '*t*'. The rise of water level in the measuring tank is noted down. Then actual discharge through the orifice,

$$Q = \frac{\text{Area of measuring tank} \times \text{rise of water level in the measuring tank}}{\text{Time } (t)}$$

Theoretical discharge, $Q_{th} = \text{Area of orifice} \times \sqrt{2gH}$

Hence, $$C_d = \frac{Q}{Q_{th}} = \frac{Q}{a \times \sqrt{2gH}} \quad ...(8.6)$$

8.5.3. Determination of Co-efficient of Contraction (C_c)

The co-efficient of contraction (C_c) can be found from the following relation:

$$C_d = C_c \times C_v$$

$$\therefore \quad C_c = \frac{C_d}{C_v} \quad ...(8.7)$$

8.5.4. Loss of head in Orifice Flow

The loss of head through an orifice can be determined by applying the Bernoulli's equation between points O and C (Fig. 8.2).

$$\frac{p_O}{w} + \frac{V_O^2}{2g} + z_O = \frac{p_C}{w} + \frac{V_C^2}{2g} + z_C + \text{losses}$$

Substituting the proper values, we get:

$$0 + 0 + H = 0 + \frac{V^2}{2g} + 0 + h_f$$

Where, V is the actual flow velocity through the orifice.

$$\therefore \quad h_f = H - \frac{V^2}{2g} = H\left(1 - \frac{V^2}{2gH}\right) \quad ...[8.8(a)]$$

$$= H(1 - C_v^2)$$

or $$h_f = \frac{V^2}{2g}\left(\frac{2gH}{V^2} - 1\right) = \frac{V^2}{2g}\left(\frac{1}{C_v^2} - 1\right) \quad ...[8.8(b)]$$

Example 8.3. *A vertical sharp-edged orifice 120 mm in diameter is discharging water at the rate of 98.2 litres/sec. under a constant head of 10 metres. A point on the jet, measured from the vena contracta of the jet has co-ordinates 4.5metres horizontal and 0.54 metre vertical. Find the following for the orifice.*

(i) *Co-efficient of velocity,* **(ii)** *Co-efficient of discharge, and*
(iii) *Co-efficient of contraction.*

Solution. Diameter of orifice, $d = 120 \text{ mm} = 0.12 \text{ m}$

$\therefore$ Area of orifice, $a = \frac{\pi}{4} \times 0.12^2 = 0.01131 \text{ m}^2$

Discharge, $Q = 98.2 \text{ litres/sec.} = \frac{98.2}{1000} = 0.0982 \text{ m}^3/\text{s}$

Head, $H = 10 \text{ m}$

Horizontal distance of a point on the jet from vena contracta, $x = 4.5$ m

Vertical distance, $y = 0.54$ m

Now theoretical velocity, $V_{th} = \sqrt{2gH} = \sqrt{2 \times 9.81 \times 10} = 14 \text{ m/s}$

Theoretical discharge,

$$Q_{th} = \text{Area of orifice } (a) \times V_{th}$$
$$= 0.01131 \times 14 = 0.1583 \text{ m}^3/\text{s}$$

(*i*) Co-efficient of velocity, C_v:

$$C_v = \frac{x}{\sqrt{4yH}}$$

$$= \frac{4.5}{\sqrt{4 \times 0.54 \times 10}} = \mathbf{0.968} \text{ (Ans.)}$$

(*ii*) Co-efficient of dischrge, C_d:

$$C_d = \frac{\text{Actual discharge}}{\text{Theoretical discharge}}$$

$$= \frac{0.0982}{0.1583} = \mathbf{0.62} \text{ (Ans.)}$$

(*iii*) Co-efficient of contraction, C_c:

$$= \frac{C_d}{C_v} = \frac{0.62}{0.968} = \mathbf{0.64} \text{ (Ans.)}$$

Example 8.4. *A large tank has a sharp edged circular orifice of 930 mm² area at a depth of 3 m below constant water level. The jet issues horizontally and in a horizontal distance of 2.4 m, it falls by 0.53 m, the measured discharge is 4.3 lit/s. Derermine coefficients of velocity, contraction and discharge for the orfice.*

Solution. *Given :* Area of the orifice, $a = 930 \text{ mm}^2$; $H = 3$ m; $x = 2.4$ m; $y = 0.53$ m; $Q = 4.3$ litres/sec. $= 0.0043 \text{ m}^3/\text{s}$

C_v, C_c and C_d:

Theoretical volocity, $V = \sqrt{2gH} = \sqrt{2 \times 9.81 \times 3}$

$= 7.67$ m/s

Theoretical discharge $= a \times V_{th}$

$= 930 \times 10^{-6} \times 7.67$

$= 0.00713 \text{ m}^3/\text{s}$

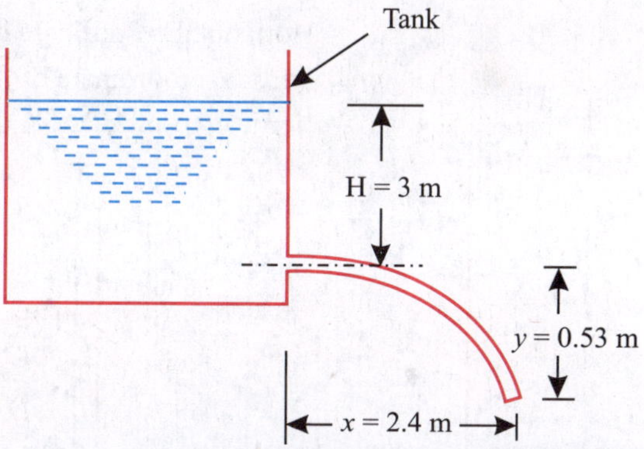

Fig. 8.3

Co-efficient of velocity,

$$C_v = \frac{x}{\sqrt{4yH}} = \frac{2.4}{\sqrt{4 \times 0.53 \times 3}}$$

$= \mathbf{0.952}$ **(Ans.)**

Co-efficient of discharge,

$$C_d = \frac{\text{Actual discharge}}{\text{Theoretical discharge}} = \frac{0.0043}{0.00713}$$

$= \mathbf{0.603}$ **(Ans.)**

Co-efficient of contraction,

$$C_c = \frac{C_d}{C_v} = \frac{0.603}{0.952} = \mathbf{0.633} \text{ (Ans.)}$$

Example 8.5. *The head of water over an orifice of diameter 100 mm is 12 m. The water coming out from the orifice is collected in a rectangular tank 2 m × 0.9 m. The rise of water level in this tank is 1.2 m in 30 seconds. Find the co-efficient of discharge.*

Solution. Head of water, $H = 12$ m

Diameter of orifice, $d = 100$ mm $= 0.1$ m

$\therefore$ Area, $a = \frac{\pi}{4} \times 0.1^2 = 0.00785 \text{ m}^2$

Area of the measuring tank, $A = 2 \times 0.9 = 1.8 \text{ m}^2$

Rise of water level (in $t = 30$ s), $h = 1.2$ m

Co-efficient of discharge, C_d

$$\text{Theoretical velocity, } V_{th} = \sqrt{2gH}$$

$$= \sqrt{2 \times 9.81 \times 12} = 15.34 \text{m/s}$$

$$\therefore \quad \text{Theoretical discharge, } Q_{th} = a \times V_{th}$$

$$= 0.00785 \times 15.34 = 0.1204 \text{ m}^3/\text{s}$$

$$\text{Actual discharge, } Q = \frac{A \times h}{t} = \frac{1.8 \times 1.2}{30} = 0.072 \text{ m}^3/\text{s}$$

$$\therefore \quad \text{Co-efficient of discharge, } C_d = \frac{Q}{Q_{th}} = \frac{0.072}{0.1204} \simeq \mathbf{0.6}$$ **(Ans.)**

Example 8.6. *A tank has two identical orifices in one of its vertical sides, The upper orifice is 1.5 m below the water surface and the lower one is 3 m below the water surface as shown in Fig. 8.4. Find the point, at which the two jets will intersect, if the co-efficient of velocity is 0.92 for both the orifices.*

Solution. Height of water above the upper orifice, $H_1 = 1.5$ m

Height of water above the lower orifice, $H_2 = 3$ m

Co-efficient of velocity, $C_v = 0.92$

Let, x = Horizontal co-ordinate of the point of intersection A,

y_1 = Vertical co-ordinate of the point of intersection A from the orifice 1,and

y_2 = Vertical co-ordinate of the point of intersection A from the orifice 2.

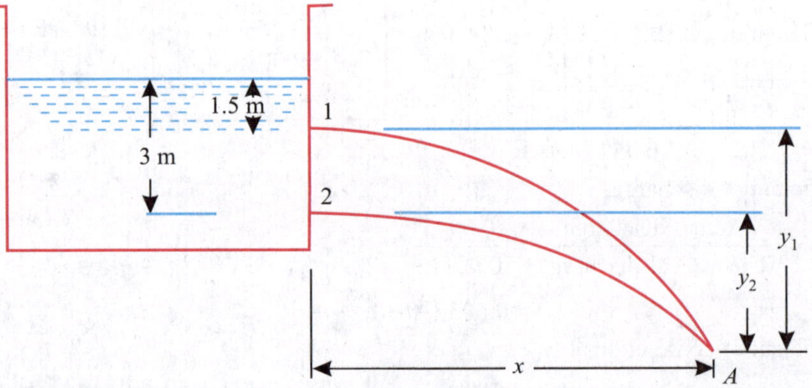

Fig. 8.4

Using the relation,

$$C_v = \sqrt{\frac{x^2}{4yH}}, \text{ with usual notations, we have:}$$

$$C_{v1} = \sqrt{\frac{x^2}{4y_1 \times 1.5}} \quad ...(i)$$

and,

$$C_{v2} = \sqrt{\frac{x^2}{4y_2 \times 3.0}} \quad ...(ii)$$

Since the two orifice are identical, therefore equating (*i*) and (*ii*), we get:

$$\sqrt{\frac{x^2}{4y_1 \times 1.5}} = \sqrt{\frac{x^2}{4y_2 \times 3.0}}$$

$$\therefore \quad y_1 = 2y_2 \quad ...(iii)$$

From the geometry of the tank, we know that,

$$y_1 = y_2 + (3 - 1.5) = y_2 + 1.5 \quad ...(iv)$$

Solving eqns. (*iii*) and (*iv*), we get:

$$y_2 = 1.5 \text{ m and } y_1 = 3 \text{ m}$$

Again, using the relation,

$$C_v = \sqrt{\frac{x^2}{4y_1 \times H_1}}, \text{ with usual notations, we get:}$$

$$0.92 = \sqrt{\frac{x^2}{4 \times 3 \times 1{\cdot}5}} = \sqrt{\frac{x^2}{18}} = \frac{x}{\sqrt{18}}$$

$$\therefore \quad x = 0.92 \times \sqrt{18} = \mathbf{3.9\ m}$$ **(Ans.)**

Example 8.7. *Explain briefly how the co-efficient of velocity of a jet issuing through an orifice can be experimentally determined.*

Find an expression for head loss in an orifice flow in terms of co-efficient of velocity and jet velocity.

The head lost in flow through a 50 mm diameter orifice under a certain head is 160 mm of water and the velocity of water in the jet is 7.0 m/s. If the co-efficient of discharge be 0.61, determine:

(*i*) *Head on the orifice causing flow;*

(*ii*) *The co-efficient of velocity;*

(*iii*) *The diameter of the jet.* **[UPSC]**

Solution. Diameter of the orifice, d = 50 mm = 0.05 m

Head of water lost in flow, h_f = 160 mm = 0.16 m

Velocity of water in the jet, V = 7.0 m/s

Co-efficient of discharge, C_d = 0.61

(*i*) Head on the orifice causing flow, H:

Bernoulli's equation between the reservoir surface and vena-contracta (see Fig. 8.1), yields:

$$H = \frac{V^2}{2g} + h_f = \frac{7^2}{2 \times 9.81} + 0.16$$

$$= \mathbf{2.66\ m\ (Ans.)}$$

(*ii*) The Co-efficient of velocity, C_v

$$C_v = \frac{V}{\sqrt{2gH}} = \frac{7}{\sqrt{2 \times 9.81 \times 2.66}}$$

$$= \mathbf{0.97\ (Ans.)}$$

(*iii*) The Diameter of the jet, d_j:

$$C_d = C_v \times C_c$$

$$\therefore \quad C_c = \frac{C_d}{C_v} = \frac{0.61}{0.97} = 0.63$$

But, $$C_c = \frac{(\pi/4) \times d_j^2}{(\pi/4) \times d^2} = \frac{d_j^2}{d^2}$$

$$\therefore \quad 0.63 = \frac{d_j^2}{(0.05)^2}$$

or, $$d_j^2 = 0.63 \times (0.05)^2 = 0.001575$$

or, $d_j = 0.0397$ m or **39.7 mm (Ans.)**

Example 8.8. *A 3 m high tank standing on the ground is kept full of water. There is a small orifice in its vertical side with its centre at depth h metres below the free surface of liquid in the tank. Find the value of h so that the liquid strikes the ground at the maximun distance from the tank. Assuming $C_v = 0.97$, calculate the maximum value of the horizontal distance.*

Solution. Height of tank/water, H = 3m

Co-efficient of velocity, C_v = 0.97

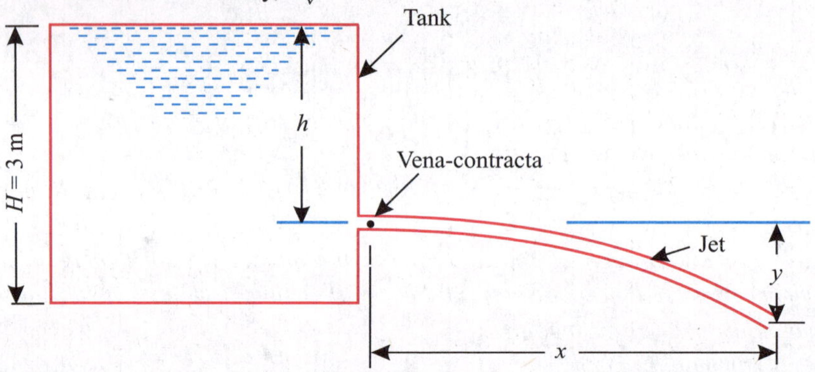

Fig. 8.5

Value of *h*:

From kinematics of flow,

$$x = Vt \quad ...(i) \qquad y = \frac{1}{2}gt^2 \quad ...(ii)$$

where, x, y = Co-ordinates, and

t = The time taken for the liquid particle to travel from the orifice to the ground.

Eliminating 't' from (i) and (ii), we get:

$$y = \frac{1}{2}g \times \left(\frac{x}{V}\right)^2$$

or, $$x^2 = \frac{2V^2 y}{g}$$

Substituting, $V = C_v \sqrt{2gh}$ and $y = (H - h)$, we get:

$$x^2 = \frac{2 \times C_v^2 \times 2gh\,(H-h)}{g}$$

$\therefore$ $$x = 2\,C_v \sqrt{h\,(H-h)} \quad ...(iii)$$

Horizontal distance x of the jet trajectory would be maximum when $h\,(H - h)$ is maximum or when,

$$\frac{d}{dh}[h\,(H-h)] = 0 \text{ or } \frac{d}{dh}(hH - h^2) = 0$$

or, $$H - 2h = 0$$

or, $$h = \frac{H}{2} = \frac{3}{2} = \mathbf{1.5\ m}\ \textbf{(Ans.)}$$

Maximum value of horizontal distance, $(x)_{max}$:

Substituting, $h = 1.5$ m and $C_v = 0.97$ in (iii), we get:

$$(x)_{max} = 2 \times 0.97 \sqrt{1.5\,(3-1.5)}$$

$$= \mathbf{2.91\ m}\ \textbf{(Ans)}$$

Example 8.9. *A tank containing water is provided with a sharp edged circular orifice of 7.5 mm diameter. The height of water in the tank is 1.44 m above the orifice. The jet strikes a wall 1.5 m away and 0.42 m vertically below the centre line of the contracted section of the jet. The actual discharge through the orifice is measured to be 35 litres in 4 minutes. Deteremine:*

(i) The orifice co-efficients; *(ii) The power loss at the orifice.*

Solution. Diameter of the orifice, $d = 7.5$ mm $= 0.0075$ m

$\therefore$ Area of the orifice, $a = \frac{\pi}{4} \times d^2 = \frac{\pi}{4} \times 0.0075^2 = 0.0000442\ m^2$

Height of water in the tank above the orifice, $H = 1.44$ m

Horizontal distance of a point on the jet from vena-contracta, $x = 1.5$ m

Vertical distance, $y = 0.42$ m

The actual discharge measured in 4 minutes = 35 litres

i.e., $$Q = \frac{35}{1000} \times \frac{1}{4 \times 60} = 1.46 \times 10^{-4}\ m^3/s$$

(i) Orifice co-efficients

$$Q = C_d \,.\, a \,.\, \sqrt{2gH}$$

or, $$1.46 \times 10^{-4} = C_d \times 0.0000442 \times \sqrt{2 \times 9.81 \times 1.44}$$

$\therefore$ $$C_d = \frac{1.46 \times 10^{-4}}{0.0000442 \times \sqrt{2 \times 9.81 \times 1.44}} = \mathbf{0.62}\ \textbf{(Ans.)}$$

From the measurement of jet co-ordinates,

$$\text{Co-efficient of velocity, } C_v = \frac{x}{\sqrt{4yH}} = \frac{1.5}{\sqrt{4 \times 0.42 \times 1.44}} = \mathbf{0.964} \text{ (Ans.)}$$

The co-efficient of contraction follows from the relation,

$$C_d = C_c \times C_v$$

$$\therefore \quad C_v = \frac{C_d}{C_v} = \frac{0.62}{0.964} = \mathbf{0.64} \text{ (Ans.)}$$

(*ii*) The power loss at the orifice:

$$\text{Loss of head, } h_f = H(1 - C_v^2) \qquad \text{[Eqn. 8.8 (a)]}$$

$$= 1.44(1 - 0.964^2) = 0.102 \text{ m}$$

The *loss co-efficient* or the *co-efficient of resistance* prescribes the ratio of loss of head in the orifice to the total head available.

$$\textit{Loss co-efficient} = \frac{h_f}{H} = \frac{0.102}{1.44} = \mathbf{0.071} \text{ (Ans.)}$$

$$\text{Power loss} = wQh_f = 9810 \times 1.46 \times 10^{-4} \times 0.102 = \mathbf{0.146\ W} \text{ (Ans.)}$$

Example 8.10. *A 100 mm diameter orifice discharge 36 litres per second of water under a constant head of 2.6 m. A flat plate held normal to the jet just downstream from the orifice requires a force of 240 N to resist the impact of the jet. Determine the hydraulic co-efficients.*

Solution. Dia. of the orifice, $d = 100$ mm $= 0.1$m

∴ Area of the orifice,

$$A = \frac{\pi}{4}d^2 = \frac{\pi}{4} \times 0.1^2 = 0.00785 \text{ m}^2$$

Discharge through the orifice,

$$Q = 36 \text{ litres/s} = \frac{36}{1000} = 0.036 \text{ m}^3/\text{s}$$

Constant head of water above the orifice,

$$H = 2.6 \text{ m}$$

Force required to resist the jet, $F = 240$ N

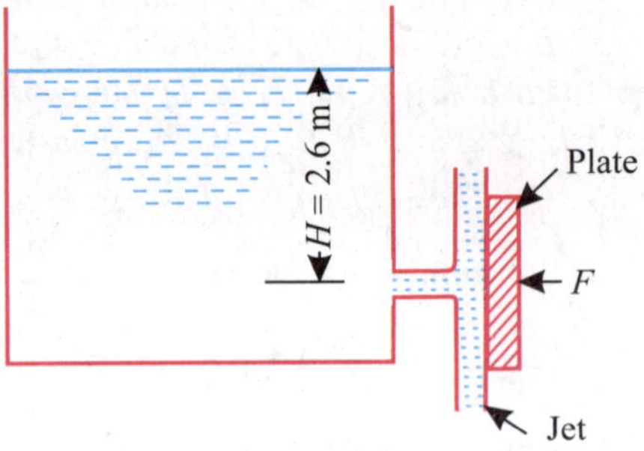

Fig. 8.6

Hydraulic co-efficients:

From momentum equation, the force (F) required to hold the plate in position is

$$F = \frac{wQ}{g}V$$

where, w = Sp. weight of water (= 9810 N/m^3), and

V = Velocity at the vena-contracta.

Substituting the values in the above equation, we get:

$$240 = \frac{9810 \times 0.036}{9.81} \times V$$

$$\therefore \quad V = \frac{240 \times 9.81}{9810 \times 0.036} = 6.66 \text{ m/s}$$

$$\text{Theoretical velocity,} \quad V_{th} = \sqrt{2gH} = \sqrt{2 \times 9.81 \times 2.6} = 7.14 \text{ m/s}$$

$\therefore$ Co-efficient of velocity, $C_v = \dfrac{V}{V_{th}} = \dfrac{6.66}{7.14} = \mathbf{0.932}$ **(Ans.)**

Theoretical discharge, $Q_{th} = a \times \sqrt{2gH} = 0.00785 \times \sqrt{2 \times 9.81 \times 2.6}$

$= 0.056\ m^3/s$

$\therefore$ Co-efficient of discharge, $C_d = \dfrac{Q}{Q_{th}} = \dfrac{0.036}{0.056} = \mathbf{0.643}$ **(Ans.)**

Co-efficient of contraction, $C_c = \dfrac{C_d}{C_v} = \dfrac{0.643}{0.932} = \mathbf{0.69}$ **(Ans.)**

Example 8.11. *A tank shown in Fig, 8.7 has a nozzle of exit deameter D_1 at a depth H_1 below the free surface. At the side opposite to that of nozzle 1, another nozzle is proposed at a depth $\frac{H_1}{2}$. What should be deameter D_2 in terms of D_1 so that the net horizontal force on the tank is zero?*

(UPTU)

Solution. Let, V = Velocity, m/s

m = Mass discharge, kg/s, and

F = Reactive force due to rate of change of momentum of the issuing jet.

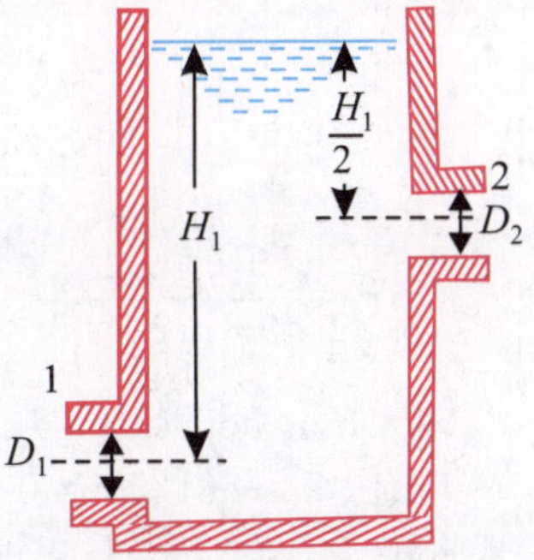

Fig. 8.7

At jet 1:

$$V_1 = \sqrt{2gH_1}$$

$$m_1 = \rho . A_1 V_1 = \rho \times \frac{\pi}{4} D_1^2 \times \sqrt{2gH_1}$$

and,

$$F_1 = m_1 V_1 = \rho \times \frac{\pi}{4} D_1^2 \sqrt{2gH_1} \times \sqrt{2gH_1}$$

$$= \rho \frac{\pi}{4} D_1^2 \times 2gH_1$$

At jet 2:

$$V_2 = \sqrt{2g\left(\frac{H_1}{2}\right)} = \sqrt{gH_1}\ ;\ m_2 = \rho A_2 V_2 = \rho \times \frac{\pi}{4} D_2^2 \times \sqrt{gH_1}$$

and,

$$F_2 = m_2 V_2 = \rho \times \frac{\pi}{4} D_2^2 \times \sqrt{gH_1} \times \sqrt{gH_1} = \rho \times \frac{\pi}{4} D_2^2 \times gH_1$$

For the net horizontal force to be zero, F_1 should be numerically equal to F_2, since both of them act in *opposite directions*.

$$\therefore \quad \rho \frac{\pi}{4} D_1^2 .2gH_1 = \rho \times \frac{\pi}{4} D_2^2 gH_1$$

or,

$$2D_1^2 = D_2^2$$

or,

$$D^2 = D_1 \sqrt{2} = \mathbf{1.414 D_1} \quad \textbf{(Ans.)}$$

Example 8.12. *A closed tank, having an orifice of diameter 20 mm at the bottom of the tank, is partially filled with water upto a height of 2.5 m. The air is pumped into the upper part of the tank. Determine the pressure required for a discharge of 5 litres per second through the orifice, Take discharge co-fficient, C_d = 0.6 for the orifice.*

Solution. Height of water above orifice, $H = 2.5$ m

Dia. of the orifice, $d = 20$ mm $= 0.02$ m

$\therefore$ Area of the orifice, $A = \frac{\pi}{4}d^2 = \frac{\pi}{4} \times (0.02)^2 = 0.000314 \text{ m}^2$

Discharge through the orifice, $Q = 5$ litres/sec.

$$= \frac{5}{1000} = 0.005 \text{ m}^3/s$$

Co-efficient of discharge, $C_d = 0.6$

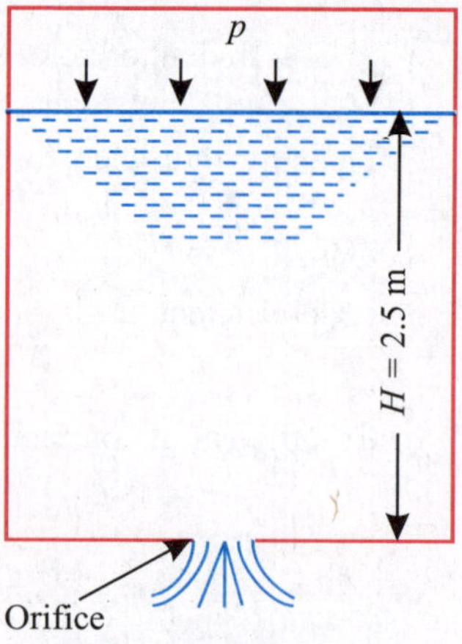

Fig. 8.8

Pressure required

Let p is the intensity of presure required above water surface in kN/m^2.

Then, pressure head of air $= \frac{p}{w} = \frac{p}{9{\cdot}81} = 0.102p$ metres of water.

If V is the velocity at outlet of orifice, then:

$$V = \sqrt{2g\left(H + \frac{p}{w}\right)} = \sqrt{2 \times 9.81\,(2.5 + 0.102p)}$$

$$\therefore \quad \text{Discharge, } Q = C_d \times a \times V$$

$$\text{or} \quad 0.005 = 0.6 \times 0.000314 \times \sqrt{2 \times 9.81\,(2.5 + 0.102p)}$$

$$\sqrt{2 \times 9.81\,(2.5 + 0.102p)} = \frac{0.005}{0.6 \times 0.000314} = 26.5$$

Squaring both sides, we get:

$$\text{or,} \quad 2 \times 9.81\,(2.5 \times 0.102p) = (26.5)^2 = 702.2$$

$$\text{or,} \quad 2.5 + 0.102\,p = \frac{702.2}{2 \times 9.81} = 35.79$$

$$\therefore \quad p = \frac{35.79 - 2.5}{0.102} = \mathbf{326.4 kN/m^2} \textbf{ (Ans.)}$$

8.6. DISCHARGE THROUGH A LARGE RECTANGULAR ORIFICE

When the available hetad of a liquid is less than 5 times the height of the orifice, the orifice is called a **large orifice.** In case of a small orifice, the velocity is considered to be constant in the entire cross- section and the discharge can be calculated by the formula $Q = C_d \times a \times \sqrt{2gH}$. But in case of a large orifice, the velocity of a liquid, flowing through the orifice, varies with the available head of the liquid and hence Q *cannot* be calculated as mentioned above (*i.e.* $Q = C_d \times a \times \sqrt{2gH}$).

Consider a large rectangular orifice in one side of the tank discharging water freely into the atmosphere, as shown in Fig. 8.9.

Let, H_1 = Height of liquid above the top of the orifice,

H_2 = Height of liquid above the bottom of the orifice,

b = Breadth of the orifice, and

C_d = Co-efficient of discharge.

Consider an elementary horizontal strip of depth 'dh' at depth of 'h' below the water level as shown in Fig. 8.9.

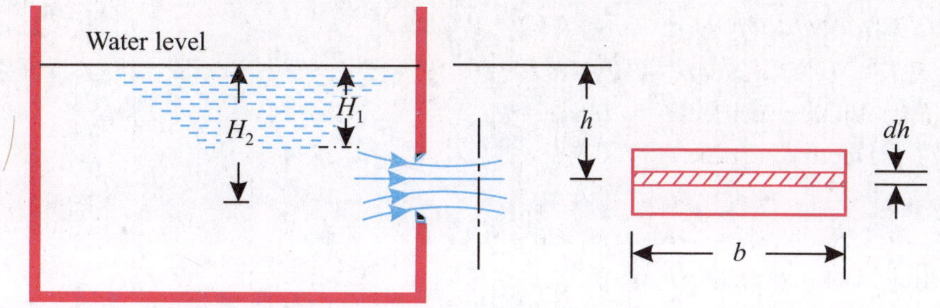

Fig. 8.9. Large rectangular orifice.

∴ Area of the strip = $b \cdot dh$

Theoretical velocity of water through the strip = $\sqrt{2gh}$

∴ Discharge through the strip,

$$dQ = C_d \times \text{area of strip} \times \text{velocity}$$
$$= C_d \times b \times dh \times \sqrt{2gh}$$
$$= Cd \cdot b \cdot dh \sqrt{2gh}$$

Total discharge through the whole orifice may be found out by integrating the above equation between the limits H_1 and H_2.

∴ $$Q = \int_{H_1}^{H_2} C_d . b . dh \sqrt{2gh}$$
$$= C_d . b \times \sqrt{2g} \int_{H_1}^{H_2} \sqrt{h}$$
$$= C_d . b \sqrt{2g} \left[\frac{h^{3/2}}{3/2} \right]_{H_1}^{H_2}$$
$$= 2/3\, C_d . b \sqrt{2g}\, (H_2^{3/2} - H_1^{3/2}) \quad \text{...(8.9)}$$

Example 8.13. *Find the discharge through a rectangular orifice 3.0 m wide and 2.0 m deep fitted to a water tank. The water level in the tank is 4·0 m above the top edge of the orifice. Take C_d = 0.62.*

Solution. Width of the orifice, b = 3.0 m

Depth of the orifice, d = 2.0 m

Height of water above the top of the orifice, H_1 = 4.0 m

∴ Height of the water above the bottom of the orifice, $H_2 = 4 + d = 4 + 2 = 6$ m

Co-efficient of discharge, C_d = 0.62

Discharge through the orifice, *Q*:

Using the relation:

$$Q = \frac{2}{3} C_d \cdot b\sqrt{2g}\, (H_2^{3/2} - H_1^{3/2}) \quad \text{with usual notations}$$
$$= \frac{2}{3} \times 0.62 \times 3.0 \times \sqrt{2 \times 9.81}\left(6^{3/2} - 4^{3/2}\right) = 36.78 \text{ m}^3/\text{s}$$

i.e. **Q = 36.78 m³/s (Ans.)**

Example 8.14. **A** *rectangular orifice 0.6 m wide and 0.8 m deep is discharging water from a vessel. The top edge of the orifice is 0.4 m below the water surface in the vessel. Find:*

(i) The discharge through the orifice if $C_d = 0.62$;
(ii) The percentage error if the orifice is treated as a small orifice.

Solution. Width of orifice, $b = 0.6$ m

Depth of orifice, $d = 0.8$ m

$H_1 = 0.4$ m

$H_2 = H_1 + d = 0.4 + 0.8 = 1.2$ m

Co-efficient of discharge, $C_d = 0.62$

(i) Discharge through the orifice, *Q*:

$$Q = \frac{2}{3} C_d \times b \times \sqrt{2g}\,(H_2^{3/2} - H_1^{3/2})$$

$$= \frac{2}{3} \times 0.62 \times 0.6 \times \sqrt{2 \times 9.81}\left[1.2^{3/2} - 0.4^{3/2}\right] \text{m}^3/\text{s}$$

$$= 1.098\,(1.314 - 0.253) = \mathbf{1.165\ m^3/s\ (Ans.)}$$

(ii) The percentage error if the orifice is treated as a small orifice:

Discharge for a small orifice,

$$Q' = C_d \times a \times \sqrt{2gh}$$

where, $$h = H_1 + \frac{d}{2} = 0.4 + \frac{0.8}{2} = 0.8 \text{ m},$$

and, $$a = b \times d = 0.6 \times 0.8 = 0.48 \text{ m}^2$$

$\therefore$ $$Q' = 0.62 \times 0.48 \times \sqrt{2 \times 9.81 \times 0.8} = 1.179 \text{ m}^3/\text{s}$$

$$\% \text{ error} = \frac{Q' - Q}{Q} = \frac{1.179 - 1.165}{1.165} = 0.012 \text{ or } \mathbf{1.2\ \%\ (Ans.)}$$

8.7. DISCHARGE THROUGH FULLY SUBMERGED ORIFICE

If an orifice has its whole of the outlet side submerged under liquid so that it discharges a jet of liquid into the liquid of the same kind then it is known as **fully submerged** (or *drowned*) **orifice.**

Consider a fully submerged orifice as shown in Fig. 8.10.

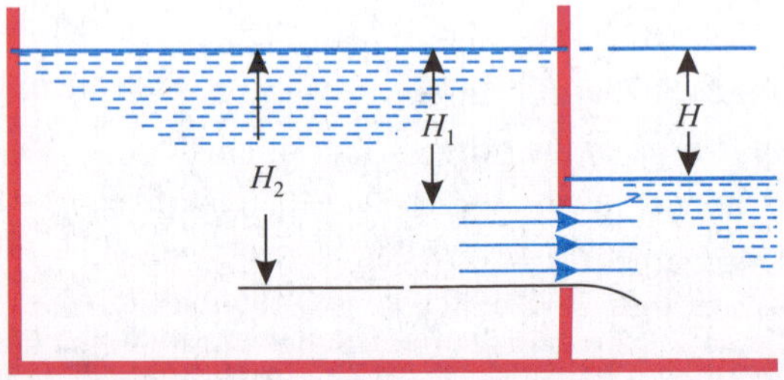

Fig. 8.10. Fully submerged orifice.

Let, H_1 = Height of water (on the upstream side) above the top of the orifice,

H_2 = Height of water (on the upstream side) above the bottom of the orifice,

H = Difference between the two water levels on either side of the orifice,

b = Width of orifice, and

C_d = Co-efficent of discharge.

$\therefore$ Area of the orifice = $b\,(H_2 - H_1)$

We know that theoretical velocity of water through the orifice = $\sqrt{2gH}$

$\therefore$ Actual velocity of water = $C_v\ \sqrt{2gH}$

Since in this case co-efficient of contraction is 1, therefore, taking C_d equal to C_v, we find that the actual velocity of water $= C_d \times \sqrt{2gH}$

$\therefore$ Discharge through the orifice,

$$Q = \text{Area of orifice} \times \text{actual velocity}$$

$$= b\,(H_2 - H_1) \times C_d\sqrt{2gH}$$

$$= C_d \cdot b\,(H_2 - H_1) \times \sqrt{2gH} \qquad \text{...(8.10)}$$

Sometimes, depth of submerged orifice (*d*) is given instead of H_1 and H_2. In such cases, the discharge,

$$Q = C_d \cdot b \cdot d\ \sqrt{2gH} \qquad \text{...(8.11)}$$

Example 8.15. *Find the discharge through a totally drowned orifice 1.5 m wide and 1 m deep, if the difference of water levels on both the sides of the orifice be 2.5 m. Take $C_d = 0.62$.*

Solution. Width of the orifice, b = 1.5 m

Difference of water levels, H = 2.5m

Depth of the orifice, d = 1 m

Co-efficient of dicsharge, C_d = 0.62

Discharge, Q:

Using the relation,

$$Q = C_d \,.\, b \,.\, d\ \sqrt{2gH}$$

$$= 0.62 \times 1.5 \times 1 \times \sqrt{2 \times 9.81 \times 2.5} = 6.513 \text{ m}^3/\text{s}$$

i.e., $\mathbf{Q = 6.513\ m^3/s}$ **(Ans.)**

8.8. DISCHARGE THROUGH PARTIALLY SUBMERGED ORIFICE

If the outlet side of an orifice is only partly submerged (or drowned) under liquid then it is known as **partially submerged** (*or drowned*) **orifice** (Fig. 8.11). The upper portion behaves as an *orifice discharging free,* while the lower portion behaves as a submerged orifice. The total discharge is determined by computing separately the discharges through the free and the submerged portions and then adding together the two discharges thus computed.

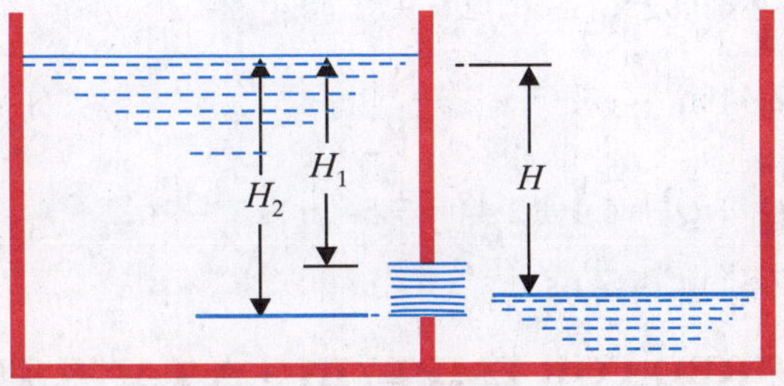

Fig. 8.11. Partially submerged orifice.

Discharge through the submerged portion,

$$Q_1 = C_d.b.(H_2 - H) \times \sqrt{2gH} \qquad \text{...(As in Art. 8.7)}$$

and, the discharge through the free portion,

$$Q_2 = \frac{2}{3} C_d \cdot b \cdot \sqrt{2g}\ (H^{3/2} - H_1^{3/2}) \qquad \text{...(As in Art. 8.6)}$$

Total discharge $\quad Q = Q_1 + Q_2$

$$= C_d.b.(H_2 - H) \times \sqrt{2gH} + \frac{2}{3}.C_d.b.\sqrt{2g}\ (H^{3/2} - H_1^{3/2}) \qquad \text{...(8.12)}$$

Example 8.16. *A rectangular orifice 1.5 m wide and 1.2 m deep is fitted in one side of a large tank. The water level on one side of the orifice is 2 m above the top edge of the orifice, while on the other side of the orifice, the water level is 0.4 m below its top edge. Calculate the discharge through the the orifice if $C_d = 0.62$.*

Solution. Width of orifice, $b = 1.5$ m

Depth of orifice, $d = 1.2$ m

Height of water level above the top of the orifice, $H_1 = 2$ m

Height of water level above the bottom of the orifice, $H_2 = 2 + 1.2 = 3.2$ m

Difference of water levels on both the sides, $H = 2.4$ m

Co-efficient of discharge, $C_d = 0.62$

Since the orifice is partially submerged, let us treat the upper portion as a free orifice and the lower portion as a submerged orifice.

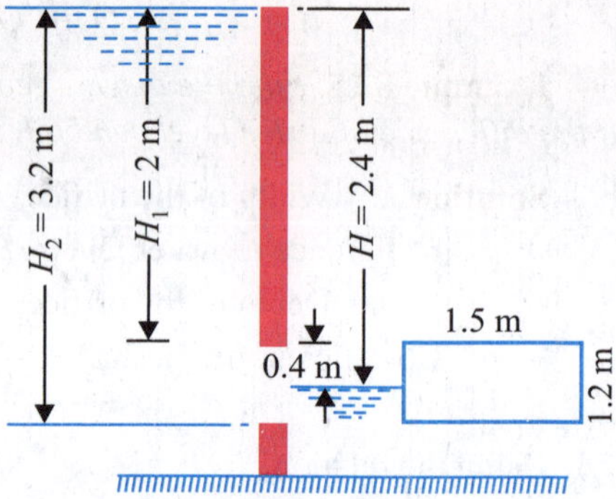

Fig. 8.12

Let, $\quad Q_1$ = Discharge through the submerged portion, and

$\quad Q_2$ = Discharge through the free portion.

Using the relation:

$$Q_1 = C_d \,.\, b \,.\, (H_2 - H) \times \sqrt{2gH} \qquad \text{...with usual notations}$$

$$= 0.62 \times 1.5\ (3.2 - 2.4) \times \sqrt{2 \times 9.81 \times 2.4} = 5.1 \text{ m}^3/\text{s}$$

Now, using the relation:

$$Q_2 = \frac{2}{3} C_d \cdot b\sqrt{2g}\ (H^{3/2} - H_1^{3/2}) \qquad \text{...with usual notations}$$

$$= \frac{2}{3} \times 0.62 \times 1.5 \times \sqrt{2 \times 9.81}\ (2.4^{3/2} - 2^{3/2})$$

$$= 2.44 \text{ m}^3/\text{s}$$

The total discharge,

$$Q = Q_1 + Q_2 = 5.1 + 2.44 = 7.54 \text{ m}^3/\text{s}$$

i.e. $\quad Q$ = **7.54 m³/s (Ans.)**

8.9. TIME REQUIRED FOR EMPTYING A TANK THROUGH AN ORIFICE AT ITS BOTTOM

Consider a tank, of uniform cross-sectional area, containing some liquid, and having an orifice at its bottom as shown in Fig. 8.13.

Let, A = Cross-sectional area of the tank,

a = Area of the orifice,

H_1 = Initial height of liquid,

H_2 = Final height of liquid

T = Time in seconds, required to bring the level from H_1 to H_2

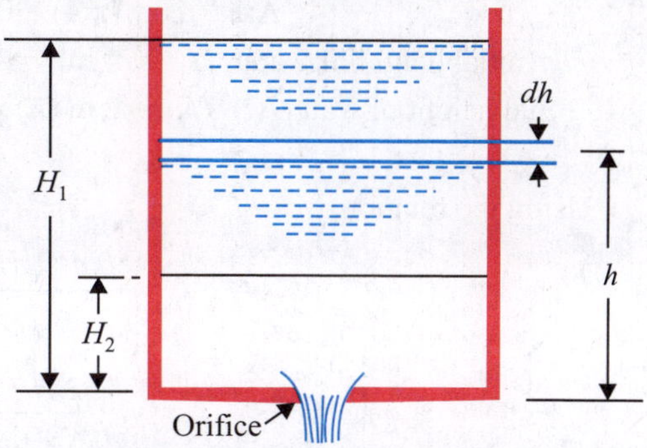

Fig. 8.13 Tank with an orifice at its bottom.

Let at some instant the height of the liquid be h above the orifice and let the liquid surface fall by an amount dh after a small interval for time dt.

Then, volume of the liquid that has passed the tank in time dt,

$$dq = -A \cdot dh \quad ...(i)$$

(– ve sign of dh is taken because the value of h decreases when the discharge increases). Also, theoretical velocity through the orifice, $v = \sqrt{2gh}$

$\therefore$ Discharge through the orifice in a small interval of time dt,

dq = Co-efficient of discharge × area × theoretical velocity × time.

$$= C_d \,.\, a \,.\, \sqrt{2gh} \,.\, dt \quad ...(ii)$$

Equating (*i*) and (*ii*), we get:

$$-A \cdot dh = C_d \,.\, a \,.\, \sqrt{2gh} \,.\, dt$$

$$\therefore \quad dt = \frac{-A.dh}{C_d.a.\sqrt{2gh}} = \frac{-A\,(h^{-1/2})\,dh}{C_d.a\sqrt{2g}}$$

Time taken (T) to lower the level from H_1 to H_2 is calculated by integrating the above equation between the limits H_1 and H_2.

i.e.
$$T = \int_{H_1}^{H_2} \frac{-A\,(h^{-1/2})dh}{C_d.a.\sqrt{2g}} = \frac{-A}{C_d.a\sqrt{2g}} \int_{H_1}^{H_2} h^{-1/2} dh$$

$$= \frac{-A}{C_d.a.\sqrt{2g}} \left[\frac{h^{1/2}}{1/2}\right]_{H_1}^{H_2} = \frac{-2A}{C_d.a\sqrt{2g}} \left[h^{1/2}\right]_{H_1}^{H_2}$$

$$= \frac{-2A}{C_d.a.\sqrt{2g}} - \left[\sqrt{H_2} - \sqrt{H_1}\right] = \frac{2A\left(\sqrt{H_1} - \sqrt{H_2}\right)}{C_d.a\sqrt{2g}} \quad ...(8.13)$$

If the tank is to be emptied completely, then $H_2 = 0$

and,
$$T = \frac{2A\sqrt{H_1}}{C_d.a\sqrt{2g}} \quad ...(8.14)$$

Example 8.17. *A circular tank of diameter 3 m contains water upto a height of 4m. The tank is provided with an orifice of diameter 0.4 m at the bottom. Find the time taken by water,*

(*i*) *to fall from 4 m to 2 m, and*

(*ii*) *for completely emptying the tank.*

Take $C_d = 0.6$

Solution. Dia. of the tank, D = 3m

$\therefore$ Area, $a = (\pi/4) \times 3^2 = 7.068 \text{ m}^2$

Dia. of the orifice, d = 0.4 m

$\therefore$ Area, $a = (\pi/4) \times 0.4^2 = 0.1257 \text{ m}^2$

Initial height of water, $H_1 = 4$ m

Final height of water, (*i*) $H_2 = 2$ m (*ii*) $H_2 = 0$

Case I. When H_2= 2 m

Using the relation,

$$T = \frac{2A(\sqrt{H_1} - \sqrt{H_2})}{C_d \cdot a \cdot \sqrt{2g}} \quad \text{...with usual notations}$$

$$= \frac{2 \times 7.068 (\sqrt{4} - \sqrt{2})}{0.6 \times 0.1257 \times \sqrt{2 \times 9.81}} = \frac{8.28}{0.334} = 24.8 \text{ s}$$

i.e. T = **24.8 s (Ans.)**

Case II. When H_2 = 0.

$$T = \frac{2A\sqrt{H_1}}{C_d \, . \, a\sqrt{2g}} = \frac{2 \times 7.068 \times \sqrt{4}}{0.6 \times 0.1257 \sqrt{2 \times 9.81}} = \frac{28.27}{0.334} = 84.6s$$

i.e. T = **84.6s (Ans.)**

Example 8.18. *A swimming pool 12 m long and 7 m wide holds water to a depth of 2 m. If the water is discharged through an opening of area 0.2 m² at the bottom of the pool, find the time required to empty the tank. Take co-efficient of discharge for the opening as 0.6.* **(UPSC)**

Solution. Area of the swimming pool, $A = 12 \times 7 = 84 \text{ m}^2$

Area of the orifice (opening) = 0.2 m^2

Co-efficient of discharge, $C_d = 0.6$

Initial height of water, $H_1 = 2$ m

Time required to empty the tank, *T*:

Using the relation: $$T = \frac{2A\sqrt{H_1}}{C_d \, . \, a\sqrt{2g}} \quad \text{[Eqn. (8.14)]}$$

Substituting the values, we get: $$T = \frac{2 \times 84 \times \sqrt{2}}{0.6 \times 0.2\sqrt{2 \times 9.81}} = \textbf{446.98 s (Ans.)}$$

Example 8.19. *A 1 m diameter circular tank contains water upto a height of 4 m. At the bottom of tank an orifice of 40 mm is provided. Find the height of water above the orifice after 1.5 minutes. Take co-efficient of discharge for the orifice $C_d = 0.6$.*

Solution. Dia. of tank, D = 1 m

$\therefore$ Area, $A = \frac{\pi}{4} D^2 = \frac{\pi}{4} \times 1^2 = 0.785 \text{ m}^2$

Dia. of orifice, d = 40 mm =0.04 m

$\therefore$ Area, $a = \frac{\pi}{4} d^2 = \frac{\pi}{4} \times 0.04^2 = 0.001257 \text{ m}^2$

Initial height of water, H_1 = 4m

Time, T = 1.5 min. = 1.5 × 60 = 90 s

Height of water above the orifice after 1.5 minutes:

Let H_2 be height of water above the orifice after 1.5 minutes.

Using the relation: $$T = \frac{2A(\sqrt{H_1} - \sqrt{H_2})}{C_d \cdot a\sqrt{2g}}$$ (Eqn.8.13)

Substituting the values, we get:

$$90 = \frac{2 \times 0.785 \times (\sqrt{4} - \sqrt{H_2})}{0.6 \times 0.001257 \times \sqrt{2 \times 9.81}}$$

$$= 469.9\,(2 - \sqrt{H_2})$$

or, $$\sqrt{H_2} = 2 - \frac{90}{469.9} = 1.808$$

$\therefore$ H_2 = **3.269m (Ans.)**

Example 8.20. *Fig. 8.14 shows a rectangular tank having the compartments 1and 2, communicating by on orifice 100 mm square, its centre being 1 m above the bottom of the tank. The horizontal cross-sections of the compartments 1 and 2 are 12 m² and 24m² respectively. At a certain instant the water stands 4 m deep in 1 and 2 m deep in 2. How soon thereafter will surface reach a common level ?*

Take the efficient of discharge, $C_d = 0.6$

Solution. Size of the orifice = 100 mm (or 0.1 m) square

$\therefore$ Area, $a = 0.1 \times 0.1 = 0.01\ m^2$

Area of compartment 1, $A_1 = 12\ m^2$

Area of compartment 2, $A_2 = 24\ m^2$

Discharge co-efficient, $C_d = 0.6$

Time taken by the surface to reach a common level, T:

Let, y = Depth of water in '1' at any instant, and

dy = Change in depth during any interval of time dT.

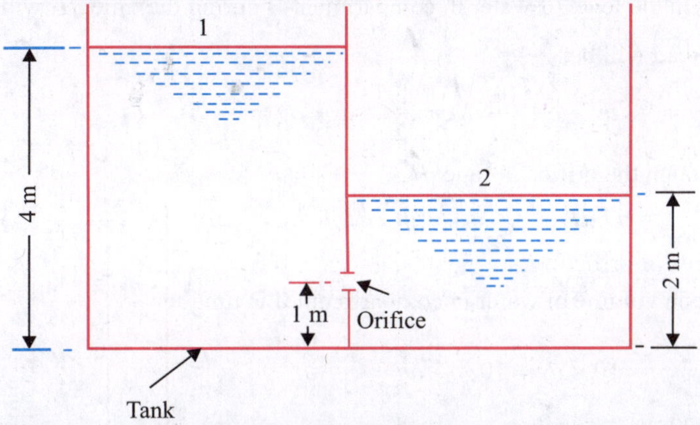

Fig. 8.14

Then, rise in 2's level during the same time will be $\frac{12}{24} \times dy$ and net change in head will be,

$$dh = dy - \left(-\frac{12}{24} \times dy\right) = \frac{3}{2}\,dy \text{ or } dy = \frac{2}{3}\,dh$$

Discharge through orifice in time dT

$$= Q \cdot dT = C_d . a. \sqrt{2gh}\ dT \qquad ...(i)$$

Also the dicrease in volume of water in time dT

$$= 12 \times dy = 12 \times \frac{2}{3} dh = 8\ dh \qquad ...(ii)$$

Equating (*i*) and (*ii*), we get:

$$-8\ dh = C_d \cdot a \cdot \sqrt{2gh} \cdot dT$$

(Negative sign is introduced as with the increase in time, the height of water in '1' decreases)

$$\therefore \quad dT = \frac{-8}{C_d \cdot a \cdot \sqrt{2g}} \cdot \frac{dh}{\sqrt{h}} = \frac{-8}{0{\cdot}6 \times 0{\cdot}01 \times \sqrt{2 \times 9{\cdot}81}} \cdot \frac{dh}{\sqrt{h}} = -301 \frac{dh}{\sqrt{h}}$$

Integrating both the sides, we get:

$$\int_0^T dT = -301 \int_2^0 \frac{dh}{\sqrt{h}} = 301 \int_0^2 h^{-1/2} dh$$

$$T = 301 \left[\frac{h^{-1/2+1}}{-1/2+1} \right]_0^2 = \left[301 \times 2\sqrt{h} \right]_0^2$$

$$= 301 \times 2 \times \sqrt{2} = \mathbf{851.35\,s\ (Ans.)}$$

Example 8.21. *A vessel has compartments A and B communicating by an orifice 150 cm², its centre being 1 m above the botton of the vessel. The cross section of A is 10 m² and that of B is 20 m² At a certain time the water stands 4 m in A and 2 m in B. How soon thereafter water will attain common level ? Assume $C_d = 0.62$.* **(MU)**

Solution. Refer to Fig, 8.15.

Let, y = Depth of water in compartment A at any instant,

and, dy = Change in depth during any interval of time dT.

Then, the rise in the level of water in compariment B during the time dT will be $\frac{10}{20} \times dy$ and the net change in head will be,

$$dh = dy - \left(-\frac{10}{20} dy \right) = \frac{3}{2} dy \ (or\ dy = \frac{2}{3} dh)$$

Discharge through the orifice in time dT

$$= Q.dT = C_d .a. \sqrt{2gh} \ . dT \qquad ...(i)$$

(where, a = area of orifice)

Also decrease in volume of water in compartment A in time dT

$$= 10 \times dy = 10 \times \frac{2}{3} dh = \frac{20}{3} dh$$

Equating (*i*) and (*ii*), we get:

$$-\frac{20}{3} dh = C_d \cdot a \cdot \sqrt{2gh} \cdot dT$$

(Negative sign is introduced as with increase in time, the height of water in compartment A decreases)

$$\therefore \quad dT = \frac{-6.667}{C_d .a. \sqrt{2g}} \times \frac{dh}{\sqrt{h}}$$

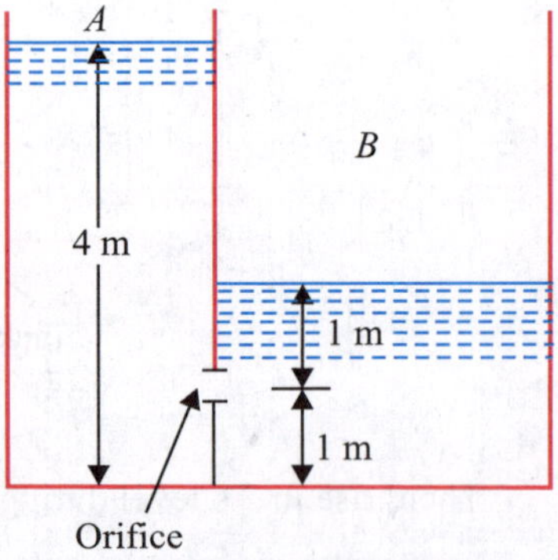

Fig. 8.15

$$= \frac{-6.667}{0.62 \times (150 \times 10^{-4}) \times \sqrt{2 \times 9.81}} \times \frac{dh}{\sqrt{h}} = -161.84 \times \frac{dh}{\sqrt{h}}$$

Integrating both sides, we get:

$$\int_0^T dT = -161.84 \int_2^0 \frac{dh}{\sqrt{h}} = 161.84 \int_0^2 h^{-1/2}\, dh$$

$$\therefore \quad T = 161.84 \left[\frac{(h)^{\frac{-1}{2}+1}}{-\frac{1}{2}+1} \right]_0^2 = 161.84\, [2\sqrt{h}]_0^2 = \mathbf{457.7\,s\ (Ans.)}$$

Example 8.22. *A cylindrical tank 3 m in diameter and 6 m high has an orifice 150 mm in diameter at the bottom centre of the tank. A constant discharge of 85 litres of water per second is fed into the tank. At the same time water is being discharged through the orifice. Determine the time taken to lower the water surface level in the tank from 5 m to 2.5 m above the centre of orifice. Take* $C_d = 0.72$. *The top of the tank is open to the atmosphere.* **[UPSC Exams.]**

Solution. Dia. of the tank, $D = 3$ m

$\therefore$ Area, $A = \frac{\pi}{4} \times 3^2 = 7.068\ \text{m}^2$

Dia. of the orifice, $d = 150$ mm $= 0.15$ m

$\therefore$ Area, $a = \frac{\pi}{4} \times 0.15^2 = 0.01767\ \text{m}^2$

Constant discharge of water fed into the tank, $q = 85$ litres/s $= 0.085\ \text{m}^3/\text{s}$

Initial height of water, $H_1 = 5$ m

Final height of water, $H_2 = 2.5$ m

Time taken to lower the water surface level:

Let, Q = Outflow *i.e.* discharge through the orifice, and

dh = The fall in water surface in the tank in time dT under the conditions of simultaneous inflow and outflow.

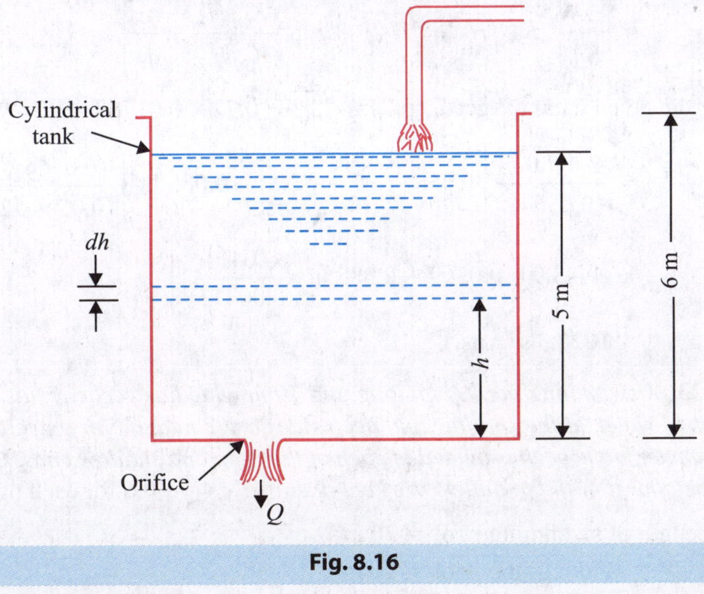

Fig. 8.16

From the principle of continuity, we have:

$$-A.dh = (Q - q)\, dT = (C_d.a.\sqrt{2gh} - q)\, dT$$

or, $$dT = -\frac{A.dh}{(C_d.a.\sqrt{2gh} - q)}$$

Let, $$Q = K\sqrt{h}$$

where, $$K = C_d.a.\sqrt{2g}$$

and, $$(K\sqrt{h} - q) = x,$$

then, $$dx = \frac{Kdh}{2\sqrt{h}}\left(or\ dh = \frac{2\sqrt{h} \times dx}{K}\right)$$

Time taken to lower the water surface from a height, H_1 to H_2

$$T = -\int_{H_1}^{H_2} \frac{A.dh}{(K\sqrt{h} - q)} = -\int_{H_1}^{H_2} \frac{A \times 2\sqrt{h}.dx}{K\,(K\sqrt{h} - q)} \quad \text{(substituting the value of } dh\text{)}$$

Multiplying the numerator and denominator by K, we get:

$$= -\int_{H_1}^{H_2} \frac{A.2\sqrt{h}.dx.K}{K^2(K\sqrt{h} - q)} = -\frac{2A}{K^2}\int (x + q)\frac{dx}{x} \qquad (\because K\sqrt{h} = x + q)$$

$$= -\frac{2A}{K^2}\int\left(1 + \frac{q}{x}\right)dx = -\frac{2A}{K^2}[x + q\ \ln(x)]$$

$$= -\frac{2A}{K^2}\left[(K\sqrt{h} - q) + q\ \ln(K\sqrt{h} - q)\right]_{H_1}^{H_2}$$

$$= \frac{2A}{K^2}\left[(K\sqrt{h} - q) + q\ \ln(K\sqrt{h} - q)\right]_{H_2}^{H_1}$$

$$= \frac{2A}{K^2}\left[K(\sqrt{H_1} - \sqrt{H_2}) + q\ \ln\frac{(K\sqrt{H_1} - q)}{(K\sqrt{H_2} - q)}\right]$$

Substituting the given data, we get $K = C_d.a.\sqrt{2g} = 0.72 \times 0.01767 \times \sqrt{2 \times 9.81} = 0.0564$

$$= \frac{2 \times 7.068}{(0.0564)^2}\left[0.0564\,(\sqrt{5} - \sqrt{2.5}) + 0.085\ \ln\left\{\frac{(0.0564\sqrt{5} - 0.085)}{(0.0564\sqrt{2.5} - 0.085)}\right\}\right]$$

$$= 4443.94\left[0.0369 + 0.085\ \ln\left(\frac{0.0411}{0.00417}\right)\right]$$

$= \mathbf{1028.3\ s}$ **(Ans.)**

Example 8.23. *A swimming pool 30 m long and 10 m wide has vertical sides and bottom at a slope. The depths of water at the shallow and deep sides are 2 m and 5 m repectively. Two outlets, each of 0.4 m diameter, have been provided at each of the deep and shallow ends. Calculate the time taken to empty the pool if both the outlets are kept open. Take* $C_d = 0.6$ for each opening.

Solution. Length of swimming pool = 30 m

Width of the pool = 10 m

$\therefore$ Area of the pool $A = 30 \times 10 = 300 \text{ m}^2$

Diameter of each outlet, $d = 0.4$ m

$\therefore$ Area, $a = \frac{\pi}{4} \times 0.4^2 = 0.1256 \text{ m}^2$

Discharge co-efficient for each opening, $C_d = 0.6$

Time taken to empty the pool, T:

Let, T_1 = Time required to bring the water level from LM to NP, and

T_2 = Time taken to empty the triangular element NPS.

Then, $T = T_1 + T_2$

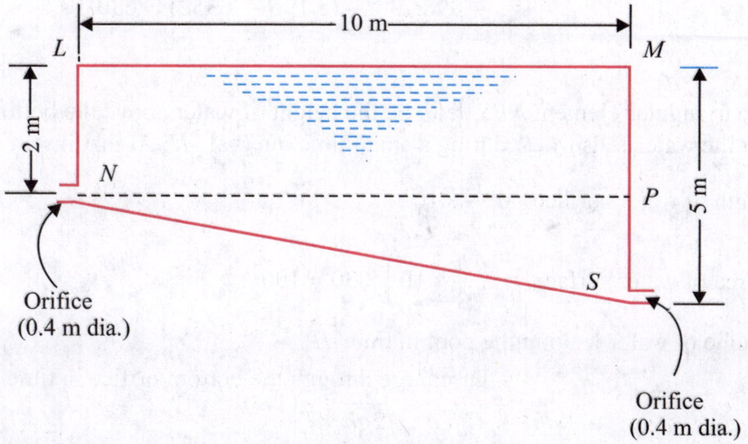

Fig. 8.17

(i) Time T_1:

Refer to Fig. 8.17. The section NP corresponds to centre of the top orifice/opening. Let us consider an instant when the height of water above the centre of the top orifice is h metres. At that instant, the height of water above the bottom orifice equals $(h + 3)$ metres. If during a small time interval dT the water level falls by dh, then:

Volume of water leaving the pool in time dT

= Discharge through the two orifices in time dT

i.e.,
$$-A.dh = C_d.a.\sqrt{2g\,(h+3)}\;dT + C_d.a.\sqrt{2gh}.\;dT$$

or,
$$dT = \frac{-A\,dh}{C_d.a.\sqrt{2gh}\;(\sqrt{h+3)} + \sqrt{h})}$$

$$\int_0^{T_1} dT = \frac{-A}{C_d.a.\sqrt{2g}} \int_{h=2}^{h=0} \frac{dh}{\sqrt{(h+3} + \sqrt{h}}$$

$$T_1 = \frac{-A}{C_d.a.\sqrt{2g}} \int_{h=2}^{h=0} \frac{\left[\sqrt{(h+3)} - \sqrt{h}\right]}{\left[\sqrt{(h+3)} + \sqrt{h}\right]\left[\sqrt{(h+3)} - \sqrt{h}\right]}.dh$$

$$= \frac{-A}{C_d.a.\sqrt{2g}} \int_{h=2}^{h=0} \frac{\left[\sqrt{(h+3)} - \sqrt{h}\right]}{3}.dh$$

$$= \frac{-A}{C_d.a.\sqrt{2g}} \times \frac{1}{3}\left[\frac{(h+3)^{3/2}}{3/2} - \frac{h^{3/2}}{3/2}\right]_2^0$$

$$= \frac{-A}{C_d.a.\sqrt{2g}} \times \frac{1}{3} \times \frac{2}{3}\left[(h+3)^{3/2} - h^{3/2}\right]_2^0$$

Substituting the values, we get:

$$= \frac{-300}{0.6 \times 0.1256 \times \sqrt{2 \times 9.81}} \times \frac{2}{9}\left[(3)^{3/2} - \{(2+3)^{3/2} - 2^{3/2}\}\right]$$

$$= -898.73 \times \frac{2}{9}(5.196 - 8.352) = 630.3 \text{ s}$$

(ii) Time T_2:

Within the triangular element *NPS,* let h be the height of water above the bottom orifice at any instant; and let the water falls by dh during a small time interval dT. At that instant:

$$\text{Width of water surface} = \frac{h}{3} \times 10$$

$$\text{Area of water surface} = \left(\frac{h}{3} \times 10\right) \times 30 = 100\,h$$

Now, Volume of water leaving the pool in time dT

$$= \text{Discharge through the bottom orifice in time } dT$$

$$-A.dh = C_d \cdot a \cdot \sqrt{2gh} \cdot dT$$

or

$$dT = \frac{-A.dh}{C_d.a.\sqrt{2gh}} = \frac{-100h.\,dh}{C_d.a.\sqrt{2gh}}$$

$$= \frac{-100}{C_d \cdot a \cdot \sqrt{2g}}\, h^{1/2} \cdot dh$$

$$\therefore \quad \int_0^{T_2} dT = \frac{-100}{C_d.a.\sqrt{2g}} \int_{h=3}^{h=0} h^{1/2}.dh$$

Substituting values, we get:

$$T_2 = \frac{-100}{0.6 \times 0.1256 \times \sqrt{2 \times 9.81}}\left[\frac{2}{3} \times h^{3/2}\right]_3^0$$

$$= -299.57\left[\frac{2}{3} \times (0 - 3^{3/2})\right] = 1037.7s$$

$\therefore$ Total time, $T = T_1 + T_2 = 630.3 + 1037.7 =$ **1668 s (Ans.)**

Example 8.24. *Fig 8.18 shows a truncated cone having vertex angle θ = 60°. How long does it take to draw the liquid surface from y = 3 m to y = 1 m ? Take C_d = 0.85* **[IIT Bombay]**

Solution. Dia. of the orifice, $d = 0.1$ m

$$\therefore \quad \text{Area, } a = \frac{\pi}{4} \times 0.1^2 = 0.007854 \text{ m}^2$$

$$\text{Vertex angle, } \theta = 60°$$

Discharge co-efficient, $C_d = 0.85$

Time required, T:

From the geometry of the truncated cone,

$$\frac{0.5}{x} = \tan 30° = \frac{1}{\sqrt{3}}$$

or, $$x = 0.5 \times \sqrt{3} = 0.866 \text{ m}$$

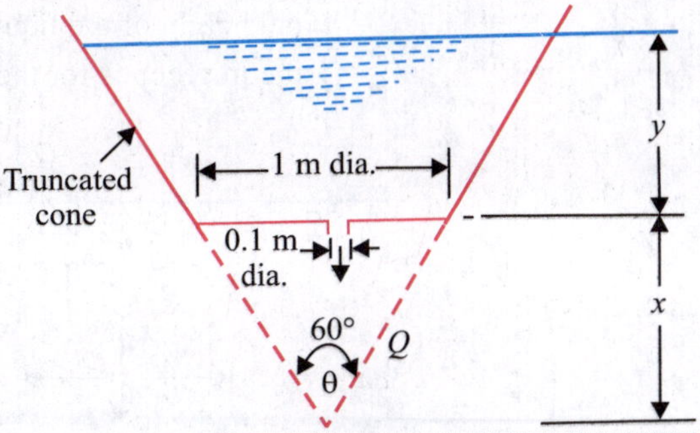

Fig. 8.18

Let r = Radius of truncated cone at a distance $(x + y)$ from the vertex.

Then, $$\frac{r}{x+y} = \tan 30°$$

or $$r = (0.866 + y) \tan 30° = \frac{(0.866 + y)}{\sqrt{3}}$$

Further, let the liquid surface falls a distance dy in time dT. Then from the continuity principle, we have:

$$\pi r^2 (-dy) = Q.dT = C_d.a.\sqrt{2gy}\,.dT$$

or, $$-\pi (0.866 + y)^2 \times \frac{1}{2} dy = 0.85 \times 0.007854 \times \sqrt{2 \times 9.81 \times y \times dT}$$

or, $$-1.047 (0.866 + y^2)\, dy = 0.0296 \sqrt{y} \times dT$$

or, $$dT = \frac{1.047\,(0.866 + y)^2\, dy}{0.0296\sqrt{y}} = -35.37 \times \frac{(0.866 + y)^2}{\sqrt{y}} \cdot dy$$

The time required to empty the cone from $y = 3$ m to 1 m ,

$$T = 35.37 \int_3^1 \frac{(0.866 + y)^2}{\sqrt{y}} .dy = -35.37 \int_3^1 \frac{(0.75 + y^2 + 1.732y)}{\sqrt{y}} .dy$$

$$= 35.37 \int_1^3 \left(\frac{0.75}{\sqrt{y}} + y^{3/2} + 1.732 y^{1/2} \right) dy$$

$$= 35.37 \left[0.75 \times \frac{y^{-1/2+1}}{-1/2+1} + \frac{y^{3/2+1}}{3/2+1} + 1.732 \times \frac{y^{1/2+1}}{1/2+1} \right]_1^3$$

$$= = 35.37 \left[1.5 y^{1/2} + \frac{2}{5} y^{5/2} + 1.732 \times 2/3\, y^{3/2} \right]_1^3$$

$$= 35.37 \left[1.5 (3^{1/2} - 1) + \frac{2}{5} (3^{5/2} - 1) + 1.155 (3^{3/2} - 1) \right]$$

$$= 35.37 (1.098 + 5.835 + 4.846) = \mathbf{416.6 \text{ s}} \text{ (Ans.)}$$

8.10. TIME REQUIRED FOR EMPTYING A HEMISPHERICAL TANK

Consider a hemispherical tank containing some liquid and fitted with an orifice at its bottom as shown in the Fig. 8.19.

Let, R = Radius of the tank,

a = Area of the orifice,
H_1 = Initial height of the liquid,
H_2 = Final height of the liquid, and
T = Time in seconds for the liquid to fall from height H_1 to H_2.

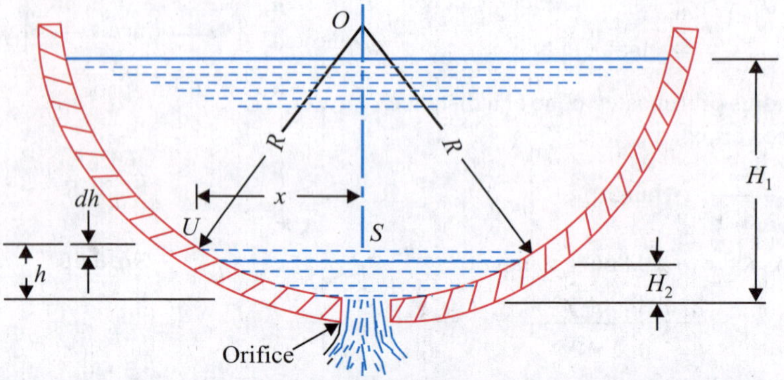

Fig. 8.19. Hemispherical tank.

Let at any instant of time, the height of liquid over the orifice is h and x be the radius of the liquid surface.

Then, area of liquid surface, $A = \pi x^2$

Theoretical velocity of liquid $= \sqrt{2gh}$

Let the height of liquid decrease by dh in a small interval of time dT. Then,

Volume of liquid leaving the tank in time dT

$$= A.dh = \pi x^2 \times dh \qquad ...(i)$$

Also, volume of liquid flowing through the orifice in time dT

$$= C_d \times \text{area of orifice} \times \text{velocity} \times dT$$

$$= C_d \,.\, a \,.\, \sqrt{2gh} \times dT \qquad ...(ii)$$

Equating (i) and (ii), we get:

$$\pi x^2 (-dh) = C_d \,.\, a\sqrt{2gh} \times dT$$

The negative sign accounts for the *decrease in head* on the orifice with *increase in time interval.*

$$dT = \frac{-\pi x^2 \cdot dh}{C_d \cdot a \cdot \sqrt{2gh}} \qquad ..(iii)$$

From Fig. 8.19, we have:

$$OU = R \text{ and } OS = (R - h)$$

$$\therefore \quad x = US = \sqrt{OU^2 - OS^2} = \sqrt{R^2 - (R-h)^2}$$

$$= \sqrt{R^2 - R^2 - h^2 + 2Rh} = \sqrt{2Rh - h^2}$$

or $\quad x^2 = (2RH - h^2)$

Substituting this value of x^2 in eqn. (iii), we get:

$$dT = \frac{-\pi (2Rh - h^2)\, dh}{C_d . a . \sqrt{2gh}}$$

$$= \frac{-\pi}{C_d . a . \sqrt{2g}} = (2Rh - h^2)\, h^{-1/2}\, dh$$

$$= \frac{-\pi}{C_d . a . \sqrt{2g}} (2Rh^{1/2} - h^{3/2})\, dh$$

The total time T required to bring the liquid level from H_1 to H_2 is obtained by integrating the above equation between the limits H_1 to H_2 .

$$\int_0^T dT = \int_{H_1}^{H_2} \frac{-\pi}{C_d . a \sqrt{2g}} (2Rh^{1/2} - h^{3/2})\, dh$$

$$T = \frac{-\pi}{C_d . a \sqrt{2g}} \int_{H_1}^{H_2} (2Rh^{1/2} - h^{3/2})\, dh$$

$$= \frac{-\pi}{C_d . a \sqrt{2g}} \left[2R \times \frac{h^{1/2+1}}{\frac{1}{2}+1} - \frac{h^{3/2+1}}{\frac{3}{2}+1} \right]_{H_1}^{H_2}$$

$$= \frac{-\pi}{C_d . a \sqrt{2g}} \left[\frac{2}{3} \times 2R\, h^{3/2} - \frac{2}{5} h^{5/2} \right]_{H_1}^{H_2}$$

$$= \frac{-\pi}{C_d . a \sqrt{2g}} \left[\frac{4}{3} R \left(H_2^{3/2} - H_1^{3/2} \right) - \frac{2}{5} \left(H_2^{5/2} - H_1^{5/2} \right) \right]$$

or
$$T = \frac{\pi}{C_d . a . \sqrt{2g}} \left[\frac{4}{3} R \left(H_1^{3/2} - H_2^{3/2} \right) - \frac{2}{5} \left(H_1^{5/2} - H_2^{5/2} \right) \right] \quad ...(8.15)$$

For emptying the tank completely, $H_2 = 0$ and hence,

$$T = \frac{\pi}{C_d . a . \sqrt{2g}} \left[\frac{4}{3} R H_1^{3/2} - \frac{2}{5} H_1^{5/2} \right] \quad ...(8.16)$$

Example 8.25. *A hemispherical tank of 2 m radius is provided with an orifice of 40 mm at its bottom. It contains water upto a height of 1.8 m. Find the time required by water*

(i) to fall from 1.8 m to 1.2 m, and

(ii) for completely emptying the tank.

Take $C_d = 0.62$.

Solution. Radius of tank, R = 2 m

Diameter of the orifice, d = 40 mm = 0.04 m

∴ Area, $a = \frac{\pi}{4} \times 0.04^2 = 1.2566 \times 10^{-3}\, m^2$

Initial height of water, H_1 = 1.8 m

Co-efficient of discharge for the orifice, C_d = 0.62

(i) Time required by water to fall from 1.8 m to 1.2 m:

In this case, $H_1 = 1.8$ m and $H_2 = 1.2$ m

Time T is given by :

$$T = \frac{\pi}{C_d . a . \sqrt{2g}} \left[\frac{4}{3} R \left(H_1^{3/2} - H_2^{3/2} \right) - \frac{2}{5} \left(H_1^{5/2} - H_2^{5/2} \right) \right] \quad ...(Eqn. 8.15)$$

$$= \frac{\pi}{0.62 \times 1.2566 \times 10^{-3} \times \sqrt{2 \times 9.81}}\left[\frac{4}{3} \times 2\left(1.8^{3/2} - 1.2^{3/2}\right) - \frac{2}{5}\left(1.8^{5/2} - 1.2^{5/2}\right)\right]$$

$= 910.36\ [2.934 - 1.107] = 1663$ seconds

= 27 min. 43 sec. (Ans.)

(*ii*) Time required by water for completely emptying the tank:

Here $H_1 = 1.8$ m and $H_2 = 0$

Time T is given by: $$T = \frac{\pi}{C_d \cdot a\sqrt{2g}}\left(\frac{4}{3} R H_1^{3/2} - \frac{2}{5} H_1^{5/2}\right) \quad \text{...Eqn. (8.16)}$$

$$= \frac{\pi}{0.62 \times 1.2566 \times 10^{-3} \times \sqrt{2 \times 9.81}}\left(\frac{4}{3} \times 2 \times 1.8^{3/2} - \frac{2}{5} \times 1.8^{5/2}\right)$$

$= 910.36\ (6.44 - 1.738) = 4280.5$ seconds

= 71 min. 20.5 sec. (Ans.)

Example 8.26. *A tank has an upper cylindrical portion of 1.25 m radius and 3 m height with hemispherical base. The tank is provided with an orifice of 150 mm diameter at its bottom. Find the time required to empty it if it is initially full of water.*

Take C_d =0.62 for the orifice.

Solution. Radius of the tank, $R = 1.25$ m

$\therefore$ Area, $A = \pi R^2 = \pi \times 1.25^2 = 4.908\ \text{m}^2$

Dia. of orifice, $d = 150$ mm $= 0.15$ m

$\therefore$ Area, $a = \frac{\pi}{4} \times 0.15^2 = 0.01767\ \text{m}^2$

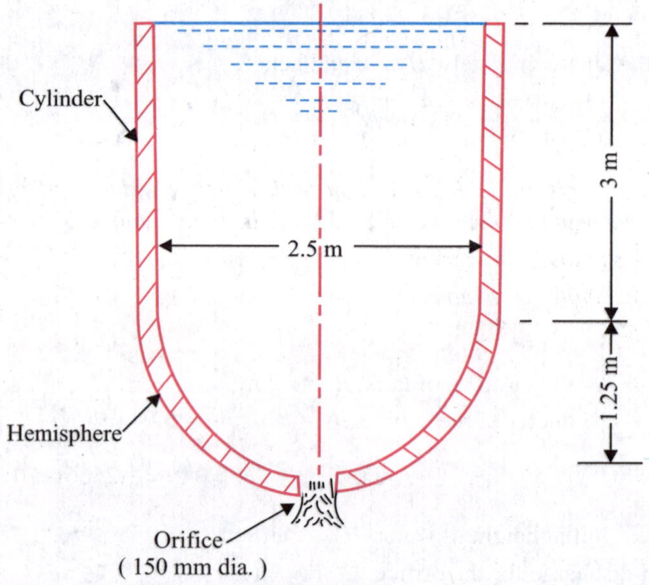

Fig. 8.20

The tank consists of two portions, cylindrical and hemispherical (Fig. 8.20).

Let, T_1 = Time required to empty the upper cylindrical portion, and

T_2 = Time required to empty the hemispherical portion.

Then, total time, $= T_1 + T_2$.

For cylindrical portion :

$$H_1 = 3 + 1.25 = 4.25 \text{ m}, H_2 = 3 \text{ m}$$

Using the relation: $$T_1 = \frac{2A\left(\sqrt{H_1} - \sqrt{H_2}\right)}{C_d.a.\sqrt{2g}} \quad \text{...(Eqn. 8.13)}$$

$$= \frac{2 \times 4.908\ (\sqrt{4.25} - \sqrt{1.25})}{0.62 \times 0.01767 \times \sqrt{2 \times 9.81}}$$

$$= \frac{9.816\ (2.061 - 1.118)}{0.0485} = 190.85 \text{ s}$$

For hemispherical portion:

$$H_1 = 1.25 \text{ m}, H_2 = 0$$

Using the relation:

$$T_2 = \frac{\pi}{C_d.a.\sqrt{2g}}\left[\frac{4}{3}RH_1^{3/2} - \frac{2}{5}H_1^{5/2}\right] \quad \text{...(Eqn.8.16)}$$

Substituting the values, we get:

$$T_2 = \frac{\pi}{0.62 \times 0.01767 \times \sqrt{2 \times 9.81}}\left[\frac{4}{3} \times 1.25 \times 1.25^{3/2} - \frac{2}{5} \times 1.25^{5/2}\right]$$

$$= 64.74\ (2.329 - 0.698) = 105.6 \text{ s}$$

∴ Total time taken to empty the tank,

$$T = T_1 + T_2 = 190.85 + 105.6 = \mathbf{296.45\ s\ (Ans.)}$$

8.11. TIME REQUIRED FOR EMPTYING A CIRCULAR HORIZONTAL TANK

Consider a circular horizontal tank having an orifice at its bottom and containing some liquid.

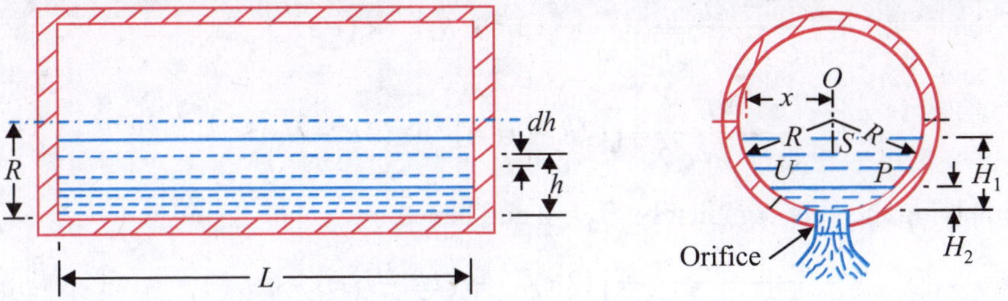

Fig. 8.21

Let, R = Radius of the tank,

L = Length of the tank,

H_1 = Initial height of the liquid,

H_2 = Final height of the liquid, and

T = Time in seconds for the liquid to fall from height H_1 to H_2.

Let at any time, the height of liquid over the orifice is h and it decreases dh in a small interval of time dT. Further, let x be the radius of liquid surface at this instant. Then,

Volume of liquid leaving the tank in time $dT = A.dh$ ...(*i*)

$= A.dh = UP \times L \times dh = 2xL.dh \quad (\because UP = 2x)$

(where, A = surface area)

Velocity of liquid through the orifice = $\sqrt{2gh}$

Volume of liquid flowing through the orifice in time dT

$$= C_d \times a \times \sqrt{2gh} \times dT \qquad ...(ii)$$

Volume of liquid leaving the tank equals the volume of liquid flowing through the orifice.

i.e. $\quad -2x\,L.dh = C_d \times a \times \sqrt{2gh} \times dT$

The negative sign accounts for the decrease in head on the orifice with increase in time interval.

$$\therefore \quad dT = \frac{-2x\,L \cdot dh}{C_d \cdot a \cdot \sqrt{2gh}} \qquad ...(iii)$$

From Fig. 8.21, we have:

$$OU = R \text{ and } OS = (R - h)$$

$$\therefore \quad x = US = \sqrt{OU^2 - OS^2} = \sqrt{R^2 - (R-h)^2} = \sqrt{2Rh - h^2}$$

Substituting this value of x in eqn. (*iii*), we get:

$$dT = \frac{-2\sqrt{(2Rh - h^2)} \times L \times dh}{C_d.a.\sqrt{2gh}} = \frac{-2L\sqrt{(2R-h)}.dh}{C_d.a.\sqrt{2g}} \quad \text{(Taking } \sqrt{h} \text{ common)}$$

The total time T required to bring the liquid level from height H_1 to H_2 can be found out by integrating the above equation within the limits H_1 and H_2.

$$\therefore \quad \int_0^T dT = \int_{H_1}^{H_2} \frac{-2L\sqrt{(2R-h)} \cdot dh}{C_d.a.\sqrt{2g}}$$

or, $$T = \frac{-2L}{C_d.a.\sqrt{2g}} \int_{H_1}^{H_2} (2R - h)^{1/2}\, dh$$

$$= \frac{-2L}{C_d.a.\sqrt{2g}} \times \frac{2}{3} \times \left[(2R - h)^{3/2} \times (-1\right]_{H_1}^{H_2}$$

or, $$T = \frac{4L}{3C_d.a\sqrt{2g}}\left[(2R - H_2)^{3/2} - (2R - H_1)^{3/2}\right] \qquad ...(8.17)$$

For emptying the tank completely, $H_2 = 0$ and hence,

$$T = \frac{4L}{3C_d.a.\sqrt{2g}}\left[(2R)^{3/2} - (2R - H_1)^{3/2}\right] \qquad ...(8.18)$$

Example 8.27. *A horizontal boiler drum 6 m long and 3 m in diameter is provided with an orifice 100 mm in diameter at its bottom. It contains water upto a height of 2.4 m. Calculate the tiime taken to empty the drum. Take discharge co-efficient, C_d = 0.6.*

Solution. Length of the drum, L = 6 m

Diameter of the drum, D = 3.0 m

$\therefore$ Radius, R = 1.5 m

Dia. of the orifice, d = 100 mm = 0.1 m

$\therefore$ Area, $a = \frac{\pi}{4} \times 0.1^2 = 7.854 \times 10^{-3}$ m^2

Initial height of water, H_1 = 2.4 m

Final height of water, $H_2 = 0$

Time taken to empty the drum, *T*:

Using the relation: $T = \dfrac{4L}{3C_d \cdot a \cdot \sqrt{2g}}\left[(2R)^{3/2} - (2R - H_1)^{3/2}\right]$ (Eqn.8.18)

$$= \frac{4 \times 6}{3 \times 0.6 \times 7.854 \times 10^{-3} \times \sqrt{2 \times 9.81}}\left[(2 \times 1.5)^{3/2} - (2 \times 1.5 - 2.4)^{3/2}\right]$$

$= 383.26\ (5.196 - 0.464) = 1813.6$ s

$=$ **30 min. 13.6 sec. (Ans.)**

Example 8.28. (Tank with two orifices). *A 600 mm diameter cylindrical tank (vertical) contains water to a depth of 2.5 m. There are two orifices in the tank, one at the bottom and the other in one of the vertical sides at a height of 1.5 m above the bottom. if the area of each orifice is 12 cm² and discharge co-efficient 0.6, calculate the time required to empty the tank.*

Solution. Dia, of the tank, $D = 600$ mm $= 0.6$ m

$\therefore$ Area, $A = \dfrac{\pi}{4} \times 0.6^2 = 0.2827 \text{m}^2$

Area of each orifice,

$a = 12 \text{ cm}^2 = 0.0012 \text{ m}^2$

Discharge co-efficient for each orifice, $C_d = 0.6$.

Time required to empty the tank, T:

Let, T_1 = Time required to bring the water level from *LM* to *NP*, and

T_2 = Time required to empty the portion below the section *NP*.

Total time, $T = T_1 + T_2$

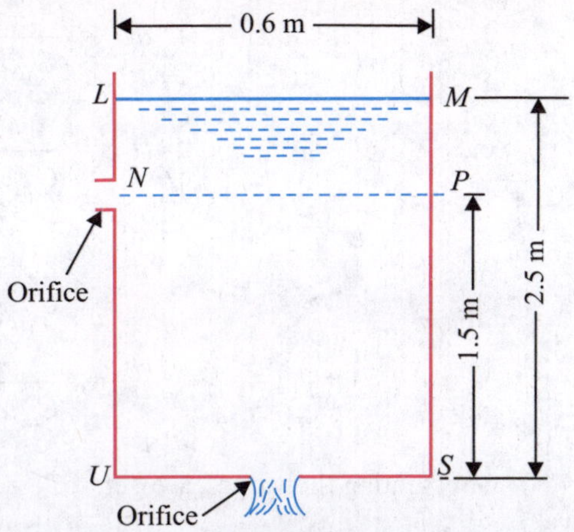

Fig. 8.22

For time T_1:

Let us consider an instant when the height of water above the center of upper orifice is *h* metres. Then the height of water above the bottom, at that instant, equals $(h + 1.5)$ meters. If the water level falls by *dh* during a small time interval *dT*, then:

Volume of the water leaving the tank in time dT = Discharge through the two orifices in time *dT*.

$$-A \cdot dh = C_d \cdot a \cdot \sqrt{2g(h + 1{\cdot}5)} \cdot dT + C_d \cdot a \cdot \sqrt{2gh} \cdot dT$$

$$\therefore \quad dT = \frac{-A \cdot dh}{C_d \cdot a\sqrt{2g}\left[\sqrt{(h + 1.5)} + \sqrt{h}\right]}$$

$$\therefore \quad \int_0^{T_1} dT = \frac{-A}{C_d \cdot a\sqrt{2g}} \int_{h=1}^{0} \frac{dh}{\sqrt{(h + 1{\cdot}5)} + \sqrt{h}}$$

$$T_1 = \frac{-A}{C_d \cdot a\sqrt{2g}} \int_{h=1}^{h=0} \frac{\left[\sqrt{(h + 1.5)} - \sqrt{h}\right]}{\left[\sqrt{(h + 1.5)} + \sqrt{h}\right]\left[\sqrt{(h + 1.5)} - \sqrt{h}\right]} \cdot dh$$

$$T_1 = \frac{-A}{C_d \cdot a \cdot \sqrt{2g}} \int_{h=1}^{h=0} \frac{\sqrt{(h + 1.5)} - \sqrt{h}}{1.5} \cdot dh$$

$$= \frac{-A}{C_d \cdot a \cdot \sqrt{2g}} \times \frac{1}{1{\cdot}5}\left[\frac{(h + 1.5)^{3/2}}{3/2} - \frac{h^{3/2}}{3/2}\right]_1^0$$

Substituting the values, we get:

$$T_1 = \frac{-0.2827}{0.6 \times 0.0012 \times \sqrt{2 \times 9.81}} \times \frac{1}{1.5} \times \frac{2}{3}\left[(h+1.5)^{3/2} - h^{3/2}\right]_1^0$$

$$= -39{\cdot}39\left[(1{\cdot}5)^{3/2} - \left\{(2{\cdot}5)^{3/2} - (1)^{3/2}\right\}\right]$$

$$= -39.39\,(1.837 - 3.953 + 1) = 43.96 \text{ s}$$

For time T_2:

Below the section *NP*, let *h* be the height of water above the bottom orifice at any instant, and let the water be leaving in a small time interval *dT*, then:

Volume of water leaving the tank is time *dT*

= Discharge through the bottom orifice in time *dT*

$$-A.\,dh = C_d \,.\, a \,.\, \sqrt{2gh} \cdot dT$$

$$\therefore \quad dT = \frac{-A.dh}{C_d.a.\sqrt{2gh}}$$

or,
$$\int_0^{T2} dT = \frac{-A}{C_d \,.\, a \,.\, \sqrt{2g}} \int_{h=1{\cdot}5}^{0} h^{-1/2}\, dh$$

or,
$$T_2 = \frac{-A}{C_d.a.\sqrt{2g}}\left[\frac{h^{1/2}}{1/2}\right]_{1{\cdot}5}^{0}$$

$$= \frac{-2A}{C_d.a.\sqrt{2g}}\left[h^{1/2}\right]_{1.5}^{0}$$

Substituting the values, we get:
$$T_2 = \frac{-2 \times 0.2827}{0.6 \times 0.0012 \times \sqrt{2 \times 9.81}}\,(0 - 1.5^{1/2})$$

$$= 177.28 \times 1.5^{1/2} = 217.12 \text{ s}$$

Total time, $T = T_1 + T_2 = 43.96 + 217.12 =$ **261.08 s (Ans.)**

8.12. CLASSIFICATION OF MOUTHPIECES

The mouthpieces may be classified as follows :

1. *According to the position of the mouthpiece* :

(*i*) Internal mouthpiece. (*ii*) External mouthpiece.

2. *According to the shape of the mouthpiece:*

(*i*) Cylindrical mouthpiece. (*ii*) Convergent mouthpiece.

(*iii*) Convergent - divergent mouthpiece.

3. *According to nature of discharge:*

(*i*) Mouthpiece running full. (*ii*) Mouthpiece running free.

Note : A mouthpiece is said to be *running free* if the jet of liquid aftter contraction does not touch the sides of the mouthpiece. But if the jet after contraction expands and fills the whole mouthpiece it is known as *running full.*

8.13. DISCHARGE THROUGH AN EXTERNAL MOUTHPIECE

A **mouthpiece** *is a small tube (two or three times its diameter in length) attached to an orifice.* An external mouthpiece is attached to the vessel such that it projects outside. Fig.8.23 shows a tank to which is attached an external cylindrical mouthpiece.

Let, a_1 = Area of mouthpiece at outlet,
v_1 = Velocity of liquid at outlet,
a_c = Area of flow at vena-contracta,
v_c = Velocity of liquid at C-C section,
H = Height of liquid above the centre of the mouthpiece, and
C_c = Co-efficient of contraction.

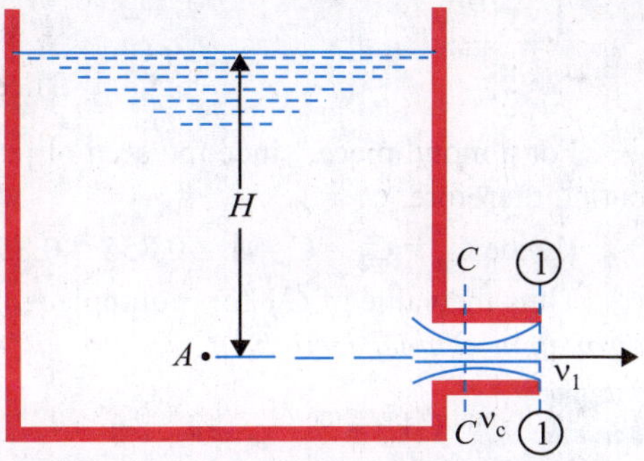

Fig. 8.23. External cylindrical mouthpiece.

Applying continuity equation at C-C and 1-1, we get:

$$a_c v_c = a_1 v_1$$

$$\therefore \quad V_c = \frac{a_1 v_1}{a_c} = \frac{v_1}{a_c / a} = \frac{v_1}{C_c}$$

(where $a_c / a = C_c$ = co-efficient of contraction)

Taking $C_c = 0.62$, we get: $v_c = \dfrac{v_1}{0.62}$

From section C–C the jet of liquid suddenly enlarges at section 1–1; the loss of head due to sudden enlargement is given by:

$$h_L = \frac{(v_c - v_1)^2}{2g}$$

$$= \frac{\left(\frac{v_1}{0.62} - v_1\right)^2}{2g} \qquad \left(\because v_c = \frac{v_1}{0.62}\right)$$

$$= \frac{v_1^2}{2g}\left(\frac{1}{0.62} - 1\right)^2$$

$$= \frac{0.375\, v_1^2}{2g}$$

(Please refer to Art. 12.4.1 for loss of head due to sudden enlargement)

Applying Bernoulli's equation to point A and 1 -1, we get:

$$\frac{P_A}{w} + \frac{v_A^2}{2g} + z_A = \frac{p_1}{w} + \frac{v_1^2}{2g} + z_1 + h_L$$

But $z_A = z_1$, $\dfrac{p_1}{w}$ = atmospheric pressure = 0, and v_A is negligible.

$$\therefore \quad H + 0 = 0 + \frac{v_1^2}{2g} + \frac{0.375 v_1^2}{2g}$$

$$\text{or,} \quad H = \frac{1.375 v_1^2}{2g} \quad \text{or} \quad v_1 = \sqrt{\frac{2gH}{1.375}} = 0.855\sqrt{2gH}$$

Theoretical velocity of liquid at outlet, $v_{th} = \sqrt{2gH}$

∴ Co-efficient of velocity for mouthpiece,

$$C_v = \frac{\text{Actual velocity}}{\text{Theoretical velocity}} = \frac{0.855\sqrt{2gH}}{\sqrt{2gH}} = 0.855$$

For a mouthpiece, since the area of jet of liquid at outlet is equal to the area of mouthpiece at outlet, therefore, $C_c = 1$.

Hence $C_d = C_c \times C_v = 1 \times 0.855 = 0.855$

Thus the value of C_d for mouthpiece is more than the value of C_d for orifice, and so *discharge through mouthpiece will be more.*

Note: In actual practice $C_v = C_d \approx 0.82$.

Example 8.29. *Find the discharge from a 80 m diameter external mouthpiece, fitted to a side of a large vessel, if the head over the mouthpiece is 6 m.*

Solution. Dia. of the mouthpiece = 80 mm = 0.08 mm

$\therefore$ Area, $a = \frac{\pi}{4} \times 0.08^2 = 0.005026 \text{ m}^2$

Head over the mouthpiece, $H = 6$ m

C_d for the mouthpiece = 0.855

$\therefore$ Discharge, $Q = C_d \times \text{area} \times \text{velocity}$

$= C_d \times a \times \sqrt{2gH}$

$= 0.855 \times 0.005026 \times \sqrt{2 \times 9.81 \times 6} =$ **0.0466 m³/s (Ans.)**

Example 8.30. *An external cylindrical mouthpiece of diameter 120 mm is discharging water under a constant head of 6 m. If C_c for vena-contracta = 0.62, C_d = 0.86 and atmospheric pressure head = 10·3 m of water, find :*

(i) *Discharge through the mouthpiece, and*

(ii) *Absolute pressure head of water at vena-contracta.*

Solution. Diameter of mouthpiece, d = 120 mm = 0.12 m

$\therefore$ Area, $a = \frac{\pi}{4} \times 0.12^2 = 0.0113 \text{ m}^2$

Head, $H = 6$ m

C_c for vena-contracta = 0.62

Discharge co-efficient, C_d = 0.86

Atmospheric pressure head, H_a = 10.3 m

(*i*) Discharge through mouthpiece, *Q*:

Discharge, $Q = C_d \cdot a \cdot \sqrt{2gH} = 0.86 \times 0.0113 \times \sqrt{2 \times 9.81 \times 6}$

= **0.1054 m³/s (Ans.)**

(*ii*) Absolute pressure head at vena-contracta, H_c:

Refer to Fig. 8·24. Applying Bernoulli's equation at *A* and *C-C,* we get:

$$\frac{p_A}{w} + \frac{v_A^2}{2g} + z_A = \frac{p_c}{w} + \frac{v_c^2}{2g} + z_c$$

But, $\frac{p_A}{w} = H_a + H,\ v_A = 0$ and $z_A = z_c$

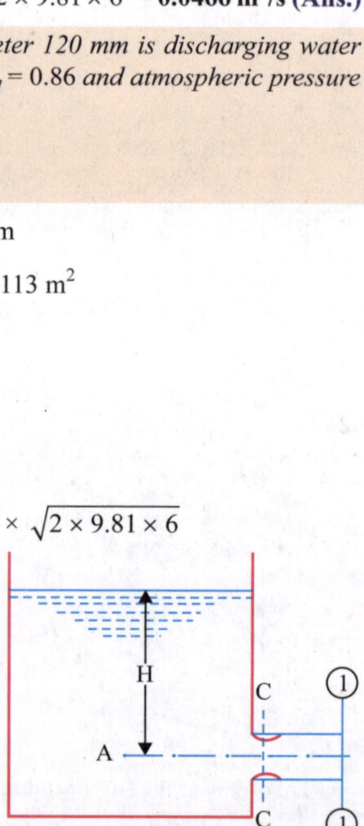

Fig. 8.24

$$\therefore \quad (H_a + H) + 0 = \frac{p_c}{w} + \frac{v_c^2}{2g} = H_c + \frac{v_c^2}{2g}$$

$$\therefore \quad H_c = H_a + H - \frac{v_c^2}{2g}$$

But, $$v_c = \frac{v_1}{0.62}$$

$$\therefore \quad H_c = H_a + H - \left(\frac{v_1}{0.62}\right)^2 \times \frac{1}{2g} = H_a + H - \frac{v_1^2}{2g} \times \frac{1}{(0.62)^2}$$

But, $$H = 1.375 \frac{v_1^2}{2g} \text{ or } \frac{v_1^2}{2g} = \frac{H}{1.375} = 0.7272H$$

$$\therefore \quad H_c = H_a + H - 0.7272\, H \times \frac{1}{(0.62)^2}$$

$$= H_a = H - 1.89\, H = H_a - 0.89\, H$$

$$= 10.3 - 0.89 \times 6 = \mathbf{4.96\ m\ (absolute)}$$ **(Ans.)**

8.14. DISCHARGE THROUGH A CONVERGENT-DIVERGENT MOUTHPIECE

Fig. 8.25. shows a convergent-divergent mouthpiece (which converges upto vena-contracta and then diverges). In this mouthpiece since there is no sudden enlargement of the jet, therefore, the loss of energy due to sudden enlargement is eliminated. For this mouthpiece. $C_d = 1$.

Let, H = Head of liquid over the mouthpiece,

H_a = Atmospheric pressure head, and

H_c = Absolute pressure head at vena-contracta.

Applying Bernoulli's equation at the free water surface and section C-C, we get:

$$\frac{p}{w} + \frac{v^2}{2g} + z = \frac{p_c}{w} + \frac{v_c^2}{2g} + z_c$$

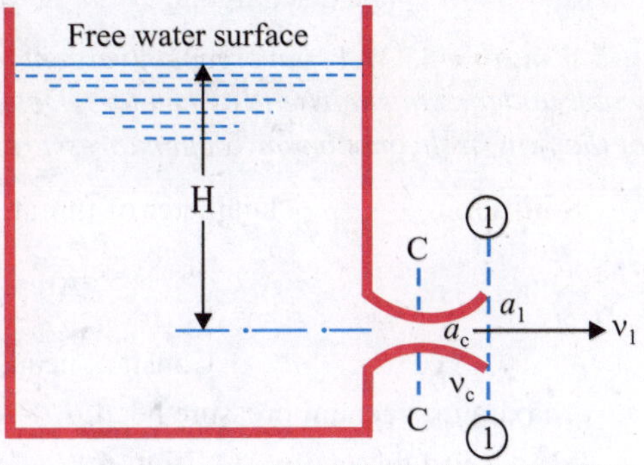

Fig. 8.25. Convergent-divergent mouthpiece.

Assuming that datum passes through the centre of the mouthpiece, we have:

$$\frac{p}{w} = H_a,\ v = 0,\ \frac{p_c}{w} = H,\ z_c = 0$$

$$\therefore \quad H_a + 0 + H = H_c + \frac{v_c^2}{2g} + 0 \qquad ...(i)$$

or, $$\frac{v_c^2}{2g} = H_a + H - H_c \qquad ...(ii)$$

or, $$v_c = \sqrt{2g\,(H_a + H - H_c)}$$

Now applying Bernoulli's equation at sections C-C and 1-1, we get:

$$\frac{p_c}{w} + \frac{v_c^2}{2g} + z_c = \frac{p_1}{w} + \frac{v_1^2}{2g} + z_1$$

But, $$z_c = z_1 \text{ and } \frac{p_1}{w} = H_a$$

$$\therefore \quad H_c + \frac{v_c^2}{2g} = H_a + \frac{v_1^2}{2g}$$

Also from eqn. (*i*), we have:

$$H_c + \frac{v_c^2}{2g} = H_a + H$$

$$\therefore \quad H_a + \frac{v_1^2}{2g} = H_a + H$$

$$\therefore \quad v_1 = \sqrt{2gH}$$

By continuity equation, we have: $a_c v_c = a_1 v_1$

or, $$\frac{a_1}{a_c} = \frac{v_c}{v_1} = \frac{\sqrt{2g(H_a + H - H_c)}}{\sqrt{2gH}} = \sqrt{\frac{H_a}{H} + 1 - \frac{H_c}{H}}$$

i.e. $$\frac{a_1}{a_c} = \sqrt{1 + \frac{H_a - H_c}{H}} \quad ...(8.19)$$

The discharge, $Q = a_c \times \sqrt{2gH}$ ...(8.20)

Example 8.31. *A convergent-divergent mouthpiece having throat diameter 40 mm is dischrging water under a constant head of 4 meters. Determine the maximum outlet diameter to avoid separation of the flow, if the maximum vacuum pressure is 8·5 meters of water. Find the discharge also.*

Solution. Diameter of throat, d_c = 40 mm = 0.04 m

$$\therefore \quad \text{Area, } a_c = \frac{\pi}{4} \times 0.04^2 = 0.001257 \text{ m}^2$$

Constant head, H = 4 m

Maximum vacuum pressure head, $H_a - H_c$ = 8·5 m

Maximum deameter at outlet, d_1:

Using the relation:

$$\frac{a_1}{a_c} = \sqrt{1 + \frac{H_a - H_c}{H}}$$ with usual notations, we have:

$$\frac{\frac{\pi}{4} \times d_1^2}{\frac{\pi}{4} \times d_c^2} = \sqrt{1 + \frac{8.5}{4}} = 1.767 \text{ or } \frac{d_1}{d_c} = 1.329$$

or, $$d_1 = 1.329 \times d_c = 1.329 \times 40 \simeq \textbf{53 mm (Ans.)}$$

Discharge, Q:

Using the relation,

$$Q = a_c \times \sqrt{2gH}$$ with usual notations, we get:

$$Q = 0.001257 \times \sqrt{2 \times 9.81 \times 4} = \mathbf{0.01113\ m^3/s}\ \textbf{(Ans.)}$$

Example 8.32. *The diametres of the throat and exit of a convergent-divergent mouthpiece are 40 mm and 80 mm respectively. It is fitted to the vertical side of a tank, containing water. If the maximum vacuum pressure is 7.5 m of water find the maximum head of water for steady flow. Take atmospheric pressure = 10.3 m of water.*

Solution. Dia. of throat, d_c = 40 mm = 0.04 m

Dia. of exit, d_1 = 80 mm = 0.08 m

Atmospheric pressure head, H_a = 10.3 m of water

The maximum vacuum pressure will be at *throat only,* therefore, pressure head at throat = 7.5 m

or, $H_c = H_a - 7.5$ (absolute)

$= 10.3 - 7.5 = 2.8$ m (absolute)

Maximum head of water:

Let the maximum head of water over mouthpiece = H metres of water

Using the relation:

$$\frac{a_1}{a_c} = \sqrt{1 + \frac{H_a - H_c}{H}} \qquad \text{...(Eqn.8.19)}$$

$$\frac{\frac{\pi}{4} d_1^2}{\frac{\pi}{4} d_c^2} = \sqrt{1 + \frac{10.3 - 2.8}{H}} \quad \text{or} \quad \frac{0.08^2}{0.04^2} = \sqrt{1 + \frac{7.5}{H}}$$

or, $$4 = \sqrt{1 + \frac{7.5}{H}} \quad \text{or } 16 = 1 + \frac{7.5}{H}$$

or, $\mathbf{H = 0.5\ m\ of\ water}$ **(Ans.)**

Example 8.33. *A convergent-divergent mouthpiece is fitted to the side of a tank. It is discharging 5.5 litres/sec. of water under a constant head of 2.0 m. If the head lost in the divergent portion is $\frac{1}{10}$th of the kinetic head at outlet and the separation pressure is 2.5 m, find the throat and exit diameters. Take atmospheric pressure = 10.3 m of water.*

Solution. Diascharge through the mouthpiece, Q = 5.5 litres/sec. = 0.0055 m^3/s

Constant head, H = 2.0 m

Head lost in divergent portion = 0.1 × kinetic head at outlet

H_c or H_{sep} = 2.5 m (abs.)

Atmospheric pressure head, = H_a = 10.3 m. of water

Diameter at throat; d_c:

Refer to Fig. 8.25. Applying Bernoulli's equation to the free water surface and throat section, we get:

$$\frac{p}{w} + \frac{v^2}{2g} + z = \frac{p_c}{w} + \frac{v_c^2}{2g} + z_c$$

Assuming that datum passes through the centre of the mouthpiece, we have:

$$H_a + 0 + H = H_c + \frac{v_c^2}{2g}$$

$$\therefore \quad \frac{v^2}{2g} = H_a + H - H_c = 10.3 + 2.0 - 2.5 = 9.8 \text{ m of water}$$

$$\therefore \quad v_c = \sqrt{2 \times 9.81 \times 9.8} = 13.866 \text{ m/s}$$

Now, $$Q = a_c \times v_c$$

or, $$0.0055 = \frac{\pi}{4} d_c^2 \times 13.866$$

or, $$d_c = \left(\frac{0.0055 \times 4}{\pi \times 13.866}\right)^{1/2} = 0.0225 \text{ m} = \mathbf{22.5\ mm\ (Ans.)}$$

Diameter at outlet, d_1:

Refer to Fig. 8.25. Applying Bernoulli's equation to the free water surface and outlet of mouthpiece, we get:

$$\frac{p}{w} + \frac{v^2}{2g} + z = \frac{p_1}{w} + \frac{v_1^2}{2g} + z_1 + h_L$$

$$H_a + 0 + H = H_a + \frac{v_1^2}{2g} + 0 + 0.1 \times \frac{v_1^2}{2g} \qquad \left(\because \frac{p_1}{w} = H_a\right)$$

$$\therefore \quad \text{H} = \frac{v_1^2}{2g} + 0.1 \times \frac{v_1^2}{2g} = 1.1 \frac{v_1^2}{2g}$$

or, $$v_1^2 = \frac{2gH}{1.1} = \frac{2 \times 9.81 \times 2}{1.1} = 35.673$$

$$\therefore \quad v_1 = 5.97 \text{ m/s}$$

Now, $$Q = a_1 v_1$$

or, $$0.0055 = \frac{\pi}{4} d_1^2 \times v_1 = \frac{\pi}{4} d_1^2 \times 5.97$$

$$\therefore \quad d_1 = \left(\frac{0.0055 \times 4}{\pi \times 5{\cdot}97}\right)^{1/2} = 0.03425 \text{ m} = \mathbf{34.25\ mm\ (Ans.)}$$

8.15. DISCHARGE THROUGH AN INTERNAL MOUTHPIECE (OR RE-ENTRANT OR BORDA'S MOUTHPIECE)

An **internal mouthpiece** is *short cylindrical tube attached to an orifice in such a way that it (tube) projects inwardly to a tank.* If the length of the tube is *equal to diameter,* the jet of liquid comes out from mouthpiece without touching the sides of the tube (Fig. 8.26); the mouthpiece is known as ***running free***. But *if the length of the tube is about 3 times its diameter*, the *jet comes out with its diameter equal to the diameter of mouthpiece at the outlet* (Fig. 8.27); *the mouthpiece is said to be* ***running full***.

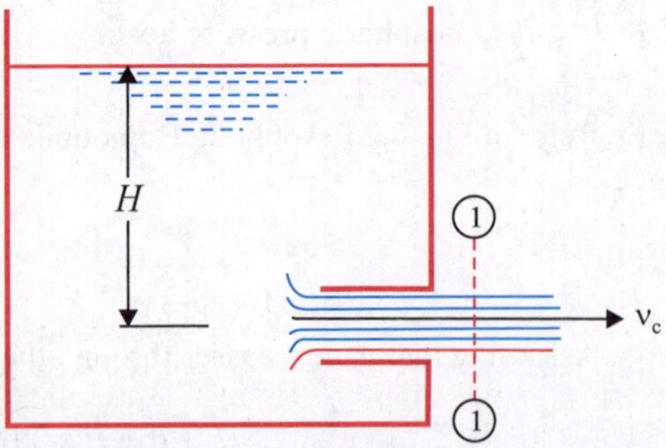

Fig. 8.26. Mouthpiece running free.

8.15.1. Mouthpiece Running Free

Consider a mouthpiece *running free* as shown in Fig. 8.26.

Let, H = Height of the liquid above the mouthpiece,

a = Area of orifice or mouthpiece,

a_c = Area of contracted jet, and

v_c = Velocity through mouthpiece.

$\therefore$ Pressure of the liquid on the mouthpiece, $p = wH$

and, force acting on the mouthpiece

$$= \text{Pressure} \times \text{area}$$

$$= wH \times a \qquad ...(i)$$

Mass of liquid flowing per second $= \dfrac{wa_c v_c}{g}$

Momentum of flowing liquid/sec.

$$= \text{Mass} \times \text{velocity} = \frac{wa_c v_c \times v_c}{g}$$

$$= \frac{wa_c v_c^2}{g} \qquad ...(ii)$$

Since the water is initially at rest, therefore initial momentum = 0

$$\therefore \quad \text{Change of momentum} = \frac{wa_c v_c^2}{g}$$

As per Newton's second law of motion, the force is equal to the rate of change of momentum. Therefore equating (*i*) and (*ii*), we get:

$$wH \times a = \frac{wa_c v_c^2}{g}$$

$$H \times a = \frac{a_c v_c^2}{g}$$

$$\frac{v_c^2}{2g} \times a = \frac{a_c v_c^2}{g} \qquad \left(\because H = \frac{v_c^2}{2g}\right)$$

$$\therefore \quad a = 2a_c \text{ or } \frac{a_c}{a} = \frac{1}{2} = 0.5$$

$$\therefore \quad \text{Co-efficient of contraction, } C_c = \frac{a_c}{a} = 0.5$$

Since there is no loss of head, co-efficient of velocity, $C_v = 1.0$

$$\therefore \quad \text{Co-efficient of discharge, } C_d = C_c \times C_v = 0.5 \times 1 = 0.5$$

$$\therefore \quad \text{Discharge, } Q = C_d \times a \times \sqrt{2gH}$$

$$= 0.5 \times a \times \sqrt{2gH} \qquad ...(8.21)$$

8.15.2 Mouthpiece Running Full

Consider a mouthpiece *running full* as shown in Fig. 8.27.

Let, a_c = Area at vena-contracta,

a = Area of orifice or mouthpiece,

v_c = Velocity of the liquid at *C-C* (vena-contracta),

v_1 = Velocity of the liquid at 1-1 (or outlet), and

H = Height of liquid above the mouthpiece.

Since the liquid is flowing continuosly, therefore from the continuity equation, we have:

$$a_c v_c = a_1 v_1 \qquad (a_1 = a)$$

$$v_c = \frac{a_1 v}{a_c} \qquad ...(i)$$

We know that the co-efficient of contraction for an internal mouthpiece is 0.5. Substituting this value of $C_c \left(= \frac{a_c}{a_1}\right) = 0.5$ in (*i*), we get:

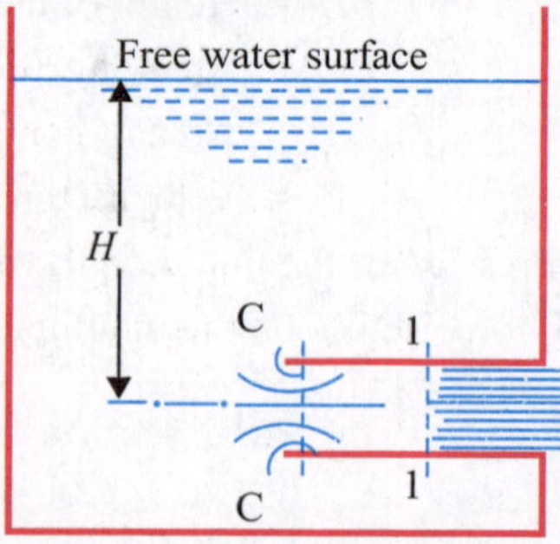

Fig. 8.27. Mouthpiece running full.

$$v_c = 2v_1 \qquad ...(ii)$$

The jet of liquid after passing through *C–C*, suddenly enlarges at section 1–1. Therefore, there will be loss of head due to sudden enlargement,

$$h_L = \frac{(v_c - v_1)^2}{2g} = \frac{(2v_1 - v_1)^2}{2g} \qquad (\because v_c = 2v_1)$$

$$= \frac{v_1^2}{2g}$$

Applying Bernoulli's equation to free water surface in tank and section 1–1 (or outlet),we get:

$$\frac{p}{w} + \frac{v^2}{2g} + z = \frac{p_1}{w} + \frac{v_1^2}{2g} + z_1 + h_L$$

Assuming datum line passing through the centre line of mouthpiece

$$0 + 0 + H = 0 + \frac{v_1^2}{2g} + 0 + \frac{v_1^2}{2g}$$

$$\therefore \qquad H = \frac{v_1^2}{2g} + \frac{v_1^2}{2g} = \frac{v_1^2}{g} \quad \text{or} \quad v_1 = \sqrt{gH}$$

Here v_1 is the actual velocity as losses have been taken into account.

But throretical velocity,

$$v_{th} = \sqrt{2gH}$$

$\therefore$ Co-efficient of velocity, $C_v = \frac{v_1}{v_{th}} = \frac{\sqrt{gH}}{\sqrt{2gH}} = \frac{1}{\sqrt{2}}$

As the area of the jet at outlet is equal to the area of the mouthpiece, hence co-efficient of contraction = 1

$$\therefore \qquad C_d = C_c \times C_v = 1 \times \frac{1}{\sqrt{2}} = \frac{1}{\sqrt{2}} = 0.707$$

$$\therefore \qquad \text{Discharge, } Q = C_d \times a \times \sqrt{2gH} = 0.707 \times a \times \sqrt{2gH} \qquad ...(8.22)$$

Example 8.34. *An internal mouthpiece of 100 mm diameter is discharging water under a constant head of 5 m. Find the discharge through mouthpiece, when :*

(*i*) *The mouthpiece is running free, and*

(*ii*) *The mouthpiece is running full.*

Solution. Dia. of mouthpiece, $d = 100 \text{ mm} = 0{\cdot}1 \text{ m}$

$\therefore$ Area, $a = \frac{\pi}{4} \times 0.1^2 = 0.00785 \text{ m}^2$

Constant head, $H = 5$ m

Discharge, Q:

(i) When mouthpiece is running free:

Using the relation:

$$Q = 0.5 \times a \times \sqrt{2gH} \quad \text{...[Eqn. (8.21)]}$$

$$= 0.5 \times 0.00785 \times \sqrt{2 \times 9.81 \times 5}$$

$$= \mathbf{0{\cdot}0388 \text{ m}^3/\text{s}} \text{ (Ans.)}$$

(ii) When mouthpiece is running full:

Using the relation:

$$Q = 0.707 \times a \times \sqrt{2gH} \quad \text{...[Eqn. (8.22)]}$$

$$= 0.707 \times 0.00785 \times \sqrt{2 \times 9.81 \times 5}$$

$$= \mathbf{0.0549 \text{ m}^3/\text{s}} \text{ (Ans.)}$$

Example 8.35. *An external mouthpiece converges from inlet up to the vena-contracta to the shape of the jet and then diverges gradually. The diameter at vena-contracta is 20 mm and the head over the centre of the mouthpiece is 1·44 m. The head loss in the contraction may be taken as 1% and that in the divergent portion 5% of the total energy head before the inlet. What is the maximun discharge that can be drawn through the outlet and what should be the corresponding diameter at the outlet ?*

Assume that the pressure in the system may be permitted to fall upto 8 m below atmosphere, the liquid conveyed being water. **[UPSC Exam, Fluid Mech.]**

Solution. The dia. of mouthpiece at vena-contracta,

$d_c = 20 \text{ mm} = 0.02 \text{ m}$

$\therefore$ Area, $a_c = \frac{\pi}{4} \times 0.02^2 = 3.141 \times 10^{-4} \text{ m}^2$

Head over the centre of the mouthpiece, $H = 1.44$ m

Head loss in the contraction

$$= \frac{1}{100} \times H = \frac{1}{100} \times 1.44 = 0.0144 \text{ m}$$

Head loss in the divergent portion

$$= \frac{5}{100} H = \frac{5}{100} \times 1.44 = 0.072 \text{ m}$$

Head at the vena-contracta, $H_c = -8$ m

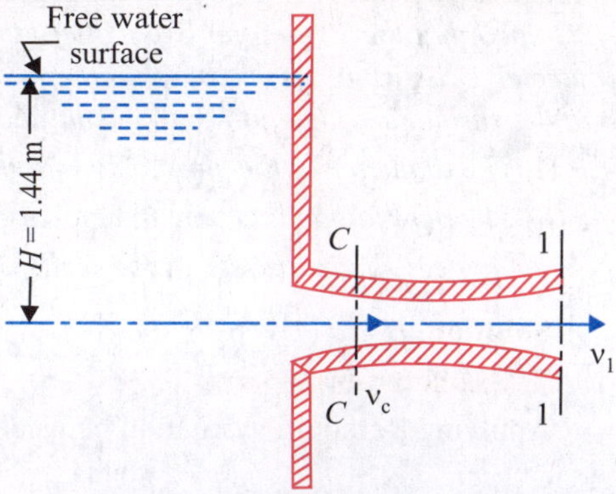

Fig. 8.28

Maximum discharge, Q:

Applying Bernoulli's equation at the free water surface and section *C-C.*,we get:

$$\frac{p}{w} + \frac{v^2}{2g} + z = \frac{p_c}{w} + \frac{v_c^2}{2g} + z_c + \text{head loss in the contraction}$$

Assuming that datum passes through the centre of the mouthpiece, we have:

$$0 + 0 + 1.44 = -8.0 + \frac{v_c^2}{2g} + 0 + 0.0144$$

or, $$\frac{v_c^2}{2g} = 1.44 + 8 - 0.0144 = 9.426$$

∴ $$v_c = (2 \times 9.81 \times 9.426)^{1/2} = 13.6 \text{ m/s.}$$

Maximum discharge, $$Q = a_c \cdot v_c$$

$$= 3.141 \times 10^{-4} \times 13.6 = 4.272 \times 10^{-3} \text{ m}^3\text{/s} \quad \text{or} \quad \mathbf{4.272 \text{ litres/s (Ans.)}}$$

Diameter at the outlet, d_1:

Now applying Bernoulli's equation at the free water surface and the exit end of the mouthpiece, we get:

$$\frac{p}{w} + \frac{v^2}{2g} + z = \frac{p_1}{w} + \frac{v_1^2}{2g} + z_1 + \text{total head loss in the contraction and divergent portion}$$

or, $$0 + 0 + 1.44 = 0 + \frac{v_1^2}{2g} + 0 + (0.0144 + 0.072)$$

∴ $$\frac{v_1^2}{2g} = 1.44 - (0.0144 + 0.072) = 1.354$$

or $$v_1 = (2 \times 9.81 \times 1.354)^{1/2} = 5.15 \text{ m/s}$$

Also, Discharge $Q = a_1 \cdot v_1$ or $4.27 \times 10^{-3} = \frac{\pi}{4} \times d_1^2 \times 5.15$

∴ $$d_1 = \left(\frac{4.272 \times 10^{-3} \times 4}{\pi \times 5.15}\right)^{1/2} = 0.0325 \text{ m} = \mathbf{32.5 \text{ mm (Ans.)}}$$

Example 8.36. *A streamlined nozzle of diameter d is supplied at constant head, the magnitude of the head being larger compared to d. The nozzle discharges directly into the atmoshphere and is so shaped that the issuing jet is parallel at the nozzle exit. To increase the flow rate a shroud of the diameter D is firmly secured to the nozzle as shown in Fig. 8·29 .The jet expands to fill the shroud and the shroud is long enough to ensure that the flow leaving is steady and parallel. Determine:*

(i) *The diameter of the shroud so that the flow rate is maximised, and*

(ii) *The percentage increase in discharge.*

Neglect shear stresses at the walls of the shroud. **[UPSC Fluid Mech. and FluidM/C.]**

Solution. $H > d$ (given).

(i)* Diameter of the shroud, *D

Applying Bernoulli's equation between section (1) and (2), we get:

$$\frac{p_1}{w} + \frac{v_1^2}{2g} + z_1 = \frac{p_2}{w} + \frac{v_2^2}{2g} + z_2 + \text{loss due to sudden expansion}$$

$$\frac{p_1}{w} + \frac{v_1^2}{2g} = 0 + \frac{v_2^2}{2g} + \frac{(v_1 - v_2)^2}{2g} \qquad (\because z_2 = z_2) \quad ...(i)$$

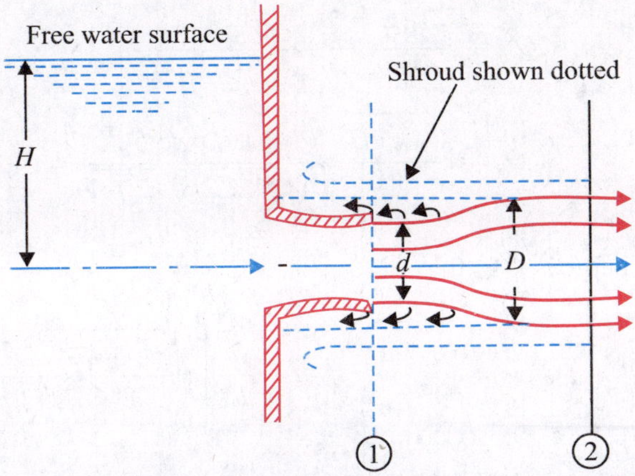

Fig. 8.29

Now, applying Bernoulli's equation between free water surface and section (1), we get:

$$\frac{p}{w} + \frac{v^2}{2g} + z = \frac{p_1}{w} + \frac{v_1^2}{2g} + z_1$$

$$0 + 0 + H = \frac{p_1}{w} + \frac{v_1^2}{2g} + 0$$

or, $$H = \frac{p_1}{w} + \frac{v_1^2}{2g} \quad \text{...}(ii)$$

From continuity equation, we have:

$$Q = a_1 v_1 = a_2 v_2$$

or, $$Q = \frac{\pi}{4} \times d^2 \times v_1 = \frac{\pi}{4} \times D^2 \times v_2 \quad \text{...}(iii)$$

Eliminating p_1 between eqns. (*i*) and (*ii*) and using eqn. (*iii*), we get:

$$H = \frac{v_2^2}{2g} + \frac{(v_1 - v_2)^2}{2g}$$

$$= \frac{1}{2g}\left(\frac{4Q}{\pi D^2}\right) + \frac{1}{2g}\left(\frac{4Q}{\pi d^2} - \frac{4Q}{\pi D^2}\right)^2$$

$$= \frac{8Q^2}{\pi^2 g}\left[\frac{1}{D^4} + \left(\frac{1}{d^2} - \frac{1}{D^2}\right)^2\right]$$

$$= \frac{8Q^2}{\pi^2 g}\left[\frac{1}{D^4} + \frac{1}{d^4} + \frac{1}{D^4} - \frac{2}{D^2 d^2}\right]$$

$$= \frac{8Q^2}{\pi^2 g}\left[\frac{1}{D^4} + \frac{1}{d^4} - \frac{2}{D^2 d^2}\right] = \frac{8Q^2}{\pi^2 g}\left[\frac{2d^4 + D^4 - 2D^2 d^2}{D^4 d^4}\right]$$

$$= \frac{8Q^2}{\pi^2 g}\left[\frac{d^4 + d^4 + D^4 - 2D^2 d^2}{D^4 d^4}\right] = \frac{8Q^2}{\pi^2 g}\left[\frac{d^4 + (D^2 - d^2)^2}{D^4 d^4}\right]$$

or, $$Q^2 = \frac{\pi^2 gH}{8}\left[\frac{D^4 d^4}{d^4 + (D^2 - d^2)^2}\right]$$

$\therefore$ $$Q = \frac{\sqrt{\pi^2 gH}}{8} \times \frac{D^2 d^2}{\sqrt{d^4 + (D^2 - d^2)^2}} \quad \text{...}(iv)$$

For maximum Discharge, $\frac{dQ}{dD} = 0$

or, $$\frac{d}{dD}\left[\sqrt{\frac{\pi^2 gH}{8}} \times \frac{D^2 d^2}{\sqrt{d^4 + (D^2 - d^2)^2}}\right] = 0$$

or, $$\frac{1}{\sqrt{d^4 + (D^2 - d^2)^2}} \times (2Dd^2) + D^2 d^2\left[-\frac{1}{2}\{d^4 + (D^2 - d^2)^2\}^{-3/2}\right] 2(D^2 - d^2)\cdot 2D = 0$$

or, $$\frac{1}{\sqrt{d^4 + (D^2 - d^2)^2}} \times 2d^2 - 2D^2 d^2\left[\frac{1}{\left\{d^4 + (D^2 - d^2)^2\right\}^{3/2}}\right] \times (D^2 - d^2) = 0$$

or, $$2d^2 - 2D^2 d^2 (D^2 - d^2) \times \frac{1}{\left[d^4 + (D^2 - d^2)^2\right]} = 0$$

or, $$2d^2[d^4 + (D^2 - d^2)^2] - 2D^2 d^2 (D^2 - d^2) = 0$$

or, $$d^4 + (D^2 - d^2)^2 - D^2(D^2 - d^2) = 0$$

or, $$d^4 + (D^2 - d^2)^2 = D^2(D^2 - d^2)$$

or, $$d^4 + D^4 + d^4 - 2D^2 d^2 = D^4 - D^2 d^2$$

or, $$2d^4 = D^2 d^2$$

or, $$\mathbf{D} = \sqrt{2}\mathbf{d} \textbf{ (Ans.)}$$

***(ii)* Percentage increase in discharge:**

The maximum discharge,

$$Q_{max} = \sqrt{\frac{\pi^2 gH}{8}} \times \frac{(\sqrt{2}d)^2 d^2}{\sqrt{d^4 + (2d^2 - d^2)^2}}$$ [Substituting $D = \sqrt{2}\,d$ in eqn.(*iv*)]

$$= \frac{\pi d^2}{2\sqrt{2}}\sqrt{2gH}$$

$\therefore$ Percentage increase in discharge

$$= \frac{Q_{max} - Q}{Q} \times 100 = \frac{\frac{\pi d^2}{2\sqrt{2}}\sqrt{2gH} - \frac{\pi d^2}{4}\sqrt{2gH}}{\frac{\pi d^2}{4}\sqrt{2gH}} \times 100$$

$$= \left(\sqrt{2} - 1\right) \times 100 = \mathbf{41.42\%} \textbf{ (Ans.)}$$

HIGHLIGHTS

1. An *orifice* is an opening in the wall or base of a vessel through which the fluid flows. The top edge of the orifice is always *below* the free surface.
2. A *mouthpiece* in an attachment in the form of a small tube or pipe fixed to the orifice (the length of pipe extension is usually 2 to 3 times the orifice diameter) and is used to increase the amount of discharge.
3. Theoretical velocity of jet of water from orifice is given as: $V = \sqrt{2gH}$
4. There are three important hydraulic co-efficients namely

   (*i*) Co-efficient of contraction, $C_c = \dfrac{\text{Area of jet at vena-contracta}}{\text{Area of orifice}}$

   (*ii*) Co-efficient of velocity, $C_v = \dfrac{\text{Actual velocity at vena-contracta}}{\text{Theoretical velocity}}$

   $$= \frac{x}{\sqrt{4yH}}.$$

   (where, x and y are the co-ordinates of any point of jet of water from vena-contracta)

   (*iii*) Co-efficient of discharge, $C_d = \dfrac{\text{Actual discharge}}{\text{Theoretical discharge}} = C_c \times C_v$

5. Discharge through a *large rectangular orifice*,

   $$Q = \frac{2}{3} C_d \times b \times \sqrt{2g}\left[H_2^{3/2} - H_1^{3/2}\right]$$

   where, C_d = Discharge co-efficient for the orifice,
   b = Width of orifice,
   H_1 = Height of liquid above top adge of orifice, and
   H_2 = Height of liquid above bottom edge of orifice.

   (A large orifice is one, where the head of liquid above the centre of orifice is *less* than 5 times the depth of orifice)

6. Discharge through *fully submerged orifice*,

   $$Q = C_d \times b \times (H_2 - H_1) \times \sqrt{2gH}$$

   where, C_d = Discharge co-efficient for the orifice,
   b = Width of orifice,
   H_2 = Height of liquid above bottom edge of orifice on upstream side
   H_1 = Height of liquid above top edge of orifice on upstream side, and
   H = Difference of liquid levels on both sides of the orifice.

7. Discharge through *partially submerged orifice*,

   $$Q = C_d . b. (H_2 - H)\sqrt{2gH} + \frac{2}{3} C_d . b. \sqrt{2g}\,(H^{3/2} - H_1^{3/2})$$

   where C_d, b, H, H_1, H_2 have usual meanings.

8. Time of emptying a tank through an orifice at its bottom,

$$T = \frac{2A(\sqrt{H_1} - \sqrt{H_2})}{C_d.a.\sqrt{2g}}$$

where, A = Area of tank,
a = Area of orifice,
H_1 = Initial height of liquid in tank,
H_2 = Final height of liquid in tank, and
C_d = Co-efficent of orifice.

If the tank is to be completely emptied, then:

$$T = \frac{2A\sqrt{H}}{C_d.a.\sqrt{2g}}$$

9. Time of emptying a hemispherical tank by an orifice fitted at its bottom,

$$T = \frac{\pi}{C_d.a.\sqrt{2g}}\left[\frac{4}{3}R(H_1^{3/2} - H_2^{3/2}) - \frac{2}{5}(H_1^{5/2} - H_2^{5/2})\right]$$

and for completely emptying the tank,

$$T = \frac{\pi}{C_d.a.\sqrt{2g}}\left[\frac{4}{3}R\,H_1^{3/2} - \frac{2}{5}H_1^{5/2}\right]$$

where, a = Area of orifice,
R = Radius of the hemispherical tank,
H_1 = Initial height of liquid,
H_2 = Final height of liquid, and
C_d = Co-efficient of discharge.

10. Time of emptying a circular horizontal tank by an orifice at the bottom of the tank,

$$T = \frac{4L}{3\,C_d.a.\sqrt{2g}}\left[(2R - H_2^{3/2}) - (2R - H_1)^{3/2}\right]$$

and for completely emptying the tank,

$$T = \frac{4L}{3\,C_d.a.\sqrt{2g}}\left[(2R)^{3/2} - (2R - H_1)^{3/2}\right]$$

where, L = length of horizontal tank.

11. *Co-efficient of discharge* C_d

(*i*) External mouthpiece = 0.855

(*ii*) Internal mouthpiece; running full, = 0.707
running free = 0.50

(*iii*) Convergent - divergent mouthpiece = 1.0

12. Absolute pressure head, for an external mouthpiece, at vena-contracta,

$$H_c = H_a - 0.89\,H$$

where, H_a = Atmospheric pressure head = 10.3 m of water, and
H = Head of liquid above the mouthpiece.

13. In case of a convergent-divergent mouthpiece, the ratio of areas at outlet and at vena-contracta is given by:

$$\frac{a_1}{a_c} = \sqrt{1 + \frac{H_a - H_c}{H}}$$

where, a_1 = Area of mouthpiece at outlet,
a_c = Area of mouthpiece at vena-contracta,
H_a = Atmospheric pressure head,
H_c = Absolute pressure head at vena-contracta, and
H = Height of liquid above mouthpiece.

OBJECTIVE TYPE QUESTIONS

Fill in the Blanks/Choose the Correct Answer

1. An ...... is an opening in the wall or base of a vessel through which the fluid flows.

2. The top edge of the orifice is always below/above the free surface.

3. A mouthpiece is used to decrease /increase the amount of discharge.

4. An orifice is said to be submerged/discharging free when it discharges into another liquid.

5. In orifice it is convenient to work in terms of gauge/absolute pressures.

6. Co-efficient of contraction (C_c) is equal to
(*a*) a_c/a (*b*) a/a_c
(*c*) $a \times a_c$ (*d*) $\sqrt{a_c / a}$.

7. For sharp-edged orifices the value of C_v is taken as,
(*a*) 0.82 (*b*) 0.84
(*c*) 0.9 (*d*) 0.98.

8. The value of C_d varies from,
(*a*) 0.2 to 0.3 (*b*) 0.3 to 0.4
(*c*) 0.4 to 0.5 (*d*) 0.6 to 0.65.

9. The discharge through a large rectangular orifice is given by

(*a*) $\frac{1}{3} C_d . b . \sqrt{2g} \, (\sqrt{H_2} - \sqrt{H_1})$

(*b*) $\frac{2}{3} C_d . b . 2g \, (\sqrt{H_2} - \sqrt{H_1})$

(*c*) $\frac{2}{3} C_d . b . \sqrt{2g} (H_2^{3/2} - H_1^{3/2})$

(*d*) $\frac{2}{3} C_d . \sqrt{b} . 2g \, (\sqrt{H_2} - \sqrt{H_1})$.

10. The discharge through a fully submerged orifice is given by,
(*a*) $C_d \cdot b \cdot (H_2 - H_1) \times 2gH$
(*b*) $C_d . \sqrt{b} . (H_2 - H_1) \times \sqrt{2gH}$
(*c*) $C_d . b^2 \, (H_2 - H_1) \times \sqrt{2gH}$
(*d*) $C_d . b . (H_2 - H_1) \times \sqrt{2gH}$.

11. Time of emptying a tank through an orifice at its bottom is given by,
(*a*) $\frac{2A\sqrt{H_1}}{C_d . a^2 . 2g}$ (*b*) $\frac{2A\sqrt{H_1}}{C_d . a . \sqrt{2g}}$
(*c*) $\frac{A\sqrt{H_1}}{C_d . a \sqrt{2g}}$ (*d*) $\frac{4A\sqrt{H_1}}{C_d . a \sqrt{2g}}$.

12. Discharge through an internal mouthpiece running free is given by
(*a*) $0.5 \times a \times \sqrt{2gH}$
(*b*) $0.4 \times a^2 \times \sqrt{2gH}$
(*c*) $0.707 \times a \times \sqrt{2gH}$
(*d*) $0.3 \times a^2 \times \sqrt{2gH}$.

ANSWERS

1. Orifice	**2.** Below	**3.** Increase	**4.** Submerged	**5.** Gauge	**6.** (*a*)
7. (*d*)	**8.** (*d*)	**9.** (*c*)	**10.** (*d*)	**11.** (*b*)	**12.** (*a*).

THEORETICAL QUESTIONS

1. What is an orifice? How are the orifices classified ?
2. What is a mouthpiece ?
3. What is Torricelli's theorem?
4. Name and explain briefly the hydraulic co-efficients.
5. Derive the expression $C_d = C_c \times C_v$.
6. How is vena contracta defined ?
7. How are hydraulic co-efficients determined experimentally ?
8. What is the difference between a small and a large orifice ?
9. Obtain an expression for discharge through a large orifice.
10. State the difference between a wholly submerged orifice and a partially submerged orifice.
11. Derive an expression for discharge through fully submerged orifice.
12. Obtain an expression for time of emptying a tank through an orifice at its bottom.
13. Derive an expression for time of emptying a circular hemispherical tank.
14. Obtain an expression for time of emptying a circular horizontal tank.
15. How are mouthpieces classified ?
16. Obtain an expression for absolute pressure head at vena contracta for an external mouthpiece.
17. Derive an experssion for the ratio of diameters at outlet and at vena-contracta for a convergent-divergent mouthpiece in terms of absolute pressure head at vena-contracta, head of liquid above mouthpiece and atmospheric pressure head.

UNSOLVED EXAMPLES

ORIFICES

1. An orifice 60 mm in diameter is discharging water under a head of 9 metres. If $C_d = 0.6$ and $C_v = 0.9$ find :
   (*i*) Actual discharge, and
   (*ii*) Actual velocity of the jet at vena-contracta.
   [Ans. (*i*) 0.02254 m^3/s, (*ii*) 11.26 m/s]
2. The head of water over the centre of an orifice of diameter 20 mm is 1 m. The actual discharge through the orifice is 0·85 litres/s. Find the co-efficient of discharge. **[Ans.** 0.61]
3. A jet of water issues from a circular orifice of 25 mm diameter, under a constant head of 1metre. It falls 35 mm vertically down and strikes the ground at a distance of 350 mm from the center of the vena contracta. If the discharge through the jet is 1.35 litres/s find:
   (*i*) Co-efficient of discharge;
   (*ii*) Co-efficient of velocity;
   (*iii*) Co-efficient of contraction.
   [Ans. (*i*) 0.625, (*ii*) 0.935. (*iii*) 0.668]
4. The water is coming out of an orifice of diameter 100 mm under a head of 10 m. It is collected in a circular tank of diameter 1.5 m. The rise of water level in this tank is 1.0 m. in 25 seconds. Also the co-ordinates of a point on the jet, measured from venacontracta are 4.3 m horizontal and 0.5 m vertical. Find the hydraulic co-efficients (*i.e.*co-efficient of discharge, co-efficient of velocity and co-efficient of contraction).
   [Ans. 0.643; 0.96; 0.669]
5. The head of water over an orifice of diameter 100 mm is 10 m The water coming out from orifice is collected in circular tank of diameter 1·5 m. The rise of water level in this tank is 1·0 m in 25 seconds. Find the co-efficient of discharge. **[Ans.** 0·643]
6. An orifice, 60 mm in diameter, is discharging water under a head of 9 metres. Calculate the discharge and actual velocity of the jet at vena contracta, if $C_d = 0{\cdot}6$ and $C_v = 0{\cdot}9$.
   [Ans. 0·02254 m^3/s; 11·96 m/s]
7. A tank has two identical orifices in one of its vertical sides. The upper orifice is 2 metres below the water surface. and the lower one is 4 metres below the water surface. If the value of C_v for each orifice is 0·9, find the point of intersection of the two jets. **[Ans.** 5·1m]
8. A closed tank has water to a height of 0·9 m, above 15 mm diameter sharp-edged orifice privided at the bottom of the tank. To what pressure air must be pumped into the tank above water if the discharge is to be 1·5 litres/sec. ?
   Take discharge co-efficient, $C_d = 0{\cdot}62$ for the orifice. **[Ans.** 91·25 kN/m^2]
9. A 100 mm diameter orifice discharges 45 litres/sec. of water under a head of 2.75 metres. A flat plate held normal to the jet just downstream from the vena contracta requires a force of 310 N to resist the impact of jet. Find C_c,C_v,C_d.
   [Ans. 0.84, 0.927, 0.78]
10. A rectangular orifice 1.5 m wide and 1.0 m deep is discharging water from a tank. If the water level in the tank is 3.0 m above the top edge

of the orifice, find the discharge through the orifice. Take $C_d = 0.6$ **[Ans.** 7.45 m^3/s]

11. A submerged orifice 1 meter wide has height of water from the bottom and top of the orifice as 2.25 metres respectively. Find the discharge through the orifice, if the difference of water levles on both the sides of the orifice be 375 mm. Take $C_d = 0.62$ **[Ans.** 0.42m^3/s]

12. An orifice, in one side of a large tank, is rectangular is shape 2 m broad and 1 m deep. The water level on one side of the orifice is 4 m above its top edge. The water level on the other side of the orifice is 0.5 m below its top edge. Calculate the discharge through the orifice per second, if $C_d = 0.625$ **[Ans.** 11.58 m^3/s]

13. A circular tank, of diameter 4 m contains water upto a height of 5 m. The tank is provided with an orifice if diameter 0.5 m at the bottom. Find the time taken by water,

(*i*) to fall from 5 m to 2 m, and

(*ii*) for completely emptying the tank.

Take $C_d = 0.6$.**[Ans.** (*i*)39.6 s, (*ii*) 107.7s]

14. A 1.25 m diameter circular tank contains water upto a height of 5 m . At the bottom of the tank an orifice of 50 mm is provided. Find the height of water above the orifice after 1.5 minutes. Take $C_d = 0.62$. **[Ans.** 4.154 m]

15. A hemispherical cistern of 6 m radius is full of water. It is fitted with a 75 mm diameter sharp edged orifice at the bottom. Calculate the time required to lower the level in the cistern by 2 meters. Assume co-efficient of discharge for the orifice as 0.6. **[Ans.** 2 h 18 min 42 s]

16. A tank has an upper cylindrical portion of 5 m diameter and 4 m high with hemispherical base. Find the time required to empty it through an orifice of 200 mm diameter at its bottom, if the tank is intially full of water. Take $C_d = 0.6$ for the orifice. **[Ans.** 1078 s]

17. A horizontal boiler 5 m long and 3 m in diameter is half full of water. It is provided with a 100 mm diameter orifice at its bottom. Calculate the time taken to empty the drum.

Take $C_d = 0.6$ **[Ans.** 17 min 50 sec.]

18. A 30 m long and 10 m wide swimming pool has vertical sides and bottom at a slope. The depth of water at the shallow and deep sides are 2 m and 5 m respectively. Two outlets, each 0.3 m diameter, have been provided at each of the deep and shallow ends. Calculate the time taken to empty the pool if both the outlets are kept open. Take $C_d = 0.62$ for each opening. **[Ans.** 2871 s]

19. A 750 mm diameter vertical cylindrical tank contains water to a depth of 2.5 m. There are two orifices in the tank; one at the bottom and the other in one of the vertical sides at a height of 1.5 m above the bottom, If the area of each orifice is 15cm^2 and discharge co-efficient 0.6, calculate the time required to empty the tank.

[Ans. 326.3 s]

MOUTHPIECES

20. Find the discharge from a 100 mm diameter external mouthpiece, fitted to a side of a vessel, if the head over the mouthpiece is 4 m.

[Ans. 0.595 m^3/s]

21. An external cylindrical mouthpiece of diameter 150 mm is discharging water under a constant head of 6 m. If C_c for vena-contracta = 0.62,C_d = 0.855 and atmospheric pressure head = 10.3 m of water, find:

(*i*) Discharge through the mouthpiece, and

(*ii*) Absolute pressure head of water at vena contracta.

[Ans. (*i*) 0.1639 m^3/s, (*ii*) 496 m (abs.)]

22. A convergent-divergent mouthpiece having throat diameter of 40 mm is discharging water under a constant head of 2 m. Determine the maximum outlet diameter for maximum discharge. Find the maximum discharge also. Take H_a = 10.3 m of water and H_{sep} = 2.5 m absolute.

[Ans. 59.5 mm; 0.00787 m^3/s]

23. An internal mouthpiece of 80 mm diameter is discharging under a constant head of 8 m. Find the discharge through the mouthpiece, when (*i*) the mouthpiece is running free and (*ii*) the mouthpiece is running full.

[Ans. (*i*) 0.02226 m^3/s, (*ii*) 0.03147 m^3/s]

24. A convergent-divergent mouthpiece is fitted into the vertical side of a tank containing water. Assumming that there are no losses in the convergent part of the mouthpiece, and that the losses in the divergent part are equivalent to 0.2 times the velocity head at exit and that the maximum absolute pressure head at the throat is 2.44 m of water for a barometric pressure of 760 mm of mercury, determine the throat and exit diameters of the mouthpiece when the discharge is 4.25 lit./sec. for a head of 1.52 metres. **[UPSC Exams.]**

[Ans. 20 mm, 33 mm]

Chapter 9

FLOW OVER NOTCHES AND WEIRS

9.1. DEFINITIONS

Notch. A **notch** *may be defined as an opening provided in the side of a tank or vessel such that the liquid surface in the tank is below the top edge of the opening*. A notch may be regarded as an *orifice* with the water surface *below its upper edge*. It is generally made of *metallic plate. It is used for measuring the rate of flow of a liquid through a small channel or a tank.*

Weir. A **weir** *may be defined as any regular obstruction in an open stream over which the flow takes place*. It is made of *masonry or concrete*. The conditions of flow in the case of a weir are practically the same as those of a rectangular notch. That is why, a notch is sometimes called as a weir and vice versa.

Weirs may be used for *measuring the rate of flow of water in rivers or streams.*

— *Nappe or vein*. The sheet of water flowing through a notch or over a weir is known as the *nappe* or *vein*.

— *Sill or crest*. The top of the weir over which the water flows is known as the *sill* or *crest*.

Note. The main difference between a notch and a weir is that the *notch is of small size*, but the weir is of a *bigger one*. Moreover a notch is usually made in a *plate*, whereas a weir is usually made of *masonry or concrete*.

9.2. TYPES/CLASSIFICATION OF NOTCHES AND WEIRS

9·2·1 Types of Notches

There are several types of notches, depending upon their shapes. However, the following are important from subject point of view:

1. Rectangular notch,
2. Triangular notch,
3. Trapezoidal notch, and
4. Stepped notch.

9·2·2 Types of Weirs

There are several types of weirs depending upon their shapes, nature of discharge, width of crest or nature of crest. However, the following are important from subject point of view:

1. *According to shape:*
   (*i*) Rectangular weir, and
   (*ii*) Cippoletti weir.
2. *According to nature of discharge:*
   (*i*) Ordinary weir, and
   (*ii*) Submerged or drowned weir.
3. *According to the width of crest:*
   (*i*) Narrow-crested weir, and
   (*ii*) Broad-crested weir.
4. *According to the nature of crest:*
   (*i*) Sharp-crested weir, and
   (*ii*) Ogee weir.

9.3. DISCHARGE OVER A RECTANGULAR NOTCH OR WEIR

Consider a rectangular notch or weir provided in a channel carrying water as shown in Fig. 9·1.

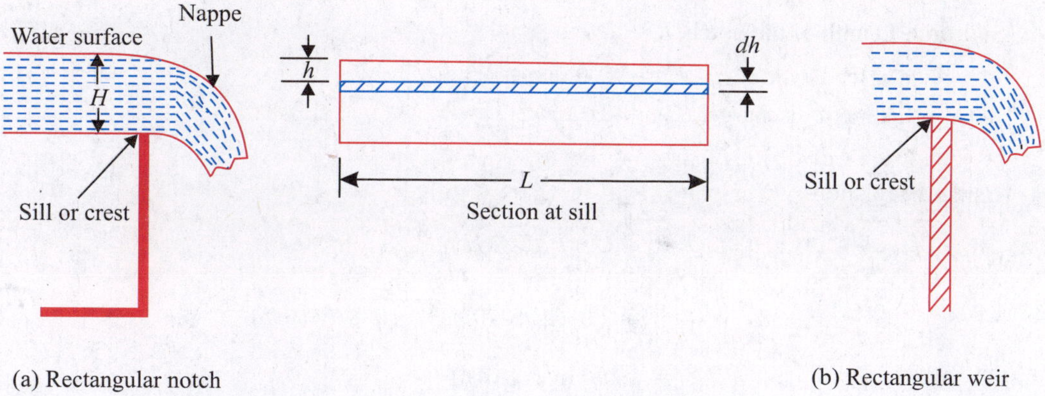

Fig. 9.1. Rectangular notch and weir.

Let, H = Height of water above sill of the notch,
L = Length of notch or weir, and
C_d = Co-efficient of discharge.

Let us consider a horizontal strip of water of thickness dh at a depth h from the water level as shown in Fig. 9·1.

$$\text{Area of strip} = L \times dh$$

Theoretical velocity of water flowing through strip

$$= \sqrt{2gh}$$

The discharge through the strip,

$$dQ = C_d \times \text{area of strip} \times \text{theoretical velocity}$$

$$= C_d \times L \times dh \times \sqrt{2gh} \qquad ...(i)$$

The total discharge, over the whole notch, may be found out by integrating the above equation within the limits 0 and H.

$$\therefore \qquad Q = \int_0^H C_d \times L \times \sqrt{2gh} \times dh$$

$$= C_d \times L \times \sqrt{2g} \int_0^H (h)^{1/2}\, dh$$

$$= C_d \times L \times \sqrt{2g} \left[\frac{h^{1/2+1}}{\frac{1}{2}+1}\right]_0^H$$

$$= C_d \times L \times \sqrt{2g} \left[\frac{h^{3/2}}{3/2}\right]_0^H$$

$$= 2/3 \times C_d \times L \times \sqrt{2g}\, (H)^{3/2}$$

i.e.

$$Q = \frac{2}{3} C_d \,.\, L \sqrt{2g}\, (H)^{3/2} \qquad ...(9\cdot 1)$$

Note. The expression for discharge over a rectangular notch or weir is *same*.

Example. 9.1. *A rectangular notch 2·0 m wide has a constant head of 500 mm. Find the discharge over the notch, if co-efficient of discharge for the notch is 0·62.*

Solution. Length of the notch, L = 2·0 m

Head over notch, H = 500 mm = 0·5 m

Co-efficient of discharge, C_d = 0·62

Discharge, Q:

Using the relation,

$$Q = \frac{2}{3} C_d \,.\, L\sqrt{2g}\, (H)^{3/2}$$

$$= \frac{2}{3} \times 0\cdot 62 \times 2\cdot 0 \times \sqrt{2 \times 9\cdot 81} \times (0\cdot 5)^{3/2}$$

$$= \mathbf{1\cdot 294\ m^3/s}$$ **(Ans.)**

Example. 9.2. *A rectangular notch has a discharge of 0·24 m³/s, when head of water is 800 mm. Find the length of the notch. Assume C_d = 0·6.*

Solution. Discharge, Q = 0·24 m^3/s

Head over notch, H = 800 mm = 0·8 m

Co-efficient of discharge, C_d = 0·6

Length of the notch, L:

Using the relation :

$$Q = \frac{2}{3} C_d \,.\, L \times \sqrt{2g}\, (H)^{3/2}$$

$$0\cdot 24 = \frac{2}{3} \times 0\cdot 6 \times L \times \sqrt{2 \times 9\cdot 81}\, (0\cdot 8)^{3/2} = 1\cdot 267\, L$$

$$\therefore \qquad L = \frac{0\cdot 24}{1\cdot 267} = 0\cdot 189 \text{ m or } 189 \text{ mm}$$

i.e. **L = 189 mm (Ans.)**

9.4. DISCHARGE OVER A TRIANGULAR NOTCH OR WEIR

Refer to Fig. 9·2. *A* triangular notch is also called a *V*-notch.

Let, H = Head of water above the apex of the notch,

θ = Angle of the notch, and

C_d = Co-efficient of discharge.

Consider a horizontal strip of water of thickness *dh*, and at a depth *h* from the water surface as shown in Fig. 9·2.

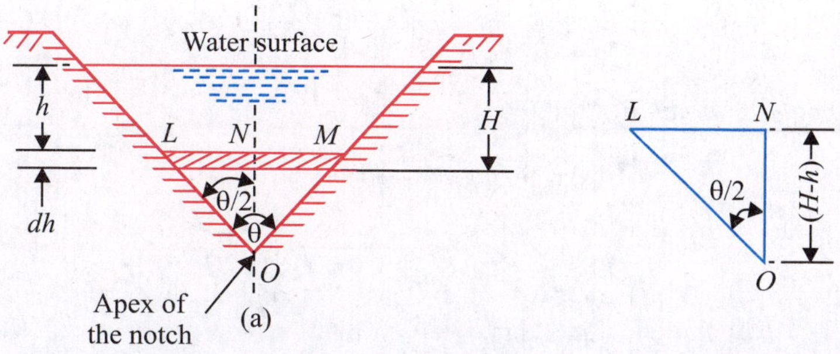

Fig. 9.2. The triangular notch.

From Fig. 9·2 (*b*), we have:

$$\tan\frac{\theta}{2} = \frac{LN}{ON} = \frac{LN}{H-h}$$

$$\therefore \quad LN = (H-h)\tan\frac{\theta}{2}$$

$$\text{Width of strip} = LM = 2LN = 2(H-h)\tan\frac{\theta}{2}$$

$$\therefore \quad \text{Area of the strip} = 2(H-h)\tan\frac{\theta}{2}\times dh$$

We know that theoretical velocity of water through the strip

$$= \sqrt{2gh}$$

$\therefore$ Discharge through the strip,

$$dQ = C_d \times \text{area of strip} \times \text{theoretical velocity}$$

$$= C_d \times 2(H-h)\tan\frac{\theta}{2}\times dh \times \sqrt{2gh}$$

The total discharge, over the whole notch, may be found out by integrating the above equation, within the limits 0 and H.

$$\therefore \quad Q = \int_0^H C_d \times 2(H-h)\tan\frac{\theta}{2}\times\sqrt{2gh}\cdot dh$$

$$= 2\,C_d\sqrt{2g}\tan\frac{\theta}{2}\int_0^H (H-h)\sqrt{h}\cdot dh$$

$$= 2\,C_d\sqrt{2g}\tan\frac{\theta}{2}\int_0^H \left[Hh^{1/2} - h^{3/2}\right] dh$$

$$= 2\,C_d\sqrt{2g}\tan\frac{\theta}{2}\left[\frac{H\cdot h^{3/2}}{3/2} - \frac{h^{5/2}}{5/2}\right]_0^H$$

$$= 2C_d\sqrt{2g}\,\tan\frac{\theta}{2}\left[\frac{2}{3}H\cdot H^{3/2}-\frac{2}{5}H^{5/2}\right]$$

$$= 2\,C_d\sqrt{2g}\,\tan\frac{\theta}{2}\left[\frac{2}{3}H^{5/2}-\frac{2}{5}H^{5/2}\right]$$

$$= 2\,C_d\sqrt{2g}\,\tan\frac{\theta}{2}\left[\frac{4}{15}H^{5/2}\right]$$

$$= \frac{8}{15}C_d\sqrt{2g}\,\tan\frac{\theta}{2}H^{5/2} \quad \text{...(9·2)}$$

For a *right angled V-notch*, if $C_d = 0{\cdot}6$,

$$\left(\theta = 90°,\ \therefore\ \tan\frac{\theta}{2} = 1\right)$$

Then,

$$Q = \frac{8}{15}\times 0{\cdot}6\sqrt{2\times 9{\cdot}81}\times 1\times H^{5/2}$$

$$= 1{\cdot}417\,H^{5/2} \quad \text{...(9·3)}$$

Advantages of a triangular notch over a rectangular notch:

A triangular notch claims the following *advantages* over a rectangular notch:

1. For a right angled *V*-notch or weir the expression for the computation of discharge is *very simple*.
2. For low discharges a triangular notch gives *more accurate results* than a rectangular notch.
3. In a given triangular notch, only one reading *i.e.*, head (*H*) is required to be taken for the measurement of discharge.
4. Ventilation of a triangular notch is not necessary.
5. The same triangular notch can measure a wide range of flows accurately.

Example 9.3. *Find the discharge over a triangular notch of angle 60° when the head over the triangular notch is 0·2 m. Assume $C_d = 0{\cdot}6$.*

Solution. Angle of notch, $\theta = 60°$

Depth of water, $H = 0{\cdot}2$ m

Co-efficient of discharge, $C_d = 0{\cdot}6$

Discharge, Q:

Using the relation :

$$Q = \frac{8}{15}C_d\sqrt{2g}\,\tan\frac{\theta}{2}\times H^{5/2}$$

$$= \frac{8}{15}\times 0{\cdot}6\times\sqrt{2\times 9{\cdot}81}\times\tan\frac{60°}{2}\times(0{\cdot}2)^{5/2}$$

$$= \frac{8}{15}\times 0{\cdot}6\times 4{\cdot}429\times 0{\cdot}577\times 0{\cdot}01788$$

$$= \mathbf{0{\cdot}01462\ m^3/s}$$ **(Ans.)**

Example 9.4. *During an experiment in a laboratory, 0·05 m³ of water flowing over a right-angled notch was collected in one minute. If the head of the sill is 50 mm calculate the co-efficient of discharge of the notch.*

Solution. Discharge, $Q = 0{\cdot}05\ \text{m}^3/\text{min} = 0{\cdot}000833\ \text{m}^3/\text{s}$

Angle of notch, $\theta = 90°$

Head of the sill, $H = 50 \text{ mm} = 0{\cdot}05 \text{ m}$

Co-efficient of discharge, C_d:

Using the relation:

$$Q = \frac{8}{15} C_d \sqrt{2g} \tan\frac{\theta}{2} \times H^{5/2}$$

$$0{\cdot}000833 = \frac{8}{15} \times C_d \times \sqrt{2 \times 9{\cdot}81} \times \tan\left(\frac{90°}{2}\right) \times (0{\cdot}05)^{5/2}$$

$$= \frac{8}{15} \times C_d \times 4{\cdot}429 \times 1 \times 0{\cdot}000559 = 0{\cdot}00132\, C_d$$

$$\therefore \quad C_d = \frac{0{\cdot}000833}{0{\cdot}00132} = \mathbf{0{\cdot}63} \textbf{ (Ans.)}$$

Example 9.5. *A rectangular channel 1·5 m wide has a discharge of 0·2 m³/s, which is measured by a right-angled V-notch-weir. Find the position of the apex of the notch from the bed of the channel if the maximum depth of water is not to exceed 1 m. Assume C_d = 0·62.*

Solution. Width of the rectangular channel, $L = 1{\cdot}5$ m

Discharge, $Q = 0{\cdot}2 \text{ m}^3/\text{s}$

Depth of water in the channel = 1·0 m

Co-efficient of discharge, $C_d = 0{\cdot}62$

Angle of the notch, $\theta = 90°$

Position of the apex of the notch :

Using the relation :

$$Q = \frac{8}{15} C_d \sqrt{2g} \tan\frac{\theta}{2} \times H^{5/2}$$

$$0{\cdot}2 = \frac{8}{15} \times 0{\cdot}62 \times \sqrt{2 \times 9{\cdot}81} \times \tan\left(\frac{90°}{2}\right) \times H^{5/2}$$

$$= 1{\cdot}465\, H^{5/2}$$

$$\therefore \quad H = \left(\frac{0{\cdot}2}{1{\cdot}465}\right)^{2/5} = 0{\cdot}45 \text{ m}$$

Position of apex of the notch from the bed of channel

= Depth of water in channel – height of water over V-notch

= 1 – 0·45 = **0·55 m (Ans.)**

9.5. DISCHARGE OVER A TRAPEZOIDAL NOTCH OR WEIR

Fig. 9·3 shows a trapezoidal notch or weir which is a combination of a rectangular and a triangular notch or weir. As such the discharge over such a notch or weir will be the *sum of the discharges over the rectangular and triangular notches or weirs.*

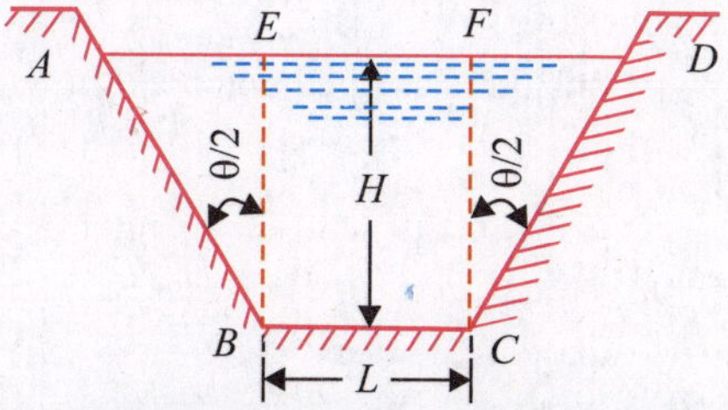

Fig. 9.3 The trapezoidal notch.

Let, H = Height of water over the notch,

L = Length of the rectangular portion (or crest) of the notch.,

C_{d1} = Co-efficient of discharge for the rectangular portion, and

C_{d2} = Co-efficient of discharge for the triangular portion.

The discharge through the rectangular portion *BCFE* is given by (Eqn. 9·1),

$$Q_1 = \frac{2}{3} C_{d1} L \sqrt{2g}\, H^{3/2}$$

The discharge through two triangular notches *ABE* and *FCD* is equal to the discharge through a single triangular notch of angle θ and is given by [Eqn. 9.2],

$$Q_2 = \frac{8}{15} C_d \sqrt{2g} \tan\frac{\theta}{2} \times H^{5/2}$$

∴ Discharge through trapezoidal notch or weir *ABCDA*,

$$Q = Q_1 + Q_2$$

$$= \frac{2}{3} C_{d1} L \sqrt{2g}\, H^{3/2} + \frac{8}{15} C_{d2} \sqrt{2g} \tan\frac{\theta}{2} \times H^{5/2} \quad ...(9·4)$$

Example 9.6. *Find the discharge through a trapezoidal notch which is 1·2 m wide at the top and 0·50 m at the bottom and is 0·4 m in height. The head of water on the notch is 0·3 m. Assume C_d for rectangular portion = 0·62, while for triangular portion = 0·60.*

Solution.

Top width = 1·2 m

Base width, L = 0·5 m

Head of water, H = 0·3 m

For rectangular portion, C_{d1} = 0·62

For triangular portion, C_{d2} = 0·60

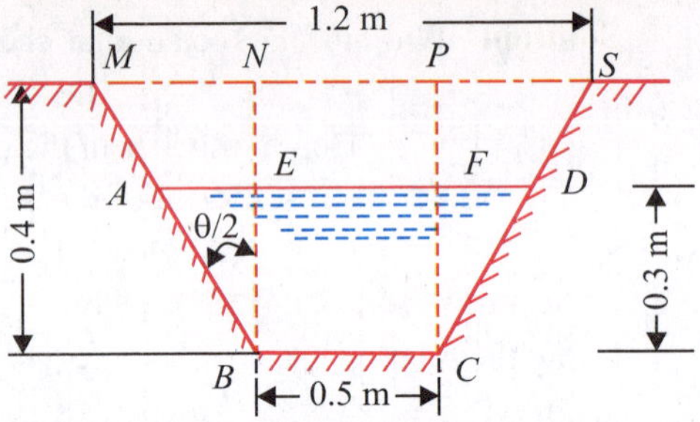

Fig. 9.4

Discharge, Q:

From Δ *MNB*, we have:

$$\tan\frac{\theta}{2} = \frac{MN}{NB} = \frac{(MS - NP)/2}{NB}$$

$$= \frac{(1·2 - 0·5)/2}{0·4}$$

$$= 0·875$$

Discharge through the trapezoidal notch is given by,

$$Q = \frac{2}{3} C_{d1} \cdot L \sqrt{2g}\, H^{3/2} + \frac{8}{15} C_{d2} \sqrt{2g} \tan\frac{\theta}{2} \times H^{5/2}$$

$$= \frac{2}{3} \times 0·62 \times 0·5 \times \sqrt{2 \times 9·81} \times 0·3^{3/2} + \frac{8}{15} \times 0·6 \times \sqrt{2 \times 9·81} \times 0·875 \times (0·3)^{5/2}$$

$$= 0·1504 + 0·0611 = \mathbf{0·2115\ m^3/s\ (Ans.)}$$

9.6. DISCHARGE OVER A STEPPED NOTCH

A **stepped notch** is *a combination of rectangular notches* as shown in Fig. 9·5. The discharge through a stepped notch is equal to the sum of the discharges through the different rectangular notches.

Consider a stepped notch as shown in Fig. 9·5.

Let,

H_1 = Height of water above sill of notch 1,

L_1 = Length of notch 1,

H_2, L_2 = Corresponding values for notch 2,

H_3, L_3 = Corresponding values for notch 3, and

C_d = Co-efficient of discharge for all notches.

The discharge over the notch 1,

$$Q_1 = \frac{2}{3} C_d \,.\, L_1 \sqrt{2g}\; H_1^{3/2}$$

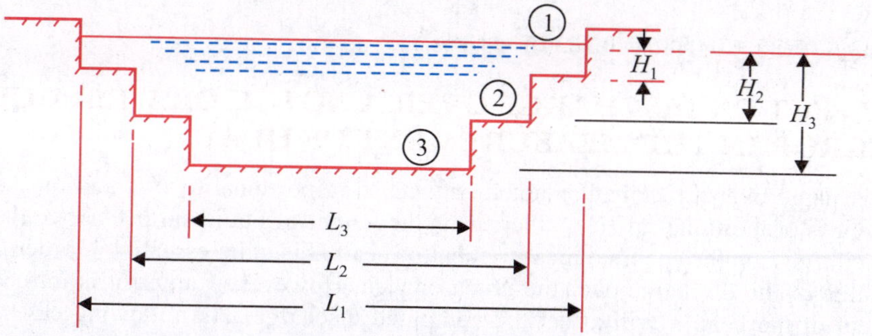

Fig. 9.5. The stepped notch.

Similarly, discharge over the notch 2,

$$Q_2 = \frac{2}{3} C_d \,.\, L_2 \sqrt{2g}\left[H_2^{3/2} - H_1^{3/2}\right]$$

and, discharge over the notch 3,

$$Q_3 = \frac{2}{3} C_d \cdot L_3 \sqrt{2g}\left[H_3^{3/2} - H_2^{3/2}\right]$$

$\therefore$ Total discharge, $Q = Q_1 + Q_2 + Q_3$

Example 9.7. *Find the discharge over a stepped rectangular notch, as shown in Fig. 9·6. Take co-efficient of discharge for all the portions as 0·62.*

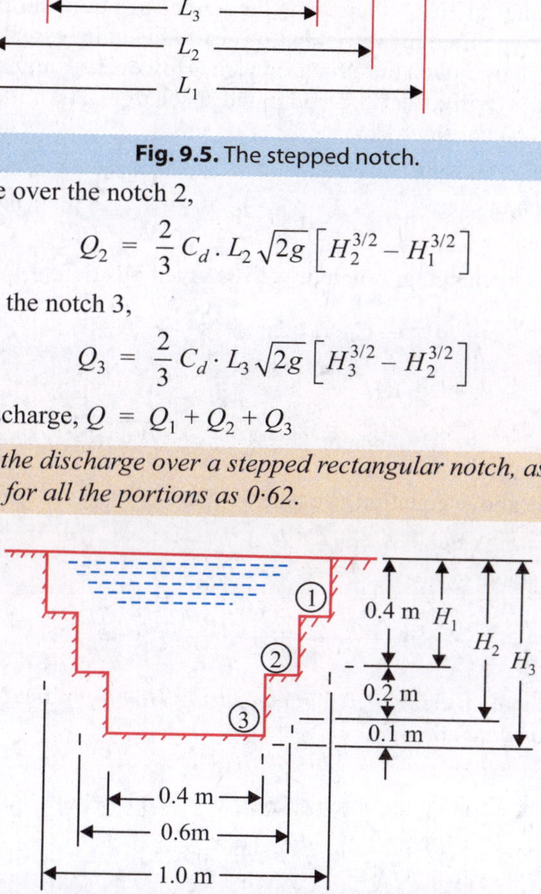

Fig. 9.6

Solution. Co-efficient of discharge, $C_d = 0{\cdot}62$

Let, Q_1 = Discharge over the top portion,

Q_2 = Discharge over the middle portion, and

Q_3 = Discharge over the bottom portion.

The total discharge over the notch,

$$Q = Q_1 + Q_2 + Q_3$$

$$= \frac{2}{3} C_d \,.\, L_1 \sqrt{2g}\; H_1^{3/2} + \frac{2}{3} C_d \,.\, L_2 \sqrt{2g}\left[H_2^{3/2} - H_1^{3/2}\right] + \frac{2}{3} C_d \,.\, L_3 \sqrt{2g}\left[H_3^{3/2} - H_2^{3/2}\right]$$

$$= \frac{2}{3} \times 0\cdot62 \times 1\cdot0 \times \sqrt{2 \times 9\cdot81} \times (0\cdot4)^{3/2} + \frac{2}{3} \times 0\cdot62 \times 0\cdot6 \sqrt{2 \times 9\cdot81}\left[0\cdot6^{3/2} - 0\cdot4^{3/2}\right]$$

$$+ \frac{2}{3} \times 0\cdot62 \times 0\cdot4 \times \sqrt{2 \times 9\cdot81}\left[0\cdot7^{3/2} - 0\cdot6^{3/2}\right]$$

$= 0{\cdot}463 + 0{\cdot}232 + 0{\cdot}0885 =$ **$0{\cdot}783$ m^3/s (Ans.)**

9.7. EFFECT ON DISCHARGE OVER A NOTCH OR WEIR DUE TO ERROR IN THE MEASUREMENT OF HEAD

The discharge over a rectangular notch or weir is proportional to $H^{3/2}$ and over a triangular notch or weir is proportional to $H^{5/2}$, where H is the height of liquid surface above the sill of the notch or weir. As such the accurate measurement of head H is quite essential in order to obtain an accurate value of the discharge over the notch or weir. However, if an error is introduced in the measurement of the head it will affect the computed discharge. The following cases of error in measurement of head will be considered:

(*i*) For rectangular notch or weir.

(*ii*) For triangular notch or weir.

(*i*) Rectangular Notch or Weir :

The discharge for a rectangular notch or weir is given by (Eqn. 9·1),

$$Q = \frac{2}{3} C_d . L \sqrt{2g}\ H^{3/2}$$

$$= KH^{3/2} \quad \text{...}(i)$$

$$\left(\text{where } K = \frac{2}{3} C_d . L \sqrt{2g}\right)$$

Differentiating the above equation, we get:

$$dQ = K \times 3/2 \times H^{1/2}\ dH \quad \text{...}(ii)$$

Dividing (*ii*) by (*i*), we get:

$$\frac{dQ}{Q} = \frac{K \times 3/2 \times H^{1/2}\ dH}{KH^{3/2}} = \frac{3}{2}\frac{dH}{H} \quad \text{...}(9{\cdot}5)$$

Eqn. (9·5) shows that an *error of 1% in measuring H will produce* 1·5 % *error in discharge over a rectangular notch or weir.*

(*ii*) Triangular Notch or Weir :

The discharge over a triangular notch or weir is given by (Eqn. 9·2),

$$Q = \frac{8}{15} C_d \sqrt{2g}\ \tan\frac{\theta}{2} \times H^{5/2} \quad \text{...}(iii)$$

$$= K \times H^{5/2}$$

$$\left(\text{where, } K = \frac{8}{15} C_d \sqrt{2g}\ \tan\frac{\theta}{2}\right)$$

Differentiating Eqn. (*iii*), we get:

$$dQ = K \times 5/2 \times H^{3/2}\ dH \quad \text{...}(iv)$$

Dividing (*iv*) by (*iii*), we get:

$$\frac{dQ}{Q} = \frac{K \times 5/2 \times H^{3/2}\ dH}{K \times H^{5/2}} = \frac{5}{2}\frac{dH}{H} \quad \text{...}(9{\cdot}6)$$

Eqn. (9·6) shows that an error or *1% in measuring H will produce 2·5% error in discharge over a triangular notch or weir.*

Example 9.8. *A rectangular notch 0·5 m long is used for measuring a discharge of 0·04 m^3/s. An error of 2 mm was made in measuring the head over the notch. Calculate the percentage error in the discharge. Take C_d = 0·6.*

Solution. Length of notch, $L = 0{\cdot}5$ m

Discharge, $Q = 0{\cdot}04\ m^3/s$

Error in head, $dH = 2\ mm = 0{\cdot}002$ m

Let, H = Height of water over rectangular notch.

Error in discharge, $\frac{dQ}{Q}$:

The discharge through a rectangular notch is given by,

$$Q = \frac{2}{3} C_d . L \sqrt{2g}\ H^{3/2}$$

$$0 \cdot 04 = \frac{2}{3} \times 0 \cdot 6 \times 0 \cdot 5 \times \sqrt{2 \times 9 \cdot 81} \times H^{3/2}$$

$$= 0{\cdot}886\ H^{3/2}$$

$$\therefore \quad H = \left(\frac{0 \cdot 04}{0 \cdot 886}\right)^{2/3} = 0 \cdot 126 \text{ m}$$

Using the relation:

$$\frac{dQ}{Q} = \frac{3}{2} \times \frac{dH}{H}$$

$$= \frac{3}{2} \times \frac{0 \cdot 002}{0 \cdot 126} = 0 \cdot 0238 \quad \text{or} \quad \mathbf{2{\cdot}38\ \%\ (Ans.)}$$

Example 9.9. *A discharge of 0·06 m^3/s was measured over a right-angled notch. While measuring the head over the notch, an error of 1·5 mm was made. Determine the percentage error in the discharge, if the co-efficient of discharge for the notch is 0·6.*

Solution. Discharge, $Q = 0{\cdot}06\ m^3/s$

Angle of notch, $\theta = 90°$

Error in measurement of head, $dH = 1{\cdot}5\ mm = 0{\cdot}0015$ m.

Co-efficient of discharge, $C_d = 0{\cdot}6$

Let, H = Height of water, above the apex of the notch.

Error in discharge, $\frac{dQ}{Q}$:

Using the relation:

$$Q = \frac{8}{15} C_d \sqrt{2g}\ \tan \frac{\theta}{2}\ H^{5/2}$$

$$0 \cdot 06 = \frac{8}{15} \times 0 \cdot 6 \times \sqrt{2 \times 9 \cdot 81} \times \tan\left(\frac{90°}{2}\right) \times H^{5/2}$$

$$= 1{\cdot}417\ H^{5/2}$$

$$\therefore \quad H = \left(\frac{0 \cdot 06}{1 \cdot 417}\right)^{2/5} = 0 \cdot 282 \text{ m}$$

Now, using the relation:

$$\frac{dQ}{Q} = \frac{5}{2} \times \frac{dH}{H} = \frac{5}{2} \times \frac{0 \cdot 0015}{0 \cdot 282}$$

$$= 0{\cdot}0133 \text{ or } \mathbf{1{\cdot}33\ \%\ (Ans.)}$$

9.8. VELOCITY OF APPROACH

The velocity with which the water approaches or reaches the weir or notch before it flows over it is known as '**velocity of approach**'. Thus if V_a is the velocity of approach, then an additional head $H_a \left(= \frac{V_a^2}{2g}\right)$ due to the velocity of approach, is acting on water flowing over the notch or weir. Then initial and final height of water over the notch or weir will be $(H + H_a)$ and H_a respectively.

The velocity of approach (V_a) is determined by finding the discharge over the weir or notch neglecting velocity of approach,

Let, Q = Discharge over weir or notch, and

A = Cross-sectional area of channel on the upstream side of the weir or notch.

Then the velocity of approach,

$$V_a = \frac{Q}{A}$$

This velocity of approach is used to find an additional head $\left(H_a = \frac{V_a^2}{2g}\right)$. Again the discharge is calculated and above process is repeated for more accurate discharge.

Discharge over a rectangular weir, with velocity of approach

$$= \frac{2}{3} C_d . L \sqrt{2g} \left[(H_1 + H_a)^{3/2} - (H_a)^{3/2}\right] \quad ...(9.7)$$

Example 9.10. *Find the discharge over a rectangular weir of length 80 m. The head of water over the weir is 1·2 m. The velocity of approach is given as 1·5 m/s. Take $C_d = 0·6$.*

Solution. Length of weir, L = 80 m

Head of water, H = 1·2 m

Velocity of approach, V_a = 1·5 m/s

Co-efficient of discharge, C_d = 0·6

Discharge, Q:

The head due to velocity of approach,

$$H_a = \frac{V_a^2}{2g} = \frac{1 \cdot 5^2}{2 \times 9 \cdot 81} = 0 \cdot 1146 \text{ m}$$

Using the relation:

$$Q = \frac{2}{3} C_d \cdot L \sqrt{2g} \left[(H + H_a)^{3/2} - H_a^{3/2}\right]$$

$$= \frac{2}{3} \times 0 \cdot 6 \times 80 \times \sqrt{2 \times 9 \cdot 81} \left[(1 \cdot 2 + 0 \cdot 1146)^{3/2} - (0 \cdot 1146)^{3/2}\right]$$

$$= 141 \cdot 74 \, (1 \cdot 507 - 0 \cdot 0388) = \mathbf{208 \cdot 1 \ m^3/s} \text{ (Ans.)}$$

9.9. EMPIRICAL FORMULAE FOR DISCHARGE OVER RECTANGULAR WEIR

The discharge over a rectangular weir,

$$Q = \frac{2}{3} C_d . L \sqrt{2g} \, H^{3/2} \quad \text{... *without* velocity of approach ...}(i)$$

$$= \frac{2}{3} C_d . L \sqrt{2g} \left[(H + H_a)^{3/2} - H_a^{3/2}\right] \quad \text{... *with* velocity of approach ...}(ii)$$

The equations (*i*) and (*ii*) are applicable to the weir or notch for which the *crest/sill length is equal to the width of the channel*; this type of weir is called **Suppressed weir.**

When the weir is not suppressed, the effect of end contractions is considered.

1. Francis's Formula:

On the basis of experimental analysis Francis established that:

— The end contraction decreases the effective length of the crest of weir and hence decreases the discharge.

— Each end contraction reduces the crest length by 0·1 *H*, where *H* is the head over the weir.

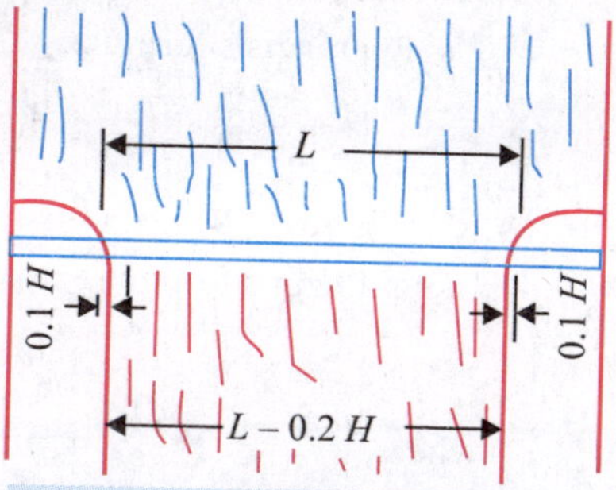

Fig. 9.7

For a rectangular weir there are *two end contractions only* and hence *effective length*

$$= L - 0{\cdot}1 \times 2 \times H = L - 0{\cdot}2\,H$$

and discharge,

$$Q = \frac{2}{3} \times C_d \times (L - 0{\cdot}2\,H) \times \sqrt{2g}\;H^{3/2} \qquad ...(9{\cdot}8)$$

[If there are *n* end contractions, we may write the empirical formula proposed by Francis as:

$$Q = \frac{2}{3} \times C_d \times (L - 0{\cdot}1\,nH) \times \sqrt{2g}\;H^{3/2} \qquad ...\ 9{\cdot}8\ (a)$$]

When $C_d = 0{\cdot}623$ and $g = 9{\cdot}81\ \text{m/s}^2$, then:

$$Q = \frac{2}{3} \times 0.623 \times (L - 0.2H) \times \sqrt{2 \times 9.81}\;H^{3/2}$$

$$= 1{\cdot}84\,(L - 0{\cdot}2\,H)\,H^{3/2} \qquad ...(9{\cdot}9)$$

— When end contractions are *suppressed*, we have:

$$Q = 1{\cdot}84\,LH^{3/2} \qquad ...(9{\cdot}10)$$

(When end contractions are *suppressed*, the value of *n* is taken as *zero*.)

When velocity of approach is considered, we have:

$$Q = 1{\cdot}84\,L\left[(H + H_a)^{3/2} - H_a^{3/2}\right] \qquad ...(9{\cdot}11)$$

2. Bazin's Formula:

Bazin's formula for the discharge (*Q*) over a rectangular weir is given as follows:

$$\left.\begin{aligned} Q &= m \times L \times \sqrt{2g} \times H^{3/2} \\ m &= \frac{2}{3} \times C_d = 0{\cdot}405 + \frac{0{\cdot}003}{H} \end{aligned}\right\} \qquad ...(9{\cdot}12)$$

where, H = Height of water over the weir.

When velocity of approach is considered, we have:

where,

$$\left.\begin{aligned} Q &= m_1 \times L \times \sqrt{2g} \times (H + H_a)^{3/2} \\ m_1 &= 0{\cdot}405 + \frac{0{\cdot}003}{(H + H_a)} \end{aligned}\right\} \qquad ...(9{\cdot}13)$$

Example 9.11. *The head of water over a rectangular weir is 500 mm. If the length of the crest of the weir with end contractions suppressed is 1·4 m, find the discharge using the following formulae:*

(*i*) *Francis's formula, and*

(*ii*) *Bazin's formula.*

Solution. Head of water over the weir, $H = 500 \text{ mm} = 0{\cdot}5 \text{ m}$

Length of the weir, $L = 1{\cdot}4 \text{ m}$

(i) Discharge by Francis's formula, Q:

Using Francis's formula,

$$Q = 1{\cdot}84\, LH^{3/2} = 1{\cdot}84 \times 1{\cdot}4 \times (0{\cdot}5)^{3/2}$$

$$= \mathbf{0{\cdot}91\ m^3/s.\ (Ans.)}$$

(ii) Discharge by Bazin's formula, Q:

Using Bazin's formula,

$$Q = m \times L \times \sqrt{2g}\ H^{3/2}$$

where, $$m = 0{\cdot}405 + \frac{0{\cdot}003}{H} = 0{\cdot}405 + \frac{0{\cdot}003}{0{\cdot}50} = 0{\cdot}411$$

$\therefore$ $$Q = 0{\cdot}411 \times 1{\cdot}4 \times \sqrt{2 \times 9{\cdot}81} \times (0{\cdot}5)^{3/2}$$

$$= \mathbf{0{\cdot}901\ m^3/s\ (Ans.)}$$

Example 9.12. *A 30 metres long weir is divided into 10 equal bays by vertical posts, each 0·6 m wide. Using Francis's formula, calculate the discharge over the weir under an effective head of 1 metre.*

Solution. Length of the weir $= 30$ m

Number of bays $= 10$

$\therefore$ Number of vertical posts $= 10 - 1 = 9$

Width of each post $= 0{\cdot}6$ m

$\therefore$ Effective length, $L = 30 - 9 \times 0{\cdot}6 = 24{\cdot}6$ m

Number of end contractions, $n = 2 \times 10 = 20$

(*one bay has two end contractions*)

Head of water, $H = 1$ m

Discharge, Q:

Using Francis's formula,

$$Q = 1{\cdot}84\,(L - 0{\cdot}1 n H)\, H^{3/2}$$

$$= 1{\cdot}84\,(24{\cdot}6 - 0{\cdot}1 \times 20 \times 1) \times (1)^{3/2}$$

$$= \mathbf{41{\cdot}58\ m^3/s\ (Ans.)}$$

Example 9.13. *A 40 metres long weir is divided into 12 equal bays by vertical posts, each 0·6 m wide. Using Francis's formula, calculate the discharge over the weir if the head over the crest is 1·20 m and velocity of approach is 2 m/s.*

Solution. Length of the weir $= 40$ m

Number of bays $= 12$

$\therefore$ Number of vertical post $= 12 - 1 = 11$

Width of each post $= 0{\cdot}6$ m

$\therefore$ Effective length, $L = 40 - 11 \times 0{\cdot}6 = 33{\cdot}4$ m

Number of end contractions, $n = 2 \times 12 = 24$

Head on weir, $H = 1{\cdot}2$ m

Velocity of approach, $V_a = 2$ m/s

$\therefore$ Head due to V_a, $H_a = \dfrac{V_a^2}{2g} = \dfrac{2^2}{2 \times 9{\cdot}81} = 0{\cdot}2038$ m

Discharge (Q) by Francis's formula with end contractions and velocity of approach is given by:

$$Q = 1{\cdot}84\,[L - 0{\cdot}1\,n(H + H_a)]\,[(H + H_a)^{3/2} - H_a^{3/2}]$$
$$= 1{\cdot}84\,[33{\cdot}4 - 0{\cdot}1 \times 24 \times (1{\cdot}2 + 0{\cdot}2038)]\,[(1{\cdot}2 + 0{\cdot}2038)^{3/2} - (0{\cdot}2038)^{3/2}]$$
$$= 1{\cdot}84\,[33{\cdot}4 - 3{\cdot}369]\,[1{\cdot}663 - 0{\cdot}092]$$
$$= \mathbf{86{\cdot}8\ m^3/s}\ \textbf{(Ans.)}$$

9.10. CIPPOLETTI WEIR OR NOTCH

The Cippoletti weir is *trapezoidal weir*, having side slopes of 1 horizontal to 4 vertical as shown in Fig. 9·8. By providing slope on the sides, an increase in discharge through the triangular portions (*AED* and *FBC*) is obtained; without this slope the weir would be a rectangular one, and due to end contraction, the discharge would decrease. Thus the advantage of this weir is that the *factor of end contraction is not required* (while using Francis's formula).

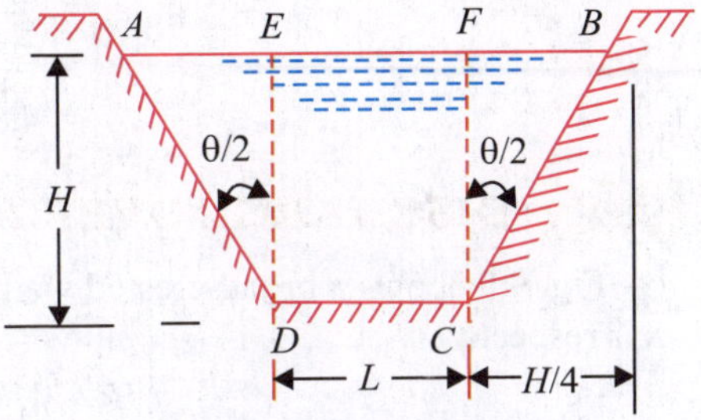

Fig. 9.8 Cippoletti weir.

Let us split the trapezoidal weir into the following:

(*i*) Rectangular weir, and

(*ii*) Triangular notch

The discharge over a rectangular weir (with two end contractions),

$$Q_1 = \frac{2}{3} \times C_d \times (L - 0{\cdot}2\,H)\sqrt{2g}\,H^{3/2} \quad ...(i)$$

and discharge over the triangular notch,

$$Q_2 = \frac{8}{15}\,C_d\sqrt{2g}\,\tan\frac{\theta}{2} \times (H)^{5/2} \quad ...(ii)$$

∴ Total discharge,

$$Q = Q_1 + Q_2$$
$$= \frac{2}{3}\,C_d\,(L - 0{\cdot}2\,H)\sqrt{2g}\,H^{3/2} + \frac{8}{15}\,C_d\sqrt{2g}\,\tan\frac{\theta}{2} \times H^{5/2} \quad ...(9{\cdot}14)$$

To avoid the factor of end contraction, Cippoletti gave the formula for discharge,

$$Q = \frac{2}{3}\,C_d\,L\sqrt{2g} \times H^{3/2} \quad ...(9{\cdot}15)$$

Equating the eqns. (9·14) and (9·15), we get:

$$\frac{2}{3}\,C_d\,L\sqrt{2g}\,H^{3/2} = \frac{2}{3}\,C_d\,(L - 0{\cdot}2H)\sqrt{2g}\,H^{3/2} + \frac{8}{15}\,C_d\sqrt{2g}\,\tan\frac{\theta}{2} \times H^{5/2}$$

Dividing both sides by $\frac{2}{3}\,C_d\sqrt{2g}\,H^{3/2}$, we have:

$$L = L - 0.2H + \frac{4}{5}\tan\frac{\theta}{2} \times H$$

or, $$\frac{4}{5}\tan\frac{\theta}{2} \times H = 0.2H$$

∴ $$\tan\frac{\theta}{2} = 0{\cdot}2 \times \frac{5}{4} = \frac{1}{4}$$

The above relation indicates that in a trapezoidal weir having side slopes 1 horizontal to 4 vertical the factor of end contraction is *not* required for discharge, while using Francis's formula.

Example 9.14. *Find the discharge over a Cippoletti weir of length 1·8 m when the head over the weir is 1·2 m. Take* $C_d = 0{\cdot}62$

Solution. Length of weir, $L = 1.8$ m

Head of water, $H = 1.2$ m

Co-efficient of discharge, $C_d = 0.62$

Discharge over the weir, Q:

Using the relation:

$$Q = \frac{2}{3} C_d L \sqrt{2g}\, H^{3/2}$$

$$= \frac{2}{3} \times 0.62 \times 1.8 \times \sqrt{2 \times 9.81} \times (1.2)^{3/2}$$

$$= \mathbf{4.33\ m^3/s}$$ **(Ans.)**

9.11. DISCHARGE OVER A BROAD CRESTED WEIR

Fig. 9·9 shows a broad-crested weir. Let 1 and 2 be the upstream and downstream ends of the weir respectively.

Let, H = Head of water in the upstream side of the weir,

h = Head of water on the downstream side of the weir,

v = Velocity of the water on the downstream side of the weir,

L = Length of the weir, and

C_d = Co-efficient of discharge.

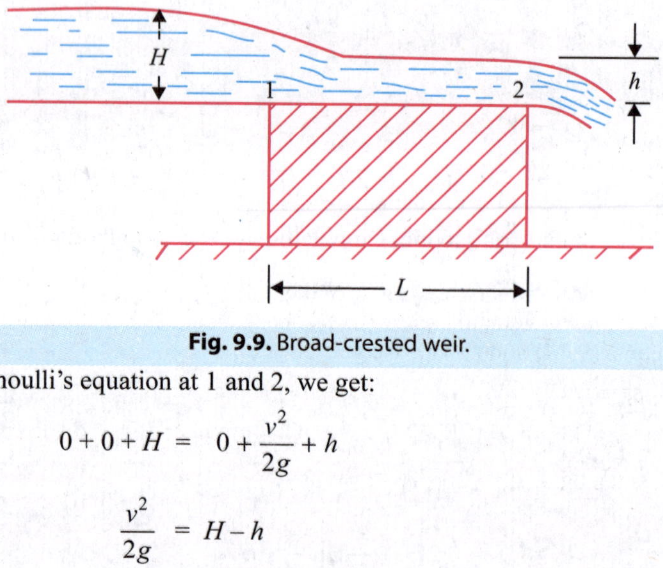

Fig. 9.9. Broad-crested weir.

Applying Bernoulli's equation at 1 and 2, we get:

$$0 + 0 + H = 0 + \frac{v^2}{2g} + h$$

$$\therefore \quad \frac{v^2}{2g} = H - h$$

$$\text{or,} \quad v = \sqrt{2g(H-h)}$$

$\therefore$ The discharge over weir, $Q = C_d \times$ area of flow $\times$ velocity

$$= C_d \times L \times h \times v$$

$$= C_d \times L \times h \times \sqrt{2g(H-h)}$$

$$= C_d \times L \times \sqrt{2g}\, \sqrt{Hh^2 - h^3} \quad \text{...(9·16)}$$

The discharge will be *maximum*, if $(Hh^2 - h^3)$ is maximum.

$$\text{or,} \quad \frac{d}{dh}(Hh^2 - h^3) = 0$$

$$\text{or,} \quad 2hH - 3h^2 = 0$$

$$\text{or,} \quad 2H = 3h$$

$$\therefore \quad h = \frac{2}{3}H$$

Substituting the value of h in eqn. (9·16), we get:

$$Q_{max} = C_d \times L \times \sqrt{2g}\sqrt{H \times \left(\frac{2}{3}H\right)^2 - \left(\frac{2}{3}H\right)^3}$$

$$= C_d \times L \times \sqrt{2g}\sqrt{\frac{4}{9}H^3 - \frac{9}{27}H^3}$$

$$= C_d \times L \times \sqrt{2g}\sqrt{\frac{4}{27}H^3}$$

$$= C_d \times L \times \sqrt{2g} \times \frac{2}{3}H\sqrt{\frac{H}{3}}$$

$$= \frac{2}{3\sqrt{3}}C_d \times L \times \sqrt{2g} \times H^{3/2}$$

$$= 0{\cdot}3849 \times C_d \times L \times \sqrt{2 \times 9{\cdot}81} \times H^{3/2}$$

$$= 1{\cdot}705 \times C_d \times L \times H^{3/2} \quad \text{...(9·17)}$$

9.12. DISCHARGE OVER A NARROW-CRESTED WEIR

In case of a narrow-crested weir, $2L < H$. This weir is similar to a rectangular weir or notch and hence, Q is given by:

$$Q = \frac{2}{3} \times C_d \times L \times \sqrt{2g} \times H^{3/2} \quad \text{...(9·18)}$$

9.13. DISCHARGE OVER AN OGEE WEIR

In the Fig. 9·10 is shown an Ogee weir, in which the crest of the weir rises upto maximum height of 1·115 H and then falls as shown (where, H = height of water above inlet of the weir). The discharge over an Ogee weir is the same as that of a rectangular weir and is given by:

$$Q = \frac{2}{3} \times C_d \times L \times \sqrt{2g} \times H^{3/2} \quad \text{...(9·18)}$$

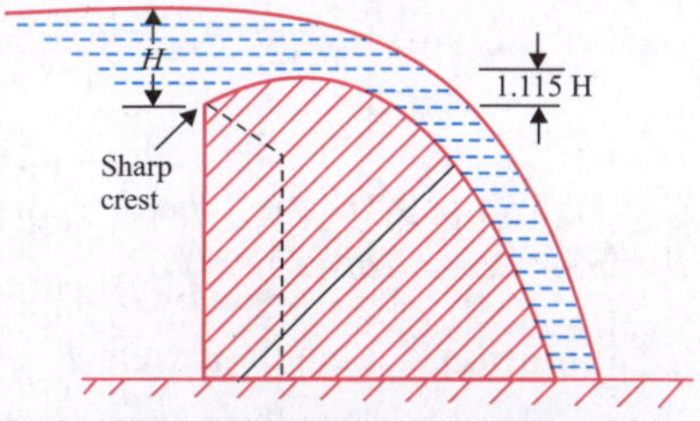

Fig. 9.10. An Ogee weir.

9.14. DISCHARGE OVER SUBMERGED OR DROWNED WEIR

A *weir is said to be* **submerged** *or* **drowned weir** *if the water level on its downstream side is above its crest*. Such a weir is shown in Fig. 9·11. The total discharge over the weir is obtained by dividing the weir into *two parts*. *The portion between upstream and downstream water surfaces may be treated as* **free weir** and portion between downstream water surface and crest as a **drowned weir.**

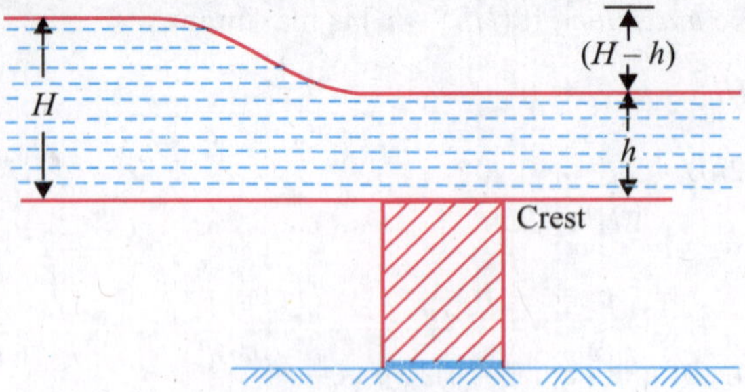

Fig. 9.11. Submerged weir.

Let, H = Height of water on the upstream side of the weir, and

h = Height of water on the downstream side of the weir.

Then, Q_1 = Discharge over upper portion

$$= \frac{2}{3}.C_{d1}.L.\sqrt{2g}\ (H - h)^{3/2}$$

and, Q_2 = Discharge through drowned portion

$= C_{d2} \times$ area of flow $\times$ velocity of flow

$$= C_{d2}.L.h.\sqrt{2g\ (H - h)}$$

where, C_{d1} and C_{d2} are the respective discharge co-efficients.

$\therefore$ Total discharge, $Q = Q_1 + Q_2$

$$= \frac{2}{3}.\ C_{d1}.\ L.\ \sqrt{2g}\ (H - h)^{3/2} + C_{d2}.L.\ h.\ \sqrt{2g\ (H - h)} \quad ...(9{\cdot}19)$$

Example 9.15. *A 45 m long broad-crested weir has 0·5 m of water above its crest. Find the maximum discharge over the weir. Take C_d = 0·62. Neglect velocity of approach.*

Solution. Length of the weir, L = 45 m

Head of water, H = 0.5 m

C_d = 0.62

Maximum discharge, Q_{max}:

$$Q_{max} = 1.705\ C_d \times L \times H^{3/2}$$

$$= 1.705 \times 0.62 \times 45 \times (0.5)^{3/2}$$

$$= \mathbf{16.82\ m^3/s}\ \textbf{(Ans.)}$$

Example 9.16. *Find the discharge over an narrow-crested weir 6 m long and having a head of 0·4 m of water. Take C_d = 0.62.*

Solution. Length of weir, L = 6 m

Head of water, H = 0·4 m

Discharge co-efficient, C_d = 0·62

Discharge, Q:

$$Q = \frac{2}{3} \times C_d \times L \times \sqrt{2g} \times H^{3/2} \quad ...[\text{Eqn. } 9{\cdot}18]$$

$$= \frac{2}{3} \times 0{\cdot}62 \times 6 \times \sqrt{2 \times 9{\cdot}81} \times 0{\cdot}4^{3/2} = \mathbf{2{\cdot}779\ m^3/s}\ \textbf{(Ans.)}$$

Example 9.17. *In a submerged weir of 2·5 m length the heights of water on the upstream and downstream sides are 0·2 m and 0·1 m respectively. Find the discharge over the weir if discharge co-efficients for free and drowned portions are 0·62 and 0·8 respectively.*

Solution. Length of weir, $L = 25$ m

Height of water on upstream side, $H = 0.2$ m

Height of water on downstream side, $h = 0.1$ m

$C_{d1} = 0.62$

$C_{d2} = 0.8$

Discharge over the weir, Q:

Total discharge, $Q = Q_1$ (discharge through free portion) + Q_2 (discharge through the drowned portion)

$$= \frac{2}{3} C_{d1} \times L \times \sqrt{2g}\,(H-h)^{3/2} + C_{d2} \times L \times h \times \sqrt{2g\,(H-h)} \quad \text{...[Eqn. (9·19)]}$$

$$= \frac{2}{3} \times 0 \cdot 62 \times 2 \cdot 5 \times \sqrt{2 \times 9 \cdot 81}\,(0 \cdot 2 - 0 \cdot 1)^{3/2} + 0 \cdot 8 \times 2 \cdot 5 \times 0 \cdot 1 \times \sqrt{2 \times 9 \cdot 81\,(0 \cdot 2 - 0 \cdot 1)}$$

$= 0{\cdot}1447 + 0{\cdot}2801 =$ **0·4248 m³/s (Ans.)**

Example 9.18. *Water flows over a rectangular sharp-crested weir 1 m long, the head over the sill of the weir being 0·66 m. The approach channel is 1·4 m wide and depth of flow in the channel is 1·2 m. Starting from first principles, determine the rate of discharge over the weir. Consider also the velocity of approach and the effect of end contractions. Take the co-efficient of discharge for the weir as 0·6.* **[UPSC Exams.]**

Solution. Length of weir, $L = 1$ m

Head of water, $H = 0{\cdot}66$ m

Co-efficient of discharge, $C_d = 0{\cdot}6$

Rate of discharge, Q:

(i) Neglecting velocity of approach:

The discharge over a rectangular sharp-crested contracted weir is given by Eqn. (9·8),

$$Q = \frac{2}{3} C_d (L - 0 \cdot 1\, nH) \sqrt{2g}\; H^{3/2}$$

(where, n = no. of end contractions)

$$= \frac{2}{3} \times 0 \cdot 6\,(1 - 0 \cdot 1 \times 2 \times 0 \cdot 66) \times \sqrt{2 \times 9 \cdot 81} \times (0 \cdot 66)^{3/2}$$

$= 0{\cdot}3472 \times 4{\cdot}429 \times 0{\cdot}536 =$ **0·824 m³/s (Ans.)**

(ii) Taking velocity of approach into consideration:

$$\text{Velocity of approach, } V_a = \frac{Q}{A} = \frac{0 \cdot 824}{1 \cdot 4 \times 1 \cdot 2} = 0 \cdot 49 \text{ m/s}$$

$$\text{Head due to } V_a,\ h_a = \frac{V_a^2}{2g} = \frac{0 \cdot 49^2}{2 \times 9 \cdot 81} = 0 \cdot 0122 \text{ m}$$

$$H + h_a = 0{\cdot}66 + 0{\cdot}0122 = 0{\cdot}6722 \text{ m}$$

Discharge considering the velocity of approach,

$$Q = \frac{2}{3} C_d \left[L - 0 \cdot 1\, n\,(H + h_a)\right] \times \sqrt{2g} \times \left[(H + h_a)^{3/2} - (h_a)^{3/2}\right]$$

$$= \frac{2}{3} \times 0 \cdot 6\,(1 - 0 \cdot 1 \times 2 \times 0 \cdot 6722) \times \sqrt{2 \times 9 \cdot 81}\left[(0 \cdot 6722)^{3/2} - (0 \cdot 0122)^{3/2}\right]$$

$$= 0 \cdot 3462 \times 4 \cdot 429\,(0 \cdot 551 - 0 \cdot 001347)$$

$$= \mathbf{0 \cdot 8428\ m^3/s}$$ **(Ans.)**

9.15. TIME REQUIRED TO EMPTY A RESERVOIR OR A TANK WITH RECTANGULAR AND TRIANGULAR WEIRS OR NOTCHES

(*a*) Rectangular weir or notch :

Consider a reservior or a tank provided with a rectangular weir or notch in one of its sides.

Let, A = Uniform cross-sectional area of the tank,

L = Length of crest of the weir or notch,

H_1 = Initial height of liquid above the crest of notch,

H_2 = Final height of liquid above the crest of notch,

C_d = Co-efficient of discharge, and

T = Time required in seconds to lower the height of liquid from H_1 to H_2.

Further, let h = The height of liquid surface above the crest of weir or notch at any instant, and

dh = The fall of liquid surface in a small time dT.

Then,

$$-A.dh = Q \times dT$$

$$= \frac{2}{3} C_d \,.\, L \,.\, \sqrt{2g} \,.\, h^{3/2}\, dT$$

(Negative sign indicates that as T increases, h decreases.)

or,

$$dT = \frac{-A\, dh}{\frac{2}{3} C_d \,.\, L \,.\, \sqrt{2g} \,.\, h^{3/2}}$$

To obtain total time T, the above eqn. is integrated between the limits H_1 to H_2.

$$\therefore \quad \int_0^T dT = \int_{H_1}^{H_2} \frac{-Adh}{\frac{2}{3} C_d \,.\, L \,.\, \sqrt{2g} \times h^{3/2}}$$

or,

$$T = \frac{-A}{\frac{2}{3} C_d \,.\, L \,.\, \sqrt{2g}} \int_{H_1}^{H_2} h^{-3/2}\, dh$$

$$= \frac{-3A}{2\, C_d \,.\, L \,.\, \sqrt{2g}} \left[\frac{h^{-3/2+1}}{(-3/2)+1}\right]_{H_1}^{H_2}$$

$$= \frac{-3A}{2\, C_d \,.\, L \,.\, \sqrt{2g}} \left(-\frac{2}{1}\right) \left[\frac{1}{\sqrt{h}}\right]_{H_1}^{H_2}$$

$$= \frac{3A}{C_d \,.\, L \,.\, \sqrt{2g}} \left[\frac{1}{\sqrt{H_2}} - \frac{1}{\sqrt{H_1}}\right] \quad \text{...(9·20)}$$

(*b*) Triangular weir or notch:

Consider a reservoir or a tank provided with a triangular weir or notch in one of its sides.

Let, A = Uniform cross-sectional area of the tank,

θ = Angle of the notch,

H_1 = Initial height of liquid above the apex of notch,

H_2 = Final height of liquid above the apex of notch, and

C_d = Co-efficient of discharge.

Further, let, h = The height of liquid surface above the crest of weir or notch at any instant; and,

dh = The fall of liquid surface in a small time dT.

Then,
$$-A.\,dh = Q \times dT$$
$$= \frac{8}{15} C_d \times \tan\frac{\theta}{2} \times \sqrt{2g} \times h^{5/2}\, dT$$

or,
$$dT = \frac{-A.dh}{\frac{8}{15} C_d \times \tan\frac{\theta}{2} \times \sqrt{2g} \times h^{5/2}}$$

To obtain total time T, the above eqn. is integrated between the limits H_1 to H_2.

$\therefore$
$$\int_0^T dT = \int_{H_1}^{H_2} \frac{-A.dh}{\frac{8}{15} C_d \times \tan\frac{\theta}{2} \times \sqrt{2g} \times h^{5/2}}$$

or,
$$T = \frac{-A}{\frac{8}{15} \times C_d \times \tan\frac{\theta}{2} \times \sqrt{2g}} \int_{H_1}^{H_2} h^{-5/2}\, dh$$

$$= -\frac{-15A}{8 \times C_d \times \tan\frac{\theta}{2} \times \sqrt{2g}} \left[\frac{h^{-3/2}}{-3/2}\right]_{H_1}^{H_2}$$

$$= \frac{-15A}{8 \times C_d \times \tan\frac{\theta}{2} \times \sqrt{2g}} (-2/3) \left[\frac{1}{h^{3/2}}\right]_{H_1}^{H_2}$$

$$= \frac{5A}{4 \times C_d \times \tan\frac{\theta}{2} \times \sqrt{2g}} \left[\frac{1}{H_2^{3/2}} - \frac{1}{H_1^{3/2}}\right] \quad \text{...(9·21)}$$

Example 9.19. *Find the time required to lower the water level from 3 m to 2 m in a reservoir of dimensions 70 m × 70 m, by*

(i) a rectangular notch of length 1·2 m;

(ii) a right angled V-notch.

Take C_d = 0·62

Solution. Dimensions of the reservoir = 70 m × 70 m

$\therefore$ Area, A = 70 × 70 = 4900 m²

Length of rectangular notch, L = 1·2 m

Angle of notch, θ = 90°

Co-efficient of discharge, C_d = 0·62

Initial height of water, H_1 = 3 m

Final height of water, H_2 = 2 m

Time required, T:

(i) Rectangular notch:

$$T = \frac{3A}{C_d \cdot L \cdot \sqrt{2g}}\left[\frac{1}{\sqrt{H_2}} - \frac{1}{\sqrt{H_1}}\right] \quad \text{...[Eqn. 9·20]}$$

Substituting the values, we get:

$$T = \frac{3 \times 4900}{0 \cdot 62 \times 1 \cdot 2 \times \sqrt{2 \times 9 \cdot 81}}\left[\frac{1}{\sqrt{2}} - \frac{1}{\sqrt{3}}\right]$$

$$= 4460{\cdot}62\,(0{\cdot}707 - 0{\cdot}577) = \mathbf{579{\cdot}88\ s\ (Ans.)}$$

(ii) A right angled V-notch:

$$T = \frac{5A}{4 \times C_d \times \tan\frac{\theta}{2} \times \sqrt{2g}}\left[\frac{1}{H_2^{3/2}} - \frac{1}{H_1^{3/2}}\right] \quad \text{...[Eqn. 9·21]}$$

$$= \frac{5 \times 4900}{4 \times 0 \cdot 62 \times \tan\frac{90°}{2} \times \sqrt{2 \times 9 \cdot 81}}\left[\frac{1}{2^{3/2}} - \frac{1}{3^{3/2}}\right]$$

$$= 2230{\cdot}3\,(0{\cdot}3535 - 0{\cdot}1924) = \mathbf{359.3\ s\ (Ans.)}$$

HIGHLIGHTS

1. A *notch* may be defined as an opening provided in the side of a tank or vessel such that the liquid surface in the tank is *below the top edge of the opening*.
2. A *weir* may be defined as any regular obstruction is an open stream over which the flow takes place.
3. Discharge through a rectangular notch or weir is given by,

$$Q = \frac{2}{3} C_d \times L \times \sqrt{2g} \times H^{3/2}$$

where, C_d = Co-efficient of discharge,

L = Length of notch or weir, and

H = Head of water over the notch or weir.

4. Discharge through a triangular notch or weir is given by,

$$Q = \frac{8}{15} \times C_d \times \sqrt{2g} \times \tan\frac{\theta}{2} \times H^{5/2}$$

where, θ = angle of the notch.

5. Discharge through a trapezoidal notch or weir is given by,

$$Q = \frac{2}{3} C_{d1} \times L \times \sqrt{2g} \times H^{3/2} + \frac{8}{5} C_{d2} \sqrt{2g} \times \tan\frac{\theta}{2} \times H^{5/2}$$

where, C_{d1} = Co-efficient of discharge for rectangular notch,

Cd_2 = Co-efficient of discharge for triangular notch, and

$\frac{\theta}{2}$ = Slope of the side of trapezoidal notch.

6. The error in discharge due to the error in the measurement of head over a rectangular or a triangular notch or weir is given by

$$\frac{dQ}{Q} = \frac{3}{2} \times \frac{dH}{H} \quad \text{... for a } \textit{rectangular notch or weir}$$

$$= \frac{5}{2} \times \frac{dH}{H} \quad \text{... for a triangular notch or weir}$$

where, Q = Discharge through rectangular or triangular notch or weir, and

H = Head over the notch or weir.

7. The velocity with which the water approaches or reaches the weir or notch before it flows over it is known as '*Velocity of approach*'. It is denoted by V_a and is given by:

$$V_a = \frac{\text{Discharge over the notch or weir}}{\text{Cross–sectional area of channel}}$$

8. The head due to velocity of approach is given by,

$$H_a = \frac{V_a^2}{2g}$$

9. The discharge over a rectangular weir,

$$Q = \frac{2}{3} C_d . L . \sqrt{2g} . H^{3/2} \quad \text{... without velocity of approach}$$

$$= \frac{2}{3} C_d . L . \sqrt{2g} \, [(H + H_a^{3/2}) - (H_a)^{3/2}] \quad \text{... with velocity of approach}$$

10. *Francis's formula* for discharge over a rectangular weir is given by:

$$Q = \frac{2}{3} C_d \times (L - 0{\cdot}1\, nH) \sqrt{2g}\, H^{3/2} \quad \text{... for } n \text{ end contractions}$$

$$= 1{\cdot}84\, (L - 0{\cdot}2\, H)\, H^{3/2} \quad \text{... for two end contractions}$$

$$= 1{\cdot}84\, LH^{3/2} \quad \text{... if end contractions are suppressed}$$

$$= 1{\cdot}84\, L\, [(H + H_a)^{3/2} - H_a^{3/2}] \quad \text{... if velocity of approach is considered}$$

(when $C_d = 0{\cdot}623$, $g = 9{\cdot}81$ m/s^2)

11. *Bazin's formula* for discharge over a rectangular weir,

$$Q = m\, L \sqrt{2g}\, H^{3/2} \quad \text{... without velocity of approach}$$

$$= m\, L \sqrt{2g}\, [(H + H_a)^{3/2}] \quad \text{... with velocity of approach}$$

where $$m = = \frac{2}{3} C_d = 0{\cdot}405 + \frac{0{\cdot}003}{H} \quad \text{... without velocity of approach}$$

$$= 0{\cdot}405 + \frac{0{\cdot}003}{(H + H_a)}] \quad \text{... with velocity of approach}$$

12. The *Cippoletti weir* is a trapezoidal weir, having side slopes of 1 horizontal to 4 vertical. The discharge through the weir is given by,

$$Q = \frac{2}{3} C_d . L . \sqrt{2g}\, H^{3/2} \quad \text{... without velocity of approach}$$

$$= \frac{2}{3} C_d . L . \sqrt{2g} \left[(H + H_a)^{3/2} - H_a^{3/2} \right] \quad \text{... with velocity of approach.}$$

13. Discharge over a *broad-crested weir* is given by,

$$Q = C_d . L . \sqrt{2g} \sqrt{Hh^2 - h^3}$$

where, L = Length of the weir,

H = Height of water, above crest, and

h = Head of water on the downstream of the weir.

The condition for maximum discharge is

$$h = \frac{2}{3} H, \text{ and maximum discharge is given by,}$$

$$Q_{max} = 1\cdot705\ C_d.\ L.\ H^{3/2}$$

14. Discharge over an *Ogee weir* is given by,

$$Q = \frac{2}{3} C_d.\ L.\ \sqrt{2g} \times H^{3/2}$$

15. Discharge over *submerged or drowned weir* is given by,

$$Q = \text{Discharge over upper portion + discharge through drowned portion}$$

$$= \frac{2}{3} C_{d1}.\ L.\ \sqrt{2g}\ (H-h)^{3/2} + C_{d2}.\ L.\ h.\ \sqrt{2g\ (H-h)}$$

16. The time required to *empty a reservoir or a tank* by a rectangular or a triangular notch is given by,

$$T = \frac{3A}{C_d.\ L.\ \sqrt{2g}} \left[\frac{1}{\sqrt{H_2}} - \frac{1}{\sqrt{H_1}}\right] \quad \text{... by a } \textit{rectangular notch}$$

$$= \frac{5A}{4\ C_d \times \tan\frac{\theta}{2} \times \sqrt{2g}} \left[\frac{1}{H_2^{3/2}} - \frac{1}{H_1^{3/2}}\right] \quad \text{... by a } \textit{triangular notch}$$

where, A = Cross-sectional area of a tank or a reservoir,
H_1 = Initial height of liquid above the apex of notch, and
H_2 = Final height of liquid above the apex of notch.

OBJECTIVE TYPE QUESTIONS

Choose the Correct Answer:

1. An opening provided in the side of a tank or vessel such that the liquid surface in the tank is below the top edge of the opening is known as
(*a*) weir (*b*) notch
(*c*) orifice (*d*) none of the above.

2. A notch is generally made of
(*a*) masonary or concrete (*b*) metallic plate
(*c*) plastic plate (*d*) any of these.

3. Any regular obstruction in an open stream over which the flow takes place is known as
(*a*) notch (*b*) orifice
(*c*) weir (*d*) any of these.

4. Which or the following may be used for measuring the rate of flow of water in rivers or streams?
(*a*) Notches (*b*) Orifices
(*c*) Weir (*d*) Any of these.

5. Discharge over a rectangular notch or weir is given by
(*a*) $\frac{1}{2} C_d.\ L.\sqrt{2g}\ (H)^{3/2}$
(*b*) $\frac{3}{4} C_d.\ L.\sqrt{2g}\ (H)^{3/2}$
(*c*) $C_d.\ L.\sqrt{2g}\ (H)^{5/2}$
(*d*) $\frac{2}{3} C_d.\ L.\sqrt{2g}\ (H)^{3/2}$.

where, C_d = Co-efficient of discharge,
L = Length of notch or weir, and
H = Height of water above sill of the notch.

6. Discharge, (Q) over a triangular notch or weir is given by
(*a*) $\frac{2}{3} C_d.\sqrt{2g}\ \tan\frac{\theta}{2}.\ H^{3/2}$
(*b*) $C_d.\sqrt{2g}\ \tan\frac{\theta}{2}.\ H^{5/2}$

(c) $\frac{1}{2} C_d.\sqrt{2g} \tan\theta H^{5/2}$

(d) $\frac{8}{15} C_d.\sqrt{2g} \tan\frac{\theta}{2}. H^{5/2}$

where, θ is the angule of notch.

7. Discharge over a trapezoidal notch or weir is given by

(a) $C_{d1}.L.\sqrt{2g}\, H^{3/2} + \frac{8}{15} C_{d2}.\sqrt{2g} \tan\frac{\theta}{2}.H^{3/2}$

(b) $\frac{2}{3} C_{d1}.L.\sqrt{2g}\, H^{3/2} + C_{d2}.\sqrt{2g} \tan\theta\, H^{5/2}$

(c) $\frac{2}{3} C_{d1}.L.\sqrt{2g}\, H^{3/2} + \frac{8}{15} C_{d2}\sqrt{2g} \tan\frac{\theta}{2}.H^{5/2}$

(d) $\frac{1}{2} C_{d1}.L.\sqrt{2g}\, H^{3/2}$

$+ \frac{8}{15} C_{d2}.\sqrt{2g} \tan\frac{\theta}{2}.H^{5/2}$

Where C_{d_1} = Co-efficient of discharge for the rectangular portion, and

C_{d_2} = Co-efficient of discharge for the traiangular portion.

8. An error of 1% in measuring H will produce ... error in discharge over a rectangular notch or weir.

(a) 1% (b) 1·5%
(c) 2% (d) 2·5%.

9. An error of 1% in measuring H will produce ... error in discharge over a triangular notch or weir

(a) 1% (b) 1·5%
(c) 2% (d) 2·5%.

10. The error in discharge due to the error in the measurement of head over a rectangular notch or weir is given by

(a) $\frac{dQ}{Q} = \frac{1}{2}\frac{dH}{H}$ (b) $\frac{dQ}{Q} = \frac{3}{2}\frac{dH}{H}$

(c) $\frac{dQ}{Q} = \frac{3}{4}\frac{dH}{H}$ (d) none of these.

11. The error in discharge due to the error in the measurement of head over a triangular notch or weir is given by

(a) $\frac{dQ}{Q} = \frac{1}{2}\frac{dH}{H}$ (b) $\frac{dQ}{Q} = \frac{dH}{H}$

(c) $\frac{dQ}{Q} = \frac{3}{2}\frac{dH}{H}$ (d) $\frac{dQ}{Q} = \frac{5}{2}\frac{dH}{H}$.

12. The discharge over a rectangular weir, considering velocity of approach, is given by

(a) $Q = \frac{2}{3} C_d.L.\sqrt{2g}\, H^{3/2}$

(b) $Q = \frac{2}{3} C_d.L.\sqrt{2g}\left[(H+H_a)^{3/2} - (H_a)^{3/2}\right]$

(c) $Q = \frac{2}{3} C_d.L.\sqrt{2g}\left[(H+H_a)^{1/2} - (H_a)^{1/2}\right]$

(d) none of these.

where H_a is the additional head due to velocity of approach.

13. Francis's formula for a rectangular weir with n end contractions is given by

(a) $Q = \frac{2}{3} C_d.(L - 0{\cdot}1\, nH)\sqrt{2g}.H^{3/2}$

(b) $Q = \frac{3}{2} C_d.(L - 0{\cdot}1\, nH)\sqrt{2g}.H^{5/2}$

(c) $Q = C_d.(L - 0{\cdot}1\, nH)\sqrt{2g}.H^{3/2}$

(d) none of these.

14. Discharge over a broad-crested weir is given by

(a) $Q = C_d.L.\sqrt{2g}\sqrt{H-h}$

(b) $Q = \frac{2}{3} C_d.L.\sqrt{2g}\sqrt{H-h}$

(c) $Q = \frac{3}{4} C_d.L.\sqrt{2g}\sqrt{H-h}$

(d) $Q = C_d.L.\sqrt{2g}\sqrt{Hh^2 - h^3}$

where, H = Head of water on the up-stream side of the weir,
h = Head of water on the down-stream side of the weir,
L = Length of the weir, and
C_d = Co-efficient of discharge.

15. Maximum discharge over a broad-crested weir is given by.

(a) $Q = C_d.L.H^{3/2}$
(b) $Q = 0{\cdot}5\, C_d.L.H^{5/2}$
(c) $Q = 1{\cdot}705\, C_d.L.H^{3/2}$
(d) $Q = 1{\cdot}705\, C_d.L.H^{5/2}$

16. The time required to empty a reservoir or a tank by a rectangular notch is given by

(a) $T = \frac{A}{C_d.L.\sqrt{2g}}\left[\frac{1}{\sqrt{H_2}} - \frac{1}{\sqrt{H_1}}\right]$

(b) $T = \frac{2A}{C_d.L.\sqrt{2g}}\left[\frac{1}{H_2^{3/2}} - \frac{1}{H_1^{3/2}}\right]$

(c) $T = \frac{3A}{C_d.L.\sqrt{2g}}\left[\frac{1}{\sqrt{H_2}} - \frac{1}{\sqrt{H_1}}\right]$

(d) none of these.

17. The time required to empty a reservoir or a tank by a triangular notch is given by

(a) $T = \dfrac{A}{4C_d . \tan \dfrac{\theta}{2} \sqrt{2g}} \left[\dfrac{1}{\sqrt{H_2}} - \dfrac{1}{\sqrt{H_1}} \right]$

(b) $T = \dfrac{3A}{4C_d . \tan \theta \sqrt{2g}} \left[\dfrac{1}{\sqrt{H_2}} - \dfrac{1}{\sqrt{H_1}} \right]$

(c) $T = \dfrac{5A}{4C_d . \tan \dfrac{\theta}{2} \sqrt{2g}} \left[\dfrac{1}{H_2^{3/2}} - \dfrac{1}{H_1^{3/2}} \right]$

(d) none of these.

ANSWERS

1. (b)	2. (b)	3. (c)	4. (c)	5. (d)	6. (d)
7. (c)	8. (b)	9. (d)	10. (b)	11. (d)	12. (b)
13. (a)	14. (d)	15. (c)	16. (c)	17. (c).	

THEORETICAL QUESTIONS

1. Define the following terms:
(i) Notch, (ii) Weir,
(iii) Nappe or vein (iv) Sill or crest.

2. What is the main difference between a notch and a weir ?

3. How are notches and weirs classified ?

4. Derive an expression for the discharge over a rectangular notch or weir in terms of head of water over the crest of the notch or weir.

5. Find an expression for the discharge over a triangular notch or weir in terms of head of water over the crest of the notch or weir.

6. Prove that the error in discharge due to error in the measurement of head over a triangular notch or weir is given by

$$\frac{dQ}{Q} = \frac{5}{2} \frac{dH}{H}$$

where, Q = Discharge through the triangular notch, and
H = Head over the triangular notch.

7. What are the advantages of a triangular notch over a rectangular notch ?

8. What is 'velocity of approach' ?

9. Derive an expression for the discharge over a rectangular weir with velocity of approach.

10. What do you understand by 'end contraction' of a weir ?

11. What is the effect of end contraction on the discharge through a weir ?

12. Find an expression for the discharge over a Cippoletti weir ?

13. Derive an expression for the maximum discharge over a broad-crested weir.

14. Write short notes on the following:
(i) Narrow-crested weir
(ii) Ogee weir.
(iii) Submerged or drowned weir.

15. Derive an expression for the time required to empty a tank with a rectangular notch.

16. Prove that the time (T) required to empty a tank with a triangular notch is given by

$$T = \frac{5A}{4C_d . \tan \frac{\theta}{2} \sqrt{2g}} \left[\frac{1}{H_2^{3/2}} - \frac{1}{H_1^{3/2}} \right]$$

Where, A = Uniform cross-sectional area of the tank,
θ = Angle of notch,
H_1 = Initial height of liquid above the apex of notch,
H_2 = Final height of liquid above the apex of notch, and
C_d = Co-efficient of discharge.

UNSOLVED EXAMPLES

1. Find the discharge of water flowing over a rectangular notch of 2·5 m length when the constant head over the notch is 400 mm. Take $C_d = 0{\cdot}62$. **[Ans.** 1·16 m^3/s]

2. The head of water over a rectangular notch is 900 mm. The discharge is 0·3 m^3/s. Find the length of the notch when $C_d = 0{\cdot}62$. **[Ans.** 192 mm]

3. Find the discharge over a triangular notch of angle 60° when the head over the V-notch is 0·3 m. Take $C_d = 0{\cdot}6$. **[Ans.** 0·04 m^3/s]

4. A rectangular channel 2·0 m wide has a discharge of 0·25 m^3/s, which is measured by a right-angled V-notch. Find the position of the apex of the notch from the bed of the channel if the maximum depth of water is not to exceed 1·3 m. Assume $C_d = 0{\cdot}62$. **[Ans.** 0·807 m]

5. Find the discharge through a trapezoidal notch which is 1 m wide at the top and 0·4 m at the bottom and is 0·3 m in height. The head of water on the notch is 0·2 m. Assume C_d for rectangular portion = 0·62 while for triangular portion = 0·6. **[Ans.** 0·09084 m^3/s]

6. Find the discharge over a stepped rectangular notch, as shown in Fig. 9·12. Take co-efficient of discharge for all the portions as 0·64. **[Ans.** 0·712 m^3/s]

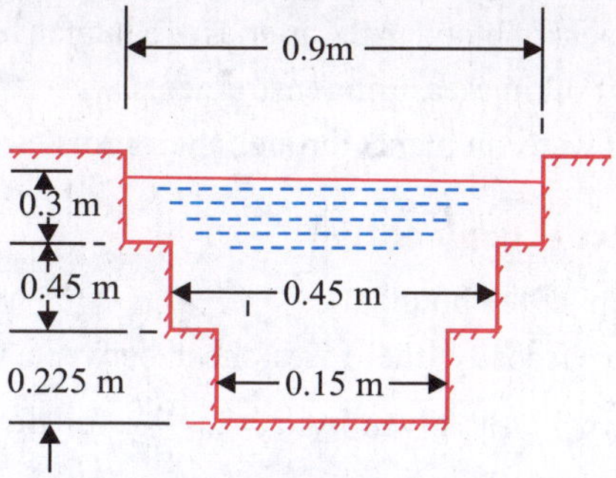

Fig. 9.12

7. A rectangular notch 400 mm long is used for measuring a discharge of 0·03 m^3/s. An error of 1·5 mm was made, while measuring the head over the notch. Calculate the precentage error in the discharge. Assume $C_d = 0{\cdot}6$. **[Ans.** 1·85%]

8. A right angled V-notch is used for measuring a discharge of 0·03 m^3/s. An error of 1·5 mm was made while measuring the head over the notch. Calculate the percentage error in the discharge. Assume $C_d = 0{\cdot}62$. **[Ans.** 1·77%]

9. A discharge of 0·15 m^3/s was measured over a V-notch under a constant head of 1 metre. Determine the percentage error, in the measurement of discharge, if an error of 10 mm has taken place while measuring the head of water. **[Ans.** 2·5%]

10. Find the discharge over a rectangular weir of length 100 m. The head of water over the weir is 1·5 m. The velocity of approach is given as 0·5 m/s. Assume $C_d = 0{\cdot}6$. **[Ans.** 329·35 m^3/s]

11. The head of water over a rectangular weir is 400 mm. The length of the crest of the weir with end contraction suppressed is 1·5 m. Find the discharge using the following formulae:
   (*i*) Francis's formula, and
   (*ii*) Bazin's formula
   [Ans. (*i*) 0·6982 m^3/s, (*ii*) 0·6932 m^3/s]

12. A weir 36 metres long is divided into 12 equal bays by vertical posts, each 0·6 m wide. Determine the discharge over the weir if the head over the crest is 1·20 m and velocity of approach is 1·2 m/s. Use Francis's formula. **[Ans.** 75·246 m^3/s]

13. Water is flowing over a Cippoletti weir 4 metres long under a head of 1 metre. Calculate the discharge, if the co-efficient of discharge for the weir is 0·6. **[Ans.** 7·086 m^3/s]

14. A 40 m long broad-creasted weir has 0·4 m height of water above its crest. Find the maximum discharge. Take $C_d = 0{\cdot}6$. Neglect velocity of approach. **[Ans.** 10·35 m^3/s]

15. In a submerged weir of 3 m length the heights of water on the upstream and downstream sides are 0·2 m and 0·1 m respectively. Find the discharge over the weir if the discharge co-efficients for free and drowned portions are 0·6 and 0·8 respectively. **[Ans.** 0·504 m^3/s]

Chapter 10

LAMINAR FLOW

10.1. INTRODUCTION

So far, in the preceding chapters, primarily the flow of an ideal fluid has been discussed. In the case of Newtonian fluid, the flows can be classified as (*i*) laminar (or viscous), and (*ii*) turbulent, depending on characteristic Reynolds number $\frac{\rho V l}{\mu}$, where l is the characteristic length.

Examples of laminar/viscous flow:

(*i*) Flow past tiny bodies.

(*ii*) Underground flow.

(*iii*) Movement of blood in the arteries of a human body.

(*iv*) Flow of oil in measuring instruments.

(*v*) Rise of water in plants through their roots etc.

Characteristics of laminar flow:

(*i*) 'No slip' at the boundary.

(*ii*) Due to viscosity, there is a shear between fluid layers, which is given by $\tau = \mu \cdot \frac{du}{dy}$ for flow in X-direction.

(*iii*) The flow is rotational.

(*iv*) Due to viscous shear, there is continuous *dissipation of energy* and for maintaining the flow energy must be supplied externally.

(*v*) Loss of energy is proportional to *first power of velocity* and *first power of viscosity*.

(*vi*) No mixing between different fluid layers (except by molecular motion, which is very small).

(*vii*) The flow remains laminar as long as $\frac{\rho V l}{\mu}$ is *less* than critical value of Reynolds number.

10.2. REYNOLDS EXPERIMENT

Osborne Reynolds in 1883, with the help of a simple experiment (see Fig. 10.1), demonstrated the existence of the following two types of flows:

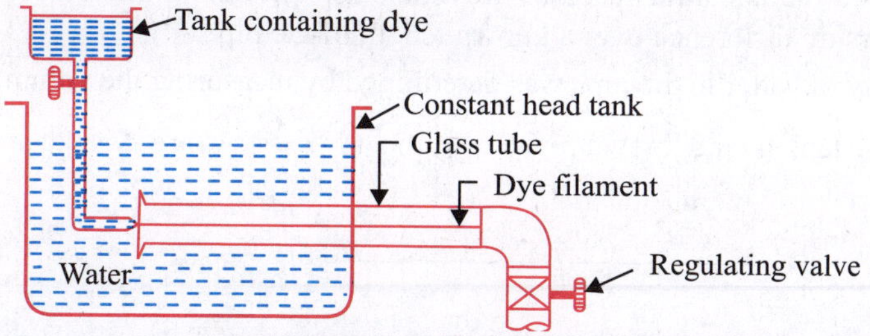

Fig.10.1. Reynolds apparatus.

1. Laminar flow (Reynolds number, $Re < 2000$)
2. Turbulent flow (Reynolds number, $Re > 4000$)

(Re between 2000 and 4000 indicates *transition from laminar to turbulent flow*)

Reynolds experiment:

***Apparatus*:**

Refer to Fig. 10.1. Reynolds experiment apparatus consisted essentially of the following:

1. A constant head tank filled with water,
2. A small tank containing dye (sp. weight of dye same as that of water),
3. A horizontal glass tube provided with a bell mouthed entrance, and
4. A regulating valve.

Procedure followed:

The water was made to flow from the tank through the glass tube into the atmosphere and the velocity of flow was varied by adjusting valve. The liquid dye was introduced into the flow at the bell mouth through a small tube as shown in Fig. 10.1.

Observations made:

1. When the *velocity* of flow was *low*, the dye remained in the form of a *straight* and *stable filament* passing through the glass tube so steadily that it scarecely seemed to be in motion. This was a case of **laminar flow** as shown in Fig. 10.2 (*a*).
2. With the increase of velocity a critical state was reached at which the dye filament showed irregularities and began to waver (see Fig. 10.2 *b*). This shows that the flow is no longer a laminar one. This was a **transitional state**.
3. With further increase in velocity of flow the fluctuations in the filament of dye became more intense and ultimately the dye diffused over the entire cross-section of the tube, due to the intermingling of the particles of the flowing fluid. This was the case of a **turbulent flow** as shown in Fig. 10.2 (*c*).

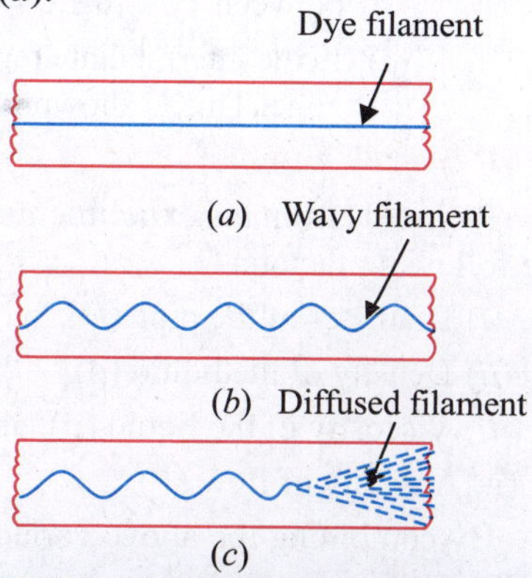

Fig. 10.2. Appearance of dye filament in (*a*) laminar flow, (*b*) transition, and (*c*) turbulent flow.

On the basis of his experiment Reynolds discovered that:

(*i*) In case of **laminar flow:** The loss of pressure head ∝ velocity.

(*ii*) In case of **turbulent flow:** The loss of head is approximately ∝ V^2

[More exactly the loss of head ∝ V^n where *n* varies from 1.75 to 2.0]

Fig. 10.3 shows the apparatus used by Reynolds for estimating the loss of head in a pipe by measuring the pressure difference over a known length of the pipe.

(*i*) The velocity of water in the pipe was determined by measuring the volume of water (*Q*) collected in the tank over a known period of time ($V = \frac{Q}{A}$, where *A* is the area of cross-section of the pipe.)

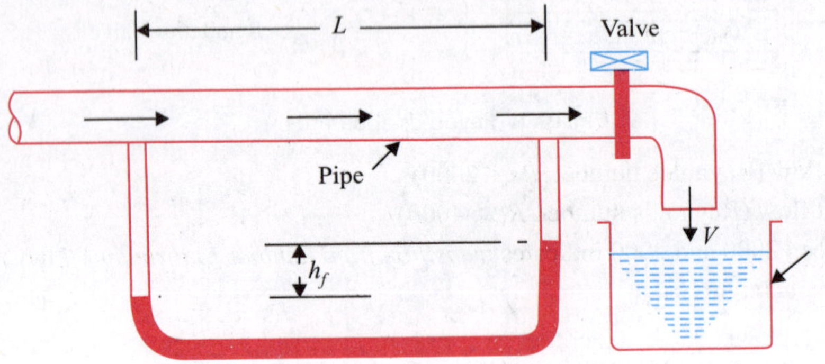

Fig. 10.3. Loss of head in a pipe.

(*ii*) The velocity of flow (*V*) was changed and corresponding values of h_f (loss of head) were obtained.

(*iii*) A graph was plotted between *V* (velocity of flow) and h_f (loss of head). Such a graph is shown in Fig. 10.4. It may be seen from the graph that:

(*a*) At *low velocities* the curve is a straight line, indicating that the h_f (loss of head) is *directly proportional to velocity*—the flow is **laminar** (or viscous),

(*b*) At *higher velocities* the curve is parabolic; in this range $h_f \alpha V^n$, where the value of *n* lies between 1.75 to 2.0 — the flow is **turbulent.**

(*c*) In the intermediate region, there is a transition zone. This is shown by *dotted line.*

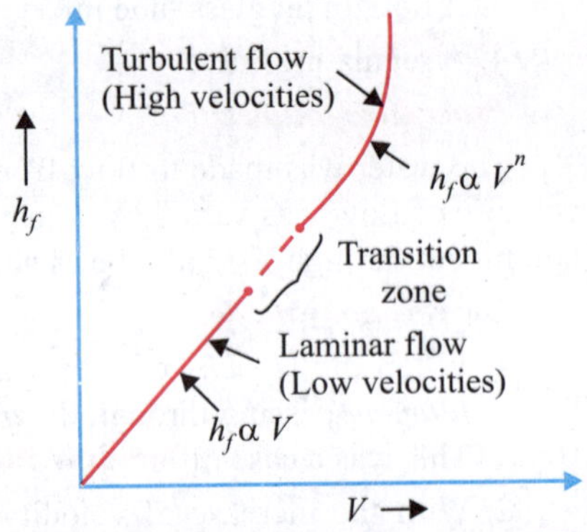

Fig. 10.4

Reynolds number :

Reynolds from his experiments found that the nature of flow in a *closed conduit* depends upon the following factors:

(*i*) Diameter of the pipe (*D*),

(*ii*) Density of the liquid (ρ),

(*iii*) Viscosity of the liquid (μ), and

(*iv*) Velocity of flow (*V*).

By combining the above variables Reynolds determined a non-dimensional quantity equal to $\frac{\rho VD}{\mu}$ which is known as ***Reynolds number*** (*Re*).

i.e. Reynolds number $$Re = \frac{\rho VD}{\mu}$$

(In general case D is replaced by L, known as characteristic length and we have, $Re = \frac{\rho VL}{\mu}$)

It may also be expressed as:

$$Re = \frac{VD}{\nu}$$

where, ν = Kinematic viscosity $\left(= \frac{\mu}{\rho}\right)$

when, $Re < 2000$ ... the flow is *laminar* (or viscous)

$Re > 4000$ ... the flow is *turbulent*.

Re between 2000 and 4000 ... the flow is *unpredictable*.

Critical Reynolds number :

- All experiments agree that a lower limit of critical value of $(Re)_{cr}$ exists (though there appears to be no definite upper limit of the critical value of $(Re)_{cr}$ which characterises full attainment of turbulence) and its value is approximately 2000 (for circular pipe). This lower critical Reynolds number is of greater engineering importance as it defines the *limit below which all turbulence, no matter how severe, entering the flow from any source will eventually be damped out by viscous action.*
- It has been observed that the upper limit of critical Reynolds number $(Re)_{cr}$ depends upon the following factors:
  - (*i*) Initial turbulence in the flow (approach),
  - (*ii*) Shape of the pipe entrance, and
  - (*iii*) Roughness of pipe.

Reynolds found the upper limit of $(Re)_{cr}$ to lie between $12000 < (Re)_{cr} < 14000$; these values are of little practical interest and we may consider the upper limit of $(Re)_{cr}$ to be defined by $2700 < (Re)_{cr} < 4000$.

— For demarcating the regimes of laminar and turbulent flows, the concept of critical Reynolds number proves quite useful.

The *lower* critical Reynolds number for some important cases are as under:

(*i*) $(Re)_{cr} = 1$ ... for sphere

(*ii*) $(Re)_{cr} = 50$ ... for open channels

(*iii*) $(Re)_{cr} = 1000$ ... for parallel plates.

10.3. NAVIER-STOKES EQUATIONS OF MOTION

Refer to Fig. 10.5.

Consider an infinitly small mass of fluid enclosed in an elemantary parallelopiped of sides dx, dy and dz. The motion of the fluid element is influenced by the following forces :

(*i*) *Normal forces due to pressure :*

The net pressure force in the X-direction

$$= p.\,dy\,.\,dz - \left[p + \frac{\partial p}{\partial x}dx\right]dy\,.\,dz = -\frac{\partial p}{\partial x}dx\,.\,dy\,.\,dz$$

(*ii*) *Gravity or body force :*

Let B be the body force *per unit mass of fluid* having components B_x, B_y and B_z in the X, Y and Z directions respectively.

Then, the body force acting on the parallelopiped in the direction of X-coordinate

$$= B_x \,.\, \rho \,.\, dx \,.\, dy \,.\, dz.$$

(iii) Inertia forces :

The inertia force acting on the fluid mass, along the *X*-co-ordinate is given by,

Mass × acceleration

$$= \rho \,.\, dx \,.\, dy \,.\, dz \,.\, \frac{du}{dt}$$

(iv) Shear forces:

Let S_x, S_y, S_z be the components of shear force per unit mass set up by viscous effects in *X*, *Y* and *Z* direction respectively. Then, the shear force acting on the parallelopied in the direction of *X*-co-ordinate is $= S_x \,.\, \rho \,.\, dx \,.\, dy \,.\, dz$

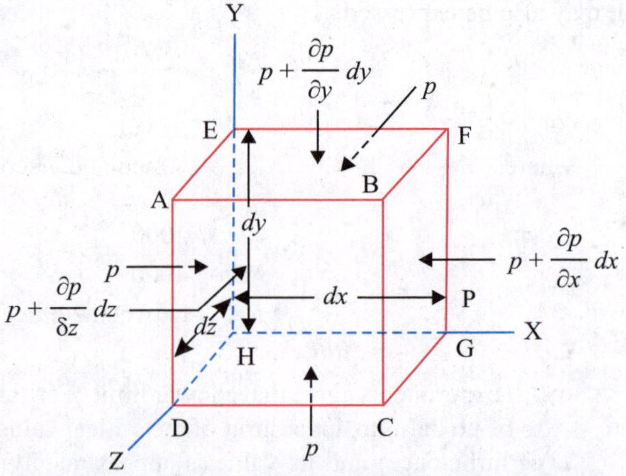

Fig. 10.5

As per Newton's second law of motion summation of forces acting in the fluid element in any direction equals the resulting inertia forces in that direction. Thus along *X*-direction:

$$-\frac{\partial p}{\partial x} dx \,.\, dy \,.\, dz + B_x \,.\, \rho \,.\, dx \,.\, dy \,.\, dz + S_x \,.\, \rho \,.\, dx \,.\, dy \,.\, dz = \rho \,.\, dx \,.\, dy \,.\, dz \,\frac{du}{dt}$$

$$B_x - \frac{1}{\rho} \cdot \frac{\partial p}{\partial x} = \frac{du}{dt} - S_x$$

Similarly, $$B_y - \frac{1}{\rho} \cdot \frac{\partial p}{\partial y} = \frac{dv}{dt} - S_y,$$

and, $$B_z - \frac{1}{\rho} \cdot \frac{\partial p}{\partial z} = \frac{dw}{dt} - S_z \qquad ...(10.1)$$

Let us now find the ***values of S_x, S_y and S_z:***

— The resistance (shear) force acting on the face AEHD $= -\mu \frac{\partial u}{\partial x} (dy \,.\, dz)$

(Resistance force due to viscosity = τ × area)

The resistance force acting on the face BFGC

$$= \mu \frac{\partial}{\partial x}\left(u + \frac{\partial u}{\partial x} \,.\, dx\right)(dy \,.\, dz) = \mu \left(\frac{\partial u}{\partial x} + \frac{\partial^2 u}{\partial x^2} dx\right)(dy \,.\, dz)$$

The resistance forces acting on the opposite faces have opposite signs. Further, *both of these forces are direced apposite to the respective opposite forces.*

The resultant force along the *X*-axis

= The algebraic sum of forces acting on the faces AEHD and BFGC

$$= -\mu \frac{\partial u}{\partial x} (dy \,.\, dz) + \mu \left(\frac{\partial u}{\partial x} + \frac{\partial^2 u}{\partial x^2} dx\right)(dy \,.\, dz)$$

$$= \mu \frac{\partial^2 u}{\partial x^2} dx \,.\, dy \,.\, dz \qquad ...(i)$$

— Similarly the *X*-component of the resistance force acting on the faces EFGH and ABCD respectively are :

$$-\ \mu \frac{\partial u}{\partial z}(dx\,.\,dy) \quad \text{and} \quad \mu\left(\frac{\partial u}{\partial z}+\frac{\partial^2 u}{\partial z^2}\,.\,dz\right)(dx\,.\,dy)$$

The resultant force along the X-axis

$$= \text{The sum of the above components} = \mu\,\frac{\partial^2 u}{\partial z^2}\,.\,dx\,.\,dy\,.\,dz \quad ...(ii)$$

— Similarly, the X-components of the resistance force acting on the faces DHGC and AEFB

$$= \mu\,\frac{\partial^2 u}{\partial y^2}\,dx\,.\,dy\,.\,dz \qquad ...(iii)$$

The total viscous force, parallel to X-axis, on all the six faces of the parallelopiped is given by the sum of the quantities (*i*), (*ii*) and (*iii*) and is

$$= \mu\cdot\frac{\partial^2 u}{\partial x^2}\cdot dx\cdot dy\cdot dz + \mu\cdot\frac{\partial^2 u}{\partial y^2}\cdot dx\cdot dy\cdot dz + \mu\cdot\frac{\partial^2 \mu}{\partial z^2}\cdot dx\cdot dy\cdot dz$$

$$= \mu\cdot\left(\frac{\partial^2 u}{\partial x^2}+\frac{\partial^2 u}{\partial y^2}+\frac{\partial^2 u}{\partial z^2}\right)dx\cdot dy\cdot dz$$

The resistance (shear) per unit mass in obtained by dividing the above quantity by $\rho\ dx\,.\,dy\,.\,dz$.

$$\therefore \qquad S_x = \frac{\mu}{\rho}\left(\frac{\partial^2 u}{\partial x^2}+\frac{\partial^2 u}{\partial y^2}+\frac{\partial^2 u}{\partial z^2}\right) = \nu\left(\frac{\partial^2 u}{\partial x^2}+\frac{\partial^2 u}{\partial y^2}+\frac{\partial^2 u}{\partial z^2}\right),$$

Similarly

$$S_y = \nu\left(\frac{\partial^2 v}{\partial x^2}+\frac{\partial^2 v}{\partial y^2}+\frac{\partial^2 v}{\partial z^2}\right), \text{ and}$$

$$S_z = \nu\left(\frac{\partial^2 w}{\partial x^2}+\frac{\partial^2 w}{\partial y^2}+\frac{\partial^2 w}{\partial z^2}\right).$$

Putting these values of S_x, S_y and S_z in eqn. (10.1), we get:

$$B_x - \frac{1}{\rho}\cdot\frac{\partial p}{\partial x} = \frac{du}{dt} - \nu\left[\frac{\partial^2 u}{\partial x^2}+\frac{\partial^2 u}{\partial y^2}+\frac{\partial^2 u}{\partial z^2}\right]$$

$$B_y - \frac{1}{\rho}\cdot\frac{\partial p}{\partial y} = \frac{dv}{dt} - \nu\left[\frac{\partial^2 v}{\partial x^2}+\frac{\partial^2 v}{\partial y^2}+\frac{\partial^2 v}{\partial z^2}\right]$$

$$B_z - \frac{1}{\rho}\cdot\frac{\partial p}{\partial z} = \frac{dw}{dt} - \nu\left[\frac{\partial^2 w}{\partial x^2}+\frac{\partial^2 w}{\partial y^2}+\frac{\partial^2 w}{\partial z^2}\right] \qquad ...\ (10.2)$$

These equations are called **Navier-Stokes equations** *and are fundamental to general analysis of a viscous flow.*

- Navier-Stokes equations, *in vector form*, may be writtern as :

$$\frac{DV}{Dt} = B - \frac{1}{\rho}\ \text{grad.}\ p + \nu\,\nabla^2 V$$

Where ∇^2 denotes the Laplace operator,

i.e.

$$\nabla^2 = \left[\frac{\partial^2}{\partial x^2}+\frac{\partial^2}{\partial y^2}+\frac{\partial^2}{\partial z^2}\right]$$

- The number of unknown, for an incompressible flow is four *viz.* u, v, w and p. The Navier-Stokes equation plus incompressible continuity equation $\frac{\partial u}{\partial x} + \frac{\partial v}{\partial y} + \frac{\partial w}{\partial z} = 0$ are the sufficient conditions for the determination of the flow characteristics.
- Since Navier-Stokes equation is a second order non-linear differential equation, therefore, its general solution has not been yet found out (the non-linearity arises from the convective terms in $\frac{DV}{Dt}$). Thus, *the solutions are available for flow situations where the fluid characteristics such as viscosity and density are constant and boundary configuration is simple.*

Some of the *important applications of Navier-Stokes equations are:*

1. Laminar flow in circular pipes.
2. Laminar flow between concentric rotating cylinders.
3. Laminar uni-directional flow between stationary parallel plates.
4. Laminar uni-directional flow between parallel plates having relative motion.

10.4. RELATIONSHIP BETWEEN SHEAR STRESS AND PRESSURE GRADIENT

Let us consider a fluid element having the form of an elementary parallelopiped shown in Fig. 10.6 (*a*). The velocity distribution is shown in Fig. 10.6 (*b*); the velocity distribution is non-uniform due to relative motion between different layers of fluid. The motion of the fluid element will be resisted by shearing or frictional forces which must be overcome by maintaining a pressure gradient in the direction of flow. Let us assume that the pressure is uniformly distributed at both the ends of the body.

Let, τ = Shear stress on the lower face *ABCD* of the element, then

$\tau + \frac{\partial \tau}{\partial y}\delta y$ = Shear stress on the upper face *A′B′C′D′* of the element.

For two-dimensional steady flow there will be no shear stresses on the vertical faces *ABB′A′* and *CDD′C′*. Thus the only forces acting on the element in the direction of flow (*X*-axis) will be the pressure and shear forces.

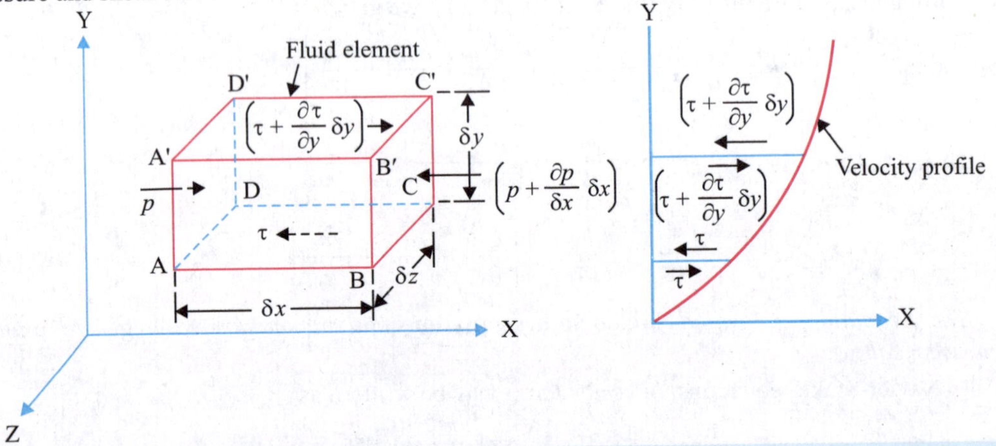

Fig. 10.6. Forces on a fluid element in laminar flow.

Net shearing force on the element

$$= \left(\tau + \frac{\partial \tau}{\partial y}\delta y\right)\delta x \cdot \delta z - \tau \cdot \delta x \cdot \delta z$$

$$= \frac{\partial \tau}{\partial y}\delta x \cdot \delta y \cdot \delta z \quad \text{...(i)}$$

Net pressure force on the element

$$= p \cdot \delta y \cdot \delta z - \left(p + \frac{\partial p}{\partial x} \cdot \delta x\right) \delta y \cdot \delta z$$

$$= -\frac{\partial p}{\partial x} \delta x \cdot \delta y \cdot \delta z \qquad \text{...}(ii)$$

For the flow to be steady and uniform, there being no acceleration, the sum of the forces must be zero.

From (*i*) and (*ii*), we have:

$$\frac{\partial \tau}{\partial y} \cdot \delta x \cdot \delta y \cdot \delta z - \frac{\partial p}{\partial x} \cdot \delta x \cdot \delta y \cdot \delta z = 0$$

or,

$$\frac{\partial \tau}{\partial y} = \frac{\partial p}{\partial x} \qquad \text{...(10.3)}$$

This equation (10.3) indicates that the *pressure gradient in the direction of flow is equal to the shear gradient in the direction normal to the direction of flow*. This equation holds good for *all types of flow* and *all types of boundary geometry*.

10.5. FLOW OF VISCOUS FLUID IN CIRCULAR PIPES—HAGEN POISEUILLE LAW

Hagen–Poiseuille theory is based on the following *assumptions*:

1. The fluid follows Newton's law of viscosity.
2. There is no slip of fluid particles at the boundary (*i.e.* the fluid particles adjacent to the pipe will have zero velocity).

Fig. 10.7 shows a horizontal circular pipe of radius R, having laminar flow of fluid through it. Consider a small concentric cylinder (fluid element) of radius r and length dx as a free body.

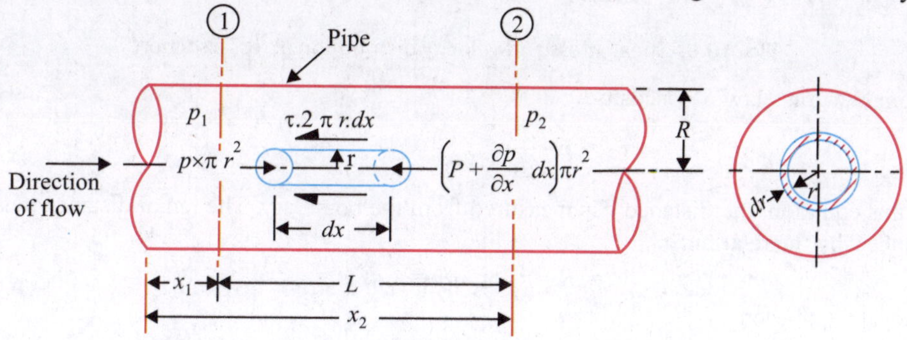

Fig. 10.7. Viscous/laminar flow through a circular pipe.

If τ is the shear stress, the shear force F is given by:

$$F = \tau \times 2\pi r \times dx$$

Let p be the intensity of pressure at left end and the intensity of pressure at the right end be $\left(p + \frac{\partial p}{\partial x} \cdot dx\right)$.

Thus the forces acting on the fluid element are:

1. The shear force, $\tau \times 2\pi r \times dx$ on the surface of fluid element.
2. The pressure force, $p \times \pi r^2$ on the left end.
3. The pressure force, $\left(p + \frac{\partial p}{\partial x} \cdot dx\right) \pi r^2$ on the right end.

For steady flow, the net force on the cylinder must be *zero*.

$$\therefore \quad \left[p \times \pi r^2 - \left(p + \frac{\partial p}{\partial x} \cdot dx \right) \pi r^2 \right] - \tau \times 2\pi r \times dx = 0$$

or,
$$-\frac{\partial p}{\partial x} \cdot dx \times \pi r^2 - \tau \times 2\pi r \times dx = 0$$

or,
$$\tau = -\frac{\partial p}{\partial x} \cdot \frac{r}{2} \qquad ...(10.4)$$

— Eqn. (10.4) shows that flow will occur only if *pressure gradient exists in the direction of flow*. The *negative sign* shows that *pressure decreases in the direction of flow*.

— Eqn. (10.2) indicates that the *shear stress* varies linearly across the section (see Fig. 10.8). Its value is zero at the centre of pipe ($r = 0$) and maximum at the pipe wall given by:

$$\tau_0 = -\frac{\partial p}{\partial x}\left(\frac{R}{2}\right) \qquad ...[10.4\,(a)]$$

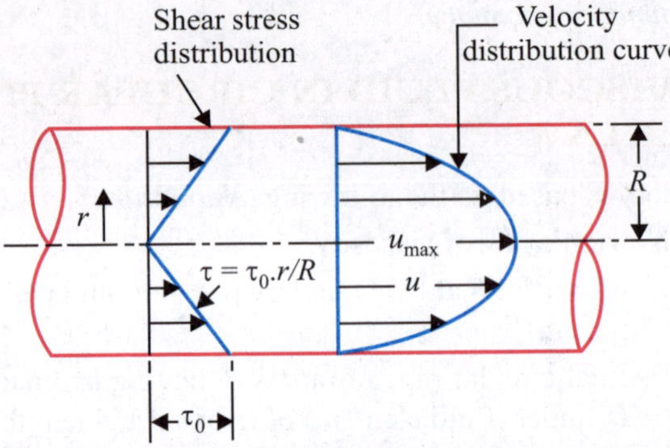

Fig. 10.8. Shear stress and velocity distribution across a section.

From Newton's law of viscosity,

$$\tau = \mu \cdot \frac{du}{dy} \qquad ...(i)$$

In this equation, the distance y is measured from the boundary. The radial distance r is related to distance y by the relation:

$$y = R - r \quad \text{or} \quad dy = -\,dr$$

The eqn. (*i*) becomes

$$\tau = -\mu \frac{du}{dr} \qquad ...(10.5)$$

Comparing two values of τ from eqns. 10.2 and 10.3, we have:

$$-\mu \frac{du}{dr} = -\frac{\partial p}{\partial x} \cdot \frac{r}{2}$$

or,
$$du = \frac{1}{2\mu}\left(\frac{\partial p}{\partial x}\right) r \cdot dr$$

Integrating the above equation w.r.t. 'r', we get:

$$u = \frac{1}{4\mu} \cdot \frac{\partial p}{\partial x} \cdot r^2 + C \qquad ...(10.6)$$

Where C is the constant of integration and its value is obtained from the boundary condition :

At, $$r = R, \ u = 0$$

$$\therefore \quad 0 = \frac{1}{4\mu} \cdot \frac{\partial p}{\partial x} R^2 + C \quad \text{or} \quad C = -\frac{1}{4\mu} \cdot \frac{\partial p}{\partial x} \cdot R^2$$

Substituting this value of C in eqn. (10.4), we get:

$$u = \frac{1}{4\mu} \cdot \frac{\partial p}{\partial x} r^2 - \frac{1}{4\mu} \cdot \frac{\partial p}{\partial x} R^2$$

or,
$$u = -\frac{1}{4\mu} \cdot \frac{\partial p}{\partial x} (R^2 - r^2) \quad \text{...(10.7)}$$

Eqn. (10.7) shows that the velocity distribution curve is a *parabola* (see Fig. 10.8). The maximum velocity occurs at the centre and is given by,

$$u_{max} = -\frac{1}{4\mu} \cdot \frac{\partial p}{\partial x} \cdot R^2 \quad \text{...(10.8)}$$

From eqns. (10.7) and (10.8), we have:

$$u = u_{max} \left[1 - \left(\frac{r}{R}\right)^2\right] \quad \text{...(10.9)}$$

Eqn. (10.9) is the *most commonly used equation for the velocity distribution for laminar flow through pipes*. This equation can be used to calculate the *discharge as* follows:

The discharge through an elementary ring of thickness dr at radial distances r is given by:

$$dQ = u \times 2\pi r \times dr$$

$$= u_{max} \left[1 - \left(\frac{r}{R}\right)^2\right] 2\pi r \cdot dr$$

Total discharge, $$Q = \int dQ$$

$$= \int_0^R u_{max} \left[1 - \left(\frac{r}{R}\right)^2\right] 2\pi r \cdot dr$$

$$= 2\pi \, u_{max} \int_0^R \left(r - \frac{r^3}{R^2}\right) dr$$

$$= 2\pi \, u_{max} \left[\frac{r^2}{2} - \frac{r^4}{4R^2}\right]_0^R = 2\pi \, u_{max} \left[\frac{R^2}{2} - \frac{R^4}{4R^2}\right]$$

$$= \frac{\pi}{2} u_{max} \, R^2$$

Average velocity of flow, $$\bar{u} = \frac{Q}{A} = \frac{\frac{\pi}{2} u_{max} \, R^2}{\pi R^2} = \frac{u_{max}}{2} \quad \text{...(10.10)}$$

Eqn. (10.10) shows that the *average velocity is one-half the maximum velocity.*

Substituting the value of u_{max} from eqn. (10.8), we have:

$$\bar{u} = -\frac{1}{8\mu} \cdot \frac{\partial p}{\partial x} \cdot R^2$$

or,
$$-\partial p = \frac{8\mu \bar{u}}{R^2} \cdot \partial x$$

The pressure difference between two sections 1 and 2 at distance x_1 and x_2 (see Fig. 10.7). is given by

$$-\int_{p_1}^{p_2} \partial p = \frac{8\mu\bar{u}}{R^2} \int_{x_1}^{x_2} \partial x$$

or,
$$(p_1 - p_2) = \frac{8\mu\bar{u}}{R^2}(x_2 - x_1) = \frac{8\mu\bar{u}L}{R^2}$$

or,
$$(p_1 - p_2) = \frac{32\mu\bar{u}\,L}{D^2} \quad \text{...(10.11)}$$

where, D is the diameter of the pipe, and L is the length.

Eqn. (10.11) is known as the **Hagen-Poiseuille equation.**

Example 10.1. *An oil of viscosity 9 poise and specific gravity 0.9 is flowing through a horizontal pipe of 60 mm diameter. If the pressure drop in 100 m length of the pipe is 1800 kN/m², determine:*

(i) *The rate of flow of oil;*

(ii) *The centre-line velocity;*

(iii) *The total frictional drag over 100 m length;*

(iv) *The power required to maintain the flow;*

(v) *The velocity gradient at the pipe wall;*

(vi) *The velocity and shear stress at 8 mm from the wall.*

Solution. Viscosity of the oil, $\mu = 9 \text{ poise} = \frac{1}{10} \times 9 = 0.9 \text{ Ns/m}^2$

Sp. gr. of the oil $= 0.9$

Diameter of the pipe, $D = 60 \text{ mm} = 0.06 \text{ m}$

$\therefore$ Area of the pipe, $A = \frac{\pi}{4} \times 0.06^2 = 0.002827 \text{ m}^2$

Pressure drop in 100 m length of the pipe, $\Delta p = 1800 \text{ kN/m}^2$

(i) The rate of flow, Q:

$$(p_1 - p_2) = \Delta p = \frac{32\mu\bar{u}\,L}{D^2} \quad \text{(where } \bar{u} = \text{average velocity)}$$

$$1800 \times 10^3 = \frac{32 \times 0{\cdot}9 \times \bar{u} \times 100}{(0{\cdot}06)^2}$$

or,
$$\bar{u} = \frac{1800 \times 10^3 \times (0{\cdot}06)^2}{32 \times 0{\cdot}9 \times 100} = 2{\cdot}25 \text{ m/s}$$

$$\text{Reynolds number, } Re = \frac{\rho VD}{\mu} = \frac{0.9 \times 1000 \times 2.25 \times 0.06}{0.9} = 135$$

As Re is less than 2000, the flow is *laminar.*

Rate of flow, $Q = A.\bar{u} = 0.002827 \times 2.25$

$= \mathbf{0.00636\ m^3/s}$ **or 6.36 lit./s. (Ans.)**

(ii) The centre-line velocity, u_{max}:

$u_{max} = 2\bar{u} = 2 \times 2.25 =$ **4.5 m/s (Ans.)**

(*iii*) The total frictional drag over 100 m length, F_D:

Wall shear stress,

$$\tau_0 = -\frac{\partial p}{\partial x} \cdot \frac{R}{2} \qquad \text{...[Eqn. 10.2 (a)]}$$

Now,
$$-\frac{\partial p}{\partial x} = -\frac{p_2 - p_1}{x_2 - x_1} = \frac{p_1 - p_2}{L} = \frac{\Delta p}{L} = \frac{1800 \times 10^3}{100} = 18000$$

$\therefore$
$$\tau_0 = 18000 \times \frac{0 \cdot 06/2}{2} = 270 \text{ N/m}^2$$

$\therefore$ Frictional drag for 100 m length,

$$F_D = \tau_0 \times \pi DL = 270 \times \pi \times 0.06 \times 100 = 5089 \text{ N or } \mathbf{5.089 \text{ kN}} \text{ (Ans.)}$$

(*iv*) The power required to maintain the flow, *P*:

$$P = F_D \times \bar{u}$$
$$= 5.089 \times 2.25 = \mathbf{11.45 \text{ kW}} \text{ (Ans.)}$$

[Alternatively, $P = Q \,.\, \Delta p = 0.00636 \times 1800 = 11.45$ kW]

(*v*) The velocity gradient at the pipe wall, $\left(\frac{du}{dy}\right)_{y=0}$:

$$\tau_0 = \mu \cdot \left(\frac{\partial u}{dy}\right)_{y=0}$$

or,
$$\left(\frac{\partial u}{dy}\right)_{y=0} = \frac{\tau_0}{\mu} = \frac{270}{0.9} = \mathbf{300 \text{ s}^{-1}} \text{ (Ans.)}$$

(*vi*) The velocity and shear stress at 8 mm from the wall :

$$u = -\frac{1}{4\mu} \cdot \frac{\partial p}{\partial x}(R^2 - r^2) \qquad \text{...[Eqn. (10.5)]}$$

Here, $y = 8 \text{ mm} = 0.008$ m

But, $y = R - r$

$\therefore$ $0.008 = 0.03 - r$ or $r = 0.022$ m

$\therefore$
$$u_{(8\,mm)} = -\frac{1}{4 \times 0.9} \times \frac{1800 \times 10^3}{100}(0.03^2 - 0.022^2)$$
$$= \mathbf{2.08 \text{ m/s}} \text{ (Ans.)}$$

Also,
$$\frac{\tau}{r} = \frac{\tau_0}{R} \qquad \text{(Refer to Fig. 10.9)}$$

$\therefore$
$$\tau_{(8\,mm)} = r \times \frac{\tau_0}{R} = 0.022 \times \frac{270}{0.03}$$
$$= \mathbf{198 \text{ kN/m}^2} \text{ (Ans.)}$$

Example 10.2. *Oil of absolute viscosity 1.5 poise and density 848.3 kg/m^3 flows through a 30 cm I.D. pipe. If the head loss in 3000 m length of pipe is 20 m, assuming a laminar flow, determine* **(i)** *the velocity,* **(ii)** *Reynolds number and* **(iii)** *friction factor (Fanning's).* **(UPTU)**

Solution. *Given* : $\mu = 1.5$ poise $= 1.5 \times \frac{1}{10} = 0.15$ N-s/m^2, $\rho = 848.3$ kg/m^3; $D = 30$ cm $= 0.3$ m; $h_f = 20$ m; $L = 3000$ m; Flow-*laminar.*

(*i*) The velocity:

We know that,
$$\Delta p = \frac{32\mu\bar{u}L}{D^2} \quad \text{(where, } \bar{u} = \text{average velocity)}$$

or, $$\Delta p = \rho g h_f = \frac{32\mu \bar{u} L}{D^2}$$

or, $$\bar{u} = \frac{\rho g h_f D^2}{32\,\mu L} = \frac{848.3 \times 9.81 \times 20 \times 0.3^2}{32 \times 0.15 \times 3000} = \textbf{1.04 m/s (Ans.)}$$

***(ii)* Reynolds number; *Re* :**

$$Re = \frac{\rho \bar{u} D}{\mu} = \frac{848.3 \times 1.04 \times 0.3}{0.15} = \textbf{1764.5 (Ans.)}$$

***(iii)* Friction coefficient, *f* :**

$$f = \frac{16}{Re} = \frac{16}{1764.5} = \textbf{0.00907 (Ans.)} \quad \text{[Eqn. (10.11)]}$$

Example 10.3. *A crude oil of viscosity 0.9 poise and relative density 0.9 is flowing through a horizontal circular pipe of diameter 120 mm and length 12 m. Calculate the difference of pressure at the two ends of the pipe, if 785 N of the oil is collected in a tank in 25 seconds.*

Solution. Viscosity of the crude oil, μ = 0.9 poise = 0.09 Ns/m^2

Relative density = 0.9

$\therefore$ Weight density = 0.9 × 9810 = 8829 N/m^3

Diameter of the pipe, D = 120 mm = 0.12 m

Length of the pipe, L = 12 m

Weight of the oil collected in 25 s = 785 N

Difference of pressure, $(p_1 - p_2)$:

The difference of pressure for viscous or laminar flow is given by

$$(p_1 - p_2) = \frac{32\mu\, \bar{u}\, L}{D^2}$$

Now, weight of oil collected/sec. $= \frac{785}{25} = 31.4 \text{ N/s} = w \times Q$

$$\therefore \quad Q = \frac{31.4}{8829} = 0.00355 \text{ m}^3/\text{s}$$

$$\text{Average velocity, } \bar{u} = \frac{Q}{\text{Area}} = \frac{0.00355}{(\pi/4)D^2} = \frac{0.00355}{(\pi/4) \times 0.12^2} = 0.314 \text{ m/s}$$

$$\text{Reynolds number, } Re = \frac{\rho V D}{\mu} = \frac{(0.9 \times 1000) \times 0.314 \times 0.12}{0.09} = 376.8$$

Since $Re < 2000$, therefore, the flow is *laminar/viscous*.

Substituting the values in eqn. (*i*), we get

$$(p_1 - p_2) = \frac{32 \times 0.09 \times 0.314 \times 12}{(0.12)^2} = \textbf{753.6 N/m}^2 \textbf{ (Ans.)}$$

Example 10.4. *A liquid with a specific gravity 2.8 and a viscosity 0.8 poise flows through a smooth pipe of unknown diameter, resulting in a pressure drop of 800 N/m^2 in 2 km length of the pipe. What is the pipe diameter if the mass flow rate is 2500 kg/h.* **(NU)**

Solution. *Given:* Sp. gravity = 2.8, μ = 0.8 × 0.1 = 0.08 Ns/m^2; Δp = 800 N/m^2;

$$L = 2 \text{ km} = 2000 \text{ m}; \; m = 2500 \text{ kg/h} = \frac{2500}{3600} = 0.6944 \text{ kg/s}$$

Pipe diameter, D :

$$m = \rho A\bar{u} \quad \text{or} \quad \bar{u} = \frac{m}{\rho A}$$

or,
$$\bar{u} = \frac{0.6944}{(2.8 \times 1000) \times \frac{\pi}{4} D^2} = \frac{3.158 \times 10^{-4}}{D^2}$$

Assuming flow to be laminar, we have:

$$\Delta p = \frac{32\mu\bar{u}L}{D^2} \quad \text{(where, } \bar{u} = \text{average velocity)} \qquad \text{...[Eqn. 10.11]}$$

$$800 = \frac{32 \times 0.08 \times 3.158 \times 10^{-4} \times 2000}{D^2 \times D^2}$$

or,
$$D = \left(\frac{32 \times 0.08 \times 3.158 \times 10^{-4} \times 2000}{800}\right)^{1/4} = \mathbf{0.212 \text{ m (Ans.)}}$$

Check for laminar flow,

$$Re = \frac{\rho\bar{u}D}{\mu} = \frac{(2.8 \times 1000) \times 3.158 \times 10^{-4} \times D}{D^2 \times 0.08} = \frac{2800 \times 3.158 \times 10^{-4}}{0.212 \times 0.08} = 52,$$ which confirms that flow is laminar ($Re < 2000$).

Example 10.5. *A fluid of viscosity 8 poise and specific gravity 1.2 is flowing through a circular pipe of diameter 100 mm. The maximum shear stress at the pipe wall is 210 N/m². Find:*

(i) *The pressure gradient,*

(ii) *The average velocity, and*

(iii) *Reynolds number of flow.*

Solution. Viscosity of fluid, μ = 8 poise = 0.8 Ns/m²

Specific gravity = 1.2

∴ Mass density, ρ = 1.2 × 1000 = 1200 kg/m³

Diameter of the pipe, D = 100 mm = 0.1 m

Maximum shear stress, τ_0 = 210 N/m²

(*i*) The pressure gradient, $\frac{\partial p}{\partial x}$:

We know,
$$\tau_0 = -\frac{\partial p}{\partial x} \cdot \frac{R}{2}$$

or,
$$210 = -\frac{\partial p}{\partial x} \times \frac{(0.1/2)}{2}$$

∴
$$\frac{\partial p}{\partial x} = -\frac{210 \times 4}{0 \cdot 1} = \mathbf{-8400 \text{ N/m}^2 \text{ per m (Ans.)}}$$

(*ii*) The average velocity, $\bar{u}$:

We know,
$$\bar{u} = \frac{1}{2} u_{max}$$
$$= \frac{1}{2}\left[-\frac{1}{4\mu} \cdot \frac{\partial p}{\partial x} \cdot R^2\right] \qquad \text{...[Eqn. (10.8)]}$$
$$= \frac{1}{2}\left[-\frac{1}{4 \times 0.8} \times (-8400) \times (0.1/2)^2\right]$$
$$= \mathbf{3.28 \text{ m/s (Ans.)}}$$

(iii) Reynolds number, Re:

$$Re = \frac{\rho VD}{\mu} = \frac{1200 \times 3.28 \times 0.1}{0.8} = \mathbf{492\ (Ans.)}$$

Example 10.6. *A fluid of density 1200 kg/m^3 and viscosity 0.5 poise is flowing at a rate of 5m^3/min in a circular pipe of cross-section of 1 m^2. Is the flow laminar or turbulent? Can you predict the maximum velocity of the fluid in the pipe ?*

Solution. *Given:* $\rho = 1200$ kg/m^3; $\mu = 0.5$ poise $= 0.5 \times \frac{1}{10} = 0.05$ Ns/m^2

$$A = 1\ \text{m}^2;\quad Q = 5\ \text{m}^3/\text{min}$$

$$Q = AV = 1 \times \frac{5}{60}\ \text{m}^3/\text{s}$$

$$V_{av} = \bar{u} = \frac{Q}{A} = \frac{5/60}{1} = \frac{5}{60}\ \text{m/s}$$

$$A = 1 = \frac{\pi}{4}D^2 \quad \text{or} \quad D = 1.128\ \text{m}$$

$$\text{Reynolds number, } Re = \frac{\rho \bar{u} D}{\mu} = \frac{1200 \times (5/60) \times 1.128}{0.05} = 2256$$

Since $Re < 2300$, therefore the flow is **laminar. (Ans.)**

The velocity profile is parabolic, hence

$$u_{max} = 2\bar{u} = 2 \times \frac{5}{60} = \mathbf{0.1667\ m/s\ (Ans.)}$$

Example 10.7. *A lubricating oil of viscosity 1 poise and specific gravity 0.9 is pumped through a 30 mm diameter pipe. If the pressure drop per metre length of pipe is 20 kN/m^2, determine:*

(i) The mass flow rate in kg/min,

(ii) The shear stress at the pipe wall,

(iii) The Reynolds number of flow, and

(iv) The power required per 50 m length of the pipe to maintain the flow.

Solution. Viscosity of oil, $\mu = 1$ poise $= 0.1$ Ns/m^2

Sp. gr. of oil, $= 0.9$

$\therefore$ Weight density, $w = 0.9 \times 9810 = 8829$ N/m^3

Diameter of pipe, $D = 30$ mm $= 0.03$ m

$$\text{Area, } A = \frac{\pi}{4} \times 0.03^2 = 7.068 \times 10^{-4}\ \text{m}^2$$

Pressure drop per metre length of pipe, $(p_1 - p_2) = 20$ kN/m^2

(i) Mass flow rate:

Pressure drop for laminar flow through a pipeline is given by,

$$(p_1 - p_2) = \frac{32\mu\bar{u}L}{D^2}$$

$$\therefore \quad 20 \times 10^3 = \frac{32 \times 0.01 \times \bar{u} \times 1}{(0.03)^2}$$

(where, $\bar{u}$ = average velocity of flow)

$$\text{or,} \quad \bar{u} = \frac{20 \times 10^3 \times (0.03)^2}{32 \times 0.1 \times 1} = 5.625\ \text{m/s}$$

$$\text{Flow rate, } Q = A \times \bar{u} = 7.068 \times 10^{-4} \times 5.625 = 0.003975 \text{ m}^3/\text{s}$$

$$\therefore \quad \text{Mass flow rate} = (0.9 \times 1000) \times 0.003975 \times 60$$

$$= \mathbf{214.65\ kg/min.\ (Ans.)}$$

(*ii*) Shear stress at the wall, τ_0:

$$\tau_0 = -\frac{\partial p}{\partial x} \cdot \frac{R}{2} = 20 \times 10^3 \times \frac{(0.03/2)}{2} = \mathbf{150\ N/m^2\ (Ans.)}$$

(*iii*) Reynolds number of flow, Re:

$$Re = \frac{\rho V D}{\mu} = \frac{(0.9 \times 1000) \times 5.625 \times 0.03}{0.1} = \mathbf{1518.7\ (Ans.)}$$

(where, $V = \bar{u} = 5.625$ m/s)

This is less than 2000 and hence the flow is *laminar*.

(*iv*) Power required, *P*:

$$\text{Loss of head, } h_f = \frac{p_1 - p_2}{w} = \frac{20 \times 10^3}{8829} = 2.265 \text{ m of oil}$$

$$\text{Power reqd. per metre} = w\,Q h_f = 8829 \times 0.003975 \times 2.265\ W = 79.49\ W$$

For 50 *m* length, power required,

$$P = 79.49 \times 50 = 3974.5\ W \text{ or } \mathbf{3.974\ kW\ (Ans.)}$$

Example 10.8. *In a pipe of 300 mm diameter the maximum velocity of flow is found to be 2 m/s. If the flow in the pipe is laminar, find:*

*(**i**) The average velocity and the radius at which it occurs, and*

*(**ii**) The velocity at 50 mm from the wall of the pipe.*

Solution. Diameter of the pipe, D = 300 mm = 0.3 m

Maximum velocity, u_{max} = 2 m/s

(*i*) Average velocity, $\bar{u}$:

We know, $$\bar{u} = \frac{1}{2} u_{max}$$

$$\therefore \quad \bar{u} = \frac{2}{2} = \mathbf{1\ m/s\ (Ans.)}$$

Radius at which $\bar{u}$ occurs :

The velocity, u at any radius r is given by

$$u = -\frac{1}{4\mu}\frac{\partial p}{\partial x}(R^2 - r^2) \quad \text{...[Eqn. (10.7)]}$$

$$= -\frac{1}{4\mu}\frac{\partial p}{\partial x} R^2 \left[1 - \frac{r^2}{R^2}\right]$$

Also, $$u_{max} = -\frac{1}{4\mu} \cdot \frac{\partial p}{\partial x} \cdot R^2 \quad \text{...[Eqn. (10.8)]}$$

$$\therefore \quad u = u_{max}\left[1 - \left(\frac{r}{R}\right)^2\right] \quad \text{...(i)}$$

Here, $$u = \bar{u} = 1 \text{ m/s}$$

$$\therefore \quad 1 = 2\left[1 - \left(\frac{r}{0.15}\right)^2\right] \quad \left(\because R = \frac{0.3}{2} = 0.15 \text{ m}\right)$$

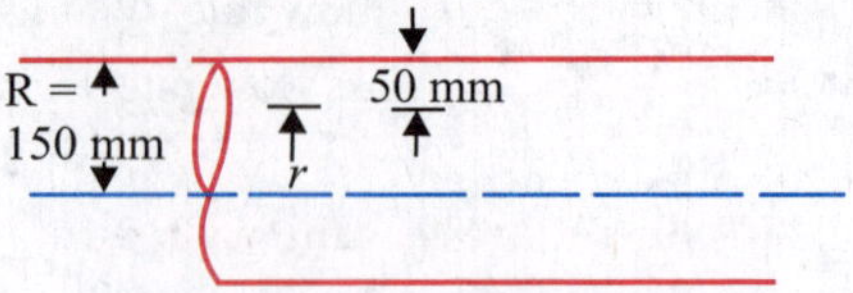

Fig. 10.9

or, $$\frac{1}{2} = 1 - \left(\frac{r}{0 \cdot 15}\right)^2$$

or, $$\left(\frac{r}{0 \cdot 15}\right)^2 = 0.5$$

or, $$\frac{r}{0.15} = \sqrt{0.5} = 0.707$$

$\therefore$ $r = 0.106$ m or **106 mm (Ans.)**

(*ii*) Velocity at 50 mm from the wall :

$$r = 150 - 50 = 100 \text{ mm} = 0.1 \text{ m}$$

$\therefore$ Velocity at a radius 0.1 m or 50 mm from the pipe wall is given by [eqn. (*i*)]:

$$u = u_{max}\left[1 - \left(\frac{r}{R}\right)^2\right]$$

$$= 2\left[1 - \left(\frac{0.1}{0.15}\right)^2\right] = \mathbf{1.11 \text{ m/s}} \textbf{ (Ans.)}$$

Example 10.9. *An oil of viscosity 0.15 Ns/m² and specific gravity 0.9 is flowing through a circular pipe of diameter 30 mm and of length 3 m at $\frac{1}{10}$th of critical velocity for which Reynolds number is 2450. Find:*

(*i*) *The velocity of flow through the pipe,*

(*ii*) *The head in metres of oil across the pipe length required to maintain the flow, and*

(*iii*) *The power required to overcome viscous resistance to flow of oil.*

Solution. Viscosity of the oil, $\mu = 0.15$ Ns/m²

Specific gravity = 0.9

$\therefore$ Mass density, $\rho = 0.9 \times 1000 = 900$ kg/m³

Diameter of the pipe, $D = 30$ mm $= 0.03$ m

Length of the pipe, $L = 3$ m

Velocity of flow, $\bar{u} = \frac{1}{10} \times$ critical velocity (at Reynolds number 2450)

(*i*) Velocity of flow, $\bar{u}$:

We know, $$(Re)_{cr} = \frac{\rho V_{cr} D}{\mu}$$

(where, V_{cr} = critical velocity)

or, $$2450 = \frac{900 \times V_{cr} \times 0.03}{0.15}$$

or, $$V_{cr} = \frac{2450 \times 0.15}{900 \times 0.03} = 13.61 \text{ m/s}$$

$\therefore$ Velocity of flow through the pipe,

$$\bar{u} = \frac{1}{10} \times 13.61 = \mathbf{1.361 \text{ m/s}} \textbf{ (Ans.)}$$

(*ii*) Head required to maintain the flow:

For laminar flow through a pipeline,

$$p_1 - p_2 = \frac{32 \mu \bar{u} L}{D^2}$$

or, Loss of head, $h_f = \frac{p_1 - p_2}{w} = \frac{32\mu\bar{u}L}{wD^2} = \frac{32\mu\bar{u}L}{(\rho g)D^2}$

$\therefore \quad h_f = \frac{32 \times 0.15 \times 1.361 \times 3}{900 \times 9.81 \times 0.03^2} =$ **2.466 m (Ans.)**

(*iii*) Power required, *P*:

The power required to overcome viscous resistance to flow of oil,

$$P = w\,Q\,h_f = (900 \times 9.81) \times \left(\frac{\pi}{4} \times 0.03^2 \times 1.361\right) \times 2.466$$

$= \mathbf{20.9\ W}$ **(Ans.)**

Example 10.10. *An oil* ($\mu = 20$ cP, $\rho = 1200$ kg/m^3) *flows through a 2.5 cm I.D. pipe 250 m long.*

(*i*) *What is the maximum flow in* m^3/s *that will ensure laminar flow ?*

(*ii*) *What would be the pressure drop for this flow?* **(Bombay University)**

Solution. *Given:* $\mu = 20$ c.P. $= 20 \times 10^{-2}$ poise $= 20 \times 10^{-2} \times \frac{1}{10}$ Ns/m^2 = 0.02 Ns/m^2; $\rho = 1200$ kg/m^3; $D_1 = 2.5$ cm = 0.025 m; $L = 250$ m.

Flow will be *laminar flow* if Reynolds number is less than 2000.

Now, $Re = \frac{\rho V D}{\mu}$

or, $2000 = \frac{1200 \times V \times 0.025}{0.02}$ or $V = \frac{2000 \times 0.02}{1200 \times 0.025} = 1.33$ m/s

(*i*) Maximum flow that will ensure laminar flow:

$$\text{Discharge} = A \times V = \frac{\pi}{4} \times (0.025)^2 \times 1.33 = \mathbf{6.528 \times 10^{-4}\ m^3/s}$$ **(Ans.)**

(*ii*) Pressure drop :

Coefficient of friction, $f = \frac{16}{Re} = \frac{16}{2000} = 0.008$

Head lost due to friction, $h_f = \frac{4fLV^2}{D \times 2g}$

$= \frac{4 \times 0.008 \times 250 \times 1.33^2}{0.025 \times 2 \times 9.81} = 28.85$ m

Pressure drop for the flow $= wh_f = (\rho g) \times h_f$

$= 1200 \times 9.81 \times 28.85$ N/m^2

$= 339622.2$ N/m^2 = **3.396 bar (Ans.)** ($\because$ 1 bar = 10^5 N/m^2).

Example 10.11. *Crude oil of* $\mu = 1.5$ *poise and relative density 0.9 flows through a 20 mm diameter vertical pipe. The pressure gauges fixed 20 m apart read 600 kN/m^2 and 200 kN/m^2, as shown in Fig. 10.10. Find the direction and rate of flow through the pipe.* **[PTU]**

Solution. Dynamic viscosity, μ = 1.5 poise = 0.15 Ns/m^2

Relative density = 0.9

$\therefore$ Weight density of oil, w = $0.9 \times 9.81 = 8.829$ kN/m^3

Diameter of the pipe, D = 20 mm = 0.02 m

Length, L = 20 m

Pressure at A, p_A = 600 kN/m^2

Pressure at B, p_B = 200 kN/m^2

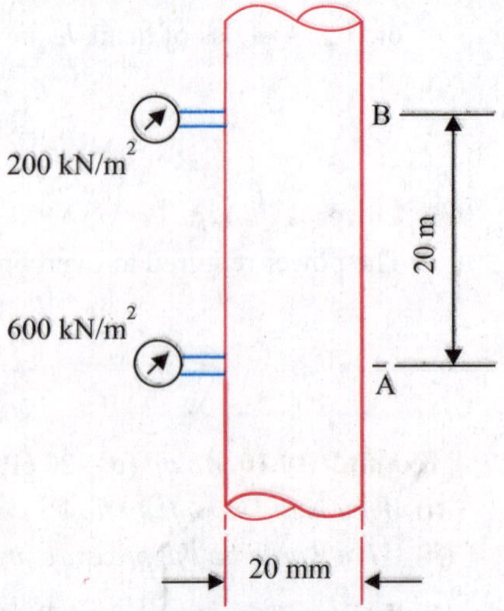

Fig. 10.10

Direction of flow:

Since the pipe is of uniform diameter, *velocity head would be same* and as such flow direction will be indicated by the values of *piezometric head* at sections A and B. Taking the level at A as datum, we have:

Piezometric head at A

$$= \frac{p_A}{w} + z_A = \frac{600}{8 \cdot 829} + 0 = 67 \cdot 96 \text{ m}$$

Piezometric head at B

$$= \frac{p_B}{w} + z_B = \frac{200}{8 \cdot 829} + 20 = 42 \cdot 65 \text{ m}$$

Since piezometric head at A is greater than that at B, hence, flow takes place **from A to B** (*i.e. upwards*) **(Ans.)**

Rate of flow:

Loss of piezometric head = h_f = 67.96 – 42.65 = 25.31 m

But the loss of pressure head for viscous flow through circular pipe is given by the Hagen-Poiseuille relation,

$$h_f = \frac{32\, \mu\, \bar{u}\, L}{wD^2}$$

or,
$$25.31 = \frac{32 \times 0.15 \times \bar{u} \times 20}{(8.829 \times 10^3) \times (0.02)^2}$$

or,
$$\bar{u} = \frac{25.31 \times (8.829 \times 10^3) \times (0.02)^2}{32 \times 0.15 \times 20} = 0.931 \text{ m/s}$$

$$\text{Reynolds number, } Re = \frac{\rho V D}{\mu} = \frac{(0.9 \times 1000) \times 0.931 \times 0.02}{0.15} = 111.72 \qquad (\because V = \bar{u})$$

As Reynolds number is less than 2000, the flow is *laminar*.

$\therefore$ Flow rate, Q = Average velocity × area

$= \bar{u} \times \pi/4 \times D^2 = 0.931 \times \pi/4 \times 0.02^2$

$=$ **2.925×10^{-4} m^3/s** or **0.2925 litres/sec. (Ans.)**

Example 10.12. *Oil of specific gravity 0.82 is pumped through a horizontal pipeline 150 mm in diameter and 3 km long at the rate of 0.015 m^3/s. The pump has an efficiency of 68% and requires 7.5 kW to pump the oil.*

(i) What is the dynamic viscosity of the oil?

(ii) Is the flow laminar? **[Panjabi University]**

Solution. Sp. gr. of the oil = 0.82

Diameter of pipe, D = 150 mm = 0.15 m

$\therefore$ Area, A = $(\pi/4) \times 0.15^2 = 0.01767$ m^2

Length of pipe, L = 3 km = 3000 m

Discharge, Q = 0.015 m^3/s

Efficiency of pump, η = 68%

Power required to pump the oil, P = 7.5 kW

(i) Dynamic viscosity of oil, μ:

$$\text{Average velocity, } \bar{u} = \frac{Q}{A} = \frac{0.015}{0.01767} = 0.849 \text{ m/s}$$

If h_f represents the loss of head, then:

$$w\,Qh_f = \eta \times P$$

or, $$h_f = \frac{\eta \times P}{wQ} = \frac{0.68 \times (7.5 \times 10^3)}{(0.82 \times 9810) \times 0.015} = 42.26 \text{ m}$$

Again, for viscous/laminar flow through a pipeline,

$$(p_1 - p_2) = \frac{32\,\mu\,\bar{u}\,L}{D^2}$$

or, $$\text{Loss of head, } h_f = \left(\frac{p_1 - p_2}{w}\right) = \frac{32\,\mu\bar{u}L}{wD^2}$$

or, $$42.26 = \frac{32 \times \mu \times 0.849 \times 3000}{(0.82 \times 9810) \times 0.15^2}$$

or, $$\mu = \frac{42.26 \times (0.82 \times 9810) \times 0.15^2}{32 \times 0.849 \times 3000} = \mathbf{0.0938\ Nsm/m^2}\ \textbf{(Ans.)}$$

(ii) Is the flow laminar?

Reynolds number, $$Re = \frac{\rho VD}{\mu} = \frac{(0.82 \times 1000) \times 0.849 \times 0.15}{0.0938} \qquad (\because V = \bar{u})$$

or, $Re = 1113.3$

This is less than 2000 and hence the flow is **laminar (Ans.)**

Example 10.13. *A pipe 60 mm diameter and 450 m long slopes upwards at 1 in 50. An oil of viscosity 0.9 Ns/m² and specific gravity 0.9 is required to be pumped at the rate of 5 litres/sec.*

(i) Is the flow laminar?

(ii) What pressure difference is required to attain this condition?

(iii) What is the power of the pump required assuming an overall efficient of 65%?

(iv) What is the centre-line velocity and the velocity gradient at pipe wall? **(MU)**

Solution. Diameter of the pipe, D = 60 mm = 0.06 m

∴ Area of the pipe = $\frac{\pi}{4} \times 0.06^2 = 0.00283 \text{ m}^2$

Length of the pipe, L = 450 m

Slope = 1 in 50

Viscosity of oil, μ = 0.9 Ns/m²

Weight density, w = $0.9 \times 9810 = 8829 \text{ N/m}^3$

Discharge, Q = 5 litres/sec.

= $0.005 \text{ m}^3/\text{s}$.

Overall efficiency, η_0 = 65%

(i) Is the flow laminar?

$$\text{Average velocity, } \bar{u} = \frac{Q}{A} = \frac{0.005}{0.00283} = 1.767 \text{ m/s}$$

∴ $$\text{Reynolds number, } Re = \frac{\rho VD}{\mu} = \frac{(0.9 \times 1000) \times 1.767 \times 0.06}{0.9} = 106$$

Since $Re < 2000$, therefore, **flow is laminar. (Ans.)**

(*ii*) Pressure difference required:

Applying Bernoulli's equation between section (1) and (2), we get:

$$\frac{p_1}{w} + \frac{V_1^2}{2g} + z_1 = \frac{p_2}{w} + \frac{V_2^2}{2g} + z_2 + h_f$$

or, $$\frac{p_1}{w} + \frac{V_1^2}{2g} + 0 = \frac{p_2}{w} + \frac{V_2^2}{2g} + \frac{1}{50} \times 450 + \frac{32\mu\bar{u}L}{D^2 \times w}$$

or, $$\left(\frac{p_1 - p_2}{w}\right) = 9 + \frac{32\mu\bar{u}\,L}{D^2 \times w} \qquad (\because V_1 = V_2 \text{ and } z_1 = 0)$$

or, $$p_1 - p_2 = 9w + \frac{32\mu\bar{u}L}{D^2}$$

$$= 9 \times 8829 + \frac{32 \times 0.9 \times 1.767 \times 450}{0.06^2}$$

$$= 79461 + 6.36 \times 10^6 = 6.44 \times 10^6 \text{ N/m}^2 \text{ or } \mathbf{6.44\ MN/m^2}$$ **(Ans.)**

(*iii*) Power of the pump:

$$P = Q\,(p_1 - p_2) = 0.005 \times 6.44 \times 10^3 = 32.2 \text{ kW}$$

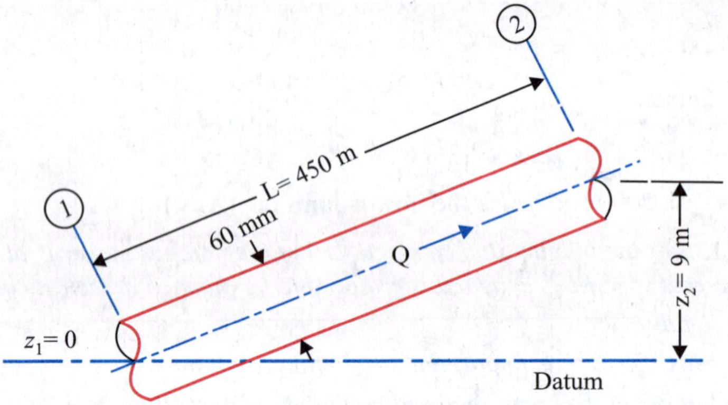

Fig. 10.11

$$\text{Power of the pump} = \frac{32.2}{\eta_0} = \frac{32.2}{0.65} = 49.54 \text{ kW}$$ **(Ans.)**

(*iv*) Centre-line velocity, u_{max}:

$$u_{max} = 2\bar{u} = 2 \times 1.767 = \mathbf{3.534\ m/s}$$ **(Ans.)**

Velocity gradient at the pipe wall:

$$\tau_0 = -\frac{\partial p}{\partial x} \cdot \frac{R}{2}$$

$$= \frac{6.44 \times 10^6}{450} \times \frac{0.03}{2} = 214.67 \text{ N/m}^2$$

But, $$\tau_0 = \mu \cdot \left(\frac{\partial u}{\partial y}\right)_{y=0}$$

or, $$\left(\frac{\partial u}{\partial y}\right)_{y=0} = \frac{\tau_0}{\mu} = \frac{214.67}{0.9} = \mathbf{238.5\ s^{-1}}$$ **(Ans.)**

Example 10.14. *A total of 12 litres per second of oil is pumped through two pipes in parallel, one 12 cm in diameter and the other 10 cm in diameter, both pipes being 1000 metres long. The specific gravity of the oil is 0.97 and the kinematic viscosity 9 cm² per second. Calculate the flow rate through each pipe and the power of the pump.* **[UPSC Exam, Fluid Machines]**

Solution. Total discharge of oil through the two pipes,

Q = 12 litres/sec.

= 0.012 m³/s

Diameter of pipe 1,

D_1 = 12 cm = 0.12 m

Diameter of pipe 2,

D_2 = 10 cm = 0.1 m

$L_1 = L_2 = L$ = 1000 m

(where, L_1 and L_2 are the lengths of the pipes 1 and 2 respectively)

Specific gravity of the oil = 0.97

Kinematic viscosity of the oil,

ν = 9 cm²/s

= 9 × 10⁻⁴ m²/s.

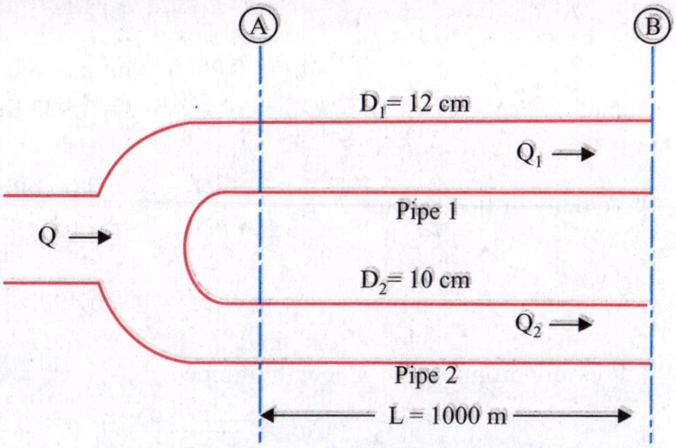

Fig. 10.12

Let, Q_1 = Discharge in pipe 1, and

Q_2 = Discharge in pipe 2.

Since the pipes are in parallel, the total discharge Q is distributed in both the pipes. From the principle of continuity, we have

$$Q = Q_1 + Q_2$$

or,
$$0.012 = Q_1 + Q_2 \quad ...(i)$$

Flow rate through each pipe, Q_1 and Q_2:

Assuming laminar flow in both the pipes, the pressure difference between sections 'A' and 'B' is the same in both the pipes,

$$\Delta p = \frac{32\mu V_1 L}{D_1^2} = \frac{32\mu V_2 L}{D_2^2} \quad ...(ii)$$

(where, V_1 and V_2 are the velocities of flow in the pipes 1 and 2 respectively).

From the continuity equation, we have:

$$V_1 = \frac{Q_1}{A_1} = \frac{Q_1}{\frac{\pi}{4} D_1^2} = \frac{4Q_1}{\pi D_1^2}$$

and,
$$V_2 = \frac{Q_2}{A_2} = \frac{Q_2}{\frac{\pi}{4} D_2^2} = \frac{4Q_2}{\pi D_2^2}$$

From eqn. (*ii*), we have:

$$\frac{V_1}{D_1^2} = \frac{V_2}{D_2^2}$$

∴
$$\frac{4Q_1}{\pi D_1^4} = \frac{4Q_2}{\pi D_2^4}$$

From which,
$$\frac{Q_1}{Q_2} = \left(\frac{D_1}{D_2}\right)^4 \quad \text{or} \quad Q_2 = Q_1\left(\frac{D_2}{D_1}\right)^4$$

Substituting the value of Q_2 in eqn. (*i*), we get:

$$0.012 = Q_1 + Q_1\left(\frac{D_2}{D_1}\right)^4 = Q_1\left[1+\left(\frac{D_2}{D_1}\right)^4\right]$$

$$= Q_1\left[1+\left(\frac{0.1}{0.12}\right)^4\right] = 1.482\ Q_1$$

$\therefore$ $Q_1 = 0.008097\ \text{m}^3/\text{s}$ or **8.097 litres/sec. (Ans.)**

and, $Q_2 = 12 - 8.097 =$ **3.903 litres/sec. (Ans.)**

Power of the pump, P:

Velocity of flow in pipe 2, $V_2 = \dfrac{4Q_2}{\pi D_2^2} = \dfrac{4 \times 0.003903}{\pi \times (0.1)^2} = 0.497\ \text{m/s}$

Velocity of flow in pipe 1, $V_1 = V_2\left(\dfrac{D_2}{D_1}\right)^2 = 0.497 \times \left(\dfrac{0.1}{0.12}\right)^2 = 0.345\ \text{m/s}$

Pressure drop in 1000 m length of pipe 2,

$$\Delta p = \frac{32\mu V_2 L}{D_2^2}$$

$$\text{Loss of head, } h_f = \frac{\Delta p}{w} = \frac{32\left(\frac{\mu}{\rho}\right)V_2 L}{g D_2^2}$$

$$= \frac{32 \times 9 \times 10^{-4} \times 0.497 \times 1000}{9{\cdot}81 \times (0.1)^2} = 145.9 \text{ m of oil}$$

Power lost in viscous friction,

$$P = w\,Q\,h_f = (0.97 \times 9.81) \times 0.012 \times 145.9 = 16.66 \text{ kW}$$

Assuming the overall efficiency of the pump as 62%, the power of pump

$$= \frac{16.66}{0.62} = \mathbf{26.87\ kW}\ \textbf{(Ans.)}$$

$$\text{Reynolds number, } Re_2 = \frac{V_2 D_2}{\nu} = \frac{0.497 \times 0.1}{9 \times 10^{-4}} = 55.2$$

$$Re_1 = \frac{V_1 D_1}{\nu} = \frac{0.345 \times 0.12}{9 \times 10^{-4}} = 46$$

Since the Reynolds numbers in both the pipes are less than 2000, the assumption of laminar flow in both the pipes is *valid*.

Example 10.15. *It is required to pump glycerine at the rate of 25 litres/sec. from a sump and deliver it freely at a point 120 m away and 8 m above the level of sump through a 150 mm pipe, Fig. 10.13.*

(*i*) *What is the power of the pump required assuming an overall efficiency of 65% ?*

(*ii*) *What would be the rate of rise of temperature due to viscous dissipation if the pipe is completely insulated ?*

Sp. gr. of glycerine = 1.26; viscosity = 15 poise, specific heat = 248 J/N °C;

K.E. correction factor, $\alpha = 2$.

Solution. Rate of flow of glycerine, $Q = 25$ litres/sec. $= 0.025\ m^3/s$

Diameter of the pipe, $D = 150$ mm $= 0.15$ m

$\therefore$ Area, $A = \frac{\pi}{4} \times 0.15^2 = 0.01767\ m^2$

Overall efficiency, $\eta_0 = 65\ \%$

Specific gravity of glycerine $= 1.26$

$\therefore$ Weight density, $w = 1.26 \times 9810 = 12361\ N/m^3$

Viscosity, $\mu = 15$ poise $= 1.5\ Ns/m^2$

Specific heat $= 248$ J/N °C

K.E. Correction factor, $\alpha = 2$.

(*i*) Power of the pump required, P:

$$\text{Velocity of flow, } V = \frac{Q}{A} = \frac{0.025}{0.01767} = 1.415 \text{ m/s}$$

$$\text{Reynolds number, } Re = \frac{\rho VD}{\mu} = \frac{(1.26 \times 1000) \times 1.415 \times 0.15}{1.5} = 178.3$$

Since the Reynolds number is less than 2000, the flow is *laminar*.

Applying Bernoulli's equation at sump (1) and free delivery point (2), we get:

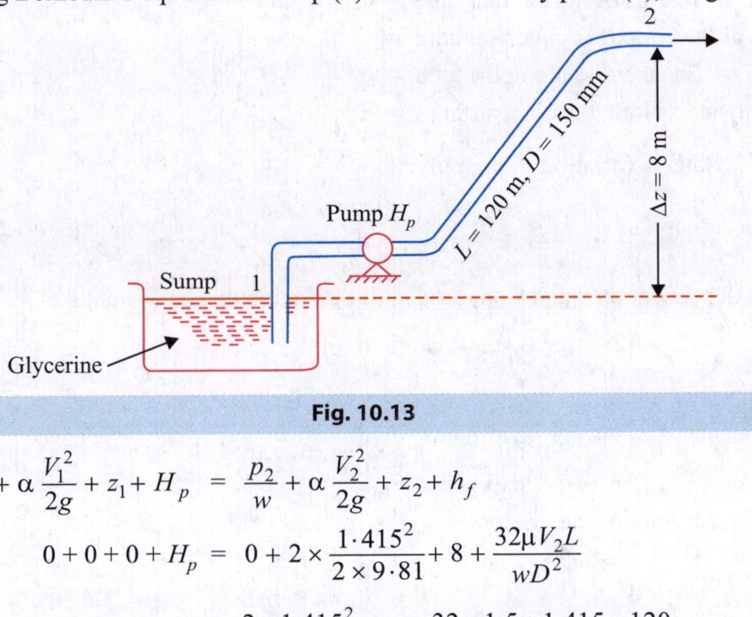

Fig. 10.13

$$\frac{p_1}{w} + \alpha \frac{V_1^2}{2g} + z_1 + H_p = \frac{p_2}{w} + \alpha \frac{V_2^2}{2g} + z_2 + h_f$$

$$0 + 0 + 0 + H_p = 0 + 2 \times \frac{1 \cdot 415^2}{2 \times 9 \cdot 81} + 8 + \frac{32 \mu V_2 L}{wD^2}$$

or,

$$H_p = \frac{2 \times 1.415^2}{2 \times 9.81} + 8 + \frac{32 \times 1.5 \times 1.415 \times 120}{12361 \times 0.15^2} = 37.51 \text{ m}$$

Power of the pump required,

$$P = \frac{wQH_p}{\eta_0} = \frac{12361 \times 0.025 \times 37.51}{0.65 \times 1000} \text{ kW} = \mathbf{17.83\ kW}$$ **(Ans.)**

(*ii*) Rate of rise of temperature:

Dissipation of energy per N per second

= (Energy on the discharge side of the pump–energy at the point of delivery) per N per second

$$= h_f \times \frac{V}{L}$$

(since h_f is energy lost per unit weight (N) of the fluid in a length L)

$$= \frac{32\,\mu\,VL}{wD^2} \times \frac{V \text{ N.m}}{L \text{ N.s}} \text{ or } \frac{\text{J}}{\text{s.N}}$$

$$= \frac{32 \times 1.5 \times 1.415^2}{12361 \times 0.15^2} = 0.345\,\frac{\text{J}}{\text{s.N}}$$

∴ Rate of rise of temperature

$$= \frac{0.345}{248} \times 60 \times 60 = \mathbf{5°C/h} \textbf{ (Ans.)}$$

Example 10.16. *A horizontal circular tube of radius "a" has a fixed co-axial cylindrical core of radius b. τ_a and τ_b are the shear stresses along the tube and core surfaces when a viscous liquid is flowing through the annulus. The flow is laminar and the rate of variation of pressure along the length of the passage is* $\left(-\frac{\partial p}{\partial l}\right)$. *Show that :*

$$\alpha\,\tau_a - b\,.\,\tau_b = \frac{1}{2}(a^2 - b^2)\left(\frac{\partial p}{\partial l}\right)$$

[UPSC Exams., Fluid Mech. & Fluid Machines]

Solution. Radius of the circular tube $= a$

Radius of the co-axial cylindrical core $= b$

Shear stress along the tube $= \tau_a$

Shear stress along the core surfaces $= \tau_b$

Rate of variation of pressure $= -\frac{\partial p}{\partial l}$

We know, $$\frac{\partial p}{\partial x} + \frac{\partial \tau}{\partial r} + \frac{\tau}{r} = 0 \qquad \text{...Eqn. [10.12 (a)]}$$

Since p is dependent on x and τ on r, the above equation can be written as:

$$\frac{\partial p}{\partial x} + \frac{1}{r} \cdot \frac{\partial}{\partial r}(\tau \cdot r) = 0$$

Integrating, w.r.t. r, we get:

$$\frac{r^2}{2} \cdot \frac{\partial p}{\partial x} + \tau \cdot r = C$$

(where, C = constant of integration)

At, $r = a, \quad \tau = \tau_a$

At, $r = b, \quad \tau = \tau_b$

Also, $$\frac{\partial p}{\partial x} = -\frac{\partial p}{\partial l}$$

Substituting the above values, we get:

$$\frac{a^2}{2}\left(-\frac{\partial p}{\partial l}\right) + a \cdot \tau_a = C \qquad \text{...(i)}$$

and, $$\frac{b^2}{2}\left(-\frac{\partial p}{\partial l}\right) + b \cdot \tau_b = C \qquad \text{...(ii)}$$

Subtracting (*ii*) from (*i*), we get:

$$\frac{1}{2}(a^2 - b^2)\left(-\frac{\partial p}{\partial l}\right) + a \cdot \tau_a - b \cdot \tau_b = 0$$

or, $$a.\tau_a - b.\tau_b = \frac{1}{2}(a^2 - b^2)\left(\frac{\partial p}{\partial l}\right)$$ ...(**Proved**)

Example 10.17. *Crude oil is pumped through a 150 mm diameter smooth pipe which is subjected to seasonal changes in temperature. At the maximum temperature of 38°C, when the kinematic viscosity is 0.28 stokes, a power input of 2.3 kW per 300 m is required to maintain a flow of 30 litres/sec. What power input would be required to maintain the same rate of flow at the minimum temperature of 0°C if the viscosity of the oil is then 10 times great ?*

Assume a specific gravity of 0.9 at both temperatures. **[Roorkee University]**

Solution. Diameter of the pipe, $D = 150 \text{ mm} = 0.15 \text{ m}$

Kinematic viscosity of the oil, $\nu = 0.28 \text{ stokes} = 0.28 \times 10^{-4} \text{ m}^2/\text{s}$

Length of pipe considered, $L = 300 \text{ m}$

Specific gravity $= 0.9$

Rate of flow, $Q = 30 \text{ litres/sec.} = 0.03 \text{ m}^3/\text{s}$

Specific gravity of the oil $= 0.9$

Power input required, P:

Reynolds number at 38°C, $(Re)_{38°C} = \frac{VD}{\nu}$

$$\left(\text{where velocity, } V = \frac{Q}{A} = \frac{0.03}{(\pi/4) \times 0.15^2} = 1{\cdot}697 \text{ m/s}\right)$$

or, $$(Re)_{38°C} = \frac{1.697 \times 0.15}{0.28 \times 10^{-4}} = 9091$$

$\therefore$ Reynolds number at 0°C, $(Re)_{0°C} = \frac{1}{10} \times 9091 = 909.1$

It is thus obvious that the flow at 38°C is turbulent, while at 0°C, it is *laminar* (since $Re < 2000$).

Pressure drop in laminar flow is given by,

$$p_1 - p_2 = \frac{32\mu\bar{u}L}{D^2} = \frac{32 \times (\rho\nu \times 10)\,\bar{u}\,L}{D^2} \qquad [\because (\mu)_{0°C} = 10 \times (\mu)_{38°C}]$$

Here, $\bar{u} = V = 1.697 \text{ m/s}, L = 300 \text{ m}, D = 0.15 \text{ m}$

$\rho = 0.9 \times 1000 = 900 \text{ kg/m}^3$, and $\nu = 0.28 \times 10^{-4}$

Substituting the values, we get:

$$p_1 - p_2 = \frac{32 \times (800 \times 0.28 \times 10^{-4} \times 10) \times 1.697 \times 300}{(0.15)^2}$$

$$= 182461 \text{ N/m}^2 \text{ or } 182.46 \text{ kN/m}^2$$

Power required to maintain flow

$= Q(p_1 - p_2) = 0.03 \times 182.46 =$ **5.474 kW (Ans.)**

Example 10.18. *A pipe of diameter 100 mm and length 1000 m is used to pump oil of viscosity 0.85 Ns/m² and specific gravity 0.92 at the rate of 1.2 m³/min. The first 300 m of pipe is laid along the ground sloping upwards 10° to the horizontal and the remaining pipe is laid on the ground sloping upwards at 15° to the horizontal.*

(i) *State whether the flow is laminar or turbulent ?*

(ii) *Determine the pressure to be developed by the pump and the power of the driving motor if the pump efficiency is 65%.*

Assume suitable data for friction factor, f, if required

[UPSC Exams., Fluid Mechanics and Hydraulic Machines]

Solution. Diameter of the pipe, $D = 100 \text{ mm} = 0.1 \text{ m}$

Length of the pipe, $L = 1000 \text{ m}$

Viscosity of the oil, $\mu = 0.85 \text{ Ns/m}^2$

Specific gravity $= 0.92$

Discharge, $Q = 1.2 \text{ m}^3\text{/min.}$

Pump efficiency, $\eta_p = 65\%$

(*i*) Flow–laminar or turbulent?

Reynolds number of flow,

$$Re = \frac{\rho V D}{\mu}$$

where,
$$V = \frac{Q}{\frac{\pi}{4} \times D^2} = \frac{(1.2/60)}{\frac{\pi}{4} \times 0.1^2} = 2.546 \text{ m/s}$$

$$\rho = 0.92 \times 1000 = 920 \text{ kg/m}^3$$

$$Re = \frac{920 \times 2.546 \times 0.1}{0.85} = 275.6$$

Since $Re < 2000$, therefore, the flow is **laminar. (Ans.)**

(*ii*) Pressure to be developed by the pump, *p*:

Height of the end point *B* of the pipline above the pump centre *P*

$$= 300 \sin 10° + 700 \sin 15° = 233.26 \text{ m.}$$

The *friction factor*, for laminar flow, is given by:

$$f = \frac{64}{Re} = \frac{64}{275.6} = 0.2322$$

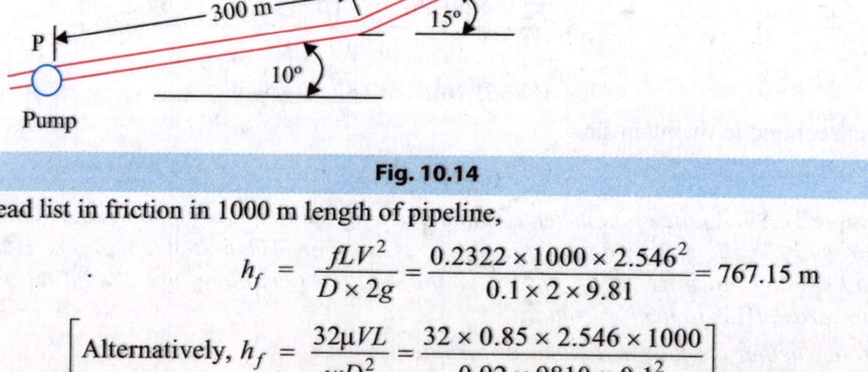

Fig. 10.14

Head list in friction in 1000 m length of pipeline,

$$h_f = \frac{fLV^2}{D \times 2g} = \frac{0.2322 \times 1000 \times 2.546^2}{0.1 \times 2 \times 9.81} = 767.15 \text{ m}$$

$$\left[\text{Alternatively, } h_f = \frac{32 \mu V L}{w D^2} = \frac{32 \times 0.85 \times 2.546 \times 1000}{0.92 \times 9810 \times 0.1^2} = 767.3 \text{ m} \right]$$

Assuming pressure in the pipeline at B as atmospheric, taking horizontal through the pump centre as the datum and applying Bernoulli's equation between the pump outlet and the end of the pipeline, we get:

$$\frac{p}{w} + \frac{V^2}{2g} + 0 = 0 + \frac{V^2}{2g} + 2.33.26 + h_f$$

$$= 0 + \frac{V^2}{2g} + 233.26 + 767.15 = \frac{V^2}{2g} + 1000.41$$

(where, p = pressure just at the pump outlet)

or, $\frac{p}{w} = 1000.41$ or $p = 0.92 \times 9.81 \times 1000.41 =$ **9028.9 kN/m²** **(Ans.)**

Power of the driving motor,

$$P = \frac{wQh}{\eta_p} = \frac{w \times Q \times p}{w \times \eta_p} = \frac{Q \times p}{0.65} = \frac{(1.2/60) \times 9028.9}{0.65}$$

$$= \textbf{277.8 kW} \textbf{ (Ans.)}$$

Example 10.19. *Derive a relation for the torque required to rotate the cone at a constant angular velocity ω for the conical thrust bearing shown in Fig. 10.15. For one such bearing, 120 W gets dissipated when a shaft with maximum cone radius 100 mm turns with 620 r.p.m. over a uniform fluid layer of thickness 1.2 mm. If semi-angle for the conical bearing is 30°, find the dynamic viscosity of the fluid.* **(Anna university)**

Solution. Refer to Fig. 10.15.

Consider an elementary ring of bearing surface of radius r and thickness dh at a distance h from the cone apex.

Then, $r = h \tan \alpha$, and bearing surface of the elementary ring, $dA = 2\pi r\,(dh \sec \alpha) = 2\pi h \tan \alpha . dh \sec \alpha$.

Shear stress (viscous),

$$\tau = \mu \frac{du}{dy} = \mu \frac{V}{t}$$

But, V (linear velocity) $= \omega r = \omega . h \tan \alpha$

$$\therefore \quad \tau = \frac{\mu \omega h \tan \alpha}{t}$$

(where, t is the thickness of the oil film)

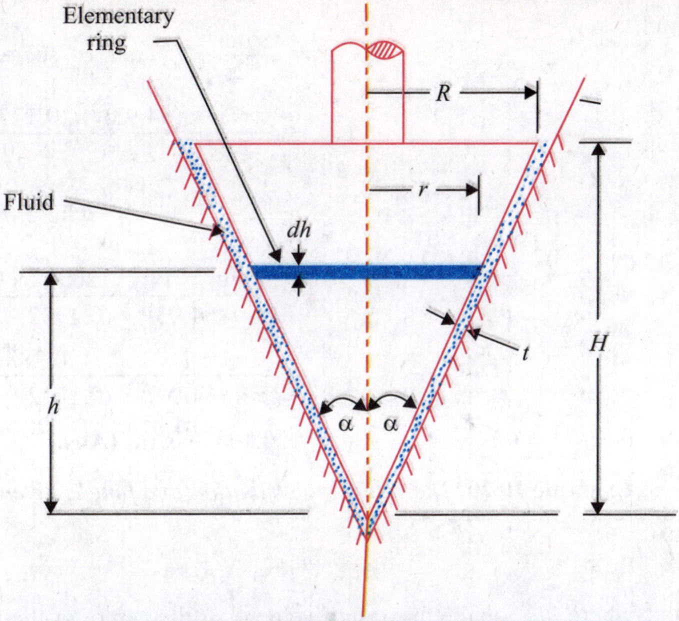

Fig. 10.15. Conical thrust bearing.

Tangential resistance on the ring,

$$dF = \text{Shear stress} \times \text{area of the ring}$$

$$= \frac{\mu \omega h \tan \alpha}{t} \times 2\pi h . \tan \alpha . dh . \sec \alpha$$

$$= 2\pi \mu \tan^2 \alpha . \sec \alpha . \frac{\omega}{t} h^2 . dh$$

and, $\quad$ torque $= dF \times r = dF.h \tan \alpha$

$$\therefore \quad dT = 2\,\pi\,\mu \tan^3 \alpha \,.\, \sec \alpha \,.\, \frac{\omega}{t}\, h^3\, dh$$

$$\text{Torque, } T = 2\,\pi\,\mu \tan^3 \alpha \,.\, \sec \alpha \,.\, \frac{\omega}{t} \int_0^H h^3\, dh$$

$$= 2\,\pi\,\mu \tan^3 \alpha \,.\, \sec \alpha \,.\, \frac{\omega}{t} \times \frac{H^4}{4}$$

or,
$$T = \frac{\pi \mu \omega}{2t} H^4 \tan^3 \alpha \cdot \sec \alpha \qquad ...(i)$$

Given : Power dissipated, P = 120 W

Maximum cone radius, R = 100 mm = 0.1 m

Speed, N = 620 r.p.m.

$$\therefore \quad \text{Angular velocity} = \frac{2\pi N}{60} = \frac{2\pi \times 620}{60} = 64.93 \text{ rad./s}$$

Thickness of fluid layer, t = 1.2 mm = 0.0012 m

Semi-angle for conical bearing, α = 30°

Dynamic viscosity, μ:

$$\text{Power, } P = T \,.\, \omega$$

where,
$$T = \frac{\pi \mu \omega}{2t} H^4 \cdot \tan^3 \alpha \cdot \sec \alpha$$

$$\therefore \quad P = \frac{\pi \mu \omega^2}{2\tau} H^4 \cdot \tan^3 \alpha \cdot \sec \alpha$$

$$120 = \frac{\pi \times \mu \times (64.93)^2 \times (0.1732)^4 \times (\tan 30°)^3 \times \sec 30°}{2 \times 0.0012}$$

$$\left(\text{where, } H = \frac{R}{\tan \alpha} = \frac{0.1}{\tan 30°} = 0.1732 \text{ m}\right)$$

or,
$$\mu = \frac{120 \times 2 \times 0.0012}{\pi \times (64.93)^2 \times (0.1732)^4 \times (\tan 30°)^3 \times \sec 30°}$$

$$= \frac{0.288}{\pi \times (64.93)^2 \times (0.1732)^4 \times 0.1924 \times 1.1547}$$

or, μ = **0.1087 Ns/m² (Ans.)**

Example 10.20. *The velocity distribution in a pipe is given by,*

$$\frac{u}{u_{\max}} = 1 - \left(\frac{r}{R}\right)^n$$

where, u_{max} is the maximum velocity at the centre of the pipe, u is the velocity at a distance r from the centre and R is the pipe radius. Obtain an expression for mean velocity in terms of u_{max} and n. **(PTU)**

Solution. The velocity distribution in a pipe is:

$$\frac{u}{u_{\max}} = 1 - \left(\frac{r}{R}\right)^n \qquad \text{... (given)}$$

where, u = Velocity at a distance r from the centre,

u_{max} = Maximum velocity at the centre of pipe, and

R = Pipe radius.

Now discharge Q passing through any cross-section of the circular pipe can be obtained by integrating a small discharge passing through an elementary ring of the thickness dr at a distance, r.

$$dQ = u \times (2\pi r)\, dr = u_{max}\left[1-\left(\frac{r}{R}\right)^n\right] 2\pi r \,.\, dr$$

Integrating, we get:

$$Q = \int_0^R u_{max}\left[1-\left(\frac{r}{R}\right)^n\right] 2\pi r \,.\, dr$$

$$= 2\pi\, u_{max}\int_0^R \left[r - \frac{(r)^{n+1}}{R^n}\right] dr$$

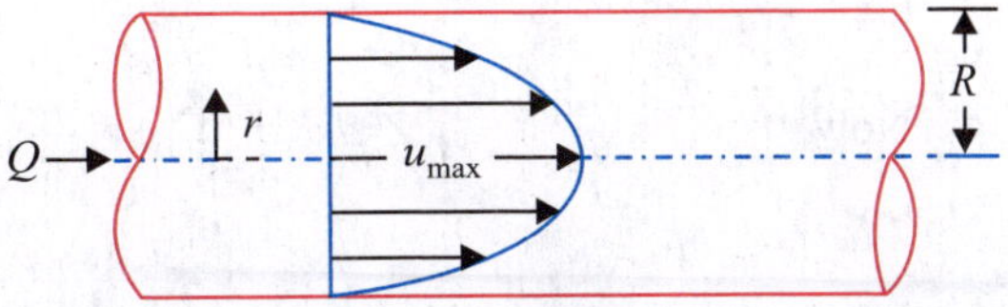

Fig. 10.16

$$= 2\pi\, u_{max}\left[\frac{r^2}{2} - \frac{(r)^{n+2}}{(n+2)\,R^n}\right]_0^R$$

$$= 2\pi\, u_{max}\left[\frac{R^2}{2} - \frac{(R)^{n+2}}{(n+2)\,R^n}\right]$$

$$= 2\pi\, u_{max}\left[\frac{R^2}{2} - \frac{R^2}{n+2}\right]$$

$$= \pi R^2 \times u_{max}\left[\frac{n}{n+2}\right]$$

$$= A \times u_{max}\left[\frac{n}{n+2}\right]$$

[where, A (= πR^2) is cross-sectional area of the pipe]

$\therefore$ Mean velocity, $\bar{u} = \frac{Q}{A} = \boldsymbol{u_{max}\left(\frac{n}{n+2}\right)}$ **(Ans.)**

Example 10.21. **(*a*)** *The radial velocity profile in a pipe is given by* $u = u_{max}\left(1-\frac{r}{R}\right)^n$ *where u is the velocity at a radial distance r,* u_{max} *is the maximum velocity and R is the radius of the pipe. Derive an equation for the average velocity in the pipe.*

(*b*) *For incompressible fluid in laminar flow prove that* $f = \frac{16}{Re}$, *where f is the Fanning friction coefficient and Re is the Reynolds number.* **(MDU, Haryana)**

Solution. (*a*) $u = u_{max}\left(1-\frac{r}{R}\right)^n$ ... Given

Average velocity, $\bar{u} = \frac{1}{\pi R^2}\int_0^R u \times 2\pi r\, dr = \frac{2}{R^2}\int_0^R ur\, dr$

$$= \frac{2}{R^2}\int_0^R u_{max}\left(1-\frac{r}{R}\right)^n r\, dr\,]$$

$$= \frac{2u_{max}}{R^2}\int_0^R r\left(1-\frac{r}{R}\right)^n dr$$

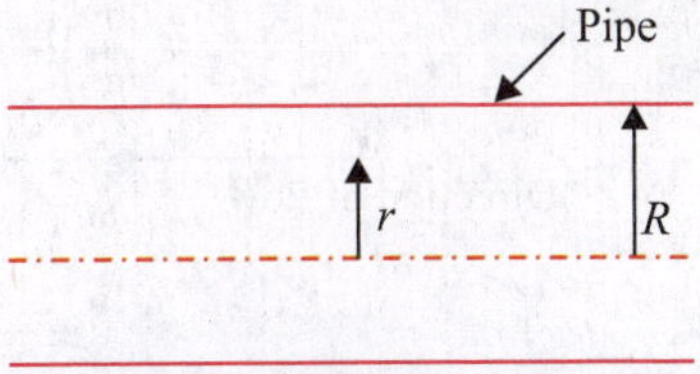

Fig. 10.17

The integral is evaluated first.

$$I = \int r\left(1-\frac{r}{R}\right)^n dr$$

Put, $$\left(1-\frac{r}{R}\right)^n = Z$$

$$I = r\int Z\,dr - \int \frac{dr}{dr}\left(\int Zdr\right) dr = r\int Z\,dr - \int\left(\int Zdr\right) dr$$

Now, $$\int Z\,dr = \int\left(1-\frac{r}{R}\right)^n dr$$

Let, $$1-\frac{r}{R} = t, \text{ then } \frac{-dr}{R} = dt \text{ or } dr = -Rdt$$

Hence, $$\int Z\,dr = \int(-Rt^n)\,dt = \frac{-Rt^{n+1}}{n+1}$$

$\therefore$ $$I = \frac{-rRt^{n+1}}{n+1} - \int\left[\left(\frac{-Rt^{n+1}}{n+1}\right)(-Rdt)\right]$$

$$= -\frac{R}{n+1}\left[rt^{n+1} + \int Rt^{n+1}dt\right]$$

$$= -\frac{R}{n+1}\left[r\left(1-\frac{r}{R}\right)^{n+1} + \frac{R}{n+2}\left(1-\frac{r}{R}\right)^{n+2}\right]$$

$\therefore$ $$\bar{u} = \frac{2u_{max}}{R^2}\left(-\frac{R}{n+1}\right)\left[r\left(1-\frac{r}{R}\right)^{n+1} + \frac{R}{n+2}\left(1-\frac{r}{R}\right)^{n+2}\right]_0^R$$

$$= \frac{2u_{max}}{R\,(n+1)}(-1)\left[-\frac{R}{n+2}\right]$$

or, $$\bar{u} = \frac{2u_{max}}{(n+1)\,(n+2)}$$ **(Ans.)**

(*b*) Refer to article 10.10.

Example 10.22. *Show that the momentum correction factor and energy correction factor for laminar flow through a circular pipe are $\frac{4}{3}$ and 2 respectively.*

Solution. (*i*) Momentum correction factor, β:

In a circular pipe, for laminar flow, the velocity distribution at any radius r is given by eqn. (10.7)

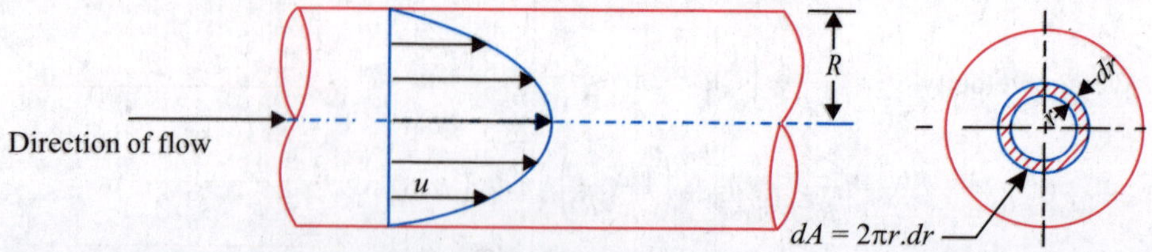

Fig. 10.18

$$u = -\frac{1}{4\mu}\cdot\frac{\partial p}{\partial x}(R^2 - r^2) \qquad ...(i)$$

Consider an elementary area dA in the form of a ring (Fig. 10.18) at a radius r and of width dr then

$$dA = 2\pi r \,.\, dr$$

Discharge through the ring, $dQ = u \times 2\pi r.dr$

Momentum of the fluid through the ring per second

$$= \text{Mass of fluid} \times \text{velocity of flow}$$
$$= (\rho \,.\, dQ) \times u$$
$$= (\rho \times u \times 2\pi r \,.\, dr) \times u$$
$$= 2\pi\, \rho\, u^2\, r \,.\, dr$$

Total actual momentum of the fluid per second across the section

$$= \int_0^R 2\pi\, \rho u^2 r \cdot dr$$

Substituting the value of u from (i), we have:

Actual momentum of the fluid per second

$$= 2\pi\rho \int_0^R \left[-\frac{1}{4\mu}\cdot\frac{\partial p}{\partial x}(R^2 - r^2)\right]^2 r \cdot dr$$

$$= 2\pi\rho \left[\frac{1}{4\mu}\left(\frac{\partial p}{\partial x}\right)\right]^2 \int_0^R (R^2 - r^2)^2 r \cdot dr$$

$$= \frac{2\pi\rho}{16\mu^2}\left(\frac{\partial p}{\partial x}\right)^2 \int_0^R (R^4 + r^4 - 2R^2 r^2)\, r \cdot dr$$

$$= \frac{\pi\rho}{8\mu^2}\left(\frac{\partial p}{\partial x}\right)^2 \int_0^R (R^4 r + r^5 - 2R^2 r^3)\, dr$$

$$= \frac{\pi\rho}{8\mu^2}\left(\frac{\partial p}{\partial x}\right)^2 \left[\frac{R^4 r^2}{2} + \frac{r^6}{6} - \frac{2R^2 r^4}{4}\right]_0^R$$

$$= \frac{\pi\rho}{8\mu^2}\left(\frac{\partial p}{\partial x}\right)^2 \left[\frac{R^6}{2} + \frac{R^6}{6} - \frac{2R^6}{4}\right]$$

$$= \frac{\pi\rho}{8\mu^2}\left(\frac{\partial p}{\partial x}\right)^2 \left(\frac{6R^6 + 2R^6 - 6R^6}{12}\right)$$

$$= \frac{\pi\rho}{48\mu^2}\left(\frac{\partial p}{\partial x}\right)^2 R^6 \qquad ...(ii)$$

Momentum of the fluid per second based on *average velocity*

$$= \text{Mass of fluid/sec.} \times \text{average velocity}$$
$$= \rho A\bar{u} \times \bar{u} = \rho A\bar{u}^2$$

where, A = Area of cross-section = πR^2

$\bar{u}$ = Average velocity = $\dfrac{u_{max}}{2}$

$$= \frac{1}{2}\left[-\frac{1}{4\mu}\left(\frac{\partial p}{\partial x}\right)\right]R^2 \qquad \left[\because u_{max} = -\frac{1}{4\mu}\cdot\left(\frac{\partial p}{\partial x}\right)R^2\right]$$

$$= -\frac{1}{8\mu}\left(\frac{\partial p}{\partial x}\right)R^2$$

∴ Momentum of the fluid per second based on average velocity

$$= \rho \times \pi R^2 \times \left[-\frac{1}{8\mu}\left(\frac{\partial p}{\partial x}\right)R^2\right]^2$$

$$= \rho\pi \times \frac{1}{64\mu^2}\left(\frac{\partial p}{\partial x}\right)^2 R^6 \qquad ...(iii)$$

$$\therefore \qquad \beta = \frac{\text{Momentum/sec. based on actual velocity}}{\text{Momentum/sec. based on average velocity}}$$

$$= \frac{\frac{\pi\rho}{48\mu^2}\left(\frac{\partial p}{\partial x}\right)^2 R^6}{\frac{\pi\rho}{64\mu^2}\left(\frac{\partial p}{\partial x}\right)^2 R^6} = \mathbf{\frac{4}{3}} \textbf{ (Ans.)}$$

(*ii*) Energy correction factor, α:

K.E. of the fluid flowing through the elementary ring of radius *r* and thickness *dr* per second

$$= \frac{1}{2} \times \text{mass} \times (\text{velocity})^2$$

$$= \frac{1}{2} \times (\rho.dQ) \times u^2$$

$$= \frac{1}{2}\rho\,(u \times 2\pi r \times dr) \times u^2$$

$$= \frac{1}{2}\rho \times 2\pi r\, u^3\, dr$$

Total actual K.E. of flow per second

$$= \int_0^R \rho\pi\, ru^3\, dr$$

$$= \int_0^R \rho\pi r\left[-\frac{1}{4\mu}\left(\frac{\partial p}{\partial x}\right)(R^2 - r^2)\right]^3 dr$$

$$= \rho\pi\left[-\frac{1}{4\mu}\left(\frac{\partial p}{\partial x}\right)\right]^3 \int_0^R (R^2 - r^2)^3\, dr$$

$$= -\rho\pi \times \frac{1}{64\,\mu^3}\left(\frac{\partial p}{\partial x}\right)^3 \int_0^R (R^6 - r^6 - 3R^4r^2 + 3R^2r^4)\, r\, dr$$

$$= -\frac{\rho\pi}{64\mu^3}\left(\frac{\partial p}{\partial x}\right)^3\left[\frac{R^6r^2}{2} - \frac{r^8}{8} - \frac{3R^4r^4}{4} + \frac{3R^2r^6}{6}\right]_0^R$$

$$= -\frac{\rho\pi}{64\,\mu^3}\left(\frac{\partial p}{\partial x}\right)^3\left[\frac{R^8}{2} - \frac{R^8}{8} - \frac{3R^8}{4} + \frac{3R^8}{6}\right]$$

$$= \frac{\rho\pi}{512\,\mu^3}\left(\frac{\partial p}{\partial x}\right)^3 R^8 \qquad \text{...(iv)}$$

K.E. of the flow based on average velocity

$$= \frac{1}{2} \times \text{mass} \times (\text{average velocity})^2$$

$$= \frac{1}{2} \times \rho A\bar{u} \times \bar{u}^2 = \frac{1}{2}\,\rho A\bar{u}^3$$

$$= \frac{1}{2}\,\rho \times \pi R^2 \times \left[-\frac{1}{8\mu}\cdot\left(\frac{\partial p}{\partial x}\right) R^2\right]^3$$

$$\left[\because\ A = \pi R^2 \text{ and } \bar{u} = -\frac{1}{8\mu}\left(\frac{\partial p}{\partial x}\right) R^2\right]$$

$$= -\frac{1}{2} \times \rho \times \pi R^2 \times \frac{1}{512\,\mu^3}\left(\frac{\partial p}{\partial x}\right)^3 \times R^6$$

$$= -\frac{\rho\pi}{1024}\cdot\left(\frac{\partial p}{\partial x}\right)^3 \times R^8 \qquad \text{...(v)}$$

$$\therefore \quad \alpha = \frac{\text{K.E./sec. based on actual velocity}}{\text{K.E./sec. based on average velocity}}$$

$$= \frac{-\dfrac{\rho\pi}{512\,\mu^3}\left(\dfrac{\partial p}{\partial x}\right)^3 \times R^8}{-\dfrac{\rho\pi}{1024}\left(\dfrac{\partial p}{\partial x}\right)^3 \times R^8} = \mathbf{2\cdot 0\ (Ans.)}$$

10.6. FLOW OF VISCOUS FLUID THROUGH AN ANNULUS

Let us consider an annulus (horizontal) of outer radius R_1 and inner radius R_2 through which steady laminar flow of an incompressible fluid is taking place. A fluid element having a shape of small concentric cylindrical sleeve of length dx and thickness dr considered at a radial distance r is chosen as a free body. The forces acting on the fluid element as shown in Fig. 10.19, in the direction of flow, are:

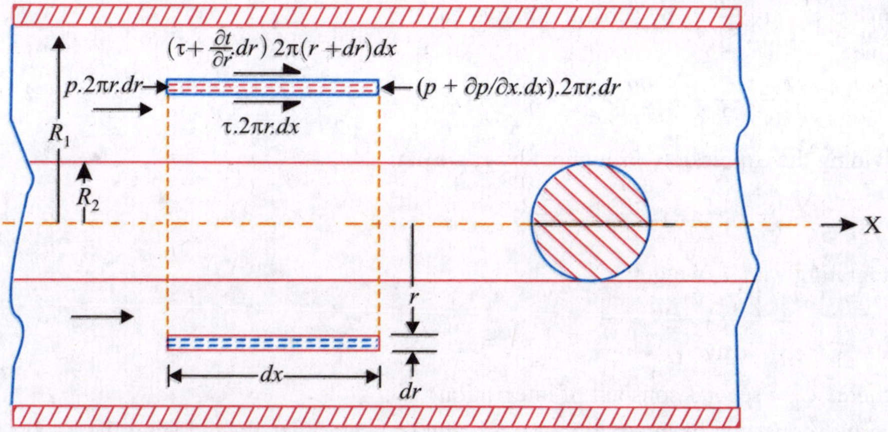

Fig. 10.19. Laminar flow through an annulus.

1. Normal pressure forces over the end areas,

$$p.2\pi r.dr; \text{ and, } \left(p + \frac{\partial p}{\partial x} \cdot dx\right) 2\pi r \cdot dr$$

2. Shear forces over the inner and outer curved surfaces,

$$\tau \,.\, 2\pi r \,.\, dx, \text{ and, } \left(\tau + \frac{\partial \tau}{\partial r} \cdot dr\right) 2\pi\,(r + dr)\cdot dx$$

Since the flow is steady and uniform, the summation of the forces on the free body in the direction of flow must be *zero*.

$$\therefore\ p\cdot 2\pi r\cdot dr - \left[\left(p + \frac{\partial p}{\partial x}\cdot dx\right) 2\pi r\cdot dr\right] + \tau\cdot 2\pi r\cdot dx - \left[\left(\tau + \frac{\partial \tau}{\partial r}\cdot dr\right) 2\pi (r + dr)\,dx\right] = 0$$

Simplifying, we get:

$$\left(-\frac{\partial p}{\partial x}\cdot dx\right) 2\pi\, r\cdot dr - 2\pi\,\tau\cdot dr\cdot dx - 2\pi\,\frac{\partial \tau}{\partial r}\,dr\cdot r\cdot dx - 2\pi\,\frac{\partial \tau}{\partial r}\cdot dr\cdot dr\cdot dx = 0$$

Neglecting the last term which is of higher order, and dividing throughout by the volume of the element $2\pi r.dr.dx$, we get:

$$-\frac{\partial p}{\partial x} - \frac{\tau}{r} - \frac{\partial \tau}{\partial r} = 0$$

or, $$\frac{\partial p}{\partial x} + \frac{\partial \tau}{\partial r} + \frac{\tau}{r} = 0 \qquad \text{...[10.12 (a)]}$$

Since p is dependent on x and τ on r, the above equation may be expressed as:

$$\frac{\partial p}{\partial x} + \frac{1}{r}\frac{\partial}{\partial r}(\tau r) = 0 \qquad \text{...[10.12 (b)]}$$

Integrating w.r.t. r, we get:

$$\frac{\partial p}{\partial x}\int r\cdot dr + \int \frac{d}{dr}(\tau r)\cdot dr = C_1$$

(where, C_1 = constant of integration)

$$\left(\frac{\partial p}{\partial x}\right)\frac{r^2}{2} + \tau\cdot r = C_1$$

Since $\tau = -\mu\cdot\left(\frac{\partial u}{\partial r}\right)$, by substitution, we have:

$$\left(\frac{\partial p}{\partial x}\right)\frac{r^2}{2} - \mu\cdot\frac{\partial u}{\partial r}\cdot r = C_1$$

Dividing the expression throughout by r, we get:

$$\left(\frac{\partial p}{\partial x}\right)\frac{r}{2} - \mu\cdot\frac{\partial u}{\partial r} = \frac{C_1}{r}$$

Integrating w.r.t. r, we get:

$$\left(\frac{\partial p}{\partial x}\right)\frac{r^2}{4} - \mu\, u = C_1 \log_e r + C_2 \qquad \text{...(10.13)}$$

(where, C_2 = second constant of integration).

The two constants of integration (*i.e.* C_1 and C_2) can be evaluated from the known boundary conditions;

i.e. at $r = R_1$ $u = 0$, and

$$r = R_2 \quad u = 0$$

After substituting these conditions and solving for C_1 and C_2, we obtain the velocity distribution as:

$$u = -\frac{1}{4\,\mu}\left(\frac{\partial p}{\partial x}\right)\left[R_1^2 - r^2 - \frac{R_1^2 - R_2^2}{\ln\left(\frac{R_1}{R_2}\right)} \cdot \ln\left(\frac{R_1}{r}\right)\right] \qquad ...(10.14)$$

In order to locate the point where maximum velocity occurs we differentiate eqn. (10.14) w.r.t. r and equate it to zero. Thus, we have

$$\frac{\partial u}{\partial r} = 0 = -\frac{1}{4\mu}\left(\frac{\partial p}{\partial x}\right)\left[-2r + \frac{1}{r}\frac{(R_1^2 - R_2^2)}{\ln\left(\frac{R_1}{R_2}\right)}\right]$$

$$\therefore \quad r = \left[\frac{R_1^2 - R_2^2}{2\ln\left(\frac{R_1}{R_2}\right)}\right]^{1/2} \qquad ...(10.15)$$

By substituting this value of r in eqn. (10.14), the value of maximum velocity may be obtained.

The discharge through the annulus,

$$\mathbf{Q} = \int_{R_2}^{R_1} 2\pi r \cdot dr \cdot u$$

$$= -\frac{\pi}{8\mu}\left(\frac{\partial p}{\partial x}\right)\left[R_1^4 - R_2^4 - \frac{(R_1^2 - R_2^2)^2}{\ln\left(\frac{R_1}{R_2}\right)}\right] \qquad ...(10.16)$$

The average velocity of flow through the annulus is given by,

$$\bar{\mathbf{u}} = \frac{Q}{\pi\,(R_1^2 - R_2^2)}$$

$$= -\frac{1}{8\mu}\left(\frac{\partial p}{\partial x}\right)\left[(R_1^2 + R_2^2) - \frac{(R_1^2 - R_2^2)}{\ln\left(\frac{R_1}{R_2}\right)}\right] \qquad ...(10.17)$$

The shear stress is given by,

$$\tau = -\mu \cdot \frac{du}{dr}$$

From eqn. (10.14), the velocity gradient may be obtained as:

$$\frac{du}{dr} = -\frac{1}{4\mu}\left(\frac{\partial p}{\partial x}\right)\left[-2r - \frac{R_1^2 - R_2^2}{\ln\left(\frac{R_1}{R_2}\right)}\left(-\frac{1}{r}\right)\right]$$

$$= -\frac{1}{4\mu}\left(-\frac{\partial p}{\partial x}\right)\left(2r - \frac{1}{r} \cdot \frac{R_1^2 - R_2^2}{\ln\left(\frac{R_1}{R_2}\right)}\right)$$

$\therefore$ **Shear stress distribution** is given by:

$$\tau = -\mu \cdot \frac{\partial u}{\partial r}$$

or,

$$= \frac{1}{4}\left(-\frac{\partial p}{\partial x}\right)\left[2r - \frac{1}{r} \cdot \frac{R_1^2 - R_2^2}{\ln\left(\frac{R_1}{R_2}\right)}\right] \qquad ...(10.18)$$

Example 10.23. *A uniform circular tube of bore radius R_1 has a fixed co-axial cylindrical solid core of radius R_2. An incompressible viscous fluid flows through the annular passage under a pressure gradient $\left(-\frac{\partial p}{\partial x}\right)$. Determine the radius at which shear stress in the stream is zero given that the flow is laminar under steady state condition.* **[GATE]**

Solution. Bore radius of circular tube $= R_1$

Radius of the solid core $= R_2$

Pressure gradient $= \left(-\frac{\partial p}{\partial x}\right)$

Radius at which shear stress is zero:

The shear stress distribution is given by,

$$\tau = \frac{1}{4}\left(-\frac{\partial p}{\partial x}\right)\left[2r - \frac{1}{r}\cdot\frac{R_1^2 - R_2^2}{\ln\left(\frac{R_1}{R_2}\right)}\right] \qquad \text{...[Eqn. (10.18)]}$$

For zero shear stress, $\tau = 0$ and we have:

$$2r - \frac{1}{r}\cdot\frac{R_1^2 - R_2^2}{\ln\left(\frac{R_1}{R_2}\right)} = 0$$

or,
$$2r^2 = \frac{R_1^2 - R_2^2}{\ln\left(\frac{R_1}{R_2}\right)}$$

or,
$$r = \left[\frac{1}{2}\left(\frac{R_1^2 - R_2^2}{\ln\left(\frac{R_1}{R_2}\right)}\right)\right]^{1/2} \quad \textbf{(Ans.)}$$

10.7. FLOW OF VISCOUS FLUID BETWEEN TWO PARALLEL PLATES

10.7.1. One Plate Moving and Other at Rest—Couette Flow

Let us consider laminar flow between two parallel flat plates located at a distance b apart such that the lower plate is at rest and the upper plate moves uniformly with a constant velocity U as shown in Fig. 10.20. A small rectangular element of fluid of length dx, thickness dy and unit width is considered as a free body (see Fig. 10.20). The forces acting on the fluid element are:

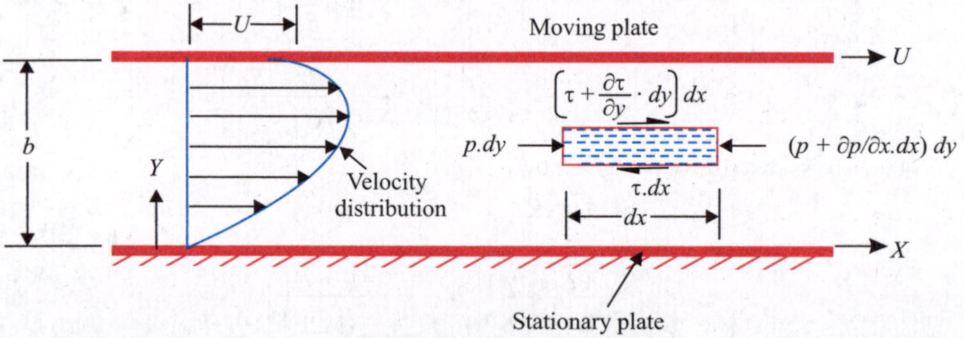

Fig. 10.20. Couette flow.

1. The pressure force, $p.dy \times 1$ on the left end,

2. The pressure force, $\left(p + \frac{\partial p}{\partial x} \cdot dx\right) dy \times 1$ on the right end,

3. The shear force, $\tau.dx \times 1$ on the lower surface, and

4. The shear force, $\left(\tau + \frac{\partial \tau}{\partial y} \cdot dy\right) dx \times 1$ on the upper surface.

For steady and uniform flow, there is no acceleration and hence the resultant force in the direction of flow is *zero*.

$$\therefore \quad p.dy - \left(p + \frac{\partial p}{\partial x} \cdot dx\right) dy - \tau\, dx + \left(\tau + \frac{\partial \tau}{\partial y} \cdot dy\right) dx = 0$$

or,

$$-\frac{\partial p}{\partial x} \cdot dx \cdot dy + \frac{\partial \tau}{\partial y} \cdot dy \cdot dx = 0$$

Dividing by the volume of the element $dx.dy$, we get:

$$\frac{\partial p}{\partial x} = \frac{\partial \tau}{\partial y} \qquad \text{...(10.19)}$$

Eqn. (10.19) shows the interdependence of shear and pressure gradients and is *applicable for laminar as well as turbulent flow*. Accordingly the pressure gradient, in the direction of flow, is *equal* to the shear gradient across the flow.

According to Newton's law of viscosity for laminar flow the shear stress, $\tau = \mu \cdot \frac{du}{dy}$. Substituting for τ in eqn. (10.19), we get:

$$\frac{\partial p}{\partial x} = \mu \cdot \frac{\partial^2 u}{\partial y^2}$$

Since $\frac{\partial p}{\partial x}$ is independent of y, integrating the above equation twice w.r.t. y gives:

$$u = \frac{1}{2\mu} \cdot \frac{\partial p}{\partial x} y^2 + C_1 y + C_2 \qquad \text{...(10.20)}$$

where, C_1 and C_2 are the constants of integration to be evaluated from the known boundary conditions. In the present case the boundary conditions are:

At $\quad y = 0, u = 0$, and at $y = b, u = U$

$$\therefore \quad C_2 = 0, \quad \text{and} \quad C_1 = \frac{U}{b} - \frac{1}{2\mu}\left(\frac{\partial p}{\partial x}\right) b$$

Hence, substituting the values of C_1 and C_2 in eqn. (10.20), it yields the following equation for the *velocity distribution* for generalised *Couette flow:*

$$u = \frac{U}{b} y - \frac{1}{2\mu} \cdot \frac{\partial p}{\partial x} (by - y^2) \qquad \text{...(10.21)}$$

The eqn. (10.21) indicates that the velocity distribution in Couette flow depends on both U and $\left(\frac{\partial p}{\partial x}\right)$. However, the pressure gradient $\left(\frac{\partial p}{\partial x}\right)$ in this case may be either positive or negative. In a particular case when $\left(\frac{\partial p}{\partial x}\right)$ equals *zero*, there is no pressure gradient in the direction of flow, then, we have $u = U \cdot \frac{y}{b}$ which indicates that the velocity distribution is *linear*. This particular case is known as *simple* (*or plain*) *Couette flow or simple shear flow.*

The discharge per unit width (q) may be obtained as follows:

$$q = \int_0^b u \cdot dy = \int_0^b \left[\frac{U}{b} y - \frac{1}{2\mu} \cdot \frac{\partial p}{\partial x} (by - y^2) \right] dy$$

$$= U \cdot \frac{b}{2} - \frac{b^3}{12\mu} \cdot \frac{\partial p}{\partial x} \quad ...(10.22)$$

The *distribution of shear stress* across any section may be determined by using Newton's law of viscosity. Thus,

$$\tau = \mu \cdot \frac{\partial u}{\partial y} = \mu \left[\frac{U}{b} - \frac{1}{2\mu} \cdot \frac{\partial p}{\partial x} (b - 2y) \right]$$

$$= \mu \cdot \frac{U}{b} - \frac{1}{2} \cdot \frac{\partial p}{\partial x} (b - 2y) \quad ...(10.23)$$

The type of flow discussed above (*i.e.* flow of viscous fluid between two plates-one *stationary* and the other *moving*) is known as **generalised Couette flow.**

10.7.2. Both Plates at Rest

In this case the equations for velocity, discharge q and the shear stress can be obtained from similar equations for generalised Couette flow by putting $U = 0$. Thus for flow between two stationary parallel plates, shown in Fig. 10.21, we have:

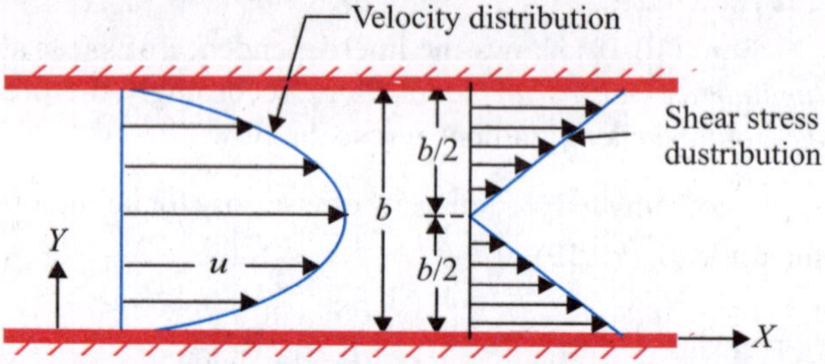

Fig. 10.21. Flow between stationary plates.

Velocity,

$$u = -\frac{1}{2\mu} \cdot \frac{\partial p}{\partial x} (by - y^2) \quad ...(10.24)$$

[Eqn. (10.24) represents the plane *Poiseuille flow*]

Discharge per unit width,

$$q = -\frac{b^3}{12\,\mu} \cdot \frac{\partial p}{\partial x} \quad ...(10.25)$$

$$\text{Shear stress, } \tau = -\frac{1}{2} \cdot \frac{\partial p}{\partial x} (b - 2y) \quad ...(10.26)$$

10.7.3. Both Plates Moving in Opposite Directions

For flow between parallel plates, the velocity distribution is given by:

$$u = \frac{1}{2\mu} \cdot \frac{\partial p}{\partial x} \cdot y^2 + C_1 y + C_2 \quad ...\text{Eqn. (10.20)}$$

In the present case the boundary conditions are:

At, $y = 0, u = -V$, and

At, $y = b, u = U$

Substituting these boundary conditions in eqn. (10.20), we get:

$$-V = C_2 \quad i.e. \quad C_2 = -V$$

and, $$U = \frac{1}{2\mu} \cdot \frac{\partial p}{\partial x} b^2 + C_1 b - V$$

or, $$U+V = \frac{1}{2u}\cdot\frac{\partial p}{\partial x}b^2 + C_1 b$$

$$\therefore \quad C_1 = (U+V)\frac{1}{b} - \frac{1}{2\mu}\frac{\partial p}{\partial x}\cdot b$$

Hence the eqn. (10.20) becomes:

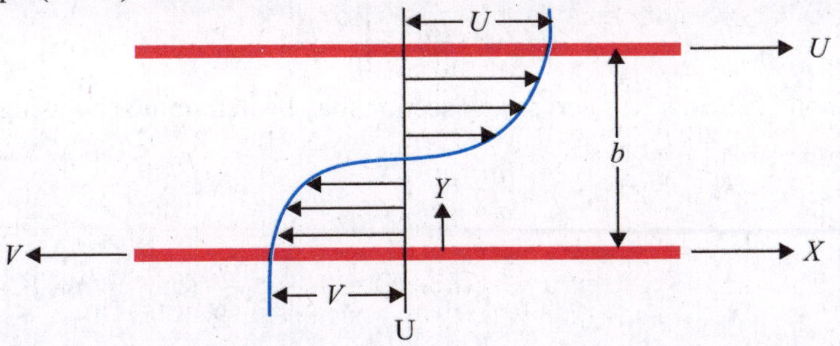

Fig. 10.22. Flow between parallel horizontal plates, both the plates moving in opposite directions.

$$u = \frac{1}{2\mu}\cdot\frac{\partial p}{\partial x}\cdot y^2 + \left[(U+V)\frac{1}{b} - \frac{1}{2\mu}\cdot\frac{\partial p}{\partial x}\cdot b\right]y - V$$

$$\therefore \quad u = (U+V)\frac{y}{b} - \frac{1}{2\mu}\cdot\frac{\partial p}{\partial x}(by - y^2) - V \qquad ...(10.27)$$

The distance y at which the velocity u is zero may be determined as follows:

$$(U+V)\frac{y}{b} - \frac{1}{2\mu}\cdot\frac{\partial p}{\partial x}(by - y^2) - V = 0$$

Rearranging the above equation, we have:

$$\frac{1}{2\mu}\cdot\frac{\partial p}{\partial x}y^2 + \left(\frac{U+V}{b} - \frac{1}{2\mu}\cdot\frac{\partial p}{\partial x}\cdot b\right)y - V = 0$$

Solving this quadratic equation, we have:

$$y = \frac{-\left[\frac{U+V}{b} - \frac{1}{2\mu}\cdot\frac{\partial p}{\partial x}\cdot b\right] \pm \sqrt{\left(\frac{U+V}{b} - \frac{1}{2\mu}\cdot\frac{\partial p}{\partial x}\cdot b\right)^2 + 4\cdot\frac{1}{2\mu}\cdot\frac{\partial p}{\partial x}\cdot V}}{2\times\frac{1}{2\mu}\cdot\frac{\partial p}{\partial x}}$$

$$= \frac{-\left[\frac{U+V}{b} - \frac{1}{2\mu}\cdot\frac{\partial p}{\partial x}\cdot b\right] \pm \sqrt{\left(\frac{U+V}{b}\right)^2 + \frac{1}{4\mu^2}\left(\frac{\partial p}{\partial x}\right)^2 b^2 - \frac{(U-V)}{\mu}\cdot\frac{\partial p}{\partial x}}}{\frac{1}{\mu}\cdot\frac{\partial p}{\partial x}}$$

The above equation will yield two values of y, one which is $+ve$ and less than b will be accepted and the other one rejected.

The discharge per unit width of plates is given by,

$$q = \int_0^b u\, dy$$

$$= \int_0^b \left[(U+V)\frac{y}{b} - \frac{1}{2\mu}\frac{\partial p}{\partial x}(by - y^2) - V\right]dy$$

$$= (U + V)\left[\frac{y^2}{2b}\right]_0^b - \frac{1}{2\,\mu}\cdot\frac{\partial p}{\partial x}\left[b\cdot\frac{y^2}{2} - \frac{y^3}{3}\right] - V\,[y]_0^b$$

$$= (U + V)\frac{b}{2} - \frac{1}{2\mu}\cdot\frac{\partial p}{\partial x}\left(\frac{b^3}{2} - \frac{b^3}{3}\right) - Vb$$

$$= (U - V)\frac{b}{2} - \frac{1}{12\mu}\frac{\partial p}{\partial x}b^3 \qquad \text{...(10.28)}$$

The distribution of shear stress across any section may be determined by using Newton's law of viscosity. Thus,

$$\tau = \mu\cdot\frac{du}{dy}$$

$$= \mu\frac{d}{dy}\left[(U+V)\frac{y}{b} - \frac{1}{2\mu}\cdot\frac{\partial p}{\partial x}(by - y^2) - V\right]$$

$$= \mu\left[\frac{U+V}{b} - \frac{1}{2\mu}\cdot\frac{\partial p}{\partial x}(b - 2y)\right]$$

$$= \mu\left(\frac{U+V}{b}\right) - \frac{1}{2}\frac{\partial p}{\partial x}(b - 2y)$$

$$= (U+V)\frac{\mu}{b} - \frac{\partial p}{\partial x}\left(\frac{b}{2} - y\right) \qquad \text{...(10.29)}$$

The distance y at which the shear stress will be zero is obtained by putting eqn. (10.29) to zero. Thus,

$$(U+V)\frac{\mu}{b} - \frac{\partial p}{\partial x}\left(\frac{b}{2} - y\right) = 0$$

or,
$$\frac{\partial p}{\partial x}\left(\frac{b}{2} - y\right) = (U+V)\frac{\mu}{b}$$

or,
$$\frac{b}{2} - y = \frac{(U+V)\frac{\mu}{b}}{\frac{\partial p}{\partial x}}$$

$$\therefore \qquad y = \frac{b}{2} - \frac{\mu}{b}\left(\frac{U+V}{\partial p/\partial x}\right) \qquad \text{...(10.30)}$$

Example 10.24. *Determine the direction and amount of flow per metre width between two parallel plates when one is moving relative to the other with a velocity of 3 m/s in the negative direction, if* $\frac{\partial p}{\partial x} = -100 \times 10^6$ *N/m³ and* $\mu = 0.4$ *poise and distance between the plates is 1 mm.*

(MGU, Kerala)

Solution. *Given:* $U = -3$ m/s; $\frac{dp}{dx} = -100 \times 10^6$ N/m³, $\mu = 0.4$ poise $= 0.4 \times \frac{1}{10} = 0.04$ Ns/m²; $b = 1$ mm $= 0.001$ m.

We know that,
$$q = U\cdot\frac{b}{2} - \frac{b^3}{12\mu}\cdot\frac{\partial p}{\partial x} \qquad \text{[Eqn. (10.22)]}$$

Substituting the values, we have:

$$q = -3 \times \frac{0.001}{2} - \frac{0.001^3}{12 \times 0.04} \times (-100 \times 10^6) = 0.2068 \text{ m}^3/\text{s}$$

Hence, *amount of flow per metre width* = **0.2068 m³/s. (Ans.)**

Positive direction (*i.e.* in the direction opposite to that of the moving plate). **(Ans.)**

Example 10.25. *Two parallel plates kept 100 mm apart have laminar flow of oil between them with a maximum velocity of 1.5 m/s. Calculate:*

(*i*) *The discharge per metre width,*

(*ii*) *The shear stress at the plates,*

(*iii*) *The difference in pressure between two points 20 m apart,*

(*iv*) *The velocity gradient at the plates, and*

(*v*) *The velocity at 20 mm from the plate.*

Assume viscosity of oil to be 24.5 poise.

Solution. Distance between the parallel plates, $b = 100 \text{ mm} = 0.1 \text{ m}$

Maximum velocity of the oil, $u_{max} = 1.5 \text{ m/s}$

Viscosity of the oil, $\mu = 24.5 \text{ poise} = 2.45 \text{ Ns/m}^2$

(*i*) The discharge per metre width, q:

In this case the average velocity of flow,

$$\bar{u} = \frac{2}{3} u_{max} = \frac{2}{3} \times 1.5 = 1.0 \text{ m/s}$$

$$\therefore \quad q = \bar{u} \times b = 1.0 \times 0.1 = \mathbf{0.1 \ m^3/s \ per \ m} \ \textbf{(Ans.)}$$

(*ii*) The shear stress at the plates τ_0 :

We know,

$$q = \frac{b^3}{12\mu}\left(-\frac{\partial p}{\partial x}\right) \quad \text{...[Eqn. (10.25)]}$$

Substituting the values, we have:

$$0.1 = \frac{0.1^3}{12 \times 2.45}\left(-\frac{\partial p}{\partial x}\right)$$

or,

$$\left(-\frac{\partial p}{\partial x}\right) = \frac{0.1 \times 12 \times 2.45}{0.1^3} = 2940 \text{ N/m}^2\text{/m}$$

The shear stress across any section is given by:

$$\tau = \frac{1}{2}\left(-\frac{\partial p}{\partial x}\right)(b - 2y) \quad \text{...[Eqn. (10.26)]}$$

The shear stress at the plates is obtained by putting $y = 0$ in the above equation. Thus,

$$\tau_0 = \frac{1}{2}\left(-\frac{\partial p}{\partial x}\right) b$$

$$= \frac{1}{2} \times 2940 \times 0.1 = \mathbf{147 \ N/m^2} \ \textbf{(Ans.)}$$

(*iii*) Pressure difference between two points 20 m apart:

We know,

$$-\frac{\partial p}{\partial x} = 2940$$

or,

$$-\partial p = 2940 \, \partial x$$

Integrating w.r.t. x, we get:

$$\int_{p_1}^{p_2} (-\partial p) = \int_{x_1}^{x_2} 2940 \, (\partial x)$$

or,

$$p_1 - p_2 = 2940 \, (x_2 - x_1)$$

$$= 2940 \times 20 = 58800 \text{ N/m}^2 \text{ or } \mathbf{58.8 \ kN/m^2} \ \textbf{(Ans.)}$$

(iv) The velocity gradient at the plates, $\left(\frac{\partial u}{\partial y}\right)_{y=0}$:

$$\tau_0 = \mu \cdot \left(\frac{\partial u}{\partial y}\right)_{y=0}$$

or,
$$\left(\frac{\partial u}{\partial y}\right)_{y=0} = \frac{\tau_0}{\mu} = \frac{147}{2.45} = 60 \text{ s}^{-1} \textbf{ (Ans.)}$$

(v) The velocity at 20 mm from the plate:

$$u = \frac{1}{2\mu} \cdot \left(\frac{-\partial p}{\partial x}\right)(by - y^2) \qquad \text{...[Eqn. (10.24)]}$$

$$= \frac{1}{2 \times 2 \cdot 45} \times 2940\,(0.1 \times 0.02 - 0.02^2)$$

$(\because y = 20 \text{ mm} = 0.02 \text{ m})$

$$= \textbf{0.96 m/s (Ans.)}$$

Example 10.26. *A liquid of viscosity of 0.9 poise is filled between two horizontal plates 10 mm apart. If the upper plate is moving at 1 m/s with respect to the lower plate which is stationary and the pressure difference between two sections 60 m apart is 60 kN/m², determine:*

(i) The velocity distribution,

(ii) The discharge per unit width, and

(iii) The shear stress on the upper plate.

Solution. Viscosity of the liquid,

$\mu = 0.9$ poise $= 0.09$ Ns/m²

Distance between the plates,

$b = 10$ mm $= 0.01$ m

Velocity of the upper plate, $U = 1$ m/s

Pressure difference between the sections 60 m apart = 60 kN/m²

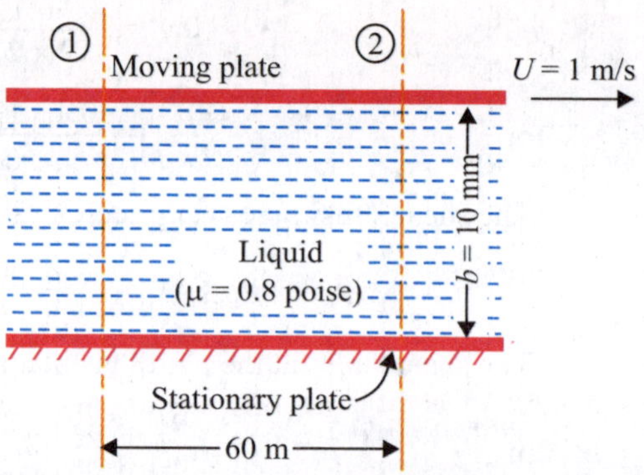

Fig. 10.23

$$\therefore \quad \left(-\frac{\partial p}{\partial x}\right) = \frac{60 \times 10^3}{60}$$

$$= 103 \text{ N/m}^2\text{/m}$$

(i) The velocity distribution:

The system corresponds to Couette flow for which the velocity distribution is given as:

$$u = \frac{U}{b}y + \frac{1}{2\mu}\left(-\frac{\partial p}{\partial x}\right)(by - y^2) \qquad \text{...[Eqn. (10.21)]}$$

$$= \frac{1}{0.01}y + \frac{1}{2 \times 0.09} \times 10^3 (0.01 \times y - y^2)$$

$$= y\,(100 + 55.55 - 5555.55\,y)$$

$$= y\,(155.55 - 5555.55\,y)$$

Hence, the *velocity distribution is*: $\boldsymbol{u = y\,(155.55 - 5555.55\,y)}$ **(Ans.)**

(*ii*) Discharge per unit width, *q*:

$$q = \int_0^b u\, dy$$

$$= \int_0^{0.01} (155.55\, y - 5555.55\, y^2)\, dy$$

$$= \left[155.55 \times \frac{y^2}{2} - 5555.55 \times \frac{y^3}{3}\right]_0^{0.01}$$

$$= \left[155.55 \times \frac{0.01^2}{2} - 5555.55 \times \frac{0.01^3}{3}\right]$$

$$= (0.007777 - 0.001852) = \mathbf{0.005925\ m^3/s}$$ **(Ans.)**

(*iii*) The shear stress on the upper plate, τ_0 :

$$\text{Shear stress, } \tau = \mu \cdot \left(\frac{\partial u}{\partial y}\right) = \mu \frac{\partial}{\partial y} (155.55\, y - 5555.55\, y^2)$$

$$= 0.09\,(155.55 - 11111.1\, y)$$

For the top plate, $y = 0.01$ m

$$\therefore \quad \tau_0 = 0.09\,(155.55 - 11111.1 \times 0.01) \simeq \mathbf{4\ N/m^2}$$ **(Ans.)**

Example 10.27. *Fluid is in laminar motion between two parallel plates under the action of motion of one of the plates and also under the presence of a pressure gradient in such a way that the net forward discharge across any section is zero.*

(i) Find out the point where minimum velocity occurs and its magnitude.

(ii) Draw the velocity distribution graph across any section.

Solution. In the given case of flow, the velocity distribution is given by:

$$u = \frac{U}{b}\, y - \frac{1}{2\mu} \frac{\partial p}{\partial x} (by - y^2) \qquad \text{...[Eqn. (10.21)]}$$

and, the discharge per unit width,

$$q = \frac{Ub}{2} - \frac{b^3}{12\mu} \cdot \frac{\partial p}{\partial x} \qquad \text{...[Eqn. (10.22)]}$$

Net forward discharge,

$$q = 0 \qquad \text{...(Given)}$$

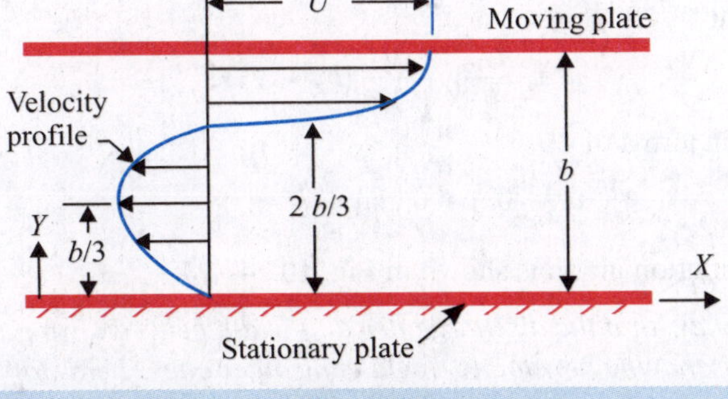

Fig. 10.24

$$\therefore \quad 0 = \frac{Ub}{2} - \frac{b^3}{12\mu} \cdot \frac{\partial p}{\partial x}$$

or,
$$\frac{\partial p}{\partial x} = \frac{Ub}{2} \times \frac{12\mu}{b^3} = \frac{6\mu U}{b^2}$$

Minimum velocity occurs where,

$$\frac{\partial u}{\partial y} = 0$$

Thus,
$$\frac{\partial}{\partial y}\left[\frac{U}{b} \cdot y - \frac{1}{2\mu}\frac{\partial p}{\partial x}(by - y^2)\right] = 0$$

or,
$$\frac{U}{b} - \frac{1}{2\mu}\frac{\partial p}{\partial x}(b - 2y) = 0$$

or,
$$\frac{U}{b} = \frac{1}{2\mu}\frac{\partial p}{\partial x}(b - 2y)$$

or,
$$(b - 2y) = \frac{(U/b) \times 2\mu}{(\partial p/\partial x)}$$

or,
$$2y = b - \frac{(U/b) \times 2\mu}{(\partial p/\partial x)}$$

or,
$$y = \frac{b}{2} - \frac{(U/b) \times \mu}{6\mu U/b^2} = \frac{b}{3} \qquad \left(\because \frac{\partial p}{\partial x} = \frac{6\mu U}{b^2}\right)$$

Hence, *minimum velocity occurs at a distance* $\boldsymbol{\frac{b}{3}}$ *from the fixed plate.* **(Ans.)**

The *magnitude of minimum velocity* is obtained by putting $y = \frac{b}{3}$ in the equation of velocity distribution. Thus,

$$u = \frac{U}{b} \cdot y - \frac{1}{2\mu}\frac{\partial p}{\partial x}(by - y^2)$$

or,
$$u_{min} = \frac{U}{b} \times \frac{b}{3} - \frac{1}{2\mu} \times \frac{6\mu U}{b^2}\left(b \times \frac{b}{3} - \frac{b^2}{9}\right)$$

$$= \frac{U}{3} - \frac{2U}{3} = -\frac{U}{3} \quad \textbf{(Ans.)}$$

(*ii*) Velocity distribution graph:

The velocity distribution graph may be drawn by substituting arbitrary values of y such as $0.1b$, $0.2b$, $0.3b$ etc. in the equation,

$$u = \frac{U}{b}y - \frac{3U}{b^2}(by - y^2),$$

and computing u in terms of U.

Also, when $u = 0, y = 0$ and $\frac{2}{3}b$

The velocity distribution graph is shown in Fig. 10.24.

Example 10.28. *Show that the discharge per unit width between two parallel plates distance b apart, when one plate is moving at velocity U while the other one is held stationary, for the condition of zero shear stress at the fixed plate is* $q = \frac{Ub}{3}$

Solution. The given case of flow corresponds to Couette flow for which the velocity distribution given by:

$$u = \frac{U}{b} \cdot y + \frac{1}{2\mu}\left(-\frac{\partial p}{\partial x}\right)(by - y^2)$$

$\therefore$ Discharge per unit width,

$$q = \int_0^b u \cdot dy = \int_0^b \left[\frac{U}{b} \cdot y + \frac{1}{2\mu}\left(-\frac{\partial p}{\partial x}\right)(by - y^2)\right] dy$$

$$= \left[\frac{U}{b} \cdot \frac{y^2}{2} + \frac{1}{2\mu}\left(-\frac{\partial p}{\partial x}\right)\left(b \cdot \frac{y^2}{2} - \frac{y^3}{3}\right)\right]_0^b$$

$$= \frac{U}{b} \cdot \frac{b^2}{2} + \frac{1}{2\mu}\left(-\frac{\partial p}{\partial x}\right)\left(\frac{b^3}{2} - \frac{b^3}{3}\right)$$

$$= \frac{Ub}{2} + \frac{1}{2\mu}\left(-\frac{\partial p}{\partial x}\right)\frac{b^3}{6} \quad \text{...}(i)$$

$$\text{Stress, } \tau = \mu \cdot \frac{\partial u}{\partial y}$$

$$= \mu \frac{d}{dy}\left[\frac{Uy}{b} + \frac{1}{2\mu}\left(-\frac{\partial p}{\partial x}\right)(by - y^2)\right]$$

$$= \mu\left[\frac{U}{b} + \frac{1}{2\mu}\left(-\frac{\partial p}{\partial x}\right)(b - 2y)\right]$$

But shear stress at the surface of fixed plate ($y = 0$) = 0 ... (*Given*)

$$\therefore \quad 0 = \mu\left[\frac{U}{b} + \frac{1}{2\mu}\left(-\frac{\partial p}{\partial x}\right)b\right]$$

or,
$$\frac{U}{b} + \frac{1}{2\mu}\left(-\frac{\partial p}{\partial x}\right)b = 0$$

or,
$$\frac{1}{2\mu}\left(-\frac{\partial p}{\partial x}\right) = -\frac{U}{b^2}$$

Making substitution for this expression in (*i*), we get:

$$q = \frac{Ub}{2} - \frac{U}{b^2} \times \frac{b^3}{6} = \mathbf{\frac{Ub}{3}} \quad \text{...(Proved)}$$

Example 10.29. *Laminar flow of a fluid of viscosity 0.9 Ns/m² and specific gravity 1.26 occurs between a pair of parallel plates of extensive width, inclined at 45° to the horizontal, the plates being 10 mm apart. The upper plate moves with a velocity of 2.0 m/s relative to the lower plate and in a direction opposite to the fluid flow. Pressure gauges mounted at two points 1 m vertically apart on the upper plate record pressures of 250 kN/m² and 80 kN/m² respectively. Determine:*

(*i*) *The velocity and shear stress distribution between the plates,*

(*ii*) *The maximum flow velocity, and*

(*iii*) *The shear stress on the upper plate.* **[MU]**

Solution. Viscosity of the fluid, $\mu = 0.9 \text{ Ns/m}^2$

Specific gravity of the fluid = 1.26

Distance between the plates, b = 10 mm = 0.01 m

Velocity of upper (moving) plate, $U = -2.0$ m/s

Pressure, $p_1 = 250$ kN/m^2

Pressure, $p_2 = 80$ kN/m^2.

(i) The velocity and shear stress distribution between the plates:

Considering sections 1 and 2, we have:

$$h_1 - h_2 = \left(\frac{p_1}{w} + z_1\right) - \left(\frac{p_2}{w} + z_2\right)$$

$$= \left(\frac{250 \times 10^3}{1.26 \times 9810} + 1\right) - \left(\frac{80 \times 10^3}{1.26 \times 9810}\right) + 0$$

or,
$$h_1 - h_2 = 21.225 - 6.47$$

$$= 14.755 \text{ m in } \sqrt{2} \text{ m or } 1.414 \text{ m}$$

Since $h_1 > h_2$, flow will be in *downward* direction.

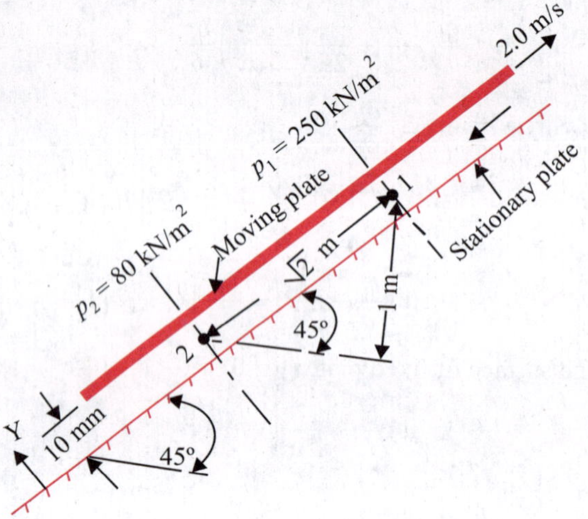

Fig. 10.25

$$\frac{\partial h}{\partial x} = -\frac{14.755}{1.414} = -10.435$$

and,
$$\frac{\partial p}{\partial x} = w\frac{\partial h}{\partial x} = (1.26 \times 9810) \times (-10.435)$$

$$= -128983 \text{ N/m}^2 \text{ or } -128.983 \text{ kN/m}^2$$

The velocity distribution in this case of flow is given by:

$$u = \frac{U}{b} \cdot y - \frac{1}{2\mu} \cdot \left(\frac{\partial p}{\partial x}\right)(by - y^2) \quad \text{[Eqn. (10.21)]}$$

Substituting the values, we get:

$$u = -\frac{2.0}{0.01}y - \frac{1}{2 \times 0.9} \times (-128.983 \times 10^3)(0.01y - y^2)$$

$$= -200y + 716.57y - 71657y^2$$

$$= 516.57y - 71657y^2$$

Hence, velocity distribution is given by:

$$\mathbf{u = 516.57y - 71657y^2} \textbf{ (Ans.)}$$

The shear stress distribution is given by:

$$\tau = \mu \cdot \frac{U}{b} - \frac{1}{2}\frac{\partial p}{\partial x}(b - 2y) \quad \text{...[Eqn. (10.21)]}$$

$$= 0.9 \times \left(\frac{-2}{0.01}\right) - \frac{1}{2} \times (-128.983 \times 10^3)(0.01 - 2y)$$

$$= -180 + 644.91 - 128982y = 464.91 - 128982y$$

Hence, the shear stress distribution is given by:

$$\tau = \mathbf{464.91 - 128982\, y} \text{ (Ans.)}$$

(*ii*) Maximum flow velocity, u_{max}:

For maximum velocity, $\frac{du}{dy} = 0$

or, $\frac{d}{dy}(516.57y - 71657y^2) = 0$

or, $516.57 - 143314y = 0$

or, $y = 3.604 \times 10^{-3}$ m

∴ Maximum velocity, $u_{max} = 516.57 \times 3.604 \times 10^{-3} - 71657 \times (3.604 \times 10^{-3})^2$

$= 1.862 - 0.931 = \mathbf{0.931\ m/s}$ **(Ans.)**

(*iii*) The shear stress on the upper plate:

$$(\tau)_{0.01} = 464.91 - 128982 \times 0.01 = \mathbf{-824.91\ N/m^2} \text{ (Ans.)}$$

Example 10.30. *A large thin plate is pulled at constant velocity U through a narrow gap of height h. On one side of the plate is oil of viscosity μ and on the other side oil of viscosity αμ, where α is a constant. Calculate the position of the plate so that the drag force on it will be minimum.*

(UPTU)

Solution. Refer to Fig. 10.26. Let a be the distance of the thin plate from the top surface.

Shear stress on *top portion*;

$$\tau_1 = \mu_1 \frac{du}{dy} = \mu \frac{U}{a}$$

Shear stress on the *bottom portion*;

$$\tau_2 = \mu \frac{du}{dy} = \alpha\mu \frac{U}{(h-a)}$$

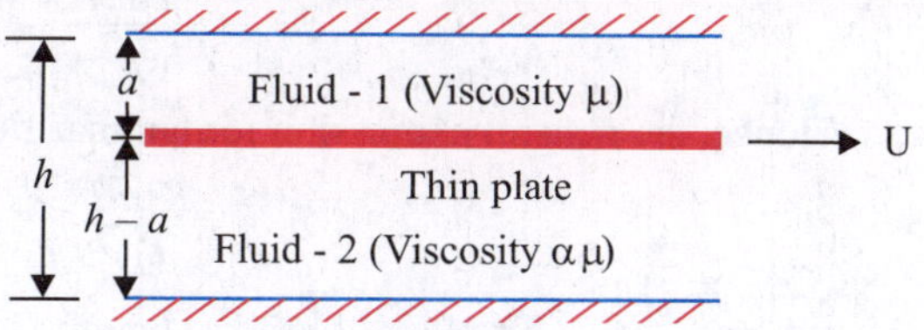

Fig. 10.26

Total drag force on the plate,

$$F = A(\tau_1 + \tau_2)$$

$$= A\left[\mu\frac{U}{a} + \alpha\mu\frac{U}{(h-a)}\right]$$

$$= AU\left(\frac{\mu}{a} + \frac{\alpha\mu}{h-a}\right)$$

$$= AU\mu\left(\frac{1}{a} + \frac{\alpha}{h-a}\right)$$

For F to be *minimum*:

$$\frac{dF}{da} = -\frac{1}{a^2} + \frac{\alpha}{(h-a)^2} = 0$$

or, $$\frac{\alpha}{(h-a)^2} = \frac{1}{a^2}$$

or, $$\frac{\sqrt{\alpha}}{h-a} = \frac{1}{a}$$

or, $$a\sqrt{x} = h-a$$

or, $$a(1+\sqrt{\alpha}) = h$$

or, $$\boldsymbol{a = \frac{h}{1+\sqrt{\alpha}}}$$

which gives the position of the plate for *minimum drag* **(Ans.)**

10.8. LAMINAR FLOW THROUGH POROUS MEDIA

It was established by Darcy through experiments that the velocity of a fluid through a porous media varies *linearly* with the loss of head h_f, which indicates that the flow through the porous media is *laminar*.

Consider a circular pipe of length L and diameter D completely filled with porous material of grain diameter d_s. The flow takes places through the interstices of the porous material. If porosity is n, the diameter of the passage through the particles is nd_s. The loss of head when liquid flows through a porous media can be determined by using the general expression for head loss in laminar flow.

The loss of head for laminar/viscous flow *through a pipe* is given by:

$$h_f = \frac{32\,\mu\bar{u}L}{wD^2}$$

Similarly, the loss of head for laminar flow *through parallel plates* is given by:

$$h_f = \frac{12\mu\bar{u}L}{wb^2}$$

Hence, the general expression for laminar flow may be expressed as:

$$h_f = \frac{K\mu\bar{u}L}{wD^2} \qquad ...(10.31)$$

where, h_f = The loss of head in length L,

K = A constant, the value of which depends on the shape of the passage,

μ = Dynamic viscosity of the fluid,

$\bar{u}$ = Average velocity of flow,

w = Weight density of the fluid, and

D = A characteristic length representing the geometry of the passage.

Eqn. (10.31) can be used for laminar flow through porous media. The *diameter of the passage through particles* is given by:

$$d = n\,d_s$$

Substituting this value of d for D in eqn. (10.31), we get:

$$h_f = \frac{K\,\mu\bar{u}L}{wn^2\,d_s^2}$$

or, $$\bar{u} = \frac{wn^2 d_s^2}{K\mu}\left(\frac{h_f}{L}\right)$$

or, $$\bar{u} = ki \qquad ...(10.32)$$

where, k = A constant, called the *co-efficient of permeability*, and

i = The hydraulic gradient $\left(= \frac{h_f}{L}\right)$

Eqn. (10.32) is the well known Darcy's equation for flow of water through soil.

— The equation is applicable for the Reynolds number < 1.

— The equation is normally valid (according to Ehrenberger) for velocities $\bar{u}$ less than 3 to 4.5 mm/s.

Example 10.31. *Water at a rate of 0.0006 litre/sec. is flowing through a sandy specimen of 8 cm height and 45 cm² cross-sectional area under a constant head of 7 cm. Determine the co-efficient of permeability.*

Solution. Discharge through sandy specimen, Q = 0.0006 litre/sec.

Area of cross-section, A = 45 cm²

Height of specimen, L = 8 cm

Constant head, h_f = 7 cm

Co-efficient of permeability, *k*:

$$\text{Average velocity, } \bar{u} = \frac{Q}{A} = \frac{0.0006 \times 10^3}{45} = 0.0133 \text{ cm/s}$$

Using the relation :

$$\bar{u} = ki = k\left(\frac{h_f}{L}\right), \text{ we get:}$$

$$0.0133 = k \times \frac{7}{8}$$

or $$k = \frac{0.0133 \times 8}{7} = \mathbf{0.0152 \text{ cm/s}} \text{ (Ans.)}$$

10.9. POWER ABSORBED IN BEARINGS

In a bearing, a very thin film of lubricating oil is maintained between its stationary surface and the surface of the rotating shaft. The lubricating oils are viscous and hence the theory of laminar/viscous flow can be applied to the theory of lubrication. A very viscous oil leads to greater resistance and causes great power loss; a light oil, on the other hand, may not be able to maintain the required film between the metal surfaces and wear of the surfaces will take place. The expressions for power absorbed due to viscous resistance in different types of bearing are derived as given below.

10.9.1. Journal Bearing

Fig. 10.27 shows a journal bearing in which a shaft is rotating. A lubricating oil is filled in the annular space between the shaft and the bearing.

Let, D = Diameter of the shaft,

t = Thickness of oil film,

L = Length of the bearing, and

N = Speed of the shaft in r.p.m.

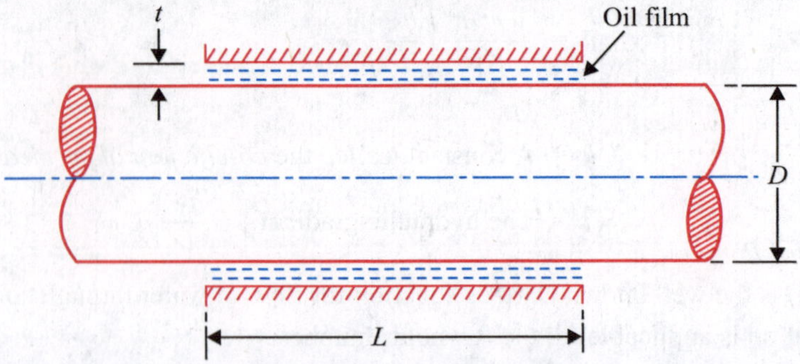

Fig. 10.27. Journal bearing.

∴ Angular speed,

$$\omega = \frac{2\pi N}{60} \text{ rad/s}$$

Tangential speed of the shaft,

$$V = \omega R$$

or,

$$V = \frac{2\pi N}{60} \times \frac{D}{2} = \frac{\pi DN}{60} \text{ m/s.}$$

As the thickness 't' of the oil film is very small, a linear velocity distribution can be presumed.

Hence,

$$\frac{du}{dy} = \frac{V-0}{t} = \frac{V}{t} = \frac{\pi DN}{60 \times t}$$

∴ Shear stress, $\tau = \mu \times \dfrac{\pi DN}{60 \times t}$

Shear force or viscous resistance,

$$F = \tau \times \text{area of surface of the shaft}$$

$$= \frac{\mu\pi DN}{60t} \times \pi DL = \frac{\mu\pi^2 D^2 NL}{60t}$$

∴ Torque required to overcome the viscous resistance of the whole of the bearing,

$$T = F \times \frac{D}{2} = \frac{\mu\pi^2 D^2 NL}{60t} \times \frac{D}{2} = \frac{\mu\pi^2 D^3 NL}{120t} \quad \text{...(10.33)}$$

∴ Power absorbed in overcoming the resistance,

$$P = T.\omega = \frac{2\pi NT}{60} \text{ watts} \quad \text{...(10.34)}$$

$$\left(\text{where } T = \frac{\mu\pi^2 D^3 NL}{120\, t}\right)$$

Example 10.32. *A shaft of 100 mm diameter rotates at 60 r.p.m. in a 200 mm long bearing. Taking that the two surfaces are uniformly separated by a distance of 0.5 mm and taking linear velocity distribution in the lubricating oil having dynamic viscosity 0.04 poise, find the power absorbed in bearing.* **[PTU]**

Solution. Diameter of the shaft, D = 100 mm = 0.1 m

Speed of the shaft, N = 60 r.p.m.

Length of the bearing, L = 200 mm = 0.2 m

Thickness of oil film, t = 0.5 mm = 0.0005 m

Dynamic viscosity, μ = 0.04 poise = 0.004 Ns/m^2

Power absorbed, P:

The torque required to overcome viscous resistance in a journal bearing is given by:

$$T = \frac{\mu\pi^2 D^3 NL}{120t} = \frac{0.004 \times \pi^2 \times 0.1^3 \times 60 \times 0.2}{120 \times 0.0005} = 0.00789 \text{ Nm}$$

$$\therefore \quad \text{Power absorbed} = \frac{2\pi NT}{60} = \frac{2\pi \times 60 \times 0.00789}{60}$$

$$= \mathbf{0.0496\ W\ (Ans.)}$$

10.9.2. Foot-step Bearing

Fig. 10.28 shows a foot-step bearing at the end of a vertical shaft. The space between the surface of the shaft and bearing is filled with oil of viscosity μ.

Let, R = Radius of the shaft,

N = Speed of the shaft, and

t = Thickness of oil film.

Consider an elementary circular ring of radius r and thickness dr as shown in the Fig. 10.28.

Area of the elementary ring $= 2\pi r.dr$

$$\text{The shear stress, } \tau = \mu \cdot \frac{\partial u}{\partial y} = \mu \cdot \frac{V}{t}$$

where, V is the tangential velocity of shaft at radius r and is equal to

$$\omega r = \frac{2\pi N}{60} \times r$$

∴ Shear force on the elementary ring,

$$dF = \tau \times \text{area of the ring}$$

$$= \mu \times \frac{2\pi N}{60} \times \frac{r}{t} \times 2\pi r \cdot dr$$

$$= \frac{u}{15} \times \frac{\pi^2 N r^2}{t} \cdot dr$$

$$\text{Torque on the ring, } dT = dF \times r = \frac{\mu}{15t} \cdot \pi^2 N r^2 \cdot dr \cdot r$$

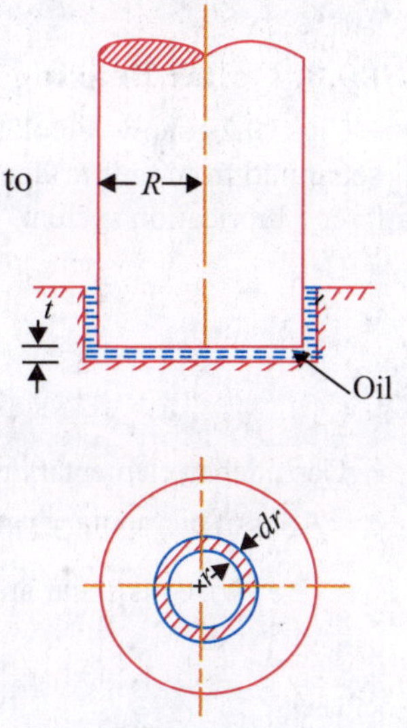

Fig. 10.28. Foot-step bearing.

∴ Total torque required to overcome viscous resistance,

$$T = \int_0^R \frac{\mu}{15t} \cdot \pi^2 N r^3 \cdot dr = \frac{\mu}{15t} \cdot \pi^2 \cdot N \int_0^R r^3 dr$$

$$= \frac{\mu}{15t} \cdot \pi^2 \cdot N \left[\frac{r^4}{4}\right]_0^R = \frac{\mu}{15t} \cdot \pi^2 \cdot N \cdot \frac{R^4}{4}$$

or, $$T = \frac{\mu}{60t} \cdot \pi^2 \cdot N R^4 \qquad ...(10.35)$$

∴ Power absorbed by the entire bearing,

$$P = T.\omega = \frac{2\pi NT}{60} \text{ watts}$$

$$\left(\text{where, } T = \frac{\mu}{60t} \cdot \pi^2 \cdot N \cdot R^4\right)$$

Example 10.33. *Find the power required to rotate a vertical shaft of diameter 100 mm at 750 r.p.m. The lower end of the shaft rests in a foot-step bearing. The end of the shaft and surface of the bearing are both flat and are separated by an oil film of thickness 0.5 mm. The viscosity of the oil is 1.5 poise.* **[Delhi University]**

Solution. Diameter of the shaft, D = 100 mm = 0.1 m

Speed of the shaft, N = 750 r.p.m.

Thickness of the film, t = 0.5 mm = 0.0005 m

The viscosity of the oil, μ = 1.5 poise = 0.15 Ns/m^2

Power required, P:

The torque required to overcome the viscous resistance in a foot-step bearing is given by:

$$T = \frac{\mu}{60t} \cdot \pi^2 \cdot N \cdot R^4 = \frac{0.15}{60 \times 0.0005} \times \pi^2 \times 750 \times \left(\frac{0.1}{2}\right)^4$$

$$= 0.2313 \text{ Nm}$$

$\therefore$ Power required to rotate the shaft,

$$P = \frac{2\pi NT}{60} = \frac{2\pi \times 750 \times 0.2313}{60} = \textbf{18.16 W (Ans.)}$$

10.9.3. Collar Bearing

Fig. 10.29 shows a collar bearing which takes up an axial thrust of shaft. The face of the collar is separated from the surface of the bearing with a film of uniform thickness which is maintained by a forced lubrication system.

Let, R_1 = Internal radius of the collar,

R_2 = External radius of the collar,

t = Thickness of oil film, and

N = Speed of the shaft in r.p.m.

Consider an elementary ring of bearing surface of radius r and thickness dr as shown in Fig. 10.29.

Area of elementary ring, $dA = 2\pi r \,.\, dr$

Viscous shear stress, $\tau = \mu \cdot \dfrac{\partial u}{\partial y} = \mu \cdot \dfrac{V}{t}$

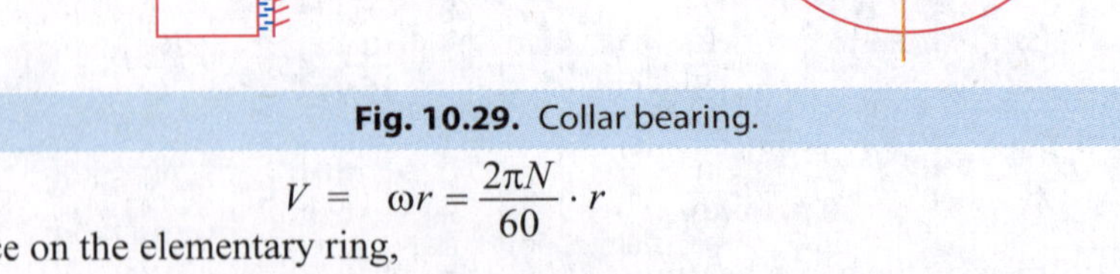

Fig. 10.29. Collar bearing.

where, $V = \omega r = \dfrac{2\pi N}{60} \cdot r$

Shear force on the elementary ring,

$$dF = \text{Viscous shear stress} \times \text{area of the ring}$$

$$= \tau \times 2\pi r \cdot dr = \mu \times \frac{2\pi N r}{60t} \times 2\pi r \cdot dr$$

$$= \frac{\mu}{15} \frac{\pi^2 N r^2}{t} \cdot dr$$

Torque on the elementary ring, $dT = dF \times r$

$$= \frac{\mu}{15t} \cdot \pi^2 N r^2 \cdot dr \cdot r$$

∴ Total torque required to overcome the viscous resistance,

$$T = \int_{R_1}^{R_2} \frac{\mu}{15t} \cdot \pi^2 N r^3 dr = \frac{\mu}{15t} \pi^2 N \int_{R_1}^{R_2} r^3 \, dr$$

$$= \frac{\mu}{15t} \pi^2 N \left[\frac{r^4}{4}\right]_{R_1}^{R_2}$$

$$T = \frac{\mu}{60t} \pi^2 N \left(R_2^4 - R_1^4\right) \quad \text{...(10.36)}$$

∴ Power absorbed by the entire bearing,

$$P = \frac{2\pi NT}{60} \text{ watts.}$$

Example 10.34. *A collar bearing having external and internal diameters 240 mm and 180 mm respectively is used to take the thrust of a shaft. An oil film of thickness 0.25 mm and of viscosity 0.8 poise is maintained between the collar surface and the bearing. Find the power lost in overcoming the viscous resistance of oil when the shaft is running at 300 r.p.m.*

Solution. External radius, $R_2 = \frac{240}{2} = 120 \text{ mm} = 0.12 \text{ m}$

Internal radius, $R_1 = \frac{180}{2} = 90 \text{ mm} = 0.09 \text{ m}$

Thickness of oil film, $t = 0.25 \text{ mm} = 0.00025 \text{ m}$

Viscosity of the oil, $\mu = 0.8 \text{ poise} = 0.08 \text{ Ns/m}^2$

Speed of the shaft, $N = 300$ r.p.m.

Power lost in viscous resistance, P:

Torque required to overcome the viscous resistance,

$$T = \frac{\mu}{60t} \pi^2 N \left(R_2^4 - R_1^4\right) \quad \text{...[Eqn. (10.36)]}$$

$$= \frac{0.08}{60 \times 0.00025} \pi^2 \times 300 \left(0.12^4 - 0.09^4\right) = 2.238 \text{ Nm}$$

∴ Power lost in viscous resistance,

$$P = \frac{2\pi NT}{60} = \frac{2\pi \times 300 \times 2.238}{60} = \mathbf{70.31 \text{ W}} \text{ (Ans.)}$$

10.10. LOSS OF HEAD DUE TO FRICTION IN VISCOUS FLOW

In a pipe of diameter D in which a viscous fluid of viscosity μ is flowing with a velocity $\overline{u}$, the loss of pressure head, h_f, is given by eqn. (10.11) as:

$$h_f = \frac{32 \mu \overline{u} L}{w D^2} \quad \text{...(i)}$$

where, L = Length of the pipe, and

w = Weight density of the fluid.

The loss of head due to friction is given by:

$$h_f = \frac{4fLV^2}{D \times 2g} = \frac{4fL\bar{u}^2}{D \times 2g} \qquad ...(ii)$$

where, f is the co-efficient of friction between pipe and fluid, and $V = \bar{u}$.

(Note : For derivation of this formula, please refer to Art 11.2)

From eqn. (*i*) and (*ii*), we have:

$$\frac{32\ \mu\bar{u}L}{wD^2} = \frac{4fL\bar{u}^2}{D \times 2g}$$

or,
$$f = \frac{32\ \mu\bar{u}L \times D \times 2g}{4\ L\bar{u}^2 \rho.gD^2} = \frac{16\mu}{\bar{u}\rho D} \qquad (\because\ w = \rho.g)$$

$$= \frac{16\mu}{\rho VD} = 16 \times \frac{1}{Re} \qquad (\because\ \bar{u} = V)$$

$$\left[\text{where, } Re \left(= \frac{\rho VD}{\mu}\right) \text{ is the Reynolds number}\right]$$

i.e.
$$f = \frac{16}{Re} \qquad ...(10.37)$$

Example 10.35. *In a pipe of 200 mm diameter in which water is flowing, there is a shear stress of 0.12 kN/m² at a point distant 30 mm from the pipe axis. If the co-efficient of friction between the pipe and the fluid is 0.04, calculate the shear stress at the pipe wall.* **[Nagpur University]**

Solution. Diameter of the pipe, D = 200 mm = 0.2 m

Co-efficient of friction, f = 0.04

Shear stress at r = 30 mm, $\tau = 0.12$ kN/m²

Shear stress at the pipe wall, τ_0:

$$\text{Co-efficient of friction, } f = \frac{16}{Re} \qquad ...[\text{Eqn. (10.37)}]$$

or,
$$Re = \frac{16}{f} = \frac{16}{0.04} = 400$$

Since $Re < 2000$, hence the flow is *viscous/ laminar*.

The shear stress in case of viscous flow through a pipe is given as:

$$\tau = -\frac{\partial p}{\partial x} \cdot \frac{r}{2} \qquad ...[\text{Eqn. (10.4)}]$$

But $\frac{\partial p}{\partial x}$ is constant across a section, therefore, $\tau \,\alpha\, r$

Shear stress at the pipe wall ($r = 0.1$ m) is τ_0.

$$\therefore \quad \frac{\tau}{r} = \frac{\tau_0}{0.1} \text{ or } \frac{0.12}{0.03} = \frac{\tau_0}{0.1}$$

or,
$$\tau_0 = \frac{0.012 \times 0.1}{0.03} = \mathbf{0.4\ kN/m^2\ (Ans.)}$$

Example 10.36. *A pipe 240 mm in diameter and 10000 m long is laid at a slope of 1 in 180. An oil of specific gravity 0.85 and viscosity 1.5 poise is pumped up at the rate of 0.02 m³/s. Find:*

(i) Head lost due to friction, and

(ii) Power required to pump the oil.

Solution. Diameter of the pipe, D = 240 mm = 0.24 m

$\therefore$ Area, $A = (\pi/4) \times 0.24^2 = 0.04524$ m²

Length of the pipe, $L = 10000$ m
Slope ot the pipe, i = 1 in 180
Specific gravity of oil, $S = 0.85$
Viscosity of oil, $\mu = 1.5$ poise $= 0.15$ Ns/m^2
Discharge, $Q = 0.02$ m^3/s

(*ii*) Head lost due to friction, h_f:

$$\text{Velocity of flow, } \bar{u} = \frac{Q}{A} = \frac{0.02}{0.04524} = 0.442 \text{ m/s}$$

$$\text{Reynolds number, } Re = \frac{\rho VD}{\mu} = \frac{(0.85 \times 1000) \times 0.442 \times 0.24}{0.15} = 601$$

As $Re < 2000$, the flow is *viscous/laminar*.

$$\text{The co-efficient of friction, } f = \frac{16}{Re} \qquad \text{...[Eqn. (10.37)]}$$

$$= \frac{16}{601} = 0.02662$$

$\therefore$ Head lost due to friction,

$$hf = \frac{4 fL\bar{u}^2}{D \times 2g} = \frac{4 \times 0.02662 \times 10000 \times 0.442^2}{0.24 \times 2 \times 9.81} = 44.17 \text{ m}$$

Height through which oil is to be raised by the pump

$$= \text{Slope} \times \text{length of pipe}$$

$$= i \times L = \frac{1}{180} \times 10000 = 55.55 \text{ m}$$

Total head against which pump is to work,

$$H = h_f + i \times L = 44.17 + 55.55 = 99.72 \text{ m}$$

$\therefore$ Power required to pump the oil,

$$P = \frac{wQH}{1000} kW = \frac{(0.85 \times 9810) \times 0.02 \times 99.72}{1000}$$

$$= \mathbf{16.63 \ kW} \text{ (Ans.)}$$

10.11. MOVEMENT OF PISTON IN DASHPOT

A **dashpot** *is a device employed for damping vibrations of machines* (Fig. 10.30). It consists of piston that moves in a concentric cylinder, the diameter of which is only slightly greater than that of the piston. The cylinder contains a viscous oil, the quantity of which should be sufficient to cover the top of the piston. The piston is connected with the machine element whose motion is to be restrained. On the downward movement of piston, under the load W, the oil is displaced from the underneath and it moves to the space above the piston through the small annular clearance between the piston and the cylinder. Conversely, during the upward movement of the piston the oil is displaced downwards. It is due to this aspect that the mechanical vibrations of the machine element (connected to the piston) are damped.

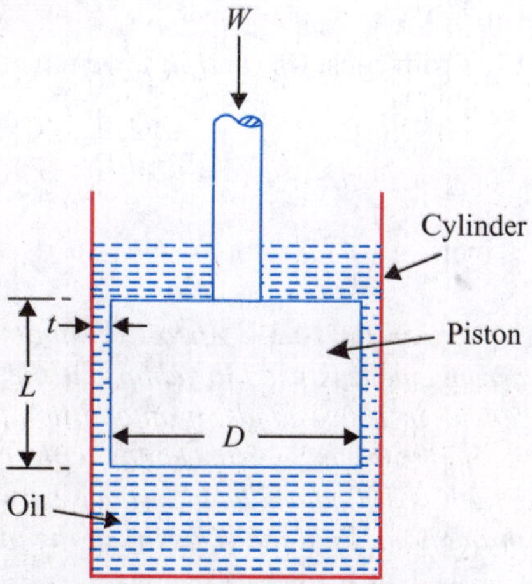

Fig. 10.30 Dashpot mechanism.

Let, D = Diameter of the piston,
L = Length of the piston,
μ = Viscosity of the oil,
V = Velocity of the piston,
$\bar{u}$ = Average velocity of oil in clearance,
t = Clearance between dashpot and piston, and
Δp = Difference of pressure intensities between the two ends of the piston.

$$= \frac{W}{\frac{\pi}{4} D^2} = \frac{4W}{\pi D^2} \quad ...(i)$$

The flow of oil through the clearance space is similar to the viscous/laminar flow between parallel plates and as such the following relation holds good,

$$\Delta p = \frac{12\mu \bar{u} L}{t^2} \quad ...(ii)$$

From eqns. (*i*) and (*ii*), we have:

$$\frac{4W}{\pi D^2} = \frac{12\mu \bar{u} L}{t^2}$$

or,

$$\bar{u} = \frac{Wt^2}{3\pi\mu L D^2} \quad ...(iii)$$

The rate of oil flow in dash pot

$$= V \times \frac{\pi}{4} D^2$$

(where, V = velocity of piston or the velocity of oil in dashpot in contact with piston)

Rate of flow through clearance

$$= \bar{u} \times \pi D \,.\, t$$

By continuity equation, we have:

$$\bar{u} \times \Delta D \,.\, t = V \times \frac{\pi}{4} D^2$$

or,

$$\bar{u} = V \times \frac{\pi}{4} D^2 \times \frac{1}{\pi D \cdot t} = \frac{VD}{4t} \quad ...(iv)$$

From eqns. (*iii*) and (*iv*), we have:

$$\frac{Wt^2}{3\pi\mu L D^2} = \frac{VD}{4t}$$

or,

$$\mu = \frac{4Wt^3}{3\pi L D^3 V} \quad ...(10.38)$$

Example 10.37. *An oil dashpot consists of a piston moving in a cylinder having oil. This arrangement is used to damp out the vibrations. The piston falls with uniform speed and covers 50 mm in 100 seconds. If an additional weight of 1.334 N is placed on the top of the piston, it falls through 50 mm in 86 seconds with unifrom speed. The diameter of the piston is 75 mm and its length is 100 mm. The clearance between the piston and the cylinder is 1.2 mm which is uniform throughout. Find the viscosity of the oil.* **[UPTU]**

Solution. Diameter of the piston, D = 75 mm = 0.075 m
Length of the piston, L = 100 mm = 0.1 m

Clearance, t = 1.2 mm = 0.0012 m

Additional weight = 1.334 N

Viscosity of oil, μ:

Let, W = Weight of the piston,

V = Velocity of piston without additional weight, and

V' = Velocity of piston with the additional weight.

Using eqn. (10.38), we have:

$$\mu = \frac{4Wt^3}{3\pi LD^3 V} = \frac{4\,(W+1.334)\,t^3}{3\pi LD^3 V'}$$

or, $$\frac{W}{V} = \frac{W+1.334}{V'}$$

or, $$\frac{V}{V'} = \frac{W}{W+1.334} \quad ...(i)$$

But, $$V = \frac{50}{100} = 0.50 \text{ mm/s}$$

and, $$V' = \frac{50}{86} = 0.581 \text{ mm/s}$$ (Data given)

$$\therefore \quad \frac{V}{V'} = \frac{0.5\times10^{-3}}{0.581\times10^{-3}} = 0.86 \quad ...(ii)$$

From eqns. (*i*) and (*ii*), we have:

$$\frac{W}{W+1.334} = 0.86$$

or, $$W = 0.86\,(W+1.334) = 0.86\,W + 1.147$$

or, $$W = 8.19\ N$$

Now, $$\mu = \frac{4Wt^3}{3\pi LD^3 V} \quad ...[\text{Eqn. (10.38)}]$$

$$= \frac{4\times8.19\times(0.0012)^3}{3\pi\times0.1\times(0.075)^3\times\left(\frac{50}{1000}\times\frac{1}{100}\right)}$$

$$= \mathbf{0.2847\ Ns/m^2}$$ **(Ans.)**

10.12. MEASUREMENT OF VISCOSITY

To determine the co-efficient of viscosity of a liquid the following experimental methods are used:

1. Rotating cylinder method
2. Falling sphere method
3. Capillary tube
4. Efflux viscometers.

The devices used for measurement of viscosity are known as **Viscometers.**

10.12.1. Rotating Cylinder Method

In this method Newton's law of viscosity is used to measure the viscosity of a fluid. Fig. 10.31 shows a rotating cylinder viscometer. It consists of two concentric cylinders, the annular space between them is filled with the liquid whose viscosity is to be determined. The outer cylinder is rotated at a constant angular velocity ω with respect to the inner stationary cylinder. The torque transmitted by the enclosed liquid to the stationary cylinder is measured by the torsional strain of the restraining spring attached to the top of the inner cylinder.

According to Newton's law of viscosity,

$$\text{Shear stress } (\tau) = \mu \times \text{velocity gradient} \left(\frac{du}{dy}\right)$$

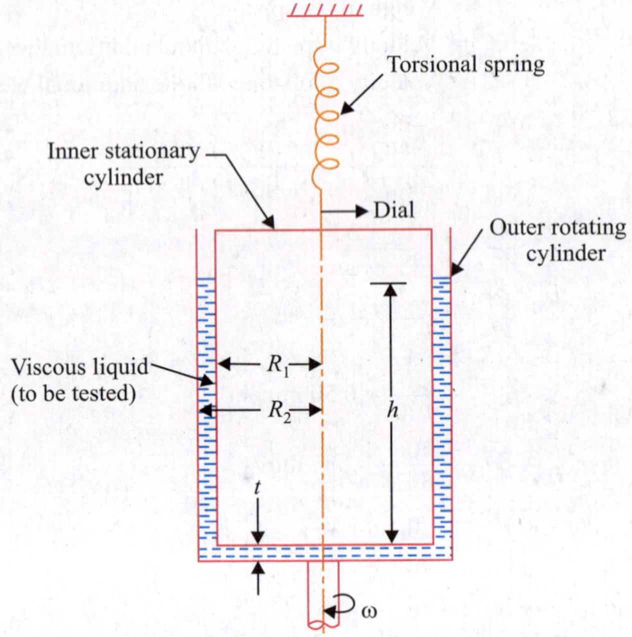

Fig. 10.31. Rotating cylinder viscometer.

Since the annular space $t = (R_2 - R_1)$ is quite small (where R_2 and R_1 are the radii of the outer and inner cylinders respectively), the velocity gradient,

$$\frac{du}{dy} = \frac{V}{t} = \frac{2\pi R_2 N}{60t}$$

(where, N = the rotational speed of the outer cylinder in r.p.m.)

$$\therefore \quad \text{Shear stress } (\tau) = \mu \times \frac{2\pi R_2 N}{60\, t}$$

$$\text{Viscous drag} = \text{Shear stress} \times \text{area}$$

$$= \mu \times \frac{2\pi R_2 N}{60t} \times 2\pi R_1 h$$

(where, h = height of liquid)

$$\text{Viscous torque} = \text{Viscous drag} \times \text{radius}$$

$$= \left(\mu \times \frac{2\pi R_2 N}{60\, t} \times 2\pi R_1 h\right) \times R_1 = \frac{\mu\pi^2 R_1^2 R_2 h N}{15t}$$

Viscous torque must equal the torque T exerted by the torquemeter.

$$\therefore \quad T = \frac{\mu\pi^2 R_1^2 R_2 \cdot hN}{15t}$$

$$\text{or,} \quad \mu = \frac{15\, T t}{\pi^2 R_1^2 R_2 h N} \qquad \text{...(10.37)}$$

Thus a rotational type viscometer can be calibrated to directly give μ for given speed of rotation N.

Example 10.38. *In a rotating cylinder viscometer, the radii of the cylinder are 32 mm and 30 mm, and the outer cylinder is rotated steadily at 200 r.p.m. For a certain liquid filled in the annular space to a depth 80 mm, the torque produced on the inner cylinder is 0.9 × 10^{-4} Nm. Calculate the viscosity of the liquid.*

Assume the velocity distribution to be linear.

Solution. Radius of the outer rotating cylinder, R_2 = 32 mm = 0.032 m

Radius of the inner stationary cylinder, R_1 = 30 mm = 0.03 m

Height of liquid, h = 80 mm = 0.08 m

Speed of the outer cylinder, N = 200 r.p.m.

Torque produced on the inner cylinder T = 0.9×10^{-4} Nm

Viscosity of the liquid, μ:

$$\text{The tangential velocity, } V = \frac{2\pi R_2 N}{60} = \frac{2\pi \times 0.032 \times 200}{60} = 0.67 \text{ m/s}$$

Since the velocity distribution is linear, therefore,

$$\frac{du}{dy} = \frac{V}{t} = \frac{0.67}{(R_2 - R_1)} = \frac{0.67}{(0.032 - 0.03)} = 335 \text{ s}^{-1}$$

$$\text{Viscous shear stress, } \tau = \mu \frac{V}{t} = 335\ \mu$$

$$\text{Viscous force/drag} = 335\ \mu \times 2\pi R_1 h$$

$$= 335\ \mu \times 2\pi \times 0.03 \times 0.08 = 5.05\ \mu$$

$$\text{Viscous torque} = 5.05\ \mu \times R_1$$

$$= 5.05\ \mu \times 0.03 = 0.1515\ \mu$$

But, Viscous torque = Torque (T) measured by the torquemeter

∴ $0.1515\ \mu = 0.9 \times 10^{-4}$

or, $$\mu = \frac{0.9 \times 10^{-4}}{0.1515} = \mathbf{5.94 \times 10^{-4}\ Ns/m^2}$$ **(Ans.)**

Example 10.39. *In a torsion viscometer, the outer cylinder of 150.5 mm diameter is rotated by turning the shaft at a constant speed of 100 r.p.m. Owing to its viscosity, the liquid under test transmits a torque of 540 Nm to the inner cylinder of 150 mm diameter, which is suspended by torsion wire fixed at its upper end. If the liquid is 130 mm deep, find its viscosity.*

(MGU, Kerala)

Solution. Refer to Fig. 10.31.

Given : $R_2 = \frac{150.5}{2} = 75.25$ mm = 0.07525 m; $R_1 = \frac{150}{2} = 75$ mm = 0.075 m; N = 100 r.p.m; T = 540 Nm; $h + t$ = 130 mm = 0.13 m

Viscosity of the liquid, μ:

Let us assume that the clearance at the bottom of the two cylinder is 0.25 mm, *i.e.* the difference between radii of two cylinders, then,

$$t = 0.25 \text{ mm} = 0.00025 \text{ m}$$

∴ $$h = 0.13 - 0.00025 = 0.12975 \text{ m}$$

We know that, $$\mu = \frac{15Tt}{\pi^2 R_1^2 R_2 h N}$$ ...[Eqn. (10.39)]

Substituting the values, we get:

$$\mu = \frac{15 \times 540 \times 0.00025}{\pi^2 \times 0.075^2 \times 0.07525 \times 0.12975 \times 100} = \mathbf{37.36\ Ns/m^2}$$ **(Ans.)**

10.12.2. Falling Sphere Method

Falling sphere method of measuring viscosity of a liquid is based on '*Stokes*' *law*.

Fig. 10.32 shows a falling sphere viscometer. A small spherical ball is released into the liquid to be tested and it accelerates under the gravitational force until it reaches a maximum/terminal velocity V when the *buoyant and viscous drag forces balance the gravity force.*

Let,
d = Diameter of the spherical ball,
l = Distance travelled by the sphere in viscous liquid,
t = Time taken by the sphere to cover distance l,
ρ_s = Density of sphere,
ρ_f = Density of fluid/liquid,
W = Weight of sphere,
F_B = Buoyant force, acting on the sphere
F_D = Drag force, and
μ = Dynamic viscosity of the liquid under test.

The forces acting on the sphere are:

1. Weight, W...... acting vertically *downwards*
2. Buoyant force, F_B...... acting vertically *upwards*
3. Drag force, F_D...... acting vertically *upwards*

$$W = \text{Volume} \times \text{density of sphere} \times g$$

$$= \frac{\pi}{6} d^3 \times \rho_s \times g \qquad \left(\because \text{Volume of sphere} = \frac{\pi}{6} d^3\right)$$

$$F_B = \text{Weight of liquid displaced}$$

$$= \text{Volume of liquid displaced} \times \text{density of liquid} \times g$$

$$= \frac{\pi}{6} d^3 \times \rho_f \times g$$

($\because$ Volume of liquid displaced = volume of sphere)

$$F_D = 3\pi \mu V D \qquad \text{... (Stokes law)}$$

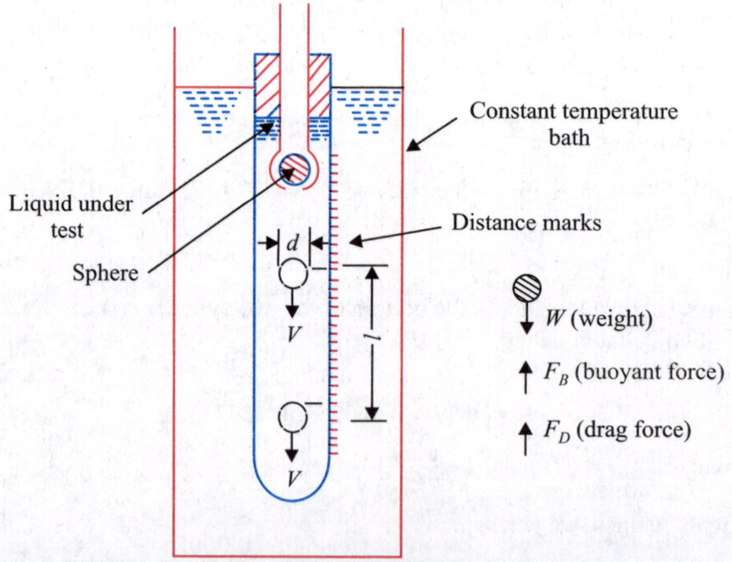

Fig. 10.32. Falling sphere viscometer.

For equilibrium,

$$F_D + F_B = W$$

or,
$$F_D = W - F_B$$

$$3\pi\mu VD = \frac{\pi}{6}d^3 \times \rho_s \times g - \frac{\pi}{6}d^3 \times \rho_f \times g \quad \text{(substituting the values)}$$

$$= \frac{\pi}{6}d^3 \times g\,(\rho_s - \rho_f)$$

or,μ
$$\mu = \frac{\pi}{6} \cdot \frac{d^3 \times g\,(\rho_s - \rho_f)}{3\pi Vd} = \frac{gd^2}{18V}(\rho_s - \rho_f) \quad \text{...(10.40)}$$

From the above equation the value of dynamic viscosity μ can be determined.

Note. Stokes' law is essentially valid for Reynolds number below 0.1 where the wall has no effect on the terminal fall velocity V.

Example 10.40. *In a falling sphere viscometer, a lubricating oil of density 900 kg/m³ was placed in a 80 mm inside diameter tube. A 10 mm diameter steel ball of density 8000 kg/m³ was found to travel a distance of 950 mm in 19 seconds. Determine the viscosity of the oil.*

Solution. Density of lubricating oil, $\rho_f = 900$ kg/m³

Diameter of the sphere, $d = 10$ mm $= 0.01$ m

Density of steel ball, $\rho_s = 8000$ kg/m³

Distance travelled in 19 seconds $= 950$ mm $= 0.95$ m

Viscosity of the oil, μ:

$$\text{Weight of the ball, } W = \frac{\pi}{6}d^3 \times \rho_s \times g = \frac{\pi}{6} \times 0.01^3 \times 8000 \times 9.81 = 0.0411 \text{ N}$$

$$\text{Buoyant force, } F_B = \frac{\pi}{6}d^3 \times \rho_f \times g = \frac{\pi}{6} \times 0.01^3 \times 900 \times 9.81 = 0.00462 \text{ N}$$

$$\text{Drag force, } F_D = 3\pi\mu Vd = 3\pi \times \mu \times \left(\frac{0.95}{19}\right) \times 0.01 = 0.00471\,\mu \text{ N}$$

For equilibrium:

$$F_D + F_B = W$$

or,
$$F_D = W - F_B$$

or,
$$0.00471\,\mu = 0.0411 - 0.00462 = 0.0365$$

or,
$$\mu = \frac{0.0365}{0.00471} = \mathbf{7.75 \text{ Ns/m}^2} \textbf{ (Ans.)}$$

Let us check the Reynolds number, Re.

$$Re = \frac{\rho Vd}{\mu} = \frac{900 \times (0.95/19) \times 0.01}{7.75} = 0.058 < 0.1$$

10.12.3. Capillary Tube Method

This method makes use of Hagen-Poiseuille equation for laminar flow through circular tubes. Fig. 10.33 shows a capillary tube viscometer. It consists of a tank in which the liquid whose viscosity is to be determined is filled. A capillary tube of diameter D and length L is attached horizontally very close to the bottom of tank. The tube is allowed to discharge freely into the atmosphere. The liquid is collected in a measuring tank for a given time. Then the rate of liquid collected in the tank per second is determined. The pressure head is measured at a point far away from the tank.

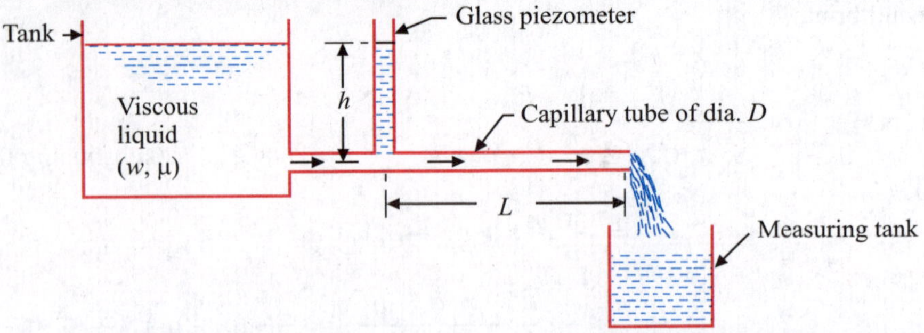

Fig. 10.33. Capillary tube viscometer.

Let, h = Difference of pressure head for length L,

μ = Co-efficient of viscosity, and

w = Weight density of the liquid.

According to Hagen-Poiseuilli's equation, we have:

$$h = \frac{32\mu \bar{u} L}{wD^2}$$

But,

$$\bar{u} = \frac{Q}{\frac{\pi}{4} D^2}$$

(where, Q = discharge of liquid through the tube)

$$\therefore \quad h = \frac{32\,\mu \times \dfrac{Q}{(\pi/4) \times D^2} \times L}{wD^2} = \frac{128\,\mu\, QL}{\pi w D^4}$$

or,

$$\mu = \frac{\pi w h\, D^4}{128\, QL} \quad ...(10.41)$$

Example 10.41. *The viscosity of an oil of specific gravity 0.8 is measured by a capillary tube of diameter 40 mm. The difference of pressure head between two points 1.2 m apart is 0.3 m of water. The weight of oil collected in a measuring tank is 400 N in 100 seconds. Find the viscosity of oil.*

Solution. Sp. gr. of oil = 0.8

∴ Weight density of oil = $0.8 \times 9810 = 7848$ N/m^3

Dia. of the capillary tube, D = 40 mm = 0.04 m

Length of the tube, L = 1.2 m

Difference of pressure head, h = 0.3 m of water

Weight of oil collected, W = 400 N

Time, t = 100 s.

Viscosity of the oil, μ :

$$\text{Discharge, } Q = \frac{\text{Weight of oil collected/sec}}{\text{Weight density}} = \frac{(400/100)}{7848} = 0.000509 \text{ m}^3/\text{s}$$

We know,

$$\mu = \frac{\pi w h D^4}{128\, QL}$$

$$= \frac{\pi \times 7848 \times 0.3 \times (0.04)^4}{128 \times 0.000509 \times 1.2} = \mathbf{0.242\ Ns/m^2}\ \textbf{(Ans.)}$$

10.12.4. Efflux Viscometers

In Efflux viscometers the *viscosity is determined by noting the time of efflux, under specific conditions, for a fixed volume of fluid through a specific capillary or aperture* (standardized nozzle or orifice). The operation of *Saybolt, Redwood* and *Engler* is based on this principle.

Fig. 10.34 shows a **Saybolt viscometer.** It consists of a tank in the bottom of which is a short capillary tube. The tank is filled with the liquid whose viscosity is to be determined; a constant temperature both surrounds this tank to ensure that the liquid remains at uniform constant temperature during the test run. The viscosity is determined by measuring the time required for 60 cm^3 of liquid at a known temperature to flow out of the reservoir through the tube. The initial level of the liquid in the reservoir is previously adjusted to a standard height. From the time measurement, the kinematic viscosity of the liquid can be determined by the use of empirical formula or the calibration chart.

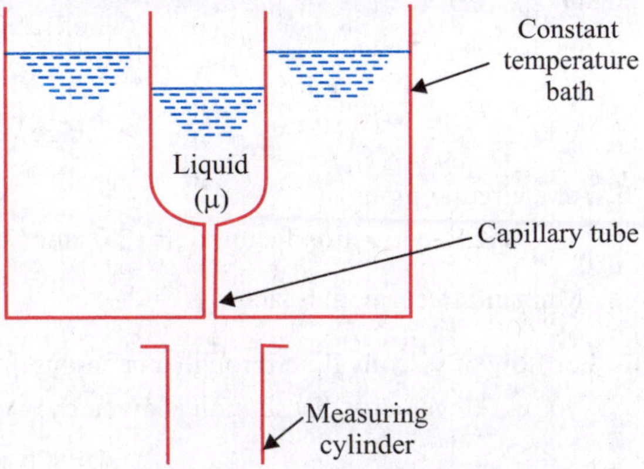

Fig. 10.34. Saybolt viscometer.

These viscometers (laboratory instruments) are widely employed in *petroleum and allied industries*.

HIGHLIGHTS

1. Reynolds number, $Re < 2000$ ...Laminar flow

   Reynolds number, $Re > 4000$ ...Turbulent flow

2. In case of laminar flow : The loss of head $\propto V$, where V is the velocity of flow.

   In case of turbulent flow : The loss of head $\propto V^2$ (approx).

   $\propto V^n$ (more exactly), where n varies from 1.75 to 2.0.

3. Relationship between shear stress and pressure gradient:

$$\frac{\partial \tau}{\partial y} = \frac{\partial p}{\partial x}$$

   This equation indicates that the pressure gradient in the direction of flow is equal to the shear gradient in the direction normal to the direction of flow.

4. In case of viscous flow through circular pipes, we have:

   (*i*) Shear stress, $\tau = -\frac{\partial p}{\partial x} \cdot \frac{r}{2}$

   (*ii*) Velocity, $u = -\frac{1}{4\mu} \cdot \frac{\partial p}{\partial x} (R^2 - r^2)$

   Max. velocity, $u_{max} = -\frac{1}{4\mu} \cdot \frac{\partial p}{\partial x} R^2$

   Average velocity, $\bar{u} = \frac{u_{max}}{2}$

   Again, $u = u_{max}\left[1 - \left(\frac{r}{R}\right)^2\right]$

(*iii*) Loss of pressure head, $h_f = \frac{32\,\mu\bar{u}L}{w \cdot D^2}$

where, r = Radius at any point,

R = Radius of the pipe,

D = Diameter of the pipe,

μ = Co-efficient of viscosity,

w = Weight density ($\rho.g$), and

$\bar{u}$ = Average velocity $= \frac{Q}{\pi R^2}$.

5. For a circular pipe:

K.E. correction factor, $\alpha = 2.0$, and

Momentum correction factor, $\beta = \frac{4}{3}$.

6. For flow of viscous fluid through an annulus:

(*i*) The velocity distribution is given by:

$$u = -\frac{1}{4\mu}\left(\frac{\partial p}{\partial x}\right)\left[R_1^2 - r^2 - \frac{R_1^2 - R_2^2}{\ln\left(\frac{R_1}{R_2}\right)} \cdot \ln\left(\frac{R_1}{r}\right)\right]$$

Velocity will be maximum, when

$$r = \left[\frac{R_1^2 - R_2^2}{2\ln\left(\frac{R_1}{R_2}\right)}\right]^{1/2}$$

The discharge through annulus,

$$Q = -\frac{\pi}{8\mu}\left(\frac{\partial p}{\partial x}\right)\left[R_1^4 - R_2^4 - \frac{(R_1^2 - R_2^2)^2}{\ln\left(\frac{R_1}{R_2}\right)}\right]$$

The average velocity of flow through the annulus is given by,

$$\bar{u} = -\frac{1}{8\mu}\left(\frac{\partial p}{\partial x}\right)\left[R_1^2 + R_2^2 - \frac{(R_1^2 - R_2^2)}{\ln\left(\frac{R_1}{R_2}\right)}\right]$$

(*iii*) The shear stress distribution is given by:

$$\tau = \frac{1}{4}\left(-\frac{\partial p}{\partial x}\right)\left[2r - \frac{1}{r} \cdot \frac{R_1^2 - R_2^2}{\ln\left(\frac{R_1}{R_2}\right)}\right]$$

(where, R_1 and R_2 are the outer and inner radii of the annulus respectively)

7. For the viscous flow between *two parallel plates*:

Case I. *One plate moving and the other at rest - Couette flow:*

Velocity distribution: $u = \frac{U}{b}y - \frac{1}{2\mu} \cdot \frac{\partial p}{\partial x}(by - y^2)$

The Discharge per unit width, $q = \frac{U \cdot b}{2} - \frac{b^3}{12\mu} \cdot \frac{\partial p}{\partial x}$

Shear stress distribution: $\tau = \mu \cdot \dfrac{U}{b} - \dfrac{1}{2} \cdot \dfrac{\partial p}{\partial x}(b - 2y)$

Case II. *Both plates at rest:*

$$u = -\frac{1}{2\mu} \cdot \frac{\partial p}{\partial x}(by - y^2)$$

$$q = -\frac{b^3}{12\mu} \cdot \frac{\partial p}{\partial x}, \text{ and}$$

$$t = -\frac{1}{2} \cdot \frac{\partial p}{\partial x}(b - 2y)$$

Case III. *Both plates moving in opposite directions:*

$$u = (U + V)\frac{y}{b} - \frac{1}{2\mu} \cdot \frac{\partial p}{\partial x}(by - y^2) - V$$

$$q = (U - V)\frac{b}{2} - \frac{1}{12\mu} \cdot \frac{\partial p}{\partial x} \cdot b^3$$

$$\tau = (U + V)\frac{\mu}{b} - \frac{\partial p}{\partial x}\left(\frac{b}{2} - y\right)$$

The shear stress (τ) will be zero at,

$$y = \frac{b}{2} - \frac{\mu}{b}\left[\frac{U + V}{(\partial p / \partial x)}\right]$$

where, U and V = The velocities (in opposite directions) of the upper and lower plates respectively.

b = Distance between the parallel plates, and

μ = Co-efficient of viscosity of the fluid.

8. Laminar flow through *porous media*:

$$\text{Loss of head, } h_f = \frac{K\mu\bar{u}L}{wn^2 d_s^2}$$

where, k = A constant, the value of which depends on the shape of the passage,

μ = Co-efficient of viscosity,

$\bar{u}$ = Average velocity,

L = Length,

w = Weight density of the fluid,

n = Porosity, and

d_s = Grain diameter-porosity material.

(nd_s = diameter of the passage through the particles)

From the above eqn. we have, $\bar{u} = ki$ ... known as Darcy's equation.

where, k = a constant, called the co-efficient of permeability, and

i = the hydraulic gradient $\left(\dfrac{h_f}{L}\right)$

9. *Power absorbed in bearings* (P) is given by:

$$P = T \cdot \omega = \frac{2\pi NT}{60} \text{ watts, where } T \text{ is in Nm.}$$

where, T = Torque required to overcome the viscous resistance of the whole of bearing,

ω = Angular speed of the shaft $\left(=\frac{2\pi N}{60}\right)$, and

N = Speed of the shaft in r.p.m.

For various bearings, the values of T are given by:

$$T = \frac{\mu\pi^2 D^3 NL}{120t} \quad \text{...Journal bearing}$$

$$T = \frac{\mu}{60t}\pi^2 NR^4 \quad \text{...Foot-step bearing}$$

$$T = \frac{\mu}{60}\pi^2 N\,(R_2^4 - R_1^4) \quad \text{...Collar bearing}$$

where, t = thickness of oil film.

10. For the viscous flow the co-efficient of friction is given by:

$$f = \frac{16}{Re}$$

where, Re = Reynolds number = $\frac{\rho VD}{\mu} = \frac{VD}{\nu}$

11. In a dashpot arragngement, the co-efficient of viscosity is given by:

$$\mu = \frac{4Wt^3}{3\pi LD^3 V}$$

where, W = Weight of piston/force on piston,
t = Clearance between dashpot and piston,
L = Length of the piston,
D = Diameter of the piston, and
V = Velocity of the piston.

12. The co-efficient of viscosity may be determined by the following methods:

***(i)* Rotating cylinder method:** $\mu = \frac{15Tt}{\pi^2 R_1^2 R_2 hN}$

where, T = Torque,
t = Annular space,
R_1 = Radius of inner stationary cylinder,
R_2 = Radius of the outer rotating cylinder,
h = Height of liquid, and
N = Speed of the rotating cylinder in r.p.m.

***(ii)* Falling sphere method:** $\mu = \frac{gd^2}{18V}(\rho_s - \rho_f)$

where, d = Diameter of the sphere,
V = Velocity of sphere,
ρ_s = Density of sphere, and
ρ_f = Density of fluid/liquid.

***(iii)* Capillary tube method:** $\mu = \frac{\pi whD^4}{128\,QL}$

where, w = Weight density of the liquid,
h = Difference of pressure head for length L,
D = Diameter of the capillary tube, and
Q = Discharge of liquid through the capillary tube.

OBJECTIVE TYPE QUESTIONS

Choose the Correct Answer:

1. The laminar/viscous flow is characterised by Reynolds number which is
(*a*) less than the critical value
(*b*) equal to critical value
(*c*) more than critical value
(*d*) none of the above.

2. The laminar flow is characterised by
(*a*) existence of eddies
(*b*) irregular motion of fluid particles
(*c*) fluid particles moving in layers parallel to the boundary surface
(*d*) none of the above.

3. Which of the following is an example of laminar flow?
(*a*) Underground flow
(*a*) Flow past tiny bodies
(*c*) Flow of oil in measureing instruments
(*a*) All of the above
(*e*) None of the above.

4. In case of laminar flow, the loss of pressure head is proportional to
(*a*) velocity, (*b*) velocity^2
(*c*) velocity^3 (*d*) none of the above.

5. The pressure gradient in the direction of flow is equal to the shear gradient in the direction
(*a*) parallel to the direction of flow
(*a*) normal to the direction of flow
(*a*) either of the above
(*a*) none of the above.

6. ... studied the laminar flow through a circular tube experimentally
(*a*) Prandtl
(*b*) Pascal
(*c*) Hagen and Poiseuille
(*d*) None of the above.

7. ... is the most commonly used equation for the velocity distribution for laminar flow through pipes.
(*a*) $u = u_{max}\left[1 - \frac{r}{R}\right]$
(*b*) $u = u_{max}\left[1 - \left(\frac{r}{R}\right)^2\right]$
(*c*) $u = u_{max}\left[1 - \left(\frac{r}{R}\right)^3\right]$
(*d*) $u = u_{max}^2\left[1 - \left(\frac{r}{R}\right)^2\right]$.

8. In laminar flow the pressure drop per unit length of pipe ($\Delta p/L$) is given as
(*a*) $\frac{32\mu\bar{u}}{D^2}$ (*b*) $\frac{2\mu\bar{u}}{D^2}$
(*c*) $\frac{32\mu\bar{u}}{D^3}$ (*d*) none of above.

9. The K.E. correction factor a for a circular pipe is equal to
(*a*) 2 (*b*) 3
(*c*) 4 (*d*) 6.

10. The momentum correction factor b for a circular pipe is to equal to
(*a*) $\frac{1}{3}$ (*b*) $\frac{2}{3}$
(*c*) $\frac{4}{3}$ (*d*) $\frac{5}{3}$.

11. The flow through a porous media is governed by well known Darcy's law which relates the velocity with the head loss and is usually expressed as
(*a*) $u = \frac{kh_f}{L}$ (*b*) $u = \frac{kL}{h_f}$
(*c*) $u = k \cdot \left(\frac{h_f}{L}\right)^2$ (*d*) $u = k\left(\frac{L}{h_f}\right)^3$.

12. The shear stress distribution in pipe flow is given as
(*a*) $\tau = -\left(\frac{\partial p}{\partial x}\right)\frac{r}{2}$ (*b*) $\tau = r \cdot \left(\frac{\partial p}{\partial x}\right)$
(*c*) $\tau = -2r\left(\frac{\partial p}{\partial x}\right)$ (d) none of the above.

13. For viscous flow the co-efficient of friction is given by

(*a*) $f = \frac{8}{Re}$ (*b*) $f = \frac{16}{Re}$

(*c*) $f = \frac{32}{Re}$ (*d*) $f = \frac{60}{Re}$.

14. In case of viscous flow through circular pipes

(*a*) $\bar{u} = 2\,u_{max}$ (*b*) $\bar{u} = \frac{3}{2} u_{max}$

(*c*) $\bar{u} = \frac{u_{max}}{2}$ (*d*) none of the above.

15. The maximum velocity in a circular pipe when flow is laminar occurs at

(*a*) the top of the pipe

(*b*) the bottom of the pipe

(*c*) the centre of the pipe

(*d*) not necessarily at the centre.

ANSWERS

1. (*a*)	**2.** (*c*)	**3.** (*d*)	**4.** (*a*)	**5.** (*b*)	**6.** (*c*)
7. (*b*)	**8.** (*a*)	**9.** (*a*)	**10.** (*c*)	**11.** (*a*)	**12.** (*a*)
13. (*b*)	**14.** (*b*)	**15.** (*c*)			

THEORETICAL QUESTIONS

1. What is the difference between a laminar flow and a turbulent flow?

2. What are the characteristics of a laminar flow?

3. Enumerate examples of laminar flow.

4. Draw a neat sketch of the Reynolds apparatus, and explain how the laminar flow can be demonstrated with the help of the apparatus.

5. Derive a relationship between shear stress and pressure gradient.

6. Derive an expression for the velocity distribution for viscous flow through a circular pipe. Also sketch the distribution of velocity and shear stress across a section of the pipe.

7. For a steady laminar flow through a circular pipe prove that the velocity distribution across the section is parabolic and the average velocity is half of the maximum local velocity.

8. What factors account for the loss of energy in laminar flow? How does the energy loss vary with velocity of flow?

9. Derive Hagen-Poiseuille equation and state the assumptions made.

10. For flow of viscous fluid through an annulus derive expressions for the following:

(*i*) Discharge through the annulus,

(*ii*) Average velocity of flow, and

(*iii*) Shear stress distribution.

11. What is a Couette flow?

12. For a viscous flow through a circular pipe prove that the kinetic energy correction factor is equal to 2.

13. Find an expression for the power absorbed in overcoming viscous resistance in case of a collar bearing.

14. Show that the value of co-efficient of friction for viscous flow through a circular pipe is given by,

$f = \frac{16}{Re}$, where Re = Reynolds number.

15. Derive an expression for the co-efficient of viscosity in case of a dashpot arrangement.

16. Describe briefly any two methods of determining the co-efficient of viscosity of a liquid.

UNSOLVED EXAMPLES

1. An oil of 8 poise and specific gravity 0.9 is flowing through a horizontal pipe of 50 mm diameter. If the pressure drop in 100 m length of the pipe is 2000 kN/m^2, determine: (*i*) Rate of flow of oil (*ii*) Centre-line velocity; (*iii*) Total frictional drag over 100 m length of pipe; (*iv*) Power required to maintain the flow; (*v*) Velocity gradient at the pipe wall; (*vi*) Velocity and shear stress at 10 mm from the wall.

[Ans. (*a*) 3.83 lit./s; (*ii*) 3.9 m/s; (*iii*) 3.93 kN; (*iv*) 7.65 kW (*v*) 312 s^{-1}; (*vi*) 2.5 m/s; 150 N/m^2**]**

2. An oil of viscosity 1 poise and relative density 0.9 is flowing through a circular pipe of diameter 50 mm and of length 300 m. The rate of flow of liquid is 0.0035 m^3/s. Find the pressure drop in a length of 300 m and shear stress at the wall.

[Ans. 684.3 kN/m^2, 28·5 N/m^2]

3. In a circular pipe of diameter 100 mm a fluid of viscosity 7 poise and sp. gr. 1.3 is flowing. If the maximum shear stress at the wall of the pipe is 196.2 N/m^2, find:
   (*i*) The pressure gradient,
   (*ii*) The average velocity, and
   (*iii*) Reynolds number of flow.
   [Ans. (*i*) 7848 N/m^2 per m; (*ii*) 3.5 m/s; (*iii*) 650]

4. An oil of viscosity 0.02 poise and sp. gr. 0.8 is flowing through 50 mm diameter pipe of length 500 m at the rate of 0.19 lit./sec. Determine:
   (*i*) Reynolds number of flow,
   (*ii*) Centre-line velocity,
   (*iii*) Pressure gradient,
   (*iv*) Wall shear stress, and
   (*v*) Power required to maintain the flow.
   [Ans. (*i*) 1936.3; (*ii*) 0.1936 m/s; (*iii*) 2.478 N/m^2; (*iv*) 0.031 N/m^2; (*v*) 0.2354 W]

5. What power is required per km of a line to overcome the viscous resistance to the flow of glycerine through a horizontal pipe of diameter 100 mm at the rate of 10 lit./s? Take $\mu = 8$ poise and kinematic visosity (ν) = 6.0 stokes.
   [Delhi University]
   [Ans. 32.5 kW]

6. In a pipe of 200 mm diameter the maximum velocity of flow is found to be 1.5 m/s. If flow in the pipe is laminar, find:
   (*i*) The average velocity and the radius at which it occurs, and
   (*ii*) The velocity at 40 mm from the wall of the pipe.
   [Ans. (*i*) 0.75 m/s; 70.7 mm; (*ii*) 0.96 m/s]

7. An oil of viscosity 0.143 Ns/m2 and specific gravity 0.9 is flowing through a circular pipe of diameter 25 mm and of length 3 m at $\frac{1}{10}$ th of critical velocity for which Reynolds number is 2500. Find:
   (*i*) The velocity of flow through the pipe,
   (*ii*) The head in metres of oil across the pipe length required to maintain the flow, and
   (*iii*) The power required to overcome viscous resistance to flow of oil.
   [Ans. (*i*) 1.589 m/s, (*ii*) 3.593 m, (*iii*) 24.73 W]

8. In a laboratory a horizontal pipe of 500 mm diameter was used to measure the viscosity of a crude oil having specific weight of 9 kN/m^3. During the test a pressure difference of 18 kN/m^2 was recorded from two pressure gauges located 6 m apart on the pipe. The oil was allowed to discharge into a weighing tank and 5 kN of oil was collected in 3 minutes. Find the dynamic viscosity of the oil. **[Ans.** 1.49 poise]

9. The fixed parallel plates kept at 80 mm apart have laminar flow of oil between them with a maximum velocity 1.5 m/s. Taking dynamic viscosity of oil to be m = 19.62 poise, calculate;
   (*i*) The discharge per metre width,
   (*ii*) The shear stress at the plates,
   (*iii*) The pressure difference between two points 25 m apart,
   (*iv*) The velocity at 20 mm from the plate, and
   (*v*) The velocity gradient at the plates end.
   [Ans. (*i*) 0.08 m^3/s; (*ii*) 147 N/m^2; (*iii*) 91.97 kN/m^2; (*iv*) 1.125 m/s; (*v*) 75s– 1]

10. A liquid of viscosity 0.1 Ns/m^2 and sp. gr. 0.9 is filled between two horizontal plates 10 mm apart. If the upper plate is moving at 2 m/s and the pressure difference between two sections 10 m apart is 9.81 kN/m^2, determine the shear stress on the plate. **[Ans.15 N/m^2]**

11. Water at a rate of 0.0008 litre/sec. is flowing through a sandy specimen of 10 cm height and 50 cm^2 cross-sectional area under constant head of 8 cm. Calculate the co-efficient of permeability.
    [Ans. 0.02 cm/s]

12. Find the torque and power absorbed to rotate a shaft of diameter 50 mm, at 1200 r.p.m. concentrically within a sleeve 50.17 mm in diameter and 90 mm long, flooded with oil for which m = 0.8 poise. **[Ans.1.045 Nm, 0.1313 kW]**

    $$\left(\textbf{Hint.}\text{ Thickness of oil film, } t = \frac{50{\cdot}17 - 50}{2} = 0{\cdot}085\text{ mm}\right)$$

13. Find the power required to rotate a circular disc of diameter 200 mm at 100 r.p.m. The circular disc has a clearance of 0.4 mm from the bottom flat plate and clearance contain oil of viscosity 0.11 Ns/m^2 **[Ans. 473.48 W]**

14. A collar bearing having external and internal diameters 150 mm and 100 mm respectively is used to take the thrust of a shaft. An oil film of thickness 0.25 mm and of viscosity 0.8 poise is maintained between the collar surface and the bearing. Find the power lost in overcoming the viscous resistance of oil when the shaft is running at 300 r.p.m. **[Ans. 12.54 W]**

15. Water is flowing through a 240 mm diameter pipe with co-efficient of friction $f = 0.042$. The shear stress at a point 48 mm from the pipe axis is 0.1 kN/m^2. Calculate the shear stress at the pipe wall. **[Ans. 0.25 kN/m^2]**

16. A pipe 200 mm in diameter and 10000 m long is laid at a slope of 1 in 200. An oil of specific gravity 0.9 and viscosity 0.15 Ns/m^2 is pumped up at the rate of 0.02 m^2/s. Find:

(*i*) Head lost due to friction, and

(*ii*) Power required to pump the oil.

[**Ans.** (*i*) 86.5 m; (*ii*) 24.09 kW]

17. In a rotating cylinder viscometer, the radii of the cylinders are 32 mm and 30 mm, and the outer cylinder is rotated steadily at 180 r.p.m. For a certain liquid filled in the annular space to a depth 75 mm, the torque produced on the inner cylinder is 1.2×10^{-4} Nm. Calculate the viscosity of the liquid.[**Ans.** 9.39×10^{-4} Ns/m^2]

18. In order to determine the viscosity of a lubricating oil by falling-sphere method, a steel spherical ball of specific gravity 7.7 and diameter 2 mm is allowed to fall freely under gravity through a distance of 140 mm in 215 seconds. The sp. gr. of the oil is 0.8. Determine the viscosity of the oil. [**Ans.** 2.31 Ns/m^2]

19. A fluid of sp.gr. 1.02 was made to pass through an accurate tube, length 35 cm and bore 0.1 cm under a head of 18 cm. A discharge equilvalent to 40 cm^3 was collected in a period of 400 seconds. Find the dynamic viscosity of the fluid.

[**Ans.** 1.266×10^{-3} Ns/m^2]

Chapter

11

TURBULENT FLOW IN PIPES

11.1. INTRODUCTION

In a pipe, a laminar flow occurs when Reynolds number (*Re*) is less than 2000 and a turbulent flow occurs when $Re > 4000$. In a turbulent flow, the fluid motion is irregular and chaotic and there is complete mixing of fluid due to collision of fluid masses with one another. The fluid masses are interchanged between adjacent layers. As the fluid masses in adjacent layers have different velocities, interchange of fluid masses between the adjacent layers is accompanied by a transfer of momentum which causes additional shear stresses of high magnitude between adjacent layers. *The shear in turbulent flow is mainly due to momentum transfer.* The contribution of fluid viscosity to total shear is small and is usually neglected. In case of laminar flow, because of definite functional relationship 'between shear stress due to viscosity and velocity' it has been possible to derive a mathematical relationship for evaluation of energy dissipation or frictional head but such a simple relationship does not exist for turbulent flow. However to solve some of the practical problems, efforts have been made to evolve semi-empirical theories of turbulence.

Following points are worth noting about turbulent flow:

(*i*) The velocity distribution in turbulent flow is more uniform than in laminar flow.

(*ii*) In turbulent flow the velocity gradients near the boundary shall be quite large resulting in more shear.

(*iii*) In turbulent flow the flatness of velocity distribution curve in the core region away from the wall is because of the *mixing of fluid layers and exchange of momentum between them*.

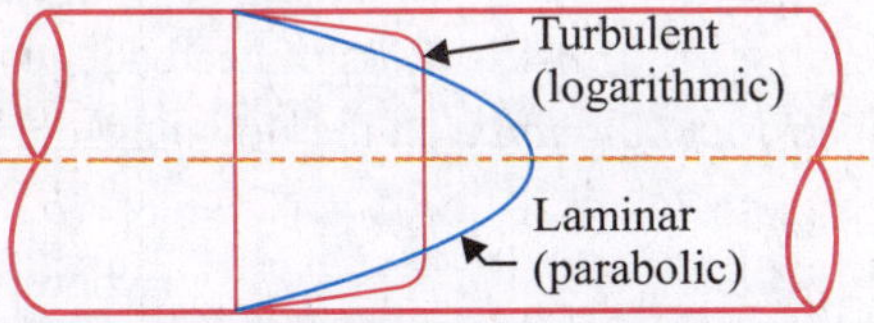

Fig. 11.1. Shows the velocity distribution curves for laminar and turbulent flows in a pipe.

(*iv*) The velocity distribution which is paraboloid in laminar flow, tends to follow power law and logarithmic law in turbulent flow.

(*v*) Random orientation of fluid particles in a turbulent flow gives rise to additional stresses, called the ***Reynolds stresses.***

(*vi*) Formation of eddies, mixing and curving of path lines in a turbulent flow results in much greater frictional losses for the same rate of discharge, viscosity and pipe size.

The turbulent motion can be *classified* as follows:

1. ***Wall turbulence.*** It occurs in immediate vicinity of solid surfaces and in the boundary layer flows where the fluid has a negligible mean acceleration.
2. ***Free turbulence.*** It occurs in jets, wakes, mixing layers etc.
3. ***Convective turbulence.*** It takes place where there is conversion of P.E into K.E. by the process of mixing (*e.g.* the turbulent flow in the annular space between the concentric rotating cylinder, conventional flow between parallel horizontal plates etc.).

11.2. LOSS OF HEAD DUE TO FRICTION IN PIPE FLOW–DARCY EQUATION

In case of turbulent flow through pipes it has been observed through experiments that the viscous friction effects associated with fluid are proportional to:

(*i*) The length of the pipe, L,

(*ii*) The wetted perimeter, P, and

(*iii*) V^n, where V is the average velocity of flow and n is an index varying from 1·5 to 2 (depending on the material and nature of the pipe surface); for commercial pipes $\simeq 2$ (with turbulent flow).

Fig. 11·2. shows a horizontal pipe having steady flow. Consider control volume enclosed between sections 1 and 2 of the pipe.

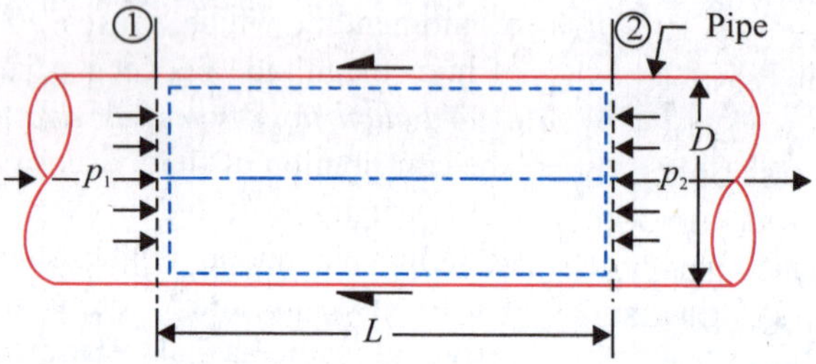

Fig. 11.2. Forces on a control volume in a pipe flow.

Let, p_1 = Intensity of pressure at section 1,

p_2 = Intensity of pressure at section 2,

L = Length of the pipe, between sections 1 and 2,

D = Diameter of the pipe,

f' = Non-dimensional factor (whose value depends upon the material and nature of the pipe surface), and

h_f = Loss of head due to friction.

Propelling force on the flowing fluid between the two sections is

$$= (p_1 - p_2)\, A$$

(where, A = area of cross-section of the pipe)

Frictional resistance force $= f'\, PLV^2$

where, P = Wetted perimeter, and

V = Average flow velocity.

Under equilibrium conditions:

$$\text{Propelling force} = \text{Frictional resistance force}$$

i.e. $$(p_1 - p_2) A = f' PLV^2$$

Dividing both sides by weight density w, we have:

$$\left(\frac{p_1 - p_2}{w}\right) A = \frac{f'}{w} PLV^2$$

or, $$h_f = \frac{f'}{w}\left(\frac{P}{A}\right) LV^2$$

or, $$h_f = \frac{2gf'}{w}\left(\frac{P}{A}\right)\frac{LV^2}{2g} = \frac{2gf'}{w} \times \frac{L}{m} \times \frac{V^2}{2g} \quad ...(11\cdot1)$$

The ratio $\frac{A}{P}$ *is called the* **hydraulic mean depth or hydraulic radius**, denoted by m (or R).

The term $\left(\frac{L}{m} \times \frac{V^2}{2g}\right)$ has dimensions of h_f and thus the term $\frac{2gf'}{w}$ is a non-dimensional quantity and let us replace it by another constant f.

$$\therefore \quad h_f = f \times \frac{L}{m} \times \frac{V^2}{2g} \quad ...[11.1(a)]$$

In case of a circular pipe,

$$\text{Hydraulic mean depth, } m = \frac{A}{P} = \frac{\frac{\pi}{4} \times D^2}{\pi D} = \frac{D}{4}$$

Substituting this value in eqn. (11·1 (*a*)), we get:

$$h_f = f \times \frac{L}{D/4} \times \frac{V^2}{2g} = \frac{4fLV^2}{D \times 2g} \quad ...(11\cdot2)$$

(The factor f is known as *Darcy coefficient of friction.*)

Eqn. (11·2) is known as **Darcy-Weisbach equation** and it *holds good for all types of flows provided a proper value of f is chosen.*

Sometimes eqn. (11·2) is written as:

$$h_f = \frac{f_1 LV^2}{D \times 2g}$$

where, f_1 is *known as* **friction factor** ($f_1 = 4f$)

Expression for co-efficient of friction in terms of shear stress:

Refer to Fig. 11.2,

$$(p_1 - p_2) A = \text{Force due to shear stress, } \tau_0$$

$$(\text{where, } \tau_0 = \text{shear stress at the pipe wall})$$

$$= \text{Shear stress } (\tau_0) \times \text{surface area}$$

$$= \tau_0 \times \pi DL$$

or, $$(p_1 - p_2)\frac{\pi}{4} D^2 = \tau_0 \times \pi DL$$

or, $$(p_1 - p_2)\frac{D}{4} = \tau_0 L$$

or, $$(p_1 - p_2) = \frac{4\tau_0 \times L}{D} \quad ...(11\cdot3)$$

Eqn. (11·2) can be written as:

$$h_f = \frac{p_1 - p_2}{w} = \frac{4fLV^2}{D \times 2g}$$

or, $$(p_1 - p_2) = \frac{4fLV^2}{D \times 2g} \times w \qquad ...(11·4)$$

Equating eqns. (11·3) and (11·4), we get:

$$\frac{4\tau_0 L}{D} = \frac{4fLV^2}{D \times 2g} \times w$$

or, $$\tau_0 = \frac{fV^2 \times w}{2g} = \frac{fV^2 \times \rho g}{2g} = \frac{f\rho V^2}{2} \qquad ...[11·5\,(a)]$$

or, $$f = \frac{2\tau_0}{\rho V^2} \qquad ...[11·5\,(b)]$$

11.3. CHARACTERISTICS OF TURBULENT FLOW

The turbulent flow is characterised by *random, irregular and haphazard movement of fluid particles*. It has been observed during experimentation that at any fixed point in turbulent field, the velocity and consequently the pressure fluctuates with time about a mean value.

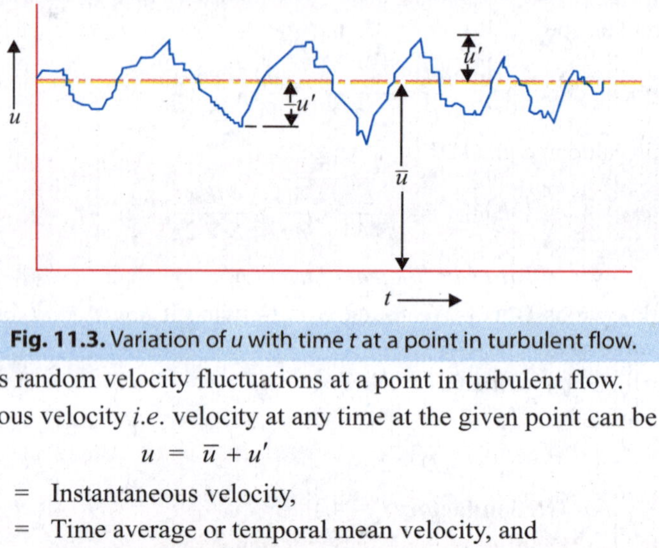

Fig. 11.3. Variation of *u* with time *t* at a point in turbulent flow.

Fig. 11·3 shows random velocity fluctuations at a point in turbulent flow.

The instantaneous velocity *i.e.* velocity at any time at the given point can be expressed as:

$$u = \bar{u} + u' \qquad ...(11·6)$$

where, u = Instantaneous velocity,

$\bar{u}$ = Time average or temporal mean velocity, and

u' = Velocity fluctuation (fluctuating component).

Similarly, $v = \bar{v} + v'$,

$w = \bar{w} + w'$,

and, $p = \bar{p} + p'$ ...(11·7)

From the definition of average-velocities, we have:

$$\left.\begin{aligned} \frac{1}{T}\int_0^T u\,dt = \bar{u}; \quad \frac{1}{T}\int_0^T v\,dt = \bar{v}; \\ \frac{1}{T}\int_0^T w\,dt = \bar{w}; \quad \frac{1}{T}\int_0^T p\,dt = \bar{p} \end{aligned}\right\} \qquad ...(11·8)$$

and,
$$\left.\begin{aligned} \frac{1}{T}\int_0^T u'dt = \overline{u}' = 0; \quad \frac{1}{T}\int_0^T v'dt = \overline{v}' = 0; \\ \frac{1}{T}\int_0^T w'dt = \overline{w}' = 0; \quad \frac{1}{T}\int_0^T p'dt = \overline{p}' = 0 \end{aligned}\right\} \quad ...(11\cdot9)$$

where, T = Large interval of time.

Magnitude of turbulence = Arithmetic mean of root-mean square value of turbulent fluctuations in the three directions

$$= \sqrt{\left(\frac{\overline{u'^2} + \overline{v'^2} + \overline{w'^2}}{3}\right)} \quad ...(11\cdot10)$$

Intensity of turbulence

$$= \frac{\sqrt{\dfrac{\overline{u'^2} + \overline{v'^2} + \overline{w'^2}}{3}}}{\overline{V}} \quad ...(11\cdot11)$$

where, $\overline{V}$ = Line average resultant velocity at the point.

For describing the turbulence fully, besides the intensity of turbulence, the average size of the eddy is also necessary which can be obtained from the curve of velocity variation with time (as shown in Fig. 11·3) by multiplying the average time interval at which the curve crosses the mean value, with the average velocity of flow.

11.4. SHEAR STRESSES IN TURBULENT FLOW

In turbulent flow, as stated earlier, velocity fluctuations cause momentum transport which results in developing additional shear stresses of high magnitude between adjacent layers of the fluid. In order to determine the magnitude of the turbulent shear stress a number of semi-empirical theories have been developed some of which are discussed below.

11·4·1 Boussinesq's Theory

According to this theory (1877), the expression for the shear stress, τ_t for the turbulent flow can be written as :

$$\tau_t = \eta \cdot \frac{d\overline{u}}{dy} \quad ...(11\cdot12)$$

where η (eta) is called "*eddy*" *viscosity*, and $\overline{u}$ is the temporal mean velocity in the direction of flow at a point at distance y from the solid boundary.

Similar to kinematic viscosity $\nu = \frac{\mu}{\rho}$, the "*eddy*" *kinematic viscosity* $\in$ (Greek 'epsilon') is also obtained by dividing eddy viscosity η, by the mass density of the fluid ρ, thus,

$$\in = \frac{\eta}{\rho}$$

When viscous action is also included, the total shear stress may be expressed as :

$$\tau = \tau_\upsilon + \tau_t$$

(where τ_υ = shear stress due to viscosity)

or,
$$\tau = \mu \frac{du}{dy} + \eta \frac{d\overline{u}}{dy} \quad ...(11\cdot13)$$

The magnitude of η may vary from zero (if the flow is laminar) to several thousand times that of μ. As the values of η and $\in$ cannot be predicted, the Boussinesq's equation has a *limited use*.

11·4·2 Reynolds Theory

According to this theory (1886), the turbulent shear stress between two layers of a fluid at a small distance apart is given as:

$$\tau = \rho u' \upsilon' \qquad ...(11·14)$$

where u' and υ' are the fluctuating components of velocity in the directions of x and y due to turbulence.

Since both u' and υ' vary and subsequently τ also varies, therefore, to find the shear stress, the time average is taken and eqn. (11·14) becomes:

$$\bar{\tau} = \overline{\rho u' \upsilon'} \qquad ...(11·15)$$

11·4·3 Prandtl's Mixing Length Theory

According to Prandtl (1925), the **mixing length** (l) is *defined as* the *average lateral distance through which a small mass of fluid particles would move from one layer to the other adjacent layers before acquiring the velocity of the new layer*. He assumed that components u' and υ' are of the same order and the velocity fluctuation in X-direction is related to the mixing length as:

$$u' = l\frac{du}{dy}$$

$$\therefore \qquad \overline{u' \times \upsilon'} = \overline{u' \upsilon'} = \left(l\frac{du}{dy}\right) \times \left(l\frac{du}{dy}\right) = l^2\left(\frac{du}{dy}\right)^2 \qquad \left(\because \upsilon' = l\frac{du}{dy}\right)$$

Substituting the value of $\overline{u' \upsilon'}$ in eqn. (11·15), we get:

$$\bar{\tau} = \rho l^2\left(\frac{du}{dy}\right)^2 \qquad ...(11·16)$$

When the viscous action is also included the total shear stress may be expressed as :

$$\bar{\tau} = \mu\frac{du}{dy} + \rho l^2\left(\frac{du}{dy}\right)^2 \qquad ...(11·17)$$

Eqn. (11·17) is used for most of the turbulent flow problems for determining the shear stress (viscous shear stress is negligible except near the boundary).

11.5. UNIVERSAL VELOCITY DISTRIBUTION EQUATION

Assuming the viscous shear stress to be negligible near the boundary the shear stress in turbulent flow is given by the eqn. (11·16).

i.e. $$\bar{\tau} = \rho l^2\left(\frac{du}{dy}\right)^2$$

From this equation, we can obtain velocity distribution if the relation between l, the mixing length, and y is known.

Also $l \propto y$ (from the pipe wall) ...*Prandtl's hypothesis*

or, $$l = \lambda y$$

where, λ = a constant of proportionality, known as '***Karman universal constant***' (= 0·4).

Substituting the values of l in eqn. (11·16), we get:

$$\bar{\tau} \text{ or } \tau = \rho \times (\lambda y)^2 \times \left(\frac{du}{dy}\right)^2 = \rho\lambda^2 y^2\left(\frac{du}{dy}\right)^2 \qquad ...(i)$$

Assuming that the turbulent shear stress remains constant in the vicinity of wall, we have

$$\tau = \tau_0 \quad (\tau_0 = \text{the boundary shear stress})$$

The eqn. (*i*) becomes:

$$\tau_0 = \rho\,\lambda^2 y^2 \left(\frac{du}{dy}\right)^2$$

or, $$\frac{du}{dy} = \frac{1}{\lambda y}\sqrt{\frac{\tau_0}{\rho}} = u_f\left(\frac{1}{\lambda y}\right) \quad ...(ii)$$

$$\left[\text{where, } u_f = \textit{shear friction velocity} \text{ or } \textbf{shear velocity} = \sqrt{\frac{\tau_0}{\rho}}\right]$$

or, $$du = u_f\left(\frac{1}{\lambda y}\right) dy \quad ...(iii)$$

(u_f is *constant* for a given case of turbulent flow)

Integrating the other equation, we get:

$$u = \frac{u_f}{\lambda}\ln(y) + C \quad ...(11\cdot18)$$

(where, C = constant of integration)

Eqn. (11·18) shows that velocity distribution in turbulent flow is *logarithmic* in nature.

The constant of integration C is determined by the boundary condition.

At $y = R$ (radius of the pipe), $u = u_{max}$

By substituting the above values in eqn. (11·18), we have:

$$u_{max} = \frac{u_f}{\lambda}\ln(R) + C$$

or $$C = u_{max} - \frac{u_f}{\lambda}\ln(R)$$

Substituting this value of C in eqn. (11·18), we get:

$$u = \frac{u_f}{\lambda}\ln(y) + u_{max} - \frac{u_f}{\lambda}\ln(R)$$

$$= u_{max} + \frac{u_f}{\lambda}[\ln(y) - \ln(R)]$$

or, $$u = u_{max} + \frac{u_f}{\lambda}\ln\left(\frac{y}{R}\right)$$

Taking $\lambda = 0\cdot4$, we get:

$$\boldsymbol{u = u_{max} + 2\cdot5\, u_f \ln\left(\frac{y}{R}\right)} \quad ...(11\cdot19)$$

Eqn. (11·19) is called **Prandtl's universal distribution equation.** This equation is applicable to *smooth as well as rough boundaries*.

This equation (11·19) may be written in *non-dimensional form*:

$$\frac{u_{max} - u}{u_f} = 2\cdot5\ln\left(\frac{R}{y}\right)$$

$$= 5\cdot75\log_{10}\left(\frac{R}{y}\right)$$

i.e.
$$\frac{u_{max} - u}{u_f} = 5 \cdot 75 \log_{10}\left(\frac{R}{y}\right) \quad ...(11 \cdot 20)$$

The difference ($u_{max} - u$) is known as the **velocity defect.**

Example 11·1. *In a pipe of 360 mm diameter having turbulent flow, the centre-line velocity is 7 m/s and that at 60 mm from the pipe wall is 6 m/s. Calculate the shear friction velocity.*

Solution. Radius of the pipe $= \frac{360}{2} = 180 \text{ mm} = 0 \cdot 18 \text{ m}$

Centre-line velocity, $u_{max} = 7$ m/s

Velocity at 60 mm (*i.e.* distance y), $u = 6$ m/s

Shear velocity, u_f:

We know,
$$\frac{u_{max} - u}{u_f} = 5 \cdot 75 \log_{10}\left(\frac{R}{y}\right) \quad ...[\text{Eqn. } (11 \cdot 20)]$$

$$\therefore \quad \frac{7-6}{u_f} = 5 \cdot 75 \log_{10}\left(\frac{0 \cdot 18}{0 \cdot 06}\right) = 2 \cdot 743$$

$$\therefore \quad u_f = \mathbf{0 \cdot 36 \text{ m/s (Ans.)}}$$

Example 11·2. *A pipe of 100 mm diameter is carrying water. If the velocities at the pipe centre and 30 mm from the pipe centre are 2.0 m/s and 1.5 m/s respectively and flow in the pipe is turbulent, calculate the wall shearing stress.* **(Anna University)**

Solution. *Given :* $R = \frac{100}{2} = 50 \text{ mm} = 0.05 \text{ m}$; $u_{max} = 2.0$ m/s;

Velocity at $r = 30$ mm or $y = R - r = 50 - 30 = 20$ mm, $u = 1.5$ m/s.

Wall shearing stress, τ_0:

$$\frac{u_{max} - u}{u_f} = 5.75 \log_{10}\left(\frac{R}{y}\right) \quad ...[\text{Eqn. } (11 \cdot 20)]$$

(where, u_f = shear velocity)

Substituting the values, we get:
$$\frac{2.0 - 1.5}{u_f} = 5.75 \log_{10}\left(\frac{0.05}{0.02}\right) = 2.288$$

$$u_f = \frac{(2.0 - 1.5)}{2.288} = 0.218 \text{ m/s}$$

Using the relation:
$$u_f = \sqrt{\frac{\tau_0}{\rho}}$$

or,
$$0.218 = \sqrt{\frac{\tau_0}{1000}} \quad (\because \rho \text{ for water} = 1000 \text{ kg/m}^3)$$

or,
$$\tau_0 = \mathbf{47.524 \text{ N/m}^2 \text{ (Ans.)}}$$

11.6. HYDRODYNAMICALLY SMOOTH AND ROUGH BOUNDARIES

Refer to Fig. 11·4. If k is the average height of the irregularities of the surface of a boundary, then in general, the boundary is said to be **rough** if value of k is *high* and **smooth** if k is *low*. However, for proper classification of smooth and rough boundaries, besides the boundary characteristics, the flow and fluid characteristics need to be considered.

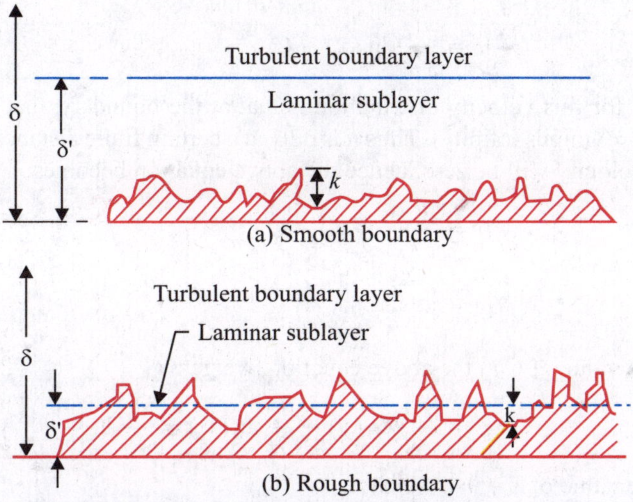

Fig. 11.4. Smooth and rough boundaries

As shown in Fig. 11·4 when the average height k of the irregularities (projecting from its surface) is *much less than* the thickness of the laminars sublayer δ' the flow outside the laminar sublayer is turbulent; the eddies of various sizes present, try to penetrate the laminar sublayer. *These eddies cannot reach the surface irregularities/projections due to greater thickness of the laminar sublayer and so the boundary acts as a* **smooth boundary.** As the Reynolds number (*Re*) *increases the thickness of the sublayer decreases (can even become much less than k), the irregularities will then project through the laminar sublayer and eventually the laminar sublayer is destroyed completely.* Subsequently, the eddies will come in contact with the surface irregularities and there will be a *large amount of energy loss. This type of boundary is known as hydrodynamically* **rough boundary.**

Through experiments Nikuradse found that the boundary behaves as:

(*i*)Hydrodynamically smooth boundary ...when $\left(\frac{k}{\delta'}\right) < 0\cdot25$,

(*ii*) Hydrodynamically rough boundary ...when $\left(\frac{k}{\delta'}\right) > 6\cdot0$, and

(*iii*) Boundary in transition ...when $0\cdot25 < \left(\frac{k}{\delta'}\right) < 6\cdot0$.

In terms of roughness Reynolds number $\frac{u_f k}{\nu}$:

(*i*) For smooth boundary ... $\frac{u_f k}{\nu} < 4$,

(*ii*) For rough boundary ... $\frac{u_f k}{\nu} > 100$, and

(*iii*) For boundary in transition stage ... $\frac{u_f k}{\nu}$ lies between 4 and 100.

Note : It may be noted that the thickness of laminar sublayer δ' is *not* a fixed quantity. It *depends upon the Reynolds number*; it is just possible that a pipe may behave as smooth at low Reynolds number and rough at high Reynolds number. *The height of roughness projection, however, remains constant.*

11·6·1. Velocity Distribution for Turbulent Flow in Smooth Pipes

The velocity distribution for turbulent flow in pipes in given by Eqn. 11·18 as :

$$u = \frac{u_f}{\lambda} \ln(y) + C$$

The peculiarity for this velocity distribution is that at the boundary, that is for $y = 0$, it gives velocity u equal to $-\infty$ (minus infinity). Thus it is only at a certain finite distance above the boundary say $y = y'$, that the velocity will be zero, hence the above equation becomes:

$$0 = \frac{u_f}{\lambda} \ln(y') + C$$

or, $$C = -\frac{u_f}{\lambda} \ln(y')$$

Substituting the value of C in the above equation, we get:

$$u = \frac{u_f}{\lambda} \ln(y) - \frac{u_f}{\lambda} \ln(y') = \frac{u_f}{\lambda} \ln\left(\frac{y}{y'}\right)$$

Substituting the value of $\lambda = 0{\cdot}4$, we have:

$$u = \frac{u_f}{0{\cdot}4} \ln\left(\frac{y}{y'}\right) = 2{\cdot}5\, u_f \ln\left(\frac{y}{y'}\right)$$

or, $$\frac{u}{u_f} = 2{\cdot}5 \times 2{\cdot}3 \log_{10}\left(\frac{y}{y'}\right)$$

or, $$\frac{u}{u_f} = 5{\cdot}75 \log_{10}\left(\frac{y}{y'}\right) \qquad \text{...(11·21)}$$

It has been observed from Nikuradse's experimental studies of turbulent flow in smooth pipes that for turbulent flow in smooth pipes of any size the value of the parameter $\left(\frac{u_f y}{\nu}\right)$ for $y = \delta'$ is approximately 11·6 and for $y = y'$ it is approximately 0·108.

i.e. $$\frac{u_f \delta'}{\nu} = 11{\cdot}6 \quad \text{or} \quad \delta' = \frac{11{\cdot}6\nu}{u_f} \qquad \text{...(11·22)}$$

and, $$\frac{u_f y'}{\nu} = 0.108$$

or, $$y' = \frac{0{\cdot}108\nu}{u_f}\left(= \frac{\delta'}{107}\right) \qquad \text{...(11·23)}$$

Substituting the value of $y'\left(= \frac{0{\cdot}108\,\nu}{u_f}\right)$ in eqn. 11·21, we get:

$$\frac{u}{u_f} = 5{\cdot}75 \log_{10}\left(\frac{y}{\frac{0.108\nu}{u_f}}\right)$$

$$= 5{\cdot}75 \log_{10}\left(\frac{u_f \cdot y}{0{\cdot}108\nu}\right) = 5{\cdot}75 \log_{10}\left(\frac{u_f \cdot y}{\nu}\right) = 5.75 \log_{10}(0.108)$$

or, $$\boldsymbol{\frac{u}{u_f} = 5{\cdot}75 \log_{10}\left(\frac{u_f \cdot y}{\nu}\right) + 5{\cdot}5} \qquad \text{...(11·24)}$$

The eqn. (11·24) is known as **Karman-Prandtl equation** *for the velocity distribution near hydrodynamically* ***smooth boundaries.***

11·6·2 Velocity Distribution for Turbulent Flow in Rough Pipes

As shown in Fig. 11·4 (*b*), the thickness of laminar sublayer is very small, the surface irregularities are above the laminar sublayer and hence the laminar sublayer is completely destroyed. From the experiments conducted by Nikuradse and others, using pipes artificially roughened by cemented coatings of sand grains (irregularities/projections) of diameter k, it has been found that y' is directly found proportional to k and $y' = \frac{k}{30}$.

Substituting this value of y' in eqn. (11·24), we get:

$$\frac{u}{u_f} = 5\cdot75 \log_{10}\left(\frac{y}{k/30}\right) = 5\cdot75\,[\log_{10}(y/k) \times 30]$$

$$= 5\cdot75 \log_{10}(y/k) + 5\cdot75 \log_{10} 30$$

or,
$$\mathbf{\frac{u}{u_f} = 5\cdot75 \log_{10}(y/k) + 8\cdot5} \qquad ...(11\cdot25)$$

The eqn. (11·25) is known as **Karman-Prandtl equation** *for the velocity distribution near hydrodynamically* ***rough boundaries.***

Example 11·3. *The velocity of flow in a badly corroded 7·5 cm pipe is found to increase 20 percent as a pitot tube is moved from a point 1 cm from the wall to a point 2 cm from the wall. Estimate the height of roughness elements.* **[Roorkee University]**

Solution. The velocity distribution near the rough boundaries is given by:

$$\frac{u}{u_f} = 5.75 \log_{10}\left(\frac{y}{k}\right) + 8.5 \qquad ...[\text{Eqn. } (11\cdot25)]$$

where, k = Average height of roughness elements, and

u_f = Shear friction velocity.

Let, u = The velocity at a distance (y) of 1 cm from the pipe wall, and $1\cdot2u$ = the velocity at a distance of 2 cm from the pipe wall (given),

then,
$$\frac{u}{u_f} = 5.75 \log_{10}\left(\frac{1}{k}\right) + 8.5 \qquad ...(i)$$

and,
$$\frac{1.2u}{u_f} = 5.75 \log_{10}\left(\frac{2}{k}\right) + 8.5 \qquad ...(ii)$$

Dividing (*i*) by (*ii*), we get:

$$\frac{1}{1.2} = \frac{5.75 \log_{10}\left(\frac{1}{k}\right) + 8.5}{5.75 \log_{10}\left(\frac{2}{k}\right) + 8.5}$$

or,
$$5.75 \log_{10}\left(\frac{2}{k}\right) + 8.5 = 1.2\left[5.75 \log_{10}\left(\frac{1}{k}\right) + 8.5\right]$$

$$5.75 \log_{10}\left(\frac{2}{k}\right) + 8.5 = 6.9 \log_{10}\left(\frac{1}{k}\right) + 10.2$$

$$5\cdot75 \log_{10}(2) - 5\cdot75 \log_{10} k + 8\cdot5 = 6\cdot9 \log_{10} 1 - 6\cdot9 \log_{10} k + 10\cdot2$$

$$1\cdot73 - 5\cdot75 \log_{10} k + 8\cdot5 = 0 - 6\cdot9 \log_{10} k + 10\cdot2$$

$$1\cdot15 \log_{10} k = -0\cdot03$$

or,
$$\log_{10} k = -\frac{0.03}{1.15} = -0.0261$$

$\therefore$
$$k = \mathbf{0\cdot942\ cm} \text{ (Ans.)}$$

Example 11.4. *A pipeline carrying water has surface protrusions of average height of 0·10 mm. If the shear stress developed is 8·2 N/m² determine whether the pipe surface acts as smooth, rough or in transition. For water take ρ = 1000 kg/m³ and kinematic viscosity ν = 0·0093 stokes.* **[Bangalore University]**

Solution. Average height of surface protrusions,

$$k = 0{\cdot}10 \text{ mm} = 0{\cdot}1 \times 10^{-3} \text{ m}$$

Shear stress developed, $\tau_0 = 8{\cdot}2 \text{ N/m}^2$

Density of water, $\rho = 1000 \text{ kg/m}^3$

Kinematic viscosity, $\nu = 0{\cdot}0093 \text{ stokes} = 0{\cdot}0093 \times 10^{-4} \text{ m}^2\text{/s}$

Shear velocity is given by,

$$u_f = \sqrt{\frac{\tau_0}{\rho}}$$

$$\therefore \quad u_f = \sqrt{\frac{8{\cdot}2}{1000}} = 0{\cdot}0906 \text{ m/s}$$

Roughness Reynolds number is

$$= \frac{u_f k}{\nu} = \frac{0.0906 \times (0.1 \times 10^{-3})}{0.0093 \times 10^{-4}} = 9.74$$

Since $\dfrac{u_f k}{\nu}$ lies between 4 and 100 the pipe surface behaves as in **transition. (Ans.)**

Example 11.5. *In a pipe of diameter 100 mm, carrying water, the velocities at the pipe centre and 30 mm from the pipe centre are found to be 2·5 m/s and 2.2 m/s respectively. Find the wall shearing stress.*

Solution. Radius of the pipe, $R = \frac{100}{2} = 50 \text{ mm} = 0.05 \text{ m}$

Velocity at the centre, $u_{max} = 2{\cdot}5$ m/s

Velocity at 30 mm from the centre = 2.2 m/s.

Wall shearing stress, τ_0:

Using the equation:

$$\frac{u_{max} - u}{u_f} = 5.75 \log_{10}\left(\frac{R}{y}\right)$$

(where, u_f = shear friction velocity)

where, $u = 2.2$ m/s at $y = (R - 30)$ mm = (50 – 30) mm = 0·02 m

$$\therefore \quad \frac{2.5 - 2.2}{u_f} = 5.75 \log_{10}\left(\frac{0.05}{0.02}\right) = 2.288$$

or, $$\frac{0.3}{u_f} = 2.88 \quad \text{or} \quad u_f = 0{\cdot}1311$$

Now using the relation:

$$u_f = \sqrt{\frac{\tau_0}{\rho}}, \text{ we have:}$$

$$0.1311 = \sqrt{\frac{\tau_0}{1000}} \quad \text{or} \quad \frac{\tau_0}{1000} = (0.1311)^2 = 0.01719$$

$$\therefore \quad \tau_0 = \mathbf{17{\cdot}19 \text{ N/m}^2} \textbf{ (Ans.)}$$

Example 11.6. *A smooth pipe of 80 mm diameter and 1000 m long is carrying water at the rate of 8 litres/sec. If the kinematic viscosity of water is 0·015 stokes and the value of co-efficient of friction 'f' is given by the relation* $f = \dfrac{0\cdot 0791}{(Re)^{1/4}}$*, where Re is Reynolds number, calculate:*

(i) *Loss of head,*

(ii) *Wall shearing stress,*

(iii) *Centre-line velocity,*

(iv) *Velocity and shear stress at 20 mm from the pipe wall, and*

(v) *Thickness of laminar sublayer.*

Solution. Diameter of the pipe, $D = 80 \text{ mm} = 0.08 \text{ m}$

Length of the pipe, $L = 1000 \text{ m}$

Discharge, $Q = 8 \text{ litres/sec.} = 0.008 \text{ m}^3/\text{s}$

Kinematic viscosity of water, $\nu = 0\cdot 015 \text{ stokes}$

$$= 0.015 \times 10^{-4} \text{ m}^2/\text{s}$$

$$\text{Mean velocity, } V = \frac{Q}{A} = \frac{0.008}{\frac{\pi}{4} \times (0.08)^2} = 1.59 \text{ m/s}$$

$$\therefore \quad \text{Reynolds number, } Re = \frac{VD}{\nu} = \frac{1.59 \times 0.08}{0.015 \times 10^{-4}} = 84800$$

$$\text{Co-efficient of friction, } f = \frac{0.0791}{(Re)^{1/4}} = \frac{0.0791}{(84800)^{1/4}} = 0.004635$$

(i) Loss of head, h_f:

$$h_f = \frac{4fLV^2}{D \times 2g} = \frac{4 \times 0.004635 \times 1000 \times 1.59^2}{0.08 \times 2 \times 9.81} = \mathbf{29.98 \text{ m}} \textbf{ (Ans.)}$$

(ii) Wall shearing stress, τ_0:

$$\tau_0 = \frac{fV^2\rho}{2} \qquad \text{[Eqn. 11·5 } (a)\text{]}$$

$$= \frac{0.004635 \times 1.59^2 \times 1000}{2} = \mathbf{5.86 \text{ N/m}^2} \textbf{ (Ans.)}$$

(iii) Centre-line velocity, u_{max}:

$$\frac{u}{u_f} = 5.75 \log_{10}\left(\frac{u_f y}{\nu}\right) + 5.5 \qquad \text{...}(i) \text{ [Eqn. (11·24)]}$$

where, u_f = shear friction velocity

$$= \sqrt{\frac{\tau_0}{\rho}} = \sqrt{\frac{5\cdot 86}{1000}} = 0\cdot 0765 \text{ m/s}$$

The velocity will be maximum where $y = \dfrac{D}{2} = \dfrac{0.08}{2} = 0.04$ m

Hence, at $y = 0\cdot 04$ m $u = u_{max}$; substituting these values in (*i*), we get:

$$\frac{u_{max}}{0.0765} = 5.75 \log_{10}\left(\frac{0.0765 \times 0.04}{0.015 \times 10^{-4}}\right) + 5.5 = 24.53$$

$$\therefore \quad u_{max} = 0.0765 \times 24.53 = \mathbf{1.876 \text{ m/s}} \textbf{ (Ans.)}$$

(*iv*) **Velocity and shear stress at 20 mm from the pipe wall:**

The shear stress (τ) at any point is given by:

$$\tau = -\frac{\partial p}{\partial x} \times \frac{r}{2} \quad ...(ii)$$

where, r = distance from the centre of the pipe.

∴ Shear stress at pipe wall (where $r = R$),

$$\tau_0 = -\frac{\partial p}{\partial x} \times \frac{R}{2} \quad ...(iii)$$

Dividing (*ii*) by (*iii*), we get:

$$\frac{\tau}{\tau_0} = \frac{r}{R}$$

∴ Shear stress, $\tau = \tau_0 \times \frac{r}{R}$

where, $r = 40 - 20 = 20 \text{ mm} = 0.02 \text{ m}$

∴ $\tau = 5.86 \times \frac{0.02}{0.04} = \mathbf{2.93\ N/m^2}$ **(Ans.)**

Again, $\frac{u}{u_f} = 5.75 \log_{10}\left(\frac{u_f \cdot y}{\nu}\right) + 5.5$

where, $u_f = 0.0765$ m/s and $y = 0.2$ m from the pipe wall

∴ $\frac{u}{0.0765} = 5.75 \log_{10}\left(\frac{0.0765 \times 0.02}{0.015 \times 10^{-4}}\right) + 5.5 = 22.80$

or $\mathbf{u = 1.744\ m/s}$ **(Ans.)**

(*v*) **Thickness of laminar sublayer, δ′ :**

Thickness of laminar sublayer is given by,

$$\delta' = \frac{11.6\, \nu}{u_f} \quad \text{[Eqn. (11·22)]}$$

$$= \frac{11.6 \times 0.015 \times 10^{-4}}{0.765} \times 10^3 \text{ mm} = \mathbf{0.227\ mm} \ \textbf{(Ans.)}$$

11.7. COMMON EQUATION FOR VELOCITY DISTRIBUTION FOR BOTH SMOOTH AND ROUGH PIPES

Refer Fig. 11·5. Consider an elementary circular ring of radius r and thickness dr as shown in Fig. 11·5. The distance of the ring from the pipe wall,

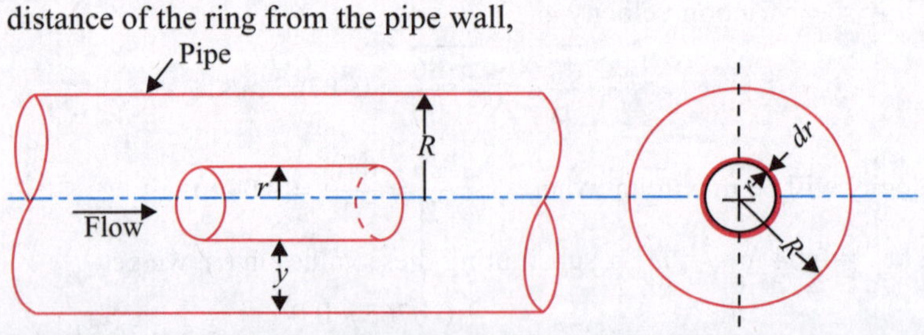

Fig. 11.5. Average velocity for turbulent flow.

$$y = R - r$$

(where, R = radius of the pipe).

The discharge through the ring is given by:

$$dQ = \text{Area of the ring} \times \text{velocity} = 2\pi r \cdot dr \times u$$

$$\therefore \quad \text{Total discharge, } Q = \int dQ = \int_0^R u \times 2\pi r \cdot dr$$

(i) For smooth pipes:

In the case of smooth pipes the velocity distribution is given by [Eqn. (11·24)] as:

$$\frac{u}{u_f} = 5.75 \log_{10}\left(\frac{u_f \cdot y}{\nu}\right) + 5.5$$

$$M = \left[5.75 \log_{10} \frac{u_f (R-r)}{\nu} + 5.5\right] \times u_f$$

Substituting the value of u in eqn. (11·26), we get:

$$Q = \int_0^R \left[5.75 \log_{10} \frac{u_f (R-r)}{\nu} + 5.5\right] u_f \times 2\pi r \,.\, dr$$

$$\therefore \quad \text{Average velocity, } \bar{U} = \frac{Q}{A} = \frac{Q}{\pi R^2}$$

$$\bar{U} = \frac{1}{\pi R^2} \int_0^R \left[5.75 \log_{10} \frac{u_f (R-r)}{\nu} + 5.5\right] u_f \times 2\pi r \,.\, dr$$

After integration and simplification, we have:

$$\frac{\bar{U}}{u_f} = 5.75 \log_{10} \frac{u_f R}{\nu} + 1.75 \quad \text{...(11·27)}$$

(ii) For rough pipes:

In case of rough pipes, the velocity at any point in the turbulent flow is given by eqn. (11·25) as:

$$\frac{u}{u_f} = 5.75 \log_{10} (y/k) + 8.5 = 5.75 \log_{10}\left(\frac{R-r}{k}\right) + 8.5 \quad (\because y = R - r)$$

or,

$$u = u_f \left[5.75 \log_{10}\left(\frac{R-r}{k}\right) + 8.5\right]$$

Substituting the value of u in eqn. (11·26), we get:

$$Q = \int_0^R u_f \left[5.75 \log_{10}\left(\frac{R-r}{k}\right) + 8.\right] 2\pi r \cdot dr$$

$$\therefore \quad \text{Average velocity, } \bar{U} = \frac{Q}{\pi R^2} = \frac{1}{\pi R^2} \int_0^R u_f \left[5.75 \log_{10}\left(\frac{R-r}{k}\right) + 8.5\right] 2\pi r \cdot dr$$

After integration and simplication, we have:

$$\frac{\bar{U}}{u_f} = 575 \log_{10}\left(\frac{R}{k}\right) + 4.75 \quad \text{...(11.28)}$$

From eqns. (11·24) and (11·27) by subtraction, we have:

$$\frac{u}{u_f} - \frac{\bar{U}}{u_f} = \left[5.75 \log_{10}\left(\frac{u_f \cdot y}{\nu}\right) + 5.5\right] - \left[5.75 \log_{10} \frac{u_f R}{\nu} + 1.75\right]$$

$$\text{or,}\qquad \frac{u-\bar{U}}{u_f} = 3.75 - 5.75 \log_{10}\left(\frac{u_f R}{\nu} \times \frac{\nu}{u_f y}\right)$$

$$= 3{\cdot}75 - 5{\cdot}75 \log_{10}\left(\frac{R}{y}\right)$$

$$\text{or,}\qquad \frac{u-\bar{U}}{u_f} = 5.75 \log_{10}\left(\frac{y}{R}\right) + 3.75 \qquad \text{...}(i)$$

Similarly, from eqns. (11·25) and (11·28), we get:

$$\frac{u}{u_f} - \frac{\bar{U}}{u_f} = \left[5.75 \log_{10}\left(\frac{y}{k}\right) + 8.5\right] - \left[5.75 \log_{10}\left(\frac{R}{k}\right) + 4.75\right]$$

$$\frac{u-\bar{U}}{u_f} = 5.75 \log_{10}\left(\frac{y}{R}\right) + 3.75 \qquad \text{...}(ii)$$

As eqns. (*i*) and (*ii*) are identical, the ***velocity distribution in both types of pipes is the same.***

$$\therefore \qquad \frac{u-\bar{U}}{u_f} = 5.75 \log_{10}\left(\frac{y}{R}\right) + 3.75 \qquad \text{...(11·29)}$$

The common equation holds good for both types of pipes due to the reason that the *velocity distribution for the turbulent core is identical in both cases.*

Example 11.7. *Find the distance from the pipe wall at which the local velocity is equal to the average velocity for turbulent flow in pipes.*

Solution. Local velocity at a point = Average velocity ...(*Given*)

i.e. $u = \bar{U}$

Using the relation:

$$\frac{u-\bar{U}}{u_f} = 5.75 \log_{10}\left(\frac{y}{R}\right) + 3.75 \qquad \text{[Eqn. (11·29)]}$$

$$\text{or,}\qquad 5.75 \log_{10}\left(\frac{y}{R}\right) + 3.75 = 0 \qquad (\because\ u = \bar{U})$$

$$\text{or,}\qquad 5.75 \log_{10}\left(\frac{y}{R}\right) = -3.75$$

$$\text{or,}\qquad \log_{10}\left(\frac{y}{R}\right) = -\frac{3.75}{5.75} = -\,0.652$$

or, $\frac{y}{R} = 0.223$ or $y = 0{\cdot}223\,R$ **(Ans.)**

11.8. VELOCITY DISTRIBUTION FOR TURBULENT FLOW IN SMOOTH PIPES BY POWER LAW

The eqns. (11·20), (11·24) and (11·25) of velocity distribution for turbulent flow are inconvenient to use, being *logarithmic* in nature. Nikuradse, through experiments, established the following velocity distribution law (exponential form) for smooth pipes:

$$\frac{u}{u_{max}} = \left(\frac{y}{R}\right)^{\frac{1}{n}} \qquad \text{...(11·30)}$$

where, exponent $\frac{1}{n}$ depends on Reynolds number (*Re*) and it *decreases* with the *increasing Re*.

For:
$$Re = 400, \frac{1}{n} = \frac{1}{6}$$
$$Re = 1.1 \times 10^5, \frac{1}{n} = \frac{1}{7}$$
$$Re \geq 2 \times 10^6, \frac{1}{n} = \frac{1}{10}$$

Therefore, for $\frac{1}{n} = \frac{1}{7}$, the velocity distribution law becomes:

$$\frac{u}{u_{max}} = \left(\frac{y}{R}\right)^{1/7} \quad ...(11\cdot31)$$

Eqn. (11·31) is known as $\frac{1}{7}$ **th power law** *of velocity distribution for smooth pipes.*

11.9. RESISTANCE TO FLOW OF FLUID IN SMOOTH AND ROUGH PIPES

When a fluid flows through a pipe frictional resistance is offered to the motion of the fluid and the loss of head due to friction is expressed by Darcy-Weisbach equation, $h_f = \frac{4fLV^2}{D \times 2g}$. But the loss of head can be predicted correctly only if the friction co-efficient can be evaluated accurately. It can be shown by dimensional analysis that the friction co-efficient f depends upon the Reynolds number $\left(\frac{\rho VD}{\mu}\right)$ and the ratio k/D.

Thus,
$$f = \phi\left[\left(\frac{\rho VD}{\mu}\right), \frac{k}{D}\right] \quad ...(11\cdot32)$$

where, D = Diameter of the pipe,
ρ = Density of the fluid,
μ = Dynamic viscosity of the fluid, and
k = Average height of pipe wall roughness protrusions.

(The term $\frac{k}{D}$ is commonly known as *relative roughness*).

The eqn. (11·32) is a *general equation which is applicable to laminar as well as turbulent flows in pipes*.

(*a*) Variation of friction co-efficient '*f*' for "laminar flow":

As derived in previous chapter the co-efficient of friction '*f*' for laminar flow in pipes is given by:

$$f = \frac{16}{Re} \quad ...(11\cdot33)$$

The eqn. (11·33) shows that for laminar flow the friction coefficient f varies inversely with Re and it is independent of $\left(\frac{k}{D}\right)$ ratio.

(*b*) Variation of '*f*' for "turbulent flow":

For the fully developed turbulent flow the friction coefficient '*f*' is a function of Re or k/D ratio or both, depending on whether the boundary is hydrodynamically smooth or rough or it is in transition.

(*i*) Variation of friction co-efficient '*f*' "for smooth pipes":

The coefficient of friction '*f*' for turbulent flow in smooth pipes is a function of Reynolds number (Re) only, and is independent of relative roughness k/D. The value of '*f*' for smooth pipes for Re varying from 4000 to 1×10^5 is given by the following empirical relation (*developed by* ***Blasius***):

$$f = \frac{0.0791}{(Re)^{1/4}} \qquad ...(11\cdot34)$$

The value of 'f' for $Re > 10^5$ is obtained from eqn. (11·27),

$$\frac{\bar{U}}{u_f} = 5.75 \log_{10} \frac{u_f R}{\nu} + 1.75 \qquad ...(\text{Eqn. } 11\cdot27)$$

Also,
$$f = \frac{2\tau_0}{\rho V^2} \qquad ...[\text{Eqn. } 11\cdot5\ (b)]$$

(where, V = average velocity)

$$\therefore \quad f = \frac{2\tau_0}{\rho \bar{U}^2} = \frac{2}{\bar{U}^2} \times u_f^2 \qquad \left[\because \sqrt{\frac{\tau_0}{\rho}} = u_f\right]$$

or,
$$u_f^2 = \frac{f\bar{U}^2}{2}$$

or,
$$u_f = \bar{U}\sqrt{\frac{f}{2}}$$

Substituting the value of u_f in eqn. (11·27), we get:

$$\frac{\bar{U}}{\bar{U}\sqrt{\frac{f}{2}}} = 5.75 \log_{10}\left(\frac{\bar{U}}{\nu}\sqrt{\frac{f}{2}}\right) R + 1.75$$

or,
$$\frac{1}{\sqrt{f/2}} = 5.75 \log_{10}\left(\frac{\bar{U} R}{\nu}\sqrt{f/2}\right) + 1.75$$

Substituting $R = D/2$ and simplifying, we get:

$$\frac{1}{\sqrt{4f}} = 2.03 \log_{10}\left(\frac{\bar{U}D}{\nu}\sqrt{4f}\right) - 0.91$$

But,
$$\frac{\bar{U}D}{\nu} = Re$$

$$\frac{1}{\sqrt{4f}} = 2.03 \log_{10}(Re\sqrt{4f}) - 0.91 \qquad ...(11\cdot35)$$

Eqn. (11·35) is valid upto $Re = 4 \times 10^6$

Karman-Prandtl resistance equation *for turbulent flow in smooth pipes* is given by:

$$\frac{1}{\sqrt{4f}} = 2.0 \log_{10}(Re\sqrt{4f}) - 0.8 \qquad ...(11\cdot36)$$

From Nikuradse's experimental measurements eqn. (11·36) has been found to be valid from $Re = 5 \times 10^4$ to Re as high as 4×10^7. The eqn. (11·36) *can be solved by hit and trial method.* However the following empirical relationship given by Nikuradse for 'f' can be used directly:

$$f = 0.0008 + \frac{0.05525}{(Re)^{0.237}} \qquad ...(11\cdot37)$$

(*ii*) Variation of friction co-efficient '*f*' for "rough pipes":

For turbulent flow in rough pipes the friction co-efficient 'f' depends only on relative roughness (k/D) and is independent of Reynolds number (Re). An expression for 'f' is obtained as follows:

For turbulent flow in rough pipes the mean velocity $\bar{U}$ of flow has been expressed by the eqn. 11·28,

$$\frac{\bar{U}}{u_f} = 5.75 \log_{10}\left(\frac{R}{k}\right) + 4.75 \quad \text{...(Eqn. 11·28)}$$

But, $$u_f = \bar{U}\sqrt{\frac{f}{2}}$$

$$\therefore \quad \frac{\bar{U}}{\bar{U}\sqrt{f/2}} = 5.75 \log_{10}(R/k) + 4.75$$

On simplification, we get:

$$\frac{1}{\sqrt{4f}} = 2.03 \log_{10}(R/k) + 1.68 \quad \text{...(11·38)}$$

The experimental results obtained by Nikuradse follow closely the trend of the following equation, (instead of eqn. 11·38):

$$\frac{1}{\sqrt{4f}} = 2.0 \log_{10}(R/k) + 1.74 \quad \text{...(11·39)}$$

(*iii*) **Value of friction factor for "commercial pipes":**

Colebrook and White developed an empirical equation of the following form to predict the friction factor for commercial pipes,

$$\frac{1}{\sqrt{f_1}} - 2.0 \log_{10}\left(\frac{R}{k}\right) = 1.74 - 2.0 \log_{10}\left[1 + 18.7\,\frac{(R/k)}{Re\sqrt{f_1}}\right] \quad \text{...(11·40)}$$

where, f_1 (friction factor) = $4f$ (friction coefficient).

Example 11·8. *In a rough pipe of diameter 0·6 m and length 4500 m water is flowing at the rate of 0·6 m³/s. If the average height of roughness is 0·48 mm find the power required to maintain this flow.*

Solution. Diameter of the pipe, $D = 0·6$ m

$\therefore$ Radius, $R = \frac{0.6}{2} = 0.3$ m

Length of the pipe, $L = 4500$ m

Discharge, $Q = 0·6\ m^3/s$

Average height of roughness, $k = 0·48$ mm $= 0·48 \times 10^{-3}$ m

Power required to maintain the flow, P:

Power required, $P = wQh_f$ ...(*i*)

where, $$h_f = \frac{4fLV^2}{D \times 2g}$$

where, f = Co-efficient of friction,

V = Average velocity of flow, and

w = Weight density of water (= 9·81 kN/m³).

Let us first calculate the value of 'f'.

For a rough pipe, the value of 'f' is given by:

$$\frac{1}{\sqrt{4f}} = 2.0 \log_{10}\left(\frac{R}{k}\right) + 1.74 \quad \text{...[Eqn. (11·39)]}$$

$$= 2.0 \log_{10}\left(\frac{0.3}{0.48 \times 10^{-3}}\right) + 1.74 = 7.331$$

or, $\sqrt{4f} = \dfrac{1}{7.331} = 0.1364$

or, $f = 0{\cdot}00465$

Also, average velocity, $V = \dfrac{Q}{(\frac{\pi}{4} \times D^2)} = \dfrac{0.6}{\frac{\pi}{4} \times 0.6^2} = 2.122$ m/s

$\therefore$ Head lost in friction, $h_f = \dfrac{4fLV^2}{D \times 2g} = \dfrac{4 \times 0.00465 \times 4500 \times (2.122)^2}{0.6 \times 2 \times 9.81} = 32$ m

Substituting the values in eqn. (*i*), we get:

$P = 9{\cdot}81 \times 0{\cdot}6 \times 32 =$ **188·35 kW (Ans.)**

Example 11.9. *The friction for turbulent flow through rough pipes can be determined by Kaman-Prandtl equation*

$$\frac{1}{\sqrt{f}} = 2 \log_{10} (R_0 / k) + 1.74$$

where, f = friction factor, R_0 = pipe radius and k = average roughness.

Two reservoirs with a surface level difference of 20 metres are to be connected by 1 metre diameter pipe 6 km long.

(*i*) *What will be the discharge when a cast-iron pipe of roughness k = 0·3 mm is used ?*

(*ii*) *What will be the percentage increase in discharge if the cast-iron pipe is replaced by a steel pipe of roughness k = 0·1 mm ?*

Neglect all local losses. **[Delhi University]**

Solution. Difference in levels, $h = 20$ m

Diameter of the pipe, $D = 1$ m

$\therefore$ Radius, $R_0 = {\cdot}5$ m

Length of the pipe, $L = 6$ km $= 6 \times 1000 = 6000$ m

Roughness of C.I. pipe, $k = 0{\cdot}3$ mm $= 0{\cdot}3 \times 10^{-3}$ m

Roughness of steel pipe, $k = 0{\cdot}1$ mm $= 0{\cdot}1 \times 10^{-3}$ m

(*i*) Discharge with C.I. pipe, $Q_{C.I.}$:

$$\frac{1}{\sqrt{f}} = 2 \log_{10} (R_0 / k) + 1.74 \quad \text{...(Given)} \qquad \text{...(i)}$$

$$= 2 \log_{10} [0.5/(0.3 \times 10^{-3})] + 1.74 = 8.1837$$

$$f = \left(\frac{1}{8.1837}\right)^2 = 0.0149$$

Head loss due to friction,

$$h_f = \frac{fLV^2}{D \times 2g}$$

[where, f = friction factor (= 4 × friction coefficient)]

$$20 = \frac{0.0149 \times 6000 \times V^2}{1 \times 2 \times 9.81} \qquad \text{(neglecting all local losses)}$$

or, $V = 2{\cdot}095$ m/s

$\therefore$ Discharge through C.I. pipe,

$Q_{C.I} = (\pi/4) \times 1^2 \times 2{\cdot}095 =$ **1·645 m³/s (Ans.)**

(*ii*) **Percentage increase in discharge :**

For steel pipe : $k = 0{\cdot}1 \times 10^{-3}\ m, R_0 = 0{\cdot}5$ m

Substituting the values is eqn. (*i*), we get:

$$\frac{1}{\sqrt{f}} = 2 \log_{10} [0{\cdot}5/(0{\cdot}1 \times 10^{-3})] + 1{\cdot}74 = 9{\cdot}1379 \quad \text{or} \quad f = 0{\cdot}0119$$

Head lost due to friction,

$$20 = \frac{fLV^2}{D \times 2g}$$

or,
$$20 = \frac{0.0119 \times 6000 \times V^2}{1 \times 2 \times 9.81}$$

or,
$$V = 2{\cdot}344 \text{ m/s}$$

∴ Discharge through steel pipe,

$$Q_S = (\pi/4) \times 1^2 \times 2{\cdot}344 = 1{\cdot}841 \text{ m}^3\text{/s}$$

∴ % age increase is discharge

$$= \frac{Q_S - Q_{C.I.}}{Q_{C.I.}} \times 100 = \frac{1.841 - 1.645}{1.645} \times 100 = \mathbf{11.91\%} \text{ (Ans.)}$$

Example 11.10. *A smooth pipeline of 100 mm diameter carries 2.27 m³ per minute of water at 20°C with kinematic viscosity of 0.009 stokes, calculate:*

(*i*) *Friction factor:* **(*ii*)** *Maximum velocity;*

(*iii*) *Shear stress at the boundary.* **(UPTU)**

Solution. *Given:* $R = \frac{100}{2} = 50$ mm = 0.05 m; $Q = \frac{2.27}{60} = 0.0378$ m³/s;

$\nu = 0.0098$ stokes = 0.0098 cm²/s = 0.0098×10^{-4} m²/s

Average velocity, $\bar{U} = \frac{Q}{\text{Area}} = \frac{0.0378}{\pi R^2} = \frac{0.0378}{\pi \times 0.05^2} = 4.81$ m/s

∴ Reynolds number, $Re = \frac{\bar{U}D}{\nu} = \frac{4.81 \times 0.1}{0.0098 \times 10^{-4}} = 4.91 \times 10^5$

The flow is *turbulent* as $Re > 10^5$. Hence for smooth pipe, the coefficient of friction '*f*' is obtained from the equation,

$$\frac{1}{\sqrt{4f}} = 2.0 \log_{10} (Re\sqrt{4f}) - 0.8 \qquad \text{... [Eqn. (11·36)]}$$

or,
$$\frac{1}{\sqrt{4f}} = 2.0 \log_{10} (4.9 \times 10^5 \times \sqrt{4f}) - 0.8$$
$$= 2.0\left[\log_{10} (4.91 \times 10^5) + \log_{10} \sqrt{4f}\right] - 0.8$$
$$= 2.0\,[5.6911 + \log_{10} \sqrt{4f}] - 0.8$$
$$= 2 \times 5.6911 + 2 \log_{10} \sqrt{4f} - 0.8$$
$$= 11.382 + \log_{10} (\sqrt{4f})^2 - 0.8 = 10.582 + \log_{10} (4f)$$

or,
$$\frac{1}{\sqrt{4f}} - \log_{10} (4f) = 10.582 \qquad \text{...(i)}$$

(*i*) **Friction factor, f_1:**

Friction factor $f_1 = 4 \times$ coefficient of friction $= 4f$

Substituting the value of '4f' in (*i*), we get:

$$\frac{1}{\sqrt{f_1}} - \log_{10}(f_1) = 10.582 \qquad ...(ii)$$

Solving by *hit and trial method,* we get f_1 = **0.013 (Ans.)**

(*ii*) **Maximum velocity, u_{max}:**

$$f = \frac{f_1}{4} = \frac{0.013}{4} = 0.00325$$

Also,
$$u_f = \bar{U}\frac{\sqrt{f}}{2} = 4.81 \times \frac{\sqrt{0.00325}}{2} = 0.194 \text{ m/s}$$

For smooth pipe, the velocity at any point is given by:

$$u = u_f\left[5.75 \log_{10}\left(\frac{u_f \times y}{\nu}\right) + 5.5\right] \qquad ...[\text{Eqn. } (11{\cdot}24)]$$

The velocity will be maximum at the centre of the pipe where $y = R = 0.05$ m *i.e.* radius of the pipe. Hence, the above equation becomes:

$$u_{max} = u_f\left[5.75 \log_{10}\left(\frac{u_f \times R}{\nu}\right) + 5.5\right]$$

$$= 0.194\left[5.75 \log_{10}\left(\frac{0.194 \times 0.05}{0.0098 \times 10^{-4}}\right) + 5.5\right] = \mathbf{5.524 \text{ m/s}} \textbf{ (Ans.)}$$

(*iii*) **Shear stress at the boundary, τ_0:**

$$u_f = \frac{\sqrt{\tau_0}}{\rho} \quad \text{or} \quad (u_f)^2 = \frac{\tau_0}{\rho}$$

$$\tau_0 = \rho\,(u_f)^2 = 1000 \times (0.194)^2 = \mathbf{37.64 \text{ N/m}^2} \textbf{ (Ans.)}$$

Example 11.11. *In a pipe of diameter 300 mm the centre-line velocity and the velocity at a point 100 mm from the centre, as measured by pitot tube, are 2·4 m/s and 2·0 m/s respectively. Assuming the flow in the pipe to be turbulent, find:*

(*i*) *Discharge through the pipe,* **(*ii*)** *Co-efficient of friction, and*

(*iii*) *Height of roughness projections.*

Solution. Diameter of the pipe, D = 300 mm = 0·3 m

∴ Radius, $R = \frac{0.3}{2} = 0.15$ m

Centre-line velocity, u_{max} = 2·4 m/s

Velocity at r = 100 mm or $y = 150 - 100 = 50$ mm, $u = 2{\cdot}0$ m/s

(*i*) **Discharge through the pipe, Q:**

$$\frac{u_{max} - u}{u_f} = 5.75 \log_{10}\left(\frac{R}{y}\right) \qquad ...[\text{Eqn. } (11{\cdot}20)]$$

(where u_f is shear velocity)

Substituting the values, we get:

$$\frac{2.4 - 2.0}{u_f} = 5.75 \log_{10}\left(\frac{0.15}{0.05}\right) = 2.743$$

or,
$$u_f = 0{\cdot}146 \text{ m/s}$$

Using the equation :

$$\frac{u - \overline{U}}{u_f} = 5.75 \log_{10}\left(\frac{y}{R}\right) + 3.75, \text{ we have:} \qquad \text{...[Eqn. (11·29)]}$$

At, $y = R, \quad u = u_{max}$

$$\therefore \quad \frac{u_{max} - \overline{U}}{u_f} = 5.75 \log_{10}\left(\frac{R}{R}\right) + 3.75 = 5.75 \times 0 + 3.75 = 3.75$$

But, $u_{max} = 2·4$ m/s and $u_f = 0·146$ m/s

$$\therefore \quad \frac{2.4 - \overline{U}}{0.146} = 3.75$$

or, $\overline{U} = 2·4 - 0·146 \times 3·75 = 1·85$ m/s

∴ Discharge, Q = Area × average velocity

$= (\pi/4) \times 0·3^2 \times 1·85 =$ **0·1307 m³/s (Ans.)**

(*ii*) **Co-efficient of friction, '*f*':**

We have, $u_f = \overline{U}\sqrt{\frac{f}{2}}$

or, $0.146 = 1·85\sqrt{\frac{f}{2}}$

or, $\sqrt{\frac{f}{2}} = \frac{0.146}{1.85} = 0.0789$

∴ $f =$ **0·0124 (Ans.)**

(*iii*) **Height of roughness projections, k:**

We know that $\frac{1}{\sqrt{4f}} = 2.0 \log_{10}(R/k) + 1.74$ ...[Eqn. (11·39)]

$$\frac{1}{\sqrt{4 \times 0.0124}} = 2.0 \log_{10}\left(\frac{0.15}{k}\right) + 1.74$$

$$4.49 = 2.0 \log_{10}\left(\frac{0.15}{k}\right) + 1.74$$

or, $\log_{10}\left(\frac{0.15}{k}\right) = \frac{4.49 - 1.74}{2} = 1.375$

or, $\frac{0.15}{k} = 23.71$

or, $k = 0·00633$ m or **6·33 mm (Ans.)**

Example 11·12. *A rough plastic pipe 500 mm in diameter and 300 m in length carrying water with a velocity of 3 m/s, has an absolute roughness of 0·25 mm and a kinematic viscosity of 0·9 centistokes,*

(*i*) *Is the flow turbulent or laminar?* (*ii*) *What is the head lost in friction?*

For laminar flow, $f = \frac{64}{Re}$

For turbulent flow, $\frac{1}{\sqrt{f}} = 2 \log_{10}\frac{R}{k} + 1.74$ **[UPSC Civil Services (IAS) Exams.]**

(f = friction factor)

Solution. Diameter of the pipe, D = 500 mm = 0·5 m

Length of the pipe, L = 300 m

Velocity of water, V = 3 m/s

Absolute roughness, k = 0·25 mm = $0·25 \times 10^{-3}$ m

Kinematic viscosity, ν = 0·9 centistokes = $0·9 \times 10^{-6}$ m²/s.

(*i*) **Is the flow turbulent or laminar?**

Reynolds number of flow, $Re = \frac{VD}{\nu} = \frac{3 \times 0.5}{0.9 \times 10^{-6}} = 1.667 \times 10^6$

Since $Re > 2000$, therefore, the flow is **turbulent. (Ans.)**

(*ii*) **Head lost in friction:**

Friction factor (f) for turbulent flow in rough pipes is given by :

$$\frac{1}{\sqrt{f}} = 2 \log_{10} \frac{R}{k} + 1.74 \qquad \text{...(Given)}$$

$$= 2 \log_{10} \frac{0.25}{0.25 \times 10^{-3}} + 1.74 = 7.74$$

$$\therefore \qquad f = \left(\frac{1}{7.74}\right)^2 = 0.0167$$

Head lost in friction,

$$h_f = \frac{fLV^2}{D \times 2g} = \frac{0·0167 \times 300 \times 3^2}{0·5 \times 2 \times 9·81} = \mathbf{4·59\ m}\ \textbf{(Ans.)}$$

Example. 11.13. *In a smooth pipe of diameter 0·5 m and length 1000 m water is flowing at the rate of 0·05 m³/s. Assuming the kinematic viscosity of water as 0·02 stokes, find:*

(*i*) *Head lost due to friction,*

(*ii*) *Wall shear stress,*

(*iii*) *Centre-line velocity, and*

(*iv*) *Thickness of laminar sublayer.*

Solution. Diameter of smooth pipe, D = 0·5 m

$\therefore$ Radius, $R = \frac{0.5}{2} = 0.25$ m

Length of the pipe, L = 1000 m

Discharge through the pipe, Q = 0.05 m³/s

Kinematic viscosity of water, ν = $0·02 \times 10^{-4}$ m²/s

$$\text{Average velocity, } \overline{U} = \frac{Q}{\text{Area}} = \frac{0.05}{\frac{\pi}{4} \times (0.5)^2} = 0.2546 \text{ m/s}$$

$$\therefore \qquad \text{Reynolds number, } Re = \frac{V \times D}{\nu} = \frac{\overline{U} \times D}{\nu} = \frac{0.2546 \times 0.5}{0.02 \times 10^{-4}} = 6.365 \times 10^4$$

Since $Re > 4000$, the flow is *turbulent*.

We know that,
$$f = \frac{0.0791}{(Re)^{1/4}} \qquad \text{...[Eqn. (11·34)]}$$

$$= \frac{0.0791}{(6.365 \times 10^4)^{1/4}} = 0.00498$$

(*i*) **Head lost due to friction, h_f:**

$$h_f = \frac{4fL\bar{V}^2}{D \times 2g} = \frac{4fL\bar{U}^2}{D \times 2g} = \frac{4 \times 0.00498 \times 1000 \times (0.2546)^2}{0.5 \times 2 \times 9.81}$$

$$= \mathbf{0.1316\ m\ (Ans.)}$$

(*ii*) **Wall shear stress, τ_0:**

We know that,
$$\tau_0 = \frac{f\rho V^2}{2} = \frac{f\rho\bar{U}^2}{2} \qquad \text{...[Eqn. 11·5 (a)]}$$

$$= \frac{0.00498 \times 1000 \times (10.2546)^2}{2} = \mathbf{0.1614\ N/m^2\ (Ans.)}$$

(*iii*) **Centre-line velocity, u_{max}:**

We know that,
$$\frac{u}{u_f} = 5.75 \log_{10}\left(\frac{u_f y}{\nu}\right) + 5.5 \qquad \text{...[Eqn. (11·24)]}$$

At,
$$y = R, \quad u = u_{max}$$

$$\therefore \qquad \frac{u_{max}}{u_f} = 5.75 \log_{10}\left(\frac{u_f \, . \, R}{\nu}\right) + 5.5$$

where,
$$u_f = \sqrt{\frac{\tau_0}{\rho}} = \sqrt{\frac{0.1614}{1000}} = 0.0127 \text{ m/s}$$

Substituting the values in the above eqn., we get:

$$\frac{u_{max}}{0.0127} = 5.75 \log_{10}\left(\frac{0.0127 \times 0.25}{0.02 \times 10^{-4}}\right) + 5.5 = 23.9$$

or,
$$u_{max} = \mathbf{0{\cdot}303\ m/s\ (Ans.)}$$

(*iv*) **Thickness of laminar sublayer, δ':**

We know that,
$$\delta' = \frac{11.6 \times \nu}{u_f} \qquad \text{...[Eqn (11·22)]}$$

$$= \frac{11.6 \times 0.02 \times 10^{-4}}{0.0127} = 0.001826 \text{ m} = \mathbf{1{\cdot}826\ mm\ (Ans.)}$$

Example 11.14. *Water is flowing in a rough pipe of 0·5 m diameter and 800 m length at the rate of 0·5 m^3/s. Assuming the average height of roughness as 0·15 mm, determine:*

(*i*) *Co-efficient of friction,*

(*ii*) *Wall shear stress, and*

(*iii*) *Centre-line velocity and velocity at a distance of 200 mm from the pipe wall.*

Solution. Diameter of the pipe, $D = 0{\cdot}5$ m

Radius, $R = \frac{0.5}{2} = 0.25$ m

Length of the pipe, $L = 800$ m

Discharge, $Q = 0{\cdot}5 \text{ m}^3/\text{s}$

Average height of roughness, $k = 0{\cdot}015 \text{ mm} = 0{\cdot}015 \times 10^{-3}$ m

(*i*) **Co-efficient of friction, *f*:**

Using the equation:

$$\frac{1}{\sqrt{4f}} = 2.0 \log_{10}\left(\frac{R}{k}\right) + 1.74 \qquad \text{...[Eqn. (11·39)]}$$

or, $$\frac{1}{\sqrt{4f}} = 2.0 \log_{10}\left(\frac{0.25}{0.015 \times 10^{-3}}\right) + 1.74 = 10.184$$

$$\sqrt{4f} = \frac{1}{10.184} = 0.0982$$

$$f = \mathbf{0{\cdot}00241} \text{ (Ans.)}$$

(ii) **Wall shear stress, τ_0:**

$$\tau_0 = \frac{f\rho V^2}{2} \quad \text{...[Eqn. 11·5 (a)]}$$

where, $$V = \frac{\text{Discharge}}{\text{Area}} = \frac{0\cdot 5}{\frac{\pi}{4} \times 0\cdot 5^2} = 2\cdot 546 \text{ m/s}$$

$$\therefore \quad \tau_0 = \frac{0.00241 \times 1000 \times (2.546)^2}{2} = \mathbf{7.81\ N/m^2} \text{ (Ans.)}$$

(iii) **Centre-line velocity, u_{max}:**

For rough pipe: $$\frac{u}{u_f} = 5.75 \log_{10}\left(\frac{y}{k}\right) + 8.5 \quad \text{...[Eqn. (11·25)]}$$

At $$y = R,\ u = u_{max}$$

$$\therefore \quad \frac{u_{max}}{u_f} = 5.75 \log_{10}\left(\frac{R}{k}\right) + 8.5 \quad \text{...(i)}$$

where, $$u_f = \sqrt{\frac{\tau_0}{\rho}} = \sqrt{\frac{7.81}{1000}} = 0.0884 \text{ m/s}$$

Substituting the values of u_f, R and k in eqn. (*i*), we get:

$$\frac{u}{0.0884} = 5.75 \log_{10}\left(\frac{0.2}{0.015 \times 10^{-3}}\right) + 8.5 = 32.77$$

$$\therefore \quad u_{max} = 0{\cdot}0884 \times 32{\cdot}77 = \mathbf{2{\cdot}897\ m/s} \text{ (Ans.)}$$

Velocity at a distance of 200 mm from the pipe wall, *u*:

For a rough pipe: $$\frac{u}{u_f} = 5.75 \log_{10}\left(\frac{y}{k}\right) + 8.5$$

where, $$u_f = 0{\cdot}0884 \text{ m/s},\ y = 200 \text{ mm} = 0{\cdot}2 \text{ m and } k = 0{\cdot}015 \times 10^{-3} \text{ m}$$

$$\therefore \quad \frac{u}{0.0884} = 5.75 \log_{10}\left(\frac{0.2}{0.015 \times 10^{-3}}\right) + 8.5 = 32.22$$

or, $$u = 0{\cdot}00884 \times 32{\cdot}22 = \mathbf{2{\cdot}848\ m/s} \text{ (Ans.)}$$

Example 11.15. *Hydrodynamically smooth pipe carries water at the rate of 300 l/s at 20° C ($\rho = 1000$ kg/m^3, $\nu = 10^{-6}$ m^2/s) with a head loss of 3 m in 100 m length of pipe. Determine the pipe diameter. Use $f = 0.0032 + \frac{0.221}{(Re)^{0.237}}$ equation for f, where $h_f = \frac{f \times L \times V^2}{D \times 2g}$ and $Re = \frac{\rho VD}{\mu}$.*

(Anna University)

Solution. *Given:* $Q = 300$ l/s $= 0.3$ m^3/s; $\rho = 1000$ kg/m^3; $\nu = 10^{-6}$ m^2/s; $h_f = 3$ m;

$L = 100$ m; Friction factor, $f = 0.0032 + \frac{0.221}{(Re)^{0.237}}$.

Diameter of the pipe, D:

$$h_f = \frac{fLV^2}{D \times 2g}$$

or, $$3 = \frac{f \times 100 \times V^2}{D \times 2 \times 9.81} \quad \text{or} \quad f = \frac{0.5886D}{V^2}$$

Now, $$Q = A \times V$$

or, $$0.3 = \frac{\pi}{4} \times D^2 \times V \quad \text{or} \quad D^2\, V = 0.382$$

∴ $$V = \frac{0.382}{D^2}$$

Also, $$f = 0.0032 + \frac{0.221}{(Re)^{0.237}} \qquad ...(Given)$$

or, $$\frac{0.5886D}{V^2} = 0.0032 + \frac{0.221}{(V \times D \times 10^6)^{0.237}}$$

or, $$\frac{0.5886D}{(0.382/D^2)^2} = 0.0032 + \frac{0.221}{\left[\frac{0.382}{D^2} \times D \times 10^6\right]^{0.237}}$$

or, $$\frac{0.5886D^5}{(0.382)^2} = 0.0032 + \frac{0.221}{\left(\frac{0.382 \times 10^6}{D}\right)^{0.237}}$$

or, $$4.034\, D^5 = 0.0032 + 0.0105 \times D^{0.237}$$

or, $$4.034\, D^5 - 0.0105\, D^{0.237} - 0.0032 = 0$$

Solving by hit and trial method, we get:

$$D \simeq 0.308 \text{ m} \quad \textbf{(Ans.)}$$

Example 11.16. *Design the diameter of a steel pipe to carry water having kinematic viscosity $\nu = 10^{-6}$ m^2/s with a mean velocity of 1 m/s. The head loss is to be limited to 5 m per 100 m length of pipe. Consider the equivalent sand roughness height of pipe, $k_s = 45 \times 10^{-4}$ cm. Assume that the Darcy-Weisbach friction co-efficient over the whole range of turbulent flow can be expressed as*

$$f = 0.0055\left[1 + \left(20 \times 10^3 \frac{k_s}{D} + \frac{10^6}{Re}\right)^{1/3}\right]$$

where, D = Diameter of pipe and Re = Reynolds number. **(Delhi University)**

Solution. *Given :* $\nu = 10^{-6}$ m²/s; $\overline{U} = 1$ m/s; $h_f = 5$ m in a length 100 m (L);

$k = 45 \times 10^{-4}$ cm $= 45 \times 10^{-6}$ m

$$\text{Friction factor, } f = 0.0055\left[1 + \left(20 \times 10^3 \frac{k_s}{D} + \frac{10^6}{Re}\right)^{1/3}\right] \qquad ...(i)$$

Diameter of the steel pipe, *D*:

Using Darcy-Weisbach equation: $h_f = \dfrac{4fL\overline{U}^2}{D \times 2g}$, we have:

$$f = \frac{h_f \times D \times 2g}{4L\overline{U}^2} = \frac{5 \times D \times 2 \times 9.81}{4 \times 100 \times 1^2} = 0.2452D$$

$$\text{Reynolds number, } Re = \frac{\rho \overline{U} D}{\mu} = \frac{\overline{U} D}{\nu} = \frac{1 \times D}{10^{-6}} = 10^6 D$$

Substituting the values in (*i*), we get:

$$0.2452\, D = 0.0055 \left[1 + \left(20 \times 10^3 \times \frac{45 \times 10^{-6}}{D} + \frac{10^6}{10^6 D} \right)^{1/3} \right]$$

$$\text{or,} \quad \frac{0.2452D}{0.0055} = \left[1 + \left(\frac{0.9}{D} + \frac{1}{D} \right)^{1/3} \right]$$

$$\text{or,} \quad 44.58D = \left[1 + \left(\frac{1.9}{D} \right)^{1/3} \right] \quad \text{or} \quad (44.58D - 1) = \left(\frac{1.9}{D} \right)^{1/3}$$

$$\text{or,} \quad (44.58D - 1)^3 = \frac{1.9}{D} \qquad ...(ii)$$

$$\text{or,} \quad D\,(44{\cdot}58\, D - 1)^3 = 1.9$$

Solving by *hit and trial method*, we get $D =$ **0.0854 m (Ans.)**

Example 11.17. *Water flows through a horizontal conical pipe, 2 m long and having a diameter of 200 mm at the inlet and 150 mm at the discharge end. A constant discharge of 0·4 m³/s flows through the pipe. Starting from first principles determine the loss of head due to pipe friction. Take friction factor = 0·04.* **[UPSC Exams, Hydraulic and Hydraulic m/cs]**

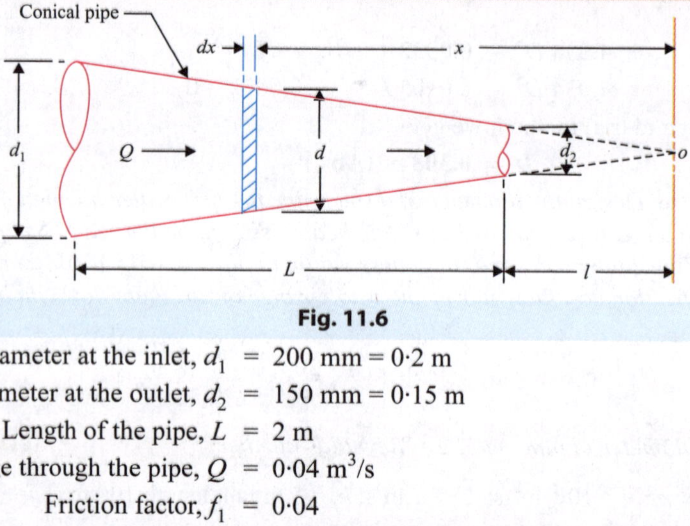

Fig. 11.6

Solution. Diameter at the inlet, $d_1 = 200 \text{ mm} = 0{\cdot}2 \text{ m}$

Diameter at the outlet, $d_2 = 150 \text{ mm} = 0{\cdot}15 \text{ m}$

Length of the pipe, $L = 2 \text{ m}$

Discharge through the pipe, $Q = 0{\cdot}04 \text{ m}^3/\text{s}$

Friction factor, $f_1 = 0{\cdot}04$

Let us first derive the expression for loss of head due to friction in a tapering pipe as follows:
The Darcy-Weisbach equation in differential form can be written as:

$$dh_f = \frac{f_1 \cdot dx \cdot V^2}{d \times 2g} \qquad ...(i)$$

where, f_1 = Friction factor, and

V = Velocity of flow (at the section considered)

Refer to Fig. 11·6. From the geometry of the cone we can write,

$$\frac{d_1}{L + l} = \frac{d_2}{l} = \frac{d}{x}$$

(where, d = diameter at a distance x from O)

or, $$d = \frac{x}{L}(d_1 - d_2)$$

The velocity, $$V = \frac{Q}{\frac{\pi}{4} d^2} = \frac{4Q}{\pi d^2} = \frac{4Q}{\pi \left\{\frac{x}{L}(d_1 - d_2)\right\}^2}$$

Substituting for d and V in eqn. (i), we get:

$$dh_f = \frac{f_1 L \cdot dx}{x(d_1 - d_2)} \cdot \frac{1}{2g}\left\{\frac{4QL^2}{\pi x^2 (d_1 - d_2)^2}\right\}^2$$

$$= \left\{\frac{8 f_1 Q^2 L^5}{g\,\pi^2 (d_1 - d_2)^5}\right\}\frac{dx}{x^5}$$

Assuming f_1 to be constant, the friction loss in the conical pipe,

$$h_f = \frac{g f_1 Q^2 L^5}{g\,\pi^2 (d_1 - d_2)^5}\int_l^{(L+l)} \frac{d}{x^5} = \frac{8 f_1 Q^2 L^5}{g\,\pi^2 (d_1 - d_2)^5}\left[-\frac{1}{4x^4}\right]_l^{L+l}$$

$$h_f = \frac{2 f_1 Q^2 L}{g\pi^2 (d_1 - d_2)}\left(\frac{1}{d_2^4} - \frac{1}{d_1^4}\right)$$

Substituting the values, we get:

$$h_f = \frac{2 \times 0.04 \times 0.04^2 \times 2}{9.81 \times \pi^2 (0.2 - 0.15)}\left(\frac{1}{0.15^4} - \frac{1}{0.20^4}\right)$$

$$= \mathbf{0{\cdot}0714\ m}$$ **(Ans.)**

HIGHLIGHTS

1. The flow is turbulent when Reynolds number (Re) is more than 4000. The turbulent flow is characterised by random, irregular and haphazard movement of fluid particles.
2. The shear in turbulent flow is mainly due to momentum transfer.
3. Loss of head due to friction in pipe flow is given by

$$h_f = \frac{4 fLV^2}{D \times 2g}, \text{ where } f \text{ is the friction co-efficient}$$

$$= \frac{f_1 LV^2}{D \times 2g}, \text{ where } f_1\ (= 4f) \text{ is the friction factor.}$$

4. Co-efficient of friction in terms of shear stress is expressed as $f = \frac{2\tau_0}{\rho V^2}$

where, τ_0 = Shear stress,
ρ = Mass density of fluid, and
V = Average/mean velocity of flow.

5. In turbulent flow the shear stress (τ) is the sum of shear stress due to viscosity (τ_υ) and shear stress due to turbulence (τ_t) *i.e.*,

$$\tau = \tau_\upsilon + \tau_t = \mu\frac{du}{dy} + \eta\frac{d\bar{u}}{dy}$$

6. According to Reynolds theory the shear stress (τ) is given as:

$$\tau = \rho u'\upsilon'$$

where u' and υ' are the fluctuating components of velocity.

7. According to Prandtl's mixing theory the shear stress (τ) is given as:

$$\tau = \rho l^2 \left(\frac{du}{dy}\right)^2$$

8. Prandtl's universal velocity distribution equation is expressed as:

$$u = u_{max} + 2{\cdot}5\, u_f \ln\left(\frac{y}{R}\right)$$

where, u_{max} = Centre-line velocity,

y = Distance from the pipe wall,

R = Radius of the pipe, and

u_f = Shear friction velocity $\sqrt{\frac{\tau_0}{\rho}}$

9. *Velocity defect* is the difference between the maximum velocity (u_{max}) and local velocity (u) at any point and is given by:

$$(u_{max} - u) = u_f \times 5{\cdot}75 \log_{10} (R/y)$$

10. If 'k' is the average height of the irregularities of the surface of a boundary, then in general, the boundary is said to the *rough* if the value of 'k' compared to the thickness of the laminar sublayer δ' is high and *smooth* if 'k' is low (in comparison with δ').

Boundary is smooth ....when $\frac{k}{\delta'} < 0{\cdot}25$

Boundary is rough ....when $\frac{k}{\delta'} > 6{\cdot}0$

Boundary is in transition ....when $\frac{k}{\delta'}$ lies between 0.25 to 6·0.

11. For turbulent flow, the velocity distribution is given as:

For smooth pipes: $\frac{u}{u_f} = 5.75 \log_{10}\left(\frac{u_f y}{\nu}\right) + 5.5$

For rough pipes: $\frac{u}{u_f} = 5.75 \log_{10}\left(\frac{y}{k}\right) + 8.5$

where, u_f = Shear friction velocity $= \sqrt{\frac{\tau_0}{\rho}}$,

ν = Kinematic viscosity of the fluid,

y = Distance from the pipe wall, and

k = Roughness factor.

12. For turbulent flow the velocity distribution in terms of average velocity is given as:

For smooth pipes: $\frac{\overline{U}}{u_f} = 5.75 \log_{10}\left(\frac{u + R}{\nu}\right) + 1.75$

For rough pipes: $\frac{\overline{U}}{u_f} = 5{\cdot}75 \log_{10} (R/k) + 4{\cdot}75$

13. The difference of local velocity and average velocity for smooth and rough pipes is given by:

$$\frac{u - \overline{U}}{u_f} = 5.75 \log_{10} (y/R) + 3.75$$

14. Velocity distribution for turbulent flow in smooth pipes by *power law* is given as : $\frac{u}{u_{max}} = \left(\frac{y}{R}\right)^{1/n}$ where exponent $\frac{1}{n}$ depends on Reynolds number (*Re*) and it decreases with the increasing *Re*.

15. The co-efficient of friction is given by:

$$f = \frac{16}{Re} \quad \text{...for laminar flow}$$

$$= \frac{0.0791}{(Re)^{1/4}} \quad \text{for turbulent flow in smooth pipes}$$

for $Re \geq 4000$ but $\leq 10^5$

$$= 0.0008 + \frac{0.05525}{(Re)^{0.237}} \quad \text{for } Re \geq 10^5 \text{ but } \leq 4 \times 10^7$$

$$\frac{1}{\sqrt{4f}} = 2 \log_{10} (R/k) + 1{\cdot}74 \quad \text{for rough pipes} \quad \text{(where, } Re = \text{Reynolds number)}$$

OBJECTIVE TYPE QUESTIONS

Choose the Correct Answers:

1. The flow is said to be turbulent when Reynolds number is
(*a*) less than 1000
(*b*) equal to 2000
(*c*) greater than 4000
(*d*) between 1000 to 4000.

2. The shear in turbulent flow is mainly due to
(*a*) heat transfer
(*b*) mass transfer
(*c*) momentum transfer
(*d*) all of the above.

3. Which of the following statements is *correct?* Wall turbulence occurs
(*a*) in immediate vicinity of solid surfaces and in the boundary layer flows where the fluid has a negligible mean acceleration
(*b*) in jets, wakes, mixing layer etc.
(*c*) where there is conversion of potential energy into kinetic energy by the process of mixing
(*d*) none of the above.

4. Turbulence in flow is characterised by which of the following?
(*a*) Fluctuating components of velocities
(*b*) High Reynolds number
(*c*) Cross currents and eddies with intermixing of particles
(*d*) Excess energy dissipation with rise in temperature
(*e*) All to the above.

5. The flow in town water supply pipes is generally
(*a*) laminar (*b*) turbulent
(*c*) transition (*d*) any of the above.

6. The most essential feature of a turbulent flow is
(*a*) high velocity
(*b*) velocity at a point remains constant with time
(*c*) large discharge
(*d*) Velocity and pressure at a point exhibit irregular fluctuations of high frequency.

7. In turbulent flow the velocity distribution is a function of the distance y measured from the boundary surface and shear friction velocity u_f, and follows a
(*a*) linear law (*b*) hyperbolic law
(*c*) parabolic law (*d*) logarithmic law.

8. A turbulent flow is considered steady when
(*a*) the algebraic sum of velocity fluctuations is zero
(*b*) the velocity at a point does not change with time

(*c*) temporal mean velocity at a point remains constant with time
(*d*) the discharge remains constant.

9. The Darcy-Weisbach friction factor f which is a direct measure of resistance to flow in pipes depends on which of the following?
(*a*) Relative roughness, velocity and viscosity
(*b*) Relative roughness, diameter and viscosity
(*c*) Roughness height, diameter and velocity
(*d*) Roughness height, diameter, velocity and kinematic viscosity.

10. Commercial cast-iron and steel pipes carrying fluids under pressure are regarded as hydraulically smooth when
(*a*) the laminar layer is thin as compared to the average height of roughness elements
(*b*) the height of the roughness projections is low
(*c*) the roughness elements are all completely covered by the laminar sublayer
(*d*) none of the above.

11. Intensity of turbulence is
(*a*) the average K.E. of turbulence
(*b*) the violence of turbulent fluctuations and is measured by the root mean square value of velocity fluctuations
(*c*) the mean time interval between the reversals in the sign of velocity fluctuation
(*d*) none of the above.

12. Which of the following factors determine the friction factor for turbulent flow in a rough pipe?
(*a*) Mach number and relative roughness
(*b*) Froude's number and Mach's number
(*c*) Reynolds number and relative roughness
(*d*) Froude's number and relative roughness.

13. In case of turbulent flow of a fluid through a circular tube (as compared to the case of laminar flow at the same flow rate) the maximum velocity is ....., shear stress at the wall is ....., and the pressure drop across a given length is ....., the correct words for the blanks are, respectively
(*a*) lower, higher, lower
(*b*) lower, higher, higher
(*c*) higher, lower, lower
(*d*) higher, higher, higher.

14. Prandtl's universal equation is given as:
(*a*) $u = u_{max} + 2 \cdot 5\, u_f \log_e \left(\frac{y}{R}\right)$
(*b*) $u = u_{max} + 3 \cdot 5\, u_f \log_e \left(\frac{y}{R}\right)$
(*c*) $u = u_{max} + 4 \cdot 5\, u_f \log_e \left(\frac{y}{R}\right)$
(*d*) $u = u_{max} + 5 \cdot 5\, u_f \log_e \left(\frac{y}{R}\right)$

where, u_f = Shear friction velocity,
y= Distance from the pipe wall, and
R= Radius of the pipe.

ANSWERS

1. (*c*)	**2.** (*c*)	**3.** (*a*)	**4.** (*e*)	**5.** (*b*)	**6.** (*d*)
7. (*d*)	**8.** (*c*)	**9.** (*d*)	**10.** (*c*)	**11.** (*b*)	**12.** (*c*)
13. (*b*)	**14.** (*a*).				

THEORETICAL QUESTIONS

1. Enumerate the factors which influence the stability of laminar flow.
2. What is turbulence ?
3. How is turbulent motion classified?
4. What are the characteristics of a turbulent flow?
5. What do you understand by wall turbulent and free turbulence?
6. Derive an expression for the loss of head due to friction in pipes.
7. Define 'shear velocity' for turbulent flow in circular pipes.
8. Obtain an expression for the co-efficient of friction in terms of shear stress.
9. Derive an expression for shear stress on the basis of 'Prandtl Mixing Length Theory'.
10. Obtain an expression for the Prandtl's universal velocity distribution for turbulent flow in pipes. Why this velocity distribution is called universal?
11. In what way does the flow through a rough pipe differ from that in smooth pipe?
12. What is meant by a smooth boundary and a rough boundary?
13. Explain why the hydraulic loss in a pipe is influenced by the surface roughness only at higher Reynolds numbers.

14. Derive an expression for the velocity distribution for turbulent flow in smooth pipes.

15. Show that velocity distribution for turbulent flow through rough pipes is given as:

$$\frac{u}{u_f} = 5{\cdot}75 \log_{10} (y/k) + 8{\cdot}5$$

where, u_f = Shear velocity,
y = Distance from pipe wall, and
k = Roughness factor.

16. Derive expressions for velocity distribution in terms of average velocity for (*i*) smooth pipe and, (*ii*) rough pipe.

17. Prove that the difference of local velocity (u) and average velocity ($\overline{U}$) for turbulent flow through rough or smooth pipes is given by:

$$\frac{u - \overline{U}}{u_f} = 5{\cdot}75 \log_{10} (y/R) + 3{\cdot}75.$$

UNSOLVED EXAMPLES

1. In a pipe of 300 mm diameter having turbulent flow, the centre-line velocity is 6 m/s and that at 50 mm from the pipe wall is 5 m/s. Calculate the shear friction velocity. [**Ans.** 0·36 m/s]

2. A pipeline carrying water has surface protrusions of average height of 0·15 mm. If the shear stress developed is 4·9 N/m^2 determine whether the pipe surface acts as smooth, rough or in transition. The kinematic viscosity of water may be taken as 0·01 stokes. [**Ans.** Transition]

3. The velocity of flow in a badly corroded 8 cm pipe is found to increase 30 percent as a pitot tube is moved from a point 1 cm from the wall to 3 cm from the wall. Estimate the height of the roughness elements. [**Ans.** 0·773 cm]

4. Motor having dynamic viscosity of 0·01 poise flows in a 75 mm diameter smooth pipe at the rate of 0·007 m^3/sec. Calculate:

(*i*) The shear friction velocity,
(*ii*) The velocity at 25 mm from the pipe centre, and
(*iii*) The thickness of laminar sublayer.
Take friction factor = 0·018.

[**Ans.** (*i*) 0·0752 m/s; (*ii*) 1·7 m/s; (*iii*) 0·155 mm]

5. A smooth pipe 100 mm in diameter and 1000 m long carries water at the rate of 0·0075 m^3/s. If the kinematic viscosity of water is 0·02 stokes, calculate:

(*i*) Head lost, (*ii*) Wall shearing stress,
(*iii*) Centre-line velocity,
(*iv*) Shear stress and velocity at 40 mm from the centre-line, and
(*v*) Thickness of the laminar sublayer.

[**Ans.** (*i*) 9·96 m; (*ii*) 2·45 N/m^2; (*iii*) 1·15 m/s; (*iv*) 1·96 N/m^2; 0·95 m/s; (*v*) 0·47 mm]

6. A 300 mm diameter pipe is carrying water. If the velocities at the pipe centre and at a point 100 mm from the pipe centre are respectively 3 m/s and 2·5 m/s, determine the wall shearing stress. Assume the flow to be turbulent.

[**Ans.** 32·96 N/m^2]

7. In a rough pipe of diameter 500 mm and length 3500 m water is flowing at the rate of 0·5 m^3/s. If the average height of roughness is 0·40 mm find the power required to maintain this flow.

[**Ans.** 210·9 kW]

8. In a pipe of diameter 300 mm the centre-line velocity and the velocity at a point 100 mm from the centre as measured by pitot-tube are 2·0 m/s and 1·6 m/s respectively. Assuming the flow in the pipe to be turbulent, find:

(*i*) Discharge through the pipe,
(*ii*) Co-efficient of friction, and
(*iii*) Height of roughness projections.

[**Ans.** (*i*) 0·1027 m^3/s; (*ii*) 0·02; (*iii*) 18·98 mm]

9. In a smooth pipe of diameter 0·4 m and length 800 m water is flowing at the rate of 0·04 m^3/s. Assuming the kinematic viscosity of water as 0·018 stokes, find:

(*i*) Head lost due to friction,
(*ii*) Wall shear stress,
(*iii*) Centre-line velocity, and
(*iv*) Thickness of laminar sublayer.

[**Ans.** (*i*) 0·2 m; (*ii*) 0·245 N/m^2; (*iii*) 0·0377 m/s; (*iv*) 1·338 mm]

10. Water is flowing in a rough pipe of 400 mm diameter and 1000 m long at the rate of 400 litres/sec. Assuming the average height of roughness as 0·012 mm, determine:

(*i*) Co-efficient of friction,
(*ii*) Wall shear stress,
(*iii*) Centre-line velocity and velocity at a distance of 150 mm from the pipe wall.

[**Ans.** (*i*) 0·00241; (*ii*) 12·2 N/m^2; (*iii*) 3·6 m/s; 3·52 m/s]

Chapter 12

FLOW THROUGH PIPES

12.1. INTRODUCTION

A **pipe** *is a closed conduit* (generally of circular section) *which is used for carrying fluids under pressure.* The flow in a pipe is termed *pipe flow* only when the fluid *completely fills the cross-section and there is no free surface of fluid. The pipe running partially full* (in such a case *atmospheric pressure exists* inside the pipe) *behaves like an* ***open channel***.

12.2. LOSS OF ENERGY (OR HEAD) IN PIPES

When water flows in a pipe, it experiences some resistance to its motion, due to which its velocity and ultimately the head of water available is reduced. This loss of energy (or head) is classified as follows :

A. Major Energy Losses

This loss is due to *friction.*

B. Minor Energy Losses

These losses are due to :

1. Sudden enlargement of pipe,
2. Sudden contraction of pipe,
3. Bend of pipe,
4. An obstruction in pipe,
5. Pipe fittings, etc.

12.3. MAJOR ENERGY LOSSES

These losses which are *due to friction* are calculated by :

1. Darcy-Weisbach formula
2. Chezy's formula.

12·3·1 Darcy-Weisbach Formula

The loss of head (or energy) in pipes due to friction is calculated from Darcy-Weisbach formula (derived in chapter 11 Art. 11·2) which is given by:

$$h_f = \frac{4fLV^2}{D \times 2g} \quad \text{...(12·1)}$$

where, h_f = Loss of head due to friction,

f = Co-efficient of friction, (a function of Reynolds number, Re)

$h = \frac{0.0791}{(Re)^{1/4}}$ for Re varying from 4000 to 10^6

$= \frac{16}{Re}$ for $Re < 2000$ (laminar/viscous flow)

L = Length of the pipe,

V = Mean velocity of flow, and

D = Diameter of the pipe.

12·3·2 Chezy's Formula for Loss of Head due to Friction

Refer to Fig. 11·2. An equilibrium between the propelling force due to pressure difference and the frictional resistance gives :

$$(p_1 - p_2)\, A = f'\, PLV^2$$

or
$$\frac{(p_1 - p_2)}{w} \cdot A = \frac{f'}{w} PLV^2 \quad \text{[Refer to Art. 11.2]}$$

or
$$h_f = \frac{f'}{w} \frac{P}{A} LV^2$$

$\therefore$ Mean velocity, $V = \sqrt{\frac{w}{f'}} \times \sqrt{\frac{A}{P} \times \frac{h_f}{L}}$

where, the factor $\sqrt{\frac{w}{f}}$, is called the Chezy's constant, C;

the ratio $\frac{A}{P}\left(= \frac{\text{area of flow}}{\text{wetted perimeter}}\right)$ is called the ***hydraulic mean depth*** or ***hydraulic radius*** and denoted by m (or R);

the ratio $\frac{h_f}{L}$ prescribes the *loss of head per unit length of pipe* and is denoted by **i or S** (slope).

$\therefore$ Mean velocity, $V = C\sqrt{m\, i}$ ...(12·2)

Eqn. (12·2) is *known as* **Chezy's formula.** This formula helps to find the head loss due to friction if the mean flow velocity through the pipe and also the value of Chezy's constant C are known.

Note : (*i*) Darcy-Weisbach formula (for loss of head) is generally used for the flow through *pipes.*

(*ii*) Chezy's formula (for loss of head) is generally used for the flow through *open channels.*

(*iii*) The values of hydraulic mean depth for a *circular pipe,*

$$m = \frac{D}{4} \left[\because m = \frac{\text{Area}}{\text{Perimeter}} = \frac{\frac{\pi}{4} \times D^2}{\pi D} = \frac{D}{4}\right]$$

Example 12.1. *In a pipe of diameter 350 mm and length 75 m water is flowing at a velocity of 2·8 m/s. Find the head lost due to friction using :*

(*i*) *Darcy-Weisbach formula;* (*ii*) *Chezy's formula for which C = 55.*

Assume kinematic viscosity of water as 0·012 stoke.

Solution. Diameter of the pipe, $D = 350 \text{ mm} = 0{\cdot}35 \text{ m}$

Length of the pipe, $L = 75$ m

Velocity of flow, $V = 2{\cdot}8$ m/s

Chezy's constant, $C = 55$

Kinematic viscocity of water, $v = 0{\cdot}012 \text{ stoke} = 0{\cdot}012 \times 10^{-4} \text{ m}^2/\text{s}$.

Head lost due to friction, h_f :

(*i*) **Darcy-Weisbach fomula :**

Darcy-Weisbach formula is given by:

$$h_f = \frac{4fLV^2}{D \times 2g}$$

where, f = coefficient of friction (a function of Reynolds number, Re)

$$Re = \frac{V \times D}{v} = \frac{2{\cdot}8 \times 0{\cdot}35}{0{\cdot}012 \times 10^{-4}} = 8{\cdot}167 \times 10^5$$

$$\therefore \quad f = \frac{0.0791}{(Re)^{1/4}} = \frac{0.0791}{(8.167 \times 10^5)^{1/4}} = 0.00263$$

$\therefore$ Head lost due to friction,

$$h_f = \frac{4 \times 0.00263 \times 75 \times (2.8)^2}{0.35 \times 2 \times 9.81} = \mathbf{0.9\ m} \quad \textbf{(Ans.)}$$

(*ii*) **Chezy's formula :**

$$V = C\sqrt{m\,i}$$

where, $$C = 55,\ m = \frac{A}{p} = \frac{\frac{\pi}{4} \times D^2}{\pi D} = \frac{D}{4} = \frac{0.35}{4} = 0.0875 \text{ m}$$

$$\therefore \quad 2.8 = 55\sqrt{0.0875 \times i}$$

or, $$0.0875 \times i = \left(\frac{2.8}{55}\right)^2 = 0.00259$$

or, $$i = 0.0296$$

But, $$i = \frac{h_f}{L} = 0.0296$$

$$\therefore \quad \frac{h_f}{75} = 0.0296$$

or, $$h_f = 75 \times 0{\cdot}0296 = \mathbf{2{\cdot}22\ m} \quad \textbf{(Ans.)}$$

Example 12.2. *Water flows through a pipe of diameter 300 mm with a velocity of 5 m/s. If the co-efficient of friction is given by* $f = 0.015 + \frac{0.08}{Re^{0.3}}$ *where Re is the Reynolds number, find the head lost due to friction for a length of 10 m. Take kinematic viscosity of water as 0·01 stoke.*

Solution. Diameter of the pipe, $D = 300 \text{ mm} = 0{\cdot}3 \text{ m}$

Velocity of water $V = 5$ m/s

Length of the pipe, $L = 10$ m

Viscosity of water, $v = 0{\cdot}01 \text{ stoke} = 0{\cdot}01 \times 10^{-4} \text{ m}^2/\text{s}$. $(\because 1 \text{ stoke} = 1 \text{ cm}^2/\text{s} = 1 \times 10^{-4} \text{ m}^2/\text{s})$

Head lost due to friction h_f :

$$\text{Co-efficient of friction, } f = 0.015 + \frac{0.08}{(Re)^{0.3}} \quad \text{...(given)}$$

$$\text{But, Reynolds number, } Re = \frac{\rho VD}{\mu} = \frac{VD}{\nu} = \frac{5 \times 0.3}{0.01 \times 10^{-4}} = 1.5 \times 10^6$$

$$\therefore \quad f = 0.015 + \frac{0.08}{(1.5 \times 10^6)^{0.3}} = 0.0161$$

∴ Head lost due to friction,

$$h_f = \frac{4fLV^2}{D \times 2g} = \frac{4 \times 0.0161 \times 10 \times 5^2}{0.3 \times 2 \times 9.81}$$

$$= \mathbf{2.735\ m}\ \textbf{(Ans.)}$$

Example 12.3. *In a pipe of 300 mm diameter and 800 m length an oil of specific gravity 0·8 is flowing at the rate of 0·45 m³/s. Find :*

(i) Head lost due to friction, and

(ii) Power required to maintain the flow.

Take kinematic viscosity of oil as 0·3 stoke.

Solution. Diameter of the pipe, D = 300 mm = 0·3 m

Length of the pipe, L = 800 m

Specific gravity of oil = 0·8

Kinematic viscosity of oil, ν = 0·3 stoke = $0{\cdot}3 \times 10^{-4}$ m²/s

Discharge, Q = 0·45 m³/s.

(*i*) **Head lost due to friction, h_f :**

$$\text{Velocity, } V = \frac{Q}{\text{Area}} = \frac{0.45}{\frac{\pi}{4} \times 0.3^2} = 6.366 \text{ m/s}$$

$$\therefore \quad \text{Reynolds number, } Re = \frac{V \times D}{\nu} = \frac{6.366 \times 0.3}{0.3 \times 10^{-4}} = 6.366 \times 10^4$$

$$\therefore \text{ Co-efficient of friction, } f = \frac{0.0791}{(Re)^{1/4}} = \frac{0.0791}{(6.366 \times 10^4)^{1/4}} = 0.00498$$

$$\therefore \quad h_f = \frac{4fLV^2}{D \times 2g} = \frac{4 \times 0.00498 \times 800 \times (6.366)^2}{0.3 \times 2 \times 9.81}$$

$$= \mathbf{109.72\ m}\ \textbf{(Ans.)}$$

(*ii*) **Power required, P :**

Power required to maintain the flow, $P = wQh_f$

where, $w = 0{\cdot}8 \times 9{\cdot}81 = 7{\cdot}848$ kN/m³

$h_f = 109{\cdot}72$ m, $Q = 0{\cdot}45$ m³/s

∴ $P = 7{\cdot}848 \times 0{\cdot}45 \times 109{\cdot}72 =$ **387·48 kW (Ans.)**

Example 12.4. *Water is to be supplied to the inhabitants of a college campus through a supply main. The following data is given :*

Distance of the reservoir from the campus = 3000 m

Number of inhabitants = 4000

Consumption of water per day of each inhabitant = 180 litres

Loss of head due to friction = 18 m

Co-efficient of friction for the pipe, $f = 0{\cdot}007$

If the half of the daily supply is pumped in 8 hours, determine the size of the supply main.

Solution. Distance of the reservoir from the college campus = 3000 m

Number of inhabitants = 4000

Consumption per day per inhabitant = 180 litres = $0{\cdot}18$ m^3

$\therefore$ Total supply per day = $4000 \times 0{\cdot}18 = 720$ m^3

Since half of this supply is to be pumped in 8 hours, therefore maximum flow for which the pipe is to be designed,

$$Q = \frac{720}{2 \times 8 \times 3600} = 0.0125 \text{ m}^3/\text{s}$$

Loss of head due to friction, $h_f = 18$ m

Co-efficient of friction, $f = 0{\cdot}007$

Diameter of the supply line, *D* :

Using the relation :

$$h_f = \frac{4fLV^2}{D \times 2g}$$

where,
$$V = \frac{Q}{A} = \frac{0.0125}{\frac{\pi}{4} \times D^2} = \frac{0.0159}{D^2}$$

$$\therefore \quad 18 = \frac{4 \times 0.007 \times 3000 \times (0.159/D^2)^2}{D \times 2 \times 9.81}$$

or,
$$D^5 = \frac{4 \times 0.007 \times 3000 \times 0.0159^2}{18 \times 2 \times 9.81} = 6.013 \times 10^{-5}$$

$\therefore$ $D = 0{\cdot}143$ m or **143 mm (Ans.)**

Example 12.5. *Water flows through a pipeline whose diameter varies from 25 cm to 15 cm in a length of 10 m. If the Darcy-Weisbach friction factor is assumed constant at $0{\cdot}018$ for the whole pipe, determine the head loss in friction when the pipe is flowing full with a discharge of $0{\cdot}06$ m^3/s.*

Solution. *Given :* $D_1 = 25$ cm $= 0{\cdot}25$ m; $D_2 = 15$ cm $= 0{\cdot}15$ m, $L = 10$ m; $f = 0{\cdot}018$; $Q = 0{\cdot}06$ m^3/s

Consider a stretch of length dx at a distance x from the 25 cm diameter end (Fig. 12.1).

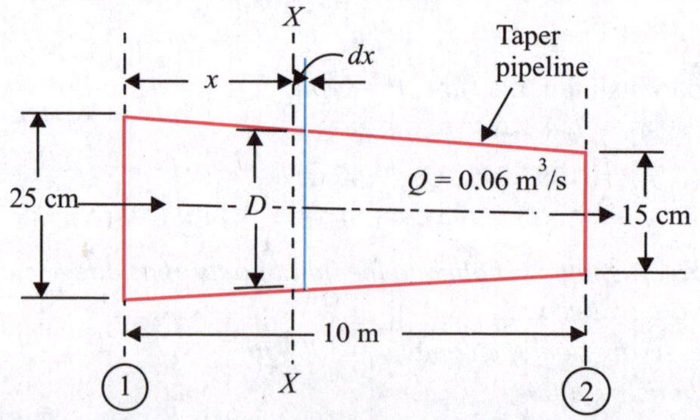

Fig. 12.1

$$dh_{fx} = \frac{fdxV^2}{D \times 2g}$$

$$= \frac{fdx\left[Q \div \left(\frac{\pi}{4} \times D^2\right)\right]^2}{D \times 2g} = \frac{fQ^2 dx}{2g\left(\frac{\pi}{4}\right)^2 D^5}$$

$$= 0.08263 \times \frac{fQ^2 dx}{D^5}$$

where, D = Diameter at the section XX

$$D = \left[0.25 - \left(\frac{0.25 - 0.15}{10}\right)x\right] = \frac{1}{100}(25 - x) \text{ m}$$

Hence, $$dh_{fx} = 0.08263 \times 0.018\,(0.06)^2 \times (100)^5 \times \frac{dx}{(25 - x)^5}$$

$$= 53544 \times \frac{dx}{(25 - x)^5}$$

Total head loss, $$h_f = \int_0^{10} dh_{fx}$$

$$= 53544 \int_0^{10} (25 - x)^{-5}\, dx = 53544 \left[\frac{1}{4\,(25 - x)^4}\right]_0^{10}$$

$$= \frac{53544}{4}\left[\frac{1}{(15)^4} - \frac{1}{(25)^4}\right] = \mathbf{0.23\ m}$$ **(Ans.)**

Example. 12.6. *A pipeline 50 cm diameter takes off from a reservoir whose water surface elevation is 145 m above datum. The pipe is 4500 m long and is laid completely at the datum level. In the last 1000 m of the pipe, water is withdrawn by a series of pipes at a uniform rate of 0·075 m^3/s per 250 m. Find the pressure at the end of the pipeline.*

Assume f (friction factor) = 0·018 and the pipe to have a dead end. **(UPSC)**

Solution. *Given* : Diameter of pipeline, D = 50 cm = 0·5 m; L = 4500 m; L_0 = 1000 m; f = 0·018.

First an expression for loss of head in a pipe having a uniform withdrawal of q^* m^3/s per metre length is derived.

Refer to Fig. 12.2. Consider a section at a distance x from the start of the uniform withdrawal at q^* per metre length.

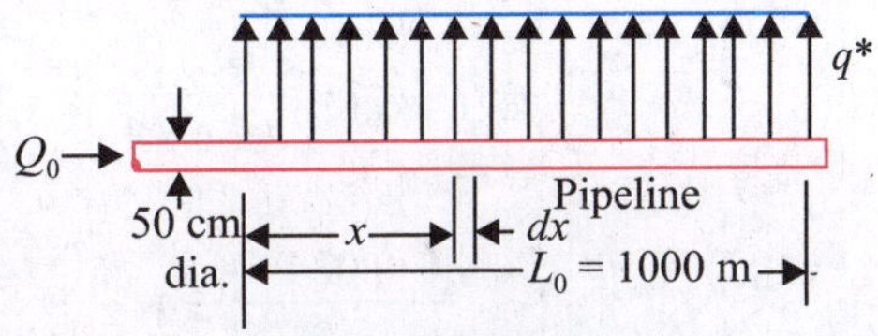

Fig. 12.2

Discharge, $Q_x = Q_0 - q^*x$

In a small distance dx,

$$dh_f = \frac{fLV^2}{D \times 2g} = \frac{f}{2g} \times \left(\frac{Q_0 - q^*x}{\frac{\pi}{4}D^2}\right)^2 \times \frac{1}{D} \times dx = \frac{8f}{\pi^2 g D^5}(Q_0 - q^*x)^2\, dx$$

$\therefore$ $$h_f = \int_0^{L_0} dh_f = \frac{-8f}{3\pi^2 g D^5} \times \frac{1}{q^*} \times \left[(Q_0 - q^*x)^3\right]_0^{L_0}$$

or, $$h_f = \frac{8f}{3\pi^2 gD^5} \times \frac{1}{q^*} \times \left[Q_0^3 - (Q_0 - q^*L_0)^3\right]$$

Here, $$Q_0 = \frac{1000}{250} \times 0.075 = 0.3 \text{ m}^3/\text{s}$$

$$q^* = \frac{0.075}{250} = 0.0003 \text{ m}^3/\text{s}$$

$$L_0 = 1000 \text{ m}$$

H_L = Total head lost = [Head lost in first (4500 – 1000) m with a discharge Q_d = 0·3 m^3/s] + [Head lost in 1000 m with a uniform withdrawal of q^*]

$$= h_{f1} + h_{f2}$$

$$h_{f1} = \frac{0.018 \times 3500 \times \left[0.3 \div \left(\frac{\pi}{4} \times 0.5\right)^2\right]^2}{0.5 \times 2 \times 9.81} = 24.3 \text{ m}$$

$$h_{f2} = \frac{8f}{3\pi^2 gD^5} \times \frac{1}{q^*} \times \left[Q_0^3 - (Q_0 - q^*L_0)^3\right]$$

$$= \frac{8 \times 0.018}{3\pi^2 \times 9.81 \times (0.5)^5} \times \frac{1}{0.0003}\left[(0.3)^3 - (0.3 - 0.0003 \times 1000)^3\right]$$

$$= 1·43 \text{ m}$$

Total head loss = 24·3 + 1·43 = 25·73 m

Residual head at the dead end = 145 – 25·73 = **119·27 m (Ans.)**

Example 12.7. *A pump delivers water from a tank A (water surface elevation = 110 m) to tank B (water surface elevation = 170 m). The suction pipe is 45 m long (friction factor, f = 0·024) and 35 cm in diameter. The delivery pipe is 950 m long (f = 0·022) and 25 cm in diameter. The head discharge relationship for the pump is given by H_p = (90 – 8000 Q^2), where H_p is in metres and Q in m^3/s. Calculate :*

(i) The discharge in the pipeline. *(ii) The power delivered by the pump.*

Solution. Refer to Fig. 12·3.

Given: D_1 = 35 cm = 0·35 m; L_1 = 45 m; D_2 = 25 cm = 0·25 m; L_2 = 950 m; f_1 = 0·024; f_2 = 0·022; $H_p = 90 - 8000\,Q^2$

Suction pipe :

Head loss, $$= h_{L1} = \frac{f_1 L_1 V_1^2}{D_1 \times 2g}$$

$$= \frac{0.024 \times 45}{0.35} \times \frac{V_1^2}{2g} = 3.086 \frac{V_1^2}{2g}$$

Delivery pipe :

Head loss, $$h_{L2} = \frac{f_2 L_2 V_2^2}{D_2 \times 2g}$$

$$= \frac{0.022 \times 950}{0.25} \times \frac{V_2^2}{2g} = 83.6 \frac{V_2^2}{2g}$$

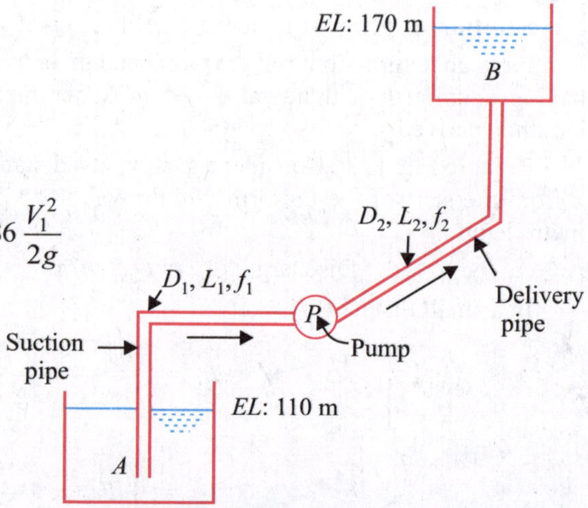

Fig. 12.3

$$\text{Total head loss, } H_L = 3.086\frac{V_1^2}{2g} + 83.6\frac{V_2^2}{2g}$$

By continuity equation,

$$A_1V_1 = A_2V_2$$

$$\frac{\pi}{4}\times(0.35)^2\times V_1 = \frac{\pi}{4}\times(0.25)^2\times V_2$$

or,

$$V_1 = 0{\cdot}51\,V_2$$

$$\frac{V_1^2}{2g} = 0.26\frac{V_2^2}{2g}$$

$$\therefore \quad H_L = 3.086\times 0.26\frac{V_2^2}{2g} + 83.6\frac{V_2^2}{2g} = 84.4\frac{V_2^2}{2g}$$

$$\text{Static head} = 170 - 110 = 60\text{ m}$$

H_P = Head delivered by the pump = Static head + friction head

$$= 60 + 84{\cdot}4\frac{V_2^2}{2g}$$

$$= 60 + 84.4\times\left(\frac{Q}{\frac{\pi}{4}\times(0.25)^2}\right)^2\times\frac{1}{2\times 9.81}$$

$$= 60 + 1785{\cdot}3\,Q^2$$

Also, $H_P = 90 - 8000\,Q^2$ ...(*Given*)

$$\therefore \quad 90 - 8000\,Q^2 = 60 + 1785{\cdot}3\,Q^2$$

or, $Q = 0{\cdot}05537\text{ m}^3/\text{s}$

$$\therefore \quad H_P = 60 + 1785{\cdot}3\times(0{\cdot}05537)^2 = 65{\cdot}47\text{ m}$$

Hence, power delivered by the pump,

$$\mathbf{P} = wQH_P = 9{\cdot}81\times 0{\cdot}05537\times 65{\cdot}47 = \mathbf{35{\cdot}56\ kW}\ \textbf{(Ans.)}$$

12.4. MINOR ENERGY LOSSES

Whereas the major loss of energy or head is due to friction, the minor loss of energy (or head) includes the following cases :

1. Loss of head due to sudden enlargement,
2. Loss of head due to sudden contraction,
3. Loss of head due to an obstruction in the pipe,
4. Loss of head at the entrance to a pipe,
5. Loss of head at the exit of a pipe,
6. Loss of head due to bend in the pipe, and
7. Loss of head in various pipe fittings.

12·4·1 Loss of Head due to Sudden Enlargement

Fig. 12·4. shows a liquid flowing through a pipe which has *sudden enlargement*. Due to sudden enlargement, the flow is decelerated abruptly and eddies are developed resulting in loss of energy (or head).

Consider two sections 1 – 1(before enlargement) and 2 – 2 (after enlargement).

Let, A_1 = Area of pipe at section 1–1.

$= \frac{\pi}{4} D_1^2$ (where D_1 is the diameter of the pipe),

p_1 = Intensity of pressure at section 1–1,

V_1 = Velocity of flow at section 1–1,

$A_2 \left(= \frac{\pi}{4} D_2^2\right)$, p_2 and V_2 = Corresponding values at section 2–2,

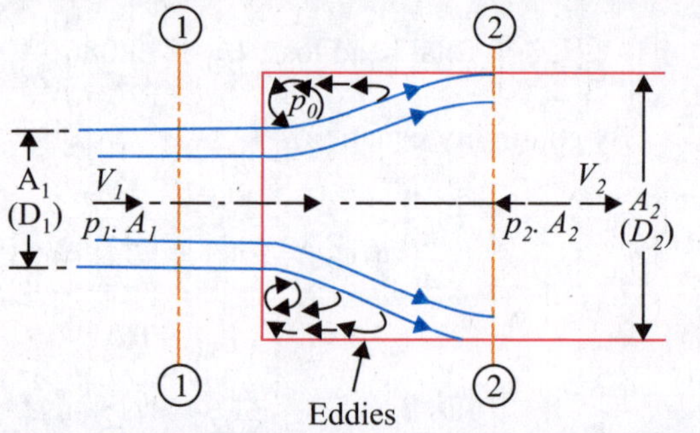

Fig. 12.4. Loss of head due to sudden enlargement.

p_0 = Intensity of pressure of the liquid eddies on the area $(A_2 - A_1)$, and

h_e = Loss of head due to sudden enlargement.

Applying Bernoulli's equation to sections 1–1 and 2–2, we have:

$$\frac{p_1}{w} + \frac{V_1^2}{2g} + z_1 = \frac{p_2}{w} + \frac{V_2^2}{2g} + z_2 + \text{Loss of head due to sudden enlargement } (h_e)$$

But, $z_1 = z_2$ ...pipe being horizontal

$$\therefore \quad \frac{p_1}{w} + \frac{V_1^2}{2g} = \frac{p_2}{w} + \frac{V_2^2}{2g} + h_e$$

or, $$h_e = \left(\frac{p_1}{w} - \frac{p_2}{w}\right) + \left(\frac{V_1^2}{2g} - \frac{V_2^2}{2g}\right) \quad ...(i)$$

Now, the force acting on liquid in the control volume (between sections 1–1 and 2–2) in the flow direction is given by :

$$F_x = p_1 \cdot A_1 + p_0 (A_2 - A_1) - p_2 \cdot A_2$$

Assuming $p_0 \simeq p_1$, we have:

$$F_x = p_1 \cdot A_1 + p_1 (A_2 - A_1) - p_2 \cdot A_2$$

$$= p_1 A_2 - p_2 A_2 = (p_1 - p_2) A_2 \quad ...(ii)$$

Consider **momentum** of liquid at the sections 1–1 and 2–2; momentum of liquid /sec at

section 1–1 = Mass × velocity.

$$= \rho A_1 V_1 \times V_1 = p A_1 V_1^2$$

Momentum of liquid/sec. at section 2–2 $= \rho A_2 V_2 \times V_2 = \rho A_2 V_2^2$

∴ Change of momentum of liquid/sec.

$$= \rho A_2 V_2^2 - \rho A_1 V_1^2$$

But from continuity equation, we have:

$$A_1 V_1 = A_2 V_2$$

or, $$A_1 = \frac{A_2 V_2}{V_1}$$

∴ Change of momentum/sec.

$$= \rho A_2 V_2^2 - \rho \times \frac{A_2 V_2}{V_1} \times V_1^2$$

$$= \rho A_2 V_2^2 - \rho A_2 V_1 V_2$$

$$= \rho A_2 (V_2^2 - V_1 V_2) \quad ...(iii)$$

Now, Net force = Change of momentum

$$\therefore \quad (p_1 - p_2) A_2 = \rho A_2 (V_2^2 - V_1 V_2)$$

or, $$\frac{p_1 - p_2}{\rho} = V_2^2 - V_1 V_2$$

Dividing both sides by g, we get:

$$\frac{p_1 - p_2}{\rho g} = \frac{V_2^2 - V_1 V_2}{g}$$

or, $$\frac{p_1}{w} - \frac{p_2}{w} = \frac{V_2^2 - V_1 V_2}{g} \qquad (\because \rho g = w)$$

Substituting the value of $\left(\frac{p_1}{w} - \frac{p_2}{w}\right)$ in eqn. (*i*), we get:

$$h_e = \frac{V_2^2 - V_1 V_2}{g} + \frac{V_1^2}{2g} - \frac{V_2^2}{2g}$$

$$= \frac{2V_2^2 - 2V_1V_2 + V_1^2 - V_2^2}{2g} = \frac{V_1^2 + V_2^2 - 2V_1V_2}{2g} = \frac{(V_1 - V_2)^2}{2g}$$

$$\therefore \quad h_e = \frac{(V_1 - V_2)^2}{2g} \qquad ...(12\cdot2)$$

Example 12.8. *At a sudden enlargement of a water main from 240 mm to 480 mm diameter, the hydraulic gradient rises by 10 mm. Calculate the rate of flow.* **[MDU, Haryana]**

Solution. Diameter of the smaller pipe, D_1 = 240 = mm = 0·24 m

Diameter of larger pipe, D_2 = 480 mm = 0·48 m

Rise of hydraulic gradient, *i.e.*

$$\left(\frac{p_2}{w} + z_2\right) - \left(\frac{p_1}{w} + z_1\right) = 10 \text{ mm} = 0\cdot01 \text{ m}$$

[The term $\left(\frac{p}{w} + z\right)$ prescribes the hydraulic gradient]

Rate of flow, Q:

Applying Bernoulli's equation to small and large pipe sections (1–1 and 2–2), we get:

$$\frac{p_1}{w} + \frac{V_1^2}{2g} + z_1 = \frac{p_2}{w} + \frac{V_2^2}{2g} + z_2 + h_e \text{ (i.e., head lost due to sudden enlargement)} \qquad ...(i)$$

But, $$h_e = \frac{(V_1 - V_2)^2}{2g} \qquad ...(ii)$$

From continuity equation, we have:

$$A_1 V_1 = A_2 V_2$$

$$\therefore \quad V_1 = \frac{A_2 V_2}{A_1} = \frac{\frac{\pi}{4} \times D_2^2}{\frac{\pi}{4} \times D_1^2} \times V_2 = \left(\frac{D_2}{D_1}\right)^2 \times V_2$$

or, $$V_1 = \left(\frac{0.48}{0.24}\right)^2 \times V_2 = 4V_2$$

Substituting this value of V_1 in eqn. (*ii*), we get:

$$h_e = \frac{(4V_2 - V_2)^2}{2g} = \frac{9V_2^2}{2g}$$

Now, substituting the values of he and V_1 in eqn. (*i*), we have:

$$\frac{p_1}{w} + \frac{(4V_2)^2}{2g} + z_1 = \frac{p_2}{w} + \frac{V_2^2}{2g} + z_2 + \frac{9V_2^2}{2g}$$

or,
$$\frac{16V_2^2}{2g} - \frac{V_2^2}{2g} - \frac{9V_2^2}{2g} = \left(\frac{p_2}{w} + z_2\right) - \left(\frac{p_1}{w} + z_1\right)$$

or,
$$\frac{6V_2^2}{2g} = 0.01$$

or,
$$V_2 = \left(\frac{0.01 \times 2 \times 9.81}{6}\right)^{1/2} = 0.181 \text{ m/s}$$

$\therefore$ Rate of flow, $Q = A_2V_2 = \frac{\pi}{4} \times 0.48^2 \times 0.181 =$ **0.03275 m³/s (Ans.)**

Example 12.9. *A horizontal pipe 150 mm in diameter is joined by sudden enlargement to a 225 mm diameter pipe. Water is flowing through it at the rate of 0·05 m³/s. Find :*

(i) Loss of head due to abrupt expansion,

(ii) Pressure difference in the two pipes, and

(iii) Change in pressure if the change of section is gradual without any loss.

Solution. Diameter of the smaller pipe, D_1 = 150 mm = 0·15 m

$\therefore$ Area, $A_1 = \frac{\pi}{4} \times 0.15^2 = 0.01767 \text{ m}^2$

Diameter of the larger pipe, D_2 = 225 mm = 0·225 m

$\therefore$ Area, $A_2 = \frac{\pi}{4} \times 0.225^2 = 0.03976 \text{ m}^2$

Discharge, Q = 0·05 m³/s

(*i*) Loss of head due to abrupt expansion, h_e :

$$h_e = \frac{(V_1 - V_2)^2}{2g}$$

where, V_1 and V_2 are the velocities of flow in the smaller and larger diameter pipes respectively.

$$V_1 = \frac{Q}{A_1} = \frac{0.05}{0.01767} = 2.83 \text{ m/s}$$

$$V_2 = \frac{Q}{A_2} = \frac{0.05}{0.03976} = 1.26 \text{ m/s}$$

Hence,
$$h_e = \frac{(2.83 - 1.26)^2}{2 \times 9.81} = \mathbf{0.1256 \text{ m}} \textbf{ (Ans.)}$$

(*ii*) Pressure difference in the two pipes :

Applying Bernoulli's equation at the smaller and the larger pipe sections, we get:

$$\frac{p_1}{w} + \frac{V_1^2}{2g} + z_1 = \frac{p_2}{w} + \frac{V_2^2}{2g} + z_2 + h_e$$

or,
$$\left(\frac{p_2 - p_1}{w}\right) = \frac{V_1^2 - V_2^2}{2g} - h_e \qquad [\because z_1 = z_2, \text{ the pipe being horizontal}]$$

or, $$\left(\frac{p_2 - p_1}{w}\right) = \frac{2.83^2 - 1.26^2}{2 \times 9.81} - 0.1256 = \mathbf{0.202 \text{ m of water}} \text{ (Ans.)}$$

The positive sign indicates that there is *gain* in pressure. Thus, although there is an energy loss, the pressure increases across a sudden flow of expansion.

(*iii*) Change in pressure with gradual change of section :

If the change of section is gradual *without loss,* then, gain in pressure,

$$\frac{p_2 - p_1}{w} = \frac{V_1^2 - V_2^2}{2g} = \frac{2.83^2 - 1.26^2}{2 \times 9.81} = \mathbf{0.327 \text{ m of water}} \text{ (Ans.)}$$

Example 12.10. *The diameter of a horizontal pipe which is 300 mm is suddenly enlarged to 600 mm. The rate of flow of water through this pipe is 0·4 m³/s. If the intensity of pressure in the smaller pipe is 125 kN/m², determine.*

(*i*) *Loss of head, due to sudden enlargement,*

(*ii*) *Intensity of pressure in the larger pipe, and*

(*iii*) *Power lost due to enlargement.*

Solution. Diameter of the smaller pipe, D_1 = 300 mm = 0·03 m

$$\text{Area, } A_1 = \frac{\pi}{4} \times 0.3^2 = 0.0707 \text{ m}^2$$

Diameter of the longer pipe, D_2 = 600 mm = ·06 m

$$\text{Area, } A_2 = \frac{\pi}{4} \times 0.06^2 = 0.2828 \text{ m}^2$$

Rate of flow of water, Q = 0·4 m³/s

Intensity of pressure in the smaller pipe, p_1 = 125 kN/m²

$$\text{Now velocity, } V_1 = \frac{Q}{A_1} = \frac{0.4}{0.0707} = 5.66 \text{ m/s}$$

$$\text{Velocity, } V_2 = \frac{Q}{A_2} = \frac{0{\cdot}4}{0{\cdot}2828} = 1.414 \text{ m/s}$$

(*i*) Loss of head due to sudden enlargement, h_e :

Loss of head due to sudden enlargement,

$$h_e = \frac{(V_1 - V_2)^2}{2g}$$

$$= \frac{(5.66 - 1.414)^2}{2 \times 9.81} = \mathbf{0.918 \text{ m}} \text{ (Ans.)}$$

(*ii*) Intensity of pressure in the large pipe, p_2 :

Applying Bernoulli's equation before and after sudden enlargement, we get:

$$\frac{p_1}{w} + \frac{V_1^2}{2g} + z_1 = \frac{p_2}{w} + \frac{V_2^2}{2g} + z_2 + h_e$$

But, $z_1 = z_2$ ...because pipe is horizontal

$$\therefore \quad \frac{p_1}{w} + \frac{V_1^2}{2g} = \frac{p_2}{w} + \frac{V_2^2}{2g} + h_e$$

or, $$\frac{p_2}{w} = \frac{p_1}{w} + \frac{V_1^2}{2g} - \frac{V_2^2}{2g} - h_e$$

$$= \frac{125}{9.81} + \frac{5.66^2}{2 \times 9.81} - \frac{1.414^2}{2 \times 9.81} - 0.918$$

$$= 12{\cdot}74 + 1{\cdot}63 - 0{\cdot}1 - 0{\cdot}918 = 13{\cdot}35 \text{ m}$$

$$\therefore \quad p_2 = w \times 13{\cdot}35 = 9{\cdot}81 \times 13{\cdot}35$$

$$= \mathbf{130{\cdot}9 \ kN/m^2} \quad \textbf{(Ans.)}$$

(*iii*) Power lost due to sudden enlargement, P_{lost} :

$$P_{lost} = \frac{wQh_e}{1000} \ kW$$

where, $w = 9.81 \times 1000 \text{ N/m}^2$,

$Q = 0.4 \text{ m}^3/\text{s}$, and

$h_e = 0{\cdot}918$ m

$$\therefore \quad P_{lost} = \frac{(9.81 \times 1000) \times 0.4 \times 0.918}{1000}$$

$$= \mathbf{3.6 \ kW} \quad \textbf{(Ans.)}$$

Example 12.11. *In a 80 mm diameter pipeline an oil of specific gravity 0·8 is flowing at the rate of 0·0125 m³/s. A sudden expansion takes place into a second pipeline of such diameter that maximum pressure rise is obtained. Find :*

(*i*) *Loss of energy in sudden expansion,*

(*ii*) *Differential gauge length indicated by an oil-mercury manometer connected between the two pipes.* **[PTU]**

Solution. Diameter of the smaller pipe, $D_1 = 80 \text{ mm} = 0{\cdot}08$ m

Specific gravity of oil, $S = 0{\cdot}8$

Discharge, $Q = 0{\cdot}0125 \text{ m}^3/\text{s}$.

(*i*) Loss of energy in sudden expansion :

$$\text{Velocity of flow, } V = \frac{Q}{\text{Area}} = \frac{0.0125}{\frac{\pi}{4} \times 0.08^2} = 2.49 \text{ m/s}$$

The *pressure rise will be maximum* when:

$$\frac{D_1}{D_2} = \frac{1}{\sqrt{2}} \qquad \text{(where, } D_2 = \text{diameter of the larger pipe)}$$

[For derivation of the formula, refer to Example 12·12]

or, $$D_2 = \sqrt{2}\, D_1 = \sqrt{2} \times 0.08 = 0.1131 \text{ m}$$

$$\therefore \quad V_2 = \frac{0.0125}{\frac{\pi}{4} \times (0.1131)^2} = 1.244 \text{ m/s}$$

Loss of energy (or head) in sudden expansion,

$$h_2 = \frac{(V_1 - V_2)^2}{2g} = \frac{(2.49 - 1.244)^2}{2 \times 9.81} = \mathbf{0.079 \ m \ of \ oil} \quad \textbf{(Ans.)}$$

(*iii*) Reading of the manometer :

The energy equation is given as:

$$\frac{p_1}{w} + \frac{V_1^2}{2g} + z_1 = \frac{p_2}{w} + \frac{V_2^2}{2g} + z_2 + h_e \qquad (z_1 = z_2, \text{ the pipe being horizontal})$$

$$\left(\frac{p_2 - p_1}{w}\right) = \frac{V_1^2}{2g} - \frac{V_2^2}{2g} - h_e$$

$$= \frac{2.49^2}{2 \times 9.81} - \frac{1.244^2}{2 \times 9.81} - 0.079 = 0.158 \text{ of oil}$$

Let, h = Reading of the U-tube oil-mercury manometer where limbs are connected across the expanded transition:

Then, $$\frac{p_2 - p_1}{w} = h\left(\frac{S_m}{S_0} - 1\right)$$

[where, S_m = specific gravity of mercury (= 13·6)]

or, $$0.158 = h\left(\frac{13.6}{0.8} - 1\right) = 16\,h$$

or, $$h = \frac{0.158}{16} = 0.009875 \text{ m} \quad \text{or} \quad \mathbf{9{\cdot}875\ mm}$$ **(Ans.)**

Example 12.12. *For sudden expansion in a pipe flow, work out the optimum ratio between the diameter of the pipe before expansion and the diameter of pipe after expansion so that pressure rise is maximum ? Also find the maximum pressure rise.* **(UPSC Exams.)**

Solution. Applying Bernoulli's equation at sections 1 – 1 and 2 – 2, we have:

$$\frac{p_1}{w} + \frac{V_1^2}{2g} + z_1 = \frac{p_2}{w} + \frac{V_2^2}{2g} + z_2 + h_e$$

where, h_e (energy loss due to sudden expansion) $= \dfrac{(V_1 - V_2)^2}{2g}$

$$\therefore \quad \frac{p_1}{w} + \frac{V_1^2}{2g} = \frac{p_2}{w} + \frac{V_2^2}{2g} + \frac{(V_1 - V_2)^2}{2g} \quad (\because z_1 = z_2, \text{ the pipe being horizontal})$$

$$\text{Pressure rise, } \Delta p = (p_2 - p_1) = w\left[\frac{V_1^2}{2g} - \frac{V_2^2}{2g} - \frac{(V_1 - V_2)^2}{2g}\right]$$

From continuity consideration,

$$A_1 V_1 = A_2 V_2$$

$$V_2 = \frac{A_1 V_1}{A_2} = \left(\frac{D_1}{D_2}\right)^2 V_1$$

$$\therefore \quad \Delta p = w \times \frac{V_1^2}{2g}\left[1 - \left(\frac{D_1}{D_2}\right)^4 - \left\{1 - \left(\frac{D_1}{D_2}\right)^2\right\}^2\right]$$

or $$\Delta p = w \times \frac{V_1^2}{2g}\left[2\left(\frac{D_1}{D_2}\right)^2 - 2\left(\frac{D_1}{D_2}\right)^4\right]$$

There is only one value or ratio $\left(\dfrac{D_1}{D_2}\right)$ which will provide the maximum pressure rise.

$\therefore$ For maximum pressure rise, $\dfrac{d\,(\Delta p)}{d\,(D_1/D_2)} = 0$

or, $$\frac{d\,(\Delta p)}{d\,(D_1/D_2)} = \left[4\left(\frac{D_1}{D_2}\right) - 8\left(\frac{D_1}{D_2}\right)^3\right] = 0$$

From which $\left(\frac{D_1}{D_2}\right)^2 = \frac{1}{2}$ or $\frac{D_1}{D_2} = \frac{1}{\sqrt{2}}$

∴ *Diameter ratio for the maximum pressure rise is:*

$$\boldsymbol{\frac{D_1}{D_2} = \frac{1}{\sqrt{2}}} \textbf{ (Ans.)}$$

Maximum pressure rise is:

$$(\Delta p)_{max} = w \times \frac{V_1^2}{2g}\left[2 \times \left(\frac{1}{\sqrt{2}}\right)^2 - 2\left(\frac{1}{\sqrt{2}}\right)^4\right]$$

$$= \frac{wV_1^2}{2g}(1 - 0.5) = \boldsymbol{\frac{0.5wV_1^2}{2g}} \textbf{ (Ans.)}$$

12·4·2. Loss of Head due to Sudden Contraction

Due to sudden contraction, the stream lines converge to a minimum cross-section called the *vena-contracta* and then expand to fill the downstream pipe (Fig. 12·5.)

Let, A_c = Area of flow at section C–C,

V_c = Velocity of flow at section C–C,

A_2 = Area of flow at section 2–2,

V_2 = Velocity of flow at section 2–2, and

h_c = Loss of head due to sudden contraction.

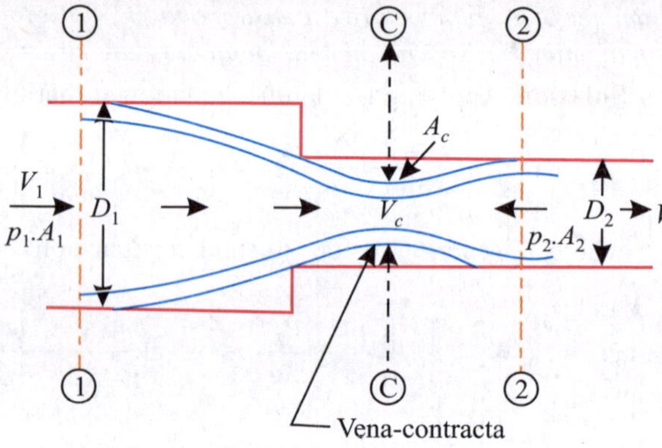

Fig. 12.5

Loss of head due to sudden contraction = Loss up to vena-contracta + loss due to sudden enlargement beyond vena-contracta

or, $$h_c = \text{Negligibly small} + \frac{(V_c - V_2)^2}{2g} \quad ...(i)$$

From continuity equation, we have:

$$A_c V_c = A_2 V_2$$

or, $$\frac{V_c}{V_2} = \frac{A_2}{A_c} = \frac{1}{(A_c / A_2)} = \frac{1}{C_c} \quad \left(\because C_c = \frac{A_c}{A_2}\right)$$

or, $$V_c = \frac{V_2}{C_c}$$

Substituting the value of V_c in eqn. (*i*), we get:

$$h_c = \frac{\left(\frac{V_2}{C_c} - V_2\right)^2}{2g} = \frac{V_2^2}{2g}\left(\frac{1}{C_c} - 1\right)^2$$

i.e., $$\boldsymbol{h_c = \frac{V_2^2}{2g}\left(\frac{1}{C_c} - 1\right)^2} \quad ...(12·3)$$

In general, $$h_c = k \frac{V_2^2}{2g}$$

where, $$k = \left(\frac{1}{C_c} - 1\right)^2$$

From experiments : $C_c = 0.62 + 0.38\left(\frac{A_2}{A_1}\right)^3$

and thus the loss co-efficient k is a function of ratio

$$\frac{A_1}{A_2} \text{ or } \frac{D_2}{D_1}$$

and, $k = 0{\cdot}375$ for $C_c = 0{\cdot}62$.

For gradual contraction (conical reducers) k is a function of cone angle and $\simeq 0{\cdot}1$.

Note : If the value of C_c is not given then loss of head due to contraction may be taken as $0{\cdot}5 \frac{V_2^2}{2g}$

i.e., $$h_e = 0.5 \frac{V_2^2}{2g} \quad ...(12{\cdot}4)$$

Example 12.13. *A horizontal pipe carries water at the rate of 0·04 m³/s. Its diameter, which is 300 mm reduces abruptly to 150 mm. Calculate the pressure loss across the contraction. Take the co-efficient of contraction = 0·62.*

Solution. Diameter of the large pipe, $D_1 = 300 \text{ mm} = 0{\cdot}3 \text{ m}$

$\therefore$ Area, $A_1 = \frac{\pi}{4} \times 0.3^2 = 0.0707 \text{ m}^2$

Diameter of the small pipe, $D_2 = 150 \text{ mm} = 0{\cdot}15 \text{ m}$

$\therefore$ Area, $A_2 = \frac{\pi}{4} \times 0.15^2 = 0.1767 \text{ m}^2$

Discharge, $Q = 0{\cdot}04 \text{ m}^3/\text{s}$.

Co-efficient of contraction, $C_c = 0{\cdot}62$

Pressure loss across the contraction, $(p_1 - p_2)$:

From continuity equation, we have:

$$A_1V_1 = A_2V_2 = Q$$

$$\therefore \quad V_1 = \frac{Q}{A_1} = \frac{0.04}{0.0707} = 0.566 \text{ m/s}$$

and, $$V_2 = \frac{Q}{A_2} = \frac{0.04}{0.01767} = 2.26 \text{ m/s}$$

Applying Bernoulli's equation before and after contraction, we get:

$$\frac{p_1}{w} + \frac{V_1^2}{2g} + z_1 = \frac{p_2}{w} + \frac{V_2^2}{2g} + z_2 + h_c \quad ...(i)$$

But, $z_1 = z_2$ ...because the pipe is horizontal and head loss due to contraction (h_c) is given as :

$$h_c = \left[\frac{1}{C_c} - 1\right]^2 \frac{V_2^2}{2g} = \left[\frac{1}{0.62} - 1\right]^2 \times \frac{2.26^2}{2 \times 9.81} = 0.0978$$

Substituting these values in eqn. (*i*), we get:

$$\frac{p_1}{w} + \frac{0.566^2}{2 \times 9.81} = \frac{p_2}{w} + \frac{2.26^2}{2 \times 9.81} + 0.0978$$

$$\therefore \quad \frac{p_1}{w} - \frac{p_2}{w} = \frac{2.26^2}{2 \times 9.81} + 0.0978 - \frac{0.566^2}{2 \times 9.81}$$

$$= 0{\cdot}26 + 0{\cdot}0978 - 0{\cdot}016 = 0{\cdot}3418$$

Hence, $p_1 - p_2 = w \times 0{\cdot}3418 = 9{\cdot}81 \times 0{\cdot}3418$

$= \mathbf{3{\cdot}35\ kN/m^2}$ **(Ans.)**

Example 12.14. *A pipe of diameter 225 mm is attached to a 150 mm diameter pipe by means of a flange in such a manner that the axes of the two pipes are in a straight line. Water flows through the arrangement at the rate of 0·05 m^3/s. The pressure loss at the transition as indicated by differential gauge length on a water-mercury manometer connected between two pipes equals 35 mm. Calculate :*

(i) *The loss of head due to contraction, and*

(ii) *The co-efficient of contraction.*

Solution. Diameter of the large pipe, D_1 = 225 mm = 0·225 m

$\therefore$ Area, $A_1 = \frac{\pi}{4} \times 0.225^2 = 0.03976\ m^2$

Diameter of the small pipe, D_2 = 150 mm = 0·15 m

$\therefore$ Area, $A_2 = \frac{\pi}{4} \times 0.15^2 = 0.01767\ m^2$

Discharge, $Q = 0{\cdot}05\ m^3/s$

Reading of the differential gauge, h = 35 mm = 0·035 m

(*i*) Loss of head due to contraction h_c :

When the water-mercury manometer is connected across the contracted transition, then

$$\frac{p_1 - p_2}{w} = h\left(\frac{S_m}{S_w} - 1\right)$$

where, S_m = Sp. gr. of mercury (= 13·6), and

S_w = Sp. gr. of water (= 1).

Substituting the values in the above eqn., we get:

$$\frac{p_1 - p_2}{w} = 0.035\left(\frac{13.6}{1.0} - 1\right) = 0.441 \text{ m}$$

Let V_1 and V_2 be the velocities of flow in the large diameter and small diameter pipes respectively, then:

$$V_1 = \frac{Q}{A_1} = \frac{0.05}{0.03976} = 1.26 \text{ m/s, and}$$

$$V_2 = \frac{Q}{A_2} = \frac{0.05}{0.01767} = 2.83 \text{ m/s}$$

Invoking Bernoulli's equation, we have:

$$\frac{p_1}{w} + \frac{V_1^2}{2g} + z_1 = \frac{p_2}{w} + \frac{V_2^2}{2g} + z_2 + h_c$$

[where, h_c = head loss due to contraction, and $z_1 = z_2$ ....the pipe being horizontal]

or, $$h_c = \left(\frac{p_1 - p_2}{w}\right) + \frac{V_1^2 - V_2^2}{2g}$$

$$= 0.441 + \frac{(1.26)^2 - (2.83)^2}{2 \times 9.81} = \textbf{0.114 m of water (Ans.)}$$

(ii) The co-efficient of contraction, C_c :

The loss of head due to contraction is given by:

$$h_c = \left(\frac{1}{C_c} - 1\right)^2 \times \frac{V_2^2}{2g}$$

or,
$$0.114 = \left(\frac{1}{C_c} - 1\right)^2 \times \frac{2.83^2}{2 \times 9.81}$$

From which, C_c = **0·65 (Ans.)**

Example 12.15. *When a sudden contraction is introduced in a horizontal pipeline from 500 mm diameter to 250 mm diameter, the pressure changes from 105 kN/m² to 69 kN/m². If the co-efficient of contraction is assumed to be 0·65, calculate the water flow rate.*

Following this if there is sudden enlargement from 250 mm to 500 mm and if the pressure at the 250 mm section is 69 kN/m², what is the pressure at the 500 mm enlarged portion ? **[Roorkee University]**

Solution. Diameter of the large pipe, D_1 = 500 m = 0·5 m

$\therefore$ Area, $A_1 = \frac{\pi}{4} \times 0.5^2 = 0.1963 \text{ m}^3$

Diameter fo the small pipe, D_2 = 250 mm = 0·025 m

$\therefore$ Area, $A_2 = \frac{\pi}{4} \times 0.25^2 = 0.04908 \text{ m}^2$

Pressure inside the large pipe, p_1 = 105 kN/m²

Pressure inside the small pipe, p_2 = 69 kN/m²

Co-efficient of contraction, C_c = 0·65

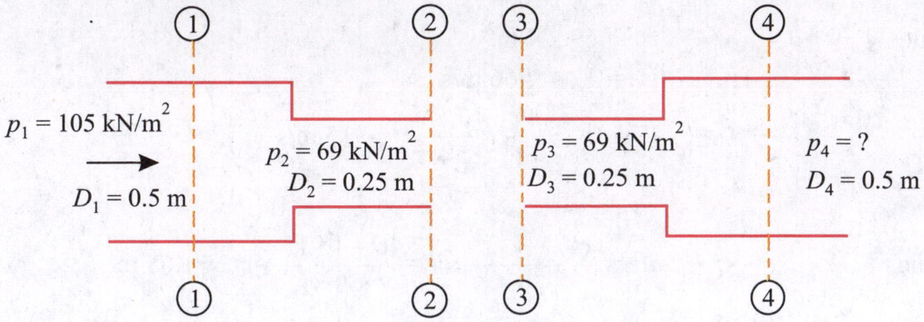

Fig. 12.6

(i) Flow rate, Q :

Head lost due to contraction is given by:

$$h_c = \frac{V_2^2}{2g}\left(\frac{1}{0.65} - 1.0\right)^2 = \frac{V_2^2}{2g}\left[\frac{1}{0.65} - 1.0\right]^2 \qquad \text{[Eqn. (12·3)]}$$

$$= 0.2899 \frac{V_2^2}{2g} \qquad ...(i)$$

From continuity considerations, we have:

$$A_1 V_1 = A_2 V_2$$

$$V_1 = \frac{A_2}{A_1} \times V_2 = \frac{(\pi/4) \times D_2^2}{(\pi/4) \times D_1^2} \times V_2$$

or, $$V_1 = \left(\frac{0.25}{0.50}\right)^2 \times V_2 = \frac{V_2}{4}$$

Applying Bernoulli's equation at 1-1 and 2-2, we get:

$$\frac{p_1}{w} + \frac{V_1^2}{2g} + z_1 = \frac{p_2}{w} + \frac{V_2^2}{2g} + z_2 + h_c$$

But, $z_1 = z_2$ ...the pipe being horizontal.

$$\therefore \quad \frac{p_1}{w} + \frac{V_1^2}{2g} = \frac{p_2}{w} + \frac{V_2^2}{2g} + h_c$$

Substituting the values, we get:

$$\frac{105}{9.81} + \frac{(V_2/4)^2}{2 \times 9.81} = \frac{69}{9.81} + \frac{V_2^2}{2 \times 9.81} + 0.2899 \frac{V_2^2}{2 \times 9.81}$$

or, $$210 + \frac{V_2^2}{16} = 138 + V_2^2 + 0.2899\, V_2^2$$

or, $$72 = 1.2899\, V_2^2 - \frac{V_2^2}{16} = 1.2274\, V_2^2$$

$$V_2 = 7{\cdot}66 \text{ m/s}$$

Hence, rate of flow, $Q = A_2V_2 = 0{\cdot}04908 \times 7{\cdot}66 = \mathbf{0{\cdot}376\ m^3/s}$ **(Ans.)**

(*ii*) **Pressure at the enlarged section, p_4 :**

Applying Bernoulli's equation at the sections 3-3 and 4-4, we get:

$$\frac{p_3}{w} + \frac{V_3^2}{2g} + z_3 = \frac{p_4}{w} + \frac{V_4^2}{2g} + z_4 + h_e \text{ (loss of head due to sudden enlargement)}$$

But, $p_3 = 69 \text{ kN/m}^2$

$$V_3 = V_2 = 7{\cdot}66 \text{ m/s}$$

$$V_4 = V_1 = \frac{V_2}{4} = \frac{7.66}{4} = 1.915 \text{ m/s}$$

$$z_3 = z_4$$

And, $$h_e = \frac{(V_3 - V_4)^2}{2g} = \frac{(7.66 - 1.915)^2}{2 \times 9.81} \text{ m} = 1.68 \text{ m}$$

Substituting the values in the above equation, we get:

$$\frac{69}{9.81} + \frac{7.66^2}{2 \times 9.81} = \frac{p_4}{9.81} + \frac{(1.915)^2}{2 \times 9.81} + 1.68$$

$$7.033 + 2.99 = \frac{p_4}{9.81} + 0.187 + 1.68$$

or, $p_4 = \mathbf{80\ kN/m^2}$ **(Ans.)**

12·4·3 Loss of Head due to Obstruction in Pipe

Refer to Fig. 12·7. The loss of energy due to an obstruction in pipe takes place on account of the reduction in the cross-sectional area of the pipe by the presence of obstruction which is followed by an abrupt enlargement of the stream beyond the obstruction.

Head loss due to obstruction ($h_{obs.}$) is given by the relation :

$$h_{obs.} = \left[\frac{A}{C_c (A-a)}\right]^2 \frac{V^2}{2g} \quad ...(12.5)$$

where, A = Area of the pipe,

a = Maximum area of obstruction, and

V = Velocity of liquid in pipe.

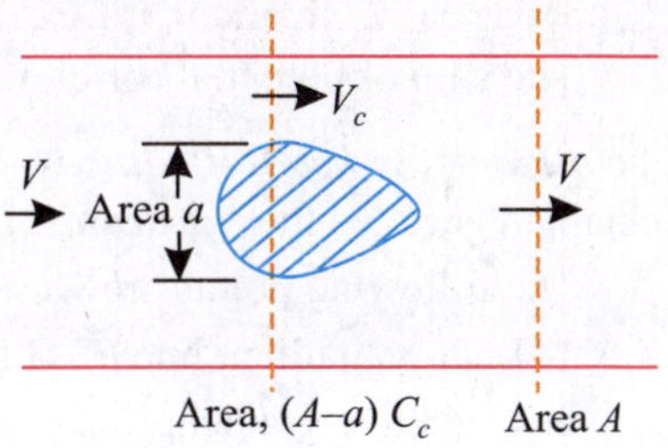

Fig. 12.7

12·4·4 Loss of Head at the Entrance to Pipe

Loss of head at the entrance to pipe (h_i) is given by the relation :

$$h_i = 0.5 \frac{V^2}{2g} \quad ...(12.6)$$

where, V = Velocity of liquid in pipe.

12·4·5 Loss of Head at the Exit of a Pipe

Loss of head at the exit of a pipe is denoted by h_0 and is given by the relation:

$$h_0 = \frac{V^2}{2g} \quad ...(12.7)$$

where, V = Velocity at outlet of pipe.

12·4·6 Loss of Head due to Bend in the Pipe

In general the loss of head in bends (h_b) provided in pipes may be expressed as :

$$h_0 = k \frac{V^2}{2g} \quad ...(12.8)$$

where, V = Mean velocity of flow of fluid, and

and, k = Co-efficient of bend; it depends upon *angle of bend, radius of curvature of bend* and *diameter of pipe.*

12·4·7 Loss of Head in Various Pipe Fittings

The loss of head in the various pipe fittings (such as valves, couplings, etc.) may also be represented as :

$$h_{\text{fittings}} = k \frac{V^2}{2g}$$

where, V = Mean velocity flow in the pipe, and k = value of the co-efficient; it depends on the type of the pipe fitting.

12.5. HYDRAULIC GRADIENT AND TOTAL ENERGY LINES

The concept of hydraulic gradient line and total energy line is quite useful in the study of flow of fluid in pipes. These lines may be obtained as indicated below.

Total Energy Line (T.E.L. or E.G.L.):

It is known that the *total head* (which is also total energy per unit weight) with respect to any arbitrary datum, is the sum of the elevation (potential) head, pressure head and velocity head, *i.e.,*

$$\text{Total head} = \frac{p}{w} + z + \frac{V^2}{2g}$$

When the fluid flows along the pipe, there is loss of head (energy) and the total energy decreases in the direction of flow. If the total energy at various points along the axis of the pipe is plotted and joined by a line, the line so obtained is called the **'*Energy gradient line*' (E.G.L.).**

In literature, energy gradient line (E.G.L.) is *also known as* **'*Total energy line*' (*T.E.L.*).**

Hydraulic Gradient Line (H.G.L.):

The sum of potential (or elevation) head and the pressure head $\left(\frac{p}{w}+z\right)$ at any point is called the *piezometric head. If a line is drawn joining the piezometric levels at various points,* the line so obtained is called the ***'Hydraulic gradient line.'***

The following points are worth noting :

1. Energy gradient line (E.G.L.) *always drops in the direction of flow because of loss of head.*
2. Hydraulic gradient line (H.G.L.) may *rise* or *fall* depending on the pressure changes.
3. Hydraulic gradient line (H.G.L.) is *always below the energy gradient line (E.G.L.)* and the vertical intercept between the two is equal to the velocity head $\left(\frac{V^2}{2g}\right)$.
4. For a pipe of *uniform cross-section the slope of the hydraulic gradient line is equal to the slope of energy gradient line.*
5. *There is no relation whatsoever between the slope of energy gradient line and the slope of the axis of the pipe.*

Example 12.16. *A horizontal pipe line 40 m long is connected to a water tank at one end and discharges freely into the atmosphere at the other end. For the first 25 m of its length from the tank, the pipe is 150 mm diameter and its diameter is suddenly enlarged to 300 mm. The height of water level in the tank is 8 m above the centre of the pipe. Considering all losses of head which occur,*

(i) Determine the rate of flow.

(ii) Draw the hydraulic gradient and energy gradient lines. Take f = 0·01 for both sections of the pipe. **[M.U.]**

Solution. Total length of the horizontal pipeline, L = 40 m.

Length of first pipe L_1 = 25 m

Diameter of first pipe D_1 = 50 mm = 0·15 m

Length of second pipe, L_2 = 40 – 25 = 15 m

Diameter of second pipe, D_2 = 00 mm = 0·3 m

Height of water, H = 8 m

Co-efficient of friction, f = 0·01

(i) Rate of flow, Q :

Applying Bernoulli's equation to the free water surface (F.W.S.) in the tank and outlet of the pipe as shown in Fig. 12·8., we get:

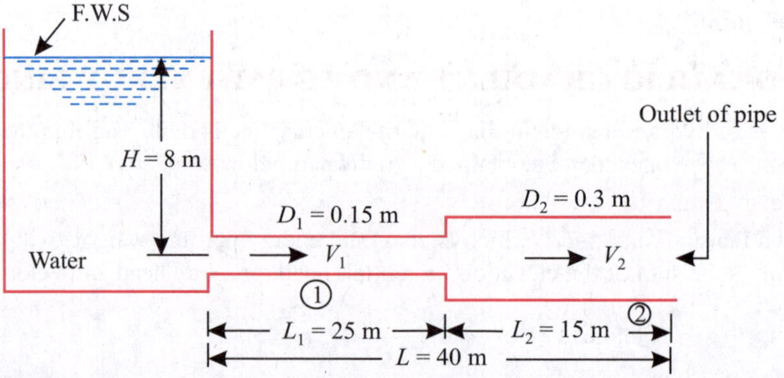

Fig. 12.8

$$\frac{p_1}{w}+\frac{V_1^2}{2g}+z_1 = \frac{p_2}{w}+\frac{V_2^2}{2g}+z_2+\text{all losses}$$

$$0 + 0 + 8.0 = 0 + \frac{V_2^2}{2g} + 0 + h_i + h_{f_1} + h_e + h_{f_2} \quad ...(i)$$

where, V_2 = Velocity of water at the outlet of pipe,

h_i = Loss of head at entrance $= 0.5\,\frac{V_1^2}{2g}$,

h_{f_1} = Head lost due to friction in pipe 1 $= \frac{4fL_1V_1^2}{D_1 \times 2g}$,

h_e = Loss of head due to sudden enlargement $= \frac{(V_1 - V_2)^2}{2g}$, and

h_{f_2} = Head lost due to friction in pipe 2 $= \frac{4fL_2V_2^2}{D_2 \times 2g}$

From continuity equation, we have:

$$A_1V_1 = A_2V_2$$

$$\therefore \quad V_1 = \frac{A_2V_2}{A_1} = \frac{(\pi/4) \times D_2^2 \times V_2}{(\pi/4) \times D_1^2}$$

$$= \left(\frac{D_2}{D_1}\right)^2 \times V_2 = \left(\frac{0{\cdot}3}{0{\cdot}15}\right)^2 \times V_2 = 4V_2$$

Substituting the value of V_1 in different head losses, we have:

$$h_1 = \frac{0.5\,V_1^2}{2g} = \frac{0.5\,(4 \times V_2)^2}{2g} = \frac{8V_2^2}{2g}$$

$$h_{f_1} = \frac{4fL_1V_1^2}{D_1 \times 2g} = \frac{4 \times 0.01 \times 25 \times (4 \times V_2)^2}{0.15 \times 2g} = 106.6\,\frac{V_2^2}{2g}$$

$$h_e = \frac{(V_1 - V_2)^2}{2g} = \frac{(4V_2 - V_2)^2}{2g} = \frac{9V_2^2}{2g}$$

$$h_{f_2} = \frac{4fL_2V_2^2}{D_2 \times 2g} = \frac{4 \times 0.01 \times 15 \times V_2^2}{0.3 \times 2g} = \frac{2V_2^2}{2g}$$

Substituting the values of these losses in eqn. (*i*), we get:

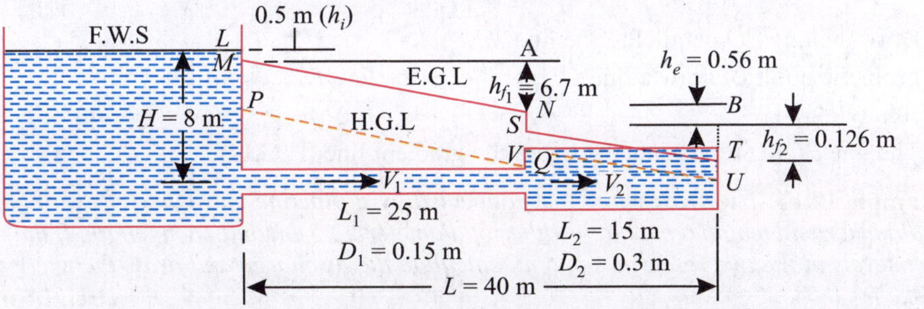

Fig. 12.9

$$8 = \frac{V_2^2}{2g} + \frac{8V_2^2}{2g} + \frac{106.6\,V_2^2}{2g} + \frac{9V_2^2}{2g} + \frac{2V_2^2}{2g}$$

$$= \frac{V_2^2}{2g}(1 + 8 + 106.6 + 9 + 2) = 126.6\,\frac{V_2^2}{2g}$$

$$\therefore \qquad V_2 = \sqrt{\frac{8 \times 2g}{126.6}} = \sqrt{\frac{8 \times 2 \times 9.81}{126.6}} = 1.11 \text{ m/s}$$

Hence, Rate of flow, $Q = A_2V_2 = \frac{\pi}{4} \times 0.3^2 \times 1.11 = \mathbf{0.078\ m^3/s}$ **(Ans.)**

***(ii)* E.G.L. and H.G.L. :**

The various head losses are : (Refer to Fig. 12·9)

$$h_i = \frac{8V_2^2}{2g} = \frac{8 \times (1.11)^2}{2 \times 9.81} = 0.5 \text{ m}$$

$$h_{f1} = 106.6\frac{V_2^2}{2g} = \frac{106.6 \times (1.11)^2}{2 \times 9.81} = 6.7 \text{ m}$$

$$h_e = \frac{9V_2^2}{2g} = \frac{9 \times (1.11)^2}{2 \times 9.81} = 0.56 \text{ m}$$

$$h_{f2} = \frac{2V_2^2}{2g} = \frac{2 \times (1.11)^2}{2 \times 9.81} = 0.126 \text{ m}$$

To draw E.G.L. and H.G.L. the following *procedure* is followed.

E.G.L. (Energy gradient line) :

The point *L* lies on F.W.S. (free water surface).

— Take $LM = h_i = 0{\cdot}5$ m

— From *M* draw a horizontal line. Taking *MA* equal to the length of the pipe (*i.e.*, L_1) draw a vertical line downward from the point *A*. Cut $AN = h_{f_1} = 6{\cdot}7$ m

— Join *MN*

— From *N*, draw a line *NS* vertically downward equal to h_e (= 0·56 m)

— From *S*, draw *SB* horizontal and from point *U* (which is lying on the centre of the pipe) draw a vertical line in the upward direction, meeting at *B*. From *B* take $BT = h_{f_2} = 0{\cdot}126$ m.

— Join *ST*

— The line *LMNST* represents the energy gradient line (E.G.L.)

H.G.L. (Hydraulic gradient line) :

— From *M*, take $MP = \frac{V_1^2}{2g} = \frac{(4 \times 1.11)^2}{2 \times 9.81} = 1.0$ m $\qquad (\because V_1 = 4V_2)$

— Draw the line *PQ* parallel to the line *MN*

— From the point *U*, draw a line *UV* parallel to the line *TS*

— Join *QV*

— The line *PQVU* represents the hydraulic gradient line (H.G.L.).

Example 12.17. *Two reservoirs are connected by a pipeline consisting of two pipes, one of 15 cm diameter and length 6 m and the other of diameter 22·5 cm and 16 m length. If the difference of water levels in the two reservoirs is 6 m, calculate the discharge and draw the energy gradient line. Take f = 0·04.* **(Delhi University)**

Solution. Refer to Fig. 12·10. *Given :* D_1 = 15 cm = 0·15 m; L_1 = 6 m; D_2 = 22·5 cm = 0·225 m; L_2 = 16 m; total losses = 6 m; *f* = 0·04.

From the continuing equation, we have: $A_1V_1 = A_2V_2$

or, $\frac{\pi}{4} \times 0.15^2 \times V_1 = \frac{\pi}{4} \times 0.225^2 \times V_2 \qquad \therefore V_1 = 2{\cdot}25\ V_2 \qquad ...(i)$

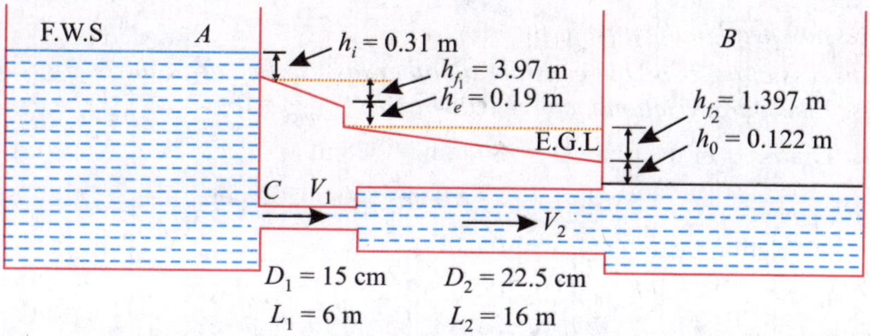

Fig. 12.10

Loss of head at entrance to a pipe, $h_i = \dfrac{0.5\,V_1^2}{2g}$

Loss of head due to friction in pipe *AB*,

$$h_{f_1} = \frac{4\,fL_1V_1^2}{D_1 \times 2g} = \frac{4 \times 0.04 \times 6 \times V_1^2}{0.15 \times 2g} = 6.4\,\frac{V_1^2}{2g}$$

Loss of head due to sudden enlargement,

$$h_e = \frac{(V_1 - V_2)^2}{2g} = \frac{\left(V_1 - \dfrac{V_1}{2.25}\right)^2}{2g} = 0.308\,\frac{V_1^2}{2g}$$

Loss of head due to friction in the pipe, *BC*,

$$h_{f_2} = \frac{4\,fL_2V^2}{D_2 \times 2g} = \frac{4 \times 0.04 \times 16 \times \left(\dfrac{V_1}{2.25}\right)^2}{0.225 \times 2g} = 2.25\,\frac{V_1^2}{2g}$$

Loss of head due to friction in the pipe *BC*,

$$h_0 = \frac{V_2^2}{2g} = \left(\frac{V_1}{2.25}\right)^2 \times \frac{1}{2g} = 0.197\,\frac{V_1^2}{2g}$$

Applying Bernoulli's equation to free water surface (F.W.S.) in the two tanks , we have:

$$\frac{p_A}{w} + \frac{V_A^2}{2g} + z_A = \frac{p_B^2}{w} + \frac{V_B^2}{2g} + z_B + \text{losses}$$

i.e., $p_A = p_B = 0,\ V_A = V_B = 0,\ z_A - z_B = 6$ m

Hence, Total losses $= 6$ m

i.e., $h_i + h_{f_1} + h_e + h_{f_2} + h_0 = 6$

$$\frac{0.5V_1^2}{2g} + 6.4\,\frac{V_1^2}{2g} + 0.308\,\frac{V_1^2}{2g} + 2.25\,\frac{V_1^2}{2g} + 0.197\,\frac{V_1^2}{2g} = 6$$

$$V_1 = 3{\cdot}49 \text{ m}$$

$$\text{Discharge, } Q = A_1V_1 = \frac{\pi}{4} \times 0.15^2 \times 3.49 = \mathbf{0.0617\ m^3/s} \quad \textbf{(Ans.)}$$

Energy gradient line is shown in the Fig. 12·10.

Example 12.18. *A pipe ABC connecting two reservoirs is 80 mm in diameter. From A to B the pipe is horizontal as shown in Fig. 12·11. and from B to C it falls by 3·5 metres. The lengths AB and BC are 25 m and 15 m respectively. If the water surface in the reservoir at A is 4 m above the centre-line of the pipe and at C 1 m above the line of the pipe, calculate :*

(i) The rate of flow, and

(ii) The pressure head in the pipe at B.

Neglect the loss at the bend but consider all other losses. Also draw the energy and hydraulic gradient lines. Take Darcy friction factor = 0·024 and $K_{entrance}$ = 0·5. **[IIT Delhi]**

Solution. Diameter of the pipe, D = 80 mm = 0·08 m

$$\text{Area, } A = \frac{\pi}{4} \times 0.08^2 = 0.005026 \text{ m}^2$$

$$\text{Friction factor } (= 4f) = 0{\cdot}024$$

$$K_{entrance} = 0{\cdot}5$$

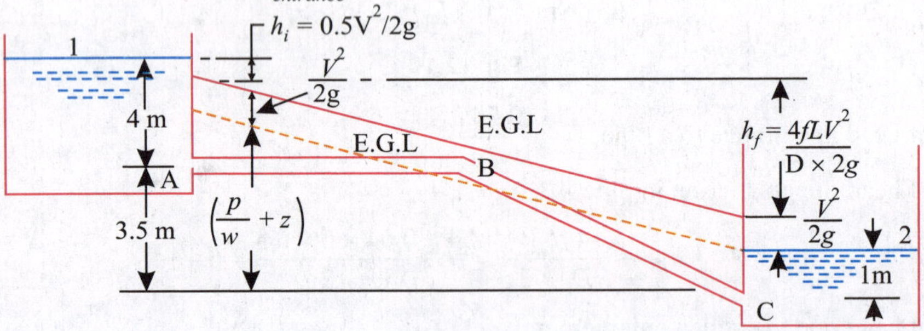

Fig. 12.11

(*i*) **The rate of flow, *Q* :**

Applying Bernoulli's equation between the water surfaces 1 and 2 in the two reservoirs (considering horizontal plane through C as datum), we get:

$$\frac{p_1}{w} + \frac{V_1^2}{2g} + z_1 = \frac{p_2}{w} + \frac{V_2^2}{2g} + z_2 + \text{loss at entrance} + h_f \text{ (loss due to friction)} + \frac{V^2}{2g}$$

$$0 + 0\,(4 + 3.5 - 1) = 0 + 0 + 0 + \frac{0{\cdot}5\,V^2}{2g} + \frac{4\,fLV^2}{D \times 2g} + \frac{V^2}{2g}$$

(where, V = velocity of flow in the pipe)

or, $$6.5 = \frac{0.5\,V^2}{2g} + \frac{0.024 \times (25 + 15) \times V^2}{0.08 \times 2g} + \frac{V^2}{2g}$$

or, $$= \frac{V^2}{2g}(0.5 + 12 + 1) + 13.5\frac{V^2}{2g}$$

or, $$V^2 = \frac{6.5 \times 2 \times 9.81}{13.5} = 9.446$$

or, $$\mathbf{V = 3{\cdot}073 \text{ m/s}} \quad \textbf{(Ans.)}$$

∴ Flow rate $= A \times V = 0{\cdot}005026 \times 3{\cdot}073 = \mathbf{0{\cdot}01544 \text{ m}^3/\text{s}}$ **(Ans.)**

(*ii*) **Pressure head in the pipe at B, $\frac{p_B}{w}$:**

Applying Bernoulli's equation at A and B, we get:

$$\frac{p_1}{w} + \frac{V_1^2}{2g} + z_1 = \frac{p_B}{w} + \frac{V_B^2}{2g} + z_B + \frac{0.5\,V_B^2}{2g} + h_f$$

$$0 + 0 + = \frac{p_B}{w} + \frac{V^2}{2g} + 0 + \frac{0{\cdot}5\,V^2}{2g} + \frac{4\,fL_{AB}V^2}{D \times 2g}$$

$$4 = \frac{p_B}{w} + \frac{V^2}{2g} + \frac{0.5V^2}{2g} + \frac{0.024 \times 25 \times V^2}{0.08 \times 2g} \quad (\because\ V_B = V = 3{\cdot}073 \text{ m/s})$$

$$4 = \frac{p_B}{w} + \frac{V^2}{2g} + \frac{0.5V^2}{2g} + \frac{7.5V^2}{2g}$$

$$= \frac{p_B}{w} + \frac{9V^2}{2g}$$

or,
$$\frac{p_B}{w} = 4 - \frac{9V^2}{2g} = 4 - \frac{9 \times (3.073)^2}{2 \times 9.81}$$

$$= -\mathbf{0{\cdot}33\ m\ of\ water}\ \text{(below atmosphere)}\ \textbf{(Ans.)}$$

Energy gradient and hydraulic gradient lines (E.G.L. and H.G.L.) :

— For plotting E.G.L. and H.G.L., we require the velocity head, (same throughout)

$$\frac{V^2}{2g} = \frac{(3.073)^2}{2 \times 9.81} = 0.481 \text{ m}$$

— Total energy at B w.r.t. horizontal datum through C

$$= 3.5 + \frac{p_B}{w} + \frac{V^2}{2g} = 3.5 - 0.33 + \frac{(3.073)^2}{2 \times 9.81} = 3{\cdot}65 \text{ m}$$

Energy gradient and hydraulic gradient lines are shown firm and dotted respectively in the Fig. 12·11; H.G.L. *below the pipeline* near *B* indicates that pressure is *negative.*

Example 12.19. *Two reservoirs A and C having a difference of level of 15·5 m are connected by a pipeline ABC, the elevation of point B being 4·0 m below the level of water in reservoir A. The length AB of the pipeline is 250 m, the pipe being made of mild steel having a friction co-efficient* f_1, *while the length BC is 450 m, the pipe having made of cast-iron having a friction co-efficient* f_2. *Both the lengths AB and BC have a diameter of 200 mm. A partially closed valve is located in the length BC at a distance of 150 m from reservoir C.*

If the flow through the pipeline is 3 m^3*/min, the pressure head at B is 0·5 m and the head loss at the valve is 5·0 m.*

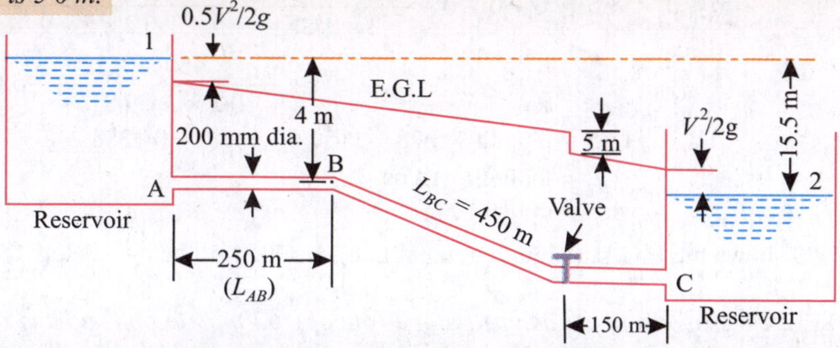

Fig. 12.12

(i) Find the friction coefficients f_1 *and* f_2.

(ii) Draw the hydraulic grade line of the pipeline and indicate on the diagram head loss values at significant points. Take into account head loss at entrance and exit points of the pipeline.

[UPTU]

Solution. Difference of water level between two reservoirs = 15·5 m

Diameter of the pipe ABC, D = 200 mm = 0·2 m

Length AB, L_{AB} = 250 m

Length BC, L_{BC} = 450 m

Discharge through the pipe, $Q = 3\ m^3/min = 0{\cdot}05\ m^3/s$

Pressure head at B, $h_B = \left(= \frac{p_B}{w}\right) = 0.5$ m

Head loss at the valve $= 5{\cdot}0$ m

(*i*) Friction co-efficients f_1 and f_2 :

Velocity in the pipe ABC, $V = \frac{Q}{\text{Area}} = \frac{0.05}{\frac{\pi}{4} \times 0.2^2} = 1.59$ m/s

Applying Bernoulli's equation at '1' and at 'B', we get:

$$\frac{p_1}{w} + \frac{V_1^2}{2g} + z_1 = \frac{p_B}{w} + \frac{V_B^2}{2g} + z_2 + \frac{0.5V_B^2}{2g} + (h_f)_{AB}$$

$$0 + 0 + 4 = 0.5 + \frac{V_B^2}{2g} + 0 + \frac{0.5V_B^2}{2g} + \frac{4f_1L_{AB}V_B^2}{D \times 2g}$$

$$4 = 0.5 + \frac{V^2}{2g} + \frac{0.5V^2}{2g} + \frac{4f_1 \times 250 \times V^2}{0.2 \times 2g} \qquad (\because V_B = V)$$

or,
$$4 = 0.5 + \frac{(1.59)^2}{2 \times 9.81} + \frac{0.5 \times (1.59)^2}{2 \times 9.81} + \frac{4f_1 \times 250 \times (1.59)^2}{0.2 \times 2 \times 9.81}$$

$$= 0{\cdot}5 + 0{\cdot}129 + 0{\cdot}0644 + 644{\cdot}3\,f_1$$

or, $f_1 = \mathbf{0{\cdot}0051}$ **(Ans.)**

Applying Bernoulli's equation between '1' and '2' and considering all losses in the pipeline ABC including the exit loss, we have:

$$\frac{p_1}{w} + \frac{V_1^2}{2g} + z_1 = \frac{p_2}{w} + \frac{V_2^2}{2g} + z_2 + \frac{0.5V^2}{2g} + \frac{4f_1L_{AB}V^2}{D \times 2g} + \frac{4f_2L_{BC}V^2}{D \times 2g} + 5.0 + \frac{V^2}{2g}$$

$$0 + 0 + 15.5 = 0 + 0 + 0 + \frac{0.5 \times (1.59)^2}{2 \times 9.81} + \frac{4 \times 0.0051 \times 250 \times (1.59)^2}{0.2 \times 2 \times 9.81}$$

$$+ \frac{4f_2 \times 450 \times (1.59)^2}{0.2 \times 2 \times 9.81} + 5.0 + \frac{(1.59)^2}{2 \times 9.81}$$

or, $15{\cdot}5 = 0{\cdot}0644 + 3{\cdot}28 + 1159{\cdot}6\,f_2 + 5{\cdot}0 + 0{\cdot}1288$

or, $f_2 = \mathbf{0{\cdot}00606}$ **(Ans.)**

(*ii*) H.G.L. (hydraulic gradient line) :

Fig. 12.9 shows the E.G.L. (energy gradient line), H.G.L. will be $\frac{V^2}{2g}$ below the E.G.L.

Example 12.20. *Water is being pumped at the rate of 0·02 m³/s to an overhead tank through a 150 mm diameter 300 m long delivery pipe. In the tank, the pipe discharges freely at height of 15 m above the pump. If the Darcy-Weisbach friction factor = 0·03 for the pipe, determine :*

(i) The pressure developed by the pump on its delivery side, and

(ii) The power delivered to water by the pump.

Draw also the hydraulic gradient from the pump to the tank. Assume that the first 285 m of the delivery pipe is horizontal and the rest is vertical. **[Delhi University]**

Solution. Rate of flow, $Q = 0{\cdot}02\ m^3/s$

Diameter of the pipe, $D = 150$ mm $= 0{\cdot}15$ m

Length of the pipe, $L = 300$ m

Darcy-Weisbach friction factor $(4f) = 0{\cdot}03$

(i) The pressure developed by the pump on its delivery side :

$$\text{Velocity of flow, } V = \frac{Q}{\text{Area}} = \frac{0.02}{\frac{\pi}{4} \times 0.15^2} = 1.132 \text{ m/s}$$

Let, p = Pressure (gauge) just on the delivery side of the pump.

Applying Bernoulli's equation to the section just on the delivery side of the pump and to the discharge end of the pipeline where the gauge pressure is zero *i.e.,* sections 1 and 2, we have:

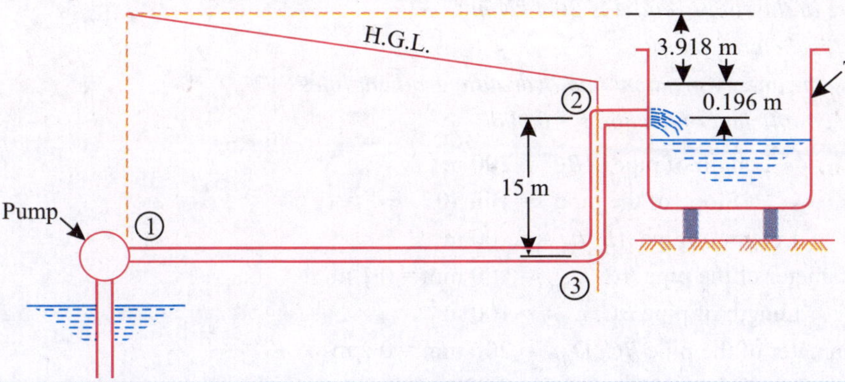

Fig. 12.13

$$\frac{p_1}{w} + \frac{V_1^2}{2g} + z_1 = \frac{p_2}{w} + \frac{V_2^2}{2g} + z_2 + h_f \qquad (h_f = \text{head loss due to friction})$$

$$\frac{p_1}{w} + \frac{(1.132)^2}{2 \times 9.81} + 0 = 0 + \frac{(1.132)^2}{2 \times 9.81} + 15 + \frac{0.03 \times 300 \times (1.132)^2}{0.15 \times 2 \times 9.81}$$

$$\left(\because \; h_f = \frac{fLV^2}{D \times 2g} \text{ where, } L = 285 + 15 = 300 \text{ m} \right)$$

$$\frac{p_1}{w} + 0.0653 = 0.0653 + 15 + 3.918$$

or, $$\frac{p_1}{w} = 18.918 \text{ m}$$

Hence, the pressure developed by the pump on the delivery side

= **18·918 m of water (Ans.)**

(ii) The power delivered to water by the pump, P :

$$P = wQh_f = 9{\cdot}81 \times 0{\cdot}02 \times 3{\cdot}918 \text{ kW}$$

$$= \mathbf{0{\cdot}768 \text{ kW}} \quad \textbf{(Ans.)}$$

[**Note:** The power required to drive the pump $= \frac{wQh_f}{\eta}$, where η is the efficiency of the pump.]

H.G.L. (hydraulic gradient line) :

Head loss in 15 m vertical length of pipeline

$$= \frac{h_f}{300} \times 15 = \frac{3.918}{300} \times 15 = 0.196 \text{ m}$$

Now piezometric head $\left(\frac{p}{w} + z \right)$ at:

Section 1 = 19·114 m (*i.e.,* 18·918 + 0·196 = 19·114 m)

Section 2 = 15·196 m (*i.e.,* 19·114 – 3·198 = 15·196 m)

Section 3 = 15 m (*i.e.,* 15·196 – 0·196 = 15 m)

The HGL from the pump to the overhead tank is plotted by marking the ordinates of piezometric heads at 1, 2 and 3 (as above) and joining these by straight lines as shown in Fig. 12·13.

Example 12.21. *A pipeline ABC 200 m long, is laid on an upward slope of 1 in 40. The length of the portion AB is 100 m and its diameter is 100 mm. At B the pipe section suddenly enlarges to 200 mm diameter and remains so for the remainder of its length BC, 100 m. A flow of 0·02 m^3/s. is pumped into the pipe at its lower end A and is discharged at the upper end C into a closed tank. The pressure at the supply end A is 200 kN/m^2.*

(i) What is the pressure at C?

(ii) Draw the energy gradient and hydraulic gradient lines.

Assume co-efficient of friction f = 0·008.

Solution. Length of pipe, ABC = 200 m

Slope of the pipe, = 1 in 40

Length of pipe AB, L_{AB} = 100 m

Diameter of the pipe AB, D_{AB} = 100 mm = 0·1 m

Length of pipe BC, L_{BC} = 100 m

Diameter of the pipe BC, D_{BC} = 200 mm = 0·2 m

Co-efficient of friction, f = 0·008

Discharge, Q = 0·02 m^3/s

The pressure at the supply end, p_A = 200 kN/m^2

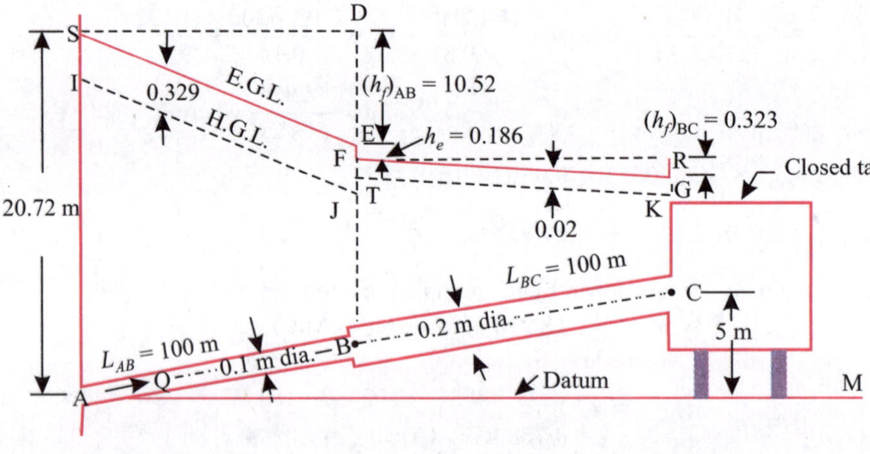

Fig. 12.14

(i) Pressure at C, p_c :

$$\text{Velocity of flow in pipe } AB, V_{AB} = \frac{0.02}{(\pi/4) \times 0.1^2} = 2.54 \text{ m/s}$$

$$\text{Velocity of flow in pipe } BC, V_{BC} = \frac{0.02}{(\pi/4) \times 0.2^2} = 0.63 \text{ m/s}$$

Invoking Bernoulli's equation at points A and C, we have:

$$\frac{p_A}{w} + \frac{V_A^2}{2g} + z_A = \frac{p_C}{w} + \frac{V_C^2}{2g} + z_C + (h_f)_{AB} + h_e + (h_f)_{BC} \quad ...(i)$$

where, $$(h_f)_{AB} = \frac{4fL_{AB}V_{AB}^2}{D_{AB} \times 2g} = \frac{4 \times 0.008 \times 100 \times 2.54^2}{0.1 \times 2 \times 9.81} = 10.52 \text{ m}$$

Loss of head due to sudden enlargement,

$$h_e = \frac{(V_{AB} - V_{BC})^2}{2g} = \frac{(2.54 - 0.63)^2}{2 \times 9.81} = 0.186 \text{ m}$$

$$(h_f)_{BC} = \frac{4fL_{BC}V_{BC}^2}{D_{BC} \times 2g} = \frac{4 \times 0.008 \times 100 \times 0.63^2}{0.2 \times 2 \times 9.81} = 0.323 \text{ m}$$

Substituting the values in eqn. (*i*), we get:

$$\frac{200}{9.81} + \frac{(2.54)^2}{2 \times 9.81} + 0 = \frac{p_C}{w} + \frac{0.63^2}{2 \times 9.81} + 5.0 + 10.52 + 0.186 + 0.323$$

$$20.38 + 0.329 = \frac{p_C}{w} + 0.02 + 16.03$$

or, $$\frac{p_C}{w} = 4.659 \text{ m}$$

or, $$p_C = 9{\cdot}81 \times 4{\cdot}659 = \mathbf{45{\cdot}7\ kN/m^2}$$ **(Ans.)**

(*ii*) Energy gradient and hydraulic gradient lines :

Pipe AB : Assuming the datum line passing through *A*, then total energy at *A*

$$= \frac{p_A}{w} + \frac{V_A^2}{2g} + z_A = \frac{200}{9.81} + \frac{(2.54)^2}{2 \times 9.81} + 0 \simeq 20.72 \text{ m}$$

Total energy at *B* = Total energy at $A - (h_f)_{AB}$

$$= 20{\cdot}72 - 10{\cdot}52 = 10{\cdot}2 \text{ m}$$

Also, $$\frac{V_C^2}{2g} = \frac{(0.63)^2}{2 \times 9.81} = 0.02 \text{ m}$$

Energy gradient line (E.G.L.)

— Draw a horizontal line *AM* as shown in Fig. 12·14.

— Draw the centreline of the pipe in such a way that slope of the pipe is 1 in 40. Thus, point *C* will be at a height of $\frac{1}{40} \times 200 = 5$ m from the line *AM*.

— Draw a vertical line *AS* equal to total energy at *A i.e.*, *AS* = 20·72 m

— From point *S*, draw a horizontal line and from point *B*, a vertical line, meeting at *D*.

— From *D*, take vertical distance $DE = (h_f)_{AB} = 10{\cdot}52$ m. Join *SE*.

— From *E* take $EF = h_e = 0{\cdot}186$ m

— From *F* draw a hroizontal line and from *C*, a vertical line meeting at *R*. From *R* take $RG = (h_f)$ *BC* = 0·323 m. Joint *F* to *G*. Then SEFG represents the ***energy gradient*** *or* ***total energy line.***

Hydraulic gradient line (H.G.L.)

— Draw the line *IJ* parallel to the line *SE* at a distance of $\frac{V_{AB}^2}{2g} = \frac{(2.54)^2}{2 \times 9.81} = 0.329$ m in the downward direction.

— Draw the line *KT* parallel to the line *GF* at a distance of $\frac{V_C^2}{2g} = \frac{(0.63)^2}{2 \times 9.81} = 0.02$ m. Join *J* to *T*.

The line IJTK represents the ***hydraulic gradient line.***

12.6. PIPES IN SERIES OR COMPOUND PIPES

Fig. 12·15 shows a system of pipes in series.

Let, D_1, D_2, D_3 = Diameters of pipes 1, 2 and 3 respectively,

L_1, L_2, L_3 = Lengths of pipes 1, 2 and 3 respectively,

V_1, V_2, V_3 = Velocities of flow through pipes 1, 2 and 3 respectively

f_1, f_2, f_3 = Co-efficients of friction for pipes 1, 2 and 3 respectively, and

H = Difference of water level in the two tanks.

As the rate of flow (Q) of water through each pipe is same, therefore,

$$Q = A_1V_1 = A_2V_2 = A_3V_3$$

Also, The difference in liquid surface levels = Sum of the various head losses in the pipes

i.e.,
$$H = h_i + h_{f_1} + h_c + h_{f_2} + h_e + h_{f_3} + \frac{V_3^3}{2g} \quad ...(i)$$

where,

h_i = Head loss at entrance $= \dfrac{0.5V_1^2}{2g}$

h_{f_1} = Head loss due to friction in pipe 1 $= \dfrac{4f_1L_1V_1^2}{D_1 \times 2g}$

h_c = Head loss at contraction $= \dfrac{0.5V_2^2}{2g}$

h_{f_2} = Head loss due to friction in pipe 2 $= \dfrac{4f_2L_2V_2^2}{D_2 \times 2g}$

h_e = Head loss due to enlargement $= \dfrac{(V_2 - V_3)^2}{2g}$

h_{f_3} = Head loss due to friction in pipe 3 $= \dfrac{4f_3L_3V_3^2}{D_3 \times 2g}$

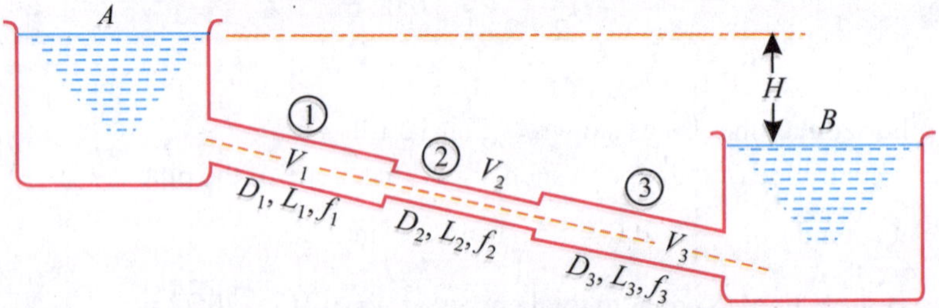

Fig. 12.15. Pipes in series.

Substituting the values in (i), we have:

$$H = h_i + h_{f_1} + h_c + h_{f_2} + h_e + h_{f_3} + \frac{V_3^2}{2g}$$

$$= \frac{0.5V_1^2}{2g} + \frac{4f_1L_1V_1^2}{D_1 \times 2g} + \frac{0.5V_2^2}{2g} + \frac{4f_2L_2V_2^2}{D_2 \times 2g} + \frac{(V_2 - V_3)^2}{2g} + \frac{4f_3L_3V_3^2}{D_3 \times 2g} + \frac{V_3^2}{2g} \quad ...(12·9)$$

If *minor losses are neglected*, then above equation becomes:

$$H = \frac{4f_1L_1V_1^2}{D_1 \times 2g} + \frac{4f_2L_2V_2^2}{D_2 \times 2g} + \frac{4f_3L_3V_3^2}{D_3 \times 2g} \quad ...(12·10)$$

If, $f_1 = f_2 = f_3 = f$, then:

$$H = \frac{4fL_1V_1^2}{D_1\times 2g} + \frac{4fL_2V_2^2}{D_2\times 2g} + \frac{4fL_3V_3^2}{D_3\times 2g}$$

$$= \frac{4f}{2g}\left[\frac{L_1V_1^2}{D_1} + \frac{L_2V_2^2}{D_2} + \frac{L_3V_3^2}{D_3}\right] \quad ...(12\cdot11)$$

Example 12.22. *Three pipes of diameters 300 mm, 200 mm and 400 mm and lengths 450 m, 255 m and 315 m respectively are connected in series. The difference in water surface levels in two tanks is 18 m. Determine the rate of flow of water if co-efficients of friction are 0·0075, 0·0078 and 0·0072 respectively considering :*

(i) Minor losses also, and

(ii) Neglecting minor losses.

Solution. Pipe 1 : $L_1 = 450$ m, $= D_1 = 300$ mm $= 0\cdot3$ m, $f_1 = 0\cdot0075$

Pipe 2 : $L_2 = 255$ m, $D_2 = 200$ mm $= 0\cdot2$ m, $f_2 = 0\cdot0078$

Pipe 3 : $L_3 = 315$ m, $D_3 = 400$ mm $= 0\cdot4$ m, $f_3 = 0\cdot0072$

Difference of water level, $H = 18$ m.

(i) Considering minor losses :

Let V_1, V_2 and V_3 be the velocities in Ist, 2nd, and 3rd pipe respectively.

From continuity considerations, we have:

$$A_1V_1 = A_2V_2 = A_3V_3$$

$$\therefore \quad V_2 = \frac{A_1V_1}{A_2} = \frac{(\pi/4)\times D_1^2}{(\pi/4)\times D_2^2}\times V_1 = \frac{D_1^2}{D_2^2}\times V_1 = \left(\frac{0.3}{0.2}\right)^2 V_1 = 2.25\,V_1$$

and,

$$V_3 = \frac{A_1V_1}{A_3} = \frac{(\pi/4)\times D_1^2}{(\pi/4)\times D_3^2}\times V_1 = \frac{D_1^2}{D_3^2}\times V_1 = \left(\frac{0.3}{0.4}\right)^2 V_1 = 0.5625\,V_1$$

We know that:

$$H = \frac{0.5V_1^2}{2g} + \frac{4f_1L_1V_1^2}{D_1\times 2g} + \frac{0.5V_2^2}{2g} + \frac{4f_2L_2V_2^2}{D_2\times 2g} + \frac{(V_2-V_3)^2}{2g} + \frac{4f_3L_3V_3^2}{D_3\times 2g} + \frac{V_3^2}{2g} \quad ...[\text{Eqn. } (12\cdot9)]$$

$$18 = \frac{0\cdot5V_1^2}{2g} + \frac{4\times 0.0075\times 450\times V_1^2}{0.3\times 2g} + \frac{0.5\times(2.25\,V_1)^2}{2g} + \frac{4\times 0.0078\times 255\times(2.25V_1)^2}{0.2\times 2g}$$
$$+ \frac{(2.25\,V_1 - 0.5625\,V_1)^2}{2g} + \frac{4\times 0.0072\times 315\times(0.5625\,V_1)^2}{0.4\times 2g} + \frac{(0.5625\,V_1)^2}{2g}$$

$$18 = \frac{V_1^2}{2g}(0.5 + 45 + 2.53 + 201.4 + 2.847 + 7.176 + 0.316)$$

$$= 259.77\,\frac{V_1^2}{2g}$$

or,

$$V_1 = \sqrt{\frac{18\times 2\times 9.81}{259.77}} = 1.166 \text{ m/s}$$

$\therefore$ Rate of flow, $Q = A_1\times V_1 = (\pi/4)\times 0\cdot3^2\times 1\cdot166 =$ **0·0824 m³/s (Ans.)**

(ii) Neglecting minor losses :

We know that,

$$H = \frac{4f_1L_1V_1^2}{D_1\times 2g} + \frac{4f_2L_2V_2^2}{D_2\times 2g} + \frac{4f_3L_3V_3^2}{D_3\times 2g} \quad ...[\text{Eqn. } (12\cdot10)]$$

$$18 = \frac{V_1^2}{2g}\left(\frac{4 \times 0.0075 \times 450}{0\cdot3} + \frac{4 \times 0.0078 \times 255 \times 2.25^2}{0\cdot2} + \frac{4 \times 0.0072 \times 315 \times (0.5625)^2}{0\cdot4}\right)$$

$$= \frac{V_1^2}{2g}(45 + 201.4 + 7.176) = 253.57 \times \frac{V_1^2}{2g}$$

or, $$V_1 = \sqrt{\frac{18 \times 2 \times 9.81}{253.57}} = 1.18 \text{ m}$$

$\therefore$ Discharge, $Q = A_1 V_1 = (\pi/4) \times 0\cdot3^2 \times 1\cdot18 =$ **$0\cdot0834$ m^3/s (Ans.)**

Example 12.23. *Two reservoirs with a difference in elevation of 15 m are connected by the three pipes in series. The pipes are 300 m long of diameter 30 cm, 150 m long of 20 cm diameter, and 200 m long of 25 cm diameter respectively. The friction factors (f) in the relation*

$$h_f = \frac{fLV^2}{D \times 2g}$$

for the three pipes are, respectively, 0·018, 0·020 and 0·019, and which account for friction and all losses. Further the contractions and expansions are sudden. Determine the flow rate in l/s. The loss co-efficient for sudden contraction from dia. 30 cm to 20 cm = 0·24. **(PTU)**

Solution. Refer to Fig. 12.16. *Given :* $D_1 = 30$ cm $= 0\cdot3$ m; $L_1 = 300$ m; $D_2 = 20$ cm $= 0\cdot2$ m; $L_2 = 150$ m; $D_3 = 25$ cm $= 0\cdot25$ m; $L_3 = 200$ m; $f_1 = 0\cdot018$; $f_2 = 0\cdot020$, $f_3 = 0\cdot019$.

Loss co-efficient for sudden contraction $= 0\cdot24$

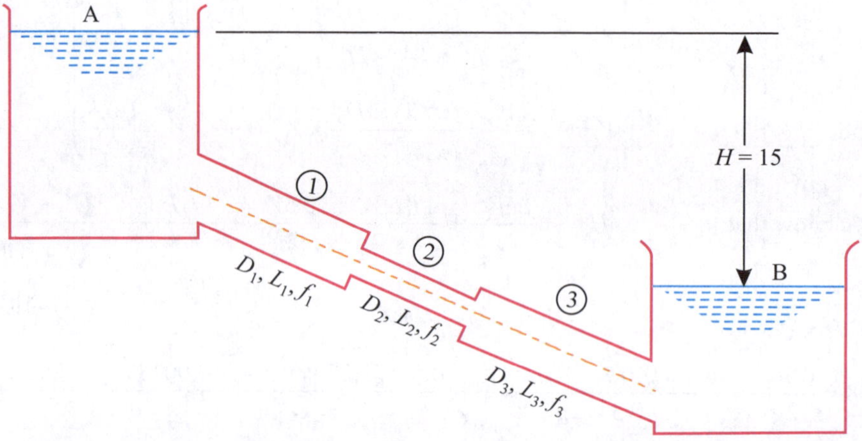

Fig. 12.16

Flow rate in l/s, Q :

Various types of losses which occur in the pipelines 1, 2 and 3 are :

(*i*) Head loss at entrance, $h_i = 0.5 \times \frac{V_1^2}{2g} = \frac{0.5}{2 \times 9.81} \times \left[\frac{4Q}{\pi \times 0.30^2}\right] = 5.1\, Q^2$

(*ii*) Head loss due to friction in pipe 1, $h_{f_1} = \frac{f_1 L_1 V_1^2}{D_1 \times 2g} = \frac{f_1 \times L_1}{D_1 \times 2g}\left[\frac{4Q}{\pi D_1^2}\right]^2$

$$= \frac{0.018 \times 300}{0.3 \times 2 \times 9.81}\left[\frac{4Q}{\pi \times 0.3^2}\right]^2 = 183.6\, Q^2$$

(*iii*) Head loss at contraction, $h_c = 0.24\frac{V_2^2}{2g} = \frac{0.24}{2g}\left[\frac{4Q}{\pi D_2^2}\right]^2$

$$= \frac{0.24}{2 \times 9.81}\left[\frac{4Q}{\pi \times 0.2^2}\right]^2 = 12.394\,Q^2$$

(*iv*) Head loss due to friction in pipe 2, $h_{f_2} = \frac{f_2 L_2 V_2^2}{D_2 \times 2g} = \frac{f_2 \times L_2}{D_2 \times 2g}\left[\frac{4Q}{\pi D_2^2}\right]^2$

$$= \frac{0.02 \times 150}{0.2 \times 2 \times 9.81}\left[\frac{4Q}{\pi \times 0.2^2}\right]^2 = 774.267\,Q^2$$

(*v*) Head loss due to sudden enlargement, $h_e = \frac{(V_2 - V_3)^2}{2g} = \frac{1}{2g}\left[\frac{4Q}{\pi D_2^2} - \frac{4Q}{\pi D_3^2}\right]^2$

$$= \frac{16Q^2}{2 \times 9.81 \times \pi^2}\left[\frac{1}{0.2^2} - \frac{1}{0.25^2}\right]^2 = 6.69\,Q^2$$

(*vi*) Head loss due to friction in pipe 3, $h_{f_3} = \frac{f_3 L_3 V_3^2}{D_3 \times 2g} = \frac{f_3 L_3}{D_3 \times 2g}\left[\frac{4Q}{\pi D_3^2}\right]^2$

$$= \frac{0.019 \times 200}{0.25 \times 2 \times 9.81}\left[\frac{4Q}{\pi \times 0.25^2}\right]^2 = 321.518\,Q^2$$

(*vii*) Head loss at the exit, $h_0 = \frac{V_3^2}{2g} = \frac{1}{2g}\left[\frac{4Q}{\pi D_3^2}\right]^2 = \frac{1}{2 \times 9.81}\left[\frac{4Q}{\pi \times 0.25^2}\right]^2 = 21.152\,Q^2$

Applying the Bernoulli's equation between the water surfaces of the two reservoirs, we get:

$$\frac{p_A}{w} + \frac{V_A^2}{2g} + z_A = \frac{p_B}{w} + \frac{V_B^2}{2g} + z_B + \text{all losses.}$$

$$0 + 0 + 15 = 0 + 0 + 0 + (5{\cdot}1 + 183{\cdot}6 + 12{\cdot}394 + 774{\cdot}267 + 6{\cdot}69 + 321{\cdot}518 + 21{\cdot}152)\,Q^2$$

or, $Q = 0{\cdot}1064$ m³/s or **106·4 *l*/s** **(Ans.)**

12.7. EQUIVALENT PIPE

An **equivalent pipe** *is defined as the pipe of uniform diameter having loss of head and discharge equal to the loss of head and discharge of a compound pipe consisting of several pipes of different lengths and diameters.* The uniform diameter of the equivalent pipe is known as the *equivalent diameter* of the series or compound pipe.

Let, $L_1, L_2, L_3,$ etc. = Lengths of pipes 1, 2, 3, etc.

$D_1, D_2, D_3,$ etc. = Diameters of pipes 1, 2, 3, etc.,

H = Total head loss,

L = Length of the equivalent pipe, and

D = Diameter of the equivalent pipe.

Then, neglecting minor losses, total head loss,

$$h_f = h_{f_1} + h_{f_2} + h_{f_3} + \ldots$$

or,

$$H = \frac{4 f_1 L_1 V_1^2}{D_1 \times 2g} + \frac{4 f_2 L_2 V_2^2}{D_2 \times 2g} + \frac{4 f_3 L_3 V_3^2}{D_3 \times 2g} + \ldots \quad \ldots(12{\cdot}12)$$

(where, f_1, f_2 and f_3, etc. are co-efficients of friction)

Also, from continuity considerations:

$$Q = A_1 V_1 = A_2 V_2 = A_3 V_3$$

$$= \frac{\pi}{4} \times D_1^2 V_1 = \frac{\pi}{4} \times D_2^2 V_2 = \frac{\pi}{4} \times D_3^2 V_3$$

$$\therefore \quad V_1 = \frac{4Q}{\pi D_1^2},\ V_2 = \frac{4Q}{\pi D_2^2},\ V_3 = \frac{4Q}{\pi D_3^2}$$

Substituting these values in eqn. (12·12), assuming $f_1 = f_2 = f_3$, etc. $= f$, we get:

$$H = \frac{4fL_1 \times \left(\frac{4Q}{\pi D_1^2}\right)^2}{D_1 \times 2g} + \frac{4fL_2 \times \left(\frac{4Q}{\pi D_2^2}\right)^2}{D_2 \times 2g} + \frac{4fL_3 \times \left(\frac{4Q}{\pi D_3^2}\right)^2}{D_3 \times 2g} + ...$$

$$= \frac{4 \times 16 fQ^2}{\pi^2 \times 2g}\left(\frac{L_1}{D_1^5} + \frac{L_2}{D_2^5} + \frac{L_3}{D_3^5} + ...\right) \quad ...(12·13)$$

Head loss in the equivalent pipe,

$$H = \frac{4fLV^2}{D \times 2g} \text{ (assuming the same value of } f \text{ as in compound pipe)}$$

where, $V = \frac{Q}{A} = \frac{Q}{\frac{\pi}{4} \times D^2} = \frac{4Q}{\pi D^2}$

$$\therefore \quad H = \frac{4fL\left(\frac{4Q}{\pi D^2}\right)^2}{D \times 2g} = \frac{4 \times 16 fQ^2 f}{\pi^2 \times 2g}\left[\frac{L}{D^5}\right] \quad ...(12·14)$$

From eqns. (12·13) and (12·14), we have:

$$\frac{4 \times 16 fQ^2}{\pi^2 \times 2g}\left(\frac{L_1}{D_1^5} + \frac{L_2}{D_2^5} + \frac{L_3}{D_3^5} + ...\right) = \frac{4 \times 16 fQ^2}{\pi^2 \times 2g}\left(\frac{L}{D^5}\right)$$

or,
$$\frac{L}{D^5} = \frac{L_1}{D_1^5} + \frac{L_2}{D_2^5} + \frac{L_3}{D_3^5} + ... \quad ...(12.15)$$

Eqn. 12·15 is known as **Dupit's equation.** If the length of the equivalent pipe is equal to the length of the compound pipe *i.e.*, $L = (L_1 + L_2 + L_3 + ...)$, the diameter D of the equivalent pipe may be determined by using this equation. Sometimes a pipe of a given diameter D which is available may be required to be used as equivalent pipe to replace a compound pipe; in this case the length of the equivalent pipe may be required to be determined and the same may also be determined by using eqn. (12·15).

Example 12.24. *A piping system consists of three pipes arranged in series; the lengths of the pipes are 1200 m, 750 m and 600 m and diameters 750 mm, 600 mm and 450 mm respectively.*

(i) Transform the system to an equivalent 450 mm diameter pipe, and

(ii) Determine an equivalent diameter for the pipe, 2550 m long.

Solution. *Pipe 1*: L_1 = 200 m; D_1 = 750 mm = 0·75 m

Pipe 2: L_2 = 750 m; D_2 = 600 mm = 0·6 m

Pipe 3: L_3 = 600 m; D_3 = 450 mm = 0·45 m

(*i*) Equivalent length, *L* :

Diameter of the equivalent pipe, D = 450 mm = 0·45 m (*Given*)

Using the relation :

$$\frac{L}{D^5} = \frac{L_1}{D_1^5} + \frac{L_2}{D_2^5} + \frac{L_3}{D_3^5}$$

$$= \frac{1200}{(0.75)^5} + \frac{750}{(0.6)^5} + \frac{600}{(0.45)^5}, \text{ we have:}$$

$$\frac{L}{(0.45)^5} = 5056.8 + 9645 + 32515.4 = 47217.2$$

or, $$L = 47217{\cdot}2 \times (0{\cdot}45)^5 = \mathbf{871{\cdot}3\ m}\ \textbf{(Ans.)}$$

(*ii*) **Equivalent diameter, *D* :**

Length of the equivalent pipe, $L = 2550$ m (*Given*)

Now, $$\frac{L}{D^5} = \frac{L_1}{D_1^5} + \frac{L_2}{D_2^5} + \frac{L_3}{D_3^5}$$

or, $$\frac{2550}{D^5} = \frac{1200}{(0.75)^5} + \frac{750}{(0.6)^5} + \frac{600}{(0.45)^5}$$

$$= 5056.8 + 9645 + 32515.4 = 47217.2$$

or, $$D = \left(\frac{2550}{47217.2}\right)^{1/5} = 0.5578 \text{ m or } \mathbf{557.8\ mm}\ \textbf{(Ans.)}$$

Example. 12.25. *A compound piping system consists of 1800 m of 50 cm diameter, 1200 m of 40 cm diameter and 600 m of 30 cm diameter pipes of the same material connected in series. What is the equivalent length of a 40 cm diameter pipe of the same material ? State clearly the assumption (s) made.* **(PEC)**

Solution. *Given :* = L_1 = 1800 m; D_1 = 50 cm = 0·5 m; L_2 = 1200 m; D_2 = 40 cm = 0·4 m; L_3 = 600 m; D_3 = 30 cm = 0·3 m.

Equivalent length of a 0·4 m diameter pipe of the same material, *L* :

Refer to Fig. 12·17.

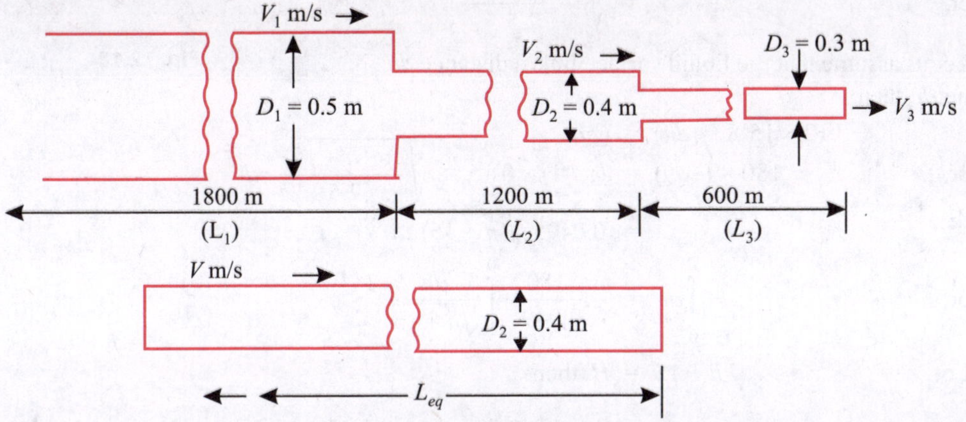

Fig. 12.17

Assumptions : 1. *f* is constant, and is the same for all the pipes.

2. The head loss due to contraction is ignored.

Using the relation : $$\frac{L}{D^5} = \frac{L_1}{D_1^5} + \frac{L_2}{D_2^5} + \frac{L_3}{D_3^5} \quad ..[\text{Eqn. } (12{\cdot}15)]$$

or, $$\frac{L}{(0.4)^5} = \frac{1800}{(0.5)^5} + \frac{1200}{(0.4)^5} + \frac{600}{(0.3)^5}$$

$$L = 1800 \times \left(\frac{0.4}{0.5}\right)^5 + 1200 + 600\left(\frac{0.4}{0.3}\right)^5$$

$$= 589{\cdot}82 + 1200 + 2528{\cdot}39 = \mathbf{4318{\cdot}2\ m}\ \textbf{(Ans.)}$$

Example 12.26. *A pipe 150 mm in diameter and 15 m long is connected to the bottom of a tank, 15 metres long by 12 metres wide. The original head over the open end of the pipe is 5 metres. Find the time of emptying the tank, assuming the entrance to the pipe is sharp-edged.*

Assume $f = 0{\cdot}01$ *in* $h_f = \dfrac{fLV^2}{D \times 2g}$. **[GATE]**

Solution. Diameter of the pipe, $D = 150$ mm $= 0{\cdot}15$ m

Length of the pipe, $L = 15$ m

Area of the tank, $= 12 \times 15 = 180\ m^2$

Friction factor, $f = 0{\cdot}01$

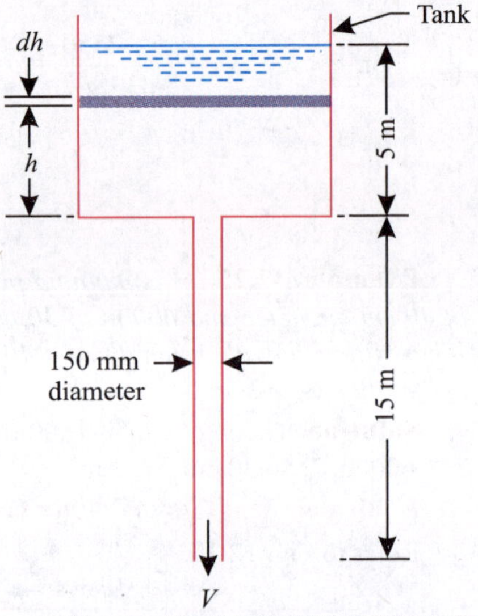

Fig. 12.18

Writing the Bernoulli's equation between the liquid surface at height '*h*' and the lower end of the pipe, considering the entrance and the friction losses, we get:

$$h + 15 = 0.5\frac{V^2}{2g} + \frac{V^2}{2g} + h_f$$

$$= 0.5\frac{V^2}{2g} + \frac{V^2}{2g} + \frac{0.01 \times 15 \times V^2}{0.15 \times 2g}$$

(where, V = velocity of flow in pipe)

$$= \frac{2.5V^2}{2g}$$

or, $$V = \sqrt{\frac{2g\,(h+15)}{2.5}}$$

Let us assume that the liquid surface falls a distance dh in time dt, then:

$$12 \times 15 \times (-\,dh) = Q{\cdot}dt$$

or, $$180 \times (-dh) = (\pi/4) \times 0.15^2 \times \sqrt{\frac{2g\,(h+15)}{2.5}}\ .\ dt$$

$$= 0.0495\sqrt{(h+15)}\ dt$$

or, $$\int_0^T dt = -\frac{180}{0.0495}\int_5^0 \frac{dh}{\sqrt{h+15}}$$

Let, $h + 15 = H$, then:

$$T = -3636\int_{20}^{15}\frac{dh}{\sqrt{H}} = -3636 \times 2\left[\sqrt{H}\right]_{20}^{15} = -3636 \times 2(\sqrt{15} - \sqrt{20})$$

$$= 4357 \text{ s or } \mathbf{1{\cdot}21\ hours}\ \textbf{(Ans.)}$$

12.8. PIPES IN PARALLEL

The pipes are said to be in *parallel* (Fig. 12·19) when a main line divides into two or more parallel pipes which again join together downstream and continues as a main line.

It may be seen from Fig. 12·19 that the rate of discharge in the main line is equal to the pipes.

Thus, $$Q = Q_1 + Q_2 \qquad ...(12{\cdot}16)$$

When the pipes are arranged in parallel, the *loss of head in each pipe (branch) is same.*

∴ Loss of head in pipe 1 = Loss of head in pipe 2.

or, $$h_f = \frac{4 f_1 L_1 V_1^2}{D_1 \times 2g} = \frac{4 f_2 L_2 V_2^2}{D_2 \times 2g} \quad ...(12\cdot17)$$

When, $f_1 = f_2$, then:

$$\frac{L_1 V_1^2}{D_1 \times 2g} = \frac{L_2 V_2^2}{D_2 \times 2g} \quad ...(12\cdot18)$$

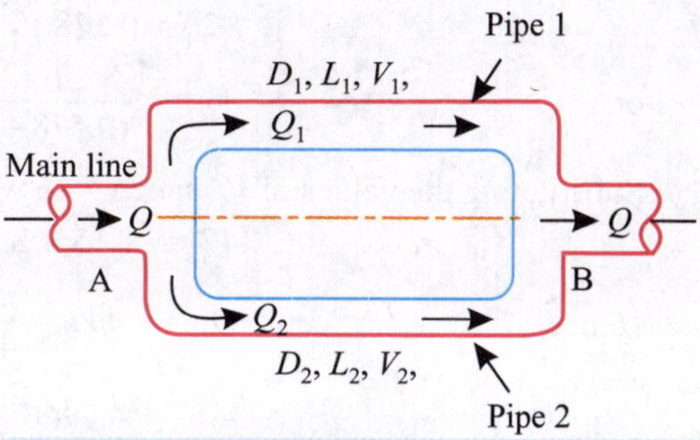

Fig. 12.19

Example 12.27. *The main pipe divides into two parallel pipes which again forms one pipe as shown in Fig. 12·19. The data is as follows :*

First parallel pipe : Length = 1000 m, diameter = 0·8 m

Second parallel pipe : Length = 1000 m, diameter = 0·6 m

Co-efficient of friction for each parallel pipe = 0·005

If the total rate of flow in the main is 2m^3/s find the rate of flow in each parallel pipe.

Solution. Length of pipe 1, L_1 = 1000 m

Diameter of pipe 1, D_1 = 0·8 m

Length of pipe 2, L_2 = 1000 m

Diameter of pipe 2, D_2 = 0·6 m

Total rate of flow, Q = 2 m^3/s

Co-efficients of friction, $f_1 = f_2 = 0\cdot005$

Rate of flow in each pipe :

Let, Q_1 = Rate of flow in pipe 1,

Q_2 = Rate of flow in pipe 2, and

Q = Total rate of flow (in main line).

Then, $Q = Q_1 + Q_2$ (Eqn. 12·16)

Also, $$h_f = \frac{4 f_1 L_1 V_1^2}{D_1 \times 2g} = \frac{4 f_2 L_2 V_2^2}{D_2 \times 2g} \quad ...[\text{Eqn. } 12\cdot17]$$

$$f_1 = f_2 \,(= 0\cdot005) \text{ and } L_1 = L_2 \,(= 1000 \text{ m})$$

The above equation reduces to :

$$\frac{V_1^2}{D_1} = \frac{V_2^2}{D_2} \quad \text{or} \quad \frac{V_1^2}{0.8} = \frac{V_2^2}{0.6}$$

or, $$V_1 = \sqrt{\frac{0.8}{0.6} \times V_2^2} = 1.15\, V_2 \quad ...(ii)$$

Now, $$Q_1 = \frac{\pi}{4} \times D_1^2 \times V_1$$

$$= \frac{\pi}{4} \times 0.8^2 \times 1.15\, V_2 = 0.578\, V_2$$

and, $$Q_2 = \frac{\pi}{4} \times D_2^2 \times V_2 = \frac{\pi}{4} \times 0.6^2 \times V_2 = 0.283\, V_2$$

Substituting the values of Q_1 and Q_2 in eqn. (*i*), we get:

$$2 = 0{\cdot}578\, V_2 + 0{\cdot}283\, V_2$$

or, $$V_2 = \frac{2}{(0.578 + 0.283)} = 2.32 \text{ m/s}$$

Substituting the values of V_2 in eqn. (*ii*), we get:

$$V_1 = 1.15 \times 2.32 = 2.67 \text{ m/s}$$

Hence, $$Q_1 = A_1V_1 = \frac{\pi}{4} \times 0.8^2 \times 2.67 = \mathbf{1.342\ m^3/s}\ \textbf{(Ans.)}$$

$\therefore$ $$Q_2 = Q - Q_1 = 2 - 1{\cdot}342$$
$$= \mathbf{0{\cdot}658\ m^3/s}\ \textbf{(Ans.)}$$

Example 12.28. *A pipeline of 600 mm diameter is 1·5 km long. To increase the discharge another line of the same diameter is introduced parallel to the first in the second-half of the length. If f = 0·01 and head at inlet is 300 mm calculate the increase in discharge. Neglect minor losses.* **[M.U.]**

Solution. Diameter of the pipeline, $D = 0{\cdot}6$ m

Length of the pipeline, $L = 1{\cdot}5$ km $= 1{\cdot}5 \times 1000 = 1500$ m.

Co-efficient of friction, $f = 0{\cdot}01$

Head at inlet, $h = 0{\cdot}3$ m

Head at outlet (= atmospheric head) = 0

$\therefore$ Head lost, $h_f = 0{\cdot}3$

Length of another parallel pipe, $L_2\ (= L_1) = \frac{1500}{2} = 750$ m

Diameter of another parallel pipe, $D_2\ (= D_1) = 0{\cdot}6$ m

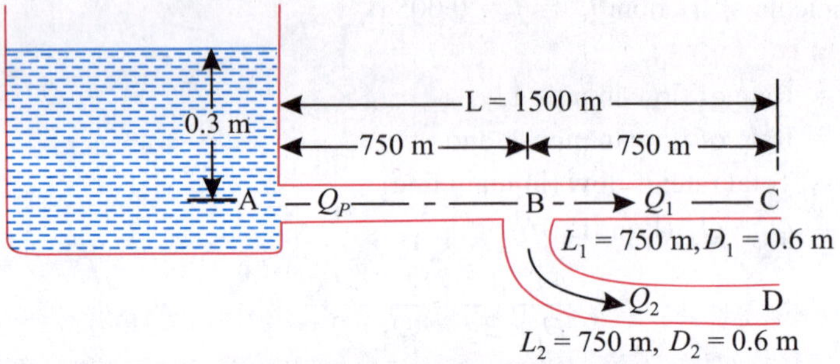

Fig. 12.20

The arrangement of the pipe system is shown in Fig. 12·20.

Increase in discharge :

Case. I. *Discharge (Q) for a single pipe of length 1500 m and diameter 0·6 m:*

The head lost due to friction in single pipe is given as :

$$h_f = \frac{4fLV^2}{D \times 2g}$$

(where, V = velocity of flow for a single pipe)

$\therefore$ $$0.3 = \frac{4 \times 0.01 \times 1500 \times V^2}{0.6 \times 2 \times 9.81}$$

or, $$V = \left[\frac{0.3 \times 0.6 \times 2 \times 9.81}{4 \times 0.01 \times 1500}\right]^{\frac{1}{2}} = 0.243 \text{ m/s}$$

∴ Discharge $$Q = A \times V = \frac{\pi}{4} \times 0.6^2 \times 0.243 = 0.0687 \text{ m}^3/\text{s} \quad ...(i)$$

Case. II. *When an additional pipe of length 750 m and diameter 0·6 m is connected in parallel with the last half length of the pipe:*

Let, Q_1 = Discharge in first parallel pipe,

Q_2 = Discharge in second parallel pipe,

Q_p = Discharge in the main pipe (when pipes are connected in parallel).

Then, $$Q_p = Q_1 + Q_2 \quad ...(\text{Fig. } 12{\cdot}20)$$

As the pipes in parallel have the same diameter and length,

$$\therefore \quad Q_1 = Q_2 = \frac{Q_p}{2}$$

Consider the flow through ABC or ABD.

Head lost (due to friction) in *ABC*

$$= \text{Head lost in } AB + \text{head lost in } BC \quad ...(ii)$$

$$\text{Head lost in } ABC = 0{\cdot}3 \text{ m } (given)$$

Now, $$\text{Head lost in } AB = \frac{4 \times 0.01 \times 750 \times V_{AB}^2}{0.6 \times 2 \times 9.81}$$

But, $$V_{AB} = \frac{Q_p}{\text{Area}} = \frac{Q_p}{(\pi/4) \times 0.6^2} = 3.54\, Q_p$$

∴ *Head Lost (due to friction) in AB*

$$= \frac{4 \times 0.01 \times 750 \times (3.54\, Q_p)^2}{0.6 \times 2 \times 9.81} = 31.9\, Q_p^2$$

Head lost due to friction through *BC*

$$= \frac{4 f L_1 V_{BC}^2}{D_1 \times 2g}$$

$$= \frac{4 \times 0.01 \times 750 \times (1.77\, Q_p)^2}{0.6 \times 2 \times 9.81}$$

$$= 7{\cdot}98\, Q_p^2 \qquad \left[\because V_{BC} = \frac{(Q_p/2)}{\text{area}} = \frac{(Q_p/2)}{(\pi/4) \times 0.6^2} = 1.77\, Q_p\right]$$

Substituting these values in eqn. (*ii*), we get:

$$0.3 = 31.9\, Q_p^2 + 7.98\, Q_p^2$$

or, $$Q_p = \left[\frac{0.3}{31.9 + 7.98}\right]^{1/2} = 0.087 \text{ m}^3/\text{s}$$

∴ $$\text{Increase in discharge} = Q_p - Q$$

$$= 0{\cdot}087 - 0{\cdot}0687 = \mathbf{0{\cdot}0183 \text{ m}^3/\text{s}} \quad \textbf{(Ans.)}$$

Example 12.29. *Two sharp ended pipes of diameters 50 mm and 100 mm respectively, each of length 100 m respectively, are connected in parallel between two reservoirs which have a difference of level of 10 m. If the friction factor for each pipe is 0·32, calculate :*

(i) Rate of flow for each pipe, and

(ii) The diameter of a single pipe 100 m long which would give the same discharge, if it were subsitutued for the original two pipes. **[Allahabad University]**

Solution. Diameter of pipe 1, D_1 = 50 mm = 0·05 m
Diameter of pipe 2, D_2 = 100 mm = 0·1 m
Length of pipe 1, L_1 = 100 m
Length of pipe 2, L_2 = 100 m
Difference in level, h = 10 m
Friction factor, $(4f)$ = 0·32

(*i*) Rate of flow for each pipe :

Let, V_1 = Velocity of flow in pipe 1, and
V_2 = Velocity of flow in pipe 2.

Since the pipes are connected in *parallel*, therefore the *loss of head will be same* in both the pipes.

For the *pipe 1,* the loss of head,

$$10 = h_f = \frac{4fL_1V_1^2}{D_1 \times 2g} = \frac{0.32 \times 100 \times V_1^2}{0.05 \times 2 \times 9.81} = 32.62 V_1^2 \qquad (\because 4f = 0{\cdot}32)$$

or, $$10 = 32.62\, V_1^2$$

or, $$V_1 = \left(\frac{10}{32.62}\right)^{1/2} = 0.55 \text{ m/s}$$

∴ Rate of flow in pipe 1,

$$Q_1 = A_1V_1 = \frac{\pi}{4} \times (0.05)^2 \times 0.55$$

$$= \mathbf{0{\cdot}00108\ m^3/s} \quad \textbf{(Ans.)}$$

For the *pipe* 2 the loss of head is given by:

$$10 = \frac{4fL_2V_2^2}{D_2 \times 2g} = \frac{0.32 \times 100 \times V_2^2}{0.1 \times 2 \times 9.81} = 16.31\, V_2^2$$

or, $$V_2 = \left(\frac{10}{16.31}\right)^{1/2} = 0.78 \text{ m/s}$$

∴ Rate of flow in pipe 2,

$$Q_2 = A_2V_2 = \frac{\pi}{4} \times 0.1^2 \times 0.78 = \mathbf{0.00613\ m^3/s}\ \textbf{(Ans.)}$$

(*ii*) Diameter of the single pipe, D :

Let, D = Diameter of the single pipe,
L = Length of the single pipe = 100 m,
V = Velocity of liquid in the single pipe, and
Q = Discharge through the single pipe.

Now, $$Q = Q_1 + Q_2$$
$$= 0.00108 + 0.00613 = 0.00721 \text{ m}^3\text{/s}$$

∴ $$V = \frac{Q}{A} = \frac{0.00721}{(\pi/4) \times D^2} = \frac{0.00918}{D^2} \text{ m/s}$$

Loss of head through the single pipe,

$$10 = h_f = \frac{4fLV^2}{D \times 2g} = \frac{0.32 \times 100 \times \left(\frac{0.00918}{D^2}\right)^2}{D \times 2 \times 9.81}$$

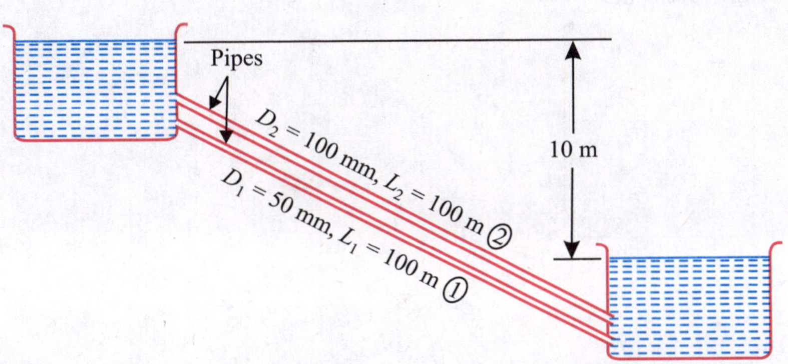

Fig. 12.21

or,
$$10 = \frac{0.32 \times 100 \times (0.00918)^2}{2 \times 9.81 \times D^5} = \frac{0.0001375}{D^5}$$

or
$$D = \left[\frac{0.0001375}{10}\right]^{1/5} = 0.1066 \text{ m} = 106.6 \text{ mm}$$

i.e., $D =$ **106·6 mm (Ans.)**

Example 12.30. *A 250 mm diameter, 3 km long straight pipe runs between two reservoirs of surface elevations 135 m and 60 m. A 1·5 km long, 300 mm diameter pipe is laid parallel to the 250 mm diameter pipe from its mid-point to the lower reservoir. Neglecting all minor losses and assuming a friction factor of 0·02 for both pipes, find the increase in discharge caused by addition of 300 diameter pipe.* **(Anna University)**

Solution. Neglecting minor losses, the application of Bernoulli's equation between the water surfaces of the two reservoirs yields: $(135 - 60) = \dfrac{fLV^2}{D \times 2g} = \dfrac{0.02 \times 3000 \times V^2}{0.25 \times 2 \times 9.81}$

or,
$$V = \left[\frac{(135 - 60) \times 0.25 \times 2 \times 9.81}{0.02 \times 3000}\right]^{1/2} = 2.476 \text{ m/s}$$

The discharge through the pipeline,

$$Q = \frac{\pi}{4} \times (0.25)^2 \times 2.476 = 0.1215 \text{ m}^3\text{/s}$$

In case of altered pipeline (see fig. 12·22) the discharge through pipe section *AB* is the sum of the discharges through sections *BC* and *BD*, or

$$Q_1 = Q_2 + Q_3$$

or,
$$\frac{\pi}{4} D_1^2 V_1 = \frac{\pi}{4} D_2^2 V_2 + \frac{\pi}{4} D_3^2 V_3$$

$$D_1^2 V_1 = D_2^2 V_2 + D_3^2 V_3$$

$$= D_1^2 V_2 + D_3^2 V_3 \quad ...(i)$$

Also, as the end points of sections *BC* and *CD* are same (they are in parallel.),

$$h_{f_2} = h_{f_3}$$

or,
$$\frac{f\,(L/2)\,V_2^2}{D_2 \times 2g} = \frac{f\,(L/2)\,V_3^2}{D_3 \times 2g}$$

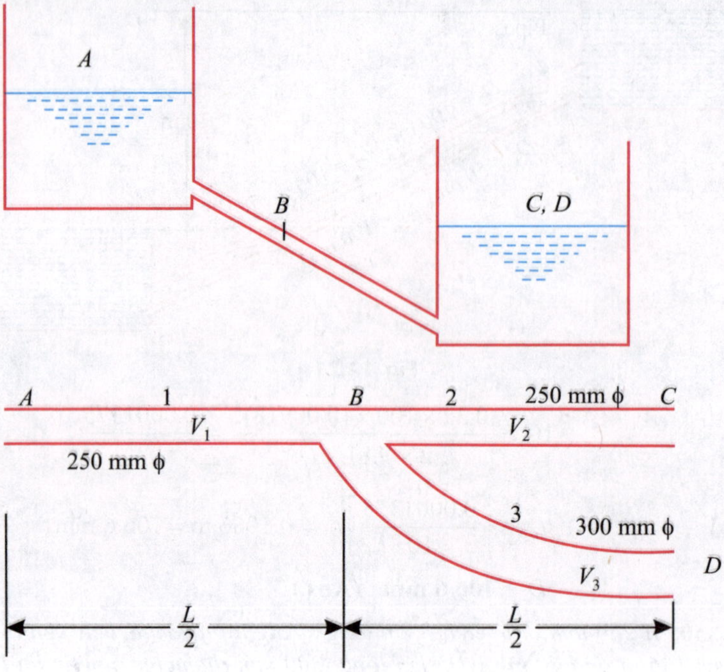

Fig. 12.22

or, $$\frac{V_2^2}{D_2} = \frac{V_3^2}{D_3}$$

or, $$V_3 = \left[V_2^2 \times \frac{D_3}{D_2}\right]^{1/2}$$

$$= \left[V_2^2 \times \frac{300}{250}\right]^{1/2}$$

$$= \sqrt{\frac{300}{250}}\, V_2 \qquad \text{...}(ii)$$

Substituting for V_3 in (i), we get:

or, $$(250)^2\, V_1 = (250)^2\, V_2 + (300)^2 \times \sqrt{\frac{300}{250}}\, V_2$$

or, $$(250)^2\, (V_1 - V_2) = (300)^2 \times \sqrt{\frac{300}{250}}\, V_2$$

or, $$V_1 - V_2 = 1{\cdot}5774\, V_2$$

or, $$V_1 = 2{\cdot}5774\, V_2 \quad \text{or} \quad V_2 = 0{\cdot}388\, V_1$$

Again, applying Bernoulli's equation between the water surfaces of the two reservoirs through *ABC*, we get:

$$(135 - 60) = \frac{f\,(L/2)V_1^2}{D_1 \times 2g} + \frac{f\,(L/2)V_2^2}{D_2 \times 2g}$$

$$75 = \frac{f\,(L/2)}{D_1 \times 2g}\,(V_1^2 + V_2^2) \qquad (\because D_1 = D_2)$$

$$= \frac{0.02 \times 1500}{0.25 \times 2 \times 9.81} \{V_1^2 + (0.388\, V_1)^2\} = 6.116 \times 1.1505\, V_1^2$$

or, $$V_1 = \left(\frac{75}{6.116 \times 1.1505}\right)^{1/2} = 3.26 \text{ m/s}$$

$\therefore$ $$\text{Discharge} = \frac{\pi}{4} D_1^2 V_1 = \frac{\pi}{4} \times 0.25^2 \times 3.26 = 0.16 \text{ m}^3/\text{s}$$

$\therefore$ Increase in discharge = 0·16 – 0·1215 = **0·0385 m³/s** or **31·7 % (Ans.)**

Example 12.31. *A farmer wishes to connect two pipes of different lengths and diameters to a common header supplied with 8 × 10⁻³ m³/s of water from a pump. One pipe is 100 m long and 5 cm in diameter. The other pipe is 800 m long. Determine the diameter of the second pipe such that both pipes have the same flow rate. Assume the pipes to be laid on level ground and friction co-efficient for both pipes as 0·02. Also determine the head loss in metres of water in the pipes.* **(GATE)**

Solution. Refer to Fig. 12·23. *Given :* $Q = 8 \times 10^{-3}$ m³/s; D_1 = 5 cm = 0·05 m; L_1 = 100 m; L_2 = 800 m; Friction co-efficient, f = 0·02.

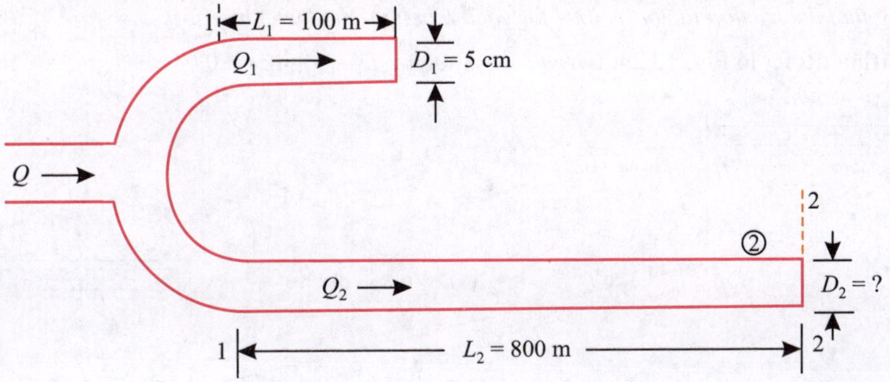

Fig. 12.23

Diameter, D_2 :

$$Q = Q_1 + Q_2 \quad \left[\text{where, } Q_1 = Q_2 = \frac{8 \times 10^{-3}}{2} = 4 \times 10^{-3} \text{ m}^3/\text{s } (Given)\right]$$

For pipe 1, $$h_{f_1} = \frac{4 f L_1 V_1^2}{D_1 \times 2g}$$

where, $$V_1 = \frac{Q_1}{(\pi/4) \times D_1^2} = \frac{4Q_1}{\pi D_1^2}$$

$\therefore$ $$h_{f_1} = \frac{4 f L_1 \times \left[\frac{4Q_1}{\pi D_1^2}\right]^2}{D_1 \times 2g} = \frac{32\, f L_1 Q_1^2}{\pi^2 \times D_1^5 \times g}$$

Similarly, *for pipe 2,* $$h_{f_2} = \frac{32\, f L_2 Q_2^2}{\pi^2 \times D_2^5 \times g} \qquad ...(ii)$$

Equating (*i*) and (*ii*) [since $h_{f_1} = h_{f_2}$], we get:

$$\frac{32\, f L_1 Q_1^2}{\pi^2 \times D_1^5 \times g} = \frac{32\, f L_2 Q_2^2}{\pi^2 \times D_2^5 \times g}$$

or, $$\frac{Q_1^2}{Q_2^2} = \frac{L_2 D_1^5}{L_1 D_2^5}$$

But, $$Q_1 = Q_2$$ ...(Given)

∴ $$L_2 D_1^5 = L_1 D_2^5$$

or, $$D_2 = \left(\frac{L_2 D_1^5}{L_1}\right)^{1/5} = \left[\frac{800 \times (0.05)^5}{100}\right]^{1/5}$$

$$= 0.7578 \text{ m} = \mathbf{7.578 \text{ cm}} \text{ (Ans.)}$$

Head loss :

$$h_{f1} (= h_{f2}) = \frac{32\, fL_1 Q_1^2}{\pi^2 \times D_1^5 \times g} = \frac{32 \times 0.02 \times 100 \times (4 \times 10^{-3})^2}{\pi^2 \times (0.05)^5 \times 9.81} = \mathbf{33.84 \text{ m}} \text{ (Ans.)}$$

Example 12.32. *A pipeline with diameter 0·8 m and length 3000 m connects two open reservoirs of water which have their water surfaces of elevations of 100 m and 70 m above a datum. In order to increase the rate of flow between the reservoirs by 20 % it is decided to lay an additional 0·8 m diameter pipeline from the upper reservoir. The second pipeline is to be parallel to the original pipeline and is to be connected to the latter at some suitable point. Determine the point of connection, assuming that the friction factor is 0·04 for each pipeline. Neglect minor losses.* **(PEC)**

Solution. Refer to Fig. 12·24. *Given* : $L = 3000$ m; $D = 0{\cdot}8$ m; $f = 0{\cdot}04$

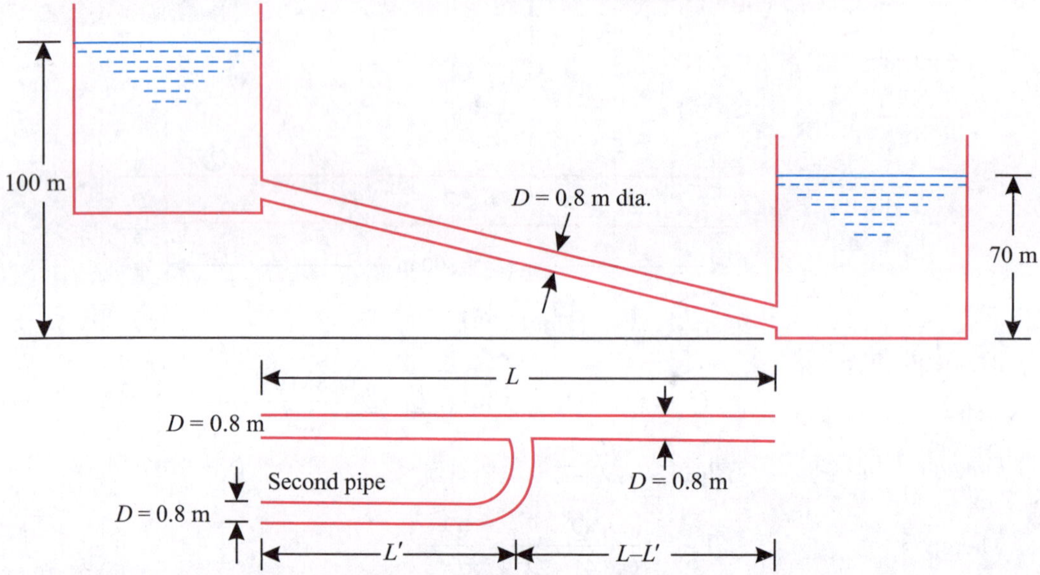

Fig. 12.24

Point of connection of second pipe, *L'*:

Head at inlet of pipe = 100 – 70 = 30 m

Case I. *Discharge (Q_1) for a single pipe length 3000 m and diameter 0·8 m:*

The head lost due to friction in single pipe is given as :

$$h_f = \frac{fLV_1^2}{D \times 2g}$$

[where, f = friction factor (= 4 × co-efficient of friction)]

where, $$V_1 = \frac{Q_1}{A_1} = \frac{Q_1}{\frac{\pi}{4} \times D^2} = \frac{4Q_1}{\pi D^2}$$

$$\therefore \qquad h_f = \frac{fL \times \left(\frac{4Q_1}{\pi D^2}\right)^2}{D \times 2g} = \frac{8fLQ_1^2}{\pi^2 D^5 \times g} = \frac{fLQ_1^2}{12D^5}$$

Substituting the values, we get:

$$30 = \frac{0.04 \times 3000 \times Q_1^2}{12 \times (0.8)^5}$$

or,
$$Q_1 = \left[\frac{30 \times 12 \times (0.8)^5}{0.04 \times 3000}\right]^{1/2} = 0.99 \text{ m}^3/\text{s}$$

Case II. *When another pipeline of length L' is added :*

Total discharge, $Q_2 = 1{\cdot}2\ Q_1 = 1{\cdot}2 \times 0{\cdot}99 = 1{\cdot}188 \text{ m}^3/\text{s}$

Discharge through each pipeline $= \frac{Q_2}{2}$

In this case, Total head loss = Sum of head losses in two pipes

i.e.,
$$h_f = \frac{fL'V_1^2}{D \times 2g} + \frac{f(L - L')V_2^2}{D \times 2g}$$

or,
$$30 = \frac{fL' \times \left(\frac{Q_2}{2}\right)^2}{12\ D^5} + \frac{f(L - L')Q_2^2}{12\ D^5}$$

or,
$$30 = \frac{fL'Q_2^2}{4 \times 12\ D^5} + \frac{f(L - L')Q_2^2}{12\ D^5}$$

Substituting the values, we get:

or,
$$\frac{30 \times 12 \times (0.8)^5}{0.04 \times (1.188)^2} = \frac{L'}{4} - L' + 3000$$

$$2089.6 = \frac{L'}{4} - L' + 3000$$

or,
$$L' - \frac{L'}{4} = 3000 - 2089.7 = 910.4$$

$$\therefore \qquad L' = \mathbf{1213{\cdot}87\ m}$$ **(Ans.)**

Example 12.33. *Two reservoirs have a constant difference of levels of 70 m and are connected by a 250 mm diameter pipe which is 4 km long. The pipe is tapped mid-way between the reservoirs and water is drawn at the rate of 0·04 m³/s. Assuming friction factor = 0·04, determine the rate at which water enters the lower reservoir.*

Solution. Diameter of the pipe, $D = 250 \text{ mm} = 0{\cdot}25 \text{ m}$

Difference of level, $h = 70 \text{ m}$

Friction factor, $4f = 0{\cdot}04$

Rate at which water enters the lower reservoir :

Let, Q = Discharge entering the lower reservoir.

Then, Discharge at the inlet $= (Q + 0{\cdot}04) \text{ m}^3/\text{s}$.

Now, from the application of Bernoulli's equation, we have:

$$h = h_{f_1} + h_{f_2}$$

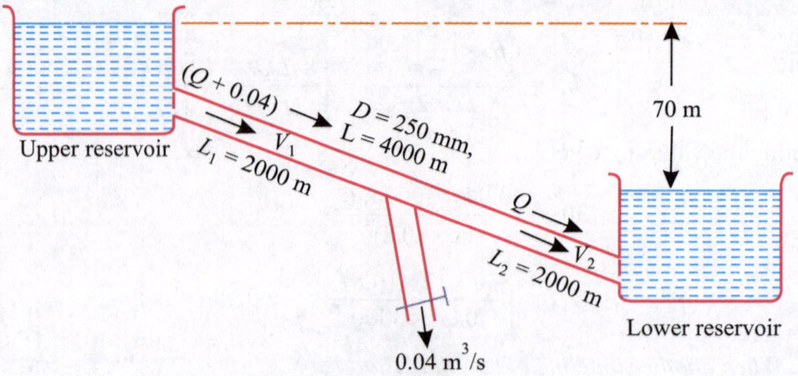

Fig. 12.25

$$70 = \frac{4fL_1V_1^2}{D \times 2g} + \frac{4fL_2V_2^2}{D \times 2g}$$

$$= \frac{0.04 \times 2000 \times V_1^2}{0.25 \times 2g} + \frac{0.04 \times 2000 \times V_2^2}{0.25 \times 2g} \qquad (\because 4f = 0{\cdot}04)$$

or, $$70 = \frac{320}{2g}(V_1^2 + V_2^2)$$

Substituting :

$$V_1 = \frac{Q + 0.04}{A} = \frac{(Q + 0.04)}{(\pi/4) \times 0.25^2} = 20.37\,(Q + 0.04)$$

and, $$V_2 = \frac{Q}{A} = \frac{Q}{(\pi/4) \times 0{\cdot}25^2} = 20{\cdot}37\,Q$$

Eqn. (*i*) becomes :

$$70 = \frac{320}{2 \times 9.81}\left[\{20.37\,(Q + 0.04)\}^2 + (20.37Q)^2\right]$$

or, $$70 = \frac{320 \times 20.37^2}{2 \times 9.81}\left[(Q + 0.04)^2 + Q^2\right]$$

or, $$70 = 6768\,(Q^2 + 0{\cdot}0016 + 0{\cdot}08Q + Q^2)$$

or, $$2Q^2 + 0{\cdot}08Q + 0{\cdot}0016 = 0{\cdot}0103$$

or, $$Q^2 + 0{\cdot}04Q - 0{\cdot}0043 = 0$$

or, $$Q = \frac{-0.04 \pm \sqrt{0.0016 + 0.0172}}{2}$$

$$= \frac{-0.04 \pm 0.137}{2}$$

$$= \frac{0.097}{2} = 0.0485\ m^3/s$$

Hence, *the rate at which water enters the lower reservoir* = **0·0485 m³/s** **(Ans.)**

Example 12.34. *Two pipes of diameters 400 mm and 200 mm are each 300 m long. When the pipes are connected in series the discharsge through the pipeline is 0·10 m³/s, find the loss of head incurred. What would be the loss of head in the system to pass the same total discharge when the pipes are connected in parallel ? Take friction factor = 0·0075 for each pipe.* **[Nagpur University]**

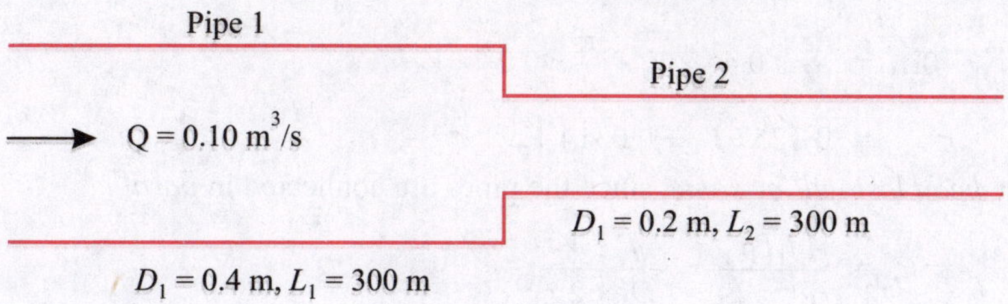

Fig. 12.26

Solution. Diameter of the pipe 1, D_1 = 400 mm = 0·4 m

Length of the pipe 1, L_1 = 300 m

Diameter of the pipe 2, D_2 = 200 mm = 0·2 m

Length of the pipe 2, L_2 = 300 m

Friction factor for each pipe $(4f)$ = 0·0075

Discharge, Q = 0.1 m³/s

(*i*) Pipes connected in series – Loss of head :

$$\text{Velocity of flow in pipe 1, } V_1 = \frac{0.1}{(\pi/4)\times 0.4^2} = 0.796 \text{ m/s}$$

$$\text{Velocity of flow in pipe 2, } V_2 = \frac{0.1}{(\pi/4)\times 0.2^2} = 3.183 \text{ m/s}$$

$$\text{Head lost due to friction in pipe 1} = \frac{4f_1L_1V_1^2}{D_1\times 2g} = \frac{0.0075\times 300\times 0.796^2}{0.4\times 2\times 9.81} = 0.1816 \text{ m}$$

Assuming head lost due to contraction,

$$h_c = k\frac{V_2^2}{2g}$$

or,

$$h_c = 0.33\frac{V_2^2}{2g}\left[\text{for}\frac{D_2}{D_1} = 0.5, k = 0.33 \text{ ...(from tables)}\right]$$

$$= \frac{0.33\times 3.183^2}{2\times 9.81} = 0.17 \text{ m}$$

$$\text{Head lost due to friction in pipe 2} = \frac{4f_2L_2V_2^2}{D_2\times 2g} = \frac{0.0075\times 300\times 3.183^2}{0.2\times 2\times 9.81}$$

$$= 5{\cdot}809 \text{ m}$$

∴ Head lost in the pipeline = 0·1816 + 0·17 + 5·809 = **6·16 m** **(Ans.)**

(*ii*) Pipes in Parallel–Loss of head :

From continuity consideration, we have:

$$Q = Q_1 + Q_2$$

$$0.1 = Q_1 + Q_2 \quad \text{...(Given)}$$

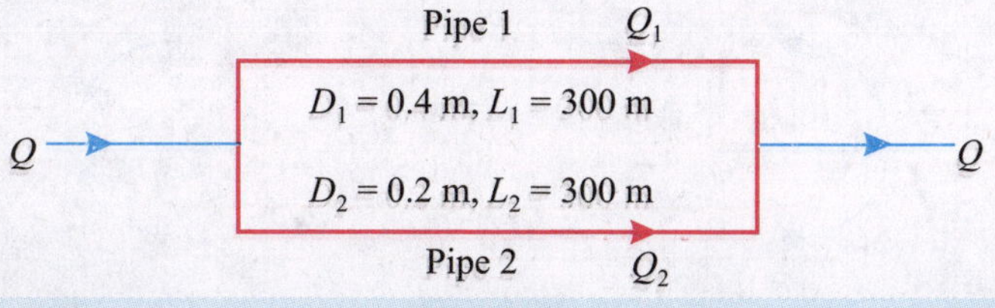

Fig. 12.27

or, $$0.1 = \frac{\pi}{4} \times 0.4^2 \times V_1 + \frac{\pi}{4} \times 0.2^2 \times V_2$$

$$= 0{\cdot}1257\, V_1 + 0{\cdot}0314\, V_2 \quad ...(1)$$

Also, *head lost will be same*, since the pipes are connected in *parallel*.

$$\therefore \quad h_f = \frac{4 f_1 L_1 V_1^2}{D_1 \times 2g} = \frac{4 f_2 L_2 V_2^2}{D_2 \times 2g}$$

But, $f_1 = f_2$ and $L_1 = L_2$

$$\therefore \quad \frac{V_1^2}{D_1} = \frac{V_2^2}{D_2} \quad \text{or} \quad \frac{V_1^2}{V_2^2} = \frac{D_1}{D_2} = \frac{0.4}{0.2} = 2$$

or, $$V_1^2 = 2V_2^2 \quad ...(2)$$

Substituting the value of V_2 from (1) in (2), we get:

$$V_1^2 = 2\left[\frac{0.1 - 0.1257\, V_1}{0.0314}\right]^2 = 2\,(3.185 - 4V_1)^2 = 20.29 + 32V_1^2 - 50.96V_1$$

or, $$31V_1^2 - 50{\cdot}96V_1 + 20{\cdot}29 = 0$$

or, $$V_1 = \frac{50.96 \pm \sqrt{50.96^2 - 4 \times 31 \times 20.29}}{2 \times 31} = 0.97 \text{ m/s},\ 0{\cdot}677 \text{ m/s}$$

Using $V_1 = 0{\cdot}97$ m/s, we have:

$$Q_1 = (\pi/4) \times 0{\cdot}4^2 \times 0{\cdot}97 = 0{\cdot}1219 \text{ m}^3/\text{s}$$

Since $Q_1 > Q$, $V_1 = 0{\cdot}97$ m/s is not *realistic*.

Using $V_1 = 0{\cdot}677$ m/s, we have:

$$Q_1 = (\pi/4) \times 0{\cdot}4^2 \times 0{\cdot}677 = 0{\cdot}085 \text{ m}^3/\text{s}$$

$$Q_2 = 0{\cdot}1 - 0{\cdot}085 = 0{\cdot}015 \text{ m}^3/\text{s}$$

$$\text{Head lost} = \frac{4 f_1 L_1 V_1^2}{D_1 \times 2g} = \frac{0.0075 \times 300 \times 0.677^2}{0.4 \times 2 \times 9.81} = \mathbf{0.131\ m}$$ **(Ans.)**

Example 12.35. *The pipes of diameter D and d of equal length L are considered. If the pipes are arranged in parallel, the loss of head for either pipe for a flow of Q is h. If the pipes are arranged in series and the same quantity Q flows through them, the loss of head is H. If d = 0·5 D, find the percentage of total flow through each pipe when placed in parallel and the ratio of H to h neglecting minor losses and assuming friction co-efficient to be constant.* **[UPSC Exams.]**

Solution. Diameter of pipe 1, $D_1 = D$

Length of pipe 1, $L_1 = L$

Diameter of pipe 2, $D_2 = d$

Length of pipe 2, $L_2 = L$

Total discharge $= Q$

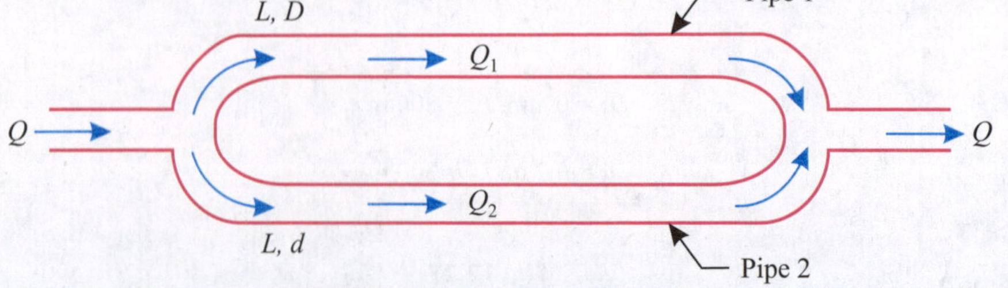

Fig. 12.28. Pipes connected in parallel.

Head lost when pipes are arranged in parallel $= h$

Head lost when pipe are arranged in series $= H$

$d = 0{\cdot}5\, D$ and f is constant.

Case I. Pipes connected in "parallel" :

When pipes are connected in *parallel*,

$$Q = Q_1 + Q_2 \quad ...(i)$$

Loss of head in each pipe $= h$

For pipe 1 :

$$h = \frac{4 f L_1 V_1^2}{D \times 2g}$$

where,

$$V_1 = \frac{Q_1}{A_1} = \frac{Q_1}{(\pi/4) \times D^2} = \frac{4Q_1}{\pi D^2}$$

$$\therefore \quad h = \frac{4 fL \times \left(\frac{4Q_1}{\pi D^2}\right)^2}{D \times 2g} = \frac{32 fLQ_1^2}{\pi^2 D^5 \times g} \quad ...(ii) \qquad (\because L_1 = L)$$

For pipe 2 :

$$h = \frac{32 fLQ_2^2}{\pi^2 d^5 \times g} \quad ...(iii)$$

From eqns. (*ii*) and (*iii*), we have:

$$\frac{32 fLQ_1^2}{\pi^2 D^5 \times g} = \frac{32 fLQ_2^2}{\pi^2 d^5 \times g}$$

or,

$$\frac{Q_1^2}{D^5} = \frac{Q_2^2}{d^5}$$

or,

$$\left(\frac{Q_1}{Q_2}\right)^2 = \left(\frac{D}{d}\right)^5 = \left(\frac{D}{0.5D}\right)^5 = 32 \qquad (\because d = 0{\cdot}5D ... Given)$$

or,

$$\frac{Q_1}{Q_2} = 5.567 \quad \text{or} \quad Q_1 = 5{\cdot}567\, Q_2$$

Substituting the value of Q_1 in eqn. (*i*), we get:

$$Q = 5{\cdot}567 Q_2 + Q_2 = 6{\cdot}657 Q_2$$

$$\therefore \quad Q_2 = \frac{Q}{6.657} = 0.15Q \quad ...(iv)$$

and,

$$Q_1 = Q - 0{\cdot}15\, Q = 0{\cdot}85\, Q \quad ...[\text{From } (i)] \quad ...(v)$$

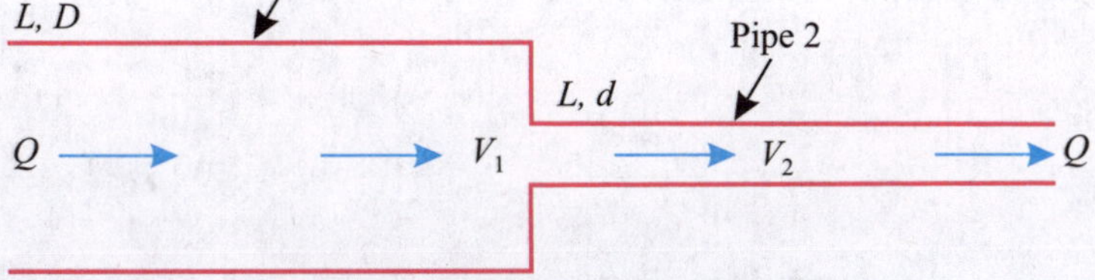

Fig. 12.29. Pipes connected in series.

Case II. Pipes connected in "series" :

In this case, Total loss = Sum of head losses in the two pipes

$$\therefore \quad H = \frac{4 fLV_1^2}{D \times 2g} + \frac{4 fLV_2^2}{d \times 2g}$$

where, $$V_1 = \frac{Q}{(\pi/4) \times D^2} = \frac{4Q}{\pi D^2}$$

$$V_2 = \frac{Q}{(\pi/4) \times d^2} = \frac{4Q}{\pi d^2}$$

$$\therefore \quad H = \frac{4fL \times \left(\frac{4Q}{\pi D^2}\right)^2}{D \times 2g} + \frac{4fL \times \left(\frac{4Q}{\pi d^2}\right)^2}{d \times 2g} \quad ...(vi)$$

or, $$H = \frac{32 fLQ^2}{\pi^2 D^5 \times g} + \frac{32 fLQ^2}{\pi^2 d^5 \times g}$$

From eqn. (*ii*) $$\frac{32 fL}{\pi^2 D^5 \times g} = \frac{h}{Q_1^2}$$

and, from eqn. (*iii*) $$\frac{32 fL}{\pi^2 d^5 \times g} = \frac{h}{Q_2^2}$$

Substituting these values in eqn. (*vi*), we get:

$$H = Q^2 \times \frac{h}{Q_1^2} + Q^2 \times \frac{h}{Q_2^2} = h\left(\frac{Q^2}{Q_1^2} + \frac{Q^2}{Q_2^2}\right)$$

$$\therefore \quad \frac{H}{h} = \frac{Q^2}{Q_1^2} + \frac{Q^2}{Q_2^2}$$

But from eqns. (*iv*) and (*v*),

$$Q_1 = 0{\cdot}85\, Q \text{ and } Q_2 = 0{\cdot}15\, Q$$

$$\therefore \quad \frac{H}{h} = \frac{Q^2}{(0.85Q)^2} + \frac{Q^2}{(0.15Q)^2} = \mathbf{45.828}$$ **(Ans.)**

Example 12.36. *A pumping plant forces water through a 600 mm diameter main, the friction head being 27 m. In order to reduce the power consumption, it is proposed to lay another main of appropriate diameter along the side of the existing one, so that the two pipes may work in parallel for the entire length and reduce the friction head to 9·6 m only. Find the diameter of the new main if with the exception of diameter, it is similar to the existing one in every respect.* **[Delhi University]**

Solution. Diameter of single main pipe, D = 600 mm = 0·6 m

Friction head, h_f = 27 m

Friction head for two parallel pipes = 9·6 m

Diameter of the new main :

Case I. *Single main :*

$$h_f = \frac{4fLV^2}{D \times 2g}$$

$$27 = \frac{4fLV^2}{0.6 \times 2 \times 9.81}$$

$$fLV^2 = \frac{27 \times 0.6 \times 2 \times 9.81}{4} = 79.461$$

But, $$V = \frac{Q}{A}$$

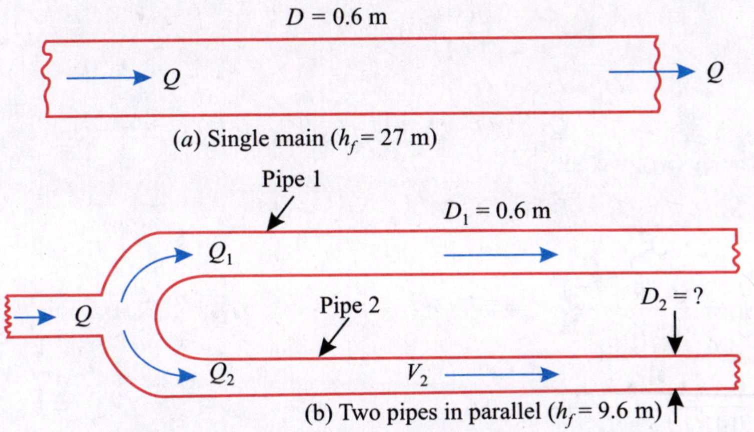

Fig. 12.30

$$\therefore \quad fL\frac{Q^2}{A^2} = 79.461 \quad \text{...}(i)$$

Case II. *Two pipes in parallel :*

$$\text{Loss of head, } h_f = 9{\cdot}6 \text{ m}$$

For pipe 1 :

$$h_{f_1} = \frac{4fL_1V_1^2}{D_1 \times 2g} = 9{\cdot}6$$

But, $$L_1 = L,\ V_1 = \frac{Q_1}{A_1} = \frac{Q_1}{A} \quad (\because A_1 = A)$$

$$D_1 = D = 0{\cdot}6 \text{ m}$$

$$\therefore \quad \frac{4fL}{0.6 \times 2 \times 9.81} \times \frac{Q_1^2}{A^2} = 9.6$$

or, $$fL\frac{Q_1^2}{A^2} = \frac{9.6 \times 0.6 \times 2 \times 9.81}{4} = 28.25 \quad \text{...}(ii)$$

For pipe 2 :

$$h_{f_2} = \frac{4fL_2V_2^2}{D_2 \times 2g} = 9.6$$

where, $$L_2 = L,\ V_2 = \frac{Q_2}{A_2}$$

$$\therefore \quad \frac{4fLQ_2^2}{D_2 \times 2g \times A_2^2} = 9.6$$

or, $$\frac{fLQ_2^2}{D_2A_2^2} = \frac{9.6 \times 2 \times 9.81}{4} = 47.09 \quad \text{...}(iii)$$

Dividing (*i*) by (*iii*), we get:

$$\frac{Q^2}{Q_1^2} = \frac{79.461}{28.25} = 2.81$$

or, $$\frac{Q}{Q_1} = 1.67$$

or, $$Q_1 = \frac{Q}{1.67} = 0.59\,Q$$

But, $$Q_1 + Q_2 = Q$$

$\therefore$ $$Q_2 = Q - Q_1 = Q - 0{\cdot}59Q = 0{\cdot}41Q$$

Dividing (*ii*) by (*iii*), we get:

$$\frac{Q_1^2 \times D_2 \times A_2^2}{Q_2^2 \times A^2} = \frac{28.25}{47.09} = 0.6$$

or, $$\frac{Q_1 \times D_2 \times (\pi/4 \times D_2^2)^2}{Q_2^2 \times \left[\pi/4 \times (0{\cdot}6)^2\right]^2} = 0.6$$

$$\left(\frac{0{\cdot}59Q}{0{\cdot}41Q}\right)^2 \times \frac{D_2^5}{(0{\cdot}36)^2} = 0.6$$

or, $$D_2^5 = 0.6 \times (0.36)^2 \times \left(\frac{0.41}{0.59}\right)^2 = 0.03755$$

or, $$D_2 = 0{\cdot}518 \text{ m} = \mathbf{518\ mm}\ \textbf{(Ans.)}$$

Example 12.37. *Two pipes A and B are connected in parallel between two points. Pipe A is 180 m long and has a diameter of 12 cm. Pipe B is 120 m long and has a diameter of 10 cm. Both the pipes have the same friction factor of 0·017. A partially closed valve in pipe A causes the discharge in the two pipes to be the same (Fig. 12·31.). Neglecting all other minor losses, calculate the value of the valve co-efficient.*

Solution. *Given* : $L_A = 180$ m; $D_A = 12$ cm $= 0{\cdot}12$ m; $L_B = 120$ m; $D_B = 10$ cm $= 0{\cdot}1$ m; Friction factor; $f = 0{\cdot}017$.

Value of the valve co-efficient, K_v :

Since the discharges are same in both the pipes,

$$A_A V_A = A_B V_B$$

or, $$\frac{\pi}{4} \times (0.12)^2 \times V_A = \frac{\pi}{4} \times (0.1)^2 \times V_B$$

$\therefore$ $$V_B = 1{\cdot}44\ V_A$$

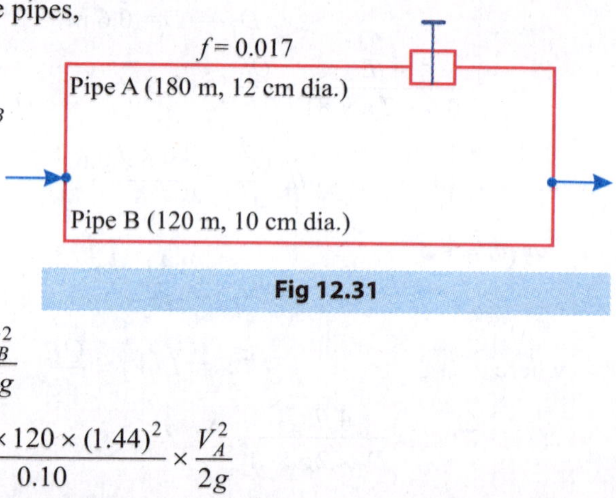

Fig 12.31

Let the losses in the valve be $K_v \dfrac{V_A^2}{2g}$.

Head losses in both the pipes are same.

Hence, $$\frac{f_A L_A V_A^2}{D_A \times 2g} + \frac{K_v V_A^2}{2g} = \frac{f_B L_B V_B^2}{D_B \times 2g}$$

$$\frac{0.017 \times 180}{0.12} \times \frac{V_A^2}{2g} + K_v \frac{V_A^2}{2g} = \frac{0.017 \times 120 \times (1.44)^2}{0.10} \times \frac{V_A^2}{2g}$$

$$25.5 + K_v = 42.30$$

$\therefore$ $$K_v = \mathbf{16.8}\ \textbf{(Ans.)}$$

Example 12.38. *Two pipes 1 and 2, each of 12 cm diameter branch off from a point A in a pipeline and rejoin at B. Pipe 1 is 480 m long and pipe 2 is 720 m long. So total head at A is 36 m. A short pipe 10 cm diameter is fitted at B and the flow is discharged into atmosphere through it as shown in Fig. 12·32. Assuming f = 0·018 for both the pipes, Calculate :*

(*i*) *Total discharge, and*

(*ii*) *Distribution of discharge in pipes 1 and 2.*

Solution. *Given* : $D_1 = 12$ cm $= 0{\cdot}12$ m; $L_1 = 480$ m; $D_2 = 12$ cm $= 0{\cdot}12$ m, $L_2 = 720$ m; $D_3 = 10$ cm $= 0{\cdot}1$ m; $f = 0{\cdot}018$.

(*i*) Total discharge, Q :

As 10 cm diameter pipe is short, the friction loss in it can be neglected.

$$H_B \text{ (= Head at } B) = \frac{V_3^2}{g}$$

$$H_A - H_B = 36 - \frac{V_3^2}{2g}$$

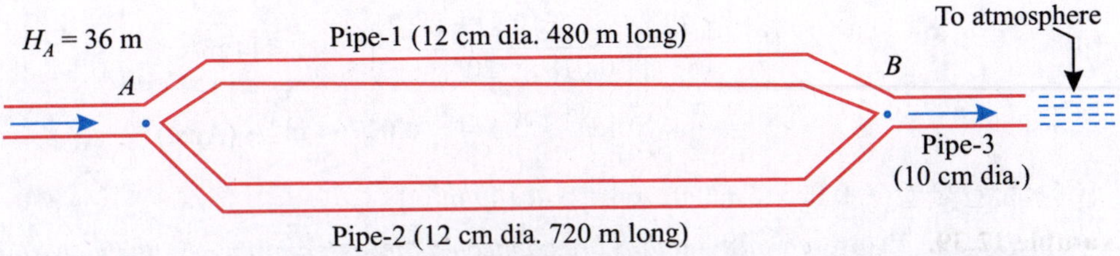

Fig. 12.32

Consider an equivalent pipe $D_{eq.} = 0{\cdot}1$ m and $f_{eq.} = 0{\cdot}018$ to replace the parallel pipes 1 and 2. Then,

$$\left(\frac{D_{eq.}^5}{f_{eq.}\, L_{eq.}}\right)^{\frac{1}{2}} = \left(\frac{D_1^5}{f_1\, L_1}\right)^{\frac{1}{2}} + \left(\frac{D_2^5}{f_2\, L_2}\right)^{\frac{1}{2}}$$

Since, $f_{eq} = f_1 = f_2$ and $D_1 = D_2 = 0{\cdot}12$ m

$$\therefore \quad \frac{(0.10)^{5/2}}{(L_{eq.})^{1/2}} = (0.12)^{5/2}\left[\frac{1}{\sqrt{480}} + \frac{1}{\sqrt{720}}\right]$$

$$= 0{\cdot}004988\,(0{\cdot}04564 + 0{\cdot}03727) = 0{\cdot}0004136$$

$$\therefore \quad L_{eq.} = \left[\frac{(0.10)^{5/2}}{0.0004136}\right]^2 = 58.46 \text{ m}$$

As $D_{eq.} = 0{\cdot}1$ m, velocity in this pipe $= V_3 = V_{eq.}$

$$\therefore \quad \text{Head loss} = H_A - H_B = 36 - \frac{V_3^2}{2g} = \frac{f_{eq.}\, L_{eq.}\, V_{eq.}^2}{D_{eq.} \times 2g}$$

$$= \frac{0.018 \times 58.46}{0.1} \times \frac{V_3^2}{2g} = 10.52\,\frac{V_3^2}{2g}$$

$$\therefore \quad \frac{V_3^2}{2g} = (10.52 + 1) = 36$$

$$V_3 = \left(\frac{36}{11.52} \times 2 \times 9.81\right)^{1/2} = 7.83 \text{ m/s}$$

Total discharge, $Q = \dfrac{\pi}{4} \times (0.10)^2 \times 7.83 = \mathbf{0.06149\ m^3/s}$ **(Ans.)**

(*ii*) Division of discharge in pipes 1 and 2; Q_1, Q_2:

$$H_A - H_B = 36 - \frac{(7.83)^2}{2 \times 9.81} = 32.875 \text{ m} = h_{f_1} = h_{f_2}$$

$$\therefore \quad \frac{f_1 L_1 V_1^2}{D_1 \times 2g} = \frac{0.018 \times 480}{0.12} \times \frac{V_1^2}{2g} = 32.875$$

$$\therefore \quad V_1 = \left(\frac{32.875 \times 2 \times 9.81 \times 0.12}{0.018 \times 480}\right)^{1/2} = 2.993 \text{ m/s}$$

$$\therefore \quad Q_1 = \frac{\pi}{4} \times (0.12)^2 \times 2.993 = \mathbf{0.03385\ m^3/s\ (Ans.)}$$

Again,
$$\frac{f_2 L_2}{D_2} \times \frac{V_2^2}{2g} = \frac{0.018 \times 720}{0.12} \times \frac{V_2^2}{2g} = 32.875$$

or,
$$V_2 = \left(\frac{32.875 \times 2 \times 9.81 \times 0.12}{0.018 \times 720}\right)^{1/2} = 2.444 \text{ m/s}$$

$$\therefore \quad Q_2 = \frac{\pi}{4} \times (0.12)^2 \times 2.444 = \mathbf{0.02764\ m^3/s\ (Ans.)}$$

[*Check* : $Q_1 + Q_2 = 0{\cdot}03385 + 0{\cdot}02764 = 0{\cdot}06149$ m^3/s]

Example 12.39. *Two reservoirs A and B are connected through a piping system consisting of 50 cm diameter pipe, 450 m long branching two pipes of 35 cm diameter and 25 cm diameter, each 650 m long. A pump situated at reservoir A pumps 0·35 m³/s of water through this pipe system to reservoir B whose water surface elevation is 50 m above that of A. Assuming pump efficiency as 60 percent and f= 0·018, determine the input power for the pump.*

Solution. Refer to Fig. 12·33. *Given* : D_1 = 50 cm = 0·5 m, L_1 = 450 m; D_2 = 35 cm = 0·35 m, L_2 = 650 m; D_3 = 25 cm = 0·25 m, L_3 = 650 m, Q = 0·35 m^3/s; η_{pump} = 60 %; f = 0·018.

Consider equivalent pipe of diameter 0·5 m to replace the two parallel pipes. The equivalent pipe ($D_{eq.}$, $L_{eq.}$, $f_{eq.}$) to replace a set of parallel pipes (D_2, L_2, f_2) and (D_3, L_3, f_3) is given by:

$$\left(\frac{D_{eq.}^5}{f_{eq.} L_{eq.}}\right)^{1/2} = \left(\frac{D_2^5}{f_2 L_2}\right)^{1/2} + \left(\frac{D_3^5}{f_3 L_3}\right)^{1/2}$$

Here,
$$f_{eq.} = f_1 = f_2$$

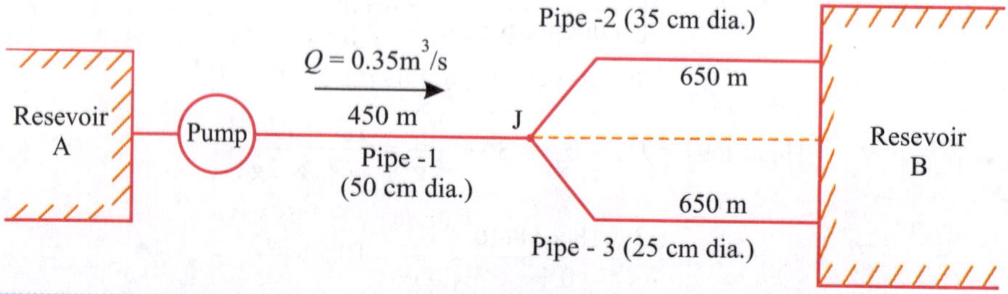

Fig. 12.33

Substituting the various values in the above eqn., we get:

$$\left[\frac{(0.5)^5}{L_{eq.}}\right]^{1/2} = \left[\frac{(0.35)^5}{650}\right]^{1/2} + \left[\frac{(0.25)^5}{650}\right]^{1/2}$$

or,
$$\frac{0.1768}{(L_{eq.})^{1/2}} = 0.002843 + 0.001226$$

or, $L_{eq.}$ = 1888 m = Equivalent length of 0·5 m diameter pipe to replace the parallel pipes.

The total equivalent length of 0·5 m pipe is now

$$= 450 + 1888 = 2338 \text{ m}$$

$$V = \frac{Q}{A} = \frac{0.35}{\frac{\pi}{4} \times (0.5)^2} = 1.78 \text{ m/s}$$

$$h_f = \frac{f_{eq.}\, L_{eq.}\, V^2}{D \times 2g} = \frac{0.018 \times 2338 \times (1.78)^2}{0.5 \times 2 \times 9.81} = 13.59 \text{ m}$$

h_t = Total pumping head $= 50 + 13{\cdot}59 = 63{\cdot}59$ m

Power input for the pump,

$$P = \frac{wQh_f}{\eta_{pump}} = \frac{9{\cdot}81 \times 0{\cdot}35 \times 63{\cdot}59}{0{\cdot}6} = \mathbf{363{\cdot}9\ kW}$$ **(Ans.)**

Note : This question could also be solved without considering the equivalent pipe. First the discharge through the each pipe is determined and then the total frictional loss is calculated. However, the calculations are definitely less with the equivalent pipe method.

Example 12.40. (Flow through branched pipes). *The water levels in the two reservoirs A and B are 104·5 m and 100 m respectively above the daum. A pipe joins each to a common point D, where pressure is 98·1 kN/m² gauge and height is 83·5 m above datum. Another pipe connects D to another tank C. What will be the height of water level in C assuming the same value of 'f' for all pipes. Take friction co-efficient = 0·0075. The diameters of the pipes AD, BD and CD are 300 mm, 450 mm, 600 mm respectively and their lengths are 240 m, 270 m, 300 m respectively.* **[IIT Delhi]**

Solution. For pipe AD : $D_{AD} = 300 \text{ mm} = 0{\cdot}3 \text{ m}$

$L_{AD} = 240$ m

For pipe BD : $D_{BD} = 450 \text{ mm} = 0{\cdot}45 \text{ m}$

$L_{BD} = 270$ m

For pipe CD : $D_{CD} = 600 \text{ mm} = 0{\cdot}6 \text{ m}$

$L_{CD} = 300$ m

Friction co-efficient for each pipe, $f = 0{\cdot}0075$

Pressure at D, $p_0 = 98{\cdot}1 \text{ kN/m}^2$

Height of water level in tank C :

$$\text{The pressure head at } D = \frac{p_D}{w} = \frac{98.1}{9.81} = 10 \text{ m of water}$$

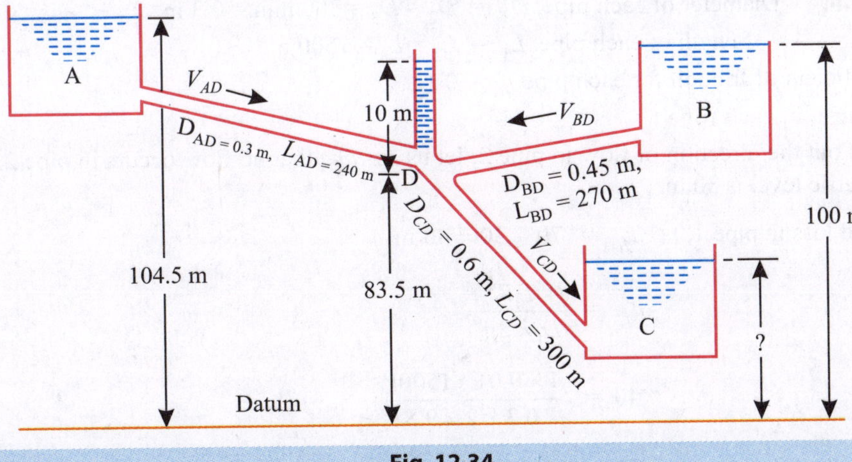

Fig. 12.34

$\therefore$ The piezometric head at D = $83{\cdot}5 + 10 = 93{\cdot}5$ m

Head loss between A and D = $104{\cdot}5 - 93{\cdot}5 = 11{\cdot}0$ m

Head loss between B and D = $100 - 93{\cdot}5 = 6{\cdot}5$ m

Using Darcy-Weisbach equation, we get:

For pipe AD :
$$11 = \frac{4fL_{AD}V_{AD}^2}{D_{AD} \times 2g} = \frac{4 \times 0.0075 \times 240 \times V_{AD}^2}{0.3 \times 2 \times 9.81}$$

or,
$$V_{AD}^2 = \frac{11 \times 0.3 \times 2 \times 9.81}{4 \times 0.0075 \times 240} = 8.99$$

or,
$$V_{AD} = 3 \text{ m/s}$$

For pipe BD :
$$6.5 = \frac{4fL_{BD}V_{BD}^2}{D_{BD} \times 2g} = \frac{4 \times 0.0075 \times 270 \times V_{BD}^2}{0.45 \times 2 \times 9.81}$$

or,
$$V_{BD}^2 = \frac{6.5 \times 0.45 \times 2 \times 9.81}{4 \times 0.0075 \times 270} = 7.085$$

or,
$$V_{BD} = 2{\cdot}66 \text{ m/s}$$

From continuity considerations, we have:

$$Q_{AD} + Q_{BD} = Q_{CD}$$

or,
$$Q_{CD} = (\pi/4) \times D_{AD}^2 \times V_{AD} + (\pi/4) \times D_{BD}^2 \times V_{BD}$$
$$= (\pi/4) \times (0.3)^2 \times 3 + (\pi/4) \times (0.45)^2 \times 2.66 = 0.635 \text{ m}^3/\text{s}$$

$\therefore$ Velocity of flow in pipe CD,

$$V_{CD} = \frac{Q_{CD}}{(\pi/4) \times D_{CD}^2} = \frac{0.635}{(\pi/4) \times 0.6^2} = 2.24 \text{ m/s}$$

$$\text{Head loss in pipe } CD = \frac{4fL_{CD}V_{CD}^2}{D_{CD} \times 2g} = \frac{4 \times 0.0075 \times 300 \times 2.24^2}{0.6 \times 2 \times 9.81} = 3.84 \text{ m}$$

$\therefore$ Water level in tank C = $93{\cdot}5 - 3{\cdot}84 =$ **89·66 m (Ans.)**

Example 12.41. (Flow through branched pipes). *Fig. 12·35 shows three reservoirs connected by pipes. Each pipe is 300 mm in diameter and 1500 m long. Assuming co-efficient of friction for each pipe, f = 0·01 find the discharge in each pipe.*

Solution. Diameter of each pipe, $D_1 = D_2 = D_3 = 300$ mm $= 0{\cdot}3$ m

Length of each pipe, $L_1 = L_2 = L_3 = 1500$ m

Co-efficient of friction for each pipe, $f = 0{\cdot}1$

Discharge in each pipe :

To find out the direction of flow in pipe 2, let us *assume* that no flow occurs in pipe 2. That is, the piezometric level is 30 m.

$\therefore$ Head loss in pipe 1, $h_{f_1} = 70 - 30 = 40$ m

Also,
$$h_{f_1} = \frac{4fL_1V_1^2}{D_1 \times 2g}$$

$\therefore$
$$40 = \frac{4 \times 0.01 \times 1500V_1^2}{0.3 \times 2 \times 9.81}$$

or,
$$V_1^2 = \frac{40 \times 0.3 \times 2 \times 9.81}{4 \times 0.01 \times 1500} = 3.924$$

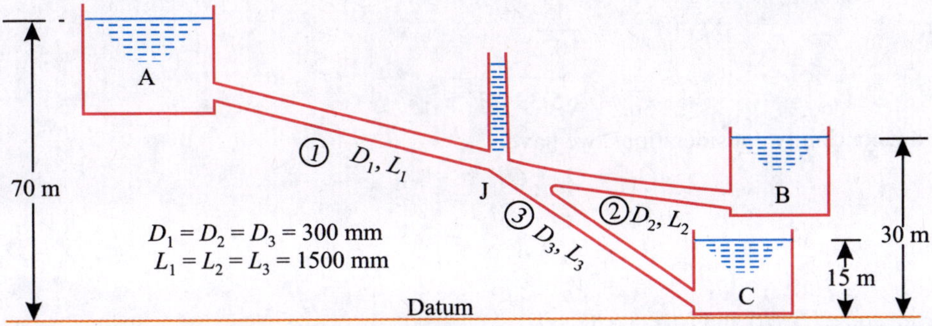

Fig. 12.35

or, $$V_1 = 1{\cdot}981 \text{ m/s}$$

∴ Discharge through the pipe 1,

$$Q_1 = A_1V_1 = \frac{\pi}{4} \times 0{\cdot}3^2 \times 1{\cdot}981 = 0{\cdot}14 \text{ m}^3\text{/s}$$

Again, head loss in pipe 3, $h_{f_3} = 30 - 15 = 15$ m

But, $$h_{f_3} = \frac{4fL_3V_3^2}{D_3 \times 2g}$$

∴ $$15 = \frac{4 \times 0.01 \times 1500 \times V_3^2}{0.3 \times 2 \times 9.81}$$

or, $$V_3^2 = \frac{15 \times 0.3 \times 2 \times 9.81}{4 \times 0.01 \times 1500} = 1.471$$

or, $$V_3 = 1{\cdot}213 \text{ m/s}$$

∴ Discharge through the pipe 3,

$$Q_3 = A_3V_3 = \frac{\pi}{4} \times 0{\cdot}3^2 \times 1{\cdot}213 = 0{\cdot}0857 \text{ m}^3\text{/s}$$

Since $Q_1 > Q_3$, the *direction of flow is from J to B*.

Considering the flow from reservoir *A* and *B*, we have:

(70 – 30) = Head loss in pipe 1 + head loss in pipe 2

or, $$40 = h_{f_1} + h_{f_2} = \frac{4fL_1V_1^2}{D_1 \times 2g} + \frac{4fL_2V_2^2}{D_2 \times 2g}$$

$$40 = \frac{4 \times 0.01 \times 1500 \times V_1^2}{0.3 \times 2 \times 9.81} + \frac{4 \times 0.01 \times 1500 \times V_2^2}{0.3 \times 2 \times 9.81}$$

or, $$40 = 10.2\,(V_1^2 + V_2^2)$$

or, $$V_1^2 + V_2^2 = \frac{40}{10.2} = 3.92$$

or, $$V_2 = \sqrt{3.92 - V_1^2} \qquad \ldots(i)$$

Similarly, considering the flow from reservoir *A* to *C*, we have:

$$70 - 15 = h_{f_1} + h_{f_3}$$

$$= \frac{4fL_1V_1^2}{D_1 \times 2g} + \frac{4fL_3V_3^2}{D_3 \times 2g} = \frac{4 \times 0.01 \times 1500 \times V_1^2}{0.3 \times 2 \times 9.81} + \frac{4 \times 0.01 \times 1500 \times V_3^2}{0.3 \times 2 \times 9.81}$$

or, $$55 = 10.2\,(V_1^2 + V_3^2)$$

or, $$V_1^2 + V_3^2 = \frac{55}{10.2} = 5.39$$

or, $$V_3 = \sqrt{5.39 - V_1^2} \qquad ...(ii)$$

From continuity considerations, we have:

$$Q_1 = Q_2 + Q_3$$

$$A_1V_1 = A_2V_2 + A_3V_3$$

But, $$A_1 = A_2 = A_3 \qquad (\because D_1 = D_2 = D_3)$$

$\therefore$ $$V_1 = V_2 + V_3 \qquad ...(iii)$$

From eqns. (*i*), (*ii*) and (*iii*), we have:

$$V_1 = \sqrt{3.92 - V_1^2} + \sqrt{5.39 - V_1^2} \qquad ...(iv)$$

By *trial and error*, we get, $V_1 \simeq 1{\cdot}9$ m/s

From eqn. (*i*) : $$V_2 = \sqrt{3.92 - 1.9^2} = 0.56 \text{ m/s}$$

From (*ii*) : $$V_3 = \sqrt{5.39 - 1.9^2} = 1.34 \text{ m/s}$$

Thus, $$Q_1 = (\pi/4) \times 0{\cdot}3^2 \times 1{\cdot}9 = \mathbf{0{\cdot}134\ m^3/s} \quad \textbf{(Ans.)}$$

$$Q_2 = (\pi/4) \times 0{\cdot}3^2 \times 0{\cdot}56 = \mathbf{0{\cdot}0396\ m^3/s} \quad \textbf{(Ans.)}$$

$$Q_3 = (\pi/4) \times 0{\cdot}3^2 \times 1{\cdot}34 = \mathbf{0{\cdot}0947\ m^3/s} \quad \textbf{(Ans.)}$$

Example 12.42. *Fig. 12·36 shows a pump supplying water from a sump at elevation 20 m to a reservoir at elevation 30 m through a pipeline of 0·5 m diameter and length 1000 m, f = 0·005. At mid-length a branch pipe 0·3 diameter, 500 m long, f = 0·005, discharges free at elevation 25 m at the rate of 0·25 m³/s. Determine :*

(i) *The discharge into the reservoir,*

(ii) *The pressure to be maintained by the pump, and*

(iii) *The power of the pump assuming an overall efficiency of 70 per cent.*

Solution. Refer to Fig. 12·36.

Given :

$D_1 = 0{\cdot}5$ m, $L_1 = 500$ m

$D_2 = 0{\cdot}5$ m, $L_2 = 500$ m

$D_3 = 0{\cdot}3$ m, $L_3 = 500$ m

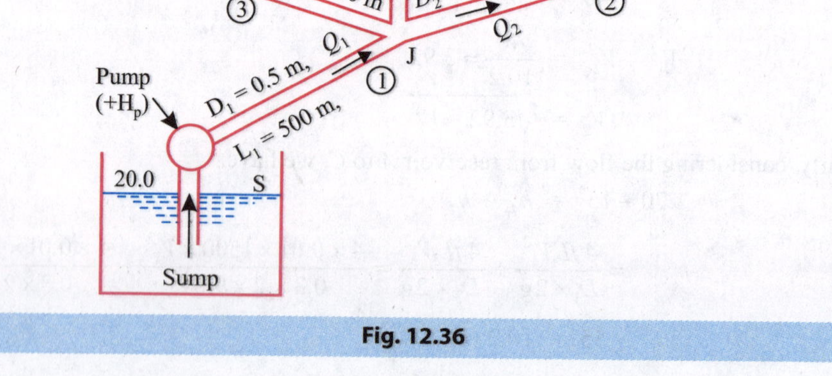

Fig. 12.36

Co-efficient of friction, $f_1 = f_2 = f_3 = f = 0{\cdot}005$
Discharge through pipe 3, $Q_3 = 0{\cdot}25 \text{ m}^3/\text{s}$
Overall efficiency, $\eta_0 = 70\%$.

(*i*) The discharge into the reservoir, Q_2 :

Energy at the joint J,

$$E_J = E_B \text{ (energy at } B) + (h_f)_{JB}$$

$$= \left(\frac{p_B}{w} + \frac{V_3^2}{2g} + z_B\right) + (h_f)_{JB}$$

$$= \frac{p_B}{w} + \frac{V_3^2}{2g} + z_B + \frac{4 f_3 L_3 V_3^2}{D_3 \times 2g}$$

$$= 0 + \frac{V_3^2}{2g}\left(1 + \frac{4 f_3 L_3}{D_3}\right) + 25$$

$$= \left(\frac{0.25}{(\pi/4) \times 0.3^2}\right)^2 \times \frac{1}{2 \times 9.81}\left(1 + \frac{4 \times 0.005 \times 500}{0.3}\right) + 25$$

$$= 0{\cdot}637\,(1 + 33{\cdot}33) + 25 = 46{\cdot}87 \text{ m}$$

Head loss, $h_{f_2} = 46.87 - 30 = 16.87$ m

i.e. $$16.87 = \frac{4 f_2 L_2 V_2^2}{D_2 \times 2g} = \frac{4 \times 0.005 \times 500 \times V_2^2}{0.5 \times 2 \times 9.81}$$

or, $$V_2 = \left(\frac{16.87 \times 0.5 \times 2 \times 9.81}{4 \times 0.005 \times 500}\right)^{1/2} = 4.07 \text{ m/s}$$

$\therefore$ $$Q_2 = (\pi/4) \times 0{\cdot}5^2 \times 4{\cdot}07 = \mathbf{0{\cdot}8 \text{ m}^3/\text{s}} \quad \textbf{(Ans.)}$$

$$Q_1 = Q_2 + Q_3 = 0{\cdot}8 + 0{\cdot}25 = 1{\cdot}05 \text{ m}^3/\text{s}$$

Head loss, $$h_{f_1} = \frac{4 f_1 L_1 V_1^2}{D_1 \times 2g} = \frac{4 \times 0.005 \times 500 \times (5.35)^2}{0.5 \times 2 \times 9.81} = 29.17 \text{ m}$$

$$\left(\because V_1 = \frac{Q_1}{A_1} = \frac{1.05}{(\pi/4) \times 0.5^2} = 5.35 \text{ m/s}\right)$$

Applying energy equation between the sump (S) and the junction (J), we have:

$$E_S + H_p = h_{f_1}$$

$$0 + 0 + 20 + H_p = 46.87 + 29.17 = 76.04 \text{ m}$$

$$H_p = 56.04 \text{ m}$$

(*i*) The pressure to be maintained by the pump, p :

$$p = wH_p = 9{\cdot}81 \times 56{\cdot}04 = \mathbf{549{\cdot}7 \text{ kN/m}^2} \quad \textbf{(Ans.)}$$

(*ii*) The power of pump, P :

$$P = \frac{wQ_1 H_p}{\eta_0} = \frac{9.81 \times 1.05 \times 56.04}{0.7} = \mathbf{824.6 \text{ kW}} \quad \textbf{(Ans.)}$$

Example 12.43. (Pipe networks). *Fig. 12·37 shows a network in which Q and h_f refer to discharges and pressure drops respectively. Subscripts 1, 2, 3, 4 and 5 designate respective values in pipe lengths AC, BC, CD, DA and AC. Subscripts A, B, C and D designate discharges entering or leaving the junction points A, B, C and D respectively.*

By sticking to the values given in the figure find the following discharges Q_B, Q_2, Q_4 and Q_5; and pressure drops h_{f_4} and h_{f_5} and give these computed values at their respective places on a neat sketch of the network along with flow directions. **[GATE]**

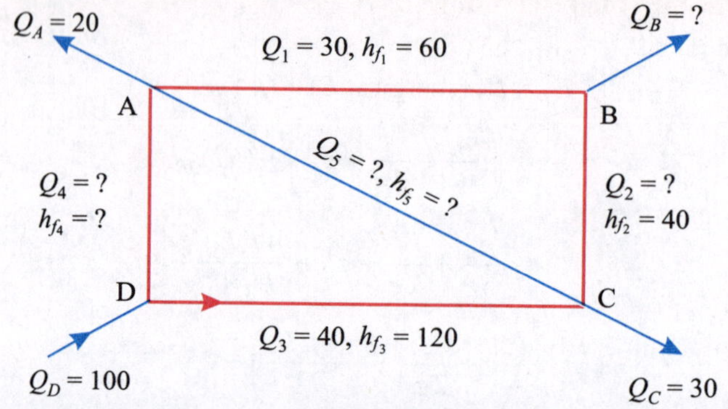

Fig. 12.37

Solution. At junctions, $\Sigma \mathbf{Q} = \mathbf{0}$

i.e., Discharge entering the junction = Discharge leaving the junction

At junction D :

$$Q_D = Q_3 + Q_4$$

or, $100 = 40 + Q_4$

or, $\mathbf{Q_4} = 100 - 40 = \mathbf{60}$ ...leaving the junction

At junction A :

$$Q_4 = Q_A + Q_1 + Q_5$$

$$60 = 20 + 30 + Q_5$$

$\therefore$ $\mathbf{Q_5} = 60 - 20 - 30 = \mathbf{10}$ ...leaving the junction

At junction C : $Q_3 + Q_5 + Q_2 = Q_c$

$$40 + 10 + Q_2 = 30$$

$\therefore$ $\mathbf{Q_2} = 30 - 40 - 10 = \mathbf{-20}$ ...leaving the junction *C*

At junction B : $Q_1 + Q_2 = Q_B$

$$30 + 20 = Q_B$$

i.e., $\mathbf{Q_B} = \mathbf{50}$ ...leaving the junction *B*

For each elementary circuit, $\Sigma \mathbf{h_f} = \mathbf{0}$

Circuit ABC :

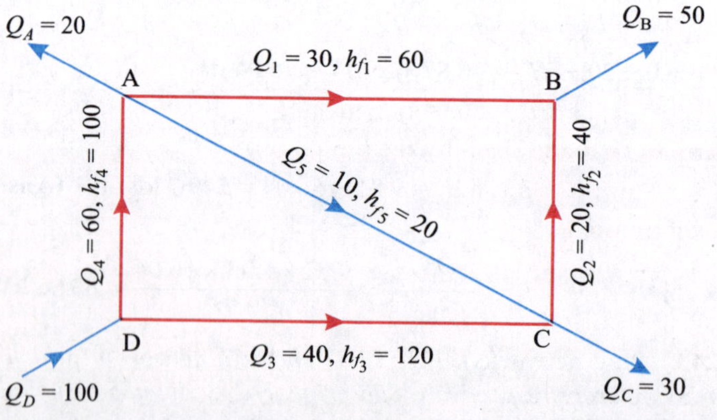

Fig. 12.38

$$h_{f_1} - h_{f_2} - h_{f_5} = 0$$

$$60 - 40 - h_{f_5} = 0$$

$$\therefore \quad h_{f_5} = 20$$

Circuit ACD :

$$h_{f_5} - h_{f_3} + h_{f_4} = 0$$

$$20 - 120 + h_{f_4} = 0$$

$$\therefore \quad h_{f_4} = 100$$

The calculated vlaues and the flow directions are shown in Fig. 12·38.

12.9. SYPHON

A **syphon** *is a long bent pipe employed for carrying water from a reservoir at a higher elevation to another reservoir at a lower elevation when the two reservoirs are separated by a hill or high level ground in between* as shown in Fig. 12·39.

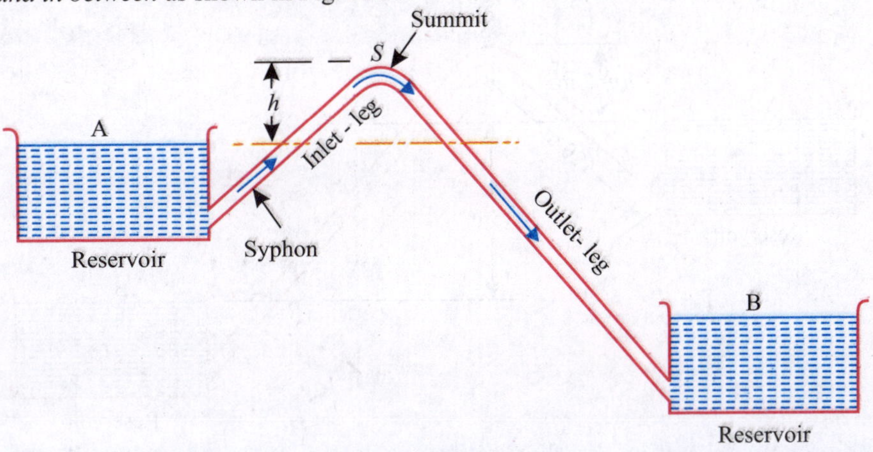

Fig. 12.39. Syphon.

The highest point (*S*) of the syphon is called the **summit.** The pressure at the point *S* is **less** *than atmospheric pressure* (since *S* lies above the free water surface in the tank *A*). The pressure at *S* can be reduced theoretically to – 10·3 m of water but in actual practice this pressure is only – 7·6 m of water (or 10·3 – 7·6 = 2·7 m of water *absolute*). When the pressure at *S* becomes less than 2·7 m of water absolute, the dissolved air and other gases would come out from water and collect at the summit. *Therefore syphon should be so laid that no section of the pipe will be more than 7·6 m above the hydraulic gradient at that section.* Moreover, in order to limit the reduction of the pressure at the summit the length of the *inlet-leg* (rising portion of the syphon) of the syphon is also required to be limited (this is so because, if the *inlet leg* is very long a considerable loss of head due to friction is caused, resulting in further reduction of the pressure at the summit).

Example 12.44. *Two reservoirs, having a difference in elevation of 15 m, are connected by a 200 mm diameter syphon. The length of the syphon is 400 m and the summit is 3 m above the water level in the upper reservoir. The length of the pipe from upper reservoir to the summit is 120 m. If the co-efficient of friction is 0·005, determine :*

(i) Discharge through the syphon, and

(ii) Pressure at the summit.

Neglect minor losses.

Solution. Diameter of the syphon, D = 200 mm = 0·2 m

Length of the syphon, L = 400 m

Difference in level of the two reservoirs, H = 15 m

Height of the summit from upper reservoir, h = 3 m

Co-efficient of friction, f = 0·005

(*i*) Discharge through the syphon, Q :

Applying Bernoulli's equation to points A and B, we get:

$$\frac{p_A}{w} + \frac{V_A^2}{2g} + z_A = \frac{p_B}{w} + \frac{V_B^2}{2g} + z_B + \text{loss of head due to friction from } A \text{ to } B$$

or, $$0 + 0 + z_A = 0 + 0 + z_B + h_f$$

$[\because p_A = p_B = \text{atmospheric pressure, and } V_A = V_B = 0]$

or, $$z_A - z_B = h_f = 15$$

But, $$h_f = \frac{4fLV^2}{D \times 2g}$$ (where, V = velocity of water in the pipe)

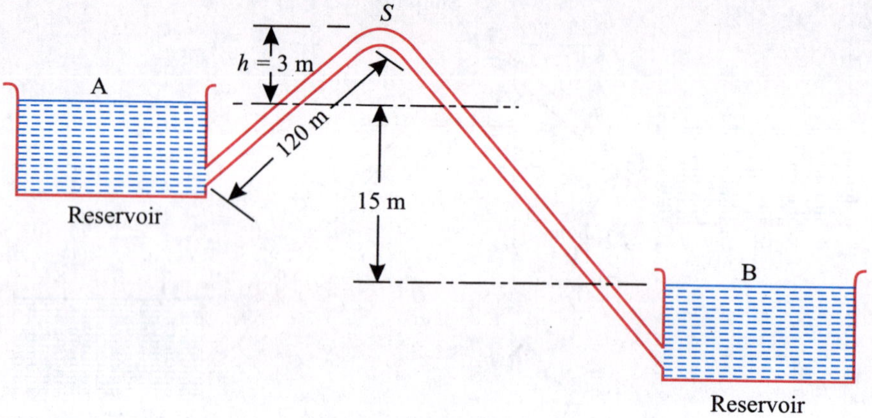

Fig. 12.40

$\therefore$ $$15 = \frac{4 \times 0.005 \times 400 \times V^2}{0.2 \times 2 \times 9.81}$$

or, $$V^2 = \frac{15 \times 0.2 \times 2 \times 9.81}{4 \times 0.005 \times 400}$$

or, $$V = 2{\cdot}7 \text{ m/s}$$

$\therefore$ Discharge, Q = Area × velocity

$$= \frac{\pi}{4} \times 0.2^2 \times 2.7 = \mathbf{0.0848\ m^3/s}$$ **(Ans.)**

(*ii*) Pressure at summit :

Applying Bernoulli's equation to points A and S, we get:

$$\frac{p_A}{w} + \frac{V_A^2}{2g} + z_A = \frac{p_S}{w} + \frac{V_S^2}{2g} + z_S$$

+ loss of head due to friction between A and S

(... assuming datum line passing through A)

$$0+0+0 = \frac{p_S}{w} + \frac{2.7^2}{2\times 9.81} + 3 + \frac{4\times 0.005\times 120\times (2.7)^2}{0.2\times 2\times 9.81}$$

$$0 = \frac{p_S}{w} + 0.37 + 3 + 4.46 = \frac{p_S}{w} + 7.83$$

$$\frac{p_S}{w} = \textbf{7.83 m of water (Ans.)}$$

Example 12.45. *A 200 mm diameter pipe, 4000 m long connects two reservoirs whose surface levels differ by 40 m. At a distance of 400 m from the upper reservoir, the pipe crosses a ridge the summit of which is 9 m above the level of water in the upper reservoir. Determine :*

(i) The minimum depth of the pipe below the summit of the ridge, if the absolute pressure head at the summit of syphon is not to fall below 3·0 m of the water (absolute).

(ii) The discharge through the pipe.

Take co-efficient of friction f = 0·006 and atmospheric head = 10·3 m of water. Neglect minor losses.

Solution. Diameter of the pipe, D = 200 mm = 0·2 m

Total length of the pipe, L = 4000 m

Length of syphon from upper reservoir to the summit, L_1 = 400 m

Difference in levels of two reservoirs = 40 m

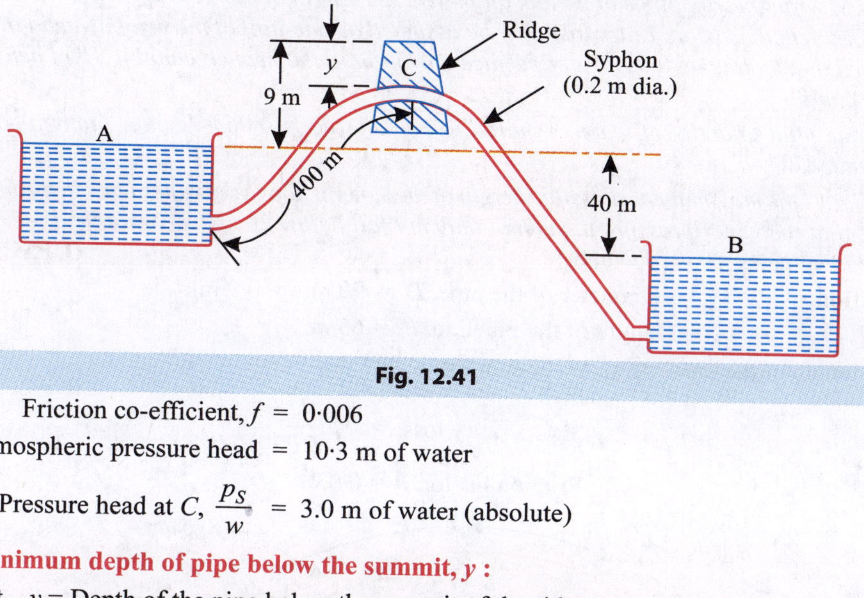

Fig. 12.41

Friction co-efficient, f = 0·006

Atmospheric pressure head = 10·3 m of water

Pressure head at C, $\frac{p_S}{w}$ = 3.0 m of water (absolute)

(i) Minimum depth of pipe below the summit, y :

Let, y = Depth of the pipe below the summit of the ridge.

Then, height of syphon from the water surface in the upper reservoir = (9 – y)

Applying Bernoulli's equation at A and B (taking datum line passing through B), we have:

$$\frac{p_A}{w} + \frac{V_A^2}{2g} + z_A = \frac{p_B}{w} + \frac{V_B^2}{2g} + z_B + (h_f)_{A-B}$$

$$0 + 0 + 40 = 0 + 0 + 0 + \frac{4fLV^2}{D\times 2g} \qquad (\because V_A = V_B = 0)$$

or, $$40 = \frac{4\times 0.006\times 4000\times V^2}{0.2\times 2\times 9.81}$$

$$\therefore \quad V = \left(\frac{40 \times 0.2 \times 2 \times 9.81}{40 \times 0.006 \times 4000}\right)^{1/2} = 1.278 \text{ m/s}$$

Now applying Bernoulli's equation at A and C (assuming datum line passing through A), we have:

$$\frac{p_A}{w} + \frac{V_A^2}{2g} + z_A = \frac{p_C}{w} + \frac{V_C^2}{2g} + z_C + (h_f)_{A-C}$$

$$10.3 + 0 + 0 = 3.0 + \frac{V^2}{2g} + (9 - y) + \frac{4 f L_1 V^2}{D \times 2g}$$

or,
$$10.3 = 3 + \frac{(1.278)^2}{2 \times 9.81} + (9 - y) + \frac{4 \times 0.006 \times 400 \times (1.278)^2}{0.2 \times 2 \times 9.81}$$

$$= 3 + 0.0832 + (9 - y) + 3.99$$

or,
$$y = 5.77 \text{ m} \quad \textbf{(Ans.)}$$

***(ii)* The discharge through the pipe, Q:**

$$Q = A \times V = \frac{\pi}{4} \times 0{\cdot}2^2 \times 1{\cdot}278$$

$$= 0{\cdot}04 \text{ m}^3/\text{s} \quad \textbf{(Ans.)}$$

Example 12.46. *Water from a main canal is syphoned to a branch canal over an embankment by means of wrought iron pipes of 90 mm diameter. The length of pipeline up to the summit is 25 m and the total length is 65 m. Entry loss may be assumed as one-half of the velocity head in the pipe. Assume friction factor, $f = 0{\cdot}03$. Water surface elevation in the branch canal is 10 m below that of the main canal.*

(i) If the total quantity of water required to be coneyed is $0{\cdot}06 m^3/s$, how many pipelines are needed ?

(ii) What is the maximum permissible height of the summit above the water level in the main canal so that the water pressure at summit may not fall below 20 kN/m^2 absolute, the barometric reading being 10 m of water ? **(UPSC Exams.)**

Solution. Diameter of the pipe, $D = 90 \text{ mm} = 0{\cdot}9$ m

Total length of the pipeline, $L = 65$ m

The length of the pipeline up to the summit, $L_1 = 25$ m

Entry loss $= 0{\cdot}5 \dfrac{V^2}{2g}$

Friction Factor, $f = 0{\cdot}03$

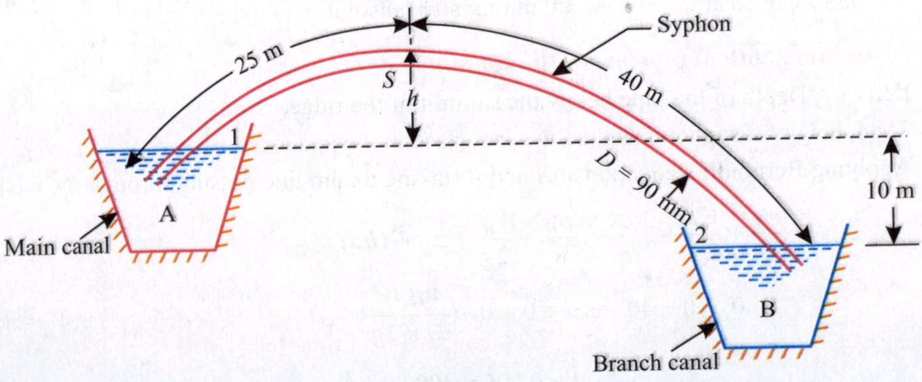

Fig. 12.42

Total discharge $Q = 0{\cdot}06\ m^3/s$

Pressure at the summit, $p_S = 20\ kN/m^2$ absolute

Atmospheric pressure head = 10 m of water.

(i) Number of pipelines needed :

Applying Bernoulli's equation between water surfaces (1 and 2) of two canals, we have:

$$\frac{p_1}{w}+\frac{V_1^2}{2g}+z_1=\frac{p_2}{w}+\frac{V_2^2}{2g}+z_2+0.5\frac{V^2}{2g}+\frac{fLV^2}{D\times 2g}+\frac{V^2}{2g}$$

$$0+0+10=0+0+0+1.5\frac{V^2}{2g}+\frac{0.03\times 65\times V^2}{0.09\times 2g}$$

or, $$10=\frac{23.17\,V^2}{2g} \qquad (\because V_1=V_2=0)$$

or, $$V=\left(\frac{10\times 2\times 9.81}{23.17}\right)^{1/2}=2.91\ m/s$$

(where, V = velocity of flow through the pipe)

Discharge through a 90 mm diameter pipe,

$$=\frac{\pi}{4}\times 0{\cdot}09^2\times 2{\cdot}91=0{\cdot}0185\ m^3/s$$

Number of 90 mm diameter pipes required to convey $0{\cdot}06\ m^3/s$

$$=\frac{0.06}{0.185}=3.24,\ \text{say } \mathbf{4}$$ **(Ans.)**

(ii) Height of the summit, h :

Invoking Bernoulli's equation between water surface1 and the summit point *S*, we have:

$$\frac{p_1}{w}+\frac{V_1^2}{2g}+z_1=\frac{p_S}{w}+\frac{V_S^2}{2g}+z_S+\frac{0.5V^2}{2g}+\frac{fL_1V^2}{D\times 2g}$$

$$10+0+0=\frac{20}{9.81}+\frac{V^2}{2g}+h+\frac{0.5V^2}{2g}+\frac{0.03\times 25\times V^2}{0.09\times 2g}$$

or, $$10=2.038+\frac{1.5\times 2.91^2}{2\times 9.81}+h+\frac{0.03\times 25\times (2.91)^2}{0.09\times 2\times 9.81}$$

or, $$10=2.038+0.647+h+3.596$$

or, $$h=\mathbf{3.72\ m}$$ **(Ans.)**

12.10. POWER TRANSMISSION THROUGH PIPES

The transmission of power through pipes carrying water or other liquids is commonly used for working of several hydraulic machines. The hydruaulic power transmitted by a pipe however depends on (*i*) the *discharge* passing through the pipe and (*ii*) the *total head of water* (or liquid). Consider a pipe AB *connected to a high level storage tank as shown in Fig. 12·43.*

Let, H = Head of water available at the inlet of pipe, m,

L = Length of the pipe, m,

D = Diameter of the pipe, m,

V = Velocity of water in the pipe m/s,

f = Co-efficient of friction, and

h_f = Loss of head in the pipe AB, due to friction, m.

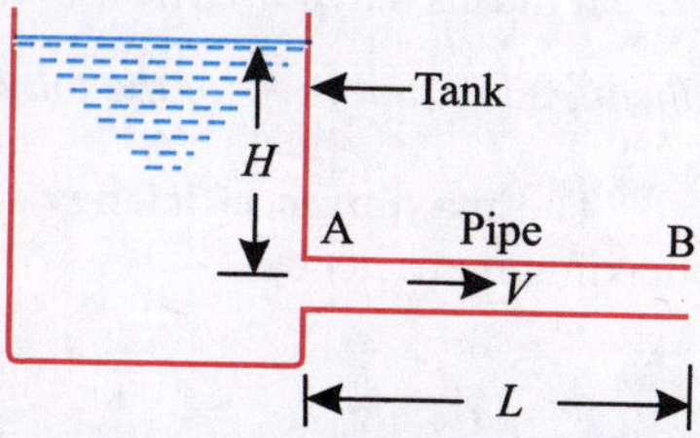

Fig. 12.43

Weight of water flowing through the pipe per second

$$= wQ = wAV \qquad ...(i)$$

(where, Q = discharge of water through the pipe, m^3/s)

and, net head of water available at B (neglecting minor losses)

$$= H - h_f = H - \frac{4fLV^2}{D \times 2g}$$

Also, The **efficiency of transmission,**

$$\eta = \frac{H - h_f}{H}$$

And, **Power, P** $= \dfrac{\left\{\begin{matrix}\text{Weight of water flowing/sec.} \\ \times \text{ head of water}\end{matrix}\right\}}{1000}$ kW

$$= wQ\,(H - h_f) \text{ kW}$$

(where, $w = 9{\cdot}81$ kN/m^3 for water)

$$= wAV\left(H - \frac{4fLV^2}{D \times 2g}\right) \text{kW}$$

$$= wA\left(HV - \frac{4fLV^3}{D \times 2g}\right) \text{kW} \quad ...(iii)$$

It is evident from eqn. (*iii*) that power transmitted depends upon the velocity of water (V), as the other things are constant.

∴ Power transmitted will be *maximum*, when:

$$\frac{d(P)}{dV} = 0$$

or, $$\frac{d}{dV}\left[wA\left(HV - \frac{4fLV^3}{D \times 2g}\right)\right] = 0$$

or, $$wA\left(H - \frac{4 \times 3fLV^2}{D \times 2g}\right) = 0$$

or, $$H - 3 \times \frac{4fLV^2}{D \times 2g} = 0$$

or, $$H - 3h_f = 0 \qquad \left[\because h_f = \frac{4fLV^2}{D \times 2g}\right]$$

or, $$H = 3h_f$$

or, $$\boldsymbol{h_f = \frac{H}{3}}$$

It means that *power transmitted through the pipe is maximum, when head lost due to friction in the pipe is equal to $\frac{1}{3}$ of the total supply head.*

The **maximum efficiency** would correspond to the maximum power transmitted and hence maximum efficiency,

$$\eta = \frac{H - \frac{H}{3}}{H} = \frac{\frac{2}{3}H}{H} = \frac{2}{3} \text{ or } \mathbf{66{\cdot}7\%}$$

Example 12.47. *A 2500 m long pipeline is used for transmission of power. 120 kW power is to be transmitted through the pipe in which water having a pressure of 4000 kN/m² at inlet is flowing. If the pressure drop over the length of pipe is 800 kN/m² and f = 0·006, find :*

(i) *Diameter of the pipe, and*

(ii) *Efficiency of transmission.*

Solution. Length of the pipeline, $L = 2500$ m

Power transmitted, $P = 120$ kW

Pressure at inlet, $p = 4000$ kN/m²

$$H = \frac{p}{w} = \frac{4000}{9.81} = 407.7 \text{ m}$$

Pressure drop $= 800$ kN/m²

$\therefore$ Loss of head, $h_f = \dfrac{800}{9.81} = 81.5$ m

$\therefore$ Co-efficient of friction, $f = 0{\cdot}006$.

(*i*) Diameter of the pipe, D :

Head available at the end of the pipe, $H - h_f = 407{\cdot}7 - 81{\cdot}5 = 326{\cdot}2$ m

Now, power transmitted is given by : $P = wQ\,(H - h_f)$ kW

$$120 = 9{\cdot}81 \times Q \times 326{\cdot}2$$

where, Q = Discharge through the pipe in m³/s, and

and, w = Specific weight of water = 9·81 kN/m³

$$\therefore \quad Q = \frac{120}{9.81 \times 326.2} = 0.0375 \text{ m}^3/\text{s}$$

But, $$Q = \frac{\pi}{4} D^2 \times V$$

$$\therefore \quad 0.0375 = \frac{\pi}{4} D^2 \times V$$

or, $$V = \frac{0.0375 \times 4}{\pi D^2} = \frac{0.0477}{D^2} \qquad ...(i)$$

The head lost due to friction, $h_f = \dfrac{4fLV^2}{D \times 2g}$

But, $h_f = 81{\cdot}5$ m (calculated above)

$$\therefore \quad 81.5 = \frac{4 \times 0.006 \times 2500 \times (0.0477/D^2)^2}{D \times 2 \times 9.81}$$

or, $$81.5 = \frac{4 \times 0.006 \times 2500 \times (0.0477)^2}{D^5 \times 2 \times 9.81}$$

or, $$D^5 = \frac{4 \times 0.006 \times 2500 \times (0.0477)^2}{81.5 \times 2 \times 9.81}$$

or, $D = 0{\cdot}1535$ m or **153·5 mm** **(Ans.)**

(*ii*) Efficiency of transmission, η :

$$\eta = \frac{H - h_f}{H} = \frac{407.7 - 81.5}{407.7} = 0.8 \text{ or } \mathbf{80\%} \quad \textbf{(Ans.)}$$

12.11. FLOW THROUGH NOZZLE AT THE END OF A PIPE

Refer to Fig. 12·44. A **nozzle** *is a tapering mouthpiece, which is fitted to the outlet end of a pipe*. The total energy at the end of the pipe consists of pressure energy and kinetic energy. By fitting the nozzle at the end of a pipe, the total energy is converted into *kinetic energy.* A high velocity is required in the fields of power development, fire fighting, mining, etc.

Fig. 12·44 shows a nozzle fitted at the end of a pipe connected to a reservoir.

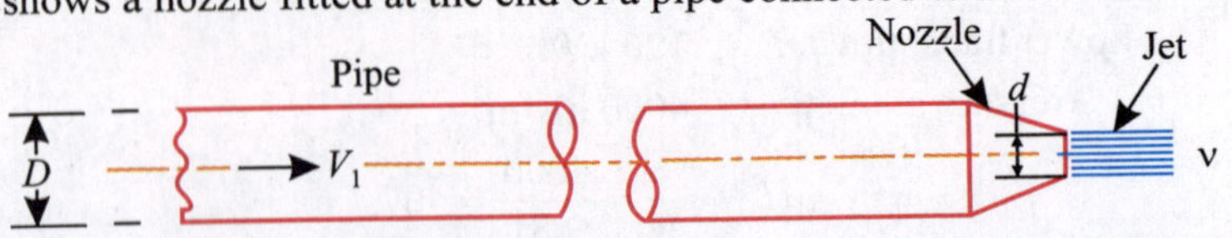

Fig. 12.44

Let, D = Diameter of the pipe,

L = Length of the pipe,

d = Diameter of the nozzle,

V = Velocity of flow in pipe,

v = Velocity of flow at the outlet of the nozzle,

f = Co-efficient of friction for the pipe, and

H = Height of water level in the reservoir above the centre-line of the nozzle.

Head lost due to friction in pipe,

$$h_f = \frac{4fLV^2}{D \times 2g}$$

∴ Head available at the base of the nozzle

$$= H - h_f = H - \frac{4fLV^2}{D \times 2g}$$

Assuming the minor losses and losses in the nozzle to be negligible, we have:

$$\text{Total head at the nozzle outlet} = \frac{v^2}{2g}$$

$$\therefore \quad H = h_f + \frac{v^2}{2g} = \frac{4fLV^2}{D \times 2g} + \frac{v^2}{2g} \quad \text{...}(i)$$

From continuity consideration, we have:

$$AV = av$$

(where A and a are the areas of the pipe and area of the nozzle at outlet respectively)

or,

$$V = \frac{av}{A}$$

Substituting the value of V in eqn. (i), we get:

$$H = \frac{4fLa^2v^2}{D \times 2g \times A^2} + \frac{v^2}{2g}$$

$$= \frac{v^2}{2g}\left(\frac{1 + 4fLa^2}{D \times A^2}\right)$$

$$\therefore \quad v = \sqrt{\frac{2gH}{1 + \frac{4fL}{D} \times \frac{a^2}{A^2}}} \quad \text{...(12.20)}$$

∴ Discharge through the nozzle $= a \times v$

12·11·1 Power Transmitted through the Nozzle

Mass of liquid flowing per second at the outlet ofthe nozzle, $m = \rho av$

The K.E. of the jet at outlet of the nozzle

$$= \frac{1}{2} mv^2 = \frac{1}{2} \times \rho av \times v^2 = \frac{1}{2} \rho av^3$$

$\therefore$ Power available at the outlet of nozzle $= \frac{1}{2} \rho av^3$ watts

Also, power available at the inlet of pipe $= wQH$

$\therefore$ Efficiency of power transmission through the nozzle,

$$\eta = \frac{\text{Power available at the outlet of nozzle}}{\text{Power available at the inlet of pipe}} = \frac{\frac{1}{2} \rho av^3}{wQH}$$

But, $w = \rho g$ and $Q = av$

$$\therefore \quad \eta = \frac{\frac{1}{2} \rho av^3}{\rho g \times av \times H} = \frac{v^2}{2gH} = \left[\frac{1}{1 + \frac{4fL}{D} \times \frac{a^2}{A^2}} \right] \quad \text{...(12·21)}$$

$$\left[\because v = \sqrt{\frac{2gH}{1 + \frac{4fL}{D} \times \frac{a^2}{A^2}}} \quad \text{...eqn. (12·20)} \right]$$

12·11·2 Condition for Transmission of Maximum Power Through Nozzle

We know that, $$H = h_f + \frac{v^2}{2g} = \frac{4fLV^2}{D \times 2g} + \frac{v^2}{2g}$$

or, $$\frac{v^2}{2g} = H - \frac{4fLV^2}{D \times 2g}$$

But power transmitted through the nozzle,

$$P = \frac{1}{2} \rho av^3 = \frac{1}{2} \rho av \times v^2$$

$$= \frac{1}{2} \rho av \left[2g \left(H - \frac{4fLV^2}{D \times 2g} \right) \right]$$

$$= wav \left(H - \frac{4fLV^2}{D \times 2g} \right) \quad \text{...(12·22)}$$

From continuity consideration, we have:

$$AV = av \text{ or } V = \frac{av}{A}$$

Substituting the value of V in eqn. (12·22), we get:

Power transmitted through nozzle, $$P = wav \left(H - \frac{4fL \times a^2 v^2}{D \times 2g \times A^2} \right) \quad \text{...[12·22(a)]}$$

Power transmitted will be *maximum*, when $\frac{dP}{dv} = 0$

$$\frac{d}{dv}\left[wav\left(H - \frac{4fL}{D \times 2g} \times \frac{a^2v^2}{A^2}\right)\right] = 0$$

or,
$$\frac{d}{dv}\left[wa\left(Hv - \frac{4fL}{D \times 2g} \times \frac{a^2v^3}{A^2}\right)\right] = 0$$

or,
$$H - 3 \times \frac{4fL}{D \times 2g} \times V^2 = 0 \qquad \left(\because \frac{a^2v^2}{A^2} = V^2\right)$$

or,
$$H - 3h_f = 0 \qquad \left(\because h_f = \frac{4fLV^2}{D \times 2g}\right)$$

or,
$$\boldsymbol{h_f = \frac{H}{3}} \qquad ...(12{\cdot}23)$$

The eqn. (12·23) indicates that the *power transmitted by a nozzle is maximum when the head lost due to friction in pipe is equal to one-third the total head supplied at the inlet of pipe.*

12·11·3 Diameter of the Nozzle for Transmitting Maximum Power

We know that,
$$H = h_f + \frac{v^2}{2g}$$

But,
$$H = 3h_f \qquad \text{[From eqn. (12·22)]}$$

$\therefore$
$$3h_f = h_f + \frac{v^2}{2g} \quad \text{or} \quad 2h_f = \frac{v^2}{2g}$$

$$\frac{2 \times 4fLV^2}{D \times 2g} = \frac{v^2}{2g}$$

For *continuity* considerations, we have:

$$AV = av \quad \text{or} \quad V = \frac{av}{A}$$

$\therefore$
$$\frac{2 \times 4fL \times a^2v^2}{D \times 2g \times A^2} = \frac{v^2}{2g}$$

or,
$$\frac{A^2}{a^2} = \frac{8fL}{D} \quad \text{or} \quad \boldsymbol{\frac{A}{a} = \sqrt{\frac{8fL}{D}}} \qquad ...(12{\cdot}24)$$

Eqn. (12·24) gives the *ratio* between the areas of the supply pipe and the nozzle for maximum power transmission.

Substituting the values of A and a in eqn. (12·24) and squaring both sides, we have:

$$\left(\frac{\frac{\pi}{4} \times D^2}{\frac{\pi}{4} \times d^2}\right)^2 = \frac{8fL}{D}$$

or,
$$\frac{D^4}{d^4} = \frac{8fL}{D} \quad \text{or} \quad D^5 = 8fLd^4$$

$\therefore$
$$\boldsymbol{d = \left(\frac{D^5}{8fL}\right)^{1/4}} \qquad ...(12{\cdot}25)$$

Example 12.48. *A nozzle is fitted to a pipe120 mm in diameter and 250 m long, with co-efficient of friction as 0·01. If the available head at the nozzle is 100 m find the diameter of the nozzle and the maximum power transmitted by a jet of water discharging freely out of a nozzle.*

Solution. Diameter of the pipe, D = 120 mm = 0·12 m

Length of the pipe, L = 250 m

Co-efficient of friction, f = 0·01

Head of water, H = 100 m.

(*i*) Diameter of the nozzle for maximum power, d :

Using the relation :

$$d = \left[\frac{D^5}{8fL}\right]^{1/4} \quad \text{...[Eqn. (12.25)]}$$

$$= \left[\frac{0.12^5}{8 \times 0.01 \times 250}\right]^{1/4} = 0.0334 \text{ m or } \mathbf{33{\cdot}4 \text{ mm}}$$

i.e., d = **33·4 mm (Ans.)**

(*ii*) Maximum power transmitted by the jet, P :

We know that for the maximum transmission of power, the head lost due to friction $= \dfrac{H}{3}$

$\therefore$ Available head, $h = 100 - \dfrac{100}{3} = \dfrac{200}{3} = 66.67$ m

$\therefore$ Velocity of water through the nozzle,

$$v = \sqrt{2gh} = \sqrt{2 \times 9.81 \times 66.67} = 36.2 \text{ m/s}$$

Now using the relation, $P = wQH$, we have: $(\because Q = a.v)$

$$P = wavH$$

$$= 9.81 \times \frac{\pi}{4} \times 0.0334^2 \times 36.2 \times 66.67 = 20.74 \text{ kW}$$

i.e., P = **20·74 kW (Ans.)**

Example 12.49. *Find the maximum power transmitted by a jet of water discharging freely out of nozzle fitted to a pipe 300 m long and 100 mm diameter with co-efficient of friction as 00·01. The available head at the nozzzle is 90 m.* **[Delhi University]**

Solution. Length of the pipe, L = 300 m

Diameter of the pipe, D = 100 mm = 0·1 m

Area of the pipe, $A = \dfrac{\pi}{4} \times 0{\cdot}1^2 = 0{\cdot}007854 \text{ m}^2$

Co-efficient of friction, f = 0·01

Head available at the nozzle, h = 90 m

Maximum power transmitted, *P* :

Let, a = Area of the nozzle.

Also, $$\frac{A}{a} = \sqrt{\frac{8fL}{D}}$$

$$\therefore \quad \frac{0.007854}{a} = \sqrt{\frac{8 \times 0.01 \times 300}{0.1}} = 15.492$$

or, $$a = \frac{0.007854}{15.492} = 0.0005069 \text{ m}^2$$

Also, $$h = \frac{v^2}{2g}$$

$\therefore$ $$90 = \frac{v^2}{2g} \quad \text{or} \quad v = \sqrt{90 \times 2 \times 9.81} = 42.02 \text{ m/s}$$

Discharge through the nozzle, $Q = av = 0{\cdot}0005069 \times 42{\cdot}02 = 0{\cdot}0213 \text{ m}^3\text{/s}$

$\therefore$ Maximum power transmitted,

$$P = wQh = 9{\cdot}81 \times 0{\cdot}0213 \times 90 \text{ kW} = \mathbf{18{\cdot}8 \text{ kW}} \quad \textbf{(Ans.)}$$

$$(\because w = 9{\cdot}81 \text{ kN/m}^3)$$

Example 12.50. *A fire engine supplies water to a hosepipe, 75 m long and 0·075 m in diameter, at a pressure of 294 kN/m² (gauge). The discharge end of the hosepipe has a nozzle of diameter d fixed to it. Taking friction factor as 0·032, determine the diameter d of the nozzle, so that the momentum of the issuing jet may be a maximum.* **(UPSC Exams.)**

Solution. Diameter of the hosepipe, $D = 0{\cdot}75$ m

Length of the hosepipe, $L = 75$ m

Pressure of water, $p = 294 \text{ kN/m}^2$ (gauge)

Friction factor $(= 4f) = 0{\cdot}032$

Diameter of the nozzle, d :

Head lost in the hosepipe, $$h_f = \frac{4fLV^2}{D \times 2g} = \frac{0.032 \times 75 \times V^2}{0.075 \times 2g} = \frac{32V^2}{2g}$$

Applying the continuity equation to the pipe and the jet, we get:

$$Q = AV = av$$

or, $$v = \frac{AV}{a} = \frac{\frac{\pi}{4} \times D^2 \times V}{\frac{\pi}{4} \times d^2} = \left(\frac{0.0075}{d}\right)^2 V$$

where, d = Diameter of the nozzle,

a = Area of the jet, and

A = Area of the hosepipe.

Applying Bernoulli's equation to the hosepipe at the fire engine and to the nozzle jet, considering the hosepipe and the nozzle to be in the horizontal plane, we have:

$$\frac{294}{9{\cdot}81} + \frac{V^2}{2g} + 0 = 0 + \frac{v^2}{2g} + 0 + h_f \text{ (head lost in the hosepipe)}$$

(Neglecting the energy loss in the nozzle, being very small)

or, $$30 + \frac{V^2}{2g} = \left(\frac{0.075}{d}\right)^4 \frac{V^2}{2g} + \frac{32V^2}{2g}$$

or, $$30 = \frac{V^2}{2g}\left[32 + \left(\frac{0.075}{d}\right)^4 - 1\right]$$

or, $$V = \sqrt{\frac{30 \times 2 \times 9.81}{31 + \left(\frac{0.075}{d}\right)^4}}$$

Momentum of issuing jet,

$$M = \rho Q v = 1000 \times \left\{\left(\frac{\pi}{4}\right) \times (0.075)^2 \times V\right\}\left(\frac{0.075}{d}\right)^2 V = 0.0248\frac{V^2}{d^2}$$

Substituting for V, we get:

$$M = \frac{0.0248}{d^2}\left[\frac{30 \times 2 \times 9.81}{31 + (0.075/d)^4}\right] = \frac{14.6}{d^2\,[31 + (0.075/d)^4]}$$

For *momentum to be maximum,* $\frac{dM}{dd} = 0$

$$\frac{d}{dd}\left[d^2\left\{31 + \left(\frac{0.075}{d}\right)^4\right\}\right] = 0$$

or,
$$\frac{d}{dd}\left[31\,d^2 + \frac{0.075^4}{d^2}\right] = 0$$

or,
$$62d - \frac{2 \times 0.075^4}{d^3} = 0$$

or,
$$62d^4 - 6{\cdot}328 \times 10^{-5} = 0$$

or,
$$d = \left(\frac{6.328 \times 10^{-5}}{62}\right)^{1/4} = 0.03178 \text{ m} \quad \text{or} \quad \mathbf{31{\cdot}78\ mm}\ \textbf{(Ans.)}$$

12.12. WATER HAMMER IN PIPES

In a long pipe, when the *flowing water is suddenly brought to rest by closing the valve or by any similar cause*, there will be a *sudden rise in pressure* due to the momentum of water being destroyed. A pressure wave is transmitted along the pipe. A sudden rise in pressure has the effect of hammering action on the walls of the pipe. This *phenomenon of sudden rise in presssure is known as* **water hammer** or **hammer blow.** The magnitude of pressure rise depends on :

(*i*) *The speed at which valve is closed,*

(*ii*) *The velocity of flow,*

(*iii*) *The length of pipe, and*

(*iv*) *The elastic properties of the pipe material as well as that of the flowing fluid.*

The rise in pressure in some cases may be so large that the pipe may even burst and therefore it is essential to take into account this pressure rise in the design of the pipes.

12·12·1 Gradual Closure of Valve

Consider a long pipe carrying liquid (Fig. (12·45)) and provided with a valve which is closed gradually.

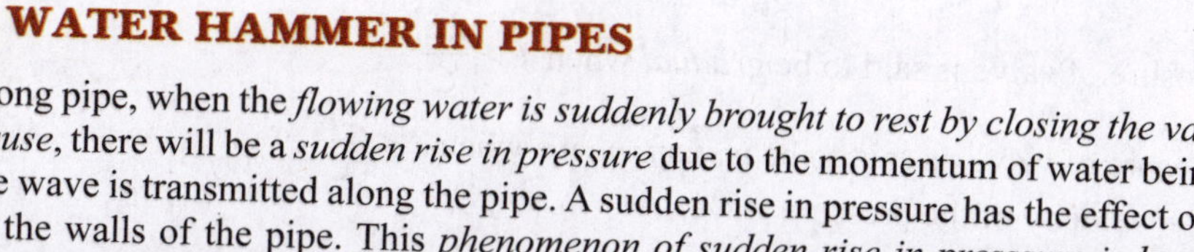

Fig. 12.45. Water hammer.

Let, A = Area of cross-section of the pipe,

L = Length of the pipe,

V = Velocity of flow of water in the pipe,

t = Time required to close the valve (in seconds), and

p = Intensity of pressure wave produced.

The mass of liquid contained in the pipe is $= \rho AL$

Assuming that the rate of closure of the valve is so adjusted that the liquid column in the pipe is brought to rest with a uniform retardation; from an intial velocity V to zero in time t seconds, we have:

$$\text{Retardation of water} = \frac{V-0}{t} = \frac{V}{t}$$

∴ The axial force available for producing retardation

$$= \text{Mass} \times \text{retardation}$$

$$= \rho AL \times \frac{V}{t} \quad ...(i)$$

Also, force due to pressure wave is $= p.A$ ...(*ii*)

Equating the two forces given by eqns. (*i*) and (*ii*), we have:

$$\rho AL \times \frac{V}{t} = p \times A$$

or,
$$p = \frac{\rho LV}{t} \quad ...(12{\cdot}26)$$

∴
$$\text{Head of pressure, } H = \frac{p}{w} = \frac{\rho LV}{w \times t} = \frac{\rho LV}{\rho{\cdot}g{\cdot}t} = \frac{LV}{gt}$$

i.e.,
$$H = \frac{LV}{gt} \quad ...(12{\cdot}27)$$

(*i*) The closure of valve is said to be *gradual* when $t > \frac{2L}{C}$ ...(12·28)

(*ii*) The closure of valve is said to be *instantaneous* when $t < \frac{2L}{C}$ ...(12·29)

where, C = velocity of the pressure wave.

12·12·2 Instantaneous Closure of Valve in Rigid Pipes

Eqn. (11·26) indicates that when the valve is closed instantaneously (*i.e.*, $t = 0$), the inertia head should rise to infinity. However, in practice, it is not possible to close the valve instantaneously, as it always takes some time. Thus, even for a very rapid closure of the valve, as observed during experimentation, the pressure rise is quite finite and measurable. Moreover, eqn. (12·26) has been derived on the *assumption that the liquid is incompressible.* This assumption is *incorrect,* because at very high pressures even liquids get compressed to *some extent* and *behave like cmpressible fluids.*

Consider a pipe of length L and area of cross-section A (Fig. 12·45) carrying water which is flowing through it at a velocity V. When the valve is closed instantaneously the K.E. of the flowing water is converted into strain energy of water (neglecting effect of friction and assuming the pipe wall to be perfectly rigid).

$$\text{Loss of } K.E. = \frac{1}{2} mV^2 = \frac{1}{2} \rho AL \times V^2 \qquad (\because m = \rho \times A \times L)$$

$$\text{Gain of strain energy} = \frac{1}{2}\left(\frac{p^2}{K}\right) \times \text{volume} = \frac{1}{2}\frac{p^2}{K} \times AL$$

[where, k = Bulk modulus of elasticity of water, and
p = Intensity of pressure wave produced.]

Equating the loss of *K.E.* to the gain of strain energy, we get:

$$\frac{1}{2}\rho AL \times V^2 = \frac{1}{2}\frac{p^2}{K} \times AL$$

or,
$$p^2 = \frac{1}{2}\rho ALV^2 \times \frac{2K}{AL} = \rho KV^2$$

$$\therefore \qquad p = \sqrt{\rho K V^2} = V\sqrt{\rho K} = V\sqrt{\frac{K\rho^2}{\rho}}$$

or,
$$p = V\rho C \qquad ...(12{\cdot}30)$$

$$\left(\text{where, } C = \sqrt{\frac{K}{\rho}}, C \text{ being the } \textit{velocity of pressure wave.}\right)$$

12·12·3 Instantaneous Closure of Valve in Elastic Pipes

As shown in Fig. 12·45, consider a pipe of length L, diameter D, thickness t (small compared to diameter).

Let, p = Increase of pressure due to water hammer,

E = Modulus of elasticity of pipe material, and

$\frac{1}{m}$ = Poisson's ratio for pipe material.

When the valve is closed intantaneously, rise of pressure takes place due to which circumferential and longitudinal stresses are produced in the pipe wall; these stresses are given as (from knowledge of strength of materials):

$$\sigma_c = \frac{pD}{2t} \quad \text{and} \quad \sigma_l = \frac{pD}{4t}$$

where, σ_c = Circumferential stress, and

σ_l = Longitudinal stress.

Also, strain energy stored in the pipe material per unit volume is

$$= \frac{1}{2E}\left(\sigma_c^2 + \sigma_l^2 - \frac{2\sigma_c\sigma_l}{m}\right)$$

$$= \frac{1}{2E}\left[\left(\frac{pD}{2t}\right)^2 + \left(\frac{pD}{4t}\right)^2 - \frac{2 \times \frac{pD}{2t} \times \frac{pD}{4t}}{m}\right]$$

$$= \frac{1}{2E}\left[\frac{p^2D^2}{4t^2} + \frac{p^2D^2}{16t^2} - \frac{p^2D^2}{4mt^2}\right]$$

Assuming, $\frac{1}{m}$ = 1/4, we have:

$$\text{Strain energy per unit volume} = \frac{1}{2E}\left[\frac{p^2D^2}{4t^2} + \frac{p^2D^2}{16t^2} - \frac{p^2D^2}{16t^2}\right] = \frac{p^2D^2}{8Et^2}$$

Total strain energy stored in pipe material

$$= \frac{p^2D^2}{8Et^2} \times \text{total volume of pipe material}$$

$$= \frac{p^2D^2}{8Et^2} \times \pi\, Dt \times L = \frac{p^2 \times D^3L}{8Et}$$

$$= \frac{p^2 \times \pi D^2 \times DL}{8Et} = \frac{p^2 ADL}{2Et} \qquad \left[\because A \text{ (area of the pipe)} = \frac{\pi}{4} \times D^2\right]$$

$$\text{Loss of K.E. of water} = \frac{1}{2}mV^2 = \frac{1}{2}\rho AL \times V^2$$

$$\text{Gain of strain energy in water} = \frac{1}{2}\left(\frac{p^2}{K}\right) \times \text{volume} = \frac{1}{2}\frac{p^2}{K} \times AL$$

Also, The loss of K.E. of water = Gain of strain energy in water + strain energy stored in material.

$$\therefore \quad \frac{1}{2}\rho AL \times V^2 = \frac{1}{2}\frac{p^2}{K} \times AL + \frac{p^2 ADL}{2Et}$$

Dividing both sides by $\frac{AL}{2}$, we get:

$$\rho V^2 = \frac{p^2}{K} + \frac{p^2 D}{Et} = p^2\left(\frac{1}{K} + \frac{D}{Et}\right)$$

$$\therefore \quad p^2 = \frac{\rho V^2}{\left(\frac{1}{K} + \frac{D}{Et}\right)}$$

or,
$$p = \sqrt{\frac{\rho V^2}{\left(\frac{1}{K} + \frac{D}{Et}\right)}} = V \times \sqrt{\frac{\rho}{\left(\frac{1}{K} + \frac{D}{Et}\right)}} \quad \text{...(12·31)}$$

12·12·4 Time required by Pressure Wave to travel from the Valve to the Tank and from Tank to Valve

$$\text{Time taken, } t = \frac{\text{Distance travelled from valve to tank and back}}{\text{Velocity of pressure wave}}$$

$$= \frac{L + L}{C} = \frac{2L}{C} \quad \textit{i.e.,} \quad t = \frac{2L}{C} \quad \text{...(12·32)}$$

where, L = Length of the pipe, and

C = Velocity of pressure wave.

Example 12.51. *In a pipe 600 mm diameter and 3000 m length, provided with a valve at its end, water is flowing with a velocity of 2 m/s. Assuming velocity of pressure wave C = 1500 m/s, find :*

(i) The rise in pressure if the valve is closed in 20 seconds, and

(ii) The rise in pressure if the valve is closed in 2·5 seconds. Assume the pipe to be rigid one and take bulk modulus of water as 2 GN/m².

Solution. Diameter of the pipe, D = 600 mm = 0·6 m

Length of the pipe, L = 300 m

Velocity of water, V = 2 m/s

Velocity of pressure wave, C = 1500 m/s.

(i) Rise in pressure, p :

Time taken to close the valve, t = 20 s

Now, The ratio, $\frac{2L}{C} = \frac{2 \times 3000}{1500} = 4$

The close of valve is said to be *gradual* if,

$$t > \frac{2L}{C} \quad \text{...[Eqn. (12·28)]}$$

Hence, the valve is closed *gradually*.

The rise in pressure (p), for gradual closure of valve, is given by:

$$p = \frac{\rho LV}{t} \quad \text{...[Eqn. (12·26)]}$$

$$= \frac{1000 \times 3000 \times 2}{20} = 300 \times 10^3 \text{ N/m}^2 \text{ or } \mathbf{300\ kN/m^2}\ \textbf{(Ans.)}$$

(ii) Rise in pressure, p :

Time taken to close the valve, $t = 2{\cdot}5$ s

Bulk modulus of water, $K = 2$ GN/m^2

Velocity of pressure wave is given by,

$$C = \sqrt{\frac{K}{\rho}} = \sqrt{\frac{2 \times 10^9}{1000}} = 1414.2 \text{ m/s}$$

$$\text{The ratio, } \frac{2L}{C} = \frac{2 \times 3000}{1414.2} = 4.24 \text{ s}$$

$$\therefore \quad t < \frac{2L}{C}$$

Thus, the valve is closed *intantaneously* [From eqn. (12·29)]

When pipe is rigid, the rise in pressure due to instantaneous closure of the valve is given by (eqn. 12·30),

$$p = V\rho C = 2 \times 1000 \times 1414{\cdot}2 \text{ N/m}^2 \text{ or } \mathbf{2828{\cdot}4 \text{ kN/m}^2} \textbf{ (Ans.)}$$

Example 12.52. *Water is flowing in a pipe of 150 mm diameter with a velocity of 2·5 m/s when it is suddenly brought to rest by closing the valve. Find the pressure rise assuming pipe is elastic, E = 206 GN/m², Poisson's ratio = 0·25 and K for water = 2·06 GN/m². Pipe wall is 5 mm thick.*

Solution. Diameter of the pipe, D = 150 mm = 0·15 m

Thickness of the pipe, t = 5 mm = 0·005 m

Velocity of water, V = 2·5 m/s

Modulus of elasticity, E = 206 GN/m^2

Bulk modulus of water, K = 2·06 GN/m^2

Poisson's ratio, $\frac{1}{m}$ = 1/4

Pressure rise, p :

Using the relation :

$$p = V\sqrt{\frac{\rho}{\left(\frac{1}{K} + \frac{D}{Et}\right)}} \qquad \text{...[Eqn. (12·31)]}$$

$$= 2.5\sqrt{\frac{1000}{\left(\frac{1}{2.06 \times 10^9} + \frac{0{\cdot}15}{2.06 \times 10^9 \times 0.005}\right)}} = 2.5\sqrt{\frac{10^{12}}{0.485 + 0.1456}}$$

$$= \mathbf{3148 \text{ kN/m}^2} \textbf{ (Ans.)}$$

Example 12.53. *In a pressure penstock 4500 m long water is flowing at 4 m/s. If the velocity of the pressure wave travelling in the pipe due to sudden complete closure of a valve at the downstream end is given as 1500 m/s, find :*

(i) The maximum pressure rise, and

(ii) The period of oscillation.

Show how the pressure changes with time at the middle point of the penstock length. All friction losses may be neglected. **(UPSC Exams.)**

Solution. Length of the penstock, L = 4500 m

Velocity of water, V = 4 m/s

Velocity of the pressure wave, C = 1500 m/s

(*i*) **The maximum pressure rise :**

Maximum pressure is given by:

$$p = V\rho C \quad \text{...[Eqn. (12·39)]}$$

$$= 4 \times 1000 \times 1500 \text{ N/m}^2 \text{ or } \mathbf{6 \text{ MN/m}^2} \text{ (Ans.)}$$

(*ii*) **The period of oscillation :**

$$\text{The period of oscillation} = \frac{2L}{C} = \frac{2 \times 4500}{1500} = \mathbf{6 \text{ seconds}} \text{ (Ans.)}$$

Pressure changes with time at the middle point of the penstock length :

The pressure wave reaches at the middle point of the penstock length in 1.5 s $\left(\frac{4500}{2 \times 1500} = 1.5 \text{ s}\right)$; at this instant the pressure at the middle point rises by 6 MN/m^2 and remains unchanged until the pressure wave returns as a wave of rarefaction of negative pressure. This happens at 4·5 s after the closure of the valve when the pressure in the penstock at the middle point is reduced by an equal amount. Fig. 12·46 shows the pressure changes at the middle point with respect to time.

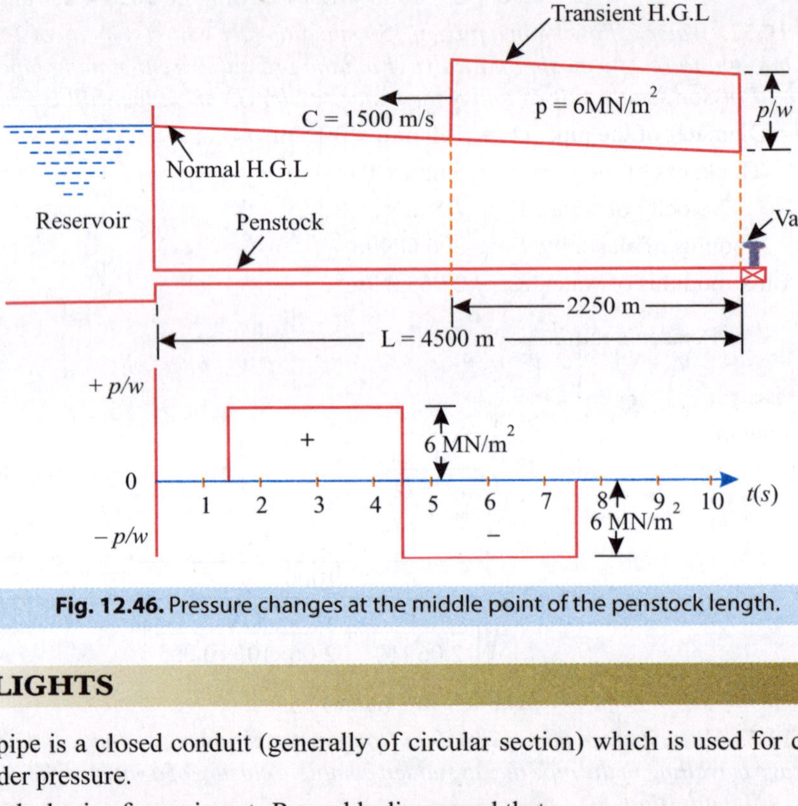

Fig. 12.46. Pressure changes at the middle point of the penstock length.

HIGHLIGHTS

1. A pipe is a closed conduit (generally of circular section) which is used for carrying fluids under pressure.
2. On the basis of experiments Reynolds discovered that :
   (*i*) In case of *laminar flow* : The loss of pressure head $\propto$ velocity (V)
   (*ii*) In case of *turbulent flow* : the loss of pressure head $\propto V^2$ (approximately)
3. *Energy (or head) losses :*
   A. *Major energy losses.......due to frictrion.*
   B. *Minor energy loses.*

   These losses are due to:

(*i*) Sudden enlargement of pipe
(*ii*) Sudden contraction of pipe,
(*iii*) Bend in pipe,
(*iv*) An obstruction in pipe, and
(*v*) Pipe fittings, etc.

4. Major energy losses (due to friction), Important formulae :

(*i*) *Darcy-Weisbach formula* (for loss of head due to friction)

$$h_f = \frac{4fLV^2}{D \times 2g} = \frac{f_1 LV^2}{D \times 2g}$$

where, f = co-efficient of friction, f_1 = friction factor (= $4f$)

(*ii*) Chezy's formula (for loss of head due to friction)

$$V = C\sqrt{mi}\left(\text{where, } i = \frac{h_f}{L}\right)$$

[$\therefore h_f = i \times L$, where i is obtained from Chezy's formula.]

5. Minor energy losses; Important formulae :

(*i*) Loss of head due to *sudden enlargement*

$$h_e = \frac{(V_1 - V_2)^2}{2g}$$

(*ii*) Loss of head due to *sudden contraction.*

$$h_c = \frac{V_2^2}{2g}\left[\frac{1}{C_c} - 1\right]^2$$

(*iii*) Loss of head due to *obstruction in pipe,*

$$h_{obs.} = \left[\frac{A}{C_c\,(A - a)} - 1\right]^2 \frac{V^2}{2g}$$

where, a = Maximum area of obstruction, and
A = Area of the pipe.

(*iv*) Loss of head at the entrance to pipe,

$$h_i = 0.5\,\frac{V^2}{2g}$$ where, V = velocity of liquid in pipe.

(*v*) Loss of head at the *exit of pipe,*

$$h_0 = \frac{V^2}{2g}$$ where, V = velocity at outlet of pipe.

(*vi*) Loss of head due to *bend in the pipe,*

$$h_b = k\,\frac{V^2}{2g}$$ where, k = co-efficient of bend.

(*vii*) Loss of head in *various pipe fittings,*

$$h_{\text{fittings}} = k\,\frac{V^2}{2g}$$

where, k = value of co-efficient; it depends on the type of pipe fittings.

6. *Energy gradient line* (E.G.L.). If the total energy at various points along the axis of the pipe is plotted and joined by a line, the line so obtained is called the '*Eenergy gradient line*'.

7. *Hydraulic gradient line* (H.G.L.). If a line is drawn joining the piezometric levels at various points, the line so obtained is called the '*Hydraulic gradient line*'.
8. *Equivalent pipe.* It is defined as the pipe of uniform diameter having loss of head and discharge equal to the loss of head and discharge of a compound pipe consisting of several pipes of different lengths and diameters. To determine the size of the equivalent pipe Dupit's equation, given below, is used :

$$\frac{L}{D^5} = \left| \frac{L_1}{D_1^5} + \frac{L_2}{D_2^5} + \frac{L_3}{D_3^5} + ... \right|$$

9. In case of *parallel pipes* :

   (*i*) Rate of discharge in the main line = Sum of the discharges in each of the parallel pipes.

   i.e., $Q = Q_1 + Q_2 + ...$

   (*ii*) The loss of head in each pipe is same.
10. A *syphon* is a long bent pipe employed for carrying water from a reservoir at a higher elevation to another reservoir at lower elevation when the two reservoirs are separated by a hill or high level ground in between.
11. *Power transmission through pipes :*

$$\text{Efficiency, } \eta = \frac{H - h_f}{H}$$

$$\text{Power, } P = wQ\,(H - h_f) \text{ kW} \qquad \text{(where, } w = 9{\cdot}81 \text{ kN/m}^3 \text{ for water)}$$

Power transmitted will be *maximum* when, $h_f = \dfrac{H}{3}$

Then, $$\eta_{max} = \frac{H - H/3}{H} = 66.7\%$$

12. *Flow through nozzles*; Important formulae :

   (*i*) Velocity, $v = \sqrt{\dfrac{2gh}{1 + \dfrac{4fL}{D} \cdot \dfrac{a^2}{A^2}}}$

   (*ii*) Power, $P = wav\left[H - \dfrac{4fL}{D \times 2g}\left(\dfrac{a^2v^2}{A^2}\right)\right]$ kW (where, $w = 9{\cdot}81$ kN/m^3 for water)

   (*iii*) Condition for *maximum power transmission* : $h_f = \dfrac{H}{3}$

   (*iv*) Diameter of nozzle for maximum power transmission,

$$d = \left(\frac{D^5}{8fL}\right)^{1/4}$$

13. *Water hammer in pipes.* The phenomenon of sudden rise in pressure in a pipe when water flowing in it is suddenly brought to rest by closing the valve is known as *water hammer* or *hammer blow.*
14. Valve closure is *gradual* when $t > \dfrac{2L}{C}$

   Valve closure is *sudden* when $t < \dfrac{2L}{C}$

   where, $C = \sqrt{\dfrac{K}{\rho}}$, C being the velocity of of pressure wave produced due to water hammer.

15. The intensity of pressure rise due to water hammer is given by, $p = \frac{\rho L V}{t}$ ... when valve is *closed gradually* (where, t = time required to close the valve),

$p = V\sqrt{\rho K}$ ...when the valve is *closed suddenly* and pipe is assumed *rigid,* and

$p = V \times \sqrt{\frac{\rho}{\left(\frac{1}{K} + \frac{D}{Et}\right)}}$ ...when valve is *closed suddenly* and the pipe is *elastic.*

(where, t = Thickness of pipewall)

where, L = Length of pipe,
V = Velocity of flow,
K = Bulk modulus of water, and
E = Modulus of elasticity for pipe material.

OBJECTIVE TYPE QUESTIONS

Choose the Correct Answer :

1. The pipe running partially/completely full behaves like an open channel.

2. In a laminar flow, Reynold's number is
(*a*) less than 2000
(*b*) more than 2000
(*c*) more than 2000 but less than 4000
(*d*) none of the above.

3. In a turbulent flow, Reynold's number is
(*a*) less than 4000
(*b*) more than 4000
(*c*) between 2000 and 4000
(*d*) none of the above.

4. In case of a laminar flow, the loss of pressure head is
(*a*) proportional to $(\text{velocity})^2$
(*b*) proportional to velocity
(*c*) proportional to $(\text{velocity})^{1/2}$
(*d*) none of the above.

5. In case of a turbulent flow, the loss of head is approximately proportional to
(*a*) velocity (*b*) $(\text{velocity})^{1/2}$
(*c*) $(\text{velocity})^{3/4}$ (*d*) $(\text{velocity})^2$

6. Darcy-Weisbach equation is used to find loss of head due to :
(*a*) sudden enlargement
(*b*) sudden contraction
(*c*) friction
(*d*) none of the above.

7. Chezy's formula is given as
(*a*) $V = C\sqrt{m^2 i}$ (*b*) $V = C^2\sqrt{mi^2}$
(*c*) $V = C\sqrt{mi}$ (*d*) $V = C\sqrt{m^2 i^3}$

8. Loss of head due to sudden enlargement is given as
(*a*) $\frac{(V_1 - V_2)^3}{2g}$ (*b*) $\frac{(V_1 - V_2)^2}{2g}$
(*c*) $\frac{V_1^2 - V_2^2}{2g}$ (*c*) $\frac{\sqrt{V_1 - V_2}}{2g}$

9. Loss of head due to sudden contraction is given as
(*a*) $\frac{V^2}{g}\left(\frac{1}{C_c} - 1\right)^2$ (*b*) $\frac{V_2^2}{2g}\left(\frac{1}{C_c} - 1\right)^2$
(*c*) $\frac{V_2}{g^2}\left(\frac{1}{C_c} - 1\right)^2$ (*d*) $\frac{V_2^2}{2g}\left(\frac{1}{C_c} - 1\right)$.

10. Loss of head due to an obstruction is given as
(*a*) $\left[\frac{A}{A - a} - 1\right]^2 \frac{V^2}{2g}$
(*b*) $\left[\frac{A}{C_c (A - a)} - 1\right] \frac{V^2}{2g}$
(*c*) $\left[\frac{A}{C_c a} - 1\right]^2 \frac{V^2}{2g}$
(*d*) $\left[\frac{A^2}{A - a} - 1\right]^2 \frac{V^2}{2g}$.

11. Loss of head at entrance to a pipe is given as

(*a*) $\frac{V^2}{2g}$ (*b*) $\frac{V}{g}$

(*c*) $0{\cdot}5\frac{V^2}{2g}$ (*d*) $\frac{V^3}{2g}$

12. Loss of head at exit of a pipe is given as

(*a*) $\frac{V^2}{2g}$ (*b*) $\frac{V^2}{g}$

(*c*) $\frac{V^3}{g}$ (*d*) $\frac{V^3}{2g}$

13. There is specific relation/no relation between the slope of the energy gradient line and the slope of the axis of the pipe.

14. The pipes are said to be in series/parallel when a main pipe line divides into two or more parallel pipes which again join together downstream and continue as a mainline.

15. The power transmitted through the pipe is maximum when head lost due to friction in the pipe is equal to

(*a*) $\frac{1}{3}$ rd of the total supply head

(*b*) $\frac{1}{4}$ th of the total supply head

(*c*) $\frac{1}{5}$ th of the total supply head

(*d*) $\frac{1}{8}$ th of the total supply head.

16. Diameter of nozzle (*d*) for maximum transmission of power is equal to

(*a*) $\left(\frac{D^5}{4fL}\right)^{1/4}$ (*b*) $\left(\frac{D^5}{8fL}\right)^{1/4}$

(*c*) $\left(\frac{D^4}{8fL}\right)^{1/4}$ (*d*) $\left(\frac{D^3}{8fL}\right)^{1/4}$

17. The energy loss in a pipeline is due to

(*a*) surface roughness only

(*b*) viscous action only

(*c*) friction offered by pipe wall as well as by viscous function

(*d*) none of the above.

18. In a pipe flow the minor losses are those

(*a*) which depend on the length of the pipeline

(*b*) caused by friction and are thus also called friction losses.

(*c*) which have a small magnitude

(*d*) which are caused on account of total disturbance produced by such fittings as valves, bends, etc.

19. In flow through pipe bends the pressures on inner and out radii

(*a*) stand at the same level increasing gradually towards the pipe centre.

(*b*) vary, it being more on the inner core.

(*c*) are different, pressure increases with increse in radius and is, therfore, more at the outer radius.

(*d*) do not vary and are the same as at the centre of the pipe.

20. The condition for maximum transmission of power through a pipeline is that one-third of the available head must be consumed in friction. The corresponding efficiency of the pipeline is

(*a*) 33·3% (*b*) 66·67%

(*c*) 90% (*d*) 100%.

21. For achieving continuous flow through a system, no position of the pipe should be higher than

(*a*) 20 (*b*) 6 m

(*c*) 7·6 m (*d*) 10 m.

measured above the hydraulic gradient line.

22. For turbulent flow in smooth pipes, the entrance length is taken as

(*a*) 20 (*b*) 50

(*c*) 80 (*d*) 115.

23. The entrace length or length of establishment of flow is

(*a*) the length in which the boundry layer remains uniform

(*b*) the pipe length inside the reservoir

(*c*) the length of pipe from its entrance in which the flow may be assumed irrotational

(*d*) the initial length in which the flow develops fully such that the velocity profile does not change downstream.

24. Due to which of the following phenomena water hammer is caused ?

(*a*) Incompressibility of fluid

(*b*) Sudden opening of a valve in a pipeline

(*c*) The material of the pipe being elastic

(*d*) Sudden closure (partial or complete) of a valve in pipe flow.

25. Under which of the following conditions the closure of valve is considered rapid ?

(*a*) the duration of valve closure is greater than $\frac{2L}{C}$

(*b*) the duration of valve closure is less than $\frac{L}{C}$

(*c*) the duration of valve closure is less than $\frac{2L}{C}$

(*d*) none of the above.

(where L = length of pipe, C = velocity of pressure wave produced due to water hammer.)

ANSWERS

1. Partially	**2.** (*a*)	**3.** (*b*)	**4.** (*b*)	**5.** (*d*)	**6.** (*c*)
7. (*c*)	**8.** (*b*)	**9.** (*b*)	**10.** (*b*)	**11.** (*c*)	**12.** (*a*)
13. No relation	**14.** Parallel	**15.** (*a*)	**16.** (*b*)	**17.** (*c*)	**18.** (*d*)
19. (*d*)	**20.** (*b*)	**21.** (*c*)	**22.** (*b*)	**23.** (*d*)	**24.** (*d*)
25. (*c*).					

THEORETICAL QUESTIONS

1. Differentiate between a laminar flow and a turbulent flow.

2. Define the terms : Major energy losses and minor energy losses in pipe.

3. Derive Darcy-Weisbach formula for calculating loss of head due to fricton in a pipe.

4. Derive Chezy's formulae for loss of head due to friction in a pipe

5. Derive formulae for calculating loss of head due to
(*i*) Sudden enlargement, and
(*ii*) Sudden contraction.

6. Explain briefly the following :
(*i*) Hydraulic gradient line (H.G.L.)
(*ii*) Energy gradient line (E.G.L.)

7. What is an equivalent pipe ?

8. What is syphon ? Where is it used ?

9. Derive an expression for the power transmission through the pipes. Find also the condition for maximum transmission of power and corresponding efficiency of transmission.

10. Find an expression for the ratio of the outlet area of the nozzle to the area of the pipe for maximum transmission of power.

11. Show that the diameter of the nozzle for maximum transmission of power is given by

$$d = \left(\frac{D^5}{8fL}\right)^{1/4}$$

where, D = Diameter of the pipe
L = Length of the pipe, and
f = Friction co-efficient.

12. What is meant by water hammer ? Derive an expression for the rise of pressure when the flowing water in a pipe is brought to rest by closing the valve gradually.

13. Obtain a formula for rise in pressure in a thin plastic pipe of circular section in which the flow of water is stopped by sudden closure of a valve.

UNSOLVED EXAMPLES

1. Find the head lost due to friction in a pipe of diameter 200 mm and length 60 m, through which water is flowing at a velocity of 2·5 m/s using :
(*i*) Darcy-Weisbach formula (assuming $f = 0{\cdot}005$), and
(*ii*) Chezy's formula for which $C = 55$.
[Ans. (*i*) 1·91 m; (*ii*) 2·48 m]

2. Water is flowing through a pipe of diameter 200 mm with a velocity of 3 m/s. If the co-efficient of friction is given by $f = 0.002 + \frac{0.09}{(Re)^{0.3}}$, where *Re* is Reynolds number, find the head lost due to friction for a length of 5 m. Take kinematic viscosity of water = 0·01 stoke.
[Ans. (0·99 m)]

3. In a pipe of diameter 200 mm and length 500 m, an oil of specific gravity 0·9 and viscosity 0·06 poise is flowing at the rate of 0·06 m^3/s. Find :
(*i*) The head lost due to friction, and
(*ii*) Power required to maintain the flow.
[Ans. (*i*) 9·48 m of waterl; (*ii*) 5·016 kW]

4. A horizontal pipe of 100 mm diameter is joined by sudden enlargement to a 150 mm diameter pipe. Water is flowing though it at the rate of 2 m^3/min. Find :
(*i*) Loss of head due to abrupt expansion,
(*ii*) Pressure difference in two pipes, and
(*iii*) Change in pressure if the change of section is gradual, without any loss.
[Ans. (*i*) 0·286 m of water; (*ii*) 0·455 m of water; (*iii*) 0·74 m of water]

5. The discharge of water through a horizontal pipe is $0{\cdot}25\ m^3/s$. Its diameter, which is 200 mm, suddenly enlarges to 400 mm. If the intensity of pressure of water in the smaller pipe is 120 kN/m^2, determine :

(*i*) Loss of head due to sudden enlargement,

(*ii*) Intensity of pressure in the large pipe, and

(*iii*) Power lost due to enlargement.

[Ans. (*i*) 1·816 m; (*ii*) 132 kN/m^2; (*iii*) 4·45 kW]

6. A horizontal pipe carries water at a rate of 0·03 m^3/s. Its diameter reduces abruptly from 150 mm to 100 mm. If the co-efficient of friction is 0·6 find the pressure loss across the contraction. **[Ans.** 9·3 kN/m^2]

7. A pipe of 150 mm diameter is attached to a 100 mm diameter pipe by means of a flange in such a manner that axes of the two pipes are in a straight line. Water flows through the arrangement at a rate of 2 m^3/min. The pressure loss at the transition as indicated by differential gauge length on a water-mercury manometer connected between the two pipes equals 80 mm. Calculate :

(*i*) The loss of head due to contraction, and

(*ii*) The co-efficient of contraction.

[Ans. (*i*) 0·268 m of water; (*ii*) 0·65]

8. Three pipes of diameters 300 mm, 200 mm and 400 mm and lengths 300 m, 170 m and 210 m respectively are connected in series. The difference in water surface levels in two tanks is 12 m. Determine the rate of flow if co-efficients of frictions are 0·005, 0·0052 and 0·0048 respectively, considering :

(*i*) Minor losses also, and

(*ii*) Neglecting minor losses.

[Ans. (*i*) 0·9945m^3/s, (*ii*) 0·1021 m^3/s]

9. A pipeline *ABC* 180 m long is laid on an upward slope of 1 in 60. The length of the portion *AB* is 90m and its diameter is 150 mm. At *B* the pipe section suddenly enlarges to 300 mm diameter and remains so for the remainder of its length *BC*, 90 m. A flow of 0·05 m^3/s is pumped into the pipe at its lower end *A* and is discharged at the upper end *C* into a closed tank. The pressure at the supply end *A* is 140 kN/m^2.

(*i*) Find the pressure at the discharge end *C*;

(*ii*) Draw energy gradient line and hydraulic gradient line. **[Ans.** 61 kN/m^2]

10. Two reservoirs are connected by two pipes of the same length laid in parallel . The diameters of the pipes are 100 mm and 300 mm respectively. If the discharge through 100 mm diameter pipe is 0·01 m^3/s, what will be the discharge through 300 mm pipe ? Assume that f is same for both pipes. **[Ans.** 0·156 m^3/s]

11. A main pipe divides into two parallel pipes which again forms one pipe. The length and diameter for the first parallel pipe are 2000 m and 1·0 m respectively, while the length and diameter of the second pipe are 2000 m and 0·8 m respectively. If the total flow in the main is 3 m^3/s and the co-efficient of friction for each paralell pipe is same and equal to 0·005, find the rate of flow in each parallel pipe.

[Ans. (*i*) 1·906 m^3/s; 1·094 m^3/s]

12. Two reservoirs are connected by a pipeline consisting of two pipes, one of 150 mm diameter and length 6 m and the other of diameter 225 mm and 16 m length. If the difference of levels in the reservoir is 6 m, calculate the discharge and draw the energy gradient line. Take friction factor = 0·04. **[Ans.** 0·018 m^3/s]

13. Two reservoirs have difference of water levels of 6 m. They are connected by a pipe system which consists of a single pipe of 600 mm diameter for the first 3000 m and then two pipes in parallel, each of 300 mm diameter and 3000 m in length. Calculate the rate of flow. Assume friction factor = 0·04. **[Ans.** 0·0725m^3/s]

14. A compound pipeline 1650 m long made up of pipes 450 mm diameter for 900 m, 375 mm for 450 m and 300 mm for 300 m, is required to be replaced by a pipe of uniform diameter. Find the diameter of the new pipe, assuming the length to remain the same. **[Ans.** 372 mm]

15. A pipeline of 600 mm diameter and 4 km length connects two reservoirs. The difference of water levels in the reservoirs is 20 m. At a distance of 1 km from the upper reservoir, a small pipe is connected to the pipeline. The water can be taken from the small pipe. Find the discharge to the lower reservoir if (*i*) No water is taken from the small pipe, and (*ii*) 0·1 m^3/s of water is taken from small pipe. Take co-efficient of friction = 0·005 and neglect minor losses.

[Ans. (*i*) 0·485 m^3/s; (*ii*) 0·458 m^3/s]

16. An existing 300 mm diameter pipeline of 3200 length connects two reservoirs with 13 m difference in their water levels. Calculate the discharge Q_1. If a parallel pipe 300 mm diameter is attached to last 1600 m length of the existing pipeline, find the new discharge Q_2. Take only wall frictoin into account. Assume friction factor = 0·04 in Darcy-Weiabach formula.

[Ans. 0.547 m³/s; 0.698 m³/s]

[IIT Madras]

17. A pipeline of 0·6 diameter is 1·5 km long. To augment the discharge, another pipeline of the same diameter is introduced parallel to the first in the second half of its length. Find the increase in discharge if the friction factor is 0·04 and head at the inlet is 30 m. **(Ans. 0·1808 m³/s)**

[UPSC Exams.]

18. A pipe of 400 mm diameter and 2 km long is connected to a reservoir at one end. The other end of the pipe is connected to junction from which two pipes each of length 1 km and diameter 300 mm run in parallel. These parallel pipes are connected to another reservoir, which is having level of water 10 m below the water level of the above reservoir. Determine the total discharge if the friction factor = 0·06.

Neglect minor losses. **[Ans. 0·0822 m³/s]**

19. The rate of flow of water pumped into a pipe ABC, which is 180 m long, is 0·05 m³/s. The pipe is laid on an upward slope of 1 in 60. The length of the portion *AB* is 90 m and its diameter is 150 mm, while the length of the portion *BC* is also 90 m but its diameter is 300 mm. The change of diameter at *B* is sudden. The flow is taking place from *A* to *C* where the pressure at *A* is 137·34 kN/m² and end *C* is connected to a closed end tank. Find the pressure at the discharge end *C* and sketch the total energy and the hydraulic gradient lines.

[Ans. 59·84 kN/m²]

20. A pipeline of 500 mm diameter and 4·5 km length connects two reservoirs whose constant difference of water level is 12 m. A branch pipe 1·25 km long and taken from a point distance 1·5 km from reservoir *A*, leads to the reservoir *C* whose water level is 15 m below that of reservoir A. Find the diameter of the branch pipe, so that the flow into both the reservoirs is same.

Assume co-efficient of friction for each pipe, $f = 0·0075$. **[Ans. 375 mm]**

21. A 200 mm diameter pipe, 8000 m long connects two reservoirs whose surface levels differ by 40 m. At a distance of 500 m from the upper reservoir, the pipe crosses a ridge the summit of which is 8 m above the level of water in the upper reservoir. Determine :

(*i*) The minimum depth of the pipe below the summit of the ridge, if the absolute pressure head at the summit of system is not to fall below 3·0 m of water, and

(*ii*) The discharge through the pipe.

Take friction co-efficient, $f = 0·006$ and atmospheric head = 10·3 m of water, Neglect minor losses.

[Ans. (*i*) 3·24 m, (*ii*) 0·02883 m³/s]

22. A pipe of 1 m diameter connects two reservoirs having a difference of levels of 6 m. The total length of the pipe is 800 m and rises to a maximum height of 3 m above the level of water in the higher reservoir at a distance of 200 m from the entrance. Find :

(*i*) Discharge in the pipe, and

(*ii*) Pressure at the highest point.

Take friction factor = 0·04, and neglect minor losses.

[Ans. – 4·69 m of water]

23. A syphon of diameter 200 mm connects two reservoirs having a difference in elevation of 15 m. The total length of the syphon is 600 m and the summit is 4 m above the water level in the upper reservoir. If the sepration takes place at 2·8 m of water absolute, find the maximum length of the syphon from the upper reservoir to the summit.

Take friction factor = 0·016 and atmospheric pressure head = 10·3 m of water.

[Ans. 128·6 m]

24. A pipeline 2000 m long is used for power transmission. 110 kW is to be transmitted through the pipe in which water having a pressure of 5000 kN/m² at inlet is flowing. If the pressure drop over the length of the pipe is 1000 kN/m² and co-efficient of friction is 0·0065, find :

(*i*) The diameter of the pipe, and

(*ii*) Efficiency of transmission.

[Ans. (*i*) 128 mm (*ii*) 80%]

25. Calculate the diameter of the nozzle and the maximum power transmitted by a jet of water discharging freely out of a nozzle, fitted to a pipe 300 m long and 100 mm diameter with co-efficient of friction as 0·01. The available head at the nozzle is 90 m.

[Ans. (*i*) 25·4 mm; (*ii*) 10·29 kW]

26. A horizontal pipe of 150 mm diameter and 200 m length conveys water from a reservoir to a nozzle 50 mm in diameter. What would be the power of the jet if thelevel of water in the reservoir is

15 m above the axis of the pipe ? Take friction co-efficient = 0·01.

Neglect losses in the nozzle. [**Ans.** 2·31 kW]

27. In a pipe of 500 mm diameter and 2500 m length, provided with a valve at its end, water is flowing with a velocity of 1·5 m/s. Assuming velocity of pressure wave = 1460 m/s, find :

(*i*) The rise in pressure if the valve is closed in 25 seconds, and

(*ii*) The rise in pressure if the valve is closed in 2 seconds. Assume the pipe to be rigid one and take bulk modulus of water as 1·962 GN/m^2.

[**Ans.** (*i*) 150 kN/m^2; (*ii*) 2101 kN/m^2]

28. Water is flowing through a cast-iron pipe of diameter 150 mm and thickness 10 mm which is provided with a valve at its end. Water is suddenly stopped by closing the valve. Find the maximum velocity of water, when the rise of pressure due to sudden closure of valve is 1·962 MN/m^2.

Take K for water = 1·962 GN/m^2 and E for cast-iron pipe = 117·7 GN/m^2.

[**Ans.** 1·57 m/s]

Chapter 13

BOUNDARY LAYER THEORY

13.1. INTRODUCTION

The concept of boundary layer was first introduced by L. Prandtl in 1904 and since then it has been applied to several fluid flow problems.

When a real fluid (viscous fluid) flows past a stationary solid boundary, a layer of fluid which comes in contact with the boundary surface, adheres to it (on account of viscosity) and condition of no slip occurs (The *no-slip* condition implies that the velocity of fluid at a solid boundary must be same as that of boundary itself). Thus the layer of fluid which cannot slip away from the boundary surface undergoes retardation; this retarded layer further causes retardation for the adjacent layers of the fluid, thereby developing a small region in the immediate vicinity of the boundary surface in which the velocity of the flowing fluid increases rapidly from *zero at the boundary surface and approaches the velocity of main stream*. The *layer adjacent to the boundary is known as* **boundary layer**. *Boundary layer is formed whenever there is relative motion between the boundary and the fluid.* Since $\tau_0 = \mu \left(\frac{\partial u}{\partial y}\right)_{y=0}$, the fluid exerts a shear stress on the boundary and boundary exerts an equal and opposite force on fluid known as the *shear resistance*.

According to boundary layer theory the extensive fluid medium around bodies moving in fluids can be divided into following two regions:

(*i*) A thin layer adjoining the boundary is called the *boundary layer* where the *viscous shear takes place*.

(*ii*) A region outside the boundary layer where the flow behaviour is quite like that of an *ideal fluid and the potential flow theory is applicable*.

13.2. BOUNDARY LAYER DEFINITIONS AND CHARACTERISTICS

Consider the boundary layer formed on a flat plate kept parallel to flow of fluid of velocity U (Fig. 13.1) (Though the growth of a boundary layer depends upon the *body shape*, flow over a flat plate aligned in the direction of flow is considered, since most of the flow surfaces can be *approximated to a flat plate and for simplicity*).

— The edge facing the direction of flow is called *leading edge*.

— The rear edge is called the *trailing edge*.

— Near the leading edge of a flat plate, the boundary layer is wholly *laminar*. For a laminar boundary layer, the velocity distribution is *parabolic*.

— The thickness of the boundary layer (δ) increases with distance from the leading edge x, as more and more fluid is slowed down by the viscous boundary, becomes unstable and breaks into *turbulent boundary layer* over a transition region.

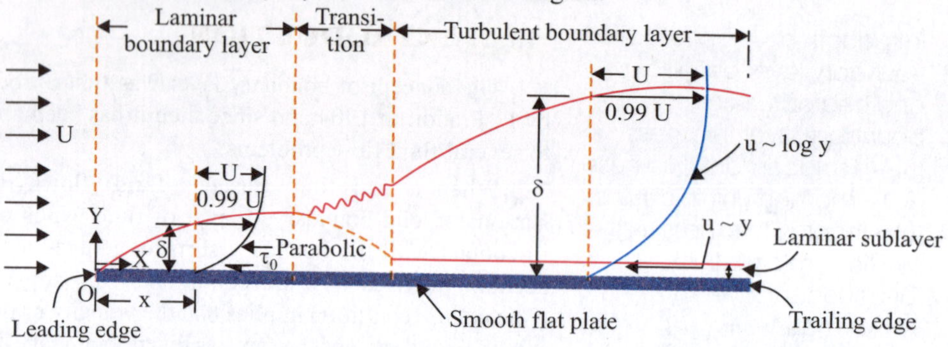

Fig. 13.1. Boundary layer on a flat plate.

For a turbulent boundary layer, if the boundary is smooth, the roughness projections are covered by a very thin layer which remains laminar, called *laminar sublayer*. The velocity distribution in the turbulent boundary layer is given by *Log law* or *Prandtl's one-seventh power law*.

The *characteristics* of a boundary layer may be summarised as follows:

(*i*) δ (thickness of boundary layer) increases as distance from leading edge x increases.

(*ii*) δ decreases as U increases.

(*iii*) δ increases as kinematic viscosity (ν) increases.

(*iv*) $\tau_0 \approx \mu\left(\dfrac{U}{\delta}\right)$; hence τ_0 decreases as x increases. However, when boundary layer becomes turbulent, it shows a sudden increase and then decreases with increasing x.

(*v*) When U increases in the downward direction, boundary layer growth is reduced.

(*vi*) When U decreases in the downward direction, flow near the boundary is further retarded, boundary layer growth is faster and is susceptible to separation.

(*vii*) The various characteristics of the boundary layer on flat plate (e.g variation of δ, τ_0 or force F) are governed by inertial and viscous forces; hence they are functions of either $\dfrac{Ux}{\nu}$ or $\dfrac{UL}{\nu}$.

(*viii*) If $\dfrac{Ux}{\nu} < 5 \times 10^5$ ... boundary layer is *laminar* (velocity distribution is *parabolic*).

If $\dfrac{Ux}{\nu} > 5 \times 10^5$ ... boundary layer is *turbulent* on that portion (velocity distribution follows *Log law* or a *power law*).

(*ix*) Critical value of $\frac{Ux}{\nu}$ at which boundary layer changes from laminar to turbulent depends on:

— turbulence in ambient flow,
— surface roughness,
— pressure gradient,
— plate curvature, and
— temperature difference between fluid and boundary.

(*x*) Though the velocity distribution would be a parabolic curve in the laminar sub-layer zone, but in view of the very small thickness we can reasonably assume that velocity distribution is linear and so the velocity gradient can be considered constant.

13.2.1. Boundary Layer Thickness (δ)

The velocity within the boundary layer increases from zero at the boundary surface to the velocity of the main stream asymptotically. Therefore the thickness of the boundary layer is arbitrarily defined as *that distance from the boundary in which the velocity reaches 99 per cent of the velocity of the free stream* ($u = 0.99U$). *It is denoted by the symbol* δ. *This definition however gives an approximate value of the boundary layer thickness* and hence δ is generally termed as **nominal thickness** *of the boundary layer.*

The boundary layer thickness for *greater accuracy* is defined in terms of certain mathematical expressions which are the measure of the boundary layer on the flow. The commonly adopted definitions of the boundary layer thickness are:

1. Displacement thickness (δ^*)
2. Momentum thickness (θ)
3. Energy thickness (δ_e).

13.2.2. Displacement Thickness (δ^*)

The *displacement thickness* can be defined as follows:

"It is the distance, measured perpendicular to the boundary, by which the main/free stream is displaced on account of formation of boundary layer."

Or

"It is an additional "wall thickness" that would have to be added to compensate for the reduction in flow rate on account of boundary layer formation".

The displacement thickness is denoted by δ^*.

Let fluid of density ρ flow past a stationary plate with velocity U as shown in the Fig. 13.2. Consider an elementary strip of thickness dy at a distance y from the plate.

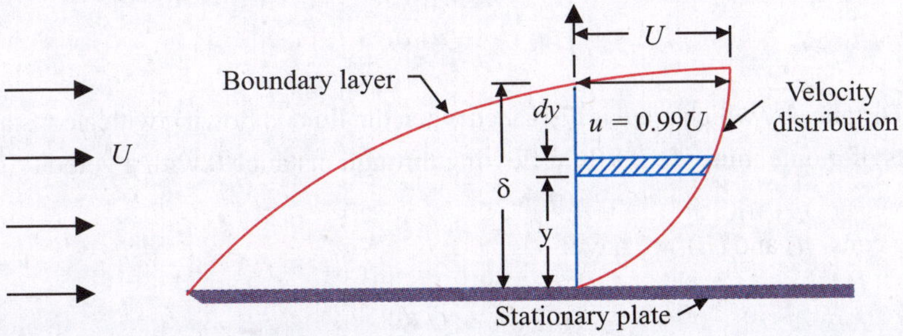

Fig. 13.2. Displacement thickness.

Assuming *unit width*, the mass flow per second through the elementary strip

$$= \rho u dy$$

Mass flow per second through the elementary strip (unit width) if the plate were not there

$$= \rho\, U \cdot dy \qquad \text{...(ii)}$$

Reduction of mass flow rate through the elementary strip

$$= \rho\,(U - u)\, dy$$

[The difference $(U - u)$ is called **velocity of defect**].

Total reduction of mass flow rate due to introduction of plate

$$= \int_0^{\delta} \rho\,(U - u)\, dy \qquad \text{...(iii)}$$

(if the fluid is incompressible)

Let the plate is displaced by a distance δ^* and velocity of flow for the distance δ^* is equal to the main/free stream velocity (*i.e.* U). Then, loss of the mass of the fluid/sec. flowing through the distance δ^*.

$$= \rho U \delta^* \qquad \text{...(iv)}$$

Equating eqns. (*iii*) and (*iv*), we get:

$$\rho U \delta^* = \int_0^{\delta} \rho\,(U - u)\, dy$$

or,

$$\delta^* = \int_0^{\delta} \left(1 - \frac{u}{U}\right) dy \qquad \text{...(13.1)}$$

13.2.3. Momentum Thickness (θ)

Momentum thickness *is defined as* the *distance through which the total loss of momentum per second be equal to if it were passing a stationary plate*. It is denoted by θ.

It may also be defined as the *distance, measured perpendicular to the boundary of the solid body, by which the boundary should be displaced to compensate for reduction in momentum of the flowing fluid on account of boundary layer formation.*

Refer to fig. 13.2. Mass of flow per second through the elementary strip = $\rho u dy$

Momentum/sec. of this fluid inside the boundary layer = $\rho u dy \times u = \rho u^2 dy$

Momentum/sec. of the same mass of fluid before entering boundary layer = $\rho u U dy$

Loss of momentum/sec. $= \rho u U dy - \rho u^2 dy = \rho u\,(U - u)\, dy$

∴ Total loss of momentum/sec.

$$= \int_0^{\delta} \rho u\,(U - u)\, dy \qquad \text{...(i)}$$

Let, θ = Distance by which plate is displaced when the fluid is flowing with a constant velocity U.

Then loss of momentum/sec. of fluid flowing through distance θ with a velocity U

$$= \rho \theta U^2 \qquad \text{...(ii)}$$

Equating eqns. (*i*) and (*ii*), we have:

$$\rho \theta U^2 = \int_0^{\delta} \rho u\,(U - u)\, dy$$

or, $$\theta = \int_0^\delta \frac{u}{U}\left(1 - \frac{u}{U}\right) dy \qquad ...(13.2)$$

The momentum thickness is useful in *kinetics*.

13.2.4. Energy Thickness (δ_e)

Energy thickness *is defined as the distance, measured perpendicular to the boundary of the solid body, by which the boundary should be displaced to compensate for the reduction in K.E. of the flowing fluid on account of boundary layer formation.* It is denoted by δ_e.

Refer to Fig. 13.2. Mass of flow per second through the elementary strip = $\rho u dy$

K.E. of this fluid inside the boundary layer

$$= \frac{1}{2} mu^2 = \frac{1}{2} (\rho u dy)\, u^2$$

K.E. of the same mass of fluid before entering the boundary layer

$$= \frac{1}{2} (\rho u dy)\, U^2$$

Loss of K.E. through elementary strip

$$= \frac{1}{2} (\rho u dy)\, U^2 - \frac{1}{2} (\rho u dy)\, u^2 = \frac{1}{2} \rho u\, (U^2 - u^2)\, dy \qquad ...(i)$$

$\therefore$ Total loss of K.E. of fluid $= \int_0^\delta \frac{1}{2} \rho u\, (U^2 - u^2)\, dy$

Let, δ_e = Distance by which the plate is displaced to compensate for the reduction in K.E.

Then, loss of K.E. through δ_e of fluid flowing with velocity U

$$= \frac{1}{2} (\rho U \delta_e)\, U^2 \qquad ...(ii)$$

Equating eqns. (*i*) and (*ii*), we have:

$$\frac{1}{2} (\rho U \delta_e)\, U^2 = \int_0^\delta \frac{1}{2} \rho\, u\, (U^2 - u^2)\, dy$$

or, $$\delta_e = \frac{1}{U^3} \int_0^\delta u\, (U^2 - u^2)\, dy$$

$\therefore$ $$\delta_e = \int_0^\delta \frac{u}{U}\left(1 - \frac{u^2}{U^2}\right) dy \qquad ...(13.3)$$

Example 13.1. *The velocity distribution in the boundary layer is given by:* $\frac{u}{U} = \frac{y}{\delta}$, *where u is the velocity at a distance y from the plate and u = U at y = δ, δ being boundary layer thickness. Find :*

(*i*) *The displacement thickness,* **(*ii*)** *The momentum thickness,*

(*iii*) *The energy thickness, and* **(*iv*)** *The value of* $\frac{\delta^*}{\theta}$.

Solution. Velocity distribution: $\frac{u}{U} = \frac{y}{\delta}$ ...(*Given*)

(*i*) The displacement thickness, δ^*

$$\delta^* = \int_0^\delta \left(1 - \frac{u}{U}\right) dy \qquad \text{...[Eqn. (13.1)]}$$

$$= \int_0^\delta \left(1 - \frac{y}{\delta}\right) dy \qquad \left(\because \frac{u}{U} = \frac{y}{\delta}\right)$$

$$= \left[y - \frac{y^2}{2\delta}\right]_0^\delta$$

$$\delta^* = \left(\delta - \frac{\delta^2}{2\delta}\right) = \delta - \frac{\delta}{2} = \frac{\boldsymbol{\delta}}{\mathbf{2}} \textbf{ (Ans.)}$$

(*ii*) The momentum thickness, θ

$$\theta = \int_0^\delta \frac{u}{U}\left(1 - \frac{u}{U}\right) dy \qquad \text{...[Eqn. (13.2)]}$$

$$= \int_0^\delta \frac{y}{\delta}\left(1 - \frac{y}{\delta}\right) dy = \int_0^\delta \left(\frac{y}{\delta} - \frac{y^2}{\delta^2}\right) dy$$

or,

$$\theta = \left[\frac{y^2}{2\delta} - \frac{y^3}{3\delta^2}\right]_0^\delta = \frac{\delta^2}{2\delta} - \frac{\delta^3}{3\delta^2} = \frac{\delta}{2} - \frac{\delta}{3} = \frac{\boldsymbol{\delta}}{\mathbf{6}} \textbf{ (Ans.)}$$

(*iii*) The energy thickness, δ_e

$$\delta_e = \int_0^\delta \frac{u}{U}\left(1 - \frac{u^2}{U^2}\right) dy \qquad \text{...[Eqn. (13.3)]}$$

$$= \int_0^\delta \frac{y}{\delta}\left(1 - \frac{y^2}{\delta^2}\right) dy = \int_0^\delta \left(\frac{y}{\delta} - \frac{y^3}{\delta^3}\right) dy$$

$$= \left[\frac{y^2}{2\delta} - \frac{y^4}{4\delta^3}\right]_0^\delta = \frac{\delta^2}{2\delta} - \frac{\delta^4}{4\delta^3} = \frac{\delta}{2} - \frac{\delta}{4} = \frac{\delta}{4}$$

i.e.

$$\delta_e = \frac{\boldsymbol{\delta}}{\mathbf{4}} \textbf{ (Ans.)}$$

(*iv*) The value of $\frac{\delta^*}{\theta}$:

$$\frac{\delta^*}{\theta} = \frac{\delta/2}{\delta/6} = \textbf{3.0 (Ans.)}$$

Example 13.2. *The velocity distribution in the boundary layer is given by* $\frac{u}{U} = \frac{3}{2}\frac{y}{\delta} - \frac{1}{2}\frac{y^2}{\delta^2}$, *$\delta$ being boundary layer thickness.*

Calculate the following:

(*i*) *The ratio of displacement thickness to boundary layer thickness* $\left(\frac{\delta^*}{\delta}\right)$, (*ii*) *The ratio of momentum thickness to boundary layer thickness* $\left(\frac{\theta}{\delta}\right)$.

Solution. Velocity distribution : $\frac{u}{U} = \frac{3}{2}\frac{y}{\delta} - \frac{1}{2}\frac{y^2}{\delta^2}$ ...(*Given*)

(*i*) δ^*/δ:

$$\delta^* = \int_0^\delta \left(1 - \frac{u}{U}\right) dy = \int_0^\delta \left(1 - \frac{3}{2}\frac{y}{\delta} + \frac{1}{2}\frac{y^2}{\delta^2}\right) dy$$

$$= \left[y - \frac{3}{2} \times \frac{y^2}{2\delta} + \frac{1}{2} \times \frac{y^3}{3\delta^2}\right]_0^\delta$$

$$= \left[\delta - \frac{3}{4} . \frac{\delta^2}{\delta} + \frac{1}{2} \times \frac{\delta^3}{3\delta^2}\right] = \left(\delta - \frac{3}{4}\delta + \frac{\delta}{6}\right) = \frac{5}{12}\delta$$

$$\therefore \quad \frac{\delta^*}{\delta} = \mathbf{\frac{5}{12}} \textbf{ (Ans.)}$$

(*ii*) θ/δ:

$$\theta = \int_0^\delta \frac{u}{U}\left(1 - \frac{u}{U}\right) dy$$

$$= \int_0^\delta \left(\frac{3}{2}\frac{y}{\delta} - \frac{1}{2}\frac{y^2}{\delta^2}\right)\left(1 - \frac{3}{2}\frac{y}{\delta} + \frac{1}{2}\frac{y^2}{\delta^2}\right) dy$$

$$= \int_0^\delta \left(\frac{3}{2}\frac{y}{\delta} - \frac{9}{4}\frac{y^2}{\delta^2} + \frac{3}{4} . \frac{y^3}{\delta^3} - \frac{1}{2}\frac{y^2}{\delta^2} + \frac{3}{4}\frac{y^3}{\delta^3} - \frac{1}{4}\frac{y^4}{\delta^4}\right) dy$$

$$= \int_0^\delta \left[\frac{3}{2}\frac{y}{\delta} - \left(\frac{9}{4}\frac{y^2}{\delta^2} + \frac{1}{2}\frac{y^2}{\delta^2}\right) + \left(\frac{3}{4}\frac{y^3}{\delta^3} + \frac{3}{4} \cdot \frac{y^3}{\delta^3}\right) - \frac{1}{4}\frac{y^4}{\delta^4}\right] dy$$

$$= \int_0^\delta \left[\frac{3}{2}\frac{y}{\delta} - \frac{11}{4}\frac{y^2}{\delta^2} + \frac{3}{2}\frac{y^3}{\delta^3} - \frac{1}{4}\frac{y^4}{\delta^4}\right] dy$$

$$= \left[\frac{3}{2} \times \frac{y^2}{2\delta} - \frac{11}{4} \times \frac{y^3}{3\delta^2} + \frac{3}{2} \times \frac{y^4}{4\delta^3} - \frac{1}{4} \times \frac{y^5}{5\delta^4}\right]_0^\delta$$

$$= \left[\frac{3}{2} \times \frac{\delta^2}{2\delta} - \frac{11}{4} \times \frac{\delta^3}{3\delta^2} + \frac{3}{2} \times \frac{\delta^4}{4\delta^3} - \frac{1}{4} \times \frac{\delta^5}{5\delta^4}\right]_0^\delta$$

$$= \left(\frac{3}{4}\delta - \frac{11}{12}\delta + \frac{3}{8}\delta - \frac{1}{20}\delta\right) = \frac{19}{120}\delta$$

or, $$\frac{\theta}{\delta} = \mathbf{\frac{19}{120}} \textbf{ (Ans.)}$$

Example 13.3. *The velocity distribution in the boundary layer is given by*

$$\frac{u}{U} = 2\left(\frac{y}{\delta}\right) - \left(\frac{y}{\delta}\right)^2, \ \delta \text{ being boundary layer thickness.}$$

Calculate the following:

(i) *Displacement thickness,*

(ii) *Momentum thickness, and*

(iii) *Energy thickness.*

Solution. *(i)* **Displacement thickness, δ^***

$$\delta^* = \int_0^\delta \left(1 - \frac{u}{U}\right) dy$$

$$= \int_0^\delta \left[1 - \left\{2\left(\frac{y}{\delta}\right) - \left(\frac{y}{\delta}\right)^2\right\}\right] dy$$

$$= \int_0^\delta \left[1 - 2\left(\frac{y}{\delta}\right) + \left(\frac{y}{\delta}\right)^2\right] dy$$

$$= \left[y - \frac{2}{2} \times \frac{y^2}{\delta} + \frac{y^3}{3\delta^2}\right]_0^\delta = \left[\delta - \frac{\delta^2}{\delta} + \frac{\delta^3}{3\delta^2}\right]$$

$$= \delta - \delta + \frac{\delta}{3} = \frac{\delta}{3} \text{ (Ans.)}$$

(ii) **Momentum thickness, θ**

$$\theta = \int_0^\delta \frac{u}{U}\left(1 - \frac{u}{U}\right) dy$$

$$= \int_0^\delta \left(\frac{2y}{\delta} - \frac{y^2}{\delta^2}\right)\left[1 - \left(\frac{2y}{\delta} - \frac{y^2}{\delta^2}\right)\right] dy$$

$$= \int_0^\delta \left(\frac{2y}{\delta} - \frac{y^2}{\delta^2}\right)\left[1 - \frac{2y}{\delta} + \frac{y^2}{\delta^2}\right] dy$$

$$= \int_0^\delta \left[\frac{2y}{\delta} - \frac{4y^2}{\delta^2} + \frac{2y^3}{\delta^3} - \frac{y^2}{\delta^2} + \frac{2y^3}{\delta^3} - \frac{y^4}{\delta^4}\right] dy$$

$$= \int_0^\delta \left[\frac{2y}{\delta} - \frac{5y^2}{\delta^2} + \frac{4y^3}{\delta^3} - \frac{y^4}{\delta^4}\right] dy$$

$$= \left[\frac{2}{2} \times \frac{y^2}{\delta} - \frac{5}{3} \times \frac{y^3}{\delta^2} + \frac{4}{4} \times \frac{y^4}{\delta^3} - \frac{1}{5} \times \frac{y^5}{\delta^4}\right]_0^\delta$$

$$= \left[\delta - \frac{5}{3}\delta + \delta - \frac{1}{5}\delta\right] = \frac{2}{15}\delta \text{ (Ans.)}$$

(iii) **Energy thickness, δ_e**

$$\delta_e = \int_0^\delta \frac{u}{U}\left(1 - \frac{u^2}{U^2}\right) dy$$

$$= \int_0^\delta \left(\frac{2y}{\delta} - \frac{y^2}{\delta^2}\right)\left[1 - \left(\frac{2y}{\delta} - \frac{y^2}{\delta^2}\right)^2\right] dy$$

$$= \int_0^\delta \left(\frac{2y}{\delta} - \frac{y^2}{\delta^2}\right)\left[1 - \left(\frac{4y^2}{\delta^2} + \frac{y^4}{\delta^4} - \frac{4y^3}{\delta^3}\right)\right] dy$$

$$= \int_0^\delta \left(\frac{2y}{\delta} - \frac{y^2}{\delta^2}\right)\left[1 - \frac{4y^2}{\delta^2} - \frac{y^4}{\delta^4} + \frac{4y^3}{\delta^3}\right] dy$$

$$= \int_0^\delta \left[\frac{2y}{\delta} - \frac{8y^3}{\delta^3} - \frac{2y^5}{\delta^5} + \frac{8y^4}{\delta^4} - \frac{y^2}{\delta^2} + \frac{4y^4}{\delta^4} + \frac{y^6}{\delta^6} - \frac{4y^5}{\delta^5}\right] dy$$

$$= \int_0^\delta \left[\frac{2y}{\delta} - \frac{y^2}{\delta^2} - \frac{8y^3}{\delta^3} + 12 \times \frac{y^4}{\delta^4} - 6 \times \frac{y^5}{\delta^5} + \frac{y^6}{\delta^6}\right] dy$$

$$= \int_0^\delta \left[\frac{2y}{\delta} - \frac{y^2}{\delta^2} - \frac{8y^3}{\delta^3} + 12 \times \frac{y^4}{\delta^4} - 6 \times \frac{y^5}{\delta^5} + \frac{y^6}{\delta^6}\right] dy$$

$$= \int_0^\delta \left[\frac{2}{2} \times \frac{y^2}{\delta} - \frac{1}{3} \times \frac{y^3}{\delta^2} - \frac{8}{4} \times \frac{y^4}{\delta^3} + \frac{12}{5} \times \frac{y^5}{\delta^4} - \frac{6}{6} \times \frac{y^6}{\delta^5} + \frac{1}{7} \times \frac{y^7}{\delta^6}\right]_0^\delta$$

$$= \left(\delta - \frac{\delta}{3} - 2\delta + \frac{12\delta}{5} - \delta + \frac{\delta}{7}\right) = \frac{\mathbf{22\delta}}{\mathbf{105}} \quad \textbf{(Ans.)}$$

Example 13.4. *If velocity distribution in laminar boundary layer over a flat plate is assumed to be given by second order polynomial $u = a + by + cy^2$, determine its form using the necessary boundary conditions.*

Solution. Velocity distribution: $u = a + by + cy^2$

The following *boundary conditions* must be satisfied:

(*i*) At $y = 0, u = 0$

$\therefore \quad u = a + by + cy^2$

$0 = a + 0 + 0 \qquad \therefore \quad a = 0$

(*ii*) At $y = \delta, u = U$

$\therefore \quad U = b\delta + c\delta^2$ ...(*i*)

(*iii*) At $y = \delta, \dfrac{du}{dy} = 0$

$$\therefore \quad \left(\frac{du}{dy}\right)_{y=\delta} = \frac{d}{dy}(a + by + cy^2) = b + 2cy = b + 2c\delta = 0 \qquad ...(ii)$$

Substituting the value of b ($= -2c\delta$) from (*ii*) in (*i*), we get:

$$U = (-2c\delta)\delta + c\delta^2 = -2c\delta^2 + c\delta^2 = -c\delta^2$$

or,
$$c = -\frac{U}{\delta^2}$$

$$\therefore \quad b = -2c\delta = -2 \times \left(-\frac{U}{\delta^2}\right)\delta = \frac{2U}{\delta}$$

Hence, *form of the velocity distribution is:*

$$u = \frac{2U}{\delta} y - \frac{U}{\delta^2} y^2$$

or,
$$\frac{u}{U} = 2\left(\frac{y}{\delta}\right) - \left(\frac{y}{\delta}\right)^2 \quad \textbf{(Ans.)}$$

Example 13.5. *The velocity distribution in the boundary layer is given by*

$$\frac{u}{U} = \left(\frac{y}{\delta}\right)^{1/7}$$

Calculate the following

(i) Displacement thickness,

(ii) Momentum thickness,

(iii) Shape factor,

(iv) Energy thickness, and

(v) Energy loss due to boundary layer if at a particular section, the boundary layer thickness is 25 mm and the free stream velocity is 15 m/s. If the discharge through the boundary layer region is 6 m^3/s per metre width, express this energy loss in terms of metres of head. Take $\rho = 1{\cdot}2$ kg/m^3.

Solution. Velocity distribution: $\frac{u}{U} = \left(\frac{y}{\delta}\right)^{1/7}$ ...(*Given*)

(i) Displacement thickness, δ^*:

$$\delta^* = \int_0^\delta \left(1 - \frac{u}{U}\right) dy$$

$$= \int_0^\delta \left[1 - \left(\frac{y}{\delta}\right)^{1/7}\right] dy = \left[y - \frac{7}{8}\frac{y^{8/7}}{\delta^{1/7}}\right]_0^\delta = \left[\delta - \frac{7}{8} \times \frac{\delta^{8/7}}{\delta^{1/7}}\right]$$

$$= \frac{\boldsymbol{\delta}}{\mathbf{8}} \quad \textbf{(Ans.)}$$

(ii) Momentum thickness, θ:

$$\theta = \int_0^\delta \frac{u}{U}\left(1 - \frac{u}{U}\right) dy$$

$$= \int_0^\delta \left(\frac{y}{\delta}\right)^{1/7}\left[1 - \left(\frac{y}{\delta}\right)^{1/7}\right] dy = \int_0^\delta \left[\left(\frac{y}{\delta}\right)^{1/7} - \left(\frac{y}{\delta}\right)^{2/7}\right] dy$$

$$= \left[\frac{7}{8}\frac{y^{8/7}}{\delta^{1/7}} - \frac{7}{9}\cdot\frac{y^{9/7}}{\delta^{2/7}}\right]_0^\delta = \left[\frac{7}{8}\frac{\delta^{8/7}}{\delta^{1/7}} - \frac{7}{9}\frac{\delta^{9/7}}{\delta^{2/7}}\right]$$

$$= \left(\frac{7}{8}\delta - \frac{7}{9}\delta\right) = \frac{\mathbf{7}}{\mathbf{72}}\boldsymbol{\delta} \quad \textbf{(Ans.)}$$

(iii) Shape factor:

$$\text{Shape factor} : = \frac{\delta^*}{\theta} = \frac{\delta/8}{7\delta/72} = \frac{\delta}{8} \times \frac{72}{7\delta} = \mathbf{1.286} \quad \textbf{(Ans.)}$$

(iv) Energy thickness, δ_e:

$$\delta_e = \int_0^\delta \frac{u}{U}\left[\left(1 - \frac{u^2}{U^2}\right)\right] dy$$

$$= \int_0^{\delta} \left(\frac{y}{\delta}\right)^{1/7} \left[1 - \left(\frac{y}{\delta}\right)^{2/7}\right] dy = \int_0^{\delta} \left[\left(\frac{y}{\delta}\right)^{1/7} - \left(\frac{y}{\delta}\right)^{3/7}\right] dy$$

$$= \left[\frac{7}{8} \times \frac{y^{8/7}}{\delta^{1/7}} - \frac{7}{10} \times \frac{y^{10/7}}{\delta^{3/7}}\right]_0^{\delta} = \left[\frac{7}{8}\delta - \frac{7}{10}\delta\right] = \frac{7}{40}\delta \text{ (Ans.)}$$

(v) Energy loss

Given: Boundary layer thickness, $\delta^* = 25$ mm

Free stream velocity, $U = 15$ m/s

Discharge per metre width, $q = 6$ m^3/s

Density of fluid, $\rho = 1.2$ kg/m^3

Now, energy thickness, $\delta_e = \frac{7}{40}\delta = \frac{7}{40} \times 25 = 4.375$ mm

Energy loss per unit width, due to boundary layer

$$= \frac{1}{2}(\rho\delta_e U) \times U^2 = \frac{1}{2} \times 1.2 \times \left(\frac{4.375}{1000}\right) \times 15^3 = \mathbf{8.859\ Nm/s} \text{ (Ans.)}$$

Let, h_1 = Energy loss (per unit width) in terms of metres of head.

Then, $\rho q h_1 = 8.859$

or, $h_1 = \frac{8.859}{\rho q} = \frac{8.859}{1.2 \times 6} = \mathbf{1.23\ m}$ **(Ans.)**

Example 13.6. *Explain what you understand by boundary layer thickness and displacement thickness. Determine the relationship between the two for a boundary layer which is (i) laminar throughout, and (ii) turbulent throughout. Assume (1) in the laminar boundary layer the flow obeys the law, shear stress $\tau = \mu \frac{du}{dy}$, where μ is the viscosity, which leads to the velocity profile $(U - u) = k(\delta - y)^2$ where U is the free stream velocity, u is the velocity at a distance y above the plate and k is a constant; (2) the velocity distribution in the turbulent boundary layer is given by $\frac{u}{U} = \left(\frac{y}{\delta}\right)^{1/7}$.*

(UPSC)

Solution. (*a*) **Boundary layer thickness.** *It is defined as the distance from the boundary of solid body measured in Y-direction to the point, where the velocity of fluid is approximately equal to 0.99 times the free stream (U) velocity of floud.*

Displacement thickness. *It is defined as the distance, measured perpendicular to the boundary of the solid body by which the boundary should be displaced to compensate for the reduction in flow rate on account of boundary layer formation.*

(*i*) ***When the flow is laminar throughout:***

Velocity profile: $(U - u) = k(\delta - y)^2$ ...(1)

$$\tau = \mu \frac{du}{dy}$$

where, U = Free stream velocity,

u = Veloctiy at a distance y above plate, and

k = Constant.

Let, δ^* = Displacement thickness, and

δ = Boundary layer thickness.

$$\delta^* = \int_0^\delta \left(1 - \frac{u}{U}\right) dy$$

Dividing eqn. (1) by U, we get:

$$1 - \frac{u}{U} = \frac{k}{U}(\delta - y)^2$$

$$\therefore \quad \delta^* = \int_0^\delta \frac{k}{U}(\delta - y)^2\, dy = \left[-\frac{k}{U} \times \frac{(\delta - y)^3}{3}\right]_0^\delta = \left[\frac{k\,(\delta - y)^3}{3U}\right]_\delta^0 = \frac{k\delta^3}{3U} \qquad \text{...(2)}$$

When $y = 0$, $u = 0$ *i.e.* on the surface of the plate.

Substituting these parameters in eqn. (1), we get $U = k\delta^2$ ...(3)

Substituting the value of U from (3) in (2), we get:

$$\delta^* = \frac{k\delta^3}{3k\delta^2} = \frac{\delta}{3} \quad \textbf{(Ans.)}$$

(*ii*) ***When the flow is turbulent throughout***

Velocity profile: $\frac{u}{U} = \left(\frac{y}{\delta}\right)^{1/7}$

$$\delta^* = \int_0^\delta \left(1 - \frac{u}{U}\right) dy = \int_0^\delta \left[1 - \left(\frac{y}{\delta}\right)^{1/7}\right] dy$$

$$\left[y - \frac{7}{8}\frac{y^{8/7}}{\delta^{1/7}}\right]_0^\delta = \frac{1}{8}\delta \quad \textbf{(Ans.)}$$

Example 13.7. *In the boundary layer over the face of a high spillway, the velocity distribution was observed to have the following form :*

$$\frac{u}{U} = \left(\frac{y}{\delta}\right)^{0.22}$$

The free stream velocity U at a certain section was observed to be 30 m/s and a boundary layer thickness of 60 mm was estimated from the velocity distribution measured at the section. The discharge passing over the spillway was 6 m³/s per metre length of spillway. Calculate :

(*i*) *The displacement thickness,*

(*ii*) *The energy thickness, and*

(*iii*) *The loss of energy upto the section under consideration.*

Solution. Velocity distribution: $\frac{u}{U} = \left(\frac{y}{\delta}\right)^{0.22}$

The free stream velocity at a certain section, $U = 30$ m/s

Thickness of the boundary layer, $\delta = 60$ mm

The discharge passing over the spillway, $q = 6\ \text{m}^3/\text{s}$ per metre length of the spillway.

(*i*) **The displacement thickness, δ^***

$$\delta^* = \int_0^\delta \left(1 - \frac{u}{U}\right) dy = \int_0^\delta \left[1 - \left(\frac{y}{\delta}\right)^{0\cdot22}\right] dy$$

$$= \left[y - \frac{y^{1.22}}{1.22 \times \delta^{0.22}}\right]_0^\delta = \left(\delta - \frac{\delta^{1.22}}{1.22 \times \delta^{0.22}}\right) = \delta\left(1 - \frac{1}{1.22}\right)$$

$$= 0.18\delta = 0.18 \times 60 \text{ mm} = \mathbf{10.8\ mm}\ \textbf{(Ans.)}$$

(*ii*) **The energy thickness, δ_e**

$$\delta_e = \int_0^\delta \frac{u}{U}\left(1 - \frac{u^2}{U^2}\right) dy$$

$$= \int_0^\delta \left(\frac{y}{\delta}\right)^{0.22} \left[1 - \left(\frac{y}{\delta}\right)^{0.44}\right] dy$$

$$= \int_0^\delta \left[\left(\frac{y}{\delta}\right)^{0.22} - \left(\frac{y}{\delta}\right)^{0.66}\right] dy$$

$$= \left[\frac{y^{1.22}}{1.22 \times \delta^{0.22}} - \frac{\delta^{1.66}}{1.66\ \delta^{0.66}}\right]_0^\delta = \left[\frac{\delta^{1.22}}{1.22 \times \delta^{0.22}} - \frac{\delta^{1.66}}{1.66 \times \delta^{0.66}}\right]$$

$$= \left[\frac{\delta}{1.22} - \frac{\delta}{1.66}\right] = 0.217\ \delta = 0.217 \times 60 = \mathbf{13.02\ mm}\ \textbf{(Ans.)}$$

(*iii*) **The loss of energy:**

The energy loss *per metre length* of spillway is,

$$E_L = \frac{1}{2} \times (\rho \times \delta_e \times U) \times U^2 = \frac{1}{2}\rho \cdot \delta_e U^3 = \frac{1}{2} \times 1000 \times \frac{13.02}{1000} \times (30)^3$$

$$= \mathbf{175.77\ kNm/s}\ \textbf{(Ans.)}$$

Energy loss (*per metre length*) in terms of metres of head

$$= \frac{E_L}{wq} = \frac{175.77}{9.81 \times 6} = \mathbf{2.986\ m}\ \textbf{(Ans.)}$$

Example 13.8. *The velocity distribution in the boundary layer over the face of a spillway was observed to be:*

$$\frac{u}{U} = \left(\frac{y}{\delta}\right)^{0.22}$$

The free stream velocity U is 20 m/s and boundary layer thickness 5 cm at a certain section. The discharge is 5 m³/s per meter length of spillway. Calculate displacement thickness, energy thickness and loss of energy up to section under consideration. **(Delhi University)**

Solution. *Given* : Velocity distribution: $\frac{u}{U} = \left(\frac{y}{\delta}\right)^{022}$

$U = 20$ m/s; $\delta = 5$ cm; $Q = 5\ m^3/s$ per metre length of spillway,

$$\delta^*, \delta_e, E_L$$

The *displacement thickness* is given by the equation:

$$\delta^* = \int_0^\delta \left(1 - \frac{u}{U}\right) dy = \int_0^\delta \left\{1 - \left(\frac{y}{\delta}\right)^{0.22}\right\} dy = \left[y - \frac{1}{(\delta)^{0.22}} \times \frac{(y)^{0.22+1}}{1.22}\right]_0^\delta$$

$$= \delta - \frac{\delta}{1.22} = \frac{0.22}{1.22}\delta = \frac{0.22}{1.22} \times 5 = \mathbf{0.9016\ cm}\ \textbf{(Ans.)}$$

The *energy thickness* is given by the equation:

$$\delta_e = \int_0^\delta \frac{u}{U}\left\{1 - \left(\frac{u}{U}\right)^2\right\} = \int_0^\delta \left\{\frac{u}{U} - \left(\frac{u}{U}\right)^3\right\} dy = \int_0^\delta \left\{\left(\frac{y}{\delta}\right)^{0.22} - \left(\frac{y}{\delta}\right)^{0.66}\right\} dy$$

$$= \int_0^\delta \left[\frac{1}{(\delta)^{0.22}} \times \frac{(y)^{0.22+1}}{1.22} - \frac{1}{(\delta)^{0.66}} \times \frac{(y)^{0.66+1}}{1.66}\right]_0^\delta$$

$$= \frac{8}{1.22} - \frac{\delta}{1.66} = \delta\left(\frac{1}{1.22} - \frac{1}{1.66}\right) = 5\left(\frac{1.66 - 1.22}{1.22 \times 1.66}\right) = \mathbf{1.086\ cm}\ \textbf{(Ans.)}$$

The *energy loss per m length* of spillway is,

$$E_L = \frac{1}{2}(\rho \times \delta_e \times U) \times U^2 = \frac{1}{2}\rho\delta_e U^3$$

$$\therefore \quad E_L = \frac{1}{2} \times 1000 \times \left(\frac{1.086}{100}\right) \times (20)^3 \times 10^{-3}\ \text{kNm/s} = 43.44\ \text{kNm/s}$$

Energy loss in terms of *m* of head

$$= \frac{E_L}{\rho Q g} = \frac{43.44 \times 1000}{1000 \times 5 \times 9.81} = \mathbf{0.8856\ m}\ \textbf{(Ans.)}$$

Example 13.9. *For steady Poiseuille flow in a pipe of radius R, obtain an expression for ratio of the displacement thickness* (δ^*) *to momentum thickness* (θ). **[Roorkee University]**

Solution. Radius of the pipe = R

$$\frac{\delta^*}{\theta}:$$

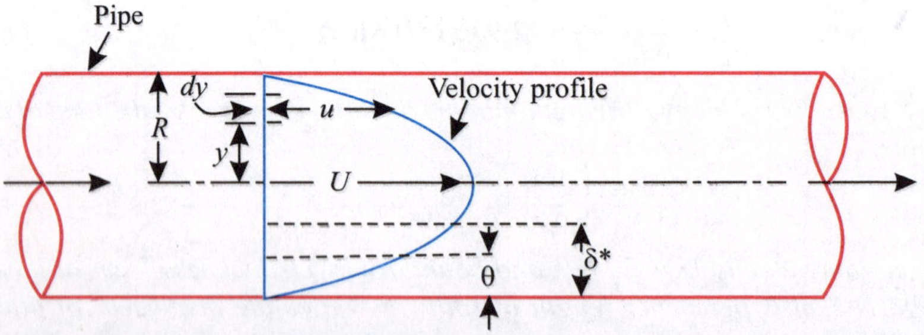

Fig. 13.3

For steady Poiseuille flow in a circular pipe, the velocity distribution is given by,

$$u = -\frac{1}{4\mu} \cdot \frac{\partial p}{\partial x}(R^2 - y^2) \qquad ...(i)$$

where y being measured from the centre of the pipe.

At, $\quad y = 0,\ u = U$ (maximum velocity)

$$\therefore \qquad U = -\frac{1}{4\mu}\cdot\frac{\partial p}{\partial x}R^2 \qquad ...(ii)$$

From the definition of displacement thickness, we have:

$$[\pi R^2 - \pi(R-\delta^*)^2]U = \int_0^R 2\pi y\,(U-u)\,dy$$

or,

$$2\pi R\delta^* U = \int_0^R 2\pi y\,(U-u)\,dy$$

[neglecting the term containing $(\delta^*)^2$, since δ^* is very small.]

or,

$$\delta^* = \frac{1}{R}\int_0^R \left(1-\frac{u}{U}\right) y\,dy = \frac{1}{R}\int_0^R \frac{y^2}{R^2}\,y\,dy = \frac{R}{4}$$

$$\left[\text{Dividing } (i) \text{ by } (ii), \text{ we have: } \quad \frac{u}{U} = \frac{R^2-y^2}{R^2} = 1-\frac{y^2}{R^2} \text{ or } \left(1-\frac{u}{U}\right) = \frac{y^2}{R^2}\right]$$

From the definition of momentum thickness, we have:

$$[\rho\,\{\pi R^2 - \pi(R-\theta)^2\}]U = \int_0^R \rho 2\pi y.dy.u\,(U-u)$$

On simplification, we get:

$$2\pi R\theta U^2 = \int_0^R 2\pi\, yu\,(U-u)\,dy$$

$$\theta = \frac{1}{R}\int_0^R \frac{u}{U}\left(1-\frac{u}{U}\right) y\,dy$$

$$= \frac{1}{R}\int_0^R \left(1-\frac{y^2}{R^2}\right)\frac{y^2}{R^2}\,y\,dy = \frac{1}{R}\int_0^R \left(\frac{y^3}{R^2}-\frac{y^5}{R^4}\right)dy$$

$$= \frac{1}{R}\left[\frac{y^4}{4R^2}-\frac{y^6}{6R^4}\right]_0^R = \frac{1}{R}\left[\frac{R^4}{4R^2}-\frac{R^6}{6R^4}\right] = \frac{1}{R}\left[\frac{R^2}{4}-\frac{R^2}{6}\right] = \frac{R}{12}$$

$$\therefore \qquad \frac{\delta^*}{\theta} = \frac{R/4}{R/12} = 3 \ \textbf{(Ans.)}$$

13.3. MOMENTUM EQUATION FOR BOUNDARY LAYER BY VON KARMAN

Von Karman suggested a method based on the *momentum equation* by the use of which the growth of a boundary layer along a flat plate, the wall shear stress and the drag force could be determined (when the velocity distribution in the boundary layer is known). Starting from the beginning of the plate, the method can be used for *both laminar and turbulent boundary layers*.

Fig. 13.4. shows a fluid flowing over a thin plate (placed at zero incidence) with a free stream velocity equal to U. Consider a small length dx of the plate at a distance x from the leading edge as shown in Fig. 13.4 (a); the enlarged view of the small length of the plate is shown in Fig. 13.4 (b). Consider *unit width* of plate perpendicular to the direction of flow.

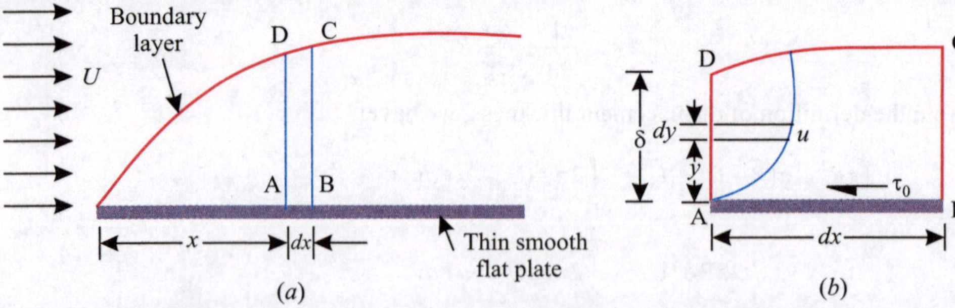

Fig. 13.4. Momentum equation for boundary layer by Von Karman.

Let *ABCD* be a small element of a boundary layer (the edge *DC* represents the outer edge of the boundary layer).

Mass rate of fluid entering through *AD*

$$= \int_0^\delta \rho u dy$$

Mass rate of fluid leaving through *BC*

$$= \int_0^\delta \rho u dy + \frac{d}{dx}\left[\int_0^\delta \rho u dy\right] dx$$

∴ Mass rate of fluid entering the control volume through the surface *DC*

= Mass rate of fluid through *BC* – mass rate of fluid through *AD*

$$= \int_0^\delta \rho u dy + \frac{d}{dx}\left[\int_0^\delta \rho u dy\right] dx - \int_0^\delta \rho u dy = \frac{d}{dx}\left[\int_0^\delta \rho u dy\right] dx$$

The fluid is entering through *DC* with a uniform velocity *U*.

Momentum rate of fluid entering the control volume in *X*-direction through *AD*

$$= \int_0^\delta \rho u^2 dy$$

Momentum rate of fluid leaving the control volume in *X*-direction through *BC*

$$= \int_0^\delta \rho u^2 dy + \frac{d}{dx}\left[\int_0^\delta \rho u^2 dy\right] dx$$

Momentum rate of fluid entering the control volume through *DC* in *X*-direction

$$= \frac{d}{dx}\left[\int_0^\delta \rho u dy\right] dx \times U \qquad (\because \text{Velocity} = U)$$

$$= \frac{d}{dx}\left[\int_0^\delta \rho u U dy\right] dx$$

∴ Rate of change of momentum of control volume

= Momentum rate of fluid through *BC* – momentum rate of fluid through *AD* – momentum rate of fluid through *DC*

$$= \int_0^\delta \rho u^2 dy + \frac{d}{dx}\left[\int_0^\delta \rho u^2\, dy\right] dx - \int_0^\delta \rho u^2\, dy - \frac{d}{dx}\left[\int_0^\delta \rho u U dy\right] dx$$

$$= \frac{d}{dx}\left[\int_0^\delta \rho u^2\, dy - \int_0^\delta \rho u\, U\, dy\right] dx$$

$$= \frac{d}{dx}\left[\int_0^\delta (\rho u^2\, dy - \rho u\, U\, dy)\right] dx$$

$$= \frac{d}{dx}\left[\rho \int_0^\delta (u^2 - uU)\, dy\right] dx$$

(ρ is constant for incompressible fluid)

$$= \rho \frac{d}{dx}\left[\int_0^\delta (u^2 - uU)\, dy\right] dx \qquad \text{...(13.4)}$$

As per momentum principle the rate of change of momentum on the control volume *ABCD* must be equal to the total force on the control volume in the same direction. The only external force acting on the control volume is the shear force acting on the side *AB* in the direction *B* to *A* (Fig. 13.4 *b*). The value of this force (*drag force*) is given by,

$$\Delta F_D = \tau_0 \times dx$$

Thus the total external force in the direction of rate of change of momentum

$$= -\tau_0 \times dx \qquad \text{...(13.5)}$$

Equating the eqns. (13.4) and (13.5), we have:

$$-\tau_0 \times dx = \rho \frac{d}{dx}\left[\int_0^\delta (u^2 - uU)\, dy\right] dx$$

or,

$$\tau_0 = -\rho \frac{d}{dx}\left[\int_0^\delta (u^2 - uU)\, dy\right]$$

or,

$$= \rho \frac{d}{dx}\left[\int_0^\delta (uU - u^2)\, dy\right]$$

$$= \rho \frac{d}{dx}\left[\int_0^\delta U^2\left(\frac{u}{U} - \frac{u^2}{U^2}\right) dy\right]$$

$$= \rho U^2 \frac{d}{dx}\left[\int_0^\delta \frac{u}{U}\left(1 - \frac{u}{U}\right) dy\right]$$

or,

$$\frac{\tau_0}{\rho U^2} = \frac{d}{dx}\left[\int_0^\delta \frac{u}{U}\left(1 - \frac{u}{U}\right) dy\right] \qquad \text{...(13.6)}$$

But, $\int_0^\delta \frac{u}{U}\left(1 - \frac{u}{U}\right) dy$ = momentum thickness (θ)

$\therefore$

$$\frac{\tau_0}{\rho U^2} = \frac{d\theta}{dx} \qquad \text{...(13.7)}$$

Eqn. (13.7) is *known as* **Von Karman momentum equation** *for boundary layer flow, and is used to find out the frictional drag on smooth flat plate for both laminar and turbulent boundary layers.*

The following *boundary conditions* must be satisfied for any *assumed velocity distribution:*

(*i*) *At the surface of the plate:* $y = 0, \quad u = 0, \quad \frac{du}{dy}$ = finite value

(*ii*) *At the outer edge of boundary layer:* $y = \delta, \; u = U$

$$y = \delta, \frac{du}{dy} = 0$$

The shear stress, τ_0 for a given velocity profile in laminar, transition or turbulent zone is obtained from eqn. (13·6) or (13·7). Then drag force on a small distance dx of a plate is given by,

$$\Delta F_D = \text{Shear stress} \times \text{area}$$

$$= \tau_0 \times (B \times dx) = \tau_0 \times B \times dx \text{[assuming width of plate as } unity\text{]}$$

(where, B = width of the plate)

∴ Total drag on the plate of length L one side,

$$F_D = \int \Delta F_D = \int_0^L \tau_0 \times B \times dx \quad \text{...(13.8)}$$

—The ratio of the shear stress τ_0 to the quantity $\frac{1}{2}\rho U^2$ is known as the "***Local co-efficient of drag***" (or ***co-efficient of skin friction***) and is denoted by C_D^*

i.e.

$$C_D^* = \frac{\tau_0}{\frac{1}{2}\rho U^2} \quad \text{...(13.9)}$$

— The ratio of the total drag force to the quantity $\frac{1}{2}\rho A U^2$ is called '***Average co-efficient of drag***' and is denoted by C_D

i.e.

$$C_D = \frac{F_D}{\frac{1}{2}\rho A U^2} \quad \text{...(13.10)}$$

where, ρ = Mass density of fluid,

A = Area of surface/plate, and

U = Free stream velocity.

13.4. LAMINAR BOUNDARY LAYER

Let us find out boundary layer thickness (δ), shear stress (τ_0), local co-efficient of drag (C_D^*) and co-efficient of drag (C_D) for the following velocity distribution in the laminar boundary layer:

1. $\frac{u}{U} = 2\left(\frac{y}{\delta}\right) - \left(\frac{y}{\delta}\right)^2$

2. $\frac{u}{U} = \frac{3}{2}\left(\frac{y}{\delta}\right) - \frac{1}{2}\left(\frac{y}{\delta}\right)^3$ ...Prandtl's velocity distribution.

3. $\frac{u}{U} = 2\left(\frac{y}{\delta}\right) - 2\left(\frac{y}{\delta}\right)^3 + \left(\frac{y}{\delta}\right)^4$

4. $\frac{u}{U} = \sin\left(\frac{\pi}{2}\frac{y}{\delta}\right)$

Case 1. *Velocity distribution*: $\dfrac{u}{U} = 2\left(\dfrac{y}{\delta}\right) - \left(\dfrac{y}{\delta}\right)^2$ ...(*i*)

(*i*) Boundary layer thickness

We know,
$$\frac{\tau_0}{\rho U^2} = \frac{d}{dx}\left[\int_0^\delta \frac{u}{U}\left(1 - \frac{u}{U}\right) dy\right] \qquad \text{[Eqn. (13.6)]}$$

Substituting the value of $\dfrac{u}{U}$, we get:

$$\frac{\tau_0}{\rho U^2} = \frac{d}{dx}\left[\int_0^\delta \left\{\frac{2y}{\delta} - \frac{y^2}{\delta^2}\right\}\left\{1 - \left(\frac{2y}{\delta} - \frac{y^2}{\delta^2}\right)\right\} dy\right]$$
$$= \frac{d}{dx}\left[\int_0^\delta \left\{\frac{2y}{\delta} - \frac{y^2}{\delta^2}\right\}\left\{1 - \frac{2y}{\delta} + \frac{y^2}{\delta^2}\right\} dy\right]$$
$$= \frac{d}{dx}\left[\int_0^\delta \left\{\frac{2y}{\delta} - \frac{4y^2}{\delta^2} + \frac{2y^3}{\delta^3} - \frac{y^2}{\delta^2} + \frac{2y^3}{\delta^3} - \frac{y^4}{\delta^4}\right\} dy\right]$$
$$= \frac{d}{dx}\left[\int_0^\delta \left\{\frac{2y}{\delta} - \frac{5y^2}{\delta^2} + \frac{4y^3}{\delta^3} - \frac{y^4}{\delta^4}\right\} dy\right]$$
$$= \frac{d}{dx}\left[\frac{2}{2}\frac{y^2}{\delta} - \frac{5}{3}\frac{y^3}{\delta^2} + \frac{4}{4}\frac{y^4}{\delta^3} - \frac{1}{5}\frac{y^5}{\delta^4}\right]_0^\delta$$
$$= \frac{d}{dx}\left[\delta - \frac{5}{3}\delta + \delta - \frac{1}{5}\delta\right] = \frac{d}{dx}\left(\frac{2}{15}\delta\right)$$

$\therefore$
$$\tau_0 = \rho U^2 \times \frac{d}{dx}\left(\frac{2}{15}\delta\right) = \frac{2}{15}\rho U^2 \frac{d\delta}{dx} \qquad \text{...(13.11)}$$

Also, according to Newton's law of viscosity,

$$\tau_0 = \mu\left(\frac{du}{dy}\right)_{y=0} \qquad \text{...}(ii)$$

But,
$$u = U\left(\frac{2y}{\delta} - \frac{y^2}{\delta^2}\right) \qquad \text{...[From eqn. }(i)]$$

and,
$$\frac{du}{dy} = U\left(\frac{2}{\delta} - \frac{2y}{\delta^2}\right), \; U \text{ being constant}$$

$\therefore$
$$\left(\frac{du}{dy}\right)_{y=0} = U\left(\frac{2}{\delta} - 0\right) = \frac{2U}{\delta}$$

Substituting this value in (*ii*), we get:

$$\tau_0 = \frac{2\mu U}{\delta} \qquad \text{...(13.12)}$$

Equating the values of τ_0 given by eqns. (13.11) and (13.12), we get:

$$\frac{2}{15}\rho U^2 \frac{d\delta}{dx} = \frac{2\mu U}{\delta}$$

or,
$$\delta \cdot \frac{d\delta}{dx} = \frac{15\mu U}{\rho U^2} = \frac{15\mu}{\rho U}$$

or,
$$\delta \cdot d\delta = \frac{15\ \mu}{\rho U}\ dx$$

Integrating both sides, we get:

$$\frac{\delta^2}{2} = \frac{15\ \mu}{\rho U}\ x + C \qquad \text{(where, } C = \text{constant of integration)}$$

At, $x = 0, \delta = 0 \qquad \therefore C = 0$

$$\therefore \quad \frac{\delta^2}{2} = \frac{15\mu x}{\rho U}$$

or,
$$\delta = \sqrt{\frac{2 \times 15\mu x}{\rho U}} = 5 \cdot 48 \sqrt{\frac{\mu x}{\rho U}}$$

$$= 5.48 \sqrt{\frac{\mu x \times x}{\rho U \times x}} = 5.48 \sqrt{\frac{x^2}{Re_x}}$$

$$\left(\text{where, } Re_x = \frac{\rho U x}{\mu}\right)$$

or,
$$\boldsymbol{\delta} = 5.48 \frac{x}{\sqrt{Re_x}} \qquad \text{...(13.13)}$$

***(ii)* Shear stress τ_0**

From eqn. (13.12), we have:

$$\tau_0 = \frac{2\mu U}{\delta}$$

But,
$$\delta = 5.48 \frac{x}{\sqrt{Re_x}} \qquad \text{[Eqn. (13.12)]}$$

$$\therefore \quad \boldsymbol{\tau_0} = \frac{2\mu U}{5.48 \dfrac{x}{\sqrt{Re_x}}} = \frac{2uU\sqrt{Re_x}}{5.48\ x} = \mathbf{0.365}\ \frac{\boldsymbol{\mu U}}{\boldsymbol{x}} \sqrt{\boldsymbol{Re_x}} \qquad \text{...(13.14)}$$

***(iii)* Local co-efficient of drag, C_D^***

$$\tau_0 = 0.365 \frac{\mu U}{x} \sqrt{Re_x} \qquad \text{...[Eqn. (13.14)]}$$

Also,
$$\tau_0 = C_D^* \frac{\rho U^2}{2} \qquad \text{...[Eqn. (13.9)]}$$

(where, C_D^* = local co-efficient of drag)

Equating the two values of τ_0, given by eqns. (13.14) and (13.9), we get:

$$C_D^* = 0.365 \frac{\mu U}{x} \sqrt{Re_x} \quad \text{or} \quad C_D^* = 0.365 \times 2 \times \frac{\sqrt{Re_x}}{\frac{\rho U x}{\mu}} = \frac{0.73}{\sqrt{Re_x}}$$

Hence, $$\boldsymbol{C_D^* = \frac{0.73}{\sqrt{Re_x}}} \quad \text{...(13.15)}$$

(*iv*) Co-efficient of drag, C_D:

We know that, $$C_D = \frac{F_D}{\frac{1}{2}\rho A U^2} \quad \text{...[Eqn. (13.10)]}$$

where, $$F_D = \int_0^L \tau_0 \times B \times dx \quad \text{...[Eqn. (13·8)]}$$

$$= \int_0^L 0.365 \frac{\mu U}{x} \sqrt{Re_x} \times B \times dx = \int_0^L \frac{\mu U}{x} \sqrt{\frac{\rho U x}{\mu}} \times B \times dx \quad \left(\because Re_x = \frac{\rho U x}{\mu}\right)$$

$$= 0.365 \int_0^L \mu U \sqrt{\frac{\rho U}{\mu}} \times \frac{1}{\sqrt{x}} \times B \times dx = 0.365\, \mu U \sqrt{\frac{\rho U}{\mu}} \times B \int_0^L x^{-1/2} \times dx$$

$$= 0.365 \mu U \sqrt{\frac{\rho U}{\mu}} \times B \left[\frac{x^{1/2}}{1/2}\right]_0^L = 0.365 \times 2 \mu U \sqrt{\frac{\rho U}{\mu}} \times B\sqrt{L}$$

or, $$F_D = 0.73 \mu U B \sqrt{\frac{\rho U L}{\mu}} \quad \text{...(13.16)}$$

$$\therefore \quad C_D = \frac{0.73 \mu U B \sqrt{\frac{\rho U L}{\mu}}}{\frac{1}{2}\rho A U^2}$$

(where, A = area of plate = $L \times B$, L and B being length and width of the plate respectively)

$$\therefore \quad \boldsymbol{C_D} = \frac{0.73 \mu U B \sqrt{\frac{\rho U L}{\mu}}}{\frac{1}{2}\rho \times L \times B \times U^2} = \frac{1.46 \mu}{\rho L U} \sqrt{\frac{\rho U L}{\mu}}$$

$$= \frac{1.46\sqrt{\mu}}{\sqrt{\rho U L}} = 1.46 \sqrt{\frac{\mu}{\rho U L}} = \boldsymbol{\frac{1.46}{\sqrt{Re_L}}} \quad \text{...(13.17)}$$

Case 2. *Velocity distribution*: $\frac{u}{U} = \frac{3}{2}\left(\frac{y}{\delta}\right) - \frac{1}{2}\left(\frac{y}{\delta}\right)^3$

(*i*) Boundary layer thickness, δ:

$$\frac{\tau_0}{\rho U^2} = \frac{d}{dx}\left[\int_0^\delta \frac{u}{U}\left(1 - \frac{u}{U}\right) dy\right] \quad \text{[Eqn. (13.6)]}$$

Substituting the value of $\frac{u}{U}$, we get:

$$\frac{\tau_0}{\rho U^2} = \frac{d}{dx}\left[\int_0^\delta \left(\frac{3}{2}\frac{y}{\delta} - \frac{1}{2}\frac{y^3}{\delta^3}\right)\left\{1 - \frac{3}{2}\frac{y}{\delta} + \frac{1}{2}\frac{y^3}{\delta^3}\right\} dy\right]$$

$$= \left[\int_0^\delta \left(\frac{3}{2}\frac{y}{\delta} - \frac{9}{4}\frac{y^2}{\delta^2} + \frac{3}{4}\frac{y^4}{\delta^4} - \frac{1}{2}\frac{y^3}{\delta^3} + \frac{3}{4}\frac{y^4}{\delta^4} - \frac{1}{4}\frac{y^6}{\delta^6}\right) dy\right]$$

$$= \frac{d}{dx}\left[\frac{3}{2}\times\frac{1}{2}\frac{y^2}{\delta} - \frac{9}{4}\times\frac{1}{3}\frac{y^3}{\delta^2} + \frac{3}{4}\times\frac{1}{5}\frac{y^5}{\delta^4} - \frac{1}{2}\times\frac{1}{4}\frac{y^4}{\delta^3} + \frac{3}{4}\times\frac{1}{5}\frac{y^5}{\delta^4} - \frac{1}{4}\times\frac{1}{7}\frac{y^7}{\delta^6}\right]_0^\delta$$

$$= \frac{d}{dx}\left[\frac{3}{4}\delta - \frac{3}{4}\delta + \frac{3}{20}\delta + \frac{3}{20}\delta - \frac{1}{8}\delta - \frac{1}{28}\delta\right] = \frac{39}{280}\frac{d\delta}{dx}$$

or, $$\tau_0 = \rho U^2 \times \frac{39}{280}\frac{d\delta}{dx} = \frac{39}{280}\rho U^2 \frac{d\delta}{dx} \quad \text{...(13.18)}$$

Also, $$\tau_0 = \mu\left(\frac{du}{dy}\right)_{y=0}$$

But, $$u = U\left[\frac{3}{2}\left(\frac{y}{\delta}\right) - \frac{1}{2}\left(\frac{y}{\delta}\right)^3\right]$$

and, $$\frac{du}{dy} = U\left(\frac{3}{2\delta} - \frac{3}{2}\frac{y^2}{\delta^3}\right)$$

$\therefore$ $$\tau_0 = \mu\left(\frac{du}{dy}\right)_{y=0} = \mu U\left(\frac{3}{2\delta} - 0\right) = \frac{3\mu U}{2\delta} \quad \text{...(13.19)}$$

Equating the two values of τ_0 given by eqns. (13.18) and (13.19), we get:

$$\frac{3\rho}{280}\rho U^2\frac{d\delta}{dx} = \frac{3\mu U}{2\delta}$$

$\therefore$ $$\delta \cdot d\delta = \frac{3}{2}\mu U \times \frac{280}{39} \times \frac{dx}{\rho U^2} = \frac{420}{39}\frac{\mu}{\rho U}dx$$

Integrating both sides, we get:

$$\delta^2 = \frac{420}{39}\frac{\mu}{\rho U}x + C$$

(where, C = constant of integration)

When, $x = 0, \delta = 0 \therefore C = 0$

$\therefore$ $$\frac{\delta^2}{2} = \frac{420}{39}\frac{\mu}{\rho U}x$$

or, $$\delta = \sqrt{\frac{420 \times 2}{39} \cdot \frac{\mu}{\rho U}x} = 4.64\sqrt{\frac{\mu x}{\rho U}}$$

$$= 4.64\sqrt{\frac{\mu x}{\rho U} \times \frac{x}{x}} = 4.64\sqrt{\frac{\mu}{\rho U x}} \cdot x = \mathbf{\frac{4.64\,x}{\sqrt{Re_x}}} \quad \text{...(13.20)}$$

(ii) Shear stress, τ_0

$$\tau_0 = \frac{3\mu U}{2\delta}$$

But, $$\delta = \frac{4.64\,x}{\sqrt{Re_x}} \qquad \text{[Eqn. (13.19)]}$$

$$\therefore \quad \tau_0 = \frac{3\mu U}{2 \times \dfrac{4.64x}{\sqrt{Re_x}}} = \frac{3}{9.28}\,\frac{\mu U\sqrt{Re_x}}{x} = \mathbf{0.323\,\frac{\mu U}{x}\sqrt{Re_x}} \qquad ...(13.21)$$

(iii) Local co-efficient of drag, C_D^*

$$\tau_0 = 0.323\,\frac{\mu U}{x}\sqrt{Re_x}$$

Also, $$\tau_0 = C_D^*\,\frac{\rho U^2}{2}$$

$$\therefore \quad C_D^*\,\frac{\rho U^2}{2} = 0.323\,\frac{\mu U}{x}\sqrt{Re_x} \quad \text{or} \quad \mathbf{C_D^* = \frac{0.646}{\sqrt{Re_x}}} \qquad ...(13.22)$$

(iv) Co-efficient of drag (C_D):

$$C_D = \frac{F_D}{\frac{1}{2}\rho A U^2} \qquad \text{[Eqn. (13.10)]}$$

where, $$F_D = \int_0^L \tau_0 \times B \times dx \qquad \text{[Eqn. (13.8)]}$$

$$= \int_0^L \frac{\mu U}{x}\,Re_x \times B \times dx = 0.0323\int_0^L \frac{\mu U}{x}\sqrt{\frac{\rho U x}{\mu}} \times B \times dx$$

$$= 0.323\,\mu U\sqrt{\frac{\rho U}{\mu}} \times B\int_0^L x^{-1/2}\,dx = 0.323\,\mu U\sqrt{\frac{\rho U}{\mu}} \times B\left[\frac{x^{1/2}}{1/2}\right]_0^L$$

$$= 0.323 \times 2\mu U\sqrt{\frac{\rho U}{\mu}} \times B \times \sqrt{L}$$

or, $$F_D = 0.646\,\mu U\sqrt{\frac{\rho U L}{\mu}} \times B \qquad ...(13.23)$$

$$\therefore \quad C_D = \frac{0.646\,\mu U B\sqrt{\dfrac{\rho U L}{\mu}}}{\frac{1}{2}\rho A U^2} \qquad \text{(where, } A = L \times B\text{)}$$

$$= \frac{0.646\,\mu U B\sqrt{\dfrac{\rho U L}{\mu}}}{\frac{1}{2}\rho \times L \times B \times U^2} = 0.646 \times 2 \times \frac{\mu}{\rho U L} \times \sqrt{\frac{\rho U L}{\mu}} = \frac{1292}{\sqrt{\dfrac{\rho U L}{\mu}}}$$

or, $$C_D = \frac{\mathbf{1.292}}{\sqrt{Re_L}} \quad \text{...(13.24)}$$

$$\left(\text{where, } Re_L = \sqrt{\frac{\rho UL}{\mu}}\right)$$

Case 3. *Velocity distribution:* $\frac{\tau_0}{\rho U^2} = \frac{d}{dx}\left[\int_0^\delta \frac{u}{U}\left(1 - \frac{u}{U}\right) dy\right]$

***(i)* Boundary layer thickness, δ**

$$\frac{\tau_0}{\rho U^2} = \frac{d}{dx}\left[\int_0^\delta \frac{u}{U}\left(1 - \frac{u}{U}\right) dy\right] \quad \text{[Eqn. (13.6)]}$$

Substituting the value of $\frac{u}{U}$, we get:

$$\tau_0 = \frac{d}{dx}\left[\int_0^\delta \left(\frac{2y}{\delta} - \frac{2y^3}{\delta^3} + \frac{y^4}{\delta^4}\right)\left(1 - \frac{2y}{\delta} + \frac{2y^3}{\delta^3} - \frac{y^4}{\delta^4}\right) dy\right]$$

$$= \frac{d}{dx}\left[\int_0^\delta \left(\frac{2y}{\delta} - \frac{4y^2}{\delta^2} + \frac{4y^4}{\delta^4} - \frac{2y^5}{\delta^5} - \frac{2y^3}{\delta^3} + \frac{4y^4}{\delta^4} - \frac{4y^6}{\delta^6} + \frac{2y^7}{\delta^7} + \frac{y^4}{\delta^4} - \frac{2y^5}{\delta^5} + \frac{2y^7}{\delta^7} - \frac{y^8}{\delta^8}\right) dy\right]$$

$$= \frac{d}{dx}\left[\frac{2}{2}\times\frac{y^2}{\delta} - \frac{4}{3}\frac{y^3}{\delta^2} + \frac{4}{5}\frac{y^5}{\delta^4} - \frac{2}{6}\times\frac{y^6}{\delta^5} - \frac{2}{4}\frac{y^4}{\delta^3} + \frac{4}{5}\frac{y^5}{\delta^4} - \frac{4}{7}\frac{y^7}{\delta^6} + \frac{2}{8}\frac{y^8}{\delta^7} + \frac{1}{5}\frac{y^5}{\delta^4} - \frac{2}{6}\frac{y^6}{\delta^5} + \frac{2}{8}\frac{y^8}{\delta^7} - \frac{1}{9}\frac{y^9}{\delta^8}\right]_0^\delta$$

$$= \frac{d}{dx}\left[\delta - \frac{4}{3}\delta + \frac{4}{5}\delta - \frac{1}{3}\delta - \frac{1}{2}\delta + \frac{4}{5}\delta - \frac{4}{7}\delta + \frac{1}{4}\delta + \frac{1}{5}\delta - \frac{1}{3}\delta + \frac{1}{4}\delta - \frac{1}{9}\delta\right]$$

$$= \frac{d\delta}{dx}\left[1 - \frac{4}{3} + \frac{4}{5} - \frac{1}{3} - \frac{1}{2} + \frac{4}{5} - \frac{4}{7} + \frac{1}{4} + \frac{1}{5} - \frac{1}{3} + \frac{1}{4} - \frac{1}{9}\right]$$

$$= \frac{d\delta}{dx}\left[1 - \left(\frac{4}{3} + \frac{1}{3} + \frac{1}{3}\right) + \left(\frac{4}{5} + \frac{4}{5} + \frac{1}{5}\right) + \left(\frac{1}{4} + \frac{1}{4} - \frac{1}{2}\right) - \left(\frac{4}{7} + \frac{1}{9}\right)\right]$$

$$= \frac{d\delta}{dx}\left(1 - 2 + \frac{9}{5} + 0 - \frac{43}{63}\right) = \frac{d\delta}{dx}\left(-1 + \frac{9}{5} - \frac{43}{63}\right)$$

$$= \frac{d\delta}{dx}\left(\frac{-315 + 567 - 215}{315}\right) = \frac{37}{315}\frac{d\delta}{dx}$$

$$\therefore \quad \tau_0 = \frac{37}{315}\rho U^2 \frac{d\delta}{dx} \quad \text{...(13.25)}$$

Also, $$\tau_0 = \mu\left(\frac{du}{dy}\right)_{y=0}$$

But, $$u = U\left[\frac{2y}{\delta} - \frac{2y^3}{\delta^3} + \frac{y^4}{\delta^4}\right]$$

and, $$\frac{du}{dy} = U\left(\frac{2}{\delta} - \frac{6y^2}{\delta^3} + \frac{4y^3}{\delta^4}\right)$$

$$\therefore \qquad \tau_0 = \mu\left(\frac{du}{dy}\right)_{y=0} = \mu U\left(\frac{2}{\delta}\right) = \frac{2\mu U}{\delta} \qquad ...(13.26)$$

Equating the two values of τ_0 given by eqns. (13.25) and (13.26), we get:

$$\frac{37}{315}\rho U^2 \frac{d\delta}{dx} = \frac{2\mu U}{\delta}$$

or, $$\delta \cdot d\delta = \frac{315}{37} \times \frac{2\mu U}{\rho U^2} dx = \frac{630}{37}\frac{\mu}{\rho U} dx$$

Integrating both sides, we get:

$$\frac{\delta^2}{2} = \frac{630}{37}\frac{\mu}{\rho U} x + C$$

(where, C = constant of integration)

At, $x = 0, \delta = 0 \therefore C = 0$

$$\therefore \qquad \frac{\delta^2}{2} = \frac{630}{37}\frac{\mu}{\rho U} x$$

$$\therefore \qquad \delta = \sqrt{\frac{630 \times 2}{37}\frac{\mu}{\rho U}} x = 5.84\sqrt{\frac{\mu x}{\rho U}} = 5.84\sqrt{\frac{\mu x}{\rho U} \times \frac{x}{x}}$$

or, $$\boldsymbol{\delta} = 5.84\sqrt{\frac{\mu}{\rho U x}} \times x = \frac{\mathbf{5.84}\boldsymbol{x}}{\sqrt{\boldsymbol{Re_x}}} \qquad ...(13.27)$$

(*ii*) Shear stress, τ_0:

$$\tau_0 = \frac{2\mu U}{\delta}$$

But, $$\delta = \frac{5.84x}{\sqrt{Re_x}} \qquad ...[\text{Eqn. } (13.27)]$$

$$\therefore \qquad \boldsymbol{\tau_0} = \frac{2\mu U}{\frac{5.84x}{\sqrt{Re_x}}} = \frac{2\mu U}{5.84x}\sqrt{Re_x} = \mathbf{0.343}\frac{\boldsymbol{\mu U}}{\boldsymbol{x}}\sqrt{\boldsymbol{Re_x}} \qquad ...(13.28)$$

(*iii*) Local co-efficient of drag, C_D^*:

$$\tau_0 = 0.343\frac{\mu U}{x}\sqrt{Re_x}$$

Also, $$\tau_0 = C_D^* \frac{\rho U^2}{2}$$

$$\therefore \qquad C_D^* \frac{\rho U^2}{2} = 0.343\frac{\mu U}{x}\sqrt{Re_x}$$

or, $$\boldsymbol{C_D^*} = \frac{\mathbf{0.686}}{\sqrt{\boldsymbol{Re_x}}} \qquad ...(13.29)$$

(*iv*) Co-efficient of drag (C_D):

$$C_D = \frac{F_D}{\frac{1}{2}\rho A U^2} \qquad [\text{Eqn. } (13.10)]$$

where, $$F_D = \int_0^L \tau_0 \times B \times dx \qquad \text{[Eqn. (13.8)]}$$

$$= \int_0^L 0.343 \frac{\mu U}{x} \sqrt{Re_x} \times B \times dx = 0.343 \int_0^L \frac{\mu U}{x} \sqrt{\frac{\rho U x}{\mu}} \times B \times dx$$

$$= 0.343\, \mu U \sqrt{\frac{\rho U}{\mu}} \times B \int_0^L x^{-1/2}\, dx = 0.343\, \mu U \sqrt{\frac{\rho U}{\mu}} \times B \left[\frac{x^{1/2}}{1/2}\right]_0^L$$

$$= 0.343 \times 2\mu U \sqrt{\frac{\rho U}{\mu}} \times B \sqrt{L}$$

or, $$F_D = 0.686\, \mu U B \sqrt{\frac{\rho U L}{\mu}} \qquad \text{...(13.30)}$$

$$\therefore \quad C_D = \frac{0.686\, \mu U B \sqrt{\frac{\rho U L}{\mu}}}{\frac{1}{2} \rho A U^2} = \frac{0.686 \mu\, U B \sqrt{\frac{\rho U L}{\mu}}}{\frac{1}{2} \rho \times L \times B \times U^2}$$

(where, $A = L \times B$)

$$= 0.686 \times 2 \times \frac{\mu}{\rho U L} \times \sqrt{\frac{\rho U L}{\mu}} = 1.372 \frac{1}{\sqrt{\frac{\rho U L}{\mu}}}$$

or, $$\mathbf{C_D = \frac{1.372}{\sqrt{Re_L}}} \qquad \text{...(13.31)}$$

Case 4. *Velocity distribution* : $\frac{u}{U} = \sin\left(\frac{\pi}{2}\frac{y}{\delta}\right)$

(*i*) Boundary layer thickness, δ:

$$\frac{\tau_0}{\rho U^2} = \frac{d}{dx}\left[\int_0^\delta \frac{u}{U}\left(1 - \frac{u}{U}\right) dy\right] \qquad \text{[Eqn. (13.6)]}$$

Substituting the value of $\frac{u}{U}$, we get:

$$\frac{\tau_0}{\rho U^2} = \frac{d}{dx}\left[\int_0^\delta \sin\left(\frac{\pi}{2}\frac{y}{\delta}\right)\left\{1 - \sin\left(\frac{\pi}{2}\frac{y}{\delta}\right)\right\} dy\right]$$

$$= \frac{d}{dx}\left[\int_0^\delta \left\{\sin\left(\frac{\pi}{2}\frac{y}{\delta}\right) - \sin^2\left(\frac{\pi}{2}\frac{y}{\delta}\right)\right\} dy\right]$$

$$= \frac{d}{dx}\left[\int_0^\delta \left\{\sin\left(\frac{\pi}{2}\frac{y}{\delta}\right) - \frac{1 - \cos\left(\frac{\pi y}{\delta}\right)}{2}\right\} dy\right]$$

$$\left(\because \sin^2\theta = \frac{1 - \cos 2\theta}{2}\right)$$

$$= \frac{d}{dx}\left[\frac{-\cos\left(\frac{\pi y}{2\,\delta}\right)}{\frac{\pi}{2\delta}} - \frac{y}{2} + \frac{\sin\left(\frac{\pi y}{\delta}\right)}{\frac{\pi}{\delta}}\right]_0^\delta$$

$$= \frac{d}{dx}\left[\left\{\frac{-\cos\left(\frac{\pi\delta}{2\delta}\right)}{\frac{\pi}{2\delta}} + \frac{\cos\left(\frac{\pi}{2\delta}\times 0\right)}{\frac{\pi}{2\delta}}\right\} - \frac{\delta}{2} + \left\{\frac{\sin\left(\frac{\pi}{\delta}\times\delta\right)}{\frac{\pi}{\delta}} - \frac{\sin\left(\frac{\pi}{\delta}\times 0\right)}{\frac{\pi}{\delta}}\right\}\right]$$

$$= \frac{d}{dx}\left[\left(0 + \frac{1}{\frac{\pi}{2\delta}}\right) - \frac{\delta}{2} + 0\right] = \frac{d}{dx}\left(\frac{2\delta}{\pi} - \frac{\delta}{2}\right) = \left(\frac{4-\pi}{2\pi}\right)\frac{d\delta}{dx}$$

$$\therefore \quad \tau_0 = \left(\frac{4-\pi}{2\pi}\right)\rho U^2 \frac{d\delta}{dx} \qquad ...(13.32)$$

Also, $\tau_0 = \mu\left(\frac{du}{dy}\right)_{y=0}$

But, $u = U\left[\sin\left(\frac{\pi}{2}\frac{y}{\delta}\right)\right]$

and, $\frac{du}{dy} = U\left[\cos\left(\frac{\pi}{2}\frac{y}{\delta}\right)\right] \times \frac{\pi}{2\,\delta}$

$$\therefore \quad \tau_0 = \mu\left(\frac{du}{dy}\right)_{y=0} = \mu U\left[\cos\left(\frac{\pi}{2}\times\frac{0}{\delta}\right)\right] \times \frac{\pi}{2\delta} = \frac{\mu U \pi}{2\delta} \qquad ...(13.33)$$

Equating the two values of τ_0 given by eqns. (13.32) and (13.33), we get:

$$\left(\frac{4-\pi}{2\pi}\right)\rho U^2 \frac{d\delta}{dx} = \frac{\mu U \pi}{2\,\delta}$$

or, $$\delta \cdot d\delta = \frac{\mu U \pi}{2} \times \left(\frac{2\pi}{4-\pi}\right) \times \frac{1}{\rho U^2} \times dx = \frac{\pi^2}{(4-\pi)} \cdot \frac{\mu U}{\rho U^2} \cdot dx$$

or, $$\delta \cdot d\delta = 11.4975\,\frac{\mu}{\rho U}\,dx$$

Integrating both sides, we get:

$$\frac{\delta^2}{2} = 11.4975\,\frac{\mu}{\rho U}\,x + C$$

(where, C = constant of integration)

At, $x = 0, \delta = 0$ $\quad \therefore C = 0$

$$\therefore \quad \frac{\delta^2}{2} = 11.4975\,\frac{\mu}{\rho U}\,x$$

$$\therefore \qquad \delta = \sqrt{2 \times 11.4975 \times \frac{\mu}{\rho U}\, x} = 4.795\sqrt{\frac{\mu}{\rho U}\, x} = 4.795\sqrt{\frac{\mu}{\rho U x}} \times x$$

$$= \frac{\mathbf{4.795\, x}}{\sqrt{\boldsymbol{Re_x}}} \qquad ...(13.34)$$

(*ii*) **Shear stress, τ_0:**

$$\tau_0 = \frac{\mu U \pi}{2\delta}$$

But,
$$\delta = \frac{4.795x}{\sqrt{Re_x}} \qquad \text{[Eqn. (13.31)]}$$

$$\therefore \qquad \boldsymbol{\tau_0} = \frac{\mu U \pi}{2 \times \dfrac{4.795x}{\sqrt{Re_x}}} = \frac{\mu U \pi \sqrt{Re_x}}{2 \times 4.795x} = \mathbf{0.327}\, \frac{\boldsymbol{\mu U}}{\boldsymbol{x}} \sqrt{\boldsymbol{Re_x}} \qquad ...(13.35)$$

(*iii*) **Local co-efficient of drag, C_D:**

$$\tau_0 = 0.327\, \frac{\mu U}{x} \sqrt{Re_x}$$

Also,
$$\tau_0 = C_D^* \cdot \frac{\rho U^2}{2}$$

$$\therefore \qquad C_D^* \frac{\rho U^2}{2} = 0.327\, \frac{\mu U}{x} \sqrt{Re_x}$$

or,
$$\boldsymbol{C_D^*} = \frac{\mathbf{0.654}}{\sqrt{\boldsymbol{Re_x}}} \qquad ...(13.36)$$

(*iv*) **Co-efficient of drag, C_D:**

$$C_D = \frac{F_D}{\frac{1}{2}\rho A U^2} \qquad \text{[Eqn. (13.10)]}$$

where,
$$F_D = \int_0^L \tau_0 \times B \times dx \qquad \text{[Eqn. (13.8)]}$$

$$= \int_0^L 0.327\, \frac{\mu U}{x} \sqrt{Re_x} \times B \times dx = 0.327 \int_0^L \frac{\mu U}{x} \sqrt{\frac{\rho U x}{\mu}} \times B \times dx$$

$$= 0.327\, \mu U \sqrt{\frac{\rho U}{\mu}} \times B \int_0^L x^{-1/2}\, dx = 0.327\, \mu U \sqrt{\frac{\rho U}{\mu}} \times B \left[\frac{x^{1/2}}{1/2}\right]_0^L$$

$$= 0.327 \times 2\, \mu U \sqrt{\frac{\rho U}{\mu}} \times B \times \sqrt{L}$$

or,
$$F_D = 0.654\, \mu U B \sqrt{\frac{\rho U L}{\mu}} \qquad ...(13.37)$$

$$\therefore \qquad C_D = \frac{0.654\,\mu UB\sqrt{\frac{\rho UL}{\mu}}}{\frac{1}{2}\rho AU^2} = \frac{0.654\,\mu UB\sqrt{\frac{\rho UL}{\mu}}}{\frac{1}{2}\rho \times L \times B \times U^2} = 1.31\frac{\mu}{\rho LU}\sqrt{\frac{\rho UL}{\mu}}$$

(where, $A = L \times B$)

$$\text{or,} \qquad C_D = 1.31 \times \frac{1}{\sqrt{\frac{\rho UL}{\mu}}} = \frac{1.31}{\sqrt{Re_L}} \qquad \text{...(13.38)}$$

Table 13.1 shows the values of δ (boundary layer thickness), C_D^* (local co-efficient of drag), C_D (average co-efficient of drag) in terms of Reynolds number (Re) for various velocity profiles/ distributions.

Table 13.1. Values of δ, C_D^* and C_D in terms of Re

S. No.		δ	C_D^*	C_D
1.	$\frac{u}{U} = 2\left(\frac{y}{\delta}\right) - \left(\frac{y}{\delta}\right)^2$	$\frac{5.48x}{\sqrt{Re_x}}$	$\frac{0.73}{\sqrt{Re_x}}$	$\frac{1.46}{\sqrt{Re_L}}$
2.	$\frac{u}{U} = \frac{3}{2}\left(\frac{y}{\delta}\right) - \frac{1}{2}\left(\frac{y}{\delta}\right)^3$	$\frac{4.64x}{\sqrt{Re_x}}$	$\frac{0.646}{\sqrt{Re_x}}$	$\frac{1.292}{\sqrt{Re_L}}$
3.	$\frac{u}{U} = 2\left(\frac{y}{\delta}\right) - 2\left(\frac{y}{\delta}\right)^3 + \left(\frac{y}{\delta}\right)^4$	$\frac{5.84x}{\sqrt{Re_e}}$	$\frac{0.686}{\sqrt{Re_x}}$	$\frac{1.372}{\sqrt{Re_L}}$
4.	$\frac{u}{U} = \sin\left(\frac{\pi}{2}\frac{y}{\delta}\right)$	$\frac{4.795\,x}{\sqrt{Re_x}}$	$\frac{0.654}{\sqrt{Re_x}}$	$\frac{1.31\,x}{\sqrt{Re_L}}$
5.	Blasius results ($Re < 3.2 \times 10^5$)	$\frac{5x}{\sqrt{Re_x}}$	$\frac{0.664}{\sqrt{Re_x}}$	$\frac{1.328}{\sqrt{Re_L}}$

Example 13.10. *The boundary layer thickness at a distance of 1 m from the leading edge of a flat plate kept over zero angle of incidence to the flow direction is 1 mm. The velocity outside the boundary layer is 25 m/s. The boundary layer thickness at a distance of 4 m is (i) 4 mm, (ii) 2 mm, (iii) 1 mm*

Select the correct answer. Assume that the boundary layer is entirely laminar

[UPTU]

Solution. Free stream velocity, $U = 25$ m/s

The boundary layer thickness at $x_1 = 1$ m, $\delta_1 = 1$ mm

The boundary layer thickness at a distance of 4 m, δ_2:

Thickness of boundary layer is given by,

$$\delta = \frac{5x}{\sqrt{Re_x}} = \frac{5x}{\sqrt{\frac{Ux}{\nu}}} = 5\sqrt{\frac{\nu x}{U}}$$

$$\therefore \qquad \delta_1 = 5\sqrt{\frac{\nu x_1}{U}}$$

and,
$$\delta_2 = 5\sqrt{\frac{\nu x_2}{U}}$$

or,
$$\frac{\delta_1}{\delta_2} = \sqrt{\frac{x_1}{x_2}},$$

or,
$$\frac{1}{\delta_2} = \sqrt{1/4} \text{ or } \delta_2 = \mathbf{2\ mm\ (Ans.)}$$

Example 13.11. *A smooth plate 2 m wide and 2.5 m long is towed in oil (sp. gr. = 0.8) at a velocity of 1.5 m/s along its length. Find the thickness of boundary layer and shear stress at the trailing edge of the plate.* $\nu_{oil} = 10^{-4}$ *m^2/s.*

Solution. *Given* : $B = 2$ m; $L = 2.5$ m; Sp. gravity = 0.8; $U = 1.5$ m/s, $\nu_{oil} = 10^{-4}$ m^2/s.

Thickness of boundary layer, δ_L:

$$R_{eL} = \frac{UL}{\nu} = \frac{1.5 \times 2.5}{10^{-4}} = 37500$$

Since Re_L is less than 5×10^5, so the boundary layer at the trailing edge is *laminar*, and Blasius equation gives,

$$\delta_x = \frac{5x}{Re_x}$$

At the trailing edge $x = L$,

$$\therefore \quad \delta_L = \frac{5 \times 2.5}{\sqrt{37500}} = 0.0645 \text{ m } = \mathbf{64.55\ mm\ (Ans.)}$$

Shear stress at the trailing edge, τ_L:

According to Blasius average co-efficient of drag (C_D^*) is given by:

$$C_D^* = \frac{0.664}{\sqrt{Re_x}} = \frac{0.664}{\sqrt{Re_L}} = \frac{0.664}{\sqrt{37500}}$$

$$\therefore \quad \tau_L = C_D^* \times \frac{1}{2}\rho U^2$$

$$= \frac{0.664}{\sqrt{37500}} \times \frac{1}{2} \times (0.8 \times 1000) \times 1.5^2 = \mathbf{3.086\ N/m^2\ (Ans.)}$$

Example 13.12. *For the velocity profile in laminar boundary layer as,*

$$\frac{u}{U} = \frac{3}{2}\left(\frac{y}{\delta}\right) - \frac{1}{2}\left(\frac{y}{\delta}\right)^3$$

find the thickness of the boundary layer and the shear stress 1.5 m from the leading edge of a plate. The plate is 2 m long and 1.4 m wide and is placed in water which is moving with a velocity of 200 mm per second. Find the total drag force on the plate if μ for water = .01 poise.

(Delhi University)

Solution. *Given* : $x = 1.5$ m; $L = 2$ m; $B = 1.4$ m; $U = 200$ mm/s = 0.2 m/s;

$$\mu = 0.01 \text{ poise} = \frac{0.01}{10} = 0.001 \text{ Ns/m}^2.$$

Velocity profile:
$$\frac{u}{U} = \frac{3}{2}\left(\frac{y}{\delta}\right) - \frac{1}{2}\left(\frac{y}{\delta}\right)^3$$

For the given profile, $\delta = \frac{4.64x}{\sqrt{Re_x}}$ ...[Eqn. (13.20)]

$$\left[\text{Here, } Re_x = \frac{\rho U x}{\mu} = \frac{1000 \times 0.2 \times 1.5}{0.001} = 3 \times 10^5 \right]$$

$$\delta = \frac{4.64 \times 1.5}{\sqrt{3 \times 10^5}} = 0.0127 \text{ m} = \mathbf{12.7 \text{ mm}} \textbf{ (Ans.)}$$

Shear stress (τ_0) is given by,

$$\tau_0 = 0.323 \frac{\mu U}{x} \sqrt{R_{ex}}$$ ...[Eqn. (3.21)]

or

$$\tau_0 = 0.323 \times \frac{0.001 \times 0.2}{1.5} \times \sqrt{3 \times 10^5} = \mathbf{0.0236 \text{ N/m}^2} \textbf{ (Ans.)}$$

Drag force (F_0) on one side of the plate is given as:

$$F_D = 0.646 \mu U \sqrt{\frac{\rho U L}{\mu}} \times B$$ ...[Eqn. (13.23)]

$$= 0.646 \times 0.001 \times 0.2 \sqrt{\frac{1000 \times 0.2 \times 2}{0.001}} \times 1.4 = 0.114 \text{ N}$$

∴ **Total Drag force** = Drag force on both sides of the plate = 2 × 0.114 = **0.228 N (Ans.)**

Example 13.13. *A plate 450 mm × 150 mm has been placed longitudinally in a stream of crude oil (specific gravity 0.925 and kinematic viscosity of 0.9 stoke) which flows with velocity of 6 m/s. Calculate:*

(i) *The friction drag on the plate,*

(ii) *Thickness of the boundary layer at the trailing edge, and*

(iii) *Shear stress at the trailing edge.* **[PTU]**

Solution. Length of the plate, L = 450 mm = 0.45 m

Width of the plate, B = 150 mm = 0.15 m

Specific gravity of oil, S = 0.925

Kinematic viscosity of oil, ν = 0.9 stoke = 0.9×10^{-4} m²/s

Velocity of oil, U = 6 m/s

(*i*) The friction drag on the plate, F_D:

Reynolds number at the end of plate,

$$Re_L = \frac{UL}{\nu} = \frac{6 \times 0.45}{0.9 \times 10^{-4}} = 30000$$

Since $Re_L < 5 \times 10^5$, the flow over the plate is *entirely laminar.*

∴ Average co-efficient of drag,

$$C_D = \frac{1.328}{\sqrt{Re_L}} = \frac{1.328}{\sqrt{30000}} = 0.007667$$

Drag on the *one side* of the plate,

$$F_D = C_D \times \frac{1}{2} \rho A U^2 = 0{\cdot}007667 \times \frac{1}{2} \times (0.925 \times 1000) \times (0.45 \times 0{\cdot}15) \times 6^2$$

(where, A = area of the plate)

$$= \mathbf{8.62\ N\ (Ans.)}$$

(*ii*) The thickness of boundary layer at the trailing edge, δ:

The thickness of boundary in the laminar range is given by,

$$\delta = \frac{5x}{\sqrt{Re_x}}$$

∴ Thickness at the trailing edge ($x = 0.45$ m),

$$\delta = \frac{5 \times 0.45}{\sqrt{30000}} = 0.013 \text{ m} = \mathbf{13\ mm\ (Ans.)}$$

(*iii*) Shear stress at the trailing edge, τ_0:

$$\text{Local co-efficient of drag, } C_D^* = \frac{0.664}{\sqrt{Re_x}} = \frac{0.664}{\sqrt{30000}} = 0.00383$$

By definition,

$$C_D^* = \frac{\tau_0}{\frac{1}{2}\rho U^2}$$

$$\therefore \quad \tau_0 = C_D^* \times \frac{1}{2}\rho U^2 = 0.00383 \times \frac{1}{2} \times (0.925 \times 1000) \times 6^2$$

$$= \mathbf{63.77\ N/m^2\ (Ans.)}$$

Example 13.14. *The velocity profile for laminar boundary is in the form given below:*

$$\frac{u}{U} = 2\left(\frac{y}{\delta}\right) - \left(\frac{y}{\delta}\right)^2$$

Find the thickness of boundary layer at the end of the plate and the drag force on one side of a plate 1.5 m long and 1 m wide when placed in water flowing with a velocity of 0.12 m/s. Calculate the value of co-efficient of drag also.

Take μ for water = 0.001 Ns/m²

Solution. Velocity distribution $\frac{u}{U} = 2\left(\frac{y}{\delta}\right) - \left(\frac{y}{\delta}\right)^2$ ...(*i*) (*Given*)

The length of the plate, L = 1.5 m

The width of the plate, B = 1 m

Free stream velocity, U = 0.12 m/s.

μ for water = 0.001 Ns/m²

Thickness of the boundary layer, δ:

Reynolds number at the end of the plate (*i.e.* at a distance of 1.5 m from the leading edge) is given by,

$$Re_L = \frac{\rho UL}{\mu} = \frac{1000 \times 0.12 \times 1.5}{0.001} = 180000$$

Since $Re_L < 5 \times 10^5$, therefore, this is the case of *laminar* boundary layer. Thickness of boundary layer at a distance of 1.5 m is given by:

$$\delta = \frac{5.48x}{\sqrt{Re_x}} \qquad \text{...[Eqn. (13.13)]}$$

$$= \frac{5.48 \times 1.5}{\sqrt{180000}} = 0.01937 \text{ m} \quad \text{or} \quad \mathbf{19.37\ mm\ (Ans.)}$$

Drag force on one side of the plate, F_D:

$$F_D = 0.73\,\mu UB\sqrt{\frac{\rho UL}{\mu}} \qquad \text{...[Eqn. (13.16)]}$$

$$= 0.73 \times 0.001 \times 0.12 \times 1 \times \sqrt{\frac{1000 \times 0.12 \times 1.5}{0.001}} = \mathbf{0.0372\ N\ (Ans.)}$$

Co-efficient of drag, C_D:

$$= \frac{1.46}{\sqrt{R_{eL}}} = \frac{1.46}{\sqrt{180000}} = \mathbf{0.00344\ (Ans.)} \qquad \text{...[Eqn. (13.17)]}$$

Example 13.15. *Air is flowing over a smooth flat plate with a velocity of 12 m/s. The velocity profile is in the form:*

$$\frac{u}{U} = 2\left(\frac{y}{\delta}\right) - \left(\frac{y}{\delta}\right)^2$$

The length of the plate is 1.1 m and width 0.9 m. If laminar boundary layer exists upto a value of Re = 2×10^5 and kinematic viscosity of air is 0.15 stoke, find:

(i) The maximum distance from the leading edge upto which laminar boundary layer exists, and

(ii) The maximum thickness of boundary layer.

Solution. Velocity distribution: $\frac{u}{U} = 2\left(\frac{y}{\delta}\right) - \left(\frac{y}{\delta}\right)^2$

Velocity of air, U = 12 m/s

Length of plate, L = 1.1 m

Width of plate, B = 0.9 m

Reynolds number upto which laminar boundary exists, $Re = 2 \times 10^5$

Kinematic viscosity of air, ν = 0.15 stokes = 0.15×10^{-4} m²/s

(i) The maximum distance from the leading edge upto which laminar boundary layer exists, x:

$$R_{e_x} = \frac{Ux}{\nu} \quad \text{or} \quad 2 \times 10^5 = \frac{12 \times x}{0.15 \times 10^{-4}}$$

or,

$$x = \frac{2 \times 10^5 \times 0.15 \times 10^{-4}}{12} = \mathbf{0.25\ m\ (Ans.)}$$

(ii) The maximum thickness of boundary layer, δ

For the given velocity profile, the maximum thickness of boundary layer is given by:

$$\delta = \frac{5.48x}{\sqrt{Re_x}} \qquad \text{...[Eqn. (13.13)]}$$

$$= \frac{5.48 \times 0.25}{\sqrt{2 \times 10^5}} = 0.00306\ \text{m or } \mathbf{3.06\ mm\ (Ans.)}$$

Example 13.16. *Atmospheric air at 20°C is flowing parallel to a flat plate at a velocity of 2.8 m/s. Assuming cubic velocity profile and using exact Blasius solution estimate the boundary layer thickness and the local co-efficient of drag (or skin friction) at x = 1.2 m from the leading edge of the plate. Also find the deviation of the approximate solution from the exact solution.*

Take the kinematic viscosity of air at 20°C = 15.4×10^{-6} m²/s.

Solution. Velocity of air, $U = 2.8$ m/s

Distance from the leading edge of the plate, $x = 1.2$ m

$$\text{Reynolds number, } R_{e_x} = \frac{Ux}{\nu} = \frac{2.8 \times 1.2}{15.4 \times 10^{-6}} = 2.18 \times 10^5$$

Blasius solution:

$$\text{Boundary layer thickness, } \delta = \frac{5x}{\sqrt{R_{ex}}} = \frac{5 \times 1.2}{\sqrt{2.18 \times 10^5}} = 0.01285 \text{ m} = \mathbf{12.85\ mm\ (Ans.)}$$

$$\text{Local co-efficient of drag, } C_D^* = \frac{0.664}{\sqrt{R_{ex}}} = \frac{0.664}{\sqrt{2.18 \times 10^5}} = 0.001422$$

Approximate solution (*with assumption of cubic velocity profile*):

$$\delta = \frac{4.64x}{\sqrt{R_{ex}}} = \frac{4.64 \times 1.2}{\sqrt{2.18 \times 10^5}} = 0.0119 \text{ m} = 11.92 \text{ mm}$$

$$C_D^* = \frac{0.646}{\sqrt{R_{ex}}} = \frac{0.646}{\sqrt{2.18 \times 10^5}} = 0.001383$$

The approximate solution deviates from the exact solution by:

$$\textbf{Deviation for } \delta\textbf{:} \ \frac{12.85 - 11.92}{12.85} \times 100 = \mathbf{7.24\%\ (Ans.)}$$

$$\textbf{Deviation for } C_D^* = \frac{0.001422 - 0.001383}{0.001422} \times 100 = \mathbf{2.74\%\ (Ans.)}$$

Example 13.17. *Air is flowing over a flat plate 5 m long and 2.5 m wide with a velocity of 4 m/s at 15°C. If $\rho = 1.208$ kg/m^3 and $\nu = 1.47 \times 10^{-5}$ m^2/s, calculate:*

(*i*) *Length of plate over which the boundary layer is laminar, and thickness of the boundary layer (laminar),*

(*ii*) *Shear stress at the location where boundary layer ceases to be laminar, and*

(*iii*) *Total drag force on both sides on that portion of plate where boundary layer is laminar.*

Solution. Length of the plate, $L = 5$ m

Width of the plate, $B = 2.5$ m

Velocity of air, $U = 4$ m/s

Density of air, $\rho = 1.208$ kg/m^3

Kinematic viscosity of air, $\nu = 1.47 \times 10^{-5}$ m^2/s

(*i*) Length of plate over which the boundary layer is laminar:

$$\text{Reynolds number, } R_{e_L} = \frac{UL}{\nu} = \frac{4 \times 5}{1.47 \times 10^{-5}} = 1.361 \times 10^6$$

Hence on the front portion, boundary layer is laminar and on the rear, it is turbulent.

$$R_{e_x} = \frac{Ux}{\nu} = 5 \times 10^5$$

$$\therefore \quad \frac{4 \times x}{1.47 \times 10^{-5}} = 5 \times 10^5$$

or $$x = \frac{5 \times 10^5 \times 1.47 \times 10^{-5}}{4} = 1.837 \text{ m}$$

Hence the boundary layer is **laminar on 1.837 m length of the plate. (Ans.)**

Thickness of the boundary layer (laminar), δ

$$\delta = \frac{5x}{\sqrt{Re_x}} = \frac{5 \times 1.837}{\sqrt{5 \times 10^5}} = 0.01299 \text{ m or } \mathbf{12.99 \text{ mm (Ans.)}}$$

(*ii*) Shear stress at the location where boundary layer ceases to be laminar, τ_0:

Local co-efficient of drag, $C_d^* = \frac{0.664}{\sqrt{5 \times 10^5}} = 0.000939$

$$\therefore \quad = C_D^* \times \frac{1}{2}\rho U^2 = 0.000939 \times \frac{1}{2} \times 1.208 \times 4^2 = \mathbf{0.00907 \text{ N/m}^2 \text{ (Ans.)}}$$

(*iii*) Total drag force on both sides of plate, F_D:

$$F_D = 2 \times C_D \times \frac{1}{2} \times \rho A U^2$$

where, C_D = Average co-efficient of drag $= \frac{1.328}{\sqrt{5 \times 10^5}} = 1.878 \times 10^{-3}$

and, A = Area of the plate $= 1.837 \times 2.5 = 4.59 \text{ m}^2$

$$\therefore \quad F_D = 2 \times 1.878 \times 10^{-3} \times \frac{1}{2} \times 1.208 \times 4.59 \times 4^2 = \mathbf{0.167 \text{ N (Ans.)}}$$

Example 13.18. *Air flows over a plate 0·5 m long and 0·6 m wide with a velocity of 4 m/s. The velocity profile is in the form.*

$$\frac{u}{U} = \sin\left(\frac{\pi}{2}\frac{y}{\delta}\right)$$

If $\rho = 1.24$ kg/m^3 and $\nu = 0.15 \times 10^{-4}$ m^2/s, calculate:

(*i*) *Boundary layer thickness at the end of the plate,*

(*ii*) *Shear stress at 250 mm from the leading edge, and*

(*iii*) *Drag force on one side of the plate.* **[Delhi University]**

Solution. Length of plate, $L = 0.5$ m

Width of plate, $B = 0.6$ m

Velocity of air, $U = 4$ m/s

Density of air, $\rho = 1.24$ kg/m^3

Kinematic viscosity of air, $\nu = 0.15 \times 10^{-4}$ m^2/s

Velocity profile : $$\frac{u}{U} = \sin\left(\frac{\pi}{2}\frac{y}{\delta}\right)$$

(*i*) Boundary layer thickness at the end of the plate, δ:

Reynolds number, $Re_x = \frac{Ux}{\nu} = \frac{4 \times 0.5}{0.15 \times 10^{-4}} = 1.33 \times 10^5$

Since $Re_x < 5 \times 10^5$, therefore, the boundary layer is *laminar over the entire length of the plate.*

We know, $$\delta = \frac{4.795x}{\sqrt{Re_x}} = \frac{4.795L}{\sqrt{Re_x}} = \frac{4.795 \times 0.5}{\sqrt{1.33 \times 10^5}}$$

$$= 0.00657 \text{ m} = \mathbf{6.57 \text{ mm (Ans.)}}$$

(*ii*) Shear stress at 250 mm from the leading edge, τ_0:

$$\tau_0 = C_D^* \times \frac{\rho U^2}{2} \quad \text{...[Eqn. (13.9)]}$$

But,
$$C_D^* = \frac{0.654}{\sqrt{Re_x}} = \frac{0.654}{\sqrt{\frac{Ux}{\nu}}} = \frac{0.654}{\sqrt{\frac{4 \times 0.25}{0.15 \times 10^{-4}}}} = 0.002533$$

$$\therefore \quad (\tau_0)_{x = 0.25 \text{ m}} = 0.002533 \times \frac{1.24 \times 4^2}{2} = \mathbf{0.025 \text{ N/m}^2 \text{ (Ans.)}}$$

(*iii*) Drag force on one side of the plate, F_D:

$$F_D = C_D \times \frac{1}{2} \rho A U^2$$

where,
$$C_D = \frac{1.31}{\sqrt{R_{eL}}} = \frac{1.31}{\sqrt{1.33 \times 10^5}} = 0.003592$$

and, A = area of the plate $= L \times B = 0.5 \times 0.6 = 0.3 \text{ m}^2$

$$\therefore \quad F_D = 0.003592 \times \frac{1}{2} \times 1.24 \times 0.3 \times 4^2 = \mathbf{0.01069 \text{ N (Ans.)}}$$

Example 13.19. *Find the ratio of friction drag on the front half and rear half of the flat plate kept at zero incidence in a stream of uniform velocity, if the boundary layer is laminar over the whole plate.*

Solution. Let, L = Length of the plate,

U = Velocity of the fluid, and

ν = Kinematic viscosity of the fluid.

Ratio of friction drag on the front half and rear half, $\frac{F_{D_1}}{F_{D_2}}$:

Reynolds number of whole plate $= \frac{UL}{\nu}$

Reynolds number for the front half $= \frac{UL}{2\nu}$

Average co-efficient of drag for total plate, $C_D = \frac{1.328}{\sqrt{\frac{UL}{\nu}}}$

$$\therefore \quad C_{D_1} \text{ for front half} = \frac{1.328}{\sqrt{\frac{UL}{2\nu}}} = \frac{1.328 \times \sqrt{2}}{\sqrt{\frac{UL}{\nu}}} = \frac{1.878}{\sqrt{\frac{UL}{\nu}}}$$

Friction drag on total plate,
$$F_D = C_D \times \frac{1}{2} \rho A U^2 = C_D \times \frac{1}{2} \rho \times LBU^2$$

$$= \frac{1.328}{\sqrt{\frac{UL}{\nu}}} \times \frac{1}{2} \rho LBU^2 = \frac{0.664}{\sqrt{\frac{UL}{\nu}}} \times \rho LBU^2$$

Friction drag on front half, $F_{D_1} = C_{D_1} \times \frac{1}{2} \rho A U^2 = C_{D_1} \times \frac{1}{2} \rho \times \frac{L}{2} BU^2$

$$= \frac{1.878}{\sqrt{\frac{UL}{\nu}}} \times \frac{1}{4} \times LBU^2 = \frac{0.4695}{\sqrt{\frac{UL}{\nu}}} \times \rho LBU^2$$

∴ Friction drag on rear half, $F_{D_2} = F_D - F_{D_1}$

$$= \frac{0.664}{\sqrt{\frac{UL}{\nu}}} \times \rho LBU^2 - \frac{0.4695}{\sqrt{\frac{UL}{\nu}}} \times \rho LBU^2$$

$$= \frac{0.1945}{\sqrt{\frac{UL}{\nu}}} \times \rho LBU^2$$

∴ Ratio, $\frac{F_{D_1}}{F_{D_2}} = \frac{\frac{0.4695}{\sqrt{UL/\nu}} \times \rho LBU^2}{\frac{0.1945}{\sqrt{UL/\nu}} \times \rho LBU^2} = \mathbf{2.414}$ **(Ans.)**

Example 13.20. *Air at standard conditions is flowing over a flat plate which is 1 m long and 0.3 m wide. The flow is uniform at the leading edge of the plate. The velocity profile in the boundary layer is assumed to be* $\frac{u}{U} = 2\left(\frac{y}{\delta}\right) - \left(\frac{y}{\delta}\right)^2$ *as the free stream velocity is U = 30 m/s. Assume that the flow conditions are independent of Z. Using control volume abcd, shown by dashed line, calculate the mass flow rate across the surface ab. [Density of air may be taken as 1.23 kg/m³, refer to Fig. 13.5]* **(GATE)**

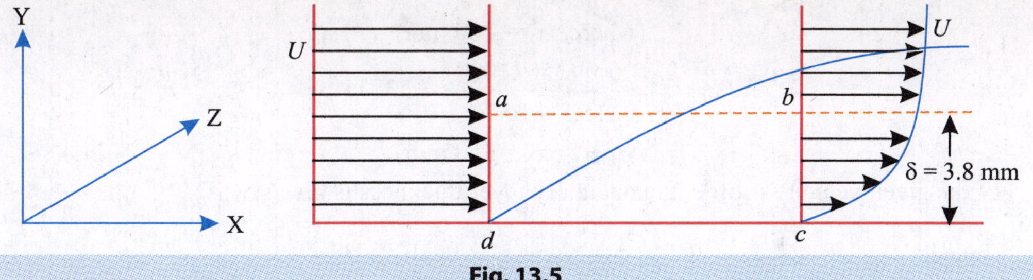

Fig. 13.5

Solution. By continuity equation for a volume *abcd*,

{Mass rate of flow across '*ad*' – mass rate of flow across '*bc*'} = mass rate of flow across '*ab*'.

$$= \rho U \times 3.8 \times 10^{-3} \times 0.3 - \rho U \times 0.3 \times \int_0^{\infty} \left\{ 2\left(\frac{y}{\delta}\right) - \left(\frac{y}{\delta}\right)^2 \right\} dy$$

$$= \rho U \times 3.8 \times 10^{-3} \times 0.3 - \rho U \times 0.3 \left[\frac{2}{\delta} \cdot \frac{y^2}{2} - \frac{y^3}{3\delta^2} \right]_0^{\delta}$$

$$= \rho U \times 3.8 \times 10^{-3} \times 0.3 - \rho U \times 0.3 \left[\delta - \frac{\delta}{3} \right]_0^{3.8 \times 10^{-3}}$$

$$= \rho U \times 3.8 \times 10^{-3} \times 0.3 \left(1 - \frac{2}{3} \right)$$

$$= 1.23 \times 30 \times 3.8 \times 10^{-3} \times 0.3 \times 0.3333 = \mathbf{0.014\ kg/s}\ \textbf{(Ans.)}$$

Example 13.21. *Air at 20°C and 1 bar flows over a flat plate at 1.5 m/s. The velocity profile for the laminar boundary layer is in the form*

$$\frac{u}{U} = \frac{3}{2}\left(\frac{y}{\delta}\right) - \frac{1}{2}\left(\frac{y}{\delta}\right)^3$$

If the kinematic viscosity of air at 20°C = 15.5 × 10^{-6} m²/s, calculate:

(i) *The boundary layer thickness at distances of 200 mm and 350 mm, and*

(ii) *The mass entrainment between the above two sections.*

Solution. Temperature of air, $T = 20 + 273 = 293\ K$

Pressure of air, $p = 1 \text{ bar} = 1 \times 10^5 \text{ N/m}^2$

Velocity of air, $U = 1.5$ m/s

Kinematic viscosity of air, $\nu = 15.5 \times 10^{-6} \text{ m}^2/\text{s}$

We know that, $pV = mRT$

or, $$p = \frac{m}{V}RT = \rho RT$$

∴ $$\rho = \frac{p}{RT} = \frac{1 \times 10^5}{287 \times 293} = 1.189 \text{ kg/m}^3$$

(The characteristic gas constant, $R = 287$ J/kg K)

(*i*) The boundary layer thickness (at x = 200 mm and x = 350 mm) δ_1, δ_2:

The Reynolds number, $$Re_x = \frac{Ux}{\nu}$$

∴ $$Re_{x_1} = \frac{1.5 \times (200/1000)}{15.5 \times 10^{-6}} = 19355$$

(where, $x_1 = 200$ mm)

$$Re_{x_2} = \frac{1.5 \times (350/1000)}{15.5 \times 10^{-6}} = 33871$$

(where, $x_2 = 350$ mm)

For the given velocity profile, the boundary layer thickness is given by:

$$\delta = \frac{4.64x}{\sqrt{Re_x}}$$

∴ $$\delta_1 = \frac{4.64 \times 200}{\sqrt{Re_{x_1}}} = \frac{4.64 \times 200}{\sqrt{19355}} = \textbf{6.67 mm} \quad \textbf{(Ans.)}$$

and, $$\delta_2 = \frac{4.64 \times 300}{\sqrt{Re_{x_2}}} = \frac{4.64 \times 300}{\sqrt{33871}} = \textbf{8.824 mm} \quad \textbf{(Ans.)}$$

(*ii*) The mass entrainment between the two sections:

The mass flow in the boundary layer, at any position, is given by the integral

$$m_x = \int_0^\delta \rho u\,dy \qquad \text{...}(i)$$

Also, $$u = U\left[\frac{3}{2}\left(\frac{y}{\delta}\right) - \frac{1}{2}\left(\frac{y}{\delta}\right)^3\right]$$

(From the given velocity profile)

Substituting the value of u in eqn. (i) and integrating, we get:

$$m_x = \int_0^\delta \rho \left[U \left\{ \frac{3y}{2\delta} - \frac{1}{2}\frac{y^3}{\delta^3} \right\} \right] dy = \rho U \left[\frac{3}{2} \times \frac{y^2}{2\delta} - \frac{1}{2} \times \frac{y^4}{4\,\delta^3} \right]_0^\delta$$

$$= \rho U \left[\frac{3}{4} \times \frac{\delta^2}{\delta} - \frac{1}{8} \times \frac{\delta^4}{\delta^3} \right] = \rho U \left(\frac{3}{4}\delta - \frac{1}{8}\delta \right) = \frac{5}{8} \rho U \delta$$

∴ The mass entrainment between the two sections

$$= \frac{5}{8} \rho U (\delta_2 - \delta_1) = \frac{5}{8} \times 1.189 \times 1.5 \,(8.824 \times 10^{-3} - 6.67 \times 10^{-3})$$

$= 0.0024$ kg/s or **8.64 kg/h (Ans.)**

Example 13.22. **(*a*)** *Water flows over a flat plate at a free stream velocity of 0.15 m/s. There is no pressure gradient and laminar boundary layer at a location is 6 mm thick. Assume a sinusoidal velocity profile given by*

$$\frac{u}{U} = \sin \frac{\pi}{2}\left(\frac{y}{\delta}\right)$$

where, δ is the boundary layer thickness, U is the free stream velocity, and u is the velocity at a distance y from the wall. Calculate the local shear stress and the skin friction co-efficient on the plate if

$$\mu = 1.02 \times 10^{-3} \text{ Ns/m}^2$$

$$\rho = 1000 \text{ kg/m}^3.$$

(*b*) *During flow over a flat plate, the laminar boundary layer undergoes a transition to turbulent boundary layer as the flow proceeds in the downstream. If the 1/7th power law turbulent velocity profile at a section is given by*

$$\frac{\bar{u}}{U} = \left(\frac{y}{\delta}\right)^{1/7} = (\eta)^{1/7}$$

find out the momentum flux within the turbulent boundary layer. The width of the boundary layer is a. The boundary layer thickness is δ. **(Delhi University)**

Solution. (*a*) *Given* : $U = 0.15$ m/s; $\delta = 6$ mm $= 0.006$ m; $\mu = 1.02 \times 10^{-3}$; $\rho = 1000$ kg/m³

Velocity profile: $$\frac{u}{U} = \sin\left[\frac{\pi}{2}\left(\frac{y}{\delta}\right)\right]$$

Local shear stress, τ_0:

From the given profile, we have:

$$u = U \sin\left[\frac{\pi}{2}\left(\frac{y}{\delta}\right)\right]$$

Differenting the above equation *w.r.t y*, we have:

$$\frac{du}{dy} = U \cos\left[\frac{\pi}{2}\left(\frac{y}{\delta}\right)\right] \times \frac{\pi}{2\delta}$$

Local shear stress, $$\tau_0 = \mu \left.\frac{du}{dy}\right|_{y=0}$$

or, $$\tau_0 = \mu U \frac{\pi}{2\delta} = \frac{(1.02 \times 10^{-3}) \times 0.15 \times \pi}{2 \times 0.006} = \mathbf{0.04\ N/m^2}\ \textbf{(Ans.)}$$

Skin friction co-efficient, C_D^*

$$C_D^* = \frac{\tau_0}{\frac{1}{2}\rho U^2} \quad \text{...[Eqn. (13.9)]}$$

$$= \frac{0.04}{\frac{1}{2} \times 1000 \times (0.15)^2} = \mathbf{0.00356}\ \textbf{(Ans.)}$$

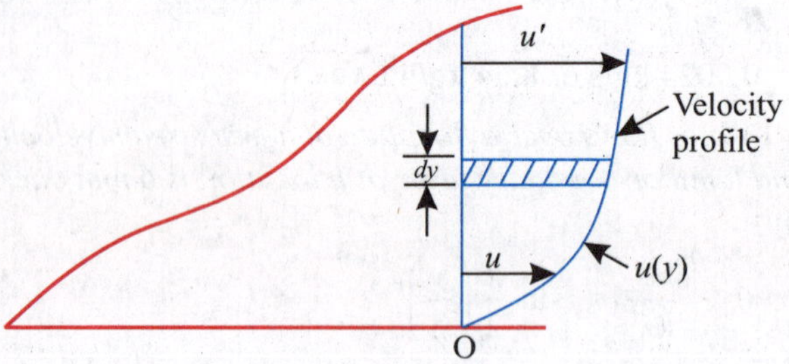

Fig. 13.6

(*b*) *Given:* Velocity profile: $\frac{u}{U} = \left(\frac{y}{\delta}\right)^{1/7}$; width of boundary layer = a; thickness of boundary layer = δ.

Momentum flux within the turbulent boundary layer:

$$\text{The momentum flux} = \int_0^\delta \text{(Mass flow through the strip } dy) \times u$$

$$= \int_0^\delta (\rho a\, dy \,.\, u)\, u = a\rho \int_0^\delta u^2 \,.\, dy = a\rho \left[\int_0^\delta U \left(\frac{y}{\delta}\right)^{1/7}\right]^2 dy$$

$$= a\rho U^2 \int_0^\delta \left(\frac{y}{\delta}\right)^{2/7} dy = a\rho \frac{U^2}{(\delta)^{2/7}} \left[\frac{(y)^{\frac{2}{7}+1}}{\left(\frac{2}{7}+1\right)}\right]_0^\delta$$

$$= \frac{a\rho U^2}{(\delta)^{2/7}} \times \frac{(\delta)^{2/7+1}}{\left(\frac{9}{7}\right)} = \frac{\mathbf{7}}{\mathbf{9}}\, \boldsymbol{a\rho U^2 \delta}\ \textbf{(Ans.)}$$

Example 13.23. *A plate 25 m long × 1.25 m wide is moving under water in the direction of its length. The drag force on the two sides of the plate is estimated to be 8500 N. Calculate:*

(*i*) *The velocity of the plate,*

(*ii*) *The boundary layer thickness at the trailing edge of the plate, and*

(*iii*) *The distance x_c at which the laminar boundary layer existing at the leading edge transforms into turbulent boundary layer. Take for water: $\rho = 1000\ kg/m^3$; $\nu = 1 \times 10^{-6}\ m^2/s$.*

Solution. Length of the plate, $L = 25$ m

Width of the plate, $B = 1.25$ m

Drag force on the two sides of the plate, $F_D = 8500\ N$

Density of water, $\rho = 1000\ \text{kg/m}^3$

Kinematic viscosity of water, $\nu = 1 \times 10^{-6}\ \text{m}^2/\text{s}$

(*i*) Velocity of the plate, U:

Since U is not known, Re_L cannot be computed. Hence assume any reasonable value of C_D between 0.005 and 0.001. Let us assume $C_D = 0.002$.

$$\text{Drag force (both sides), } F_D = C_D \times \frac{1}{2}\rho A U^2 = C_D \times \frac{1}{2}\rho\,(2 \times L \times B)\,U^2$$

$$8500 = C_D \times \frac{1}{2} \times 1000 \times (2 \times 25 \times 1.25)\,U^2$$

or,
$$U^2 = \frac{0.272}{C_D} = \frac{0.272}{0.002} = 136$$

$$\therefore \quad U = 11.66\ \text{m/s}$$

Reynolds number,
$$Re_L = \frac{UL}{\nu} = \frac{11.66 \times 25}{1 \times 10^{-6}} = 291.5 \times 10^6 \text{ (turbulent range assumed)}$$

$$C_D = \frac{0.455}{[\log_{10}(291.5 \times 10^6)]^{2.58}} = 0.00184$$

Thus recalculation gives: $U^2 = \dfrac{0.272}{0.00184} = 14782$ or $U = 12.16$ m/s

By another trial, we get:

$$Re_L = \frac{12.16 \times 25}{1 \times 10^{-6}} = 304 \times 10^6$$

$$C_D = \frac{0.455}{[\log_{10}(304 \times 10^6)]^{2.58}} = 0.001829$$

$$U^2 = \frac{0.272}{0.001829} = 148.715 \quad \text{or} \quad U = 1219 \text{ m/s}$$

i.e., $U = 12.19$ m/s *which is within reasonable accuracy.*

(*ii*) The boundary layer thickness, δ:

The thickness of boundary layer for turbulent flow is given by eqn. (13.43),

$$\delta = \frac{0.371L}{(R_{eL})^{1/5}} = \frac{0.371 \times 25}{(304 \times 10^6)^{1/5}} = \mathbf{0.1865\ m\ (Ans.)}$$

(*iii*) The distance, x_c:

Transition from laminar to turbulent boundary may be assumed to occur at

$$(Re)x_c = 5 \times 10^5$$

$$(Re)x_c = \frac{Ux_c}{\nu} = 5 \times 10^5$$

$$\therefore \quad x_c = \frac{5 \times 10^5 \times \nu}{U} = \frac{5 \times 10^5 \times 1 \times 10^{-6}}{12.19} = 0.041 \text{ m or } \mathbf{41\ mm\ (Ans.)}$$

13.5. TURBULENT BOUNDARY LAYER

As compared to laminar boundary layers, the turbulent boundary layers are *thicker*. Further in a turbulent boundary layer the velocity distribution is much more *uniform*, than in a laminar boundary layer, due to intermingling of fluid particles between different layers of the fluid. The velocity distribution in a turbulent boundary layer follows a logarithmic law *i.e.* $u \sim \log y$, which can also be represented by a *power law of the type,*

$$\frac{u}{U} = \left(\frac{y}{\delta}\right)^n \qquad ...(13.39)$$

where, $n = \frac{1}{7}$ (approx.) for $Re < 10^7$ but $> 5 \times 10^5$

$$\therefore \quad \frac{u}{U} = \left(\frac{y}{\delta}\right)^{1/7} \qquad ...(13.40)$$

This is known as **one-seventh power law.**

The eqn. (13·40), however, cannot be applied at the boundary itself because at $y = 0, \left(\frac{\delta u}{\delta y}\right) = \frac{1}{7} U\delta^{-1/7}\, y^{-6/7} = \infty$. This difficulty is circumvented by considering the *velocity in the viscous laminar sublayer to be linear* and *tangential to the seventh-root profile* at the point, where the laminar sublayer merges with the turbulent part of the boundary layer.

Blasius suggested the following relation for viscous shear stress:

$$\tau_0 = 0.0226\, \rho U^2 \left(\frac{\mu}{\rho U \delta}\right)^{1/4} \qquad ...(13·41)$$

(for Re ranging from 5×10^5 to 10^7)

Let us now find the values of δ, τ_0, C_D^*, F_D and C_d for the velocity distribution given by eqn. (13.40) $\left[i.e.\ \frac{u}{U} = \left(\frac{y}{\delta}\right)^{1/7} \right]$

(*i*) Boundary layer thickness, δ:

Substituting the value of $\frac{u}{U}$ in Von Karman integral eqn. (13.6), we have:

$$\frac{\tau_0}{\rho U^2} = \frac{d}{dx}\left[\int_0^\delta \frac{u}{U}\left(1 - \frac{u}{U}\right) dy\right]$$

$$= \frac{d}{dx}\left[\int_0^\delta \left\{\left(\frac{y}{\delta}\right)^{1/7}\left[1 - \left(\frac{y}{\delta}\right)^{1/7}\right]\right\} dy\right]$$

$$= \frac{d}{dx}\left[\int_0^\delta \left\{\left(\frac{y}{\delta}\right)^{1/7} - \left(\frac{y}{\delta}\right)^{2/7}\right\} dy\right]$$

$$= \frac{d}{dx}\left[\frac{7}{8}\frac{y^{8/7}}{\delta^{1/7}} - \frac{7}{9}\frac{y^{9/7}}{\delta^{2/7}}\right]_0^\delta = \frac{d}{dx}\left[\frac{7}{8}\delta - \frac{7}{9}\delta\right] = \frac{7}{72}\frac{d\delta}{dx}$$

[In the expression above, the limits have been taken from 0 to δ instead of δ′ to δ since the laminar sublayer (δ′) is very thin]

$$\therefore \quad \tau_0 = \frac{7}{72} \rho U^2 \frac{d\delta}{dx} \quad ...(13.42)$$

$$\text{Also,} \quad \tau_0 = 0.0225 \rho U^2 \left(\frac{\mu}{\rho U \delta}\right)^{1/4} \quad ...[\text{Eqn. } (13.27)]$$

Now equating the eqns. (13.42) and (13.41), we have:

$$\frac{7}{72} \rho U^2 \frac{d\delta}{dx} = 0.0225 \rho U^2 \left(\frac{\mu}{\rho U \delta}\right)^{1/4}$$

$$\text{or,} \quad \frac{7}{72} \frac{d\delta}{dx} = 0.0225 \left(\frac{\mu}{\rho U}\right)^{1/4} \times \frac{1}{(\delta)^{1/4}} \quad (\text{cancelling } \rho U^2 \text{ on both sides})$$

$$\text{or,} \quad \delta^{1/4} d\delta = 0.0225 \times \frac{72}{7} \times \left(\frac{\mu}{\rho U}\right)^{1/4} dx$$

$$\text{or,} \quad \delta^{1/4} d\delta = 0.2314 \left(\frac{\mu}{\rho U}\right)^{1/4} dx$$

Integrating both sides, we have:

$$\frac{4}{5} \delta^{5/4} = 0.2314 \left(\frac{\mu}{\rho U}\right)^{1/4} x + C \quad (\text{where, } C = \text{constant of integration})$$

Let boundary layer be *assumed to be turbulent over the entire length of plate.*

Hence, at $x = 0, \delta = 0 \quad \therefore C = 0$

$$\therefore \quad \frac{4}{5} \delta^{5/4} = 0.2314 \left(\frac{\mu}{\rho U}\right)^{1/4} \times x$$

$$\text{or,} \quad \delta^{5/4} = (5/4 \times 0.2314) \left(\frac{\mu}{\rho U}\right)^{1/4} \times x$$

$$\text{or,} \quad \delta = [5/4 \times 0.02314]^{4/5} \left(\frac{\mu}{\rho U}\right)^{1/5} \times x^{4/5}$$

$$= 0.371 \left(\frac{\mu}{\rho U x}\right)^{1/5} x^{1/5} \times x^{4/5} = 0.0371 \left(\frac{1}{Re_x}\right)^{1/5} \times x = \frac{0.71x}{(Re_x)^{1/5}}$$

$$\text{i.e.} \quad \boldsymbol{\delta = \frac{0.371x}{(Re_x)^{1/5}}} \quad ...(13.43)$$

(*ii*) Shear stress, τ_0:

$$\tau_0 = 0.0225 \rho U^2 \left(\frac{\mu}{\rho U \delta}\right)^{1/4} \quad [\text{Eqn. } (13.41)]$$

Substituting the value of δ from eqn. (13.43), we get:

$$\tau_0 = 0.0225 \rho U^2 \left(\frac{\mu}{\rho U \times \frac{0 \cdot 371x}{(Re_x)^{1/5}}}\right)^{1/4}$$

$$= \frac{0.0225}{(0.371)^{1/4}} \rho U^2 \left[\frac{\mu}{\rho U x} \times (Re_x)^{1/5}\right]^{1/4} = 0.0288\, \rho U^2 \left[\frac{(Re_x)^{1/5}}{Re_x}\right]^{1/4}$$

$$\left(\because Re_x = \frac{\mu}{\rho U x}\right)$$

or, $$\boldsymbol{\tau_0 = \frac{\rho U^2}{2} \times \frac{0.0576}{(Re_x)^{1/5}}} \quad ...(13.44)$$

(*iii*) Local co-efficient of drag, C_D^*:

We know $$\tau_0 = \frac{\rho U^2}{2} \times \frac{0.0576}{(Re_x)^{1/5}} \quad \text{[Eqn. (13.44)]}$$

Also, $$\tau_0 = C_D^* \times \frac{1}{2} \rho U^2 \quad \text{[Eqn. (13.9)]}$$

Now equating the eqns. (13.44) and (13.9), we have:

$$C_D^* \times \frac{1}{2} \rho U^2 = \frac{\rho U^2}{2} \times \frac{0.0576}{(Re_x)^{1/5}}$$

or, $$\boldsymbol{C_D^* = \frac{0.0576}{(Re_x)^{1/5}}} \quad ...(13.45)$$

(*iv*) Drag force, F_D:

The total drag force (F_D) on one side of the plate of width B and length L is given by,

$$F_D = \int_0^L \tau_0 \times B \times dx \quad ...\text{[Eqn. (13.8)]}$$

$$= \int_0^L \frac{\rho U^2}{2} \times \frac{0.0576}{(Re_x)^{1/5}} \times B \times dx = \int_0^L \frac{\rho U^2}{2} \times \frac{0.0576}{\left(\frac{\rho U x}{\mu}\right)^{1/5}} B \times dx$$

$$= \frac{\rho U^2}{2} \times \frac{0.0576}{\left(\frac{\rho U}{\mu}\right)^{1/5}} B \int_0^L x^{-1/5}\, dx = \frac{\rho U^2}{2} \times \frac{0.0576}{\left(\frac{\rho U}{\mu}\right)^{1/5}} B \left[\frac{5}{4} \times x^{4/5}\right]_0^L$$

$$= \frac{\rho U^2}{2} \times \frac{0.0576}{\left(\frac{\rho U}{\mu}\right)^{1/5}} \times B \times \frac{5}{4} (L)^{4/5} = \frac{\rho U^2}{2} \times \frac{0.072}{\left(\frac{\rho U L}{\mu}\right)^{1/5}} \times B \times L$$

or, $$\boldsymbol{F_D = \frac{\rho U^2}{2} \times \frac{0.072}{(Re_L)^{1/5}} \times B \times L} \quad ...(13.46)$$

(*v*) Co-efficient of drag, C_D:

We know, $$F_D = C_D \times \frac{1}{2} \rho A V^2 \quad ...\text{[Eqn. (13.10)]}$$

Now equating eqns. (13.10) and (13.46), we have:

$$C_D \times \frac{1}{2} \rho \times B \times L \times U^2 = \frac{\rho U^2}{2} \times \frac{0.072}{(Re_L)^{1/5}} \times B \times L \quad (\because \text{Area of the plate, } A = B \times L)$$

or,
$$C_D = \frac{0.072}{(Re_L)^{1/5}} \quad ...(13.42)$$

This is valid for $5 \times 10^5 < Re_L < 10^7$.

For Reynolds number *between* 10^7 *and* 10^9 the following relationship suggested by Prandtl and Schlichting holds good,

$$C_D = \frac{0.455}{(\log_{10} Re_L)^{2.58}} \quad ...(13.48)$$

13.6. TOTAL DRAG DUE TO LAMINAR AND TURBULENT LAYERS

When the leading edge is not very rough, the turbulent boundary layer does not begin at the leading edge, it is usually preceded by the laminar boundary layer. *The point of transition from laminar to turbulent layer depends upon the intensity of turbulence.* The distance x_c (Fig. 13.7) of the transition from the leading edge can be obtained from critical Reynolds number which normally ranges from 3×10^5 to 3×10^6.

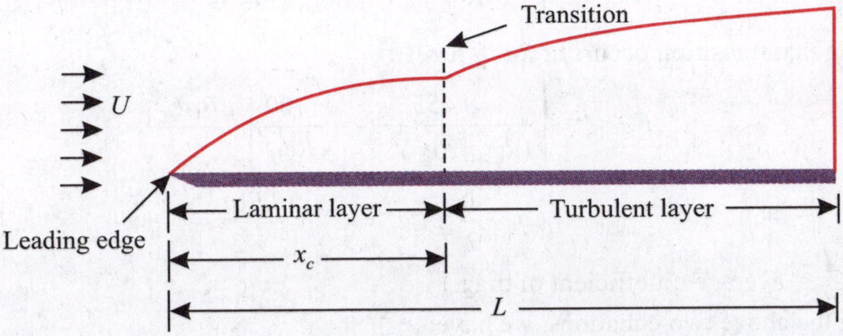

Fig. 13.7. Drag due to laminar and turbulent boundary layers.

Drag force ($F_D = F$) for the turbulent boundary layer can be estimated from the following relation:

$$F_{turb.} = (F_{turb})_{total} - (F_{turb.})_{x_c}$$

where, $(F_{turb.})_{total}$ = The drag which would occur if a turbulent boundary extends along the entire length of the plate, and

$(F_{turb.})_{x_c}$ = The drag due to fictitious turbulent boundary layer from the leading edge to a distance x_c.

Let us assume that the plate is long enough so that Reynolds number is greater than 10^7, then the turbulent drag is given by,

$$F_{turb} = \frac{0.455}{(\log_{10} Re_L)^{2.58}} \times \frac{\rho U^2}{2} \times L \times B - \frac{0.072}{(Re_c)^{1/5}} \times \frac{\rho U^2}{2} \times x_c \times B \quad ...(i)$$

where, L = Length of the plate,

B = Width of the plate, and

U = Free stream velocity.

The laminar boundary layer prevails within the length x_c and its contribution to drag force is given by:

$$F_{\text{laminar}} = \frac{1.328}{\sqrt{Re_c}} \times \frac{\rho U^2}{2} \times x_c \times B = \frac{1.328\, x_c}{\sqrt{Re_c}} \times B \times \frac{\rho U^2}{2} \qquad ...(ii)$$

$$\therefore \quad F_{\text{total}} = F_{\text{laminar}} + F_{\text{turb.}}$$

$$F_{\text{total}} = \frac{1.328\, x_c}{\sqrt{Re_c}} \times B \times \frac{\rho U^2}{2} + \left[\frac{0.455 L}{(\log_{10} Re_L)^{2.58}} \times B \times \frac{\rho U^2}{2} - \frac{0.072\, x_c}{(Re_c)^{1/5}} \times B \times \frac{\rho U^2}{2}\right].$$

$$= \left[\frac{1.328\, x_c}{\sqrt{Re_c}} + \frac{0.455\, L}{(\log_{10} Re_L)^{2.58}} - \frac{0.072 x_c}{(Re_c)^{1/5}}\right] \frac{B\rho U^2}{2} \qquad ...(iii)$$

Also, $$\frac{Re_c}{Re_L} = \frac{(\rho U x_c / \mu)}{(\rho U L / \mu)} = \frac{x_c}{L}$$

or, $$x_c = \frac{Re_c L}{Re_L}$$

Substituting the value of x_c in eqn (*iii*), we have:

$$F_{\text{total}} = \left[\frac{1.328\sqrt{Re_c}}{Re_L} + \frac{0.455}{(\log_{10} Re_L)^{2.58}} - \frac{0.072\, Re_c^{0.8}}{Re_L}\right] \frac{L B \rho U^2}{2}$$

Assuming that transition occurs at $Re_c = 5 \times 10^5$,

$$F_{\text{total}} = \left[\frac{0.455}{(\log_{10} Re_L)^{2.58}} - \frac{1700}{Re_L}\right] \frac{L B \rho U^2}{2} \qquad ...(13.49)$$

Also, $$F_{\text{total}} = C_D \times \frac{1}{2} \rho A U^2 = C_D \times \frac{L B \rho U^2}{2} \qquad ...[\text{Eqn. } (13.10)]$$

(where, C_D = average co-efficient of drag.)

Equating the above two equations, we have:

$$\mathbf{C_D = \frac{0.455}{(\log_{10} Re_L)^{2.58}} - \frac{1700}{Re_L}} \qquad ...(13.50)$$

Example 13.24. *A submarine can be assumed to have cylindrical shape with rounded nose. Assuming its length to be 50 m and diameter 5·0 m, determine the total power required to overcome boundary friction if it cruises at 8 m/s velocity in sea water at 20°C (ρ = 1030 kg/m³), ν = 1 × 10⁻⁶ m²/s.*

Solution. Length of submarine, $L = 50$ m

Diameter of submarine, $D = 5.0$ m

Velocity of submarine, $U = 8$ m/s

Density of sea water, $\rho = 1030$ kg/m^3

Kinematic viscosity of sea water, $\nu = 1 \times 10^{-6}$ m^2/s

Total power required to overcome boundary friction, *P*:

Reynolds number, $$Re_L = \frac{UL}{\nu} = \frac{8 \times 50}{1 \times 10^{-6}} = 4 \times 10^8$$

The length over which boundary layer will be laminar is given by,

$$\frac{Ux}{\nu} = 5 \times 10^5 \text{ or } x = \frac{5 \times 10^5 \times \nu}{U}$$

or, $$x = \frac{5 \times 10^5 \times 1 \times 10^{-6}}{8} = 0.0625 \text{ m}$$

This being very small, contribution to total drag from laminar boundary layer is negligible; hence C_D is given by,

$$C_D = \frac{0.455}{(\log_{10} Re_L)^{2.58}} = \frac{0.455}{\left[\log_{10}(4 \times 10^8)\right]^{2.58}} = 0.001765$$

$$\text{Area, } A = \pi DL = \pi \times 5 \times 50 = 785.4 \text{ m}^2$$

$$\therefore \quad \text{Drag force, } F_D = C_D \times \frac{1}{2}\rho A U^2 = 0.001765 \times \frac{1}{2} \times 1030 \times 785.4 \times 8^2 = 45690.2 \text{ N}$$

Hence, total power required to overcome boundary friction,

$$P = \frac{F_D U}{1000} \text{ kW} = \frac{45690.2 \times 8}{1000} = \mathbf{365.52 \text{ kW (Ans.)}}$$

Example 13.25. *12000 kW power is required to cruise a passenger ship of 300 m length and 12.0 m draft at 40 km/h. If ρ = 1030 kg/m³ and ν = 1 × 10⁻⁶ m²/s, determine the combined form and wave resistance of the ship.*

Solution. Power required to cruise the ship, $P = 12000$ kW

Length of the ship $= 300$ m

Draft of the ship $= 12$ m

$$\text{Speed of the ship, } U = 40 \text{ km/h} = \frac{40 \times 1000}{3600} = 11.11 \text{ m/s}$$

Density of water, $\rho = 1030 \text{ kg/m}^3$

Kinematic viscosity of water, $\nu = 1 \times 10^{-6} \text{ m}^2/\text{s}$

Combined form and wave resistance:

$$\text{Reynolds number, } Re_L = \frac{UL}{\nu} = \frac{11.11 \times 300}{1 \times 10^{-6}} = 3.333 \times 10^9$$

At this Reynolds number, the boundary layer will be turbulent on almost the whole length; hence, C_D is given by:

$$C_D = \frac{0.455}{(\log_{10} Re_L)^{2.58}} = \frac{0.455}{[\log_{10}(3.333 \times 10^9)]^{2.58}} = 0.001358$$

$$F_{friction} = 2 \times C_D \times \frac{1}{2}\rho A U^2 = 2 \times 0.001358 \times \frac{1}{2} \times 1030 \times 300 \times 12 \times (11.11)^2$$

$$= 621538 \text{ } N \quad \text{or} \quad 621.54 \text{ kN}$$

$$\text{Total power required, } P = FU$$

$$\therefore \quad \text{Total force, } F = \frac{P}{U} = \frac{12000}{11.11} = 1080 \text{ kN}$$

Also, $$F = F_{friction} + (F_{form} + F_{wave})$$

$$\therefore \quad (F_{form} + F_{wave}) = 1080 - F_{friction} = 1080 - 621.54 = \mathbf{458.46 \text{ kN (Ans.)}}$$

Example 13.26. *Find the ratio of friction drag on the front half and rear half of the flat plate kept at zero incidence in a stream of uniform velocity, if the boundary layer is turbulent over the whole plate.*

Solution. The average co-efficient of drag (C_D) for turbulent boundary layer is given by:

$$C_D = \frac{0.072}{(Re_L)^{1/5}} \quad \text{...[Eqn. (13.47)]}$$

For the entire plate, $Re_L = \frac{UL}{\nu}$

For the first half of the plate, $Re_x = \frac{Ux}{\nu} = \frac{UL}{2\nu}$

Drag force per unit width for the entire plate is,

$$F_D = C_D \times \frac{\rho U^2}{2} \times \text{area per unit width}$$

$$= \frac{0.072}{\left(\frac{UL}{\nu}\right)^{1/5}} \times \frac{\rho U^2}{2} \times L$$

Similarly the drag force per unit width for the front half portion of the plate is,

$$F_1 = \frac{0.072}{\left(\frac{UL}{2\,\nu}\right)^{1/5}} \times \frac{\rho U^2}{2} \times \frac{L}{2} = \frac{0.072}{\left(\frac{UL}{\nu}\right)^{1/5}} \times \frac{\rho U^2}{2} \times \frac{L}{2}\,(2)^{1/5}$$

∴ Drag force for the rear half portion of the plate is,

$$F_2 = F - F_1 = \frac{0.072L}{\left(\frac{UL}{\nu}\right)^{1/2}} \times \frac{\rho U^2}{2}\left[1 - \frac{1}{2}\,(2)^{1/5}\right]$$

Hence,

$$\frac{F_1}{F_2} = \frac{\frac{1}{2} \times (2)^{1/5}}{1 - \frac{1}{2}\,(2)^{1/5}} = \frac{0.574}{1 - 0.574} = \mathbf{1.347} \textbf{ (Ans.)}$$

Example 13.27. *A streamlined train is 200 m long with a typical cross-section having a perimeter of 9 m above the wheels. If the kinematic viscosity of air at the prevailing temperature is* 1.5×10^{-5} m^2/s *and density* 1.24 kg/m^3, *determine the approximate surface drag (friction drag) of the train when running at 90 km/h.*

Make allowance for the fact that boundary layer changes from laminar to turbulent on the train surface.

Solution. Length of the train, $L = 200$ m

Perimeter of cross-section of the train above wheels, $P = 9$ m

∴ Surface area, $A = L \times P = 200 \times 9 = 1800 \text{ m}^2$

Kinematic viscosity of air, $\nu = 1.5 \times 10^{-5} \text{ m}^2/\text{s}$

Density of air, $\rho = 1.24 \text{ kg/m}^3$

Free stream velocity, $U = 90 \text{ km/h} = \frac{90 \times 1000}{3600} = 25 \text{ m/s}$

Approximate friction drag, F_D

The Reynolds number with length of the train as the characteristic length,

$$Re_L = \frac{UL}{\nu} = \frac{25 \times 200}{1.5 \times 10^{-5}} = 3.333 \times 10^8$$

Obviously the boundary layer is *turbulent*.

Assuming that the abrupt transition from laminar to turbulent flow occurs at a Reynolds number of 5×10^5, the average co-efficient of drag,

$$C_D = \frac{0.455}{(\log_{10} Re_L)^{2.58}} - \frac{1700}{Re_L} \quad \text{[Eqn. (13.50)]}$$

$$= \frac{0.455}{[\log_{10} (3.333 \times 10^8)]^{2.58}} - \frac{1700}{3.333 \times 10^8}$$

$$= 0.001807 - 5.1 \times 10^{-6} = 0.0018$$

The approximate friction drag over the train surface,

$$F_D = C_D \times \frac{1}{2} \rho A U^2 = 0.0018 \times \frac{1}{2} \times 1.24 \times 1800 \times 25^2 = \mathbf{1255.5\ N\ (Ans.)}$$

Example 13.28. *A barge with a rectangular bottom surface 30 m long × 10 m wide is travelling down a river with a velocity of 0.6 m/s. A laminar boundary layer exists upto a Reynolds number equivalent to 5 × 10^5 and subsequently abrupt transition occurs to turbulent boundary layer. Calculate:*

(i) *The maximum distance from the leading edge upto which laminar boundary layer persists and the maximum boundary layer thickness at that point.*

(ii) *The total drag force on the flat bottom surface of the barge, and*

(iii) *The power required to push the bottom surface through water at the given velocity.*

For water ρ = 998 kg/m^3 and ν = 1 × 10^{-6} m^2/s.

Solution. Length of the bottom surface, L = 30 m

Width of the bottom surface, B = 10 m

∴ Area, $A = L \times B = 30 \times 10 = 300\ m^2$

Velocity, U = 0.6 m/s

Density of water, ρ = 998 kg/m^3

kinematic viscosity, $\nu = 1 \times 10^{-6}\ m^2/s$

(*i*) The maximum distance up to which laminar boundary layer persists, x_c:

$$(Re)_{x_c} = \frac{U x_c}{\nu} = 5 \times 10^5$$

$$\therefore \quad x_c = \frac{5 \times 10^5 \times \nu}{U} = \frac{5 \times 10^5 \times 1 \times 10^{-6}}{0.6} = \mathbf{0.833\ m\ (Ans.)}$$

Maximum boundary layer (laminar) thickness, δ:

$$\delta = \frac{5 x_c}{\sqrt{(R_e)_{x_c}}} = \frac{5 \times 0.833}{\sqrt{5 \times 10^5}} = 5.89 \times 10^{-3}\ \text{m or } \mathbf{5.89\ mm\ (Ans.)}$$

(*ii*) The total drag force F_D:

$$R_{eL} = \frac{UL}{\nu} = \frac{0.6 \times 30}{1 \times 10^{-6}} = 1.8 \times 10^7$$

The average co-efficient of drag,

$$C_D = \frac{0.455}{(\log_{10} R_{eL})^{2.58}} - \frac{1700}{R_{eL}} \qquad \text{...[Eqn. (13.50)]}$$

$$= \frac{0.455}{[\log_{10} (1.8 \times 10^7)]^{2.58}} - \frac{1700}{1.8 \times 10^7} = 0.002644$$

∴ Drag force on the bottom surface of the barge,

$$F_D = C_D \times \frac{1}{2} \rho A U^2 = 0{\cdot}002644 \times \frac{1}{2} \times 998 \times 300 \times (0.6)^2$$

$$= \mathbf{142.49\ N\ (Ans.)}$$

***(iii)* The power required, *P*:**

The power required to push the bottom surface through water at the given velocity,

$$P = F_D \times U = 142.49 \times 0.6 = \mathbf{85.49\ W\ (Ans.)}$$

13.7. BOUNDARY LAYER SEPARATION AND ITS CONTROL

In a flowing fluid when a solid body is immersed, a thin layer of fluid called the boundary layer is formed adjacent to the solid body. The forces acting on the fluid in the boundary layer are:

(*i*) Inertia forces, (*ii*) Viscous forces, and (*iii*) Pressure forces.

— When the pressure gradient in the direction of flow is negative $\left(\frac{dp}{dx} < 0\right)$ *i.e.* when the pressure *decreases* in the direction of flow, the flow is accelerated. In this case, the pressure force and inertia force add together and jointly tend to reduce the effect of viscous forces in the boundary layer. This results in a decrease in the thickness of boundary layer in the direction of flow, as a consequence of which there are *low losses* and *high efficiencies in accelerating flows*.

— When the pressure increases in the direction of flow $\left(\frac{dp}{dx} > 0\right)$, the pressure forces act *opposite* to the direction of flow and further increase the retarding effect of the viscous forces. Subsequently the thickness of the boundary layer increases rapidly in the direction of flow. *If these forces act over a long stretch,* the *boundary layer gets separated from the surface and moves into the main stream. This phenomenon is called* **separation**. *The point of the body at which the boundary layer is on the verge of separation from the surface is called* ***"point of separation"*.**

Consider a flow of fluid over a curved surface as shown in Fig. 13·8.

— As the fluid flows round the surface (the area of flow decreases) it is accelerated over the left hand section until at point *B* the velocity just outside the boundary is maximum and the pressure is minimum (as shown by the graph below the surface). Thus from *A* and *B* the pressure gradient is *negative*. As long as $\frac{dp}{dx} < 0$, the entire boundary layer *moves forward.*

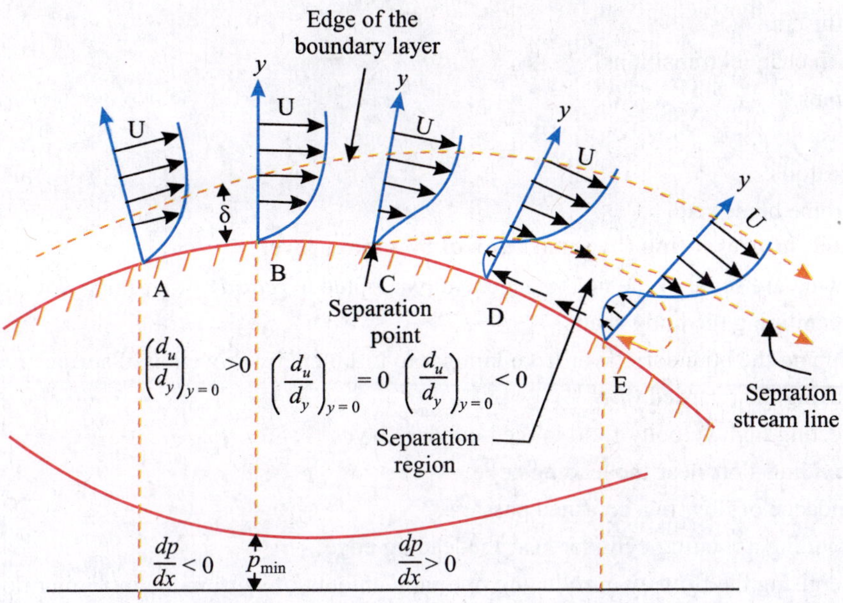

Fig. 13.8. Separation of boundary layer.

— Beyond *B* (*i.e.* along the region *BCDE*), the area of flow increases and hence velocity of flow decreases; due to decrease of velocity the pressure increases (in the direction of flow) and hence the pressure gradient $\frac{dp}{dx}$ is *positive i.e.* $\frac{dp}{dx} > 0$. The value of the velocity gradient $\left(\frac{du}{dy}\right)$ at the boundary is *zero* at the point *C*, this point is known as a **separation point** (the boundary layer starts separating from the surface because further retardation of flow near the surface is physically impossible). Large *turbulent eddies* are formed downstream of the point of separation. *The disturbed region in which the eddies are formed is called* **turbulent wake.**

The *flow separation* depends upon *factors* such as:

(*i*) *The curvature of the surface;*

(*ii*) *The Reynolds number of flow;*

(*iii*) *The roughness of the surface.*

The velocity gradient, for a given velocity profile, exhibits the following characteristics for the flow to remain *attached*, get *detached* or be on the *verge of separation*:

1. $\left(\frac{\partial u}{\partial y}\right)_{y=0}$ is + *ve* ...*Attached flow* (The flow will not separate)

2. $\left(\frac{\partial u}{\partial y}\right)_{y=0}$ is *zero* ...The flow is on the *verge of separation*

3. $\left(\frac{\partial u}{\partial y}\right)_{y=0}$ is – *ve* ...*Separated flow.*

— *Boundary layer separation is unstable, inefficient process and entails large losses due to appreciable eddying region.*

- ***Separation** occurs in the following cases:*

(*i*) Diffusers,

(*ii*) Open channel transitions,

(*iii*) Pumps,

(*iv*) Fans,

(*v*) Aerofoils,

(*vi*) Turbine blades etc.

Methods of preventing the separation of boundary layer:

Following are some of the methods generally adopted to *retard or arrest the flow separation*:

1. Streamlining the body shape.
2. Tripping the boundary layer from laminar to turbulent by provision of surface roughness.
3. Sucking the retarded flow.
4. Injecting high velocity fluid in the boundary layer.
5. Providing slots near the leading edge.
6. Guidance of flow in a confined passage.
7. Providing a rotating cylinder near the leading edge.
8. Energising the flow by introducing optimum amount of swirl in the incoming flow.

Note: Refer to Example 13.29 also.

Example 13.29. *Explain what is meant by separation of boundary layer. Describe with sketches the methods to control separation.* **(PEC)**

Solution. When a solid body is immersed in a flowing fluid, a thin layer of fluid called *boundary layer* is formed, adjacent to the solid body. In this thin layer of fluid, the velocity varies from *zero to free stream velocity* in the direction normal to the solid body. Along the length of the solid body, the thickness of the boundary layer increases. *The fluid layer adjacent to the solid surface has to do work against surface friction at the expense of kinetic energy. This loss of kinetic energy is recovered from the immediate fluid layer in contact with the layer adjacent to the solid surface through momentum exchange process. Thus the velocity of the layer goes on decreasing*. Along the length of solid body, *at a certain point a stage may come when the boundary layer may not be able to keep sticking to the solid body, if it cannot provide kinetic energy to overcome the resistance offered by the solid body.* In other words, the boundary layer will be *separated from the surface*. This phenomenon is called the **boundary layer separation**. *The point on the body at which the boundary layer is on the verge of separation from the surface is called* **point of separation.**

Methods to control separation

1. *Motion of solid boundary:*

By rotating a circular cylinder lying in a stream of fluid, so that the upper side of cylinder where the fluid as well as the cylinder move in the *same direction, the boundary layer does not form*. However on the lower side of cylinder where the fluid *motion is opposite* to that of cylinder *separation would occur* (Fig. 13.9).

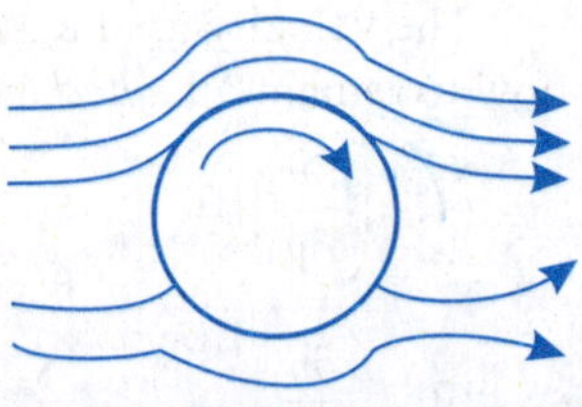

Fig. 13.9

2. *Acceleration of fluid in the boundary layer:*

This method of controlling separation consists of *supplying additional energy to particles of fluid which are being retarded in the boundary layer. This may be achieved either by injecting the fluid into the region of boundary layer from the interior of the body with the help of some available device as shown in Fig. 13.10 or by diverting a portion of fluid of the main stream from the region of high pressure to the retarded region of boundary layer through a slot provided in the body* (Fig. 13.11)

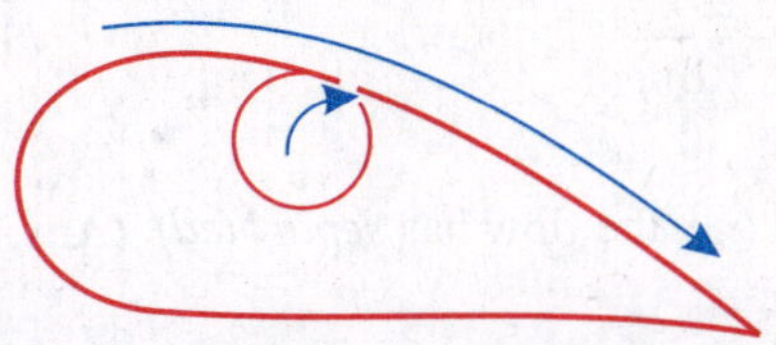

Fig. 13.10. Injecting fluid into boundary layer.

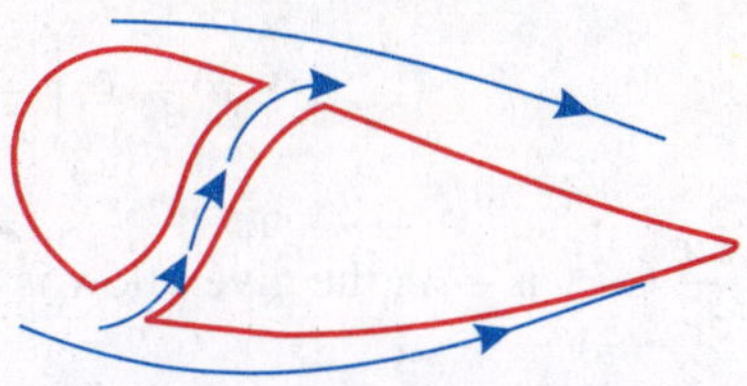

Fig. 13.11. Slotting wing.

3. *Suction of fluid from the boundary layer:*

In this method, the slow moving fluid in the boundary layer is removed by suction through slots or through a porous surface as shown in the Fig. 13.12.

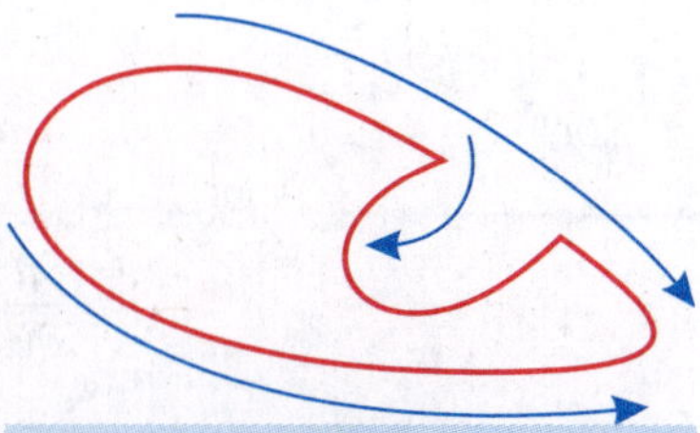

Fig. 13.12

4. *Streamlining of body shapes:*

By the use of suitably shaped bodies, the point of transition of the boundary layer from laminar to turbulent can be *moved downstream which results in the reduction of the skin friction* drag. Further more by *streamlining of body shapes, the separation may be eliminated.*

Example 13.30. *For the following velocity profiles determine whether flow is attached or detached or on the verge of separation*:

(*i*) $\frac{u}{U} = 2\left(\frac{y}{\delta}\right) - \left(\frac{y}{\delta}\right)^2$

(*ii*) $\frac{u}{U} = -2\left(\frac{y}{\delta}\right) + \left(\frac{y}{\delta}\right)^3 + 2\left(\frac{y}{\delta}\right)^4$

(*iii*) $\frac{u}{U} = 2\left(\frac{y}{\delta}\right)^2 + \left(\frac{y}{\delta}\right)^3 - 2\left(\frac{y}{\delta}\right)^4$ **[Nagpur University]**

Solution. (*i*) $\frac{u}{U} = 2\left(\frac{y}{\delta}\right) - \left(\frac{y}{\delta}\right)^2$ or $u = 2U\left(\frac{y}{\delta}\right) - U\left(\frac{y}{\delta}\right)^2$

Differentiating w.r.t. *y* the above equation, we get:

$$\frac{du}{dy} = 2U\left(\frac{1}{\delta}\right) - 2U\left(\frac{y}{\delta}\right) \times \frac{1}{\delta}$$

At, $y = 0, \left(\frac{\partial u}{\delta y}\right)_{y=0} = \frac{2U}{\delta}$

As $\left(\frac{\partial u}{\delta y}\right)_{y=0}$ is + *ve*, the given flow is **attached (Ans.)**

(*ii*)
$$\frac{u}{U} = -2\left(\frac{y}{\delta}\right) + \left(\frac{y}{\delta}\right)^3 + 2\left(\frac{y}{\delta}\right)^4$$

or,
$$u = -2U\left(\frac{y}{\delta}\right) + U\left(\frac{y}{\delta}\right)^3 + 2U\left(\frac{y}{\delta}\right)^4$$

$\therefore$
$$\frac{\partial u}{\partial y} = -2U\left(\frac{1}{\delta}\right) + 3U\left(\frac{y}{\delta}\right)^2 \times \frac{1}{\delta} + 8U\left(\frac{y}{\delta}\right)^3 \times \frac{1}{\delta}$$

At, $y = 0, \left(\frac{\partial u}{\partial y}\right)_{y=0} = -\frac{2U}{\delta}$

As $\left(\frac{\partial u}{\partial y}\right)_{y=0}$ is – *ve*, the given flow is **detached** (*i.e.* the flow has *separated*). **(Ans.)**

(iii) $$\frac{u}{U} = \left(\frac{y}{\delta}\right)^2 + \left(\frac{y}{\delta}\right)^3 - 2\left(\frac{y}{\delta}\right)^4$$

or, $$u = 2U\left(\frac{y}{\delta}\right)^2 + U\left(\frac{y}{\delta}\right)^3 - 2U\left(\frac{y}{\delta}\right)^4$$

$\therefore$ $$\frac{\partial u}{\partial y} = 4U\left(\frac{y}{\delta}\right) \times \frac{1}{\delta} + 3U\left(\frac{y}{\delta}\right)^2 \times \frac{1}{\delta} - 8U\left(\frac{y}{\delta}\right)^3 \times \frac{1}{\delta}$$

At, $y = 0, \left(\frac{\partial u}{\partial y}\right)_{y=0} = 0$

As $\left(\frac{\partial u}{\partial y}\right)_{y=0} = 0$, the given flow is **on the verge of separation.** **(Ans.)**

HIGHLIGHTS

1. When a viscous fluid flows past an immersed body, a thin boundary layer is formed in the immediate neighbourhood of solid surface. In the boundary layer, the velocity gradient $\left(\frac{\partial u}{\partial y}\right)$ is very high.
2. The resistance due to viscosity is confined only in the boundary layer. The fluid outside the boundary layer may be considered as ideal.
3. Near the leading edge of a flat plate, the boundary layer is wholly laminar. For a boundary layer, the velocity distribution is parabolic. The thickness of the boundary layer (δ) increases with distance from the leading edge, as more and more fluid is slowed down by the viscous boundary, becomes unstable and breaks into turbulent boundary layer over a transition region.
4. For a turbulent boundary layer, if the boundary is smooth, the roughness projections are covered by a very thin layer which remains laminar, called *laminar sublayer*. The velocity distribution in the turbulent boundary layer is given by *Log law* or *Prandtl's one-seventh power law*.
5. For a flow, when $Re = \frac{Ux}{\nu} < 5 \times 10^5$ ... boundary layer is laminar, and

   when, $Re = \frac{Ux}{\nu} > 5 \times 10^5$ ... boundary layer is called turbulent.

   where, U = Free stream velocity,

   x = Distance from the leading edge, and

   ν = Kinematic viscosity of fluid.
6. The *thickness of the boundary layer* is arbitrarily defined as that distance from the boundary in which the velocity reaches 99 percent of the velocity of the free stream. It is denoted by the symbol δ.

7. *Displacement thickness,* $\delta^* = \int_0^\delta \left(1 - \frac{u}{U}\right) dy$

8. *Momentum thickness,* $\delta = \int_0^\delta \frac{u}{U}\left(1 - \frac{u}{U}\right) dy$

9. *Energy thickness,* $\delta_e = \int_0^\delta \frac{u}{U}\left(1 - \frac{u^2}{U^2}\right) dy$

10. Von Karman momentum integral equation is given as:

$$\frac{\tau_0}{\rho U^2} = \frac{d\theta}{dx}$$

where, $\theta = \int_0^\delta \frac{u}{U}\left(1 - \frac{u}{U}\right) dy$, and

τ_0 = Shear stress at surface.

This equation is applicable to laminar, transition and turbulent boundary layer flows.

11. As per Blasius results:

The thickness of laminar boundary layer, $\delta = \frac{5x}{\sqrt{Re_x}}$ (where, Re_x = Reynolds number)

Average co-efficient of drag, $C_D = \frac{1.328}{\sqrt{Re_x}}$

12. For turbulent boundary layer, the velocity profile is given as :

$$\frac{u}{U} = \left(\frac{y}{\delta}\right)^{1/7}$$

This equation is *not valid very near the boundary where laminar sublayer exists.*

13. For turbulent boundary layer over a flat plate, the shear stress at the boundary is given as

$$\tau_0 = 0.0225\, \rho U^2 \left(\frac{\mu}{\rho U \delta}\right)^{1/4}$$

14. In case of a turbulent boundary layer:

For $5 \times 10^5 < Re < 10^7$:

$$\delta = \frac{0.371x}{(Re_x)^{1/5}}, \quad \text{and} \quad C_D = \frac{0.072}{(Re_L)^{1/5}}$$

For $10^7 < Re < 10^9$:

$$C_D = \frac{0.455}{(\log_{10} Re_L)^{2.58}} \quad \text{... Prandtl-Schlichting empirical equation}$$

15. Total drag on a flat plate due to laminar and turbulent layers:

$$F_{total} = \left[\frac{0.455}{(\log_{10} Re_L)^{2.58}} - \frac{1700}{Re_x}\right] \frac{LB\rho U^2}{2}$$

Average co-efficient of drag, $C_D = \frac{0.455}{(\log_{10} Re_L)^{2.58}} - \frac{1700}{Re_L}$

16. The velocity gradient, for a given velocity profile, exhibits the following characteristic for the flow to remain attached, get detached or be on the verge of separation.

(*i*) $\left(\dfrac{\partial u}{\partial y}\right)_{y=0}$ is + ve ... *Attached flow* (The flow will not separate)

(*ii*) $\left(\dfrac{\partial u}{\partial y}\right)_{y=0}$ is zero ... The flow is *on the verge of separation*

(*iii*) $\left(\dfrac{\partial u}{\partial y}\right)_{y=0}$ is – ve ... *Separated flow.*

OBJECTIVE TYPE QUESTIONS

1. In turbulent flow the velocity
(*a*) varies with time and space
(*b*) varies with time only, the patterns of fluctuation, with respect to time, being same at all points
(*c*) is constant at every point
(*d*) none of the above.

2. In a turbulent flow the shear stress is mainly due to the
(*a*) density of the fluid
(*b*) dynamic viscosity of the fluid
(*c*) kinematic viscosity of the fluid
(*d*) eddy viscosity of the fluid
(*e*) all of the above.

3. For which of the following flows Blasius equation is used?
(*a*) Laminar flow
(*b*) Turbulent flow in rough pipes
(*c*) Turbulent flow in smooth pipes for any Reynolds number
(*d*) Turbulent flow in smooth pipes for $Re < 10^5$
(*e*) none of the above.

4. In turbulent flow, which of the following gives the exact velocity distribution?
(*a*) Logarithmic distribution
(*b*) Blasius equation
(*c*) Power law with index varying
(*d*) Prandtl's one-seventh power.

5. The boundary layer exists in which of the following?
(*a*) Flow of real fluids
(*b*) Flow of ideal fluids
(*c*) Flow over flat surfaces only
(*d*) Pipe-flow only.

6. On account of which of the following boundary layer exists?
(*a*) Surface tension
(*b*) Gravitational effect
(*c*) Viscosity of fluid
(*d*) None of the above.

7. On account of which of the following L. Prandtl is regarded as the father of modern fluid mechanics?
(*a*) His pioneering research on flow of low-viscosity fluids bringing forward a new concept of boundary layer
(*b*) His new interpretations on fluid resistance
(*c*) His fundamental research in the field of aircraft-engineering
(*d*) None of the above.

8. The displacement thickness is
(*a*) the layer in which the loss of energy is minimum
(*b*) the layer which represents reduction in momentum caused by the boundary layer
(*c*) the thickness upto which the velocity approaches 99% of the free-stream velocity
(*d*) the distance measured perpendicular to the boundary by which the free-stream is displaced on account of formation of boundary layer.

9. Over a long flat plate, the laminar boundary-layer becomes unstable and changes flow characteristics from laminar to turbulent when the plate Reynolds number approaches a value between
(*a*) 3×10^4 to 5×10^4
(*b*) 3×10^5 to 6×10^5
(*c*) 2×10^6 to 5×10^6
(*d*) 5×10^6 to 8×10^6.

10. When the fluid flows along the solid boundary, more and more fluid gets retarded in the vicinity of the boundary; this deceleration is due to

(*a*) high velocity of the fluid
(*b*) high velocity flow outside the boundary layer
(*c*) high velocity gradients which exist at and near the boundary
(*d*) none of the above.

11. Momentum thickness is given by which of the following relations?

(*a*) $\int_0^\delta \left(1 - \frac{u}{U}\right) dy$ (*b*) $\int_0^\delta \frac{u}{U}\left(1 - \frac{u}{U}\right) dy$

(*c*) $\int_0^\delta \frac{u}{U}\left(1 - \frac{u^2}{U^2}\right) dy$ (*d*) none of the above.

12. The boundary layer separation occurs when

(*a*) $\frac{dp}{dx} < 0$ (*b*) $\left(\frac{\partial u}{\partial y}\right)_{y=0} = 0$

(*c*) $\left(\frac{\delta u}{\delta y}\right)_{y=0} > 0$ (*d*) none of the above.

13. Which of the following is the condition for detached flow?

(*a*) $\left(\frac{\partial u}{\partial y}\right)_{y=0} = 0$ (*b*) $\left(\frac{\partial u}{\partial y}\right)_{y=0} > 0$

(*c*) $\left(\frac{\partial u}{\partial y}\right)_{y=0} < 0$ (*d*) none of the above.

14. Von Karman momentum integral equation $\left(\frac{\tau_0}{\rho U^2} = \frac{\partial \theta}{\partial x}\right)$ is applicable to

(*a*) laminar boundary layer flow only
(*b*) turbulent boundary layer flow only
(*c*) transition boundary layer flow only
(*d*) laminar, transition and turbulent boundary layer flows.

15. If the Reynolds number is more than 5×10^5, the boundary layer is called

(*a*) laminar boundary layer
(*b*) turbulent boundary layer
(*c*) either of the above
(*d*) none of the above.

16. The separation of boundary can be prevented by

(*a*) providing small divergence in a diffuser
(*b*) providing a trip-wire ring in the laminar region for the flow over a sphere
(*c*) providing a bypass in the slotted wing
(*d*) suction of the slow moving fluid by a suction slot
(*e*) all of the above.

17. The ratio of mean velocity to the maximum velocity in a pipe depends on which of the following factors?

(*a*) Reynolds number of flow
(*b*) The pressure drop in the pipe
(*c*) The friction factor
(*d*) The density of the fluid
(*e*) The relative roughness of pipe
(*f*) All of the above.

18. The critical value of Reynolds number at which boundary layer changes from laminar to turbulent depends on which of the following?

(*a*) Turbulence in ambient flow
(*b*) Surface roughness
(*c*) Pressure gradient
(*d*) Plate curvature
(*e*) All of the above.

19. ...... thickness is the distance through which the total loss of momentum per second be equal to if it were passing a stationary plate.

(*a*) Displacement (*b*) Momentum
(*c*) Energy (*d*) None of above.

20. Ageing of pipes implies which of the following?

(*a*) A decrease in the value of friction factor
(*b*) Increase in absolute roughness linearly with time and hence friction factor
(*c*) Pipe becoming smoother with time
(*d*) None of the above.

ANSWERS

1. (*b*)	**2.** (*d*)	**3.** (*d*)	**4.** (*a*)	**5.** (*a*)	**6.** (*c*)
7. (*a*)	**8.** (*d*)	**9.** (*b*)	**10.** (*c*)	**11.** (*b*)	**12.** (*b*)
13. (*c*)	**14.** (*d*)	**15.** (*b*)	**16.** (*e*)	**17.** (*f*)	**18.** (*e*)
19. (*b*)	**20.** (*b*).				

THEORETICAL QUESTIONS

1. Explain briefly the term boundary layer.
2. Give four examples in everyday life where formation of boundary layer is important.
3. What is the 'slip condition' at the boundary?
4. What boundary condition must be satisfied by the velocity distribution in laminar boundary layer over a plate?
5. Why is the flow in the boundary layer analysed on the principles of viscous flow theory?
6. What is the physical significance of displacement thickness of boundary layer?
7. Define momentum thickness and energy thickness.
8. Define boundary layer and explain the fundamental causes of its existence.
9. Explain the characteristics of laminar and turbulent boundary layers.
10. Will the laminar boundary layer on a flat plate held at zero incidence always turn into turbulent boundary layer at $Re_x = 5 \times 10^5$? Explain.
11. Why is it necessary to control the growth of boundary layer on most of the bodies? What methods are used for such a control?
12. Is the flow within the boundary layer rotational or irrotational?
13. It is stated that the pressure distribution within the boundary layer is determined by the outside flow which can be treated as inviscid. Explain.
14. How are the thickness of boundary layer, shear stress and the drag force along the flat plate determined by Von Karman momentum equation?
15. Obtain an expression for the boundary shear stress in terms of momentum thickness.
16. How will you find the drag on a flat plate due to laminar and turbulent boundary layers?
17. How will you determine whether a boundary layer flow is attached flow, detached flow or on the verge of separation?
18. What is a boundary layer? Why does it increase with distance from the upstream edge?
19. Obtain Von Karman momentum integral equation.
20. Prove that the momentum thickness and energy thickness for boundary layer flows are given by

$$\theta = \int_0^\delta \frac{u}{U}\left(1 - \frac{u}{U}\right) dy$$

and, $$\delta_e = \int_0^\delta \frac{u}{U}\left(1 - \frac{u^2}{U^2}\right) dy$$

21. Define the following terms:
    (*i*) Laminar boundary layer
    (*ii*) Turbulent boundary layer
    (*iii*) Laminar sublayer
    (*iv*) Boundary layer thickness.
22. What is Blasius one-seventh power law of velocity distribution?
23. What is mean by average drag co-efficient C_D? How does it differ from the local drag co-efficient, C_D^*?
24. What is laminar sublayer? How is the concept of laminar sublayer useful?

UNSOLVED EXAMPLES

1. Show that for velocity distribution,

$$\frac{u}{U} = 2\left(\frac{y}{\delta}\right) - \left(\frac{y}{\delta}\right)^2,$$

the ratio of $\delta/\delta^* = 3$

2. The velocity distribution in the boundary layer over a high spillway face was found to have the following form:

$$\frac{u}{U} = \left(\frac{y}{\delta}\right)^{0.22}$$

Prove that the displacement thickness, the momentum thickness and the energy thickness in terms of δ, the boundary layer thickness, can be expressed as

$$\frac{\delta^*}{\delta} = 0.18;\ \frac{\theta}{\delta} = 0.125;\ \frac{\delta_e}{\delta} = 0.127$$

(Ravi Shanker University)

3. Find the ratio of displacement thickness to momentum thickness and momentum thick ness to energy thickness for the velocity distribution in the boundary layer given by

$$\frac{u}{U} = 2\,(y/\delta) - (y/\delta)^2$$ **[Ans. 2.5, 7/11]**

4. For the velocity profile in laminar layer given as

$$\frac{u}{U} = 2\left(\frac{y}{\delta}\right) - \left(\frac{y}{\delta}\right)^2$$

find the thickness of boundary layer at the end of the plate and the drag force on the side of the plate 1 m long and 0.8 m wide when placed in water flowing with a velocity of 0.15 m/s. Calculate the value of co-efficient of drag also. Take μ for water = 0.·001 Ns/m^2

[Ans. 14.15 mm, 0.0338 N, 0.00376]

5. Air flows over a smooth flat flate with a velocity of 10 m/s. The velocity profile is in the form

$$\frac{u}{U} = 2\left(\frac{y}{\delta}\right) - \left(\frac{y}{\delta}\right)^2$$

The length of the plate is 1.2 m and width 0.9 m. If laminar boundary layer exists upto a value of $Re = 2 \times 10^5$ and kinematic viscosity of air = 0.15 stokes, find: (*i*) The maximum distance from the leading edge upto which laminar boundary layer exists, and (*ii*) The maximum thickness of boundary layer.

[Ans. (*i*) 0.3 m; (*ii*) 3.67 mm]

6. A plate of length 500 mm and width 250 mm has been placed longitudinally in a stream of crude oil which flows with a velocity of 6 m/s. If the oil has a specific gravity of 0.9 and kinematic viscosity of 1 stoke, calculate:

(*i*) Boundary layer thickness at the middle of plate,

(*ii*) Shear stress at the middle of plate, and

(*iii*) Friction drag on one side of the plate.

[Ans. (*i*) 10.5 mm, (*ii*) 87.8 N/m^2, (*iii*) 12.36 N]

7. Atmospheric air at 20°C is flowing parallel to a flat plate at a velocity of 3 m/s. Assuming cubic velocity profile and using exact Blasius solution estimate the boundary layer thickness and the local co-efficient of drag at x = 1 m from the leading edge of the plate. Also find the deviation of the approximate solution from the exact solution.

[Ans. 11.376 mm; 1.511 × 10^{-3}; 7.2%, 2.78%]

8. Air is flowing over a plate 4 m × 2 m with a velocity of 5 m/s at 15°C. If ρ = 1.208 kg/m^3 and $\nu = 1.47 \times 10^{-5}$ m^2/s, calculate:

(*i*) Length of plate over which the boundary layer is laminar and thickness of the laminar boundary layer,

(*ii*) Shear stress at the location where boundary layer ceases to be laminar, and

(*iii*) Total force on both sides on that portion of plate where boundary layer is laminar.

[Ans. (*i*) 1.47 m; 10.39 mm; (*ii*) 0.01418 N/m^2; (*iii*) 0.1662 N]

9. A submarine can be assumed to have cylindrical shape with rounded nose. Assuming its length to be 55 m and diameter, 6·0 m, determine the total power required to overcome boundary friction if it cruises at 8·0 m/s velocity in water at 20°C Take ρ = 1030 kg/m^3; $\nu = 1 \times 10^{-6}$ m^2/s

[Ans. 476.5 kW]

10. A 2 m wide and 5.0 m long plate when towed through water at 20°C experiences a drag of 30.38 N on both the sides. Determine the velocity of the plate and the length over which the boundary layer is laminar.

[Ans. 1.0 m/s; 0.5 m]

11. If the velocity distribution in laminar boundary layer is given by $\frac{u}{U} = \frac{y}{\delta}$, obtain values/ expressions for $\frac{\theta}{\delta}, \frac{\delta}{x}, \frac{\delta^*}{\theta}$

$$\left[\textbf{Ans. } 0.333, \frac{3.64}{\sqrt{Re_x}}, 2.998\right]$$

12. Assume velocity distribution in laminar boundary layer over a flat plate to follow the law:

$$\frac{u}{U} = \sin\left(\frac{\pi}{2}\frac{y}{\delta}\right)$$

Obtain expressions for $\frac{\delta^*}{\theta}$ and $\frac{\delta}{x}$.

$$\left[\textbf{Ans. } \frac{2(\pi-2)}{(4-\pi)}, \frac{4.80}{\sqrt{Re_x}}\right]$$

13. A plate 300 mm × 100 mm is immersed in a liquid of density 998 kg/m^3 and kinematic viscosity 1×10^{-6} m^2/s. The water is moving with a velocity of 15.0 m/s parallel to it. Calculate:

(*i*) Drag force on that portion of the plate over which the boundary layer is laminar,

(*ii*) Total drag force on both sides of plate.

[Ans. (*i*) 1.39 N; (*ii*) 20.73 N]

14. A passenger ship of 300 m length and 12 m draft is travelling at 45 km/h. Assuming the ship's surface to act as flat plate, determine:

(*i*) The total friction drag, and

(*ii*) The power required to overcome this resistance.

Take ρ = 1000 kg/m^3 and $\nu = 1 \times 10^{-6}$ m^2/s.

[Ans. (*i*) 751.68 kN, (*ii*) 9396 kW]

15. The average drag co-efficient for turbulent layer flow past a thin plate is given by:

$$C_D = \frac{0.455}{(\log_{10} Re_L)^{2.58}}$$

where Re_L is the Reynolds number based on plate length. A plate 500 mm wide and 5 m long is kept parallel to the flow of water with free stream velocity 3 m/s. Calculate the drag force on both sides of the plate. Total $\nu = 0.01$ stoke. **[Ans.** 63.37 N]

16. A streamlined train is 250 m long with a typical cross-section having a perimeter of 8 m above the wheels. If the kinematic viscosity of air at the prevailing temperature is 1.5×10^{-5} m²/s and density is 1.24 kg/m³ determine the appropriate surface drag (friction drag) of the train when running at 80 km/h. Make allowance for the fact that boundary layer changes from laminar to turbulent on the train surface. **[Ans.** 1088.5 N]

17. A barge with a rectangular bottom surface 25 m long × 8 m wide is travelling down a river with a velocity of 0.5 m/s. A laminar boundary layer exists upto Reynolds number equivalent to 5×10^5 and subsequently abrupt transition occurs to turbulent boundary layer. Calculate:
   (*i*) The maximum distance from the leading edge upto which laminar boundary layer persists and maximum boundary layer thickness at that point,
   (*ii*) The total drag force on the flat bottom surface of the barge, and
   (*iii*) The power required to push the bottom surface through water, at the given velocity.

   For water $\rho = 998$ kg/m³ and $\nu = 1 \times 10^{-6}$ m²/s.
   [Ans. (*i*) 1 m; 7.07 mm (*ii*) 69.68 N; (*iii*) 34.84 W]

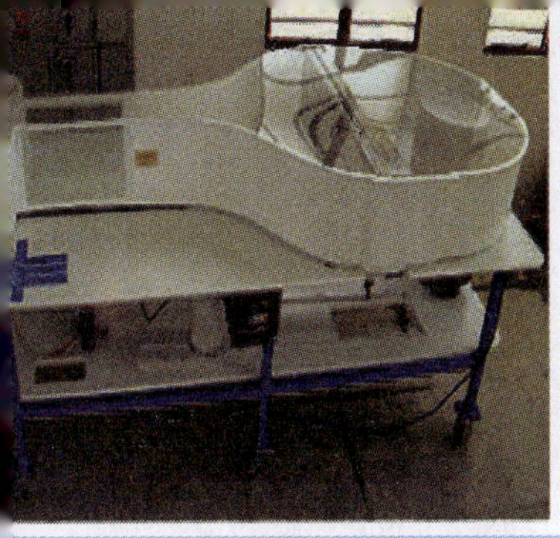

Chapter 14

FLOW AROUND SUBMERGED BODIES-DRAG AND LIFT

14.1. INTRODUCTION

In various engineering fields we encounter with the problems which involve the flow of fluid around submerged bodies/objects. In such problems either a fluid may be flowing around a stationary submerged body or a body may be flowing through a large mass of stationary fluid or both the body and the fluid may be in motion. Some of the *examples* are:

(*i*) Motion of very small objects/bodies such as fine sand particles in air or water,

(*ii*) Very large bodies such as airplanes, submarines, automobiles, ships etc. moving through air or water, and

(*iii*) The structures such as buildings, bridges etc. which are submerged in air or water,

14.2. FORCE EXERTED BY A FLOWING FLUID ON A BODY

Whenever there is relative motion between a real fluid and a body, the fluid exerts a force on the body. The body exerts an equal and opposite force on the fluid. If the body is moving at a constant velocity in a stationary fluid, the fluid motion is unsteady, because at a given point in space, the velocity changes with time. However if the body is stationary and fluid flows at a constant velocity, it is steady motion. *The magnitude of the force is same in both the cases.*

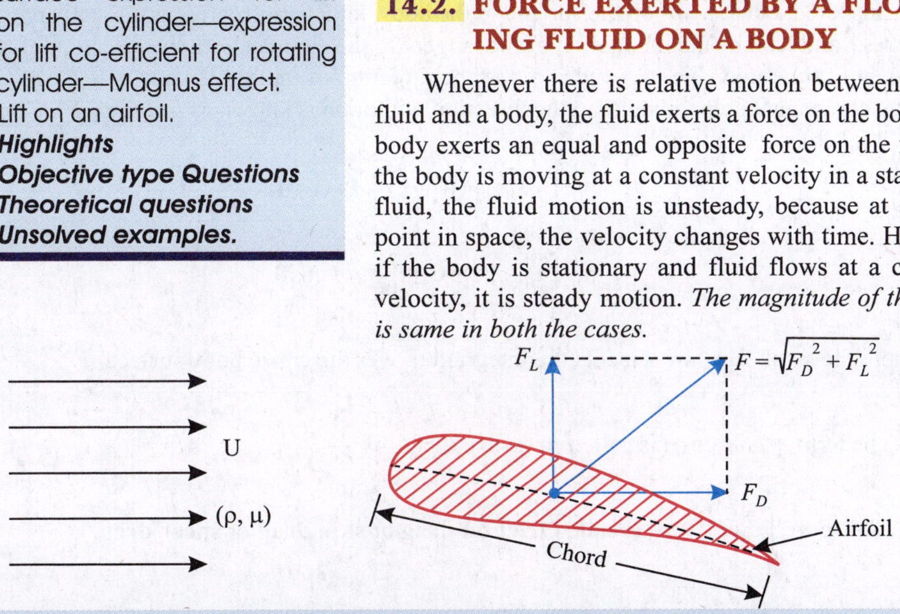

Fig. 14.1. Lift and drag on an airfoil.

A body wholly immersed in a real fluid may be subjected to fllowing two kinds of forces due to relative motion between the body and the fluid (Fig. 14.1); these are:

(*i*) **Drag force.** *The component of force in the direction of flow (free stream) on a submerged body is called the* ***drag force,*** F_D ;

(*ii*) **Lift force.** *The component of force at right angles to the direction of flow is called the* ***lift force,*** F_L.

When a free stream approaches the body *along* the axis of symmetry, the force acting on the body is only the drag force, in the direction of flow and there is no lift force. The *production of lift force requires asymmetry of flow, while drag force exists always. It is possible to create drag without lift but impossbile to create lift without drag.*

The fluid *viscosity* affects the flow around the body in three ways to cause the force on the body:

(*i*) At *low Reynolds number (Re) the fluid is deformed in very wide zone around the body causing pressure force and frictional force.*

(*ii*) As *Renolds number increases,* viscous effects are confined to the boundary layers causing predominantly *only friction force on the boundary.*

(*iii*) For certain body shapes, the *boundary layer can separate causing additional pressure.*

14.3. EXPRESSIONS FOR DRAG AND LIFT

Fig.14.2 shows a body held stationary in a stream of real fluid moving at a uniform velocity, *U.*

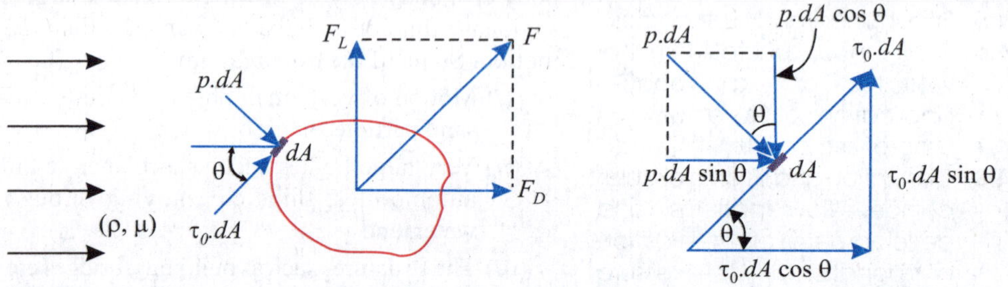

Fig. 14.2. Pressure and frictional forces on an elementary surface of an immersed body.

On an element of area *dA* on the surface of the body, let *P* and τ represent the static pressure and shear stress, and let θ be the inclination of the tangent to the element with the direction of flow. The component of the force, due to *p* and τ, along the direction of motion is known as *Drag force* F_D, while the component prependicular to the direction of motion is known as *Lift force* F_L. Considering the Fig. 14.2 (b), we can write:

$$F_D = \int_A p.dA \sin\theta + \int_A \tau_0.dA \cos\theta \qquad (14.1)$$

$$F_L = \int_A \tau_0.dA \sin\theta - \int_A p.dA \cos\theta \qquad (14.2)$$

where the symbol $\int_A$ repersents the integration over the entire body surface.

— The term $\int_A pdA \cos\theta$ is called **pressure drag.**

— The term $\int_A \tau_0.dA \sin\theta$ is called **friction drag** or **skin drag** or **shear drag.**

The contribution of *shear stresses to the lift may be neglected since shear stresses are small as compared to the pressure* and act in direction roughly perpendicular to F_L. For a body moving through a fluid of mass density ρ, at a uniform velocity U, the mathematical expression for the calculation of the drag and the lift may also be written as follows:

$$F_D = C_D\, A \frac{\rho U^2}{2} \qquad (14.3)$$

$$F_L = C_L\, A \frac{\rho U^2}{2} \qquad (14.4)$$

where, C_D = Co-efficient of drag (dimensionless),
C_L = Co-efficient of lift (dimensionless),
ρ = Density of fluid,
U = Relative velocity of fluid w.r.t. the body
A = Some characteristic area.

— For calculating the drag force (F_D), usually the *area A* is taken as the *area projected on the plane perpendicular to the relative motion of the fluid.*

— For calculating the lift force (F_1), the area A is taken as the *projected area of the body on a plane at right angles to the direction of lift force.*

— In the case of airfoil, the projection is conventionally taken on the plane of the chord, *i.e.*the area of the wing itself, independent of its inclination to the direction of flow.

$$\text{Area, } (A) = \text{Span } (l) \times \text{mean chord } (c) \qquad (14.5)$$

Examples of immersed bodies having drag and/or lift forces:

(*i*) A tall chimney exposed to wind;
(*ii*) Flow of water past a bridge pier;
(*iii*) Flow of fluids past blades in fans, blowers, compressors, turbines etc.;
(*iv*) Motion of aeroplanes, submarines, torpedoes etc.

Examples of bodies where both drag and lift forces are produced:

(*i*) Propeller blades; (*ii*) Aerofoils;
(*iii*) Hydrofiles; (*iv*) Rotating cylindrical bodies;
(*v*) Kites etc.

Following points are worth noting:

1. In contrast to drag, the lift forces may exist even in ideal fluids by the presence of circulation.
2. Real fluids also require vortices or circulation around the body for producing lift.
3. In motion of arifoils with finite spans, there is another kind of drag force associated with the lift force, called the "*induced drag*".

Pressure drag and friction drag:

The relative contribution of *pressure drag* $\left(\int p.dA \cos\theta\right)$ and *friction drag* $\left(\int \tau_0.dA \sin\theta\right)$ to the total drag depends on the following:

(*i*) Characteristics of fluid,
(*ii*) Shape of body, and
(*iii*) Orientation of the body immersed in the fluid.

- When a thin plate is placed *parallel* to the direction of flow (Fig. 14.3), the pressure drag will be *zero* ($\theta = 90°$) and the total drag is *entirely due to shear stresses* (and thus equal to friction drag or shear drag).

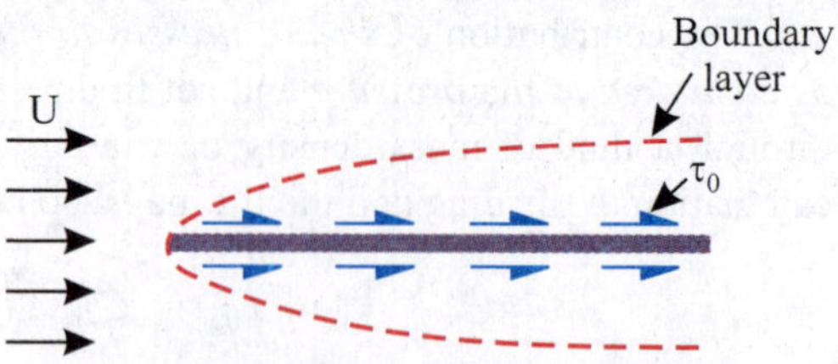

Fig. 14.3. Thin plate parallel to flow.

- When the same plate is held with its axis *normal* to flow direction (Fig. 14.4), the friction drag will be zero ($\theta = 0$) and *the flow separates at the edge forming a turbulent wake behind the plate*. In this case the total drag will be *due to the pressure force only*.
- When the plate is held *at an angle* with the direction of flow, the total drag will be equal to the *sum of pressure drag and friction drag*.

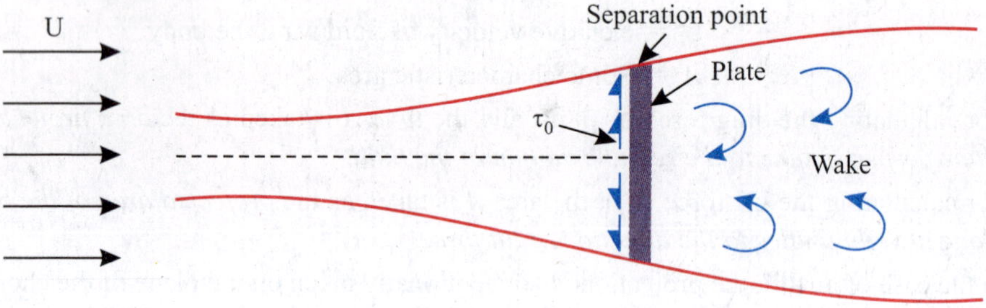

Fig. 14.4. Thin plate placed perpendicular to flow.

14.4. DIMENSIONAL ANALYSIS OF DRAG AND LIFT

For any given body shape, it is not possible to calculate the magnitude of the force, F, or its components F_D and F_L, theoretically. As such in almost all the cases the general practice is to evaluate forces experimentally. In order to plan the experiments properly and to analyse the results correctly, dimensional analysis of the problem is carried out as given below.

Let us consider an object of characteristic length L be placed in a fluid stream of velocity U, of density ρ, of viscosity μ and modulus of elasticity E. Then the force F exerted on the body could be written as :

$$F = f(L, \rho, \mu, E, U, g) \qquad (14.6)$$

By adopting any of the methods of dimensional analysis eqn. (14.6) may be transformed to the following dimensionless form:

$$\frac{F}{\rho L^2 U^2} = f\left(\frac{\rho UL}{\mu}, \frac{U}{\sqrt{E/\rho}}, \frac{U}{\sqrt{gL}}\right)$$

But, $$\frac{\rho UL}{\mu} = Re, \quad \text{Reynolds number of flow}$$

$$\frac{U}{\sqrt{E/\rho}} = M, \quad \text{Mach's number}$$

$$\frac{U}{\sqrt{gL}} = Fr, \quad \text{Froude's number}$$

$$\therefore \quad \frac{F}{\rho L^2 U^2} = f(Re, M, Fr) \qquad (14.7)$$

— At low speeds ($M \leq 0.3$) the change in density is insignificant and so the *effect of Mach's number is negligible.*

— When the body is submerged fully in surrounding fluid the *Froude's number has no effect.*

Under the above circumstances the eqn. (14.7) can be rewritten as:

$$\frac{F}{\rho L^2 U^2} = f(Re) \quad (14.8)$$

The parameter L^2 represents area of the body, and parameter $\frac{\rho U^2}{2}$ represents the dynamic pressure of the undisturbed flow stream.

Further, eqn. (14.8) applies equally to both lift and drag which can thus be expressed in dimensionless terms by the definition of drag and lift co-efficients as :

$$\text{Co-efficient of drag, } C_D = \frac{F_D}{\frac{1}{2}\rho U^2 \times A} \quad (14.9)$$

$$\text{Co-efficient of lift, } C_L = \frac{F_L}{\frac{1}{2}\rho U^2 \times A} \quad (14.10)$$

The co-efficients C_D and C_L are of paramount importance and are invariably used for *correlating aerodynamic lift forces.*

Example 14.1. *A truck having a projected area of 6.5 m² travelling at 70 km/h has a total resistance of 2000 N. Of this 20 percent is due to rolling friction and 10 percent due to surface friction. The rest is due to form drag. Make calculations for the co-efficients of form drag. Take ρ = 1.22 kg/m³ for air.* **[PTU]**

Solution. Projected area, $A = 6.5 \text{ m}^2$

Speed of the truck, $U = 70 \text{ km/h} = \frac{70 \times 1000}{60 \times 60} = 19.44 \text{ m/s}$

Density of air, $\rho = 1.22 \text{ kg/m}^3$

Total resistance $= 2000$ N

Resistance due to rolling friction $= \frac{20}{100} \times 2000 = 400\text{N}$

Resistance due to surface friction $= \frac{10}{100} \times 2000 = 200\text{N}$

Resistance due to form drag $= 2000 - 400 - 200 = 1400$ N

Co-efficient of form drag, C_D:

Now, form drag $= C_D \times \frac{\rho U^2}{2} \times A$

$$1400 = C_D \times \frac{1.22 \times (19.44)^2}{2} \times 6.5$$

$$\therefore \quad C_D = \frac{1400 \times 2}{1.22 \times (19.44)^2 \times 6.5} = \mathbf{0.934} \textbf{ (Ans.)}$$

Example 14.2. *On a flat plate of 2 m (length) × 1 m (width), experiments were conducted in a wind tunnel with a wind speed of 50 km/h. The plate is kept at such an angle that the co-efficients of drag and lift ate 0.18 and 0.9 respectively.*

Determine:

(i) Drag force,

(ii) Lift force,

(iii) Resultant force, and

(iv) Power exerted by the air stream on the plate.

Take density of air $= 1.15 \text{ kg/m}^3$

Solution. Area of the plate, $A = 2 \times 1 = 2 \text{ m}^2$

Speed of wind, $U = 50 \text{ km/h} = \dfrac{50 \times 1000}{60 \times 60} = 13.89 \text{m/s}$

Density of air, $\rho = 1.15 \text{ kg/m}^3$

Co-efficient of drag, $C_D = 0.18$

Co-efficient of lift, $C_L = 0.9$.

(*i*) Drag force, F_D:

$$F_D = C_D \times \frac{\rho U^2}{2} \times A$$

$$= 0.18 \times \frac{1.15 \times 13.89^2}{2} \times 2 = 39.94 \text{ N } \textbf{(Ans.)}$$

(*ii*) Lift force, F_L:

$$F_L = C_L \times \frac{\rho U^2}{2} \times A$$

$$= 0.9 \times \frac{1.15 \times 13.89^2}{2} \times 2 = \textbf{199.7 N (Ans.)}$$

(*iii*) Resultant force, F: $F = \sqrt{F_D^2 + F_L^2} = \sqrt{(39.94)^2 + (199.7)^2} = \textbf{203.65 N (Ans.)}$

Inclination with the velocity of air, $\theta = \tan^{-1} \dfrac{F_L}{F_D} = \tan^{-1} \dfrac{199.7}{39.94} = \mathbf{78.69^\circ}$ **(Ans.)**

(*iv*) Power extered by the air stream on the plate, P:

$$P = F_D \times \text{U}$$

$$= 39.94 \times 13.89 = \textbf{554.7 W (Ans.)}$$

Example 14.3. *Assuming the cross-sectional area of a passenger car to be 2.7 m² with a drag co-efficient of 0.6, estimate the energy requirment at a speed of 60 km/h. Assume the weight of car to be 30 kN and co-efficient of friction 0.012. Assume ρ to be 1.208 kg/m³.*

Solution. Cross-sectional area of passenger car, $A = 2.7 \text{m}^2$

Co-efficient of drag, $C_D = 0.6$

Speed of the passenger car, $U = 60 \text{ km/h } \dfrac{60 \times 1000}{60 \times 60} = 16.67 \text{ m/s}$

Weight of the car, $W = 30 \text{ kN}$

Co-efficient of friction, $\mu' = 0.012$

Energy requirement, P:

Total resisting force, (F) = Aerodynamic drag on the car + friction at the road surface

$$\therefore \quad F = C_D \frac{\rho U^2}{2} \times A + \mu' W$$

$$= 0.6 \times \frac{1.208 \times 16.67^2}{2} \times 2.7 + 0.012 \times (30 \times 1000)$$

$$= 217.9 + 360 = 631.9 \text{ N}$$

Now, $$P = F \times U$$

$$= 631.9 \times 16.67 = 10553 \text{ W or } \mathbf{10.53\ kW}$$ **(Ans.)**

(This is the power required at the wheels)

Example 14.4. *The vertical component of the landing speed of a parachute is 6 m/s. Treat the parachute as an open hemisphere (Fig. 14.5) and determine its diameter if the total weight to be carried is 1200 N. Take* $\rho = 1.208$ *kg/m*^{3} *and* $C_D = 1.33$.

Solution. Speed of parachute, $U = 6$ m/s

Weight to be carried, $W = 1200$ N

Density of air, $\rho = 1.208$ kg/m^3

Co-efficient of drag, $C_D = 1.33$

Diameter of parachute, *D*:

Projected area of the hemispherical parachute,

$$A = \frac{\pi}{4} D^2$$

Drag force, $F_D = W = 1200$ N

Using the equation:

$$F_D = C_D \times \frac{\rho U^2}{2} \times A, \text{ we get:}$$

$$1200 = 1.33 \times \frac{1.208 \times 6^2}{2} \times \frac{\pi}{4} D^2$$

or, $$D^2 = \frac{1200 \times 2 \times 4}{1.33 \times 1.208 \times \pi \times 36} = 52.83$$

or, $$D = \mathbf{7.72\ m/s}$$ **(Ans.)**

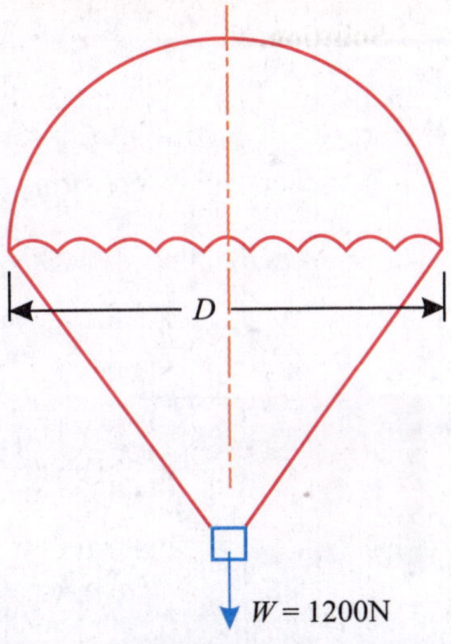

Fig. 14.5. Parachute.

Example 14.5. *Experiments were conducted in a wind tunnel at 50 kmph on a flat plate of size 2 m × 1 m. The specific weight of air is 11.28 N/m*^{3}. *The plate is kept at such an angle that the co-efficients of lift and drag are 0.75 and 0.15, respectively. Determine lift force, drag force, resulting force and power exerted by air stream on the plate.* **(Delhi University)**

Solution. *Given :* $$U = 50 \text{ kmph} = \frac{50 \times 100}{60 \times 60} = 13.89 \text{ m/s}; A = 2 \times 1 = 2\text{m}^2;$$

$$w = 11.28 \text{ N/m}^3; C_L = 0.75; C_D = 0.15$$

***F_D, F_L, F_R, P*:**

$$\rho = \frac{w}{g} = \frac{11.28}{9.8} = 1.15 \text{ kg/m}^3$$

Lift force, $$F_L = C_L \times \frac{\rho U^2}{2} \times A$$ [Eqn. (14.3)]

$$= 0.75 \times \frac{1.15 \times (13.89)^2}{2} \times 2 = \mathbf{166.4\ N}$$ **(Ans.)**

Drag force, $$F_D = C_D \times \frac{\rho U^2}{2} \times A = 0.15 \times \frac{1.15 \times (13.89)^2}{2} \times 2 = \mathbf{33.28\ N}$$ **(Ans.)**

Resultant force, $F_R = \sqrt{F_L^2 + F_D^2} = \sqrt{(166.4)^2 + (33.28)^2} = $ **169.69 N (Ans.)**

Inclination with the main stream, $\theta = \tan^{-1}\left(\frac{166.4}{33.28}\right) = $ **78.69° (Ans.)**

Power exerted by the air stream on the plate,

$$P = F_D \times U = 33.28 \times 13.89 = 462.26 \text{ Nm/s} = \textbf{462.26 W (Ans.)}$$

Example 14.6. *A kite weighing 9.8 N and having an area 1 m² makes an angle of 7° to horizontal when flying in a wind of 36 km/h. If pull on the string attached to the kite is 49 N and it is inclined to the horizontal at 45°, calculate the lift and drag co-efficients. Take ρ for air = 1.2 kg/m³.* **[Anna University]**

Solution. Weight of the kite = 9.8 N

Projected area of the kite, $A = 1 \text{ m}^2$

Angle made by the kite with the horizontal = 7°

Angle made by the string with the horizontal = 45°

Pull on the string, P = 49 N.

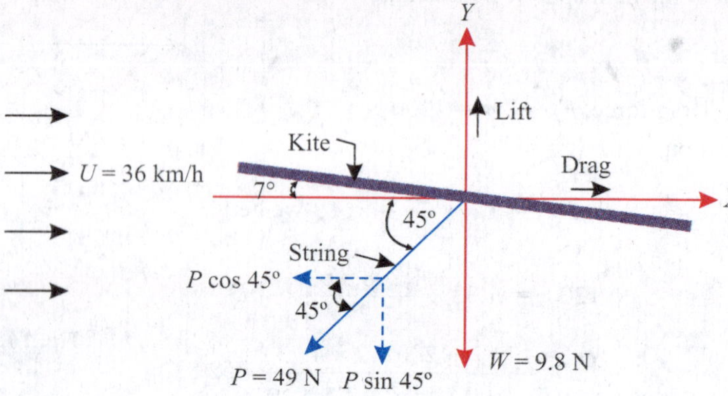

Fig. 14.6. Forces on a flying kite.

Speed of the wind, $U = 36 \text{ km/h} = \frac{36 \times 1000}{60 \times 60} = 10 \text{ m/s}$

Density of air, $\rho = 1.0 \text{ kg/m}^3$

The forces acting on the kite taken as free body are shown in Fig 14.6.

Drag forces, F_D = Force exerted by wind on the kite in the direction of motion, *i.e.* in the X-direction

= Components of pull along X- direction

= $P \cos 45° = 49 \cos 45° = 34.65$ N

Drag co-efficient, C_D:

$$F_D = C_D \times \frac{\rho U^2}{2} \times A$$

$$34.65 = C_D \times \frac{1.2 \times 10^2}{2} \times 1 = 60\, C_D$$

or C_D = **0.577 (Ans.)**

Lift co-efficient, C_L:

Lift force, F_L = Force exerted by wind on the kite perpendicular to the direction of motion *i.e.*,along Y-direction

$$= \text{Component of } P \text{ in vertically downward direction + weight of kite}$$

$$= P \sin 45° + 9.8 = 49 \sin 45° + 9.8 = 44.45 \text{ N}$$

Also, $$F_L = C_L \times \frac{\rho U^2}{2} \times A$$

$\therefore$ $$44.45 = C_L \times \frac{1.2 \times 10^2}{2} \times 1 = 60\, C_L$$

or, $$C_L = \frac{44.45}{60} = \mathbf{0.741\ (Ans.)}$$

Example 14.7. *A kite of dimensions 0.8 m × 0.8 m and weighing 6 N is maintained in air at an angle of 10° to the horizontal. The string attached to the kite makes an angle at 45° to the horizontal and at this position, the drag and lift co-efficients are estimated to be 0.6 and 0.8 respectively. Determine;*

(i) *Wind speed, and* ***(ii)*** *Tension in the string.*

Take ρ for air = 1.2 kg/m³

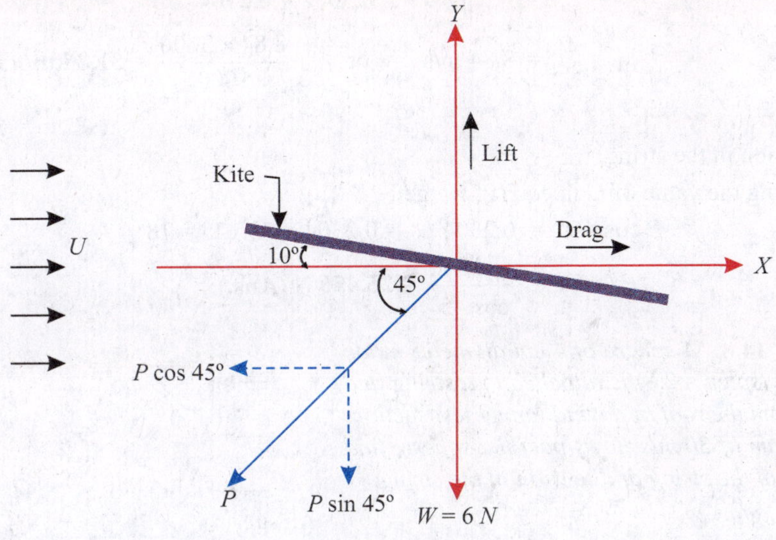

Fig. 14.7

Solution. Projected area of the kite, $A = 0.8 \times 0.8 = 0.64 \text{ m}^2$,

Weight of kite, $W = 6$ N,

Angle made by kite with horizontal = 10°,

Angle made by the string with horizontal = 45°,

Co-efficient of drag, $C_D = 0.6$,

Co-efficient of lift, $C_L = 0.8$.

(*i*) Wind speed, *U*:

Drag force, F_D = Component of string force P in the X-direction

$$= P \cos 45°$$

Also, $$F_D = C_D \times \frac{\rho U^2}{2} \times A$$

$$\therefore \quad P\cos 45° = 0.6 \times \frac{1.2U^2}{2} \times 0.64$$

$$\text{or,} \quad P\cos 45° = 0.2304\,U^2 \qquad (i)$$

$$\text{Lift force,} \quad F_L = \text{Component of string force } P \text{ vertically downwards + weight of kite}$$

$$= P\sin 45° + 6$$

$$\text{Also,} \quad F_L = C_L \times \frac{\rho U^2}{2} \times A$$

$$\text{or,} \quad P\sin 45° + 6 = 0.8 \times \frac{1.2 \times U^2}{2} \times 0.64 = 0.3071\,U^2$$

$$\text{or,} \quad P\sin 45° = 0.3071\,U^2 - 6 \qquad (ii)$$

$$\text{But,} \quad P\sin 45° = P\cos 45° \qquad (\because \sin 45° = \cos 45°)$$

$$\therefore \quad 0.2304\,U^2 = 0.3072\,U^2 - 6 \qquad [\text{equating eqns. } (i) \text{ and } (ii)]$$

$$\text{or,} \quad U^2(0.3072 - 0.2304) = 6 \quad \text{or} \quad U^2 = \frac{6}{0.3072 - 0.2304} = 78.125$$

$$\therefore \quad U = 8.84 \text{ m/s} \quad \text{or} \quad \frac{8.84 \times 3600}{1000} = \mathbf{31.8\ km/h\ (Ans.)}$$

(*ii*) Tension in the string, *T* (= *P*):

Here tension in the string, $T = P$

Substituting the value of U in eqn (*i*), we get:

$$P\cos 45° = 0.2304\,U^2 = 0.2304 \times 78.125 = 18$$

$$P(=T) = \frac{18}{\cos 45°} = \mathbf{25.456\ N\ (Ans.)}$$

Example 14.8. *A sphere of 4 cm diameter made of aluminium (sp.gr. =2.8) is attached to a string and suspended from the roof of a wind tunnel test section. If an air stream of 30 m/s flows past the sphere, find the incliaton of the string and tension in the string.*

$\rho_a = 1.2$ kg/m^3

$v_a = 1.5 \times 10^{-5}$ m^2/s

$C_D = 0.5,\ 10^4 < Re \le 3 \times 10^5, = 0.2,\ Re > 3 \times 10^5$

(Neglect drag on string). **(UPTU)**

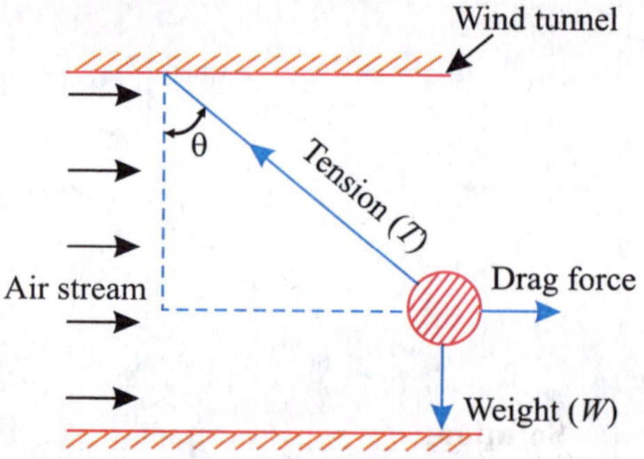

Fig. 14.8

Solution. *Given:* Dia. of sphere,

$$D = 4 \text{ cm} = 0.04 \text{ m},$$

$$\text{sp. gravity} = 2.8: U = 30 \text{ m/s};\ \rho_a = 1.2 \text{ kg/m}^3;$$

$$v_a = 1.5 \times 10^{-5} \text{ m}^2/\text{s};$$

$$C_D = 0.5,\ 10^4\ Re \le 3 \times 10^5, = 0.2,\ Re > 3 \times 10^5$$

θ, *T*:

$$\text{Weight} = \frac{4}{3}\pi R^3 \times \rho \times g = \frac{4}{3}\pi \times \left(\frac{0.04}{2}\right)^3 \times (2.8 \times 1000) \times 9.81 = 0.92 \text{ N}$$

$$Re = \frac{UD}{v_a} = \frac{30 \times 0.04}{1.5 \times 10^{-5}} = 0.8 \times 10^5$$

$\therefore \quad C_D = 0.5$

$$\text{Drag force, } F_D = C_D \times \frac{\rho_a U^2}{2} \times A = 0.5 \times \frac{1.2 \times (30)^2}{2} \times \left[\pi \times \left(\frac{0.04}{2}\right)^2\right]$$

$$= \mathbf{0.339\ N\ (Ans.)}$$

$$\tan\theta = \frac{\text{Drag force}}{\text{Weight}} = \frac{F_D}{W} = \frac{0.339}{0.92}$$

$$\therefore \quad \theta = \tan^{-1}\left(\frac{0.339}{0.92}\right) = \mathbf{20.22°\ (Ans).}$$

$$\text{Tension in the string, } T = \sqrt{F_D^2 + W^2} = \sqrt{0.339^2 + 0.92^2} = \mathbf{0.98\ N\ (Ans.)}$$

Example 14.9. *Air blows over a cylinder of diameter 60 mm and finite length with a velocity of 0.12 m/s. Find the total drag, shear drag and pressure drag on 1 m length of the cylinder if the total drag and shear drag co-efficients are 1.25 and 0.18 respectively. Take ρ for air = 1.25 kg/m³.*

Solution. Diameter of cylinder, D = mm = 0.06 m

Length of cylinder, L = 1 m

Velocity of air, U = 0.12 m/s

Total drag co-efficient, C_{DT} = 1.25

Shear drag co-efficient, C_{DS} = 0.18

Density of air, ρ = 1.25 kg/m³

Total drag,

$$F_{DT} = C_{DT} \times \frac{\rho U^2}{2} \times A$$

(where, A = projected area = $1 \times 0.06 = 0.06$ m²)

or,

$$F_{DT} = 1.25 \times \frac{1.25 \times 0.12^2}{2} \times 0.06 = \mathbf{6.75 \times 10^{-4}\ N\ \ (Ans.)}$$

Shear drag,

$$F_{DS} = C_{DS} \times \frac{\rho U^2}{2} \times A = 0.18 \times \frac{1.25 \times 0.12^2}{2} \times 0.06$$

$$= \mathbf{9.72 \times 10^{-5}\ N\ (Ans.)}$$

Also, Total drag = Pressure drag + shear drag

$\therefore$ **Pressure drag** = Total drag – shear drag

$$= 6.75 \times 10^{-4} - 9.72 \times 10^{-5} = \mathbf{5.778 \times 10^{-4}\ N\ (Ans.)}$$

Example 14.10. *A 2.5 m long body having a projected area of 2.4 m² normal to the dirction of motion, is moving through water which is having a viscosity of 0.0012 Ns/m². Find the drag on the body if it has drag co-efficient 0.45 for Reynolds number of 7× 10⁶.*

Solution. Length of body, L = 25 m

Projected area of body, A = 2.4 m²

Viscocity of water, μ = 0.0012 Ns/m²

Drag co-efficient, C_D = 0.45

Reynolds number, Re = 7×10^6

Drag on the body, F_D:

Let us first find from the given Reynolds number the velocity with which the body is moving in water.

Now,

$$Re = \frac{\rho U L}{\mu}$$

$$\text{or,} \quad 7 \times 10^6 = \frac{1000 \times U \times 2.5}{0.0012} \quad \text{or} \quad U = \frac{7 \times 10^6 \times 0.0012}{1000 \times 2.5} = 3.36 \text{ m/s}$$

Drag on the body (F_D) is given by:

$$F_D = C_D \times \frac{\rho U^2}{2} \times A = 0.45 \times \frac{1000 \times 3.36^2}{2} \times 2.4$$

$$= \mathbf{6096.4 \text{ N (Ans.)}}$$

Example 14.11. *A cup anemometer shown in Fig. 14.9 rotates freely without air friction. Calculate the speed of rotation against a wind speed of 54 km/h. Take for hemisphere: For hollow upstream, $C_D = 1.33$; for hollow downstream, $C_D = 0.34$.*

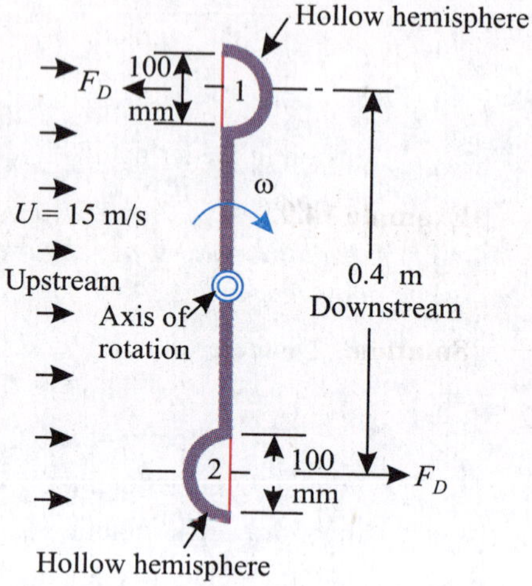

Fig. 14.9

Solution. Wind speed,

$$U = 54 \text{ km/h} = \frac{54 \times 1000}{60 \times 60} = 15 \text{ m/s}$$

Speed of rotation, N (r.p.m.):

If the anemometer revolves at a uniform angular velocity ω, for steady rotation, net torque *about the axis of rotation must be zero.*

Fluid velocity relative to cup 1 = 15 – 0.2 ω

Fluid velocity relative to cup 2 = 15 + 0.2 ω

Corresponding drag forces on 1 and 2 are:

$$F_D = 1.33 \times \frac{A\rho}{2} (150 - 0.2\omega)^2$$

$$F_D = 1.34 \times \frac{A\rho}{2} (15 + 0.2\omega)^2 \qquad \left[\because F_D = C_D \times \frac{A\rho U^2}{2}\right]$$

Now, $$\text{Torque} = (F_{D_1} - F_{D_2})\, r = 0$$

or, $$F_{D_1} = F_{D_2} \qquad (\because r \neq 0)$$

or, $$1.33 \frac{A\rho}{2} (15 - 0.2\omega)^2 = 0.34 \times \frac{A\rho}{2} (15 + 0.2\omega)^2$$

or, $$\left(\frac{15 - 0.2\omega}{15 + 0.2\omega}\right)^2 = \frac{0.34}{1.33} \quad \text{or} \quad \frac{15 - 0.2\omega}{15 + 0.2\omega} = 0.5056$$

or, $$15 - 0.2\,\omega = 0.5056\,(15 + 0.2\,\omega) = 7.584 + 0.101\omega$$

or, $$0.301\,\omega = 7.146, \quad \text{or} \quad \omega = \frac{7.416}{0.301} = 24.64 \text{ rad/s.}$$

But, $$\omega = \frac{2\pi N}{60} = 24.64$$

$$\therefore \quad N = \frac{24{\cdot}64 \times 60}{2\pi} = \mathbf{235.3 \text{ r.p.m. (Ans.)}}$$

Example 14.12. *A.mixer consists of two circular discs each 120 mm in diameter. These discs are spaced 1.2 m apart on the two ends of a horizontal rod whose centre has a vertical shaft attachement to it. The mixer is used to rotate in a solution having a density $\rho = 930$ kg/m^3 and kinematic viscosity $\nu = 0.8$ stoke. Neglecting the resistance of the rod and shaft, find the power required by the shaft revolving at 50 r. p.m. For 3000 < Re <5000, take $C_D = 1.15$.*

Solution. Diameter of each circular disc, $D = 120$ m $= 0.12$ m

Distance between the disc $=$ 1.2 m

Density of solution, $\rho = 930 \text{ kg/ m}^3$

Kinematic viscosity of the solution,

$\nu = 0.8$ stoke $= 0.8 \times 10^{-4} \text{ m}^2/\text{s}$

Speed of the shaft, $N = 50$ r. p .m.

Co-effiecient of drag, $C_D = 1.15$

(for $3000 < Re < 5000$)

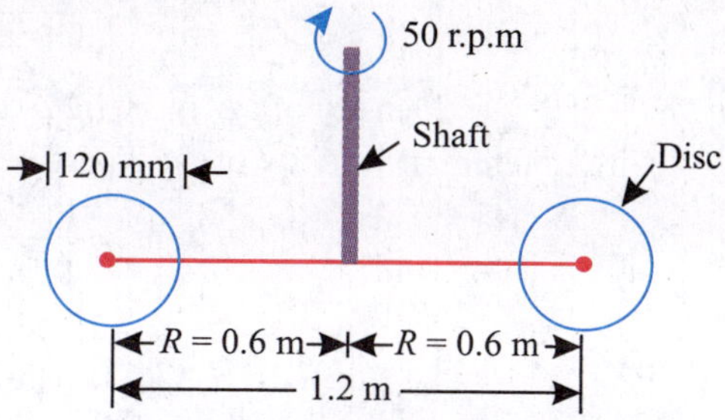

Fig. 14.10

Power required, *P*:

Linear velocity of each disc,

$$U = \frac{\pi DN}{60} = \frac{\pi \times 1.2 \times 50}{60} = 3.14 \text{ m/s}$$

$$\text{Reynolds number, } Re = \frac{UD}{\nu}$$

$$= \frac{3.14 \times 0.12}{0.8 \times 10^{-4}} = 4710$$

As Re lies between 3000 and 5000, therefore, coefficient of drag, $C_D = 1.15$

$$\text{The drag on each disc, } F_D = C_D \times \frac{\rho U^2}{2} \times A$$

$$= 1.15 \times \frac{930 \times 3.14^2}{2} \times (\pi/4) \times 0.12^2 = 59.63 \text{ N}$$

$\therefore$ Torque produced by the drag on the two discs

$$= 2 F_D \times R = 2 \times 59.63 \times 0.6 = 71.55 \text{ Nm}$$

$$\text{Power required, } P = \frac{2\pi NT}{60} \text{ watts} = \frac{2\pi \times 50 \times 71.55}{60} = \mathbf{374.6 W} \textbf{ (Ans.)}$$

[Alternatively: $P = 2 \times F_D \times U = 2 \times 59.63 \times 3.14 =$ **374.5 W (Ans.)**

Example 14.13. *A ship is propelled by two cylindrical rotors each of diameter 2.5 m and length 7.5 m revolving at 150 r. p. m. about their axes which are horizontal. Estimate the force exerted upon the rotors in the direction of motion when the relative wind velocity is 40 km/h at an angle of 30° to the horizontal. Assume ρ for air as 1.22 kg/m³.*

Solution. Diameter of each rotor, $D = 2.5$ m

Length of each rotor, $L = 7.5$ m

Speed of each rotor,

$N = 150$ r. p. m.

Relative wind velocity,

$U = 40$ km/h

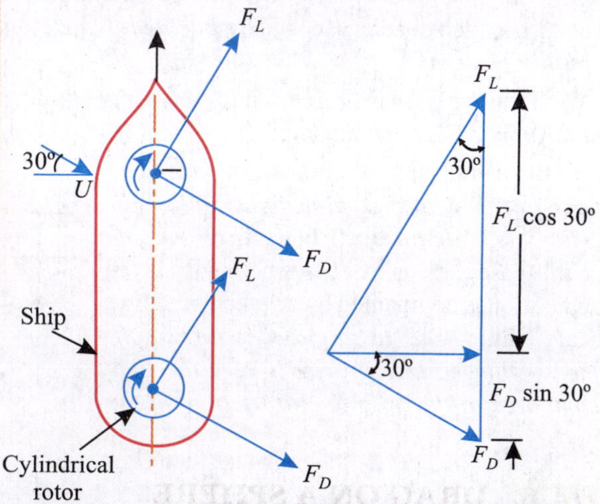

Fig. 14.11. Estimation of force on a ship propelled by two rotors.

$$= \frac{40 \times 1000}{600 \times 60} = 11.11 \text{ m/s}$$

Density of air, $\rho = 1.22 \text{ kg/m}^3$

Circumferential velocity of the rotors,

$$u_c = \frac{\pi DN}{60} = \frac{\pi \times 2.5 \times 150}{60} = 19.63 \text{ m/s}$$

$$\therefore \quad \text{Ratio, } \frac{u_c}{U} = \frac{19.63}{11.11} = 1.77$$

From Fig. 14.20, the corresponding values of drag and lift co-efficients are:

$C_L \simeq 4.4$ and $C_D \simeq 1.5$

Lift force for each rotor,

$$F_L = C_L \times \frac{\rho U^2}{2} \times A = 4{\cdot}4 \times \frac{1{\cdot}22 \times 11{\cdot}11^2}{2} \times (18{\cdot}75) = 6211{\cdot}7 \text{ N}$$

(where, A = Projected area = 7.5 m × 2.5 m = 18.75m²)

Drag force for each rotor,

$$F_D = C_D \times \frac{\rho U^2}{2} \times A = 1{\cdot}5 \times \frac{1{\cdot}22 \times 11{\cdot}11^2}{2} \times 18{\cdot}75 = 2117{\cdot}6 \text{ N}$$

Total force in the direction of motion,

$$F = 2\,(F_L \cos 30° - F_D \sin 30°)$$
$$= 2\,(6211.7 \cos 30° - 2117.6 \sin 30°) = \mathbf{8641 \ N \ (Ans.)}$$

14.5. STREAMLINED AND BLUFF BODIES

Streamlined body. *A body whose surface coincides with the stream lines when placed in a flow, is called a* **streamlined body** (Fig. 14.12). In this case flow separation takes place only at the trailling edge or rearmost part of the body. The wake formation zone behind a streamlined body is very small, as a consequence of which the pressure drag will be very small. In such a body although due to *greater surface* of the body the skin friction increases but the net effect is a *significant reduction of total drag.* A body may be streamlined at *low velocites but may not be so at higher velocities,* also when placed in *a particular position in flow but may not be so when placed in another position.*

Streamlined shapes are used for the *wings of aeroplanes* and for the *blades of marine propellers and rotary axial* flow machines.

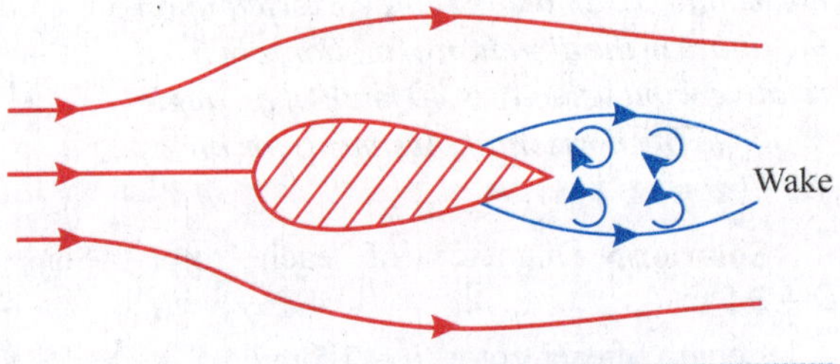

Fig. 14.12. Streamlined body.

Bluff body. *A body whose surface does not coincide with streamlines when placed in a flow, is called a* **bluff body** *(Fig. 14.13).* In this case there is extensive boundary layer separation accompanied by a wake with large scale eddies. *Due to large wake formation, the resulting pressure drag is very large as compared to the drag due to friction on the body.*

14.6. DRAG ON A SPHERE

It has been observed that in the case of an ideal fluid flowing past a sphere (or any other object) there is no drag.

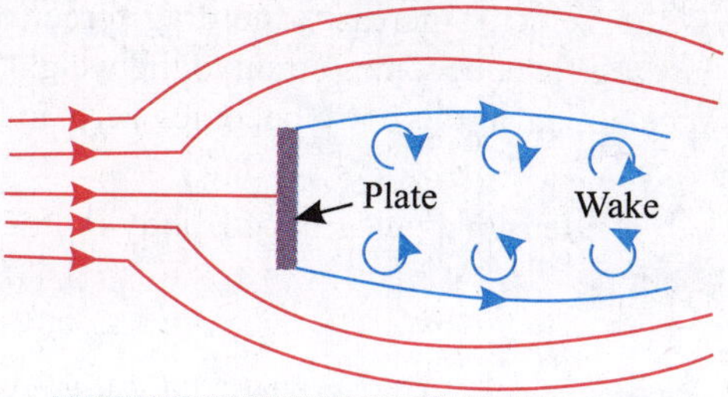

Fig. 14.13. Bluff body.

Let us consider a case when real fluid flows past a sphere. Let D be the diameter of the sphere, V be the velocity of flow of fluid of mass density ρ and viscosity μ.

(*i*) **For $Re \le 0.2$:** When the velocity of flow is very small or the fluid is very viscous such that the Reynolds number is very small, being as low as 0.2 $\left(i.e.\ Re = \frac{\rho UD}{\mu} \le 0.2 \right)$ or even less then the *viscous forces are much more predominant than the intertial forces.* C.G. Stokes analysed theoretically the flow around a sphere under very low velocities, such that $Re < 0.2$.Stokes found that the total drag force is given by:

$$F_D = 3\,\pi\,\mu DU \tag{14.11}$$

He further found out that out of the total drag given by eqn. (14.11), *two-thirds* is contributed by *skin friction* and *one-third* by the *pressure difference.* Thus:

$$\text{Skin friction drag} = \frac{2}{3} F_D = \frac{2}{3} \times 3\pi\mu DU = 2\pi\mu DU$$

$$\text{Pressure drag} = \frac{1}{3} F_D = \frac{1}{3} \times 3\pi\mu DU = \pi\mu DU$$

Also, the total drag is given by:

$$F_D = C_D \times \frac{\rho U^2}{2} \times A \qquad \text{[Eqn. (14.9)]}$$

(where, A = projected area of the sphere $= \frac{\pi}{4} D^2$)

From eqns. (14.11) and (14.9), we have:

$$3\pi\mu DU = C_D \times \frac{\rho U^2}{2} \times \frac{\pi}{4} \times D^2$$

$$\therefore \quad C_D = \frac{3\pi\mu DU}{\frac{\rho U^2}{2} \times \frac{\pi}{4} D^2} = \frac{24\mu}{\rho UD} = \frac{24}{Re} \tag{14.12}$$

Eqn. (14.12) is generally called **'Stokes law'.**

(*ii*) **For Re between 0.2 and 5:** Oseen made an improvement to the Stokes' solution by *partly* taking into account the *effect of inertial terms.*He found that

$$C_D = \frac{24}{Re}\left(1 + \frac{3}{16Re}\right) \tag{14.13}$$

(*iii*) **For $5 \le Re \le 1000$:** The value of C_D for Re between 5 to 1000 is equal to 0.4

(*iv*) **For $1000 \le Re \le 100000$:** The value of C_D in the range is more or less independent of Reynolds number, and may be taken as 0.5.

(*v*) **For $Re > 10^5$:** For Reynolds mumber greater than 10^5 the value of C_D is approximately equal to 0.2.

14.6.1. Terminal velocity of a body

The **terminal velocity** *is the maximum velocity attained by a falling body.* When a body is allowed to fall from rest in the atmosphere its velocity increases due to gravitational acceleration.

As the velocity increases the drag force (opposing the motion of the body) also increases. When the drag force becomes equal to the weight of the body, the acceleration ceases and the net external force acting in the body becomes zero and the body will move at constant speed (called terminal velocity).

The terminal velocity of a body falling through a liquid at rest is calculated from the following relation:

$$W = F_D + F_B \tag{14.14}$$

where, W = Weight of the body, acting downward,

F_D = Drag force, acting vertically upward, and

F_B = Buoyant force, acting vertically upward.

The terminal velocity of a sphere falling through a liquid at rest is calculated as follows:

$$W = F_D + F_B$$

$$\frac{\pi}{6} D^3 \times w_s = 3\pi\mu DU + \frac{\pi}{6} D^3 \times w_f$$

[where, D = Diameter of the sphere,

w_s = Specific weight of the material of sphere,

w_f = Specific weight of the fluid,

D = Diameter of the sphere, and

U = Terminal velocity.]

or,
$$3\pi\mu DU = \frac{\pi}{6} D^3 (w_s - w_f)$$

or,
$$U = \frac{D^2}{18\mu}(w_s - w_f) \tag{14.15}$$

$$\left[\text{or, } \mu = \frac{D^2}{18U}(w_s - w_f)\right] \tag{14.15(a)}$$

14.6.2. Applications of Stokes' Law

The following are the *applications of Stokes' low:*

1. To calculate the terminal velocity of a falling sphere and hence the viscosity of the fluid.
2. Desilting river flow.
3. Separating the coolant from metal chips in machining operations.
4. Sanitary engineering—treatment of raw water and sewerage etc.

Example 14.14. *A ball of 70 mm diameter is supported in a vertical air stream which is flowing at a velocity of 6.5 m/s. Calculate the weight of the ball. Take for air: $\rho = 1.25$ kg/m^3 and $\nu = 1.4$ stokes.*

Solution. Diameter of the ball, D = 70 mm = 0.07 m.

Velocity of air, U = 6.5 m/s

Density of air, ρ = 1.25 kg/m^3

Kinematic viscosity of air,

$$\nu = 1.4 \text{ stokes} = 1.4 \times 10^{-4} \text{ m}^2/\text{s}.$$

Weight of the ball, W:

$$\text{Reynolds number, } Re = \frac{UD}{\nu} = \frac{6.5 \times 0.07}{1.4 \times 10^{-4}} = 3250$$

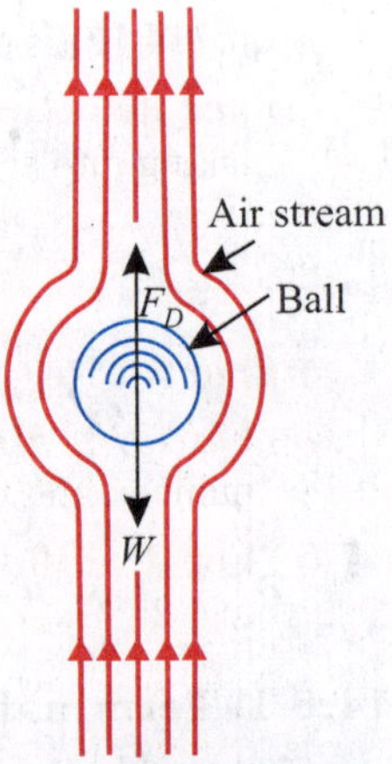

Fig. 14.14

Thus the value of Re lies between 1000 and 10000 and hence $C_D = 0.5$.

When the ball is just supported in stream, its weight is equal to the drag force (Fig. 14.14), neglecting buoyant force being very small.

But, Drag force, $F_D = C_D \times \dfrac{\rho U^2}{2} \times A$

where, A = Projected area of the ball

$$= \frac{\pi}{4} \times D^2 = \frac{\pi}{4} \times 0.07^2 = 0.003848 \text{ m}^2$$

$$\therefore \quad F_D = 0.5 \times \frac{1.25 \times 6.5^2}{2} \times 0.003848 = 0.0508 \text{ N}$$

Hence, weight of the ball, $W = F_D =$ **0.0508 N (Ans.)**

Example 14.15. *A steel sphere of 4 mm diameter falls in glycerine at a terminal velocity of 0.04 m/s. Assuming Stokes' law is applicable, determine:*

(i) *Dynamic viscosity of glycerine,*

(ii) *Drag force, and*

(iii) *Drag co-efficient for the sphere.*

Take specific weights of steel and glycerine as 75 kN/m³ and 12.5 kN/m³ respectively.

Solution. Diameter of the sphere, D = 4 mm = 0.004 m

Terminal velocity, U = 0.04 m/s

Specific weight of steel, w_s = 75 kN/m³

Specific weight of glycerine, w_f = 12.5 kN/m³

(*i*) Dynamic viscosity of glycerine, μ:

$$\text{Weight of sphere, } W = \frac{\pi}{6} D^3 \times w_s = \frac{\pi}{6} \times (0.004)^3 \times (75 \times 10^3) = 0.0025\,13 \text{ N}$$

$$\text{Buoyant force on sphere, } F_B = \frac{\pi}{6} D^3 \times w_f = \frac{\pi}{6} \times (0.004)^2 \times (12.5 \times 10^3) = 0.0004188 \text{ N}$$

$$\text{Drag force on sphere, } F_D = 3\pi\mu DV = 3\pi \times \mu \times 0.004 \times 0.04 = 0.001508\ \mu \text{ N}$$

But, $W = F_D + F_B$

$$\therefore \quad 0.002513 = 0.001508\mu + 0.0004188$$

or, $$\mu = \left(\frac{0.002503 - 0.0004188}{0.001508}\right) = 1.388 \text{ Ns/m}^2$$

$$\left(Re = \frac{\rho UD}{\mu} = \frac{12.5 \times 10^3 \times 0.04 \times 0.004}{9.81 \times 1.388} \right.$$

$$\left. = 0.147; \text{ Since } Re < 0.2, \text{ therefore, the expression } F_D = 3\pi\mu DU \text{ is valid} \right)$$

$$\left[\text{Also, } \mu = \frac{D^2}{18U}(w_s - w_f) = \frac{0.004^2}{18 \times 0.04}(75 - 12.5) \times 10^3 = 1.388 \text{ Ns/m}^2 \right]$$

[Eqn. 14.15 (a)]

(*ii*) Drag force, F_D:

$F_D = 3\pi\mu DU = 3\pi \times 1.388 \times 0.004 \times 0.04 =$ **0.00209 N (Ans.)**

(ii) Drag co-efficient for sphere, C_D :

$$C_D = \frac{24}{Re} \quad \text{[Eqn. 14.12]}$$

$$= \frac{24}{0.147} = \mathbf{163.26} \ \textbf{(Ans.)}$$

Example 14.16. *Determine the velocity of fall of rain drops of 0.3 mm diameter in atmospheric air having density 12 kg/m³ and kinematic viscosity 0.15 stokes. Assume stokes' law holds good.*

Solution. Diameter of the rain drop, $D = 0.3 \text{ mm} = 0.3 \times 10^{-3}$ m

Density of water (rain drops), $\rho = 1.2 \text{ kg/m}^3$

Kinematic viscosity, $\nu = 0.15 \text{ stokes} = 0.15 \times 10^{-4} \text{ m}^2\text{/s}$

∴ Dynamic viscosty, $\mu = \rho\nu = 1.2 \times 0.15 \times 10^{-4} = 1.8 \times 10^{-5} \text{ Ns/m}^2$

The terminal velocity of a spherical rain drop in laminar motion in air of large extent is given by (Stokes' law),

$$U = \frac{D^2}{18\,\mu}(w_s - w_f) \quad \text{[Eqn. (14.15)]}$$

where, w_s = Specific weight of spherical rain drop (= 9810 N/m³), and

w_s = Specific weight of fluid (air) = (1.2 × 9.81 N/m³)

$$\therefore \quad U = \frac{(0{\cdot}3 \times 10^{-3})^2}{18 \times 1{\cdot}8 \times 10^{-5}}(9810 - 1{\cdot}2 \times 9{\cdot}81) = \mathbf{2{\cdot}72 \ m/s} \ \textbf{(Ans.)}$$

Example 14.17. *A 2 mm diameter metallic ball of specific gravity 11 is allowed to fall in a fluid of specific gravity 0.9 and viscosity 1.4 Ns/m². Determine:*

(i) Drag force (exerted by the fluid on the ball),

(ii) Pressure drag and skin friction drag, and

(iii) Terminal velocity of ball in fluid.

Solution. Diameter of the ball, $D = 2 \text{ mm} = 2 \times 10^{-3}$ m

Specific gravity of metallic ball = 11

∴ Specific weight, $w_s = 11 \times 9.81 \text{ kN/m}^3 = 107.91 \text{ kN/m}^3$

Specific gravity of fluid, = 0.9

∴ Specific weight, $w_f = 0.9 \times 9.81 = 8.83 \text{ kN/m}^3$

Dynamic viscosity of fluid, $\mu = 1.4 \text{ Ns/m}^2$.

(i) Drag force, F_D :

$$\text{Weight of the ball, } w = \frac{\pi}{6} D^3 \times w_s = \frac{\pi}{6} \times (2 \times 10^{-3})^3 \times (107.91 \times 10^3)$$

$$= 4.52 \times 10^{-4} \text{ N}$$

$$\text{Buoyant force, } F_B = (\pi/6) \times D^3 \times w_f = (\pi/6) \times (2 \times 10^{-3})^3 \times (8.83 \times 10^3)$$

$$= 3.69 \times 10^{-5} \text{ N}$$

When the ball attains the terminal velocity, we have:

$$W = F_D + F_B$$

or, $$F_D = W - F_B = 4.52 \times 10^{-4} - 3.69 \times 10^{-5} = \mathbf{4.151 \times 10^{-4} \ N} \ \textbf{(Ans.)}$$

(ii) Pressure drag, skin friction drag:

$$\text{Pressure drag} = \frac{1}{3} F_D = \frac{1}{3} \times 4{\cdot}151 \times 10^{-4} = \mathbf{1{\cdot}384 \times 10^{-4} \ N} \ \textbf{(Ans.)}$$

$$\text{Skin friction drag} = \frac{2}{3} F_D = \frac{2}{3} \times 4{\cdot}151 \times 10^{-4} = \mathbf{2{\cdot}767 \times 10^{-4}\ N\ (Ans.)}$$

(*iii*) Terminal velocity of the ball U:

$$F_D = 3\ \pi\mu DU \qquad \text{[Eqn. (14.11)]}$$

$$\therefore \quad 4.151 \times 10^{-4} = 3\pi \times 1.4 \times 2 \times 10^{-3} \times U$$

or,
$$U = \frac{4.151 \times 10^{-4}}{3\pi \times 1.4 \times 2 \times 10^{-3}} = \mathbf{0.0157\ m/s\ (Ans.)}$$

Now let us check the Reynolds number, *Re*.

$$Re = \frac{\rho UD}{\mu} = \frac{(8.83 \times 10^3) \times 0.0157 \times 2 \times 10^{-3}}{9.81 \times 1.4} = 0.02$$

Since $Re < 0.2$, therefore, the expression $F_D = 3\ \pi\mu DU$ for the calculating the terminal velocity is valid,

Example 14.18. *Stokes derived the drag F_D experienced by a sphere of diameter D moving at a uniform velocity U through a fluid of visosity μ to be $F_D = 3\ \pi\mu DU$. State the validity of this expression in relation to the particular Reynolds number. Derive the co-efficient of drag C_D from Stokes' law.* **[MDU, Haryana]**

Solution. Stokes derived the expression for total drag,

$$F_D = 3\ \pi\mu DU \qquad ...(i)$$

on a sphere immersed in a flowing fluid for which Reynolds number is upto 0.2, so that inertia forces may be assumed negligible. In that case the various forces are much more important and predominant than inertia forces.

Drag is also given by the expression:

$$F_D = C_D \times A \times \rho\frac{U^2}{2} \qquad ...(ii)$$

where, *A* (= projected area of sphere) $= \frac{\pi}{4}D^2$, and C_D = co-efficient of drag.

From (*i*) and (*ii*), we have:

$$3\pi\mu DU = C_D \times \frac{\pi}{4}D^2 \times \frac{\rho U^2}{2}$$

or,
$$C_D = \frac{3\pi\mu DU}{\frac{\pi}{4}D^2 \times \frac{\rho U^2}{2}} = \frac{24\mu}{\rho UD} = \mathbf{\frac{24}{Re}}\ \textbf{(Ans.)}$$

Example 14.19. *Determine the largest diameter and corresponding terminal velocity of a polystyrene spherical particle settling in air. It obeys Stokes' law.*

Density of polystyrene particle = 1047.9 kg/m³
Density of air = 1.2 kg/m³
Kinematic viscosity of air = 1.5 × 10⁻⁵ m²/s **(M.U.)**

Solution. *Given:* $\rho_s = 1047.9\ kg/m^3$; $\rho_a = 1.2\ kg/m^3$, $\nu_a = 1.5 \times 10^{-5}\ m^2/s$

***D, U* :**

The Stokes' law is valid upto *Re* =1.0. For maximum size particle that obeys Stokes' law,

$$Re_{max} = 1 = \frac{UD}{\nu_a} \quad \text{or} \quad U = \frac{\nu_a}{D}$$

Stokes' law would give: $U = \frac{D^2}{18\mu}(w_s - w_f)$ [Eqn. (14.15)]

(where, suffices s and f stand for sphere and fluid respectively)

$$\frac{v_a}{D} = \frac{D^2}{18\mu}(\rho_s \times g - \rho_a \times g)$$

$$\mu = \mu_a = v_a \times \rho_a$$
$$= 1.5 \times 10^{-5} \times 1.2$$
$$= 1.8 \times 10^{-5}$$

Substituting the values, we get:

$$\frac{1.5 \times 10^{-5}}{D} = \frac{D^2}{18 \times 1.8 \times 10^{-5}}(1047.9 \times 9.81 - 1.2 \times 9.81)$$

or,
$$D = \left[\frac{1.5 \times 10^{-5} \times 18 \times 1.8 \times 10^{-5}}{9.81\,(1047.9 \times 1.2)}\right]^{\frac{1}{3}}$$
$$= 7.793 \times 10^{-5} \text{ m} = \mathbf{0.0779\ mm\ (Ans)}$$

$\therefore$ Terminal Velocity, $U = \frac{v_a}{D} = \frac{1.5 \times 10^{-5}}{0.0779 \times 10^{-3}} = \mathbf{0.1926\ m/s}$ **(Ans.)**

14.7. DRAG ON A CYLINDER

Consider a real fluid flowing past a cylinder of a diameter D and length L (length being perpendicular to the direction of flow), with a uniform velocity U.

(*i*) For $Re < 1$:

— When $Re < 0.2$, the inertia force is negligibly small as compared to viscous force and hence flow pattern will be *symmetrical.*

— Also, when $Re < 1$, $F_D \propto U$ and $C_D \propto \frac{1}{Re}$.

(*ii*) For $Re = 1$ to 2000; C_D decreases and attains a minimum value of 0.95 at $Re = 2000$.

(*iii*) For $Re = 2000$ to 3×10^4 : C_D increase and becomes 1.2 at $Re = 3 \times 10^4$.

(*iv*) For $Re = 3 \times 10^4$ to 3×10^5 : C_D decreases and its value bocomes 0.3 at $Re = 3 \times 10^5$

(*v*) For $Re = 3 \times 10^6$: C_D increases and attains a value of 0.7 in the end.

14.8. CIRCULATION AND LIFT ON A CIRCULAR CYLINDER

14.8.1. Flow Patterns and Development of Lift

Case I. Stationary cylinder. Consider an ideal fluid flowing over a *stationary cylinder* of radius R , with a uniform velocity U. In this case flow pattern will be symmetrical (Fig.14.15) and the velocity u at any point on the surface of the cylinder is given by,

$$u_\theta = 2\,U \sin\theta \qquad (14.16)$$

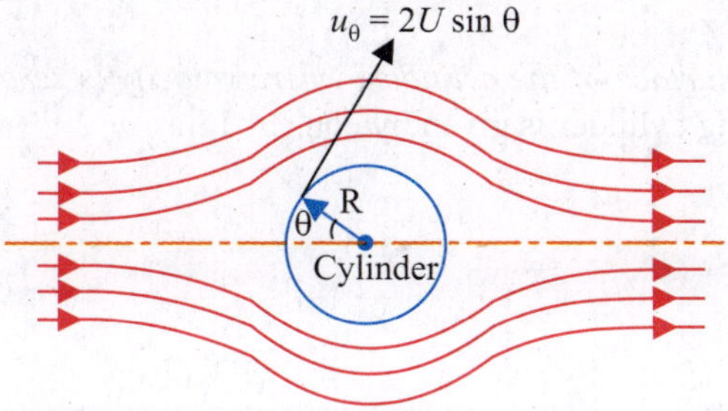

Fig. 14.15. Flow of ideal fluid over stationary cylinder.

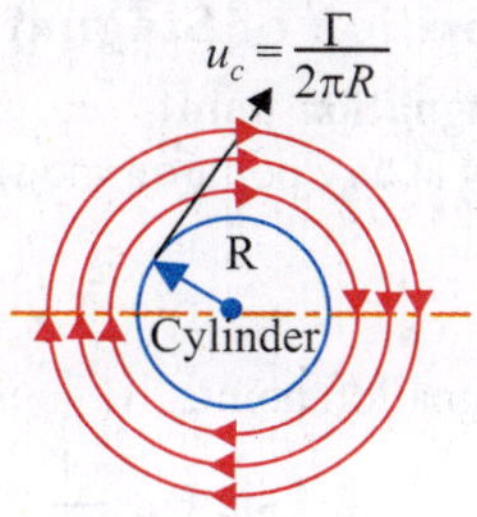

Fig. 14.16. Stream lines for free vortex.

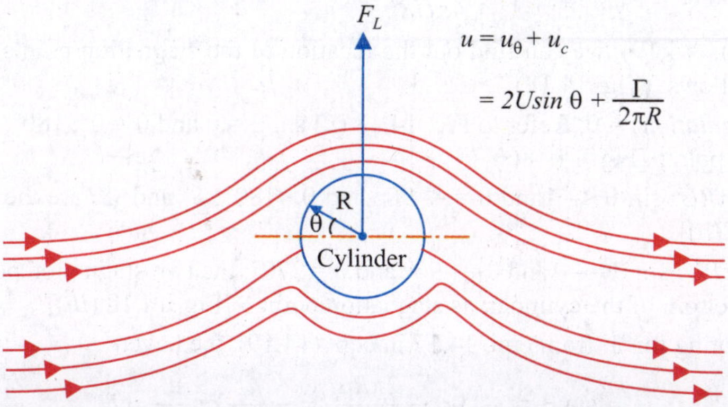

Fig. 14.17. Flow pattern over a rotating cylinder and development of lift on cylinder due to circulation.

where, θ = The angular distance of the point from the forward stagnation point.

In this case, since the flow pattern is symmetrical about the horizontal axis, the pressure distributions on the upper and lower halves of the cylinder are *identical,* and hence there is *no lift* acting on the cylinder.

Case II. Constant circulation imparted to the cylinder. When a constant circulation Γ is imparted to the same cylinder, the flow pattern around the cylinder consists of stream lines which are series of *concentric circles* (Fig. 14.16). The peripheral velocity on the surface of the cylinder due to circulation is given by,

$$\mu_c = \frac{\Gamma}{2\pi R} \qquad (14.17)$$

Case III. Composite flow pattern. If the above two flow patterns are superimposed one over the other, then a composite flow pattern as shown in Fig. 14.17 will be obtained. The flow pattern is now unsymmetrical about the horizontal axis. The velocity at any point on the surface of the cylinder is obtained by adding eqns. (14.16) and (14.17) as:

$$u = u_\theta + u_c = 2U \sin \theta + \frac{\Gamma}{2\pi R} \qquad (14.18)$$

As the circulation Γ has been taken as *clockwise,* the superimposition causes the velocity around the *upper half* portion of the cylinder to be *higher* than that around the lower half portion (this is so because around the upper half portion of the cylinder the velocity of flow and the velocity due to circulation being in the same direction are *added* together, while around the lower half portion of the cylinder both velocities being in opposite direction are *subtracted*). Hence on the lower half portion of the cylinder, where velocity is less, pressure will be more than the pressure on the upper half portion of the cylinder. As such a pressure force acts on the upward direction and obviously a *lift force* is exerted on the cylinder, However, *since the flow is symmetrical about the vertical axis, the cylinder is not subjected to any drag.*

14.8.2. Position of Stagnation Points

The **stagnation points** *are those points on the surface of the cylinder, where velocity* is *zero.* The velocity at any point on the surface of the rotating cylinder is given by eqn. 14.18 as:

$$u = 2U \sin\theta + \frac{\Gamma}{2\pi R}$$

For stagnation point, $\quad u = 0$

$$\therefore \quad 2U \sin\theta + \frac{\Gamma}{2\pi R} = 0$$

or,

$$\sin\theta = -\frac{\Gamma}{4\pi UR} \qquad (14.19)$$

From this eqn. (14.19), we can find out the location of the stagnation points on the surface of the cylinder, as follows: (Fig. 14.18)

(*i*) *For* Γ (*circulation*) = 0; Refer to Fig. 14.18 (*i*.) $\sin\theta = 0$ and $\theta = 0°, 180°$; S_1 and S_2 are the stagnation points [Fig. 14.18(*i*)]

(*ii*) *For* $\Gamma < 4\pi RU$: $\sin\theta <- 1$and $\theta = <-90°$ and $\theta > 180°$; S_1 and S_2 are the stagnation points [Fig. 14.18(*ii*)].

(*iii*) *For* $\Gamma = 4\pi RU$: $\sin\theta = -1$and $\theta = -90°$ and $\theta = 270°$; the two stagnation points coincide and lie at the bottom of the cylinder, as stagnation point *S* [Fig. 14.18 (*iii*)].

By substituting for Γ from eqn. 14.17 in eqn. (14.19), we have:

$$\sin\theta = -1 = -\frac{2\pi R u_c}{4\pi UR} = -\frac{u_c}{2U} \text{ or } \frac{u_c}{U} = 2$$

(*iv*) *For* $\Gamma > 4\pi RU$: $\sin\theta > -1$ which is not feasible. In this case stagnation points do not occur on the cylinder surface, they detach from the cylinder and lie into the fluid stream below the point – 90° and 270° [Fig. 14.18 (*iv*)]

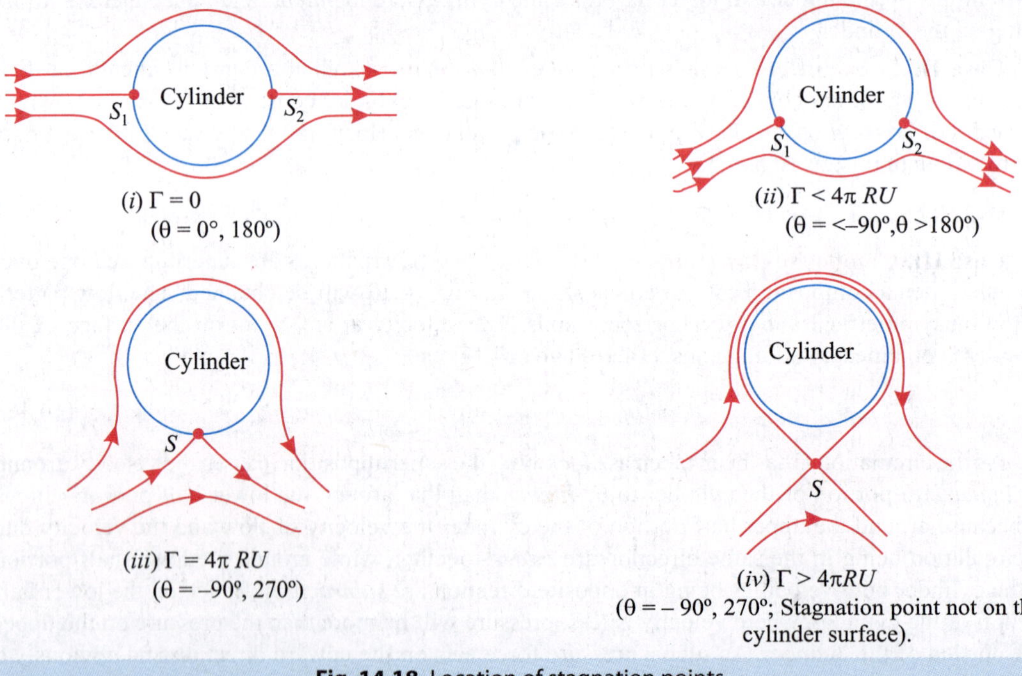

(*i*) $\Gamma = 0$ ($\theta = 0°, 180°$)

(*ii*) $\Gamma < 4\pi RU$ ($\theta = <-90°, \theta > 180°$)

(*iii*) $\Gamma = 4\pi RU$ ($\theta = -90°, 270°$)

(*iv*) $\Gamma > 4\pi RU$ ($\theta = -90°, 270°$; Stagnation point not on the cylinder surface).

Fig. 14.18. Location of stagnation points.

14.8.3. Pressure at any Point on the Cylinder Surface

The magnitude of the lift exerted on the cylinder due to the composite flow pattern may be determined by integrating over the entire surface of the cylinder, the components of the pressure forces on elementary surface areas normal to the direction of uniform flow. The pressure at any point on the cylinder is obtained by applying Bernoulli's equation between any point in the unaffected flow (upstream condition) and any point on the surface of the cylinder. Thus,

$$p_0 + \frac{1}{2}\rho U^2 = p + \frac{1}{2}\rho u^2 \tag{14.20}$$

where, P_0 = Pressure in the uniform flow at some distance ahead of cylinder ,

U = Velocity of uniform flow,

p = Pressure at any point on the cylinder, and

u = The velocity at any point on the surface of the cylinder

$= 2U \sin\theta + \dfrac{\Gamma}{2\pi R}$.

Substituting the value of u in eqn. (14.20), we get:

$$p_0 + \frac{1}{2}\rho U^2 = p + \frac{1}{2}\rho\left(2U\sin\theta + \frac{\Gamma}{2\pi R}\right)^2$$

or,

$$p = p_0 + \frac{1}{2}\rho U^2\left[1 - \left(2\sin\theta + \frac{\Gamma}{2\pi UR}\right)^2\right] \tag{14.21}$$

14.8.4. Expression for Lift on Cylinder (Kutta- Joukowski Theorem)

Consider a cylinder rotating in a uniform flow field. To determine the lift force on the cylinder, consider a small length of the element on the surface of the cylinder as shown in Fig. 14.19.

Let, R = Radius of the cylinder,

ds = Length of the element (= $Rd\theta$),

$d\theta$ = Angle made by the length ds at the centre of the cylinder,

p = Pressure on the surface of the element on cylinder,

p_0 = Pressure of the fluid (in the uniform flow) at some distance ahead of cylinder,

U = Velocity of uniform flow,

u = Velocity of fluid on the surface of the cylinder, and

L = Length of the cylinder.

Area of the small element *per unit length* of the cylinder, $dA = Rd\theta.\ L$

∴ Force acting on the element (directed towards the centre), $dF = p.Rd\theta.\ L$

Resolving this force into the horizontal and vertical directions, we get the drag (dF_D) and lift (dF_L) components as follows:

$$dF_D = p.Rd\theta.\ L.\cos\theta;\quad dF_L = -\,p.Rd\theta.\ L\sin\theta$$

By integrating the respective differential forces over the entire surface of the cylinder, we obtain the total drag and lift on the cylinder.

Thus,

$$F_L = -\int_0^{2\pi} pRL\sin\theta.d\theta$$

But, $$p = p_0 + \frac{1}{2}\rho U^2\left[1 - \left(2\sin\theta + \frac{\Gamma}{2\pi UR}\right)^2\right] \qquad \text{[Eqn. (14.21)]}$$

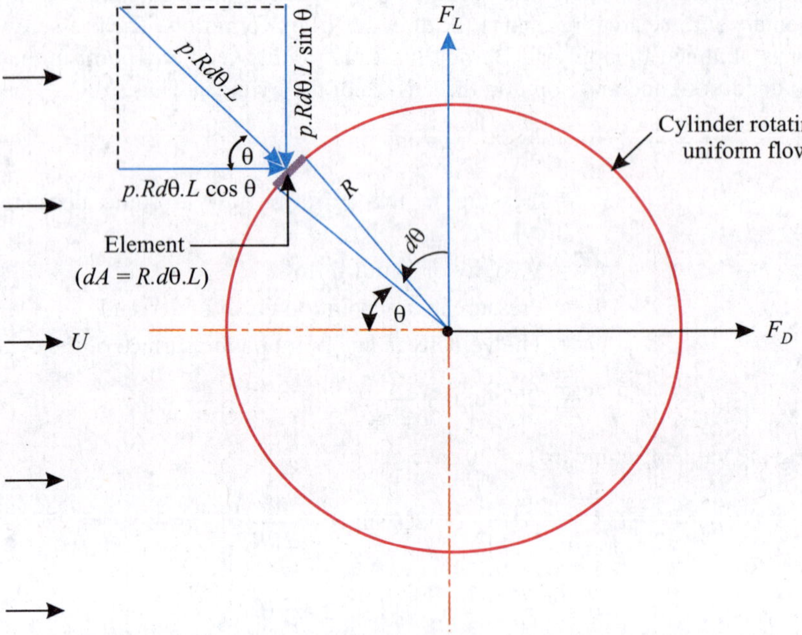

Fig. 14.19. Lift on a rotating cylinder.

$$\therefore F_L = -R_L\left[\int_0^{2\pi} p_0 \sin\theta.d\theta + \int_0^{2\pi}\frac{1}{2}\rho U^2 \sin\theta.d\theta - \int_0^{2\pi}\frac{1}{2}\rho U^2\left(2\sin\theta + \frac{\Gamma}{2\pi UR}\right)^2 \sin\theta.d\theta\right]$$

$$= -RL\left[\int_0^{2\pi} p_0 \sin\theta.d\theta + \int_0^{2\pi}\frac{1}{2}\rho U^2 \sin\theta.d\theta - \frac{1}{2}\rho U^2\left\{\int_0^{2\pi} 4\sin^3\theta.d\theta\right.\right.$$

$$\left.\left. + \int_0^{2\pi}\frac{2\Gamma}{\pi UR}\sin^2\theta.d\theta + \int_0^{2\pi}\frac{\Gamma^2}{4\pi^2 U^2 R^2}\sin\theta.d\theta\right\}\right]$$

But $\int_0^{2\pi} \sin^n\theta.d\theta = 0$ when n is *odd*, therefore, the above expression reduces to:

$$F_L = R.L\left(\frac{1}{2}\rho U^2 \times \frac{2\Gamma}{\pi UR}\right)\int_0^{2\pi}\sin^2\theta.d\theta$$

$$= \frac{\rho LU\Gamma}{\pi}\int_0^{2\pi}\left(\frac{1-\cos 2\theta}{2}\right)d\theta$$

$$= \frac{\rho U\Gamma}{\pi}\left[\frac{1}{2}\theta - \frac{\sin\theta}{2}\right]_0^{2\pi} = \rho ULT \text{ per unit length of cylinder.}$$

Hence the total lift of a cylinder of length L is given by:

$$F_L = \rho LU\Gamma \qquad (14.22)$$

Eqn. (14.22) is known as **Kutta-Joukowski equation;** it applies *not only to circular cylinder but also to other bodies of any shape* (including an airfoil) as well.

The resulting flow pattern for a rotating cylinder in a uniform flow field is shown in Fig. 14.17; it is symmetrical about the vertical axis of the cylinder. Hence the velocity distribution and pressure distribution is symmetrical about the vertical axis and as such *there will be no drag on the cylinder* $\left(i.e. \int_0^{2\pi} p\, Rd\theta . L . \cos\theta = 0 \right)$. *The concept of zero drag on bodies immersed in a steady flow of ideal fluid is called* **D'Alembert's paradox.**

14.8.5. Expression for Lift Coefficient for Rotating Cylinder

The lift coefficient (C_L) defined by eqn. (14.4) is given as:

$$F_L = C_L \frac{\rho U^2}{2} \times A \quad \text{or} \quad C_L = \frac{2F_L}{\rho U^2 A}$$

Also, $$F_L = \rho L U \Gamma \qquad \text{Eqn. (14.22)}$$

$$\therefore \quad C_L = \frac{2 \times \rho L U \Gamma}{\rho U^2 A} = \frac{2\rho L U \Gamma}{\rho U^2 \times 2RL} = \frac{\Gamma}{UR} \qquad (14.23)$$

(where, A = projected area = $2RL$)

From, eqn. (14.17), we have:

$$u_c = \frac{\Gamma}{2\pi R} \quad \text{or} \quad \frac{\Gamma}{R} = 2\pi u_c$$

Substituting this value of $\frac{\Gamma}{R}$ in eqn. (14.22),we get:

$$C_L = 2\pi \frac{u_c}{U} \qquad (14.24)$$

(where, u_c = peripheral speed of the cylinder due to circulation)

Thus lift co-efficient depends on the ratio $\frac{u_c}{U}$.

Fig. 14.20 shows the variation of C_L and C_D with $\frac{u_c}{U}$ for a rotating circular cylinder in a fluid. The following observations are worth nothing:

1. For a circular cylinder rotating in an *ideal fluid,* the theoretical function $C_L = 2\pi \frac{u_c}{U}$ is shown as a broken line; when $\frac{u_c}{U} = 2$, the stagnation points meet at the cylinder's bottom (Fig. 14.18 (*iii*) and $C_L = 2\pi \times 2 = 4\pi = 12.56$ which is the *theoretical maximum* of the lift co-efficient.

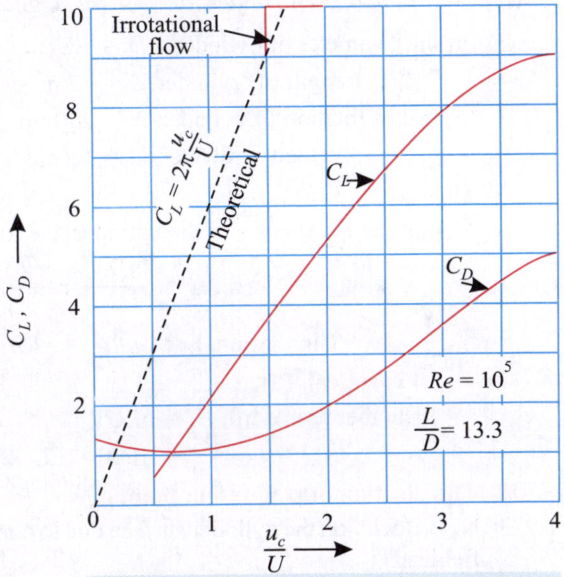

Fig. 14.20. C_L, C_D for a rotating cylinder.

2. For a circular cylinder rotating in a *real fluid* it can be seen that:

(*i*) C_L becomes maximum $\frac{u_0}{U} = 4$ and C_D increases quite rapidly beyond $\frac{u_c}{U} = 1.5$.

The experimental values of C_L differ from the theoretical values due to the following factors:

(*a*) Effect of viscosity,

(*b*) Circulation around a rotating cylinder not being exactly the same as that due to an irrotational vortex, and

(*c*) Effect of length.

(*ii*) For a short cylinder, $\frac{L}{D} < 10$, C_L is reduced;

For $\frac{L}{D} < 5$, C_L is about half of that for a long cylinder, due to flow around ends.

14.8.6. Magnus Effect

The generation of lift by spinning cylinder in a fluid stream is called **Magnus effect.** The phenomenon of the lift produced by circulation around a cylinder of circular cross-section placed in a uniform stream of fluid, was first investigated experimentally by a German Physicist H.G. Magnus in 1852 and hence the name is given as *Magnus effect.*

- This effect has been successfully employed in the *propulsion of ships.*
- The Magnus effect may also be used with advantage in the *games like table tennis, golf, cricket etc.*

Example 14.20. *A cylinder 1.8 m in diameter and 12 m long rotates at 240 r.p.m. with its axis perpendicular to the stream of water flowing at a velocity of 15 m/s. Assuming no slip between the cylinder and the circulating flow, determine:*

(*i*) *The circulation,*

(*ii*) *The theoretical lift,*

(*iii*) *The position of stagnation points, and*

(*iv*) *The r.p.m. of the cylinder for a single stagnation point.*

Solution. Diameter of cylinder, $D = 1.8$ m

Length of cylinder, $L = 12$ m

Speed of rotation of cylinder, $N = 240$ r.p.m.

Velocity of water, $U = 15$ m/s

(*i*) The circulation, Γ :

Velocity at the surface of the cylinder due to circulation alone,

$$u_c = \frac{\pi DN}{60} = \frac{\pi \times 1.8 \times 240}{60} = 22.6 \text{ m/s}$$

$$\text{Circulation, } \Gamma = 2\pi R u_c = \pi D u_c = \pi \times 1.8 \times 22.6 = \mathbf{127.8\ m^2/s}$$

(*ii*) The theoretical, lift:

$$\text{The theoretical lift, } F_L = \rho L U \Gamma$$

$$= 1000 \times 12 \times 22.6 \times 127.8 = \mathbf{34.66 \times 10^6\ N\ (Ans.)}$$

(*iii*) The position of stagnation points:

Net velocity on the cylinder surface due to combination of circulation and free stream velocity field is,

$$u = 2U \sin\theta + \frac{\Gamma}{2\pi R}$$

At stagnation points, $u = 0$

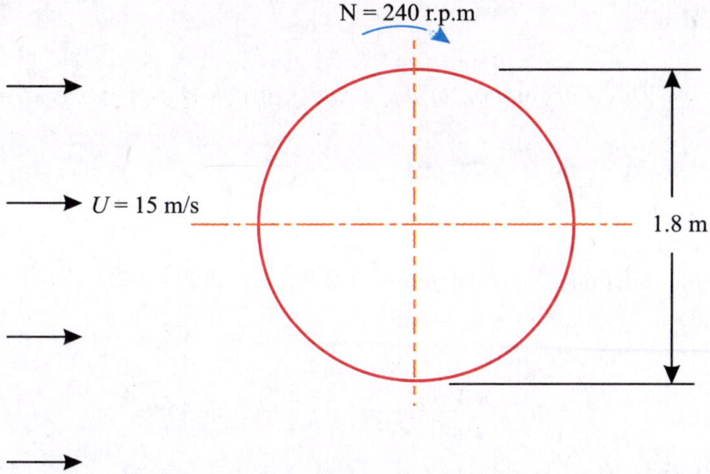

Fig. 14.21

$$2U.\sin\theta + \frac{\Gamma}{2\pi R} = 0 \quad \text{or} \quad 2U\sin\theta = -\frac{\Gamma}{2\pi R}$$

or, $\Gamma = -4\pi RU\sin\theta$

or, $\sin\theta = -\dfrac{\Gamma}{4\pi RU} = -\dfrac{127.8}{4\pi \times 0.9 \times 15} = -0.753$

$= -\sin(48.85°)$

$= \sin(180° + 48.85°)$ and $\sin(360° - 48.85°)$

∴ $\theta = (180° + 48.85°)$ and $(360° - 48.85°)$

$=$ **228.85°** and **311.15° (Ans.)**

The position of stagnation points is shown in Fig. 14.22

(*iv*) The r.p. m. of the cylinder for single stagnation point, N:

For a single stagnation point, we have:

$$\Gamma = 4\pi UR = 4\pi \times 15 \times 0.9 = 169.65 \text{ m}^2/\text{s}$$

Also, $u_c = \dfrac{\Gamma}{2\pi R}$

$= \dfrac{169.65}{2\pi \times 0.9} = 30\text{m/s}$

But, $u_c = \dfrac{\pi DN}{60}$ or $N = \dfrac{60u_c}{\pi D} = \dfrac{60 \times 30}{\pi \times 1.8}$

= **318.3 r.p.m. (Ans.)**

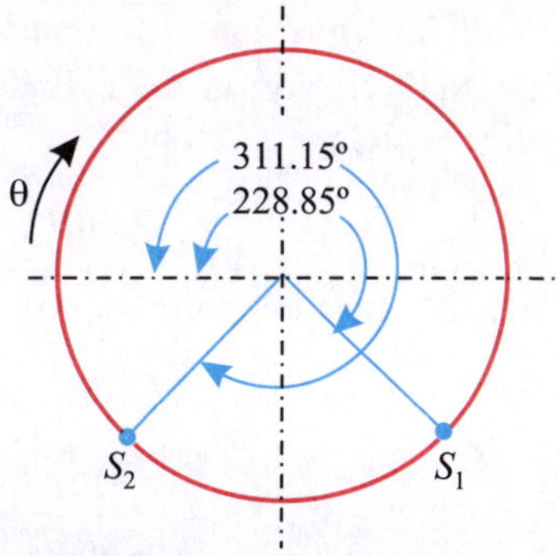

Fig. 14.22

Example 14.21. *A cylinder whose axis is perpendicular to the stream of air having a velocity of 20 m/s rotates at 300 r.p.m. The cylinder is 2 m in diameter and 10 m long. Find:*

(*i*) *The circulation,*

(*ii*) *The theoretical lift force per unit length,*

(*iii*) *The position of stagnation points, and*

(*iv*) *The actual lift, drag and direction of resultant force.*

Take density of air = 1.24 kg/m^3. *For actual drag and lift, take* C_L = 3.4, C_D = 0.65 and $\frac{u_c}{U} = 1.57$.

(*v*) *Find also the speed of rotation of the cylinder, which will give only a single stagnation point.* **[PTU]**

Solution. Velocity of air, U = 20 m/s

Speed of rotation, N = 300 r.p.m.

Diameter of cylinder, D = 2 m

Length of cylinder, L = 10 m

Density of air, ρ = 1.24 kg/ m^3

Peripheral velocity due to cylinder rotation,

$$u_c = \frac{\pi DN}{60} = \frac{\pi \times 2 \times 300}{60} = 31.4 \text{ m/s}$$

(*i*) The circulation, Γ:

Circulation = Circumference × peripheral velocity

or, $$\Gamma = 2\pi R u_c \qquad \text{[Eqn. (14.17)]}$$

or, $$\Gamma = 2\pi \times \left(\frac{2}{2}\right) \times 31{\cdot}4 = \mathbf{197{\cdot}3 \text{ m}^2/\text{s}} \text{ (Ans.)}$$

(*ii*) Theoretical lift force per unit length:

Theoretical lift is given by:

$$F_L = \rho L U \Gamma \qquad \text{[Eqn. (14.22)]}$$

∴ *Theoretical lift per unit length*

$$= \frac{F_L}{L} = \frac{\rho LUT}{L} = \rho U\Gamma = 1.24 \times 20 \times 197.3$$

= **4893 N/m length (Ans.)**

(*iii*) The position of stagnation points:

Net velocity on the cylinder surface (u) due to combination of circulation and free stream velocity field is given by:

$$u = 2U \sin\theta + \frac{\Gamma}{2\pi R}$$

At stagnation points, $u = 0$

$$\therefore \quad 0 = 2U \sin\theta + \frac{\Gamma}{2\pi R}$$

or, $$\sin\theta = -\frac{\Gamma}{2\pi RU} = -\frac{197.3}{4\pi \times \left(\frac{2}{2}\right) \times 20}$$

$$= -0.785 = -\sin(51.72°)$$

$$= \sin(180° + 51.72°) \quad \text{and} \quad \sin(360° - 51.72°)$$

∴ θ = **231.72°** and **308.28° (Ans.)**

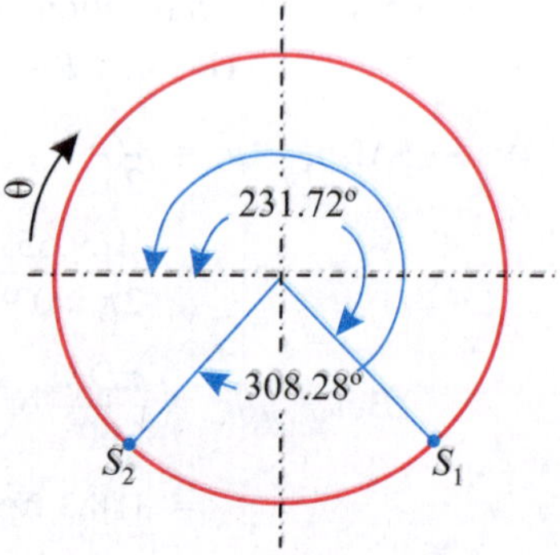

Fiig. 14.23

The position of stagnation points is shown in Fig. 14.23.

(*iv*) The actual lift, drag and direction of resultant force:

For actual lift and drag, $C_L = 3.4$, $C_D = 0.65$ and $\frac{u_c}{U} = 1.57$

The ratio of $\frac{u_c}{U}$ from theoretical consideration is given as:

$$\frac{u_c}{U} = \frac{31.4}{20} = 1.57$$

Now actual lift is given by:

$$F_L = C_L \times \frac{\rho U^2}{2} \times A = 3.4 \times \frac{1.24 \times 20^2}{2} \times 20 = \mathbf{16864\,N} \textbf{ (Ans.)}$$

(where, A = projected area of cylinder = length × diameter = 10 m × 2 m = 20 m^2)

Actual drag force,

$$F_D = C_D \times \frac{\rho U^2}{2} \times A = 0.65 \times \frac{1.24 \times 20^2}{2} \times 20 = \mathbf{3224\ N} \textbf{ (Ans.)}$$

$$\text{Resultant force, } F = \sqrt{F_L^2 + F_D^2} = \sqrt{16864^2 + 3224^2} = \mathbf{17169.4\ N} \textbf{ (Ans.)}$$

The inclination (α) of the resultant force with the horizontal is given by:

$$\tan\alpha = \frac{F_L}{F_D} = \frac{16864}{3224} = 5.23 \quad \text{or} \quad \alpha = \mathbf{79.2^\circ} \textbf{ (Ans.)}$$

(*v*) Speed of rotation of the cylinder for single stagnation point, N:

For a single stagnation point, we have:

$$\Gamma = 4\pi UR$$

$$= 4\pi \times 20 \times \left(\frac{2}{2}\right) = 251.32 \text{ m}^2/\text{s}$$

Also, $$u_c = \frac{\Gamma}{2\pi R} = \frac{251.32}{2\pi \times \left(\frac{2}{2}\right)} = 40 \text{ m/s}$$

But, $$u_c = \frac{\pi D N}{60}$$

$\therefore$ $$40 = \frac{\pi \times 2 \times N}{60} \quad \text{or} \quad N = \frac{40 \times 60}{\pi \times 2} \simeq \mathbf{382\ r.p.m.} \textbf{ (Ans.)}$$

Example 14.22. *Air having a velocity of 40 m/s is flowing over a cylinder of diameter 1.5 m and length 10 m, when the axis of the cylinder is perpendicular to the air stream. Find the speed at which the cylinder is to be rotated about its axis so that a lift force of 7 kN/m length of the cylinder is devloped. Also determine the location of the stagnation points. Assume density of air as 1.25 kg/m^3.* **(UPTU)**

Solution. *Given:* U = 40 m/s; D = 1.5 m; L = 10 m; F_L = 7 kN/m length; ρ = 1.25 kg/m^3.

Speed N:

Using the relation: $$F_L = \rho L U \Gamma \quad \text{[Eqn. (14.22)]}$$

or, $$\text{Circulation, } \Gamma = \frac{(F_L/L)}{\rho U} = \frac{(7 \times 1000)}{1.25 \times 40} = 140 \text{ m}^2/\text{s}$$

$$\text{Circulation} = \text{Circumference} \times \text{peripheral velocity}$$

i.e. $$\Gamma = 2\pi R \times u_c \quad \text{[Eqn, (14.17)]}$$

or, $$140 = 2\pi \times \frac{1.5}{2} \times u_c$$

or, $u_c = 29.71 \text{ m/s} = \omega R$

$$\therefore \quad \omega = \frac{u_c}{R} = \frac{29.71}{(1.5/2)} = 39.61 \text{ rad/s} = \frac{2\pi N}{60}$$

or, $$N = \frac{39.61 \times 60}{2\pi} = \textbf{378.2 r.p.m (Ans.)}$$

Position of stagnation points :

The net velocity on the cylinder surface (u) due to combination of circulation and force stream velocity field is given by :

$$u = 2U \sin\theta + \frac{\Gamma}{2\pi R}$$

At stagnation point, $u = 0$

$$0 = 2U \sin\theta + \frac{\Gamma}{2\pi R}$$

or, $$\sin\theta = -\frac{\Gamma}{4\pi RU} = -\frac{140}{4\pi \times 0.75 \times 40} = -0.3714$$

$$= -\sin(21.8°)$$

$$= \sin(180 + 21.8°) \text{ and } \sin(360 - 21.8°)$$

$$\theta = \textbf{201.8° and 338.2° (Ans.)}$$

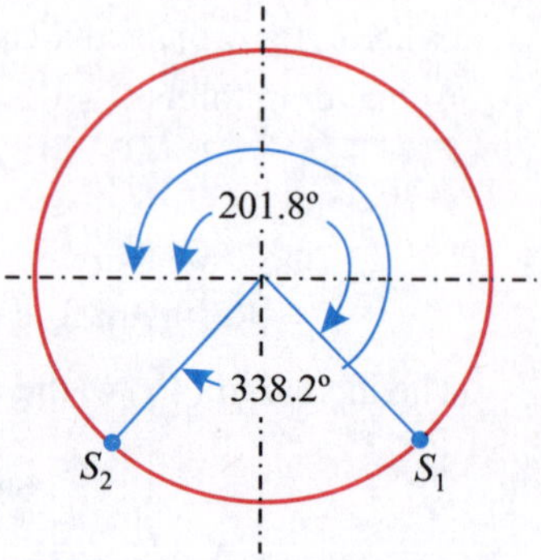

Fig. 14.24

The position of the stagnation points (($S_1$and S_2) is shown in Fig. 14.24.

Example 14.23. *As an application of the Magnus effect,a ship is built having two vertical rotors 10 m high and 3 m in diameter. The rotors are spun at 250 r.p.m. On a day when the air temperature is 20°C and the relative motion of the air to the ship results in 54 kmph wind, calculate the force emitted by the spinning rotors on the ship. Take ρ for air as 1.25 kg/m³.* **[IIT Madras]**

Solution. Diameter of each rotor, $D = 3$ m

Height of each rotor, $H (= L) = 10$ m

Speed of each rotor, $N = 250$ r.p.m.

Wind velocity, $$U = 54 \text{ km/h} = \frac{54 \times 1000}{60 \times 60} = 15 \text{ m/s}$$

Force emitted by the spinning rotors, F_L:

Circulation (Γ) generated by the rotation of cylinder is given by:

$$\Gamma = 2\pi R u_c \qquad \text{[Eqn. (14.17)]}$$

where, $$u_c = \frac{\pi DN}{60} = \frac{\pi \times 3 \times 250}{60} = 39.27 \text{ m/s}$$

$$\therefore \quad \Gamma = 2\pi \times (3/2) \times 39.27 = 370.1 \text{ m}^2/\text{s}$$

Transverse force (perpendicular to the wind direction) developed by each rotating cylinder is given by:

$$F_L = \rho L U \Gamma$$

or, $$F_L = 1.25 \times 10 \times 15 \times 370.1$$

$$= 69393.75\ N \simeq 69.4 \text{ kN}$$

∴ Total force emitted by the spinning rotors

$$= 2 \times 69.4 = \textbf{138.8 kN (Ans.)}$$

14.9. LIFT ON AN AIRFOIL

An airfoil or aerofoil is a streamlined body which may be either symmetrical or unsymmetrical, as shown in Fig. 14.25.

Some of the *definitions* relating airfoil are given below:

1. **Chord line.** *It is the line joining the leading and trailing edges of the airfoil. The length of the line is known as "chord of airfoil."*
2. **Profile centreline.** *It is the line joining the midpoints of the profile.*
3. **Angle of attack.** *It is angle between the chordline and direction of the fluid stream.*
4. **Camber.** *It is the curvature of an airfoil.*
5. **Stall.** An airfoil is said to be in *stall condition* when the angle of attack of an airfoil is *greater* than the angle of attack at maximum lift. *At stall the air separates from the airfoil or wing and eddies are formed, as a consequence of which there is a considerable increase in the drag co-efficient.*

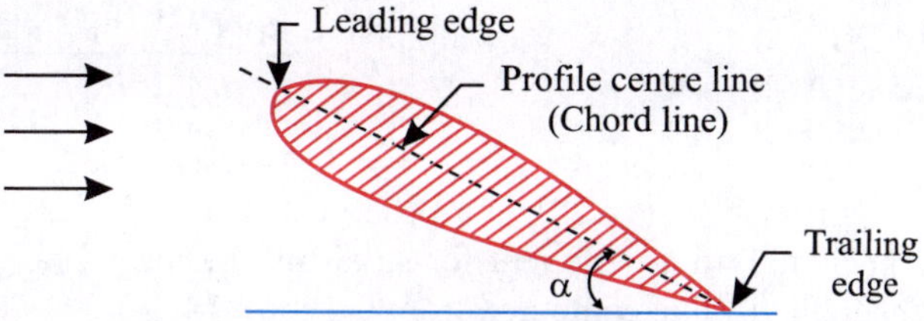

(*a*) Symmetrical

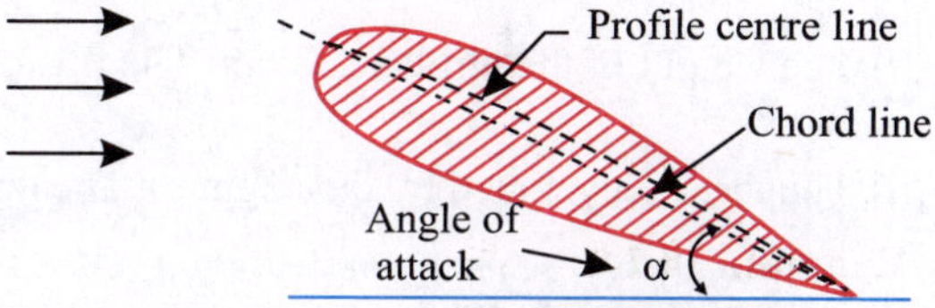

(*b*) Unsymmetrical

Fig. 14.25 Airfoil.

6. **Aspect ratio (A.R.)** *The ratio of span of the wing to its mean chord is called the* **aspect ratio** *of a wing.*

i.e.
$$A.R. = \frac{l}{c} \tag{14.25}$$

where, l = Span of the wing, and

c = Mean chord.

Normally the wings are not rectangle when viewed from the above ; in this case aspect ratio is given by:

$$\text{A.R.} = \frac{l}{c} = \frac{l}{A/l} = \frac{l^2}{A} \tag{14.26}$$

$$(\text{when } A = l \times c \quad \text{or} \quad c = A/l)$$

— From the theoretical analysis, the circulation Γ developed on the airfoil so that the stream line at the trailing edge of the airfoil is tangential to the airfoil is given as:

$$\Gamma = \pi\, cU \sin \alpha \tag{14.26}$$

where, c = Chord length,

α = Angle of attack, and

U = Free stream velocity of airfoil.

Also lift force, F_L is given as:

$$F_L = \rho L U \Gamma$$

$$\therefore \quad F_L = \rho L U \times \pi\, cU \sin \alpha = \pi \rho c L U^2 \sin \alpha \quad (\because \Gamma = \pi\, cU \sin \alpha)$$

The lift force is also given by:

$$F_L = C_L \times \frac{\rho U^2}{2} \times A = C_L \times \frac{\rho U^2}{2} \times c \times L \tag{14.27}$$

Equating the two values of lift force given by eqns. (14.26), and (14.27), we get:

$$\pi \rho c L U^2 \sin\alpha = C_L \times \frac{\rho U^2}{2} \times c \times L$$

$$\therefore \quad C_L = \frac{\pi \rho c L U^2 \sin\alpha \times 2}{\rho U^2 \times c \times L} = 2\pi \sin\alpha$$

i.e. $C_L = 2\pi \sin\alpha$ (14.28)

From eqn. (14.28), we observe that co-efficient of lift depends upon the angle of attack. The actual lift co-efficient for an airfoil, in normal range of operation, is about 95 *per cent* of the theoretical value computed from the eqn. (14.28).

With real fluids, the airfoil creates its own circulation or vortex field in order to experience lift.

— When a flying object such as an airplane is in a *steady-state,* then:

(*i*) The weight of the airplane, (W) = The lift force $\left(C_L \times \frac{\rho U^2}{2} \times A\right)$,

(*ii*) The thrust developed by the engine = The drag force.

Example 14.24. *A jet plane weighing 24.5 kN and having a wing area of 16.7 m² flies at a velocity of 950 km/h. When the engine delivers 6125 kW, 65 percent of the power is used to overcome the drag resistance of the wing. Calculate the co-efficients of lift and drag for the wing. Take density of the atmospheric air = 1.208 kg/m³*

Solution. Weight of the jet plane, W = 24.5 kN

Wing area, A = 16.7 m²

Velocity of the plane, U = 950 km/h = $\frac{950 \times 1000}{60 \times 60} \simeq 264$ m/s.

Power delivered by the engine = 6125 kW

Percentage of the power used to overcome the drag resistance = 65%

Density of atmospheric air, ρ = 1.208 kg/m³

Co-efficients of lift and drag, C_L and C_D:

Lift force, F_L = Weight of the jet plane

$$\text{or,} \quad C_L \times \frac{\rho U^2}{2} \times A = 24.5 \times 10^3$$

$$\text{or,} \quad C_L \times \frac{1.208 \times 264^2}{2} \times 16.7 = 24.5 \times 10^3 \text{ N}$$

$$\text{or,} \quad C_L \times \frac{2 \times 24.5 \times 10^3}{1.208 \times 264^2 \times 16.7} = \mathbf{0.0348\ (Ans.)}$$

Power required to overcome drag resistance

$$= F_D \times U = 0.65 \times (6125 \times 10^3) \qquad \textit{(Given)}$$

$$\text{But,} \quad F_D \text{ (drag force)} = C_D \times \frac{\rho U^2}{2} \times A$$

$$\therefore \quad C_D \times \frac{\rho U^2}{2} \times A \times U = 0.65 \times (6125 \times 10^3)$$

$$\text{or,} \quad C_D \times \frac{1.208 \times 264^2}{2} \times 16.7 \times 264 = 0.65 \times (6125 \times 10^3)$$

$$\therefore \qquad C_D = \frac{2 \times 0.65 \times (6125 \times 10^3)}{1.208 \times 264^2 \times 16.7 \times 264} = \mathbf{0.0214 \ (Ans.)}$$

Example 14.25. *An aeroplane weighing 39.24 kN is flying in a horizontal direction at 360 km/h. The plane spans 15 m and has a wing surface area of 35 m^2. If drag co-efficient C_D = 0.03 and for air ρ = 1.22 kg/m^3, determine:*

(i) Co-efficient of lift,

(ii) Power required to drive the plane, and

(iii) Theoretical value of the boundary layer circulation. **[Delhi University]**

Solution. Weight of the aeroplane, $W = 39.24$ kN

Speed of the aeroplane, $U = 360 \text{ km/h} = \frac{360 \times 1000}{60 \times 60} = 100 \text{ m/s}$

Span of the aeroplane, $L = 15$ m

Wing surface area, $A = 35 \text{ m}^2$

Co-efficient of drag, $C_D = 0.03$

Density of air, $\rho = 1.22 \text{ kg/m}^3$.

(i) Co-efficient of lift, C_L:

For equilibrium in vertical direction, lift equals the weight of the aeroplane.

$$\therefore \qquad W = C_L \times \frac{\rho U^2}{2} \times A$$

$$\text{or,} \qquad 39.24 \times 10^3 = C_L \times \frac{1{\cdot}2 \times 100^2}{2} \times 35$$

$$\text{or,} \qquad C_L = \frac{2 \times 39.24 \times 10^3}{1.2 \times 100^2 \times 35} = \mathbf{0.187 \ (Ans.)}$$

(ii) Power required to drive the plane, P:

$$\text{Drag force, } F_D = C_D \times \frac{\rho U^2}{2} \times A$$

$$= 0.03 \times \frac{1.20 \times 100^2}{2} \times 35 = 6300 \text{ N}$$

Power required, $P = F_D \times U = 6300 \times 100 \times 10^{-3}$ kW = **630 kW (Ans.)**

(iii) Theoretical value of boundary layer circulation, Γ:

Lift force, $F_L = \rho L U \Gamma$

$$\text{or,} \qquad 39.24 \times 10^3 = 1.22 \times 15 \times 100 \times \Gamma$$

$$\text{or,} \qquad \Gamma = \frac{39.24 \times 10^3}{1.22 \times 15 \times 100} = \mathbf{21.4 \ m^2/s \ (Ans.)}$$

Example 14.26. *A wing of a small aeroplane is rectangular in plan having a span of 12 m and chord of 1.8 m.. In a horizontal flight at 200 km/h the total aerodynamic force acting on the wing is 28 kN. If the lift-drag ratio is 10, determine:*

(i) Co-efficients of lift and drag,

(ii) Total weight the aeroplane can carry, and

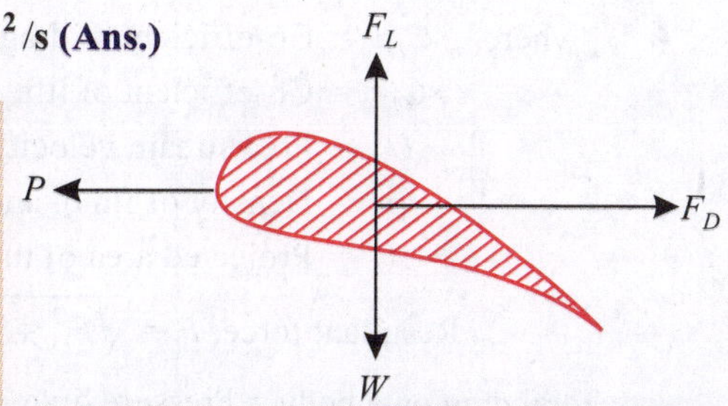

Fig. 14.26

(iii) Power required for the flight.
Take ρ for air = 1.2 kg/m³

Solution. Span, $l = 12$ m
Chord, $c = 1.8$ m

Speed of the aeroplane,

$$U = 200 \text{ km/h} = \frac{200 \times 1000}{60 \times 60} = 55.55 \text{ m/s}$$

Aerodynamic force, $F_L = 28$ kN

(*i*) Co-efficients of lift and drag:

For horizontal flight (Fig. 14.26):

$$F_L \uparrow = W \downarrow, \; F_D = C_D \, A \frac{\rho U^2}{2}, \; A = l \times c$$

Now, $$\frac{F_L}{F_D} = 10 \qquad \textit{(Given)}$$

$$\therefore \quad \frac{F_L}{F_D} = 10 = \frac{28 \times 1000}{C_D \times (12 \times 1.8) \times \dfrac{1.2 \times 55.55^2}{2}}$$

or, $$C_D = \frac{28 \times 1000 \times 2}{10 \times (12 \times 1.8) \times 1.2 \times 55.55^2} = \mathbf{0.07} \textbf{ (Ans.)}$$

(*ii*) Total weight the aeroplane can carry, W:

$$W = F_L = \mathbf{28 \text{ kN}} \textbf{ (Ans.)}$$

(*iii*) Power required for flight, *P*:

$$P = F_D \times U = \frac{F_L}{10} \times U = \frac{28}{10} \times 55.55 \qquad \left(\because \frac{F_L}{F_D} = 10\right)$$

$$= \mathbf{155.54 \text{ kN}} \textbf{ (Ans.)}$$

HIGHLIGHTS

1. A body wholly immersed in a real fluid may be subjected to the following forces:
   Drag force (F_D): It is the force exerted by fluid in the direction of flow (free stream).
   Lift force (F_L): It is the force exerted by fluid at right angles to the direction of flow.
2. The mathematical expressions for F_D and F_L are:

$$F_D = C_D \times \frac{\rho U^2}{2} \times A \text{ and } F_L = C_L \times \frac{\rho U^2}{2} \times A$$

where, C_D = Co-efficient of drag,
C_L = Co-efficient of lift,
U = Free stream velocity of fluid,
ρ = Density of fluid, and
A = Projected area of the body.

Resultant force, $F = \sqrt{F_D^2 + F_L^2}$

3. Total drag on a body = Pressure drag + friction drag

4. A body whose surface coincides with the stream lines when placed in a flow, is called a *streamlined* body. If the surface of the body does not coincide with the streamlines, the body in called *bluff* body.

5. Stokes found out that for $Re < 0.2$ the total drag on a sphere is given by

$F_D = 3\pi\mu DU$; and of the total drag

$$\text{Skin Friction drag} = \frac{2}{3} \times 3\pi\mu Du = 2\pi\mu DU \text{ , and}$$

$$\text{Pressure drag} = \frac{1}{3} \times 3\pi\mu DU = \pi\mu DU$$

6. For sphere, the values of C_D for different Reynolds number are:

Reynolds number (*Re*)	C_D
(*i*) Lesss than 0.2	$\frac{24}{Re}$
(*ii*) Between 0.2 and 5.0	$\frac{24}{Re}\left(1+\frac{3}{16Re}\right)$
(*iii*) Between 5 and 1000	0.4
(*iv*) Between 1000 and 10^5	0.5
(*v*) Greater than 10^5	0.2

7. The *terminal velocity* is the maximum velocity attained by a fallling body. The terminal velocity of a body falling through a liquid at rest is calculated from the following relation:

$$W = F_D + F_B$$

where, F_D and F_B are the drag force and buoyant force respectively, acting vertically upward.

8. The velocity of ideal fluid at any point on the surface of the cylinder is given by $u_\theta = 2U \sin\theta$

where, u_θ = Tangential velocity on the surface of the cylinder,
U = Uniform velocity (or free stream velocity),
θ = The angular distance of the point from the forward stagnation point.

9. The peripheral velocity on the surface of the cylinder due to circulation (u_c) is given by :

$$u_c = \frac{\Gamma}{2\pi R}$$

where, Γ = circulation, and R = radius of the cylinder.

10. The resultant velocity in a circular cylinder which is rotated at a constant speed in a uniform flow field is given by:

$$u = u_\theta + u_c = 2U \sin\theta + \frac{\Gamma}{2\pi R}$$

11. The position of stagnation points is given by:

$$\sin\theta = \frac{\Gamma}{4\pi R}$$

For a single stagnation point, the condition is:

$\Gamma = 4\pi UR$ ...in terms of circulation

$u_c = 2U$ ...in terms of tangential velocity.

12. The pressure at any point on the cylinder surface (p) is given by:

$$p = p_o + \frac{1}{2}\rho U^2 \left[1 - \left(2\sin\theta + \frac{\Gamma}{2\pi UR}\right)^2\right]$$

where, p_o = The pressure in the uniform flow at some distance ahead of cylinder.

13. When a circular cylinder is rotated in a uniform flow, a lift force (F_L) is produced on the cylinder, the magnitude of which is given by:

$$F_L = \rho L U \Gamma$$

This equation is known as **Kutta - Joukowski equation.**

14. The expression for lift co-efficient for a rotating cylinder in a uniform flow is given by:

$$C_L = \frac{\Gamma}{UR} \quad \text{...in terms of circulation}$$

$$C_L = 2\pi \frac{u_c}{U} \quad \text{...in terms of tangential velocity.}$$

15. The generation of lift by spinning cylinder in a fluid stream is called **Magnus effect.**

16. Circulation developed on the airfoil is given by:

$$\Gamma = \pi c\, U \sin \alpha$$

where, c = Chord length, α = Angle of attack.

17. The expression for co-efficient of lift for an airfoil is given by:

$$C = 2\pi \sin \alpha$$

18. When an aeroplane is in steady-state:

(*i*) The weight of aeroplane (W) = The lift force $\left(C_L \times \frac{\rho U^2}{2} \times A \right)$

(*ii*) The thrust developed by the engine = The drag force.

OBJECTIVE TYPE QUESTIONS

Choose the Correct Answer:

1. The pressure drag depends upon
   (*a*) the characteristics of the oncoming flow
   (*b*) the boundary layer formation
   (*c*) the separation of boundary layer and the size of the wake
   (*d*) the shear stresses generated on the body surface.
2. In case of airfoils, the profile drag is one which is caused by
   (*a*) the compressibilty effects
   (*b*) the shape and orientation of airfoil
   (*c*) the circulation induced around the airfoil
   (*d*) none of the above.
3. The friction drag is primarily due to
   (*a*) separation of boundary layer
   (*b*) weight component in the direction of flow
   (*c*) shear stresses generated due to viscous acion
   (*d*) none of the above.
4. For a perfectly streamlined body which of the following statements is *incorrect?*
   (*a*) The pressure drag is very small
   (*b*) The boundary layer remains thin over the entire surface and does not separate
   (*c*) The flow separation points and a wake region is formed
   (*d*) The streamline pattern and pressure distribution are nearly the same as for an irrotational flow.
5. The drag force is given by
   (a) $C_D \rho U^2 A$ (*b*) $C_D \rho^2 U^2 A$
   (*c*) $C_D \rho U^2 A$ (*d*) $C_D \frac{\rho U^2}{2} A$
6. The shape of a streamlined body is such as to
   (*a*) fix the separation points as much ahead as possible
   (*b*) shift the boundary layer separation to the rearmost part thereby considerably reducing the wake-size
   (*c*) make the streamline pattern symmetrical
   (*d*) none of the above.
7. Which of following statements is *correct* for bluff bodies?
   (*a*) The total drag is considerably larger as compared to that for streamlined bodies

(b) The friction drag is greater than the pressure drag
(c) The total drag is much less as compared to that for streamlined bodies.
(d) None of the above.

8. The drag force experienced by an object is
(a) the component of resultant fluid dynamic force in the flow direction
(b) the horizontal force due to pressure variation over the surface of object
(c) the resultant fluid dynamics force acting on the object
(d) none of the above.

9. The drag and lift forces experienced by an object placed in a fluid stream are due to
(a) pressure and turbulence
(b) viscosity and turbulence
(c) pressure and viscosity
(d) pressure and gravity.

10. The lift force that may act on an object is
(a) the component force due to the fluid displaced by the body
(b) the component of resultant fluid dynamic force in a direction normal to the general direction of flow
(c) the force due to shear stress that acts on the body surface
(d) none of the above.

11. Which of the following conditions/requirements is necessary to induce lift on an object ?
(a) The object should be so shaped that there are zones if high and low velocities resulting in pressure difference between upperside and bottomside of the object.
(b) The object should be so designed that pressure distribution over its surface is symmetrical
(c) The shape of the object should be sym- metrical and the axis of the symmetry be aligned parallel to the flow direction
(d) None of the above.

12. A strreamlined body is defined as a body about which
(a) the drag is zero
(b) the flow is laminar
(c) the flow is along streamlines
(d) the flow separation is suppressed.

13. When a circular cylinder is rotated in a uniform flow, a lift force is produced on the cylinder which is caused by
(a) the pressure difference between the two halves, the bottom-half being subjected to a higher pressure
(b) the symmetrical streamline patterns
(c) the shear stresses.due to viscous action
(d) none of the above.

14. The location of stagnation points is found from the relation
(a) $\sin\theta = -\dfrac{\Gamma}{4\pi UR^2}$
(b) $\sin\theta = -\dfrac{\Gamma^2}{4\pi UR}$
(c) $\sin\theta = -\dfrac{\Gamma^2}{4\pi UR}$
(d) $\sin\theta = -\dfrac{\Gamma}{4\pi UR}$.

15. For a single stagnation point, the condition is
(a) $\Gamma = 4\pi U R$ (b) $\Gamma = 2\pi U R$
(c) $\Gamma = 4\pi U^2 R$ (d) $\Gamma = 4\pi U R^2$.

16. The expression for co-efficient of lift for an airfoil is given by
(a) $C_L = 2\pi \sin^2 \alpha$ (b) $C_L = 4\pi \sin \alpha$
(c) $C_L = 2\pi \sin \alpha$ (c) none of the above.

17. The experssion for lift co-efficient for a rotating cylinder in a uniform flow is given by
(a) $C_L = \dfrac{\Gamma}{R^2U}$ (b) $C_L = \dfrac{\Gamma}{RU^2}$
(c) $C_L = \dfrac{\Gamma}{RU}$ (d) none of the above.

18. The velocity of ideal fluid at any point on the surface of the cylinder is given by
(a) $U \sin\theta$ (b) $2U \sin\theta$
(b) $3U \sin\theta$ (d) $4U \sin\theta$.

19. The drag on a sphere for Reynolds number less than 0.2 is given by
(a) $\pi\mu DU$ (b) $2\pi\mu DU$
(c) $3\pi\mu DU$ (d) none of the above.

20. The mathematical expression for lift force is given by
(a) $F_L = C_L\rho AU$
(b) $F_L = C_L \dfrac{\rho U^2}{2} A$
(c) $F_L = C_L\rho AU^2A$
(d) none of the obove.

21. The lift force on an airfoil is due to
(a) the circulation of air around it
(b) the pressure difference of the top and bottom surface
(c) the formation of tip vortices
(d) the angle of attack.

22. the terminal velocity of a small sphere settling in a viscous fluid varies as
(*a*) the Reynolds number
(*b*) the square of its diameter
(*c*) directly proportional to the viscosity of the fluid
(*d*) its diameter.

23. At the stall point for the airfoil
(*a*) the boundary layer separates at the leading edge
(*b*) the lift is maximum and the drag is minimum
(*c*) the lift is zero and the drag is maximum
(*d*) the lift is maximum and the drag in creases sharply beyond it.

24. The velocity at the top of spinning ball is
(*a*) less than that at bottom
(*b*) greater than that at bottom
(*c*) equal to that at the bottom
(*d*) independent of spinning.

25. The circulation around an airfoil required for lift is produced
(*a*) when the airfoil is kept inclined to flow direction
(*b*) due to tip vortices
(*c*) by rotation of airfoil
(*d*) because of surface discontinuity formed at the trailling edge.

26. The terminal velocity of a body in a stationary mass of fluid corresponds to the situation when the
(*a*) body acquires a constant velocity in any direction
(*b*) net force acting on the body equals zero
(*c*) weight of the body equals the buoyancy force acting on it
(*d*) net force acting on the body acts in vertical direction.

ANSWERS

1. (*c*)	**2.** (*b*)	**3.** (*c*)	**4.** (*c*)	**5.** (*d*)	**6.** (*b*)
7. (*a*)	**8.** (*a*)	**9.** (*c*)	**10.** (*b*)	**11.** (*a*)	**12.** (*d*)
13. (*a*)	**14.** (*d*)	**15.** (*a*)	**16.** (*c*)	**17.** (*c*)	**18.** (*b*)
19. (*c*)	**20.** (*b*)	**21.** (*a*)	**22.** (*b*)	**23.** (*d*)	**24.** (*b*)
25. (*b*)	**26.** (*b*)				

THEORETICAL QUESTIONS

1. Define drag force and lift force of an object immersed in a fluid.
2. Distinguish between teh friction drag and the pressure drag.
3. When are the factors on which the total drag of a body fully immersed in a fluid depend?
4. Define co-efficient of drag and lift and state the factors on which these co-efficients depend.
5. Differentiate between a streamlined body and bluff body.
6. What is the expression for the drag on a sphere, when Reynolds number (*Re*) is upto 0.2 ? Hence prove that the drag co-efficient for sphere for this renge of *Re* is given by

$$C_D = \frac{24}{Re}$$

7. What do you mean by terminal velocity of a body ?
8. Describe with the help of a sketch, the variation of drag co-efficeint for a cylinder over a wide range of Reynolds number.
9. Why should circulation superimposed on flow past a body cause a lift ?
10. Draw and explain the approximate flow pattern and the pressure distribution around a flat plate placed perpendicular in a stream flow.
11. What is meant by Magnus effect ?
12. Derive an expression for the lift produced on a rotating cylinder placed in a uniform flow field such that the axis of the cylinder is perpendicular to the direction of flow.
13. Obtain an expression for co-efficient of lift for a rotating cylinder placed in a uniform flow.
14. Define stagnation points.
15. How is the position if the stagnation points for a rotating cylinder in a uniform flow determined?
16. Define the following terms for an airfoil.
(*i*) Chord line
(*ii*) Angle of attack
(*iii*) Camber
(*iv*) Profile centre line.

UNSOLVED EXAMPLES

1. In a wind tunnel experiments were conducted with a wind speed of 50 km/h on a flat plate of size 2 m long and 1 m wide. The mass density of air is 1.15 kg/m^3 The plate is kept at such an angle that co-efficients of lift and drag are 0.75 and 0.15 respectively.Determine: (*i*) Lift force, (*ii*) Drag force, (*iii*) Resultant Force, and (*iv*) Power exerted by the airstream on the plate.

[**Ans.** (*i*) 166.28 N; (*ii*)33.25 N; (*iii*)169.6 N;θ = 78.69°; (*iv*) 461.89 W]

2. A passenger car has a weight of 30 kN and the co-efficient of friction between the road and tyers is 0.01. Assuming the cross-sectional area of the car to be 2.25 m^2 with a drag co-efficient of 0.60 estimate the energy requirement at a speed of 60 km/h. [**Ans.** 8.78 kW]

3. A man weighing 981 N descends to the ground from an aeroplane with the help of a parachute against the resistance of air. The shape of the parachute is hemispherical of 2 m diameter. Find the velocity of the parachute with which it comes down. Assume C_D = 0.5 and ρ for air = 1.25 kg/m^3 and ν = 0.015 stoke

[**Ans.** 31.6 m/s]

4. A kite 0.8 × 0.8 m weighing 3.924 N assumes an angle of 12° ot the horizontal .The string attached to the kite makes an angle of 45° to the horizontal. The pull on the string is 24.525 N when the wind is flowing at a speed of 30 km/h. Find the corresponding co-efficients of drag and lift, Take ρ for air = 1.25 kg/m^3.

[**Ans.** C_D = 0.624, C_L = 0.765]

5. A kite weighing 7.85 N has an effective area of 0.8 m^2 .It is maintained in air at an angle of 10° to the horizontal. The string attached to the kite makes an angle of 45° ot the horizontal and at this position the values of co-efficients of drag and lift are 0.6 and 0.8 respectively. Determine:

(*i*) The speed of wind, and

(*ii*) The tension in the string.

Take ρ for air = 1.25 kg/m^3

[**Ans.** 31.9 km/h; 33.25 N]

6. A submarine assumed to approximate a cylinder 4 m in diameter and 20 m long is travelling submerged at 1.3 m/s in sea water. Find the drag exerted on it, if the drag co-efficient for Reynolds number greater than 10^5 may be taken as 0.75 Take for water, ρ = 1035 kg/m^3 and ν = 0.015 stoke. [**Ans.** 52.47 kN]

7. A ball of 80 mm diameter is supported in vertical air stream which is flowing at a velocity of 7 m/s. If the density and kinematic viscosity of air are 1.25 kg/m^3 and 1.5 stokes respectively, calculate the weight of the ball.

[**Ans.** 0.0769 N]

8. A steel sphere of 3 mm diameter falls in glycerine at a terminal velocity of 0.035 m/s. If specific weights of steel and glycerine are 75 kN/m^3 and 12.5 kN /m^3 determine: (*i*) Dynamic viscosity of glycerine, (*ii*) Drag force, and (*iii*)Drag coefficient for the sphere.

[**Ans.** (*i*) 0.893 Ns/m^2, (*ii*)8.837 × 10^{-4} N, (*iii*) 160.2]

9. A metallic ball (sp. gr. = 12) of 2 mm diameter is allowed to fall in fluid of specific gravity 0.95 and kinematic viscosity 1.5 Ns/m^2. Determine: (*i*) Drag force, (*ii*) Pressure drag and skin friction drag, and (*iii*) terminal velocity of ball in fluid.

[**Ans.** (*i*) 4.54 × 10^{-4} N; (*ii*) 1.514 × 10^{-4} N; 3.026 × 10^{-4} N; (*iii*) 0.016 m/s]

10. A wing of a small aeroplane is rectangular in plan having a span of 10 m and chord of 1.6 m. In a horizontal flight at 2.2 km/h the total aerodynamic force acting of the wing is 25 kN. If the lift-drag ratio is 10, determine; (*i*)The co-efficient of lift and drag; (*ii*) The total weight the aeroplane can carry, and (*iii*) The power required for the flight.

[**Ans.** (*i*)0.7, 0.07; (*ii*) 25 kN; (*iii*)153 kW]

11. A cylinder 1.2 m in diameter and 8 m long rotates of 90 r.p.m. with its axis perpendicular to an air stream with a wind velocity of 30 m/s. Assuming no slip condition between the cylinder and circulatory flow, find: (*i*) The magnitude of circulation, (*ii*) the transverse or lift force, and (*iii*)the position of stagnation points. Take specific weight of air as 12.25 N/m^3.

[**Ans.** (*i*) 21.3 m^2/s; (*ii*) 6.33 kN; (*iii*)185.4°; 354.6°]

12. A cylinder 1.2 m diameter and 8 m long rotates at 160 r.p.m. with its axis perpendicular to the stream of water flowing at a velocity of 10 m/s. Assuming no slip between the cylinder and the circulatory flow, ditermine:

(*i*) The circulation,

(*ii*) The theoretical lift,

(*iii*) The position of stagnation points, and

(*iv*) The speed of cylinder (in r.p.m.) for a single stagnation point:

[**Ans.** (*i*) 38 m^2/s; (*ii*)3.04 × 10^6N; (*iii*)210.2°; 329.8°; (*iv*)318 r.p.m.]

13. A circular cylinder of 1.0 m diameter and 10 m length is rotated at 420 r. p.m. about its axis when it is kept is air stream with 11.0 m/s velocity perpendicular to its axis. Determine:

(*i*) Circulation around the cylinder,

(*ii*) Theoretical lift and lift co-efficient,

(*iii*) Position if stagnation points,

(*iv*) Actual drag and lift force on the cylinder, and

(*v*) Actual resultant force and its direction.

Take ρ = 1.208 kg/m^3, and experimental values of C_D and C_L as 1.5 and 5.1 respectively.

[**Ans.** (*i*) 69.1 m^2/s; (*ii*) 9182.67 N; 12.565 (*iii*) – 90°; (*iv*) 1096.26 N; 3727.28 N; (*v*)3885.15 N; 73.61°]

14. A ship is propelled by two cylindrical rotors turming at 250 r. p.m. about their axes which are vertical. Each rotor is 6 m long and 2 m in diameter. Estimate the force exerted upon the rotors in the direction of motion when the relative wind velocity is 60 km/h at an angle of 60° opposing the direction of motion. Assume ρ for air is 1.25 kg/m^3.

[**Ans.** 10098 N]

15. A jet plane weighing 29.4 kN and having a wing area of 20 m^2 flies at a velocity of 950 km/h. When the engine delivers 7350 kW,65 percent of the power is used to overcome the drag resistance of the wing. Calculate the co-efficient of lift and drag for the wing. Take density of atmospheric air 1.208 kg/m^3.

[**Ans.** 0.0349; 0.0215]

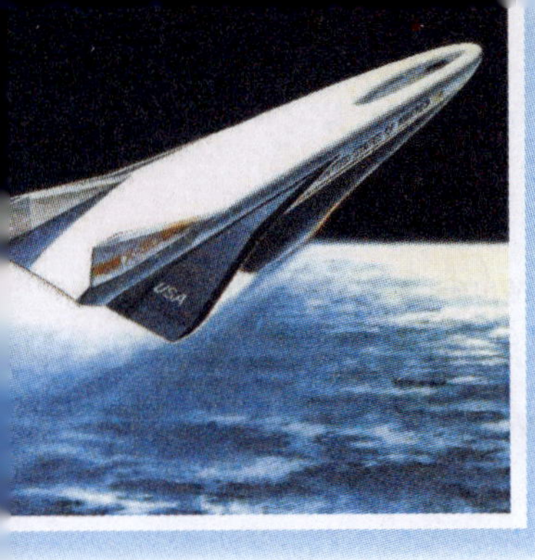

Chapter 15

COMPRESSIBLE FLOW

15.1. INTRODUCTION

A compressible flow *is that flow in which the density of the fluid changes during flow.* All real fluids are compressible to some extent and therefore their density will change with change in pressure or temperature. If the relative change in density $\Delta \rho/\rho$ is small, the fluid can be treated as incompressible. A compressible fluid, such as air, can be considered as incompressible with constant ρ if *changes in elevation are small, acceleration is small,* and/or *temperature changes are negligible.* In other words, if Mach's number U/C, where C is the sonic velocity, is small, compressible fluid can be treated as incompressible.

The gases are treated as compressible fluids and study of this type of flow is often referred to as '*Gas dynamics*'.

Some important problems where *compressibility effect* has to be considered are :

(*i*) Flow of gases through nozzles, orifices ;

(*ii*) Compressors ;

(*iii*) Flight of aeroplanes and projectiles moving at higher altitudes;

(*iv*) Water hammer and accoustics.

'***Compressibility***' *affects the drag co-efficients of bodies by formation of shock waves, discharge co-efficients of measuring devies such as orificemeters, venturimeters and pitot tubes, stagnation pressure and flows in converging-diverging sections.*

15.2. BASIC THERMODYNAMIC RELATIONS

15.2.1. The Characteristics Equation of State

At temperatures that are considerably in excess of critical temperature of a fluid, and also at very low pressure, the vapour of fluid tends to obey the equation:

$$\frac{pv}{T} = \text{constant} = R \left(\text{or } \frac{p}{\rho} = RT \right)$$

In practice, no gas obeys this law rigidly, but many gases tend towards it. An imaginary ideal gas which obeys this law is called a *perfect gas,* and the equation $\frac{pv}{T} = R$, is called the *characteristic equation of a state of a perfect gas.* The constant R is called the *gas constant.* Each perfect gas has a different gas constant.

Units of R are Nm/kg K or kJ/kg K

Usually, the characteristic equation is written as :

$$pv = RT \qquad \text{...(15.1)}$$

or, for m kg, occupying V m^3,

$$pV = mRT \qquad \text{...(15.2)}$$

or,

$$p = \frac{m}{V} RT = \rho RT \qquad \text{...(15.2 (a))}$$

Taking log on both sides, we get:

$$\ln (p) = \ln (\rho) + \ln (R) + \ln (T)$$

Upon differentiation, we have:

$$\frac{dp}{p} = \frac{d\rho}{\rho} + \frac{dR}{R} + \frac{dT}{T}$$

Since R is constant for a particular gas, its derivative is zero.

$$\therefore \quad \frac{dp}{p} - \frac{d\rho}{\rho} - \frac{dT}{T} = 0 \qquad \text{...(15.3)}$$

Eqn. (15.3) is the *differential equation of a perfect gas.*

15.2.2. Specific Heats

— The specific heat of a solid or liquid is usually defined as *the heat required to raise unit mass through one degree temperature rise.*

— For a gas there are an infinite number of ways in which heat may be added between any two temperatures, and hence a gas could have an infinite number of specific heats. However, only two specific heats for gases are defined.

(*i*) Specific heat at constant volume, c_v

(*ii*) Specific head at constant pressure, c_p.

(In case of real gases, c_p and c_v *vary with temperature,* but a suitable *average value* may be used for most practical purposes.)

$$c_p = c_v + R \qquad \text{...(15.4)}$$

$$\frac{c_p}{c_v} = \gamma \text{ (gamma)} \qquad \text{...(15.5)}$$

15.2.3. Internal Energy

It is the heat energy stored in a gas. If a certain amount of heat is supplied to a gas the result is that temperature of gas may increase or volume of gas may increase thereby doing some external work or both temperature and volume may increase. *If during heating of a gas the temperature increases its internal energy will also increase.*

Joule's law *of internal energy states that the internal energy of a perfect gas is a function of temperature only.* In other words, internal energy of a gas is dependent on the *temperature change only* and is *not affected by the change in pressure and volume.*

We do not know how to find the absolute quantity of internal energy in any substance, however, what is needed in engineering is the change of internal energy (ΔU).

15.2.4. Enthalpy

One of the fundamental quantities which occurs invariably in thermodynamics is the *sum of internal energy (u) and pressure volume product (pv). This sum is called* **Enthalpy (h).**

i.e. $$h = u + pu$$

The total enthalpy of mass, *m, of a fluid is given by,*

$$H = U + pV, \text{ where } H = mh$$

15.2.5. Energy, Work and Heat

Energy. Energy is a general term embracing *energy in transition and stored energy.* The stored energy of a substance may be in the forms of *mechanical energy* and *internal energy* (other forms of stored energy may be chemical energy and electrical energy). Part of the stored energy may take the form of either potential energy or kinetic energy due to velocity. The balance part of the energy is known as *internal energy.*

Heat and work. These are the forms of energy in transition and are the only forms in which energy can cross the boundaries of a system. Neither heat nor work can exist as stored energy.

Work. Work is said to be done when a *force moves through a distance.* If a part of the boundary of a system undergoes a displacement under the action of a pressure, the work done W is the product of the force (pressure × area) and the distance it moves in the direction of the force.

Work is a transient quantity which only appears at the boundary while a change of state is taking place within a system. Work is 'something' which appears at the boundary when a system changes its state due to the movement of a part of the boundary under the action of a force.

Work output of the system $= + W$

Work input to system $= - W$

Heat. Heat (denoted by the symbol Q) may be defined in an analogous way to work as follows:

"*Heat is something which appears at the boundary when a system changes its state due to a difference in temperature between the system and its surroundings*".

Heat, like work, is a transient quantity which only appears at the boundary while a change is taking place within the system.

Heat received by the system $= + Q$

Heat rejected or given up by the system $= - Q$

15.3. BASIC THERMODYNAMIC PROCESSES

The basic thermodynamic processes are given below :

1. **Constant volume (isochoric) process (v = constant).** A change in the state of system at constant volume is called *isochoric process.* An isochoric process results when the gas system is heated or cooled in an *enclosed space* (*e.g.* a rigid vessel).

   Formulae (for unit mass) :

   $$\text{Heat added, } Q = c_v (T_2 - T_1) \quad ...(15.7)$$

   $$\text{Work done, } W = 0 \quad ...(15.8)$$

   $$p, v, T \text{ relations : } \frac{T_2}{T_1} = \frac{p_2}{p_1} \quad ...(15.9)$$

   where suffix 1 and suffix 2 represent the 'start' and 'finish' points of the process respectively.

2. **Constant pressure (isobaric) process (p = constant).** In this process a change in the state of the gas (working fluid) takes place at *constant pressure.* For a constant pressure process, the boundary must move against an external resistance as heat is supplied; for instance a gas in a cylinder behind a piston can be made to undergo a constant pressure process. Since the piston is pushed through a certain distance by the force exerted by the gas, then the work is done on its surroundings.

Formulae (for unit mass) :

$$\text{Head added, } Q = c_p\,(T_2 - T_1) \qquad \text{...(15.10)}$$

$$\text{Work done, } W = p\,(v_2 - v_1) \qquad \text{...(15.11)}$$

$$p, v, T \text{ relations : } \frac{T_2}{T_1} = \frac{v_2}{v_1} \qquad \text{...(15.12)}$$

3. **Isothermal process pv or $\frac{p}{\rho}$ = constant, T = constant).** A process at a constant temperature is called an *isothermal process. When a working substance in a cylinder behind a piston expands from a high pressure there is a tendency for the temperature to fall. In an isothermal expansion heat must be added continuously in order to keep the temperature at the initial value. Similarly in an isothermal compression heat must be removed from the working substance continuously during the process.*

Formulae (for unit mass) :

$$\text{Heat added, } \quad Q = p_1 v_1 \ln\left(\frac{v_2}{v_1}\right) = RT_1 \ln\left(\frac{\rho_1}{\rho_2}\right) \qquad \text{...(15.13)}$$

$$\text{Work done, } \quad W = p_1 v_1 \ln\left(\frac{v_2}{v_1}\right) = RT_1 \ln\left(\frac{\rho_1}{\rho_2}\right) \qquad \text{...(15.14)}$$

$$p, v, T, \text{ relations : } \quad p_1 v_1 = \left(\text{or } \frac{p_1}{\rho_1} = \frac{p_2}{\rho_2}\right) \qquad \text{...(15.15)}$$

4. **Adiabatic process (pv^γ or $\frac{p}{\rho^\gamma}$ = constant).** An adiabatic process is one *in which no heat is transferred to or from the gas* during the process. Such a process can be reversible or irreversible. *For an adiabatic process to take place, perfect thermal insulation for the system must be available.*

Formulae (for unit mass) :

$$\text{Heat added, } Q = 0 \qquad \text{...(15.16)}$$

$$\text{Work done, } W = \frac{p_1 v_1 - p_2 v_2}{\gamma - 1} = \frac{R\,(T_1 - T_2)}{\gamma - 1} \qquad \text{...(15.17)}$$

$$p, v, T, \text{ relations : } p_1 v_1^\gamma = p_2 v_2^\gamma \qquad \text{...(15.18)}$$

$$\frac{T_2}{T_1} = \left(\frac{v_1}{v_2}\right)^{\gamma - 1} = \left(\frac{p_2}{p_1}\right)^{\frac{\gamma - 1}{\gamma}} \qquad \text{...(15.19)}$$

If the adiabatic process is *reversible* (or frictionless), it is known as *isentropic process.* In case the pressure and density are related in such a way that $\gamma \neq \frac{c_p}{c_v}$ but is equal to some positive value then the process is known as *polytropic,* according to which $\frac{p}{\rho^n}$ = constant ($n \neq \gamma$).

15.4. BASIC EQUATIONS OF COMPRESSIBLE FLUID FLOW

The basic equations of compressible fluid flow are : (*i*) Continuity equation, (*ii*) Momentum equation, (*iii*) Energy equation, and (*iv*) Equation of state.

The only change from incompressible fluid cases is that thermodynamic laws are applied in addition to the basic principle of conservation of mass, energy and momentum.

15.4.1. Continuity Equation

In case of *one-dimensional flow,* mass per second = ρAV

(where, ρ = mass density, A = area of cross-section, V = velocity)

Since the mass or mass per second is constant according to law of conservation of mass, therefore,

$$\rho AV = \text{Constant} \qquad ...(15.20)$$

Differentiating the above equation, we get:

$$d(\rho AV) = 0 \quad \text{or} \quad \rho d(AV) + AVd\rho = 0$$

or,
$$\rho(AdV + VdA) + AVd\rho = 0 \quad \text{or} \quad \rho AdV + \rho VdA + AVd\rho = 0$$

Dividing both sides by ρAV, and rearranging we get:

$$\frac{d\rho}{\rho} + \frac{dA}{A} + \frac{dV}{V} = 0 \qquad ...(15.21)$$

Eqn. (15.18) is also known as equation of continuity in *differential form.*

15.4.2. Momentum Equation

The momentum equation for compressible fluids is similar to the one for incompressible fluids. This is because in momentum equation the *change in momentum flux is equated to force required to cause this change.*

Momentum flux = Mass flux × velocity = $\rho AV \times V$

But the mass flux *i.e.* ρAV = constant ...By continuity equation

Thus the momentum equation is completely independent of the compressibility effects and hence for compressible fluids too the momentum equation, say X-direction, may be expressed as :

$$\Sigma F_x = (\rho AVV_x)_2 - (\rho AVV_x)_1 \qquad ...(15.22)$$

15.4.3. Bernoulli's or Energy Equation

In chapter 6 Bernoulli's equation for an incompressible fluid has been derived and the same procedure is followed. As the flow of compressible fluid is steady, the same Euler equation (Eqn. 6.) is obtained as :

$$\frac{dp}{\rho} + VdV + gdz = 0 \qquad ...(15.23)$$

Integrating both sides, we get:

$$\int \frac{dp}{\rho} + \int VdV + \int gdz = \text{constant}$$

or,
$$\int \frac{dp}{\rho} + \frac{V^2}{2} + gz = \text{constant} \qquad ...(15.24)$$

In compressible flow since ρ is not constant it cannot be taken outside the integration sign. In compressible fluids the pressure (p) changes with change of density (ρ), depending on the type of process. Let us find out the Bernoulli's equation for isothermal and adiabatic processes.

(*a*) Bernoulli's equation for isothermal process :

In case of an *isothermal process*

$$pv = \text{constant} \quad \text{or} \quad \frac{p}{\rho} = \text{constant} = c_1 \ (say)$$

(where v = specific volume = $1/\rho$)

$$\therefore \quad \rho = \frac{p}{c}$$

Hence, $\int \frac{dp}{\rho} = \int \frac{dp}{p/c_1} = \int \frac{c_1 dp}{p} = c_1 \int \frac{dp}{p} = c_1 \ln(p) = \frac{p}{\rho} \ln(p) \quad \left(\because \ c_1 = \frac{p}{\rho}\right)$

Substituting the value of $\int \frac{dp}{\rho}$ in eqn. (15.24), we get

$$\frac{p}{\rho} \ln(p) + \frac{V^2}{2} + gz = \text{constant}$$

Dividing both sides by g, we get

$$\frac{p}{\rho g} \ln(p) + \frac{V^2}{2g} + z = \text{constant} \qquad ...(15.25)$$

Eqn. (15.25) is the *Bernoulli's equation for compressible flow undergoing isothermal process.*

(*b*) Bernoulli's equation for adiabatic process :

In case of an *adiabatic process*:

$$pv^\gamma = \text{constant} \quad \text{or} \quad \frac{p}{\rho^\gamma} = \text{constant} = c_2 \ (say)$$

$$\therefore \quad \rho^\gamma = \frac{p}{c_2} \quad \text{or} \quad \rho = \left(\frac{p}{c_2}\right)^{1/\gamma}$$

Hence,

$$\int \frac{dp}{\rho} = \int \frac{dp}{(p/c_2)^{1/\gamma}} = (c_2)^{1/\gamma} \int \frac{1}{p^{1/\gamma}} dp = (c_2)^{1/\gamma} \int p^{-1/\gamma} dp$$

$$= (c_2)^{1/\gamma} \left[\frac{p^{-\frac{1}{\gamma}+1}}{\left(-\frac{1}{\gamma}+1\right)} \right] = \frac{(c_2)^{1/\gamma} (p)^{\left(\frac{\gamma-1}{\gamma}\right)}}{\left(\frac{\gamma-1}{\gamma}\right)} = \frac{\gamma}{\gamma-1} c_2^{1/\gamma} (p)^{\left(\frac{\gamma-1}{\gamma}\right)}$$

$$= \left(\frac{\gamma}{\gamma-1}\right)\left(\frac{p}{\rho^\gamma}\right)^{1/\gamma} (p)^{\left(\frac{\gamma-1}{\gamma}\right)} \qquad \left(\because c_2 = \frac{p}{\rho^\gamma}\right)$$

$$= \left(\frac{\gamma}{\gamma-1}\right)\left(\frac{p^{1/\gamma}}{\rho^{\gamma \times \frac{1}{\gamma}}}\right) (p)^{\left(\frac{\gamma-1}{\gamma}\right)}$$

$$= \left(\frac{\gamma}{\gamma-1}\right) \frac{p^{\left(\frac{1}{\gamma}+\frac{\gamma-1}{\gamma}\right)}}{\rho} = \left(\frac{\gamma}{\gamma-1}\right) \frac{p}{\rho}$$

Substituting the value of $\int \frac{dp}{\rho}$ in eqn. (15.24), we get

$$\left(\frac{\gamma}{\gamma-1}\right)\frac{p}{\rho}+\frac{V^2}{2}+gz = \text{constant}$$

Dividing both sides by g, we get

$$\left(\frac{\gamma}{\gamma-1}\right)\frac{p}{\rho g}+\frac{V^2}{2g}+z = \text{constant} \quad ...(15.26)$$

Eqn. (15.26) is the *Bernoulli's equation for compressible flow undergoing adiabatic process.*

Example 15.1. *A gas is flowing through a horizontal pipe. On a section where cross-section area is 50 cm², the pressure and temperature are found to be 3 bar (gauge)and 20°C respectively. At another section where the area of cross-section is 25 cm², the pressure is recorded 2 bar (gauge). If the mass rate of flow of gas through the pipe is 0.6 kg/s find the velocities of the gas at these sections, assuming an isothermal change.*

Take R = 287 J/kg K, and atmospheric pressure = 1 bar.

Solution.

Section 1: Area, $A_1 = 50\text{ cm}^2 = 50 \times 10^{-4}\text{ m}^2$

Pressure, $p_1 = 3$ bar (gauge) $= 3 + 1 = 4$ bar $= 4 \times 10^5$ N/m² (abs.)

Temperature, $T_1 = 20 + 273 = 293\ K$

Section 2: Area, $A_2 = 25\text{ cm}^2 = 25 \times 10^{-4}\text{ m}^2$

Pressure, $p_2 = 2$ bar (gauge) $= 2 + 1 = 3$ bar $= 3 \times 10^5$ N/m² (abs.)

Mass rate of flow of gas, $m = 0.6$ kg/s

Characteristic gas constant, $R = 287$ J/kg K

Atmospheric pressure = 1 bar

Velocities at the sections V_1, V_2 :

The characteristic equation is written as :

$$p = \rho RT \quad ...[\text{Eqn. 15.2 } (a)]$$

Section 1: $p_1 = \rho_1 RT_1$ or $\rho_1 = \frac{p_1}{RT_1} = \frac{4 \times 10^5}{287 \times 293} = 4.757\text{ kg/m}^3$

Also, $m = \rho_1 A_1 V_1$

or, $V_1 = \frac{m}{\rho_1 A_1} = \frac{0.6}{4.757 \times 50 \times 10^{-4}} = \mathbf{25.22\ m/s}$

Section 2: $\rho^2 = \frac{p_2}{RT_2} = \frac{3 \times 10^5}{287 \times 293} = 3.567\text{ kg/m}^3 \quad (\because T_1 = T_2 = 293\ K)$

Also, $m = \rho_2 A_2 V_2$

$\therefore$ $V_2 = \frac{m}{\rho_2 A_2} = \frac{0.6}{3.567 \times 25 \times 10^{-4}} = \mathbf{67.28\ m/s}$ **(Ans.)**

Example 15.2. *Fig. 15.1 shows a horizontal pipe in which gas is flowing at a temperature of 6°C. The pressures at the sections 1 and 2 are 4 bar (gauge) and 3 bar (gauge) respectively. If R = 287 J/kg K and atmospheric pressure is 1 bar find the velocities of the gas at these sections.*

Solution. Refer to Fig. 15.1.

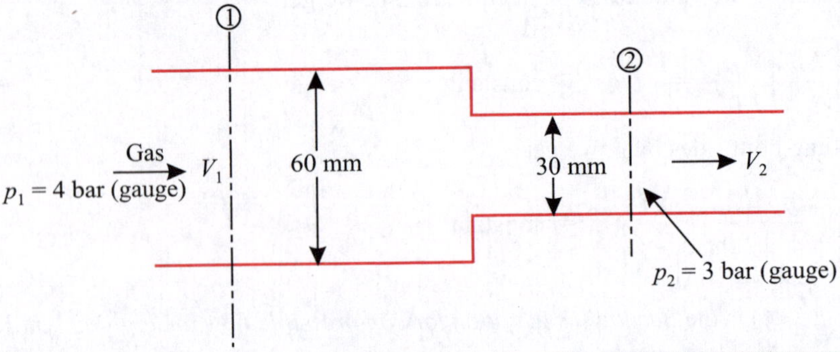

Fig. 15.1

Section 1: Diameter of pipe, $D_1 = 60$ mm $= 0.06$ m

$$\therefore \quad \text{Area, } A_1 = \frac{\pi}{4} \times 0.06^2 = 2.827 \times 10^{-3}\ \text{m}^2$$

$$\text{Pressure, } p_1 = 4 \text{ bar (gauge)} = 4 + 1 = 5 \text{ bar (abs.)} = 5 \times 10^5\ \text{N/m}^2 \text{ (abs.)}$$

$$\text{Temperature, } T_1 = 6 + 273 = 279\ \text{K}$$

Section 2: Diameter of pipe, $D_2 = 30$ mm $= 0.03$ m

$$\therefore \quad \text{Area, } A_2 = \frac{\pi}{4} \times 0.3^2 = 7.0686 \times 10^{-4}\ \text{m}^2$$

$$\text{Pressure, } p_2 = 3 \text{ bar (gauge)}$$

$$= 3 + 1 = 4 \text{ bar (abs.)} = 4 \times 10^5\ \text{N/m}^2 \text{ (abs.)}$$

$$\text{Gas constant, } R = 287\ \text{J/kg K}$$

Velocities of the gas at sections 1 and 2, V_1, V_2:

Applying continuity equation at 1 and 2, we get:

$$\rho_1 A_1 V_1 = \rho_2 A_2 V_2 \quad \text{or} \quad \frac{V_2}{V_1} = \frac{\rho_1 A_1}{\rho_2 A_2} = \frac{\rho_1 \times 2{\cdot}827 \times 10^{-3}}{\rho_2 \times 7{\cdot}0686 \times 10^{-4}} = 4 \times \frac{\rho_1}{\rho_2} \quad ...(i)$$

For *an isothermal process,* we have:

$$\frac{p_1}{\rho_1} = \frac{p_2}{\rho_2} \quad \text{or} \quad \frac{\rho_1}{\rho_2} = \frac{p_1}{p_2} = \frac{5 \times 10^5}{4 \times 10^5} = 1.25$$

Substituting the value of $\frac{\rho_1}{\rho_2} = 1.25$ in eqn. (*i*), we get:

$$\frac{V_2}{V_1} = 4 \times 1.25 = 5 \quad \text{or} \quad V_2 = 5V_1 \quad ...(ii)$$

Applying Bernoulli's equation at sections 1 and 2 for isothermal process (Eqn. 15.25), we have:

$$\frac{p_1}{\rho_1 g} \ln(p_1) + \frac{V_1^2}{2g} + z_1 = \frac{p_2}{\rho_2} \ln(p_2) + \frac{V_2^2}{2g} + z_2$$

But, $\quad z_1 = z_2$, since the pipe is horizontal,

$$\therefore \quad \frac{p_1}{\rho_1 g} \ln(p_1) + \frac{V_1^2}{2g} = \frac{p_2}{\rho_2} \ln(p_2) + \frac{V_2^2}{2g}$$

$$\text{or, } \frac{p_1}{\rho_1 g} \ln(p_1) - \frac{p_2}{\rho_2 g} \ln(p_2) = \frac{V_2^2}{2g} - \frac{V_1^2}{2g}$$

But, $\frac{p_1}{\rho_1} = \frac{p_2}{\rho_2}$ (for an *isothermal process*),

$$\therefore \quad \frac{p_1}{\rho_1 g}\ln(p_1) - \frac{p_1}{\rho_1 g}\ln(p_2) = \frac{V_2^2}{2g} - \frac{V_1^2}{2g}$$

or,
$$\frac{p_1}{\rho_1 g}\ln\left(\frac{p_1}{p_2}\right) = \frac{(5V_1)^2}{2g} - \frac{V_1^2}{2g} = \frac{24V_1^2}{2g} = \frac{12V_1^2}{g} \qquad (\because V_2 = 5V_1)$$

or,
$$\frac{p_1}{\rho_1 g}\ln\left(\frac{5\times10^5}{4\times10^5}\right) = \frac{12V_1^2}{g} \quad \text{or} \quad 0.223\,\frac{p_1}{\rho_1 g} = \frac{12V_1^2}{g}$$

or,
$$\frac{p_1}{\rho_1} = \frac{12V_1^2}{0.223} = 53.8V_1^2 \qquad ...(iii)$$

From equation of state, we have:

$$p_1 = \rho_1 RT_1 \quad \text{...Section 1} \quad \text{or} \quad \frac{p_1}{\rho_1} = RT_1 = 287 \times 279 = 80073$$

Substituting the valve of $\frac{p_1}{\rho_1}$ in eqn. (*iii*), we get:

$$53.8\,V_1^2 = 80073 \quad \text{or} \quad V_1^2 = \frac{80073}{53.8} = 1488.34$$

or, $\mathbf{V_1 = 38.58\ m/s}$ **(Ans.)**

From eqn. (*ii*) we have: $V_2 = 5\,V_1 = 5 \times 38.58 =$ **192.9 m/s** **(Ans.)**

Example 15.3. *A 120 mm diameter pipe reduces to 60 mm diameter through a sudden contraction. When it carries air at 25°C under isothermal condition, the absolute pressures observed in the two pipes just before and after the contraction are 480 kN/m² and 384 kN/m² respectively. Determine:*

(*i*) *Densities at the two sections,*

(*ii*) *Velocities at the two sections, and*

(*iii*) *Mass rate of flow through the pipe.*

Take R = 287 J/kg K

Solution. Section 1: Diameter of the pipe,

$$D_1 = 120 \text{ mm} = 0.12 \text{ m}$$

$$\therefore \quad \text{Area, } A_1 = \frac{\pi}{4} \times 0.12^2 = 0.01131 \text{ m}^2$$

Pressure, $p_1 = 480 \text{ kN/m}^2$

Temperature, $T_1 = 25 + 273 = 298$ K

Section 2: Diameter of the pipe,

$$D_2 = 60 \text{ mm} = 0.06 \text{ m}$$

$$\therefore \quad \text{Area, } A_2 = \frac{\pi}{4} \times 0.06^2 = 2.827 \times 10^{-3} \text{ m}^2$$

Pressure, $p_2 = 384 \text{ kN/m}^2$

Temperature, $T_2 = T_1 = 298\ K$ (since the condition is *isothermal*)

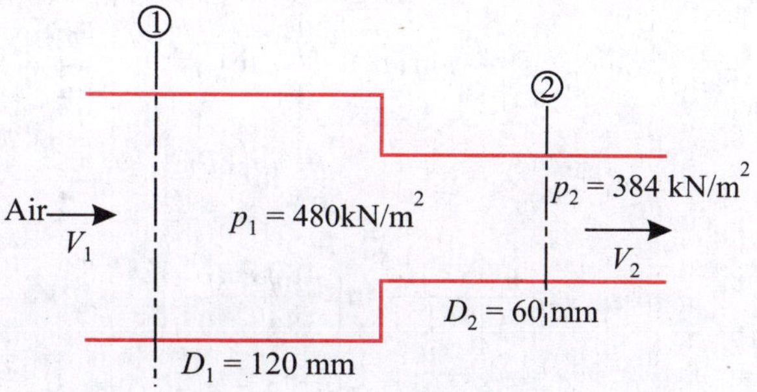

Fig. 15.2

(i) Densities, ρ_1 and ρ_2 :

For isothermal condition, $\frac{p_1}{\rho_1} = \frac{p_2}{\rho_2}$ [Eqn. (15.15)]

or, $$\frac{p_1}{p_2} = \frac{\rho_1}{\rho_2} \quad \text{or} \quad \frac{480}{384} = \frac{\rho_1}{\rho_2} = 1.25$$

Also $$p_1 = \rho_1 RT_1 \quad \text{or} \quad \rho_1 = \frac{p_1}{RT_1}$$

or, $$\rho_1 = \frac{480 \times 10^3}{287 \times 298} = \mathbf{5.61\ kg/m^3}$$ **(Ans.)**

$\therefore$ $$\rho_2 = \frac{\rho_1}{1.25} = \frac{5.61}{1.25} = \mathbf{4.488\ kg/m^3}$$ **(Ans.)**

(ii) Velocities, V_1 and V_2 :

According to continuity equation:

$$\rho_1 A_1 V_1 = \rho_2 A_2 V_2$$

or, $$\frac{V_2}{V_1} = \frac{\rho_1 A_1}{\rho_2 A_2} = 1.25 \times \frac{0.01131}{2.827 \times 10^{-3}} = 5.0$$

Applying Bernoulli's equation at sections 1 and 2 for isothermal condition, we get:

$$\frac{p_1}{\rho_1 g} \ln(p_1) + \frac{V_1^2}{2g} + z_1 = \frac{p_2}{\rho_2 g} \ln(p_2) + \frac{V_2^2}{2g} + z_2$$

Assuming $z_1 = z_2$, we have:

$$\frac{p_1}{\rho_1 g} \ln(p_1) + \frac{V_1^2}{2g} = \frac{p_2}{\rho_2 g} \ln(p_2) + \frac{V_2^2}{2g}$$

or, $$\frac{p_1}{\rho_1 g} \ln(p_1) - \frac{p_2}{\rho_2 g} \ln(p_2) = \frac{V_2^2}{2g} - \frac{V_1^2}{2g}$$

Cancelling 'g' on both the sides, we get:

$$\frac{p_1}{\rho_1} \ln(p_1) - \frac{p_2}{\rho_2} \ln(p_2) = \frac{V_2^2}{2g} - \frac{V_1^2}{2g}$$

or, $$\frac{p_1}{\rho_1} \ln(p_1) - \frac{p_1}{\rho_1} \ln(p_2) = \frac{V_2^2}{2} - \frac{V_1^2}{2} \qquad \left(\because \frac{p_1}{\rho_1} = \frac{p_2}{\rho_2}\right)$$

or, $$\frac{p_1}{\rho_1} \ln\left(\frac{p_1}{p_2}\right) = \frac{V_2^2}{2} - \frac{V_1^2}{2} = \frac{(5V_1)^2}{2} - \frac{V_1^2}{2} = 12V_1^2 \qquad (\because V_2 = 5V_1)$$

or, $$\frac{480 \times 10^3}{5{\cdot}61} \ln\left(\frac{480 \times 10^3}{384 \times 10^3}\right) = 12V_1^2$$

or, $85561.5 \times 0.223 = 12V_1^2$ or $V_1^2 = 1590$ or $V_1 = \mathbf{39.87\ m/s}$ **(Ans.)**

$\therefore$ $V_2 = 5V_1 = 5 \times 39.87 = \mathbf{199.35\ m/s}$ **(Ans.)**

(iii) Mass rate of flow through the pipe, m :

$m = \rho_1 A_1 V_1\ (= \rho_2 A_2 V_2)$ or $m = 5.61 \times 0.01131 \times 39.87 = \mathbf{2.53\ kg/s}$ **(Ans.)**

Example 15.4. *A gas with a velocity of 300 m/s is flowing through a horizontal pipe at a section where pressure is 78 kN/m² absolute and temperature 40° C. The pipe changes in diameter and at this section, the pressure is 117 kN/m² absolute. Find the velocity of the gas at this section if the flow of the gas is adiabatic. Take R = 287 J/kg K and γ = 1.4.* **[Delhi University]**

Solution.

Section 1: Velocity of the gas, $V = 300$ m/s

Pressure, $p_1 = 78$ kN/m²

Temperature, $T_1 = 40 + 273 = 313$ K

Section 2: Pressure, $p_2 = 117$ kN/m²

$R = 287$ J/kg K, $\gamma = 1.4$

Velocity of gas at section 2, V_2 :

Applying Bernoulli's equations at sections 1 and 2 for *adiabatic process,* we have:

$$\left(\frac{\gamma}{\gamma-1}\right)\frac{p_1}{\rho_1 g}+\frac{V_1^2}{2g}+z_1 = \left(\frac{\gamma}{\gamma-1}\right)\frac{p_2}{\rho_2 g}+\frac{V_2^2}{2g}+z_2 \qquad \text{[Eqn. (15.26)]}$$

But, $z_1 = z_2$, since the pipe is horizontal.

$$\therefore \quad \left(\frac{\gamma}{\gamma-1}\right)\frac{p_1}{\rho_1 g}+\frac{V_1^2}{2g} = \left(\frac{\gamma}{\gamma-1}\right)\frac{p_2}{\rho_2 g}+\frac{V_2^2}{2g}$$

Cancelling '*g*' on both sides, we get:

$$\left(\frac{\gamma}{\gamma-1}\right)\left(\frac{p_1}{\rho_1}-\frac{p_2}{\rho_2}\right) = \frac{V_2^2}{2}-\frac{V_1^2}{2}$$

$$\text{or,} \quad \left(\frac{\gamma}{\gamma-1}\right)\frac{p_1}{\rho_1}\left(1-\frac{p_2}{\rho_2}\times\frac{\rho_1}{p_1}\right) = \frac{V_2^2}{2}-\frac{V_1^2}{2}$$

$$\therefore \quad \left(\frac{\gamma}{\gamma-1}\right)\frac{p_1}{\rho_1}\left(1-\frac{p_2}{p_1}\times\frac{\rho_1}{\rho_2}\right) = \frac{V_2^2}{2}-\frac{V_1^2}{2} \qquad \text{...}(i)$$

For an adiabatic flow : $\dfrac{p_1}{\rho_1^\gamma} = \dfrac{p_2}{\rho_2^\gamma}$ or $\dfrac{p_1}{p_2} = \left(\dfrac{\rho_1}{\rho_2}\right)^\gamma$ or $\dfrac{\rho_1}{\rho_2} = \left(\dfrac{p_1}{p_2}\right)^{\frac{1}{\gamma}}$

Substituting the value of $\dfrac{\rho_1}{\rho_2}$ in eqn. (*i*), we get:

$$\left(\frac{\gamma}{\gamma-1}\right)\frac{p_1}{\rho_1}\left\{1-\frac{p_2}{p_1}\times\left(\frac{p_1}{p_2}\right)^{\frac{1}{\gamma}}\right\} = \frac{V_2^2}{2}-\frac{V_1^2}{2}$$

$$\left(\frac{\gamma}{\gamma-1}\right)\frac{p_1}{\rho_1}\left\{1-\left(\frac{p_2}{p_1}\right)^{1-\frac{1}{\gamma}}\right\} = \frac{V_2^2}{2}-\frac{V_1^2}{2}$$

$$\text{or,} \quad \left(\frac{\gamma}{\gamma-1}\right)\frac{p_1}{\rho_1}\left\{1-\left(\frac{p_2}{p_1}\right)^{\frac{\gamma-1}{\gamma}}\right\} = \frac{V_2^2-V_1^2}{2} \qquad \text{...}(ii)$$

At section 1 : $\dfrac{p_1}{\rho_1} = RT_1 = 287 \times 313 = 89831,$

$$\frac{p_2}{p_1} = \frac{117}{78} = 1.5, \quad \text{and} \quad V_1 = 300 \text{ m/s}$$

Substituting the values in eqn. (*ii*), we get:

$$\left(\frac{1.4}{1.4-1}\right) \times 89831 \left\{1-(1.5)^{\frac{1.4-1}{1.4}}\right\} = \frac{V_2^2}{2} - \frac{300^2}{2}$$

$$314408.5\,(1 - 1.1228) = \frac{V_2^2}{2} - 45000$$

or,
$$-38609.4 = \frac{V_2^2}{2} - 45000$$

or,
$$V_2^2 = 12781.2 \quad \text{or} \quad V_2 = 113.05 \text{ m/s} \quad \textbf{(Ans.)}$$

Example 15.5. *In the case of air flow in a conduit transition, the pressure, velocity and temperature at the upstream section are 35 kN/m², 30 m/s and 150°C respectively. If at the downstream section the velocity is 150 m/s, determine the pressure and the temperature if the process followed is isentropiic. Take $\gamma = 1.4$, $R = 290$ J/kg K.*

Solution.

Section 1 (upstream) : Pressure, $p_1 = 35$ kN/m²,

Velocity, $V_1 = 30$ m/s

Temperature, $T_1 = 150 + 273 = 423$ K

Velocity, $V_2 = 150$ m/s

$R = 290$ J/kg K, $\gamma = 1.4$

Section 2 (downstream) :

Pressure, p_2 :

Applying Bernoulli's equation at sections 1 and 2 for *isentropic* (*reversible adiabatic*) *process*, we have:

$$\left(\frac{\gamma}{\gamma-1}\right)\frac{p_1}{\rho_1 g} + \frac{V_1^2}{2g} + z_1 = \left(\frac{\gamma}{\gamma-1}\right)\frac{p_2}{\rho_2 g} + \frac{V_2^2}{2g} + z_2$$

Assuming $z_1 = z_2$, we have:

$$\left(\frac{\gamma}{\gamma-1}\right)\frac{p_1}{\rho_1 g} + \frac{V_1^2}{2g} = \left(\frac{\gamma}{\gamma-1}\right)\frac{p_2}{\rho_2 g} + \frac{V_2^2}{2g}$$

Cancelling '*g*' on both the sides, and rearranging we get:

$$\left(\frac{\gamma}{\gamma-1}\right)\frac{p_1}{\rho_1}\left(1 - \frac{p_2}{p_1} \times \frac{\rho_1}{\rho_2}\right) = \frac{V_2^2}{2} - \frac{V_1^2}{2} \quad ...(i)$$

For an isentropic flow: $\frac{p_1}{\rho_1^\gamma} = \frac{p_2}{\rho_2^\gamma}$ or $\frac{p_1}{p_2} = \left(\frac{\rho_1}{\rho_2}\right)^\gamma$ or $\frac{\rho_1}{\rho_2} = \left(\frac{p_1}{p_2}\right)^{\frac{1}{\gamma}}$

Substituting the value of $\frac{\rho_1}{\rho_2}$ in eqn. (*i*), we have:

$$\left(\frac{\gamma}{\gamma-1}\right)\frac{p_1}{\rho_1}\left\{1 - \frac{p_2}{p_1} \times \left(\frac{p_1}{p_2}\right)^{\frac{1}{\gamma}}\right\} = \frac{V_2^2}{2} - \frac{V_1^2}{2}$$

$$\left(\frac{\gamma}{\gamma-1}\right)\frac{p_1}{\rho_1}\left\{1 - \left(\frac{p_2}{p_1}\right)^{1-\frac{1}{\gamma}}\right\} = \frac{V_2^2}{2} - \frac{V_1^2}{2}$$

$$\left(\frac{\gamma}{\gamma-1}\right)\frac{p_1}{\rho_1}\left\{1 - \left(\frac{p_2}{p_1}\right)^{\frac{\gamma-1}{\gamma}}\right\} = \frac{V_2^2}{2} - \frac{V_1^2}{2}$$

Substituting the values, we get:

$$\frac{1.4}{1.4-1} \times 122670 \left\{1 - \left(\frac{p_2}{p_1}\right)^{\frac{1.4-1}{1.4}}\right\} = \frac{150^2}{2} - \frac{30^2}{2} = 10800$$

$$\left(\because \frac{p_1}{\rho_1} = RT_1 = 290 \times 423 = 122670\right)$$

$$429345 \left\{1 - \left(\frac{p_2}{p_1}\right)^{0.2857}\right\} = 10800$$

or, $$\left(\frac{p_2}{p_1}\right)^{0.2857} = 1 - \frac{10800}{429345} = 0.9748$$

or, $$\frac{p_2}{p_1} = (0.9748)^{1/02857} = (0.9748)^{3.5} = 0.9145$$

or, $$p_2 = 35 \times 0.9145 = \mathbf{32\ kN/m^2}\ \textbf{(Ans.)}$$

Temperature, T_2:

For an *isentropic process*, we have:

$$\frac{T_2}{T_1} = \left(\frac{p_2}{p_1}\right)^{\frac{\gamma-1}{\gamma}} = (0.9145)^{\frac{1.4-1}{1.4}} = (0.9145)^{0.2857} = 0.9748$$

$$\therefore \quad T_2 = 423 \times 0.9748 = 412.3\ \text{K or } t_2 = 412.3 - 273 = \mathbf{139.3°\ C}\ \textbf{(Ans.)}$$

15.5. PROPAGATION OF DISTURBANCES IN FLUID AND VELOCITY OF SOUND

The solids as well as fluids consist of molecules. Whereas the molecules in solids are close together , these are relatively apart in fluids. Consequently whenever there is a minor disturbance, it travels instantaneously in case of solids; but in case of fluid the molecules change in position before the transmission or propagation of the disturbance depends upon its *elastic properties. The velocity of disturbance depends upon the changes of pressure and density of the fluid.*

The propagation of disturbance is similar to the propagation of sound through a media. The *speed of propagation of sound in a media* is known as **acoustic or sonic velocity** and depends upon the difference of pressure. Incompressible flow, velocity of sound (sonic velocity) is of paramount importance.

15.5.1. Derivation of Sonic Velocity (velocity of sound)

Consider a one-dimentional flow through long straight rigid pipe of uniform cross-sectional area fitted with a frictionless piston at one end as shown in Fig. 15.3. The tube is filled with a compressible fluid initially at rest. If the piston is moved suddenly to the right with velocity, a *pressure wave* would be propagated through the fluid with a velocity of sound wave.

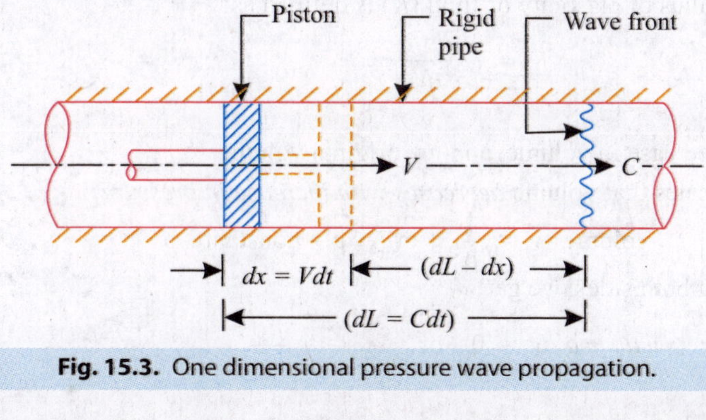

Fig. 15.3. One dimensional pressure wave propagation.

Let, A = Cross-sectional area of the pipe,
V = Piston velocity,
p = Fluid pressure in the pipe before the piston movement,
ρ = Fluid density before the piston movement,
dt = A small interval of time during which piston moves, and
C = Velocity of pressure wave or sound wave (travelling in the fluid).

Before the movement of the poston the length dL has an initial density ρ, and its total mass

$$= \rho \times dL \times A$$

When the piston moves through a distance dx, the fluid density within the compressed region of length $(dL - dx)$ will be increased and becomes $(\rho + d\rho)$ and subsequently the total mass of fluid in the compressed region $= (\rho + d\rho)(dL - dx) \times A$

$$\therefore \quad \rho \times dL \times A = (\rho + d\rho)(dL - dx) \times A \quad \text{...by } \textit{principle of continuity.}$$

But, $dL = C\,dt$ and $dx = Vdt$; therefore, the above equation becomes:

$$\rho C dt = (\rho + d\rho)(C - V)\,dt$$

or, $$\rho C = (\rho + d\rho)(C - V) \quad \text{or} \quad \rho C = \rho C - \rho V + d\rho.C - d\rho.V$$

or, $$0 = -\rho V + d\rho.C - d\rho.V$$

Neglecting the term $d\rho.V$ (V being much smaller than C), we get:

$$d\rho.C = \rho V \quad \text{or} \quad C = \frac{\rho V}{d\rho} \quad \text{...(15.27)}$$

Further in the region of compressed fluid, the fluid particles have attained a velocity which is apparently equal to V (velocity of the piston), accompanied by an increase in pressure dp due to sudden motion of the piston. Applying inpulse-momentum equation for the fluid in the compressed region during dt, we get:

$$dp \times A \times dt = \rho \times dL \times A\,(V - 0)$$

(Force on the fluid) (Rate of change of momentum)

or, $$dp = \rho \frac{dL}{dt} V = \rho \times \frac{Cdt}{dt} \times V = \rho CV \quad (\because dL = Cdt)$$

or, $$C = \frac{dp}{\rho V} \quad \text{...(15.28)}$$

Multiplying eqns. (15.2) and (15.3), we get:

$$C^2 = \frac{\rho V}{dl} \times \frac{dp}{\rho V} = \frac{dp}{d\rho}$$

$$\therefore \quad C = \sqrt{\frac{dp}{d\rho}} \quad \text{...(15.29)}$$

15.5.2. Sonic Velocity in terms of Bulk Modulus

The bulk modulus of elasticity of fluid (K) is defined as:

$$K = \frac{dp}{\left(-\frac{dv}{v}\right)} \quad \text{...}(i)$$

where, dv = decrease in volume, and v = original volume.

(–*ve* sign indicates that volume *decreases with increase in pressure*)

Also, volume $v \propto \frac{1}{\rho}$, or $v\rho$ = constant

Differentiating both sides, we get

$$v\,d\rho + \rho\,dv = 0 \quad \text{or} \quad -\frac{dv}{v} = \frac{d\rho}{\rho}$$

Substituting the value of $-\dfrac{dv}{v}\left(=\dfrac{dp}{K}\right)$ from eqn. (*i*), we get:

$$\frac{dp}{K} = \frac{d\rho}{\rho} \quad \text{or} \quad \frac{dp}{d\rho} = \frac{K}{\rho}$$

Substituting this value of $\dfrac{dp}{d\rho}$ in eqn. (15.29), we get

$$C = \sqrt{\frac{K}{\rho}} \qquad ...(15.30)$$

Eqn. (15.30) *is applicable for liquids and gases.*

15.5.3. Sonic Velocity for Isothermal Process

For is tothermal process : $\dfrac{p}{\rho}$ = constant

Differentiating both sides, we get:

$$\frac{\rho\,.\,dp - p\,.\,d\rho}{\rho^2} = 0 \quad \text{or} \quad \frac{dp}{\rho} - \frac{p.d\rho}{\rho^2} = 0$$

or,

$$\frac{dp}{\rho} = \frac{p\,.\,d\rho}{\rho^2} \quad \text{or} \quad \frac{dp}{d\rho} = \frac{p}{\rho} = RT \qquad ...(15.31)$$

$$\left(\frac{p}{\rho} = RT \quad \text{...equation of state}\right)$$

Substituting the value of $\dfrac{dp}{d\rho}$ in eqn. (15.29), we get:

$$C = \sqrt{\frac{p}{\rho}} = \sqrt{RT} \qquad ...(15.32)$$

15.5.4 Sonic Velocity for Adiabatic Process

For isentropic (reversible adiabatic) process: $\dfrac{p}{\rho^\gamma}$ = constant

or, $\quad p\,.\,\rho^{-\gamma}$ = Constant

Differentiating both sides, we have $p\,(-\gamma)\,.\,\rho^{-\gamma-1}\,d\rho + \rho^{-\gamma}\,dp = 0$

Dividing both sides by $\rho^{-\gamma}$, we get: $\quad -p\,\gamma\,\rho^{-1}\,d\rho + dp = 0 \quad$ or $\quad dp = p\,\gamma\,\rho^{-1}\,d\rho$

or,

$$\frac{dp}{d\rho} = \frac{p}{\rho}\gamma = \gamma RT \qquad \left(\because \frac{p}{\rho} = RT\right)$$

Substituting the value of $\dfrac{dp}{d\rho}$ in eqn. (15.29), we get:

$$C = \sqrt{\gamma RT} \qquad ...(15.33)$$

The following points are worth noting :

(*i*) The process is assumed to be *adiabatic* when minor disturbaces are to be propagated through air; due to *very high velocity* of disturbances/pressure waves appreciable heat transfer does not take place.

(*ii*) For calculation of velocity of the sound/pressure waves, **isothermal process** *is considered only when it is mentioned in the numerical problem* (that the process is isothermal). *When no process is mentioned in the problem, calculations are made assuming the process to be* **adiabatic.**

15.6. MACH NUMBER

The **Mach number** *is an important parameter in dealing with the flow of compressible fluids, when elastic forces become important and predominant.*

Mach number *is defined as the square root of the ratio of the inertia force of a fluid to the elastic force.*

$$\therefore \text{ Mach number, } M = \sqrt{\frac{\text{Inertia force}}{\text{Elastic force}}} = \sqrt{\frac{\rho A V^2}{KA}} = \sqrt{\frac{V^2}{K/\rho}} = \frac{V}{\sqrt{K/\rho}} = \frac{V}{C} \quad \left[\because \sqrt{K/\rho} = C \;\; \text{...eqn. (15.30)}\right]$$

i.e.

$$M = \frac{V}{C} \qquad \text{...(15.34)}$$

Thus,

$$M = \frac{\text{Velocity at a point in a fluid}}{\text{Velocity of sound at that point at a given instant of time}}$$

Depending on the value of Mach number, the flow can be *classified* as follows :

1. *Subsonic flow* : Mach number is *less* than 1.0 (or $M < 1$); in this case $V < C$.
2. *Sonic flow* : Mach number is equal to 1.0 (or $M = 1$); in this case $V = C$.
3. *Supersonic flow* : Mach number is *greater* than 1.0 (or $M > 1$); in this case $V > C$.

When the Mach number in flow region is slightly less to sightly greater than 1.0, the flow is termed as **transonic flow.**

The following points are worth noting :

(*i*) Mach number is important in those problems in which the *flow velocity is comparable with the sonic velocity* (velocity of sound). It may happen in case of airplanes travelling at very high speed, projectiles, bullets etc.

(*ii*) If for any flow system the *Mach number is less than about 0.4 the effects of compressibility may be neglected (for that flow system).*

Example 15.6. *Find the sonic velocity for the following fluids :*

(i) Crude oil of specific gravity 0.8 and bulk modulus 1.5 GN/m².

(ii) Mercury having a bulk modulus of 27 GN/m². **(Delhi University)**

Solution. *Crude oil:* Specific gravity = 0.8

$\therefore$ Density of oil, $\rho = 0.8 \times 1000 = 800 \text{ kg/m}^3$

Bulk modulus, $K = 1.5 \text{ GN/m}^2$

Mercury : Bulk modulus, $K = 27 \text{ GN/m}^2$

Density of mercury, $\rho = 13.6 \times 1000 = 13600 \text{ kg/m}^3$

Sonic velocity, C_{oil}, C_{Hg} :

Sonic velocity is given by the relation :

$$C = \sqrt{\frac{K}{\rho}} \qquad \text{...[Eqn. (15.30)]}$$

$$\therefore \quad C_{oil} = \sqrt{\frac{1.5 \times 10^9}{800}} = \mathbf{1369.3 \text{ m/s}} \quad \textbf{(Ans.)}$$

$$C_{Hg} = \sqrt{\frac{27 \times 10^9}{13600}} = \mathbf{1409 \text{ m/s}} \quad \textbf{(Ans.)}$$

Example 15.7. *An aeroplane is flying at a height of 14 km where temperature is – 45°C. The speed of the plane is corresponding to M = 2. Find the speed of the plane if R = 287 J/kg K and γ = 1.4.*

Solution. Temperature (at a height of 14 km), $t = -45°C$.

$$T = -45 + 273 = 228\ K$$

Mach number, $M = 2$

Gas constant, $R = 287$ J/kg K

$\gamma = 1.4$

Speed of the plane, V :

Sonic velocity, (C) is given by:

$$C = \sqrt{\gamma RT} \quad \text{(assuming the process to be } adiabatic\text{)} \qquad \text{...[Eqn. (15.33)]}$$

$$= \sqrt{1.4 \times 287 \times 228} = 302.67 \text{ m/s}$$

Also,
$$M = \frac{V}{C} \qquad \text{...[Eqn. (15.34)]}$$

or,
$$2 = \frac{V}{302.67}$$

or,
$$V = 2 \times 302.67 = 605.34 \text{ m/s} = \frac{605.34 \times 3600}{1000} = \mathbf{2179.2\ km/h} \text{ (Ans.)}$$

15.7. PROPAGATION OF DISTURBANCE IN COMPRESSIBLE FLUID

When some disturbance is created in a compressible fluid (elastic or pressure waves are also generated), it is propagated in all directions with sonic velocity (= C) and its nature of propagation depends upon the Mach number (M). Such disturbance may be created when an object moves in a relatively stationary compressible fluid or when a compressible fluid flows past a stationary object.

Consider a tiny projectile moving in a straight line with velocity V through a compressible fluid which is stationary. Let the projectile is at A when time $t = 0$, then in time t it will move through a distance $AB = Vt$. During this time the disturbance which originated from the projectile when it was at A will grow into the surface of sphere of radius Ct as shown in Fig. 15.4, which also shows the growth of the other disturbances which will originate from the projectile at every $t/4$ interval of time as the projectile moves from A to B.

Let us find nature of propagation of the disturbance for different Mach numbers.

Case I : When $M < 1$ (*i.e.* $V < C$). In this case since $V < C$ the projectile lags behind the disturbance/pressure wave and hence as shown in Fig. 15.4 (a) the projectile at point B lies inside the sphere of radius Ct and also inside other spheres formed by the disturbances/waves started at intermediate points.

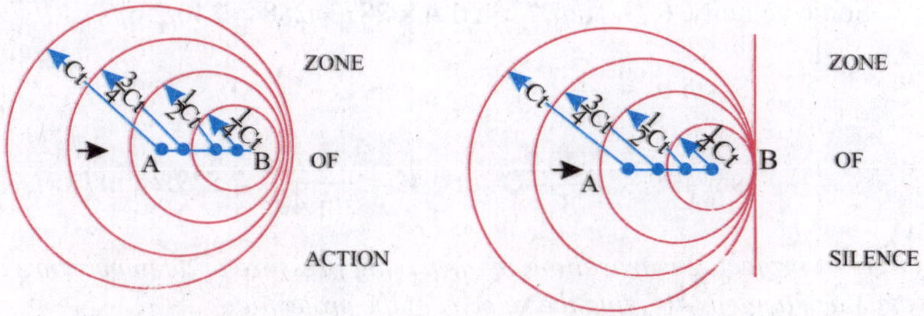

(a) M < 1 (V < C)
Subsonic

(b) M = 1 (V = C)
Sonic motion

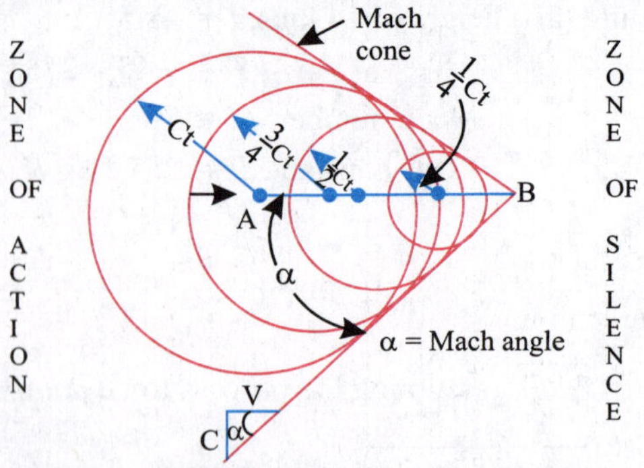

Fig. 15.4. Nature of propagation of disturbances in compressible flow.

Case II: When $M = 1$ (*i.e.* $V = C$). In this case, the disturbance always travels with the projectile as shown in Fig. 15.4 (*b*). The circle drawn with centre *A* will pass through *B*.

Case III: When $M > 1$ (*i.e.* $V > C$). In this case the projectile travels faster than the disturbance. Thus the distance *AB* (which the projectile has travelled) is more than *Ct*, and hence the projectile at point '*B*' is outside the spheres formed due to formation and growth of disturbance at $t = 0$ and at the intermediate points (Fig. 15.3 (*c*)). If the tangents are drawn (from the point *B*) to the circles, the spherical pressure waves form a cone with its vertex at *B*. It is known as ***Mach cone***. The semi-vertex angle α of the cone is known as ***Mach angle*** which is given by:

$$\sin \alpha = \frac{Ct}{Vt} = \frac{C}{V} = \frac{1}{M} \qquad ...(15.35)$$

In such a case (M > 1), the effect of the disturbance is felt only in region inside the Mach cone, this region is called *zone of action*. The region outside the Mach cone is called *zone of silence*.

It has been observed that when an *aeroplane is moving with supersonic speed, its noise is heard only after the plane has already passed over us*.

Example 15.8. *Find the velocity of a bullet fired in standard air if its Mach angle is 40°.*

Solution. Mach angle, $\alpha = 40°$

$\gamma = 1.4$

For standard air: $R = 287$ J/kg K, $t = 15°$C or $T = 15 + 273 = 288$ K

Velocity of the bullet, *V*:

Sonic velocity, $C = \sqrt{\gamma RT} = \sqrt{1.4 \times 287 \times 288} = 340.2$ m/s

Now, $\sin \alpha = \dfrac{C}{V}$

or, $\sin 40° = \dfrac{340.2}{V}$ or $V = \dfrac{340.2}{\sin 40°} = $ **529.26 m/s (Ans.)**

Example 15.9. *A projectile is travelling in air having pressure and temperature as 88.3 kN/m^2 and – 2°C. If the Mach angle is 40°, find the velocity of the projectile.*

Take $\gamma = 1.4$ and $R = 287$ J/kg K. **[M.U.]**

Solution. Pressure, $p = 88.3 \text{ kN/m}^2$

Temperature, $T = -2 + 273 = 271 \text{ K}$

Mach angle, $M = 40°$

$\gamma = 1.4, R = 287 \text{ J/kg K}$

Velocity of the projectile, *V*:

Sonic velocity, $C = \sqrt{\gamma RT} = \sqrt{1{\cdot}4 \times 287 \times 271} \simeq 330 \text{ m/s}$

Now, $$\sin \alpha = \frac{C}{V} \quad \text{or} \quad \sin 40° = \frac{330}{V}$$

or, $$V = \frac{330}{\sin 40°} = \mathbf{513.4 \text{ m/s}} \textbf{ (Ans.)}$$

Example 15.10. *A supersonic aircraft flies at an altitude of 1.8 km where temperature is 4°C. Determine the speed of the aircraft if its sound is heard 4 seconds after its passage over the head of an observer. Take $R = 287$ J/kg K and $\gamma = 1.4$.*

Solution. Altitude of the aircraft = 1.8 km = 1800 m

Temperature, $T = 4 + 273 = 277 \text{ K}$

Time, $t = 4s$

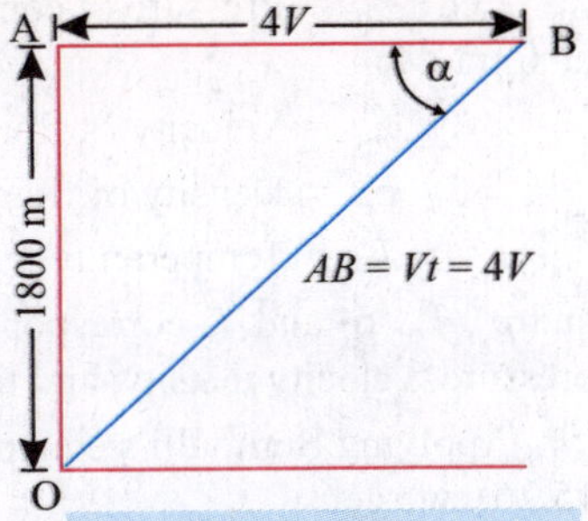

Fig. 15.5

Speed of the aircraft, *V*:

Refer to Fig. 15.5. Let *O* represent the observer and *A* the position of the aircraft just vertically over the observer. After 4 seconds, the aircraft reaches the position represented by the point *B*. Line *AB* represents the wave front and α the Mach angle.

From Fig. 15.5, we have :

$$\tan \alpha = \frac{1800}{4V} = \frac{450}{V} \quad ...(i)$$

But, Mach number $$M = \frac{V}{C} = \frac{1}{\sin \alpha}$$

or, $$V = \frac{C}{\sin \alpha} \quad ...(ii)$$

Substituting the value of *V* in eqn. (*i*), we get:

$$\tan \alpha = \frac{450}{(C/\sin \alpha)} = \frac{450 \sin \alpha}{C}$$

or, $$\frac{\sin \alpha}{\cos \alpha} = \frac{450 \sin \alpha}{C} \quad \text{or} \quad \cos \alpha = \frac{C}{450} \quad ...(iii)$$

But, $C = \sqrt{\gamma RT}$, where *C* is the sonic velocity

$R = 287 \text{ J/kg K and } \gamma = 1.4$ ...(Given)

$\therefore \quad C = \sqrt{1.4 \times 287 \times 277} = 333.6 \text{ m/s}$

Substituting the value of *C* in eqn. (*ii*), we get:

$$\cos \alpha = \frac{333.6}{450} = 0.7413$$

$$\therefore \quad \sin \alpha = \sqrt{1 - \cos^2 \alpha} = \sqrt{1 - 0.7413^2} = 0.6712$$

Substituting the value of sin α in eqn. (*ii*), we get:

$$V = \frac{C}{\sin\alpha} = \frac{333.6}{0.6712} = 497\text{ m/s} = \frac{497 \times 3600}{1000} = \mathbf{1789.2\,km/h}\ \textbf{(Ans.)}$$

15.8. STAGNATION PROPERTIES

The point on the immersed body where the velocity is zero is called **stagnation point**. At this point velocity head is converted into pressure head. The values of pressure (p_s), temperature (T_s) and density (ρ_s) at stagnation point are called ***stagnation properties.***

15.8.1 Expression for Stagnation Pressure (p_s) in Compressible Flow

Consider the flow of compressible fluid past an immersed body where the velocity becomes zero. Consider *frictionless adiabatic* (*isentropic*) condition. Let us consider two points, O in the free stream and the stagnation point S as shown in the Fig. 15.6.

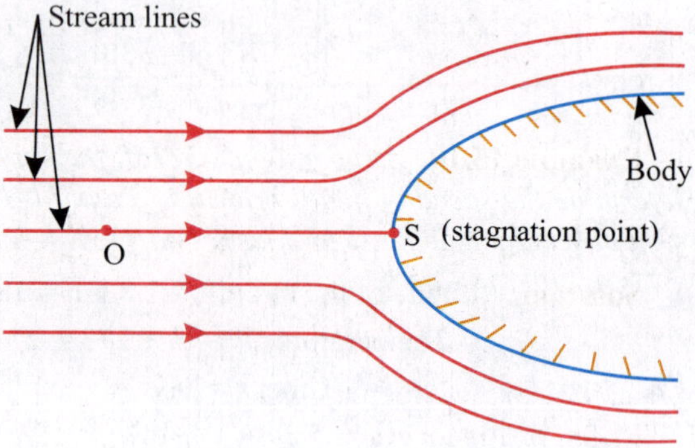

Fig. 15.6 Stagnation properties.

Let, p_0 = Pressure of compressible fluid at point O,

V_0 = Velocity of fluid at O,

ρ_0 = Density of fluid at O,

T_0 = Temperature of fluid at O,

and p_s, V_s, ρ_s and T_s corresponding values of pressure, velocity density, and temperature at point S.

Applying Bernoulli's equation for adiabatic (frictionless) flow at points O and S, (given by eqn. 15.26), we get:

$$\left(\frac{\gamma}{\gamma-1}\right)\frac{p_0}{\rho_0 g} + \frac{V_0^2}{2g} + z_0 = \left(\frac{\gamma}{\gamma-1}\right)\frac{p_s}{\rho_s g} + \frac{V_s^2}{2g} + z_s$$

But $z_0 = z_s$; the above equation reduces to:

$$\left(\frac{\gamma}{\gamma-1}\right)\frac{p_0}{\rho_0 g} + \frac{V_0^2}{2g} = \left(\frac{\gamma}{\gamma-1}\right)\frac{p_s}{\rho_s g} + \frac{V_s^2}{2g}$$

Cancelling 'g' on both the sides, we have:

$$\left(\frac{\gamma}{\gamma-1}\right)\frac{p_0}{\rho_0} + \frac{V_0^2}{2} = \left(\frac{\gamma}{\gamma-1}\right)\frac{p_s}{\rho_s} + \frac{V_s^2}{2}$$

At point S the velocity is zero, i.e. $V_s = 0$; the above equation becomes:

$$\left(\frac{\gamma}{\gamma-1}\right)\left(\frac{p_0}{\rho_0} - \frac{p_s}{\rho_s}\right) = -\frac{V_0^2}{2}$$

or, $$\left(\frac{\gamma}{\gamma-1}\right)\frac{p_0}{\rho_0}\left(1 - \frac{p_s}{\rho_s} \times \frac{\rho_0}{p_0}\right) = -\frac{V_0^2}{2}$$

or, $$\left(\frac{\gamma}{\gamma-1}\right)\frac{p_0}{\rho_0}\left(1 - \frac{p_s}{p_0} \times \frac{\rho_0}{\rho_s}\right) = -\frac{V_0^2}{2} \quad \ldots(i)$$

For adiabatic process:

$$\frac{p_0}{\rho_0^\gamma} = \frac{p_s}{\rho_s^\gamma} \quad \text{or} \quad \frac{p_0}{p_s} = \frac{\rho_0^\gamma}{\rho_s^\gamma}$$

or, $$\frac{\rho_0}{\rho_s} = \left(\frac{p_0}{p_s}\right)^{\frac{1}{\gamma}} \quad ...(ii)$$

Substituting the value of $\frac{\rho_0}{\rho_s}$ in eqn. (*i*), we get:

$$\left(\frac{\gamma}{\gamma-1}\right)\frac{p_0}{\rho_0}\left[1-\frac{p_s}{p_0}\times\left(\frac{p_0}{p_s}\right)^{\frac{1}{\gamma}}\right] = -\frac{V_0^2}{2}$$

or, $$\left(\frac{\gamma}{\gamma-1}\right)\frac{p_0}{\rho_0}\left[1-\left(\frac{p_s}{p_0}\right)^{1-\frac{1}{\gamma}}\right] = -\frac{V_0^2}{2}$$

or, $$\left[1-\left(\frac{p_s}{p_0}\right)^{\frac{\gamma-1}{\gamma}}\right] = -\frac{V_0^2}{2}\left(\frac{\gamma-1}{\gamma}\right)\frac{\rho_0}{p_0}$$

or, $$1+\frac{V_0^2}{2}\left(\frac{\gamma-1}{\gamma}\right)\frac{\rho_0}{p_0} = \left(\frac{p_s}{p_0}\right)^{\frac{\gamma-1}{\gamma}} \quad ...(iii)$$

For adiabatic process, the sonic velocity is given by:

$$C = \sqrt{\gamma RT} = \sqrt{\gamma\frac{p}{\rho}} \qquad \left(\because \frac{p}{\rho} = RT\right)$$

For point 0, $$C_0 = \sqrt{\gamma\frac{p_0}{\rho_0}} \quad \text{or} \quad C_0^2 = \gamma\frac{p_0}{\rho_0}$$

Substituting the value of $\frac{\gamma p_0}{\rho_0} = C_0^2$ in eqn. (*iii*), we get:

$$1+\frac{V_0^2}{2}(\gamma-1)\times\frac{1}{C_0^2} = \left(\frac{p_s}{p_0}\right)^{\frac{\gamma-1}{\gamma}}$$

or, $$1+\frac{V_0^2}{2C_0^2}(\gamma-1) = \left(\frac{p_s}{p_0}\right)^{\frac{\gamma-1}{\gamma}}$$

$$1+\frac{M_0^2}{2}(\gamma-1) = \left(\frac{p_s}{p_0}\right)^{\frac{\gamma-1}{\gamma}} \qquad \left(\because \frac{V_0^2}{C_0^2} = M_0^2\right)$$

or, $$\left(\frac{p_s}{p_0}\right)^{\frac{\gamma-1}{\gamma}} = \left[1+\left(\frac{\gamma-1}{2}\right)M_0^2\right]$$

or, $$\frac{p_s}{p_0} = \left[1+\left(\frac{\gamma-1}{2}\right)M_0^2\right]^{\frac{\gamma}{\gamma-1}} \quad ...(iv)$$

or, $$\boldsymbol{p_s = p_0\left[1+\left(\frac{\gamma-1}{2}\right)M_0^2\right]^{\frac{\gamma}{\gamma-1}}} \quad ...(15.36)$$

Eqn. (15.36) gives the value of ***stagnation pressure.***

Compressibility correction factor:

If the right hand side of Eqn. (15.36) is expanded by the binomial theorem, we get:

$$p_s = p_0\left[1+\frac{\gamma}{2}M_0^2+\frac{\gamma}{8}M_0^4+\frac{\gamma(2-\gamma)}{48}M_0^6\right]$$

$$= p_0\left[1+\frac{\gamma M_0^2}{2}\left(1+\frac{M^2}{4}+\frac{2-\gamma}{24}M_0^4+...\right)\right]$$

or, $$p_s = p_0+\frac{p_0\gamma M_0^2}{2}\left(1+\frac{M_0^2}{4}+\frac{2-\gamma}{24}M_0^4+...\right) \quad ...(15.37)$$

But, $$M_0^2 = \frac{V_0^2}{C_0^2}=\frac{V_0^2}{\left(\frac{\gamma p_0}{\rho_0}\right)}=\frac{V_0^2\rho_0}{\gamma p_0} \qquad \left(\because C_0^2=\frac{\gamma p_0}{\rho_0}\right)$$

Substituting the value of M_0^2 in eqn. 15.37, we get:

$$p_s = p_0+\frac{p_0\gamma}{2}\times\frac{V_0^2\rho_0}{\gamma p_0}\left(1+\frac{M_0^2}{4}+\frac{2-\gamma}{24}M_0^4+...\right)$$

or, $$p_s = p_0+\frac{\rho_0 V_0^2}{2}\left(1+\frac{M_0^2}{4}+\frac{2-\gamma}{24}M_0^4+...\right) \quad ...(15.38)$$

Also, $$p_s = p_0+\frac{\rho_0 V_0^2}{2} \text{ (when compressibility effects are neglected)} \quad ...(15.39)$$

The comparison of eqns. (15.38) and (15.39) shows that the effects of compressibility are isolated in the bracketed quantity and that these effects *depend only* upon the *Mach number*. The bracketed quantity $\left[i.e., \left(1+\frac{M_0^2}{4}+\frac{2-\gamma}{24}M_0^4+...\right)\right]$ may thus be considered as a **compressibility correction factor**. It is worth noting that :

- For $M < 0.2$, the compressibility affects the pressure difference $(p_s - p_0)$ by *less than 1 per cent* and the simple formula for flow at constant density is then sufficiently accurate.
- *For larger value of M*, as the terms of binomial expansion become significant, the *compressibility effect must be taken into account.*
- When the Mach number exceeds a value of about 0.3 the *Pitot-static tube used for measuring aircraft speed needs calibration to take into account the compressibility effects.*

15.8.2. Expression for Stagnation Density (ρ_s)

From eqn. (*ii*), we have:

$$\frac{\rho_0}{\rho_s}=\left(\frac{p_0}{p_s}\right)^{\frac{1}{\gamma}} \quad \text{or} \quad \frac{\rho_s}{\rho_0}=\left(\frac{p_s}{p_0}\right)^{\frac{1}{\gamma}} \quad \text{or} \quad \rho_s=\rho_0\left(\frac{p_s}{p_0}\right)^{\frac{1}{\gamma}}$$

Substituting the value of $\left(\frac{p_s}{p_0}\right)$ from eqn. (*iv*), we get:

$$\rho_s = \rho_0\left[\left\{1+\left(\frac{\gamma-1}{2}\right)M_0^2\right\}^{\frac{\gamma}{\gamma-1}}\right]^{\frac{1}{\gamma}}$$

or, $$\rho_s = \rho_0 \left[1 + \left(\frac{\gamma - 1}{2}\right) M_0^2\right]^{\frac{1}{\gamma - 1}} \quad ...(15.40)$$

15.8.3 Expression for stagnation temperature (T_s)

The equation of state is given by : $\frac{p}{\rho} = RT$

For stagnation point, the equation of state may be written as :

$$\frac{p_s}{\rho_s} = RT_s \quad \text{or} \quad T_s = \frac{1}{R}\frac{p_s}{\rho_s}$$

Substituting the values of p_s and ρ_s from eqns. (15.36) and (15.37), we get:

$$T_s = \frac{1}{R} \frac{p_0 \left[1 + \left(\frac{\gamma - 1}{2}\right) M_0^2\right]^{\frac{\gamma}{\gamma - 1}}}{\rho_0 \left[1 + \left(\frac{\gamma - 1}{2}\right) M_0^2\right]^{\frac{1}{\gamma - 1}}}$$

$$= \frac{1}{R}\frac{p_0}{\rho_0} \left[1 + \left(\frac{\gamma - 1}{2}\right) M_0^2\right]^{\left(\frac{\gamma}{\gamma - 1} - \frac{1}{\gamma - 1}\right)}$$

$$= \frac{1}{R}\frac{p_0}{\rho_0} \left[1 + \left(\frac{\gamma - 1}{2}\right) M_0^2\right]^{\left(\frac{\gamma - 1}{\gamma - 1}\right)}$$

or, $$T_s = T_0 \left[1 + \left(\frac{\gamma - 1}{2}\right) M_0^2\right] \quad ...(15.41)$$

$$\left(\because \frac{p_0}{\rho_0} = RT_0\right)$$

Example 15.11. *An aeroplane is flying at 1000 km/h through still air having a pressure of 78.5 kN/m² (abs.) and temperature – 8° C . Calculate on the stagnation point on the nose of the plane :*

(i) Stagnation pressure,

(ii) Stagnation temperature, and

(iii) Stagnation density.

Take for air : $R = 287$ J/kg K and $\gamma = 1.4$.

Solution. Speed of aeroplane,

$$V = 1000 \text{ km/h} = \frac{1000 \times 1000}{60 \times 60} = 277{\cdot}77 \text{ m/s}$$

Pressure of air, $p_0 = 78.5$ kN/m²

Temperature of air, $T_0 = -8 + 273 = 265$ K

For air : $R = 287$ J/kg K, $\gamma = 1.4$

The sonic velocity for adiabatic flow is given by:

$$C_0 = \sqrt{\gamma R T_0} = \sqrt{1.4 \times 287 \times 265} = 326.31 \text{ m/s}$$

$\therefore$ Mach number, $$M_0 = \frac{V_0}{C_0} = \frac{277.77}{326.31} = 0.851$$

(i) Stagnation pressure, p_s :

The stagnation pressure (p_s) is given by the relation:

$$p_s = p_0\left[1+\left(\frac{\gamma-1}{2}\right)M_0^2\right]^{\frac{\gamma}{\gamma-1}} \quad \text{...[Eqn. (15.36)]}$$

or,

$$p_s = 78.5\left[1+\left(\frac{1.4-1}{2}\right)\times 0.851^2\right]^{\frac{1.4}{1.4-1}}$$

$$= 78.5\,(1.145)^{3.5} = \mathbf{126.1\ kN/m^2} \quad \textbf{(Ans.)}$$

(ii) Stagnation temperature, T_s :

The stagnation temperature is given by:

$$T_s = T_0\left[1+\left(\frac{\gamma-1}{2}\right)M_0^2\right] \quad \text{...[Eqn. (15.41)]}$$

$$= 265\left[1+\frac{1.4-1}{2}\times 0.851^2\right] = 303.4\ \text{K} \quad \text{or} \quad \mathbf{30.4°\ C} \quad \textbf{(Ans.)}$$

(iii) Stagnation density, ρ_s :

The stagnation density (ρ_s) is given by:

$$\frac{p_s}{\rho_s} = RT_s \quad \text{or} \quad \rho_s = \frac{p_s}{RT_s}$$

or,

$$\rho_s = \frac{126.1\times 10^3}{287\times 303.4} = \mathbf{1.448\ kg/m^3} \quad \textbf{(Ans.)}$$

Example 15.12. *Air has a velocity of 1000 km/h at a pressure of 9.81 kN/m² vacuum and a temperature of 47°C. Compute its stagnation properties and the local Mach number. Take atmospheric pressure = 98.1 kN/m², R = 287 J/kg K and γ = 1.4.*

What would be the compressibility correction factor for a pitot-static tube to measure the velocity at a Mach number of 0.8. **[PEC]**

Solution. Velocity of air, $V_0 = 1000\ \text{km/h} = \frac{1000\times 1000}{60\times 60} = 277{\cdot}78\ \text{m/s}$

Temperature of air, $T_0 = 47 + 273 = 320\ \text{K}$

Atmospheric pressure, $p_{atm} = 98.1\ \text{kN/m}^2$

Pressure of air (static), $p_0 = 98.1 - 9.81 = 88.29\ \text{kN/m}^2$

$R = 287\ \text{J/kg K}, \gamma = 1.4$

Sonic velocity, $C_0 = \sqrt{\gamma RT_0} = \sqrt{1.4\times 287\times 320} = 358.6\ \text{m/s}$

∴ Mach number, $M_0 = \frac{V_0}{C_0} = \frac{277.78}{358.6} = 0.7746$

Stagnation pressure, (p_s) :

The stagnation pressure is given by:

$$p_s = p_0\left[1+\left(\frac{\gamma-1}{2}\right)M_0^2\right]^{\frac{\gamma}{\gamma-1}} \quad \text{...[Eqn. (15.36)]}$$

or,

$$p_s = 88.29\left[1+\frac{1.4-1}{2}\times 0.7746^2\right]^{\frac{1.4}{1.4-1}}$$

$$= 88.29\,(1.12)^{3.5} = \mathbf{131.27\ kN/m^2} \quad \textbf{(Ans.)}$$

Stagnation temperature, T_s :

$$T_s = T_0\left[1+\left(\frac{\gamma-1}{2}\right)M_0^2\right] \quad \text{...[Eqn. (15.41)]}$$

or,
$$T_s = 320\left[1+\frac{1.4-1}{2}\times 0.7746^2\right] = 358.4\ K \text{ or } \mathbf{85.4°C} \ \textbf{(Ans.)}$$

Stagnation density, ρ_s :

$$\rho_s = \frac{p_s}{RT_s} = \frac{131.27\times 10^3}{287\times 358.4} = \mathbf{1.276\ kg/m^3} \ \textbf{(Ans.)}$$

Compressibility factor at $M = 0.8$:

Compressibility factor
$$= 1+\frac{M_0^2}{4}+\frac{2-\gamma}{24}M_0^4+...$$
$$= 1+\frac{0.8^2}{4}+\frac{2-1.4}{24}\times 0.8^4 = \mathbf{1.1702} \ \textbf{(Ans.)}$$

Example 15.13. *Air at a pressure of 220 kN/m² and temperature 27°C is moving at a velocity of 200 m/s. Calculate the stagnation pressure if*

(i) Compressibility is neglected; (ii) Compressibility is accounted for.

For air, take $R = 287$ *J/kg K,* $\gamma = 1.4$

Solution. Pressure of air, $p_0 = 200$ kN/m²

Temperature of air, $T_0 = 27 + 233 = 300$ K

Velocity of air, $V_0 = 200$ m/s

Stagnation pressure, p_s :

(i) Compressibility is neglected :

$$p_s = p_0 + \frac{\rho_0 V_0^2}{2}$$

where,
$$\rho_0 = \frac{p_0}{RT_0} = \frac{220\times 10^3}{287\times 300} = 2.555 \text{ kg/m}^3$$

∴
$$p_s = 220+\frac{2.555\times 200^2}{2}\times 10^{-3}\,(\text{kN/m}^2) = \mathbf{271.1\,kN/m^2} \ \textbf{(Ans.)}$$

(ii) Compressibility is accounted for :

The stagnation pressure, when compressibility is accounted for, is given by:

$$p_s = p_0 + \frac{\rho_0 V_0^2}{2}\left(1+\frac{M_0^2}{4}+\frac{2-\gamma}{24}M_0^4+...\right) \quad \text{...[Eqn. (13.38)]}$$

Mach number,
$$M_0 = \frac{V_0}{C_0} = \frac{200}{\sqrt{\gamma RT_0}} = \frac{200}{\sqrt{1.4\times 287\times 300}} = 0.576$$

Whence,
$$p_s = 220+\frac{2.555\times 200^2}{2}\times 10^{-3}\left(1+\frac{0.576^2}{4}+\frac{2-1.4}{24}\times 0.576^4\right)$$

or,
$$p_s = 220 + 51.1\,(1 + 0.0829 + 0.00275) = \mathbf{275.47\ kN/m^2} \ \textbf{(Ans.)}$$

Example 15.14. *In aircraft flying at an altitude where the pressure was 35 kPa and temperature – 38°C, stagnation pressure measured was 65.4 kPa. Calculate the speed of the aircraft. Take molecular weight of air as 28.* **(UPSC)**

Solution. Pressure of air, $p_0 = 35 \text{ kPa} = 35 \times 10^3 \text{ N/m}^2$

Temperature of air, $T_0 = -38 + 273 = 235 \text{ K}$

Stagnation pressure, $p_s = 65.4 \text{ kPa} = 65.4 \times 10^3 \text{ N/m}^2$

Speed of the aircraft, V_a :

$$p_0 V = mRT_0 = m \times \left(\frac{R_0}{M}\right) T_0$$

or,
$$\rho_0 = \frac{m}{V} = \frac{p_0 M}{R_0 T_0}$$

where,
R = Characteristic gas constant,
R_0 = Universal gas constant = 8314 Nm/mole K,
M = Molecular weight, for air = 28, and
ρ_0 = Density of air.

Substituting the values, we get:

$$\rho_0 = \frac{(35 \times 10^3) \times 28}{8314 \times 235} = 0.5 \text{ kg/m}^3$$

Now, using the relation:
$$p_s = p_0 + \frac{\rho_0 V_a^2}{2} \quad \text{... [(Eqn. 15.39)]}$$

or,
$$V_a = \sqrt{\frac{2(p_s - p)}{\rho_0}} = \sqrt{\frac{2(65.4 \times 10^3 - 35 \times 10^3)}{0.5}}$$

$$= \textbf{348.7 m/s} \quad \textbf{(Ans.)}$$

15.9. AREA-VELOCITY RELATIONSHIP AND EFFECT OF VARIATION OF AREA FOR SUBSONIC, SONIC AND SUPERSONIC FLOWS

For an *incompressible flow* the continuity equation may be expressed as :

AV = Constant, which when differentiated gives,

$$AdC + VdA = 0$$

or,
$$\frac{dA}{A} = -\frac{dV}{V} \quad \text{...(15.42)}$$

But in case of *compressible flow*, the continuity equation is given by:

ρAV = Constant, which can be differentiated to give

$$\rho d(AV) + AVd\rho = 0$$

or, $$\rho(AdV + VdA) + AVd\rho = 0$$

or, $$\rho AdV + \rho VdA + AVd\rho = 0$$

Dividing both sides by ρAV, we get:

$$\frac{dV}{V} + \frac{dA}{A} + \frac{d\rho}{\rho} = 0 \quad \text{...(15.93)}$$

or,
$$\frac{dA}{A} = -\frac{dV}{V} - \frac{d\rho}{\rho} \quad \text{...(15.43 (a)}$$

The Euler's equation for compressible fluid is given by:

$$\frac{dp}{\rho} + VdV + gdz = 0$$

Neglecting the z terms the above equation reduces to:

$$\frac{dp}{\rho} + VdV = 0$$

This equation can also be expressed as:

$$\frac{dp}{\rho} \times \frac{d\rho}{d\rho} + VdV = 0$$

or, $$\frac{dp}{d\rho} \times \frac{d\rho}{\rho} + VdV = 0$$

But, $$\frac{dp}{d\rho} = C^2 \quad \text{...[Eqn. (15.29)]}$$

$\therefore$ $$C^2 \times \frac{d\rho}{\rho} + VdV = 0$$

or, $$C^2 \frac{d\rho}{\rho} = -VdV \quad \text{or} \quad \frac{d\rho}{\rho} = -\frac{VdV}{C^2}$$

Substituting the value of $\frac{d\rho}{\rho}$ in eqn. (15.43), we get:

$$\frac{dV}{V} + \frac{dA}{A} - \frac{VdV}{C^2} = 0$$

or, $$\frac{dA}{A} = \frac{VdV}{C^2} - \frac{dV}{V} = \frac{dV}{V}\left(\frac{V^2}{C^2} - 1\right)$$

$\therefore$ $$\boldsymbol{\frac{dA}{A} = \frac{dV}{V}\left(M^2 - 1\right)} \quad \left(\because M = \frac{V}{C}\right) \quad \text{...(15.44)}$$

This important equation is due to ***Hugoniot.***

Eqns. (15.42) and (15.44) give variation of $\left(\frac{dA}{A}\right)$ for the flow of incompressible and compressible fluids respectively. The ratios $\left(\frac{dA}{A}\right)$ and $\left(\frac{dV}{V}\right)$ are respectively fractional variations in the values of area and flow velocity in the flow passage.

Further, in order to study the variation of pressure with the change in flow area, an expression similar to eqn. (15.44), as given below, can be obtained:

$$dp = \rho V^2 \left(\frac{1}{1 - M^2}\right)\frac{dA}{A} \quad \text{...(15.45)}$$

From eqns. (15.44) and (15.45), it is possible to formulate the following *conclusions* of practical significance:

(*i*) For subsonic flow ($M < 1$) :

$$\frac{dV}{V} > 0 ; \frac{dA}{A} < 0 ; dp < 0 \text{ (convergent nozzle)}$$

$$\frac{dV}{V} < 0 ; \frac{dA}{A} > 0 ; dp > 0 \text{ (divergent diffuser)}$$

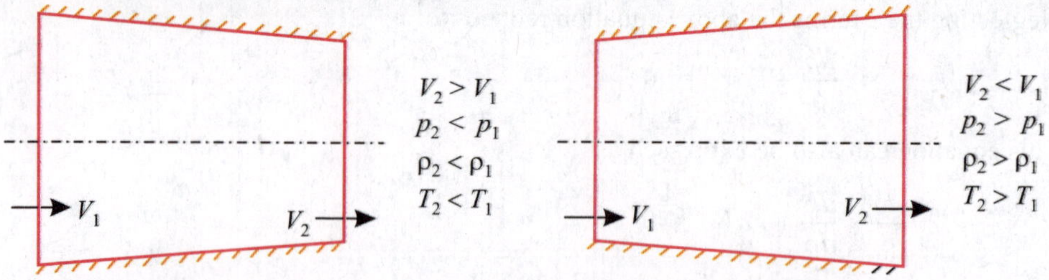

(*a*) Convergent nozzle. (*b*) Divergent diffuser

Fig. 15.7. Subsonic flow (M < 1).

(*ii*) For supersonic flow ($M > 1$) :

$$\frac{dV}{V} > 0 \; ; \frac{dA}{A} > 0 \; ; dp < 0 \quad \text{(divergent nozzle)}$$

$$\frac{dV}{V} < 0 \; ; \frac{dA}{A} < 0 \; ; dp > 0 \quad \text{(convergent diffuser)}$$

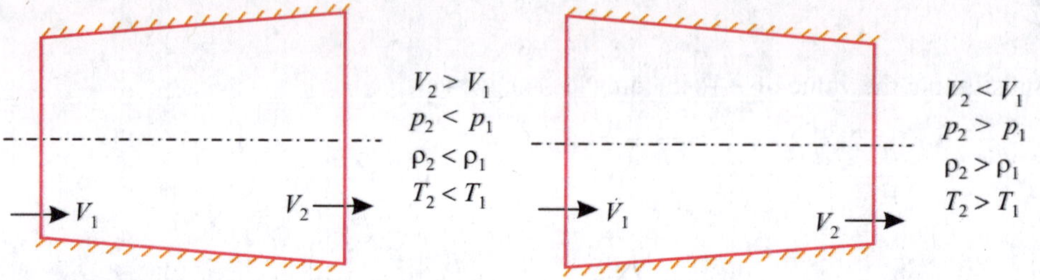

(*a*) Divergent nozzle (*a*) Convergent diffuser.

Fig. 15.8. Supersonic flow (M > 1).

(*iii*) For sonic flow ($M = 1$) :

$$\frac{dA}{A} = 0$$ (straight flow passage since dA must be zero)

and, dp = (zero/zero) *i.e.* indeterminate, but when evaluated, the change of pressure $dp = 0$, since $dA = 0$ and the flow is frictionless.

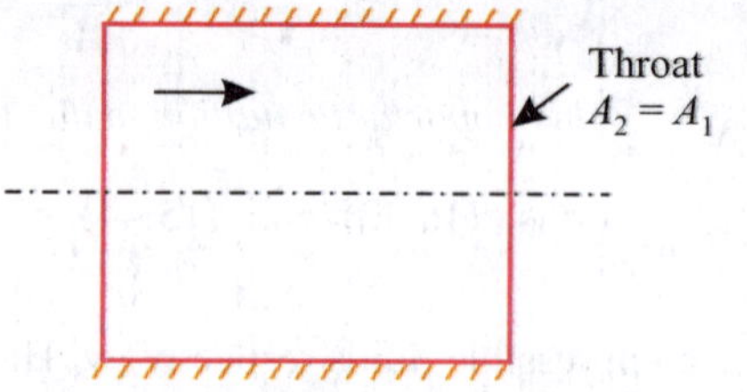

Fig. 15.9. Sonic Flow (M = 1)

15.10. FLOW OF COMPRESSIBLE FLUID THROUGH A CONVERGENT NOZZLE

Fig. 15.10 shows a large tank/vessel fitted with a short convergent nozzle and containing a compressible fluid. Consider two points 1 and 2 inside the tank and exit of the nozzle respectively.

Let, p_1 = Pressure of fluid at the point 1,

V_1 = Velocity of fluid in the tank (= 0),

T_1 = Temperature of fluid at point 1,

ρ_1 = Density of fluid at point 1, and

p_2, V_2, T_2 and ρ_2 = Corresponding values of pressure, velocity, temperature and density at point 2.

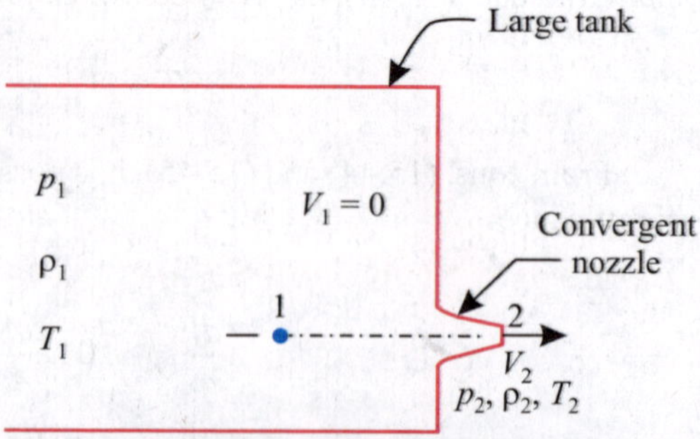

Fig. 15.10. Flow of fluid through a convergent nozzle.

Assuming the flow to take place *adiabatically*, then by using Bernoulli's equation (for adiabatic flow), we have:

$$\left(\frac{\gamma}{\gamma-1}\right)\frac{p_1}{\rho_1 g}+\frac{V_1^2}{2g}+z_1 = \left(\frac{\gamma}{\gamma-1}\right)\frac{p_2}{\rho_2 g}+\frac{V_2^2}{2g}+z_2 \qquad \text{[Eqn. (15.26)]}$$

But $z_1 = z_2$ and $V_1 = 0$

$$\therefore \quad \frac{\gamma}{\gamma-1}\frac{p_1}{\rho_1 g} = \left(\frac{\gamma}{\gamma-1}\right)\frac{p_2}{\rho_2 g}+\frac{V_2^2}{2g}$$

or,
$$\left(\frac{\gamma}{\gamma-1}\right)\left[\frac{p_1}{\rho_1 g}-\frac{p_2}{\rho_2 g}\right] = \frac{V_2^2}{2g}$$

or,
$$\frac{\gamma}{\gamma-1}\left(\frac{p_1}{\rho_1}-\frac{p_2}{\rho_2}\right) = \frac{V_2^2}{2}$$

or,
$$V_2 = \sqrt{\frac{2\gamma}{(\gamma-1)}\left(\frac{p_1}{\rho_1}-\frac{p_2}{\rho_2}\right)}$$

or,
$$V_2 = \sqrt{\frac{2\gamma}{(\gamma-1)}\frac{p_1}{\rho_1}\left(1-\frac{p_2}{\rho_2}\times\frac{\rho_1}{p_1}\right)} \qquad ...(1)$$

For adiabatic flow :
$$\frac{p_1}{\rho_1^\gamma} = \frac{p_2}{\rho_2^\gamma} \quad \text{or} \quad \frac{p_1}{p_2} = \left(\frac{\rho_1}{\rho_2}\right)^\gamma$$

or,
$$\frac{\rho_1}{\rho_2} = \left(\frac{p_1}{p_2}\right)^{\frac{1}{\gamma}} \qquad ...(i)$$

Substituting the value of $\frac{\rho_1}{\rho_2}$ in eqn. (1), we get:

$$V_2 = \sqrt{\frac{2\gamma}{(\gamma-1)}\frac{p_1}{\rho_1}\left[1-\frac{p_2}{p_1}\times\left(\frac{p_1}{p_2}\right)^{\frac{1}{\gamma}}\right]} = \sqrt{\frac{2\gamma}{(\gamma-1)}\frac{p_1}{\rho_1}\left[1-\left(\frac{p_2}{p_1}\right)^{1-\frac{1}{\gamma}}\right]}$$

or,
$$V_2 = \sqrt{\frac{2\gamma}{(\gamma-1)}\frac{p_1}{\rho_1}\left[1-\left(\frac{p_2}{p_1}\right)^{\frac{\gamma-1}{\gamma}}\right]} \qquad ...(15.46)$$

The mass rate of flow of the compressible fluid,

$$m = \rho_2 A_2 V_2 \qquad (A_2 \text{ being the area of the nozzle at the exit})$$

$$= \rho_2 A_2\sqrt{\frac{2\gamma}{(\gamma-1)}\frac{p_1}{\rho_1}\left[1-\left(\frac{p_2}{p_1}\right)^{\frac{\gamma-1}{\gamma}}\right]}, \qquad \text{[substituting } V_2 \text{ from eqn. (15.46)]}$$

or,
$$m = A_2\sqrt{\frac{2\gamma}{(\gamma-1)}\frac{p_1}{\rho_1}\times\rho_2^2\left[1-\left(\frac{p_2}{p_1}\right)^{\frac{\gamma-1}{\gamma}}\right]}$$

From eqn. (*i*), we have:

$$\rho_2 = \frac{\rho_1}{(p_1/p_2)^{1/\gamma}} = \rho_1\left(\frac{p_2}{p_1}\right)^{\frac{1}{\gamma}}$$

$$\therefore \qquad \rho_2^2 = \rho_1^2 \left(\frac{p_1}{p_2}\right)^{2/\gamma}$$

Substituting this value in the above equation, we get:

$$m = A_2 \sqrt{\frac{2\gamma}{\gamma-1}\frac{p_1}{\rho_1} \times \rho_1^2 \left(\frac{p_2}{p_1}\right)^{2/\gamma} \left[1 - \left(\frac{p_2}{p_1}\right)^{\frac{\gamma-1}{\gamma}}\right]}$$

$$= A_2 \sqrt{\frac{2\gamma}{\gamma-1} p_1\rho_1 \left[\left(\frac{p_2}{p_1}\right)^{2/\gamma} - \left(\frac{p_2}{p_1}\right)^{\frac{\gamma-1}{\gamma}+\frac{2}{\gamma}}\right]}$$

$$m = A_2 \sqrt{\frac{2\gamma}{\gamma-1} p_1\rho_1 \left[\left(\frac{p_2}{p_1}\right)^{2/\gamma} - \left(\frac{p_2}{p_1}\right)^{\frac{\gamma+1}{\gamma}}\right]} \qquad ...(15.47)$$

The mass rate of flow (m) depends on the value of $\frac{p_2}{p_1}$ (for the given values of p_1 and ρ_1 at point 1).

Value of $\frac{p_2}{p_1}$ for maximum value of mass rate of flow:

For maximum value of m we have: $\dfrac{dm}{d\left(\frac{p_2}{p_1}\right)} = 0$

As other quantities except the ratio $\frac{p_2}{p_1}$ are constant, therefore:

$$\frac{d}{d\left(\frac{p_2}{p_1}\right)} = \left[\left(\frac{p_2}{p_1}\right)^{2/\gamma} - \left(\frac{p_2}{p_1}\right)^{\frac{\gamma+1}{\gamma}}\right] = 0$$

or, $$\frac{2}{\gamma}\left(\frac{p_2}{p_1}\right)^{\frac{2}{\gamma}-1} - \left(\frac{\gamma+1}{\gamma}\right)\left(\frac{p_2}{p_1}\right)^{\frac{\gamma+1}{\gamma}-1} = 0$$

or, $$\left(\frac{p_2}{p_1}\right)^{\frac{2}{\gamma}-1} = \frac{\gamma+1}{2}\left(\frac{p_2}{p_1}\right)^{\frac{1}{\gamma}} \quad \text{or} \quad \left(\frac{p_2}{p_1}\right)^{\frac{2-\gamma}{\gamma}} = \frac{\gamma+1}{2}\left(\frac{p_2}{p_1}\right)^{\frac{1}{\gamma}}$$

or, $$\left(\frac{p_2}{p_1}\right)^{2-\gamma} = \left(\frac{\gamma+1}{2}\right)^{\gamma}\left(\frac{p_2}{p_1}\right)$$

or, $$\left(\frac{p_2}{p_1}\right)^{2-\gamma-1} = \left(\frac{\gamma+1}{2}\right)^{\gamma} \quad \text{or} \quad \left(\frac{p_2}{p_1}\right)^{1-\gamma} = \left(\frac{\gamma+1}{2}\right)^{\gamma}$$

or, $$\left(\frac{p_2}{p_1}\right)^{\gamma-1} = \left(\frac{2}{\gamma+1}\right)^{\gamma} \quad \text{or} \quad \boldsymbol{\left(\frac{p_2}{p_1}\right) = \left(\frac{2}{\gamma+1}\right)^{\frac{\gamma}{\gamma-1}}} \qquad ...(15.48)$$

Eqn. (15.48) is the *condition for maximum mass flow rate through the nozzle.*

- *It may be pointed out that a convergent nozzle is employed when the exit pressure is equal to or more than the critical pressure, and a convergent-divergent nozzle is used when the discharge pressure is less than the critical pressure.*

For air with $\gamma = 1.4$, the *critical pressure ratio,*

$$\frac{p_2}{p_1} = \left(\frac{2}{1.4+1}\right)^{\frac{1.4}{1.4-1}} = 0.528 \qquad ...(15.49)$$

Relevant relations for critical density and temperature are :

$$\frac{\rho_2}{\rho_1} = \left(\frac{2}{\gamma+1}\right)^{\frac{1}{\gamma-1}} \qquad ...[15.49(a)]$$

$$\frac{T_2}{T_1} = \frac{2}{\gamma+1} \qquad ...[15.49(b)]$$

Value of V_2 for maximum rate of flow of fluid:

Substituting the value of $\frac{p_2}{p_1}$ from eqn. (15.48) in eqn. (15.46), we get:

$$V_2 = \sqrt{\frac{2\gamma}{\gamma-1}\frac{p_1}{\rho_1}\left[1-\left(\frac{2}{\gamma+1}\right)^{\frac{\gamma}{\gamma-1}\times\frac{\gamma-1}{\gamma}}\right]} = \sqrt{\frac{2\gamma}{\gamma-1}\frac{p_1}{\rho_1}\left(1-\frac{2}{\gamma+1}\right)}$$

$$= \sqrt{\frac{2\gamma}{\gamma-1}\frac{p_1}{\rho_1}\left(\frac{\gamma+1-2}{\gamma+1}\right)} = \sqrt{\frac{2\gamma}{\gamma-1}\frac{p_1}{\rho_1}\left(\frac{\gamma-1}{\gamma+1}\right)}$$

or, $$V_2 = \sqrt{\frac{2\gamma}{\gamma+1}\frac{p_1}{\rho_1}}\ (= C_2) \qquad ...(15.50)$$

Maximum rate of flow of fluid through nozzle, m_{max}:

Substituting the value of $\frac{p_2}{p_1}$ From eqn. (15.49) in eqn. (15.47), we get:

$$m_{max} = A_2\sqrt{\left(\frac{2\gamma}{\gamma-1}\right)p_1\rho_1\left[\left(\frac{2}{\gamma+1}\right)^{\frac{\gamma}{\gamma+1}\times\frac{2}{\gamma}} - \left(\frac{2}{\gamma+1}\right)^{\frac{\gamma}{\gamma-1}\times\frac{\gamma+1}{\gamma}}\right]}$$

$$= A_2\sqrt{\left(\frac{2\gamma}{\gamma-1}\right)p_1\rho_1\left[\left(\frac{2}{\gamma+1}\right)^{\frac{2}{\gamma-1}} - \left(\frac{2}{\gamma+1}\right)^{\frac{\gamma+1}{\gamma-1}}\right]}$$

For air, $\gamma = 1.4$,

$$\therefore \quad m_{max} = A_2\sqrt{\left(\frac{2\times1.4}{1.4-1}\right)p_1\rho_1\left[\left(\frac{2}{1.4+1}\right)^{\frac{2}{1.4-1}} - \left(\frac{2}{1.4+1}\right)^{\frac{1.4+1}{1.4-1}}\right]}$$

$$= A_2\sqrt{7\,p_1\,\rho_1\,(0.4018-0.3348)}$$

or, $$\boldsymbol{m_{max} = 0.685\,A_2\sqrt{p_1\rho_1}} \qquad ...(15.51)$$

Variation of mass flow rate of compressible fluid with pressure ratio $\left(\frac{p_2}{p_1}\right)$:

A passage in which the sonic velocity has been reached and thus in which the mass flow rate is maximum is often said to be ***choked*** *or in* ***chocking conditions***. It is evident from eqn. (15.47) that for a fixed value of inlet pressure the mass flow depends on nozzle exit pressure.

Fig. 15.11 depicts the variation of actual and theoretical mass flow rate versus $\frac{p_2}{p_1}$. Following points are *worth noting* :

(*i*) The flow rate increases with a decrease in the pressure ratio $\frac{p_2}{p_1}$ and attains the maximum value of the critical pressure ratio $\frac{p_2}{p_1} = 0.528$ for air.

(*ii*) With further decrease in exit pressure below the critical value, the theoretical mass flow rate decreases. This is contrary to the actual results where the mass flow rate remains constant after attaining the maximum value. This may be explained as follows :

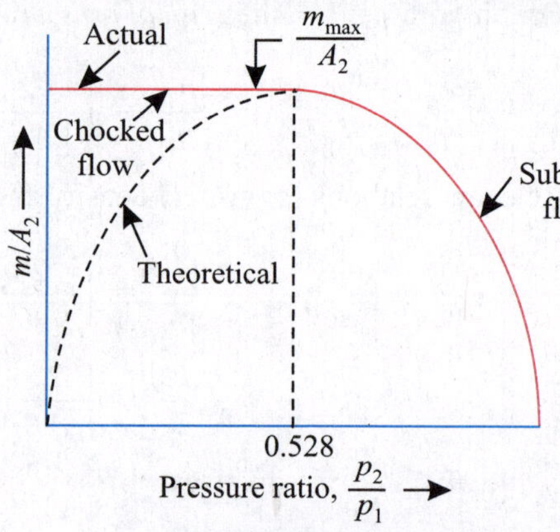

Fig. 15.11. Mass flow rate through a convergent nozzle.

At critical pressure ratio, the velocity V_2 at the throat is equal to the sonic speed (derived below). For an accelerating flow of a compressible fluid in a convergent nozzle the velocity of flow within the nozzle is subsonic with a maximum velocity equal to the sonic velocity at the throat. Thus once the velocity V_2 at the throat has attained the sonic speed at the critical pressure ratio, it remains at the same value for all the values of $\left(\frac{p_2}{p_1}\right)$ less than critical pressure ratio, since the flow in the nozzle is being continuously accelerated with the reduction in the throat pressure below the critical values and hence the velocity cannot reduce. Thus, the mass flow rate for all values of $\left(\frac{p_2}{p_1}\right)$ less than critical pressure ratio remains constant at the maximum value (indicated by the solid horizontal line in Fig. 15.11). This fact has been verified experimentally too.

Velocity at outlet of nozzle for maximum flow rate :

The velocity at outlet of nozzle for *maximum flow rate* is given by:

$$V_2 = \sqrt{\left(\frac{2\gamma}{\gamma+1}\right)\frac{p_1}{\rho_1}} \qquad \text{...[Eqn. (15.50)}$$

Now pressure ratio,
$$\frac{p_2}{p_1} = \left(\frac{2}{\gamma+1}\right)^{\frac{\gamma}{\gamma-1}}$$

$$\therefore \quad p_1 = \frac{p_2}{\left(\frac{2}{\gamma+1}\right)^{\frac{\gamma}{\gamma-1}}} = p_2\left(\frac{2}{\gamma+1}\right)^{\frac{\gamma}{\gamma-1}}$$

For adiabatic flow:
$$\frac{p_1}{\rho_1^\gamma} = \frac{p_2}{\rho_2^\gamma} \quad \text{or} \quad \frac{p_1}{p_2} = \left(\frac{\rho_1}{\rho_2}\right)^\gamma$$

or,
$$\frac{\rho_1}{\rho_2} = \left(\frac{p_1}{p_2}\right)^{\frac{1}{\gamma}} = \left(\frac{p_2}{p_1}\right)^{-\frac{1}{\gamma}}$$

$$\therefore \quad \rho_1 = \rho_2\left(\frac{p_2}{p_1}\right)^{-\frac{1}{\gamma}} \text{ or } \rho_2\left(\frac{2}{\gamma+1}\right)^{\frac{\gamma}{\gamma-1}\times\frac{-1}{\gamma}} \text{ or } \rho_2\left(\frac{2}{\gamma+1}\right)^{\frac{1}{1-\gamma}}$$

Substituting the values of p_1 and ρ_1 in the above eqn. (15.50), we get:

$$V_2 = \sqrt{\left(\frac{2\gamma}{\gamma+1}\right) \times p_2 \left(\frac{2}{\gamma+1}\right)^{\frac{\gamma}{1-\gamma}} \times \left\{\frac{1}{\rho_2} \times \left(\frac{2}{\gamma+1}\right)^{\frac{1}{\gamma-1}}\right\}}$$

$$= \sqrt{\left(\frac{2\gamma}{\gamma+1}\right) \times \frac{p_2}{\rho_2} \times \left(\frac{2}{\gamma+1}\right)^{\frac{\gamma}{1-\gamma}+\frac{1}{\gamma-1}}} = \sqrt{\left(\frac{2}{\gamma+1}\right) \times \frac{p_2}{\rho_2}\left(\frac{2}{\gamma+1}\right)^{-1}}$$

or,
$$V_2 = \sqrt{\left(\frac{2\gamma}{\gamma+1}\right) \times \frac{p_2}{\rho_2}\left(\frac{\gamma+1}{2}\right)} = \sqrt{\frac{\gamma p_2}{\rho_2}} = C_2$$

i.e.
$$V_2 = C_2 \qquad \text{...(15.52)}$$

Hence, the *velocity* at the outlet of nozzle for *maximum flow rate equals sonic velocity.*

15.11. VARIABLES OF FLOW IN TERMS OF MACH NUMBER

In order to obtain relationship involving change in velocity, pressure, temperature and density in terms of the Mach number use is made of the continuity, perfect gas, isentropic flow and energy equations.

For *continuity equation,* we have:

$$\rho AV = \text{constant}$$

Differentiating the above equation, we get:

$$\rho\,[AdV + VdA] + AVd\rho = 0$$

Dividing throughout by ρAV, we have:

$$\frac{dV}{V} + \frac{dA}{A} + \frac{d\rho}{\rho} = 0$$

From *isentropic flow,* we have:

$$\frac{p}{\rho^\gamma} = \text{constant} \quad \text{or} \quad \frac{dp}{p} = \gamma\,\frac{dp}{p}$$

For *perfect gas,* we have: $p = \rho RT$

or,
$$\frac{dp}{p} = \frac{d\rho}{\rho} + \frac{dT}{T}$$

From *energy equation,* we have: $c_pT + \frac{V^2}{2} + \text{constant}$

Differentiating throughout, we get:

$$c_p dT + VdV = 0$$

or,
$$\left(\frac{\gamma R}{\gamma-1}\right) dT + VdV = 0 \qquad \left(\because c_p = \frac{\gamma R}{\gamma-1}\right)$$

or,
$$\frac{\gamma R}{\gamma-1}\,\frac{dT}{V^2} + \frac{dV}{V} = 0 \qquad \text{...}(i)$$

Also, Sonic velocity, $C = \sqrt{\gamma RT} \quad \therefore \gamma R = \frac{C^2}{T}$

Substituting the value of $\gamma R = \frac{C^2}{T}$ in eqn. (*i*), we get:

$$\frac{C^2}{(\gamma-1)\,T} \times \frac{dT}{V^2} + \frac{dV}{V} = 0$$

or, $$\frac{1}{(\gamma-1)\,M^2}\,\frac{dT}{T} + \frac{dV}{V} = 0 \qquad \left(\because M = \frac{V}{C}\right) \qquad \text{...(15.52)}$$

From the Mach number relationship:

$$M = \frac{V}{\sqrt{\gamma RT}} \qquad \text{(where } \sqrt{\gamma RT} = C\text{)}$$

$$\frac{dM}{M} = \frac{dV}{V} - \frac{1}{2}\frac{dT}{T} \qquad \text{...(15.53)}$$

Substituting the value of $\frac{dT}{T}$ from eqn. (15.52) in eqn. (15.53), we get:

$$\frac{dM}{M} = \frac{dV}{V} - \frac{1}{2}\left[-\frac{dV}{V} \times (\gamma-1)\,M^2\right]$$

$$= \frac{dV}{V} + \frac{1}{2}\frac{dV}{V} \times (\gamma-1)\,M^2$$

or, $$\frac{dM}{M} = \frac{dV}{V}\left[1 + \frac{\gamma-1}{2}M^2\right]$$

or, $$\frac{dV}{V} = \frac{1}{\left[1+\left(\frac{\gamma-1}{2}\right)M^2\right]}\frac{dM}{M} \qquad \text{...(15.54)}$$

Since the quantity within the bracket is *always positive, the trend of variation of velocity and Mach number is similar. For temperature variation, one can write:*

$$\frac{dT}{T} = \left[\frac{-(\gamma-1)\,M^2}{1+\left(\frac{\gamma-1}{2}\right)M^2}\right]\frac{dM}{M} \qquad \text{...(15.55)}$$

Since the right hand side is *negative* the *temperature changes follow an opposite trend to that of Mach number.* Similarly for *pressure* and *density,* we have:

$$\frac{dp}{p} = \left[\frac{-\gamma \cdot M^2}{1+\left(\frac{\gamma-1}{2}\right)M^2}\right]\frac{dM}{M} \qquad \text{...(15.56)}$$

and, $$\frac{d\rho}{\rho} = \left[\frac{-M^2}{1+\left(\frac{\gamma-1}{2}\right)M^2}\right]\frac{dM}{M} \qquad \text{...(15.57)}$$

For changes in *area* we have:

$$\frac{dA}{A} = \left[\frac{-(1-M^2)}{1+\left(\frac{\gamma-1}{2}\right)M^2}\right]\frac{dM}{M} \qquad \text{...(15.58)}$$

The quantity within the brackets may be *positive* or *negative* depending upon the *magnitude of Mach number*. By integrating eqn. (15.58), we can obtain a relationship between the critical throat area A_c, where Mach number is *unity* and the area A at any section where $M \gtrless 1$,

$$\frac{A}{A_c} = \frac{1}{M}\left[\frac{2+(\gamma-1)\,M^2}{\gamma+1}\right]^{\frac{\gamma+1}{2(\gamma-1)}} \quad ...(15.59)$$

Example 15.15. *The pressure leads from Pitot-static tube mounted on an aircraft were connected to a pressure gauge in the cockpit. The dial of the pressure gauge is calibrated to read the aircraft speed in m/s. The calibration is done on the ground by applying a known pressure across the gauge and calculating the equivalent velocity using incompressible Bernoulli's equation and assuming that the density is 1.224 kg/m³.*

The gauge having been calibrated in this way the aircraft is flown at 9200 m, where the density is 0.454 kg/m³ and ambient pressure is 30 kN/m². The gauge indicates a velocity of 152 m/s. What is the true speed of the aircraft ? **[UPSC Fluid Mechanics.]**

Solution. Bernoulli's equation for an *incompressible flow* is given by:

$$p + \frac{\rho V^2}{2} = \text{constant}$$

The stagnation pressure (p_s) created at Pitot-static tube,

$$p_s = p_0 + \frac{\rho_0 V_0^2}{2} \quad \text{(neglecting compressibility effects)} \quad ...(i)$$

Here, $p_0 = 30 \text{ kN/m}^2,\ V_0 = 152 \text{ m/s},\ \rho_0 = 1.224 \text{ kg/m}^3$ ...(*Given*)

$$\therefore \quad p_s = 30 + \frac{1.224 \times 152^2}{2} \times 10^{-3} = 44.139 \text{ kN/m}^2$$

Neglecting *compressibility effect*, the speed of the aircraft when

$\rho_0 = 0.454 \text{ kg/m}^3$ is given by [using eqn. (*i*)]:

$$44.139 \times 10^3 = 30 \times 10^3 + \frac{0.454 \times V_0^2}{2}$$

or,
$$V_0^2 = \frac{(44.139 - 30) \times 10^3 \times 2}{0.454} = 62286.34$$

$$\therefore \quad V_0 = 249.57 \text{ m/s}$$

$$\text{Sonic velocity, } C_0 = \sqrt{\gamma R T_0} = \sqrt{\gamma \frac{p_0}{\rho_0}} = \sqrt{1.4 \times \frac{30 \times 10^3}{0.454}} = 304.16 \text{ m/s}$$

$$\text{Mach number, } M_0 = \frac{V_0}{C_0} = \frac{249.57}{304.16} = 0.82$$

Compressibility correction factor $= \left(1 + \frac{M_0^2}{4}\right)$, neglecting the terms containing higher powers of M_0 (from eqn 15.38)

$$= \left(1 + \frac{0.82^2}{4}\right) = 1.168$$

$$\therefore \text{ True speed of aircraft} = \frac{249.57}{\sqrt{1.168}} = 230.9 \text{ m/s}$$

Hence, *true speed of aircraft* = **230.9 m/s (Ans.)**

Example 15.16. ***(a)*** *In case of isentropic flow of a compressible fluid through a variable duct, show that*

$$\frac{A}{A_c} = \frac{1}{M}\left[\frac{1+\frac{1}{2}(\gamma-1)M^2}{\frac{1}{2}(\gamma+1)}\right]^{\frac{\gamma+1}{2(\gamma-1)}}.$$

where γ is the ratio of specific heats, M is the Mach number at a section whose area is A and A_c *is the critical area of flow.*

(b) *A supersonic nozzle is to be designed for air flow with Mach number 3 at the exit section which is 200 mm in diameter. The pressure and temperature of air at the nozzle exit are to be 7.85 kN/m² and 200 K respectively. Determine the reservoir pressure and temperature and the throat area. Take : γ = 1.4.* **[UPSC Exams Fluid Mechanics.]**

Solution. (*a*) Refer to Art. 15.11.

(*b*) Mach number, $M = 3$

Area at the exit section, $A = \frac{\pi}{4} \times 0.2^2 = 0.0314 \text{ m}^2$

Pressure of air at the nozzle, $(p)_{nozzle} = 7.85 \text{ kN/m}^2$

Temperature of air at the nozzle, $(T)_{nozzle} = 200 \text{ K}$

Reservoir pressure, $(p)_{res.}$:

From eqn. (15.36), $$(p)_{res.} = (p)_{nozzle}\left[1+\left(\frac{\gamma-1}{2}\right)M^2\right]^{\left(\frac{\gamma}{\gamma-1}\right)}$$

or, $$(p)_{res.} = 7.85\left[1+\left(\frac{1.4-1}{2}\right)\times 3^2\right]^{\left(\frac{1.4}{1.4-1}\right)} = \mathbf{288.35 \text{ kN/m}^2} \text{ (Ans.)}$$

Reservoir temperature, $(T)_{res.}$:

From eqn. (15.41), $$(T)_{res.} = (T)_{nozzle} = \left[1+\left(\frac{\gamma-1}{2}\right)M^2\right]$$

or, $$(T)_{res.} = 200\left[1+\left(\frac{1.4-1}{2}\right)\times 3^2\right] = \mathbf{560 \text{ K}} \text{ (Ans.)}$$

Throat area (critical), A_c :

From eqn. (15.59), $$\frac{A}{A_c} = \frac{1}{M}\left[\frac{2+(\gamma-1)M^2}{\gamma+1}\right]^{\frac{\gamma+1}{2(\gamma-1)}}$$

or, $$\frac{0.0314}{A_c} = \frac{1}{3}\left[\frac{2+(1.4-1)3^2}{1.4+1}\right]^{\frac{1.4+1}{2(1.4-1)}}$$

or, $$\frac{0.0314}{A_c} = \frac{1}{3}(2.333)^3 = 4.23$$

or, $$A_c = \frac{0.0314}{4.23} = \mathbf{0.00742 \text{ m}^2} \text{ (Ans.)}$$

15.12. FLOW THROUGH LAVAL NOZZLE (CONVERGENT-DIVERGENT NOZZLE)

Laval nozzle is a convergent-divergent nozzle (named after de Laval, the swedish scientist who invented it) in which *subsonic flow prevails in the converging section, critical or transonic conditions in the throat and supersonic flow in the diverging section.*

Let, p_2 (= p_c) = Pressure in the throat when the flow is sonic for given pressure p_1.

— When the pressure in the receiver, $p_3 = p_1$, there will be no flow through the nozzle, this is shown by line *a* in Fig. 15.12 (*b*).

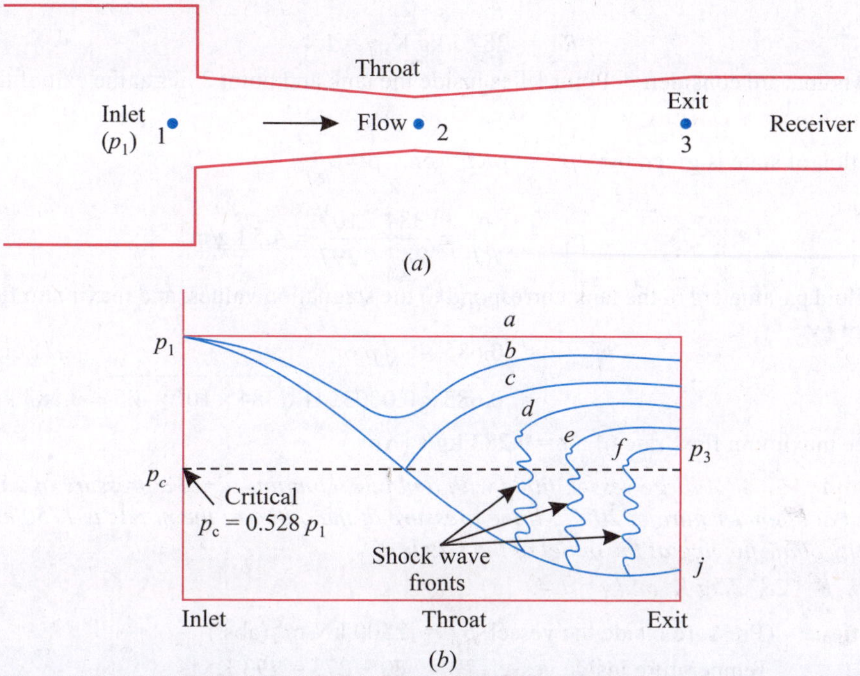

Fig. 15.12. (*a*) Lavel nozzle (convergent-divergent nozzle); (b) Pressure distribution through a converge-divergent nozzle with flow of compressible fluid.

— When the receiver pressure is reduced, flow will occur through the nozzle. As long as the value of p_3 is such that throat pressure p_2 is greater than the critical pressure 0.528 p_1, the flow in the converging and diverging sections will be subsonic. This condition is shown by line '*b*'.

— With further reduction in p_3, a stage is reached when p_2 is equal to critical pressure p_c = 0.528 p_1, at this line $M = 1$ in the throat. This condition is shown by line '*c*'. Flow is subsonic on the upstream as well the downstream of the throat. The flow is also *isentropic.*

— If p_3 *is further reduced, it does not effect the flow in convergent section. The flow in throat is sonic, downstream it is supersonic*. Somewhere in the diverging section a shock wave occurs and flow changes to subsonic (curve *d*). The flow *across the shock is non-isentropic. Downstream of the shock wave the flow is subsonic and decelerates.*

— If the value of p_3 is further reduced, the shock wave forms somewhat downstream (curve *e*).

— For p_3 equal to p_j, the shock wave will occur just at the exit of divergent section.

— If the value of p_3 lies before p_f and p_j oblique waves are formed at the exit :

Example 15.17. *A large tank contains air at 284 kN/m² gauge pressure and 24°C temperature. The air flows from the tank to the atmosphere through a convergent nozzle. If the diameter at the outlet of the nozzle is 20 mm, find the maximum flow rate of air.*

Take: R = 287 J/kg K, γ = 1.4 and atmospheric pressure = 100 kN/m². **[Roorkee University]**

Solution. Pressure in the tank, p_1 = 284 kN/m² (gauge) = 284 + 100 = 384 kN/m² (absolute)

Temperature in the tank, T_1 = 24 + 273 = 297 K

Diameter at the outlet of the nozzle,

$$D = 20 \text{ mm} = 0.02 \text{ m}$$

$$\therefore \quad \text{Area, } A_2 = \frac{\pi}{4} \times 0.02^2 = 0.0003141 \text{ m}^2$$

$$R = 287 \text{ J/kg K}, \gamma = 1.4$$

(Two points are considered. Point 1 lies inside the tank and point 2 lies at the exit of the nozzle)

Maximum flow rate, m_{max}:

Equation of state is given by: $p = \rho RT$ or $\rho = \dfrac{p}{RT}$

$$\therefore \quad \rho_1 = \frac{p_1}{RT_1} = \frac{384 \times 10^3}{287 \times 297} = 4.5 \text{ kg/m}^3$$

The fluid parameters in the tank correspond to the stagnation values, and maximum flow rate of air is given by:

$$m_{max} = 0.685\, A_2 \sqrt{p_1 \rho_1} \quad \text{...[Eqn. (15.51)]}$$

$$= 0.685 \times 0.0003141 \sqrt{384 \times 10^3 \times 4.5} = 0.283 \text{ kg/s}$$

Hence maximum flow rate of air = **0.283 kg/s (Ans.)**

Example 15.18. *A large vessel, fitted with a nozzle, contains air at a pressure of 2500 kN/m² (abs.) and at a temperature of 20°C. If the pressure at the outlet of the nozzle is 1750 kN/m² find the velocity of air flowing at the outlet of the nozzle.*

Take : R = 287 J/kg K, and γ = 1.4.

Solution. Pressure inside the vessel, $p_1 = 2500 \text{ kN/m}^2$ (abs.)

Temperature inside vessel, $T_1 = 20 + 273 = 293 \text{ K}$

Pressure at the outlet of the nozzle, $p_2 = 1750 \text{ kN/m}^2$ (abs.)

$R = 287 \text{ J/kg K}, \gamma = 1.4$

Velocity of air, V_2:

$$V_2 = \sqrt{\left(\frac{2\gamma}{\gamma - 1}\right) \frac{p_1}{\rho_1} \left[1 - \left(\frac{p_2}{p_1}\right)^{\frac{\gamma - 1}{\gamma}}\right]} \quad \text{...[Eqn. (15.46)]}$$

where, $\rho_1 = \dfrac{p_1}{RT_1}$ (From equation of state : $\dfrac{p}{\rho} = RT$)

$$= \frac{2500 \times 10^3}{287 \times 293} = 29.73 \text{ kg/m}^3$$

Substituting the values in the above equation, we get:

$$V_2 = \sqrt{\left(\frac{2 \times 1.4}{1.4 - 1}\right) \times \frac{2500 \times 10^3}{29.73} \left[1 - \left(\frac{1750}{2500}\right)^{\frac{1.4 - 1}{1.4}}\right]}$$

$$= \sqrt{7 \times 84090\,(1 - 0.903)} = 238.9 \text{ m/s}$$

i.e. V_2 = **238.9 m/s (Ans.)**

Example 15.19. *A tank fitted with a convergent nozzle contains air at a temperature of 20 °C. The diameter at the outlet of the nozzle is 25 mm. Assuming adiabatic flow, find the mass rate of flow of air through the nozzle to the atmosphere when the pressure in the tank is :*

(i) *140 kN/m² (abs.);* **(ii)** *300 kN/m².*

Take for air : R = 287 J/kg K and γ = 1.4. Barometric pressure = 100 kN/m²

Solution. Temperature of air in the tank,

$$T_1 = 20 + 273 = 293 \text{ K}$$

Diameter at the outlet of the nozzle,

$$D_2 = 25 \text{ mm} = 0.025 \text{ m}$$

$$\text{Area, } A_2 = \frac{\pi}{4} \times 0.025^2 = 0.0004908 \text{ m}^2$$

$$R = 287 \text{ J/kg K}, \gamma = 1.4$$

(*i*) Mass rate of flow of air when pressure in the tank is 140 kN/m² (abs.), m :

$$\rho_1 = \frac{p_1}{RT_1} = \frac{140 \times 10^3}{287 \times 293} = 1.665 \text{ kg/m}^3$$

$$p_1 = 140 \text{ kN/m}^2 \text{ (abs.)}$$

$$\text{Pressure at the nozzle, } p_2 = \text{Atmospheric pressure} = 100 \text{ kN/m}^2$$

$$\therefore \quad \text{Pressure ratio, } \frac{p_2}{p_1} = \frac{100}{140} = 0.7143$$

Since the pressure ratio is more than the critical value, flow in the nozzle will be *subsonic*, hence mass rate of flow of air is given by eqn. 15.47, as:

$$m = A_2 \sqrt{\frac{2\gamma}{\gamma - 1} p_1 \rho_1 \left[\left(\frac{p_2}{p_1}\right)^{\frac{2}{\gamma}} - \left(\frac{p_2}{p_1}\right)^{\frac{\gamma+1}{\gamma}} \right]}$$

$$= 0.0004908 \sqrt{\left(\frac{2 \times 1.4}{1.4 - 1}\right) \times 140 \times 10^3 \times 1.665 \left[(0.7143)^{\frac{2}{1.4}} - (0.7143)^{\frac{1.4+1}{1.4}} \right]}$$

$$= 0.0004908 \sqrt{1631700 \, (0.7143)^{1.4285} - (0.7143)^{1.7142}}$$

$$\text{or,} \quad m = 0.0004908 \sqrt{1631700 \, (0.6184 - 0.5617)} = \mathbf{0.1493 \text{ kg/s}} \quad \textbf{(Ans.)}$$

(*ii*) Mass rate of flow of air when pressure in the tank is 300 kN/m² (abs.) :

$$p_1 = 300 \text{ kN/m}^2 \text{ (abs.)}$$

$$p_2 = \text{Pressure at the nozzle} = \text{atmospheric pressure} = 100 \text{ kN/m}^2$$

$$\therefore \quad \text{Pressure ratio, } \frac{p_2}{p_1} = \frac{100}{300} = 0.33$$

The pressure ratio being less than the critical ratio 0.528, the flow in the nozzle will be *sonic*, the flow rate is *maximum* and is given by eqn. (5.51), as:

$$m_{max} = 0.685 \, A_2 \sqrt{p_1 \rho_1}$$

$$\text{where,} \quad \rho_1 = \frac{p_1}{RT_1} = \frac{300 \times 10^3}{287 \times 293} = 3{\cdot}567 \text{ kg/m}^3$$

$$m_{max} = 0.685 \times 0.0004908 \sqrt{300 \times 10^3 \times 3.567} = \mathbf{0.3477 \text{ kg/s}} \quad \textbf{(Ans.)}$$

Example 15.20. *At some section in the convergent-divergent nozzle, in which air is flowing, pressure, velocity, temperature and cross-sectional area are 200 kN/m², 170 m/s, 200°C and 1000 mm² respectively. If the flow conditions are isentropic, determine :*

(i) Stagnation temperature and stagnation pressure.

(ii) Sonic velocity and Mach number at this section.

(iii) *Velocity, Mach number and flow area at outlet section where pressure is 110 kN/m^2.*

(iv) *Pressure, temperature, velocity and flow area at throat of the nozzle.*

Take for air : $R = 287$ J/kg K, $c_p = 1.0$ kJ/kg K, and $\gamma = 1.4$.

Solution. Let subscripts 1, 2 and t refer to the conditions at given section, outlet section and throat section of the nozzle respectively.

Pressure in the nozzle, $p_1 = 200$ kN/m^2

Velocity of air, $V_1 = 170$ m/s

Temperature, $T_1 = 200 + 273 = 473$ K

Cross-sectional area, $A_1 = 1000 \text{ mm}^2 = 1000 \times 10^{-6} = 0.001 \text{ m}^2$

For air : $R = 87$ J/kg K; $c_p = 1.0$ kJ/kg K; $\gamma = 1.4$

(*i*) Stagnation temperature (T_s) and stagnation pressure (p_s) :

$$\text{Stagnation temperature, } T_s = T_1 + \frac{V_1^2}{2 \times c_p}$$

$$= 473 + \frac{170^2}{2 \times (1.0 \times 1000)} = \mathbf{487.45\ K} \quad \textbf{(or 214.45°C) (Ans.)}$$

Also,
$$\frac{p_s}{p_1} = \left(\frac{T_s}{T_1}\right)^{\frac{\gamma}{\gamma-1}} = \left(\frac{487.45}{473}\right)^{\frac{1.4}{1.4-1}} = 1.111$$

$\therefore$ Stagnation pressure, $p_s = 200 \times 1.111 = \mathbf{222.2\ kN/m^2}$ **(Ans.)**

(*ii*) Sonic velocity and Mach number at this section :

$$\text{Sonic velocity, } C_1 = \sqrt{\gamma R T_1} = \sqrt{1.4 \times 287 \times 473} = \mathbf{435.9\ m/s} \textbf{ (Ans.)}$$

$$\text{Mach number, } M_1 = \frac{V_1}{C_1} = \frac{170}{435.9} = \mathbf{0.39} \textbf{ (Ans.)}$$

(*iii*) Velocity, Mach number and flow area at outlet section where pressure is 110 kN/m^2 :

Pressure at outlet section, $p_2 = 110$ kN/m^2 ...(*Given*)

From eqn (15.36),
$$\frac{p_s}{p_2} = \left[1 + \left(\frac{\gamma-1}{2}\right) M_2^2\right]^{\frac{\gamma}{\gamma-1}}$$

$$\frac{222.2}{110} = \left[1 + \left(\frac{1.4-1}{2}\right) M_2^2\right]^{\frac{1.4}{1.4-1}} = (1 + 0.2\, M_0^2)^{3.5}$$

or,
$$(1 + 0.2\, M_2^2) = \left(\frac{222.2}{110}\right)^{\frac{1}{3.5}} = 1.222$$

or,
$$M_2 = \left(\frac{1.222 - 1}{0.2}\right)^{1/2} = \mathbf{1.05} \textbf{ (Ans.)}$$

Also,
$$\frac{T_2}{T_s} = \left(\frac{p_2}{p_s}\right)^{\frac{\gamma-1}{\gamma}} = \left(\frac{110}{222.2}\right)^{\frac{1.4-1}{1.4}} = 0.818$$

or, $T_2 = 0.818 \times 487.45 = 398.7$ K

Sonic velocity at outlet section, $C_2 = \sqrt{\gamma R T_2} = \sqrt{1.4 \times 287 \times 398.7} = 400.25$ m/s

$\therefore$ Velocity at outlet section, $V_2 = M_2 \times C_2 = 1.05 \times 400.25 = \mathbf{420.26\ m/s}$ **(Ans.)**

Now, Mass flow at the given section = Mass flow at outlet section (exit)

... *Continuity equation*

i.e. $$\rho_1 A_1 V_1 = \rho_2 A_2 V_2 \quad \text{or} \quad \frac{p_1}{RT_1} A_1 V_1 = \frac{p_2}{RT_2} A_2 V_2$$

∴ Flow area at the outlet section,

$$A_2 = \frac{p_1 A_1 V_1 T_2}{T_1 p_1 V_2} = \frac{200 \times 0.001 \times 170 \times 398.7}{473 \times 110 \times 420.26}$$

$$= 6.199 \times 10^{-4} \text{ m}^2$$

Hence, $A_2 = 6.199 \times 10^{-4}$ m^2 or **619.9 mm^2 (Ans.)**

***(iv)* Pressure (p_t), temperature (T_t), velocity (V_t), and flow area (A_t) at throat of the nozzle :**

At throat, *critical conditions prevail, i.e.* the flow velocity becomes *equal to the sonic velocity* and *Mach number attains* a unit value.

From eqn. (15.41), $$\frac{T_s}{T_t} = \left[1 + \left(\frac{\gamma - 1}{2}\right) M_t^2\right]$$

or, $$\frac{487.45}{T_t} \left[1 + \left(\frac{1.4-1}{2}\right) \times 1^2\right] = 1.2 \quad \text{or} \quad T_t = 406.2 \text{ K}$$

Hence, T_t = **406.2 K (or 133.2°C) (Ans.)**

Also, $$\frac{p_t}{p_s} = \left(\frac{T_t}{T_s}\right)^{\frac{\gamma}{\gamma - 1}}$$

or, $$\frac{p_t}{222.2} = \left(\frac{406.2}{487.45}\right)^{\frac{1.4}{1.4-1}} = 0.528$$

or, $p_t = 222.2 \times 0.528 =$ **117.32 kN/m^2 (Ans.)**

Sonic velocity (corresponding to throat conditions),

$$C_t = \sqrt{\gamma R T_t} = \sqrt{1.4 \times 287 \times 406.2} = 404 \text{ m/s}$$

∴ Flow velocity, $V_t = M_t \times C_t = 1 \times 404 = 404$ m/s

By continuity equation, we have :

$$\rho_1 A_1 V_1 = \rho_t A_t V_t$$

or, $$\frac{p_1}{RT_1} A_1 V_1 = \frac{p_t}{RT_t} A_t V_t$$

∴ Flow area at throat, $$A_t = \frac{p_1 A_1 V_1 T_t}{T_1 p_t V_t} = \frac{200 \times 0.001 \times 170 \times 406.2}{473 \times 117.32 \times 404} = 6.16 \times 10^{-4} \text{ m}^2$$

Hence, $A_t = 6.16 \times 10^{-4}$ m^2 or **616 mm^2 (Ans.)**

15.13. SHOCK WAVES

Whenever a supersonic flow (compressible) abruptly changes to subsonic flow, a shock wave (analogous to hydraulic jump in an open channel) *is produced, resulting in a sudden rise in pressure, density, temperature and entropy.* This occurs due to pressure differentials and when the Mach number of the approaching flow $M_1 > 1$. A shock wave is a pressure wave of finite thickness, of the order of 10^{-2} to 10^{-4} mm in the atmospheric pressure. A shock wave takes place in the *diverging section of a nozzle, in a diffuser, throat of a supersonic wind tunnel, in front of sharp-nosed bodies.*

Shock waves are of two types :

1. Normal shocks which are almost perpendicular to the flow.
2. Oblique shocks which are inclined to the flow direction.

15.13.1 Normal shock wave

Consider a duct having a compressible sonic flow (See Fig. 15.13)

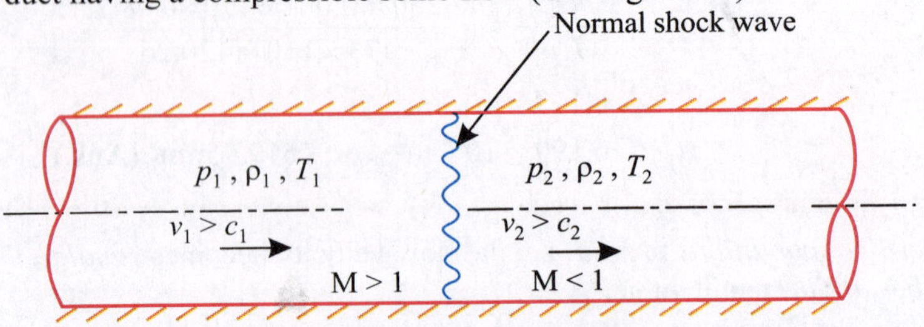

Fig. 15.13. Normal shock wave.

Let p_1, ρ_1, T_1, and V_1 be the pressure, density, temperature and velocity of the flow ($M_1 > 1$) and p_2, ρ_2, T_2 and V_2 the corresponding values of pressure, density, temperature and velocity after a shock wave takes place ($M_2 < 1$).

For analysing a normal shock wave, use will be made of the *continuity, momentum* and *energy equations*.

Assume unit area cross-section, $A_1 = A_2 = 1$.

Continuity equation : $$m = \rho_1 V_1 = \rho_2 V_2 \quad ...(i)$$

Momentum equation : $$\Sigma F_x = p_1 A_1 - p_2 A_2 = m(V_2 - V_1) = \rho_2 A_2 V_2^2 - \rho_1 A_1 V_1^2$$

for $A_1 = A_2 = 1$, the pressure drop across the shock wave,

$$p_1 - p_2 = \rho_2 V_2^2 - \rho_1 V_1^2 \quad ...(ii)$$

$$p_1 + \rho_1 V_1^2 = p_2 + \rho_2 V_2^2$$

Consider the flow across the shock wave as adiabatic.

Energy equation : $$\left(\frac{\gamma}{\gamma - 1}\right)\frac{p_1}{\rho_1} + \frac{V_1^2}{2} = \left(\frac{\gamma}{\gamma - 1}\right)\frac{p_2}{\rho_2} + \frac{V_2^2}{2} \quad ...[\text{Eqn. (15.26)}]$$

($z_1 = z_2$, duct being in horizontal position)

or, $$\frac{\gamma}{\gamma - 1}\left(\frac{p_2}{\rho_2} - \frac{p_1}{\rho_1}\right) = \frac{V_1^2 - V_2^2}{2} \quad ...(iii)$$

Combining continuity and momentum equations [refer to eqns. (*i*) and (*ii*)], we get:

$$p_1 + \frac{(\rho_1 V_1)^2}{\rho_1} = p_2 + \frac{(\rho_2 V_2)^2}{\rho_2} \quad ...(15.60)$$

This equation is known as **Rankine Line Equation.**

Now combining continuity and energy equations [refer to eqns. (*i*) and (*iii*)], we get:

$$\frac{\gamma}{\gamma - 1}\left(\frac{p_1}{\rho_1}\right) + \frac{(\rho_1 V_1)^2}{2\rho_1^2} = \frac{\gamma}{\gamma - 1}\left(\frac{p_2}{\rho_2}\right) + \frac{(\rho_2 V_2)^2}{2\rho_2^2} \quad ...(15.61)$$

This equation is called **Fanno Line Equation.**

Further combining eqns. (*i*), (*ii*) and (*iii*) and solving for $\frac{p_2}{p_1}$, we get:

$$\frac{p_2}{p_1} = \frac{\left(\frac{\gamma+1}{\gamma-1}\right)\frac{\rho_2}{\rho_1} - 1}{\left(\frac{\gamma+1}{\gamma-1}\right) - \frac{\rho_2}{\rho_1}} \qquad ...(15.62)$$

Solving for density ratio $\frac{\rho_2}{\rho_1}$, the same equations yield:

$$\frac{\rho_2}{\rho_1} = \frac{V_1}{V_2} = \frac{1 + \left(\frac{\gamma+1}{\gamma-1}\right)\frac{p_2}{p_1}}{\left(\frac{\gamma+1}{\gamma-1}\right) + \frac{p_2}{p_1}} \qquad ...(15.63)$$

The eqns. (15.62) and (15.63) are called **Rankine-Hugoniot equations.**

One can also express $\frac{p_2}{p_1}, \frac{V_2}{V_1}, \frac{\rho_2}{\rho_1}$ and $\frac{T_2}{T_1}$ in terms of Mach number as follows :

$$\frac{p_2}{p_1} = \frac{2\gamma M_1^2 - (\gamma - 1)}{(\gamma + 1)} \qquad ...(15.64)$$

$$\frac{V_1}{V_2} = \frac{\rho_2}{\rho_1} = \frac{(\gamma+1) M_1^2}{(\gamma-1) M_1^2 + 2} \qquad ...(15.65)$$

$$\frac{T_2}{T_1} = \frac{[(\gamma-1) M_1^2 + 2][2\gamma M_1^2 - (\gamma-1)]}{(\gamma+1)^2 M_1^2} \qquad ...(15.66)$$

By algebraic manipulation the following equation between M_1 and M_2 can be obtained:

$$M_2^2 = \frac{(\gamma-1) M_1^2 + 2}{2\gamma M_1^2 - (\gamma-1)} \qquad ...(15.67)$$

Example 15.21. *For a normal shock wave in air Mach number is 2. If the atmospheric pressure and air density are 26.5 kN/m² and 0.413 kg/m³ respectively, determine the flow conditions before and after the shock wave. Take γ = 1.4.*

Solution. Let subscripts 1 and 2 represent the flow conditions before and after the shock wave.

Mach number, $M_1 = 2$

Atmospheric pressure, $p_1 = 26.5 \text{ kN/m}^2$

Air density, $\rho_1 = 0.413 \text{ kg/m}^3$.

Mach number, M_2 :

$$M_2^2 = \frac{(\gamma-1) M_1^2 + 2}{2\gamma M_1^2 - (\gamma-1)} \qquad ...[\text{Eqn. 15.67})]$$

$$= \frac{(1.4-1)\times 2^2 + 2}{2\times 1.4 \times 2^2 - (1.4-1)} = \frac{3.6}{11.2 - 0.4} = 0.333$$

$\therefore$ $M_2 = \mathbf{0.577}$ **(Ans.)**

Pressure, p_2 :

$$\frac{p_2}{p_1} = \frac{2\gamma M_1^2 - (\gamma-1)}{(\gamma+1)} \qquad ...[\text{Eqn. (15.64)}]$$

$$= \frac{2\times 1.4\times 2^2 - (1.4-1)}{(1.4+1)} = \frac{11.2 - 0.4}{2.4} = 4.5$$

$\therefore$ $p_2 = 26.5 \times 4.5 = \mathbf{119.25 \text{ kN/m}^2}$ **(Ans.)**

Density, ρ_2 :

$$\frac{\rho_2}{\rho_1} = \frac{(\gamma+1)\,M_1^2}{(\gamma-1)\,M_1^2+2} \qquad \text{...[Eqn. (15.65)]}$$

$$= \frac{(1.4+1)\,2^2}{(1.4-1)\,2^2+2} = \frac{9.6}{1.6+2} = 2.667$$

$\therefore$ $$\rho = 0.413 \times 2.667 = \mathbf{1.101\ kg/m^3}\ \textbf{(Ans.)}$$

Temperature, T_1:

Since, $$p_1 = \rho_1 RT_1,$$

$\therefore$ $$T_1 = \frac{p_1}{\rho_1 R} = \frac{26.5 \times 10^3}{0.413 \times 287} = 223.6\ \text{K} \quad \text{or} \quad \mathbf{-49.4°C}\ \textbf{(Ans.)}$$

Temperature, T_2:

$$\frac{T_2}{T_1} = \frac{[(\gamma-1)\,M_1^2+2]\,[2\gamma M_1^2-(\gamma-1)]}{(\gamma+1)^2\,M_1^2}$$

$$= \frac{[(1.4-1)\,2^2+2]\,[2 \times 1.4 \times 2^2-(1.4-1)]}{(1.4+1)^2 \times 2^2}$$

$$= \frac{(1.6+2)\,(11.2-0.4)}{23.04} = 1.6875$$

$\therefore$ $$T_2 = 223.6 \times 1.6875 = 377.3\ \text{K} \quad \text{or} \quad \mathbf{104.3°C}\ \textbf{(Ans.)}$$

Velocity, V_1 :

$$C_1 = \sqrt{\gamma RT_1} = \sqrt{1.4 \times 287 \times 223.6} = 299.7\ \text{m/s}$$

Since $$\frac{V_1}{C_1} = M_1 = 2$$

$\therefore$ $$V_1 = 299.7 \times 2 = \mathbf{599.4\ m/s}\ \textbf{(Ans.)}$$

Velocity, V_2 :

$$C_2 = \sqrt{\gamma RT_2} = \sqrt{1.4 \times 287 \times 377.3} = 389.35\ \text{m/s}$$

Since, $$\frac{V_2}{C_2} = M_2 = 0.577$$

$\therefore$ $$V_2 = 389.35 \times 0.577 = \mathbf{224.6\ m/s}\ \textbf{(Ans.)}$$

15.13.2. Oblique Shock Wave

As shown in Fig. 15.14, when a supersonic flow undergoes a sudden turn through a small angle α (positive), an oblique wave is established at the corner. In comparison with normal shock waves, the *oblique shock waves, being weaker, are preferred.*

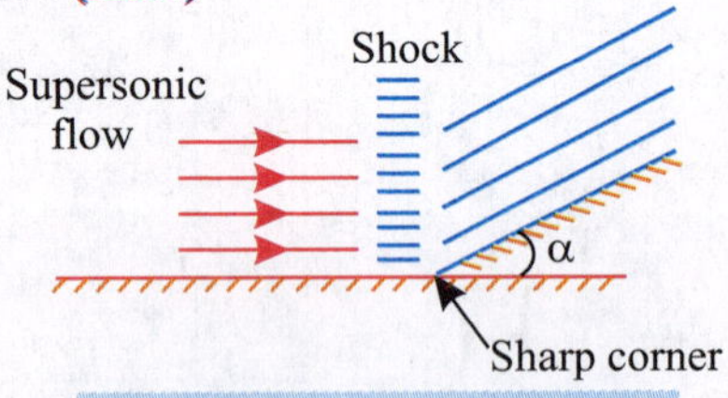

Fig. 15.14. Oblique shock wave.

The shock waves should be avoided or made as weak as possible, since during a shock wave conversion of mechanical energy into heat energy takes place.

15.13.3. Shock Strength

The **strength of shock** *is defined as the ratio of pressure rise across the shock to the upstream pressure.*

i.e. Strength of shock $= \dfrac{p_2 - p_1}{p_1} = \dfrac{p_2}{p_1} - 1$

$$= \frac{2\gamma M_1^2 - (\gamma - 1)}{\gamma + 1} - 1 = \frac{2\gamma M_1^2 - (\gamma - 1) - (\gamma + 1)}{\gamma + 1}$$

$$= \frac{2\gamma M_1^2 - \gamma + 1 - \gamma - 1}{\gamma + 1} = \frac{2\gamma M_1^2 - 2\gamma}{\gamma + 1} = \frac{2\gamma}{\gamma + 1}(M_1^2 - 1)$$

Hence, *strength of shock* $= \dfrac{2\gamma}{\gamma + 1}(M_1^2 - 1)$ ...(15.68)

Example 15.22. *In a duct in which air is flowing, a normal shock wave occurs at a Mach number of 1.5 . The static pressure and temperature upstream of the shock wave are 170 kN/m² and 23°C respectively. Determine :*

(i) Pressure, temperature and Mach number downstream of the shock, and

(ii) Strength of shock.

Take $\gamma = 1.4$

Solution. Let subscripts 1 and 2 represent flow conditions upstream and downstream of the shock wave respectively.

Mach number, $M_1 = 1.5$

Upstream pressure, $p_1 = 170$ kN/m²

Upstream temperature, $T_1 = 23 + 273 = 296$ K

$\gamma = 1.4$

(*i*) Pressure, temperature and Mach number downstream of the shock :

$$\frac{p_2}{p_1} = \frac{2\gamma M_1^2 - (\gamma - 1)}{\gamma + 1} \quad \text{...[Eqn. (15.64)]}$$

$$= \frac{2 \times 1.4 \times 1.5^2 - (1.4 - 1)}{1.4 + 1} = \frac{6.3 - 0.4}{2.4} = 2.458$$

$\therefore$ $p_2 = 170 \times 2.458 =$ **417.86 kN/m² (Ans.)**

$$\frac{T_2}{T_1} = \frac{[(\gamma - 1)M_1^2 + 2][2\gamma M_1^2 - (\gamma - 1)]}{(\gamma + 1)^2 M_1^2} \quad \text{...[Eqn. (15.66)]}$$

$$= \frac{[(1.4-1)\times 1.5^2 + 2][2\times 1.4\times 1.5^2 - (1.4-1)]}{(1.4 + 1)^2 \times 1.5^2} = \frac{2.9 \times 5.9}{12.96} = 1.32$$

$\therefore$ $T_2 = 296 \times 1.32 =$ **390.72 K** or **117.72°C (Ans.)**

$$M_2^2 = \frac{(\gamma - 1)M_1^2 + 2}{2\gamma M_1^2 - (\gamma - 1)} \quad \text{...[Eqn. (15.67)]}$$

$$= \frac{(1.4 - 1) \times 1.5^2 + 2}{2 \times 1.4 \times 1.5^2 - (1.4 - 1)} = \frac{2.9}{5.9} = 0.49$$

$\therefore$ $M_2 =$ **0.7 (Ans.)**

(*ii*) Strength of shock :

Strength of shock $= \dfrac{p_1}{p_2} - 1 = 2.458 - 1 =$ **1.458 (Ans.)**

15.14. MEASUREMENT OF COMPRESSIBLE FLOW

A. Measurement of discharge (flow rate) :

1. Convergent nozzle.
2. Orificemeter.
3. Convergent-divergent nozzle.
4. Venturimeter—If the *pressure drop* between the entrance and the throat is *small*, the flow computation may be made considering it as an *isothermal process*; if *pressure drop is appreciable*, the flow will be *adiabatic with a rapid fall of temperature at the throat :*

B. Measurement of velocity :

1. Pitot tube....*works on the principle of stagnation pressure.*
2. Hot-wire anemometer—*works on the principle that the rate of heat loss varies with the flow velocity;*
   — Particularly used in a *supersonic wind tunnel.*
   — Constant-current hot-wire anemometer, because of its high sensitivity, is especially suitable for flow in which velocity fluctuations are small.
   — Since it responds very rapidly to fluctuations of velocity it is widely used in conjunction with oscilloscopes and similar electronic instruments for measuring the intensity of turbulence.

C. Measurement of flow direction :

The instruments which may be used to determine both the magnitudes as well as the direction of the velocity are :

1. Pitot cylinder...suitable for determination of both magnitude and direction of velocity in a *two-dimensional flow.*
2. Pitot sphere....may be used to determine the magnitude and direction of the velocity in a *three-dimensional flow.*

15.15. FLOW OF COMPRESSIBLE FLUID THROUGH VENTURIMETER

Consider a compressible fluid thowing through a horizontal venturimeter. Let suffices 1 and 2 denote main and throat diameters of venturimeter respectively. Considering the flow to be *adiabatic*, we have:

$$\left(\frac{\gamma}{\gamma-1}\right)\frac{p_1}{\rho_1 g}+\frac{V_1^2}{2g}+z_1 = \left(\frac{\gamma}{\gamma-1}\right)\frac{p_2}{\rho_2 g}+\frac{V_2^2}{2g}+z_2 \quad \text{...[Eqn. (15.26)]}$$

Taking $z_1 = z_2$ (venturimeter being horizontal) and cancelling 'g' we get:

$$\left(\frac{\gamma}{\gamma-1}\right)\frac{p_1}{\rho_1}+\frac{V_1^2}{2} = \left(\frac{\gamma}{\gamma-1}\right)\frac{p_2}{\rho_2}+\frac{V_2^2}{2}$$

or,
$$\frac{\gamma}{\gamma-1}\left[\frac{p_1}{\rho_1}-\frac{p_2}{\rho_2}\right] = \frac{V_2^2}{2}-\frac{V_1^2}{2}$$

or,
$$\left(\frac{\gamma}{\gamma-1}\right)\frac{p_1}{\rho_1}\left[1-\frac{p_2}{\rho_2}\times\frac{\rho_1}{p_1}\right] = \frac{V_2^2}{2}-\frac{V_1^2}{2} \quad \text{...}(i)$$

For adiabatic flow :
$$\frac{p_1}{\rho_1^{\gamma}} = \frac{p_2}{\rho_2^{\gamma}}$$

$$\therefore \quad \frac{p_1}{p_2} = \left(\frac{\rho_1}{\rho_2}\right)^{\gamma}$$

$$\text{or,} \quad \frac{\rho_1}{\rho_2} = \left(\frac{p_1}{p_2}\right)^{\frac{1}{\gamma}} \quad \text{...(ii)}$$

Substituting this value of $\frac{\rho_1}{\rho_2}$ in eqn. (*i*), we get:

$$\text{or,} \quad \left(\frac{\gamma}{\gamma-1}\right)\frac{p_1}{\rho_1}\left[1 - \frac{p_2}{p_1} \times \left(\frac{p_2}{p_1}\right)^{-\frac{1}{\gamma}}\right] = \frac{V_2^2}{2} - \frac{V_1^2}{2}$$

$$\text{or,} \quad \left(\frac{\gamma}{\gamma-1}\right)\frac{p_1}{\rho_1}\left[1 - \left(\frac{p_2}{p_1}\right)^{1-\frac{1}{\gamma}}\right] = \frac{V_2^2}{2} - \frac{V_1^2}{2}$$

$$\text{or,} \quad \left(\frac{\gamma}{\gamma-1}\right)\frac{p_1}{\rho_1}\left[1 - \left(\frac{p_2}{p_1}\right)^{\frac{\gamma-1}{\gamma}}\right] = \frac{V_2^2}{2} - \frac{V_1^2}{2} \quad \text{...(iii)}$$

$$\text{Also,} \quad \rho_1 A_1 V_1 = \rho_2 A_2 V_2 \quad \text{...Continuity equation}$$

$$\therefore \quad V_1 = \frac{\rho_2 A_2 V_2}{\rho_1 A_1}$$

Substituting the value of V_1 in eqn. (*iii*), we get:

$$\left(\frac{\gamma}{\gamma-1}\right)\frac{p_1}{\rho_1}\left[1 - \left(\frac{p_2}{p_1}\right)^{\frac{\gamma-1}{\gamma}}\right] = \frac{V_2^2}{2} - \left(\frac{\rho_2 A_2 V_2}{\rho_1 A_1}\right)^2 \times \frac{1}{2} = \frac{V_2^2}{2}\left[1 - \frac{\rho_2^2 A_2^2}{\rho_1^2 A_1^2}\right] \quad \text{...(iv)}$$

$$\text{But from eqn. (ii)} \quad \left(\frac{\rho_2}{\rho_1}\right)^2 = \left(\frac{p_2}{p_1}\right)^{2/\gamma}$$

Substituting this value in eqn. (*iv*), we get:

$$\left(\frac{\gamma}{\gamma-1}\right)\frac{p_1}{\rho_1}\left[1 - \left(\frac{p_2}{p_1}\right)^{\frac{\gamma-1}{\gamma}}\right] = \frac{V_2^2}{2}\left[1 - \left(\frac{p_2}{p_1}\right)^{\frac{2}{\gamma}} \times \frac{A_2^2}{A_1^2}\right] \quad \text{...(iv)}$$

$$\therefore \quad V_2^2 = \frac{\left(\frac{2\gamma}{\gamma-1}\right)\frac{p_1}{\rho_1}\left[1 - \left(\frac{p_2}{p_1}\right)^{\frac{\gamma-1}{\gamma}}\right]}{\left[1 - \left(\frac{p_2}{p_1}\right)^{\frac{2}{\gamma}} \times \frac{A_2^2}{A_1^2}\right]}$$

$$\therefore \quad V_2 = \sqrt{\frac{\left(\frac{2\gamma}{\gamma-1}\right)\frac{p_1}{\rho_1}\left[1 - \left(\frac{p_2}{p_1}\right)^{\frac{\gamma-1}{\gamma}}\right]}{1 - \left(\frac{p_2}{p_1}\right)^{\frac{2}{\gamma}} \times \frac{A_2^2}{A_1^2}}}$$

∴ Mass rate of flow through venturimeter,

$$m = \rho_2 A_2 V_2 = \rho_2 A_2 \sqrt{\frac{\left(\frac{2\gamma}{\gamma-1}\right)\frac{p_1}{\rho_1}\left[1-\left(\frac{p_2}{p_1}\right)^{\frac{\gamma-1}{\gamma}}\right]}{1-\left(\frac{p_2}{p_1}\right)^{\frac{2}{\gamma}}\times\left(\frac{A_2}{A_1}\right)^2}} \quad \text{...(15.69)}$$

Example 15.23. *Find the mass rate of flow of air through a venturimeter having inlet diameter 300 mm and throat diameter 150 mm. The pressure and temperature of air at inlet section of the venturimeter are 137 kN/m² absolute and 15°C respectively, and the pressure at the throat is 127 kN/m² absolute. Take R = 287 J/kg K and adiabatic exponent γ = 1.4.* **[Delhi University]**

Solution. Let suffices 1 and 2 represent the conditions at the inlet and throat sections of venturimeter.

Diameter at inlet, $D_1 = 300 \text{ mm} = 0.3 \text{ m}$

∴ Area, $A_1 = \frac{\pi}{4} \times 0.3^2 = 0.07068 \text{ m}^2$

Diameter of throat, $D_2 = 150 \text{ mm} = 0.15 \text{ m}$

∴ Area, $A_2 = \frac{\pi}{4} \times 0.15^2 = 0.01767 \text{ m}^2$

Pressure, $p_1 = 137 \text{ kN/m}^2$ (*abs.*)

Temperature, $T_1 = 15 + 273 = 288 \text{ K}$

Pressure, $p_2 = 127 \text{ kN/m}^2$

$R = 287 \text{ J/kg K}, \gamma = 1.4$

Mass rate of flow, m :

$$\rho_1 = \frac{p_1}{RT_1} = \frac{137 \times 10^3}{287 \times 288} = 1.657 \text{ kg/m}^3$$

$$\frac{\rho_2}{\rho_1} = \left(\frac{p_2}{p_1}\right)^{\frac{1}{\gamma}}$$

or,

$$\rho_2 = \rho_1 \times \left(\frac{p_2}{p_1}\right)^{\frac{1}{\gamma}} = 1.657 \times \left(\frac{127}{137}\right)^{\frac{1}{1.4}} = 1.57 \text{ kg/m}^3$$

Mass flow rate through a venturimeter is given by:

$$m = \rho_2 A_2 \sqrt{\frac{\left(\frac{2\gamma}{\gamma-1}\right)\frac{p_1}{\rho_1}\left[1-\left(\frac{p_2}{p_1}\right)^{\frac{\gamma-1}{\gamma}}\right]}{1-\left(\frac{p_2}{p_1}\right)^{\frac{2}{\gamma}}\times\left(\frac{A_2}{A_1}\right)^2}} \quad \text{...[Eqn. (15.69)]}$$

$$m = 1.57 \times 0.01767 \sqrt{\frac{\left(\frac{2\times1.4}{1.4-1}\right)\times\frac{137\times10^3}{1.657}\left[1-\left(\frac{127}{137}\right)^{\frac{1.4-1}{1.4}}\right]}{1-\left(\frac{127}{137}\right)^{\frac{2}{1.4}}\times\left(\frac{0.01767}{0.07068}\right)^2}}$$

or, $$m = 0.02774\sqrt{\frac{7\times 82.68\times 10^3(1-.09786)}{1-0.897\times 0.0625}} = \mathbf{3.177\ kg/s}\ \textbf{(Ans.)}$$

HIGHLIGHTS

1. A compressible flow is that flow in which the density of the fluid changes during flow.

2. The characteristic equation of state is given by :

$$\frac{p}{\rho} = RT$$

where, p = Absolute pressure, N/m^2,
ρ = Density of gas, kg/m^3,
R = Characteristic gas constant, J/kg K, and
R = Absolute temperature (= t°C + 273).

3. The pressure and density of a gas are related as :

For isothermal process $\frac{p}{\rho}$ = constant

For adiabatic process : $\frac{p}{\rho^\gamma}$ = constant

4. The continuity equation for compressible flow is given as :

$$\rho AV = \text{constant}$$

$$\frac{d\rho}{\rho} + \frac{dA}{A} + \frac{dV}{V} = 0 \qquad \text{...in differential form.}$$

5. For compressible fluids Bernoulli's equation is given as :

$$\frac{p}{\rho g}\ln(p) + \frac{V^2}{2g} + z = \text{constant} \qquad \text{... for isothermal process}$$

$$\left(\frac{\gamma}{\gamma-1}\right)\frac{p}{\rho g} + \frac{V^2}{2g} + z = \text{constant} \qquad \text{... for adiabatic process}$$

6. Sonic velocity is given by :

$$C = \sqrt{\frac{dp}{d\rho}} = \sqrt{\frac{K}{\rho}} \qquad \text{... in terms of bulk modulus}$$

$$C = \sqrt{\frac{p}{\rho}} = \sqrt{RT} \qquad \text{... for isothermal process}$$

$$C = \sqrt{\frac{\gamma p}{\rho}} = \sqrt{\gamma RT} \qquad \text{... for adiabatic process.}$$

7. Mach number, $M = \frac{V}{C}$

(*i*) Subsonic flow : $M < 1$, $V < C$ ... disturbance always moves ahead of the projectile
(*ii*) Sonic flow : $M = 1$, $V = C$ ... disturbance moves along the projectile
(*iii*) Supersonic flow : $M > 1$, $V > C$ ... The projectile always moves ahead of the disturbance.

Mach angle is given by: $\sin\alpha = \frac{C}{V} = \frac{1}{M}$

8. The pressure, temperature and density at a point where velocity is zero are called stagnation pressure (p_s), temperature, (T_s) and stagnation density ρ_s. Their values are given as :

$$p_s = p_0 \left[1 + \left(\frac{\gamma - 1}{2}\right) M_0^2\right]^{\frac{\gamma}{\gamma - 1}}$$

$$\rho_s = \rho_0 \left[1 + \left(\frac{\gamma - 1}{2}\right) M_0^2\right]^{\frac{1}{\gamma - 1}}$$

$$T_s = T_0 \left[1 + \left(\frac{\gamma - 1}{2}\right) M_0^2\right]$$

where p_0, ρ_0 and T_0 are the pressure, density and temperature at any point O in the flow.

9. Area-velocity relationship for compressible fluid is given as :

$$\frac{dA}{A} = \frac{dV}{V}(M^2 - 1)$$

(*i*) Subsonic flow ($M < 1$) : $\frac{dV}{V} > 0; \frac{dA}{A} < 0; dp < 0$ (convergent nozzle)

$\frac{dV}{V} < 0; \frac{dA}{A} > 0; dp > 0$ (divergent diffuser)

(*ii*) Supersonic flow ($M > 1$) : $\frac{dV}{V} > 0; \frac{dA}{A} > 0; dp < 0$ (divergent nozzle)

$\frac{dV}{V} < 0; \frac{dA}{A} < 0; dp > 0$ (convergent diffuser)

(*iii*) Sonic flow ($M = 1$) : $\frac{dA}{A} = 0$ (straight flow passage since dA must be zero)

$dp = \frac{zero}{zero}$ *i.e.* indeterminate, but when evaluated, the change of pressure $dp = 0$, since $dA = 0$ and the flow is frictionless.

10. Flow of compressible fluid through a convergent nozzle :

(*i*) Velocity through a nozzle or orifice fitted to a large tank :

$$V_2 = \sqrt{\left(\frac{2\gamma}{\gamma - 1}\right)\frac{p_1}{\rho_1}\left[1 - \left(\frac{p_2}{p_1}\right)^{\frac{\gamma}{\gamma - 1}}\right]}$$

(*ii*) The mass rate of flow is given by :

$$m = A_2 \sqrt{\left(\frac{2\gamma}{\gamma - 1}\right) p_1 \rho_1 \left[\left(\frac{p_2}{p_1}\right)^{\frac{2}{\gamma}} - \left(\frac{p_2}{p_1}\right)^{\frac{\gamma + 1}{\gamma}}\right]}$$

(*iii*) Value of $\left(\frac{p_2}{p_1}\right)$ for maximum value of mass rate of flow is given by :

$$\left(\frac{p_2}{p_1}\right) = \left(\frac{2}{\gamma + 1}\right)^{\frac{\gamma}{\gamma - 1}} = 0.528 \quad (\text{when } \gamma = 1.4)$$

(*iv*) Value of V_2 for maximum rate of flow of liquid is given as:

$$V_2 = \sqrt{\left(\frac{2\gamma}{\gamma + 1}\right)\frac{p_1}{\rho_1}} \; (= C_2)$$

(*v*) Maximum rate of flow of fluid through nozzle,

$$m_{max} = A_2 \sqrt{\left(\frac{2\gamma}{\gamma - 1}\right) p_1\rho_1 \left[\left(\frac{2}{\gamma + 1}\right)^{\frac{2}{\gamma - 1}} - \left(\frac{2}{\gamma + 1}\right)^{\frac{\gamma + 1}{\gamma - 1}}\right]}$$

For air, substituting $\gamma = 1.4$, we get:

$$m_{max} = 0.685\, A_2 \sqrt{p_1\rho_1}$$

If the pressure ratio is less than 0.528, the mass rate of flow of the fluid is always corresponding to the pressure ratio of 0.528. But if the pressure ratio is more than 0.528, the mass rate of flow of fluid is corresponding to the given pressure ratio.

11. Whenever a supersonic flow (compressible) changes to subsonic flow, a shock wave (analogous to hydraulic jump in an open channel) is produced, resulting in a sudden rise in pressure, density, temperature and entropy.

$$p_1 + \frac{(\rho_1 V_1)^2}{\rho_1} = p_2 + \frac{(\rho_2 V_2)^2}{\rho_2} \qquad \text{... Ranking Line Equation}$$

$$\frac{\gamma}{\gamma - 1}\left(\frac{p_1}{\rho_1}\right) + \frac{(\rho_1 V_1)^2}{2\rho_1^2} = \frac{\gamma}{\gamma - 1}\left(\frac{p_2}{\rho_2}\right) + \frac{(\rho_2 V_2)^2}{2\rho_2^2} \qquad \text{... Fanno Line Equation}$$

$$\left.\begin{aligned} \frac{p_2}{p_1} &= \frac{\left(\frac{\gamma + 1}{\gamma - 1}\right)\frac{\rho_2}{\rho_1} - 1}{\left(\frac{\gamma + 1}{\gamma - 1}\right) - \frac{\rho_2}{\rho_1}} \\ \frac{\rho_2}{\rho_1} = \frac{V_1}{V_2} &= \frac{1 + \left(\frac{\gamma + 1}{\gamma - 1}\right)\frac{p_2}{p_1}}{\left(\frac{\gamma + 1}{\gamma - 1}\right) + \frac{p_2}{p_1}} \end{aligned}\right\} \qquad \text{...Ranking-Hugoniot Equations}$$

One can also express $\frac{p_2}{p_1}, \frac{V_2}{V_1}, \frac{\rho_2}{\rho_1}$, and $\frac{T_2}{T_1}$ in terms of Mach number as follows :

$$\frac{p_2}{p_1} = \frac{2\gamma M_1^2 - (\gamma - 1)}{\gamma + 1} \qquad \text{...(i)}$$

$$\frac{V_1}{V_2} = \frac{\rho_2}{\rho_1} = \frac{(\gamma + 1)\, M_1^2}{(\gamma - 1)\, M_1^2 + 2} \qquad \text{...(ii)}$$

$$\frac{T_2}{T_1} = \frac{[(\gamma - 1)\, M_1^2 + 2]\,[2\gamma M_1^2 - (\gamma - 1)]}{(\gamma + 1)^2\, M_1^2} \qquad \text{...(iii)}$$

Also,

$$M_2^2 = \frac{(\gamma - 1)\, M_1^2 + 2}{2\gamma M_1^2 - (\gamma - 1)}$$

12. Mass rate of flow through venturimeter,

$$m = \rho_2 A_2 \sqrt{\frac{\left(\frac{2\gamma}{\gamma - 1}\right)\frac{p_1}{\rho_1}\left[1 - \left(\frac{p_2}{p_1}\right)^{\frac{\gamma - 1}{\gamma}}\right]}{1 - \left(\frac{p_2}{p_1}\right)^{\frac{2}{\gamma}} \times \left(\frac{A_2}{A_1}\right)^2}}$$

OBJECTIVE TYPE QUESTIONS

Choose the Correct Answer :

1. All real fluids are
   (*a*) incompressible
   (*b*) compressible to some extent
   (*c*) compressible to any extent
   (*d*) none of the above.
2. A change in the state of a system at constant volume is called
   (*a*) isobaric process
   (*b*) isochoric process
   (*c*) isothermal process
   (*d*) adiabatic process.
3. A process during which no heat is transferred to or from the gas is called an
   (*a*) isochoric process
   (*b*) isobaric process
   (*c*) adiabatic process
   (*d*) isothermal process.
4. An adiabatic process is one which follows the relation
   (*a*) $\frac{p}{\rho}$ = constant
   (*b*) $\frac{p}{\rho^\gamma}$ = constant
   (*c*) $\frac{p}{\rho^n}$ = constant ($n \neq \gamma$)
   (*d*) v = constant.
5. An isentropic flow is one which is
   (*a*) isothermal
   (*b*) adiabatic
   (*c*) adiabatic and irreversible
   (*d*) adiabatic and reversible.
6. Indicate upto what Mach number can a fluid flow be considered incompressible ?
   (*a*) 0·1 (*b*) 0·3
   (*c*) 0·8 (*d*) 1·0.
7. Which of the following is the basic equation of compressible fluid flow ?
   (*a*) Continuity equation
   (*b*) Momentum equation
   (*c*) Energy equation
   (*d*) Equation of state
   (*e*) All of the above.
8. The velocity of disturbance in case of fluids is ..... the velocity of the disturbance in solids.
   (*a*) less than (*b*) equal to
   (*c*) more than (*d*) none of the above.
9. Sonic velocity (*C*) for adiabatic process is given as
   (*a*) $C = \sqrt{\gamma RT^3}$ (*b*) $C = \sqrt{\gamma RT}$
   (*c*) $C = \sqrt{\gamma^2 RT}$ (*d*) $C = \gamma RT$.
   where γ = ratio of specific heats, R = gas constant, T = temperature.
10. The flow is said to be subsonic when Mach number is
    (*a*) equal to unity (*b*) less than unity
    (*c*) greater than unity (*d*) none of above.
11. The region outside the Mach cone is called
    (*a*) zone of action (*b*) zone of silence
    (*c*) control volume (*d*) none of the above.
12. A stagnation point is the point on the immersed body where the magnitude of velocity is
    (*a*) small (*b*) large
    (*c*) zero (*d*) none of the above.
13. A convergent-divergent nozzle is used when the discharge pressure is
    (*a*) less than the critical pressure
    (*b*) equal to the critical pressure
    (*c*) more than the critical pressure
    (*d*) none of the above.
14. At critical pressure ratio, the velocity at the throat of a nozzle is
    (*a*) equal to the sonic speed
    (*b*) less than the sonic speed
    (*c*) more than the sonic speed
    (*d*) none of the above.
15. Laval nozzle is a
    (*a*) convergent nozzle
    (*b*) divergent nozzle
    (*c*) convergent-divergent nozzle
    (*d*) any of the above.
16. A shock wave is produced when
    (*a*) a subsonic flow changes to sonic flow
    (*b*) a sonic flow changes to supersonic flow
    (*c*) a supersonic flow changes to subsonic flow
    (*d*) none of the above.
17. The sonic velocity in a fluid medium is directly proportional to
    (*a*) Mach number
    (*b*) pressure
    (*c*) square root of temperature
    (*d*) none of the above.

18. The stagnation pressure (p_s) and temperature (T_s) are
(*a*) less than their ambient counterparts
(*b*) more than their ambient counterparts
(*c*) the same as in ambient flow
(*d*) none of the above.

19. Across a normal shock
(*a*) the entropy remains constant
(*b*) the pressure and the temperature rise
(*c*) the velocity and pressure decrease
(*d*) the density and temperature decrease.

20. A normal shock wave
(*a*) is reversible
(*b*) is irreversible
(*c*) is isentropic
(*d*) occurs when approaching flow is supersonic.

21. The sonic speed in an ideal gas varies
(*a*) inversely as bulk modulus
(*b*) directly as the absolute pressure
(*c*) inversely as the absolute temperature
(*d*) none of the above.

22. In a supersonic flow, a diffuser is a conduit having
(*a*) gradually decreasing area
(*b*) converging-diverging passage
(*c*) constant area throughout its length
(*d*) none of the above.

23. Choking of a nozzle fitted to a pressure tank containing gas implies
(*a*) sonic velocity at the throat
(*b*) increase of the mass flow rate
(*c*) obstruction of flow
(*d*) all of the above.

24. A shock wave which occurs in a supersonic flow represents a region in which
(*a*) a zone of silence exists
(*b*) there is no change in pressure, tempera- ture and density
(*c*) there is sudden change in pressure, temperature and density
(*d*) velocity is zero.

25. Which of the following statements regarding a normal shock is correct ?
(*a*) It occurs when an abrupt change takes place from supersonic into subsonic flow condition
(*b*) It causes a disruption and reversal of flow pattern
(*c*) It may occur in sonic or supersonic flow
(*d*) None of the above.

26. For compressible fluid flow the area-velocity relationship is
(*a*) $\frac{dA}{A} = \frac{dV}{V}(1 - M^2)$
(*b*) $\frac{dA}{A} = \frac{dV}{V}(C^2 - 1)$
(*c*) $\frac{dA}{A} = \frac{dV}{V}(M^2 - 1)$
(*d*) $\frac{dA}{A} = \frac{dV}{V}(1 - V^2)$

27. The sonic velocity is largest in which of the following ?
(*a*) Water (*b*) Steel
(*c*) Kerosene (*d*) Air.

28. Which of the following expressions does not represent the speed of sound in a medium ?
(*a*) $\sqrt{\frac{K}{\rho}}$ (*b*) $\sqrt{\gamma RT}$
(*c*) $\sqrt{K\frac{p}{\rho}}$ (*d*) $\sqrt{\frac{dp}{d\rho}}$.

29. The differential for energy in isentropic flow is of the form
(*a*) $\frac{dV}{V} + \frac{dp}{\rho} + \frac{dA}{A} = 0$
(*b*) $VdV + \frac{dp}{\rho} = 0$
(*c*) $2VdV + \frac{dp}{\rho} = 0$
(*d*) $dp + d(\rho V^2) = 0$.

30. Which of the following statements is *incorrect* ?
(*a*) A shock wave occurs in divergent section of a nozzle when the compressible flow changes abruptly from supersonic to subsonic state.
(*b*) A plane moving at supersonic state is not heard by the stationary observer on the ground until it passes him because zone of disturbance in Mach cone trails behind the plane
(*c*) A divergent section is added to a convergent nozzle to obtain supersonic velocity at the throat.
(*d*) none of above.

ANSWERS

1. (*b*)	2. (*b*)	3. (*c*)	4. (*b*)	5. (*d*)	6. (*b*)
7. (*e*)	8. (*a*)	9. (*b*)	10. (*b*)	11. (*b*)	12. (*c*)
13. (*a*)	14. (*a*)	15. (*c*)	16. (*c*)	17. (*c*)	18. (*b*)
19. (*b*)	20. (*d*)	21. (*d*)	22. (*a*)	23. (*d*)	24. (*c*)
25. (*a*)	26. (*c*)	27. (*b*)	28. (*c*)	29. (*b*)	30. (*c*).

THEORETICAL QUESTIONS

1. Differentiate between compressible and incompressible flows.
2. Give the examples when liquid is treated as a compressible fluid.
3. When is the compressibility of fluid important ?
4. What is the difference between isentropic and adiabatic flows ?
5. What is the relation between pressure and density of a compressible fluid for (*a*) isothermal process (*b*) adiabatic process ?
6. Obtain an expression in differential form for continuity equation for one-dimensional compressible flow.
7. Derive an expression for Bernoulli's equation when the process is adiabatic.
8. How are the disturbances in compressible fluid propagated ?
9. What is sonic velocity ? On what factors does it depend ?
10. What is Mach number ? Why is this parameter so important for the study of flow of compressible fluids ?
11. Prove that velocity of sound wave in a compressible fluid is given by : $C = \sqrt{k/\rho}$ where, k and ρ are the bulk modulus and density of fluid respectively.
12. Define the following terms :
    (*i*) Subsonic flow (*ii*) Sonic flow
    (*iii*) Supersonic flow (*iv*) Mach cone.
13. What is silence zone during the disturbance which propagates when an object moves in still air ?
14. What is stagnation point of an object immersed in fluid ?
15. What is stagnation pressure ?
16. What are static and stagnation temperatures ?
17. Derive an expression for mass flow rate of compressible fluid through an orifice or nozzle fitted to a large tank. What is the condition for maximum rate of flow ?
18. What is the critical pressure ratio for a compressible flow through a nozzle? On what factors does it depend ?
19. Describe compressible flow through a convergent-divergent nozzle. How and where does the shock wave occur in the nozzle ?
20. What do you mean by compressibility correction factor ?
21. How is a shock wave produced in a compressible fluid ? What do you mean by the term "Shock strength" ?
22. Derive an expression for mass rate of flow through a venturimeter.

UNSOLVED EXAMPLES

1. A 100 mm diameter pipe reduces to 50 mm diameter through a sudden contraction. When it carries air at 20·16°C under isothermal conditions, the absolute pressures observed in the two pipes just before and after the contraction are 400 kN/m^2 and 320 kN/m^2 respectively. Determine the densities and velocities at the two sections. Take R = 290 J/kg K.
   [Ans. 4·7 kg/m^3; 3·76 kg/m^3; 39·7 m/s; 198·5 m/s]
2. A gas with a velocity of 300 m/s is flowing through a horizontal pipe at a section where pressure is 60 kN/m^2 (abs.) and temperature 40°C. The pipe changes in diameter and at this section the pressure is 90 kN/m^2. If the flow of gas is adiabatic find the velocity of gas at this section.
   Take R = 287 J/kgK and γ = 1·4.
   [Ans. 113 m/s]

3. An aeroplane is flying at 21·5 m/s at a low altitude where the velocity of sound is 325 m/s. At a certain point just outside the boundary layer of the wings, the velocity of air relative to the plane is 305 m/s. If the flow is frictionless adiabatic determine the pressure drop on the wing surface near this position.
Assume $\gamma = 1{\cdot}4$, pressure of ambient air = 102 kN/m^2. [**Ans.** 28·46 kN/m^2]

4. A jet propelled aircraft is flying at 1100 km/h. at sea level. Calculate the Mach number at a point on the aircraft where air temperature is 20°C. Take : $R = 287$ J/kg K and $\gamma = 1{\cdot}4$.
[**Ans.** 0·89]

5. An aeroplane is flying at an height of 20 km where the temperature is – 40°C. The speed of the plane is corresponding to $M = 1{\cdot}8$. Find the speed of the plane.
Take : $R = 287$ J/kg K, $\gamma = 1{\cdot}4$.
[**Ans.** 1982·6 km/h]

6. Find the velocity of bullet fired in standard air if its Mach angle is 30°. [**Ans.** 680·4 m/s]

7. Air, thermodynamic state of which is given by pressure $p = 230$ kN/m^2 and temperature = 300 K is moving at a velocity $V = 250$ m/s. Calculate the stagnation pressure if (*i*) compressibility is neglected and (*ii*) compressibility is accounted for.
Take $\gamma = 1{\cdot}4$, and $R = 287$ J/kg K.
[**Ans.** 313 kN/m^2, 323 kN/m^2]

8. A large vessel, fitted with a nozzle, contains air at a pressure of 2943 kN/m^2 (abs.) and at a temperature of 20°C. If the pressure at the outlet of the nozzle is 2060 kN/m^2 (abs.) find the velocity of air flowing at the outlet of the nozzle.
Take : $R = 287$ J/kgK, and $\gamma = 1{\cdot}4$
[**Ans.** 239·2 m/s]

9. Nitrogen gas ($\gamma = 1{\cdot}4$) is released through a 10 mm orifice on the side of a large tank in which the gas is at a pressure of 10 bar and temperature 20°C. Determine the mass flow rate if (*i*) the gas escapes to atmosphere (1 bar); (*ii*) the gas is released to another tank at (*a*) 5 bar, (*b*) 6 bar.
[**Ans.** (*i*) 0·183 kg/s; (*ii*) 0·183 kg/s; 0·167 kg/s]

10. Air is released from one tank to another through a convergent-divergent nozzle at the rate of 12 N/s. The supply tank is at a pressure of 400 kN/m^2 and temperature 110°C, and the pressure in the receiving tank is 100 kN/m^2. Determine: (*i*) The pressure, temperature, and Mach number in the constriction, (*ii*) The required diameter of constriction, (*iii*) The diameter of the nozzle at the exit for full expansion, and the Mach number.
[**Ans.** (*i*) 210 kN/m^2; 319 K, (*ii*) 43·5 mm; (*iii*) 48 mm; 1·56]

11. Oxygen flows in a conduit at an absolute pressure of 170 kN/m^2. If the absolute pressure and temperature at the nose of small object in the stream are 200 kN/m^2 and 70·16°C respectively, determine the velocity in the conduit. Take $\gamma = 1{\cdot}4$ and $R = 281{\cdot}43$ J/kg K.
[**Ans.** 175·3 m/s]

12. Air at a velocity of 1400 km/h has a pressure of 10 kN/m^2 vacuum and temperature of 50·16°C. Calculate local Mach number and stagnation pressure, density and temperature.
Take $\gamma = 1{\cdot}4$, $R = 281{\cdot}43$ J/kg K and barometric pressure = 101·325 kN/m^2
[**Ans.** 1·089; 192·358 kN/m^2; 1·708 kg/m^3; 399·8 K]

13. A normal shock wave occurs in a diverging section when air is flowing at a velocity of 420 m/s, pressure 100 kN/m^2, and temperature 10°C. Determine : (*i*) The Mach number before and after the shock, (*ii*) The pressure rise, and (*iii*) The velocity and temperature after the shock.
[**Ans.** (*i*) 1·25; 0·91; (*ii*) 66 kN/m^2, (*iii*) 292 m/s; 54°C]

14. A normal shock wave occurs in air flowing at a Mach number of 1·5. The static pressure and temperature of the air upstream of the shock wave are 100 kN/m^2 and 300 K. Determine the Mach number, pressure and temperature downstream of the stockwave. Also estimate the shock strength.
[**Ans.** 0·7; 246 kN/m^2; 396·17 K; 1·46]

15. A 25 mm diameter venturimeter is fixed in a 75 mm diameter pipe to measure the rate of flow of gas. If the absolute pressure at the inlet and the throat of venturimeter are equivalent to 1010 mm and 910 mm of mercury, determine the volumetric flow rate of gas. Assume the flow to be isentropic, $\gamma = 1{\cdot}4$ and $\rho_1 = 1{\cdot}6$ kg/m^3.
[**Ans.** 0·0599 m^3/s]

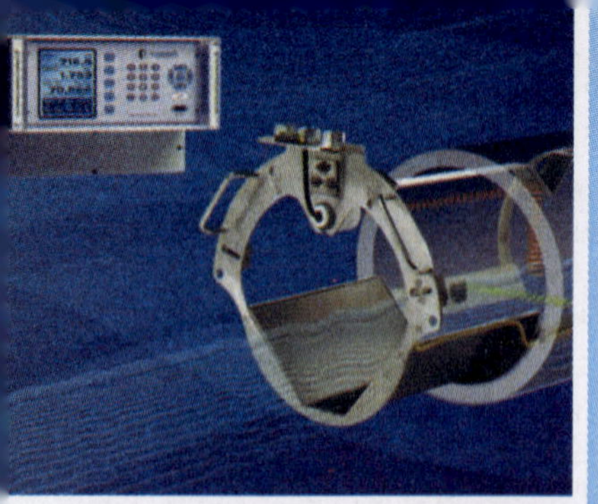

Chapter 16

FLOW IN OPEN CHANNELS

A. UNIFORM FLOW

16.1. INTRODUCTION

16.1.1 Definition of an Open Channel.

An **open channel** *may be defined as a passage in which liquid flows with its upper surface exposed to atmosphere.* In open channels the flow is due to *gravity*, thus the flow conditions are greatly influenced by the *slope* of the channel.

16.1.2 Comparison between Open Channel and Pipe Flow

The important points of *difference* between the two types of flows are given below:

S.No.	Aspects	Open channel flow	Pipe flow
1.	*Cause of flow*	Gravity force (provided by sloping bottom)	The pipe runs full and the flow, in general, takes place at *the expense of hydraulic pressure*; the pressure continously decreases in the direction of flow.
2.	*Geometry of cross-section*	Open channels may have any shape: triangular, rectangular, trapezoidal, parabolic, circular etc.	Pipes ...generally round in cross-section ... cross-section of flow is fixed, since the flowing liquid entirely fills the pipe section.
3.	*Surface roughness*	Varies between wide limits, the hydraulic roughness varies with depth of flow.	Roughness co-efficient varies from a low value to a very high value, depending upon the material of the pipe.

4.	*Piezometric head*	$(z + y)$, where y is the depth of flow. H.G.L. coincides with the water surface.	$\left(z + \frac{p}{w}\right)$, where p is the pressure in the pipe. H.G.L. does not coincide with water surface.
5.	*Velocity distribution*	The maximum velocity occurs at a little distance below the water surface. The shape of the velocity profile is dependent on the channel roughness.	The velocity distribution is symmetrical about the pipe axis, maximum velocity occuring at the pipe centre and the velocity at the pipe wall reducing to zero.

16.1.3 Types of Channels

The various types of channels are:

1. **Natural channel.** It is the one which has irregular sections of varying shapes, developed in a natural way.

   Examples: Rivers, streams etc.

2. **Artificial channel.** It is the one which is built artificially for carrying water for various purposes. They have the cross-sections with regular geometrical shapes (which usually remain same throughout the length of the channel).

   Examples: Rectangular channel, trapezoidal channel, parabolic channel etc.

3. **Open channel.** A channel without any cover at the top is known as an *open channel.*

   Examples: Irrigation canals, rivers, streams, flumes and water falls.

4. **Covered or closed channels.** The channel having a cover at the top is known as a *covered* or *closed channel.*

   Examples: Partly filled conduits carrying public water supply such as sewerage lines, underground drains, tunnels etc. not running full of water.

5. **Prismatic channel.** A channel with constant bed slope and the same cross-section along its length is known as a *prismatic channel.*

   The prismatic channels can be further subdivided as:

   (*i*) ***Exponential channel.*** It is the one in which area of cross-section of flow is directly proportional to any power of depth of flow in channel.

   Examples: Rectangular, triangular and parabolic channels.

   (*ii*) ***Non-exponential channel.*** Trapezoidal and circular channels are non-exponential channels.

16.2. TYPES OF FLOW IN CHANNELS

The flow in channels is classified into the following types, *depending upon the change in the depth of flow with respect to space and time:*

1. Steady flow and unsteady flow
2. Uniform flow and non-uniform (or varied) flow
3. Laminar flow and turbulent flow
4. Subcritical flow, critical flow and supercritical flow.

16.2.1 Steady Flow and Unsteady Flow

- When the flow characteristics (such as depth of flow, flow velocity and the flow rate at any cross-section) do not change with respect to time, the flow in a channel is said to be *steady*.

  Mathematically, $\frac{\partial y}{\partial t} = 0, \frac{\partial V}{\partial t} = 0,$ or $\frac{\partial Q}{\partial t} = 0$

  where y, V and Q are depth of flow, velocity and rate of flow respectively.
- The flow is said to be *unsteady flow* when these flow parameters vary with time.

  Mathematically, $\frac{\partial y}{\partial t} \neq 0; \frac{\partial V}{\partial t} \neq 0$ or $\frac{\partial Q}{\partial t} \neq 0.$

16.2.2 Uniform and Non-uniform (or varied) Flow

- Flow in a channel is said to be *uniform* if the depth, slope, cross-section and velocity *remain constant* over a given length of the channel.

  Mathematically, $\frac{\partial y}{\partial l} = 0, \frac{\partial V}{\partial l} = 0$

  Uniform flows are possible only in prismatic channels only. A uniform flow may be either steady or unsteady, depending upon whether or not the discharge varies with time; *unsteady uniform flow is rare in practice.*
- Flow in a channel is said to be *non-uniform* (*or varied*) when the channel depth *varies* continuously from one section to another.

  Mathematically, $\frac{\partial y}{\partial l} \neq 0, \frac{\partial V}{\partial l} \neq 0$

  Varied flow may be further classified as:

  (*i*) *Rapidly varied flow* (*R.V.F.*). In this type of flow depth of flow *changes abruptly over a comparatively small length of channel.*

  Examples: Hydraulic jump and the hydraulic drop.

  (*ii*) *Gradually varied flow* (*G.V.F.*). In this case the change in depth of flow takes place gradually in a long length of the channel.

16.2.3 Laminar Flow and Turbulent Flow

The flow in the open channel may be characterised as laminar or turbulent depending upon the value of Reynolds number, defined as:

$$Re = \frac{\rho VR}{\mu} \quad ...(16.1)$$

where, V = Average velocity of flow in the channel, and

R = Hydraulic radius (defined as the ratio of area of flow to wetted perimeter)

When $Re < 500$ ...flow is *laminar*

$Re > 2000$ ...flow is *turbulent*

$500 < Re < 2000$ ...flow is *transitional*.

16.2.4 Subcritical flow, Critical Flow and Supercritical Flow

Since gravitational force is a predominant force in the case of channel flow, therefore Froude number, $Fr = \frac{V}{\sqrt{gD}}$ (where V and D are the mean velocity of flow and hydraulic depth of the channel respectively) is an important parameter for analysing open channel flows. Depending upon Froude number the channel flow may be characterised as:

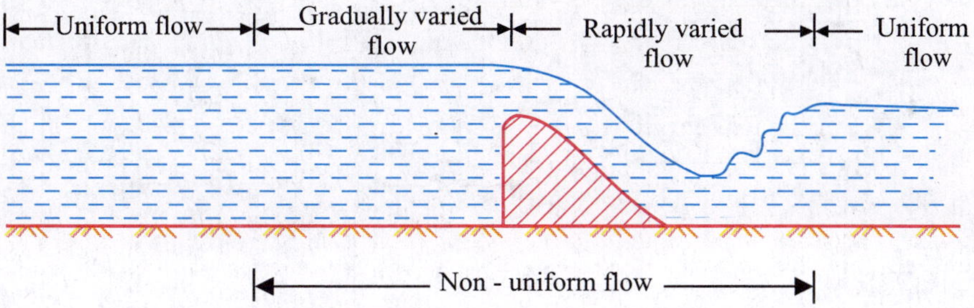

Fig. 16.1. Uniform and non-uniform flow.

(*i*) When $Fr < 1$ (or $V < \sqrt{gD}$): The flow is described as *subcritical* (or *tranquil* or streaming)

(*ii*) When $Fr = 1$: The flow is said to be in a *critical* state.

(*iii*) When $Fr > 1$: The flow is said to be *supercritical* (or *rapid* or *shooting* or *torrential*)

Some of the types of channel flow are shown in Fig. 16.1

16.3. DEFINITIONS

1. **Depth of flow (*y*).** It is the vertical distance of the lowest point of a channel section (bed of the channel) from the free *surface*.
2. **Depth of flow section.** It is the depth of flow normal to the bed of the channel.

$$d = y \cos \theta \qquad ...(16.2)$$

where, θ = The angle which the channel bed makes with the horizontal.

Since the slopes of the channels are very small,

$$\cos\theta \simeq 1 \text{ and } d \simeq y.$$

The depth of flow and depth of flow section are assumed equal, unless mentioned otherwise.

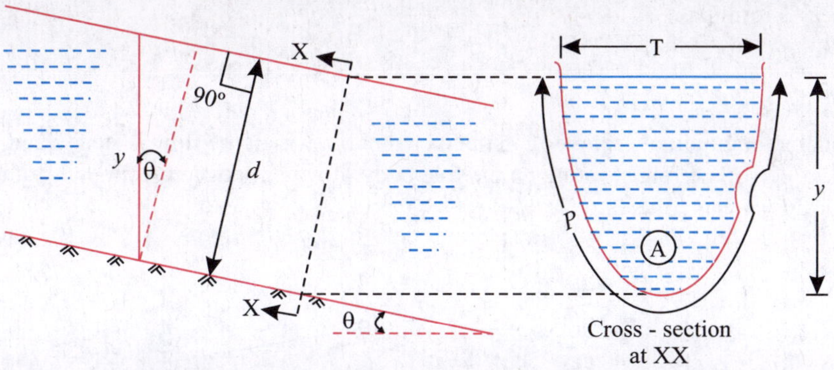

Fig. 16.2. Terms related to flow through open channel.

3. **Top width (T).** It is the width of the channel section at the free surface (*i.e.* the width of the liquid surface exposed to the atmospheric pressure.
4. **Wetted area (A).** It is the cross-sectional area of the flow section of the channel.
5. **Wetted perimeter (P).** It is the length of the channel boundary in contact with the flowing water at any section.
6. **Hydraulic radius (R).** It is ratio of the cross-sectional area of flow to wetted perimeter. It is also called *hydraulic mean depth*.

i.e.
$$R = \frac{A}{P} \qquad ...(16.3)$$

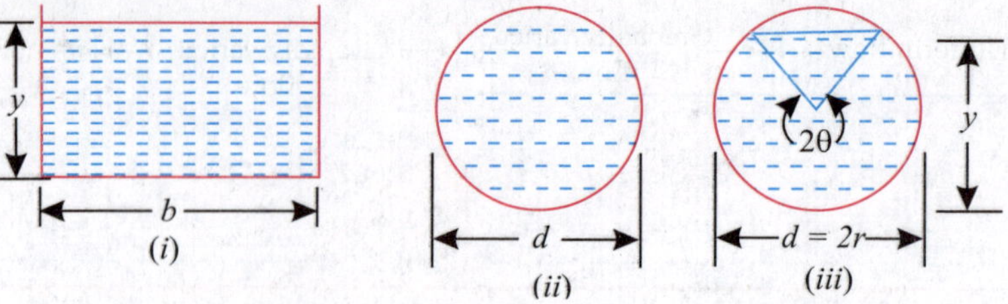

Fig. 16.3.

Examples: (*i*) Rectangular open channel:

$$R = \frac{A}{P} = \frac{b \times y}{b + 2y} \quad ...(16.4)$$

(*ii*) Pipe running full:

$$R = \frac{A}{P} = \frac{(\pi / 4) \times d^2}{\pi d} = \frac{d}{4} \quad ...(16.5)$$

(*iii*) Pipe not running full:

$$R = \frac{A}{P} = \frac{\frac{r^2}{2}(2\theta - \sin 2\theta)}{2r\,\theta} \quad ...(16.6)$$

7. **Hydraulic depth (D).** It is the ratio of the wetted area A to the top width T.

i.e. $$D = \frac{A}{T} \quad ...(16.7)$$

16.4. OPEN CHANNEL FORMULAE FOR UNIFORM FLOW

For uniform flow in open channels, the following formulae will be discussed:

1. Chezy's formula
2. Manning's formula.

16.4.1 Chezy's Formula

Consider a longitudinal section of an open channel in which the flow is steady and uniform, as shown in Fig. 16.4. The forces acting on the free body of water between sections 1-1 and 2-2 in the direction of flow are as follows:

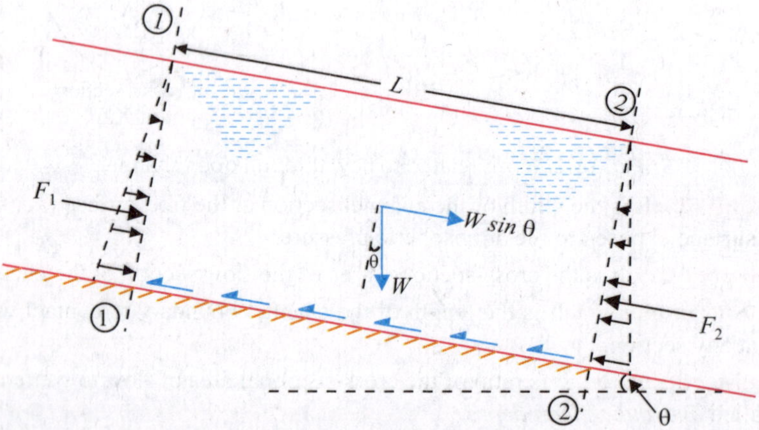

Fig. 16.4. Uniform flow in open channel.

(*i*) Pressure forces F_1 and F_2 acting on the two ends of the body; these forces balance each other since the depth of channel remains constant.

(*ii*) The component of weight of the water in the direction of flow, which is

$$= W \sin \theta = wAL \sin \theta$$

where, w = Specific weight of water,

A = Wetted cross-sectional area of channel,

L = Length of the channel considered, and

θ = Angle of inclination of channel bottom with the horizontal.

(*iii*) Frictional resistance offered by the sides of the channel which is = $\tau_0 PL$, where P is the wetted perimeter of the channel and τ_0 is the average shear stress at the channel boundary.

As the flow is steady and uniform, it is neither accelerating nor decelerating; the liquid mass is in equilibrium and the frictional resistance to flow equals the weight of liquid mass acting along the line of fluid motion. Thus

$$wAL \sin \theta = \tau_0 PL$$

Since frictional resistance τ_0 varies with (velocity)^2, τ_0 may be expressed as fV^2 where f is a *non-dimensional factor* whose value depends upon the *material* and *nature of flow surface.*

$$\therefore \quad wAL \sin \theta = fV^2 PL$$

or,
$$V_2 = \frac{wAL \sin \theta}{fPL} \quad \text{or} \quad V = \sqrt{\frac{w}{f}} \times \sqrt{\frac{A}{P} \sin \theta}$$

Since $\frac{A}{P}$ is the hydraulic radius (or hydraulic mean depth) and θ is the slope of the channel bed (S), we may write:

$$V = C\sqrt{RS} \qquad \text{...(16.8)}$$

where $C = \sqrt{\frac{w}{f}}$ (a *variable which depends on the roughness of the channel surface and the flow Reynolds number*).

Eqn. (16.8) is known as ***Chezy's formula*** (named after the French engineer Antoine Chezy who developed this formula in 1775). The term C is known as *Chezy's constant*.

Discharge through the channel, Q = Area × velocity

$$= AC\sqrt{RS}$$

which can be written as:

$$Q = K\sqrt{S} \qquad \text{...(16.9)}$$

where, $K = AC\sqrt{R}$

The factor K is called the **conveyance** of the channel section, and is a *measure of the carrying capacity of the channel*. For a channel of constant slope, the conveyance is directly proportional to discharge Q.

Empirical relations for the Chezy's constant C:

Although Chezy's equation is quite simple, the selection of a correct value of C is rather difficult. Some of the important formulae developed for Chezy's constant C are:

(*a*) Bazin's formula:

A French hydraulician H. Bazin's (1897) proposed the following empirical formula for Chezy's constant:

$$C = \frac{157.6}{181 + \frac{K}{\sqrt{R}}} \qquad \text{...(16.10)}$$

where, R is the hydraulic radius and K is the Bazin's constant whose value depends on surface roughness. Some typical values of K are:

S.No.	*Surface of channel*	*Bazin's constant (K)*
1.	Smooth cement plaster or planed wood	0.11
2.	Concrete, brick, or unplaned wood	0.21
3.	Smooth rubble masonry or poor brickwork	0.83
4.	Earth channels in very good condition	1.54
5.	Earth channels in rough condition	3.17
6.	Dredged earth channels, average condition	2.36

(*b*) Kutter's formula:

Two Swiss engineers Ganguillet and Kutter proposed the following empirical formula (1869) for the determination of Chezy's constant C.

$$C = \frac{23 + \frac{0.00155}{S} + \frac{1}{N}}{1 + \left(23 + \frac{0.00155}{S}\right)\frac{N}{\sqrt{R}}} \qquad \text{...(16.11)}$$

where N is the Kutter's constant whose value depends upon the type of the channel surface. Some typical values of N are given below:

S.No.	*Surface of channel*	N *(Kutter's/Manning's constant)*
1.	Smooth cement plaster or planed wood	0.010
2.	Very smooth concrete and planed timber	0.011
3.	Smooth concrete	0.012
4.	Glazed brickwork	0.013
5.	Vitrified clay	0.014
6.	Brick surface lined with cement mortar	0.015
7.	Earth channels in best condition	0.017
8.	Straight unlined earth channels in good condition	0.020
9.	Rivers and earth channels in fair condition	0.025
10.	Canal and river of rough surface with weeds	0.030

(*c*) Manning's formula:

Rober Manning (an Irish engineer) gave the following empirical relation for determination of Chezy's constant C (1889), which is *simplest* of all used for uniform open channel flow:

$$C = \frac{1}{N} \cdot R^{1/6}$$

where N is the Manning's constant (also known as ***rugosity co-efficient***—a term generally used by British engineers) whose value depends on the channel surface.

Example 16.1. *Find the rate of flow and conveyance for a rectangular channel 7.5 m wide for uniform flow at a depth of 2.25 m. The channel is having bed slope as 1 in 1000. Take Chezy's constant C = 55.*

Also state whether the flow is tranquil or rapid.

Solution. Width of the rectangular channel, $b = 7.5$ m

Depth of flow, $y = 2.25$ m

$\therefore$ Area of flow, $A = b \times y = 7.5 \times 2.25 = 16.875 \text{ m}^2$

Bed slope, $S = \dfrac{1}{1000}$

Chezy's constant, $C = 55$

Wetted perimeter, $P = b + 2y = 7.5 + 2 \times 2.25 = 12.0$ m

$\therefore$ Hydraulic radius (or hydraulic mean depth), $R = \dfrac{A}{P} = \dfrac{16.875}{12.0} = 1.406$ m

Rate of flow, Q:

Using Chezy's formula, average velocity,

$$V = C\sqrt{RS} = 55\sqrt{1.406 \times \frac{1}{1000}} = 2.06 \text{ m/s}$$

$\therefore$ *Discharge*, $Q = AV = 16.875 \times 2.06 =$ **34.76 m³/s (Ans.)**

Conveyance, K:

$$K = AC\sqrt{R} = 16.875 \times 55 \times \sqrt{1.406} = \mathbf{1100.5} \text{ (Ans.)}$$

State of flow (tranquil or rapid):

$$\text{Froude number, } Fr = \frac{V}{\sqrt{gy}} = \frac{2.06}{\sqrt{9.81 \times 2.25}} = 0.438$$

Since $Fr < 1.0$, the flow in the channel is **tranquil** in nature. **(Ans.)**

Example 16.2. *A triangular gutter, whose sides include an angle of 60°, conveys water at a uniform depth of 250 mm. If the discharge is 0.04 m³/s, determine the gradient of the trough. Use the Chezy's formula assuming that C = 52.* **[Delhi University]**

Solution. Depth of flow = 250 mm = 0.25 m.

Discharge through the gutter, $Q = 0.04 \text{ m}^3/\text{s}$

Chezy's constant, $C = 52$

Bed slope, S:

Refer to Fig. 16.5. From $\Delta\, ACO$,

$$\frac{CO}{AO} = \cos 30° \quad \text{or} \quad AO = \frac{CO}{\cos 30°}$$

$$= \frac{0.25}{\cos 30°} = 0.288 \text{ m}$$

i.e. $AO = BO = 0.288$ m

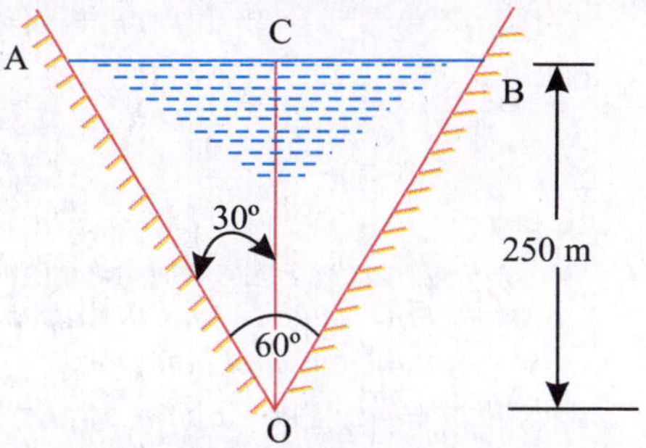

Fig. 16.5

Further $\dfrac{AC}{CO} = \tan 30°$

or, $AC = CO \tan 30° = 0.25 \times 0.577 = 0.144$ m

or, $AB = 2AC = 0.288$ m

$\therefore$ Area of flow, $A = \dfrac{1}{2} \times AB \times CO = \dfrac{1}{2} \times 0.288 \times 0.25 = 0.036 \text{ m}^2$

Wetted perimeter, $P = AO + BO = 0.288 + 0.288 = 0.576$ m

Hydraulic radius, $R = \dfrac{A}{P} = \dfrac{0.036}{0.576} = 0.0625$ m

Using Chezy's formula, we have:

$$Q = AV = AC\sqrt{RS} \quad \text{or} \quad 0.04 = 0.036 \times 52 \times \sqrt{0.0625 \times S}$$

or, $$\sqrt{0.0625 \times S} = \frac{0.04}{0.036 \times 52} = 0.02137$$

or, $$S = \frac{0.02137^2}{0.0625} = \frac{1}{137} \quad \text{(Squaring both sides)}$$

Hence, *gradient of the trough (or bed slope) is* **1 in 137 (Ans.)**

Example 16.3. *Find the discharge of water through the channel shown in Fig. 16.6. Take the value of Chezy's constant = 60 and slope of the bed as 1 in 950.* **[UPTU]**

Solution. Chezy's constant, $C = 60$

Bed slope, $S = \frac{1}{950}$

Discharge, Q:

Refer to Fig. 16.6.

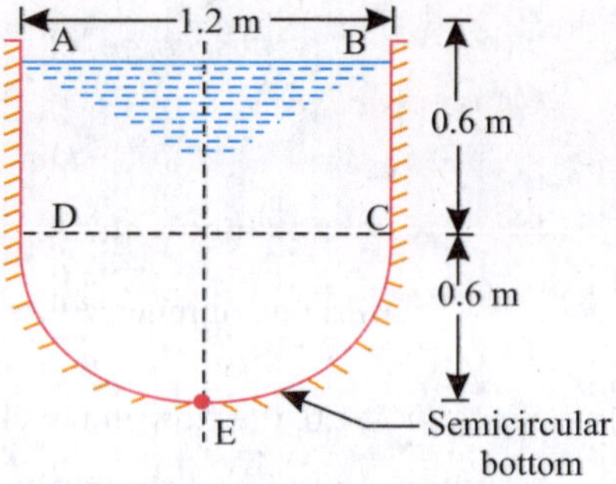

Fig. 16.6

Area of flow, A = Area $ABCD$ + area DEC

$$= 1.2 \times 0.6 + \frac{\pi \times 0.6^2}{2} = 1.285 \text{ m}^2$$

Wetted perimeter, $P = AD + DEC + CB$

$$= 0.6 + \pi \times 0.6 + 0.6 = 3.085 \text{ m}$$

∴ Hydraulic mean radius,

$$R = \frac{A}{P} = \frac{1.285}{3.085} = 0.416 \text{ m}$$

Using Chezy's formula, we have:

$$Q = AV = AC\sqrt{RS}$$

$$= 1.285 \times 60 \times \sqrt{0.416 \times \frac{1}{950}} = \mathbf{1.613\ m^3/s} \text{ (Ans.)}$$

Example 16.4. *A canal of trapezoidal section has bed width of 8 m and bed slope of 1 in 4000. If the depth of flow is 2.4 m and side slopes of the channel are 1 horizontal to 3 vertical, determine the average flow velocity and the discharge carried by the channel. Also compute the average shear stress at the channel boundary.*

Take value of Chezy's constant = 55.

Solution. Width of the channel bed, $b = 8$ m

Bed slope, $S = \frac{1}{4000}$

Side slopes = 1 horizontal to 3 vertical

Depth of flow, $y = 2.4$ m

Chezy's constant, $C = 55$

Horizontal distance $EA = BF = ny$

where, n = side slope (1 vertical to n horizontal)

Top width $CD = AB + 2BF = b + 2ny$

Slant side $AD = BC = \sqrt{y^2 + n^2 y^2}$

$$= y\sqrt{n^2+1}$$

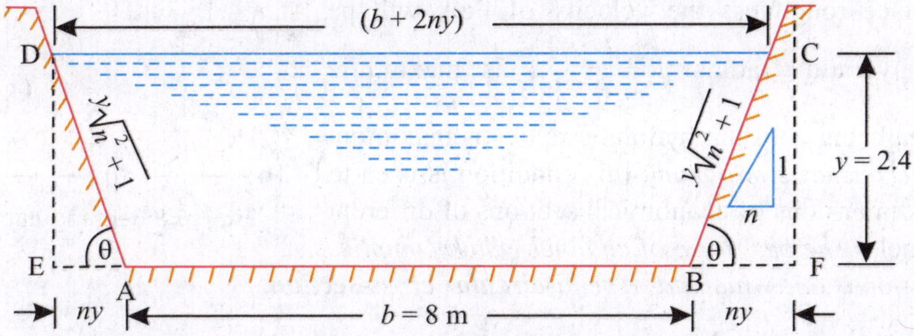

Fig. 16.7

$\therefore$ Wetted perimeter, $P = AB + AD + BC$

$$= 8 + 2y\sqrt{n^2+1} = 8+2\times2.4\sqrt{\left(\frac{1}{3}\right)^2+1} = 13.06 \text{ m} \quad (\because n = 1/3)$$

Area of flow $= \left(\dfrac{\text{Top width + bottom width}}{2}\right) \times \text{height} = \dfrac{(b+2ny)+b}{2} \times y = y\,(b+ny)$

$$= 2.4\left(8 + \frac{1}{3}\times 2.4\right) = 21.12 \text{ m}^2$$

Hydraulic radius, $R = \dfrac{A}{P} = \dfrac{21.12}{13.06} = 1.617$ m

Average flow velocity:

Average flow velocity, $V = C\sqrt{RS}$

$$= 55\sqrt{1.617 \times \frac{1}{4000}} = \mathbf{1.106 \text{ m/s}} \text{ (Ans.)}$$

Discharge, Q :

Discharge through the channel, $Q = AV = 21.12 \times 1.106 = \mathbf{23.36 \text{ m}^3/\text{s}}$ **(Ans.)**

Shear stress at channel boundary, τ_0:

Under equilibrium conditions, the frictional resistance to flow equals the weight of liquid mass acting along the line of fluid motion,

i.e. $\tau_0 LP = wAL \sin\theta$

$\therefore$ *Shear stress at the channel boundary,*

$$\tau_0 = \frac{wAL\sin\theta}{LP} = w\frac{A}{P}\sin\theta = w \times R \times S \qquad (\because S = \sin\theta)$$

$$= 9810 \times 1.617 \times \frac{1}{4000} = \mathbf{3.96 \text{ N/m}^2} \text{ (Ans.)}$$

16.5. MOST ECONOMICAL SECTION OF A CHANNEL

The **most economical section** (also called the *best section or most efficient section) is one which gives the maximum discharge for a given amount of excavation.*

From continuity equation it is evident that discharge is maximum when velocity is maximum, the area of cross-section of channel remaining constant. From Chezy's formula and Manning's formula it can be seen that for a given value of slope and surface roughness the velocity of flow will be maximum if hydraulic radius $R = \left(= \frac{A}{P}\right)$ is maximum.

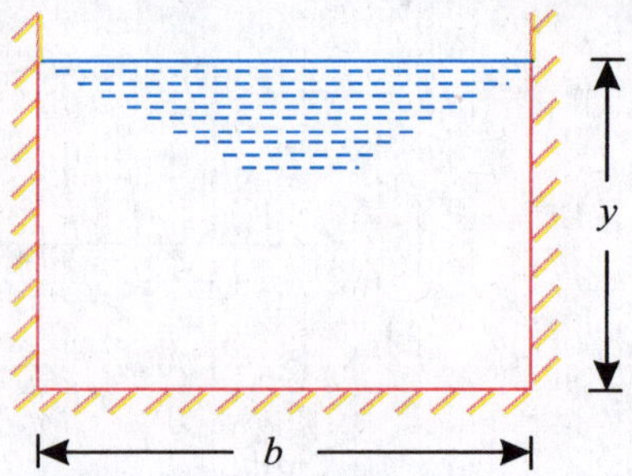

Fig. 16.8 Rectangular channel.

Further the area being constant hydraulic radius is maximum if the *wetted perimeter is minimum*; this condition is used to determine the dimensions of economical sections of different forms of channels. *The best form of channel which complies with this condition is one which has a* ***semi-circular cross-section.***

16.5.1 Most Economical Rectangular Channel Section

Fig. 16.8 shows the cross-section of a rectangular channel. Let b and y be the base width and depth of flow respectively.

$$\text{Area of flow, } A = b \times y, \quad \text{...(i)}$$

$$\text{Wetted perimeter, } P = b + 2y \quad \text{...(ii)}$$

Substituting the value of $b \left(= \frac{A}{y}\right)$ from eqn. (*i*) in eqn. (*ii*), we get:

$$P = \frac{A}{y} + 2y$$

For the section to be most economical/efficient, the wetted perimeter P must be a *minimum*.

i.e.
$$\frac{dP}{dy} = 0 \quad \text{or} \quad \frac{d}{dy}\left[\frac{A}{y} + 2y\right] = 0$$

or,
$$-\frac{A}{y^2} + 2 = 0 \quad \text{or} \quad A = 2y^2 \quad \text{or} \quad b \times y = 2y^2 \qquad [\because A = b \times y]$$

or,
$$b = 2y \quad \text{or} \quad y = b/2 \quad \text{...(16.12)}$$

Hydraulic radius, *R*:

$$\text{Hydraulic radius, } R = \frac{A}{P} = \frac{b \times y}{b + 2y}$$

$$= \frac{2y \times y}{2y + 2y} = \frac{2y^2}{4y} = \frac{y}{2} \qquad (\because b = 2y)$$

i.e.
$$R = \frac{y}{2} \quad \text{...(16.13)}$$

Thus the rectangular channel section will be most economical when:

(*i*) *The depth of flow is equal to half the base width* $\left(y = \frac{b}{2}\right)$, or

(*ii*) *Hydraulic radius is equal to half the depth of flow* $\left(R = \frac{y}{2}\right)$.

Example 16.5. *A rectangular channel is to be dug in the rocky portion of a soil. Find its most economical cross-section if it is to convey 12 m^3/s of water with an average velocity of 3 m/s. Take Chezy's constant C = 50.*

Solution. Discharge, $Q = 12 \text{ m}^3/\text{s}$

Average velocity, $V = 3$ m/s

Chezy's constant, $C = 50$

The geometric relations for *optimum discharge* through a rectangular channel are:

$$b = 2y \quad \text{and} \quad R = \frac{y}{2}, \text{ then area } A = b \times y = 2y^2$$

where b, y and R are base width of the channel, depth of flow and hydraulic radius respectively.

Now, $Q = A \times V = 2y^2 \times V$ or $12 = 2y^2 \times 3$ or $y = 1.414$ m

i.e. Flow depth, $y = 1.414$ m

∴ Base width of the channel, $b = 2y = 2 \times 1.414 = 2.828$ m

Hydraulic radius, $R = \frac{y}{2} = \frac{1.414}{2} = 0.707$ m

Also, $V = C\sqrt{RS}$ ...Chezy's formula

or, $S = \frac{V^2}{C^2 R} = \frac{3^2}{50^2 \times 0.707} = \frac{1}{196}$

(where S = slope bed)

Hence, $b = 2.828$ m, $y = 1.414$ m, $S = \frac{1}{196}$ **(Ans.)**

Example 16.6. *Determine the most economical section of a rectangular channel carrying water at the rate of 0.5 m^3/s; the bed slope of the channels being 1 in 2000. Take Chezy's constant C = 50.*

Solution. Discharge, $Q = 0.5 \text{ m}^3/\text{s}$

Bed slope, $S = \frac{1}{2000}$

Chezy's constant, $C = 50$

Most economical section:

The rectangular channel section will be most economical when:

(*i*) Base width, $b = 2y$

(*ii*) Hydraulic radius, $R = \frac{y}{2}$ (where, y = depth of flow)

Area of flow, $A = b \times y = 2y \times y = 2y^2$

Now, Discharge $Q = AC\sqrt{RS}$ ...Chezy's formula

$$0.5 = 2y^2 \times 50\sqrt{\frac{y}{2} \times \frac{1}{2000}}$$

$$= 100\sqrt{\frac{1}{4000}} \times y^{5/2} = 1.581\, y^{5/2}$$

∴ $y^{5/2} = \frac{0.5}{1.581} = 0.316$ or $y = (0.316)^{2/5} = 0.63$ m

and, $b = 2y = 2 \times 0.63 = 1.26$ m

Hence, $\mathbf{b = 1.26}$ **m and** $\mathbf{y = 0.63}$ **m (Ans.)**

Example 16.7. *A rectangular channel 4 m wide has depth of water 1.5 m. The slope of the bed of the channel is 1 in 1000 and value of Chezy's constant C = 55. It is desired to increase the* *discharge to a maximum by changing the dimensions of the section for constant area of cross-section, slope of the bed and roughness of the channel. Find the new dimensions of the channel and increase in discharge.* **[PTU]**

Solution. Base width of the channel, $b = 4$ m

Depth of flow, $y = 1.5$ m

Bed slope, $S = \frac{1}{1000}$

Chezy's constant, $C = 55$

New dimensions of the channel and increase in discharge:

Area of flow, $A = b \times y = 4 \times 1.5 = 6 \text{ m}^2$

Wetted perimeter, $P = b + 2y = 4 + 2 \times 1.5 = 7.0$ m

Hydraulic radius, $R = \frac{A}{P} = \frac{6}{7} = 0.857$

Discharge, $Q = AC\sqrt{RS} = 6 \times 55\sqrt{0.857 \times \frac{1}{1000}} = 9.66 \text{ m}^3\text{/s}$

For determining maximum discharge, for given area of cross-section, slope of the bed and roughness of the channel, we follow the procedure given below:

Let b' = New base width of the channel, and

y' = New depth of flow,

Then, area $A = b' \times y'$, where $A = 6.0 \text{ m}^2$ (= constant)

$\therefore \quad b' \times y' = 6$

Also for maximum discharge, $b' = 2y'$

$\therefore \quad 2y' \times y' = 6$ or $y'^2 = 3$ or $y' = \sqrt{3} = 1.732$ m,

and, $\quad b' = 2y' = 2 \times 1.732 = 3.464$ m

Hence *new dimensions* of the channel are: $\boldsymbol{b' = 3.464}$ **m** and $\boldsymbol{y' = 1.732}$ **m (Ans.)**

Wetted perimeter, $P' = b' + 2y' = 3.464 + 2 \times 1.732 = 6.928$ m

$\therefore$ Hydraulic radius, $R' = \frac{A}{P'} = \frac{6}{6.928} = 0.866$ m

[Alternatively $R' = \frac{y'}{2} = \frac{1.732}{2} = 0.866$ m (maximum discharge conditional)]

Maximum discharge, $Q' = AC\sqrt{R'S} = 6 \times 55 \times \sqrt{0.866 \times \frac{1}{1000}} = 9.71 \text{ m}^3\text{/s}$

$\therefore$ *Increase in discharge* $= Q' - Q = 9.71 - 9.66 =$ **0.05 m³/s (Ans.)**

16.5.2 Most Economical Trapezoidal Channel Section

Fig 16.9 shows the cross-section of a trapezoidal channel.

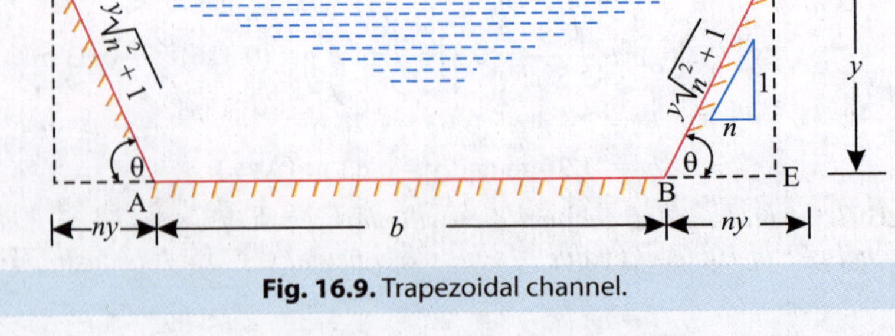

Fig. 16.9. Trapezoidal channel.

Let b = Base width of the channel,

y = Depth of flow, and

θ = Angle made by the sides with horizontal.

Side slope = 1 vertical to n horizontal.

$$\text{Area of flow, } A = \left(\frac{AB + CD}{2}\right) \times y = \frac{b + (b + 2ny)}{2} \times y = (b + ny)\, y \quad ...(i)$$

$$\therefore \quad \frac{A}{y} = b + ny$$

$$\text{or,} \quad b = \frac{A}{y} - ny \quad ...(ii)$$

$$\text{Wetted perimeter, } P = AD + AB + BC = AB + 2BC \quad (\because AD = BC)$$

$$= b + 2\sqrt{BE^2 + CE^2}$$

$$= b + 2\sqrt{n^2 y^2 + y^2}$$

$$\text{or,} \quad P = b + 2y\sqrt{n^2 + 1} \quad ...(iii)$$

Substituting the value of b from eqn. (*ii*) in eqn. (*iii*), we get:

$$P = \frac{A}{y} - ny + 2y\sqrt{n^2 + 1} \quad ...(iv)$$

The section of the channel will be *most economical* when its wetted perimeter (P) is *minimum*,

i.e. $\dfrac{dP}{dy} = 0$

$$\text{or,} \quad \frac{d}{dy}\left[\frac{A}{y} - ny + 2y\sqrt{n^2 + 1}\right] = 0$$

$$\text{or,} \quad -\frac{A}{y^2} - n + 2\sqrt{n^2 + 1} = 0 \quad (\because n \text{ is constant})$$

$$\text{or,} \quad \frac{A}{y^2} + n = 2\sqrt{n^2 + 1}$$

Substituting the value of A from eqn. (*i*), in the above equation, we get:

$$\frac{(b + ny)\, y}{y^2} + n = 2\sqrt{n^2 + 1}$$

$$\text{or,} \quad \frac{(b + ny)}{y} + n = 2\sqrt{n^2 + 1}$$

$$\text{or,} \quad \frac{b + ny + ny}{y} + 2\sqrt{n^2 + 1} \quad \text{or} \quad \frac{b + 2ny}{y} = 2\sqrt{n^2 + 1}$$

$$\text{or,} \quad \frac{b + 2ny}{2} = y\sqrt{n^2 + 1} \quad ...(16.14)$$

[*i.e. Half of top width = One of the sloping sides* ... Fig 16.9]

Hydraulic radius, *R*:

Hydraulic radius, $R = \dfrac{A}{P}$

$$A = (b + ny) \times y \qquad \text{[From eqn. } (i)]$$

$$P = b + 2y\sqrt{n^2+1} \qquad \text{[From eqn. } (iii)]$$

But, $$2y\sqrt{n^2+1} = b + 2ny \qquad \text{[From eqn. (16.14)]}$$

$\therefore$ $$P = b + (b + 2ny) = 2\,(b + ny)$$

$\therefore$ Hydraulic radius, $$R = \frac{(b+ny)\,y}{2\,(b+ny)} = \frac{y}{2} \qquad ...(16.15)$$

i.e., The hydraulic radius equals half the flow depth.

Fig. 16.10 shows a trapezoidal channel of most economical section.

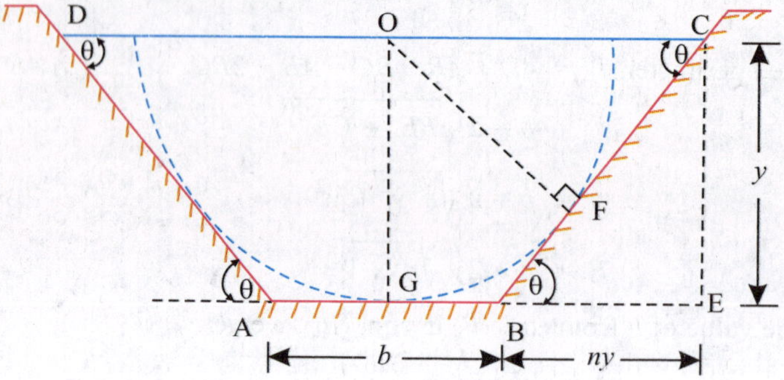

Fig. 16.10. Most economical section of a trapezoidal channel.

Let, θ = Angle made by the sloping side with the horizontal,

O = Centre of the top width *DC*, and

OF = A perpendicular to the sloping side *BC*.

The Δ *OCF* is then a right angled triangle with $\angle OCF = \theta$

$\therefore$ $$\sin\theta = \frac{OF}{OC} \quad \text{or} \quad OF = OC\sin\theta \qquad ...(v)$$

Also, from Δ *BCE*, $$\sin\theta = \frac{CE}{BC} = \frac{y}{\sqrt{y^2+n^2y^2}} = \frac{y}{y\sqrt{n^2+1}} = \frac{1}{\sqrt{n^2+1}}$$

Substituting the value of sin θ in eqn. (*iv*), we have

$$OF = OC \times \frac{1}{\sqrt{n^2+1}} = y\sqrt{n^2+1} \times \frac{1}{\sqrt{n^2+1}} = y, \text{ depth of flow}$$

$$\left[\because OC = \text{Half of top width} = \frac{b+2ny}{2} = y\sqrt{n^2+1} \text{ ...Eqn. (16·14)}\right]$$

Thus a circle with centre *O* and radius equal to the depth of flow will be *tangential* to the three sides of a most economical trapezoidal section; this condition stipulates that the most economical section of a trapezoidal channel will be a *half-hexagon*.

Hence *conditions for most economical trapezoidal section are:*

1. $\dfrac{b+2ny}{2} = y\sqrt{n^2+1}$ (*i.e.* Half of top width = One of the sloping sides)

2. Hydraulic radius, $R = \dfrac{y}{2}$

3. A semicircle drawn from *O* with radius equal to depth of flow will touch the three sides of the trapezoidal channel.

Best side slope for most economical trapezoidal section:

Side slope will be the best when the section is most-economical or when the wetted perimeter is minimum. For that $\frac{dP}{dn} = 0$

$$\therefore \quad \frac{d}{dn}\left[\frac{A}{y} - ny + 2y\sqrt{n^2+1}\right] = 0$$

$$\left[\because P = \frac{A}{y} - ny + 2y\sqrt{n^2+1} \text{ ...From eqn. } (iv)\right]$$

or,
$$-y + 2y \times \frac{1}{2}(n^2+1)^{\frac{1}{2}-1} \times 2n = 0$$

$$-y + 2ny \times \frac{1}{\sqrt{n^2+1}} = 0$$

Cancelling y and rearranging, we have:

$$2n = \sqrt{n^2+1}$$

Squaring both sides, we have:

$$4n^2 = n^2 + 1 \quad \text{or} \quad 3n^2 = 1$$

or,
$$n = \frac{1}{\sqrt{3}} \qquad \text{...(16.16)}$$

If the sloping side makes an angle θ with the horizontal, then

$$\tan\theta = \frac{1}{n} = \sqrt{3} = \tan 60°$$

$$\therefore \quad \theta = 60° \qquad \text{...(16.17)}$$

Hence *best side slope is at 60° to the horizontal.*

For the most economical section,

$$\text{Half of top width} = \text{Length of the sloping side}$$

$$\frac{b+2ny}{2} = y\sqrt{n^2+1}$$

Substituting the value of side slope $n = \frac{1}{\sqrt{3}}$ in the above eqn. we get:

$$\frac{b + 2 \times \frac{1}{\sqrt{3}}y}{2} = y\sqrt{(1/\sqrt{3})^2+1} = \frac{2y}{\sqrt{3}}$$

or,
$$\frac{\sqrt{3}\,b + 2y}{2 \times \sqrt{3}} = \frac{2y}{\sqrt{3}}$$

or,
$$\sqrt{3}\,b + 2y = 4y \quad \text{or} \quad b = \frac{2y}{\sqrt{3}} \qquad \text{...}(vi)$$

Now, wetted perimeter, $P = b + 2y\sqrt{n^2+1}$

$$= \frac{2y}{\sqrt{3}} + 2y\sqrt{\left(\frac{1}{\sqrt{3}}\right)^2 + 1} \qquad \left(\because b = \frac{2y}{\sqrt{3}} \text{ and } n = \frac{1}{\sqrt{3}}\right)$$

$$= \frac{2y}{\sqrt{3}} + 2y \times \frac{2}{\sqrt{3}} = \frac{6y}{\sqrt{3}} = 3 \times \frac{2y}{\sqrt{3}} = 3b$$

i.e. $\quad P = 3b \qquad \left(\because b = \frac{2y}{\sqrt{3}}\right)$

Thus for a *side slope of 60°, the length of sloping side is equal to the base width of the trapezoidal section.*

Example 16.8. *A trapezoidal channel has side slopes of 3 horizontal to 4 vertical and the slope of its bed is 1 in 2000. Determine the optimum dimensions of the channel if it is to carry water at 0.5 m³/s. Take Chezy's constant as 80.* **[RGPV, Bhopal]**

Solution. Side slope, $n = \frac{\text{Horizontal}}{\text{Vertical}} = \frac{3}{4}$

Bed slope, $S = \frac{1}{2000}$

Discharge, $Q = 0.5 \text{ m}^3/\text{s}$

Chezy's constant, $C = 80$

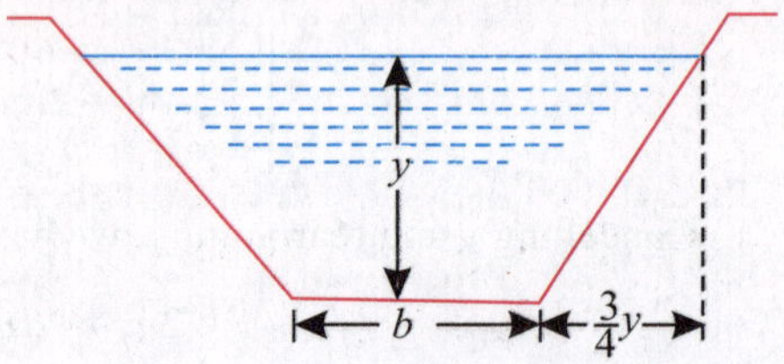

Fig. 16.11

Optimum dimensions of the channel:

For the most economical section, using eqn. (16.14), we have:

$$\frac{b + 2ny}{2} = y\sqrt{n^2 + 1}$$

[where, b = base width of the channel section, and y = depth of flow.]

or, $$\frac{b \times 2 \times \frac{3}{4}y}{2} = y\sqrt{\left(\frac{3}{4}\right)^2 + 1} = \frac{5}{4}y$$

or, $$\frac{b + 1.5y}{2} = 1.25y \quad \text{or} \quad b = 2 \times 1.25y - 1.5y = y$$

i.e. $\quad b = y \qquad ...(i)$

Also discharge, $\quad Q = AC\sqrt{RS}$

[where, R = hydraulic radius, and S = bed slope]

$$0.5 = A \times 80\sqrt{\frac{y}{2} \times \frac{1}{2000}} \qquad \left(\because R = \frac{y}{2}\right)$$

But area, $$A = (b + ny) \times y$$

$$= \left(y + \frac{3}{4}y\right) \times y = 1.75y^2 \qquad [\because b = y \text{ ...eqn. } (i)]$$

$$\therefore \quad 0.5 = 1.75y^2 \times 80\sqrt{\frac{y}{2} \times \frac{1}{2000}} = 2.2136y^{5/2}$$

$$\therefore \quad y = \left(\frac{0.5}{2.2136}\right)^{2/5} = \mathbf{0.55\ m}\ \textbf{(Ans.)}$$

$b = y =$ **0.55 m (Ans.)**

∴ Optimum dimensions of the channel are:

Width (b) = Depth of flow (y) = **0.55 m (Ans.)**

Example 16.9. *A trapezoidal channel having the side slope equal to 60° with the horizontal and laid on a slope of 1 in 750, carries a discharge of 10 m³/s. Find the width at the base and depth of flow for most economical section. Take the value of Chezy's resitance co-efficient C = 66.* **[AMIE]**

Solution. Bed slope, $S = \frac{1}{750}$

Discharge, $Q = 10 \text{ m}^3/\text{s}$

Chezy's constant, $C = 66$

Side slope with the horizontal $= 60°$

Dimensions for most economical section, b and y:

For a trapezoidal channel of most economical (optimum) cross-section, the geometric parameters have the following proportions:

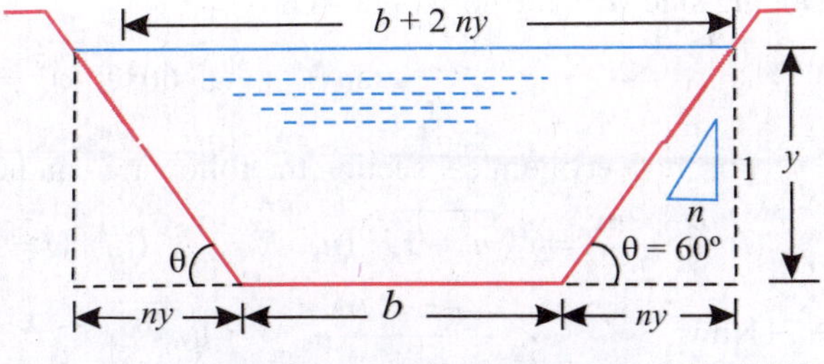

Fig. 16.12

(*i*) $\frac{b + 2ny}{2} = y\sqrt{n^2 + 1}$,

(*ii*) $R = \frac{y}{2}$

(*iii*) $\tan\theta = \tan 60° = \sqrt{3} = \frac{1}{n}$ or $n = \frac{1}{\sqrt{3}}$

Thus from (*i*) and (*iii*), we have:

$$\frac{b + 2 \times \frac{1}{\sqrt{3}} y}{2} = y\sqrt{\left(\frac{1}{\sqrt{3}}\right)^2 + 1}; \quad \frac{\sqrt{3}b + 2y}{2\sqrt{3}} = \frac{2y}{\sqrt{3}} \text{ or } \sqrt{3}b + 2y = 4y \text{ or } b = \frac{2}{\sqrt{3}} y$$

Area of flow, $A = (b + ny)\, y = \left(b + \frac{1}{\sqrt{3}} y\right) y = \left(\frac{2}{\sqrt{3}} y + \frac{1}{\sqrt{3}} y\right) y = \sqrt{3} y^2$

Also, discharge, $Q = AC\sqrt{RS}$

(where, R = hydraulic radius)

$$10 = \sqrt{3}\, y^2 \times 66 \sqrt{\frac{y}{2} \times \frac{1}{750}} = 2.95\, y^{5/2}$$

$\therefore$ *Depth of flow*, $y = \left(\frac{10}{2.95}\right)^{2/5}$ $=$ **1.63 m (Ans.)**

Base width, $b = \frac{2}{\sqrt{3}} y = \frac{2}{\sqrt{3}} \times 1.63 =$ **1.88 m (Ans.)**

Example 16.10. *An open channel of most economical section, having the form of a half hexagon with horizontal bottom is required to give a maximum discharge of 20.2 m³/s of water. The slope of the channel bottom is 1 in 2500. Taking Chezy's constant, C = 60 in Chezy's equation, determine the dimensions of the cross-section.*

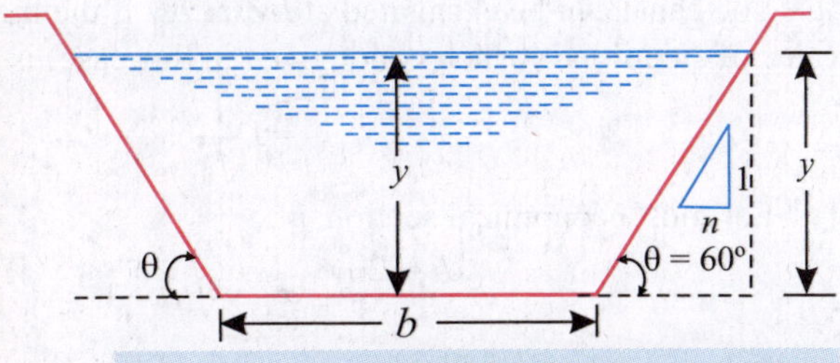

Fig. 16.13

Solution. Maximum Discharge,

$$Q = 20.2 \text{ m}^3/\text{s}$$

$$\text{Bed slope, } S = \frac{1}{2500}$$

$$\text{Chezy's constant } C = 60$$

Dimensions of the cross-section:

Since the channel has a form of a *half hexagon* (Fig. 16.13), therefore, the angle made by the sloping side with the horizontal is 60°.

$$\therefore \quad \tan\theta = \tan 60° = \sqrt{3} = \frac{1}{n} \quad \text{or} \quad n = \frac{1}{\sqrt{3}}$$

For most economical section the following conditions should be satisfied:

$$(i)\ \frac{b+2ny}{2} = y\sqrt{n^2+1}, \quad (ii)\ R = \frac{y}{2}, \quad (iii)\ n = \frac{1}{\sqrt{3}}$$

Now,
$$\frac{b+2ny}{2} = y\sqrt{n^2+1}$$

or,
$$\frac{b+2\times\frac{1}{\sqrt{3}}y}{2} = y\sqrt{\left(\frac{1}{\sqrt{3}}\right)^2+1} \text{ or } \frac{\sqrt{3}\,b+2y}{2\sqrt{3}} = \frac{2y}{\sqrt{3}} \text{ or } b = \frac{2}{\sqrt{3}}y$$

$$\text{Area of flow, } A = (b+ny)\,y = \left(b+\frac{1}{\sqrt{3}}y\right)y = \left(\frac{2}{\sqrt{3}}y+\frac{1}{\sqrt{3}}y\right)y = \sqrt{3}y^2$$

Also, discharge, $Q = AC\sqrt{RS}$, where R is hydraulic radius;

$$\therefore \quad 20.2 = \sqrt{3}y^2\times 60\sqrt{\frac{y}{2}\times\frac{1}{2500}} = 1.47\,y^{5/2}$$

or,
$$y = \left(\frac{20.2}{1.47}\right)^{2/5} = \mathbf{2.852} \textbf{ (Ans.)}$$

$$b = \frac{2}{\sqrt{3}}y = \frac{2}{\sqrt{3}}\times 2.852 = \mathbf{3.29\ m} \textbf{ (Ans.)}$$

Example 16.11. *A power canal of trapezoidal section has to be excavated through hard clay at least cost. Determine the dimensions of the channel, given, discharge equal to 14 m³/s, bed slope 1:2500 and Manning's N = 0.02.* **[M.U.]**

Solution. Discharge, $Q = 14 \text{ m}^3/\text{s}$

$$\text{Bed slope, } S = \frac{1}{2500}$$

$$\text{Manning's } N = 0.02.$$

The canal can be excavated at *least cost* if the trapezoidal section is the *most economical*. The value of side slope (which is not given in this case) is given by (for most economical section),

$$n = \frac{1}{\sqrt{3}} \qquad \text{...[Eqn. (16.16)]}$$

For most economical section:

$$\frac{b+2ny}{2} = y\sqrt{n^2+1} \qquad \text{...[Eqn. (16.14)]}$$

(where b = base width, and y = depth of flow)

$$\therefore \qquad \frac{b+2\times\frac{1}{\sqrt{3}}y}{2} = y\sqrt{\left(\frac{1}{\sqrt{3}}\right)^2+1} = \frac{2}{\sqrt{3}}y \qquad \left(\because\ n=\frac{1}{\sqrt{3}}\right)$$

or,
$$b = \frac{2}{\sqrt{3}}y\times 2-\frac{2}{\sqrt{3}}y = \frac{2}{\sqrt{3}}y \qquad ...(i)$$

$$\text{Area of flow, } A = (b+ny)\,y = \left(\frac{2}{\sqrt{3}}y+\frac{1}{\sqrt{3}}y\right)y = \sqrt{3}\,y^2$$

Now, discharge, Q is given by:

$$Q = AC\sqrt{RS}, \quad \text{where } C = \frac{1}{N}R^{1/6}$$

or,
$$Q = \sqrt{3}y^2\times\frac{1}{N}R^{1/6}\sqrt{RS} = \sqrt{3}y^2\times\frac{1}{N}R^{2/3}S^{1/2}$$

or,
$$14.0 = \sqrt{3}\,y^2\times\frac{1}{0.02}\times\left(\frac{y}{2}\right)^{2/3}\times\sqrt{\frac{1}{2500}}$$

or,
$$14.0 = 1.732y^2\times y^{2/3}\times\frac{1}{(2)^{2/3}} = 1.09\,y^{8/3}$$

or,
$$y = \left(\frac{14}{1.09}\right)^{3/8} = \mathbf{2.6\ m}\ \textbf{(Ans.)}$$

$$b = \frac{2}{\sqrt{3}}y = \frac{2}{\sqrt{3}}\times 2.6 = \mathbf{3.0\ m}\ \textbf{(Ans.)}$$

Example 16.12. *Design an earthen trapezoidal channel for water having a velocity of 0.6 m/s. Side slope of the channel is 1:1.5 and quantity of water flowing is 3 m^3/s. Assume C in Chezy's formula as 65.* **[Delhi University]**

Solution. Velocity of flow, $V = 0.6$ m/s

$$\text{Side slope, } n = \frac{\text{Horizontal}}{\text{Vertical}} = \frac{1.5}{1} = 1.5$$

Discharge, $Q = 3\ m^3/s$

Chezy's constant, $C = 65$

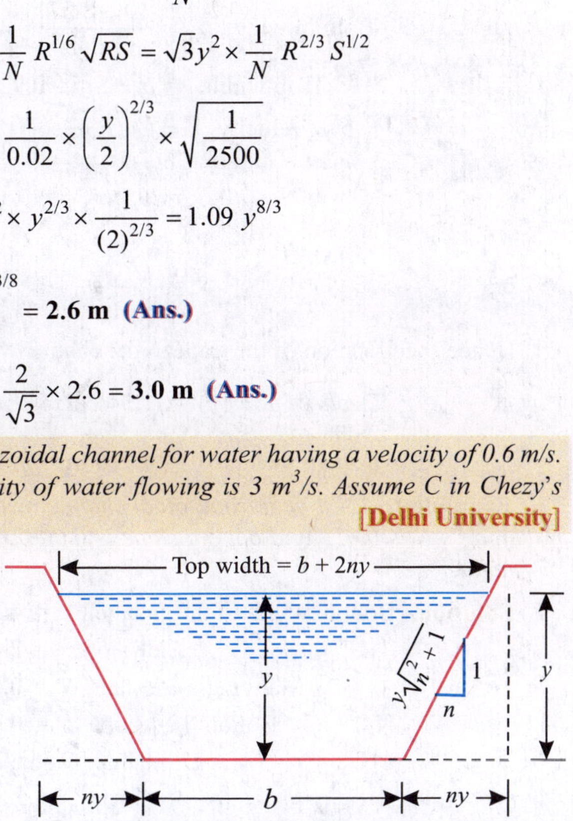

Fig. 16.14

For design, the most economical trapezoidal section is used, for which the following condition may be used:

$$\text{Hydraulic radius, } R = \frac{y}{2}$$

$$\text{Area of flow, } A = \frac{Q}{V} = \frac{3}{0.6} = 5\ m^2$$

$$\text{Wetted perimeter, } P = b+2y\sqrt{n^2+1}$$

Also,
$$R = \frac{A}{P} = \frac{5}{b+2y\sqrt{n^2+1}} = \frac{y}{2} \qquad \left(\because\ R=\frac{y}{2}\right)$$

or,
$$10 = y\left[b+2y\sqrt{1.5^2+1}\right] = y\,(b+3.6\,y) \text{ or } by+3.6y^2$$

i.e. $10 = by + 3.6y^2$ ...(i)

Also, $A = (b + ny)\, y$

or, $S = (b + 1.5y)\, y$ or $by + 1.5y^2$

or, $by = 5 - 1.5y^2$ ...(ii)

Substituting (ii) in (i), we get:

$$10 = 5 - 1.5y^2 + 3.6y^2 = 5 + 2.1y^2$$

or, $$y = \left(\frac{5}{2.1}\right)^{1/2} = 1.543 \text{ m}$$

Substituting the value of y (= 1.543 m) in eqn. (i), we get:

$$10 = b \times 1.543 + 3.6 \times (1.543)^2 = 1.543b + 8.571$$

$\therefore$ Bottom width, $$b = \frac{10 - 8.571}{1.543} = 0.926 \text{ m}$$

Top width, $= b + 2ny = 0.926 + 2 \times 1.5 \times 1.543 = 5.555$ m

Velocity, $V = C\sqrt{RS}$ ... Chezy's formula

$$0.6 = 65\sqrt{\frac{y}{2}S} \quad \text{or} \quad 0.6 = 65\sqrt{\frac{1.543}{2} \times S} = 57.09\sqrt{S}$$

or, $$S = \left(\frac{0.6}{57.09}\right)^2 = 1.104 \times 10^{-4} \quad \text{or} \quad \frac{1}{9054}$$

Hence specification of the trapezoidal channel would be:

Depth of flow (y) = **1.543 m**; *Slope of the bed* (S) = $\mathbf{\frac{1}{9054}}$

Bottom width (b) = **0.926 m**; *Top width* = **5.555 m (Ans.)**

Example 16.13. *For a trapezoidal channel with bottom width 40 m and side slopes 2H : 1V, Manning's N is 0.015 and bottom slope is 0.0002. If it carries 60 m³/s discharge, determine the normal depth.* **[MDU, Haryana]**

Solution. Bottom width of the channel, $b = 40$ m

Side slopes $= 2\,H : 1\,V$ i.e. $n = 2$

Manning's constant, $N = 0.015$

Bottom/bed slope, $S = 0.0002$

Discharge, $Q = 60 \text{ m}^3/\text{s}$

Normal depth, y:

Now, area $A = (b + ny)\, y = (40 + 2y) \times y$

and, Perimeter, $P = b + 2y\sqrt{n^2 + 1} = 40 + 2y\sqrt{2^2 + 1} = 40 + 2\sqrt{5}y = 40 + 4.472y$

$\therefore$ Hydraulic radius, $$R = \frac{A}{P} = \frac{(40 + 2y) \times y}{40 + 4.472d}$$

Discharge, $Q = A \times V = A \times C\sqrt{RS}$ where, Chezy's constant, $C = \frac{1}{N} R^{1/6}$

$\therefore$ $$Q = A \times \frac{1}{N} R^{1/6} \sqrt{RS} = A \times \frac{1}{N} \times R^{2/3} \times S^{1/2}$$

or, $$60 = (40 + 2y)\, y \times \frac{1}{0.015} \times \left[\frac{(40 + 2y) \times y}{40 + 4.472y}\right]^{2/3} \times (0.0002)^{1/2}$$

$$= \frac{[(40 + 2y) \times y]^{5/3}}{0.015 \times (40 + 4.472)^{2/3}} \times 0.01414$$

$$\therefore \quad \frac{60 \times 0.015 \times (40 + 4.472y)^{2/3}}{0.01414} = [(40 + 2y) \times y]^{5/3}$$

or, $\quad 63.65\,(40 + 4.472\,y)^{2/3} = [(40 + 2y) \times y]^{5/3}$

or, $\quad (40y + 2y^2)^{5/3} - 63.65\,(40 + 40.472y)^{2/3} = 0$

By hit and trial method, we get:

y = **1.31 m (Ans.)**

Example 16.14. *A trapezoidal channel with side slopes of 1:1 has to be designed to convey 10 m³/s at a velocity of 2 m/s, so that the amount of concrete lining for the bed and sides is minimum.*

(i) *Calculate the area of lining required for one metre length of the canal.*

(ii) *If the rugosity co-efficient N = 0.015, calculate the bed slope of the canal for uniform flow.*

[UPSC Exams.]

Solution. Side slope, $n = 1$

Discharge, $Q = 10\ \text{m}^3/\text{s}$

Velocity, $V = 2\ \text{m/s}$

Rugosity/Manning's co-efficient, $N = 0.015$

Area of flow, $\dfrac{Q}{V} = \dfrac{10}{2} = 5\ \text{m}^2$

(i) Lining required for one metre length of the canal:

For minimum amount of concrete lining, the wetted perimeter must be minimum; for this condition we have (for a trapezoidal channel):

(i) $\dfrac{b+2ny}{2} = y\sqrt{n^2+1}$ and (ii) $R = \dfrac{y}{2}$

(where b = base width, y = depth of flow, and R = hydraulic radius)

$$\therefore \quad \frac{b + 2 \times 1 \times y}{2} = y\sqrt{1+1} = \sqrt{2}\,y$$

or, $\quad b + 2y = 2\sqrt{2}y \quad$ or $\quad b = 2y(\sqrt{2} - 1) = 0.828y$

Area of flow, $A = (b + ny)\,y$

or, $\quad 5 = (0.828\,y + y)\,y = 1.828y^2$

or, $\quad y = \left(\dfrac{5}{1.828}\right)^{1/2} = 1.65\ \text{m}$

$b = 0.828y = 0.828 \times 1.65 = 1.37\ \text{m}$

Area of lining per metre length

$= P \times 1 = (b + 2y\sqrt{n^2 \times 1}) \times 1 \quad (\because P = b + 2y\sqrt{n^2+1})$

$= 1.37 + 2 \times 1.65\sqrt{1+1}$ = **6.04 m (Ans.)**

(ii) Bed slope of the canal, S:

$$Q = AC\sqrt{RS}, \quad \text{where} \quad C = \frac{1}{N}R^{1/6}$$

or, $$Q = A \times \frac{1}{N}R^{1/6}\sqrt{RS} = A \times \frac{1}{N}R^{2/3}S^{1/2}$$

or, $10 = 5 \times \frac{1}{0.015} \times \left(\frac{1.65}{2}\right)^{2/3} S^{1/2} = 293.2\, S^{1/2}$

$\therefore$ $S = \left(\frac{10}{293.2}\right)^2 = 1.163 \times 10^{-3}$

or, **1 in 860 (Ans.)**

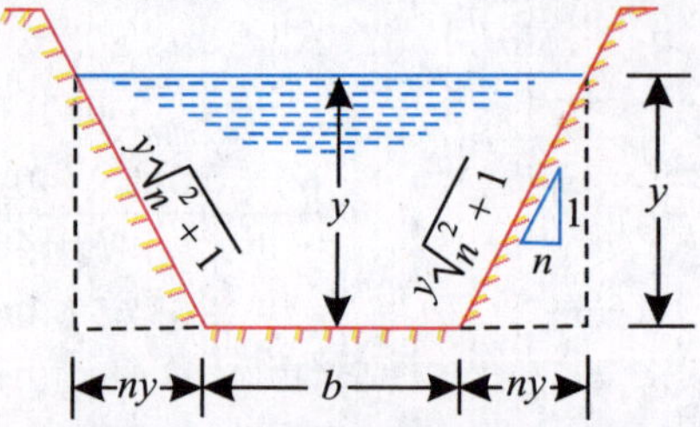

Fig. 16.15

Example 16.15. *A trapezoidal channel is required to carry 8 m³/s of water at a velocity of 2 m/s. Find the most economical cross-section if the channel has side slopes 1 horizontal to 2 vertical. For the same discharge what saving in power would result if this trapezoidal section is replaced by a rectangular section 1.5 m deep and 4 m wide. Take Chezy's constant C = 55.*

Solution. For trapezoidal channel:

Discharge, $Q = 8\ m^3/s$

Velocity of flow, $V = 2$ m/s

$\therefore$ Area of flow, $A = Q/V = 8/2 = 4\ m^2$

Side slope, $n = \frac{\text{Horizontal}}{\text{Vertical}} = \frac{1}{2}$

Chezy's constant $C = 55$.

The trapezoidal channel section will be *most economical*, when:

Half of top width = Length of one sloping side

or, $\frac{b + 2ny}{2} = y\sqrt{n^2 + 1}$

(where b = base width, y = depth of flow)

or, $\frac{b + 2 \times \frac{1}{2} y}{2} = y\sqrt{\left(\frac{1}{2}\right)^2 + 1} = \frac{\sqrt{5}}{2} y$

or, $b + y = \sqrt{5}\, y$ or $b = y(\sqrt{5} - 1) = 1.236y$ ...(*i*)

Area of flow, $A = (b + ny)\,y = \left(b + \frac{1}{2} y\right) y$

or, $4 = (1.236y + 0.5y)\,y = 1.732y^2$

or, $y = \left(\frac{4}{1.736}\right)^{1/2}$ = **1.52 m (Ans.)**

$\boldsymbol{b}$ = $1.236y = 1.236 \times 1.52$ = **1.88 m (Ans.)**

Also hydraulic radius, R (for most economical section) $= y/2 = \frac{1.52}{2} = 0.76$ m

Now, velocity, $V = C\sqrt{RS}$, where S is the bed slope

$\therefore$ $2 = 55\sqrt{0.76 \times S}$ or $S = \left(\frac{2}{55}\right)^2 \times \frac{1}{0.76} = 1.739 \times 10^{-3} \simeq 1 \text{ in } 575$

For rectangular channel:

Base width, $b = 4$ m

Depth of flow, $y = 1.5$ m

$\therefore$ Area of flow, $A = b \times y = 4 \times 1.5 = 6.0 \text{ m}^2$

Wetted perimeter, $P = b + 2y = 4 + 2 \times 1.5 = 7 \text{ m}$

Hydraulic radius, $R = \dfrac{A}{P} = \dfrac{6}{7} = 0.857 \text{ m}$

Flow velocity, $V = \dfrac{Q}{A} = \dfrac{8}{6} = 1.333 \text{ m/s}$

From Chezy's formula, $V = C\sqrt{RS}$

or, $1.333 = 55\sqrt{0.857 \times S}$

or, $S = \left(\dfrac{1.333}{55}\right)^2 \times \dfrac{1}{0.857} = 6.854 \times 10^{-4} \simeq 1 \text{ in } 1459$

$\therefore$ Saving in head *per kilometre of channel run*

$$h = (1.739 \times 10^{-3} - 6.854 \times 10^{-4}) \times 1000 = 1.054 \text{ m}$$

Hence, *saving in power* $= \dfrac{wQh}{1000} \text{ kW} = \dfrac{9810 \times 8 \times 1.054}{1000} = \mathbf{82.7\ kW}$ **(Ans.)**

Example 16.16. *A hydraulically efficient trapezoidal channel has side slopes of 1:1. It is required to discharge 14 m^3/s with a gradient (channel slope) of 1 in 1000. If unlined, the value of Chezy's C is 45. If lined with concrete, the value is 70. If the least cost per m^3 of excavation is three times the cost m^2 of lining, will the lined or the unlined channel be cheaper?* **[Anna University]**

Solution. Side slope, $n = \dfrac{1}{1} = 1$

Discharge, $Q = 14 \text{ m}^3/\text{s}$

Bed slope, $S = \dfrac{1}{1000}$

Chezy's constant C: Unlined channel = 45,

Channel lined with concrete = 70.

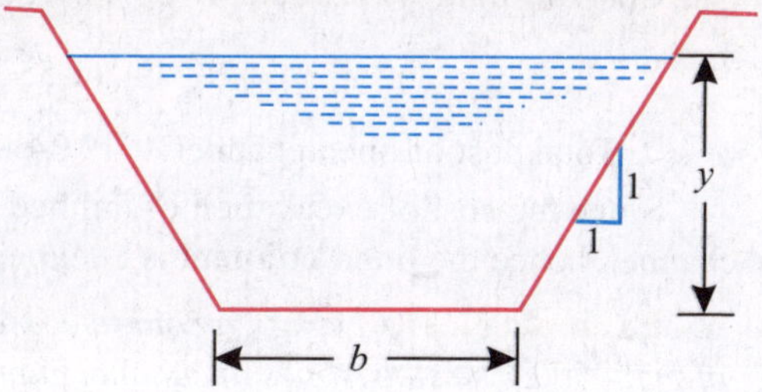

Fig. 16.16

Hydraulically efficient trapezoidal channel must satisfy the following *conditions*:

(*i*) $\dfrac{b + 2ny}{2} = y\sqrt{n^2 + 1}$, and (*ii*) $R = \dfrac{y}{2}$

where, b = Base width of channel,

y = Depth of flow, and

R = Hydraulic radius

or, $\dfrac{b + 2y}{2} = y\sqrt{1 + 1} = \sqrt{2}\,y$ or $b + 2y = 2\sqrt{2}\,y$

or, $b = 2y(\sqrt{2} - 1) = 0.828\,y$

Unlined channel:

$$Q = AC\sqrt{RS} = (b + ny)\, y \times C\sqrt{\frac{y}{2} S}$$

$$14 = (0.828y + y)\, y \times 45 \times \sqrt{\frac{y}{2} \times \frac{1}{1000}} = 1.839\, y^{5/2} \quad (\because n = 1)$$

or, $y = \left(\dfrac{14}{1.839}\right)^{2/5} = 2.25 \text{ m}$

$$b = 0.828\,y = 0.828 \times 2.25 = 1.863 \text{ m}$$

Let, cost of lining per m^2 of the channel surface = K

Then, cost of excavation per m^3 = 3 K ...(*Given*)

Consider one metre length of channel.

Amount of excavation = $A \times 1 = (b + ny)\,y \times 1 = (1.863 + 1 \times 2.25) \times 2.25 \times 1 = 9.254 \text{ m}^2$

$\therefore$ The cost of excavation $= 3 \text{ K} \times 9.254 = 27.76 \text{ K}$

Lined channel:

$$Q = AC\sqrt{RS} = (b + ny)\; y \times C\sqrt{\frac{y}{2} S}$$

or,
$$14 = (0.828y + y)\; y \times 70 \times \sqrt{\frac{y}{2} \times \frac{1}{1000}} = 2.86\, y^{5/2}$$

or,
$$y = \left(\frac{14}{2.86}\right)^{2/5} = 1.88 \text{ m}$$

$$b = 0.828y = 0.828 \times 1.88 = 1.55 \text{ m}$$

Considering one metre length of channel, cost of excavation

$$= A \times 1 \times 3\text{K} = (b + ny)\, y \times 3\text{K} = (1.55 + 1 \times 1.88\,) \times 1.88 \times 3\text{K}$$
$$= 19.34 \text{ K}$$

Cost of lining = Perimeter (P) $\times 1 \times \text{K} = (b + 2y\,\sqrt{n^2 + 1}\,) \times 1 \times \text{K}$

$$= (1.55 + 2 \times 1.88\,\sqrt{1 + 1}\,)\,\text{K} = 6.86 \text{ K}$$

$\therefore$ Total cost of lined channel $= 19.34 \text{ K} + 6.86\text{K} = 26.2\text{K}$

Since the cost of excavation of unlined channel (27.76K) is greater than the total cost of lined channel, hence the **lined channel is cheaper. (Ans.)**

Example 16.17. *Design a concrete lined channel to carry a discharge of 500 m³/s at a slope of 1 in 4000. The side slopes of channel may be taken as 1:1. The Manning's roughness co-efficient for the lining is 0.014. Assume the permissible velocity in the section as 2.5 m/s.* **[UPSC Exams.]**

Solution. Discharge, $Q = 500 \text{ m}^3\text{/s}$

Bed slope, $S = \dfrac{1}{4000}$

Side slope, $n = \dfrac{1}{1} = 1$

Manning's roughness co-efficient, $N = 0.0014$

Permissible velocity, $V = 2.5$ m/s

Base width (b) and depth of flow (y):

$$\text{Area of flow, } A = \frac{Q}{V} = \frac{500}{2.5} = 200 \text{ m}^2$$

Also,
$$A = (b + ny)y = (b + y)y \qquad (\because n = 1)$$

or,
$$A = (b + y)\,y = 200 \qquad ...(i)$$

$$\text{Perimeter, } P = b + 2y\sqrt{n^2 + 1} = b + 2y\sqrt{1 + 1} = b + 2\sqrt{2}\,y$$

$$\text{Hydraulic radius, } R = \frac{A}{P} = \frac{200}{b + 2\sqrt{2}y}$$

$$\text{Discharge, } Q = AC\sqrt{RS}\text{, where } C = \frac{1}{N}R^{1/6}$$

or, $$Q = A \times \frac{1}{N}R^{1/6}\sqrt{RS} = A \times \frac{1}{N}R^{2/3}\sqrt{S}$$

Substituting the values, we get:

$$500 = 200 \times \frac{1}{0.014} \times \left(\frac{200}{b + 2\sqrt{2}y}\right)^{2/3} \times \sqrt{\frac{1}{4000}} = \frac{7724.88}{(b + 2\sqrt{2}y)^{2/3}}$$

or, $$b + 2\sqrt{2}y = \left(\frac{7724.88}{500}\right)^{3/2} = 60.73 \qquad ...(ii)$$

From eqn. (*i*), $$(b + y) = \frac{200}{y} \quad \text{or} \quad b = \frac{200}{y} - y$$

Substituting this value of b in eqn. (*ii*), we get:

$$\frac{200}{y} - y + 2\sqrt{2}y = 60.73 \quad \text{or} \quad 200 - y^2 + 2\sqrt{2}y^2 = 60.73y$$

or, $y^2(2\sqrt{2} - 1) - 60.73y + 200 = 0$ or $1.828y^2 - 60.73y + 200 = 0$

or, $y^2 - 33.22y + 109.41 = 0$

or, $$y = \frac{33.22 \pm \sqrt{(33.22)^2 - 4 \times 109.41}}{2} = \frac{33.22 \pm 25.8}{2} = 29.51 \text{ m, } 3.71 \text{ m}$$

$y = 3.71$ m (rejecting the first value, being impracticable)

and, $$b = \frac{200}{y} - y = \frac{200}{3.71} - 3.71 = 50.2 \text{ m}$$

Hence, *width of the channel*, **b = 50.2 m (Ans.)**

and, *depth of flow*, **y = 3.71 m (Ans.)**

Example 16.18. *A trapezoidal canal is to carry 45 m³/s with a mean velocity of 0.6 m/s. One side of canal is vertical and the other has a slope of 2 horizontal to 1 vertical. Find the minimum hydraulic slope, if Manning's N = 0.013.* **(PTU)**

Solution. *Given:* $Q = 45$ m³/s, $V_{mean} = 0.6$ m/s; $n = 2$, Manning's $N = 0.013$

Minimum hydraulic slope, S:

Refer to Fig. 16.17.

Area of flow, $$A = \left(\frac{AB + CD}{2}\right) \times y = \left(\frac{b + (b + ny)}{2}\right)y$$

$$= \left[\frac{b + (b + 2y)}{2}\right]y = (b + y)\,y$$

But, $$A = \frac{Q}{V_{mean}} = \frac{45}{0.6} = 75 \text{ m}^2$$

$\therefore \quad (b + y)\,y = 75$

or, $$b = \frac{75}{y} - y \qquad ...(i)$$

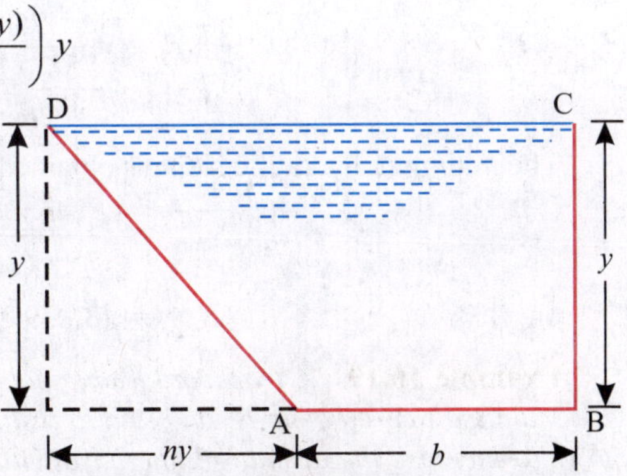

Fig. 16.17

Wetted perimeter, $P = b + y\sqrt{n^2 + 1} + y$

$$= b + y\{\sqrt{n^2+1} + 1\}$$

or, $$P = b + y(\sqrt{5} + 1) \qquad (\because n = 2)$$

$$\text{Hydraulic radius, } R = \frac{A}{P} = \frac{75}{b + y(\sqrt{5}+1)}$$

$$= \frac{75}{\left(\frac{75}{y} - y\right) + y\sqrt{5} + y}$$

$$= \frac{75}{\frac{75}{y} + y\sqrt{5}}$$

Now, discharge (Q) is given by:

$$Q = AC\sqrt{RS} \quad \text{where, } C = \frac{1}{N}(R)^{\frac{1}{6}}$$

or, $$Q = A\times\frac{1}{N}(R)^{1/6}\sqrt{RS} = A\times\frac{1}{N}(R)^{\left(\frac{1}{6}+\frac{1}{2}\right)}\sqrt{S} = A\times\frac{1}{N}(R)^{2/3}\sqrt{S}$$

or, $$\sqrt{S} = \frac{QN}{A(R)^{2/3}} = \frac{45\times 0.013}{75(R)^{2/3}} \qquad ...(i)$$

For S to be minimum, R has to be maximum.

or, $$\frac{75}{\frac{75}{y} + y\sqrt{5}} \text{ is to be maximum}$$

or, $$\frac{75}{y} + y\sqrt{5} \text{ is to be minimum}$$

or, $$\frac{d}{dy}\left[\frac{75}{y} + y\sqrt{5}\right] = 0$$

$$-\frac{75}{y^2} + \sqrt{5} = 0 \text{ or } y^2 = \frac{75}{\sqrt{5}}$$

or, $$y = 5.79 \text{ m}$$

Hence, for minimum slope,

$$R = \frac{75}{\frac{75}{y} + y\sqrt{5}} = \frac{75}{\frac{75}{5.79} + 5.79\sqrt{5}} = 2.896 \text{ m}$$

The minimum hydraulic slope is obtained by substituting their value of R in (*i*).

$$\therefore \quad \sqrt{S_{min}} = \frac{45\times 0.013}{75\times(2.896)^{2/3}} = 3.839\times 10^{-3}$$

or, $$S_{min} = (3.839\times 10^{-3})^2 = \mathbf{1.474\times 10^{-5}} \textbf{ (Ans.)}$$

Example 16.19. *A trapezoidal channel having a cross-sectional area A_1, wetted perimeter P_1, Manning's co-efficient N, and laid to a slope S carries a discharge Q, at a depth of flow equal to y. To increase the discharge, the base width of the channel is widened by x, keeping all other parameters same. Prove that*

$$\left(\frac{Q_2}{Q_1}\right)^3 \times \left(1+\frac{x}{P_1}\right)^2 = \left(1+\frac{xy}{A_1}\right)^5$$

where, Q_2 is the new discharge in the channel. **[UPSC Exams.]**

Solution. The Chezy's constant (C), using Manning's formula, is given by:

$$C = \frac{1}{N}(R)^{1/6}$$

$\therefore$ Velocity of flow, $V = C\sqrt{RS} = \frac{1}{N}R^{1/6} \times (RS)^{1/2} = \frac{R^{2/3}S^{1/2}}{N}$

where, R = Hydraulic radius (or hydraulic mean depth), and

S = Slope of the channel bed.

$$\text{Discharge, } Q = AV = A \times \frac{R^{2/3}S^{1/2}}{N}$$

$$= KAR^{2/3} = KA\left(\frac{A}{P}\right)^{2/3} = K\frac{A^{5/3}}{P^{2/3}} \qquad \left(\because R = \frac{A}{P}\right) \qquad ...(i)$$

where, K (*a* constant) $= \frac{S^{1/2}}{N}$ (S and N kept constant)

Area of cross-section of the widened canal $A_2 = (A_1 + xy)$

Wetted perimeter of the original channel, $P_2 = (P_1 + x)$

Where A_1 and P_1 are the area of cross-section and wetted perimeter respectively of the original channel.

Then from expression (*i*), we have:

$$Q_1 = K\frac{A_1^{5/3}}{P_1^{2/3}} \quad \text{and} \quad Q_2 = K\frac{A_2^{5/3}}{P_2^{2/3}}$$

$$\therefore \quad \frac{Q_2}{Q_1} = \left(\frac{A_2}{A_1}\right)^{5/3} \times \left(\frac{P_1}{P_2}\right)^{2/3}$$

Substituting the values of A_2 and P_2 in the above equation, we have:

$$\frac{Q_2}{Q_1} = \left(\frac{A_1 + xy}{A_1}\right)^{5/3} \times \left(\frac{P_1}{P_1 + x}\right)^{2/3}$$

$$= \left(1+\frac{xy}{A_1}\right)^{5/3} \times \left(\frac{1}{1+\frac{x}{P_1}}\right)^{2/3}$$

Taking cube on both sides, we get:

$$\left(\frac{Q_2}{Q_1}\right)^3 = \left(1+\frac{xy}{A_1}\right)^5 \times \left(\frac{1}{1+\frac{x}{P_1}}\right)^2$$

or,

$$\left(\frac{Q_2}{Q_1}\right)^3 \times \left(1+\frac{x}{P_1}\right)^2 = \left(1+\frac{xy}{A_1}\right)^5 \qquad \textbf{...Proved}$$

16.5.3 Most Economical Triangular Channel Section

Fig. 16.18 shows a triangular channel. The side slopes are n (horizontal) to 1 (vertical)

Let, y = Depth of flow, and

θ = Angle made by the sides with the vertical.

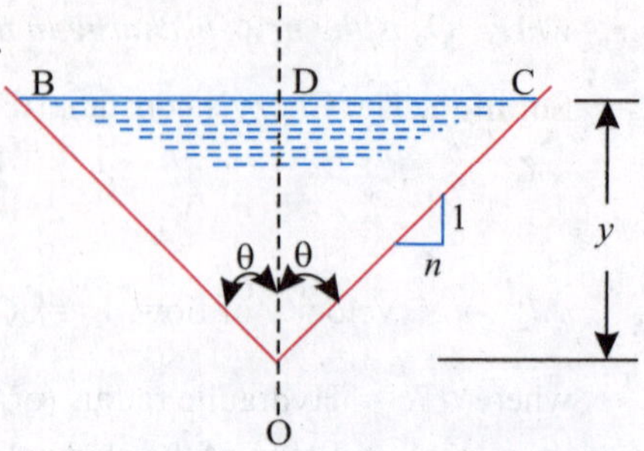

Fig. 16.18. Triangular channel.

From ΔODC, $\dfrac{CD}{DO} = \tan\theta$ or $\dfrac{CD}{y} = \tan\theta$

or, $CD = y\tan\theta$

Also, $\dfrac{DO}{CO} = \cos\theta$ or $\dfrac{y}{CO} = \cos\theta$

or, $CO = y\sec\theta$

Area of flow,

$$A = \frac{1}{2}\times BC\times DO = \frac{1}{2}\times 2CD\times DO$$

$$= \frac{1}{2}\times 2y\tan\theta\times y = y^2\tan\theta$$

i.e. $A = y^2\tan\theta$ ...(i)

Perimeter, $P = BO + OC = 2OC = 2y\sec\theta$ $(\because\ BO = OC)$ ...(ii)

Substituting the value of $y\left(=\sqrt{\dfrac{A}{\tan\theta}}\right)$ from eqn. (i) in eqn. (ii), we get:

$$P = 2\sqrt{\frac{A}{\tan\theta}}\sec\theta = 2\frac{\sqrt{A}}{\sqrt{\tan\theta}}(\sec\theta) \quad ...(iii)$$

Assuming the area to be constant, eqn. (iii) can be differentiated with respect to θ and equated to zero for obtaining the condition for minimum P.

i.e. $$\frac{dP}{d\theta} = \frac{d}{d\theta}\left[2\frac{\sqrt{A}}{\sqrt{\tan\theta}}(\sec\theta)\right] = 0$$

$$= 2\sqrt{A}\left[\frac{\sqrt{\tan\theta}\times\sec\theta.\tan\theta - \sec\theta\times\frac{1}{2}(\tan\theta)^{-1/2}\sec^2\theta}{\tan\theta}\right] = 0$$

$$= 2\sqrt{A}\left[\frac{\sec\theta\tan\theta}{\sqrt{\tan\theta}} - \frac{\sec^3\theta}{2(\tan\theta)^{3/2}}\right] = 0$$

or, $\sec\theta\,(2\tan^2\theta - \sec^2\theta) = 0$

Since $\sec\theta \neq 0$,

$\therefore$ $2\tan^2\theta - \sec^2\theta = 0$ or $2\tan^2\theta = \sec^2\theta$

or, $\sqrt{2}\tan\theta = \sec\theta$

$\therefore$ $\theta = 45°$; and $n = 1$ ...(16.18)

Hence, a triangular channel section will be most economical when each of its sloping sides makes an angle of 45° with the vertical.

Hydraulic radius, $R = \dfrac{A}{P} = \dfrac{y^2\tan\theta}{2y\sec\theta}$

Substituting the value of θ from eqn. (16.18) in the above eqn., we get:

$$R = \frac{y^2 \tan 45°}{2y \sec 45°} = \frac{y^2}{2y \times \sqrt{2}} = \frac{y}{2\sqrt{2}} \quad \text{...(16.19)}$$

Thus it can be seen that the *most economical triangular channel section will be a half square described on a diagonal and having equal sloping sides.*

Example 16.20. *Water flows in a channel of the shape of isosceles triangle of bed width 'a' and sides making an angle of 45° with the bed. Determine the relation between depth of flow 'd' and the bed width 'a' for maximum velocity condition and for maximum discharge condition. Use Manning's formula and note that 'd' is less than 0.5 a.* **[UPSC, CES, Exams.]**

Solution. Bed width of the channel $= a$

Angle of sides with the bed $= 45°$

Depth of flow $= d\ (d < 0.5a)$

Velocity, $V = C\sqrt{RS}$

But $C = \frac{1}{N} R^{1/6}$, where N is Manning's constant

$$\therefore \quad V = \frac{1}{N} R^{1/6} \sqrt{RS} = \frac{1}{N} R^{2/3} S^{1/2} \quad \text{...}(i)$$

where, R = hydraulic radius, S = bed slope.

Area of flow, $A = \left(\frac{GH + BC}{2}\right) \times d$

But $GH = BC - 2JC = a - 2d$

$$\left[\because \frac{HJ}{JC} = \tan 45° = 1 \quad \text{or} \quad \frac{d}{JC} = 1 \text{ or } JC = d\right]$$

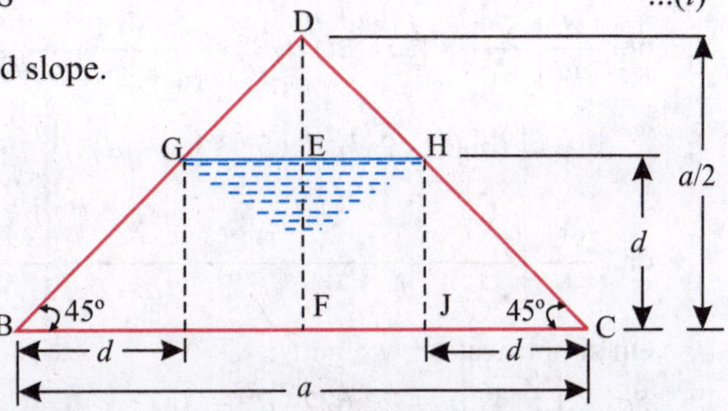

Fig. 16.19

$$\therefore A = \left[\frac{(a - 2d) + a}{2}\right] \times d = (a - d)\, d$$

Wetted perimeter, $P = BC + BG + HC = BC + 2BG \qquad (\because BG = HC)$

But $BG = \sqrt{d^2 + d^2} = d\sqrt{2}$

$$\therefore \quad P = a + 2\sqrt{2}\, d$$

Hydraulic radius, $R = \frac{A}{P} = \frac{(a - d)\, d}{a + 2\sqrt{2}\, d}$

$$\therefore \quad V = \frac{1}{N} \left[\frac{(a - d)\, d}{a + 2\sqrt{2}\, d}\right]^{2/3} S^{1/2}$$

For maximum velocity, $\frac{dV}{dd} = 0$

$$\frac{d}{dd}\left[\frac{S^{1/2}}{N}\left\{\frac{(a - d)\, d}{a + 2\sqrt{2}\, d}\right\}^{2/3}\right] = 0$$

$$\frac{S^{1/2}}{N}\left[\frac{2}{3}\left\{\frac{(a - d)\, d}{a + 2\sqrt{2}\, d}\right\}^{-\frac{1}{3}} \left\{\frac{(a + 2\sqrt{2}\, d)(a - 2d) - (a - d)\, d \times 2\sqrt{2}}{(a + 2\sqrt{2}\, d)^2}\right\}\right] = 0$$

On simplification, we have:

$$a^2 - 2ad - 2\sqrt{2}\,d^2 = 0$$

or,
$$a = \frac{2d \pm \sqrt{4d^2 + 8\sqrt{2}\,d^2}}{2} = \frac{2d \pm 3.91\,d}{2} = 2.955\,d$$

(neglecting –*ve* value)

or,
$$\frac{d}{a} = \frac{1}{2.955} = \mathbf{0.338\ (Ans.)}$$

For maximum discharge, $\frac{dQ}{dd} = 0$

$$Q = A.V = (a-d)\,d \times \frac{1}{N}\left\{\frac{(a-d)\,d}{a + 2\sqrt{2}\,d}\right\}^{2/3} S^{1/2}$$

$$\therefore \quad \frac{d}{dd}\left[(a-d)\,d \times \frac{1}{N}\left\{\frac{(a-d)\,d}{a + 2\sqrt{2}\,d}\right\}^{2/3} S^{1/2}\right] = 0$$

or,
$$\frac{d}{dd}\left[\frac{S^{1/2}}{N} \times \{(a-d)\,d\}^{5/3} \times \frac{1}{(a + 2\sqrt{2}\,d)^{2/3}}\right] = 0$$

or,
$$\frac{S^{1/2}}{N}\left[\frac{(a + 2\sqrt{2}\,d)^{2/3} \times 5/3\,\{(a-d)\,d\}^{2/3} \times (a - 2d) - \{(a-d)\,d\}^{5/3} \times \left\{\frac{2}{3}(a + 2\sqrt{2}\,d)^{-1/3} \times 2\sqrt{2}\right\}}{(a + 2\sqrt{2}\,d)^{4/3}}\right] = 0$$

On simplification, we get:

$$5a^2 - 1.5147\,ad - 22.6274\,d^2 = 0$$

or,
$$a = \frac{1.5147\,d \pm d\,\sqrt{(1.5147)^2 + 4 \times 5 \times 22.6274}}{10}$$

$$= \frac{1.5147\,d \pm 21.327\,d}{10} = 2.284\,d \text{ (neglecting –}ve\text{ value)}$$

or,
$$\frac{d}{a} = \frac{1}{2.284} = \mathbf{0.4378\ (Ans.)}$$

16.5.4. Most Economical Circular Channel Section

Circular pipes and culverts which are partly filled are treated as channels. In case of conduits the condition of area remaining constant does not hold good since both the wetted perimeter and wetted area vary with depth of flow. The most economical section (optimum section) is designed *both for conditions of maximum mean velocity and maximum flow rate.*

$$\text{Velocity of flow, } V = C\sqrt{RS} = C\sqrt{\frac{A}{P}\,S} \qquad \text{...Chezy's formula}$$

$$\text{Discharge, } Q = AV = AC\sqrt{RS} = C\sqrt{\left(\frac{A^3}{P}\right)S}$$

Thus the *flow velocity* will have a maximum value when hydraulic radius $\left(\frac{A}{P}\right)$ is *maximum,* and a maximum discharge is obtained when $\left(\frac{A^3}{P}\right)$ is *maximum.*

Fig. 16.20 shows a circular channel through which water is flowing.

Let, y = Depth of flow,

r = Radius of the channel, and

2θ = Angle subtended by water surface AB at the centre in radians.

Wetted perimeter, P = Length of arc AD

$$= \frac{2\pi r}{2\pi} \times 2\theta = 2r\theta$$

i.e. $$P = 2r\theta \qquad \text{... (16.20)}$$

Wetted area, A = Area $ADBA$

= Area of sector $OADBO$ – area of ΔOAB

$$= \frac{\pi r^2}{2\pi} \times 2\theta - \frac{1}{2} AB \times CO$$

$$= r^2\theta - \frac{1}{2} \times 2BC \times CO \qquad (\because AB = 2BC)$$

$$= r^2\theta - \frac{1}{2} \times 2 \times r \sin\theta \times r\cos\theta$$

$(\because BC = r\sin\theta,\ CO = r\cos\theta)$

$$= r^2\theta - \frac{1}{2} r^2 \times 2\sin\theta\cos\theta$$

or, $$A = r^2\left(\theta - \frac{\sin 2\theta}{2}\right) \qquad \text{...(16.21)}$$

$(\because 2\sin\theta\cos\theta = \sin 2\theta)$

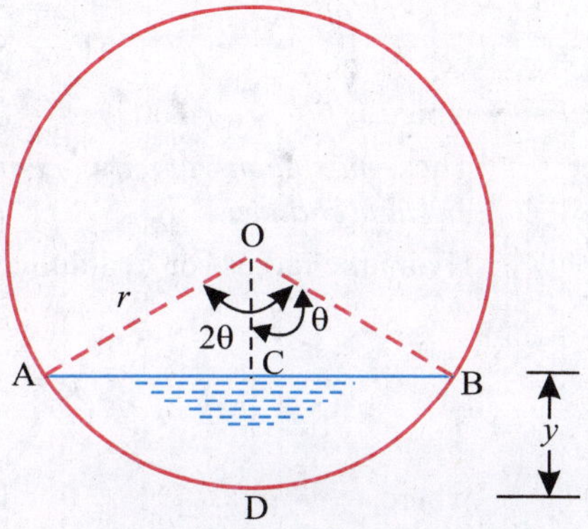

Fig. 16.20. Circular channel.

(*i*) Condition for maximum velocity:

The *velocity will be maximum* when:

$$\frac{d}{d\theta}\left(\frac{A}{P}\right) = 0$$

(where, A and P both are functions of θ).

or, $$\frac{P\dfrac{dA}{d\theta} - A\cdot\dfrac{dP}{d\theta}}{P^2} = 0 \quad \text{or} \quad P\frac{dA}{d\theta} - A\cdot\frac{dP}{d\theta} = 0 \qquad \text{...}(i)$$

Now, $$A = r^2\left(\theta - \frac{\sin 2\theta}{2}\right) \qquad \text{[Eqn. (16.21)]}$$

$$\frac{dA}{d\theta} = r^2\left(1 - \frac{\cos 2\theta}{2} \times 2\right) = r^2(1 - \cos 2\theta)$$

Again, $$P = 2r\theta \qquad \text{[Eqn. (16.20)}$$

$$\frac{dP}{d\theta} = 2r$$

Substituting the values of A, P, $\frac{dA}{d\theta}$ and $\frac{dP}{d\theta}$ in eqn. (*i*), we get:

$$2r\theta\,[r^2(1 - \cos 2\theta)] - r^2\left(\theta - \frac{\sin 2\theta}{2}\right) \times 2r = 0$$

or, $$2r^3\theta(1 - \cos 2\theta) - 2r^3\left(\theta - \frac{\sin 2\theta}{2}\right) = 0$$

or, $\theta(1-\cos 2\theta) = \left(\theta - \frac{\sin 2\theta}{2}\right) = 0$ (cancelling $2r^3$)

or, $\theta - \theta.\cos 2\theta - \theta + \frac{\sin 2\theta}{2} = 0$

or, $\theta.\cos 2\theta = \frac{\sin 2\theta}{2}$

$\therefore \quad \tan 2\theta = 2\theta$

Solution gives : **2 θ = 257.5°** (approximately) ... by hit and trial method, or **θ = 128.75°**

Depth of flow, $y = OD - OC = r - r\cos\theta$ (Fig. 16.16)

$= r(1 - \cos\theta) = r(1 - \cos 128.75°) \simeq 1.62\,r \simeq 0.81d$

i.e. $\mathbf{y \simeq 0.81\, d}$ ...(16.22)

where, d = Diameter of the circular channel.

Thus, *maximum velocity occurs when the depth of flow is 0.81 times the diameter of the circular channel.*

Hydraulic radius (or hydraulic mean depth) for maximum velocity,

$$R = \frac{A}{P} = \frac{r^2\left(\theta - \frac{\sin 2\theta}{2}\right)}{2r\theta} = \frac{r}{2\theta}\left(\theta - \frac{\sin 2\theta}{2}\right) \quad ...(16.23)$$

where, $\theta = 128.75° = 128.75 \times \frac{\pi}{180} = 2.247$ radians

$$\therefore \quad R = \frac{r}{2 \times 2.247}\left(2.247 - \frac{\sin 257.5°}{2}\right)$$

or, $\mathbf{R} \simeq 0.6086r \simeq \mathbf{0.305d}$ ...(16.24)

Thus, for *maximum mean velocity in a channel of circular section hydraulic radius equals* 0.305 *times the channel diameter.*

(*ii*) Condition for maximum discharge:

The *discharge will be maximum* when:

$$\frac{d}{d\theta}\left(\frac{A^3}{P}\right) = 0 \quad \text{or} \quad \frac{P \times 3A^2\frac{dA}{d\theta} - A^3\frac{dP}{d\theta}}{P^2} = 0$$

or, $$3PA^2\frac{dA}{d\theta} - A^3\frac{dP}{d\theta} = 0$$

Dividing, both sides by A^2, we get:

or, $$3P\frac{dA}{d\theta} - A\frac{dP}{d\theta} = 0 \quad ...(i)$$

$P = 2r\theta$ (Eqn. 16.20)

$\therefore \quad \frac{dP}{d\theta} = 2r$

$A = r^2\left(\theta - \frac{\sin 2\theta}{2}\right)$ (Eqn. 16.21)

$\therefore \quad \frac{dA}{d\theta} = r^2(1 - \cos 2\theta)$

Substituting the values of P, A, $\frac{dP}{d\theta}$ and $\frac{dA}{d\theta}$ in eqn. (*i*), we have:

$$3 \times 2r\theta \times r^2 (1 - \cos 2\theta) - r^2 \left(\theta - \frac{\sin 2\theta}{2}\right) \times 2r = 0$$

or, $$6r^3\theta (1 - \cos 2\theta) - 2r^3 \left(\theta - \frac{\sin 2\theta}{2}\right) = 0$$

Dividing by $2r^3$, we get:

or, $$3\theta (1 - \cos 2\theta) - \left(\theta - \frac{\sin 2\theta}{2}\right) = 0$$

or, $$3\theta - 3\theta \cos 2\theta - \theta + \frac{\sin 2\theta}{2} = 0$$

or, $$2\theta - 3\theta \cos 2\theta + \frac{\sin 2\theta}{2} = 0$$

or, $$4\theta - 6\theta \cos 2\theta + \sin 2\theta = 0$$

Solution gives: $2\theta = 308°$ ... by hit and trial method

$$\theta = \frac{308}{2} = \mathbf{154°}$$

Depth of flow for maximum discharge,

$$y = r(1 - \cos\theta) \qquad \text{[Fig. 16.16]}$$

$$= r(1 \cos 154°) \simeq 1.9r \simeq 0.95d$$

i.e. $$y \simeq \mathbf{0.95d} \qquad (16.25)$$

where, d is the diameter of the circular channel.

Thus *for maximum discharge through a circular channel, the depth of flow is equal to 0.95 times its diameter.*

Hydraulic radius for maximum discharge,

$$R = \frac{A}{P} = \frac{r^2\left(\theta - \frac{\sin 2\theta}{2}\right)}{2r\theta} = \frac{r}{2\theta}\left(\theta - \frac{\sin 2\theta}{2}\right)$$

where, $$\theta = 154° = 154 \times \frac{\pi}{180} = 2.687 \text{ radians}$$

$\therefore$ $$R = \frac{r}{2 \times 2.687}\left(2.687 - \frac{\sin 308°}{2}\right)$$

or, $$R \simeq 0.573r \simeq \mathbf{0.29d} \qquad ...(16.26)$$

Thus *for maximum discharge through a circular channel, the hydraulic radius equals 0.29 times channel diameter.*

Example 16.21. *A concrete lined circular channel of 3.6 m diameter has a bed slope of 1 in 600. Determine the velocity and flow rate for the conditions of:*

(i) Maximum velocity, and *(ii) discharge.*

Take Chezy's constant, C = 50.

Solution. Diameter of the circular channel, $d = 3.6$ m

$$\text{Bed slope, } S = \frac{1}{600}$$

$$\text{Chezy's constant, } C = 50$$

Let 2θ = Total angle subtended by the water surface at the centre of the channel.

Flow velocity, V; flow rate, Q:

(i) Maximum velocity condition:

For maximum velocity condition,

$$2\theta = 257.5° = 257.5 \times \frac{\pi}{180} = 4.49 \text{ radians}$$

$$\text{Depth of flow, } y = 0.81d = 0.81 \times 3.6 \simeq 2.92 \text{ m}$$

$$\text{Area of flow, } A = \frac{r^2}{2}(2\theta - \sin 2\theta)$$

$$= \frac{1.8^2}{2}(4.49 - \sin 257.5°) = 8.85 \text{ m}^2$$

$$\text{Wetted perimeter, } P = 2\,r\theta = r \times 2\theta = 1.8 \times 4.49 = 8.08 \text{ m}$$

$$\text{Hydraulic radius, } R = \frac{A}{P} = \frac{8.85}{8.08} = 1.095$$

$$\therefore \quad \text{Flow velocity, } V = C\sqrt{RS} = 50\sqrt{1.095 \times \frac{1}{600}} \simeq \mathbf{2.14 \text{ m/s}} \text{ (Ans.)}$$

$$\text{Flow rate, } Q = AV = 8.85 \times 2.14 = \mathbf{18.94 \text{ m}^3\text{/s}} \text{ (Ans.)}$$

(ii) Maximum discharge condition:

For maximum discharge condition,

$$2\theta = 308° = 308 \times \frac{\pi}{180} = 5.375 \text{ radians}$$

$$\text{Depth of flow, } y = 0.95d = 0.95 \times 3.6 = 3.42 \text{ m}$$

$$\text{Area of flow, } A = \frac{r^2}{2}(2\theta - \sin 2\theta)$$

$$= \frac{1.8^2}{2}(5.375 - \sin 308°) = 6.984 \text{ m}^2$$

$$\text{Wetted perimeter, } P = 2r\theta = r \times 2\theta = 1.8 \times 5.375 = 9.675 \text{ m}$$

$$\text{Hydraulic radius, } R = \frac{A}{P} = \frac{9.984}{9.675} = 1.032 \text{ m}$$

$$\therefore \quad \text{Flow velocity, } V = C\sqrt{RS} = 50\sqrt{1.032 \times \frac{1}{600}} = \mathbf{2.07 \text{ m/s}} \text{ (Ans.)}$$

$$\text{Flow rate, } Q = AV = 9.984 \times 2.07 = \mathbf{20.66 \text{ m}^3\text{/s}} \text{ (Ans.)}$$

16.6. OPEN CHANNEL SECTION FOR CONSTANT VELOCITY AT ALL DEPTHS OF FLOW

It has been observed that according to Chezy's or Manning's formulae the hydraulic radius is the sole shape parameter on which the velocity of flow in a channel laid on a constant bottom slope depends. Thus, *if the hydraulic radius is constant for any depth of flow the velocity of flow will be constant.*

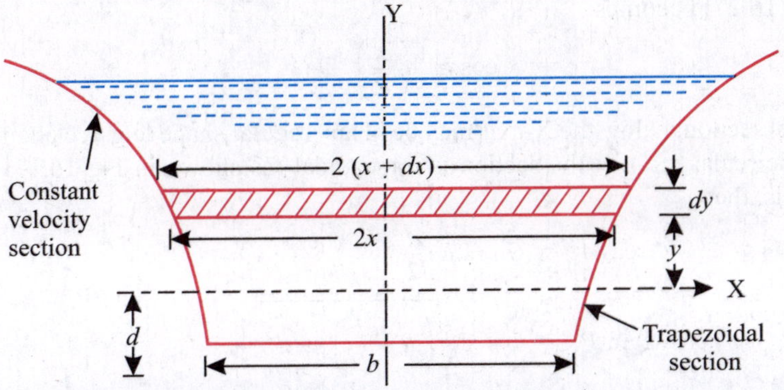

Fig. 16.21. Channel section for constant velocity at all depths.

Consider a profile of channel section (shown in Fig. 16.21) having a constant hydraulic radius R for any depth of flow. For constant velocity V, hydraulic radius has to be constant, which means that $\frac{dA}{dP}$ must remain constant at all depth of flow.

i.e.,
$$\frac{dA}{dP} = R$$

where, cross-sectional area, $dA = 2xdy$

and, wetted perimeter, $dP = 2\sqrt{(dx)^2 + (dy)^2}$

For a small portion of the channel section considered at a depth of y and dy in thickness, as shown in Fig. 16·21.

$$\therefore \quad \frac{2xdy}{2\sqrt{(dx)^2 + (dy)^2}} = R \quad \text{or} \quad x^2 (dy)^2 = R^2 [(dx)^2 + (dy)^2]$$

Dividing both sides by $(dx)^2$, we get:

$$x^2\left(\frac{dy}{dx}\right)^2 = R^2\left[1 + \left(\frac{dy}{dx}\right)^2\right] \quad \text{or} \quad x^2\left(\frac{dy}{dx}\right)^2 = R^2 + R^2\left(\frac{dy}{dx}\right)^2$$

or,
$$\left(\frac{dy}{dx}\right)^2 (x^2 - R^2) = R^2 \quad \left(\frac{dy}{dx}\right)^2 = \frac{R^2}{x^2 - R^2}$$

or,
$$\frac{dy}{dx} = \frac{R}{\sqrt{x^2 - R^2}} \quad \text{or} \quad dy = \frac{R}{\sqrt{x^2 - R^2}} \cdot dx$$

Integrating both sides, we get the following two forms:

$$y = R \cos h^{-1}\left(\frac{x}{R}\right) + C \qquad ...(16.27)$$

or,
$$y = R \ln (x + \sqrt{x^2 - R^2}) + C_1 \qquad ...(16.27\ (a))$$

where, C and C_1 are the constants of integration.

However, we shall consider the first form.

The eqn. (16.27) is the equation of curves forming the sides of the section, the channel is bottomless. The value of C can be obtained if the width of the section of X-axis is known. Let the width be $2R$ at $y = 0$ *i.e.* $x = R$ at $y = 0$

$$\therefore \quad 0 = R \cos h^{-1}\left(\frac{R}{R}\right) + C \qquad \text{(From eqn. 16.27)}$$

or,
$$C = 0$$

Thus eqn. (16.27) becomes:

$$y = R \cos h^{-1}\left(\frac{x}{R}\right) \quad ...(16.28)$$

The channel section, below the X-axis may be of any regular shape (e.g. rectangular, trapezoidal, triangular, semicircular etc.). If the section is trapezoidal (as shown in Fig 16.17) for the section below the X-axis, then:

$$\text{Area, } A_1 = (b + 2R)\frac{d}{2}$$

$$\text{Perimeter, } P_1 = b + 2\sqrt{\left(R - \frac{b}{2}\right)^2 + d^2}$$

It has been observed in *the case of an open channel that the velocity increases with the increase in depth of flow, thereby causing damage (scouring of the bed and sides) to the channel section.* On the contrary if the *depth of flow decreases, the velocity decreases* which *may cause silting of the suspended matter* in the liquid. Both these defects are removed by having ***constant velocity channels*** (where in the *large fluctuations in the velocity are avoided*).

Channel sections of constant velocity are designed particularly in the case of large sewers in which the discharge ranges from a certain minimum value that flows daily to a very large value during rainy season. In such sewers, the bottom portion (triangular or trapezoidal) is designed for the minimum discharge which flows during lean period, when the discharge increases further, the *constant-velocity section becomes effective and discharges the increased flow at the constant velocity.*

Example 16.22. *It is required to design a channel to give a constant mean velocity of flow of 1.8 m/s at all depths of flow. The lower portion of the channel to carry the minimum discharge is rectangular and has the best proportion, the bottom width being 1.5 m. Determine:*

(i) The channel bed slope;

(ii) The depth of flow when the width of water surface is 9 m.

Take Manning's N = 0.015.

Solution. Velocity of flow at all depths, $V = 1.8$ m/s

Bottom width, $b = 1.5$ m

Manning's $N = 0.015$

Width of water surface = 9 m

The bottom portion is rectangular and has the best proportion, thus $b = 2d$, where b and d are the base width and depth of flow respectively.

or, $1.5 = 2d; \quad \therefore \ d = 0.75$ m

Also for the best channel section, $R = \frac{d}{2} = \frac{0.75}{2} = 0.375$ m

(*i*) The channel bed slope, S:

Using Manning's formula, $V = \frac{1}{N} R^{2/3} S^{1/2}$

(where, R = hydraulic radius)

or, $$1.8 = \frac{1}{0.015} \times (0.375)^{2/3} S^{1/2}$$

or, $$S^{1/2} = \frac{1.8 \times 0.015}{(0.375)^{2/3}} = 0.05192 \quad \text{or} \quad S = 0.0027 \text{ or } 1 \text{ in } 370$$

Hence, the channel bed slope = 1 in 370 (Ans.)

(*ii*) **Depth of flow:**

$$y = R \ln[x + \sqrt{x^2 - R^2}] + C \qquad \text{[Ean. 16.27 (a)]}$$

When, $x = \frac{1.5}{2} = 0.75 \text{ m}, y = 0$

$$\therefore \qquad C = -R \ln[0.75 + \sqrt{0.75^2 - R^2}]$$

Substituting this value of C in the above eqn., we have:

$$y = R \ln[x + \sqrt{x^2 + R^2}] - R \ln[0.75 + \sqrt{0.75^2 - R^2}]$$

or,

$$y = R \ln\left[\frac{x + \sqrt{x^2 - R^2}}{0.75 + \sqrt{0.75^2 - R^2}}\right]$$

When, $x = \frac{9}{2} = 4.5$ m (given), $R = 0.375$ m (calculated earlier), substituting these values, we have:

$$y = 0.375 \ln\left[\frac{4.5 + \sqrt{4.5^2 - 0.375^2}}{0.75 + \sqrt{0.75^2 - 0.375^2}}\right] = 0.375 \ln\left[\frac{4.5 + 4.484}{0.75 + 0.694}\right] = 0.697 \text{ m}$$

$\therefore$ Total depth of flow $= d + y = 0.75 + 0.697 =$ **1.447 m (Ans.)**

B. NON-UNIFORM FLOW

16.7. NON-UNIFORM FLOW THROUGH OPEN CHANNELS

Whereas in *uniform flow* the gravity force on the flowing liquid just *balances* the frictional force between the flowing liquid and that inside surface of the channel which is in contact with this liquid, the friction force and gravity force are *not in balance* in case of *a steady non-uniform flow*. Non-uniform flow may be *caused by*:

(*i*) The change in width, depth, bed slope etc. of a channel;

(*ii*) An obstruction, constructed across a channel of uniform width.

- *Waves and surges in open channel produce unsteady non-uniform flow.*

Non-uniform flow is also known as the *flow of varying depth or, the varied flow*. The varied flow may be:

(*i*) *Gradually varied flow (G.V.F.).* In this case of flow the depth of flow increases or decreases *gradually* in the direction of flow; this change from one depth of flow to another occurs gradually in a distance of *appreciable length*.

(*ii*) *Rapidly varied flow (R.V.F.).* In this case a sudden change of depth occurs at a particular point of a channel and the change from one depth to another takes place in a distance of *very short length*.

16.8. SPECIFIC ENERGY AND SPECIFIC ENERGY CURVE

The total energy of flow per *unit weight* of liquid is given by:

$$\text{Total energy} = z + y + \frac{V^2}{2g}$$

where, z = Elevation of the channel bottom above the horizontal bottom,

y = Depth of flow, and

V = Average velocity of flow.

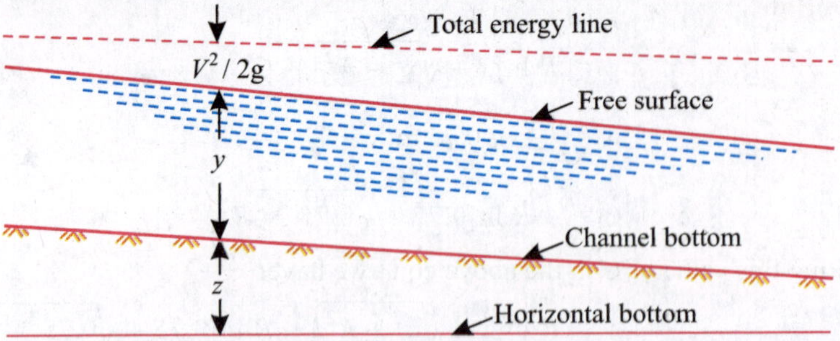

Fig. 16.22. Specific energy.

If the channel bottom itself is taken as the datum (Fig. 16.22), then total energy for unit weight of liquid,

$$E = y + \frac{V^2}{2g} \qquad ...(16.29)$$

The energy E given by eqn. (16.29) is known as *specific energy*. Thus **specific energy** *is defined as the energy per unit weight of flowing liquid above the channel bottom.* Although the total (or Bernoulli's) energy is reduced by friction, the specific energy can *increase* or *decrease from* section to section if the *bed elevation changes; however, for uniform flow the specific energy remains constant along the flow.*

It is evident from eqn. (16.29) that specific energy comprises:

(*i*) Potential energy of flow (E_p), y, and

(*ii*) Kinetic energy of flow (E_k), $\frac{V^2}{2g}$.

i.e.
$$E = y + \frac{V^2}{2g}$$
$$= E_p + E_k$$

For the sake of simplicity let us consider a channel of *rectangular section*.

Let, b = Width of channel,

y = Depth of flow, and

Q = Discharge through the channel.

Now, Velocity of flow, $V = \frac{\text{Discharge}}{\text{Area}} = \frac{Q}{b \times y} = \frac{q}{y}$ ...(16.30)

(where q = discharge per unit width)

$\therefore$ Specific energy, $E = y + \frac{(q/y)^2}{2g}$

or,
$$E = y + \frac{q^2}{2gy^2} = E_p + E_k \qquad ...(16.31)$$

For a given channel section and discharge, eqn. (16.31) can be represented graphically as a plot of specific energy E against the depth of flow. Such a plot is called the *specific energy curve/ diagram* and it consists of a family of similar curves each representing a given unit discharge.

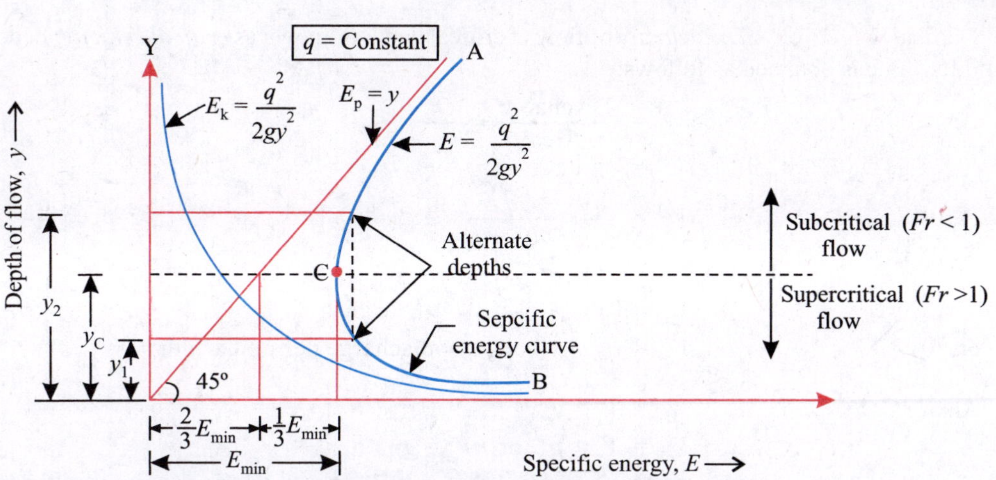

Fig. 16.23. Specific energy curve.

The specific energy plot of Fig. 16.23 entails the following information:

(*i*) The curve for potential energy (*i.e.* $E_p = y$) is a *straight line* passing through the origin, making an angle of 45° with each of the two axes (*X* and *Y*),

(*ii*) The *curve* for kinetic energy is a *parabola*. Plot for *specific energy is obtained by adding kinetic energy to potential energy.*

(*iii*) Specific energy is asymptotic to the horizontal axis for small values of *y* and asymptotic to 45° line for high values of *y*.

(*iv*) At a certain depth y_c, called the *critical depth*, the specific energy curve has a point of *minimum specific energy*, the corresponding flow velocity is called the critical velocity V_c.

(*v*) For every value of specific energy other than minimum there are two possible depths of flow (y_1 and y_2), one greater and other less than critical depth y_c; these two depths (for same specific energy) are referred to as *alternate or conjugate depths*.

Critical depth, y_c. It can be seen from the specific energy curve *ACB* (Fig 16.23) that, there is one point *C* on the curve which has a *minimum specific energy*, thereby indicating that below this value of specific energy the given discharge cannot occur. *The depth of flow at which the specific energy is minimum is called* ***critical depth*** y_c.

The mathematical expression for critical depth can be obtained by differentiating the specific energy equation, $E = y + \frac{q^2}{2gy^2}$ with respect to *y* and equating the derivative to zero. Thus:

$$\frac{dE}{dy} = \frac{d}{dy}\left[y + \frac{q^2}{2gy^2}\right] = 0$$

or, $$1 + \frac{q^2}{2g}\left(-\frac{2}{y^3}\right) = 0 \quad \text{or} \quad 1 = \frac{2q^2}{2gy^3}$$

or, $$y = \left(\frac{q^2}{g}\right)^{1/3}$$

But when the specific energy is minimum the depth of flow is critical, denoted by y_c.

$$\therefore \quad y_c = \left(\frac{q^2}{g}\right)^{1/3} \quad \text{...(16.32)}$$

Critical velocity, V_c. *The velocity* of flow at critical depth is known as *critical velocity;* denoted by V_c. Its value is obtained as follows:

$$\text{Velocity} = \frac{\text{Discharge}}{\text{Area}} = \frac{Q}{b \cdot y} = \frac{q}{y}$$

$$\therefore \quad V_c = \frac{q}{y_c} = \frac{q}{\left(\frac{q^2}{g}\right)^{1/3}} = q^{1/3} g^{1/3} \quad \left[\because y_c = \left(\frac{q^2}{g}\right)^{1/3}\right]$$

$$\text{or,} \quad V_c^3 = qg \quad \left(\text{where, } q = \text{discharge per unit width} = \frac{Q}{b}\right)$$

$$\text{Also} \quad q = V_c \times y_c$$

$$\therefore \quad V_c^3 = V_c y_c g \quad \text{or} \quad V_c^2 = g y_c$$

$$\text{or,} \quad V_c = \sqrt{g y_c} \qquad \text{...(16.33)}$$

Minimum specific energy in terms of critical depth. The specific energy is given by:

$$E = y + \frac{q^2}{2gy^2} \qquad \text{(Eqn. 16.31)}$$

The specific energy is *minimum* when *depth of flow is critical* and hence the above equation becomes:

$$E_{min} = y_c + \frac{q^2}{2gy_c^2}$$

$$\text{But,} \quad y_c = \left(\frac{q^2}{g}\right)^{1/3} \quad \text{or } y_c^3 = \frac{q^2}{g} \qquad \text{(Eqn. 16.32)}$$

$$\therefore \quad E_{min} = y_c + \frac{y_c^3}{2y_c^2} = y_c + \frac{y_c}{2} = \frac{3y_c}{2} \qquad \text{(Eqn. 16.34)}$$

$$\left(\text{or } y_c = \frac{2}{3} E_{min}\right)$$

Critical flow. Refer to Fig. 16.23. *A critical flow is one in which specific energy is minimum.* A flow *corresponding to critical depth is also known as* ***critical flow.***

From eqn. (16.33), we have:

$$V_c = \sqrt{g y_c} \quad \text{or} \quad \frac{V_c}{\sqrt{g y_c}} = 1$$

$$\text{But,} \quad \frac{V_c}{\sqrt{g y_c}} = \text{Froude number } (Fr)$$

$$\therefore \quad Fr = 1 \text{ for critical flow.}$$

Subcritical flow. The flow is *subcritical* (or *streaming* or *tranquil*) when the depth of flow in a channel is *greater than the critical depth* (y_c). In this type of flow, $Fr < 1$.

Supercritical flow. The flow is *supercritical* (or *shooting* or *torrential*) when the depth of flow in a channel is *less than the critical depth* (y_c). In this case $Fr > 1$.

Condition for maximum discharge for a given value of specific energy:

The specific energy (E) at any section of a channel is given by:

$$E = y + \frac{V^2}{2g}, \quad \text{where,} \quad V = \frac{Q}{A} = \frac{Q}{b \times y}$$

$$\therefore \quad E = y + \frac{Q^2}{b^2 y^2} \times \frac{1}{2g} = y + \frac{Q^2}{2gb^2 y^2}$$

or, $$Q^2 = 2gb^2y^2 (E - y)$$

or, $$Q = b\sqrt{2g\,(Ey^2 - y^3)}$$

For discharge Q to be maximum the expression $(Ey^2 - y^3)$ should be *maximum*.

i.e. $$\frac{d}{dy}(Ey^2 - y^3) = 0$$

or, $$2Ey - 3y^2 = 0 \qquad (\because E \text{ is constant})$$

or, $$2Ey = 3y^2$$

or, $$y = \frac{2}{3}E \qquad ...(16.35)$$

or, $$E = \frac{3y}{2} \qquad ...[16.35\,(a)]$$

According to eqn. (16.34) specific energy is *minimum* when it is equal to $\frac{3}{2}$ times the value of depth of critical flow. Here according to eqn. [16.35 (*a*)] the specific energy is equal to $\frac{3}{2}$ times the depth of flow. Thus eqn. [16.35 (*a*)] represents minimum specific energy and y is the critical depth. Hence the *condition for maximum discharge for given value of specific energy* is that the *depth of flow should be critical*.

Fig. 16.24 shows the discharge curve.

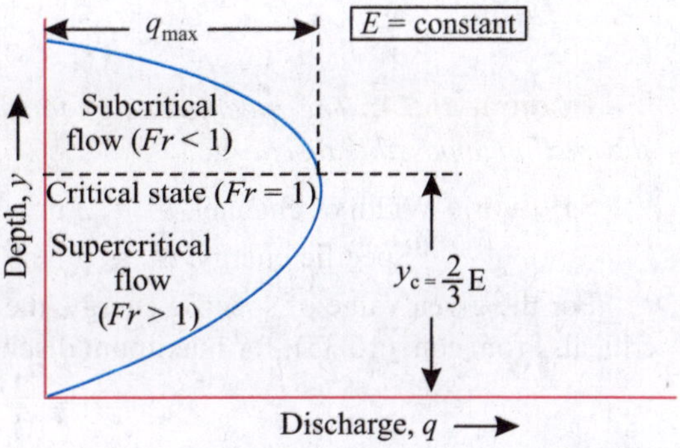

Fig. 16.24. Discharge curve.

Example 16.23. *A 8 m wide channel conveys 15 m³/s of water at a depth of 1.2 m. Calculate:*
(*i*) *Specific energy of the flowing water;*
(*ii*) *Critical depth, critical velocity and minimum specific energy;*
(*iii*) *Froude number and state whether flow is subcritical or supercritical.*

Solution. Width of the channel, $b = 8$ m

Discharge, $Q = 15 \text{ m}^3/\text{s}$

Depth of flow, $y = 1.2$ m

(*i*) Specific energy of the flowing water:

Average flow velocity,

$$V = \frac{Q}{b \times y} = \frac{15}{8 \times 1.2} = 1.5625 \text{ m/s}$$

Discharge per unit width,

$$q = \frac{Q}{b} = \frac{15}{8} = 1.875 \text{ m}^3/\text{s per m}$$

∴ Specific energy,

$$E = y + \frac{V^2}{2g} = 1.2 + \frac{1.5625^2}{2 \times 9.81} = \mathbf{1.324\ m\ (Ans.)}$$

(*ii*) Critical depth (y_c), critical velocity (V_c) and E_{min}.:

Critical depth, $$y_c = \left(\frac{q^2}{g}\right)^{1/3} = \left(\frac{1.875^2}{9.81}\right)^{1/3} = \mathbf{0.71\ m/s\ (Ans.)}$$

Critical velocity, $$V_c = \sqrt{gy_c} = \sqrt{9.81 \times 0.71} = \mathbf{2.64\ m/s\ (Ans.)}$$

Minimum specific energy, $$E_{min} = \frac{3}{2} y_c = \frac{3}{2} \times 0.71 = \mathbf{1.065\ m\ (Ans.)}$$

$$\left(\text{Alternatively: } E_{min} = y_c + \frac{V_c^2}{2g} = 0.71 + \frac{2.64^2}{2 \times 9.81} = 1.065\ \text{m}\right)$$

(*iii*) Froude number and nature of flow:

Froude number, $$Fr = \frac{V}{\sqrt{gy}} = \frac{1.5625}{\sqrt{9.81 \times 1.2}} = 0.455$$

Since $Fr < 1$, the flow is *subcritical* or *tranquil state*. This is also evident from the fact that $y > y_c$ *i.e.*, $\frac{y}{y_c} > 1$.

Example 16.24. *The specific energy for a 3 m wide channel is to be 3 Nm/N. What would be the maximum possible discharge?* **[PTU]**

Solution. Width of channel, $b = 3$ m

Specific energy, $E = 3$ Nm/N

For the given value of specific energy, the discharge will be maximum, when depth of flow is critical. From eqn. (16.35), for maximum discharge, we have:

$$y_c = y = \frac{2}{3} E = \frac{2}{3} \times 3 = 2\ \text{m}$$

∴ Maximum discharge, Q_{max} = Area × velocity

$= (b \times y_c) \times V_c$

(∵ At critical depth, y_c, the velocity will be critical.)

But, $V_c = \sqrt{gy_c} = \sqrt{9.81 \times 2} = 4.43$ m/s

Substituting the values, we have:

$$Q_{max} = 3 \times 2 \times 4.43 = \mathbf{26.58\ m^3/s\ (Ans.)}$$

Example 16.25. *Water flows at a steady and uniform depth of 2 m in an open channel of rectangular cross-section having base width equal to 5 m and laid at a slope of 1 in 1000. It is desired to obtain critical flow in the channel by providing a hump in the bed. Calculate the height of the hump and sketch the flow profile. Consider the value of Manning's rugosity co-efficient N = 0.02 for the channel surface.* **[UPSC Exams.]**

Solution. Depth of flow, $y = 2$ m

Base width of channel, $b = 5$ m

Bed slope, S = 1 in 1000

Manning's co-efficient, $N = 0.02$

Height of the hump, h:

For rectangular channel : Area, $A = b \times y$, and

Perimeter, $P = b + 2y$

$\therefore$ Hydraulic radius, $R = \dfrac{A}{P} = \dfrac{b \times y}{b + 2y} = \dfrac{5 \times 2}{5 + 2 \times 2} = 1.111$ m

Discharge, $Q = A \times V = A \times C\sqrt{RS}$

where, Chezy's constant $C = \dfrac{1}{N} R^{1/6}$

$$\therefore \quad Q = A \times \frac{1}{N} R^{1/6}\sqrt{RS} = \frac{A}{N} R^{2/3} S^{1/2}$$

$$= \frac{(5 \times 2)}{0.02} \times (1.111)^{2/3} \times \left(\frac{1}{1000}\right)^{1/2} \quad \text{(substituting the values)}$$

$$= 16.96 \text{ m}^3/\text{s}$$

Discharge per unit width, $q = \dfrac{Q}{b} = \dfrac{16.95}{5} = 3.392 \text{ m}^3/\text{s}$

Critical depth, $y_c = \left(\dfrac{q^2}{g}\right)^{1/3} = \left(\dfrac{3.392^2}{9.81}\right)^{1/3} = 1.055$ m

Minimum specific energy, $E_{min} = \dfrac{3}{2} \times 1.055 = 1.5825$ m

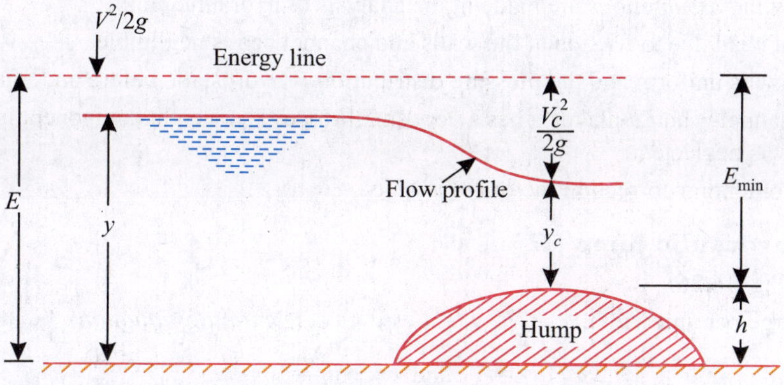

Fig. 16.25.

Specific energy in normal flow,

$$E = y + \frac{V^2}{2g} = 2 + \frac{1.696^2}{2 \times 9.81} = 2.147 \text{ m}$$

where, $V = \dfrac{1}{N} R^{2/3} S^{1/2} = \dfrac{1}{0.02} \times (1.111)^{2/3} \times \left(\dfrac{1}{1000}\right)^{1/2} = 1.696$ m/s

Height of hump provided, $h = E - E_{min} = 2.147 - 1.5825 =$ **0.5645 m (Ans.)**

The flow profile has been shown in Fig. 16.25.

16.9. HYDRAULIC JUMP OR STANDING WAVE

In an open channel when rapidly flowing stream abruptly changes to slowly flowing stream, a distinct rise or jump in the elevation of liquid surface takes place, this phenomenon is known as

hydraulic jump (which is analogous to shock wave in compressible fluids). The hydraulic jump *converts kinetic energy of stream rapidly flowing into potential energy*. Due to this there is a *loss of kinetic energy*. At the place where hydraulic jump occurs *rollers of turbulent water* (eddying turbulences) form, which *cause dissipation of energy*. A hydraulic jump occurs in practice at the toe of *spillways* or *below a sluice gate where the velocity is very high*.

The hydraulic jump is also known as a **standing wave** *because it is, in essence, a wave which is stationary (i.e., at stand-still) at one place*. Such a standing wave is shown in Fig. 16.26.

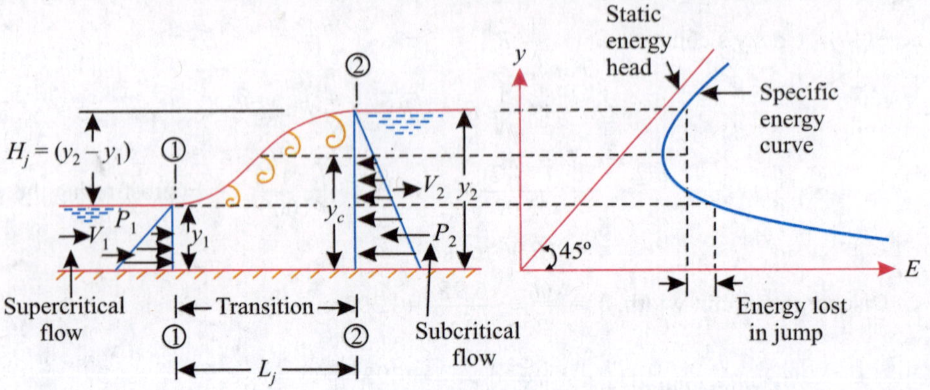

Fig. 16.26. Hydraulic jump.

Analysis of hydraulic jump:

The following *assumptions* are made in the analysis of hydraulic jump:

1. Loss of head due to friction at the walls and channel bed is negligible.
2. The flow is uniform and the pressure distribution is hydrostatic before and after the jump.
3. The channel is horizontal or it has a very small slope. The weight component in the direction of flow is neglected.
4. The momentum correction factor (β) is unity.

Height of hydraulic jump (H_j):

Refer to Fig. 16.26.

Discharge per unit width, $q = V_1 y_1 = V_2 y_2$ ...*Continuity equation*   ...(*i*)

$$\therefore \quad V_1 = \frac{q}{y_1} \quad \text{and} \quad V_2 = \frac{q}{y_2}$$

In case of hydrostatic pressure distribution, the pressure force at any section,

$$P = wA\bar{y}$$

where, $\bar{y}$ = Vertical depth of centroid of wetted area from the liquid surface.

$$\therefore \quad P_1 = w \times (y_1 \times 1) \times \frac{y_1}{2} = \frac{wy_1^2}{2} \quad \text{...Pressure force at section 1-1}$$

$$P_2 = w \times (y_2 \times 1) \times \frac{y_2}{2} = \frac{wy_2^2}{2} \quad \text{...Pressure force at section 2-2}$$

Net force acting on mass of water between 1-1 and 2-2

$$= P_2 - P_1 = \frac{wy_2^2}{2} - \frac{wy_1^2}{2} = \frac{w}{2}(y_2^2 - y_1^2) \quad \text{...(ii)}$$

$[\because P_2 > P_1 \text{ as } y_2 > y_1]$

Now, change in linear momentum $= \rho q (V_1 - V_2)$ ...(*iii*)

But, according to *impulse-momentum equation*:

Net force acting on a mass of fluid = Rate of change of momentum in the same direction

$$\therefore \quad P_2 - P_1 = \rho q (V_1 - V_2) \quad \text{or} \quad \frac{w}{2}(y_2^2 - y_1^2) = \rho q (V_1 - V_2)$$

Substituting, $V_1 = \dfrac{q}{y_1}$ and $V_2 = \dfrac{q}{y_2}$, we have:

$$\frac{\rho g}{2}(y_2^2 - y_1^2) = \rho q\left(\frac{q}{y_1} - \frac{q}{y_2}\right) = \rho q^2\left(\frac{1}{y_1} - \frac{1}{y_2}\right) \qquad (\because w = \rho g)$$

$$\frac{g}{2}(y_2 + y_1)(y_2 - y_1) = q^2\left(\frac{1}{y_1} - \frac{1}{y_2}\right) = q^2\left(\frac{y_2 - y_1}{y_1 y_2}\right)$$

Dividing both sides by $(y_2 - y_1)$, we get:

$$\frac{g}{2}(y_2 + y_1) = \frac{q^2}{y_1 y_2} \quad \text{or} \quad (y_2 + y_1) = \frac{2q^2}{g y_1 y_2} \qquad ...(iv)$$

Multiplying both sides by y_2, we have:

$$y_2^2 + y_1 y_2 = \frac{2q^2}{g y_1} \quad \text{or} \quad y_2^2 + y_1 y_2 - \frac{2q^2}{g y_1} = 0 \qquad ...(v)$$

or,
$$y_2 = \frac{-y_1 \pm \sqrt{y_1^2 + 4 \times 1 \times \dfrac{2q^2}{g y_1}}}{2} = -\frac{y_1}{2} \pm \sqrt{\frac{y_1^2}{4} + \frac{2q^2}{g y_1}}$$

or,
$$y_2 = -\frac{y_1}{2} + \sqrt{\frac{y_1^2}{4} + \frac{2q^2}{g y_1}} \quad \text{or} \quad -\frac{y_1}{2} - \sqrt{\frac{y_1^2}{4} + \frac{2q^2}{g y_1}}$$

Neglecting the second root (being impossible, *–ve* depth), we have:

$$y_2 = -\frac{y_1}{2} + \sqrt{\frac{y_1^2}{4} + \frac{2q^2}{g y_1}} \qquad ...(16.36)$$

$$= -\frac{y_1}{2} + \sqrt{\frac{y_1^2}{4} + \frac{2 \times (V_1 y_1)^2}{g y_1}} \qquad (\because q = V_1 y_1)$$

or,
$$y_2 = -\frac{y_1}{2} + \sqrt{\frac{y_1^2}{4} + \frac{2 V_1^2 y_1}{g}} \qquad ...(16.37)$$

Expression of y_2 in terms of Froude number (Fr):

Eqn. (16.37) can be written as:

$$y_2 = -\frac{y_1}{2} + \sqrt{\frac{y_1^2}{4}\left(1 + \frac{8V_1^2}{g y_1}\right)}$$

or,
$$y_2 = -\frac{y_1}{2} + \frac{y_1}{2}\sqrt{1 + \frac{8V_1^2}{g y_1}} \qquad ...(vi)$$

But,
$$F_{r_1} = \frac{V_1}{\sqrt{g y_1}} \quad \text{or} \quad (F_{r_1})^2 = \frac{V_1^2}{g y_1}$$

$\therefore$ Substituting this value in expression (*vi*), we have:

$$y_2 = -\frac{y_1}{2} + \frac{y_1}{2}\sqrt{1 + 8\,(Fr_1)^2}$$

or, $$y_2 = \frac{y_1}{2}\left(\sqrt{1+8\,(Fr_1)^2} - 1\right) \qquad ...(16.38)$$

$\therefore$ Height of hydraulic jump, $H_j = y_2 - y_1$ ...(16.39)

Length of hydraulic jump (L_j). Length of hydraulic jump represents *that short distance over which the jump occurs* (Refer Fig. 16.26). For rectangular channels with horizontal floor, length of a jump has been found to vary between *5 to 7 times the height of the jump.*

i.e., $$L_j = 5 \text{ to } 7\, H_j \qquad ...(16.40)$$

Loss of energy due to hydraulic jump:

The loss of energy due to hydraulic jump is equal to the difference of specific energies at the upstream (1-1) and downstream (2-2) sections.

i.e. $$E_2 = E_1 - E_2$$

$$= \left(y_1 + \frac{V_1^2}{2g}\right) - \left(y_2 + \frac{V_2^2}{2g}\right) = \left(\frac{V_1^2}{2g} - \frac{V_2^2}{2g}\right) - (y_2 - y_1)$$

$$= \left(\frac{q^2}{2gy_1^2} - \frac{q^2}{2gy_2^2}\right) - (y_2 - y_1) \qquad \left(\because V_1 = \frac{q}{y_1},\ V_2 = \frac{q}{y_2}\right)$$

or, $$= \frac{q^2}{2g}\left(\frac{1}{y_1^2} - \frac{1}{y_2^2}\right) - (y_2 - y_1) \qquad ...(vii)$$

or, $$E_L = \frac{q^2}{2g}\left(\frac{y_2^2 - y_1^2}{y_1^2\, y_2^2}\right) - (y_2 - y_1)$$

But, $$q^2 = gy_1y_2\left(\frac{y_2 + y_1}{2}\right) \qquad ...(\text{From expression } iv)$$

$\therefore$ Loss of energy, $$E_L = gy_1y_2\left(\frac{y_2 + y_1}{2}\right) \times \frac{(y_2^2 - y_1^2)}{2\,gy_1^2y_2^2} - (y_2 - y_1)$$

$$= \frac{(y_2 + y_1)(y_2^2 - y_1^2)}{4y_1\,y_2} - (y_2 - y_1)$$

$$= \frac{(y_2 + y_1)(y_2 + y_1)(y_2 - y_1)}{4y_1y_2} - (y_2 - y_1)$$

$$= (y_2 - y_1)\left[\frac{(y_2 + y_1)^2}{4y_1y_2} - 1\right]$$

$$= (y_2 - y_1)\left[\frac{y_2^2 + y_1^2 + 2y_1y_2 - 4y_1y_2}{4y_1y_2}\right]$$

$$= (y_2 - y_1)\left[\frac{(y_1 - y_2)^2}{4y_1\,y_2}\right]$$

or, $$E_L = \frac{(y_2 - y_1)^3}{4y_1y_2} \qquad ...(16.41)$$

Example 16.26. *A sluice gate discharges water into horizontal rectangular channel with a velocity of 10 m/s and depth of flow of 1 m. Determine the depth of flow of water after the jump and consequent loss in total head* **[NU]**

Solution. Velocity of flow before hydraulic jump, $V_1 = 10$ m/s.

Depth of flow before hydraulic jump, $y_1 = 1$ m

Depth of flow after the jump, y_2:

Discharge *per unit width,* $q = V_1 \times y_1 = 10 \times 1 = 10$ m³/s per m

The depth of flow after the jump is given by:

$$y_2 = -\frac{y_1}{2} + \sqrt{\frac{y_1^2}{4} + \frac{2q^2}{gy_1}} \quad \text{...[Eqn. (16.36)]}$$

or,

$$y_2 = -\frac{1}{2} + \sqrt{\frac{1^2}{4} + \frac{2 \times 10^2}{9.81 \times 1}} = \mathbf{4.043\ m\ (Ans.)}$$

Loss in total head, E_L:

Loss in total head is given by:

$$E_L = \frac{(y_2 - y_1)^3}{4y_1y_2} \quad \text{...[Eqn. (16.31)]}$$

or,

$$E_L = \frac{(4.043 - 1)^3}{4 \times 1 \times 4.043} = \mathbf{1.742\ m\ (Ans.)}$$

Example 16.27. *A 3.6 m wide rectangular channel conveys 9.0 m³/s of water with a velocity of 6 m/s.*

(i) *Is there a condition for hydraulic jump to occur? If so, calculate the height, length and strength of the jump.*

(ii) *What is loss of energy per kg of water?*

Solution. Width of channel, $b = 3.6$ m

Discharge, $Q = 9.0$ m³/s

Velocity of flow before jump, $V_1 = 6$ m/s

(*i*) Is there a condition for hydraulic jump to occur?

$$\text{Depth of water before jump, } y_1 = \frac{Q}{b \times V_1} = \frac{9.0}{3.6 \times 6} = 0.4167 \text{ m}$$

$$\text{Discharge per unit width, } q = \frac{Q}{b} = \frac{9.0}{3.6} = 2.5 \text{ m}^3\text{/s per m}$$

$$\text{Critical depth, } y_c = \left(\frac{q^2}{g}\right)^{1/3} = \left(\frac{2.5^2}{9.81}\right)^{1/3} = 0.86 \text{ m}$$

Since $y_1 < y_c$, a jump would occur. (Ans.)

Froude number ahead of jump,

$$Fr_1 = \frac{V_1}{\sqrt{gy_1}} = \frac{6}{\sqrt{9.81 \times 0.4167}} = 2.967$$

Depth of water downstream the jump,

$$y_2 = \frac{y_1}{2}\left[\sqrt{1 + 8(Fr_1)^2} - 1\right] \quad \text{...(Eqn. 16.38)}$$

$$y_2 = \frac{0.4167}{2}\left[\sqrt{1 + 8 \times 2.967^2} - 1\right] = 1.5525 \text{ m}$$

∴ **Height of jump, H_j** $= y_2 - y_1 = 1.5525 - 0.4167 = \mathbf{1.1358\ m}$ **(Ans.)**

Length of jump, L_j $= 6(y_2 - y_1) = 6 \times 1.1358 =$ **6.8148 m (Ans.)**

Strength of jump $= \frac{y_2}{y_1} = \frac{1.5525}{0.4167} =$ **3.726 (Ans.)**

(*ii*) **Loss of energy per kg of water, E_L:**

Velocity before jump, $V_1 = 6$ m/s ...(*Given*)

Velocity after jump, $V_2 = \frac{q}{y_2} = \frac{2.5}{1.5525} = 1.61$ m/s

$$E_1 = y_1 + \frac{V_1^2}{2g} = 0.4167 + \frac{6^2}{2 \times 9.81} = 2.25 \text{ m}$$

$$E_2 = y_2 + \frac{V_2^2}{2g} = 1.5525 + \frac{1.61^2}{2 \times 9.81} = 1.68 \text{ m}$$

∴ Loss of energy in the jump, $E_L = E_1 - E_2 = 2.25 - 1.68 =$ **0.57 m (Ans.)**

$$\left[\text{Alternatively, } E_L = \frac{(y_2 - y_1)^3}{4y_1y_2} = \frac{(1.5525 - 0.4167)^3}{4 \times 1.5525 \times 0.4167} = \mathbf{0.57\ m}\right]$$

Example 16.28. *In a rectangular channel of 0.5 m width, a hydraulic jump occurs at a point where depth of water flow is 0.15 m and Froude number is 2.5. Determine:*

(*i*) *The specific energy;* (*ii*) *The critical and subsequent depths,*

(*iii*) *Loss of head, and;* (*iv*) *Energy dissipated.*

Solution. Width of the channel, $b = 0.5$ m

Depth of flow, $y_1 = 0.15$ m

Froude number, $Fr = 2.5$

Now, $Fr = \frac{V_1}{\sqrt{gy_1}}$, where V_1 is the upstream velocity

∴ $2.5 = \frac{V_1}{\sqrt{9.81 \times 0.15}}$ or $V_1 = 3.03$ m/s

Discharge per unit width, $q = V_1y_1 = 3.03 \times 0.15 = 0.4545$ m³/s per m

(*i*) **Specific energy, E:**

$$E = y_1 + \frac{V_1^2}{2g} = 0.15 + \frac{3.03^2}{2 \times 9.81} = \mathbf{0.618\ m\ (Ans.)}$$

(*ii*) **Critical depth, y_c:**

$$y_c = \left(\frac{q^2}{g}\right)^{1/3} = \left[\frac{0.4545^2}{9.81}\right]^{1/3} = \mathbf{0.276\ m\ (Ans.)}$$

Subsequent depth, $y_2 = \frac{y_1}{2}\left[\sqrt{1 + 8(Fr_1)^2} - 1\right]$

or, $y_2 = \frac{0.15}{2}\left[\sqrt{1 + 8 \times 2.5^2} - 1\right] =$ **0.461 m (Ans.)**

(*iii*) **Loss head, E_L:**

$$E_L = \frac{(y_2 - y_1)^3}{4y_1y_2} = \frac{(0.461 - 0.15)^3}{4 \times 0.15 \times 0.461} = \mathbf{0.108\ m\ (Ans.)}$$

(*iv*) **Power dissipated, P:**

$$P = wQE_L$$

where $Q = A_1 V_1 = (b \times y_1)\, V_1 = (0.5 \times 0.15) \times 3.03 = 0.227 \text{ m}^3/\text{s}$

$\therefore$ $P = 9810 \times 0.227 \times 0.108 = $ **240.5 W (Ans.)**

Example 16.29. *Find in terms of specific energy E, an expression for the critical depth in a trapezoidal channel with bottom width b and side slope 1 vertical to n horizontal.*

[MDU, Haryana]

Solution. The specific energy (E) of a channel is given as:

$$E = y + \frac{V^2}{2g} = y + \frac{Q^2}{2gA^2} \qquad (\because V = Q/A)$$

where,
y = Depth of flow,
V = Average velocity of flow,
Q = Discharge, and
A = Area of cross-section of the channel.

The condition for minimum specific energy (F_{min}) can be obtained by differentiating the specific energy equation with respect to y and equating the derivative to zero. Thus:

$$\frac{dE}{dy} = \frac{d}{dy}\left[y + \frac{Q^2}{2g\,A^2}\right] = 0$$

$$= 1 + \frac{Q^2}{2g} \times \left(-2 \times A^{-3} \cdot \frac{dA}{dy}\right) = 1 - \frac{Q^2}{gA^3} \times \frac{dA}{dy} = 0$$

$(\because Q = \text{constant})$

$$\therefore \quad \frac{dA}{dy} = \frac{gA^3}{Q^2} = \frac{gA_c^3}{Q^2}, \quad \text{for critical condition} \qquad ...(i)$$

In case of a trapezoidal channel,

$$A = (b + ny)\,y = by + ny^2$$

$$\frac{dA}{dy} = b + 2ny = b + 2ny_c, \quad \text{for critical condition} \qquad ...(ii)$$

From expressions (*i*) and (*ii*), we have:

$$\frac{gA_c^3}{Q^2} = b + 2ny_c \quad \text{or} \quad \frac{Q^2}{g} = \frac{A_c^3}{b + 2ny_c} \qquad ...(iii)$$

The specific energy for critical conditions becomes:

$$E = y_c + \frac{Q^2}{2gA_c^2}$$

Substituting the value of $\frac{Q^2}{g}$ from expression (*iii*), we get:

$$E = y_c + \frac{A_c^3}{2A_c^2\,(b + 2ny_c)} = y_c + \frac{A_c}{2(b + 2ny_c)}$$

or,
$$E = y_c + \frac{(b + ny_c)\,y_c}{2\,(b + 2ny_c)} \qquad ...(iv)$$

or,
$$E \times 2\,(b + 2ny_c) = y_c \times 2\,(b + 2ny_c) + (b + ny_c)\,y_c$$

or,
$$2bE + 4nEy_c = 2by_c + 4ny_c^2 + by_c + ny_c^2$$

Rearranging the above equation, we have:

$$5ny_c^2 + (3b - 4nE)\,y_c - 2bE = 0$$

or,
$$y_c = \frac{-(3b - 4nE) \pm \sqrt{(3b - 4nE)^2 - 4 \times 5n \times (-2bE)}}{2 \times 5n}$$

or,
$$y_c = \frac{(4nE - 3b) \pm \sqrt{(3b - 4nE)^2 + 40nbE}}{10n} \quad \textbf{(Ans.)}$$

Note : When $n = 0$, the expression (*iv*) becomes:

$$E = y_c + \frac{b \cdot y_c}{2b} = y_c + \frac{y_c}{2} = \frac{3y_c}{2} \quad \text{or} \quad y_c = \frac{2}{3}E$$

which is the condition for maximum discharge for a given value of specific energy in a *rectangular channel.*

Example 16.30. (Flow in venturiflume) *A venturiflume is 1.30 m wide at entrance and 0.65 m in the throat. Neglecting hydraulic losses in the flume, calculate the flow if the depths at the entrance and throat are 0.65 m and 0.60 m respectively. A hump is now installed at the throat, of height 200 mm, so that a standing wave (hydraulic jump) is formed beyond the throat. What is the increase in the upstream depth when the same flow as before passes through the flume?*

[Roorkee University]

Solution. Width of venturiflume at entrance, $b_1 = 1.3$ m

Width at throat, $b_2 = 0.65$ m

Depth of flow at section 1, $y_1 = 0.65$ m

Depth of flow at section 2, $y_2 = 0.6$ m

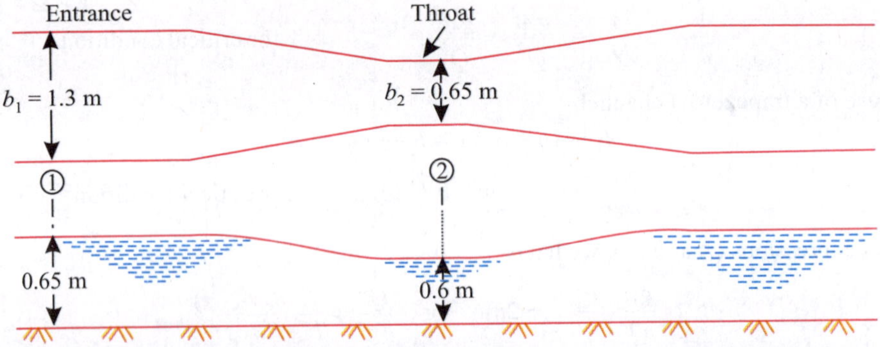

Fig. 16.27. Flow in venturiflume.

Using continuity equation, we have:

$$\text{Discharge, } Q = b_1 y_1 V_1 = b_2 y_2 V_2$$

or,
$$Q = 1.3 \times 0.65 \times V_1 = 0.65 \times 0.6 V_2, \; \therefore \; V_2 = \frac{1.3 \times 0.65 V_1}{0.65 \times 0.6} = 2.17 V_1$$

Neglecting losses, Specific energy at (1) = Specific energy at (2)

i.e.
$$y_1 + \frac{V_1^2}{2g} = y_2 + \frac{V_2^2}{2g}$$

$$0.65 + \frac{V_1^2}{2g} = 0.6 + \frac{(2.17V_1)^2}{2g}$$

or
$$\frac{(2.17V_1)^2}{2g} - \frac{V_1^2}{2g} = 0.65 - 0.6 = 0.05$$

or, $$\frac{V_1^2}{2g}(2.17^2 - 1) = 0.05$$

or, $$V_1^2 = \frac{0.05 \times 2g}{(2.17^2 - 1)} = \frac{0.05 \times 2 \times 9.81}{2.17^2 - 1}$$

or, $$V_1 = 0.514 \text{ m/s}$$

The discharge, $Q = b_1 y_1 V_1 = 1.3 \times 0.65 \times 0.514 = 0.434 \text{ m}^3/\text{s}$

Critical depth in contracted portion,

$$y_c = \left(\frac{q^2}{g}\right)^{1/3}$$

where, $$q = \frac{Q}{b_1} = \frac{0.434}{0.65} = 0.67 \text{ m}^3/\text{s per m}$$

$\therefore$ $$y_c = \left(\frac{0.67^2}{9.81}\right)^{1/3} = 0.357 \text{ m}$$

The new specific energy corresponding to critical flow at the throat when hump of height h is installed,

$$y_c = h + y_c + \frac{V_c^2}{2g} = h + \frac{3}{2}y_c = 0.2 + \frac{3}{2} \times 0.357 = 0.735 \text{ m}$$

(where, $h = 200$ mm $= 0.2$ m) ...(*Given*)

The upstream surface will rise till the upstream specific energy equals 0.735 m.

$$0.735 = y_1 + \frac{V_1^2}{2g}$$

$$= y_1 + \frac{[Q/(b_1 \times y_1)]^2}{2g}$$

or, $$0.735 = y_1 + \frac{Q^2}{2g \times (1.3y_1)^2} = y_1 + \frac{0.435^2}{2 \times 9.81 \times 1.69 y_1^2} = y_1 + \frac{0.0057}{y_1^2}$$

i.e. $y_1^3 \, 0.735 \, y_1^2 + 0.0057 = 0$

Solving by trial and error, $y_1 = 0.72$ m

The increase in the upstream depth $= 0.72 - 0.65 = 0.07$ m $=$ **70 mm** **(Ans.)**

Example 16.31. *A sluice across a channel 7.2 m wide discharges a stream 1.2 m deep. What is the flow rate when the depth upstream of the sluice is 8.4 m ? On the downstream side concrete blocks have been placed to create condition for hydraulic jump to occur. Calculate the force on the blocks if the downstream depth is 3.6 m.*

Solution. Refer to Fig. 16.28.

Applying continuity equation at sections (1-1), (2-2) and (3-3), we have:

Discharge, $$Q = (b_1 \times y_1) V_1 = (b_2 \times y_2) V_2 = (b_3 \times y_3) V_3$$

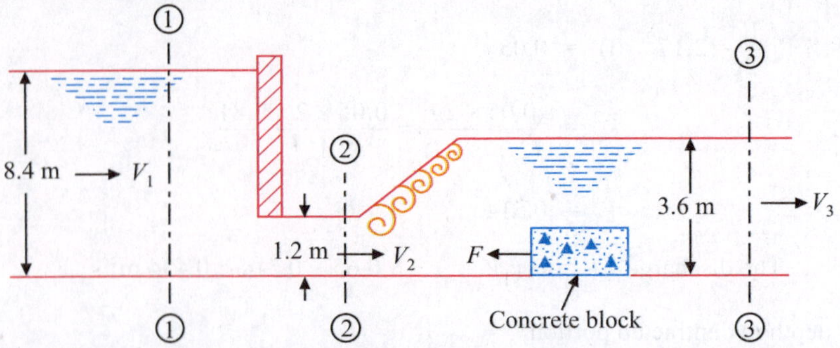

Fig. 16.28

But, $b_1 = b_2 = b_3 = 7.2$ m, $y_1 = 8.4$ m, $y_2 = 1.2$ m, $y_3 = 3.6$ m

$\therefore$ $Q = (7.2 \times 8.4)\, V_1 = (7.2 \times 1.2)\, V_2 = (7.2 \times 3.6)\, V_3$

From which, $V_2 = 7V_1$ and $V_3 = 2.333V_1$

Neglecting frictional losses between sections (1-1) and (2-2), the specific energies at (1-1) and (2-2) are equal.

or,
$$y_1 + \frac{V_1^2}{2g} = y_2 + \frac{V_2^2}{2g}$$

or,
$$8.4 + \frac{V_1^2}{2g} = 1.2 + \frac{(7V_1)^2}{2g} = 1.2 + \frac{49V_1^2}{2g} \qquad (\because V_2 = 7V_1)$$

or,
$$\frac{48V_1^2}{2g} = 7.2 \quad \text{or} \quad V_1^2 = \frac{7.2 \times 2 \times 9.81}{48} = 2.943$$

$\therefore$
$$V_1 = 1.715 \text{ m/s}$$

Flow rate, Q:

$$Q = (b_1 y_1)\, V_1 = 7.2 \times 8.4 \times 1.715 = \mathbf{103.72\ m^3/s}\ \textbf{(Ans.)}$$

Force on the blocks, F:

Applying momentum equation to sections (2-2) and (3-3), neglecting the boundary friction, we have:

$$P_2 - F - P_3 = \frac{wQ}{g}(V_3 - V_2)$$

$$w\, A_2\, \bar{y}_2 - F - w\, A_3\, \bar{y}_3 = \frac{w\,Q}{g}(V_3 - V_2)$$

$$9810 \times (7.2 \times 1.2) \times \frac{1.2}{2} - F - 9810 \times (7.2 \times 3.6) \times \frac{3.6}{2} = \frac{9810 \times 103.72}{9.81}(2.333\ V_1 - 7V_1)$$

$$50855 - F - 457695 = 103720\,(-4.667 \times 1.715)$$

or,
$$F = 50855 - 457695 + 103720\,(4.667 \times 1.715)$$
$$= 423325 \text{ N} \quad \text{or} \quad 423.325 \text{ kN}$$

Hence, the force on the concrete blocks = **423.325 kN** which acts in a direction *opposite* to *F* **(Ans.)**

Example 16.32. *Uniform flow occurs at a depth of 1.5 m in a long rectangular channel 3 m wide and laid to a slope of 0.0009. If Manning's N = 0.015 calculate:*

(i) *Maximum height of hump on the floor to produce critical depth.*

(ii) *Width of contraction which will produce critical depth without increasing the upstream depth of flow.* **[IIT Madras]**

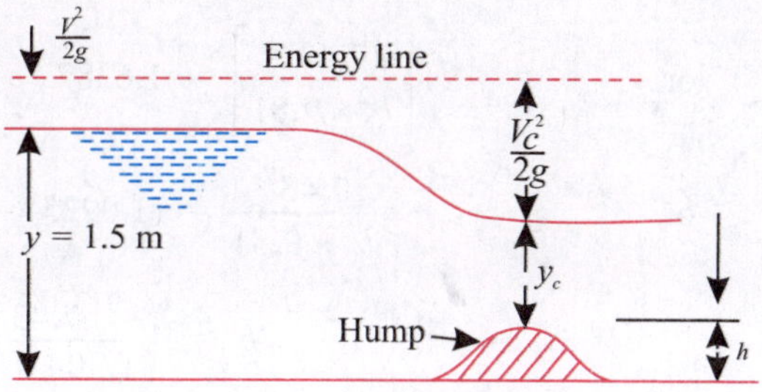

Fig. 16.29

Solution. Depth of flow, $y = 1.5$ m

Width of channel, $b = 3$ m

Bed slope, $S = 0.0009$

Manning's $N = 0.015$

Height of the hump, h:

Discharge, $Q = A \times V = A \times C\sqrt{RS}$

where, C (Chezy's constant) $= \frac{1}{N} R^{1/6}$

$$\therefore \quad Q = A \times \frac{1}{N} R^{1/6} \sqrt{RS} \qquad ...(i)$$

$$= A \times \frac{1}{N} R^{2/3} S^{1/2}$$

(where, V = average velocity of flow, and

R = hydraulic radius)

Here, area, $A = b \times y = 3 \times 1.5 = 4.5 \text{ m}^2$

Perimeter, $P = b + 2y = 3 + 2 \times 1.5 = 6$ m and $R = \frac{A}{P} = \frac{4.5}{6} = 0.75$ m

Substituting the values in expression (*i*), we get:

$$Q = 4.5 \times \frac{1}{0.015} \times (0.75)^{2/3} \times (0.0009)^{1/2} = 7.43 \text{ m}^3/\text{s}$$

Discharge per unit width, $q = \frac{Q}{b} = \frac{7.43}{3} = 2.477 \text{ m}^3/\text{s per m}$

Critical depth, $y_c = \left(\frac{q^2}{g}\right)^{1/3} = \left(\frac{2.477^2}{9.81}\right)^{1/3} = 0.855$ m

Now, equating the specific energies upstream and at the hump, we get:

$$1.5 + \frac{V^2}{2g} = h + y_c + \frac{V_c^2}{2g} \qquad ...(ii)$$

Here, $V = \frac{Q}{A} = \frac{7.43}{4.5} = 1.65$ m/s, and

$$V_c = \sqrt{gy_c} \text{ or } V_c^2 gy_c \text{ or } y_c = \frac{V_c^2}{g} \text{ or } \frac{V_c^2}{2g} = \frac{y_c}{2}$$

Substituting the values in expression (*ii*), we have:

$$1.5 + \frac{1.65^2}{2 \times 9.81} = h + 0.855 + \frac{0.855}{2} \quad \text{or} \quad 1.6387 = h + 1.2825$$

$$\therefore \quad \mathbf{h = 0.3562 \text{ m}} \text{ (Ans.)}$$

(*ii*) Width of contraction:

Let, b_c = Width at the contracted portion to produce critical depth.

Now, Upstream specific energy = Specific energy at the contracted portion.

$$1.6387 = y_c + \frac{V_c^2}{2g} = y_c + \frac{y_c}{2} = \frac{3}{2} y_c$$

$$= \frac{3}{2}\left[\frac{q^2}{g}\right]^{1/3} = \frac{3}{2}\left[\frac{(Q/b_c)^2}{g}\right]^{1/3} = \frac{3}{2}\left[\frac{(7.43)^2}{b_c^2 \times 9.81}\right]^{1/3}$$

or, $$\left[\frac{(7.43)^2}{b_c^2 \times 9.81}\right] = 1.6387 \times \frac{2}{3} = 1.0925$$

or, $$\frac{7.43^2}{b_c^2 \times 9.81} = (1.0925)^3 = 1.304$$

$$\therefore \quad b_c = \left(\frac{7.43^2}{1.304 \times 9.81}\right)^{\frac{1}{2}} = \mathbf{2.077\ m\ (Ans.)}$$

Example 16.33. *Water flows at a velocity of 1 m/s and a depth of 2 m in an open channel of rectangular cross-section, 3 m wide. At a certain section the width is reduced to 1.8 m and the bed is raised by 0.65 m. Will the upstream depth be affected? If so, to what extent?*

[UPSC, CES Exams.]

Solution. Velocity of flow, $V = 1$ m/s

Depth of flow, $y = 2$ m

Width of channel, $b = 3$ m

Width of contracted section, $b_c = 1.8$ m

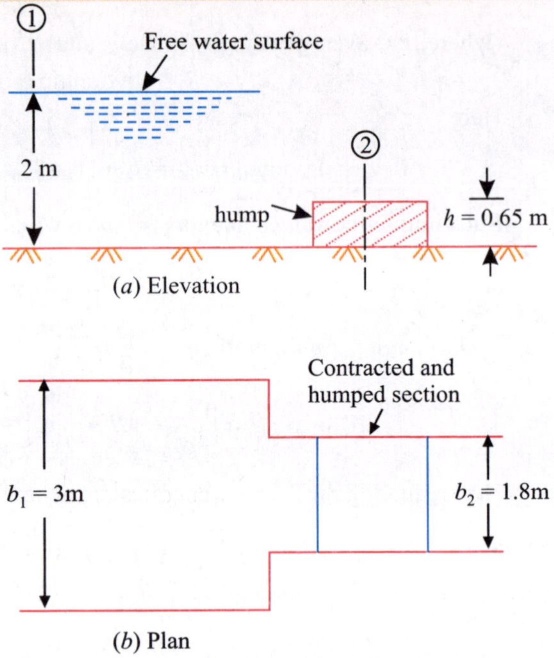

Fig. 16.30

At section (1): Refer to Fig. 16.30.

Specific energy at the section,

$$E_1 = y_1 + \frac{V_1^2}{2g} = 2 + \frac{(1)^2}{2 \times 9.81} = 2.051 \text{ m}$$

Discharge, $Q = A.V = (b_1 \times y_1) \times V_1$
$= (3 \times 2) \times 1 = 6 \text{ m}^3/\text{s}$

Discharge per unit width,

$$q_1 = \frac{Q}{b_1} = \frac{6}{3} = 2 \text{ m}^3/\text{s per m}$$

Critical depth,

$$(y_c)_1 = \left(\frac{q_1^2}{g}\right)^{1/3} = \left[\frac{2^2}{9.81}\right]^{1/3} = 0.7415 \text{ m}$$

Since $y_1 > y_c$, the flow in the channel is *sub-critical.*

Minimum specific energy at section 1,

$$(E_{min})_1 = \frac{3}{2}(y_c)_1 = \frac{3}{2} \times 0.7415 = 1.1122 \text{ m}$$

At the section (2) (contracted and humped section):

Discharge per unit width, $$q_2 = \frac{Q}{b_2} = \frac{6}{1.8} = 3.333 \text{ m}^3/\text{per m}$$

Critical depth,

$$(y_c)_2 = \left(\frac{q_2^2}{g}\right)^{1/3} = \left(\frac{3.333^2}{9.81}\right)^{1/3} = 1.0423 \text{ m}$$

Minimum specific energy,

$$(E_{min})_2 = \frac{3}{2}(y_c)_2 = \frac{3}{2} \times 1.0423 = 1.5634 \text{ m}$$

Specific energy w.r.t. channel bed at section (2),

$$E_2 = (E_{min})_2 + h = 1.5634 + 0.65 = 2.2134 \text{ m}$$

Since $E_2 > E_1$ the upstream depth will be affected. The flow will be possible only when the upstream water level is increased such that:

$$E_1 = E_2 \quad \text{or} \quad y_1 + \frac{V_1^2}{2g} = 2.2134 \qquad ...(i)$$

Also

$$Q = b_1 y_1 \times V_1 \qquad \text{...Continuity equation}$$

$$6 = 3 \times y_1 \times V_1 \quad \text{or} \quad V_1 y_1 = 2 \qquad ...(ii)$$

From expressions (*i*) and (*ii*), we have:

$$y_1 + \frac{(2/y_1)^2}{2g} = 2.2134$$

or,

$$y_1 + \frac{4}{2g \times y_1^2} = 2.2134$$

or,

$$y_1 + \frac{0.204}{y_1^2} = 2.2134 \quad \text{or} \quad y_1^3 = 2.2134\, y_1^2 + 0.204 = 0$$

Solving by trial and error, we get $y_1 = 2.17$ m

Hence the water level on the upstream side will be headed up by,

$$(2.17 - 2) = 0.17 \text{ m or } \mathbf{170 \text{ mm}} \text{ (Ans.)}$$

Example 16.34. *A hydraulic jump occurs in a V-shaped channel having sides sloping at 45°. Derive an equation relating the two depths and the flow rate.*

If the depths before and after the jump in the above channel are 0.50 m and 1.0 m, determine:

(i) The flow rate;

(ii) Froude numbers before and after the jump. **[Roorkee University]**

Solution. Let,
y_1 = Depth of flow *before* hydraulic jump,
V_1 = Velocity of flow *before* hydraulic jump, and
y_2, V_2 = Depth of flow and velocity of flow respectively *after* hydraulic jump.

Refer to Fig. 16.31:

According to impulse-momentum equation:

Net force acting on a mass of fluid = Rate of change of momentum in the same direction

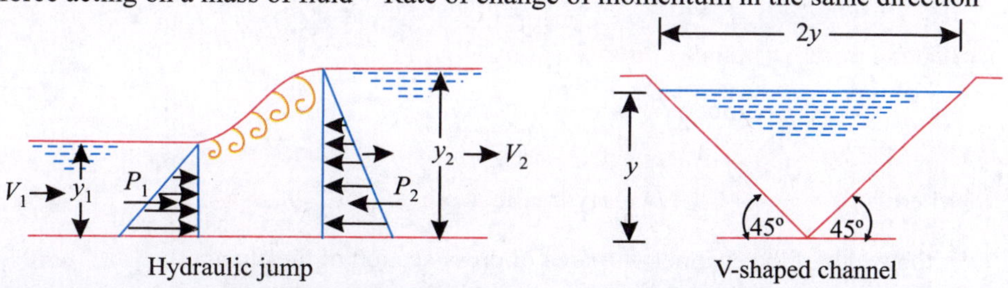

Fig. 16.31. Hydraulic jump – V-shaped channel.

$$P_1 - P_1 = \frac{wQ}{g}(V_1 - V_2)$$

(where, Q = discharge or flow rate)

$$\text{Area, } A = \frac{1}{2} \times 2y \times y = y^2 \quad \text{and} \quad \bar{y} = \frac{1}{3} y$$

$$\therefore \qquad P_1 = wA_1\bar{y}_1 = w \times y_1^2 \times \left(\frac{1}{3}y_1\right) = \frac{1}{3}wy_1^3$$

and,
$$P_2 = wA_2\bar{y}_2 = w \times y_2^2 \times \left(\frac{1}{3}y_2\right) = \frac{1}{3}wy_2^3$$

From continuity equation, we have:

$$Q = A_1V_1 = A_2V_2; \quad V_1 = \frac{Q}{A_1} = \frac{Q}{y_1^2} \quad \text{and} \quad V_2 = \frac{Q}{A_2} = \frac{Q}{y_2^2}$$

Substituting these quantities in expression (*i*), we have:

$$\frac{1}{3}wy_2^3 - \frac{1}{3}wy_1^3 = \frac{wQ}{g}\left(\frac{Q}{y_1^2} - \frac{Q}{y_2^2}\right)$$

or,
$$\frac{1}{3}(y_2^3 - y_1^3) = \frac{Q^2}{g}\left(\frac{1}{y_1^2} - \frac{1}{y_2^2}\right) \quad \text{(cancelling } w \text{ on both sides)}$$

or,
$$\frac{1}{3}(y_2^3 - y_1^3) = \frac{Q^2}{g}\left(\frac{y_2^2 - y_1^2}{y_1^2 y_2^2}\right)$$

or,
$$Q^2 = \frac{g}{3} \times y_1^2 y_2^2 \left(\frac{y_2^3 - y_1^3}{y_2^2 - y_1^2}\right)$$

or,
$$Q = y_1 y_2 \sqrt{\frac{g}{3}\left(\frac{y_2^3 - y_1^3}{y_2^2 - y_1^2}\right)}$$

This is the required equation relating the two depths and the flow rate.

Depths: $y_1 = 0.5$ m, $y_2 = 1.0$ m ...(*Given*)

(*i*) Flow rate, Q:

$$Q = y_1 y_2 \sqrt{\frac{g}{3}\left(\frac{y_2^3 - y_1^3}{y_2^2 - y_1^2}\right)}$$

or
$$Q = 0.5 \times 1.0\sqrt{\frac{9.81}{3}\left(\frac{1^3 - 0.5^3}{1^2 - 0.5^2}\right)} = 0.5\sqrt{3.27\left(\frac{1 - 0.125}{1 - 0.25}\right)} = \mathbf{0.977\ m^3/s} \ \textbf{(Ans.)}$$

(*ii*) Froude number before and after jump, Fr_1, Fr_2:

$$\text{Froude number, } F_r = \frac{V}{\sqrt{g\,D}}$$

where,
$$D = \text{Hydraulic depth} = \frac{A}{T}$$

(T = top width of the channel, A = area of cross-section of the channel)

$$V_1 = \frac{Q}{y_1^2} = \frac{0.977}{0.5^2} = 3.91 \text{ m/s}$$

$$V_2 = \frac{Q}{y_2^2} = \frac{0.977}{1^2} = 0.977 \text{ m/s}$$

$$D_1 = \frac{A_1}{T} = \frac{y_1^2}{2y_1} = \frac{y_1}{2} = \frac{0.5}{2} = 0.25 \text{ m}$$

$$D_2 = \frac{A_2}{T} = \frac{y_2^2}{2y_2} = \frac{y_2}{2} = \frac{1.0}{2} = \mathbf{0.5\ m}$$

$$Fr_1 = \frac{V_1}{\sqrt{gD_1}} = \frac{3.91}{\sqrt{9.81 \times 0.25}} = \mathbf{2.5\ m/s\ (Ans.)}$$

$$Fr_1 = \frac{V_2}{\sqrt{gD_2}} = \frac{0.977}{\sqrt{9.81 \times 0.5}} = \mathbf{0.44\ (Ans.)}$$

Example 16.35. (Surges in open channels). *A horizontal rectangular channel of 3 m width and 2 m water depth conveys water at 18 m³/s. If the flow rate is suddenly reduced to $\frac{2}{3}$ of its original value, compute the magnitude and speed of the upstream surge.*

Assume that the front of the surge is rectangular and friction in the channel is neglected.

[UPSC Exams.]

Solution. Width of channel, $b = 3$ m

Depth of water, $y_1 = 2$ m

The flow rate or discharge, $Q_1 = 18\ m^3/s$

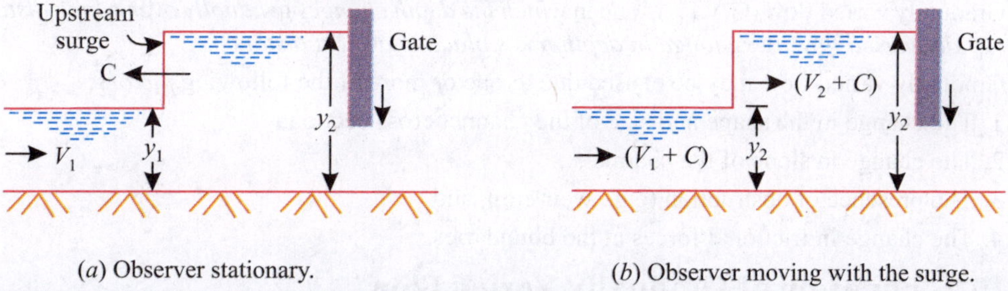

Fig. 16.32

In a channel, when discharge is suddenly reduced by operating a gate, an upstream surge will be developed which will move with a constant velocity C (also known as *celerity* of the wave) as shown in Fig. 16.32 (*a*). An observer standing on the canal bank will notice the surge moving upstream. This unsteady flow case can be transformed into a steady one by *superimposing* flow with velocity C in opposite direction as shown in Fig. 16.32 (*b*)

Also, $$by_1 (V_1 + C) = by_2 (V_2 + C) \quad \text{...Continuity equation}$$

or, $$y_1 (V_1 + C) = y_2 (V_2 + C)$$

Again, $$\frac{wb}{2}(y_2^2 - y_1^2) = \frac{wb}{g} y_1 (V_1 + C)(V_1 - V_2) \quad \text{Momentum equation}$$

or, $$(y_2^2 - y_1^2) = \frac{2y_1}{g}(V_1 + C)(V_1 - V_2) \quad \text{...(i)}$$

Now, $$V_1 = \frac{Q_1}{b \times y_1} = \frac{18}{3 \times 2} = 3\ m/s$$

$$Q_2 = \frac{2}{3} Q_1 \quad \text{...(Given)}$$

∴ $$Q_2 = \frac{2}{3} \times 18 = 12\ m^3/s$$

$$Q_2 = (b_2 \times y_2)\, V_2 = b_2 \times V_2 y_2$$

∴ $$V_2 y_2 = \frac{Q_2}{b_2} = \frac{12}{3} = 4\ m^2/s \text{ per m}$$

Now, $V_1 y_1 = V_2 y_2 + C(y_2 - y_1)$ ...*Continuity equation*

$$3 \times 2 = 4 + C(y_2 - 2)$$

or, $$C = \frac{2}{y_2 - 2}$$

Substituting the values in expression (*i*) we have:

$$(y_2^2 - 2^2) = \frac{2 \times 2}{9.81}\left(3 + \frac{2}{y_2 - 2}\right)(3 - V_2)$$

$$(y_2^2 - 4) = 0.41\left(3 + \frac{2}{y_2 - 2}\right)\left(3 - \frac{4}{y_2}\right) \quad \left[\because V_2 y_2 = 4 \text{ or } V_2 = 4/y_2\right]$$

Solving by trial and error, $y_2 = 2.8$ m and

Height of the surge $= y_2 - y_1 = 2.8 - 2 = \mathbf{0.8}$ **m (Ans.)**

Velocity of the upstream surge, $C = \frac{2}{y_2 - 2} = \frac{2}{2.8 - 2} = \mathbf{2.5}$ **m/s (Ans.)**

16.10. GRADUALLY VARIED FLOW

Gradually varied flow (G.V.F.) is one in *which the depth changes gradually over a long distance.* In a *rapidly varied flow,* the *change in depth takes place in a short distance.*

Gradually varied flow may be caused due to one or more of the following *factors*:

1. The change in the shape and size of the channel cross-section,
2. The change in slope of the channel,
3. The presence of obstruction (e.g., weir etc.), and
4. The change in frictional forces at the boundaries.

16.10.1. Equation of Gradually Varied Flow

The following *assumptions* are made for analysing gradually varied flow:

1. The channel is a prismatic (a channel with constant section and alignment).
2. The bed slope is small.
3. The flow is steady and hence discharge is constant.
4. The pressure distribution over the channel section is hydrostatic *i.e.* stream lines are practically straight and parallel.
5. The energy correction factor (α) is unity.
6. The roughness co-efficient is constant for the length of the channel and it does not depend on the depth of flow.
7. The Chezy and Manning correlations are equally applicable to gradually varied flow for determining the slope of energy line.

Consider a rectangular channel having gradually varied flow (Fig. 16.33), the depth of flow gradually decreasing in the direction of flow.

Let, b = Width of the channel,

Q = Discharge through the channel,

z = Height of bottom of channel above datum,

y = Depth of flow,

V = Mean velocity of flow,

S_b = $\tan i \simeq i$ = slope of the channel bed, and

S_e = $\tan j \simeq j$ = slope of energy line.

According to Bernoulli's equation, the energy equation at any section is given by:

$$E = z + y + \frac{V^2}{2g} \qquad \ldots(i)$$

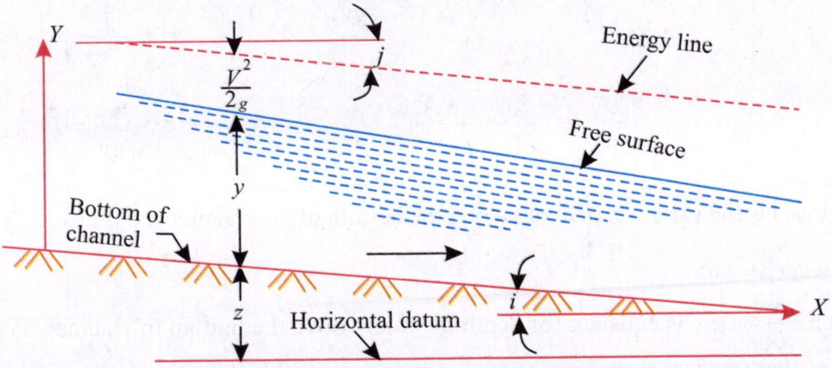

Fig. 16.33. Gradually varied flow in a channel.

Taking the bottom of the channel on the *X*-axis and the vertically upwards direction measured from the channel bottom, as the *Y*-axis, differentiation of eqn. (*i*), with respect to *x* yields:

$$\frac{dE}{dx} = \frac{dz}{dx} + \frac{dy}{dx} + \frac{d}{dx}\left(\frac{V^2}{2g}\right) \qquad \ldots(ii)$$

Now, $$\frac{d}{dx}\left(\frac{V^2}{2g}\right) = \frac{d}{dx}\left[\frac{(Q/A)^2}{2g}\right] = \frac{d}{dx}\left[\frac{\{Q/(b\cdot y)\}^2}{2g}\right] \qquad \left[\because V = \frac{Q}{A} \text{ and } A = b\cdot y\right]$$

$$= \frac{d}{dx}\left[\frac{Q^2}{b^2\cdot y^2 \times 2g}\right] = \frac{Q^2}{b^2 \times 2g}\frac{d}{dx}\left(\frac{1}{y^2}\right) \qquad \left[\because Q, b \text{ and } y \text{ are constant}\right]$$

$$= \frac{Q^2}{b^2 \times 2g}\frac{d}{dy}\left(\frac{1}{y^2}\right)\frac{dy}{dx}$$

$$= \frac{Q^2}{b^2 \times 2g}\left(-\frac{2}{y^3}\right)\frac{dy}{dx} = \frac{-2Q^2}{b^2 \times 2gy^3}\frac{dy}{dx}$$

or, $$\frac{d}{dx}\left(\frac{V^2}{2g}\right) = \frac{-Q^2}{b^2\cdot y^2 \times gy}\frac{dy}{dx} = -\frac{V^2}{gy}\frac{dy}{dx} \qquad \left(\because \frac{Q}{b\cdot y} = V\right)$$

Substituting the value of $\frac{d}{dx}\left(\frac{V^2}{2g}\right)$ in expression (*ii*), we get:

$$\frac{dE}{dx} = \frac{dz}{dx} + \frac{dy}{dx} - \frac{V^2}{gy}\frac{dy}{dx}$$

or, $$\frac{dE}{dx} = \frac{dz}{dx} + \frac{dy}{dx}\left(1 - \frac{V^2}{gy}\right) \qquad \ldots(iii)$$

Now, $$\frac{dE}{dx} = \text{Slope of energy line} = -S_e$$

and, $$\frac{dz}{dx} = \text{Slope of bed of the channel} = -S_b$$

– ve signs with S_e and S_b indicate that the values of *E* and *z* *decrease* with the *increase* of *x*.

Substituting the values of $\frac{dE}{dx}$ and $\frac{dz}{dx}$ in expression (*iii*), we get:

$$-S_e = -S_b + \frac{dy}{dx}\left(1 - \frac{V^2}{gy}\right) \quad \text{or} \quad \frac{dy}{dx} = \frac{(S_b - S_e)}{\left(1 - \frac{V^2}{gy}\right)} \quad \text{...(16.42)}$$

or,
$$\frac{dy}{dx} = \frac{(S_b - S_e)}{\left[1 - (Fr)^2\right]} \quad \left(\because \frac{V}{\sqrt{gy}} = Fr\right) \quad \text{...(16.43)}$$

$\frac{dy}{dx}$ represents the variation of depth along the bottom of the channel and is also called the *slope of the free water surface.*

(*i*) When $\frac{dy}{dx} = 0$: y is constant (or depth of water above the bottom of channel is *constant*); it means that *free water surface is parallel to the channel bed.*

(*ii*) When $\frac{dy}{dx} > 0 \left(or \ \frac{dy}{dx} \ is \ +ve\right)$: *It indicates that the depth of water increases in the direction of flow, the profile of water so obtained is called* **back water curve.**

(*iii*) When $\frac{dy}{dx} < 0$ *or* $\frac{dy}{dx}$ *is – ve* : *It indicates that the depth of water decreases* in the direction of flow. The profile of water so obtained is known as **drop down curve**.

16.10.2. Back Water Curve and Afflux

In an open channel when the flow is uniform, the flow has constant depth at all the sections and the surface of the free water lies parallel to bed of the channel. But when an obstruction like a dam, weir etc. comes across the channel width the water level rises and it has maximum depth from the bed at some section (Fig. 16.34). If y_1 is the depth of water at the point, where the water starts rising up and y_2 is the maximum height of rising water from the bed, then this increase in depth (*i.e.* $y_2 - y_1$) is known as **'afflux'** and the curved surface of the liquid with its *concavity* upwards, is known as **'back water curve'**.

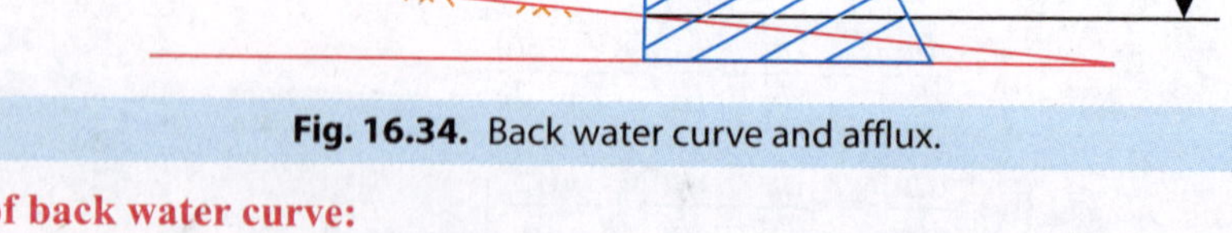

Fig. 16.34. Back water curve and afflux.

Length of back water curve:

The length of back water curve is the distance along the bed of the channel between the section where water starts rising to the section and where water has maximum depth.

Consider a channel in which a back water curve is formed as shown in Fig. 16.35. Let two sections 1-1 and 2-2 are so chosen that distance between them represents the length of backwater curve.

Let, y_1 = Depth of flow at section 1-1,

V_1 = Velocity of flow at section 1-1,

y_2 = Depth of flow at section 2-2,

V_2 = Velocity of flow at section 2-2,

S_b = Bed slope,

S_e = Energy line slope, and

l = Length of back water curve.

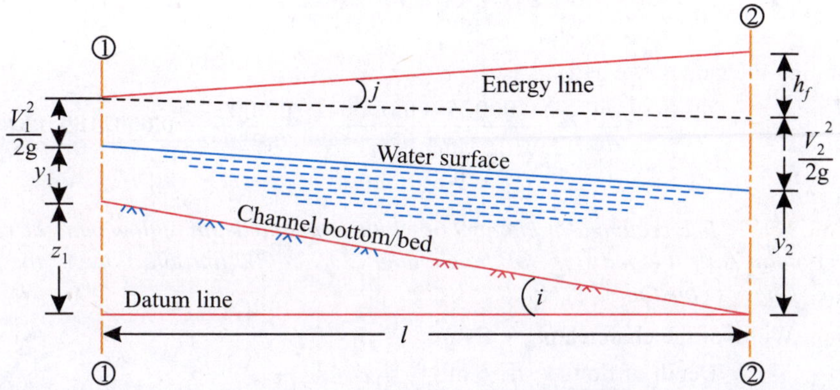

Fig. 16.35. Length of back water curve.

Applying Bernoulli's equation at the two sections with channel bed at section 2-2 as the datum for potential head, we have:

$$z_1 + y_1 + \frac{V_1^2}{2g} = y_2 + \frac{V_2^2}{2g} + h_f \qquad (\because z_2 = 0)$$

where, h_f = Loss of head due to friction = $S_e \times l$, and $z_1 = S_b \times l$

$$\therefore \quad S_b \times l + y_1 + \frac{V_1^2}{2g} = y_2 + \frac{V_2^2}{2g} + S_e \times l$$

or,
$$S_b \times l - S_e \times l = \left(y_2 + \frac{V_2^2}{2g}\right) - \left(y_1 + \frac{V_1^2}{2g}\right)$$

or,
$$l\,(S_b - S_e) = E_2 - E_1 \quad \left(\text{where } E_2 = y_2 + \frac{V_2^2}{2g},\ E_1 = y_1 + \frac{V_1^2}{2g}\right)$$

$$\therefore \quad l = \frac{E_2 - E_1}{S_b - S_e} \qquad \text{...(16.43)}$$

where, E_1 and E_2 represent the specific energies at the beginning and end of the backwater curve. The value of S_e (slope of energy line) is determined by Manning's formula or Chezy's formula corresponding to flow conditions at mean/average depth of flow.

Example 16.36. *In a rectangular channel 12 m wide and 3.6 m deep water is flowing with a velocity of 1.2 m/s. The bed slope of the channel is 1 in 4000. If flow of water through the channel is regulated in such a way that energy line is having a slope of 0.00004 find the rate of change of depth of water in the channel.*

Solution. Width of channel, b = 12 m

Depth of the channel, y = 3.6 m

Velocity of flow, V = 1.2 m/s

Bed slope, $S_b = \frac{1}{4000} = 0.00025$

Slope of the energy line, $S_e = 0.00004$

Rate of change of depth of water, $\frac{dy}{dx}$:

$$\frac{dy}{dx} = \frac{S_b - S_e}{\left(1 - \frac{V^2}{gy}\right)} \quad \text{...[Eqn. (16.42)]}$$

Substituting the values, we get:

$$\frac{dy}{dx} = \frac{0.00025 - 0.00004}{\left(1 - \frac{1.2^2}{9.81 \times 3.6}\right)} = \frac{0.00021}{0.9592} = \mathbf{0.0002189} \ \textbf{(Ans.)}$$

Example 16.37. *In a rectangular channel of width 24 m and depth of flow 6 m, the rate of flow of water is 86.4 m³/s. If the bed slope of the channel is 1 in 4000 find the slope of the free water surface. Take Chezy's constant C = 60.*

Solution. Width of the channel, $b = 24$ m

Depth of flow, $y = 6$ m

Rate of flow or discharge, $Q = 86.4 \text{ m}^3/\text{s}$

Bed slope, $S_b = \frac{1}{4000} = 0.00025$

Chezy's constant, $C = 60.$

Slope of the free water surface, $\frac{dy}{dx}$:

Discharge, $Q = A \times V = A \times C\sqrt{RS_b}$

where, A = Area of flow $= b \times y = 24 \times 6 = 144 \text{ m}^2$

Hydraulic radius $= \frac{A}{P} = \frac{144}{b + 2y} = \frac{144}{24 + 2 \times 6} = 4$ m

The slope of the energy line (S_e) is determined from Chezy's formula.

$\therefore \quad 86.4 = 144 \times 60\sqrt{4 \times S_e} = 17280\sqrt{S_e}$ [Art. 16.10, point 7]

or $\quad S_e = \left(\frac{86.4}{17280}\right)^2 = 0.000025$

Now, $\quad \frac{dy}{dx} = \frac{S_b - S_e}{1 - \frac{V^2}{gy}} = \frac{0.00025 - 0.000025}{1 - \frac{0.6^2}{9.81 \times 6}}$

$$\left(V = \frac{Q}{b \times y} = \frac{86.4}{24 \times 6} = 0.6 \text{ m/s}\right)$$

Hence, slope of the free water surface = **0.000226 (Ans.)**

Example 16.38. *A wide channel laid to a slope of 1 in 1000 carries a discharge of 3.5 m³/s per metre width at a depth of 1.6 m. Find out the value of Chezy's constant C. Consider the flow to be uniform.*

If the actual depth varies from 1.5 m at an upstream location to 1.7 m at a location 300 m downstream or in other words the flow is gradually varied, what will be the value of Chezy's co-efficient C. **[Roorkee University]**

Solution. Bed slope of channel, $S_b = \frac{1}{1000}$

Discharge, $q = 3.5 \text{ m}^3/\text{s}$ per metre width

Depth of water, $y = 1.6$ m

$\therefore$ Velocity of flow $= \frac{q}{y} = \frac{3.5}{1.6} = 2.1875$ m/s

Hydraulic radius, $R = \frac{A}{P} = \frac{b \times y}{b + 2y}$

For a wide channel, the width b of the stream is large in comparison with depth of flow y. Therefore,

$$R \simeq \frac{b \times y}{b} = y = 1.6 \text{ m}$$

(*i*) Uniform flow:

$$V = C\sqrt{RS_b} \qquad \text{...Chezy's formula}$$

$$\therefore \quad 2.1875 = C\sqrt{1.6 \times \frac{1}{1000}} = 0.04\,C$$

$$\therefore \quad C = \frac{2.1875}{0.04} = \mathbf{54.68} \textbf{ (Ans.)}$$

(*ii*) Gradually varied flow:

Slope of the free water surface, $\frac{dy}{dl} = \frac{1.7 - 1.5}{300} = 0.000667$

Average flow depth, $y = \frac{y_1 + y_2}{2} = \frac{1.7 + 1.5}{2} = 1.6$ m

Velocity at average flow depth, $V = \frac{q}{y} = \frac{3.5}{1.6} = 2.1875$ m

Hydraulic radius, $R \simeq y = 1.6$ m

The rate of change of depth is given by:

$$\frac{dy}{dl} = \frac{S_b - S_e}{1 - \frac{V^2}{gy}}$$

or,
$$0.000667 = \frac{0.001 - S_e}{1 - \frac{2.1875^2}{9.81 \times 1.6}} = \frac{0.001 - S_e}{0.695}$$

or,
$$S_e = 0.001 - 0.000667 \times 0.695 = 0.000536$$

Now,
$$V = C\sqrt{RS_e} \qquad \text{...Chezy's formula}$$

$$2.1875 = C\sqrt{1.6 \times 0.000536} = 0.0293\,C$$

or,
$$C = \frac{2.1875}{0.0293} = \mathbf{74.65} \textbf{ (Ans.)}$$

Example 16.39. *The normal depth of flow of water, in a rectangular channel 1.5 m wide, is one metre. The bed slope of the channel is 0.0006 and Manning's rugosity co-efficient N 0.012. Find the critical depth.*

At a certain section of the same channel the depth is 0.92 m while at a second section the depth is 0.86 m. Find the distance between the two sections. Also find whether the section is located downstream or upstream with respect to the first section. **[UPSC Exams.]**

Solution. Width of the channel, $b = 1.5$ m

Normal depth of water, $y_n = 1$ m

$\therefore$ Area of flow, $A = b \times y_n = 1.5 \times 1 = 1.5 \text{ m}^2$

Perimeter, $P = b + 2y_n = 1.5 + 2 \times 1 = 3.5$ m

$\therefore$ Hydraulic radius, $R = \dfrac{A}{P} = \dfrac{1.5}{3.5} = 0.4286$ m

Manning's co-efficient, $N = 0.012$

Bed slope, $S_b = 0.0006$

Critical depth:

$$\text{Discharge, } Q = A \times V = A \times C\sqrt{RS_b} = A \times \frac{1}{N} R^{1/6}\sqrt{RS_b} = A \times \frac{1}{N} R^{2/3}\sqrt{S_b}$$

(where, Chezy's constant, $C = \dfrac{1}{N} R^{1/6}$)

or,
$$Q = 1.5 \times \frac{1}{0 \cdot 012} \times (0.4286)^{2/3} \times (0.0006)^{1/2} = 1.74 \text{ m}^3/\text{s}$$

$$\text{Discharge per unit width, } q = \frac{Q}{b} = \frac{1.74}{1.5} = 1.16 \text{ m}^3/\text{s per m}$$

$$\text{The critical depth, } y_c = \left(\frac{q^2}{g}\right)^{1/3} = \left[\frac{1.16^2}{9.81}\right]^{1/3} = \mathbf{0.516 \text{ m}} \textbf{ (Ans.)}$$

Specific energy at 0.92 m depth:

$$E_1 = 0.92 + \frac{V_1^2}{2g}$$

where,
$$V_1 = \frac{Q}{b \times 0.92} = \frac{1.74}{1.5 \times 0.92} = 1.26 \text{ m/s}$$

$$\therefore \quad E_1 = \frac{1.26^2}{2 \times 9.81} = 1.0 \text{ m}$$

Specific energy at 0.86 m depth:

$$E_2 = 0.86 + \frac{V_2^2}{2g}$$

where,
$$V_2 = \frac{Q}{b \times 0.86} = \frac{1.74}{1.5 \times 0.86} = 1.35 \text{ m/s}$$

$$\therefore \quad E_2 = \frac{1.35^2}{2 \times 9.81} = 0.953 \text{ m}$$

Slope of energy line (S_e) at the mean section:

$$y = \frac{y_1 + y_2}{2} = \frac{0.92 + 0.86}{2} = 0.89 \text{ m}$$

Now, $$Q = A \times \frac{1}{N} R^{2/3} (S_e)^{1/2} \quad \text{or} \quad Q^2 = A^2 \times \frac{R^{4/3}}{N^2} S_e$$

$$\therefore \quad S_e = \frac{Q^2 N^2}{A^2 R^{4/3}} = \frac{1.74^2 \times 0.012^2}{(1.5 \times 0.89)^2 \times (0.407)^{4/3}} = 8.11 \times 10^{-4} = 0.000811$$

$$\left(\because R = \frac{A}{P} = \frac{1.5 \times 0.89}{1.5 + 2 \times 0.89} = 0.407 \right)$$

Distance between the two sections,

$$\Delta x = \frac{E_2 - E_1}{S_b - S_e} = \frac{0.953 - 1.0}{0.0006 - 0.000811} = \mathbf{222.75\ m}\ \textbf{(Ans.)}$$

Slope of water surface, $$\frac{dy}{dx} = \frac{S_b - S_e}{1 - \frac{V^2}{gy}}$$

Average depth of flow = 0.89 m (calculated above)

Velocity at mean section, $$V = \frac{Q}{1.5 \times 0.89} = \frac{1.74}{1.5 \times 0.89} = 1.3 \text{ m/s}$$

$$\therefore \quad \frac{dy}{dx} = \frac{0.0006 - 0.000811}{1 - \frac{1.3^2}{9.81 \times 0.89}} = -2.616 \times 10^{-4}$$

Since $\frac{dy}{dx}$ is –*ve*, therefore, the second section is **downstream (Ans.)**

Example 16.40. (Length of backwater curve). *Draw the specific energy diagram for various constant discharges and show the alternate and critical depths.*

A weir is installed across a rectangular open channel thereby raising the flow depth from 1.5 m in a normal flow to 2.5 m at the weir. The width of the channel is 10 m and it is laid to a slope of 1 in 10000. Find an approximate length of the backwater curve considering the average velocity, average depth and average slope midway between the two sections. Take the value of Manning's rugosity co-efficient equal to 0.02. **[Delhi University]**

Solution. ***Upstream section 1-1*:**

Width of the channel, $b_1 = 10$ m

Depth of flow, $y_1 = 1.5$ m

$\therefore$ Area of flow, $A_1 = b_1 \times y_1 = 10 \times 1.5 = 15 \text{ m}^2$

Wetted perimeter, $P_1 = b_1 + 2y_1 = 10 + 2 \times 1.5 = 13$ m

$\therefore$ Hydraulic radius, $$R_1 = \frac{A_1}{P_1} = \frac{15}{13} = 1.154 \text{ m}$$

Chezy's constant, $$C_1 = \frac{1}{N}(R)^{1/6} = \frac{1}{0.02} \times (1.154)^{1/6} = 51.2$$

(where, $N = 0.02$ ... *Given*)

Velocity of flow, $$V_1 = C_1\sqrt{RS_b} = 51.2\sqrt{1.154 \times \frac{1}{10000}} = 0.55 \text{ m/s}$$

(where, slope of the channel bed, $S_b = \frac{1}{10000}$ ...*Given*)

Specific energy, $$E_1 = y_1 + \frac{V_1^2}{2g} = 1.5 + \frac{0.55^2}{2 \times 9.81} = 1.515 \text{ m}$$

Downstream section 2-2:

$$\text{Width of the channel, } b_2 = b_1 = 10 \text{ m}$$

$$\text{Depth of flow, } y_2 = 2.5 \text{ m}$$

$$\text{Area of flow, } A_2 = b_2 \times y_2 = 10 \times 2.5 = 25 \text{ m}^2$$

$$\text{Wetted perimeter, } P_2 = b_2 + 2y_2 = 10 + 2 \times 2.5 = 15 \text{ m}$$

$$\therefore \quad \text{Hydraulic radius, } R_2 = \frac{A_2}{P_2} = \frac{25}{15} = 1.667 \text{ m}$$

Also, $A_1V_1 = A_2V_2$ ...*Continuity equation*

$$\therefore \quad V_2 = \frac{A_1V_1}{A_2} = \frac{15 \times 0.55}{25} = 0.33 \text{ m/s}$$

$$\text{Specific energy, } E_2 = y_2 + \frac{V_2^2}{2g} = 2.5 + \frac{0.33^2}{2 \times 9.81} = 2.505 \text{ m}$$

The value of S_e (slope of energy line) is calculated by Chezy's formula corresponding to flow *conditions at the average depth of flow.*

$$\text{Average depth of flow, } y = \frac{y_1 + y_2}{2} = \frac{1.5 + 2.5}{2} = 2 \text{ m}$$

At the average depth of flow:

$$\text{Area of flow, } A = b \times y = 10 \times 2 = 20 \text{ m}^2 \qquad (\because b_1 = b_2 = b = 10 \text{ m})$$

$$\text{Wetted perimeter, } P = b + 2y = 10 + 2 \times 2 = 14 \text{ m}$$

$$\therefore \quad \text{Hydraulic radius, } R = \frac{A}{P} = \frac{20}{14} = 1.428 \text{ m}$$

Again, $AV = A_1V_1$

$$\therefore \quad \text{Velocity of flow, } V = \frac{A_1V_1}{A} = \frac{15 \times 0.55}{20} = 0.4125 \text{ m/s}$$

$$\text{Chezy's constant, } C = \frac{1}{N}(R)^{1/6} = \frac{1}{0.02} \times (1.428)^{1/6} = 53.06$$

$$\text{Velocity, } V = C\sqrt{R \times S_e}$$

or, $$0.4125 = 53.06\sqrt{1.428 \times S_e} = 63.4\sqrt{S_e}$$

or, $$S_e = \left(\frac{0.4125}{63.4}\right)^2 = 0.0000423$$

Length of back water curve,

$$l = \frac{E_2 - E_1}{S_b - S_e}, \text{ where } S_b \text{ is the slope of channel bed}$$

$$= \frac{2.505 - 1.515}{0.0001 - 0.0000423} = 17157 \text{ or } \mathbf{17.157 \text{ km}} \text{ (Ans.)}$$

Example 16.41. (Back water curve). *A river 45 m wide has a normal depth of flow of 3 m and an average bed slope of 1 in 10000. A weir is built across the river raising the water surface level at the weir site to 5 m above the bottom of the river. Assuming that the back water curve is an arc of circle, calculate the approximate length of the backwater curve. Consider that the river is prismatic. Take the value of N in Manning's formula as 0.025.* **[UPSC Exams.]**

Solution. Width of the bed, $b = 45$ m

Depth of flow (normal), $y_n = 3$ m

Average bed slope, $S_b = \frac{1}{10000} = 0.0001$

Depth of flow at weir site, $y = 5$ m

Manning's co-efficient, $N = 0.025$

Afflux, $h = y - y_n = 5 - 3 = 2$ m

Length of back water curve, *l*:

Length of backwater curve, *by circular arc method,* is given as:

$$l = \frac{2h}{dy/dx} \quad ...(i)$$

Area of flow, $A = 45 \times 3 = 135 \text{ m}^2$

Perimeter, $P = 45 + 2 \times 3 = 51$ m

Hydraulic radius, $R = \frac{A}{P} = \frac{135}{51} = 2.65$ m

$$\text{Discharge, } Q = A \times V = A \times C\sqrt{RS_b} = A \times \frac{1}{N} R^{1/6}\sqrt{RS_b} = A \times \frac{1}{N} R^{2/3} S_b^{1/2}$$

(where, Chezy's constant, $C = \frac{1}{N} \times R^{1/6}$)

or, $$Q = 135 \times \frac{1}{0.025} \times (2.65)^{2/3} \times (0.0001)^{1/2} = 103.4 \text{ m}^3/\text{s}$$

At the weir site:

$$y = 5 \text{ m}, V = \frac{Q}{45 \times 5} = \frac{103.4}{45 \times 5} = 0.46 \text{ m/s}$$

$$\text{Hydraulic radius, } R = \frac{A}{P} = \frac{45 \times 5}{45 + (2 \times 5)} = 4.09 \text{ m}$$

Slope of water surface at the weir,

$$\frac{dy}{dx} = \frac{S_b - S_e}{1 - \frac{V^2}{gy}}$$

where, S_e is the slope of the total energy line at the weir, V and y are the velocity and depth of flow respectively at the weir.

$$S_e = \frac{Q^2N^2}{A^2R^{4/3}} \quad \text{(Refer to example 16.39)}$$

$$= \frac{V^2N^2}{R^{4/3}} = \frac{0.46^2 \times 0.025^2}{(4.09)^{4/3}} = 2.02 \times 10^{-5} = 0.0000202$$

$$\frac{V^2}{gy} = \frac{0.46^2}{9.81 \times 5} = 0.0043$$

$$\therefore \quad \frac{dy}{dx} = \frac{0.0001 - 0.0000202}{1 - 0.0043}$$

Substituting the value of $\frac{dy}{dx}$ in expression (*i*), we have:

$$l = \frac{2 \times 2}{0.00008} = 50000$$ or **50 km (Ans.)**

16.11. MEASUREMENT OF FLOW OF IRREGULAR CHANNELS

The term "*irregular channels*" includes *large rivers* and *small streams*. In case of a small stream it is possible to obtain the quantity of flow *by fitting a notch or weir across the stream*; the *discharge may then be calculated by measuring the head over the notch*. However, this method cannot be employed for large rivers on account of the expense and the obstruction which may be caused to navigation. In order to obtain the discharge through a large river (or irregular channel), we require: (*i*) Area of flow, and (*ii*) Mean velocity of flow. By knowing this data discharge is calculated as follows:

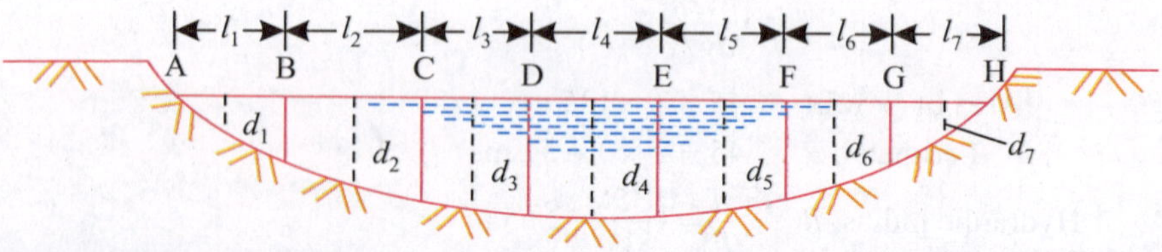

Fig. 16.36. Cross-section of river with unequal segments (Segments method).

16.11.1. Area of Flow

The area of flow may be *calculated* by the several methods but the following are important ones:

1. Simple segments method. 2. Simpson's rule.

1. Simple segments method :

In this method, the cross-section of the river is divided into a number of segments *AB*, *BC*, *CD*, etc. as shown in Fig. 16.36.

Let, l_1, l_2, l_3 ... = Lengths of the segments *AB*, *BC*, *CD* ... respectively, and

d_1, d_2, d_3 ... = Mean depths of the respective segment.

Then, Area of flow, A = Area of segment *AB* + area of segment *BC* + area of segment *CD* + ...

$$= l_1 d_1 + l_2 d_2 + l_3 d_3 + \ldots$$

2. Simpson's rule:

A greater accuracy in the computation of discharge may be obtained by using *Simpson's rule*. In this method the whole river width is divided into an *even number of equal segments* so that there are *odd* number of depths taken at the end of each segment as shown in Fig. 16.28. Then area of flow,

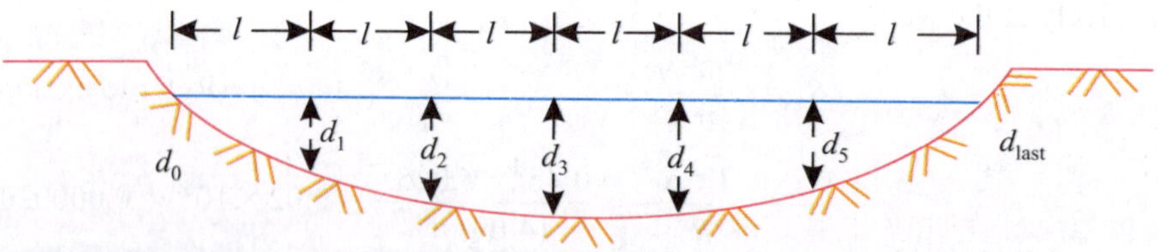

Fig. 16.37. Cross-section of river with equal segments (Simpson's) rule.

$$A = \frac{l}{3}(d_0 + d_{last}) + 2(d_1 + d_3 + d_5) + 4(d_2 + d_4 + d_6)$$

where, l = Length of each segment, and

d_0, d_1, d_2 ..... = Depths taken at the end of segments.

16.11.2. Mean Velocity of Flow

The mean velocity of flow may be *measured* by the following methods :

1. Pitot tube 2. Floats 3. Current meter.

1. Pitot tube. A pitot tube is a simple device used for measuring the velocity of flow at the required point in the flowing stream. In its simplest form it consists of a glass tube (large enough for capillary effects to be negligible) bent at *right angle*. The tube is dipped vertically in the flowing stream with its lower open end facing the direction of flow and upper open end projecting above the water surface in the stream as shown in the Fig. 16.38. The water rises up in the tube, due to pressure exerted by the flowing water. By measuring the rise of water in the tube, the velocity of water (V) is calculated by using the following relation:

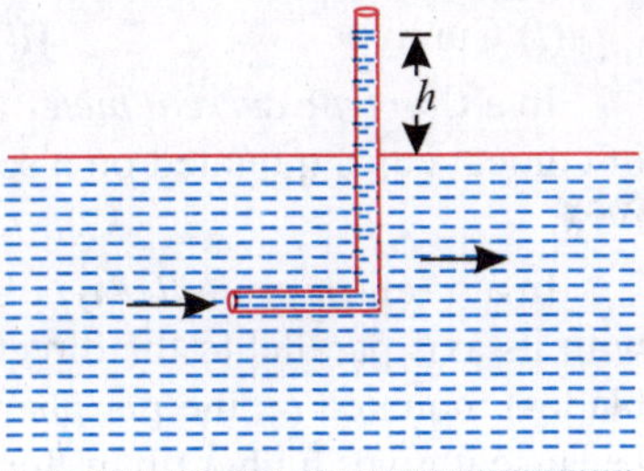

Fig. 16.38. Pitot tube.

$$V = \sqrt{2gh}$$

where, h = Height of water in the tube above the water surface, and

g = Acceleration due to gravity.

2. Floats. The velocity of flow can be measured in a simple way by means of *floats*. A float is a small object made of wood or other suitable material which is lighter than water and thus capable of floating on the surface. The *surface velocity at any section may be obtained by using* a ***single float***. The time taken by the float to traverse a known distance is measured; the velocity is then calculated by dividing the distance travelled (by the float) by the time taken to travel that distance. Since the mean velocity of flow is equal to 0.8 to 0.95 times the surface velocity, the approximate value of the mean velocity of flow may then be determined from the known value of the surface velocity.

A better method is to use ***double floats.*** A double float consists of a *surface float* on to which is attached a *hollow metal sphere*, heavier than water, and suspended from it by a cord of known length (Fig. 16.39). The depth of the lower float may be regulated by the length of the cord. The velocity is then obtained by noting the time taken by the float to traverse a known distance (as explained in the previous case of single float)

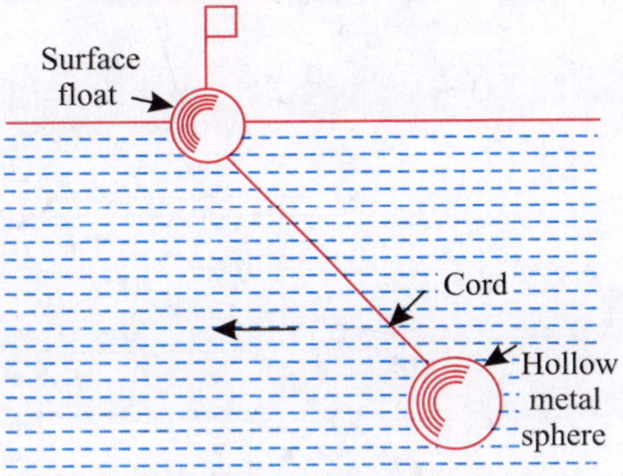

Fig. 16.39. Double float.

The double float method *directly* gives the value of mean velocity of flow.

The *best type of float* is the ***rod float*** (Fig. 16.40). It consists of a vertical wooden rod which is weighted at the bottom to keep it vertical. The length of the rod is so adjusted that it reaches the bottom of stream (without touching the weeds, sand or mud at the bottom of the river) and its top should be above the water surface. Some types of rod are made telescopic, so that length may be adjusted to suit any depth. *The rod will travel with a velocity equal to the mean velocity of the section.*

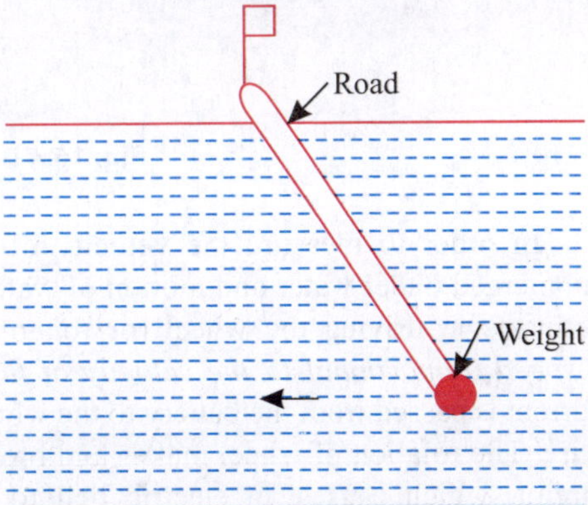

Fig. 16.40. Rod float.

3. Current meter. A current meter is an instrument used to measure the velocity of flow at a required point in the flowing stream. In general it consists of a *wheel or revolving element containing blades or cups, and a tail on which flat vanes or fins are fixed.* The current meters, according to the shape of the revolving element, may be classified as follows:

(*i*) Cup type (*ii*) Screw type or propeller type.

In a *Cup type current meter* (Fig. 16.41) the wheel or revolving element has the form of a series of conical cups, mounted on a spindle. The spindle is held vertical at right angle to the direction of flow.

In a *screw or propeller type current meter* (Fig. 16.42) the revolving element consists of a shaft, with its axis parallel to the direction of flow, which carries a number of curved vanes (or propeller blades) mounted on the periphery of the shaft. This type of meter is more sensitive than cup type because it gives higher r.p.m. for the same velocity of flow.

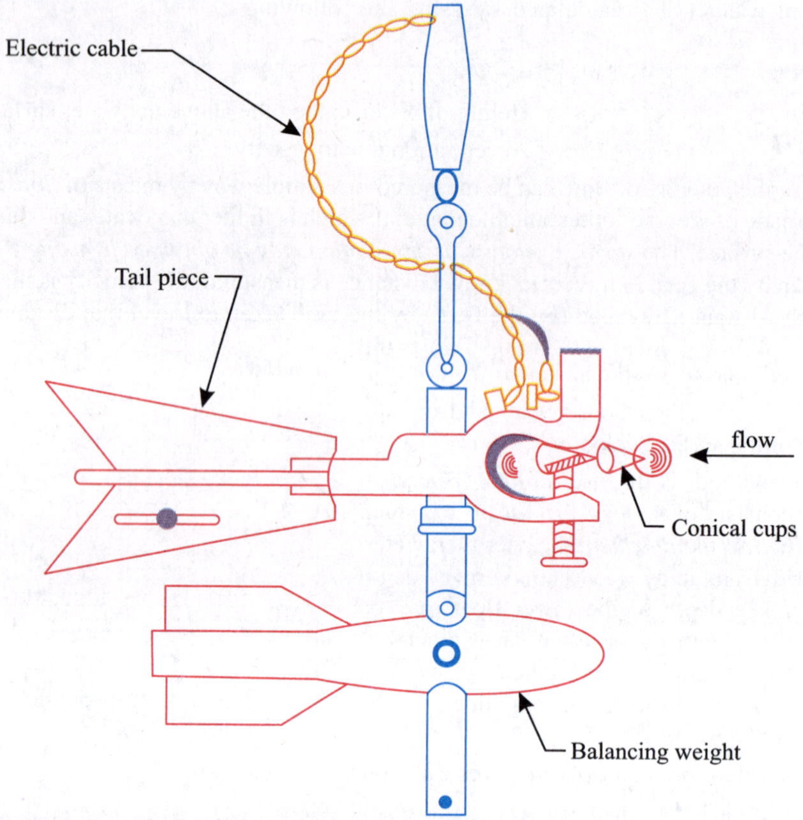

Fig. 16.41. Cup type current meter.

In order to measure the velocity of flow, meter is submerged under water and motion of water in the stream activates it, driving the wheel (or rotatory elements) at a *speed proportional to the velocity of flow*. An electric current is passed from the battery to the wheel by means of wire. The rotation of wheel makes and breaks the electric circuit, which causes an electric bell to ring. Thus by counting the ringing of bell, the rotations of the wheel and hence the velocity of flowing water is obtained.

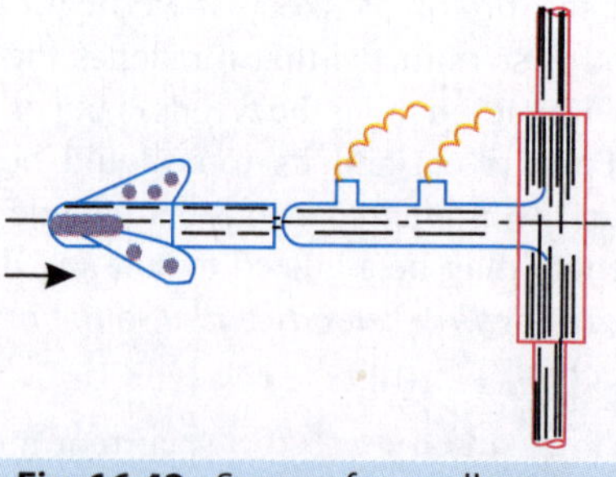

Fig. 16.42. Screw of propeller type current meter.

HIGHLIGHTS

1. An *open channel* may be defined as a passage in which liquid flows with its upper surface exposed to atmoshpere.
2. Flow in a channel is said to be *uniform,* if the depth, slope, cross-section and velocity remain constant over a given length of the channel. Flow in a channel is said to be *non-uniform* (or varied) when the channel depth *varies* continuously from one section to another.
3. The flow in the open channel may be characterised as laminar or turbulent depending upon the value of Reynolds number:

   When $Re < 500$...flow is laminar;

   When $Re > 2000$...flow is turbulent.

   When $500 < Re < 2000$ ...flow is transitional.
4. If Froude number (Fr) is less than 1.0, the flow is subcritical or streaming. If Fr is equal to 1.0, the flow is critical. If Fr is greater than 1.0, the flow is supercritical or shooting.
5. Velocity by Chezy's formula is given by

$$V = C\sqrt{RS}$$

where, C = Chezy's constant,

R = Hydraulic radius (or hydraulic mean depth)

$$= \frac{A \text{ (area)}}{P \text{ (wetted perimeter)}}, \text{ and}$$

S = Slope of the bed.

6. Empirical relations for the Chezy's constant, C

(*i*) $$C = \frac{157.6}{1.81 + \frac{K}{\sqrt{R}}} \quad \text{...Bazin's formula}$$

where, K = Bazin's constant,

R = Hydraulic radius (or hydraulic mean depth)

(*ii*) $$C = \frac{23 + \frac{0.00155}{S} + \frac{1}{N}}{1\left(23 + \frac{0.00155}{S}\right)\frac{N}{\sqrt{R}}} \quad \text{...Kutter's formula}$$

where, N = Kutter's constant, and S = bed slope.

(*iii*) $$C = \frac{1}{N}R^{1/6} \quad \text{....Manning's formula}$$

where, N = Manning's constant = Kutter's constant.

7. The *most economical section* (also called the best section or most efficient section) is one which gives the maximum discharge for a given amount of excavation.
8. *Conditions for maximum discharge* through different channel sections:

   (*a*) *Rectangular section:*

   (*i*) $b = 2y$; (*ii*) $R = \frac{y}{2}$

   (*b*) *Trapezoidal section:*

   (*i*) Half top width = Sloping side

   or, $$\frac{b + 2ny}{2} = y\sqrt{n^2 + 1}$$

(*ii*) $$R = \frac{y}{2}$$

(*iii*) A semicircle drawn from the mid-point of the top width with radius equal to depth of flow will touch the three sides of the channel. *Best side slope* for most economical trapezoidal section is

$$\theta = 60° \quad \text{or} \quad n = \frac{1}{\sqrt{3}} = \frac{1}{\tan\theta}$$

(*c*) *Triangular section:*

(*i*) Each sloping side makes an angle of 45° with the vertical.

(*ii*) Hydraulic radius, $R = \frac{y}{2\sqrt{2}}$.

(*d*) *Circular section:*

(*i*) Condition for *maximum discharge*:
Depth of flow, $y = 0.95$ diameter of circular channel;
Hydraulic radius, $R = 0.29$ times channel diameter.

(*ii*) Condition for *maximum velocity*:
Depth of flow, $y = 0.81$ diameter of circular channel;
Hydraulic radius, $R = 0.305$ diameter.

9. For a *circular channel*:

$$\text{Area of flow, } A = r^2\left(\theta - \frac{\sin 2\theta}{2}\right)$$

Wetted perimeter, $P = 2r\,\theta$

where, r = Radius of circular channel, and
θ = Half the angle subtended by the water surface at the centre.

10. Channel sections of constant velocity are designed particularly in the case of large sewers in which the discharge ranges from a certain minimum value that flows daily to a very large value during rainy season.

11. The total energy of flow per unit weight of liquid is given by:

$$\text{Total energy} = z + y + \frac{V^2}{2g}$$

12. Specific energy of a flowing liquid per unit weight,

$$E = y + \frac{V^2}{2g}$$

13. The depth of flow at which specific energy is minimum is called *criticial depth*, which is given by $y_c = \left(\frac{q^2}{g}\right)^{1/3}$, where q = discharge per unit width.

14. The velocity of flow at critical depth is known as *critical velocity*, which is given by:

$$V_c = \sqrt{g \times y_c}$$

15. Minimum specific energy is given by:

$$E_{min} = \frac{3}{2} y_c, \quad \text{where} \quad y_c = \text{critical depth.}$$

16. (*i*) A flow corresponding to critical depth (or when Froude number, $Fr = 1$) is known as *critical flow*.

(*ii*) When the depth of flow in a channel is greater than critical depth (when $Fr < 1$) the flow is said to be *sub-critical or streaming flow.*

(*iii*) The flow is *supercritical* (or shooting or torrential) when the depth of flow in a channel is less than the critical depth (when $Fr > 1$).

17. The condition for maximum discharge for given value of specific energy is that the depth of flow should be *critical*.

18. Hydraulic jump. In an open channel when rapidly flowing stream abruptly changes to slowly flowing stream, a distinct rise or jump in the elevation of liquid surface takes place, this phenomenon is known as *hydraulic jump*. The hydraulic jump is also known as '*standing wave*'.

The depth of flow after the jump is given by:

$$y_2 = -\frac{y_1}{2} + \sqrt{\frac{y_1^2}{4} + \frac{2q^2}{2gy_1}} \quad \text{...(in terms of } q)$$

$$= -\frac{y_1}{2} + \sqrt{\frac{y_1^2}{4} + \frac{2V_1^2 y_1}{g}} \quad \text{...(in terms of } V_1)$$

$$= \frac{y_1}{2}\left(\sqrt{1 + 8Fr_1^2} - 1\right) \quad \text{...(in terms of } Fr_1)$$

(where, y_1 = depth of flow of water before the jump)

Height of hydraulic jump, $H_j = y_2 - y_1$

Length of hydraulic jump, L_j = 5 to 7 H_j

Loss of energy due to hydraulic jump, $E_L = \dfrac{(y_2 - y_1)^3}{4y_1y_2}$

19. Gradually varied flow (G.V.F.) is one in which the depth changes gradually over a long distance. Equation of gradually varied flow is given by:

$$\frac{dy}{dx} = \frac{S_b - S_e}{\left(1 - \dfrac{V^2}{gy}\right)} \quad \text{...(in terms of } V)$$

$$= \frac{S_b - S_e}{(1 - Fr^2)} \quad \text{...(in terms of } Fr)$$

where, $\dfrac{dy}{dx}$ = Slope of free water surface,

S_b = Slope of the channel bed,

S_e = Slope of the energy line, and

V = Velocity of flow.

20. Afflux is the increase in water level due to some obstruction across the flowing liquid; the curved surface of the liquid with its concavity upwards, is known as **back water curve**.

Length of back water curve, $l = \dfrac{E_2 - E_1}{S_b - S_e}$

where, $E_1\left(= y_1 + \dfrac{V_1^2}{2g}\right)$ and $E_2\left(= y_2 + \dfrac{V_2^2}{2g}\right)$ represent the specific energies at the beginning and end of back water curve.

OBJECTIVE TYPE QUESTIONS

Choose the Correct Answer:

1. Which of the following is the most essential condition for a hydraulic jump to form?
   (*a*) The constancy of specific energy
   (*b*) The existence of subcritical flow before the jump
   (*c*) The existence of supercritical flow before the jump
   (*d*) None of the above.
2. In a hydraulic jump the energy loss is expressed as
   (*a*) $\frac{(y_2 - y_1)^2}{4y_1y_2}$ (*b*) $\frac{(y_2 - y_1)^3}{4y_1y_2}$
   (*c*) $\frac{(y_2 - y_1)}{4y_1y_2}$ (*d*) $\frac{\sqrt{(y_2 - y_1)}}{4y_1 y_2}$.
3. The water surface slope $\frac{dy}{dx}$, in case of uniform flow in the channel, is equal to
   (*a*) 0 (*b*) 1
   (*c*) 1000 (*d*) ∞.
4. In open channels, gradually varied flow is caused
   (*a*) when the channel slope is equal to the normal slope
   (*b*) when the pressure forces and the change of momentum are different from each other
   (*c*) when the force causing the flow is not equal to the resistance force
   (*d*) when there is an equilibrium between the forces causing the flow and those opposing it.
5. In a channel, the alternate depths of flow are the depths
   (*a*) which occur at the same specific energy
   (*b*) at which total energies are same
   (*c*) for the same specific force
   (*d*) none of the above.
6. The critical depth is the depth of flow at which
   (*a*) the Froude number is less than unity
   (*b*) the specific energy is maximum
   (*c*) the specific energy is minimum
   (*d*) the unit discharge is minimum.
7. In a rectangular channel, the critical depth is given by
   (*a*) $\left(\frac{q^2}{g}\right)^{1/2}$ (*b*) $\left(\frac{q^2}{g}\right)^{1/3}$
   (*c*) $\left(\frac{q^2}{g}\right)^{1/4}$ (*d*) $\left(\frac{q^3}{g}\right)^{1/3}$.
8. In open channels, the specific energy is
   (*a*) the total energy per unit discharge
   (*b*) the total energy measured above a horizontal datum
   (*c*) the total energy measured with respect to the channel bottom which is taken as datum
   (*d*) the kinetic energy plotted above the free-surface.
9. An open channel flow is one in which
   (*a*) the soild boundaries confining the flow are open at the top
   (*b*) the liquid flowing in a closed conduit has a free-surface
   (*c*) a closed conduit is full of flowing liquid
   (*d*) none of the above.
10. In case of open channels, uniform flow is characterised by
   (*a*) a constant slope of channel bottom
   (*b*) a constant depth of flow
   (*c*) a changing depth of flow
   (*d*) none of the above.
11. For flow in open channels, the Manning's equation is expressed as
   (*a*) $C = \frac{1}{N} R^{1/4}$
   (*b*) $V = C\sqrt{RS}$
   (*c*) $V = \frac{1}{N} R^{2/3} S^{1/2}$
   (*d*) $C = 87/(1 + m/\sqrt{R})$.
12. The maximum velocity in open channels occurs
   (*a*) near the channel bottom
   (*b*) a little below the free-surface
   (*c*) at the free surface
   (*d*) none of the above.
13. Under which of the following conditions steady non-uniform flow in open channels occurs?
   (*a*) When the discharge and depth both vary along the channel length
   (*b*) When a constant discharge flows at the constant depth of flow
   (*c*) When a constant discharge flows in a channel laid at a fixed slope
   (*d*) When for a constant discharge the liquid depth in the channel varies along its length.
14. Hydraulically efficient channel cross-section is one

(*a*) which carries maximum discharge under given conditions of slope, roughness and flow area
(*b*) which has the minimum hydraulic radius
(*c*) which has the maximum wetted perimeter
(*d*) none of the above.

15. The equation of gradually varied flow is expressed by
(*a*) $\frac{dy}{dx} = \frac{S_b - S_e}{1 - Fr^2}$ (*b*) $\frac{dy}{dx} = \frac{S_b - S_e}{1 + Fr^2}$
(*c*) $\frac{dy}{dx} = \frac{S_b - S_e}{1 - Fr^3}$ (*d*) $\frac{dy}{dx} = \frac{S_b - S_e}{1 - \sqrt{Fr}}$.

16. A channel without any cover at the top is known as
(*a*) natural channel (*b*) open channel
(*c*) artificial channel (*d*) none of above.

17. A channel with constant bed slope and the same cross-section along its length is known as
(*a*) natural channel
(*b*) artificial channel
(*c*) prismatric channel
(*d*) open channel.

18. The flow in the open channel may be characterised as laminar when
(*a*) $Re < 500$ (*b*) $Re > 2000$
(*c*) $500 < Re < 2000$ (*d*) none of the above.

19. The channel flow is subcritical when
(*a*) $Fr < 1$ (*b*) $Fr = 1$
(*c*) $Fr > 1$ (*d*) any of the above.

20. Non-uniform flow may be caused by
(*a*) the change in width, depth, bed slope etc. of a channel
(*b*) An obstruction, constructed across a channel of uniform width
(*c*) both (*a*) and (*b*)
(*d*) none of the above.

21. Prismatic channels are those which have
(*a*) a constant bed slope downstream
(*b*) the same cross-section and bed slope throughout
(*c*) the shape of a prism
(*d*) a uniform cross-section throughout.

22. For the best trapezoidal section
(*a*) depth of flow = half the bed width
(*b*) side slope is 45°
(*c*) the shape is of a half hexagon
(*d*) none of the above.

23. For the best rectangular section
(*a*) $y = b/3$ (*b*) $y = b$
(*c*) $y = \frac{b}{2}$ (*d*) $y = \frac{b}{4}$

24. Manning and Chezy formulae are valid for
(*a*) steady
(*b*) steady uniform flow
(*c*) steady non-uniform flow
(*d*) unsteady uniform flow.

25. The hydraulic jump occurs in a channel when
(*a*) the bed slope is adverse
(*b*) the bed slope changes from steep to mild
(*c*) flow changes from subcritical to super-critical
(*d*) none of the above.

26. In an open channel flow, shooting flow cannot
(*a*) occur just after a hydraulic jump
(*b*) be gradually varied
(*c*) follow tranquil flow
(*d*) none of the above.

27. When Froude's number is equal to unity, the flow in an open channel is called
(*a*) critical flow (*b*) tranquil flow
(*c*) streaming flow (*d*) shooting flow.

28. The cross-section of a channel is said to be best, if the
(*a*) hydraulic mean depth is maximum
(*b*) section has the least perimeter for a given area
(*c*) roughness co-efficient is maximum
(*d*) section gives maximum area for a given flow.

29. The strength of a jump is governed by the
(*a*) upstream velocity
(*b*) downstream velocity
(*c*) upstream Froude number
(*d*) bed slope.

30. For maximum discharge through a circular channel, the depth of flow should be equal to
(*a*) 0.6 times the diameter of the channel
(*b*) 0.8 times the diameter of the channel
(*c*) 0.95 times the diameter of the channel
(*d*) 1.2 times the diameter of the channel.

ANSWER

1. (c)	2. (b)	3. (a)	4. (c)	5. (a)	6. (c)
7. (b)	8. (c)	9. (b)	10. (b)	11. (c)	12. (b)
13. (d)	14. (a)	15. (a)	16. (b)	17. (c)	18. (a)
19. (a)	20. (c)	21. (b)	22. (c)	23. (c)	24. (a)
25. (b)	26. (a)	27. (a)	28. (b)	29. (c)	30. (c).

THEORETICAL QUESTIONS

1. What is an open channel ?

2. What are the different types of channels? Give examples in each case.

3. What is the purpose of providing bed slope in open channels?

4. Explain briefly the following:
(*i*) Uniform and non-uniform flows,
(*ii*) Laminar and turbulent flows,
(*iii*) Steady and unsteady flows, and
(*iv*) Subcritical and supercritical flows.

5. State the conditions under which uniform and non-uniform flows are produced.

6. Differentiate between 'Gradually varied flow' and 'Rapidly varied flow'.

7. What is Chezy's formula? How is it derived ? **[UPSC]**

8. How does the roughness of channel affect the Chezy's constant? **[BHU]**

9. What is Bazin's formula and how is it used ? **[UPSC]**

10. State the following formulae for the values of C:
(*i*) Bazin's formula, (*ii*) Kutter's formula, and
(*iii*) Manning's formula.

11. What do you mean by 'Most-economical section' of an open channel? How is it deter- mined?

12. What are the conditions for the rectangular channel of best section?

13. Show that the hydraulic mean depth of a trapezoidal channel having the best proportion is half of the minimum depth. **[IIT Kharagpur]**

14. Define the following terms :
(*i*) Hydraulic radius, (*ii*) Wetted perimeter, and
(*iii*) Slope of the bed

15. For a trapezoidal channel of most economical section, prove that:
(*i*) Half of top width = Length of one of the sloping sides;
(*ii*) Hydraulic mean depth = $\frac{1}{2}$ × depth of flow.

16. State and prove the condition under which the trapezoidal section of an open channel will be most economical.

17. State and prove the conditions of maximum discharge and maximum velocity for circular channel.

18. What is a specific energy curve?

19. What do you understand by critical depth of an open channel when the flow in it is not uniform? **(IIT Kharagpur)**

20. Derive expressions for critical depth and critical velocity?

21. (*a*) What is mean by 'Hydraulic jump' in an open channel?
(*b*) Determine from first principle the conditions required for the formation of such a jump in the case of a rectangular channel of constant width and calculate the loss of head in terms of depth just before and after the jump. **[UPSC]**

22. Derive an expression for loss of energy head for a hydraulic jump.

23. Define the terms: (*i*) Afflux and (*ii*) Back water curve.
Prove that the length of the backwater curve is given by

$$l = \frac{E_2 - E_1}{S_b - S_e}$$

where, l = length of backwater curve, E_2 = specific energy at the end of backwater curve, E_1 = specific energy at the section where water starts rising, S_b = slope of bed, and S_e = slope of energy gradient.

UNSOLVED EXAMPLES

1. Find the rate of flow and conveyance for a rectangular channel 5.0 m wide for uniform flow at a depth of 1.5 m. The channel is having bed slope of 1 in 1000. Take Chezy's constant $C = 50$. Also state whether the flow is tranquil or rapid.

   [**Ans.** 11.48 m^3/s; 363.09, tranquil]

2. A flow of water of 100 litres per second flows down in a rectangular flume of width 60 cm having adjustable bottom slope. If the Chezy's constant C is 56, find the bottom slope necessary for uniform flow with a depth of flow of 30 cm. Also find the conveyance K of the flume.

   $$\left[\textbf{Ans. } \frac{1}{1524};\ 3.9\ m^3/s\right]$$

3. A triangular gutter, whose sides include an angle of 60°, conveys water at a uniform depth of 4 m. If the slope of the bed is 1 in 1000 find the rate of flow of water. Take Chezy's constant $C = 55$.

   [**Ans.** 16.066 m^3/s]

4. Calculate the discharge of water in such a channel having semicircular bottom of 3 m diameter and two sides as vertical when the depth of flow is 2.7 m. Take Chezy's constant equal to 60 and slope of the bed as 1 in 2000. [**Ans.** 9.585 m^3/s]

5. Determine the discharge through a trapezoidal channel of width of 8 m and side slopes of 1 horizontal to 3 vertical. The depth of flow of water is 2.4 m and the slope of the bed is 1 in 4000. Take Chezy's constant $C = 60$.

   [**Ans.** 25.47 m^3/s]

6. Find the most economical cross-section of a rectangular channel which is to be dug in the rocky portion of a soil. The channel is to convey 8 m3/s of water with an average velocity of 2 m/s. Take Chezy's constant $C = 65$.

   $$\left[\textbf{Ans. } b = 2.828\text{ m};\ y = 1.414\text{ m},\ S = \frac{1}{746}\right]$$

7. Determine the most economical section of a rectangular channel carrying water at the rate of 0.4 m3/s; The bed slope of the channel being 1 in 2000. Take Chezy's constant $C = 50$.

   [**Ans.** b = 1.154 m; y = 0.577 m]

8. A trapezoidal channel carries a discharge of 2.5 m^3/s. Design the section if the slope is 1 in 1200 and the side slopes are 1 in 1. Use Chezy's formula, $C = 55$. [**Ans.** $b = 0.9$ m; $y = 1.085$ m]

9. Determine the dimensions of the most economical trapezoidal earth-lined channel (Manning's $N = 0.020$) to carry 14 m^3/s at a slope of 1 in 2500. [**Ans.** $b = 2.98$ m; $y = 2.58$ m]

   $$\left[\textbf{Hint. } \text{Take } n = \frac{1}{\sqrt{3}}\right]$$

10. A trapezoidal channel has side slopes of 1 horizontal to 2 vertical and the slope of the bed is 1 in 1500. The area of the section is 40 m^2. If Chezy's constant $C = 60$, determine:

    (*i*) The dimensions of the section if it is most economical, and

    (*ii*) Discharge of the most economical section.

    [Ans. (*i*) $b = 5.93$ m; $y = 4.8$ m (*ii*) 96 m^3/s]

11. Design a trapezoidal channel for carrying 30 m^3/s of water. The bed slope of the channel is 1:1800 and side slope of horizontal to 1 vertical. Assume C in Chezy's formula as 50.

    [Rajputana University]

    [**Ans.** $b = 1.872$ m; $y = 3.12$ m]

12. A concrete lined circular channel of 3 m diameter has a bed slope of 1 in 500. Determine the velocity and the flow rate for the condition of (*i*) maximum velocity, and (*ii*) maximum discharge. Take Chezy's constant $C = 50$.

    [**Ans.** (*i*) 2.13 m/s, 13.11 m^3/s
    (*ii*) 2.073 m/s; 14.37 m^3/s]

13. A 3 m wide rectangular channel conveys 12 m^3/s of water at a depth of 2 m. Calculate:

    (*i*) Specific energy of flowing fluid;

    (*ii*) Critical depth, critical velocity and the minimum specific energy;

    (*iii*) Froude number and state whether flow is subcritical or supercritical.

    [**Ans.** (*i*) 2.2038 m; (*ii*) 1.177 m; 3.398 m/s; 1.765 m; (*iii*) 0.453; subcritical]

14. Calculate the specific energy of 12 m^3/s of water flowing with a velocity of 1.5 m/s in a rectangular channel 7.5 m wide. Find the depth of water in the channel when the specific energy would be minimum. What would be the value of critical velocity as well as minimum specific energy?

    [**Ans.** 1.1825 m, 0.639 m; 2.5 m/s; 0.0958 m]

15. A 3.6 m wide rectangular channel carries water to a depth of 1.8 m. In order to measure the discharge, the channel width is reduced to 2.4 m and a hump of 0.30 m height is provided at the bottom. Calculate the discharge if water surface in the contracted section drops by 0.15 m. Assume no losses.

    [UPSC, CES Exams.]

    [**Ans.** 6.418 m^3/s]

16. A control sluice spanning the entry of a 4.0 m wide rectangular channel having a mild slope admits water at the rate of 16.0 m^3/s and at a velocity of 3.0 m/s. Find whether a hydraulic jump is expected in the channel downstream from the sluice. **[UPSC Exams.]**

[**Ans.** Jump not expected.]

17. Water flows at the rate of 1 m^3/s along a channel of rectangular section, 1.75 metres in width. Calculate the critical depth. If a hydraulic jump is formed at a point where the upstream depth is 0.25 m, what would be the rise in water level and power lost in the jump? **[IIT Delhi]**

[**Ans.** 0.322 m; 0.158 m; 90.15 W]

18. A hydraulic jump occurs in a rectangular channel and the depths of flow before and after the jump are 0.5 m and 2.0 m respectively. Calculate the critical depth of flow. **(Roorkee University)**

[**Ans.** 1.077 m]

19. In a rectangular channel, 10 m wide and 3 m deep, water is flowing with a velocity of 1 m/s. The bed slope of the channel is 1 in 4000. If flow of water through the channel is regulated in such a way that energy line is having a slope of 0.00004 find the rate of change of depth of water in the channel. [**Ans.** 0.000217]

20. In a rectangular channel of width 20 m and depth of flow 5 m, the rate of flow of water is 50 m^3/s. If the bed slope of the channel is 1 in 4000 find the slope of the free water surface. Take Chezy's constant $C = 60$.

21. A concrete lined rectangular channel 5.5 m wide carries water at a rate of 10 m^3/s. Calculate the critical depth, critical velocity and the corresponding minimum specific energy. Would the flow be subcritical or supercritical at a point where the flow depth is 0.5 m. Also find the slope of free water surface at this point if the channel bed is having a slope of 1 in 2000. Take Manning's constant N = 0.01.

[**Ans.** 0.696 m; 2.613 m/s; 1.044 m; supercritical; 0.00216]

22. Find the length of the backwater curve caused by an afflux of 2.0 m, in a rectangular channel of width 40 m and depth 2.5 m. The slope of the bed is given as 1 in 11000. Take Manning's $N = 0.03$.

Hint : Afflux $= y_2 - y_1 = 2.0$ m; $y_1 = 2.5$ m

[**Ans.** 33.584 km]

Chapter 17

"Universities' Questions (Latest) with *Solutions*"

SECTION-A: SHORT ANSWER QUESTIONS

Q. 1. *What is 'Continuum'?*

Ans. A continuous and homogeneous medium is called *'Continuum'*. From the continuum view point, the overall properties and behaviour of fluids can be studied without regard for its atomic and molecular structure.

Q. 2. *What is 'viscosity'?*

Ans. ***Viscosity*** may be defined as the property of a fluid which determines its resistance to shearing stresses. Viscosity of fluids is due to cohesion and interaction between particles. An 'ideal fluid' has no viscosity.

Q. 3. *What is 'hyrostatic law'?*

Ans. The hydrostatic law states : "The rate of increase of pressure in a vertically downward direction must be equal to the specific weight of the fluid at that point."

This law is used to determine the pressure at any point.

Q. 4. *What is 'Standard atmospheric pressure'?*

Ans. The atmospheric pressure at sea level (above absolute zero) is called 'Standard atmospheric pressure'.

It has the following equivalent values:

101.3 kN/m^2 or 101.3 kPa; 10.3 m of water; 760 mm of mercury; 1013 mb (millibar); $\simeq$ 1 bar $\simeq$ 100 kPa = 10^5 N/m^2.

Q. 5. *What is 'gauge pressure'?*

Ans. It is the pressure measured with the help of pressure measuring instrument in which the atmospheric pressure is taken as datum. The atmospheric pressure on the scale is marked as zero.

Q. 6. *What is a 'differential manometer'?*

Ans. It is a device used to measure the difference in pressures between two points in a pipe, or in two different pipes. In its simplest form a differntial manometer consists of a *U*-tube, containing a heavy liquid, whose two ends are connected to the points, whose difference of pressures is required to be found out.

Q. 7. *What is the use of a micromanometer?*

Ans. It is used for measuring small pressure differences. It utilizes two manometer liquids which are inmiscible with each other and also with the fluid whose pressure difference is to be measured.

Q. 8. *How does 'total pressure' differ from 'centre of pressure'?*

Ans. ***Total pressure*** is defined as the force exerted by static fluid on a surface (either plane or curved) when the fluid comes in contact with the surface. This force is always at right angle (or normal) to the surface.

Centre of pressure is defined as the point of application of the total pressure on the surface.

Q. 9. *List the possibilities of dam failure?*

Ans. The possibilities of dam failure are :

(*i*) Failure due to sliding along its base.

(*ii*) Failure due to tension or compression.

(*iii*) Failure due to shear at the weakest section.

(*iv*) Failure due to overturning.

Q. 10. *What is 'buoyancy'?*

Ans. Whenever a body is immersed wholly or partially in a fluid it is subjected to an upward force which tends to lift (or buoy) it up. This tendency for an immersed body to be lifted up in the fluid, due to an upward force opposite to action of gravity is known as ***buoyancy.***

Q. 11. *What is 'centre of buoyancy'?*

Ans. The point of application of the force of buoyancy on the body is known as the ***centre of buoyancy.*** It is always the centre of gravity of the volume of fluid displaced.

Q. 12. *Define the term 'metacentre'?*

Ans. ***Metacentre*** may be defined as a point of intersection of the axis of the body passing through e.g. (G) and original centre of buoyancy (B) and a vertical line passing through the centre of buoyancy (B_1) of the tilted position of the body (floating). The position of the centre (M) remains practically constant for the small angle of tilt θ.

Q. 13. *What do you mean by 'unstable equilibrium'?*

Ans. If the body does not return to its original prosition from the slightly displaced angular position and heels farther away, when given a small angular displacement, such an equilibrium is called an ***unstable equilibrium.***

Q. 14. *What is the difference between 'steady and unsteady flows'?*

Ans. The type of flow in which the fluid characteristics like velocity, pressure, density, etc. at a point *do not change* with time is called ***steady flow.***

An ***unsteady flow*** is that type of flow in which the velocity, pressure or density at a point *change* w.r.t. time.

Q. 15. *What is a 'non-uniform flow'? Give two examples.*

Ans. A ***non-uniform flow*** is that type of flow in which the velocity at any given time *changes* with respect to space.

Examples: (*i*) Flow through a non-prismatic conduit;

(*ii*) Flow around a uniform pipe-bend or canal bend.

Q. 16. *Name the type of flow in the following cases :*

(*i*) Ground water flow.

(*ii*) Flow in a converging or diverging pipe or channel.

(*iii*) Flow over a drain hole of a stationary tank or wash basin.

(*iv*) Subsonic aerodynamics

Ans. (*i*) Laminar flow;

(*ii*) Three dimensional flow;

(*iii*) Irrotational flow;

(*iv*) Incompressible flow

Q. 17. *What is the difference between 'path line and 'stream line'?*

Ans. A ***path line*** is the path followed by a fluid particle in motion, whereas, a ***stream line*** is an imaginary line within the flow so that the tangent at any point on it indicates the velocity at the point.

Q. 18. *What is a 'stream tube'? Give examples.*

Ans. A ***stream tube*** is a fluid mass bounded by a group of stream lines. The contents of a stream tube are known as 'current flament'.

Examples: Pipes and nozzles.

Q. 19. *What is 'continuity equation'?*

Ans. A 'continuity equation' is based on the principle of conservation of mass. It states as follows: "If no fluid is added or removed from the pipe in any length then the mass passing across different sections shall be same".

Q. 20. *What do you mean by the terms 'circulation' and 'vorticity'?*

Ans. ***Circulation*** is defined mathematically as the line integral of the tangential velocity about a closed path (contour). Circulation around regular curves can be obtained by integration.

Vorticity is defined as the circulation per unit of enclosed area. If a flow posesses vorticity, it is rotational.

Q. 21. *State 'Bernoulli's equation' and list its practical applications?*

Ans. ***Bernoulli's equation*** states: "In an ideal incommpressible fluid when the flow is steady and continuous, the sum of pressure energy, kinetic energy and potential (or datum) energy is constant along a stream line."

Practical applications: (*i*) Venturimeter; (*ii*) Orificemeter; (*iii*) Rotameter and elbow meter; (*iv*) Pilot tube.

Q. 22. *What is a 'venturimeter'?*

Ans. A ***venturimeter*** is a device which is inserted into a pipeline to measure incompressible fluid flow rates. It consists of a convergent section which reduces the diameter to between one-half to one-fourth of the pipe diameters. This is followed by a divergent section. The pressure difference between the position just before the venturi and the throat of the venturi is measured by a differential manometer. The working of the venturimeter is based on the Bernoulli's principle, that when the velocity head increases in an accelerated flow, there is a corresponding reduction in the piezometric head.

Q. 23. *What are the main points of difference between a veturimeter and orificemeter?*

Ans. Following are the main points of difference :

(*i*) The venturimeter can be used for measuring the flow rates of all incompressible flows, whereas orifice meters are generally used for measuring the flow rates of liquids; (*ii*) Venturimeter is installed in pipeline only, and the accelerated flow through the apparatus is subsequently decelerated to the original velocity at the outlet of the venturimeter. The flow continues through the pipeline. In the orificemeter the entire potential energy of the fluid is converted to kinetic energy and the jet discharges freely into the open atmosphere; (*iii*) In the venturimeter, the flow velocity is measured by noting the pressure difference between the inlet and throat of venturimeter, whereas in the orificemeter the discharge velocity is measured by using pitot tube or by trajectory method.

Q. 24. *What assumptions are made while deriving Bernoulli's equation?*

Ans. The following assumptions are made while deriving Bernoulli's equation :

(*i*) The liquid is ideal and incompressible;

(*ii*) The flow is steady and continuous;

(*iii*) The flow is along stream lines, *i.e.*, one dimensional;

(*iv*) The velocity is uniform over the section and is equal to the mean velocity;

(*v*) The only forces acting on the fluid are the gravity forces and pressure forces.

Q. 25. *What is a Pitot tube? On what principle does it work?*

Ans. ***Pitot tube*** is one of the most accurate devices for velocity measurement.

It works on the principle that if the velocity of flow at a point becomes zero, the pressure there is increased due to conversion of kinetic energy into pressure energy.

It consists of a glass tube in the form of 90° bend of short length open at both its ends. It is placed in the flow with its bent leg directed upstream so that a stagnation point is created immediately in the front of the opening. The kinetic energy at this point gets converted into pressure energy causing the liquid to rise in the vertical limb, to a height equal to the stagnation pressure.

Q. 26. *What is 'Impulse-momentum equation"? What are its applications?*

Ans. ***Impulse-momemtum equation*** states: "The momentum of a force *F* acting on a fluid mass '*m*' in a short interval of time *dt* is equal to the change of momentum *d* (*mv*) in the direction of force."

Applications: This equation is used to the following types of problems:

1. To determine the resultant force acting on the boundary of flow passage by a stream of fluid as the stream changes its direction, magnitude or both. Problems of this type are :

(*i*) Pipe bends; (*ii*) Reducers; (*iii*) Moving values; (*iv*) Jet propulsion, etc.

2. To determine the characteristic of flow when there is an abrupt change of flow section. Problems of this type are :

(*i*) Sudden enlargement in a pipe; (*ii*) Hydraulic jump in a channel, etc.

Q. 27. *Define kinetic energy and momentum correction factors (Coriolis coefficients).*

Ans. ***Kinetic energy correction factor:*** It is defined as the ratio of the kinetic energy of flow per second based on actual velocity across a section to the kinetic energy of flow per second based on average velocity across the same section. It is denoted by 'α'.

Momentum correction factor: It is defined as the ratio of momentum of the flow per second based on actual velocity to the momentum of the flow per second based on average velocity across a section. It is denoted by 'β'.

Q. 28. *What is moment of momentum principle?*

Ans. ***Moment of momentum principle*** states: "The resulting torque acting on a rotating fluid is equal to the rate of change of moment of momentum."

When the moment of momentum of flow leaving a control volume is different from that entering it, the result is a torque acting over the control volume.

Q. 29. *What is 'vortex motion'? How is it characterised?*

Ans. The ***vortex motion*** is defined as a motion in which the whole fluid mass rotates about an axis.

A vortex motion is characterised by a flow pattern wherein the stream lines are curved. When fluid flows between curved stream lines, centrifigal forces are set up and these are counter-balanced by the pressure force acting in the redial direction.

Q. 30. *What is 'dimensional analysis'?*

Ans. ***Dimensional analysis*** is a mathematical technique which makes use of the study of the dimensions for solving several engineering problems. It is based on the 'principle of dimensional homogeneity' and uses the dimensions of relevant variables affecting the phenomenon.

It is specially useful in presenting experimental results in a concise form.

Q. 31. *What are the applications of dimensional homogeneity?*

Ans. The applications of dimensional homogeneity are :

(*i*) It facilitates to determine the dimensions of a physical quantity;

(*ii*) It helps to check whether an equation of any physical phenomenon is dimensionally homogeneous or not;

(*iii*) It facilitates conversion of units from one form system to another;

(*iv*) It provides a step towards dimensional analysis which is fruitfully employed to plan experiments and to present the results meaningfully.

Q. 32. *What is the difference between 'model' and 'prototype'?*

Ans. The ***model*** is the small scale replica of the actual structure or machine. The actual structure of machine is called ***prototype.***

The models are not always smaller than the prototype, in some cases a model may be even larger or of the same size as prototype depending upon the need and purpose (*e.g.*, the working of a wrist watch or a carburettor can be studied in a large scale model).

Q. 33. *Enumerate the forces which influence hydraulic phenomena.*

Ans. (*i*) Inertia force; (*ii*) Viscous force; (*iii*) Gravity force; (*iv*) Pressure force; (*v*) Surface tension force; (*vi*) Elastic force.

Q. 34. *What is Mach number?*

Ans. It is defined as the square root of the ratio of inertia force to the elastic force.

Q. 35. *What is a 'distorted model'?*

Ans. A ***distorted model*** is one which is not geometrically similar to its prototype. In such a model different scale ratios for linear dimensions are adopted. For example in case of a wide and shallow river it is not possible to obtain the same horizontal and vertical scale ratios, however, if these ratios are taken to be same then because of the small depth of flow the vertical dimensions of the model will become too less in comparison to its horizontal length. Thus in distorted models the plan form is geometrically similar to that of prototype but the cross-section is distorted.

Q. 36. *What do you understand by 'Scale effect in models'?*

Ans. By model testing it is not possible to predict the exact behaviour of the prototype. The behaviour of the prototype as predicted by two models with different scale ratios is generally not the same. Such a discrepancy or difference in the prediction of behaviour of the prototype is termed as ***scale effect.*** The magnitude of the scale effect is affected by the type of the problem and the scale ratio used for the performance of experiments on models. The scale effect can be positive and negative and when applied to the results accordingly, the corrected results then hold good for prototype.

Scale effect can be known by testing a number of models using different scale ratios, and the exact behaviour of the prototype can then be predicted.

Q. 37. *What are the limitations of model investigation / hydraulic similitude?*

Ans. 'Model investigation', although very important and valuable, may not provide ready solution to all problems. It has the following 'limitations':

(*i*) The model results, in general, are qualitative but not quantitative;

(*ii*) As compared to the cost of analytical work, models are usually expensive;

(*iii*) Transferring results to the prototype requires some judgement (the scale effect should be allowed for);

(*iv*) The selection of size of a model is a matter of experience.

Q. 38. *What is the difference between an 'orifice' and a 'mouthpiece'?*

Ans. An ***orifice*** is an opening in the wall or base of a vessel through which the fluid flows. The top edge of the orifice is always *below* the free surface (If the free surface is below the top edge of the orifice, becomes a weir).

A ***mouthpiece*** is an attachment in the form of a small tube or pipe fixed to the orifice (the length of pipe extension is usually 2 to 3 times the orifice diameter) and is used to increase the amount of discharge.

Orifices as well as mouthpieces are used to measure the discharge.

Q. 39. *What is 'coefficient of resistance'?*

Ans. The ratio of loss of head (or loss of kinetic energy) in the orifice to the head of water (actual kinetic energy) available at the exit of the orifice is known as ***Coefficient of resistance.*** It is denoted by C_r.

The loss of head in the orifice takes place, because the walls of the orifice offer some resistance to the liquid, as it comes out. While solving numerical problems C_r is generally neglected.

Q. 40. *What is the difference between a 'notch' and a 'weir'?*

Ans. A ***notch*** may be defined as an opening provided in the side of a tank or vessel such that the liquid surface in the tank is below the top edge of the opening. It is generally made of metallic plate and is used for measuring the rate of flow of a liquid through a small channel or a tank.

A ***weir*** may be defined as any regular obstruction in an open stream over which the flow takes place. It is made of masonry or concrete. The conditions of flow, in the case of a weir are practically the same, as those of a rectangular notch. That is why, a notch is sometimes called as a weir or vise versa.

Q. 41. *What is the formula for calculating discharge over a triangular notch?*

Ans. The formula for calculating discharge (Q) over a triangular notch is given by :

$$Q = \frac{8}{15} C_d \sqrt{2g} \tan \frac{\theta}{2} H^{5/2}$$

where, H = Head of water above the apex of the notch,

θ = Angle of notch, and

C_d = Coefficient of discharge.

Q. 42. *What is velocity of approach?*

Ans. The velocity with which the water approaches or reaches the weir or notch before it flow over is known as ***velocity of approach.*** Thus if V_a is the velocity of approach, then an additional head $H_a \left(= \frac{V_a^2}{2g}\right)$ due to the velocity of approach is acting on water flowing over the notch or weir. Then initial and final heights of water over the notch or weir will be $(H + H_a)$ and H_a respectively.

Q. 43. *Name the type of flow for each of the following Reynolds (Re) numbers :*

(*i*) Re < 2000; (*ii*) Re > 4000; (*iii*) Re between 2000 and 4000.

Ans. (*i*) Laminar flow; (*ii*) Turbulent flow; (*iii*) Unpredictable flow.

Q. 44. *What are the important applications of Navier-Stokes equations?*

Ans. The important applications of Navier-stokes equations are :

(*i*) Laminar flow in circular pipes;

(*ii*) Laminar flow between concentric rotating cylinders;

(*iii*) Laminar uni-directional flow between stationary parallel plates;

(*iv*) Laminar uni-directional flow between parallel plates having relative motion.

Q. 45. *How is loss of head due to friction in pipe flow expressed?*

Ans. Loss of head (h_f) due to friction in pipe flow is given by :

$$h_f = \frac{4fLV^2}{D \times 2g} = \frac{f_1 LV^2}{D \times 2g}$$

where, f = Friction coefficient; f_1 (= $4f$) = friction factor,

L = Length of the pipe between the two sections considered,

D = Diameter of the pipe, and

V = Average flow velocity.

Q. 46. *When does a pipe behave like an open channel?*

Ans. A pipe is a closed conduit (generally of circular cross-section) which is used for carrying fluids under pressure. The flow in a pipe is termed pipe flow only when the fluid *completely fills* the cross-section and there is no free surface of liquid. The pipe running *partially full* (in such a case atmospheric pressure exists inside the pipe) behaves like an open channel.

Q. 47. *What is the difference between 'Energy' and 'Hydraulic' gradient lines?*

Ans. ***'Energy gradient line (E.G.L.):*** If the total energy at various points along the axis of the pipe is plotted and joined by a line, the line so obtained is called the 'Energy gradient line'.

Hydraulic gradient line: If a line is drawn joining the piezometric levels at various points, the line so obtained is called the 'Hydraulic gradient line'.

Q. 48. *What do you mean by water hammer in pipes?*

Ans. The phenomenon of sudden rise in pressure in a pipe when water flowing in it is suddenly brought to rest by closing the valve is known as ***water hammer*** or ***hammer blow.***

Q. 49. *What is a boundary layer?*

Ans. The layer adjacent to the boundary is known as ***boundary layer.*** Boundary layer is formed whenever there is relative motion between the boundary and the fluid.

According to boundary layer theory the extensive fluid medium around bodies moving in the fluids can be divided into following two regions :

(*i*) A thin layer adjoining the boundary is called the 'boundary layer' where the viscous shear takes place.

(*ii*) A region outside the boundary layer where the flow behaviour is quite like that of an ideal fluid and the potential flow theory is applicable.

Q. 50. *What is boundary layer thickness?*

Ans. The velocity within the boundary layer increases from zero at the boundary surface to the velocity of the main stream asymptotically. Therefore the ***thickness boundary layer*** is arbitrarily defined as that distance from the boundary in which the velocity reaches 99 per cent of the velocity of the free stream ($u = 0.99U$). It is defined by the symbol δ. This definition however gives an approximate value of the boundary layer thickness and hence δ is generally termed as 'nominal thickness' of boundary layer.

The commonly adopted definitions of the boundary layer thickness are : (*i*) Displacement thickness (δ^*); (*ii*) Momentum thickness (θ); (*iii*) Energy thickness (δ_e).

Q. 51. *How does 'displacement thickness (δ*)' differ from momentum thickness (θ)?*

Ans. ***Displacement thickness*** is the distance measured perpendicular to the boundary, by which the main/free stream is displaced on account of formation of boundary layer (δ).

Momentum thickness is the distance through which the total loss of momentum per second be equal to it if it were passing a stationary plate. The momentum thickness is useful in kinetics.

Q. 52. *What is 'Von Karman momentum equation'? What is the use of this equation?*

Ans. ***Von Karman momentum equation*** is given by :

$$\frac{\tau_0}{\rho U^2} = \frac{d\theta}{dx}$$

where,

$$\theta = \int_0^{\delta} \frac{u}{U}\left(1 - \frac{u}{U}\right) dy, \text{ and}$$

τ_0 = Shear stress at the surface,

ρ = Density of fluid,

u = Velocity at the section considered,

U = Free stream velocity, and

dy = Thickness of the section considered.

This equation is used to find out the frictional drag on smooth flat plate for both laminar and turbulent boundary layers.

Q. 53. *On what factors does the flow separation depends?*

Ans. The flow separation depends on the following factors :

(*i*) The curvature of the surface, (*ii*) The Reynolds number, and (*iii*) Roughness of surface.

Q. 54. *Name the methods used to control separation.*

Ans. The following methods are used to control separation:

(*i*) Motion of boundary layer, (*ii*) Acceleration of fluid in the boundary layer, (*iii*) Suction of fluid from the boundary layer, and (*iv*) Streamlining of body shapes.

Q. 55. *Name the forces to which a body wholly immersed in a real fluid may be subjected to?*

Ans. A body wholly immersed in a real fluid may be subjected to the following forces:

(*i*) Drag force (F_D): It is the force exerted by the fluid in the direction of flow (free stream).

(*ii*) Lift force (F_L): It is the force exerted by fluid at right angles to the direction of flow.

Q. 56. *What is the difference between a 'streamlined body' and a 'bluff body'?*

Ans. A body whose surface *coincides* with the stream lines when placed in a flow, is called a ***streamlined body.*** If the surface of the body *does not coincide* with the stream lines the body is called ***bluff body.***

Q. 57. *What is the 'terminal velocity' in relation to the falling body? What is the formula for calculating it for a sphere falling through a liquid at rest.*

Ans. The ***terminal velocity*** is the maximum velocity attained by a falling body. The terminal velocity (U) of a sphere falling through a liquid at rest is calculated from the following relation:

$$U = \frac{D^2}{18\mu}(w_s - w_f)$$

where, D = Diameter of the sphere, μ = Dynamic viscosity of the fluid, w_s = Specific weight of the material of sphere, and w_f = Specific weight of fluid.

Q. 58. *What is D'Alembert's paradox?*

Ans. The concept of zero drag on bodies immersed in a steady flow of ideal fluid is called ***D'Alembert's paradox.***

Q. 59. *What is 'Magnus effect'? What are it uses?*

Ans. The generation of lift by spinning cylinder in a fluid stream is called ***Magnus effect.***

Uses :

(*i*) This effect has been successfully employed in the propulsion of ships;

(*ii*) The Magnus effect may also be used with advantage in the games like table tennis, golf, cricket etc.

Q. 60. *How is Kutta-Joukowski equation expressed?*

Ans. According to ***Kutta-Jowkowski equation,*** the total lift (F_L) of a cylinder of length L is given by :

$$F_L = \rho L U \Gamma$$

where, ρ = Density of fluid,

L = Length of the cylinder,

U = Velocity of uniform flow, and

Γ = Circulation.

Q. 61. *What do you mean by stagnation point and stagnation properties?*

Ans. The point on the immersed body where the velocity is zero is called ***stagnation point.*** At this point velocity head is converted into pressure head. The values of pressure (p_s), temperature (T_s) and density (ρ_s) at stagnation point are called ***stagnation properties.***

Q. 62. *What are shock waves in compressible flow?*

Ans. Whenever a supersonic flow (compressible) abruptly changes to subsonic flow, a shock wave (analogous to hydraulic jump in an open channel) is produced resulting in a sudden rise in pressure, density, temperature and entropy. This occurs due to pressure differentials and when the Mach number of the approaching flow is greater than one (*i.e.,* $M > 1$).

Q. 63. *What is an open channel?*

Ans. An ***open channel*** may be defined as a passage in which liquid flows with its upper surface exposed to atmosphere. In open channels the flow is due to gravity, thus the flow conditions are greatly influenced by the slope of the channel.

Q. 64. *What is hydraulic radius (R)?*

Ans. ***Hydraulic radius*** is the ratio of the cross-sectional area of flow to wetted parameter. It is also called 'hydraulic mean depth'.

Q. 65. *What do you mean by most economical section of a channel?*

Ans. The ***most economical section*** (also called the best section or most efficient section) is one which gives the maximum discharge for a given amount of excavation.

Q. 66. *What is a 'hydraulic jump' or 'standing wave'?*

Ans. In an open channel when rapidly flowing stream abruptly changes to slowly flowing stream, a distinct rise or jump in the elevation of fluid surface takes place, this phenomenon is known as ***hydraulic jump*** (which is analogous to shock wave in compressible fluids). The hydraulic jump converts kinetic energy of stream rapidly flowing into potential energy. Due to this there is a loss of kinetic energy. At the place where hydraulic jump occurs rollers of turbulent water (eddying turbulences) form, which cause dissipation of energy. A hydraulic jump occurs in practice at the toe of spillways or below a sluice gate where the *velocity is very high.*

The hydraulic jump is also known as a ***standing wave*** because it is, in essence, a *wave which is stationary* (*i.e.,* at stand-still) at one place.

Q. 67. *How does 'afflux' differ from' back water curve'?*

Ans. ***Afflux*** is the increase in water level due to some obstruction across the flowing liquid; the curved surface of the liquid with its concavity upwards, is known as ***back water curve.***

SECTION-B: "QUESTIONS WITH SOLUTIONS"

Q. 1. *A circular pipe 100 mm in diameter has a 2.5 m length which is porous. In this porous section the velocity of exit is known to be constant (Fig. 1). If the velocities at inlet and outlet of the porous section are 1.8 m/s and 1.1 m/s respectively, calculate :*

(i) The discharge emitted out through walls of the porous pipe, and

(ii) The average velocity of this emitted discharge.

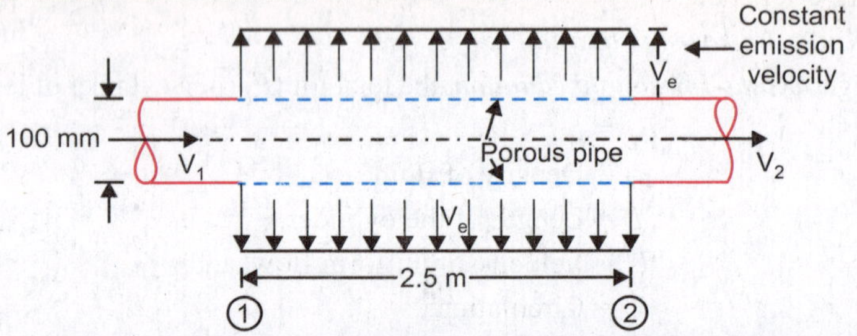

Fig. 1

Solution. *Given:* Dia. of the pipe, $D = 100\ mm = 0.1\ m$; Length, $L = 2.5\ m$; Velocities at inlet and outlet of the porous pipe, $V_1, V_2 = 1.8\ m/s$ and $1.1\ m/s$ respectively.

Area of the pipe cross-section, $A = \frac{\pi}{4} \times (0.1)^2 = 7.854 \times 10^{-3}\ m^2$

(i) The discharge emitted out through walls of the porous pipe, Q_e:

Inlet discharge, $Q_1 = AV_1 = 7.854 \times 10^{-3} \times 1.8 = 0.014137\ m^3/s$

Outlet discharge, $Q_2 = AV_2 = 7.854 \times 10^{-3} \times 1.1 = 0.0086394\ m^3/s$

∴ Discharge emitted through walls of the porous pipe,

$$Q_e = Q_1 - Q_2 = 0.014137 - 0.0086394 = \mathbf{0.0054976\ m^3/s}\ \textbf{(Ans.)}$$

(ii) The average velocity of the emitted discharge V_e :

Surface area of the emission, $A_e = \pi DL$

$$= \pi \times 0.1 \times 2.5 = 0.7854\ m^2$$

Velocity of emission, $V_e = \frac{Q_e}{A_e} = \frac{0.0054976}{0.7854} = \mathbf{0.007\ m/s}$ **(Ans)**

Q.2. *Fig. 2. shows a standard lined triangular section. The section consists of a triangular section of side slope 'n' horizontal : 1 vertical with its bottom being rounded off by a circular curve of radius equal to the full supply depth. For such a channel calculate fully supply depth corresponding to a full supply discharge of 20 m³/s. The side slopes are 2 horizontal : 1 vertical, the longitudinal slope is 1 in 2500 and Manning's N = 0.018.*

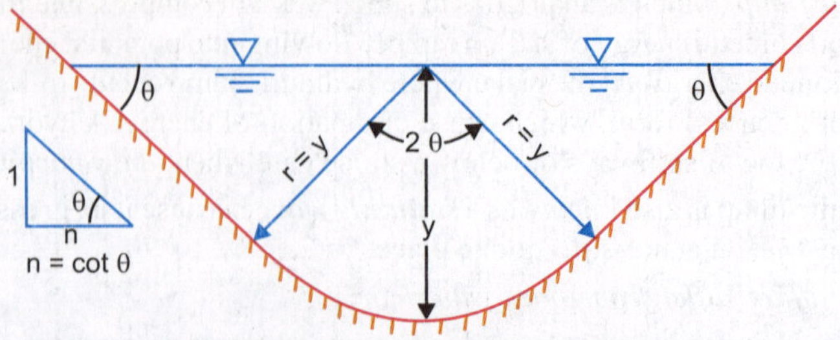

Fig. 2. Standard lined triangular canal section.

Sultion. *Given:* Full supply discharge, $Q = 20\ m^3$; Side slopes = 2 horizontal : 1 vertical; Longitudinal slopes = 1 in 2500; Manning's $N = 0.018$.

Full supply depth, *y* :

Let y_0 = Normal (or full supply) depth = r

θ = Inclination of the sides to the horizontal,

$$\cot\theta = n, \quad \text{or,} \quad \theta = \tan^{-1}\frac{1}{n}$$

$$\text{Area, } A = 2\left(\frac{1}{2}y^2\cot\theta\right) + \frac{1}{2}y^2 \cdot 2\theta$$

$$= y^2(\theta + \cot\theta) \quad \text{...(i)}$$

$$= \varepsilon y^2, \text{ where, } \varepsilon = \theta + \cot\theta = \left(\tan^{-1}\frac{1}{n} + n\right)$$

$$\text{Wetted perimeter, } P = 2y\cot\theta + 2y\theta$$

$$= 2y(\cot\theta + \theta) = 2\varepsilon y \quad \text{...(ii)}$$

$$\text{Hydraulic radius, } R = \frac{A}{P} = \frac{\varepsilon y^2}{2\varepsilon y} = \frac{y}{2} \quad \text{...(iii)}$$

In the present case, $n = 2$

and, $$\tan^{-1}\frac{1}{n} = \tan^{-1}\frac{1}{2} = 26.565 \times \frac{\pi}{180} = 0.4636 \text{ rad}$$

$\therefore$ $$\varepsilon = \theta + \cot\theta = \tan^{-1}\frac{1}{n} + n$$

$$= 0.4636 + 2 = 2.4636$$

and, $$A = \varepsilon y^2 = 2.4636\,y^2 \quad \text{[from (i)]}$$

$$R = 0.5\,y \quad \text{[from (iii)]}$$

By using Manning's equation, we have :

$$Q = A \times \frac{1}{N} R^{2/3} S^{1/2}$$

$$20 = 2.4636\,y^2 \times \frac{1}{0.018} \times (0.5\,y)^{2/3} \times \left(\frac{1}{2500}\right)^{1/2}$$

$$20 = 1.7244\,y^{8/3}$$

or, $$y = \left(\frac{20}{1.7244}\right)^{3/8} = \mathbf{2.507\ m}\ \textbf{(Ans.)}$$

Q. 3. *In Fig. 3 is shown a standard lined trapezoidal section which has a bottom width of 30 m and side slopes of 1.5 horizontal : 1 vertical. The longitudinal slope is 1 in 4500 and the Manning's N can be assumed to be 0.017. Determine the discharge if the full supply depth y is 3.2 m.*

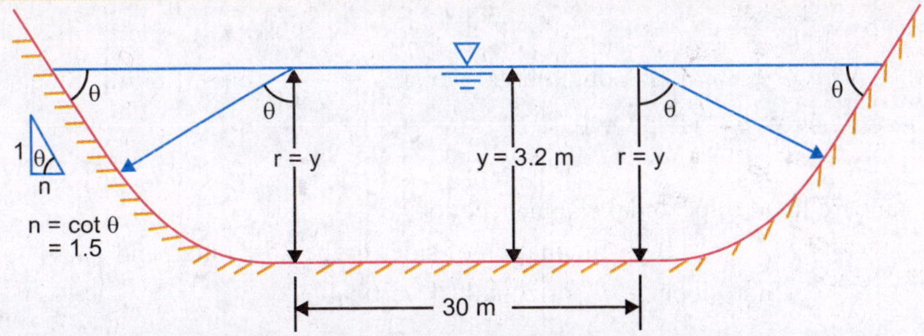

Fig. 3. Standard lined trapezoidal section.

Solution. *Given:* Bottom width, $b = 30$ m; Side slopes = 1.5 horizontal : 1 vertical ($n = 1.5$);

Longitudinal slope; $S = \frac{1}{4500}$; Supply depth, $y = 3.2$ *m*; Manning's $N = 0.017$.

Discharge with full supply width, *Q*:

Let the side slopes be *n* horizontal : 1 vertical. If θ is the inclination of side to the horizontal, then:

$$\cot\theta = n, \quad \text{and} \quad \theta = \tan^{-1}\frac{1}{n}$$

If, $$\varepsilon = \cot\theta + \theta = n + \tan^{-1}\frac{1}{n}\left(= 1.5 + \tan^{-1}\frac{1}{1.5}\times\frac{\pi}{80} = 2.088\right), \text{ then}$$

$$\text{Area, } A = by + y^2(\cot\theta + \theta) = (b + \varepsilon y)\,y$$

$$\text{Perimeter, } P = b + 2y(\cot\theta + \theta) = b + 2y\varepsilon$$

Inserting the values, we get :

$$A = (b + \varepsilon y)\,y = (32 + 2.088 \times 3.2) \times 3.2 = 123.78 \text{ m}^2$$

and, $$P = b + 2y\varepsilon = 32 + 2 \times 3.2 \times 2.088 = 45.363 \text{ m}$$

and, $$\text{hydraulic radius, } R = \frac{A}{P} = \frac{123.78}{45.363} = 2.729 \text{ m}$$

By using Manning's formula, we get :

$$\text{Discharge, } Q = A \times V = A \times \frac{1}{N} R^{2/3} S^{1/2}$$

$$= 123.78 \times \frac{1}{0.017} \times (2.729)^{2/3} \times \left(\frac{1}{4500}\right)^{1/2} = \mathbf{211.96\ m^3/s} \text{ (Ans.)}$$

Q. 4. *Fig. 4, shows a standard lined trapezoidal channel section. For such a channel determine the bed width 'b' and depth of flow 'y' to carry 85 m^3/s of discharge on a slope of 1 in 2500. The velocity of flow is to be 1.8 m/s and the side slopes are 1.2 horizontal : 1 vertical.*

Manning's N can be taken as 0.016.

Also b > y.

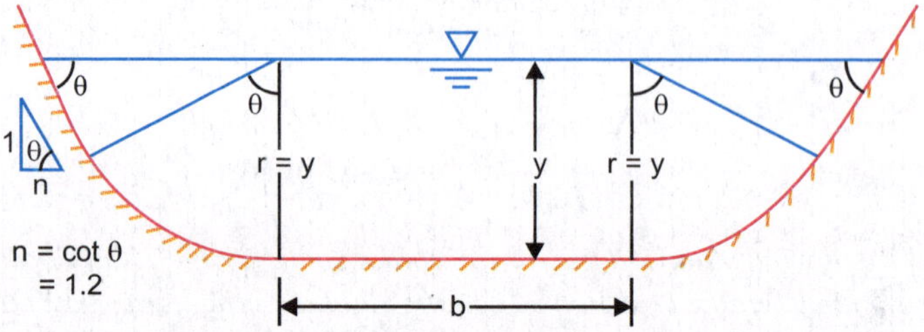

Fig. 4

Solution. *Given:* $Q = 85$ m^3/s; Longitudinal slope, $S = \frac{1}{2500}$; $V = 1.8$ *m/s*; Side slopes = 1.2 horizontal : 1 vertical (or, $n = 1.2$); $N = 0.016$.

Bed width, *b*; Depth of flow, *y*:

For the standard lined trapezoidal channel section,

Let, θ = Inclination of sides to the horizontal, and

Side slope = *n* horizontal : 1 vertical

Then, $\cot\theta = n$, or, $\theta = \tan^{-1}\frac{1}{n}$

Further, let $\cot\theta + \theta = n + \tan^{-1}\frac{1}{n} = \varepsilon$, then :

$$\text{Area, } A = by + y^2(\cot\theta + \theta) = by + \varepsilon y^2 = (b + \varepsilon y)y$$

$$\text{Perimeter, } P = b + 2y(\cot\theta + \theta) = b + 2y\varepsilon$$

Inserting the values, we get :

$$\varepsilon = 1.2 + \left(\tan^{-1}\frac{1}{1.2} \times \frac{\pi}{180}\right) = 1.895$$

Area, $$A = \frac{Q}{V} = \frac{85}{1.8} = 47.22 \text{ m}^2$$

Also, $$A = by + 1.895\,y^2 = 47.22 \quad ...(1)$$

By, Manning's formula,

$$V = \frac{1}{N} R^{2/3} S^{1/2}$$

or, $$1.8 = \frac{1}{0.016} \times R^{2/3} \times \left(\frac{1}{2500}\right)^{1/2} = 1.25\,R^{2/3}$$

$\therefore$ $$R = \left(\frac{1.8}{1.25}\right)^{3/2} = 1.728$$

Also, $$R = \frac{A}{P} = \frac{47.22}{b + 2y \times 1.895} = \frac{47.22}{b + 3.79y} = 1.728 \text{ (as above)}$$

or, $$b + 3.79\,y = \frac{47.22}{1.728} = 27.327$$

or, $$b = 27.327 - 3.79\,y \quad ...(2)$$

Substituting for b in (1), we get :

$$A = (27.327 - 3.79\,y)\,y + 1.895\,y^2 = 47.22$$

$$= 27.327y - 3.79\,y^2 + 1.895\,y^2 = 47.22$$

or, $$-1.895\,y^2 + 27.327\,y - 47.22 = 0$$

or, $$1.895\,y^2 - 27.327\,y + 47.22 = 0$$

or, $$y^2 - 14.42\,y + 24.92 = 0$$

Solving for y and *noting* $b > y$, we have :

$$y = \frac{14.42 - \sqrt{(14.42)^2 - 4 \times 24.92}}{2} = \frac{14.42 - 10.40}{2}$$

$$= \mathbf{2.01\ m} \text{ (Ans)}$$

Now, $$b = 27.327 - 3.79 \times 2.01 = \mathbf{19.7\ m} \text{ (Ans.)}$$

Q. 5. *For a triangular channel having a vertex angle of 110°, calculate the critical depth for a discharge 2.8 m³/s.*

Solution. Refer to Fig. 5.

Given: $2\theta = 110°$; $Q = 2.8\ m^3/s$

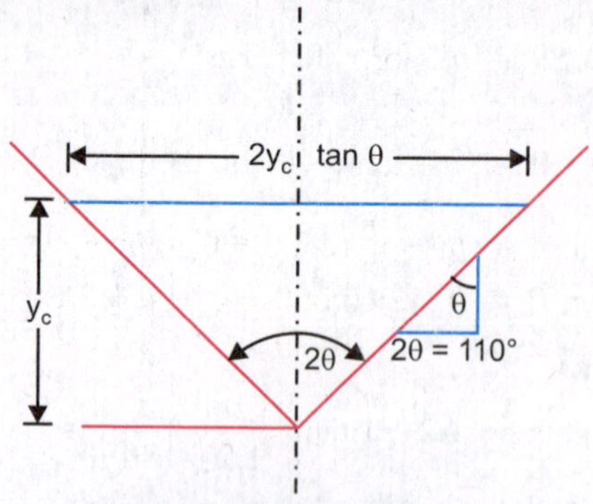

Fig. 5. Triangular channel.

Critical depth, y_c:

$$\text{Top width, } b_{top} = 2y_c \tan\theta$$

$$\text{Area, } A_c = \frac{1}{2} \times 2y_c \tan\theta \times y_c$$

$$= y_c^2 \tan\theta$$

At critical depth,

$$\frac{Q^2}{g} = \frac{A_c^3}{b_{top}} = \frac{y_c^6 \tan^3\theta}{2y_c \tan\theta} = \frac{1}{2} y_c^5 \tan^2\theta$$

or,

$$y_c = \left(\frac{2Q^2}{g} \times \frac{1}{\tan^2\theta}\right)^{1/5}$$

$$= \left[\frac{2 \times (2.8)^2}{9.81} \times \frac{1}{(\tan 55°)^2}\right]^{1/5} = \mathbf{0.952\ m}\ \textbf{(Ans.)}$$

Q. 6. *An overflow spillway has its crest at elevation 133 m and horizontal apron at an elevation 103 m on the downstream side. Estimate the tailwater elevation required to form an hydraulic jump when the elevation of the energy line just upstream of the spillway crest is 135 m. Assume C_d = 0.74 for the spillway. Neglect energy loss due to flow over the spillway.*

Solution. Refer to Fig. 6

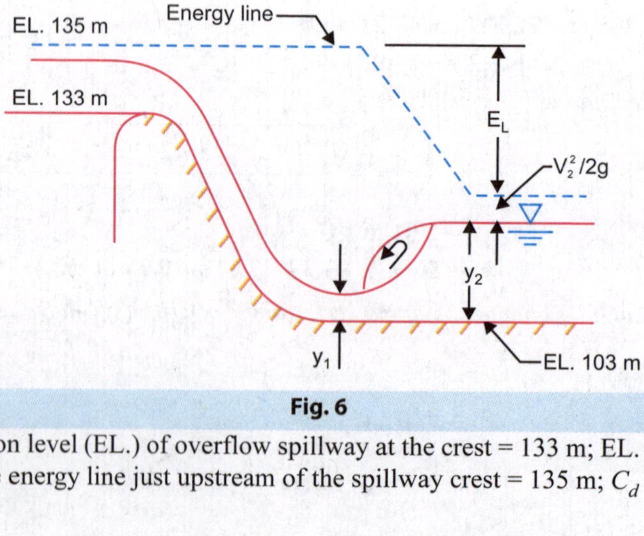

Fig. 6

Given: Elevation level (EL.) of overflow spillway at the crest = 133 m; EL. of horizontal apron = 103 m; EL. of the energy line just upstream of the spillway crest = 135 m; C_d = 0.74.

Tailwater elevation required to form an hydraulic jump:

We know that, $Q = \frac{2}{3} C_d \sqrt{2g}\, H^{3/2}$

Hence, $H = 135 - 133 = 2$ m

$\therefore \quad Q = \frac{2}{3} \times 0.74 \times \sqrt{2 \times 9.81} \times (2)^{3/2} = 6.18 \text{ m}^3/\text{s}$

$E_1 = 135 - 103 = 32$ m

Also, $E_1 = y_1 + \frac{V_1^2}{2g} = y_1 + \frac{Q^2}{2g\, y_1^2}$ $\left[\because Q = A_1 \times V_1 \text{ or, } V_1 = \frac{Q}{A_1} = \frac{Q}{1 \times y_1}\right]$

$= y_1 + \frac{(6.18)^2}{2 \times 9.81 y_1^2}$

Hence, $y_1 + \frac{1.947}{y_1^2} = 32 \text{ m } (i.e.\ 135 - 103)$

By trial and error, $y_1 = 0.2475\ m$

Now, $V_1 = \frac{Q}{y_1} = \frac{6.18}{0.2475} = 24.97$ m/s

and, Froud number, $F_{r1} = \frac{V_1}{\sqrt{g y_1}} = \frac{24.97}{\sqrt{9.81 \times 0.2475}} = 16.025$

We know that, $y_2 = \frac{y_1}{2}\left[\sqrt{1 + 8(F_{r1})^2} - 1\right]$ ...[Eq. (16.38)]

or, $y_2 = \frac{0.2475}{2}\left[\sqrt{1 + 8(16.025)^2} - 1\right] = 5.487$ m

Hence, required tailwater elevation = 103 + 5.487 = **108.487 m** **(Ans.)**

Q. 7. *The space between two square flat parallel plates is filled with oil. Each side of the plate is 680 mm. The thickness of the oil film is 12 mm. The upper plate which moves at 2.8 m/s requires a force of 105 N to maintain the speed. Determine :*

(i) *The dynamic viscosity of the oil;* ***(ii)*** *The kinetic viscosity of oil if the specific gravity of oil is 0.92.*

Solution. *Given:* Each side of a square plate = 680 mm = 0.68 m;

The thickness of oil, dy = 12 mm = 0.012 m; Velocity of upper plate = 2.8 m/s; Force required to maintain the speed = 105 N; Specific gravity of oil = 0.92.

Now shear stress, $\tau = \frac{\text{Force}}{\text{Area}} = \frac{105}{0.68 \times 0.68} = 227.1 \text{ N/m}^2$

(*i*) Dynamic viscosity μ:

We know that, $\tau = \mu \cdot \frac{du}{dy}, \quad 227.1 = \mu \times \frac{(2.8 - 0)}{0.012}$

$\therefore \quad \mu = \frac{227.1 \times 0.012}{2.8} = \mathbf{0.097\ Ns/m^2}$ **(Ans)**

(*ii*) Kinematic viscosity, ν:

Weight density of oil, $w = 0.92 \times 9.81 \text{ kN/m}^3$

$= 9.025 \text{ kN/m}^3 \text{ or } 9025 \text{ N/m}^3$

Mass density of oil, $\rho = \frac{w}{g} = \frac{9025}{9.81} \simeq 920$

Using the relation : $\nu = \frac{\mu}{\rho} = \frac{0.97}{920} = \mathbf{0.00105\ m^2/s}$ **(Ans).**

Q. 8. *Fig. 7 shows a U-tube differential manometer connecting two pressure pipes at A and B. The pipe A contains a liquid of specific gravity 1.5 under a pressure of 105 kN/m². The pipe B contains oil of specific gravity 0.78 under a pressure of 190 kN/m².*

Determine the difference of pressure measured by mercury at fluid filling U-tube.

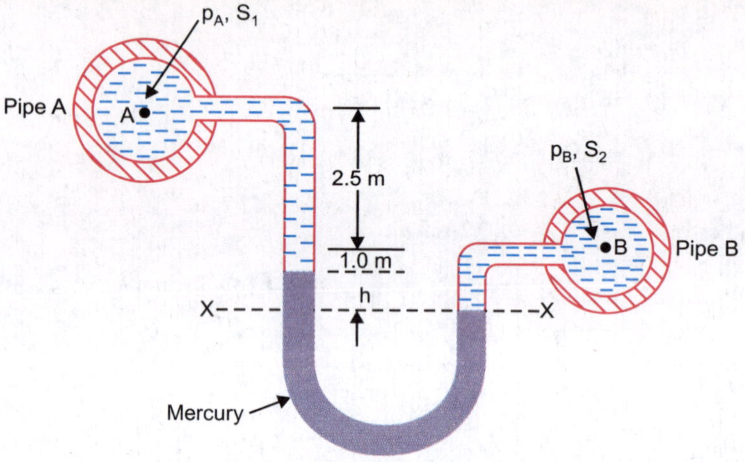

Fig. 7

Solution. Refer to Fig. 7. *Given:* Specific gravity of liquid at *A*, $S_1 = 1.5$; Pressure at *A*, $p_A = 105$ kN/m²; Specific gravity of liquid at *B*, $S_2 = 0.78$; Pressure at *B*, $p_B = 190$ kN/m².

Difference of pressure measured by mercury, *h*:

Pressure heat at *A*, $h_A = \frac{p_A}{w} = \frac{105}{9.81} = 10.7$ m of water

Pressure heat at *B*, $h_B = \frac{p_B}{w} = \frac{190}{9.81} = 19.37$ m of water

Taking *X–X* as the datum line :

Pressure head above *X–X* in the *left limb*

$= h_A + (2.5 + 1.0)\, S_1 + h \times 13.6$ m of water.

Pressure head above *X–X* in the *right limb*

$= h_B + (1.0 + h) \times S_2$ m of water.

Equating the above pressure heads we get :

$$h_A + (2.5 + 1.0)\, S_1 + h \times 13.6 = h_B + (1.0 + h) \times S_2$$

or, $$10.7 + 3.5 \times 1.5 + 13.6\,h = 19.37 + (1.0 + h) \times 0.78$$

or, $$15.95 + 13.6\,h = 20.15 + 0.78\,h$$

From which, $h = 0.327$ m, or, **327 mm (Ans.)**

Q. 9. *A trapezoidal 2.5 m wide at the bottom and 1.2 m deep has side slopes 1 : 1. Determine : **(i)** Total pressure; **(ii)** Centre of pressure on the vertical gate closing the channel when it is full of water.*

Solution. Refer to Fig. 8.

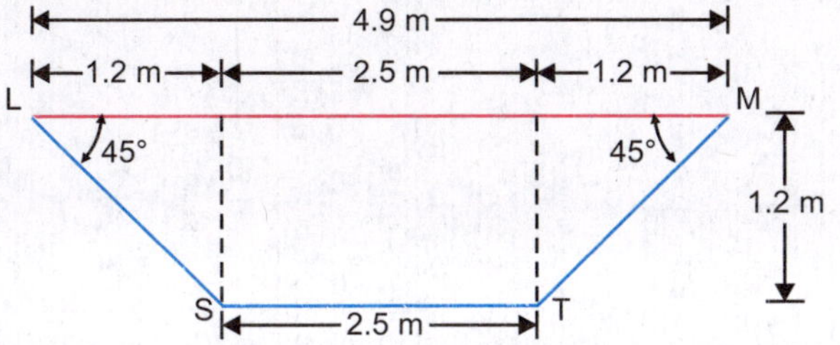

Fig. 8

(*i*) Total pressure, *P*:

For rectangle :

$$\text{Area, } A_1 = 2.5 \times 1.2 = 3.0 \text{ m}^2$$

$$\bar{x} = \frac{1.2}{2} = 0.6 \text{ m}$$

$$P_1 = wA\bar{x} = 9.81 \times 3.0 \times 0.6 = 17.66 \text{ kN}$$

This acts at a depth $\bar{h}_1$.

But, $$\bar{h}_1 = \frac{I_G}{A\bar{x}} + \bar{x} = \frac{\left[\left(2.5 \times 1.2^3\right)/12\right]}{3.0 \times 0.6} + 0.6 = 0.8 \text{ m}$$

For triangles:

$$\text{Area, } A_2 = 2 \times \frac{1}{2} \times 1.2 \times 1.2 = 1.44 \text{ m}^2 \text{ (For two triangles);}$$

$$\bar{x} = \frac{1.2}{3} = 0.4 \text{ m}$$

$$P_2 = wA\bar{x} = 9.81 \times 1.44 \times 0.4 = 5.65 \text{ kN}$$

This acts at a depth of $\bar{h}_2$.

But, $$\bar{h}_2 = \frac{I_G}{A\bar{x}} + \bar{x} = \frac{\left[\left(2.4 \times 1.2^3\right)/36\right]}{1.44 \times 0.4} + 0.4 = 0.6 \text{ m}$$

Total pressure, $P = P_1 + P_2 = 17.66 + 5.65 =$ **23.31 kN (Ans.)**

(*ii*) Centre of pressure, $\bar{h}$:

Taking moments about the top, we get :

$$P \times \bar{h} = P_1 \times \bar{h}_1 + P_2 \times \bar{h}_2$$

or, $$\bar{h} = \frac{P_1 \bar{h}_1 + P_2 \bar{h}_2}{P} = \frac{17.66 \times 0.8 + 5.651 \times 0.6}{23.31}$$

$$= \mathbf{0.75 \text{ m}} \text{ (Ans)}$$

Q. 10. *A wooden block of specific gravity 0.8 floats in water. If the size of the block is 1.6 m × 0.8 m × 0.6 m, find its metacentric height.*

Solution. Refer to Fig. 9.

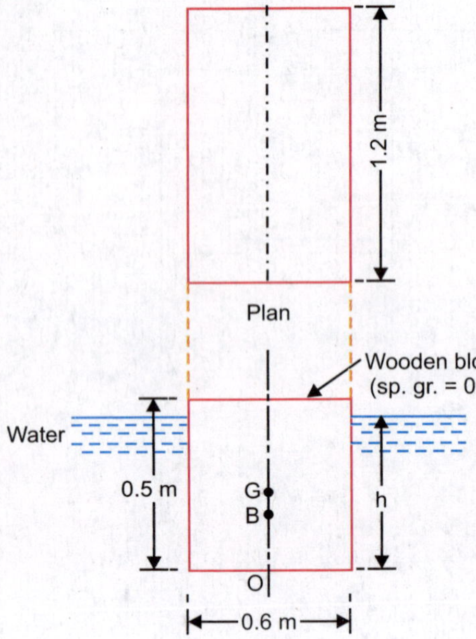

Fig. 9

Given: Size/dimensions of the block = 1.6 *m* × 0.8 *m* × 0.6 *m*; Specific gravity of wood, $\rho = 0.8$.

Metacentric height:

$$\text{Specific weight, } w = \rho \times g = 0.8 \times 9.81 = 7.85 \text{ kN/m}^3$$

$$\text{Weight of wooden block} = \text{Specific weight} \times \text{volume}$$

$$= 7.85 \times (1.2 \times 0.6 \times 0.5) = 2.83 \text{ kN}$$

$$\text{Let depth of immersion} = h \text{ metre}$$

$$\text{Weight of water displaced} = \text{Specific weight of water} \times \text{volume of the wood submerged in water}$$

$$= 9.81 \times 1.2 \times 0.6 \times h = 7.06 \text{ h}$$

Now for equilibrium,

$$\text{Weight of wooden block} = \text{Weight of water displaced}$$

i.e., $$7.06\,h = 2.83$$

or, $$h = \frac{2.83}{7.06} = 0.4 \text{ m}$$

Distance of centre of buoyancy from the bottom *i.e.,*

$$OB = \frac{h}{2} = \frac{0.4}{2} = 0.2 \text{ m}$$

and, $$OG = \frac{0.5}{2} = 0.25 \text{ m}$$

∴ $$BG = OG - OB = 0.25 - 0.2 = 0.05 \text{ m}$$

Also, $$BM = \frac{I}{V}$$

Where, I = Moment of inertia of a rectangular section

$$= \frac{1.2 \times 0.6^3}{12} = 0.0216 \text{ m}^4$$

and, V = Volume of water displaced, or, volume of wood in water

$$= 1.2 \times 0.6 \times h = 1.2 \times 0.6 \times 0.4 = 0.288 \text{ m}^3$$

$$\therefore \qquad BM = \frac{I}{V} = \frac{0.0216}{0.288} = 0.075 \text{ m}$$

We know that the metacentric height,

$$GM = BM - BG \quad (\because G \text{ is above } B)$$

$$= 0.075 - 0.05 = \mathbf{0.025\ m} \text{ (Ans)}$$

Q. 11. *A pipe 240 m long slopes down 1 in 80 and tapers from 500 mm diameter at the higher end to 250 mm diameter at the lower end, and carries 80 litres / sec. of oil (sp. gr. 0.75). If the pressure gauge at the higher end reads 55 kN/m², determine:*

(i) Velocities at the two ends; (ii) Pressure at the lower end.

Neglect all losses.

Solution. Refer to Fig. 10.

Given: $l = 240$ m; $D_1 = 500$ mm $= 0.5$ m; $D_2 = 250$ mm $= 0.25$ m; Slope : 1 in 80; $p_1 = 55$ kN/m², Rate of oil flow, $Q = 80$ litres/sec. $= 0.08$ m³/s; Sp. gr. $= 0.75$.

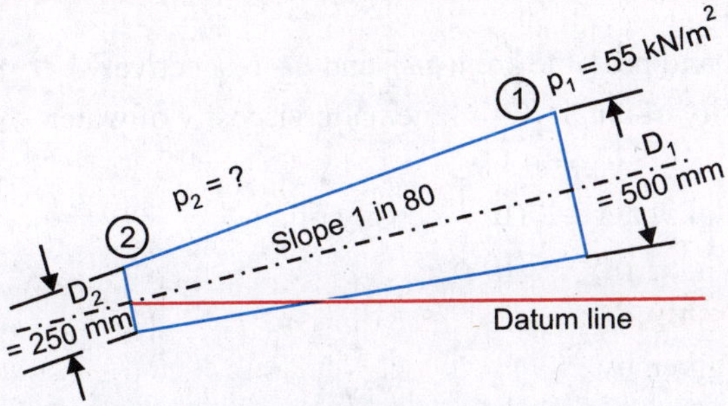

Fig. 10

(i) Velocities, V_1, V_2 :

$$\text{Area, } A_1 = \frac{\pi}{4} \times D_1^2 = \frac{\pi}{4} \times 0.5^2 = 0.196 \text{ m}^2$$

$$\text{Area, } A_2 = \frac{\pi}{4} \times D_2^2 = \frac{\pi}{4} \times 0.25^2 = 0.049 \text{ m}^2$$

Height of the higher end, above datum,

$$z_1 = \frac{1}{80} \times 240 = 3 \text{ m}$$

Height of the lower end, above datum,

$$z_2 = 0$$

Now, $\qquad Q = A_1 V_1 = A_2 V_2$

where, V_1 and V_2 are the velocities at the higher and lower ends respectively.

$$V_1 = \frac{Q}{A_1} = \frac{0.08}{0.196} = \mathbf{0.408\ m/s} \text{ (Ans)}$$

and, $$V_2 = \frac{Q}{A_2} = \frac{0.08}{0.049} = \mathbf{1.632\ m/s} \text{ (Ans)}$$

(ii) Pressure at the lower end, p_2:

Using Bernoulli's equation for both ends of the pipe, we have :

$$\frac{p_1}{w} + \frac{V_1^2}{2g} + z_1 = \frac{p_2}{w} + \frac{V_2^2}{2g} + z_2$$

or, $$\frac{55}{0.75 \times 9.81} + \frac{(0.408)^2}{2 \times 9.81} + 3 = \frac{p_2}{0.75 \times 9.81} + \frac{(1.632)^2}{2 \times 9.81} + 0$$

or, $$7.475 + 0.00848 + 3 = \frac{p_2}{7.36} + 0.136$$

or, $$p_2 = \mathbf{76.16\ kN/m^2\ (Ans.)}$$

Q. 12. *Resistance R to the motion of a completely submerged body is given by* $R = \rho V^2 L^2 \phi \left(\frac{VL}{\nu}\right)$, *where ρ and ν are density and kinematic viscosity of the fluid while L is the length of the body and V is the velocity of flow. If resistance of a one-sixth scale airship model when tested in water at 10 m/s is 230 N, what will be the resistance in air of the airship at the corresponding speed? Kinematic viscosity of air is 13 times that of water and density of water is 810 times of air.*

Solution. *Given:* Scale ratio $= \frac{L_m}{L_p} = \frac{1}{6}$; Velocity of model, $V_m = 10$ *m/s*; Resistance of model, $R_m = 230$ N.

The fluids for model and prototpe are *water* and *air* respectively.

∴ Kinematic viscosity of air = 13 × kinematic viscosity of water

or, $$\nu_p = 13\ \nu_m$$

Density of water = 810 × density of air

or, $$\rho_m = 810\ \rho_p$$

Resistance of the airship, R_p:

The resistance, *R*, is given by :

$$R = \rho V^2 L^2 \phi \left(\frac{VL}{\nu}\right)$$

From the above equation it is obvious that flow in the model will be dynamically similar if the Reynolds numbers are equal in both the systems. Thus, if,

$$\left(\frac{VL}{\nu}\right)_m = \left(\frac{VL}{\nu}\right)_p \qquad \ldots(i)$$

Then, $$\left(\frac{R}{\rho V^2 L^2}\right)_m = \left(\frac{R}{\rho V^2 L^2}\right)_p \qquad \ldots(ii)$$

From eqn. (*i*), we have :

$$\frac{V_m L_m}{\nu_m} = \frac{V_p L_p}{\nu_p}$$

or, $$V_p = V_m \times \frac{L_m}{L_p} \times \frac{\nu_p}{\nu_m} = 10 \times \frac{1}{6} \times 13 = 21.67 \text{ m/s}$$

At this prototype velocity, the resistance of the airship is obtained from eqn. (*ii*) as follows :

$$\frac{R_m}{\rho_m V_m^2 L_m^2} = \frac{R_p}{\rho_p V_p^2 L_p^2}$$

or, $$R_p = R_m \times \frac{\rho_p}{\rho_m} \times \frac{V_p^2}{V_m^2} \times \frac{L_p^2}{L_m^2}$$

$$= 230 \times \frac{1}{810} \times \left(\frac{21.67}{10}\right)^2 \times (6)^2 = \mathbf{48\ N\ (Ans.)}$$

Q. 13. *A rectangular channel 1.6 m wide has a discharge of 0.24 m^3/s, which is measured by a right angled V-notch-weir. Find the position of the apex of the notch from the bed of the channel if the maximum depth of water is not to exceed 1.1 m. Assume $C_d = 0.63$.*

Solution. *Given:* Width of the rectangular channel, $L = 1.6$ m; Discharge, $Q = 0.24\ m^3/s$; Depth of water in the channel = 1.1 m; Coefficient of discharge, $C_d = 0.63$; Angle of notch, $\theta = 90°$.

Position of the apex of the notch:

Using the following relation for discharge over a triangular notch, we get :

$$Q = \frac{8}{15} C_d \sqrt{2g} \tan\frac{\theta}{2} \times H^{5/2} \qquad \text{...[Eqn. (9.2)]}$$

where, H is head of water above the apex of the notch.

Inserting the various values in the above eqn. we have:

$$0.24 = \frac{8}{15} \times 0.63 \times \sqrt{2 \times 9.81} \times \tan\left(\frac{90°}{2}\right) \times H^{5/2}$$

$$= 1.488\ H^{5/2}$$

or, $$H = \left(\frac{0.24}{1.488}\right)^{2/5} = 0.48 \text{ m}$$

Position of the apex of the notch from the bed of channel

= Depth of water in the channel – height of water over the notch

= 1.1 – 0.48 = 0.62 m **(Ans.)**

Q. 14. *It is required to pump glycerine at the rate of 22 litres/sec. from a sump and deliver it freely at a point 105 m away and 7 m above the level of sump through a 150 mm pipe (Fig. 11).*

(i) What is the power of the pump required assuming an overall efficiency of 70 percent?

(ii) What should be the rate of rise of temperature due to viscous dissipation if the pipe is completely insulated?

Sp. gr. of glycerine = 1.26; Viscosity = 15 poise; Specific heat = 250 J/N°C; K.E. correction factor, α = 2.

Solution. *Given:* Rate of flow of glycerine = 22 litres/sec = 0.022 m^3/s; Diameter of the pipe, D = 150 mm = 0.15 m; L = 105 m; Overall efficiency $\eta_0 = 70\%$; Sp. gr. of glycerine = 1.26, Viscosity, μ = 15 poise = 1.5 Ns/m^2; Specific heat = 250 *J/N°C,* K.E. correction factor, α = 2.

(i) Power of the pump required, *P*:

$$\text{Velocity of flow, } V = \frac{Q}{A} = \frac{0.022}{\frac{\pi}{4} \times (0.15)^2} = 1.245 \text{ m/s}$$

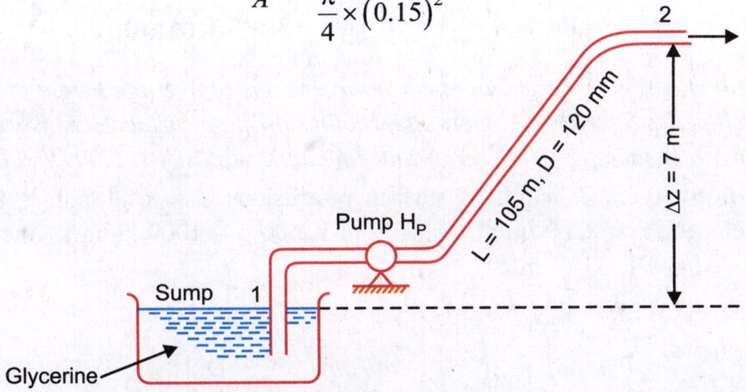

Fig. 11

$$\text{Reynolds number, } Re = \frac{\rho VD}{\mu} = \frac{(1.26\times 1000)\times 1.245\times 0.15}{1.5} = 156.9$$

Since the Reyolds number is *less* than 2000, the flow is *laminar*.

Applying Bernoulli's equation at sump (1) and free delivery point (2), we get :

$$\frac{p_1}{w}+\frac{V_1^2}{2g}+z_1+H_p = \frac{p_2}{w}+\alpha\frac{V_2^2}{2g}+z_2+h_f$$

$$0+0+0+H_p = 0+2\times\frac{(1.245)^2}{2\times 9.81}+7+\frac{32\,\mu V_2 L}{wD^2}$$

(where, H_p = Head developed by the pump, w = weight density of glycerine = (1.26 × 1000) × 9.81 = 12361 N/m^3, and h_f = loss of head due to friction)

or, $$H_p = 2\times\frac{(1.245)^2}{2\times 9.81}+7+\frac{32\times 1.5\times 1.245\times 105}{12361\times(0.15)^2}$$

$$= 0.158+7+22.561 = 29.72 \text{ m}$$

Power of the pump required,

$$P = \frac{wQH_p}{\eta_0} = \frac{12361\times 0.022\times 29.72}{0.7\times 1000}\text{ kW}$$

$$= \mathbf{11.54\ kW\ (Ans)}$$

(*ii*) Rate of rise of temperature:

Dissipation of energy per N per second

= (Energy on the discharge side of the pump – energy at the point of delivery) per N per second

$$= h_f\times\frac{V}{L}$$

(since h_f is energy lost per unit weight (N) of the fluid at a length L)

$$= \frac{32\,\mu VL}{wD^2}\times\frac{V}{L}\ \frac{N.m}{N.s}\ \text{ or }\ \frac{J}{s.N}$$

$$= \frac{32\times 1.5\times(1.245)^2}{12361\times(0.15)^2} = 0.267\,\frac{J}{s.N}$$

∴ Rise of temperature $= \frac{0.267}{250}\times 60\times 60 = \mathbf{3.8°C/h}$ **(Ans.)**

Q. 15. *A pipline carrying water has surface protrusions of average height of 0.11 mm. If the shear stress developed is 8.5 N/mm^2, determine whether the pipe surface acts as smooth, rough or in transition. For water take ρ = 1000 kg/m^3 and kinematic viscosity = 0.0091 stokes.*

Solution. *Given:* Average height of surface protrusions, k = 0.11 mm = 0.11 × 10^{-3} m; Shear stress developed, τ_0 = 8.5 N/mm^2; Density of water, ρ = 1000 kg/m^3; Kinematic viscosity, ν = 0.0091 stokes = 0.0091 × 10^{-4} m^2/s

Shear velocity (u_f) is given by :

$$u_f = \sqrt{\frac{\tau_0}{\rho}}$$

or, $$u_f = \sqrt{\frac{8.5}{1000}} = 0.0922 \text{ m/s}$$

Roughness Reynolds number $$= \frac{u_f k}{\nu} = \frac{0.0922 \times (0.11 \times 10^{-3})}{0.0091 \times 10^{-4}} = 11.14$$

Since $\frac{u_f k}{\nu}$ lies between 4 and 100 the pipe surface behaves as in **transition (Ans).**

Q. 16. *In a 100 mm diameter pipeline an oil of specific gravity 0.75 is flowing at the rate of 0.0145 m³/s. A sudden expansion takes place into a second pipeline of such diameter that maximum pressure rise is obtained. Determine :*

(i) Loss of energy in sudden expansion; (ii) Differential gauge length indicated by an oil-mercury manometer connected between the two pipes.

Solution. *Given:* Diameter of the smaller pipe, D_1 = 100 mm = 0.1 m; Specific gravity of oil, S_0 = 0.75; Discharge, Q = 0.0145 m³/s.

(i) Loss of energy in sudden expansion, h_e:

Velocity of flow, $$V_1 = \frac{Q}{\text{Area}} = \frac{0.0145}{\frac{\pi}{4} \times 0.1^2} = 1.85 \text{ m/s}$$

The *pressure will be maximum* when,

$$\frac{D_1}{D_2} = \frac{1}{\sqrt{2}}$$ (where, D_2 = diameter of the larger pipe)

(*Note:* For derivation of the formula, refer to Example 12.12)

or, $$D_2 = \sqrt{2}\, D_1 = \sqrt{2} \times 0.1 = 0.1414 \text{ m}$$

∴ $$V_2 = \frac{0.0145}{\frac{\pi}{4} \times (0.1414)^2} = 0.92 \text{ m/s}$$

Loss of energy (or head) in sudden expansion,

$$h_e = \frac{(V_1 - V_2)^2}{2g} = \frac{(1.85 - 0.92)^2}{2 \times 9.81} = \mathbf{0.044 \text{ m of oil}} \text{ (Ans)}$$

(ii) Reading of the manometer:

The energy equation is given as :

$$\frac{p_1}{w} + \frac{V_1^2}{2g} + z_1 = \frac{p_2}{w} + \frac{V_2^2}{2g} + z_2 + h_e$$ ($z_1 = z_2$, the pipe being horizontal)

or, $$\frac{p_2}{w} - \frac{p_1}{w} = \frac{V_1^2}{2g} - \frac{V_2^2}{2g} - h_e$$

$$= \frac{(1.85)^2}{2 \times 9.81} - \frac{(0.92)^2}{2 \times 9.81} - 0.044 = 0.087 \text{ m of oil}$$

Let, h = Reading of the U-tube oil-mercury manometer where limbs are connected across the expanded transition,

Then, $$\frac{p_2 - p_1}{w} = h\left(\frac{S_m}{S_0} - 1\right)$$

[Where, S_m = specific gravity of mercury (= 13.6)]

or, $$0.087 = h\left(\frac{13.6}{0.8}-1\right) = 16\,h$$

or, $$h = \frac{0.087}{16} = 0.005437 \text{ m or } \mathbf{5.437\ mm}$$ **(Ans.)**

Q. 17. *For the velocity profile in laminar boundary layer as,*

$$\frac{u}{U} = \frac{3}{2}\left(\frac{y}{\delta}\right)-\frac{1}{2}\left(\frac{y}{\delta}\right)^3$$

find the thickness of the boundary layer and the shear stress 1.4 m from the leading edge of a plate. The plate is 1.8 m long and 1.2 m wide and is placed in water which is moving with a velocity of 180 mm per second.

Determine the total drag force on the plate if μ for water = 0.01 poise.

Solution. *Given:* x = 1.4 m; L = 1.8 m; U = 180 mm/s = 0.18 m/s; $\mu = 0.01 \text{ poise} = \frac{0.01}{10}$

$= 0.001 \text{ Ns/m}^2$ $\left(\because 1 \text{ poise} = \frac{1}{10} \text{ Ns/m}^2\right)$

Velocity profile : $$\frac{u}{U} = \frac{3}{2}\left(\frac{y}{\delta}\right)-\frac{1}{2}\left(\frac{y}{\delta}\right)^3$$

For the given profile, $$\delta = \frac{4.64x}{\sqrt{Re_x}}$$ ...[Eqn. (13.20)]

[Here, $$Re_x = \frac{\rho U_x}{\mu} = \frac{1000\times 0.18\times 1.4}{0.001} = 2.52\times 10^5\,]$$

Thickness of the boundary layer,

$$\delta = \frac{4.64\times 1.4}{\sqrt{2.52\times 10^5}} = 0.0129 \text{ m} = \mathbf{12.9\ mm}$$ **(Ans.)**

Shear stress (τ_0) is given by :

$$\tau_0 = 0.323\frac{\mu U}{x}\sqrt{Re_x}$$ ...[Eqn. (13.21)

or, $$\tau_0 = 0.323\times\frac{0.001\times 0.18}{1.4}\times\sqrt{2.52\times 10^5}$$

$$= \mathbf{0.0208\ N/m^2}$$ **(Ans)**

Drag force (F_D) on one side of the plate is given as :

$$F_D = 0.646\,\mu U\sqrt{\frac{\rho UL}{\mu}}\times B$$ ...[Eqn. (13.23)]

$$= 0.646\times 0.001\times 0.18\sqrt{\frac{1000\times 0.18\times 1.8}{0.001}}\times 1.4 = 0.093\,N$$

∴ Total *drag force* = Drag force on both sides of the plate

= 2 × 0.093 = **0.186 N (Ans.)**

Q. 18. *Determine the largest diameter and correspnoding terminal velocity of a polystyrene spherical particle settling in air. It obeys Stokes' law.*

Take : Density of polystyrene spherical particle = 1050 kg/m³;
Density of air = 1.2 kg/m³; kinematic viscosity of air = 1.48 × 10⁻⁵ m²/s

Solution. *Given:* $\rho_s = 1050$ kg/m^3; $\rho_a = 1.2$ kg/m^3; $\nu_a = 1.48 \times 10^{-5}$ m^2/s

D.U:

The stoke's law is valid upto $Re = 1.0$. For maximum size particle that obeys stoke's law,

$$Re_{max} = 1 = \frac{UD}{\nu_a}, \quad \text{or,} \quad U = \frac{\nu_a}{D}$$

Stoke's law is given by :

$$U = \frac{D^2}{18\mu}(w_s - w_f) \qquad \text{...[Eqn. (14.15)]}$$

(where, suffices *s* and *f* stand for sphere and fluid respectively)

Now,
$$\frac{\nu_a}{D} = \frac{D^2}{18\mu}(\rho_s \times g - \rho_f \times g)$$

(Here, $\mu = \mu_a = \nu_a \times \rho_a = 1.48 \times 10^{-5} \times 1.2 = 1.78 \times 10^{-5}$)

Substituting the values, we get :

$$\frac{1.48 \times 10^{-5}}{D} = \frac{D^2}{18 \times 1.78 \times 10^{-5}}(1050 \times 9.81 - 1.2 \times 9.81)$$

or,
$$D = \left[\frac{1.48 \times 10^{-5} \times 18 \times 1.78 \times 10^{-5}}{9.81(1050 - 1.2)}\right]^{1/3} = 7.724 \times 10^{-5} \text{ m}$$

$$= \mathbf{0.0772\ mm\ (Ans.)}$$

Q.19. *The temperature of the earth's atmosphere drops about 5° C for every 1000 m of elevation above the earth's surface. If the air temperature at the ground level is 18°C and the pressure is 760 mm Hg, at what elevation is the pressure 410 mm Hg? Assume that air behaves as an ideal gas.*

Solution. *Given:* $T_0 = 18 + 273 = 291\ K$; $p_0 = 760$ mm Hg; $p = 410$ mm Hg;

$$\frac{dT}{dZ} = -\frac{5}{1000}\ °C/m$$

Elevation *Z* :

Temperature lapse-rate,
$$L = \frac{dT}{dZ} = -\frac{g}{R}\left(\frac{\gamma - 1}{\gamma}\right)$$

$\therefore$
$$L = -\frac{5}{1000} = -\frac{g}{R}\left(\frac{\gamma - 1}{\gamma}\right)$$

or,
$$\frac{5}{1000} = \frac{9.81}{287}\left(\frac{\gamma - 1}{\gamma}\right)$$

(where, R = Gas constant = 287 J/kg K for air)

$\therefore$
$$\frac{\gamma - 1}{\gamma} = \frac{5 \times 287}{1000 \times 9.81} = 0.1463$$

Using the relation :
$$p = p_0\left[1 - \frac{\gamma - 1}{\gamma} k \frac{gz}{RT_0}\right]^{\frac{\gamma}{\gamma - 1}} \qquad \text{...[Eqn. (2.18)]}$$

or, $$410 = 760\left[1-0.1463\times\frac{9.81\times Z}{287\times 291}\right]^{\frac{1}{0.1463}}$$

or, $$\left(\frac{410}{760}\right)^{0.1463} = 1-0.1463\times\frac{9.81\times Z}{287\times 291} = 1-1.718\times 10^{-5}\,Z$$

or, $$1.718\times 10^{-5}\,Z = 1-\left(\frac{410}{760}\right)^{0.1463} = 0.0863$$

or, $$Z = \frac{0.0863}{1.718\times 10^{-5}} = \mathbf{5023\ m\ (Ans.)}$$

Q. 20. *A tank of 0.8 m length and of cross-section shown in Fig. 12, contains water. The tank is made of 3 mm steel plates. Determine :*

(i) *The force on the bottom due to water;* ***(ii)*** *The longitudinal tensile stresses in the side walls AB if (a) the tank is suspended from the top, and (b) it is supported at the bottom.*

Solution. Refer to Fig. 12.

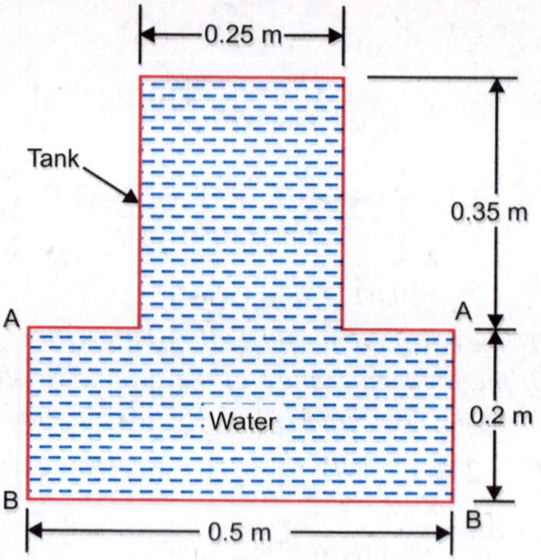

Fig. 12

***(i)* Force on the bottom:**

Force on the bottom due to water,

$$P_{bottom} = wA\bar{x}$$
$$= 9.81\times(0.5\times 0.8)\times(0.2+0.35)$$
$$= \mathbf{2.158\ kN\ (Ans.)}$$

***(ii)* Longitudinal tensile stresses:**

Force on the surface *AA*,

$$P_{AA} = 9.81\times(0.25\times 0.8)\times 0.35 = 0.687\ \text{kN}$$

(*a*) *When suspended from the top* the stress on the side walls,

$$\sigma = \frac{2.158}{(0.5+0.5+0.8+0.8)\times\frac{3}{1000}} = \mathbf{276.66\ kN/m^2\ (Ans)}$$

(*b*) *When supported from the bottom* the stress on the side walls,

$$\sigma = \frac{0.687}{(0.5+0.5+0.8+0.8)\times\frac{3}{100}} = \mathbf{80.08\ kN/m^2}\ \textbf{(Ans.)}$$

Q. 21. *A hollow wooden cylinder of specific gravity 0.58 has an outer diameter of 500 mm and inner diameter of 250 mm. It is required to float in oil of specific gravity 0.85. Calculate :*

(i) The maximum length (height) of the cylinder so that it shall be stable when floating with its axis vertical;

(ii) The depth to which it will sink.

Solution. Refer to Fig. 13.

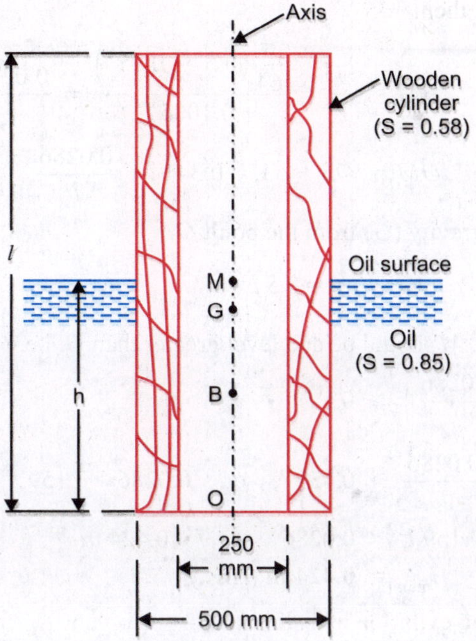

Fig. 13

Given: Outer diameter of the cylinder, D = 500 mm = 0.5 m; Inner diameter of cylinder, d = 250 mm = 0.25 m; Specific weight of wood = 0.58 × 9.81 = 5.69 kN/m^3; Specific weight of oil = 0.85 × 9.81 = 8.34 kN/m^3

(i) Maximum length of cylinder for stability, l_{max}:

$$\therefore \quad \text{Weight of cylinder} = \text{Volume of cylinder} \times \text{specific weight}$$

$$= \frac{\pi}{4}(D^2 - d^2) \times l \times 5.69$$

$$= \frac{\pi}{4}(0.5^2 - 0.25^2) \times l \times 5.69$$

$$= 0.838\, l\ kN$$

(where, l = length/height of the cylinder)

This also represents the weight of oil displaced.

∴ Volume of oil displaced,

$$V = \frac{\text{Weight of oil displaced}}{\text{Specific weight of oil}} = \frac{0.838\, l}{8.34} = 0.1005\, l$$

i.e., Volume of cylinder immersed in oil, $V = 0.1005\, l$

$$\therefore \quad \text{Depth of immersion, } h = \frac{\text{Volume of cylinder under oil}}{\text{Cross-section area of cylinder}}$$

$$= \frac{0.1005\, l}{\frac{\pi}{4}\left(0.5^2 - 0.25^2\right)} = 0.682\, l$$

Height of centre of buoyancy (B) from O,

$$\text{i.e.,} \quad OB = \frac{h}{2} = \frac{0.682\, l}{2} = 0.341\, l$$

If M is the metacentre, then:

$$BM = \frac{I}{V} = \frac{\frac{\pi}{64}\left(0.5^4 - 0.25^4\right)}{0.1005\, l} = \frac{0.0286}{l}$$

$$OM = OB + BM = 0.341\, l + \frac{0.0286}{l}$$

Distance of centre of gravity (G) from the ponit O,

$$OG = \frac{l}{2} = 0.5\, l$$

For stable equilibrium, M should be at a level greater than G, i.e. $OM > OG$

$$\text{or,} \quad \left(0.341\, l + \frac{0.0286}{l}\right) > 0.5\, l$$

$$\text{or,} \quad \frac{0.0286}{l} > 0.159\, l; \quad \text{or,} \quad 0.0286 > 0.159\, l^2$$

$$\text{or,} \quad 0.159\, l^2 < 0.0286 \quad \text{or} \quad l < 0.424\, m$$

$$\therefore \quad l_{max} = \mathbf{0.424\ m}\ \textbf{(Ans.)}$$

(*ii*) Depth to which the cylinder will sink *h*:

$$h = 0.682\, l = 0.682 \times 0.424 = \mathbf{0.289\ m}\ \textbf{(Ans.)}$$

Q. 22. *The velocity components in x and y directions are given as* $u = \frac{xy^3}{3} - x^2y$ and $v = xy^2 - \frac{yx^3}{3}$. Indicate whether the given distribution is a possible field of flow or not a possible field of flow.

Solution. *Given:* $u = \frac{xy^3}{3} - x^2y,\ v = xy^2 - \frac{yx^3}{3}$ ...Velocity components

A possible flow field (two-dimensional) must satisfy the continuity equation :

$$\frac{\partial u}{\partial x} + \frac{\partial v}{\partial y} = 0 \qquad ...(i)$$

$$\text{Now,} \quad \frac{\partial u}{dx} = \frac{y^3}{3} - 2xy, \quad \frac{dv}{dy} = 2xy - \frac{x^3}{3}$$

Substituting these values in eqn. (*i*), we get :

$$\left(\frac{y^3}{3} - 2xy\right) + \left(2xy - \frac{x^3}{3}\right) = \frac{1}{3}\,(y^3 - x^3)$$

Since the continuity equation is *not* satisfied, the given velocity components, therefore, **do not represent a possible case of flow. (Ans.)**

Q. 23. *A siphon consisting of a pipe of 100 mm diameter is used to empty kerosene oil (sp. qr. = 0.75) from the tank A. The siphon discharges to the atmosphere at an elevation of 1.4 m. The oil surface in the tank is at an elevation of 4.4 m. The centre line of the siphon pipe at its highest point C is at an elevation of 5.8 m. Determine :*

***(i)** The discharge in the pipe; **(ii)** The pressure at point C.*

The losses in the pipe may be assumed to be 0.42 m upto summit, 1.24 m from the summit to outlet.

Solution. Consider points 1 and 2 at the surface of the oil in the tank *A* and at the outlet as shown in Fig. 14. The velocity V_1 can be assumed to be zero. Applying Bernoulli's equation at points 1 and 2, we get :

$$\frac{p_1}{w} + \frac{V_1^2}{2g} + z_1 = \frac{p_2}{w} + \frac{V_2^2}{2g} + z_2 + \underset{\text{(losses)}}{h_{f\,(1-2)}}$$

$$0 + 0 + 4.4 = 0 + \frac{V_2^2}{2g} + 1.4 + (0.42 + 1.24)$$

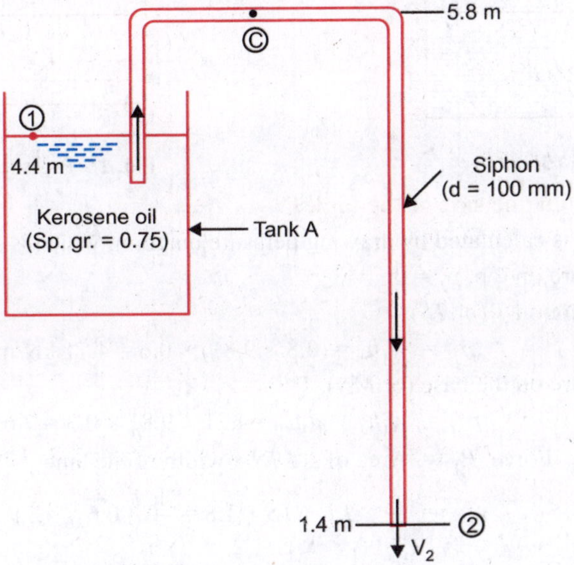

Fig. 14

or, $V_2 = 5.13$ m/s

(i) The discharge in pipe, *Q*:

$$Q = A_2V_2 = \frac{\pi}{4} \times \left(\frac{100}{1000}\right)^2 \times 5.13 = \mathbf{0.04\ m^3/s\ (Ans.)}$$

(ii) The pressure at point *C*:

Applying Bernoulli's equation at points 1 and *C*, we get :

$$\frac{p_1}{w} + \frac{V_1^2}{2g} + z_1 = \frac{p_C}{w} + \frac{V_C^2}{2g} + z_C + h_{f(1-C)}$$

$$0 + 0 + 4.4 = \frac{p_C}{w} + \frac{(5.13)^2}{2 \times 9.81} + 5.8 + 0.42$$

or, $\frac{p_C}{w} = -3.16$ m

or, $p_C = (0.75 \times 9.81) \times (-3.16) = -23.25$ kN/m^2 or $-$ **23.25 kPa (gauge) (Ans.)**

Q. 24. *Fig. 15 shows a tank containing water and liquid (sp. gr. = 0.8) upto a height of 0.3 m and 0.6 m respectively. Calculate :*

*(i) Total pressure on the side of the tank; **(ii)** The position of centre of pressure from one side of the tank, which is 1.8 m wide.*

Solution. *Given:* Depth of liquid, $h_1 = 0.6$ m; Depth of water, $h_2 = 0.3$ m; Sp. gr. of liquid, S = 0.8, Width of the tank = 1.8 m.

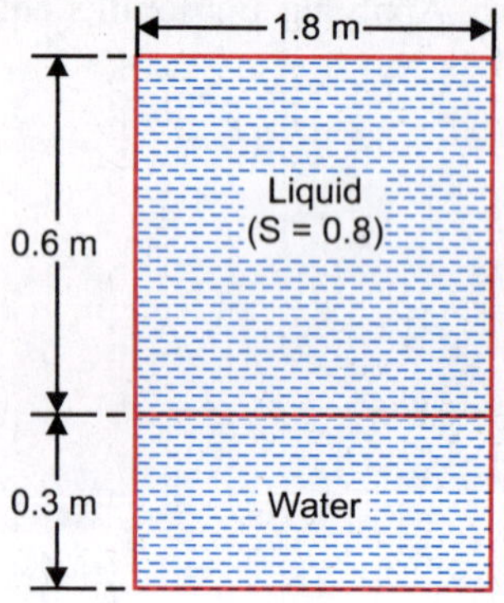

Fig. 15

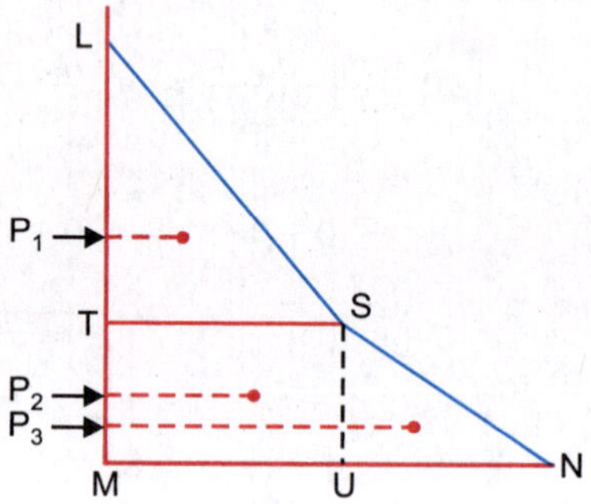

Fig. 16. Pressure diagram

(i) Total pressure on one side of the tank *P*:

Total pressure (P) is calculated by drawing perssure diagram, which is shown in Fig. 16.

Intensity of pressure on top, $p_L = 0$

Intensity of pressure on T (or TS),

$$p_T = w_1 h_1 = (0.8 \times 9.81) \times 0.6 = 4.71 \text{ kN/m}^2$$

Intensity of pressure on the base (or MN),

$$p_M = w_1 h_1 + w_2 h_2 = 4.71 + 9.81 \times 0.3 = 7.65 \text{ kN/m}^2$$

Now, Force, P_1 = Area of $\Delta\, LTS$ × width of the tank

$$= \frac{1}{2} \times LT \times TS \times 1.8 = \frac{1}{2} \times 0.6 \times 4.71 \times 1.8 = 2.54 \text{ kN}$$

Force, P_2 = Area of rectangle $MTSU$ × width of the tank

$$= MT \times TS \times 1.8$$

$$= 0.3 \times 4.71 \times 1.8 = 2.54 \; kN$$

P_3 = Area of $\Delta\, SUN$ × width of the tank

$$= \frac{1}{2} \times SU \times UN \times 1.8$$

$$= \frac{1}{2} \times 0.3 \times (9.81 \times 0.3) \times 1.8 = 0.79 \text{ kN}$$

($\because$ $UN = w_2 h_2 = 9.81 \times 0.3$)

Total pressure,

$$P = P_1 + P_2 + P_3 = 2.54 + 2.54 + 0.79 = 5.87 \text{ kN}$$

(ii) Centre of pressure, $\bar{h}$:

Taking moments of all the forces about L, we get :

$$P \times \bar{h} = P_1 \times \frac{2}{3} LT + P_2 \times \left(LT + \frac{1}{2} TM \right) + P_3 \times \left(LT + \frac{2}{3} MT \right)$$

$$5.87\,\bar{h} = 2.54 \times \frac{2}{3} \times 0.6 + 2.54 \left(0.6 + \frac{1}{2} \times 0.3 \right) + 0.79 \times \left(0.6 + \frac{2}{3} \times 0.3 \right)$$

$$= 1.016 + 1.905 + 0.632 = 3.553$$

or, $\bar{h}$ = **0.605 m from the top (Ans.)**

Q.25. *A solid cube of side 600 mm each is made of a material of relative density 0.52. The cube floats in a liquid of relative density 0.92 with two of its faces horizontal. Examine its stability.*

Solution. Refer to Fig. 17.

Given: Side of the cube = 600 mm = 0.6 m;

Sp. gr. of cube material = 0.52; Relative density of liquid = 0.92.

$$\text{Depth of cube is liquid, } h = \frac{0.6 \times 0.52}{0.92} = 0.339 \text{ m}$$

Distance of centre of buoyance (B) from O,

$$OB = \frac{h}{2} = \frac{0.339}{2} = 0.1695 \text{ m}$$

Distance of centre of gravity (G) from O,

$$OG = \frac{0.6}{2} = 0.3 \text{ m}$$

$$BG = OG - OB = 0.3 - 0.1695 = 0.1305 \text{ m}$$

B lies below G.

$$BM = \frac{I}{V}$$

where, I = Moment of inertia of the plane of the body about $YY = \frac{1}{12}(0.6)(0.6)^3 = 0.0108 \text{ m}^4$

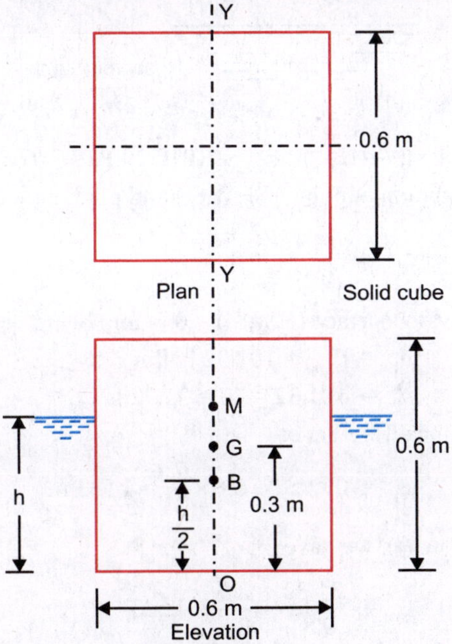

Fig. 17

and, V = Volume of liquid displaced

$= 0.6 \times 0.6 \times 0.339 = 0.122 \text{ m}^3$

$$\therefore \quad BM = \frac{I}{V} = \frac{0.0108}{0.122} = 0.0885 \text{ m}$$

Metacentric height, $GM = BM - BG = 0.0885 - 0.1305 = -0.042$ m

–ve sign means that the metacentre (M) is below the centre of gravity (G). Thus the cube will be **unstable. (Ans.)**

Q.26. *The suction pipe of a pump rises at a slope of 2 vertical in 3 along the pipe which is 100 mm in diameter. The pipe is 6.8 m long; its lower end being just below the water surface in the reservoir. For design reasons, it is desirable that pressure at inlet to the pump shall fall to more than 70 kPa below atmospheric pressure. Neglecting friction, determine the maximum discharge that the pump may deliver. Take atmospheric pressure as 101.32 kPa.*

Solution. Refer to Fig. 18.

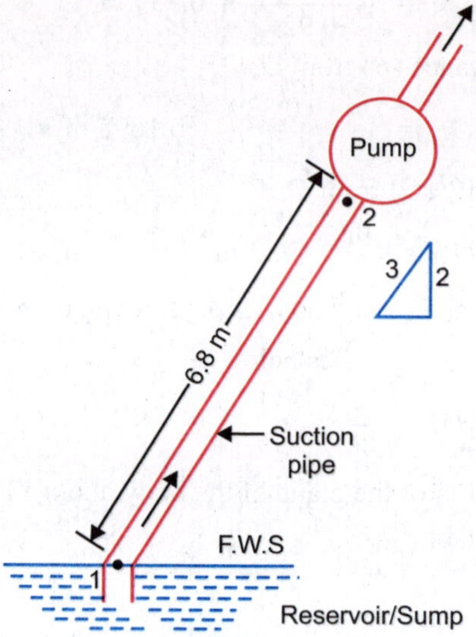

Fig. 18

Given: $d = 100$ mm $= 0.1$ m; $l = 6.8$ m; $p_{atm} = 101.32$ kPa $= 101.32$ kN/m^2.

Applying Bernoulli's equation at point 1 (F.W.S.) and point 2 (suction point to pump), we get:

$$\frac{p_1}{w} + \frac{V_1^2}{2g} + z_1 = \frac{p_2}{w} + \frac{V_2^2}{2g} + z_2 \quad \ldots(i)$$

Velocity V_1 on the free water surface (F.W.S.) = 0 (sump being very large)

$$p_1 = p_{atm} = 101.32 \text{ kN/m}^2;$$

$$p_2 = 101.32 - 70 = 31.32 \text{ kN/m}^2$$

Taking point 1 as datum head, we have:

$$z_1 = 0; \quad z_2 = 6.8 \times \frac{2}{3} = 4.533 \text{ m}$$

Inserting the values in eqn. (i), we have:

$$\frac{101.32}{9.81} + 0 + 0 = \frac{31.32}{9.81} + \frac{V_2^2}{2g} + 4.533$$

or, $V_2 = 7.15$ m/s

∴ The maximum discharge the pump may deliver,

$$Q = A_2 \times V_2 = \frac{\pi}{4} \times (0.1)^2 \times 7.15 = \mathbf{0.056\ m^3/s\ (Ans.)}$$

Q. 27. *In a falling sphere viscometer, a lubricating oil of density 850 kg/m³ was placed in a 90 mm inside diameter tube. A 10 mm diameter steel ball of density 8200 kg/m³ was found to travel a distance of 920 mm is 18 seconds. Determine the viscosity of the oil.*

Solution. *Given:* Density of lubricating oil, $\rho_f = 850$ kg/m³; Diameter of the sphere = 10 mm = 0.01 m; Density of steel ball, $\rho_s = 8200$ kg/m³; Distance travelled in 18 seconds = 920 mm = 0.92 m.

Viscosity of the oil μ:

$$\text{Weight of the ball, } W = \frac{\pi}{6} d^3 \times \rho_s \times g = \frac{\pi}{6} \times (0.01)^3 \times 8200 \times 9.81 = 0.042 \text{ N}$$

$$\text{Buoyancy force, } F_B = \frac{\pi}{6} d^3 \times \rho_f \times g = \frac{\pi}{6} \times (0.01)^3 \times 850 \times 9.81 = 0.00437 \text{ N}$$

$$\text{Drag force, } F_D = 3\pi\mu Vd = 3\pi \times \mu \times \left(\frac{0.92}{18}\right) \times 0.01 = 0.00482\ \mu\text{N}$$

For equilibrium,

$$F_D + F_B = W$$

or, $$F_D = W - F_B$$

or, $$0.00482\ \mu = 0.042 - 0.00437$$

or, $$\mu = \mathbf{7.8\ Ns/m^2\ (Ans.)}$$

Let us check the Reynolds number, *Re*:

$$Re = \frac{\rho V d}{\mu} = \frac{850 \times (0.92/18) \times 0.01}{7.8} = 0.0557 < 0.1$$

Q. 28. *The main pipe divides into two parallel pipes which again form one pipe as shown in Fig. 19. The data is as follows :*

First parallel pipe; Length = 900 m; diameter = 0.7 m; Second parallel pipe : Length = 900 m; diameter = 0.5 m; Coefficient of friction for each parallel pipe = 0.0045.

If the total rate of flow in the main is 1.8 m³/s find the rate of flow in each parallel pipe.

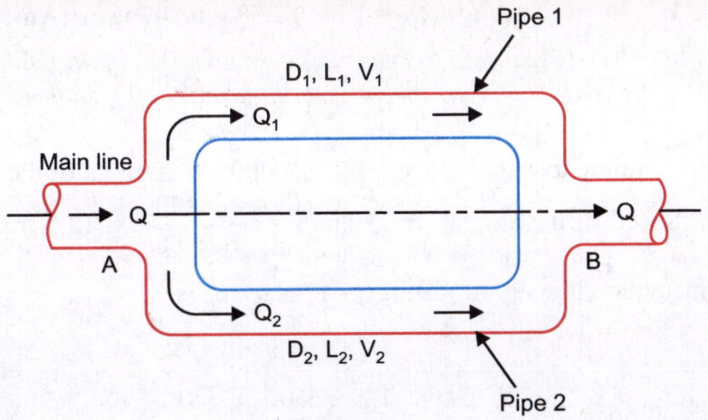

Fig. 19

Solution. Refer to Fig. 19.

Given: $D_1 = 0.7$ m; $L_1 = 900$ m; $D_2 = 0.5$ m; $L_2 = 900$ m; Total rate of flow, $Q = 1.8$ m³/s; Coefficient's of friction, $f_1 = f_2 = 0.0045$.

Rate of flow in each pipe:

Let Q_1 = Rate of flow in pipe 1,

Q_2 = Rate of flow in pipe 2, and

Q = Total rate of flow (in main line),

Then, $$Q = Q_1 + Q_2 \quad \text{...(i) [Eqn. (12.6)]}$$

Also, $$h_f = \frac{4f_1L_1V_1^2}{D_1 \times 2g} = \frac{4f_2L_2V_2^2}{D_2 \times 2g}$$

The above equation reduces to:

$$\frac{V_1^2}{D_1} = \frac{V_2^2}{D_2} \text{ or } \frac{V_1^2}{0.7} = \frac{V_2^2}{0.5}$$

or, $$V_1 = \sqrt{\frac{0.7}{0.5} \times V_2^2} = 1.18\, V_2 \quad \text{...(ii)}$$

Now, $$Q_1 = \frac{\pi}{4} \times D_1^2 \times V_1 = \frac{\pi}{4} \times (0.7)^2 \times 1.18\, V_2 = 0.454\, V_2$$

and, $$Q_2 = \frac{\pi}{4} \times D_2^2 \times V_2 = \frac{\pi}{4} \times 0.5^2 \times V_2 = 0.196\, V_2$$

Substituting the values of Q_1 and Q_2 in eqn. (*i*), we get :

$$1.8 = 0.454\, V_2 + 0.196\, V_2$$

or, $$V_2 = 2.77 \text{ m/s}$$

Substituting the value of V_2 in eqn. (*ii*), we have :

$$V_1 = 1.18 \times 2.77 = 3.27 \text{ m/s}$$

Hence, $$Q_1 = A_1V_1 = \frac{\pi}{4} \times 0.7^2 \times 3.27 = \mathbf{1.258\ m^3/s\ (Ans.)}$$

and $$Q_2 = Q - Q_1 = 1.8 - 1.258 = \mathbf{0.542\ m^3/s\ (Ans.)}$$

Q. 29. *10000 kW power is required to cruise a passenger ship of 260 m length, 10 m draft at 45 km/h. If ρ = 1020 kg/m³ and ν = 1 × 10⁻⁶ m²/s, determine the combined form and wave resistance of the ship.*

Solution. Power required to cruise the ship, P = 10000 kW; Length of the ship = 260 m; Draft of the ship = 10 m; Speed of the ship, U = 45 km/h = $\frac{45 \times 1000}{60 \times 60}$ = 12.5 m/s; Density of water, $\rho = 1020$ kg/m³; Kinematic viscosity of water, $\nu = 1 \times 10^{-6}$ m²/s

Combined form and wave resistance :

$$\text{Reynolds number, } Re_L = \frac{UL}{\nu} = \frac{125 \times 260}{1 \times 10^{-6}} = 3.25 \times 10^9$$

At this Reynolds number, the boundary layer will be turbulent on almost the whole length; C_D is given by:

$$C_D = \frac{0.455}{(\log_{10} Re_L)^{2.58}} = \frac{0.455}{\left[\log_{10}\left(3.25 \times 10^9\right)\right]^{2.58}} = 0.001362$$

$$F_{\text{friction}} = 2 \times C_D \times \frac{1}{2}\rho A U^2$$

$$= 2 \times 0.001362 \times \frac{1}{2} \times 1020 \times (260 \times 10) \times (12.5)^2$$

$$= 564378 \text{ N or } 564.38 \text{ kN}$$

Total power required, $P = FU$

Total force, $F = \frac{P}{U} = \frac{10000}{12.5} = 800$ kN

Also, $F = F_{\text{friction}} + (F_{\text{form}} + F_{\text{wave}})$

$(F_{\text{form}} + F_{\text{wave}}) = F - \text{Friction}$

$= 800 - 564.38 =$ **235.62 kN (Ans.)**

Q. 30. *Air having a velocity of 35 m/s is flowing over a cylinder of diameter 1.2 m and length 8 m, when the axis of the cylinder is perpendicular to the stream. Find the speed at which the cylinder is to be rotated about its axis so that a lift force of 6 kN/m length of the cylinder is developed. Also determine the location of the stagnation points. Assume density of air as 1.24 kg/m^3.*

Solution. *Given:* $U = 35$ m/s; $D = 1.2$ m; $L = 8$ m; $F_L = 6$ kN/m; $\rho = 1.24$ kg/m^3

Speed N:

Using the relation: $F_L = \rho L U \Gamma$ [Eqn. (14.22)]

or, Circulation, $\Gamma = \frac{(F_L/L)}{\rho U} = \frac{6 \times 1000}{1.24 \times 35} = 138$ m/s

Circulation = Circumference × peripheral velocity

$\Gamma = 2\pi R \times u_c$ [Eqn. (14.17)]

or, $138 = 2\pi \times \frac{1.2}{2} \times u_c$

or, $u_c = 36.6$ m/s

Angular velocity, $w = \frac{u_c}{R} = \frac{36.6}{(1.2/2)} = 61 \text{ rad/s} = \frac{2\pi N}{60}$

or, $N = \frac{61 \times 60}{2\pi} =$ **582.5 r.p.m. (Ans.)**

Position of stagnation points:

The net velocity on the cylinder surface (u) due to combination of circulation and force stream velocity field in given by :

$$u = 2\,U \sin\theta + \frac{\Gamma}{2\pi R}$$

At stagnation point, $u = 0 \quad \therefore \quad 0 = 2\,U \sin\theta + \frac{\Gamma}{2\pi R}$

or, $\sin\theta = -\frac{\Gamma}{4\pi R U} = -\frac{138}{4\pi \times (1.2/.2) \times 35} = -0.523 = -\sin(31.5°)$

$$= \sin(180° + 31.5°) \text{ and } \sin(360° - 31.5°)$$

or, θ = **211.5° and 328.5° (Ans.)**

The position of stagnation points (S_1 and S_2) is shown in Fig. 20.

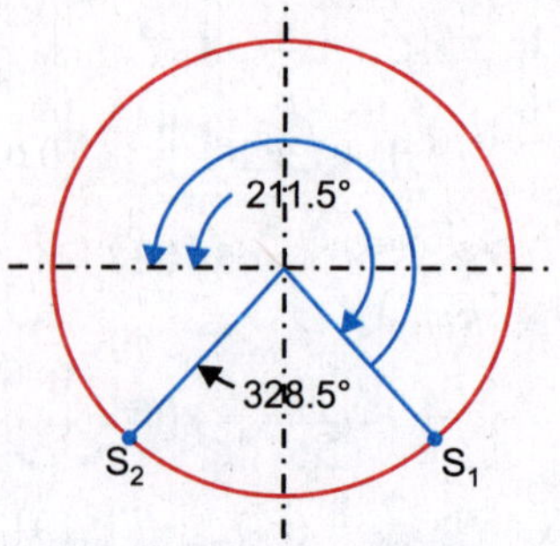

Fig. 20

GATE and UPSC Examinations' Questions with Answers/Solutions

Chapter 18

A. Conventional Questions with Answers/Solutions

B. Multiple-choice Questions with Answers and *'Explanations'*

A. CONVENTIONAL QUESTIONS WITH ANSWERS/SOLUTIONS

Q. 18.1. ***(Hydrostatic forces on surfaces)*** *A tank with the vertical sides measuring 3 m × 3 m contains water to a depth of 1.2 m. An oil of density 900 kg/m³ was poured in the tank up to a depth of 0.8 m. The vertical wall can withstand the thrust of 58 kN. Calculate the actual thrust on the wall and centre of pressure. If the oil level is increased up to 0.9 m, what will be stability of the wall?* **(GATE)**

Solution. *Given:* Tank's vertical sides measurement = 3 m × 3 m; Depth of water = 1.2 m; Depth of liquid (ρ = 900 kg/m³) = 0.8 m; Thrust which vertical side can withstand = 58 kN.

Refer to Fig. 18.1

Actual thrust on the wall, P_{act} :

Thrust or total pressure due to 0.8 m of *oil,*

$$P_1 = A \times w\bar{x} = (0.8 \times 3) \times (\rho.g) \times \frac{0.8}{2}$$

$$= (0.8 \times 3) \times (900 \times 9.81) \times 0.4 \times 10^{-3}$$

$$= 8.476 \text{ kN}$$

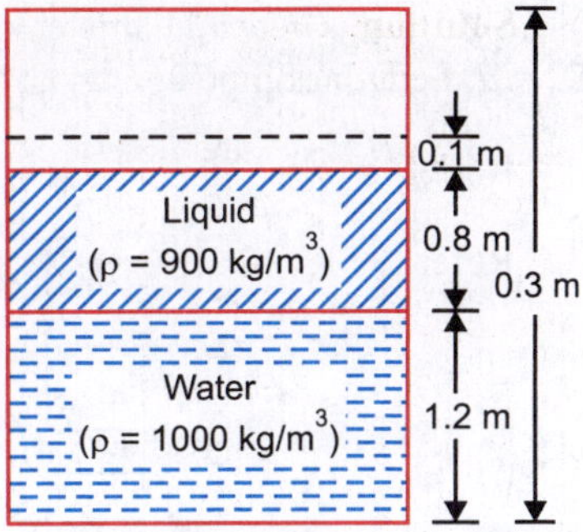

Fig. 18.1

Centre of pressure,
$$\bar{h}_1 = \bar{x} + \frac{I_G}{A\bar{x}}$$

$$= 0.4 + \frac{3 \times 0.8^3}{12 \times (0.8 \times 3) \times 0.4}$$

$$= 0.533 \text{ m}$$

Intensity of pressure at the top surface of water

$$= \rho_{oil} \times g \times h_{oil} = 900 \times 9.81 \times 0.8 \times 10^{-3} = 7.063 \text{ kN/m}^2 \text{ or kPa}$$

Thrust or total pressure due to water,

$$P_2 = A \times (\rho g\bar{x} + 7.063)$$

$$= \left[(1.2 \times 3) \times (1000 \times 9.81 \times \frac{1.2}{2} + 7.063 \times 10^3)\right] \times 10^{-3}$$

$$= 46.616 \text{ kN}$$

Centre of pressure,
$$\bar{h}_2 = \bar{x} + \frac{I_G}{A\bar{x}}$$

$$= 0.6 + \frac{3 \times 1.2^3}{12 \times (1.2 \times 3) \times 0.6}$$

$= 0.8$ m from water surface

$= 0.8 \text{ m} + 0.8 \text{ m} = 1.6$ m from oil surface

Hence, overall centre of pressure,

$$\bar{h} = \frac{P_1 \bar{h}_1 + P_2 \bar{h}_2}{(P_1 + P_2)} = \frac{8.476 \times 0.533 + 46.616 \times 1.6}{8.476 + 46.616}$$

$= 1.436$ from oil surface

Total thrust or pressure $= P_1 + P_2 = 8.476 + 46.616 = 55.092$ kN

When height of *oil* column is 0.9 m:

Thrust due to oil $= (0.9 \times 3) \times (900 \times 9.81 \times 0.45) \times 10^{-3} = 10.727$ kN

Intensity of pressure on top surface of water

$= 900 \times 9.81 \times 0.9 \times 10^{-3} = 7.946 \text{ kN/m}^2$

Thrust or total pressure due to *water*

$= (1.2 \times 3) [(1000 \times 9.81 \times 0.6 \times 10^{-3} + 7.946] = 49.795$ kN

Total thrust $= 49.795 + 10.727 = 60.522$ kN

Since the calculated total thrust on the wall *i.e.,* 60.522 kN is *greater* than the given value of 58 kN, therefore, the wall will *not* be able to stand the combine thrust and will *topple*. **(Ans.)**

Q. 18.2. *(Flow through pipes)* *Two pipes have length L each. One of them has a diameter of D and other d. If the pipes are arranged in parallel, the head loss is h for a discharge of Q m³/s. When the pipes are connected in series, the head lost is H for same discharge. Find the ratio of H to h, for D = 2.25 d. (All dimensions in m)* **(IES)**

Solution. *Given:* Diameter of pipe 1, $D_1 = D$; Length of pipe; $L_1 = L$; Diameter of pipe 2, $D_2 = d$, Length of pipe 2, $L_2 = L$; Total discharge $= Q$.

Ratio $\frac{H}{G}$

Refer to Fig. 18.2.

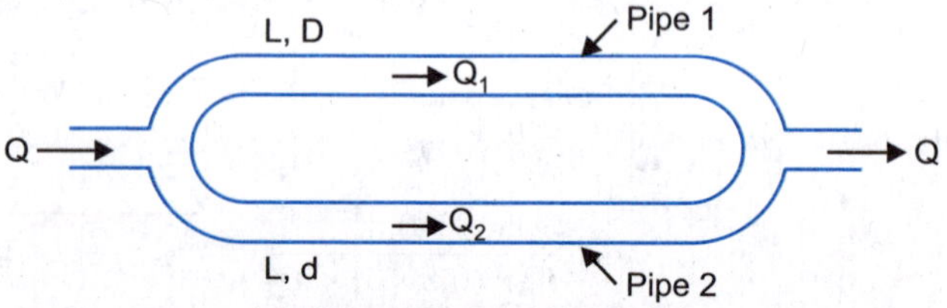

(a) Pipes connected in parallel

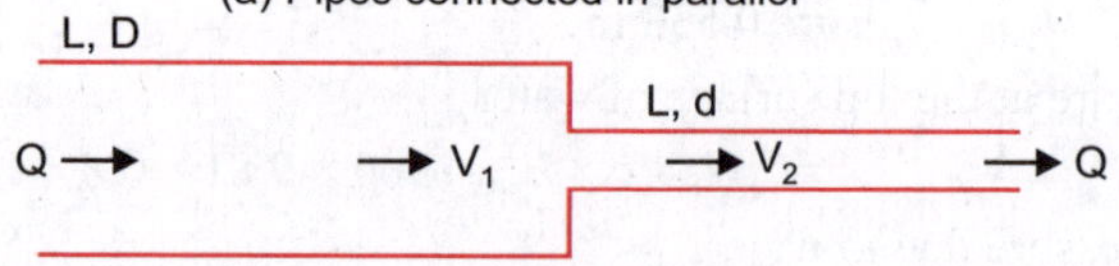

(b) Pipes connected in series

Fig. 18.2

Case I *When pipes are connected in "parallel"*: Refer to Fig. 18.2 (a).

When pipes are connected in *parallel*,

$$Q = Q_1 + Q_2 \quad \text{...}(i)$$

Loss of head in each pipe = h

For pipe 1: $$h = \frac{4 f L_1 V_1^2}{D \times 2g}$$

where, $$V_1 = \frac{Q_1}{A_1} = \frac{Q_1}{(\pi/4) \times D^2} = \frac{4Q_1}{\pi D^2}$$

$\therefore$ $$h = \frac{4 fL \times \left(\frac{4Q_1}{\pi D^2}\right)^2}{D \times 2g} = \frac{32 f LQ_1^2}{\pi^2 D^5 \times g} \quad (\because L_1 = L) \quad \text{...}(ii)$$

For pipe 2: $$h = \frac{32 f LQ_2^2}{\pi^2 d^5 \times g} \quad \text{...}(iii)$$

From equal (*ii*) and (*iii*), we get:

$$\frac{32 f LQ_1^2}{\pi^2 D^5 \times g} = \frac{32 f LQ_2^2}{\pi^2 d^5 \times g}$$

or, $$\frac{Q_1^2}{D^5} = \frac{Q_2^2}{d^5}$$

or, $$\left(\frac{Q_1}{Q_2}\right)^2 = \left(\frac{D}{d}\right)^5 = \left(\frac{2.25\, d}{d}\right)^5 = 57.665 \quad (D = 2.25\, d \text{ ...given})$$

or, $$\frac{Q_1}{Q_2} = 7.594 \quad \text{or} \quad Q_1 = 7.594\, Q_2$$

Substituting the value of Q_1 in eqn. (*i*), we have:

$$Q = 7.594\, Q_2 + Q_2 = 8.594\, Q_2$$

or, $$Q_2 = 0.116\, Q \quad \text{...}(iv)$$

and, $$Q_1 = 7.594 \times 0.116\, Q = 0.881\, Q \quad \text{...}(v)$$

Case II *Pipes convected in "series"*: Refer to Fig. 18.2 (*b*).

In this case, Total loss = Sum of head losses in two pipes

or $$H = \frac{4 f LV_1^2}{D \times 2g} + \frac{4 f LV_2^2}{d \times 2g}$$

where, $$V_1 = \frac{Q}{(\pi/4) \times D^2} = \frac{4Q}{\pi D^2}$$

and, $$V_2 = \frac{Q}{(\pi/4) \times d^2} = \frac{4Q}{\pi d^2}$$

$$H = \frac{4 f L \times \left(\frac{4Q}{\pi D^2}\right)^2}{D \times 2g} + \frac{4 f L \times \left(\frac{4Q}{\pi d^2}\right)^2}{d \times 2g}$$

or, $$H = \frac{32 f LQ^2}{D \times 2g} + \frac{32 f LQ^2}{d \times 2g} \quad \text{...}(vi)$$

From eqn. (*ii*), $$\frac{32fL}{\pi^2 D^5 \times g} = \frac{h}{Q_1^2}$$

and, From eqn. (*iii*) $$\frac{32fL}{\pi^2 d^5 \times g} = \frac{h}{Q_2^2}$$

Inserting these values in eqn. (*vi*), we get:

$$H = Q^2 \times \frac{h}{Q_1^2} + Q^2 \times \frac{h}{Q_2^2} = h\left(\frac{Q^2}{Q_1^2} + \frac{Q^2}{Q_2^2}\right)$$

or, $$\frac{H}{h} = \frac{Q^2}{Q_1^2} + \frac{Q^2}{Q_2^2}$$

From eqns (*iv*) and (*v*), we have:

$$Q_1 = 0.881\,Q \quad \text{and} \quad Q_2 = 0.116\,Q$$

$$\therefore \quad \frac{H}{h} = \frac{Q^2}{(0.881\,Q)^2} + \frac{Q^2}{(0.116\,Q)^2} = 1.288 + 74.316 = \mathbf{75.6}\ \textbf{(Ans.)}$$

Q. 18.3. *(Triangular weir)* *Develop (in general terms) the expression for the per cent of error in Q over a triangular weir if there is a small error in the measurement of the vertex angle. Assume there is no error in the weir coefficient. Compute the per cent error in Q, if there is a 1° error in the measurement of total vertex angle of a triangular weir which is having a total vertex angle of 60°.* **(GATE)**

Solution. *Given*: Error in measurement, $dQ = 1°$; Total vertex angle, $1Q = 60°$

Percentage error in Q:

In case of triangular weir,

$$Q = \frac{8}{15} C_d \sqrt{2g} \,.\, \tan\frac{\theta}{2} \,.\, H^{5/2}$$

If C_d and H are constant, then:

$$Q = k.\tan\frac{\theta}{2}, \quad \text{where } k \text{ is constant}$$

$$\log Q = \log k + \log \tan\frac{\theta}{2}$$

Differentiating both sides, we get:

$$\frac{dQ}{Q} = 0 + \frac{\sec^2\left(\frac{\theta}{2}\right)}{\tan\left(\frac{\theta}{2}\right)} \cdot \frac{d\theta}{2} \qquad \ldots(i)$$

When θ is *very small* or $\theta \to 0$

$$\sec\theta \to 1, \qquad \tan\theta \to 0$$

Now eqn. (*i*) reduces to:

$$\frac{dQ}{Q} = \frac{1}{\left(\frac{\theta}{2}\right)} \cdot \frac{d\theta}{2} = \frac{d\theta}{\theta}$$

For, $d\theta = 1°$ and $\theta = 60°$, we have:

$$\frac{dQ}{Q} = \frac{1}{60} = 0.0167 \quad \text{or} \quad \mathbf{1.67\%}\ \textbf{(Ans.)}$$

Q. 18.4. ***(Fluid kinematics)*** *A flow field is defined by $u = 2y$ and $v = xy$. Derive expressions for the acceleration components. Find the magnitude of the velocity and acceleration at the point (2, 3). Specify units in terms of L and T.* **(IES)**

Solution. *Given*: $u = 2y$; $v = xy$

Expressions for the acceleration components:

$$a_x = u\frac{\partial u}{\partial x} + v\frac{\partial u}{\partial y}$$

$$= 2y \times 0 + xy \times 2 = 2xy = 2 \times 2 \times 3 = 12$$

$$a_y = u\frac{\partial v}{\partial x} + v\frac{\partial v}{\partial y}$$

$$= 2y \times y + xy \times x = xy^2 + x^2y = 2 \times 3^2 + 2^2 \times 3 = 30$$

Magnitude of acceleration $= \sqrt{a_x^2 + a_y^2} = \sqrt{(12)^2 + (30)^2}$

$= 32.31 \text{ m/s}^2$ or $\mathbf{32.31\ LT^{-2}}$ **(Ans.)**

Magnitude of velocity $= \sqrt{u^2 + v^2} = \sqrt{(2 \times 3)^2 + (2 \times 3)^2}$

$= 8.48 \text{ m/s}$ or $\mathbf{8.48\ LT^{-1}}$ **(Ans.)**

Q. 18.5. ***(Boundary layer thickness)*** *For the velocity distribution prescribed by $u/u_0 = (y/\delta)^{1/7}$, show that the ratio of displacement thickness (δ*) to momentum thickness (θ) is 1.285.* **(GATE)**

Solution. *Given*: $\dfrac{u}{u_0} = \left(\dfrac{y}{\delta}\right)^{1/7}$

$\mathbf{\dfrac{\delta^*}{\theta}}$:

Displacement thickness, δ:

$$\delta^* = \int_0^\delta \left(1 - \frac{u}{u_0}\right) dy$$

$$= \int_0^\delta \left[1 - \left(\frac{y}{\delta}\right)^{1/7}\right] dy = \left[y - \frac{7}{8}\frac{y^{8/7}}{\delta^{1/7}}\right]_0^\delta = \left[\delta - \frac{7}{8} \times \frac{\delta^{8/7}}{\delta^{1/7}}\right] = \frac{\delta}{8}$$

Momentum thickness, θ:

$$\theta = \int_0^\delta \frac{u}{u_0}\left(1 - \frac{u}{u_0}\right) dy$$

$$= \int_0^\delta \left(\frac{y}{\delta}\right)^{1/7} \left[1 - \left(\frac{y}{\delta}\right)^{1/7}\right] dy = \int_0^\delta \left[\left(\frac{y}{\delta}\right)^{1/7} - \left(\frac{y}{\delta}\right)^{2/7}\right] dy$$

$$= \left[\frac{7}{8} \cdot \frac{y^{8/7}}{\delta^{1/7}} - \frac{7}{9} \cdot \frac{y^{9/7}}{\delta^{2/7}}\right]_0^\delta = \left[\frac{7}{8} \cdot \frac{\delta^{8/7}}{\delta^{1/7}} - \frac{7}{9} \cdot \frac{\delta^{9/7}}{\delta^{2/7}}\right]$$

$$= \left[\frac{7}{8}\delta - \frac{7}{9}\delta\right] = \frac{7}{72}\delta$$

$$\therefore \quad \frac{\delta^*}{\theta} = \frac{(\delta/8)}{\left(\frac{7}{72}\delta\right)} = 1.285........$$ **Proved (Ans.)**

Q. 18.6. (Venturimeter) *For a rate of flow exceeding certain value, the coefficient of discharge for a venturimeter used for measuring the discharge of an incompressible fluid is found to be constant. Prove that loss of head in the convergent portion of the venturi can be expressed as KQ^2 under these conditions, where K is a constant (function of C_d, areas of the venturimeter) and Q is flow rate in m^3/s. What will be the value of K, assuming the C_d constant?* **(IES)**

Solution. *Given:* C_d = constant

Refer to fig. 6.29 (Venturimeter).

Applying Bernoulli's equation at section 1 and 2, we get.

$$\frac{p_1}{w} + \frac{V_1^2}{2g} + z_1 = \frac{p_2}{w} + \frac{V_2^2}{2g} + z_2$$

$$\frac{V_2^2 - V_1^2}{2g} = h_2 - h_1 = \Delta h$$

where, $$h = \frac{p}{w} + z = \text{piezometric head}$$

Applying continuity equation at sections 1 and 2, we have:

$$A_1 V_1 = A_2 V_2 \quad \text{or} \quad V_1 = \frac{A_2}{A_1} V_2$$

or, $$\frac{V_2^2 - \left(\frac{A_2}{A_1} V_2\right)^2}{2g} = \Delta h$$

or, $$V_2^2 \left[1 - \left(\frac{A_2}{A_2}\right)^2\right] = 2g\Delta h$$

or, $$V_2 = \sqrt{\frac{2g.\Delta h}{\left[1 - \left(\frac{A_2}{A_1}\right)^2\right]}}$$

Now, $$Q = \frac{C_d\, A_2 \sqrt{2g\Delta h}}{\sqrt{1 - \left(\frac{D_2}{D_1}\right)^2}} \quad \text{or} \quad \Delta h = \frac{Q^2}{2gA_2^2.C_d^2}\left\{1 - \left(\frac{D_2}{D_1}\right)^4\right\}$$

Head lost between inlet and thrust is given by:

$$H = \frac{V_2^2}{2g}\left(\frac{1}{C_d^2} - 1\right)\left\{1 - \left(\frac{D_2}{D_1}\right)^4\right\}$$

$$= (1 - C_d^2)\frac{\left\{1 - \left(\frac{D_2}{D_1}\right)^4\right\} V_2^2}{2g\, C_d^2}$$

or, $$H = (1 - C_d^2)\, \Delta h$$

or, $$H = \frac{1 - C_d^2}{C_d^2} \cdot \frac{Q^2}{2g\, A_2^2}\left\{1 - \left(\frac{D_2}{D_1}\right)^4\right\}$$

As C_d, g, A_2, D_2, D_1 are constant, therefore,

$$H = KQ^2 \text{.... Proved} \qquad \textbf{(Ans.)}$$

Now, $$H = (1 - C_d^2)\,\Delta h = KQ^2$$

$\therefore$ $$K = \frac{1 - C_d^2}{Q^2}\,\Delta h \qquad \textbf{(Ans.)}$$

Q. 18.7. ***(Flow through orifices)*** *A cylindrical water tank of 50 cm diameter and 120 cm height is initially filled with water. The top of the tank is open to the atmosphere. A discharge plug is fitted at the bottom of the tank. When the plug near the bottom of the tank is pulled out, a water jet streams out of the tank with a jet diameter of 1 cm. The mean velocity of the jet is given by* $V = \sqrt{2gh}$ *where h is the height of the water in the tank measured from the centre of the hole. Determine how long will it take for the water level in the tank to drop to 60 cm level from the bottom. Neglect the distance between the bottom of the tank and the centre of the hole compared to the total water height.* **(GATE)**

Solution. *Given:* D = 50 cm = 0.5 m; H_1 = 120 cm = 1.2 m; d = 1 cm = 0.01 m; H_2 = 600 cm = 0.6 m.

Refer to Fig. 18.3.

Time taken for water level to drop to 0.6 m:

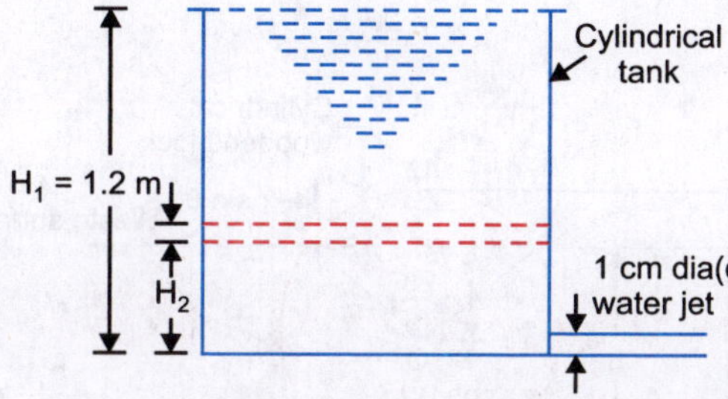

Fig. 18.3

When the height of water level above the orifice is H, then velocity of jet (V) is given by:

$$V = \sqrt{2gH}$$

If the water level in the tank lowers by dH, in a time t,

then the volume of water $= -\left(\frac{\pi}{4} D^2\right) dH$ ...(*i*)

Volume of water flowed out of orifice

$$= V \times a \times dt = V \times \left[\frac{\pi}{4} \times d^2\right] \times dt \qquad \text{...(ii)}$$

Equating both volumes (*i.e.*, (*i*) and (*ii*)) we get:

$$-\left(\frac{\pi}{4} D^2\right) dH = V \times \left(\frac{\pi}{4} d^2\right) \times dt = \sqrt{2gH} \times \left(\frac{\pi}{4} d^2\right) \times dt$$

or, $$\frac{dH}{\sqrt{2gH}} = -\frac{d^2}{D^2}\,dt$$

Integrating both sides we have:

$$\frac{1}{\sqrt{2g}}\int_{H_1=1.2\text{ m}}^{H_2=0.6\text{ m}}\frac{dH}{(H)^{1/2}} = \int_0^T -\frac{0.01^2}{0.5^2}\times dt = -0.0004\,dt$$

or
$$\int_{H_1}^{H_2}\frac{dH}{(H)^{1/2}} = -\int_0^T\sqrt{2\times 9.81\times 0.0004}\,dt = -\int_0^T 0.00177\,dt$$

or
$$\int_{H_1}^{H_2}\frac{H^{1/2}}{\left(\frac{1}{2}\right)} = -\int_0^T 0.00177\,dt \quad\text{or}\quad \left[H_2^{1/2}-H_1^{1/2}\right]_{1.2}^{0.6} = -0.00177\,T$$

or,
$$T = \left[\frac{2\{(0.6)^{1/2}-(1.2)^{1/2}\}}{0.00177}\right] = 362\text{ s} = \mathbf{6.04\ minutes\ (Ans.)}$$

Q. 18.8. ***(Buoyancy and floatation)*** *Determine the position in which a solid cylindrical block of wood of diameter 0.3 m and length 0.4 m will float in water. Take specific gravity of wood as 0.5.* **(IES)**

Solution. *Given:* $d = 0.3$ m; $l = 0.4$ m; $S = 0.5$.

Refer to Fig. 18.4.

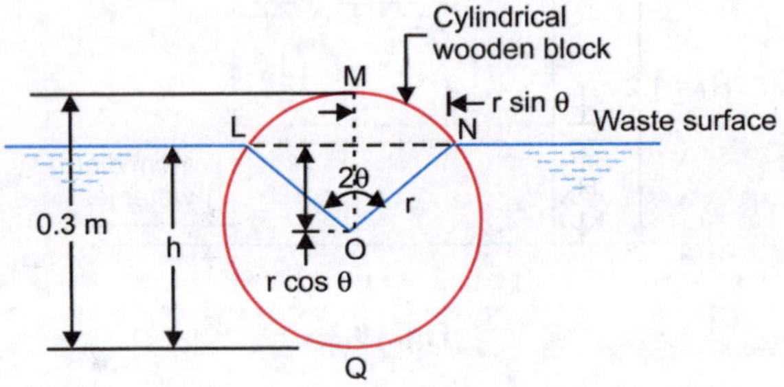

Fig. 18.4

$$\text{Weight of the wooden block} = (0.5\times 9.81)\times\frac{\pi}{4}d^2 l$$

$$= (0.5\times 9.81)\times\frac{\pi}{4}\times 0.3^2\times 0.4 = 0.1387\text{ kN}$$

This also represents the weight of water displaced.

$$\therefore \text{Volume of water displaced} = \frac{0.1387}{9.81} = 0.01414\text{ m}^3$$

Let, h = Depth of immersion

$\therefore$ Volume of wooden block inside water

= Volume of water displaced = 0.01414 m^3

Now, 0.01414 = Area $LQNL \times 0.4$

or, $$\text{Area } LQNL = \frac{0.01414}{0.4} = 0.03535\text{ m}^3$$

Also, Area $LQNL$ = Area $LQNOL$ + Area LON

$$= \pi r^2 \left[\frac{360 - 2\theta}{360}\right] + \frac{1}{2} \times 2r \sin\theta \times r \cos\theta$$

$$= \pi r^2 \left(1 - \frac{\theta}{180}\right) + r^2 \sin\theta \cos\theta$$

or, $$0.03535 = \pi \times 0.15^2 \left(1 - \frac{\theta}{180}\right) + (0.15)^2 \sin\theta \cos\theta$$

or, $$0.03535 = 0.0707 - 0.0003927\,\theta + 0.000225 \sin\theta \cos\theta$$

or, $$0.0003927\,\theta - 0.0225 \sin\theta \cos\theta = 0.03535$$

or, $$\theta - 57.3 \sin\theta \cos\theta = 90.02$$

By trial and error, we get $\theta \simeq 90.1°$

Depth of wooden block in water,

$$h = r + r \cos\theta$$

$$= 0.15 + 0.15 \times \cos 90.1° = \mathbf{0.1497\ m}$$ **(Ans.)**

Q. 18.9. (Turbulent flow in rough pipe) *A rough pipe of diameter 0.1 m carries water at 20°C at the rate of 50 L/S. If the average height of the roughness projections on the pipe surface is 0.15 mm, determine:*

(i) Friction factor.

(ii) Shear velocity.

(iii) Shear stress at the pipe surface.

(iv) Maximum velocity.

Take for water at 20°C

γ = Kinematic viscosity = 1×10^{-6} m²/s.

ρ = Mass density = 1000 kg/m³. **(IES)**

Solution. *Given:* $D = 0.1$ m; $Q = 50$ litres/s $= 0.05$ m³/s; $k = 0.15$ mm $= 0.15 \times 10^{-3}$ m; $\gamma = 1 \times 10^{-6}$ m²/s; $\rho = 1000$ kg/m³.

(i) Friction factor f_1:

Mean velocity of water, $$\bar{U} = \frac{Q}{A} = \frac{0.05}{\frac{\pi}{4} \times 0.1^2} = 6.37 \text{ m/s}$$

Reynolds number, $$Re = \frac{\bar{U}D}{\gamma} = \frac{6.37 \times 0.1}{1 \times 10^{-6}} = 6.37 \times 10^5$$

Since $Re > 10^5$, therefore the flow is *turbulent* in the rough pipe.

We know that for rough turbulent flow,

$$\frac{1}{\sqrt{f_1}} = 2.0 \log_{10}\left(\frac{R}{k}\right) + 1.74 \qquad \text{...[Eqn. (11.39)]}$$

or, $$\frac{1}{\sqrt{f_1}} = 2.0 \log_{10}\left(\frac{0.05}{0.15 \times 10^{-3}}\right) + 1.74 = 6.78$$

$\therefore$ $$f_1 = \left(\frac{1}{6.78}\right)^2 = \mathbf{0.0217}$$ **(Ans.)**

(ii) Shear velocity, u_f:

Friction coefficient $$f = \frac{f_1}{4} = \frac{0.0217}{4} = 0.00542$$

Also, $u_f = \bar{U}\sqrt{\frac{f}{2}} = 6.37 \times \sqrt{\frac{0.00542}{2}}$ = **0.332 m/s (Ans.)**

(iii) Shear stress at pipe surface, τ_0:

We know that, $f = \frac{2\tau_0}{\rho \bar{U}^2}$ ...[Eqn. 11.5(*b*)]

or, $\tau_0 = \frac{f\rho\bar{U}^2}{2} = \frac{0.00542 \times 1000 \times (6.37)^2}{2}$ = **109.96 N/m² (Ans.)**

(iv) Maximum velocity, U_{max}:

$$\frac{U_{max}}{u_f} = 5.75 \log_{10}(y/k) + 8.5$$ ...[Eqn. (11.25)]

(This equation is known as Karman-Prandtl equation for the velocity distribution near hydrodynamically *rough* boundaries).

or, $\frac{U_{max}}{0.332} = 5.75 \log_{10}\left(\frac{0.05}{0.15 \times 10^{-13}}\right) + 8.5$ $(\because y = R = 0.05 \text{ m})$

or, $U_{max} = 0.332 \times \left[5.75 \log_{10}\left(\frac{0.05}{0.15 \times 10^{-3}}\right) + 8.5\right]$ = **7.64 m/s (Ans.)**

Q. 18.10. *(Laminar flow)* *Show that the friction factor is inversely proportional to the Reynolds number in case of Laminar flow in circular pipes.* **(GATE)**

Solution. The loss of head for energy (h_f) in pipes due to friction is calculated from Darcy-Weisbach formula which is given by:

$$h_f = \frac{f_1 L\bar{u}^2}{D \times 2g} \quad \text{(where } f_1 \text{ is the friction factor)} \quad ...(i)$$

From Hagen-Poiseuille formula, the loss of pressure head due to flow of viscous fluid is given as:

$$h_f = \frac{32\mu\bar{u}L}{\rho g D^2} \quad ...(ii)$$

From eqns. (*i*) and (*ii*), we get:

$$\frac{f_1 L\bar{u}^2}{D \times 2g} = \frac{32\mu\bar{u}L}{\rho g D^2}$$

or, $$f_1 = \frac{(D \times 2g) \times 32\mu\bar{u}L}{L\bar{u}^2 \times \rho g D^2} = \frac{64\mu\bar{u}}{\rho\bar{u}^2 D} = \frac{64}{\left(\frac{\rho\bar{u}D}{\mu}\right)} = \frac{64}{Re}$$

i.e., $f_1 \propto \frac{1}{\text{Re}}$ **......Proved (Ans.)**

Q. 18.11. *(Compressible flow)* *An airplane flies at an altitude with a velocity of 800 km/hr. The pressure and temperature at that altitude are 1.206 × 10⁴ N/m² and 217 K respectively. Calculate:*

(i) The maximum possible temperature on the airplane skin.

(ii) The maximum possible pressure intensity on the airplane body.

(iii) The critical velocity of air relative to the airplane.

(iv) The maximum possible velocity of the air relative to the airplane. **(IES)**

Solution. *Given:* Velocity of air plane, $V_1 = 800 \text{ km/h} = \frac{800 \times 1000}{3600} = 222.22 \text{ m/s}$;

$p_1 = 1.206 \times 10^4 \text{ N/m}^2$; $T_1 = 217$ K.

(i) Maximum possible temperature on the airplane skin, T_0 :

T_0 will be stagnation temperature because velocity of air also gets converted to temperature.

Now,
$$T_0 = T_1 + \frac{V_1^2}{2c_p}$$
$$= 217 + \frac{(222.22)^2}{2 \times 1.005 \times 10^3} = \mathbf{241.57 \text{ K (Ans.)}}$$

(ii) Maximum possible pressure intensity on the airplane body, p_0 :

$$\frac{T_0}{T_1} = \left(\frac{p_0}{p_1}\right)^{\frac{\gamma - 1}{\gamma}}$$

or,
$$\frac{p_0}{p_1} = \left(\frac{T_0}{T_1}\right)^{\frac{\gamma}{\gamma - 1}} \quad \text{or} \quad p_0 = p_1 \left(\frac{T_0}{T_1}\right)^{\frac{\gamma}{\gamma - 1}}$$

or,
$$p_0 = 1.206 \times 10^4 \left(\frac{241.57}{217}\right)^{\frac{1.4}{0.4}} = \mathbf{1.755 \times 10^4 \text{ N/m}^2 \text{ (Ans.)}}$$

(iii) Critical velocity of air relative to airplane, C :

$$C = \sqrt{\gamma R T_1} = \sqrt{1.4 \times 287 \times 217} = \mathbf{295.28 \text{ m/s (Ans.)}}$$

(iv) Maximum possible velocity of air relative to the airplane :

$$\text{Maximum possible velocity} = \sqrt{\gamma R T_0}$$
$$= \sqrt{1.4 \times 287 \times 241.57}$$
$$= 311.55 \text{ m/s} \quad \text{or} \quad \mathbf{1121.58 \text{ km/h (Ans.)}}$$

Q. 18.12. ***(Flow through pipes)*** *Develop an expression for the pressure loss across a conical contraction of diameter D_1 and D_2 in a given length L for a laminar flow.* **(IES)**

Solution. Refer to Fig. 18.5.

Expression for pressure loss, $(p_1 - p_2)$:

Consider a stretch of length dx at a distance x from D_1 diameter end.

Diameter at the section XX,

$$D = D_1 - \left(\frac{D_1 - D_2}{L}\right) x$$

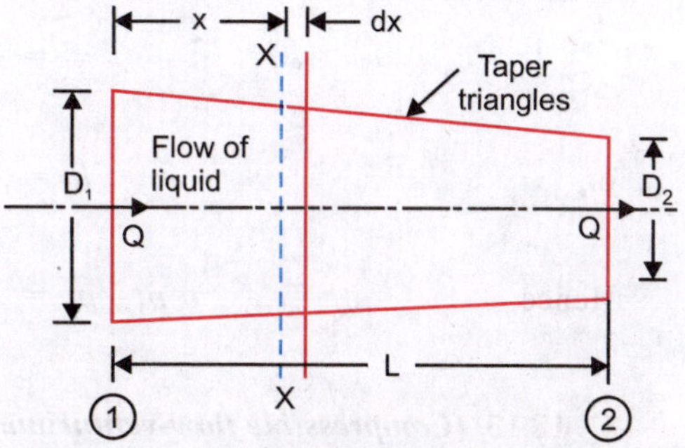

Fig. 18.5

The head loss due to friction in pipes of uniform diameter D and length L in given by :

$$h_f = \frac{fLV^2}{D \times 2g} \quad \text{...Darcy-Weisback equation}$$

Where, 'f' is the friction factor.

Now, loss of head (dh_f) through the small stretch dx,

$$dh_f = \frac{f.(dx).V^2}{\left[D_1 - \left(\frac{D_1 - D_2}{L}\right)x\right]2g} \qquad ...(i)$$

We know that, $\quad f\text{(friction factor)} = \frac{64}{Re} = \frac{64\mu}{\rho VD}$

Let, $\quad \frac{D_1 - D_2}{L} = k$

Then, $\quad f = \frac{64\mu}{[\rho V(D_1 - kx)]}$

[*i.e.,* diameter at a distance x becomes $(D_1 - kx)$]

Let, $\quad D_1 - kx = D'$

Then, $\quad f = \frac{64\mu}{\rho VD'} = \frac{64\mu}{\rho\left[Q \div \left(\frac{\pi}{4}D'^2\right)\right]D'} = \frac{16\pi\mu D'}{\rho Q}$

Substituting this value in eqn. (i), we get:

$$dh_f = \frac{16\pi\mu D'}{\rho QD' \times 2g} \times \left[\frac{Q}{\frac{\pi}{4}D'^2}\right]^2 \times dx$$

$$\left[\because D_1 - \left(\frac{D_1 - D_2}{2}\right)x = D_1 - kx = D'\right]$$

or, $\quad dh_f = \frac{128\gamma Q}{\pi g} \cdot \frac{dx}{(D')^4} \qquad \left(\because \frac{\mu}{\rho} = \gamma\right)$

or, $\quad dh_f = \frac{128\gamma Q}{\pi g} \times \frac{dx}{(D_1 - kx)^4}$

Integrating both sides, we get:

$$h_f = \int_0^{h_f} dh_f = \int_0^L \frac{128\gamma Q}{\pi g} \times \frac{dx}{(D_1 - kx)^4}$$

$$= \frac{128\gamma QL}{\pi g \cdot (D_1 - D_2)}\left[\frac{1}{D_2^3} - \frac{1}{D_1^3}\right] \times \frac{1}{3}$$

or, $\quad h_f = \frac{p_1 - p_2}{\rho g} = \frac{128\mu QL}{\pi\rho g(D_1 - D_2)}\left[\frac{1}{D_2^3} - \frac{1}{D_1^3}\right] \times \frac{1}{3}$

Hence, $\quad p_1 - p_2 = \frac{128\mu QL}{3\pi(D_1 - D_2)}\left[\frac{1}{D_2^3} - \frac{1}{D_1^3}\right]$ **Ans.**

Q. 18.13. *(Compressible flow-venturimeter)* *Calculate the mass flow rate of oxygen through a 100 mm diameter horizontal pipe if the inlet pressure is 1.06 m of mercury. The diameter at the throat is 30 mm. The ratio of pressure between the venturimeter and the inlet is 0.9. Take $\gamma = 1.4$ and density of oxygen gas is 1.429 kg/m^3.* **(IES)**

Solution. *Given*: Pipe diameter, $D_1 = 100$ mm = 0.1 m; Throat diameter, $D_2 = 30$ mm = 0.03 m; Pressure at inlet $p_1 = 1.06$ m of Hg = (13.6 × 1000) × 9.81 × 1.06 = 1.414 × 10^5 N/m^2; $\frac{p_2}{p_1} = 0.9$; $\gamma = 1.4$; Density of oxygen gas, $\rho_1 = 1.429$ kg/m^3.

Refer to Fig. 18.6.

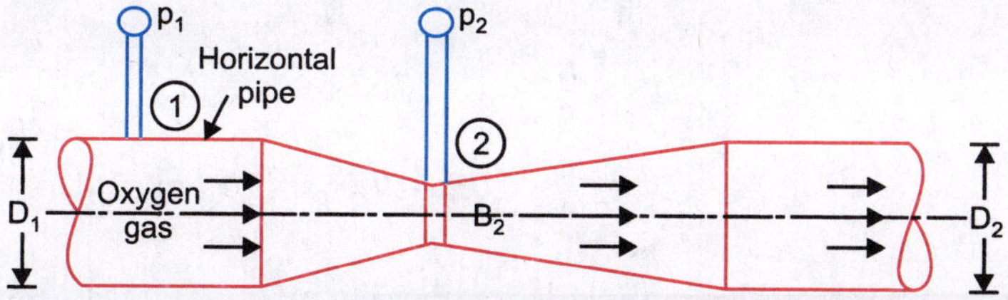

Fig. 18.6. Venturimeter.

Mass flow rate of Oxygen, *m* :

Applying Bernoulli's equation at points 1 and 2, we get:

$$\left(\frac{\gamma}{\gamma-1}\right)\frac{p_1}{\rho_1 g} + \frac{V_1^2}{2g} + z_1 = \left(\frac{\gamma}{\gamma-1}\right)\frac{p_2}{\rho_2 g} + \frac{V_2^2}{2g} + z_2$$

or, $$\left(\frac{\gamma}{\gamma-1}\right)\frac{p_1}{\rho_1} + \frac{V_1^2}{2} = \left(\frac{\gamma}{\gamma-1}\right)\frac{p_2}{\rho_2} + \frac{V_2^2}{2} \quad (\because z_1 = z_2, \text{ pipe being horizontal})$$

or, $$\frac{\gamma}{\gamma-1}\left(\frac{p_1}{\rho_1} - \frac{p_2}{\rho_2}\right) = \frac{V_2^2}{2} - \frac{V_1^2}{2} \quad \ldots(i)$$

For compressible fluids,

$$\rho_1 A_1 V_1 = \rho_2 A_2 V_2 \text{ or } V_1 = \frac{\rho_2 A_2 V_2}{\rho_1 A_1}$$

For adiabatic flow,

$$\frac{p_1}{\rho_1^r} = \frac{p_2}{\rho_2^r} \text{ or } \frac{\rho_2}{\rho_1} = \left(\frac{p_2}{p_1}\right)^{\frac{1}{r}}$$

Substituting the values in eqn. (*i*), we have:

$$\frac{\gamma}{\gamma-1}\left(\frac{p_1}{\rho_1} - \frac{p_2}{\rho_2}\right) = \left[\frac{V_2^2}{2} - \frac{1}{2}\left(\frac{\rho_2 A_2 V_2}{\rho_1 A_1}\right)^2\right]$$

or, $$= \frac{V_2^2}{2}\left[1 - \left(\frac{p_2}{p_1}\right)^{2/\gamma} \times \frac{A_2^2}{A_1^2}\right]$$

or, $$V_2 = \sqrt{\frac{\frac{2\gamma}{\gamma-1}\cdot\frac{p_1}{\rho_1}\left[1 - \left(\frac{p_2}{p_1}\right)^{\frac{\gamma-1}{\gamma}}\right]}{\left[1 - \left(\frac{p_2}{p_1}\right)^{2/\gamma}\frac{A_2^2}{A_1^2}\right]}}$$

Mass flow rate, $m = \rho A_2 V_2$

or,
$$m = \rho_2 A_2 \sqrt{\frac{\frac{2\gamma}{\gamma-1}\cdot\frac{p_1}{\rho_1}\left[1-\left(\frac{p_2}{p_1}\right)^{\frac{\gamma-1}{\gamma}}\right]}{\left[1-\frac{A_2^2}{A_1^2}\left(\frac{p_2}{p_1}\right)^{2/\gamma}\right]}} \quad ...(ii)$$

Now,
$$A_1 = \frac{\pi}{4}D_1^2 = \frac{\pi}{4}\times 0.1^2 = 7.854\times 10^{-3}\ \text{m}^2$$

$$A_2 = \frac{\pi}{4}D_2^2 = \frac{\pi}{4}\times 0.03^2 = 7.068\times 10^{-4}\ \text{m}^2$$

$$\rho_2 = \rho_1\left(\frac{p_2}{p_1}\right)^{1/\gamma} = 1.429\times(0.9)^{\frac{1}{1.4}} = 1.325\ \text{kg/m}^3$$

$$\left[\because \frac{\rho_2}{\rho_1} = \left(\frac{p_2}{p_1}\right)^{\frac{1}{\gamma}}\right]$$

Inserting the various values in eqn. (*ii*) we get:

$$\boldsymbol{m} = 1.325\times(7.068\times10^{-4})\sqrt{\frac{\left[\frac{2\times1.4}{(1.4-1)}\cdot\frac{1.414\times10^5}{1.429}\left\{1-(0.9)^{\frac{1.4-1}{1.4}}\right\}\right]}{\left[1-\left(\frac{7.068\times10^{-4}}{7.854\times10^{-3}}\right)^2\times(0.9)^{\frac{2}{1.4}}\right]}}$$

$$= 9.365\times10^{-4}\sqrt{\left[\frac{(6.926\times10^5)\times0.0296}{0.993}\right]} = \mathbf{0.1346\ kg/s\ (Ans.)}$$

Q. 18.14. ***(Model analysis)*** *Show that for a flow governed only by gravity, inertia, and pressure forces, the ratio of rates of flow in two dynamically similar systems equal to the* $\frac{5}{2}$ *power of the length ratio.* **(GATE)**

Solution. According to Froude model law:

$$(F_r)_m = (F_r)_p$$

or,
$$\frac{V_m}{\sqrt{g_m L_m}} = \frac{V_p}{\sqrt{g_p L_p}} \quad ...[\text{Eqn. (7.22)}]$$

or,
$$\frac{V_p}{V_m} = \sqrt{\frac{L_p}{L_m}} = \sqrt{L_r} \quad V_r \qquad (\because g_m = g_p)$$

Flow rate ratio,
$$Q_r = \frac{Q_p}{Q_m} = \frac{A_p V_p}{A_m V_m} = L_r^2 V_r$$

$$= L_r^2\times L_r = \boldsymbol{(L_r)^{5/2}}\ \textbf{(Ans.)}$$

Q. 18.15. ***(Laminar flow)*** *Oil of viscosity 0.97 poise and 0.9 specific gravity flows through a horizontal circular pipe of 100 mm diameter and 10 m length. Calculate the pressure difference between the ends of the pipe. What is the type of flow?*

Solution. *Given:* μ = 0.97 = 0.097 Ns/m^2; $S = 0.9$, $D = 100$ mm = 0.1 m; $L = 10$ m.

$p_1 - p_2$:

We know that : $$p_1 - p_2 = \frac{32\mu \bar{u} L}{D^2}$$ ...[Eqn. (10.11)]

Where $\bar{u}$ is an average velocity.

Now, $$Q = \bar{u} \times A \quad or \quad \bar{u} = \frac{Q}{A} = \frac{Q}{\frac{\pi}{4}\times 0.1^2} = 127.3\,Q$$

$$\therefore \quad p_1 - p_2 = \frac{32\times 0.097\times (127.3\,Q)\times 10}{0.1^2} = \mathbf{39.5 \times 10^4 Q} \textbf{ (Ans.)}$$

Type of flow:

Since discharge Q is not given, $\bar{u}$ *cannot* be found, therefore, type of flow cannot be found, which depends on the value of Reynolds number Re, where $Re = \frac{\rho \bar{u} D}{\mu}$ **(Ans.)**

Q. 18.16. ***(Flow through pipes)*** *A pipe of 300 mm diameter and 1000 m length connects two reservoirs kept at 15 m level difference. Find the flow through the pipe. If an additional length of 500 m of 300 mm diameter pipe is connected at the later half of the existing pipe, find the increase in discharge. Neglect minor losses. Take f = (coefficient of friction) = 0.005.* **(GATE)**

Solution. *Given*: $D = 300$ mm = 0.3 m; $L = 1000$ m; $h_1 = h_2 = 500$ m; $D_2 = D_1 = 300$ mm = 0.3 m; $f = 0.005$; $h_f = 15$ m.

All losses are negligible except friction.

Increase in discharge:

Refer to Fig. 18.7.

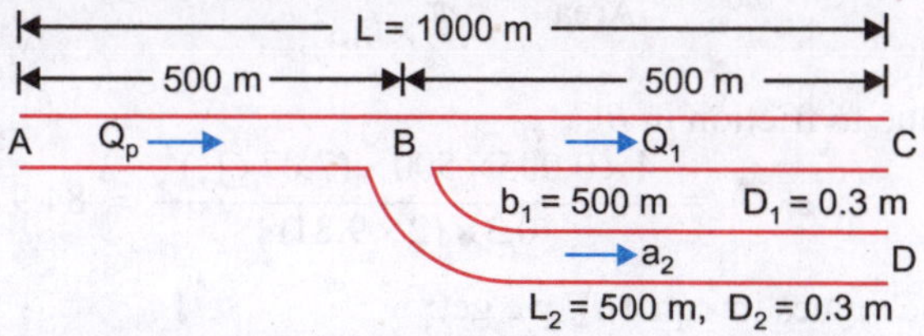

Fig. 18.7

Case I: *Discharge Q for a single pipe of length 1000 m and diameter 0.3 m:*

The head lost due to friction in a single pipe is given as:

$$h_f = \frac{4fLV^2}{D\times 2g},$$ where V is the velocity of flow in a single pipe

or, $$15 = \frac{4\times 0.005\times 1000\times V^2}{0.3\times 2\times 9.81}$$

or, $$V^2 = \left(\frac{15\times 0.3\times 2\times 9.81}{4\times 0.005\times 1000}\right)^{1/2} = 2.1 \text{ m/s}$$

$$\therefore \quad \text{Discharge, } Q = A\times V = \frac{\pi}{4}\times 0.3^2\times 2.1 = 0.1484 \text{ m}^3\text{/s} \quad ...(i)$$

Case II: *When an additional pipe of length 500 m and diameter 0.3 m is connected in parallel with the last half length of the pipe:*

Let, Q_1 = Discharge in first parallel pipe,

Q_2 = Discharge in second parallel pipe, and

Q_p = Discharge in the main pipe (when pipes are connected in parallel)

Then, $Q_p = Q_1 + Q_2$

As the pipes in *parallel* have the *same length and diameter*, therefore,

$$Q_1 = Q_2 = \frac{Q_p}{2}$$

Consider the flow through ABC or ABD:

Head lost (due to friction) in ABC = Head lost in AB + Head lost in BC ...(*ii*)

Head lost in ABC = 15 m (given)

Now, $$\text{Head lost in } AB = \frac{4 \times 0.005 \times 500 \times V_{AB}^2}{0.3 \times (2 \times 9.81)}$$

But, $$V_{AB} = \frac{Q_p}{\text{Area}} = \frac{Q_p}{\frac{\pi}{4} \times 0.3^2} = 14.15\, Q_p$$

$$\therefore \text{ Head lost in friction in } AB = \frac{4 \times 0.005 \times 500 \times (14.15\, Q_p)^2}{0.3 \times (2 \times 9.81)} = 340.2\, Q_p^2$$

Head lost due to friction in BC

$$= \frac{4 \times 0.005 \times 500 \times V_{BC}^2}{0.3 \times (2 \times 9.81)}$$

But, $$V_{BC} = \frac{(Q_p/2)}{\text{Area}} = \frac{(Q_p/2)}{\frac{\pi}{4} \times 0.3^2} = 7.07\, Q_p$$

$\therefore$ Head lost due to friction in BC

$$= \frac{4 \times 0.005 \times 500 \times (7.07\, Q_p)^2}{0.3 \times (2 \times 9.81)} = 84.9\, Q_p^2$$

Substituting the values in eqn. (*ii*), we get:

$$15 = 340.2\, Q_p^2 + 84.9\, Q_p^2 = 425.1\, Q_p^2$$

or, $$Q_p = \left(\frac{15}{425.1}\right)^{1/2} = 0.1878 \text{ m}^3/\text{s}$$

Hence, *increase in discharge* = $Q_p - Q$ = 0.1878 – 0.1484 = **0.0394 m³/s** **(Ans.)**

Q. 18.17. ***(Venturimeter)*** *Determine the throat diameter of a venturimeter in a installation of 100 mm diameter pipe carrying water. The maximum range available in water-Hg differential pressure gauge is 50 cm of Hg deflection. Find the maximum throat diameter which will induce full gauge deflection when the flow rate is 20 l/s. Assume C_d = 0.984.* **(IES)**

Solution. *Given*: Diameter of the main pipe, D = 100 mm = 0.1 m; Difference of pressure head, y = 50 cm of Hg = 0.5 m of Hg; Flow rate, Q = 20 litres/sec = 0.02 m³/s; C_d = 0.984.

Maximum throat diameter, d:

We know that: $$h = y\left[\frac{S_{Hg}}{S_{\text{water}}} - 1\right] = 0.5\left[\frac{13.6}{1} - 1\right] = 6.3 \text{ m}$$

Also, $$Q = C_d \times \frac{A_1 A_2}{\sqrt{A_1^2 - A_2^2}} \times \sqrt{2gh} \quad \text{...[Eqn. (6.6)]}$$

$$0.02 = 0.984 \times \frac{\left(\frac{\pi}{4}\times 0.1^2\right)\times\left(\frac{\pi}{4}\times d^2\right)}{\sqrt{\left(\frac{\pi}{4}\right)^2 [0.1^4 - d^4]}} \times \sqrt{2\times 9.81\times 6.3}$$

$$= \frac{0.08592\, d^2}{\sqrt{0.1^4 - d^4}}$$

Squaring both sides, we get:

$$(0.02)^2 = \frac{(0.08592)^2\, d^4}{(0.1)^4 - d^4} = \frac{0.738\times 10^{-3}\, d^4}{1\times 10^{-4} - d^4}$$

or, $4 \times 10^{-4} (1 \times 10^{-4} - d^4) = 0.738 \times 10^{-3} d^4$

or, $4 \times 10^{-8} = d^4 (4 \times 10^{-4} + 0.738 \times 10^{-3})$

$$d = \left[\frac{4\times 10^{-8}}{4\times 10^{-4} + 0.738\times 10^{-3}}\right]^{1/4} = 0.0476 \text{ m} \quad \text{or} \quad \mathbf{47.6\ mm\ (Ans.)}$$

Q. 18.18. ***(Flow through pipes)*** *A reservoir supplies 45,000 m^3 of water in 8 hours. During this time, the level of water in the reservoir drops from 125 m to 75 m. The head loss in the pipeline is 15 m. Determine the diameter of the supply pipeline using 4f = 0.04 in Darcy-Weisback equation.* **(GATE)**

Solution. *Given*: $Q = 45{,}000 \text{ m}^3$; Drop in level of water = 125 – 75 = 50 m.

Diameter of supply line d:

Head loss in pipeline is 15 m so the net driving potential for velocity at any time = $(h - 15)$ m

Area of cross-section of tank, $A = \frac{45000}{50} = 900 \text{ m}^2$

We know that: $$\frac{dQ}{dt} = -A\frac{dh}{dt} = C_d.a.\sqrt{2g(h-15)} \quad (\because \text{'}h\text{' decreases})$$

Assuming, $C_d = 1$, we get:

$$\frac{dh}{\sqrt{h-15}} = -\frac{a}{A}\sqrt{2g}.dt$$

$$\int_{h_1=125}^{h_2=75} \frac{dh}{\sqrt{h-15}} = -\frac{a}{A}\sqrt{2g}.\int_0^t dt = -\frac{a}{A}.\sqrt{2g}.t$$

or, $$2\left[\sqrt{125-15} - \sqrt{75-15}\right] = \frac{a\times\sqrt{2\times 9.81}}{900}\times(8\times 3600)$$

or, $5.484 = a \times 141.74$ *i.e.,* $a = 0.0387 \text{ m}^2$

or, $\frac{\pi}{4} d^2 = 0.0387$ or $d = 0.222$ m or **22.2 cm (Ans.)**

Q. 18.19. ***(Hydrostatic forces on surfaces)*** *A ship is sailing in the ocean. The captain of the ship observes an iceberg floating in the sea at a distance and he estimates the visible volume of the iceberg above sea level as 600 m^3. If the density of the iceberg is 915 kg/m^3, determine the total volume and weight of the iceberg. The density of the sea water may be taken as 1025 kg/m^3.* **(GATE)**

Solution. *Given*: Volume of iceberg above seak level = 600 m^3; Density of iceberg, ρ_i = 915 kg/m^3; Density of sea water, ρ_s = 1025 kg/m^3.

Total volume of iceberg, *V*:

$$\text{Volume of ice } in \text{ sea water} = (V - 600) \text{ m}^3$$

Now, Weight of iceberg = Weight of water displaced by ice

or, $$\rho_i \times V \times g = \rho_s (V - 600) \times g$$

or, $$V = \frac{\rho_s}{\rho_i}(V - 600) = \frac{1025}{915}(V - 600) = 1.1202 (V - 600)$$

or, $$V = 1.1202\,V - 672.12 \quad \text{or} \quad V \simeq \mathbf{5592\ m^3}\ \textbf{(Ans.)}$$

Weight of iceberg, W_i:

$$W_i = \rho_i \times V \times g = 915 \times 5592 \times 9.81 = \mathbf{50.194 \times 10^6\ N}\ \textbf{(Ans.)}$$

Q. 18.20. ***(Fluid dynamics-Forced vertex flow)*** *A circular cylinder of height 200 mm and radius 80 mm is open at the top. It is fixed on the table at its center which can be rotated by a motor. Determine the speed of rotation of table so that one-third of the area of the bottom of cylinder gets exposed. At the beginning of rotation the cylinder was filled with liquid.* ***(IES)***

Solution. *Given*: Height of cylinder = 200 mm = 0.2 m; Radius of cylinder, r_1 = 80 mm = 0.08 m.

Speed of rotation, *N*:

Refer to Fig. 18.8.

Let *N* be the speed of rotation at which $\frac{1}{3}$rd bottom of cylinder gets exposed.

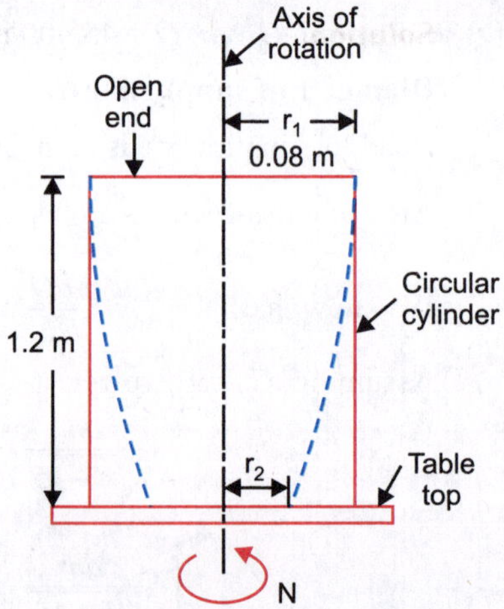

Fig. 18.8

Then: $$\pi r_2^2 = \frac{1}{3}\pi r_1^2 = \frac{1}{3}\pi \times (0.08)^2$$

or, $$r_2^2 = 0.04619 \text{ m}$$

The equation for *forced vertex flow* is given as:

$$z_2 - z_1 = \frac{v_2^2 - v_1^2}{2g} = \frac{\omega^2 (r_2^2 - r_1^2)}{2g}$$

or, $$z_1 - z_2 = \frac{\omega^2 (r_1^2 - r_2^2)}{2g} = \frac{\omega^2 [(0.08)^2 - (0.04619)^2]}{2 \times 9.81}$$

or, $$0.2 = 2.174 \times 10^{-4}\,\omega^2$$

or, $$\omega^2 = \frac{0.2}{2.174 \times 10^{-4}} = 919.96$$

or, $$\left(\frac{2\pi N}{60}\right)^2 = 919.96 \quad \text{or} \quad 0.01097\, N^2 = 919.96$$

or, $$N = \left(\frac{919.96}{0.01097}\right)^{1/2} = \mathbf{289.6\ rpm\ (Ans.)}$$

Q. 18.21. *Describe the working principle of a Pitot-static tube with the help of a neat sketch and explain how it can be used to measure the flow rate.* **(IES)**

Ans. Refer to *Article* **6.6.4.**

Q. 18.22. *Derive Darcy-Weisback equation for head loss in pipe due to friction.* **(IES)**

Ans. Refer to *Article* **12.3.1.**

Q. 18.23. *What is physical significance of Reynolds number and Mach number? Give examples of their area of applications.* **(GATE)**

Ans. Refer to *Article* **7.8.1** and **7.8.5**.

Q. 18.24. *Give an expression for discharge through an orifice meter.* **(GATE)**

Ans. Refer to *Article* **6.6.2.**

Q. 18.25. *Distinguish, with the help of neat sketches, between a hydrodynamically rough surface and a hydrodynamically smooth surface.* **(IES)**

Ans. Refer to *Article* **11.6.**

B. MULTIPLE-CHOICE QUESTIONS WITH ANSWERS AND "*EXPLANATIONS*"

Q.18.1. A fluid flow is represented by the velocity field $\vec{V} = a x\vec{i} + a y\vec{j}$, where a is a constant. The equation of streamline passing through a point (1, 2) is

(*a*) $x - 2y = 0$ (*b*) $2x + y = 0$ (*c*) $2x - y = 0$ (*d*) $x + 2y = 0$.

Ans. (*c*)

EXPLANATION:

Given: $\vec{V} = ax\hat{i} + ay\hat{j}$

i.e. $u_x = ax$ and $u_y = ay$

Equation of stream line is given by:

$$\frac{dx}{u_x} = \frac{dy}{u_y}$$

or, $\frac{dx}{ax} = \frac{dy}{ay}$

or, $\frac{dx}{x} = \frac{dy}{y}$

Integrating both sides, we get:

$$\ln(x) = \ln(y) + \ln(c)$$

(where c is constant of integration)

$\therefore$ $x = cy$

Since the streamline passes through point (1, 2), therefore,

$$1 = 2c$$

$$c = 1/2$$

Hence, equation of stream line is:

$$x = \frac{1}{2}y$$

or, $2x - y = 0$ **(Ans.)**

Q.18.2. An incompressible fluid (kinematic viscosity, 7.4×10^{-7} m²/s, specific gravity, 0.88) is held between two parallel plates. If the top plate is moved with a velocity of 0.5 m/s while the bottom one is held stationary, the fluid attains a linear velocity profile in the gap of 0.5 mm between these plates; the shear stress in Pascals on the surface of top plate is

(*a*) 0.651×10^{-3} (*b*) 0.651 (*c*) 6.51 (*d*) 0.651×10^{3}.

Ans. (*b*)

EXPLANATION: Refer to Fig. 18.9.

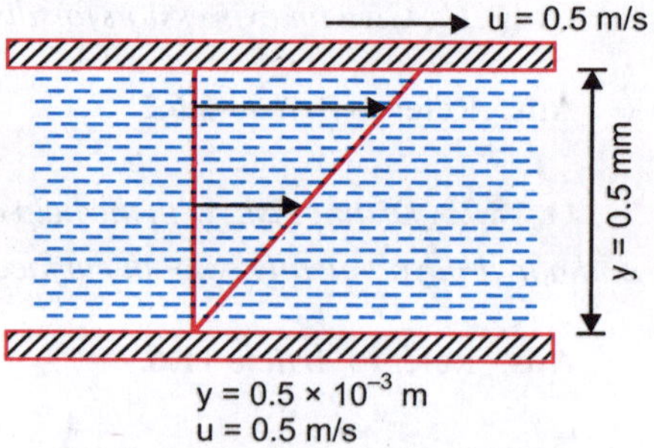

Fig. 18.9

Shear stress $\tau = \mu\frac{du}{dy}$

For linear velocity profile,

$$\tau = \mu \cdot \frac{u}{y}$$

Now, $\nu = \frac{\mu}{\rho}$

or, $\mu = \nu \times \rho$

$$= 7.4 \times 10^{-7} \times (0.88 \times 1000)$$

$$= 6.512 \times 10^{-4} \text{ Pa-s}$$

$\therefore$ $\tau = 6.512 \times 10^{-4} \times \frac{0.5}{0.5 \times 10^{-3}}$

$$= 0.6512 \text{ N/m}^2 \textbf{ (Ans.)}$$

Q.18.3. A cylindrical body of cross-sectional area A, height H and density ρ_s, is immersed to a depth h in a liquid of density ρ, and tied to the bottom with a string. The tension in the string is

(*a*) ρghA (*b*) $(\rho_s - \rho)\, ghA$

(*c*) $(\rho - \rho_s)\, ghA$ (*d*) $(\rho h - \rho_s H)gA$

Ans. (*d*)

EXPLANATION: Refer to Fig. 18.10.

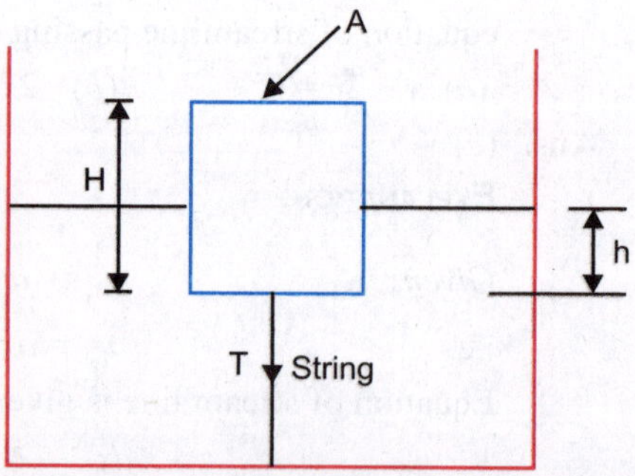

Fig. 18.10

$$T + Mg = \text{Buoyancy force}$$

$$T + \rho_S HAg = \rho hAg$$

$$\therefore \quad T = gA(\rho h - \rho_S H) \text{ (Ans.)}$$

Q.18.4. A water container is kept on a weighing balance. Water from a tap is falling vertically into the container with a volume flow rate of Q; the velocity of the water when it hits the water surface is U. At a particular instant of time the total mass of the container and water is m. The force registered by the weighing balance at this instant of time is

(*a*) $mg + \rho QU$ (*b*) $mg + 2\rho QU$ (*c*) $mg + \rho QU^2/2$ (*d*) $\rho QU^2/2$.

Ans. (*a*)

EXPLANATION:

Mass of water hitting the surface = ρQ

Force on weighing balance due to water strike

= Initial momentum – final momentum

$= \rho QU - 0$

$= \rho QU$

Weight of container and water = mg

∴ Total force on weighing balance

$= mg + \rho QU$ **(Ans.)**

Q.18.5. Air flows through a venturi and into atmosphere (Fig. 18.11). Air density is ρ; atmospheric pressure is ρ_a; throat diameter is D_t; exit diameter is D and exit velocity is U. The throat is connected to a cylinder containing a frictionless piston attached to a spring. The spring constant is k. The bottom surface of the piston is exposed to atmosphere. Due to the flow, the piston moves by distance x. Assuming incompressible frictionless flow, x is

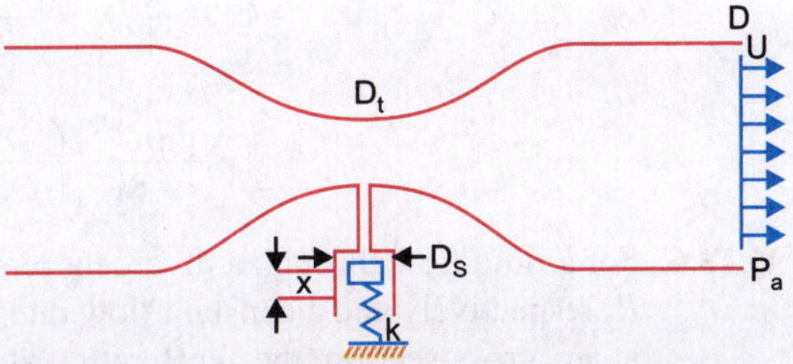

Fig. 18.11

(*a*) $(\rho U^2/2k)\pi D_S^2$ (*b*) $(\rho U^2/8k)\left(\dfrac{D^2}{D_t^2} - 1\right)\pi D_s^2$

(*c*) $(\rho U^2/2k)\left(\dfrac{D^2}{D_t^2} - 1\right)\pi D_s^2$ (*c*) $(\rho U^2/8k)\left(\dfrac{D^4}{D_t^4} - 1\right)\pi D_s^2$.

Ans. (*d*)

EXPLANATION: Refer to Fig. 18.12

Applying continuity equation, we get:

$$A_1 V_1 = A_2 V_2$$

$$V_1 = \left(\frac{A_2}{A_1}\right) V_2 = \left(\frac{\frac{\pi}{4} D^2}{\frac{\pi}{4} D_t^2}\right) U$$

$$V_1 = \left(\frac{D}{D_t}\right)^2 U \quad \text{...}(i)$$

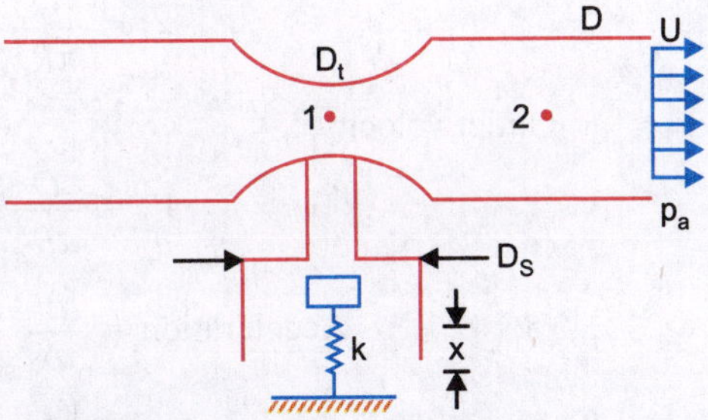

Fig. 18.12

Applying Bernoulli's equation:

$$\frac{p_1}{\rho g}+\frac{V_1^2}{2g} = \frac{p_2}{\rho g}+\frac{V_2^2}{2g}$$

$[z_1 = z_2$, because venturi is *horizontal*]

$$\frac{p_1-p_2}{\rho g} = \frac{V_2^2-V_1^2}{2g}$$

$$\therefore \quad p_1-p_2 = \frac{\rho}{2}(V_2^2-V_1^2)$$

From equation (*i*),

$$p_1-p_2=\frac{\rho}{2}\left[U^2-\left(\frac{D}{D_t}\right)^4 U^2\right]$$

$$=\frac{\rho}{2}U^2\left[1-\left(\frac{D}{D_t}\right)^4\right] \quad ...(ii)$$

Since, Spring force = Pressure force due to air

$$-kx = \frac{\pi}{4}D_s^2\times(p_1-p_2)$$

From equation (*ii*):

$$-kx = \frac{\pi}{4}D_s^2\times\frac{\rho U^2}{2}\left[1-\left(\frac{D}{D_t}\right)^4\right]$$

$$\therefore \quad x = \frac{\rho U^2}{8k}\left[\left(\frac{D}{D_t}\right)^4-1\right]\pi D_s^2 \quad \textbf{(Ans.)}$$

Q.18.6. For a fluid flow through a divergent pipe of length L having inlet and outlet radii of R_1 and R_2 respectively and a constant flow rate of Q, assuming the velocity to be axial and uniform at any cross-section, the acceleration at the exit is

(*a*) $\dfrac{2Q(R_1-R_2)}{\pi R_2^3 L}$ (*b*) $\dfrac{2Q^2(R_1-R_2)}{\pi R_2^3 L}$

(*c*) $\dfrac{2Q^2(R_1-R_2)}{\pi^2 R_2^5 L}$ (*c*) $\dfrac{2Q^2(R_2-R_1)}{\pi^2 R_2^5 L}$.

Ans. (*c*)

Explanation: Refer to Fig. 18.13

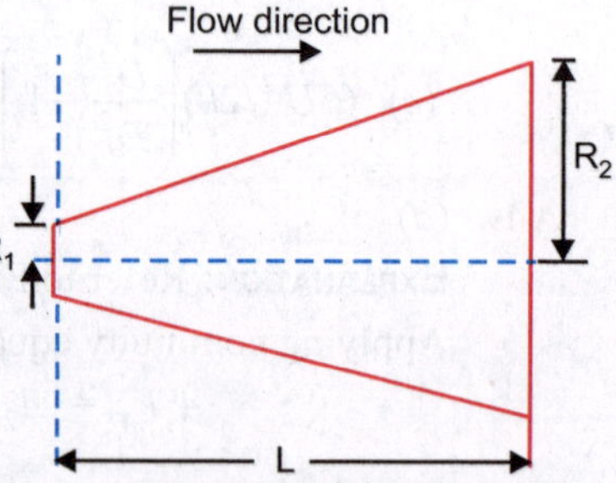

Fig. 18.13

Inlet velocity,

$$V_1 = \frac{Q}{\pi R_1^2}$$

Outlet velocity,

$$V_2 = \frac{Q}{\pi R_2^2}$$

$$\text{Acceleration} = \frac{dV}{dx}$$

$$= \frac{V_2-V_1}{L} = \frac{Q}{\pi L}\left[\frac{1}{R_2^2}-\frac{1}{R_1^2}\right]$$

$$\text{Acceleration at exit} = V_2 \frac{dV}{dx} = \frac{Q}{\pi R_2^2} \frac{Q}{\pi L}\left[\frac{R_1^2 - R_2^2}{R_1^2 R_2^2}\right]$$

$$= \frac{Q^2}{\pi^2 R_2^2 L}\left[\frac{(R_1 - R_2)(R_1 + R_2)}{R_1^2 R_2^2}\right]$$

Consider limiting case *i.e.* $R_1 \to R_2$, Then,

Acceleration at the exit

$$= \frac{Q^2}{\pi^2 R_2^2 L}\left[\frac{(R_1 - R_2)2R_2}{R_2^4}\right]$$

$$= \frac{2Q^2(R_1 - R_2)}{\pi^2 R_2^5 L} \quad \textbf{(Ans.)}$$

Q.18.7. A closed cylinder having a radius R and height H is filled with oil of density ρ. If the cylinder is rotated about its axis at an angular velocity of ω, the thrust at the bottom of the cylinder is

(*a*) $\pi R^2 \rho g H$ (*b*) $\pi R^2 \dfrac{\rho\omega^2 R^2}{4}$

(*c*) $\pi R^2(\rho\omega^2 R^2 + \rho g H)$ (*d*) $\pi R^2\left(\dfrac{\rho\omega^2 R^2}{4} + \rho g H\right)$

Ans. (*d*)

EXPLANATION: Refer to Fig. 18.14

We know that:

$$\frac{\partial p}{\partial r} = \frac{\rho v^2}{r} = \rho\omega^2 r$$

$$\int_0^r \partial p = \int_0^r \rho\omega^2 r\,dr$$

$$\therefore \quad p = \frac{\rho\omega^2 r^2}{2}$$

Area of circular ring $= 2\pi r dr$

Force on elementary ring = Intensity of pressure × Area of ring

$$= \frac{\rho}{2}\omega^2 r^2 2\pi r dr$$

∴ Total force on the top of the cylinder

$$\int_0^R \frac{\rho\omega^2 r^2}{2} 2\pi r dr = \frac{\rho}{2}\omega^2 \cdot 2\pi \int_0^R r^3 dr$$

$$= \pi\omega^2\rho\left[\frac{r^4}{4}\right]_0^R$$

$$= \rho\omega^2 \cdot \frac{\pi R^4}{4}$$

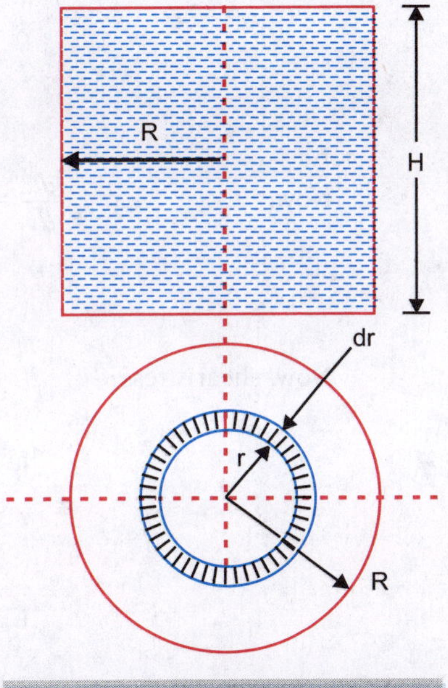

Fig. 18.14

Thrust at the bottom of the cylinder = Weight of water in cylinder + total force on the top of cylinder

$$= \rho g \times \pi R^2 \times H + \rho\omega^2 \times \frac{\pi R^4}{4}$$

$$= \pi R^2 \left[\rho g H + \frac{\rho\omega^2 R^2}{4} \right] \textbf{ (Ans.)}$$

Q.18.8. For air flow over a flat plate, velocity (U) and boundary layer thickness (δ) can be expressed respectively as

$$\frac{U}{U_\infty} = \frac{3}{2}\frac{y}{\delta} - \frac{1}{2}\left(\frac{y}{\delta}\right); \delta = \frac{4.64x}{\sqrt{\text{Re}_x}}$$

If the free stream velocity is 2 m/s, and air has kinematic viscosity of 1.5×10^{-5} m²/s and density of 1.23 kg/m³, the wall shear stress at $x = 1$ m, is

(*a*) 2.36×10^2 N/m² (*b*) 43.6×10^{-3} N/m²

(*c*) 4.36×10^{-3} N/m² (*d*) 2.18×10^{-3} N/m².

Ans. (*c*)

EXPLANATION:

Reynold number,

$$Re_x = \frac{ux}{v}$$

$$= \frac{2 \times 1}{1.5 \times 10^{-5}} = 1.33 \times 10^5$$

$$\delta = \frac{4.64x}{\sqrt{\text{Re}_x}} = \frac{4.64 \times 1}{\sqrt{1.33 \times 10^5}}$$

$$= 0.0127$$

Now,

$$\frac{du}{dy} = U\left[\frac{3}{2}\cdot\frac{1}{\delta} - \frac{3}{2}\left(\frac{y^2}{\delta^3}\right)\right]$$

$$= \left.\frac{du}{dy}\right|_{y=0} = \frac{3U}{2\delta}$$

Now, shear stress,

$$\tau_0 = \mu\left(\frac{du}{dy}\right)_{y=0}$$

$$= \mu \times \frac{3U}{2\delta}$$

$$= \frac{3U \times \nu \times \rho}{2\delta} \qquad (\because \mu = \nu\rho)$$

$$= \frac{3 \times 2 \times 1.5 \times 10 \quad \times 1.23}{2 \times 0.0127}$$

$$= 4.36 \times 10^{-3} \text{ N/m}^2 \textbf{ (Ans.)}$$

Q.18.9. A centrifugal pump is required to pump water to an open water tank situated 4 km away from the location of the pump through a pipe of diameter 0.2 m having Darcy's friction factor of 0.01. The average speed of water in the pipe is 2 m/s. If it is to maintain a constant head of 5 m in the tank, neglecting other minor losses, the absolute discharge pressure at the pump exit is

(*a*) 0.449 bar (*b*) 5.503 bar

(*c*) 44.911 bar (*d*) 55.203 bar.

Ans. (*b*)

EXPLANATION:

Head loss due to friction

$$h_f = \frac{fLV^2}{2gd}$$

$$= \frac{0.01 \times 4000 \times (2)^2}{2 \times 9.81 \times 0.2}$$

$$= 40.78 \text{ m}$$

Pressure corresponding to this head

$$= \rho g(h_f + h + h_{atm})$$

$$= 1000 \times 9.81\ (40.78 + 5 + 10.3)$$

$$= 5.50 \times 10^5 \text{ N/m}^2$$

$$= 5.50 \text{ bar } \textbf{(Ans.)}$$

Q.18.10. The pressure gauges G_1 and G_2 installed on the system show pressure of $P_{G1} = 5.00$ bar and $P_{G2} = 1.00$ bar. The value of unknown pressure P is

(Atmospheric pressure = 1.01 bar]

(*a*) 1.01 bar (*b*) 2.01 bar

(*c*) 5.00 bar (*d*) 7.01 bar

Ans. (*d*)

EXPLANATION: Refer to Fig. 18.15

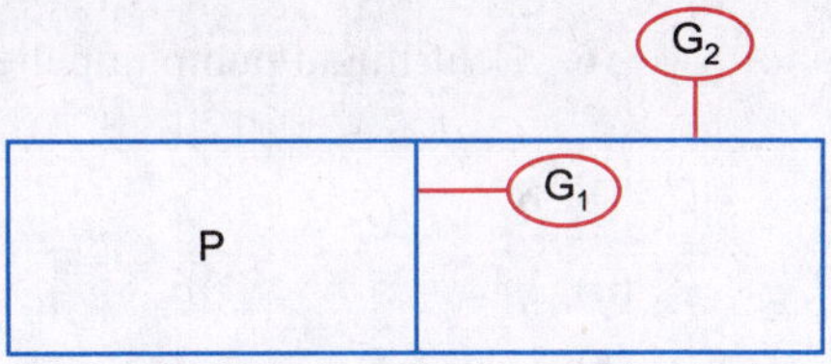

Fig. 18.15

Absolute pressure of $G_2 = 1 + 1.01 = 2.01$ bar

Absolute pressure of G_1 = Pressure of P

$= 5 + 2.01$

$= 7.01$ bar **(Ans.)**

Q.18.11. At a hydro electric power plant site, available head and flow rate are 24.5 m and 10.1 m³/s respectively. If the turbine to be installed is required to run at 4.0 revolutions per second (rps) with an overall efficiency of 90%, the suitable type of turbine for this site is

(*a*) Francis (*b*) Kaplan

(*c*) Pelton (*d*) Propeller.

Ans. (*a*)

EXPLANATION:

Given: $H = 24.5$ m,

$Q = 10.1$ m³/s,

$N = 4$ rev/sec

$$= 4 \times 60 = 240 \text{ rpm, and}$$

$$\eta_0 = 0.90$$

$$\text{Power generated} = \rho g H \times 0.9 \times Q$$

$$= 1000 \times 9.81 \times 10.1 \times 24.5 \times 0.9$$

$$= 2184.74 \text{ kW}$$

$$N_S = \frac{N\sqrt{P}}{H^{5/4}} = \frac{240\sqrt{2184.7}}{(24.5)^{5/4}}$$

$$= 205.80$$

Hence, turbine is *Francis*. **(Ans.)**

Q.18.12. Match List-I with List-II and select the correct answer using the codes given below the lists:

List-I

P. Reciprocating pump

Q. Axial flow pump

R. Microhydel plant

S. Backward curved vanes

List-II

1. Plant with power output below 100 kW

2. Plant with power output between 100 kW to 1 MW

3. Positive displacement

4. Draft tube

5. High flow rate, low pressure ratio

6. Centrifugal pump impeller

Codes:

	P	*Q*	*R*	*S*
(*a*)	3	5	6	2
(*b*)	3	5	2	6
(*c*)	3	5	1	6
(*d*)	4	5	1	6

Ans. (*b*)

Explanation:

(*P*) Reciprocating pump — Positive displacement

(*Q*) Axial flow pump — High flow rate, low pressure ratio

(*R*) Microhydel plant — Power output between 100 kW to 1 MW

(*S*) Backward curved vanes — centrifugal pump impeller **(Ans.)**

Q.18.13. The velocity components in the *x* and *y* directions of a two dimensional potential flow are *u* and *v*, respectively. Then, $\frac{\partial u}{\partial x}$ is equal to

(*a*) $\frac{\partial v}{\partial x}$ (*b*) $-\frac{\partial v}{\partial x}$

(*c*) $\frac{\partial v}{\partial y}$ (*d*) $-\frac{\partial v}{\partial y}$.

Ans. (*d*)

EXPLANATION:

For two dimensional flow, continuity equation should be satisfied.

i.e. $$\frac{\partial u}{\partial x} + \frac{\partial v}{\partial y} = 0$$

$$\frac{\partial u}{dx} = -\frac{\partial v}{\partial y} \quad \textbf{(Ans.)}$$

Q.18.14. For a Newtonian fluid

(*a*) shear stress is proportional to shear strain

(*b*) rate of shear stress is proportional to shear strain

(*c*) shear stress is proportional to rate of shear strain

(*d*) rate of shear stress is proportional to rate of shear strain

Ans. (*c*) For a Newtonian fluid,

$$\tau \propto \frac{du}{dy}$$

$$\tau = \mu \frac{du}{dy}$$

where, τ is shear stress

$\frac{du}{dy}$ → rate of shear strain **(Ans.)**

Q.18.15. In a two-dimensional velocity field with velocities u and v along the x and y directions respectively, the convective acceleration along the x-direction is given by

(*a*) $u\frac{\partial v}{\partial x} + v\frac{\partial u}{\partial y}$ (*b*) $u\frac{\partial u}{\partial x} + v\frac{\partial v}{\partial y}$

(*c*) $u\frac{\partial u}{\partial x} + v\frac{\partial u}{\partial y}$ (*d*) $v\frac{\partial u}{\partial x} + u\frac{\partial u}{\partial y}$

Ans. (*c*)

EXPLANATION:

$$a_x = \frac{du}{dt} = u\frac{du}{dx} + v\frac{du}{dy} \quad \textbf{(Ans.)}$$

Q.18.16. A two-dimensional flow field has velocities along the x and y directions given by $u = x^2t$ and $v = -2\,xyt$ respectively, where t is time. The equation of streamline is

(*a*) x^2y = constant (*b*) xy^2 = constant

(*c*) xy = constant (*d*) not possible to determine.

Ans. (*d*)

EXPLANATION:

We know that:

$$\frac{du}{dy} = -u = -x^2t \qquad ...(i)$$

and, $$\frac{du}{dx} = v = -2xyt \qquad ...(ii)$$

Integrating the equation (*i*) we get:

$$\therefore \quad \psi = -x^2yt + f(x) \qquad ...(iii)$$

Now differenting with respect to x, we get:

$$\frac{d\psi}{dx} = -2xyt + f'(x)$$

From equation (*ii*), we get:

$$-2xyt = -2xyt + f'(x)$$

$$\therefore \quad f'(x) = 0$$

Integrating $\quad f(x) = C$

$\therefore$ From equation (*iii*),

$$\psi = -x^2y\,t + C$$

The line for which stream function 'ψ' is constant called as streamline.

i.e. $\quad x^2y\,t = C$

If 't' is constant, then equation of stream line is x^2y = constant. If 't' is variant then from this it is not possible to determine equation of stream line. **(Ans.)**

Q.18.17. The velocity profile in fully developed laminar flow in a pipe of diameter D is given by $u = u_0(1 - 4r^2/D^2)$, where r is the radial distance from the center. If the viscosity of the fluid is μ, the pressure drop across a length L of the pipe is

(*a*) $\frac{\mu u_0 L}{D^2}$ (*b*) $\frac{4\mu u_0 L}{D^2}$ (*c*) $\frac{8\mu u_0 L}{D^2}$ (*d*) $\frac{16\mu u_0 L}{D^2}$

Ans. (*d*)

EXPLANATION:

We know that:

Pressure drop across a length L of pipe is,

$$\Delta p = \frac{32\mu u_{av} L}{D^2} \qquad ...(i)$$

and

$$u_{av} = \frac{u_0}{2} \qquad ...(ii)$$

From equation (*i*) and (*ii*)

$$\Delta p = \frac{16\mu u_0 L}{D^2} \text{ (Ans.)}$$

Q.18.18. A siphon draws water from a reservoir and discharges it out at atmospheric pressure (Fig. 18.16). Assuming ideal fluid and the reservoir is large, the velocity at point P in the siphon tube is

(*a*) $\sqrt{2gh_1}$ (*b*) $\sqrt{2gh_2}$

(*c*) $\sqrt{2g(h_2 - h_1)}$ (*d*) $\sqrt{2g(h_2 + h_1)}$.

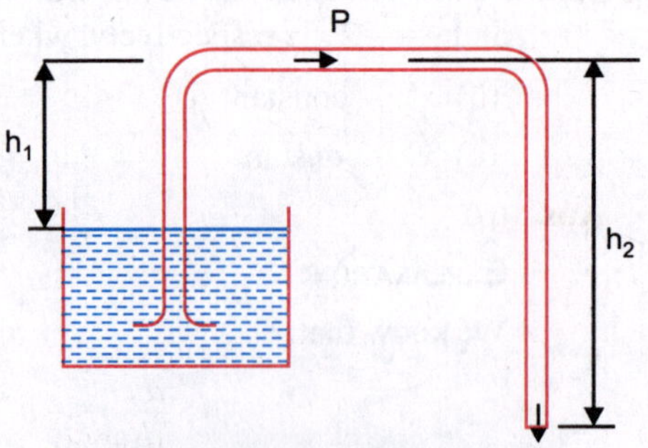

Fig. 18.16

Ans. (*c*)

EXPLANATION:

Refer to Fig. 18.17.

Applying Bernoulli's equation between (1) and (2), we get:

$$\frac{p_1}{\rho g}+\frac{V_1^2}{2g}+z_1 = \frac{p_2}{\rho g}+\frac{V_2^2}{2g}+z_2$$

or, $$\frac{p_{atm}}{\rho g}+0+(h_2-h_1) = \frac{p_{atm}}{\rho g}+\frac{V_2^2}{2g}+0$$

∴ $$(h_2-h_1) = \frac{V_2^2}{2g}$$

∴ $$V_2 = \sqrt{2g(h_2-h_1)}$$

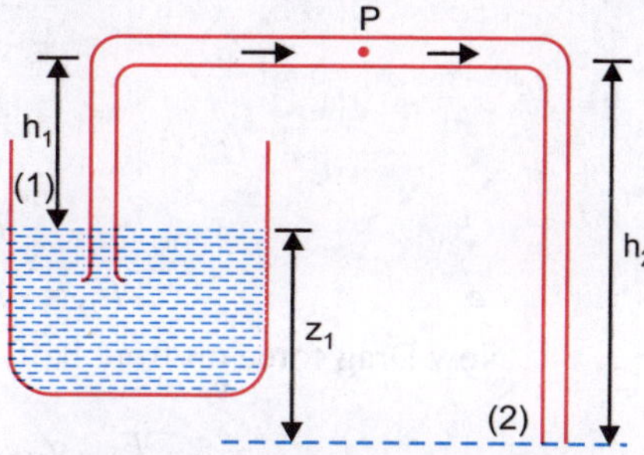

Fig. 18.17

Velocity of fluid inside the tube is same,

$$V_p = V_2 = \sqrt{2g(h_2-h_1)}$$ **(Ans.)**

Q.18.19. A horizontal-shaft centrifugal pump lifts water at 65° C. The suction nozzle is one metre below pump centerline. The pressure at his point equals 200 kPa gauge and velocity is 3m/s. Steam tables show saturation pressure at 65° C as 25 kPa, and specific volume of the saturated liquid is 0.001020 m^3/kg. The pump Net Positive Suction Head (NPSH) in metres is

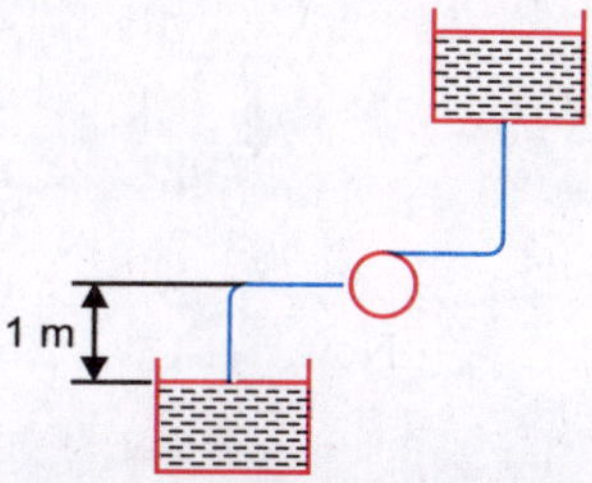

Fig. 18.18

(*a*) 24 (*b*) 26

(*c*) 28 (*d*) 30.

Ans. (*a*)

EXPLANATION: Refer to Fig. 18.18.

Net pressure difference = 200 – (– 25) kPa

= 225 kPa = 2.25 bar

$$= \frac{2.25\times 10.33}{1.013} \text{ m of water}$$

= 22.95 m of water

Static head = 1 m

∴ Total net positive suction head (NPSH)

= Pressure head + static head

= 22.95 + 1

= 23.95 ≈ 24 m of water **(Ans.)**

Q.18.20. Consider an incompressible laminar boundary layer flow over a flat plate of length L, aligned with the direction of an incoming uniform free stream. If F is the ratio of the drag force on the front half of the plate to the drag force on the rear half, then

(*a*) $F < 1/2$ (*b*) $F = 1/2$

(*c*) $F = 1$ (*d*) $F > 1$.

Ans. (*d*)

EXPLANATION:

Drag force $$F_D = C_f \times \frac{1}{2}\rho A V^2$$

$$= \frac{1.328}{\sqrt{Re_L}} \times \frac{1}{2}\rho A V^2$$

$$= \frac{1.328}{\sqrt{\frac{\rho L V}{\mu}}} \times \frac{1}{2}\rho \times A \times L \times V^2$$

i.e. $F_D \propto \sqrt{L}$

Now Drag force on front half,

$$F_{D/2} \propto \sqrt{\frac{L}{2}}$$

$\therefore$ $$F_{D/2} \propto \frac{F_D}{\sqrt{2}}$$

Drag force on rear half,

$$F'_{D/2} = F_D - F_{D/2}$$

$$= \left(1 - \frac{1}{\sqrt{2}}\right) F_D$$

Now, $$F = \frac{F_{D/2}}{F'_{D/2}}$$

$$= \frac{\frac{F_D}{\sqrt{2}}}{\left(1 - \frac{1}{\sqrt{2}}\right) F_D} = \frac{1}{\sqrt{2} - 1} > 1$$

$\therefore$ $F > 1$ **(Ans.)**

Q.18.21. In a steady flow through a nozzle, the flow velocity on the nozzle axis is given by $v = u_0(1 + 3x/L)$, where x is the distance along the axis of the nozzle from its inlet plane and L is the length of the nozzle. The time required for a fluid particle on the axis to travel from the inlet to the exit plane of the nozzle is

(*a*) $\frac{L}{u_0}$ (*b*) $\frac{L}{3u_0}\ln(4)$

(*c*) $\frac{L}{4u_0}$ (*d*) $\frac{L}{2.5u_0}$.

Ans. (*b*)

EXPLANATION:

We know that :

Velocity, $$v = \frac{dx}{dt}$$

$\therefore$ $$\frac{dx}{dt} = u_0\left(1 + \frac{3x}{L}\right)$$

$\Rightarrow$ $$u_0 . dt = \frac{dx}{\left(1 + \frac{3x}{L}\right)}$$

Integrating both sides, we get:

$$u_0\int_0^t dt = u_0\int_0^L \frac{dx}{\left(1+\dfrac{3x}{L}\right)}$$

$$u_0 t = \frac{L}{3}\left[\ln\left(1+\frac{3x}{L}\right)\right]_0^L$$

$$u_0 t = \frac{L}{3}\ln(4)$$

$$\therefore \qquad t = \frac{L}{3u_0}\ln(4) \quad \textbf{(Ans.)}$$

Q.18.22. Consider steady laminar incompressible axi-symmetric fully developed viscous flow through a straight circular pipe of constant cross-sectional area at a Reynolds number of 5. The ratio of inertia force to viscous force on a fluid particle is

(*a*) 5 (*b*) 1/5

(*c*) 0 (*d*) ∞.

Ans. (*a*)

EXPLANATION:

$$\text{Reynolds number} = \frac{\text{Inertia force}}{\text{viscous force}} = 5 \ \textbf{(Ans.)}$$

Q.18.23. The ratio V_m/U_0 is (Fig. 18.19)

(*a*) $\dfrac{1}{1-2(\delta/H)}$ (*b*) 1

(*c*) $\dfrac{1}{1-(\delta/H)}$ (*d*) $\dfrac{1}{1+(\delta/H)}$

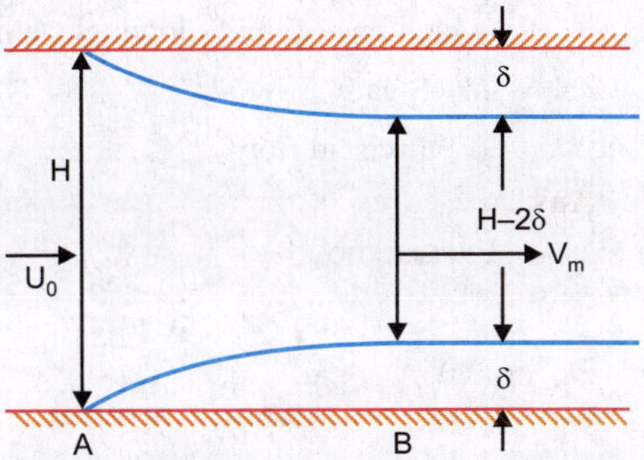

Fig. 18.19

Ans. (*a*)

EXPLANATION:

Assume width of channel is b. Applying continuity equation at A and B, we have:

$$U_0(H \times b) = V_m(H-2\delta) \times b$$

or,
$$\frac{V_m}{U_0} = \frac{H}{H-2\delta} = \frac{1}{1-\dfrac{2\delta}{H}} \quad \textbf{(Ans.)}$$

Q.18.24. The ratio $\dfrac{p_A - p_B}{\frac{1}{2}\rho U_0^2}$ (where p_A and p_B are the pressures at section A and B, respectively, and ρ is the density of the fluid) is

(*a*) $\dfrac{1}{[1+(\delta/H)]^2}$ (*b*) $\dfrac{1}{[1-(\delta/H)]^2}$ (*c*) $\dfrac{1}{(1-(2\delta/H)^2}-1$ (*d*) $\dfrac{1}{1+(\delta/H)}$

Ans. (*c*)

EXPLANATION:

Applying Bernoulli's equation at A and B, we get:

$$\frac{p_A}{\rho g} + \frac{V_A^2}{2g} = \frac{p_B}{\rho g} + \frac{V_B^2}{2g}$$

or,
$$\frac{p_A - p_B}{\rho g} = \frac{V_B^2 - V_A^2}{2g}$$

or,
$$\frac{p_A - p_B}{\rho} = \frac{V_m^2 - U_o^2}{2}$$

or,
$$\frac{p_A - p_B}{\frac{1}{2}\rho U_0^2} = \left(\frac{V_m}{U_o}\right)^2 - 1$$

Using the value of $\frac{V_m}{U_0}$ from Q. 18.23, we get:

$$\frac{p_A - p_B}{\frac{1}{2}\rho U_0^2} = \frac{1}{\left(1 - \frac{2\delta}{H}\right)^2} - 1 \text{ (Ans.)}$$

Q.18.25. For the continuity equation given by $\vec{\Delta}\cdot\vec{V} = 0$ to be valid, where $\vec{V}$ is the velocity vector, which one of the following is a necessary condition ?

(*a*) Steady flow (*b*) Irrotational flow

(*c*) Inviscid flow (*b*) Incompressible flow.

Ans. (*d*)

EXPLANATION:

$$\vec{\Delta}\cdot\vec{V} = 0$$

$$\frac{\partial u}{\partial x} + \frac{\partial v}{\partial y} + \frac{\partial w}{\partial z} = 0$$

So the above equation represents *incompressible flow* **(Ans.)**

Q.18.26. Consider steady, incompressible and irrotational flow through a reducer in a horizontal pipe where the dimater is reduced from 20 cm to 10 cm. The pressure in the 20 cm pipe just upstream of the reducer is 150 kPa. The fluid has a vapour pressure of 50 kPa and specific weight of 5 kN/m^3. Neglecting frictional effects, the maximum discharge in m^3/s) that can pass through the reducer without causing cavitation is

(*a*) 0.05 (*b*) 0.16

(*c*) 0.27 (*d*) 0.38.

Ans. (*b*)

EXPLANATION:

Refer to Fig. 18.20

Vapour pressure, $p_v = 50$ kPa

Specific weight, $w = \gamma = \rho g = 5$ kN/m^3

Consider steady, incompressible and irrotational flow and neglect frictional effect.

From continuity equation:

$$A_1V_1 = A_2V_2$$

or, $$\frac{\pi}{4}D_1^2V_1 = \frac{\pi}{4}D_2^2V_2$$

or, $$(20)^2V_1 = (10)^2V_2$$

or, $$V_2 = 4\,V_1$$

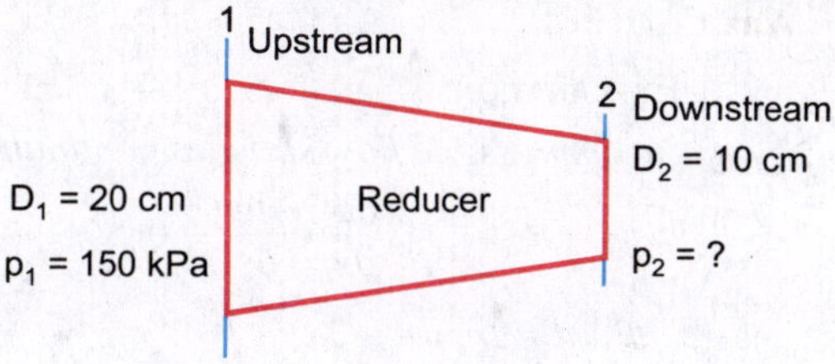

Fig. 18.20

The maximum pressure in downstream of reducer should be greater than or equal to vapour pressure (p_v = 50 kPa) to avoid cavitation. Therefore, for maximum discharge,

$$p_2 = 50 \text{ kPa}$$

Applying Bernoulli's equation between upstream and downstream, we get:

$$\frac{p_1}{w} + \frac{V_1^2}{2g} + z_1 = \frac{p_2}{w} + \frac{V_2^2}{2g} + z_2 \quad (z_1 = z_2 \text{ for horizontal pipe})$$

$$\frac{150}{5} + \frac{V_1^2}{2g} = \frac{50}{5} + \frac{(4V_1)^2}{2g}$$

$$\frac{(16-1)V_1^2}{2g} = \frac{150-50}{5} = \frac{100}{5} = 20$$

$$V_1 = \sqrt{\frac{20 \times 2g}{15}}$$

$$= \sqrt{\frac{20 \times 2 \times 9.81}{15}}$$

$$= 5.114 \text{ m/s}$$

The maximum discharge,

$$Q_{max} = A_1V_1$$

or, $$Q = \frac{\pi}{4}D_1^2V_1$$

or, $$Q = \frac{\pi}{4}(20 \times 10^{-2})^2(5.114)$$

or, $$Q_{max} = 0.161 \text{ m}^3\text{/sec} \textbf{ (Ans.)}$$

Q.18.27. You are asked to evaluate assorted fluid flows for their suitability in a given laboratory application. The following three flow choices, expressed in terms of the two-dimensional velocity fields in the *xy*-plane, are made available.

P. $u = 2y,\ v = -3x$

Q. $u = 3xy,\ v = 0$

R. $u = -2x,\ v = 2y$

Which flow(*s*) should be recommended when the application requires the flow to be incompressible and irrotational?

(*a*) *P* and *R* (*b*) *Q*

(*c*) *Q* and *R* (*d*) *R*

Ans. (*d*)

EXPLANATION:

Incompressible flow satisfies continuity equation:

$$\frac{\partial u}{\partial x} + \frac{\partial v}{\partial y} = 0$$

P. $u = 2y, v = -3x$

$$\frac{\partial(2y)}{\partial x} + \frac{\partial(-3x)}{\partial y}$$

or, $0 + 0 = 0$ ...*Incompressible flow*

Q. $u = 3xy, v = 0$

$$\frac{\partial(3xy)}{\partial x} + \frac{\partial(0)}{\partial y}$$

$3y + 0 \neq 0$ ...*Compressible flow*

R. $u = -2x, v = 2y$

$$\frac{\partial(-2x)}{\partial x} + \frac{\partial(2y)}{\partial y}$$

$-2 + 2 = 0$ ...*Incompressible flow*

For irrotational flow condition is

$$w_z = \frac{1}{2}\left(\frac{\partial v}{\partial x} - \frac{\partial u}{\partial y}\right) = 0$$

For *P*: $u = 2y, v = -3x$

$$w_z = \frac{1}{2}\left[\frac{\partial(-3x)}{\partial x} - \frac{\partial(2y)}{\partial y}\right]$$

$$= \frac{1}{2}[-3 - 2] \neq 0$$ ...*Rotational flow*

For *Q*: $u = 3xy, v = 0$

$$w_z = \frac{1}{2}\left[\frac{\partial(0)}{\partial x} - \frac{\partial(3xy)}{\partial y}\right]$$

$$= \frac{1}{2}[0 - 3x] \neq 0$$ ...*Rotational flow*

For *R*: $u = -2x, v = 2y$

$$w_z = \frac{1}{2}\left[\frac{\partial(2y)}{\partial x} - \frac{\partial(-2x)}{\partial y}\right]$$

$$= \frac{1}{2}[0 - 0] = 0$$ ...*Irrotational flow*

Q.18.28. Water at 25° C is flowing through a 1.0 km long G.I. pipe of 200 mm diameter at the rate of 0.07 m^3/s. If value of Darcy friction factor for this pipe is 0.02 and density of water is 1000 kg/m^3, the pumping power (in (kW) required to maintain the flow is

(*a*) 1.8
(*b*) 17.5
(*c*) 20.5
(*d*) 41.0.

Ans. (*b*)

EXPLANATION:

Given, pipe length, L = 1000 m

Pipe diameter, D = 200 mm = 0.2 m

Flow rate, $Q = 0.07\ m^3/s$

Density, $\rho = 1000\ kg/m^3$

Friction factor, $f = 0.02$

Head loss,
$$h_f = \frac{fLV^2}{2gD} = \frac{fLQ^2}{12D^5}$$
$$= \frac{0.02 \times 1000 \times (0.07)^2}{12 \times (0.2)^5}$$
$$= 25.52\ \text{m}$$

Pumping power required,
$$P = \rho g Q h_f$$
or,
$$P = 1000 \times 9.81 \times 0.07 \times 25.52$$
$$= 17524.5\ \text{W}$$
$$= 17.52\ \text{kW}\ \textbf{(Ans.)}$$

Q.18.29. The velocity profile of a full developed laminar flow in a straight circular pipe, as shown in Fig. 18.21 is given by the expression

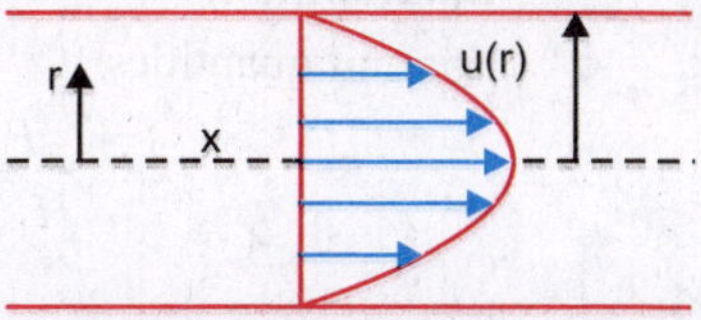

Fig. 18.21

$$u(r) = -\frac{R^2}{4\mu}\left(\frac{dp}{dx}\right)\left(1 - \frac{r^2}{R^2}\right)$$

where $\frac{dp}{dx}$ is a constant

The average velocity of fluid in the pipe is

(*a*) $-\frac{R^2}{8\mu}\left(\frac{dp}{dx}\right)$ (*b*) $-\frac{R^2}{4\mu}\left(\frac{dp}{dx}\right)$ (*c*) $-\frac{R^2}{2\mu}\left(\frac{dp}{dx}\right)$ (*d*) $-\frac{R^2}{\mu}\left(\frac{dp}{dx}\right)$

Ans. (*a*)

EXPLANATION:

The velocity profile of a fully developed laminar flow in a straight circular pipe, as shown in Fig. 13, is given by the expression:

$$u(r) = -\frac{R^2}{4\mu}\left(\frac{dp}{dx}\right)\left[1 - \frac{r^2}{R^2}\right]$$
$$= U_{max}\left[1 - \frac{r^2}{R^2}\right]$$

where,
$$U_{max} = -\frac{R^2}{4\mu}\left(\frac{dp}{dx}\right)$$

where, $\frac{dp}{dx}$ is a constant

The *average velocity* of fluid in the pipe is

$$V_{avg} = \frac{U_{max}}{2} = -\frac{R^2}{8\mu}\left(\frac{dp}{dx}\right) \textbf{ (Ans.)}$$

Q.18.30. The maximum velocity of a one-dimensional incompressible fully developed viscous flow, between two fixed parallel plates, is 6 ms^{-1}. The mean velocity (in ms^{-1}) of the flow is

(*a*) 2 (*b*) 3 (*c*) 4 (*d*) 5

Ans. (*c*)

EXPLANATION:

Ratio of maximum velocity to average velocity for one dimensional incompressible flow between two fixed plate is given as:

$$\frac{U_{max}}{U_{mean}} = \frac{3}{2}$$

or, $$U_{mean} = \frac{6\times 2}{3} = 4 \text{ m/s } \textbf{(Ans.)}$$

Q.18.31. A hydraulic turbine develops 1000 kW power of a head of 40 m. If the head is reduced to 20 m, the power developed (in kW) is

(*a*) 177 (*b*) 354 (*c*) 500 (*d*) 707.

Ans. (*b*)

EXPLANATION:

For unit quantities

$$\frac{P_1}{H_1^{3/2}} = \frac{P_2}{H_2^{3/2}}$$

$$P_2 = P_1\left(\frac{H_2}{H_1}\right)^{3/2}$$

$$= 1000\times\left(\frac{20}{40}\right)^{3/2} = 353.6 \approx 354 \text{ kW } \textbf{(Ans.)}$$

Q.18.32. A smooth pipe of diameter 200 mm carries water. The pressure in the pipe at section S_1 (elevation: 10 m) is 50 kPa. At section S_2 (elevation : 12 m) the pressure is 20 kPa and velocity is 2 ms^{-1}. Density of water is 1000 kgm^{-3} and acceleration due to water is 1000 kgm^{-3} and acceleration due to gravity is 9.8 ms^{-2}, which of the following is TRUE?

(*a*) flow is from S_1 and S_2 and head loss is 0.53 m

(*b*) flow is from S_2 to S_1 and head loss is 0.53 m

(*c*) flow is from S_1 to S_2 and head loss is 1.06 m

(*d*) flow is from S_2 to S_1 and head loss is 1.06 m.

Ans. (*c*)

EXPLANATION: Refer to Fig. 18.22

Applying Bernoulli's equation between section S_1 and S_2, we get:

$$\frac{p_1}{\rho g} + \frac{V_1^2}{2g} + z_1 = \frac{p_2}{\rho g} + \frac{V_2^2}{2g} + z_2 + h_L$$

As area is constant, velocity head will be same.

Inserting the values, we get:

$$\therefore \quad h_L = \frac{(50-20)\times 10^3}{1000\times 9.81} - 2$$

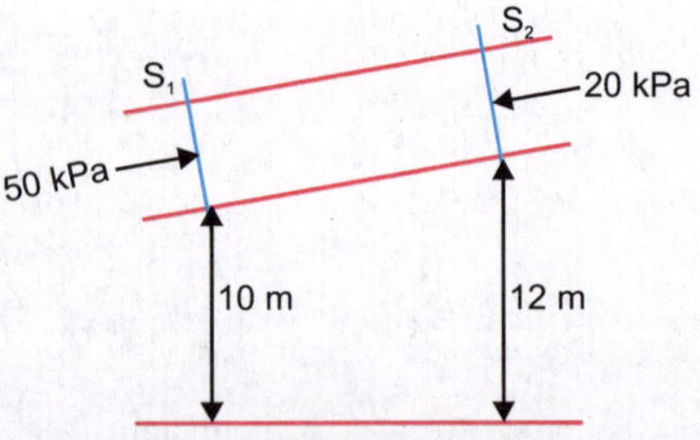

Fig. 18.22

$= 3.058 - 2$
$= 1.06$ m

Thus, flow from S_1 to S_2 and head loss is 1.06 m. **(Ans.)**

Q.18.33. A streamline and an equipotential line in a flow field

(*a*) are parallel to each other (*b*) are perpendicular to each other
(*c*) intersect at an acute angle (*d*) are identical.

Ans. (*b*)

EXPLANATION:

Streamline and equipotential line in flow field are perpendicular to each other. **(Ans.)**

Q.18.34. Figure 18.23 shows the schematic for the measure-ment of velocity of air (density = 1.2 kg/m^3) through a constant-area duct using a pitot tube and a water tube manometer. The differential head of water (density = 1000 kg/m^3) in the two columns of the manometer is 100 mm. Take acceleration due to gravity as 9.8 m/s^2. The velocity of air in m/s is

(*a*) 6.4 (*b*) 9.0
(*c*) 12.8 (*d*) 25.6.

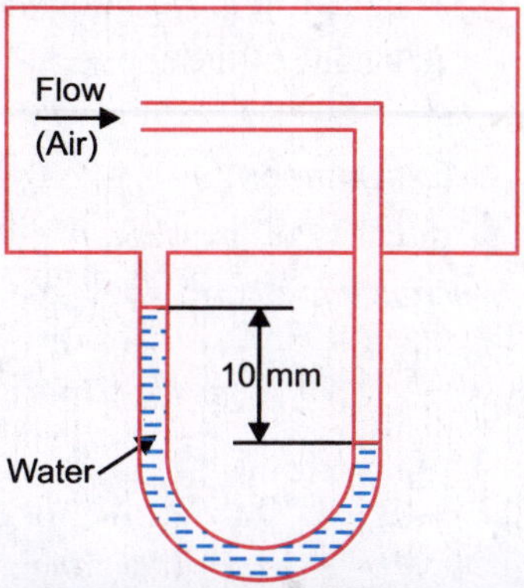

Fig. 18.23

Ans. (*c*)

EXPLANATION:

Use $\rho_1 h_1 = \rho_2 h_2$

where, ρ_1 and ρ_2 are densities of fluids

$$\therefore \quad h_2 = \frac{\rho_1 h_1}{\rho_2} = \frac{1000 \times 10 \times 10^{-3}}{1.2}$$

$$h_2 = 8.33 \text{ m}$$

$$\therefore \quad \text{Velocity of air} = \sqrt{2 \times g \times H}$$

$$= \sqrt{2 \times 9.81 \times 8.33}$$

$$= 12.78 \text{ m/s} \ \textbf{(Ans.)}$$

Q.18.35. Calculate the specific weight, specific mass and specific gravity of a liquid having a volume of 6 m^3 and weight of 44 kN.

(*a*) 5.33 kN/m^3, 547.5 kg/m^3, 0.447
(*b*) 6.33 kN/m^3, 647.5 kg/m, 0.547
(*c*) 7.333 kN/m^3, 747.5 kg/m^3, 0.747
(*d*) none of the above.

Ans. (*c*)

EXPLANATION:

Volume of liquid = 6 m^3; Weight of the liquid = 44 kN

Specific weight, $w = \dfrac{\text{Weight of liquid}}{\text{Volume of liquid}} = \dfrac{44}{6}$

$= 7.333$ kN/m^3 **(Ans.)**

Specific mass or mass density, $\rho = \dfrac{w}{g} = \dfrac{7.333 \times 1000}{9.81}$

$= 747.5 \text{ kg/m}^3$ **(Ans.)**

Specific gravity, $S = \frac{w_{liquid}}{w_{water}} = \frac{7.333}{9.81} = 0.747$ **(Ans.)**

Q.18.36. Specific gravity of mercury = 13.6;
Intensity of pressure = 400 kPa
The intensity of pressure (gauge) in various units (S.I.) is
(*a*) 0.3 bar, 3.077 m of water, 0.15 m of mercury
(*b*) 0.4 bar, 4.077 m of water, 0.299 m of mercury
(*c*) 0.5 bar, 5.077 m of water, 0.399 m of mercury
(*d*) none of the above.

Ans. (*b*)

EXPLANATION:

Intensity of pressure, $p = 400$ kPa

Gauge pressure:

(*i*) $p = 400 \text{ kPa} = 400 \text{ kN/m}^2$
$= 0.4 \times 10^5 \text{ N/m}^2$ $\quad (\because 1 \text{ bar} = 10^5 \text{ N/m}^2)$
$= 0.4$ bar **(Ans.)**

(*ii*) $h = \frac{p}{w} = \frac{0.4 \times 10^5}{9.81 \times 10^3}$
$= 4.077$ m of water **(Ans.)**

(*iii*) $h = \frac{p}{w} = \frac{0.4 \times 10^5}{9.81 \times 10^3 \times 13.6}$
$= 0.299$ m of mercury **(Ans.)**

$$\left[\begin{array}{l}\text{where } w = \text{specific weight} \\ \text{For water: } w = 9.81 \text{ kN/m}^3 \\ \text{For mercury}: w = 9.81 \times 13.6 \text{ mN/m}^3\end{array}\right]$$

Q.18.37. An isosceles triangular plate of base 3 m and altitude 3 m is immersed vertical in an oil of specific gravity 0.8. The base of the plate coincides with the free surface of oil.
The total pressure on the plate, and centre of pressure are
(*a*) 25.3 kN,. 1.1 m
(*b*) 35.3 kN, 1.5 m
(*c*) 45.3 kN, 2.5 m
(*d*) none of the above.

Ans. (*b*)

EXPLANATION: Refer to Fig. 18.24

Base of the plate, $b = 3$ m

Height of the plate, $h = 3$ m

$\therefore$ Area, $A = \frac{b \times h}{2} = \frac{3 \times 3}{2} = 4.5 \text{ m}^2$

Specific gravity of oil, $S = 0.8$

The distance of C.G. from the free surface of oil,

$$\bar{x} = \frac{1}{3} h = \frac{1}{3} \times 3$$

$= 1$ m

(*i*) *Total pressure on the plate, P:*

We know that, $P = wA\bar{x}$

$P = (0.8 \times 9.81) \times 4.5 \times 1 = 35.3$ kN **(Ans.)**

(*ii*) *Centre of pressure, h:*

Centre of pressure is given by the relation,

$$\bar{h} = \frac{I_G}{A\bar{x}} + \bar{x} = \frac{(bh^3/36)}{A\bar{x}} + \bar{x}$$

$$= \frac{(3 \times 3^3/36)}{4.5 \times 1} + 1$$

$= 1.5$ m **(Ans.)**

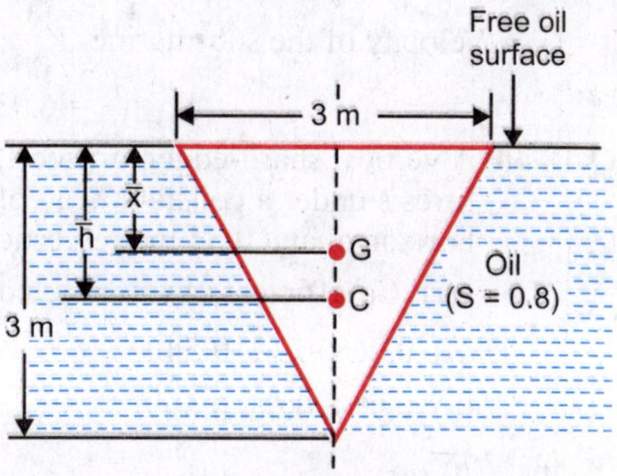

Fig. 18.24

Q.18.38. In a pipe of 90 mm diameter water is flowing with a mean velocity of 2 m/s and a gauge pressure of 350 kN/m^2. The total head, if pipe is 8 metres above the datum line.

(*a*) 23.88 m (*b*) 33.88 m

(*c*) 43.88 m (*d*) 53.88 m

Ans. (*c*)

EXPLANATION:

Diameter of the pipe = 90 mm

Pressure, $p = 350$ kN/m^2; velocity of water, $V = 2$ m/s

Datum head, $z = 8$ m; Specific weight of water, $w = 9.81$ N/m^3

Total head of water, *H*: Using the relation,

$$H = z + \frac{V^2}{2g} + \frac{p}{w}, \quad \text{neglecting friction}$$

$$H = 8 + \frac{2^2}{2 \times 9.81} + \frac{350}{9.81}$$

$= 43.88$ m **(Ans.)**

Q.18.39. A sub-marine fitted with a pitot tube moves horizontally in sea. Its axis is 12 m below the surface of water. The pitot tube fixed in front of the sub-marine and along its axis is connected to the two limbs of a U-tube containing mercury, the reading or which is found to be 200 mm. The speed of the sub-marine is

(Take the specific-gravity of sea water = 1.025 times fresh water.)

(*a*) 24.9 km/h (*b*) 34.9 km/h

(*c*) 44.9 km/h (*d*) none of the above.

Ans. (*a*)

EXPLANATION:

Reading of the manometer, $y = 200$ mm $= 0.2$ m of mercury

Sp. gravity of mercury, $S_h = 13.6$; Sp. gravity of sea water, $S_l = 1.025$

$$h = y\left(\frac{S_h}{S_l} - 1\right) = 0.2\left(\frac{13.6}{1.025} - 1\right) = 2.45 \text{ m}$$

Velocity of the sub-marine, $V = \sqrt{2gh} = \sqrt{2 \times 9.81 \times 2.45}$

$= 6.93$ m/s or 24.9 km/h **(Ans.)**

Q.18.40. A vertical sharp-edged orifice 120 mm in diameter is discharging water at the rate of 98.2 litres/s under a constant head of 10 metres. A point, on the jet has co-ordinate 4.5 metres horizontal and 0.54 metre vertical. For the orifice.

(*i*) Co-efficient of velocity, co-efficient of discharge, and co-efficient of contraction are:

(*a*) 0.868, 0.52, 0.54 (*b*) 0.968, 0.62, 0.64

(*c*) 0.989, 0.66, 0.69 (*d*) none of the above.

Ans. (*b*)

EXPLANATION:

Diameter of orifice, $d = 120$ mm $= 0.12$ m

Area of orifice, $a = \frac{\pi}{4} \times 0.12^2 = 0.01131\text{ m}^2$

Discharge, $Q = 98.2$ litres/s

$= \frac{98.2}{1000} = 0.0982\text{ m}^3/\text{s}$

Head, $H = 10$ m

Horizontal distance of a point on the jet from vena-contracta

$x = 4.5$ m

Vertical distance, $y = 0.54$ m

Now, theoretical velocity, $V_{th} = \sqrt{2gh}$

$= \sqrt{2 \times 9.81 \times 10} = 14$ m/s

Theoretical discharge, Q_{th} = Area of orifice (a) × V_{th}

$= 0.01131 \times 14 = 0.1583\text{ m}^3/\text{s}$

(*i*) *Co-efficient of velocity, C_v:*

$$C_v = \frac{x}{\sqrt{4yH}} = \frac{4.5}{\sqrt{4 \times 0.54 \times 10}} = 0.068 \textbf{ (Ans.)}$$

(*ii*) *Co-efficient of discharge, C_d:*

$$C_d = \frac{\text{Actual discharge}}{\text{Theoretical discharge}}$$

$$= \frac{0.0982}{0.1583} = 0.62 \textbf{ (Ans.)}$$

(*iii*) *Co-efficient of contraction, C_c:*

$$C_c = \frac{C_d}{C_v} = \frac{0.62}{0.968} = 0.64 \textbf{ (Ans.)}$$

Q.18.41. What is the discharge through a rectangular orifice 3.0 m wide and 2.0 deep fitted to a water tank? The water level in the tank is 4.0 m above the top edge of orifice. Take $C_d = 0.62$

(*a*) 36.76 m^3/s (*b*) 46.76 m^3/s

(*c*) 56.76 m^3/s (*d*) none of the above

Ans. (*a*)

EXPLANATION:

Width of the orifice, $b = 3.0$ m

Depth of the orifice = 2.0 m

Height of water above the top of the orifice, $H_1 = 4.0$ m

$\therefore$ Height of the water above the bottom of the orifice, $H_2 = 4 + 2 = 6$ m

Co-efficient of discharge, $C_d = 0.62$

Discharge through the orifice, Q:

Using the relation,

$$Q = \frac{2}{3}C_d b\sqrt{2g}(H_2^{3/2} - H_1^{3/2}) \text{ with usual notations}$$

$$= \frac{2}{3}\times 0.62\times 3.0\times \sqrt{2\times 9.81}(6^{3/2} - 4^{3/2}) = 36.76 \text{ m}^3/\text{s}$$

i.e. $Q = 36.76 \text{ m}^3/\text{s}$ **(Ans.)**

Q.18.42. A shaft of 100 mm diameter rotates at 60 r.p.m. in a 200 mm long bearing. Taking that the two surfaces are uniformly separated by a distance of 0.5 mm and taking linear velocity distribution in the lubricating oil having dynamic viscosity 0.04 paise, find the power absorbed in hearing.

(*a*) 0.0196 W (*b*) 0.0296 W

(*c*) 0.0396 W (*d*) 0.0496 W.

Ans. (*d*)

EXPLANATION:

Diameter of the shaft, $D = 100$ mm = 0.1 m

Speed of the shaft, $N = 60$ r.p.m.

Length of the bearing, $L = 200$ mm = 0.2 m

Thickness of oil film, $t = 0.5$ mm = 0.005 m

Dynamic viscosity, $\mu = 0.04$ poise = 0.04 Ns/m^2

Power absorbed, P:

The torque required to overcome viscous resistance in a journal bearing is given by:

$$T = \frac{\mu\pi^2 D^3 NL}{120t} = \frac{0.004\times\pi^2\times 0.1^3\times 60\times 0.2}{120\times 0.0005} = 0.00798 \text{ N}$$

$$\therefore \quad \text{Power absorbed} = \frac{2\pi NT}{60} = \frac{2\pi\times 60\times 0.00789}{60} = 0.0496 \text{ W } \textbf{(Ans.)}$$

Q.18.43. In a smooth pipe of diameter 0.5 m and length 1000 m water is flowing at the rate of 0.05 m^3/s. Assuming the kinematic viscosity of water as 0.02 stokes, find head lost due to friction

(*a*) 0.1316 m (*b*) 0.1416 m

(*c*) 0.1516 m (*d*) 0.1616 m

Ans. (*a*)

EXPLANATION:

Diameter of smooth pipe, $D = 0.5$ m

$$\therefore \quad \text{Radius} = \frac{0.5}{2} = 0.25 \text{ m}$$

Length of the pipe, $L = 1000$ m

Discharge through the pipe, $Q = 0.05\ m^3/s$

Kinematic viscosity of water, $\nu = 0.02 \times 10^{-4}\ m^2/s$

$$\text{Average velocity, } \bar{u} = \frac{Q}{\text{area}} = \frac{0.05}{\frac{\pi}{4}\times(0.5)^2} = 0.2546 \text{ m/s}$$

$$\therefore \text{ Reynolds number, Re} = \frac{V\times D}{\nu} = \frac{\bar{u}\times D}{\nu} = \frac{0.2546\times 0.5}{0.02\times 10^{-4}} = 6.365 \times 10^4$$

Since $Re > 4000$, the flow is *turbulent*.

$$\text{We know that } \quad f = \frac{0.0791}{(\text{Re})^{1/4}} = \frac{0.0791}{(6.365\times 10^4)^{1/4}} = 0.00498$$

Head lost the to friction, h_f:

$$h_f = \frac{4fLV^2}{D\times 2g} = \frac{4fL\bar{U}^2}{D\times 2g} = \frac{4\times 0.00498\times 1000\times(0.2546)^2}{0.5\times 2\times 9.81}$$

$$= 0.1316 \text{ m } \textbf{(Ans.)}$$

Q.18.44. The diameter of a horizontal pipe which is 300 mm is suddenly enlarged to 600 mm. If the rate of flow of water through this pipe is 0.4 m^3/s determine the loss of head, due to sudden enlargement,

(*a*) 0.618 m (*b*) 0.718 m

(c) 0.1818 (*d*) 0.918 m

Ans. (*d*)

EXPLANATION :

Diameter of the smaller pipe $D_i = 300$ mm = 0.3 m

$$\text{Area, } \quad A_1 = \frac{\pi}{4}\times 0.3^2 = 0.0707 \text{ m}^2$$

Diameter of longer pipe $D_2 = 600$ mm = 0.6 m

$$\text{Area, } \quad A_2 = \frac{\pi}{4}\times 0.6^2 = 0.2828 \text{ m}^2$$

Rate of flow of water, $Q = 0.4\ m^3/s$

$$\text{Now, Velocity } \quad V_1 = \frac{Q}{A_1} = \frac{0.4}{0.0707} = 5.66 \text{ m/s}$$

$$\text{Velocity } \quad V_2 = \frac{Q}{A_2} = \frac{0.4}{0.2828} = 1.414 \text{ m/s}$$

$$\text{Loss of head due to sudden enlargement, } h_c = \frac{(V_1 - V_2)^2}{2g} = \frac{(5.66-1.414)^2}{2\times 9.81} = 0.918 \text{ m } \textbf{(Ans.)}$$

Q.18.45. Air flows over a plate 0.5 m long and 0.6 m wide with a velocity of 4 m/s. The velocity profile is in the form $\frac{u}{U} = \sin\left(\frac{\pi}{2}\frac{y}{8}\right)$

If $\rho = 1.24\ kg/m^3$ and $\nu = 0.15 \times 10^{-4}\ m^2/s$, the boundary layer thickness at the end of the plate is:

(*a*) 5.57 mm (*b*) 6.57 mm

(*c*) 7.57 mm (*d*) 8.57 mm

Ans. (*b*)

EXPLANATION:

Length of plate, $L = 0.5$ m

Width of plate, $B = 0.6$ m

Velocity of air, $U = 4$ m/s

Density of air, $\rho = 1.24$ kg/m^3

Kinematic viscosity of air, $\nu = 0.15 \times 15 \times 10^{-4}$ m^2/s

Velocity profile, $\frac{u}{U} = \sin\left(\frac{\pi}{2}\frac{y}{\delta}\right)$

Boundary layer thickness at the end of the plate, δ:

Reynolds number, $Re_x = \frac{Ux}{\nu} = \frac{4 \times 0.5}{0.15 \times 10^{-4}} = 1.33 \times 10^5$

Since $Re_x < 5 \times 10^5$, therefore, the boundary layer in laminar over the entire length of the plate.

We know, $\delta = \frac{4.795x}{\sqrt{\text{Re}_x}} = \frac{4.795L}{\sqrt{\text{Re}_L}} = \frac{4.795 \times 0.5}{\sqrt{1.33 \times 10^5}} = 0.00657$ m $= 6.57$ mm **(Ans.)**

Q.18.46. A truck having a projected area of 6.5 m^2 travelling at 70 km/h has a total resistance of 2000 N. Of this 20 percent is due to rolling friction and 10 percent due to surface friction. The rest is due to form drag. The co-efficient of form drag (Take $\rho = 1.22$ kg/m^3 for air) is

(*a*) 0.734 (*b*) 0.834

(*c*) 0.934 (*d*) none of the above.

Ans. (*c*)

EXPLANATION:

Projected area, $A = 6.5$ m^2

Speed of the truck, $U = 70 \text{ km/h} = \frac{70 \times 1000}{60 \times 60} = 19.44$ m/s

Density of air, $\rho = 1.22$ kg/m^2

Total resistance = 2000 N

Resistance due to rolling friction = $\frac{20}{100} \times 2000 = 400$ N

Resistance due to surface friction = $\frac{10}{100} \times 2000 = 200$ N

Resistance due to form drag = 2000 – 400 – 200 = 1400 N

Coefficient of form drag, C_D:

Now, Form drag $= C_D \times \frac{\rho U^2}{2} \times A$

$$\therefore \quad 1400 = C_D \times \frac{1.22 \times (19.44)^2}{2} \times 6.5$$

$$\therefore \quad C_D = \frac{1400 \times 2}{1.22 \times (19.44)^2 \times 6.5} = 0.934 \textbf{ (Ans.)}$$

Q.18.47. An aeroplane is flying at an height of 14 km where temperature is – 45° C. The speed of the plane is corresponding to $M = 2$. If $R = 287$ J/kg K and $\gamma = 1.4$, the speed of the plane is:

(*a*) 2179 km/h (*b*) 3010 km/h (*c*) 3250 km/h (*d*) 3379 km/h.

Ans. (*a*)

EXPLANATION:

Temperature (at a height of 14 km)

$$t = -45° \text{ C}$$

$$T = -45 + 273 = 228 \text{ K}$$

Mach number $M = 2$

Gas constant, $R = 287$ J/kg K

$$\gamma = 1.4$$

Speed of the plane, V:

Sonic velocity (*C*) is given by:

$$C = \sqrt{\gamma RT} \quad \text{(assuming the process to be adiabatic)}$$

$$\sqrt{1.4 \times 287 \times 228} = 302.67 \text{ m/s}$$

Also, $M = \dfrac{V}{C}$

or, $M = \dfrac{V}{302.67}$

or, $V = 2 \times 302.67 = 605.34 \text{ m/s} = \dfrac{605.34 \times 3600}{1000} = 2179$ km/h **(Ans.)**

Q.18.48. Find the velocity of a bullet fired in standard air if its mach angle is 40°.

(*a*) 429 m/s (*b*) 529 m/s

(*c*) 629 m/s (*d*) 729 m/s

Ans. (*b*)

EXPLANATION:

Mach angle, $\alpha = 40°$

$$\gamma = 1.4$$

For standard air: $R = 287$ J/kgK, $t = 15°$ C or $T = 15 + 273 = 288$ K

Velocity of the bullet, V:

Sonic velocity, $C = \sqrt{\gamma RT} = \sqrt{1.4 \times 287 \times 288} = 340.2$ m/s

Now, $\sin \alpha = \dfrac{C}{V}$

or, $\sin 40° = \dfrac{340.2}{V}$ or $V = \dfrac{340.2}{\sin 40°} = 529$ m/s **(Ans.)**

Q.18.49. A rectangular channel is to be dug in the rocky portion of a soil. What is the most economical cross-section if it is to convey 12 m^3/s of water with an average velocity of 3 m/s? Take Chezy's constant $C = 50$

(*a*) $b = 1.828$ m, $y = 0.914$ m, $S = \dfrac{1}{190}$

(*b*) $b = 2.828$ m, $y = 1.414$ m, $S = \dfrac{1}{196}$

(*c*) $b = 4.2$ m, $y = 2.1$ m, $S = \dfrac{1}{176}$

(*d*) none of the above

Ans. (*b*)

EXPLANATION:

Discharge, $Q = 12\ m^3/s$

Average velocity, $V = 3$ m/s

Chezy's constant, $C = 50$

The geometric relations for *optimum discharge* through a rectangular channel are:

$$b = 2y \text{ and } R = \frac{y}{2}, \text{ then area } A = b.y = 2y^2$$

Where b, y and R are base width of the channel, depth of flow and hydraulic radius respectively.

Now, $Q = A.V. = 2y^2 \times V$ or $12 = 2y^2 \times 3$ or $y = 1.414$ m

i.e., Flow depth, $y = 1.414$ m

∴ Base width of the channel, $b = 2y = 2 \times 1.414 = 2.828$ m

Hydraulic radius, $R = \frac{y}{2} = \frac{1.414}{2} = 0.707$ m

Also $V = C\sqrt{RS}$ ... Chezy's formula

or, $S = \frac{V^2}{C^2R} = \frac{3^2}{50^2 \times 0.707} = \frac{1}{196}$ (where S = slope bed)

Hence, $b = 2.828$ m, $y = 1.414$ m, $S = \frac{1}{196}$ **(Ans.)**

Q.18.50. A sluice gate discharges water into horizontal rectangular channel with a velocity of 10 m/s and depth of flow of 1 m. What is the depth of flow of water after the jump and consequent loss in total head?

(*a*) 2.2 m, 1.2 m (*b*) 3.2 m, 1.4 m

(*c*) 4.043 m, 1.742 m (*d*) 5.043 m, 2.742 m.

Ans. (*c*)

EXPLANATION:

Velocity of flow before hydraulic jump, $V_1 = 10$ m/s

Depth of flow before hydraulic jump, $y_1 = 1$ m

Depth of flow after the jump, y_2:

Discharge per unit width, $q = V_1 \times y_1 = 10 \times 1 = 10\ m^3/s$ per m

The depth of flow water the jump is given by:

$$y_2 = -\frac{y_1}{2} + \sqrt{\frac{y_1^2}{4} + \frac{2q^2}{gy_1}}$$

or, $$y_2 = -\frac{1}{2} + \sqrt{\frac{1^2}{4} + \frac{2 \times 10^2}{9.81 \times 1}} = 4.042 \text{ m } \textbf{(Ans.)}$$

Loss in total head, E_L:

Loss in total head is given by:

$$E_L = \frac{(y_2 - y_1)^3}{4y_1y_2}$$

or, $$E_L = \frac{(4.043 - 1)^3}{4 \times 1 \times 4.043} = 1.7432 \text{ m } \textbf{(Ans.)}$$

Q.18.51. Flow takes place at Reynolds Number of 1500 in two different pipes with relative roughness of 0.001 and 0.002. The friction factor

(*a*) will be higher in the case of pipe with relative roughness of 0.001
(*b*) will be higher in the case of pipe having relative roughness of 0.002
(*c*) will be the same in both the pipes
(*d*) in the two pipes cannot be compared on the basis of data given.

Ans. (*c*)

EXPLANATION:

The friction factor will be the same for both the pipes because for *Re* < 1500, *i.e.*, laminar flow, it is independent of relative roughness of pope. Thus (*c*) is the correct choice.

Q.18.52. Decrease in temperature, in general results in

(*a*) an increase in viscosities of both gases and liquids
(*b*) a decrease in the viscosities of both liquids and gases
(*c*) an increase in the viscosity of liquids and a decrease in that of gases
(*d*) a decrease in the viscosity of liquids and an increase in that of gases.

Ans. (*c*)

EXPLANATION:

Viscosity for water, $\mu_1 = [0.001793/(1 + 0.03368\,t + 0.000221\,t^2)$, and
Viscosity for air, $\mu_1 = [0.000001702\,(1 + 0.00329\,t + 0.000007\,t^2]$
From above it is evident that with decrease in temperature, the viscosity of water increases while that of air decreases. Thus, decrease in temperature, in general, results in an increase in the viscosity of liquids and a decrease in that of gases.
Thus the correct choice is (*c*).

Q.18.53. The energy loss between sections (1) and (2) of the pipe shown in Fig. 18.25 is

(*a*) 1.276 kg-m
(*b*) 1.00 kg-m
(*c*) 0.725 kg-m
(*d*) 0.15 kg-m.

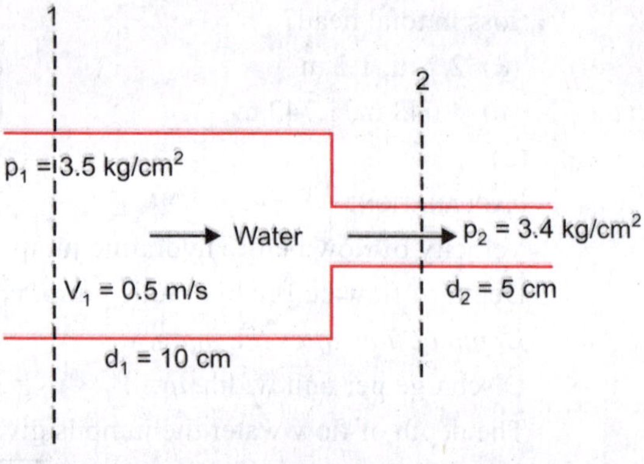

Fig. 18.25

Ans. (*c*)

EXPLANATION:

$$A_1V_1 = A_2V_2 \text{ or } \frac{\pi}{4}\times 0.1^2 \times 0.6 = \frac{\pi}{4}\times 0.05^2 \times V_2$$

or, $V_2 = 2.4$ m/s

Invoking Bernoulli's equation at sections 1 and 2, we have:

$$\frac{p_1}{w} + \frac{V_1^2}{2g} + z_1 = \frac{p_2}{w} + \frac{V_2^2}{2g} + z_2 + h_c \text{ (energy loss)}$$

$$h_c = \left(\frac{p_1 - p_2}{w}\right) + \left(\frac{V_1^2 - V_2^2}{2g}\right) \quad (z_1 = z_2\text{, the pipe being horizontal})$$

$$= \frac{(3.5 - 3.4)\times 10^4}{1000} + \frac{0.6^2 - 2.4^2}{2\times 9.81} = 1.0 - 0.275 = 0.725 \text{ kg m } \textbf{(Ans.)}$$

Q.18.54. The reading of the pressure gauge fitted on a vessel is 25 bar. The atmospheric pressure is 1.03 bar and the value of g is 9.81 m/s^2. The absolute pressure in the vessel is

(*a*) 23.97 bar (*b*) 25.00 bar (*c*) 26.03 bar (*d*) 34.84 bar

Ans. (*c*)

EXPLANATION:

$$p_{abs} = p_{gauge} + p_{atm.} = 25 + 1.03 = 26.03 \text{ bar } \textbf{(Ans.)}$$

Thus (*c*) is the correct choice.

Q.18.55. In a pipe flow, the head lost due to friction is 6 m. If the power transmitted through the pipe has to be the maximum, then the total head at the inlet of the pipe will have to be maintained at

(*a*) 36 m (*b*) 30 m (*c*) 24 m (*d*) 18 m

Ans. (*d*)

EXPLANATION:

Head lost due to friction, $h_f = 6$ m

For maximum power transmission, the supply head (H) should be equal to $3h_f$

$$\therefore \quad H = 3 \times 6 = 18 \text{ m } \textbf{(Ans.)}$$

Thus (*d*) is the correct choice.

Q.18.56. The speed of the air emerging from the blades of a running table fan is intended to be measured as a function of time. The point of measurement is very close to the blade and the time period of the speed fluctuation is four times the time taken by the blade to complete one revolution. The appropriate method of measurement would involve the use of

(*a*) a Pitot tube (*b*) a hot wire anemometer

(*c*) high speed photography (*d*) a Schlieren system.

Ans. (*d*)

EXPLANATION:

(*d*) is the correct choice since other instruments (choices) are used under the following conditions:

Pitot tube ..... for measuring speed in closed duct/pipe

Hot wire anemometer ... for measuring speed over a period of time (does not respond to fact changes as mentioned in the question.)

High speed photography .... for measuring blade speed (not or air)

Q.18.57. A fluid jet is discharging from a 100 mm nozzle and the vena-contracta formed has a diameter of 90 mm. If the coefficient of velocity is 0.95, then the coefficient of discharge for a nozzle is

(*a*) 0.855 (*b*) 0.81 (*c*) 0.9025 (*d*) 0.7695.

Ans. (*d*)

EXPLANATION:

Co-efficient of contraction, $C_c = \dfrac{A_c}{A} = \dfrac{\frac{\pi}{4} \times 90^2}{\frac{\pi}{4} \times 100^2} = 0.8$, co-efficient of velocity, $C_v = 0.95$.

$\therefore$ Co-efficient of discharge, $C_d = C_c \times C_v = 0.81 \times 0.95 = 0.7695$ **(Ans.)**

Q.18.58. A circular disc of radius 'r' is submerged vertically in a static fluid upto a depth 'h' from the free surface. If $h > r$, then the position of centre pressure will

(*a*) be directly proportional to h (*b*) be inversely proportional to h

(*c*) be directly proportional to r (*d*) not be a function of h or r.

Ans. (*d*)

EXPLANATION:

(*d*) is the correct choice, since centre of pressure $\left(\frac{I_G}{A\bar{x}} + \bar{x}\right)$ is below c.g., and as such it is not a function of *h* or *r* alone.

Q.18.59. If a cylindrical wooden pole, 20 cm in diameter, and 1 m in height is placed in a pool of water in a vertical position (the specific gravity of wood is 0.6), then it will

(*a*) float in stable equilibrium
(*b*) float in unstable equilibrium
(*c*) float in neutral equilibrium
(*d*) start moving horizontally.

Ans. (*b*)

EXPLANATION:

Under the given conditions the pole will float with 0.6 m inside water and 0.4 m above water surface; metacentre is below *c.g.* and as such the pole will float in unstable equilibrium. Thus (*b*) is the correct choice. **(Ans.)**

Q.18.60. Drag on cylinders and spheres decreases when the Reynolds number is in the region of 2×10^5 since

(*a*) flow separation occurs due to transition to turbulence
(*b*) flow separation is delayed due to onset of turbulence
(*c*) flow separation is advanced due to transition to turbulence
(*d*) flow reattachment occurs.

Ans. (*d*)

EXPLANATION:

When the Reynolds number is in the region of 2×10^5 the boundary layer on the cylinder and spheres starts becoming unstable and thus boundary layer is said to reattach; as a result of flow reattachment, there is a recovery of pressure over the back side and consequently there is a reduction in drag force.

Thus (*d*) is the correct choice.

Q.18.61. In turbomachinery, the relevant parameters are volume flow rate, density viscosity, bulk modulus, pressure difference, power consumption, rotational speed and a characteristic dimension. According to Buckingham pi (π) theorem, the number of independent non-dimensional groups for this case is

(*a*) 3 (*b*) 4 (*c*) 5 (*d*) 6.

Ans. (*c*)

EXPLANATION:

The number of physical quantities, in the present case, $n = 8$

Number of fundamental dimensions, $m = 3$

$\therefore$ Number of independent non-dimensional groups = $n - m = 8 - 3 = 5$ **(Ans.)**

Q.18.62. An open tank contains water to a depth of 2 m and oil over it to a depth of 1 m. If the specific gravity of oil 0.8, then the pressure intensity at the interface of the two fluid layers will be

(*a*) 7848 N/m^2 (*b*) 8720 N/m^2 (*c*) 9347 N/m^2 (*d*) 9750 N/m^2

Ans. (*a*)

EXPLANATION:

Pressure intensity at the interface of the two liquids

$$= \rho g h = 1000 \times 9.81 \times (1 \times 0.8) = 7848 \text{ N/m}^2$$ **(Ans.)**

Q.18.63. An inclined manometer, inclined at 30° to the horizontal, measures the pressure differential between two locations of a pipe carrying water. If the manometric liquid is mercury (specific gravity 13.6) and the manometer showed a level difference of 20 cm, then the pressure head difference of water between the two tapping will be

(*a*) 1.26 m (*b*) 1.36 m (*c*) 2.52 m (*d*) 2.72 m

Ans. (*b*)

EXPLANATION:

Vertical level of mercry = 20 × sin 30° 10 cm or 0.1 m

Pressure head difference of water between the two tapping = 0.1 × 13.6 = 1.36 m. Thus (*b*) is the correct choice.

Q.18.64. The pressure gauge reading in metre of water column shown in Fig. 18.26 will be

(*a*) 3.20 m (*b*) 2.72 m

(c) 2.52 m (*d*) 1.52 m.

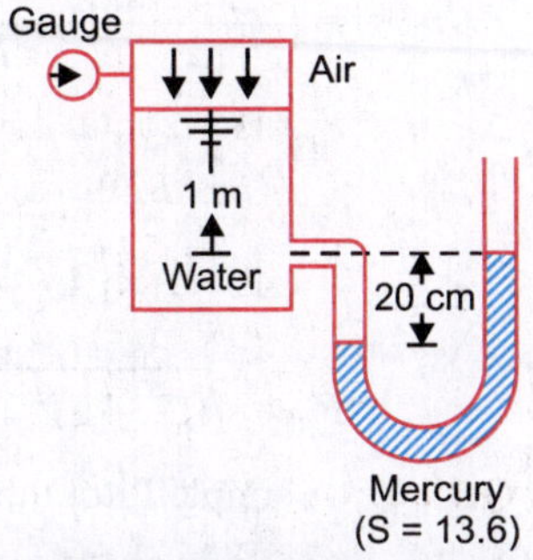

Fig. 18.26

Ans. (*d*)

EXPLANATION:

The pressure gauge reading (p) in *metres of water* may be calculated as follows:

$$p+1+\frac{20}{100} = \frac{20}{100}\times 13.6$$

or, $$p + 1.2 = 2.72$$

or, $$p = 1.52 \text{ m } \textbf{(Ans.)}$$

Q.18.65. Two pipe lines at different pressures, p_A and p_B, each carrying the same liquid of specific gravity S_1, are connected to a U-tube with a liquid of specific gravity S_2 resulting in the level differences h_1, h_2 and h_3 as shown in the Fig. 18.27. The difference in pressure head between points A and B in terms of head of water is

(*a*) $h_1S_2 + h_2S_1 + h_3S_1$

(*b*) $h_1S_1 + h_2S_2 - h_3S_1$

(*c*) $h_1S_1 - h_2S_2 - h_3S_1$

(*d*) $h_1S_1 + h_2S_2 + h_3S_1$

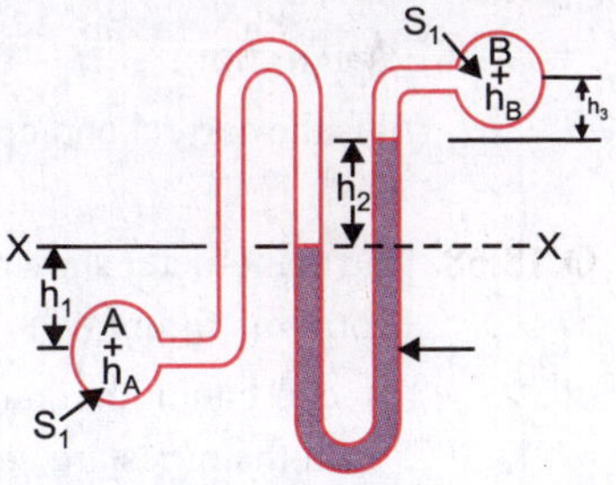

Fig. 18.27

Ans. (*d*)

EXPLANATION: Refer to Fig. 19

With reference to datum XX :

New pressure on left side = $h_A - h_1S_1$ (the pressure due to × inverted portion being equal)

Net pressure on right side = $h_B + h_3S_1 + h_2 S_2$

$$\therefore \quad h_A - h_1 S_1 = h_B + h_3S_1 + h_2S_2$$

or $$h_A - h_B = h_1S_1 + h_2S_2 + h_3S_1$$

Thus (*d*) is the correct choice.

Q.18.66. In the situation shown in the Fig. 18.28, the length BC is 3 m and M is the mid-point of BC. The hydrostatic force on BC measured per unit width (width being perpendicular to the plane of the paper) with 'g' being the acceleration due to gravity, will be

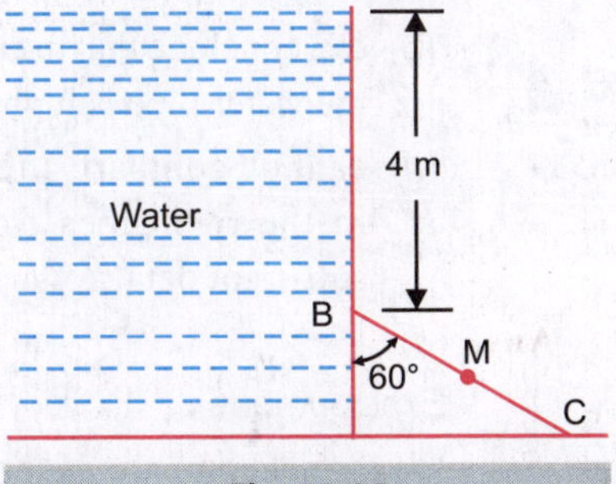

Fig. 18.28

(*a*) 16500 g N/m passing through *M*

(*b*) 16500 g N/m passing through a point between *M* and *C*

(*c*) 14250 g N/m passing through *M*

(*d*) 14250 g N/m passing through a point between *M* and *C*.

Ans. (*d*)

EXPLANATION: Refer to Fig. 18.29.

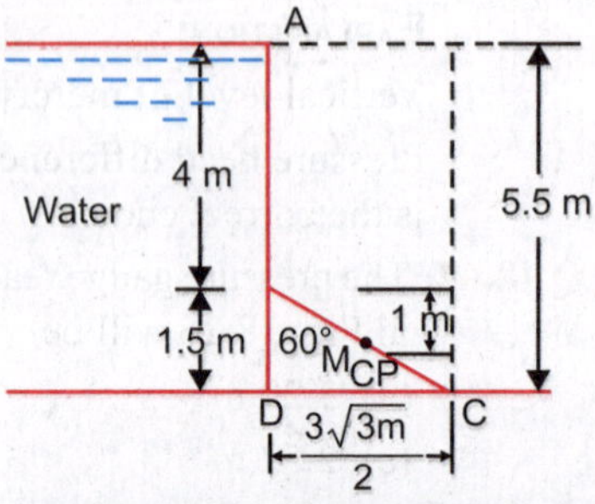

Fig. 18.29

Hydrostatic force on *BC*, $F_{BC} = \sqrt{F_V^2 + F_H^2}$

where, F_v = Vertical component = weight over area BC

$$= \left(\frac{5.5 + 4.0}{2}\right) \times \frac{3\sqrt{3}}{2} \times 1 \times 1000 \times g = 12340 \text{ gN/m}$$

F_H=Horizontal component = projected area of *BC*

(*i.e.*, *BD*) × depth upto centre of *BD* × (1000 × *g*)

$$= (.15 \times 1) \times \left(4 + \frac{1.5}{2}\right) \times (1000 \times g) = 7125 \text{ g N/m}$$

$\therefore$ $F_{BC} = \sqrt{(1234\,g)^2 + (7125\,g)^2}$ ≈ 14250 g N/m between *M* and *C* **(Ans.)**

Q.18.67. A simple Pitot tube can be used to measure which of the following quantities ?

1. Static head
2. Datum head
3. Dynamic head
4. Friction head
5. Total head

Select the correct answer using the codes given below

Codes:

(*a*) 1, 2 and 4 (*b*) 1, 3 and 5 (*c*) 2, 3 and 4 (*d*) 2, 3 and 5.

Ans. (*b*)

EXPLANATION:

(*b*) is the correct choice since a simple pitot tube can measure static, dynamic and total heads. **(Ans.)**

Q.18.68. The manometer shown in Fig. 18.30 connects two pipes, carrying oil and water respectively. From this figure one

(*a*) can conclude that the pressures in the pipes are equal

(*b*) can conclude that the pressure in the oil pipe is higher

(*c*) can conclude that the pressure in the water pipe is higher

(*d*) cannot compare the pressure in the two pipes for want of sufficient data

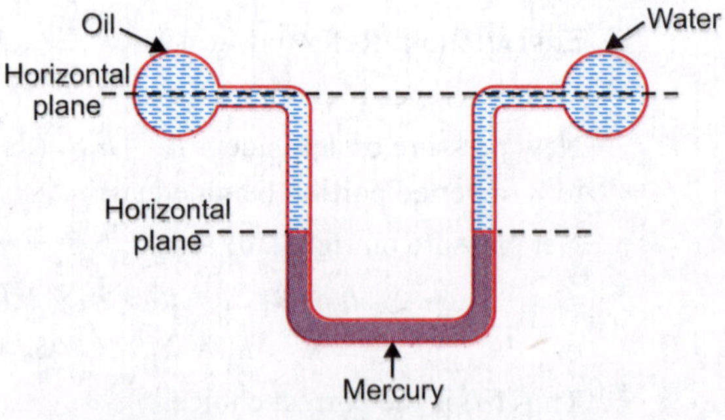

Fig. 18.30

Ans. (*d*)

EXPLANATION:

We cannot compare the pressure in the two pipes since the specific gravity of the fluids is not given. **(Ans.)**

Q.18.69. At the point of boundary layer separation

(*a*) shear stress is maximum (*b*) shear stress is zero

(*b*) velocity is negative (*d*) density variation is maximum.

Ans. (*b*)

EXPLANATION:

At the verge of separation, $\left(\frac{\partial u}{\partial y}\right)_{y=0}$ is zero,

$\therefore$ Shear stress, $\tau = \mu\left(\frac{\partial u}{\partial y}\right)_{y=0}$ is also zero. **(Ans.)**

Q.18.70. The turbulent boundary-layer thickness varies as

(*a*) $x^{4/5}$ (*b*) $x^{1/2}$

(*c*) $x^{1/5}$ (*d*) $x^{1/7}$.

Ans. (*a*)

EXPLANATION:

Turbulent boundary layer thickness varies as $\frac{\delta}{x} = \frac{0.477}{x^{0.2}}$ or $\delta \alpha x^{4/5}$ **(Ans.)**

Q.18.71. A tank has in its side a very small horizontal cylinder fitted with a frictionless piston. The head of liquid above the piston is '*h*' and the piston area '*a*', the liquid having a specific weight γ. What is the force that must be exerted on the piston to hold it in position against the hydrostatic pressure?

(*a*) $2\gamma ha$ (*b*) γha

(*c*) $\frac{2\gamma ha}{3}$ (*d*) $\frac{\gamma ha}{2}$.

Ans. (*b*)

EXPLANATION:

The pressure of liquid above the piston = γh.

$\therefore$ Force exerted on the piston to hold it in position

$= \gamma h \times$ piston area $(a) = \gamma ha$ **(Ans.)**

Q.18.72. A jet of oil with relative density 0.7 strikes normally a plate with a velocity of 10 m/s. The jet has an area of 0.03 cm^2. The force exerted on the plate by the jet is

(*a*) 210 N (*b*) 2.1 kN

(*c*) 20.6 kN (*d*) 20.6 N.

Ans. (*b*)

EXPLANATION:

Force exerted by a jet of oil striking normally on a stationary plate,

$$F = \rho a V^2 = (0.7 \times 10^3) \times 0.03 \times 10^2 = 2100 \text{ N or } 2.1 \text{ kN } \textbf{(Ans.)}$$

Q.18.73. The parameters which determine the friction for turbulent flow in a rough pipe are:

(*a*) Froude number and relative roughness

(*b*) Froude number and Mach number

(*c*) Reynolds number and relative roughness

(*d*) Mach number and relative rouchness.

Ans. (*c*)

EXPLANATION:

Whereas in a 'laminar flow' friction factor depends only on Reynolds number (*Re*), but in case of '*turbulent flow*', the friction factor depends *both on Re and roughness factor.* **(Ans.)**

Q.18.74. An oil of kinematic viscosity 0.5 stoke is flowing through a pipe of 5 cm diameter. The flow through the pipe becomes critical at velocity of

(*a*) 0.2 m/s (*b*) 2 m/s

(*c*) 2.5 m/s (*d*) 4 m/s.

Ans. (*b*)

EXPLANATION:

Given: $\gamma = 0.5$ stoke $= 0.5 \times 10^{-4}$; $D = 5$ cm $= 0.05$ m

$$\text{Critical value of } (Re)_{cr} = 2000 = \frac{VD}{\gamma} = \frac{V \times 0.05}{0.5 \times 10^{-4}}$$

$$\therefore \quad V = \frac{2000 \times (0.5 \times 10^{-4})}{0.05} = 2 \text{ m/s } \textbf{(Ans.)}$$

Q.18.75. The head loss in a sudden expansion from 6 cm diameter pipe to 12 cm diameter pipe in terms of velocity V_1 in the smaller diameter pipe is

(*a*) $\frac{3}{16} \cdot \frac{V_1^2}{2g}$ (*b*) $\frac{5}{16} \cdot \frac{V_1^2}{2g}$

(*c*) $\frac{7}{16} \cdot \frac{V_1^2}{2g}$ (*d*) $\frac{9}{16} \cdot \frac{V_1^2}{2g}$

Ans. (*d*)

EXPLANATION:

Refer to Fig. 18.31.

Losses due to sudden enlargement,

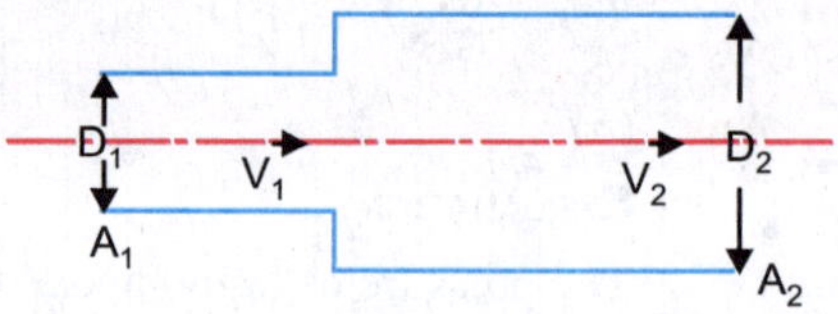

Fig. 18.31

$$h_e = \frac{(V_1 - V_2)^2}{2g}$$

Also, $A_1 V_1 = A_2 V_2$ ...Continuity equation

$$\text{or,} \quad V_2 = \frac{A_1 V_1}{A_2} = \frac{\frac{\pi}{4} \times 0.06^2}{\frac{\pi}{4} \times 0.12^2} \times V_1 = \frac{V_1}{4}$$

$$\therefore \quad h_e = \frac{1}{2g}\left(V_1 - \frac{V_1}{4}\right)^2 = \frac{9}{16} \frac{V_1^2}{2g} \textbf{ (Ans.)}$$

Q.18.76. Air (density 1.2 kg/m^3 and kinematic viscosity 15 centistokes) flows over a flat plate at zero angle of incidence, at a velocity of 20 m/s. If Reynolds number at transition is taken as 2.5×10^5, maximum distance from leading edge up to which the boundary layer remains laminar is

(*a*) 375 mm (*b*) 93.75 mm

(*c*) 187.5 mm (*d*) 250 mm

Ans. (*c*)

EXPLANATION:

Given: $\rho = 1.2$ kg/m^3; $\gamma = 15 \times 10^{-6}$ m^2/s; $U_\infty = 20$ m/s

As transition taken place at $(Re)_{cr} = 2.5 \times 10^5$, therefore,

$$2.5 \times 10^5 = \frac{20 \times x}{15 \times 10^{-6}}$$ (where x is the maximum distance from leading edge upto which boundary layer remains laminar)

or, $$x = \frac{2.5 \times 10^5 \times 15 \times 10^{-6}}{20} = 0.1875 \text{ m} \quad \text{or } 187.5 \text{ mm}$$ **(Ans.)**

Q.18.77. The discharge, over a rectangular weir of width 100 m when the head of water over the weir is 1.5 m and the head due to velocity of approach is 0.02 m, is given by

(*a*) 842.5 m^3/s (*b*) 653.4 m^3/s

(*c*) 814.5 m^3/s (*d*) 552.5 m^3/s.

Ans. (*d*)

EXPLANATION:

The discharge over a rectangular weir is given by:

$$Q = \frac{2}{3} C_d \,.\, L \,.\, \sqrt{2g} \left[(H + H_a)^{3/2} - (H_a)^{3/2}\right]$$ ...with velocity of approach

$$= \frac{2}{3} \times 1 \times 100 \times \sqrt{2 \times 9.81} \left[(1.5 + 0.02)^{3/2} - (0.02)^{3/2}\right]$$

$$= 295.3 \times 1.871 = 552.5$$ **(Ans.)**

Q.18.78. The velocity potential function is given by an expression $\phi = -\frac{xy^3}{3} - x^2 + \frac{x^3 y}{3} + y^2$. The velocity component in x direction is

(*a*) $xy^2 - \frac{x^3}{3} - 2y$ (*b*) $\frac{y^3}{3} + 2x - x^2 y$

(*c*) $3x^2 y + 2x - xy^2$ (*d*) $x^3 y^2 + 2x^2 - y^2 x$.

Ans. (*b*)

EXPLANATION:

Velocity potential function $\phi = -\frac{xy^3}{3} - x^2 + \frac{x^3 y}{3} + y^2$ ...Given

Velocity component in x direction,

$$u = -\frac{\partial \phi}{\partial x} = -\frac{\partial}{\partial x}\left[-\frac{xy^3}{3} - x^2 + \frac{x^3 y}{3} + y^2\right]$$

$$= \frac{y^3}{3} + 2x - x^2 y$$ **(Ans.)**

Q.18.79. The stream function in a two-dimensional flow field is given by $\psi = x^2 - y^2$. Then the magnitude of velocity at point (1, 1) is

(*a*) 2 (*b*) $2\sqrt{2}$

(*c*) 4 (*d*) 8.

Ans. (*b*)

EXPLANATION:

Stream function, $\psi = x^2 - y^2$ ...Given

$$u = \frac{\partial \psi}{\partial x} = \frac{\partial}{\partial y}(x^2 - y^2) = -2y$$

$$v = -\frac{\partial \psi}{\partial x} = -\frac{\partial}{\partial x}(x^2 - y^2) = -2x$$

Resultant velocity, $V = \sqrt{u^2 + v^2} = \sqrt{(-2y)^2 + (-2x)^2} = 2\sqrt{(x^2 + y^2)}$

Velocity at (1, 1) = $2\sqrt{1^2 + 1^2} = 2\sqrt{2}$ **(Ans.)**

Q.18.80. Consider the following statements:

1. Increasing the metacentric height of a ship causes increase in the period of rolling.
2. The frequency of pitching can be reduced by adding more loads along the length of a ship below its centre of gravity.
3. A ship has different metacentres in rolling and pitching.
4. Stability can be improved by increasing the width and reducing the draft.

Which of these statements are correct?

(*a*) 1, 2, 3 and 4 (*b*) 1, 2 and 4 only (*c*) 1, 2 and 3 only (*d*) 2, 3 and 4 only

Ans. (*d*)

EXPLANATION:

Time period of rolling (*i.e.*, one complete oscillation) '*T*' is given by:

$$T = 2\pi\sqrt{\frac{k^2}{GM.g}} \quad \text{or} \quad 7\alpha\frac{1}{\sqrt{GM}} \qquad ...(i)$$

where, k = radius of gyration about G;

GM = metacentric height of the body.

From eqn. (*i*) it is evident that period of rolling '*decreases*' with the *increase* in the metacentric height. **(Ans.)**

Q.18.81. Consider the following statements related to the stability of floating bodies:

1. The metacentre should be above the centre of gravity of the floating body for stable equilibrium during small oscillations.
2. For a floating body, stability is not determined simply by the relative positions of centre of gravity and centre buoyancy.
3. The position of metacentre of a floating body is fixed irrespective of the axis of oscillations.
4. Large value of metacentric height reduces the period of roll of the vessel.

Which of these statements are correct?

(*a*) 1 and 3 only (*b*) 2 and 4 only

(*c*) 1, 2 and 4 only (*d*) 1, 2, 3 and 4

Ans. (*c*)

EXPLANATION:

The position of metacentre of a floating body is *not* fixed; it changes with the change of axis of oscillation. **(Ans.)**

Q.18.82. A circular area of 1.2 m diameter is immersed vertically in a liquid of unit weight 800 N/m^3 with its top edge just on the liquid surface. The depth of centre of pressure on one side, measured below the liquid surface, is

(*a*) 0.80 m (*b*) 0.75 m

(*c*) 0.60 m (*d*) 0.64 m

Ans. (*b*)

EXPLANATION:

Refer to Fig. 18.32.

The position of the centre of pressure,

$$\bar{h} = \bar{x} + \frac{I_G}{A\bar{x}}$$

$$= \frac{d}{2} + \frac{\frac{\pi}{64} \times d^4}{\frac{\pi}{4} \times d^2 \times \frac{d}{2}} = \frac{d}{2} + \frac{d}{8} = \frac{5d}{8}$$

$$= \frac{5}{8} \times 1.2 = 0.75 \text{ (Ans.)}$$

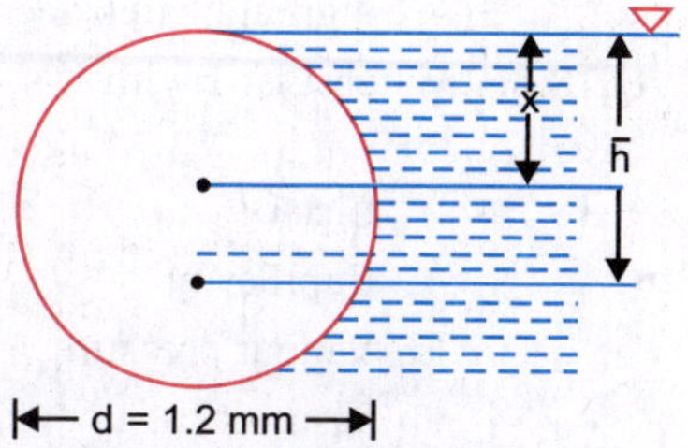

Fig. 18.32

Q.18.83. If angle of contact of a drop of liquid is acute then

(*a*) adhesion is more than cohesion

(*b*) cohesion is more than adhesion

(*c*) cohesion is equal to adhesion

(*d*) adhesion and cohesion have no bearing with angle of contact.

Ans. (*a*)

EXPLANATION:

When *adhesion* > *cohesion* (missicive-an concave) the angle of contact is *acute.*

– For *wetting liquid* (water): $\theta < \frac{\pi}{2}$.

For water: θ = 0 when pure water is the contact with glass. But θ becomes as high as 25° when water is slightly contaminated.

– For *non-wetting liquid* (mercury): $\theta > \frac{\pi}{2}$.

(For mercury : θ varies between 130° to 150°) **(Ans.)**

Q.18.84. Pascal's law states that pressure at a point is equal to all directions in a

(*a*) Liquid at rest (*b*) Fluid at rest

(*c*) Laminar flow (*d*) Turbulent flow.

Ans. (*b*)

EXPLANATION:

The Pascal's law states as follows:

"The intensity of pressure at any point in a fluid at rest is the same in all directions." **(Ans.)**

Q.18.85. With increase in pressure the bulk modulus of elasticity

(*a*) Decreases (*b*) Increases

(*c*) Remains constant (*d*) None of the above.

Ans. (*b*)

EXPLANATION:

Bulk modulus, $K = \dfrac{dp \text{ (increase of pressure)}}{-dV/V \text{ (Volumetric strain)}}$

i.e., $K = \dfrac{dp}{-dV/V}$ *i.e., K increases* with *increase* in pressure.

(–ve sign indicates decrease in volume with increase in pressure) **(Ans.)**

Q.18.86. Match List-I with List-II and select the correct answer using the code as given below the Lists:

List-I	List-II
A. Capillarity	1. Cavitation
B. Vapour pressure	2. Density of water
C. Viscosity	3. Shear forces
D. Specific gravity	4. Surface tension

Codes:

	A	B	C	D
(*a*)	2	3	1	4
(*b*)	4	3	1	2
(*c*)	2	1	3	4
(*d*)	4	1	3	2.

Ans. (*d*)

EXPLANATION:

Capillarity → 4; Vapour pressure → 1; Viscosity → 3; Specific gravity → 2,

i.e., d (4, 1, 3, 2) **(Ans.)**

Q.18.87. The stability of a floating body is obtained when its

(*a*) Centre of gravity is below the centre of buoyancy

(*b*) Metacentric height is negative

(*c*) Metacentric height is positive

(*d*) Metacentric height is zero.

Ans. (*c*)

EXPLANATION:

The distance between the centre of gravity (*G*) of a floating body and the metacentre (*M*) *i.e.,* distance *GM* is called metacentric height *GM*.

For *stable equilibrium*, the position of *M* remains higher than G, *i.e., GM* is +ve. **(Ans.)**

Q.18.88. The stream function of a two-dimensional flow is $\psi = 2xy$. The flow is

(*a*) Rotational (*b*) Irrotational

(*c*) Vortex flow (*d*) Unsteady pulsating flow.

Ans. (*b*)

EXPLANATION:

$$\psi = 2xy \quad \text{...(Given)}$$

Now, $$\frac{\partial \psi}{\partial x} = 2y, \quad \frac{\partial \psi}{\partial y} = -2x$$

and, $$\frac{\partial^2 \psi}{\partial x} = 0 \quad \frac{\partial^2 \psi}{\partial y} = 0 \quad \frac{\partial^2 \psi}{\partial x^2} + \frac{\partial^2 \psi}{\partial y^2} = 0$$

Hence, $\psi = 2xy$ represents a possible *irrotational* flow **(Ans.)**

Q.18.89. Consider the following statements pertaining to kinematics and dynamics of fluid flow:

1. For $\psi = x^2 - y^2$, velocity at (1, 1) is $2\sqrt{2}$.
2. For all types of flow, stream and potential functions exist.
3. Bernoulli's equation is not valid for real fluid flow.

Which of these statements are correct?

(*a*) 1, 2 and 3 (*b*) 1 and 2 only

(*c*) 2 and 3 only (*d*) 1 and 3 only

Ans. (*d*)

EXPLANATION:

For all types of flow, stream and potential functions *do not exist*. 'Potential function' (ϕ) exists only for *irrotational flow* while 'stream function (ψ)' applies both to rotational or irrotational flows (which are steady and incompressible). **(Ans.)**

Q.18.90. The flow past the cylinder with the vortex motion causes a net transverse motion. This transverse force is known as

(*a*) Magnus effect

(*b*) Robin effect

(*c*) D'Alembert's Pradox

(*d*) Rankine doublet.

Ans. (*a*)

EXPLANATION:

The generation of lift & transverse force by spinning cylinder in a fluid stream is called 'Magnus effect'. **(Ans.)**

Q.18.91. The conditions in which Bernoulli's equation applies are

1. The flow must be inviscid.
2. The fluid may be compressible or incompressible.
3. The flow must be steady.
4. There should be only one stream line in the flow.

(*a*) 1, 2, 3 and 4 (*b*) 1, 2 and 3 only

(*c*) 1, 3 and 4 only (*d*) 2, 3 and 4 only

Ans. (*c*)

EXPLANATION:

The statement '2' is wrong because as per assumption of Bernoulli's equation the fluid is ideal and incompressible. **(Ans.)**

Q.18.92. Which one of the following instruments is a rate meter?

(*a*) Disk meter (*b*) hot wire anemometer

(*c*) Pitot tube (*d*) Venturimeter.

Ans. (*d*)

EXPLANATION:

Venturimeter is known as a 'rate meter'. It is an instrument used to measure the rate of discharge in a pipeline and is often fixed permanently at different sections of the pipeline to know the discharge there. **(Ans.)**

Q.18.93. For laminar flow through a pipe, the discharge varies

(*a*) Linearly as the diameter (*b*) Inversely as the square of diameter

(*c*) As the inverse of viscosity (*d*) Inversely as the pressure gradient.

Ans. (*c*)

EXPLANATION:

For laminar flow through pipe, $Q \propto \frac{1}{\mu}$ *i.e.,* discharge varies inversely as the *inverse* of viscosity. **(Ans.)**

Q.18.94. A thin plate has been placed parallel to flow direction. The relative magnitude of friction and pressure drags will be

(*a*) Negligible friction as well as pressure drag

(*b*) Negligible pressure drag and maximum friction drag

(*c*) Maximum pressure drag and negligible friction drag

(*d*) Pressure drag equals to friction drag.

Ans. (*b*)

EXPLANATION:

When a thin plate is placed parallel to the flow direction, the relative magnitude of 'pressure drag' will be *negligible* and that of friction drag will be *maximum.* **(Ans.)**

Q.18.95. At what depth below the free surface of oil having a density of 784 kg/m^3 will the pressure be very nearly equal to 1 bar?

(*a*) 10 metres (*b*) 14 metres

(*c*) 13 metres (*d*) 7.84 metres.

Ans. (*c*)

EXPLANATION:

$$p = wh = \rho gh$$

or, $$1 \times 10^5 = 784 \times 9.81 \times h$$

or, $$h = \frac{1 \times 10^5}{784 \times 9.81} = 13 \text{ m} \quad \textbf{(Ans.)}$$

Q.18.96. The Reynolds number of a fluid flowing over a flat plate at a distance of 16 cm from the leading edge is 25600. The thickness of the boundary layer at this point will be

(*a*) 5 mm (*b*) 7.5 mm (*c*) 10 mm (*d*) 10.5 mm.

Ans. (*a*)

EXPLANATION:

Thickness of boundary larger is given by:

$$\delta = \frac{5x}{\sqrt{\text{Re}_x}} = \frac{5 \times 16}{\sqrt{25600}} = 0.5 \text{ cm} = 5 \text{ mm} \quad \textbf{(Ans.)}$$

Q.18.97. A flat plate of 4 m length is kept parallel to air flowing at 5 m/s at 15°C. Assuming the density of air to be 1.2 kg/m^3 and dynamic viscosity to be 1.76×10^{-5} kg/m-s, and knowing that the flow becomes turbulent when Reynolds number exceeds 5×10^5, the flow will become turbulent at

(*a*) 1.25 m (*b*) 1.47 m

(*c*) 1.52 m (*d*) 1.74 m.

Ans. (*b*)

EXPLANATION:

$$Re_x = \frac{Ux}{\gamma} = \frac{\rho Ux}{\mu}$$

The flow will turbulent when $Re = 5 \times 10^5$

$$\therefore \quad 5 \times 10^5 = \frac{1.2 \times 5 \times x}{1.76 \times 10^{-5}} \quad \text{or,} \quad x = 1.47 \text{ m} \quad \textbf{(Ans.)}$$

Q.18.98. The flow in a pipe whose valve is being opened or closed gradually is an example of

(*a*) steady flow (*b*) nonsteady flow

(*c*) steady uniform flow (*d*) steady nonuniform flow.

Ans. (*b*)

EXPLANATION:

The flow in a pipe whose valve is being opened or closed gradually is an example of *non steady* flow. **(Ans.)**

Q.18.99. A velocity potential function exists only for

(*a*) steady flow (*b*) uniform flow

(*c*) irrotational flow (*d*) compressible flow.

Ans. (*c*)

EXPLANATION:

Potential function (ϕ) exists *only for irrotation flow.* **(Ans.)**

PART – II

HYDRAULIC MACHINES

(Fluid Power Engineering)

Chapter 1

IMPACT OF FREE JETS

1.1. INTRODUCTION

A fluid **jet** *is a stream of fluid issuing from a nozzle with a high velocity and hence a high kinetic energy.* When a jet impinges on a plate or vane, it exerts a force on it (due to change in momentum). This force (hydrodynamic) can be evaluated by using '*Impulse-momentum principle*'. This chapter deals with the application of the impulse-momentum equation for evaluating the hydrodynamic force on the stationary and moving vanes. The following cases of impact of jet will be considered:

A. Force exerted by the jet on the stationary plate:

1. When flat plate is held normal to the jet;
2. When flat plate is held inclined to the jet;
3. When plate is curved.

B. Force exerted by the jet on the moving plate:

1. When plate is held normal to the jet;
2. When plate is held inclined to the jet;
3. When plate is curved.

A. FORCE EXERTED BY THE JET ON THE STATIONARY PLATE

1.2. FORCE EXERTED ON A STATIONARY FLAT PLATE HELD NORMAL TO THE JET

Fig. 1.1 shows a fluid jet striking a stationary flat plate held perpendicular to the flow direction. Let a and V be cross-sectional area and velocity of the jet respectively. The jet, after striking this plate (vertical), will get its direction changed through 90°; but, it will move on and off the plate with velocity V, if we *neglect* the friction between the jet and the plate as is possible when the plate is *smooth*. If the *friction is considered*, the velocity of liquid coming off the plate will be *slightly less* than V.

The force exerted by the jet on the plate (assuming it *smooth*) in the direction of jet (*X*-direction),

F_x = Rate of change of momentum (in the direction of force)

= (Initial momentum – final momentum) ... *Impulse-momentum principle.*

= (Mass/sec) × [velocity of jet before striking the plate – velocity of jet after striking the plate]

$= \rho a V (V - 0)$ [$\because$ Mass/second $= \rho a V$]

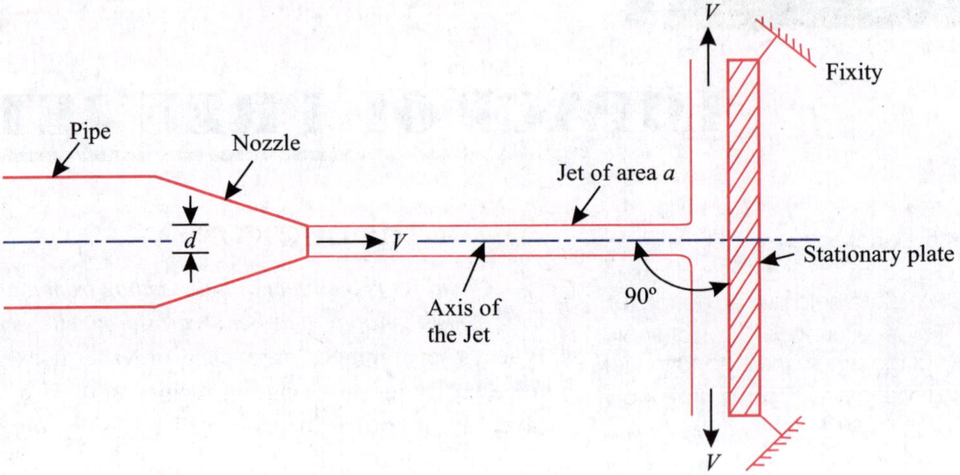

Fig. 1.1. Fluid jet striking a stationary plate.

or, $F_x = \rho a V^2$ ...(1.1)

(where, ρ = mass density of liquid; *a* = area of jet $= \frac{\pi}{4} d^2$, *d* being diameter of the jet).

It may be noted that a jet leaves in the direction normal to X-axis, the final velocity in the X-direction is *zero.*

Since the plate is *stationary*, therefore, the *work done on the plate is zero.*

1.3. FORCE EXERTED ON A STATIONARY FLAT PLATE HELD INCLINED TO THE JET

Fig. 1.2 shows the stationary flat plate inclined at θ° to the direction of the horizontal jet. If *a* and *V* are the cross-sectional area and velocity of the jet respectively, then the mass of liquid per second striking the plate

$= \rho \times aV$ (where $a = \frac{\pi}{4} d^2$, *d* being diameter of the jet)

After striking the plate (assuming it *smooth*), the jet leaves the plate with a velocity equal to initial velocity (*V*).

Let us apply the *impulse- momentum equation* in the direction normal to the plate.

Force in normal direction, $F_n = \rho a V (V \sin \theta - 0)$

$= \rho a V^2 \sin \theta$ ...(1.2)

This normal force can be resolved into two components; component F_x, *parallel* to the direction of jet and component F_y, *normal* to the direction of jet.

$F_x = F_n \sin \theta = \rho a V^2 \sin \theta \times \sin \theta = \rho a V^2 \sin^2 \theta$ ...(1.3)

$$F_y = F_n \cos\theta = \rho a V^2 \sin\theta \times \cos\theta = \rho a V^2 \sin\theta \cos\theta \qquad ...(1.4)$$

In this case also, the work done is *zero* as the plate is stationary. When the fluid strikes the plate, it gets divided into two streams Q_1 and Q_2. Since the frictional resistance has been assumed to be negligible, the resultant force in the direction tangential to the plate is zero. Applying the impulse-momentum equation in the direction tangential to the plate, we obtain:

$$(\rho Q_1 V - \rho Q_2 V) - \rho Q V \cos\theta = 0$$

$$Q_1 - Q_2 - Q \cos\theta = 0 \qquad ...(i)$$

Also, $$Q_1 + Q_2 = Q \qquad (\textit{Continuity equation}) \quad ...(ii)$$

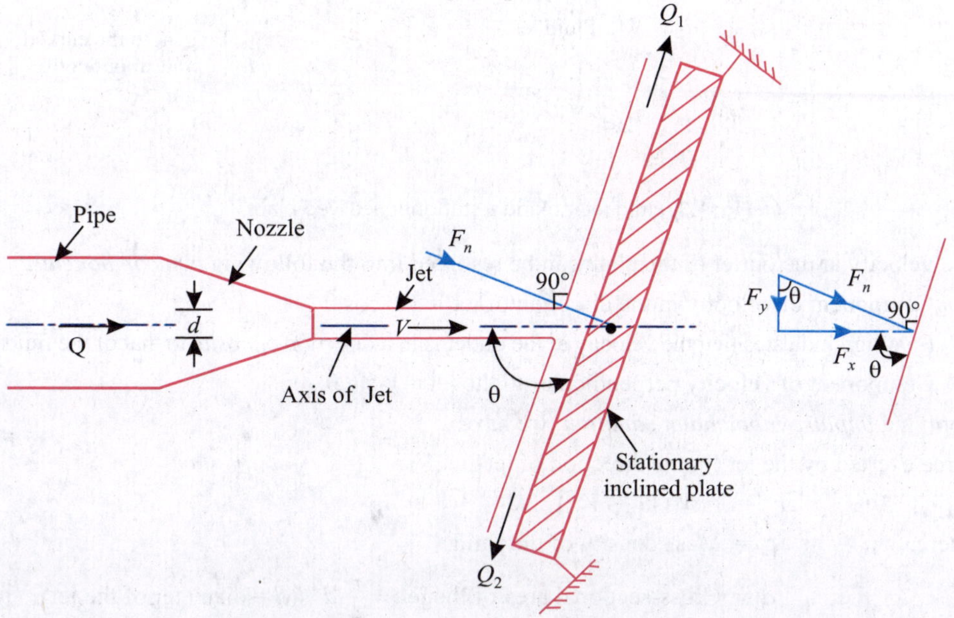

Fig. 1.2. Fluid jet striking a stationary inclined plate.

Solving eqns. (*i*) and (*ii*), we get:

$$Q_1 = \frac{Q}{2}(1 + \cos\theta) \qquad ...(1.5)$$

and, $$Q_2 = \frac{Q}{2}(1 - \cos\theta) \qquad ...(1.6)$$

Ratio of discharges, $$\frac{Q_1}{Q_2} = \frac{1 + \cos\theta}{1 - \cos\theta} \qquad ...(1.7)$$

1.4. FORCE EXERTED ON STATIONARY CURVED PLATE

Case I. Jet strikes the curved plate at the centre:

Cosider a fluid jet striking a stationary curved plate (*smooth*) at the centre as shown in Fig. 1.3. The jet after striking the plate comes out with the same velocity, in the tangential direction of the curved plate.

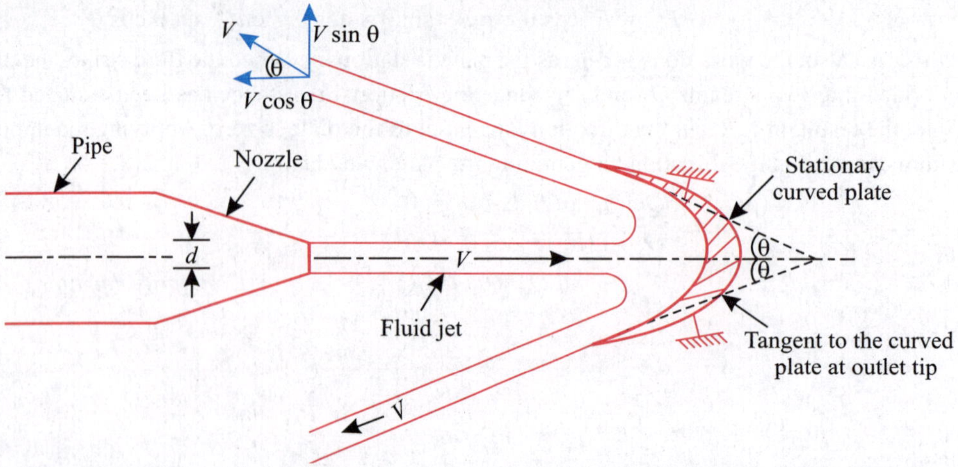

Fig. 1.3. Fluid jet striking a stationary curved plate.

The velocity at the outlet of the plate can be resolved into the following *two components*:

(*i*) Component of velocity in the direction of jet = $-V\cos\theta$

(–ve sign indicates that the velocity at the outlet is in a direction *opposite* to that of the fluid jet)

(*ii*) Component of velocity perpendicular to the jet = $V\sin\theta$

Applying *impulse-momentum equation*, we have:

Force exerted by the jet (in the direction of jet),

$$F_x = \rho a V(V_{1x} - V_{2x})$$

where, ρ = Mass density of the fluid,

a = Cross-sectional area of the jet $= \frac{\pi}{4} d^2$ (d = diameter of the jet),

V = Velocity of the jet,

V_{1x} = Initial velocity in the direction of jet = V

V_{2x} = Final velocity in the direction of jet = $-V\cos\theta$

$$\therefore \quad F_x = \rho a V[V-(-V\cos\theta)] = \rho a V[V + V\cos\theta]$$

or,
$$F_x = \rho a V^2(1+\cos\theta) \qquad \text{...(1.8)}$$

Similarly,
$$F_x = \rho a V(V_{1y} - V_{2y})$$

where, V_{1y} = Initial velocity in the direction of $y = 0$

V_{2y} = Final velocity in the direction of $y = V\sin\theta$

$$\therefore \quad F_y = \rho a V(0 - V\sin\theta) = -\rho a V^2 \sin\theta \qquad \text{...(1.9)}$$

–ve sign indicates that force is acting in the *downward* direction.

Note: The angle of defection of the jet = (180° – θ).

Case II. Jet strikes the curved plate at one end tangentially when the plate is symmetrical:

Fig. 1.4 shows a fluid jet striking a stationary symmetrical curved plate (*smooth*) at one end tangentially, the plate is symmetrical about X-axis. Let V be the velocity of the jet and θ be the angle made the jet with X-axis at inlet tip of the curved plate. The velocity of fluid at outlet tip of the curved plate will be equal to V (since the curved plate is assumed smooth).

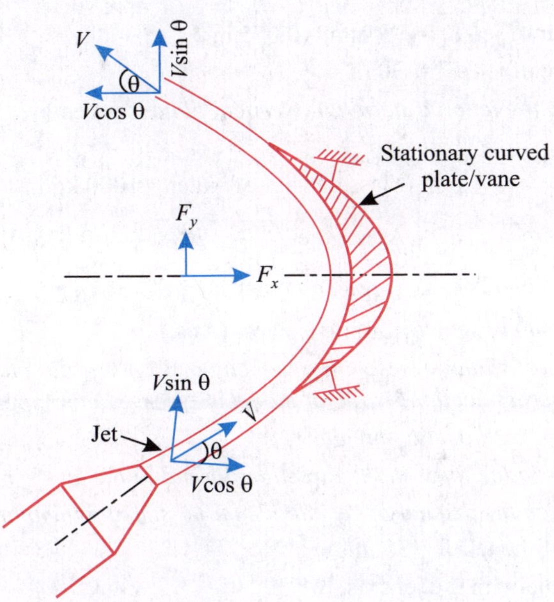

Fig. 1.4. Fluid jet striking stationary curved plate/vane.

The forces exerted by the fluid jet in X and Y directions are:

$$F_x = \rho a V (V_{1x} - V_{2x})$$

$$= \rho a V [V \cos\theta - (-V \cos\theta)]$$

$$= \rho a V (V \cos\theta + V \cos\theta) = \rho a V \times 2V \cos\theta$$

or, $$F_x = 2\rho a V^2 \cos\theta \qquad ...(1.10)$$

$$F_y = \rho a V (V_{1y} - V_{2y})$$

$$= \rho a V [V \sin\theta - V \sin\theta] = 0$$

i.e., $$F_y = 0$$

Case III. Jet strikes the curved plate or vane at one end tangentially when the plate is unsymmetrical:

In this case, as the plate is *unsymmetrical* about X-axis, therefore, the angles made by the tangents drawn at inlet and outlet tips of the plate with X-axis will be *different*. Let θ and ϕ be the angles made by the tangents at inlet tip and outlet tip respectively with X-axis.

∴ Components of velocity at inlet: $V_{1x} = V\cos\theta$; $V_{1y} = V\sin\theta$

Components of velocity at outlet: $V_{2x} = -V\cos\phi$; $V_{2y} = V\sin\phi$

Now, the forces exerted by the fluid jet in X and Y direction are:

$$F_x = \rho a V (V_{1x} - V_{2x})$$

$$F_x = \rho a V [V \cos\theta - (-V \cos\phi)] = \rho a V (V \cos\theta + V \cos\phi)$$

or $$F_x = \rho a V^2 (\cos\theta + \cos\phi) \qquad ...(1.11)$$

and, $$F_y = \rho a V (V_{1y} - V_{2y})$$

$$= \rho a V (V \sin\theta - V \sin\phi)$$

or $$F_y = \rho a V^2 (\sin\theta - \sin\phi) \qquad ...(1.12)$$

Example 1.1. *A jet of water, 75 mm in diameter, issues with a velocity of 30 m/s and impinges on a stationary flat plate which destroys its forward motion. FInd the force exerted by the jet on the plate and work done.*

Solution. Diameter of jet, $d = 75 \text{ mm} = 0.075 \text{ m}$

Velocity of jet, $V = 30 \text{ m/s}$

The *force exerted by the jet on a stationary vertical plate* is given by:

$$F = \rho a V^2$$

where, ρ = Mass density of water = 1000 kg/m^3

$$a = \text{Area of jet} = \frac{\pi}{4} \times d^2 = \frac{\pi}{4} \times 0.075^2 = 0.004418 \text{ m}^2$$

$$\therefore \quad F = 1000 \times 0.004418 \times 30^2 = \mathbf{3976.2 \text{ N}} \text{ (Ans.)}$$

As the plate is *stationary*, the **work done is zero. (Ans.)**

Example 1.2. *A jet of water srikes with a velocity of 35 m/s a flat plate inclined at 30° with the axis of the jet. If the cross-sectional area of the jet is 25 cm², determine:*

(i) The force exerted by the jet on the plate,

(ii) The components of the force in the direction normal to the jet

(iii) The ratio in which the discharge gets divided after striking the plate.

Solution. Velocity of the jet, $V = 35$ m/s

Inclination of the plate with the jet axis, $\theta = 30°$

Area of the jet, $a = 25 \text{ cm}^2 = 25 \times 10^{-4} \text{ m}^2$

(i) The force exerted by the jet, F :

$$F = \rho a V^2 \sin\theta \qquad \text{[Eqn. (1.3)]}$$

$$= 1000 \times (25 \times 10^{-4}) \times 35^2 \times \sin 30° = \mathbf{1531.25 \text{ N}} \text{ (Ans.)}$$

(ii) The components of the force, F :

$$F_x = F \sin\theta = 1531.25 \times \sin 30° = \mathbf{765.625 \text{ N}} \text{ (Ans.)}$$

$$F_y = F \cos\theta = 1531.25 \times \cos 30° = \mathbf{1326.1 \text{ N}} \text{ (Ans.)}$$

(iii) The ratio in which the discharge gets divided :

$$\frac{Q_1}{Q_2} = \frac{1 + \cos\theta}{1 - \cos\theta} \qquad \text{[Eqn. (1.7)]}$$

or

$$\frac{Q_1}{Q_2} = \frac{1 + \cos 30°}{1 - \cos 30°} = \frac{1 + 0.866}{1 - 0.866} = \mathbf{13.925} \text{ (Ans.)}$$

Example 1.3. *A jet of water of diameter 40 mm moving with a velocity of 30 m/s, strikes a curved fixed symmetrical plate at the centre. Find the force exerted by the jet water in the direction of the jet if the jet is deflected through an angle of 120 ° at the outlet of the curved plate.*

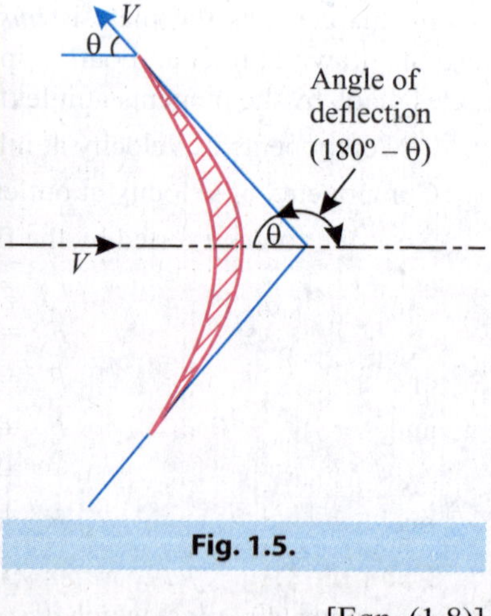

Fig. 1.5.

Solution. Diameter of jet, $d = 40 \text{ mm} = 0.04 \text{ m}$

$$\therefore \quad \text{Area of jet, } a = \frac{\pi}{4} \times d^2 = \frac{\pi}{4} \times 0.04^2$$

$$= 0.001256 \text{ m}^2$$

Velocity of jet, $V = 30$ m/s

Angle of deflection = 120°, or, $180 - \theta = 120°$

$$\therefore \quad \theta = 180° - 120° = 60°$$

Force exerted by the jet of water in the direction of jet,

$$F_x = \rho a V^2 (1 + \cos\theta) \qquad \text{[Eqn. (1.8)]}$$

$$= 1000 \times 0.001256 \times 30^2 (1 + \cos 60°)$$

$$= \mathbf{1695.6\ N\ (Ans.)}$$

Example 1.4. *A jet of water of 20 mm diameter and moving at 15 m/s, strikes upon the centre of a symmetrical vane. After impingement, the jet gets deflected through 160° by the vane. Presuming vane to be smooth determine:*

(i) The force exerted by jet on the vane, and

(ii) The ratio of velocity at outlet to that at inlet if actual reaction of the vane is 127 N.

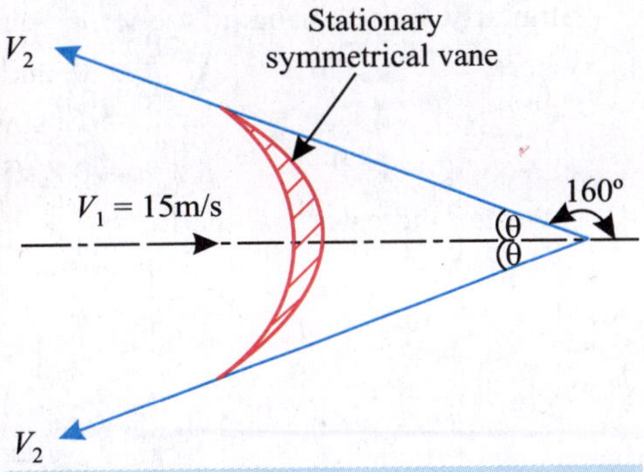

Fig. 1.6.

Solution. Diameter of the jet, $d = 20$ mm $= 0.02$ m

Velocity of jets, $V = 15$ m/s

Angle of deflection $= 160°$.

(i) The force exerted by the jet on the vane, F :

Refer to Fig 1.6.

$$160° = 180 - \theta, \text{ or, } \theta = 180 - 160 = 20°$$

For *smooth vane*, the theoretical force (or thrust) exerted by the jet on the vane is,

$$F = \rho a V^2 (1 + \cos \theta) \quad ...(i)$$

$$= 1000 \times (\frac{\pi}{4} \times 0.02^2) \times 15^2 (1 + \cos 20°)$$

$$= \mathbf{137.1\ N\ (Ans.)}$$

(ii) $\frac{V_2}{V_1}$ **:**

Actual reaction of the vane = 127 N (*Given*)

If the vane is *not smooth*, then outgoing velocity at the vane tip is less than the incoming velocity, *i.e.*, $\frac{V_2}{V_1} = K$ where $K < 1$. The eqn. (*i*) gets modified to

$$F = \rho a V^2 (1 + K \cos \theta)$$

$$127 = 1000 \times (\frac{\pi}{4} \times 0.02^2) \times 15^2 (1 + K \cos 20°)$$

or, $$1 + K \cos 20° = \frac{127}{1000 \times (\frac{\pi}{4} \times 0.02^2) \times 15^2} = 1.796$$

or, $$K = \frac{1.796 - 1}{\cos 20°} = \mathbf{0.847\ (Ans.)}$$

Example 1.5. *A jet of water from a nozzle is deflected through 60° from its original direction by curved plate which it enters tangentially without shock with a velocity of 30 m/s and leaves with a mean velocity of 25 m/s. If the discharge form the nozzle is 0.8 kg/s, calculate the magnitude and direction of the resultant force on the vane, if the vane is stationary.* **[UPTU]**

Solution. Velocity at inlet, $V_1 = 30$ m/s

Velocity at outlet, $V_2 = 25$ m/s

Mass per second $= 0.8$ kg/s

Force in the direction of jet, F_x = Mass per sec. $\times (V_{1x} - V_{2x})$

where, $$V_{1x} = V_1 = 30 \text{ m/s}$$

$$V_{2x} = V_2 \cos 60° = 25 \cos 60° = 12.5 \text{ m/s}$$

$$\therefore \quad F_x = 0.8\,(30 - 12.5) = 14 \text{ N}$$

Similarly, force normal to the jet, F_y = mass per sec. × $(V_{1y} - V_{2x})$

where, $V_{1y} = 0$, and

$$V_{2y} = V_2 \sin 60° = 25 \sin 60° = 21.65 \text{ N}$$

$$\therefore \quad F_y = 0.8\,(0 - 21.65) = -17.32 \text{ N}$$

(–ve sign indicates that the force F_y *is acting in the vertically downward direction*)

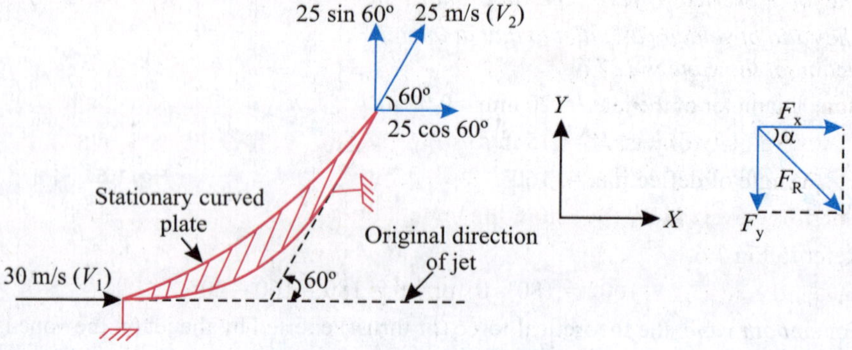

Fig. 1.7.

∴ Resultant force in the curved plate,

$$F_R = \sqrt{F_x^2 + F_y^2} = \sqrt{14^2 + 17.32^2} = \mathbf{22.27\ N\ (Ans.)}$$

The angle made by the resultant force with X-axis (Refer to Fig. 1.7),

$$\tan \alpha = \frac{F_y}{F_x} = \frac{17.32}{14} = 1.237$$

$$\therefore \quad \alpha = \tan^{-1} 1.237 \simeq \mathbf{51° \ (Ans.)}$$

Example 1.6. *A jet of water of diameter 60 mm moving with a velocity of 40 m/s, strikes a curved fixed plate tangentially at one end at an angle of 30° to horizontal. The jet leaves the plate at an angle of 20° to the horizontal. Find the force exerted by the jet on the plate in the horizontal and vertical directions.*

Solution. Diameter of jet, d = 60 mm = 0.06 m

$$\therefore \quad \text{Area, } a = \frac{\pi}{4} \times d^2 = \frac{\pi}{4} \times 0.06^2 = 0.002827 \text{ m}^2$$

Velocity of the jet, V = 40 m/s

Angle made by the jet at inlet tip with horizontal, $\theta = 30°$

Angle made by the jet at outlet tip with horizontal, $\phi = 20°$.

Force exerted by the jet :

Force exerted by the jet in *X*-direction,

$$F_x = \rho a V^2 (\cos \theta + \cos \phi) \qquad \text{[Eqn. (1.11)]}$$

$$= 1000 \times 0.002827 \times 40^2 (\cos 30° + \cos 20°) = \mathbf{8167.6\ N\ (Ans.)}$$

Force exerted by the jet in *Y*-direction,

$$F_y = \rho a V^2 (\sin \theta - \sin \phi) \qquad \text{[Eqn. (1.12)]}$$

$$= 1000 \times 0.002827 \times 40^2 (\sin 30° - \sin 20°) = \mathbf{714.57\ N\ (Ans.)}$$

Example 1.7. *A rectangular plate, weighing 60 N is suspended vertically by a hinge on the top horizontal edge. The centre of gravity of the plate is 100 mm from the hinge. A horizontal jet of* *water 20 mm diameter, whose axis is 150 mm below the hinge impinges normally on the plate with a velocity of 5 m/s. Determine:*

(i) The horizontal force applied at the centre of gravity to maintain the plate in its vertical portion.

(ii) The corresponding velocity of the jet, if the plate is deflected through 30° and the same force continues to act at the centre of gravity of the plate. **[Delhi University]**

Solution. Weight of plate, $W = 60$ N

Distance of weight W from hinge, $x = 100$ mm $= 0.1$ m

Diameter of the jet, $d = 20$ mm $= 0.02$ m

$$\therefore \quad \text{Area, } a = \frac{\pi}{4} \times d^2 = \frac{\pi}{4} \times (0.02)^2 = 0.000314 \text{ m}^2$$

Distance of the axis of the jet from hinge $= 150$ mm $= 0.15$ m

Velocity of jet, $V = 15$ m/s

Refer to Fig. 1.8 for the plate and its orientation in the vertical and deflected positions.

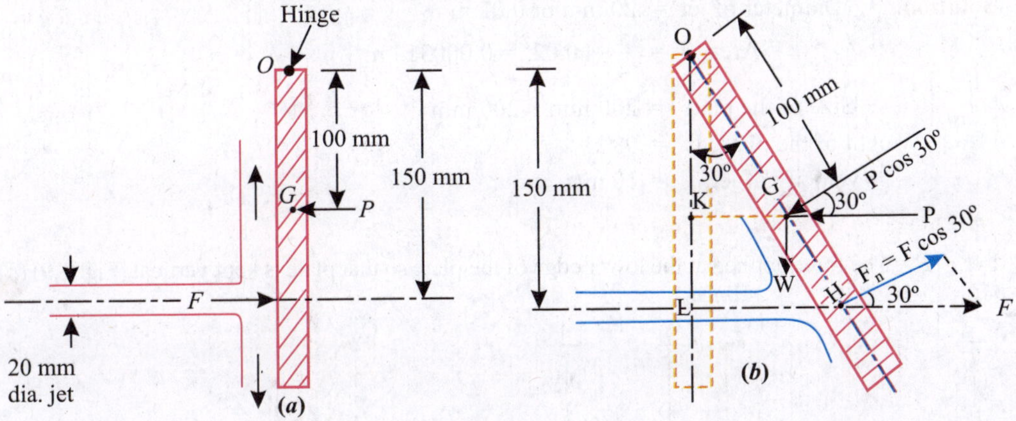

Fig. 1.8.

(i) Horizontal force, P :

Normal force exerted by the jet on plate,

$$F = \rho a V^2 = 1000 \times 0.000314 \times 5^2 = 7.85 \text{ N}$$

Let P be the force to be applied at the centre of gravity G [Fig. 1.8 (*a*)] to keep the plate in its vertical position. Then taking moments about the hinge point O, we get:

$$F \times 150 = P \times 100$$

or,
$$P = \frac{F \times 150}{100} = \frac{7.85 \times 150}{100} = \mathbf{11.77} \text{ (Ans.)}$$

(ii) Velocity of the jet :

Let, V = Velocity of the jet, if the plate is deflected through 30° and the same force continues to act at the centre of gravity of the plate.

Refer to Fig. 1.8. (*b*). Taking moments about the hinge point O, we get

$$W \times GK + P \cos 30° \times OG = F \cos 30° \times OH \quad \text{...(i)}$$

But,
$$GK = 0.1 \sin 30° = 0.05 \text{ m}, OG = 0.1 \text{ m}; OH = \frac{OL}{\cos 30°} = \frac{0.15}{\cos 30°} = 0.1732 \text{ m}$$

Substituting the various values, we get

$$60 \times 0.05 + 11.77 \times 0.866 \times 0.1 = F \times 0.1732$$

$$3 + 1.02 = 0.15\,F$$

$$\therefore \quad F = 26.8 \text{ N}$$

Now, jet force, $F = \rho a V^2$, or, $26.8 = 1000 \times 0.000314 \times V^2$

$$\therefore \quad V = \left(\frac{26.8}{1000 \times 0.000314}\right)^{1/2} = \textbf{9.24 m/s (Ans.)}$$

Example 1.8. *A jet of water of diameter 20 mm strikes a 200 mm × 200 mm square plate of uniform thickness with a velocity of 10 m/s at the centre of the plate which is suspended vertically by a hinge on its top horizontal edge. The weight of the plate is 98 N. The jet strikes normal to the plate.*

(i) What force must be applied at the lower edge of the plate so that plate is kept vertical ?

(ii) If the plate is allowed to deflect freely, what will be the inclination of the plate with vertical due to the force exerted by jet water?

Solution. Diameter of jet = 20 mm or 0.02 m

$$\therefore \quad \text{Area, } a = \frac{\pi}{4} \times 0.02^2 = 0.000314 \text{ m}^2$$

Size of the plate = 200 mm × 200 mm

Weight of the plate, W = 98 N

Velocity of jet, V = 10 m/s

(i) Force to be applied at lower edge, P :

Let, P = The force applied at the lower edge of the plate so that plate is kept vertical [Fig. 1.9) (*a*)].

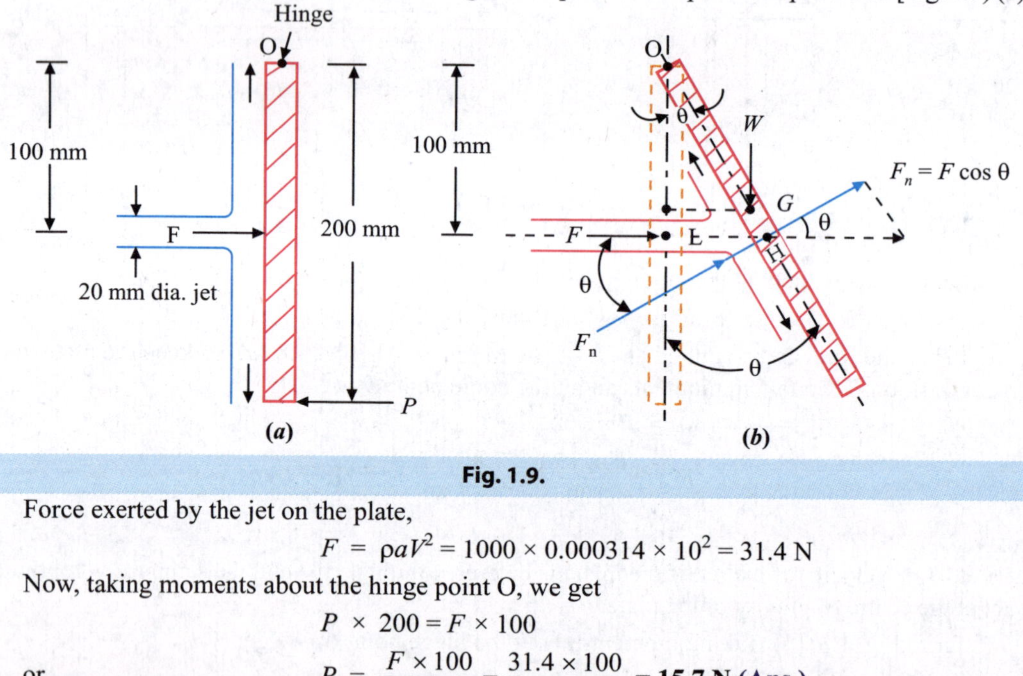

Fig. 1.9.

Force exerted by the jet on the plate,

$$F = \rho a V^2 = 1000 \times 0.000314 \times 10^2 = 31.4 \text{ N}$$

Now, taking moments about the hinge point O, we get

$$P \times 200 = F \times 100$$

or,

$$P = \frac{F \times 100}{200} = \frac{31.4 \times 100}{200} = \textbf{15.7 N (Ans.)}$$

(ii) Inclination of the plate :

Let, θ = Inclination of the plate with vertical due to force exerted by the jet [Fig. 1.9 (*b*)].

Force exerted by water normal to the plate is given by:

$$F_n = F\cos\theta = \rho a V^2 \cos\theta = 31.4 \cos\theta$$

[$\because$ $\rho a V^2 = 31.4$ N, calculated earlier]

Taking moments about the hinge point O, we get:

$$F_n \times OH = W \times GK \quad ...(i)$$

where, $OH = \dfrac{OL}{\cos\theta} = \dfrac{0.1}{\cos\theta}$ m, $GK = 0.1 \sin\theta$ m

Substituting the values in eqn. (*i*), we have

$$31.4\cos\theta \times \frac{0.1}{\cos\theta} = 98 \times 0.1 \sin\theta$$

$$\therefore \quad \sin\theta = \frac{31.4}{98} = 0.32$$

Hence, $\theta = \sin^{-1} 0.32 =$ **18.66°** **(Ans.)**

B. FORCE EXERTED BY THE JET ON THE MOVING PLATE

1.5. FORCE EXERTED ON MOVING FLAT PLATE HELD NORMAL TO JET

Fig. 1.10 shows a fluid jet striking a flat vertical plate moving with a uniform velocity away from the jet.

Let, V = Absolute velocity of the jet,

a = Cross-sectional area of the jet, and

u = Velocity of the flat plate held normal to the jet.

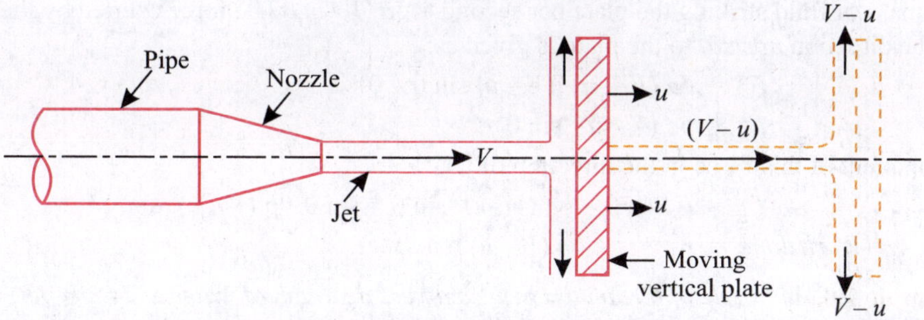

Fig. 1.10. Fluid jet striking a moving plate.

The relative velocity with which the jet strikes the plate is $(V - u)$.

Mass of water striking the plate per second = $\rho a (V - u)$

$\therefore$ Force exerted by the jet on the plate in the direction of jet,

F_x = Mass of water striking the plate/sec × (initial velocity with which water strikes–final velocity)

$= \rho a (V - u) [(V - u) - 0]$ ($\because$ Final velocity in the diction of jet = 0)

or, $$F_x = \rho a (V - u)^2 \quad ...(1.13)$$

The work done = Force × the distance through which the body moves in the direction of force.

$$\therefore \quad \textit{Work done} = \rho a (V - u)^2 \times u \quad ...(1.14)$$

Note : This case is not practically feasible because the distance between the nozzle and the plate will go on increasing. However, if a series of plates is fitted on the wheel, there is always a plate facing the jet. Thus, the entire fluid issuing from the jet strikes the plates.

1.6. FORCE EXERTED ON A MOVING PLATE HELD INCLINED TO THE DIRECTION OF JET

Fig. 1.11 shows a fluid jet striking an inclined plate, which is moving with uniform velocity in the direction of the jet.

Let, V = Absolute velocity of the jet,

u = Velocity of plate in the direction of jet

a = Cross-sectional area of jet, and

θ = Angle between jet and the plate.

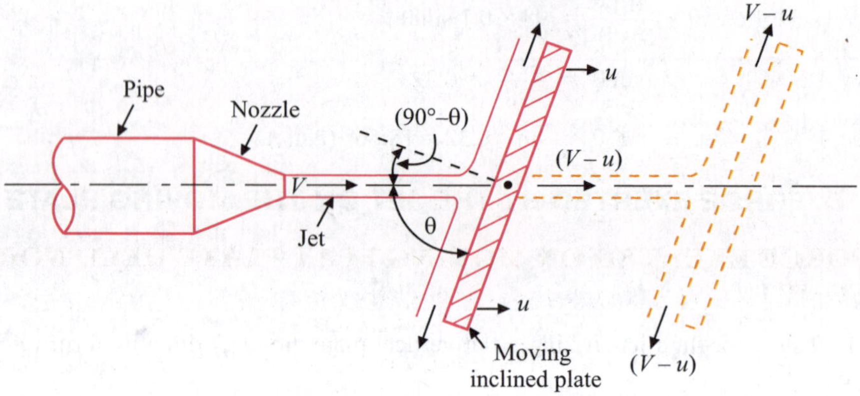

Fig. 1.11. Fluid jet striking a moving plate held inclined to the direction of jet.

Relative velocity with which the jet strikes the plate = $(V - u)$

The mass of fluid striking the plate per second = $\rho a\,(V - u)$. The force exerted by the jet on the plate in the direction *normal* to the plate is given as:

$$F_n = \rho a\,(V - u)\,[(V - u)\sin\theta - 0]$$

or, $$F_n = \rho a\,(V - u)^2 \sin\theta \quad ...(1.15)$$

Component of this force in the direction of jet,

$$F_x = F_n \sin\theta = \rho a\,(V - u)^2 \sin\theta \times \sin\theta = \rho\,(V - u)^2 \sin^2\theta \quad ...(1.16)$$

$\therefore$ $$\textit{Work done} = F_x \times u = \rho a\,(V - u)^2 \sin\theta \times u \quad ...(1.17)$$

Example 1.9. *A nozzle of 60 mm diameter delivers a stream of water at 24 m/s perpendicular to a plate that moves away from the jet at 6 m/s.*

Find: (*i*) *The force on the plate,*

(*ii*) *The work done, and*

(*iii*) *The efficiency of the jet.*

Solution. Diameter of the nozzle/jet, $d = 60$ mm $= 0.06$ m

Velocity of water, $V = 24$ m/s

Velocity of the plate, $u = 6$ m/s

(*i*) The force on the plate, F :

$$F = \rho a\,(V - u)^2 \quad \text{[Eqn. (1.13)]}$$

$$= 1000 \times \left(\frac{\pi}{4} \times 0.06^2\right) \times (24 - 6)^2 = \mathbf{916\ N}\ \textbf{(Ans.)}$$

(*ii*) The work done :

$$\textit{Work done} = F \times u = 916 \times 6 = \mathbf{5496\ Nm/s}\ \textbf{(Ans.)}$$

(iii) The efficiency of jet, η_{jet} :

$$\text{Kinetic energy of issuing jet} = \frac{1}{2} mV^2 = \frac{1}{2} (\rho aV) \times V^2 \qquad (\because \text{Mass, } m = \rho aV)$$

$$= \frac{1}{2} (1000 \times \frac{\pi}{4} \times 0.06^2 \times 24) \times 24^2 = 19543.2 \text{ Nm/s}$$

$$\therefore \quad \eta_{jet} = \frac{\text{Work done}}{\text{Kinetic energy of issuing jet}}$$

$$= \frac{5496}{19543.2} = 0{\cdot}281 \text{ or } \mathbf{28.1\%} \textbf{ (Ans.)}$$

Example 1.10. *A 75 mm diameter jet having a velocity of 30 m/s strikes a flat plate, the normal of which is inclined at 45° to the axis of the jet. Find the normal pressure on the plate,*

(i) When the plate is stationary;

(ii) When the plate is moving with a velocity of 15 m/s in the direction of jet, away from the jet. Also determine the power and efficiency of the jet when the plate is moving.

[Allahabad University]

Solution. Diameter of the jet, $d = 75$ mm $= 0.075$ m

$$\therefore \quad \text{Area, } a = \frac{\pi}{4} \times 0.075^2 = 0.004418 \text{ m}^2$$

Angle between the jet and the plate, $\theta = 90° - 45° = 45°$

Velocity of the jet, $V = 30$ m/s

(i) *When the plate is stationary,* the normal force on the plate is:

$$F_n = \rho a V^2 \sin\theta \qquad \text{[Eqn. (1.2)]}$$

$$= 1000 \times 0.004418 \times 30^2 \times \sin 45° = \mathbf{2811.6 \text{ N}} \textbf{ (Ans.)}$$

(ii) *When the plate is moving with a velocity of 15 m/s and moving away from the jet,* the normal force on the plate is

$$F_n = \rho a (V - u)^2 \sin\theta \quad (\text{where, } u = 15 \text{ m/s}) \qquad \text{[Eqn. 1.15]}$$

$$= 1000 \times 0.004418 (30 - 15)^2 \times \sin 45° = \mathbf{702.9 \text{ N}} \textbf{ (Ans.)}$$

Work done per second by the jet

= Force in the direction of jet × distance moved by the plate in the direction of jet/sec.

$$= F_n \times u$$

where, $F_x = F_n \sin\theta = 702.9 \times \sin 45° = 497$ N

$\therefore$ Work done $= 497 \times 15 = 7455$ Nm/s

$\therefore$ *Power of the jet* $= 7455$ J/s $= 7455$ W $=$ **7.455 kW (Ans.)**

$$\textit{Efficiency of the jet} = \frac{\text{Work done on the plate}}{\text{Kinetic energy supplied by the jet}}$$

$$= \frac{7455}{\frac{1}{2}(\rho aV) \times V^2} = \frac{7455}{\frac{1}{2} \times (1000 \times 0{\cdot}004418 \times 30) \times 30^2}$$

$$= 0.125 \text{ or } \mathbf{12.5\%} \textbf{ (Ans.)}$$

Example 1.11. *A 75 mm diameter water jet having a velocity of 12 m/s impinges on a plane, smooth plate at an angle of 60° to the normal to the plate. What will be the impact when (i) the plate is stationary, and (ii) the plate is moving in the direction of the jet at 6 m/s? Estimate the work done per unit time by the jet on the plate in each case. Take the density of water as 998 kg/m³.* **[N.U.]**

Solution. Given: $d = 75$ mm $= 0.075$ m; $V = 12$ m/s; $\theta = 90 - 60° = 30°$; $u = 6$ m/s; $\rho = 998$ kg/m^3.

Force on the plate and work done :

(*i*) *When the plate is stationary :*

Force on the plate, $F = (\rho a V) V \sin 30°$

$$= \left[998 \times \frac{\pi}{4} \times (0.075)^2 \times 12 \times 12 \sin 30°\right] = \mathbf{317.45\ N(Ans.)}$$

Work done = **0**, since the plate is stationary **(Ans.)**

(*ii*) *When the plate is moving :*

Normal force on the plate, $F_n = [\rho a (V - u)] \times (V - u) \sin 30°$

$$= \rho a (V - u)^2 \sin 30° = 998 \times \frac{\pi}{4} \times (0.075)^2 \times (12 - 6)^2 \times 0.5 = \mathbf{79.36\ N}\ \ \textbf{(Ans.)}$$

Work done on the plate $= F_n \sin \theta \times u$

$= 79.36 \sin 30° \times 6 = \mathbf{238.08\ Nm/s}$ **(Ans.)**

Example 1.12. (*a*) *Derive the following expression for force F exerted by a jet of area 'a' which strikes a flat plate at an angle θ to the normal to the plate with velocity V. The plate itself is moving with velocity u in the direction of normal to the plate surface.*

$$F = \rho a \frac{(V \cos\theta - u)^2}{\cos\theta}$$

(*b*) *A 40 mm diameter jet having a velocity of 20 m/s strikes a flat plate, the normal of which is inclined at 30° to the axis of jet. If the plate itself is moving with a velocity of 8 m/s parallel to itself and in the direction of normal to its surface, calculate:*

(*i*) *Normal force exerted on the plate,*

(*ii*) *Work done per second, and*

(*iii*) *Efficiency of the jet* **[Punjab University]**

Solution. (*a*) Fig 1.12 shows the orientation of the jet and the arrangement of the plate.

Component of plate velocity in the direction of jet $= \dfrac{u}{\cos\theta}$

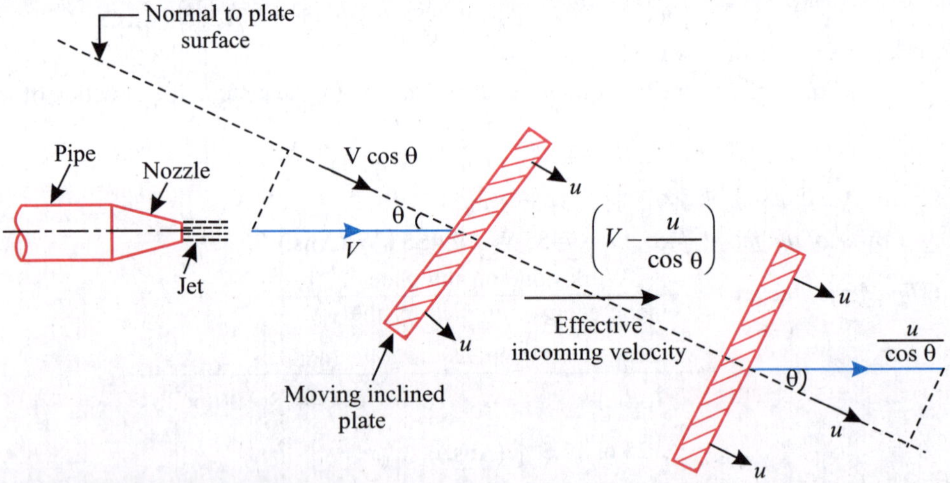

Fig. 1.12. Fluid jet and an inclined plate—plate moves in a direction normal to its surface.

∴ Effective incoming velocity $= V - \dfrac{u}{\cos\theta}$

Mass of fluid striking the plate $= \rho a \left(V - \dfrac{u}{\cos\theta}\right) = \rho a \left(\dfrac{V \cos\theta - u}{\cos\theta}\right)$

Component of absolute velocity of jet *normal* to plate = $V \cos \theta$

$\therefore$ Change of velocity *normal* to plate = $(V \cos \theta - u)$

Force exerted on the plate (F) = Mass × change of velocity

or, $$F = \rho a \left(\frac{V \cos \theta - u}{\cos \theta} \right) \times (V \cos \theta - u)$$

or, $$F = \rho a \frac{(V \cos \theta - u)^2}{\cos \theta}$$ **Proved.**

(*b*) Diameter of the jet, d = 40 mm = 0.04 m

$\therefore$ $$\text{Area, } a = \frac{\pi}{4} \times d^2 = \frac{\pi}{4} \times 0.04^2 = 0.001256 \text{ m}^2$$

Velocity of jet (absolute), V = 20 m/s

Velocity of the plate, u = 8 m/s

The inclination of the normal to the plate with the axis of jet, $\theta = 30°$

(*i*) Normal force exerted on the plate, F :

$$F = \rho a \frac{(V \cos \theta - u)^2}{\cos \theta} = 1000 \times 0{\cdot}001256 \times \frac{(20 \cos 30° - 8)^2}{\cos 30°} = \mathbf{125{\cdot}98 \text{ N}}$$ **(Ans.)**

(*ii*) Work done per second :

Work done/sec = Normal force exerted on the plate × distance moved by the plate

= 125.98 × 8 = **1007.84 Nm/s (Ans.)**

(*iii*) Efficiency of the jet, η_{jet} :

$$\eta_{jet} = \frac{\text{Work done}}{\text{Kinetic energy of issuing jet}} = \frac{1007.84}{\frac{1}{2} mV^2}$$

$$= \frac{1007.84}{\frac{1}{2}(\rho a V)V^2} = \frac{1007.84}{\frac{1}{2}(1000 \times 0.001256 \times 20) \times 20^2} = 0.20 \textit{ or } \mathbf{20\%}$$ **(Ans.)**

1.7. FORCE EXERTED ON A CURVED PLATE (OR VANE) WHEN THE PLATE (OR VANE) IS MOVING IN THE DIRECTION OF JET

A. Single vane:

Fig. 1.13 shows a fluid jet striking at the centre of curved vane moving with a uniform velocity in the direction of jet.

Let, V = Absolute velocity of the jet,

a = Area of jet, and

u = Velocity of the plate in the direction of the jet.

When the jet strikes the moving vane, the effective velocity is the relative velocity $(V - u)$. The component of this velocity [*i.e.*, $(V - u)$] in the direction of jet

$$= -(V - u) \cos \theta$$

(– ve sign indicates that the component is in the direction *opposite* to that of the jet.)

Mass of fluid striking the plate = $\rho a (V - u)$

$\therefore$ Force exerted by the jet on the vane,

F_x = Mass striking per sec × (initial velocity with which the jet strikes the vane in the direction of jet – final velocity)

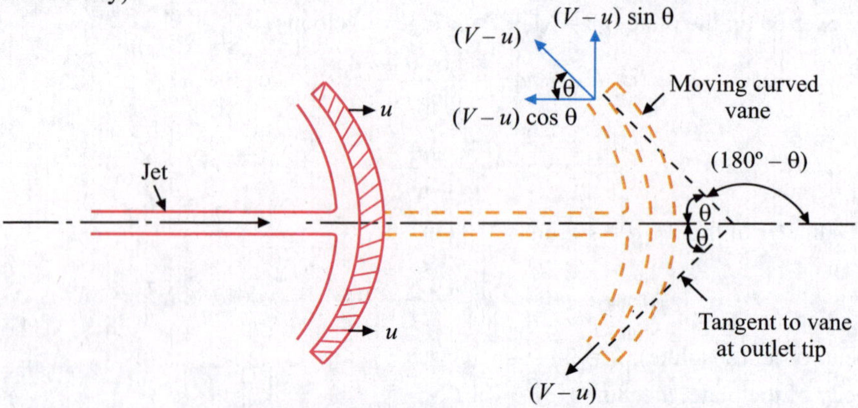

Fig. 1.13. Jet striking a curved moving vane.

$$= \rho a (V-u) [(V-u) - \{-(V-u)\cos\theta\}]$$

$$= \rho a (V-u) [(V-u) + (V-u)\cos\theta]$$

or, $$F_x = \rho a (V-u)^2 (1+\cos\theta) \qquad ...(1.18)$$

Work done on the vane per second

$$= F_x \times u = \rho a (V-u)^2 (1+\cos\theta) \times u \qquad ...(1.19)$$

Kinetic energy of issuing jet $= \frac{1}{2} mV^2 = \frac{1}{2} (\rho a V) V^2 = \frac{1}{2} \rho a V^3$

$$\text{Efficiency, } \eta = \frac{\text{Work done}}{\text{Kinetic energy supplied by the jet}}$$

$$= \frac{\rho a (V-u)^2 (1+\cos\theta) \times u}{\frac{1}{2} \rho a V^3}$$

or, $$\eta = \frac{2(V-u)^2 (1+\cos\theta) u}{V^3} \qquad ...(1.20)$$

For a given jet velocity, the efficiency will be *maximum* when

$$\frac{d\eta}{du} = 0$$

or, $$\frac{d}{du}\left[\frac{2(V-u)^2 (1+\cos\theta) u}{V^3}\right] = 0$$

or, $$\frac{2}{V^3}(1+\cos\theta) \frac{d}{du}[(V-u)^2 \times u] = 0$$

or, $$\frac{2}{V^3}(1+\cos\theta) \frac{d}{du}[(V^2+u^2-2Vu)u] = 0$$

or, $$\frac{2}{V^3}(1+\cos\theta) \frac{d}{du}(V^2 u + u^3 - 2Vu^2) = 0$$

or, $$\frac{2}{V^3}(1+\cos\theta)(V^2 + 3u^2 - 4Vu) = 0$$

For a given system $\frac{2}{V^3}(1 + \cos\theta) \neq 0$

$$\therefore \quad V^2 + 3u^2 - 4Vu = 0$$

or, $$(V - u)(V - 3u) = 0$$

i.e., $$u = V \text{ or } u = \frac{V}{3} \qquad ...(1.21)$$

When $u = V$, the work done becomes zero. Thus, for maximum efficiency $u = V/3$, *i.e., vane velocity is 1/3 rd of the jet velocity.*

B. Series of vanes:

In this case, there is always one vane or the other facing the jet (e.g., curved vanes mounted equidistantly around the periphery of a wheel) and the entire fluid is utilized. The mass of fluid striking the vanes per second equals ρaV.

Thrust exerted by the jet on the vane,

$$F_x = \rho aV[(V-u) - \{-(V-u)\cos\theta\}]$$

$$= \rho aV[(V-u) + (V-u)\cos\theta]$$

or, $$F_x = \rho aV(V-u)(1+\cos\theta) \qquad ...(1.22)$$

$$\text{Work done per second} = F_x \times u$$

$$= \rho aV[(V-u)(1+\cos\theta) \times u \qquad ...(1.23)$$

Kinetic energy supplied by the jet

$$= \frac{1}{2}(\rho aV)V^2 = \frac{1}{2}\rho aV^3$$

$$\therefore \quad \text{Efficiency, } \eta = \frac{\text{Work done on the wheel}}{\text{Kinetic energy supplied by the jet}}$$

$$= \frac{\rho aV(V-u)(1+\cos\theta) \times u}{\frac{1}{2}\rho aV^3}$$

or, $$\eta = \frac{2u(V-u)(1+\cos\theta)}{V^2} \qquad ...(1.24)$$

The efficiency is *maximum* if

$$\frac{d\eta}{du} = 0$$

or, $$\frac{d}{du}\left[\frac{2u(V-u)(1+\cos\theta)}{V^2}\right] = 0$$

or, $$\frac{2(1+\cos\theta)}{V^2} \times \frac{d}{du}(uV - u^2) = 0$$

or, $$\frac{2(1+\cos\theta)}{V^2}(V - 2u) = 0$$

For a given system, $\frac{2(1+\cos\theta)}{V^2} \neq 0$ and therefore

$$V - 2u = 0 \text{ or } u = \frac{V}{2} \qquad ...(1.25)$$

Hence for the *maximum efficiency of the wheel, the peripheral speed (u) is one-half the velocity of jet.*

$$\text{Maximum efficiency, } \eta_{max} = \frac{2\left(\frac{V}{2}\right)\left(V - \frac{V}{2}\right)(1 + \cos\theta)}{V^2}$$

$$\left[\text{Substituting } u = \frac{V}{2} \text{ in eqn. (1.24)}\right]$$

or,
$$\eta_{max} = \frac{1 + \cos\theta}{2} \quad \text{...(1.26)}$$

When $\theta = 0$, *i.e.* the vanes are *semicircular,* $\eta_{max} = \frac{1+1}{2} = 1$ or 100%. Thus, the theoretical maximum efficiency of the wheel is 100%. This concept (of having vanes of semicircular configuration) is utilized in the design of buckets for Pelton wheel. The buckets are, however not exactly semicircular. The angle of deflection is limited to 160° – 170° depending upon a particular design. This *ensures that the jet coming out of a bucket does not interfere with the jet striking the bucket.*

Example 1.13. *A jet of water, 60 mm in diameter, strikes a curved vane at its centre with a velocity of 18 m/s. The curved vane is moving with a velocity of 6 m/s in the direction of the jet. The jet is deflected through an angle of 165°. Assuming the plate to be smooth, find:*

(i) Thrust on the plate in the direction of jet,

(ii) Power of the jet, and

(iii) Efficiency of the jet.

Solution. Diameter of the jet, $d = 60 \text{ mm} = 0.06 \text{ m}$

$$\therefore \quad \text{Area, } a = \frac{\pi}{4} \times d^2 = \frac{\pi}{4} \times 0.06^2 = 0.002827 \text{ m}^2$$

Velocity of the jet, $V = 18$ m/s

Velocity of the vane, $u = 6$ m/s

Angle of deflection of the jet = 165°

∴ Angle made by the relative velocity at the outlet of the vane,

$$\theta = 180 - 165 = 15°$$

(i) Thrust on the plate :

Thrust on the plate in the direction of the jet,

$$F_x = \rho a (V - u)^2 (1 + \cos\theta) \quad \text{...[Eqn. 1.18]}$$

$$= 1000 \times 0.002827 (18 - 6)^2 (1 + \cos 15°) = \mathbf{800.3\ N} \text{ (Ans.)}$$

(ii) Power of the jet :

Work done by the jet on the vane per second

$$= F_x \times u = 800.3 \times 6 = 4801.8 \text{ Nm/s}$$

$$\therefore \quad \textit{Power of the jet} = 4801.8 \text{ J/s} = 4801.8 \text{ W} \simeq \mathbf{4.8\ kW} \text{ (Ans.)}$$

(iii) Efficiency of the jet, η_{jet} :

$$\eta_{jet} = \frac{\text{Work done by the jet/sec.}}{\text{Kinetic energy of the jet/sec.}}$$

$$= \frac{4801.8}{\frac{1}{2}(\rho a V) \times V^2} = \frac{4801.8}{\frac{1}{2}(1000 \times 0.002827 \times 18) \times 18^2} = 0.5825 \text{ or } \mathbf{58.25\ \%} \text{ (Ans.)}$$

Example 1.14. **(a)** *A stationary vane having an inlet angle of zero degree and an outlet angle of 25° receives water at velocity of 50 m/s. Determine the components of force acting on it in the direction of the jet velocity and normal to it. Also find the resultant force in magnitude and direction per kg of flow.*

(b) *If the vane stated above is moving with a velocity of 20 m/s in the direction of the jet, calculate the force components in the direction of the vane velocity and across it, also the resultant force in magnitude and direction. Calculate the work done and power developed per kg of flow.*

[UPTU]

Solution.

(a) Stationary vane :

Inlet angle of the vane = 0°

Outlet angle of the vane = 25°

Velocity of water jet, V = 50 m/s

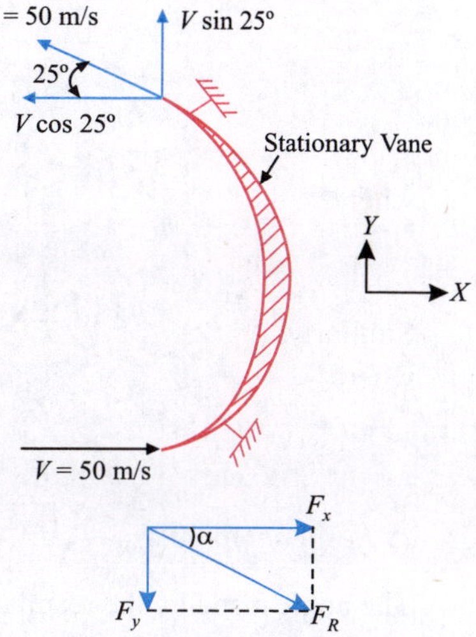

Fig. 1.14. Stationary Vane.

The force in the direction of jet per kg of flow,

$$F_x = 1 \times (V_{1x} - V_{2x})$$

where, V_{1x} = 50 m/s

$$V_{2x} = -V\cos 25° = -50 \cos 25° = -45.315 \text{ m/s}$$

$\therefore$ $F_x = 1 \times [50 - (-45.315)] = 95.315$ N

Similarly, the force exerted by the jet in the direction perpendicular to the direction of the jet per kg of flow,

$$F_y = 1 \times (V_{1y} - V_{2y})$$

where, V_{1y} = 0, and

$$V_{2y} = V\sin 25° = 50 \sin 25° = 21.13 \text{ m/s}$$

$\therefore$ $F_y = 1\,(0 - 21.13) = -21.13$ N

(– ve sign indicates that F_y is acting in the *downward direction.*)

$\therefore$ Resulting force per N of water (Refer to Fig. 1.14),

$$F_R = \sqrt{F_x^2 + F_y^2} = \sqrt{95.315^2 + 21.13^2} = \mathbf{97.63\ N} \text{ (Ans.)}$$

The angle made by the resultant with X-axis,

$$\tan\alpha = \frac{F_y}{F_x} = \frac{21.13}{95.315} = 0.2217$$

$\therefore$ $\alpha = \tan^{-1} 0.2217 = \mathbf{12.5°}$ **(Ans.)**

(b) Moving vane :

Velocity of the vane, u = 20 m/s

The force exerted by the jet on the moving vane in the direction of jet,

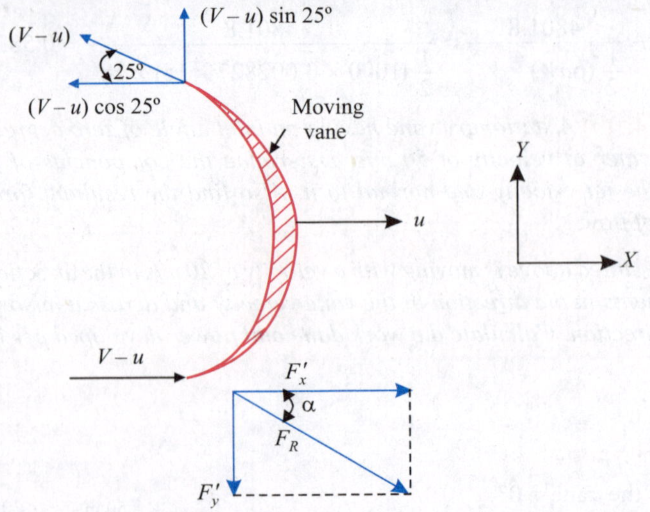

Fig. 1.15. Moving Vane.

$$F'_x = 1 \times (V_{1x} - V_{2x})$$

where, $V_{1x} = V - u = 50 - 20 = 30$ m/s

$V_{2x} = -(V-u)\cos 25° = -(50-20)\cos 25° = -27.19$ m/s

∴ $F'_x = 1 \times [30 - (-27.19)] =$ **57.19 N (Ans.)**

Similarly, $F'_y = 1 \times (V_{1y} - V_{2y})$

where $V_{1y} = 0$,

$V_{2y} = (V-u)\sin 25° = (50-20)\sin 25° = 12.67$ m/s

$F'_y = 1 \times (0 - 12.67) =$ **– 12.67 N (Ans.)**

∴ *Resultant force*, $F_R = \sqrt{F'^2_x + F'^2_y} = \sqrt{57.19^2 + 12.67^2} =$ **58.57 N (Ans.)**

The angle made by the resultant with X-axis,

$$\tan\alpha = \frac{F'_y}{F'_x} = \frac{12.67}{57.19} = 0.2215$$

or, $\alpha = \tan^{-1} 0.2215 =$ **12.5° (Ans.)**

Work done per second $= F'_x \times u = 57.19 \times 20 =$ **1143.8 Nm/s (Ans.)**

∴ *Power developed* = 1143.8 J/s or *W* or **1.1438 kW (Ans.)**

Example 1.15. *A jet of water 80 mm diameter and having a velocity of 20 m/s impinges at the centre of hemispherical vane. The linear velocity of vane is 10 m/s in the direction of jet. Find the force exerted on the vane. How this force would change if the jet impinges on a series of vanes attached to the circumference of wheel ?*

Solution. Diameter of the jet, $d = 80$ mm $= 0.08$ m

∴ Area, $a = \frac{\pi}{4} \times 0.08^2 = 0.005026$ m^3

Velocity of the jet, $V = 20$ m/s

Velocity of the vane, $u = 10$ m/s

When the jet strikes at the centre of a moving vane, then effective incoming velocity = $V - u$

Force exerted on the vane, $F = \rho a (V-u)^2 (1 + \cos\theta)$ ...[Eqn. (1.18)]

For a hemispherical vane, $\theta = 0$

$$\therefore \quad F = \rho a (V-u)^2 (1 + \cos 0°) = \rho a (V-u)^2 \times 2 = 2\rho a (V-u)^2$$
$$= 2 \times 1000 \times 0.005026 (20-10)^2 = \mathbf{1005.2\ N\ (Ans.)}$$

When the jet impinges on a *series of vanes,* the entire fluid mass issuing from the jet ($m = \rho a V$) hits the vane and the force exerted by the jet on the vane system is

$$F = \rho a V (V-u)(1+\cos\theta) \qquad \text{...[Eqn. (1.22)]}$$
$$= \rho a V (V-u)(1+\cos 0°)$$
$$= 2\rho a V (V-u) \qquad (\because \theta = 0°)$$
$$= 2 \times 1000 \times 0.005026 \times 20 \times (20-10) = \mathbf{2010.4\ N\ (Ans.)}$$

Example 1.16. *A jet strikes tangentially a smooth curved vane moving in the same direction as the jet, and the jet gets reversed in the direction. Show that the maximum efficiency is slightly less than 60 per cent.*

Solution. Refer to Fig 1.16.

Let, V = Velocity of the jet, and

u = Velocity of the vane.

($V > u$ for impact)

The force exerted by jet in the direction of motion of the vane,

$$F_x = \text{Mass/sec} \times \text{change in velocity}$$
$$= \rho a (V-u)[(V-u) - \{-(V-u)\}]$$

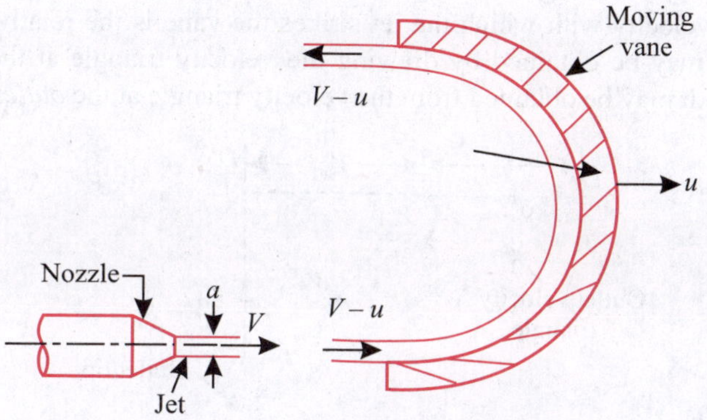

Fig. 1.16.

$$= \rho a (V-u)[(V-u) + (V-u)]$$
$$= 2\rho a (V-u)^2$$

$$\text{Work done} = F_x \times u = 2\rho a (V-u)^2 \times u$$

$$\eta = \frac{\text{Work done on the vane}}{\text{Kinetic energy of the jet}}$$

$$= \frac{2\rho a (V-u)^2 \times u}{\frac{1}{2}(\rho a V) V^2} = 4 \times \frac{u (V-u)^2}{V^3} \qquad \text{...}(i)$$

For *maximum efficiency,* $\dfrac{d\eta}{dV} = 0$

or, $$\frac{d}{dV}\left[\frac{4u (V-u)^2}{V^3}\right] = 4u\left[\frac{V^3 \times 2(V-u) - (V-u)^2 \times 3V^2}{V^6}\right] = 0$$

or, $$\frac{2V^3 (V-u) - (V-u)^2 \times 3V^2}{V^6} = 0 \qquad (\because u \neq 0)$$

or, $$2V(V-u) - 3(V-u)^2 = 0$$

or, $$(V-u)[2V - 3(V-u)] = 0$$

or, $$(V-u)(2V - 3V + 3u) = 0$$

or, $$(V-u)(3u - V) = 0, \ (V-u) \neq 0, \text{ for impact,}$$

$$\therefore \quad 3u - V = 0 \text{ or } u = \frac{V}{3}$$

Substituting this value of $u \left(= \frac{V}{3}\right)$ in expression (i), we get

$$\eta_{max} = 4 \times \frac{V/3\left(V - \frac{V}{3}\right)^2}{V^3} = \frac{16}{27} = 0.593 \text{ or } \mathbf{59.3\%}$$

which is slightly less than 60%. **(Ans.)**

1.8. JET STRIKING A MOVING CURVED VANE TANGENTIALLY AT ONE TIP AND LEAVING AT THE OTHER

A. Single vane:

Fig. 1.17, shows a jet striking a moving curved vane tangentially at one tip and leaving at the other. The effective velocity with which the jet strikes the vane is the relative velocity (V_{r1}). The relative velocity V_{r1} may be obtained by drawing the velocity triangle at the *inlet.* The absolute velocity (V_2) at the exit may be obtained from the velocity triangle at the *outlet.* Fig. 1.17 shows the velocity triangles.

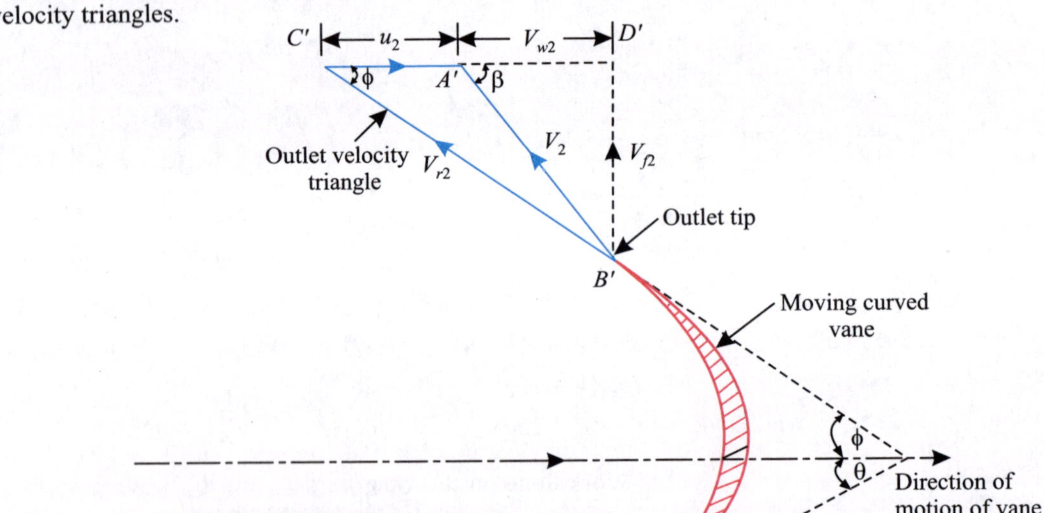

Fig. 1.17. Jet striking a moving curved vane tangentially at one tip and leaving at the other.

Let, V_1, V_2 = Absolute velocities of the jet at the inlet and outlet respectively,
u_1, u_2 = Peripheral velocities of the vane at the inlet and outlet respectively,
V_{r1}, V_{r2} = Relative velocities at the inlet and outlet respectively,
V_{f1}, V_{f2} = Velocities of the flow at the inlet and outlet respectively,
V_{w1}, V_{w2} = Velocities of the whirl at the inlet and outlet respectively,
θ, ϕ = Tip angles at the inlet and outlet respectively,
α, β = Angles which the absolute velocities make at the inlet and outlet respectively.

It may be *noted* that:

- All angles are measured with the direction of motion of vane,
- The velocity of whirl is the component of the absolute velocity in the direction of motion.
- The velocity of flow is the component of the absolute velocity normal to the direction of motion.

The triangles ABD and $B'C'D'$ are called *inlet* and *outlet velocity triangles* and are drawn as follows:

1. Inlet velocity triangle:

- Take any point A and draw a line $AB = V_1$ (in magnitude), making an angle α with the horizontal line AD.
- Draw a line $AC = u_1$ and join C to B, CB then represents relative velocity (V_{r1}) of the jet at inlet. If the loss of energy at inlet due to *impact is zero,* then CB *must be in the tangential direction* to the vane at inlet.
- From B draw a perpendicular BD meeting the horizontal line AC produced at D. Then BD represents the velocity of flow at Inlet (V_{f1}). AD represents the velocity of whirl at inlet (V_{w1}). $\angle BCD = \theta$ = vane angle at inlet.

2. Outlet velocity triangle:

If the vane surface is assumed *smooth,* the energy loss due to friction will be zero and thus $V_{r1} = V_{r2}$ will be in tangential direction to the vane at outlet.

- Draw $B'C'$ in the tangential direction of the vane at outlet and cut $B'C' = V_{r2}$.
- From C' draw a line $C'A'$ in the direction of vane at outlet and equal to u_2 (the velocity of vane at outlet). Join $B'A'$. Then $B'A'$ represents the absolute velocity of the jet (V_2) at outlet in magnitude and direction.
- From B' draw a perpendicular $B'D'$ to meet the line $C'A'$ produced at D'. Then $B'D'$ and $A'D'$ represent the velocity of flow (V_{f2}) and velocity of whirl (V_{w2}) at outlet respectively.
- ϕ = angle of vane at outlet, β = angle made by V_2 with the direction of motion of vane at outlet.

If vane is *smooth* and is having velocity in the direction of motion at inlet and outlet *equal,* then

$$u_1 = u_2 = u \text{ (velocity in the direction of motion), and } V_{r1} = V_{r2}$$

Mass of water striking the vane per second = $\rho a V_{r1}$

(where, a = area of jet water)

∴ Force exerted in the direction of motion,

F_x = Mass of water striking the vane per second × (Initial velocity with which the jet strikes in the *direction of motion* – final velocity)

$$= \rho a V_{r1}[V_{r1}\cos\theta - (-V_{r2}\cos\phi)]$$

But, $V_{r1}\cos\theta = (V_{w1} - u_1)$, and $V_{r2}\cos\phi = (u_2 + V_{w2})$ (Refer to Fig. 1.17)

$$\therefore \quad F_x = \rho a V_{r1}[(V_{w1} - u_1) - \{-(u_2 + V_{w2})\}]$$

$$= \rho a V_{r1}[V_{w1} - u_1 + u_2 + V_{w2}]$$

or, $F_x = \rho a V_{r1} (V_{w1} + V_{w2})$ $(\because u_1 = u_2)$ ...(*i*)

The eqn. (*i*) is *true only when* β *is an actue angle* (See Fig. 1.17), When β = 90°, $V_{w2} = 0$ the eqn. (*i*) reduces to

$$F_x = \rho a V_{r1} (V_{w1})$$

If β is an *obtuse angle,* the expression for F_x will become

$$F_x = \rho a V_{r1} (V_{w1} - V_{w2})$$

Thus, in general F_x is written as:

$$F_x = \rho a V_{r1} (V_{w1} \pm V_{w2}) \qquad ...(1.27)$$

Work done per second by the jet on the vane

$$= F_x \times u = \rho a V_{r1} (V_{w1} \pm V_{w2}) \times u \qquad ...(1.28)$$

∴ Work done per second per unit weight of fluid striking

$$= \frac{\rho a V_{r1} (V_{w1} \pm V_{w2}) \times u}{\text{Weight of fluid striking}}$$

$$= \frac{\rho a V_{r1} (V_{w1} \pm V_{w2}) \times u}{\rho a V_{r1} \times g}$$

$$= \frac{1}{g} (V_{w1} \pm V_{w2}) \times u \qquad ...(1.29)$$

B. Force exerted on a series of radial curved vanes :

Consider a series of radial curved vanes mounted on a wheel as shown in Fig. 1.18. The jet water impinges upon the vanes and the wheel starts rotating at a constant angular speed.

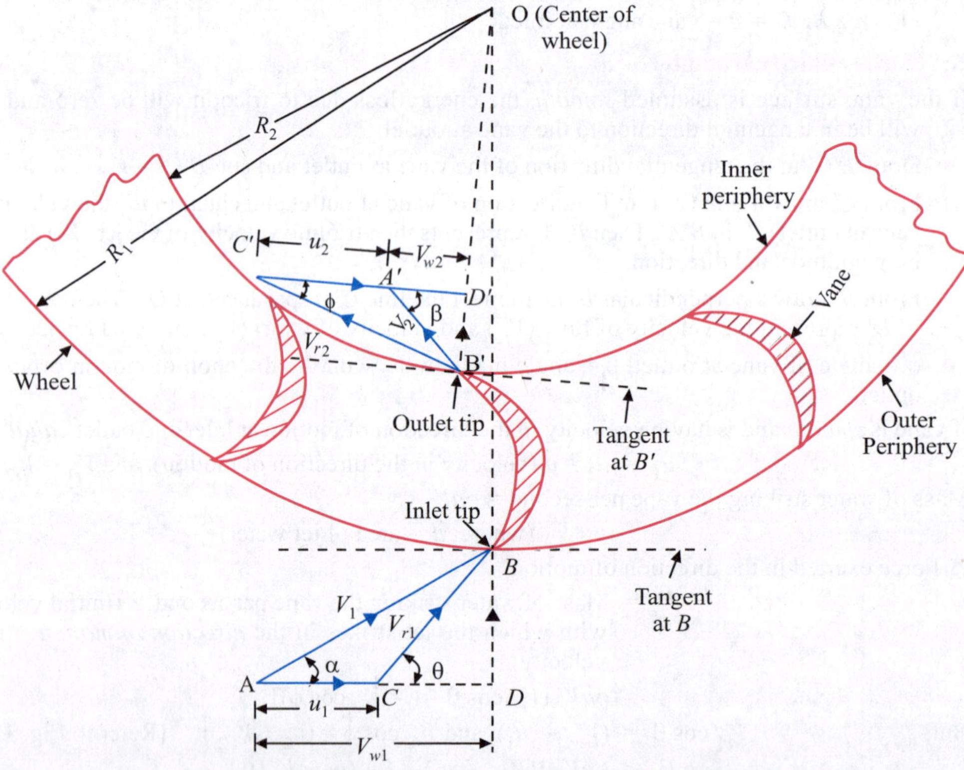

Fig. 1.18. Series of radially curved vanes mounted on a wheel.

Let, ω = Angular speed of the wheel, and

R_1, R_2 = Radii of the wheel at the inlet and outlet of the vane respectively.

As the vanes are situated radially round the wheel the blade velocities at the inlet and outlet tips of the vane would be different, *i.e.,*

$$u_1 = \omega R_1 \quad \text{and} \quad u_2 = \omega R_2$$

The flow system is inward or outward, depending upon whether the jet enters the outer periphery or the inner periphery.

The inlet and outlet triangles are shown in Fig. 1.18.

The mass of water striking per second (for a series of vanes)

= Mass of water issuing from the nozzle per second

= $\rho a V_1$ (where, a = area of jet, V_1 = velocity of jet).

Momentum of water striking the vanes (in tangential direction) per second *at inlet*

$$= (\rho a V_1) \times V_{w1}$$

[where, V_{w1} (= $V_1 \cos \alpha$) = component of V_1 in the *tangential direction.*]

Similarly, momentum of water per second at outlet

$$= \rho a V_1 \times (-V_{w2}) = -\rho a V_1 \times V_{w2}$$

[where, $V_{w2} = (V_2 \cos \beta)$ = component of V_2 in tangential direction]

–ve sign is taken as V_2 at outlet is in opposite direction.

Now, angular momentum per second at *inlet* = momentum at inlet × radius at inlet.

$$= (\rho a V_1) \times V_{w1} \times R_1$$

Angular momentum per second at outlet = $-(\rho a V_1) \times V_{w2} \times R_2$

Torque exerted by water on the wheel,

T = Rate of change of angular momentum

= (initial angular momentum per second – final angular momentum per second)

$$= \rho a V_1 \times V_{w1} \times R_1 - \{-(\rho a V_1 \times V_{w2} \times R_2)\}$$

$$= \rho a V_1 (V_{w1} \times R_1 + V_{w2} \times R_2)$$

Work done per second on the wheel = $T \times \omega$

$$= \rho a V_1 (V_{w1} \times R_1 + V_{w2} \times R_2) \times \omega$$

$$= \rho a V_1 (V_{w1} \times \omega R_1 + V_{w2} \times \omega R_2)$$

$$= \rho a V_1 (V_{w1} \times u_1 + V_{w2} \times u_2)$$

$$(\because u_1 = \omega R_1 \quad \text{and} \quad u_2 = \omega R_2)$$

In case β is an *obtuse angle* (Fig. 1.18) then work done per second is

$$= \rho a V_1 (V_{w1} u_1 - V_{w2} u_2)$$

$\therefore$ The general expression for the work done per second on the wheel

$$= \rho a V_1 (V_{w1} u_1 \pm V_{w2} u_2) \qquad ...(1.30)$$

If the discharge is radial at outlet, then $\beta = 90°$ and work done is

$$= \rho a V_1 (V_{w1} u_1) \qquad (\because V_{w_2} = 0)$$

Efficiency of the radial curved vane, η_{vane}:

$$\eta_{\text{vane}} = \frac{\text{Work done per second}}{\text{Kinetic energy per second}}$$

$$= \frac{\rho a V_1 [V_{w1} u_1 \pm V_{w2} u_2]}{\frac{1}{2}(\rho a V_1) \times V_1^2}$$

$$= \frac{2\,[V_{w1}u_1 \pm V_{w2}u_2]}{V_1^2} \quad ...(1.31)$$

Example 1.17. *A jet of water having a velocity of 40 m/s strikes a curved vane, which is moving with a velocity of 20 m/s. The jet makes an angle of 30° with the direction of motion of vane at inlet and leaves at an angle of 90° to the direction of motion of vane at outlet. Draw the velocity triangles at inlet and outlet and determine the vane angles at inlet and outlet so that the water enters and leaves the vane without shock.*

[Delhi University]

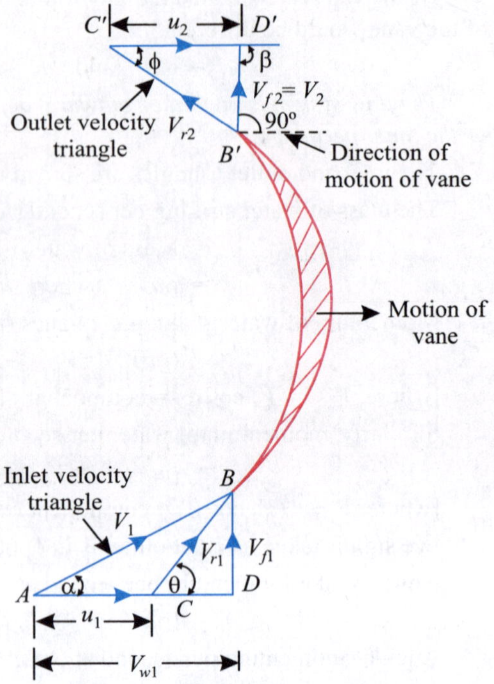

Fig. 1.19.

Solution. Velocity of jet, $V_1 = 40$ m/s

Velocity of vane, $u_1 = 20$ m/s

Angle made by the jet at inlet, $\alpha = 30°$

Angle made by the jet at outlet = 90°

$\therefore \quad \beta = 180° - 90° = 90°$

Here, we have $u_1 = u_2 = u = 20$ m/s

Vane angles at inlet and outlet:

Vane angles at inlet and outlet are θ and φ respectively.

From Δ *BCD*, we have

$$\tan\theta = \frac{BD}{CD} = \frac{BD}{AD - AC} = \frac{V_{f1}}{V_{w1} - u_1}$$

where,

$$V_{f1} = V_1 \sin\alpha = 40 \times \sin 30° = 20 \text{ m/s}$$

$$V_{w1} = V_1 \cos\alpha = 40 \times \cos 30° = 34.64 \text{ m/s}$$

$$u_1 = 20 \text{ m/s} \quad \textit{(Given)}$$

$$\because \quad \tan\theta = \frac{20}{34.64 - 20} = 1.366$$

or, $\theta = \tan^{-1}(1.366) = $ **53.79° (Ans.)**

Again form Δ *BCD*, we have:

$$\sin\theta = \frac{V_{f1}}{V_{r1}}, \text{ or, } V_{r1} = \frac{V_{f1}}{\sin\theta} = \frac{20}{\sin 53.79°} = 24.78 \text{ m/s}$$

But, $V_{r2} = V_{r1} = 24.78$ m/s

Hence from Δ *B'C'D'*, we have:

$$\cos\phi = \frac{u_2}{V_{r2}} = \frac{20}{24.78} = 0.8071$$

or, $\phi = \cos^{-1}(0.8071) = $ **36.18° (Ans.)**

Example 1.18. *A jet of water having a velocity of 45 m/s impinges without shock on a series of vanes moving at 15 m/s. The direction of motion of the vanes is inclined at 20° to that of jet. The relative velocity at outlet is 0.9 of that at inlet, and absolute velocity of water at exit is to be normal to the motion of vanes. Find:*

(i) Vane angles at inlet and outlet,

(ii) Work done on vanes per N (newton) of water supplied by the jet, and

(iii) Hydraulic efficiency. **[UPTU]**

Solution. Velocity of the jet, $V_1 = 45$ m/s

Velocity of vane, $u_1 = u_2 = (u =)$ 15 m/s

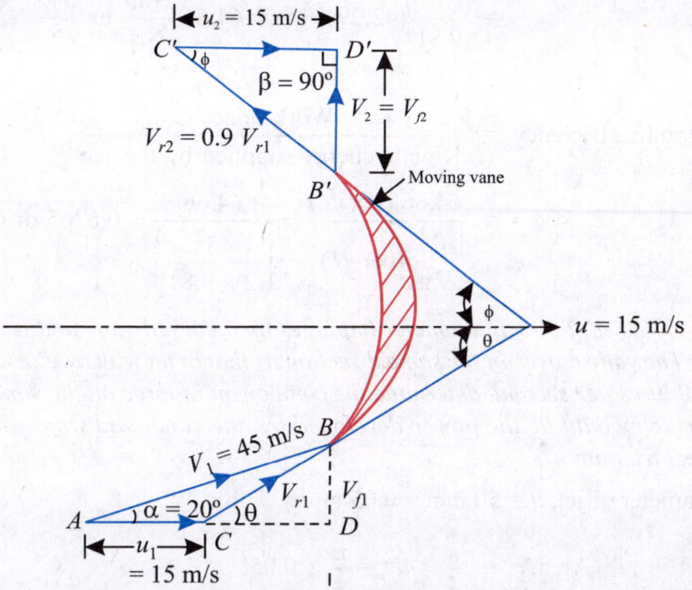

Fig. 1.20.

Angle made by jet at inlet, with direction of motion of vane, $\alpha = 20°$

Relative velocity at outlet, $V_{r2} = 0.9V_{r1}$ (relative velocity at inlet).

(i) Vane angles at inlet and outlet :

Vane angles at inlet and outlet are θ and ϕ.

$$\text{In } \Delta\ BCD,\ \tan\theta = \frac{V_{f1}}{(V_{w1} - u_1)}$$

where,

$$V_{f1} = V_1 \sin\alpha = 45° \sin 20° = 15.39 \text{ m/s}$$

$$V_{w1} = V_1 \cos\alpha = 45 \cos 20° = 42.29 \text{ m/s}$$

$$\therefore \quad \tan\theta = \frac{15.39}{42.29 - 15} = 0.564$$

or,

$$\theta = \tan^{-1} 0.564 = \mathbf{29.42°} \text{ (Ans.)}$$

$$\text{Again from } \Delta\ BCD,\ \frac{V_{f1}}{V_{r1}} = \sin\theta \quad \text{or} \quad V_{r1} = \frac{V_{f1}}{\sin\theta} = \frac{15.39}{\sin 29.42°} = 31.33 \text{ m/s}$$

$$\therefore \quad V_{r2} = 0.9\ V_{r1} = 0.9 \times 31.33 = 28.2 \text{ m/s}$$

From $\Delta\ B'C'D'$, we have:

$$\cos\phi = \frac{u_2}{V_{r2}} = \frac{15}{28.2} = 0.5319$$

$$\therefore \quad \phi = \cos^{-1} 0.5319 = \mathbf{57.87°} \text{ (Ans.)}$$

(ii) Work done on vanes per N of water :

Work done per second per N of water striking

$$= \frac{1}{g}(V_{w1}\,u_1 + V_{w2}\,u_2) = \frac{1}{g}(V_{w1}\,u_1) \qquad [\because V_{w2} = 0]$$

$$= \frac{1}{9.81}(42.29 \times 15) = \mathbf{64.66}\ \frac{\textbf{N.m}}{\textbf{N.s}}\ \textbf{or}\ \frac{\textbf{J / s}}{\textbf{N}}\ \textbf{(Ans.)}$$

(iii) Hydraulic efficiency :

$$\text{Hydraulic efficiency} = \frac{\text{Work done}}{\text{Kinetic energy supplied by the jet}}$$

$$= \frac{64.66\ (\text{per } N)}{\frac{V_1^2}{2g}\ (\text{per } N)} = \frac{64.66}{\left(\frac{45^2}{2 \times 9.81}\right)} = 0.6265 \text{ or } \mathbf{62.65\%}\ \textbf{(Ans.)}$$

Example 1.19. *A jet of 50 mm diameter impinges on a curved vane and is deflected through an angle of 175°. The vane moves in the same direction as that of jet with a velocity of 35 m/s. If the rate of flow is 170 litres per second, determine the component of force on the vane in the direction of motion. How much would be the power developed by the vane and what would be the water efficiency? Neglect friction.* **[Punjab University]**

Solution. Diameter of jet, $d = 50$ mm $= 0.05$ m

$$\therefore \quad \text{Area, } a = \frac{\pi}{4} \times d^2 = \frac{\pi}{4} \times 0.05^2$$

$$= 0.001963 \text{ m}^2$$

Angle of deflection = 175°

Velocity of the vane, $u_1 = u_2\ (= u) = 35$ m/s.

Rate of flow, Q = 170 litres = 0.17 m³/s

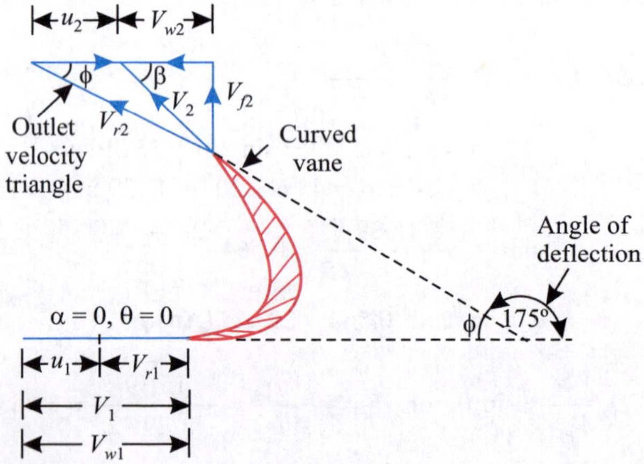

Fig. 1.21.

Since the jet of water moves in the same direction as that of vane, $\alpha = \theta = 0$ and, therefore, the inlet velocity triangle will be a *straight line* with,

$$V_1 = \frac{Q}{a} = \frac{0.17}{0.001963} = 86{\cdot}6 \text{ m/s}$$

$$V_{r1} = V_1 - u_1 = 86.6 - 35 = 51.6 \text{ m/s}$$

and, $$V_{w1} = V_1 = 86.6 \text{ m/s}$$

Corresponding to outlet velocity triangle,

$$\phi = 180° - 175° = 5°$$

Further, since the vane is *smooth*, therefore,

$$V_{r2} = V_{r1} = 51.6 \text{ m/s}$$

$$V_{w2} = V_{r2} \cos \phi - u_2$$

$$= 51.6 \times \cos 5° - 35 = 16.4 \text{ m/s}$$

Power developed by the vane :

Force exerted by the jet on the vane in the direction of motion,

$$F = \rho a V_{r1} (V_{w1} + V_{w2})$$

$$= 1000 \times 0.001963 \times 51.6 (86.6 + 16.4) = 10432.9 \text{ N}$$

$$\text{Work done} = \text{Force} \times \text{velocity}$$

$$= 10432.9 \times 35 = 365151 \text{ Nm/s or J/s}$$

Hence, *power developed by the vane* = 365151 J/s or W or **365.151 kW (Ans.)**

$$\textit{Efficiency of vane (water efficiency)} = \frac{\text{Work done on the vane}}{\text{Kinetic energy supplied by the jet}}$$

$$= \frac{365151}{\frac{1}{2}\rho Q V_1^2} = \frac{365151}{\frac{1}{2} \times 1000 \times 0.17 \times 86.6^2} = 0.573 \text{ or } \mathbf{57.3\%} \text{ (Ans.)}$$

Example 1.20. *A jet of water moving at 12 m/s impinges on a concave shaped vane to deflect the jet through 120° when stationary. The vane is moving at 5 m/s. Find:*

(i) The angle of jet so that there is no shock at inlet,

(ii) The absolute velocity of the jet at exit both in magnitude and direction, and

(iii) The work done per second per N of water.

Assume that vane is smooth. **[Anna University]**

Solution. Velocity at jet, $V_1 = 12$ m/s

Velocity of vane, $u_1 = u_2 (= u) = 5$ m/s

Angle of deflection of the jet = 120°

(i) The angle of the jet at inlet of the vane, α :

Assuming vane to be symmetrical, we have

$$\theta = \phi$$

Now, $$120° = 180 - (\theta + \phi)$$

∴ $$\theta + \phi = (180° - 120°) = 60° \quad \therefore \theta = \phi = 30°$$

Applying sine rule to Δ *ABC,* we have:

$$\frac{AB}{\sin (180° - \theta)} = \frac{AC}{\sin (\theta - \alpha)}, \text{ or, } \frac{V_1}{\sin \theta} = \frac{u_1}{\sin (\theta - \alpha)}$$

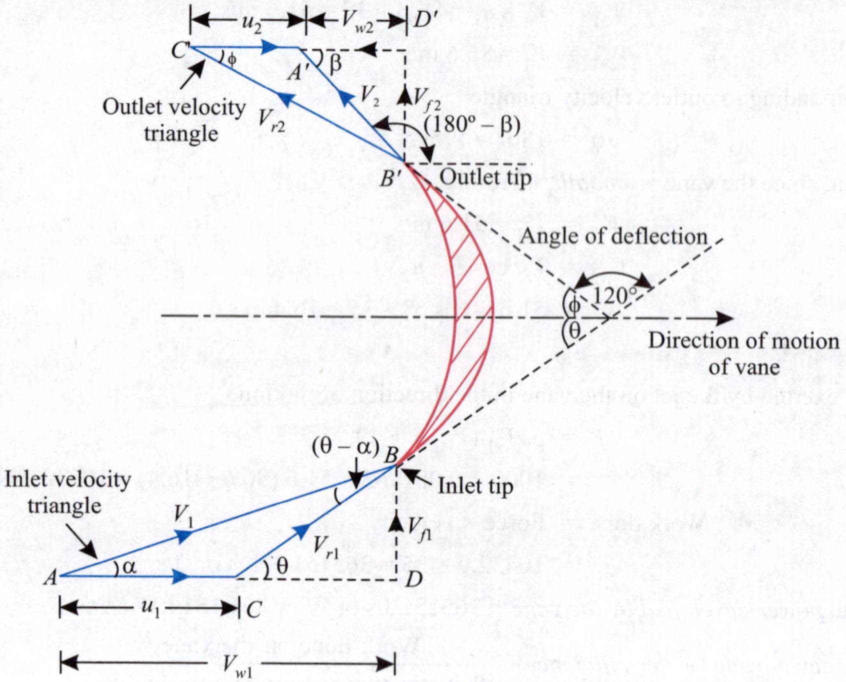

Fig. 1.22.

or, $$\frac{12}{\sin 30°} = \frac{5}{\sin (30° - \alpha)}, \text{ or, } \sin (30° - \alpha) = \frac{5 \times \sin 30°}{12} = 0.2083$$

∴ $$30° - \alpha = \sin^{-1} 0.2083 = 12°$$

or, $$\alpha = 30° - 12° = \mathbf{18° \text{ (Ans.)}}$$

***(ii)* The absolute velocity of the jet at exit; V_2:**

Again applying sine rule to ΔABC, we have:

$$\frac{V_1}{\sin (180° - \theta)} = \frac{V_{r1}}{\sin \alpha}, \text{ or, } \frac{12}{\sin \theta} = \frac{V_{r1}}{\sin 18°}$$

∴ $$V_{r1} = \frac{12 \times \sin 18°}{\sin \theta} = \frac{12 \times \sin 18°}{\sin 30°} = 7.42 \text{ m/s}$$

In ΔABD: $V_{w1} = V_1 \cos \alpha = 12 \cos 18° = 11.41$ m/s

Now, since the vane is *smooth,* therefore,

$$V_{r2} = V_{r1} = 7.42 \text{ m/s}$$

At *outlet,* from $\Delta B'C'D'$, we have:

$$V_{r2} \cos \phi = u_2 + V_{w2}$$

∴ $$V_{w2} = V_{r2} \cos \phi - u_2 = 7.42 \cos 30° - 5 = 1.42 \text{ m/s}$$

Also, $$V_{f2} = V_{r2} \sin \phi = 7.42 \sin 30° = 3.71 \text{ m/s}$$

Now, $$\tan \beta = \frac{V_{f2}}{V_{w2}} = \frac{3.71}{1.42} = 2.613$$

∴ Angle of jet at outlet, $\beta = \tan^{-1} 2.613 = 69.06°$

Hence, angle made by V_2 at oulet with direction of motion of vane is

$$= 180° - \beta = 180° - 69.06° = \mathbf{110.94°}\ \textbf{(Ans.)}$$

Absolute velocity of jet at exit, $V_2 = \sqrt{V_{w2}^2 + V_{f2}^2}$

$$= \sqrt{1.42^2 + 3.71^2} = \mathbf{3.97\ m/s}\ \textbf{(Ans.)}$$

(iii) The work done per second per N of water :

The work done per second per N of water

$$= \frac{1}{g}(V_{w1}u_1 + V_{w2}u_2) = \frac{1}{g}(V_{w1} + V_{w2}) \times u \quad [\because \beta < 90°]$$

$$= \frac{9}{9.81}(11.41 + 1.42) \times 5 = \mathbf{6.539\ Nm}\ \textbf{(Ans.)}$$

Example 1.21. *A jet of water having a velocity of 35 m/s impinges on a series of vanes moving with a velocity of 20 m/s. The jet makes an angle of 30° to the direction of motion of vanes when entering and leaves at an angle of 120°. Draw the triangles of velocities at inlet and outlet and find:*

(i) The angles of vanes tips so that water enters and leaves without shock,

(ii) The work done per N of water entering the vanes, and

(iii) The efficiency. **[AMIE, Fluid Power Engg.]**

Solution. Velocity of jet, $V_1 = 35$ m/s

Velocity of vane, $u_1 = u_2 (= u) = 20$ m/s

Angle made by jet at inlet, $\alpha = 30°$

Angle made by the jet at outlet $= 120°$ (with the direction of motion of vane)

$\therefore$ $\beta = 180 - 120 = 60°$ (See Fig. 1.23)

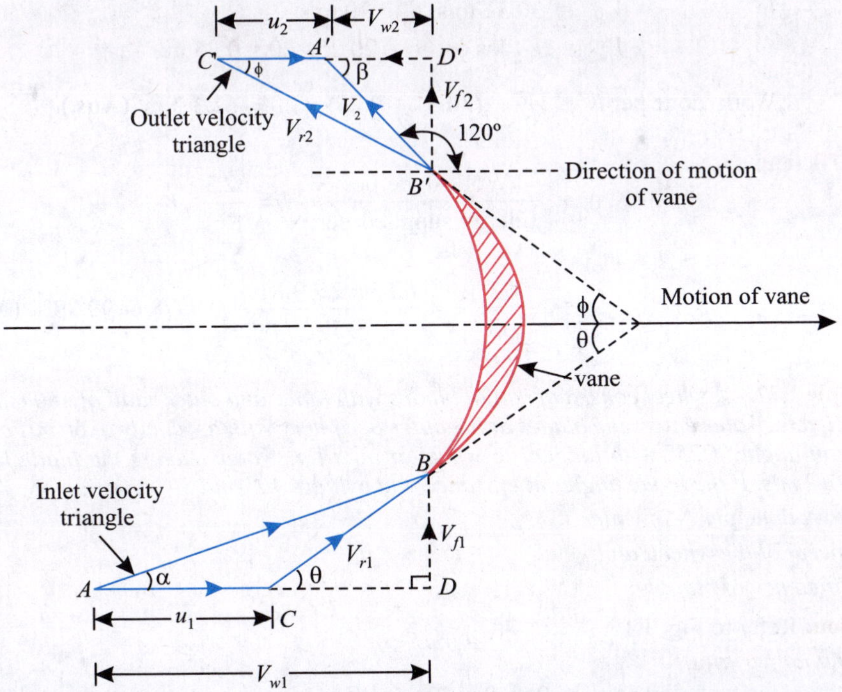

Fig. 1.23.

(i) Angles of vane tips :

From inlet triangle, we have:

$$V_{w1} = V_1 \cos\alpha = 35 \cos 30° = 30.31 \text{ m/s}$$

$$V_{f1} = V_1 \sin\alpha = 35 \sin 30° = 17.50 \text{ m/s}$$

$$\tan\theta = \frac{V_{f1}}{V_{w1} - u_1} = \frac{17.5}{30.31 - 20} = 1.697$$

$$\therefore \quad \theta = \tan^{-1} 1.697 \simeq \mathbf{60°} \textbf{ (Ans.)}$$

Applying sine rule to inlet velocity triangle, we have:

$$\frac{V_{r1}}{\sin 90°} = \frac{V_{f1}}{\sin\theta} \quad \text{or} \quad \frac{V_{r1}}{1} = \frac{17.50}{\sin 60°} \quad \text{or} \quad V_{r1} = 20.25 \text{ m/s}$$

Now, $V_{r2} = V_{r1} = 20.25$ m/s

Applying sine rule to outlet velocity triangle, we have:

$$\frac{V_{r2}}{\sin 120°} = \frac{u_2}{\sin(60° - \phi)}, \quad \text{or,} \quad \frac{20.25}{\sin 120°} = \frac{20}{\sin(60° - \phi)}$$

or,
$$\sin(60° - \phi) = \frac{20 \times \sin 120°}{20.25} = 0.855$$

or,
$$60° - \phi = \sin^{-1}(0.855) \quad \text{or} \quad \phi = 58.75°$$

$$\therefore \quad \phi = 60° - 58.75° = \mathbf{1.25°} \textbf{ (Ans.)}$$

(ii) Work done per N of water entering the vanes :

Work done per N of water entering the vanes

$$= \frac{1}{g}(V_{w1} + V_{w2}) \times u_1 \qquad [\because \beta < 90°]$$

$$V_{w1} = 30.31 \text{ m/s}, \; u_1 = 20 \text{ m/s}$$

$$V_{w2} = V_{r2}\cos\phi - u_2 = 20.25 - 20 = 0.25 \text{ m/s}$$

$$\therefore \quad \text{Work done per } N = \frac{1}{9.81}(30.31 + 0.25) \times 20 = \mathbf{62.3 \text{ Nm}} \textbf{ (Ans.)}$$

(iii) Efficiency, η :

$$\eta = \frac{\text{Work done per N}}{\text{Energy supplied per N}} = \frac{62.3}{\frac{V_1^2}{2g}}$$

$$= \frac{62.3}{\frac{35^2}{2 \times 9.81}} = \frac{62.3 \times 2 \times 9.81}{35^2} = 0.9978 \text{ or } \mathbf{99.78\%} \textbf{ (Ans.)}$$

Example 1.22. *A wheel consist of radial blades with inner and outer radii of 360 mm and 720 mm respectively. Water enters the blades at the outer periphery with a velocity of 60 m/s and supply jet makes an angle of 25° with tangent to wheel at inlet tip. Water leaving the blade has a flow velocity of 12 m/s. If the blade angles at entrance and exit are 40° and 30° respectively, determine:*

(i) Work done per N of water,

(ii) Speed of the wheel, and

(iii) Efficiency of blading.

Solution. Refer to Fig. 1.18.

Inlet velocity triangle :

$$\alpha = 25°, \theta = 40° \text{ and } V_1 = 60 \text{ m/s}$$

$$V_{f1} = V_1 \sin\alpha = 60 \sin 25° = 25.36 \text{ m/s}$$

$$V_{w1} = V_1 \cos \alpha = 60 \cos 25° = 54.38 \text{ m/s}$$

$$u_1 = V_{w1} - \frac{V_{f1}}{\tan \theta} = 54.38 - \frac{25.36}{\tan 40°} = 24.16 \text{ m}$$

Outlet velocity triangle :

$$\phi = 30°, V_{f2} = 12 \text{ m/s}$$

Since, $u_1 = \omega R_1$ and $u_2 = \omega R_2$

$$\therefore \quad u_2 = u_1 \times \frac{R_2}{R_1} = 24.16 \times \frac{0.36}{0.72} = 12.08 \text{ m/s}$$

$(\because R_2 = 360 \text{ mm} = 0.36 \text{ m}$ and $R_1 = 720 \text{ mm} = 0.72 \text{ m})$

$$V_{w2} = \frac{V_{f2}}{\tan 30°} - u_2 = \frac{12}{\tan 30°} - 12.08 = 8.70 \text{ m/s}$$

(*i*) Work done per N of water :

The work done per second per N of water

$$= \frac{1}{g}(V_{w1} u_1 + V_{w2} u_2) \qquad [\because \beta < 90°]$$

$$= \frac{1}{9.81}(54.38 \times 24.16 + 8.70 \times 12.08) = \mathbf{144.6 \text{ Nm}} \text{ (Ans.)}$$

(*ii*) Speed of the wheel :

$$\text{Angular velocity, } \omega = \frac{u_1}{R_1} = \frac{24.16}{0.72} = 38.55 \text{ rad/s}$$

But, $\omega = \dfrac{2\pi N}{60}$ where N is the speed of the wheel.

$$\therefore \quad N = \frac{\omega \times 60}{2\pi} = \frac{33.55 \times 60}{2\pi} \ \mathbf{320.38 \text{ r.p.m.}} \text{ (Ans.)}$$

(*iii*) Efficiency of blading, η :

$$\eta = \frac{\text{Work done}}{\text{Energy supplied by jet}} = \frac{144.6}{\frac{V_1^2}{2g}\text{(per N of water)}}$$

$$= \frac{144.6}{\frac{60^2}{2 \times 9.81}} = \frac{144.6 \times 2 \times 9.81}{60^2} = 0.788 \text{ or } \mathbf{78.8\%} \text{ (Ans.)}$$

Example 1.23. *A jet of water having a velocity of 18 m/s strikes a curved vane which is moving with a velocity of 6 m/s. The vane is symmetrical and so shaped that the jet is deflected through 120°. Determine:*

(*i*) *The angle of the jet at inlet of the vane so that there is no shock,*

(*ii*) *The absolute velocity of the jet at outlet in magnitude and direction, and*

(*iii*) *The work done per N of water.*

Solution. Velocity of jet, $V_1 = 18$ m/s

Velocity of vane, $u_1 = u_2 (= u) = 6$ m/s

Refer to Fig 1.24.

(i) The angle of jet at inlet of the vane, α :

As the vane is *symmetrical*, hence $\theta = \phi$

Angle of deflection of jet = 120° (*Given*)

$$120° = 180° - (\theta + \phi) \quad \text{or} \quad \theta + \phi = 180° - 120° = 60°$$

$$\therefore \quad \theta = \phi = 30°$$

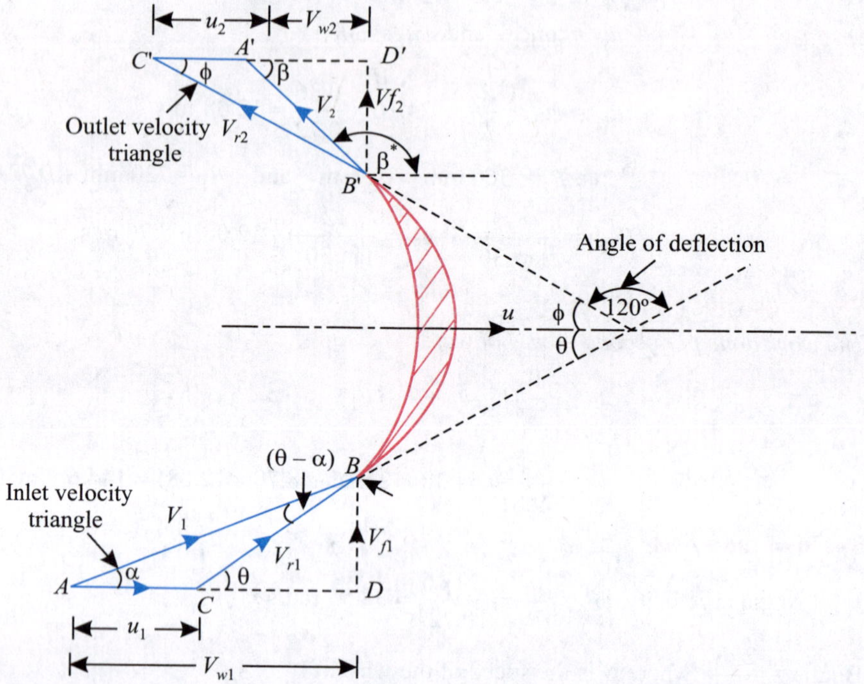

Fig. 1.24.

Applying sine rule to Δ *ABC,* we have:

$$\frac{AC}{\sin(\theta - \alpha)} = \frac{AB}{\sin(180° - 30°)}$$

or,
$$\frac{u_1}{\sin(30° - \alpha)} = \frac{V_1}{\sin 30°}$$

or,
$$\frac{6}{\sin(30° - \alpha)} = \frac{18}{\sin 30°}$$

or,
$$\sin(30° - \alpha) = \frac{6 \times \sin 30°}{18} = 0.1667$$

or,
$$30° - \alpha = \sin^{-1}(0.1667) = 9.6°$$

$$\therefore \quad \alpha = 30° - 9.6° = \mathbf{20.4°} \text{ (Ans.)}$$

(ii) The absolute velocity of jet at outlet, V_2 :

$$V_{r1} = V_{r2} \qquad (\because \text{ Vane is smooth.})$$

Again, applying sine rule to Δ *ABC,* we have:

$$\frac{AB}{\sin(180° - \theta)} = \frac{BC}{\sin \alpha}, \quad \text{or,} \quad \frac{V_1}{\sin(180° - 30°)} = \frac{V_{r1}}{\sin 20.4°}$$

or, $\dfrac{18}{\sin 30°} = \dfrac{V_{r1}}{\sin 20.4°}$ or $V_{r1} = \dfrac{18 \times \sin 20.4°}{\sin 30°} = 12.55$ m/s

$\therefore \quad V_{r2} = V_{r1} = 12.55$ m/s

From outlet velocity triangle $B'C'D'$, we have:

$$V_{r2} \cos \phi = u_2 + V_{w2}$$

$$12.55 \cos 30° = 5 + V_{w2}$$

or, $V_{w2} = 12.55 \cos 30° - 6 = 4.87$ m/s

Also, $V_{f2} = V_{r2} \sin \phi = 12.55 \times \sin 30° = 6.27$ m/s

From $\Delta B'A'D'$, we have:

$$V_2 = \sqrt{V_{w2}^2 + V_{f2}^2} = \sqrt{(4.87)^2 + (6.27)^2} = \mathbf{7.94\ m/s}\ \textbf{(Ans.)}$$

$$\tan \beta = \frac{V_{f2}}{V_{w2}} = \frac{6.27}{4.87} = 1.287$$

$\therefore \quad \beta = \tan^{-1} 1.287 = 52.15°$

$\therefore$ *Angle made by absolute velocity at outlet with the direction of motion,*

$$\beta^* = 180 - \beta = 180° - 52.15° = \mathbf{127.85°}\ \textbf{(Ans.)}$$

(*iii*) The work done per N of water :

The work done per *N* of water

$$= \frac{1}{g} (V_{w1} + V_{w2}) \times u \qquad (\because \beta < 90°)$$

$$= \frac{1}{9.81} (V_1 \cos \alpha + V_{w2}) \times u \qquad (\because V_{w1} = V_1 \cos \alpha)$$

$$= \frac{1}{9.81} (18 \cos 20.4° + 4.87) \times 6 = \mathbf{13.3\ Nm/s}\ \textbf{(Ans.)}$$

Example 1.24. *A jet of water having a velocity of 36 m/s strikes a series of radial curved vanes mounted on a wheel which is rotating at 240 r.p.m. The jet makes an angle of 20° with the tangent to the wheel at inlet and leaves the wheel with a velocity of 6 m/s at an angle of 130° to the tangent to the wheel at outlet. Water is flowing from outward in a radial direction. The outer and inner radii of the wheel are 500 mm and 250 mm respectively. Determine:*

(*i*) *Vane angles at inlet and outlet,*

(*ii*) *Work done per second per N of water, and*

(*iii*) *Efficiency of the wheel.*

Solution. Velocity of jet, $V_1 = 36$ m/s

Speed of wheel, $N = 240$ r.p.m.

$\therefore$ Angular speed, $\omega = \dfrac{2\pi N}{60} = \dfrac{2\pi \times 240}{60} = 25.13$ rad./s

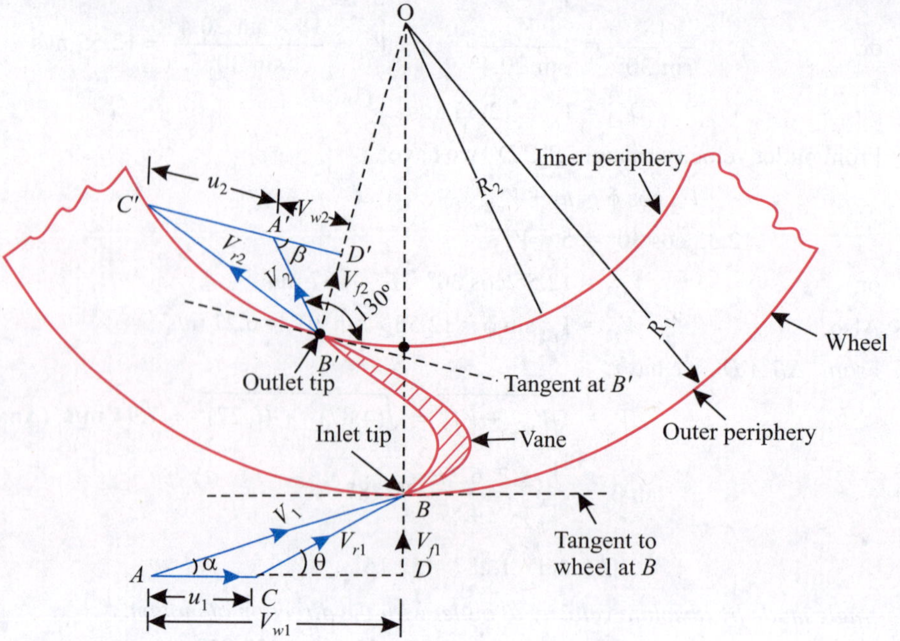

Fig. 1.25.

Angle of jet inlet, $\alpha = 20°$

Velocity of jet at outlet, $V_2 = 6$ m/s

Angle made by the jet at outlet with the tangent to wheel = 130°

$\therefore$ Angle, $\beta = 180 - 130° = 50°$

Outer radius, $R_1 = 500$ mm = 0.5 m

Inner radius, $R_2 = 250$ mm = 0.25 m

$\therefore$ Velocity, $u_1 = \omega R_1 = 25.13 \times 0.5 = 12.56$ m/s

and, $u_2 = \omega R_2 = 25.13 \times 0.25 = 6.28$ m/s

(*i*) Vane angles at inlet and outlet, θ and ϕ :

From ΔABD, we have:

$$V_{w1} = V_1 \cos \alpha = 36 \times \cos 20° = 33.83 \text{ m/s}$$

$$V_{f1} = V_1 \sin \alpha = 36 \times \sin 20° = 12.31 \text{ m/s}$$

In ΔCBD, $\tan \theta = \dfrac{BD}{CD} = \dfrac{BD}{AD - AC} = \dfrac{V_{f1}}{V_{w1} - u_1} = \dfrac{12.31}{33.83 - 12.56} = 0.578$

$\therefore$ $\theta = \tan^{-1} 0.578 =$ **30° (Ans.)**

From outlet velocity triangle, we have:

$$V_{w2} = V_2 \cos \beta = 6 \cos 50° = 3.86 \text{ m/s}$$

$$V_{f2} = V_2 \sin \beta = 6 \sin 50° = 4.59 \text{ m/s}$$

In $\Delta B'C'D'$, $\tan \phi = \dfrac{V_{f2}}{u_2 + V_{w2}} = \dfrac{4.59}{6.28 + 3.86} = 0.4527$

$\therefore$ $\phi = \tan^{-1} (0.4527) =$ **24.35° (Ans.)**

(ii) Work done per second per N of water :

$$\text{Work done per second} = \frac{1}{g}(V_{w1}u_1 + V_{w2}u_2) \qquad (\because \beta < 90°)$$

$$= \frac{1}{9.81}(33.83 \times 12.56 + 3.86 \times 6.28) = \mathbf{45.78\ Nm}\ \textbf{(Ans.)}$$

(iii) Efficiency of the wheel, η :

$$\eta = \frac{2(V_{w1}u_1 + V_{w2}u_2)}{V_1^2} \qquad \text{[Eqn. (1.31)]}$$

$$= \frac{2(33.83 \times 12.56 + 3.86 \times 6.28)}{36^2} = 0.693 \text{ or } \mathbf{69.3\%}\ \textbf{(Ans.)}$$

Example 1.25. *A 30 mm diameter jet strikes without shock on a series of vanes. The jet velocity is 60 m/s and the vanes move in the same direction as the jet. The shape of each vane is such that, when stationary, it would deflect the jet through an angle of 150°. The friction reduces the relative velocity by 10% as water flows across the vanes and there is a further windage loss given by* $\frac{u^2}{2}$ *Nm/kg of water, where u is the vane speed. Determine:*

(i) The velocity of vanes corresponding to maximum efficiency, and

(ii) The corresponding thrust on the vanes in the direction of motion.

Solution. Diameter of the jet, $d = 30 \text{ mm} = 0.03 \text{ m}$

$\therefore$ Area, $a = \frac{\pi}{4} \times d^2 = \frac{\pi}{4} \times 0.03^2 = 0.0007068 \text{ m}^2$

Velocity of jet, $V_1 = 60$ m/s.

Reduction in relative velocity due to friction = 10%

$\therefore$ $V_{r2} = (1 - 0.1)V_{r1} = 0.9 V_{r1}$

Deflection of jet = 150°

Windage loss $= \frac{u^2}{2}$ Nm/kg of water, where u is the vane speed.

(i) The velocity of vanes corresponding to maximum efficiency :

Refer to Fig. 1.26 for inlet and outlet velocity tringles.

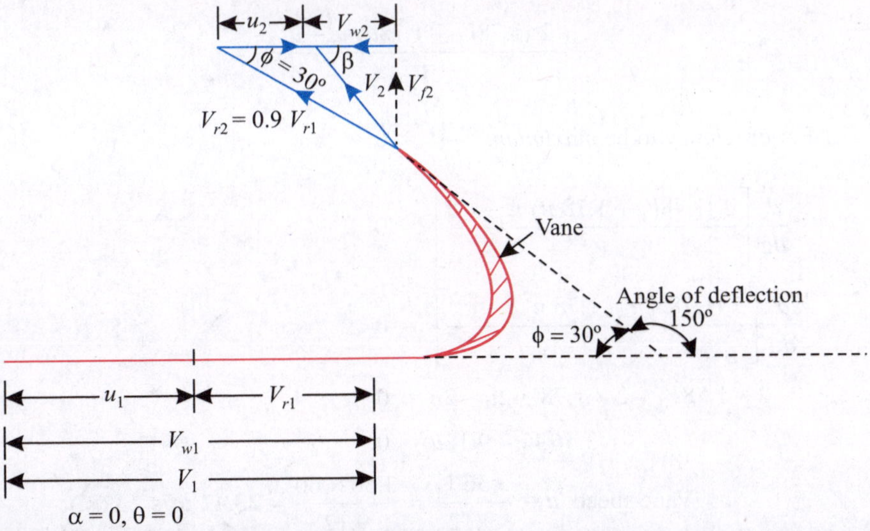

Fig. 1.26.

$$V_{w1} = V_1 = 60 \text{ m/s}; u_1 = u_2 = u$$
$$V_{r1} = V_1 - u; \phi = 180° - 150° = 30°$$
$$V_{r2} = 0.9\ V_{r1} = 0.9\ (V_1 - u)$$
$$V_{w2} = V_{r2} \cos \phi - u$$
$$= 0.9\ (V_1 - u) \cos 30° - u = 0.78\ (V_1 - u) - u$$

When series of such vanes are fixed to the wheel, the entire fluid of mass $\rho a V_1$ issuing from the jet is utilized in striking the vanes.

Thrust or force on the vane in the direction of its motion,

$$F = \rho a V_1 (V_{w1} + V_{w2}) \qquad (\because \beta < 90°)$$
$$= \rho a V_1 [V_1 + 0.78\ (V_1 - u) - u]$$
$$= \rho a V_1 (1.78\ V_1 - 1.78\ u) \qquad \text{...}(i)$$

$$\text{Work done per second} = F \times u = \rho a V_1 (1.78\ V_1 - 1.78\ u)\ u$$

$$\text{Windage loss} = \frac{u^2}{2} \text{ Nm per unit mass of water}$$
$$= \rho a V_1 \times \frac{u^2}{2}$$

$$\therefore \quad \text{Useful work done} = \rho a V_1 (1.78\ V_1 - 1.78\ u)\ u - \rho a V_1 \times \frac{u^2}{2}$$

Energy supplied by the water jet

$$= \frac{1}{2} m V_1^2 = \frac{1}{2} \rho a V_1 \times V_1^2$$

Now,
$$\text{efficiency, } \eta = \frac{\text{Useful work done}}{\text{Energy supplied}}$$

$$= \frac{\rho a V_1 (1.78\ V_1 - 1.78\ u)\ u - \rho a V_1 \times \frac{u^2}{2}}{\frac{1}{2} \rho a V_1 \times V_1^2}$$

$$= \frac{2\ (1.78 V_1 - 1.78 u)\ u - u^2}{V_1^2}$$

For efficiency to be *maximum*, $\frac{d\eta}{du} = 0$

$$\therefore \quad \frac{d}{du}\left[\frac{2\ (1.78 V_1 - 1.78\ u)\ u - u^2}{V_1^2}\right] = 0$$

or,
$$\frac{d}{du}\left[\frac{2\ (1.78 V_1 u - 1.78\ u^2) - u^2}{V_1^2}\right] = 0$$

or,
$$2 \times 1.78 V_1 - 2 \times 1.78 \times 2u - 2u = 0$$

or,
$$3.56\ V_1 - 9.12u = 0$$

or,
$$\text{Vane speed, } u = \frac{3.56\ V_1}{9.12} = \frac{3.56 \times 60}{9.12} = \mathbf{23.42\ m/s\ (Ans.)}$$

(ii) The corresponding thrust on the vanes, F :

Substituting the relavent data in eqn (i), we get

$$F = 1000 \times 0.0007068 \times 60\,(1.78 \times 60 - 1.78 \times 23.42) = \mathbf{2761.2\ N}\ \textbf{(Ans.)}$$

Example 1.26. *The rotor of inward flow hydraulic turbine has a diameter over the tips of the moving vanes of 1.2 m. The diameter at the bottom of the vanes is 0.72 m. The speed is 300 r.p.m. The water is supplied through fixed vanes at 10° to the tangent to the outer circumference of the rotor, the velocity of water being 12 m/s. If the water leaves the moving vanes with the velocity entirely radial and equal to 4.2 m/s, determime:*

(i) The blade angles at entry and exit, so that the water may enter and leave the moving blades without shock.

(ii) The velocity of water relative to the vanes at the exit.

Solution. Radius of the wheel at inlet of the vane, $R_1 = \dfrac{1.2}{2} = 0.6$ m

Radius of the wheel at outlet of the vane, $R_2 = \dfrac{0.72}{2} = 0.36$ m

Speed of the wheel, $N = 300$ r.p.m.

$\therefore$ Angular speed, $\omega = \dfrac{2\pi N}{60} = \dfrac{2\pi \times 300}{60} = 10\pi$ rad./s

Then, tangential velocity at inlet tip of this blade, $u_1 = \omega R_1 = 10\pi \times 0.6 = 18.85$ m/s,

and, tangential velocity at outlet tip of the blade, $u_2 = \omega R_2 = 10\pi \times 0.36 = 11.31$ m/s

Angle at inlet, $\alpha = 10°$

Absolute velocity of jet at inlet, $V_1 = 12$ m/s

Absolute velocity of jet at outlet, $V_2 = 4.2$ m/s

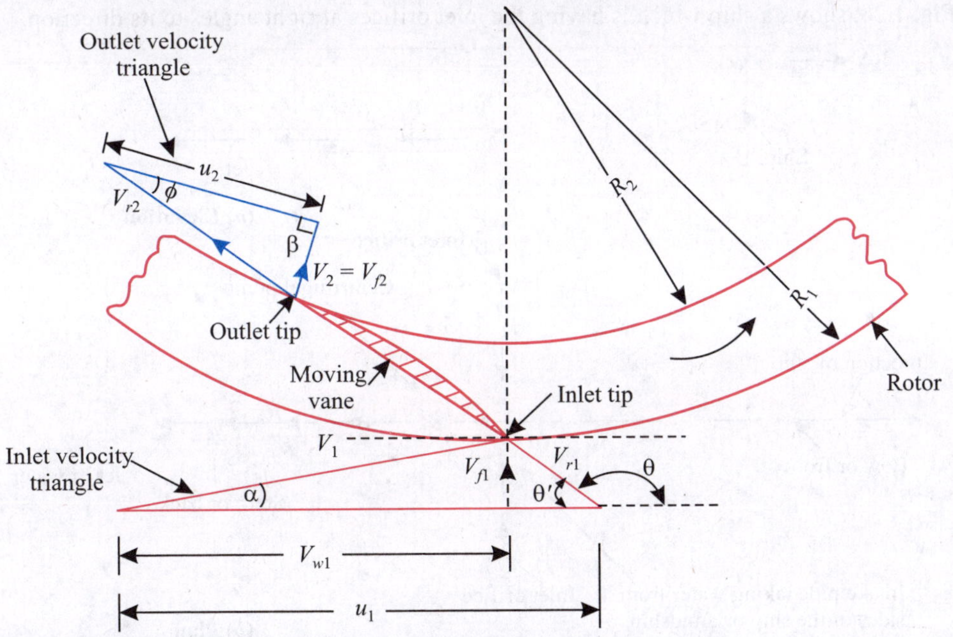

Fig. 1.27.

(i) The blade angles at entry and exit, θ and φ :

From inlet velocity triangle, we have :

$$V_{w1} = V_1 \cos \alpha = 12 \cos 10° = 11.82 \text{ m/s}$$

$$V_{f1} = V_1 \sin \alpha = 12 \sin 10° = 2.08 \text{ m/s}$$

$$\therefore \quad \tan \theta' = \frac{V_{f1}}{u_1 - V_{w1}} = \frac{2.08}{18.85 - 11.82} = 0.295$$

or, $$\theta' = \tan^{-1} 0.295 = 16.43°$$

∴ *Blade angle at inlet*, $\theta = 180° - \theta' = 180° - 16.43° =$ **163.57° (Ans.)**

From outlet triangle, we have:

$$\tan \phi = \frac{V_2}{u_2} = \frac{4.2}{11.31} = 0.3713$$

or, $\phi = \tan^{-1} 0.3713 =$ **20.37° (Ans.)**

(ii) The velocity of water relative to the moving vanes, V_{r2} :

From outlet velocity triangle, we have:

$$\frac{V_2}{V_{r2}} = \sin \phi, \quad \text{or,} \quad V_{r2} = \frac{V_2}{\sin \phi} = \frac{4.2}{\sin 20.37°} = \mathbf{12.06 \text{ m/s}} \textbf{ (Ans.)}$$

1.9. JET PROPULSION OF SHIPS

One of the applications of the *impulse-momentum equation* is **'jet propulsion'** wherein the reaction of a high velocity jet issuing from a nozzle provides the necessary thrust. This principle is employed in propelling the ships, aircrafts and missiles.

Case I. When the inlet orifices are at right angles to the direction of the motion of the ship.

Fig. 1.28. shows a ship which is having the inlet orifices at right angles to its direction.

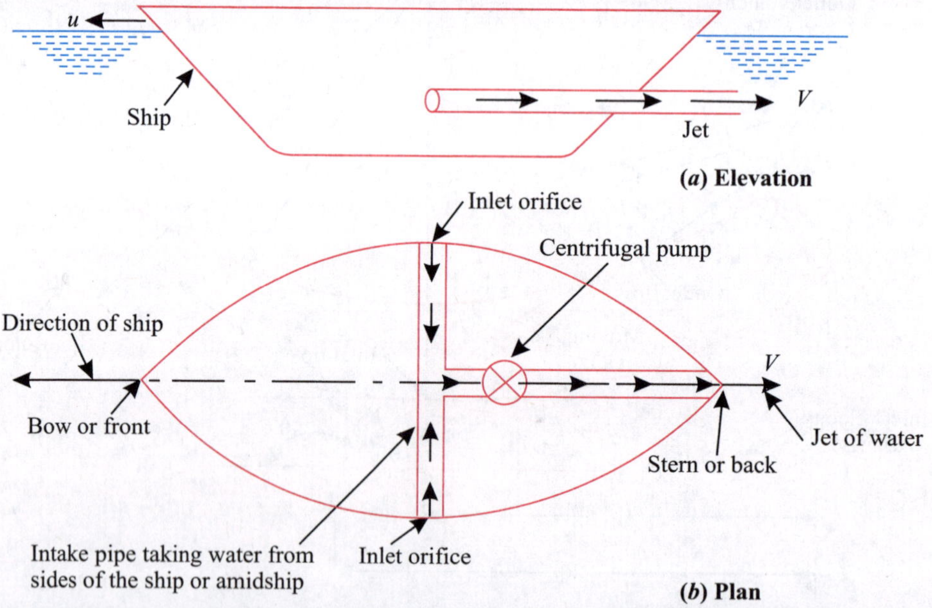

Fig. 1.28. Inlet orifices at right angles to the ship motion.

The ship carries a centrifugal pump which takes water from the sea and discharges it through nozzle at the rear of the ship.

Let, V = Absolute velocity of the issuing jet,

u = Velocity of the moving ship,

V_r = Relative velocity of the jet with respect to ship

= $V - (-u) = V + u$ (since the ship velocity is in a direction opposite to that of absolute jet velocity), and

a = Area of orifices.

Mass of water issuing from the orifice at the back of the ship = $\rho a V_r = \rho a (V + u)$

∴ Propulsive force exerted on the ship,

$$F = \text{Mass flow rate of water} \times \text{change in jet velocity}$$

$$= \rho a (V+u)(V_r - u) = \rho a (V+u)[(V+u) - u] = \rho a (V+u) \times V \quad ...[1.32]$$

Thrust or propulsive work per second = Forward thrust × speed of ship

$$= F \times u = \rho a (V+u) \times V \times u \quad ...[1.33]$$

As the intake is at right angles to the direction of motion, inlet velocity of water is zero; hence the outlet velocity equals V_r and hence the kinetic energy supplied by the jet per second is

$$= \frac{1}{2}(\rho a V_r) \times V_r^2 = \frac{1}{2}\rho a V_r^3 = \frac{1}{2}\rho a (V+u)^3 \quad ...[1.34]$$

$$\therefore \text{ Efficiency of propulsion, } \eta = \frac{\text{Propulsive work}}{\text{Kinetic energy supplied by the jet}}$$

$$= \frac{\rho a (V+u) \times V \times u}{\frac{1}{2}\rho a (V+u)^2} = \frac{2Vu}{(V+u)^2} \quad ...[1.35]$$

For a given jet velocity V, the condition for *maximum efficiency of propulsion* is given by, $\frac{d\eta}{du} = 0$

i.e., $$\frac{d}{du}\left(\frac{2Vu}{(V+u)^2}\right) = 0$$

or, $$\frac{(V+u)^2 \times 2V - 2Vu \times 2(V+u)}{(V+u)^4} = 0$$

or, $$(V+u)^2 \times 2V - 2Vu \times 2(V+u) = 0$$

or, $$(V+u)[(V+u)2V - 4Vu] = 0$$

$$(V+u)2V - 4Vu = 0 \quad (\because V \neq -u)$$

or, $$2V(V+u-2u) = 0 \quad (\because V \neq -u)$$

or, $$V - u = 0$$

$$\therefore \quad u = V \quad ...[1.36]$$

Hence for *maximum efficiency of propulsion, u* = V and by substitution,

$$\eta_{max} = \frac{2 \times u \times u}{(u+u)^2} = \frac{2u^2}{(2u)^2} = 05 \text{ or } \mathbf{50\%}$$

(Neglecting loss of head due to friction, etc. in the intake and ejecting pipes.)

Case II. When the inlet orifices face the direction of motion of the ship.

Fig. 1.29 shows a ship which is having the inlet orifices *facing the direcion of the motion of the ship.* The water is drawn in by a longitudinal (intake) pipe from bow (front) of the ship and is discharged at the stern (back).

For this case the expressions for propulsive force and work done per second will be the *same* as those for the case I *i.e.,* when the inlet orifices are at right angles to the ship motion. But the energy supplied by the jet will be different, as in this case the water enters with a velocity equal to the velocity of the ship (u).

$$\therefore \quad \text{Kinetic energy supplied by the jet} = \frac{1}{2} \text{ mass of water supplied per second} \times (V_r^2 - u^2)$$

$$= \frac{1}{2} \rho a V_r \, (V_r^2 - u^2)$$

But, $V_r = V + u$ (as in case I)

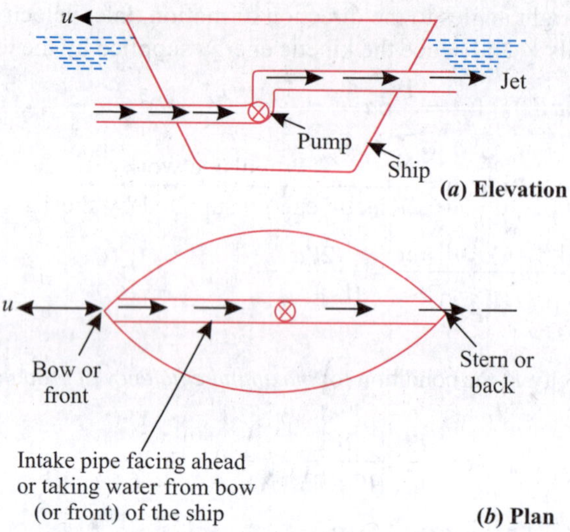

Fig. 1.29. Inlet orifices facing the direction of ship.

$$\therefore \text{ Kinetic energy supplied by the jet} = \frac{1}{2} \rho a \, (V + u) \, [\, (V + u)^2 - u^2] \qquad \text{...(1.37)}$$

$\therefore$ Efficiency of propulsion,

$$\eta = \frac{\text{Work done per second by jet}}{\text{Energy supplied by the jet}}$$

$$= \frac{\rho a \, (V + u) \times V \times u}{\frac{1}{2} \rho a \, (V + u) \, [\, (V + u)^2 - u^2]}$$

[Work done = $\rho a \, (V + u) \times V \times u$] ...from eqn. (1.33)

$$= \frac{2Vu}{(V + u)^2 - u^2} = \frac{2Vu}{V^2 + u^2 + 2Vu - u^2} = \frac{2Vu}{V^2 + 2Vu} = \frac{2u}{V + 2u} \qquad \text{...(1.38)}$$

In this case, however it is not possible to derive a practical condition for maximum efficiency. But for $u = V$, which is the condition for the maximum efficiency in the previous case (*i.e.,* case I), corresponding value of the efficiency for this case will be:

$$\eta = \frac{2u}{V + 2u} = \frac{2u}{u + 2u} = \frac{2}{3} \text{ or } 0.6667 = \mathbf{66.67\%}$$

In actual practice, since the velocity of ship u will normally be *less* than the velocity of jet V, and therefore the *limiting value of u is equal to V*. Hence the above obtained value of the efficiency may be *cosidered as the maximum possible efficiency for this case.*

Note: The propulsion of ships is also known as ***water rocket.*** In practice, jet propulsion is used only in small life boats. For large ships, the screw propulsion is generally perferred because of *high overall efficiency of screw propulsion.*

Example 1.27. *A ship driven by reaction jets and discharging astern is found to have resistance to motion of 2950 N when moving at 30 km/h. The velocity of jet relative to ship is 18 m/s. Determine:*

(*i*) *The number of jets if each jet has an area of 85 cm²;*

(*ii*) *The power required to work the pump and the propulsive efficiency for the following cases:*

(*a*) *Inlet orifices at right angles to ship motion;*

(*b*) *Inlet orifices face the direction of ship motion.*

Solution. Resistance to motion = 2950 N

$$\text{Velocity of the ship, } u = 30 \text{ km/h} = \frac{30 \times 1000}{60 \times 60} = 8.33 \text{ m/s}$$

Velcoity of the jet relative to the ship, $V_r = (V + u) = 18$ m/s

∴ Absolute velocity of the jet, $V = V_r - u = 18 - 8.33 = 9.67$ m/s

Area of each jet, $a = 85 \text{ cm}^2 = 85 \times 10^{-4} \text{ m}^2$

(*i*) **Number of jets required :**

Thrust force exerted on the ship, $F = \rho a\,(V + u) \times V$ ...[Eqn. (1.32)]

Since thrust equals the resistance to motion of ship, therefore,

$$2950 = 1000 \times a \times 18 \times 9.67, \text{ or, } a = \frac{2950}{1000 \times 18 \times 9.67} = 0.01695 \text{ m}^2$$

$$\therefore \quad \text{Number of jets} = \frac{\text{Total area of jets}}{\text{Area of each jet}} = \frac{0.01695}{85 \times 10^{-4}} = \mathbf{2} \textbf{ (Ans.)}$$

(*ii*) **Power required to drive the pump and propulsive efficiency :**

Propulsive work = Thrust × forward velocity = 2950 × 8.33 = 24573.5 Nm/s

∴ *Power required* = 24573.5 J/s or W or **24.573kW (Ans.)**

This will be same for both the cases (*a*) and (*b*).

(*a*) When intake orifices are at right angles to motion of ship, then kinetic energy supplied by jets

$$= \frac{1}{2}\rho\, a\,(V + u)^3 \quad \text{...[Eqn. 1.34]}$$

$$= \frac{1}{2} \times 1000 \times 0.01695 \times 18^3 = 49426.2 \text{ Nm/s}$$

∴ *Propulsive efficiency*

$$= \frac{\text{Propulsive work}}{\text{Kinetic energy supplied by the jet}} = \frac{24573.5}{49426.2} = 0.497 \text{ or } \mathbf{49.7\%} \textbf{ (Ans.)}$$

[Alternatively,
Propulsive efficiency $= \dfrac{2Vu}{(V+u)^2} = \dfrac{2 \times 9.67 \times 8.33}{18^2} = 0.497$ or **49.7%**]

(*b*) When intake orifices face the direction of ship motion, then kinetic energy supplied by the jet,

$$= \frac{1}{2} \rho a (V+u) [(V+u)^2 - u^2] \quad \text{...[Eqn. (1.37)]}$$

$$= \frac{1}{2} \times 1000 \times 0.016695 \times 18 (18^2 - 8.33^2) = 38840.9 \text{ Nm/s}$$

$$\therefore \text{ Propulsive efficiency} = \frac{\text{Propulsive work}}{\text{Kinetic energy supplied by the jet}}$$

$$= \frac{24573.5}{38840.9} = 0.6326 \text{ or } \mathbf{63.26\%} \text{ (Ans.)}$$

Example 1.28. *A small ship is fitted with jets of total area 0.65 m². The velocity through the jet is 9 m/s and speed of the ship is 18 km/h in sea water. The efficiencies of the engine and the pump are 85% and 65% and respectively. If the water is taken amidship, determine:*

(*i*) *Propelling force, and*

(*ii*) *Overall efficiency.*

Assume the pipe losses to be 10% of the kinetic energy of the jets.

[MDU Haryana]

Solution. Total area of jets, $a = 0.65 \text{ m}^2$

Velocity of jet relative to ship, $V_r = 9$ km/s

Speed of the ship, $u = 18 \text{ km/h} = \dfrac{18 \times 1000}{60 \times 60} = 5$ m/s

Efficiency of the engine, $\eta_E = 85\%$

Efficiency of the pump, $\eta_P = 65\%$

Pipe losses, $h_f = 10\%$ of K.E. of jets

$$= \frac{10}{100} \times \frac{V_r^2}{2} = \frac{V_r^2}{20}$$

Now, $V_r = V + u$

or, $V = V_r - u = 9 - 5 = 4$ m/s

(where, V = absolute velocity of jet)

(*i*) **Propelling force, F :**

$$F = \rho a (V+u) V \quad \text{...[Eqn. (1.32)]}$$

$$= 1000 \times 0.65 (4+5) \times 4 = \mathbf{23400 \text{ N}} \text{ (Ans.)}$$

(*ii*) **Overall efficiency, $\eta_{overall}$:**

Work done by the jets per second

$$= F \times u = 23400 \times 5 = 117000 \text{ Nm/s}$$

The output of the pump should be such as to give the jet a relative velocity V_r and also overcome the pipe losses.

∴ Output of the pump per kg of water

$= \text{K.E. of jet} + \text{pipe losses}$

$$= \frac{V_r^2}{2} + \frac{V_r^2}{20} = \frac{V_r^2}{2}(1 + 0.1) = 1.1\frac{V_r^2}{2}$$

$$\text{Input to the pump per kg of water} = \frac{\text{Output of the pump}}{\text{Efficiency of the pump}(\eta_p)}$$

$$= \frac{1.1V_r^2}{2 \times 0.65}$$

The input to the pump = Output of the engine

$$\therefore \text{ Input to the engine per kg of water} = \frac{1.1V_r^2}{2 \times 0.65 \times \eta_E}$$

$$= \frac{1.1 \times 9^2}{2 \times 0.65 \times 0.85} = 80.63 \text{ Nm}$$

$\therefore$ Total input to the engine = Mass of water × input per kg of water

$= (\rho a V_r) \times 80.63$

$= 1000 \times 0.65 \times 9 \times 80.63 = 471685.5$ Nm

$$\therefore \qquad \eta_{overall} = \frac{\text{Work done by jets}}{\text{Total input to engine}} = \frac{117000}{471685.5} = 0.248 \text{ or } \mathbf{24.8\%} \text{ (Ans.)}$$

Example 1.29. *A jet propelled boat, moving with a velocity of 6 m/s, draws water amidship. The total area of the jet is 424 cm^2. If the total resistance offered to the motion of the boat is 5890 N, determine:*

(i) Volume of water drawn by the pump per second, and

(ii) Efficiency of the jet propulsion.

Solution. Velocity of boat, $u = 6$ m/s

Total area of jets, $a = 424 \text{ cm}^2 = 424 \times 10^{-4} = 0.0424 \text{ m}^2$

Total resistance to motion $= 5890$ N

Since the propelling force must be equal to the resistance to the motion, therefore,

Propelling force, $F = 5890$ N

But propelling force, $F = \rho a (V + u) V$ ...[Eqn. (1.32)]

$\therefore \quad \rho a (V + u) V = 5890$

or, $1000 \times 0.0424 (V + 6) \times V = 5890$

$$\text{or,} \qquad (V + 6) V = \frac{5890}{1000 \times 0.0424} = 138.9$$

$$\text{or,} \qquad V^2 + 6V - 138.9 = 0$$

$$V = \frac{-6 \pm \sqrt{6^2 + 4 \times 138.9}}{2} \cdot \frac{-6 \pm 24.32}{2} = 916 \text{ m/s}$$

(i) Volume of water drawn by the pump per second :

= Volume of water discharged through orifices at the back in the form of the jets

$= aV_r = a(V + u) = 0.0424 (9.16 + 6) = \mathbf{0.643 \ m^3/s}$ **(Ans.)**

(*ii*) **Efficiency of the jet propulsion :**

$$\eta = \frac{2Vu}{(V+u)^2} \qquad \text{...Eqn. (1.35)}$$

$$= \frac{2 \times 9.16 \times 6}{(9.16+6)^2} = 0.478 \text{ or } \mathbf{47.8\%} \text{ (Ans.)}$$

Example 1.30. (*a*) *A small ship driven by reaction jets and discharging astern is estimated to have a relative velocity of 12 m/s when moving at 30 km/h. The cross-sectional area of the jets at discharge is 240 cm². Find resistance to the motion of ship and propulsive work.*

(*b*) *If water enters through orifices facing the direction of motion of ship and pump is 85 per cent efficient and frictional losses in the pipe are equivalent to 3.6 m of water head, find:*

(*i*) *Power required to drive the pump, and*

(*ii*) *Overall efficiency of propulsion.*

Solution. Relative velocity of ship, $V_r = 12$ m/s

$$\text{Speed of the ship, } u = 30 \text{ km/h} = \frac{30 \times 1000}{60 \times 60} = 8.33 \text{ m/s}$$

The cross-sectional area of the jet at discharge, $a = 240 \text{ cm}^2 = 0.024 \text{ m}^2$

Efficiency of pump, $\eta_p = 85\%$

Frictional losses, $h_f = 3.6$ m of water head.

(*a*) **Resistance to motion and propulsive work :**

Thrust or propulsive force, $F = \rho a (V + u)V$ ...[Eqn. (1.32)]

Now, $V_r = V + u$ or $V = V_r - u = 12 - 8.33 = 3.67$ m/s

(where, V = absolute velocity of the jet)

$\therefore$ $F = 1000 \times 0.024 \times 12 \times 3.67 = 1057$ N

Hence, *resistance to motion* = F = **1057 N (Ans.)**

Propulsive work = Thrust × forward velocity

= 1057 × 8.33 = 8804.8 Nm/s

= 8804.8 J/s or W or **8.8 kW (Ans.)**

(*b*) When the intake of water is at the front end and the water enters with the boat speed u and discharges astern (back) with relative velocity V_r, then,

$$\text{Energy supplied by the jet} = \frac{1}{2} m (V_r^2 - u^2)$$

Actual energy supplied to water, considering frictional loss in the pipes

$$= \frac{1}{2} m (V_r^2 - u^2) + mgh_f = \frac{1}{2} \rho a V_r (V_r^2 - u^2) + (\rho a V_r)\, gh_f$$

$$= \rho a V_r \left[\frac{1}{2}(V_r^2 - u^2) + gh_f\right]$$

$$= 1000 \times 0.024 \times 12 \left[\frac{1}{2}(12^2 - 8.33^2) + 9.81 \times 3.6\right] = 20913 \text{ Nm/s} \simeq 20.9 \text{ kW}$$

This is equal to the *output of the pump.*

(*i*) **Power required to drive the pump :**

$$\text{Power required ro drive the pump} = \frac{\text{Output of the pump}}{\eta_p} = \frac{20.9}{0.85} = \mathbf{24.58 \text{ kW}} \text{ (Ans.)}$$

(ii) Overall efficiency of propulsion, $\eta_{overall}$:

$$\eta_{overall} = \frac{\text{Propulsive power}}{\text{Power supplied to the pump}}$$

$$= \frac{8.8}{24.58} = 0.358 \text{ or } \mathbf{35.8\%} \text{ (Ans.)}$$

Example 1.31. *A jet-propelled boat discharges water through a jet of area 240 cm^2; the water being drawn from inlet openings facing the direction of motion. The total drag is estimated to be 21.2 u^2 N where u is the speed of the boat in m/s. If the boat moves at 64.8 km/h, determine:*

(i) *Relative velocity of jet,*

(ii) *Energy supplied by the jet,*

(iii) *Power of the motor required to work the pumps, and*

(iv) *Efficiency of propulsion.* **[Anna University]**

Take efficiency of pump set as 80% and density of water 1020 kg/m^3.

Solution. Area of jet, $a = 240 \text{ cm}^2 = 0.024 \text{ m}^2$

Total drag $= 21.2\, u^2 N$, where u is the speed of boat in m/s.

Velocity of the boat, $u = 64.8$ km/h

$$= \frac{64.8 \times 1000}{60 \times 60} = 18 \text{ m/s}$$

Efficiency of the pump, $\eta_p = 80\%$

(i) Relative velocity of jet, V_r :

Thrust force on the boat $= \rho a V_r (V_r - u)$

Also, resistance to the motion of ship (drag) equals the thrust force,

$$\therefore \quad 21.2u^2 = \rho a V_r (V_r - u)$$

or, $$21.2 \times 18^2 = 1020 \times 0.024\, V_r (V_r - 18)$$

or, $$6868.8 = 24.48\, V_r (V_r - 18)$$

or, $$V_r (V_r - 18) = \frac{6868.8}{24.48} = 280.6$$

or, $$V_r^2 - 18V_r - 280.6 = 0$$

or, $$V_r = \frac{18 \pm \sqrt{18^2 + 4 \times 280.6}}{2}$$

$$= \frac{18 + 38.03}{2} = \mathbf{28 \text{ m/s}} \text{ (Ans.)} \text{ (–ve value is not possible.)}$$

(ii) Energy supplied by the jet :

Mass of water discharged $= \rho a V_r$

$\therefore$ Kinetic energy supplied by the jet

$$= \frac{1}{2} (\rho a V_r)(V_r^2 - u^2)$$

$$= \frac{1}{2}(1020 \times 0.024 \times 28)(28^2 - 18^2) = 157651.2 \text{ N m/s}$$

(iii) Power of motor :

Power of the motor required to work the pumps

$$= \frac{157651.2}{0.8} = 197064 \text{ Nm/s or } 197064 \text{ J/s or W or} \simeq \mathbf{197\ kW}\ \textbf{(Ans.)}$$

(iv) Efficiency of propulsion, η_{prop} :

$$\eta_{prop.} = \frac{2u}{V + 2u} \quad \text{...[Eqn. (1.38)].}$$

$$= \frac{2u}{V_r + u} = \frac{2 \times 18}{28 + 18} = 0.7826 \text{ or } \mathbf{78.26\%}\ \textbf{(Ans.)} (\because V + u = V_r)$$

HIGHLIGHTS

1. A fluid jet is a stream of fluid issuing from a nozzle with a high velocity and hence a high kinetic energy.
2. The force exerted by a jet of water on a "*stationary plate*" (**F_x**):

   $F_x = \rho a V^2$ ...for a vertical plate,

   $= \rho a V^2 \sin^2 \theta$ ...for an inclined plate,

   $= \rho a V^2 (1 + \cos \theta)$ ...for a curved plate and jet strikes at the centre,

   $= 2\, \rho a V^2 \cos \theta$ ...for a curved plate and jet strikes at one of the tips of the jet.

   where, V = Velocity of the jet,

   θ = Angle between the jet and the plate for inclined plate, and

   = Angle made by the jet with the direction of motion for curved plates.
3. The force exerted by a jet of water on a *moving plate* in the direction of the motion of the plate (F_x):

   $F_x = \rho a (V - u)^2$ ...for a moving vertical plate,

   $= \rho a (V - u)^2 \sin^2 \theta$ ...for an inclined moving plate, and

   $= \rho a (V - u)^2 (1 + \cos \theta)$ ...when jet strikes the curved plate at the centre.
4. When a jet of water strikes a curved moving vane at one of its tips and comes curved out at the other tip, the force exerted and work done are given by (from inlet and outlet velocity triangles):

   Force exerted, $F_x = \rho a V_{r1} (V_{w1} \pm V_{w2})$

   Work done per second $= \rho a V_{r1} (V_{w1} \pm V_{w2}) \times u$

   + ve sign is taken ...when $\beta < 90°$ (*i.e.*, β is an acute angle)

   – ve sign is taken ...when $\beta > 90°$ (*i.e.*, β is an obtuse angle)

   $V_{w2} = 0$ ...when $\beta = 90°$

   Work done per second per N of fluid

   $$= \frac{1}{g} (V_{w1} + V_{w2}) \times u$$

   For series of vanes:

   Force exerted, $F_x = \rho a V_1 (V_{w1} \pm V_{w2})$

   Work done per sec $= \rho a V_1 (V_{w1} \pm V_{w2}) \times u$

   Work done per sec per N of fluid $= \frac{1}{g} (V_{w1} + V_{w2}) \times u$

where, V_1 = Absolute velocity of jet at inlet,
V_{w1} = Velocity of whirl at inlet,
V_{w2} = Velocity of whirl at outlet, and
u = Velocity of the vane.

5. *For seires of radial curved vanes:*

Work done per second on the wheel

$$= \rho a V_1 (V_{w1} \times u_1 \pm V_{w2} \times u_2)$$

Efficiency of the radial curved vane,

$$\eta_{\text{vane}} = \frac{\rho a V_1 \, (V_{w1} u_1 \pm V_{w2} u_2)}{\frac{1}{2} (\rho a V_1) \times V_1^2} = \frac{2 \, (V_{w1} u_1 \pm V_{w2} u_2)}{V_1^2}$$

where, u_1 = Tangential velocity of vane at inlet, and
u_2 = Tangential velocity of vane at outlet.

6. *Jet propulsion of ships:*

Case I. When the inlet orifices are at right angles to the direction of motion of the ships.

Efficiency of propulsion, $\eta = \dfrac{2Vu}{(V+u)^2}$

Conditions for maximum efficiency, $\dfrac{d\eta}{du} = 0$, *i.e.*, $u = V$

η_{max} = 50% (neglecting loss of head due to friction, etc. in the intake and ejecting pipes)

Case II. When the inlet orifices face the direction of motion of the ship.

Efficiency of propulsion, $\eta = \dfrac{2u}{V + 2u}$

OBJECTIVE TYPE QUESTIONS

Choose the Correct Answer:

1. The force exerted by a jet of water on a stationary vertical plate in the direction of jet is given by
   (*a*) ρaV (*b*) ρaV^2
   (*c*) $\rho a^2 V$ (*c*) ρaV^3.
2. The force exerted by a jet of water on a moving vertical plate, in the direction of motion of plate is given by
   (*a*) ρaV^2 (*b*) ρaV^3
   (*c*) $\rho a\,(V-u)^2$ (*d*) $\rho a\,(V-u)^3$.
3. When a steady jet impinges on a fixed inclined surface
   (*a*) the flow is divided into parts proportional to the angle of inclination of the surface
   (*b*) no force is exerted by the jet on the vane
   (*c*) the momentum component is unchanged parallel to the surface
   (*d*) none of the above.
4. For maximum efficiency of a series of curved vanes, the speed is
   (*a*) equal to the jet speed
   (*b*) $\frac{3}{4}$ of the jet speed
   (*c*) $\frac{1}{2}$ of the jet speed
   (*d*) $\frac{1}{3}$ of the jet speed.
5. The efficiency of jet propulsion with inlet orifices at right angles to the direction of motion of ship is given by
   (*a*) $\dfrac{2u}{V+u}$ (*b*) $\dfrac{2V}{(V+u)^2}$
   (*c*) $\dfrac{2Vu}{(V+u)^2}$ (*d*) $\dfrac{2u(V-u)}{V^3}$.

6. The efficiency of jet propulsion when the inlet orifices face the direction of motion of the ship is given by

(a) $\frac{2V}{V+u}$ (b) $\frac{2u}{V+2u}$.

(c) $\frac{2Vu}{V+u}$ (d) $\frac{2V}{V+u}$.

ANSWERS

1. (b) 2. (c) 3. (a) 4. (c) 5. (c) 6. (b).

THEORETICAL QUESTIONS

1. Derive an expression for the force exerted by a jet of water on a fixed vertical plate in the direction of the jet.
2. Show that the force exerted by a jet of water on moving inclined plate in the direction of jet is given by

$$F_x = \rho a (V-u)^2 \sin^2 \theta$$

where, a = Area of jet,
V = Velocity of the jet, and
θ = Inclination of the plate with the jet.

3. Prove that for a curved radial vane the efficiency is given by

$$\eta = \frac{2 (V_{w1}\, u_1 \pm V_{w2}\, u_2)}{V_1^2}$$

4. Show that efficiency of propulsion when the inlet orifices face the direction of motion of the ship is given by, $\eta = \frac{2u}{V + 2u}$, where V is absolute velocity of issuing jet and u is the velocity of the ship.

UNSOLVED EXAMPLES

1. A jet of water, 50 mm in diameter, issues with a velocity of 10 m/s and impinges on a stationary flat plate which destroys its forward motion. Find the force exerted by the jet on the plate and the work done. **[Ans.** 196.35 N]
2. A jet of water of diameter 75 mm moving with a velocity of 20 m/s strikes a fixed plate in such a way that the angle between the jet and the plate is 60°. Find the force exerted by the jet on the plate.
   (*i*) in the direction normal to the plate, and
   (*ii*) in the direction of jet.
   [Ans. (*i*) 1530 N; (*ii*) 1325 N]
3. A jet of water of diameter 60 mm moving with a velocity of 40 m/s, strikes a curved fixed symmetrical plate at the centre. Find the force exerted by the jet of water in the direction of the jet, if the jet is deflected through an angle of 120° at the outlet of the curved plate. **[Ans.** 6785.8 N]
4. A jet of water of diameter 70 mm moving with a velocity of 40 m/s, strikes a curved fixed plate tangentially at one end at an angle of 30° to the horizontal. The jet leaves the plate at an angle 20° to the horizontal. Find the force exerted by the jet on the plate in the horizontal and vertical directions. **[Ans.** 11117 N; 972.61 N]
5. A rectangular plate weighing 60 N is suspended vertically by a hinge on the top horizontal edge. The centre of gravity of the plate is 100 mm from the hinge. A horizontal jet of water of 25 mm diameter, whose axis is 150 mm below the hinge, impinges normally to the plate with a velocity of 6 m/s. Find:
   (*i*) The horizontal force applied at the centre of gravity to maintain the plate in vertical position, and
   (*ii*) The change in velocity of jet if the plate is deflected through 30° and the same horizontal force continues to act at the centre of gravity of the plate.
   [Ans. (*i*) 26.49 N, (*ii*) 2.48 m/s (increase)]
6. A square plate weighing 117.72 N and of uniform thickness and 300 mm edge is hung so that horizontal jet 20 mm dimater and having a velocity of 15 m/s impinges on the plate. The centre line of the jet is 150 mm below the upper edge of the plate, and when the plate is vertical the jet strikes the plate normally and at its centre.
   (*i*) Find what force must be applied at the lower edge of the plate in order to keep the plate vertical.

(*ii*) If the plate is allowed to swing freely, find the inclination to the vertical which the plate will assume under the action of jet.

[Ans. (*i*) 35.32 N, (*ii*) 36.87°]

7. A nozzle of 50 mm diameter delivers a stream of water at 20 m/s prependicular to a plate that moves away from the jet at 5 m/s. Find:

(*i*) The force on the plate,

(*ii*) The work done, and

(*iii*) The efficiency of jet.

[Ans. (*i*) 441.45 N; (*ii*) 2207 Nm/s (*iii*) 28.1%]

8. A jet of water of 75 mm diameter strikes a curved vane at its centre with a velocity of 20 m/s. The curved vane is moving with a velocity of 8 m/s in the direction of jet. Find the force exerted on the plate in the direction of the jet, power and efficiency of the jet.

Assume the plate to be smooth.

[Ans. 1250.4 N; 10 kW (app.), 56.4%]

9. A jet of water 100 mm diameter and having a velocity of 30 m/s strikes tangentially on a wheel which deflects the jet through an angle of 120°. Calculate the thrust on the vane when

(*i*) The axis of symmetry of the vane is horizontal.

(*ii*) The tangent at inlet tip is horizontal.

[Ans. 1958 N; 30°, (*ii*) 1958 N; 30°]

10. A jet of water 100 mm diameter and having a velocity of 15 m/s impinges at the centre of a hemispherical vane. The linear velocity of vane is 5 m/s in the direction of the jet. Find the force exerted on the vane. How this force would change if the jet impinges on a series of vanes attached to the circumference of a wheel ?

[Ans. 1569.6 N, 2354.4 N]

11. A jet of water moving with a velocity of 30 m/s impinges on series of curved vanes moving with a velocity of 15 m/s. The jet makes an angle of 20° with the direction of motion of vanes. Assuming $K = 0{\cdot}9$, and that the absolute velocity of water at exit is normal to the direction of motion of vanes, determine:

(*i*) Vane angles at entrance and exit,

(*ii*) Work done on the vanes per N of water, and

(*iii*) Efficiency of the system.

[Ans. (*i*) 37.85°, 3.8°; (*ii*) 43.2 Nm/s; (*iii*) 94%]

12. A jet of water moving with a velocity of 20 m/s impinges on a curved vane, which is moving with a velocity of 10 m/s. The jet makes an angle of 20° with the direction of motion of vane at inlet and leaves at angle of 130° to the direction of motion of vane at outlet. Determine:

(*i*) The angles of curved vane tips so that water enters and leaves without shock;

(*ii*) The work done per N of water entering the vane.

[Ans. (*i*) $\theta = 37.87°$; $\phi = 6.56°$; (*ii*) 20.24 Nm/s or W]

13. A wheel consists of radial blades with inner and outer radii of 300 mm and 600 mm respectively. Water enters the blades at the outer periphery with a velocity of 50 m/s and the supply jet makes an angle of 25° with tangent to wheel at inlet tip. Water leaving the blade has a flow velocity of 10 m/s. If the blade angles at entrance and exit are 40° and 30° respectively, determine:

(*i*) Work done per N of water,

(*ii*) Speed of the wheel, and

(*iii*) Efficiency of blading.

[Ans. (*i*) 100.43 Nm; (*ii*) 320.38 r.p.m., (*iii*) 78.8%]

14. In a jet propelled boat water is drawn amidship and discharged at the back with an absolute velocity of 20 m/s. If the cross-sectional area of the jet is 200 cm^2 and the boat is moving in sea water with a speed of 8·33 m/s determine: (*i*) The propelling force on the boat, (*ii*) Power required to drive the pump, and (*iii*) Efficiency of jet propulsion.

[Ans. 11332 N; (*ii*) 94.3 kW; (*iii*) 41.5%]

15. A jet propelled boat is discharging water at a speed of 10 m/s relative to the ship in a jet of 0·02 m^2 corss-sectional area. If the boat moves through water with a velocity of 20 km/h, determine:

(*i*) The resistance of the vessel and power exerted by the jet, and

(*ii*) The efficiency of jet apart from losses in pumping machinery.

Assume that inlet orifices face the direction of flow.

[Ans. (*i*) 890 N; (*ii*) 6.91 kW; 71.4%]

16. A jet-propelled boat discharges water through a jet of area 200 cm^2; the water being drawn form inlet openings facing the direction of motion. The total drag is estimated to be $17{\cdot}66\,u^2$ N where u is the speed of the boat in m/s. If the boat moves at 54 km/h, determine:

(*i*) Relative velocity of jet,

(*ii*) Energy supplied by the jet,

(*iii*) Power of motor required to work the pumps, and

(*iv*) Efficiency of propulsion.

Assume: Efficiency of pump-set = 75 per cent, and density of water = 1020 kg/m^3.

[Ans. (*i*) 23.34 m/s; (*ii*) 76125 Nm/s; (*iii*) 101.4 kW; (*iv*) 78.2%]

Chapter
2

HYDRAULIC TURBINES

2.1. INTRODUCTION

A **hydraulic turbine** is a *prime mover* (a machine which uses the raw energy of a substance and converts it into mechanical energy) *that uses the energy of flowing water and converts it into the mechanical energy* (*in the form of rotation of the runner*). This mechanical energy is used in running an electric generator which is directly coupled to the shaft of the hydraulic turbine; from this electric generator, we get electric power which can be transmitted over long distances by means of transmission lines and transmission towers. The hydraulic turbines are also known as '*water turbines*' since the fluid medium used in them is water.

First hydroelectric station was probably started in America in 1882 and thereafter development took place very rapidly. In India, the first major hydroelectric power plant of 4.5 MW capacity named as Sivasamudram Scheme in Mysore was commissioned in 1902.

Hydro (water) power is a conventional renewable source of energy which is clean, free from pollution and generally has a good environment effect. However, the following factors are major obstacles in the utilisation of hydropower resources:

(*i*) Large investments,

(*ii*) Long gestation period, and

(*iii*) Increased cost of power transmission.

Fig. 2.1 shows the flow sheet of hydroelectric power plant.

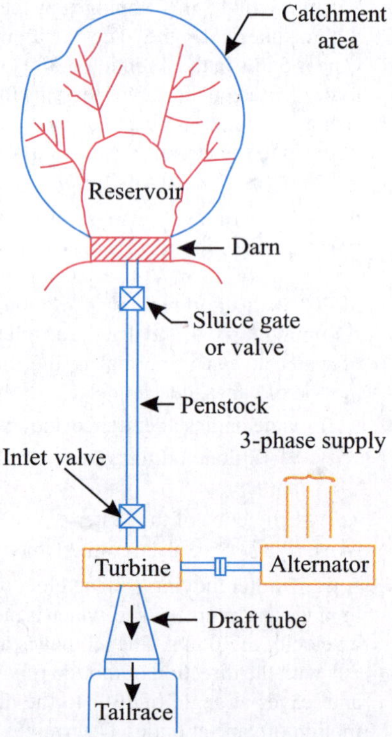

Fig. 2.1. Flow sheet of hydroelectric power plant.

2.2. CLASSIFICATION OF HYDRAULIC TURBINES

The hydraulic turbines are *classified* as follows :

1. According to the head and quantity of water available.
2. According to the name of the originator.
3. According to the action of water on moving blades.
4. According to the direction of flow of water in the runner.
5. According to the disposition of the turbine shaft.
6. According to the specific speed *N*.

1. According to the head and quantity of water avaliable :

(*i*) *Impulse turbine* ... requires *high head* and *small quantity of flow.*

(*ii*) *Reaction turbine* ... requires *low head* and *high rate of flow.*

Actually there are two types of reaction turbines, one for medium head and medium flow and the other for low head and large flow.

2. According to the name of the originator :

(*i*) *Pelton turbine* ... named after Lester Allen Pelton of California (U.S.A.). It is an impulse type of turbine and is used for *high head and low discharge.*

(*ii*) *Francis turbine* ... named after James Bichens Francis. It is a reaction type of turbine from *medium high to medium low heads and medium small to medium large quantites of water.*

(*iii*) *Kalpan turbine* ... named after Dr. Victor Kaplan. It is a reaction *type of turbine for low heads and large quanties of flow.*

3. According to action of water on the moving blades :

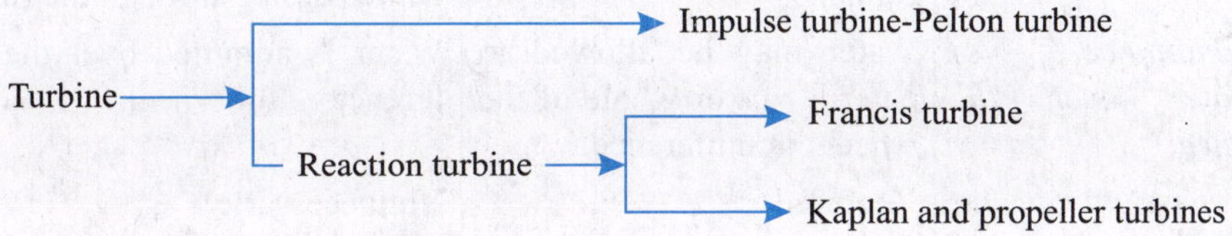

4. According to direction of flow of water in the runner :

(*i*) Tangential flow turbines (Pelton turbine)

(*ii*) Radial flow turbine (no more used)

(*iii*) Axial flow turbine (Kaplan turbine)

(*iv*) Mixed (radial and axial) flow turbine (Francis turbine).

In *tangential flow* turbine of Pelton type the water strikes the runner tangential to the path of rotation.

In *axial flow* turbine water flows parallel to the axis of the turbine shaft. Kaplan turbine is an axial flow turbine. In Kaplan turbine the runner blades are *adjustable and can be rotated* about pivots fixed to the boss of the runner. If the runner blades of the axial flow turbines are *fixed,* these are called "*propeller turbines*".

In *mixed flow* turbines the water enters the blades radially and comes out axially, parallel to the turbine shaft. *Modern Francis turbines have mixed flow runners.*

5. According to the disposition of the turbine shaft :

Turbine shaft may be either vertical or horizontal. In modern practice, Pelton turbines usually have horizontal shafts whereas the rest, especially the large units, have vertical shafts.

6. According to specific speed :

The *specific speed* of a turbine is defined as the speed of a geometrically similar turbine that would develop *1 kW* under *1 m* head. All geometrically similar turbines (irrespective of the sizes) will have the same specific speeds when operating under the same head.

$$\text{Specific speed, } N_s = \frac{N\sqrt{P}}{H^{5/4}}$$

where, N = The normal working speed,

P = Power output of the turbine, and

H = The net or effective head in metres.

Turbines with low specific speeds work under high head and low discharge conditions, while high specific speed turbines work under low head and high discharge conditions.

The following table gives the comparison between the impulse and reaction turbines with regard to their operation and application.

Table 2.1. Comparison between Impulse and Reaction Turbines

S. No.	Aspects	Impulse turbine	Reaction turbine
1.	*Conversion of fluid energy*	The available fluid energy is converted into K.E. by a nozzle.	The energy of the fluid is partly transformed into K.E. before it (fluid) enters the runner of the turbine.
2.	*Changes in pressure and velocity*	The pressure remains same (atmospheric) throughout the action of water on the runner.	After entering the runner with an excess pressure, water undergoes changes both in velocity and pressure while passing through the runner.
3.	*Admittance of water over the wheel*	Water may be allowed to enter a part or whole of the wheel circumference.	Water is admitted over the circumference of the wheel.
4.	*Water-tight causing*	Required	Not necessary.
5.	*Extent to which the water fills the wheel/ turbine*	The wheel/turbine does not run full and air has a free access to the buckets.	Water completely fills all the passages between the blades and while flowing between inlet and outlet sections does work on the blades.
6.	*Installation of unit*	Always installed above the tail race. No draft tube is used.	Unit may be installed above or below the tail race, use of a draft tube is made.
7.	*Relative velocity of water*	Either remaining constant or reduces slightly due to friction.	Due to continuous drop in pressure during flow through the blade, the relative velocity increases.
8.	*Flow regulation*	— By means of a needle valve fitted into the nozzle. — Impossible without loss.	— By means of a guide-vane assembly. — Always accompanied by loss.

2.3. IMPULSE TURBINES—PELTON WHEEL

In an impulse turbine the *pressure energy of water is converted into kinetic energy* when passed through the nozzle and forms the high velocity jet of water. The formed water jet is used for driving the wheel.

Pelton wheel (named after the American engineer Lester Allen Pelton), among the various impulse turbines that have been designed and utilized, is by far the important. The Pelton wheel or Pelton turbine is a *tangential flow impulse turbine.*

Important Pelton turbine installations in India :

S. No.	*Scheme/Project*	*Location (State)*	*Source of water*
1.	Koyana hydroelectric project	Koyana (Maharashtra)	Koyana river
2.	Mahatama Gandhi hydroelectric works	Sharavathi (Karnataka)	Sharavathi river
3.	Mandi hydroelectric scheme	Joginder Nagar (Himachal Pradesh)	Uhl river
4.	Pallivasal power station	Pallivasal (Kerala)	Mudirapuzle river
5.	Pykara hydroelectric scheme	Pykara (Tamil Nadu)	Pykara river.

2.3.1. Construction and working of Pelton Wheel/Turbine

A Pelton wheel/turbine consists of a **rotor**, at the periphery of which are mounted equally spaced *double hemispherical or double ellipsoidal buckets.* Water is transferred from a high head source through penstock which is fitted with a **nozzle**, through which the water flows out at a *high speed jet.* **A needle spear** moving inside the nozzle *controls the water flow through the nozzle* and the same time, provides a smooth flow with negligible energy loss. All the available *potential energy is thus converted into kinetic energy* before the jet strikes the **buckets** of the **runner**. *The pressure all over the wheel is constant and equal to atmosphere, so that energy transfer occurs due to purely impulse action.*

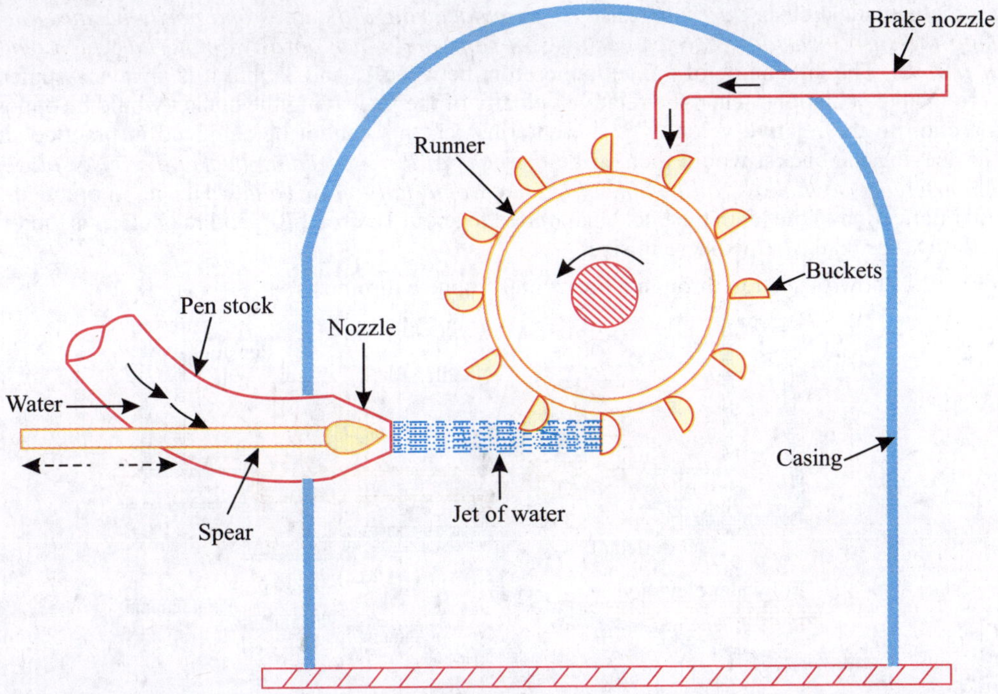

Fig. 2.2. Pelton wheel.

The Pelton turbine is provided with a **casing** the function of which is to *prevent the splashing of water and to discharge water to the tail race.*

When the nozzle is completely closed by moving the spear in the forward direction the amount of water striking the runner is reduced to zero but the runner due to inertia continues revolving for a long time. In order to bring the runner to rest in a short time, a nozzle (brake) is provided which directs the jet of water on the back of buckets; this jet of water is called **braking jet.**

Speed of the turbine runner is kept constant by a **governing mechanism** *that automatically regulates the quantity of water flowing through the runner in accordance with any variation of load.*

Fig. 2.2 shows a schematic diagram of a Pelton wheel, while Fig. 2.3 shows two views of its bucket.

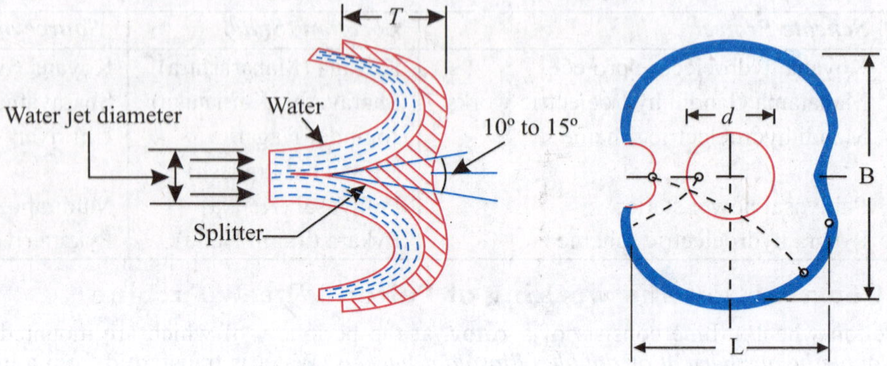

$$\frac{L}{d} = 2 \text{ to } 3; \quad \frac{B}{d} = 3 \text{ to } 4; \quad \frac{D}{d} = 11 \text{ to } 16; \quad \frac{T}{d} = 0.8 \text{ to } 1.2; \quad \text{notch (width)} = 1.1d + 5 \text{ mm}$$

Fig. 2.3. The bucket dimensions.

The jet emerging from the nozzle hits the splitter symmetrically and is equally distributed into the two halves of hemispherical bucket as shown. The bucket centre line cannot be made exactly like a mathematical cusp, *partly because of manufacturing difficulties and partly because the jet striking the cusp invariably carries particles of sand and other abrasive material which tend to wear it down.* The inlet angle of the jet is therefore between 1° and 3°, but it is always assumed to be zero in all calculations. Then the relative velocity of the jet leaving the bucket would be opposite in direction to the relative velocity of the entering jet; this cannot be achieved in practice since the jet leaving the bucket would then strike *the back of the succeeding bucket to cause splashing and interference so that overall turbine efficiency would fall to low values.* Hence, in practice, the angular deflection of the jet in the bucket is limited to about 165° or 170°, and the bucket is therefore *slightly smaller* than a hemisphere in size.

Fig. 2.4 shows a section through a horizontal-impulse turbine.

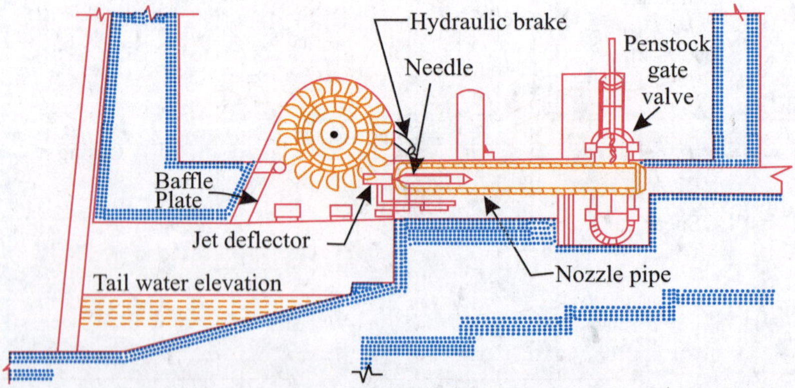

Fig. 2.4. Section through a horizontal-impulse turbine.

2.3.2. Work done and Efficiency of a Pelton Wheel

Fig. 2.5 shows the velocity triangles.

Let, N = Speed of wheel in r.p.m.,

D = Diameter of the wheel,

d = Diameter of the jet,

u = Peripheral (or circumferential) velocity of runner. It will be same at inlet and outlet of the runners at the mean pitch. (*i.e.* $u = u_1 = u_2$)

$$= \frac{\pi DN}{60},$$

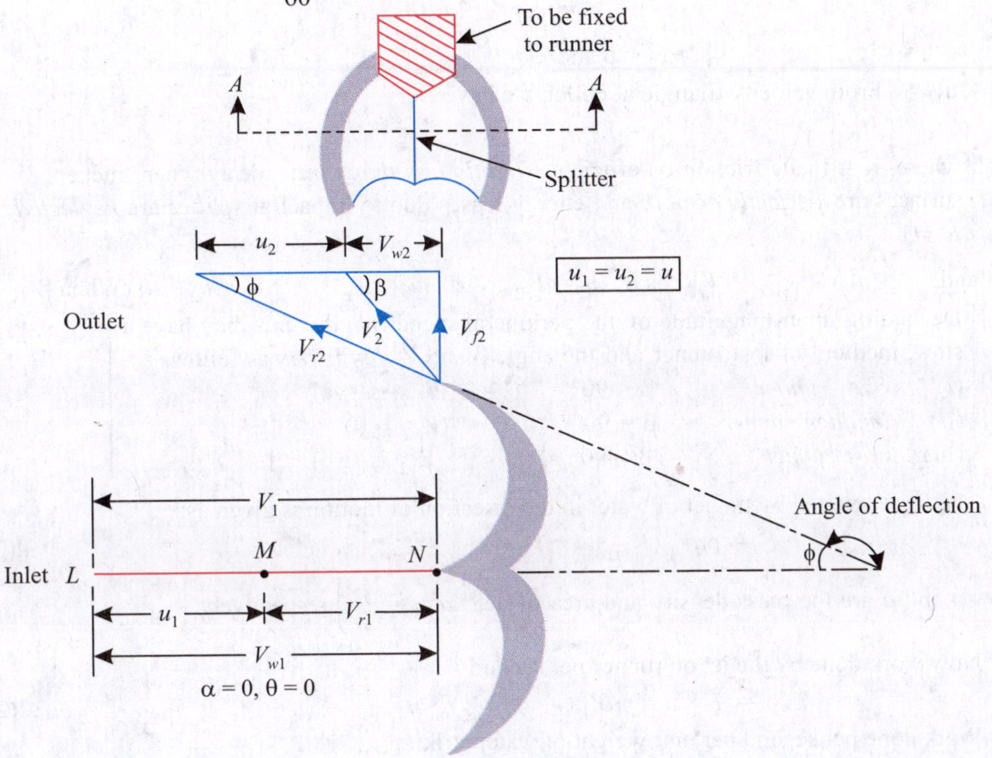

Fig. 2.5. Velocity triangles.

V_1 = Absolute velocity of water at inlet,

V_{r1} = Jet velocity relative to vane/bucket at inlet,

α = Angle between the direction of the jet and direction of motion of the vane/bucket (also called *guide angle*),

θ = Angle made by the relative velocity (V_{r1}) with the direction of motion at inlet (also called *vane angle at inlet*),

V_{w1} and V_{f1} = The components of the velocity of the jet V_1, in direction of motion and perpendicular to the direction of motion of the vane respectively;

V_{w1} is also known as *velocity of whirl* at inlet,

V_{f1} is also known as *velocity of flow* at inlet,

V_2 = Velocity of jet, leaving the vane or velocity of jet at outlet of the vane,

V_{r2} = Relative velocity of the jet with respect to the vane at outlet,

ϕ = Angle made by the relative velocity V_{r2} with the direction of motion of the vane at outlet and also called *vane angle at outlet*,

β = Angle made by the velocity V_2 with the direction of motion of the vane at outlet, and

V_{w2} and V_{f2} = Components of the velocity V_2, in the direction of motion of vane and perpendicular to the direction of motion of vane at outlet;
V_{w2} is also called the *velocity of whirl at outlet*, and
V_{f2} is also called the *velocity of flow at outlet*.

Inlet. The velocity triangle at *inlet* will be a *straight line* where

$$V_{r1} = V_1 - u_1 = V_1 - u, \; V_{w1} = V_1 \qquad (\because u_1 = u_2 = u)$$

$$\alpha = 0 \text{ and } \theta = 0$$

Outlet : From velocity triangle at outlet, we have

$$V_{r2} = KV_{r1},$$

[where, K = blade friction co-efficient, *slightly less than unity*. Idealy when bucket surfaces are *perfectly smooth* and energy losses due to impact at splitter are *neglected*, $K = 1$]

and, $$V_{w2} = V_{r2} \cos\phi - u_2 = V_{r2} \cos\phi - u \qquad (\because u_1 = u_2 = u) \text{ (When } \beta < 90°)$$

[Depending upon magnitude of the peripheral speed (u), the unit may have a slow, medium or fast runner and the angle β and V_{w2} will vary as follows :

(*i*)	*Slow runner*	$\beta < 90°$	(V_{w2} is –ve)
(*ii*)	*Medium runner*	$\beta = 90°$	($V_{w2} = 0$)
(*iii*)	*Fast runner*	$\beta > 90°$	(V_{w2} is +ve)

]

The force exerted by the jet of water in the direction of motion is given as:

$$F = \rho a V_1 (V_{w1} + V_{w2}) \qquad \text{...(2.1)}$$

[ρ and a are the mass density and area of jet $\left(a = \frac{\pi}{4} d^2\right)$ respecitvely.]

Now work done by the jet on runner per second

$$= F \times u = \rho a V_1 (V_{w1} + V_{w2}) \times u \qquad \text{...(2.2)}$$

Work done per second per unit weight of water striking

$$= \frac{\rho a V_1 (V_{w1} + V_{w2}) \times u}{\text{Weight of water striking}} = \frac{\rho a V_1 (V_{w1} + V_{w2}) \times u}{\rho a V_1 \times g}$$

$$= \frac{1}{g} (V_{w1} + V_{w2})\, u \qquad \text{...[2.2 (a)]}$$

The energy supplied to the jet at inlet is in the form of K.E. and is equal to $\frac{1}{2} m V_1^2$.

$\therefore$ Kinetic energy (K.E.) of jet per second = $\frac{1}{2} (\rho a V_1) \times V_1^2$

$\therefore$ Hydraulic efficiency, $$\eta_h = \frac{\text{Work done per second}}{\text{K.E. of jet per second}} = \frac{\rho a V_1 (V_{w1} + V_{w2}) \times u}{\frac{1}{2} (\rho a V_1) \times V_1^2}$$

or, $$\eta_h = \frac{2 (V_{w1} + V_{w2}) \times u}{V_1^2} \qquad \text{...(2.3)}$$

From inlet and outlet velocity triangles, we have:

$$V_{w1} = V_1, V_{r1} = V_1 - u_1 = V_1 - u$$

$$V_{w2} = V_{r2} \cos\phi - u_2 = V_{r2}\cos\phi - u = KV_{r1}\cos\phi - u = K(V_1 - u)\cos\phi - u$$

Substituting the values of V_{w1} and V_{w2} in eqn (2.3), we have:

$$\eta_h = \frac{2[V_1 + K(V - u)\cos\phi - u]u}{V_1^2} = \frac{2[(V_1 - u)(1 + K\cos\phi)]u}{V_1^2} \quad \text{...(2.4)}$$

The hydraulic efficiency will be *maximum* for given value of V_1 when,

$$\frac{d}{du}(\eta_h) = 0$$

i.e.,

$$\frac{d}{du}\left[\frac{2(V_1 - u)(1 + \cos\phi)u}{V_1^2}\right] = 0$$

or,

$$\frac{2(1 + K\cos\phi)}{V_1^2} \times \frac{d}{du}(V_1 u - u^2) = 0$$

Since,

$$\frac{2(1 + K\cos\phi)}{V_1^2} \neq 0, \therefore \frac{d}{du}(V_1 u - u^2) = 0$$

or,

$$V_1 - 2u = 0, \text{ or, } u = \frac{V_1}{2} \quad \text{...(2.5)}$$

The above equation states that *hydraulic efficiency of a Pelton wheel is maximum when the velocity of the wheel is half the velocity of jet of water at inlet.* The maximum efficiency can be obtained by substituting the value of $u = \frac{V_1}{2}$ in eqn. (2.4).

$$(\eta_h)_{max} = \frac{2\left(V_1 - \frac{V_1}{2}\right)(1 + K\cos\phi)\frac{V_1}{2}}{V_1^2} = \frac{2 \times \frac{V_1}{2}(1 + K\cos\phi) \times \frac{V_1}{2}}{V_1^2}$$

or,

$$(\eta_h)_{max} = \frac{(1 + K\cos\phi)}{2} \quad \text{...(2.6)}$$

If friction factor, $K = 1$ (*i.e.,* assuming *no friction*), we have

$$(\eta_h)_{max} = \frac{1 + \cos\phi}{2} \quad \text{...[2.6(a)]}$$

2.3.3. Definitions of Heads and Efficiencies

Fig. 2.6 shows a general layout of a hydroelectric power plant using an impulse turbine (Pelton wheel).

1. Gross head. The gross (total) head is the difference between the water level at the reservoir (also known as the *head race*) and the water level at the tail race. It is denoted by H_g.

2. Net or effective head. The head available at the inlet of the turbine is known as net or effective head. It is denoted by H and is given by:

$$H = H_g - h_f - h$$

where, h_f = Total loss of head between the head race and entrance of the turbine

$$= \frac{4fLV^2}{D \times 2g}$$ (L = length of penstock, D = diameter of penstock,

V = velocity of flow in penstock), and

h = Height of nozzle above the tail race.

3. Efficiencies. The following are the important *efficiencies of turbine* :

(i) Hydraulic efficiency (η_h). It is defined as the *ratio of power developed by the runner to the power supplied by the jet at entrance to the turbine.*

Mathematically,
$$\eta_h = \frac{\text{Power developed by the runner}}{\text{Power supplied at the inlet of turbine}}$$

$$= \frac{\rho Q_a (V_{w1} \pm V_{w2})\, u}{w Q_a H} = \frac{\left(\frac{w}{g}\right) Q_a (V_{w1} \pm V_{w2})\, u}{w Q_a H}$$

$$= \frac{(V_{w1} \pm V_{w2})\, u}{gH} = \frac{H_r}{H} \quad \text{...(2.7)}$$

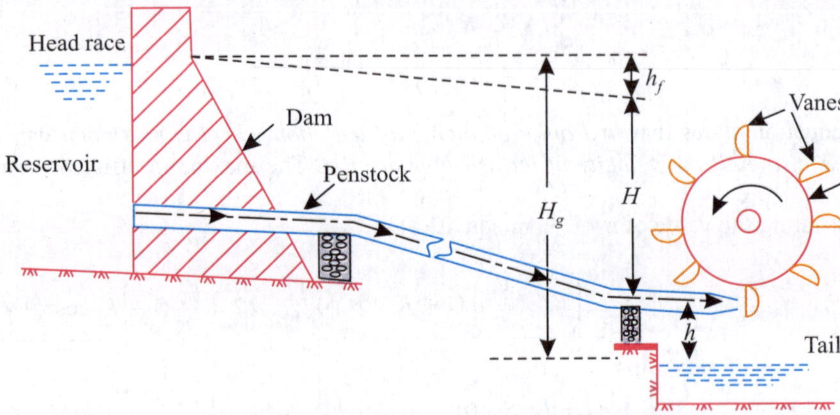

Fig. 2.6. Layout of hydroelectric power plant using an impulse turbine (Pelton wheel).

where, V_{w1}, V_{w2} = Velocities of whirl at inlet and outlet respectively,

u = Tangential velocity of vane,

H = Net head on the turbine, and

Q_a = Actual flow rate to turbine runner (bucket).

The parameter, $H_r = \frac{1}{g}(V_{w1} + V_{w2})\, u$ represents the energy transfer per unit weight of water and is referred to as the '*runner head*' or '*Euler head*'.

$H - H_r = \Delta H$ = Hydraulic losses within the turbine.

(ii) Mechanical efficiency (η_m). It is defined as the *ratio of the power obtained from the shaft of the turbine to the power developed by the runner.* These two powers differ by the amount of mechanical losses, *viz.,* bearing friction, etc.

Mathematically,
$$\eta_h = \frac{\text{Power available at the turbine shaft}}{\text{Power developed by turbine runner}} = \frac{\text{Shaft power}}{\text{Bucket power}}$$

$$= \frac{P}{wQ_a\left(\frac{V_{w1}+V_{w2}}{g}\right)u} = \frac{P}{wQ_aH_r} \quad ...(2.8)$$

Values of mechanical efficiency for a Pelton wheel usually lie between *97 to 99 percent depending on size and capacity of the unit.*

(*iii*) Volumetric efficiency (η_v). The volumetric efficiency is the *ratio of the volume of water actually striking the runner to the volume of water supplied by the jet to the turbine.* That is,

$$\eta_v = \frac{\text{Volume of water actually striking the runner } (Q_a)}{\text{Total water supplied by the jet to the turbine } (Q)} \quad ...(2.9)$$

For Pelton turbines, $\eta_v \simeq 0.97$ to 0.99.

(*iv*) Overall efficiency (η_o). It is defined as the *ratio of power available at the turbine shaft to the power supplied by the water jet.* That is

$$\eta_0 = \frac{\text{Power available at the turbine shaft}}{\text{Power available from the water jet}} = \frac{\text{Shaft power}}{\text{Water power}} = \frac{P}{wQH} \quad ...(2.10)$$

(where, Q = the total discharge in m^3/s supplied by the jet.)

The values of overall efficiency for a Pelton wheel lie between 0.85 to 0.90.

The individual efficiencies may be combined to give,

$$\eta_0 = \eta_h \times \eta_m \times \eta_v$$

$$= \frac{H_r}{H} \times \frac{P}{wQ_aH_r} \times \frac{Q_a}{Q} = \frac{P}{wQH}, \text{ which is the same as defined vide eqn. (2.10)}$$

If η_g is the efficiency of a generator, then power output of hydrounit (turbine + hydrogenerators)

$$= (wQH) \times \eta_0 \times \eta_g$$

The product $\eta_0 \times \eta_g$ is known as *hydroelectric plant efficiency.*

2.3.4. Design Aspects of Pelton wheel

The following points should be considered while *designing a Pelton wheel* :

1. Velocity of jet. The velocity of jet at inlet is given by,

$$V_1 = C_v\sqrt{2gH} \quad ...(2.11)$$

where, C_v = Co-efficient of velocity (= 0·98 or 0·99), and

H = Net head on turbine.

2. Velocity of wheel. The velocity of wheel (u) is given by,

$$u = K_u\sqrt{2gH} \quad ...(2.12)$$

where, K_u = Speed ratio. It varies from 0.43 to 0.48.

3. Angle of deflection of the jet. The angle of deflection of the jet through the buckets is taken as 165° if no angle of deflection is given.

4. Mean diameter of the wheel (*D*). The mean diameter or pitch diameter D of the Pelton wheel is given by,

$$u = \frac{\pi DN}{60} \text{ or } D = \frac{60\,u}{\pi N} \quad ...(2.13)$$

5. Jet ratio (m). It is defined as the *ratio of the pitch diameter* (*D*) *of the Pelton wheel to the diameter of the jet* (*d*). It is denoted by '*m*' and is given as :

$$m = \frac{D}{d} \text{ (lies between 11 and 16 for maximum hydraulic efficiency)} \quad ...(2.14)$$

Normally, the jet ratio is adopted as 12 in practice.

6. Bucket dimensions. Some of the main dimensions of the bucket of a Pelton wheel are as follows :

Refer to Fig. 2.3 : $B = 3$ to $4d$; $L = 2$ to $3d$; $T = 0.8$ to $1.2d$.

7. Number of jets. Normally a Pelton wheel has one nozzle or one jet. However, a number of nozzles may be employed when more power is to be produced with the same wheel. Theoretically *six nozzles* can be used on Pelton wheel. However, practical considerations limit the use of not more than two jets per runner for a vertical runner and not more than four jets per runner if it is of horizontal configuration.

Number of jets is obtained by *dividing the total rate of flow through the turbine by the rate of flow of water through a single jet.*

8. Number of buckets (Z). The number of buckets for a Pelton wheel should be such that the jet is always completely intercepted by the buckets so that volumetric efficiency of the turbine is very close to unity. Number of buckets on a runner is given by,

$$Z = 15 + \frac{D}{2d} = 15 + 0.5\text{ m} \quad ...(2.15)$$

Example 2.1. *A Pelton wheel is receiving water from a penstock with a gross head of 510 m. One-third of gross head is lost in friction in the penstock. The rate of flow through the nozzle fitted at the end of the penstock is 2·2 m³/s. The angle of deflection of the jet is 165°. Determine :*

(i) The power given by water to the runner, and

(ii) Hydraulic efficiency of the Pelton wheel.

Take C_v (co-efficient of velocity) = 1·0 and speed ratio = 0·45.

Solution. Gross head, $H_g = 510$ m

Head lost in friction, $h_f = \frac{H_g}{3} = \frac{510}{3} = 170$ m

∴ Net head, $H = H_g - h_f = 510 - 170 = 340$ m

Discharge, $Q = 2{\cdot}2\ \text{m}^3/\text{s}$

Angle of deflection = 165°

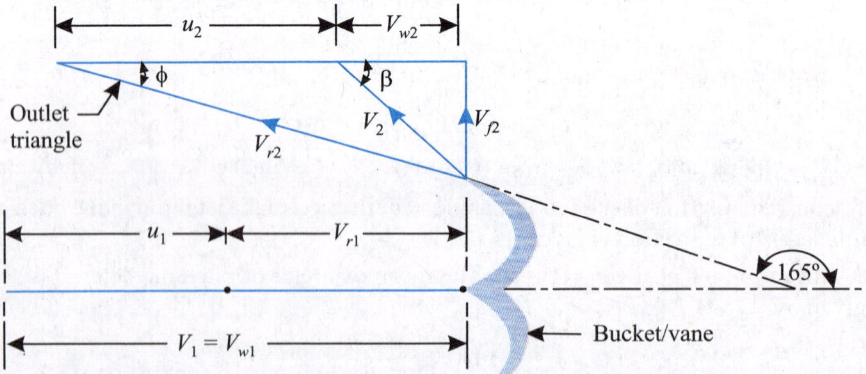

Fig. 2.7

$\therefore$ Angle, $\phi = 180° - 165° = 15°$

Co-efficient of velocity, $C_v = 1.0$

Speed ratio, $K_u = 0.45$

(i) The power given by water to the runner :

Velocity of jet, $V_1 = C_v \sqrt{2gH} = 1.0\sqrt{2 \times 9.81 \times 340} = 81.67$ m/s

Velocity of wheel, $u = K_u \sqrt{2gH} = 0.45\sqrt{2 \times 9.81 \times 340} = 36.75$ m/s

Refer to fig. 2.7. $V_{r1} = V_1 - u_1 = V_1 - u = 81.67 - 36.75 = 44.92$ m/s $(\because u_1 = u_2 = u)$

Also, $V_{w1} = V_1 = 81.67$ m/s

From outlet velocity triangle, we have:

$$V_{r2} = V_{r1} = 44.92 \text{ m/s}$$

Also, $V_{r2} \cos\phi = u_2 + V_{w2} = u + V_{w2}$

or, $V_{w2} = V_{r2} \cos\phi - u = 44.92 \cos 15° - 36.75 = 6.64$ m/s

Work done by the jet on the runner per second

$= \rho Q (V_{w1} + V_{w2}) \times u$ ...[Eqn (2.2)]

$= 1000 \times 2.2\,(81.67 + 6.64) \times 36.75 = 7139863$ Nm/s

$\therefore$ Power given by water to the runner = 7139863 J/s

or, $W \simeq$ **7139.8 kW (Ans.)**

(ii) Hydraulic efficiency of the Pelton wheel, η_h :

$$\eta_h = \frac{2\,(V_{w1} + V_{w2}) \times u}{V_1^2} \quad \text{...[Eqn (2.3)]}$$

$$= \frac{2\,(81.67 + 6.64) \times 36.75}{(81.67)^2} = 0.973 \text{ or } \mathbf{97.3\ \%\ (Ans.)}$$

Alternatively :

$$\eta_h = \frac{(V_{w1} + V_{w2})\,u}{gH} \quad \text{...[Eqn (2.7)]}$$

$$= \frac{(18.67 + 6.64) \times 36.75}{9.81 \times 340} = 0.973 \text{ or } \mathbf{97.3\ \%\ (Ans.)}$$

Example 2.2. *A Pelton wheel having a mean bucket diameter of 1·2 m is running at 1000 r.p.m. The net head on the Pelton wheel is 840 m. If the side clearance angle is 15° and discharge through the nozzle is 0·12 m³/s, determine :*

(i) Power available at the nozzle, and

(ii) Hydraulic efficiency of the turbine.

Solution. Mean diameter of Pelton wheel, $D = 1.2$ m

Speed of wheel, $N = 1000$ r.p.m.

$\therefore$ Tangential velocity of the wheel, $u = \dfrac{\pi DN}{60} = \dfrac{\pi \times 1.2 \times 1000}{60} = 62.83$ m/s

Net head on the turbine, $H = 840$ m

Side clearance angle, $\theta = 15°$

Discharge $Q = 0.12\ m^3/s$

(i) Power available at the nozzle :

Velocity of jet at inlet, $V_1 = C_v\sqrt{2gH}$

$$= 1.0\sqrt{2 \times 9.81 \times 840} = 128.38 \text{ m/s}$$

(Assume $C_v = 1.0$ if not given)

∴ Power available at nozzle

$$= wQH = 9810 \times 0.12 \times 840 = 988848 \text{ Nm/s or J/s or W} \simeq \mathbf{988.85\ kW}$$ **(Ans.)**

(ii) Hydraulic efficiency, η_h :

$$\eta_h = \frac{2(V_1 - u)(1 + K\cos\phi)u}{V_1^2} \qquad \text{...[Eqn. (2.4)]}$$

$$= \frac{2(128.38 - 62.83)(1 + \cos 15°) \times 62.83}{(128.38)^2} = \frac{131.1(1 + 0.966) \times 62.83}{(128.38)^2}$$

(Assume $K = 1$)

$= 0.982$ or **98.2 % (Ans.)**

Example 2.3. *A Pelton wheel is to be designed for the following specifications :*

Power (brake or shaft)	*... 9560 kW*
Head	*... 350 metres*
Speed	*... 750 r.p.m.*
Overall efficiency	*... 85%*
Jet diameter	*... not to exceed 1/6 th of the wheel diameter*

Determine the following :

(i) The wheel diameter, *(ii) Diameter of the jet, and*

(iii) The number of jets required.

Take $C_v = 0{\cdot}985$, Speed ratio = 0.45. **[UPTU]**

Solution. Shaft or brake power = 9560 kW

Head, H = 350 m

Speed, N = 750 r.p.m.

Overall efficiency, η_0 = 85%

Ratio of jet diameter to wheel, $\dfrac{d}{D} = \dfrac{1}{6}$

Co-efficient of velocity, C_v = 0.985

Speed ratio, K_u = 0.45

(i) The wheel diameter, D :

$$\text{Velocity of jet, } V_1 = C_v\sqrt{2gH} = 0.985\sqrt{2 \times 9.81 \times 350} = 81.62 \text{ m/s}$$

The velocity of wheel, $u = u_1 = u_2$

$$= K_u \times \sqrt{2gH} = 0.45\sqrt{2 \times 9.81 \times 350} = 37.3 \text{ m/s}$$

But, $$u = \frac{\pi DN}{60}$$

∴ $$37.3 = \frac{\pi D \times 750}{60}, \quad \text{or,} \quad D = \frac{37.3 \times 60}{\pi \times 750} = \mathbf{0.95\ m}$$ **(Ans.)**

(*ii*) Diameter of the jet, *d* :

$$\frac{d}{D} = \frac{1}{6}$$

$$\therefore \quad d = \frac{D}{6} = \frac{0.95}{6} = \mathbf{0.158\ m}\ \textbf{(Ans.)}$$

(*iii*) The number of jets required :

$$\text{Discharge of one jet, } q = \text{Area of jet} \times \text{velocity of jet}$$

$$= \frac{\pi}{4} d^2 \times V_1 = \frac{\pi}{4} \times 0.158^2 \times 81.62 = 1.6\ \text{m}^3/\text{s}$$

Now, overall efficiency, $\eta_0 = \dfrac{\text{Shaft power}}{\text{Water power}} = \dfrac{9560}{wQH}$

or, $0.85 = \dfrac{9560}{9.81 \times Q \times 350}$ $\quad (\because w = 9.81\ \text{kN/m}^3)$

$$\therefore \quad \text{Total discharge, } Q = \frac{9560}{0.85 \times 9.81 \times 350} = 3.27\ \text{m}^3/\text{s}$$

$$\therefore \quad \text{Number of jets} = \frac{\text{Total discharge}}{\text{Discharge of one jet}} = \frac{Q}{q} = \frac{3.27}{1.6} = \mathbf{2\ jets}\ \textbf{(Ans.)}$$

Example 2.4. *A Pelton wheel nozzle, for which* $C_v = 0{\cdot}97$, *is 400 m below the water surface of a lake. The jet diameter is 80 mm, the pipe diameter is 0·6 m, its length is 4 km, and* $f = 0.032$ *in the formula* $h_f = \dfrac{fLV^2}{D \times 2g}$. *The buckets deflect the jet through 165° and they run at 0·48 times the jet speed, bucket friction reducing the velocity at outlet by 15 per cent of the relative velocity at inlet. Mechanical efficiency = 90%. Determine* :

(*i*) *The flow rate, and*

(*ii*) *The shaft power developed by the turbine.* **[MDU Haryana]**

Solution. Co-efficient of velocity, $C_v = 0.97$

Gross head, $H_g = 400$ m

Diameter of jet, $d = 80$ mm $= 0.08$ m

Diameter of pipe, $D = 0.6$ m

Length of pipe, $L = 4$ km $= 4000$ m

Friction factor, $f = 0.32$

Angle, $\phi = 180° - 165° = 15°$

Bucket speed, $u = 0.48$ times the jet speed

Relative velocity at the outlet (V_{r2}) $= 0.85$ times the relative velocity at inlet V_{r1}.

(*i*) The flow rate, *Q* :

Let, V = Velocity of water in pipe, and

V_1 = Velocity of jet of water.

Also, $AV = aV_1$ ...*Continuity equation*

(where, A = area of pipe, and a = area of jet)

or, $$\frac{\pi}{4} \times D^2 \times V = \frac{\pi}{4} \times d^2 \times V_1$$

$$V = \frac{d^2}{D^2} \times V_1 = \left(\frac{0.08}{0.6}\right)^2 \times V_1 = 00177\ V_1 \quad \text{...}(i)$$

Applying Bernoulli's equation to free surface of water in the reservoir and the outlet of the nozzle, we have:

Head at reservoir = Kinetic head of jet of water + head lost due to friction in pipe + head lost in nozzle

$$= \frac{V_1^2}{2g} + \frac{fLV^2}{D \times 2g} + \text{head lost in nozzle,} \quad \text{...}(ii)$$

Let, $(V_1)_{th}$ = Theoretical velocity at outlet of nozzle, and

V_1 = Actual velocity of jet of water.

Then, $$\frac{V_1}{(V_1)_{th}} = C_v \text{ or, } (V_1)_{\text{th}} = \frac{V_1}{C_v}$$

Now, Head lost in nozzle = Head corresponding to $(V_1)_{th}$ – head corresponding to V_1

$$= \frac{(V_1)_{th}^2}{2g} - \frac{V_1^2}{2g} = \left(\frac{V_1}{C_v}\right)^2 \times \frac{1}{2g} - \frac{V_1^2}{2g}$$

$$= \frac{V_1^2}{2g}\left(\frac{1}{C_v^2} - 1\right)$$

Substituting this value in eqn. (*ii*), we get:

$$\text{Head at reservoir} = \frac{V_1^2}{2g} + \frac{fLV^2}{D \times 2g} + \frac{V_1^2}{2g}\left(\frac{1}{C_v^2} - 1\right)$$

or, $$400 = \frac{V_1^2}{2g} + \frac{0.032 \times 4000V^2}{0.6 \times 2 \times 9.81} + \frac{V_1^2}{2 \times 9.81} + \frac{V_1^2}{2g} \times \frac{1}{C_v^2} - \frac{V_1^2}{2g}$$

$$= \frac{0.032 \times 4000 \times (0.0177V_1)^2}{0.6 \times 2 \times 9.81} + \frac{V_1^2}{2 \times 9.81} \times \frac{1}{(0.97)^2} \quad (\because V = 0.0177\text{V}_1)$$

$$= 0.0034\ V_1^2 + 0.054\ V_1^2 = 0.0574\ V_1^2$$

$$V_1 = \left(\frac{400}{0.0574}\right)^{1/2} = 83.48 \text{ m/s}$$

∴ Flow rate = Area of jet × velocity of jet

$$= \frac{\pi}{4} \times (0.08)^2 \times 83.48 = \mathbf{0.419\ m^3/s}\ \textbf{(Ans.)}$$

(*ii*) The shaft power :

Velocity of bucket, $u_1 = 0{\cdot}48V_1 = 0{\cdot}48 \times 83{\cdot}48 = 40{\cdot}07$ m/s

Refer to Fig. 2.8. $V_{r1} = V_1 - u_1 = 83.47 - 40.07 = 43.4$ m/s

$V_{w1} = V_1 = 83.48$ m/s

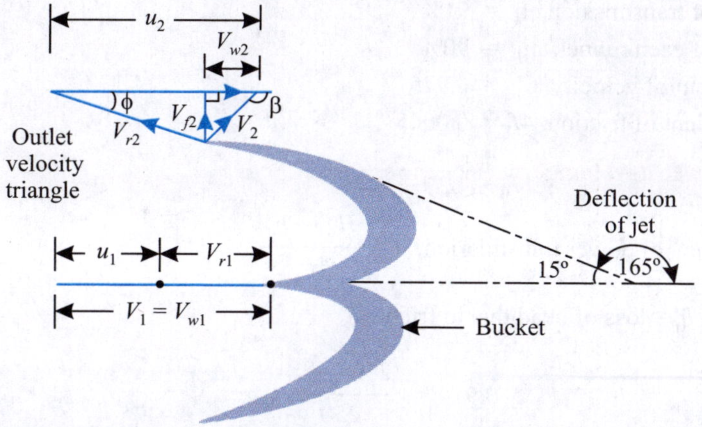

Fig. 2.8

From the outlet velocity triangle, we have:

$$V_{r2} = 0.85 V_{r1} = 0.85 \times 43.4 = 36.89 \text{ m/s}$$

$$V_{w2} = u_2 - V_{r2} \cos \phi$$

$$= 40.07 - 36.89 \times \cos 15° = 4.44 \text{ m/s}$$

Mechanical efficiency,

$$\eta_m = \frac{\text{Shaft power}}{\text{Power given to runner}}$$

∴ Shaft power, $= \eta_m \times$ power given to runner

But power given to runner

$$= \frac{w}{g} Q (V_{w1} - V_{w2}) \times u$$

[Here –ve sign is taken since $\beta > 90°$ (*i.e.*, V_{w1} and V_{w2} are in the *same direction*)]

$$\therefore \quad \text{Shaft power} = \eta_m \times \frac{w}{g} Q (V_{w1} - V_{w2}) \times u_1$$

$$= 0.9 \times \frac{9.81}{9.81} \times 0.419 (83.48 - 4.44) \times 40.07 \text{ kW} \qquad (\because w = 9.81 \text{ kN/m}^3)$$

$$= \textbf{1194.3 kW (Ans.)}$$

Example 2.5. *The water available for a Pelton wheel is 4 m^3/s and the total head from the reservoir to the nozzle is 250 m. The turbine has two runners with two jets per runner. All the four jets have the same diameters. The pipe is 3 km long. The efficiency of transmission through the pipeline and the nozzle is 91 % and efficiency of each runner is 90 %. The velocity co-efficient of each nozzle is 0·975 and co-efficient of friction '4f' for the pipe is 0·0045. Determine :*

(i) *The power developed by the turbine,*

(ii) *The diameter of the jet, and*

(iii) *The diameter of the pipeline.* **[M.U]**

Solution. Rate of flow, $Q = 4 \text{ m}^3/\text{s}$

Total or gross head, $H_g = 250$ m

Total number of jets $= 2 \times 2 = 4$

Length of pipe, $L = 3 \text{ km} = 3000$ m

Efficiency of transmission, η = 91%
Efficiency of each runner, η_h = 90%
Co-efficient of velocity, C_v = 0.975
Co-efficient of friction, $4f$ = 0.0045

(i) The power developed by the runner :

Efficiency of power transmission, $\eta = \dfrac{H_g - h_f}{H_g}$

(where, h_f = loss of head due to friction)

or, $0.91 = \dfrac{250 - h_f}{250}$

$\therefore \quad h_f = 250 - 250 \times 0.91 = 22.5$ m

$\therefore$ Net head on the turbine, $H = H_g - h_f = 250 - 22.5 = 227.5$ m

Velocity of jet, $V_1 = C_v\sqrt{2gH} = 0.975\sqrt{2 \times 9.81 \times 227.5} = 65.14$ m/s

Now, Water power = Kinetic energy of the jet

$$\frac{1}{2}mV_1^2 = \frac{1}{2}\rho Q V_1^2 = \frac{1}{2} \times 1000 \times 4 \times 65.14^2 = 8486439 \text{ Nm/s}$$

$= 8486439$ J/s or $W \simeq 8486.44$ kW

But, hydraulic efficiency, $\eta_h = \dfrac{\text{Power developed by the turbine}}{\text{Water power}}$

or, $0.9 = \dfrac{\text{Power developed by the turbine}}{8486.44}$

$\therefore$ Power developed by the turbine

$= 0.9 \times 8486.44 =$ **7637.8 kW (Ans.)**

(ii) The diameter of the jet, d :

Discharge per jet, $q = \dfrac{\text{Total discharge}}{\text{No. of jets}} = \dfrac{4}{4} = 1.0 \text{ m}^3/\text{s}$

But, $q = \dfrac{\pi}{4} \times d^2 \times V_1$

$\therefore \quad 1.0 = \dfrac{\pi}{4} \times d^2 \times 65.14$ or $d = \left(\dfrac{1.0 \times 4}{\pi \times 65.14}\right)^{1/2} \simeq$ **0.14 m (Ans.)**

(iii) The diameter of the pipeline, D :

Head lost due to friction, $h_f = \dfrac{4fLV^2}{D \times 2g}$

where, V = velocity through pipe $= \dfrac{Q}{\text{Area}} = \dfrac{Q}{(\pi/4) \times D^2} = \dfrac{4Q}{\pi D^2}$

$$\therefore \quad h_f = \frac{0.0045 \times 3000 \times \left(\frac{4Q}{\pi D^2}\right)^2}{D \times 2g}$$

$$\text{or,} \quad 22.5 = \frac{0.0045 \times 3000 \times 16Q^2}{D \times 2 \times 9.81 \times \pi^2 \times D^4}$$

$$= \frac{0.0045 \times 3000 \times 16 \times (4)^2}{D^5 \times 2 \times 9.81 \times \pi^2} = \frac{17.85}{D^5}$$

$$\text{or,} \quad D^5 = \frac{12.85}{22.5} \quad \text{or} \quad D = \left(\frac{17.85}{22.5}\right)^{1/5} = 0.955 \text{ m}$$

Hence, *the diameter of the pipeline, D* = **0.955 m (Ans.)**

Example 2.6. *A single jet Pelton wheel runs at 300 r.p.m. under a head of 510 m. The jet diameter is 200 mm, its deflection inside the bucket is 165° and its relative velocity is reduced by 15% due to friction. Determine* :

(i) *Water power,*

(ii) *Resultant force on the bucket, and*

(iii) *Overall efficiency.*

Take: Mechanical losses = 3%, co-efficient of velocity = 0.98, and speed ratio = 0.46.

[PTU]

Solution. Speed of the wheel, N = 300 r.p.m.

Diameter of jet, d = 200 mm = 0.2 m

Net head, H = 510 m

Angle of deflection of jet = 165°

Reduction of relative velocity due to friction = 15%

Mechanical losses = 3%

Co-efficient of velocity, C_v = 0.98

Speed ratio, K_u = 0.46.

***(i)* Water power :**

$$\text{Velocity of jet, } V_1 = C_v\sqrt{2gH} = 0.98\sqrt{2 \times 9.81 \times 510} = 98 \text{ m/s}$$

∴ Discharge through the Pelton wheel,

$$Q = \text{Area of jet } (a) \times \text{velocity } (V_1)$$

$$= \frac{\pi}{4} \times (0.2)^2 \times 98 = 3.078 \text{ m}^3/\text{s}$$

$$\text{Water power} = wQH = 9.81 \times 3.078 \times 510 \text{ kW} = \mathbf{15399.5 \text{ kW}} \textbf{ (Ans.)}$$

***(ii)* Resultant force on the bucket :**

$$\text{Peripheral speed of the wheel, } u = K_u\sqrt{2gH} = 0.46\sqrt{2 \times 9.81 \times 510} = 46 \text{ m/s}$$

Refer to fig. 2.8. *At inlet to turbine* :

$$V_{w1} = V_1 = 98 \text{ m/s}$$

$$V_{r1} = (V_1 - u_1) = 98 - 46 = 52 \text{ m/s}$$

At exit from the turbine :

The blade angle at exit, $\phi = 180° - 165° = 15°$

$V_{r2} = 0.85\ V_{r1}$ ...(*Given*)

or, $V_{r2} = 0.85 \times 52 = 44.2$ m/s

As $V_{r2} \cos \phi$ is *less* than blade speed u, the velocity triangle at outlet will be as shown in Fig. 2.8 ($\beta > 90°$)

$$V_{w2} = u_2 - V_{r2} \cos \phi = 46 \qquad (\because u_1 = u_2 = u)$$
$$= 46 - 44.2 \cos 15° = 3.31 \text{ m/s}$$

∴ Resultant force on the bucket,

$$F = \rho Q (V_{w1} - V_{w2}) \qquad (\because \beta > 90°)$$
$$= 1000 \times 3.078\ (98 - 3.31) = \mathbf{291455.8\ N\ (Ans.)}$$

(*iii*) Brake power, P :

Power developed by the wheel $= F \times u = 291455.8 \times 46$ Nm/s or J/s or W

$= 291455.8 \times 46 \times 10^{-3}$ kW

$= 13406.97$ kW

∴ Brake power (power produced at the shaft),

$$P = 13406.97 \times (1 - 0.03) = \mathbf{13004.76\ kW\ (Ans.)}$$

(*iv*) Overall efficiency, η_o :

$$\eta_0 = \frac{\text{Brake power}}{\text{Water power}}$$

$$= \frac{13004.76}{15399.5} = 0.844 \text{ or } \mathbf{84.4\%\ (Ans.)}$$

Example 2.7. *A Pelton wheel running at 480 r.p.m. and operating under an available head of 420 m is required to develop 4800 kW. There are two equal jets and the bucket deflection angle is 165°. The overall efficiency is 85 percent when the water is discharged from the wheel in a direction parallel to the axis of rotation. The co-efficient of velocity of nozzle = 0·97 and blade speed ratio = 0·46. The relative velocity of water at exit from the bucket is 0·86 times the relative velocity at inlet. Calculate the following :*

(*i*) *Cross-sectional area of each jet,*

(*ii*) *Bucket pitch circle diameter, and*

(*iii*) *Hydraulic efficiency of the turbine.*

Solution. Speed of the wheel, N = 480 r.p.m.

Available head, H = 420 m

Shaft power, P = 4800 kW

Angle of deflection of jet = 165°

Overall efficiency, η_0 = 85%

Co-efficient of velocity of nozzle, C_v = 0.97

Blade speed ratio, K_u = 0.46

Relative velocity of water at exit = 0·86 times the relative velocity at inlet

(*i*) Cross-sectional area of each jet, a :

$$\text{Shaft power, } P = wQH \times \eta_0$$
$$4800 = 9.81 \times Q \times 420 \times 0.85$$

$\therefore$ Total discharge through the wheel, $Q = \dfrac{4800}{9.81 \times 420 \times 0.85} = 1.37 \text{ m}^3/\text{s}$

Velocity of jet, $V_1 = C_v \sqrt{2gH} = 0.97\sqrt{2 \times 9.81 \times 420} = 88.05$ m/s

Now, total discharge Q = No. of jets × area of each nozzle (a) × velocity of jet (V_1)

or, $1.37 = 2 \times a \times 88.05$

$\therefore \quad a = \dfrac{1.37}{2 \times 88.05} = \mathbf{7.779 \times 10^{-3}\ m^2}$ **(Ans.)**

(ii) Bucket pitch circle diameter, D :

Velocity of bucket, $u = K_u \sqrt{2gH} = 0.46\sqrt{2 \times 9.81 \times 420} = 41.76$ m/s

Also, $u = \dfrac{\pi D N}{60}$; $41.76 = \dfrac{\pi D \times 480}{60}$;

$\therefore \quad D = \dfrac{41.76 \times 60}{\pi \times 480} = \mathbf{1.66\ m}$ **(Ans.)**

(iii) Hydraulic efficiency of the turbine, η_h :

$$\eta_h = \frac{2(V_1 - u)(1 + K\cos\phi)\,u}{V_1^2} \qquad \text{...[Eqn. (2.4)]}$$

The blade angle at exit; $\phi = 180° - 165° = 15°$

Substituting the relevant data in the above eqn. we get:

$$\eta_h = \frac{2 \times (88.05 - 41.76)(1 + 0.86 \times \cos 15°) \times 41.76}{(88.05)^2} \qquad (\because K = 0.86)$$

$$= \frac{2 \times 46.29\,(1 + 0.86 \times 0.966) \times 41.76}{7752.8} = 0.913 \text{ or } \mathbf{91.3\%}\ \textbf{(Ans.)}$$

Example 2.8. *The following data relate to a Pelton wheel :*

Head at the base of the nozzle = 82 m; diameter of the jet = 100 mm; discharge of the nozzle = 0.30 m³/s; shaft power = 206 kW; power absorbed in mechanical resistance = 4.5 kW. Determine :

(i) Power lost in nozzle, and

(ii) Power lost due to hydraulic resistance in water.

Solution. Head at the base of the nozzle, $H_1 = 82$ m

Diameter of the jet, $d = 100$ mm $= 0.1$ m

$\therefore$ Area of the jet, $a = \dfrac{\pi}{4} \times 0.1^2 = 0.007854 \text{ m}^2$

Discharge of the nozzle, $Q = 0.30 \text{ m}^3/\text{s}$

Shaft power, $P = 206$ kW

Power absorbed in mechanical resistance = 4.5 kW.

(i) Power lost in nozzle :

Discharge, Q = Area of jet × velocity of jet

$0.30 = 0.007854 \times V_1$

$\therefore \qquad V_1 = \dfrac{0.30}{0.007854} = 38.2$ m/s

Power available at the base of the nozzle

$$wQH_1 = 9.81 \times 0.30 \times 82 = 241.3 \text{ kW} \qquad [\because w = 9.81 \text{ kN/m}^3]$$

Power corresponding to K.E. of the jet,

$$\frac{1}{2}\left(\frac{wQ}{g}\right)V_1^2 = \frac{1}{2} \times \left(\frac{9.81 \times 0.30}{9.81}\right) \times 38.2^2 = 218.9 \text{ kW}$$

$\therefore$ Power lost in nozzle = Power available at the nozzle base – power corresponding to K.E. of the jet

= 241.3 – 218.9 = **22.4 kW (Ans.)**

***(ii)* Power lost due to hydraulic resistance in water :**

Power at the base of the nozzle = Shaft power + power lost in runner + power lost in nozzle

241.3 = 206 + power lost in runner + 22.4

$\therefore$ Power lost in runner = 241.3 – 206 – 23.4 = **12.9 kW (Ans.)**

Example 2.9. *A single jet Pelton turbine is required to drive a generator to develop 10000 kW. The available head at the nozzle is 760 m. Assuming electric generation efficiency 95 percent, Pelton wheel efficiency 87 percent, co-efficient of velocity for nozzle 0·97, mean bucket velocity 0·46 of jet velocity, outlet angle of bucket 15° and the relative velocity of the water leaving the buckets 0·85 of that inlet, find :*

(i) The flow in m³/s,

(ii) The diameter of jet,

(iii) The force exerted by the jet on the buckets, and

(iv) The best synchronous speed for generation at 50 Hz and the corresponding mean diameter if the ratio of the mean bucket circle diameter to the jet diameter is not to be less than 10.

[N.U.]

Solution. Output of generator = 10000 kW

Generator efficiency = 95%

Availavble head at the nozzle, H = 760 *m*

Pelton wheel efficiency = 87%

Co-efficient of velocity, C_v = 0.97

Bucket velocity, u = 0.46 × jet velocity

Relative velocity of water at outlet = 0.85 × relative velocity at inlet

Outlet angle of bucket, ϕ = 15°

***(i)* The flow in m³/s :**

Output of turbine, P_t = Input of generator

$$= \frac{\text{Output of the generator}}{\text{Generator efficiency}}$$

$$= \frac{10000}{0.95} = 10526.3 \text{ kW}$$

Available power of the turbine $= wQH = \dfrac{P_t}{\text{Pelton wheel efficiency}}$

or, $$9.81 \times Q \times 760 = \frac{10526.3}{0.87}$$

$$\therefore \quad Q = \frac{10526.3}{9.81 \times 760 \times 0.87} = \mathbf{1.62\ m^3/s}\ \textbf{(Ans.)}$$

(ii) The diameter of jet d :

$$Q = \frac{\pi}{4} \times d^2 \times V_1$$

where, $$V_1 = \text{Velocity of jet} = C_v \times \sqrt{2gH}$$

$$= 0.97 \times \sqrt{2 \times 9.81 \times 760} = 118.45 \text{ m/s}$$

$$\therefore \quad 1.62 = \frac{\pi}{4} \times d^2 \times 118.45$$

or, $$d = \left(\frac{1.62 \times 4}{\pi \times 118.45}\right)^{1/2} = 0.132 \text{ m or } \mathbf{132\ mm}\ \textbf{(Ans.)}$$

(iii) The force exerted by the jet on the buckets :

Bucket velocity, $u = 0.46 V_1 = 0.46 \times 118.45 = 54.5$ m/s

At inlet : $V_{w1} = V_1 = 118.45$ m/s

$u_1 = u_2 = 54.5$ m/s

$V_{r1} = V_1 - u_1 = 118.45 - 54.5 \simeq 64$ m/s

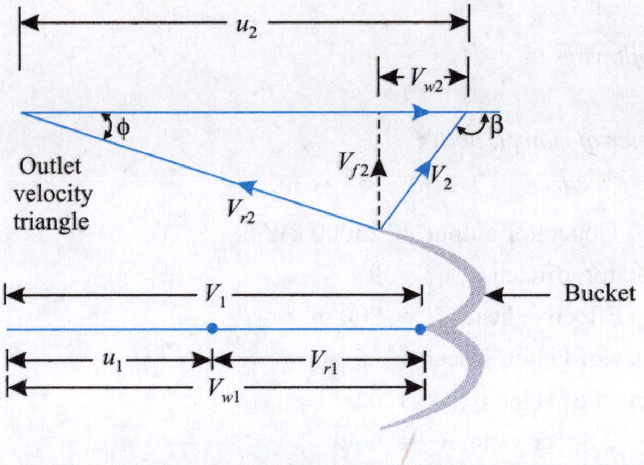

Fig. 2.9

At outlet :

$$V_{r2} = 0.85\, V_{r1} = 0.85 \times 64 = 54.4 \text{ m/s}$$

$$V_{w2} = u_2 - V_{r2} \cos\phi = 54.5 - 54.4 \times \cos 15° = 1.95 \text{ m/s}$$

$\therefore$ Force exerted by jet on water,

$$F = \rho Q (V_{w1} - V_{w2}) \qquad (\because \beta > 90°)$$

$$= 1000 \times 1.62\,(118.5 - 1.95)$$

$$= 188811 \text{ N} \simeq \mathbf{188.8\ kN}\ \textbf{(Ans.)}$$

(iv) Best synchronous speed (N_{syn}); mean bucket diameter (D) :

Now, $\frac{D}{d} = 10$, where D is the mean bucket diameter

$\therefore$ $D = 10 \times d = 10 \times 132 = 1320$ mm or 1.32 m

$$u = \frac{\pi DN}{60} \text{ or } N = \frac{60u}{\pi D} = \frac{60 \times 54.5}{\pi \times 1.32} \simeq 788 \text{ r.p.m.}$$

Frequency of generator, $f = \frac{N_{syn.} P}{120}$, where P = no. of poles.

If $P = 8$, $N_{syn.} = \frac{120 f}{P} = \frac{120 \times 50}{8} = 750$ r.p.m. which is nearest to 788 r.p.m.

$\therefore$ $D_{(revised)} = \frac{1320 \times 788}{750} = 1387$ mm or **1.387 m (Ans.)**

Example 2.10. *The following data relate to a double overhung Pelton unit :*

Output of generator	*...25000 kW*
Generator efficiency	*...93 %*
Effective head at the base of nozzle	*...300 m*
Pelton wheel efficiency	*...85 %*
Co-efficient of velocity	*...0·97*
Speed ratio	*...0·46*
Jet ratio	*...12*

Determine the following :

(i) Size of jet,

(ii) Mean diameter of runner, and

(iii) Synchronous speed.

Solution. Generator output = 25000 kW

Generator efficiency, η_g = 93 %

Effective head, H = 300 m

Efficiency of Pelton wheel = 85 %

Co-efficient of velocity, C_v = 0.97

Speed ratio, K_u = 0.46

Jet ratio, $m = \frac{D}{d} = 12$

(i) Size of jet, *d* :

There are two runners keyed on the two ends of the shaft, and the generator lies between them. Each runner is to be considered as one complete turbine. Thus, two Pelton turbines are feeding the generator.

$\therefore$ Output of each turbine, $P_t = \frac{25000}{2 \times \eta_g} = \frac{25000}{2 \times 0.93} = 13440.8$ kW

Power developed by each turbine $= \dfrac{P_t}{\text{Pelton wheel efficiency}} = \dfrac{13440.8}{0.85} = 15812.7$ kW

But, $15812.7 = wQH$

$$\therefore \quad Q = \frac{15812.7}{wH} = \frac{15812.7}{9.81 \times 300} = 5.37 \text{ m}^3/\text{s}$$

Velocity of jet, $V_1 = C_v\sqrt{2gH} = 0.97\sqrt{2 \times 9.81 \times 300} = 74.4$ m/s

Also, Q = Area of jet × velocity of jet $= a \times V_1 = \dfrac{\pi}{4} \times d^2 \times V_1$

or, $5.37 = \dfrac{\pi}{4} \times d^2 \times 74.4$

$$\therefore \quad d = \left(\frac{5.37 \times 4}{\pi \times 74.4}\right)^{1/2} = 0.3 \text{ m or } \mathbf{300\ mm}\ \textbf{(Ans.)}$$

(*ii*) Mean diameter of runner, D :

$$m = \frac{D}{d} = 12$$

or, $D = 12d = 12 \times 0.3 = $ **3.6 m (Ans.)**

(*iii*) Synchronous speed ($N_{syn.}$) :

Peripheral speed, $V = K_u \times \sqrt{2gH} = 0.46\sqrt{2 \times 9.81 \times 300} = 35.3$ m/s

But, $u = \dfrac{\pi DN}{60} \quad \therefore N = \dfrac{60u}{\pi D} = \dfrac{60 \times 35.3}{\pi \times 3.6} = 187.3$ r.p.m.

Frequency of generator, $f = \dfrac{N_{syn.} \times P}{120}$

$$\therefore \quad N_{syn.} = \frac{120f}{P} = \frac{120 \times 50}{P} = \frac{6000}{P}$$

[where, f = frequency = 50 Hz (given), and P = no. of poles]

Assuming $P = 32$, we have:

$$D_{syn.} = \frac{6000}{32} = \mathbf{187.5\ r.p.m.}\ \textbf{(Ans.)}$$

$$D_{(revised)} = \frac{3.6 \times 187.3}{187.5} \simeq \mathbf{3.6\ m}\ \textbf{(Ans.)}$$

Example 2.11. *The following data relate to a Pelton wheel :*

Head	*... 72 m*
Speed of the wheel	*... 240 r.p.m.*
Shaft power of the wheel	*...115 kW*
Speed ratio	*... 0·45*
Co-efficient of velocity	*... 0·98*
Overall efficiency	*... 85%*

Design the Pelton wheel.

Solution. Effective head, H = 72 m

Speed of the wheel, N = 240 r.p.m.

Shaft power, P = 115 kW

Speed ratio, K_u = 0·45

Co-efficient of velocity, C_v = 0·98

Overall efficiency, η_0 = 85%

Design the Pelton wheel; it means to find diameter of the wheel D, diameter of jet (d), width and depth of buckets and number of buckets on the wheel.

(*i*) Diameter of wheel, *D*:

$$\text{Velocity of jet, } V_1 = C_v\sqrt{2gH} = 0.98\sqrt{2 \times 9.81 \times 72} = 36.8 \text{ m/s}$$

$$\therefore \text{ Bucket velocity, } u\ (=u_1 = u_2) = K_u \times V_1 = 0.45 \times 36.8 = 16.56 \text{ m/s}$$

But,
$$u = \frac{\pi DN}{60}, \text{ or, } D = \frac{60u}{\pi N} = \frac{60 \times 16.56}{\pi \times 240} = \mathbf{1.32\ m}\ \textbf{(Ans.)}$$

(*ii*) Diameter of jet, *d*:

$$\text{Overall efficiency, } \eta_0 = \frac{\text{Shaft power}}{\text{Water power}} = \frac{P}{wQH}$$

or,
$$0.85 = \frac{115}{9.81 \times Q \times 72}$$

or,
$$Q = \frac{115}{0.85 \times 9.81 \times 72} = 0.1915 \text{ m}^3/\text{s}$$

But,
$$Q = \text{Area of jet} \times \text{velocity of jet}$$

$$0.1915 = \frac{\pi}{4} \times d^2 \times V_1 = \frac{\pi}{4} d^2 \times 36.8$$

$$\therefore \quad d = \left(\frac{0.1915 \times 4}{\pi \times 36.8}\right)^{1/2} = 0.0814 \text{ m or } \mathbf{81.4\ mm}\ \textbf{(Ans.)}$$

(*iii*) Size of buckets:

Width of the bucket, B = 3 to 4 times jet diameter (d)

$\simeq 3.5\,d = 3.5 \times 81.4 =$ **285 mm (Ans.)**

Radial length of bucket, L = 2 to 3 times jet diameter (d)

$\simeq 2.5\,d = 2.5 \times 81.4 =$ **203.5 mm (Ans.)**

Depth of bucket, T = 0.8 to 1.2 times jet diameter (d)

$\simeq 1.0\,d =$ **81.4 mm (Ans.)**

(*iv*) Number of buckets on the wheel, Z :

$$Z = 15 + \frac{D}{2d} = 15 + \frac{1.32 \times 1000}{2 \times 81.4} = \mathbf{23}\ \textbf{(Ans.)}$$

Example 2.12. *A Pelton wheel of 1.1 m mean bucket diameter works under a head of 500 m. The deflection of jet is 165° and its relative velocity is reduced over the bucket by 15 per cent due to friction. If the diameter of jet is 100 mm and the water is to leave the bucket without any whirl, determine :*

(*i*) *Rotational speed of wheel,*
(*ii*) *Ratio of bucket speed to jet velocity,*
(*iii*) *Impulsive force and power developed by the wheel,*
(*iv*) *Available power (water power),*
(*v*) *Power input to buckets, and*
(*vi*) *Efficiency of the wheel with power input to bucket as reference input.*
Take $C_v = 0.97$. **[UPSC]**

Solution. Mean bucket diameter, $D = 1.1$ m

Net head, $H = 500$ m

Deflection of jet = 165°

Reduction of relative velocity due to friction = 15%

Diameter of jet, $d = 100$ mm = 0.1 m

Co-efficient of velocity, $C_v = 0.97$

(*i*) **Rotational speed of wheel, N :**

Velocity of jet, $V_1 = C_v\sqrt{2gH} = 0.97\sqrt{2 \times 9.81 \times 500} = 96.07$ m/s

Let, bucket speed $u_1 = u_2 = u$

Relative velocity at inlet, $V_{r1} = V_1 - u_1 = (96.07 - u)$

Relative velocity at outlet, $V_{r2} = 0.85\ V_{r1}$

$= 0.85\ (96.07 - u)$ ...(*i*)

The blade angle at exit, $\phi = 180° - 165° = 15°$

As the jet leaves the bucket *without any whirl,* the velocity triangle at outlet will be as shown in Fig. 2.10 ($\beta = 90°$)

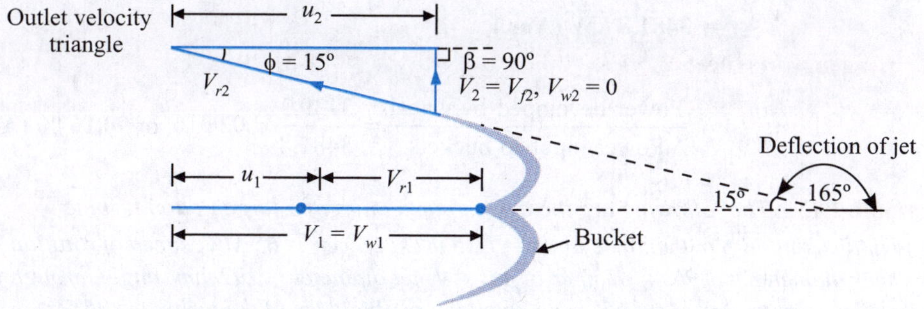

Fig. 2.10

$V_{r2} \cos\phi = u$, or, $V_{r2} \cos 15° = u$ ...(*ii*)

From (*i*) and (*ii*), we get:

$0.85\ (96.07 - u) \cos 15° = u$

or, $0.85\ (96.07 - u) \times 0.966 = u$

or, $78.88 - 0.821\ u = u$

or, $u = 43.31$ m/s

Also, $u = \dfrac{\pi DN}{60}$, or, $43.31 = \dfrac{\pi \times 1.1 \times N}{60}$

$\therefore$ Rotational speed of wheel, $N = \dfrac{43.31 \times 60}{\pi \times 1.1} \simeq$ **752 r.p.m. (Ans.)**

(ii) Ratio of bucket speed to jet velocity :

$$\frac{u}{V_1} = \frac{43.31}{96.07} = \mathbf{0.4508} \text{ (Ans.)}$$

(iii) Impulsive force and power developed by the wheel :

Discharge through the wheel,

$$Q = \frac{\pi}{4} \times d^2 \times V_1 = \frac{\pi}{4} \times (0.1)^2 \times 96.07 = 0.7545 \text{ m}^3/\text{s}$$

Impulsive force on the buckets,

$$F = \rho Q (V_{w1} \pm V_{w2}) = \rho Q (V_{w1}) \qquad (\because V_{w2} = 0)$$

$$= 1000 \times 0.7545 \times 96.07 \qquad (\because V_{w1} = V_1)$$

$$= \mathbf{72484.8 \text{ N}} \text{ (Ans.)}$$

Power developed by the wheel,

$$= F \times u = 72484.8 \times 43.31 = 3139316.7 \text{ Nm/s or J/s or W}$$

$$= \mathbf{3139.3 \text{ kW}} \text{ (Ans.)}$$

(iv) Available power (water power) :

$$\text{Available power (water power)} = wQH$$

$$= 9.81 \times 0.7545 \times 500 = \mathbf{3700.8 \text{ kW}} \text{ (Ans.)}$$

(v) Power input to buckets :

$$\text{Power input to buckets} = \frac{1}{2} m V_1^2 = \frac{1}{2} (\rho Q) \times V_1^2$$

$$= \frac{1}{2} \times 1000 \times 0.7545 \times (96.07)^2 = 3481808 \text{ Nm/s or J/s or W}$$

$$= \mathbf{3481.8 \text{ kW}} \text{ (Ans.)}$$

(vi) Efficiency of wheel η_{wheel} :

$$\eta_{wheel} = \frac{\text{Power developed by wheel}}{\text{Power input to buckets}} = \frac{3139.3}{3481.8} = 0.9016 \text{ or } \mathbf{90.16\ \%} \text{ (Ans.)}$$

Example 2.13. *The following are the design particulars of a large Pelton turbine :*

Head at distributor = 630 m; discharge = 12.5 m³/s; power = 65 MW; speed of rotation = 500 r.p.m; runner diameter = 1.96 m; number of jets = 4; jet diameter = 192 mm; angle through which the jet is defleted by the buket = 165°; and mechanical efficiency of the turbine = 96%.

Determine the hydraulic power losses in the distributor nozzle assembly and the buckets.

[UPSC]

Solution. Head at distributor, H = 630 m

Discharge, Q = 12.5 m³/s

Shaft power, P = 65 MW = 65000 kW

Speed of rotation, N = 500 r.p.m.

Runner diameter, D = 1.96 m

Number of jets = 4

Jet diameter, d = 192 mm = 0.192 m

Angle of deflection = 165°

Mechanical efficiency of the turbine, η_m = 96%

Hydraulic power losses in nozzle assembly and buckets :

$$\text{Mechanical efficiency, } \eta_m = \frac{\text{Shaft power}}{\text{Power developed by the runner}}$$

or,
$$0.96 = \frac{65000}{\text{Power developed by the runner}}$$

or,
$$\text{Power developed by the runner} = \frac{65000}{0.96} = 67708 \text{ kW}$$

$\therefore$
$$\text{Power developed per jet} = \frac{67708}{4} = 16927 \text{ kW}$$

$$\text{Discharge per jet, } q = \frac{Q}{4} = \frac{12.5}{4} = 3.125 \text{ m}^3/\text{s}$$

But
$$q\,(= 3.125) = \text{Area of jet } (a) \times \text{velocity of jet } (V_1)$$

or,
$$3.125 = \frac{\pi}{4} \times d^2 \times V_1 = \frac{\pi}{4} \times 0.192^2 \times V_1$$

$\therefore$
$$= \frac{3.125 \times 4}{\pi \times 0.192^2} = 107.93 \text{ m/s}$$

Also,
$$\text{peripheral speed of runner, } u = \frac{\pi DN}{60} = \frac{\pi \times 1.96 \times 500}{60} = 51.31 \text{ m/s}$$

$$\text{Blade angle at outlet, } \phi = 180° - 165° = 15°$$

$$\text{Work developed per jet} = \frac{wQ}{g}(V_1 - u)(1 + K \cos\phi)\, u$$

(where, K = blade friction co-efficient)

$\therefore$
$$\frac{wq}{g}(V_1 - u)(1 + K\cos\phi)\, u = 16927$$

or,
$$\frac{9.81 \times 3.125}{9.81}(107.93 - 51.31)(1 + K\cos 15°) \times 51.31 = 16927$$

or,
$$9078.7\,(1 + K\cos 15°) = 16927$$

or,
$$K\cos 15° = \frac{16927}{9078.7} - 1 = 0.8644$$

$\therefore$
$$K = \frac{0.8644}{\cos 15°} = 0.895$$

Also,
$$V_{r2} = KV_{r1}$$

But,
$$V_{r1} = (V_1 - u_1) = (V_1 - u)$$

$\therefore$
$$V_{r2} = K(V_1 - u)$$

$$\text{Theoretical velocity of jet } (V_1)_{\text{th}} = \sqrt{2gH}$$

$$\text{Actual velocity of jet } V_1 = C_v \times (V_1)_{th} = C_v\sqrt{2gH}$$

$\therefore$
$$\text{Head lost in nozzle } V_1 = \frac{(V_1)_{th}^2 - V_1^2}{2g} = \frac{2gH - C_v^2\,(2gH)}{2g}$$

$$= (1 - C_v^2)H$$

But, $$C_v = \frac{V_1}{\sqrt{2gH}} = \frac{107.93}{\sqrt{2 \times 9.81 \times 630}} = 0.97$$

$\therefore$ Head lost in nozzle $= (1 - 0.97^2) \times 630 = 37.23$ m

Head lost in buckets $$= \frac{V_{r1}^2 - V_{r2}^2}{2g} = \frac{V_{r1}^2 - K^2 V_{r1}^2}{2g} = \frac{V_{r1}^2}{2g}(1 - K^2)$$

$$= \frac{(V_1 - u)^2}{2g}(1 - K^2) = \frac{(107.93 - 51.31)^2}{2 \times 9.81} \times (1 - 0.895^2) = 32.5 \text{ m}$$

$\therefore$ The head lost in nozzle and buckets,

$$H_L = 37.23 + 32.5 = 69.73 \text{ m}$$

Power loss $= wQH_L = 9.81 \times 12.5 \times 69.73 =$ **8550.6 kW (Ans.)**

Example 2.14. *Show that in Pelton wheel, where the buckets deflect the water through* (180° – ϕ), *the hydraulic efficiency of the wheel is given by:*

$$\eta_h = \frac{2u\,(V - u)\,(1 + \cos\phi)}{V^2}$$

where, V is the velocity of the jet and u is the velocity of the wheel at the pitch radius.

[UPSC]

Solution. Refer to Article 2.3.2.

Example 2.15. *Prove that the maximum efficiency of Pelton wheel occurs when the ratio of bucket velocity u to the velocity V is given by the expression.*

$$\frac{u}{V} = \frac{1 - \cos\theta + K_1}{2\,(1 - \cos\theta) + K_1 + K_2}$$

where K_1 *and* K_2 *are the constants.*

Loss due to bucket friction and shock $= \dfrac{K_1\,(V - u)^2}{2g}$

Loss due to bearing friction and windage losses $= K_2 \dfrac{u^2}{2g}$

θ = *bucket angle at outlet* = (180° – ϕ) *i.e., angle of deflection of jet.*

Volumetric losses to be considered negligible.

Solution. The net amount of work done per unit weight of water (taking into account the losses given)

$$= \frac{1}{g}[(V - u)\,(1 - \cos\theta)]\,u - K_1 \frac{(V - u)^2}{2g} - K_2 \frac{u^2}{2g}$$

$\therefore$ Efficiency,
$$\eta = \frac{\frac{1}{g}[(V - u)\,(1 - \cos\theta)]\,u - K_1 \frac{(V - u)^2}{2g} - K_2 \frac{u^2}{2g}}{(V^2/2g)}$$

$$= \frac{2\,[(V-u)\,u \times (1-\cos\theta)] - K_1\,(V-u)^2 - K_2 u^2}{V^2}$$

The efficiency to be *maximum*, $\frac{d\eta}{du} = 0.$

$$\therefore \quad \frac{d\eta}{du} = \frac{2\,(V-2u)\,(1-\cos\theta) + 2K_1\,(V-u) - 2K_2 u}{V^2} = 0$$

or, $(V-2u)\,(1-\cos\theta) + K_1\,(V-u) - K_2 u = 0$

or, $V(1-\cos\theta) - 2u\,(1-\cos\theta) + K_1 V - K_1 u - K_2 u = 0$

or, $V(1-\cos\theta + K_1) = u\,[2\,(1-\cos\theta) + K_1 + K_2]$

$$\therefore \quad \frac{u}{V} = \frac{1-\cos\theta + K_1}{2\,(1-\cos\theta) + K_1 + K_2} \quad \textbf{...(Proved)}$$

2.4. REACTION TURBINES

In reaction turbines, the *runner utilizes both potential and kinetic energies*. As the water flows through the stationary parts of the turbine, whole of its pressure energy is *not* transformed to kinetic energy and when the water flows through the moving parts, there is a *change both in pressure and in the direction and velocity of flow of water*. As the water gives up its energy to the runner, both its pressure and absolute velocity get reduced. The water which acts on the runner blades is under a pressure *above atmospheric and the runner passages are always completely filled with water.*

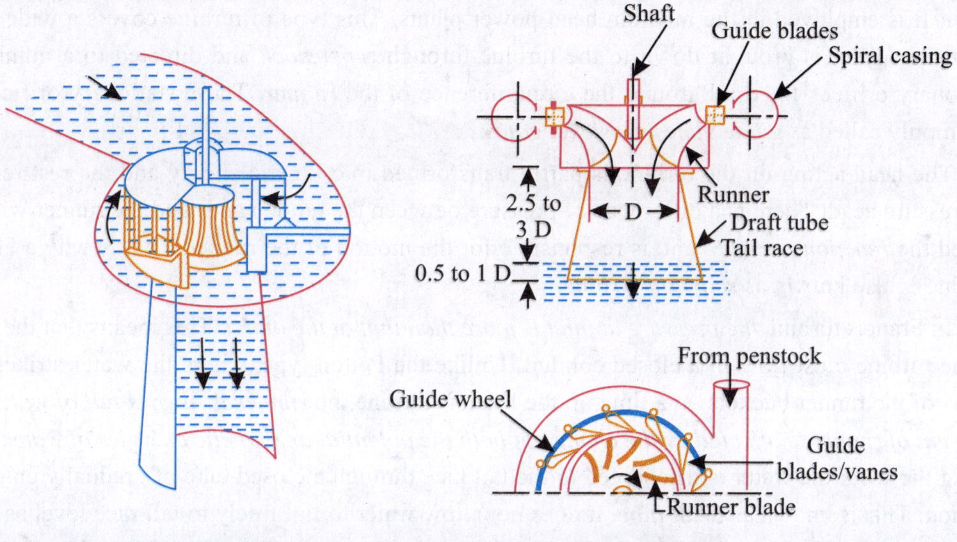

Fig. 2.11. Schematic diagram of a Francis turbine.

Important reaction turbines are *Francis*, *Kaplan* and *Propeller*.

2.4.1. Francis Turbine

Fig. 2.11 shows a schematic diagram of a Francis turbine. The *main parts of a Francis turbine are:*

1. *Penstock ...* It is a large size conduit which conveys water from the upstream of the dam/reservoir to the turbine runner.

2. *Spiral/scroll casing* ... It constitutes a closed passage whose cross-sectional area gradually decreases along the flow direction, area is maximum at inlet and nearly zero at exit.
3. *Guide vanes/wicket gates* ... These vanes direct the water onto the runner at an angle appropriate to the design. The motion to them is given by means of a hand wheel or automatically by a governor.
4. *Governing mechanism* ... It changes the position of the guide blades/vanes to affect a variation in water flow rate, when the load conditions on the turbine change.
5. *Runner and runner blades* ... — The driving force on the runner is both due to impulse and reaction effects;

   — The number of runner blades usually varies between 16 to 24.
6. *Draft tube* ... It is a gradually expanding tube which discharges water, passing through the runner, to the tail race.

The modern Francis turbine is an *inward mixed flow reaction turbine* (in the earlier stages of development, Francis turbine had a purely radial flow runner), *i.e. water under pressure, enters the runner from the guide vanes towards the centre in radial direction and discharges out of the runner axially.* The Francis turbine operates under *medium heads* and also requires *medium quantity* of water. It is employed in the medium head power plants. This type of turbine covers a wide range of heads. Water is brought down to the turbine through a *penstock* and directed to a number of stationary orifices fixed all around the circumference of the *runner*. These stationary orifices are commonly called as *guide vanes* or *wicket gates*.

The head acting on the turbine is partly transformed into kinetic energy and the rest remains as pressure head. There is a difference of pressure between the guide vanes and the runner which is called the *reaction pressure* and is responsible for the motion of the runner. That is why a Francis turbine is also known as *reaction turbine*.

In Francis turbine *the pressure at inlet is more than that at the outlet*. This means that the water in the turbine must flow in a closed conduit. Unlike the Pelton type, where the water strikes only a few of the runner buckets at a time, in the Francis turbine the *runner is always full of water. The moment of runner is affected by the change of both the potential and kinetic energies of water.* After doing the work the water is discharged to the tail race through a closed tube of gradually enlarging section. This is known as *draft tube*. It does not allow water to fall freely to tail race level as in the Pelton turbine. The free end of the draft tube is submerged deep in tail water making, thus, the entire water passage, right from the head race up to the tail race, *totally enclosed*.

Fig. 2.12 shows general layout of a hydroelectric power plant *using a reaction turbine*.

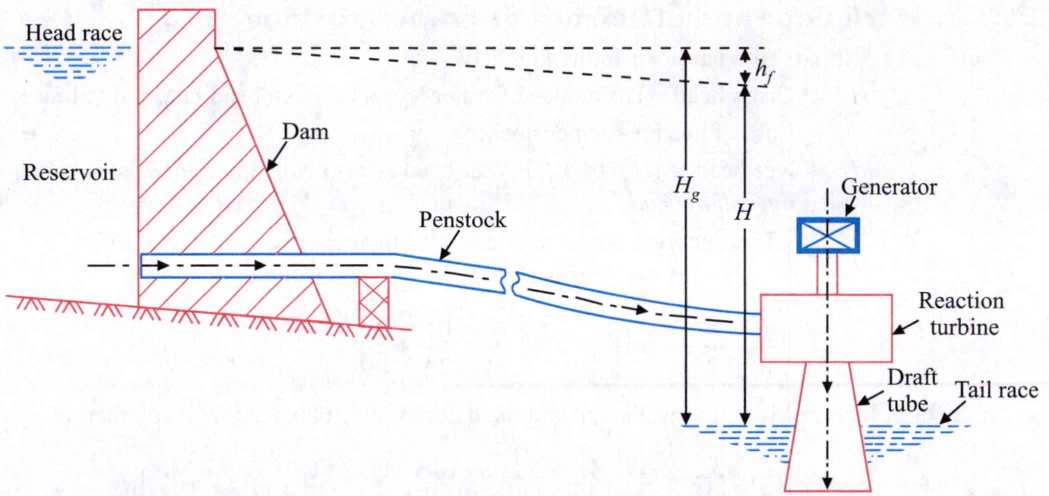

Fig. 2.12. General layout of a hydroelectric power plant using a reaction turbine.

Important Francis Turbine Installations in India :

S.No.	Scheme/Project	Location (State)	Source of water
1.	Bhakhra dam project	Bhakra (Punjab)	Sutlej river
2.	Cauvery hydroelectric scheme	Siva Samudram (Karnataka)	Cauvery river
3.	Chambal hydroelectric scheme	Gandhi sagar (Rajasthan)	Chambal river
4.	Hirakud dam project	Hirakud (Orissa)	Hirakud river
5.	Rihand dam project	Rihand (Uttar Pradesh)	Rihand river

Important differences between Inward and Outward Flow Reaction Turbines :

The following are the important differences between inward and outward flow reaction turbines :

S.No.	Aspects	Inward flow reaction turbine	Outward flow reaction turbine
1	*Entry of water*	Water enters at the outer periphery, flows inward and towards the centre of the turbine and discharges at the outer periphery.	Water enters at the inner periphery flows outward and discharges at the outer periphery.
2	*Centrifugal head imparted*	Negative (negative centrifugal head reduces the relative velocity of water at the outlet).	Positive (Positive centrifugal head increases the relative velocity of water at the outlet).
3	*Discharge*	Does not increase.	The discharge increases.
4	*Speed control*	Easy and effective.	Very difficult.
5	*Tendency of the wheel to race*	Nil. The turbine adjusts the speed by itself.	If the turbine speed increases the wheel tends to race; the turbine cannot adjust the speed by itself.
6	*Suitability*	Quite suitable for medium high heads; best suitable for large outputs and units.	Quite suitable for low or medium heads.
7	*Application*	For power projects.	Practically obsolete.

2.4.1.1. Work done and efficiency of Francis turbine

Net head at the turbine runner : In the Fig. 2.12,

H_g = Gross head = Difference of water levels between head race and tail race;

h_f = Loss of head in the penstock;

H = Net head = $(H_g - h_f)$. The net head is also called *available* or *working* or *operation head.*

$$\text{Also,} \quad H = \left[\begin{array}{c}\text{Total energy available at exit}\\ \text{from the penstock}\end{array}\right] - \left[\begin{array}{c}\text{total energy available at exit}\\ \text{from the draft tube}\end{array}\right]$$

$$= \left(\frac{p}{w} + \frac{V^2}{2g} + z\right)_{\text{penstock}} - \left(\frac{p}{w} + \frac{V^2}{2g} + z\right)_{\text{draft tube}}$$

If the draft tube exit is at tail race level, and the datum is also taken at that level, then,

$$H = \left(\frac{p}{w} + \frac{V^2}{2g} + z\right)_{\text{penstock}} - \frac{V_d^2}{2g}$$

(where, V_d = velocity at the exit of the draft tube)

Neglecting the velocity at the draft tube exit (V_d), we have:

$$H = \left(\frac{p}{w} + \frac{V^2}{2g} + z\right) \quad \text{...(2.16)}$$

Work done by the runner :

Fig. 2.13 shows the runner and the velocity diagrams (inlet and outlet) for an inward flow reaction turbine. The general expression for the work done with usual notations according to the Euler momentum equation, is given by,

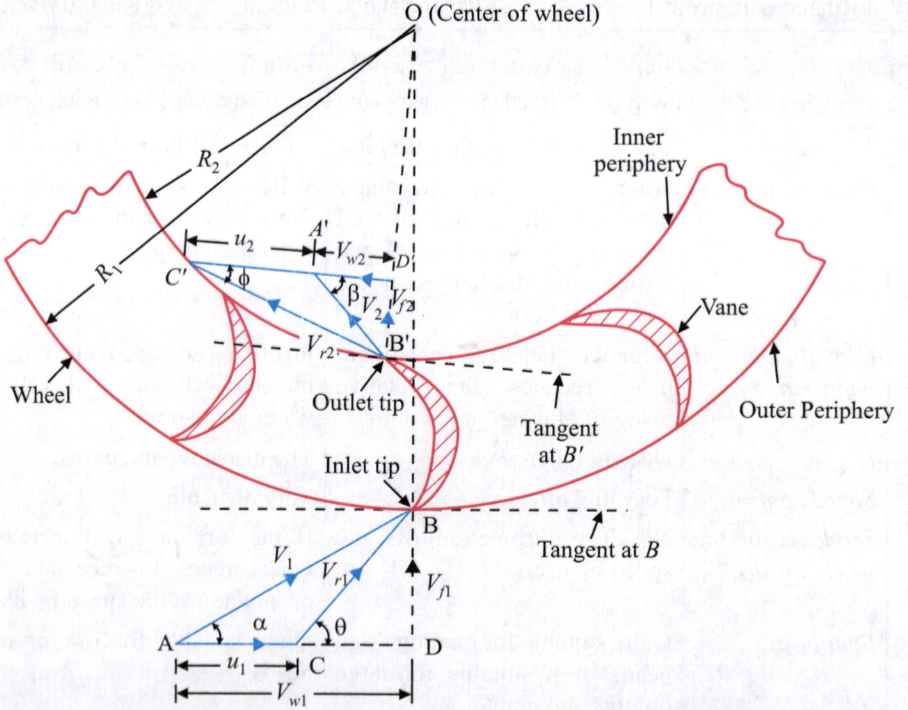

Fig. 2.13. Velocity diagrams for an inward flow reaction turbine.

$$\text{Work done} = \rho Q (V_{w1} u_1 \pm V_{w2} u_2)$$

$$= \frac{wQ}{g} (V_{w1} u_1 \pm V_{w2} u_2) \quad ...(2.17)$$

where, Q = Discharge through the runner, m^3/s.

The maximum output under given conditions is obtained when $V_{w2} = 0$.

Thus, the maximum work done is given by,

$$\text{Work done} = \frac{wQ}{g} (V_{w1} u_1) \quad ...(2.18)$$

This *discharge in this case is radial*. For radial discharge, the *absolute velocity at exit is radial.*

Hydraulic efficiency, η_h :

If H is the net head, then input to the turbine = wQH.

$$\eta_h = \frac{\text{Power developed by the runner}}{\text{Power supplied to the turbine (water power)}} = \frac{\frac{wQ}{g}(V_{w1} u_1)}{wQH}$$

or, $$\eta_h = \frac{V_{w1} u_1}{gH} \quad ...(2.19)$$

[However, if the velocity of whirl at the exit is *not* zero, then

$$\eta_h = \frac{V_{w1} u_1 \pm V_{w2} u_2}{gH} \quad ...[2.19(a)]$$]

The hydraulic efficiency of the Francis turbine varies from 85 to 90 percent.

Mechanical efficiency, η_m :

The mechanical efficiency is given by:

$$\eta_m = \frac{\text{Shaft power (P)}}{\text{Power developed by the runner}} \quad ...(2.20)$$

Overall efficiency, η_0 :

The overall efficiency is given as:

$$\eta_0 = \frac{\text{Shaft water}}{\text{Water power}} = \frac{P}{wQH} \quad ...(2.21)$$

and, $$\eta_0 = \eta_h \times \eta_m \quad [2.21(a)]$$

The overall efficiency varies from 80 to 90 percent.

2.4.1.2. Working proportions of a Francis turbine

The following working proportions pertain to a Francis turbine :

1. Ratio of width to diameter $\left(\frac{B}{D}\right)$:

The ratio of width (B_1) to the diameter of the wheel (D_1) at inlet is represented by n. Thus,

$$n = \frac{B_1}{D_1}$$

The value of n varies from 0.10 to 0.45.

2. Flow ratio (K_f) :

Flow ratio is the *ratio of the velocity of flow at inlet to the theoretical jet velocity*. Thus,

$$\text{Flow ratio, } K_f = \frac{V_{f1}}{\sqrt{2gH}} \qquad \text{...(2.23)}$$

The value of K_f varies from 0.15 to 0.30.

3. Speed ratio (K_u)

Speed ratio is the ratio of the peripheral speed at inlet to the theoretical jet velocity. Thus,

$$\text{Speed ratio, } K_u = \frac{u}{\sqrt{2gH}}$$

The value of K_u ranges from 0.6 to 0.9.

2.4.1.3. Design of Francis turbine runner

The runner of a Francis turbine is required to be designed to develop a known power P, when running at a known speed N r.p.m. under a known head H. The design of the runner involves the determination of its *size* and the *vane angles*.

The design of a Francis turbine runner is carried out as follows :

1. Assume suitable values of η_0, η_h, n, K_f and K_t.
2. Determine the required discharged Q from the relation:

$$P = \eta_0 \times wQH \qquad \text{...(2.24)}$$

3. Obtain the velocity of flow from the discharge and flow area.

Let B_1, D_1 and t_1 respectively be the width, diameter and thickness of runner vane at inlet (Fig. 2.14).

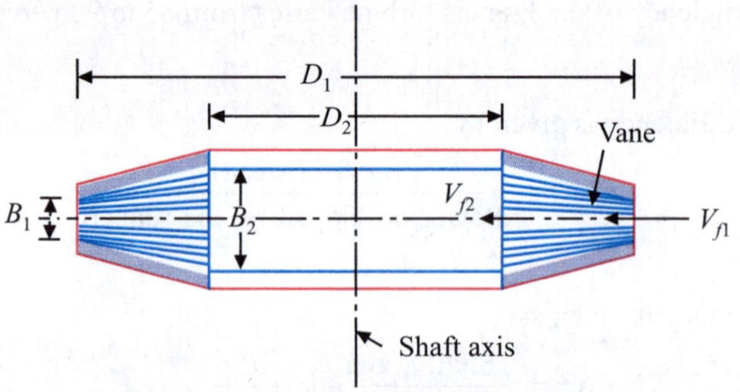

Fig. 2.14. Entry of flow to runner vane.

Then, total area at the outer periphery (*i.e.*, at the runner inlet),

$$A = (\pi D_1 - Z_{t1})\, B_1 = K_{t1} \pi D_1 B_1 \qquad \text{...(2.25)}$$

where K_{t1} is known as *vane thickness factor/co-efficient*; its value is *always less than unity* (usually of the order of 0.95 or so).

$$\text{Discharge} = \text{Area of flow} \times \text{velocity of flow}$$

i.e.,
$$Q = K_{t1} \pi D_1 B_1 \times V_{f1} \qquad \text{...(2.26)}$$

$$\therefore \quad \text{Flow velocity, } V_{f1} = \frac{Q}{K_{t1}\pi D_1 B_1} = \frac{Q}{K_t \pi n D_1^2} \quad (\because B_1 = nD_1) \qquad \text{...[2.26(a)]}$$

Also,
$$V_{f1} = K_f \sqrt{2gH}, \quad \therefore \; K_f \sqrt{2gH} = \frac{Q}{K_t \pi n D_1^2}$$

or, $$D_1 = \left[\frac{Q}{(K_f\sqrt{2gH})\,K_t\pi n}\right]^{1/2} \qquad ...(2.27)$$

Then, width $B_1 = nD_1$ [Eqn. (2.22)]

4. Find the rim velocity (tangential velocity) u_1 from the relation:

$$u_1 = \frac{\pi D_1 N}{60}$$

5. Find the velocity of whirl at inlet (V_{w1}) from Eq [2.19)

$$\eta_h = \frac{V_{w1}\,u_1}{gH}, \quad \text{or,} \quad V_{w1} = \frac{\eta_h gH}{u_1} \qquad ...(2.28)$$

6. Obtain the guide vane angle (α) and the runner vane angle (θ) from the following relations obtained from inlet velocity triangle (Fig. 2.13):

$$\tan\alpha = \frac{V_{f1}}{V_{w1}} \qquad ...(2.29)$$

and, $$\tan\theta = \frac{V_{f1}}{V_{w1} - u_1} \qquad ...(2.30)$$

7. Assume runner diameter D_2 at the outlet to be approximately one-half the diameter at inlet.

Thus, $$D_2 = \frac{D_1}{2} \text{ and } u_2 = \frac{u_1}{2}.$$

8. The velocity of flow at the exit (V_{f2}) is obtained as follows :

$$Q = K_{t1}\pi D_1 B_1 V_{f1} = K_{t2}\pi D_2 B_2 V_{f2} \qquad ...\textit{Continuity equation}$$

Thus, $$\frac{V_{f1}}{V_{f2}} = \frac{K_{t2}\pi D_2 B_2}{K_{t1}\pi D_1 B_1}$$

Usually, it is presumed that $V_{f1} = V_{f2}$ and $K_{t1} = k_{t2}$, that gives $B_2 = 2B_1$

9. Find the runner vane angle at exit (ϕ) from the velocity outlet triangle, assuming the discharge at the runner exit to be radial ($\beta = 90°$). Thus,

$$\tan\theta = \frac{V_{f2}}{u_2} \qquad ...(2.31)$$

10. The number of vanes varies from 16 to 24. In order to *avoid periodic impulse, the number of vanes should be either one more or one less than the number of guide vanes.*

2.4.1.4. Advantages and disadvantages of a Francis turbine over a Pelton wheel

Advantages :

The Francis turbine claims the following *advantages* over Pelton wheel :

1. In Francis turbine the variation in the operating head can be more easily controlled.
2. In Francis turbine the ratio of maximum and minimum operating heads can be even two.
3. The operating head can be utilized even when the variation in the tail water level is relatively large when compared to the total head.
4. The mechanical efficiency of Pelton wheel decreases faster with wear than Francis turbine.

5. The size of the runner, generator and power house required is small and economical if the Francis turbine is used instead of Pelton wheel for same power generation.

Disadvantages/Drawbacks :

As compared with Pelton wheel, the Francis turbine has the following *drawbacks/ shortcomings*:

1. Water which is not clean can cause very rapid wear in high head Francis turbine.
2. The overhaul and inspection is much more difficult comparatively,
3. Cavitation is an ever-present danger.
4. The water hammer effect is more troublesome with Francis turbine.
5. If Francis turbine is run below 50 percent head for a long period it will not only lose its efficiency but also the cavitation danger will become more serious.

Example 2.16. *An inward flow reaction turbine has external and internal diameters as 1·08 m and 0.54 m. The turbine is running at 200 r.p.m. The width of the turbine at inlet is 240 mm and velocity of flow through the runner is constant and is equal to 2.16 m/s. The guide blades make an angle of 10° to the tangent of the wheel and discharge at the outlet of the turbine is radial. Draw the inlet and outlet velocity triangles and determine :*

(*i*) *The absolute velocity of water at inlet of the runner,*
(*ii*) *The velocity of whirl at inlet,*
(*iii*) *The relative velocity at inlet,*
(*iv*) *The runner blade angles,*
(*v*) *Width of runner at outlet,*
(*vi*) *Weight of water flowing through the runner per second,*
(*vii*) *Head at inlet of the turbine,*
(*viii*) *Power developed, and*
(*ix*) *Hydraulic efficiency of the turbine.*

Solution. External diameter, $D_1 = 1.08$ m

Internal diameter, $D_2 = 0.54$ m

Speed, $N = 200$ r.p.m.

Width at inlet, $B_1 = 240$ mm $= 0.24$ m

Velocity of flow, $V_{f1} = V_{f2} = 2.16$ m/s

Guide blade angle, $\alpha = 10°$

Discharge at outlet .... radial

$$\therefore \quad \beta = 90° \text{ and } V_{w2} = 0$$

$$\text{Tangential velocity of wheel at inlet, } u_1 = \frac{\pi D_1 N}{60} = \frac{\pi \times 1.08 \times 200}{60} = 11.31 \text{ m/s}$$

$$\text{Tangential velocity of wheel at outlet, } u_2 = \frac{\pi D_2 N}{60} = \frac{\pi \times 0.54 \times 200}{60} = 5.65 \text{ m/s}$$

(*i*) Absolute velocity of water at inlet of the runner, V_1 :

From inlet velocity triangle, we have:

$$V_1 \sin \alpha = V_{f1}$$

$$\therefore \quad V_1 = \frac{V_{f1}}{\sin \alpha} = \frac{2.16}{\sin 10°} = \mathbf{12.44 \text{ m/s (Ans.)}}$$

(ii) Velocity of whirl at inlet, V_{w1} :

$$V_{w1} = V_1 \cos\alpha = 12.44 \times \cos 10° = \mathbf{12.25\ m/s\ (Ans.)}$$

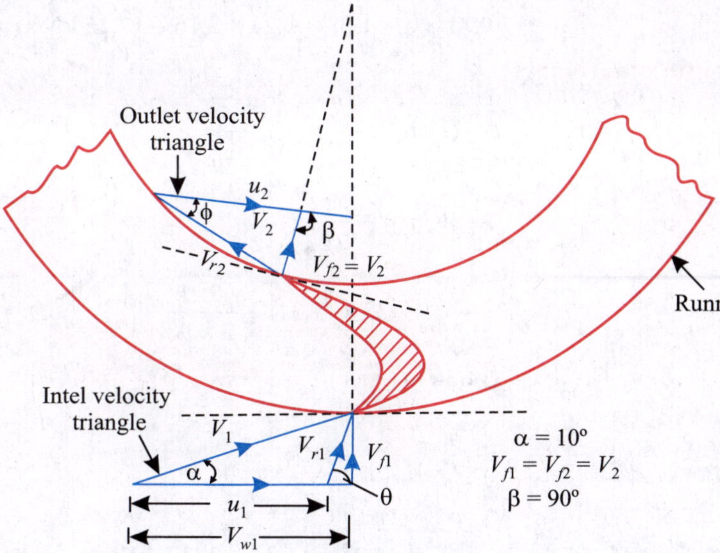

Fig. 2.15

(iii) Relative velocity at inlet, V_{r1} :

$$V_{r1} = \sqrt{(V_{w1} - u_1)^2 + V_{f1}^{\ 2}}$$

$$= \sqrt{(12{\cdot}25 - 11.31)^2 + (2.16)^2} = \mathbf{2.35\ m/s\ (Ans.)}$$

(iv) Runner blade angles, θ, ϕ :

Again, from inlet velocity triangle, we have:

$$\tan\theta = \frac{V_{f1}}{V_{w1} - u_1} = \frac{2.16}{12.25 - 11.31} = 2.298$$

$$\therefore \quad \theta = \tan^{-1} 2.298 = \mathbf{66.48°\ (Ans.)}$$

From the outlet velocity triangle, we have:

$$\tan\theta = \frac{V_{f2}}{u_2} = \frac{2.16}{5.65} = 0.382$$

$$\therefore \quad \phi = \tan^{-1} 0.382 = \mathbf{20.9°\ (Ans.)}$$

(v) Width of runner at outlet, B_2 :

$$\pi D_1 B_1 V_{f1} = \pi D_2 B_2 V_{f2} (= Q) \qquad \textit{...Continuity equation}$$

or,
$$D_1 B_1 = D_2 B_2 \qquad (\because V_{f1} = V_{f2})$$

$$\therefore \quad B_2 = \frac{D_1 B_1}{D_2} = \frac{1.08 \times 0.24}{0.54} = 0.48 \text{ m or } \mathbf{480\ mm\ (Ans.)}$$

(vi) Weight of water flowing through the runner per second :

Weight of water flowing per second

$$= wQ = w \times \pi D_1 B_1 V_{f1}$$

$$= 9.81 \times \pi \times 1.08 \times 0.24 \times 2.16 = \textbf{17.25 kN/s (Ans.)}$$

(vii) Head at inlet of turbine, H :

$$= \frac{1}{g}(V_{w1}u_1 \pm V_{w2}u_2) + \frac{V_2^2}{2g}$$

$$= \frac{1}{g}(V_{w1}u_1) + \frac{V_2^2}{2g} \qquad (\because V_{w2} = 0)$$

$$= \frac{1}{9.81}(12.25 \times 11.31) + \frac{2.16^2}{2 \times 9.81} \qquad (\because V_2 = V_{f2})$$

$$= \textbf{14.36 m (Ans.)}$$

(viii) Power developed :

$$\textit{Power developed} = \rho Q \times V_{w1}u_1 = \frac{wQ}{g} \times V_{w1}u_1$$

$$= \frac{17.25}{9.81} \times 12.25 \times 11.31 = \textbf{243.6 kW (Ans.)}$$

(ix) Hydraulic efficiency, η_h :

$$\eta_h = \frac{V_{w1}u_1}{gH} \qquad \text{...[Eqn (2.19)]}$$

$$= \frac{12.25 \times 11.31}{9.81 \times 14.36} = 0.9835 \quad \text{or} \quad \textbf{98.35\% (Ans.)}$$

Example 2.17. *A reaction turbine works at 450 r.p.m. under a head of 120 m. Its diameter at inlet is 1.2 m and the flow area is 0.4 m^2. The angles made by absolute and relative velocities at inlet are 20° and 60° respectively with the tangential velocity. Determine :*

(i) The volume flow rate,

(ii) The power developed, and

(iii) The hydraulic efficiency. **[PTU]**

Solution.

Speed of turbine, N = 450 r.p.m

Head, H = 120 m

Diameter at inlet, D_1 = 1.2 m

Flow area, $\pi D_1 B_1$ = 0.4 m^2

Angle made by absolute velocity, α = 20°

Angle made by the relative velocity at inlet, θ = 60°

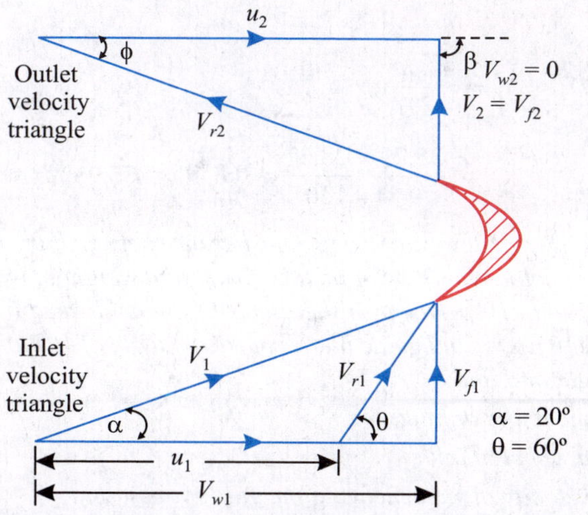

Fig. 2.16

(i) The volume flow rate, Q :

Tangential velocity of the turbine,

$$u_1 = \frac{\pi D_1 N}{60} = \frac{\pi \times 1.2 \times 450}{60} = 28.27 \text{ m/s}$$

From inlet velocity triangle, we have:

$$\tan \alpha = \frac{V_{f1}}{V_{w1}}, \quad \text{or,} \quad \tan 20° = \frac{V_{f1}}{V_{w1}}$$

$$\therefore \quad V_{f1} = V_{w1} \tan 20° = 0.364\ V_{w1} \qquad ...(i)$$

Also,

$$\tan \theta = \frac{V_{f1}}{V_{w1} - u_1} = \frac{0.364\ V_{w1}}{V_{w1} - 28.27} \qquad (\because V_{f1} = 0.364\ V_{w1})$$

or,

$$\tan 60° = \frac{0.364\ V_{w1}}{V_{w1} - 28.27}, \text{ or, } 1.732 = \frac{0.364\ V_{w1}}{V_{w1} - 28.27}$$

or, $1.732 (V_{w1} - 28.27) = 0.364\ V_{w1}$, or , $1.732\ V_{w1} - 48.96 = 0.364\ V_{w1}$

$$\therefore \quad V_{w1} = \frac{48.96}{(1.732 - 0.364)} = 35.79 \text{ m/s}$$

From eqn. (*i*), we have:

$$V_{f1} = 0.364 \times 35.79 = 13.027 \text{ m/s}$$

$\therefore$ Volume flow rate, $Q = \pi D_1 B_1 \times V_{f1}$

But, $\pi D_1 B_1 = 0.4 \text{ m}^2$ ...(*Given*)

$\therefore$ $Q = 0.4 \times 13.027 =$ **$5.211 \text{ m}^3\text{/s}$ (Ans.)**

(ii) Power developed :

Work done per second $= \rho Q (V_{w1} u_1)$ $[\because V_{w2} = 0$ ...Given]

$= 1000 \times 5.211 \times 35.79 \times 28.27 = 5272402$ Nm/s or J/s

$\therefore$ Power developed $= 5272402$ J/s, or, $W =$ **5272.4 kW (Ans.)**

(iii) The hydraulic efficiency, η_h :

$$\eta_h = \frac{V_{w1}u_1}{gH} \qquad \text{...[Eqn (2.19)]}$$

$$= \frac{35.79 \times 28.27}{9.81 \times 120} = 0.8595 = \mathbf{85.95\%} \text{ (Ans.)}$$

Example 2.18. *An inward flow reaction turbine has an external diameter of 1 m and its breadth at inlet is 250 mm. If the velocity of flow at inlet is 2 m/s, find weight of water passing through the turbine per second. Assume 10 per cent of the area of flow is blocked by blade thickness. If the speed of the runner is 210 r.p.m. and guide blades make an angle of 10° to the wheel tangent, draw the inlet velocity triangle and find :*

(i) *The runner vane angle at inlet,*

(ii) *The velocity of wheel at inlet,*

(iii) *The absolute velocity of water leaving the guide vanes, and*

(iv) *The relative velocity of water entering the runner blade.* **[Rookee University]**

Solution. External diameter, D_1 = 1 m

Breadth of inlet, B_1 = 250 m = 0·25 m

Velocity of flow at inlet, V_{f1} = 2.0 m/s

Area of flow blocked by blade thickness = 10 %

Speed of the runner, N = 210 r.p.m.

Guide blade angle, α = 10°

Weight of water passing through the turbine :

$$\text{Area blocked by vane thickness} = \frac{10}{100} \times \pi D_1 B_1 = 0.1\, \pi D_1 B_1$$

∴ Actual area through which flow takes place,

$$A = \pi D_1 B_1 - 0.1\, \pi D_1 B_1 = 0.9\, \pi D_1 B_1$$

$$= 0.9\, \pi \times 1 \times 0.25 = 0.7068 \text{ m}^2$$

∴ Weight of water passing per second through the turbine

$$= w \times A \times V_{f1} = 9.81 \times 0.7068 \times 2$$

$$= \mathbf{13.68 \text{ kN/s}} \text{ (Ans.)}$$

Inlet velocity triangle is shown in Fig 2.17.

(i) The runner vane angle at inlet, θ :

Tangential velocity of wheel at inlet,

$$u_1 = \frac{\pi D_1 N}{60} = \frac{\pi \times 1 \times 10}{60} = 10.99 \text{ m/s}$$

From inlet velocity triangle, we have:

$$\tan\alpha = \frac{V_{f1}}{V_{w1}} = \frac{2.0}{V_{w1}}, \text{ or, } V_{w1} = \frac{2.0}{\tan\alpha} = \frac{2.0}{\tan 10°} = 11.34 \text{ m/s}$$

$$\tan\theta = \frac{V_{f1}}{V_{f1} - u_1} = \frac{2.0}{11.34 - 10.99} = 5.714$$

or,

$$\theta = \tan^{-1} 5.714$$

$$= \mathbf{80.07°} \text{ (Ans.)}$$

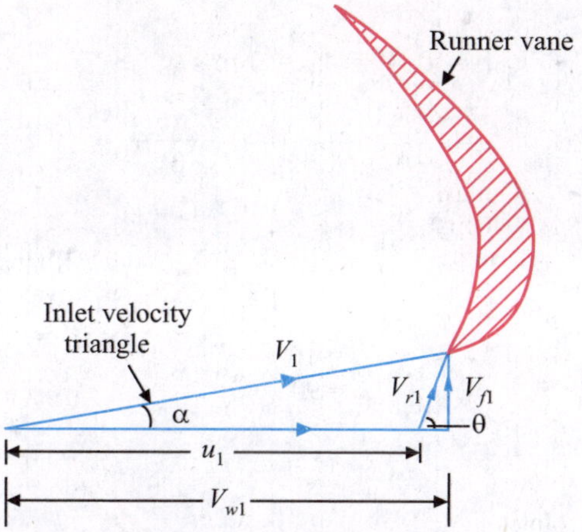

Fig. 2.17

(ii) The velocity of wheel at inlet u_1 :

The velocity of wheel at inlet = $\boldsymbol{u_1}$ **= 10.99 m/s (Ans.)**

(iii) The absolute velocity of water leaving the guide vanes, V_1 :

Again, from inlet velocity triangle , we have:

$$\sin\alpha = \frac{V_{f1}}{V_1}, \quad \text{or,} \quad \sin 10° = \frac{2{\cdot}0}{V_1}$$

$$\therefore \quad V_1 = \frac{2.0}{\sin 10°} = \mathbf{11.52\ m/s\ (Ans.)}$$

(iv) The relative velocity of water entering the runner blade, V_{r1} :

$$\sin\theta = \frac{V_{f1}}{V_{r1}}, \quad \text{or,} \quad \sin 80.07° = \frac{2.0}{V_{r1}}$$

$$\therefore \quad V_{r1} = \frac{2.0}{\sin 80.07°} = \mathbf{2.03\ m/s\ (Ans.)}$$

Example 2.19. *In an inward flow reaction turbine the head on the turbine is 32 m. The external and internal diameters are 1.44 m and 0.72 m respectively. The velocity of flow through the runner is constant and equal to 3 m/s. The guide blade angle is 10° and the runner vanes are rigid at inlet. If the discharge at outlet is radial, determine :*

(i) The speed of the turbine,

(ii) The vane angle at outlet of the runner, and

(iii) Hydraulic efficiency.

Solution. Head on the turbine, H = 32 m

External diameter, D_1 = 1.44 m

Internal diameter, D_2 = 0.72 m

Velocity of flow, V_f = constant; $V_{f1} = V_{f2} = 3$ m/s

The guide blade angle, α = 10°

Runner vanes are *radial at inlet,*

$$\therefore \quad \theta = 90°; \quad \therefore \quad V_{w1} = u_1$$

Discharge is radial,

$$\therefore \quad V_{w2} = 0, \; V_2 = V_{f2} = 3 \text{ m/s}$$

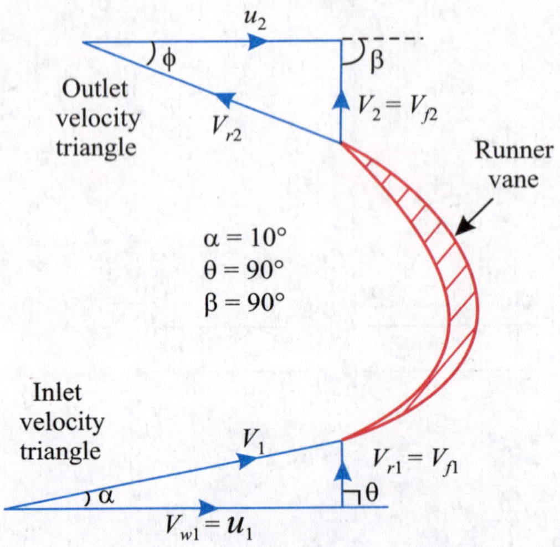

Fig. 2.18

***(i)* The speed of the turbine, *N* :**

From inlet velocity triangle, we have:

$$\tan\alpha = \frac{V_{f1}}{u_1}, \quad \text{or,} \quad u_1 = \frac{V_{f1}}{\tan\alpha} = \frac{3}{\tan 10°}$$

or, $$u_1 = 17.01 \text{ m/s}$$

Also, $$u_1 = \frac{\pi D_1 N}{60}, \quad \text{or,} \quad N = \frac{60\, u_1}{\pi D_1}$$

or, $$N = \frac{60 \times 17.01}{\pi \times 1.44} = \mathbf{225.6 \text{ r.p.m.}} \; \textbf{(Ans.)}$$

***(ii)* The vane angle at outlet of the runner, ϕ :**

$$u_2 = \frac{\pi D_2 N}{60} = \frac{\pi \times 0.72 \times 225.6}{60} = 8.505 \text{ m/s}$$

From the outlet velocity triangle, we have:

$$\tan\phi = \frac{V_{f2}}{u_2} = \frac{3.0}{8.505} = 0.3527$$

$$\therefore \quad \phi = \tan^{-1} 0.3527 = \mathbf{19.43°} \; \textbf{(Ans.)}$$

***(iii)* Hydraulic efficiency, η_h :**

$$\eta_h = \frac{V_{w1} u_1}{gH} \quad [V_{w2} = 0, \text{ the discharge being } \textit{radial} \text{ at outlet.}]$$

$$= \frac{17.01 \times 17.01}{9.81 \times 32} = 0.9217 \text{ or } \mathbf{92.17\%} \; \textbf{(Ans.)} \quad \left[\because V_{w1} = u_1, \text{ the runner } V \text{ at inlet being radial}\right]$$

Example 2.20. *An inward flow reaction turbine is supplied 0·233 m³/s of water under a head of 11 m. The wheel vanes are radial at inlet and the inlet diameter is twice the outlet diameter. The velocity of flow is constant and equal to 1.83 m/s. The wheel makes 370 r.p.m. Determine :*

(i) *Guide vane angle,*
(ii) *Inlet and outlet diameters of the wheel, and*
(iii) *The width of the wheel at inlet and exit.*
Assume that the discharge is radial and there are no losses in wheel.
Take speed ratio = 0.7
Neglect the thickness of the vanes. **[Anna University]**

Solution.

Flow rate, $Q = 0.233\ m^3/s$

Head, $H = 11$ m

Velocity of flow = constant; $V_{f1} = V_{f2} = 1.83$ m/s

Speed of the wheel = 370 r.p.m

Speed ratio, $K = 0.7$

Wheel vanes are radial at inlet, thus $\theta = 90°$, $V_{r1} = V_{f1}$

Inlet diameter = 2 × outlet diameter *i.e.*, $D_1 = 2D_2$

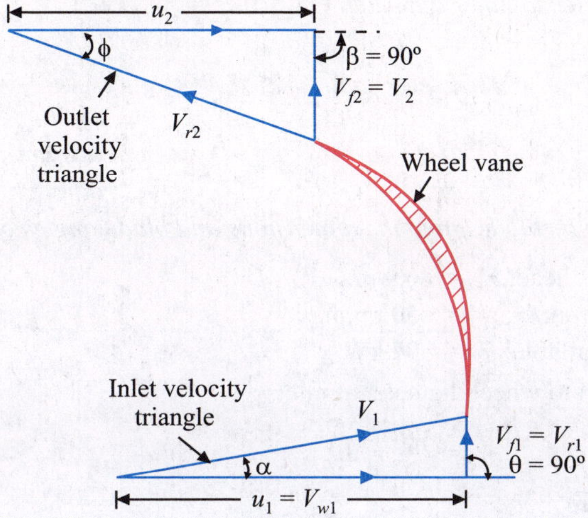

Fig. 2.19

(i) Guide vane angle, α :

$$u_1 = K_u\sqrt{2gH} = 0.7\sqrt{2gH}$$

$$= 0.7 \times \sqrt{2 \times 9.81 \times 11} = 10.28 \text{ m/s}$$

From inlet velocity triangle, we have:

$$\tan\alpha = \frac{V_{f1}}{u_1} = \frac{1.83}{10.28} = 0.178$$

$$\therefore \quad \alpha = \tan^{-1} 0.178 = \mathbf{10.09°} \text{ (Ans.)}$$

(ii) Inlet and outlet diameters of the wheel, D_1 and D_2 :

$$u_1 = \frac{\pi D_1 N}{60}, \quad \text{or,} \quad 10.28 = \frac{\pi D_1 \times 370}{60}$$

$$\therefore \quad \text{Inlet diameter, } D_1 = \frac{10.28 \times 60}{\pi \times 370} = \mathbf{0.53\ m} \text{ (Ans.)}$$

$$\text{Outlet diameter, } D_2 = \frac{D_1}{2} = \frac{0.53}{2} = \mathbf{0.265\ m} \text{ (Ans.)}$$

(iii) The width of the wheel at inlet and outlet, B_1 and B_2 :

$$Q = \pi D_1 B_1 V_{f1} = \pi D_2 B_2 V_{f2} \quad \text{...Continuity equation}$$

or, $$D_1 B_1 = D_2 B_2 \quad (\because V_{f1} = V_{f2})$$

Now, $$Q = \pi D_1 B_1 V_{f1}, \text{ or, } 0.233 = \pi \times 0.53 \times B_1 \times 1.83$$

or, $$B_1 = \frac{0.233}{\pi \times 0.53 \times 1.83} = 0.0765 \text{ m, or, } \mathbf{76.5\ mm\ (Ans.)}$$

$$B_2 = 2B_1 = 2 \times 76.5 = \mathbf{153\ mm\ (Ans.)}$$

Example 2.21. *The following data pertain to an inward flow reaction turbine :*

Net head	*... 86.4 m*
Speed of the runner	*... 650 r.p.m*
Shaft power available	*.... 397 kW*
Ratio of wheel width to wheel diameter at inlet	*... 0·10*
Ratio of outer diameter to inner diameter	*.... 0.5*
Flow ratio	*... 0.17*
Hydraulic efficiency	*... 95 %*
Overall efficiency	*.... 85 %*
Flow velocity	*... constant.*
Discharge	*... radial*

Neglecting blockage by blades, find the dimensions and blade angles of the turbine.

Solution. Net head, H = 86.4 m.

Speed of the runner, N = 650 r.p.m.

Shaft power available, P = 397 kW

Ratio of wheel width to wheel diameter at inlet,

$$n = \frac{B_1}{D_1} = 0.1$$

Ratio of outer diameter to inner diameter = 0.5

Flow ratio, K_f = 0.17

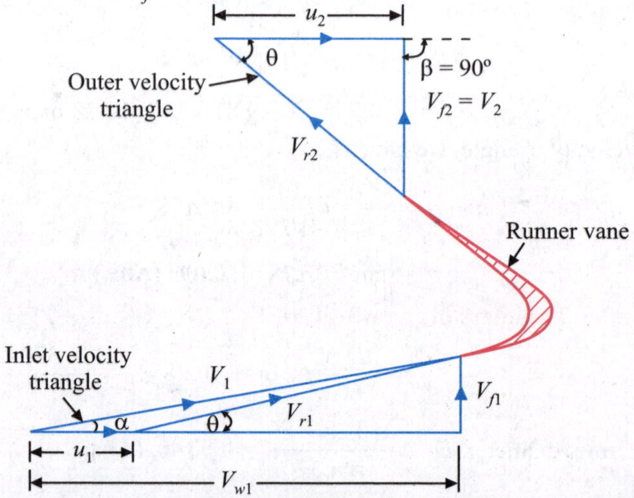

Fig. 2.20

Hydraulic efficiency, η_h = 95%

Overall efficiency, η_0 = 85%

Flow velocity = constant *i.e.*, $V_{f1} = V_{f2}$

Discharge is radial *i.e.*, β = 90° or $V_2 = V_{f2}$

Main dimensions of the turbine :

$$\text{Flow velocity, } V_{f1} = K_f \sqrt{2gH}$$

$$= 0.17\sqrt{2 \times 9.81 \times 85.4} = 7.0 \text{ m/s}$$

$$\therefore \quad V_{f1} = V_{f2} = 7.0 \text{ m/s}$$

The shaft power available from the turbine,

$$P = wQH \times \eta_0$$

or, $$397 = 9.81 \times Q \times 86.4 \times 0.85$$

$$\therefore \quad \text{Discharge, } Q = \frac{397}{9.81 \times 86.4 \times 0.85} = 0.551 \text{ m}^3/\text{s}$$

Also $Q = \pi D_1 B_1 V_{f1}$ (Neglecting blockage by blades)

[where, D_1 and B_1 are the diameter and width of the wheel at the inlet respectively.]

or, $$0.551 = \pi D_1 \times 0.1 D_1 \times 7.0 \qquad \left[\because \frac{B_1}{D_1} = 0.1 \text{ ...Given}\right]$$

$$\therefore \quad D_1 = \left(\frac{0.551}{\pi \times 0.1 \times 7.0}\right)^{1/2} = \mathbf{0.5 \text{ m}} \textbf{ (Ans.)}$$

$$B_1 = 0.1 D_1 = 0.1 \times 0.5 = \mathbf{0.05 \text{ m}} \textbf{ (Ans.)}$$

Diameter of wheel at outlet, $D_2 = 0.5\, D_1 = 0.5 \times 0.5 =$ **0.25 m (Ans.)**

($\because D_2 = 0.5\, D_1$ ...*Given*)

Since the discharge of water at inlet and outlet tips is same, therefore,

$$Q = \pi D_1 B_1 V_{f1} = \pi D_2 B_2 V_{f2} \qquad \text{....Continuity equation}$$

or, $$D_1 B_1 = D_2 B_2 \qquad (\because V_{f1} = V_{f2})$$

or, $$B_2 = \frac{D_1 B_1}{D_2} = \frac{D_1 B_1}{0.5 D_1} = 2B_1 = 2 \times 0.05 = \mathbf{0.1 \text{ m}} \textbf{ (Ans.)}$$

Refer to Fig 2.20.

Angles at inlet :

$$\text{Peripheral velocity at inlet, } u_1 = \frac{\pi D_1 N}{60} = \frac{\pi \times 0.5 \times 650}{60} = 17.0 \text{ m/s}$$

$$\text{Hydraulic efficiency, } \eta_h = \frac{V_{w1} u_1}{gH} \qquad \left[\because V_{w2} = 0, \text{ the discharge being radial at outlet.}\right]$$

$$0.95 = \frac{V_{w1} \times 17.0}{9.81 \times 86.4}$$

or, $$V_{w1} = \frac{0.95 \times 9.81 \times 86.4}{17.0} = 47.36 \text{ m/s}$$

Since $u_1 < V_{w1}$ the inlet triangle will be as shown in Fig 2.20.

From inlet triangle, we have:

$$\tan \alpha = \frac{V_{f1}}{V_{w1}} = \frac{7.0}{47.36} = 0.1478$$

∴ Guide vane angle, $\alpha = \tan^{-1} 0.1478 =$ **8.4° (Ans.)**

Again,

$$\tan \theta = \frac{V_{f1}}{V_{w1} - u_1} = \frac{7.0}{47.36 - 17.0} = 0.23$$

∴ Vane inlet angle, $\theta = \tan^{-1} 0.23 =$ **12.95° (Ans.)**

Angles at outlet :

From outlet triangle, we have:

$$u_2 = \frac{\pi D_2 N}{60} = \frac{\pi \times 0.25 \times 650}{60} = 8.5 \text{ m/s}$$

$$\tan \phi = \frac{V_{f2}}{u_2} = \frac{7.0}{8.5} = 0.823$$

∴ Vane angle at outlet, $\phi = \tan^{-1} 0.823 =$ **39.45° (Ans.)**

$\beta = 90°$ (∵ Discharge is *radial*.) **(Ans.)**

Example 2.22. *The following data pertain to an inward flow reaction turbine :*
Diameter of wheel at inner periphery = 540 mm
Width of wheel at inner periphery = 60 mm
Diameter of wheel at outer periphery = 360 mm
Width of wheel at outer periphery = 90 mm
Area occupied by the vanes = 8% of the periphery
Guide vane angle = 25° to the tangent to the runner
Moving vane angle at inlet = 95° (vane inclined forward to the direction of motion)
Exit angle = 30°
Hydraulic losses = 10% of the supply head
Mechanical friction losses = 5% of the supply head
Pressure in the outer casing = 66 m more than that at discharge from the runner.
Determine the following :
(i) Speed of the runner (for no shocks at entry), and
(ii) Power available at the turbine shaft.

Solution. At inner periphery : D_1 = 540 mm or 0.54 m; B_1 = 60 mm or 0.06 m
At outer periphery : D_2 = 360 mm = 0.36 m; B_2 = 90 mm = 0.09 m
Guide vane angle, α = 25° to the tangent to the runner
Moving vane angle at inlet = 95° (vanes inclined forward to the direction of motion)
Exit angle ϕ = 30°
Hydraulic losses = 10% of the supply head
Mechanical losses = 5% of the supply head
Pressure in the outer casing = 66 m more than that at discharge from the runner.

(i) Speed of the runner, N :

Refer to Fig. 2.21.

$$Q = K_{f1}\pi D_1 B_1 \times V_{f1} = K_{f2}\pi D_2 B_2 \times V_{f2} \quad \text{...Continuity equation}$$

Taking, $K_{t1} = K_{t2}$; $V_{f1} = \frac{D_2}{D_1} \times \frac{B_2}{B_1} \times V_{f2} = \frac{0.36}{0.54} \times \frac{0.09}{0.06} \times V_{f2} = V_{f2}$

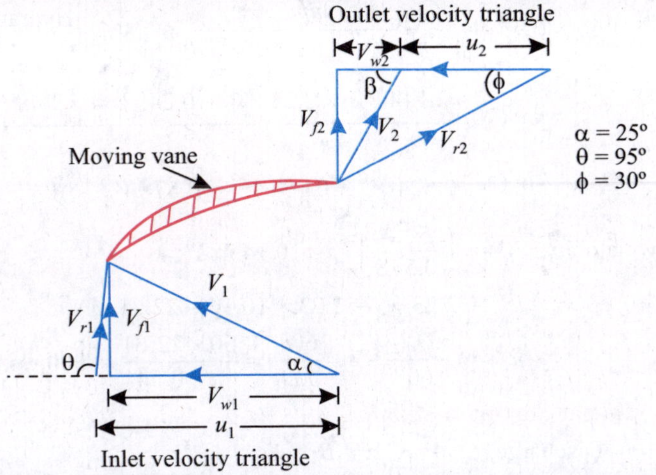

Fig. 2.21

$\therefore \quad V_{f1} = V_{f2} = V_f$

From *inlet velocity triangle*, we have:

$$\tan\alpha = \frac{V_{f1}}{V_{w1}}, \quad \text{or,} \quad V_{w1} = \frac{V_{f1}}{\tan\alpha} = \frac{V_{f1}}{\tan 25°}$$

$$= 2.144\, V_{f1} \quad \text{...(i)}$$

$$\tan(180° - \theta) = \frac{V_{f1}}{u_1 - V_{w1}};$$

$$\tan(180° - 95°) = \frac{V_{f1}}{u_1 - 2.144 V_{f1}} \quad (\because V_{w1} = 2.144\, V_{f1})$$

or, $$\frac{V_{f1}}{u_1 - 2.144\, V_{f1}} = 11.43$$

or, $$V_{f1} = 11.43\,(u_1 - 2.144\, V_{f1}) = 11.43\, u_1 - 24.5\, V_{f1}$$

or, $$25.5\, V_{f1} = 11.43\, u_1, \text{ or, } u_1 = 2.23\, V_{f1}$$

From outlet *velocity triangle*, we have:

Since blade speed is proportional to diameter, therefore,

$$u_2 = u_1 \times \frac{D_2}{D_1} = 2.23 V_{f1} \times \frac{0.36}{0.54} = 1.49 V_{f1}$$

$$\frac{V_{f2}}{V_{w2} + u_2} = \tan\phi, \quad \text{or,} \quad \frac{V_{f2}}{V_{w2} + 1.49 V_{f1}} = \tan 30° = 0.577$$

or, $$\frac{V_{f2}}{V_{w2} + 1.49 V_{f2}} = 0.577 \quad (\because V_{f1} = V_{f2})$$

or, $V_{f2} = 0.577\, V_{w2} + 0.86\, V_{f2}$, or, $V_{w2} = 0.243\, V_{f2}$

Absolute velocity of water at outlet,

$$V_2 = \sqrt{V_{f_2}^2 + V_{w2}^2} = \sqrt{V_{f2}^2 + (0.243V_{f2})^2} = 1.03V_{f2}$$

Now, Head supplied = Head utilised (*i.e.,* work done) + energy or head at outlet (neglecting loss of head in the runner)

$$66 \times 0.9^* = \frac{V_{w1}u_1 + V_{w2}u_2}{g} + \frac{V_2^2}{2g} \qquad \left[\because {}^*\text{Hydraulic losses} = 10\% \ \ldots\textit{Given}\right]$$

$$59.4 = \frac{2.144\, V_{f1} \times 2.23\, V_{f1} + 0.243\, V_{f2} \times 1.49\, V_{f2}}{g} + \frac{(1.03\, V_{f2})^2}{2g}$$

$$59.4 = 0.524\, V_{f1}^2 + 0.054\, V_{f1}^2 = 0.578\, V_{f1}^2 \qquad (\because V_{f1} = V_{f2})$$

$\therefore$ Flow velocity, $V_{f1} = \left(\dfrac{59.4}{0.578}\right)^{1/2} = 10.14$ m/s

Now, $u_1 = 2.23\, V_{f1} = 2.23 \times 10.14 = 22.61$ m/s

Also, $u_1 = \dfrac{\pi D_1 N}{60}$; $N = \dfrac{60u_1}{\pi D_1} = \dfrac{60 \times 22.61}{\pi \times 0.54}$ = **800 r.p.m. (Ans.)**

(*ii*) Power available at the turbine shaft, *P* :

$$\text{Discharge, } Q = K_{t1}\pi D_1 B_1 \times V_{f1}$$

$$= (1- 0.08)\, \pi \times 0.54 \times 0.06 \times 10.14 = 0.949 \text{ m}^3\text{/s}$$

$$\text{Power developed by the turbine} = wQ \times \left(\frac{V_{w1}u_1 + V_{w1}u_2}{g}\right)$$

$$= 9.81 \times 0.949 \times 0{\cdot}524\, V_{f1}^2$$

$$\left[\because \frac{V_{w1}u_1 + V_{w2}u_2}{g} = 0.524\, V_{f1}^2, \text{ as calculated above}\right]$$

$$= 9.81 \times 0.949 \times 0.524 \times (10.14)^2 = 501.6 \text{ kW}$$

As the mechanical losses amount to 5 percent,

Shaft/brake power, $P = 501.6 \times 0.95$ = **476.5 kW (Ans.)**

Example 2.23. *An inward flow reaction turbine (vertical shaft) running at 400 r.p.m requiring a discharge of 15.0 m³/s has an overall efficiency of 90 per cent. The velocity at inlet of the spiral casing is 8·5 m/s and pressure head at this point 230 m. The centre-line of the spiral casing inlet is 2.5 m above the tail water level. The diameter of the runner at inlet is 2.0 m and width at inlet is 0.25 m. If the hydraulic efficiency is 94 per cent and the flow is radial at the outlet from the runner, determine:*

(*i*) *Power developed by the turbine,*

(*ii*) *Specific speed,*

(*iii*) *Guide vane angle,*

(*iv*) *Runner blade angle at inlet, and*

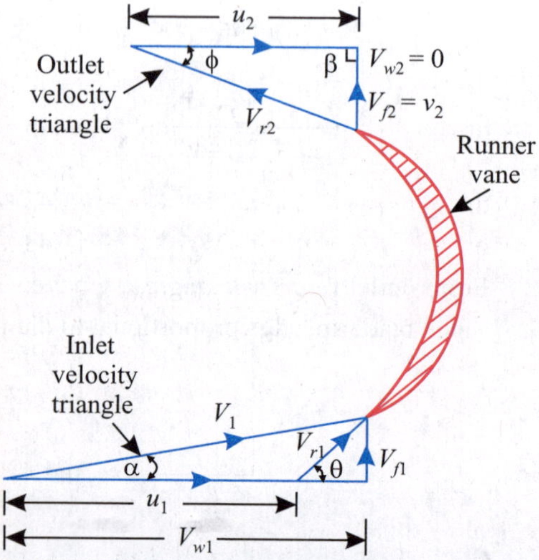

Fig. 2.22

(*v*) *Percentage of net head which is kinetic at entry to the runner.*
Assume the thickness of the blades to be negligible.

Solution. Speed of the turbine/runner, N = 400 r.p.m.

Flow rate/discharge, Q = 15.0 m^3/s

Overall efficiency, η_0 = 90 %

Velocity at inlet of spiral casing = 8.5 m/s

Pressure head = 230 m

Diameter of the runner at inlet, D_1 = 2.0 m

Width at inlet, B_1 = 0.25 m

Hydraulic efficiency, η_h = 94 %.

(*i*) Power developed by the turbine :

Head at inlet to the spiral casing,

$$H = 230 + \frac{8.5^2}{2 \times 9.81} + 2.5 = 236.2 \text{ m}$$

$$\text{Overall efficiency, } \eta_0 = \frac{\text{Power developed by the turbine}}{wQH}$$

or,
$$0.9 = \frac{\text{Power developed by the turbine}}{9.81 \times 15.0 \times 236.2}$$

∴ Power developed by the turbine

$$= 0.9 \times 9.81 \times 15.0 \times 236.2 = \mathbf{31281\ kW\ (Ans.)}$$

(*ii*) Specific speed, N_s :

$$N_s = \frac{N\sqrt{P}}{H^{5/4}} = \frac{400 \times \sqrt{31281}}{(236.2)^{5/4}} = \mathbf{76.4\ (Ans.)}$$

(*iii*) Guide vane angle, α :

$$\text{Discharge, } Q = \pi D_1 B_1 V_{f1}, \text{ or, } 15.0 = \pi \times 2.0 \times 0.25 \times V_{f1}$$

$$\therefore \text{ Velocity of flow at inlet, } V_{f1} = \frac{15.0}{\pi \times 2.0 \times 0.25} = 9.55 \text{ m/s}$$

Peripheral velocity of blade at inlet,

$$u_1 = \frac{\pi D_1 N}{60} = \frac{\pi \times 2.0 \times 400}{60} = 41.88 \text{ m/s}$$

Also $V_{w2} = 0$, since the discharge is *radial*.

$$\text{Hydraulic efficiency, } \eta_h = \frac{V_{w1} u_1}{gH} \qquad [\because V_{w2} = 0]$$

or,
$$0.94 = \frac{V_{w1} \times 41.88}{9.81 \times 236.2}$$

$$\therefore \text{ Velocity of whirl at inlet, } V_{w1} = \frac{0.94 \times 9.81 \times 236.2}{41.88} = 52.0 \text{ m/s}$$

From *inlet velocity triangle*, we have:

$$\tan \alpha = \frac{V_{f1}}{V_{w1}} = \frac{9.55}{52.0} = 0.1836$$

$$\therefore \quad \alpha = \tan^{-1} 0.1836 = \mathbf{10.4^\circ} \textbf{ (Ans.)}$$

(*iv*) Runner blade angle at inlet, θ :

Again, from inlet velocity triangle, we have :

$$\tan \theta = \frac{V_{f1}}{V_{w1} - u_1} = \frac{9.55}{52.0 - 41.88} = 0.9436$$

$$\therefore \quad \theta = \tan^{-1} 0.9436 = \mathbf{43.34^\circ} \textbf{ (Ans.)}$$

(*v*) Kinetic head as percentage of net head :

$$\text{Absolute velocity at inlet, } V_1 = \frac{V_{w1}}{\cos \alpha} = \frac{52.0}{\cos 10.4^\circ} = 52.87 \text{ m/s}$$

Percentage of net head which is kinetic at entry to the runner

$$= \frac{V_1^2 / 2g}{H} = \frac{V_1^2}{2gH} = \frac{52.87^2}{2 \times 9.81 \times 236.2} = 0.603 \text{ or } \mathbf{60.3\%} \textbf{ (Ans.)}$$

Example 2.24. *In an inward flow reaction turbine the diameter of the outer periphery is two times the diameter of inner one, and the turbine operates under a head of 20 m. The turbine has radial tips at the inlet while at the exit the blades make an angle of 30° with the forward tangent. Assuming a constant radial velocity of flow and that the blade friction accounts for a dissipation of energy equivalent to 10 per cent of kinetic energy at the outlet, determine :*

(i) Runner velocity at the rim, and

(ii) Hydraulic efficiency of the turbine.

Assume the turbine discharges radially at the outlet.

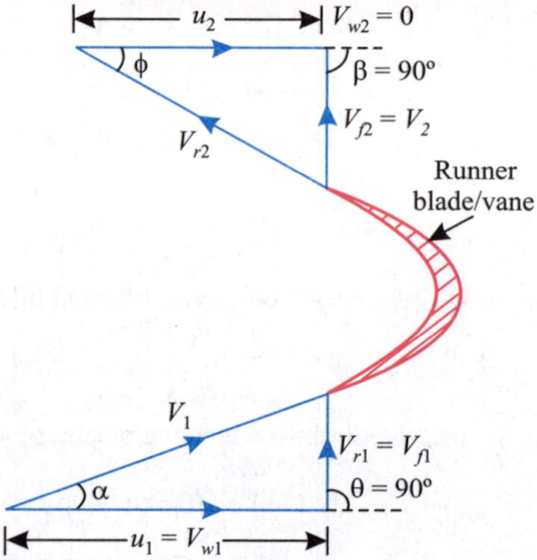

Fig. 2.23

Solution. Diameter of the outer periphery, $D_1 = 2D_2$ (diameter of the inner periphery)

Head under which the turbine operates, $H = 20$ m

Tips at inlet = radial *i.e.*, θ = 90°

Blade angle at the outlet, φ = 30° (with the forward tangent)

Dissipation of energy (due to blade friction) = 10 percent of K.E. at the outlet

Turbine discharge is radial *i.e.*, β = 90°

Constant radial velocity of flow *i.e.*, $V_{f1} = V_{f2} = V_f$

(*i*) Runner velocity at the rim, u_1 :

From energy considerations, we have:

Energy supplied = Energy transferred to the runner + energy lost in blade friction + K.E. at outlet

$$H = \frac{V_{w1} u_1}{g} + 0.1 \frac{V_2^2}{2g} + \frac{V_2^2}{2g} = \frac{u_1^2}{2g} + 1.1 \frac{V_2^2}{2g} \qquad (\because V_{w1} = u_1)$$

From outlet velocity triangle (Fig. 2.23),

$$\tan\phi = \frac{V_{f2}}{u_2}, \quad \text{or,} \quad V_{f2} = u_2 \tan\phi = u_2 \tan 30°$$

$$\therefore \qquad H = \frac{u_1^2}{2g} + 1.1\frac{(u_2 \tan 30°)^2}{2g} \qquad (\because V_{f2} = V_2)$$

Also, $u_1 = \omega R_1$ and $u_2 = \omega R_2$

$$\therefore \qquad \frac{u_1}{u_2} = \frac{\omega R_1}{\omega R_2} = \frac{\omega D_1}{\omega D_2} = 2, \text{ or, } \quad u_1 = 2u_2 \qquad [\because D_1 = 2D_2 \text{ ...Given}]$$

$$\therefore \qquad H = \frac{(2u_2)^2}{g} + 1.1\frac{(0.577u_2)^2}{2g} = \frac{4u_2^2}{g} + \frac{0.183u_2^2}{g} = \frac{4.183u_2^2}{9.81} = 0.426u_2^2$$

$$\text{or,} \qquad 20 = 0.426\,u_2^2, \text{ or, } u_2 = \left(\frac{20}{0426}\right)^{1/2} = 6.85 \text{ m/s}$$

∴ Runner velocity at the rim,

$$u_1 = 2u_2 = 2 \times 6.85 = \mathbf{13.70\ m/s}\ \textbf{(Ans.)}$$

(*ii*) Hydraulic efficiency, η_h :

$$\eta_h = \frac{V_{w1}u_1}{gH} = \frac{u_1^2}{gH} = \frac{13.70^2}{9.81 \times 20} = 0.9566 \text{ or } \mathbf{95.66\%}\ \textbf{(Ans.)} \qquad \left[\because \begin{aligned} V_{w2} &= 0; \\ V_{w1} &= u_1 \end{aligned}\right]$$

Example 2.25. *A Francis turbine with an overall efficiency of 76% is required to produce 150 kW. It is working under a head of 8 m. The peripheral velocity = $0.25\sqrt{2gH}$ and the radial velocity of flow at inlet is $0.95\sqrt{2gH}$. The wheel runs at 150 r.p.m. and the hydraulic losses in the turbine are 20% of the available energy. Assuming radial discharge, determine :*

(*i*) *The guide blade angle,*

(*ii*) *The wheel vane angle at inlet,*

(*iii*) *Diameter of the wheel at inlet, and*

(*iv*) *Width of the wheel at inlet.*

Solution. Overall efficiency, $\eta_0 = 76\%$

Shaft power produced, $P = 150$ kW.

Head, $H = 8$ m

Peripheral velocity, $u = 0.25\sqrt{2gH}$

Radial velocity of flow at inlet, $V_{f1} = 0.95\sqrt{2gH}$

Wheel speed, $N = 150$ r.p.m.

Since discharge at the outlet is *radial;* $V_{w2} = 0$, $V_{f2} = V_2$

Hydraulic losses in the turbine = 20% of available energy

$$\text{Now,} \qquad u_1 = 0.25\sqrt{2 \times 9.81 \times 8} = 3.13 \text{ m/s}$$

$$V_{f1} = 0.95\sqrt{2 \times 9.81 \times 8} = 11.9 \text{ m/s}$$

$$\text{Hydraulic efficiency, } \eta_h = \frac{\text{Total head at inlet} - \text{hydraulic losses}}{\text{Total head at inlet}}$$

$$= \frac{H - 0.2H}{H} = 0.8$$

Also, $$\eta_h = \frac{V_{w1} u_1}{gH} \qquad [\because V_{w2} = 0]$$

$$\therefore \quad 0.8 = \frac{V_{w1} \times 3.13}{9.81 \times 8}, \text{ or, } V_{w1} = \frac{0.8 \times 9.81 \times 8}{3.13} = 20.0 \text{ m/s}$$

***(i)* The guide blade angle, α :**

From inlet velocity triangle (Fig. 2.24),

$$\tan \alpha = \frac{V_{f1}}{V_{w1}} = \frac{11.9}{20.0} = 0.595$$

$$\alpha = \tan^{-1} 0.595 = \mathbf{30.75°} \textbf{ (Ans.)}$$

***(ii)* The wheel vane angle at inlet, θ :**

$$\tan \theta = \frac{V_{f1}}{(V_{w1} - u_1)} = \frac{11.9}{(20.0 - 3.13)} = 0.705$$

$$\therefore \quad \theta = \tan^{-1} 0.705 = \mathbf{35.18°} \textbf{ (Ans.)}$$

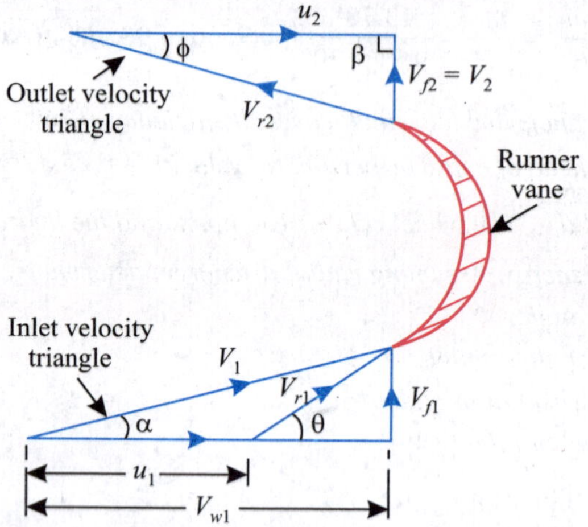

Fig. 2.24

***(iii)* Diameter of the wheel at inlet, D_1 :**

Using the relation, $u_1 = \dfrac{\pi D_1 N}{60}$, we get:

$$D_1 = \frac{60 u_1}{\pi N} = \frac{60 \times 3.13}{\pi \times 150} = \mathbf{0.398 \text{ m}} \textbf{ (Ans.)}$$

***(iv)* Width of the wheel at inlet, B_1 :**

Overall efficiency,

$$\eta_0 = \frac{\text{Shaft power}}{\text{Water power}} = \frac{P}{wQH}$$

or, $$0.76 = \frac{150}{9.81 \times Q \times 8}$$

or, $$Q = \frac{150}{0.76 \times 9.81 \times 8} = 2.515 \text{ m}^3/\text{s}$$

Also, $$Q = \pi D_1 B_1 \times V_{f1}$$

$$2.515 = \pi \times 0.398 \times B_1 \times 11.9$$

$$\therefore \quad B_1 = \frac{2.515}{\pi \times 0398 \times 11.9} = \mathbf{0.169 \ m} \ \textbf{(Ans.)}$$

Example 2.26. *The following data pertain to a Francis turbine :*

Net head	*... 70 m*
Speed	*... 700 r.p.m.*
Shaft power	*... 330 kW*
Overall efficiency	*... 85 %*
Hydraulic efficiency	*... 92 %*
Flow ratio	*... 0·22*
Breadth ratio	*... 0·1*
Outer diameter of runner	*... 2 × inner diameter of runner*
Velocity of flow	*... constant*
Outlet discharge	*... radial*

The thickness of vanes occupy 6 per cent of circumferential area of the runner.

Determine:

(*i*) *Diameters of runner at inlet and outlet,*
(*ii*) *Width of the wheel at inlet,*
(*iii*) *Guide blade angle, and*
(*iv*) *Runner vane angles at inlet and outlet.*

Solution. Net head, $H = 70$ m; Speed, $N = 700$ r.p.m.;

Shaft power = 330 kW; Overall efficiency, $\eta_0 = 85\%$;

Hydraulic efficiency, $\eta_h = 92\%$;

Flow ratio = 0.22; Breadth ratio, $\frac{B_1}{D_1} = 0.1$;

D_1 (outer diameter) = $2D_2$ (inner diameter);

Thickness of vanes = 6% of circumferential area of runner;

$V_{f1} = V_{f2}$ ...Velocity of flow is constant (*Given*).

(*i*) Diameters of runner at inlet and outlet D_1, D_2 :

Now, $$\text{flow ratio} = 0.22 = \frac{V_{f1}}{\sqrt{2gH}}$$

$$\therefore \quad V_{f1} = 0.22\sqrt{2gH} = 0.22\sqrt{2 \times 9.81 \times 70} = 8.15 \text{ m/s}$$

$$\text{Actual area of flow} = \left(1 - \frac{6}{100}\right)\pi D_1 B_1 = 0.94\, \pi D_1 B_1$$

Since discharge is *radial* at outlet,

$$\therefore \quad V_{w2} = 0 \text{ and } V_{f2} = V_2$$

Using relation : $\eta_0 = \dfrac{\text{Shaft power}}{\text{Water power}}$, or, $0.85 = \dfrac{330}{wQH} = \dfrac{330}{9.81 \times Q \times 70}$

$$\therefore \quad Q = \frac{330}{0.85 \times 9.81 \times 70} = 0.565 \text{ m}^3/\text{s}$$

But, Q = Actual area of flow × velocity of flow

$= 0.94\, \pi D_1 B_1 \times V_{f1}$

$$\therefore \quad 0.565 = 0.94\, \pi D_1 \times 0.1 D_1 \times 8.15 \qquad \left[\because \frac{B_1}{D_1} = 0.1 \quad ...Given\right]$$

$$\therefore \quad D_1 = \left(\frac{0.565}{0.94\pi \times 0.1 \times 8.15}\right)^{1/2} = \mathbf{0.484\ m\ (Ans.)}$$

$$D_2 = \frac{D_1}{2} = \frac{0.484}{2} = \mathbf{0.242\ m\ (Ans.)}$$

***(ii)* Width of the wheel at inlet, B_1 :**

$$B_1 = 0.1 D_1 = 0.1 \times 0.484 = 0.0484, \text{ or, } \mathbf{48.4\ mm\ (Ans.)}$$

Tangential speed of the runner at inlet,

$$u_1 = \frac{\pi D_1 N}{60} = \frac{\pi \times 0.484 \times 700}{60} = 17.74 \text{ m/s}$$

Using relation for hydraulic efficiency,

$$\eta_h = \frac{V_{w1} u_1}{gH} \qquad [\because V_{w2} = 0]$$

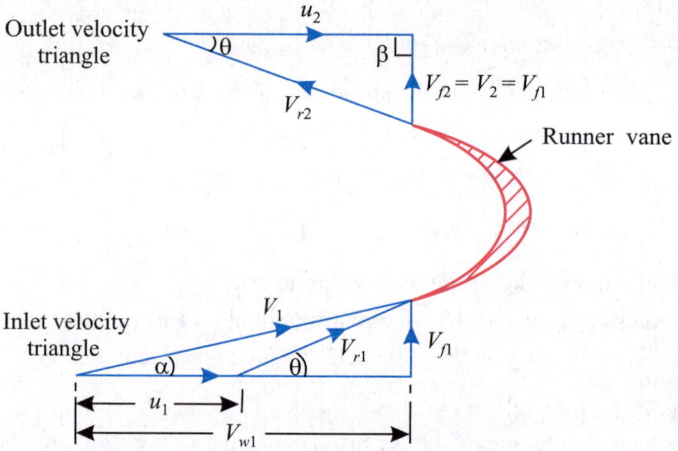

Fig. 2.25

$$\text{or,} \quad 0.92 = \frac{V_{w1} \times 17.74}{9.81 \times 70}$$

$$\text{or,} \quad V_{w1} = \frac{0.92 \times 9.81 \times 70}{17.74} = 35.6 \text{ m/s}$$

(iii) Guide blade angle, α :

From inlet velocity triangle,

$$\tan\alpha = \frac{V_{f1}}{V_{w1}} = \frac{8.15}{35.6} = 0.229$$

$$\therefore \quad \alpha = \tan^{-1}(0.229) = \mathbf{12.89°\ (Ans.)}$$

(iv) Runner vane angles at inlet and outlet θ, φ :

$$\tan\theta = \frac{V_{f1}}{V_{w1} - u_1} = \frac{8.15}{35.6 - 17.74} = 0.456$$

$$\therefore \quad \theta = \tan^{-1}(0.456) = \mathbf{24.5°\ (Ans.)}$$

From outlet velocity triangle,

$$\tan\phi = \frac{V_{f2}}{u_2} = \frac{V_{f1}}{u_2} \qquad ...(i)$$

But,

$$u_2 = \frac{\pi D_2 N}{60} = \frac{\pi \times D_1}{2} \times \frac{N}{60} \qquad \left[\because D_2 = \frac{D_1}{2} \quad ...\ Given\right]$$

$$= \frac{\pi \times 0.484 \times 700}{2 \times 60} = 8.87 \text{ m/s}$$

Putting the value of u_2 in eqn. (*i*), we get

$$\tan\phi = \frac{8.15}{8.87} = 0.9188\text{, or, } \phi = \tan^{-1}(0.9188) = \mathbf{42.58°\ (Ans.)}$$

Example 2.27. (*a*) *Show that the hydraulic efficiency for a Francis turbine having velocity of flow through runner as constant, is given by the relation:*

$$\eta_h = \cfrac{1}{1 = \cfrac{\frac{1}{2}\tan^2\alpha}{\left(1 - \cfrac{\tan\alpha}{\tan\theta}\right)}}$$

where, α = guide blade angle, θ = runner vane angle at inlet.

The turbine is having radial discharge at outlet.

(*b*) *If the vanes are radial at inlet, then show that,*

$$\eta_h = \frac{2}{2 + \tan^2\alpha}$$

Solution. Velocity of flow is constant *i.e.*, $V_{f1} = V_{f2}$

Discharge is radial at outlet *i.e.*, $V_{w2} = 0$, $V_{f2} = V_2$

From *inlet velocity triangle* : $\tan\alpha = \dfrac{V_{f1}}{V_{w1}}$

$$\therefore \quad V_{f1} = V_{w1}\tan\alpha \qquad ...(i)$$

Also, $\tan\theta = \dfrac{V_{f1}}{V_{w1} - u_1}$, or, $V_{w1} - u_1 = \dfrac{V_{f1}}{\tan\theta}$

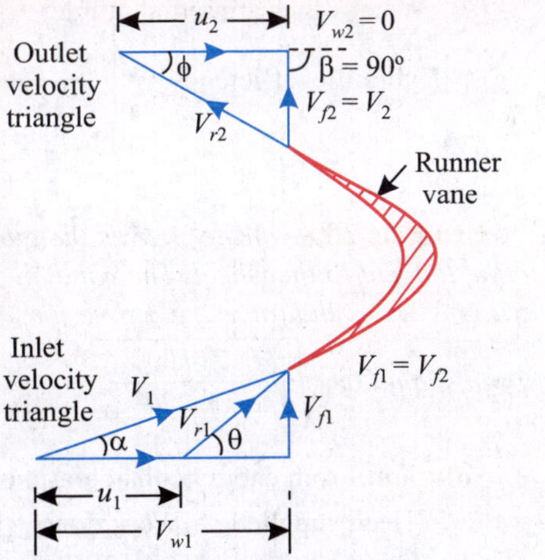

Fig. 2.26

or, $$V_{w1} - u_1 = \frac{V_{w1} \tan \alpha}{\tan \theta}$$

$$\therefore \quad u_1 = V_{w1} - \frac{V_{w1} \tan \alpha}{\tan \theta} = V_{w1}\left(1 - \frac{\tan \alpha}{\tan \theta}\right) \quad ...(ii)$$

Head under which turbine is working,

$$H = \frac{V_{w1} u_1}{g} + \frac{V_2^2}{2g} \quad [\because V_{w2} = 0]$$

or, $$H = \frac{V_{w1} u_1}{g} + \frac{V_{f1}^2}{2g} \quad [\because V_2 = V_{f2} = V_{f1}]$$

Substituting the values of V_{f1} and u_1 from eqns. (*i*) and (*ii*), we get:

$$H = \frac{V_{w1}}{g} \times V_{w1}\left(1 - \frac{\tan \alpha}{\tan \theta}\right) + \frac{(V_{w1} \tan \alpha)^2}{2g}$$

$$= \frac{V_{w1}^2}{g}\left(1 - \frac{\tan \alpha}{\tan \theta}\right) + \frac{V_{w1}^2}{2g} \tan^2 \alpha = \frac{V_{w1}^2}{g}\left(1 - \frac{\tan \alpha}{\tan \theta} + \frac{\tan^2 \alpha}{2}\right)$$

Using relation for hydraulic efficiency, we have:

$$\eta_h = \frac{V_{w1} u_1}{gH} = \frac{V_{w1} \times V_{w1}\left(1 - \frac{\tan \alpha}{\tan \theta}\right)}{g \times \frac{V_{w1}^2}{g}\left(1 - \frac{\tan \alpha}{\tan \theta} + \frac{\tan^2 \alpha}{2}\right)} = \frac{\left(1 - \frac{\tan \alpha}{\tan \theta}\right)}{\left(1 - \frac{\tan \alpha}{\tan \theta} + \frac{\tan^2 \alpha}{2}\right)}$$

or, $$\eta_h = \frac{1}{1 + \frac{\frac{1}{2}\tan^2 \alpha}{\left(1 - \frac{\tan \alpha}{\tan \theta}\right)}} \quad \left[\text{Dividing numerator and denominator by } \left(1 - \frac{\tan \alpha}{\tan \theta}\right)\right]$$ **...(Proved)**

(*b*) When vanes are radial at inlet, $\theta = 90°$

$\therefore$ Hydraulic efficiency, $$\eta_h = \frac{1}{1 + \frac{\frac{1}{2}\tan^2 \alpha}{(1-0)}} = \frac{2}{2 + \tan^2 \alpha}$$ **...(Proved)**

Example 2.28. *Water leaves the guide vanes of an inward radial flow turbine at an angle* α *to the tangent to the wheel. The vane angle at entry to the wheel is 90° and the velocity of flow at exit is K times that at entry. Prove that for maximum efficiency under a head H, the peripheral speed should be* $\sqrt{\frac{2gH}{2 + K^2 \tan^2 \alpha}}$.

Solution. From energy considerations,

Head supplied = Work done + kinetic head at exit

$$H = \frac{V_{w1} u_1 \pm V_{w2} u_2}{g} + \frac{V_2^2}{2g}$$

(Assuming the *losses* within the runner to be *negligible*)

From inlet velocity triangle, we have:

$u_1 = V_{w1}$, and , $V_{f1} = u_1 \tan\alpha$

($\because$ Flow at inlet is *radial*.)

For conditions of maximum efficiency, the flow leaves the runner *radially*, *i.e.*, $V_{w2} = 0$

Also, $V_2 = V_{f2} = KV_{f1} = Ku_1 \tan\alpha$

$$\therefore\ H = \frac{V_{w1}u_1}{g} + \frac{V_2^2}{2g}$$

$$\text{or, } H = \frac{u_1^2}{g} + \frac{K^2 u_1^2 \tan^2\alpha_1}{2g} = \frac{u_1^2}{2g}(2 + K^2 \tan^2\alpha)$$

$\therefore$ Peripheral speed,

$$u_1 = \sqrt{\frac{2gH}{2 + K^2 \tan\alpha}} \quad \text{...(Proved)}$$

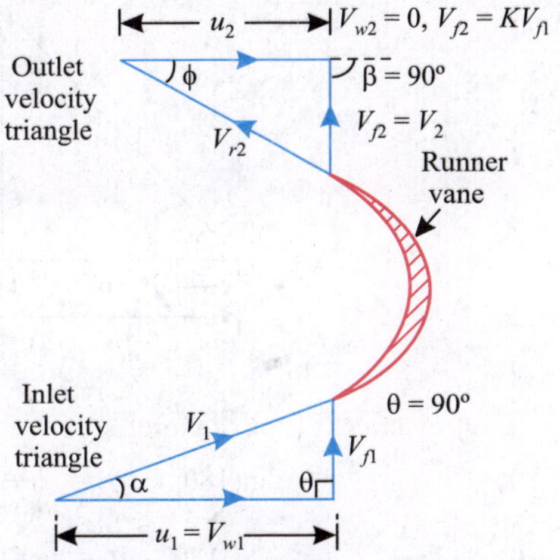

Fig. 2.27

Example 2.29. *A vertical shaft Francis turbine runs at 420 r.p.m. while the discharge is 15 m³/s. The velocity and pressure head at entrance of the runner are 10 m/s and 230 m respectively. The elevation above the tail race is 5 m. The diameter of the runner is 2 m and the width at the inlet is 270 mm. The overall and hydraulic efficiencies are 92% and 98% respectively. Calculate :*

(*i*) *Total head across the turbine;*

(*ii*) *Power output;*

(*iii*) *The guide vane angle;*

(*iv*) *Vane angle at the inlet.*

Density of water may be taken as 1000 kg/m³. **[GATE]**

Solution. *Given* : $N = 420$ r.p.m.; $Q = 15\ \text{m}^3/\text{s}$; $V_1 = 10$ m/s; Head at the entrance = 230 m; Elevation above the tail race, $z = 5$ m; $D_1 = 2$ m; $B_1 = 270$ mm = 0.27 m; $\eta_0 = 92$ %; $\eta_h = 98$ %.

(*i*) Total head across the turbine :

$$h = 230 + \frac{V_1^2}{2g} + z = 230 + \frac{10^2}{2 \times 9.81} + 5 = \textbf{240.09 m (Ans.)}$$

(*ii*) Power output = η_0 × power delivered to the fluid

$= 0.92 \times wQH$

$= 0.92 \times (1000 \times 9.81) \times 15 \times 240.09 \times 10^{-6}$ MW = **32.5 MW (Ans.)**

(*iii*) Guide vane angle, α : Refer to Fig. 2.28.

$$u_1 = \frac{\pi D_1 N}{60} = \frac{\pi \times 2 \times 420}{60} = 43.98 \text{ m/s}$$

Now discharge, $Q = \pi D_1 B_1 \times V_{f1}$

or, $15 = \pi \times 2 \times 0.27 \times V_{f1}$

$$\text{or,}\quad V_{f1} = \frac{15}{\pi \times 2 \times 0.27} = 8.84 \text{ m/s}$$

$$\sin\alpha = \frac{V_{f1}}{V_1} = \frac{8.84}{10} = 0.884$$

$$\therefore \quad \alpha = \sin^{-1}(0.884) = \mathbf{62.13° \ (Ans.)}$$

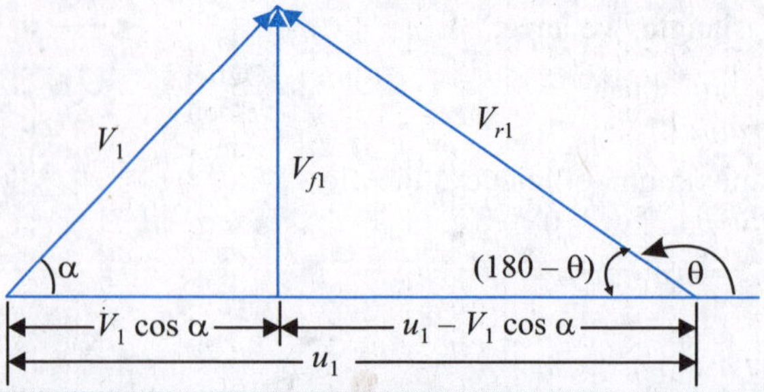

Fig. 2.28

(iv) Vane angle at the inlet, θ :

$$\tan(180° - \theta) = \frac{V_{f1}}{u_1 - V_1 \cos\alpha} = \frac{8.84}{43.98 - 10\cos(62.13°)} = 0.2249$$

$$\therefore \quad 180° - \theta = \tan^{-1}(0.2249) = 12.67°$$

$$\therefore \quad \theta = 180° - 12.67° = \mathbf{167.33° \ (Ans.)}$$

Example 2.30. *An inward flow turbine runner has an outer diameter of 0.6 m and an inner diameter of 0.3 m and runs at 750 r.p.m. The radial velocity of flow at inlet and exit is 6 m/s. Water enters the runner making an angle of 12° to the direction of motion of the blades at inlet. It leaves the runner radially. The mass flow rate is 1 kg/s. Calculate :*

(i) Power developed.

(ii) Angle between the relative velocity of water and tangential velocity of the runner at exit.

[UPTU]

Solution. *Given* : $D_1 = 0.6$ m; $D_2 = 0.3$ m; $N = 750$ r.p.m.; $V_{f1} = V_{f2} = 6$ m/s; $\alpha = 12°$; $\beta = 90°$; $m = 1$ kg/s.

Refer to Fig. 2.29.

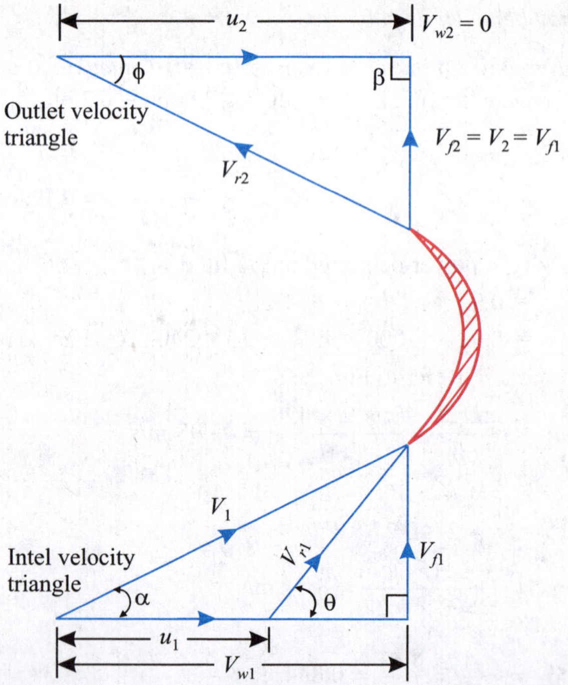

Fig. 2.29

(*i*) Power developed, *P* :

Peripheral velocity at inlet,

$$u_1 = \frac{\pi D_1 N}{60} = \frac{\pi \times 0.6 \times 750}{60} = 23.56 \text{ m/s}$$

Peripheral velocity at exit:

$$u_2 = \frac{\pi D_2 N}{60} = \frac{\pi \times 0.3 \times 750}{60} = 11.78 \text{ m/s}$$

From *inlet velocity triangle*, we get

$$\tan \alpha = \frac{V_{f1}}{V_{w1}}$$

or, $$\tan 12° = \frac{6}{V_{w1}}, \quad \text{or,} \quad V_{w1} = \frac{6}{\tan 12°} = 28.23 \text{ m/s}$$

Power developed by the turbine,

$$P = wQ \times \left(\frac{V_{w1}u_1 + V_{w2}u_2}{g}\right)$$

$$= wQ \times \frac{V_{w1}u_1}{g} \qquad (\because V_{w2} = 0)$$

$$\therefore \quad P = mg \times \frac{V_{w1}u_1}{g}$$

$$= 1 \times 9.81 \times \frac{28.23 \times 23.56}{9.81} = \mathbf{666.09\ W}\ \textbf{(Ans.)}$$

(*ii*) Angle ϕ :

From *outlet velocity triangle*, we have:

$$\tan \phi = \frac{V_{f2}}{u_2} = \frac{6}{11.78} = 0.5093$$

$$\therefore \quad \phi = \tan^{-1}(0.5093) \simeq \mathbf{27°}\ \textbf{(Ans.)}$$

Example 2.31. *An inward flow reaction turbine operating under 30 m head, develops 4000 kW while running at 300 r.p.m. The overall efficiency of the turbine is 0.85; the hydraulic efficiency is 0.9; and the radial velocity of flow at inlet is 7 m/s; the inlet guide vane angle at full gate opening is 30°. Calculate the diameter and width of the runner at inlet. Blade thickness co-efficient is 5%.* **[UPSC]**

Solution. *Given*: H = 30 m; Power developed = 4000 kW; N = 300 r.p.m.; η_0 = 0.85; η_h = 0.9; V_{f1} = 7 m/s, α = 30°, Vane thickness co-efficient,

$$K_{t_1} = \left(1 - \frac{5}{100}\right) = 0.95$$

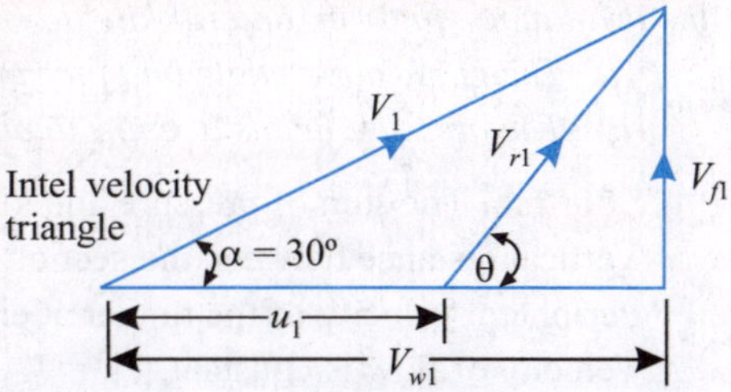

Fig. 2.30

Diameter and width of the runner at the inlet (D_1, B_1):

$$\text{Overall efficiency, } \eta_0 = \frac{\text{Output power}}{\text{Power of water supplied}} = \frac{4000 \times 1000}{w \times Q \times H}$$

$$0.85 = \frac{4000 \times 1000}{9810 \times Q \times 30}$$

or, $$Q = \frac{4000 \times 1000}{0.85 \times 9810 \times 30} = 15.99 \text{ m}^3/\text{s}$$

Hydraulic efficiency, $$\eta_h = \frac{V_{w1} \times u_1}{gH} \quad \text{...[Eqn. 2.19]}$$

Now, from *inlet velocity triangle* (Refer to Fig. 2.30), we get:

$$\frac{V_{f1}}{V_{w1}} = \tan 30°, \quad \text{or,} \quad V_{w1} = \frac{V_{f1}}{\tan 30°} = \frac{7}{\tan 30°} = 12.12 \text{ m/s}$$

Now, substituting the values in the above eqn., we get:

$$0.9 = \frac{12.12 \times u_1}{9.81 \times 30}$$

or, $$u_1 = \frac{0.9 \times 9.81 \times 30}{12.12} = 21.85 \text{ m}$$

Also, $$u_1 = \frac{\pi D_1 N}{60}, \quad \text{or,} \quad 21.85 = \frac{\pi \times D_1 \times 300}{60}$$

or, $$D_1 = \frac{21.85 \times 60}{\pi \times 300} = \mathbf{1.39 \text{ m}} \textbf{ (Ans.)}$$

Further, discharge $Q = K_{t1} \pi D_1 B_1 V_{f1}$

Substituting the values, we get:

$$15.99 = 0.95\, \pi \times 1.39 \times B_1 \times 7$$

$$\therefore \quad B_1 = \frac{15.99}{0.95\, \pi \times 1.37 \times 7} = \mathbf{0.55 \text{ m}} \textbf{ (Ans.)}$$

Example 2.32. *In an inward flow reaction turbine (vertical shaft) the sum of the pressure and kinetic heads at entrance to the spiral casing is 132 m and vertical distance between this section and the tail race level is 3·3 m. The peripheral velocity of the runner at entry is 33 m/s, the radial component of velocity of water (velocity of flow) is constant at 11·0 m/s and the discharge from the runner is without whirl, i.e. radial discharge. The hydraulic losses are: (a) losses between turbine entrance and discharge from guide vanes = 4·95 m, (b) losses in the runner = 8·8 m, (c) losses in the draft tube = 0·88 m, and (d) kinetic energy rejected to the tail race = 0·55 m. Determine :*

(i) The guide vane angle and the runner blade angle at inlet;

(ii) The pressure heads at entry to and discharge from the runner.

Solution. The sum of pressure and kinetic heads at entrance to the spiral casing = 132 m

Vertical distance between the section (entrance) and the tail race level = 3.3 m

Peripheral velocity of the runner at entry, $u_1 = 33$ m/s.

Velocity of flow is constant, $V_{f1} = V_{f2} = 11.0$ m/s

Discharge is radial, $V_{w2} = 0$

Losses between turbine entrance and discharge from guide vanes = 4.95 m

Losses in the runner = 8.8 m

Losses in the draft tube = 0.88 m

Kinetic energy rejected to the tail race = 0.55 m.

(i) The guide vane angle (α), the runner blade angle, (θ) :

Head utilized by the runner, $H = 132 + 3.3 - \text{hydraulic losses}$

$= 132 + 3.3 - (4.95 + 8.8 + 0.88 + 0.55) = 120.12$ m

Head utilized by the runner is given by,

$$H = \frac{V_{w1} u_1}{g} \qquad (\because V_{w2} = 0)$$

$$\therefore \quad V_{w1} = \frac{gH}{u_1} = \frac{9.81 \times 120.12}{33} = 35.71 \text{ m/s}$$

From *inlet velocity triangle*, we have:

$$\tan\alpha = \frac{V_{f1}}{V_{w1}} = \frac{11.0}{35.71} = 0.308$$

$$\therefore \quad \alpha = \tan^{-1} 0.308 = \mathbf{17.12°} \textbf{ (Ans.)}$$

Again, $$\tan\theta = \frac{V_{f1}}{V_{w1} - u_1} = \frac{11.0}{35.71 - 33} = 4.06$$

$$\therefore \quad \theta = \tan^{-1} 4.06 = \mathbf{76.16} \textbf{ (Ans.)}$$

(ii) The pressure heads at entry and discharge from the runner :

Taking tail race as datum, applying Bernoulli's equation to the turbine inlet and the runner, we obtain :

$$132 + 3.3 = \frac{V_1^2}{2g} + \frac{p_1}{w} + z_1 + 4.95$$

Substituting $z_1 = 3{\cdot}3$ m, and,

$$V_1 = \frac{V_{f1}}{\sin\alpha} = \frac{11.0}{\sin 17.12°} = 37.37 \text{ m/s, we have :}$$

The *pressure head at inlet,*

$$\frac{p_1}{w} = (132 + 3.3) - \frac{37.37^2}{2 \times 9.81} - 3.3 - 4.95$$

$$= \mathbf{55.87 \text{ m}} \textbf{ (Ans.)}$$

Now, applying Bernoulli's equation to the turbine entrance and *runner outlet*, we get:

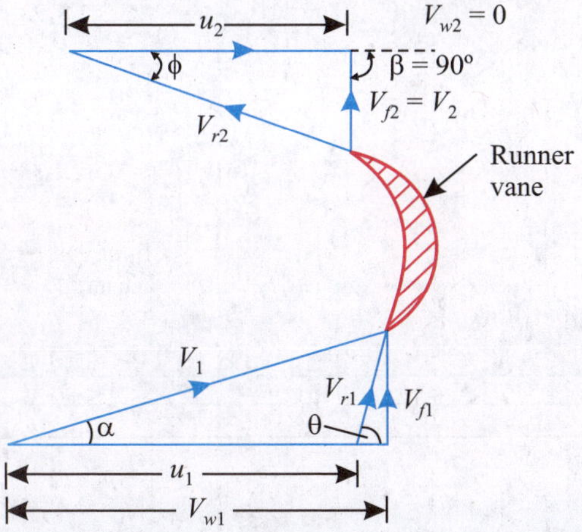

Fig. 2.31

$$132 + 3.3 = \frac{V_2^2}{2g} + \frac{p_2}{w} + z_2 + H + 4{\cdot}95 + 8.8$$

Substituting, $V_2 = 11.0$ m/s, $z_2 = 3.3$ *m*, $H = 120.12$ m, we get:

$$135.3 = \frac{11.0^2}{2 \times 9.81} + \frac{p_2}{w} + 3.3 + 120.12 + 4.95 + 8.8$$

$$= 6.17 + \frac{p_2}{w} + 137.17$$

$$\therefore \quad \frac{p_2}{w} = 135.3 - 61.7 - 137.17 = -\mathbf{8.04\ m}$$ **(Ans.)**

Example 2.33. *The following data pertain to a vertical shaft inward flow reaction turbine :*
Net head under which the turbine operates = 24.5 m
Discharge through the turbine = 10.5 m³/s
Speed of the turbine = 225 r.p.m
Inlet angle of the runner vane = 115° (measured from the direction of runner rotation)
Velocity of flow at inlet to runner = 6.5 m/s
Velocity with which water enters the draft tube without swirl = 6 m/s
Discharge velocity from the exit of draft tube = 2.5 m/s
The mean height of the runner entry surface = 1.5 m } *above tail race level*
The mean height of entrance to the draft tube = 1.2 m } *above tail race level*
Hydraulic efficiency = 90 %
Determine the following :

(i) *Diameter of the runner at entry surface, and*

(ii) *Pressure head at entry to the runner and at entrance to the draft tube; friction loss in the runner is 0·9 m and that in the draft tube 0·6 m of water.*

Solution. Refer to Fig. 2.32. Inlet angle of runner vane, $\theta = 115°$

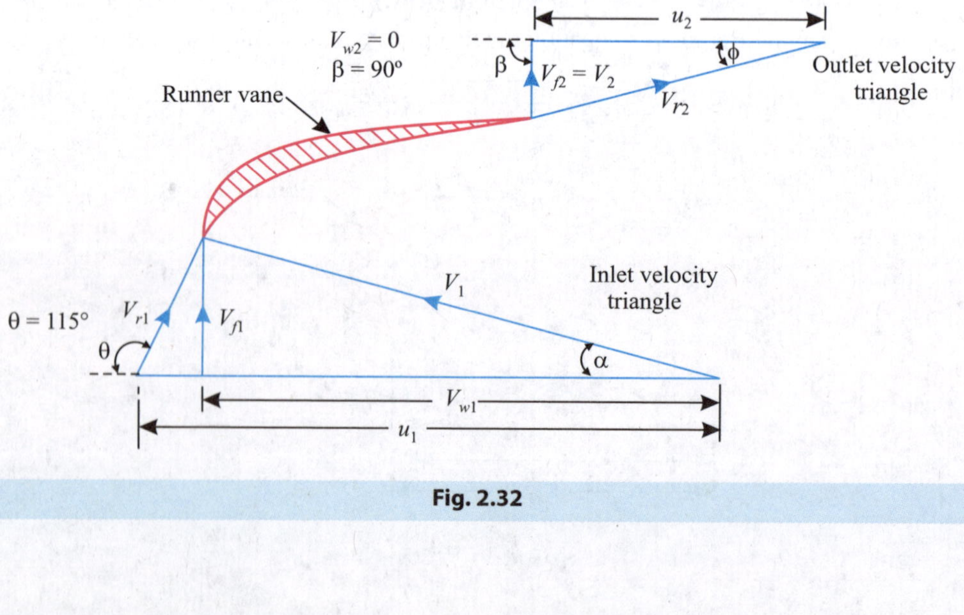

Fig. 2.32

From *inlet velocity triangle*, we have:

$$\frac{V_{f1}}{(u_1 - V_{w1})} \tan(180° - 115°), \quad \text{or,} \quad u_1 - V_{w1} = \frac{V_{f1}}{\tan(180° - 115°)} = \frac{6.5}{0.466} = 3.03$$

$$\therefore \quad u_1 = V_{w1} + 3.03 \qquad \text{...}(i)$$

Hydraulic efficiency, $\eta_h = \frac{V_{w1} u_1}{gH}$ $[\because V_{w2} = 0 \text{ ... } Given]$

$$0.9 = \frac{V_{w1} u_1}{9.81 \times 24.5}, \quad \text{or,} \quad V_{w1} u_1 = 0.9 \times 9.81 \times 24.5 = 216.31$$

i.e., $V_{w1} u_1 = 216.31$ ...(*ii*)

From eqns. (*i*) and (*ii*), we obtain

$$V_{w1}(V_{w1} + 3.03) = 216.31$$

$$\text{or,} \quad V_{w1}^2 + 3.03\, V_{w1} - 216.31 = 0$$

$$\text{or,} \quad V_{w1} = \frac{-3.03 \pm \sqrt{3.03^2 + 4 \times 216.31}}{2} = \frac{-3.03 \pm 29.57}{2} = 13.27 \text{ m/s}$$

$$\therefore \quad u_1 = 13.27 + 3.03 = 16.3 \text{ m/s} \qquad \text{(neglecting –ve sign)}$$

(*i*) Diameter of the runner at entry surface, D_1 :

$$u_1 = \frac{\pi D_1 N}{60} = \frac{\pi D_1 \times 225}{60}$$

$$\therefore \quad D_1 = \frac{60\, u_1}{\pi \times 225} = \frac{60 \times 16.3}{\pi \times 225} = \mathbf{1.38 \text{ m}} \textbf{ (Ans.)}$$

(*ii*) Pressure head at entry to the runner (p_1/w) and at entrance to the draft tube (p_2/w) :

Absolute velocity at entry to runner,

$$V_1 = \sqrt{V_{f1}^2 + V_{w1}^2} = \sqrt{6.5^2 + 13.27^2} = 14.78 \text{ m/s}$$

Taking tail race as datum, the total head across the turbine,

$$H = \frac{p_1}{w} + \frac{V_1^2}{2g} + z_1 \qquad \text{...}(i)$$

(neglecting losses in scroll and guide blades and the velocity head with which the water comes out of the draft tube)

∴ *Pressure head at entry to turbine runner,*

$$\frac{p_1}{w} = H - \frac{V_1^2}{2g} - z_1 = 24.5 - \frac{14.78^2}{2 \times 9.81} - 1.5 = \mathbf{11.87 \text{ m of water}} \textbf{ (Ans.)}$$

From *energy considerations* at the inlet and outlet of the turbine runner, we have:

$$\frac{p_1}{w} + \frac{V_1^2}{2g} + z_1 = \frac{p_2}{w} + \frac{V_2^2}{2g} + z_2 + \text{work done} + \text{losses in runner} \qquad \text{...}(ii)$$

Now, work done (or head utilized) = 0.9 H (since, $\eta_h = 90\%$ ...*Given*)

Also, $\frac{p_1}{w} + \frac{V_1^2}{2g} + z_1 = 24.5$ ...From eqn. (*i*)

Substituting the above value in eqn. (*ii*), we obtain:

$$24.5 = \frac{p_2}{w} + \frac{V_2^2}{2g} + z_2 + 22.05 + 0.9$$

or, $$\frac{p_2}{w} + \frac{V_2^2}{2g} + z_2 = 24.5 - (22.05 + 0.9) = 1.55 \text{ m}$$

∴ *Pressure head at exit from the turbine runner* (or at inlet to draft tube),

$$\frac{p_2}{w} = 1.55 - \frac{V_2^2}{2g} - z_2 = 1.55 - \frac{6^2}{2 \times 9.81} - 1.2 = -\mathbf{1.485\ m}\ \textbf{(Ans.)}$$

[∵ $V_2 = 6$ m/s ... *Given*]

Example 2.34. *In a vertical shaft inward flow reaction turbine, water enters the runner from the guide blades at an angle of 155° with the runner blade angle at entry being 100°. Both these angle are measured from the tangent at runner periphery drawn in the direction of runner rotation. The flow velocity through the runner is constant, water enters the draft tube from the runner without whirl and the discharge from the draft tube into the tail race takes place with a velocity of 3.0 m/s. The runner has the dimensions of 480 mm external diameter and 45.6 mm inlet width. The turbine works with a net head of 50·4 m and the loss of head in the turbine due to fluid resistance is 5.76 m of water. Determine :*

(*i*) *Speed of the runner;*

(*ii*) *Runner blade angle at a point on the outlet edge where the radius of rotation is 108 mm;*

(*iii*) *Power generated by the turbine and its specific speed;*

(*iv*) *Inlet diameter of the draft tube.*

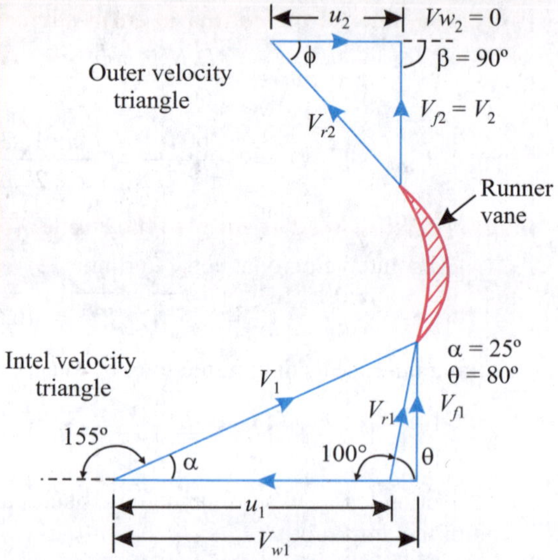

Fig. 2.33

Solution. External diameter of the runner, $D_1 = 480$ mm $= 0.48$ m

Inlet width of the runner, $B_1 = 45.6$ mm $= 0.0456$ m

Net head, $H = 50.4$ m

Loss of head in the turbine due to fluid resistance $= 5.76$ m

Refer to Fig. 2.33. From the *inlet velocity triangle*,

$$\alpha = 180° - 155° = 25° \ ; \ \theta = 180° - 100° = 80°$$

Also, $$\frac{V_{f1}}{V_{w1}} = \tan\alpha, \text{ or, } V_{w1} = \frac{V_{f1}}{\tan\alpha}$$

∴ $$V_{w1} = \frac{V_{f1}}{\tan 25°} = 2.144\, V_{f1}$$

Again, $$\tan\theta = \frac{V_{f1}}{V_{w1} - u_1}, \text{ or, } V_{w1} - u_1 = \frac{V_{f1}}{\tan\theta}$$

or, $$u_1 = V_{w1} - \frac{V_{f1}}{\tan 80°}$$

$$= 2.144V_{f1} - 0.1763V_{f1} = 1.968V_{f1}$$

Since the discharge is *radial,* therefore,

$$V_{w2} = 0$$

Now, from energy considerations, we have:

Head supplied = Work done + kinetic head at exit + losses in the runner

$$50.4 = \frac{V_{w1}u_1}{g} + \frac{V_2^2}{2g} + 4.8$$

$$50.4 = \frac{2.144\,V_{f1} \times 1.968\,V_{f1}}{9.81} + \frac{3.0^2}{2 \times 9.81} + 5.76 = 0.43\,V_{f1}^2 + 0.459 + 5.76$$

$$\therefore \quad 0.43\,V_{f1}^2 = 44.18, \quad \text{or,} \quad V_{f1} = \left(\frac{44.18}{0.43}\right)^{1/2} = 10.14 \text{ m/s}$$

$$u_1 = 1.968\,V_{f1} = 1.968 \times 10.14 = 19.95 \text{ m/s}$$

(*i*) Speed of the runner, N :

$$u_1 = \frac{\pi D_1 N}{60}, \quad \text{or,} \quad N = \frac{60\,u_1}{\pi D_1} = \frac{60 \times 19.95}{\pi \times 0.48} = \mathbf{794\ r.p.m.}\ \text{(Ans.)}$$

(*ii*) Runner blade angle at a point on the outlet edge where the radius of rotation is 108 mm, ϕ :

In the *outlet velocity triangle,* $V_2 = V_{f2} = V_{f1} = 10{\cdot}14$ m/s

Periphery velocity of the outer edge at 108 mm radius,

$$u_2 = u_1 \times \frac{R_2}{R_1} = 19.95 \times \frac{108}{(480/2)} = 8.97 \text{ m/s}$$

$$\tan\phi = \frac{V_{f2}}{u_2} = \frac{10.14}{8.97} = 1.13$$

$$\therefore \quad \phi = \tan^{-1}(1.13) = \mathbf{48.5°}\ \text{(Ans.)}$$

(*iii*) Power generated by the turbine and its specific speed :

$$\text{Power developed by the turbine} = wQ \times \frac{V_{w1}u_1}{g}$$

where, Q = Discharge through the turbine

$$= \pi D_1 B_1 \times V_{f1} = \pi \times 0.48 \times 0.0456 \times 10.14 = 0.697 \text{ m}^3\text{/s};$$

and

$$\frac{V_{w1}u_1}{g} = \frac{2.144\,V_{f1} \times 1.968\,V_{f1}}{9.81} = 0.43\,V_{f1}^2 = 0.43 \times (10.14)^2 = 44.2$$

$\therefore$ Power developed by the turbine = 9.81 × 6.97 × 44.2 = **302.2 kW** **(Ans.)**

Assuming a mechanical efficiency of 97%,

Power available at the turbine shaft, P = 302.2 × 0.97 = 293.13 kW

$$\text{Specific speed, } N_s = \frac{N\sqrt{P}}{H^{5/4}} = \frac{794 \times \sqrt{293.13}}{(50.4)^{5/4}} = \mathbf{101.23}\ \text{(Ans.)}$$

(*iv*) Inlet diameter of the draft tube, d_i :

$$\text{Inlet area of draft tube} = \frac{\text{Discharge}}{\text{Flow velocity}} = \frac{0.697}{10.14} = 0.0687 \text{ m}^2$$

$$\therefore \quad \frac{\pi}{4} d_i^2 = 0.0687, \quad \text{or,} \quad d_i = \left(\frac{0.0687 \times 4}{\pi}\right)^{1/2} = \mathbf{0.295\ m\ (Ans.)}$$

Example 2.35. *A Francis turbine supplied through a 6 m diameter penstock has the following particulars :*

Output of installation = 63500 kW; Flow = 117 m³/s; Speed = 150 r.p.m. Hydraulic efficiency = 92 per cent; Mean diameter of turbine at entry = 4 m; Mean blade height at entry = 1 m; Entry diameter of draft tube = 4·2 m; Velocity in tail race = 2·4 m/s.

The static pressure head in the penstock measured just before entry to the runner is 57·4 m. The point of measurement is 3 m above the level of the tail race. The loss in the draft tube is equivalent to 30 percent of the velocity head at entry to it. The exit plane of the runner is 2 m above the tail race and the flow leaves the runner without swirl. Determine :

(i) Overall efficiency;

(ii) Direction of flow relative to the runner at inlet;

(iii) Pressure head at entry to the draft tube. **[M.U.]**

Solution. Output of installation, $P = 63500$ kW

Diameter of the penstock, $D_p = 6$ m

Discharge through the turbine, $Q = 117\ m^3/s$

Speed, $N = 150$ r.p.m.

Hydraulic efficiency, $\eta_h = 92\%$

Mean diameter of turbine at inlet, $D_1 = 4$ m

Mean blade height at entry, $B_1 = 1$m

Entry diameter of draft tube, $d_i = 4{\cdot}2$ m

Velocity in the tail race, $V_{tr} = 2{\cdot}4$ m/s

The static pressure head in the penstock just before entry to the runner = 57·4 m

Loss of head in the draft tube = 30 per cent of the velocity head at entry to it.

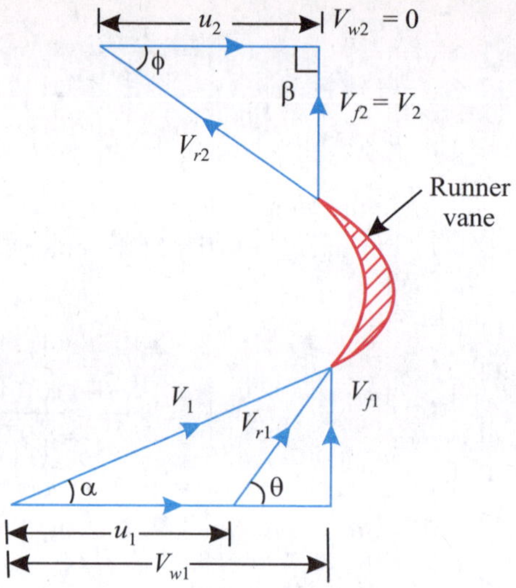

Fig. 2.34

(i) Overall efficiency, η_0 :

Velocity in the penstock,

$$V_p = \frac{Q}{\frac{\pi}{4} \times D_p^2} = \frac{117}{\frac{\pi}{4} \times 6^2} = 4.138 \text{ m/s}$$

Velocity at entry to the draft tube,

$$V_{ed} = \frac{Q}{\frac{\pi}{4} \times d_i^2} = \frac{117}{\frac{\pi}{4} \times 4.2^2} = 8.44 \text{ m/s}$$

Head just before entry to the runner

$$\frac{p}{w} + \frac{V^2}{2g} + z = 57.4 + \frac{4.138^2}{2 \times 9.81} + 3 = 61.27 \text{ m}$$

(where $z = 3$ m ...*Given*)

Net or effective head, H = Head at entry to runner – kinetic energy in tail race

$$= 61.27 - \frac{V_{tr}^2}{2g}$$

$$\therefore \quad H = 61.27 - \frac{2.4^2}{2 \times 9.81} = 60.97 \text{ m}$$

$$\text{Overall efficiency, } \eta_0 = \frac{\text{Output power}}{\text{Input power}} = \frac{63500}{wQH} = \frac{63500}{9.81 \times 117 \times 60.97}$$

$$= 0.907 \text{ or } \mathbf{90.7\% \text{ (Ans.)}}$$

(*ii*) Direction of flow relative to the runner at inlet, θ :

$$\text{Hydraulic efficiency, } \eta_h = \frac{V_{w1} u_1}{gH}$$

[$\because V_{w2} = 0$, since the flow leaves the runner without swirl]

$$\text{or,} \quad V_{w1} = \frac{\eta_h \times gH}{u_1}$$

$$\text{where,} \quad u_1 = \frac{\pi D_1 N}{60} = \frac{\pi \times 4 \times 150}{60} = 31.41 \text{ m/s}$$

$$\therefore \quad V_{w1} = \frac{0.92 \times 9.81 \times 60.97}{31.41} = 17.52 \text{ m/s}$$

From *inlet velocity triangle*, we have : $\tan \theta = \dfrac{V_{f1}}{V_{w1} - u_1}$

$$\text{But,} \quad V_{f1} = \frac{Q}{\pi D_1 B_1} = \frac{117}{\pi \times 4 \times 1} = 9.3 \text{ m/s} \qquad (\because Q = \pi D_1 B_1 \times V_{f1})$$

$$\therefore \quad \tan \theta = \frac{9.31}{17.52 - 31.41} = -0.67 \text{ m/s}$$

$$\therefore \quad = \tan^{-1}(-0.67) = 180° - 33.82° = \mathbf{146.18° \text{ (Ans.)}}$$

(Fig. 2.34 to be modified accordingly)

(*iii*) Pressure head at entry to the draft tube, (p_2/w) :

Applying Bernoulli's equation between the entrance to the draft tube and the tail race, we obtain:

$$\frac{p_2}{w} + \frac{V_2^2}{2g} + z_2 = 0 + \frac{V_{tr}^2}{2g} + 0.3 \times \frac{V_2^2}{2g}$$

$$\text{or,} \quad \frac{p_2}{w} = -z_2 - 0.7\frac{V_2^2}{2g} + \frac{V_{tr}^2}{2g} = -2 - 07 \times \frac{8.44^2}{2 \times 9.81} + \frac{2.4^2}{2 \times 9.81}$$

[$\because V_2 = V_{ed} = 8{\cdot}44$ m/s]

$$= -2 - 2.54 + 0.29 = \mathbf{-4.25 \text{ m (Ans.)}}$$

Example 2.36. (Outward flow reaction turbine). (*a*) *What are the disadvantages of an onward-flow radial turbine as compared with a radial inward-flow turbine.*

(*b*) *An outward reaction turbine is running at 300 r.p.m. and the rate of flow of water through the turbine is 7.2 m^3/s. The internal and external diameters of the turbine are 2 m and 2.75 m* *respectively. The width of the runner is constant at inlet and outlet and is equal to 300 mm. The head on the turbine is 216 m. The discharge at the outlet is radial. Neglecting thickness of the vanes, determine :*

(i) *Velocities of flow at inlet and outlet, and*

(ii) *Vane angles at inlet and outlet.* **[Anna University]**

Solution. (a) At inlet and exit of the turbine, the relative velocities (V_{r1}, V_{r2}) and blade velocities (u_1, u_2) are related as follows :

$$\frac{V_{r2}^2 - V_{r1}^2}{2g} = \frac{u_2^2 - u_1^2}{2g}, \text{ or, } \frac{V_{r2}^2}{2g} = \frac{V_{r1}^2}{2g} + \frac{(u_2 - u_1)^2}{2g}$$

In case of an inward flow turbine the relative velocity *decreases* at exit from the turbine since $u_2 < u_1$. But in an outward flow turbine the relative velocity increases at outlet as $u_2 > u_1$; this aspect makes the task of speed control of an outward flow turbine more difficult than that of an inward flow turbine.

(b) Speed of the turbine, $N = 300$ r.p.m.

Rate of flow of water, $Q = 7{\cdot}2 \text{ m}^3/\text{s}$

Internal diameter, $D_1 = 2$ m

External diameter, $D_2 = 2.75$ m

Width of runner = constant, $B_1 = B_2 = 300$ mm = 0.3 m

Head, $H = 216$ m

Discharge at outlet = radial, $V_{w2} = 0$, $V_{f2} = V_2$

Tangential velocity at inlet,

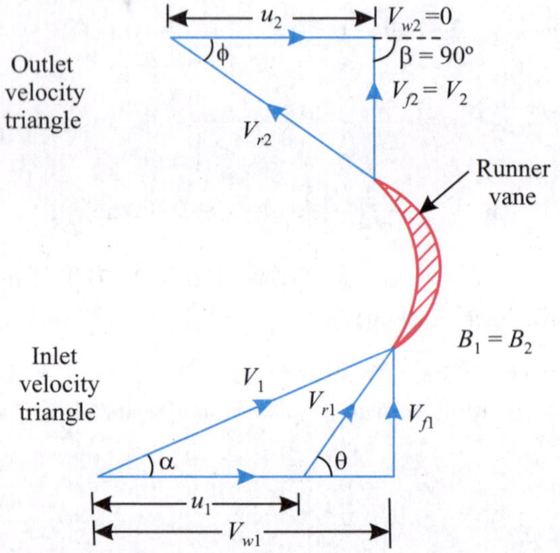

Fig. 2.35

$$u_1 = \frac{\pi D_1 N}{60} = \frac{\pi \times 2 \times 300}{60} = 31.4 \text{ m/s}$$

Tangential velocity at outlet,

$$u_2 = \frac{\pi D_2 N}{60} = \frac{\pi \times 2.75 \times 300}{60} = 43.19 \text{ m/s}$$

(i) Velocities of flow at inlet and outlet V_{f1}, V_{f2} :

The discharge (Q) through the turbine is given by,

$$Q = \pi D_1 B_1 V_{f1} = \pi D_2 B_2 V_{f2}$$

$$\therefore \quad V_{f1} = \frac{Q}{\pi D_1 B_1} = \frac{7.2}{\pi \times 2 \times 0.3} = \mathbf{3.82\ m/s\ (Ans.)}$$

and,
$$V_{f2} = \frac{Q}{\pi D_2 B_2} = \frac{7.2}{\pi \times 2.75 \times 0.3} = \mathbf{2.77\ m/s\ (Ans.)}$$

Now,
$$\text{head, } H = \frac{V_{w1}u_1}{g} + \frac{V_2^2}{2g} = \frac{V_{w1}u_1}{g} + \frac{V_{f2}^2}{2g} \qquad (\because V_{w2} = 0, V_2 = V_{f2})$$

$$216 = \frac{V_{w1} \times 31.4}{981} + \frac{2.77^2}{2 \times 9.81}, \quad \text{or,} \quad 216 = 3.2\,V_{w1} + 0.391$$

$$\therefore \quad V_{w1} = \frac{(216 - 0.391)}{3.2} = 67.38 \text{ m/s}$$

(*ii*) Vane angles at inlet and outlet, θ, φ :

From *inlet velocity triangle,*
$$\tan\theta = \frac{V_{f1}}{V_{w1} - u_1} = \frac{3.82}{67.38 - 31.4} = 0.1062$$

$$\therefore \quad \theta = \tan^{-1}(0.1062) = \mathbf{6.06^\circ\ (Ans.)}$$

From *outlet velocity triangle,*
$$\tan\phi = \frac{V_{f2}}{u_2} = \frac{2.77}{43.9} = 0.0641$$

$$\therefore \quad \phi = \tan^{-1}(0.0641) = \mathbf{3.66^\circ\ (Ans.)}$$

2.4.2. Propeller and Kaplan turbines-Axial Flow Reaction Turbines

It has been observed that with *increasing specific speed* the flow tends to be *axial*. If water flows parallel to the axis of the rotation of the shaft, the turbine is known as *axial flow turbine*; when the head at inlet of the turbine is the sum of pressure energy and kinetic energy and during the flow of water through runner a part of the pressure energy is converted into kinetic energy, the turbine is known as *reaction turbine*. The shaft of an axial flow reaction turbine is *vertical*. The lower end of the shaft is made larger which is known as '*hub*' or '*boss*'. The vanes are fixed on the hub and it acts as runner for axial flow reaction turbine. Two important axial flow reaction turbines are:

(*i*) *Propeller turbine*, and

(*ii*) *Kaplan turbine*.

In these turbines all parts such as *spiral casing*, *stay vanes*, *guide vanes*, *control vanes*, *and draft tube* are similar to mixed-flow turbines in design. But the *water enters the runner in an axial direction* and during the process of energy transfer, it travels across the blade passage in axial direction and *leaves axially*. *The pressure at the inlet of the blades is larger than the pressure at the exit of the blades. The energy transfer is due to the reaction effect, i.e. the change in the magnitude of relative velocity across the blades.*

In an axial flow turbine the number of blades are *fewer* and hence the *loading on the blade is larger. Smaller contact area causes less frictional loss compared to mixed flow turbines*, but the peripheral speed of the turbine is *larger*. Axial flow rotors *do not have a rim at the outer end* like the Francis rotors; but the *blades are enclosed in a cylindrical casing.*

The tip clearance between the blades and the cylindrical casing is small; hence the flow past blades can be considered *two-dimensional*. The water coming out from the guide vanes undergoes a whirl which is assumed to satisfy the law of free vortex ($V_w = C/r$). Accordingly the *whirl is largest near the hub and smallest at the outer end of blade*. Hence the *blade is twisted along its axis.*

2.4.2.1. Propeller turbine

The need to utilize *low heads where large volume of water is available* makes it essential to provide a large flow area and to run the machine at very low speeds. The propeller turbine is a reaction turbine used for heads between 4 m and 80 m. It is purely *axial-flow* device providing the largest possible flow area that will *utilize a large volume of water and still obtain flow velocities which are not too large.*

The propeller turbine (Fig. 2.36) consists of an axial-flow runner with four to six or at the most ten blades of air-foil shape. The runner is generally kept horizontal, *i.e* the shaft is vertical. The blades resemble the propeller of a ship. In the propeller turbine, as in Francis turbine, the runner blades *are fixed* and *non-adjustable*. The *spiral casing* and *guide blades* are similar to those in Francis turbine. The *guide mechanism* is similar to that in a Francis turbine.

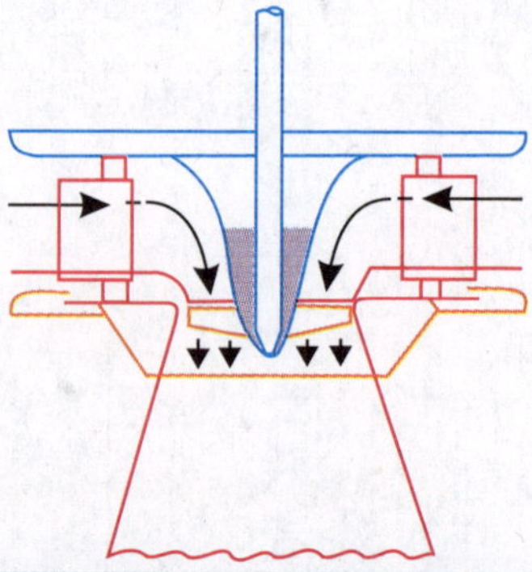

Fig. 2.36. Propeller turbine.

2.4.2.2. Kaplan turbine

A propeller turbine is quite suitable when the *load on the turbine remains constant*. At *part load* its efficiency is very low; since the blades are *fixed*, the water *enters with shock* (at part load) and *eddies are formed which reduce the efficiency*. This defect of the propeller turbine is removed in Kaplan turbine. In a Kaplan turbine the *runner blades are adjustable* and *can be rotated about pivots fixed to the boss of the runner*. The *blades are adjusted automatically by servomechanism so that at all loads the flow enters them without shock*. Thus, *a high efficiency is maintained even at part load.* The servomotor cylinder is usually accommodated in the hub. Figs. 2.37 and 2.38 show the Kaplan turbine runner and Kaplan turbine (schematic diagram) respectively.

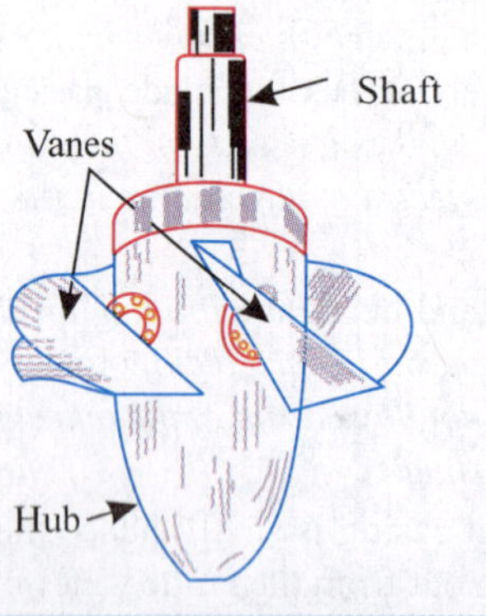

Fig. 2.37. Kaplan turbine runner.

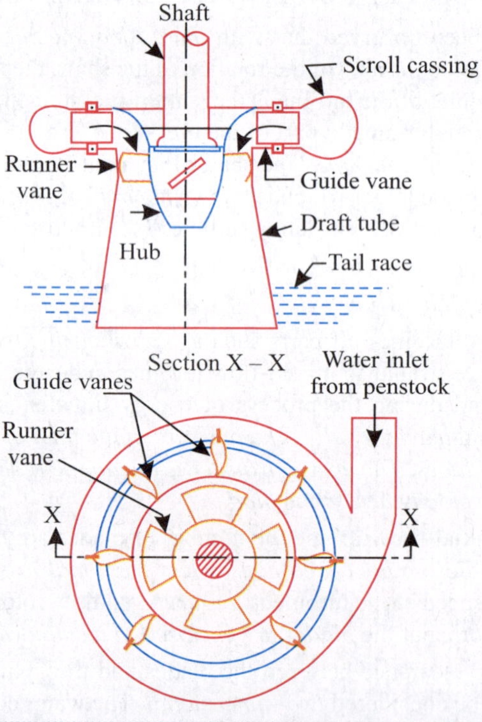

Fig. 2.38

The Kaplan turbine has *purely axial flow*. Usually it has 4 to 6 blades having no outside rim. It is also known as a *variable-pitch propeller turbine* since the pitch of the turbine can be changed because of adjustable vanes. The Kaplan turbine behaves like a propeller turbine at full-load conditions.

The scroll casing, guide mechanism and draft tube are similar to that in the Francis turbine. The shape of runner blades is different from that of Francis turbine. The blades of Kaplan turbine are made of *stainless steel*.

Kaplan turbine, like every propeller turbine, is a *high speed turbine* and is used for smaller heads; as the speed is high, the number of runner-vanes is small.

Kaplan turbines have taken the place of Francis turbines for certain medium head installations. Kaplan turbines with sloping guide vanes to reduce the overall dimensions are being used.

Important Kaplan Turbine Installations in India :

S.No.	Scheme/Project	Location (State)	Source of water
1	Bhakra-Nangal Project	Gangwal & Kota (Punjab)	Nangal hydel
2	Hirakud Dam Project	Hirakud (Orissa)	Mahanadi river
3	Nizam Sagar Project	Nizam Sagar (Andhra Pradesh)	Nanjira river
4	Radhanagri Hydroelectric Scheme	Kolhapur (Maharashtra)	Bhagvati river
5	Tungbhadra Hydroelectric Scheme	Tungbadhra (Karnataka)	Tungbadhra river

Differences between Francis Turbine and Kaplan Turbine :

S.No.	Aspects	Francis turbine	Kaplan turbine
1.	*Type of turbine*	Radially inward or mixed flow.	Partially axial flow.
2.	*Disposition of shaft*	Horizontal or vertical	Only vertical.
3.	*Adjustability of runner vanes*	Runner vanes are *not* adjustable.	Runner vanes are adjustable.
4.	*Number of vanes*	Large, 16 to 24 blades	Small, 3 to 8 blades
5.	*Resistance to be overcome*	Large, (owing to large number of vanes and greater area of contact with water)	Less (owing to fewer number of vanes and less wetted area)
6.	*Head*	Medium (60 m to 250 m)	Low (up to 30 m)
7.	*Flow rate*	Medium	Large
8.	*Specific speed*	50-250	250-850
9.	*Type of governor*	Ordinary	Heavy duty

Working proportions :

The expressions for work done, efficiency and power developed by axial flow propeller and Kaplan turbines are identical to those of a Francis turbine, and the working proportions are obtained in an identical fashion. However, the following *deviations need to be noted carefully*:

1. In case of a propeller/Kaplan turbine, the ratio n is taken as $\frac{D_b}{D_0}\left(\text{and not } \frac{B}{D}\right)$

where, D_0 = Outside diameter of the runner, and

D_b = Diameter of boss (or hub).

Discharge, Q = Area of flow × velocity of flow

$$= \frac{\pi}{4}(D_0^2 - D_b^2) \times V_f$$

$$= \frac{\pi}{4}(D_0^2 - D_b^2) \times K_f\sqrt{2gH} \quad \text{(where, } K_f = \text{flow ratio)}$$

or, $$Q = \frac{\pi}{4} D_0^2 (1 - n^2) \times K_f \sqrt{2gH} \quad ...(2.31)$$

$$\left(\because n = \frac{D_b}{D_0}, \quad \text{or,} \quad D_b = nD_0 \right)$$

The value of n ranges from 0.35 to 0.60.

The value of $K_f = 0.70$.

2. The peripheral velocity u of the runner vanes depends upon the radius of the point under consideration and thus the blade angles vary from the rim to the boss and the vanes are *warped*; this is necessary to *ensure shock free entry and exit.*

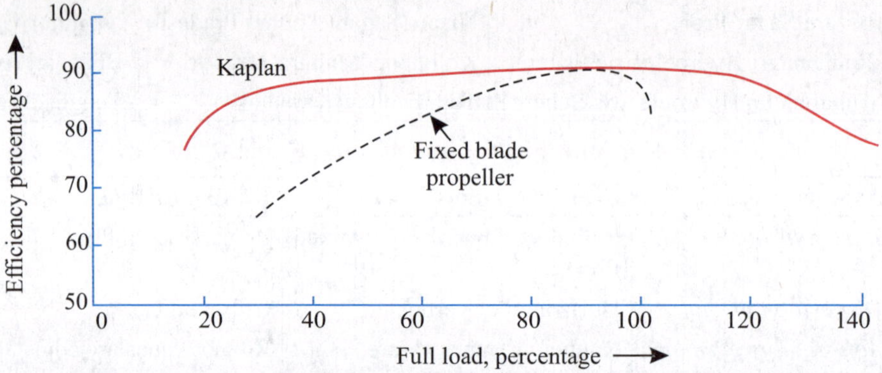

Fig. 2.39. Comparison of efficiencies of propeller (fixed blades) and Kaplan turbines.

3. The *velocity of flow remains constant throughout.*

Fig. 2.39 shows the comparison of efficiencies of propeller (fixed blades) and Kaplan turbines.

2.4.2.3. Kaplan turbine versus Francis turbine :

Kaplan turbine claims the following *advantages* over Francis turbine :

1. For the same power developed Kaplan turbine is more compact in construction and smaller in size.
2. Part-load efficiency is considerably high.
3. Low frictional losses (because of small number of blades used).

Example 2.37. *A Kaplan turbine develops 22000 kW at an average head of 35 m. Assuming a speed ratio of 2, flow ratio of 0.6, diameter of the boss equal to 0·35 times the diameter of the runner and an overall efficiency of 88 per cent, calculate the diameter, speed and specific speed of the turbine.*

Solution. Shaft power, P = 22000 kW; Head, H = 35 m;

Speed ratio, K_u = 2.0; Flow ratio, K_f = 0.6;

Diameter of boss (D_b) = 0.35 × diameter of the runner (D_0), *i.e.* $D_b = 0.35D_0$;

Overall efficiency, η_0 = 88 per cent.

Diameter of the runner, D_0 :

$$K_u = \frac{u_1}{\sqrt{2gH}} = 2.0;\ u_1 = 2.0 \times \sqrt{2gH} = 2.0 \times \sqrt{2 \times 9.81 \times 35} = 52.4 \text{ m/s}$$

$$K_f = \frac{V_{f1}}{\sqrt{2gH}} = 0.6, \quad \text{or,} \quad V_{f1} = 0.6 \times \sqrt{2gH}$$

$$= 0.6 \times \sqrt{2 \times 9.81 \times 35} = 15.7 \text{ m/s}$$

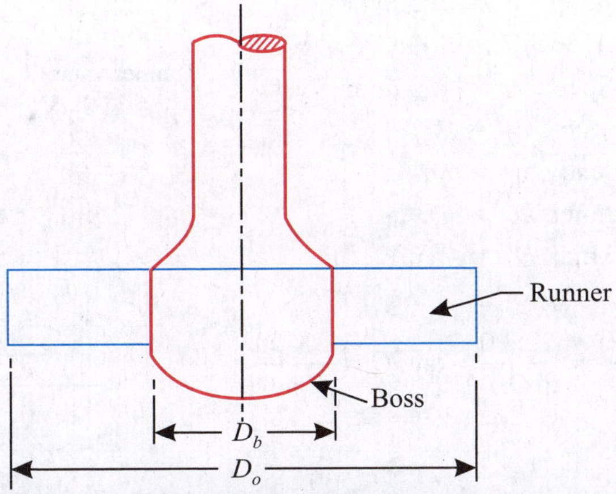

Fig. 2.40

Overall efficiency,

$$\eta_0 = \frac{\text{Shaft power (P)}}{\text{Water power}} = \frac{22000}{wQH}$$

or, $$0.88 = \frac{22000}{9.81 \times Q \times 35}$$

$$Q = \frac{22000}{0.88 \times 9.81 \times 35} = 72.8 \text{ m}^3/\text{s}$$

Also $$Q = \text{Area of flow} \times \text{velocity of flow}$$

$$= \frac{\pi}{4} \times (D_0^2 - D_b^2) \times V_{f1}$$

or, $$72.8 = \frac{\pi}{4}[D_0^2 - (0.35D_0)^2] \times 15.7 \qquad [\because D_b = 0.35\, D_0]$$

$$= \frac{\pi}{4} D_0^2\,[1 - 0.35^2] \times 15.7 = 10.82 D_0^2$$

$\therefore$ $$D_0 = \left(\frac{72.8}{10.82}\right)^{1/2} \simeq \mathbf{2.6\ m\ (Ans.)}$$

Speed of the turbine, N :

$$u_1 = \frac{\pi D_0 N}{60}, \quad \text{or,} \quad N = \frac{60\, u_1}{\pi D_0} = \frac{60 \times 52.4}{\pi \times 2.6} = \mathbf{384.9\ r.p.m.\ (Ans.)}$$

Specific speed of the turbine, N_s :

$$N_s = \frac{N\sqrt{P}}{H^{5/4}} = \frac{384.9 \times \sqrt{22000}}{(35)^{5/4}} = \mathbf{670.6\ (Ans.)}$$

Example 2.38. *The following data pertain to a Kaplan turbine :*

Power available at shaft = 22500 kW; Head = 20 m; Speed = 150 r.p.m. Hydraulic efficiency = 95 %; Overall efficiency = 88 %; Outer diameter of runner = 4·5 m; Diameter of the hub = 2 m.

Assuming that the turbine discharges without whirl at exit, determine the runner vane angles at the hub and at the outer periphery.

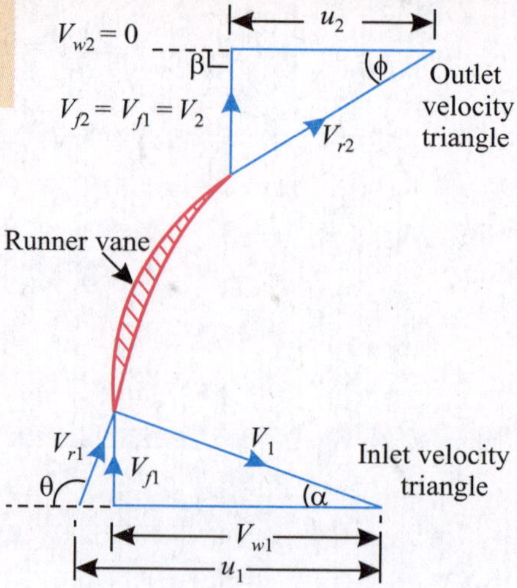

Fig. 2.41

Solution. Shaft power, $P = 22500$ kW

Head, $H = 20$ m

Speed, $N = 150$ r.p.m.

Hydraulic efficiency, $\eta_h = 95\%$

Overall efficiency, $\eta_0 = 88\%$

Outer diameter of runner, $D_0 = 4{\cdot}5$ m

Diameter of the hub, $D_b = 2$ m

Overall efficiency,

$$\eta_0 = \frac{\text{Shaft power (P)}}{\text{Water power}} = \frac{22500}{wQH}, \quad \text{or,} \quad Q = \frac{22500}{\eta_0 wH}$$

∴ Discharge,

$$Q = \frac{22500}{0.88 \times 9.81 \times 20} = 130.32 \text{ m}^3/\text{s}$$

Also,

$$Q = \frac{\pi}{4}(D_0^2 - D_b^2) \times V_{f1}$$

or,

$$130.32 = \frac{\pi}{4}(4.5^2 - 2^2) \times V_{f1}$$

∴

$$V_{f1} = \frac{130.32}{\frac{\pi}{4} \times (4.5 - 2^2)} = 10.21 \text{ m/s}$$

Vane angles at hub :

$$u_1 = \frac{\pi D_b N}{60} = \frac{\pi \times 2 \times 150}{60} = 15.7 \text{ m/s}$$

Hydraulic efficiency,

$$\eta_h = \frac{V_{w1} u_1}{gH}, \quad \text{or,} \quad V_{w1} = \frac{\eta_h gH}{u_1} = \frac{0.95 \times 9.81 \times 20}{15.7} = 11.87 \text{ m/s}$$

From *inlet velocity triangle*, $\tan(180° - \theta) = \frac{V_{f1}}{u - V_{w1}} = \frac{10.21}{15.7 - 11.87} = 2.26$

∴ $180° - \theta = \tan^{-1}(2.66) = 69.4°$

∴ Runner vane angle at inlet, $\theta = 180° - 69.4° =$ **110.6° (Ans.)**

From *outlet velocity triangle*, $\tan\phi = \frac{V_{f2}}{u_2} = \frac{V_{f1}}{u_1} = \frac{10.21}{15.7} = 0.6503$

∴ Runner vane angle at exit, $\phi = \tan^{-1}(0.6503) =$ **33.03° (Ans.)**

Vane angles at extreme edge of the runner (outer periphery) :

$$u_1 = \frac{\pi D_0 N}{60} = \frac{\pi \times 4.5 \times 150}{60} = 35.34 \text{ m/s}$$

$$\text{Hydraulic efficiency, } \eta_h = \frac{V_{w1} u_1}{gH}$$

$$0.95 = \frac{V_{w1} \times 35.34}{9.81 \times 20}, \quad \text{or, } V_{w1} = \frac{0.95 \times 9.81 \times 20}{35.34} = 5.27 \text{ m/s}$$

From *inlet velocity triangle*, $\tan(180° - \theta) = \frac{V_{f1}}{u_1 - V_{w1}} = \frac{10.21}{35.34 - 5.27} = 0.339$

or, $(180° - \theta) = \tan^{-1}(0.339) = 18.72°$

∴ Runner vane angle at inlet, $\theta = 180° - 18.72° =$ **161.28° (Ans.)**

From *outlet velocity triangle*, $\tan\phi = \frac{V_{f2}}{u_2} = \frac{V_{f1}}{u_1} = \frac{10.21}{35.34} = 0.2889$

∴ Runner vane angle at exit, $\phi = \tan^{-1}(0.2889) =$ **16.11° (Ans.)**

Example 2.39. *Calculate the diameter and speed of the runner of a Kaplan turbine developing 6000 kW under an effective head of 5 m. Overall efficiency of the turbine is 90%. The diameter of the boss is 0·4 times the external diameter of the runner. The turbine speed ratio is 2·0 and flow ratio 0·6. What is the specific speed of the turbine?* **[UPSC]**

Solution. *Given* : Power developed, $P = 6000$ kW; $H = 5$m; $\eta_0 = 90\%$;
$D_b = 0.4D_0$; Speed ratio, $K_u = 2.0$; Flow ratio, $K_f = 0.6$.

Diameter (D_0) and speed (N) of the runner :

$$K_u = 2.0 = \frac{u_1}{\sqrt{2gH}}, \quad \text{or, } u_1 = 2\sqrt{2 \times 9.81 \times 5} = 19.81 \text{ m/s}$$

$$K_f = 0.6 = \frac{V_{f1}}{\sqrt{2gH}}, \quad \text{or, } V_{f1} = 0.6\sqrt{2 \times 9.81 \times 5} = 5.94 \text{ m/s}$$

Also, $$\eta_0 = \frac{P}{wQH}$$

or, $$Q = \frac{P}{\eta_0 wH} = \frac{6000 \times 1000}{0.9 \times 9810 \times 5} = 135.9 \text{ m}^3/\text{s}$$

But, $$Q = \frac{\pi}{4}(D_0^2 - D_b^2) \times V_{f1}$$

or, $$135.9 = \frac{\pi}{4}\left[D_0^2 - (0.4\, D_0)^2\right] \times 5.94 = \frac{\pi}{4} D_0^2 (1 - 0.16) \times 5.94$$

∴ $$D_0 = \left[\frac{135.9 \times 4}{\pi(1 - 0.16) \times 5.94}\right]^{1/2} = \mathbf{5.89 \text{ m}} \textbf{ (Ans.)}$$

Now, $$u_1 = \frac{\pi D_0 N}{60}$$

or, $$N = \frac{u_1 \times 60}{\pi D_0} = \frac{19.81 \times 60}{\pi \times 5.89} = \mathbf{64.23\ r.p.m.}\ \textbf{(Ans.)}$$

Specific speed of the turbine, N_s :

$$N_s = \frac{N\sqrt{P}}{H^{5/4}}$$

$$= \frac{64.23\sqrt{6000}}{(5)^{5/4}} = \mathbf{665.4}\ \textbf{(Ans.)}$$

Example 2.40. *The propeller reaction turbine of runner diameter 4.5 m is running at 48 r.p.m. The guide blade angle at inlet is 145° and the runner blade angle at outlet is 25° to the direction of vane. The axial flow area of water through the runner is 30 m². If the runner blade angle at inlet is radial, determine :*

(i) *Hydraulic efficiency of the turbine,*

(ii) *Discharge through the turbine, and*

(iii) *Power developed by the runner.* **[Roorkee University]**

Solution. Diameter of the runner, $D_0 = 4{\cdot}5$ m

Speed of the runner, $N = 48$ r.p.m.

Guide blade angle, $\alpha = 145°$

Runner blade angle at inlet is radial *i.e.* $\theta = 90°$, $V_{f1} = V_{r1}$

Runner blade angle at outlet, $\phi = 25°$

Area of flow, $A_f = 30\ m^2$

(i) Hydraulic efficiency of the turbine, η_h :

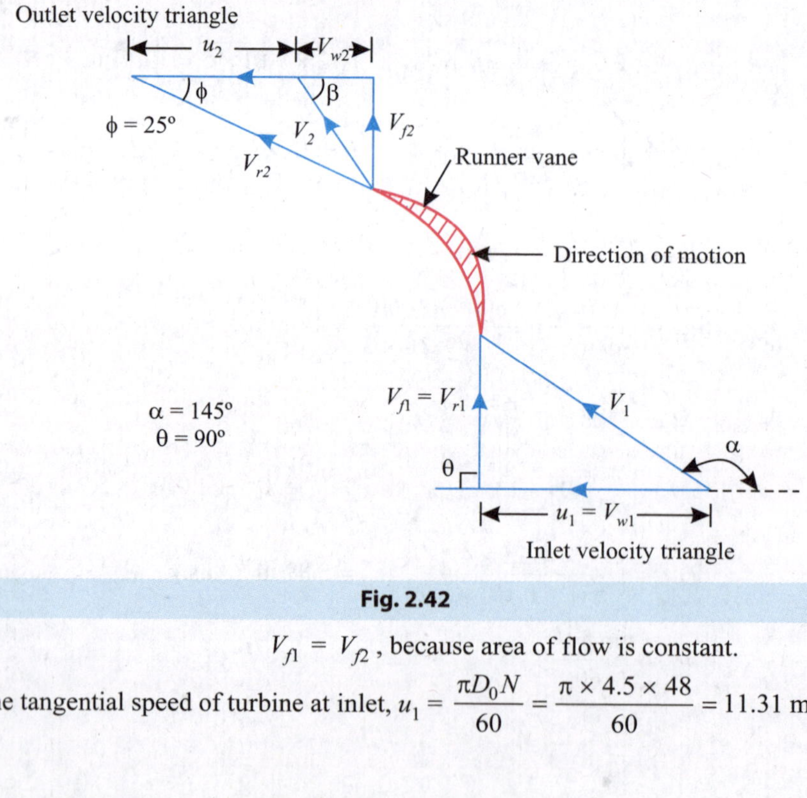

Fig. 2.42

$V_{f1} = V_{f2}$, because area of flow is constant.

The tangential speed of turbine at inlet, $u_1 = \frac{\pi D_0 N}{60} = \frac{\pi \times 4.5 \times 48}{60} = 11.31$ m/s

Also, $u_2 = u_1 = 11.31$ m/s

From *inlet velocity triangle*, we have:

$$\tan(180° - \alpha) = \frac{V_{f1}}{u_1}, \quad \text{or,} \quad \tan(180° - 145°) = \frac{V_{f1}}{u_1}$$

$$\therefore \quad V_{f1} = u_1 \times \tan 35° = 11.31 \times \tan 35° = 7.92 \text{ m/s}$$

Also, $V_{w1} = u_1 = 11.31$ m/s

From *outlet velocity triangle*, we have:

$$\tan\phi = \frac{V_{f2}}{u_2 + V_{w2}} = \frac{7.92}{11.31 + V_{w2}} \qquad (V_{f2} = V_{f1};\ u_2 = u_1)$$

$$\therefore \quad \tan 25° = \frac{7.92}{11.31 + V_{w2}}, \quad \text{or,} \quad 11.31 + V_{w2} = \frac{7.92}{\tan 25°} = 16.98$$

$$\therefore \quad V_{w2} = 16.98 - 11.31 = 5.67 \text{ m/s}$$

$$\therefore \quad V_2 = \sqrt{V_{f2}^2 + V_{w2}^2} = \sqrt{7.92^2 + 5.67^2} = 9.74 \text{ m/s}$$

Also,

$$H = \frac{1}{g}(V_{w1}u_1 - V_{w2}u_2) + \frac{V_2^2}{2g}$$

(Negative sign is taken since the absolute velocities at inlet and outlet are in the same direction and so are the velocities of whirl).

$$\therefore \quad H = \frac{1}{9.8}(11.31 \times 11.31 - 5.67 \times 11.31) + \frac{9.74^2}{2 \times 9.81} = 6.5 + 4.83 = 11.33 \text{ m}$$

$\therefore$ Hydraulic efficiency,

$$\eta_h = \frac{V_{w1}u_1 - V_{w2}u_2}{gH}$$

$$= \frac{(11.31 \times 11.31 - 5.67 \times 11.31)}{9.81 \times 11.33} = 0.575 \text{ or } \mathbf{57.5\%} \textbf{ (Ans.)}$$

(*ii*) Discharge through the turbine, Q :

$$Q = \text{Area of flow} \times \text{velocity of flow} = A_f \times V_{f1}$$

$$= 30 \times 7.92 = \mathbf{237.6\ m^3/s} \textbf{ (Ans.)}$$

(*iii*) Power developed by the turbine :

$$\text{Power developed by the turbine} = \frac{wQ}{g}(V_{w1}u_1 - V_{w2}u_2)$$

$$= \frac{9.81 \times 237.6}{9.81}(11.31 \times 11.31 - 5.67 \times 11.31) = \mathbf{15156.12\ kW} \textbf{ (Ans.)}$$

2.5. DERIAZ TURBINE

Fig. 2.43 shows a schematic view of a Deriaz (or diagonal) turbine which is a reaction turbine. It is named in the honour of its inventor P. Deriaz. This turbine is intermediate between the mixed-flow and the axial-flow turbines, because the flow of water as it passes through the runner is at an angle of 45° to axis and hence it is also known as *Diagonal turbine*. Deriaz turbine has the following *features* :

- It can be employed for the heads varying from 30 m to 150 m.
- The blades of the runner are pivoted to the hub and unlike in the Kaplan turbines, the axes of the blades are inclined to the axis of shaft. The direction of flow of water is as in the Francis runner.
- Guide vanes are provided ahead of the blades to regulate and direct the flow.
- The runner has no outer rim connecting all the blades as these blades are movable.

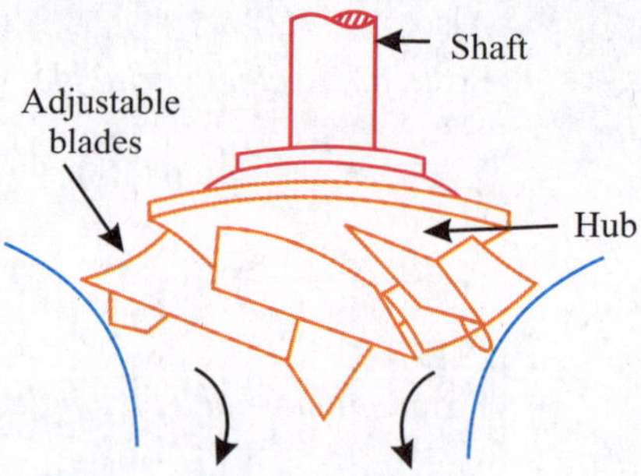

Fig. 2.43. Deriaz turbine.

- The casing of the turbine (not shown in Fig. 2.43) is so shaped that there is only small clearance between the blade tips and the casing to reduce leakage loss.

The runner of the Deriaz turbine is so shaped that it can be used both as a *turbine as well as a pump* and hence it may be classified as a *reversible type turbine*. As such Deriaz turbines are amply suitable for *pumped storage hydropower plants*.

Advantages of Deriaz turbine :

The Deriaz turbine entails the following *advantages* :

1. Improved part load efficiency.
2. Can be conveniently used as a pump-turbine unit.
3. By adjusting the runner to shut position the starting torque under water can be reduced.
4. Unlike axial flow turbines at shut position the flow area is completely closed.
5. Due to oblique location of blades the loading on the outer trunnion journal bearing is reduced.
6. The arrangement for varying the blade angle can be housed with greater convenience as compared to the Kaplan turbine.

2.6. TUBULAR OR BULB TURBINES

Invariably the electric generator coupled to the Kaplan turbine is enclosed and works *inside a straight passage* having the shape of a *bulb*. The *water tight bulb* is submerged directly into a stream of water, and the bends at inlet to casing, draft tube, etc. which are *responsible for the loss of head are dispensed with*. The unit then needs *less installation space* with a consequent *reduction in excavation and other civil engineering works*. These turbines are referred to as **tubular or bulb turbines**. The tubular turbine, a modified axial flow turbine, was developed in Germany by Arno Fischer in 1937. The economical harnessing of fairly low heads on major rivers is now possible with high-output bulb turbines. The following **features** are worth noting :

- A *tubular or bulb turbine* is an axial flow turbine with either adjustable or non-adjustable runner vanes (and hence similar to Kaplan or propeller turbines).
- In such a turbine the scroll casing is *not* provided but the runner is placed in a tube extending from head water to the tail water (and hence it is called tubular turbine).
- It is a low head turbine and is employed for heads varying from 3 m to 15 m.
- The disposition of shaft in a tubular turbine may be vertical, or inclined or horizontal.

The turbo-generator set using tubular turbine has an outer casing having the shape of a bulb. Such a set is now termed as **bulb set** and the turbine used for the set is called a *bulb turbine* (Fig. 2.44). The *advantages* and *disadvantages* of bulb sets *compared to Kaplan turbines* are as follows :

Advantages :

The bulb sets claim the following *advantages* over the Kaplan turbines.

1. Due to absence of spiral casing the plant width is small.
2. Can be used for the sites having very low head.
3. Because of almost straight flow and straight draft tube the maximum turbine efficiency is increased by about 3 per cent.
4. Bulb units can pass higher discharge (than conventional Kaplan turbine) under equivalent conditions.
5. At part loads there is reduced loss of efficiency.
6. Quite suitable for operation on widely varying heads.
7. Because of small dimensions of the power house there is saving in excavation and civil engineering works.

Disadvantages :

1. Leakage of water into generator chamber and condensation are source of trouble (leading to gradual deterioration of electrical insulation).
2. The erection techniques may be time consuming.

The use of bulb turbines offers the saving in the equipment of low head developments and great flexibility of operation and hence are highly suitable for ***tidal power station.***

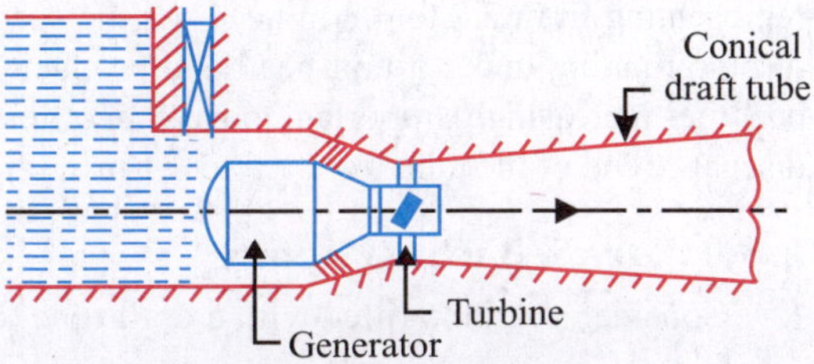

Fig. 2.44. Bulb turbine.

2.7. RUNAWAY SPEED

Runaway speed *is the maximum speed, governor being disengaged, at which a turbine would run when there is no external load but operating under design head and discharge.* All the rotating parts including the rotor of alternator should be designed for the centrifugal stresses caused by this maximum speed.

The practical values of run away speeds for various turbines with respect to their rated speed N are as follows :

Pelton wheel	...1.8 to 1.9 N
Francis turbine (mixed flow)	...2.0 to 2.2 N
Kaplan turbine (axial flow)	...2.5 to 3.0 N

2.8. DRAFT TUBE

In the case of mixed and axial flow turbines only a part of available energy is converted into velocity energy at the inlet to the runner; the rest is in the form of pressure energy. This residual pressure is converted into velocity in the runner, as a consequence of which the outlet velocity increases. With the increase in the value of specific speed N_s, the exit velocity energy $\frac{V_2^2}{2g}$ increases compared with H (the available energy).

In the *Pelton wheel* all the available energy is converted into velocity energy before it strikes the wheel. As such it works under *atmospheric conditions* and the wheel *has to be placed above the maximum tail water level*. The loss of energy due to exit velocity varies from 1 to 4% .

In the case of *mixed and axial flow turbines* a large portion of the energy is associated with the water as it leaves the runner. This exit energy varies from 4 to 25% for mixed flow turbines and from 20 to 50% of the total head for axial flow turbines. As this energy cannot be used in the runner, therefore, it becomes necessary to find a way out to extract this energy. *An expanding pressure conduit hermetically fixed at runner outlet and having the other end below the minimum tail water level helps to convert the velocity head into pressure or potential head. This expanding device is called* **draft tube.** Draft tube is an *integral part* of mixed and axial flow turbines. Because of the draft tube *it is possible to have the pressure at runner outlet much below the atmospheric pressure.*

The draft tube serves the following two *purposes* :

1. *It allows the turbine to be set above tail-water level, without loss of head, to facilitate inspection and maintenance.*
2. *It regains, by diffuse action, the major portion of the kinetic energy delivered to it from the runner.*

At rated load, the velocity at the upstream end of the tube for modern units ranges from 7 to 9 m/s, representing from 2.7 to 4.8 m head. As the specific speed (it is the speed of a geometrically similar turbine running under a unit head and producing unit power) is increased and the head reduced, it becomes increasingly important to have an efficient draft tube. Good practice limits the velocity at the discharge end of the tube from 1.5 to 2.1 m/s, representing less than 0·3 m velocity head loss.

2.8.1. Draft Tube Theory

Consider a turbine fitted with a draft tube (conical) as shown in Fig. 2.45.

Let, y = Distance of the bottom of draft tube from tail race, and

p_a = Atmospheric pressure at the surface of tail race.

Applying Bernoulli's equation to the section 2-2 (representing the runner exit or inlet of the draft tube) and the section 3-3 (representing the draft tube exit); assuming section 3-3 as the datum line, we have:

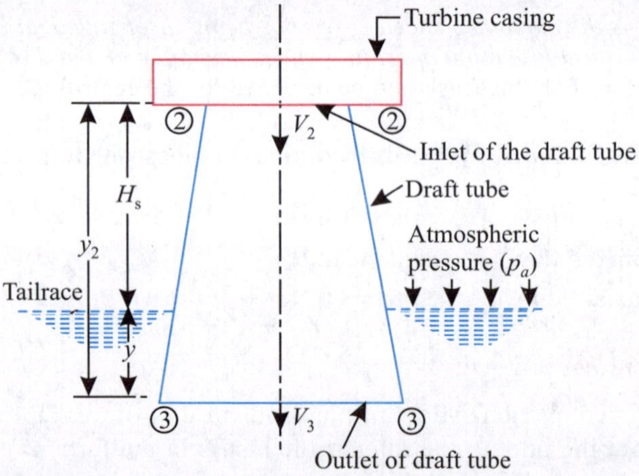

Fig. 2.45. Draft tube theory.

$$\frac{p_2}{w} + \frac{V_2^2}{2g} + y_2 = \frac{p_3}{w} + \frac{V_3^2}{2g} + 0 + h_f \qquad ...(i)$$

where, h_f = Loss of energy between sections 2-2 and 3-3.

Rewriting the above expression (*i*) for $\frac{p_2}{w}$, we obtain:

$$\frac{p_2}{w} = \frac{p_3}{w} - y_2 - \left(\frac{V_2^2 - V_3^2}{2g} - h_f\right) \quad \text{...(ii)}$$

Substituting $\frac{p_3}{w} = \frac{p_a}{w} + y$ in expression (*ii*), we get:

$$\frac{p_2}{w} = \frac{p_a}{w} + (y - y_2) - \left(\frac{V_2^2 - V_3^2}{2g} - h_f\right)$$

The term $(y_2 - y)$ which represents the vertical distance between the runner exit and the tail water level is called the **suction head of draft tube** and is denoted by H_s. Correspondingly the factor $\frac{V_2^2 - V_3^2}{2g}$ is called the **dynamic head.**

$$\therefore \quad \frac{p_2}{w} = \frac{p_a}{w} - H_s - \left(\frac{V_2^2 - V_3^2}{2g} - h_f\right) \quad \text{...(2.32)}$$

In eqn. (2.32), $\frac{p_2}{w}$ is *less than atmospheric pressure.*

The **efficiency of a draft tube** (η_d) is defined as the *ratio of net gain in pressure head to the velocity head at entrance of draft tube.* Thus,

$$\eta_d = \frac{\text{Net gain in pressure head}}{\text{Velocity head at entrance of draft tube}}$$

$$= \frac{\left(\frac{V_2^2 - V_3^2}{2g} - h_f\right)}{\frac{V_2^2}{2g}} \quad \text{...(2.33)}$$

where, V_2 = Velocity of water at section 2-2 (inlet of draft tube), and

V_3 = Velocity of water at section 3-3 (outlet of draft tube).

$$\left[h_f = \frac{V_2^2 - V_3^2}{2g} - \eta_d \times \frac{V_2^2}{2g}\right] \quad \text{...2.33 (a)}$$

2.8.2. Types of Draft Tubes

The following two types of draft tubes are commonly used :

1. The straight conical or concentric tube.
2. The elbow type.

Properly designed, the two types are about equally efficient, *over 85 per cent.*

1. Conical type. The conical type draft tube is *generally* used on *low-powered units for all specific speeds, frequently, on large-head units*. The side angle of flare ranges from 4 to 6°, the length from 3 to 4 times the diameter and the discharge area from four to five times the throat area. Fig. 2.46 shows a straight *conical* draft tube.

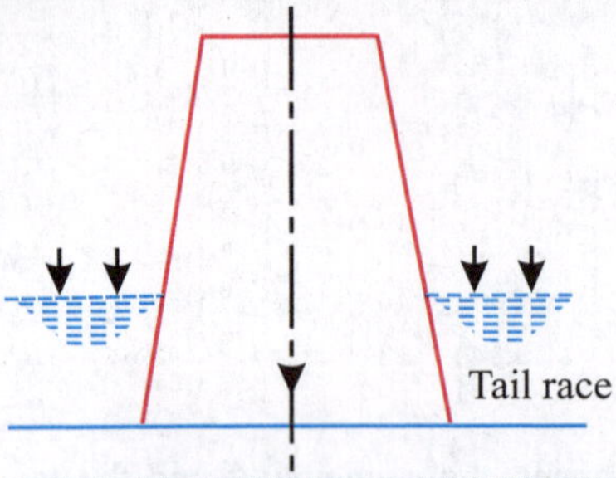

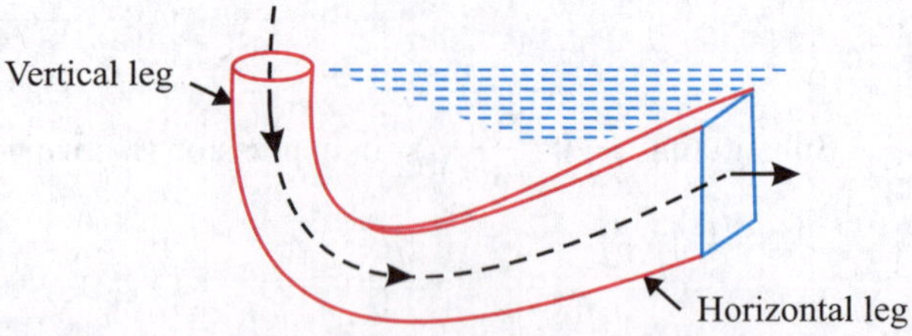

Fig. 2.46. Straight conical draft tube.

Fig. 2.47. Elbow type draft tube.

2. Elbow type. The elbow type of tube is used with *most* turbine installations. This type of draft tube is designed to turn the water from the *vertical to the horizontal direction with a minimum depth of excavation and at the same time having a high efficiency*. The transition from a circular section in the vertical leg to a rectangular section in the horizontal leg takes place in the bend. The horizontal portion of the draft tube is generally *inclined upwards to lead the water gradually to the level of the tail race and to prevent entry of air from the exit end*. The *exit* end of the draft tube *must be totally immersed in water*. Fig. 2.47 shows an elbow type draft tube. One or two vertical piers are placed in the horizontal portion of the tube, for structural and hydraulic reasons.

Moody's spreading draft tube. Fig. 2.48 shows a *Moody's spreading draft tube*. It is provided with a *solid central core* of conical shape which *reduces whirling action of discharged water*. The efficiency of such a draft tube is about 85%. It is suited particularly for helical flows which occur when the water leaves the runner with a whirl component.

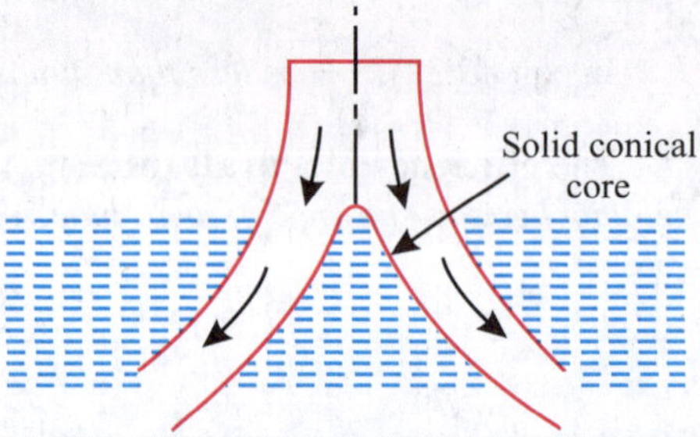

Fig. 2. 48. Moody's spreading draft tube or 'Hydrocone'.

Example 2.41. *A Kaplan turbine develops 1500 kW under a head of 6 m. The turbine is set 2.5 m above the tail race level. A vacuum gauge inserted at the turbine outlet records a suction head of 3·1 m. If the hydraulic efficiency is 82 per cent, what would be the efficiency of draft tube having inlet diameter of 3 m ?*

What will be the reading of suction gauge if power developed is reduced to 750 kW, the head and speed remaining constant.

Solution. Power developed = 1500 kW; Head, $H = 6$ m

Height of turbine above tail race level = 2·5 m; Hydraulic efficiency, $\eta_h = 82\%$

Draft tube inlet diameter, $d_i = 3$ m.

Efficiency of draft tube, η_d :

$$\text{Hydraulic efficiency, } \eta_h = \frac{\text{Power developed}}{\text{Water power}} = \frac{\text{Power developed}}{wQH}$$

$$\therefore \quad \text{Power developed} = wQH \times \eta_h$$

$$1500 = 9.81 \times Q \times 6 \times 0.82, \text{ or, } Q = \frac{1500}{9.81 \times 6 \times 0.82} = 31.08 \text{ m}^3/\text{s}$$

Velocity of water at inlet of draft tube,

$$V_2 = \frac{Q}{\frac{\pi}{4} d_i^2} = \frac{31.08}{\frac{\pi}{4} \times 3^2} = 4.397 \text{ m/s}$$

$$\text{Pressure head required} = 3.1 - 2.5 = 0.6 \text{ m}$$

$$\therefore \text{ Efficiency of draft tube, } \eta_d = \frac{0.6}{\frac{V_2^2}{2g}} = \frac{0.6}{\frac{4.397^2}{2 \times 9.81}} = 0.6088 \text{ or } \mathbf{60.88\%} \text{ (Ans.)}$$

Reading of suction gauge :

For reduced output of 750 kW assuming constant efficiency, we have:

$$\text{Discharge, } Q_1 = \frac{Q}{2} = \frac{31.08}{2} = 15.54 \text{ m}^3/\text{s}$$

Also,

$$V_2 = \frac{15.54}{\frac{\pi}{4} \times 3^2} = 2.198 \text{ m/s}$$

$$\text{Head gained in draft tube} = \eta_d \times \frac{2.198^2}{2g}$$

$$= 0.6088 \times \frac{2.198^2}{2 \times 9.81} \simeq 0.15 \text{ m}$$

$\therefore$ Reading of gauge $= 2.5 + 0.15 =$ **2.65 m (Ans.)**

Example 2.42. *Determine the overall efficiency of a Kaplan turbine developing 2850 kW under a head of 5·2 m. It is provided with a draft tube with its inlet (diameter 3 m) set 1·8 m above the tail race level. A vacuum gauge connected to the draft tube indicates a reading of 5·2 m of water. Assume draft tube efficiency as 75 per cent.*

Solution. Power developed = 2850 kW; Head, $H = 5.2$ m

Height of draft inlet tube above tail race level, $H_s = 1.8$ m

Reading of the gauge = – 5.2 m

Draft tube efficiency, $\eta_d = 75\%$

Overall efficiency of the turbine, η_0 :

$$\frac{p_2}{w} = \frac{p_a}{w} - H_s - \left(\frac{V_2^2 - V_3^2}{2g} - h_f\right) \quad \text{...[Eqn. (2.32)]}$$

$$-5.2 = 0 - 1.8 - \left(\frac{V_2^2 - V_3^2}{2g}\right), \text{ neglecting } h_f \text{ (head loss in draft tube)}$$

or,

$$\frac{V_2^2 - V_3^2}{2g} = 3.4$$

Also,

$$\eta_d = \frac{(V_2^2 - V_3^2)/2g}{(V_2^2/2g)} \quad \text{...[Eqn. (2.33)]}$$

or,

$$0.75 = \frac{3.4}{(V_2^2/2g)}, \text{ or, } \frac{V_2^2}{2g} = \frac{3.4}{0.75} = 4.533$$

$$\therefore \quad V_2 = \sqrt{4.533 \times 2g} = \sqrt{4.533 \times 2 \times 9.81} = 9.43 \text{ m/s}$$

$$\text{Discharge, } Q = \frac{\pi}{4} \times 3^2 \times 9.43 = 66.65 \text{ m}^3/\text{s}$$

$$\therefore \text{ Overall efficiency, } \eta_0 = \frac{\text{Power developed}}{\text{Water power}} = \frac{2850}{wQH}$$

$$= \frac{2850}{9.81 \times 66.65 \times 5.2} = 0.8382 \quad \text{or} \quad \mathbf{83.82\%\ (Ans.)}$$

Example 2.43. *A conical draft tube having inlet and outlet diameters 1.2 m and 1.8 m discharges water at outlet with a velocity of 3 m/s. The total length of the draft tube is 7.2 m and 1·44 m of the length of draft tube is immersed in water. If the atmospheric pressure head is 10.3 m of water and loss of head due to friction in the draft tube is equal to 0.2 × velocity head at outlet of the tube, determine :*

(i) Pressure head at inlet, and

(ii) Efficiency of the draft tube.

Solution. Inlet diameter of the draft tube, $d_i = 1.2$ m

Outlet diameter, $d_0 = 1.8$ m

Velocity at outlet, $V_3 = 3$ m/s

Total length of draft tube, $H_s + y = 7.2$ m

Length of draft tube in water, $y = 1.44$ m

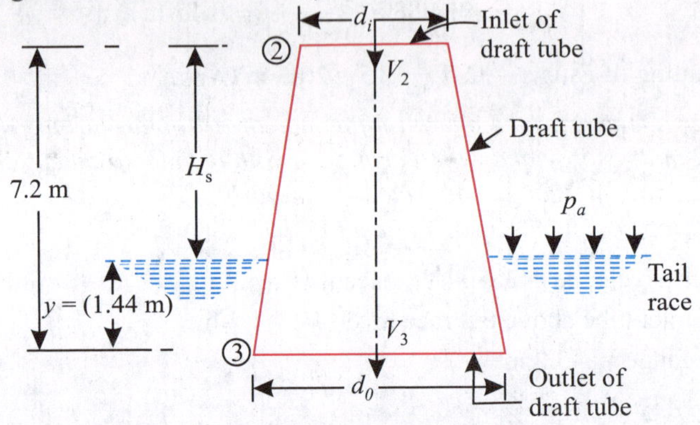

Fig. 2.49

$\therefore$ $$H_s = 7.2 - 1.44 = 5.76 \text{ m}$$

Atmospheric pressure head, $\frac{p_a}{w} = 10.3$ m

Loss of head due to friction,

$$h_f = 0.2 \times \text{velocity head at outlet}$$

$$= 0.2\,\frac{V_3^2}{2g}$$

(*i*) Pressure head at inlet, $\frac{p_2}{w}$:

Discharge through the draft tube,

$$Q = A_3V_3 = \frac{\pi}{4} \times d_0^2 \times V_3 = \frac{\pi}{4} \times 1.8^2 \times 3 = 7.634 \text{ m/s}$$

$$\text{Velocity of inlet, } V_2 = \frac{Q}{A_2} = \frac{7.634}{\frac{\pi}{4}\,d_i^2} = \frac{7.634}{\frac{\pi}{4} \times 1.2^2} = 6.75 \text{ m/s}$$

Using eqn. (2.32),

$$\frac{p_2}{w} = \frac{p_a}{w} - H_s - \left(\frac{V_2^2 - V_3^2}{2g} - h_f\right) = \frac{p_a}{w} - H_s - \left(\frac{V_2^2 - V_3^2}{2g} - 0.2\frac{V_3^2}{2g}\right)$$

$$= 10.3 - 5.76 - \left(\frac{6.75^2 - 3^2}{2 \times 9.81} - 0.2 \times \frac{3^2}{2 \times 9.81}\right)$$

or, $$\frac{p_2}{w} = 4.54 - (1.863 - 0.092) = \mathbf{2.769\ m\ (abs)}\ \textbf{(Ans.)}$$

(ii) Efficiency of the draft tube, η_d :

$$\eta_d = \frac{\left(\frac{V_2^2 - V_3^2}{2g} - h_f\right)}{\frac{V_2^2}{2g}} = \frac{\frac{V_2^2 - V_3^2}{2g} - 0.2\frac{V_3^2}{2g}}{\frac{V_2^2}{2g}} = \frac{\frac{V_2^2}{2g} - \left(\frac{V_3^2}{2g} + 0.2\frac{V_3^2}{2g}\right)}{\frac{V_2^2}{2g}}$$

$$= 1 - 1.2\left(\frac{V_3}{V_2}\right)^2 = 1 - 1.2\left(\frac{3}{6.75}\right)^2 = 0.763,\ \text{or,}\ \mathbf{76.3\ \%}\ \textbf{(Ans.)}$$

Example 2.44. *A reaction turbine and its draft tube have a vertical axis. The pressure head in the spiral casing at inlet is 48 m above atmospheric pressure and the velocity of water is 6 m/s. The water flow through the tube is 2.1 m³/s, and the hydraulic and overall efficiencies are 83 per cent and 80 per cent respectively. The top of the draft tube is 1.2 m below the centre line of the spiral casing while the tail race is 3.9 m below the top of the draft tube. The diameter of the draft tube at inlet is 0·75 m and that at the tail race level 1.05 m. Determine :*

(i) *Total head across the turbine,* **(ii)** *Shaft power,*

(iii) *Head lost in friction in turbine and draft tube, and*

(iv) *Power lost in mechanical friction.*

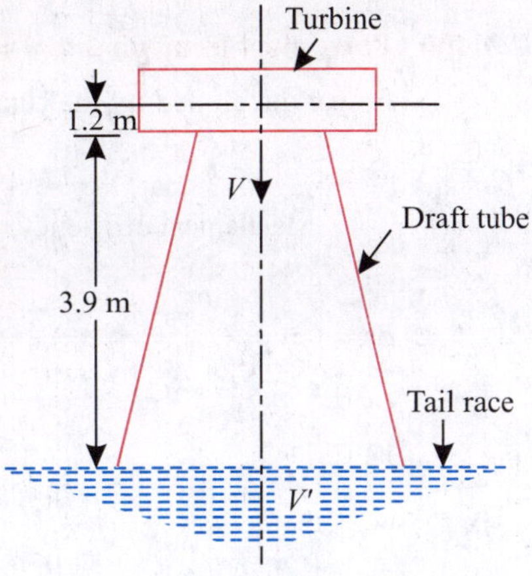

Fig. 2.50

Solution. Pressure head in the spiral casing = 48 m (above atmospheric pressure)

Velocity of water, $V = 6$ m/s

Discharge through the draft tube, $Q = 2.1\ m^3/s$

Hydraulic efficiency, $\eta_h = 83\%$

Overall efficiency, $\eta_0 = 80\%$

Inlet diameter of draft tube, $d_i = 0.75$ m

Outlet Diameter, $d_0 = 1.05$ m

(i) Total head across the turbine :

Total head across the turbine above the tail race level = Total head in the spiral casing measured above the tail race.

or, $$H = \frac{p}{w} + \frac{V^2}{2g} + (1.2 + 3.9)$$

$$= 48 + \frac{6^2}{2 \times 9.81} + (1.2 + 3.9) = \mathbf{54.93\ m}\ \textbf{(Ans.)}$$

(ii) Shaft power, P :

$$P = \eta_0 \times wQH = 0.8 \times 9.81 \times 2.1 \times 54.93$$
$$= \mathbf{905.3\ kW\ (Ans.)}$$

(iii) Head lost in friction in turbine and draft tube, $(h_{ft} + h_{fd})$:

$$V' = \frac{Q}{\frac{\pi}{4} d_0^2} = \frac{4Q}{\pi d_0^2} = \frac{4 \times 2.1}{\pi \times 1.05^2} = 2.425 \text{ m/s}$$

Head utilized by the turbine $H - h_{ft} - h_{fd} - \dfrac{V'^2}{2g}$

$$= 54.93 - (h_{ft} + h_{fd}) - \frac{2.425^2}{2 \times 9.81} = 54.63 - (h_{ft} + h_{fd})$$

(where, h_{ft} and h_{fd} are the heads lost due to friction in the turbine and draft tube respectively.)

$$\text{Hydraulic efficiency, } \eta_h = \frac{\text{Head utilized by the turbine}}{\text{Head supplied to the turbine}}$$

$$0.83 = \frac{54.63 - (h_{ft} + h_{fd})}{54.93}$$

or, $$h_{ft} + h_{fd} = 54.63 - 0.8 \times 54.93 = \mathbf{10.68\ m\ (Ans.)}$$

(iv) Power lost in mechanical friction, P_f :

Power developed by the runner = Shaft power (P) + power lost in mechanical friction (P_f)
$$= P + P_f$$

$$\text{Mechanical efficiency, } \eta_m = \frac{\text{Shaft power}}{\text{Power developed by the runner}}$$

or, $$\eta_m = \frac{P}{P + P_f}$$

But, $$\eta_0 = \eta_h \times \eta_m, \quad \text{or,} \quad \eta_m = \frac{\eta_0}{\eta_h} = \frac{0.8}{0.83} = 0.9638$$

∴ $$0.9638 = \frac{905.3}{905.3 + P_f}, \quad \text{or,} \quad 0.9638\,(905.3 + P_f) = 905.3$$

or, $$P_f = \frac{905.3}{0.9638} - 905.3 = \mathbf{34\ kW\ (Ans.)}$$

2.9. SPECIFIC SPEED

The **specific speed** *of a turbine is defined as the speed of a turbine which is identical in shape, geometrical dimensions, blade angles, gate opening, etc. which would develop unit power when working under a unit head.*

The specific speed may be *derived* as follows :

The overall efficiency (η_0) of any turbine is given by,

$$\eta_0 = \frac{\text{Power available at the shaft of the turbine (shaft power)}}{\text{Power supplied at the inlet of the turbine (water power)}}$$

$$= \frac{P}{wQH} \qquad ...(i)$$

where, P = Shaft power,

Q = Discharge through turbine,

H = Head under which turbine is working, and

w = Weight density of water.

From eqn. (*i*), $P = \eta_0 \times wQH$

or, $P \propto Q \times H$ (as η_0 and w are constant.) ...(*ii*)

Now, let D = Diameter of actual turbine,

N = Speed of actual turbine,

u = Tangential velocity of the turbine,

N_s = Specific speed of the turbine, and

V = Absolute velocity of water.

Then relation between V, u and H is as given below :

$$u \propto V \text{ where, } V \propto \sqrt{H}$$

or, $$u \propto \sqrt{H} \qquad ...(iii)$$

But the tangential velocity u is given by:

$$u = \frac{\pi DN}{60}$$

or, $$u \propto DN \qquad ...(iv)$$

$\therefore$ From eqns. (*iii*) and (*iv*), we have:

$$\sqrt{H} \propto DN$$

or, $$D = \frac{\sqrt{H}}{N} \qquad ...(v)$$

The discharge (Q) through the turbine is given by:

$$Q = \text{Area} \times \text{velocity}$$

But, Area $\propto B \times D$ (where, B = width)

$\therefore$ $\propto D^2$ $(\because B \propto D)$

$\therefore$ $$Q \propto D^2 \sqrt{H}$$

$$\propto \left(\frac{\sqrt{H}}{N}\right)^2 \sqrt{H} \qquad \left[\because \text{From eqn. } (v), D \propto \frac{\sqrt{H}}{N}\right]$$

$$\propto \frac{H}{N^2} \sqrt{H} \propto \frac{H^{3/2}}{N^2}$$

Substituting the value of Q in eqn. (*i*), we get:

$$P \propto \frac{H^{3/2}}{N^2} \times H \propto \frac{H^{5/2}}{N^2}$$

$\therefore$ $$P = K \frac{H^{5/2}}{N^2}$$ where, K = constant of proportionality.

If, $P = 1$ kW and $H = 1$ m, the speed N = specific speed N_s, then by substituting these values in the above equation, we get:

$$1 = \frac{K \times (1)^{5/2}}{N_s^2}, \text{ or, } N_s^2 = K$$

$$\therefore \quad P = N_s^2 \frac{H^{5/2}}{N^2}, \text{ or, } N_s^2 = \frac{N^2 P}{H^{5/2}}$$

$$\therefore \quad N_s = \frac{N\sqrt{P}}{H^{5/4}} \qquad ...(2.33)$$

where, P is in kW and H in metres.

[N_s (S.I units) = 0.86 N_s (metric)]

- Specific speed plays an important role in the *selection of the type of turbine*. By knowing the specific speed of turbine the *performance of the turbine can also be predicted.*
- If a runner of *high specific speed* is used for a given head and power output, the *overall cost of installation is lower*. The selection of too high specific speed reaction runner would reduce the size of the runner to such an extent that the discharge velocity of water into the throat of draft tube would be excessive. This is objectionable because a *vacuum* may be created in the extreme case.
- The runner of *too high specific speed* with high available head *increases the cost of turbine* on account of high mechanical strength required. The runner of *too low specific speed* with low available head increases the cost of generator due to the low turbine speed.
- *An increase in specific speed of turbine is accompanied by lower maximum efficiency and greater depth of excavation of the draft tube*. In choosing a high specific speed turbine, an increase in cost of excavation of foundation and draft tube should be considered in addition to the efficiency. The weighted *efficiency over the operating range of turbine is more important in the selection of a turbine instead of maximum efficiency.*

Note : For N_s –range refer to Table 2.2. (P-163).

Example 2.45. *A turbine is to operate under a head of 25 m at 200 r.p.m . The discharge is 9 m^3/s. If the overall efficiency is 90 per cent, determine :*

(i) Power generated; *(ii) Specific speed of the turbine;*

(iii) Type of turbine. **[N.U.]**

Solution. Head, $H = 25$ m; Speed, $N = 200$ r.p.m.;

Discharge, $Q = 9$ m^3/s; Overall efficiency, $\eta_0 = 90\%$.

(i) Power generated, P :

$$P = \eta_0 \times wQH = 0.9 \times 9.81 \times 9 \times 25 = \mathbf{1986.5\ kW\ (Ans.)}$$

(ii) Specific speed of the turbine, N_s :

$$N_s = \frac{N\sqrt{P}}{H^{5/4}} = \frac{200 \times \sqrt{1986.5}}{(25)^{5/4}} = \mathbf{159.4\ r.p.m.\ (Ans.)}$$

(iii) Type of Turbine :

As the specific speed lies between 80 and 400 (Refer to table 2.2), the turbine is a **Francis turbine. (Ans.)**

Example 2.46. *A Pelton wheel generates 8000 kW under a net head of 130 m at a speed of 200 r.p.m. Assuming the co-efficient of velocity for the nozzle 0.98, hydraulic efficiency 87 percent, speed ratio 0.46, and jet diameter to wheel diameter ratio* $\frac{1}{9}$, *determine :*

(i) Discharge required, *(ii) Diameter of the wheel,*
(iii) Diameter and number of jets required, and *(iv) Specific speed.*
Mechanical efficiency is 75 per cent. **[GATE]**

Solution. Power generated (shaft power), $P = 8000$ kW

Net head, $H = 130$ m

Speed, $N = 200$ r.p.m.

Co-efficient of velocity, $C_v = 0.98$

Hydraulic efficiency, $\eta_h = 87\%$

Speed ratio, $K_u = 0.46$

Jet diameter to wheel diameter, $\frac{d}{D} = \frac{1}{9}$

Mechanical efficiency, $\eta_m = 75\ \%$

(i) Discharge required, Q :

Overall efficiency, $\eta_0 = \eta_h \times \eta_m = 0.87 \times 0.75 = 0.6525$

Also, $$\eta_0 = \frac{\text{Shaft power}}{\text{Water power}} = \frac{P}{wQH}$$

$$\therefore \quad Q = \frac{P}{\eta_0 wH} = \frac{8000}{0.6525 \times 9.81 \times 130} = \mathbf{9.614\ m^3/s}\ \textbf{(Ans.)}$$

(ii) Diameter of the wheel, D :

$$\text{Speed ratio, } K_u = \frac{u_1}{\sqrt{2gH}}, \quad \text{or,} \quad 0.46 = \frac{u_1}{\sqrt{2 \times 9.81 \times 130}}$$

$$\therefore \quad u_1 = 0.46\sqrt{2 \times 9.81 \times 130} = 23.23 \text{ m/s}$$

Also, $$u_1 = \frac{\pi DN}{60}, \quad \text{or,} \quad D = \frac{60\, u_1}{\pi N}$$

or, $$D = \frac{60 \times 23.23}{\pi \times 200} = \mathbf{2.218\ m}\ \textbf{(Ans.)}$$

(iii) Diameter and number of jets required :

$$\frac{d}{D} = \frac{1}{9};\ d = \frac{D}{9} = \frac{2.218}{9} = 0.2464 \text{ m or } \mathbf{246.4\ mm}\ \textbf{(Ans.)}$$

$$\therefore \quad \text{Area of jet, } a = \frac{\pi}{4} \times d^2 = \frac{\pi}{4} \times (0.2464)^2 = 0.04768 \text{ m}^2$$

$$\text{Velocity of the jet, } V = C_v\sqrt{2gH} = 0.98\sqrt{2 \times 9.81 \times 130} \simeq 49.5 \text{ m/s}$$

$\therefore$ Discharge through one jet, $q = a \times V = 0.04768 \times 49.5 = 2.36 \text{ m}^3/\text{s}$

$$\therefore \quad \text{Number of jets} = \frac{Q}{q} = \frac{9.614}{2.36} = 4.07 \text{ say } \mathbf{4}\ \textbf{(Ans.)}$$

(iv) Specific speed, N_s :

$$N_s = \frac{N\sqrt{P}}{H^{5/4}} = \frac{200 \times \sqrt{8000}}{(130)^{5/4}} = \textbf{40.75 r.p.m. (Ans.)}$$

Example 2.47. *Give the range of specific speed values of the Kaplan, Francis turbines and Pelton wheels. What factors decide whether Kaplan, Francis or a Pelton wheel type turbine would be used in a hydroelectric project.* **[UPSC]**

Solution. • The **specific speed** *of a turbine is defined* as *the speed of a turbine which is identical in shape, geometrical dimensions, blade angles, gate opening, etc. which would develop unit power when working under a unit head.*

- Based on specific speed, the turbines for the project are selected as shown in the Fig. 2.51.
- In general, the selection of a turbine for hydroelectric project is based on the following considerations :

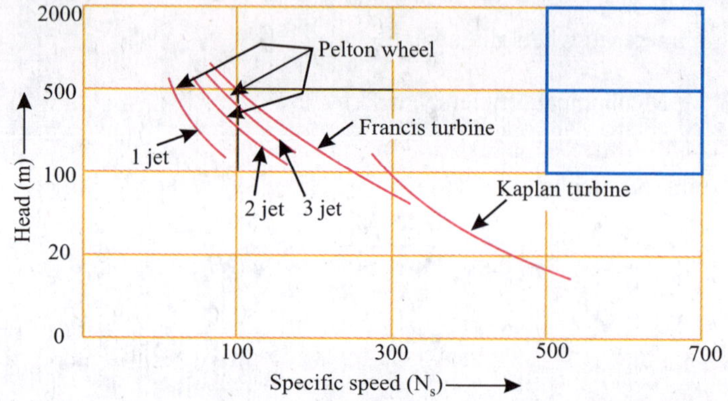

Fig. 2.51

1. For *high heads*, *Pelton wheels* are invariably selected.
2. For *intermediate heads*, *Francis turbines* are selected.
3. For *low head* and *high discharge*, Kaplan turbines are selected.

Example 2.48. *In a hydroelectric station, water is available at the rate of 175 m^3/s under a head of 18 m. The turbines run at a speed of 150 r.p.m. with overall efficiency of 82%. Find the number of turbines required if they have the maximum specific speed of 460.* **[GATE]**

Solution. *Given* : $Q = 175\ m^3/s$; $H = 18$ m; $N = 150$ r.p.m.; $\eta_0 = 82\%$; $N_s = 460$.

Number of turbines required :

$$\text{Specific speed of the turbine,} = \frac{N\sqrt{P}}{H^{5/4}} \quad ...[\text{Eqn. (2.33)}]$$

$$460 = \frac{150\sqrt{P}}{(18)^{5/4}} \quad \text{(where, P is in kW and H is in metres.)}$$

$$\text{or, Power available at turbine shaft, } P = \left[\frac{460 \times (18)^{5/4}}{150}\right]^2 = 12927.5 \text{ kW}$$

$$\text{Power available from turbines} = wQH \times \eta_0 = 9.81 \times 175 \times 18 \times 0.82 = 25339.23 \text{ kW}$$

$$\textit{No. of turbines required} = \frac{25339.23}{12927.5} = 1.96 \text{ say } \mathbf{2} \text{ (Ans.)}$$

2.10. UNIT QUANTITIES

Let us consider a *single unit*. When the head on the unit is changed/varied then the speed of an ungoverned turbine changes. The velocities at various points do not change direction but their magnitudes vary in proportion to the *square root of the head.*

At a given point in the turbine under a head H, let

V = Absolute velocity,

V_r = Relative velocity,

u = Peripheral velocity, and

V', V_r', u' = Corresponding values at a different head H', then as velocity is proportional to $\sqrt{H}$, we have

$$\frac{u}{u'} = \frac{V_r}{V_r'} = \frac{V}{V'} = \frac{\sqrt{H}}{\sqrt{H'}} \quad ...(2.34)$$

If the discharges are Q and Q' then,

$$\frac{Q}{Q'} = \frac{V}{V'} = \frac{N}{N'} = \frac{\sqrt{H}}{\sqrt{H'}} \quad ...(2.35)$$

If the power outputs are P and P' then,

$$\frac{P}{P'} = \frac{QH}{Q'H'} = \frac{\sqrt{H}}{\sqrt{H'}} \times \frac{H}{H'} = \left(\frac{H}{H'}\right)^{3/2} \quad ...(2.36)$$

$$\left(\because \frac{Q}{Q'} = \frac{\sqrt{H}}{\sqrt{H'}}\right)$$

The hydraulic efficiency of the turbine under these two heads may be considered to be nearly same, as the velocity triangles at these heads are similar at a point.

If the various quantities are *reduced to a theoretical one metre head* the comparison of performance data and computations of experimental values on a single unit are *considerably simplified.*

Then,

$$N_u = \frac{N}{\sqrt{H}} \quad ...(2.37)$$

$$Q_u = \frac{Q}{\sqrt{H}} \quad ...(2.38)$$

$$P_u = \frac{P}{H^{3/2}} \quad ...(2.39)$$

The above quantities are called **unit quantities** of a turbine. *Unit speed is the hypothetical speed of the turbine operating under one metre head.* Similarly, other proportionality constants in Eqns. 2.38 and 2.39 are defined.

For presenting the performance of geometrically similar turbines independent of the actual head, discharge and power output the ***unit characteristics*** prove quite helpful. **Geometrically similar turbines will have the same unit characteristics under similar operating conditions.** Thus with the help of a model the performance of a prototype can be predicted within certain limits.

If a turbine is working under different heads the behaviour of the turbine can be easily known from the values of the *unit quantities* as follows :

Let, H_1, H_2 = Heads under which a turbine works,

N_1, N_2 = Corresponding speeds,

Q_1, Q_2 = Corresponding discharges, and

P_1, P_2 = Corresponding powers developed.

Then using eqns. (2.37), (2.38), (2.39), respectively, we obtain

$$N_u = \frac{N_1}{\sqrt{H_1}} = \frac{N_2}{\sqrt{H_2}} \quad ...(2.40)$$

$$Q_u = \frac{Q_1}{\sqrt{H_1}} = \frac{Q_2}{\sqrt{H_2}} \quad ...(2.41)$$

$$P_u = \frac{P_1}{H_1^{3/2}} = \frac{P_2}{H_2^{3/2}} \quad ...(2.42)$$

Example 2.49. *A turbine is to operate under a head of 25 m at 200 r.p.m. The discharge is 9 m³/s. If the efficiency is 90 per cent determine the performance of the turbine under a head of 20 m.* **[M.U]**

Solution. Head under which turbine works, H_1 = 25 m

Speed of the turbine, N_1 = 200 r.p.m.

Discharge through the turbine, Q_1 = 9 m³/s

Efficiency (overall), η_0 = 90%

Performance of turbine under a head of 20 m; N_2, Q_2, P_2 :

Performance of the turbine under a head, H_2 = 20 m means to find speed (N_2), discharge (Q_2), and power generated (P_2) by the turbine when working under a head of 20 m.

Overall efficiency,

$$\eta_0 = \frac{\text{Shaft power}}{\text{Water power}} = \frac{P}{wQH} = \frac{P_1}{wQ_1H_1}$$

$$\therefore \quad P_1 = \eta_0 \times wQ_1H_1 = 0.9 \times 9.81 \times 9 \times 25 = 1986.5 \text{ kW}$$

Now,

$$\frac{N_1}{\sqrt{H_1}} = \frac{N_2}{\sqrt{H_2}} \quad ...[\text{Eqn. (2.40)}]$$

$$\therefore \quad N_2 = \frac{N_1\sqrt{H_2}}{\sqrt{H_1}} = \frac{200 \times \sqrt{20}}{\sqrt{25}} = \mathbf{178.88 \text{ r.p.m.}} \text{ (Ans.)}$$

and,

$$\frac{Q_1}{\sqrt{H_1}} = \frac{Q_2}{\sqrt{H_2}} \quad ...[\text{Eqn. (2.41)}]$$

$$\therefore \quad Q_2 = \frac{Q_1\sqrt{H_2}}{\sqrt{H_1}} = \frac{9 \times \sqrt{20}}{\sqrt{25}} = \mathbf{8.05 \text{ m}^3/\text{s}} \text{ (Ans.)}$$

and,

$$\frac{P_1}{H_1^{3/2}} = \frac{P_2}{(H_2)^{3/2}} \quad ...[\text{Eqn (2.42)}]$$

$$\therefore \quad P_2 = \frac{P_1 \times (H_2)^{3/2}}{(H_1)^{3/2}} = \frac{1986.5 \times (20)^{3/2}}{(25)^{3/2}} = \mathbf{1421.4 \text{ kW}} \text{ (Ans.)}$$

2.11. MODEL RELATIONSHIP

(i) Head co-efficient, C_H :

The tangential velocity of the runner, $u = K_u\sqrt{2gH} = \dfrac{\pi DN}{60}$

or, $$N = \frac{60K_u\sqrt{2gH}}{\pi D}, \text{ or, } N \propto \frac{\sqrt{H}}{D}$$

$\therefore$ $$ND = \sqrt{H}, \text{ or, } \frac{H}{N^2D^2} = \text{constant} \qquad ...(2.43)$$

The parameter $\dfrac{H}{N^2D^2}$ is called **head co-efficient, C_H.**

(ii) Capacity or flow co-efficient, C_Q :

Discharge through the turbine, Q = Area × velocity = $A \times V_f$

But, $$A \propto D^2, \text{ and, } V_f = K_f\sqrt{2gH} \propto \sqrt{H}$$

$\therefore$ $$Q \propto D^2\sqrt{H}$$

Substituting the value of Q in eqn. (2.43), we obtain:

$$Q \propto D_2 \times ND \propto ND^3$$

or, $$\frac{Q}{ND^3} = \text{constant} \qquad ...(2.44)$$

The parameter, $\dfrac{Q}{ND^3}$ is called the **capacity or flow co-efficient, C_Q.**

(iii) Power co-efficient C_P :

The shaft power available from a turbine,

$$P = \eta_0 \times wQH \propto QH$$

But, $Q \propto ND^3$ and $H \propto N^2D^2$ $\therefore$ $P \propto ND^3 \times N^2D^2$, or, $\propto N^3D^5$

or, $$\frac{P}{N^3D^5} = \text{constant} \qquad ...(2.45)$$

The parameter $\dfrac{P}{N^3D^5}$ is called the **power co-efficient, C_P.**

With the use of above relations it is possible to present the behaviour of a prototype from the test runs made on a geometrically similar model; the model is presumed to have the same values of speed ratio K_u, flow ratio K_f and specific speed N_s. A group of geometrically similar machines are said to belong to a homologous series. All machines of such a series have the same values of C_H, C_Q or C_P or their combinations.

Example 2.50. *A hydro-turbine is required to give 25 MW at 50 m head and 90 r.p.m. runner speed. The laboratory facilities available permit testing of 20 kW model at 5 m head. What should be the model runner speed and model to prototype scale ratio?* **[UPTU]**

Solution. *Given* : P_p = 25 MW; H_p = 50 m; N_p = 90 r.p.m.; P_m = 20 kW; H_m = 5 m

$$\mathbf{N_m; \frac{D_p}{D_m} (= L_r):}$$

Prototype specific speed, $(N_s)_p = \dfrac{N_p\sqrt{P_p}}{(H_p)^{5/4}}$ (where, P is in kW)

$$= \frac{90 \times \sqrt{25 \times 10^3}}{(50)^{5/4}} = 107$$

For model, $$107 = \frac{N_m\sqrt{P_m}}{(H_m)^{5/4}} \qquad [\because (N_s)_p = (N_s)_m]$$

or, $$N_m = \frac{107 \times (H_m)^{5/4}}{\sqrt{P_m}} = \frac{107 \times (5)^{5/4}}{\sqrt{20}} = \mathbf{178.89\ r.p.m.}\ \textbf{(Ans.)}$$

For similar turbines $\dfrac{P}{H^{3/2}D^2}$ should be equal.

$$\therefore \quad \frac{P_p}{H_p^{3/2}D_p^2} = \frac{P_m}{H_m^{3/2}D_m^2}$$

or, $$\frac{D_p}{D_m}(= L_r) = \sqrt{\frac{P_p}{P_m} \times \left(\frac{H_m}{H_p}\right)^{3/2}} = \sqrt{\frac{25 \times 10^3}{20} \times \left(\frac{5}{50}\right)^{3/2}} = \mathbf{6.287}\ \textbf{(Ans.)}$$

Example 2.51. *A water turbine delivering 10 MW power is to be tested with the help of a geometrically similar 1 : 8 model, which runs at the same speed as the prototype.*

(i) *Find the power developed by the model assuming the efficiencies of the model and the prototype are equal.*

(ii) *Find the ratio of the heads and the ratio of mass flow rates between the prototype and the model.* **[PTU]**

Solution. *Given* : $P_p = 10$ MW; $N_p = N_m$; $\dfrac{L_m}{L_p} = \dfrac{D_m}{D_p} = \dfrac{1}{8}$; $\eta_p = \eta_m$.

(i) Power developed by the model, P_m:

We know that, $P \propto N^3 \times D^5$ ... [Eqn. (2.45)]

(where, N is the speed and D is the diameter.)

$$\therefore \quad P_p \propto N_p^3 D_p^5, \text{ and, } P_m \propto N_m^3 D_m^5$$

or, $$\frac{P_p}{P_m} = \left(\frac{N_p}{N_m}\right)^3 \times \left(\frac{D_p}{D_m}\right)^5 = (1)^3 \times \left(\frac{8}{1}\right)^5 = 8^5 \qquad (\because N_p = N_m)$$

$$\therefore \quad P_m = \frac{P_p}{(8)^5} = \frac{10 \times 10^6}{(8)^5} = \mathbf{305.2\ W}\ \textbf{(Ans.)}$$

(ii) Ratio of heads $\left(\dfrac{H_p}{H_m}\right)$ and ratio of mass flow rates $\left(\dfrac{m_p}{m_m}\right)$:

We know that, $H \propto N^2D^2$ ... [Eq. (2.43)]

$$\therefore \quad \frac{H_p}{H_m} = \left(\frac{N_p}{N_m}\right)^2 \times \left(\frac{D_p}{D_m}\right)^2 = (1)^2 \times (8)^2 = \mathbf{64}\ \textbf{(Ans.)}$$

Also, discharge, $Q \propto ND^3$ ... [Eqn. (2.47)]

$\therefore$ Ratio of mass flow rates, $\dfrac{Q_p}{Q_m} = \dfrac{m_p}{m_m} = \left(\dfrac{N_p}{N_m}\right)\left(\dfrac{D_p}{D_m}\right)^3 = 1 \times (8)^3 = \mathbf{512}$ **(Ans.)**

Example 2.52. *Obtain an expression for the specific speed of a hydraulic tubine and explain its significance. Give the range of speed values of the Kaplan, Francis tubines and Pelton wheels.* **[UPSC]**

Solution. Refer to Article 2.9 and Table 2.2.

Example 2.53. *A 1/5 scale model of a centrifugal pump absorbs 20 kW when pumping against a test head of 8 m at its best speed of 400 r.p.m. If the actual pump works against 32 m head, find the speed and power required for the actual pump. Determine also the quantities of water discharged by the two pumps.* **[UPSC]**

Solution. *Given* : $L_r = \dfrac{D_p}{D_m} = 5$; $P_m = 20$ kW; $H_m = 8$ m, $N_m = 4000$ r.p.m.;

$$H_p = 32 \text{ m}.$$

N_p, P_p; Q_p, Q_m :

Now, $\dfrac{\sqrt{H_p}}{D_p N_p} = \dfrac{\sqrt{H_m}}{D_m N_m}$ (where, suffix p stands for prototype and suffix m for model)

$$\therefore \quad N_p = N_m \times \frac{D_m}{D_p}\sqrt{\frac{H_p}{H_m}} = 400 \times \frac{1}{5} \times \sqrt{\frac{32}{8}} = \mathbf{160\ r.p.m.}\ \textbf{(Ans.)}$$

Also, $\dfrac{P_p}{D_p^5 N_p^3} = \dfrac{P_m}{D_m^5 N_m^3}$

$$\therefore \quad P_p = \left(\frac{D_p}{D_m}\right)^5 \times \left(\frac{N_p}{N_m}\right)^3 \times P_m = (5)^5 \times \left(\frac{160}{400}\right)^3 \times 20 = \mathbf{4000\ kW}\ \textbf{(Ans.)}$$

We know that $P_m = w_m Q_m H_m$

or, $20 \times 20^3 = 9810 \times Q_m \times 8$

$$\therefore \quad Q_m = \frac{20 \times 10^3}{9810 \times 8} = \mathbf{0.255\ m^3/s}\ \textbf{(Ans.)}$$

Also, $\dfrac{Q_p}{D_p^3 N_p} = \dfrac{Q_m}{D_m^3 N_m}$

or, $Q_p = \left(\dfrac{D_p}{D_m}\right)^3 \times \dfrac{N_p}{N_m} \times Q_m = (5)^3 \times \dfrac{160}{400} \times 0.255 = \mathbf{12.75\ m^3/s}$ **(Ans.)**

Example 2.54. *A hydraulic turbine is to develop 1015 kW when running at 120 r.p.m. under a net head of 12 m. Work out the maximum flow rate and specific speed for the turbine if the overall efficiency at the best operating point is 92 per cent. In order to predict its performance, a 1 : 10 scale model is tested under a head of 7.2 m. What would be the speed, power output and water consumption of the model if it runs under the conditions similar to the prototype ?*

Solution. Shaft power, $P = 1015$ kW; Speed, $N = 120$ r.p.m.
Overall efficiency, $\eta_0 = 92\ \%$; Head, $H = 12$ m

Flow rate (Q), Specific speed (N_s) :

$$\eta_0 = \frac{\text{Shaft power}}{\text{Water power}} = \frac{P}{wQH};\ Q = \frac{P}{\eta_0 wH}$$

or, $$\text{Flow rate, } Q = \frac{1015}{0.92 \times 9.81 \times 12} = \mathbf{9.372\ m^3/s}\ \textbf{(Ans.)}$$

$$\text{Specific speed, } N_s = \frac{N\sqrt{P}}{H^{5/4}} = \frac{120\sqrt{1015}}{(12)^{5/4}} = \mathbf{171.2\ r.p.m.}\ \textbf{(Ans.)}$$

Model scale = 1 : 10 (*Given*)

Head under which under model is tested, $H_m = 7.2$ m (*Given*)

N_m, P_m, Q_m :

For similar turbines each of the following parameters must be same for both model and prototype:

(*i*) $$\text{Head co-efficient, } C_H = \frac{H}{N^2D^2};$$

(*ii*) $$\text{Flow co-efficient, } C_Q = \frac{Q}{ND^3}$$

(*iii*) $$\text{Power co-efficient, } C_p = \frac{P}{N^3D^5}$$

(*i*) $$\left(\frac{H}{N^2D^2}\right)_m = \left(\frac{H}{N^2D^2}\right)_p, \text{ or, } \frac{H_m}{N_m^2D_m^2} = \frac{H_p}{N_p^2D_p^2}, \text{ or, } N_m^2 = N_p^2\,\frac{D_p^2}{D_m^2} \times \frac{H_m}{H_p}$$

$$\therefore \textit{ Model speed, } N_m = N_p \times \frac{D_p}{D_m} \times \left(\frac{H_m}{H_p}\right)^{1/2} = 120 \times 10 \times \left(\frac{7.2}{12}\right)^{1/2} = \mathbf{929.5\ r.p.m.}\ \textbf{(Ans.)}$$

(*ii*) $$\left(\frac{Q}{ND^3}\right)_m = \left(\frac{Q}{ND_3}\right)_p, \text{ or, } \frac{Q_m}{N_mD_m^3} = \frac{Q_p}{N_pD_p^3}$$

$\therefore$ *Discharge in the model,*

$$Q_m = Q_p \times \frac{N_m}{N_p} \times \left(\frac{D_m}{D_p}\right)^3 = 9.372 \times \frac{929.5}{120} \times \left(\frac{1}{10}\right)^3 = \mathbf{0.0726\ m^3/s}\ \textbf{(Ans.)}$$

(*iii*) $$\left(\frac{P}{N^3D^5}\right)_m = \left(\frac{P}{N^3D^5}\right)_p, \text{ or, } \frac{P_m}{N_m^3D_m^5} = \frac{P_p}{N_p^3D_p^5}$$

$\therefore$ *Power produced by the model,*

$$P_m = P_p \times \left(\frac{N_m}{N_p}\right)^3 \times \left(\frac{D_m}{D_p}\right)^5 = 1015 \times \left(\frac{929.5}{120}\right)^3 \times \left(\frac{1}{10}\right)^5 = \mathbf{4.72\ kW}\ \textbf{(Ans.)}$$

Example 2.55. *In a hydroelectric generating plant there are four similar turbines of total output 220000 kW. Each turbine is 90 per cent efficient and runs at 100 r.p.m. under a head of 65 m. It is proposed to test the model of the above turbine in a flume where discharge is 0.4 m³/s under a head of 4 m . Determine the size (scale ratio) of the model. Also calculate the model speed and power results expected from the model.* **[P.E.C.]**

Solution. Power available from each turbine $= \dfrac{220000}{4} = 55000$ kW

$$\begin{aligned} \text{Efficiency (overall) of each turbine, } \eta_0 &= 90\% \\ \text{Speed of the turbine, } N &= 100 \text{ r.p.m.} \\ \text{Head, } H &= 65 \text{ m} \\ \text{Discharge through the model, } Q_m &= 0.4 \text{ m}^3/\text{s} \\ \text{Head under which model is tested, } H_m &= 4 \text{ m} \end{aligned}$$

Scale ratio :

Using the relation, $P = \eta_0 \times wQH$, or, $Q = \dfrac{P}{\eta_0 wH} = \dfrac{55000}{0.9 \times 9.81 \times 65} = 95.84 \text{ m}^3/\text{s}$

For similar turbines the following dimensionless parameters must be same for model and prototype :

(*i*) Head co-efficient, $C_H = \dfrac{H}{N^2 D^2}$; (*ii*) Flow co-efficient, $C_Q = \dfrac{Q}{ND^3}$;

(*iii*) Power co-efficient, $C_P = \dfrac{P}{N^3 D^5}$

From the head co-efficient and flow co-efficient it follows that:

$$\frac{Q}{D^2\sqrt{H}} = \text{Constant}; \left(\frac{Q}{D^2\sqrt{H}}\right)_m = \left(\frac{Q}{D^2\sqrt{H}}\right)_p, \text{ or, } \frac{Q_m}{D_m^2\sqrt{H_m}} = \frac{Q_p}{D_p^2\sqrt{H_p}}$$

∴ **Scale ratio :**

$$\frac{D_m}{D_p} = \left[\left(\frac{Q_m}{Q_p}\right)\left(\frac{H_p}{H_m}\right)^{1/2}\right]^{1/2} = \left[\left(\frac{0.4}{95.84}\right)\left(\frac{65}{4}\right)^{1/2}\right]^{1/2} = 0.1297 \text{ or } \mathbf{1 : 7{\cdot}71} \textbf{ (Ans.)}$$

Speed of the model, N_m :

$$\left(\frac{H}{N^2D^2}\right)_m = \left(\frac{H}{N^2D^2}\right)_p, \text{ or, } \frac{H_m}{N_m^2 D_m^2} = \frac{H_p}{N_p^2 D_p^2}, \text{ or, } \frac{N_m^2}{N_p^2} = \frac{H_m}{H_p} \times \frac{D_p^2}{D_m^2}$$

$$\therefore \quad N_m = N_p\sqrt{\frac{H_m}{H_p}} \times \frac{D_p}{D_m} = 100\sqrt{\frac{4}{65}} \times \left(\frac{1}{0.1297}\right) = \mathbf{191.26 \text{ r.p.m.}}$$

Power available from the model P_m :

$$\left(\frac{P}{N^3D^5}\right)_m = \left(\frac{P}{N^3D^5}\right)_p, \text{ or, } \frac{P_m}{N_m^3 D_m^5} = \frac{P_p}{N_p^3 D_p^5}$$

$$P_m = P_p \times \left(\frac{N_m}{N_p}\right)^3 \times \left(\frac{D_m}{D_p}\right)^5 = 55000\left(\frac{191.26}{100}\right)^3 \times (0.1297)^5 = \mathbf{14.12 \text{ kW}}$$

Example 2.56. **(*a*)** *Prove that specific speed can be expressed as* $N_s = 3.13 N_u \sqrt{Q_u \eta_0}$, *where,* N_u = *unit speed,* Q_u = *unit discharge, and* η_0 = *overall efficiency.*

(*b*) *A Kaplan turbine working under a head of 10 m and at a design speed of 250 r.p.m. has a flow rate of 24* m^3/s. *The diameters of the runner and boss/hub are 2 m and 1 m respectively. The inlet and outlet diameters of the draft tube are 2 m and 3 m respectively. The pressure recorded at inlet to the draft tube is 3 m vacuum. The vapour and barometric pressures are 1·6 m and 10 m respectively. The efficiency of the draft tube is 80 per cent. The Thoma's cavitation factor for the turbine is given by the relation,* $\sigma = \eta_d K_f^2 + \lambda K_u^2$, *in which* η_d *is the efficiency of the draft tube,* K_f *is the flow ratio,* K_u *is the speed ratio and* λ *is a dimensionless factor defined by* $\lambda = (p_2 / w - p_{min}/w)/(u^2/2g)$ *in which u is the tangential velocity,* (p_2/w) *is the pressure head at inlet to draft tube, and* (p_{min}/w) *is the minimum pressure head at a point on the blade. If overall efficiency is 90 per cent determine :*

(*i*) *The minimum pressure on the blade;*

(*ii*) *The value of* N_s.

Solution. (*a*) Specific speed (N_s) is given by : $N_s = \dfrac{N\sqrt{P}}{H^{5/4}}$ ...(*i*)

Also power output (shaft power), $P = wQH \times \eta_0 = 9.81\ QH\eta_0$ kW

Substituting the value of P in eqn. (*i*), we get:

$$N_s = \frac{N}{H^{5/4}}\sqrt{9.81\ QH\eta_0} = 3.13\frac{N}{H^{5/4}}\sqrt{QH\eta_0}$$

$$= 3.13 \times \frac{N}{\sqrt{H}} \times \sqrt{\frac{Q}{\sqrt{H}} \times \eta_0} = 3.13\ N_u \sqrt{Q_u \eta_0} \quad \text{...(Proved)}$$

$$\left(\because N_u = \frac{N}{\sqrt{H}},\ Q_u = \frac{Q}{\sqrt{H}}\right)$$

(*b*) Head under which the turbine is working, H = 10 m

Speed of the turbine runner, N = 250 r.p.m.

Flow rate, Q = 24 m^3/s

Runner Diameter, D_0 = 2 m

Diameter of the boss/hub, D_b = 1 m

Inlet diameter of the draft tube, d_i = 2 m

Outlet diameter of the tube, d_0 = 3 m

Vapour pressure, H_v = 1.6 m

Barometric pressure, $\dfrac{p_a}{w}$ = 10 m

The pressure head inlet to the draft tube, $\dfrac{p_2}{w}$ = 3 m vacuum

Efficiency of draft tube, η_d = 80%

Overall efficiency, η_0 = 90%

(*i*) The minimum pressure on the blade, p_{min} :

Discharge, $$Q = \frac{\pi}{4}(D_0^2 - D_b^2) \times V_f = \frac{\pi}{4}(D_0^2 - D_b^2)\, K_f \sqrt{2gH}$$

or, $$= \frac{\pi}{4}(2^2 - 1^2) \times K_f \times \sqrt{2 \times 9.81 \times 10} = 33.0 K_f$$

$\therefore$ $$K_f = \frac{24}{33.0} = 0.727$$

Also, $$u = \frac{\pi D_0 N}{60} = K_u \sqrt{2gH}, \text{ or, } \frac{\pi \times 2 \times 250}{60} = K_u \times \sqrt{2 \times 9.81 \times 10}$$

$\therefore$ $$K_u = \frac{\pi \times 2 \times 250}{60\sqrt{2 \times 9.81 \times 10}} = 1.87$$

Also, $$u = \frac{\pi D_0 N}{60} = \frac{\pi \times 2 \times 250}{60} = 26.18 \text{ m/s}$$

Using the Eqn. (2.32), we have:

$$\frac{p_2}{w} = \frac{p_a}{w} - H_s - \left(\frac{V_2^2 - V_3^2}{2g} - h_f\right)$$

But h_f (head lost in draft tube) $= \dfrac{V_2^2 - V_3^2}{2g} - \eta_d \dfrac{V_2^2}{2g}$ ...[Eqn. (2.33 (*a*)]

$\therefore$ $$\frac{p_2}{w} = \frac{p_a}{w} - H_s - \left[\frac{V_2^2 - V_3^2}{2g} - \left(\frac{V_2^2 - V_3^2}{2g} - \eta_d \frac{V_2^2}{2g}\right)\right] \quad \text{(By substitution)}$$

or, $$\frac{p_2}{w} = \frac{p_a}{w} - H_s - \eta_d \frac{V_2^2}{2g}$$

where, $$\frac{p_2}{w} = -3 + 10 = 7 \text{ m absolute, and}$$

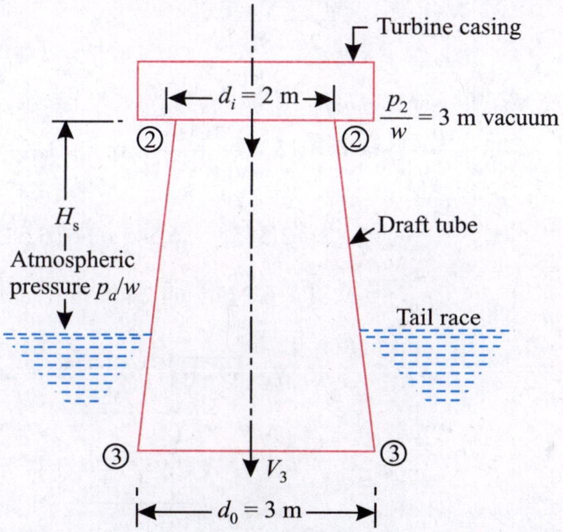

Fig. 2.52

$$V_2 = \frac{Q}{\frac{\pi}{4} d_i^2} = \frac{24}{\frac{\pi}{4} \times 2^2} = 7.64 \text{ m/s}$$

By substituting these values in the above equation, we get:

$$7 = 10 - H_s - 0.8 \times \frac{7.64^2}{2 \times 9.81}$$

$$\therefore \quad H_s = 10 - 7 - 0.8 \times \frac{7.64^2}{2 \times 9.81} = 0.62 \text{ m}$$

The cavitation factor (σ) is given by:

$$\sigma = \frac{H_a - H_v - H_s}{H} \qquad \text{...[Eqn. (2.48)]}$$

By substituting the values, we get:

$$\sigma = \frac{10 - 1.6 - 0.62}{10} = 0.778$$

Also, $\sigma = \eta_d K_f^2 + \lambda K_u^2$ ...*(Given)*

Thus, by substituting the values, we obtain:

$$0.778 = 0.8 \times 0.727^2 + \lambda \times 1.87^2$$

or, $$0.778 = 0.423 + 3.497\lambda$$

$$\therefore \quad \lambda = \frac{0.778 - 0.423}{3.497} = 0.1015$$

But, $$\lambda = \frac{\frac{p_2}{w} - \frac{p_{min}}{w}}{\left(\frac{u^2}{2g}\right)} \qquad \text{...(Given)}$$

or, $$0.1015 = \frac{-3 - \frac{p_{min}}{w}}{\frac{(26.18)^2}{2 \times 9.81}}$$

or, $$-3 - \frac{p_{min}}{w} = 0.1015 \times \frac{(26.18)^2}{2 \times 9.81}, \text{ or, } -3 - \frac{p_{min}}{w} = 3.545$$

or, $$\frac{p_{min}}{w} = -3 - 3.545 = -6.545 \text{ m, or } 6.545 \text{ m (vacuum)}$$

or, $p_{min} = 9.81 \times 6.545 =$ **64.2 kN/m²** *(vacuum)* **(Ans.)**

(ii) The value of N_s :

$$N_s = 3.13\, N_u \sqrt{Q_u}\, \eta_0 \qquad \text{...[Proved at } (a)\text{]}$$

$$= 3.13 \times \frac{N}{\sqrt{H}} \sqrt{\frac{Q}{\sqrt{H}}} \times \eta_0$$

$$= 3.13 \times \frac{250}{\sqrt{10}} \sqrt{\frac{24}{\sqrt{10}}} \times 0.9 = 646.7$$ **(Ans.)**

2.12. SCALE EFFECT

However smooth a model is made, the geometric similarity between the prototype and model cannot be extended to surface roughness. This variation of surfaceness with respect to the size of turbine will cause a *small but appreciable variation in the proportion of the effective head lost due to hydraulic friction*. Thus, the *efficiency of prototype will be different from the corresponding model efficiency*. This aspect is referred to as **scale effect**. It has been observed that with increase in size a geometrically similar mixed or axial flow turbine has greater efficiency than that of the model operating under hydraulically similar conditions.

In order to express the difference of efficiencies as found in tests of model and prototypes, various laws have been proposed. One of the earliest and most generally accepted is the semi-empirical formula suggested by Moody;

$$\frac{1-\eta_p}{1-\eta_m} = \left(\frac{D_m}{D_p}\right)^{0.2} \quad ...(2.46)$$

Ackert suggested the following formula, *considering the frictional loss as a function of Reynolds number*,

$$\frac{1-\eta_p}{1-\eta_m} = \frac{1}{2}\left[1+\left(\frac{D_m}{D_p}\right)^{0.2}\left(\frac{H_m}{H_p}\right)^{01}\right] \quad ...(2.47)$$

where, η_p = Overall efficiency of the prototype,

D_p = Linear dimension of the prototype,

H_p = Head of the prototype,

and, η_m, D_m, H_m = Corresponding values of overall efficiency, linear dimension and head of the model.

These formulae are applicable for the *point of best efficiency.*

Note : (*i*) Moody's formula is based on the assumptions that all losses are due to fluid friction only and the flow is completely turbulent (and that eliminates any effect of Reynolds number).

(*ii*) No scale effect has been observed in the case of Pelton wheel; this may be due to the deterioration in the smoothness of the jet with increasing size, which offsets the benefits due to reduced frictional losses.

Example 2.57. *A model turbine constructed to a scale of 1:10 when tested under a head of 8 m at 400 r.p.m. gave an efficiency of 77 per cent. Determine the r.p.m. of the prototype and the ratio of powers developed by the model and prototype if the prototype works under a head of 100 m. What will be the efficiency of the prototype if scale effect is considered ?*

[Anna University]

Solution. *Given* : Scale ratio = 1 : 10; $\frac{D_p}{D_m} = 10$; $H_m = 8$ m; $N_m = 400$ r.p.m.; $\eta_m = 77\%$;

$H_p = 100$ m.

Speed of the prototype, N_p:

For similarity between model and prototype :

$$\left(\frac{H}{N^2D^2}\right)_m = \left(\frac{H}{N^2D^2}\right)_p, \text{ or, } \frac{H_m}{N_m^2D_m^2} = \frac{H_p}{N_p^2D_p^2}, \text{ or, } N_p^2 = N_m^2 \times \frac{D_m^2}{D_p^2} \times \frac{H_p}{H_m}$$

$$\therefore \quad N_p = N_m \times \frac{D_m}{D_p} \times \left(\frac{H_p}{H_m}\right)^{1/2} = 400 \times \frac{1}{10} \times \left(\frac{100}{8}\right)^{1/2} = \mathbf{141.42\ r.p.m.}\ \textbf{(Ans.)}$$

Ratio of powers developed, $\frac{P_p}{P_m}$:

$$\therefore \quad \left(\frac{P}{N^3 D^5}\right)_m = \left(\frac{P}{N^3 D^5}\right)_p, \text{ or, } \frac{P_m}{N_m^3 D_m^5} = \frac{P_p}{N_p^3 D_p^5}$$

$$\therefore \quad \frac{P_p}{P_m} = \left(\frac{N_p}{N_m}\right)^3 \times \left(\frac{D_p}{D_m}\right)^5 = \left(\frac{141.42}{400}\right)^3 \times (10)^5 = \mathbf{4419.3}\ \textbf{(Ans.)}$$

Efficiency of the prototype when scale effect is considered :

The efficiencies are related by:

$$\frac{N_p}{N_m} = \frac{D_m}{D_p}\sqrt{\frac{H_p}{H_m}}\sqrt{\frac{\eta_p}{\eta_m}}$$

$$\frac{\eta_p}{\eta_m} = \left(\frac{N_p}{N_m}\right)^2 \left(\frac{D_p}{D_m}\right)^2 \frac{H_m}{H_p} = \left(\frac{141.42}{400}\right)^2 (10)^2 \times \frac{8}{100} = 0.9999$$

$$\therefore \quad \eta_p = \eta_m \times 0.9999 = 0.77 \times 0.9999 = 0.7699 \text{ or } \mathbf{76.99\%}\ \textbf{(Ans.)}$$

2.13. PERFORMANCE CHARACTERISTICS OF HYDRAULIC TURBINES

The turbines are normally designed for specific values of head, speed, discharge, power and efficiency (known as the *designed conditions*). But oftenly turbines may be required to operate under conditions different from those for which these have been designed. Thus, to know about their exact behaviour under varying conditions it becomes necessary to conduct tests either on the actual turbines at the site or on their small scale models in a research laboratory. The results so obtained are usually represented graphically and the curves obtained are known as "*Characteristic curves*". These curves are usually plotted in terms of unit quantities (for sake of convenience). The characteristic curves are of the following types :

1. Main or constant head characteristic curves.
2. Operating or constant speed characteristic curves.
3. Constant efficiency or iso-efficiency or Muschel curves.

2.13.1. Main or Constant Head Characteristic Curves

- *Head and gate opening are maintained constant.*
- *Speed is varied* by allowing a variable quantity of water to flow through the inlet opening.
- The brake power (P) is then measured mechanically by means of a dynamometer.
- The overall efficiency and unit quantities are then calculated by using the basic data; these are then plotted *against unit speed as abscissa.*

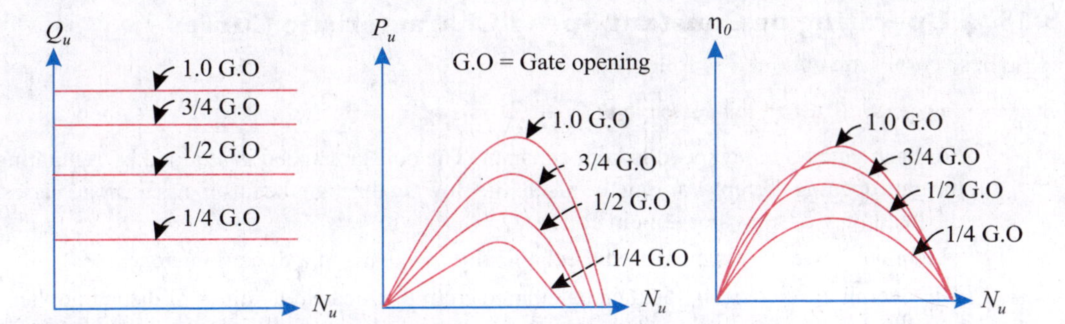

Fig. 2.53. Main characteristic curves of Pelton wheel.

Figs. 2.53, 2.54 and 2.55 show the main characteristic curves of Pelton wheel, Francis turbine and Kaplan turbine respectively.

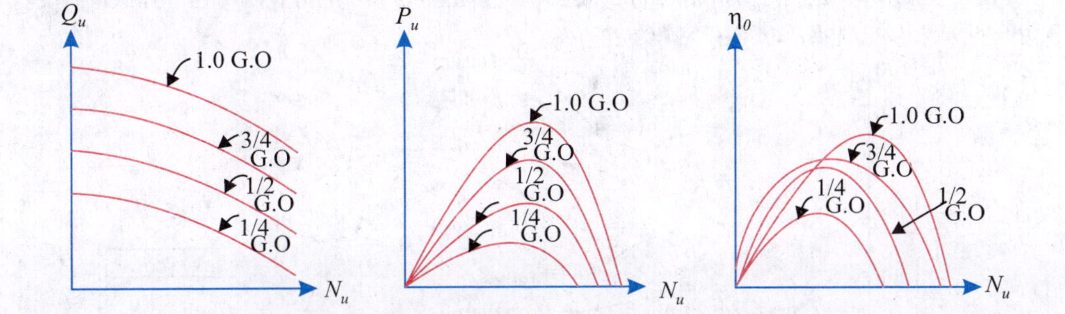

Fig. 2.54. Main characteristic curves of Francis turbine.

The main characteristic curves yield the following information :

- The discharge Q_u for a *Pelton wheel* depends only upon the gate opening and is independent of N_u; the curves for Q_u are horizontal.
- The curves between Q_u and N_u for a *Francis turbine are falling curves*. This is due to the fact that a *centrifugal head develops which* acts outwards and *opposes* the external head causing flow, eventually decreasing the discharge as the speed increases.
- The curves between Q_u and N_u for a *Kaplan turbine* are *rising curves*; the discharge increases with the increase in speed.

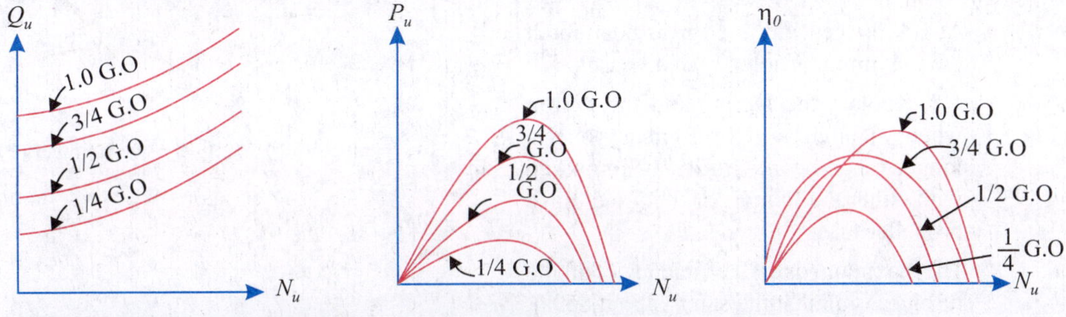

Fig. 2.55. Main characteristic curves of Kaplan turbine.

- The curves between P_u and N_u and those between η_0 and N_u indicate that at a particular speed the efficiency is maximum.

The maximum efficiency for a *Pelton wheel* usually occurs at the *same speed for all gate openings; this speed usually corresponds to a speed ratio of 0.45 . However, the maximum efficiency for a reaction turbine usually occurs at different speeds for different gate openings.*

2.13.2. Operating or Constant Speed Characteristic Curves

These curves are obtained as follows :

(a) Percentage of full load v/s overall efficiency (η_0) curves :

- For each gate opening speed is kept constant. The constant speed is attained by regulating the gate opening thereby varying the discharge flowing through the turbine as the load varies; the head may or may not remain constant.
- The brake power (P) is measured mechanically by means of a dynamometer.
- The overall efficiency (η_0) is then calculated from the measured values of discharge, head and power.
- Further knowing the total load capacity of the turbine the percentage of full load is computed from the measured power and a plot of η_0 *v/s* percentage of full load is prepared.

Fig. 2.56 shows the graphs plotted between *percentage of full load v/s* η_0 for different types of turbines. The following *points are worth noting* :

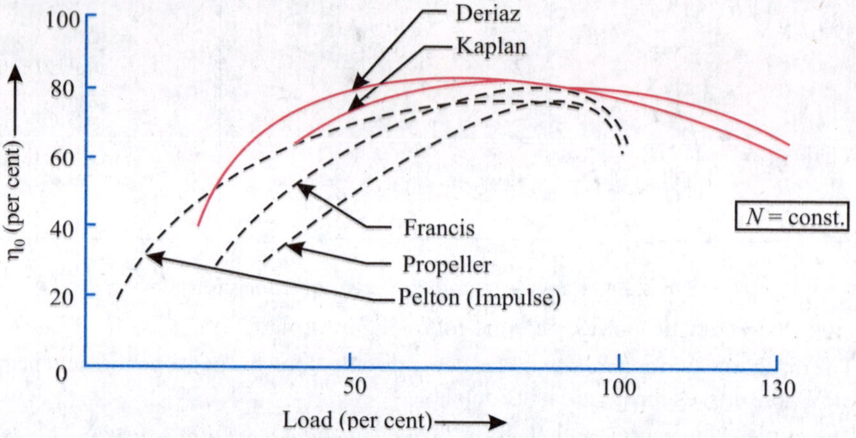

Fig. 2.56. Percentage of full load v/s η_0 curves for hydraulic turbines.

- As the percentage full load increases η_0 also increases (In other words, at reduced loads η_0 is also less).
- At 100 per cent full load η_0 is near about the maximum efficiency in all cases.
- The Kaplan, the Deriaz and the Pelton wheel maintain a high efficiency over a longer range of *part load* as compared with either the Francis or the fixed blade propeller turbine.
- The maximum overall efficiency of all the turbines is almost the same (about 85%).

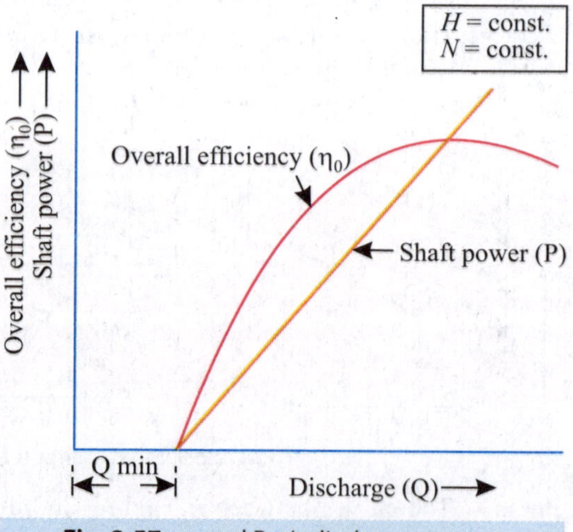

Fig. 2.57. η_0 and P v/s discharge curves.

(b) Overall efficiency (η_0) and output (shaft) power (P) v/s discharge (Q) curves:

Fig. 2.57 shows overall efficiency (η_0) and shaft power (P) *v/s* discharge curves. Q_{min} is the minimum discharge required to set the turbine runner into motion from its state of rest. These curves yield the following information :

- Shaft power or output power (P) is a straight line, since $P \propto Q$ if H (head) is constant.
- η_0 *v/s* discharge (Q) graph is curvilinear and η_0 increases with Q and remains *nearly* constant beyond a particular value of discharge.

2.13.3. Constant efficiency or iso-efficiency or Muschel curves

Refer to Fig. 2.58. As η–N curve is of parabolic nature, there exits two speeds for one value of efficiency except for maximum efficiency which occurs at one speed only. Corresponding to these values of speeds there are also two values of discharge for each value of efficiency (Q-N curve). Hence on Q-N curve we can plot two points for each value of efficiency and one point for maximum efficiency. By adopting this procedure for different gate openings or heads we can get number of Q-N curves and we can plot on them efficiency points (as described above). The points denoting the same efficiency can now be joined to get constant iso-efficiency curves or Muschel curves (The German word 'Muschel' means shell, indicating shape of curve). The diagram showing these curves is also called Hill diagram (since it looks like top view of a hill). In actual practice unit speed and unit discharge are taken along the co-ordinate axes.

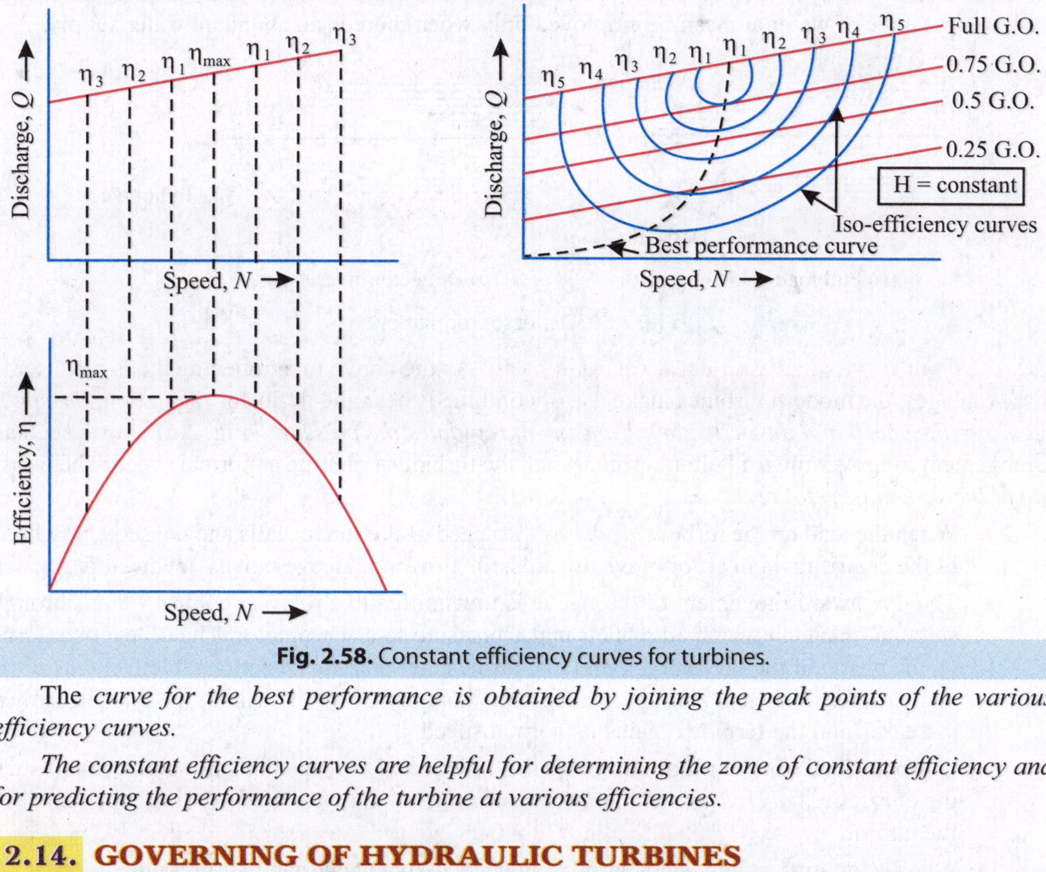

Fig. 2.58. Constant efficiency curves for turbines.

The *curve for the best performance is obtained by joining the peak points of the various efficiency curves.*

The constant efficiency curves are helpful for determining the zone of constant efficiency and for predicting the performance of the turbine at various efficiencies.

2.14. GOVERNING OF HYDRAULIC TURBINES

Governing of hydraulic turbine means *speed regulation*. Governing of a turbine is necessary as a turbine is directly coupled to an electric generator, which is required to run at constant speed under all fluctuating load conditions. This is achieved by means of a *governor* called oil pressure governor.

2.14.1. Governing of Impulse Turbines

In order to regulate the quantity of water rejected from the turbine nozzle and from striking the buckets one of the following methods of regulation may be adapted :

1. Spear regulation. 2. Deflector regulation. 3. Combined spear and deflector regulation.

1. Spear regulation. Refer to Fig. 2.59. In this method the rate of flow is regulated by altering the cross-sectional area of stream by moving the spear to and from inside nozzle. This method of speed regulation is suitable when the *fluctuation of load is small and a relatively large penstock feeds a small turbine*. The disadvantages of this method is that when the load falls all of sudden, the turbine nozzle has to close suddenly which may cause water *hammer* in the *penstock*.

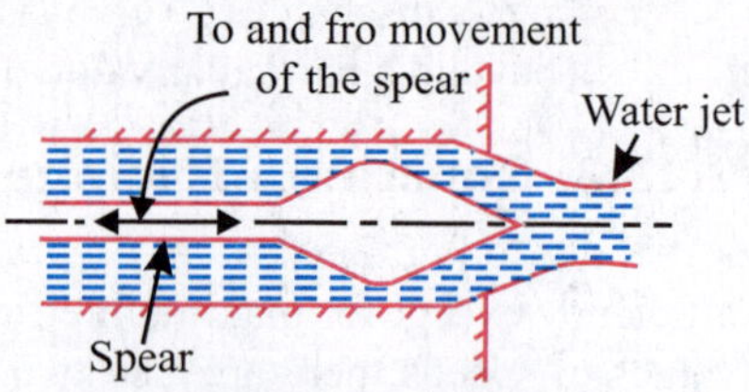

Fig. 2.59. Spear regulation in Pelton wheel.

2. Deflector regulation. Refer to Fig. 2.60. The deflector is generally a plate connected to the oil pressure governor by means of levers. When necessity arises to deflect the jet, the plate can be brought in between the nozzle and buckets, thereby diverting the water away from the runner and directing into the tail race. The use of deflector regulation is restored to *when the supply of water is constant* but the *load fluctuates*. The position of spear can be adjusted by hand. As the nozzle has always a constant opening, it results in wastage of water and can be employed only when there is an abundant water supply.

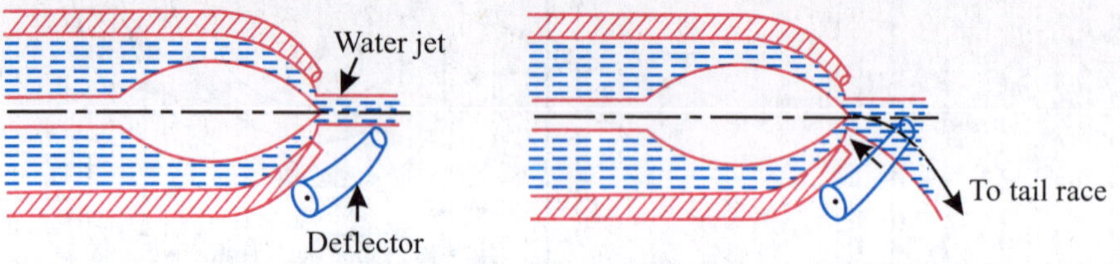

(*a*) Full load (*b*) Deflector diverts part of the jet.

Fig. 2.60. Deflector regulation.

3. Combined spear and deflector regulation. As the above mentioned methods have some disadvantages, the modern turbines make use of combined spear and deflector regulation; *the spear regulates the speed and the deflector arrangement regulates the pressure*. Fig. 2.61 shows such an arrangement for governing of Pelton turbine when the turbine is running at normal speed. The *working of the system is as follows* :

- When the load on the turbine *increases* the speed of the runner falls and consequently balls of the centrifugal governor move inwards; the governor sleeve moves downwards.
- The downward movement of the sleeve is transmitted to a relay or control valve (through suitable linkages) which admits oil under pressure to a servomotor. The oil exerts a force on the piston of the servomotor, and that pushes the spear to a position which *increases* the annular area of the nozzle flow passage; the quantity of water striking the buckets is then increased and the turbine regains its normal speed.
- When the load on the turbine *decreases* the direction of movement of the servomotor is such the nozzle area *decreases* and that allows a smaller quantity of water to strike the runner of the turbine.
- A deflector arrangement safeguards against excessive water hammer pressure.

2.14.2. Governing of Reaction Turbines

In a reaction turbine the discharge is controlled *by varying the area of flow between adjacent guide vanes*. The guide vanes are connected to the regulating ring through links. The regulating ring is connected to the regulating lever through two regulating rods. The regulating ring is thus connected to the regulating shaft which is operated by a servomotor (Fig. 2.62). The servomotor, oil sump, control valve and system of pipes, etc. are similar to that in the governing arrangement of an impulse turbine. The component parts are, however, stronger as the greater energy is required to move the gates as compared to the spear in the nozzle of a Pelton turbine.

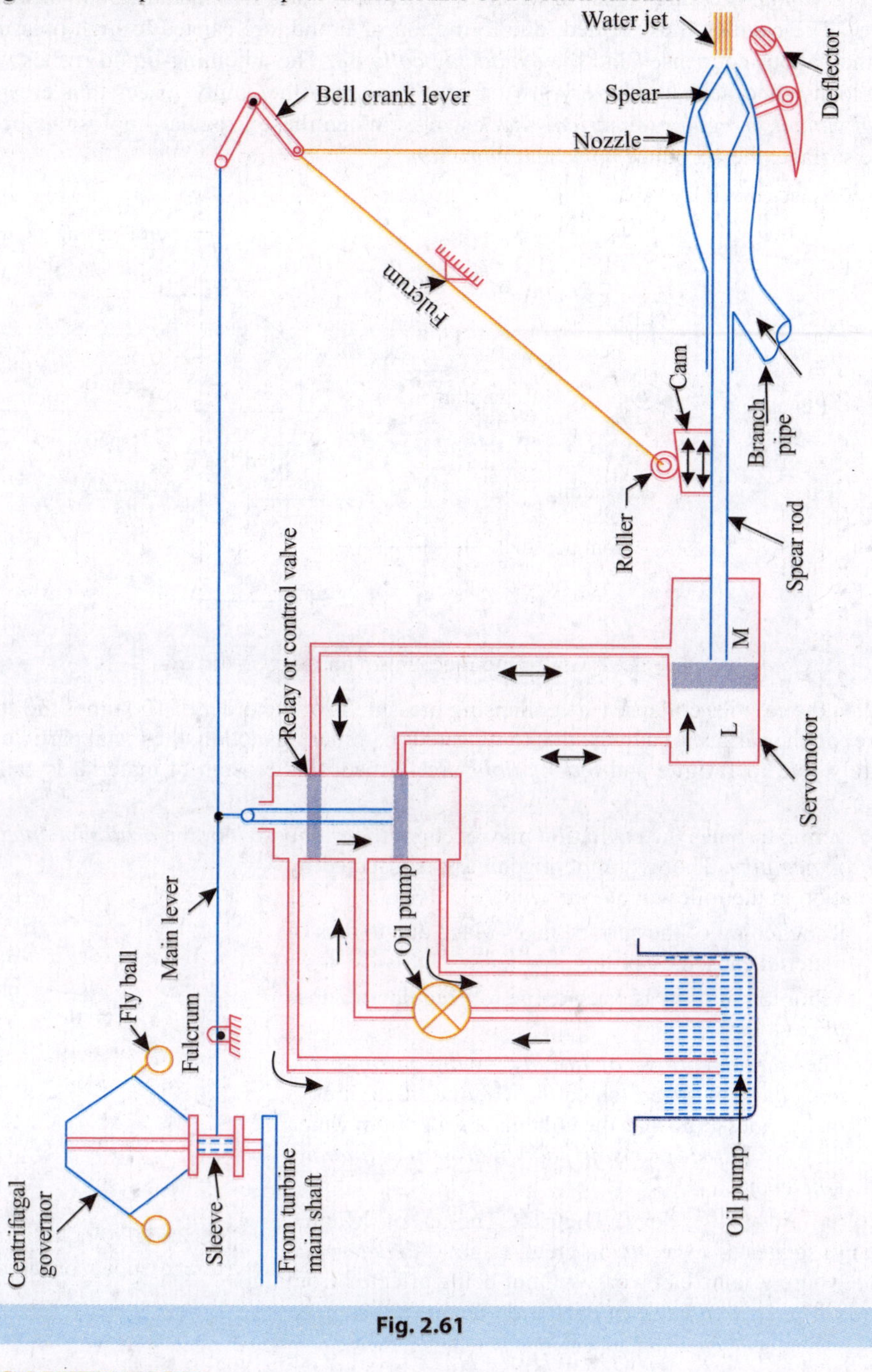

Fig. 2.61

2.15. CAVITATION

The formation, growth, and collapse of vapour filled cavities or bubbles in a flowing liquid due to local fall in fluid pressure is called **cavitation**. When the pressure at any point in a flow field equals the vapour pressure of the liquid at that temperature vapour cavities (bubbles of vapour) begin to appear. It is presumed that a vapour cavity is formed around a dust nuclei which is in the liquid (The vapour pressure values of water at 15° and 20° C are 1.74 m and 2.38 m of water column absolute). The cavities thus formed, due to motion of liquid, are carried to high pressure regions where the vapour condenses and they *suddenly collapse*. The adjoining liquid rushes with a very great velocity (and hence with very great force) to occupy the empty spaces thus created, *causes series of violent, irregular, spherical shock waves*. When these irregular implosions occur on the metallic surface, they produce *noise* and *vibration*.

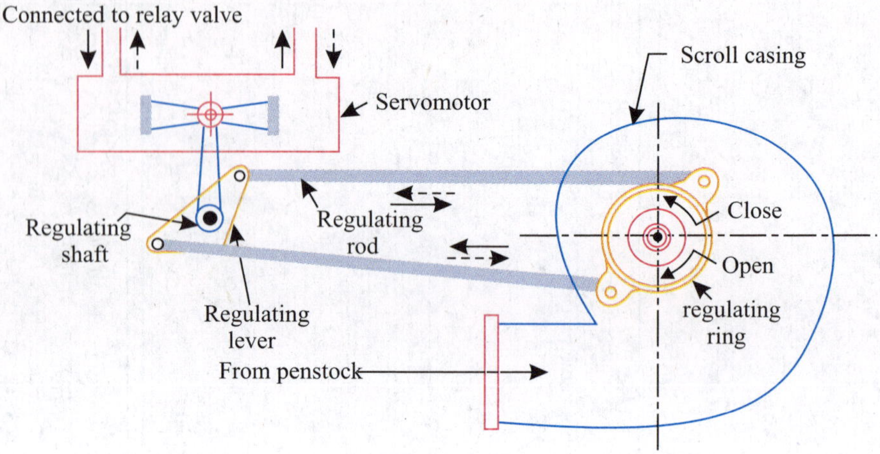

Fig. 2.62. Governing mechanism for reaction turbines.

When the cavities collapse (the collapsing pressure is of the order of 100 times the atmospheric pressure) on the surface of a body, due to repeated 'hammering' action, the metal particle gives way ultimately due to fatigue and *indentations* are formed; this erosion of material is called **pitting** (Fig. 2.63).

In reaction turbines the cavitation may occur at the *runner exit* or the *draft tube inlet* where the *pressure is negative*. The hydraulic machinery is affected by the cavitation in the following *three ways* :

1. Roughening of the surface takes place due to loss of material caused by pitting.
2. Vibration of parts is caused due to irregular collapse of cavities.
3. The *actual volume of liquid flowing through the machine is reduced* (since the volume of cavities is many times more than the volume of water from which they are formed) *causing sudden drop in output and efficiency*.

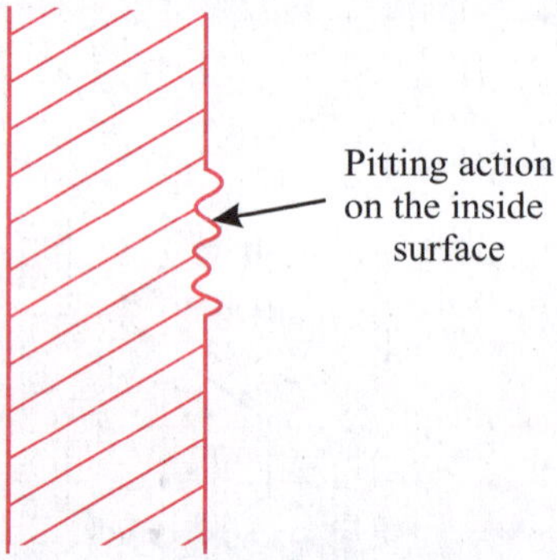

Fig. 2.63. Pitting action on the surface (shown on large scale).

Cavitation factor. Prof. Dietrich Thoma of Munich (Germany) suggested a cavitation factor (sigma) to *determine the zone* where turbine can work without being affected from cavitation. The *critical* value of cavitation factor (σ_c) is given by,

$$\sigma_c = \frac{(H_a - H_v) - H_s}{H} \quad ...(2.48)$$

where, H_a = Atmospheric pressure head in metres of water,

H_v = Vapour pressure in metres of water corresponding to the water temperature,

H = Working head of turbine (difference between head race and tail race level in metres), and

H_s = Suction pressure head (or height of turbine outlet above tail race level in metres).

The values of critical factor *depends upon the specific speed of the turbine.*

The value for σ_c for different materials may be determined with the help of the following empirical relations :

For Francis turbine : $$\sigma_c = 0.625\left(\frac{N_s}{380.78}\right)^2 \quad ...(2.49)$$

For propeller turbine : $$\sigma_c = 0.28 + \left[\frac{1}{7.5}\left(\frac{N_s}{380.78}\right)^3\right] \quad ...(2.50)$$

For Kaplan turbines, values of σ_c obtained by eqn. (2.50) should be *increased by* 10%.

(In the above expressions N_s is in (r.p.m., kW, m) units.

Suction specific speed $(N_s)_{suc.}$: In addition to Thoma's criterion the consideration of suction specific speed provides very useful criterion for *establishing similarity in respect of cavitation in the turbines. The* **suction speed** *may be defined as the speed of a geometrically similar turbine such that when it is developing a power equal to 1 kW, the total suction head H_{sv}* is equal to 1 m (absolute units). It can be proved that specific speed is given by:

$$(N_s)_{suc.} = \frac{N\sqrt{P}}{(\sigma H)^{4/5}} \quad ...(2.51(a))$$

$$\sigma = \left[\frac{N_s}{(N_s)_{suc.}}\right]^{4/5} \quad ...(2.51(b))$$

The eqns. 2.51(a) and (b) give the relation between the two parameters σ and $(N_s)_{suc.}$, both of which are useful for establishing a similarity in respect of cavitation in the model and prototype turbines. The *concept of suction speed, however, is more commonly used in pumps.*

Methods to avoid cavitation :

The following methods may be used to *avoid cavitation* :

1. Runner/turbine may be *kept under water*. But it is not advisable as the inspection and repair of the turbine is difficult. The other method to avoid cavitation zone without keeping the runner under water is *to use the runner of low specific speed.*
2. The *cavitation free runner* may be designed to fulfil the given conditions with extensive research.
3. It is possible to reduce the cavitation effect by *selecting materials which resist better the cavitation effect*. The cast steel is better than cast iron and stainless steel or alloy steel is still better than cast steel.
4. The cavitation effect can be reduced by *polishing* the surface. That is why the cast steel runners and blades are coated with stainless steel.
5. The cavitation may be avoided by selecting a runner of proper specific speed for given head.

Example 2.58. *A Francis turbine works under a head of 25 m and produces 11800 kW while running at 120 r.p.m. The turbine has been installed at a station where atmospheric pressure is 10 m of water and vapour pressure is 0·2 m of water. Calculate the maximum height of the straight draft tube for the turbine.*

Solution. Head under which the turbine works, $H = 25$ m

Power output, $P = 11800$ kW

Speed of the turbine, $N = 120$ r.p.m.

Atmospheric pressure, $p_a = 10$ m of water

Vapour pressure, $H_v = 0.2$ m.

Maximum height of the draft tube, H_s :

$$\text{Specific speed, } N_s = \frac{N\sqrt{P}}{H^{5/4}} = \frac{120\sqrt{11800}}{(25)^{5/4}} = 233.2 \text{ r.p.m.}$$

Critical value of Thoma's cavitation factor for a Francis turbine

$$\sigma_c = 0.625\left(\frac{N_s}{380.78}\right)^2 \qquad \text{...[Eqn. (2.49)]}$$

$$= 0.625\left(\frac{233.2}{380.78}\right)^2 = 0.2344$$

Also,
$$\sigma_c = \frac{H_c - H_v - H_s}{H} \qquad \text{...By definition}$$

or,
$$0.2344 = \frac{10 - 0.2 - H_s}{25}, \text{ or, } 0.2344 \times 25 = 10 - 0.2 - H_s$$

$\therefore$
$$H_s = 10 - 0.2 - 0.2344 \times 25 = 3.94 \text{ m}$$

Hence, *maximum permissible height of the draft tube* = **3.94 m (Ans.)**

2.16. SELECTION OF HYDRAULIC TURBINES

The following points should be considered while selecting right type of hydraulic turbines for hydroelectric power plant :

1. Specific speed. High specific speed is essential where head is low and output is large, because otherwise the rotational speed will be low which means cost of turbo-generator and power- house will be high. On the other hand, there is practically no need of chosing a high value of specific speed for high installations, because even with low specific speed high rotational speed can be attained with medium capacity plants. Refer to Table 2.2.

2. Rotational speed. Rotational speed depends on specific speed. Also the rotational speed of an electrical generator with which the turbine is to be directly coupled, depends on the frequency and number of pair of poles. The *value of specific speed adopted should be such that it will give the synchronous speed of the generator.*

3. Efficiency. The turbine selected should be such that it gives the *highest overall efficiency for various operating conditions.*

4. Partload operation. In general the efficiency at partloads and overloads is less than normal. For the sake of economy the turbine should always run with maximum possible efficiency to get more revenue.

When the turbine has to run at part or overload conditions *Deriaz turbine* is employed. Similarly, for low heads, Kaplan turbine will be useful for such purposes in place of propeller turbine.

5. Cavitation. The installation of water turbines of reaction type over the tail race is affected by *cavitation*. The critical value of cavitation factor must be obtained to see that the turbine works in *safe zone*. Such a value of cavitation factor also affects the design of turbine, especially of Kaplan, propeller and bulb types.

6. Disposition of turbine shaft. Experience has shown that the *vertical shaft* arrangement is better for large-sized reaction turbines, therefore, it is *almost universally adopted.* In case of *large size impulse turbines*, *horizontal shaft arrangement* is mostly employed.

7. Head. (*i*) *Very high heads* (*350 m and above*). For heads greater than 350 m, Pelton turbine is generally employed and there is practically no choice except in very special cases.

(*ii*) *High heads* (*150 m to 350 m*). In this range either Pelton or Francis turbine may be employed. *For higher specific speeds Francis turbine is more compact and economical than the Pelton turbine* which for the same working conditions would have to be much bigger and rather cumbersome.

(*iii*) *Medium heads* (*60 m to 150 m*). A Francis turbine is usually employed in this range. Whether a high or low specific speed unit would be used depends on the selection of the speed.

(*iv*) *Low heads* (*below 60 m*). Between 30 and 60 m heads both Francis and Kaplan turbines may be used. The latter is more expensive but yields a higher efficiency at partloads and overloads. It is therefore preferable for *variable loads. Kaplan turbine is generally employed for heads under 30 m. Propeller turbines are however, commonly used for heads up to 15 m. They are adopted only when there is practically no load variations.*

(*v*) *Very low heads.* For very low heads bulb turbines are employed these days. Although Kaplan turbines can also be used for heads from 2 m to 15 m but they are *not economical.*

Table 2.2. Criteria for Selection of Turbines

S. No.	Type of turbine	Head H(m)	Specific speed (N_s)	Speed ratio (K_u)	Maximum hydraulic efficiency (%)	Remarks
1.	*Pelton*: 1 jet 2 jets 4 jets	up to 2000 up to 1500 up to 500	12 to 30 17 to 50 24 to 70	0.43 to 0.48	89	Employed for very high head.
2.	*Francis*: High-head Medium head Low head	up to 300 50 to 150 30 to 60	80 to 150 150 to 250 250 to 400	0.6 0.9 to	93	Full load efficiency high; partload efficiency lower than Pelton wheel.
3.	*Propeller and Kaplan*	4 to 60	300 to 1000	1.4 to 2	93	High part load efficiency; high discharge with low head.
4.	*Bulb or tubular turbines*	3 to 10	1000 to 1200	6 to 8	91	Employed for very low head–*tidal power plants.*

Overall efficiency (η_0) of all turbines ≃ 85 per cent.

2.17. SURGE TANKS

A **surge tank** *is a small reservoir or tank in which the water level rises or falls to reduce the pressure swings so that they are not transmitted in full to a closed circuit.* In general a surge tank is employed to serve the following *purposes* :

1. To reduce the distance between the free water surface and turbine thereby reducing the water hammer effect (the *water hammer* is defined as the change in pressure rapidly above or below normal pressure caused by sudden changes in rate of flow through the pipe according to the demand of the prime mover) on penstock and also protect upstream tunnel from high pressure rises.
2. To serve as *supply tank* to the turbine when water in the pipe is accelerating during increased load conditions and *storage tank* when the water is decelerating during reduced load conditions.

Types of surge tanks :

The different types of surge tanks in use are :

1. Simple surge tank
2. Inclined surge tank
3. The expansion chamber and gallery type surge tank
4. Restricted orifice surge tank
5. Differential surge tank.

1. Simple surge tank. A simple surge tank is a vertical standpipe connected to the penstock as shown in Fig. 2.64. In the surge tank if the overflow is allowed, the rise in pressure can be eliminated but *overflow surge tank* is seldom satisfactory and usually uneconomical. Surge tanks are built high enough so that water cannot overflow even with a full load change on the turbine. It is always desirable to place the surge tank on ground surface, above the penstock line, at the point where the latter drops rapidly to the powerhouse as shown in Fig. 2.64. Under the circumstances when site for its location is not available the height of the tank should be increased with the help of a support.

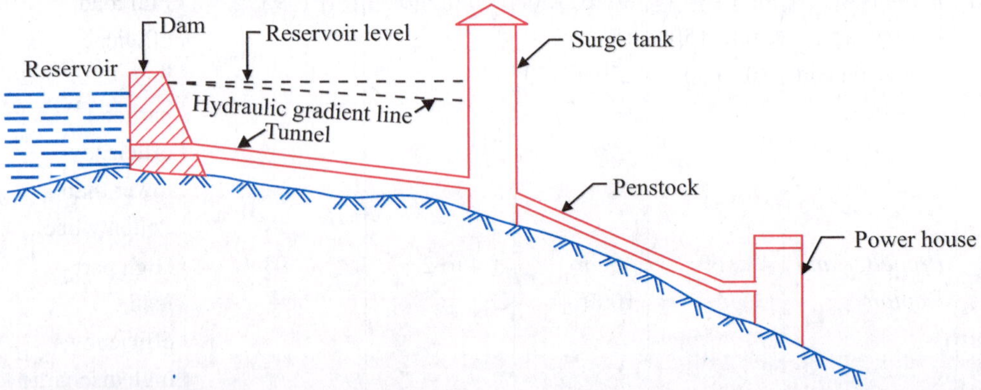

Fig. 2.64. Surge tank on ground level.

2. Inclined surge tank. When a surge tank is inclined (Fig.2.65) to the horizontal its effective water surface increases and therefore, lesser height surge tank is required of the same diameter if it is inclined or lesser diameter tank is required for the same height. But this type of surge tank is more costlier than ordinary type as construction is difficult and is rarely used unless the topographical conditions are in favour.

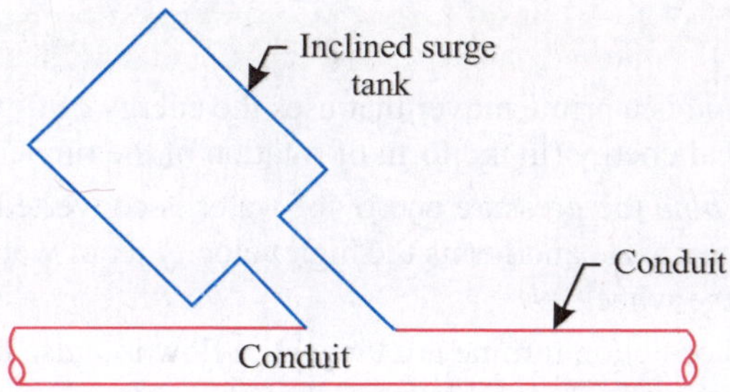

Fig. 2.65. Inclined surge tank.

3. Expansion chamber surge tank. Refer to Fig. 2.66. This type of a surge tank has an expansion tank at top and expansion gallery at the bottom; these expansions *limit the extreme* surges. The 'upper expansion chamber' must be above the maximum reservoir level and 'bottom gallery' must be *below the lowest steady running level in the surge tank*. Besides this the intermediate shaft should have stable minimum diameter.

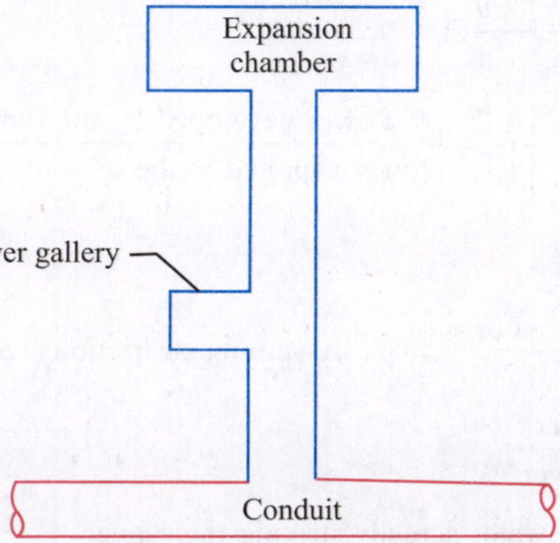

Fig. 2.66. Expansion chamber surge tank.

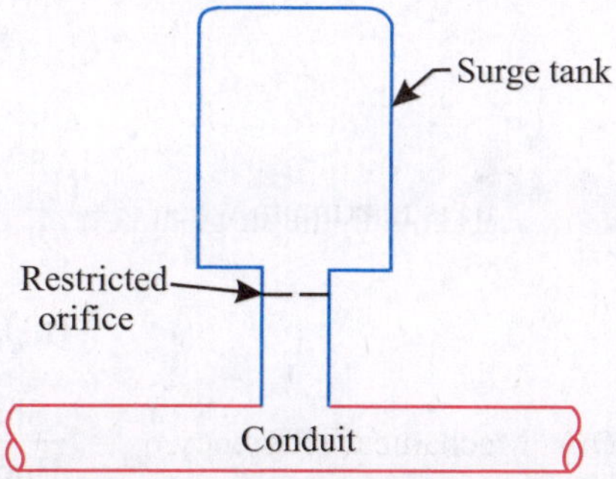

Fig. 2.67. Restricted orifice surge tank.

4. Restricted orifice surge tank. Refer to Fig. 2.67. It is also called *throttled surge tank*. The main object of providing a throttle or restricted orifice is to *create an appreciable friction loss when the water is flowing to or from the tank*. When the load on the turbine is reduced, the surplus water passes through the throttle and a retarding head equal to the loss due to throttle is built up in the conduit. The size of the throttle can be designed for any desired retarding head. *The size of the throttle adopted is usually such as the initial retarding head is equal to the rise of water surface in the tank when the full load is rejected by the turbine* (a case when there is closure of the gate valve).

Advantage. Storage function of the tank can be separated from accelerating and retarding functions.

Disadvantage. Considerable portion of water hammer pressure is transmitted directly into the low pressure conduit.

In comparison to other types of surge tanks these are *less popular*.

5. Differential surge tank. Refer to Fig. 2.68. A differential surge tank has a riser with a small hole at its lower end through which water enters in it. The function of the surge tank depends upon the area of hole.

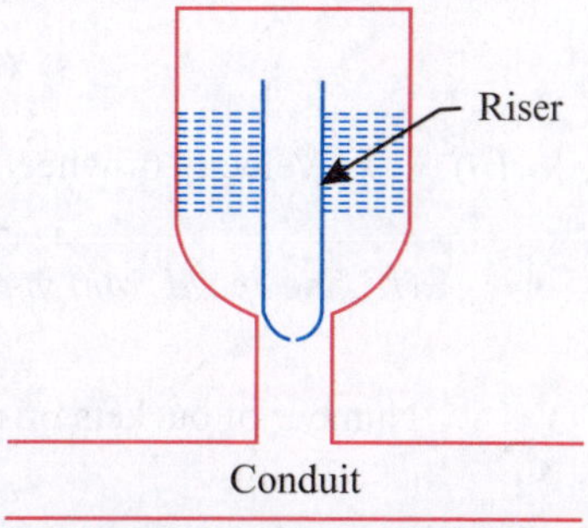

Fig. 2.68. Differential surge tank.

HIGHLIGHTS

1. A *hydraulic turbine* is a prime mover that uses the energy of flowing water and converts it into the mechanical energy (in the form of rotation of the runner).
2. In an *impulse turbine* the pressure energy of water is converted into kinetic energy when passed through the nozzle and forms the high velocity jet of water. The formed water jet is used for driving the wheel.

   The Pelton wheel or Pelton turbine is a tangential flow impulse turbine and is used for high head. Some *important formulae* relating *Pelton wheel* are :

Work done and efficiencies :

(*i*) The work done by the jet on runner per second = $\rho a V_1 (V_{w1} \pm V_{w2})$

(*ii*) The work done per second per unit weight of water striking

$$= \frac{1}{g}(V_{w1} \pm V_{w2}) \times u$$

(*iii*) Hydraulic efficiency, $\eta_h = \dfrac{2(V_{w1} \pm V_{w2}) \times u}{V_1^2}$

$$\left[\eta_h = \frac{\text{Power developed by the runner}}{\text{Power supplied at the inlet of turbine}}\right]$$

η_h is maximum when $u = \dfrac{V_1}{2}$, and

$$(\eta_h)_{max} = \frac{1 + \cos\phi}{2}$$ ...Assuming no friction (*i.e.*, $K = 1$)

(*iv*) Mechanical efficiency, $\eta_m = \dfrac{\text{Shaft power}}{\text{Bucket power}}$

(*v*) Volumetric efficiency, $\eta_v = \dfrac{\text{Volume of water actually striking the runner}}{\text{Total water supplied by the jet to the turbine}}$

(*vi*) Overall efficiency, $\eta_0 = \dfrac{\text{Shaft power}}{\text{Water power}} = \dfrac{P}{wQH}$

Also, $\eta_0 = \eta_h \times \eta_m \times \eta_v$

Design aspects :

(*i*) Velocity of jet, $V_1 = C_v\sqrt{2gH}$ $\left(\text{or, } C_v = \dfrac{V_1}{\sqrt{2gH}}\right)$

(C_v = 0.98 or 0.99)

(*ii*) Velocity of wheel, $u = (u_1 = u_2) = K_u\sqrt{2gH}$ $\left[K_u = \dfrac{u}{\sqrt{2gH}}\right]$

(K_u, the *speed ratio* varies from 0.43 to 0.48).

Number of buckets on a runner $Z = 15 + \dfrac{D}{2d} = 15 + 0.5\, m$

[Where m (jet ratio) $= \frac{D}{d}$; D and d being the pitch diameters of Pelton wheel and the jet diameter respectively. $\frac{D}{d}$ lies between 11 and 16 for maximum hydraulic efficiency; normally jet ratio is adopted as 12 in practice.]

3. In a reaction turbine the runner utilizes both potential and kinetic energies.

Formulae for various reaction turbines are as follows :

(a) Francis turbine :

(*i*) Francis turbine is an inward radial flow reaction turbine having discharge *radial* at outlet which means the angle made by absolute velocity at outlet is 90°, *i.e.* $\beta = 90°$ Then $V_{w2} = 0$ and work done by water on the runner per second per unit weight of water is

$$= \frac{1}{g} V_{w1} u_1$$

(*ii*) Flow ratio, $K_f = \dfrac{V_{f1}}{\sqrt{2gH}}$; K_f varies from 0.15 to 0.30.

(*iii*) Speed ratio, $K_u = \dfrac{u}{\sqrt{2gH}}$; K_u ranges from 0.6 to 0.9.

(*iv*) The ratio of width (B_1) to the diameter of the wheel (D_1), $n = \dfrac{B_1}{D_1}$; n varies from 0.10 to 0.45.

(*v*) Discharge, $Q = K_{t1} \pi D_1 B_1 V_{f1} = K_{t2} \pi D_2 B_2 V_{f2}$

[where K_t is known as vane thickness factor/co-efficient; its value is usually of the order of 0·95 or so (always less than unity)]

(b) Kaplan turbine :

It is an axial flow turbine in which the vanes on the hub are *adjustable*. It is used for low heads where large volumes of water are available. In this turbine a high efficiency is maintained even at partload. The peripheral velocities at inlet and outlet are equal, *i.e.* $u_1 = u_2$

$$\text{Discharge, Q} = \frac{\pi}{4} \times (D_0^2 - D_b^2) \times V_f$$

where, D_0 = Outside diameter of the runner, and
D_b = Diameter of boss (or hub).
V_f = Velocity of flow; ($V_{f1} = V_{f2} = V_f$)

4. *Deriaz turbine*. It is also known as diagonal turbine. Its runner is so shaped that it can be used both as a turbine as well as a pump and hence it may be classified as a reversible type turbine. As such these turbines are amply suitable for pumped storage hydropower plants.

5. *Tubular or bulb turbine*. It is an axial flow turbine with either adjustable or non-adjustable runner vanes. It is employed for low heads, varying from 3 m to 15 m.

6. *Runaway speed* is the maximum speed, governor being disengaged, at which a turbine would run when there is no external load but operating under design head and discharge.

7. A *draft tube* is a pipe of gradually increasing area used for discharging water from the exit of a reaction turbine. It is an integral part of mixed and axial flow turbines. The efficiency of a draft tube (η_d) is given by :

$$\eta_d = \frac{\text{Net gain in pressure head}}{\text{Velocity head at entrance of draft tube}} = \frac{\left(\frac{V_2^2 - V_3^2}{2g} - h_f\right)}{\frac{V_2^2}{2g}}$$

where, V_2 = Velocity of water at inlet of the draft tube, and

V_3 = Velocity of water at outlet of the draft tube.

$$\left[\text{or,} \quad h_f = \frac{V_2^2 - V_3^2}{2g} - \eta_d \times \frac{V_2^2}{2g}\right]$$

8. *Specific speed* (N_s) of a turbine is defined as the speed of a geometrically similar turbine which would develop unit power when working under a unit head. It is given by the relation:

$$N_s = \frac{N\sqrt{P}}{H^{5/4}}$$

where, P = Shaft power, and

H = Net head on the turbine.

Specific speed plays an important role in the *selection of the type of turbine.*

9. *Unit quantities* are the quantities which are obtained when the head on the turbine is unity. They are given as:

$$\text{Unit speed, } N_u = \frac{N}{\sqrt{H}}$$

$$\text{Unit discharge, } Q_u = \frac{Q}{\sqrt{H}}$$

$$\text{Unit power, } P_u = \frac{P}{H^{3/2}}$$

10. The important characteristic curves of a turbine are:
    (*i*) Main or constant head characteristic curves.
    (*ii*) Operating or constant speed characteristic curves.
    (*iii*) Constant efficiency or iso-efficiency or Muschel curves.

11. The formation, growth and collapse of vapour filled cavities or bubbles in a flowing liquid due to local fall in fluid pressure is called **cavitation.** The critical value of cavitation factor (σ_c) is given by

$$\sigma_c = \frac{(H_a - H_v) - H_s}{H}$$

where, H_a = Atmospheric pressure head in metres of water,

H_v = Vapour pressure in metres of water corresponding to the water temperature,

H = Working head of turbine (difference between head race and tail race levels in metres), and

H_s = Suction pressure head (or height of turbine inlet above tail race level) in metres.

The value of critical factor depends upon specific speed of the turbine.

12. A '*surge tank*' is a small reservoir or tank in which the water level rises or falls to reduce the pressure swings so that they are not transmitted in full to a closed circuit.

OBJECTIVE TYPE QUESTIONS

Choose the Correct Answer

1. For an impulse turbine which of the following statements is *correct* :
(*a*) It makes use of a draft tube
(*b*) It is not exposed to atmosphere
(*c*) It is most suited for low head installations
(*d*) It operates with initial complete conversion of pressure head to velocity head.

2. Which of the following statements is *correct* in case of a Pelton wheel :
(*a*) It can operate at optimum efficiency at all high speeds
(*b*) It is kept entirely submerged in water below the tail race.
(*c*) It gives optimum efficiency at runaway speed
(*d*) It operates by converting the available energy fully into kinetic energy before entering the rotor.

3. The effective (or net) head at the turbine is
(*a*) the sum of gross head plus head loss in penstock and the velocity head at the turbine exit.
(*b*) the difference between gross head minus the head loss in penstock
(*c*) the difference between the gross head minus head loss in penstock and the velocity head at the turbine exit
(*d*) the sum of gross head plus the head loss in the penstock.

4. The difference between the power obtained from the turbine shaft and power supplied by water at its entry to the turbine is equal to
(*a*) sum of hydraulic and mechanical losses
(*b*) sum of mechanical and volumetric losses
(*c*) mechanical losses
(*d*) hydraulic losses.

5. Which of the following statements is a definition of the hydraulic efficiency of a turbine?
(*a*) The ratio of power available at the turbine shaft to that supplied to it by runner.
(*b*) The ratio of the power supplied by the runner to the power available at the shaft.
(*c*) The ratio of power utilized by runner to that supplied by the water at entry to the turbine.
(*d*) The ratio of power supplied by water at entry to the power utilized by runner.

6. The power which appears in the expression for the specific speed is the:
(*a*) shaft power
(*b*) water power
(*c*) power into the turbine
(*d*) none of the above.

7. Which of the following statements is *correct*: Runaway speed of a hydraulic turbine is the speed
(*a*) at which there would be no damage to the turbine runner
(*b*) at which the turbine runner can be allowed to run freely without load and with wicket gates wide open
(*c*) corresponding to maximum overload permissible
(*d*) at full load.

8. The specific speed of a turbine is expressed as
(*a*) $\frac{N\sqrt{P}}{H}$ (*b*) $\frac{N\sqrt{P}}{H^2}$
(*c*) $\frac{N\sqrt{P}}{H^{3/4}}$ (*d*) $\frac{N\sqrt{P}}{H^{5/4}}$

9. Which of the following statements is *correct* for a reaction turbine?
(*a*) The outlet must be above the tail race.
(*b*) Water may be allowed to enter a part or whole of wheel circumference.
(*c*) Flow can be regulated without loss.
(*d*) There is only partial conversion of available head to velocity head before entry to rotor.

10. In a reaction turbine the function of a draft tube is to
(*a*) provide safety to turbine
(*b*) prevent air from entering
(*c*) reconvert the kinetic energy to flow energy
(*d*) increase the rate of flow.

11. Which of the following statements with respect to a reaction water turbine is *incorrect*:

(*a*) The spiral casing serves to uniformly distribute water into guide blades

(*b*) The water leaves the turbine at atmospheric pressure

(*c*) The draft tube allows setting of the turbine above the tail race with minimum reduction of available energy

(*d*) The guide vanes direct the flow at proper angle.

12. Which of the following turbines is suitable for specific speed ranging from 300 to 1000 and heads below 30 m:

(*a*) Francis (*b*) Kaplan

(*c*) Propeller (*d*) Pelton.

13. Specific speed of a turbo-machine

(*a*) relates the shape rather than the size of the machine

(*b*) remains unchanged under different conditions of operation

(*c*) has the dimensions of rotational speed

(*d*) is the speed of a machine having unit dimensions.

14. In an outward radial flow turbine energy conversion process is

(*a*) purely by reaction only

(*b*) purely by impulse only

(*c*) partly by impulse and partly by reaction

(*d*) none of the above.

15. Which of the following turbines is least efficient under part load conditions:

(*a*) Propeller (*b*) Kaplan

(*c*) Francis (*d*) Pelton.

16. A surge tank is used to

(*a*) prevent occurrence of hydraulic jump

(*b*) smoothen the flow

(*c*) relieve the pipeline of excessive pressure transients

(*d*) avoid reversal of flow.

17. Which of the following turbines is most efficient at partload operation?

(*a*) Kaplan (*b*) Propeller

(*c*) Francis (*d*) Pelton wheel.

18. With respect to a Kaplan turbine which of the following statements is *incorrect*?

(*a*) It employs large guide vane angles than is the case for a Francis turbine.

(*b*) It is designed for flow velocity of mixed flow type.

(*c*) It has blades of small camber to prevent separation.

(*d*) It can adjust both guide vane and blade angles according to rate of discharge.

19. Specific speed of an impulse turbine (Pelton wheel) ranges from

(*a*) 12 to 70 (*b*) 80 to 400

(*c*) 300 to 1000 (*d*) 1000 to 1200.

20. A turbo-machine becomes more susceptible to cavitation if

(*a*) velocity attains a high value

(*b*) pressure become very high

(*c*) temperature rises above the critical value

(*d*) Thoma's cavitation parameter exceeds a certain limit

(*e*) pressure falls below the vapour pressure.

21. Cavitation damage in turbine runner occurs near the

(*a*) inlet on the convex side of blades

(*b*) outlet on the convex side of blades

(*c*) inlet on the concave side of blades

(*d*) outlet on the concave side of blades.

22. Which of the following serious problems arise from cavitation?

(*a*) Noise and vibration.

(*b*) Damage to blade surface.

(*c*) Fall in efficiency.

(*d*) All of the above.

23. Which of the following statements is *correct*?

(*a*) Muschel curves are the performance plots pertaining to constant efficiency.

(*b*) Operating characteristics curves of a turbine refer to the performance curves drawn at constant speed.

(*c*) Main characteristic curves of a turbine are the performance curves obtained under condition of constant head.

(*d*) All of the above.

(*e*) None of the above.

24. A Kaplan turbine is

(*a*) an inward flow impulse turbine

(*b*) low head axial flow turbine

(*c*) high head axial flow turbine

(*d*) high head mixed flow turbine.

25. An impulse turbine requires

(*a*) high head and small quantity of flow

(*b*) low head and small quantity of flow

(*c*) low head and high rate of flow

(*d*) none of the above.

26. ......of a turbine is defined as the ratio of power available at the turbine shaft to the power supplied by the water jet.
(*a*) Mechanical efficiency
(*b*) Hydraulic efficiency
(*c*) Overall efficiency
(*d*) Volumetric efficiency.

27. The ratio of power developed by the runner to the power supplied by the jet at entrance to the turbine is known as
(*a*) hydraulic efficiency
(*b*) mechanical efficiency
(*c*) volumetric efficiency
(*d*) overall efficiency.

28. The water which acts on the runner blades of a reaction turbine is under a pressure
(*a*) equal to atmospheric
(*b*) below atmospheric
(*c*) above atmospheric
(*d*) none of the above.

29. The runner passages of a reaction turbine are
(*a*) partially filled with water
(*b*) always completely filled with water
(*c*) never filled with water
(*d*) none of the above.

30. The value of speed ratio (K_u) in case of a Francis turbine ranges from
(*a*) 0.2 to 0.3 (*b*) 0.4 to 0.5
(*c*) 0.6 to 0.9 (*d*) none of the above.

31. The value of flow ratio (K_f) in case of a Francis turbine varies from:
(*a*) 0.1 to 0.14 (*b*) 0.15 to 0.30
(*c*) 0.35 to 0.5 (*d*) 0.6 to 0.9.

32. A Kaplan turbine claims which of the following advantages over a Francis turbine?
(*a*) More compact in construction and smaller in size.
(*b*) Partload efficiency is considerably high.
(*c*) Low frictional losses.
(*d*) All of the above.

33. Which of the following draft tubes is suited particularly for helical flow?
(*a*) Conical type draft tube.
(*b*) Elbow type draft tube.
(*c*) Moody's spreading draft tube.
(*d*) None of the above.

34. Critical value of cavitation factor (σ_c) is given by:
(*a*) $\dfrac{(H_a + H_v) - H_s}{H}$
(*b*) $\dfrac{(H_a - H_v) + H_s}{H}$
(*c*) $\dfrac{(H_a - H_v) - H_s}{H}$
(*d*) $\dfrac{(H_a + H_v) + H_s}{H}$.

35. Which of the following surge tank is also called a throttled surge tank?
(*a*) Inclined surge tank.
(*b*) Expansion chamber surge tank.
(*c*) Restricted orifice surge tank.
(*d*) None of the above.

ANSWERS

1. (*d*)	2. (*d*)	3. (*c*)	4. (*a*)	5. (*c*)	6. (*a*)
7. (*b*)	8. (*d*)	9. (*d*)	10. (*c*)	11. (*b*)	12. (*b*)
13. (*a*)	14. (*d*)	15. (*a*)	16. (*c*)	17. (*a*)	18. (*b*)
19. (*a*)	20. (*e*)	21. (*b*)	22. (*d*)	23. (*d*)	24. (*b*)
25. (*a*)	26. (*c*)	27. (*a*)	28. (*c*)	29. (*b*)	30. (*c*)
31. (*b*)	32. (*d*)	33. (*c*)	34. (*c*)	35. (*c*).	

THEORETICAL QUESTIONS

1. What is a hydraulic turbine ?
2. How are hydraulic turbines classified ?
3. Give the comparison between impulse and reaction turbines.
4. With the help of neat diagram explain the construction and working of a Pelton wheel turbine.
5. Derive an expression for hydraulic efficiency of a Pelton wheel.
6. What is the condition for hydraulic efficiency of a Pelton wheel to be maximum ?
7. Derive an expression for maximum hydraulic efficiency of a Pelton wheel.

8. Draw a general layout of a hydroelectric power plant using an impulse turbine and define the following:
   (*i*) Gross head, (*ii*) Net head,
   (*iii*) Hydraulic efficiency, and
   (*iv*) Overall efficiency of the impulse turbine.
9. Draw a schematic diagram of a Francis turbine and explain briefly its construction and working.
10. Draw a general layout of a hydroelectric power plant using a reaction turbine.
11. State the advantages and disadvantages of a Francis turbine over a Pelton wheel.
12. What are the functions of a draft tube ?
13. Why does a Pelton wheel not possess any draft tube ?
14. How do the losses in the draft tube effect the pressure at runner exit ?
15. What is the difference between a propeller turbine and a Kaplan turbine ?
16. Where is Kaplan turbine used ?
17. State the advantages of a Kaplan turbine over Francis turbine.
18. Write a short note on Deriaz turbine.
19. What are tubular or bulb turbines ?
20. What are the advantages and disadvantages of bulb sets compared to Kaplan turbines ?
21. How is specific speed of a turbine defined ?
22. Write a short note on 'scale effect.'
23. What is cavitation? How can it be avoided in reaction turbines ?
24. On what factors does the cavitation in water turbines depend ?
25. Enumerate some methods to avoid cavitation in water turbines.
26. What is governing and how it is accomplished for different types of water turbines ?
27. Sketch and describe a modern method of regulation to maintain a constant speed for either (*a*) Pelton wheel or (*b*) Francis turbine.
28. Show with the help of a line sketch as to how the speed of a reaction water turbine is governed by servomotor ?
29. What is a surge tank ?
30. Which points should be considered while selecting right type of hydraulic turbines for hydroelectric power plant ?

UNSOLVED EXAMPLES

1. A Pelton wheel has a mean bucket speed of 10 m/s with a jet of water flowing at the rate of 0.7 m^3/s under a head of 30 m. The buckets deflect the jet through an angle of 160°. Calculate the power and the efficiency of the turbine. Assume co-efficient of velocity as 0.98.

   [Ans. 186.9 kW; 94.54%]

2. A Pelton wheel having a mean bucket diameter of 1·0 m is running at 1000 r.p.m. The net head on the Pelton wheel is 700 m. If the side clearance angle is 15° and discharge through the nozzle is 0·1 m^3/s, determine power available at the nozzle and hydraulic efficiency of the turbine.

   [Ans. 686.5 kW; 97.18%]

3. The shaft power of a Pelton wheel, the buckets of which are struck by two jets, is 15445 kW. The diameter of each jet is 200 mm. If the net head on the turbine is 400 m, find the overall efficiency of the turbine. Take $C_v = 1.0$.

   [Ans. 70.8%]

4. The jet of water coming out of nozzle strikes the buckets of a Pelton wheel which when stationary would deflect the jet through 165°. The velocity of water at exit is 0·9 times at the inlet and the bucket speed is 0·45 times the jet speed. If the speed of the Pelton wheel is 300 r.p.m. and the effective head is 150 m, determine:
   (*i*) Hydraulic efficiency, and
   (*ii*) Diameter of the Pelton wheel.
   Take co-efficient of velocity, $C_v = 0.98$

   [Ans. (*i*) 92.5%; (*ii*) 1.55 m]

5. A Pelton wheel is required to develop 9193.7 kW at the shaft when working under a head of 300 m. Assuming the values of C_v, K_u (speed ratio) and m (= D/d) as 0.98, 0.45 and 12 respectively, determine:
   (*i*) The number of jets,
   (*ii*) The diameter of the wheel,
   (*iii*) The quantity of water required, and
   (*iv*) The diameter of the jet.
   Take the speed of the wheel as 550 r.p.m. and overall efficiency as 85%.

   [Ans. (*i*) 7; (*ii*) 1.2 m; (*iii*) 3.68 m^3/s; (*iv*) 0.1 m]

6. A Pelton wheel is to be designed to develop 735.5 kW at 400 r.p.m. It is to be supplied with water from a reservoir whose level is 250 m above the wheel through a pipe 900 m long. The pipeline losses are to be 5 per cent of gross head. The co-efficient of friction is 0.005. The bucket speed is to be 0.46 of the jet speed and efficiency of wheel is 85%. Calculate :
   (*i*) Pipeline diameter,
   (*ii*) Jet diameter, and

(*iii*) Wheel diameter. **[Panjab University]**

[Ans. (*i*) 440 mm; (*ii*) 84 mm; (*iii*) 1.48 m]

7. The following data is related to a Pelton turbine:

Brake/shaft power = 126.5 kW
Head = 300 m
Speed = 600 r.p.m.
Co-efficient of velocity, $C_v = 0.98$
Speed ratio, $K_u = 0.45$
Overall efficiency, $\eta_0 = 75\%$

Determine the following :

(*i*) The discharge,
(*ii*) The least jet diameter,
(*iii*) The mean runner diameter jet ratio, and
(*iv*) The number of buckets.

[Panjab University]

[Ans. (*i*) 0.0573 m^3/s; (*ii*) 31 mm; (*iii*) 35.6; (*iv*) 33]

8. A Pelton wheel has a mean bucket speed of 12 m/s and is supplied with water at the rate of 0.7 m^3/s under a head of 30 m. If the buckets deflect the jet through an angle of 160°, find the power and the efficiency of the turbine.

[Madras University and UPSC]

[Ans. 194.12 kW; 93.4%]

9. A jet of water impinges on a series of curved vanes at an angle of 30° to the direction of motion of the vanes while entering and leaves the vanes horizontally. The head under which the jet issues from the nozzle is 30 m, the co-efficient of velocity for the nozzle is 0·9 and the diameter of the jet after leaving the nozzle is 50 mm. The speed of the vanes is 10 m/s and the relative velocity of the water at outlet is 0·8 times the relative velocity at inlet. Calculate :

(*i*) The angle of vane tips at inlet;
(*ii*) The power developed by the jet, and
(*iii*) The efficiency of the system.

[Rajputana University]

[Ans. 50.8°; 8.6 kW; 69.2 %]

10. A Pelton wheel is to be designed to the following specifications :

Power	... 11948 kW
Head	... 381 m
Speed	... 750 r.p.m.
Overall efficiency	... 86%

Jet diameter not to exceed $\frac{1}{16}$ times the wheel diameter. Determine :

(*i*) The wheel diameter.
(*ii*) The number of jets required.
(*iii*) The diameter of the jet.

[Rajasthan University]

[Ans. (*i*) 1 m; (*ii*) 4; (*iii*) 118 mm]

11. The buckets of a Pelton impulse turbine deflect the jet through a total angle of 165° and owing to surface friction the relative velocity of water leaving the bucket is 0·85 times that at entry. Draw the velocity vector diagram at entry and exit and find the ratio of bucket velocity to jet velocity in order that the water shall leave the buckets without whirl. In such a turbine the available head at the nozzle is 650 m, the co-efficient of velocity for the nozzle is 0·97, the jet diameter 100 mm and mean bucket diameter 1·2 m. Using the conditions referred to above determine :

(*i*) Best running speed in r.p.m,
(*ii*) Impulsive force of the buckets at this speed,
(*iii*) Power developed by the buckets, and
(*iv*) Efficiency of buckets.

[UPSC, Ravi Shanker University]

[Ans. (*i*) 786 r.p.m.; (*ii*) 94470 N; (*iii*) 4660 kW; (*iv*) 90.5%]

12. A Pelton wheel, 2.45 m in diameter, operates under the following conditions :

Net head = 370 m; co-efficient of velocity = 0.98; speed ratio = 0.47; relative velocity of water at outlet = 0.90 times that at inlet; deflection of jet = 160°; diameter of the jet = 0·88 m.

Determine the following :

(*i*) The input power to the shaft, and
(*ii*) The r.p.m. of the wheel.

[UPSC Exams.]

[Ans. (*i*) 7549.8 kW; (*ii*) 312.15 r.p.m.]

13. A Pelton wheel has to develop 13230 kW under a net head of 800 m while running at a speed of 600 r.p.m. If the co-efficient of the jet $C_v = 0.97$, speed ratio $K_u = 0{\cdot}46$ and the ratio of jet diameter is $\frac{1}{16}$ of wheel diameter, determine the following :

(*i*) The diameter of the pitch circle,
(*ii*) The diameter of each jet,
(*iii*) The quantity of water supplied to the wheel, and
(*iv*) The number of jets required.

Assume overall efficiency as 85 percent.

[UPSC; AMIE]

[Ans. 1.834 m; 114.6 mm; 1.254 m^3/s; 2]

14. In a Pelton wheel the buckets deflect the jet by 170° and the relative velocity is reduced by 12% due to bucket friction. For a speed ratio of 0.47, calculate from first principles the hydraulic efficiency of the wheel.

The bucket circle diameter of the wheel is 0.9 m and there is one jet for which $C_v = 0.98$. The actual efficiency of the wheel is 0.9 times its theoretical efficiency. The wheel develops 1700 kW under a head of 550 m. Calculate :

(*i*) The speed of wheel in r.p.m. and

(*ii*) The diameter of the nozzle. **[UPSC]**

[Ans. (*i*) 1035.6 r.p.m; (*ii*) 66 mm**]**

15. An inward flow reaction turbine has external and internal diameters as 0.9 m and 0.45m respectively. The turbine is running at 200 r.p.m. and width of turbine at inlet is 0.2 m. The velocity of flow through the runner is constant and is equal to 1.8 m/s. The guide blades make an angle of 10° to the tangent of the wheel and discharge at the outlet of turbine is radial. Draw the inlet and outlet velocity triangles and determine: (*i*) Relative velocity at inlet, (*ii*) The runner blade angles, (*iii*) Width of the runner at outlet, (*iv*) Head at the inlet of the turbine, (*v*) Power developed; and (*vi*) Hydraulic efficiency of the turbine.

[Ans. (*i*) 1.963 m/s; (*ii*) $\theta = 66.48°$; $\phi = 20.9°$; (*iii*) 0.4 m; (*iv*) 9.97 m; (*v*) 97.8 kW; (*vi*) 98.34%**]**

16. An inward flow reaction turbine of inlet diameter 1·2 m operates under a head of 150 m and requires a discharge of 6 m^3/s at a rotational speed of 400 r.p.m. The guide vane angle is 20° and the water leaves the runner blade axially. If the runner is 0.1 m wide at the inlet, calculate :

(*i*) The torque and power supplied to the shaft, and

(*ii*) The efficiency of the turbine.

[Ravi Shanker University]

[Ans. (*i*) 156 kNm; 6533 kW; (*ii*) 74%**]**

17. The inward flow reaction turbine develops 735 kW at 750 r.p.m. under a net head of 100 m. The guide vanes makes an angle of 15° with the tangent at inlet. The axial length of the blade at inlet is 0.1 times the outer diameter. The radial velocity of flow through the wheel is constant and the discharge from the wheel is radial. The blade thickness blocks 5 per cent of the area of flow at inlet. The hydraulic efficiency of the wheel is 88% and overall efficiency is 84%. Determine :

(*i*) The wheel diameter,

(*ii*) The wheel width, and

(*iii*) The blade angle at inlet.

[Ans. (*i*) 0.574 m; (*ii*) 0.0574 m; (*iii*) $\theta = 38.7°$**]**

18. A Francis turbine has to be designed to develop 367.5 kW under a head of H = 70 m while running at N = 750 r.p.m. Ratio of width of runner to diameter of runner, $n = 0.1$, inner diameter is half the outer diameter. Flow ratio = 0.15, hydraulic efficiency = 95%, mechanical efficiency = 84%. Four percent of the circumferential area of runner to be occupied by the thickness of vanes, velocity of flow is constant and the discharge is radial at exit. Calculate: (*i*) The diameter of the wheel, (*ii*) The quantity of water supplied, and (*iii*) The guide vane angle at inlet and runner vane angles at inlet and exit. **[UPSC Exams.]**

[Ans. (*i*) 0.633 m; (*ii*) 0.67 m^3/s; (*iii*) $\alpha = 11°\ 58'$, $\theta = 76°\ 50'$ $\phi = 24°\ 5'$**]**

19. A Francis turbine with an overall efficiency of 75 percent is required to produce 149.26 kW. It is working under a head of 7.62 m. The peripheral velocity = $0.26\sqrt{2gH}$ and the radial velocity of flow at inlet is $0.96\sqrt{2gH}$. The wheel runs at 150 r.p.m. and the hydraulic losses in the turbine are 22 percent of the available energy. Assuming radial discharge, determine :

(*i*) The guide blade angle,

(*ii*) The wheel vane angle at inlet,

(*iii*) Diameter of the wheel at inlet, and

(*iv*) Width of the wheel at inlet.

[AMIE, Fluid Power Engg.]

[Ans. (*i*) $\alpha = 32.6°$; (*ii*) $\theta = 37.7°$; (*iii*) 0.404 m; (*iv*) 0.17 m**]**

20. Design a Francis turbine runner with the following data :

Net head	... 68 m
Speed of the runner	... 750 r.p.m.
Output	... 330·9 kW.
Hydraulic efficiency	... 94%
Overall efficiency	... 85%
Flow ratio	... 0.15
Breadth ratio	... 0·1

Inner diameter of runner = $\frac{1}{2}$ × outer diameter

Also assume 5 per cent of circumferential area of the runner to be occupied by the thickness of the vanes.

Velocity of flow remains constant throughout and flow is radial at exit.

[Ans. $D_1 = 0.6$ m; $D_2 = 0.3$ m, $B_1 = 0.06$ m; $\alpha = 11°\ 38'$, $\theta = 60°\ 40'$; $\phi = 24°.57'$

21. A Francis turbine has a wheel diameter of 1 m at the entrance and 0.5 m at the exit. The vane angle at the entrance is 90° and the guide vane angle is 15°. The water at the exit leaves the vanes without any tangential velocity. The head is 30 m and the radial component of flow is constant. What would be the speed of the wheel in r.p.m. and vane angle at exit ? State whether the speed calculated is synchronous one or not. If not, what speed would you recommend to couple the turbine with an alternator of 50 Hz ?

[UPSC Exams.]

[**Ans.** 324 r.p.m; 28° 12′; 300 r.p.m.]

22. The following data pertain to an inward flow reaction turbine :

Overall efficiency	... 75%
Power given by the turbine	... 128·7 kW.
Head	... 6 m

The velocity of the periphery of wheel

$$= 0.5\sqrt{2gH}$$

Radial velocity of flow $= 0.5\sqrt{2gH}$

Speed of the wheel = 250 r.p.m.

Hydraulic losses in the turbine = 22 per cent of the available energy.

Determine the following :

(*i*) Guide blade angle at inlet,

(*ii*) The wheel vane angle at inlet,

(*iii*) The diameter of the wheel, and

(*iv*) The width of wheel at inlet.

Assume the discharge to be radial.

[Panjab University]

[**Ans.** (*i*) 34° 48′, (*ii*) 49° 36′; (*iii*) 662 mm; (*iv*) 371 mm]

23. The following data pertain to an inward flow reaction turbine:

Power to be developed	... 625 kW
Speed of the runner	... 1000 r.p.m.
Head	... 100 m
Guide vane angle	... 16°
Internal diameter = 0·6 times the external diameter	
Hydraulic efficiency	... 88%
Overall efficiency	... 86%
Allowance of blade thickness	... 5%
Axial length of blade inlet = 0·1 times the outer diameter	
Radial velocity of flow	... constant

Find the leading dimensions of the runner.

[Jadavpur University]

[**Ans.** $D_1 = 0.527$ m; $D_2 = 0.316$ m; $B_1 = 52.7$ mm; $\theta = 67.5°$; $\phi = 31° 37'$]

24. The following data pertain to a Kaplan turbine : Power available at shaft = 8850 kW; net available head = 5.5 m;

speed ratio = 2.1; flow ratio = 0.67, overall efficiency = 85%.

Assuming that hub diameter of the wheel is 0·35 times the outside diameter, determine :

(*i*) Runner diameter;

(*ii*) Runner speed.

[**Ans.** (*i*) 6.34 m; (*ii*) 65.7 r.p.m.]

25. A Kaplan turbine produces 44000 kW under a head of 24.7 m, with an overall efficiency of 90 per cent. Taking the value of speed ratio as 1.6, flow ratio as 0.5 and the hub diameter as 0.35 times the outside diameter, find the runner diameter and speed of the turbine.

[**Ans.** 5.16 m, 130.7 r.p.m.]

26. The following data pertain to a Kaplan turbine : Shaft power = 13230 kW; Speed = 75 r.p.m; Head = 8 m; Diameter of boss of runner = 0.35 times the external diameter; speed ratio = 2; Flow ratio = 0.6.

Find the efficiency of the turbine.

[**Ans.** 80.7%]

27. A Kaplan turbine develops 1471 kW under a head of 6 m. The turbine is set 2.5 m above the tail race level. A vacuum gaunge inserted at the turbine outlet records a suction head of 3.1 m. If the hydraulic efficiency is 85 per cent, what would be the efficiency of draft tube having inlet diameter of 3 m ? What will be the reading of suction gauge if power developed is reduced to half (735.5 kW), the head and speed remaining constant.

[**Ans.** 68%; 2.6496 m]

28. Calculate the efficiency of a Kaplan turbine developing 2900 kW under a net head of 5 m. It is provided with a draft tube with its inlet (diameter 3 m) set 1.6 m above the tail race level. A vacuum gauge connected to the draft tube indicates a reading of 5 m of water. Assume draft tube efficiency as 78 per cent.

[**Ans.** 90.4%]

29. A conical draft tube is discharging water at outlet with a velocity of 2.5 m/s. Its inlet and outlet diameters are 1 m and 1.5 m respectively. The total length of the draft tube is 6 m and 1.2 m of the length of draft tube is immersed in water. If the atmospheric pressure head is 10.3 m of water and loss of head due to friction in the draft tube is equal to 0.2 × velocity head at outlet of

the draft tube, find: (*i*) Pressure head at inlet, (*ii*) Efficiency of the draft tube.

[Ans. (*i*) 4·27 m (abs.); 76·3%]

30. A hydraulic turbine is to develop 845. kW when running at 100 r.p.m. under a head of 10 m. Work out the maximum flow rate and specific speed for the turbine if the overall efficiency at the best operating point is 92 per cent. In order to predict its performance, a 1:10 scale model is tested under a head of 6 m. What would be the speed, power output and water consumption of the model if it runs under the conditions similar to the prototype ?

[Ans. $Q = 9.37$ m^3/s; $N_s = 163.5$; $N_m = 774.6$ r.p.m.; $Q_m = 0.0726$ m^3/s; $P_m = 3.93$ kW]

31. Determine the maximum height of straight conical draft tube of 13240 kW Francis turbine running at 150 r.p.m., under a net head of 27 m. The turbine is installed at station where the effective atmospheric pressure is 10·6 m of water. The draft tube must sink at least 0·77 m below the tail race. **[Ans.** 2.22 m]

[Hint: Max. height of draft tube = $H_s + 0.77$]

Chapter 3

CENTRIFUGAL PUMPS

3.1. INTRODUCTION

A **pump** *is a contrivance which provides energy to a fluid in a fluid system; it assists to increase the pressure energy or kinetic energy, or both of the fluid by converting the mechanical energy.* The *basic difference* between a *turbine* and *the pump*, from hydrodynamic point of view, is that in the former flow takes place from the *high pressure side to the low pressure side,* whereas in *pump* flow takes place from the *low pressure towards the higher pressure.* Thus in a *turbine* there is *accelerated flow,* while in a *pump*, the flow is *decelerated.*

3.2. CLASSIFICATION OF PUMPS

On the basis of transfer of mechanical energy the pumps can be broadly *classified* as follows:

1. ***Rotodynamic pumps:***
   (*i*) Radial flow pumps
   (*ii*) Axial flow pumps
   (*iii*) Mixed flow pumps .
2. ***Positive displacement pumps.***

In rotodynamic pumps, *increase in energy level is due to a combination of centrifugal energy, pressure energy, and kinetic energy.*

- The energy transfer, *in a radial flow pump*, occurs mainly when the flow is in its *radial path.*
- In an *axial flow pump*, the energy transfer occurs when the flow is in its *axial direction.*
- The energy transfer in a *mixed flow pump* takes place when the flow comprises radial as well as axial components.

The radial flow type pumps are commonly called *centrifugal pumps* (only these pumps will be discussed in this chapter).

Classification of centrifugal pumps:

On the *basis of characteristic features*, the centrifugal pumps are *classified* as follows:

1. *Type of casing*:
   (*i*) Volute pumps (*ii*) Turbine pump or diffusion pump.
2. *Working head:*
   (*i*) Low lift centrifugal pumps .... they work against heads upto 15 m
   (*ii*) Medium lift centrifugal pumps .... used to build up heads as high as 40 m
   (*iii*) High lift centrifugal pumps .... employed to deliver liquids at heads above 40 m.
3. *Liquid handled:*
   (*i*) Closed impeller pump (*ii*) Semi-open impeller pump (or Non-clog pump)
   (*iii*) Open impeller pump.
4. *Number of impellers per shaft:*
   (*i*) Single stage centrifugal pump ... has *one* impeller, usually a low lift pump.
   (*ii*) Multi- stage centrifugal pump ... has *two or more* impellers and pressure is built in steps; used usually for high working heads and the number of stages depends on the head required.
5. *Number of entrances to the impeller:*
   (*i*) Single entry or single suction pump ... water is admitted on one side of the impeller.
   (*ii*) Double entry or double suction pump ... water is admitted from both sides of the impeller; axial thrust is neutralised.
   ... employed for pumping large quantities of fluid.
6. *Relative direction of flow through impeller:*
   (*i*) Radial flow pump ... normally radial flow impellers are used in *all centrifugal pumps*
   (*ii*) Axial flow pump ... designed to deliver huge quantities of water at comparatively low heads; *ideally suited for irrigation purposes.*
   (*iii*) Mixed flow pump ... mostly employed for *irrigation purposes.*

3.3. ADVANTAGES OF CENTRIFUGAL PUMP OVER DISPLACEMENT (RECIPROCATING) PUMP

The centrifugal pump claims the following *advantages* with reference to a positive displacement (reciprocating) pump.

1. The cost of a centrifugal pump is less as it has fewer parts.
2. Installation and maintenance are easier and cheaper.
3. Its discharging capacity is much greater than that of a reciprocating pump.
4. It is compact and has smaller size and weight for the same capacity and energy transfer.
5. Its performance characteristics are superior.
6. It can be employed for lifting highly viscous liquid such as paper pulp, muddy and sewage water, oil, sugar molasses etc.

7. It can be operated at very high speeds without any danger of separation and cavitation.
8. It can be directly coupled to an electric motor or an oil engine.
9. The torque on the power source is uniform, the output fron the pump is also uniform.

However, because of higher efficiency the reciprocating pumps are still employed for high heads and small discharges. A reciprocating pump can build up very high pressures (as high as 700 bar or even more) and as such these pumps are used for lifting oils from very deep oil wells.

3.4. COMPONENT PARTS OF A CENTRIFUGAL PUMP

Refer to Fig. 3.1. A centrifugal pump consists of the following *main components*:

1. Impeller 2. Casing 3. Suction pipe 4. Delivery pipe.

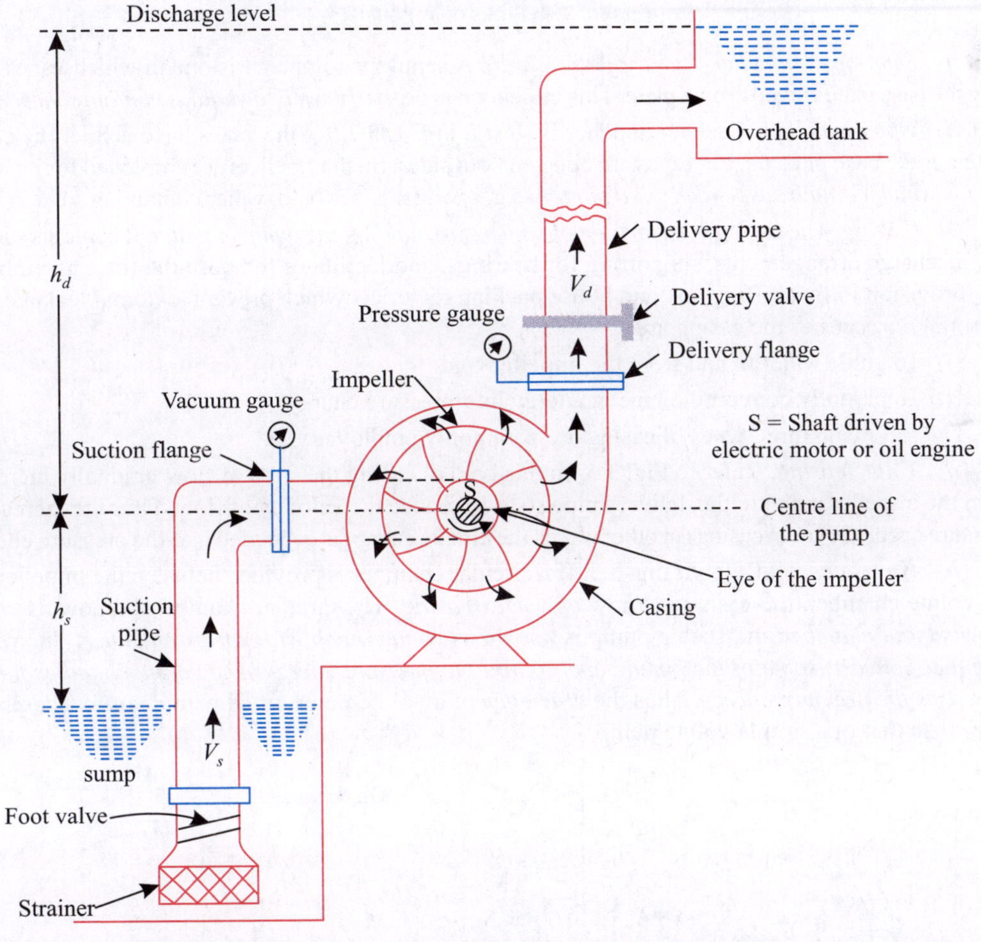

Fig. 3.1. Volute type centrifugal pump–component parts.

1. Impeller. An *impeller* is a wheel (or rotor) with a series of backward curved vanes (or blades). It is mounted on a shaft which is usually coupled to an electric motor.

The impellers are of following *three types*:

(*i*) *Shrouded or closed impeller.* Refer to Fig. 3.2 (*a*). In this type of impeller vanes are provided with metal cover plates or shrouds on both the sides. It provides better guidance for the liquid and has a high efficiency. It is employed when the *liquid to be pumped is pure and relatively free from debris.*

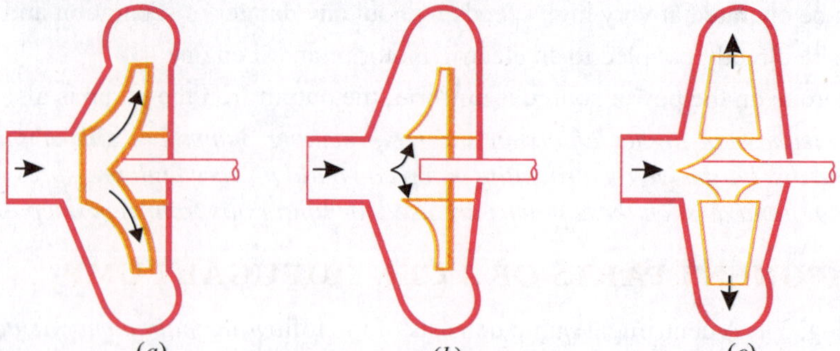

Fig. 3.2. Types of impellers.

(*ii*) *Semi-open impeller.* Refer to Fig. 3.2 (*b*). A semi-open impeller is one in which vanes have only the base plate and no crown plate. This impeller *can be used even if the liquids contain some debris.*

(*iii*) *Open impelller*. Such an impeller is shown in Fig. 3.2 (*c*); the vanes have neither the crown plate nor the base plate *i.e.* the vanes are open on both sides. Such impellers are employed for *pumping liquids which contain suspended solid matter* (e.g. sewage, paper pulp, water containing sand or grit)

2. Casing. The casing is an *airtight chamber surrounding the pump impeller.* It contains suction and discharge arrangements, supporting for bearings, and facilitates to house the rotor assembly. It has provision to fix stuffing box and house packing materials which prevent external leakage. The essential *purposes* of the casing are:

(*i*) To guide water to and from the impeller, and

(*ii*) To partially convert the kinetic energy into pressure energy.

The following three types of casing are commonly employed:

(*a*) *Volute casing*. Refer to Fig. 3.1. In this type of casing the area of flow gradually increases from the impeller outlet to the delivery pipe so as to reduce the velocity of flow. Thus the increase in pressure occurs in voute casing (in other words the kinetic energy is concerted into the pressure energy)

(*b*) *Vortex casing*. Refer to Fig. 3.3. If a circular chamber is provided between the impeller and the volute chamber, the casing is know as *vortex casing.* The circular chamber is know as *vortex or whirlpool chamber* and such a pump is known as *volute pump with vortex chamber*. The *vortex chamber converts some of the kinetic energy into the pressure energy. The volute chamber further increases the pressure energy*. Thus the *efficiency* of a volute pump fitted with a vortex chamber is *more* than that of a simple volute pump.

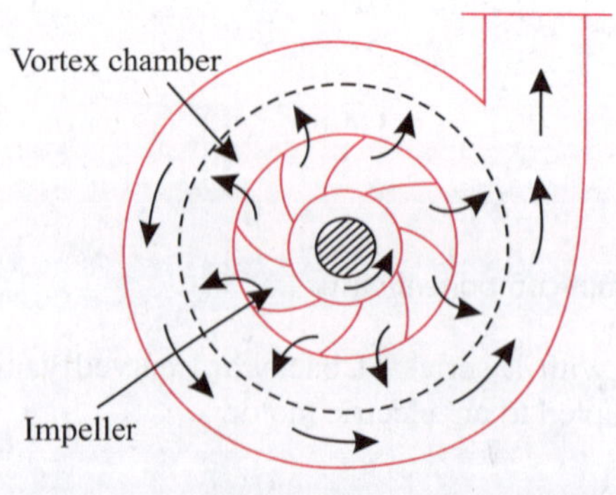

Fig. 3.3. Vortex casing.

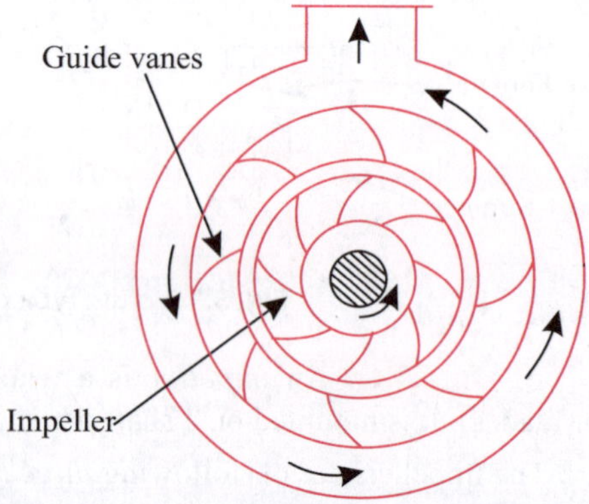

Fig. 3.4. Casing with guide blades.

(*c*) *Casing with guide blades*. Refer to Fig. 3.4. In this type of casing impeller is surrounded by a series of guide blades (or vanes) mounted on a ring which is know as a *diffuser*. The liquid leaving the impeller passes through the passage (having a gradually increasing area) between guide vanes/blades; the velocity of flow *decreases* and the kinetic energy, is converted into pressure energy. *Machines with diffuser blades have rather maximum efficiency, but are less satisfactory when a wide range of operating conditions is required. These pumps are costlier than volute pumps.*

3. Suction pipe. The pipe which connects the centre/eye of the impeller to sump from which liquid is to be lifted is known as *suction pipe.* In order to check the formation of air pockets the pipe is laid *air tight.* To prevent the entry of soid particles, debris etc. into the pump the suction pipe is provided with a strainer at its lower end. The lower end of the pipe is also fitted with a *non-return foot valve* which does not permit the liquid to drain out of the suction pipe when pump is *not working*; this also helps in *priming.*

4. Delivery pipe. The pipe which is connected at its lower end to the outlet of the pump and it delivers the liquid to the required height is known as *delivery pipe*. A *regulating valve* is provided on the delivery pipe to regulate the supply of water.

Following points, regarding *impellers, are* worth noting:

(*i*) Where it is required to pump clear and fresh water, the impeller is *cast as a single piece* and is made of *castiron.* The cast–iron impellers are *cheaper.*

(*ii*) Where *corrosion* due to salt water or chemicals is expected the impellers are made of materials such as *gunmetal, stainless steel etc.*

(*iii*) Machines (pumps) that handle *hot water,* having temperatures above 150°C have to be made of *cast steel impellers with special types of packings.*

(*iv*) Where acids are to pumped, the impeller and all inside surfaces in contact with liquid should be coated with a suitable material to withstand corrosion.

(*v*) Machines (pumps) employed in milk industry are made of *stainless steel* to prevent contamination of the liquids handled.

3.5. WORKING OF A CENTRIFUGAL PUMP

A centrifugal pump works on the *principle that when a certain mass of fluid is rotated by an external source, it is thrown away from the central axis of rotation and a centrifugal head is impressed which enables it to rise to a higher level.*

The *working /operation* of a centrifugal pump is explained *step-wise* below:

1. The delivery valve is closed and the pump is *primed* that is, *suction pipe, casing and portion of the delivery pipe upto the delivery valve are completely filled with the liquid (to be pumped) so that no air pocket is left.*

2. Keeping the delivery valve still closed the electric motor is started to rotate the impeller. The rotation of the impeller causes strong suction or vaccum just at the eye of the casing.

3. The speed of the impeller is gradually increased till the impeller rotates at its normal speed and develops normal energy required for pumping the liquid.

4. After the impeller attains the normal speed the delivery valve is opened when the liquid is continuously sucked (from sump well) up the suction pipe, it passes through the eye of casing and enters the impeller at its centre or it enters the impeller vanes at their inlet tips. This liquid is impelled out by the rotating vanes and it comes out at the outlet tips of the vanes into the casing. Due to impeller action the *pressure head as well as velocity heads of the liquid are increased* (some of this velocity heads is converted into pressure head in the casing and in the diffuser blades/vanes if they are also provided).

5. From casing, the liquid passes into pipe and is lifted to the required height (and discharged from the outlet or upper end of the delivery pipe).

6. So long as motion is given to the impeller and there is supply of liquid to be lifted the process of lifting the liquid to the required height remains continuous.

7. When pump is to be stopped the delivery valve should be first closed, otherwise there may be some backflow from the reservoir.

3.6. WORK DONE BY THE IMPELLER (OR CENTRIFUGAL PUMP) ON LIQUID

The expression for *work done* or energy supplied by the impeller of a centrifugal pump on the liquid flowing through may be derived in the same way as for turbine. Fig . 3.5 shows one vane of the impeller.

The liquid enters the impeller at its centre and leaves at its outer periphery.

Assumptions:

(*i*) Liquid enters the impeller eye in *radial direction,* the whirl component V_{w1} (of the inlet absolute velocity V_1) is *zero* and the flow component V_{f1} equals the absolute velocity itself (*i.e.* $V_{f1} = V_1$); $\alpha = 90°$.

(*ii*) No energy loss in the impeller due to friction and eddy formation.

(*iii*) No loss due to shock at entry.

(*iv*) There is uniform velocity distribution in the narrow passages formed between two adjacent vanes.

Fig. 3.5 shows a portion of the impeller of a centrifugal pump with the one vane and the velocity triangles at the inlet and the outlet tips of the vane.

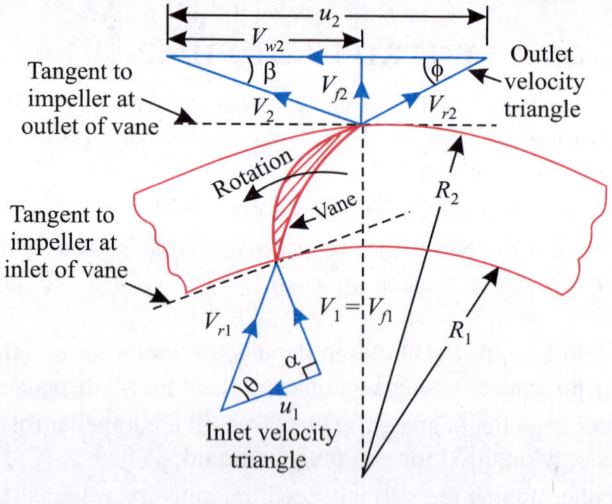

Fig. 3.5. Velocity triangles for an impeller vane.

Let,

D_1 = Diameter of the impeller at inlet ($R_1 = D_1/2$),

N = Speed of the impeller in r.p.m.,

ω = Angular velocity $\left(= \frac{2\pi N}{60} \text{ rad/s}\right)$,

u_1 = Tangential velocity of the impeller at inlet

$$= \frac{\pi D_1 N}{60} \left(= \frac{2\pi R_1 N}{60} \right) = \omega R_1,$$

D_2 = Diameter of the impeller at outlet ($R_2 = D_2/2$),

u_2 = Tangential velocity of impeller at outlet

$$= \frac{\pi D_2 N}{60} \left(= \frac{2\pi R_2 N}{60} \right) = \omega R_2,$$

V_1 = Absolute velocity of water at *inlet*,

V_{w1} = Velocity of whirl at inlet,

V_{r1} = Relative velocity of liquid at inlet,

V_{f1} = Velocity of flow at inlet,

α = Angle made by absolute velocity (V_1) at inlet with the direction of motion of vane,

θ = Angle made by the relative velocity (V_{r1}) at inlet with the direction of motion of vane, and

V_2, V_{w2}, V_{r2}, V_{f2}, β and ϕ are the corresponding values at *outlet*.

While passing through the impeller, the velocity of whirl changes and there is a change of moment of momentum.

Torque on the impeller = Rate of change of moment of momentum

Moment of momentum at inlet = 0 $(\because V_{w1} = 0)$

$$\text{Moment of momentum at outlet} = \frac{W}{g}(V_{w2}R_2)$$

$$\therefore \quad \text{Torque} = \frac{W}{g}(V_{w2}R_2)$$

Work done per second = Torque × angular velocity

$$= \frac{W}{g}(V_{w2}R_2) \times \omega = \frac{W}{g}(V_{w2}u_2) \qquad (\because u_2 = \omega R_2) \quad ...(3.1)$$

Work done per second per unit weight of liquid

$$= \frac{V_{w2}\,u_2}{g} \qquad ...[3.1\ (a)]$$

Eqn. (3.1) has been developed *assuming* flow at inlet to be *radial* (*i.e.* $V_{w1} = 0$). If the flow is *not radial*, the expression for work done may be written as :

$$\text{Work done per second} = \frac{W}{g}(V_{w2}u_2 - V_{w1}u_1)$$

or, Work done per second per unit weight of liquid

$$= \frac{1}{g}(V_{w2}u_2 - V_{w1}u_1) \qquad ...(3.2)$$

Eqn 3.2 is known as the **Euler momentum equation for centrifugal pumps.**

The term $\frac{1}{g}(V_{w2}u_2 - V_{w1}u_1)$ is referred to as ***Euler head*** $\boldsymbol{H_e}$ [*Theoretical head*] where, W = weight of liquid = $w \times Q$, and

$$Q = \text{volume of liquid} = \pi D_1 B_1 \times V_{f1} = \pi D_2 B_2 \times V_{f2}$$

where, B_1 and B_2 are the widths of impeller at inlet and outlet and V_{f1} and V_{f2} are the velocities of flow at inlet and outlet respectively.

Eqn. 3.1 stipulates that for delivering liquid at high heads the peripheral velocity u_2 must be high and vector V_{w2} must be large (so as to provide adequate whirl to the liquid). The increase in u_2 can be obtained by increasing the impeller diameter and speed of rotation. The whirl component V_{w2} however can be augmented by the providing adequate number of vanes of suitable size and shape.

Further, from *outlet triangle*, we have:

$$V_{r2}^2 = V_{f2}^2 + (u_2 - V_{w2})^2, \text{ or, } V_{f2}^2 = V_{r2}^2 - (u_2 - V_{w2})^2 \quad ...(i)$$

Also,
$$V_{f2}^2 = V_2^2 - V_{w2}^2 \quad ...(ii)$$

From expressions (*i*) and (*ii*), we have:

$$V_2^2 - V_{w2}^2 = V_{r2}^2 - (u_2 - V_{w2})^2 = V_{r2}^2 - (u_2^2 + V_{w2}^2 - 2u_2 V_{w2})$$

or,
$$V_2^2 - V_{w2}^2 = V_{r2}^2 - u_2^2 - V_{w2}^2 + 2u_2 V_{w2}$$

or,
$$u_2 V_{w2} = \frac{1}{2}(V_2^2 + u_2^2 - V_{r2}^2)$$

Similarly from *inlet triangle*, we can obtain:

$$u_1 V_{w1} = \frac{1}{2}(V_1^2 + u_1^2 - V_{r1}^2)$$

Substituting in eqn. (3.2), we get:

Work done per second per unit weight of liquid (or H_e)

$$= \frac{V_2^2 - V_1^2}{2g} + \frac{u_2^2 - u_1^2}{2g} + \frac{V_{r1}^2 - V_{r2}^2}{2g} \quad ..(3.3)$$

Eqn. (3.3) indicates that work done on the liquid consists of *three* terms:

– The *first* term $\left(\frac{V_2^2 - V_1^2}{2g}\right)$ represents the increase in kinetic energy or dynamic head.

– The *second* term $\left(\frac{u_2^2 - u_1^2}{2g}\right)$ represents an increase in static pressure.

– The *third* term $\left(\frac{V_{r1}^2 - V_{r2}^2}{2g}\right)$ indicates the change in kinetic energy due to retardation of flow relative to the impeller (this term, therefore, represents conversion of kinetic energy within the impeller itself).

Eqn. (3.3) is sometimes known as the *fundamental equation* of centrifugal pump.

3.7. HEAD OF A PUMP

The head of a centrifugal pump may be expressed in the following ways:

(*i*) Static head; (*ii*) Manometric head; (*iii*) Total, gross or effective head.

(i) **Static head.** The *sum of suction head and delivery head is known as* ***static head.*** This is represented by H_{stat} and is written as:

$$H_{stat} = h_s + h_d \qquad \text{...(3.4)}$$

where, h_s = Suction head (it is the vertical height of the centre line of the pump shaft above the liquid surface in the sump from which the liquid is being raised), and

h_d = Delivery head (it is vertical height of the liquid surface in the tank / reservoir to which the liquid is delivered above the centre line of the pump shaft).

The terms h_s and h_d are known as *static suction lift* and *static delivery lift* respectively.

(ii) **Manometric head.** *The head against which a centrifugal pump has to work is known* as the ***manometric head.*** It is the head measured across the pump inlet and outlet flanges. It is denoted by H_{mano} and is given by the following expressions:

(i) H_{mano} = Head imparted by the impeller to liquid – loss of head in the pump (*i.e.* impeller, and casing)

$$= \frac{V_{w2}u_2}{g} - (h_{Li} + h_{Lc}) \qquad \text{...(3.5)}$$

(where, h_{Li} and h_{Lc} are the losses of head in the *impeller* and *casing* respectively.)

$$= \frac{V_{w2}u_2}{g} \quad \text{...if loss of head in the pump is } \textit{zero}, \qquad \text{...(3.6)}$$

(ii)
$$H_{mano} = H_{static} + \text{losses in pipes} + \frac{V_d^2}{2g}$$

$$= (h_s + h_d) + (h_{fs} + h_{fd}) + \frac{V_d^2}{2g} \qquad \text{...(3.7)}$$

where, h_s = Suction head,

h_d = delivery head,

h_{fs} = Frictional head loss in the suction pipe,

h_{fd} = Frictional head loss in the delivery pipe, and

V_d = Velocity of liquid in delivery pipe.

(iii) H_{mano} = Total head at outlet of the pump – total head at inlet of the pump

$$= \left(\frac{p_2}{w} + \frac{V_2^2}{2g} + z_2\right) - \left(\frac{p_1}{w} + \frac{V_1^2}{2g} + z_1\right) \qquad \text{...(3.8)}$$

where, $\frac{p_2}{w}$ = Pressure head at outlet of pump = h_d,

$\frac{V_2^2}{2g}$ = Velocity head at outlet of the pump

= Velocity head in the delivery pipe = $\frac{V_d^2}{2g}$,

z_2 = Vertical height of the pump outlet from the datum line, and

$\frac{p_1}{w}, \frac{V_1^2}{2g}, z_1$ = corresponding values of pressure head, velocity head and datum head at inlet of the pump $\left(\textit{i.e.,}\ h_s, \frac{V_s^2}{2g} \text{ and } z_s \text{ respectively}\right)$.

(iii) Total, gross or effective head. *It is equal to the static head plus all the head losses occurring in flow before, through and after the impeller.*

3.8. LOSSES AND EFFICIENCIES OF A CENTRIFUGAL PUMP

3.8.1. Losses in Centrifugal Pump

When a centrifugal pump operates, the various losses which occur are as follows:

1. Hydraulic losses:

(*i*) *Hydraulic losses in the pump:*

(*a*) Shock or eddy losses at the entrance to and exit from the impeller.

(*b*) Losses due to friction in the impeller.

(*c*) Friction and eddy losses in the guide vanes/diffuser and casing.

(*ii*) *Other hydraulic losses:*

(*a*) Friction and other minor losses in the suction pipe.

(*b*) Friction and other minor losses in the delivery pipe.

2. Mechanical losses:

(*i*) Losses due to disc friction between the impeller and the liquid which fills the clearance spaces between the impeller and casing.

(*ii*) Losses pertaining to friction of the main bearing and glands.

3. Leakage loss:

The loss of energy due to leakage of liquid is known *as leakage loss.* The various losses in a centrifugal pump are shown diagramatically in Fig. 3.6.

3.8.2. Efficiencies of a Centrifugal Pump

The various *efficiencies* of a centrifugal pump are:

(*i*) Manometric efficiency (η_{mano}), (*ii*) Volumetric efficiency (η_v),

(*iii*) Mechanical efficiency (η_m), and (*iv*) Overall efficiency (η_0).

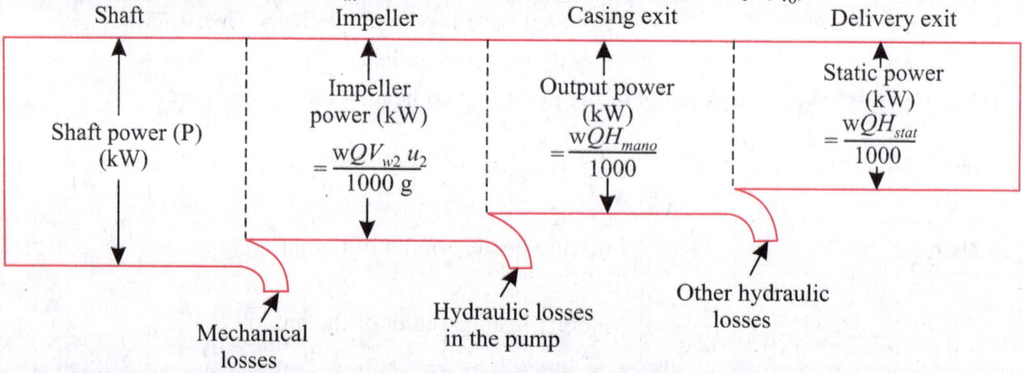

Fig. 3.6. Losses in centrifugal pump.

(i) Manometric efficiency (η_{mano}). *The ratio of the manometric head developed by the pump to the head imparted by the impeller to the liquid is known as* ***manometric efficiency.*** Thus,

$$\eta_{mano} = \frac{\text{Manometric head}}{\text{Head imparted by impeller to liquid}}$$

or,

$$\eta_{mano} = \frac{H_{mano}}{\left(\frac{V_{w2}u_2}{g}\right)} = \frac{gH_{mano}}{V_{w2}u_2} \quad ...(3.9)$$

(ii) Volumetric efficiency (η_v). *The ratio of quantity of liquid discharged per second from the pump to quantity passing per second through the impeller is known as **volumetric efficiency**.* Thus,

$$\eta_v = \frac{\text{Liquid discharged per second from the pump}}{\text{Quantity of liquid passing per second through the impeller}}$$

or,
$$\eta_v = \frac{Q}{Q+q}$$

where,
Q = Actual liquid discharged at the pump outlet per second, and

q = Leakage of liquid per second from the impeller (through the clearances between the impeller and casing).

(iii) Mechanical efficiency (η_m). *The ratio of the power delivered by the impeller to the liquid to the power input to the pump shaft is known as **mechanical efficiency**.* Thus,

$$\eta_m = \frac{\text{Power delivered by the impeller to the liquid}}{\text{Power input to the pump shaft (P)}}$$

or,
$$\eta_m = \frac{w\,(Q+q)\,(V_{w2}u_2/g)}{P} \quad \text{...(3.11)}$$

$$= \frac{P - P_{mech.loss}}{P} \quad \text{...[3.11(a)]}$$

(iv) Overall efficiency (η_0). *The ratio of power output of the pump to the power input to the pump is known as **overall efficiency**.* Thus,

$$\eta_0 = \frac{\text{Power output of the pump}}{\text{Power input to the pump / shaft}} = \frac{wQH_{mano}}{P} \quad \text{...(3.12)}$$

Also,
$$\eta_0 = \eta_{mano} \times \eta_v \times \eta_m$$

$$= \frac{H_{mano}}{(V_{w2}u_2/g)} \times \frac{Q}{(Q+q)} \times \frac{w(Q+q)\,(V_{w2}u_2/g)}{P}$$

$$= \frac{wQH_{mano}}{P}, \text{ which is the same as eqn. (3.12)}$$

3.8.3. Effect of Outlet Vane Angle (ϕ) on Manometric Efficiency

The total energy of liquid before entering the impeller, with reference to the centre of pump, is taken as zero. After leaving the impeller, the liquid has a pressure energy (H_{mano}) and kinetic energy $\left(\frac{V_2^2}{2g}\right)$. The energy supplied to the impeller is $\frac{V_{w2}u_2}{g}$. Neglecting the losses in the pump and equating the energy given to the impeller to the increase in total energy, we have:

$$\frac{V_{w2}u_2}{g} = H_{mano} + \frac{V_2^2}{2g}$$

or,
$$H_{mano} = \frac{V_{w2}u_2}{g} - \frac{V_2^2}{2g} \quad \text{...(3.13)}$$

From velocity triangle at outlet shown in Fig. 3.5, we have:

$$V_2^2 = V_{w2}^2 + V_{f2}^2, \text{ and, } V_{w2} = u_2 - \frac{V_{f2}}{\tan\phi} = u_2 - V_{f2}\cot\phi$$

Then,
$$H_{mano} = \frac{(u_2 - V_{f2}\cot\phi)\times u_2}{g} - \frac{(u_2 - V_{f2}\cot\phi)^2 + V_{f2}^2}{2g}$$
$$= \frac{2\,(u_2^2 - u_2V_{f2}\cot\phi) - [(u_2^2 + V_{f2}^2\cot^2\phi - 2u_2V_{f2}\cot\phi) + V_{f2}^2]}{2g}$$
$$= \frac{2u_2^2 - 2u_2V_{f2}\cot\phi - u_2^2 - V_{f2}^2\cot^2\phi + 2u_2V_{f2}\cot\phi - V_{f2}^2}{2g}$$
$$= \frac{u_2^2 - V_{f2}^2(1+\cot^2\phi)}{2g} = \frac{u_2^2 - V_{f2}^2\,\text{cosec}^2\theta}{2g} \qquad ...(3.14)$$

The manometric efficiency of the pump, under the ideal condition assumed above, will become:
$$\eta_{mano} = \frac{H_{mano}}{(V_{w2}u_2/g)} = \frac{gH_{mano}}{V_{w2}u_2} = \frac{u_2^2 - V_{f2}^2\text{cosec}^2\theta}{2u_2\,(u_2 - V_{f2}\cot\phi)}$$

Let us assume the flow ratio $K_f\left[=\frac{V_{f2}}{\sqrt{2gH_{mano}}}\right] = 0.25$; computing the value of u_2 in terms of H_{mano} from eqn. 3.14 for different values of ϕ, it will be observed that as the value of ϕ varies from 90° to 20° the value of η_{mano} increases from 0.47 to 0.73. A further decrease in the angle ϕ will increase the efficiency, but it is impracticable to have the angle ϕ less than 20°, as it would *result in long and narrow blades, with very high frictional losses.* As such the *minimum value of* ϕ is 20°.

Example 3.1. *The impeller of a centrifugal pump has an external diameter of 450 mm and internal diameter of 200 mm and it runs at 1440 r.p.m. Assuming a constant radial flow through the impeller at 2.5 m/s and that the vanes at exit are set back at an angle 25°, determine:*

(i) Inlet vane angle,

(ii) The angle, absolute velocity of water at exit makes with the tengent, and

(iii) The work done per N of water.

Solution. Internal diameter of the impeller, $D_1 = 200$ mm $= 0.2$ m

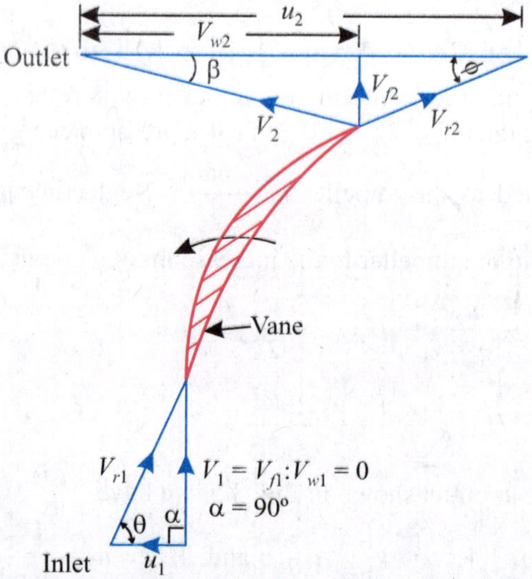

Fig. 3.7

External diameter of the impeller, D_2 = 450 mm = 0.45 m

Speed of impeller, N = 1440 r.p.m.

Velocity of flow, $V_{f1} = V_{f2} = 2.5$ m/s

Vane angle at outlet, ϕ = 25°

(i) Inlet vane angle, θ:

Tangential velocity of impeller at inlet,

$$u_1 = \frac{\pi D_1 N}{60} = \frac{\pi \times 0.2 \times 1440}{60} = 15.08 \text{ m/s}$$

From velocity triangle at *inlet,* we have:

$$\tan\theta = \frac{V_{f1}}{u_1}, \text{ or, } \tan\theta = \frac{2.5}{15.08} = 0.1658$$

$$\therefore \quad \theta = \tan^{-1} 0.1658 = \mathbf{9.4° \text{ (Ans.)}}$$

(ii) The angle, absolute velocity of water at exit makes with the tangent, β:

Tangential velocity of impeller at outlet,

$$u_2 = \frac{\pi D_2 N}{60} = \frac{\pi \times 0{\cdot}45 \times 1440}{60} = 33.93 \text{ m/s}$$

From velocity triangle at *outlet,* we have:

$$V_{w2} = u_2 - \frac{V_{f2}}{\tan\phi}, \text{ or, } V_{w2} = 33.93 - \frac{2.5}{\tan 25°} = 28.57 \text{ m/s}$$

Now,
$$\tan\beta = \frac{V_{f2}}{V_{w2}} = \frac{2.5}{28.57} = 0.0875$$

$$\therefore \quad \beta = \tan^{-1} 0.0875 = \mathbf{5° \text{ (Ans.)}}$$

(iii) Work done per N of water:

$$\textit{Work done per N of water} = \frac{V_{w2}u_2}{g} = \frac{28.57 \times 33.93}{9.81} = \mathbf{98.81 \text{ Nm (Ans.)}}$$

Example 3.2. *A centrifugal pump is to discharge 0.118 m^3/s at a speed of 1450 r.p.m against a head of 25 m. The impeller diameter is 250 mm, its width at outlet is 50 mm and manometric efficiency is 75 percent. Determine the vane angle at the outer periphery of the impeller.* **[PTU]**

Solution. Discharge, Q = 0.118 m^3/s

Speed N = 1450 r.p.m.

Speed, H_{mano} = 25 m

Diameter of impeller at outlet,

D_2 = 250 mm = 0.25 m

Width at outlet, B_2 = 50 mm = 0.05 m

Manometric efficiency, η_{mano} = 75%

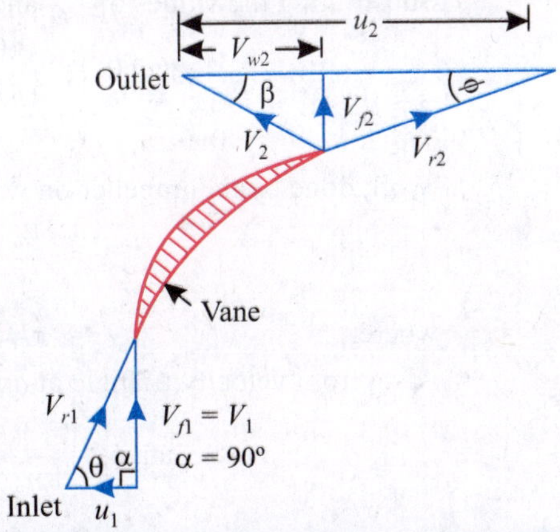

Fig. 3.8

Vane angle at outlet, ϕ:

Tangential velocity of impeller at outlet,

$$u_2 = \frac{\pi D_2 N}{60} = \frac{\pi \times 0.25 \times 1450}{60} = 18.98 \text{ m/s}$$

Discharge, $Q = \pi D_2 B_2 \times V_{f2}$

$$\therefore \quad V_{f2} = \frac{Q}{\pi D_2 B_2} = \frac{0.118}{\pi \times 0.25 \times 0.05} = 3.0 \text{ m/s}$$

Manometric efficiency, $\eta_{mano} = \dfrac{gH_{mano}}{V_{w2}u_2}$

or, $$0.75 = \frac{9.81 \times 25}{V_{w2} \times 18.98}, \quad \text{or,} \quad V_{w2} = \frac{9.81 \times 25}{0.75 \times 18.98} = 17.23 \text{ m/s}$$

From velocity triangle at *outlet,* we have:

$$\tan\phi = \frac{V_{f2}}{u_2 - V_{w2}} = \frac{3.0}{18.98 - 17.23} = 1.7143$$

$$\therefore \quad \phi = \tan^{-1} 1.7143 = \mathbf{59.74^\circ} \textbf{ (Ans.)}$$

Example 3.3. *The impeller of a centrifugal pump having external and internal diameters 500 mm and 250 mm respectively, width at outlet 50 mm and running at 1200 r.p.m. works against a head of 48 m. The velocity of flow through the impeller is constant and equal to 3.0 m/s. The vanes are set back at an angle of 40° at outlet. Determine:*

(*i*) *Inlet vane angle,*

(*ii*) *Work done by the impeller on water per second, and*

(*iii*) *Manometric efficiency.*

Solution. External diameter of impeller, D_2 = 500 mm = 0.05 m

Internal diameter, D_1 = 250 mm = 0.25 m

Width at outlet, B_2 = 50 mm = 0.05 m

Speed, N = 1200 r.p.m.

Head, H_{mano} = 48 m

Velocity of flow, $V_{f1} = V_{f2}$ = 3.0 m/s

Vane angle at outlet, ϕ = 40°

(*i*) Inlet vane angle, θ:

Refer to Fig. 3.8. From velocity triangle at *inlet*, we have:

$$\tan\theta = \frac{V_{f1}}{u_1} \quad \text{where, } u_1 = \frac{\pi D_1 N}{60} = \frac{\pi \times 0.25 \times 1200}{60} = 15.7 \text{ m/s}$$

Substituting the values of V_{f1} and u_1, we get:

$$\tan\theta = \frac{3.0}{15.7} = 0.191 \qquad \therefore \theta = \tan^{-1} 0.191 = \mathbf{10.81^\circ} \textbf{ (Ans.)}$$

(*ii*) Work done by the impeller:

Work done by the impeller on water per second is given by eqn. (3.1) as

$$= \frac{W}{g} V_{w2}u_2 = \frac{wQ}{g} \times V_{w2}u_2 \qquad \text{...(i)}$$

where, $Q = \pi D_2 B_2 \times V_{f2} = \pi \times 0.5 \times 0.05 \times 3.0 = 0.2356 \text{ m}^3\text{/s}$

Also, from velocity triangle at *outlet*, we have:

$$\tan\phi = \frac{V_{f2}}{u_2 - V_{w2}} = \frac{3.0}{31.41 - V_{w2}}, \quad \text{or,} \quad \tan 40^\circ = \frac{3.0}{31.41 - V_{w_2}}$$

$$\left(\text{where, } u_2 = \frac{\pi D_2 N}{60} = \frac{\pi \times 0.5 \times 1200}{60} = 31.41 \text{ m/s}\right)$$

or, $31.41 - V_{w2} = \dfrac{3.0}{\tan 40°}$, or, $V_{w_2} = 31.41 - \dfrac{3.0}{\tan 40°} = 27.83$ m/s

Substituting the values in eqn (*i*), we get the work done by the impeller

$$= \frac{9.81 \times 0.2356}{9.81} \times 27.83 \times 31.41 = \mathbf{205.95\ kNm}\ \textbf{(Ans.)}$$

$(\because w = 9.81 \text{ kN/m}^3)$

(*iii*) Manometric efficiency, (η_{mano}):

Manometric efficiency is given by eqn. (3.9) as:

$$\eta_{mano} = \frac{gH_{mano}}{V_{w2}u_2} = \frac{9.81 \times 48}{27.83 \times 31.41} = 0.5386 \text{ or } \mathbf{53.86\%}\ \textbf{(Ans.)}$$

Example 3.4. *A centrifugal pump running at 800 r.p.m. is working against a total head of 20.2 m. The external diameter of the impeller is 480 mm and outlet width 60 mm. If the vanes angle at outlet is 40° and manometric efficiency is 70 percent, determine:*

(*i*) *Flow velocity at outlet,*

(*ii*) *Absolute velocity of water leaving the vane,*

(*iii*) *Angle made by the absolute velocity at outlet with the dircetion of motion at outlet, and*

(*iv*) *Rate of flow through the pump.*

Solution. Speed, N = 800 r.p.m.; Head, H_{mano} = 20.2 m;

External diameter, D_2 = 480 mm = 0.48 m; Width at outlet, B_2 = 60 mm = 0.06 m;

Outlet vangle angle, ϕ = 40°; Manometric efficiency, η_{mano} = 70 %.

Refer to Fig. 3.9.

(*i*) Flow velocity at outlet, V_{f2}:

Tangential velocity of impeller at outlet,

$$u_2 = \frac{\pi D_2 N}{60} = \frac{\pi \times 0.48 \times 800}{60}$$

$$= 20.1 \text{ m/s}$$

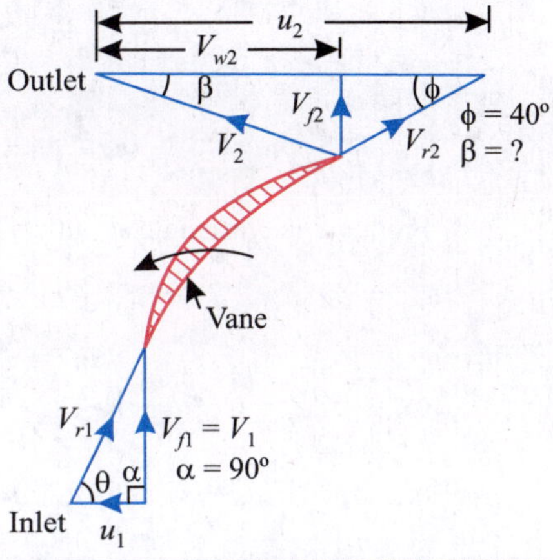

Fig. 3.9

Also, manometric efficiency is given by,

$$\eta_{mano} = \frac{gH_m}{V_{w2}u_2} \quad \text{...(Eqn 3.9)}$$

or, $$0.70 = \frac{9.81 \times 20.2}{V_{w2} \times 20.1}$$

or, $$V_{w2} = \frac{9.81 \times 20.2}{0.70 \times 20.1} = 14.08 \text{ m/s}$$

From velocity triangle at outlet, we have:

$$\tan \phi = \frac{V_{f2}}{u_2 - V_{w2}} = \frac{V_{f2}}{(20.1 - 14.08)}$$

or, $$V_{f_2} = \tan \phi\ (20.1 - 14.08)$$

$$= \tan 40°\ (20.1 - 14.08) = \mathbf{5.05\ m/s}\ \textbf{(Ans.)}$$

(*ii*) Absolute velocity of water leaving the vane, V_2:

$$V_2 = \sqrt{V_{f2}^2 + V_{w2}^2} = \sqrt{5.05^2 + 14.08^2} = \mathbf{14.96\ m/s}\ \textbf{(Ans.)}$$

(*iii*) Angle made by the absolute velocity at outlet with the direction of motion, β:

From velocity triangle at *outlet*, we have:

$$\tan\beta = \frac{V_{f2}}{V_{w2}} = \frac{5.05}{14.08} = 0.3586 \quad \therefore \ \beta = \tan^{-1}(0.3586) = \mathbf{19.7° \ (Ans.)}$$

(*iv*) Rate of flow through the pump, Q:

$$Q = \pi D_2 B_2 \times V_{f2} = \pi \times 0.48 \times 0.06 \times 5.05 = \mathbf{0.457 \ m^3/s \ (Ans.)}$$

Example 3.5. *A centrifugal pump impeller runs at 80 r.p.m. and has outlet vane angle of 60°. The velocity of flow is 2.5 m/s throughout and diameter of the impeller at exit is twice that at inlet. If the manometric head is 20 m and the manometric efficiency is 75 percent, determine:*

(*i*) *The diameter of the impeller at the exit, and*

(*ii*) *Inlet vane angle.*

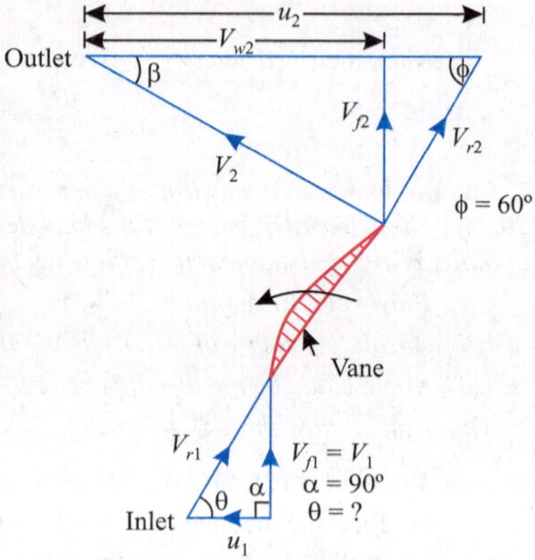

Fig. 3.10

Solution. Speed, N = 80 r.p.m.; Outlet vane angle, ϕ = 60°; Velocity of flow, $V_{f1} = V_{f2}$ = 2.5 m/s; manometric head, H_{mano} = 20 m; Manometric efficiency, η_{mano} = 75%;

Diameter of the impeller at outlet,

$$D_2 = 2D_1 \text{(diameter at inlet)}$$

(*i*) The diameter of the impeller at the exit, D_2:

$$\eta_{mano} = \frac{gH_{mano}}{V_{w2}u_2} \qquad \text{.... Eqn. (3.9)}$$

$$0.75 = \frac{9.81 \times 20}{V_{w2}u_2}, \ \text{or,} \ V_{w2}u_2 = \frac{9.81 \times 20}{0.75} = 261.6 \qquad ...(i)$$

From velocity triangle at outlet (Fig. 3.10), we have

$$\tan\phi = \frac{V_{f2}}{u_2 - V_{w2}}$$

or,
$$u_2 - V_{w2} = \frac{V_{f2}}{\tan\phi}, \ \text{or,} \ V_{w2} = u_2 - \frac{V_{f2}}{\tan\phi}$$

or,
$$V_{w2} = u_2 - \frac{2.5}{\tan 60°} = u_2 - 1.44$$

Substituting this value of V_{w2} in (*i*), we get:

$$(u_2 - 1.44)\,u_2 = 261.6, \quad \text{or} \quad u_2^2 - 1.44u_2 - 261.6 = 0$$

or,
$$u_2 = \frac{1.44 \pm \sqrt{1.44^2 + 4 \times 261.6}}{2} = \frac{1.44 \pm 32.38}{2} = 16.91 \text{ m/s (ignoring –ve sign)}$$

Also, tangential velocity of impeller at outlet, $u_2 = \dfrac{\pi D_2 N}{60}$, or, $D_2 = \dfrac{60u_2}{\pi N}$

$$\therefore \qquad D_2 = \frac{60 \times 16.91}{\pi \times 80} = 4.037 \text{ m} \simeq \mathbf{4 \ m \ (Ans.)}$$

(*ii*) Inlet vane angle, θ:

Tangential velocity of the impeller at inlet, $u_1 = \dfrac{u_2}{2} = \dfrac{16.91}{2} = 8.455$ m/s $\quad \left(\because D_1 = \dfrac{D_2}{2}\right)$

From velocity triangle at *inlet*, we have:

$$\tan\theta = \frac{V_{f1}}{u_1} = \frac{2.5}{8.455} = 0.2957$$

$$\therefore \qquad \theta = \tan^{-1}(0.2957) = \mathbf{16.47° \ (Ans.)}$$

Example 3.6. *A centrifugal pump impeller having external and intenal diameters 480 mm and 240 mm respectively is running at 100 r.p.m. The rate of flow through the pump is 0.0576 m³/s and velocity of flow is constant and equal to 2.4 m/s. The diameters of the suction and delivery pipes are 180 mm and 120 mm respectively and suction and delivery heads are 6.2 m (abs.) and 30.2 m of water respectively. If the power required to drive the pump is 23.3 kW and the outlet vane angle is 45°, determine:*

(i) Inlet vane angle,

(ii) The overall efficiency of the pump, and

(iii) The manometric efficiency of the pump.

Solution. External diameter of the impeller,

$$D_2 = 480 \text{ mm} = 0.48 \text{ m},$$

Internal diameter, $D_1 = 240 \text{ mm} = 0.24 \text{ m}$,

Speed, $N = 1000$ r.p.m.,

Discharge, $Q = 0.0567 \text{ m}^3/\text{s}$;

Velocity of flow, $V_{f1} = V_{f2} = 2.4$ m/s

The diameter of suction pipe,

$$D_s = 180 \text{ mm} = 0.18 \text{ m}$$

The diameter of delivery pipe,

$$D_d = 120 \text{ mm} = 0.12 \text{ m}$$

Suction head, $h_s = 6.2$ m (abs.)

Delivery head, $h_d = 30.2$ m (abs.)

Shaft power, $P = 23.3$ kW

Outlet vane angle, $\phi = 45°$

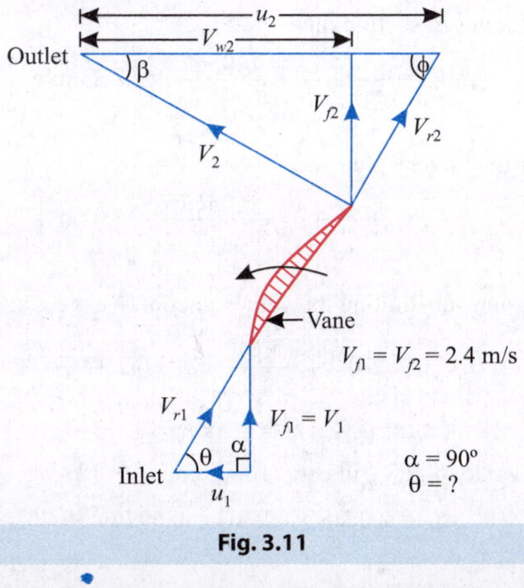

Fig. 3.11

(*i*) Inlet vane angle, θ:

Tangential velocity of impeller at *inlet*,

$$u_1 = \frac{\pi D_1 N}{60} = \frac{\pi \times 0.24 \times 1000}{60} = 12.56 \text{ m/s}$$

From velocity triangle at *inlet*, we have:

$$\tan\theta = \frac{V_{f1}}{u_1} = \frac{2.4}{12.56} = 0.191$$

$$\therefore \quad \theta = \tan^{-1}(0.191) = \mathbf{10.8° \ (Ans.)}$$

(*ii*) The overall efficiency of the pump, η_0:

The overall efficiency of a centrifugal pump is given by,

$$\eta_0 = \frac{wQH_{mano}}{P} = \frac{9.81 \times 0.0567 \times H_{mano}}{23.3} = 0.02387\, H_{mano}$$

(where, $w = 9.81$ kN/m^3)

Also H_{mano} is given by eqn. (3.8) as:

$$H_{mano} = \left(\frac{p_2}{w} + \frac{V_2^2}{2g} + z_2\right) - \left(\frac{p_1}{w} + \frac{V_1^2}{2g} + z_1\right) \quad ...(ii)$$

where, $\frac{p_2}{w}$ = Pressure head at pump outlet, $h_d = 30.2$ m,

$\frac{V_2^2}{2g}$ = Velocity head at pump outlet = $\frac{V_d^2}{2g}$,

z_2 = Vertical height of pump outlet from datum line,

$\frac{p_1}{w}$ = Pressure heat at pump inlet, $h_s = 6.2$ m (abs.),

$\frac{V_1^2}{2g}$ = Velocity head at pump inlet, $\frac{V_s^2}{2g}$, and

z_1 = Vertical height of pump inlet from datum line.

Now, velocity of water in suction pipe,

$$V_s = \frac{Q}{\frac{\pi}{4} \times D_s^2} = \frac{0.0567}{\frac{\pi}{4} \times 0.18^2} = 2.23 \text{ m/s}$$

Velocity of water in delivery pipe,

$$V_d = \frac{Q}{\frac{\pi}{4} \times D_d^2} = \frac{0.0567}{\frac{\pi}{4} \times 0.12^2} = 5.01 \text{ m/s}$$

Assuming $z_2 = z_1$ and substituting the values in eqn. (*ii*), we get:

$$H_{mano} = \left(30.2 + \frac{5.01^2}{2 \times 9.81}\right) - \left(6.2 + \frac{2.23^2}{2 \times 9.81}\right)$$

$$= 31.48 - 6.45 = 25.03 \text{ m}$$

Substituting this value of H_{mano} in eqn. (*i*), we get:

$$\eta_0 = 0.02387 \times 25.03 = 0.597 \text{ or } \mathbf{59.7\% \ (Ans.)}$$

(iii) The manometric efficiency of the pump, η_{mano}:

$$\eta_{mano} = \frac{gH_{mano}}{V_{w2}u_2} \quad \text{...Eqn. (3.9)}$$

$$u_2 = \frac{\pi D_2 N}{60} = \frac{\pi \times 0.48 \times 1000}{60} = 25.13 \text{ m/s}$$

From velocity triangle at outlet (Fig. 3.11), we have:

$$\tan\phi = \frac{V_{f2}}{u_2 - V_{w2}}, \text{ or, } \tan 45° = \frac{2.4}{25.13 - V_{w2}}, \text{ or, } 25.13 - V_{w2} = \frac{2.4}{\tan 45°} = 2.4$$

$$\therefore \quad V_{w2} = 25.13 - 2.4 = 22.73 \text{ m/s}$$

Substituting the values in the above equation, we get:

$$\eta_{mano} = \frac{9.81 \times 25.03}{22.73 \times 25.13} = 0.43 \text{ or } \mathbf{43\%} \text{ (Ans.)}$$

Example 3.7. *It is required to deliver 0.048 m^3/s of water to a height of 24 m through a 150 mm diameter pipe and 120 m long, by a centrifugal pump. If the overall efficiency of the pump is 75 percent and co-efficient of friction, $f = 0.01$ for thr pipe line, find the power required to drive the pump.*

Solution. Rate of flow, $Q = 0.048$ m^3/s; Height, $H_{stat} = h_s + h_d = 24$ m

Diameter of pipe, $D_s = D_d = D = 150$ mm, or, 0.15 m,

Length, $L_s + L_d = L = 120$ m

Overall efficiency, $\eta_o = 75\%$

Co-efficient of friction, $f = 0.01$

Power required to drive the pump, P:

$$\text{Velocity of water in pipe, } V_s = V_d = V = \frac{Q}{\text{Area of pipe}} = \frac{0.048}{\frac{\pi}{4} \times 0.15^2} = 2.7 \text{ m/s}$$

Loss of head due to friction in pipe,

$$(h_{fs} = h_{fd}) = \frac{4fLV^2}{D \times 2g} = \frac{4 \times 0.01 \times 120 \times 2.7^2}{0.15 \times 2 \times 9.81} = 11.89 \text{ m}$$

The manometric head (H_{mano}) is given by eqn. (3.7) as:

$$H_{mano} = (h_s + h_d) + (h_{fs} + h_{fd}) + \frac{V_d^2}{2g}$$

$$= 24 + 11.89 + \frac{2.7^2}{2 \times 9.81} = 36.26 \text{ m}$$

Using the relation : $$\eta_0 = \frac{wQH_{mano}}{P}, \text{ we get:}$$

$$0.75 = \frac{9.81 \times 0.048 \times 36.26}{P} \quad (\because w = 9.81 \text{ kN/m}^3)$$

or, $$P = \frac{9.81 \times 0.048 \times 36.26}{0.75} = \mathbf{22.76 \text{ kW}} \text{ (Ans.)}$$

Example 3.8. *The impeller of a centrifugal pump is of 300 mm diameter and 50 mm width at the periphery, and has blades whose tip angle incline backwards 60° from the radius. The pump delivers 17 m³/min. of water and the impeller rotates at 1000 r.p.m. Assuming that the pump is designed to admit radially, calculate:*

(i) Speed and direction of water as it leaves the impeller,

(ii) Torque exerted by the impeller on water,

(iii) Shaft power required, and

(iv) Lift of the pump.

Take, mechanical efficiency = 95% and hydraulic efficiency = 75%.

[Rajasthan University]

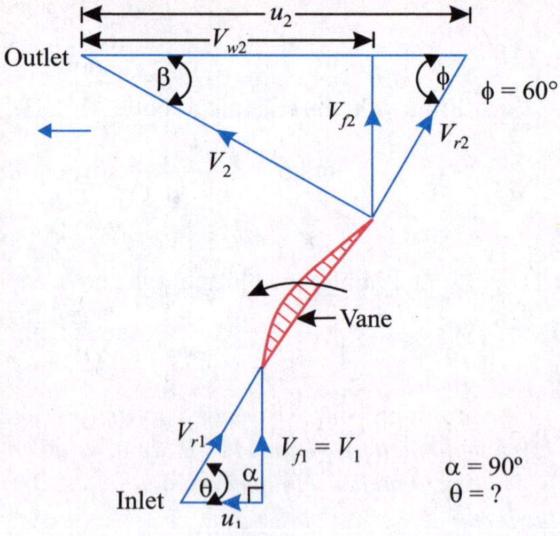

Fig. 3.12

Solution. External diameter of impeller, $D_2 = 300$ mm = 0.3 m

Width at periphery, $B_2 = 50$ mm = 0.05 m

Outlet vane angle, $\phi = 60°$

Discharge, $Q = 17$ m³/min., or, 0.2833m³/s

Speed of the impeller, $N = 1000$ r.p.m.

$\eta_m = 95\%$; $\eta_h = 70\%$.

(i) Speed and direction of water as it leaves the impeller, V_2, β:

Tangential velocity of impeller at *outlet*,

$$u_2 = \frac{\pi D_2 N}{60} = \frac{\pi \times 0.3 \times 1000}{60} = 15.71 \text{ m/s}$$

Also, $$Q = \pi D_2 B_2 \times V_{f2}, \text{ or, } V_{f2} = \frac{Q}{\pi D_2 B_2}$$

$\therefore$ $$V_{f2} = \frac{0.2833}{\pi \times 0.3 \times 0.05} = 6.01 \text{ m/s}$$

From velocity triangle at *outlet*, (Fig. 3.12), we have:

$$\tan\phi = \frac{V_{f2}}{u_2 - V_{w2}}, \text{ or, } u_2 - V_{w2} = \frac{V_{f2}}{\tan\phi}$$

or, $$V_{w2} = u_2 - \frac{V_{f2}}{\tan\phi} = 15.71 - \frac{6.01}{\tan 60°} = 12.24 \text{ m/s}$$

$\therefore$ Absolute velocity of water at outlet tip of impeller,

$$V_2 = \sqrt{V_{w2}^2 + V_{f2}^2} = \sqrt{12.24^2 + 6.01^2} = \textbf{13.63 m/s (Ans.)}$$

$$\tan\beta = \frac{V_{f2}}{V_{w2}} = \frac{6.01}{12.24} = 0.491$$

$\therefore$ The direction of outgoing velocity, $\beta = \tan^{-1}(0.491) =$ **26.15° (Ans.)**

(ii) Torque exerted by the impeller on water, T:

$$T = \frac{wQ}{g}(V_{w2} R_2)$$

$$= \frac{9.81 \times 0.2833}{9.81} \times 12.24 \times \left(\frac{0.3}{2}\right) = \mathbf{0.52\ kNm}\ \textbf{(Ans.)}$$

$$(\because w = 9.81\ \text{kN/m}^3)$$

(*iii*) Shaft power required, P:

$$\text{Impeller or rotor power} = \frac{2\pi NT}{60} = \frac{2\pi \times 1000 \times 0.52}{60} = 54.45\ \text{kW}$$

$$\eta_m = \frac{\text{Impeller power}}{\text{Shaft power}},\ \text{or, } 0.95 = \frac{54.45}{P}$$

$$P = \frac{54.45}{0.95} = \mathbf{57.31\ kW}\ \textbf{(Ans.)}$$

(*iv*) Lift of the pump:

$$\text{Impeller power} = w\,(Q + q)\,H_i$$

where, w = Weight density of water, kN/ m^3,

H_i = Ideal head, m (= theoretical head – hydraulic losses), and

q = Leakage of water, m^3/s.

Neglecting leakage effects, we obtain:

$$54.45 = 9.81 \times 0.2833 \times H_i,\ \text{or, } H_i = \frac{54.45}{9.81 \times 0.2833} = 19.59\ \text{m}$$

$$\text{Now, hydraulic efficiency, } \eta_h = \frac{\text{Actual head or lift}}{\text{Ideal head}}$$

$\therefore$ Lift of the pump $= \eta_h \times$ ideal head $(H_i) = 0.70 \times 19.59 =$ **13.71 m of water (Ans.)**

Example 3.9. *A centrifugal pump (diffusion type) has suction lift of 1.8 m and the delivery tank is 14.2 m above the pump. The velocity of water in the delivery pipe is 1.6 m/s. The radial velocity of flow through the wheel is 2.8 m/s and the tangent to the vane at the exit from the wheel makes an angle of 120° with the dirction of motion. Assuming that the water enters radially and neglecting friction and other losses, determine:*

(*i*) *Velocity of wheel at the exit,*

(*ii*) *Velocity and pressure head at exit from the wheel, and*

(*iii*) *Direction of the fixed guide vane.*

Solution. Suction lift, h_s = 1.8 m

Delivery head, h_d = 14.2 m

The velocity of water in delivery pipe, V_d = 1.6 m/s

The radial velocity of flow, $V_{f1} = V_{f2}$ = 2.8 m/s

Outlet vane angle, ϕ = 180° – 120° = 60°.

(*i*) Velocity of wheel at the exit, u_2:

Head against which pump has to work,

$$H = h_s + h_d \quad \text{(neglecting friction and other losses)}$$

$$= 1.8 + 14.2 = 16\ \text{m of water}$$

Also, $$H = \frac{V_{w2} u_2}{g} \quad \text{...Euler equation}$$

$$V_{w2} u_2 = gH = 9.81 \times 16 = 156.96 \quad \text{...}(i)$$

From velocity triangle at outlet (Fig. 3.13), we have:

$$\tan \phi = \frac{V_{f2}}{u_2 - V_{w2}}, \text{ or } u_2 - V_{w2} = \frac{V_{f2}}{\tan \phi}$$

or,
$$V_{w2} = u_2 - \frac{V_{f2}}{\tan \phi}$$

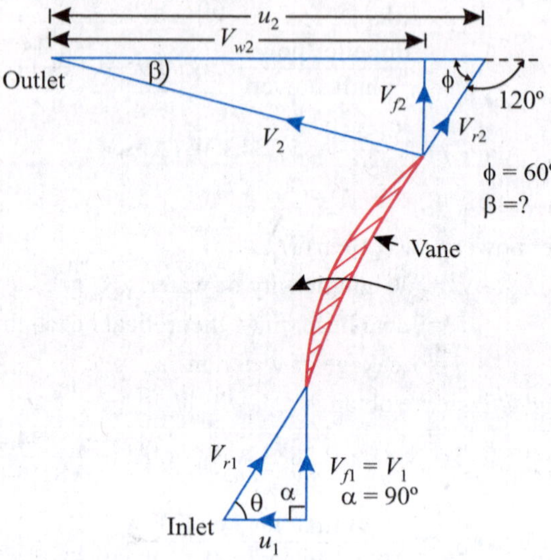

Fig. 3.13

$$\therefore \quad V_{w2} = u_2 - \frac{2.8}{\tan 60°} u_2 - 1.616 \qquad ...(ii)$$

Substituting this value of V_{w2} in (*i*), we get:

$$(u_2 - 1.616)\, u_2 = 156.96, \text{ or, } u_2^2 - 1.616\, u_2 - 156.96 = 0$$

$$\therefore \quad u_2 = \frac{1.616 \pm \sqrt{1.616^2 + 4 \times 156.96}}{2} = \frac{1.616 \pm 25.108}{2} = 13.36 \text{ m/s (ignoring –ve sign)}$$

Hence, *the velocity of wheel at exit* = **13.36 m/s (Ans.)**

(*ii*) Velocity and pressure head at exit from the wheel:

From eqn. (*i*), we have: $V_{w2} = \frac{156.96}{u_2} = \frac{156.96}{13.36} = 11.75$ m/s

Absolute velocity, $V_2 = \sqrt{V_{w2}^2 + V_{f2}^2} = \sqrt{11.75^2 + 2.8^2} = 12.08$ m/s

$\therefore$ Velocity head at exit $= \frac{V_2^2}{2g} = \frac{12.08^2}{2 \times 9.81}$ = **7.44 m of water (Ans.)**

Pressure head at exit $= \frac{p_2}{w} = h_d - \frac{V_2^2}{2g}$

$= 14.2 - 7.44$ = **6.76 m of water (Ans.)**

(*iii*) Direction of fixed guide vane, β:

$$\tan \beta = \frac{V_{f2}}{V_{w2}} = \frac{2.8}{11.75} = 0.2383$$

$\beta = \tan^{-1}(0.2383)$ = **13.4° (Ans.)**

Example 3.10. *Show that the rise of pressure in the impeller of a centrifugal pump when frictional and other losses in the impeller are neglected, is given by*

$$\frac{1}{2g}[V_{f1}^2 + u_2^2 - V_{f2}^2 \operatorname{cosec}^2 \phi]$$

where, V_{f1}, V_{f2} = *Velocities of flow at inlet and outlet respectively,*

u_2 = *Tangential velocity of impeller at outlet, and*

ϕ = *Vane angle at outlet.*

Solution. Let the values at inlet and outlet of impeller are represented by the suffices 1 and 2 respectively.

Invoking Bernoulli's equation at the inlet and outlet of the impeller, neglecting losses from inlet to outlet, we have:

$$(\text{Total energy})_{\text{inlet}} = (\text{Total energy})_{\text{outlet}} - \text{work done by impeller on water}$$

$$\frac{p_1}{w} + \frac{V_1^2}{2g} + z_1 = \left(\frac{p_2}{w} + \frac{V_2^2}{2g} + z_2\right)$$

– work done by impeller on water per unit weight of water

$$= \frac{p_2}{w} + \frac{V_2^2}{2g} + z_2 - \frac{V_{w2}u_2}{g} \quad \text{(assuming flow to be } \textit{radial at inlet}\text{)}$$

If the inlet and outlet of the impeller are at the same height (*i.e.* $z_1 = z_2$), then

$$\frac{p_1}{w} + \frac{V_1^2}{2g} = \frac{p_2}{w} + \frac{V_2^2}{2g} - \frac{V_{w2}u_2}{g}$$

$$\therefore \quad \left(\frac{p_2}{w} - \frac{p_1}{w}\right) = \frac{V_1^2}{2g} - \frac{V_2^2}{2g} + \frac{V_{w2}u_2}{g} \quad ...(i)$$

where, $\frac{p_2}{w} - \frac{p_1}{w}$ = Pressure rise in impeller.

Refer to Fig. 3.8. From velocity triangle at *inlet*, we have $V_1 = V_{f1}$ ... (*ii*)

From velocity triangle at outlet, we have:

$$\tan\phi = \frac{V_{f2}}{u_2 - V_{w2}}, \text{ or, } u_2 - V_{w2} = \frac{V_{f2}}{\tan\phi}$$

or,
$$V_{w2} = u_2 - \frac{V_{f2}}{\tan\phi} = u_2 - V_{f2}\cot\phi \quad ...(iii)$$

Also,
$$V_2^2 = V_{f2}^2 + V_{w2}^2 = V_{f2}^2 + (u_2 - V_{f2}\cot\phi)^2$$

$$= V_{f2}^2 + (u_2^2 + V_{f2}^2\cot^2\phi - 2u_2V_{f2}\cot\phi)$$

$$= V_{f2}^2 + V_{f2}^2\cot^2\phi + u_2^2 - 2u_2V_{f2}\cot\phi$$

$$= V_{f2}^2(1 + \cot^2\phi) + u_2^2 - 2u_2V_{f2}\cot\phi$$

$$= V_{f2}^2\operatorname{cosec}^2\phi + u_2^2 - 2u_2V_{f2}\cot\phi \quad ...(iv)$$

$$(\because 1 + \cot^2\phi = \operatorname{cosec}^2\phi)$$

Substituting the values of V_1, V_{w2} and V_2^2 from eqns. (*ii*), (*iii*), and (*iv*), respectively in eqn. (*i*), we get:

$$\textit{Pressure rise in impeller} = \frac{V_{f1}^2}{2g} - \frac{1}{2g}(V_{f2}^2 \text{cosec}^2\phi + u_2^2 - 2u_2V_{f2}\cot\phi) + \frac{(u_2 - V_{f2}\cot\phi)\times u_2}{g}$$

$$= \frac{1}{2g}[V_{f1}^2 - V_{f2}^2\text{cosec}^2\phi - u_2^2 + 2u_2V_{f2}\cot\phi + 2u_2^2 - 2u_2V_{f2}\cot\phi]$$

$$= \frac{1}{2g}[V_{f1}^2 + u_2^2 - V_{f2}^2\text{cosec}^2\phi] \quad ...(3.16)$$

Example 3.11. *The following data relate to a centrifugal pump:*
The diameters of the impeller at inlet and outlet = 180 mm and 360 mm respectively
The widths of the impeller at inlet and outlet = 14.4 mm and 7.2 mm respectively
The rate of flow through the pump = 17.28 litres/s
Speed of the impeller = 1500 r.p.m.
Vane angle at the outlet = 45°
The water enters the impeller radially at inlet.
Neglecting losses through the impeller, find the pressure rise in the impeller

Solution. *Given* : D_1 = 180 mm = 0.18 m; D_2 = 360 mm = 0.36 m; B_1 = 14.4 mm = 0.0144 m; B_2 = 7.2 mm = 0.0072 m; Q = 17.26 litres/s = 0.01728 m^3/s ; N =1500 r.p.m.; ϕ = 45°

Pressure rise in the impeller:

$$\text{Velocity of flow at inlet, } V_{f1} = \frac{Q}{\pi D_1B_1} = \frac{0.01728}{\pi \times 0.18 \times 0.0144} = 2.12 \text{ m/s}$$

$$\text{Velocity of flow at outlet, } V_{f2} = \frac{Q}{\pi D_2B_2} = \frac{0.01728}{\pi \times 0.36 \times 0.0072} = 2.12 \text{ m/s}$$

Tangential velocity of impeller at outlet,

$$u_2 = \frac{\pi D_2N}{60} = \frac{\pi \times 0.36 \times 1500}{60} = 28.27 \text{ m/s}$$

$$\textit{Pressure rise in impeller} = \frac{1}{2g}[V_{f1}^2 + u_2^2 - V_{f2}^2\text{cosec}^2\phi] \quad ...[\text{Eqn. } 3.16]$$

$$= \frac{1}{2\times 9.81}[2.12^2 + 28.27^2 - 2.12^2 \times \text{cosec}^2\, 45°]$$

$$= \frac{1}{2\times 9.81}(4.494 + 799.193 - 8.988) = \mathbf{40.5\ m}\ \textbf{(Ans.)}$$

Example 3.12. *A centrifugal pump impeller has at outlet a diameter of 360 mm and width 60 mm. The vanes are curved backwards at 35° to the tangent at outer periphery and thickness of vanes occupies 20 percent of the peripheral area and the velocity of flow is constant from inlet to outlet. The impeller rotates at 800 r.p.m. If the rate of flow through the pump is 0.13 m^3/s, determine:*

(i) The pressure rise in the impeller, and
(ii) The percentage of total work converted to kinetic energy.

Solution. Diameter of the impeller at outlet, D_2 = 360 mm = 0.36 m
Width of impeller at outlet, B_2 = 60 mm = 0.06 m
Outlet vane angle, ϕ = 35°
Area occupied by thickness of vanes = 20% of the peripheral area

Thickness co-efficient, $K_t = 1 - 0.2 = 0.8$

Speed of impeller, $N = 800$ r.p.m.

Rate of flow through the pump,

$$Q = 0.13 \text{ m}^3/\text{s}$$

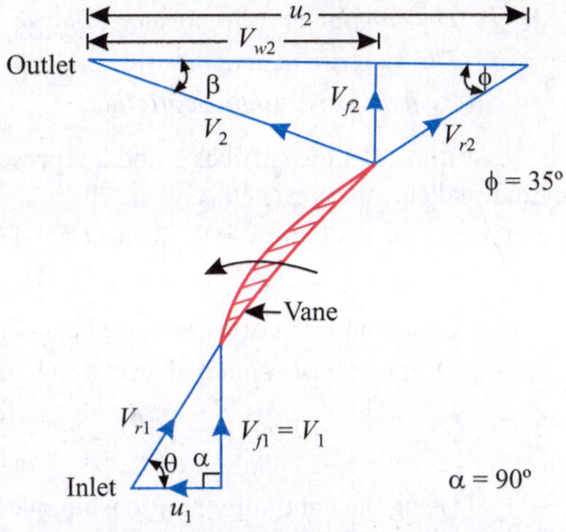

Fig. 3.14

(i) Pressure rise in the impeller:

Tangential velocity of impeller at outlet,

$$u_2 = \frac{\pi D_2 N}{60} = \frac{\pi \times 0.36 \times 800}{60} = 15.08 \text{ m/s}$$

Rate of flow, $Q = K_t \times \pi D_2 B_2 \times V_{f2}$

or, $0.13 = 0.8 \times \pi \times 0.36 \times 0.06 \times V_{f2}$

$$\therefore V_{f2} = \frac{0.13}{0.8 \times \pi \times 0.36 \times 0.06} = 2.39 \text{ m/s}$$

Since the velocity of flow is constant from inlet to outlet, $V_{f1} = V_{f2} = 2.39$ m/s

From velocity triangle at *outlet* (Fig, 3.14), we have:

$$\tan\phi = \frac{V_{f2}}{u_2 - V_{w2}}, \text{ or, } u_2 - V_{w2} = \frac{V_{f2}}{\tan\phi}, \text{ or, } V_{w2} = u_2 - \frac{V_{f2}}{\tan\phi}$$

$$\therefore \quad V_{w2} = 15.08 - \frac{2.39}{\tan 35°} = 11.66 \text{ m/s}$$

Now, Pressure rise $= \frac{1}{2g}[V_{f1}^2 + u_2^2 - V_{f2}^2 \text{ cosec}^2\phi]$ ...[Eqn. 3.16]

$$= \frac{1}{2 \times 9.81}[2.39^2 + 15.08^2 - 2.39^2 \times \text{cosec}^2 35°]$$

$$= \frac{1}{2 \times 9{\cdot}81}[5.712 + 227.406 - 17.362] \simeq \mathbf{11 \text{ m of water}} \textbf{ (Ans.)}$$

(ii) The percentage of work converted to kinetic energy:

Absolute velocity of water leaving the vane,

$$V_2 = \sqrt{V_{f2}^2 + V_{w2}^2} = \sqrt{2.39^2 + 11.66^2} = 11.9 \text{ m/s}$$

Kinetic energy per unit weight of water $= \frac{V_2^2}{2g} = \frac{11.9^2}{2 \times 9.81} = 7.217$ Nm

Work done per unit weight of water $= \frac{V_{w2} u_2}{g} = \frac{11.66 \times 15.08}{9.81} = 17.92$ Nm

$\therefore$ Percentage of work converted to kinetic energy

$$= \frac{7.217}{17.92} \times 100 = \mathbf{40.27\%} \textbf{ (Ans.)}$$

Example 3.13. *A pump impeller is 375 mm in diameter and it discharges water with velocity components of 2 m/s and 12 m/s in the radial and tangential directions respectively. The impeller is surrounded by a concentrical cylindrical chamber with parallel sides; the outer diameter being 450 mm. If the flow in the chamber is a free spiral vortex, find:*

(*i*) *The component velocities of water on leaving, and*

(*ii*) *The increase in pressure.*

Assume losses to be negligible.

Solution. Let the suffices 1 and 2 represent the conditions at inlet and outlet of the concentric cylindrical chamber respectively.

Given : $D_1 = 375$ mm $= 0.375$ m; $D_2 = 450$ mm $= 0.45$ m; $V_{f1} = 2$ m/s; $V_{w1} = 12$ m/s.

(*i*) The component velocities of water at outlet of the chamber:

Using the free vortex law, we have $V_{w1} R_1 = V_{w2} R_2$

$\therefore$ *Tangential velocity* at outlet of chamber,

$$V_{w2} = \frac{V_{w1}R_1}{R_2} = 12 \times \frac{(0.375 / 2)}{(0.45 / 2)} = \mathbf{10\ m/s}\ \textbf{(Ans.)}$$

Using the continuity relationship, we have:

$$\pi D_1 B_1 \times V_{f1} = D_2 B_2 \times Vf_2$$

(where, V_{f2} = *radial velocity* at outlet of chamber)

But, $B_1 = B_2$ ... for a parallel sided chamber

$$\therefore \quad D_1 \times V_{f1} = D_2 \times V_{f2}, \text{ or, } V_{f2} = \frac{D_1 V_{f1}}{D_2} = \frac{0.375 \times 2}{0.45} = \mathbf{1.667\ m/s}\ \textbf{(Ans.)}$$

(*ii*) The increase in pressure:

Invoking Bernoulli's equation assuming no loss of head and no change in datum, we have:

$$\frac{p_1}{w} + \frac{V_1^2}{2g} = \frac{p_2}{w} + \frac{V_2^2}{2g}$$

$\therefore$ *The increase in pressure,*

$$= \frac{p_2 - p_1}{w} = \frac{V_1^2 - V_2^2}{2g}$$

$$= \frac{(12^2 + 2^2) - (10^2 + 1.667^2)}{2 \times 9.81} = \mathbf{2.3\ m\ of\ water}\ \textbf{(Ans.)}$$

Example 3.14. *A centrifugal pump, in which water enters radially, delivers water to a height of 165 mm. The impeller has a diameter of 360 mm and width 180 mm at inlet and the corresponding dimensions at the outlet are 720 mm and 90 mm respectively; its rotational speed is 1200 r.p.m. The blades are curved backward at 30° to the tangent at exit and the discharge is 0.389 m³/s. Determine:*

(*i*) *Theoretical head developed,*

(*ii*) *Manometric efficiency*

(*iii*) *Pressure rise across the impeller assuming losses equal to 12 percent of velocity head at exit,*

(*iv*) *Pressure rise and the loss of head in the volute casing,*

(*v*) *The vane angle at inlet, and*

(*vi*) *Power required to drive the pump assuming an overall efficiency of 70%. What would be corresponding mechanical efficiency ?*

Solution. Manometric head, H_{mano} = 165 m

Diameter of impeller at inlet, D_1 = 360 mm = 0.36 m

Width at inlet, B_1 = 180 mm = 0.18 m

Diameter of impeller at outlet,

$D_2 = 720 \text{ mm} = 0.72 \text{ m}$

Width at outlet, $B_2 = 90 \text{ mm} = 0.09 \text{ m}$

Speed, $N = 1200$ r.p.m.

Outlet vane angle, $\phi = 30°$

Discharge, $Q = 0.389 \text{ m}^3/\text{s}$

$\eta_0 = 70\%$.

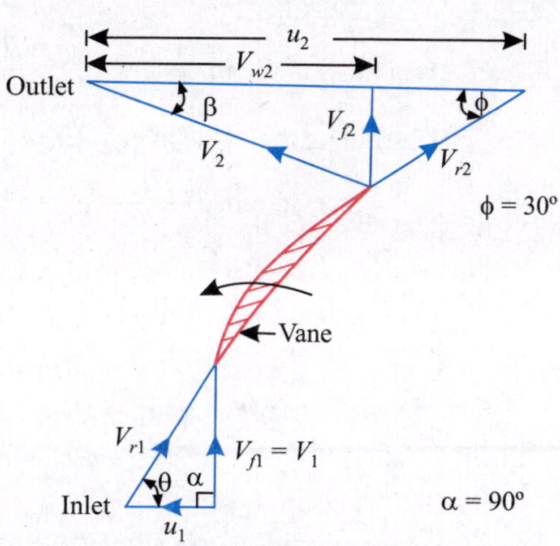

Fig. 3. 15

(i) Theoretical head developed:

In case of a centrifugal pump the Euler or outlet theoretical head is given by:

$$H_e = \frac{V_{w2}u_2 - V_{w1}u_1}{g}$$

As the flow is radial, $\alpha = 90°$, and $V_{w1} = 0$

$$\therefore \quad H_e = \frac{V_{w2}u_2}{g}$$

Now,
$$u_2 = \frac{\pi D_2 N}{60} = \frac{\pi \times 0.72 \times 1200}{60} = 45.24 \text{ m/ s}$$

$$V_{f2} = \frac{Q}{\pi D_2 B_2} = \frac{0.389}{\pi \times 0.72 \times 0.09} = 1.91 \text{ m/s}$$

From velocity triangle at *outlet* (Fig. 3.15), we have:

$$\tan\phi = \frac{V_{f2}}{u_2 - V_{w2}}, \text{ or, } u_2 - V_{w2} = \frac{V_{f2}}{\tan\phi}, \text{ or, } V_{w2} = u_2 - \frac{V_{f2}}{\tan\phi}$$

$$\therefore \quad V_{w2} = 45.24 - \frac{1.91}{\tan 30°} = 41.93 \text{ m/ s}$$

$$\therefore \quad H_e \text{ (Euler head)} = \frac{V_{w2}u_2}{g} = \frac{41.93 \times 45.24}{9.81} = \mathbf{193.4 \text{ m}} \text{ (Ans.)}$$

(ii) Manometric efficiency, η_{mano}:

$$\eta_{mano} = \frac{\text{Manometric head}}{\text{Theoretical head}} = \frac{165}{193.4} = 0.853 \text{ or } \mathbf{85.3\%} \text{ (Ans.)}$$

(iii) Pressure rise across the impeller:

Applying energy equation between the inlet (suffix 1) and outlet (suffix 2), we have

$$\frac{p_1}{w} + \frac{V_1^2}{2g} + z_1 + H_e = \frac{p_2}{w} + \frac{V_2^2}{2g} + z_2 + h_{loss}$$

(where, h_{loss} = head loss in impeller)

Pressure rise,
$$\frac{p_2 - p_1}{w} = H_e + \frac{V_1^2 - V_2^2}{2g} - h_{loss} \quad ...(i) \text{ (Assuming } z_1 = z_2)$$

where,
$$V_1^2 = V_{f1}^2 = 1.912 = 3.648$$

$$V_2^2 = V_{f1}^2 + V_{w2}^2 = 1.91^2 + 41.93^2 = 1761.77$$

$$(\because V_{f1} = V_{f2} = 1.91 \text{ m/s})$$

Head loss in the impeller, $h_{loss} = \dfrac{0.12V_2^2}{2g} = \dfrac{0.12 \times 1761.77}{2 \times 9.81} = 10.77$ m

Substituting the value in eqn. (*i*), we have:

$$\text{Pressure rise, } \frac{p_2 - p_1}{w} = 193.4 + \frac{3.648 - 1761.77}{2 \times 9.81} - 10.77 = \mathbf{93.02\ m}\ \textbf{(Ans.)}$$

(*iv*) Pressure rise and loss of head in casing:

$$\text{Pressure rise in casing} = H_{mano} - \text{pressure rise in impeller}$$
$$= 165 - 93.02 = \mathbf{71.98\ m}\ \textbf{(Ans.)}$$

$$\text{Loss of head in casing} = H_e - H_{mano} - h_{loss}$$
$$= 193.4 - 165 - 10.77 = \mathbf{17.63\ m}\ \textbf{(Ans.)}$$

(*v*) Inlet vane angle, θ:

From velocity triangle at *inlet*, we have:

$$\tan\theta = \frac{V_{f1}}{u_1} = \frac{1.91}{(\pi D_1 N/60)} = \frac{1.91}{(\pi \times 0.36 \times 1200/60)} = 0.0844$$

$$\therefore \quad \theta = \tan^{-1}(0.0844) = \mathbf{4.8^\circ}\ \textbf{(Ans.)}$$

(*vi*) Power required to drive the pump, P:

$$\text{Overall efficiency,} \quad \eta_0 = \frac{wQH_{mano}}{P}$$

$$\text{or} \quad P = \frac{wQH_{mano}}{\eta_0} = \frac{9.81 \times 0.389 \times 165}{0.7} = 899.5\ \text{kW}$$

Mechanical efficiency, η_m:

$$\text{We know that,} \quad \eta_0 = \eta_{mano} \times \eta_v \times \eta_m$$

Assuming volumetric efficiency (η_v) to be 100%, we have:

$$\eta_m = \frac{\eta_0}{\eta_{mano}} = \frac{0.7}{0.853} = 0.82 \text{ or } \mathbf{82\ \%}\ \textbf{(Ans.)}$$

Example 3.15. *A centrifugal pump lifts water under a static head of 36 m of water of which 4 m is suction lift. Suction and delivery pipes are both 150 mm in diameter. The head loss in suction pipe is 1.8 m and in delivery pipe 7 m. The impeller is 380 mm in diameter and 25 mm wide at mouth and revolves at 1200 r.p.m. Its exit blade angle is 35°. If the manometric efficiency of the pump is 82 percent determine:*

(*i*) *The discharge through the pump, and*

(*ii*) *The pressure at the suction and delivery branches of the pump.* **[M.U]**

Solution. Static head, $H_{stat} = 36$ m; Suction lift, $h_s = 4$ m;

The diameter of each of the suction and delivery pipes,

$D_s = D_d = 150$ mm or 0.15 m;

Head lost in suction pipe, $h_{fs} = 1.8$ m;

Head lost in delivery pipe, $h_{fd} = 7$ m;

Diameter of impeller at the outlet, $D_2 = 380$ mm or 0.38 m

Width of impeller at the outlet, $B_2 = 25$ mm or 0.025 m

Speed of impeller, N = 1200 r.p.m.

Outlet blade/ vane angle, ϕ = 35°

Manometric efficiency, η_{mano} = 82%

(i) The discharge through the pump, Q :

Total head to be supplied by the pump,

$$H_{mano} = (h_s + h_d) + h_{fs} + h_{fd} = 36 + 1.8 + 7 = 44.8 \text{ m}$$

[where $(h_s + h_d) = H_{stat} = 36$ m ...(*Given*)]

Tangential/periphery velocity of impeller/ wheel at outlet,

$$u_2 = \frac{\pi D_2 N}{60} = \frac{\pi \times 0.38 \times 1200}{60} = 23.87 \text{ m/s}$$

Assuming flow at the inlet to be *radial*, $\alpha = 90°$

Work done per unit weight of water $= \dfrac{V_{w2} u_2}{g}$

Manometric efficiency, $\eta_{mano} = \dfrac{H_{mano}}{\dfrac{V_{w2} u_2}{g}} = \dfrac{g H_{mano}}{V_{w2} u_2}$

$$\therefore \quad V_{w2} = \frac{g H_{mano}}{\eta_{mano} \times u_2} = \frac{9.81 \times 44.8}{0.82 \times 2387} = 22.45 \text{ m/s}$$

Now, $\tan \phi = \dfrac{V_{f2}}{u_2 - V_{w2}}$ (Refer to Fig. 3.8)

or, $\tan 35° = \dfrac{V_{f2}}{23.87 - 22.45}$, or, $V_{f2} = \tan 35° \, (23.87 - 22.45) = 0.99$ m/s

$\therefore$ Discharge, $Q = \pi D_2 B_2 \times V_{f2} = \pi \times 0.38 \times 0.025 \times 0.99 =$ **0.0295 m³/s (Ans.)**

(ii) The pressure at the suction and delivery branches of the pump :

Velocity in suction or delivery pipe, V_s or $V_d = \dfrac{Q}{\text{Area of pipe}} = \dfrac{0.0295}{\dfrac{\pi}{4} \times 0.15^2} = 1.67$ m/s

$$\text{Velocity head, } \frac{V_s^2}{2g} = \frac{V_d^2}{2g} = \frac{1.67^2}{2 \times 9.81} = 0.142 \text{ m}$$

Total effective pressure on the delivery side

$$= h_d + h_{fd} + \frac{V_d^2}{2g} = 32 + 7 + 0.142 = 39.142 \text{ m of water}$$

$= 9.81 \times 39.142$ kN/m² = **383.98 kN/m² (Ans.)**

$(\because p = wH;\ w = 9.81 \text{ kN/m}^3)$

(where $h_d = H_{stat} - h_s = 36 - 4 = 32$ m)

Pressure on the suction side $= h_s + h_{fs} + \dfrac{V_s^2}{2g} = 4 + 1.8 + 0.142 = 5.942$ m of water *vacuum*

or, $10 - 5.942 = 4.058$ m of water absolute

$= 9.81 \times 4.058$ kN/m² = **39.8 kN/m² absolute (Ans.)**

Example 3.16. *A centrifugal impeller has dimensions and blade angles as given in Fig. 3.16. Water at the rate of 60 litres per second enters the impeller radially and the radial velocity remains constant in the impeller. Determine the impeller speed and the torque produced by it.* **[GATE]**

data: $R_1 = 7.5$ cm

$R_2 = 15$ cm

$\beta_1 = \beta_2 = 30°$

Impeller inlet area, $A_1 = 250\ \text{cm}^2$.

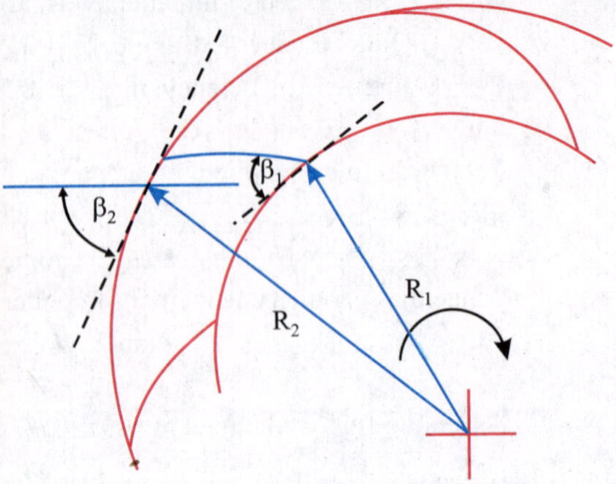

Fig. 3.16

Solution. *Given:* $Q = 60\ l/s = 0.06\ \text{m}^3/\text{s}$;

$R_1 = 7.5\ \text{cm} = 0.075\ \text{m}$;

$R_2 = 15\ \text{cm} = 0.15\ \text{m}\ \beta_1 = \beta_2 = 30°$

Impeller inlet area, $A_1 = 250\ \text{cm}^2$

$= 250 \times 10^{-4}\ \text{m}^2$

$$\therefore \quad V_1 = \frac{Q}{A} = \frac{0.06}{250 \times 10^{-4}} = 2.4\ \text{m/s}$$

If speed of the impeller is N r.p.m. then,

$$u_1 = \frac{2\pi R_1 N}{60} = \frac{2\pi \times 0.075N}{60} = 0.00785\ \text{N}$$

$$u_2 = \frac{2\pi R_2 N}{60} = \frac{2\pi \times 0.15 \times N}{60} = 0.0157\ \text{N}$$

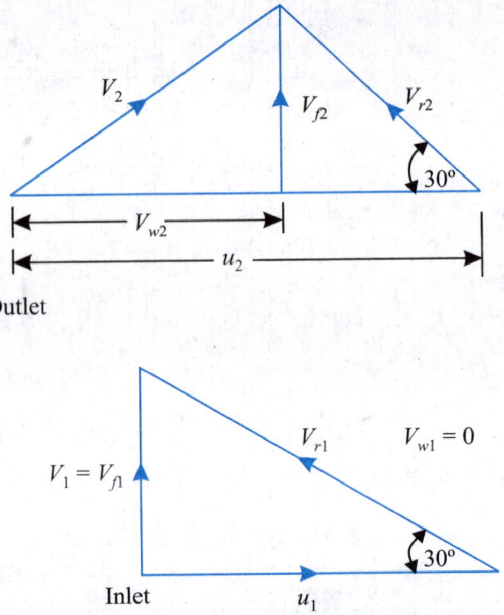

Fig. 3.17

From *inlet velocity triangle*, we have:

$$\tan 30° = \frac{V_{f1}}{u_1}, \quad \text{or,} \quad u_1 = \frac{V_{f1}}{\tan 30°}$$

$$= \frac{2.4}{\tan 30°} = 4.16\ \text{m/s}$$

$$\therefore \quad u_1 = 4.16 = 0.00785\ \text{N}$$

or, Impeller speed,

$$N = \frac{4.16}{0.00785} = \mathbf{530\ r.p.m.}\ \textbf{(Ans.)}$$

$$V_{r1} = \sqrt{V_{f1}^2 + u_1^2} = \sqrt{(2.4)^2 + (4.16)^2} = 4.8\ \text{m/s} = V_{r2}$$

$$u_2 = 0.0157\ \text{N} = 0.0157 \times 530 = 8.32\ \text{m/s}$$

From *outlet velocity triangle*, we have:

$$V_{w2} = u_2 - V_{r2}\cos 30°$$

$$= 8.32 - 4.8 \times \cos 30° = 4.16\ \text{m/s}$$

$$\text{Torque} = \frac{W}{g} \times V_{w2}R_2 = \frac{wQ}{g} \times V_{w2}R_2 = \frac{(1000 \times g) \times 0.06}{g} \times 4.16 \times 0.15 = \mathbf{37.44\ Nm}\ \textbf{(Ans.)}$$

Example 3.17. *A centrifugal pump is required to discharge 0.2 m^3 of water per second against a head of 22 m when the impeller rotates at a speed of 1500 r.p.m. The manometric efficiency is 75 percent. The loss of head in pump in metres due to fluid resistance is 0.03 V_2^2 where V_2 m/s is the velocity of water leaving the impeller. The area of the impeller outlet surface is 1.2 D_2^2 m^2, where D is the impeller diameter in m. Determine:*

(i) The impeller diameter, and (ii) The outlet vane angle.

Assume that the water enters the impeller without whirl.

Solution. Discharge through the centrifugal pump, $Q = 0.2 \text{ m}^3/\text{s}$

Manometric head, $H_{mano} = 22$ m

Speed of the impeller, $N = 1500$ r.p.m.

Manometric efficiency, $\eta_{mano} = 75\%$

Loss of head due to fluid resistance $= 0.03\, V_2^2$

Area of impeller outlet surface $= 1.2\, D_2^2$

(i) The impeller diameter, D_2 :

$$\eta_{mano} = \frac{gH_{mano}}{V_{w2}u_2} \quad \text{...[Eqn. 3.9]}$$

$$\therefore \quad = \frac{V_{w2}u_2}{g} = \frac{H_{mano}}{\eta_{mano}} = \frac{22}{0.75} = 29.33 \text{ m} \quad \text{...}(i)$$

Also,
$$H_{mano} = \frac{V_{w2}u_2}{g} - \text{loss of head in the pump} \quad \text{[Eqn. 3.5]}$$

$$\therefore \quad \text{Losses in the pump} = 29.33 - 22 = 7.33 \text{ m}$$

Thus,
$$0.03\, V_2^2 = 7.33, \quad \text{or,} \quad V_2 = \left(\frac{7.33}{0.03}\right)^{1/2} = 15.63 \text{ m/s}$$

Velocity of flow at outlet,
$$V_{f2} = \frac{Q}{\text{Area of flow}} = \frac{0.2}{1.2\, D_2^2} = \frac{0.167}{D_2^2} \text{ m/s}$$

Peripheral or tangential velocity of impeller at outlet,

$$u_2 = \frac{\pi D_2 N}{60} = \frac{\pi \times D_2 \times 1500}{60} = 78.54\, D_2$$

Substituting the value of u_2 in eqn (*i*), we have

$$V_{w2} = \frac{g \times 29.33}{u_2} = \frac{9.81 \times 29.33}{78.54 D_2} = \frac{3.66}{D_2} \text{ m/s}$$

Refer to Fig. 3.8. From velocity triangle at *outlet*, we have:

$$V_{f2} = (V_2^2 - V_{w2}^2)^{1/2}$$

or,
$$\frac{0.167}{D_2^2} = \left[(15.63)^2 - \left(\frac{3.66}{D_2}\right)^2\right]^{1/2} = \left[244.3 - \frac{13.4}{D_2^2}\right]^{1/2}$$

Squaring both sides, we have:

or,
$$\frac{0.0279}{D_2^4} = 244.3 - \frac{13.4}{D_2^2}, \quad \text{or,} \quad 0.0279 = 244.3 D_2^4 - 13.4 D_2^2$$

or, $$244.3D_2^4 - 13.4D_2^2 - 0.0279 = 0$$

$$D_2^2 = \frac{13.4 \pm \sqrt{13.4^2 + 4 \times 244.3 \times 0.0279}}{2 \times 244.3} = \frac{13.4 \pm 14.38}{2 \times 244.3} = 0.0568 \text{ m}^2 \text{ (ignoring –ve sign)}$$

$\therefore$ $$D_2 = \sqrt{0.0568} = 0.238 \text{ or } \mathbf{238\ mm}\ \textbf{(Ans.)}$$

(*ii*) Outlet vane angle, ϕ:

From velocity triangle at *outlet*, we have:

$$\tan\phi = \frac{V_{f2}}{u_2 - V_{w2}} = \frac{(0.167/0.238^2)}{(78.54 \times 0.238) - 3.66/0.238)} = \frac{2.95}{18.69 - 15.38} = 0.8912$$

$\therefore$ $$\phi = \tan^{-1}(0.8912) = \mathbf{41.7°}\ \textbf{(Ans.)}$$

Example 3.18. *The following data refer to a radial, single stage, double suction, centrifugal pump:*

Discharge at the pump outlet = 90 litres / sec; Diameter at inlet = 100 mm;

Diameter at outlet = 290 mm; Head = 36 m;

Speed of impeller = 1750 r.p.m; Width at inlet = 25 mm per side; Width at outlet = 23 mm in total;

Overall efficiency = 60 percent; Leakage losses = 2.7 litres / sec;

Mechanical losses = 1.5 kW; Contraction factor due to vane thickness = 0.87;

Outlet vane angle = 27°.

Assuming that water enters the impeller at inlet radially, determine;

(*i*) *The inlet vane angle,*

(*ii*) *The angle at which water leaves the wheel,*

(*iii*) *The speed ratio,*

(*iv*) *The absolute velocity of water leaving the impeller,*

(*v*) *The manometric efficiency,*

(*vi*) *The volumetric efficiency, and*

(*vii*) *The mechanical efficiency.*

Solution. *Given* : Q_{po} = 90 litres/sec. = 0.09 m^3/s; D_1 = 100 mm or 0.1 m; D_2 = 290 mm or 0.29 m; H_{mano} = 36 m; N = 1750 r.p.m; B_1 = 0.025 m per side;

B_2 = 0.023 m in total; η_0 = 60%;

Leakage losses, q = 2.7 litres/sec. = 0.0027 m^3/s;

Mechanical losses = 1.5 kW;

Contraction factor due to vane thickness,

K_t = 0.87; ϕ = 27°; α = 90°.

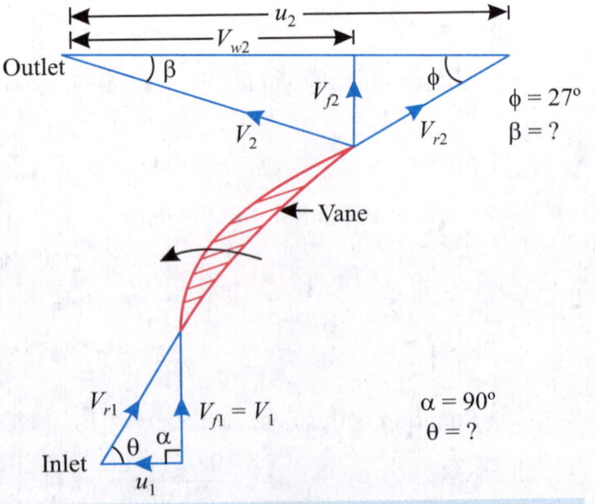

Fig. 3.18

(*i*) The quantity of water handled:

Total quantity of water handled by pump,

$$Q = Q_{po} + q = 0.09 + 0.0027 = 0.0927 \text{ m}^3/\text{s}$$

(where, Q_{po} = discharge at pump outlet)

$\therefore$ $$Q \text{ per side} = \frac{0.0927}{2} = 0.04635 \text{ m}^3/\text{s}$$

Peripheral speed at inlet,

$$u_1 = \frac{\pi D_1 N}{60} = \frac{\pi \times 0.1 \times 1750}{60} = 9.16 \text{ m/s}$$

Also, $$Q = K_t \times \pi D_1 B_1 \times V_{f1}$$

or, $$V_{f1} = \frac{Q}{K_t \times \pi D_1 B_1}$$

or, $$V_{f1} = \frac{0.04635}{0.87 \times \pi \times 0.1 \times 0.025} = 6.78 \text{ m/s}$$

From velocity triangle at *inlet* (Fig. 3.18), we have:

$$\tan\theta = \frac{V_{f1}}{u_1} = \frac{6.78}{9.16} = 0.74 \quad \therefore \theta = \tan^{-1}(0.74) = \mathbf{36.5°} \quad \textbf{(Ans.)}$$

(*ii*) The angle at which water leaves the wheel, β:

Again, $$Q = K_t \times \pi D_2 B_2 \times V_{f2}$$

$$\left(\text{where, } B_2 = \frac{0.023}{2} = 0.0115 \text{ m from one side}\right)$$

$\therefore$ Velocity of flow at outlet, $$V_{f2} = \frac{Q}{K_t \pi D_2 B_2} = \frac{0.04635}{0.87 \times \pi \times 0.29 \times 0.0115} = 5.08 \text{ m/s}$$

Peripheral speed at outlet, $$u_2 = \frac{\pi D_2 N}{60} = \frac{\pi \times 0.29 \times 1750}{60} = 26.57 \text{ m/s}$$

From velocity triangle at *outlet* (fig. 3.18), we have:

$$\tan\phi = \frac{V_{f2}}{u_2 - V_{w2}}, \quad \text{or,} \quad u_2 - V_{w2} = \frac{V_{f2}}{\tan\phi}$$

$\therefore$ $$V_{w2} = u_2 - \frac{V_{f2}}{\tan\phi} = 26.57 - \frac{5.08}{\tan 27°} = 16.6 \text{ m/s}$$

Further, $$\tan\beta = \frac{V_{f2}}{V_{w2}} = \frac{5.08}{16.6} = 0.306$$

$\therefore$ $$\beta = \tan^{-1}(0.306) = \mathbf{17°} \textbf{ (Ans.)}$$

(*iii*) The speed ratio, K_{u2}:

$$K_{u2} = \frac{u_2}{\sqrt{2gH_{mano}}} = \frac{26.57}{\sqrt{2 \times 9.81 \times 36}} \simeq \mathbf{1} \textbf{ (Ans.)}$$

(*iv*) The absolute velocity of water leaving the impeller, V_2:

Refer to Fig. 3.18: $V_2 \cos\beta = V_{w2}$, or, $$V_2 = \frac{V_{w2}}{\cos\beta} = \frac{16.6}{\cos 17°} = \mathbf{17.36 \text{ m/s}} \textbf{ (Ans.)}$$

(v) The manometric efficiency, η_{mano}:

$$\eta_{mano} = \frac{gH_{mano}}{V_{w2}u_2} \quad \text{...Eqn. (3.9)}$$

$$= \frac{9.81 \times 36}{16.6 \times 26.57} = 0.8 \text{ or } \mathbf{80\ \%\ (Ans.)}$$

(vi) The volumetric efficiency, η_v:

$$\eta_v = \frac{Q_{po}}{Q_{po} + q} = \frac{0.09}{0.09 + 0.0027} = 0.97 \text{ or } \mathbf{97\ \%\ (Ans.)}$$

(vii) The mechanical efficiency, η_m:

$$\eta_m = \frac{\text{Shaft power} - \text{mechanical losses}}{\text{Shaft power}}$$

But, shaft power $= \dfrac{wQ_{po}H_{mano}}{\eta_0} = \dfrac{9.81 \times (0.09/2) \times 36}{0.6} = 26.49 \text{ kW}$

$$\therefore \quad = \frac{26.49 - 1.5}{26.49} = 0.9433 \text{ or } \mathbf{94.33\ \%\ (Ans.)}$$

Example 3.19. *A centrifugal pump impeller, having outlet diameter 0.35 m is running at 960 r.p.m. The velocity of flow (assumed constant throughout the system) is equal to 2.4 m/s. The vane angle at outlet is 28°. The static suction lift is 4.03 m. The energy losses in suction pipe, impeller and volute casing* are *0.88 m, 0.70 m and 1.26 m of water respectively. Determine the readings of vacuum or pressure gauges placed at:*

(i) Inlet to the pump,

(ii) Impeller outlet (in clearance between impeller and outlet), and

(iii) Pump outlet or delivery flange, 0.24 m above the centreline of the pump.

Solution. Diameter of impeller at outlet, $D_2 = 0.35$ m

Speed of impeller, $N = 960$ r.p.m.

Velocity of flow, $V_{f1} = V_{f2} = 2.4$ m/s

The vane angle at outlet, $\phi = 28°$

The static suction lift, $h_s = 4.03$ m

The energy losses in suction pipe, $h_{fs} = 0.88$ m

The energy losses in impeller, $h_{Li} = 0.70$ m

The energy losses in volute casing, $h_{Lc} = 1.26$ m

(i) Reading of the vacuum gauge at inlet to the pump, p_s:

The pressure head at inlet to the pump is given by,

$$\frac{p_s}{w} = -\left[h_s + h_{fs} + \frac{V_s^2}{2g}\right] = -\left(4.03 + 0.88 + \frac{2.4^2}{2 \times 9.81}\right) = -\ \mathbf{5.2\ m\ (Ans.)}$$

(ii) Reading of the gauge at impeller outlet, $\frac{p_2}{w}$:

$$\frac{p_s}{w} + \frac{V_s^2}{2g} + \frac{V_{w2}u_2}{g} = \frac{p_2}{w} + \frac{V_2^2}{2g} + h_{Li} \quad \text{...}(i)$$

Now, $u_2 = \dfrac{\pi D_2 N}{60} = \dfrac{\pi \times 0.35 \times 960}{60} = 17.59 \text{ m/s}$

Refer to Fig. 3.8.

$$V_{w2} = u_2 - \frac{V_{f2}}{\tan\phi} = 17.59 - \frac{2.4}{\tan 28°} = 13.07 \text{ m/s}$$

$$V_2 = \sqrt{V_{w2}^2 + V_{f2}^2} = \sqrt{13.07^2 + 2.4^2} = 13.29 \text{ m/s}$$

Substituting the above values in eqn. (*i*), we have:

$$-5{\cdot}2 + \frac{2.4^2}{2 \times 9.81} + \frac{13.07 \times 17.59}{9.81} = \frac{p_2}{w} + \frac{13.29^2}{2 \times 9.81} + 0.7$$

or, $$-5.2 + 0.293 + 23.43 = \frac{p_2}{w} + 9.0 + 0.7$$

or, $$\frac{p_2}{w} = -5.2 + 0.293 + 23.43 - 9.0 - 0.7 = \mathbf{8.82\ m}$$ **(Ans.)**

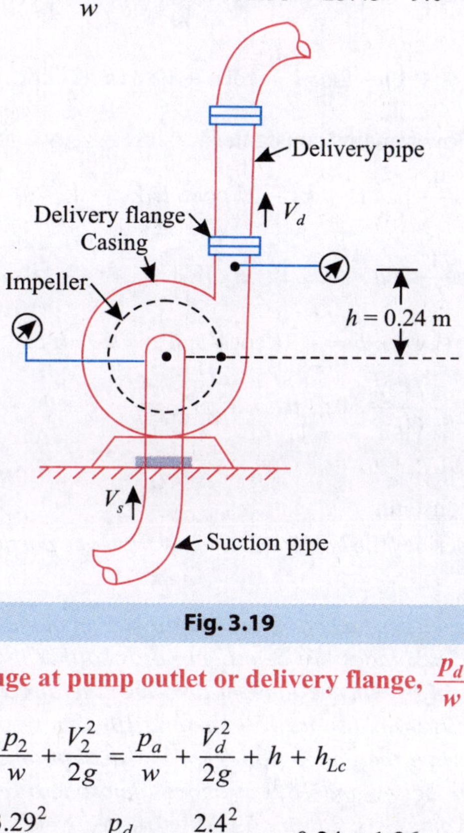

Fig. 3.19

(*iii*) **Reading of the gauge at pump outlet or delivery flange, $\frac{p_d}{w}$:**

Refer to Fig. 3.19: $$\frac{p_2}{w} + \frac{V_2^2}{2g} = \frac{p_a}{w} + \frac{V_d^2}{2g} + h + h_{Lc}$$

or, $$8.82 + \frac{13.29^2}{2 \times 9.81} = \frac{p_d}{w} + \frac{2.4^2}{2 \times 9.81} + 0.24 + 1.26$$

or, $$8.82 + 9.0 = \frac{p_d}{w} + 0.293 + 0.24 + 1.26$$

∴ $$\frac{p_d}{w} = 8.82 + 9.0 - 0.293 - 0.24 - 1.26 = \mathbf{16.03\ m}$$ **(Ans.)**

Example 3.20. *Show that, in general, for a centrifugal pump running at speed N and giving a discharge Q, the manometric head is expressible in the form:*

$$H_{mano} = AN^2 + BNQ + CQ^2$$

where A, B and C are constants.

Solution. Pressure rise, $\frac{p_2 - p_1}{w} = \frac{1}{2g}[V_{f1}^2 + u_2^2 - V_{f2}^2 \text{cosec}^2\phi]$ ...[Refer to example 3.10.]

The above relationship has been derived by neglecting gravitational effects, any friction losses, and assuming radial entry of water. Further, neglecting any loss of head in the pump, the manometric head is given by *pressure rise through the impeller together with a certain percentage of kinetic head at the impeller exit which is recovered in the volute chamber or the diffuser ring.* Thus,

$$H_{mano} = \frac{p_2 - p_1}{w} + \frac{kV_2^2}{2g}$$

where, $V_2^2 = V_{f2}^2 + V_{f2}^2 \cot^2\phi + u_2^2 - 2u_2 V_{f2} \cot\phi$ ...Refer to example 3.10

$$\therefore \quad H_{mano} = \frac{1}{2g}[V_{f1}^2 + u_2^2 - V_{f2}^2 \text{cosec}^2\phi] + \frac{k}{2g}[V_{f2}^2 + V_{f2}^2 \cot^2\phi + u_2^2 - 2u_2V_{f2}\cot\phi]$$

$$= \frac{1}{2g}[u_2^2(1+k) - 2ku_2V_{f2}\cot\phi + V_{f2}^2(k + k\cot^2\phi - \text{cosec}^2\phi) + V_{f1}^2]$$

Assuming, velocity of flow remains constant, $V_{f1} = V_{f2} = V_f$, we have:

$$H_{mano} = \frac{1}{2g}[u_2^2(1+k) - 2k\cot\phi\, u_2V_f + V_f^2(k + k\cot^2\phi - \text{cosec}^2\phi)]$$

$$= \frac{1}{2g}[au_2^2 + bu_2V_f + cV_f^2]$$

where, $a = (1 + k);\ b = -2k\cot\phi$ and $c = k + k\cot^2\phi - \text{cosec}^2\phi$

Also, $u_2 = \frac{\pi D_2 N}{60}$ *i.e.*, $u_2 \propto N;\ V_f = \frac{Q}{A}$ *i.e.* $V_f \propto Q$

$$H_{mano} = AN^2 + BNQ + CQ^2$$ **...Proved**

(where A, B and C are constants.)

The above equation prescribes the *head delivery law from one particular pump at one particular speed.*

Example 3.21. *The impeller of a centrifugal pump has an outer diameter of 250 mm and an effective area of 0.017 m². The blades are bent backwards so that the direction of outlet relative velocity makes an angle of 148° with the tangent drawn in the direction of impeller rotaton, the diameters of suction and delivery pipes are 150 mm and 100 mm respectively. The pump delivers 0.031 m³/s at 1450 r.p.m. when the gauge points on the suction and delivery pipes close to the pumps show heads of 4.6 m below and 18.0 m above atmosphere respectively. The head losses in the suction and delivery pipes are 2.0 m and 2.9 m respectively. The motor driving the pump delivers 8.67 kW. Assumimg that water enters the pump without shock and whirl, determine:*

(i) *The manometric efficiency, and*

(ii) *The overall efficiency of the pump.* **[UPSC Exams.]**

Solution. Outer diameter of impeller, D_2 = 250 mm = 0.25 m

Effiective area of flow = 0.017 m²

Outlet vane angle, ϕ = 180° – 148° = 32°

Diameter of the suction pipe, D_s = 150 mm = 0.15 m

Diameter of the delivery pipe, D_d = 100 mm = 0.1 m

Discharge through the pump, $Q = 0.031\ m^3/s$

Speed of the pump, $N = 1450$ r.p.m.

Head lost in the suction pipe, $h_{fs} = 2.0$ m

Head lost in the delivery pipe, $h_{fd} = 2.9$ m

Power delivered to the pump, $P = 8.67$ kW

(*i*) The manometric efficiency, η_{mano}:

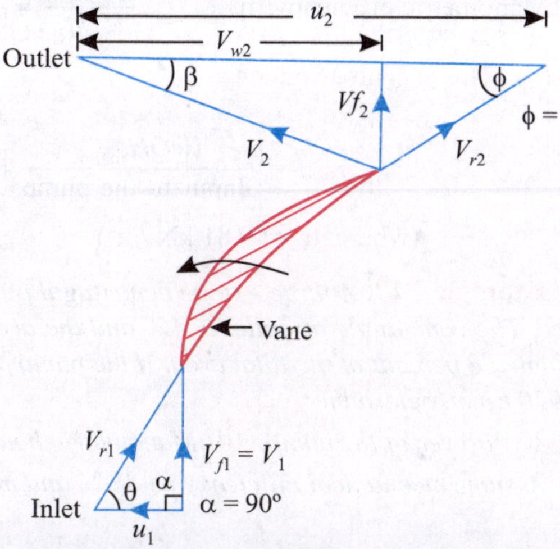

Fig. 3.20

Velocity in the suction pipe,

$$V_s = \frac{Q}{\frac{\pi}{4} \times D_s^2} = \frac{0.031}{\frac{\pi}{4} \times 0.15^2} = 1.754 \text{ m/s}$$

Invoking Bernoulli's equation between the water surface in the sump and the pump inlet where pressure gauge is fitted, we have:

$$0 = h_s + h_{fs} + \frac{p_s}{w} + \frac{V_s^2}{2g}$$

or, $$0 = h_s + 2.0 - 4.6 + \frac{(1.754)^2}{2 \times 9.81}$$

or, $$h_s = -2.0 + 4.6 - \frac{(1.754)^2}{2 \times 9.81} = 2.44 \text{ m}$$

Again, applying Bernoulli's equation between the impeller outlet where the delivery pressure gauge is fitted and outlet of the delivery pipe, we have:

$$\frac{p_d}{w} + \frac{V_d^2}{2g} = h_d + h_{fd} + \frac{V_d^2}{2g}$$

or, $$h_d = \frac{p_d}{w} - h_{fd} = 18 - 2.9 = 15.1 \text{ m}$$

From velocity triangle at *outlet* (Fig. 3.20), we have:

$$\tan\phi = \frac{V_{f2}}{u_2 - V_{w2}}, \text{ or, } u_2 - V_{w2} = \frac{V_{f2}}{\tan\phi}, \text{ or, } V_{w2} = u_2 - \frac{V_{f2}}{\tan 32°}$$

or, $$V_{w2} = u_2 - \frac{V_{f2}}{\tan 32°} = u_2 - 1.6\,V_{f2}$$

where, $$u_2 = \frac{\pi D_2 N}{60} = \frac{\pi \times 0.25 \times 1450}{60} = 18.98 \text{ m/s}$$

and, $$V_{f2} = \frac{Q}{\text{Effective area of flow}} = \frac{0.031}{0.017} = 1.82 \text{ m/s}$$

∴ $$V_{w2} = 18.98 - 1.6 \times 1.82 = 16.07 \text{ m/s}$$

Velocity in the delivery pipe, $$V_d = \frac{Q}{\frac{\pi}{4} \times D_d^2} = \frac{0.031}{\frac{\pi}{4} \times 0.1^2} = 3.95 \text{ m/s}$$

Manometric head, $H_{mano} = (h_s + h_d) + (h_{fs} + h_{fd}) + \dfrac{V_d^2}{2g}$

$$= (2.44 + 15.1) + (2.0 + 2.9) + \frac{3.95^2}{2 \times 9.81} = 23.23\,\text{m}$$

Manometric efficiency, $\eta_{mano} = \dfrac{gH_{mano}}{V_{w2}u_2} = \dfrac{9.81 \times 23.23}{16.07 \times 18.98} = 0.747$ or **74.7% (Ans.)**

(*ii*) The overall efficiency, η_0:

$$= \frac{wQH_{mano}}{\text{Input to the pump}} = \frac{9.81 \times 0.031 \times 23.23}{8.67} = 0.8148, \text{ or, } \mathbf{81.48\%}$$

(where, $w = 9.81$ kN/m^3)

Example 3.22. *A three - stage centrifugal pump has impeller 400 mm in diameter and 20 mm wide. The vane angle at outlet is 45° and the area occupied by the thickness of the vanes may be assumed 8 percent of the total area. If the pump delivers 3.6 m^3 of water per minute when running at 920 r.p.m. determine:*

(i) Power of the pump, (ii) Manometric head, and (iii) Specific speed.

Assume mechanical efficiency as 88 % and manometric efficiency as 77 percent.

[Delhi University]

Solution. Number of stage, $n = 3$

Diameter of impeller at outlet, D_2 = 400 mm = 0.4 m

Width of impeller at outlet, B_2 = 20 mm = 0.02 m

Outlet vane angle, ϕ = 45°

Area occupied by thickness of vanes = 8% of the total area

Discharge through the pump, Q = 3.6 m^3/min. = 0.06 m^3/s

Speed of the impeller, N = 920 r.p.m.

Mechanical efficiency = 88%.

Manometric efficiency = 77%.

(*i*) Manometric head $(H_{mano})_{total}$:

Peripheral or tangential velocity of impeller at outlet,

$$u_2 = \frac{\pi D_2 N}{60} = \frac{\pi \times 0.4 \times 920}{60} = 19.27 \text{ m/s}$$

$$\text{Net outlet area} = \left(1 - \frac{8}{100}\right)\pi D_2 B_2$$

$$= 0.92\pi \times 0.4 \times 0.02 = 0.02312 \text{ m}^2$$

Velocity of flow at outlet,

$$= \frac{Q}{\text{Net outlet area}} = \frac{0.06}{0.02312} = 2.59 \text{ m/s}$$

From velocity triangle at *outlet* (Fig. 3.21), we have:

$$\tan\phi = \frac{V_{f2}}{u_2 - V_{w2}}, \text{ or, } u_2 - V_{w2} = \frac{V_{f2}}{\tan\phi}$$

or, $$V_{w2} = u_2 - \frac{V_{f2}}{\tan\phi} = 19.27 - \frac{2.59}{\tan 45°} = 16.68 \text{ m/s}$$

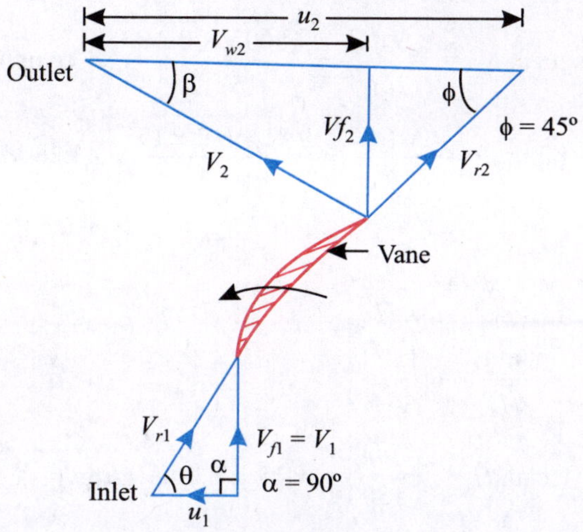

Fig. 3.21

Assuming radial entry, the head developed by each impeller,

$$H_{mano} = \eta_{mano} \times \frac{V_{w2}u_2}{g} = 0.77 \times \frac{16.68 \times 19.27}{9.81} = 25.23 \text{ m}$$

∴ Manometric head $(H_{mano})_{total}$ developed by three impeller,

$$3 \times 25.23 = \mathbf{75.69\ m}\ \textbf{(Ans.)}$$

(ii) Power of the pump, P:

$$\eta_0 = \eta_m \times \eta_{mano} = 0.88 \times 0.77 = 0.6776 \text{ (Assuming } \eta_v \text{ to be unity)}$$

Also, $$\eta_0 = \frac{wQH_{mano}}{\text{Power of pump}}$$

∴ Power of pump, $$P = \frac{wQ(H_{mano})_{total}}{\eta_0} = \frac{9810 \times 0.06 \times 75.69}{1000 \times 0.6776} = \mathbf{65.75\ kW}\ \textbf{(Ans.)}$$

(iii) Specific speed, N_s:

$$N_s = \frac{N\sqrt{Q}}{(H_{mano})^{3/4}},$$ where H_{mano} is the manometric head developed per impeller

...(Eqn. 3.25)

$$= \frac{920 \times \sqrt{0.06}}{(25.23)^{3/4}} = \mathbf{20}\ \textbf{(Ans.)}$$

Example 3.23. *A centrifugal pump rotating at 1500 r.p.m. delivers 0.2 m^3/s at a head of 15 m. Calculate the specific speed of the pump and the power input. Assume overall efficiency of the pump as 0.68.*

If this pump were to operate at 900 r.p.m. what would be the head, discharge and power required for homologous conditions? Assume overall efficiency remains unchanged at new r.p.m.

[UPTU]

Solution. *Given:* $N = 1500$ r.p.m.; $Q = 0.2\ m^3/s$; $H = 15$ m; $\eta_0 = 0.68$; N = 900 r.p.m.

At 1500 r.p.m.:

$$\text{Specific speed, } N_s = \frac{N\sqrt{Q}}{(H)^{3/4}} = \frac{1500 \times \sqrt{0.2}}{(15)^{3/4}} = \mathbf{88} \textbf{ (Ans.)}$$

$$\text{Power input, } P = \frac{wQH}{\eta_0} = \frac{9.81 \times 0.2 \times 15}{0.68} = \mathbf{43.28\ kW} \textbf{ (Ans.)}$$

At 900 r.p.m.:

$$N_u = \frac{N}{\sqrt{H}}$$

i.e.
$$\frac{900}{\sqrt{H}} = \frac{1500}{\sqrt{15}}$$

or,
$$\text{Head, } H = \left(\frac{900}{1500}\right)^2 \times 15 = \mathbf{5.4\ m} \textbf{ (Ans.)}$$

$$Q_u = \frac{Q}{\sqrt{H}}$$

i.e.
$$\frac{Q}{\sqrt{5{\cdot}4}} = \frac{0.2}{\sqrt{15}}$$

$\therefore$
$$Q = \sqrt{\frac{5.4}{15}} \times 0.2 = \mathbf{0.12\ m^3/s} \textbf{ (Ans.)}$$

$$P_u = \frac{P}{(H)^{3/2}}$$

i.e.
$$\frac{P}{(5{\cdot}4)^{3/2}} = \frac{43.28}{(15)^{3/2}}$$

$$P = \left(\frac{5.4}{15}\right)^{3/2} \times 43.28 = \mathbf{9.35\ kW} \textbf{ (Ans.)}$$

Example 3.24. *Two geometrically similar pumps are running at the same speed of 1000 r.p.m. One has an impeller diameter of 0.4 m and discharge of 30 l/s against a head of 20 m. If the other pump gives half of this discharge rate, determine the head and diameter of the second pump.*

[GATE]

Solution. Given: $N_1 = N_2 = 1000$ r.p.m.; $D_1 = 0.4$ m; $Q_1 = 30\ l/s = 0.03\ m^3/s$;

$$H_1 = 20\text{ m}; Q_2 = \frac{30}{2} = 15\, l/s = 0.015\ m^3/s.$$

H_2, D_2 :

All geometrically similar pumps will have the same specific speed.

i.e.
$$N_s = \frac{N_1\sqrt{Q_1}}{(H_1)^{3/4}} = \frac{N_2\sqrt{Q_2}}{(H_2)^{3/4}}$$

or,
$$H_2 = \left[\frac{N_2}{N_1} \times \sqrt{\frac{Q_2}{Q_1}} \times (H_1)^{3/4}\right]^{4/3}$$

$$= \left[\frac{1000}{1000} \times \sqrt{\frac{0.015}{0.030}} \times (20)^{3/4}\right]^{4/3} = \mathbf{12.6\ m}\ \textbf{(Ans.)}$$

Also, $$D \propto \frac{\sqrt{H}}{N}$$

or, $$D_1 \propto \frac{\sqrt{H_1}}{N_1}, \text{ and } D_2 \propto \frac{\sqrt{H_2}}{N_2} \qquad (\because N_1 = N_2)$$

$\therefore$ $$\frac{D_1}{D_2} = \sqrt{\frac{H_1}{H_2}} = \sqrt{\frac{20}{12.6}} = 1.256$$

or, $$D_2 = \frac{D_1}{1.256} = \frac{0.4}{1.256} = \mathbf{0.317\ m}\ \textbf{(Ans.)}$$

Example 3.25. *A centrifugal pump running at 750 r.p.m. discharges water at 0.1 m^3/s against a head of 10 m at its best efficiency. A second pump of the same homologous series, when working at 500 r.p.m., is to deliver water at 0.05 m^3/s at its best efficiency. What will be the design head of the second pump and what is the scale ratio between the first and the second ?* **[GATE]**

Solution. *Given*: N_1 = 750 r.p.m.; $Q_1 = 0.1 m^3/s$; H_1 = 10 m; N_2 = 500 r.p.m.; $Q_2 = 0.05\ m^3/s$

Design head of the second pump, H_2:

We know that, $$\frac{N_1\sqrt{Q_1}}{H_1^{3/4}} = \frac{N_2\sqrt{Q_2}}{H_2^{3/4}}$$

or, $$\frac{750 \times \sqrt{0.1}}{(10)^{3/4}} = \frac{500 \times \sqrt{0.05}}{(H_2)^{3/4}}$$

or, $$42.17 = \frac{111.8}{(H_2)^{3/4}}$$

$\therefore$ $$H_2 = \left(\frac{111.8}{42.17}\right)^{4/3} = \mathbf{3.67\ m}\ \textbf{(Ans.)}$$

(*ii*) Scale ratio, L_r:

We know that, $$\frac{Q_1}{Q_2} = (L_r)^{2.5}$$

or, $$\frac{0.1}{0.05} = (L_r)^{2.5}$$

or, $$L_r = \left(\frac{0.1}{0.05}\right)^{\frac{1}{2.5}} = \mathbf{1.32}\ \textbf{(Ans.)}$$

3.9. MINIMUM SPEED FOR STARTING A CENTRIFUGAL PUMP

When a centrifugal pump is started, it will start delivering liquid only if the pressure rise in the impeller is more than or equal to the manometric head (H_{mano}). In other words, there will be no flow of liquid until the speed of the pump is such that the required centrifugal head caused by the centrifugal force on rotating water when the impeller is rotating, but there is *no flow*

$$= \frac{u_2^2}{2g} - \frac{u_1^2}{2g} = \frac{u_2^2 - u_1^2}{2g}$$

Flow will commence only if $\frac{u_2^2 - u_1^2}{2g} \geq H_{mano}$

For *minimum speed,* we must have:

$$\frac{u_2^2 - u_1^2}{2g} = H_{mano} \quad ...(3.17)$$

Also,

$$\eta_{mano} = \frac{gH_{mano}}{V_{w2}u_2} \quad \text{[Eqn (3.9)]}$$

$$\therefore \quad H_{mano} = \eta_{mano} \times \left(\frac{V_{w2}u_2}{g}\right)$$

Also,

$$u_1 = \frac{\pi D_1 N}{60}; \quad u_2 = \frac{\pi D_2 N}{60}$$

Substituting the values in eqn. (3.17), we get:

$$\frac{1}{2g}\left[\left(\frac{\pi D_2 N}{60}\right)^2 - \left(\frac{\pi D_1 N}{60}\right)^2\right] = \eta_{mano} \times \frac{V_{w2}}{g} \times \left(\frac{\pi D_2 N}{60}\right)$$

Dividing both sides by $\frac{\pi N}{g \times 60}$, we have:

$$\frac{\pi N}{120}(D_2^2 - D_1^2) = \eta_{mano} \times (V_{w2} \times D_2)$$

$$\therefore \quad N\,(i.e.\ N_{min.}) = \frac{120 \times \eta_{mano} \times V_{w2} \times D_2}{\pi\,(D_2^2 - D_1^2)} \quad ...(3.18)$$

Example 3.26. *A centrifugal pump working in a dock pump 1565 litres per second against a mean lift of 6.1m when the impeller rotates at 200 r.p.m.The impeller diameter is 1.22 m and the area at outer periphery is 6450 cm². If the vanes are set back at an angle of 26° at the outlet, determine:*

(i) Hydraulic efficiency,

(ii) Power required to drive the pump, and

(iii) Minimum speed to start pumping if the ratio of external to internal diameter is 2.

[PTU]

Solution. Discharge through the pump, Q = 1565 litres/ sec. or 1.565 m³/s

Actual or manometric head = 6.1 m

Speed of the impeller, N = 200 r.p.m.

Diameter of the impeller at outlet, D_2 = 1.22 m

Area at the outer periphery = 6450 cm² = 0.645 m²

Outlet vane angle, ϕ = 26°

(i) Hydraulic efficiency, η_h:

Peripheral or tangential velocity of impeller at outlet,

$$u_2 = \frac{\pi D_2 N}{60} = \frac{\pi \times 1.22 \times 200}{60} = 12.77 \text{ m/s}$$

$$V_{f2} = \frac{Q}{A} = \frac{1.565}{0.645} = 2.43 \text{ m/s}$$

Refer to Fig. 3.8. $V_{w2} = u_2 - \frac{V_{f2}}{\tan\phi} = 12.77 - \frac{2.43}{\tan 26°} = 7.79 \text{ m/s}$

$$\text{Euler head, } H_e = \frac{V_{w2}u_2}{g} = \frac{7.79 \times 12.77}{9.81} = 10.14 \text{ m}$$

If the effect of slip is *neglected*, ideal head equals Euler head.

$$\therefore \text{ Hydraulic (or manometric) efficiency, } \eta_h = \frac{\text{Actual or manometric head}}{\text{Ideal or Euler head}}$$

or, $\eta_h = \frac{6.1}{10.14} = 0.6016$ or **60.16 % (Ans.)**

(ii) Power required to drive the pump:

Power required to drive the pump (neglecting mechanical losses)

$$= \frac{wQ}{1000} \times \frac{V_{w2}u_2}{g} \text{ kW}$$

$$= \frac{9810 \times 1.565 \times 7.79 \times 12.77}{1000 \times 9.81} = \mathbf{155.68 \text{ kW}} \text{ (Ans.)}$$

(iii) Minimum speed to start pumping, N_{min}:

For *minimum speed*, we must have:

$$\frac{u_2^2 - u_1^2}{2g} = H_{mano}$$

Since, $D_2 = 2D_1$ (*Given*), $\therefore u_2 = 2u_1$

$$\therefore \frac{u_2^2 - u_2^2/4}{2g} = 6.1, \text{ or, } \frac{3u_2^2}{8g}, \text{ or, } u_2 = \left(\frac{6.1 \times 8 \times 9.81}{3}\right)^{\frac{1}{2}} = 12.63 \text{ m/s}$$

Also, $u_2 = \frac{\pi D_2 N_{min}}{60}$, or, $12.63 = \frac{\pi \times 1.22 \times N_{min}}{60}$

$$\therefore N_{min} = \frac{12.63 \times 60}{\pi \times 1.22} = \mathbf{197.7 \text{ r.p.m.}} \text{ (Ans.)}$$

Example 3.27. *A centrifugal pump impeller has diameters at inlet and outlet as 360 mm and 720 mm respectively. The flow velocity at outlet is 2.4 m/s and the vanes are set back at an angle of 45° at the outlet. If the manometric efficiency is 70 percent, calculate the minimum starting speed of the pump.*

Solution. Diameter of impeller at inlet, $D_1 = 360$ mm or 0.36 m

Diameter of impeller at outlet, $D_2 = 720$ mm or 0.72 m

The flow velocity at outlet, $V_{f2} = 2.4$ m/s

Outlet vane angle, $\phi = 45°$

Manometric efficiency, $\eta_{mano} = 70$ %

Minimum starting speed of the pump, N_{min}:

Refer to Fig 3.8. From velocity triangle at *outlet*, we have:

$$\tan\phi = \frac{V_{f2}}{u_2 - V_{w2}}, \text{ or, } u_2 - V_{w2} = \frac{V_{f2}}{\tan\phi} = \frac{2.4}{\tan 45°} = 2.4 \text{ m/s}$$

$$\therefore \quad V_{w2} = u_2 - 2.4$$

But,
$$u_2 = \frac{\pi D_2 N_{min}}{60} = \frac{\pi \times 0.72 N_{min}}{60} = 0.0377\ N_{min}$$

$$\therefore \quad V_{w2} = 0.0377 N_{min} - 2.4$$

Using eqn. (3.17) for minimum starting speed, we have:

$$N_{min} = \frac{120 \times \eta_{mano} \times V_{w2} \times D_2}{\pi (D_2^2 - D_1^2)}$$

$$= \frac{120 \times 0.70 \times (0.0377 N_{min} - 2.4) \times 0.72}{\pi (0.72^2 - 0.36^2)}$$

or,
$$N_{min} = 49.51\ (0.0377 N_{min} - 2.4)$$

$$= 1.866 N_{min} - 118.824$$

or,
$$0.866 N_{min} = 118.824$$

$$\therefore \quad N_{min} = \frac{118.824}{0.866} = \mathbf{137.2\ r.p.m.}\ \textbf{(Ans.)}$$

3.10. EFFECT OF VARIATION OF DISCHARGE ON THE EFFICIENCY

When a centrifugal pump *runs and discharges at its 'designed speed', its efficiency is maximum.* If the discharge is either *increased or decreased its efficiency drops owing to loss of head due to shock at entry to impeller.*

Refer to Fig 3.22:

- *abc* is velocity triangle at *inlet* when the pump is operating under the normal conditions of flow rate (discharge). The relative velocity V_{r1} is along the contour of vane (θ is the inlet vane angle).
- With the decrease (or increase) in discharge, the flow velocity decreases (or increases) from *cb* to *cd.*
- With the pump running at the *same speed,* the peripheral velocity *ac remains unchanged* and the effective inlet velocity diagram becomes edc.
- The new relative velocity *ad* (V'_{r1}) *no longer remains parallel to the vane and consequently shock occurs at entry to impeller.* With fixed value of flow velocity *cd* (V'_{f1}) and flow taking place along the blade, the velocity vector should have the form *cde; de* is parallel to *ab. The sudden change in peripheral velocity ac brings about shock* and as a consequence of which there is a loss of head.

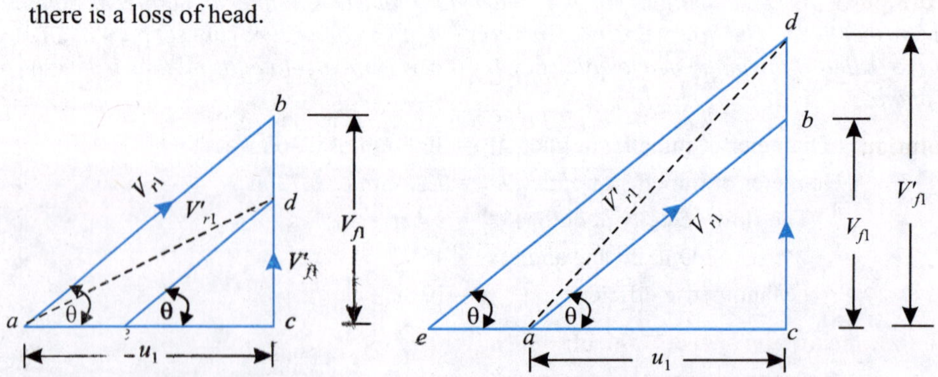

(*a*) Decrease in discharge (*b*) Increase in discharge

Fig. 3.22. Inlet velocity triangles with decrease and increase in discharge.

Loss of head (at entrance to impeller), $H_L = \frac{(\text{Change of velocity})^2}{2g} = \frac{(ae)^2}{2g}$

(*a*) *For decrease in discharge:* $H_L = \frac{(ae)^2}{2g} = \frac{(ac - ec)^2}{2g} = \frac{(u_1 - V'_{f1} \cot\theta)^2}{2g}$ ...(3.19)

(*b*) *For increase in discharge:* $H_L = \frac{(ae)^2}{2g} = \frac{(ec - ac)^2}{2g} = \frac{(V'_{f1} \cot\theta - u_1)^2}{2g}$ ...(3.20)

Example 3.28. *A centrifugal pump is delivering 0.216 m³/s of water against a head of 18 m; the speed of rotation of impeller being 600 r.p.m. The diameters at outer and inner periphery of the impeller are 600 mm and 300 mm respectively. The area of flow is constant at 0.084 m² from inlet to outlet of impeller. If the vanes of the impeller are bent at an angle of 35° to the tangent at exit, determine:*

(*i*) *Manometric efficency,*

(*ii*) *Inlet vane angle, and*

(*iii*) *Loss of head at inlet to impeller when the discharge is reduced by 35 percent.*

Solution. Discharge through the pump, $Q = 0.216 \text{ m}^3/\text{s}$

Manometric head, $H_{mano} = 18 \text{ m}$

Speed of rotation of impeller, $N = 600$ r.p.m.

Diameter of impeller at outlet, $D_1 = 600 \text{ mm} = 0.6 \text{ m}$

Diameter of impeller at inlet, $D_2 = 300 \text{ mm} = 0.3 \text{ m}$

The area of flow, $A_f = 0.084 \text{ m}^2$

Outlet vane angle, $\phi = 35°$

(*i*) Manometric efficiency, η_{mano}:

Peripheral or tangential velocities at inlet and outlet of the impeller are:

$$u_1 = \frac{\pi D_1 N}{60} = \frac{\pi \times 0.3 \times 600}{60} = 9.42 \text{ m/s}$$

$$u_2 = \frac{\pi D_2 N}{60} = \frac{\pi \times 0.6 \times 600}{60} = 18.85 \text{ m/s}$$

Flow velocity, $V_{f1} = V_{f2} = V_f = \frac{Q}{A_f} = \frac{0.216}{0.084} = 2.57 \text{ m/s}$

Refer to Fig 3.8. $V_{w2} = u_2 - \frac{V_{f2}}{\tan\phi} = 18.85 - \frac{2.57}{\tan 35°} = 15.18 \text{ m/s}$

Manometric efficiency, $\eta_{mano} = \frac{gH_{mano}}{V_{w2} u_2}$ ...[Eqn. (3.9)]

$$= \frac{9.81 \times 18}{15.18 \times 18.85} = 0.617 \text{ or } \mathbf{61.7\%} \textbf{ (Ans.)}$$

(*ii*) Inlet vane angle, θ:

Refer to Fig. 3.8. $\tan\theta = \frac{V_{f1}}{u_1} = \frac{2.57}{9.42} = 0.2728$

$\therefore$ $\theta = \tan^{-1}(0.2728) = \mathbf{15.26°}$ **(Ans.)**

(*iii*) Loss of head when the discharge is reduced by 35% :

When the discharge is reduced by 35 %, the velocity of flow,

$$V_f = V'_{f1} = 2.57 \times (1 - 0.35) = 1.67 \text{ m/s}$$

$$\text{Loss of head at inlet} = \frac{(u_1 - V'_{f1} \cot\theta)^2}{2g} \qquad \text{...[Eqn. (3.19)]}$$

$$= \frac{(9.42 - 1.67 \times \cot 15.26°)^2}{2 \times 9.81} = \mathbf{0.55 \text{ m of water}} \text{ (Ans.)}$$

3.11. EFFECT OF NUMBER OF VANES OF IMPELLER ON HEAD AND EFFICIENCY

The velocities indicated in velocity triangles (shown in Fig 3.5 and elsewhere) known as Euler's velocity triangles, can be obtained in practice only if the impeller has *very closely - spaced vanes.* Practically, it is impossible to have a very large number of vanes due to the two *reasons;* (*i*) The larger the number of vanes, the greater is the obstructed area owing to vanes thickness and consequently there is greater loss of head loss due to friction (*ii*) In order to fabricate the impeller easily, it is desirable that passages should be wider; it also minimises the possibility of pump being choked due to floating debris in the liquid.

Although, practically, the vanes are designed according to Euler's velocity triangles yet there is slight difference in the actually developed velocity triangles. The actual velocity of whirl (V_{w2}) at the outlet, *due to secondary or circulatory flow in the impeller,* is less than that in the Euler's velocity triangles. consequently, the actual head imparted (H_{actual}) by the impeller is less than the Euler head (H_e).

Thus, $$H_{actual} < H_e$$

The ratio $\left(\frac{H_{actual}}{H_e}\right)$ is known as *vane efficiency or effectiveness* ε (Greek 'epsilon')

i.e. $$\varepsilon = \frac{H_{actual}}{H_e}$$

It has been observed through experiments that as the *number of vanes is increased the* value of ε *increases and approaches unity.* The value of ε, in addition to number of vanes, depends on the shape of the vane and the outlet vane angle. In general, for radial flow pumps the value of ε varies from 0.6 to 0.8 as the number of vanes is increased from 4 to 12. However, for impeller with vanes more than 24 the value of ε may be taken as unity. Unless otherwise mentioned, the value of ε is taken as unity.

3.12. WORKING PROPORTIONS OF CENTRIFUGAL PUMPS

1. Speed ratio (K_u). *The speed ratio is the ratio of peripheral speed at exit (u_2) to the theoretical velocity of jet corresponding to manometric head (H_{mano})*. Thus,

$$K_u = \frac{u_2}{\sqrt{2gH_{mano}}}; \; K_u \text{ varies from 0.95 to 1.25}$$

2. Flow ratio, (K_f). *The flow ratio is the ratio of the velocity of flow at exit to the theoretical velocity of the jet corresponding to manometric head (H_{mano})*. Thus,

$$K_f = \frac{V_{f2}}{\sqrt{2gH_{mano}}}; \; K_f \text{ varies from 0.1 to 0.25}$$

Diameters of impellers and pipes:

(i) Outlet diameter of impeller (D_2):

Peripheral speed, $u_2 = \dfrac{\pi D_2 N}{60}$, where N is the speed of rotation of impeller.

Also, $$u_2 = K_u\left(\sqrt{2gH_{mano}}\right), \text{ where } K_u \text{ is the speed ratio.}$$

$$\therefore \quad \frac{\pi D_2 N}{60} = K_u\sqrt{2gH_{mano}}, \quad \text{or,} \quad D_2 = \frac{60\,K_u\sqrt{2gH_{mano}}}{\pi N}$$

or, $$D_2 = \frac{84.6K_u\sqrt{H_{mano}}}{N} \qquad \text{...(3.21)}$$

If D_2 and N are known, by using eqn. (3.21) we can find out the head which a pump can develop; it will serve as a cheak for existing pump.

(ii) Inlet diameter of impeller (D_1):

Depending upon specific speed (N_s) or total head (H_{mano}) the inlet diameter D_1 is kept in range; $D_1 = \frac{1}{3}D_2$ to $\frac{2}{3}D_2$. An average value of $D_1 = 0.5D_2$ is usually taken.

(iii) Least diameter of impeller:

The least or minimum diameter of an impeller can be determined on the basics of the fact that the pump will start delivering liquid only when *centrifugal head equals the total head* H_{mano}. Thus,

$$\frac{u_2^2 - u_1^2}{2g} = H_{mano}$$

or, $$\left(\frac{\pi D_2 N}{60}\right)^2 - \left(\frac{\pi D_1 N}{60}\right)^2 = 2gH_{mano}, \quad \text{or,} \quad \left(\frac{\pi N}{60}\right)^2\left(D_2^2 - D_1^2\right) = 2gH_{mano}$$

Taking $D_1 = 0.5D_2$, we obtain:

$$\left(\frac{\pi N}{60}\right)^2\left[D_2^2 - (0.5D_2)^2\right] = 2gH_{mano}, \quad \text{or,} \quad \left(\frac{\pi N}{60}\right)^2 \times 0.75D_2^2 = 2 \times 9.81\,H_{mano}$$

$$\therefore \quad D_2 = \left(\frac{2 \times 9.81H_{mano}}{0.75}\right)^{1/2} \times \frac{60}{\pi N} = \frac{97.68\sqrt{H_{mano}}}{N} \qquad \text{...(3.22)}$$

(iv) Diameter of suction pipe (D_s) :

If D_s is the diameter of the suction pipe and V_s is the velocity of flow in suction pipe (usually V_s is 1.5 to 3 m/s), then the quantity of water to be pumped is given by:

$$Q = \frac{\pi}{4}D_s^2 \times V_s, \quad \text{or,} \quad D_s^2 = \frac{4Q}{\pi V_s}$$

or, $$D_d = \sqrt{\frac{4Q}{\pi V_s}} \qquad \text{...(3.23)}$$

(v) Diameter of delivery pipe (D_d):

If D_d is the diameter of the delivery pipe and V_d is the velocity of flow in delivery pipe (usually V_d is 1.5 to 3.5 m/s), then the discharge,

$$Q = \frac{\pi}{4} \times D_d^2 \times V_d, \quad \text{or,} \quad D_d^2 = \frac{4Q}{\pi V_d}$$

$$\therefore \qquad D_d = \sqrt{\frac{4Q}{\pi V_d}} \qquad \text{...(3.24)}$$

Note : The value of V_d is generally equal to or slightly higher than that V_s.

3.13. MULTI-STAGE CENTRIFUGAL PUMPS

A multi-stage centrifugal pump is one which has *two or more identical impellers* mounted on the same shaft or on different shafts. The important functions performed by a multi-stage pump are:

1. *To produce heads greater than that permissible with a single impeller, 'discharge remaining constant'. The task can be achieved by* ***'series arrangement'*** *where in the impellers are mounted on the same shaft and enclosed in the same casing.*
2. *To discharge a large quantity of liquid, 'head remaining same'.* This task is accomplished by ***'parallel arrangement'*** wherein impellers are mounted on *separate shafts*

3.13.1. Pumps in Series

For obtaining a high head, a number of impellers are mounted in *series* or on the same shaft. Fig. 3.23 shows such an arrangment for a two-stage pump. The discharge from impeller–1 passes through a guided passage and enters the impeller–2. At the outlet of impeller–2, the pressure of water will be more than the pressure of water at outlet of impeller–1. Thus if more number of impellers are mounted on the same shaft the pressure at outlet will be increased further. If in each stage, the manometric head imposed on the liquid is H_{mano}, then for *n identical* impellers the total head developed will be; $H_{total} = nH$, however, the *discharge* passing through each impeller is *same.*

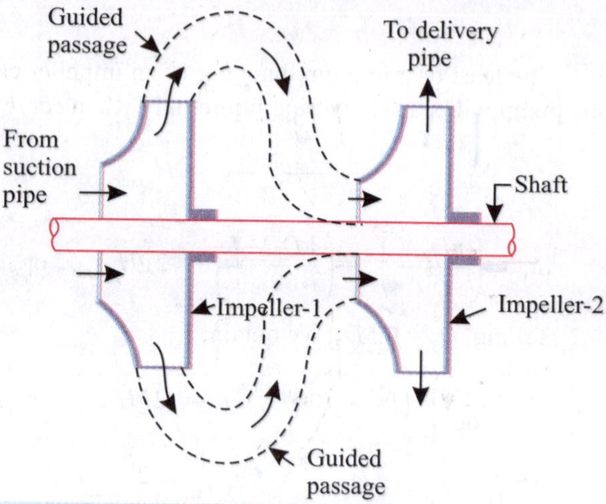

Fig. 3.23. Two-stage pump-impellers in series.

The series arrangement is employed for delivering a *relatively small quantity of liquid against very high heads.*

The *advantages* of multi–stage pumps–impellers in series over single-stage pumps are as follows:

1. Less loss due to friction.
2. Reduced stresses.
3. Small slip leakage.
4. The number of stages may be so chosen that the pump speed suits the driving motor speed.
5. By proper arrangement of impellers a thrust can be eliminated.
6. Owing to lower specific speed of individual impellers a higher suction lift is possible.

3.13.2. Pumps in Parallel

When a *large quantity of liquid* is required to be pumped against a *relatively small head* (which is impossible for a single pump to accomplish), two or more pumps are employed which are so arranged that each of these pumps working separately lifts the liquid from a common sump and delivers it to a common collecting pipe through which it is carried to required height. This arrangement is known *as pumps in parallel* (since each pump delivers the liquid against the *same head*). If Q is the discharge capacity of one pump and there are *n identical* pumps (arranged in parallel) then total discharge will be, $Q_{total} = nQ$

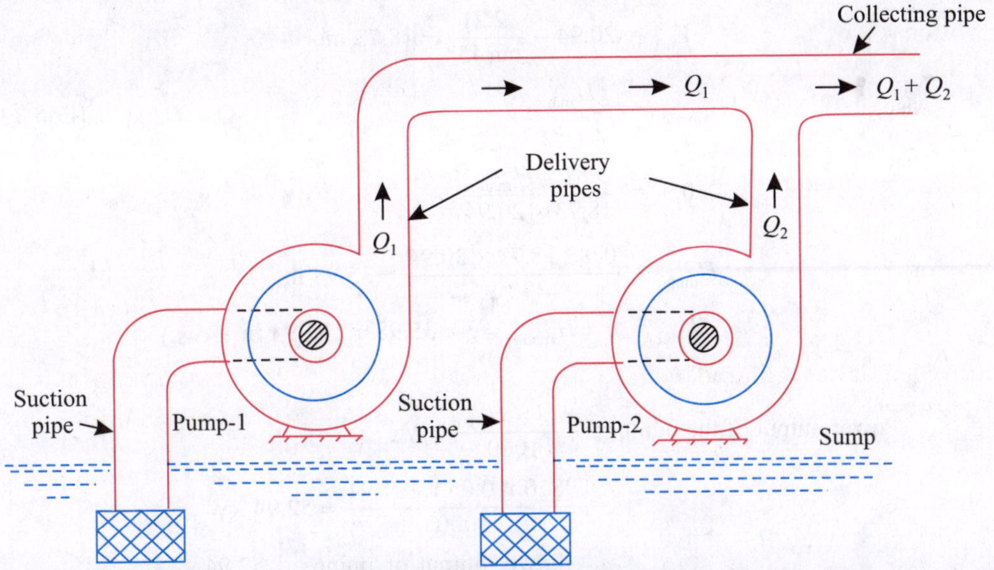

Fig. 3.24. Pumps in parallel.

Example 3.29. *A three stage centrifugal pump has impellers 400 mm in diameter and 20 mm wide at outlet. The vanes are curved back at the outlet at 45° and reduce the circumferential area by 10 percent. The manometric efficiency is 90 percent and the overall efficiency is 80 percent. The pump is running at 1000 r.p.m. and delivering 0.05 m³/s. Determine:*

(i) Head generated by the pump, and

(ii) Shaft power required to run the pump.

Solution. Number of stages, $n = 3$

Diameter of impeller at outlet, $D_2 = 400 \text{ mm} = 0.4 \text{ m}$

Width at outlet, $B_2 = 20 \text{ mm} = 0.02 \text{ m}$

Outlet vane angle, $\phi = 45°$

Reduction in area at outlet $= 10\%$

Manometric efficiency, $\eta_{mano} = 90\%$

Overall efficiency, $\eta_0 = 80\%$; Speed, $N = 1000$ r.p.m.

Discharge through the pump, $Q = 0.05 \text{ m}^3/\text{s}$.

(i) Head generated by the pump, H_{total}:

$$\text{Area of flow at outlet} = 0.9\pi D_2 B_2 = 0.9 \times \pi \times 0.4 \times 0.02 = 0.02262 \text{ m}^2$$

$$\therefore \quad \text{Velocity of flow at outlet, } V_{f2} = \frac{Q}{\text{Area of flow}} = \frac{0.05}{0.02262} = 2.21 \text{ m/s}$$

Peripheral or tangential velocity of impeller at outlet,

$$u_2 = \frac{\pi D_2 N}{60} = \frac{\pi \times 0.4 \times 1000}{60} = 20.94 \text{ m/s}$$

Refer to Fig. 3.8. From velocity triangle at *outlet*, we have:

$$\tan\phi = \frac{V_{f2}}{u_2 - V_{w2}}, \text{ or, } u_2 - V_{w2} = \frac{V_{f2}}{\tan\phi}, \text{ or, } V_{w2} = u_2 - \frac{V_{f2}}{\tan\phi}$$

or, $$V_{w2} = 20.94 - \frac{2.21}{\tan 45°} = 18.73 \text{ m/s}$$

Also, $$\eta_{mano} = \frac{gH_{mano}}{V_{w2}u_2} \quad \text{...[Eqn (3.9)]}$$

$$0.9 = \frac{9.81 \times H_{mano}}{18.73 \times 20.94}$$

or, $$H_{mano} = \frac{0.9 \times 18.73 \times 20.94}{9.81} = 35.98 \text{ m}$$

∴ $$H_{total} = n \times H_{mano} = 3 \times 35.98 = \mathbf{107.94\ m} \text{ (Ans.)}$$

(*ii*) Shaft lower required, *P*:

$$\text{Power output of the pump} = \frac{wQ \times H_{total}}{1000} \text{ kW}$$

$$= \frac{9810 \times 0.05 \times 107.94}{1000} = 52.94 \text{ kW}$$

Now, Overall efficiency, $$\eta_0 = \frac{\text{Power output of pump}}{\text{Power input to the pump}} = \frac{52.94}{P}$$

∴ $$P = \frac{52.94}{\eta_0} = \frac{52.94}{0.8} = \mathbf{66.17\ kW} \text{ (Ans.)}$$

Example 3.30. *It is required to pump water out of deep well under a total head of 90 m. A number of identical pumps of design speed 1000 r.p.m. and specific speed 30 with a rated capacity of 0.15 m^3/s are available. How many pumps are required and how should they be connected whether in series or in parallel ?*

Solution. Total head, $H_{total} = 90$ m; Design speed, $N = 1000$ r.p.m.
Specific speed, $N_s = 30$; Discharge through each pump, $Q = 0.15$ m^3/s

Number of pumps required, *n*:

Let, H_{mano} = Manometric head developed by each pump.

Now, specific speed, $$N_s = \frac{N\sqrt{Q}}{(H_{mano})^{3/4}}$$

or, $$30 = \frac{1000 \times \sqrt{0.15}}{(H_{mano})^{3/4}}, \text{ or, } H_{mano} = \left[\frac{1000 \times \sqrt{0.15}}{30}\right]^{4/3} = 30.28 \text{ m}$$

∴ $$\text{Number of pumps stages} = \frac{H_{total}}{H_{mano}} = \frac{90}{30.28} = 3$$

As the total head required to be developed is more that the head developed by each pump, the pumps should be connected in **series. (Ans.)**

3.14. SPECIFIC SPEED

The **specific speed** *of a centrifugal pump is defined as the speed of a geometrically similar pump which would deliver unit quantity (one cubic metre of liquid per second) against a unit head (one metre)*. It is denoted by N_s. The specific speed is a characteristic of pumps which can be used as a basis for *comparing the performance of different pumps.*

An expression for specific speed may be obtained as follows:

$$\text{Discharge, } Q = \text{Area} \times \text{velocity of flow}$$

$$= \pi DB \times V_f$$

or,
$$Q \propto D \times B \times V_f \qquad ...(i)$$

where, D and B are the diameter and width of the pump impeller respectively.

Now, $B \propto D$, therefore, from eqn. (*i*), we have:

$$Q \propto D^2 \times V_f \qquad ...(ii)$$

Also, the tangential velocity is given by:

$$u = \frac{\pi DN}{60}, \text{ or, } u \propto DN \qquad ...(iii)$$

Again, the tangential velocity (u) and velocity of flow (V_f) bear the following relationship with the manometric head (H_{mano}):

$$u \propto V_f \propto \sqrt{H_{mano}} \qquad ...(iv)$$

Substituting the value of u in eqn. (*iii*), we have:

$$\sqrt{H_{mano}} \propto DN, \text{ or, } D \propto \frac{\sqrt{H_{mano}}}{N}$$

Substituting the value of D in eqn. (*ii*) , we obtain:

$$Q \propto \frac{H_{mano}}{N^2} \times V_f \propto \frac{H_{mano}}{N^2} \times \sqrt{H_{mano}} \propto \frac{(H_{mano})^{3/2}}{N^2} \quad \left[\because V_f \propto \sqrt{H_{mano}} \quad ...\text{eqn.}(iv)\right]$$

$$\therefore \quad Q = K \frac{(H_{mano})^{3/2}}{N^2} \qquad ...(v)$$

(where, K = constant of proportionality)

By definition: When $H = 1$ m, and $Q = 1$ m^3/s, then N = specific speed, N_s. That is,

$$1 = K \frac{(1)^{3/2}}{N_s^2}, \text{ or, } K = N_s^2$$

Eqn. (*v*) may then be written as:

$$Q = N_s^2 \frac{(H_{mano})^{3/2}}{N^2}, \text{ or, } N_s^2 = \frac{N^2 Q}{(H_{mano})^{3/2}}$$

$$\therefore \quad \text{Specific speed, } N_s = \frac{N\sqrt{Q}}{(H_{mano})^{3/4}} \qquad ...(3.25)$$

— The values of N, H and Q are those for normal operating condition (the design point) which would generally coincide with the optimum efficiency.

— In case of a multi-stage pump the value of H_{mano} to be used in eqn. (3.25) is obtained by *dividing the total head developed by the number of stages.* For a double suction pump *half* the actual discharge delivered by the pump is taken as Q.

The ranges of specific speeds for different types of pumps are tabulated below:

Type of pump	Slow speed radial flow	Medium speed radial flow	High speed radial flow	Mixed flow (or screw type)	Axial flow (or propeller type)
Specific speed	10 to 30	30 to 50	50 to 80	80 to 160	160 to 500

— Within *limits of net positive suction head* (NPSH) is the net head in metres of liquid that is required to make the liquid flow through the suction pipe from the sump to the impeller) available, the pump with the *highest specific speed* is generally the *best choice.* Such a pump can operate at the *highest rotational speed and is of the smallest size.*

Example 3.31. *The diameter and width of a centrifugal pump impeller are 300 mm and 60 mm respectively. The pump is delivering 144 litres of liquid per second with a manometric efficiency of 85 percent. The effective outlet vane angle is 30°. If the speed of rotation is 950 r.p.m. calculate specific speed of the pump.*

Solution. Diameter of impeller at outlet, $D_2 = 300 \text{ mm} = 0.3 \text{ m}$

Width of impeller at outlet, $B_2 = 60 \text{ mm} = 0.06 \text{ m}$

Discharge through the pump, $Q = 144 \text{ litres/s} = 0.144 \text{ m}^3/\text{s}$

Manometric efficiency, $\eta_{mano} = 85\ \%$

The effective outlet vane angle, $\phi = 30°$

Speed of rotation, $N = 950$ r.p.m.

Specific speed of the pump, N_s :

Peripheral or tangential velocity at outlet of impeller,

$$u_2 = \frac{\pi D_2 N}{60} = \frac{\pi \times 0.3 \times 950}{60} = 14.92 \text{ m/s}$$

Velocity of flow, $$V_{f2} = \frac{Q}{\pi D_2 B_2} = \frac{0.144}{\pi \times 0.3 \times 0.06} = 2.55 \text{ m/s}$$

Refer to Fig. 3.8. From velocity triangle at *outlet*, we have:

$$V_{w2} = u_2 - \frac{V_{f2}}{\tan \phi} = 14.92 - \frac{2.55}{\tan 30°} = 10.5 \text{ m/s}$$

Now, manometric efficiency, $$\eta_{mano} = \frac{gH_{mano}}{V_{w2} u_2} = \frac{9.81 \times H_{mano}}{10.5 \times 14.92}$$

$$\therefore \quad H_{mano} = \frac{\eta_{mano} \times 10.5 \times 14.92}{9.81} = \frac{0.85 \times 10.5 \times 14.92}{9.81} = 13.57 \text{ m}$$

Specific speed, $$N_s = \frac{N\sqrt{Q}}{(H_{mano})^{3/4}} \qquad \text{...[Eqn. (3.25)]}$$

$$= \frac{950 \times \sqrt{0.144}}{(13.37)^{3/4}} \simeq \mathbf{51\ (Ans.)}$$

3.15. MODEL TESTING AND GEOMETRICALLY SIMILAR PUMPS

In order to know the performance of prototypes, the models of centrifugal pumps are tested. The performance of the prototype pump will be correctly predicted by its model test only if the following *conditions* are satisfied:

- Specific speed of model = Specific speed of prototype

i.e. $$(N_s)_m = (N_s)_p$$

or, $$\left[\frac{N\sqrt{Q}}{(H_{mano})^{3/4}}\right]_m = \left[\frac{N\sqrt{Q}}{(H_{mano})^{3/4}}\right]_p \quad ...(3.26)$$

- Peripheral tangential velocity, $u = \frac{\pi DN}{60}$, also $u \propto \sqrt{H_{mano}}$

$$\therefore \quad \sqrt{H_{mano}} \propto DN, \text{ or, } \frac{\sqrt{H_{mano}}}{DN} = \text{constant}$$

$\left[\frac{H_{mano}}{D^2N^2}\right.$ is called the *head or lift co-efficient*$\left.\right]$

or, $$\left(\frac{\sqrt{H_{mano}}}{DN}\right)_m = \left(\frac{\sqrt{H_{mano}}}{DN}\right)_p \quad ...(3.27)$$

- Also $$Q \propto D^2 \times V_f \quad ...(\text{Eqn } (iii) \text{ of Art. 3.7})$$

But, $$V_f \propto u \propto DN$$

$$\therefore \quad Q \propto D^2 \times DN, \text{ or, } Q \propto D^3N, \text{ or, } \frac{Q}{D^3N} = \text{constant}$$

The factor $\left[\frac{Q}{D^3N}\right.$ is called **flow co-efficient**$\left.\right]$

or, $$\left(\frac{Q}{D^3N}\right)_m = \left(\frac{Q}{D^3N}\right)_p \quad ...(3.28)$$

- Power of the pump, $P = wQH_{mano}$ (neglecting losses)

$$\therefore \quad P \propto Q \times H_{mano}$$

or, $$P \propto D^3N \times H_{mano} \quad (\because Q \propto D^3N)$$

or, $P \propto D^3N \times D^2N^2$, or, $P \propto D^5N^3$, or, $\frac{P}{D^5N^3} = \text{constant}$ $\quad (\because \sqrt{H_{mano}} \propto DN)$

$\left[\frac{P}{D^5N^3}\right.$ is called the **power co-efficient**$\left.\right]$

or, $$\left(\frac{P}{D^5N^3}\right)_m = \left(\frac{P}{D^5N^3}\right)_p \quad ...(3.29)$$

In case of *geometrically **similar** pumps* the suffix '*m*' is replaced by '1' and suffix '*p*' is replaced by '2'.

Example 3.32. *In order to predict the performance of a large centrifugal pump, a scale model of one - sixth size was made with the following specifications: Power P = 25 kW; Head H_{mano} = 7 m; Speed N = 1000 r.p.m. If the prototype pump has to work against a head of 22 m, calculate its working speed, the power required to drive it, and the ratio of the flow rates handled by the two pumps.*

Solution. Scale ratio = one – sixth

Model:	**Prototype:**
Power, P_m = 25 kW	Power, P_p = ?
Head, $(H_{mano})_m$ = 7 m	Head, $(H_{mano})_p$ = 22 m
Speed, N_m = 1000 r.p.m.	Speed, N_p = ?

Speed of prototype, N_p:

Using eqn. (3.27), $\left(\dfrac{\sqrt{H_{mano}}}{DN}\right)_m = \left(\dfrac{\sqrt{H_{mano}}}{DN}\right)_p$, we have:

$$\frac{(\sqrt{H_{mano}})_m}{D_m N_m} = \frac{(\sqrt{H_{mano}})_p}{D_p N_p}, \text{ or, } N_p = \frac{(\sqrt{H_{mano}})_p}{(\sqrt{H_{mano}})_m} \times \frac{D_m}{D_p} \times N_m$$

or
$$N_p = \frac{\sqrt{22}}{\sqrt{7}} \times \frac{1}{6} \times 1000 = \mathbf{295.47 \text{ r.p.m.}} \text{ (Ans.)}$$

Power required to drive the prototype pump, P_p:

Using eqn. (3.29), $\left(\dfrac{P}{D^5N^3}\right)_m = \left(\dfrac{P}{D^5N^3}\right)_p$, we have:

$$\frac{P_m}{D_m^5 N_m^3} = \frac{P_p}{D_p^5 N_p^3}, \text{ or, } P_p = P_m \times \frac{D_p^5 N_p^3}{D_m^5 N_m^3} = P_m \times \left(\frac{D_p}{D_m}\right)^5 \times \left(\frac{N_p}{N_m}\right)^3$$

$$= 25 \times \left(\frac{6}{1}\right)^5 \times \left(\frac{295.47}{1000}\right)^3 = \mathbf{5014.6 \text{ kW}} \text{ (Ans.)}$$

Ratio of the flow rates, $\dfrac{Q_p}{Q_m}$:

Using eqn. (3.28), $\left(\dfrac{Q}{D^3N}\right)_m = \left(\dfrac{Q}{D^3N}\right)_p$, we have :

$$\frac{Q_m}{D_m^3 N_m} = \frac{Q_p}{D_p^3 N_p}, \text{ or, } \frac{Q_p}{Q_m} = \frac{D_p^3 N_p}{D_m^3 N_m} = \left(\frac{D_p}{D_m}\right)^3 \times \frac{N_p}{N_m}$$

or,
$$\frac{Q_p}{Q_m} = \left(\frac{6}{1}\right)^3 \times \frac{295.47}{1000} = \mathbf{63.82} \text{ (Ans.)}$$

Example 3.33. *Two geometrically similar pumps are running at the same speed of 1000 r.p.m. One pump has an impeller diameter of 300 mm and lifts water at the rate of 0.02 m^3/s against a head of 15 m. Determine the head and impeller diameter of the other pump to deliver half the discharge.* **[M.U.]**

Solution. **Pump -1:** Speed, $N_1 = 1000$ r.p.m
Diameter, $D_1 = 300$ mm or 0.3 m
Head, $H_{mano_1} = 15$ m
Discharge, $Q_1 = 0.02$ m^3/s

Pump -2: Speed, $N_2 = 1000$ r.p.m.
Diameter, $D_2 = ?$
Head, $H_{mano_2} = ?$
Discharge, $Q_2 = \frac{Q_1}{2} = \frac{0.02}{2} = 0.01 \text{m}^3/\text{s}$

Head, H_{mano_2}:

Using the eqn. (3.26), $\left[\frac{N\sqrt{Q}}{(H_{mano})^{3/4}}\right]_1 = \left[\frac{N\sqrt{Q}}{(H_{mano})^{3/4}}\right]_2$, we have:

$$\frac{N_1\sqrt{Q_1}}{(H_{mano_1})^{3/4}} = \frac{N_2\sqrt{Q_2}}{(H_{mano_2})^{3/4}}$$

or, $$\frac{1000 \times \sqrt{0.02}}{(15)^{3/4}} = \frac{1000 \times \sqrt{0.01}}{(H_{mano_2})^{3/4}}$$

or, $$(H_{mano_2})^{3/4} = \frac{1000 \times \sqrt{0.01} \times (15)^{3/4}}{1000 \times \sqrt{0.02}} = 5.389$$

or, $$H_{mano_2} = (5.389)^{4/3} = \mathbf{9.45\ m}$$ **(Ans.)**

Impeller diameter, D_2:

Using the eqn. (3.27), $\left[\frac{\sqrt{H_{mano}}}{DN}\right]_1 = \left[\frac{\sqrt{H_{mano}}}{DN}\right]_2$, we have:

$$\frac{\sqrt{H_{mano_1}}}{D_1N_1} = \frac{\sqrt{H_{mano_2}}}{D_2N_2}$$

or, $$\frac{\sqrt{15}}{0.3 \times 1000} = \frac{\sqrt{9.45}}{D_2 \times \sqrt{1000}}$$

$\therefore$ $$D_2 = \frac{0.3 \times 1000 \times \sqrt{9.45}}{1000 \times \sqrt{15}} = 0.238 \text{ m or } \mathbf{238\ mm}$$ **(Ans.)**

Example 3.34. *3 m^3 of water per second is lifted to a height of 30 m with an efficiency of 75 percent by single - stage centrifugal pump. The impeller diameter is 300 mm and it is rotating at 2000 r.p.m. Find the number of stages and diameter of each impeller of a similar multi-stage pump to lift 5 m^3 of water per second to a height of 200 m when rotating at 1500 r.p.m.*

[Allahabad University]

Solution. Single-stage pump:
Discharge, $Q_1 = 3$ m^3/s
Manometric height, $H_{mano_1} = 30$ m
Diameter of impeller, $D_1 = 300$ mm or 0.3 m
Speed $N_1 = 2000$ r.p.m.

Multi-stage pump:
Discharge, $Q_2 = 5$ m^3/s
Manometric height, $H_{mano_2} = ?$ (per stage)
Diameter of each impeller, $D_2 = ?$
Speed, $N_2 = 1500$ r.p.m.

Number of stage, n:

Since specific speed should be same, therefore, applying eqn. 3.26, we have:

$$\left[\frac{N\sqrt{Q}}{(H_{mano})^{3/4}}\right]_1 = \left[\frac{N\sqrt{Q}}{(H_{mano})^{3/4}}\right]_2$$

or, $$\frac{N_1\sqrt{Q_1}}{(H_{mano_1})^{3/4}} = \frac{N_2\sqrt{Q_2}}{(H_{mano_2})^{3/4}}, \text{ or, } \frac{2000 \times \sqrt{3}}{(30)^{3/4}} = \frac{1500 \times \sqrt{5}}{(H_{mano_2})^{3/4}}$$

or, $$(H_{mano_2})^{3/4} = \frac{1500 \times \sqrt{5} \times (30)^{3/4}}{2000 \times \sqrt{3}} = 12.411, \text{ or, } H_{mano_2} = (12.411)^{4/3} = 28.71 \text{ m}$$

$$\therefore \text{ Number of stages} = \frac{\text{Total head}}{\text{Head per stage}} = \frac{200}{28.71} = \mathbf{6.966 \simeq 7} \textbf{ (Ans.)}$$

Diameter of each impeller, D_2:

Using eqn.3.27, $\left[\frac{\sqrt{H_{mano}}}{DN}\right]_1 = \left[\frac{\sqrt{H_{mano}}}{DN}\right]_2$, we have:

$$\frac{\sqrt{H_{mano_1}}}{D_1N_1} = \frac{\sqrt{H_{mano_2}}}{D_2N_2}, \text{ or, } \frac{\sqrt{30}}{0.3 \times 2000} = \frac{\sqrt{28.71}}{D_2 \times 1500}$$

or, $$D_2 = \frac{0.3 \times 2000 \times \sqrt{28.71}}{1500 \times \sqrt{30}} = 0.3913 \text{ m or } \mathbf{391.3 \text{ mm}} \textbf{ (Ans.)}$$

Example 3.35. *A centrifugal pump is discharging 0·025 m³/s of water against a total head of 18 m. The diameter of the impeller is 0.4 m and it is rotating at 1400 r.p.m. Calculate the head, discharge and ratio of powers of a geometrically similar pump of diameter 0.25 m when it is running at 2800 r.p.m.*

Solution. Centrifugal pump:

Discharge, $Q_1 = 0{\cdot}025 \text{ m}^3/\text{s}$

Head, $H_{mano_1} = 18$ m

Diameter, $D_1 = 0.4$ m

Speed, $N_1 = 1400$ r.p.m

Geometrically similar pump:

Discharge, $Q_2 = ?$

Head, $H_{mano_2} = ?$

Diameter $D_2 = 0.25$ m

Speed, $N_2 = 2800$ r.p.m.

Head, H_{mano_2}:

Using eqn. (3.27) : $\left[\frac{\sqrt{H_{mano}}}{DN}\right]_1 = \left[\frac{\sqrt{H_{mano}}}{DN}\right]_2$, we have:

$$\frac{\sqrt{H_{mano_1}}}{D_1N_1} = \frac{\sqrt{H_{mano_2}}}{D_2N_2}, \text{ or, } \frac{\sqrt{18}}{0.4 \times 1400} = \frac{\sqrt{H_{mano_2}}}{0.25 \times 2800}$$

or, $$H_{mano_2} = \left(\frac{\sqrt{18} \times 0.25 \times 2800}{0.4 \times 1400}\right)^2 = \mathbf{28.125 \text{ m}} \textbf{ (Ans.)}$$

Discharge, Q_2:

Using eqn. (3.28) : $\left(\frac{Q}{D^3N}\right)_1 = \left(\frac{Q}{D^3N}\right)_2$, we have:

$$\frac{Q_1}{D_1^3N_1} = \frac{Q_2}{D_2^3N_2}, \text{ or, } \frac{0.025}{0.4^3 \times 1400} = \frac{Q_2}{0.25^3 \times 2800}$$

or, $$Q_2 = \frac{0.025 \times 0.25^3 \times 2800}{0.4^3 \times 1400} = \mathbf{0.0122\ m^3/s}$$ **(Ans.)**

Ratio of power, $\frac{P_1}{P_2}$:

Using eqn. (3.29): $$\left(\frac{P}{D^5 N^3}\right)_1 = \left(\frac{P}{D^5 N^3}\right)_2,$$ we have

$$\frac{P_1}{D_1^5 N_1^3} = \frac{P_2}{D_2^5 N_2^3}, \text{ or, } \frac{P_1}{P_2} = \frac{D_1^5 N_1^3}{D_2^5 N_2^3} = \frac{0.4^5 \times 1400^3}{0.25^3 \times 2800^3} = \mathbf{1.31}$$ **(Ans.)**

3.16. CHARACTERISTICS OF CENTRIFUGAL PUMPS

Ordinarily a centrifugal pump is worked under its maximum efficiency conditions. However, when the pump is run at conditions different from the design conditions, it performs differently. Therefore, to predict the behaviour of the pump under varying conditions of speeds, heads, discharges or powers, tests are usually conducted. The results obtained from these tests are plotted in from of *characteristic curves;* these curves delineate useful information about the performance of a pump in its installation.

The following *four types of characteristic curves* are usually prepared for centrifugal pumps:

1. Main characteristic curves,
2. Operating characteristic curves,
3. Constant efficiency or Muschel curves, and
4. Constant head and constant discharge curves.

1. Main characteristic curves:

The main characteristic curves are obtained as follows:

- The pump is run at a *constant speed* and the *discharge is varied* over the desired range (by delivery valve)
- Measurements are taken for manometric head (H_{mano}) and shaft power (P) for each discharge(Q).
- Calculations are made for the pump overall efficiency, η_0
- The curves are plotted between Q and H_{mano}; Q and P; and Q and η_0 for that speed.
- The same procedure is repeated by running the pump at another speed.
- A family of curves is obtained as shown in Fig. 3.25.

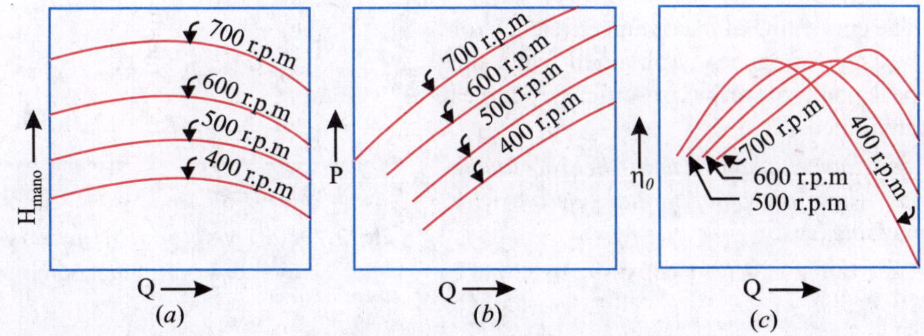

Fig. 3.25. Main characteristic curves.

2. Operating characteristic curves:

When a centrifugal pump operates at the *design speed* (same as speed of driving motor) the *maximum* efficiency occurs. Evidently for *optimum performance,* the pump needs to be operated at the design speed. To obtain *operating characteristic curves* the pump is run at the design speed and the discharge is varied, as in the case of main characteristic curves. The operating characteristic curves are shown in Fig. 3.26. The design discharge and head *are obtained from the corresponding* curves where the efficiency is maximum,

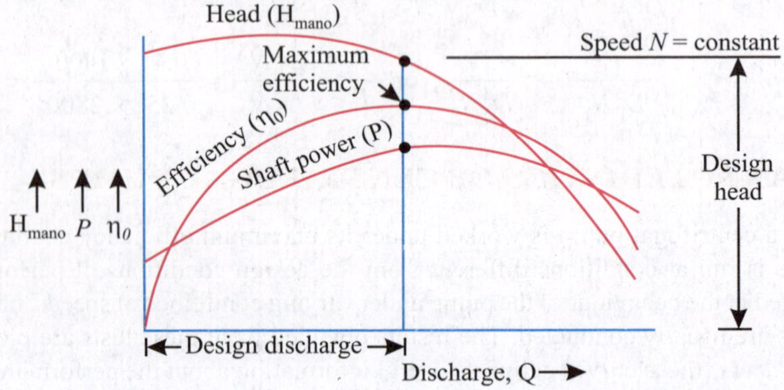

Fig. 3.26. Operating characteristic curves of a centrifugal pump.

3. Constant efficiency or Muschel curves:

The constant efficiency curves (also called iso-efficiency curves), depict the performance of a pump over its entire range of operations. These curves are obtained from main characteristic curves as follows:

- For a given efficiency, the values of discharges are obtained from Fig. (3.25) (*c*). These points are projected on the head (H_{mano}) *v/s* discharge (Q) for that speed in Fig. 3.25 (*a*).
- Similarly, for another value of efficiency and speed, the points are obtained and projected.
- The points corresponding to one efficiency are joined.
- The curves so obtained are the constant efficiency or Muschel curves.
- The curve/ line of maximum efficiency (or best performance) is obtained when the peak points of various iso-efficiency curves are joined.

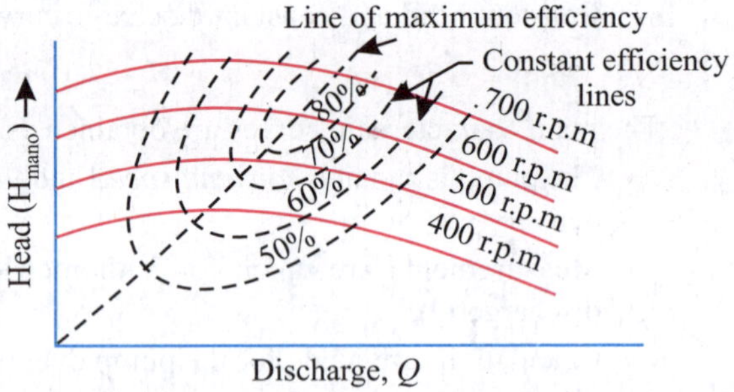

Fig. 3.27. Constant efficiency or Muschel curves

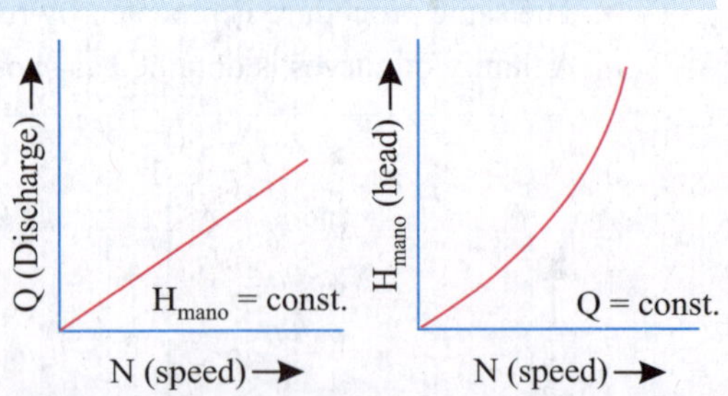

Fig. 3.28. **(*a*)** Qv/s N and **(*b*)** Hmano v/s N curves of a centrifugal pump

The constant efficiency curves help to locate the regions where the pump would operate with maximum efficiency.

4. Constant head and constant discharge curves:

The performance of a variable speed pump for which the *speed constantly varies* can be determined by these curves. When the pump has a variable speed, the plots between Q and N, and

H_{mano} and N may be obtained. In the first case H_{mano} is kept constant and in the second case, Q is kept constant. The curves are shown in Fig. 3.28.

3.17. NET POSITIVE SUCTION HEAD (NPSH)

Fig. 3.29. shows a centrifugal pump drawing liquid from a sump open to a atmosphere.

Let, h_s = Vertical distance between the centre line of the pump and the free liquid surface of the sump,

V_s = Velocity of liquid in the suction pipe,

h_{fs} = Losses in the suction pipe upto the pump inlet (1),

p_1 = Absolute static pressure at pump inlet,

p_a = Absolute atmospheric pressure, and

p_v = Vapour pressure of the liquid for a given temperature.

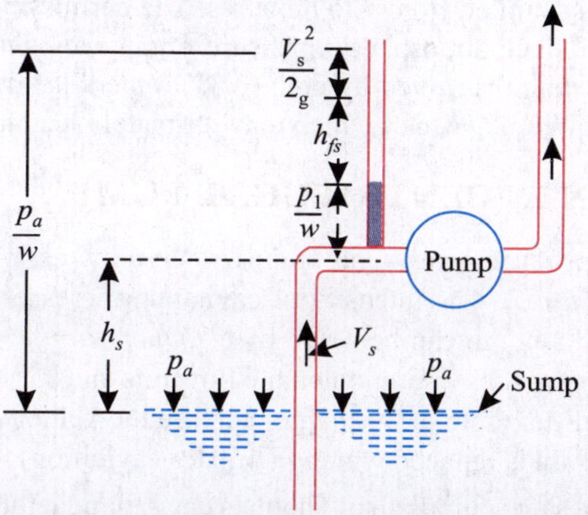

Fig. 3.29. Pressure balance at pump section.

Now the pump will work without cavitation, if p_1 is *greater than* p_v by an amount equal to that required by the liquid for the increase in velocity head when entering the impeller; if this amount be denoted by H_{sv}, we can write

$$\frac{p_1}{w} = \frac{p_v}{w} + H_{sv} \qquad ...(i)$$

Also,

$$\frac{p_1}{w} = \frac{p_a}{w} - \left(h_s + h_{fs} + \frac{V_s^2}{2g}\right) \qquad ...(ii)$$

From (*i*) and (*ii*), we have:

$$H_{sv} = \frac{p_a}{w} - \left(h_s + h_{fs} + \frac{V_s^2}{2g}\right) - \frac{p_v}{w}$$

or,

$$H_{sv} = H_a - H_s - H_v \qquad ...(3.30)$$

$$\left(H_a = \frac{p_a}{w}, \text{ and, } H_v = \frac{p_v}{w}\right)$$

where, H_s = Total suction head $= \left(h_s + h_{fs} + \frac{V_s^2}{2g}\right)$

This value of H_{sv} is frequently called the *net positive suction head* (NPSH). Thus the net positive suction head may *be defined "as the difference between the net inlet head and the head corresponding to the vapour pressure of the liquid"*. NPSH may also be defined as "*the net head (in metres of liquid) that is required to make the liquid flow through the suction pipe from the sump to the impeller.*"

This *term has significance only when cavitating liquids are handled.*

NPSH is a parameter (diamensional) that *can be used to check cavitation in pump.* The term *NPSH* is a frequently used in *pump industry.* The minimum *NPSH* depends upon the pump design, its speed and the discharge.

From eqn. (*ii*), the **limiting value of suction lift** (h_s) is given by:

$$h_s = \left(\frac{p_a - p_v}{w}\right) - h_{fs} - \frac{V_s^2}{2g}, \text{ when } p_1 = p_v \quad ...(3.31)$$

Suction height is usually limited from 7 to 8 metres. The permissible suction lift would be less at elevated pump elevation since atmospheric pressure diminishes with altitude. The suction lift should in no case be more than that given by eqn. (3.31), otherwise due to reduction in pressure, rapid vaporization of the liquid may occur, which may ultimately lead to cavitation.

3.18. CAVITATION IN CENTRIFUGAL PUMPS

Cavitation begins to appear in centrifugal pumps when the *pressure at the suction falls below the vapour pressure of the liquid.* The intensity of cavitation increases with the decrease in value of NPSH. The cavitation in a pump can be noted by a *sudden drop in efficiency, head and power requirement.* The cavitation imposes limitation on the flow rate and speed of rotation of pump (since as the speed of rotation and flow rate of discharge increase the velocity of liquid at inlet increases due to which absolute pressure is reduced which facilitates cavitation).

As in the case of turbines, for pumps also, Thoma's cavitation factor is used to indicate the onset of cavitation. For pumps *Thoma's cavitation factor* is defined as:

$$\sigma = \frac{H_a - H_s - H_v}{H_{mano}} = \frac{H_{sv}}{H_{mano}} \quad ...(3.32)$$

where,
H_a = Atmospheric pressure expressed in metres of water head,
H_v = Vapour pressure expressed in metres of water head,
H_s = Total suction head $\left(= h_s + h_{fs} + \frac{V_s^2}{2g}\right)$,
H_{sv} = Net positive suction head (NPSH), and
H_{mano} = Manometric head.

The cavitation will occur if the value of σ is less than the critical value σ_c at which the cavitation just begins. The cavitation parameter σ is a *function of specific speed, efficiency of the pump, and number of vanes.*

The *harmful effects of cavitation are:*

(*i*) Pitting and erosion of surface (due to continuous hammering action of collapsing bubbles)
(*ii*) Sudden drop in head, efficiency and the power delivered to the fluid.
(*iii*) Noise and vibration (produced by the collapse of bubbles)

The *factors which facilitate onset of cavitation are as follows:*

(*i*) Restricted suction, (*ii*) High runner speed,

(*iii*) Too high specific speed for optimum design parameters, and

(*iv*) Too high temperature of the flowing liquid.

Suction specific speed:

For geometrically similar machines (homologous),

$$Q \propto ND^3 \quad ...(i)$$

$$NPSH \propto \frac{V^2}{2g} \propto \frac{Q^2}{D^4} \quad ...(ii)$$

Eliminating the dimension D from the above expression, we have:

$$\frac{N\sqrt{Q}}{(NPSH)^{3/4}} = \text{constant} = (N_s)_{suc.} \quad ...(3.33)$$

The parameter $(N_s)_{suc}$. is called the **suction specific speed.** When the different machines have equal values of $(N_s)_{suc}$., it indicates that the machines are operating with similar degree of cavitation.

Now by eliminating $N\sqrt{Q}$ from the following expressions, we get:

$$(N_s)_{suc.} = \frac{N\sqrt{Q}}{(NPSH)^{3/4}} \quad ...\text{Suction specific speed}$$

$$N_s = \frac{N\sqrt{Q}}{(H_{mano})^{3/4}} \quad ... \text{pump specific speed (normal)}$$

$$\frac{NPSH}{H_{mano}} = \left[\frac{N_s}{(N_s)_{suc.}}\right]^{4/3}$$

or, $$\sigma = \left(\frac{N_s}{(N_s)_{suc.}}\right)^{4/3} \quad ...(3.34)$$

Example 3.36. *Tests on a pump model indicate a cavitation parameter $\sigma_c = 0.10$. A homologous unit is to be installed at a location where atmospheric pressure, $p_a = 0{\cdot}91$ bar and vapour pressure $p_v = 0{\cdot}035$ bar absolute and is to pump water against a head of 25 m. What is the maximum permissible suction head ?* **[P.E.C.]**

Solution. Cavitation paremeter, $\sigma_c = 0.10$

Atmospheric pressure, $p_a = 0.91$ bar, or, $H_a = \frac{0.91 \times 10^5}{9810} = 9.27$ m of water

Vapour pressure, $p_v = 0.035$ bar, or, $H_v = \frac{0.035 \times 10^5}{9810} = 0.356$ m of water

Manometric head, $H_{mano} = 25$ m

Maximum permissible suction head, h_s:

Using the relation: $\sigma = \frac{H_a - H_s - H_v}{H_{mano}}$, or, $\sigma_c = \frac{H_c - H_s - H_v}{H_{mano}}$, neglecting head lost due to friction

or, $$0.10 = \frac{9.27 - h_s - 0.356}{25}, \text{ or, } 0.10 \times 25 = 8.914 - h_s$$

$\therefore$ $$h_s = 8.914 - 0.10 \times 25 = \mathbf{6.41\ m\ (Ans.)}$$

Example 3.37. *Find the height from the water surface at which a centrifugal pump may be installed in the following case to avoid cavitation:*

Atmospheric pressure = 1.01 bar; vapour pressure = 0.022 bar; inlet and other losses in suction pipe = 1.42 m; effective head of pump = 49 m; and cavitation parameter = 0.115.

Solution. *Given :*

$$p_a = 1.01 \text{ bar, or, } H_a = \frac{1.01 \times 10^5}{9810} = 10.29 \text{ m}$$

$$p_v = 0.022 \text{ bar, or, } H_v = \frac{0.022 \times 10^5}{9810} = 0.224 \text{ m}$$

Inlet and other losses in suction pipe, $h_{fs} = 1.42$ m,
Effective head of pump (manometric head), $H_{mano} = 49$ m.
Cavitation parameter, $\sigma = 0.115$.

Installation height above water surface, h_s:

Cavitation factor/ parameter is given by:

$$\sigma = \frac{H_a - H_s - H_v}{H_{mano}} = \frac{H_a - (h_s + h_{fs}) - H_e}{H_{mano}}$$

or, $$0.115 = \frac{10.29 - (h_s + 1.42) - 0.224}{49} = \frac{8.646 - h_s}{49}$$

or, $$h_s = 8.646 - 0.115 \times 49 = \mathbf{3.01 \text{ m}} \text{ (Ans.)}$$

Example 3.38. *A single-stage centrifugal pump runs at 600 r.p.m. and delivers 360 m³/min.. of water against a head of 144 m. The pump impeller is 2.4 m in diameter and it has a positive suction lift (including the velocity head and friction) of 3.6 m. Laboratory tests are to be conducted on a model with 0.54 m diameter impeller and on a reduced head of 114 m. Calculate the speed, discharge and suction lift for the laboratory tests. Assume atmospheric head = 10.18 m of water and vapour head = 0·32 m of water.*

Solution. **Prototype pump:**

Speed, $N_p = 600$ r.p.m.
Discharge, $Q_p = 360$ m³/min
Manometric head, $(H_{mano})_p = 144$ m
Diameter of impeller, $D_p = 2.4$ m
Positive suction lift = 3.6 m
Vapour head, $H_v = 0{\cdot}32$ m of water.

Model pump:

Speed, $N_m = ?$
Discharge, $Q_m = ?$
Manometric head, $(H_{mano})_m = 114$ m
Diameter of impeller, $D_m = 0.54$ m
Atmospheric head, $H_a = 10.18$ m of water.

(*i*) Speed of the model pump, N_m:

Using the relation: $$\left(\frac{\sqrt{H_{mano}}}{DN}\right)_m = \left(\frac{\sqrt{H_{mano}}}{DN}\right)_p \quad \text{...[Eqn. (3.27)]}$$

or, $$\frac{(\sqrt{H_{mano}})_m}{D_m N_m} = \frac{(\sqrt{H_{mano}})_p}{D_p N_p}, \text{ or, } N_m = \frac{(\sqrt{H_{mano}})_m}{(\sqrt{H_{mano}})_p} \times \frac{D_p}{D_m} \times N_p$$

or, $$N_m = \sqrt{\frac{114}{144}} \times \frac{2.4}{0.54} \times 600 = \mathbf{2372.7 \text{ r.p.m.}} \text{ (Ans.)}$$

(*ii*) **Discharge for the model pump, Q_m:**

Using the relation: $\left(\frac{Q}{D^3N}\right)_m = \left(\frac{Q}{D^3N}\right)_p$ ...[Eqn. (3.28)]

$$\frac{Q_m}{D_m^3 N_m} = \frac{Q_p}{D_p^3 N_p}, \text{ or, } Q_m = Q_p\left(\frac{D_m}{D_p}\right)^2 \times \frac{N_m}{N_p}$$

or,
$$Q_m = 360 \times \left(\frac{0.54}{2.4}\right)^3 \times \frac{2372.7}{600} = 16.21\,\text{m}^3/\text{min}$$

(*iii*) **Positive suction lift with which model should be tested, H_s:**

Cavitation factor for the prototype,

$$\sigma_p = \frac{H_a - H_s - H_v}{(H_{mano})_p} = \frac{10.18 - 3.6 - 0.32}{144} = 0.0435$$

For cavitation similarity, $\sigma_m = \sigma_p$

$$\therefore \quad \sigma_m = \frac{10.18 - H_s - 0.32}{114}, \text{ or, } 0.0435 = \frac{9.86 - H_s}{114}$$

$\therefore H_s = 9.86 - 0.0435 \times 114 =$ **4.9 m** (*including velocity head and friction*) **(Ans.)**

3.19. PRIMING OF A CENTRIFUGAL PUMP

The operation of filling the suction pipe, casing of the pump and a portion of the delivery pipe completely from outside source with the liquid to be raised, before starting the pump, to remove any air, gas or vapour from these parts of the pump is called **priming** *of a centrifugal pump.* If a centrifugal pump is *not primed before starting, air pockets inside the impeller may give rise to vortices and cause discontinuity of flow. Further, dry running of the pump may result in rubbing and seizing of the wearing rings and cause serious damage.*

- **Small pumps** are usually primed by pouring liquid into the funnel provided for the purpose. While doing priming, the air-vent valve provided in the pump casing is opened; the air escapes through the valve. The priming is continued till all air from the suction pipe, impeller and casing has been removed.
- **Large pumps** are primed by evacuating the casing and the suction pipe by a *vacuum pump or by an ejector;* the liquid is thus drawn up the suction pipe from the sump and the pump is filled with liquid.
- The internal construction of some pumps is such that *special arrangements containing a supply of liquid are provided in the suction pipe due to which automatic priming of the pump occurs;* such pumps are known as **'self priming pumps'.**

3.20. SELECTION OF PUMPS

- The main criteria of the selection of the type of pump are values of discharge (Q), head (H) and speed (N). From these values the specific speed of the pump is calculated and subsequently the type of the pump can be decided.
- When the specific speed is low and it is possible to increase the pump speed, it is better to use multi-stage pump; the number of stages are decided on the basis of the head and the type of the pump to be used.
- The *type of impeller* is another aspect of pump selection:

(*i*) *Impeller shrounded type* ... for pumping fresh clean water.

(*ii*) *Impeller-unshrounded or propeller type* ... for pumping soild-liquid mixture or near plastic material.

(For pumping *molasses* etc. sometimes positive displacement screw pump or lobe pumps are employed.)

(*iii*) *Mixed flow impellers with diffuser vanes* ... used for *deep well or submersible pumps.*

- Axial flow pumps are employed for *very low heads* of about six metres and *for large discharges.*
- *Radial flow pumps* are used when the *head is high.*

3.21. OPERATIONAL DIFFICULTIES IN CENTRIFUGAL PUMPS

The type of operational *difficulties* commonly experienced in centrifugal pumps and their *remedies* (given in *parentheses*) are as given below:

I. Pump fails to start pumping:

1. Pump may not be properly primed – (Reprime the pump).
2. Total head against which the pump is working may be much higher than that for which the pump is designed – (Check the head with accurate gauges; reduce the head or change the pump).
3. Impeller may be clogged – (Clean the impeller).
4. The rotation of the impeller may be in the wrong direction. (Change the direction of rotation).
5. Too high suction lift (Reduce the suction lift).
6. Law speed – (Increase the speed).

II. Pump is not working upto capacity and pressure:

1. Leakage of air into the pump – (Plug the leakege).
2. Some of the parts are damaged due to excessive wear and tear – (Replace the worn out/ damaged parts).

III. Pump stops working:

1. Presence of air in suction line – (Remove the air by priming and plug the entry of air).
2. High suction lift (Reduce the suction lift).

IV. Pump has very low efficiency :

1. Speed may be too high – (Reduce the speed)
2. Head may be too low and the pump delivers the liquid in large quantity – (Reduce the discharge or change the pump).
3. Pump may be operating in wrong direction – (Correct the direction of rotation of impeller).
4. Shaft may be bent, the impeller may be touching the casing, stuffing boxes may be too tight, wearing rings may be worn – (Repair the affected parts).

HIGHLIGHTS

1. A pump is a contrivance which provides energy to a fluid in a fluid system; it assists to increase the pressure energy or kinetic energy, or both of the fluid by converting the mechanical energy.
2. (*a*) Work done per second per unit weight of liquid

$$= \frac{V_{w2}u_2}{g}, \text{ assuming flow at inlet to be } \textit{radial} \quad ...(i)$$

(*b*) If the flow is *not radial,* the expression for work done may be written as:

Work done per second per unit weight of liquid

$$= \frac{1}{g}(V_{w2}u_2 - V_{w1}u_1) \quad ...(ii)$$

Eqn. (*ii*) is known as the *Euler momentum equation for centrifugal pumps.*

The term $\frac{1}{g}(V_{w2}u_2 - V_{w1}u_1)$ is referred to as Euler head (H_e)

(*c*) Work done per second per unit weight of liquid (or H_e)

$$= \frac{V_2^2 - V_1^2}{2g} + \frac{u_2^2 - u_1^2}{2g} + \frac{V_{r1}^2 - V_{r2}^2}{2g} \quad ...(iii)$$

This equation is sometimes called the *fundamental equation of a centrifugal pump.*

3. *Suction head* (h_s). It is the vertical height of the centreline of pump shaft above the liquid surface in the sump from which the liquid is being raised.
Delivery head (h_d). It is the vertical height of the liquid surface in the tank/reservoir to which the liquid is delivered above the centreline of the pump shaft.
The sum of suction head and delivery head is known as *static head* (H_{stat}).
4. *Manometric head* (H_{mano}). The head against which a centrifugal pump has to work is known as manometric head. It is given as:

(*i*) $H_{mano} = \frac{V_{w2}u_2}{g}$ – loss of head in the pump (*i.e.* impeller and casing)

(*ii*) $$H_{mano} = H_{stat} + \text{losses in pipe} + \frac{V_d^2}{2g}$$

$$= (h_s + h_d) + (h_{fs} + h_{fd}) + \frac{V_d^2}{2g}$$

(*iii*) H_{mano} = Total head at outlet of the pump – total head at inlet of the pump

$$= \left(\frac{p_2}{w} + \frac{V_2^2}{2g} + z_2\right) - \left(\frac{p_1}{w} + \frac{V_1^2}{2g} + z_1\right)$$

5. The various efficiencies of the pump are

(*i*) Manometric efficiency, $\eta_{mano} = \frac{gH_{mano}}{V_{w2}u_2}$

(*ii*) Volumetric efficiency, $\eta_v = \frac{Q}{Q + q}$

where, Q = Actual liquid discharge at the pump outlet second, and

q = Leakage of liquid per second from the impeller (through the clearances between the impeller and casing)

(*iii*) Mechanical efficiency, $\eta_m = \dfrac{w(Q+q)\,(V_{w2}u_2/g)}{P}$

$$= \frac{P - P_{mach.loss}}{P} \text{ (where, } P = \text{shaft power)}$$

(*iv*) Overall efficiency, $\eta_0 = \dfrac{wQH_{\text{mano}}}{P}$

Also, $\eta_0 = \eta_{mano} \times \eta_v \times \eta_m$

6. The *minimum speed for starting a centrifugal pump* is given by:

$$N(i.e.\ N_{min}) = \frac{120 \times \eta_{\text{mano}} \times V_{w2} \times D_2}{\pi(D_2^2 - D_1^2)}$$

7. A multi-stage pump is one which has two or more identical impellers (mounted on the same shaft or on different shafts); to produce a *high head* the impellers are connected in *series* while to *discharge a large quantity of liquid,* the impellers are connected in *parallel.*

8. The *specific speed* (N_s) of a centrifugal pump is defined as the speed of a geometrically similar pump which would deliver unit quantity (one cubic metre of liquid per second) against a unit head (one metre). Thus.

$$N_s = \frac{N\sqrt{Q}}{(H_{\text{mano}})^{3/4}}$$

9. For complete similarity between the model and prototype/actual centrifugal pump the following conditions should be satisfied:

(*i*) $$\left[\frac{N\sqrt{Q}}{(H_{\text{mano}})^{3/4}}\right]_m = \left[\frac{N\sqrt{Q}}{(H_{\text{mano}})^{3/4}}\right]_p$$

(*ii*) $$\left(\frac{\sqrt{H_{\text{mano}}}}{DN}\right)_m = \left(\frac{\sqrt{H_{\text{mano}}}}{DN}\right)_p$$

(*iii*) $$\left(\frac{Q}{D^3N}\right)_m = \left(\frac{Q}{D^3N}\right)_p$$

(*iv*) $$\left(\frac{P}{D^5N^3}\right)_m = \left(\frac{P}{D^5N^3}\right)_p$$

10. The characteristics curves are used for predicting the behaviour and performance of a pump when it is working under different heads, speeds and rates of flow.

11. The net positive suction head (*NPSH*) may be defined as "The difference between the net inlet head and the head corresponding to the vapour pressure of the liquid"

12. *Cavitation* begins to appear in centrifugal pumps when the pressure at the suction falls below the vapour pressure of the liquid. It can be noted by *sudden drop in efficiency, head and power requirement.*

OBJECTIVE TYPE QUESTIONS

Choose the Correct Answer:

1. Which of the following types of impeller is used for centrifugal pumps dealing with muds?
   (*a*) One-side shrouded
   (*b*) Two -sides shrouded
   (*c*) Double section
   (*d*) Open.
2. Which of the following statements is *correct* with reference to an impeller with backward curved vanes?
   (*a*) It has a falling head - discharge characteristic.
   (*b*) It has rising head - discharge characteristic
   (*c*) It is easier to fabricate.
   (*d*) It cannot run at speeds other than the design speed.
3. The head developed by a centrifugal pump may be expressed as
   (*a*) $H = \frac{V_{w2}u_2 + V_{w1}u_2}{g}$
   (*b*) $H = \frac{V_{w2}u_2}{g}$
   (*c*) $H = \frac{V_{w1}u_1}{g}$
   (*d*) none of the above.
4. With reference to a centrifugal pump which of the following statements is *incorrect* ?
   (*a*) The discharge control valve is fitted in the delivery pipe.
   (*b*) The suction pipe is provided with a foot valve and a strainer.
   (*c*) The suction pipe has larger diameter as compared to the discharge pipe.
   (*d*) The discharge control valve is fitted in the suction pipe.
5. A centrifugal pump should be so installed above the water level in the sump such that
   (*a*) the negative pressures are not allowed to develop in the impeller
   (*b*) the negative pressures do not reach as low a value as the vapour pressure
   (*c*) its height is more than 10·28 m at ordinary temperature of liquid
   (*d*) none of the above.
6. The specific speed of a pump is defined as the speed of unit of such a size that it
   (*a*) produces unit power with unit head available
   (*b*) delivers unit discharge at unit head
   (*c*) requires unit power to develop unit head
   (*d*) delivers unit discharge at unit power.
7. Which of the following statements pertaining to a given centrifugal pump is *correct* ?
   (*a*) Discharge varies as the square of speed
   (*b*) Power varies as the square of speed
   (*c*) Discharge varies directly as speed
   (*d*) Head varies inversely as speed.
8. The delivery valve, while starting centrifugal pump, is kept
   (*a*) fully closed (*b*) fully open
   (*c*) half open (*d*) in any position.
9. Which of the following is *not* a dismensionless parameter ?
   (*a*) Friction factor
   (*b*) Specific speed
   (*c*) Thoma's cavitation parameter
   (*d*) Pressure co-efficient.
10. With reference to manometric head which of the following statements is *correct* ?
    (*a*) It is the head developed by the pump.
    (*b*) It is the height to which water is lifted by the pump measured above the pump centreline.
    (*c*) it is the difference in elevation between the water surface in the high level reservoir and the water level in the sump.
    (*d*) It is the difference in the piezometric heads between the points on the delivery and suction pipes as close to the pump as possible.
11. Higher specific speeds (160 to 500) of centrifugal pump indicate that the pump is of
    (*a*) radial flow type (*b*) axial flow type
    (*c*) mixed flow type (*d*) any of these types.
12. What will happen if requirements of net positive suction head (NPSH) for a given pump are not satisfied ?
    (*a*) The pump will get cavitated.
    (*b*) The pump will consume more power.
    (*c*) The pump will not develop head.
    (*d*) The pump will have a low efficiency.
13. The net positive suction head (*NPSH*) which represents the suction head at the impeller eye is given by
    (*a*) $\frac{p_a - p_v}{w} - h_s - h_{fs}$
    (*b*) $\frac{p_a - p_v}{w} - h_s + h_{fs}$

(c) $\frac{p_a - p_v}{w} + h_s + h_{fs}$

(d) $\frac{p_a - p_v}{w} + h_s - h_{fs}$.

14. To prevent cavitation, the suction lift must be considerably lower than the maximum limit expressed by

(a) $\frac{p_a - p_v}{w} + \frac{V_s^2}{2g} - h_{fs}$

(b) $\frac{p_a - p_v}{w} - \frac{V_s^2}{2g} + h_{fs}$

(c) $\frac{p_a - p_v}{w} - \frac{V_s^2}{2g} - h_{fs}$

(d) $\frac{p_a - p_v}{w} + \frac{V_s^2}{2g} + h_{fs}$.

15. In centrifugal pumps, cavitation is reduced by

(a) increasing the flow velocity

(b) reducing the discharge

(c) throttling the discharge

(d) reducing the suction head.

16. Which of the following statements pertaining to a centrifugal pump is *incorrect* ?

(a) The suction lift of a pump can be upto 10·3 m or even more.

(b) The impellers of a multi-stage pump are arranged in parallel to discharge a large quantity of liquid.

(c) The volute casing of the pump maintains the velocity of flow constant, prevents eddies and converts velocity head to pressure head.

(d) The manometric head refers to the difference between the total energy of liquid at exit from and at inlet to the pump.

17. Regarding cavitation which of the following statements in *incorrect* ?

(a) Cavitation affects the performance of a turbine to a lesser degree than that of a pump.

(b) Thoma's cavitation parameter has different expressions for turbines and pumps.

(c) With the increase in pump speed, there is increase in its minimum net positive suction head requirement.

(d) The leading edge of blades in pumps and the trailing edge of blades in water turbines are more susceptible to cavitation damage.

18. A centrifugal pump is taking much of power, the probable reason may be

(a) liquid being pumped is heavy

(b) speed of the pump is low

(c) there is leakage of air

(d) ineffective strainer and foot valve arrangement.

19. In rotodynamic pumps, the increase in energy level is due to

(a) centrifugal energy only

(b) pressure energy only

(c) kinetic energy only

(d) combination of *a*, *b* and *c*.

20. In a pump there is

(a) accelerating flow

(b) decelerated flow

(c) either of the above

(d) none of the above.

21. In a centrifugal pump the regulating valve is provided on

(a) the suction pipe (b) delivery pipe

(c) the casing (d) none of the above.

22. In a centrifugal pump the sum of suction head and delivery head is known as

(a) manometric head (b) total head

(c) static head (d) none of the above.

23. Regarding manometric head (H_{mano}) which of the following relations is *correct* ?

(a) H_{mano} = head imparted by the impeller to the liquid – loss of head in the pump

(b) H_{mano} = static head + losses in pipes + $\frac{V_d^2}{2g}$

(c) H_{mano} = total head at outlet of the pump- total head at inlet of pump

(d) All of the above.

24. The ratio of power outlet of the pump to the power input to the pump is known as

(a) mechanical efficiency

(b) overall efficiency

(c) manometric efficiency

(d) none of the above.

25. The flow ratio in case of a centrifugal pump varies from

(a) 0.1 to 0.25 (b) 0.25 to 0.40

(c) 0.40 to 0.50 (d) 0.50 to 0.65.

ANSWERS

1. (*d*)	2. (*a*)	3. (*b*)	4. (*d*)	5. (*b*)	6. (*b*)
7. (*c*)	8. (*a*)	9. (*b*)	10. (*d*)	11. (*b*)	12. (*a*)
13. (*a*)	14. (*c*)	15. (*d*)	16. (*a*)	17. (*b*)	18. (*a*)
19. (*d*)	20. (*a*)	21. (*b*)	22. (*c*)	23. (*d*)	24. (*b*)
25. (*a*).					

THEORETICAL QUESTIONS

1. What is a pump ?
2. How are pumps classified ?
3. How are centrifugal pumps classified ?
4. State the advantages of a centrifugal pump over a displacement (reciprocating) pump.
5. List the main component parts of a centrifugal pump and explain them briefly.
6. Explain the working of a single - stage centrifugal pump with a neat sketch.
7. How does a volute casing differ from a vortex casing for the centrifugal pump ?
8. Explain briefly, with neat sketches, any two of the following types of casing
   (*i*) Volute casing; (*ii*) Vortex casing;
   (*iii*) Casing with guide blades/vanes.
9. Derive an expression for the work done by the impeller of a centrifugal pump on liquid per second per unit weight of liquid.
10. What is 'Euler head' ?
11. Define the following terms
    (*i*) Static head,
    (*ii*) Manometric head, and
    (*iii*) Total head.
12. Enumerate the losses which occur when a centrifugal pump operates.
13. Explain briefly the following efficiencies of a centrifugal pump:
    (*i*) Manometric efficiency,
    (*ii*) Volumetric efficiency,
    (*iii*) Mechanical efficiency, and
    (*iv*) Overall efficiency.
14. Discuss the influence of exit blade angle on the performance and efficiency of a centrifugal pump. Assume radial flow at entrance.
15. Derive an expression for the minimum speed for starting a centrifugal pump.
16. Explain briefly the effect of variation of discharge on the efficiency.
17. What is the effect of number of vanes of impeller on head and efficiency ?
18. State the difference between single stage and multi-stage pumps.
19. Discribe multi-stage pump with (*i*) impeller in series and (*ii*) impellers in parallel.
20. Define specific speed of a centrifugal pump. Derive an expression for the same.
21. How does the specific speed of a centrifugal pump differ from that of a turbine ?
22. Write down the ranges of specific speeds for the following types of pumps:
    (*i*) Slow speed radial flow,
    (*ii*) Medium speed radial flow,
    (*iii*) High speed radial flow, and
    (*iv*) Axial flow.
23. How is the model testing of the centrifugal pumps carried out ?
24. What do you mean by 'characteristics of centrifugal pumps ?
25. What is the significance of characteristic curves?
26. What do you mean by 'net positive suction head' (*NPSH*) ?
27. What is 'cavitation' ?
28. What are the effects of cavitation ? Give the necessary precautions against cavitation.
29. List the factors which facilitate onset of cavitation.
30. Define 'suction specific speed'.
31. What is priming ? Why is it necessary ?
32. How are small and large centrifugal pumps primed ?
33. How is the selection of pumps made ?
34. Give the operational difficulties commonly experienced in centrifugal pumps and their remedies.
35. Why are centrifugal pumps used sometimes in series and sometimes in parallel ? Draw the following characteristic curves for a centrifugal pump:
    Head, power and efficiency *versus* discharge with constant speed.

UNSOLVED EXAMPLES

1. The impeller of a centrifugal pump has an external diameter of 400 mm and internal diameter of 180 mm and it runs at 1440 r.p.m. Assuming a constant radial flow through the impeller at 2·5 m/s and that the vanes at the exit are set back at an angle of 25°, determine : (*i*) Inlet vane angle, (*ii*) The angle, absolute velocity of water at the exit makes with the tangent, and (*iii*) The work done per N of water.

   [**Ans.** (*i*) 10.42° ; (*ii*) 5.75° ; (*iii*) 76.18 Nm]

2. A centrifugal pump delivers water against a net head of 14·5 m and a design speed of 1000 r.p.m. The vanes are curved back to an angle of 30° with the periphery. The impeller diameter is 300 mm and outlet width 50 mm. Determine the discharge of the pump if manometric efficiency is 95 percent.

   [**Ans.** 0.1675 m^3/s]

3. The impeller of a centrifugal pump having external and internal diameters 500 mm and 250 mm respectively, width at outlet 50 mm and running at 1000 r.p.m. works against a head of 40 m. The velocity of flow through the impeller is constant and equal to 2.5 m/s. The vanes are set back at angle of 40°at outlet. Determine: (*i*) Inlet vane angle, (*ii*) Work done by the impeller on water per second, and (*iii*) Manometric efficiency.

   [**Ans.** (*i*) 10.81°; (*ii*) 119.2 kNm; (*iii*) 64.6%]

4. Determine the head imparted to a fluid as it passes through an impeller of 250 mm outlet diameter and 100 mm inlet diameter rotated at 1440 r.p.m. The outlet vane angle is set back at an angle of 20° to the tangent. Assume radial entrance and velocity of flow as 3 m/s.

   [**Ans.** 20.4 m]

5. A centrifugal pump impeller has an outer diamter of 300 mm and width at outer periphery 12·5 mm. The pump has radial inflow and delivers 0·08 m^3/s of water against a total of 40 m. if the speed of the pump is 1500 r.p.m. and its manometric efficiency is 80 percent find the blade angle at the exit. [**Ans.** $\phi = 69°$]

6. A centrifugal pump is running at 1000 r.p.m. and working against a head of 20 m. The rate of flow through the pump is 0.2 m^3/s. The outlet vane angle of impeller is 45° and velocity of flow at outlet is 2.5 m/s. If the manometric efficiency of the pump is 80 percent, calculate the diameter and width of impeller at outlet,

   [**Ans.** (*i*) 324 mm ; (*ii*) 78.6 mm]

7. A centrifugal pump (diffusion type) has a suction lift of 1.5 m and the delivery tank is 13.5 m above the pump. The velocity of water in the delivery pipe is 1.5 m/s. The radial velocity of flow through the wheel is 3 m/s and the tangent to the vane at exit from the wheel makes an angle of 120° with the direction of motion. Assuming that the water enters radially and neglecting friction and other losses, determine : (*i*) Velocity of wheel at exit , (*ii*) Velocity and pressure head at exit from the wheel, and(*iii*) Direction of fixed guide vanes.

   [**Ans.** (*i*) 13.07 m/s; (*ii*) 6.5 m of water; (*iii*) 14.89°]

8. A centrifugal pump impeller whose external and internal diameters are 400 mm and 200 mm respectively is running at 950 r.p.m. The rate of flow through the pump is 0.035 m^3/s. The suction and delivery heads are 5 m and 25 m respectively. The diameters of the suction and delivery pipe are 120 mm and 80 mm respectively. If the outlet vane angle is 45°, the flow velocity is constant and equal to 1.8 m/s and power required to drive the pump is 15 kW, determine:

   (*i*) Inlet vane angle, (*ii*) The overall efficiency, and (*iii*) The manometric efficiency.

   [**Ans.** (*i*) 10.26°; (*ii*) 61.76 % ; (*iii*) 73.65 %]

9. A centrifugal pump impeller whose external diameter and width at the outlet are 0.8 m and 0·1m respectively is running at 550 r.p.m. The angle of impeller vanes at outlet is 40°. The pump delivers 0.98 m^3 of water per second under an effective head of 35 m. If the pump is driven by a 500 kW motor, determine : (*i*) The manometric efficiency, (*ii*) The overall efficiency, and (*iii*) The mechanical efficiency, Assume water enters the vanes radially at inlet.

   [**Ans.** (*i*) 81 %; (*ii*) 67 %; (*iii*) 83 %]

10. A centrifugal pump impeller having external and internal diameters 400 mm and 200 mm respectively is running at 1200 r.p.m. The widths of impeller at outlet and inlet are 8 mm and 16 mm respectively. The rate of flow of water through the pump is 0.015 m^3/s. The outlet vane angle of the impeller is 30°. If the loss of head through the impeller is 1.15 m find the pressure rise in the impeller.

    Assume water enters the impeller radially at inlet. [**Ans.** 30.7 m]

11. A centrifugal pump is delivering 0.04 m^3 of water per second to a height of 20 m through a 150 mm diameter 100 m long pipeline. If the inlet losses in suction pipe are equal to 0.33 m and friction factor is 0.06 for the pipeline find the power required to drive the pump.

Assume overall efficiency of the pump as 70 percent. **[Ans.** 17.4 kW]

12. A centrifugal pump with 1.2 m diameter runs at 200 r.p.m. and discharges 1880 litres/sec, the average lift being 6 m. The angle which the vanes make at exit with the tangent to the impeller is 26° and the radial velocity of flow is 2.5 m/s. Determine the manometric efficiency and the least speed to start pumping against a head of 6 m; the inner diameter of the impeller being 0.6 m . **[Ans.** 199.36 r.p.m]

13. The diameter of a centrifugal pump impeller is 300 mm and its width is 600 mm. the pump delivers 120 litres/sec with a manometric efficinecy of 85 percent. The effective outlet vane angle is 30°. If the speed of the rotation is 1000 r.p.m. calculate the specific speed of the pump.

14. A multi - stage centrifugal pump has four identical impellers, keyed to the same shaft. The width and diameter of each impeller at outlet are 50 mm and 600 mm respectively. The vanes of each impeller are having outlet angle as 45°. The speed of the pump is 400 r.p.m. and the total manometric head developed is 40 m. If the discharge through the pump is 0.2 m^3/s, find the manometric efficiency. **[Ans.** 74.82 %]

15. Find the number of pumps required to take water from a deep well under a total head of 120 m. All the pumps are identical and are running at 800 r.p.m. The specific speed of each pump is given as 25 while the rated capacity of each pump is 0.16 m^3/s **[Ans.** 4]

16. A centrifugal pump is discharging 0.03 m^3/s of water against a total head of 20 m. The diameter of the impeller is 400 mm and it is rotating at 1500 r.p.m. Calculate the head, discharge and ratio of powers of a geometrically similar pump of diameter 250 mm when it is running at 3000 r.p.m. **[Ans.** 31.25 m; 0.01465 m^3/s ; 1.31]

17. A centrifugal pump (single stage) runs at 500 r.p.m. and delivers 300 m^3/min of water against a head of 120 m. The pump impeller is 2 m in diameter and it has a positive suction lift (including the velocity head and friction) of 3 m. Laboratory tests are to be conducted on a model with 450 mm diameter impeller and on a reduced head of 95 m. Assuming atmospheric head = 10.15 m of water and vapour head = 0.34 m of water calculate the speed, discharge and suction lift for the laboratory tests. **[Ans.** 1977 r.p.m.; 13.51 m^3/min ; 4.418 m]

Chapter 4

RECIPROCATING PUMPS

4.1. INRODUCTION

The reciprocating pump is a *positive displacement pump* as it sucks and raises the liquid by actually displacing it with a piston/plunger that executes a reciprocating motion in a closely fitting cylinder. The amount of liquid pumped is equal to the volume displaced by the piston.

The pumps designed with disk pistons create pressures upto 25 bar and the plunger pumps built up still higher pressures. Discharge from these pumps is almost wholly dependent on the pump speed.

The total efficiency of a reciprocating pump is about 10 to 20% higher than a comparable centrifugal pump.

Reciprocating pumps for industrial uses have almost become *obsolete owing to their high capital cost as well as maintenance cost as compared to that of centrifugal pumps*. However, small hand-operated pumps such as cycle pumps, football pumps, kerosene pumps, village well pumps and pumps used as important parts of hydraulic jack etc. still find wide applications. *The reciprocating pump is best suited for relatively small capacities and high heads*. This type of pump is very common in *oil drilling operations*.

The reciprocating pump is generally employed for:

(*i*) Light oil pumping,

(*ii*) Feeding small boilers condensate return, and

(*iii*) Pneumatic pressure systems.

4.2. CLASSIFICATION OF RECIPROCATING PUMPS

Reciprocating pumps are *classified* as follows:

1. According to the water being in contact with piston:

(*i*) *Single-acting pump* ...water is in contact with *one side* of the piston

(*ii*) *Double-acting pump* ...water is in contact with *both sides* of the piston.

2. According to number of cylinders:

(*i*) Single cylinder pump

(*ii*) Double cylinder pump (or two throw pump)

(*iii*) Triple cylinder pump (or three throw pump)

(*iv*) Duplex double-acting pump (or four throw pump)

(*v*) Quintuplex pump or (five throw pump).

In general the reciprocating pumps having more than one cylinder are known as *multi-cylinder pumps*.

4.3. MAIN COMPONENTS AND WORKING OF A RECIPROCATING PUMP

Refer to Fig. 4.1. The **main parts** *of a reciprocating pump are:*

1. Cylinder
2. Piston
3. Suction valve
4. Delivery valve
5. Suction pipe
6. Delivery pipe
7. Crank and connecting rod mechanism operated by a power source e.g. steam engine, internal combustion engine or an electric motor.

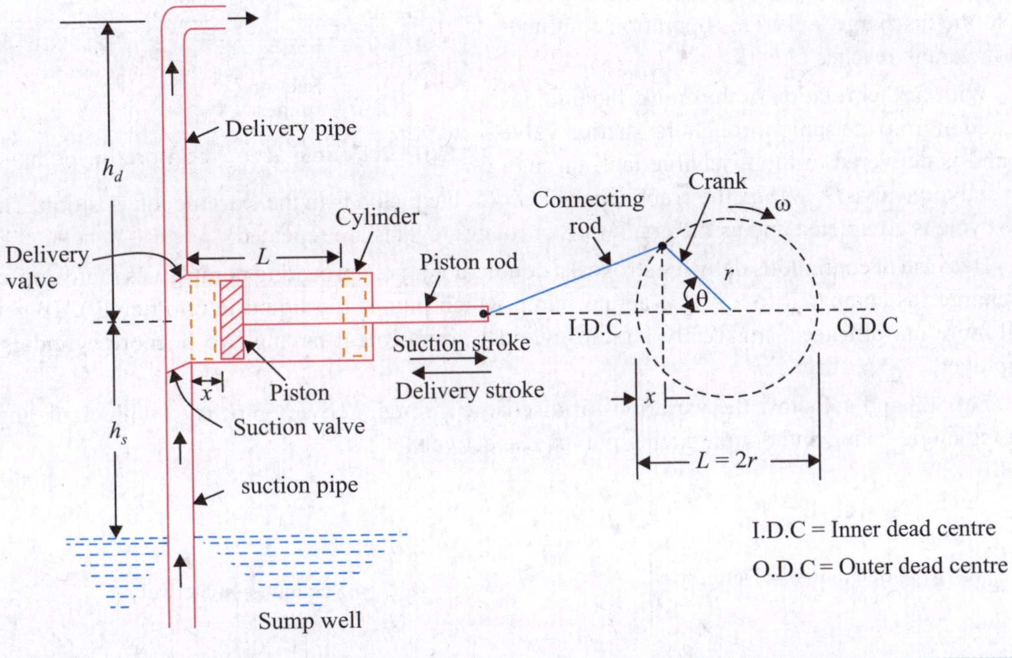

Fig. 4.1. Schematic view of single-acting reciprocating pump.

Working of a single-acting reciprocating pump:

As shown in Fig. 4.1, a single acting reciprocating pump has one suction pipe and one delivery pipe. It is usually placed above the liquid level in the sump. When the crank rotates the piston moves backward and forward inside the cylinder. The pump operates as follows:

— Let us suppose that initially the crank is at the inner dead centre (I.D.C.) and crank rotates in the clockwise direction. As the crank rotates, the piston moves towards right and a vacuum is created on the left side of the piston. This vacuum causes suction valve to open and consequently the liquid is forced from the sump into the left side of the piston. When the crank is at the outer dead centre (O.D.C) the suction stroke is completed and the left side of the cylinder is full of liquid.

— When the crank further turns from O.D.C to I.D.C., the piston moves inward to the left and high pressure is built up in the cylinder. The delivery valve opens and the liquid is forced into the delivery pipe. The liquid is carried to the discharge tank through the delivery pipe. At the end of delivery stroke the crank comes to the I.D.C and the piston is at the extreme left position.

Working of a double-acting reciprocating pump:

Refer to Fig. 4.2. In a double-acting reciprocating pump, suction and delivery *strokes occur simultaneously*. When the crank rotates from *I.D.C.* in the clockwise direction, a vacuum is created on the left side of piston and the liquid is sucked in from the sump through value S_1. At the same time, the liquid on the right side of the piston is pressed and a high pressure causes the delivery valve D_2 to open and the liquid is passed on to the discharge tank. This operation continues till the crank reaches *O.D.C.*

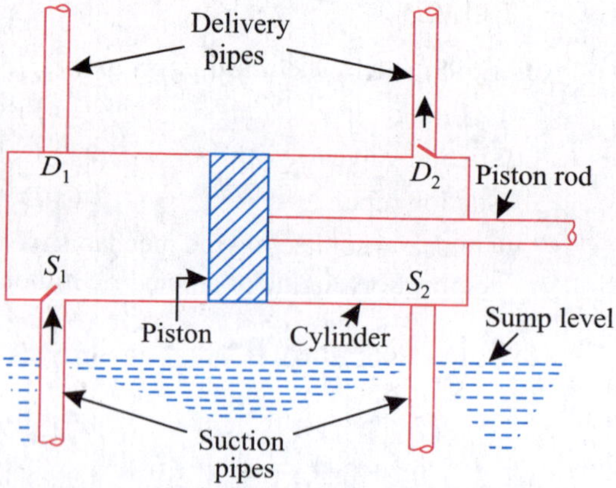

Fig. 4.2. Double-acting reciprocating pump.

With further rotation of the crank, the liquid is sucked in from the sump through the suction valve S_2 and is delivered to the discharge tank through the delivery valve D_1. When the crank reaches *I.D.C.*, the piston is in the extreme left position. Thus one cycle is completed and as the crank further rotates, cycles are repeated.

Because of continuous delivery strokes, a double-acting reciprocating pump gives more uniform discharge (as compared to a single-acting pump which pumps the liquid intermittently). To get a still more uniform feed, invariably a multi-cylinder arrangement having two or more cylinders is employed.

Fig. 4.3 and 4.4 show the variations of discharge through delivery pipe (Q_d) with crank angle (θ) for single-acting and double-acting pumps respectively.

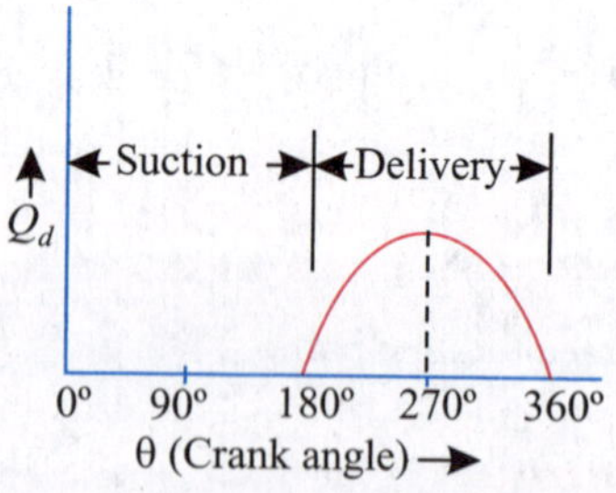

Fig. 4.3. Q_d v/s θ variations for single-acting pump.

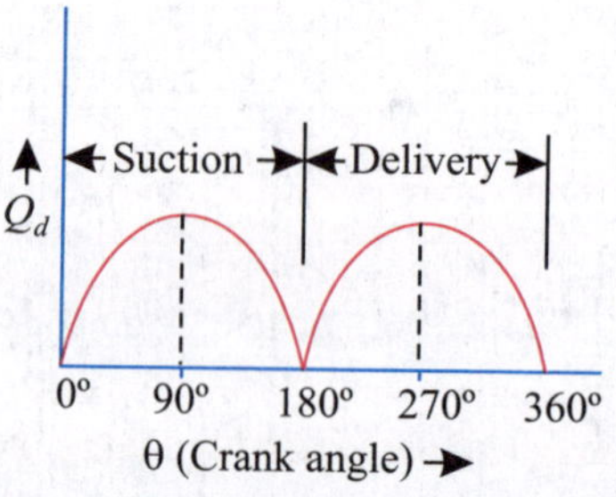

Fig. 4.4. Q_d v/s θ variations for double-acting pump.

4.4. DISCHARGE, WORK DONE AND POWER REQUIRED TO DRIVE RECIPROCATING PUMP

4.4.1. Single-acting reciprocating pump

Consider a single-acting reciprocating pump shown in Fig. 4.1

Let, D = Diameter of the cylinder, m

A = Cross-sectional area of the piston/cylinder = $\frac{\pi}{4} D^2$ m^2

r = Radius of crank, m

N = Speed of the crank, r.p.m.

L = Length of the stroke (= $2r$), m

h_s = Height of the centre of the cylinder above the liquid surface, m and

h_d = Height to which the liquid is raised above the centre of the cylinder, m.

Volume of liquid sucked in during suction stroke = $A \times L$

∴ *Discharge* of the pump per second, $Q = A \times L \times \frac{N}{60}$ ...(4.1)

Weight of water delivered per second, $W = w\,Q = \frac{wALN}{60}$ ...(4.2)

Work done per second = Weight of water lifted/sec. × total height through which liquid is lifted

$$= W(h_s + h_d) = \frac{wALN}{60}(h_s + h_d) \qquad ...(4.3)$$

∴ *Power required* to drive the pump $= \frac{wALN}{60 \times 1000}(h_s + h_d)$ kW ...(4.4)

(where, w = weight density of liquid in N/m^3)

4.4.2. Double-acting Reciprocating Pump

Refer to Fig. 4.2.

Let, D = Diameter of the piston,

d = Diameter of the piston rod,

A_{pr} = cross-sectional area of the piston rod = $\frac{\pi}{4} d^2$

Area on one side of the piston, $A = \frac{\pi}{4} D^2$

Area on other side of the piston where piston rod is connected to the piston,

$$A' = A - A_{pr} = \frac{\pi}{4} D^2 - \frac{\pi}{4} d^2 = \frac{\pi}{4}(D^2 - d^2).$$

Volume of liquid delivered in one revolution of crank

$$= A\,L + A'\,L = (A + A')\,L = \left[\frac{\pi}{4} D^2 + \frac{\pi}{4}(D^2 - d^2)\right] L$$

∴ *Discharge* of the pump per second $= \left[\frac{\pi}{4} D^2 + \frac{\pi}{4}(D^2 - d^2)\right] L \times \frac{N}{60}$ ...(4.5)

If the diameter of the piston rod '*d*' is very small as compared to the diameter of the piston '*D*' then it can be neglected and hence *discharge* of the pump per second will become

$$Q = \left(\frac{\pi}{4} D^2 + \frac{\pi}{4} D^2\right) \times \frac{LN}{60} = 2 \times \frac{\pi}{4} D^2 \times \frac{LN}{60} = \frac{2\ A\ L\ N}{60} \quad ...(4.6)$$

Evidently the output of a double acting pump is two-times that of a single acting pump.

Work done per second = Weight of water delivered × total height through which liquid is lifted

$$= \left(w \times \frac{2ALN}{60}\right) \times (h_s + h_d)$$

$$= \frac{2wALN}{60} (h_s + h_d) \quad ...(4.7)$$

Power required to drive the pump, $P = \dfrac{2wALN}{60 \times 1000} (h_s + h_d)$ kW ...(4.8)

(where, w = weight density of liquid in N/m^3)

4.5. CO-EFFICIENT OF DISCHARGE AND SLIP OF RECIPROCATING PUMP

4.5.1. Co-efficient of Discharge

In a reciprocating pump, the actual discharge ($Q_{act.}$) is always slightly different from the theoretical discharge ($Q_{th.}$) due to following *reasons*:

(*i*) Leakage through the valves, glands and piston packing,

(*ii*) Imperfect operation of the valves (suction and discharge), and

(*iii*) Partial filling of cylinder by the liquid.

The ratio between actual discharge and theoretical discharge is known as the **co-efficient of discharge (C_d) of the pump**. That is,

$$C_d = \frac{\text{Actual discharge}}{\text{Theoretical discharge}} = \frac{Q_{act.}}{Q_{th.}} \quad ...(4.9)$$

When the value of C_d is expressed in percentage, it is known as '**volumetric efficiency**' of the pump. Volumetric efficiency depends upon the dimensions of the pump and its value ranges from 85-98%.

4.5.2. Slip

The difference between the theoretical discharge and actual discharge is *called the* **slip** *of the pump*. That is

$$\text{Slip} = Q_{th.} - Q_{act.} \quad ...(4.10)$$

But the slip is oftenly expressed in percentage which is given by,

$$\%\ \text{Slip} = \frac{Q_{th.} - Q_{act.}}{Q_{th.}} \times 100 = \left(1 - \frac{Q_{act.}}{Q_{th.}}\right) \times 100 = (1 - C_d) \times 100 \quad ...(4.11)$$

The percentage of slip for the pumps maintained in *good condition is* of the order of 2% or even less.

Negative slip. In most of the reciprocating pumps $Q_{act.}$ is *less than* $Q_{th.}$; in such a case the value of C_d is *less than unity* and the *slip of the* pump is '*positive*'. However, in some cases $Q_{act.}$ may be *more* than $Q_{th.}$; in such a case C_d is more than *unity* and the *slip* will be '*negative*'. The slip *will be negative when there is a direct connection between the suction and delivery sides before the end of suction stroke. This happens if the momentum of liquid in the suction pipe is large enough to open* *the delivery valve before the beginning of delivery stroke. The negative slip is possible in case of pumps having long suction pipe and a short delivery pipe, especially when these are operating at high speeds.*

Example 4.1. *A single-acting reciprocating pump, running at 50 r.p.m. delivers 0.00736 m^3/s of water. The diameter of the piston is 200 mm and stroke length 300 mm. The suction and delivery heads are 3.5 m and 11.5 m respectively. Determine:*

(i) *Theoretical discharge,*

(ii) *Co-efficient of discharge,*

(iii) *Percentage slip of the pump, and*

(iv) *Power required to run the pump.*

Solution. Speed of the pump, $N = 50$ r.p.m.

Actual discharge, $Q_{act.} = 0.00736\ m^3/s$

Diameter of the piston, $D = 200\ mm = 0.2\ m$

$$\therefore \quad \text{Area, } A = \frac{\pi}{4} \times 0.2^2 = 0.0314\ m^2$$

Stroke length, $L = 300\ mm = 0.3\ m$

Suction head, $h_s = 3.5\ m$

Delivery head, $h_d = 11.5\ m$

(i) Theoretical discharge, $Q_{th.}$:

$$Q_{th.} = \frac{ALN}{60} = \frac{0.0314 \times 0.3 \times 50}{60} = \mathbf{0.00785\ m^3/s\ (Ans.)}$$

(ii) Co-efficient of discharge, C_d:

$$C_d = \frac{Q_{act.}}{Q_{th.}} = \frac{0.00736}{0.00785} = \mathbf{0.937\ (Ans.)}$$

(iii) Percentage slip of the pump:

$$\%\ \text{slip} = \frac{Q_{th.} - Q_{act.}}{Q_{th.}} \times 100 = \frac{0.00785 - 0.00736}{0.00785} \times 100 = \mathbf{6.24\%\ (Ans.)}$$

(iv) Power required to run the pump, P:

$$P = \frac{wALN}{60 \times 1000}(h_s + h_d)\,\text{kW} = \frac{9810 \times 0.0314 \times 0.3 \times 50}{60 \times 1000}(3.5 + 11.5) = \mathbf{1.155\ kW\ (Ans.)}$$

Example 4.2. *A single-acting reciprocating pump operating at 120 r.p.m. has a piston diameter of 200 mm and stroke of 300 mm. The suction and delivery heads are 4 m and 20 m, respectively. If the efficiency of both suction and delivery strokes is 75 percent, determine the power required by the pump.* **[UPTU]**

Solution. *Given:* $N = 120$ r.p.m.; $D = 200\ mm = 0.2\ m$; $L = 300\ mm = 0.3\ m$; $h_s = 4\ m$; $h_d = 20\ m$; $\eta_{(\text{suction and delivery strokes, each})} = 75\%$

Power require by the pump, P :

Theoretical discharge of the pump,

$$Q = \frac{ALN}{60} = \frac{\frac{\pi}{4} \times (0.2)^2 \times 0.3 \times 120}{60} = 0.0188\ m^3/s$$

Power required to drive the pump,

$$P = \frac{wQ\,(h_s + h_d)}{\eta} = \frac{9810 \times 0.0188\,(4 + 20)}{0.75} = 5901.7 \text{ W or } \mathbf{5.9\ kW}\ \textbf{(Ans.)}$$

Example 4.3. *The discharge / crank-angle characteristic for a reciprocating pump has the likeness of the top half of a sine-curve as shown in Fig. 4.5.*

Draw the quantitative characteristic curve for a system consisting of three such pumps connected in parallel and discharging at a crank phase difference of 120° from each other. Identify the magnitude and position of two consecutive maxima on that curve.

[GATE]

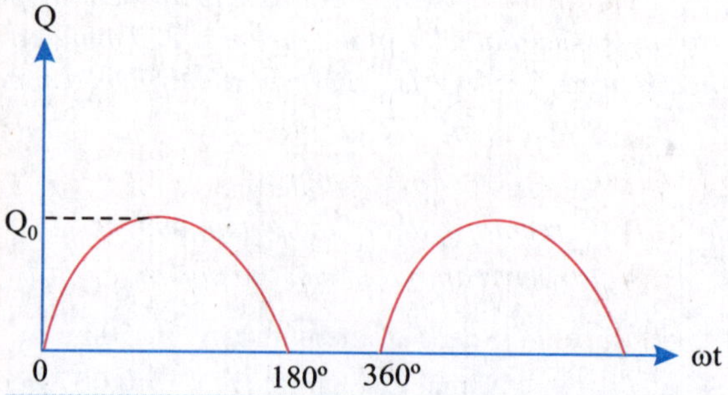

Fig. 4.5

Solution. The maximum discharge is equal to Q_0 (maximum discharge of one pump) and occurs at 60° intervals of 30°, 90°, 150°........ (See Fig. 4.6).

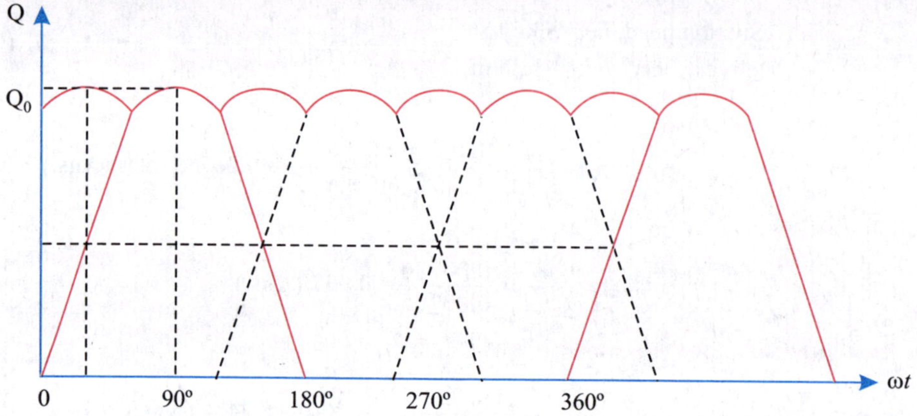

Fig. 4.6

Example 4.4. *A "three throw" pump has cylinders of 250 mm diameter and stroke of 500 mm each. The pump is required to deliver 0.1 m³/s at a head of 100 m. Friction losses are estimated to be 1 m in suction pipe and 19 m in delivery pipe. Velocity of water in delivery pipe is 1 m/s, overall efficiency is 85% and the slip is 3%. Determine:*

(i) *Speed of the pump, and*

(ii) *Power required to run the pump.*

[PTU]

Solution. Diameter of each cylinder, D = 250 mm = 0.25 m

Stroke length of each cylinder, L = 500 mm = 0.5 m

Actual discharge, $Q_{act.}$ = 0.1 m^3/s

Static head, $(h_s + h_d)$ = 100 m

Friction loss in suction pipe, h_{fs} = 1 m

Friction loss in delivery pipe, h_{fd} = 19 m

Velocity of water in delivery pipe, V_d = 1 m/s

Overall efficiency of the pump, η_0 = 85%

Percentage slip = 3%

(i) Speed of the pump, N:

A three throw pump uses three equal cylinders with rams connected to cranks at 120° apart driven by a common shaft.

For a three throw pump, the theoretical discharge is given by:

$$Q_{th} = 3 \times \frac{ALN}{60} = 3 \times \frac{\pi}{4} \times 0.25^2 \times \frac{0.5 \times N}{60} = 0.001227 \text{ N}$$

$$\therefore \text{ Actual discharge, } Q_{act} = \left(1 - \frac{3}{100}\right) Q_{th.} = 0.97 \times 0.001227 \text{ N} = 0.00119 \text{ N}$$

But, $Q_{act} = 0.1 \text{ m}^3/\text{s}$ ...(*Given*)

$$\therefore \quad 0.1 = 0.00119\,N, \quad \text{or,} \quad N = \frac{0.1}{0.00119} = \mathbf{84 \text{ r.p.m}} \text{ (Ans.)}$$

(ii) Power required to run the pump, P:

Total head against which pump has to work,

$$H = (h_s + h_d) + (h_{fs} + h_{fd}) + \frac{V_d^2}{2g}$$

$$= 100 + (1 + 19) + \frac{1.0^2}{2 \times 9.81} = 120.05 \text{ m}$$

$$\therefore \quad \text{Water power} = \frac{wQ_{act.}H}{1000} \text{ kW} = \frac{9810 \times 0.1 \times 120.05}{1000} 117.77 \text{ kW}$$

Power required to drive the shaft,

$$P = \frac{\text{Water power}}{\text{Overall efficiency}} = \frac{117.77}{0.85} = \mathbf{138.55 \text{ kW}} \text{ (Ans.)}$$

4.6. EFFECT OF ACCELERATION OF PISTON ON VELOCITY AND PRESSURE IN THE SUCTION AND DELIVERY PIPES

Refer to Fig. 4.1. If the crank rotates uniformly and the length of connecting rod is enough compared to the radius of crank, the piston makes simple harmonic motion. This causes acceleration during the first half of the stroke, and deceleration during the second half of the stroke.

Let,
A = Area of the cylinder,
a = Area of the pipe (suction or delivery),
l = Length of pipe (suction or delivery),
r = Radius of the crank, and
ω = Angular speed of the crank in rad/s.

The crank is rotating with an angular velocity ω and let in time t seconds, the crank turns through angle θ (in radians) from I.D.C. (inner dead centre). The displacement of the piston in time t is x as shown in Fig. 4.1.

Now, angle turned by the crank in time t, $\theta = \omega t = \frac{2\pi N}{60} \times t$

(where, N = rotational speed of crank in r.p.m.)

The corresponding distance (x) travelled by the piston,

$$x = r - r\cos\theta = r(1 - \cos\theta) = r(1 - \cos\omega t) \quad \text{...(4.12)}$$

$$\text{Velocity of the piston, } V = \frac{dx}{dt} = \frac{d}{dt}[r(1 - \cos\omega t)] = \frac{d}{dt}(r - r\cos\omega t)$$

or, $$V = \omega r \sin \omega t \quad ...(4.13)$$

Acceleration of the piston, $$a_p = \frac{dV}{dt} = \frac{d}{dt}(\omega r \sin \omega t) = \omega^2 r \cos \omega t \quad ...(4.14)$$

Now from continuity considerations, the *volume of liquid flowing from the pipe equals the volume of liquid flowing into the cylinder.*

∴ Velocity of liquid in the pipe (v) × area of pipe (a)

= velocity of piston (V) × area of cylinder (A)

$$\therefore \quad v = \frac{AV}{a} = \frac{A}{a}\omega r \sin \omega t \quad ...(4.15)$$

Acceleration of liquid in pipe $$= \frac{d}{dt}(v) = \frac{d}{dt}\left[\frac{A}{a}\omega r \sin \omega t\right]$$

$$= \frac{A}{a}\omega^2 r \cos \omega t \quad ...(4.16)$$

Mass of water in pipe = Density × volume of liquid in pipe = $\rho a l$

Force required to accelerate the water in the pipe = Mass × acceleration

$$= \rho a l \times \frac{A}{a}\omega^2 r \cos \omega t$$

∴ Intensity of pressure due to acceleration

$$= \frac{\text{Force required to accelerate the liquid}}{\text{Area of pipe}} = \frac{\rho a l \times \frac{A}{a}\omega^2 r \cos \omega t}{a}$$

$$= \rho l \times \frac{A}{a}\omega^2 r \cos \theta$$

∴ Pressure head due to acceleration, $$h_a = \frac{\text{Intensity of pressure}}{\text{Weight density of liquid } (w)}$$

$$= \frac{\rho l \times \frac{A}{a}\omega^2 r \cos \theta}{\rho g} \quad (\because w = \rho g)$$

$$= \frac{l}{g} \times \frac{A}{a}\omega^2 r \cos \theta \quad ...(4.17)$$

The pressure head due to acceleration in the suction and delivery pipes is obtained by using subscripts 's' and 'd' respectively in the eqn. (4.17) as follows:

$$h_{as} = \frac{l_s}{g} \times \frac{A}{a_s}\omega^2 r \cos \theta \quad ...(4.18)$$

$$h_{ad} = \frac{l_d}{g} \times \frac{A}{a_d}\omega^2 r \cos \theta \quad ...(4.19)$$

Thus the pressure head due to acceleration given by eqn. (4.17), is a *function of angular displacement* θ.

Note : It may be noted that for any stroke, *the angular displacement θ is measured from the instant of commencement of that stroke.* In case of *suction stroke* the piston moves *outward* and θ is measured from I.D.C. (inner dead centre) and during *delivery stroke* the piston moves *inward* and θ is measured from *O.D.C* (outer dead centre).

The values of 'h_a' for different values of θ are:

(*i*) When $\theta = 0°$ (*i.e.* the *beginning* of the stroke), $h_a = \frac{l}{g}\frac{A}{a}\omega^2 r$ ...(4.20)

($\because \cos 0° = 1$)

(*ii*) When $\theta = 90°$ (*i.e.* the *middle* of the stroke), $h_a = 0$ ...(4.21)

($\because \cos 90° = 0$)

(*iii*) When $\theta = 180°$ (*i.e.* the end of the stroke), $h_a = -\frac{l}{g}\frac{A}{a}\omega^2 r$ ...(4.22)

($\because \cos 180° = -1$)

∴ Maximum pressure head due to acceleration, $(h_a)_{max} = \frac{l}{g} \times \frac{A}{a}\omega^2 r$ ...(4.23)

For $0° < \theta < 90°$, h_a has +ve values and for $90° < \theta < 180°$, h_a has –ve values, thereby indicating that for the first half of the stroke there is *acceleration head* development and in the later half of the stroke *retardation head* is developed.

In case the connecting rod is *not very long as compared to crank length* then it *cannot* be assumed that the piston has a simple harmonic motion and in that case the pressure head, h_a is given by:

$$h_a = \frac{l}{g}\frac{A}{a}\omega^2 r \cos\theta \left(\cos\theta + \frac{\cos 2\theta}{n}\right) \quad ...(4.24)$$

where, n = Ratio of the length of connecting rod to the crank length.

From eqn. (4.24), we have:

(*i*) When $\theta = 0°$ (*i.e.* the *beginning* of the stroke), $h_a = \frac{l}{g}\frac{A}{a}\omega^2 r\left(1 + \frac{1}{n}\right)$ ...(4.25)

(*ii*) When $\theta = 90°$ (*i.e.* the middle of stroke), $h_a = 0$ ...(4.26)

(*iii*) When $\theta = 180°$ (*i.e.* at the *end* of the stroke), $h_a = \frac{l}{g}\frac{A}{a}\omega^2 r\left(1 - \frac{1}{n}\right)$ ...(4.27)

Effect of variation of velocity on friction in pipes:

The liquid flowing through suction and delivery pipes causes loss of head due to friction, which is given by Darcy-Weisbach equation as:

$$h_f = \frac{4 f l v^2}{d \times 2g} \quad ...(i)$$

where, f = Co-efficient of friction,

l = Length of the pipe,

d = Diameter of the pipe, and

v = Velocity of liquid in the pipe.

Also the velocity of liquid in the pipe, $v = \frac{A}{a}\omega r \sin\omega t = \frac{A}{a}\omega r \sin\theta$ ...[Eqn. (4.15)]

Substituting the value of 'v' in (*i*), we get:

$$h_f = \frac{4 fl}{d \times 2g}\left(\frac{A}{a}\omega r \sin\theta\right)^2 \quad ...(4.28)$$

The variation of h_f with θ is **parabolic.** The values of h_f for suction and delivery pipes are obtained from eqn. (4.28) by using subscripts '*s*' for suction pipe and '*d*' for delivery pipe as:

$$h_{fs} = \frac{4fl_s}{d_s \times 2g}\left(\frac{A}{a_s}\omega r \sin\theta\right)^2 \quad ...(4.29)$$

$$h_{fd} = \frac{4fl_d}{d_d \times 2g}\left(\frac{A}{a_d}\omega r \sin\theta\right)^2 \quad ...(4.30)$$

The loss of head due to friction (h_f) in pipes given by eqn. (4.28) varies with θ as:

(*i*) When θ = 0° (*i.e.* the *beginning* of the stroke), $h_f = 0$ ...(4.31)

(*ii*) When θ = 90° (*i.e.* the *middle* of the stroke), $h_f = \frac{4fl}{d \times 2g}\left(\frac{A}{a}\omega r\right)^2$ ...(4.32)

(*iii*) When θ = 180° (*i.e.* the *end* of the stroke), $h_f = 0$ ...(4.33)

∴ Maximum value of loss of head due to friction,

$$(h_f)_{max} = \frac{4fl}{d \times 2g}\left(\frac{A}{a}\omega r\right)^2 \quad ...(4.34)$$

4.7. INDICATOR DIAGRAMS

The **indicator diagram** *of a reciprocating pump is the diagram which shows the pressure head of the liquid in the cylinder corresponding to any position during the suction and delivery strokes. It is a graph between pressure head and stroke length of the piston for one complete revolution* (pressure head is taken as ordinate and stroke length as abscissa).

4.7.1. Ideal Indicator Diagram

The indicator diagram obtained by *neglecting* the loss of head due to friction in the suction and delivery pipes and the effect of acceleration of piston, is known as an *ideal indicator diagram*. Such diagram for a single-cylinder single-acting pump is shown is Fig. 4.7, the line *EF* represents the atmospheric pressure head $\left[H_{atm.} = \frac{p_a}{w}\right]$ equal to 10.3 m of water.

Let, h_s = Suction head, and

h_d = Delivery head.

- The pressure head in the cylinder (represented by line AB) during *suction stroke*, is *constant* and equal to suction head (h_s) which is below the atmospheric pressure head ($H_{atm.}$) by a height h_s. The *absolute pressure head* in cylinder during the suction stroke will be ($H_{atm.} - h_s$); it is shown by ordinate AS at the beginning of the stroke and by ordinate BT at the end of stroke and, is *uniform* throughout the stroke.
- During the *delivery stroke* the pressure head in the cylinder

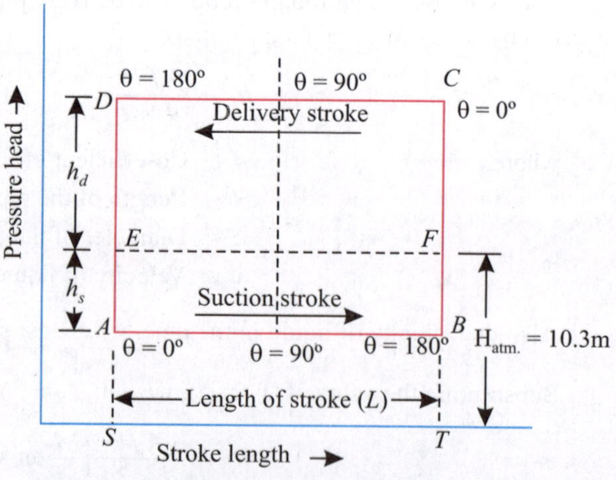

Fig. 4.7. Ideal indicator diagram.

(represented by line CD) is *constant* and equal to delivery head (h_d). The *uniform absolute pressure head* throughout the delivery stroke is ($h_d + H_{atm.}$) and is denoted by the ordinate TC or SD.

The work done by the pump per second is

$$= \frac{w \times ALN}{60} \times (h_s + h_d) \quad \text{...[Eqn. (4.3)]}$$

$$= K \times L \times (h_s + h_d) \qquad \left(\text{where, } K = \frac{wAN}{60} = \text{const.}\right)$$

$$\propto L \times (h_s + h_d)$$

But from Fig. 4.7, the area of indicator diagram *ABCDA*

$$= AB \times BC = AB\,(BF + FC) = L\,(h_s + h_d) \quad \text{...}(ii)$$

From (*i*) and (*ii*), we have:

Work done by the pump $\propto$ *area of indicator diagram*

Thus, work done by the pump per second $\frac{wAN}{60}$ × area of indicator diagram ...(4.35)

If the pump is double-acting, *neglecting* the area of the piston rod, work done per second is proportional to *twice* the area of the indicator diagram.

4.7.2. Effect of Acceleration in Suction and Delivery Pipes on Indicator Diagram

The effect of acceleration in suction and delivery pipes is discussed below:

(*a*) Effect of acceleration in the suction pipe:

As the piston (considering it as the beginning of the stroke) moves outward, it should create not only a negative pressure equal to the suction head (h_s) but it should also *accelerate the liquid.* If h_{as} is the acceleration head, then total negative pressure head at the *beginning* of the suction stroke is ($h_s + h_{as}$), the ordinate *EA'*, *absolute pressure head* at this point is denoted by ordinate *A'S*. So that separation *does not* take place, the absolute pressure at the beginning of stroke should not fall *below the vapour pressure*.

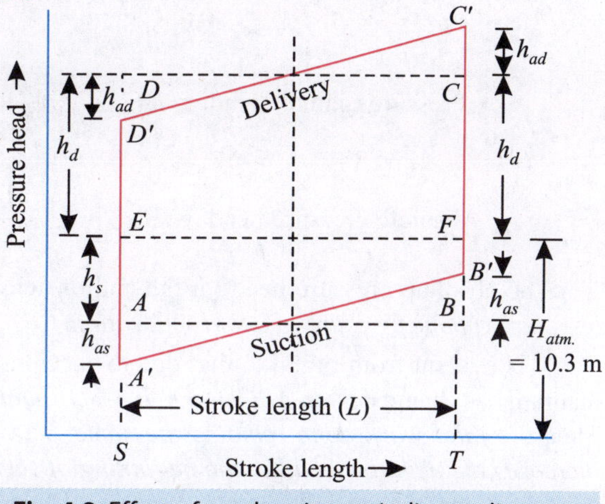

Fig. 4.8. Effect of acceleration on indicator diagram.

If l_s and a_s are length and cross-sectional area of the suction pipe respectively, then:

(*i*) At the beginning of the suction stroke:

$$\text{The accelerating head, } h_{as} = \frac{l_s}{g} \times \frac{A}{a_s}\,\omega^2 r \quad \text{...[Eqn. 4.20]}$$

$$\text{Negative pressure (vacuum) head, } h_s + h_{as} = h_s + \frac{l_s}{g} \times \frac{A}{a_s}\,\omega^2 r \quad \text{...(4.36)}$$

$$\text{Absolute pressure head} = H_{atm.} - \left(h_s + \frac{l_s}{g} \times \frac{A}{a_s}\,\omega^2 r\right)$$

(ii) At the middle of the suction stroke:

$$\text{The acceleration head, } h_{as} = 0 \qquad \text{...[Eqn. 4.20]}$$

$$\text{Negative pressure (vacuum) head} = h_s \qquad \text{...(4.37)}$$

$$\text{Absolute pressure head} = H_{atm.} - h_s$$

(iii) At the end of the suction stroke:

$$\text{The acceleration head, } h_{as} = -\frac{l_s}{g} \times \frac{A}{a_s}\,\omega^2 r \qquad \text{...[Eqn. 4.22]}$$

$$\text{Negative pressure (vacuum) head} = h_s + h_{as} = h_s - \frac{l_s}{g} \times \frac{A}{a_s}\,\omega^2 r \qquad \text{...(4.38)}$$

$$\text{Absolute pressure head} = H_{atm.} - \left(h_s - \frac{l_s}{g} \times \frac{A}{a_s}\,\omega^2 r\right)$$

(b) Effect of acceleration in the delivery pipe:

In the *beginning* of delivery stroke the liquid in the delivery pipe is *accelerated*, while at the *end* of delivery stroke the liquid is *retarded*.

If l_d and a_d are the length and cross-sectional area of the delivery pipe respectively, then:

(i) At the beginning of delivery stroke:

$$\text{Pressure head (gauge)} = h_d + h_{ad} = h_d + \frac{l_d}{g} \times \frac{A}{a_d}\,\omega^2 r \qquad \text{...(4.39)}$$

(ii) At the middle of delivery stroke:

$$\text{Pressure (gauge) head} = h_d \qquad (\because h_{ad} = 0) \qquad \text{...(4.40)}$$

(iii) At the end of delivery stroke:

$$\text{Pressure (gauge) head} = h_d - \frac{l_d}{g} \times \frac{A}{a_d} \times \omega^2 r \qquad \text{...(4.41)}$$

$$\text{Absolute pressure head} = H_{atm.} + h_d - \frac{l_d}{g} \times \frac{A}{a_d} \times \omega^2 r \qquad \text{...(4.42)}$$

The absolute pressure head (at the end of delivery stroke) given by eqn. (4.42) *should not be less than vapour pressure to avoid separation.*

It is evident from Fig. 4.8. that due to acceleration in suction and delivery pipes, the indicator diagram has changed from *ABCD* to *A' B' C' D'* *but the area of indicator diagram remains unaltered.* Thus the *total work done remains the same. The main effect of the acceleration head is that it increases the negative head at the beginning of suction stroke. If the simple harmonic motion does not take place, the straight lines A' B'* and *C' D' will become slightly curved.*

Example 4.5. *A single-acting reciprocating pump has a diameter (piston) of 150 mm and stroke length 350 mm. The centre of the pump is 3.5 m above the water surface in the sump and 22 m below the delivery water level. Both the suction and delivery pipes have the same diameter of 100 mm and are 5 m and 30 m long respectively. If the pump is working at 30 r.p.m., determine:*

(i) *The pressure heads on the piston at the beginning, middle and end of both suction and delivery strokes.*

(ii) *The power required to drive the pump.*

Take atmospheric pressure as 10.3 m of water.

Solution. Diameter of piston, $D = 150 \text{ mm} = 0.15 \text{ m}$

Stroke length $L = 350 \text{ mm} = 0.35 \text{ m}$

Suction head, $h_s = 3.5 \text{ m}$

Delivery head, $h_d = 22 \text{ m}$

Diameter of pipes, $d_s = d_d = 100 \text{ mm} = 0.1 \text{ m}$

Length of suction pipe, $l_s = 5 \text{ m}$

Length of delivery pipe, $l_d = 30 \text{ m}$

Speed of pump, $N = 30$ r.p.m.

Atmospheric pressure, $H_{atm.} = 10.3 \text{ m}$

(i) The pressure heads on the piston:

(a) Suction stroke:

The pressure head *due to acceleration* in *suction pipe* is given by:

$$h_{as} = \frac{l_s}{g} \times \frac{A}{a_s} \times \omega^2 r \cos\theta \qquad \text{...Eqn. (4.18)}$$

At the *beginning* of the stroke ($\theta = 0°$),

$$h_{as} = \frac{l_s}{g} \times \frac{A}{a_s} \times \omega^2 r = \frac{5}{9.81} \times \left[\frac{(\pi/4) \times 0.15^2}{(\pi/4) \times 0.1^2}\right] \times \left(\frac{2\pi \times 30}{60}\right)^2 \times (0.175) = 1.98 \text{ m of water}$$

$$\left(\because r = \frac{L}{2} = \frac{0.35}{2} = 0.175 \text{ m}\right)$$

At the *middle* of the stroke ($\theta = 90°$), $h_{as} = 0$

At the *end* of the stroke ($\theta = 180°$), $h_{as} = -\frac{l_s}{g} \times \frac{A}{a_s} \times \omega^2 r = -1.98$ m of water (as calculated above)

$\therefore$ Pressure heads (on the piston) in metres of water *during suction stroke*:

At *beginning* $= (h_s + h_{as}) = 3.5 + 1.98 = 5.48$ m (vacuum)

$= 10.3 - 5.48 =$ **4.82 m of water (absolute) (Ans.)**

At *middle* $= (h_s + 0) = 3.5$ m (vacuum)

$= 10.3 - 3.5 =$ **6.8 m of water (absolute) (Ans.)**

At *end* $= 3.5 - 1.98 = 1.52$ m (vacuum)

$= 10.3 - 1.52 =$ **8.78 m of water (absolute) (Ans.)**

(b) Delivery stroke:

The pressure head *due to acceleration* in *delivery pipe* is given by:

$$h_{ad} = \frac{l_d}{g} \times \frac{A}{a_d} \times \omega^2 r \cos\theta$$

At the *beginning* of the stroke ($\theta = 0°$),

$$h_{ad} = \frac{l_d}{g} \times \frac{A}{a_d} \times \omega^2 r = \frac{30}{9.81} \times \left[\frac{(\pi/4) \times 0.15^2}{(\pi/4) \times 0.1^2}\right] \times \left(\frac{2\pi \times 30}{60}\right)^2 \times 0.175 = 11.88 \text{ m}$$

At the *middle* of the stroke ($\theta = 90°$), $h_{ad} = 0$

At the *end* of the stroke ($\theta = 180°$), $h_{ad} = -\frac{l_d}{g} \times \frac{A}{a_d} \times \omega^2 r = -11.088$ m (as calculated above)

∴ Pressure heads (on the piston) in the metres of water *during delivery stroke*:

At *beginning* $= h_d + h_{ad} = 22 + 11.88 = 33.88$ m (*gauge*)

$= 10.3 + 33.88 =$ **44.18 m of water (absolute) (Ans.)**

At *middle* $= h_d + 0 = 22$ m (*gauge*)

$= 10.3 + 22 =$ **32.3 m of water (absolute) (Ans.)**

At *end* $= h_d - h_{ad} = 22 - 11.8 = 10.2$ m (*gauge*)

$= 10.3 + 10.2 =$ **20.5 m of water (absolute) (Ans.)**

(*ii*) Power required to drive the pump, P:

Theoretical discharge of the pump,

$$Q = \frac{ALN}{60} = \frac{\pi}{4} \times (0.15)^2 \times 0.35 \times 30 \times \frac{1}{60} = 0.00309 \text{ m}^3/\text{s}$$

Work done by the pump

$$= wQ\,(h_s + h_d) = 9810 \times 0.00309\,(3.5 + 22) = 772.98 \text{ Nm/s or J/s}$$

∴ *Power required to drive the pump, P* = **772.98 W (Ans.)**

Example 4.6. *A single-acting reciprocating pump has a diameter (piston) of 100 mm and stroke length 200 mm. The length and diameter of the suction pipe are 6.5 m and 50 mm respectively. If the suction lift of the pump is 3.2 m and separation occurs when pressure in the pump falls below 2.5 m of water absolute and the manometer reads 763 mm of mercury, find the maximum speed at which pump can be run without separation in the suction pipe.*

Solution. Diameter of piston, $D = 100$ mm $= 0.1$ m

∴ Area, $A = \frac{\pi}{4} \times 0.1^2 = 0.00785$ m^2

Stroke length, $L = 200$ mm $= 0.2$ m

∴ Crank radius, $r = L/2 = 0.2 = 0.1$ m

Length of suction pipe, $l_s = 6.5$ m

Diameter of suction pipe, $d_s = 50$ mm $= 0.05$ m

∴ Area of suction pipe, $a_s = \frac{\pi}{4} \times 0.05^2 = 0.001963$ m^2

The suction lift of the pump, $h_s = 3.2$ m

Separation pressure head, $h_{sep} = 2.5$ m

Maximum speed at which pump can run without separation, *N* :

$$\text{Atmospheric head, } H_{atm.} = \frac{763}{1000} \times 13.6 = 10.377 \text{ m of water}$$

During suction stroke, the possibility of separation is only at the *beginning of the stroke*. At the beginning of suction stroke $\theta = 0°$ and $\cos\theta = 1$, that gives:

$$h_{as} = \frac{l_s}{g} \times \frac{A}{a_s} \times \omega^2 r = \frac{6.5}{9.81} \times \frac{0.00785}{0.001963} \times \omega^2 \times 0.1 = 0.265\,\omega^2$$

Pressure head in the cylinder at the beginning of suction stroke

$= (h_s + h_{as})$ vacuum

$= H_{atm.} - (h_s + h_{as})$ absolute.

This absolute pressure (at the beginning of suction stroke) should not fall *below* the vapour pressure head ($h_{sep.}$) *to avoid separation*, thus, in *limiting condition*,

$$H_{atm.} - (h_s + h_{as}) = h_{sep.}$$

or, $10.377 - (3.2 + 0.265\omega^2) = 2.5$, or, $10.377 - 3.2 - 0.265\omega^2 = 2.5$

or, $\omega^2 = \dfrac{10.377 - 3.2 - 2.5}{0.265}$ ∴ Angular velocity, $\omega = 4.2$ rad./s.

But, $\omega = \dfrac{2\pi N}{60}$, or, $N = \dfrac{60\omega}{2\pi} = \dfrac{60 \times 4.2}{2 \times \pi}$ **40.1 r.p.m. (Ans.)**

Example 4.7. *The cross-sectional area of a plunger of a reciprocating pump equals 1.5 times that of a delivery pipe. The delivery pipe is 60 m long and it rises upward at a slope of 1 in 6. If the plunger has an acceleration of 2.4 m/s² at the end of the stroke and separation pressure is 2.5 m of water, find whether separation will take place and, if so, at which section of the pipe.*

Assume simple harmonic motion, and take atmospheric pressure = 10.3 m of water.

Solution. Cross-sectional area of plunger, $A = 1.5\, a_d$ (area of delivery pipe)

Length of delivery pipe, $l_d = 60$ m

Slope of the delivery pipe = 1 in 6

Acceleration of the plunger at the end of the stroke = 2.4 m/s²

Separation pressure head, $h_{sep.} = 2.5$ m

Atmospheric pressure head, $H_{atm.} = 10.3$ m

Delivery head, h_d = Slope of the delivery pipe × length of the delivery pipe

$$= \frac{1}{6} \times 60 = 10 \text{ m}$$

The possibility of separation during delivery stroke is only at the *end of the stroke* where $\theta = 180°$ and $\cos\theta = -1$; that gives the pressure head due to acceleration in the delivery pipe,

$$h_{ad} = \frac{l_d}{g} \times \frac{A}{a_d} \times \omega^2 r \cos\theta$$

$$h_{ad} = -\frac{l_d}{g} \times \frac{A}{a_d} \times \omega^2 r = -\frac{60}{9.81} \times 1.5 \times 2.4 = -22.02 \text{ m}$$

(∵ Acceleration, $\omega^2 r = 2.4$ m/s²)

∴ Pressure head in the cylinder at the end of delivery stroke

$= (h_d + h_{ad})$ *gauge*

$= H_{atm} + (h_d + h_{ad})$ absolute

$= 10.3 + (10 - 22.02) = -1.72$ m of water

Since the absolute pressure head is *less than* the allowable separation pressure head of 2.5 m of water therefore, **separation will occur. (Ans.)**

Let, l = The length of pipe upto the section where the separation occurs.

Then, $h_d = \dfrac{1}{6} \times l = 0.1667l$

$$h_{ad} = -\frac{l}{g} \times 1.5 \times 2.4 = -\frac{l}{9.81} \times 1.5 \times 2.4 = -0.367l$$

From *limiting condition for separation*, we have:

$$H_{atm.} + (h_d + h_{ad}) = h_{sep.}$$

$$10.3 + (0.1667\, l - 0.367 l) = 2.5$$

$$l = \frac{10.3 - 2.5}{(0.367 - 0.1667)} = \mathbf{38.94\ m\ (Ans.)}$$

Example 4.8. *The diameter and stroke length of a single-acting reciprocating pump are 75 mm and 150 mm respectively. It takes its supply of water from a sump 3 m below the pump through a pipe 5 m long and 40 mm in diameter. It delivers water to a tank 12 m above the pump through a pipe 30 mm in diameter and 15 m long. If separation occurs 75 kN/m² below the atmospheric pressure, find the maximum speed at which pump may be operated without separation. Assume that the piston has a simple harmonic motion.* **[Rajasthan University]**

Solution. Diameter of pump, $D = 75 \text{ mm} = 0.075 \text{ m}$

$\therefore$ Area, $A = \frac{\pi}{4} \times 0.075^2 = 0.004418 \text{ m}^2$

Stroke length, $L = 150 \text{ mm} = 0.15 \text{ m}$

$\therefore$ Crank radius, $r = \frac{0.15}{2} = 0.075 \text{ m}$

Suction head, $h_s = 3 \text{ m}$

Delivery head, $h_d = 12 \text{ m}$

Length of suction pipe, $l_s = 5 \text{ m}$

Diameter of suction pipe, $d_s = 40 \text{ mm} = 0.04 \text{ m}$

$\therefore$ Area of suction pipe, $a_s = \frac{\pi}{4} \times 0.04^2 = 0.001256 \text{ m}^2$

Length of delivery pipe, $l_d = 15 \text{ m}$

Diameter of delivery pipe, $d_d = 30 \text{ mm} = 0.03 \text{ m}$

$\therefore$ Area of delivery pipe, $a_d = \frac{\pi}{4} \times 0.03^2 = 0.0007068 \text{ m}^2$

Separation head, $h_{sep.} = -\frac{75 \times 1000}{9810} = -7.645$ m of water

Maximum speed at which pump may be operated without separation, *N*:

Speed of pump without separation during 'Suction stroke', N:

The possibility of separation, during suction stroke, is only at the *beginning of the stroke*. At the beginning of the stroke $\theta = 0°$ and $\cos\theta = 1$, that gives:

$$h_{as} = \frac{l_s}{g} \times \frac{A}{a_s} \times \omega^2 r = \frac{5}{9.81} \times \frac{0.004418}{0.001256} \times \omega^2 \times 0.075 = 0.134\, \omega^2$$

$\therefore$ Pressure head in the cylinder at the beginning of suction stroke

$$= (h_s + h_{as}) \text{ vacuum}$$

$$= H_{atm.} - (h_s + h_{as}) \text{ absolute}$$

Limiting condition for *no separation* gives:

$$H_{atm.} - (h_s + h_{as}) = h_{sep.}$$

$$H_{atm.} - (h_s + h_{as}) = (H_{atm.} - 7.645) \text{ abs.}$$

or, $7.645 = h_s + h_{as}$, or, $7.645 = 3 + 0.134\omega^2$, or, $\omega^2 = \dfrac{7 \cdot 645 - 3}{0 \cdot 134}$, or, $\omega = 5.88$ rad/s

But, $\omega = \dfrac{2\pi N}{60}$, or, $N = \dfrac{60\,\omega}{2\pi} = \dfrac{60 \times 5.88}{2 \times \pi} = \mathbf{56.15 \text{ r.p.m}}$

Speed of pump without separation during delivery stroke, N:

The pressure head due to acceleration in the delivery pipe is given as:

$$h_{ad} = \frac{l_d}{g} \times \frac{A}{a_d} \times \omega^2 r \cos\theta$$

During delivery stroke the possibility of separation is only at the end of the stroke. At the end of delivery stroke $\theta = 180°$ and $\cos\theta = -1$, that gives:

$$h_{ad} = -\frac{15}{9.81} \times \frac{0.004418}{0.0007068} \times \omega^2 \times 0.075 = -0.7168\,\omega^2$$

∴ Pressure head in the cylinder at the end of delivery stroke

$$= (h_d + h_{ad}) \text{ gauge}$$

$$= H_{atm.} + (h_d + h_{ad}) \text{ absolute}$$

Limiting condition for *no separation* gives:

$$H_{atm.} + (h_d + h_{ad}) = h_{sep.}$$

$$H_{atm.} + (h_d + h_{ad}) = (H_{atm.} - 7.645) \text{ abs.}$$

or, $7.645 = -(h_d + h_{ad})$, or, $7.645 = -(12 - 0.7168\omega^2)$, or, $0.7168\omega^2 = 19.645$

or, Angular velocity, $\omega = \left(\dfrac{19.645}{0.716}\right)^{1/2} = 5.235$ rad/s

But, $\omega = \dfrac{2\pi N}{60}$, or, $N = \dfrac{60\omega}{2\pi} = \dfrac{60 \times 5.235}{2\pi} \simeq 50$ r.p.m.

∴ Maximum permissible speed, N = **50 r.p.m.** (*minimum* of the two speeds obtained above)

(Ans.)

Example 4.9. *The bore and stroke of a reciprocating pump are 250 mm and 500 mm respectively. The pump delivers water through a 100 mm delivery pipe to a tank located at 14 m above it and 27 m horizontally from it. If separation occurs at a pressure of 22 kN/m² absolute, find the safe speed at which pump should run for the following arrangements of delivery pipe:* (*i*) *The delivery pipe is horizontal from the pump and then vertical upto the tank and* (*ii*) *The delivery pipe is vertical from the pump and then horizontal upto the tank.*

The atmospheric pressure at the pump side = 10.3 m of water and connecting rod-crank ratio = 5.

Solution. The bore of the pump, D = 250 mm = 0.25 m

∴ Area, $A = \dfrac{\pi}{4} \times 0.25^2 = 0.0491 \text{ m}^2$

Stroke length, L = 500 mm = 0.5 m

$$\therefore \quad \text{Crank radius, } r = \frac{L}{2} = \frac{0.5}{2} = 0.25 \text{ m}$$

$$\text{Diameter of delivery pipe, } d_d = 100 \text{ mm} = 0.1 \text{ m}$$

$$\therefore \quad \text{Area of delivery pipe, } a_d = \frac{\pi}{4} \times 0.1^2 = 0.007854 \text{ m}^2$$

$$\text{Length of delivery pipe, } l_d = 14 + 27 = 41 \text{ m}$$

$$\text{Separation head, } h_{sep.} = \frac{22 \times 1000}{9810} = 2.242 \text{ m}$$

Safe speed at which pump should run, *N*:

(*i*) *The delivery pipe is horizontal from the pump and then vertical upto the tank*:

Acceleration head at the end of delivery stroke,

$$h_{ad} = -\frac{l_d}{g} \times \frac{A}{a_d} \times \omega^2 r \left(1 - \frac{1}{n}\right) \qquad \text{...[Eqn.(4.27)]}$$

$$= -\frac{41}{9.81} \times \frac{0.0491}{0.007854} \times \omega^2 \times 0.25 \left(1 - \frac{1}{5}\right) = -5.22\,\omega^2$$

The separation possibility, if any, is at the bend after the horizontal portion of the delivery pipe. The entire delivery head is available at the bend.

Limiting condition for no separation gives:

$$H_{atm.} + (h_d + h_{ad}) = h_{sep.}$$

$$\text{or,} \quad 10.3 + (14 - 5.22\,\omega^2) = 2.242, \text{ or, } 5.22\,\omega^2 = 22.058$$

$$\therefore \quad \omega = \left(\frac{22.058}{5.22}\right)^{1/2} = 2.055 \text{ rad/s}$$

$$\text{But,} \quad \omega = \frac{2\pi N}{60}, \text{ or, } N = \frac{60\omega}{2\pi} = \frac{60 \times 2.055}{2\pi} = \mathbf{19.62 \text{ r.p.m.}} \text{ (Ans.)}$$

(*ii*) *The delivery pipe is vertical from the pump and then horizontal upto the tank*:

The possibility of separation is at the bend after the vertical portion of the delivery pipe. The delivery head becomes *zero* at the bend and the horizontal pipe after the bend has a considerable value of acceleration head. The *limiting condition for no separation gives*:

$$H_{atm.} + (h_d + h_{ad}) = h_{sep.}$$

$$10.3 + (0 - 5.22\omega^2) = 2.242, \text{ or, } 5.22\omega^2 = 8.058$$

$$\therefore \quad \omega = \left(\frac{8.058}{5.22}\right)^{1/2} = 1.242 \text{ rad/s}$$

$$\text{But,} \quad \omega = \frac{2\pi N}{60}, \text{ or, } N = \frac{60\omega}{2\pi} = \frac{60 \times 1.242}{2\pi} = \mathbf{11.86 \text{ r.p.m.}} \text{ (Ans.)}$$

From above calculations, it is evident that the *pump can run at a higher speed without occurrence of separation with* **arrangement (*i*).** **(Ans.)**

4.7.3. Effect of Friction in Suction and Delivery Pipes on Indicator Diagram

The head lost due to friction in suction and delivery pipes is given by eqns. (4.29) and (4.30) as:

$$h_{fs} = \frac{4fl_s}{d_s \times 2g}\left(\frac{A}{a_s}\omega r \sin\theta\right)^2, \text{ and } h_{fd} = \frac{4fl_d}{d_d \times 2g}\left(\frac{A}{a_d}\omega r \sin\theta\right)^2$$

From the above equations, it is evident that the variation of h_{fs} or h_{fd} with θ is *parabolic*.

(*i*) At the *beginning of suction or delivery stroke*: θ = 0°, sin θ = 0 and therefore $h_{fs} = 0$, $h_{fd} = 0$ *i.e.* there is no loss of head due to friction.

(*ii*) At the *middle* of the *suction or delivery stroke*: θ = 90°, sin θ = 1 and, therefore,

$$h_{fs} = \frac{4fl_s}{d_s \times 2g}\left(\frac{A}{a_s}\omega r\right)^2, \text{ and } h_{fd} = \frac{4fl_d}{d_d \times 2g}\left(\frac{A}{a_d}\omega r\right)^2$$

(*iii*) At the *end of suction or delivery stroke*: θ = 180°, sin θ = 0 and therefore h_{fs} and $h_{fd} = 0$

These results, evidently, indicate that frictional losses are zero at the beginning and end of the strokes and maximum at the mid of the strokes. Fig. 4.9 shows the effect of friction on the indicator diagram.

The work done against friction in suction and delivery pipes is given by the areas of parabolas *AGB* and *CDI*.

$$\text{Area } AGB = AB \times \frac{2}{3} GH = AB \times \frac{2}{3} h_{fs}$$

$$= L \times \frac{2}{3} h_{fs}$$

$$\left[\text{where, } h_{fs} = \frac{4fl_s}{d_s \times 2g}\left(\frac{A}{a_s}\omega r\right)^2\right]$$

$$\text{Similarly, area } CDI = CD \times \frac{2}{3} \times IJ = L \times \frac{2}{3} h_{fd}$$

$$(\because CD = AB = L)$$

$$\left[\text{where, } h_{fd} = \frac{4fl_d}{d_d \times 2g}\left(\frac{A}{a_d}\omega r\right)^2\right]$$

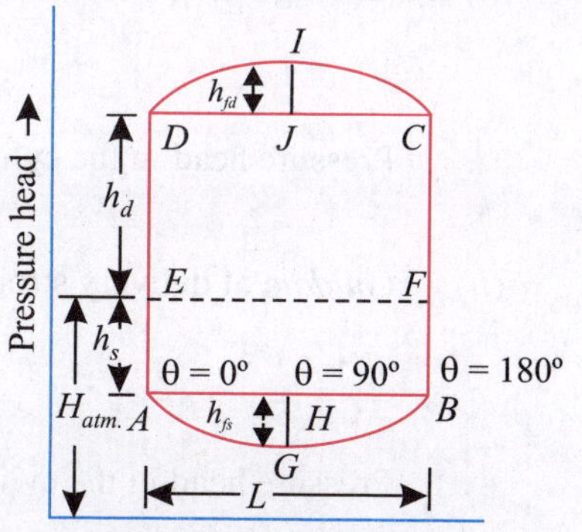

Fig. 4.9. Effect of friction on indicator diagram.

4.7.4. Effect of Acceleration and Friction in Suction and Delivery Pipes on Indicator Diagram.

The acceleration head (h_a) and friction head (h_f) at any instant of flow in the suction and delivery pipes of a reciprocating pump are given as:

$$h_a = \frac{l}{g}\frac{A}{a}\omega^2 r\cos\theta;\ h_f = \frac{4fl}{d \times 2g}\left(\frac{A}{a}\omega r \sin\theta\right)^2$$

(*a*) Suction stroke:

The pressure head on the piston during suction stroke for any angle θ of the crank = $(h_s + h_{as} + h_{fs})$

(*i*) At the *beginning* of the suction stroke, θ = 0° and we have:

$$h_{as} = \frac{l_s}{g}\frac{A}{a_s}\omega^2 r \text{ and } h_{fs} = 0$$

∴ Pressure head in the cylinder = $(h_s + h_{as})$ *below* atmospheric head

$$= H_{atm.} - (h_s + h_{as}) \text{ absolute.}$$

(*ii*) At *middle of* suction stroke, $\theta = 90°$ and we have:

$$h_{as} = 0,\ h_{fs} = \frac{4fl_s}{d_s \times 2g}\left(\frac{A}{a_s}\omega r\right)^2$$

$\therefore$ Pressure head in the cylinder $= (h_s + h_{fs})$ *below* atmospheric head

$$= H_{atm.} - (h_s + h_{fs}) \text{ absolute.}$$

(*iii*) At the *end* of suction stroke, $\theta = 180°$ and we have:

$$h_{as} = -\frac{l_s}{g}\frac{A}{a_s}\omega^2 r, \text{ or } h_{fs} = 0$$

$\therefore$ Pressure head in the cylinder $= (h_s - h_{as})$ *below* atmospheric head

$$= H_{atm.} - (h_s - h_{as}) \text{ absolute.}$$

(*b*) Delivery stroke:

The pressure head on the piston during delivery stroke for any angle θ of the crank $= (h_d + h_{ad} + h_{fd})$

(*i*) At the *beginning* of delivery stroke, $\theta = 0°$ and we have:

$$h_{ad} = \frac{l_d}{g}\frac{A}{a_d}\omega^2 r, \text{ and } h_{fd} = 0$$

$\therefore$ Pressure head in the cylinder $= (h_d + h_{ad})$ *above* atmospheric head

$$= H_{atm.} + (h_d + h_{ad}) \text{ absolute.}$$

(*ii*) At *middle* of delivery stroke, $\theta = 90°$ and we have:

$$h_{ad} = 0 \text{ and } h_{fd} = \frac{4fl_d}{d_d \times 2g}\left(\frac{A}{a_d}\omega r\right)^2$$

$\therefore$ Pressure head in the cylinder $= (h_d + h_{fd})$ *above* atmospheric head

$$= H_{atm.} + (h_d + h_{fd}) \text{ absolute}$$

(*iii*) At the *end* of delivery stroke, $\theta = 180°$ and we have:

$$h_{ad} = -\frac{l_d}{g}\frac{A}{a_d}\omega^2 r \text{ and } h_{fd} = 0$$

$\therefore$ Pressure head in the cylinder $= (h_d - h_{ad})$ *above* atmospheric head

$$= H_{atm.} + (h_d - h_{ad}) \text{ absolute.}$$

Fig. 4.10 shows a complete indicator diagram including the effects of acceleration and friction.

Area of indicator diagram

$A'GB'C'ID'$ = Area $A'HB'C'JD'$ + area of parabola $A'GB'$ + area of parabola $C'ID'$

But, Area $A'HB'C'JD'$

$$= \text{area } ABCD = (h_s + h_d) \times L$$

Area of parabola $A'GB'$

$$= A'GB' = A'B' \times \frac{2}{3} \times HK$$

$$= \frac{2}{3} \times (A'B' \times HK)$$

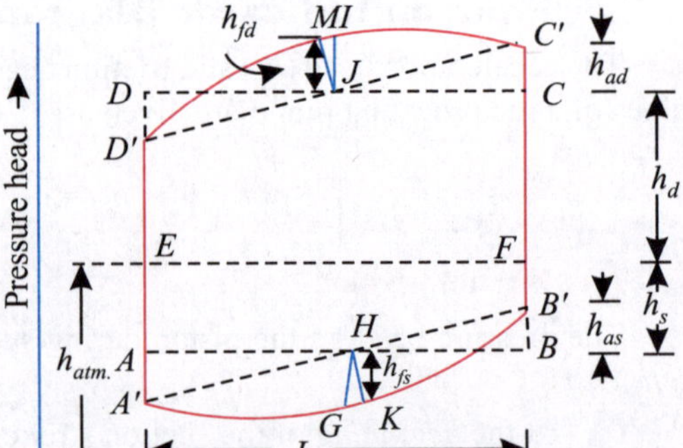

Fig. 4.10. Effect of acceleration and friction on indicator diagram.

$$= \frac{2}{3} \times (AB \times GH) = \frac{2}{3} \times L \times h_{fs}$$

Similarly, area of parabola $C'ID' = C'D' \times \frac{2}{3} JM = \frac{2}{3}(C'D' \times JM)$

$$= \frac{2}{3}(CD \times JI) = \frac{2}{3} \times L \times h_{fd}$$

$\therefore$ Area of indicator diagram $= (h_s + h_d) L + \frac{2}{3} \times L \times h_{fs} + \frac{2}{3} \times L \times h_{fd}$

$$= \left(h_s + h_d + \frac{2}{3} h_{fs} + \frac{2}{3} h_{fd}\right) L$$

As the area of the indicator diagram is proportional to work done by the pump, therefore,

Work done by pump per second $\propto \left(h_s + h_d + \frac{2}{3} h_{fs} + \frac{2}{3} h_{fd}\right) L$

$$= K \left(h_s + h_d + \frac{2}{3} h_{fs} + \frac{2}{3} h_{fd}\right) L$$

Where, K = a constant of proportionality

$$= \frac{wAN}{60} \qquad \text{...for a single-acting pump}$$

$$= \frac{2wAN}{60} \qquad \text{...for a double-acting pump.}$$

Hence, the work done per second by a *single-acting pump*

$$= \frac{wALN}{60}\left(h_s + h_d + \frac{2}{3} h_{fs} + \frac{2}{3} h_{fd}\right) \qquad \text{...(4.43)}$$

and, for a double-acting pump

$$= \frac{2wALN}{60}\left(h_s + h_d + \frac{2}{3} h_{fs} + \frac{2}{3} h_{fd}\right) \qquad \text{...(4.44)}$$

Example 4.10. *A single-acting reciprocating pump has a stroke length of 150 mm, suction pipe is 7 m long and the ratio of suction pipe diameter to the piston diameter is 3/4. The water level in the sump is 2.5 m below the axis of the pump cylinder and the pipe connecting the sump and pump cylinder is 75 mm in diameter. If the crank is running at 75 r.p.m., determine the pressure head on the piston at the beginning, middle and end of the suction stroke. Take friction co-efficient, f = 0.01.* **[Delhi University]**

Solution. Stroke length, L = 150 mm = 0.15 m

$\therefore$ Crank radius, $r = L/2 = \frac{0{\cdot}15}{2} = 0.075$ m

Length of suction pipe, l_s = 7 m

Ratio of suction pipe dia. to the piston dia $\frac{d_s}{D} = 3/4$

The water level in the sump below the axis of the pump cylinder,

$$h_s = 2.5 \text{ m}$$

Diameter of suction pipe, d_s = 75 mm = 0.075 m

Speed of the crank, N = 75 r.p.m.

Friction co-efficient, f = 0.01

Pressure head on the piston at the beginning, middle and end of the suction stroke:

$$\frac{A}{a_s} = \frac{\text{Area of piston}}{\text{Area of suction pipe}} = \frac{\frac{\pi}{4}D^2}{\frac{\pi}{4}d_s^2} = \left(\frac{D}{d_s}\right)^2 = \left(\frac{4}{3}\right)^2 = \frac{16}{9}$$

$$\left(\because \frac{d_s}{D} = 3/4 \quad \text{...Given}\right)$$

$$\text{Angular velocity, } \omega = \frac{2\pi N}{60} = \frac{2\pi \times 75}{60} = 7.85 \text{ rad/s}$$

The acceleration head (h_{as}) and friction head (h_{fs}) at any instant of flow through suction pipes are given as:

$$h_{as} = \frac{l_s}{g}\frac{A}{a_s}\omega^2 r\cos\theta = \frac{7}{9\cdot81} \times \frac{16}{9} \times 7.85^2 \times 0.075\cos\theta = 5.86\cos\theta$$

$$h_{fs} = \frac{4fl_s}{d_s \times 2g}\left(\frac{A}{a_s}\omega r\sin\theta\right)^2 = \frac{4 \times 0.01 \times 7}{0.075 \times 2 \times 9.81}\left(\frac{16}{9} \times 7.85 \times 0\cdot075 \times \sin\theta\right)^2$$

$$= 0.199\sin^2\theta$$

The pressure head on the piston during *suction stroke* for any angle θ of the crank = $h_s + h_{as} + h_{fs}$

(*i*) **At the beginning of suction stroke,** θ = 0° and we have:

$$h_{as} = 5.86 \text{ m, and, } h_{fs} = 0$$

∴ Pressure head on the piston $= H_{atm.} - (h_s + h_{as}) = H_{atm.} - (2.5 + 5.86)$

$= (H_{atm.} - 8.36 \text{ m})$ m of water *absolute*, or,

8.36 m of water vacuum. (Ans.)

(*ii*) At the *middle* of suction stroke, θ = 90° and we have:

$$h_{as} = 0 \text{ and } h_{fs} = 0.199 \text{ m}$$

∴ Pressure head on the piston $= H_{atm.} - (h_s + h_{fs}) = H_{atm.} - (2.5 + 0.199)$

$= (H_{atm.} - 2.699)$ m of water *absolute*, or,

2.699 m of water vacuum (Ans.)

(*iii*) At the *end* of suction stroke, θ = 180° and we have:

$$h_{as} = -5.86 \text{ m and } h_{fs} = 0$$

∴ Pressure head on the piston $= H_{atm.} - (h_s + h_{as}) = H_{atm.} - (2.5 - 5.86)$

$= H_{atm.} + 3.36$ m of *absolute*, or,

3.36 m of water gauge (Ans.)

Example 4.11. *The piston diameter and stroke length of a double-acting single cylinder reciprocating pump are 150 mm and 300 mm respectively. The centre of the pump is 4.5 m above the water level in the sump and 32 m below the delivery water level. Both the suction and delivery pipes have the same diameter of 75 mm and are 6 m and 36 m long respectively. If the pump is working at 30 r.p.m. determine:*

(i) *The pressure heads on the piston at the beginning, middle and end of both suction and delivery strokes,*

(ii) *The power required to drive pump if the mechanical efficiency is 80%,*

(iii) *The maximum head at any instant against which the pump has to work and its corresponding duty.*

Take atmospheric pressure head = 10.3 m of water, and Darcy's friction co-efficient for both the pipes as 0.01.

Solution. Diameter of the piston, $D = 150 \text{ mm} = 0.15 \text{ m}$

$\therefore$ Area, $A = \frac{\pi}{4} \times 0.15^2 = 0.01767 \text{ m}^2$

Stroke length, $L = 300 \text{ mm} = 0.3 \text{ m}$

$\therefore$ Crank radius, $r = L/2 = \frac{0.3}{2} = 0.15 \text{ m}$

Suction head, $h_s = 4.5 \text{ m}$

Delivery head, $h_d = 32 \text{ m}$

Diameters of suction and delivery pipes, $d_s = d_d = 75 \text{ mm} = 0.075 \text{ m}$

$\therefore$ Area, $a_s = a_d = \frac{\pi}{4} \times 0.075^2 = 0.00442 \text{ m}^2$

Length of suction pipe, $l_s = 6 \text{ m}$

Length of delivery pipe, $l_d = 36 \text{ m}$

Speed of the pump, $N = 30$ r.p.m.

$\therefore$ Angular velocity, $\omega = \frac{2\pi N}{60} = \frac{2\pi \times 30}{60} = 3.14 \text{ rad/s}$

Mechanical efficiency, $\eta_{mech} = 80\%$

(i) Pressure heads on the piston:

Suction stroke:

Acceleration head, $h_{as} = \frac{l_s}{g}\frac{A}{a_s}\omega^2 r \cos\theta$

$$= \frac{6}{9{\cdot}81} \times \frac{0{\cdot}01767}{0{\cdot}00442} \times 3.14^2 \times 0.15 \cos\theta = 3.62 \cos\theta$$

Friction head, $h_{fs} = \frac{4fl_s}{d_s \times 2g}\left(\frac{A}{a_s}\omega r \sin\theta\right)^2$

$$= \frac{4 \times 0{\cdot}01 \times 6}{0{\cdot}075 \times 2 \times 9{\cdot}81}\left(\frac{0{\cdot}01767}{0{\cdot}00442} \times 3{\cdot}14 \times 0{\cdot}15 \times \sin\theta\right)^2 = 0.578 \sin^2\theta$$

The pressure head on the piston during *suction stroke* for any angle θ of the crank $= (h_s + h_{as} + h_{fs})$

(*a*) At the *beginning* of stroke, $\theta = 0°$ and we have:

$h_{as} = 3.62 \text{ m}$ and $h_{fs} = 0$

$\therefore$ Pressure head on the piston $= H_{atm.} - (h_s + h_{as})$

$= 10.3 - (4.5 + 3.67) =$ **2.13 m of water absolute** **(Ans.)**

(*b*) At the *middle* of stroke, $\theta = 90°$ and we have:

$$h_{as} = 0 \text{ and } h_{fs} = 0.578 \text{ m}$$

$\therefore$ Pressure head on the piston $= H_{atm.} - (h_s + h_{fs}) = 10.3 - (4.5 + 0.578)$

$= \mathbf{5.22 \text{ m of water absolute}}$ **(Ans.)**

(*c*) At the *end* of stroke, $\theta = 180°$ and we have:

$$h_{as} = -3.62 \text{ m and } h_{fs} = 0$$

$\therefore$ Pressure head on the piston $= H_{atm.} - (h_s + h_{as}) = 10.3 - (4.5 - 3.62)$

$= \mathbf{9.42 \text{ m of water absolute}}$ **(Ans.)**

Delivery stroke:

$$\text{Acceleration head, } h_{ad} = \frac{l_d}{g}\frac{A}{a_d}\omega^2 r\cos\theta$$

$$= \frac{36}{9.81} \times \frac{0.01767}{0.00442} \times 3.14^2 \times 0.15\cos\theta = 21.69\cos\theta$$

$$\text{Friction head, } \frac{h}{h_{fd}} = \frac{h}{h_{fd}} = \frac{4fl_d}{d_d \times 2g}\left(\frac{A}{a_d}\omega r\sin\theta\right)^2$$

$$= \frac{4 \times 0.01 \times 36}{0.075 \times 2 \times 9.81}\left(\frac{0.01767}{0.00442} \times 3.14 \times 0.15\sin\theta\right)^2 = 3.47\sin^2\theta$$

The pressure head on the piston during delivery stroke for an angle θ of the crank $= (h_d + h_{ad} + h_{fd})$

(*a*) At the *beginning* of the stroke, $\theta = 0°$ and we have:

$$h_{ad} = 21.69 \text{ m and } h_{fd} = 0$$

$\therefore$ Pressure head on the piston $= H_{atm.} + (h_d + h_{ad}) = 10.3 + (32 + 21.69)$

$= \mathbf{63.99 \text{ m of water absolute}}$ **(Ans.)**

(*b*) At the *middle* of stroke, $\theta = 90°$ and we have:

$$h_{ad} = 0, \text{ and } h_{fd} = 3.47 \text{ m}$$

$\therefore$ Pressure head on the piston $= H_{atm.} + (h_d + h_{fd}) = 10.3 + (32 + 3.47)$

$= \mathbf{45.77 \text{ m of water absolute}}$ **(Ans.)**

(*c*) At the *end* of stroke, $\theta = 180°$ and we have:

$$h_{ad} = -21.69 \text{ m, and, } h_{fd} = 0$$

$\therefore$ Pressure head on the piston $= H_{atm.} + (h_d + h_{ad}) = 10.3 + (32 - 21.69)$

$= \mathbf{20.61 \text{ m of water absolute}}$ **(Ans.)**

(*ii*) The power required to drive the pump:

Work done by the pump (double-acting)

$$= \frac{2wALN}{60}\left(h_s + h_d + \frac{2}{3}h_{fs} + \frac{2}{3}h_{fd}\right) \qquad \text{...[Eqn. (4.44)]}$$

$$= \frac{2 \times 9810 \times 0.01767 \times 0.3 \times 30}{60}\left(4.5 + 32 + \frac{2}{3} \times 0.578 + \frac{2}{3} \times 3.47\right) = 2038.44 \text{ Nm/s}$$

$\therefore$ Power required to drive the pump $= \dfrac{\text{Work done by the pump}}{\eta_{mech.}}$

$= \dfrac{2038.44}{0.8} = 2548 \text{ W} = \mathbf{2.548 \text{ kW}}$ **(Ans.)**

(*iii*) The maximum head and power required to drive the pump:

The maximum head against which the pump has to work is larger of

(*a*) $(h_s + h_{fs}) + (h_d + h_{fd}) = (4.5 + 0.578) + (32 + 3.47)$

$= 40.548$ m (mid position of piston)

(*b*) $(h_s + h_{as}) + (h_d + h_{ad}) = (4.5 - 3.62) + (32 + 21.69)$

$= 54.57$ m (end position of piston)

Thus, *maximum head* = **54.57 m (Ans.)**

$\therefore$ The work done by the pump

$$= \frac{2wALN}{60} \times 54.57 = \frac{2 \times 9810 \times 0.01767 \times 0.3 \times 30}{60} \times 54.57 = 2837.8 \text{ N/ms.}$$

$\therefore$ *Power required to drive the pump*

$= \dfrac{2837.8}{0.8} = 3547 \text{ W} = \mathbf{3.547 \text{ kW}}$ **(Ans.)**

Example 4.12. *The bore and stroke of a double-acting single-cylinder reciprocating pump, running at 30 r.p.m., are 200 mm and 400 mm respectively. The pump draws water from a sump 1.2 m. below the pump through a suction pipe 100 mm in diameter and 3.0 m long. The water is delivered to a tank 28 m above the pump through a delivery pipe 100 mm in diameter and 38 m long. Assuming the motion of the piston to be simple harmonic determine the net force due to fluid pressure on the piston when it has moved through a distance of 100 mm from the I.D.C. (inner dead centre).*

Take friction co-efficient for both the suction and delivery pipes as 0.006. Neglect the size of the piston rod.

Solution. Bore of the pump, $D = 200 \text{ mm} = 0.2 \text{ m}$

Stroke length, $L = 400 \text{ mm} = 0.4 \text{ m}$

$\therefore$ Crank radius, $r = \dfrac{L}{2} = \dfrac{0.4}{2} = 0.2 \text{ m}$

Area of piston, $A = \dfrac{\pi}{4} \times 0.2^2 = 0.0314 \text{ m}^2$

Area of suction and delivery pipes, $a_d = a_s = \dfrac{\pi}{4} \times 0.1^2 = 0.00785 \text{ m}^2$

Speed of the pump, $N = 30$ r.p.m.

$\therefore$ Angular velocity, $\omega = \dfrac{2\pi N}{60} = \dfrac{2\pi \times 30}{60} = 3.14$ rad/s

Suction head, $h_s = 1.2$ m

Delivery head, $h_d = 28$ m

Length of suction pipe, $l_s = 3.0$ m

Length of delivery pipe, $l_d = 38$ m

Friction co-efficient for both the pipes, $f = 0.006$.

Net force on the piston:

(a) Suction side:

Distance moved by the piston from *I.D.C.*, $x = 100$ mm $= 0.1$ m ..(*Given*)

But, $x = r(1 - \cos\theta)$

$\therefore$ $0.1 = 0.2(1 - \cos\theta)$, or, $\cos\theta = 0.5$ or $\theta = 60°$

The pressure head on the piston during suction stroke for any angle θ of the crank $= (h_a + h_{as} + h_{fs})$

Now, $h_s = 1.2$ m ...(*Given*)

Acceleration head,

$$h_{as} = \frac{l_s}{g}\frac{A}{a_s}\omega^2 r\cos\theta = \frac{3}{9.81} \times \frac{0.0314}{0.00785} \times (3.14)^2 \times 0.2 \times \cos 60° = 1.206 \text{ m}$$

$$\text{Friction head, } h_{fs} = \frac{4fl_s}{d_s \times 2g}\left(\frac{A}{a_s}\omega r\sin\theta\right)^2$$

$$= \frac{4 \times 0.006 \times 3.0}{0.1 \times 2 \times 9.81}\left(\frac{0.0314}{0.00785} \times 3.14 \times 0.2 \times \sin 60°\right)^2 = 0.1737 \text{ m}$$

$\therefore$ Pressure head on the piston $= (h_s + h_{as} + h_{fs}) = 1.2 + 1.206 + 0.1737$

$= 2.579$ m of water below atmospheric head

$= 10.3 - 2.579 = 7.721$ m of water absolute

$\therefore$ Force on the piston from *suction side*

$=$ Specific weight (w) × pressure head (h) × area of piston (A)

$= 9810 \times 7.721 \times 0.0314 = 2378.3$ N

(b) Delivery side:

The angular displacement from the O.D.C. (outer dead centre) for delivery stroke (corresponding to angular displacement of 60° from the I.D.C.), $\theta = 180° - 60° = 120°$

The pressure head on the piston during delivery stroke for any angle θ of the crank $= (h_d + h_{ad} + h_{fd})$

Acceleration head,

$$h_{ad} = \frac{l_d}{g}\frac{A}{a_d}\omega^2 r\cos\theta = \frac{38}{9.81} \times \frac{0.0314}{0.00785} \times 3.14^2 \times 0.2 \times \cos 120° = -15.27 \text{ m}$$

$$\text{Friction head, } h_{fd} = \frac{4fl_d}{d_d \times 2g}\left(\frac{A}{a_d}\omega r\sin\theta\right)^2$$

$$= \frac{4 \times 0.006 \times 38}{0.1 \times 2 \times 9.81}\left(\frac{0.0314}{0.00785} \times 3.14 \times 0.2 \times \sin 120°\right)^2 = 2.2 \text{ m}$$

$\therefore$ Pressure head on the piston $= (h_d + h_{ad} + h_{fd}) = 28 - 15.27 + 2.2$

$= 14.93$ m of water above atmospheric head

$= (10.3 + 14.93) = 25.23$ m of water absolute

$\therefore$ Force on the piston from delivery side

$=$ Specific weight (w) × pressure head (h) × area of piston (A)

$= 9810 \times 25.23 \times 0.0314 = 7771.7$ N

$\therefore$ *Net force on the piston* $= 7771.7 - 2378.3 =$ **5393.4 N (Ans.)**

4.8. AIR VESSELS

An **air vessel** *is a closed chamber containing compressed air in the upper part and liquid being pumped in the lower part. One air vessel is fixed on the suction pipe just near the suction valve and one is fixed on the delivery pipe near the delivery valve. The air vessels are used for the following purposes:*

1. *To get continuous supply of liquid at a uniform rate (whatever fluctuations take place, they occur between the air vessels and the pump).*
2. *To save the power required to drive the pump* (By the use of air vessels the acceleration and friction heads are considerably reduced, thereby the work is also reduced).
3. *To run the pump at much higher speed without any danger of separation* (By fitting the air vessels as close to the pump as possible, the length of the pipe in which acceleration takes place is reduced due to which acceleration head is reduced, and pump can run at a high speed without separation).

Fig. 4.11 shows a reciprocating pump fitted with air vessels. When the liquid level in the air vessel rises, the air above is compressed, this compressed air forces the liquid as soon as the pressure in the pipe falls. The variation in air pressure may be reduced by increasing the capacity of the air vessels.

In a delivery pipe the liquid beyond the air vessel is assumed to flow with a uniform velocity (V_d). When the piston forces the liquid into the delivery pipe with a velocity *greater* than mean velocity V_d, *the additional liquid moves into the air vessel*. When the velocity is *less* than mean velocity, V_d, the liquid *flows out of the air vessel and makes up the deficiency.* The volume of liquid present in the portion of the delivery pipe between the cylinder and air vessel is *accelerated*. The same reasoning is applicable to the air vessel fitted on the suction pipe.

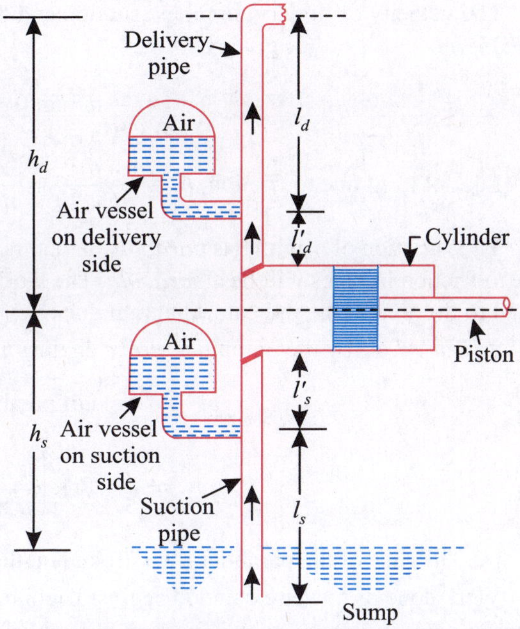

Fig. 4.11. Reciprocating pump with air vessels.

Fig. 4.12 shows the indicator diagrams without and with adequate air vessels.

Let, A = Area of cross-section of the cylinder,

a = Area of cross-section of suction or delivery pipe,

l_d = Length of delivery pipe beyond the air vessel,

l_d' = Length of delivery pipe between cylinder and air vessel,

l_s = Length of suction pipe below air vessel,

l_s' = Length of suction pipe between cylinder and air vessel,

h_{ad} = Pressure head due to acceleration in delivery pipe,

h_{as} = Pressure head due to acceleration in suction pipe,

h_{fd} = Loss of head due to friction in delivery pipe beyond the air vessel,

h'_{fd} = Loss of head due to friction in delivery pipe between cylinder and air vessel,

h_{fs} = Loss of head due to friction in suction pipe below the air vessel, and

h'_{fs} = Loss of head due to friction in suction pipe between cylinder and air vessel.

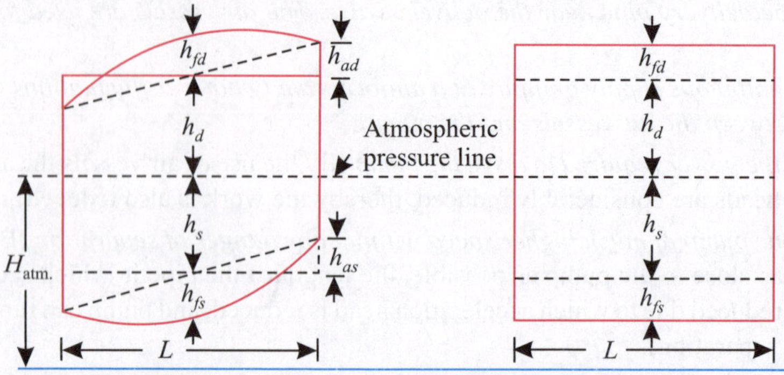

Fig. 4.12. Indicator diagrams without and with air vessels.

Case I. Work done or power expended against friction '*without air vessels*':

The velocity of flow (v) in pipes (suction and delivery), for a *single-acting* reciprocating pump *without any air vessel,* is given as:

$$v = \frac{A}{a}\omega r \sin\theta \qquad \text{...[Eqn. (4.15)]}$$

$$\text{Loss of head due to friction, } h_f = \frac{4flv^2}{d \times 2g} = \frac{4fl}{d \times 2g}\left(\frac{A}{a}\omega r \sin\theta\right)^2 \qquad \text{...(4.45)}$$

The variation of h_f with θ is *parabolic* in nature and hence indicator diagram for the loss of head due to friction in pipes will be a *parabola*. The work done by the pump against friction per stroke is equal to the area of the indicator diagram due to friction.

∴ *Work done* by the pump *per stroke* against *friction*

$$= \text{Area of parabola} = \frac{2}{3} \times \text{base} \times \text{height}$$

$$= \frac{2}{3} \times L \times \left[\frac{4fl}{d \times 2g} \times \left(\frac{A}{a}\omega r\right)^2\right] \qquad \text{...(4.46)}$$

[∵ The base of the parabola = L (stroke length), and the height = h_f at θ = 90°]

Work done or power expended against friction,

$$P_1 = \frac{wAN}{60} \times \frac{2}{3} \times L \times \frac{4fl}{d \times 2g}\left(\frac{A}{a}\omega r\right)^2$$

or,

$$P_1 = \frac{wANL}{60} \times \frac{4fl}{3d \times g}\left(\frac{A}{a}\omega r\right)^2 \qquad \text{...(4.47)}$$

Case II. Work done or Power Expended Against Friction '*with air vessels*':

When air vessels having adequate capacity are fitted on the suction and delivery pipes, the velocity of flow in pipes (suction and delivery) may be *assumed constant* and equal to the *average/mean flow velocity*.

$$\text{Mean velocity of flow, } \bar{v} = \frac{\text{Discharge}}{\text{Area of pipe}} = \frac{A \times L \times (N/60)}{a} = \frac{A \times 2r \times (\omega/2\pi)}{a} = \frac{A}{a} \times \frac{\omega r}{\pi}$$

$$\text{Loss of head due to friction, } h_f = \frac{4fl\bar{v}^2}{d \times 2g} = \frac{4fl}{d \times 2g}\left(\frac{A}{a} \times \frac{\omega r}{\pi}\right)^2 \quad \text{...(4.48)}$$

Eqn. (4.48) shows that with the fitting of air vessels, the loss of head due to friction is independent of θ and hence indicator diagram is a *rectangle*.

∴ Work done by the pump per stroke against friction

$$= \text{Area of rectangle} = \text{base} \times \text{height}$$

$$= L \times \frac{4fl}{d \times 2g}\left(\frac{A}{a} \times \frac{\omega r}{\pi}\right)^2 \quad \text{...(4.49)}$$

Work done or power expended against friction,

$$P_2 = \frac{wAN}{60} \times L \times \frac{4fl}{d \times 2g}\left(\frac{A}{a} \times \frac{\omega r}{\pi}\right)^2 \quad \text{...(4.50)}$$

Now, ratio, $\dfrac{P_2}{P_1} = \dfrac{\text{Work done or power expended against friction } \textit{with air vessels}}{\text{Work done or power expended against friction } \textit{without air vessels}}$

$$= \frac{\dfrac{wANL}{60} \times \dfrac{4fl}{d \times 2g}\left(\dfrac{A}{a} \times \dfrac{\omega r}{\pi}\right)^2}{\dfrac{wANL}{60} \times \dfrac{4fl}{3d \times g}\left(\dfrac{A}{a}\,\omega r\right)^2} = \frac{3}{2\pi^2}$$

Percentage of work saved in pipe friction by fitting air vessels

$$= \frac{P_1 - P_2}{P_1} = 1 - \frac{P_2}{P_1} = \left(1 - \frac{3}{2\pi^2}\right) = \mathbf{0.848 \text{ or } 84.8\%}$$

Work saved in a double-acting reciprocating pump:

The work done or power expended against friction in case of double-acting reciprocating pump *without air vessel* is the same as given in case of single-acting reciprocating pump, *i.e*

$$P_1 = \frac{wANL}{60} \times \frac{4fL}{3d \times g}\left(\frac{A}{a}\,\omega r\right)^2$$

The mean velocity of flow, v for double-acting pump is given by:

$$v = \frac{\text{Discharge}}{\text{Area of pipe}} = \frac{2AL \times (N/60)}{a} = \frac{2A \times 2r \times (\omega/2\pi)}{a} = \frac{2A}{a} \times \frac{\omega r}{\pi}$$

$$\text{Loss of head due to friction, } \quad h_f = \frac{4flv^2}{d \times 2g} = \frac{4fl}{d \times 2g}\left(\frac{2A}{a} \times \omega r\right)^2 \quad \text{...(4.51)}$$

Work done by the pump per stroke against friction

$$= L \times \frac{4fl}{d \times 2g}\left(\frac{2A}{a} \times \frac{\omega r}{\pi}\right)^2 \quad \text{...(4.52)}$$

Work done or power expended against friction,

$$P_2 = \frac{wAN}{60} \times L \times \frac{4fl}{d \times 2g}\left(\frac{2A}{a} \times \frac{wr}{\pi}\right)^2 \quad \text{...(4.53)}$$

Now ratio, $$\frac{P_2}{P_1} = \frac{\frac{wANL}{60} \times \frac{4fl}{d \times 2g}\left(\frac{2A}{a} \times \frac{wr}{\pi}\right)^2}{\frac{wANL}{60} \times \frac{4fl}{3d \times g}\left(\frac{A}{a}\omega r\right)^2} = \frac{6}{\pi^2}$$

Percentage of work saved in pipe friction by fitting air vessels

$$= \frac{P_1 - P_2}{P_1} = 1 - \frac{P_2}{P_1} = \left(1 - \frac{6}{\pi^2}\right) = 0.392 \text{ or } \mathbf{39.2\%}$$

Example 4.13. *A single-acting reciprocating pump is to raise a liquid of density 1200 kg/m³ through a vertical height of 11.5 m, from 2.5 m below pump axis to 9 m above it. The plunger moves with simple harmonic motion, has diameter 125 mm and stroke 225 mm. The suction and delivery pipes are of 75 mm diameter and 3.5 m and 13.5 m long respectively. There is a long vessel placed on the delivery pipe near the pump axis but there is no air vessel on the suction pipe. If separation takes place 0.88 bar below atmospheric pressure find:*

(i) Maximum speed with which the pump can run without separation taking place, and

(ii) Power required to drive the pump, if f = 0.02

Neglect slip for the pump. **[AMIE-Fluid Power Engg.]**

Solution. Density of liquid, $\rho = 1200 \text{ kg/m}^3$

Total vertical height $= 11.5$ m

Suction head, $h_s = 2.5$ m

Delivery head, $h_d = 9$ m

Diameter of plunger, $D = 125 \text{ mm} = 0.125$ m

$\therefore$ Area of plunger, $A = \frac{\pi}{4} \times 0.125^2 = 0.0123 \text{ m}^2$

Stroke length, $L = 225 \text{ mm} = 0.225 \text{ m}$, $\therefore$ Crank radius, $r = \frac{0.225}{2} = 0.1125$ m

Diameter of each pipe (suction and delivery),

$$d_s = d_d = 75 \text{ mm} = 0.075 \text{ m}$$

$$\text{Area, } a_a = a_d = \frac{\pi}{4} \times 0.075^2 = 0.00442 \text{ m}^2$$

Length of suction pipe, $l_s = 3.5$ m

Length of delivery pipe, $l_d = 13.5$ m.

Friction co-efficient, $f = 0.02$.

Since air vessel is placed on delivery side only therefore, the *velocity in the delivery pipe will be uniform* and there will be *no accelerating head* (on delivery side).

Separation pressure = 0.88 bar below atmospheric pressure

$\therefore$ Separation pressure head $= \frac{0.88 \times 10^5}{1200 \times 9.81} = 7.47$ m $\left[\because h = \frac{p}{w}, \text{ and, } w = \rho g\right]$

(*i*) Maximum speed with which pump can run without separation, *N*:

The separation can take place only *at the beginning of suction stroke*. Since no air vessel has been fitted on suction side, therefore, there will be accelerating head (on suction side).

Pressure head at the beginning of suction stroke = $(h_s + h_{as})$ below atmosphere.

Limiting condition for *no separation* gives,

$$h_s + h_{as} = 7.47, \quad \text{or,} \quad 2.5 + h_{as} = 7.47, \quad \text{or,} \quad h_{as} = 4.97 \text{ m}$$

But h_{as} (at the beginning of stroke) $= \frac{l_s}{g} \times \frac{A}{a_s}\, \omega^2 r$

$$\therefore \quad 4.97 = \frac{3.5}{9.81} \times \frac{0.0123}{0.00442} \times \omega^2 \times 0.1125$$

$$\text{or,} \quad \omega = \left(\frac{4.97 \times 9.81 \times 0.00442}{3.5 \times 0.0123 \times 0.1125}\right)^{1/2} = 6.67 \text{ rad/s}$$

$$\text{But,} \quad \omega = \frac{2\pi N}{60}, \text{ or, } N = \frac{60\omega}{2\pi} = \frac{60 \times 6.67}{2\pi}$$ **63.69 r.p.m. (Ans.)**

(*ii*) Power required to drive the pump, *P*:

In case of a single-acting pump the discharge (Q) is given by :

$$Q = \frac{ALN}{60} = \frac{0.0123 \times 0.225 \times 63.69}{60} = 0.00294 \text{ m}^3\text{/s}$$

Velocity of liquid in the delivery pipe, $v = \frac{Q}{a_d} = \frac{0.00294}{0.00442} = 0.665$ m/s

Loss of head due to friction in delivery pipe,

$$h_{fd} = \frac{4 f l_d v^2}{d_d \times 2g} = \frac{4 \times 0.02 \times 13.5 \times 0.665^2}{0.075 \times 2 \times 9.81} = 0.324 \text{ m}$$

The maximum value of h_{fs}, during suction stroke, is given by:

$$h_{fs} = \frac{4 f l_s}{d_s \times 2g} \times \left(\frac{A}{a_s} \omega r\right)^2 = \frac{4 \times 0.02 \times 3.5}{0.075 \times 2 \times 9.81} \times \left(\frac{0.0123}{0.00442} \times 6.67 \times 0.1125\right)^2 = 0.829 \text{ m}$$

Now, power required to drive the pump,

$$P = wQ\left(h_s + h_d + \frac{2}{3} h_{fs} + h_{fd}\right)$$

$$= (1200 \times 9.81) \times 0.00294 \left(2.5 + 9 + \frac{2}{3} \times 0.829 + 0.324\right)$$

$$=$$ **428.3 W (Ans.)**

Example 4.14. *The plunger diameter and stroke length of a single-acting reciprocating pump are 300 mm and 500 mm respectively. The speed of the pump is 50 r.p.m. The diameter and length of delivery pipe are 150 mm and 55 m respectively. If the pump is equipped with an air vessel on the delivery side at the centre line of the pump, find the power saved in overcoming friction in the delivery pipe.*

Take friction co-efficient, f = 0.01

Solution. Diameter of plunger, D = 300 mm = 0.3 m

$$\therefore \quad \text{Area, } A = \frac{\pi}{4} \times 0.3^2 = 0.07068 \text{ m}^2$$

Stroke length, L = 500 mm = 0.5 m,

$\therefore$ Crank radius, $r = \dfrac{0.5}{2} = 0.25$ m

Speed of the pump, $N = 50$ r.p.m.

$\therefore$ Angular velocity, $\omega = \dfrac{2\pi N}{60} = \dfrac{2\pi \times 50}{60} = 5.23$ rad/s

Diameter of delivery pipe, $d_d = 150$ mm $= 0.15$ m

$\therefore$ Area of delivery pipe, $a_d = \dfrac{\pi}{4} \times 0.15^2 = 0.01767\ \text{m}^2$

Length of delivery pipe, $l_d = 55$ m

Friction co-efficient, $f = 0.01$

Power saved in overcoming friction in the delivery pipe:

Maximum velocity of water in delivery pipe,

$$v_d = \frac{A}{a_d}\omega r = \frac{0.07068}{0.01767} \times 5.23 \times 0.25 = 5.23 \text{ m/s}$$

Maximum loss of head due to friction,

$$h_{fd} = \frac{4fl_d v_d^2}{2g \times d_d} = \frac{4 \times 0.01 \times 55 \times 5.23^2}{2 \times 9.81 \times 0.15} = 20.45 \text{ m}$$

$\therefore$ Power required to overcome friction

$$= \frac{wALN}{60} \times \left(\frac{2}{3}h_{fd}\right) = \frac{9810 \times 0.07068 \times 0.5 \times 50}{60} \times \left(\frac{2}{3} \times 20.45\right) = 3938.7 \text{ W} = \mathbf{3.938\ kW}$$

With air vessel fitted, the velocity in the delivery pipe becomes constant and is given by,

$$v_d = \frac{A}{a_d} \times \frac{\omega r}{\pi} = \frac{0.07068}{0.01767} \times \frac{5.23 \times 0.25}{\pi} = 1.66 \text{ m/s}$$

Loss of head due to friction,

$$h_{fd} = \frac{4fl_d v_d^2}{d_d \times 2g} = \frac{4 \times 0.01 \times 55 \times 1.66^2}{0.15 \times 2 \times 9.81} = 2.06 \text{ m}$$

$\therefore$ Power required to overcome friction

$$= \frac{wALN}{60} \times h_{fd} = \frac{9810 \times 0.07068 \times 0.5 \times 50}{60} \times 2.06 = 595 \text{ W or } 0.595 \text{ kW}$$

Hence, the *power saved* by fitting an air vessel

$= 3.938 - 0.595 =$ **3.343 kW (Ans.)**

Example 4.15. *The diameter and stroke of a single-acting reciprocating pump are 300 mm and 500 mm respectively. The pump takes its supply of water from sump 3.2 m below the pump axis through a pipe 9 m long and 200 mm diameter. If separation occurs at 2.4 m of water absolute, determine:*

(i) *The speed at which separation may take place at the beginning of suction stroke, and*

(ii) *The speed of the pump if an air vessel is fitted on the suction side 2.4 m above the sump water level.*

Take atmospheric pressure head = 10.3 m of water, and friction co-efficient, f = 0.01.

Solution. Diameter of piston, D = 300 mm = 0.3 m

$$\therefore \quad \text{Area, } A = \frac{\pi}{4} \times 0.3^2 = 0.07068 \text{ m}^2$$

Stroke length, L = 500 mm = 0.5 m

$$\therefore \quad \text{Crank radius, } r = \frac{0.5}{2} = 0.25 \text{ m}$$

Suction head, h_s = 3.2 m

Diameter of suction pipe, d_s = 200 mm = 0.2 m

$$\therefore \quad \text{Area of suction pipe, } a_s = \frac{\pi}{4} \times 0.2^2 = 0.0314 \text{ m}^2$$

Length of suction pipe, l_s = 9 m

Separation head, h_{sep} = 2.4 m of water absolute

Atmospheric pressure head, $H_{atm.}$ = 10.3 m of water

Friction co-efficient, f = 0.01

(*i*) The speed at which separation may take place (no air vessel fitted), *N*:

The pressure head due to acceleration in the suction pipe,

$$h_{as} = \frac{l_s}{g} \times \frac{A}{a_s} \omega^2 r \cos\theta$$

At the beginning of the suction stroke, $\theta = 0°$ and we have:

$$h_{as} = \frac{l_s}{g} \times \frac{A}{a_s} \omega^2 r = \frac{9}{9.81} \times \frac{0.07068}{0.0314} \times \omega^2 \times 0.25 = 0.516\,\omega^2$$

$\therefore$ Pressure head in the cylinder at the beginning of suction stroke

$$= (h_s + h_{as}) = (3.2 + 0.516\,\omega^2) \text{ below atmospheric head}$$

Limiting condition for *no separation* gives:

$$H_{atm.} - (h_s + h_{as}) = h_{sep.} \quad \text{or, } 10.3 - (3.2 + 0.516\,\omega^2) = 2.4$$

$$\text{or,} \quad \omega = \left(\frac{10.3 - 2.4 - 3.2}{0.516}\right)^{1/2} = 3.02 \text{ rad./s}$$

$$\text{But,} \quad \omega = \frac{2\pi N}{60}, \text{ or, } N = \frac{60\omega}{2\pi} = \frac{60 \times 3.02}{2\pi} = \mathbf{28.8 \text{ r.p.m.}} \textbf{ (Ans.)}$$

(*ii*) The speed of pump when an air vessel is fitted on suction side, *N*:

Since the air vessel is installed 2.4 m above the sump water level, therefore: (*i*) there will be a loss of head due to friction in the suction pipe for the length of $9 \times \frac{2.4}{3.2} = 6.75$ m; (*ii*) the acceleration pressure head will be restricted in the remaining (9 – 6.75) = 2.25 m length of suction pipe.

The pressure head due to acceleration (h_{as}) in the suction pipe at the beginning of suction stroke ($\theta = 0°$) is given by:

$$h_{as} = \frac{l_s}{g} \times \frac{A}{a_s} \times \omega^2 r = \frac{2.25}{9.81} \times \frac{0.07068}{0.0314} \times \omega^2 \times 0.25 = 0.129\,\omega^2$$

The velocity of water in the suction pipe *fitted with air vessel,*

$$v_s = \frac{A}{a_s} \times \frac{\omega r}{\pi} = \frac{0.07068}{0.0314} \times \frac{\omega \times 0.25}{\pi} = 0.179\ \omega$$

Loss of head due to friction, $$h_{fs} = \frac{4fl_s v_s^2}{d_s \times 2g} = \frac{4 \times 0.01 \times 6.75 \times (0.179\omega)^2}{0.2 \times 2 \times 9.81} = 0.0022\ \omega^2$$

Limiting condition for *no separation* gives:

$$H_{atm.} - (h_s + h_{as} + h_{fs}) = h_{sep.}$$

$$10.3 - (3.2 + 0.129\omega^2 + 0.0022\omega^2) = 2.4$$

or, $$10.3 - 3.2 - 0.1312\omega^2 = 2.4, \text{ or, } \omega = \left(\frac{10.3 - 3.2 - 2.4}{0.1312}\right)^{1/2} = 5.98 \text{ rad./s}$$

But, $$\omega = \frac{2\pi N}{60}, \text{ or, } N = \frac{60\omega}{2\pi} = \frac{60 \times 5.98}{2\pi} = \mathbf{57.1\ r.p.m.\ (Ans.)}$$

Evidently by *fitting an air vessel, the pump can be run at higher speeds without any chance of separation.*

Example 4.16. *A double-acting reciprocating pump is running at 30 r.p.m. Its bore and stroke are 250 mm and 400 mm respectively. The pump lifts water from a sump 3.8 m below and delivers it to tank at a height 65 m above the cylinder axis. The length of suction and delivery pipes are 6 m and 150 m respectively. The diameter of the delivery pipe is 100 mm. If an air vessel of adequate capacity has been fitted on the discharge side, determine:*

(*i*) *The minimum diameter of suction pipe to prevent cavitation assuming 2.5 m as the minimum head to prevent separation of flow which causes cavitation.*

(*ii*) *The maximum gross head against which pump has to work and the corresponding power of motor. Assume mechanical efficiency = 78% and slip = 1.5%.*

Take atmospheric pressure head (at the pump site) = 10.0 m, and friction co-efficient, f = 0.012.

Solution. The speed of the pump, $N = 30$ r.p.m.

∴ Angular velocity, $$\omega = \frac{2\pi N}{60} = \frac{2\pi \times 30}{60} = 3.14 \text{ rad/s}$$

Bore of the pump, $D = 250 \text{ mm} = 0.25 \text{ m}$

∴ Area, $$A = \frac{\pi}{4} \times 0.25^2 = 0.0491 \text{ m}^2$$

Stroke length, $L = 400 \text{ mm} = 0.4 \text{ m}$

∴ Crank radius, $$r = \frac{0.4}{2} = 0.2 \text{ m}$$

Suction head, $h_s = 3.8$ m

Delivery head, $h_d = 65$ m

Length of suction pipe, $l_s = 6$ m

Length of delivery pipe, $l_d = 150$ m

Diameter of delivery pipe, $d_d = 100 \text{ mm} = 0.1 \text{ m}$

∴ Area of delivery pipe, $$a_d = \frac{\pi}{4} \times 0.1^2 = 0.00785 \text{ m}^2$$

Separation head, $h_{sep.}$ = 2.5 m of water absolute
Mechanical efficiency, $\eta_{mech.}$ = 78%; slip = 1.5%
Atmospheric pressure head, $H_{atm.}$ = 10.0 m; friction co-efficient, $f = 0.012$.

(*i*) The minimum diameter of suction pipe, to prevent cavitation, d_s:

It is at the beginning of the suction stroke (θ = 0°) where cavitation is likely to occur and at that instant the pressure head due to acceleration is given by,

$$h_{as} = \frac{l_s}{g}\frac{A}{a_s}\omega^2 r\cos\theta = \frac{l_s}{g}\frac{A}{a_s}\omega^2 r \qquad [\because \text{ when } \theta = 0°, \cos\theta = 1]$$

$$= \frac{6}{9.81} \times \frac{0.0491}{\frac{\pi}{4}\times d_s^2} \times 3.14^2 \times 0.2 = \frac{0.0754}{d_s^2} \qquad ...(i)$$

$$\text{Friction head, } h_{fs} = \frac{4fl_s}{d_s \times 2g}\left(\frac{A}{a_s}\omega r\sin\theta\right)^2 = 0 \qquad (\because \sin\theta = \sin 0° = 0)$$

Limiting condition for *no separation* gives,

$$H_{atm.} - (h_s + h_{as}) = h_{sep.}$$

$$\text{or,} \quad 10.0 - \left(3.8 + \frac{0.0754}{d_s^2}\right) = 2.5, \text{ or, } \frac{0.0754}{d_s^2} = 10.0 - 2.5 - 3.8$$

$$\text{or,} \quad d_s = \left(\frac{0.0754}{10.0 - 2.5 - 3.8}\right)^{1/2} = 0.1427 \text{ m or } \mathbf{142.7\ mm\ (Ans.)}$$

(*ii*) Gross head and power of motor:

$$\text{The discharge, } Q = \frac{2ALN}{60} = \frac{2 \times 0.0491 \times 0.4 \times 30}{60} = 0.01964 \text{ m}^3/\text{s}$$

The total head (*H*) against which the water has to be lifted is equal to sum of various heads at *I.D.C.* (inner dead centre) position of the piston,

i.e., $$H = (h_s + h_{as} + h_{fs}) + (h_d + h_{ad} + h_{fd})$$

(*a*) Suction side: h_s = 3.8 m (*Given*)

At the beginning of the stroke, θ = 0° and we have:

$$h_{as} = \frac{l_s}{g} \times \frac{A}{a_s}\omega^2 r = \frac{0.0754}{d_s^2} \qquad [\text{as eqn. } (i)]$$

$$= \frac{0.0754}{0.1427^2} = 3.7 \text{ m}$$

$$\text{Friction head, } h_{fs} = \frac{4fl_s}{d_s \times 2g}\left(\frac{A}{a_s}\omega r\sin\theta\right)^2 = 0$$

$$(\because \sin\theta = \sin 0° = 0)$$

(*b*) Delivery side: h_d = 65 m (*Given*)

As an air vessel of adequate capacity has been installed on the delivery side, therefore acceleration is zero and velocity is no longer fluctuating (except in short length between the cylinder and air vessel). Also, since this shaft length has not been specified, the acceleration head can be assumed to be negligible.

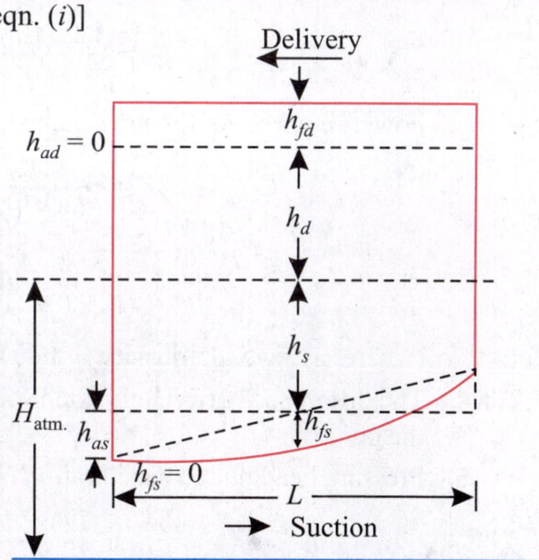

Fig. 4.13

$\therefore \quad h_{ad} = 0$

Velocity in the delivery pipe,

$$v_d = \frac{Q}{a_d} = \frac{0.01964}{0.00785} = 2.5 \text{ m/s}$$

$$\therefore \quad \text{Friction head, } h_{fd} = \frac{4 f l_d v_d^2}{d_d \times 2g} = \frac{4 \times 0.0012 \times 150 \times 2.5^2}{0.1 \times 2 \times 9.81} = 22.93 \text{ m}$$

$\therefore$ Gross head against which pump has to work,

$$H = (3.8 + 3.7 + 0) + (65 + 0 + 22.93) = 95.43 \text{ m}$$

Gross volume of water with a slip of 1.5%

$$= 0.01964 \times 1.015 = 0.01993 \text{ m}^3\text{/s}$$

$$\therefore \quad \text{Power required} = wQH = 9810 \times 0.01993 \times 95.43 = 18657.8 \text{ W} \simeq 18.66 \text{ kW}$$

$$\text{Power of motor, } P = \frac{18.66}{\eta_{mech.}} = \frac{18.66}{0.78} = \mathbf{23.92\ kW} \text{ (Ans.)}$$

HIGHLIGHTS

1. The reciprocating pump is a positive displacement pump and consists of a cylinder, a piston a suction valve, a delivery valve, a suction pipe, a delivery pipe and crank and connecting rod mechanism operated by a power source e.g. steam engine, I.C. engine or an electric motor.
2. Discharge through a pump per second is given as

$$Q = \frac{ALN}{60} \quad \text{...for a single-acting pump}$$

$$Q = \frac{2ALN}{60} \quad \text{...for a double-acting pump}$$

3. Work done by reciprocating pump per second is given as

$$= \frac{wALN}{60}(h_s + h_d) \quad \text{...for a single-acting pump}$$

$$= \frac{2wALN}{60}(h_s + h_d) \quad \text{...for a double-acting pump}$$

Power required to drive the pump

$$= \frac{wALN}{60 \times 1000}(h_s + h_d)\ kW \quad \text{...for a single-acting pump}$$

$$= \frac{2wALN}{60 \times 1000}(h_s + h_d)\ kW \quad \text{...for a double-acting pump.}$$

(where, w = weight density of liquid in N/m^3.)

4. The difference between the theoretical discharge and actual discharge is called the '*slip*' of the pump.
5. Pressure head due to acceleration (h_a) in the suction and delivery pipes is given as:

$$h_{as} = \frac{l_s}{g} \times \frac{A}{a_s}\,\omega^2 r \cos\theta \quad \text{...For suction pipe;}$$

$$h_{ad} = \frac{l_d}{g} \times \frac{A}{a_d} \omega^2 r \cos\theta \qquad \text{...For delivery pipe.}$$

6. The *indicator diagram* of a reciprocating pump is the diagram which shows the pressure head of the liquid in the pump cylinder corresponding to any position during the suction and delivery strokes. It is a graph between pressure head and stroke length of the piston for one complete revolution.
7. Work done by the pump is proportional to the area of the indicator diagram.
8. Work done by the pump per second due to acceleration and friction in suction and delivery pipes

$$= \frac{wALN}{60}\left(h_s + h_d + \frac{2}{3}h_{fs} + \frac{2}{3}h_{fd}\right) \qquad \text{...For a single-acting pump}$$

$$= \frac{2wALN}{60}\left(h_s + h_d + \frac{2}{3}h_{fs} + \frac{2}{3}h_{fd}\right) \qquad \text{...For a double-acting pump.}$$

9. An *air vessel* is a closed chamber containing compressed air in the upper part and liquid being pumped in the lower part. The air vessels are used: (*i*) To get continuous supply of liquid at a uniform rate, (*ii*) To save the power required to drive the pump and (*iii*) To run the pump at a much higher speed without any danger of separation.

OBJECTIVE TYPE QUESTIONS

Choose the correct Answer

1. With respect to a reciprocating pump which of the following statements is *incorrect* ?
   (*a*) The limiting value of separation pressure head for water is 6·8 m (absolute).
   (*b*) During suction, the separation may take place at the beginning of suction stroke.
   (*c*) During delivery, the separation may take place at the end of delivery stroke.
   (*d*) Indicator diagram shows variation of pressure head in the cylinder for one revolution of crank.
2. Reciprocating pumps are most suited where
   (*a*) constant heads are required on mains despite fluctuation in discharge
   (*b*) operating speeds are much high
   (*c*) constant supplies are required regardless of pressure fluctuations
   (*d*) none of the above.
3. Which of the following statements is *incorrect* for a reciprocating pump ?
   (*a*) The reciprocating pump is essentially a low speed machine.
   (*b*) The percentage of power saved by fitting air vessels is more in a double-acting than in a single-acting pump.
   (*c*) The reciprocating pumps can handle only low viscosity liquids free from impurities.
   (*d*) none of the above.
4. In a reciprocating pump the air vessels are used for which of the following purposes ?
   (*a*) To get continuous supply of liquid at a uniform rate.
   (*b*) To save the power required to drive the pump.
   (*c*) To run the pump at much higher speed without any danger of separation.
   (*d*) All of the above.
5. The pressure head due to acceleration in the suction pipe (h_{as}) is given as:
   (*a*) $\frac{l_s}{g} \times \frac{A}{a_s} \times \omega r \cos\theta$
   (*b*) $\frac{l_s}{2g} \times \frac{A^2}{a_s} \times \omega r \cos\theta$
   (*c*) $\frac{l_s}{g} \times \frac{A}{a_s} \times \omega^2 r \cos\theta$
   (*d*) none of the above.
6. Discharge through a double-acting reciprocating pump is given as
   (*a*) $\frac{ALN}{60}$ (*b*) $\frac{ALN}{120}$
   (*c*) $\frac{2ALN}{60}$ (*d*) $\frac{3ALN}{120}$.

ANSWERS

1. (*a*) 2. (*c*) 3. (*b*) 4. (*d*) 5. (*c*) 6. (*c*).

THEORETICAL QUESTIONS

1. Describe the principle and working of a reciprocating pump.
2. How are reciprocating pumps classified ?
3. Define slip, percentage slip and negative slip of a reciprocating pump.
4. What is negative slip in reciprocating pump ? Explain with neat sketches the function of air vessels in a reciprocating pump ? **[AMIE, Fluid Power Engg.]**
5. Obtain an expression for the pressure head due to acceleration in the suction and delivery pipes.
6. Define indicator diagram. Prove that work done by the pump is proportional to the area of indicator diagram.
7. Draw an indicator diagram, considering the effect of acceleration and friction in suction and delivery pipes. Find an expression for the work done per second in case of a single-acting reciprocating pump.
8. What is an air vessel ?
9. What are the uses of air vessels ?
10. Show from the first principles that work saved in a single-acting reciprocating pump, by fitting an air vessel, is 84.8 percent.

UNSOLVED EXAMPLES

1. A single-acting reciprocating pump, running at 60 r.p.m., delivers 0.53 m^3 of water per minute. The diameter of the piston is 200 mm and stroke length 300 mm. The suction and delivery heads are 4 m and 12 m respectively. Determine: (*i*) Theoretical discharge, (*ii*) Co-efficient of discharge, (*iii*) Percentage slip of the pump, and (*iv*) Power required to run the pump. [**Ans.** (*i*) 0.00942 m^3/s; (*ii*) 0.937; (*iii*) 6.26%; (*iv*) 1.47 kW]
2. A single-acting reciprocating pump having a bore of 150 mm and a stroke of 300 mm is raising water to height of 20 m above the sump level. The pump has an actual discharge of 0.0052 m^3/s. The efficiency of the pump is 70%. If the speed of pump is 60 r.p.m. determine: (*i*) Theoretical discharge, (*ii*) Theoretical power, (*iii*) Actual power, and (*iv*) Percentage slip. [**Ans.** (*i*) 0.0053 m^3/s; (*ii*) 1.04 kW, (*iii*) 1.48 kW; (*iv*) 1.88%]
3. A single-acting reciprocating pump has a piston diameter of 150 mm and stroke length 350 mm. The centre of the pump is 3 m above the water surface in the sump and 20 m below the delivery water level. Both the suction and delivery pipes have the same diameter of 100 mm and are 5 m and 30 m long respectively. If the pump is working at 35 r.p.m., determine:
   (*i*) Pressure heads due to acceleration at the beginning of suction and delivery strokes,
   (*ii*) Pressure heads in the cylinder at the beginning of suction and delivery strokes, and
   (*iii*) Pressure heads in the cylinder at the end of suction and delivery strokes.
   [**Ans.** (*i*) 2.695 m, 16.17 m; (*ii*) 4.605 m of water (abs.), 46.47 m of water (abs.), (*iii*) 9.99 m of water (abs.), 14.13 m (abs.)]
4. The diameter and stroke of a single-acting reciprocating pump are 125 mm and 300 mm. The pump is fed by a suction pipe 75 mm in diameter and 7 m long; the suction lift being 4 m. The separation occurs if the absolute pressure head in the cylinder during suction stroke falls below 2·5 m of water. What is the maximum speed at which pump can be run without separation in the suction pipe ?
   Take atmosphere pressure head = 10.3 m of water. [**Ans.** 34.1 r.p.m.]
5. The diameter and stroke length of single-acting reciprocating pump are 100 mm and 200 mm respectively. It takes its supply of water from a sump 4 m below the pump through a pipe 6 m long and 40 mm in diameter. It delivers water to a tank 14 m above the pump through a pipe 30 mm in diameter and 18 m long. If the separation occurs at 78.48 kN/m^2 below the atmospheric pressure, find the maximum speed at which pump may be operated without separation. Assume plunger has a simple harmonic motion. [**Ans.** 30.9 r.p.m.]

6. The cross-sectional area of plunger equals 1.65 times that of a delivery pipe. The delivery pipe is 55 m long and it rises upward at a slope of 1 in 5. If the plunger has an acceleration of 2.5 m/s^2 at the end of the stroke and separation pressure is 2.5 m of water find whether separation will take place and, if so, at which section of the pipe. Assume simple harmonic motion and take atmospheric pressure = 10·3 m of water

   [**Ans.** Separation will take place; 35.45 m]

7. The bore and stroke of a reciprocating pump are 250 mm and 500 mm respectively. The pump delivers water through 100 mm delivery pipe to a tank located at 12 m above it and 25 m horizontally from it. If the separation occurs at a pressure of 22.5 kN/m^2 absolute, find the safe speed at which the pump should run for the following arrangements of delivery pipe:
   (*i*) The delivery pipe is horizontal from the pump and then vertical upto the tank and
   (*ii*) The delivery pipe is vertical from the pump and then horizontal upto the tank.

   Take: Atmospheric pressure (at the pump site) = 10.3 m of water, connecting rod-crank ratio = 5.

   [**Ans.** (*i*) 19.68 r.p.m; (*ii*) 12.45 r.p.m.]

8. The piston diameter and stroke length of a single acting reciprocating pump are 150 mm and 300 mm respectively. The centre of the pump is 5·0 m above the water level in the sump and 33 m below the delivery water level. Both the suction and delivery pipes have the same diameter of 75 mm and are 65 m and 39 m long respectively. If the pump is working at 30 r.p.m. determine:
   (*i*) The pressure head on the piston at the beginning, middle and end of both suction and delivery strokes, and
   (*ii*) The power required to drive the pump.

   Take atmospheric pressure head = 10.3 m of water and friction co-efficient, f = 0.01 for both the pipes.

   [**Ans.** (*i*) 1.38 m (abs.); 4.672 m (abs.), 9.22 m (abs.); 66.84 m (abs.); 47.067 m (abs.); 19.76 m (abs.); (*ii*) 1.064 kW]

9. The bore and stroke of a double-acting single-cylinder reciprocating pump, running at 35 r.p.m., are 200 mm and 400 mm respectively. The pump draws water from a sump 1·0 m below the pump through a suction pipe 100 mm in diameter and 2·5 m long. The water is delivered to a tank 30 m above the pump through a delivery pipe 100 mm in diameter and 40 m long. Assuming the motion of the piston to be simple harmonic determine the net force due to fluid pressure on the piston when it has moved through a distance of 100 mm from inner dead centre (*I.D.C.*).

   Take friction co-efficient for both the suction and delivery pipes as 0.0075. Neglect the size of the piston rod. [**Ans.** 2.522 kN]

10. The plunger diameter and stroke length of a single-acting reciprocating pump are 300 mm and 500 mm respectively. The speed of the pump is 60 r.p.m. The diameter and length of delivery pipe are 150 mm and 60 m respectively. If the pump is equipped with an air vessel on the delivery side at the centre line of the pump find the power saved in overcoming friction in delivery pipe.

    Take friction co-efficient, f = 0.01.

    [**Ans.** 6.3 kW]

11. The diameter and stroke of a single-acting reciprocating pump are 300 mm and 500 mm respectively. The pump takes its supply of water from sump 3.5 m below the pump axis through a pipe 10 m long and 200 mm diameter. If separation occurs at 2.5 m of water absolute, determine:
    (*i*) The speed at which separation may take place at the beginning of suction stroke, and
    (*ii*) The speed of the pump if an air vessel is fitted on the suction side 2.5 m above the sump water level.

    Take atmospheric pressure head = 10.3 m of water and friction co-efficient, f = 0.01.

    [**Ans.** (*i*) 26.16 r.p.m; (*ii*) 48.56 r.p.m.]

Chapter 5

MISCELLANEOUS HYDRAULIC MACHINES

5.1. INTRODUCTION

There are many hydraulic devices/machines which are based on the principles of *fluid statics* and *fluid kinematics* and are used for either *storing the hydraulic energy and then transmitting when needed or magnifying the hydraulic energy several times and transmitting the same*. In all such machines power is transmitted with the help of a fluid which may be a liquid (water or oil). In this chapter following hydraulic devices/machines will be discussed.

1. Hydraulic accumulator, 2. Hydraulic intensifier,
3. Hydraulic press, 4. Hydraulic crane,
5. Hydraulic lift, 6. Hydraulic ram,
7. Hydraulic coupling,
8. Hydraulic torque converter,
9. Air lift pump, and 10. Jet pump.

5.2. HYDRAULIC ACCUMULATOR

Hydraulic accumulator *is a device used to store the energy of liquid under pressure and make this energy available* (*as a quick secondary source of power*) *to hydraulic machines, such as presses, lifts and cranes*. In case of hydraulic crane or lift, the liquid under pressure needs to be supplied during upward motion of the load only. This energy is supplied from hydraulic accumulator. But when the lift is moving downward, no large external energy is required and during that period the energy from the pump is stored in the accumulator.

The function of hydraulic accumulator is analogous to that of the flywheel of a reciprocating engine and an electric storage battery. It damps out pressure surges and shocks in the hydraulic system, and thus it functions as a *pressure regulator*.

5.2.1. Simple Hydraulic accumulator

Construction and working. Fig. 5.1 shows a *simple hydraulic accumulator*. It consists of a fixed vertical cylinder, containing a sliding ram/plunger. A load/weight is placed on the top, to create pressure in the cylinder chamber. One side of the cylinder is connected to the pump and the other side to the machine.

In the beginning, the ram is at the lowermost position. During idle periods of driven machine (say crane or lift) high pressure liquid supplied by the pump is admitted in the hollow space of the cylinder, it raises the ram, on which the heavy load is placed. Flow of more liquid continues till the ram is at its uppermost position; at this position, the cylinder is full of water and the maximum amount of pressure energy is accumulated. This accumulated energy is later discharged to the driven machine, during its working stroke (*i.e.* when it requires maximum amount of energy).

Capacity of accumulator. The *maximum amount of energy that the accumulator can store* is known as the *capacity of the accumulator*.

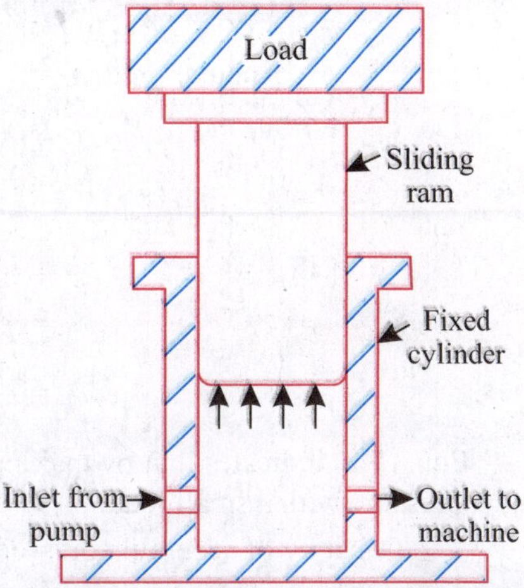

Fig. 5.1 Simple hydraulic accumulator.

Let, A = Area of the sliding ram,

L = Stroke or lift of the ram,

p = Intensity of pressure of liquid supplied by the pump, and

W = Total weight of the ram (including the weight of the load on the ram).

Then, $W = P \times A$

The work done in lifting the ram = $W \times$ lift of ram

$= W \times L$

$= p \times A \times L$ $\quad (\because W = p \times A)$

But the work done in lifting the ram = Energy stored in the accumulator = Capacity of the accumulator

$\therefore$ Capacity of the accumulator = $p \times A \times L$

$= p \times$ volume of accumulator ...(5.1)

$(\because A \times L =$ volume of accumulator)

5.2.2. Differential Hydraulic Accumulator

Fig. 5.2 shows a differential hydraulic accumulator. *The advantage of this accumulator is that liquid can be stored at a high pressure by a comparatively small load on the ram.* It consists of a fixed vertical ram/plunger inside which is provided a central liquid passage of small diameter. This fixed cylindrical ram/plunger is surrounded by closely fitting brass bush, which is surrounded by an inverted *sliding* cylinder having a circular projected collar on which weights are placed. Passages for liquid to enter and leave the unit are provided in the fixed ram, and connected to the inlet and outlet pipes, as shown in the Fig. 5.2.

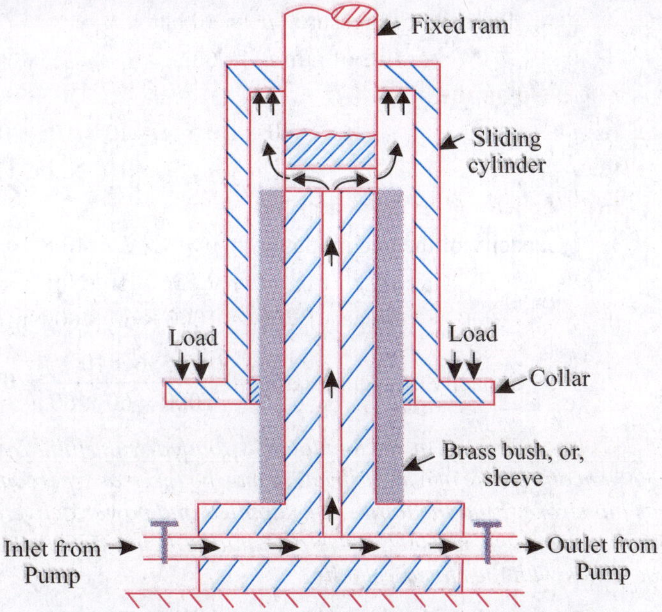

Fig. 5.2 Differential hydraulic accumulator.

The liquid supplied from the pump enters the cylinder through central vertical hole provided in the fixed ram and causes the loaded cylinder to move upwards, thus storing the hydraulic energy. When the liquid is drawn by the machine from the accumulator, the liquid leaves the cylinder through the same central hole. The liquid entering the cylinder exerts pressure on the *annular area of the cylinder which is equal to cross-sectional area (horizontal) of the brass bush or sleeve.*

Let, D = External diameter of the bush,

d = Diameter of fixed ram,

$\therefore$ Annular area, $A = \frac{\pi}{4}(D^2 - d^2)$,

L = Vertical lift of the sliding cylinder,

W = Total weight of sliding cylinder (including the weight placed on the cylinder), and

p = Intensity of pressure of liquid by pump.

Then, $W = p \times A$

$$\therefore \quad P = \frac{W}{A} \quad \text{...(5.2)}$$

Eqn. (5.2) indicates that by making the area of the bush small, it is possible to store liquid at a high pressure with a small load.

$$\text{Capacity of accumulator} = W \times L$$
$$= p \times A \times L = p \times \text{volume} \quad \text{...(5.3)}$$

Example 5.1. *An accumulator has a ram of 200 mm diameter and a lift of 6 m. If the liquid is supplied at a pressure of 40 bar, find: (i) load on the ram, and (ii) capacity of the accumulator.* **[Anna University]**

Solution. Diameter of ram, D = 200 mm = 0·2 m

$\therefore$ Area, $A = \frac{\pi}{4} \times 0.2^2 = 0.0314 \text{ m}^2$

Intensity of pressure, p = 40 bar

Lift of ram L = 6 m

(*i*) Load on the ram, *W* :

$$W = p \times A = 40 \times 10^5 \times 0.0314$$
$$= 1.256 \times 10^5 \text{ N, or, } \mathbf{125.6\ kN} \text{ (Ans.)}$$

(*ii*) Capacity of the accumulator:

$$\text{Capacity of the accumulator} = p \times A \times L = 40 \times 10^5 \times 0.0314 \times 6 \text{ Nm}$$
$$= 7.536 \times 10^5 \text{ Nm}$$

$$\text{Since 1 kWh} = 1000 \times 60 \times 60 \text{ Nm}$$

$$\therefore \quad \text{Capacity of accumulator} = \frac{7.536 \times 10^5}{1000 \times 60 \times 60} = \mathbf{0.209\ kWh} \text{ (Ans.)}$$

Example 5.2. *An accumulator is loaded with 400 kN weight. The ram has a diameter of 300 mm and stroke of 6 m. Its friction may be taken as 5 percent. It takes two minutes to fall through its full stroke. Find the total work supplied and power delivered to the hydraulic appliance by the accumulator, when 0.0075 m³/s of liquid is being delivered by a pump, while the accumulator descends with the stated velocity.* **[AMIE, Fluid Power Engg.]**

Solution. Total load on the accumulator = 400 kN

Diameter of ram, D = 300 mm = 0.3 m

$\therefore$ Area of ram, $A = \frac{\pi}{4} \times 0.3^2 = 0.07068 \text{ m}^2$

Stroke of ram, $L = 6$ m

Friction = 5 percent.

Total work supplied and power delivered:

Net load on accumulator when it descends = $400 \times 0.95 = 380$ kN

Time taken by ram to fall through full stroke, t = 2 min, or, 120 s

$\therefore$ Distance moved by ram per sec. $= \frac{1}{t} = \frac{6}{120} = 0.05$ m/s

Liquid supplied by pump = $0.0075 \text{ m}^3/\text{s}$ (*Given*)

Work done by accumulator per second

= Net load on ram × distance moved by ram per sec.

= $380 \times 0.05 = 19$ kN m/s

Intensity of pressure of water, $p = \frac{\text{Net load}}{\text{Area}} = \frac{380 \times 10^3}{0.07068} = 5376.3 \times 10^3 \text{ N/m}^2$

Pressure head, $H = \frac{p}{w} = \frac{5376.3 \times 10^3}{9810} = 548$ m

Work supplied by pump per second = Weight of water supplied per sec. × pressure head

= $wQH = 9810 \times 0.0075 \times 548$

= 40319 Nm/s, or, 40.319 kN m/s

$\therefore$ *Total work supplied to hydraulic machine*

= Work supplied by accumulator + work supplied by the pump

= $19 + 40.319 =$ **59.319 kN m/s (Ans.)**

Power delivered to the hydraulic machine = **59.319 kW (Ans.)**

Example 5.3. *It is required to transmit 25 kW power from an accumulator through a pipeline 100 mm diameter and 1500 m long. The ram is loaded with a weight of 1250 kN and the friction loss in the pipeline equals 2.5 per cent of the total power being transmitted. Determine the diameter of the ram.*

Take friction co-efficient = 0.01.

Solution. Power to be transmitted, P = 25 kW

Diameter of the pipe, d = 100 mm = 0.1 m

Length of the pipe, l = 1500 m

Load on the ram, W = 1250 kN

Friction loss in the pipeline = 2.5 percent of the total power being transmitted

$= \frac{2.5}{100} \times 25 = 0.625$ kW

Diameter of the ram, *D*:

The loss of head due to friction in pipeline is given by,

$$h_f = \frac{4flV^2}{d \times 2g} = \frac{4 \times 0.01 \times 1500 \times V^2}{0.1 \times 2 \times 9.81} = 30.58\, V^2$$

(where, V = velocity of flow through the pipeline)

$$\text{Power lost due to friction} = \frac{wQh_f}{1000} \text{ kW (where, } w = 9810 \text{ N/m}^3 \text{ for water)}$$

or, $$0.625 = \frac{9810 \times (\pi/4) \times 0.1^2 \times V \times 30.58V^2}{1000} = 2.356V^3$$

∴ $$= \left(\frac{0.625}{2.356}\right)^{1/3} = 0.64 \text{ m/s}$$

$$\text{Discharge in the pipeline} = \frac{\pi}{4} \times 0.1^2 \times 0.64 = 0.005026 \text{ m}^3\text{/s}$$

The same discharge flows through the accumulator.

$$\text{Power developed by accumulator} = \frac{wQH}{1000} \text{ kW}$$

(where, H = pressure head of water in the accumulator.)

∴ $$25 = \frac{9810 \times 0.005026 \times H}{1000},$$

or, $$H = \frac{25 \times 1000}{9810 \times 0.005026} = 507 \text{ m of water}$$

Pressure intensity in the accumulator, $p = wH$, or, $p = 9810 \times 507 = 4973670 \text{ N/m}^2$

But, $$\text{Pressure intensity} = \frac{\text{Load on the ram}}{\text{Area of the ram}} = \frac{1250 \times 10^3}{\frac{\pi}{4} \times D^2}$$

∴ $$4973670 = \frac{1250 \times 10^3}{\frac{\pi}{4} \times D^2}, \text{ or, } D^2 = \frac{1250 \times 10^3}{\frac{\pi}{4} \times 4973670} = 0.3199$$

∴ $D = 0.565$ m or **565 mm (Ans.)**

Example 5.4. *The diameters of two portions of the ram of a differential accumulator are 150 mm and 140 mm respectively, the stroke being 1·25 m. If the accumulator is supplied with water at pressure 1200 m of water, find load on the ram and the capacity.*

Solution. *Given :* $D = 150$ mm $= 0.15$ m; $d = 140$ mm $= 0.14$ m;

Stroke length = 1.25 m; Pressure head, $h = 1200$ m.

Load on the ram and the capacity:

Pressure on the ram, $p = wh = 9810 \times 1200 = 117.72 \times 10^5 \text{ N/m}^2$

Load on the ram = Pressure intensity × annular area

$$= 117.72 \times 10^5 \times \frac{\pi}{4}(0.15^2 - 0.14^2) = 0.268 \times 10^5 \text{ N or } \mathbf{26.8 \text{ kN}} \textbf{ (Ans.)}$$

Capacity of ram = Load on the ram × stroke length

$$= 26.8 \times 1.25 = 33.5 \text{ kN m}$$

∴ $$\text{Capacity in kWh} = \frac{33.5 \times 10^3}{1000 \times 60 \times 60} = \mathbf{0.0093 \text{ kWh}} \textbf{ (Ans.)}$$

Example 5.5. *The diameters of the two parts of the ram of a differential accumulator are 150 mm and 120 mm, and stroke length is 1.25 m. If the pressure of water is 7850 kN/m² when the load is at rest at the upper end of stroke or when the load is moving with uniform velocity, what will be the weight of the loaded cylinder? How much energy can be stored in the accumulator?*

Find also the diameter of the ram of an ordinary accumulator to move the same load with the help of the same water pressure.

Solution. D = 150 mm = 0.15 m; d = 120 mm = 0.12 m;

Stroke length = 1.25 m; Pressure of water = 7850 kN/m^2.

Weight of loaded cylinder:

$$\text{Weight of loaded cylinder} = \text{Pressure} \times \text{annular area}$$

$$= 7850 \times \frac{\pi}{4}(0.15^2 - 0.12^2) = \mathbf{49.94\ kN}\ \textbf{(Ans.)}$$

Energy stored in accumulator:

$$\text{Energy stored in the accumulator} = \text{Load} \times \text{displacement}$$

$$= 49.94 \times 1.25 = \mathbf{62.42\ kNm}\ \textbf{(Ans.)}$$

Diameter of the ram of an ordinary accumulator, D′:

$$\text{Load on the ram} = \text{Pressure intensity} \times \text{area}$$

$$49.94 = 7850 \times \frac{\pi}{4}(D')^2$$

$$\therefore \quad D' = \left(\frac{49.94 \times 4}{7850 \times \pi}\right)^{1/2} = 0.09 \text{ m or } \mathbf{90\ mm}\ \textbf{(Ans.)}$$

Example 5.6. *A hydraulic accumulator has sliding ram of 400 mm diameter which slides through 7.5 m in 3 minutes during its working stroke, while weight on the ram including its self weight is equivalent to 300 kN. The pump supplies water at 0.009 m^3/s rate and packing friction amounts to 4 percent of total load. Determine:*

(i) Pressure intensity of water,

(ii) Power delivered to machine supplied by accumulator,

(iii) Power required to drive the pump having efficiency 72 percent.

Solution. Diameter of sliding ram, D = 400 mm = 0·4 m

$$\therefore \quad \text{Area, } A = \frac{\pi}{4} \times 0.4^2 = 0.1256 \text{ m}^2$$

Weight on ram including self weight, W = 300 kN

Packing friction = 4% of total load

$$= \frac{4}{100} \times 300 = 12 \text{ kN}$$

∴ Discharge of water supplied by pump, q = 0.009 m^3/s

Efficiency of pump, η = 72%

(i) Pressure intensity of water, *p*:

Net load on the sliding ram = 300 – 12 = 288 kN

$$\therefore \quad \text{Pressure intensity of water} = \frac{288}{0.1256} \simeq \mathbf{2293\ kN/m^2}\ \textbf{(Ans.)}$$

(ii) Power delivered to machine supplied by accumulator, *P*:

Let Q = Total discharge of water supplied to the machine,

q = Discharge of water supplied by the pump, (= 0.009 m^3/s), and

L = Stroke length of the accumulator ram, (= 7.5 m),

Then, $AL = (Q - q)\,t$, or, $0.1256 \times 7.5 = (Q - 0.009) \times (3 \times 60)$

or, $$Q = \frac{0.1256 \times 7.5}{3 \times 60} + 0.009 = 0.0142 \text{ m}^3/\text{s}$$

∴ Power delivered to the machine $= p \times Q$

$= 2293 \times 0.0142$ kW $=$ **32.56 kW (Ans.)**

(*iii*) Power required to drive the pump:

$$\textit{Power required to drive the pump} = \frac{p \times q}{\eta} = \frac{2293 \times 0.009}{0.72} \text{ kW} = \mathbf{28.66 \text{ kW}} \text{ (Ans.)}$$

Example 5.7. *An accumulator maintains a pressure of 6000 kN/m² in a 50 mm diameter hydraulic main. A hydraulic crane situated at a distance of 250 m from the accumulator is supplied with pressure water from this main. The ram of the hydraulic crane is of 220 mm diameter. Velocity ratio of the crane hook to ram is 4 : 1. A pressure of 280 kN/m² may be assumed on the ram to account for mechanical friction of ram, pulleys etc. Calculate the load lifted when it is raised with a speed of 0.6 m/s.*

Assume a co-efficient of friction for the hydraulic main as 0.01. **[UPTU]**

Solution. Pressure in the accumulator $= 6000$ kN/m²

Diameter of hydraulic main, d $= 50$ mm $= 0.05$ m

Length of hydraulic main, l $= 250$ m

Diameter of the ram, D $= 220$ mm $= 0.22$ m

Velocity ratio of the crane hook to ram $= 4 : 1$

Pressure lost due to mechanical friction $= 280$ kN/m²

Velocity of crane hook $= 0{\cdot}6$ m/s

Co-efficient of friction for the hydraulic main, f $= 0.01$

Load lifted, *W*:

$$\text{Velocity of ram} = \frac{0.6}{4} = 0.15 \text{ m/s}$$

Let V be the velocity of water in the hydraulic main. Since the quantity of water per second flowing through the main is equal to the quantity per second in the ram cylinder, therefore,

$$\left(\frac{\pi}{4} \times 0{\cdot}05^2\right) \times V = \frac{\pi}{4} \times 0.22^2 \times 0.15, \text{ or, } V = 2.9 \text{ m/s}$$

$$\text{Head of water in accumulator} = \frac{6000}{9.81} = 611.6 \text{ m of water} \qquad (\because w = 9.81 \text{ kN/m}^3)$$

$$\text{Head lost in friction in main, } h_f = \frac{4flV^2}{d \times 2g} = \frac{4 \times 0.01 \times 250 \times 2.9^2}{0.05 \times 2 \times 9.81} = 85.7 \text{ m of water}$$

Head lost due, to mechanical friction of ram, pulleys etc.

$$= \frac{280}{9.81} = 28.5 \text{ m of water}$$

Net head available on the ram $= 611.6 - (85.7 + 28.5) = 497.4$ m of water

∴ Net intensity of pressure on ram

$= 497.4 \times 9.81$ kN/m² $= 4879.5$ kN/m² $(\because w = 9.81 \text{ kN/m}^3)$

$$\text{Load on the ram} = 4879.5 \times \left(\frac{\pi}{4} \times 0.22^2\right) = 185.48 \text{ kN}$$

$$\therefore \quad \textit{Load lifted} \text{ by the crane hook} = \frac{185.48}{4} = \mathbf{46.37\ kN\ (Ans.)}$$

Example 5.8. *A weight loaded accumulator operates certain machinery through a pipe 100 mm in diameter and 600 m long. The accumulator has a ram 300 mm diameter and 3.5 m stroke, loaded with 320 kN; it is supplied with water by a three throw pump running at 45 r.p.m., the plungers of pump having a diameter of 45 mm and a stroke of 360 mm. The slip of the pump has been estimated as 5 per cent. If the power absorbed by the machinery is 37 kW, calculate the longest period during which it may be operated continuously.*

Take co-efficient of friction for the pipe as 0·0075. **[PTU]**

Solution. Diameter of the pipe, d = 100 mm = 0.1 m

Length of the pipe, l = 600 m

Diameter of this ram, D = 300 mm = 0.3 m

Stroke of the ram, L = 360 mm = 0.36 m

Load on the ram, W = 320 kN

Diameter of each plunger of the pump = 45 mm = 0.045 m

Stroke of each plunger = 360 mm = 0.36 m

Speed of pump = 45 r.p.m.

Slip of the pump = 5%

Power absorbed by the machinery, P = 37 kW

Co-efficient of friction for the pipe, f = 0.0075.

Longest period during which machinery can be operated continuously, *t*:

$$\text{Pressure head in the accumulator} = \frac{W}{\left(\frac{\pi}{4} \times D^2\right) \times w} = \frac{320}{\frac{\pi}{4} \times 0.3^2 \times 9.81} = 461.5 \text{ m}$$

$$(\because w = 9.81 \text{ kN/m}^3)$$

$$\text{Loss of head due to friction in the pipe, } h_f = \frac{4flV^2}{d \times 2g}$$

$$= \frac{4 \times 0.0075 \times 600 \times V^2}{0.1 \times 2 \times 9.81} = 9.17\,V^2$$

$$\therefore \quad \text{Effective head at the machine, } H = (461.5 - 9.17\,V^2)$$

$$\text{Power supplied to machinery} = wQH$$

$$37 = 9.81 \times \left(\frac{\pi}{4} \times 0.1^2 \times V\right) \times (461.5 - 9.17V^2)$$

$$= 0.077V(461.5 - 9.17V^2) = 35.53\,V - 0.706V^3$$

or, $$0.706V^3 - 35.53V + 37 = 0$$

or, $$V^3 - 50.32V + 52.4 = 0$$

Solving by trial, we get V = 1.064 m/s

$\therefore$ Discharge through the pipe, $Q = \frac{\pi}{4} \times 0.1^2 \times 1.064 = 0.008357 \text{ m}^3/\text{s}$

This discharge, Q is the same as the discharge leaving the accumulator.

Also, the discharge entering the accumulator = Discharge of the three-throw pump.

$$\text{Discharge of the pump} = 3 \times \left[\frac{\pi}{4} \times 0.045^2 \times 0.36 \times \frac{45}{60}\right] = 0.001288 \text{ m}^3/\text{s}$$

$\therefore$ Water supplied from the accumulator = 0.008357 – 0.001288 = 0.00707 m^3/s

$$\text{Volume of accumulator} = \frac{\pi}{4} \times 0.3^2 \times 3.5 = 0.247 \text{ m}^3$$

$\therefore$ The longest period during which machinery may be operated continuously (t) = time in which accumulator will be emptied

$$\therefore \quad t = \frac{0.247}{0.00707} = 34.94 \text{ s} \textbf{ (Ans.)}$$

5.3. HYDRAULIC INTENSIFIER

Hydraulic intensifier *is a device which increases the intensity of pressure of a given liquid with the help of low pressure liquid of large quantity*. It finds its application at places where a liquid of very high pressure is to be developed from available low pressure. It is located between the pump and the machine (*e.g.* press, crane, lift) that needs high pressure liquid for its operation. Its action is similar to that of a step-up electrical transformer.

Construction and working. A hydraulic intensifier consists of a fixed ram surrounded by the sliding cylinder, which is itself encased in a bigger and fixed cylinder (Fig. 5·3). The sliding cylinder contains water at high pressure (which is supplied to the machine through fixed ram) whereas the fixed cylinder contains water from the main supply at a low pressure.

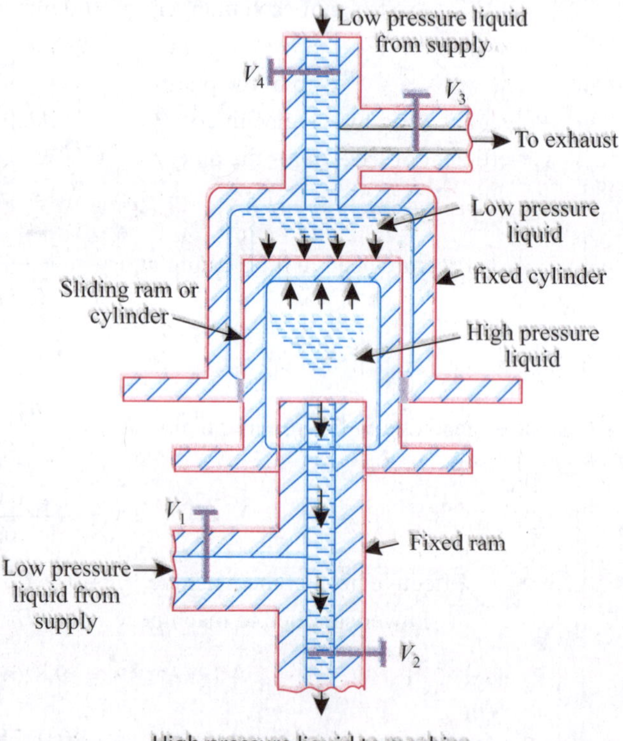

Fig. 5.3. Hydraulic intensifier.

— Initially when the sliding cylinder lies at the bottom of the stroke, the fixed cylinder is full of low pressure liquid. The valves V_2 and V_4 are then closed, the valve V_1 is opened thus admitting the low pressure liquid into the sliding cylinder; the valve V_3 is also opened which permits the low pressure liquid from the fixed cylinder to be discharged to the exhaust and the sliding cylinder to move upward. When the sliding cylinder reaches its topmost position, the inside of the sliding cylinder is full of low pressure liquid.

— The valves V_1 and V_3 are then closed and the valves V_2 and V_4 are opened. The low pressure liquid (from supply) then enters the fixed cylinder, and forces the sliding cylinder to move downward; pressure of liquid beneath is raised and the high pressure liquid is supplied to the driven machine.

The above cycle of operation is repeated.

The intensifier described above is *single-acting* (which gives supply during downward stroke only); however, *double-acting* intensifiers are also made, which give continuous supply of high pressure liquid.

— By means of an intensifier, it is possible to raise the intensity of pressure as high as 160 MN/m^2.

— Depending upon fluid used, intensifiers may also be of the following types:

(*i*) *Hydro-pneumatic intensifier*—Here air is supplied to the fixed cylinder instead of low pressure liquid.

(*ii*) *Steam intensifier*—Here steam under pressure is supplied to the fixed cylinder instead of low pressure liquid.

Let, p_1 = Pressure intensity of low pressure liquid (from supply) in the fixed cylinder,

A_1 = Cross-sectional area of sliding cylinder,

p_2 = Intensity of high pressure liquid in the fixed ram, and

A_2 = Cross-sectional area of the fixed ram.

The force exerted by low pressure liquid on the sliding cylinder in the downward direction $= p_1 \times A_1$

The force exerted by high pressure liquid on the sliding cylinder in the upward direction $= p_2 \times A_2$

For the equilibrium of the sliding cylinder at any position, we have

$$p_1 A_1 = p_2 A_2$$

∴ The intensity of high pressure liquid, $p_2 = \dfrac{p_1 A_1}{A_2}$ (neglecting friction effects) ...(5.4)

Example 5.9. *A hydraulic intensifier gets the low pressure liquid at a pressure of 40 bar and delivers it to a machine at a pressure of 160 bar. If the intensifier has a capacity of 0.021 m^3 and stroke 1.2 m, calculate the diameters of the fixed ram and the sliding cylinder to be used for this intensifier.*

Solution. Intensity of pressure of low pressure liquid, p_1 = 40 bar = 40 × 10^5 N/m^2

Intensity of pressure of high pressure liquid, p_2 = 160 bar = 160 × 10^5 N/m^2

Capacity of intensifier = 0.021 m^3

Stroke length = 1.2 m

Diameters of fixed ram (D_2) and the sliding cylinder (D_1):

Capacity of intensifier = Area of fixed ram × stroke length

$$0.021 = A_2 \times 1.2, \quad \text{or,} \quad A_2 = \frac{0.021}{1.2} = 0.0175 \text{ m}^2$$

$$\therefore \quad \frac{\pi}{4} D_2^2 = 0.0175, \text{ or, } D_2 = \left(\frac{4 \times 0.0175}{\pi}\right)^{1/2} = 0.149 \text{ m or } \mathbf{149 \text{ mm}} \text{ (Ans.)}$$

Considering equilibrium of the sliding cylinder (neglecting friction effects), we have:

$$p_1 A_1 = p_2 A_2, \text{ or, } 40 \times 10^5 \times A_1 = 160 \times 10^5 \times 0.0175, \text{ or, } A_1 = 0.07 \text{ m}^2$$

$$\therefore \quad \frac{\pi}{4} D_1^2 = 0.07, \text{ or, } d_1 = \left(\frac{4 \times 0.07}{\pi}\right)^{1/2} = 0.298 \text{ m or } \mathbf{298 \text{ mm}} \text{ (Ans.)}$$

Example 5.10. *An intensifier has a ram diameter of 150 mm and a sliding cylinder diameter of 750 mm. Calculate the pressure of water on the low pressure side of the intensifier if the pressure of water on high pressure side is 21000 kN/m². The loss due to friction at each of the packings of the intensifier is 5% of the total force on each of the packings.*

Solution. Sliding cylinder diameter, D_1 = 750 mm = 0.75 m

Ram diameter, D_2 = 150 mm = 0.15 m

Pressure of water on high pressure side, p_2 = 21000 kN/m²

Loss due to friction, k = 5% of the total force on each of the packings.

Pressure of water on low pressure side, p_1:

Considering equilibrium of the sliding cylinder, we have:

$$p_1 A_1\left(1-\frac{k}{100}\right) = \frac{p_2 A_2}{\left(1-\frac{k}{100}\right)}$$

or, $$p_1 \times \frac{\pi}{4} \times 0\cdot75^2\left(1-\frac{5}{100}\right) = 21000 \times \frac{\pi}{4} \times 0.15^2 \times \frac{1}{(1-5/100)}$$

or, $$p_1 \times \frac{\pi}{4} \times (0.75)^2 \times 0.95 = 21000 \times \frac{\pi}{4} \times 0.15^2 \times \frac{1}{0.95}$$

or, $$0.4197 p_1 = 390.6 \therefore P_1 = \frac{390.63}{0.4197} = \mathbf{930.7\ kN/m^2} \text{ (Ans.)}$$

Example 5.11. *An intensifier receives water from an overhead tank through a pipeline 60 mm in diameter and 110 m long and conveys high pressure water to a hydraulic press which has 250 mm ram diameter and exerts a force of 350 kN. The diameters of ram and sliding piston of intensifier are 0·1 m and 1 m respectively. If the level of water in the overhead tank is 15 m above the inlet to the low pressure side of the intensifier, calculate the speed with which the ram of the hydraulic press moves to exert the force.*

Take friction co-efficient, f = 0.0075 for the pipeline between the supply reservoir and the intensifier.

Solution. Diameter of sliding piston of intensifier, D_1 = 1 m

Diameter of ram of intensifier, D_2 = 0.1 m

Diameter of pipeline, d_p = 60 mm = 0.06 m

Length of pipeline, l_p = 110 m

Diameter of ram of hydraulic press, D = 250 mm = 0.25 m

Friction co-efficient, f = 0.0075

Velocity of the ram of hydraulic press, V_r:

Let, V_p = Velocity of water in the pipeline.

Loss of head due to friction,

$$h_f = \frac{4 f l_p V_p^2}{d_p \times 2g} = \frac{4 \times 0.0075 \times 110 \times V_p^2}{0.06 \times 2 \times 9.81} = 2.8 V_p^2$$

Pressure head on the low pressure side of the intensifier,

$$h_1 = (15 - 2.8\,V_p^2) \text{ m of water}$$

$\therefore$ Corresponding intensity of pressure, $p_1 = wh_1 = 9810\,(15 - 2.8\,V_p^2)$ N/m²

Pressure intensity on the high pressure side of the intensifier,

$$p_2 = p_1 \times \frac{A_1}{A_2} = 9810\,(15 - 2.8V_p^2) \times \left(\frac{\frac{\pi}{4} \times 1^2}{\frac{\pi}{4} \times 0.1^2}\right) = 9810 \times (1500 - 280V_p^2)$$

Neglecting loss of pressure between the intensifier and hydraulic press, force on the ram of hydraulic press

$$= 9810\,(1500 - 280\,V_p^2) \times \frac{\pi}{4} \times 0.25^2 \text{ ; this force } \textit{equals the load on press.}$$

$$\therefore\ 9810\,(1500 - 280\,V_p^2) \times \frac{\pi}{4} \times 0.25^2 = 350 \times 1000$$

$$\text{or,}\quad 1500 - 280\,V_p^2 = 726.8, \quad \text{or,} \quad V_p = \left(\frac{1500 - 726.8}{280}\right)^{1/2} = 1.66 \text{ m}$$

$$\text{Discharge through the pipeline} = \frac{\pi}{4} \times 0.06^2 \times 1.66 = 0.00469 \text{ m}^3\text{/s}$$

The same discharge flows to the low pressure side of the intensifier.

Discharge on the high pressure side of the intensifier

$$= 0.00469 \times \left(\frac{0.1}{1}\right)^2 = 4.69 \times 10^{-5} \text{ m}^3\text{/s}$$

$$\left[\because \quad \frac{Q_1}{Q_2} = \frac{A_1 L}{A_2 L} = \frac{A_1}{A_2}, \text{ or, } Q_2 = Q_1 \times \left(\frac{A_2}{A_1}\right) = Q_1 \left(\frac{D_2}{D_1}\right)^2\right.$$

where,
Q_1 = Rate of discharge of low pressure liquid,
Q_2 = Rate of discharge of high pressure liquid to machine, and
L = Stroke length.]

From continuity considerations, we have:

$$\frac{\pi}{4} \times 0.25^2 \times V_r = 4.69 \times 10^{-5}, \text{ or, } V_r = \frac{4.69 \times 10^{-5}}{\frac{\pi}{4} \times 0.25^2} = 0.000955 \text{ m/s}$$

$$= \mathbf{0.0573\ m/min}\ \textbf{(Ans.)}$$

5.4. HYDRAULIC PRESS

The **hydraulic press** *is a device used for lifting heavy loads by the application of much smaller force. It is based on Pascal's law, which states that intensity of pressure is transmitted equally in all directions through a mass of fluid at rest.*

Working principle. The working principle of a hydraulic press may be explained with the help of Fig. 5.4. Consider a ram and plunger, operating in two cylinders of different diameters, which are inter-connected at the bottom, through a chamber, which is filled with some liquid.

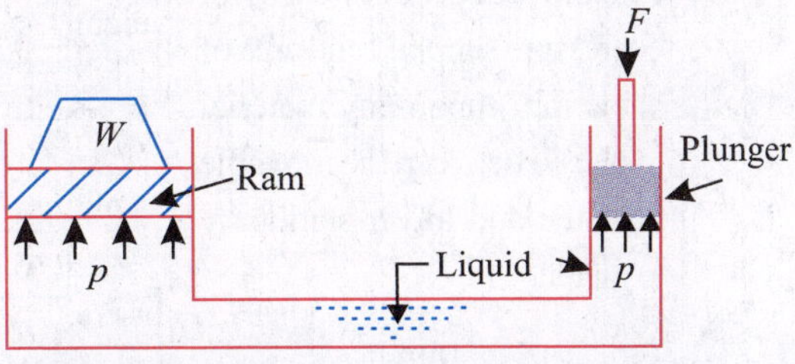

Fig. 5.4. Working principle of hydraulic press.

Let, W = Weight to be lifted,

F = Force applied on the plunger,

A = Area of ram, and

a = Area of plunger.

Pressure intensity produced by the force $F, p = \dfrac{F}{\text{Area of plunger}} = \dfrac{F}{a}$

As per Pascal's law, the above intensity p will be equally transmitted in all directions.

$\therefore$ The pressure intensity on ram $= p = \dfrac{F}{a} = \dfrac{W}{A}$

or, $$W = F \times \frac{A}{a} \quad \text{...(5.5)}$$

Eqn. (5.5) indicates that by applying a small force F on the plunger, a large force W may be developed by the ram.

Mechanical advantage of press $= \dfrac{A}{a}$

If the force in the plunger is applied by a lever which has a mechanical advantage $\dfrac{L}{l}$ (Fig. 5.5), then total mechanical advantage of machine

$$= \frac{L}{l} \times \frac{A}{a}$$

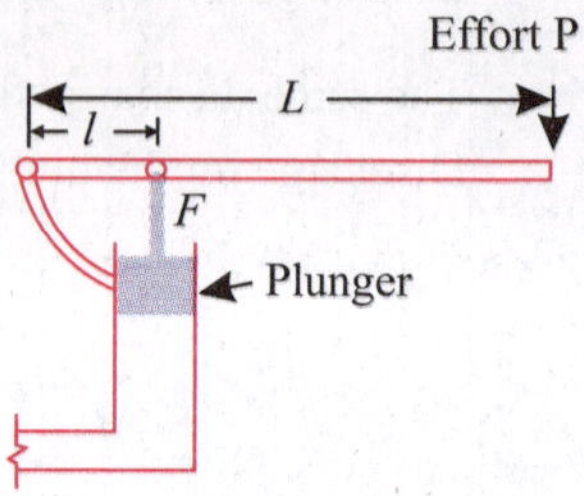

Fig. 5.5

The ratio $\dfrac{L}{l}$ is known as *leverage of press*.

Fig. 5.6 shows an '*Elementary Inverted Hydraulic Press*'.

— It consists of a cylinder (fixed) in which the ram slides. The lower end of the ram carries a movable platen which moves up and down with the ram. The upper and lower stationary platens are joined by columns.

— When liquid under high pressure is supplied to the cylinder, the ram moves downward and applies tremendous pressure (equal to the product of intensity of pressure supplied and area of the ram) upon any material placed between the movable platen and lower stationary platen.

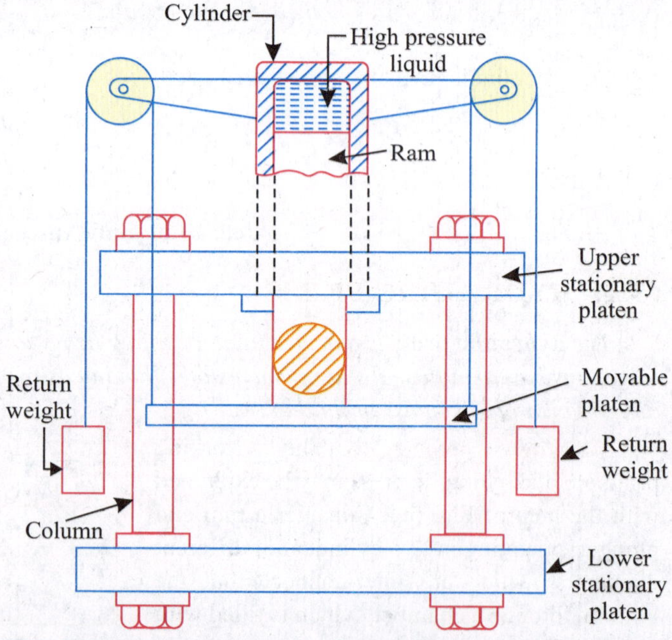

Fig. 5.6. Elementary Inverted Hydraulic Press.

For bringing the ram back in position, the liquid from the cylinder is taken out, subsequently the ram (along with movable platen) moves up by the action of return weights.

It may be noted that in some large presses it is possible to produce total thrust ranging from about 50 MN to 100 MN.

Hydraulic presses may be employed for the following jobs:

(*i*) Metal press work (to press sheet metal to any required shape).

(*ii*) Drawing and pushing rods.

(*iii*) Bending and straightening any metal piece.

(*iv*) Packing press.

(*v*) Cotton press.

(*vi*) Autoclave vulcanising press.

(*vii*) To prepare moulds and casting of bakelite (Bakelite press).

(*viii*) Forgoing press.

(*ix*) Plate press etc.

Example 5.12. *The diameters of ram and plunger of a hydraulic press are 100 mm and 12.5 mm respectively. Find the force required to be applied on the plunger to raise a load of 24 kN on the ram. If the plunger has a stroke of 200 mm, how many strokes will be required to lift the load by 500 mm. Also calculate the volume of additional liquid required. Further if the time taken to lift the load is 12 minutes, what will be power required to drive the plunger? Neglect frictional effects.*

Solution. Diameter of ram, $D = 100 \text{ mm} = 0.1 \text{ m}$.

$\therefore$ Area of ram, $A = \frac{\pi}{4} \times 0.1^2 = 0.00785 \text{ m}^2$

Diameter of plunger, $d = 12.5 \text{ mm} = 0.0125 \text{ m}$

$\therefore$ Area of plunger, $a = \frac{\pi}{4} \times 0.0125^2 = 0.0001227 \text{ m}^2$

Load to be raised, $W = 24 \text{ kN}$

Stroke of plunger $= 200 \text{ mm} = 0.2 \text{ m}$

Distance through which load is to be lifted $= 500 \text{ mm} = 0.5 \text{ m}$

Time taken to lift the load $= 12$ minutes

Force required to raise a load of 24 kN, *F*:

Since intensity of pressure is same throughout a static mass of fluid,

$$\frac{F}{a} = \frac{W}{A}, \text{ or, } \frac{F}{0.0001227} = \frac{24}{0.00785}, \text{ or, } F = \frac{24 \times 0.0001227}{0.00785} = \mathbf{0.375 \text{ kN}} \textbf{ (Ans.)}$$

Number of strokes, *n*:

Number of strokes required to lift the load by 0.5 m,

$$n = \frac{\text{Total volume of liquid to be displaced}}{\text{Volume of liquid displaced in one stroke of plunger}}$$

or,
$$n = \frac{\frac{\pi}{4} \times (0.1)^2 \times 0.5}{\frac{\pi}{4} \times (0.0125)^2 \times 0.2} = \mathbf{160} \textbf{ (Ans.)}$$

Volume of additional liquid $= \frac{\pi}{4} \times (0.1)^2 \times 0.5 = \mathbf{0.00392\ m^3}$ **(Ans.)**

Power required to drive motor, *P*:

$$\text{Work done by the press} = 24 \times 0.5 = 12 \text{ kNm (in 12 minutes)}$$

$$\text{Work done per sec.} = \frac{12}{12 \times 60} = 0.01666 \text{ kNm/s}$$

$$\therefore \quad \text{Power required, } P = 0.01666 \text{ kW or } \mathbf{16.66\ W} \text{ (Ans.)}$$

Example 5.13. *A hydraulic press has a ram of 180 mm diameter and plunger of 36 mm diameter, with stroke length of 300 mm. Weight exerted by press ram amounts to 7 kN and distance moved is 0·9 m in 15 minutes. Determine:*

(*i*) *The force applied on plunger,*

(*ii*) *The number of strokes performed by the plunger,*

(*iii*) *Work done by the press ram, and*

(*iv*) *Power required to drive the plunger.*

Solution. Diameter of ram, $D = 180 \text{ mm} = 0.18 \text{ m}$

$$\therefore \quad \text{Area of ram, } A = \frac{\pi}{4} \times 0.18^2 = 0.0254 \text{ m}^2$$

$$\text{Diameter of plunger, } d = 36 \text{ mm} = 0.036 \text{ m}$$

$$\therefore \quad \text{Area of plunger, } a = \frac{\pi}{4} \times 0.036^2 = 0.001018 \text{ m}^2$$

$$\text{Weight exerted by press ram, } W = 7 \text{ kN}$$

$$\text{Stroke length of plunger, } x = 300 \text{ mm} = 0.3 \text{ m}$$

$$\text{Distance moved by the ram, } y = 0.9 \text{ m}$$

(*i*) The force applied on plunger, *F*:

We know,

$$\frac{F}{a} = \frac{W}{A}, \text{ or, } F = \frac{a}{A} \times W = \frac{0.001018}{0.0254} \times 7 = \mathbf{0.28\ kN} \text{ (Ans.)}$$

(*ii*) The number of strokes performed by the plunger, *n* :

$$\text{Number of strokes, } n = \frac{A}{a} \times \frac{y}{x} = \frac{0.0254}{0.001018} \times \frac{0.9}{0.3} = 74.85 \simeq \mathbf{75} \text{ (Ans.)}$$

(*iii*) Work done by the press ram:

Work done by the press ram $= 7 \times 0.9 = \mathbf{6.3\ kNm}$ **(Ans.)**

(*iv*) Power required to drive the plunger, *P*:

Power required to drive the plunger = Work done by the ram per sec.

$$= \frac{6.3}{15 \times 60} \text{ kW} = 0.007 \text{ kW or } \mathbf{7\ W} \text{ (Ans.)}$$

Example 5.14. *The ram and plunger of a hydraulic press are 250 mm and 30 mm respectively, and the leverage of handle is 12 : 1. With a plunger stroke of 250 mm, the press is able to lift 180 kN through 1. 25 m in 2 minutes.*

Determine:

(i) *Force applied at the end of lever,*

(ii) *Number of strokes to be performed by the plunger in one second, and*

(iii) *Power required to drive the plunger.*

Take the packing friction of the plunger as well as the ram as 5% of the load.

Solution. Diameter of ram, $D = 250 \text{ mm} = 0.25 \text{ m}$

$\therefore$ Area of ram, $A = \frac{\pi}{4} \times 0.25^2 = 0.04908 \text{ m}^2$

Diameter of plunger, $d = 30 \text{ mm} = 0.03 \text{ m}$

$\therefore$ Area of plunger, $a = \frac{\pi}{4} \times 0.03^2 = 0.0007068 \text{ m}^2$

Leverage of handle = 12 : 1

Plunger stroke = 250 mm = 0.25 m

Load lifted, W = 180 kN

Packing friction, k = 5% of the load.

(*i*) Force applied at the end of lever, *F*′:

The effective force transmitted to create pressure on the liquid is reduced by the amount lost in overcoming friction. Also, pressure intensity in a static mass of fluid is same throughout.

$$\therefore \quad p \times a = F\left(1 - \frac{k}{100}\right), \text{ and, } W = p \times A\left(1 - \frac{k}{100}\right)$$

or, Intensity of pressure,
$$p = \frac{F\,(1 - k/100)}{a} = \frac{W}{A\,(1 - k/100)}$$

or,
$$F = \frac{Wa}{A\left(1 - \frac{k}{100}\right)^2} = \frac{180 \times 0.0007068}{0.04908 \times \left(1 - \frac{5}{100}\right)^2} = 2.87 \text{ kN}$$

Effort to be applied at the end of lever,

$$F' = \frac{F}{\text{Leverage of handle}} = \frac{2.87}{12} = \mathbf{0.239 \text{ kN}} \text{ (Ans.)}$$

(*ii*) Number of strokes per second:

$$\text{Number of strokes} = \frac{A}{a} \times \frac{\text{Distance moved by ram } (y)}{\text{Stroke length of plunger } (x)} = \frac{0.04908}{0.0007068} \times \frac{1.25}{0.25} = 348$$

$$\therefore \text{ Strokes per second} = \frac{348}{2 \times 60} \simeq \mathbf{3} \text{ (Ans.)}$$

(*iii*) Power required to drive the plunger, *P*:

Work done at plunger $= 2.87 \times 0.25 \times 349 = 248.69$ kNm (in 2 minutes)

$$\text{Work done per second} = \frac{249.69}{2 \times 60} = 2.08 \text{ kNm/s}$$

$\therefore$ *Power required, P* = **2.08 kW (Ans.)**

5.5. HYDRAULIC CRANE

Hydraulic crane *is a device which is used for lifting heavy loads (upto 25 MN)*. It is widely used in docks for loading and unloading ships, warehouses, foundary workshops and heavy industries.

Construction. A hydraulic crane (Fig. 5.7) consists of a **crane** and a hydraulic **jigger**. The crane has a central mast from which a *tie* and a *jib* are fixed. The mast is fixed on a pedestal which can revolve. The load can be lifted and moved around the crane area depending upon the length of the jib. The load is suspended by a wire rope which passes over a pulley at the end of the jib and over the tie-rod to the hydraulic jigger. The hydraulic jigger consists of a cylinder and a ram at the end of which pulleys are attached. The pulleys enable to increase the velocity ratio between the wire rope and the ram (A four sheave pulley block system will have a velocity ratio 4 : 1, thus the load suspended at one end of the wire rope will move with 4 times the speed of the ram).

Working. When the load is to be *lifted* by the crane, liquid under pressure is admitted to the cylinder of the jigger; the liquid forces the sliding ram to move vertically up. Due to the movement of the ram in the vertically upward direction, the movable pulley block (attached to the ram) also moves upward. The *distance* between the two pulley blocks *increases*, the wire or rope is pulled and the load is lifted up. *Lowering* of the load is achieved by removing the liquid from the cylinder by Jigger through the outlet valve. As the liquid leaves the cylinder, the distance between the two sets of pulleys *decreases* which results in releasing more length of the wire rope and the load gets lowered.

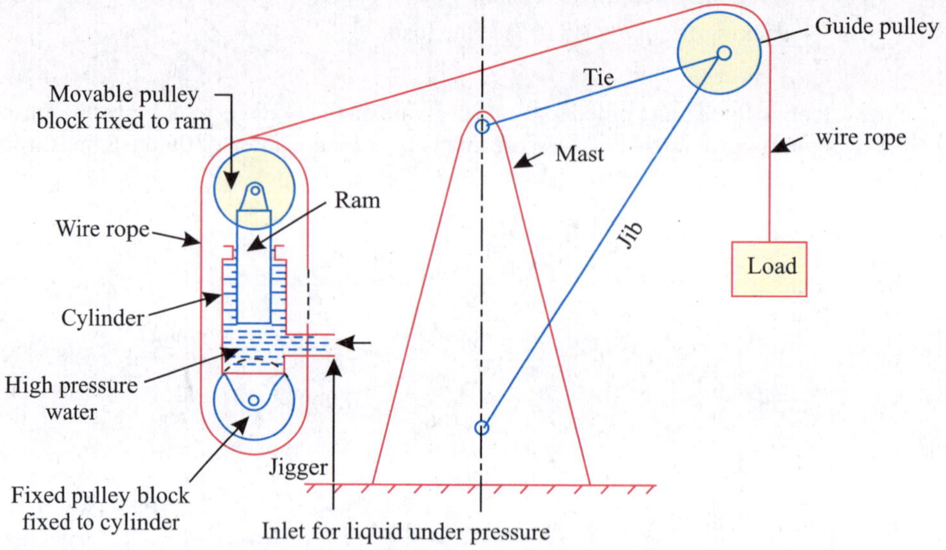

Fig. 5.7. Hydraulic crane.

The lifting speed of a modern hydraulic crane may be about 75 m per minute. However, hydraulic cranes have been replaced by the electric cranes these days.

Example 5.15. *A hydraulic crane ram has a diameter of 150 mm and the ratio between the movement of the load and the ram is 6 to 1. Water is supplied through a 40 mm diameter pipe having a length of 500 m, the pressure at the inlet end of the pipe being 7550 kN/m^2. The co-efficient of friction for the pipe is 0·01. A pressure of 440 kN/m^2 on the ram is required to overcome the mechanical losses. Determine:*

(*i*) *The maximum speed with which a load of 11 kN can be lifted, and*

(*ii*) *The load and speed of lifting which correspond to the maximum power obtained from the crane.*

Solution. Diameter of ram, D = 150 mm = 0.15 m.

The ratio between the movement of the load and the ram = 6 : 1

Diameter of pipe, d = 40 mm = 0.04 m

Length of pipe, l = 500 m

Pressure at inlet end of pipe = 7550 kN/m^2

The co-efficient of friction for the pipe, f = 0.01

Pressure required on the ram to overcome mechanical losses = 440 kN/m^2

Load to be lifted, W = 11 kN

(i) The maximum speed with which a load of 11 kN can be lifted:

$$\text{Pressure head at inlet end of pipe} = \frac{7550}{9.81} = 769.6 \text{ m} \qquad (\because w = 9.81 \text{ kN/m}^3)$$

$$\text{Pressure head required to overcome mechanical losses} = \frac{440}{9.81} = 44.8 \text{ m}$$

$$\text{Frictional loss in pipe} = \frac{4 f l V^2}{d \times 2g} = \frac{4 \times 0.01 \times 500 \times V^2}{0.04 \times 2 \times 9.81} = 25.48 V^2$$

(where, V = velocity of water in pipe)

$$\therefore \quad \text{Pressure head on the ram} = (769.6 - 44.8 - 25.48V^2) \text{ m}$$

$$\text{Pressure head required on the ram} = \frac{11 \times 6}{\frac{\pi}{4} \times 0.15^2 \times 9.81} = 380.7 \text{ m}$$

$$\therefore \quad 769.6 - 44.8 - 25.48V^2 = 380.7, \text{ or, } V^2 = \frac{769.6 - 44.8 - 380.7}{25.48} = 13.5$$

$$\therefore \quad V = 3.67 \text{ m/s}$$

$$\text{Velocity of pipe} \times \text{area} = \text{Velocity of ram} \times \text{ram area}$$

$$3.67 \times \frac{\pi}{4} \times 0.04^2 = \text{Velocity of ram} \times \frac{\pi}{4} \times 0.15^2$$

$$\text{or,} \quad \text{Velocity of ram} = 3.67 \times \left(\frac{0.04}{0.15}\right)^2 = 0.26 \text{ m/s}$$

$\therefore$ The maximum speed of the load = 0.26 × 6 = **1.56 m/s (Ans.)**

(ii) The load and speed of lifting:

For maximum transmission of power, the pressure losses in the pipeline should be $\frac{1}{3}$rd of the available head. Therefore,

$$25.48 V^2 = \frac{1}{3} \times 769.6, \text{ or, } V = \left(\frac{769.6}{3 \times 25.48}\right)^{1/2} = 3.17 \text{ m/s}$$

$$\text{Speed of lifting the head} = 3.17 \times \left(\frac{0.04}{0.15}\right)^2 \times 6 = \mathbf{1.35 \text{ m/s}} \textbf{ (Ans.)}$$

$$\text{Available head at the ram} = \left(769.6 - 44.8 - \frac{769.6}{3}\right) = 468.3 \text{ m}$$

$$= 9.81 \times 468.3 \text{ kN/m}^2 = 4594 \text{ kN/m}^2$$

$$\therefore \quad \text{The load that can be lifted} = \frac{4594}{6} \times \left(\frac{\pi}{4} \times 0.15^2\right) = \mathbf{13.53 \text{ kN}} \textbf{ (Ans.)}$$

Example 5.16. *In an installation of six hydraulic cranes, the working cycle of each of which takes 90 seconds in hoisting and lowering, each crane is fed with water at a pressure of 4900 kN/m² and is required to lift a load of 50 kN at a speed of 18 m/min, through a total height of 12 m, the jigger system giving a velocity ratio of 6. Estimate the diameter and stroke of the rams assuming an efficiency of 60 percent.*

It is assumed that all six cranes are making the working stroke at the same time. Calculate the minimum capacity of the pump feeding the installation and that of the accumulator.

[Anna University]

Solution. Number of hydraulic cranes = 6

Time taken by working cycle of each of the six cranes, t = 90 s

Pressure of water fed to each crane, p = 4900 kN/m²

Load to be lifted, W = 50 kN

Speed with which load is lifted, V = 18 m/min

Total height through which load is lifted, H = 12 m

Velocity ratio = 6

Efficiency of each ram, η = 60%

Diameter (D) and stroke of each ram (L):

Load on each ram × velocity of ram × η = Load lifted × velocity of lifting the load

$$\therefore \quad \text{Load on each ram} = \frac{W \times \text{velocity ratio}}{\eta} = \frac{50 \times 6}{0.6} = 500 \text{ kN}$$

$$\text{Area of arm} = \frac{\text{Load on ram}}{\text{Pressure } (p)} = \frac{500}{4900} = 0.102 \text{ m}^2$$

$$\therefore \quad \frac{\pi}{4} \times D^2 = 0.102, \text{ or, } D = \left(\frac{0.102 \times 4}{\pi}\right)^{1/2} = 0.36 \text{ m} = \mathbf{360 \text{ mm}} \textbf{ (Ans.)}$$

$$\text{Stroke of ram, } L = \frac{\text{Distance } (H)}{\text{Velocity ratio}} = \frac{12}{6} = \mathbf{2 \text{ m}} \textbf{ (Ans.)}$$

Minimum capacity of the pump:

$$\text{Volume swept by ram} = \text{Area of ram} \times \text{stroke} = 0.102 \times 2 = 0.204 \text{ m}^3$$

Since there are 6 cranes, volume of water supplied by the pump = 0.204 × 6 = 1.224 m³

$$\textit{Minimum capacity of the pump} = \frac{\text{Volume of water}}{\text{Time taken}} = \frac{1.224}{90} = \mathbf{0.0136 \text{ m}^3/\text{s}} \textbf{ (Ans.)}$$

Capacity of accumulator:

$$\text{Operating time of cranes} = \frac{H}{V} = \frac{12}{18} \times 60 = 40 \text{ s}$$

$$\therefore \quad \text{Idle time of crane} = 90 - 40 = 50 \text{ s}$$

But the accumulator is continuously fed by the pumps,

∴ Accumulator volume

$$= 0.0136 \times 50 = \mathbf{0.68 \text{ m}^3} \textbf{ (Ans.)}$$

$$\text{Accumulator capacity} = p \times \text{volume} = 4900 \times 0.68 = \mathbf{3332 \text{ kNm}} \textbf{ (Ans.)}$$

5.6. HYDRAULIC LIFT

Hydraulic lift *is a device used for carrying persons and loads from one floor to another, in a multi-storeyed building*. The hydraulic lifts are of the following two types:

1. Direct acting hydraulic lift, and
2. Suspended hydraulic lift.

1. Direct acting hydraulic lift. Refer to Fig. 5.8. It consists of a ram sliding in a cylinder. A platform or a cage is fitted to the top end of ram on which goods may be placed or the persons may stand. As the liquid under pressure is admitted to the cylinder, the ram moves up and the cage is lifted. The lift of the cage is equal to the stroke of the ram. The cage moves in the downward direction when the liquid from the fixed cylinder is removed.

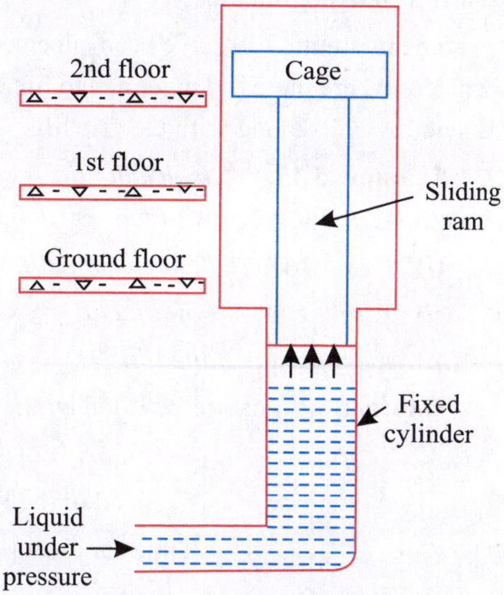

Fig. 5. 8 Direct acting hydraulic lift.

2. Suspended hydraulic lift. Refer to Fig. 5.9.

The suspended hydraulic lift is a modified form of the direct acting hydraulic lift. It is fitted with a *jigger* which is exactly same as in the case of a hydraulic crane (For the construction and operation of jigger, refer to Art. 5.5). The cage is suspended by ropes. It runs between guides of hard wood or round steel. In order to balance the weight of the cage, sliding balance weights are provided.

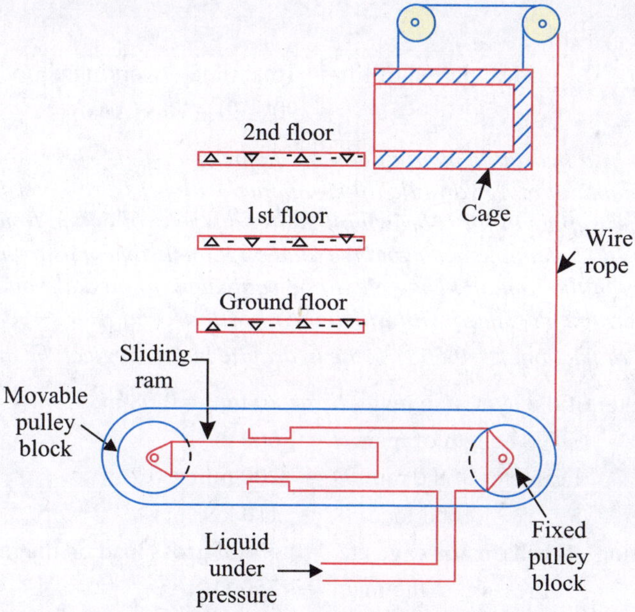

Fig. 5.9. Suspended hydraulic lift.

Modern lifts are of suspended type and have a *high velocity ratio;* the lifting speeds range from 100 to 120 m per minute.

The hydraulic lifts have been superseded by electric lifts. However hydraulic lifts are preferred in places where there is danger due to fire or explosions. The hydraulic lifts are also usually provided as standby units along with electric lifts.

Example 5.17. *A hydraulic lift is required to lift a load of 60 kN through a height of 12 m, once in every 90 seconds. If the speed of the lift is 0.6 m/s, determine:*

(i) Power required to drive the lift,

(ii) Working period of lift, and

(iii) Ideal period of the lift.

Solution. Load to be lifted by the lift, $W = 60$ kN

Height, $H = 12$ m

Speed of the lift, $V_{lift} = 0.6$ m/s

Time for one operation $= 90$ s.

(i) Power required to drive the lift, *P*:

Work done in lifting the load in 90 s $= W \times H = 60 \times 12 = 720$ kNm

$$\therefore \quad \text{Work done/sec.} = \frac{720}{90} = 8 \text{ kNm/s}$$

$\therefore$ Power required to drive the lift, $P =$ **8 kW (Ans.)**

(ii) Working period of lift:

$$\textit{Working period of lift} = \frac{\text{Height of lift } (H)}{\text{Velocity of lift } (V_{\text{lift}})} = \frac{12}{0.6} = \mathbf{20\ s.}$$

(iii) Ideal period of lift:

Ideal period of lift = Total time – working period of lift

$= 90 - 20 =$ **70 s (Ans.)**

Example 5.18. *In a hydraulic main of 80 mm diameter a steady pressure of 7500 kN/m^2 is maintained by an accumulator. A hydraulic lift is supplied with pressure water from the main, and the point at which the supply to lift is drawn off is at a distance of 640 m from the accumulator. The ram of the lift is 200 mm in diameter and the load on it, inclusive of its own weight, is 110 kN. Assuming the friction of the ram and cage etc. to be equivalent to an addition of 5% of the gross load on the ram, determine the speed with which the lift will ascend.*

Take co-efficient of friction, f = 0.008 for the hydraulic main. Neglect the minor losses.

Solution. Diameter of the hydraulic main, d = 80 mm = 0.08 m

Length of main, l = 640 m

Diameter of the ram, D = 200 mm = 0.2 m

Total load, W = 110 kN

Friction of the ram and cage etc. = 5% of gross load on the ram

Pressure in the main = 7500 kN/m^2

Co-efficient of friction for the main, f = 0.008.

Speed with which the lift will ascend, V_{lift}:

Let, V = Velocity of water in hydraulic main.

$$\text{Loss of head due to friction, } h_f = \frac{4flV^2}{d \times 2g} = \frac{4 \times 0.008 \times 640 \times V^2}{0.08 \times 2 \times 9.81} = 13.05V^2$$

Corresponding pressure intensity, $p = wh_f = 9.81 \times 13.05V^2 = 128V^2 \text{ kN/m}^2$

($\because w = 9{\cdot}81 \text{ kN/m}^3$)

$\therefore$ Pressure intensity at the lift $= (7500 - 128V^2) \text{ kN/m}^2$

Force on the ram of hydraulic lift $= (7500 - 128V^2) \times \frac{\pi}{4} \times 0.2^2$ kN

This force equals the load to be lifted during the upward motion of the lift which is

$$= \left(110 + \frac{5}{100} \times 110\right) = 115.5 \text{ kN}$$

$$\therefore \quad (7500 - 128V^2) \times \frac{\pi}{4} \times 0.2^2 = 115.5, \text{ or, } 7500 - 128V^2 = \frac{115.5 \times 4}{\pi \times 0.02^2} = 3676.48$$

or
$$V = \left(\frac{7500 - 3676.48}{128}\right)^{1/2} = 5.46 \text{ m/s}$$

$$\text{Discharge through the pipeline} = \frac{\pi}{4} \times 0.08^2 \times 5.46 = 0.02744 \text{ m}^3/\text{s}$$

Since the same discharge flows to the ram of hydraulic lift, therefore, the velocity of lift,

$$V_{lift} = \frac{0.02744}{\frac{\pi}{4} \times D^2} = \frac{0.02744}{\frac{\pi}{4} \times 0.2^2} = \mathbf{0.873 \text{ m/s}} \text{ (Ans.)}$$

Example 5.19. *A load of 120 kN is required to be lifted by a hydraulic lift through a height of 16 metres once in every 2 minutes. The lift travels up at the rate of 1.25 m /s. During working stroke of the lift, the water is supplied to it from the accumulator and the pump at a pressure intensity of 3200 kN/m². If the efficiency of the pump is 82% and that of the lift is 77% determine:*

(i) Power required to the drive the pump, and

(ii) Minimum capacity of the accumulator.

Neglect friction losses in the pipe.

Solution. Load to be lifted, W = 120 kN

Height, H = 16 m

Speed of weight, V = 1.25 m/s

Pressure intensity of water, $p = 3200 \text{ kN/m}^2$

Efficiency of the pump, η_{pump} = 82%

Efficiency of the lift, η_{lift} = 77%.

(i) Power required to drive the pump, P_{pump}:

Work done by water in raising the lift = Load lifted × distance moved per sec.

$= W \times V = 120 \times 1.25 = 150$ kNm/s

Power used at the lift = 150 kW

$$\text{Power supplied to the lift} = \frac{150}{0.77} = 194.8 \text{ kW}$$

This power has been supplied to the lift by water supplied from the pump and accumulator.

$$\text{Working period of the lift} = \frac{H}{V} = \frac{16}{1.25} = 12.8 \text{ s}$$

$$\text{Ideal period of lift} = \text{Total time} - \text{working period of lift}$$

$$= (2 \times 60) - 12.8 = 107.2 \text{ s}$$

During idle period the energy will be stored in the accumulator and during the working period the energy will be supplied to the lift from the accumulator.

Let P_{pump} be the *output of pump in kW*, then,

Energy stored in accumulator during the idle period

$$= P'_{pump} \times 107.2 \text{ kJ} \quad ...(i)$$

The above energy is supplied to the lift during the working period of 12·8 s.

$$\text{Energy supplied by the accumulator per sec.} = \frac{P'_{pump} \times 107.2}{12.8} = 8.37\, P'_{pump} \text{ kJ/s}$$

Power supplied by the accumulator = $8.37\, P'_{pump}$ kW

∴ Total power supplied by the pump and accumulator

$$= P'_{pump} + 8.37\, P'_{pump} = 9.37\, P'_{pump}$$

But power supplied to the lift = 194.8 kW

$$\therefore \quad 9.37\, P'_{pump} = 194.8, \text{ or, } P'_{pump} = \frac{194.8}{9.37} = 20.79 \text{ kW}$$

$$\therefore \text{ Power required to drive the pump, } P_{pump} = \frac{P'_{pump} \text{ (output of pump)}}{\eta'_{pump} \text{ (efficiency of pump)}}$$

$$= \frac{20.79}{0.82} = \mathbf{25.35 \text{ kW}} \text{ (Ans.)}$$

(*ii*) Minimum capacity of accumulator:

From expression (*i*), the energy stored in accumulator during the idle period

$$= P'_{pump} \times 107.2 = 20.79 \times 107.2 = 2228.69 \text{ kNm}$$

Also, the energy stored in the accumulator = p × volume of cylinder of the accumulator

∴ p × volume of cylinder of the accumulator = 2228.69

$$\therefore \text{ Volume (capacity) of the accumulator} = \frac{2228.69}{3200} = \mathbf{0.6965 \text{ m}^3} \text{ (Ans.)}$$

5.7. HYDRAULIC RAM

Hydraulic ram *is device with which small quantities of water can be pumped to higher levels from the available large quantity of water of low head.* It works on the *principle of water hammer.*

Construction. Fig. 5.10 shows the hydraulic ram. It consists of a valve box wherein low head water flows. The box contains a waste valve V_1 which opens inwards, and a delivery valve V_2, which opens outwards. Both the valves V_1 and V_2 are *non-return valves* that allow the flow only in one direction. Valve V_2 communicates with an air vessel which is connected to the delivery tank through a delivery pipe as shown in the Fig. 5.10.

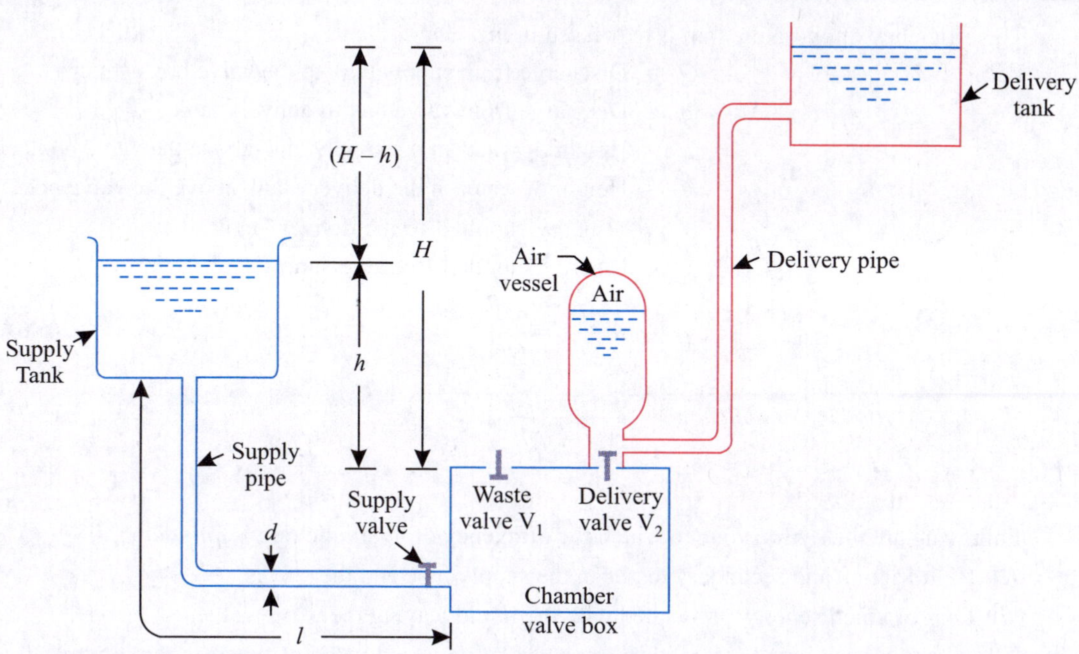

Fig. 5.10. Hydraulic ram.

Working. It works on the principle of '*water hammer*'. *When a flowing liquid is suddenly brought to rest, the change in momentum of liquid mass causes a sudden rise in pressure. This rise in pressure is utilised to raise a portion of the liquid to higher levels.*

— Initially the water flows down the supply pipe, the valve V_1 is open and water escapes through it to waste.

— As the velocity of flow in the supply pipe increases, dynamic pressure on the underside of valve V_1 becomes amply high so as to lift the valve V_1 and ultimately close it.

— Due to quick closure of valve V_1 water in the supply pipe is suddenly brought to rest and consequently pressure in the valve box increases.

— The increased high pressure lifts the valve V_2 and a part of water enters the air vessel. Subsequently air pressure inside the air vessel increases and that forces water to delivery tank through the delivery pipe.

As soon as momentum of water gets destroyed in the valve box, valve V_2 closes and the valve V_1 opens (the pressure in the valve box falls below the atmospheric pressure momentarily); the flow of water from supply tank recommences and the cycle is repeated. *The air vessel provides storage and helps to regulate the flow at the delivery end.*

Efficiency. The *efficiency* of a hydraulic ram depends upon the following:

(*i*) Losses in the pipe, (*ii*) losses in the valve box, and (*iii*) ratios $\frac{l}{h}$ and $\frac{h}{H}$.

From experiments it has been observed that, for *optimum performance*, values of $\frac{l}{H}$ and $\frac{h}{H}$ should be about 2.5 and 5 respectively. It is possible to obtain efficiencies as high as 75% *under these conditions*.

The performance of the hydraulic ram is influenced by the number of beats (openings of waste valve) which can be varied by varying the length of the travel of valve and weight of valve.

The efficiency of hydraulic ram is expressed in *two ways*:

Let, Q = Discharge from supply tank to the valve box,

q = Discharge from valve box to delivery tank,

h = Height of water in the supply tank above the valve box,

H = Height of water in the delivery tank above the valve box,

Then, *D' Aubuisson's efficiency* $= \dfrac{\text{Energy supplied to the delivery tank}}{\text{Energy supplied from the supply tank}}$

$$= \frac{wqH}{wQh} = \frac{qH}{Qh} \qquad ...(5.6)$$

Rankine's efficiency $= \dfrac{q\,(H - h)}{(Q - q)h}$ ...(5·7)

Reasons for low efficiency of hydraulic ram:

Following are the *reasons* due to which the efficiency of hydraulic ram is *quite low*:

(*i*) High friction and secondary losses in the supply pipe and the valves.

(*ii*) Loss of kinetic energy associated with the liquid leaving the waste valve.

All the above mentioned *losses vary as square of the mean velocity*, whereas *the input varies directly as the mean velocity*.

The efficiency of the ram can be improved by reducing the mean velocity. It can be accomplished by *reducing the lift of the waste valve* (this limits the maximum velocity in the supply pipe and hence the mean velocity of flow):

Working cycle of a hydraulic ram:

Let, V_{wv} = Velocity of liquid passing through waste valve just before its closure, (*wv* stands for waste valve)

d_{wv} = Diameter of waste valve,

b_{wv} = Lift of the waste valve,

W_{wv} = Weight of the waste valve,

h_{wv} = Dynamic pressure head acting on the waste valve,

d = Diameter of supply pipe,

V_{max} = Maximum velocity in the supply pipe just before the closure of the waste valve

l_s = Length of supply pipe,

t_1 = Time during which the velocity in the supply pipe builds up from zero to V_{max}, and

t_2 = Time during which the waste valve remains closed, *i.e.* the time during which delivery valve remains open in one beat (*i.e.* one complete cycle).

The dynamic pressure head, $h_{wv} = \dfrac{p_{wv}}{w} = \dfrac{V_{wv}^2}{2g}$ ...(5.8)

Also, $W_{wv} = \left(\dfrac{\pi}{4} \times d_{wv}^2\right) p_{wv}$, or, $h_{wv} = \dfrac{p_{wv}}{w} = \dfrac{4W_{wv}}{w\pi d_{wv}^2}$ ...(5.9)

Invoking continuity equation, we have:

$$(\pi \times d_{wv} \times b_{wv})V_{wv} = \frac{\pi}{4} \times d^2 \times V_{max} \quad ...(5.10)$$

The time t_1 during which the velocity in the supply pipe builds up from zero to V_{max} is also equal to the time during which the waste valve remains open in one *beat* for gradual closure of valve in rigid pipe, the rise in pressure is given by,

$$h = \frac{l_s V_{max}}{g\, t_1}, \text{ or, } t_1 = \frac{l_s V_{max}}{hg} \quad ...(5.11)$$

From water hammer equation, we have:

$$(H - h) = \frac{l_s \times V_{max}}{g \times t_2}, \text{ or, } t_2 = \frac{l_s V_{max}}{(H - h)\, g} \quad ...(5.12)$$

∴ Total time for one cycle is given by,

$$t = t_1 + t_2 = \frac{l_s V_{max}}{h\, g} + \frac{l_s V_{max}}{(H - h)\, g} = \frac{l_s V_{max}}{g}\left(\frac{1}{h} + \frac{1}{H - h}\right) \quad ...(5.13)$$

The number of beats per minute N, is equal to $(60/t)$ where, t is the time for one beat in seconds.

Let, q = Rate of discharge of water actually lifted by the ram, and

Q_{wv} = Rate of discharge of water flowing past the waste valve, then,

$$q = \left(\frac{\pi}{4} d^2\right)\left(\frac{V_{max}}{2}\right)\frac{t_2}{t} \quad ...(5.14)$$

$$Q_{wv} = \left(\frac{\pi}{4} d^2\right)\left(\frac{V_{max}}{2}\right)\frac{t_1}{t} \quad ...(5.15)$$

Fig. 5.11 shows the working cycle of hydraulic ram graphically. In Fig. 5.11 (*a*) is shown the velocity in supply pipe plotted against time, whereas Fig. 5.11 (*b*) shows the pressure head in the valve box plotted against time.

Eqns. 5.11 and 5.12 have been derived on the assumption that the loss of head due to friction is negligible. However, if loss of head due to friction in supply pipe (h_{fs}) and that in delivery pipe (h_{fd}) are taken into account, then eqns. 5.11 and 5.12 are modified as follows:

$$(h - h_{fs}) = \frac{l_s}{g} \times \frac{V_{max}}{t_1} \quad ...(5.16)$$

$$[(H - f) + h_{fd}] = \frac{l_s}{g} \times \frac{V_{max}}{t_2} \quad ....(5.17)$$

Eqn. 5.13, then, becomes:

$$t = t_1 + t_2$$

$$= \frac{l_s V_{max}}{g}\left[\frac{1}{(h - h_{fs})} + \frac{1}{\{(H - h) + h_{fd}\}}\right] \quad ...(5.18)$$

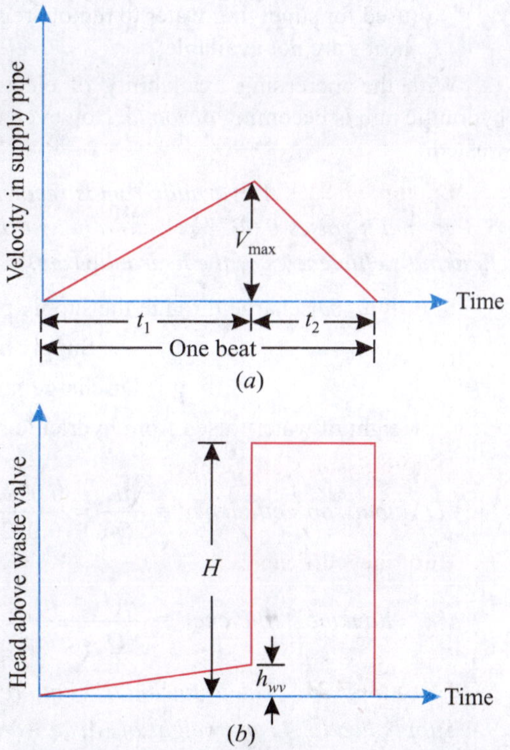

Fig. 5.11. Graphical representation of a working cycle of hydraulic ram.

Performance of hydraulic ram:

In Fig. 5.12 are shown the characteristic curves of hydraulic ram working under conditions of *constant waste-valve lift, constant supply head and varying delivery head.*

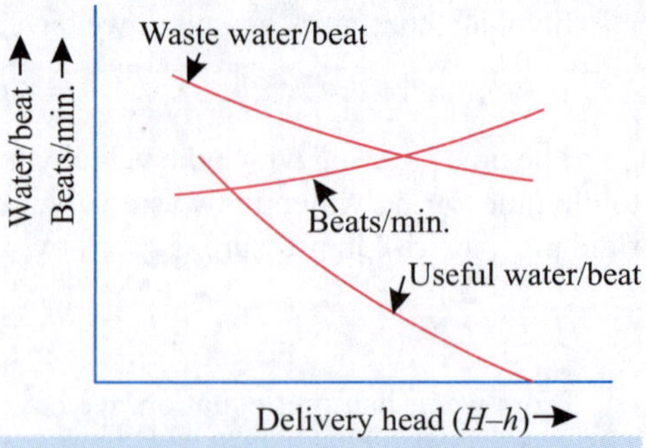

Fig. 5.12. Characteristic curves of hydraulic ram.

— With the *increase of delivery head the number of beats increases*. This is owing to the fact that as the delivery head is increased, more rapid retardation is impressed on the liquid column in the supply pipe, as a consequences of which the time taken per beat decreases and hence the number of beats per minute increases.

— Keeping the input unaltered, as *the head increases the quantity of useful water per beat decreases. With increase in head the waste water per beat decreases slightly.*

Characteristic features of hydraulic ram:

The characteristic features of hydraulic ram are as follows:

1. It works automatically and requires very little maintenance.
2. It does not need any external energy to pump water, but it works at the cost of large quantity of water.
3. Negligible running cost.
4. Due to absence of moving parts, frequent oiling is not required.
5. It is particularly suitable for pumping water from a rivulet for irrigation purposes. It can be used for supplying water to remote regions where other means of pumping water to higher heads are not available.

With the increasing availability of electric power to drive pumps even at remote places, hydraulic ram is becoming *obsolete*. However, it is used in those place where plenty of water can be wasted.

Example 5.21. *A hydraulic ram is receiving water at the rate of 0.022 m^3/s from a height of 3.3 m, and it raises 0.0022 m^3/s to a height of 5 m from the ram. Determine D'Aubuisson's and Rankine's efficiencies of the hydraulic ram.*

Solution. Discharge through the supply pipe, $Q = 0.022 \text{ m}^3/\text{s}$

Supply head, $h = 3.3$ m

Discharge raised, $q = 0.0022 \text{ m}^3/\text{s}$

Height of water raised from hydraulic ram, $H = 5$ m

D'Aubuisson's efficiency:

$$\text{D'Aubuisson's efficiency} = \frac{qH}{Qh} = \frac{0.0022 \times 21}{0.022 \times 3.3} = 0.6364 \text{ or } \mathbf{63.64\%} \text{ (Ans.)}$$

Rankine's efficiency:

$$\text{Rankine's efficiency} = \frac{q(H-h)}{(Q-q)h} = \frac{0.0022\,(21-3.3)}{(0.022-0.0022)\times 3.3} = \mathbf{0.596} \text{ or } \mathbf{59.6\%} \text{ (Ans.)}$$

Example 5.21. *The following test data refer to the hydraulic ram:*

Supply head 2.42 m; weight of waste water per minute 180 N; weight of water pumped per minute 5.4 N; and net head from the ram 44 m. Calculate D'Aubuisson's and Rankine's efficiencies.

Solution. Supply head, h = 2.42 m

Weight of waste water per minute = 180 N

Weight of water pumped per minute, W' = 5.4 N

∴ Total weight of water flowing per minute into the valve box,

$$W = 180 + 5.4 = 185.4 \text{ N}$$

Net head pumped from ram, H = 44 m

D'Aubuisson's efficiency:

$$\text{D'Aubuisson's efficiency} = \frac{qH}{Qh} = \frac{wqH}{wQh} = \frac{W'H}{Wh} = \frac{5.4 \times 44}{185.4 \times 2.42} = 0.529 \text{ or } \mathbf{52.9\%} \text{ (Ans.)}$$

[where, W' (= wq) = weight of water pumped per minute, w being weight density of water.]

$$\textit{Rankine's efficiency} = \frac{q(H-h)}{(Q-q)h} = \frac{wq\,(H-h)}{w\,(Q-q)h} = \frac{W'(H-h)}{(W-W')h}$$

$$= \frac{5.4\,(44-2.42)}{(185.4-5.4) \times 2.42} = 0.515 \text{ or } \mathbf{51.5\%} \text{ (Ans.)}$$

Example 5.22. *A hydraulic ram is being supplied water at the rate of 0.05 m^3/s from a height of 5 m, and it raises 0.005 m^3/s to a height of 35 m from the ram. The length and diameter of the pipe are 120 m and 70 mm respectively. If the co-efficient of friction is 0.009, calculate D'Aubuisson's and Rankine's efficiencies.*

Solution. Discharge through the supply pipe, Q = 0.05 m^3/s

Supply head, h = 5 m

Discharge raised, q = 0.005 m^3/s

Height of water raised from hydraulic ram, H = 35 m

Length of the pipe, l = 120 m

Diameter of the pipe, d = 75 mm = 0.075 m

Co-efficient of friction, f = 0.009.

Efficiency of the ram:

Head lost due to friction in the delivery pipe,

$$h_f = \frac{4flV^2}{d \times 2g} = \frac{4 \times 0.009 \times 120 \times V^2}{0.075 \times 2 \times 9.81}$$

But, V = Velocity of water in delivery pipe $= \dfrac{q}{\frac{\pi}{4}d^2} = \dfrac{0.005}{\frac{\pi}{4} \times 0.075^2} = 1.13$ m/s

$$\therefore \quad h_f = \frac{4 \times 0.009 \times 120 \times 1.13^2}{0.075 \times 2 \times 9.81} = 3.75 \text{ m}$$

∴ Effective head developed by the ram, $H_e = H + h_f = 35 + 3.75 = 38.75$ m

$$\textit{D'Aubuisson's efficiency} = \frac{q \times H_e}{Q \times h} = \frac{0.005 \times 38.75}{0.05 \times 5} = 0.775 \text{ or } \mathbf{77.5\%} \text{ (Ans.)}$$

$$\textit{Rankine's efficiency} = \frac{q\,(H_e - h)}{(Q-q)\,h} = \frac{0.005\,(38.75-5)}{(0.05-0.005) \times 5} = 0.75 \text{ or } \mathbf{75\%} \text{ (Ans.)}$$

Example 5.23. *Water is supplied to hydraulic ram from a height of 1.5 m by a pipe 75 mm in diameter and 12 m long. The waste valve, which is 125 mm in diameter and of weight 15 N, lifts through 6.5 mm. Determine:*

(*i*) *The number of beats per minute, and*

(*ii*) *The quantity of water delivered per minute to a tank 10 m above the waste valve.*

Solution. Supply head, h = 1.5 m

Diameter of the supply pipe, d_s = 75 mm = 0.075 m

Length of the supply pipe, l_s = 12 m

Diameter of waste valve, d_{wv} = 125 mm = 0.125 m

Weight of the waste valve, W_{wv} = 15 N

Lift of the waste valve, b_{wv} = 6.5 mm = 0.0065 m

Delivery head above the waste valve, H = 10 m

(*i*) Number of beats per minute:

The dynamic pressure head, $$h_{wv} = \frac{4W_{wv}}{w\pi d_{wv}^2} \quad \text{...[Eqn. (5.9)]}$$

$$= \frac{4 \times 15}{9810 \times \pi \times 0.125^2} = 0.1246 \text{ m of water}$$

Maximum velocity past waste valve just before closure,

$$V_{wv} = \sqrt{2gh_{wv}} = \sqrt{2 \times 9.81 \times 0.1246} = 1.56 \text{ m/s}$$

If V_{max} is the maximum velocity in the supply pipe, then from continuity consideration, we have:

$$(\pi \times d_{wv} \times b_{wv})\, V_{wv} = \left(\frac{\pi}{4} d_s^2\right) V_{max} \quad \text{...[Eqn. (5.10)]}$$

or, $$(\pi \times 0.125 \times 0.0065) \times 1.56 = \left(\frac{\pi}{4} \times 1.075^2\right) \times V_{max}$$

or, $$V_{max} = \frac{(\pi \times 0.125 \times 0.0065) \times 1.56}{\left(\frac{\pi}{4} \times 0.075^2\right)} = 0.9 \text{ m/s}$$

Let, t_1 = The time during which the velocity in the supply pipe builds up from zero to V_{max}, or, the time during which the waste valve remains *open* in one beat, and

t_2 = The time during which the waste valve remains *closed* or the time during which the delivery valve remains open in one beat and $(H - h)$ is the level of water in the delivery tank above that in the supply tank.

Then, $$t_1 = \frac{l_s \times V_{max}}{h \times g} = \frac{12 \times 0.9}{1.5 \times 9.81} = 0.734 \text{ s} \quad \text{...[Eqn (5.11)]}$$

and, $$t_2 = \frac{l_s \times V_{max}}{(H - h)\, g} = \frac{12 \times 0.9}{(10 - 1.5) \times 9.81} = 0.129 \text{ s}$$

∴ Total time for one cycle (one beat),

$$t = t_1 + t_2 = 0{\cdot}734 + 0{\cdot}129 = 0{\cdot}863 \text{ s}$$

Number of beats per minute $= \dfrac{60}{0.863} \simeq$ **69 (Ans.)**

(*ii*) **The quantity of water delivered per second to delivery tank:**

Discharge delivered to tank per second,

$$q = \left(\frac{\pi}{4} d_s^2\right) \times \frac{V_{max}}{2} \times \frac{t_2}{t} = \left(\frac{\pi}{4} \times 0.075^2\right) \times \frac{0.9}{2} \times \frac{0.129}{0.863}$$

$$= 0.000297 \text{ m}^3/\text{s}$$

$$= 0.000297 \times 60 \text{ m}^3/\text{min}$$

$$= \mathbf{0.01782 \text{ m}^3/\text{min.}} \text{ (Ans.)}$$

5.8. HYDRAULIC COUPLING

Hydraulic (or fluid) coupling *is a device which is employed for transmission of power from one shaft to another through a liquid medium.* It has no mechanical connection or face to face contact. *The magnitudes of input and output torques are equal.*

Construction. Refer to Fig. 5.13. It consists of the following two *rotating elements:*

(*i*) *Pump impeller.* It is attached to a driving shaft of the prime mover which may be an I. C. engine, a steam engine or an electric motor.

(*ii*) *Turbine runner.* It is attached to a driven shaft.

Both the above units are enclosed in a single housing filled with a liquid, usually oil, because of its lubricating power, availability and stability. This oil serves to transmit torque from the pump impeller to the turbine runner. There is no direct contact between the driving and driven parts.

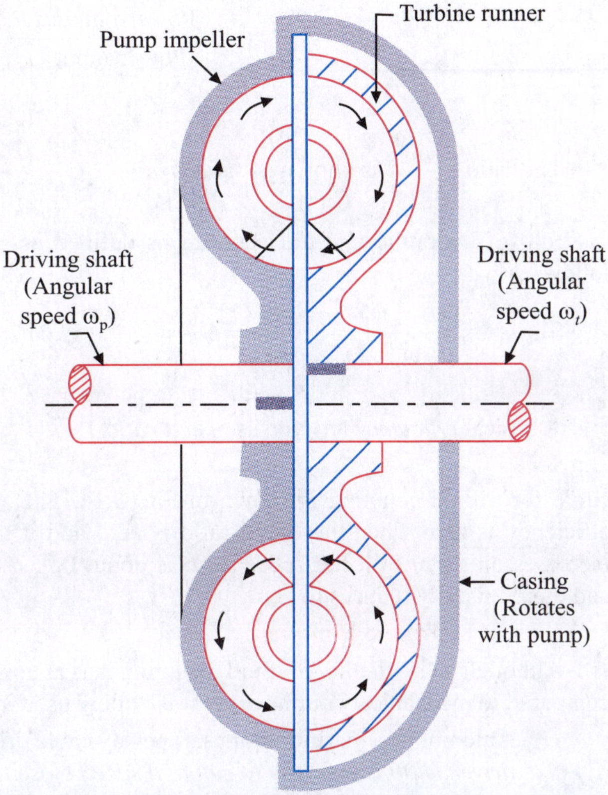

Fig. 5.13. Hydraulic coupling.

Working. As soon as the prime mover starts rotating, the pump impeller also starts rotating and throws the oil outward by centrifugal action. The oil then enters the turbine runner and exerts a force on the runner blades. The magnitude of the torque increases with an increase in the speed of the driving shaft and eventually when this torque *overcomes the inertia effects*, the turbine runner and the driven shaft begin to rotate. The oil from the runner then flows back into the pump impeller, thus a complete hydraulic (oil) circuit is established.

Expression for efficiency:

In a hydraulic coupling the power is transmitted *hydraulically* from the driving shaft to driven shaft and is free from engine vibrations. The efficiency of power transmission may be as high as 98 per cent.

Let, T_p = Torque on the pump or driving shaft '1' (*i.e.* input torque),

ω_p = Angular speed of the pump or the driving shaft '1',

T_t = Torque on the turbine or driven shaft '2' (*i.e.* output torque), and

ω_t = Angular speed of the turbine shaft or driven shaft '2'.

$\therefore$ Power input, $P_i = T_p\,\omega_p$, ...(5.19)

Power output, $P_o = T_t\,\omega_t$ ...(5.20)

Since the tangential momentum due to the velocity of whirl suffers no change as the oil passes from impeller blades to the runner blades, therefore, the torque on the driven shaft (T_t) equals that on the driving shaft (T_p), *i.e.* $T_p = T_t$.

The efficiency (η) of the hydraulic coupling is defined as the *ratio of power output to power input, i.e.*

$$= \frac{\text{Power output }(P_0)}{\text{Power input }(P_i)} = \frac{T_t\,\omega_t}{T_p\,\omega_p} = \frac{\omega_t}{\omega_p} \quad ...(5.21)$$

$$(\because T_p = T_t)$$

The ratio $\left(\frac{\omega_t}{\omega_p}\right)$ is known as *speed ratio.*

Slip of hydraulic or fluid coupling is defined as follows :

$$\text{Slip, } s = \frac{\omega_p - \omega_t}{\omega_p} = 1 - \frac{\omega_t}{\omega_p} = 1 - \eta \quad ...(5.22)$$

A typical *efficiency* (η) versus *speed ratio* $\left(\frac{\omega_t}{\omega_p}\right)$ curve for a fluid coupling is shown in Fig. 5.14. The efficiency is zero when the speed ratio is zero and it increases uniformly till the speed ratio is about 0.95, and then it rapidly reduces to zero.

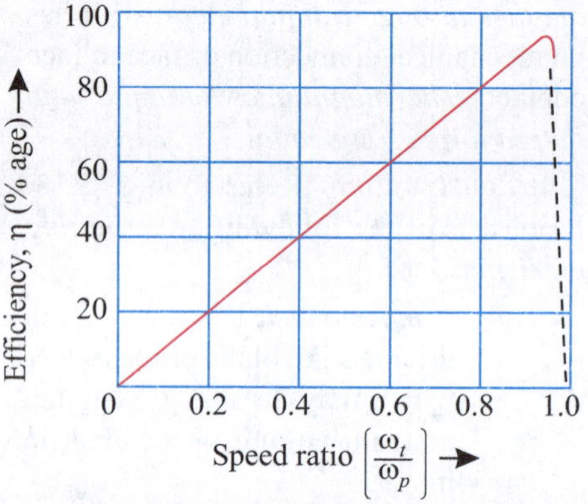

Fig. 5.14. Efficiency-speed ratio curve for hydraulic coupling.

Uses of hydraulic coupling:

Although a hydraulic or fluid coupling has a low value of transmission efficiency when compared to mechanical coupling, yet it is widely used in the following fields:

(*i*) Automobiles, marine engines, ropeway cable drive units and such other applications *where driven shaft is required to run at a speed close to that of the driving shaft.*

(*ii*) These couplings are particularly useful where *large initial loads are involved and smooth shock-free operations are required.*

5.9. HYDRAULIC TORQUE CONVERTER

Hydraulic torque converter *is a device used for transmitting increased or decreased power from one shaft to another.* A variable torque is impressed on the driven member without the use of a gear train or clutch. The torque at the driven shaft may be increased about five times the torque available at the driving shaft with an efficiency of about 90 percent.

Construction and working:

Refer to Fig. 5.15. The hydraulic torque converter consists of the following:

(*i*) Pump impeller coupled to the driving shaft,

(*ii*) Turbine runner coupled to the driven shaft, and

(*iii*) Stationary/fixed guide vanes (also known as reaction members) provided between the impeller and the turbine runner.

The liquid flowing from the pump impeller to turbine runner exerts a torque on the stationary guide vanes which change the direction of liquid, thereby making possible the transformation of torque and speed. Thus by suitably designing the stationary guide vanes the torque transmitted to the driving unit can be either increased or decreased. The torque relationship is given as :

$$T_t = T_p + T_v \quad ...(5.23)$$

where, T_t = Torque transmitted to the *turbine shaft*,

T_p = Torque of *pump impeller*, and

T_v = Variation of torque caused by *fixed guide vanes*.

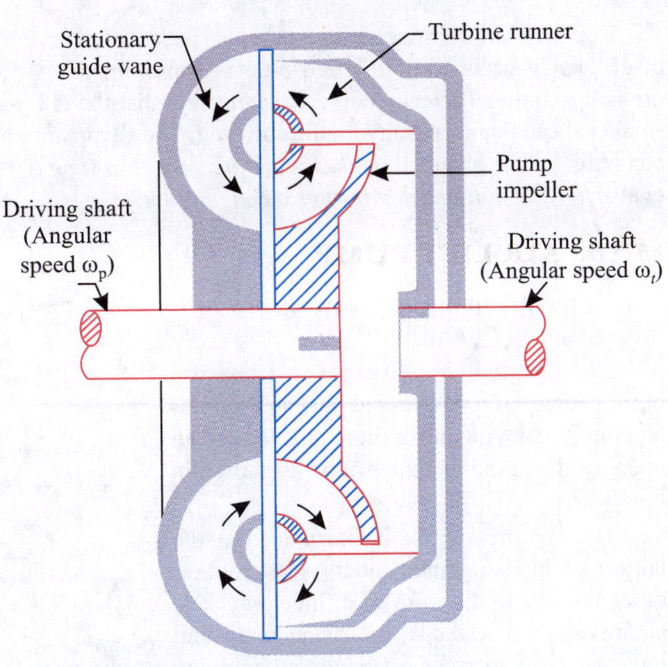

Fig. 5.15. Hydraulic torque converter.

$$\text{Power input, } P_i = T_p \, \omega_p$$

$$\text{Power output, } P_o = T_t \, \omega_t = (T_p + T_v) \, \omega t$$

$$\therefore \text{ Efficiency of torque converter, } \eta = \frac{\text{Power output } (P_o)}{\text{Power input } (P_i)} = \frac{(T_p + T_v)\,\omega_t}{T_p \omega_p}$$

$$= \frac{\omega_t}{\omega_p}\left(1 + \frac{T_v}{T_p}\right) \quad ...(5.24)$$

From equation (5.22) we find that, when there are no guide vanes, torque converter reduces to flange coupling with $T_v = 0$ and then $\eta = \dfrac{\omega_t}{\omega_p} = 1 - s$.

The torque T_v depends upon the design of the stationary guide vanes; in eqn. (5.23) it can be +ve or –ve. If the guide vanes are designed to receive a torque from the fluid which is in *opposite direction* to that exerted on the turbine (or driven) shaft, an *increased output* results. On the other hand if the shape of the guide vanes is such that they receive the torque in the *same* sense as that of driven shaft, a *torque reduction* results. Thus, since the torque in case of a hydraulic torque converter can be increased or decreased (in case of the hydraulic coupling $T_p = T_t$), therefore, it is comparable to an electric transformer. Usually the *torque converters are used for increasing the torque.*

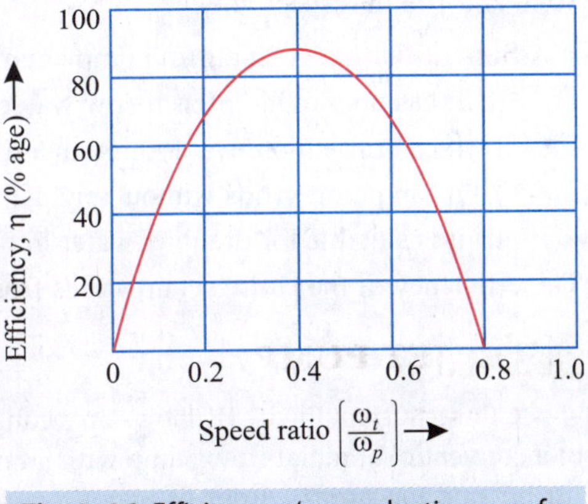

Fig. 5. 16. Efficiency v/s speed ratio curve for the hydraulic torque converter.

When a large reduction in speed ($\omega_t << \omega_p$), and a large torque is required, the hydraulic torque converters are designed which utilize two or more sets of turbine runners, and fixed guide vanes located between the turbine runners.

Fig. 5.16 shows the efficiency versus speed ratio curve for a torque converter, maximum value of efficiency occurs where speed ratio is approximately 0·5; at higher speed ratios the efficiency drops. From the efficiency curve, it is apparent that the efficiency of the torque converter is better at smaller speed than that of hydraulic coupling. The advantages of the hydraulic coupling and the torque converter can be obtained by *designing the system in such a way that at low speed ratios it acts as a converter and at high speed ratios as a coupling.*

5.10. AIR LIFT PUMP

An **air lift pump** *is a device used to lift water from a deep well or sump by utilizing the compressed air.*

Construction and working. It consists of a source of compressed air and an air pipeline fitted with one or more nozzles and an open vertical pipe or rising main as shown in Fig. 5.17.

The compressed air is introduced at the bottom of the rising main and it issues from set of air nozzles in the form of a fine spray. The air mixes with water in the rising main and *reduces the density of air-water mixture.* As soon as the pressure of the column of air-water mixture in the rising main of height H becomes less than the pressure due to the height of water column h in the bore well, the water begins to flow at the outlet of the rising main. The flow rate depends upon the density of the 'mixture' in the rising main/delivery pipe. It has been observed that best results are obtained when the value of the ratio $\left(\dfrac{h}{H-h}\right)$ is in between 4 and 1 for the values of h between 30 m and 100 m respectively.

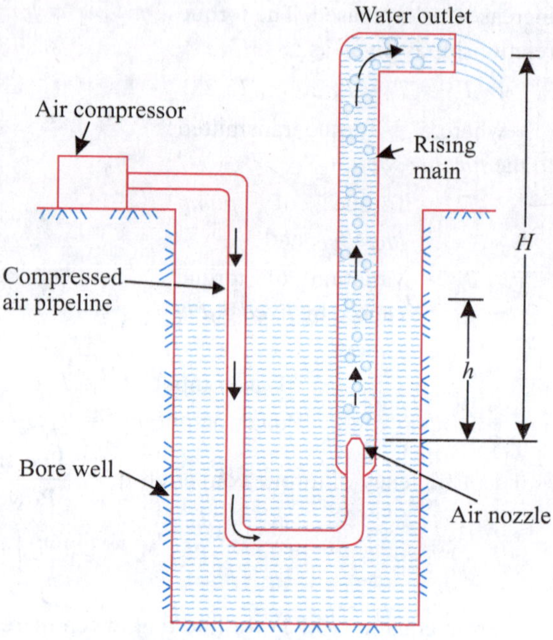

Fig. 5. 17. Air lift pump.

Salient features. An air lift pump entails the following *salient features*:

1. It has no moving parts below waterlevel and consequently no wear and tear.
2. It can raise more water through a bore hole of given diameter than any other pump.
3. It can pump solids without any damage to the system.
4. It is suitable for draining water in the mines where compressor units are already installed.

The efficiency of the entire set up varies from 20 to 40%.

5.11. JET PUMP

Construction. Fig. 5.18 shows an arrangement of a jet pump in a bore well. A jet pump consists of a conventional radial flow pump with jet nozzle at the suction end. It helps to increase the suction lift beyond the normal limit of about 8 metres of water head. With the use of jet assembly it is possible to increase the suction lift upto 60 m.

Working. The working operation of the jet pump is as follows:

—The suction side is completely filled with water and the pump is started.

— A stream of high pressure water from the delivery pipe of the pump is allowed to flow through the suction jet nozzle. The pressure energy of water is converted into kinetic energy due to which a local drop in the pressure takes place. Due to this pressure drop suction is created and water is sucked from the bore well. This action ensures a considerably large supply of low pressure water.

— When the streams with different velocities mix (in the mixing zone), some pressure rise takes place in the mixing zone.

— After the mixing zone, there is a diverging section where *further rise* of pressure occurs *due to decrease in velocity*.

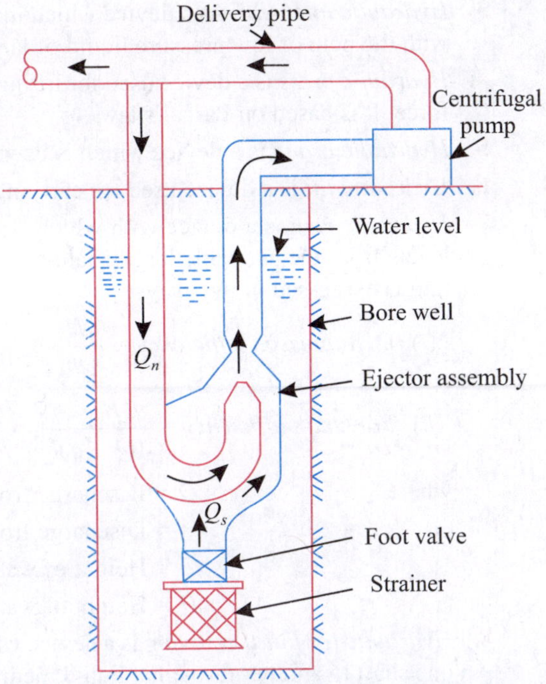

Fig. 5.18. Jet pump.

Efficiency of jet pump:

The efficiency of a jet pump is defined as:

$$\eta = \frac{Q_s (H_s + H_d)}{Q_n (H'_d - H_d)} \quad ...(5.25)$$

where,
Q_s = Discharge through the suction pipe,
Q_n = Discharge through the nozzle,
H_s = Suction head,
H_d = Delivery head, and
H'_d = Pressure head on delivery side.

The efficiency of a jet pump is very low and is of the order of 25 percent. The major losses take place in the mixing zone.

Uses. The fields of application of a jet pump are:

1. A jet pump can be used to take out muddy water from excavation trenches.
2. To lift water from wells of smaller bores.
3. Employed in mining and for pumping oil.

HIGHLIGHTS

1. The *hydraulic accumulator* is a device used to store the energy of fluid under pressure and make this energy available to hydraulic machines such as presses, lifts and cranes. Its action is similar to that of an electrical storage battery.

Capacity of hydraulic accumulator = $p \times A \times L$

[where, p = Liquid pressure supplied by pump, A = area of the sliding ram, and
L = Stroke or lift of the ram.]

2. A *differential accumulator* is a special type of accumulator that is used for storing energy at high pressure by comparatively small load on the ram.

3. *Hydraulic intensifier* is a device which increases the intensity of pressure of a given liquid with the help of low pressure liquid of large quantity.
4. *Hydraulic press* is a device used for lifting heavy loads by the application of much smalller force. It is based on Pascal's law.
5. *Hydraulic crane* is a device which is used for lifting heavy loads (upto 25 MN).
6. *Hydraulic lift* is a device used for carrying persons and loads from one floor to another.
7. *Hydraulic ram* is a device with which small quantities of water can be pumped to higher levels from the available large quantity of water of low head. The efficiency of hydraulic ram is expressed in two ways:

   (*i*) $D'Aubuisson' efficiency = \dfrac{qH}{Qh}$

   (*ii*) $Rankine's\ efficiency = \dfrac{q(H - h)}{(Q - q)h}$

   where, Q = Discharge from supply tank to the valve box,
   q = Discharge from the valve box to delivery tank,
   h = Height of water in the supply tank above the valve box, and
   H = Height of water in the delivery tank above the valve box.
8. *Hydraulic (or fluid) coupling* is a device which is employed for transmission of power from one shaft to another through a liquid medium.

   Efficiency of hydraulic coupling, $\eta = \dfrac{\omega_t}{\omega_p}$

   (where ω_t and ω_p are the angular speeds of the turbine shaft and pump shaft respectively)
   The magnitudes of input and output torque are equal.
9. *Hydraulic torque converter* is device used for transmitting increased or decreased torque from one shaft to another.

   Efficiency of torque converter, $\eta = \dfrac{\omega_t}{\omega_p}\left(1 + \dfrac{T_v}{T_p}\right)$

   (where T_v = variation of torque caused by fixed guide vanes; T_p = torque of pump impeller).
10. *Air lift pump* is a device used to lift water from a deep well or sump by utilizing the compressed air.

OBJECTIVE TYPE QUESTIONS

Choose the Correct Answer:

1. ..... is a device which increases the intensity of pressure of a given liquid with the help of low pressure liquid of large quantity.
   (*a*) Hydraulic press
   (*b*) Hydraulic crane
   (*c*) Hydraulic accumulator
   (*d*) Hydraulic intensifier.
2. Which of the following devices is used to store energy of liquid under pressure and make this energy available to hydraulic machines?
   (*a*) Hydraulic coupling
   (*b*) Hydraulic accumulator
   (*c*) Hydraulic ram
   (*d*) Hydraulic press.
3. .... is a device which is employed for transmission of power from one shaft to another through a liquid medium.
   (*a*) Hydraulic intensifier
   (*b*) Hydraulic torque converter
   (*c*) Hydraulic coupling
   (*d*) Hydraulic press.

4. Which of the following devices is used for transmitting increased or decreased torque from one shaft to another?
   (*a*) Hydraulic ram
   (*b*) Hydraulic coupling
   (*c*) Hydraulic intensifier
   (*d*) Hydraulic torque converter.
5. Efficiency of hydraulic torque converter is given by
   (*a*) $\frac{\omega_t}{\omega_p}\left(2+\frac{T_v}{T_p}\right)$ (*b*) $\frac{\omega_t}{\omega_p}\left(1+\frac{T_v}{T_p}\right)$
   (*c*) $\frac{\omega_p}{\omega_t}\left(1+\frac{T_v}{T_p}\right)$ (*d*) $\frac{\omega_t}{\omega_p}\left(1+\frac{T_p}{T_v}\right)$.
   where, ω_t = Angular speed of turbine shaft;
   ω_p = Angular speed of pump shaft;
   T_v = Variation of torque caused by fixed guide vanes;
   T_p = Torque of pump impeller.
6. ..... is a device with which small quantities of water can be pumped to higher levels from the available large quantity of water of low head.
   (*a*) Hydraulic accumulator
   (*b*) Hydraulic intensifier
   (*c*) Hydraulic ram
   (*d*) Air lift pump.
7. The function of which of the following hydraulic devices is analogous to that of the flywheel of a reciprocating engine and an electric storage battery?
   (*a*) Hydraulic ram
   (*b*) Hydraulic accumulator
   (*c*) Hydraulic intensifier
   (*d*) Hydraulic coupling.
8. Which of the following statements with regard to the purposes served by hydraulic units is *incorrect*?
   (*a*) Hydraulic torque converter is used for transmitting increased or decreased torque to the driven shaft.
   (*b*) Hydraulic ram is a pump that is used to lift small quantities of water to greater heights from large quantity of water available at small heights.
   (*c*) Hydraulic intensifier stores the energy of fluid in the form of pressure energy and is used for lifting heavy weights.
   (*d*) Hydraulic accumulator stores the energy of a fluid in the form of pressure energy; that helps to reduce the capacity of power house where there is intermittent demand for power.
9. The working of which of the following hydraulic units is based on Pascal's law?
   (*a*) Air lift pump
   (*b*) Jet pump
   (*c*) Hydraulic coupling
   (*d*) Hydraulic press.
10. With regard to hydraulic ram, which of the following statements is *incorrect*?
   (*a*) It works automatically
   (*b*) It requires very little maintenance
   (*c*) Its running cost is high
   (*d*) It has no moving parts.

ANSWERS

1. (*d*)	2. (*b*)	3. (*c*)	4. (*d*)	5. (*b*)	6. (*c*)
7. (*b*)	8. (*c*)	9. (*d*)	10. (*c*).		

THEORETICAL QUESTIONS

1. Describe with sketches the working of any two of the following hydraulic devices:
   (*i*) Hydraulic crane
   (*ii*) Hydraulic lift
   (*iii*) Hydraulic press
   (*iv*) Hydraulic coupling.
2. Describe with the aid of neat sketch the working of a hydraulic intensifier.
3. Obtain an expression for the capacity of a hydraulic accumulator.
4. What is the difference between a hydraulic accumulator and a hydraulic intensifier?
5. Describe with the aid of neat sketch the construction and working of a hydraulic ram.
6. What is the difference between a hydraulic coupling and a hydraulic torque converter?
7. Explain with neat sketch, the working of an air lift pump. Mention its advantages.
8. What is a jet pump?

9. What is the difference between a hydraulic ram and a centrifugal pump?
10. Write short notes on the following:
(*i*) Hydraulic lift,
(*ii*) Hydraulic press, and
(*iii*) Hydraulic coupling.

UNSOLVED EXAMPLES

1. An accumulator has a ram of 200 mm diameter and a lift of 6 m. If the liquid is supplied at 60 bar, find the necessary load on the ram and capacity of the accumulator.
[**Ans.** 188.49 kN; 0.314 kWh]
2. It is required to transmit 36·76 kW power from an accumulator through a pipeline 100 mm diameter and 1500 m long. The ram is loaded with a weight of 1226.25 kN and the friction loss in the pipeline equals 2 per cent of the total power being transmitted. Determine the diameter of the ram if friction co-efficient, $f = 0.01$.
[**Ans.** 493 mm]
3. The diameters of the two parts of the ram of a differential accumulator are 150 mm and 130 mm respectively, and stroke is 1.2 m. If the pressure of water is 98.1 bar when the load is either at rest at the upper end of the stroke or the load is moving with uniform velocity, what will be the weight of the loaded cylinder? How much energy can be stored in the accumulator?
Determine the diameter of the ram of an ordinary accumulator to move the same load with the help of the same water pressure?
[**Ans.** 43.16 kN; 51.8 kNm; 74.8 mm]
4. The pressure intensity of liquid supplied to an intensifier is 50 bar while the pressure intensity of liquid leaving the intensifier is 150 bar. If the intensifier has a capacity of 0.025 m^3 and stroke 1.25 m, calculate the diameters of the fixed ram and sliding cylinder to be used for this intensifier. [**Ans.** 159.6 mm; 319 mm]
5. A hydraulic press has a ram of 165 mm diameter and plunger of 33 mm diameter, with stroke length of 250 mm. Weight exerted by press ram amounts to 5.5 kN and distance moved is 1.2 m in 20 minutes. Determine:
(*i*) The force applied on plunger,
(*ii*) Number of strokes performed by the plunger,
(*iii*) Work done by the press ram, and
(*iv*) Power required to drive the plunger.
[**Ans.** (*i*) 0.22 kN; (*ii*) 120 (app.); (*iii*) 6.6 kNm; (*iv*) 5.5 W]
6. An intensifier receives water from an overhead tank through a pipeline 50 mm in diameter and 100 long and conveys high pressure water to a 600 kN hydraulic press having a ram 0·2 m diameter. The intensifier has low pressure piston diameter 1 m and high pressure ram diameter 0.1 m. If the static head on the low pressure side of the intensifier is 21 m, calculate the rate of movement of the ram when exerting its maximum force.
Take co-efficient of friction, $f = 0.0075$ for the pipeline (50 mm dia). [**Ans.** 0.026 m/min.]
7. In a hydraulic crane, the diameter of crane ram = 300 mm; length of supply pipe from accumulator = 150 m; diameter of the supply pipe = 50 mm; pressure at accumulator = 54 bar; mechanical friction of ram, pulleys etc. are equivalent to a pressure of 4.9 bar on the ram. Determine a relationship between the W kN lifted and the speed of lifting V and hence find V for $W = 50$ kN.
Take co-efficient of friction for the pipe = 0.01.
[**Ans.** $V = 0.1389\,(81.83 - 1.18\,W)^{1/2}$; 0.664 m/s]
8. A hydraulic crane is lifting a load of 11.772 kN through a height of 12 m with a speed of 0.3 m/s once in every two minutes. The crane is working under a pressure of 4905 kN/m^2 of water and has an efficiency of 65 percent. The crane is fed from an accumulator to which water is supplied by a pump. Determine: (*i*) Capacity of cylinder of the jigger, (*ii*) Capacity of accumulator, and (*iii*) Minimum power required to drive the pump.
[**Ans.** (*i*) 0.0443 m^3/s; (*ii*) 0.0295 m^3/s; (*iii*) 1.81 kW]
9. The following data refers to a hydraulic ram: Supply head 2.2 m; weight of waste water per minute 170 N; weight of water pumped per minute 5N and net head pumped from the ram 40 m.
Calculate D'Aubuisson's and Rankine's efficiencies. [**Ans.** 51.8%; 50.5%]
10. A hydraulic ram has a supply head of 2 m, the pipe being 60 mm in diameter and 5 m long. The waste valve, which is 150 mm in diameter and of weight 14.7 N, lifts through 6 mm. Determine:
(*i*) The number of beats per minute, and
(*ii*) The quantity of water delivered per minute to a tank 10 m above the ram.
[**Ans.** (*i*) 175, (*ii*) 0.0183 $m^3/min.$]

Chapter
6

WATER POWER DEVELOPMENT

6.1. HYDROLOGY

6.1.1. Definition

Hydrology *may be defined as the science which deals with the depletion and replenishment of water resources.* It deals with the surface water as well as the ground water. It is also concerned with the *transportation of water from one place to another, and from one form to another*. It helps us in determining the occurrence and avilability of water.

6.1.2. The hydrologic Cycle

The earth's water sources such as rivers, lakes, oceans and underground sources etc. mostly get their supplies from rains while the rain water itself is the evaporation from these sources. Water is lost to the atmosphere as vapour from earth, which is then precipitated back in the form of rain, snow, hail, dew, sleet or frost, etc. This evaporation and precipitation continues for ever, and thereby, a balance is maintained between the two. This process is known as *Hydrologic cycle.* It can be represented graphically as shown in Fig. 6.1 Hydrologic equation is expressed as follows:

$$P = R + E \qquad ...(6.1)$$

where, P = Precipitaion,

R = Run-off, and

E = Evaporation.

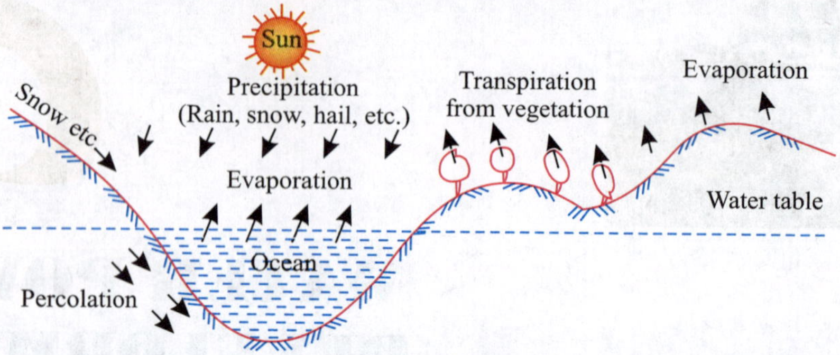

Fig. 6.1. Hydrologic cycle.

Precipitation. It includes all the water that falls from atmosphere to earth surface. Precipitation is of two types: (*i*) *Liquid precipitaion* (rain fall). (*ii*) *Solid precipitaion* (snow, hail).

Run-off and surface run-off. Run-off and surface run-off are two different terms. *Run-off* includes all the water flowing in the stream channel at any given section, while the *surface run-off* includes only the water that reaches the stream channel without first percolating down to the water table.

Run-off can, therefore, also be named as '*Discharge*' or '*Stream flow*'. *Rainfall duration, its intensity and a real distribution influence the rate and volume of run-off.*

Evaporation. Transfer of water from liquid to vapour state is called *evaporation.*

Transpiration. The process by which water is released to the atmosphere by the plants is called *transpiration.*

6.1.3. Measurement of Run-off

Run-off can be measured daily, monthly, seasonal or yearly. It can be measured by the following methods:

1. From rainfall records
2. Empirical formulae
3. Run-off curves and tables
4. Discharge observation method.

1. From rainfall records:

In this method consistent rainfall record for a sufficiently long period is taken and then average depth of rainfall over the catchment is determined. Then considering all the factors which affect run-off process, a co-efficient is arrived at for that catchment. Now a simple equation can be used to find out the run-off over the catchment.

$$\text{Run-off} = \text{Rainfall} \times \text{co-efficient.} \quad ...(6.2)$$

2. Empirical formulae:

In this method, an attempt is made to derive a direct relationship between the rainfall and subsequent run-off. For this purpose some constants are established which give fairly accurate result for a specified region. Some important formulae are given below:

(a) Khosla's formula:

$$R = P - 4.811\ T$$

where, R = Annual run-off in mm,

P = Annual rainful in mm, and

T = Mean temperature in 0°C.

(b) Inglis formulae for hilly and plain areas of Maharashtra:

For *Ghat region*

$$R = 0.88\,P - 304.8$$

For *Plain region*

$$R = \frac{(P - 177.8) \times P}{2540}$$

(c) Lacey's formula:

$$R = \frac{P}{1 + \dfrac{3084\,F}{PS}}$$

where, R = Monsoon run-off in mm,

P = Monsoon rainfall in mm,

S = Catchment area factor, and

F = Monsoon duration factor.

Values of S for various types of catchment are given below:

Type of catchment	*Value of S*
Flat, cultivated and black cotton soils	0.25
Flat, partly cultivated, various soils	0.6
Average catchment	1.00
Hills and places with little cultivation	1.70
Very hilly and steep, with hardly any cultivation	3.45

Values of F for various duration of monsoon are given below:

Class of monsoon	*Value of F*
Very short	0.50
Standard length	1.00
Very long	1.50

3. Run-off curves and tables:

Each region has its own catchment area and rainfall characteristics. Thus formulae given above and co-efficients derived there in cannot be applied universally. However, for the same region the characteristics mostly remain unchanged. Based on this fact, the run-off co-efficients are derived once for all. Then a graph is plotted in which one axis represents rainfall and the other run-off. The curves obtained are called *run-off curves.* Alternatively a table can be prepared to give the run-off for a certain value of rainfall for a particular region.

4. Discharge observation method:

The run-off over a catchment can be computed by actual measurement of discharge at an outlet of a drainage basin. The complication in this method is that the discharge of the stream at the outlet comprises surface run-off as well as sub-surface flow. To find out the sub-surface run-off it is essential to *separate* the sub surface flow from the total flow. The separation can be done on an approximate basis but with correct analysis.

Factors affecting the run-off:

The following factors affect run-off :

1. Rainfall pattern
2. Character of catchment area

3. Topography
4. Shape and size of the catchment area
5. Vegetation
6. Geology of the area
7. Weather conditions.

6.1.4. Hydrograph

Hydrograph *is defined as a graph showing discharge (run-off) of flowing water with respect to time for a specified time.* Discharge graphs are known as *flood or run-off graphs.* Each hydrograph has a reference to a particular river site. The time period for discharge hydrography may be hour, day, week or month.

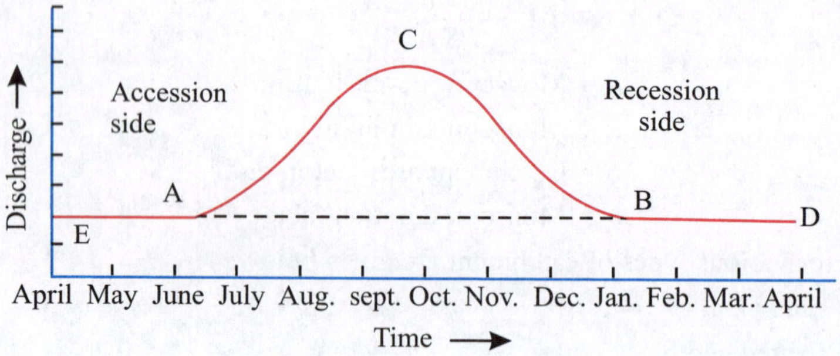

Fig. 6.2. Typical hydrograph.

Hydrograph of stream of river will depend on the characteristics of the catchment and precipitation over the catchment. Hydrograph will access the flood flow of rivers hence it is essential that anticipated hydrograph could be drawn for river for a given storm.

Hydrograph indicates the power available from the stream at different times of day, week or year.

Typical hydrographs are shown in Figs. 6.2 and 6.3.

The unit hydrograph:

The peak flow alone does not give sufficient information about the run-off since it (peak flow) represents a momentary value. Therefore it is necessary to understand the full hydrograph of flow. *The basic concept of unit hydrograph is that the hydrographs of run-off from two identical storms would be the same.* In practice identical storms occur very rarely. The rainfall generally varies in duration, amount and areal distribution. This makes it necessary to construct a typical hydrograph for a basin which could be used as a unit of measurement of run-off.

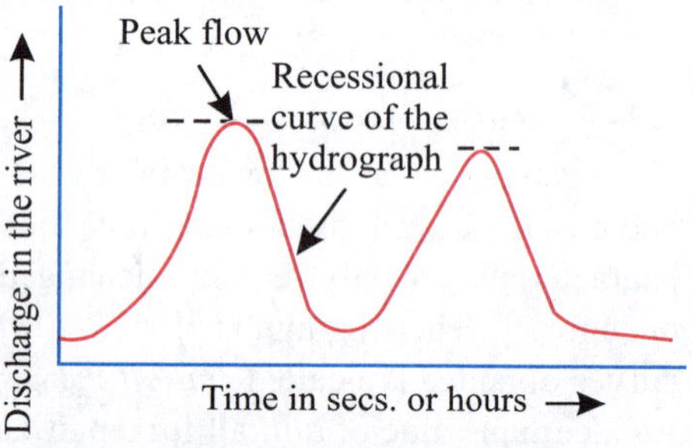

Fig. 6.3. Typical hydrograph.

A **unit hydrograph** *may be defined as a hydrograph which represents unit run-off resulted from an intense rainfall of unit duration and specific areal distribution.*

The following *steps* are used for the *construction of unit hydrograph:*

1. Choose an isolated intense rainfall of unit duration from past records.
2. Plot the discharge hydrograph for outlet from the rainfall records.
3. Deduct the base flow from stream discharge hydrograph to get hydrograph of surface run-off.

4. Find out the volume of surface run-off and convert this volume into cm of run-off over the catchment area.
5. Measure the ordinates of surface run-off hydrograph.
6. Divide these ordinates of obtained run-off in cm to get ordinates of unit hydrograph. Thus for any catchment unit hydrograph can be prepared once. Then whenever peak flow is to be found out, *multiply the maximum ordinate of unit hydrograph by the run-off value expressed in cm.* Similarly to obtain run-off hydrograph by the storm of same unit duration multiply the ordinates of the unit hydrograph by the run-off value expressed in cm. If the storm is of longer duration calculate the run-off in each unit duration of the storm. Then superimpose the run-off hydrographs in the same order giving a lag of unit period between each of them. Finally draw a summation hydrograph by adding all the overlapping ordinates. Generally the computations are done in a tabular form before the hydrograph is plotted.

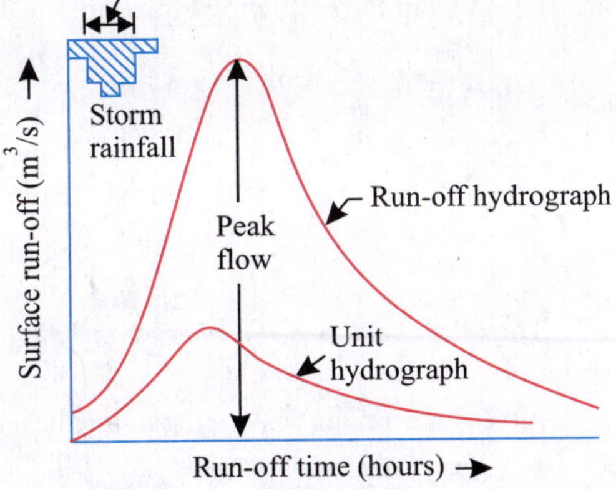

Fig. 6.4.

Fig. 6.4 shows how a run-off hydrograph is constructed from a unit hydrograph.

Limitations to the use of unit hydrograph:

1. Its use is limited to areas about 5000 sq. kilometres since similar rainfall distribution over a large area from storm to storm is rarely possible.
2. The odd-shaped basins (particularly long and narrow) have very uneven rainfall distribution. Therefore, unit hydrograph method is not adopted to such basins.
3. In mountain areas, the areal distribution is very uneven, even then unit hydrograph method is used because the distribution pattern remains same from storm to storm.

6.1.5. Flow Duration Curve

Refer to Fig. 6.5. Flow duration curve is another useful form to represent the run-off data for the given time. This curve is plotted between flow available during a period versus the fraction of time. If the magnitude on the ordinate is the potential power contained in the stream flow, the curve is known as "*power duration curve.*" This curve is a very useful tool in the analysis for the development of water power.

The flow duration curve is drawn with the help of a hydrograph from the available run-off data and here it is necessary to find out the lengths of time duration for which certain flows are available. This information either from run-off data or from hydrograph is tabulated. Now the flow duration curve taking 100 percent time on *X*-axis and run-off on *Y*-axis can be drawn.

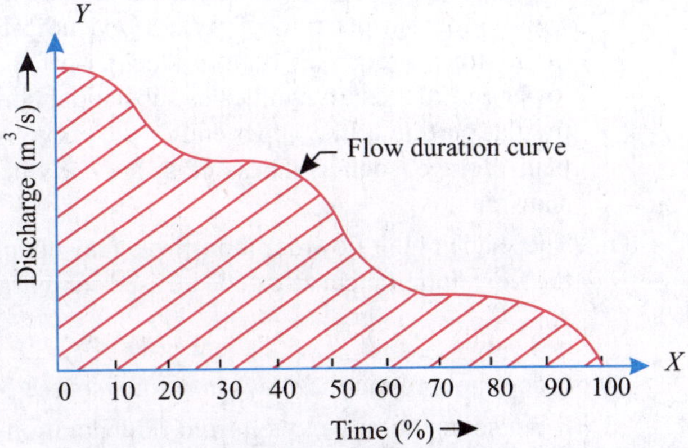

Fig. 6.5. Flow duration curve.

The area under the flow duration curve (Fig. 6.5) gives the *total quantity of run-off during that period* as the flow duration curve is representation of graph with its flows arranged in order of descending magnitude.

If the head of discharge is known, the possible power developed from water in kW can be determind from the following equation:

$$\text{Power (kW)} = \frac{wQH \times \eta_0}{1000}$$

where, Q = Discharge, m^3/s,

H = Head available, m,

w = Weight density of water, N/m^3, and

η_0 = Overall efficiency.

Thus the *flow duration curve can be converted to a power duration with some other scale on the same graph.*

Flow duration curves are most useful in the following cases:

(*i*) *For preliminary studies.*

(*ii*) *For comparison between streams.*

Uses of flow duration curve:

1. A flow duration curve allows the evaluation of low level flows.
2. It is highly useful in the planning and design of water resources projects. In particular, for hydropower studies, the flow duration curve serves to determine the potential for firm power generation. In the case of run-of the river plant, with no stroage facilities, the firm power is usually computed on the basis of flow available 90 to 97 precent of the time. The firm power is also known as the *primary power. Secondary power* is the power generated at the plant utilising water other than that used for the generation of firm power.
3. If a sediment rating curve is available for the given stream, the flow duration curve can be converted into cumulative sediment transport curve by multiplying each flow rate by its rate sediment transport. The area under this curve represents the *total amount of sediment transported.*
4. The flow duration curve also finds use in the design of drainage systems and in flood control studies.
5. A flow duration curve plotted on a log-log paper provides a qualitative description of the run-off variability in the stream. If the curve is having steep slope throughout, it indicates a stream with highly variable discharge. This is typical of the conditions where the flow is mainly from surface run-off. A *flat slope* indicates small variability which is a characteristic of the streams receiving both surface run-off and ground water run-off. A *flat-portion* at the lower end of the curve indicates substantial contribution from ground water run-off, while the flat portion at the upper end of the curve is characteristic of streams with large flood plain storage, such as lakes and swaps, or where the high flows are mainly derived from snowmelt.
6. The shape of the flow duration curve may change with the length of record. This aspect of the flow duration curve can be utilised for extrapolation of the short records.

Shortcomings/defects of flow duration curve:

1. It does not present the flows in natural source of occurrence.
2. It is also not possible to tell from flow duration curve whether the lower flows occurred in consecutive periods or were scattered throughout the considered period.

6.1.6. Mass Curve

A **mass curve** *is the graph of the cumulative values of water quantity (run-off) against time.* A mass curve is an integral curve of the hydrograph which expresses the area under the hydrograph from one time to another.

It is convenient device *to determine storage requirement* that is needed to produce a certain dependable flow from fluctuating discharge of a river by a reservoir.

Mass curve can also be used to solve *reserve problem* of determining the maximum demand rate that can be maintained by a given storage volume. However, it is a trial and error procedure.

The mass curve *will always have a positive shape* but of a greater of less degree depending upon the variations in the quantity of inflow water available. The negative inclination of mass curve would show that the amount of water flowing in the reservoir was less than the loss due to evaporation and seepage.

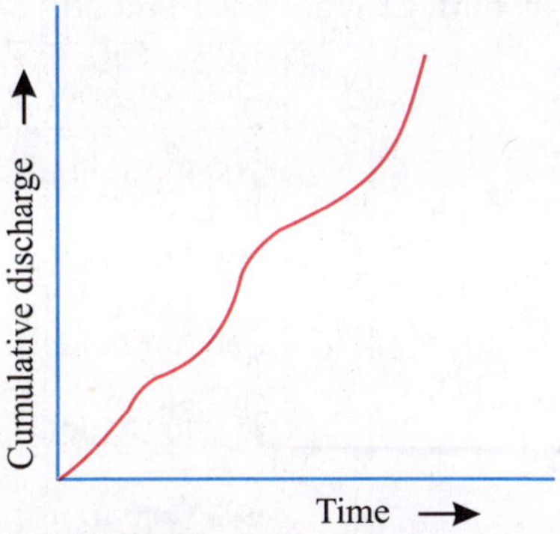

Fig. 6.6. Mass curve.

Example 6.1. *At a particular site the mean monthly discharge is as follows:*

Month	*Discharge m^3/s*	*Month*	*Discharge, m^3/s*
January	*100*	*July*	*1000*
February	*225*	*August*	*1200*
March	*300*	*September*	*900*
April	*600*	*October*	*600*
May	*750*	*November*	*400*
June	*800*	*December*	*200*

Draw the following :

(i) Hydrograph; *(ii) Flow duration curve.*

Solutions. (*i*) The **hydrogarph** is plotted between discharge (m^3/s) and time (months) as shown in Fig. 6.7.

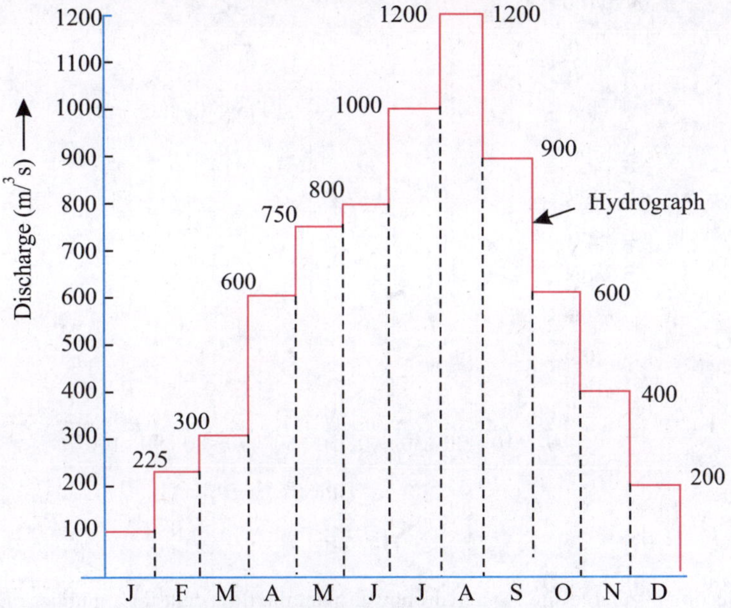

Fig. 6.7. Hydrograph.

***(ii)* Flow duration curve:**

In order to draw flow duration curve it is essential to find the length of time during which centain flows are available, e.g. 100 m^3/s is available for all 12 months, flow of 200 m^3/s for 11 months, 225 m^3/s for 10 months and so on. This information is indicated in the table below:

Discharge, m^3/s	*Length of time, months*	*%age time*
100 (and more)	12	100
200 (and more)	11	91.7
225 (and more)	10	83.3
300 (and more)	9	75.0
400 (and more)	8	66.7
600 (and more)	7	58.3
750 (and more)	5	41.7
800 (and more)	4	33.3
900 (and more)	3	25.0
1000 (and more)	2	16.7
1200 (and more)	1	8.3

The flow duration curve is then plotted as shown in Fig. 6.8

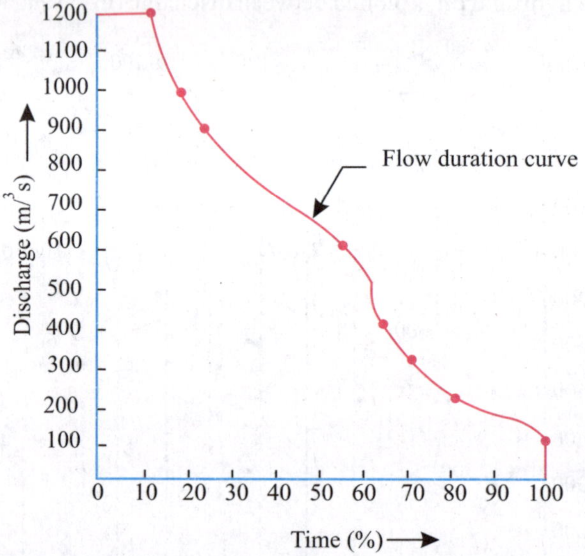

Fig. 6.8

Note: When selecting a suitable site for a hydropower plant the flow data for a number of years is collected and hydrographs and flow duration curves and the various periods are determined.

Example 6.2. *The run-off data of a river at a particular site is tabulated below:*

Month	*Mean discharge per month (millions of m^3)*	*Month*	*Mean discharge per month (millions of m^3)*
January	40	*July*	75
February	25	*August*	100
March	20	*September*	110
April	10	*October*	60
May	0	*November*	50
June	50	*December*	40

(*i*) *Draw a hydrograph and find the mean flow,*

(*ii*) *Also draw the flow duration curve, and*

(*iii*) *Find the power in MW available at mean flow if head available is 80 m and overall efficiency of generation is 85 %. Take each month of 30 days.*

Solution. (*i*) Hydrograph :

The hydrograph for the given data is drawn as shown in Fig. 6.9.

The mean discharge for the given data

$$= \frac{40 + 25 + 20 + 10 + 0 + 50 + 75 + 100 + 110 + 60 + 50 + 40}{12}$$

$$= \frac{580}{12} = 48.33 \text{ millions of m}^3\text{/month.}$$

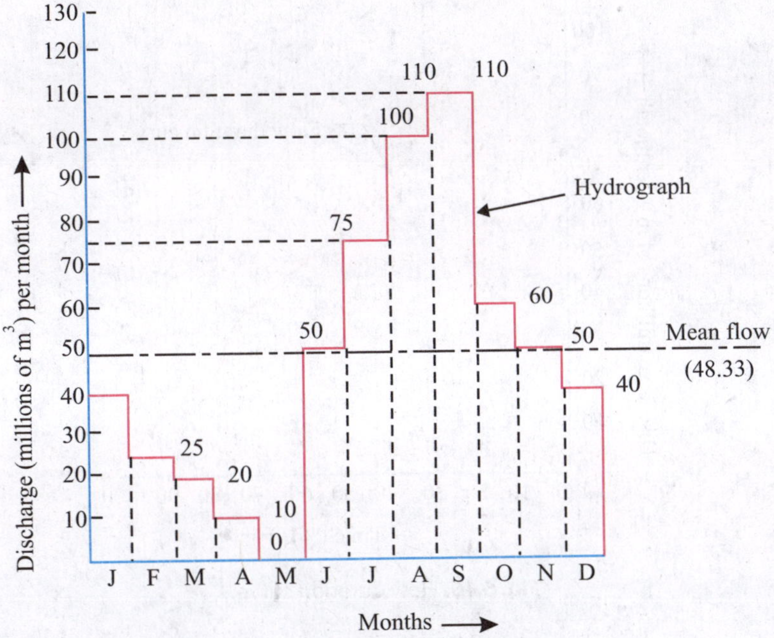

Fig. 6.9

(*ii*) Flow duration curve:

To obtain the flow duration curve, it is necessary to find the lengths of time during which certain flows are available. This information is tabulated using the hydrograph in the table as under:

Discharge per month (millions of m³)	*Total number of months during which flow is available*	*Percentage time*
0	12	100
10	11	91.7
20	10	83.3
25	9	75
40	8	66·7
50	6	50
60	4	33·3
75	3	25·0
100	2	16·7
110	1	8·3

The flow duration curve can be drawn using the data tabulated as shown in Fig. 6.10

(*iii*) Average MW energy available :

$$\textit{Average MW energy available} = \frac{wQH\eta_0}{1000}$$

$$\left[\text{where, } Q \text{ (discharge in m}^3\text{/s)} = \frac{48.33 \times 10^6}{30 \times 24 \times 3600}\right]$$

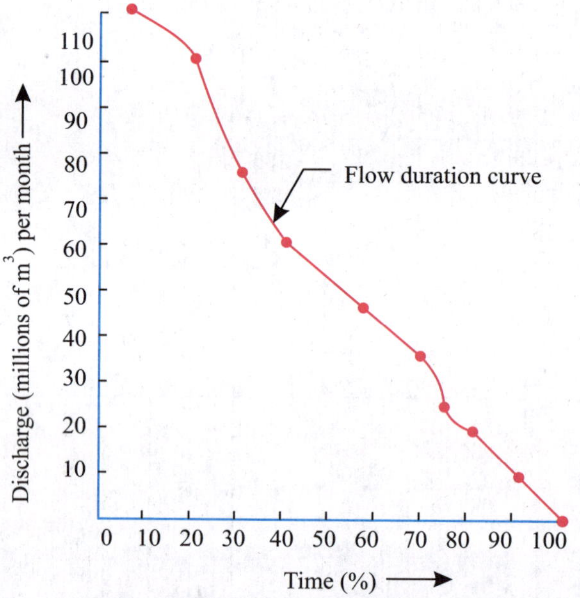

Fig. 6.10. Flow duration curve.

$$= \frac{9810 \times 48.33 \times 10^6 \times 80}{(30 \times 24 \times 3600)} \times 0.85 \times \frac{1}{1000} \text{ kW}$$

$= 12438$ kW, or, **12.438 MW** **(Ans.)**

6.2. HYDRO-POWER PLANT

6.2.1. Introduction

In hydroelectric plants, energy of water is utilised to move the turbines which in turn run the electric generators. The energy of water utilised for power generation may be kinetic or potential. The kinetic energy of water is its energy in motion and is a function of mass and velocity, while the potential energy is a function of the difference in level/head of water between two points. In either case continuous availability of water is a basic necessity; to ensure this, water collected in natural lakes and reservoirs at high altitudes may be utilised or water may be artificially stored by constructing dams across flowing stream. The ideal site is one in which a good system of natural lakes with substantial catchment area, exists at a high altitude. Rainfall is the primary source of water and depends upon such factors as temperature, humidity, cloudiness, wind etc. The usefulness of rainfall for power purposes further depends upon several complex factors which include its intensity, time distribution, topography of land etc. However it has been observed that only a small part of the rainfall can actually be utilised for power generation. A significant part is accounted for by direct evaporation, while another similar quantity seeps into the soil and forms the underground storage. Some water is also absorbed by vegetation. Thus only a part of water falling as rain actually flows over the ground surface as direct run off and forms the streams which can be utilised for hydroschemes.

First hydroelectric station was probably started in America in 1882 and thereafter development took place very rapidly. In India, the first major hydroelectric development of 4·5 MW capacity named as Sivasamudram Scheme in Mysore was commissioned in 1902. In 1914, a hydropower plant named Khopoli project of 50 MW capacity was commissioned in Maharashtra. The hydropower capacity, upto 1947, was nearly 500 MW.

Hydro (water) power is a conventional renewable source of energy which is clean, free from pollution and generally has a good environmental effect. However the following facts are *major obstacles* in the utilisation of hydropower resources :

(*i*) Large investments

(*ii*) Long gestation period

(*iii*) Increased cost of power transmission.

Next to thermal power, hydropower is important in regard to power generation. The hydroelectric power plants provide 30 percent of the total power of the world. The total hydropotential of the world is about 5000 GW. In some countries (like Norway) almost total power generation is hydrobased.

6.2.2. Application of Hydro-electric power plants

Earlier hydro-electric plants have been used as exclusive source of power, but the trend is towards use of hydro-power in an inter-connected systen with thermal stations. As a self-contained and independent power source, a hydroplant is most effective with adequate storage capacity otherwise the maximum load capacity of the station has to be based on the year. This increases the per unit cost of installation. By interconnecting hydropower with thermal (stream) power, a great deal of saving in cost can be effected due to:

(*i*) reduction in necessary reserve capacity,

(*ii*) diversity in construction programmes,

(*iii*) higher utilisation factors on hydroplants, and

(*iv*) higher capacity factors on efficient steam plants.

In an inter-connected system the base load is supplied by hydropower when the maximum flow demand is less than the stream flow while steam supplies the peak. When stream flow is lower than the maximum demand the hydroplant supplies the peak load and steam plant the base load.

6.2.3 Advantages and Disadvantages of Hydro-electric Power Plants

Advantages :

1. No fuel charges.
2. A hydroelectric plant is highly reliable.
3. Maintenance and operation charges are very low.
4. Running cost of the plant is low.
5. The plant has no standby losses.
6. The plant efficiency does not change with age.
7. It takes a few minutes to run and synchronise the plant.
8. Less supervising staff is required.
9. No fuel transportation problem.
10. No ash problem and atmosphere is not polluted since no smoke is produced in the plant.
11. In addition to power generation, these plants are also used for flood control and irrigation purposes.
12. Such a plant has comparatively a long life (100 to 125 years as against 20-45 years of a thermal plant.)
13. The number of operations required is considerably small compared with thermal power plants.
14. The machines used in hydro-electric plants are more robust and generally run at low speeds at 300 to 400 r.p.m. where as the machines used in thermal plants run at a speed 3000 to 4000 r.p.m. Therefore, there are no specialised mechanical problems or special alloys required for construction.
15. The cost of land is not a major problem since the hydroelectric stations are situated away from the developed areas.

Disadvantages :

1. The initial cost of the plant is very high.
2. It takes considerably long time for the erection of such plants.
3. Such plants are usually located in hilly areas far away from the load centre and as such they require long transmission lines and losses in them will be more.
4. Power generation by the hydro-electric plant is only dependent on the quantity of water available which in turn depends on the natural phenomenon of rain. So, if the rainfall is in time and proper and the required amount of it can be collected, the plants will function satisfactorily otherwise not.

6.2.4. Average Life of Hydroplant Components

The average life (approximate) of various components of hydro-electric power plant is given as follows:

Components	*Average life (years)*
1. Reservoirs	70–80
2. Dams	
(*i*) Earthen, concrete or masonry	150
(*ii*) Loose rock	60
3. Water ways	50–100
(*i*) Canals, tunnels	
(*ii*) Penstocks	
(*a*) Steel	40–50
(*b*) Concrete	25–50
4. Power house and equipment	
(*i*) Building	35–50
(*ii*) Generators	25
(*iii*) Transformers	30
(*iv*) Turbines (hydraulic)	5
(*v*) Pumps	20–25

6.2.5. Hydroplant controls

The various controls which are provided in a hydro-electric power plant are:

1. Hydraulic controls
2. Machine controls—starting and stopping
3. Machine controls—loading and frequency
4. Voltage control of generator and system
5. Machine protection.

6.2.6. Safety measures in hydroelectric power plants

Following safety measures need to be taken for the safe operation of a hydroelectric power plant:

1. Surge tanks
2. Screens
3. Sand traps
4. Jet dispersers
5. Pressure regulator.

Surge tanks. A surge tank is used to prevent sudden increase of pressure in the supply line or the penstock. It is placed as near as possible to the turbine. The tank may be open at the top or closed. In case, it is open at the top, it must not be lower than the level of the water in the reservoir.

Screens. These are provided to prevent logs, fishes, ice blocks and other obstructive elements from entering the pipelines and turbines.

Sand traps. Sand traps are provided to prevent the sand flowing with water in pipes since sand blast action of solid matter in the water causes rapid wear of nozzles, spears, blades etc. of the turbine.

Jet dispersers. The discharged water at the bottom of the high dams possesses large amount of energy which is likely to cause scouring of the channel below the dam and consequent damage to the dam foundation unless some means are provided to dissipate it. The possible remedies for this are either to discharge water into a cushion pool or to provide a jet disperser at the end of outlet pipe so that the end of the outlet pipe is such that the jet is broken up into a conical shower of drops and their energy is absorbed by air.

Pressure regulator. It is usually operated by a governor of the turbine. It is provided on the pipeline near the turbine inlet so that when the turbine gates are suddenly closed, pressure surges so produced are kept within the safe limits of the pipeline. The water discharge from the regulator is passed on to tailrace through a separate pipeline.

6.2.7. Preventive Maintenance to Hydroplant

The purpose of preventive maintenance is to minimise breakdown and excessive depreciation resulting from neglect. In a hydroplant (using reaction turbines) monthly, quarterly halfyearly and yearly inspection and maintenance are carried out on the following parts :

Inspection / Maintenance	*Parts*
Monthly	*Turbine cover parts* (e.g. leakage unit, drainage, holes, servomotor connections, turbine shaft and cover, oil *pump etc.) Operating ring of turbines.*
	Guide vane mechanism.
Quarterly	*Servomotor*
	Ejector cabinet
	Feedback system.
Half-yearly	*Governor machanism*
	Gauges
	Grease pumps for guide vanes and guide bearings.
	Grease pipes connected to grease pumps.
Yearly	*Turbine auxiliaries* (e.g. oil pressure tank, turbine guide bearing, turbine instruments)
	Scroll casing runner with guide vanes
	Emergency slide valve
	Pit liner
	Draft tube
	Runner blades checked for cavitational effects, cracks and wearing out.

6.2.8. Calculation of available hydro-power

The theoretical power (P_{th}) available from falling water can be calculated using the following formula:

$$P_{th} = \frac{wQH}{1000} \text{ kW} \quad \text{...(6.3)}$$

where, w = Weight density of water in N/m^3,

Q = Flow through turbine (or quantity or water available for hydropower generation) in m^3/s, and

H = Head available in metres.

The actual useful or effective output depends upon the efficiency of the various parts of the installation.

If, η_1 = Efficiency of pipelines, intake etc., and

η_2 = Efficiency of hydraulic turbine.

Then, overall efficiency $\eta_0 = \eta_1 \times \eta_2$. ...(6.4)

Since the turbine and the genertor are directly coupled on common shaft the hydro-electrical power available will be given by the equation:

$$\text{or,} \qquad P_{\text{actual}} = P_{\text{th.}} \times \eta_0 \qquad ...(6.5)$$

$$\text{or,} \qquad P_{\text{actual}} = \frac{wQH}{1000} \times \eta_0 \text{ kW} \qquad ...(6.5a)$$

6.2.9. Cost of Hydro-power Plant

The initial cost of any hydroplant is very high but the power produced by it is the cheapest. The following costs are included in development of a hydroplant :

1. Cost of land and riparian rights.
2. Cost of railways and highways required for the construction work.
3. Cost of construction.
4. Cost of engineering supervision of the project.
5. Cost of building etc.
6. Cost of equipment.
7. Cost of equipment used for power transmission.

6.2.10. Hydro-power Development in India

Hydropower is a renewable source of energy which entails many intrinsic advantages. In India, the scope of water power development is tremendous. The first hydropower station in India dates back to year 1897 when a *small* power station of 200 kW capacity was constructed at Darjeeling. Since them many big and small hydropower stations have been installed in the country.

Important hydroplants in India

State/Name of Power plant	*Installed capacity* (**MW**)
Andhra Pradesh	
Machkand (Stage I and II)	114
Upper silern	120
Lower silern	600
Srisailam	770
Nagarjun sagar pumped storage	100
Assam	
Umiam	54
Gujarat	
Ukai	300
Himachal Pradesh	
Baira suil	200
Jammu and Kashmir	
Salal	270
Karnataka	
Tungabhadra	72
Sharavati	890
Kailindi	395

Kerala	
Parambikulam-Aliyar	185
Sabarigiri	300
Idikki (Stage I)	390
Maharashtra	
Koyna (Stages I, II and III)	860
Manipur	
Loktak	70
Orissa	
Hirakud (Stage I and II)	270
Balimela	480
Punjab	
Bhakra Nangal	1084
Beas-Sutlej Link	780
Rajasthan	
Chambal	287
Uttar Pradesh	
Rihand	300
Yamuna (Stage I and II)	424
Tamil Nadu	
Kundah (Stages, I , II and III)	425
Kodiar	100

Although the present utilization of hydropower in over country is relatively small with the persent tempo of development and need for power resources it would not be long before the available potential is fully harnessed. Hydrofield provides immense scope for sophisticated study requiring application of modern mathematical and operational research techniques with the help of computers.

6.2.11. Combined Hydro and Steam Power Plants

A electrical power system should fulfil the following *objectives:*

1. To ensure an adequate and reliable electric power supply at all loads and at all times.
2. The source of energy should be such as to give the minimum overall cost of the system as a whole.

The above objectives (unless a country/region is rich either in abundant supply of cheap fuel or ample water power resources which can be developed at suitable site) can be best realised by a judicious combination of both hydro and thermal power. Hydropower represents a renewable source of energy which enjoys many intrinsic advantages as compared to thermal power. Although the cost of construction of hydropower plant is nearly same as that of a coal based steam power plant in terms of investment for MW, but hydropower plant uses water for power generation which is available in abundance in nature.

It is known that hydroplant can meet the demands of load variations more rapidly and easily. Thus, when the rate of flow of water is low, the steam plant can work at constant load producing a better efficiency and the hydroplant will work most effectively as peak load plant and its output can be varied to meet the load fluctuations.

The steam and hydroplants reverse their functions (steam plant providing the peal load and the hydroplant providing base load) when high rate of water flow is available. But even under this condition, *the steam plant output will remain constant and the hydroplant output will be varied to meet the load fluctuations.*

6.2.12. Comparison of Hydro-power Station with Thermal Power Station

The comparison between hydropower station and thermal power station is given below:

S. No.	Aspects	Hydropower station	Thermal power station
1.	*Raw material consumption,*	Nil. Water power is inexhaustible and is continuously replenished by the direct agency of sun.	Huge quantity of coal consumed, thereby exhausting "fuel reserves"
2.	*Cost of energy*	Cheaper	Costlier
3.	*Cost of energy generation.*	Immune to inflation	Very much influenced by the increase in the cost of fuel.
4.	*Life of plant*	Long useful life.	Not so long comparatively. The component parts deteriorate and become obsolete at a faster rate.
5.	*Pollution*	Free from problems of pollution.	Cause pollution and subsequently create health hazards.
6.	*Design, construction and reliability.*	Simple in design, robust in construction and reliable in operation.	Comparatively more complicated in design, less robust in construction and less reliable in operation .
7.	*Running below a certain minimum load factor.*	Can be run.	Cannot be run.
8.	*Reserve capacity and variation in power demands.*	Particularly suited to provide reserve capacity as well as meeting the exact needs of daily variation in power demands.	Comparatively not suited for the mentioned requirements.
9.	*Employment potential.*	More. Affords a relatively high employment potential and better utilization of the available local talent and resources.	Less
10.	*Man power required*	Small	Large
11.	*Labour problem*	Less	More
12.	*Foreign exchange requirement for equipment.*	Less	More
13.	*Construction time required.*	Almost same as thermal power station.	Almost same as hydropower station.
14.	*Overall capital expenditure requirements.*	Low	High

Example 6.3. *At a proposed site of hydroelectric power plant the available discharge and head are 330 m³/s and 28 m respectively. The turbine efficiency is 86%. The generator is directly coupled to the turbine. The frequency of generator is 50 Hz and number of poles used are 24. Find the least number of machines required if,*

(i) A Francis turbine with a specific speed of 260 is used;

(ii) A Kaplan turbine with a specific speed of 700 is used.

Solution. Available discharge, $Q = 330 \text{ m}^3/\text{s}$

Head, $H = 28$ m

Turbine efficiency, $\eta = 86\%$

Frequency of generation, $f = 50$ Hz

Number of poles used, $p = 24$.

As the generator is directly coupled to the turbine, the speed of turbine used must be equal to the synchronous speed of the generator.

$$N = \frac{120f}{p} = \frac{120 \times 50}{24} = 250 \text{ r.p.m}$$

$$P = \eta \times wQH = 0.86 \times 9.81 \times 330 \times 28 = 77954 \text{ kW}$$

$$(\because w = 9.81 \text{ kN/m}^3)$$

(*i*) The power capacity of each Francis turbine (P_1) can be calculated by using the following formula:

$$N_s = \frac{N\sqrt{P_1}}{H^{5/4}}, \quad \text{or,} \quad 260 = \frac{250\sqrt{P_1}}{(28)^{5/4}}$$

$$\therefore \quad P_1 = \left[\frac{260 \times (28)^{5/4}}{250}\right]^2 = 4487 \text{ kW}$$

$\therefore$ *Number of Francis turbines required* $= \frac{P}{P_1} = \frac{77954}{4487} = \mathbf{17.37 \simeq 18.}$ **(Ans.)**

(*ii*) The power capacity of each Kaplan turbine can be calculated by using the following formula:

$$N_s = \frac{N\sqrt{P_2}}{H^{5/4}}, \quad \text{or,} \quad 700 = \frac{250\sqrt{P_2}}{(28)^{5/4}}$$

$$\therefore \quad P_2 = \left[\frac{700 \times (28)^{5/4}}{250}\right]^2 = 32524.5 \text{ kW}$$

$\therefore$ *Number of Kaplan turbines required*

$$= \frac{P}{P_2} = \frac{77954}{32524{\cdot}5} = \mathbf{2.4 \simeq 3.} \text{ (Ans.)}$$

Example 6.4. *The following data relate to a proposed hydro-electric station:*

Available head = 28 m; catchment area = 420 sq. km; rainfall = 140 cm/year; percentage of total rainfall utilised = 68%; penstock efficiency = 94%; turbine efficiency = 80%; generator efficiency = 84% and load factor = 44%.

(i) Calculate the power developed, and

(ii) Suggest suitable machines and specify the same.

Solution. Head available, H = 28 m

Catchment area, A = 420 sq. km (= 420×10^6 m^2)

Rainfall = 140 cm /year (= 1.4 m/year)

Rainfall utilised, h = 68% of the total rainfall

= (0.68 × 1.4) m per year

Penstock efficiency η_p = 94%

Turbine efficiency, η_t = 80%

Generator efficiency, η_g = 84%

Load factor = 44%.

(*i*) Power developed, *P*:

Quantity of water available per year = $A \times h$

$= (420 \times 10^6) \times (0.68 \times 1.4) = 399.84 \times 10^6\ m^3$

Hence the quantity of water available per second,

$$Q = \frac{399.84 \times 10^6}{(365 \times 24) \times 3600} = 12{\cdot}6\ m^3/s.$$

$\therefore$ $P = \eta_0 \times wQH$ (where η_0 = overall efficiency = $\eta_p \times \eta_t \times \eta_g$)

$P = \eta_p \times \eta_t \times \eta_g \times wQH$

$= 0.94 \times 0.8 \times 0.84 \times 9.81 \times 12.6 \times 28 = 2186.2$ kW ($\because$ $w = 9.81\ kN/m^3$)

Hence, average output of generating units = **2186.2 kW (Ans.)**

Example 6.5. *The following data is available for a hydropower plant :*

Available head = 140 m; catchment area = 200sq. km; annual average rainfall = 145 cm; turbine efficiency = 85 % ; generator efficiency = 90 % ; Percolation and evaporation losses = 16 %.

Determine the following :

(*i*) *Power developed, and*

(*ii*) *Suggest type of turbine to be used if runner speed is to be kept below 240 r.p.m.*

Solution. Head available, H = 140 m

Catchment area, A = 200 sq. km (= 200×10^6 m^2)

Annual average rainfall, h = 145 cm (= 1.45 m)

Turbine efficiency, η_t = 85 %

Generator efficiency, η_g = 90 %

Percolation and evaporation losses, z = 16 % = 0.16

(*i*) Power developed, *P* :

Quantity of water avilable for power generation per year

$= A \times h \times (1 - z)$

$= 200 \times 10^6 \times 1.45 \times (1 - 0.16) = 2.436 \times 10^8\ m^3$ /year

Hence, quantity of water available for power generation per second,

$$Q = \frac{2.436 \times 10^8}{(365 \times 24) \times 3600} = 7.72\ m^3/s$$

$P = \eta_0 \times wQH$

$= \eta_t \times \eta_g \times wQH$

$= 0.85 \times 0.9 \times 9.81 \times 7.72 \times 140 = 8111$ kW ($w = 9.81$ kN/m^3)

or, **8.111 MW (Ans.)**

***(ii)* Type of turbine to be used:**

$$\text{Specific speed, } N_s = \frac{N\sqrt{P}}{H^{5/4}} = \frac{240\sqrt{8111}}{(140)^{5/4}} = \mathbf{44.88\ r.p.m.}\ \textbf{(Ans.)}$$

Single pelton turbine with 4 jets can be used. Further since head available is large and discharge is low, pelton turbine will work satisfactorily.

Example 6.6. *From the investigation of hydrosite the following data is avilable:*

Available head	*45 m*
Total catchment area	*60 sq. km*
Rainfall per annum	*140 cm*
Percentage of rainfall utilized	*68%*
Turbine efficiency	*82%*
Generator efficiency,	*90%*
Penstock efficiency	*74%*

Calculate the suitable capacity of a turbo- generator.

Solution. Head available, $H = 45$ m

Catchment area, $A = 60$ sq. km ($= 60 \times 10^6 \text{m}^2$)

Availabe rainfall, $h = (0.68 \times 1.4)$ m

Turbine efficiency, $\eta_t = 82$ %

Generator efficiency, $\eta_g = 90$ %

Penstock efficiency, $\eta_p = 74$ %

Quantity of water available per annum

$= A \times h = 60 \times 10^6 \times 0.68 \times 1.4 = 57.12 \times 10^6$ m^3/annum

Hence, quantity of water available per second

$$Q = \frac{57.12 \times 10^6}{(365 \times 24) \times 3600} = 1.81 \text{ m}^3\text{/s}$$

Now overall efficiency, $\eta_0 = \eta_p \times \eta_t \times \eta_g = 0.74 \times 0.82 \times 0.9 = 0.546$

$\therefore$ Power developed, $P = \eta_0 \times wQH$

$= 0.546 \times 9.81 \times 1.81 \times 45 = 436$ kW

If a load factor of 55 percent is assumed, then,

$$\text{Maximum kW} = \frac{436}{0{\cdot}55} \simeq 793 \text{ kW}$$

So a *generator of* **800 kW maximum rating** *can be selected.*

$\therefore$ *Power of the turbine* $\dfrac{793}{0.82} =$ **967 kW (Ans.)**

For a head of 45 m, which is low, *a vertical shaft Francis or Kaplan trubine may be employed.*

Example 6.7. *A hydro-electric power plant produces 27 MW under a head of 15 metres. If the overall efficiency of the plant is 72%, determine :*

(i) *Type of turbine;* **(ii)** *Synchronous speed of the generator.*

Solution.

$$\text{Power developed, } P = 27 \text{ MW } (= 27 \times 10^3 \text{ kW})$$
$$\text{Head, } H = 15 \text{ m}$$
$$\text{Overall efficiency, } \eta_0 = 72\%.$$

(*i*) Type of turbine :

$$P = \eta_0 \times wQH$$
$$27 \times 10^3 = 0.72 \times 9.81 \times Q \times 15$$
$$\therefore \quad Q = \frac{27 \times 10^3}{0.72 \times 9.81 \times 15} = 188.8 \text{ m}^3/\text{s}$$

As the head is low and discharge is high so a propeller type of turbine should be used **(Ans.)**

(*ii*) Synchronous speed of the generator, N_{syn} :

$$\text{Specific speed, } N_s = \frac{1150}{H^{1/4}} \text{ (approx.)}$$
$$= \frac{1150}{(15)^{1/4}} = 584.3 \text{ r.p.m.}$$
$$\text{Speed of rotation, } N = \frac{N_s \times H^{5/4}}{\sqrt{P}} \qquad \left(\because N_s = \frac{N\sqrt{P}}{H^{5/4}}\right)$$
$$= \frac{584.3 \times (15)^{5/4}}{\sqrt{27 \times 10^3}} \simeq 105 \text{ r.p.m}$$
$$\text{For generator, } N = \frac{120f}{p}$$
$$105 = \frac{120 \times 50}{p}$$

[where, f = frequency (= 50 Hz)]

$$\therefore \quad \text{Number of poles, } p = \frac{120 \times 50}{105} = 57.14 = 60 \text{ (say)}$$

(as the number of poles is necessarily an *even* number)

$$\text{Again, } \quad N_{syn} = \frac{120f}{p} = \frac{120 \times 50}{60} = \mathbf{100 \text{ r.p.m.}} \quad \textbf{(Ans.)}$$

Example 6.8. *Calculate the power developed in MW from a hydro-electric power plant with the following data :*

Available head	*50 m*
Catchment area	*250 sq. km*
Average annual rainfall	*120 cm*
Rainfall lost due to evaporation	*20%*
Turbine efficiency	*82%*
Generator efficiency	*84%*
Head lost in penstock	*4%.*

Solution. Head available, $H = 50$ m

Catchment area, $A = 250$ sq. km $(= 250 \times 10^6 \text{ m}^2)$

Average annual rainfall, = 120 cm (= 1.2 m)

Evaporation, = 20%

∴ Average annual rainfall available, $h = (1 - 0.2) \times 1.2 = 0.96$ m

Turbine efficiency, η_t = 82%

Generator efficiency, η_g = 84%

Penstock efficiency, η_p = 100 – 4 = 96%

Quantity of water available *per annum*

$$= A \times h = 250 \times 10^6 \times 0.96 = 2.4 \times 10^8 \text{ m}^3$$

Hence, quantity of water available *per second,*

$$Q = \frac{2.4 \times 10^8}{(365 \times 24) \times 3600} = 7.61 \text{ m}^3/\text{s}$$

Overall efficiency, $\eta_o = \eta_p \times \eta_t \times \eta_g$

$$= 0.96 \times 0.82 \times 0.84 = 0.66$$

Power developed, $P = \eta_0 \times wQH$

$$= 0.66 \times 9.81 \times 7.61 \times 50 \text{ kW}$$

$$= 2463.6 \text{ kW or } 2.463 \text{ MW}$$

Hence, power developed = **2.463 MW. (Ans.)**

Example 6.9. *In an hydro-electric power plant the reservoir is 225 m above the turbine house. The annual replenishment of reservoir is 3.5 × 10^{12} N. Calculate the energy available at the generating station bus bars if the loss of head in the hydraulic system is 25 m and the over all efficiency of the system is 85%.*

If maximum demand of 45 MW is to be supplied, determine the diameter of two steel penstocks.

Solutuion. Actual head available, $H = 225 - 25 = 200$ m

Overall efficiency, η_0 = 85%

Annual replenishment, $W = 3.5 \times 10^{12}$ N.

(*i*) Energy output :

E = Energy available at the turbine house

$$= WH = 3.5 \times 10^{12} \times 200 = 7 \times 10^{14} \text{ Nm or J}$$

$$= \frac{7 \times 10^{14}}{36 \times 10^5} = 1.944 \times 10^8 \text{ kWh} \quad [\because 1 \text{ kWh} = 36 \times 10^5 \text{ J}]$$

Energy output = $\eta_0 \times E$

$= 0.85 \times 1.944 \times 10^8 =$ **1.652×10^8 kWh. (Ans.)**

(*ii*) Diameter of steel penstock, D :

Kinetic energy of water = Loss of potential energy

$$\therefore \quad \frac{1}{2}mC^2 = mgH$$

$$\therefore \quad C = \sqrt{2gH} = \sqrt{2 \times 9.81 \times 200} = 62.64 \text{ m/s}$$

(where, C = Velocity of water in each penstock, m = mass of water in kg)

Now, $\frac{1}{2}mC^2$ = Energy to be supplied

$$\frac{1}{2} m \times (62.64)^2 = 45 \times 10^6 \text{ W}$$

$$\therefore \quad m = \frac{45 \times 10^6 \times 2}{(62.64)^2} = 22937 \text{ kg}$$

Let, A = Area of two penstocks, m^2,

A_1 = Area of each penstock = $\frac{A}{2}$ and

D = Diameter of each penstock.

Then, $m = A \times C \times \rho$

(where, ρ = Mass density of water)

$$22973 = \text{A} \times 62.64 \times 1000 \qquad \left(\rho = \frac{w}{g} = \frac{9810}{9.81} = 1000 \text{ kg/m}^3\right)$$

$$A = \frac{22973}{62.64 \times 1000} = 0.366 \text{ m}^2$$

and, $$A_1 = \frac{A}{2} = \frac{0.366}{2} = 0.183 \text{ m}^2$$

Now, $$0.183 = \frac{\pi}{4} D^2$$

$$\therefore \quad D = \left(\frac{0.183 \times 4}{\pi}\right)^{1/2} = \mathbf{0.483 \text{ m}}. \textbf{ (Ans.)}$$

Example 6.10. *It is observed that a run-of-river plant operates as peak load plant with a weekly load factor of 25%, all this capacity being firm capacity. Determine the minimum flow in river so that power plant may act as a base load plant. The following data is supplied : Rated installed capacity of generating plant = 10 MW; operating head = 16 m; Plant efficiency = 86%.*

If the stream flow is 15 m^3/s, find the daily load factor of the plant.

Solution. Weekly load factor = 25%

Rated installed capacity of generating plant = 10 MW (= 10000 kW)

Operating head H = 16 m

Plant efficiency, η_0 = 86%

Minimum flow in river in m^3/sec, Q :

$$\because \quad \text{Load factor} = \frac{\text{Average load}}{\text{Maximum demand}}$$

$$\therefore \quad \text{Average load} = \text{Load factor} \times \text{maximum demand}$$

$$= 0.25 \times 10000 = 2500 \text{ kW}$$

E = Total energy generated in one *week*

$$= 2500 \times 24 \times 7 = 42 \times 10^4 \text{ kWh}$$

Now, Power developed, $P = \eta_0 wQH$ kW

$$= 0.86 \times 9.81 \times Q \times 16 \text{ kW} = 134.98\, Q \text{ kW}$$

$\therefore$ E_1 = Total energy generated in one *week*

$$= 134.98\,Q \times 24 \times 7 = 22676.6\,Q \text{ kWh}$$

Now, $E = E_1$

$$42 \times 10^4 = 22676.6\,Q$$

$$\therefore \quad Q = \frac{42 \times 10^4}{22676.6} = 18.52 \text{ m}^3/\text{s}$$

Hence, minimum flow rate $=$ **18.52 m³/s. (Ans.)**

Power developed when stream flow is 15 m³/s,

$$P_1 = 134.98 \times 15$$

$$= 2024.7 \text{ kW}$$

Energy generated per day,

$$E_2 = P_1 \times \text{time} = 2024.7 \times 24$$

$$= 48592.8 \text{ kWh}$$

$$\therefore \quad \textit{Daily load factor} = \frac{\text{Average load}}{\text{Maximum load}}$$

$$= \frac{48592.8}{10000 \times 24} = \mathbf{0.2025 \text{ or } 20.25\%} \text{ (Ans.)}$$

Example 6.11. *Calculate the firm capacity of a run-of-river hydro-power plant to be used as 8 hours peak plant assuming daily flow in a river to be constant at 15 m³/s. Also calculate pondage factor and pondage if the head of the plant is 11 m and overall efficiency is 85%.*

Solution. Discharge, $Q = 15 \text{ m}^3/\text{s}$

Plant head, $H = 11$ m

Overall efficiency, $\eta_0 = 85\%$

Specific weight of water, $w = 9.81 \text{ kN/m}^3$

$P =$ Firm capacity without pondage

$$= \eta_0 \times wQH = 0.85 \times 9.81 \times 15 \times 11$$

$$= 1375.8 \text{ kW}$$

$$PF = \text{Pondage factor} = \frac{t_1}{t_2}$$

where, t_1 = Total hours in one day = 24, and

t_2 = Number of hours for which plant runs = 8

[***Pondage factor*** *is the ratio of total inflow hours in a given period to the total number of hours for which plant runs during the same period.*]

$$PF = \frac{24}{8} = \mathbf{3.} \text{ (Ans.)}$$

$$Q_1 = 15 \times 3 = 45 \text{ m}^3/\text{s}$$

P_1 = Firm power with pondage

$$= 1375.8 \times 3 = 4127.4 \text{ kW}$$

Pondage (*magnitude*) = (24 – 8) = 16 hours flow

$$= 16 \times 60 \times 60 \times 15 = \mathbf{8.64 \times 10^5 \text{ m}^3.} \text{ (Ans.)}$$

Example 6.12. *The following data relate to a pump storage power plant :*

Gross head	*280 m*
Dia. of head-race tunnel	*4.0 m*
Length of head-race tunnel	*620 m*
Flow velocity	*6.5 m/s*
Friction factor	*0.018*
Pumping efficiency	*85%*
Generation efficiency	*90%*

If the power plant discharges directly in the lower reservoir determine the plant efficiency.

Solution. Head, $H = 280$ m

Dia. of head-race tunnel, $D = 4.0$ m

Length of head-race tunnel, $L = 620$ m

Flow velocity $C = 6.5$ m/s

Friction factor $f = 0.018$

Pumping efficiency $\eta_p = 85\%$

Generation efficiency $\eta_g = 90\%$

Plant efficiency, η_{plant} :

Loss of head due to friction (h_f) is given by the equation :

$$h_f = \frac{fLC^2}{2gD} = \frac{0.018 \times 620 \times 6.5^2}{2 \times 9.81 \times 4.0} = 6.0 \text{ m}$$

Now, $$h_f = xH$$

or, $$6 = x \times 280 \quad \therefore x = \frac{6}{280} = 0.0214$$

$\therefore$ $$\eta_{plant} = \frac{1-x}{1+x} \times \eta_p \times \eta_g = \frac{(1-0.0214)}{(1+0.0214)} \times 0.85 \times 0.9$$

$$= \mathbf{0.7329 \text{ or } 73.29\%} \text{ (Ans.)}$$

Example 6.13. *The nature of load required for 24 hours and thermal efficiencies of the plant at the respective loads are given in the table below :*

Time period	*Load (MW)*	*Thermal efficiency (%age)*
10 A.M. to 6 P.M.	*120*	*32%*
6 P.M. to 8 P.M.	*60*	*24%*
8 P.M. to 12 A.M.	*30*	*15%*
12 A.M. to 6 A.M.	*15*	*10%*
6 A.M. to 10 A.M.	*75*	*25%*

(i) *Find the total input to the thermal plant if the load is supplied by the single thermal plant only.*

(ii) *If the above load is taken by combined thermal and pump storage plant, then find the percentage saving in the input to the plant. Thermal efficiency at full load = 32%.*

(iii) *The overall efficiencies in both cases.*

In pump storage plant, the pump and turbine are separate. The efficiency of pump is 82% and water turbine is 92%.

Solution. The load curve, drawn as per data given, is shown in Fig. 6.11.

$$\text{Total output per day} = 75 \times 4 + 120 \times 8 + 60 \times 2 + 30 \times 4 + 15 \times 6$$
$$= 300 + 960 + 120 + 120 + 90 = 1590 \text{ MWh}$$

(i) Total input to the thermal plant :

The input to the thermal plant

$$= \frac{75 \times 4}{0.25} + \frac{120 \times 8}{0.32} + \frac{60 \times 2}{0.24} + \frac{30 \times 4}{0.15} + \frac{15 \times 6}{0.1}$$
$$= 1200 + 3000 + 500 + 800 + 900 = \mathbf{6400 \text{ MWh.}} \text{ (Ans.)}$$

(ii) Percentage saving in the input to plant :

The overall efficiency of the pump storage plant

$$= 0.82 \times 0.92 = 0.7544, \text{ or, } 75.44\%.$$

Assume that the capacity of the thermal plant is x MW when it is working in combination with pump-storage plant.

The energy used from the thermal plant to pump the water of pump storage plant during off-peak period *must be equal to* the energy supplied by the pump-storage plant during peak period.

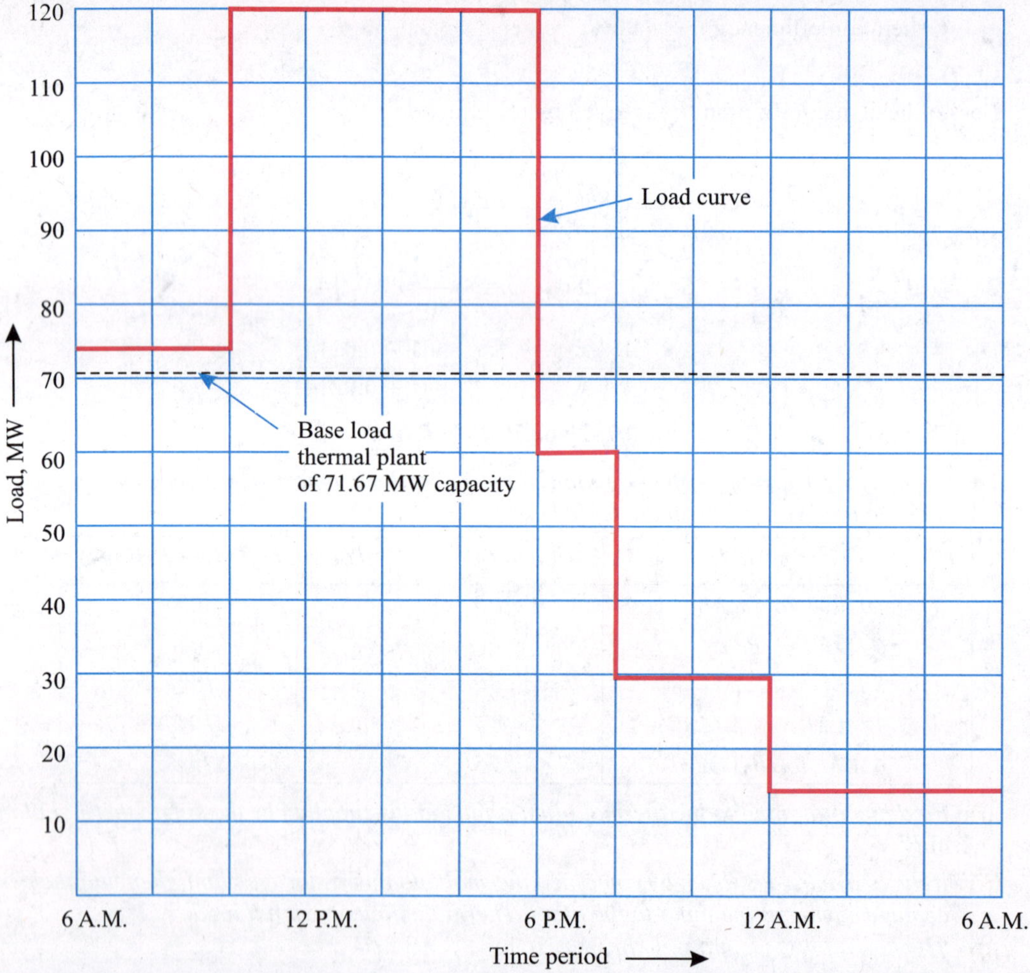

Fig. 6.11

From the Fig. 6.11, we have:

$[(x-60)\times 2+(x-30)\times 4+(x-15)\times 6]\times 0.7544=(75-x)\times 4+(120-x)\times 8$

or, $[(2x-120)+(4x-120)+(6x-90)]\times 0.7544=(300-4x)+(960-8x)$

or, $(12x-330)\times 0.7544 = 1260-12x$

or, $9.053x-248.95 = 1260-12x$

$$\therefore \quad x = \frac{1260+248.95}{(9.053+12)} = 71.67 \text{ MW}$$

The energy supplied in the second case

$$= \frac{71.67\times 24}{0.32} = 5375 \text{ MWh}$$

The percentage saving in input if the load is taken by combined thermal and pump storage plant

$$= \frac{6400-5375}{6400} = 0.16 \text{ or } \mathbf{16\%}. \textbf{ (Ans.)}$$

(*iii*) The overall efficiency in the first case :

$$= \frac{1590}{6400} = 0.2484 = \mathbf{24.84\%}. \textbf{ (Ans.)}$$

The overall efficiency in the *second case*

$$= \frac{1590}{5375} = 0.2958 \text{ or } \mathbf{29.58\%}. \textbf{ (Ans.)}$$

Example 6.14. *At a particular site of a river, the mean monthly discharge for 12 months is tabulated below :*

Month	Discharge (millions of m^3 per month)	Month	Discharge (millions of m^3 per month)
April	*250*	*Oct.*	*1000*
May	*100*	*Nov.*	*750*
June	*750*	*Dec.*	*750*
July	*1250*	*Jan.*	*500*
Aug.	*1500*	*Feb.*	*400*
Sep.	*1200*	*Mar.*	*300*

(*i*) *Draw hydrograph for the given discharges and find the average monthly flow.*

(*ii*) *Also draw the flow duration curve.*

(*iii*) *The power available at mean flow of water if available head is 90 metres at the site and overall efficiency of the generation is 82 percent.*

Take 30 days in a month.

Solution.

(*i*) Hydrograph:

The hydrograph, drawn as per data given, is shown in Fig. 6.12.

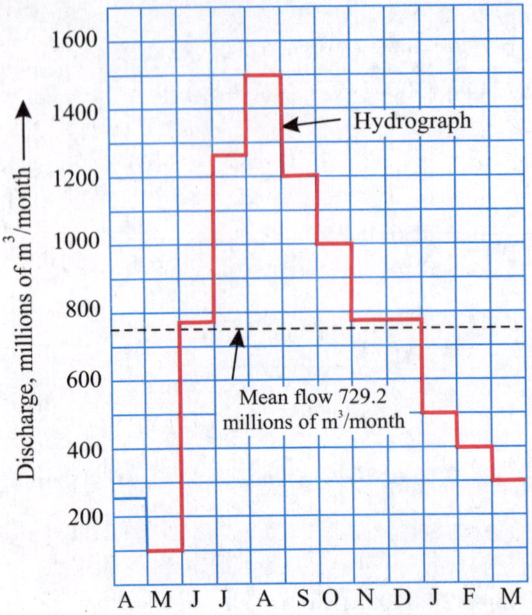

Fig. 6.12. Hydrograph.

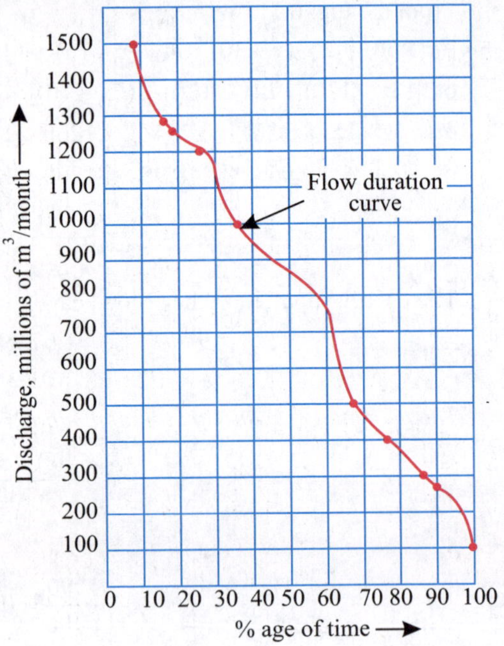

Fig. 6.13. Flow duration curve.

The average monthly flow (Refer to Fig. 6.12)

$$= \frac{250 + 100 + 750 + 1250 + 1500 + 1200 + 1000 + 750 + 750 + 500 + 400 + 300}{12}$$

$=$ **729.2 millions of m³/month. (Ans.)**

(*ii*) Flow duration curve :

In order to obtain the *flow duration curve* it is necessary to find the lengths of time during which certain flows are available. This information is tabulated, using the hydrograph, in the following table:

Discharge per month millions of m³	*Total number of months during which flow is available*	*Percentage time during which flow is available*
100	12	100
250	11	91.8
300	10	83.40
400	9	76.00
500	8	66.60
750	7	58.40
1000	4	33.30
1200	3	25.00
1250	2	16.65
1500	1	8.325

By using the above tabulated data, the *flow duration curve* can be shown in Fig. 6.13.

(*iii*) Power available at mean flow of water :

The mean/average flow available per second

$$= \frac{729.2 \times 10^6}{30 \times 24 \times 3600} = 281.3 \text{ m}^3/\text{s}$$

Average kW available at the site

$$= \frac{wQH}{1000} \times \eta_g \text{ MW} \qquad (\because w = \rho g = 1000 \times 9.81 = 9.81 \text{ kN/m}^3)$$

$$= \frac{9.81 \times 281.3 \times 90}{1000} \times 0.82 = \mathbf{203.6\ MW}. \textbf{ (Ans.)}$$

Example 6.15. *The data for a weekly flow at a particular site is given below for 12 weeks :*

Week	*Weekly flow, m³/s*	*Week*	*Weekly flow, m³/s*
1	*3000*	*7*	*600*
2	*2000*	*8*	*2250*
3	*2700*	*9*	*4000*
4	*1000*	*10*	*2000*
5	*750*	*11*	*1500*
6	*500*	*12*	*1000*

With the help of mass curve, find the size of the reservoir and the possible rate of available flow after the reservoir has been built.

Solution. In order to draw *mass curve,* we need to find the cumulative volume of water that can be stored week after week. This is done as tabulated in the table below:

Week (*a*)	*Weekly flow in m³/s* (*b*)	*Weekly flow in day-sec-metres* (*c*) = (*b*) × 7	*Cumulative volume in day-sec-metres* (*d*)
1	3000	21000	21000
2	2000	14000	35000
3	2700	18900	53900
4	1000	7000	60900
5	750	5250	66150
6	500	3500	69650
7	600	4200	73850
8	2250	15750	89600
9	4000	28000	117600
10	2000	14000	131600
11	1500	10500	142100
12	1000	7000	149100

If the *mean flow* is available in the week at the given rate, the the total flow in the week = 7 × day × m^3/s = 7 × day-sec-metres.

By using the above tabulated data, the mass curve can be drawn as shown in Fig. 6.14.

- Draw the tangent at the highest point on the mass curve from 'p' and *measure the highest distance between the tangent drawn and mass curve which gives the capacity of the reservoir.*

In this **case, capacity of the reservoir = 18 × 10³ day-sec-metres (Ans.)**

- The *slope of the line 'pq' gives the flow rate available for the given capacity reservoir.*

$$\therefore \quad \textbf{Flow rate available} = \frac{qr}{pr} = \frac{54 \times 10^3 \text{ (day-sec-metres)}}{5.5 \times 7 \text{ (days)}} = \mathbf{1402.6\ m^3\ /\ s.}\ \textbf{(Ans.)}$$

Example 6.16. *The following run-off data is collected for twelve months at a particular site :*

Month	*Flow per month, millions of m^3*	*Month*	*Flow per month, millions of m^3*
1	*50*	*7*	*95*
2	*25*	*8*	*20*
3	*10*	*9*	*15*
4	*40*	*10*	*100*
5	*5*	*11*	*85*
6	*5*	*12*	*40*

Determine the following :

(i) *The required capacity for the uniform flow of 25 millions m^3 per month throughout the year.*

(ii) *Spill-way capacity.*

(iii) *Average flow capacity if whole water is used and required capacity of the reservoir for this condition.*

Solution. In order to draw the ***mass curve,*** we need to find the cumulative volume of water that can be stored month after month. This is done as shown in the following table :

Month	*Flow per month (millions of m^3)*	*Cumulative volume, (millions of m^3)*
1	50	50
2	25	75
3	10	85
4	40	125
5	5	130
6	5	135
7	95	230
8	20	250
9	15	265
10	100	365
11	85	450
12	40	490

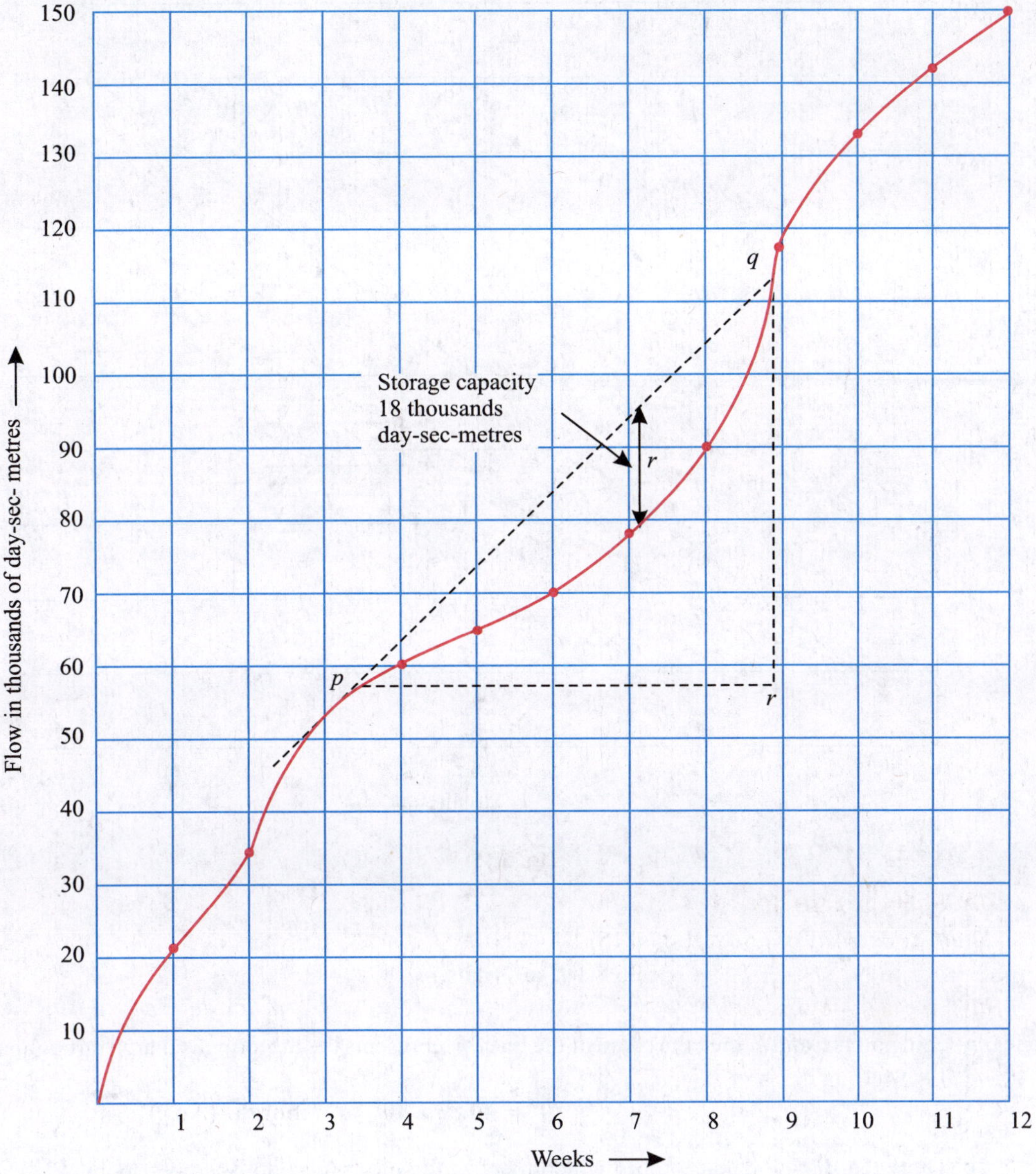

Fig. 6.14

By using the above tabulated data, the mass curve can be drawn as shown in Fig. 6.15.

(*i*) Required capacity for the uniform flow of 25 millions–m^3 per month :

- For finding the capacity of the reservoir for uniform flow of 25 millions–m^3 per month, construct the Δpqr as shown in Fig. 6.15. *qr* represents one month and *pr* represents 25 millions–m^3.
- Now draw the parallel lines to the line *pq* through the points *e* and *g* which are apex of mass curve. The greatest departure of the mass curve from these lines represents the storage capacity.

∴ *Storage capacity* = **35 × 10^6 m^3. (Ans.)**

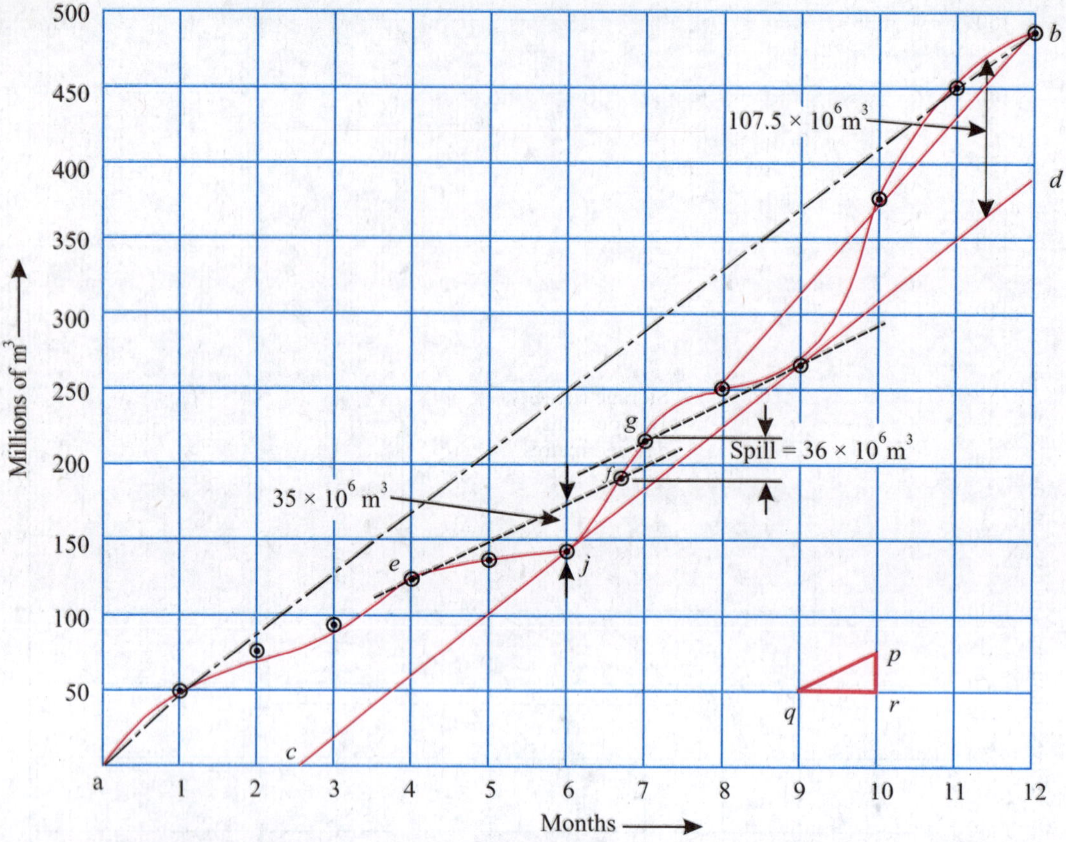

Fig. 6.15

(ii) Spillway capacity :

Spillway capacity required (Fig. 6.15)

$$= \mathbf{36 \times 10^3\ m^3.\ (Ans.)}$$

(iii) Average flow capacity

- Join points *a* and *b*, then the slope of the line *ab* represents the uniform discharge throughout the year

$$= \frac{490}{12} \times 10^6 = \mathbf{40.83 \times 10^6\ m^3 / month.\ (Ans.)}$$

- Draw the line *cd* parallel to *ab* which touches the mass curve to its lowest point '*j*'. The *maximum departure of the line cd from the mass curve represents the required* ***storage capacity*** *for the uniform supply of 40.83 × 10⁶ m³/month.* In this case, storage capacity required

$$= \mathbf{107.5 \times 10^6\ m^3.\ (Ans.)}$$

HIGHLIGHTS

1. A dam is a barrier to confine or rise water for storage or diversion to create a hydraulic head.
2. A canal is an open waterway excavated in natural ground. A flume is an open channel excavated on the surface or supported above ground on a trestle. A tunnel is a closed channel excavated through a natural obstruction such as ridge of higher land between the dam and the power house.

3. A surge tank is a small reservoir or tank in which the water level rises or falls to reduce the pressure swing so that they are not transmitted in full to a closed curcuit.
4. A draft tube serves the following two purposes :
   (*i*) It allows the turbine to set above tail-water level without loss of head, to facilitate inspection and maintenance.
   (*ii*) It regains, by diffuser action, the major portion of the kinetic energy delivered to it from the runner.
5. The plants which cater for the base load of the system are called 'base load plants' whereas the plants which can supply the power during peak loads are known as 'peak load plants'.
6. Microhydel plants (microstations) make use of standardized bulb sets with unit output rainging from 100 to 1000 kW working under heads between 1.5 to 10 metres.
7. The *specific speed* of a turbine is defined as the speed of a geometrically similar turbine that would develop one brake power under a head of one metre.
8. The Pelton turbine is a tangential flow impulse turbine. The pressure over the pelton wheel is constant and equal to atmosphere, so that energy transfer occurs due to purely impulse action.
9. The modern Francis water turbine is an inward mixed flow reaction turbine. It operates under medium heads and also requires medium quantity of water.
10. In the propeller turbine the runner blades are fixed and not-adjustable. In Kaplan turbine, which is a modification of propeller turbine the runner blades are adjustable and can be rotated about the pivots fixed to the boss of runner.
11. *Cavitation* may be defined as the phenomenon which manifests itself in the pitting of the metallic surfaces of turbine parts because of formation of cavitites.
12. *Hydrology* may be defined as the science which deal with the depletion and replenishment of water resources.
13. Run-off includes all the water flowing in the stream channel at any given section. It can be measured by the following methods:
    (*i*) From rainfall records
    (*ii*) Empirical formulae
    (*iii*) Run-off curve and tables
    (*iv*) Discharge observation method.
14. *Hydrograph* is defined as a graph showing discharge (run-off) of flowing water with respect to time for a specified time. It indicates the power available from the stream at different time of day, week or year.
15. *Flow duration curve* represents the run-off data for the given time. It is plotted between flow available during a period versus the fraction of time.

THEORETICAL QUESTIONS

1. Define hydrology.
2. Draw and explain the hydrologic cycle.
3. Define run-off. How is it measured ?
4. List the factors which affect run-off.
5. What is a hydrograph ?
6. What is a unit hydrograph ? What are the limitations to the use of unit hydrograph ?
7. What is a flow duration curve ?
8. What is a mass curve ?
9. Write a short note on hydropower development in India.

UNSOLVED EXAMPLES

1. The following data is available for a hydropower plant:

   Available head = 130 m; catchment area = 220 sq. km; annual average rainfall = 150 cm ; turbine efficiency = 86%; generator efficiency = 91% ; percolation and evaporation losses = 18%.

   Determine power developed in MW taking load factor as unity. **[Ans.** 8.563 MW]

2. From the investigation of a hydrosite the following data is available :

   Available head = 50 m; catchment area = 50 sq. km; rainfall = 150 cm per year; 70% of rainfall can be utilised; turbine efficiency 80%, generater efficiency = 91%; penstock efficiency = 75%; load factor = 60%.

   Determine the suitable capacity of a turbo-generator.

   [Ans. 750 kW (maximum rating). Francis or Kaplan turbine]

3. At a particular site the mean discharge (in millions of m^3) of a river in 12 months from January to December is respectively 80, 50, 40, 20, 0, 100, 150, 200, 220, 120, 100, 80.

   (*i*) Draw a hydrograph and find the mean flow.

   (*ii*) Also draw the flow duration curve.

   (*iii*) Find the power in MW available at mean flow if the head available is 100 m and overall efficiency of generation is 100 m and overall efficiency of generation is 80%.

   Take the each month of 30 days.

   [Ans. (*i*) 96.67 millions of m (*ii*) 29.2 MW]

Chapter 7

FLUIDICS

7.1. INTRODUCTION

The term **fluidics** relates to the combination of the two functions namely *fluid amplification and fluid logic.*

Fluidics is *defined as a control technology which makes use of fluids interaction to produce useful signals.*

- The *"field of fluidics" is the study of the performance and response characteristics of control systems, computing devices and logical switch gears based on the fluidic elements.*
- In finer control engineering, non-moving logic elements find a prominent place. *Irrespective of the development of electronics, low pressure pneumatics and fluidic elements have certain specific characteristics which put them at par with electronic controls even for modern sophisticated machines.* Various fluidic elements have been developed conforming to the need of logic functions in the industrial automation.

— The *basic principle is derived from the "Tesla's fluid-diode" and theory of "wall attachment" discovered by Coanda.*

— More and more fluid-logic elements in the form of logic gates like OR, NOR, etc. are being used along with power pneumatic circuits to offer better control and feedback to the pneumatic system. One of the major areas of their application is in the *field of sensors*. The present day state of art of pneumatic sensors is quite competitive with other form of sensors *e.g.,* fine mechanical, opto-electrical, inductive, hydraulic, ultra sound and magnetic devices etc. and are therefore widely used in various engineering tools and instruments.

History of fluidics :

- 1904 : *L. Prandtl* (German aerodynamist) suggested that in a wide angled diffuser the flow separation could be controlled by applying suction to the boundary layer.
- 1916 : — Nikola *Tesla* filed a patent for a "Valvular Conduit" for fluids in which there was an easy direction of flow and a difficult direction, owing to the interference caused by the divided branch flow opposing the intended flow-direction as can be seen in Fig. 7.1 which was granted in 1920.

— Whill Tesla claimed to have invented the first fluid device having no moving parts.

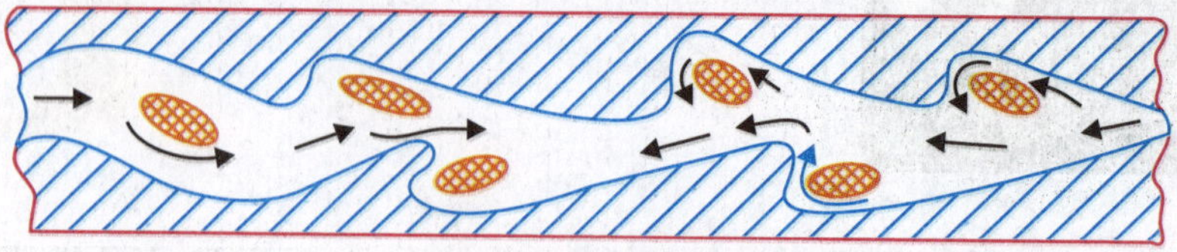

Fig. 7.1. Tesla's tube.

- 1930 : Henri *Coanda* (a Rumanian engineer) discovered that a free jet would follow an adjacent curved or inclined surface. Coanda's theory of "*wall attachment*" was a major stepping stone in the development of this field. Later this effect was used for the development of fluidic logic components.
- 1958 : Moore and Klive, working with wide angled diffusers, discovered that a jet could have two or three stable stages, depending on the angle of diffuser through which the jet was flowing.
- 1962 : Ray Auger discovered a fluidic logic element called "*Turbulence amplifier*".

7.2. ADVANTAGES, DISADVANTAGES AND APPLICATIONS OF FLUIDIC DEVICES/FLUIDICS

During the last few decades, the technology of electronic control system has leapt through milestones of innovations with various forms of transistors, ICs and the like, production costs have drastically reduced, and reliability has increased many a fold. Inspite of these developments, fluidic devices are finding wide applications and claim the following *advantages* :

Advantages :

1. More reliable.
2. Simpler in construction.
3. Smaller in size, mass or weight.
4. Offer exceptional physical and thermal stability and ruggedness.
5. Noise free.
6. Hazard free.
7. Mode of energy feeding to a fluidic system is very simple.
8. Fuidic elements are easily adaptable to logic functions in engineering applications.
9. Have good response and performance characterisitics (0.001 second).
10. Since they contain no moving parts, not much maintenance problems are encountered.

Disadvantages :

1. Unsuitable for incompressible fluids.
2. Slow speeds and low power outputs.
3. Complex systems are impracticable.
4. Inefficient in operation; they cannot be used in high-speed switching operations.
5. Not suitable for intermittent operation control systems.
6. Limited development of the field.

- The working pressure used for pneumatic fluid devices is very less within 0.05 to 0.1 bar but need not always be so. They are quite sensitive to load and position which can be easily sensed with the help of instrumentation.

Applications : The fluidic devices are used :

1. To measure flow rates;
2. To provide on-off controls;
3. To check weights;
4. To operate various types of machinery, etc.

- If used with a chemically inert gas such as nitrogen or helium, these devices are especially advantageous in cases where fire or electrical hazards are present, as in the manufacture of explosives.

7.3. FLUIDIC (OR FLUID LOGIC) ELEMENTS

7.3.1. General Aspects

The fluidic elements (also called *fuid logic elements*) were developed in the early sixties. The primary merit of these elements over all other forms of control elements is that they have a *minimum number of mechanical moving parts;* because of this, these elements are also known as "*non-moving logic*" controllers.

These element claim the following *advantages :*

1. Quite insensitive to temperature, vibration, shock, electric noise and radiation.
2. Insensitive to electromagnetic interferences etc.
3. Need no actuating force.
4. No wear and tear of elements.
5. Need very little space for mounting.

7.3.2. Coanda Effect

Physically a fluidic device is a block of material having an internal network of passages. One of the basic underlying principle of the functioning of these flow passages was given by Henri Marie Coanda (a Ramanian engineer) and is known as *"Coanda effect"* or *"Wall attachment effect"*.

This effect is explained below : Refer to Fig. 7.2.

- **Fig. 7.2. (*i*) :** A free jet of air is emitted into a confined region or orifice at a velocity high enough to *produce turbulent flow.*

  Fig. 7.2. (*ii*) : The free jet of air will continue in a given direction, pulling in with it the available air from its surroundings as it leaves the orifice. If there is greater availability of this entraining air from one side, a small vortex area (low pressure area/region) is created near the nozzle exit. This low pressure area then tends to attract the free jet, distorting it and pulling it towards the wall, because the atmospheric pressure on the other side forces the jet to cling to the surface.

  Fig. 7.3. (*iii*) : The free jet attachment continues until a small air supply is fed to the low pressure area, thus relieving the attraction of the jet to the wall. When this signal is injected, the free jet then detaches itself from the wall and resumes its normal uninterrupted flow path.

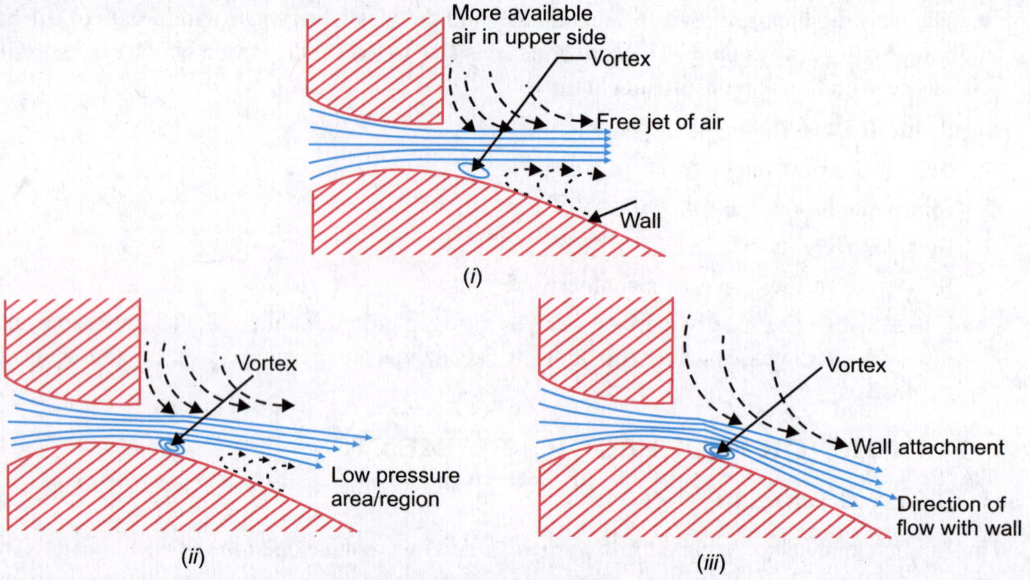

Fig. 7.2. Coanda/Wall attachment effect.

7.3.3 Classification of Fluidic Devices

Fluidic devices may be *classified* as follows :

A. 1. Digital fluidic devices :

(*i*) Wall attachment. (*ii*) Turbulence.

(*iii*) Vortex feedback.

- A *digital element* has two outputs, and flow takes place from one or other output depending upon the presence or absence of control signal. The flow never splits between two outputs; it is either fully out of one or other. It can be compared to a simple "ON-OFF" switch.
- The digital devices are of the following two categories :

(*a*) *Monostable :*

— In the absence of a signal the device always selects one of its two output states. The other state can only be selected by applying and maintaining the signal *i.e.,* when the applied signal is removed the device returns to its former state.

These devices do *not* have any *memory*.

Example : 3/2 normally operated, spring return D.C. valve.

(*b*) *Bistable :*

— The output of this device in any direction is stable, irrespective of the fact whether applied signal is present or absent.

— These devices are *equipped with memory.*

Example : 4/2 pilot operated D.C. valve.

Examples of digital fluidic devices :

(*i*) Bistable flip-flops; (*ii*) Logic gates, etc.

2. Analogue fluidic devices :

(*i*) Stream or beam deflection. (*ii*) Impact modulator.

(*iii*) Vortex.

- An "*Analogue element*" varies its output *continuously* as a function of the control output signal and gives *proportional control* (similar to an accelerator pedal of a car)

  Examples of analogue fluidic devices :

  (*i*) Fluidic position sensors; (*ii*) Fluidic vortex amplifier;
  (*iii*) Wall attachment amplifier; (*iv*) Fluidic oscillator, etc.

B. 1. Active fluidic devices :

— In an active fluidic device, the power nozzle of the device is *continuously supplied with an air pressure source.*

2. Passive fluidic devices :

— These devices intermittently receive pressure signals at the power nozzle, and this signal usually comes from the *output of preceding element in the circuit.* In other words the air only passes momentarily through the device.

C. 1. Fluid logic devices :

(*i*) Bi-stable flip-flop; (*ii*) AND gate;
(*iii*) OR-NOR gate, etc.

2. Fluidic sensors :

(*i*) Interruptible jet sensor; (*ii*) Reflex sensor;
(*iii*) Back pressure sensor.

3. Fluidic amplifiers :

(*i*) Turbulence amplifier; (*ii*) Vortex amplifiers.

7.3.4. Fluid Logic Devices

The following terms are frequently used in connection with fluid logic devices :

1. ***Logic function or gate.*** *It is defined as an assembly of one or more logic elements which produce a desired effect on satisfying certain conditions, i.e., if we apply correct input signals, we will get the required output.*
2. ***Input signal.*** *It is the pressure or flow which is directed into the input part to control the logic function or an element.*
3. ***Output signal.*** *It is the pressure or flow which is leaving the output part of a logic function or an element.*

7.3.4.1. Bi-stable flip-flop

A bi-stable flip-flop is the most common fluid logic device. It works on the principle of *Coanda effect.*

Fig. 7.3. shows this device :

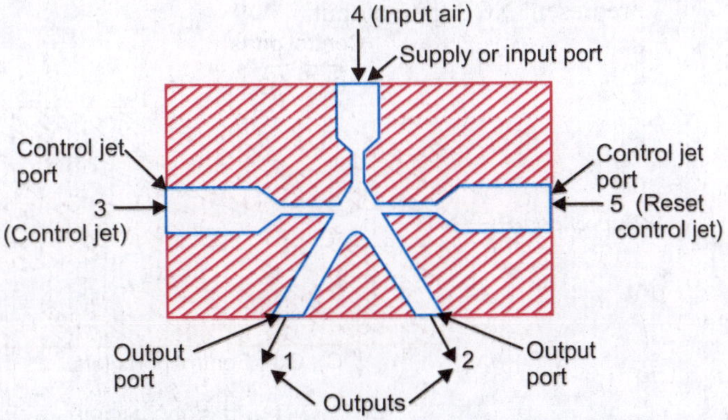

Fig. 7.3. Bi-stable flip-flop.

— In general, it consist of five ports, out of which one is supply port; two control jet ports and two output ports.

— Supply is always present on the input port (4) whereas output is dependent on the control jets (3, 5), *i.e.,* when fluid is passed from control jet 3 there will be an output – 1 and similarly when there is a supply at control jet–5 the output will be an output – 2.

- The device is suited for binary logic functions, as the output either exists or does not. The output from this device can be used as "pilot signal" for actuating various valves with low pressure actuating element.
- This device can be manufactured easily out of glass or plastic, not much larger than the size of a coin, the orifice size in such devices is of the order of 0.25 mm in diameter and the working pressure is about 0.05 to 0.1 bar. The operational speed is about 1000 cycles per second.

7.3.4.2. AND gate

Fig. 7.4. shows a fluidic AND gate/element; its operation is based on Coanda's wall attachment theory.

(*i*) Under no-control condition, output is at 0 (output–0).

(*ii*) When control jet C_1 is on, output is at 1 (output–1).

(*iii*) *When both the control jets C_1 and C_2 are on, only then there is an output at the AND gate, i.e.,* output is at 2 (output–2).

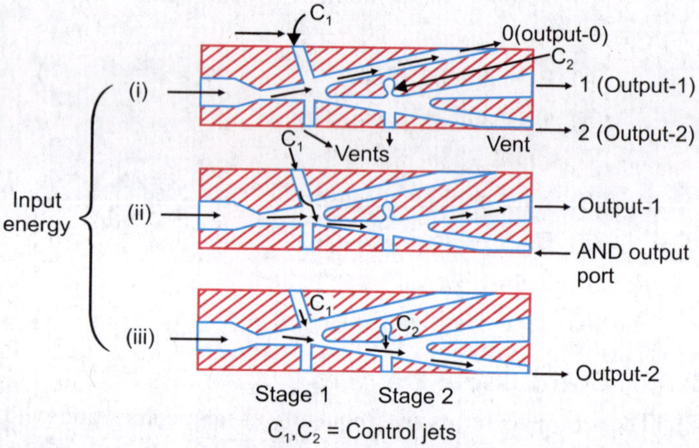

Fig. 7.4. AND gate.

7.3.4.3. OR–NOR gate

Fig. 7.5 shows fluidic OR–NOR gate.

— It consists of supply port S from which the fluid is supplied all the time. There are two control ports C_1 and C_2 and two output ports X and X_1. X represents the OR gate output while X_1 represent NOR gate output.

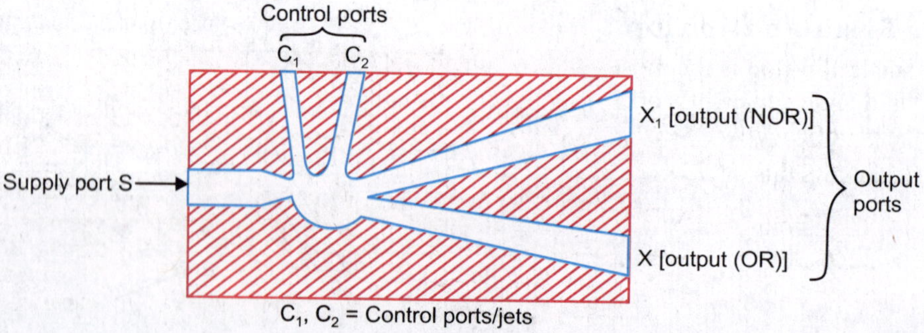

Fig. 7.5. OR–NOR gate.

— When the control jets C_1 and C_2 are absent, supply S is passed through the gate via output X_1. It implies that when there is no control input, there is an output. This is the characteristics of NOR gate and X_1 is considered as NOR output.

— When fluid stream is present at either of control jet C_1 or C_2 or both at C_1 and C_2, there will be output at X. It implies that even with one control input there is an output. This is the logic characteristic of OR gate and X output is considered as OR output.

The complete device is called as OR–NOR gate.

- Fig. 7.6 shows a circuit diagram illustrating the application of fluidic pressure for actuating a low pressure diaphragm valve.

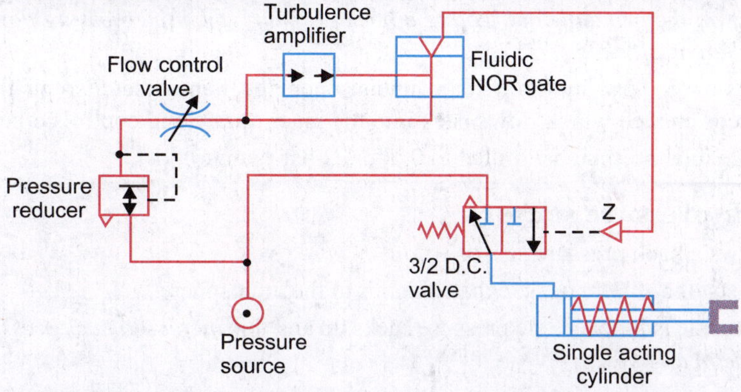

Fig. 7.6. Application of fluidic elements in pneumatic circuit.

7.3.5. Fluidic Sensors

These sensors (generally of very small size) are mainly used *to detect the presence of objects.* They are *designed to provide a signal in the form of fluid jet, to indicate the presence of an object.*

- The output of these sensors can be directly used as a *control signal for pneumatic logic circuits.* These control signals, however, need to be amplified when employed in pneumatic and hydraulic devices.

A few important fluidic sensors are described in the following subarticles.

7.3.5.1. Interruptible jet sensor

Fig. 7.7 shows an interruptible jet sensor :

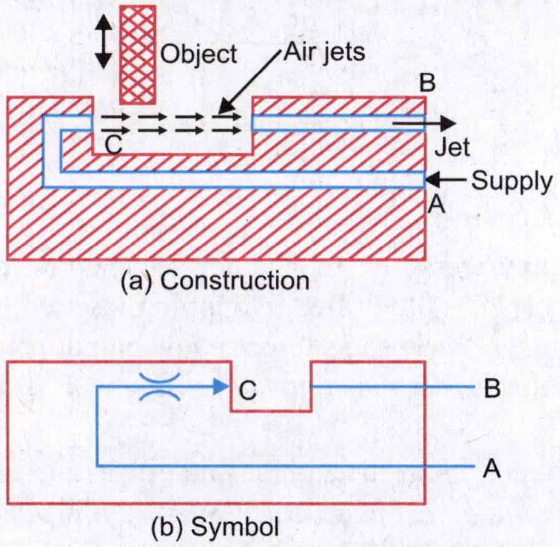

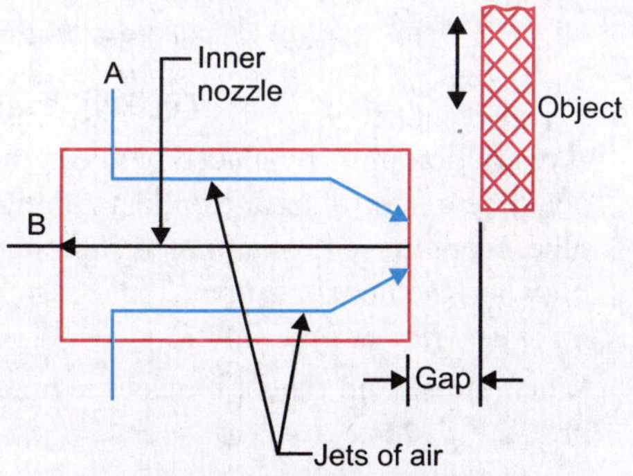

Fig. 7.7. Interruptible jet sensor. **Fig. 7.8.** Reflex sensor-symbol.

— Low pressure air is permitted to pass from A to B uninterrupted. But if a mechanical object comes between C and B, the air jets are blocked after leaving the port C and the signal at B disappears.

— The pressure at A ranges between 0.1 bar to 2 bar, but normal air-line pressure may also be used. However, in that case, it is better to throttle the air before it enters at inlet A.

— Sensing gap is limited to 5 mm.

7.3.5.2. Reflex sensor

Fig. 7.8. shows the symbol of a reflex sensor :

— It *works on the principle of creating a back pressure when the pressure flowing out to the atmosphere is blocked.*

— Two jets of air flow out through an annular opening. If an object disrupts the jets, a back pressure is created which flows back into the inner nozzle and controls other valves.

— Here, the inlet pressure is limited to 0.1 to 0.2 bar (gauge).

7.3.5.3. Back pressure sensor

Fig. 7.9 shows a back pressure sensor :

— It consists of a small nozzle exhausting air to the atmosphere.

— When nozzle is blocked, the pressure backs up and this *increased back pressure signals the presence of an object.*

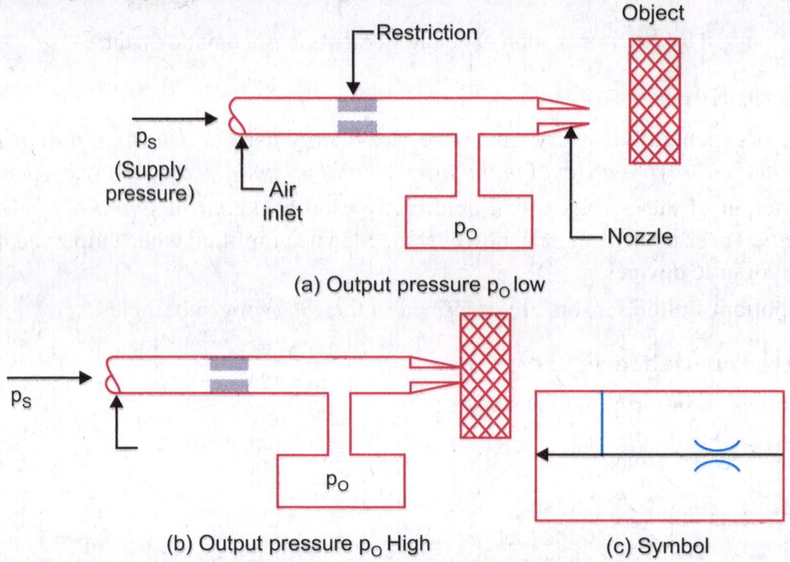

Fig. 7.9. Back pressure sensor.

— A restriction must be placed between the supply pressure inlet and nozzle. This restriction could be a short length capillary tubing or a small hole drilled into a plug inserted in the tube. Its purpose is to *produce sufficient pressure drop* so as to get a low output pressure p_o, when the nozzle is open. The reason for this is that *sensitivity of sensing will be better if the pressure is low.*

— When the sensed object blocks the nozzle outlet, the restriction has no effect, and output pressure p_o *almost equals pressure* $\mathbf{p_s}$. *Thus the object can be sensed only if practically touches the nozzle.*

7.3.6. Fluidic amplifiers

If a device gives a large change in output either pressure, flow or both, as a result of a small change in control input, the device is said to have "gain" or in other words it is an ***amplifier***.

An amplifier can be either electric, hydraulic, pneumatic, or fluidic.

- *"Fluidic amplifiers" not only control but also provide certain amplification to the fluid signals.*

7.3.6.1. Turbulence amplifier

Fig. 7.10. Illustrates a turbulence amplifier (T.A.)

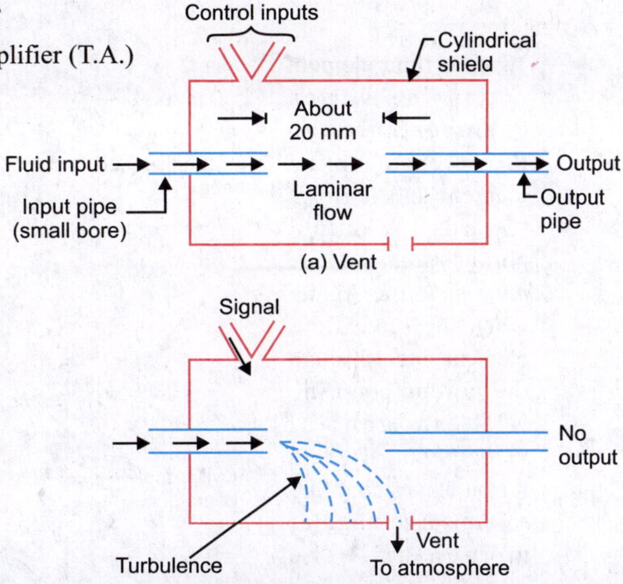

Fig. 7.10. Turbulence amplifier.

— Low pressure fluid is conducted through a long, small bore pipe to achieve *laminar flow.*

— This laminar flow issued from the inlet pipe transits the space of about 20 mm and is then collected by the outlet pipe. The space between input pipe and output pipe is protected by a cylindrical shield of diameter 20 to 30 times that of input/output pipe. This shield houses the *'control inputs'* and it is vented to atmosphere as shown in the figure.

— When there is no control input or signal, the laminar flow proceeds from input to output through the open space within the turbulence amplifier. However, if there is an input control signal, this will create a turbulence between the input and output pipes; thus the output *will not collect* any flow, hence there is *No output.*

— When the control signal is *removed,* the laminar flow is reestablished and *there will be an output.*

— There can be several control inputs and the logic function is NOR.

In these devices, the switch off time is about 4 ms (milli seconds) and the total cycle time may not exceed 6 to 7 ms.

- Following are the examples of the application of the "turbulence amplifier" to some industrial problems :

(*i*) Sensing; (*ii*) Counting;
(*iii*) Discrimination; (*iv*) Timing;
(*v*) Dispensing; (*vi*) Liquid level sensing.

7.3.6.2. Vortex amplifier

This fluidic device is used to regulate the flow of fluid by *utilising the properties of a vortex.*

Fig. 7.11. shows a vortex amplifier :

— It consists of a cylindrical disc like container, which is divided by a *cylindrical porous element* into two chambers : *Outer* chamber and *vortex* chamber.

— Supply port S is provided for fluid inlet to the cylindrical disc.

— Control jet C is provided to generate vortex in the vortex chamber. Several control jets along the circumference can be provided depending upon capacity, which throw streams of fluid in *tangential direction* and generate vortex motion in fluid.

— At the centre there is an output port X from where signal is transmitted.

Working :

— When a fluid element enters the vortex chamber through the porous coupling element and it flows towards the output port its *radial velocity must increase.* Again, when the same fluid element enters through the porous coupling with tangential velocity imparted to it as it leaves coupling to conserve angular momentum, the *angular velocity of fluid must increase* as it approaches the output port X. Thus there are two amplifying properties of vortex amplifier : (*i*) Increase in radial velocity; (*ii*) Increase in angular velocity.

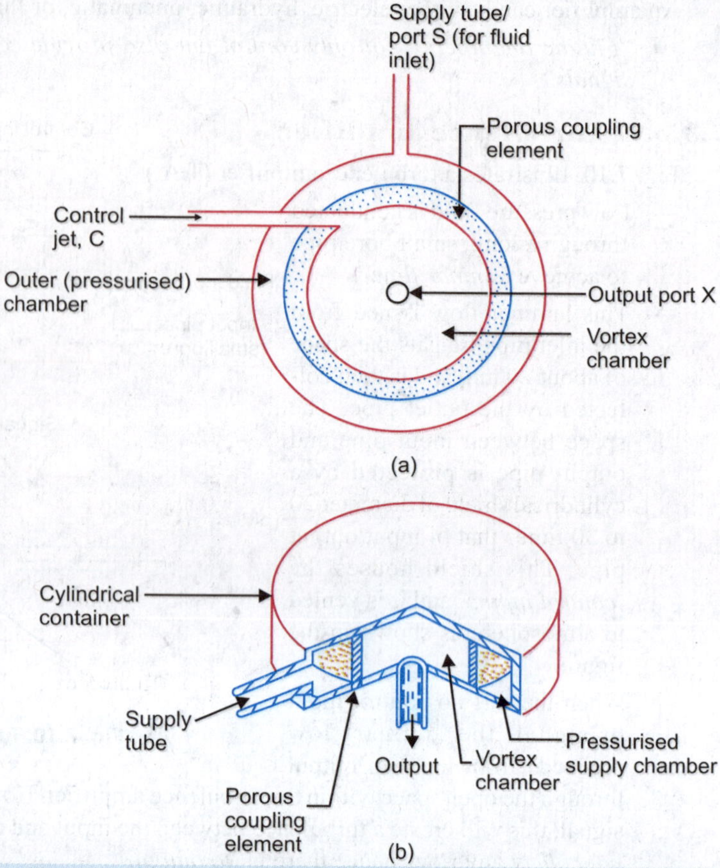

Fig. 7.11. Vortex amplifier.

— When the supply pressure is regulated, if the vortex motion of the fluid produces a centrifugal pressure drop across the vortex chamber, there is less pressure at the exit to expel the liquid, thus *less fluid flows from the exit.* The introduction of vortex motion into the chamber effectively throttles the fluid through the chamber.

It has been observed from the curves of output flow as function of the control pressure applied to vortex chamber that, the *flow is reduced with the increase of control pressure.*

— *When the control pressures are sufficiently high, the flow from supply is zero or even slightly reversed.* Centrifugal pressure increases the pressure at the inside surface of the porous coupling element so that the total pressure is *equal to or slightly higher than the supply pressure.* As a result, the control flow *can cut-off completely the flow from the supply chamber.*

The flow versus control pessure curves, for high control pressures, become tangent to the time of zero supply flow.

- *In any case, the control pressure should not be less than the supply pressure.*

7.4. COMPARISON AMONG DIFFERENT SWITCHING ELEMENTS

The comparison among different switching elements (Pneumatic valves, moving part logic elements and fluidics) is given in tabular form on the next page :

S.No.	Aspects	Pneumatic valves	Moving part logic elements	Fluidics
1.	*Air consumption*	Low	Low	High
2.	*Supply air pressure*	High	Intermediate to high	Low
3.	*Relative size*	Large	Intermediate	Intermediate
4.	*Response time*	10 to 20 ms	5 to 10 ms	1-2 ms
5.	*Sensitivity to dirt and conversion*	Good	Good	Poor
6.	*Sensitivity to shock and vibration*	Excellent	Intermediate	Excellent
7.	*Sensitivity to electric noise and radiation*	Excellent	Excellent	Excellent
8.	*Sensitivity to high temperatures*	Good	Good	Excellent
9.	*Life expectancy*	10^7 to 10^8 cycles	10^7 to 10^8 cycles	Unlimited (with clean air)

HIGHLIGHTS

1. *Fluidics* is defined as a control technology which makes use of fluids interaction to produce useful signals.
2. Fluid devices may be of following types :
   (*i*) Digital; Analogue; (*ii*) Active; passive; (*iii*) Logic devices; sensor; amplifiers.
3. Fluidics amplifiers not only control but also provide certain amplification to the fluid signals.

OBJECTIVE TYPE QUESTIONS

Fill in the Blank or Say "Yes" or "No".

1. 'Valvular conduit' was patented by ....
2. The control circuit element has a limited life.
3. A digital element has one output.
4. .... element varies its output continuously as a function of the control output signal and gives proportional control.
5. The digital devices are least important for industrial applications.
6. A device having bistable properties is also said to have ....
7. In .... device the air only passes momentarily.
8. A logic gate is a device which has inputs and outputs.
9. .... devised the first NOT gate.
10. Coanda effect was discovered in 1930 by ....
11. Bi-stable flip-flop works on the principle of .... effect.
12. The output from Bi-stable flip-flop can be used as a pilot signal for actuating various valves with low pressure actuating element.
13. Fluidic sensors are primarily used for detecting the presence of objects.

14. Vortex amplifier is used to regulate the flow of fluid by utilizing properties of a vortex.
15. The power required to turn off the turbulence amplifier is much more than the power in the output

ANSWERS

1. Nikola Tesla		**2.** No	**3.** No	**4.** Analogue
5. No	**6.** Memory	**7.** passive	**8.** Yes	**9.** Prandtl
10. Henri Coanda		**11.** Coanda	**12.** Yes	**13.** Yes
14. Yes.	**15.** No			

THEORETICAL QUESTIONS

1. Define the term 'Fluidics'.
2. Enlist the advantages, disadvantages and applications of fluidic devices/fluidics.
3. Explain briefly "Coanda effect".
4. Give the classification of fluidic devices.
5. Differentiate between the following fluidic devices :
   (*i*) Digital and analogue. (*ii*) Active and passive.
   (*iii*) Mono-stable and bi-stable.
6. Define the following terms :
   (*i*) Logic function or gate. (*ii*) Input signal.
   (*iii*) Output signal.
7. Explain briefly any two of the following fluid logic devices :
   (*i*) Bi-stable flip-flop. (*ii*) AND gate.
   (*iii*) OR-NOR gate.
8. Describe briefly the following fluidic sensors :
   (*i*) Interruptible jet sensor. (*ii*) Back pressure sensor.
9. Explain briefly air following fluidic amplifiers :
   (*i*) Turbulence amplifier. (*ii*) Vortex amplifier.
10. Give the comparison among pneumatic valves, moving part logic elements and fluidics.

Chapter 8

UNIVERSITIES' QUESTIONS (LATEST) WITH "SOLUTIONS"

SECTION A: SHORT ANSWER QUESTIONS

Q. 1. *What is a "fluid jet"?*

Ans. A ***fluid jet*** is a stream of fluid issuing from a nozzle with a high velocity and hence a high kinetic energy. When it impinges on a plate or vane, it exerts a force on it (due to change in momentum). This force (hydrodynamic) can be evaluated by using Impulse-momentum principle.

Q. 2. *Write down the formulae for the force exerted by a jet of water at a stationary plate (F_x) in the following cases: (i) Vertical plates; (ii) Inclined plate; (iii) Curved plate and jet strikes at one of tips of the jet.*

Ans. (*i*) $F_x = \rho a V^2$; (*ii*) $\rho a V^2 \sin\theta$; (*iii*) $2\rho a V^2 \cos\theta$

where, V = Velocity of the jet; θ = Angle between the jet and plate for inclined plate, and angle made by the jet with the direction of for curved plate.

Q. 3. *In case of jet propulsion of ships, what is the efficiency of propulsion when the inlet orifices face the direction of motion of the ship?*

Ans. Efficiency of propulsion, $\eta = \dfrac{2u}{V + 2u}$

where, u = Velocity of the moving ship; V = Absolute velocity of the moving jet.

Q. 4. *Point out the significance of word 'Free' in impact of free jets.*

Ans. 'Free' in impact of free jets means 'constant pressure throughout' when the jet impinges upon stationary or moving objects such as flat plates and vanes of different shapes and orientations in the study of 'impact of jets'.

Q. 5. *Explain impulse-momentum equation.*

Ans. When a force (push or pull) is applied on body it tries to change the state of rest or state of motion of that body. The amount of force applied is equal to the rate of change of momentum, where momentum is the product of mass and velocity.

Mathematically, $$F = ma = m\left(\frac{dv}{dt}\right) = \frac{d}{dt}(mv)$$

or, $$F = \frac{m}{t}(v_2 - v_1)$$

or, $$Ft = m(v_2 - v_1)$$

where, product Ft is the 'impulse' and is equal to the change in momentum.

Q. 6. *What do you mean by 'jet propulsion'?*

Ans. ***Jet propulsion*** is one of the applications of the 'impulse-moment equation' where in the reaction of high velocity jet issuing from a nozzle provides the necessary thrust. The principle is employed in propelling the ships, aircrafts and missiles.

Q. 7. *What is a dynamic machine?*

Ans. The term dynamic means power. A ***dynamic machine*** is a power machine, which receives energy from the flowing fluid in the form of momentum and converts the change in momentum into useful work.

Q. 8. *What is an impulse turbine?*

Ans. In 'impulse turbine' a high velocity jet issued from nozzle strikes a series of suitably shaped buckets fixed on the periphery of a wheel. The wheel gets resulting momentum and it gets rotated and thus we get the mechanical energy from the turbine.

Q. 9. *Classify turbines on the basis of direction of flow.*

Ans. The turbines are classified on the basis of direction of flow through the runner as follows:

(*i*) Tangential flow turbine;

(*ii*) Radial flow turbine;

(*iii*) Axial flow turbine;

(*iv*) Mixed flow turbine.

Q. 10. *What is 'scale effect'?*

Ans. However a smooth a model is made, the geometric similarity between the prototype and model cannot be extended to surface roughness. This variation of surfaceness with respect to the size of turbine will cause a small but appreciable variation in the proportion of the effective head lost due to hydraulic friction. Thus the efficiency of prototype will be different from the corresponding model efficiency. This aspect is referred to as ***scale effect***.

Q. 11. *List down some advantages of centrifugal pump over displacement pump.*

Ans. Some of the advantages claimed by centrifugal pump over displacement (reciprocating) pump are:

(*i*) The cost of a centrifugal pump is less as it has fewer parts.

(*ii*) Installation and maintenance are easier and cheaper.

(*iii*) Its discharging capacity is much greater than that of a reciprocating pump.

(*iv*) Its performance characteristics are superior.

(*v*) It can be directly coupled to an electric motor or an oil engine.

- However, because of higher efficiency the reciprocating pumps are still employed for high heads and small discharges. A reciprocating pump can build up very high pressures (as high as 700 bar or even more) and as such these pumps are made for lifting oils from very deep oil wells.

Q. 12. *What do you understand by 'specific speed' of a centrifugal pump?*

Ans. The 'specific speed' of a centrifugal pump is defined as the speed of a geometrically similar pump which would deliver unit quantity (one cubic metre of liquid per second) against a unit head (one metre).

It is denoted by N_s. The specific speed of is a characteristic of pumps which can be used as a basis for comparing the performance of different pumps.

Q. 13. *Explain the term 'negative slip' as referred to reciprocating pumps.*

Ans. In most of the reciprocating pumps $Q_{act.}$ (actual discharge) is less than $Q_{th.}$ (theoretical discharge); in such a case the value of C_d (coefficient of discharge) is less than unity and the slip of the pump is '*positive*'. However, in some cases Q_{act} may be 'more' than Q_{th} ; in such a case C_d is more than unity and the slip will be '*negative*'. The slip will be negative when there is direct connection between the suction and delivery sides before the end of the suction stroke. This happens if the momentum of liquid in the suction is large enough to open the delivery valve before the beginning of delivery stroke. The negative slip is possible in case of pumps having *long suction pipe and a short delivery pipe, especially when these are operating at high speeds.*

Q. 14. *Explain the term Net Positive Suction Head (NPSH).*

Ans. NPSH is defined as the absolute pressure head at the inlet to the pump, minus the vapour pressure head (in absolute units) plus the velocity head.

or, NPSH = Absolute pressure head at the inlet of the pump – vapour pressure head (absolute units) + velocity head.

This term is frequently used in pump industry and has significance only when cavitating liquids are used. NPSH is a parameter (dimensional) that can be used to check cavitation in pump.

The minimum NPSH depends upon the pump design, its speed and the discharge.

Q. 15. *List the various functions of surge tanks.*

Ans. Surge tank has the following functions:

(*i*) To control the pressure variations, due to rapid changes in the pipeline flow, thus eliminating water hammer possibilities.

(*ii*) To regulate the flow of water to the turbines.

(*iii*) To reduce the distance between the free water surface and turbine, thereby reducing the water hammer effect on penstock.

Q. 16. *What is a 'hydraulic ram'?*

Ans. ***Hydraulic ram*** is a device with which small quantities of water can be pumped to higher levels from the available large quantity of water of low head.

Q. 17. *What is the function of notch in Pelton turbine?*

Ans. A notch made near the edge of the outer rim of each bucket is carefully sharpened *to ensure a loss-free entry of the jet into the buckets i.e.* the path of the jet is not obstructed by incoming buckets.

Q. 18. *What are the materials used for the buckets of Pelton wheel?*

Ans. The buckets are the most important part of the Pelton turbine, they have to be designed to withstand the full force of the jet. Thus, they are made of special bronze or steel alloys with nickel, chromium or stainless steel.

Q. 19. *What is a 'draft tube'?*

Ans. A ***draft tube*** is an expanding device which has an expanding pressure conduit hermetically fixed at the runner outlet and having the other end below the minimum tail water level, that helps to convert the velocity head into pressure or potential head.

It is an integral part of mixed and axial flow turbines. Because of the draft tube it is possible to have the pressure at runner outlet *much below the atmospheric level.*

Q. 20. *What is 'priming' and why is it necessary?*

Ans. The operation of filling the suction pipe, casing of the pump and a portion of the delivery pipe completely from outside source with the liquid to be raised, before starting the pump, the remove any air, gas or vapour from these parts of the pump is called ***priming*** of a centrifugal pump.

If a centrifugal pump is not primed before starting, air pockets inside the impeller may give rise to vortices and cause discontinuity of flow. Further, dry running of the pump may result in rubbing and seizing of the wearing rings and cause serious damage.

Q. 21. *What is meant by 'degree of reaction'?*

Ans. The ***degree of reaction*** (R) is defined as the ratio of change of pressure energy in the runner to the change of total energy in the runner per kg of water.

i.e.
$$R = \frac{\text{Change in pressure energy}}{\text{Change in total energy}}$$

Q. 22. *Explain 'runaway speed'?*

Ans. The ***runaway speed*** is the maximum speed, governor being disengaged, at which a turbine would run when there is no external load but operating under design head and discharge. All the moving parts including the rotor of alternator should be designed for the centrifugal stresses caused by this maximum speed.

The practical values of runaway speed for various turbines with respect to their rated speed N are as follows:

Pelton wheel = 1.8 to 1.9 N; Francis turbine (mixed flow) = 2.0 to 2.2 N; Kaplan turbine (axial flow) = 2.5 to 3.0 N.

Q. 23. *What is a submersible pump?*

Ans. A ***submersible pump*** is a device which has a motor closely coupled to a pump body. The whole assembly is submerged in the fluid to be pumped. This *pump pushes fluid to the surface as opposed to jet pumps having pull fluids*.

The submersible pumps are more efficient than jet pumps.

Q. 24. *List the factors which influence the speed of reciprocating pump.*

Ans. Speed of reciprocating pump is influenced by:

(*i*) Asolute pressure inside the cylinder; (*ii*) Cavitation produced; (*iii*) Acceleration of piston; (*iv*) Friction in the pipes.

Q. 25. *What is a 'fluid coupling'?*

Ans. A ***fluid coupling*** is a device which is employed for transmission of power from one shaft to another through a liquid medium. It has no mechanical connection or face to face contact. The magnitudes of input and output torques are equal.

Q. 26. *Define 'Thoma's cavitation parameter'.*

Ans. Prof. Dietrich Thomas of Munich (Germany) suggested a 'cavitation factor (sigma)' to determine the zone where turbine can work without being affected from cavitation. The critical value cavitation factor (σ_c) is given by:

$$\sigma_c = \frac{(H_a - H_v) - H_s}{H}$$

where, H_a = Atmospheric pressure head in meters of water; H_v = Vapour pressure in metres of water corresponding to the water temperature, H = Working head of turbine (difference between head race and tail race level in metres), and H_s = Suction pressure head (or height of turbine outlet above tail race level in metres).

Q. 27. *What is meant by speed ratio of a Pelton wheel?*

Ans. Speed ratio $(K_u) = \dfrac{\text{The peripheral velocity of wheel } (u)}{\text{The theoretical velocity of jet } (\sqrt{2gH})}$

Q. 28. *What is the utility of an 'Air lift pump'?*

Ans. An ***air lift pump*** is a device used to lift water from a deep well or sump by utilising the compressed air.

Q. 29. *What are the salient features of an 'Air lift pump'?*

Ans. The salient features of an air lift pump are:

(*i*) It has no moving parts below water level and consequently no wear and tear.

(*ii*) It can raise more water through a bore hole of given diameter than any other pump.

(*iii*) It can pump solids without any damage to the system.

(*iv*) It is suitable for draining water in the mines where compressor units are already installed.

Q. 30. *Define the term Net or Effective head.*

Ans. The head available at the inlet of the turbine is known as ***net or effective head.*** It is denoted by H and is given by:

$$H = H_g - h_f - h$$

where, h_f = Total loss of head between the head race and entrance of the turbine

$= \dfrac{4fLV^2}{D \times 2g}$ (f = coefficient of friction, L = length of penstock,

D = diameter of penstock,

V = Velocity of flow in penstock), and

h = Height of nozzle above the tail race.

Q. 31. *What is the function of scroll casing in reaction turbines?*

Ans. A ***scroll casing*** constitutes a close passage whose cross-sectional area gradually decreases along the flow direction, area is maximum at inlet and nearly zero at exit. It provides the limited area around the runner to maintain the constant velocity of water flow around the runner.

Q. 32. *What do you mean by the capacity of Hydraulic accumulator?*

Ans. ***Hydraulic accumulator*** is a device used to store the energy of liquid under pressure and make this energy available (as a quick secondary source of power) to hydraulic machines, such as presses, lifts and cranes.

The maximum amount of energy that the accumulator can store is known as the '*capacity of the accumulator*'.

Q. 33. *What are air vessels?*

Ans. An ***air vessel*** is a closed chamber containing compressed air in the upper part and liquid being pumped in the lower part. One air vessel is fixed on the suction pipe near the suction valve and one is fixed on the delivery pipe near the delivery valve.

The air vessels are used for the following *purposes*:

(*i*) To get continuous supply of liquid at a uniform rate (whatever fluctuations take place, they occur between the air vessels and the pump).

(*ii*) To save the power required to drive the pump (By the use of air vessels the acceleration and friction heads are considerably reduced, thereby the work is also reduced).

(*iii*) To run the pump at much higher speed without any danger of separation (By fitting the air vessels as close to the pump as possible, the length of the pipe in which acceleration takes place is reduced due to which acceleration head is reduced, and pump can run at a high speed without separation.

Q. 34. *What do you understand by a 'reciprocating pump'?*

Ans. A ***reciprocating pump*** is a *positive displacement pump* as it sucks and raises the liquid by actually displacing it with a piston/plunger that executes a reciprocating motion in a closely fitting cylinder. The amount of liquid pumped with disc pistons create pressures upto 25 bar and the plunger pumps built up still higher pressures. Discharge from these pumps is almost wholly dependent on the pump speed.

The total efficiency of a reciprocating pump is about 10 to 20 per cent higher than a comparable centrifugal pump.

The reciprocating is generally employed for:

(*i*) Light oil pumping; (*ii*) Feeding small boilers, and

(*iii*) Pneumatic pressure systems.

Q. 35. *Define the draft tube efficiency.*

Ans. The 'efficiency of a draft tube (η_d)' is defined as the ratio of net gain in pressure head to the velocity head at entrance of draft tube. Thus,

$$\eta_d = \frac{\text{Net gain in pressure head}}{\text{Velocity head at entrance of draft tube}}$$

$$= \frac{\left(\dfrac{V_2^2 - V_3^2}{2g} - h_f\right)}{\dfrac{V_2^2}{2g}}$$

where, V_2 = Velocity of water at inlet of the draft tube, and

V_3 = Velocity of water at outlet of the draft tube.

$$\left[h_f = \frac{V_2^2 - V_3^2}{2g} - \eta_d \times \frac{V_2^2}{2g}\right]$$

Q. 36. *Why the draft tube is not used for Pelton turbine?*

Ans. In case of Pelton all the K.E. is lost; and draft tube is not used because the pressure value is just the atmospheric so that there is no requirement of draft tube.

Q. 37. *Define the term 'Impact of jet'.*

Ans. A fluid jet is a stream of fluid obtained from nozzle. When this jet strikes on flat or curved plate the momentum is changed and a hydrodynamic force is exerted. So 'Impact of jet' terms refer to the study of the effect when a jet strikes on the plate or vane under the various conditions.

Q. 38. *What are the functions of a draft tube?*

Ans. A draft tube performs the following functions:

(*i*) It allows the turbine to be set above tail-water level without loss of head to facilitate inspection and maintenance.

(*ii*) It regains by diffusion action, the major portion of the kinetic energy delivered to it from the runner.

Q. 39. *Define the term 'Gross head'.*

Ans. The 'Gross head' or Total head is the difference between the water level at the reservoir (also known as head race) and the level at the tail race.

Q. 40. *List the advantages of Kaplan turbine over Francis turbine.*

Ans. Kaplan turbine claims the following advantages over Francis turbine:

(*i*) For the same power developed Kaplan turbine is more compact in construction and smaller in size.

(*ii*) Part-load efficiency is considerably high.

(*iii*) Low frictional losses (because of small number of blades used).

Q. 41. *What are the bases on which hydraulic turbines are classified?*

Ans. The hydraulic turbines are classified on the following bases:

(*i*) According to the head and quantity of water available.

(*ii*) According to the name of the originator.

(*iii*) According to the action of water on moving blades.

(*iv*) According to the direction of flow of water in the runner.

(*v*) According to the disposition of the turbine shaft.

(*vi*) According to the specific speed N_s.

Q. 42. *What is the principle of working of a centrifugal pump?*

Ans. A centrifugal pump works on the principle that when a certain mass of fluid is rotated by an external source, it is thrown away from the central axis of rotation and a centrifugal head is impressed which enables it to rise to a higher level.

Q. 43. *What are the functions of a multi-stage pump?*

Ans. A multi-stage centrifugal pump is one which has two or more identical impellers mounted on the same shaft or on different shafts. The important functions performed by a multi-stage pump are:

(*i*) To *produce greater heads* than that permissible with a single impeller, discharge remaining constant. The task can be achieved by '*series arrangement*' where in the impellers are mounted on the *same shaft* and enclosed in the same casing.

(*ii*) To *discharge a large quantity of liquid*, head remaining same. This task is accomplished by '*parallel arrangement*' where in impellers are mounted on *separate shafts*.

Q. 44. *What is cavitation and how can it be avoided in reaction turbines?*

Ans. The formation, growth, and collapse of vapour filled cavities or bubbles in a flowing liquid due to local fall in fluid pressure is called ***cavitation.*** When the cavities collapse (the collapsing pressure is of order of 100 times the atmospheric pressure) on the surface of a body, due to repeated 'hammering' action, the metal particles give way ultimately due to fatigue and indentations are formed; this erosion of material is called ***pitting.***

The following methods may be used to avoid cavitation:

(*i*) Runner turbine may be kept under water. But it is not advisable as the inspection and repair of the turbine is difficult. Alternatively, the runner of low specific speed may be used.

(*ii*) It is possible to reduce the cavitation effect by selecting materials which resist better the cavitation effect. The cast steel is better than cast iron and stainless steel or alloy steel is still better than cast steel.

(*iii*) The cavitation effect can be reduced by polishing the surface. That is why the cast steel runners and blades are coated with stainless steel.

(*iv*) The cavitation may be avoided by selecting a runner of proper specific speed for given head.

Q. 45. *How are hydraulic turbines classified according to specific speed?*

Ans. The specific speed of a turbine is defined as the speed of a geometrically similar turbine that would develop 1 kW under 1 m head. All geometrically similar turbines (irrespective of the sizes) will have the same specific speeds when operating under the same head.

$$\text{Specific speed, } N_s = \frac{N\sqrt{P}}{H^{5/4}}$$

where, N = The normal speed, P = Power output of the turbine, and H = The net or effective head in metres.

Turbines with low specific speeds work under high head and low discharge conditions, while *high specific speed turbines work under low head and high discharge conditions*.

Q. 46. *Distinguish between an impulse turbine and a reaction turbine.*

Ans.

S.No.	Impulse turbine	Reaction turbine
1.	The available energy is converted into K.E. by a nozzle.	The energy of the fluid is partly transformed into K.E. before it (fluid) enters the runner of the turbine.
2.	The pressure remains same (atmospheric) throughout the action of water on the runner.	After entering the runner with an excess pressure, water undergoes changes both in velocity and pressure while passing through the runner.
3.	Always installed above the tail race. No draft tube is used.	Unit may be installed above or below the tail race, use of a draft tube is made.
4.	Water may be allowed to enter a part or whole of the wheel circumference.	Water is admitted over the circumference of the wheel.

Q. 47. *What are the functions of a surge tank?*

Ans. A ***surge tank*** is a small reservoir or tank in which the water level rises or falls to reduce the pressure swings so that they are not transmitted in full to a closed circuit. In general a surge tank is employed to serve the following *purposes*:

(*i*) To reduce the distance between the free water surface and turbine thereby reducing the water hammer effect (the water hammer is defined as the change in pressure rapidly above or below normal pressure caused by sudden changes in rate of flow through the pipe according to the demand of the prime mover) on penstock and also protect upstream tunnel from high pressure rises.

(*ii*) To serve as *supply tank* to the turbine when water in the pipe is accelerating during increased load conditions and *storage tank* when the water is decreasing during reduced load conditions.

Q. 48. *What do you understand by governing of hydraulic turbines?*

Ans. Governing of hydraulic turbine means *speed regulation*. Governing of a turbine is necessary as a turbine is directly coupled to an electric generator, which is required to run at constant speed under all fluctuating load conditions. This is achieved by a *governor* called oil pressure governor.

The power produced by water turbine is directly proportional to the available head and discharge through the turbine. The quantity of water flowing can be controlled by varying the area of flow at the turbine inlet.

In Pelton turbine, the flow area is changed by moving the spear inside the nozzle and in reaction turbine, the area of flow is varied by rotating the guide vanes with the help of governor in a controlling unit.

Q. 49. *How does a Kaplan turbine differ from a propeller turbine?*

Ans. A ***propeller turbine*** is quite suitable when the *load* on the turbine *remains constant*. At part load its efficiency is very low, since the *blades are fixed*, the water enters with shock (at part load) and eddies are formed which reduce the efficiency. This defect of the propeller turbine is removed in Kaplan turbine.

In a ***Kaplan turbine*** the runner *blades are adjustable* and can be rotated about pivots fixed to the boss of the runner. The *blades are adjusted automatically* by servomechanism so that at all loads the flow enters them *without shock*. Thus, a *high efficiency* is maintained *even at part loads*. It behaves like a propeller turbine at full-load conditions.

Q. 50. *Differentiate between Francis and Kaplan turbines.*

Ans.

S. No.	Francis Turbine	Kaplan turbine
1.	Radially inward or mixed flow.	Partially axial flow.
2.	Horizontal or vertical shaft.	Only vertical shaft.
3.	Runner vanes are not adjustable (16 to 24 blades)	Runner vanes are adjustable (3 to 8 blades)
4.	Medium head: 60 m to 250 m.	Low head: upto 30 m.
5.	Medium flow rate.	Large flow rate.
6.	Specific speed: 50–250	Specific speed: 250–850

Q. 51. *Define specific speed of turbine and write down its expression.*

Ans. The ***specific speed*** of a turbine is defined as the speed of a turbine which is identical in shape, geometrical dimensions, blade angles, gate opening, etc. which would develop unit power when working under a unit head.

Specific speed (N_s) is given by:

$$N_s = \frac{N\sqrt{P}}{H^{5/4}}$$

where, N = Speed of the runner in r.p.m., H = Head of water, and P = Power developed.

Q. 52. *What is priming of centrifugal pump?*

Ans. ***Priming*** of centrifugal pump is the operation of filling the suction pipe, casing of the pump and a portion of the delivery pipe completely from outside source with the liquid to be raised, before starting the pump, to remove any air, gas or vapour from these parts of the pump.

Q. 53. *How are various types of centrifugal pumps primed?*

Ans. ***Small pumps*** are usually primed by pouring liquid into the *funnel* provided for the purpose.

Large pumps are primed by evacuating the casing and the suction by a *vacuum pump* or by an *ejector*; the liquid is thus drawn up the suction pipe from the sump and the pump is filled with liquid.

The internal construction of some pumps is such that *special arrangements* containing a supply of liquid are provided in the suction pipe due to which automatic priming of the pump occurs; such pumps are known as ***self priming pumps***.

Q. 54. *Distinguish between the positive and non-positive displacement pumps.*

Ans. ***Positive displacement pump***: It causes a liquid to move by trapping a fixed amount of it, then forcing (displacing) that trapped volume into the discharge pipe, *e.g.* tube, gear, screw pump etc.

Non-positive displacement pump (*rotodynamic type*): It is pump in which the dynamic motion of a fluid is increased by pump action, *e.g.* centrifugal, turbine, propeller etc.

Q. 55. *Define slip for reciprocating pumps. When does negative slip occur?*

Ans. The difference between the theoretical discharge and actual discharge is called the ***slip*** of the pump

i.e., $\text{Slip} = Q_{th.} - Q_{act.}$

But the slip is oftenly expressed in percentage which is given by:

$$\%\ \text{slip} = \frac{Q_{th.} - Q_{act.}}{Q_{th.}} \times 100 = \left(1 - \frac{Q_{act.}}{Q_{th.}}\right) \times 100 = (1 - C_d) \times 100$$

where, C_d = Coefficient of discharge.

The percentage of slip for the pumps maintained in *good condition* is of the order of 2% or even less.

Negative slip. In most of the reciprocating pumps $Q_{act.}$ is *less* than $Q_{th.}$; in such a case the value of C_d is *less* than unity and the slip of the pump is 'positive'. However, in some cases $Q_{act.}$ may be *more* than $Q_{th.}$; in such a case C_d is *more* than unity and the slip will be '*negative*'. The slip will be negative when there is a *direct connection between the suction and delivery sides before the end of the suction stroke.* This happens if the momentum of liquid in the suction pipe, is large enough to open the delivery valve before the beginning of delivery stroke. The negative slip is possible in case of pumps having *long suction pipe and a short delivery pipe*, especially when these are operating at high speeds.

Q. 56. *Why is the efficiency of Kaplan turbine nearly constant irrespective of speed variation under load?*

Ans. Kaplan turbine has the concept of adjusting the runner vanes in face of changing load conditions on the turbine. With proper adjustment of blades during its running the Kaplan turbine is capable of giving a constant and high efficiency for a wide range of load conditions. The pitch of the blades is also automatically adjusted by the governor through the action of a servomotor.

Q. 57. *What is a hydraulic intensifier?*

Ans. ***Hydraulic intensifier*** is a device which increases the pressure of a given liquid with the help of low pressure liquid of large quantity.

Q. 58. *How are hydraulic pumps classified?*

Ans. Pumps may be placed in one of the two general categories:

(*i*) *Dynamic pressure pumps*: Centrifugal pump, jet pump, propeller, turbine.

(*ii*) *Positive displacement pump*: Piston plunger, gear, vane, screw pump etc.

Q. 59. *Define manometric head of a pump.*

Ans. The ***manometric head*** is defined as the head against which a centrifugal pump has to work. It is the head measured across the pump inlet and outlet flanges. It is denoted by H_{mano}.

Q. 60. *What is manometric efficiency?*

Ans. The ratio of the manometric head developed by the pump to the head imparted by the impeller to the liquid is known as '*manometric efficiency*'.

i.e.

$$\eta_{mano} = \frac{\text{Manometric head}}{\text{Head imparted by impeller to the liquid}}$$

SECTION B: QUESTIONS WITH SOLUTIONS

Q. 1. *A jet of water strikes with a velocity of 30 m/s a flat plate inclined at 45° with the axis of the jet. If the cross-sectional area of the jet is 20 cm², determine the following:*

(i) *The force exerted by the jet on the plate,*

(ii) *The components of the force in the direction of the jet, and*

(iii) *The ratio in which the discharge gets divided after striking the plate.*

Solution. *Given*: Velocity of the jet, $V = 30$ m/s, Inclination of the plate with the jet axis, $\theta = 45°$; Area of the jet, $a = 20 \text{ cm}^2 = 20 \times 10^{-4} \text{ m}^2 = 0.002 \text{ m}^2$.

(*i*) The force exerted by the jet, *F*:

$$F = \rho a V^2 \sin\theta \quad \text{[Eqn. (1.3)]}$$

$$= 1000 \times 0.002 \times 30^2 \times \sin 45° = \mathbf{1272.8\ N\ (Ans.)}$$

(*ii*) The components of the force, *F*:

$$F_x = F \sin\theta = 1272.8 \times \sin 45° = \mathbf{900\ N\ (Ans.)}$$

$$F_y = F \cos\theta = 1272.8 \times \cos 45° = \mathbf{900\ N\ (Ans.)}$$

(*iii*) The ratio in which the discharge gets divided:

$$\frac{Q_1}{Q_2} = \frac{1+\cos\theta}{1-\cos\theta} \quad \text{[Eqn. (1.7)]}$$

or,

$$\frac{Q_1}{Q_2} = \frac{1+\cos 45°}{1-\cos 45°} = \mathbf{5.83\ (Ans.)}$$

Q. 2. *A jet of water of 50 mm diameter strikes a curved vane at its centre with a velocity of 20 m/s. The curved vane is moving with a velocity of 5 m/s in the direction of the jet. The jet is deflected through an angle of 160°. Assuming the plate to be smooth, calculate:*

(i) *Thrust on the plate in the direction of the jet,*

(ii) *Power of the jet; and*

(iii) *Efficiency of the jet.*

Solution. *Given*: Diameter of the jet, $d = 50$ mm $= 0.05$ m; Velocity of the jet, $V = 20$ m/s; Velocity of the vane, $u = 5$ m/s; Angle of deflection of the jet = 160°; Angle made by the relative velocity at the outlet of the vane = 180 – 160 = 20°.

(*i*) Thrust on the plate:

$$\text{Area of the jet, } a = \frac{\pi}{4}d^2 = \frac{\pi}{4} \times 0.05^2 = 0.001963 \text{ m}^2$$

Thrust on the plate in the direction of the jet,

$$F_x = \rho a (V-u)^2 (1+\cos\theta)$$

$$= 1000 \times 0.001963\,(20-5)^2\,(1+\cos 20°) = \mathbf{856.7\ N\ (Ans.)}$$

(*ii*) Power of the jet:

Work done by the jet on the vane per second

$$= F_x \times u = 856.7 \times 5 = 4283.5 \text{ Nm/s}$$

$$\text{Power of the jet} = 4283.5 \text{ Nm/s} = 4283.5 \text{ W or } \mathbf{4.283 \text{ kW}} \textbf{ (Ans.)}$$

(*iii*) Efficiency of the jet, η_{jet}:

$$\eta_{jet} = \frac{\text{Work done by the jet/sec.}}{\text{Kinetic energy of the jet/sec.}}$$

$$= \frac{4283.5}{\frac{1}{2}(\rho a V) \times V^2} = \frac{4283.5}{\frac{1}{2}(1000 \times 0.001963 \times 20) \times 20^2}$$

$$= 0.5455 \text{ or } \mathbf{54.55\%} \textbf{ (Ans.)}$$

Q. 3. *The following data relate to a Pelton wheel:*

Heat = 80 m; Speed of wheel = 280 r.p.m.; Shaft power of wheel = 130 kW; Speed ratio = 0.48; Co-efficient of velocity = 0.97; Overall efficiency = 82%.

Design the Pelton wheel.

Solution. *Given*: Effective head, $H = 80$ m; Speed of wheel, $N = 280$ r.p.m.; Shaft power, $P = 130$ kW; Speed ratio, $K_u = 0.48$; Co-efficient of velocity, $C_v = 0.97$; Overall efficiency, $\eta_0 = 82\%$.

Design of the Pelton wheel means to find diameter of the wheel (D), diameter of the jet (d), width and depth of buckets and number of buckets on the wheel.

(*i*) Diameter of wheel, *D*:

$$\text{Velocity of jet, } V_1 = C_v\sqrt{2gH} = 0.97\sqrt{2 \times 9.81 \times 80}$$

$$= 38.4 \text{ m/s}$$

$\therefore$ Bucket velocity, $u(= u_1 = u_2) = K_u \times V_1 = 0.48 \times 38.4 = 18.4$ m/s

But, $$u = \frac{\pi DN}{60}, \textit{ or, } D = \frac{60u}{\pi N} = \frac{60 \times 18.4}{\pi \times 280} = \mathbf{1.255 \text{ m}} \textbf{ (Ans.)}$$

(*ii*) Diameter of the jet, *d*:

$$\text{Overall efficiency, } \eta_0 = \frac{\text{Shaft power}}{\text{Water power}} = \frac{P}{wQH}$$

or, $$0.82 = \frac{130}{9.81 \times Q \times 80} \qquad (\because w = 9.81 \text{ kN/m}^3)$$

or, $$\text{Discharge, } Q = \frac{130}{0.82 \times 9.81 \times 80} = 0.202 \text{ m}^3\text{/s}$$

But, $$Q = \text{Area of jet} \times \text{velocity of jet}$$

$$0.202 = \frac{\pi}{4} d^2 \times 38.4$$

or, $$d = \left(\frac{0.202 \times 4}{\pi \times 38.4}\right)^{1/2} = 0.0818 \text{ m or } \mathbf{81.8 \text{ mm}} \textbf{ (Ans.)}$$

(*iii*) Size of buckets:

Width of the bucket, $B \simeq$ 3 to 4 times jet diameter (d)

$= 3.5d = 3.5 \times 81.8 = $ **286.3 mm (Ans.)**

Radial length of bucket, $L =$ 2 to 3 times jet diameter (d)

$\simeq 2.5d = 2.5 \times 81.8 = $ **204.5 mm (Ans.)**

Depth of bucket, $T =$ 0.8 to 1.2 times jet diameter (d)

$\simeq 1.0d = $ **81.8 mm (Ans.)**

Q. 4. *A conical draft tube having inlet and outlet diameters 1.1 m and 1.7 m discharges water at outlet with a velocity of 2.8 m/s. The total length of the draft tube is 7.0 m and 1.4 m of the length of draft tube is immersed in water. If the atmospheric pressure head is 10.3 m of water and loss of head due to friction in the draft tube is equal to 0.18 × velocity head at outlet of the tube.*

Determine: (i) Pressure head at inlet, and (ii) Efficiency of the draft tube.

Solution. Refer to Fig. 1. *Given*: Inlet diameter of the draft tube, $d_i = 1.1$ m; Outlet diameter, $d_o = 1.7$ m; Velocity at outlet, $V_3 = 2.8$ m/s; Total length of draft tube, $H_s + y = 7.0$ m; Length of draft tube in water, $y = 1.4$ m; Atmospheric pressure head, $\frac{p_a}{w} = 10.3$ m; Loss of head due to friction, $h_f = 0.18 \times$ velocity head at outlet $= 0.18 \times \frac{V_1^2}{2g}$

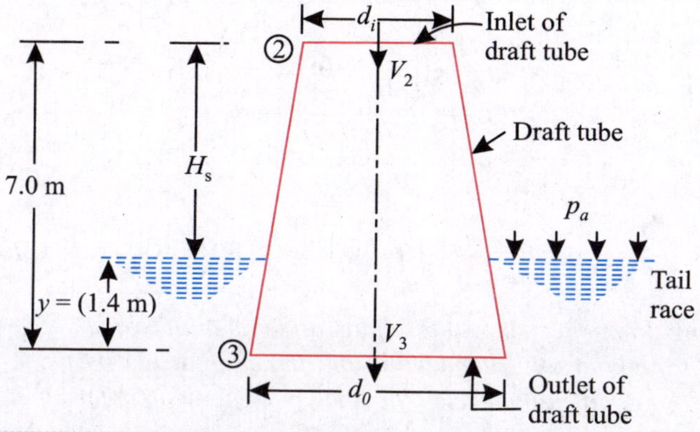

Fig. 1

***(i)* Pressure head at inlet, $\frac{p_2}{w}$:**

Discharge through the draft tube,

$$Q = A_3V_3 = \frac{\pi}{4} \times d_o^2 \times V_3 = \frac{\pi}{4} \times 1.7^2 \times 2.8 = 6.36 \text{ m/s}$$

$$\text{Velocity of inlet, } V_2 = \frac{Q}{A_2} = \frac{6.36}{\frac{\pi}{4} \times d_i^2} = \frac{6.36}{\frac{\pi}{4} \times 1.1^2} = 6.69 \text{ m/s}$$

We know that,

$$\frac{p_2}{w} = \frac{p_a}{w} - H_s - \left(\frac{V_2^2 - V_3^2}{2g} - h_f\right) \qquad \text{[Eqn. (2.32)]}$$

$$= \frac{p_a}{w} - H_s - \left(\frac{V_2^2 - V_3^2}{2g} - 0.18\frac{V_3^2}{2g}\right)$$

$$= 10.3 - (7.0 - 1.4) - \left(\frac{6.69^2 - 2.8^2}{2 \times 9.81} - 0.18 \times \frac{2.8^2}{2 \times 9.81}\right)$$

$= 4.7 - (1.88 - 0.072) =$ **2.892 m (abs.) (Ans.)**

(ii) Efficiency of the draft tube, η_d:

We know that,

$$\eta_d = \frac{\left(\frac{V_2^2 - V_3^2}{2g} - h_f\right)}{\frac{V_2^2}{2g}} \quad \text{[Eqn. (2.33)]}$$

$$= \frac{\frac{V_2^2 - V_3^2}{2g} - 0.18\frac{V_3^2}{2g}}{\frac{V_2^2}{2g}}$$

$$= \frac{\frac{V_2^2}{2g} - \left(\frac{V_3^2}{2g} + 0.18\frac{V_3^2}{2g}\right)}{\frac{V_2^2}{2g}}$$

$$= 1 - 1.18\left(\frac{V_3}{V_2}\right)^2 = 1 - 1.18\left(\frac{2.8}{6.69}\right)^2 = 0.793 \text{ or } \mathbf{79.3\%\ (Ans.)}$$

Q. 5. *A centrifugal impeller runs at 90 r.p.m. and has outlet vane angle of 62°. The velocity of flow is 2.7 m/s throughout and diameter of the impeller at exit is twice that at inlet. If the manometric head is 18 m and manometric efficiency is 74 percent, determine:*

(i) The diameter of the impeller at the exit, and (ii) Inlet vane angle.

Solution. Refer to Fig. 2.

Given: Speed, $N = 90$ r.p.m.; Outlet vane angle, $\phi = 62°$; Velocity of flow, $V_{f1} = V_{f2} = 2.7$ m/s; Manometric head, $H_{mano} = 18$ m; Manometric efficiency, $\eta_{mano} = 74\%$. Diameter of the impeller at outlet, $D_2 = 2D_1$ (diameter at inlet).

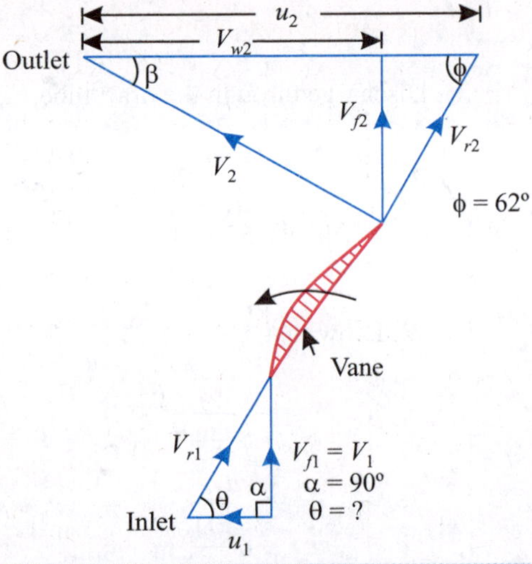

Fig. 2

(i) Diameter of the impeller at the exit, D_2:

$$\eta_{mano} = \frac{gH_{mano}}{V_{w2}u_2} \quad \text{[Eqn. (3.9)]}$$

or, $$0.74 = \frac{9.81 \times 18}{V_{w2}u_2}$$

or, $$V_{w2}u_2 = \frac{9.81 \times 18}{0.74} = 238.6 \quad ...(i)$$

From velocity triangle at outlet (Fig. 2), we get,

$$\tan\phi = \frac{V_{f2}}{u_2 - V_{w2}}$$

or, $$u_2 - V_{w2} = \frac{V_{f2}}{\tan\phi}, \text{ or, } V_{w2} = u_2 - \frac{V_{f2}}{\tan\phi}$$

or, $$V_{w2} = u_2 - \frac{2.7}{\tan 62°} = u_2 - 1.436$$

Inserting this value of V_{w2} in (*i*), we have:

$$(u_2 - 1.436)u_2 = 238.6$$

or, $$u_2^2 - 1.436u_2 - 238.6 = 0$$

or, $$u_2 = \frac{1.436 \pm \sqrt{1.436^2 + 4 \times 238.6}}{2}$$

$$= \frac{1.436 \pm 30.927}{2} = 16.18 \text{ m/s} \quad \text{(ignoring –ve sign)}$$

Also, tangential velocity of impeller at outlet,

$$u_2 = \frac{\pi D_2 N}{60}, \text{ or, } D_2 = \frac{60u_2}{\pi N}$$

$$\therefore \quad D_2 = \frac{60 \times 16.18}{\pi \times 90} = \mathbf{3.43 \text{ m (Ans.)}}$$

(*iii*) Inlet vane angle, θ:

Tangential velocity of the impeller at inlet

$$u_1 = \frac{u_2}{2} = \frac{16.18}{2} = \mathbf{8.09 \text{ m/s (Ans.)}} \quad \left(\because D_1 = \frac{D_2}{2}\right)$$

From velocity triangle at *inlet*, we get,

$$\tan\theta = \frac{V_{f1}}{u_1} = \frac{2.7}{8.09} = 0.3337$$

or, $$\theta = \tan^{-1}(0.3337) = \mathbf{18.45° \text{ (Ans.)}}$$

Q. 6. *A centrifugal pump impeller has diameters at inlet and outlet as 350 mm and 700 mm respectively. The flow velocity at outlet is 2.3 m/s and vanes are set back at an angle of 45° at the outlet. If the manometric efficiency is 75 per cent, calculate the minimum starting speed of the pump.*

Solution. *Given*: Diameter of impeller at inlet, $D_1 = 350$ mm $= 0.35$ m; Diameter of impeller at outlet, $D_2 = 700$ mm $= 0.7$ m; The flow velocity at outlet, $V_{f2} = 2.3$ m/s; Outlet vane angle, $\phi = 45°$; Manometric efficiency, $\eta_{mano} = 75\%$.

Minimum starting speed of the pump, $N_{min.}$:

Refer to Fig. 3. From velocity triangle at *outlet*, we have:

$$\tan\phi = \frac{V_{f2}}{u_2 - V_{w2}},$$

or, $$u_2 - V_{w2} = \frac{V_{f2}}{\tan\phi} = \frac{2.3}{\tan 45°} = 2.3 \text{ m/s}$$

or, $$V_{w2} = u_2 - 2.3$$

But, $$u_2 = \frac{\pi D_2 N_{min.}}{60} = \frac{\pi \times 0.7\, N_{min.}}{60}$$

$$= 0.0366\, N_{min.}$$

$$\therefore \quad V_{w2} = 0.0366\, N_{min.} - 2.3$$

For minimum speed, we have:

$$N_{min} = \frac{120 \times \eta_{mano} \times V_{w2} \times D_2}{\pi(D_2^2 - D_1^2)}$$

...[Eqn. (3.15)]

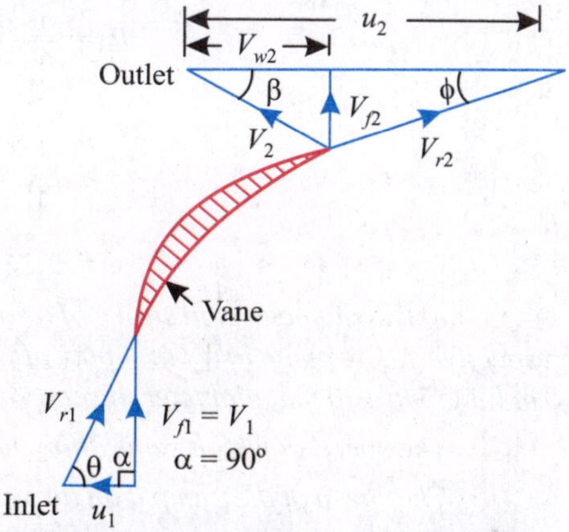

Fig. 3

$$= \frac{120 \times 0.75 \times (0.0366\, N_{min} - 2.3)}{\pi(0.7^2 - 0.35^2)}$$

or, $$N_{min.} = 77.95\,(0.0366\, N_{min} - 2.3)$$

$$= 2.853\, N_{min} - 179.285$$

or, $$1.853\, N_{min} = 179.285$$

or, $$N_{min} = \frac{179.285}{1.853} \simeq \textbf{97 r.p.m (Ans.)}$$

Q. 7. *A single acting reciprocating pump, running at 60 r.p.m., delivers 0.01518 m³/s of water. The diameter of the piston is 240 mm and stroke length 360 mm. The suction and delivery heads are 3.4 m and 11.4 m respectively. Determine:*

(i) Theoretical discharge, *(ii) Coefficient of discharge,*

(iii) Percentage slip of the pump, and *(iv) Power required to run the pump.*

Solution. *Given*: Speed of the pump, $N = 60$ r.p.m.; Actual discharge, $Q_{act.} = 0.01518$ m³/s; Diameter of the piston, $D = 240$ mm $= 0.24$ m; Stroke length, $L = 360$ mm $= 0.36$ m; Suction head, $h_s = 3.4$ m; Delivery head, $h_d = 11.4$ m.

(i) Theoretical discharge, Q_{th}:

$$Q_{th} = \frac{ALN}{60} = \frac{\left(\frac{\pi}{4} \times 0.24^2\right) \times 0.36 \times 60}{60} = \textbf{0.01629 m}^3\textbf{/s (Ans.)}$$

(ii) Coefficient of discharge, C_d:

$$C_d = \frac{Q_{act.}}{Q_{th.}} = \frac{0.01518}{0.01629} = \textbf{0.932 (Ans.)}$$

(iii) Percentage slip of the pump:

$$\%\text{ slip} = \frac{Q_{th.} - Q_{act.}}{Q_{th.}} \times 100$$

$$= \frac{0.01629 - 0.01518}{0.01629} \times 100 = \textbf{6.8\% (Ans.)}$$

(iv) Power required to run the pump, P:

$$P = \frac{w\,A\,L\,N}{60 \times 1000}\,(h_s + h_d)\ \text{k.W}$$

$$= \frac{9810 \times \left(\frac{\pi}{4} \times 0.24^2\right) \times 0.36 \times 60}{60 \times 1000}\,(3.4 + 11.4)$$

$$= \textbf{2.36 kW (Ans.)}$$

Q. 8. *The diameter and stroke of a single-acting reciprocating pump are 250 mm and 450 mm respectively. The pump takes in supply of water from sump 2.9 m below the pump and through a pipe 8 m long and 100 mm diameter. If separation occurs at 2.4 m of water absolute, determine:*

(i) The speed at which separation may take place at the beginning of suction of stroke, and

(ii) The speed of the pump if an air vessel is fitted on the suction side 2 m above the sump water level.

Take atmospheric pressure head = 10.3 m of water, and friction coefficient, $f = 0.01$.

Solution. *Given*: Diameter of piston, $D = 250$ mm $= 0.25$ m; Stroke length, $L = 450$ mm $= 0.45$ m; Crank radius, $r = \frac{0.45}{2} = 0.225$ m; Suction head, $h_s = 2.9$ m; Diameter of the suction pipe, $d_s = 200$ mm $= 0.2$ m; Length of suction pipe, $l_s = 8$ m; Separation head $= 2.4$ m of water absolute; Atmospheric pressure head, $H_{atm.} = 10.3$ m of water; Friction coefficient, $f = 0.01$.

$$\text{Area of piston, } A = \frac{\pi}{4} \times D^2 = \frac{\pi}{4} \times 0.25^2 = 0.049 \text{ m}^2$$

$$\text{Area of suction pipe, } a_s = \frac{\pi}{4} \times 0.2^2 = 0.0314 \text{ m}^2$$

(*i*) The speed at which separation may take place (no air vessel fitted), *N*:

The pressure head due to acceleration in the suction pipe, is given by:

$$h_{as} = \frac{l_s}{g} \times \frac{A}{a_s} \omega^2 r \cos\theta$$

At the beginning of the suction stroke, $\theta = 0°$, we have:

$$h_{as} = \frac{l_s}{g} \times \frac{A}{a_s} \omega^2 r = \frac{8}{9.81} \times \frac{0.049}{0.0314} \times \omega^2 \times 0.225 = 0.286\, \omega^2$$

Pressure head at the beginning of suction stroke

$$= (h_s + h_{as}) = (2.9 + 0.286\, \omega^2) \text{ below atmospheric head}$$

Limiting condition for *no separation* gives,

$$H_{atm} - (h_s + h_{as}) = h_{sep.}$$

or, $$10.3 - (2.9 + 0.286\, \omega^2) = 2.4$$

or, $$\omega = \left(\frac{10.3 - 2.4 - 2.9}{0.286}\right)^{1/2} = 4.18 \text{ rad./s}$$

But, $$\omega = \frac{2\pi N}{60}, \quad \text{or,} \quad N = \frac{60\,\omega}{2\pi} = \frac{60 \times 4.18}{2\pi} = \mathbf{39.9 \text{ r.p.m}} \text{ (Ans.)}$$

(*ii*) The speed of pump when an air vessel is fitted on suction side, *N*:

Since the air vessel is installed 2 m above the sump water level, therefore:

(*a*) There will be a loss of head due to friction in the suction pipe for the length of $8 \times \frac{2.4}{2.9} = 6.62$ m; (*ii*) the acceleration pressure head will be restricted in the remaining $(8 - 6.62)$ m $= 1.38$ m length of suction pipe.

The pressure head due to acceleration (h_{as}) in the suction pipe at the beginning of suction stroke ($\theta = 0°$) is given by:

$$h_{as} = \frac{l_s}{g} \times \frac{A}{a_s} \times \omega^2 r = \frac{1.38}{9.81} \times \frac{0.049}{0.0314} \times \omega^2 \times 0.225 = 0.049\, \omega^2$$

The velocity of water in the suction pipe **fitted with air vessel.**

$$v_s = \frac{A}{a_s} \times \frac{\omega r}{\pi} = \frac{0.049}{0.0314} \times \frac{\omega \times 0.225}{\pi} = 0.112\, \omega$$

$$\text{Loss of head due to friction, } h_{fs} = \frac{4 f\, l_s\, v_s^2}{d_s \times 2g}$$

$$= \frac{4 \times 0.01 \times 6.62 \times (0.112\,\omega)^2}{0.2 \times 2 \times 9.81} = 8.46 \times 10^{-4}\,\omega^2$$

Limiting condition for *no separation* gives:

$$H_{atm} - (h_s + h_{as} + h_{fs}) = h_{sep.}$$

or, $10.3 - (2.9 + 0.049\,\omega^2 + 8.46 \times 10^{-4}\,\omega^2) = 2.4$

or, $10.3 - 2.9 - 0.0498\,\omega^2 = 2.4$

or, $\omega = \left(\frac{10.3 - 2.9 - 2.4}{0.0498}\right)^{1/2} = 10.02$ rad/s

But, $\omega = \frac{2\pi N}{60}$ or $N = \frac{60\,\omega}{2\pi} = \frac{60 \times 10.02}{2\pi}$ = **95.7 r.p.m. (Ans.)**

Q. 9. *A hydroelectric power plant produces 30 MW under a head of 18 m. If the overall efficiency of the plant is 75%, determine:*

(i) Type of turbine; (ii) Synchronous speed of generator.

Solution. *Given*: Power developed, P = 30 MW (= 30 × 10^3 kW); Head, H = 18 m; Overall efficiency, η_0 = 75%.

(*i*) Type of turbine:

$$P = \eta_0 \times w\,Q\,H$$

$$25 \times 10^3 = 0.75 \times 9.81 \times Q \times 18$$

$$\therefore \quad Q = \frac{30 \times 10^3}{0.75 \times 9.81 \times 18} = 226.5 \text{ m}^3\text{/s}$$

As the head is low and discharge is high so "propeller type of turbine" should be used. **(Ans.)**

(*ii*) Synchronous speed of the generator, $N_{syn.}$:

$$\text{Specific speed, } N_s = \frac{1150}{(H)^{1/4}} \text{ (approx.)}$$

$$= \frac{1150}{(18)^{1/4}} = 558.3 \text{ r.p.m.}$$

$$\text{Speed of rotation, } N = \frac{N_s \times H^{5/4}}{\sqrt{P}} \qquad \left(\because N_s = \frac{N\sqrt{P}}{H^{5/4}}\right)$$

$$= \frac{558.3 \times (18)^{5/4}}{\sqrt{30 \times 10^3}} = 119.5 \text{ r.p.m.}$$

For generator, $N = \frac{120\,f}{p}$

[where, f = frequency (= 50 Hz)]

$\therefore$ Number of poles, $p = \frac{120 \times 50}{119.5}$ = **50 (Ans.)**

(Number of poles is necessarily an even number).

Q. 10. *A jet of water 24 mm diameter and moving at 12 m/s, strikes upon the centre of a symmetrical vane. After impingement, the jet gets deflected through 165° by the vane. Presuming vane to be smooth, determine:*

(i) The force exerted by jet on the vane, and

(ii) The ratio of velocity at outlet to that at inlet if actual reaction of the vane is 121 N.

Solution. *Given*: Diameter of the jet, $d = 24$ mm $= 0.024$ m; Velocity of jet, $V = 12$ m/s; Angle of deflection = 165°; Actual reaction of the vane = 121 N.

(i) The force exerted by the jet on the vane *F*:

Refer to Fig. 4.

$165° = 180 - \theta$, or, $\theta = 180 - 165 = 15°$

For *smooth vane,* the theoretical force (or thrust) exerted by the jet on the vane is, given by:

$$F = \rho a V^2 (1 + \cos\theta) \quad ...(i)$$

$$= 1000 \times \left(\frac{\pi}{4} \times 0.024^2\right) \times 12^2 (1 + \cos 15°)$$

$$= \mathbf{128\ N\ (Ans.)}$$

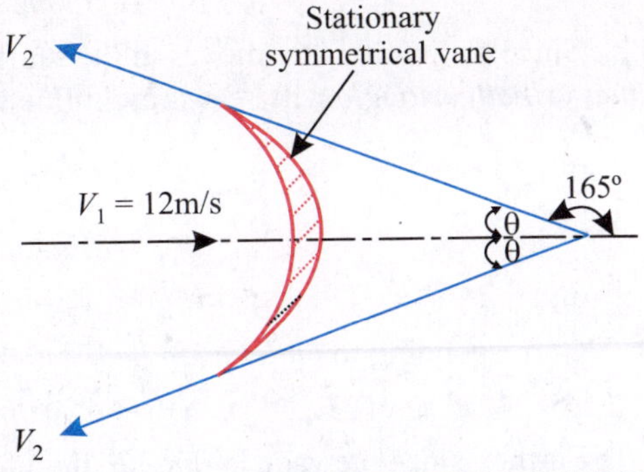

Fig. 4

(ii) $\dfrac{V_2}{V_1}$ **:**

Actual reaction of the vane = 121 N (Given)

If the vane is *not smooth,* then outgoing velocity at the vane tip is less than the incoming velocity,

i.e., $\dfrac{V_2}{V_1} = K$, where, $K < 1$. Then,

Eqn. (*i*) gets modified to:

$$F = \rho a V^2 (1 + K \cos\theta)$$

$$121 = 1000 \times \left(\frac{\pi}{4} \times 0.024^2\right) \times 12^2 (1 + K \cos 15°)$$

or $$1 + K\cos 15° = \frac{121}{1000 \times \left(\frac{\pi}{4} \times 0.024^2\right) \times 12^2} = 1.857$$

or, ∴ $$K = \frac{1.857 - 1}{\cos 15°} = \mathbf{0.887\ (Ans.)}$$

Q. 11. *A jet of 60 mm diameter impinges on a curved vane and is deflected through an angle of 165°. The vane moves in the same direction as that of jet with a velocity of 25 m/s. If the rate of flow is 180 litres per second, determine the component of force on the vane in the direction of motion. How much would be the power developed by the vane and what would be the water efficiency?*

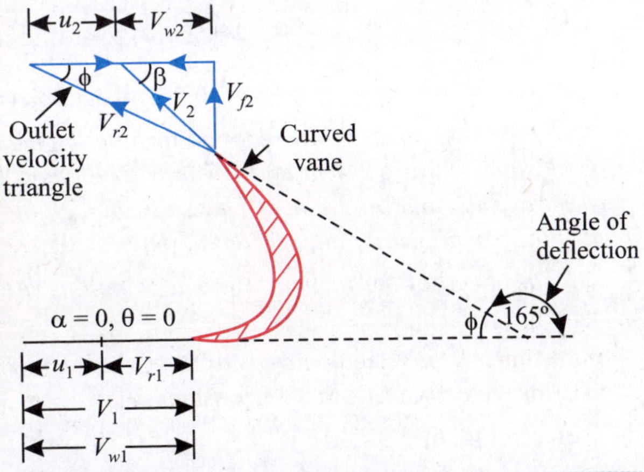

Fig. 5

Solution. *Given*: Diameter of the jet, $d = 60$ mm $= 0.06$ m; Angle of deflection = 165°; Velocity of the vane, $u_1 = u_2$ $(= u)$ = 25 m/s; Rate of flow, $Q = 180$ litres *p/s* = 0.18 m³/s.

$$\text{Area of the jet, } a = \frac{\pi}{4} d^2$$
$$= \frac{\pi}{4} \times 0.06^2$$
$$= 0.002827 \text{ m}^2$$

Since the jet of water moves in the same direction as that of vane, $\alpha = \theta = 0$ and, therefore, the *inlet velocity triangle* will be a straight line with

$$V_1 = \frac{Q}{a} = \frac{0.18}{0.002827} = 63.67 \text{ m/s}$$
$$V_{r1} = V_1 - u_1 = 63.67 - 25 = 38.67 \text{ m/s}$$

and $$V_{w1} = V_1 = 63.67 \text{ m/s}$$

Corresponding to *outlet triangle,*

$$\theta = 180° - 165° = 15°$$

Further, since the vane is *smooth,* therefore,

$$V_{r2} = V_{r1} = 38.67 \text{ m/s}$$
$$V_{w2} = V_{r2} \cos \phi - u_2$$
$$= 38.67 \cos 15° - 25 = 12.35 \text{ m/s} \qquad (\because u_1 = u_2 = 25 \text{ m/s})$$

Power developed by the vane:

Force exerted by the jet on the vane in the direction of motion,

$$F = \rho\, a\, V_{r1} (V_{w1} + V_{w2})$$
$$= 1000 \times 0.002827 \times 38.67 \times (63.67 + 12.35) = 8310.5 \text{ N}$$

$$\text{Work done} = \text{Force} \times \text{Velocity}$$
$$= 8310.3 \times 25 = 207762 \text{ Nm/s or J/s or W}$$

Hence, power developed = 207762 W or **207.8 kW (Ans.)**

Water efficiency (Efficiency of vane):

Efficiency of vane (water efficiency)

$$= \frac{\text{Work done on the vane}}{\text{Kinetic energy supplied by the jet}}$$
$$= \frac{207762}{\frac{1}{2}\rho Q V_1^2} = \frac{207762}{\frac{1}{2} \times 1000 \times 0.18 \times 63.67^2}$$
$$= 0.569 \text{ or } \mathbf{56.9\%} \text{ (Ans.)}$$

Q. 12. *In an inward flow reaction turbine the head on the turbine is 31 m. The external and internal diameters are 1.4 m and 0.7 m respectively. The velocity of flow through the remner is constant and is equal to 3.3 m/s. The guide blade angle is 11° and the runner vanes are rigid at inlet. If the discharge at outlet is rodial, determine:*

(i) *The speed of the turbine,* ***(ii)*** *The vane angle at outlet of the runner, and* ***(iii)*** *Hydraulic efficiency.*

Solution. *Given*: Head on the turbine = 31 m; External diameter, $D_1 = 1.4$ m; Internal diameter, $D_2 = 0.7$ m; Velocity of flow, V_f = constant, $V_{f1} = V_{f2} = 3.3$ m/s; Guide blade angle = 11°.

Refer to Fig. 6.

Runner vanes are *radial at inlet,*

$$\therefore \qquad \theta = 90°; \quad V_{w1} = u_1$$

Discharge is radial,

$\therefore \quad V_{w2} = 0, \quad V_2 = V_{f2} = 3.3$ m/s

(i) The speed of the turbine, N:

From inlet velocity triangle, we have:

$$\tan \alpha = \frac{V_{f1}}{u_1}$$

or, $$u_1 = \frac{V_{f_1}}{\tan \alpha} = \frac{3.3}{\tan 11°}$$

or, $$u_1 = 16.98 \text{ m/s}$$

Also, $$u_1 = \frac{\pi D_1 N}{60}$$

or, $$N = \frac{60\, u_1}{\pi D_1}$$

or, $$N = \frac{60 \times 16.98}{\pi \times 1.4} = \mathbf{231.6\ r.p.m.}\ \textbf{(Ans.)}$$

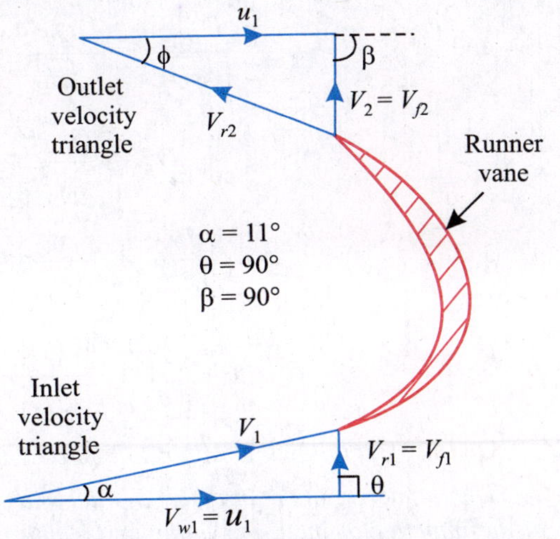

Fig. 6

(ii) The vane angle at the outlet of the runner, ϕ:

$$u_2 = \frac{\pi D_2 N}{60} = \frac{\pi \times 0.7 \times 231.6}{60} = 8.49 \text{ m/s}$$

From *outlet velocity triangle,* we have:

$$\tan \phi = \frac{V_{f2}}{u_2} = \frac{3.3}{8.49} = 0.3887$$

$$\phi = \tan^{-1}(0.3887) = \mathbf{21.2°}\ \textbf{(Ans.)}$$

(iii) Hydraulic efficiency, η_{HG}:

$$\eta_h = \frac{V_{w1}\, u_1}{g\, H} \quad (V_{w2} = 0, \text{ the discharge being radial at outlet})$$

$$= \frac{16.98 \times 16.98}{9.81 \times 31} = 0.948 \text{ or } \mathbf{94.8\%}\ \textbf{(Ans.)}$$

Q. 13. *A turbine is to operate under a head of 24 m at 180 r.p.m. The discharge is 8.5 m³/s. If the efficiency is 92 per cent, determine the performance of turbine under a head of 18 m.*

Solution. *Given*: Head under which turbine works, $H_1 = 24$ m; speed of the turbine, $N_1 = 180$ r.p.m; Discharge through the turbine, $Q_1 = 8.5$ m³/s; Efficiency (overall), $\eta_0 = 91\%$.

Performance of the turbine under a head, $H_2 = 18$ m means to find speed (N_2), discharge (Q_2) and power generated (P_2) by the turbine when working under a head of 18 m.

$$\text{Overall efficiency, } \eta_0 = \frac{\text{Shaft power}}{\text{Water power}} = \frac{P}{w\,Q\,H} = \frac{P_1}{w\,Q_1 H_1}$$

$$P_1 = \eta_0 \times w\, Q_1\, H_1 = 0.92 \times 9.81 \times 8.5 \times 24 = 1841 \text{ kW}$$

Now, $$\frac{N_1}{\sqrt{H_1}} = \frac{N_2}{\sqrt{H_2}}$$

$$\therefore \quad N_2 = \frac{N\sqrt{H_2}}{\sqrt{H_1}} = \frac{180 \times \sqrt{18}}{\sqrt{24}} = \mathbf{155.88\ r.p.m.}\ \textbf{(Ans.)}$$

and, $$\frac{Q_1}{\sqrt{H_1}} = \frac{Q_2}{\sqrt{H_2}}$$

$$\therefore \quad Q_2 = \frac{Q_1\sqrt{H_2}}{\sqrt{H_1}} = \frac{8.5 \times \sqrt{18}}{\sqrt{24}} = \mathbf{7.36\ m^3/s\ (Ans.)}$$

and, $$\frac{P_1}{H_1^{3/2}} = \frac{P_2}{(H_2)^{3/2}}$$

$$\therefore \quad P_2 = \frac{P_1 (H_2)^{3/2}}{(H_1)^{3/2}} = \frac{1841 \times (18)^{3/2}}{(24)^{3/2}} = \mathbf{1195.8\ kW\ (Ans.)}$$

Q. 14. *The following data relate to a centrifugal pump:*

The diameters of the impeller at inlet and outlet = 170 mm and 340 mm respectively; The width of the impeller at inlet and outlet = 14 mm and 7 mm respectively; The rate of flow through the pump = 16.9 litres/sec; Speed of the impeller = 1400 r.p.m. Vane angle at the outlet = 45°.

The water enters the impeller radially at inlet.

Neglecting losses through the impeller, find the pressure rise in the impeller.

Solution. *Given*: D_1 = 170 mm = 0.17 m; D_2 = 340 mm = 0.34 m; B_1 = 14 mm = 0.014 m; B_2 = 7 mm = 0.007 m; Q = 16.9 litres/s = 0.0169 m^3/s; N = 1400 r.p.m; ϕ = 45°.

Pressure rise in the impeller:

Velocity of flow at inlet,

$$V_{f1} = \frac{Q}{\pi D_1 B_1}$$

$$= \frac{0.0169}{\pi \times 0.17 \times 0.014} = 2.26 \text{ m/s}$$

Velocity of flow at outlet,

$$V_{f2} = \frac{Q}{\pi D_2 B_2}$$

$$= \frac{0.0169}{\pi \times 0.34 \times 0.007} = 2.26 \text{ m/s}$$

Tangential velocity of impeller at outlet,

$$u_2 = \frac{\pi D_2 N}{60} = \frac{\pi \times 0.34 \times 1400}{60} = 24.92 \text{ m/s}$$

Pressure rise in the impeller

$$= \frac{1}{2g}\left(V_{f1}^2 + u_2^2 - V_{f2}^2 \text{ cosec}^2\ \phi\right) \qquad \text{...[Eqn. (3.165)]}$$

$$= \frac{1}{2 \times 9.81}(2.26^2 + 24.92^2 - 2.26^2 \times \text{cosec}^2\ 45°)$$

$$= \frac{1}{2 \times 9.81}(5.108 + 621.006 - 10.215) = \mathbf{31.39\ m\ (Ans.)}$$

Q. 15. *Tests on a pump model indicate a cavitation parameter σ_c = 0.11. A homologous unit is to be installed at a location when atmospheric pressure, p_a = 0.89 bar and vapour pressure p_v = 0.034 bar absolute and is to pump water against a head of 22 m.*

Calculate the maximum permissible suction head.

Solution. *Given*: Cavitation parameter, $\sigma_c = 0.11$; Atmospheric pressure, $p_a = 0.89$ bar or $H_a = \frac{0.89 \times 10^5}{9810} = 9.07$ m of water; Vapour pressure, $p_u = 0.034$ bar or $H_v = \frac{0.034 \times 10^5}{9810} = 0.346$ m of water; Manometric head, $H_{mano} = 22$ m.

Maximum permissible suction head, h_s:

We know that,
$$\sigma = \frac{H_a - H_s - H_v}{H_{mano.}}$$

or,
$$\sigma_c = \frac{H_c - h_s - H_v}{mano.} \quad \text{neglecting head lost due to friction}$$
$$\left(\because H_s = h_s + h_{fs} + \frac{V_2^2}{2g}\right)$$

or,
$$0.11 = \frac{9.07 - h_s - 0.346}{22}$$

or,
$$0.11 \times 22 = 8.724 - h_s$$

or,
$$h_s = \mathbf{6.304\ m}\ \textbf{(Ans.)}$$

Q. 16. *A single-acting reciprocating pump has a diameter (piston) of 120 mm and stroke length 240 mm. The length and diameter of the suction pipe are 7.0 m and 60 mm respectively. If the suction lift of the pump is 3.3 m and separation occurs when pressure in the pump falls below 2.6 m of water absolute and the manometer reads 762 mm of mercury, determine the maximum speed at which pump can be run without separation in the suction pipe.*

Solution. *Given:* Piston diameter, $D = 120$ mm $= 0.12$ m, $\therefore$ Area, $A = \frac{\pi}{4} \times 0.12^2 = 0.01131\ m^2$; Stroke length, $L = 240$ mm $= 0.24$ m; Crank radius, $r = \frac{L}{2} = 0.24/2 = 0.12$ m; Length of suction pipe, $l_s = 7.0$ m; Diameter of suction pipe, $d_s = 60$ mm $= 0.06$ m, $\therefore$ Area of suction pipe, $a_s = \frac{\pi}{4} \times 0.06^2 = 0.002827\ m^2$; The suction lift of the pump, $h_s = 3.3$ m; Separation pressure head, $h_{sep.} = 2.6$ m.

Maximum speed at which pump can run without separation, N:

Atmospheric head, $H_{atm.} = \frac{762}{1000} \times 13.6 = 10.363$ m of water during suction stroke, the possibility of separation is only at the *beginning of the stroke.* At the beginning of suction stroke, $\theta = 0°$ and $\cos\theta = 1$, that gives:
$$h_{as} = \frac{l_s}{g} \times \frac{A}{a_s} \times \omega^2 r = \frac{7.0}{9.81} \times \frac{0.01131}{0.002827} \times \omega^2 \times 0.12 = 0.342\ \omega^2$$

Pressure head in the cylinder at the beginning of suction stroke
$$= (h_s + h_{as}) \text{ vacuum}$$
$$= H_{atm.} - (h_s + h_{as}) \text{ absolute}$$

This absolute pressure (at the beginning of suction stroke) *should not fall below the vapour pressure head ($h_{sep.}$) to avoid separation,* thus in the *limiting condition,*
$$H_{atm.} - (h_s + h_{as}) = h_{sep.}$$

or
$$10.363 - (3.3 + 0.342\ \omega^2) = 2.6$$

or
$$\omega^2 = \frac{10.363 - 2.6 - 3.3}{0.342}$$

or
$$\text{Angular velocity, } \omega = 3.6 \text{ rad/s}$$

But, $\omega = \dfrac{2\pi N}{60}$ or $N = \dfrac{60\,\omega}{2\pi} = \dfrac{60 \times 3.6}{2 \times \pi}$ = **34.38 r.p.m. (Ans.)**

Q. 17. *The diameters of ram and plunger of a hydraulic press are 120 mm and 15 mm respectively.*

(i) Find the force required to be applied on the plunger to raise a load of 30 kN on the ram.

(ii) If the plunger has a stroke of 220 mm, how many strokes will be required to lift the load by 450 mm. Also calculate the volume of additional liquid required.

(iii) Further, if the time taken to lift the load is 11 minutes, what will be power required to drive the plunger.

Solution. *Given*: Diameter of the ram, D = 120 mm = 0.12 m, ∴ Area of the ram = $\dfrac{\pi}{4} \times 0.12^2$ = 0.01131 m²; Diameter of the plunger, d = 15 mm = 0.015, ∴ Area of the plunger = $\dfrac{\pi}{4} \times 0.015^2$ = 0.0001767 m²; Load to be raised, W = 30 kN; Stroke of the plunger = 220 mm = 0.22 m; Distance through which load is to be lifted = 450 mm = 0.45 m; Time taken to lift the load = 11 minutes.

(i) Force required to raise a load of 30 kN, *F*:

Since pressure intensity is same throughout a static mass of fluid, therefore,

$$\frac{F}{a} = \frac{W}{A} \quad \text{or} \quad \frac{F}{0.0001767} = \frac{30}{0.01131}$$

or, $$F = \frac{30 \times 0.0001767}{0.01131} = \mathbf{0.468\ kN\ (Ans.)}$$

(ii) Number of strokes required, *n*:

Number of strokes required to lift the load by 0.45 m,

$$n = \frac{\text{Total volume of liquid to be displaced}}{\text{Volume of liquid displaced in one stroke of the plunger}}$$

$$= \frac{\frac{\pi}{4} \times (0.12)^2 \times 0.45}{\frac{\pi}{4} \times (0.015)^2 \times 0.22} = \mathbf{131\ (Ans.)}$$

Volume of additional liquid $= \dfrac{\pi}{4} \times 0.12^2 \times 0.45 = \mathbf{0.00509\ m^3\ (Ans.)}$

(iii) Power required to drive motor, *P*:

Work done by the press = 30 × 0.45 = 13.5 kNm (in 11 minutes)

Work done per second $= \dfrac{13.5}{11 \times 60}$ = 0.02045 kNm/s

∴ Power required, P = 0.02045 kW = **20.45 W (Ans.)**

Q. 18. *A 80 mm diameter jet having a velocity of 28 m/s strikes a flat plate, the normal of which is inclined at 40° to the axis of the jet. Determine the normal force on the plate:*

(i) When the plate is stationary; (ii) When the plate is moving with a velocity of 12 m/s in the direction of jet, away from the jet.

What is the power and efficiency of the jet when the plate is moving?

Solution. Diameter of the jet, d = 80 mm = 0.08 m, ∴ Area of the jet, $a = \dfrac{\pi}{4} \times 0.08^2$ = 0.00503 m²; Angle between the jet and the plate, θ = 90° – 40° = 50°; Velocity of the jet, V = 28 m/s; Velocity of the plate, u = 12 m/s.

Normal force on the plate:

(*i*) *When the plate is stationary,* the normal force on the plate is given by:

$$F_x = \rho a V^2 \sin\theta \quad \text{...[Eqn. (3.2)]}$$

$$= 1000 \times 0.00503 \times 28^2 \times \sin 50° = \mathbf{3020.9\ N\ (Ans.)}$$

(*ii*) *When the plate is moving with a velocity of 12 m/s and moving away from the jet,* the normal force on the plate is given by the relation:

$$F_n = \rho a (v - u)^2 \sin\theta$$

$$= 1000 \times 0.00503 \times (28 - 12)^2 \sin 50° = \mathbf{986.4\ N\ (Ans.)}$$

Power and efficiency of the jet when the plate is moving:

Work done per second by the jet

= Force in the direction of the jet × distance moved by the plate in the direction of the jet/sec.

$= F_x \times u$

where, $F_x = F_n \times \sin\theta = 986.4 \times \sin 50° = \mathbf{755.6\ N\ (Ans.)}$

∴ Work done $= 755.6 \times 12 = 9067.2$ Nm/s

Hence, *Power of the jet* = 9067.2 J/s = 9067.2 W = **9.067 kW (Ans.)**

$$\textit{Efficiency of the jet} = \frac{\text{Work done on the plate}}{\text{Kinetic energy supplied by the jet}}$$

$$= \frac{9067.2}{\frac{1}{2}(\rho a V) \times V^2} = \frac{9067.2}{\frac{1}{2} \times (1000 \times 0.00503 \times 28) \times 28^2}$$

= 0.1642 or **16.42% (Ans.)**

Q. 19. *A single jet Pelton wheel runs at 280 r.p.m under a head of 480 m. The jet diameter is 190 mm, its deflection inside the bucket is 160° and its relative velocity is reduced by 12 percent due to friction. Determine:*

(i) Water power; (ii) Resultant force on the bucket; and (iii) Overall efficiency.
Assume: Mechanical losses = 2.6 per cent, coefficient of velocity = 0.97; and speed ratio = 0.45.

Solution. *Given*: Speed of the wheel, $N = 280$ r.p.m.; Diameter of the jet; $d = 190$ mm = 0.19 m; Net head, $H = 480$ m; Angle of deflection of jet = 160°; Reduction of relative velocity due to friction = 12%; Mechanical losses = 2.6%; Coefficient of velocity, $C_v = 0.97$; Speed ratio, $K_u = 0.45$.

(*i*) Water power:

$$\text{Velocity of jet, } V_1 = C_v \sqrt{2\,gH} = 0.97\sqrt{2 \times 9.81 \times 480} = 94 \text{ m/s}$$

Discharge through the Pelton wheel,

$$Q = \text{Area of jet } (a) \times \text{velocity } (V_1)$$

$$= \frac{\pi}{4} \times 0.19^2 \times 94 = 2.66 \text{ m}^3/\text{s}$$

Water power $= wQH = 9.81 \times 2.66 \times 480 =$ **12525 kW (Ans.)**

(*ii*) Resultant force on the bucket:

Peripheral speed of the wheel, $u = K_u \sqrt{2\,gH} = 0.45\sqrt{2 \times 9.81 \times 480} = 43.67$ m/s

Refer to Fig. 7.

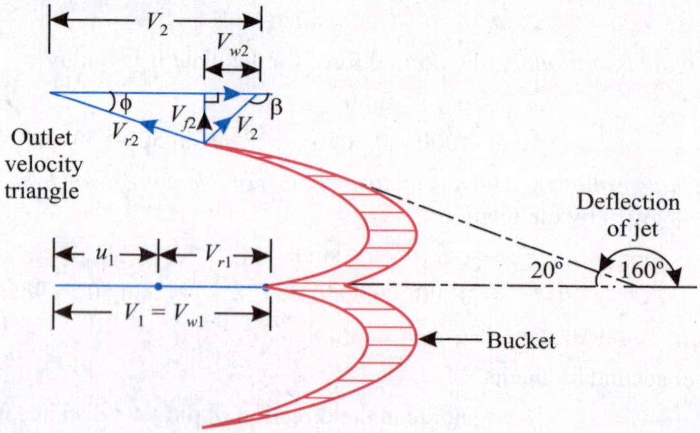

Fig. 7

At inlet to turbine:

$$V_{w1} = V_1 = 94 \text{ m/s}$$
$$V_{r1} = (V_1 - u_1) = 94 - 43.67 = 50.33 \text{ m/s}$$

At exit from the turbine:

The blade angle at exit,

$$\phi = 180° - 160° = 20°$$
$$V_{r2} = \left(100 - \frac{12}{100}\right) \times V_{r1}$$

or,
$$V_{r2} = 0.88 \times 50.33 = 44.3 \text{ m/s}$$

As $V_{r2} \cos\theta$ is less than blade speed u, the velocity triangle at outlet will be as shown in Fig. 7. ($\beta > 90°$)

$$V_{w2} = u_2 - V_{r2} \cos\phi = 43.67 - 44.3 \cos 20° = 2.04 \text{ m/s}$$

$(\because u_1 = u_2 = u)$

Resultant force on the bucket,

$$F = \rho Q (V_{w1} - V_{w2})$$
$$= 1000 \times 2.66 (94 - 2.04) = \mathbf{244614 \text{ N}} \text{ (Ans.)}$$

(*iii*) Brake power, *P*:

Power developed by the wheel

$$= F \times u$$
$$= 244614 \times 43.67 \text{ Nm/s or W}$$
$$= 244614 \times 43.67 \times 10^{-3} \text{ kW}$$
$$= \mathbf{10682 \text{ kW}} \text{ (Ans.)}$$

(*iv*) Overall efficiency, η_0:

$$\eta_0 = \frac{\text{Brake power}}{\text{Water power}}$$
$$= \frac{10682}{12525} = 0.853 \text{ or } \mathbf{85.3\%} \text{ (Ans.)}$$

Q. 20. *A Kaplan turbine develops 20 MW at average head of 32 m. Assuming a speed ratio of 2, flow ratio of 0.58, diameter of the boss equal to 0.34 times the diameter of the runner and an overall efficiency of 85 per cent, determine the diameter, speed and specific speed of the turbine.*

Solution. *Given*: Shaft power, $P = 20$ MW $= 20 \times 10^3 = 20{,}000$ kW; Head, $H = 32$ m; Speed ratio, $K_u = 2$, Flow ratio $K_f = 0.58$; Diameter of boss $(D_b) = 0.34 \times$ diameter of the runner (D_0), *i.e.*, $D_b = 0.34\, D_0$; Overall efficiency, $\eta_0 = 85\%$.

Refer to Fig. 8.

Diameter of the runner, D_0:

$$K_u = \frac{u_1}{\sqrt{2gH}} = 2, \quad u_1 = 2\times\sqrt{2gH} = 2\times\sqrt{2\times 9.81\times 32} = 50.11 \text{ m/s}$$

$$K_f = \frac{V_{f1}}{\sqrt{2gH}} = 0.58$$

or, $$V_{f1} = 0.58\times\sqrt{2gH} = 0.58\times\sqrt{2\times 9.81\times 32} = 14.5 \text{ m/s}$$

Overall efficiency,

$$\eta_0 = \frac{\text{Shafter power } (P)}{\text{Water power}} = \frac{20000}{wQH}$$

$$0.85 = \frac{20000}{9.81\times Q\times 32}$$

or, $$Q = \frac{20000}{0.85\times 9.81\times 32} = 74.9 \text{ m/s}$$

Also, Q = Area of flow × velocity of flow

$$74.9 = \frac{\pi}{4}\left(D_0^2 - D_b^2\right)\times V_{f1}$$

or, $$74.9 = \frac{\pi}{4}\left[D_0^2 - (0.34\, D_0)^2\right]\times 14.5$$

$$= \frac{\pi}{4} D_0^2\left[1 - (0.34)^2\right]\times 14.5 = 10.07\, D_0^2$$

or, $$D_0 = \left(\frac{74.9}{10.07}\right)^{1/2} = \textbf{2.73 m (Ans.)}$$

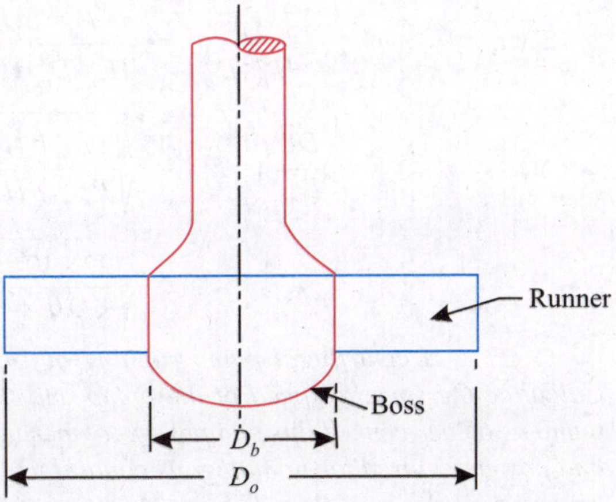

Fig. 8

Speed of the turbine, N:

$$u_1 = \frac{\pi D_0 N}{60}, \quad \text{or,} \quad N = \frac{60\, u_1}{\pi D_0} - \frac{60\times 50.11}{\pi\times 2.73} = \textbf{350.6 r.p.m. (Ans.)}$$

Specific speed of the turbine, N_s:

$$N_s = \frac{N\sqrt{P}}{H^{5/4}} = \frac{350.6\times\sqrt{20000}}{(32)^{5/4}} = \textbf{651.5 (Ans.)}$$

Q. 21. *A hydro-turbine is required to give 22 MW at 45 m head and 90 r.p.m runner speed. The laboratory facilities available permit testing of 16 kW model at 4.5 m head. What should be model runner speed and model to prototype scale ratio?*

Solution. *Given*: $P_p = 22$ MW; $H_p = 45$ m; $N_p = 90$ r.p.m.; $P_m = 16$ kW; $H_m = 4.5$ m.

N_m; $\dfrac{D_p}{D_m}$ $(= L_r)$:

Prototype specific speed, $(N_s)_p = \dfrac{N_p\sqrt{P_p}}{(H_p)^{5/4}}$ (where P is in kW)

$$= \frac{90 \times \sqrt{22 \times 10^3}}{(45)^{5/4}} = 114.5$$

For model, $$114.5 = \frac{N_m \times \sqrt{P_m}}{(H_m)^{5/4}} \qquad [\because (N_s)_p = (N_s)_m]$$

or, $$N_m = \frac{114.5 \times (H_m)^{5/4}}{\sqrt{P_m}} = \frac{114.5 \times (4.5)^{5/4}}{\sqrt{16}} = \textbf{187.6 r.p.m. (Ans.)}$$

For similar turbines $\dfrac{P}{H^{3/2}D^2}$ should be *equal*.

Then, $$\frac{P_p}{H_p^{3/2}D_p^2} = \frac{P_m}{H_m^{3/2}D_m^2}$$

or, $$\frac{D_p}{D_m}\ (= L_r) = \sqrt{\frac{P_p}{P_m} \times \left(\frac{H_m}{H_p}\right)^{3/2}}$$

$$= \sqrt{\frac{22 \times 10^3}{16} \times \left(\frac{4.5}{45}\right)^{3/2}} = \textbf{6.594 (Ans.)}$$

Q. 22. *A centrifugal pump running at 1450 r.p.m. delivers 0.18 m³/s at a head of 12 m. Calculate the specific speed of the pump and the power input. Assume overall efficiency of the pump as 65 per cent. If this pump were to operate at 800 r.p.m. what would be the head, discharge and power required for homologous conditions? Assume overall efficiency remains unchanged at new r.p.m.*

Solution. *Given*: Speed, $N = 1450$ r.p.m.; Dischange, $Q = 0.18\ m^3/s$; Head, $H = 12$ m; Overall efficiency, $\eta_0 = 65\%$; New speed, $N = 800$ r.p.m.

At 1450 r.p.m:

Specific speed, $$N_s = \frac{N\sqrt{Q}}{(H)^{3/4}} \qquad \text{...[Eqn. (3.25)]}$$

$$= \frac{1450 \times \sqrt{0.18}}{(12)^{3/4}} = \textbf{95.4 (Ans.)}$$

Power input $$= \frac{wQH}{\eta_0} = \frac{9.81 \times 0.18 \times 12}{0.65} = \textbf{32.6 kW (Ans.)}$$

At 800 r.p.m:

$$N_u = \frac{N}{\sqrt{H}}$$

i.e., $$\frac{800}{\sqrt{H}} = \frac{1450}{\sqrt{12}}$$

or, $$\text{Head, } H = \left(\frac{800}{1450}\right)^2 \times 12 = \mathbf{3.65\ m}\ \textbf{(Ans.)}$$

$$Q_u = \frac{Q}{\sqrt{H}}$$

i.e., $$\frac{Q}{\sqrt{3.65}} = \frac{0.18}{\sqrt{12}}$$

or, $$\text{Discharge, } Q = \sqrt{\frac{3.65}{12}} \times 0.18 = \mathbf{0.09927\ m^3/s}\ \textbf{(Ans.)}$$

$$P_u = \frac{P}{(H)^{3/2}}$$

i.e., $$\frac{P}{(3.65)^{3/2}} = \frac{32.6}{(12)^{3/2}}$$

or $$\text{Power input, } P = \left(\frac{3.65}{12}\right)^{3/2} \times 32.6 = \mathbf{5.469\ kW}\ \textbf{(Ans.)}$$

Q. 23. *A single-stage centrifugal pump runs at 550 r.p.m. and delivers 290 m³/min of water against a head of 135 m. The pump impeller is 2.2 m in diameter and it has a positive suction lift (including the velocity head and friction) of 3.3 m. Laboratory tests are to be conducted on a model with 0.5 m diameter impeller and on a reduced head of 105 m. Determine the speed, discharge and suction lift for the laboratory tests.*

Assume atmospheric head = 10.15 m of water, and vapour head = 0.3 m of water.

Solution.

Prototype pump:		*Model pump:*	
Speed, N_p =	550 r.p.m	Speed, N_m =	?
Discharge, Q_p =	290 m³/s	Discharge, Q_m =	?
Manometric head, $(H_{mano})_p$ =	135 m	Manometric head, $(H_{mano})_m$ =	105 m
Diameter of impeller, D_p =	2.2 m	Diameter of impeller, D_m =	0.5 m
Positive suction lift =	3.3 m	Positive suction lift, h_s =	?
Vapour head, H_v =	0.3 m of water	Atmospheric head, H_a =	10.15 m

(*i*) Speed of the model pump, N_m:

We know that: $$\left(\frac{\sqrt{H_{mano}}}{DN}\right)_m = \left(\frac{\sqrt{H_{mano}}}{DN}\right)_p \quad \text{...[Eqn. (3.27)]}$$

$$\frac{\sqrt{(H_{mano})_m}}{D_m N_m} = \frac{\sqrt{(H_{mano})_p}}{D_p N_p}$$

or, $$N_m = \frac{\sqrt{(H_{mano})_m}}{\sqrt{(H_{mano})_p}} \times \frac{D_p}{D_m} \times N_p$$

or, $$N_m = \sqrt{\frac{105}{135}} \times \frac{2.2}{0.5} \times 550 = \mathbf{2134\ r.p.m.}\ \textbf{(Ans.)}$$

(*ii*) Discharge for the model pump, Q_m:

We know that: $$\left(\frac{Q}{D^3 N}\right)_m = \left(\frac{Q}{D^3 N}\right)_p \quad \text{...Eqn. (3.28)}$$

i.e.,
$$\frac{Q_m}{D_m^3 N_m} = \frac{Q_p}{D_p^3 N_p}$$

or,
$$Q_m = Q_p \left(\frac{D_m}{D_p}\right)^3 \times \frac{N_m}{N_p}$$

or,
$$Q_m = 290\left(\frac{0.5}{2.2}\right)^3 \times \frac{2134}{550} = \mathbf{13.21\ m^3/min.\ (Ans.)}$$

(*iii*) Positive suction lift with which model should be tested, h_s:

Cavitation factor for the prototype,

$$\sigma_p = \frac{H_a - H_s - H_v}{(H_{mano})_p} = \frac{10.15 - 3.3 - 0.3}{135} = 0.0485$$

For cavitation similarity, $\sigma_m = \sigma_p$

$$\sigma_m = \frac{10.15 - H_s - 0.3}{105} = 0.0485$$

or,
$$H_s = (10.15 - 0.3) - 105 \times 0.0485$$
$$= \mathbf{4.75\ m\ (including\ velocity\ head\ and\ friction)\ (Ans.)}$$

Q. 24. *The plunger diameter and stroke length of a single-acting reciprocating pump are 250 mm and 420 mm respectively. The speed of the pump is 60 r.p.m. The diameter and length of delivery pipe are 125 mm and 50 m respectively. If the pump is equipped with an air vessel on the delivery side at the centre line of the pump, find the power saved in overcoming friction in the delivery pipe. Assume coefficient of friction, f = 0.01.*

Solution. Diameter of plunger, $D = 250$ mm $= 0.25$ m, $\therefore$ Area $A = \frac{\pi}{4} \times 0.25^2 = 0.04909\ m^2$; Stroke length, $L = 420$ mm $= 0.42$ m; Crank radius, $r = \frac{0.42}{2} = 0.21$ m; Speed of the pump, $N = 60$ r.p.m, $\therefore$ Angular velocity, $\omega = \frac{2\pi N}{60} = \frac{2\pi \times 60}{60} = 6.283$ rad/s; Diameter of delivery pipe, $d_d = 125$ mm $= 0.125$ m, $\therefore$ Area of delivery pipe, $a_d = \frac{\pi}{4} \times 0.125^2 = 0.01227\ m^2$; Length of delivery pipe, $l_d = 50$ m; Coefficient of friction, $f = 0.01$.

Power saved in overcoming friction in the delivery pipe:

Maximum velocity of water in delivery pipe,

$$v_d = \frac{A}{a_d}\omega r = \frac{0.04909}{0.01227} \times 6.283 \times 0.21 = 5.28 \text{ m/s}$$

Maximum loss of head due to friction,

$$h_{fd} = \frac{4 f\, l_d\, v_d}{2g \times d_d} = \frac{4 \times 0.01 \times 50 \times (5.28)^2}{2 \times 9.81 \times 0.125} = 22.7 \text{ m}$$

Power required to overcome friction

$$= \frac{\omega A L N}{60} \times \left(\frac{2}{3} h_{fd}\right) = \frac{9810 \times 0.04909 \times 0.42 \times 60}{60} \times \left(\frac{2}{3} \times 22.7\right)$$
$$= 3060 \text{ W or } 3.06 \text{ kW}$$

"With air vessel fitted", the velocity in the delivery pipe becomes constant and is given by:

$$v_d = \frac{A}{a_d} \times \frac{\omega r}{\pi} = \frac{0.04909}{0.01227} \times \frac{6.283 \times 0.21}{\pi} = 1.68 \text{ m/s.}$$

Loss of head due to friction,

$$h_{fd} = \frac{4 f\, l_d\, v_d^2}{2g \times d_d} = \frac{4 \times 0.01 \times 50 \times 1.68^2}{2 \times 9.81 \times 0.125} = 2.3 \text{ m}$$

Power required to overcome friction

$$= \frac{\omega A L N}{60} \times h_{fd} = \frac{9810 \times 0.04909 \times 0.42 \times 60}{60} \times 2.3 = 465 \text{ W or } 0.465 \text{ kW}$$

Hence power saved by fitting an air vessel

$= 3.06 - 0.465 =$ **2.595 kW (Ans.)**

Q. 25. *A hydraulic ram is being supplied water at the rate of 0.045 m^3/s from a height of 4.9 m and it raises 0.0045 m^3/s to a height of 32 m from the ram. The length and diameter of the pipe are 110 m and 65 mm respectively. If the coefficient of friction is 0.01, calculate D'Aubuisson's and Rankine's efficiencies.*

Solution. *Given*: Disharge through the supply pipe, $Q = 0.045$ m^3/s; Supply head, $h = 4.9$ m; Discharge raised, $q = 0.0045$ m^3/s; Height of water raised from hydraulic ram, $H = 32$ m; Length of pipe, $l = 110$ m; Diameter of the pipe, $d = 65$ mm $= 0.065$ m; Coefficient of friction, $f = 0.01$.

Efficiency of the ram:

Head lost due to friction in the delivery pipe,

$$h_f = \frac{4 f l V^2}{d \times 2g} = \frac{4 \times 0.01 \times 110 \times V^2}{0.065 \times 2 \times 9.81} = 3.45 \text{ V}^2$$

But, V = Velocity of water in delivery pipe

$$= \frac{q}{\frac{\pi}{4} d^2} = \frac{0.0045}{\frac{\pi}{4} \times 0.065^2} = 1.356 \text{ m/s}$$

$\therefore$ $h_f = 3.45 \text{ V}^2 = 3.45 \times 1.356^2 = 6.34$ m

Effective head developed by the ram,

$$H_e = H + h_f = 32 + 6.34 = 38.34 \text{ m}$$

$$\textit{D' Aubuisson's efficiency} = \frac{q \times H_e}{Q \times h} = \frac{0.0045 \times 38.34}{0.045 \times 4.9} = 0.7824 \text{ or } \mathbf{78.24\%} \textbf{ (Ans.)}$$

$$\textit{Rankine's efficiency} = \frac{q\,(H_e - h)}{(Q - q)\,h}$$

$$= \frac{0.0045\,(38.34 - 4.9)}{(0.045 - 0.0045) \times 4.9} = 0.758 \text{ or } \mathbf{75.8\%} \textbf{ (Ans.)}$$

GATE and UPSC Examinations' Questions with Answers/Solutions

Chapter 9

A. Conventional Questions with Answers/Solutions

B. Multiple-Choice Questions with Answers and "Explanations"

A. CONVENTIONAL QUESTIONS WITH ANSWERS/SOLUTIONS

Q. 9.1. ***(Centrifugal pumps)*** *Explain the effect of vane angle on manometric efficiency in a centrifugal pump. Why is vane angle in a centrifugal pump not kept at values below 20°.* **(GATE)**

Ans. Effect of outlet angle (ϕ) on manometric efficiency.

The total energy of liquid before entering the impeller, with reference to the centre of pump, is taken as zero. After leaving the impeller, the liquid has a pressure energy (H_{mano}) and kinetic energy $\left(\frac{V_2^2}{2g}\right)$. The energy supplied to the impeller is $\frac{V_{w2}u_2}{g}$. Neglecting the losses in the pump and equating the energy given to the impeller to the increase in total energy, we have:

$$\frac{V_{w2}u_2}{g} = H_{mano} + \frac{V_2^2}{2g}$$

or,

$$H_{mano} = \frac{V_{w2}u_2}{g} - \frac{V_2^2}{2g} \quad ...(i)$$

From velocity triangle at outlet shown in Fig. 9.1, we have:

$$V_2^2 = V_{w2}^2 + V_{f2}^2, \text{ and } V_{w2} = u_2 - \frac{V_{f2}}{\tan\phi} = u_2 - V_{f2}\cot\phi$$

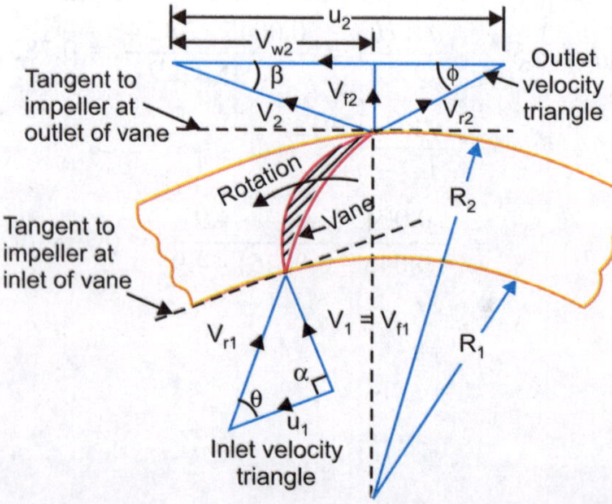

Fig. 9.1 Velocity triangles for an impeller vane.

Then, $$H_{mano} = \frac{(u_2 - V_{f2}\cot\phi)\times u_2}{g} - \frac{(u_2 - V_{f2}\cot\phi)^2 \times V_{f2}^2}{2g}$$

$$= \frac{2(u_2^2 - u_2V_{f2}\cot\phi) - [(u_2^2 + V_{f2}^2\cot^2\phi - 2u_2V_{f2}\cot\phi) + V_{f2}^2]}{2g}$$

$$= \frac{2u_2^2 - 2u_2V_{f2}\cot\phi - u_2^2 - V_{f2}^2\cot^2\phi + 2u_2V_{f2}\cot\phi - V_{f2}^2}{}$$

$$= \frac{u_2^2 - V_{f2}^2(1+\cot^2\phi)}{2g} = \frac{u_2^2 - V_{f2}^2\,\text{cosec}^2\theta}{2g} \quad \text{... (ii)}$$

The manometric efficiency of the pump, under the ideal condition assumed above, will become:

$$\eta_{mano} = \frac{H_{mano}}{(V_{w2}u_2/g)} = \frac{gH_{mano}}{V_{w2}u_2} = \frac{u_2^2 - V_{f2}^2\,\text{cosec}^2\theta}{2u_2(u_2 - V_{f2}\cot\phi)}$$

Let us assume the flow ratio $K_f \left[= \frac{V_{f2}}{\sqrt{2gH_{mano}}} \right] = 0.25$; computing the value of u_2 in terms of H_{mano} from eqn. (*ii*) for different values of ϕ, it will be observed that as the value of ϕ varies from 90° to 20° the value of η_{mano} increases from 0.47 to 0.73. A further decrease in the angle ϕ will increase the efficiency, but it is impracticable to have the angle ϕ less than 20°, as it would *result in long and narrow blades, with very high frictional losses.* As such the **minimum value** *of* ϕ is 20°.

Q. 9.2. (Hydraulic lift) *A hydraulic lift of the type commonly used for greasing automobiles consists of a 280 mm diameter ram that slides in a 280.18 mm cylinder. The annual space between the ram and cylinder is filled with oil having a kinematic viscosity of 0.00042 m²/s and specific gravity of 0.86. If the rate of travel of the ram is 0.22 m/s, find the frictional resistance when 2 m of the ram is engaged in the cylinder.* **(IES)**

Solution. *Given:* $d_r = 280$ mm, or 0.28 m; $d_{cy} = 280.18$ mm; $\nu = 0.00042$ m²/s; Specific gravity = 0.86; V = 0.22 m/s; Ram engagement = 2 m.

Now, $\nu = \frac{\mu}{\rho}$ or $\mu = \nu\rho = 0.00042 \times (0.86 \times 1000) = 0.3612$

Frictional resistance, *F*:

We know that: $$\frac{F}{A} = \mu\frac{du}{dy}$$

or, $$F = \frac{\mu AV}{dy} = \frac{0.3612\times(\pi\times0.28\times2)\times0.22}{\left(\frac{280.18-280}{2}\right)\times10^{-3}}$$

$$= \mathbf{1553.3\ N} \quad \textbf{(Ans.)}$$

Q. 9.3. (Pelton turbine) *A three jet pelton turbine is required to generate 10000 kW under a net head of 400 m. The blade angle at the outlet is 15° and the decrease in the relative velocity while passing over the blade is 5%. Determine:*

(i) *The diameter of the jet.*

(ii) *The force exerted by a single jet on the buckets.*

Given, overall efficiency of turbine = 80%

co-effecient of velocity = 0.98

speed ratio = 0.46

Further, if the jet ratio is not to be less than 10, calculate

(iii) Speed of the wheel for a frequency of 50 hertz/sec and corresponding wheel diameter. **(IES)**

Solution. *Given*: No. of jets = 3; Total power, $P = 10000$ kW; Net head, H = 400 m; Blade angle at the outlet, $\phi = 15°$; Relative velocity at the outlet, $V_{r2} = 0.95\ V_{r1}$; Overall efficiency, $\eta_0 = 80\%$, Co-efficient of velocity, $C_v = 0.98$; Speed ratio, $K_u = 0.46$; $f = 50$ hertz.

(i) Diameter of the jet, *d*:

Now, $$\eta_0 = \frac{P}{wQH}$$

or, $$0.8 = \frac{10000}{9.81 \times Q \times 400}$$

or, $$Q = \frac{10000}{0.8 \times 9.81 \times 400} = 3.18 \text{ m}^3/\text{s}$$

$\therefore$ Discharge through one nozzle $= \frac{3.18}{3} = 1.06 \text{ m}^3/\text{s}$

Also, $$1.06 = \text{Area of jet} \times \text{velocity of jet}$$

or, $$1.06 = \frac{\pi}{4} d^2 \times \left[C_v \times \sqrt{2gH}\right]$$

or, $$= \frac{\pi}{4} d^2 \times 0.98 \times \sqrt{2 \times 9.81 \times 400}$$

$\therefore$ $$d = \left[\frac{1.06 \times 4}{\pi \times 0.98 \times \sqrt{2 \times 9.81 \times 400}}\right]^{1/2} = 0.125 \text{ m or } 125 \text{ mm} \quad \textbf{(Ans.)}$$

(ii) Force exerted by a single jet on the buckets:

Refer to Fig. 2.5.

$$u_1 = K_u \times V_1 = K_u \times \sqrt{2gH} = 0.46 \times \sqrt{2 \times 9.81 \times 400} = 40.75 \text{ m/s}$$

Now, $$V_{r1} = V_1 - u_1 = C_r \sqrt{2gh} - 40.75 = 0.98\sqrt{2 \times 9.81 \times 400} - 40.75 = 46.07 \text{m/s}$$

and, $$V_{r2} = 0.95\ V_{r1} = 0.95 \times 46.07 = 43.77 \text{ m/s}$$

$$V_{w1} = V_1 = 0.98\sqrt{2 \times 9.81 \times 400} = 86.82 \text{ m/s}$$

$$V_{w2} = V_{r2} \cos\phi - u_2 = 43.77 \times \cos 15° - 40.75 = 1.53 \text{ m/s}$$

$(\because u_1 = u_2 = 40.75 \text{ m/s})$

Force exerted by a single jet on the buckets

$= \rho \times$ discharge through one jet $\times (V_{w1} + V_{w2})$

$= 1000 \times 1.06\ (86.82 + 1.53) =$ **93651 N or 93.651 kN (Ans.)**

(iii) Speed of the wheel for a frequency of 50 hertz/sec and corresponding wheel diameter:

Jet ratio = 10 or $\frac{D}{d} = 10$, $\therefore D = 10d = 10 \times 0.125 = 1.25$ m

Also, $$u_1 = \frac{\pi DN}{60}, \text{ or } N = \frac{60\mu_1}{\pi D} = \frac{60 \times 40.75}{\pi \times 1.25} = 622.6 \text{ rpm}$$

Now, frequency, $$f = \frac{Np}{60} \quad (N = \text{Speed}, p = \text{no. of poles})$$

$$p = \frac{60f}{N} = \frac{60 \times 50}{622.6} = 4.82 \text{ say } 5$$

Now, for $p = 5, N = \frac{60f}{p} = \frac{60 \times 50}{5}$ = **600 rpm** **(Ans.)**

Again, $u = \frac{\pi DN}{60}$ or $D = \frac{60u}{\pi N} = \frac{60 \times 40.75}{\pi \times 600}$ = **1.3 m** **(Ans.)**

∴ Jet ratio becomes: $\frac{D}{d} = \frac{1.3}{0.125} = 10$

Hence the given condition is *satisfied.*

Q. 9.4. (Centrifugal pump) *A centrifugal pump is to deliver 4.5 m³/s when running at 750 rpm. The diameter of the impeller at inlet is 53 cm and at outlet is 76 cm. It may be assumed that the air enters radially with a speed of 15 m/s. The vanes are set backwards at oultet at 70° to the tangent, and width at outlet is 10 cm. The volute casing gives at 30% recovery of the outlet velocity head. The losses in the impeller may be taken as equivalent to 25% of the outlet velocity head. Blade thickness effects may be naglected. Determine :*

(i) The manometric efficiency, and

(ii) The pressure at the discharge. **(IES)**

Solution. Refer to Fig. 9.2

Given: $Q = 4.5$ m³/s; $N = 750$ rpm; $D_1 = 53$ cm = 0.53 m; $D_2 = 76$ cm = 0.76 m; $V_1 = V_{f1}$ = 15 m/s; $\phi = 70°$; $B_2 = 10$ cm = 0.1 m; Volume casing recovery = 30% of V_2; Losses in impeller = 25% of the outlet velocity head = $0.25 \times \frac{V_2^2}{2g}$.

(*i*) **Manometric efficiency, η_{mano} :**

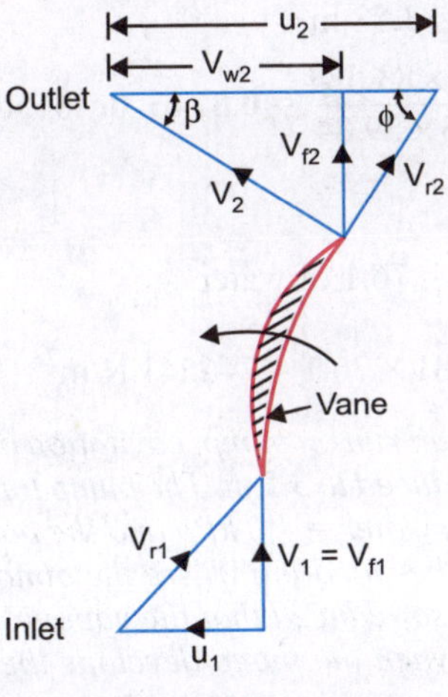

Fig. 9.2

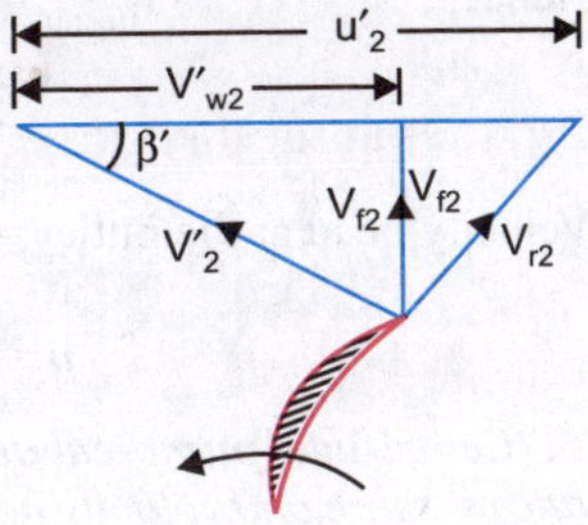

Fig. 9.3

$$u_2 = \frac{\pi D_2 N}{60} = \frac{\pi \times 0.76 \times 750}{60} = 29.84 \text{ m/s}$$

$$Q = \pi D_2 B_2 V_{f2} \quad \text{or} \quad 4.5 = \pi \times 0.76 \times 0.1 \times V_{f2}$$

or, $$V_{f2} = \frac{4.5}{\pi \times 0.76 \times 0.1} = 18.85 \text{ m/s}$$

From velocity triangle at outlet, we have :

$$\sin \phi = \frac{V_{f2}}{V_{r2}}, \text{ or } \sin 70° = \frac{18.85}{V_{r2}}$$

or, $$V_{r2} = \frac{18.85}{\sin 70°} = 20.06 \text{ m/s}$$

and, $$V_{w2} = u_2 - V_{r2} \cos \phi$$
$$= 29.84 - 20.06 \times \cos 70° = 22.98 \text{ m/s}$$

Now, $$\tan \beta = \frac{V_{f2}}{V_{w2}} = \frac{18.85}{22.98} \text{ or } \beta = 39.36°$$

Also, $$\cos \beta = \frac{V_{w2}}{V_2} \text{ or } V_2 = \frac{V_{w2}}{\cos\beta} = \frac{22.98}{\cos 39.36°} = 29.72 \text{ m/s}$$

Refer to Fig 9.3.

Since volute casing gives 30% recovery of the outlet velocity head (given), therefore,

$$V_2 = 1.3 \times 29.72 = 38.64 \text{ m}$$

∴ $$\sin\beta' = \text{—,} \frac{18.85}{38.64} = 0.4878, \text{ or } \beta' = 29.2°$$

Now, $$V'_{w2} = V'_2 \cos\beta' = 38.64 \times \cos 29.2° = 33.73 \text{ m/s}$$

Manometric head, $$H_{mano} = \frac{V_{w2}u_2}{g} - 0.25 \times \frac{V_2'^2}{2g}$$

$$= \frac{33.73 \times 29.84}{9.81} - 0.25 \times \frac{38.64^2}{2 \times 9.81}$$

$$= 102.6 - 19.02 = 83.58 \text{ m}$$

Hence, $$\eta_{mano} = \frac{gH_{mano}}{V'_{w2}u_2} = \frac{9.81 \times 83.58}{33.73 \times 29.84} = \mathbf{0.8146 \text{ or } 81.46\%} \quad \textbf{(Ans.)}$$

(*ii*) **Pressure at the discharge *p*:**

Velocity head at the outlet $= \frac{V_2'^2}{2g} = \frac{38.64^2}{2 \times 9.81} = 76.1$ of water

∴ $$p = \rho g h = 1000 \times 9.81 \times 76.1 = 746541 \text{ N/m}^2 = \mathbf{7.46 \text{ bar}} \quad \textbf{(Ans.)}$$

Q. 9.5. (*Centrifugal pump-cavitation*) *During a trail run on pump, cavitation occurred when the sum of static pressure and velocity head at inlet was reduced to 3.2 m. The pump total head was 35 m at a discharge of 0.045 m³/sec. The vapour pressure of water = 1.8 kPa and the barometer pressure = 750 mm of Hg. If the pump is to operate at some other location where the atmospheric pressure was reduced to 620 mm of Hg and the temperature is so reduced that the vapour pressure of water is 830 Pa, what is the value of caviation parameter when the pump develops the same total head and discharge? Is it necessary to reduce the height of the pump and if so, by how much?* **(GATE)**

Solution. *Given:* Total suction head, H_s = 32 m; Pump total head, H_{mano} = 35 m; $Q = 0.045$ m³/s; Vapour pressure, $H_v = 1.8$ kPa $= \frac{1.8 \times 1000}{1000 \times 9.81} = 0.183$ m or water; Atmospheric pressure, H_a = 750 mm of H_g = 750 × 13.6 × 10^{-3} = 10.2 m of water.

Thoma's cavitation factor, $$\sigma = \frac{H_a - H_s - H_a}{H_{mano}}$$

$$= \frac{10.2 - 3.2 - 0.183}{35} = 0.1948 = \sigma_c$$

This is called *critical* cavitation factor, since cavitation occurs at this location and by this arrangement at '*new location*':

$$H_a = 620 \text{ mm of Hg} = 0.62 \times 13.6 = 8.432 \text{ m of water}$$

$$H_v = \frac{830}{1000 \times 9.81} = 0.0846 \text{ m of water}$$

Again, $H_{mano} = 35$ m and $H_s = 3.2$ m ... remain the same

$$\therefore \text{ New cavitation factor, } \sigma_{new} = \frac{H_a - H_s - H_v}{H_{mano}}$$

$$= \frac{8.432 - 3.2 - 0.0846}{35} = 0.147$$

Thus, $\sigma_{new} < \sigma_c$ *i.e.*, 0.147 < 0.1948 and as such cavitation occurs.

Therefore, it is necessary to '*reduce the height of the pump*'.

If '*x*' is the new height, then we have:

$$\frac{8.432 - x - 0.0846}{35} = 0.1948$$

or, $8.3474 - x = 6.818$ or $x = 1.5294$ m

Hence, H_s must be *reduced* from 3.2 m to **1.5294** m to *avoid cavitation* **(Ans.)**

Q. 9.6. ***(Centrifugal pump)*** *A centrifugal pump is required to lift 9100 lit/s of water against a head of 6 m while running at 500 r.p.m. The velocity of flow through the wheel is 2 m/s and the manometric efficiency is 60%. The angle of vane tip with the direction of a motion is 150°. Work out the following:*

(i) *Sketch an impeller of centrifugal pump and draw the velocity triangle.*
(ii) *The diameter of impeller.*
(iii) *The width of impeller.* **(GATE)**

Solution. *Given:* $Q = 9100$ lit/s $= 9.1$ m³/s; $H_{mano} = 6$ m; $N = 500$ r.p.m., $V_{f1} = V_{f2} = 2$ m/s; $\eta_{mano} = 60\%$; $\phi = 180° - 150° = 30°$.

(*i*) Sketch of the impeller–velocity triangle (Refer to Fig. 9.4.)

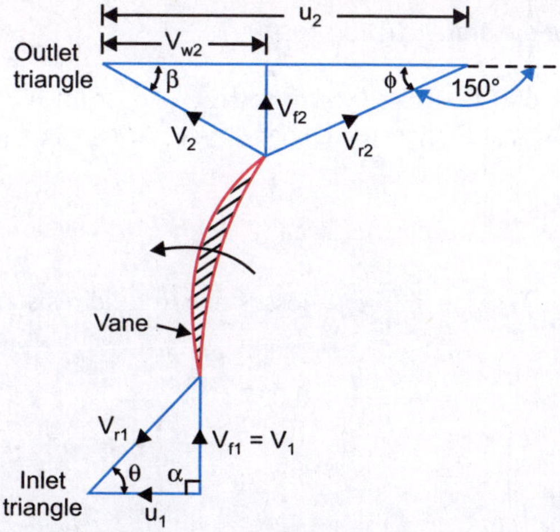

Fig. 9.4

***(ii)* Diameter of impeller, D_2:**

$$\eta_{mano} = \frac{gH_{mano}}{V_{w2}u_2} \quad \text{... [Eqn. (3.9)]}$$

$$0.6 = \frac{9.81 \times 6}{V_{w2}u_2} \text{ or } V_{w2}u_2 = \frac{9.81 \times 6}{0.6} = 98.1 \quad \text{...}(i)$$

From velocity triangle at the outlet, we have:

$$\tan\phi = \frac{V_{f2}}{(u_2 - V_{w2})} \text{ or } u_2 - V_{w2} = \frac{V_{f2}}{\tan\phi} = \frac{2}{\tan 30°} = 3.464$$

From (*i*) and (*ii*), we get:

$$u_2\,(u_2 - 30.464) = 98.1$$

or, $$u_2^{\,2} - 3.464\,u - 98.1 = 0$$

or, $$u_2 = \frac{3.464 \pm \sqrt{3.464^2 + (4 \times 98.1)}}{2} = 11.787 \text{ m/s}$$

But, $$u_2 = \frac{\pi D_2 N}{60} \text{ or } 11.787 = \frac{\pi\, D_2 \times 500}{60}$$

or, $$D_2 = \frac{11.787 \times 60}{\pi \times 500} = \mathbf{0.45\ m} \quad \textbf{(Ans.)}$$

***(iii)* Width of impeller, B_2:**

$$Q = \pi D_2 B_2 V_{f2} = \text{ or } 9.1 = \pi \times 0.45 \times B_2 \times 2$$

or, $$B_2 = \frac{9.1}{\pi \times 0.45 \times 2} = \mathbf{3.218\ m} \quad \textbf{(Ans.)}$$

Q. 9.7. *(Centrifugal pump)* *A centrifugal pump is required to discharge 600 litres of water per second and develop a head of 15 m when the impeller rotates at 750 rpm. The manometric efficiency is 80%. The loss of head in the pump due to fluid resistance being assumed to be 0.027 V^2 m of water, where V is the velocity with which water leaves the impeller. Water enters the impeller without shock or whirl and the velocity of flow is 3.2 m/sec. Determine:*

(i) The impeller diameter and outlet area.

(ii) The blade angle at the outlet edge. **(IES)**

Solution. *Given:* Q = 600 lit/sec = 0.6 m^3/s; H_{mano} = 15 m; N = 750 rpm; H_{mano} = 80%; Head loss due to fluid resistance = 0.027 V^2 = 0.027 V_2^2; $V_{f1} = V_{f2} = 3.2$ m/s.

Refer to Fig. 9.5.

(*i*) Impeller diameter (D_2) and outlet area (A_2):

$$H_{mano} = \frac{V_{w2}u_2}{g} - \text{losses due to fluid resistance}$$

$$= \frac{V_{w2}u_2}{g} - 0.027\,V^2$$

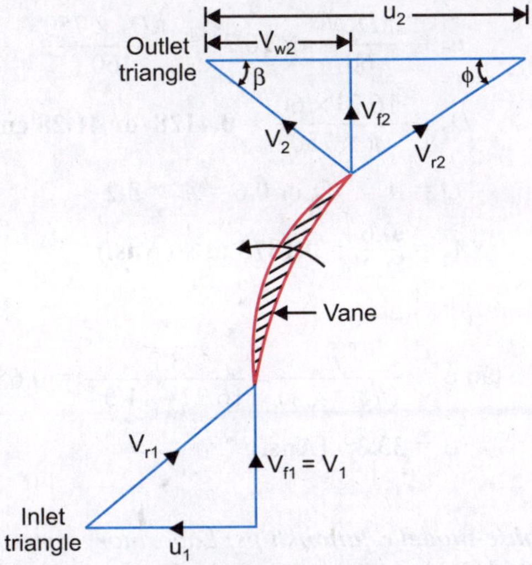

Fig. 9.5

Now, $$\eta_{mano} = \frac{H_{mano}}{(V_{w2}u_2/g)} \text{ or, } \frac{g(H_{mano})}{V_{w2}u_2} = \frac{g\left[\frac{V_{w2}u_2}{g} - 0.027\,V_2^2\right]}{V_{w2}u_2}$$

or, $$0.8 = \frac{V_{w2}u_2 - g\times 0.027\,V^2}{V_{w2}u_2} = 1 - \frac{g\times 0.027V_2^2}{V_{w2}u_2}$$

or, $$\frac{g\times 0.027V_2^2}{V_{w_2}u_2} = 0.2 \text{ or } V_{w2}u_2 = \frac{0.027V^2 g}{0.2} \quad \text{... }(i)$$

Again, $$H_{mano} = \frac{V_{w2}u_2}{g} - \text{losses}$$

or, $$15 + \text{losses} = \frac{V_{w2}u_2}{g} \quad \text{... }(ii)$$

$$15 + 0.027\,V_2^2 = \frac{V_{w2}u_2}{g} = \frac{0.027V^2 g}{0.2\times g} = 0.135\,V^2$$

or, $V_2^2\,(0.135 - 0.027) = 15$ or $V_2 = 11.78$ m/s

From velocity triangle at outlet, we have:

$$\sin\beta = \frac{V_{f2}}{V_2} = \frac{3.2}{11.78} \text{ or } \beta = 15.76°$$

and $$\cos\beta = \frac{V_{w2}}{V_2} \text{ or } \cos 15.76° = \frac{V_{w2}}{11.78}$$

or, $$V_{w2} = \cos 15.76° \times 11.78 = 11.34 \text{ m/s}$$

From (*ii*), we get: $$V_{w2}u_2 = (15 + 0.027V_2^{\,2})g$$
$$= [15 + (0.027 \times 11.78^2)] \times 9.81 = 183.9$$

or, $$u_2 = \frac{183.9}{V_{w2}} = \frac{183.9}{11.34} = 16.21 \text{ m/s}$$

Also, $u_2 = \frac{\pi D_2 N}{60}$ or $16.21 = \frac{\pi D_2 \times 750}{60}$

or, $D_2 = \frac{16.21 \times 60}{\pi \times 750} = \mathbf{0.4128}$ **or 41.28 cm (Ans.)**

We know that: $Q = A_2 \times V_{f2}$ or $0.6 = A_2 \times 3.2$

or, $A_2 = \frac{0.6}{3.2} = \mathbf{0.1875\ m^2}$ **(Ans.)**

(*ii*) **Blade angle at the outlet edge ϕ :**

$$\tan\phi = \frac{V_{f2}}{(u_2 - V_{w2})} = \frac{3.2}{16.21 - 11.34} = 0.657$$

or, $\phi = \mathbf{33.3°}$ **(Ans.)**

Q. 9.8. ***(Hydraulic turbine-model relationships)*** *Laboratory tests are required to be performed on a 1/10 scale model to find the best design for a hydraulic turbine. The turbine is required to develop 30,000 kW under a net head of 50 m running at 300 rpm. The head available at the laboratory is 12 m. Determine:*

(*i*) *The corresponding speed,*

(*ii*) *Power, and*

(*iii*) *Discharge.*

The overall efficiency is 88%. **(GATE)**

Solution. *Given:* Scale model $= \frac{D_m}{D_p} = \frac{1}{10}$; Power, $P_p = 30000$ kW; Head, $H_p = 50$ m; $N_p = 300$ rpm; $H_m = 12$ m; $\eta_0 = 88\%$.

(*i*) **Speed N_m :**

We know that: $\frac{H}{N^2 D^2}$ = constant ... [Eqn. (2.43)]

$$\therefore \quad \frac{H_p}{N_p^2 \times D_p^2} = \frac{H_m}{N_m^2 \times D_m^2}$$

or, $N_m^{\ 2} = \left(\frac{H_m}{H_p}\right) \times \left(\frac{D_p^2}{D_m^2}\right) \times N_p^2 = \frac{12}{50} \times 10^2 \times 300^2 = 2160000$

or, $N_m = 1469.7$ **rpm (Ans.)**

(*ii*) **Power, P_m :**

Also, $\frac{P}{N^3 D^5}$ = constant ... [Eqn (2.45)]

$$\therefore \quad \frac{P_p}{N_p^3 D_p^5} = \frac{P_m}{N_m^3 \times D_m^5}$$

or, $P_m = P_p \times \left(\frac{N_m}{N_p}\right)^3 \times \left(\frac{D_m}{D_p}\right)^5 = 30000 \times \left(\frac{1469.7}{300}\right)^3 \times \left(\frac{1}{10}\right)^5$

$= \mathbf{35.273\ kW}$ **(Ans.)**

***(iii)* Discharges Q_m, Q_p:**

Overall efficiency, $$\eta_0 = \frac{P_m}{\rho g Q_m H_m}$$

$$0.88 = \frac{35.273 \times 10^3}{1000 \times 9.81 \times Q_m \times 12}$$

$$\therefore \quad Q_m = \frac{35.273 \times 10^3}{0.88 \times 1000 \times 9.81 \times 12} = \mathbf{0.34\ m^3/s} \quad \textbf{(Ans.)}$$

We know that: $$\frac{Q}{ND^3} = \text{constant} \qquad \text{... [Eqn. (2.44)]}$$

$$\therefore \quad \frac{Q_p}{N_p D_p^3} = \frac{Q_m}{N_m D_m^3}$$

or, $$Q_p = Q_m \times \left(\frac{N_p}{N_m}\right) \times \left(\frac{D_p}{D_m}\right)^3$$

$$= 0.34 \times \left(\frac{300}{1469.7}\right) \times \left(\frac{10}{1}\right)^3 = \mathbf{69.4\ m^3/s} \quad \textbf{(Ans.)}$$

Q. 9.9. ***(Pelton turbine)*** *A pelton turbine is to work at the foot of dam whose reservoir level is 220 m. The head at the full opening at the turbine nozzle is 200 m and coefficient of velocity is 0.98. The turbine is to operate at 200 rpm and develop a power of 3.7 MW. Assuming blade to jet speed ratio as 0.46, estimate the wheel diameter. If the blade outlet angle is 16°, determine the blade and hydraulic efficiencies. Neglecting frictional losses.* **(IES)**

Solution. *Given:* Gross head, $H_g = 220$ m; Net or effective head, H = 200 m; Co-efficient of velocity, $C_v = 0.98$; Speed, N = 200 rpm; Power = 3.7 MW; Speed ratio, $K_u = \frac{u}{V_1} = 0.4$. Blade outlet angle, $\phi = 16°$.

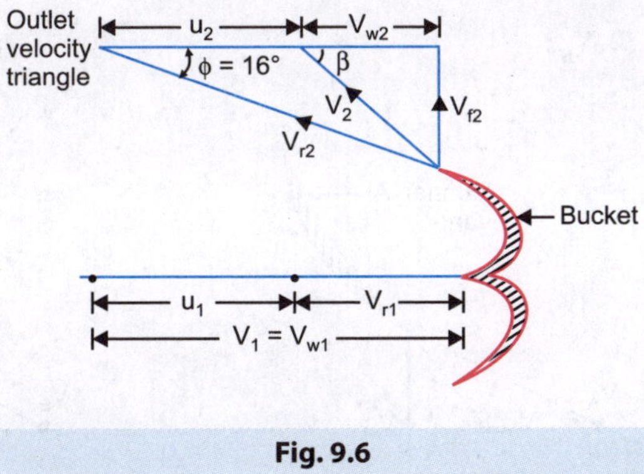

Fig. 9.6

Refer to Fig. 9.6.

Wheel diameter, *D*;

$$V_1 = C_v \sqrt{2gH} = 0.98 \times \sqrt{2 \times 9.81 \times 200} = 61.4 \text{ m/s}$$

Speed of the wheel, $u (=u_1 = u_2) = 0.46 \times V_1$

$= 0.46 \times 61.4 = 28.24$ m/s

Also, $u = \frac{\pi DN}{60}$ or $28.24 = \frac{\pi \times D \times 200}{60}$

or, $D = \frac{28.24 \times 60}{\pi \times 200} = \mathbf{2.697\ m/s}$ **(Ans.)**

Blade efficiency, η_{bl}:

$$V_{r2} = V_{r1} = V_1 - u = 61.4 - 28.24 = 33.16 \text{ m/s}$$

$$V_{w2} = V_{r2} \cos 16° - u = 33.16 \cos 16° - 28.24 = 3.635 \text{ m/s}$$

We know that: $$\eta_{bl} = \frac{2(V_{w1} + V_{w2}) \times u}{V_1^2} = \frac{2(61.4 + 3.635) \times 28.24}{(61.4)^2}$$

$= \mathbf{0.974}$ **or 97.4% (Ans.)**

Hydraulic efficiency, η_h:

$$\eta_h = \frac{(V_{w1} + V_{w2})u}{gH} \quad \text{... [Eqn. (2.7)]}$$

$$= \frac{(61.4 + 3.635) \times 28.24}{9.81 \times 200} = \mathbf{0.936 \text{ or } 93.6\%} \quad \textbf{Ans.}$$

Q. 9.10. *(Reaction turbines)* *The inward flow reaction turbines have the same diameter viz 0.7 m and the same efficiency. Both the runners work under the same head and they have the same velocity of flow, viz 5.8 m/s. One of the runner, A revolves at 500 rpm and the inlet blade angle is 65°. If the other runner, B has an inlet blade angle of 110°, at what speed should it run?*

Solution. *Given:* $D_A = D_B = 0.7$ m; $\eta_A = \eta_B$; $V_{fA} = V_{fB} = 5.8$ m/s; $N_A = 500$ rpm; Inlet blade angles: $\theta_A = 65°$, $\theta_B = 110°$.

Speed of the runner B, N_B:

Refer to Fig. 9.7.

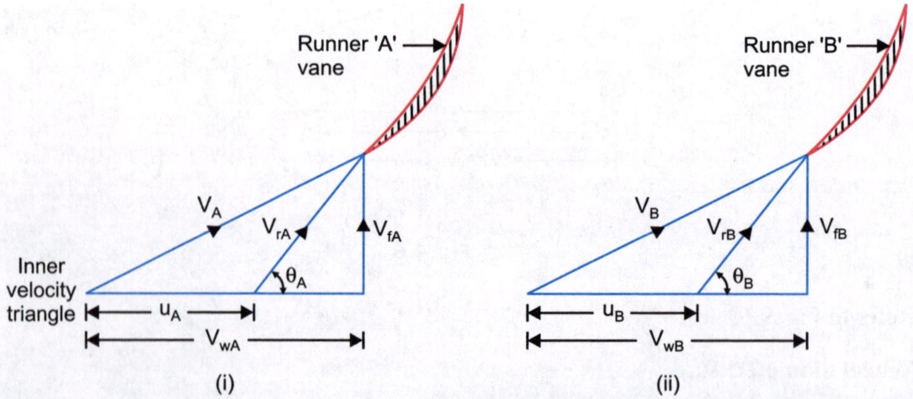

Fig. 9.7

From inner velocity triangles, we have :

$$\tan \theta_A = \frac{V_{fA}}{V_{wA} - u_A} \quad \text{... (i)}$$

$$\tan \theta_B = \frac{V_{fB}}{V_{wB} - u_B} \quad \text{... (ii)}$$

From eqns. (*i*) and (*ii*), we get:

$$\frac{\tan 65°}{\tan 110°} = \frac{V_{fA}}{V_{wA} - u_A} \times \frac{V_{wB} - u_B}{V_{fB}} = \frac{V_{wB} - u_B}{V_{wA} - u_A}$$

or, $$-0.7805 = \frac{V_{wB} - u_B}{V_{wA} - u_A}$$

or, $$0.7805 = \frac{u_B - V_{wB}}{V_{wA} - u_A} \quad \text{... (iii)}$$

Also, $$\eta_A = \eta_B \quad \text{(given)}$$

$\therefore$ $$\frac{V_{wA}\, u_A}{gH_A} = \frac{V_{wB}\, u_B}{gH_B}$$

or, $$V_{wB} = \frac{V_{wA} u_A}{u_B} \quad (\because H_A = H_B) \quad \text{... (iv)}$$

Substituting (*iv*) in (*iii*), we get:

$$0.7805 = \frac{u_B - \dfrac{V_{wA}.u_A}{u_A}}{V_{wA} - u_A} = \frac{u_B^2 - V_{wA} u_A}{u_B(V_{wA} - u_A)} \quad \text{... (v)}$$

From (*i*), $$\tan 65° = \frac{V_{fA}}{V_{wA} - u_A} = \frac{5.8}{V_{wA} - \left(\dfrac{\pi \times 0.7 \times 500}{60}\right)} = \frac{5.8}{V_{wA} - 18.32}$$

or, $$V_{wA} = \frac{5.8}{\tan 65°} + 18.32 = 21.02 \text{ m/s}$$

Inserting the various values in (*v*), we get:

$$\frac{u_B^2 - 21.02 \times 18.32}{u_B(21.02 - 18.32)} = 0.7805$$

or, $$u_B{}^2 - 385.09 = 2.107\, u_B$$

or, $$u_B{}^2 - 2.107\, u_B - 3.850.9 = 0$$

or, $$u_B = \frac{2.107 + \sqrt{2.107^2 + (4 \times 385.09)}}{2} = 20.7 \text{ m/s}$$

Also, $$u_B = \frac{\pi D_B N_B}{60} = 20.7$$

or, $$N_B = \frac{20.7 \times 60}{\pi \times 0.7} = \mathbf{564.8 \text{ rpm}} \quad \textbf{(Ans.)}$$

Q. 9.11. ***(Centrifugal pump)*** *A centrifugal pump is to discharge 0.2 m³/s at a speed of 1400 rpm against a head of 25 m. The impeller diameter is 0.3 m, its width at outlet is 0.05 m and the manometric efficiency is 80%. Determine the vane angles at the outer periphery of the impeller.* **(GATE)**

Solution. *Given:* $Q = 0.2\ \text{m}^3/\text{s}$; $N = 1400$ rpm; $H_{mano} = 25$ m; $D_2 = 0.3$ m; $B_2 = 0.05$ m; $\eta = 80\%$.

Refer to Fig. 9.8.

Vane angle at the outlet :

Tangential velocity of impeller at outlet,

$$u_2 = \frac{\pi D_2 N}{60} = \frac{\pi \times 0.3 \times 1400}{60} = 22 \text{ m/s}$$

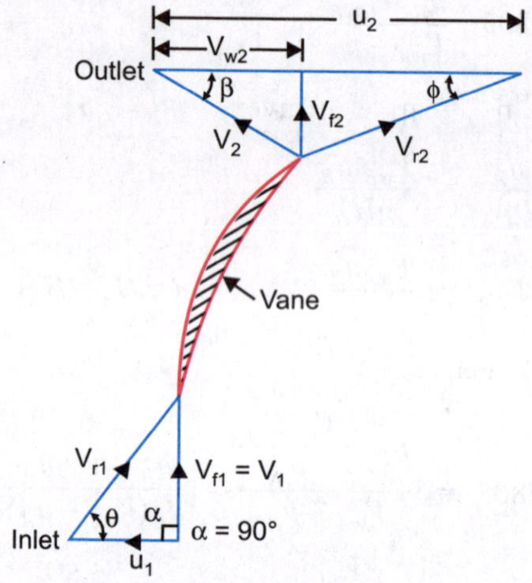

Fig. 9.8

Now, $$Q = \pi D_2 B_2 \times V_{f2}$$

or, $$V_{f2} = \frac{Q}{\pi D_2 B_2} = \frac{0.2}{\pi \times 0.3 \times 0.5} = 4.24 \text{ m/s}$$

Manometric efficiency, $$\eta_{mano} = \frac{gH_{mano}}{V_{w2} u_2}$$

or, $$V_{w2} = \frac{gH_{mano}}{\eta_{mano} \times u_2} = \frac{9.81 \times 25}{0.8 \times 22} = 13.93 \text{ m/s}$$

$$\tan \beta = \frac{V_{f2}}{V_{w2}} = \frac{4.24}{13.93} = 0.3044$$

or, $$\beta = \tan^{-1}(0.3044) = \mathbf{16.93°} \quad \textbf{(Ans.)}$$

Again, $$\tan \phi = \frac{V_{f2}}{u_2 - V_{w2}} = \frac{4.24}{22 - 13.93} = 0.5254$$

or, $$\phi = \tan^{-1}(0.5254) = \mathbf{22.71°} \quad \textbf{(Ans.)}$$

Q. 9.12. *Explain fluid coupling and torque converter and their areas of application.* **(GATE)**

Ans. Refer to Articles 5.8 and 5.9.

Q. 9.13. *Do you need priming in a gear pump? Give the reasons for your answer.* **(IES)**

Ans. In a "gear pump", *priming* is *'not'* required. The primary purpose of priming is to *remove air* from the suction pipe, casing of the pump and the delivery pipe by filling these parts with the liquid to be raised by the pump. Since the head generated by the pump is $(V_{w2}u_2/g)$ which is independent of the density of liquid, and the *density of air is very low*, the head generated will be also *very low*. In case of "gear pump" *liquid cannot slip back* into the inlet side due to the *meshing of the gear* and as such there is *no possibility for the air to get entrapped in the pump.*

Q. 9.14. *What is the necessity of governing? Explain with sketch a simple governing mechanism for a turbine.* **(GATE)**

Ans. Refer to Article 2.14.

Q. 9.15. *What is meant by cavitation and what are the methods avoiding it?* **(GATE)**

Ans. Refer to Article 2.15.

Q. 9.16. *What is the purpose of draft tube in a turbine?* **(GATE)**

Ans. Refer to Article 2.8.

B. MULTIPLE-CHOICE QUESTIONS WITH ANSWERS AND *"EXPLANATIONS"*

Q. 9.1. The specific speed of an hydraulic pump is the speed of geometrically similar pump working against a unit head and

(*a*) delivering unit quantity of water (*b*) consuming unit power
(*c*) having unit velocity of flow (*d*) having unit radial velocity.

Ans. (*a*)

EXPLANATION:

(*a*) is the correct choice, because the specific speed of hydraulic pump is the speed of geometrically similar pump working against a *unit head* and *delivering quantity of water*. **(Ans.)**

Q. 9.2. A jet of water issues from a nozzle with a velocity of 20 m/s and it impinges normally on a flat plate moving away from it at 10 m/s. If the cross-sectional area of the jet is 0.02 m^2 and the density of water is taken as 1000 kg/m^3, then the force developed on the plate will be

(*a*) 10 N (*b*) 100 N (*c*) 1000 N (*d*) 2000 N.

Ans. (*d*)

EXPLANATION:

$V = 20$ m/s, $u = 10$ m/s, $a = 0.02$ m^2, $\rho = 1000$ kg/m^3

$$\text{Force on the plate} = \rho a (V - u) \times (V - u) = 1000 \times 0.02 \times (20 - 10) \times (20 - 10)$$

$$= 2000 \text{ N}$$ **(Ans.)**

Q. 9.3. In the statement, "in a reaction turbine installation, the head of water is decreased and the speed (r.p.m.) is also decreased at a certain condition of working. The effect of each of these changes will be to X power delivered due to decrease in head and to Y power delivered due to decrease in rpm", $\frac{N\sqrt{Q}}{(H)^{5/4}}$, X and Y stand respectively for

(*a*) decrease and increase (*b*) increase and increase
(*c*) decrease and decrease (*d*) increase and decrease.

Ans. (*a*)

EXPLANATION:

In case of hydraulic reaction turbines, $P \propto H^{3/2}$, it indicates that *with the decrease in head*, there will be decrease in power. Also speed $N \propto \frac{1}{\sqrt{P}}$ or $P \propto \frac{1}{N^2}$, which means that with *decrease in speed* there will be *increase in power*. Thus (*a*) is the correct choice. **(Ans.)**

Q. 9.4. Water, having a density of 1000 kg/m^3, issues from a nozzle with a velocity of 10 m/s and the jet strikes a bucket mounted on a Pelton wheel. The wheel rotates a 10 rad/s. The mean diameter of the wheel is 1 m. The jet is split into two equal streams by the bucket, such that each stream is deflected by 120° as shown in Fig. 9.9. Friction in the bucked may be neglected. Magnitude of the torque exerted by the water on the wheel, per unit mass flow rate of the incoming jet, is

(*a*) 0 (N-m)/(kg/s) (*b*) 1.25 (N-m)/(kg/s)
(*c*) 2.5 (N-m)/(kg/s) (*d*) 7.5 (N-m)/(kg/s).

Ans. (*d*)

EXPLANATION: Refer to Fig. 9.9

$$\text{Torque} = \text{Force} \times \text{radius}$$

$$T = \rho QV(1 + \cos\theta) \times R$$

Torque per unit mass flow rate

$$= V(1 + \cos\theta)R$$
$$= 10\,(1 + \cos 60°)\,0.5$$
$$= 7.5 \text{ N-m/kg/s } \textbf{(Ans.)}$$

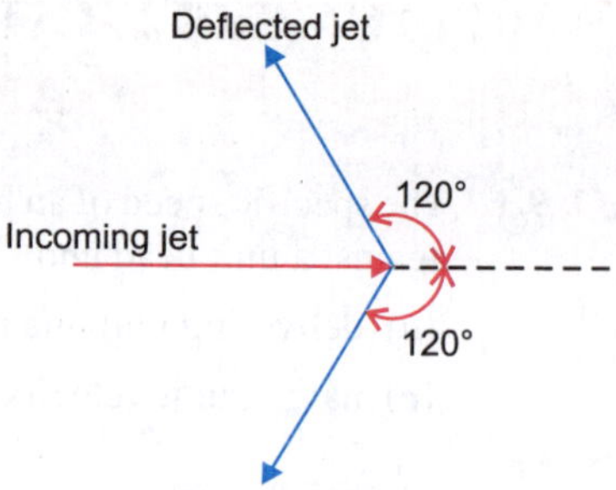

Fig. 9.9

Q. 9.5. In a Pelton wheel, the bucket peripheral speed is 10 m/s, the water jet velocity is 25 m/s and volumetric flow rate of the jet is 0.1 m^3/s. If the jet deflection angle is 120°C and the flow is ideal, the power developed is

(*a*) 7.5 kW (*b*) 15.0 kW (*c*) 22.5 kW (*d*) 37.5 kW.

Ans. (*c*)

EXPLANATION:

$$\phi = 180° - 120° = 60°$$

Power developed by pelton wheel

$$= \rho Q(V - u)\,(1 + \cos\phi).u$$
$$= 1000 \times 0.1\,(25 - 10)\,(1 + \cos 60°) \times 10$$
$$= 22500 \text{ W} = 22.5 \text{ kW } \textbf{(Ans.)}$$

Q. 9.6. The intel angle of runner blades of a Francis turbine is 90°. The blades are so shaped that the tangential component of velocity at blade outlet is zero. The flow velocity remains constant throughout the blade passage and is equal to half of the blade velocity at runner inlet. The blade efficiency of the runner is

(*a*) 25% (*b*) 50% (*c*) 80% (*d*) 89%.

Ans. (*c*)

EXPLANATION: Refer to Fig. 9.10.

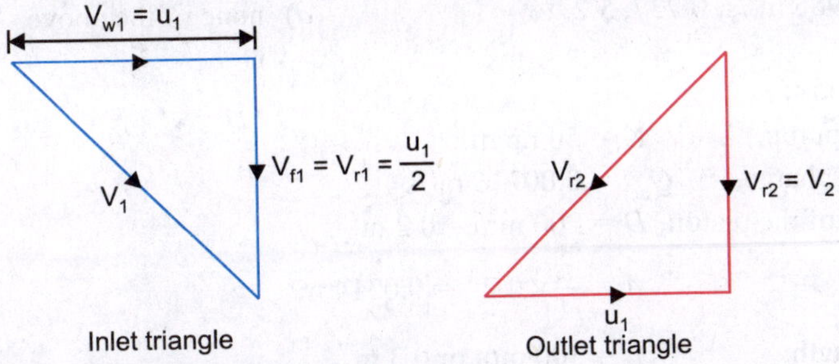

Fig. 9.10

Given:

$$V_{f1} = V_{f2} = \frac{u_1}{2}$$

$$V_2 = V_{f2} = \frac{u_1}{2}$$

$$V_1^2 = (V_{w1})^2 + (V_{f1})^2$$

$$= u_1^2 + \left(\frac{u_1}{2}\right)^2 = \frac{5}{4}u_1^2$$

$$\text{Blade efficiency} = \frac{V_1^2 - V_2^2}{V_1^2} \times 100$$

$$= \frac{\frac{5}{4}u_1^2 - \frac{u_1^2}{4}}{\frac{5}{4}u_1^2} \times 100 = \frac{4}{5} \times 100 = 80\% \textbf{ (Ans.)}$$

Q. 9.7. A large hydraulic turbine is to generate 300 kW at 1000 rpm under a head of 40 m. For initial testing, a 1 : 4 scale model of the turbine operates under a head of 10 m. The power generated by the model (in kW) will be

(*a*) 2.34 (*b*) 4.68 (*c*) 9.38 (*d*) 18.75.

Ans. (*a*)

EXPLANATION:

For similar turbines specific power will be same.

i.e.
$$\frac{P_1}{d_1^2 H_1^{3/2}} = \frac{P_2}{d_2^2 H_2^{3/2}}$$

$\therefore$
$$P_2 = P_1 \times \left(\frac{d_2}{d_1}\right)^2 \times \left(\frac{H_2}{H_1}\right)^{3/2}$$

$$= 300 \times \left(\frac{1}{4}\right)^2 \times \left(\frac{10}{40}\right)^{3/2}$$

i.e.
$$P_2 = 2.34 \text{ kW } \textbf{(Ans.)}$$

Q. 9.8. A single-acting reciprocating pump, running at 50 r.p.m. delivers 0.00736 m^3/s of water. The diameter of the piston is 200 mm and stroke length 300 mm. The suction and delivery heads are 3.5 m and 11.5 m respectively. Then,

(*i*) Theoretical discharge, (*ii*) Co-efficient of discharge, and (*iii*) Percentage slip of the pump are respectively.

(*a*) 0.00785 m^3/s, 0.937, 6.24%
(*b*) 0.00885 m^3/s, 0.837, 3.24%
(*c*) 0.00985 m^3/s, 0.737, 5.27%
(*d*) none of the above.

Ans. (*a*)

EXPLANATION:

Speed of pump, $N = 50$ r.p.m.

Actual discharge, $Q_{act} = 0.00736\ m^3/s$

Diameter of the piston, $D = 200$ mm $= 0.2$ m

$\therefore$ Area, $A = \frac{\pi}{4} \times 0.2^2 = 0.0314\ m^2$

Stroke length, $L = 300$ mm or 0.3 m

Suction head, $h_s = 3.5$ m

Delivery head, $h_d = 11.5$ m

(*i*) *Theoretical discharge,* Q_{th}:

$$Q_{th} = \frac{ALN}{60} = \frac{0.0314 \times 0.3 \times 50}{60} = 0.00785\ m^3/s \ \textbf{(Ans.)}$$

(*ii*) *Co-efficient of discharge,* C_d:

$$C_d = \frac{Q_{act.}}{Q_{th.}} = \frac{0.00736}{0.00785} = 0.937 \ \textbf{(Ans.)}$$

(*iii*) *Percentage slip of the pump:*

$$\%\ \text{slip} = \frac{Q_{th.} - Q_{act.}}{Q_{th.}} \times 100 = \frac{0.00785 - 0.00736}{0.00785} \times 100 = 6.24\% \ \textbf{(Ans.)}$$

Q. 9.9. A hydraulic intensifier gets the low pressure liquid at a pressure of 40 bar and delivers it to a machine at a pressure of 160 bar. If the intensifier has a capacity of 0.021 m^3 and stroke 1.2 m, calculate the diameters of the fixed ram and the sliding cylinder to be used for this intensifier.

(*a*) 130 mm, 260 mm
(*b*) 140 mm, 280 mm
(*c*) 149 mm, 298 mm
(*d*) none of the above.

Ans. (*c*)

EXPLANATION:

Intensity of pressure of low pressure liquid, $p_1 = 40$ bar $= 40 \times 10^5\ N/m^2$

Intensity of pressure of high pressure liquid, $p_2 = 160$ bar $= 160 \times 10^5\ N/m^2$

Capacity of intensitier = 0.021 m^3

Stroke length = 1.2 m

Diameter of fixed ram (D_2) *and the sliding cylinder* (D_1):

Capacity of intensifier = Area of fixed ram × stroke length

$$0.021 = A_2 \times 1.2 \text{ or } A_2 = \frac{0.021}{1.2} = 0.0175\ m^2$$

$$\therefore \quad \frac{\pi}{4} D_2^2 = 0.0175 \text{ or } D_2 = \left(\frac{4 \times 0.0175}{\pi}\right)^{1/2} = 0.149 \text{ m or } 149 \text{ mm} \ \textbf{(Ans.)}$$

Considering equilibrium of the sliding cylinder (neglecting friction effects), we have:

$$p_1 A_1 = p_2 A_2 \text{ or } 40 \times 10^5 \times A_1 = 160 \times 10^5 \times 0.0175 \text{ or } A_1 = 0.07 \text{ m}^2$$

$$\therefore \quad \frac{\pi}{4} D_1^2 = 0.07, \text{ or } D_1 = \left(\frac{4 \times 0.07}{\pi}\right)^{1/2} = 0.298 \text{ m or } \mathbf{298 \text{ mm (Ans.)}}$$

Q. 9.10. A hydraulic ram is receiving water at the rate of 0.022 m^3/s from a height of 3.3 m, and it raises 0.0022 m^3/s to a height of 21 m from the ram. Determine D' Aubuisson's and Rankine's efficiencies of the hydraulic ram.

(*a*) 53.64%, 49.6% (*b*) 63.64%, 59.6%

(*c*) 73.64%, 69.6% (*d*) none of the above.

Ans. (*b*)

EXPLANATION:

Discharge through the supply pipe $Q = 0.022 \text{ m}^3/\text{s}$

Supply head, $h = 3.3$ m

Discharge raised, $q = 0.0022 \text{ m}^3/\text{s}$

Height of water raised from hydraulic ram, $H = 21$ m

D' Aubuisson's efficiency:

$$\text{D' Aubuisson's efficiency} = \frac{qH}{Qh} = \frac{0.0022 \times 21}{0.002 \times 3.3} = 0.6364 \text{ or } 63.64\% \textbf{ (Ans.)}$$

Rankine's efficiency:

$$\text{Rankine's efficiency}: \frac{q(H-h)}{(Q-q)h} = \frac{0.0022(21-3.3)}{(0.022-0.0022)\times 3.3} = 0.596 \text{ or } 59.6\% \textbf{ (Ans.)}$$

Q. 9.11. A centrifugal pump is started with its delivery valve kept

(*a*) fully open (*b*) fully closed

(*c*) partially open (*d*) 50% open.

Ans. (*b*)

EXPLANATION:

A centrifugal pump is started with its valve fully closed. **(Ans.)**

Q. 9.12. As water flows through the runner of a reaction turbine, pressure acting on it would vary from

(*a*) more than atmospheric pressure to vacuum

(*b*) less than atmospheric pressure to zero gauge pressure

(*c*) atmospheric pressure to more than atmospheric pressure

(*d*) atmospheric pressure to vacuum.

Ans. (*a*)

EXPLANATION:

The pressure at 'runner inlet' of a reaction in drive is *more* than atmospheric pressure and at a 'runner outlet' it is *less* than atmospheric pressure (*i.e.*, vacuum) **(Ans.)**

Q. 9.13. Given that N = speed, P = power, H = head,

The specific speed of a hydraulic turbine is given by

(*a*) $\frac{N\sqrt{P}}{H^{4/5}}$ (*b*) $\frac{N\sqrt{P}}{H^{5/4}}$

(*c*) $\frac{P\sqrt{N}}{H^{4/5}}$ (*d*) $\frac{P\sqrt{N}}{H^{5/4}}$.

Ans. (*b*)

EXPLANATION:

The *specific speed* of a turbine is defined as the speed of the turbine which is identical in shape, geometrical in dimensions, blade angles, gate opening, etc. which would develop unit power when working under a unit head. It is given by:

$$N_B(\text{Specific speed}) = \frac{N\sqrt{P}}{H^{5/4}} \quad \textbf{(Ans.)}$$

Q. 9.14. Which one of the following turbines is used in underwater power stations?

(*a*) Pelton turbine (*b*) Deriaz turbine

(*c*) Tubular turbine (*d*) Turgo-impulse turbine.

Ans. (*c*)

EXPLANATION:

For underwater power stations, *tubular or bulb turbine* is used. A large bulb is centred in the water pipe which holds the generator, wiket gate and runner.

A tubular or bulb turbine has the following features:

- It is axial flow turbine with either adjustable or non-adjustable runner vanes (and hence similar to kaplan or propeller turbines).
- In such a turbine the scroll casing is *not* provided but the runner is placed in a tube extending from head water to the tail water (and hence it is called a tubular turbine).
- It is a low head turbine and is employed for heads varying from 3 m to 15 m.
- The disposition of the shaft may be vertical, inclined or horizontal.

Q. 9.15. A Pelton wheel is ideally suited for

(*a*) high head and low discharge (*b*) high head and high discharge

(*c*) low head and low discharge (*d*) medium head and medium discharge.

Ans. (*a*)

EXPLANATION:

The specific speed of an hydraulic turbine is given by N_s (specific speed) $= \frac{N\sqrt{P}}{H^{5/4}}$

(N = speed; P = power; H = head)

The specific speed for high head will be low and thus Pelton wheel/turbine will be suitable because N_s is the speed with which the turbine turns for a particular discharge Q, with unit head and thereby is able to produce unit power, thus for *low* N_s, *Q must be low.* **(Ans.)**

Q. 9.16. Consider the following turbines:

1. Kaplan
2. Pelton wheel
3. Francis

The correct sequence in increasing order of the specific speeds of these turbines is

(*a*) 2, 3, 1 (*b*) 2, 1, 3

(*c*) 3, 1, 2 (*d*) 1, 2, 3.

Ans. (*a*)

EXPLANATION:

The specific speed (N_s) for various types of turbines are:

Type of turbines	Specific speed
1. Propeller and Kaplan	300 – 1000
2. Pelton	12 – 70
3. Francis	80 – 400

Thus the correct sequence in increasing order of N_s is given by 2, 3, 1 *i.e.*, (*a*) is the correct answer **(Ans.)**

Q. 9.17. If the full-scale turbine is required to work under a head of 30 m and to run at 428 rpm, then a quarter-scale turbine model tested under a head of 10 m must run at

(*a*) 143 rpm (*b*) 341 rpm

(*c*) 428 rpm (*d*) 988 rpm.

Ans. (*d*)

EXPLANATION:

We know that: $$\left(\frac{\sqrt{H}}{DN}\right)_m = \left(\frac{\sqrt{H}}{DN}\right)_p \qquad \text{... [Eqn. (3.27)]}$$

or, $$\frac{\sqrt{H_m}}{D_m N_m} = \frac{\sqrt{H_p}}{D_p N_p}$$

or, $$N_m = N_p\left(\frac{D_p}{D_m}\right)\sqrt{\frac{H_m}{H_p}}$$

$$= 428 \times (4) \times \sqrt{\frac{10}{30}} = 988 \text{ rpm} \quad \textbf{(Ans.)}$$

Q. 9.18. Consider the following turbines/wheels:

1. Francis turbine
2. Pelton wheel with two or more jets
3. Pelton wheel with a single jet
4. Kaplan turbines

The correct sequence of these turbines/wheels in increasing order of their specific speeds is

(*a*) 2, 3, 1, 4 (*b*) 3, 2, 1, 4

(*c*) 2, 3, 4, 1 (*d*) 3, 2, 4, 1.

Ans. (*b*)

EXPLANATION:

The specific speed of pelton wheel with single jet is less than that of Pelton wheel with two or more jets. Furthermore, the specific speed of Francis turbines is more than Pelton wheel and less than Kaplan turbine, hence *b* is the correct answer. **(Ans.)**

Q. 9.19. Consider the following statements pertaining to a centrifugal pump:

1. The manometric head is the head developed by pump.
2. The suction pipe has, generally, a large diameter as compared to the discharge pipe.
3. The suction pipe is provided with a foot valve and a strainer.
4. The delivery pipe is provided with a foot valve and a strainer.

Which of these statements are correct?

(*a*) 1, 2, 3, and 4 (*b*) 1 and 2

(*c*) 2 and 3 (*d*) 1 and 3.

Ans. (*c*)

EXPLANATION:

The head against which a centrifugal pump has to work is known as manometric head (H_{mano}). It is given as:

$$H_{mano} - \frac{V_{w2}u_2}{g} - \text{loss of head in the pump (i.e., impeller and casing)}$$

($\frac{V_{w2}u_2}{g}$ = work done per second and per unit weight, assuming flow at inlet to be radial). **(Ans.)**

Q. 9.20. If a reciprocating pump having a mechanical efficiency of 80% delivers water at the rate of 80 kg/s with a head of 30 m, the brake power of the pump is

(*a*) 29.4 kW
(*b*) 20.8 kW
(*c*) 15.4 kW
(*d*) 10.8 kW.

Ans. (*a*)

EXPLANATION:

Power (BP) required to drive the reciprocating pump,

$$\text{P (brake)} = \frac{wQ(h_s + h_d)}{\eta} = \frac{mgH}{\eta} = \frac{80 \times 9.81 \times 30}{0.8 \times 1000}$$

$$= 29430 \text{ W} = 29.43 \text{ kW} \textbf{ (Ans.)}$$

Q. 9.21. The maximum number of jets generally employed in an impulse turbine without jet interference are

(*a*) 4
(*b*) 6
(*c*) 8
(*d*) 12.

Ans. (*b*)

EXPLANATION:

Normally a Pelton wheel has one nozzle or one jet. However, a number of nozzles may be employed when more power is to be produced with the same wheel. Theoretically *six nozzles* can be used on Pelton wheel. However, practical considerations limit the use of not more than two jets per runner for a vertical runner and not more than four jets per runner if it is of horizontal configuration. **(Ans.)**

Q. 9.22. For a water turbine, running at constant head and speed, the operating characteristic curves in the given figure 9.11 show that upto a certain discharge '*q*' both output power and efficiency remain zero.

The discharge '*q*' is required to

(*a*) overcome initial inertia
(*b*) overcome initial friction
(*c*) keep the hydraulic circuit full
(*d*) keep the turbine running at no load.

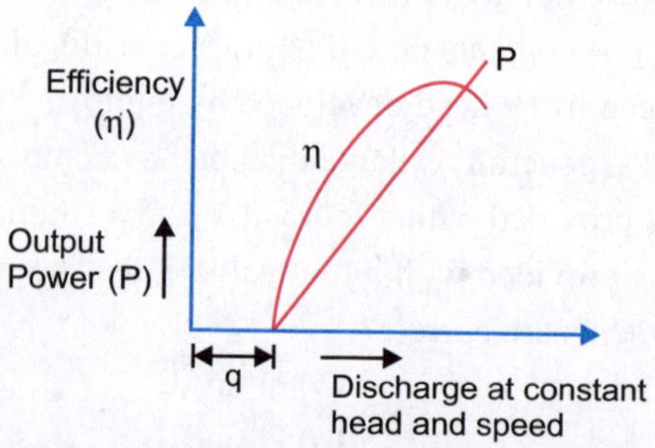

Fig. 9.11

Ans. (*b*)

EXPLANATION:

The discharge q (no load) is required to keep the turbine running under *no-load condition,* to overcome initial friction (*i.e.,* frictional losses) **(Ans.)**

Q. 9.23. The gross head on a turbine is 300 m. The length of penstock supplying water from reservoir to the turbine is 400 m. The diameter of the penstock is 1 m and velocity of water through penstock is 5 m/s. If coefficient of friction is 0.0098, the net head on the turbine would be, nearly

(*a*) 310 m (*b*) 295 m

(*c*) 200 m (*d*) 150 m.

Ans. (*b*)

EXPLANATION:

Given: Gross head, $H_g = 300$ m; L = 400 m; D = 1 m; V = 5 m/s; $f = 0.0098$

Now, Loss of head in the penstock, $h_f = \dfrac{fLV^2}{D \times 2g} = \dfrac{0.0098 \times 400 \times (5)^2}{1 \times 2 \times 9.81} = 5$ m

Hence, net head, $H = H_g - H_f = 300 - 5 = 295$ m **(Ans)**

Q. 9.24. A pump running at 1000 rpm consumes 1 kW and generates head of 10 m of water. When it is operated at 2000 rpm, its power consumption and head generated would be

(*a*) 4 kW, 50 m of water (*b*) 6 kW, 20 m of water

(*c*) 3 kW, 30 m of water (*d*) 8 kW, 40 m of water.

Ans. (*d*)

EXPLANATION:

When the diameter is constant, we have the following realtions

$$\frac{H_2}{H_1} = \left(\frac{N_2}{N_1}\right)^2 \text{ or } H_2 = H_1 \times \left(\frac{N_2}{N_1}\right)^2 = 10 \times \left(\frac{2000}{1000}\right)^2 = 40 \text{ m of water } \textbf{(Ans.)}$$

$$\text{and } \frac{P_2}{P_1} = \left(\frac{N_2}{N_1}\right)^3 \text{ or } P_2 = P_1 \times \left(\frac{N_2}{N_1}\right)^3 = 1 \times \left(\frac{2000}{1000}\right)^2 = 8 \text{ kW } \textbf{(Ans.)}$$

Q. 9.25. A centrifugal pump gives maximum efficiency when its blades are

(*a*) bent forward (*b*) bent backward

(*c*) straight (*d*) wave shaped.

Ans. (*b*)

EXPLANATION:

A centrifugal pump with its blades bent *backward* gives maximum efficiency as compared to blades with other shapes. **(Ans.)**

Q. 9.26. In utilizing scaled models in the designing of turbo-machines, which of the following relationship must be satisfied?

(*a*) $\dfrac{H}{ND^3}$ = constant; $\dfrac{Q}{N^2D^2}$ = constant

(*b*) $\dfrac{Q}{D^2\sqrt{H}}$ = constant; $\dfrac{H}{N^3D}$ = constant (*c*) $\frac{P}{QH}$ = constant; $\frac{H}{N^2D^2}$ = constant

(*d*) $\frac{NQ^{1/2}}{H^{3/2}}$ = constant; $\frac{NP^{1/2}}{H^{3/4}}$ = constant .

Ans. (*c*)

EXPLANATION:

We know that: $P = \rho QgH$, or $\frac{P}{QH}$ = constant **(Ans.)**

and, $$u = \frac{\pi DN}{60}$$

Also, $N = \frac{\sqrt{H}}{D}$ or $ND = \sqrt{H}$ or $\frac{}{N^2d^2}$ = constant **(Ans.)**

(The parameter $\frac{H}{N^2D^2}$ is called *head coefficient,* C_H)

Q. 9.27. A centrifugal pump driven by a directly coupled 3 kW motor of 1450 rpm speed, is proposed to be connected to another motor of 2900 rpm speed. The power of the motor should be

(*a*) 6 kW
(*b*) 12 kW
(*c*) 18 kW
(*d*) 24 kW.

Ans. (*d*)

EXPLANATION:

For a constant diameter, $P \propto N^3$, then

$$\frac{P_2}{P_1} = \left(\frac{N_2}{N_1}\right)^3 = \left(\frac{2900}{1450}\right)^3 = 8 \text{ or } P_2 = P_1 \times 8 = 3 \times 8 = 24 \text{ kW} \quad \textbf{(Ans.)}$$

Q. 9.28. A draft tube is used in a reaction turbine

(*a*) to guide water downstream without splashing
(*b*) to convert residual pressure energy into kinetic energy
(*c*) to convert residual kinetic energy into pressure energy
(*d*) to streamline the flow in the tail race.

Ans. (*c*)

EXPLANATION:

The draft tube serves the following two *purposes*:

1. To convert residual kinetic energy into pressure energy.
2. It allows the turbine to be set above tail water level, without loss of head, to facilitate inspection and maintenance.
   - Draft tube is an integral part of mixed and axial flow turbines.

Q. 9.29. Efficiency of Pelton wheel shall be maximum if the ratio of jet velocity to tangential velocity of the wheel is

(*a*) 1/2
(*b*) 1
(*c*) 2
(*d*) 4.

Ans. (*c*)

EXPLANATION:

The hydraulic efficiency of a Pelton wheel is maximum when the tangential velocity of wheel is *half* the velocity of jet of water at inlet **(Ans.)**

Q. 9.30. A hydraulic press has a ram of 20 cm diameter and a plunger of 5 cm diameter. The force required at the plunger to lift a weight of 16×10^4 N shall be

(*a*) 256×10^4 N (*b*) 64×10^4 N

(*c*) 4×10^4 N (*d*) 1×10^4 N.

Ans. (*d*)

EXPLANATION:

Area of ram, $A = \pi/4 \times (20)^2$ cm = $100\ \pi$ cm^2; Area of plunger, $a = \frac{\pi}{4} \times 5^2 = \frac{25\pi}{4}$ cm^2.

Load lifted, W = 16×10^4 N; force reqd. at the plunger, F = ?

$$\text{Now, } \frac{F}{a} = \frac{W}{A} \text{ or } F = \frac{a}{A} \times W = \frac{\frac{25\pi}{4}\pi}{100\pi} \times 16 \times 10^4 = 1 \times 10^4 \text{ N} \textbf{ (Ans.)}$$

Q. 9.31. Priming is necessary in

(*a*) centrifugal pumps to lift water from a greater depth

(*b*) centrifugal pumps to remove air in the suction pipe and casing

(*c*) hydraulic turbine to remove air in the turbine casing

(*d*) hydraulic turbine to increase the speed of turbine and to generate more power.

Ans. (*b*)

EXPLANATION:

The operation of filling the suction pipe, casing of the pump and a portion of the delivery pipe completely from outside source with the liquid to be raised, before starting the pump, to *remove any air, gas or vapour* form these parts of the pump is called *priming* of a centrifugal pump.

If a centrifugal pump is *not* primed before starting, air pockets inside the impeller may give rise to vortices and cause discontinuity of flow. Further dry running of the pump may result in rubbing and seizing of the wearing rings and cause serious damage.

Q. 9.32. Consider the following statements regarding air vessels provided in reciprocating pump installations:

1. The air vessels are fitted both on suction and delivery sides.
2. The air vessels are fitted far from the pump cylinder.
3. The air vessels save energy by reducing the friction loss.

Which of these statements are correct?

(*a*) 1, 2 and 3 (*b*) 1 and 2

(*c*) 2 and 3 (*d*) 1 and 3.

Ans. (*d*)

EXPLANATION:

An air vessel is a closed chamber containing compressed air in the upper part and liquid being pumped in the lower part. One air vessel is fixed on the suction pipe '*just near the suction valve*' and one is *fixed on the delivery pipe 'near delivery valve'*.

The air vessels are used for the following *purposes*:

1. To get continuous supply of liquid at a uniform rate (whatever fluctuations false place, they occur between the air vessels and the pump)
2. To save the power by reducing the friction loss required to drive the pump.
3. To run the pump at much higher speed without any danger of separation. **(Ans)**

Q. 9.33. A pump is installed at a height of 5 m above the water level in the sump. Frictional loss on the suction side is 0.6 m. If the atmospheric pressure is 10.3 m of water and vapour pressure head is 0.4 m (abs), the NPSH (Net Positive Suction Head) will be

(*a*) 3.7 m (*b*) 4 m
(*c*) 4.3 m (*d*) 4.6 m.

Ans. (*c*)

EXPLANATION:

Net Positive Suction Head, NPSH $= \frac{p_0}{w}$ – (static head + frictional head in suction + vapour pressure head)

$= 10.3 - (5 + 0.6 + 0.4) = 4.3$ m **(Ans.)**

Q. 9.34. Two Pelton wheels A and B have the same specific speed and are working under the same head. Wheel A produces 400 kW at 1000 rpm. If B produces 100 kW, then its rpm is

(*a*) 4000 (*b*) 2000
(*c*) 1500 (*d*) 1250.

Ans. (*b*)

EXPLANATION:

Specific speed, $N_B = \frac{N\sqrt{P}}{(H)^{5/4}}$

Since the Pelton wheels are having the same specific speed and are working under the same head, therefore :

$$N\sqrt{P} = \text{constant or } N_1\sqrt{P_1} = N_2\sqrt{P_2}$$

or, $$N_2 = N_1\sqrt{\frac{P_1}{P_2}} = 1000\sqrt{\frac{400}{100}} = 2000 \text{ rpm} \quad \textbf{(Ans.)}$$

Q. 9.35. A centrifugal pump needs 1000 W of power when operating at 1500 rpm. What is the power requirement if the speed of the pump is increased to 3000 rpm?

(*a*) 2000 W (*b*) 4000 W
(*c*) 6500 W (*d*) 8000 W.

Ans. (*d*)

EXPLANATION:

Now, $P \propto N^3$, where P and N are power and speed respectively.

$$\therefore \quad \frac{P_2}{P_1} = \left(\frac{N_2}{N_1}\right)^3, \text{ or } P_2 = P_1 \times \left(\frac{N_2}{N_1}\right)^3 = 1000 \times \left(\frac{3000}{1500}\right)^3 = 8000 \text{ W } \textbf{(Ans.)}$$

Q. 9.36. The centrifugal pumps have impellers with outlet dimensions of each equal to twice the inner dimensions. The inner diameter of the second impeller is three times the inner diameter of the first one. What is the speed ratio N_2/N_1 of pumps, if the pumps are required to develop the same manometric head to start delivery of water?

(*a*) 9 (*b*) 4
(*c*) 1/2 (*d*) 1/3.

Ans. (*d*)

EXPLANATION:

$$(D_0)_1 = 2\,(D_i)_1;\ (D_0)_2 = 2\,(D_i)_2;\ (D_i)_2 = 3\,(D_i)_1$$

$$\therefore \quad (D_0)_2 = 2 \times 3(D_i)_1 = 6(D_i)_1$$

Also, $N \propto \frac{1}{D}$, $\therefore \ \frac{N_2}{N_1} = \frac{(D_0)_1}{(D_0)_2} = \frac{2(D_i)_1}{6(D_i)_1} = \frac{1}{3}$ **(Ans.)**

Q. 9.37. A centrifugal pump operating at 1000 rpm develops a head of 30 m. If the speed is increased to 2000 rpm and the pump operates with the same efficiency, what is the head developed by the pump?

(*a*) 60 m (*b*) 90 m
(*c*) 120 m (*d*) 150 m.

Ans. (*c*)

EXPLANATION:

In case of a centrifugal pump, $H \alpha N^2$

$$\therefore \quad \frac{H_2}{H} = \left(\frac{N_2}{N_1}\right)^2 \text{ or, } H_2 = H_1 \times \left(\frac{N_2}{N_1}\right)^2 = 30 \times \left(\frac{2000}{1000}\right)^2 = 120 \text{ W } \textbf{(Ans.)}$$

Q. 9.38. Two centrifugal pumps A and B operate at their maximum efficiencies at 1000 rpm and 500 rpm respectively. Against the same delivery head, pump A discharges 1 m^3/s and pump B discharges 4 m^3/s respectively. What is the ratio of specific speeds $(N_S)_A : (N_S)_B$?

(*a*) 1 : 2 (*b*) 1 : 1
(*c*) 1 : 4 (*d*) 4 : 1.

Ans. (*b*)

EXPLANATION:

Specific speed (N_s) in case of a centrifugal pump is given by, $\frac{N\sqrt{Q}}{(\ )^{3/4}}$

$$\therefore \quad \frac{(N_s)_A}{(N_s)_B} = \frac{1000 \times \sqrt{1}}{500 \times \sqrt{4}} = 1 : 1 \text{ (H being same) } \textbf{(Ans.)}$$

Q. 9.39. Which one of the following pairs is not correctly matched?

(*a*) Centrifugal pump : Rotating blades in the motor create centrifugal head
(*b*) Reciprocating pump : Positive displacement pump
(*c*) Turbine pump : Centrifugal pump with guide vanes
(*d*) Gear pump : Gear teeth work like rotating blades to create centrifugal head.

Ans. (*d*)

EXPLANATION:

In a gear pump, the gear teeth do *not* create centrifugal head. A gear pump has the ability to pump highly viscous fluid. **(Ans.)**

Q. 9.40. An impulse turbine operating with a single nozzle has a specific speed of 5. What will be the approximate specific speed of the turbine if the turbine is operated with one more additional nozzle of the same size?

(*a*) 4 (*b*) 6
(*c*) 7 (*d*) 10.

Ans. (*c*)

EXPLANATION:

In case of an impulse turbine, $N_s \alpha \sqrt{Q}$

$$\therefore \quad N_s = 5\sqrt{2} \simeq 7 \quad \textbf{(Ans.)}$$

Q. 9.41. Why is a minimum of Net Positive Suction Head required for a hydraulic pump?

(*a*) To prevent cavitation (*b*) To increase discharge
(*c*) To increase suction head (*d*) To increase efficiency.

Ans. (*a*)

EXPLANATION:

The NPSH (Net Positive Suction Head) should always be *positive* to *prevent cavitation.* The term NPSH has significance only when cavitating liquids are handled. **(Ans.)**

Q. 9.42. If α is the blade angle at the outlet, then the maximum hydraulic efficiency of an ideal impulse turbine is

(*a*) $\frac{1+\cos\alpha}{2}$ (*b*) $\frac{1-\cos\alpha}{2}$

(*c*) $\frac{1-\sin\alpha}{2}$ (*d*) $\frac{1+\sin\alpha}{2}$.

Ans. (*a*)

EXPLANATION:

The maximum hydraulic efficiency of an ideal impulse turbine is given by:

$$(\eta_h)_{max} = \frac{1+\cos\alpha}{2}, \text{ where } \alpha \text{ is the blade angle } \textbf{(Ans.)}$$

Q. 9.43. In an axial flow impulse turbine, energy transfer takes place due to

(*a*) change in relative kinetic energy (*b*) change in absolute kinetic energy
(*c*) change in pressure energy (*d*) change in energy because of centrifugal force.

Ans. (*b*)

EXPLANATION:

In an axial flow impulse turbine, energy transfer takes place due to *change in absolute kinetic energy.* **(Ans.)**

Q. 9.44. The overall efficiency of Pelton turbine is 70%. If the mechanical efficiency is 85%, what is its hydraulic efficiency?

(*a*) 82.4% (*b*) 59.5%
(*c*) 72.3% (*d*) 81.5%.

Ans. (*a*)

EXPLANATION:

The overall efficiency of a pelton turbine,

$$\eta_0 = \eta_h \times \eta_m, \text{ or } 0.7 = \eta_h \times 0.85, \text{ or } \eta_h = \frac{0.7}{0.85} = 0.824 \text{ or } 82.4\% \textbf{ (Ans.)}$$

Q. 9.45. If in a pump, the discharge is halved, then assuming that the speed remains unchanged, what would be the ratio of the heads H_1/H_2?

(*a*) $\sqrt{1/3}$ (*b*) $\sqrt{2/3}$

(*c*) $\sqrt[3]{0.25}$ (*d*) $\sqrt[3]{0.5}$.

Ans. (*c*)

EXPLANATION:

In a centrifugal pump, $Q = K\dfrac{(H)^{3/2}}{N^2}$

(where, K = constant of proportionality, H = head, and N = speed)

If the speed remains constant, then: $Q \propto H^{3/2}$ or $H \propto Q^{2/3}$

$$\therefore \frac{H_1}{H_2} = \left(\frac{Q_1}{Q_2}\right)^{\frac{2}{3}} = \left(\frac{1}{2}\right)^{2/3} = \sqrt[3]{0.25} \quad \textbf{(Ans.)}$$

Q. 9.46. In a hydraulic coupling, what is the ratio of speed of the turbine runner to that of the pump impeller to maintain circulatory motion of oil?

(*a*) < 1 (*b*) = 1

(*c*) > 1 (*d*) Can be any value.

Ans. (*a*)

EXPLANATION:

In order to transmit power from pump impeller to turbine runner, circulatory motion of oil is required.

The efficiency (η) of hydraulic coupling is defined as the ratio of power output to power input, *i.e.*,

$$\eta = \frac{\text{Power output } (P_o)}{\text{Power input } (P_r)} = \frac{T_t\,\omega_t}{T_p\,\omega_p} = \frac{\omega_t}{\omega_p} \qquad (\because T_p = T_t)$$

As efficiency is always less than 1, thus $\dfrac{\omega_t}{\omega_p} < 1$ **(Ans.)**

Q. 9.47. Why is an air vessel used in a reciprocating pump?

(*a*) To obtain a continuous supply of water at uniform rate

(*b*) To reduce suction head

(*c*) To increase the delivery head

(*d*) To reduce cavitation.

Ans. (*a*)

EXPLANATION:

An air vessel are used for the following purposes:

1. To get continuous supply of liquid at a uniform rate (whatever fluctuation take place, they occur between the air vessels and the pump)
2. To save the power required to drive the pump).
3. To run the pump at such higher speed without any danger of separation. **(Ans.)**

Q. 9.48. Centrifugal pumps have which of the following advantages?

1. Low initial cost.
2. Compact, occupying less floor space.
3. Easy handling of highly viscous fluids.

Selected the correct answer using the codes given below:

(*a*) 1, 2 and 3 (*b*) 1 and 2 only

(*c*) 1 and 3 only (*d*) 2 and 3 only.

Ans. (*d*)

EXPLANATION:

Centrifugal pumps have the following advantages:

1. They are compact and occupy less floor space.
2. They can easily handle highly viscous fluids.

However, they have high initial cost. **(Ans.)**

Q. 9.49. Two pumps can operate independently at heads H_1, H_2 and discharge Q_1, Q_2 respectively. If the pumps are connected in parallel, then what are the resulting discharge (Q) and head (H)?

(*a*) $Q = Q_1 + Q_2, H = H_1 + H_2$ (*b*) $Q = Q_1 - Q_2, H = H_1 - H_2$

(*c*) $Q = Q_1 = Q_2, H = H_1 = H_2$ (*d*) $Q = Q_1 + Q_2, H = H_1 = H_2$.

Ans. (*d*)

EXPLANATION:

When the pumps are connected in *parallel*

$$Q = Q_1 + Q_2, H = H_1 = H_2 \quad \textbf{(Ans.)}$$

Q. 9.50. Which one of the following is correct for hydraulic coupling?

(*a*) It connects two shafts rotating at about the same speed

(*b*) It connects two shafts running at different speeds

(*c*) It is used to augment the torque to the driven shaft

(*d*) It is used to connect the centrifugal pump and its electrical motor for efficient operation.

Ans. (*b*)

EXPLANATION:

A hydraulic coupling connects two shafts running at *different speeds.* **(Ans.)**

FLUID MECHANICS AND HYDRAULIC MACHINES LABORATORY PRACTICALS

(Experiments : 1 to 26)

LABORATORY EXPERIMENTS

A. FLUID MECHANICS

Experiment No. 1. *To measure the pressure head of water in a pipeline by means of a* **piezometer tube.**

Experiment No. 2. *To measure the pressure head of water in a pipeline by means of a* **U-tube**.

Experiment No. 3. *To measure the difference of pressure between the two points of a pipeline by using an* **inverted U-tube.**

Experiment No. 4. *To determine the* **metacentric height** *of a ship.*

Experiment No. 5. *To verify* **Bernoulli's theorem.**

Experiment No. 6. *To find the* **coefficient 'k'** *for a given* **venturimeter**.

Experiment No. 7. *To calibrate the given* **orificemeter.**

Experiment No. 8. *To find the value of velocity head or to find the coefficient of* **pitot tube.**

Experiment No. 9. *To determine C_c (coefficient of contraction), C_v (coefficient of velocity) and C_d (coefficient of discharge) for flow through a circular/round* **orifice**.

Experiment No. 10. *To verify time for the level in a rectangular tank to fall from height H_1 to H_2 when the flow takes place through an* **orifice**.

Experiment No. 11. *To find the coefficient of discharge in an* **external mouthpiece**.

Experiment No. 12. *To find the value of k and hence coefficient of discharge in the equation $Q = kH^{5/2}$ in* **right angled triangular notch.**

Experiment No. 13. *To find the value of k and hence coefficient of discharge in the equation $Q = kH^{3/2}$ for a* **rectangular notch**.

Experiment No. 14. *To plot the flow profile over a* **broad crested weir and calibrate it**.

Experiment No. 15. *To determine different* **requires of flow** *by Reynolds experiment.*

Experiment No. 16. *To find the value of* **critical velocity in pipes** *by Reynolds experiments.*

Experiment No. 17. *To determine the* **friction factor** *for pipes of different sizes.*

Experiment No. 18. *To determine the velocity distribution in a given pipeline and obtain the* **energy and momentum correction factors**.

Experiment No. 29. *To obtain the velocity distribution in an open channel with the help of* **current meter**.

Experiment No. 20. *To verify impulse momentum principle for impact of jet on a* **stationary vane**.

Experiment No. 21. *To verify experimentally the theoretical relationship between the* **conjugate depths of a hydraulic jump** *and to determine its various elements.*

Experiment No. 22. *To visualize and plot the pattern of flow around an object in a fluid stream using* **Hele-Shaw apparatus**.

B. HYDRAULIC MACHINES

Experiment No. 23. *To study the operation and performance of a* **Pelton wheel.**

Experiment No. 24. *To study the performance of a* **Francis turbine.**

Experiment No. 25. *To study the performance characteristics of a single-stage* **centrifugal pump.**

Experiment No. 26. *To obtain the performance characteristics of a* **reciprocating pump.**

EXPERIMENTS

A. FLUID MECHANICS

***EXPERIMENT NO. 1.* To measure the pressure head of water in a pipeline by means of a piezometer tube.**

Apparatus. A horizontal pipe running full with water and fitted with a piezometer tube.

Brief theory. A *piezometer tube* is a simple glass tube used for measuring moderate pressures of liquids. It is inserted in the wall of a vessel or of a pipe, containing liquid whose pressure is to be measured. The tube extends vertically upwards to such a height that liquid can freely rise in it without overflowing. The pressure at any point in the liquid is indicated by the height of the liquid in the tube above that point, which can be read on the scale attached to it. Thus, if 'w' is the specific weight of the liquid, then pressure (p) at point A (Fig. 1) is given by the relation

$$p = wh$$

where, h = Height of the liquid in the tube above the point A.

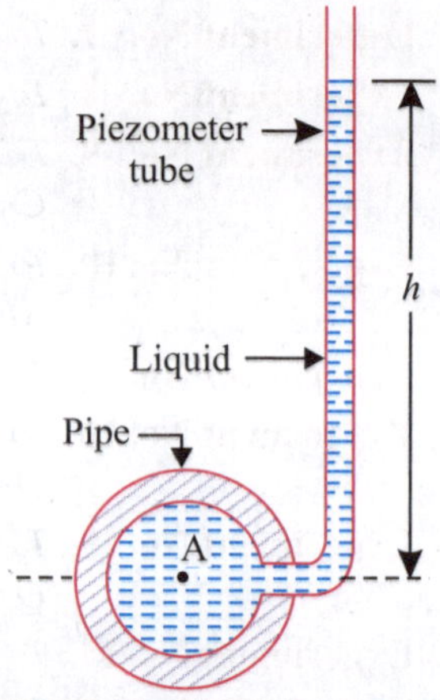

Fig. 1. Piezometer tube.

Note. A piezometer tube is not suitable for measuring negative pressure; as in such a case the air will enter in pipe through the tube.

Procedure : 1. Connect the piezometer tube into pipe.

2. Adjust the supply of water in the pipe in such a way that the water rises to a permissible height in the pipe.
3. Measure the height of water with respect to the longitudinal axis of the pipe.
4. Vary the discharge through the pipe, note down four readings (say) and tabulate as shown in Table 1.

Observations : As tabulated **(Table 1).**

Table 1. Piezometer tube – Observations

S. No.	*Pressure head, h*	*Intensity of pressure, $p = wh$ (w for water = 9810 N/m^3)*	*Remarks*
1.			
2.			
3.			
4.			

Mean pressure, p = ...

Specimen calculations : (*i*) (*ii*)

Conclusion :

Precautions. 1. The piezometer tube should be so inserted in the pipe that it is at right angles to the motion of the flow.

2. The end of the piezometer tube which is to be connected with the pipe should flush with its (pipe) inner surface and should not be rough.
3. To reduce fluctuations of water level it may be worthwhile to insert a short length of capillary tube between the pipe connection and the atmosphere surface.

EXPERIMENT NO. 2. **To measure the pressure head of water in a pipeline by means of a U-tube.**

Brief theory. Piezometer tubes cannot be employed when pressures in the lighter liquids are to be measured, since this would require very long tubes, which cannot be handled conveniently. Furthermore gas pressures cannot be measured by the piezometers because a gas forms no free atmospheric surface. These limitations can be overcome by the use of U-tube manometer.

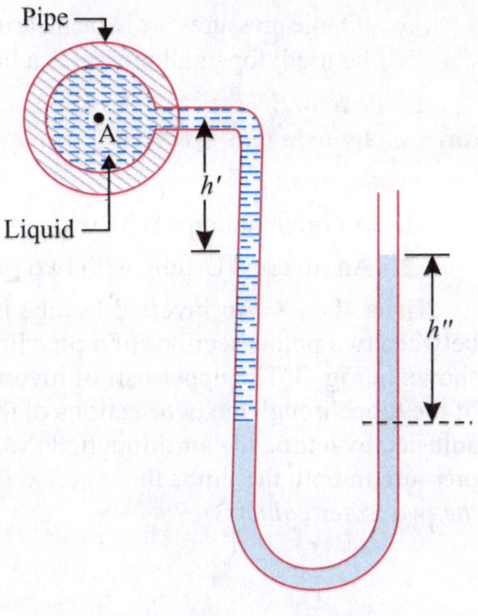

Fig. 2. U-tube.

A U-tube consists of a glass tube bent in U-shape, one end of which is connected to a point at which pressure is to be measured and other end remains open to the atmosphere as shown in Fig. 2. It contains a liquid (generally mercury) heavier than the liquid of which the pressure is to be measured.

The pressure head of liquid (h) in a pipe is found from the relation :

$$h + (h' + h'')\,S_1 = h''S_2$$

or

$$h = h''\,(S_2 - S_1) - h'S_1 \quad \text{...(General equation)}$$

where, S_1 = Sp. gr. of flowing liquid in the pipe, and

S_2 = Sp. gr. of heavier liquid in the U-tube.

If *water* ($S_1 = 1$) *is flowing through the pipe* then the above eqn. reduces to :

$$h = h''\,(S_2 - 1) - h'$$

Procedure :

1. Connect the U-tube to the pipe carrying liquid (whose pressure is to be measured).
2. Note down the readings of h' and h''.
3. Take number of readings by varying the discharge (say four) and tabulate as shown in the Table 2.

Table 2. U-tube – Observations

S. No.	*h'*	*h''*	*Pressure head* $h = h''\,(S_2 - S_1) - h'\,S_1$	*Intensity of pressure* $p = wh$ (w = *sp. wt. of liquid*)	*Remarks*
1.					
2.					
3.					
4.					

Mean pressure, p = ...

Specimen calculations : (*i*)

(*ii*)

Conclusions :

Precautions :

1. U-tube should enter the pipe at right angles to the direction in which the fluid flows.

2. The end of the U-tube which is to be connected with the pipe should flush with its (pipe) inner surface and should not be rough.
3. If large pressures are to be measured, then in U-tube heavier liquids, generally mercury, should be used; for small pressures a liquid a *little heavier* than that in the pipe should be used.

***EXPERIMENT NO. 3.* To measure the difference of pressure between the two points of a pipeline by using an inverted U-tube.**

Apparatus :

1. A horizontal pipe with two pet-cocks (at some distance apart).
2. An inverted U-tube with two rubber or plastic leads.

Brief theory. An inverted U-tube is employed for the measurement of difference of pressure between two points/sections of a pipe line carrying liquid (say water). The connections are made as shown in Fig. 3. The upper part of inverted U-tube contains air. The water enters into the two limbs of the tube through the two sections of the pipe. The height of the water columns in the tube may be adjusted by letting the air through the valve at the top. As air (trapped in the upper part) exerts equal pressure in both the limbs the *difference of pressure head is equal to the difference in the height of the two water columns.*

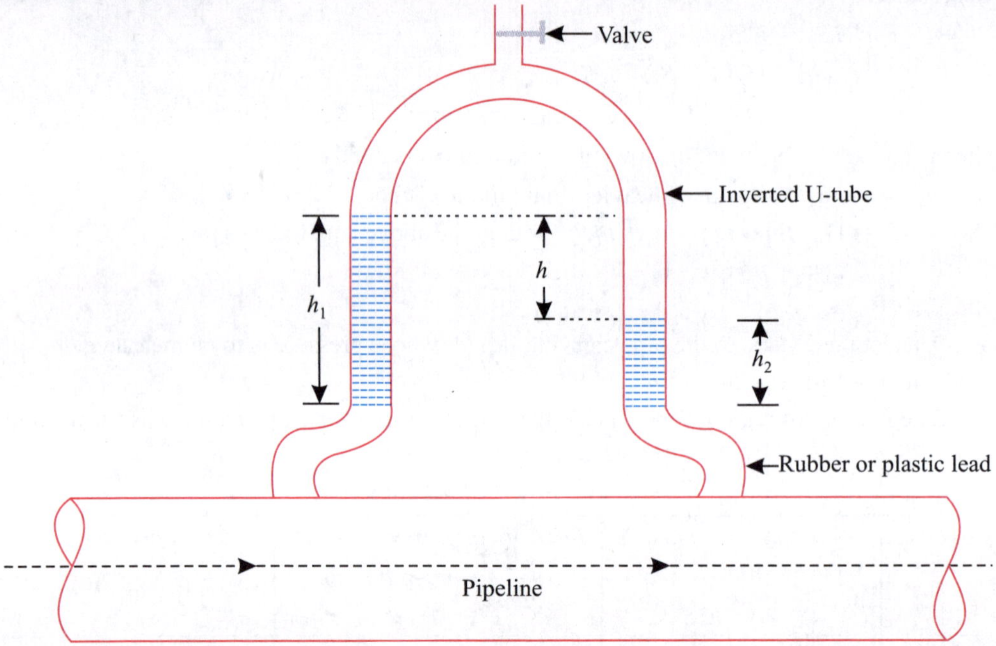

Fig. 3. Inverted U-tube.

Procedure :

1. Connect the two limbs of the inverted U-tube with the pet-cocks by means of two rubber/ plastic leads.
2. Set the pet-cocks on the 'on' position and allow the water to rise in two limbs of the tube.
3. Adjust the supply of water in such a way that the rise of water in the tube is within permissible limits.
4. Carry out minor adjustments of height of water by adjusting the air valve.
5. Note the reading on each of the two limbs.
6. Take number of reading (say four) by varying the discharge and tabulate them as given in Table 3.

Table 3. Inverted U-tube – Observations

S. No.	$\frac{p_1}{w} = h_1$	$\frac{p_2}{w} = h_2$	*Difference of pressure head* $h = (h_1 - h_2)$	*Difference of intensity of pressure,* $p = wh$	*Remarks*
1.					
2.					
3.					
4.					

Mean difference of pressure = ...

Specimen calculations : (*i*)

(*ii*)

Conclusion :

Precautions :

1. Make sure that the rubber/plastic leads are properly connected to pet-cocks.
2. While taking readings, the pet-cock levers should be put to "off" position simultaneously, so that water columns do not fluctuate and thus remain steady.

***EXPERIMENT NO. 4.* To determine metacentric height of a ship.**

Apparatus. Model of a ship. 2. Tank (containing water). 3. Weights.

Brief theory. 1. A ship model (with known c.g.) is floated in still water. A known weight (W_1) is moved across the deck (of the ship) through a certain distance (z) measured from O, consequently the ship gets tilted through a certain angle (θ) which is measured on the scale. The metacentric height (MG) is found (equating tilting and restoring moments) from the following relation.

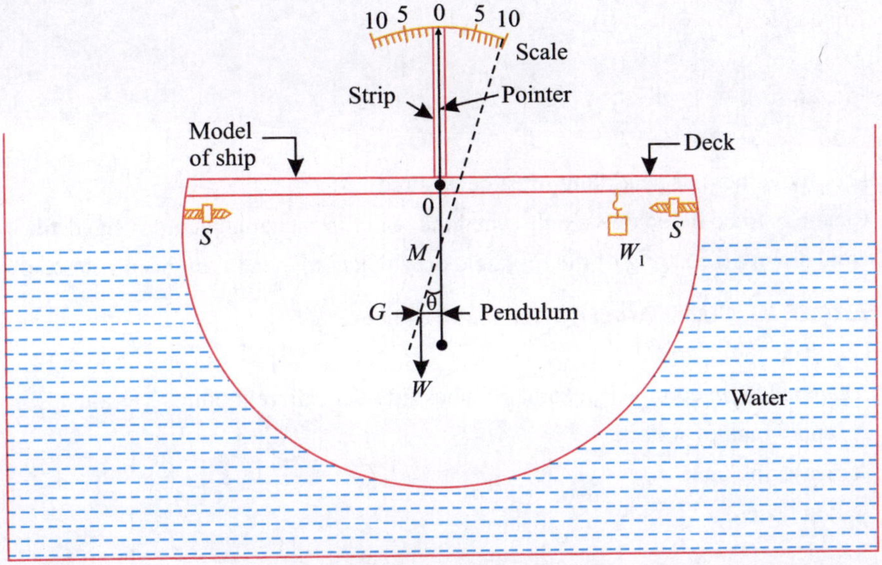

$$MG = \frac{W_1 \cdot z}{W \tan \theta}$$

S = Screws with adjustable weights (for zero adjustment)

W_1 = Known weight (hooked-movable)

W = Weight of the ship.

Fig. 4. Determination of metacentric height.

Procedure

1. Find the weight '*W*' of the model of ship outside water.
2. Place the ship model in water and with movable weight (W_1) at any position adjust the screws *S* to get zero reading on the scale.
3. Move the weight W_1 across the deck through a certain distance (z); it will result in tilting of the ship model.
4. Note down the angle of tilt 'θ'.
5. Note down more readings, by either
   (*i*) varying the load W_1 and keeping the distance 'z' constant or
   (*ii*) keeping the load W_1 constant and varying the distance 'z'.

Tabulate the readings as shown in Table 4.

Table 4. Metacentric height – Observations

S. No.	W	W_1	z	θ (degrees)	$MG = \frac{W_1 \cdot z}{W \tan\theta}$	Remarks
1.						
2.						
3.						
4.						

Mean value of $MG = \ldots\ldots\ldots$

Specimen calculations : (*i*)

(*ii*)

Conclusion :

Precautions :

1. Free movement of pendulum must be ensured.
2. Readings to be noted down only when the water in the tank becomes standstill.
3. Note down the reading of the tilt angle only when the pendulum becomes steady.

***EXPERIMENT NO. 5.* To verify Bernoulli's Theorem.**

Apparatus :

1. A tapered inclined pipe (piezometer tubes fitted at different points/sections)
2. A supply tank of water.
3. A measuring tank.
4. A stop watch.
5. A scale.

Brief theory. *Bernoulli's theorem states that in a steady flow of an ideal fluid the total energy per unit mass of fluid (at any section) remains constant along a stream line flow.* Neglecting losses, the total energy at sections 1 and 2 will have the following relation :

$$\frac{p_1}{w} + \frac{V_1^2}{2g} + z_1 = \frac{p_2}{w} + \frac{V_2^2}{2g} + z_2$$

where, $\frac{p}{w}$ = Pressure head

$\frac{V^2}{2g}$ = Velocity head, and

z = Datum head.

Procedure :

1. By slowly opening the inlet valve allow the water to flow from the supply tank.
2. Adjust the flow in such a manner that a constant head of water is available in the supply tank (*i.e.* inflow = outflow)
3. Note down the quantity of water collected (Q) in the measuring tank for a given interval of time using a stop watch.
4. Compute the areas of cross-section (A_1 and A_2) under the piezometer tubes.
5. Use the continuity equation to get V_1 and V_2 as follows :

$$Q = A_1V_1 = A_2V_2$$

$$\therefore \quad V_1 = \frac{Q}{A_1}$$

$$\text{and,} \quad V_2 = \frac{Q}{A_2}$$

6. Read the pressure head $\left(\frac{p}{w}\right)$ directly from the *piezometer tubes at the concerned sections.*
7. Note down the datum head (z) at different sections (for horizontal pipe line 'z' will be constant).
8. Tabulate the various values as shown in Table 5.

Observations :

Area at section 1, A_1 = ...

Area at section 2, A_2 = ...

Table 5. Bernoulli's theorem – Observations

S. No.	*Datum head*		*Pressure head*		*Measuring tank readings (m^3)*			*Time 't' (sec.)*	*Discharge, Q (m^3/sec.)*	*Velocity, $V = \frac{Q}{A}$*		*Velocity head, $\frac{V^2}{2g}$*		*Total head, = $\frac{p}{w} + \frac{V^2}{2g} + z$*	
	z_1	z_2	$\frac{p_1}{w}$	$\frac{p_2}{w}$	*Initial reading (a)*	*Final reading (b)*	*Quantity (m^3) (b) – (a)*			$V_1 = \frac{Q}{A_1}$	$V_2 = \frac{Q}{A_2}$	$\frac{V_1^2}{2g}$	$\frac{V_2^2}{2g}$	$\frac{p_1}{w} + \frac{V_1^2}{2g} + z_1$	$\frac{p_2}{w} + \frac{V_2^2}{2g} + z_2$
1.															
2.															
3.															
4.															
5.															

Conclusion : $\frac{p_1}{w} + \frac{V_1^2}{2g} + z_1 = \frac{p_2}{w} + \frac{V_2^2}{2g} + z_2$

Hence Bernoulli's theorem is verified.

***EXPERIMENT NO. 6.* To find the co-efficient 'k' for a given venturimeter.**

Apparatus :

1. A venturimeter (with known diameters at mouth and throat) fitted with stop cocks at mouth and throat.
2. Watermain connected to the mouth of the venturimeter through a supply valve.
3. A U-tube manometer containing mercury.
4. Water measuring tank.
5. A stop watch.

Brief theory. A venturimeter is an instrument used to measure the rate of discharge on a pipeline and is often fixed permanently at different sections of the pipeline to know the discharge there. The discharge (Q) through a venturimeter is given by the relation :

$$Q = \frac{A_1 A_2}{\sqrt{A_1^2 - A_2^2}} \sqrt{2gh} \quad ...(i)$$

(neglecting losses between the mouth and the throat)

where, A_1 = Area at the inlet,

A_2 = Area at the outlet, and

h = Difference of head (theoretical) between the two points.

The eqn. (i) may be written as:

$$Q = C\sqrt{h}$$

where, $C = \frac{A_1 A_2}{\sqrt{A_1^2 - A_2^2}} \sqrt{2g}$ = constant for the venturimeter.

The eqn. (i) gives the discharge under ideal conditions and is called the *theoretical discharge. Actual discharge* ($Q_{act.}$) is less than the theoretical discharge ($Q_{th.}$) because in actual practice some loss of head takes place due to friction and shock caused by the change of section of the pipe and subsequently the venturi head (actual difference of pressure head) becomes $k\sqrt{h}$ and $Q_{(act.)}$ is given by

$$Q_{(act.)} = C \times k\sqrt{h} \quad ...(ii)$$

or $$k = \frac{Q}{C\sqrt{h}}$$

where, k is known as venturi constant or coefficient of discharge. Its value varies from 0.96 to 0.98.

It may be noted that if liquid flowing in the venturimeter is water and the liquid in manometer is mercury (sp. gravity = 13.6), then

$$h = 12.6\, y$$

where, h = difference of head, and

y = manometer reading.

Procedure

1. Using plastic leads, connect the two limbs of the differential manometer to the mouth and throat of the venturimeter.
2. Put the stop cocks in the 'on' position and adjust the water supply valve slowly so as to get a suitable reading on the manometer.
3. Collect the quantity of water, flowing through the venturimeter, in the measuring tank and measure the discharge in time '*t*' (usually ranging from 2 min. to 5 min.)
4. Note down the corresponding reading of the difference of mercury level (y) in the two limbs of the manometer.
5. Repeat the experiment for different values of discharge (Q) and tabulate the results as shown in Table 6.

Observations :

Area at the inlet (mouth), $A_1 = \frac{\pi}{4} D_1^2 = \text{...cm}^2$

Area at the throat, $A_2 = \frac{\pi}{4} D_2^2 = \text{...cm}^2$

$$C = \frac{A_1 A_2}{\sqrt{A_1^2 - A_2^2}} \cdot \sqrt{2g}$$

Table 6. Venturimeter – Observations

S. No.	*Manometer reading 'y' (cm of Hg)*	*$h = 12.6\,y$ (cm of water)*	*Reading-measuring tank (cm^3)*			*Time 't' (sec.)*	*Discharge Q cm^3/sec*	$k = \frac{Q}{C\sqrt{h}}$	*Remarks*
			Initial reading (a)	*Final reading (b)*	*Quantity (cm^3) (b) – (a)*				

Mean value of k = ...

Specimen calculations : (*i*)
(*ii*)

Conclusion :

Precautions :

1. Before connecting the plastic leads with the manometer these should be flooded with water so that air present in them is removed.
2. All readings/measurements should be taken carefully and accurately.

***EXPERIMENT NO. 7.* To calibrate the given orifice meter**

Apparatus : (*i*) A long pipeline fitted with a sharp edged concentric circular orifice plate and having inlet and outlet valves for flow regulation.

(*ii*) A U-tube differential manometer connected to pressure tops at one diameter upstream and half diameter downstream) of the orifice plate.

(*iii*) A discharge measuring tank.

(*iv*) Stop watch.

Theory. ***Orificemeter*** or ***orifice plate*** is a device (*cheaper* than a venturimeter) employed for *measuring the discharge of fluid through a pipe.* It also works on the same principle of a venturimeter.

It consists of a flat circular plate (Fig. 5.) having a circular sharp edged hole (called orifice) concentric with the pipe. The diameter of the orifice may vary from 0.4 to 0.8 times the diameter of the pipe but its value is generally chosen as 0.5. A differential manometer is connected at section (1) which is at a distance of 1.5 to 2 times the pipe diameter upstream from the orifice plate, and at section (2) which is at a distance of about half the diameter of the orifice from the orifice plate on the downstream side.

Let, A_1 = Area of pipe at section (1),

V_1 = Velocity at section (1),

p_1 = Pressure at section (1), and

A_2, V_2 and p_2 = Corresponding values at section (2).

Applying Bernoulli's equation at section (1) and (2) we get:

$$\frac{p_1}{w} + \frac{V_1^2}{2g} + z_1 = \frac{p_2}{w} + \frac{V_2^2}{2g} + z_2$$

or, $$\left(\frac{p_1}{w} + z_1\right) - \left(\frac{p_2}{w} + z_2\right) = \frac{V_2^2}{2g} - \frac{V_1^2}{2g}$$

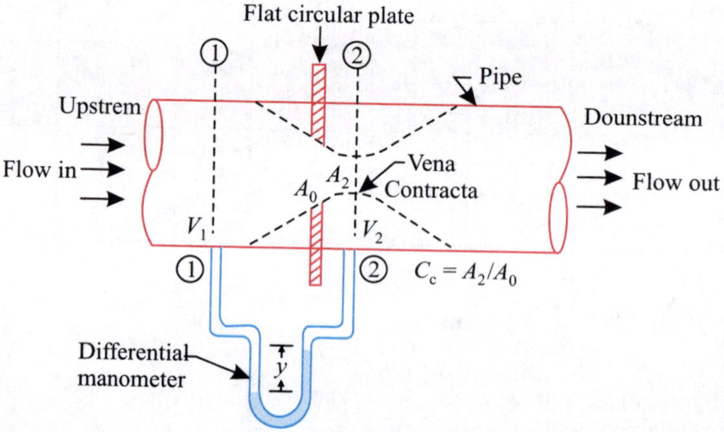

Fig. 5. Orifice meter.

or, $$h = \frac{V_2^2}{2g} - \frac{V_1^2}{2g}$$

$$\left[\because h = \left(\frac{p_1}{w} + z_1\right) - \left(\frac{p_2}{w} + z_2\right) = \text{differential head}\right]$$

or, $$\frac{V_2^2}{2g} = h + \frac{V_1^2}{2g} \quad \text{...(i)}$$

or, $$V_2 = \sqrt{2g\left(h + \frac{V_1^2}{2g}\right)} = \sqrt{2gh + V_1^2}$$

Now section (2) is at *vena-contracta* and A_2 represents the area at *vena-contracta*. If A_0 is the area of orifice then, we have

$$C_c = \frac{A_2}{A_0}$$

(where, C_c = co-efficient of contraction)

$$\therefore \quad A_2 = A_0 C_c \qquad ...(ii)$$

Using continuity equation, we get:

$$A_1 V_1 = A_2 V_2, \text{ or, } V_1 = \frac{A_2 V_2}{A_1}$$

or, $$V_1 = \frac{A_0 C_c V_2}{A_1} \qquad ...(iii)$$

Substituting the value of V_1 in eqn. (*i*) we get:

$$V_2 = \sqrt{2gh + \frac{A_0^2 C_c^2 \cdot V_2^2}{A_1^2}}$$

or, $$V_2^2 = 2gh + \left(\frac{A_0}{A_1}\right)^2 \cdot C_c^2 \cdot V_2^2$$

or, $$V_2^2 \left[1 - \left(\frac{A_0}{A_1}\right)^2 C_c^2\right] = 2gh$$

$$\therefore \quad V_2 = \frac{\sqrt{2gh}}{\sqrt{1 - (A_0/A_1)^2 C_c^2}}$$

$\therefore$ The discharge $Q = A_2 V_2 = A_0 \cdot C_c \cdot V_2$

[$\because A_2 = A_0 \cdot C_c$ ... as above eqn.(*ii*)]

$$= A_0 C_c \frac{\sqrt{2gh}}{\sqrt{1 - (A_0/A_1)^2 C_c^2}} \qquad ...(iv)$$

The above expression is simplified by using,

$$C_d = C_c \frac{\sqrt{1 - (A_0/A_1)^2}}{\sqrt{1 - (A_0/A_1)^2 C_c^2}}$$

(where, C_d = co-efficient of discharge)

$$C_c = C_d \frac{\sqrt{1 - (A_0/A_1)^2 C_c^2}}{\sqrt{1 - (A_0/A_1)^2}}$$

Substituting this value of C_c in eqn. (*iv*), we get:

$$Q = A_0 \cdot C_d \frac{\sqrt{1-(A_0/A_1)^2 C_c^2}}{\sqrt{1-(A_0/A_1)^2}} \times \frac{\sqrt{2gh}}{\sqrt{1-(A_0/A_1)^2 C_c^2}}$$

$$= \frac{C_d \cdot A_0 \cdot \sqrt{2gh}}{\sqrt{1-(A_0/A_1)^2}} = \frac{C_d \cdot A_0 \cdot A_1 \sqrt{2gh}}{\sqrt{A_1^2 - A_0^2}}$$

i.e.

$$Q = C_d \frac{A_0 \cdot A_1 \cdot \sqrt{2gh}}{\sqrt{A_1^2 - A_0^2}}$$

It may be noted that C_d (co-efficient of discharge) of an orifice meter is *much smaller than that of a venturimeter.*

Procedure :

1. Note the pipe diameter 'D_1', the orifice diameter 'D_0' and dimensions of the discharge measurement tank.
2. Adjust the inlet and outlet values for maximum discharge.
3. Allow the flow to stabilize and then note the readings in both the limbs (h_1 and h_2) of the differential manometer.
4. Determine the discharge by measuring the level rise (z) in the discharge measurement tank for a particular time (t).
5. Reduce the flow rate by closing the outlet valve slightly.
6. Repeat the steps 3 to 5 for several different discharges. Take more readings in the lower range of the discharge.

Observations :

Pipe diameter $= D_1 = \ldots\ldots.$

Orifice diameter $= D_0 = \ldots\ldots.$

Area of cross-section of pipe $= A_1 = \ldots\ldots$

Area of cross-section of orifice $= A_0 = \ldots\ldots$

Cross-sectional area of discharge measuring tank $= A_t = \ldots\ldots$

Specific gravity of manometeric fluid $= S_m = \ldots\ldots$

Specific gravity of fluid flowing through the pipe $= S = \ldots\ldots$

Table 7. Orifice meter – Observations

S. No.	*Discharge measurement*			*Manometer readings*			$Q_{th.}$ (m^3/s)	$C_d = \frac{Q_{actual}}{Q_{th.}}$
	Rise of water level in the tank z (cm)	*t (sec.)*	Q_{actual} (m^3/s)	h_1 (cm)	h_2 (cm)	*Diff. (y)* $h = y\left(\frac{S_m}{S} - 1\right)$ *(cm)*		

Calculations : For each setting of the discharge make the following set of calculations :

1. $$Q_{actual} = \frac{\text{Volume of water collected in discharge tank}}{\text{Time of collection}} = \frac{A_t\,Z}{t}$$

2. $$Q_{th} = \frac{A_0 A_1 \sqrt{2gh}}{\sqrt{A_1^2 - A_0^2}}$$

3. $$C_d = \frac{Q_{actual}}{Q_{th.}}$$

Conclusions :

Precautions :

1. Ensure that there are no air bubbles in the manometer.
2. After each change in the valve opening wait for some time for the flow to stabilize before taking readings.
3. Time interval for collection of water for discharge measurement should be large.

***EXPERIMENT NO. 8.* To find the value of velocity head or to find the coefficient of a pitot tube.**

Apparatus :

1. A pitot tube.
2. A small rectangular channel (or a pipe) with water flowing through it.

Brief theory. A pitot tube is a small open tube bent at right angle and is placed in flow such that one leg is vertical and the other leg is horizontal (Fig. 6). It is used to measure the velocity of flow at any point in a pipe or channel. *It works on the principle that if the velocity of flow at any point becomes zero, the pressure there is increased due to conversion of the kinetic energy into pressure energy.* The velocity of flow (V) is determined by measuring the rise of liquid (h) in the tube from the equation :

$$h = \frac{V^2}{2g}, \quad \text{or,} \quad V = \sqrt{2gh}$$

In actual practice, the velocity head is multiplied by a constant k the value of which depends upon the quality of the tube.

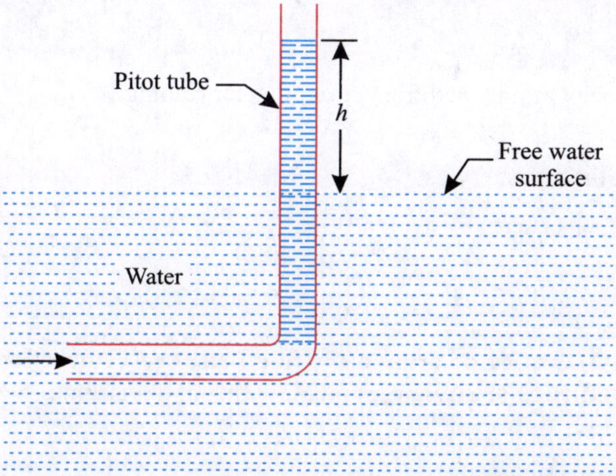

Fig. 6. Pitot tube.

$$\therefore \quad kh = \frac{V^2}{2g}$$

(The value of k is determined by actually measuring the velocity and the velocity head 'h')

Procedure :

1. Place the pitot tube in the moving water properly.
2. Note down the reading of 'h'.
3. Repeat the experiment by placing the pitot tube at different depths, find the mean value of 'h' and hence determine the velocity.
4. To find the value of 'k', measure the actual velocity of flow (V) with the help of a "current meter" and use the following relation :

$$k\frac{V^2}{2g} = \frac{V_{mean}^2}{2g}$$

The value of 'k' varies from 0.9 to 0.99.

Precautions :

1. Note down the readings accurately.
2. A pitot tube should be used preferably in pipes or channels with *shallow water* moving at *high velocity* (as good results are obtained under these conditions).

Table 8. Pitot tube/Current meter – Observations

S. No.	*Velocity head reading 'h'*	*Current meter reading*
1.		
2.		
3.		
4.		

Mean value, 'h' = ... Mean value, current meter = ...

$$\text{Now, mean velocity head,} \quad h = \frac{V_{\text{mean}}^2}{2g}$$

$$V_{\text{mean}} = \ldots\ldots.$$

Again, mean velocity as obtained from current meter reading

$$V = \ldots..$$

∴ Coefficient of the meter,

$$k = \frac{V_{\text{mean}}}{V^2}$$

Conclusion :

EXPERIMENT NO. 9. **To determine C_c (co-efficient of contraction), C_v (co-efficient of velocity) and C_d (co-efficient of discharge) for flow through a circular/round orifice.**

Apparatus :

Orifice apparatus comprises the following :

1. Supply tank provided with;
   (*a*) circular orifice
   (*b*) water inlet pipe
   (*c*) scale and sliding apparatus and
   (*d*) meter rod.
2. Measuring tank.
3. Stop watch.
4. Micrometer contraction gauge.
5. Stand for mounting the supply tank.

Brief theory. It has been observed that when a jet of water leaves an orifice it gets contracted, the maximum contraction takes place at a section slightly on the downstream side of the orifice, where the jet is more or less horizontal. Such a section is known as *vena-contracta.* The ratio of area of the jet at *vena-contracta* to the area of the orifice is known as **co-efficient of contraction** (C_c).

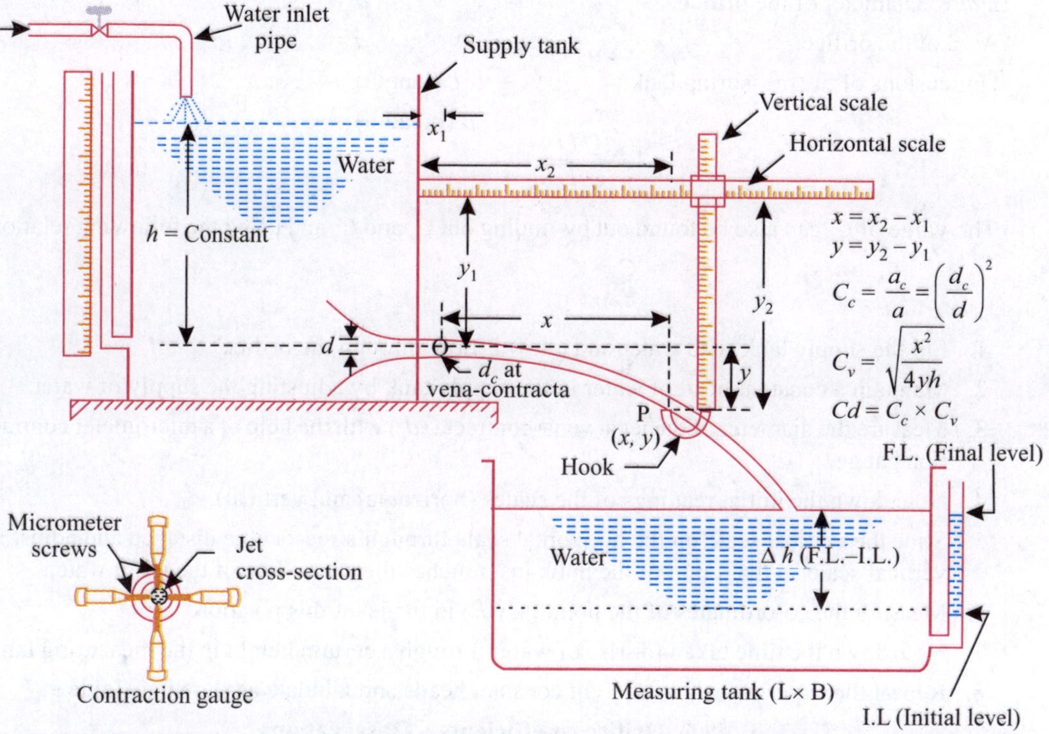

Fig. 7. Determination of co-efficients.

The ratio of actual velocity of the jet at vena-contracta to the theoretical velocity is known as **co-efficient of velocity** (C_v).

For a vertical orifice C_v can be found out by measuring the horizontal and vertical co-ordinates of a point in the jet (Refer Fig. 7.)

If, x = Horizontal ordinate of a point (say P) in the jet, in metres,

y = Vertical ordinate of the same point, in metres, and

h = Head of liquid, in metres;

then, $$C_v = \sqrt{\frac{x^2}{4yh}}$$

The ratio of actual discharge to the theoretical discharge is known as **co-efficient of discharge** (C_d).

The actual discharge may be determined by measuring the water in the measuring tank for a certain period of time 't'.

If, Q = quantity of water collected, in m^3, and

t = time, in seconds;

Then, actual discharge $= \frac{Q}{t}$ m^3/sec.

Again, if, a = Area of the orifice,

then , theoretical discharge $= a \times \sqrt{2gh}$

Data : Diameter of the orifice, d = ...

Area of the orifice, a = ...

Dimensions of the measuring tank : L (length) = ...

B (breadth) = ...

$$\therefore \quad C_d = \frac{Q/t}{a \times \sqrt{2gh}}$$

The value of C_d can also be found out by finding out C_c and C_v and using the following relation:

$$C_d = C_c \times C_v$$

Procedure :

1. Fill the supply tank with water and allow it flow through the orifice.
2. Maintain a constant head of water in the supply tank by adjusting the supply of water.
3. Measure the diameter of the jet at vena-contracta (d_c) with the help of a micrometer contraction gauge.
4. Note down the initial readings of the scales (horizontal and vertical).
5. Slide the vertical scale on the horizontal scale through a reasonable distance and adjust its vertical scale so that point of the hook just touches the centre line of the jet of water.
6. Measure the co-ordinates of the point (say P) in the jet at this position.
7. Note down the time taken for rise of water through a certain height in the measuring tank.
8. Repeat the experiment for different constant heads and tabulate as shown in Table 9.

Table 9. Orifice co-efficients – Observations

S. No.	Head 'h'	Jet dia. 'd_c'	Jet area 'a_c'	$C_c = \frac{a_c}{a}$	$x_2 - x_1 = x$	$y_2 - y_1 = y$	$C_v = \frac{x^2}{\sqrt{4yh}}$	Water level rise Δh in t sec.	$Q = L \times B \times \Delta h$	$\frac{Q}{t}$	$C_d = \frac{Q/t}{a\sqrt{2gh}}$	$C_c = \frac{C_d}{C_v}$	Remarks
1.													
2.													
3.													
4.													
5.													

Specimen calculations : (*i*)

(*ii*)

Conclusion :

Precautions :

1. In each reading head must remain constant.
2. The orifice should be completely opened.
3. The position of *vena-contracta* should be found out accurately.
4. Note down all the readings carefully.

EXPERIMENT NO. 10. **To verify time for the level in a rectangular tank to fall from height H_1 to H_2 when the flow takes place through an orifice.**

Apparatus :

1. A rectangular tank fitted with an orifice and a metre-rod (*i.e.,* graduated scale to observe the readings H_1 and H_2).
2. Callipers—to measure the orifice diameter.
3. Stop watch—to record the timings.
4. Measuring or collecting tank.

Brief theory. When water is discharged from the rectangular tank then the level of water in tank falls from height H_1 to H_2 in T seconds; this time 'T' (theoretical) is given by the relation :

$$T = \frac{2A\,(\sqrt{H_1} - \sqrt{H_2})}{a \times C_d \times \sqrt{2g}}$$

where, A = Cross-sectional (uniform) area of the supply tank,

H_1 = Initial height of water in the tank from centre of the orifice,

H_2 = Final height of water in the tank from the centre of orifice after 'T' seconds,

a = Area of the orifice, and

C_d = Co-efficient of discharge of the orifice.

Procedure :

1. Fill the tank with water to a height H_1 measured from the centre of the orifice.
2. Allow the water to discharge and press the stop watch instantaneously.
3. Note down the time taken to lower the level to H_2.
4. Similarly note down the time for different initial and final heads of water and tabulate as shown in Table 10.

Observations :

Cross-sectional area of the tank, A = ...

Diameter of the orifice, d = ...

Area of the orifice, $a = \frac{\pi}{4} d^2$ . . . . . .

Table 10. Time of emptying a tank – Observations

S. No.	Initial reading H_1	Final reading H_2	Actual time recorded T'	Theoretical time T	Error $(T' - T)$	% Error $\frac{T' - T}{T'} \times 100$	Remarks
1.							
2.							
3.							
4.							
5.							

Specimen calculations : (*i*)

(*ii*)

Conclusion :

Precautions :

1. The orifice should be opened completely.
2. The opening of the orifice and starting of the stop watch should be done simultaneously.
3. All readings should be noted carefully.

***EXPERIMENT NO. 11.* To find the co-efficient of discharge in an external mouthpiece.**

Apparatus :

1. Supply tank (with stand) fitted with an external mouthpiece, water inlet pipe and a metre rod.
2. Collecting/measuring tank.
3. Stop watch (to record time).

Brief theory. When water flows into the plain external mouthpiece (from the supply tank), the flow of water is contracted due to change in the direction of water (while entering into the mouthpiece) and it suddenly expands to fill the mouthpiece resulting in loss of head due to sudden expansion. As a result of this loss the actual velocity of water issuing from the mouthpiece becomes less than the theoretical velocity and hence actual discharge becomes less than the theoretical discharge. The co-efficient of discharge (C_d) is given by the relation :

$$C_d = \frac{\text{Actual discharge}}{\text{Theoretical discharge}} = \frac{Q}{a \times \sqrt{2gH}}$$

where, Q = Actual discharge collected,

H = Head of water, and

a = Area of the plain external mouthpiece.

Procedure

1. Fill the supply tank with water and allow it flow through an external mouthpiece (fitted to the tank).
2. Adjust the supply of water to the tank in such a way that a constant head is maintained.
3. Collect the water from the mouthpiece in the collecting/measuring tank.
4. Note the rise of water level in the tank in a certain period of time.
5. Repeat the experiment for different constant heads and the tabulate the same as shown in Table 11.

Observations :

Length of the measuring tank, $L = \ldots\ldots$

Breadth of the measuring tank, $B = \ldots\ldots$

Area of the external mouthpiece, $a = \ldots\ldots$

Table 11. External mouthpiece – Observations

S. No.	*Head H*	*Rise of water level in the measuring tank Z*	*Time taken, t*	*Discharge collected* $Q = \frac{L \times B \times Z}{t}$	$C_d = \frac{Q}{a \times \sqrt{2gH}}$
1.					
2.					
3.					
4.					
5.					

Mean value of $C_d = \ldots\ldots$

Specimen calculations : (*i*)

(*ii*)

Conclusion :

Precautions :

1. The external mouthpiece should be opened completely.
2. Throughout a reading the head must not change.
3. All readings must be taken and recorded carefully.

***EXPERIMENT NO. 12.* To find the value of *k* and hence coefficient of discharge in the equation $Q = kH^{5/2}$ in right-angled triangular notch.**

Apparatus :

1. A weir tank with baffle plates (to reduce the velocity of approach) fitted with a right-angled triangular notch and a hook-gauge.
2. A collecting/measuring tank.
3. A stop watch (to record time).

Brief theory. The discharge of water through a *triangular notch* under a constant static head H is given by the relation :

$$Q = \frac{8}{15} C_d \sqrt{2g} \tan \frac{\theta}{2} H^{5/2}$$

or,

$$Q = kH^{5/2}$$

where,

$$k = \frac{8}{15} C_d \sqrt{2g} \tan \frac{\theta}{2}$$

$$\left[\begin{array}{l} C_d = \text{Coefficient of discharge, and} \\ \theta = 90° \text{ for a right-angled notch.} \end{array} \right]$$

$\frac{8}{15} C_d \sqrt{2g}$ is almost constant for a given notch.

Procedure :

1. Open the valve (delivery) and allow the water to fill the weir tank till it first touches the apex of the notch.
2. Stop the inflow of water and adjust the pointer of the hook gauge so that it just breaks through the water surface. Note down the reading (initial) on the hook gauge (say H_1).
3. Open the valve and allow the water to pass over the notch for some time (say 2 or 3 minutes) when the head over the notch becomes constant. Note down the reading (final) on the hook gauge (say H_2).
4. Note down the time required to collect a known amount of water is the measuring tank.
5. Repeat the experiment by changing the constant head H_2 and take several readings and tabulate them as shown in the Table 12.

Observations :

Length of the measuring tank, $L = ...$

Breadth of the measuring tank, $B = ...$

Angle of the notch $\theta = 90°$

Initial reading of hook gauge $= H_1$

Table 12. Right-angled triangular notch – Observations

S. No.	*Final hook gauge reading* H_2	*Static head* $H = H_2 - H_1$	*Rise of water level in the measuring tank, 'Z'*	*Time taken,* t	*Discharge collected* $Q = \frac{L \times B \times Z}{t}$	$k = \frac{Q}{H^{5/2}}$	$C_d = \frac{k}{\frac{8}{15}\sqrt{2g}}$
1.							
2.							
3.							
4.							

Mean value of $k = ...$.

Mean value of $C_d = ...$

Specimen calculations : (*i*)

(*ii*)

Conclusion :

Precautions :

1. The head should remain constant throughout a reading.
2. Initial reading of the hook gauge should be taken when water becomes still.
3. While taking the final reading of the hook gauge it may be ensured that water surface is free from eddies or waves.
4. All the readings must be taken and recorded carefully.

***EXPERIMENT NO. 13.* To find the value of '*k*' and hence coefficient of discharge in the equation $Q = kH^{3/2}$ for a rectangular notch.**

Apparatus :

1. A weir tank with baffles.
2. Hook gauge.

3. Rectangular notch.
4. Collecting/measuring tank.
5. Stop watch.

Brief theory. The external discharge (which is always less than the theoretical discharge due to losses) through a rectangular notch is given by the relation :

$$Q = \frac{2}{3} C_d \ L \ \sqrt{2g} H^{3/2}$$

$$= k H^{3/2}$$

where, $k = \frac{2}{3} C_d \ L \ \sqrt{2g}$ which is almost constant for a given notch.

(C_d = Co-efficient of discharge)

Procedure :

1. Open the valve (delivery) and allow the water level to coincide with the sill of the weir.
2. Close the valve and adjust the pointer of the hook gauge in such a way that it touches the water level. Note down the reading (initial) on the hook gauge (say H_1).
3. Open the valve and allow the water to pass over the notch for sometime till the head over the notch becomes constant. Note down the reading (final) on the hook gauge (say H_2).
4. Note down the time required to collect a known amount of water in the collection/measuring tank.
5. Repeat the experiment by changing the constant head H_2 and take several readings and tabulate them as shown in Table 13.

Observations :

Area of the measuring tank, A = ...

Width of the rectangular notch, L = ...

Initial reading of the hook gauge, H_1 = ...

Table 13. Rectangular notch – Observations

S. No.	*Final hook gauge reading* H_2	*Static head* $H = H_2 - H_1$	*Rise of water level in the measuring tank, 'Z'*	*Time taken,* t	*Discharge collected,* $Q = \frac{A \times Z}{t}$	$k = \frac{Q}{H^{3/2}}$	$C_d = \frac{k}{\frac{2}{3} L \sqrt{2g}}$
1.							
2.							
3.							
4.							
5.							

Mean value of k = ...

Mean value of C_d = ...

Specimen calculations : (*i*)

(*ii*)

Conclusion :

Precautions :

1. The head should remain constant throughout a reading.
2. Initial reading of the hook gauge should be taken when water becomes still.
3. While taking the final reading of the hook gauge it may be ensured that water surface is free from eddies or waves.
4. All the readings must be taken and recorded carefully.

EXPERIMENT NO. 14. To plot the flow profile over a broad crested weir and calibrate it.

Apparatus :

1. A glass walled rectangular channel of sufficient length having a broad crested weir constructed sufficiently upstream of the channel outlet.
2. A pointer gauge which can be moved along the length of the channel on top rails provided on the side walls.
3. A regulated water supply.
4. A discharge measurement tank or an orifice meter in the supply line.

Theory. A weir is a device used for measurement of flow in open channels and rivers. It is nothing but a partial obstruction placed across the flow in the channel causing the liquid to backup, upstream of the obstruction, and then flows over it. When the liquid flows over the weir the depth of flow above the crest level of the weir bears a relationship with the discharge over it. Thus the discharge through an open channel can be obtained by measurement of a single parameter *i.e.,* the head of liquid above the crest of the weir.

A weir is said to be "*broad crested*" *if its crest spans all the way across the width of the channel and has substantial crest length along the direction of flow.* The length of the crest should be *greater than three times the maximum head under which the weir is to operate*, so as to ensure that the streamlines become parallel to the surface of the crest and the underside of the nappe adheres to the weir even throughout its length. The upstream edge of the weir is well rounded to prevent the separation of flow and eddy formation so as to minimise the loss of energy.

Fig. 8 shows a broad-crested weir. Let 1 and 2 be the upstream and downstream ends of the weir respectively.

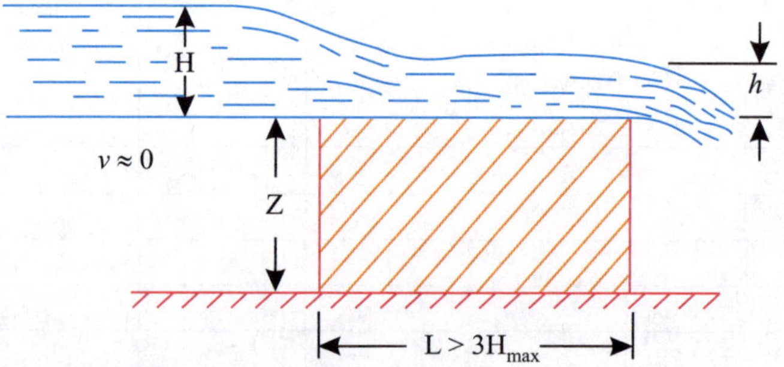

Fig. 8. Broad-crested weir.

Let, H = Head of water in the upstream side of the weir,

h = Head of water on the downstream side of the weir,

v = Velocity of the water on the downstream side of the weir,

L = Length of the weir, and

C_d = Co-efficient of discharge.

Applying Bernoulli's equation at 1 and 2, we get:

$$0 + 0 + H = 0 + \frac{v^2}{2g} + h$$

$\therefore$ $$\frac{v^2}{2g} = H - h$$

or, $$v = \sqrt{2g\,(H - h)}$$

$\therefore$ The discharge over weir,

$$Q = C_d \times \text{area of flow} \times \text{velocity}$$
$$= C_d \times L \times h \times v$$
$$= C_d \times L \times h \times \sqrt{2g\,(H - h)}$$
$$= C_d \times L \times \sqrt{2g}\,\sqrt{Hh^2 - h^3} \qquad ...(i)$$

The discharge will be *maximum*, if $(Hh^2 - h^3)$ is maximum,

or, $$\frac{d}{dh}(Hh^2 - h^3) = 0$$

or, $$2hH - 3h^2 = 0$$

or, $$2H = 3h$$

$\therefore$ $$h = \frac{2}{3}H$$

Substituting the value of h in eqn. (i)

$$Q_{\max} = C_d \times L \times \sqrt{2g}\,\sqrt{H \times (2/3\,H)^2 - (2/3\,H)^3}$$
$$= C_d \times L \times \sqrt{2g}\,\sqrt{\frac{4}{9}H^3 - \frac{8}{27}H^3}$$
$$= C_d \times L \times \sqrt{2g}\,\sqrt{\frac{4}{27}H^3}$$
$$= C_d \times L \times \sqrt{2g} \times \frac{2}{3}H\sqrt{\frac{H}{3}}$$
$$= \frac{2}{3\sqrt{3}}C_d \times L \times \sqrt{2g} \times H^{3/2}$$
$$= 0.3849 \times C_d \times L \times \sqrt{2 \times 9{\cdot}81} \times H^{3/2}$$
$$= 1.705 \times C_d \times L \times H^{3/2}$$

The above equation is not accurate due to the varied assumptions and approximations made while deriving it. Therefore it is necessary to establish experimentally a calibration equations for the weir, having the general form,

$$Q = kH^n$$

where, k and n are constants for a given weir.

This equation can be linearlised by taking logarithm on either side so that.

$$\log Q = \log k + n \log H$$

A plot of log Q *vs* log H will yield a straight line whose intercept on the log Q axis will be equal to k and whose slope corresponds to the exponent n.

Procedure :

1. Measure the length (L), width (B) and height (Z) of the broad crested weir.
2. Take the pointer readings corresponding to the bed level of the channel (Y_0) and the crest level of the weir (H_0).
3. Open the supply valve fully and allow the water to flow in the channel. Let the flow stabilize and allow the water level to become constant.
4. Starting from a section slightly upstream of the weir, move along the length of the weir in the downstream direction measuring the water surface (Y'_x) and corresponding distance from the upstream section (x) at different points right upto a section some distance downstream of the weir. Keep the interval between successive points sufficiently small so as to obtain the correct water surface profile.
5. Measure the discharge (Q_{actual}), with the help of orifice meter or discharge measurement tank.
6. Locate a section upstream of the weir (4 to 5 times the head) where the water surface level has no curvature, and take the water surface level reading (H').
7. Repeat steps 5 and 6 at least eight to ten different openings of the inlet valve, allowing the flow to stabilize before taking the readings.

Observations :

Length of the broad crested weir, L = ...

Width of the broad crested weir, B = ...

Height of the broad crested weir, Z = ...

Pointer gauge reading corresponding to the bed level of the channel = Y_0

Pointer gauge reading corresponding to the crest level of the weir = H_0

A. Observations water surface profile :

Table 14. (A) Broad crested weir – Observations

S. No.	*Distance* x *(cm)*	*Water surface level* Y'_x *(cm)*	*Depth above the bed level* $Y_x = Y'_x - Y_0$ *(cm)*
		Y_x	

B. Observations for calibration of weir :

Table 14. (B) Broad crested weir – Observations

S. No.	*Actual discharge* Q_{actual} *(m³/s)*	*Water level reading* H' *(cm)*	*Head above the weir* H *(cm)*	*Theoretical discharge* $Q_{th.}$ *(m³/S)*	$C_d = \frac{Q_{actual}}{Q_{th.}}$

Calculations :

1. For the first opening of the valve calculate the depth of water (Y_x) above the bed level at each section as

$$Y_x = Y'_x - Y_0$$

2. For all the subsequent value openings perform the following set of calculations :

   (*i*) Head above the weir, $H = H' - H_0$

   (*ii*) Theoretical discharge, $Q_{th} = 1.705\ BH^{3/2}$

   (*iii*) $C_d = \dfrac{Q_{actual}}{Q_{th.}}$

Conclusion :

Precautions :

1. Before measuring the head and discharge allow the head to become constant.
2. Measure the water surface level at a section sufficiently upstream of the weir so that the water surface is horizontal.
3. Take the pointer gauge readings when the tip of the gauge just touches the water surface. To ensure this adjust the gauge such that the tip and its image just coincide on the gauge touching the water surface.

***EXPERIMENT NO. 15.* To determine different regimes of flow by Reynolds' experiment.**

Apparatus :

1. ***Reynolds apparatus*** consisting of :
   (*i*) *Water tank* having a *glass tube* leading out of it; the glass tube has a bell mouth at entrance and a regulating valve at outlet:
   (*ii*) A *dye container* with an arrangement for injecting a fine element of dye at the entrance of the glass tube.
2. A graduated cylinder.
3. A stop watch.

Theory :

Osborne Reynolds in 1883, with the help of a simple experiment discussed below demonstrated the existence of the following two types of flows :

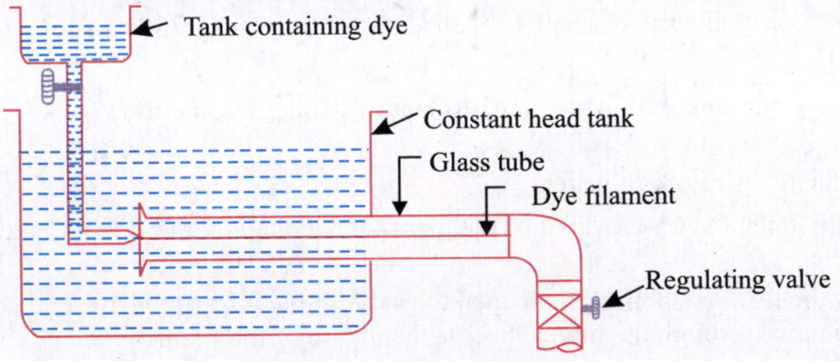

Fig. 9. Reynolds apparatus.

1. Laminar flow (Reynolds number, $Re < 2000$)
2. Turbulent flow (Reynolds number, $Re > 4000$)

   (*Re* between 2000 and 4000 indicates *transition* from laminar to turbulent flow).

Reynolds experiment :

***Apparatus* :**

Refer Fig. 9, Reynolds experiment apparatus consisted essentially of the following :

1. A constant head tank filled with water.
2. A small tank containing dye (sp. weight of dye same as that of water).
3. A horizontal glass tube provided with a bell mouthed entrance.
4. A regulating valve.

Procedure followed :

The water was made to flow from the tank through the glass tube into the atmosphere. The velocity of flow was varied by adjusting valve. The liquid dye was introduced into the bell mouth through a small tube as shown in Fig. 9.

Observations made:

1. When the *velocity* of flow was *low*, the dye remained in the form of a *straight* and *stable filament* passing through the glass tube so steadily that it scarcely seemed to be in motion. This was a case of **laminar flow** as shown in Fig. 10 (*a*).
2. With the increase of velocity a critical state was reached at which the dye filament showed irregularities and began to waver [See Fig. 10 (*b*)]. This shows that the flow is no longer a laminar one. This was a **transitional state.**
3. With further increase in velocity of flow the fluctuations in the filament of dye became more intense and ultimately the dye diffused over the entire cross-section of the tube, due to the intermingling of the particles of the flowing fluid. This was the case of a **turbulent flow** as shown in Fig. 10 (*c*).

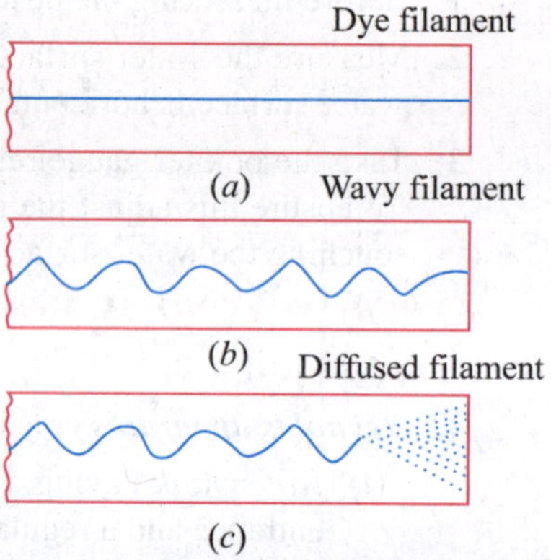

Fig. 10. Appearance of dye filament: (a) laminar flow, (b) transition flow, and (c) turbulent flow.

On the basis of his experiment Reynolds discovered that :

(*i*) In case of **laminar flow :** The loss of pressure head $\propto$ velocity.

(*ii*) In case of **turbulent flow :** The loss of head is approximately $\propto V^2$.

[More exactly the loss of head $\propto V^n$ where n varies from 1.75 to 2.0]

Procedure :

1. Fill the water tank with water and allow it to stand for some time so that the water comes to rest.
2. Note the temperature of water.
3. Partially open the outlet valve of the glass tube and allow the flow to take place at a very low rate.
4. Allow the flow to stabilize, then open the valve at the inlet of the dye injector and allow the dye to move through the tube. Observe the nature of the filament.
5. Measure the discharge by collecting water in the graduated cylinder for a certain interval of time.
6. Repeat the steps 3 and 5 for different discharges (at least three readings for each regime of flow *i.e.*, laminar, transition and turbulent).
7. Again note the temperature of water.

Observations :

Mean temperature of water, θ = ... °C

Kinematic viscosity of water, ν = ...

Diameter of glass tube, D = ...

Table 15. Flow regimes – Observations

S. No.	*Discharge measurement*			*Velocity V (m/s)*	*Reynolds No. Re*	*Observed flow regimes (Laminar, transition, turbulent)*
	Rise of water level in the graduated cylinder, h(m)	*t (sec.)*	*Q (m^3/s)*			

Calculations : Perform the following calculations for each set of readings :

(*i*) Discharge,

$$Q = \frac{\text{Volume of water collected in discharge tank}}{\text{Time of collection}} = \frac{Ah}{t}$$

where, A = Cross-sectional area of the graduated cylinder, m^2.

(*ii*) Velocity,

$$V = \frac{Q}{\frac{\pi}{4} \times D^2} = \frac{4Q}{\pi D^2}$$

(*iii*) Reynolds number,

$$Re = \frac{VD}{\gamma}$$

- Plot V *vs* Re

Conclusion :

Precautions :

1. Before starting the experiment allow the water in the tank to stand for some time.
2. After each change in the valve opening allow the flow to stabilize before taking the readings.
3. Change in velocity for each consecutive reading should be very gradual.
4. The glass pipe should run full.

***EXPERIMENT NO. 16.* To find the value of critical velocity in pipes by Reynolds experiments.**

Apparatus :

1. Reynolds apparatus consisting of piping system.
2. Measuring/collecting tank.
3. Differential manometer.
4. Stop watch.

Brief theory. The loss of head (h_f) in a pipe is obtained by measuring the fall in pressure (by using a manometer) over a known length of pipe. The velocity of flow is obtained by collecting the discharge in a measuring tank over a known time; by using the relation :

$$\text{Velocity } (v) = \frac{\text{Discharge per sec. } (Q)}{\text{Cross-sectional area of the pipe } (A)}$$

The loss of head is obtained of several velocities starting from exceedingly small value. The result obtained is plotted with velocity v as the base and h_f as the ordinate (Fig. 11). The point where the graph changes from straight line curve will give the critical velocity.

Procedure:

1. Open the supply valve and allow the water to flow through one pipe of which the diameter is measured/ noted.
2. Connect the two rubber pipe leads from the manometer to pad-locks on the pipe at certain distance apart (distance actually measured).
3. Admit water through pipe to the rubber leads and adjust the supply of water by the supply valve till a suitable reading is available on the manometer.
4. Read the loss of head on the manometer. Collect the water discharging from the pipe in the measuring tank and note the rise of water level in tank.

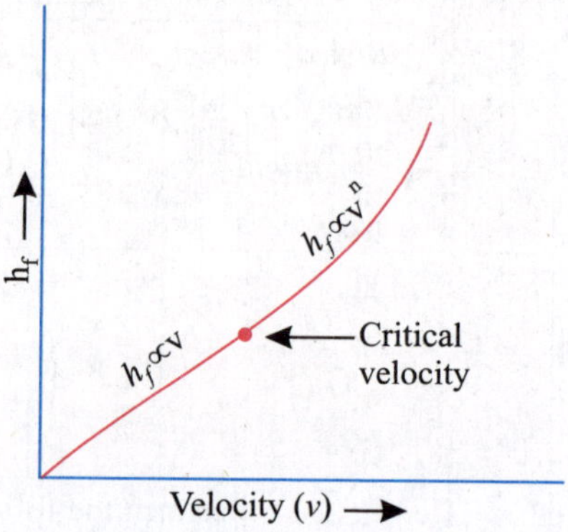

Fig. 11

5. Repeat the experiment at different velocities by varying the rate of flow of water in the pipe and tabulate the readings shown in the Table 16. Use these results to plot a curve (between h_f and v) as shown in Fig. 11. *The point where the graph changes from straight line to curve will give the critical velocity.*

Observations:

Length of pipe, l = ...

Diameter of the pipe, D = ...

Area of the pipe, $A = \frac{\pi}{4} D^2$ = ...

Length of the measuring tank, L = ...

Width of the measuring tank, B = ...

Table 16. Critical velocity in pipes – Observations

S. No.	*Loss of head (manometer reading), h_f*	*Rise of water level in the measuring tank, h*	*Time taken, t*	*Discharge, $Q = \frac{L \times B \times h}{t}$*	*Velocity $= \frac{Q}{A}$*
1.					
2.					
3.					
4.					
5.					

Specimen calculations : (*i*) Critical velocity = ...

(*ii*)

Precautions : All readings must be taken and recorded carefully.

EXPERIMENT NO. 17. To determine the friction factor for pipes of different sizes.

Apparatus :

1. Pipes of different sizes with rectangular valves at their ends, fed by the mainline through a common inlet valve at one end and outflow at the other end.
2. An inverted U-tube manometer (with water as manometric liquid) which can be connected between the two ends of any pipe.
3. Discharge measuring tank.
4. Measuring flask.
5. Stop watch.

Theory :

In case of flow through pipes, the head loss due to pipe friction is a major loss. Based on experimental observations it has been found that the loss due to friction :

(*i*) depends on pipe roughness in case of turbulent flows;

(*ii*) is directly proportional to the wetted area;

(*iii*) varies inversely as some power of the pipe diameter;

(*iv*) varies as some power of the velocity.

Combining these factors, the equation for frictional loss (h_f) is given by :

$$h_f = \frac{fLV^2}{D \times 2g}$$

where,
f = Darcy-Weisbach friction factor,
L = Length of the pipe,
V = Velocity of flow, and
D = Diameter of pipe.

Procedure:

1. Note the length of each pipe between manometer tappings, diameters of all the pipes and the size of the collecting tank.
2. Check the manometer for bubbles and remove if any.
3. Keeping the outlet valves closed, open the main inlet valve fully.
4. Open the outlet valve of one of the pipes partially, wait for a few seconds so that the flow becomes steady.
5. Note the manometer reading in both the limbs of the manometers (h_1 and h_2).
6. Make discharge measurements by measuring the level rise (z) in the discharge measurement tank for a particular interval of time (t) or if the rate of flow is very less, collect the water in the *measuring flask* for a particular interval of time.
7. Repeat the process for atleast six to eights different openings of the outlet valve.
8. Repeat steps 4 to 7 for all the pipes.

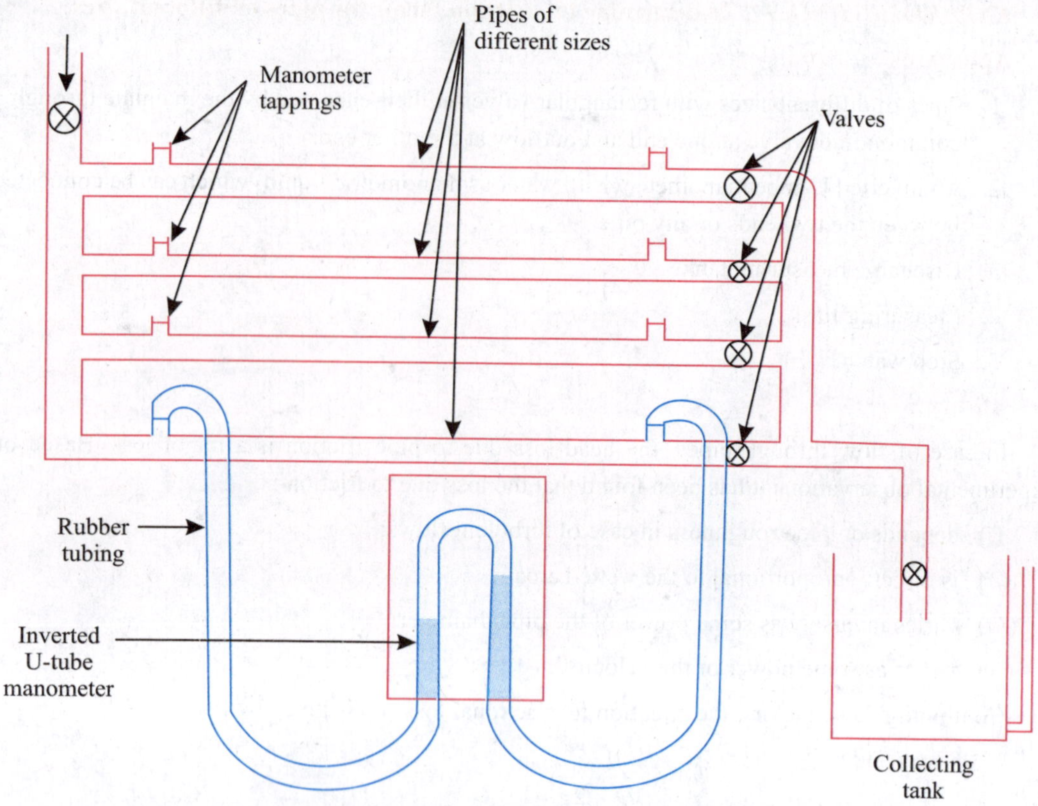

Fig. 12. Apparatus for determining friction factors.

Observations :

Length of pipelines : $L_1 = \ldots ; L_2 = \ldots ; L_3 = \ldots ; L_4 = \ldots$

Areas of cross-section of pipes : $A_1 = \ldots ; A_2 = \ldots ; A_3 = \ldots ; A_4 = \ldots$

Area of cross-section of the discharge measurement tank, $A_t = \ldots$

Temperature of water, $\theta = \ldots$ °C

Kinematic viscosity of water, $\nu = \ldots$

Table 17. Friction factor for pipes – Observations

S. No.	Pipe No.	*Manometer readings*		*Head loss* h_f *(cm)*	*Discharge measurement*			*Velocity V (m/s)*	*Friction factor, f*
		h_1 *(cm)*	h_2 *(cm)*		*Z (cm)*	*t (sec.)*	Q_{actual} *(m^3/s)*		
1.									
2.									
3.									
4.									
5.									

Calculations : For each pipe make the following calculations :

1. Discharge, $Q = \dfrac{\text{Volume collected in the discharge measuring tank}}{\text{Time of collection}} = \dfrac{A_t \times Z}{t}$

2. Velocity, $V = \dfrac{Q}{A}$, where A is the cross-sectional area of the pipe

3. Friction factor, $f = h_f \times \dfrac{D \times 2g}{LV^2}$

If the manometric liquid used is not water, then convert the manometric difference in terms of head of water to get the head loss h_f.

4. Reynolds number, $Re = \dfrac{VD}{\nu}$

5. Repeat the calculations of steps 1 to 4 for all values of discharges.

• Plot the following for each pipe :

(*i*) h_f / L vs V on log-log graph paper.

(*ii*) h_f vs D on log-log graph paper.

(*iii*) h_f vs Re on log-log graph paper.

Conclusions :

Precautions :

1. Ensure that no air bubble is present in the manometer.
2. Ensure that there is no leakage from any pipe fitting.
3. Use a sensitive manometer.
4. Keep the time for discharge measurement sufficiently large especially for low flows.

***EXPERIMENT NO. 18.* To determine the velocity distribution in a given pipeline and obtain the energy and momentum connection factors.**

Apparatus :

1. A straight pipeline having a graduated scale connected at the section where velocity distribution is to be obtained.
2. A Prandtl-Pitot tube with a differential manometer connected to it inserted in the pipeline at the section where the velocity distribution is to be obtained.
3. A pointer connected to Prandtl-Pitot tube such that it moves along the graduated scale on moving the tube.
4. A regulated water supply.
5. A discharge measurement unit in the pipeline (*viz.* venturimeter with manometer).

Theory :

While deriving Bernoulli's equation it is assumed that the velocity distribution across a single stream tube is uniform. But if there is an appreciable variation in the velocity distribution (on account of viscous and boundary resistance) correction factors α and β have to be applied to obtain the exact amount of kinetic energy or momentum available at a given cross-section.

• **Kinetic energy correction factor (α) :**

'Kinetic energy correction factor' is defined as the ratio of the kinetic energy of flow per second basd on actual velocity across a section to the kinetic energy of flow per second based on average velocity across the same section. It is denoted by α. Mathematically,

$$\alpha = \frac{\text{Kinetic energy per second based on actual velocity}}{\text{Kinetic energy per second based on average velocity}}$$

Refer to Fig. 13.

$$\alpha = \frac{1}{A}\int\left(\frac{V}{\overline{V}}\right)^3 dA \qquad ...(1)$$

where, $\overline{V}$ = Average velocity at the section LL,

V = Local or point or actual velocity,

dA = Elementary area, and

A = Area of cross-section of the pipe.

$\alpha = 1$ *for uniform velocity distribution and tends to become greater than 1 as the distribution of velocity becomes less and less uniform.*

α = 1.02 to 1.15 for *turbulent flows.*

α = 2 for *laminar flow.*

It may be noted that in most of the fluid mechanics computations, α is taken as 1 without introducing much error, since the *velocity is a small percentage of the total head.*

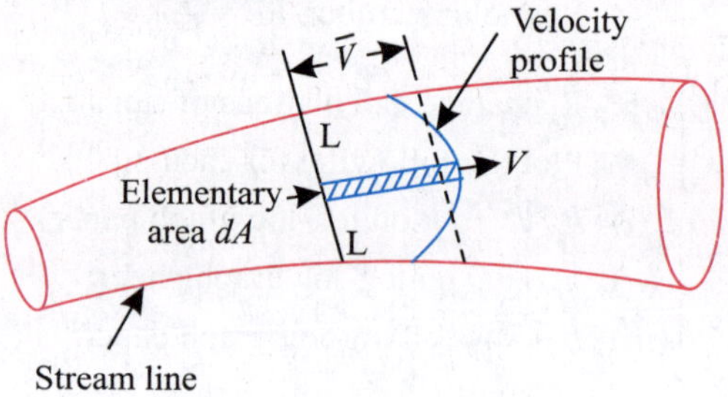

Fig. 13

- **Momentum correction factor (β)**

'*Momentum correction factor' is defined as the ratio of momentum of the flow per second based on actual velocity to the momentum of the flow per second based on average velocity across a section.* It is denoted by β. Mathematically,

$$\beta = \frac{\text{Momentum per second based on actual velocity}}{\text{Momentum per second based on average velocity}}$$

Refer to Fig. 13.

$$\beta = \frac{1}{A}\int\left(\frac{V}{\overline{V}}\right)^2 dA \qquad ...(2)$$

β = 1 for *uniform flow,*

β = 1.01 to 1.07 for *turbulent flow in pipes,* and

$\beta = \frac{4}{3}$ = 1.33 for *laminar flow in pipes.*

The value of β may be greater for open channel flow.

In most cases, β is taken as 1.

Since majority of the flow situations are turbulent in character, the usual practice is to assign *unit value* to α and β.

- The velocity distribution across a section can be obtained with the help of a Pitot-tube, which is one of the most accurate devices for velocity measurement. It consists of a glass tube in the form of a 90° bend of short length open at both its ends. It is placed in the flow with its bent leg directed upstream so that a stagnation point is created immediately in front of the opening (Fig. 14). The kinetic energy at this point gets converted into pressure energy causing the liquid to rise in the vertical limb, to a height equal to the stagnation pressure.

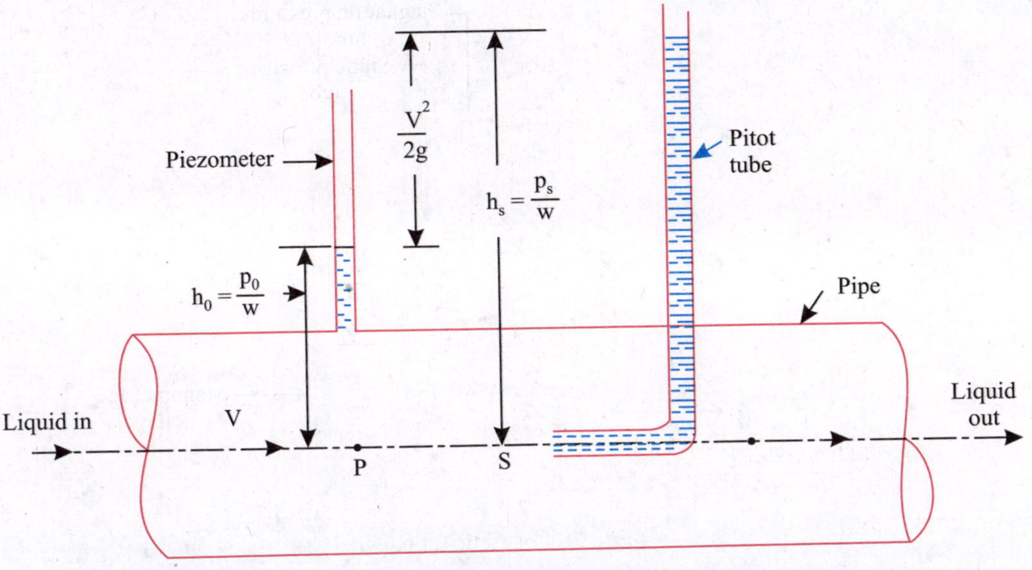

Fig. 14. Pitot tube.

Applying Bernoulli's equation between stagnation point (S) and a point (P) in the undistributed flow at the same horizontal plane, we get :

$$\frac{p_0}{w} + \frac{V^2}{2g} = \frac{p_s}{w}, \quad \text{or, } h_0 + \frac{V^2}{2g} = h_s$$

or, $$V = \sqrt{2g\,(h_s - h_0)}, \quad \text{or, } \sqrt{2g\,\Delta h} \quad \text{...(3)}$$

where, p_0 = Pressure at point '*P*' *i.e.,* static pressure,

V = Velocity at point '*P*' *i.e.,* free flow velocity,

p_s = Stagnation pressure at point 'S', and

Δh = Dynamic pressure

= Difference between stagnation pressure head (h_s) and static pressure head (h_0).

The height of liquid rise in the Pitot tube indicates the stagnation pressure head. The static pressure head may be measured separately with a piezometer (Fig. 14).

Both the static pressure as well as stagnation pressure can be measured in a device known as **Pitot-static tube** (Fig. 15).

It consists of two concentric Pitot-tubes with an annular space in between as shown in the figure. The outer tube has additional two or more holes drilled perpendicular to the direction of flow and thus the liquid level in it gives the static head, while the inner tube works as a normal Pitot-tube. If a differential manometer is connected to the tubes of a Pitot-static tube it will measure the dynamic pressure head.

If y is the manometric difference, then

$$\Delta h = y\left(\frac{S_m}{S} - 1\right)$$

where, S_m = Specific gravity of manometric liquid, and

S = Specific gravity of the liquid flowing through the pipe.

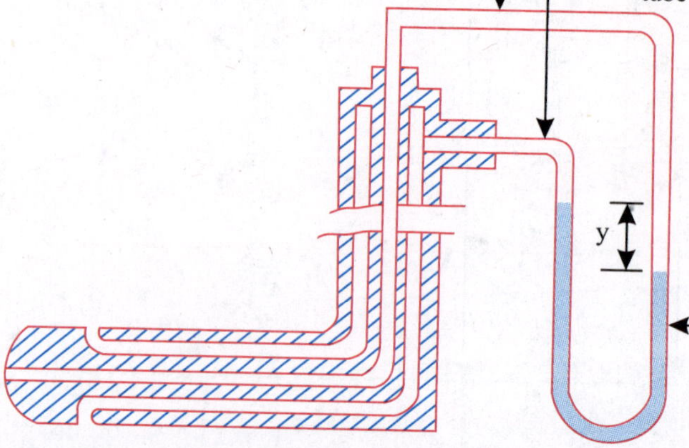

Fig. 15. Pitot-static tube.

When a Pitot-tube is placed in the fluid stream the flow along its outer surface gets accelerated and causes the static pressure to decrease. Also the stem, which is perpendicular to the flow direction, tends to produce an excess pressure head. In order to take these effects into account eqn. (3) is modified to give the actual velocity as;

$$V = C\sqrt{2g\Delta h} \quad ...(4)$$

where, C = A corrective co-efficient which takes into account the effect of stem and bent leg.

The most commonly used form of Pitot-static tube known as the *Prandtl-Pitot tube* is so designed that the effect of stem and bent leg cancel each other *i.e.*, $C = 1$.

Procedure :

1. Lower the Prandtl tube until it touches the lower wall of the pipe and note the pointer reading on the scale (G_1). Then raise it until it touches the upper wall of the pipe and note the reading (G_2).
2. Open the inlet valve fully, keeping the outlet valve closed and remove air bubbles, if any, from the manometric tube.
3. Open the outlet valve and allow the flow to take place for some time.
4. Measure the discharge (Q) through the pipeline.
5. Note the manometric readings (h_1 and h_2) and the pointer reading (G) at different positions of the Prandtl tube along the pipe diameters; the interval between successive poritions of the Prandtl tube must be kept small *i.e.,* 2–5 mm.
6. Repeat steps 3 to 5 for different openings of the valve.

Observations:

Diameter of the Pitot-static tube, d = ...

Diameter of the pipe, D = ...

Pointer reading corresponding to the lower wall of the pipe, G_1 = ...

Pointer reading corresponding to the upper wall of the pipe, G_2 = ...

Specific gravity of manometric liquid, S_m = ...

Specific gravity of liquid flowing in the pipe, S = ...

Table 18. Velocity distribution in a pipeline – Observations

S. No.	Set. No.	Pointer reading, G (cm)	Mamometer readings			Velocity $\bar{u}$ (cm/s)
			h_1 (cm)	h_2 (cm)	y (diff.). (cm)	

Calculations :

1. Calculate the pointer reading corresponding to the pipe, $G_0 = \dfrac{G_1 + G_2}{2}$
2. Corresponding to each pointer reading (G) calculate the distance of the stagnation point from the centre of the pipe, $z = G - G_0$ (negative values being below the centre point).
3. Calculate velocity (V) using eqn. (3) for all readings and plot the graph of z *vs* V.
4. Divide the whole cross-sectional area of the pipe into a number of parts as shown in Fig. 16.
5. Calculate the area of each part $dA = \pi(r_2^2 - r_1^2)$.
6. Determine the mean velocity ($\bar{V}$) for each elemental area dA *i.e.,* corresponding to $z = \dfrac{(r_1 + r_2)}{2}$ from the graph and then calculate VdA, V^2dA, V^3dA.
7. Calculate $\Sigma V^3 dA$ and $\Sigma V^2 dA$ and hence α and β using eqns. (1) and (2).
8. Calculate the average velocity of flow for the pipe section, $\bar{V} = \dfrac{Q}{A}$

Precautions :

1. Before taking the reading, check that there is no air bubble in the Pitot-tube or manometer.
2. The Pitot-tube should be placed at a sufficient distance from the regulating valve to avoid turbulence.
3. Check that the holes of the Pitot-tube are not blocked.

EXPERIMENT NO. 19. **To obtain the velocity distribution in an open channel with the help of current meter.**

Apparatus :

1. A glass walled flume of rectangular section having honeycombed walls at entrance.
2. A regulated water supply.
3. A miniature current meter.
4. A stop watch and a scale.

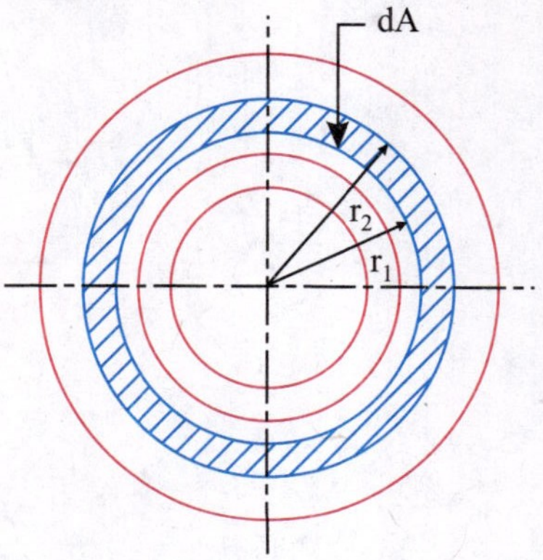

Fig. 16

Theory :

In open channels (as in the case of pipe flow) velocity does not remain constant throughout the section. Here in addition to the *retardation of velocity* at the boundaries there is retardation at the free surface also. This is due to the effects of surface tension and air resistance. In the vertical plane the velocity is minimum at the bottom and increases as we move towards the free surface, attaining a maximum value at a certain distance below the free surface (at 0.05 to 0.25 times the flow depth) after which it decreases upto the free surface (Fig. 17).

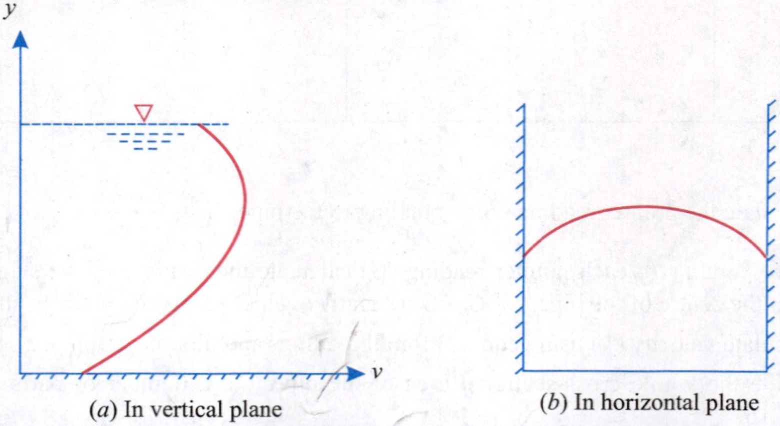

Fig. 17. Velocity distribution in a rectangular channel.

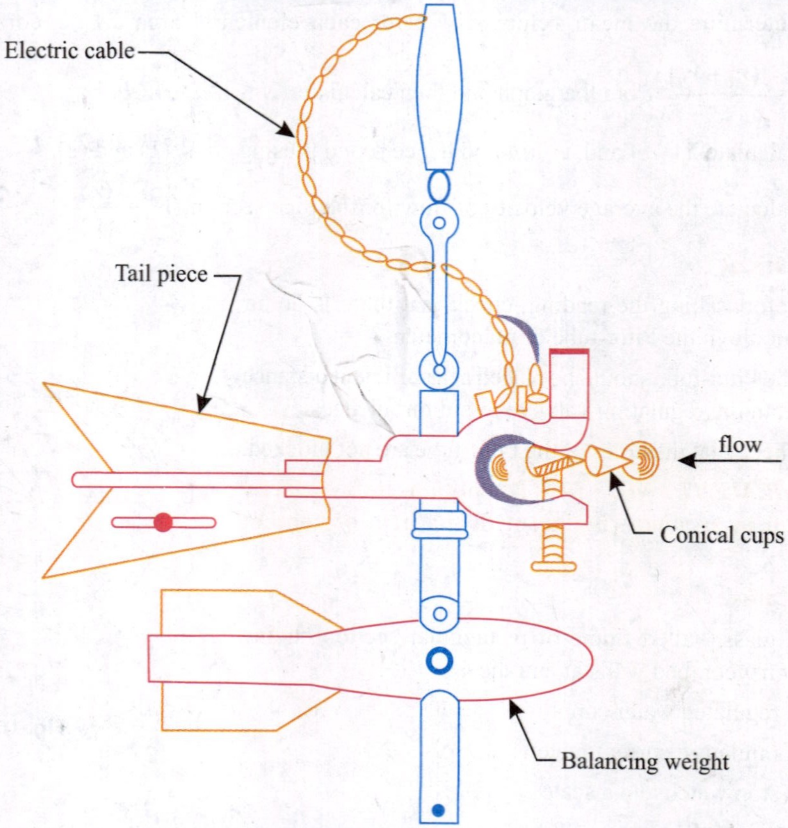

Fig. 18. Cup type current meter.

A **current meter** is *an instrument used to measure the velocity of flow at a required point in the flowing stream.* In general it consists of a *wheel or revolving element containing blades or cups, and a tail on which flat vanes or fins are fixed.* The current meters according to the shape of the revolving element, may be classified as follows :

(*i*) Cup type (*ii*) Screw type or propeller type.

In a *Cup type current meter* (Fig. 18) the wheel or revolving element has the form of a series of conical cups, mounted on a spindle. The spindle is held vertical at right angle to the direction of flow.

In a *screw or propeller current meter* (Fig. 19) the revolving element consists of a shaft, with its axis parallel to the direction of flow, which carries a number of curved vanes (or propeller blades) mounted on the periphery of the shaft. This type of meter is more sensitive than cup because it gives higher r.p.m. for the same velocity of flow.

In order to measure the velocity of flow, meter is submerged under water and motion of water in the stream activates it, driving the wheel (or rotatory elements) at a *speed proportional to the velocity of flow.* An electric current is passed from the battery to the wheel by means of wire. The rotation of wheel makes and breaks the electric circuit, which causes an electric bell to ring. Thus by counting the ringing of bell, the rotations of the wheel and hence the velocity of flowing water is obtained.

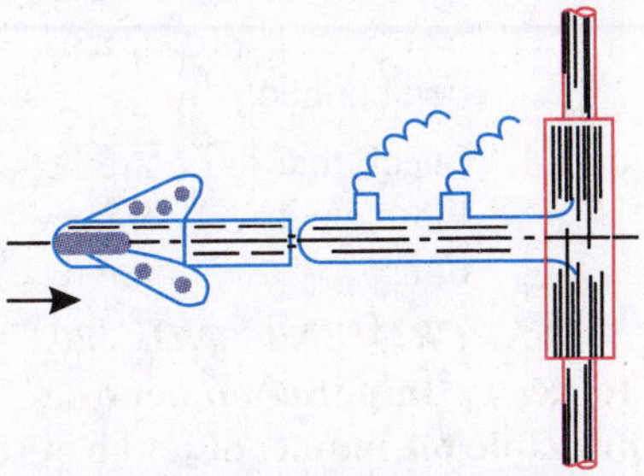

Fig. 19. Screw or propeller type current meter.

Procedure :

1. Open the supply valve fully and allow the maximum discharge to take place. Let the flow stabilize for some time.
2. Divide the channel along its width into three (or more) sections.
3. Lower the current meter along the centre line of any one section right-up to the bottom of the channel with its rotating element facing the upstream. Switch on the revolution counter and note the number of the revolutions (N) for a certain time (t).
4. Take a number of readings by placing the current meter at different suitably spaced level along the centre line of the section.
5. Repeat steps 3 and 4 for all the sections.

Observations :

Table 19. Velocity distribution in an open channel – Observations

S. No.	*Section-I*			*Section-II*			*Section-III*		
	Rev., N	*Time, t (secs.)*	*Vel. (m/s)*	*Rev., N*	*Time, t (secs.)*	*Vel. (m/s)*	*Rev. (N)*	*Time, t (secs.)*	*Vel. (m/s)*

- Plot the velocity *vs* depth graph of flow for all three sections.

Result/Conclusion :

Precautions :

1. While immersing the current meter in water the rotating element (*i.e.*, propeller/cups) should face upstream.
2. Readings should be taken after the flow becomes steady.
3. Readings should be taken at suitably spaced points along the vertical direction so that the correct velocity profile may be obtained.
4. Check that there are no loose electrical connections.

EXPERIMENT NO. 20.

To verify Impulse-momentum principle for impact of jet on a stationary vane.

Apparatus : Refer to Fig. 20.

The apparatus consists of a pipe with nozzle at one end and a regulating valve at the other end, a vane with an arrangement for measuring the force of jet coming on it (either a lever arm with a hanger for weight at one end or a platform for directly putting weight on it). The vane and nozzle are enclosed in a transparent container such that the jet strikes the vane centrally. The container has an outlet leading to a discharge measurement tank.

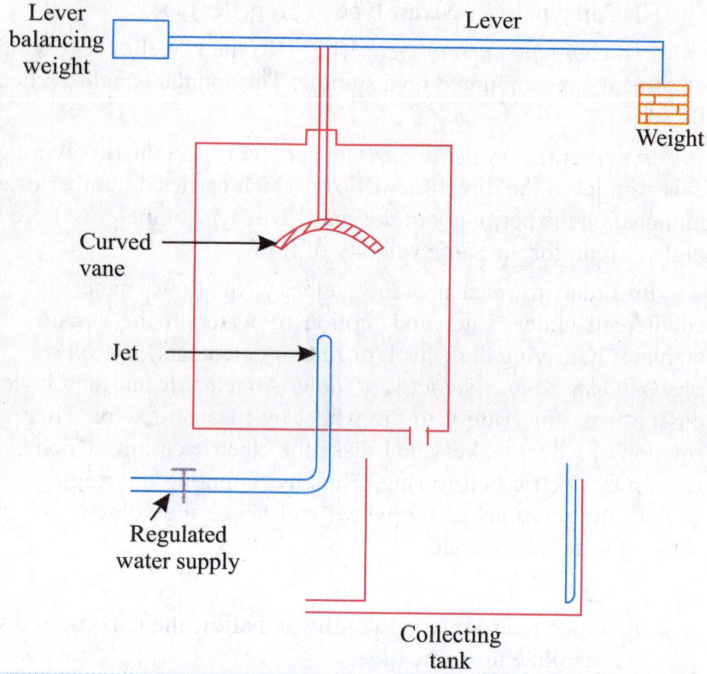

Fig. 20. Schematic arrangement of apparatus for verification of impulse-momentum principle.

Theory :

The **impulse-momentum equation** is one of the basic tools (other being Continuity and Bernoulli's equations) for the solution of flow problems. Its application leads to the solution of problems in fluid mechanics which cannot be solved by energy principles alone. Sometimes it is used in conjunction with the energy equation to obtain complete solution of engineering problems.

The momentum equation is based on the *law of conservation of momentum* or *momentum principle* which states as follows :

"*The net force acting on a mass of fluid is equal to the change in momentum of flow per unit time in that direction.*"

As per Newton's second law of motion,

$$F = ma$$

where, m = Mass of fluid,

F = Force acting on the fluid, and

a = Acceleration (acting in the same direction as F)

But acceleration, $$a = \frac{dv}{dt}$$

$$\therefore \quad F = m \cdot \frac{dv}{dt} = \frac{d\,(mv)}{dt}$$

('*m*' is taken inside the differential, being constant)

This equation is known as *momentum principle.* It can also be written as :

$$F \,.\, dt = d\,(mv)$$

This equation is known as **Impulse-momentum equation.** It may be stated as follows:

"The impulse of a force F acting on a fluid mass 'm' in a short interval of time dt is equal to the change of momentum d (mv) in the direction of force."

The impulse-momentum equation are often called simply momentum equations.

Consider a fluid jet striking a stationary curved plate (smooth) at the centre as shown in Fig. 20. The jet after striking the plate comes out with the same velocity, in the tangential direction of the curved plate.

Component of velocity V in the direction of jet $= -V\cos\theta$

(– ve sign indicates that the velocity at the outlet is in a direction *opposite* to that of the fluid jet).

Applying impulse-momentum equation, we have :

Force exerted by the jet (in the direction of jet),

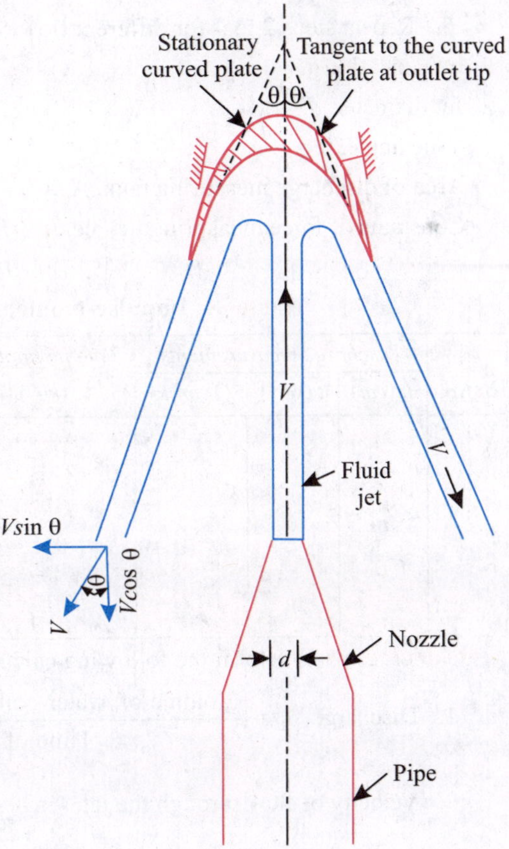

Fig. 21

$$F_y = \rho a V (V_{1y} - V_{2y})$$

where, ρ = Mass density of the fluid,

a = Cross-sectional area of the jet $= \frac{\pi}{4} d^2$ (d = diameter of the jet),

V = Velocity of the jet,

V_{1y} = Initial velocity in the direction of jet $= V$

V_{2y} = Final velocity in the direction of jet $= -V\cos\theta$

$$F_y = \rho a V [V - (-V\cos\theta)] = \rho a V (V + V\cos\theta)$$

or $$F_y = F_{th.} = \rho a V^2 (1 + \cos\theta)$$

Procedure :

1. Note the jet diameter (d), vane angle (θ), constants of force measuring device and dimensions of the discharge measurement tank.
2. Open the regulating valve and allow a low flow jet to impinge on the vane displacing it from its position.

3. Apply external weights to bring back the vane to equilibrium position and note the total weight.
4. Measure the discharge by measuring the water level rise (h) in the discharge measurement tank for a particular time (t).
5. Repeat steps 2 to 4 for different flow rates.

Observations :

Jet diameter, $d = \ldots\ldots$

Vane angle, $\theta = \ldots\ldots$

Area of discharge measuring tank, A = ...

Constants of force measuring device, (*i*)

(*ii*)

Table 20. Impulse-momentum Principle – Observations

S. No.	*Discharge measurements*			*Weights applied,* (kg_f)	*Actual force,* F_{actual} (kg_f)	*Theoretical force,* $F_{th.}$ (kg_f)	*% Error*
	h (cm)	*t (sec.)*	Q (m^3/s)				

Calculations : Perform the following calculations for each set of reading :

1. Discharge, $Q = \dfrac{\text{Volume of water collected in discharge tank}}{\text{Time of collection}} = \dfrac{A \times h}{t}$
2. Velocity of flow through the jet, $V = \dfrac{Q}{\dfrac{\pi}{4} \times d^2}$
3. $F_{th.} = \rho A V^2 (1 + \cos\theta)$
4. Calculate the actual force F_{actual} using the weights applied.
5. Calculate the % error $= \dfrac{F_{th.} - F_{actual}}{F_{th.}} \times 100$

Result/Conclusion :

- Plot the graph of $F_{th.}$ vs F_{actual}.

Precautions :

1. The discharge should be changed gradually so as not to imbalance the vane suddenly.
2. Before taking the readings ensure that the vane is perfectly and freely balanced.

***EXPERIMENT NO. 21.* To verify experimentally the theoretical relationship between the conjugate depths of a hydraulic jump and to determine the various elements.**

Apparatus :

1. A glass walled rectangular channel of sufficient length equipped with head and tail gates.
2. A pointer gauge which can be moved along the length of the channel on top rails provided on the side walls.

3. A regulated water supply with a discharge measurement unit (*i.e.,* orifice meter or venturimeter) in the supply line.

Theory :

In an open channel when rapidly flowing stream abruptly changes to slowly flowing stream, a distinct rise or jump in the elevation of liquid surface takes place, this *phenomenon* is known as **'*hydraulic jump*'** (which is analogous to shock wave in compressible fluids). The hydraulic jump *converts kinetic energy of stream rapidly flowing into potential energy.* Due to this there is a *loss of kinetic energy.* At the place where hydraulic jump occurs *rollers of turbulent water* (eddying turbulences) form, which *cause dissipation of energy.* A hydraulic jump occurs in practice at the toe of *spillways* or *below a sluice gate where the velocity is very high.*

The hydraulic jump is also known as a **'*standing wave*'** because it is, in essence, a wave which is stationary (*i.e.,* at stand-still) at one place. Such a standing wave is shown in Fig. 22.

The hydraulic jump can be analysed by the continuity and momentum equations between the pre-jump and post-jump sections. On analysing the hydraulic jump in a rectangular channel with horizontal bed (Fig. 22) a relationship between pre-jump (or initial) depth y_1 and the post (or sequent) depth y_2 is obtained as follows :

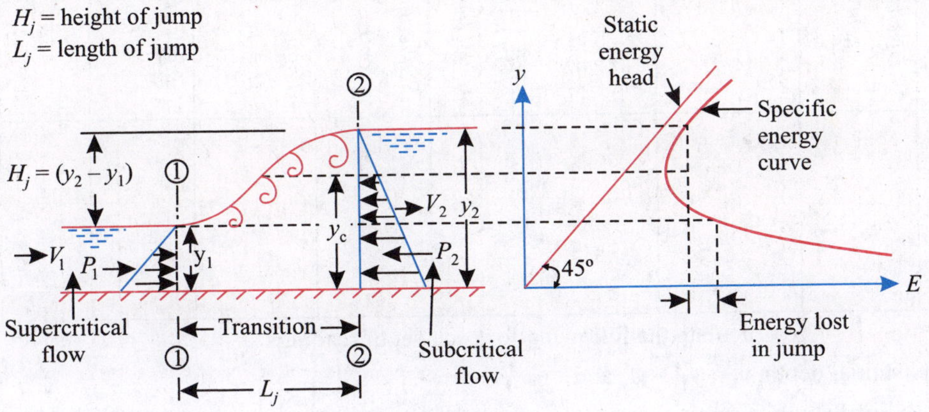

Fig. 22. Hydraulic jump.

$$\frac{y_1}{y_2} = \frac{1}{2}\left[\sqrt{1 + 8\,(F_{r1})^2} - 1\right] \quad ...(1)$$

where, $F_{r1} = \dfrac{V_1}{\sqrt{gy_1}}$ = Froude's number corresponding to the pre-jump depth.

The other *elements* of the jump are :

Height of jump, $H_j = y_2 - y_1$ ...(2)

Length of jump, $L_j \simeq 5H_j$ ...(3)

Loss of energy head occurring in the jump, $E_L = \dfrac{(y_2 - y_1)^3}{4\,y_1 y_2}$ ...(4)

Procedure :

1. Take pointer gauge reading corresponding to the bed level of the channel (y_0).
2. Open the supply valves fully and allow the water to flow in the channel. Allow the flow to stabilize, and measure the discharge Q_{actual} with the help of orifice meter.

3. Adjust the depth of flow with the help of head gate such that it is less than the critical depth *i.e.*, $F_{r1} > 1$.
4. Adjust the height of the tail gate to set up a hydraulic jump approximately midway along the channel.
5. Let the jump stabilize and take the pointer readings corresponding to the water surface just upstream (y_1') and downstream (y_2') of the jump.
6. Measure the length of the jump L_j.
7. Repeat steps 3 to 6 for different values of F_{r1} always keeping it greater than one by adjusting the opening of the head gate.

Observations :

Width of the channel, $B = \ldots.$

Pointer gauge reading corresponding to bed level, $y_0 = \ldots.$

Table 21. Hydraulic jump – Observations

S. No.	*Discharge* Q *(m³/s)*	*Pointer gauge readings*		*Initial depth* y_1 *(cm)*	*Sequent depth* y_2 *(cm)*	*Height of jump* $H_j = (y_2 - y_1)$	*Length of jump* L_j *(cm)*	$(y_2/y_1)_{actual}$	$(y_2/y_1)_{th.}$
		y_1' (cm)	y_2' (cm)						

Calculations : Calculate the following for each set of readings :

1. Initial depth, $y_1 = y_1' - y_0$, and
   Final depth, $y_2 = y_2' - y_0$
2. $\left(\dfrac{y_2}{y_1}\right)_{actual}$ using y_1 and y_2 calculated above.
3. $F_{r1} = \dfrac{Q}{B\sqrt{(g\,y_1^3)}}$
4. Calculate $\left(\dfrac{y_2}{y_1}\right)_{th.}$ using eqn. (1) and compare with the actual value obtained in step 2.
5. $H_j = y_2 - y_1$
6. $E_L = \dfrac{(y_2 - y_1)^3}{4\,y_1\,y_2}$

- Plot the following curves :

(*i*) y_2/y_1 *vs* F_{r_1}

(*ii*) L/y_2 *vs* F_{r_1}

(*iii*) E_L *vs* F_{r_1}

Conclusions :

Precautions :

1. Pointer gauge readings must be taken only after the jump stabilizes.
2. Pointer gauge readings upstream and downstream of the jump should be taken at the sections where the water surface is tranquil.

***EXPERIMENT NO. 22.* To visualize and plot the pattern of flow around an object in a fluid stream using Hele-Shaw apparatus.**

Apparatus :

1. Hele-Shaw apparatus.
2. The object around which the flow pattern is to be determined.
3. Dye, tracing paper and water supply.

The Hele-Shaw apparatus consists of two closely spaced parallel, transparent, flat plates. The narrow gap is of the order of 1.5 mm. They are connected to small transparent reservoirs at two opposite ends (Fig. 23), one being the inlet reservoir and the other outlet reservoir. At the other two sides the gap is sealed at the edges by means of clamps to prevent outflow. The level of liquid in both the inlet and outlet reservoirs is maintained as steady during the experiment. An arrangement for injection of dye is provided at various equally spaced points on the inlet side. The object around which the flow pattern is to be determined is placed centrally in the gap between the plates. When the dye is injected in the flow between the plates, the dye filaments form streamlines depicting the flow pattern around the object.

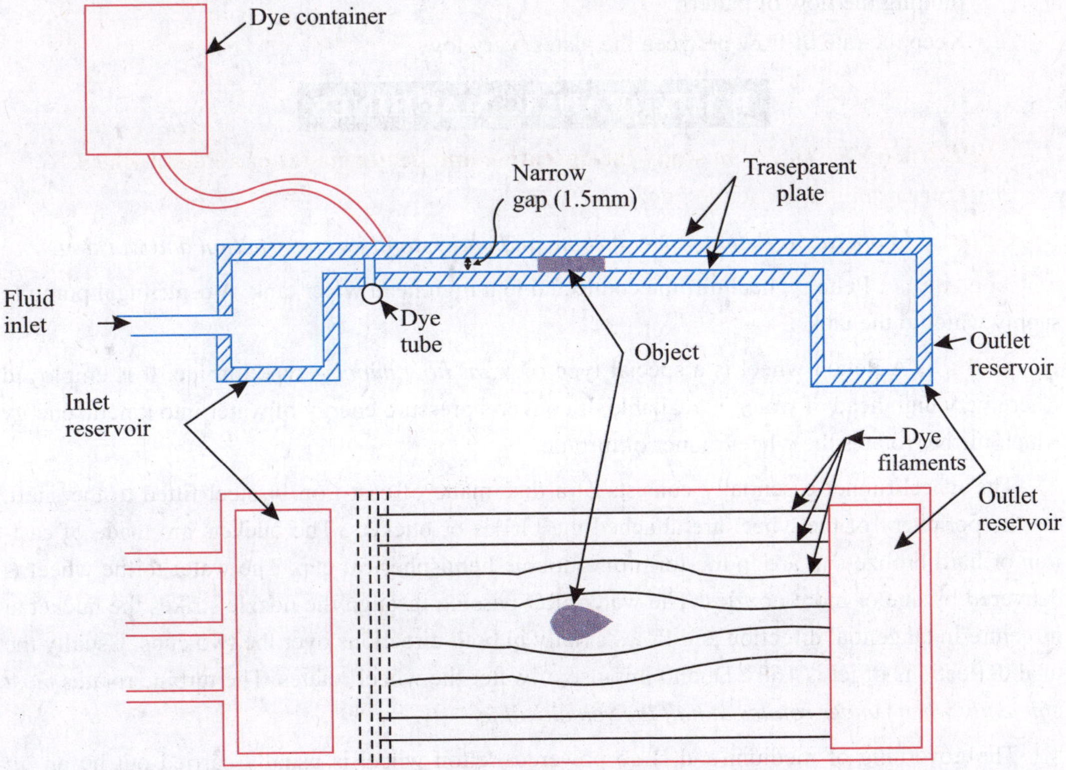

Fig. 23. Hele-Shaw apparatus.

Theory :

In order to understand flows of complex nature it is often necessary to have a mental picture of the qualitative pattern of the flow (especially for the cases which are too complex to handle through conformal transformation); this can be obtained by means of flow visualisation techniques. One such technique, developed by Hele-Shaw, stimulates the streamline patterns of two-dimensional flow based on the principle of viscous flow between parallel plates. It is well known that any potential flow pattern depends solely upon the geometrical form of the boundaries regardless of the acting forces. The apparatus developed by Hele-Shaw takes advantage of this fact to trace streamlines in two dimensional flows.

Procedure :

1. Insert the object between the plates centrally.
2. Put water in the inlet reservoir and let it flow through the gap between the parallel plates until the inlet and outlet reservoirs attain steady levels.
3. Introduce dye into the flow and wait until a well defined pattern of streamlines is observed.
4. Fix a tracing paper over the glass plate, between the inlet and outlet reservoir and trace the pattern of the streamlines and the geometry of the given object.

Result/Conclusion :

Precautions :

1. Ensure that the levels of the liquid in the inlet and outlet reservoirs remain steady while plotting the flow of pattern.
2. Keep the rate of flow between the plates, very low.

B. HYDRAULIC MACHINES

EXPERIMENT NO. 23. **To study the operation and performance of a Pelton wheel.**

A. Operation of a Pelton Wheel

Object : *To operate a Pelton-wheel turbine and understand its construction and working.*

Apparatus : Pelton wheel/turbine connected to a high head water tank. A centrifugal pump to supply water to the tank.

Theory : A Pelton wheel is a special type of *axial flow impulse* type turbine. It is employed where very high head of water is available. It converts pressure energy of water into kinetic energy which further rotates the wheel/runner of turbine.

The wheel/runner essentially consists of a disc made of cast-iron or steel fitted to the shaft. On the periphery of the wheel are attached the blades or buckets. The buckets are made of cast-iron or hard bronze and are in the form of a double hemispherical cup. The water to the wheel is delivered by one or more nozzles. The water after passing through the nozzle strikes the bucket at its centre in tangential direction and flows axially in both directions over the two cups. Usually the total deflections of jet is 160°. Due to impulse of water the wheel rotates. The turbine rotates *most efficiently when runner rotates at half the velocity of jet.*

The governing of medium and large powered Pelton wheel is usually carried out by an *oil pressure governor.* The shaft type governor is restricted to turbines of relatively low output.

Operating procedure : Refer to Fig. 24.

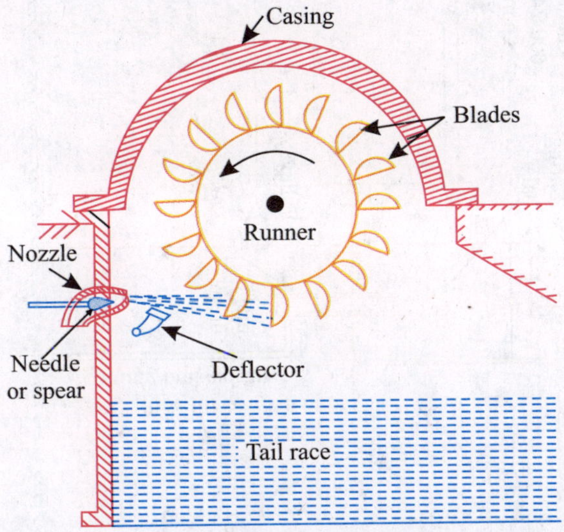

Fig. 24. Pelton wheel.

The procedure of operating a Pelton wheel includes the following steps :

1. To run the turbine; **2.** To slow down the turbine; **3.** To stop the turbine.

1. To run the turbine. (*i*) In case high head water tank receives water from a centrifugal pump, then ensure first that tank is adequately filled before running the turbine.

(*ii*) Open the supply valve of the tank slowly.

(*iii*) Open the nozzle slowly by operating the spear valve and further adjust the spear valve till required speed of the runner is obtained.

2. To slow down the turbine. (*i*) For reducing the speed of runner (*i.e.* slowing down) suddenly, deflector is used to divert the jet by the required amount.

(*ii*) Close the spear valve slowly to the required extent.

(*iii*) Remove the deflector away from jet.

3. To stop the turbine. (*i*) In order to stop the turbine, divert the jet completely with the help of a jet deflector and employ a braking device, if any, to bring the runner to stand still.

(*ii*) Close the supply valve of the tank slowly.

(*iii*) Close spear valve of the nozzle.

Precautions :

(*i*) Locate the runner/wheel in such a way that when it revolves the buckets do not splash into the tail race.

(*ii*) Do not close the main jet instantaneously as it can burst the pipe line due to '*water hammer*' effect.

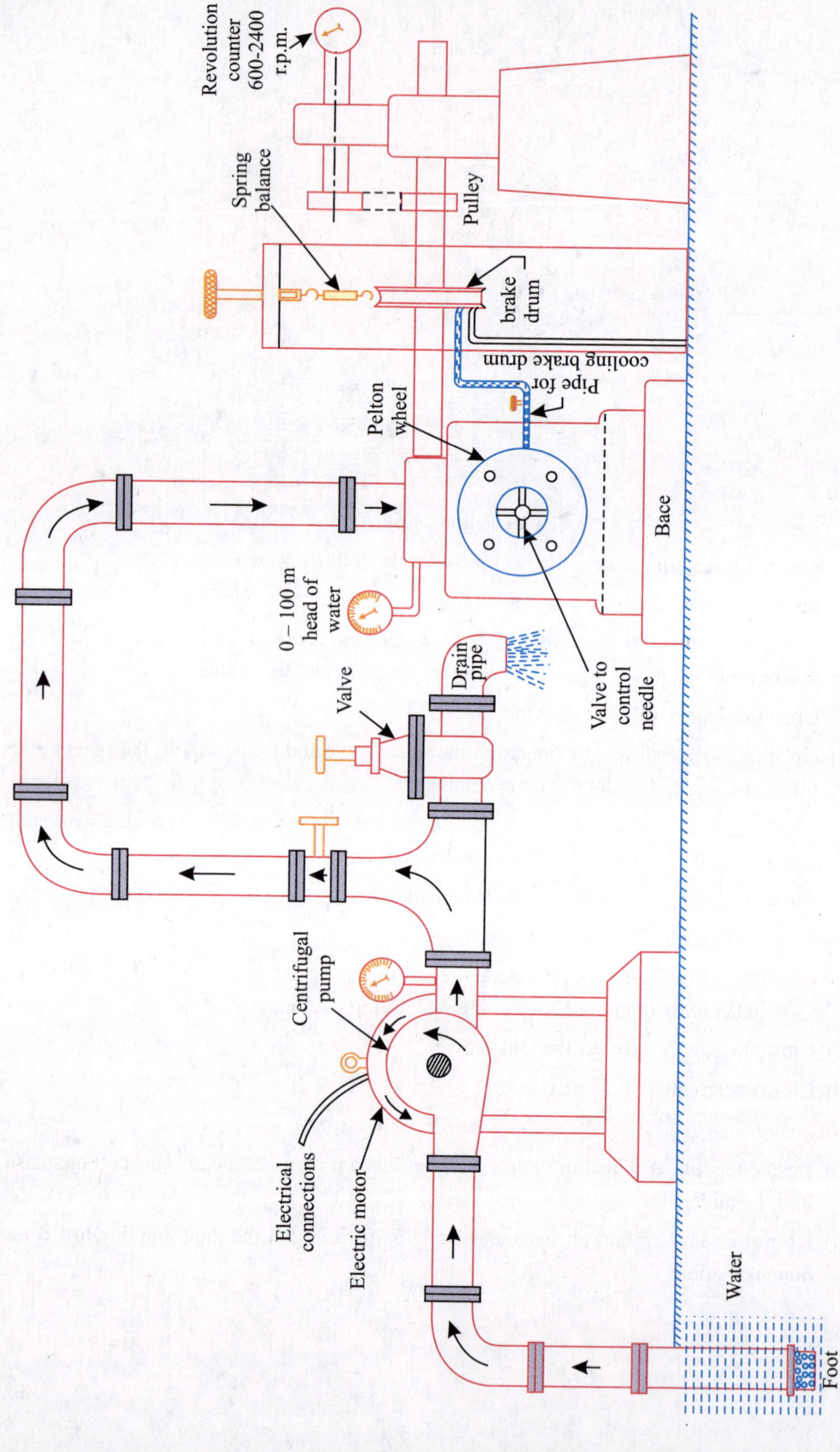

Fig. 25. Typical layout of a Pelton wheel (turbine).

Fig. 25 shows a typical layout of a Pelton wheel/turbine.

B. Performance of a Pelton Wheel

Object. *To draw operating characteristics of Pelton wheel.*

Apparatus. Pelton wheel, Scale, weights, tachometer etc.

Brief theory. A constant speed is maintained by varying the discharge (by changing spear position) as the load changes. From the measured discharge (Q), head (almost constant), power developed (P) and overall efficiency (η_0) are calculated and curves are plotted between efficiency (η_0) power (P) and the discharge (Q).

The operating characteristic curves are also known as constant speed characteristic curves. Fig. 26 shows the variation of efficiency and power with respect to discharge.

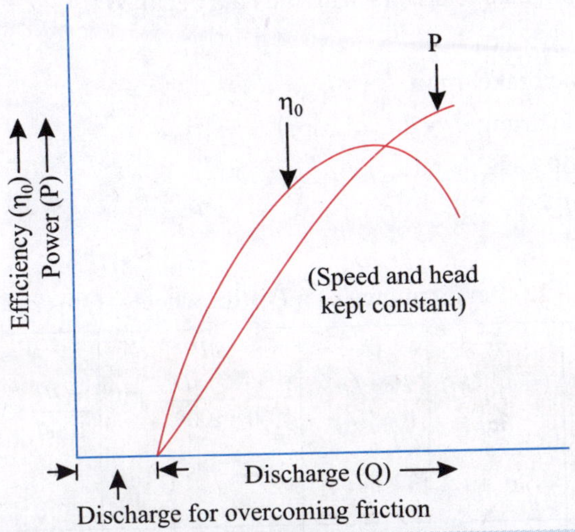

Fig. 26. Operating characteristic curves.

Formulae:

1. Discharge, $Q = 1.84\, Lh^{3/2}$ (app.)

   where, L = Length of the weir, and

   h = Head over the weir.

2. Shaft power developed (S.P.)

$$P = (W - S) \times D/2 \times 2\,\pi\, N$$

$$= (W - S)\,\pi\, DN \text{ watts}$$

$$= \frac{(W - S)\,\pi\, DN}{60 \times 1000} \text{ kW}$$

   where, W = Load applied on the brake drum (N),

   S = Spring balance reading (N),

   D = Mean diameter of the brake drum (m), and

   N = Speed in r.p.m.

3. Water power (W.P.) $= \dfrac{wQH}{1000}$ kW

   where, w = Specific weight of water (= 9810 N/m^3),

   Q = Discharge in m^3/s (as calculated at 1), and

   H = Head (of water) acting on Pelton wheel, m.

4. Overall efficiency, $\eta_0 = \dfrac{S.P.}{W.P.}$

Procedure :

1. Change the load on the hanger (*W*) and note the reading of the spring balance (*S*).
2. Adjust the delivery valve of centrifugal pump to keep head (*H*) same and adjust spear position to keep the speed (r.p.m.) same.
3. With constant speed and almost constant head note sill level reading (hook gauge reading).
4. By using the above mentioned procedure change the loads from no load to full load and tabulate the readings as given in Table 22.
5. Plot the operating characteristics with the data detained.

Observations :

Mean diameter of the brake drum, $D\ (= D_d + d_r)$ = ... m

[D_d = diameter of the drum, d_r = dia. of rope]

Sill level (initial hook gauge reading), h_1 = ... m

Length of the weir, L = ... m

Speed, (r.p.m.), N = ...

Table 22. Performance of a Pelton wheel – Observations

S. No	W	S	H	Final hook gauge reading (h_2)	h $(= h_2 - h_1)$ (m)	$Q = 1{\cdot}84\, Lh^{3/2}$ (m^3/s)	S.P. = $\dfrac{(W - S)\pi DN}{60 \times 1000}$ kW	W.P. = $\dfrac{wQH}{1000}$ kW	$\eta_0 = \dfrac{S.P.}{W.P.}$	Remarks
1.										
2.										
3.										
4.										
5.										
6.										

Note : The constency of units shall be maintained carefully.

Specimen calculations : (*i*)

(*ii*)

Conclusions :

Precautions :

1. Head over the Pelton wheel should be kept constant
2. All the readings must be taken and recorded accurately.

***EXPERIMENT NO. 24.* To study the performance of a Francis turbine.**

Apparatus :

1. A Francis turbine with an arrangement for adjusting the guide vane positions (hand wheel with suitable link mechanisms).
2. Supply pump unit.

3. Flow measurement unit (*viz.* venturimeter with manometer.)
4. Tachometer.
5. Pressure gauges at the inlet and outlet of turbine.
6. Rope brake dynamometer with spring balance connected to the turbine shaft.

Theory :

Fig. 27 shows a schematic diagram of a Francis turbine.

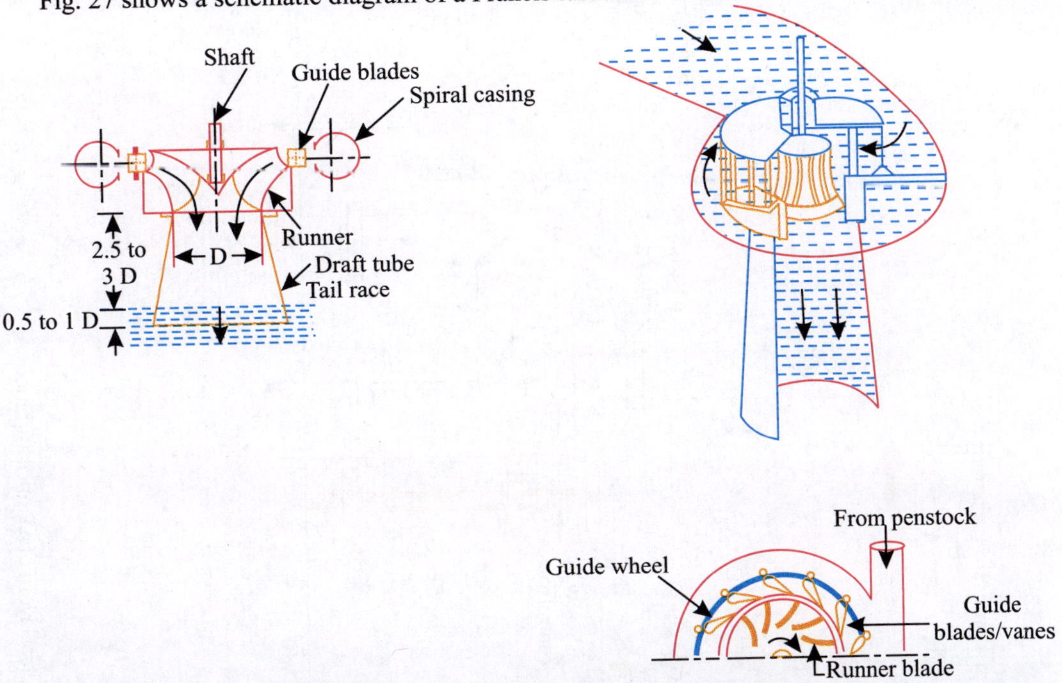

Fig. 27. Schematic diagram of a Francis turbine.

The main parts of a Francis turbine are:

1. *Penstock* ... It is a large size conduit which conveys water from the up-stream of the dam/reservoir to the turbine runner.
2. *Spiral/scroll casing* ... It constitutes a closed passage whose cross-sectional area gradually decreases along the flow direction, area is maximum at inlet and nearly zero at exit.
3. *Guide vanes/wicket gates* ... These vanes direct the water onto the runner at an angle appropriate to the design. The motion to them is given by means of a hand wheel or automatically by a governor.
4. *Governing mechanism* ... It changes the position of the guide blades/vanes to affect a variation in water flow rate, when the load conditions on the turbine change.
5. *Runner and runner blades* ... The driving force on the runner is both due to impulse reac-tions effects;

   The number of runner blades usually varies between 16 to 24.
6. *Draft tube* ... It is a gradually expanding tube which discharges water, passing through the runner, to the tail race.

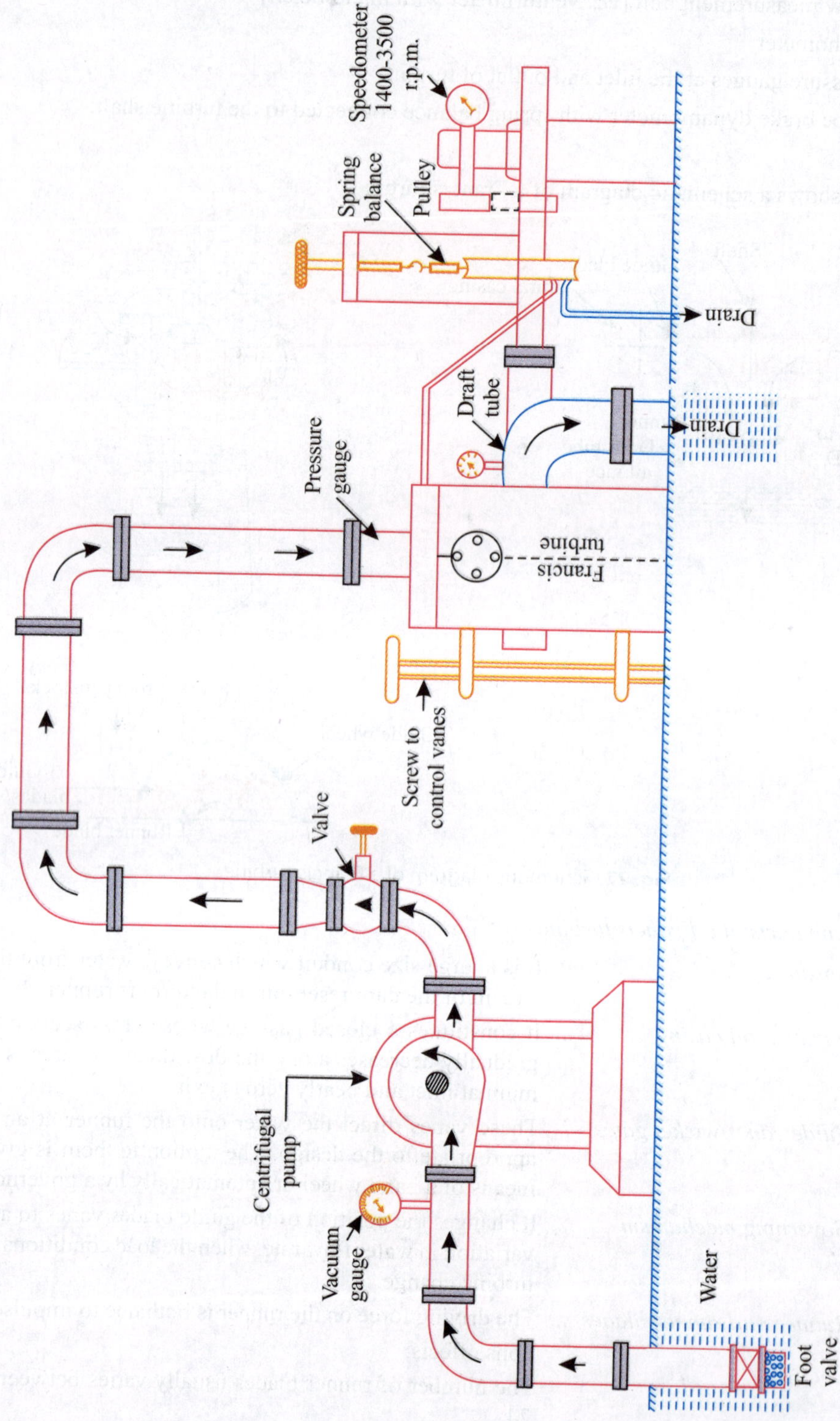

Fig. 28. Typical layout of a Francis turbine.

The modern Francis turbine is an *inward mixed flow reaction turbine* (in the earlier stages of development, Francis turbine had a purely radial flow runner) *i.e., water under pressure, enters the runner from the guide vanes towards the centre in radial direction and discharges out of the runner axially.* The Francis turbine operates under *medium heads* and also requires *medium quantity* of water. It is employed in the medium head power plants. This type of turbine covers a wide range of heads. Water is brought down to the turbine through a *penstock* and directed to a number of stationary orifices fixed all around the circumference of the *runner.* These stationary orifices are commonly called as guide *vanes* or *wicket gates*.

The head acting on the turbine is partly transformed into kinetic energy and the rest remains as pressure head. There is a difference of pressure between the guide vanes and the runner which is called the *reaction pressure* and is responsible for the motion of the runner. That is why a Francis turbine is also known as *reaction turbine.*

In Francis turbine *the pressure at inlet is more than that at the outlet.* This means that the water in the turbine must flow in a closed conduit. Unlike the Pelton type, where the water strikes only a few of the runner buckets at a time, in the Francis turbine the *runner is always full of water. The moment of runner is affected by the change of both the potential and kinetic energies of water.* After doing the work the water is discharged to the tail race through a closed tube of gradually enlarging section. This is known as *draft tube.* It does not allow water to fall freely to tail race level as in the Pelton turbine. The free end of the draft tube is submerged deep in tail water making, thus, the entire water passage, right from the head race upto the tail race, *totally enclosed.*

Fig. 28 shows the typical layout of a Francis turbine.

Procedure :

1. Note the inlet and outlet pipe diameters and measure the brake drum diameter and z_1 and z_2 *i.e.,* the distances of inlet and outlet pressure gauge tappings from the centreline of the turbine.
2. Start the supply pump, keeping the guide vanes completely closed.
3. Open the guide vanes partially (*e.g.* $\frac{1}{4}$ *th* or $\frac{1}{2}$ of total opening), simultaneously adjusting the load on the brake drum so that the speed of turbine is within limits.
4. Measure the discharge (Q).
5. Note the readings of the pressure gauges (p_1, p_2).
6. Note the readings of W (load on the hanger) and S (spring balance) and the shaft speed N.
7. Vary the speed of the turbine by varying the load (*i.e., W* and *S*) on the brake drum and take six to seven readings in the allowable range of speed.
8. Change the guide vane opening and repeat steps 4 to 7.

Observations :

Brake drum diameter (mean), D = ...

Distance of inlet pressure gauge from turbine axis, z_1 = ...

Distance of outlet pressure gauge from turbine axis, z_2 = . . .

Diameter of inlet pipe, d_1 = ...

Diameter of outlet pipe, d_2 = ...

Table 23. Performance of a Francis turbine – Observations.

S. No.	G.V. opening	Discharge Q (m^3/s)	Pressure gauge readings		Speed	Rope tension		Input	Output	η
			p_1 (kg/cm^2)	p_2 (kg/cm^2)	N (r.p.m.)	W (kgf)	S (kgf)	P_i (H.P.)	P_o (H.P.)	%

Note : The consistency of units shall be maintained carefully.

Calculations :

For each opening of the guide vane perform the following calculations :

1. $V_1 = \dfrac{Q}{(\pi/4)\, d_1^2}$, and $V_2 = \dfrac{Q}{(\pi/4)\, d_2^2}$

2. $H = \left(\dfrac{p_1}{w} - \dfrac{p_2}{w}\right) + \left(\dfrac{V_1^2 - V_2^2}{2g}\right) + (z_1 - z_2)$

3. Input power, $P_i = \dfrac{wQH}{75}$

4. Output power (B.H.P.), $P_0 = \dfrac{(W - S)\, \pi DN}{4500}$

(3 and 4) MKS system (may be calculated using S.I. Units, keeping the consistency of the units).

5. $\eta = \dfrac{P_0}{P_i} \times 100$

- Plot the curves of :
  (*i*) η *vs* N ;
  (*ii*) B.H.P. *vs* N.

Result/Conclusion :

Precautions :

1. Keep the guide vanes completely closed until the supply pump develops the rated head.
2. The turbine should be loaded gradually.
3. Always keep the speed of the turbine within limits.
4. Before switching off the supply pump remove the load on the dynamometer.

***EXPERIMENT NO. 25.* To study the performance characteristics of a single stage centrifugal pump.**

Apparatus :

1. A centrifugal pump (or a working model of centrifugal pump) with all the necessary components (*e.g.*, suction pipe, delivery pipe, foot valve, strainer etc.)
2. An electronic motor coupled to the pump shaft; wattmeter.
3. Pressure gauges connected to the delivery and suction pipes as near to pump as possible.
4. Discharge measuring unit (*viz.* venturimeter with manometer).

Brief theory :

- The *centrifugal pump* is a rotodynamic machine, which increases the pressure energy of a liquid with the help of centrifugal action. In this type of pump the liquid is imparted a whirling motion due to the rotation of the impeller which creates a centrifugal head or dynamic pressure. This pressure head enables the lifting of liquid from a lower level to a higher level.

The *main parts* of a centrifugal pump are : Refer to Fig. 29.

1. **Impeller.** It is a rotating element which is provided with a number of vanes.
2. **Casing or chamber.** It surrounds the impeller and forms a passage for flow of water.
3. **Suction pipe.** It connects the inlet of the pump to the sump from which the water is to be pumped.
4. **Strainer.** It is provided at the lower end of the suction pipe which prevents the solid bodies and debris from entering the pump which if not prevented will result in damaging the impeller.
5. **Foot valve.** It is a one way valve provided above the strainer. It keeps the suction pipe filled with water when the pump is stopped. Such an arrangement helps the pump in starting which otherwise will not be possible without priming (*i.e.,* filling the pipe and pump with liquid.)
6. **Delivery pipe.** It leads water from the outlet of the pump to the desired point.
7. **Delivery valve.** It is provided on the delivery pipe just near the outlet of the pump. Its purpose is to control the flow into the delivery pipe.
8. **Prime mover.** It drives the shaft of an impeller. It may be an I.C. engine or electric motor.

Operation of a centrifugal pump :

The operation of a centrifugal pump involves the following steps :

(*i*) *Prime the pump.* Priming means filling the suction pipe, casing of the pump and a portion of the delivery pipe upto the delivery valve with the liquid to be pumped so that the air is completely driven out of these elements.

(*ii*) After priming, keeping the delivery valve still closed, start an electric motor or an engine to rotate the impeller. The rotation of the impeller inside the casing, which is full of liquid, will produce a vortex which is a responsible for imparting a centrifugal head to the water. It will also cause a *reduction of pressure* at the centre of the impeller and thus liquid will rush through the suction pipe.

(*iii*) When the impeller attains a normal speed, the delivery valve is opened to give a continuous supply of water through the delivery pipe.

- ***Troubles and their causes :***

The common troubles and their causes experienced in a centrifugal pump are given as under :

1. **Trouble.** *Insufficient capacity or pressure and failure to deliver water/liquid.*

Causes. (*i*) Improper priming of the pump.

(*ii*) Too low a speed.

(*iii*) Too high a discharge head.

(*iv*) Too high a suction lift.

(*v*) Wrong direction of rotation.

(*vi*) Air leakage in the inlet pipe.

(*vii*) Foot valve clogged with foreign matter.

(*viii*) Mechanical defects.

(*ix*) Foot valve too small.

(*x*) Foot valve not immersed deep enough.

2. Trouble. *Pump loses water/liquid after starting.*

Causes. (*i*) Leaky suction.

(*ii*) Lift too high.

(*iii*) Excess amount of air or gases in water/liquid.

3. Trouble. *Pump takes too much power.*

Causes. (*i*) Speed too high.

(*ii*) Pumping too much water/liquid.

(*iii*) Liquids pumped of different specific gravities and viscosities than those for which the pump is designed.

(*iv*) Mechanical defects.

4. Trouble. *Pump vibrates and produces noise.*

Causes. (*i*) Misalignment.

(*ii*) Cavitation.

(*iii*) Mechanical defects (*e.g.*, bent shaft; worn out bearings etc.).

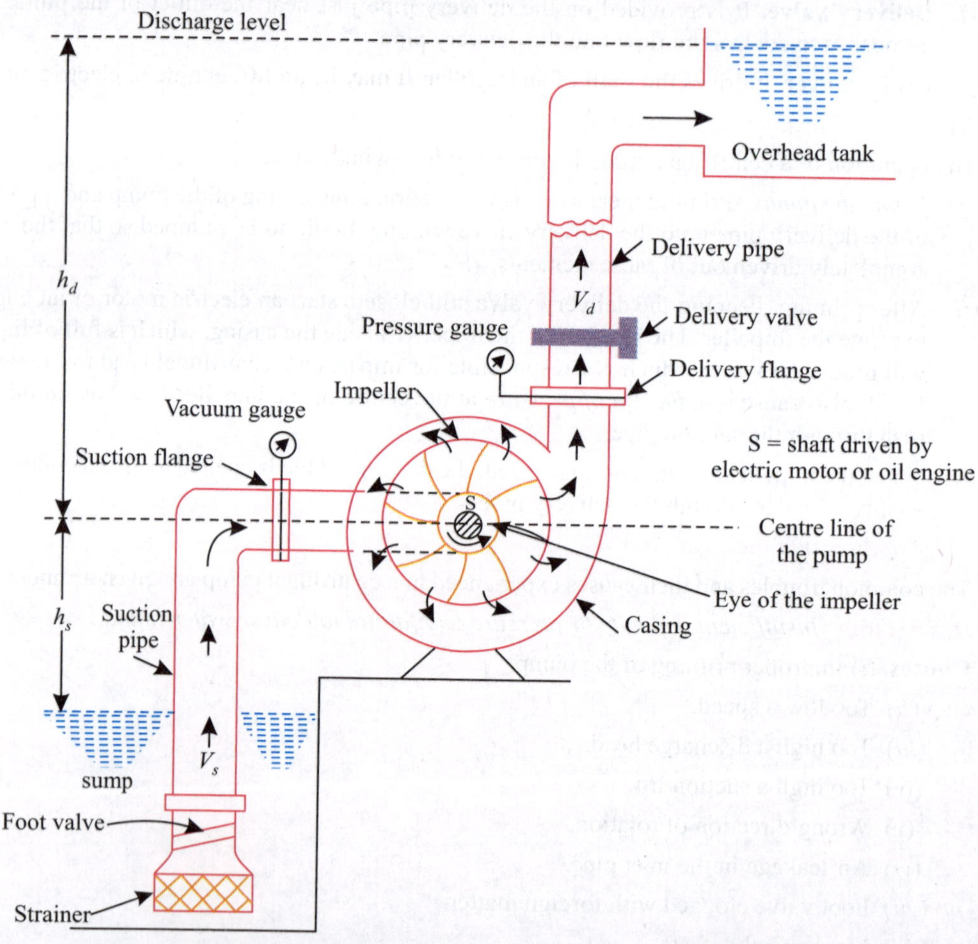

Fig. 29. Volute type centrifugal pump–component parts.

- The output power delivered by the pump is given by :

$$P_o = \frac{wQH_m}{75}$$

where, P_o = Output power in H.P.

w = Specific weight of liquid, being pumped, kg_f/m^3,

Q = Discharge of the pump, m^3/s,

H_m = Manometric head of the pump

$$= \left(\frac{p_d}{w} + \frac{V_d^2}{2g} + z_d\right) - \left(\frac{p_s}{w} + \frac{V_s^2}{2g} + z_s\right), \quad ...(1)$$

where, p_d = Pressure on the delivery side,

p_s = Pressure on the suction side,

V_d = Velocity of flow on the delivery side,

V_s = Velocity of flow on the suction side,

z_d = Distance of the pressure gauge tapping on the delivery side from the pump axis, and

z_s = Distance of the pressure gauge tapping on the suction side from the pump axis.

If the net power input to the pump (*i.e.*, after taking into account all the losses) from the prime mover is P_i then, the overall efficiency is given by :

$$\% \eta = \frac{P_o}{P_i} \times 100$$

Procedure :

1. Note down the diameters of the suction and delivery pipes, wattmeter constant, overall efficiency of the prime mover, distances of the pressure gauge tappings from the pump axis.
2. Keeping the delivery valve closed prime the pump so that the suction pipe, casing and the portion of the delivery pipe upto the delivery valve are completely filled with liquid.
3. Start the motor and then open the delivery valve fully.
4. Allow the flow to stabilize and then measure the discharge (Q).
5. Note down the pressure gauge readings (p_d and p_s) and the wattmeter reading (X)
6. Change the opening of the delivery pipe.
7. Repeat steps 4 to 6 for at least ten openings of the delivery valve ranging from maximum to minimum discharge.

Observations :

Diameter of the suction pipe, d_s = ...

Diameter of the delivery pipe, d_d = ...

Distance of the pressure gauge on delivery side from the pump axis, z_d = ...

Distance of the pressure gauge on suction side from the pump axis, z_s = ...

Wattmeter constant, k = ...

Overall efficiency of the prime mover, η_p = ...

Table 24. Performance of a single stage pump – Observations

S.No.	Discharge (m^3/s)	Pressure gauge readings				Wattmeter readings X (watts)	Manometric head H_m (m)	Output P_0 (H.P.)	Input P_i (H.P.)	η (%)
		p_d (kg/cm^2)	H_d (m)	p_s (kg/cm^2)	H_s (m)					

Note : The consistency of units shall be maintained carefully.

Calculations : Perform the following calculations for each opening of the delivery valve.

1. $V_d = \dfrac{Q}{(\pi/4)\, d_d^2}$; $V_s = \dfrac{Q}{(\pi/4)\, d_s^2}$

2. $H_d = \dfrac{p_d}{w}$; $H_s = \dfrac{p_s}{w}$

3. H_m from eqn. (1).

4. $P_o = \dfrac{wQH_m}{75}$ H.P.

5. $P_i = \dfrac{\eta_p\, k\, X}{0{\cdot}736}$ H.P.

6. $\eta_o = \dfrac{P_o}{P_i} \times 100$

- Plot the following graphs on the same axes :
  (*i*) H_m *vs* Q;
  (*ii*) η_o *vs* Q;
  (*iii*) P_i *vs* Q.

Precautions :

1. Prime the pump to remove the air completely before starting the pump.
2. After each change in the valve opening let the flow stabilize before taking readings.

EXPERIMENT NO. 26. **To obtain the performance characteristics of a reciprocating pump.**

Apparatus :

1. A double-acting reciprocating pump with all the necessary components (*i.e.*, suction and delivery pipes, no return valves, foot valves etc.).

2. An electric motor coupled to the pump shaft; wattmeter connected to the driving motor.
3. A vacuum gauge (or U-tube manometer) and a pressure gauge connected to the suction and delivery pipes respectively as near to the pump as possible.
4. A discharge measurement unit (*viz.* venturimeter with manometer) connected to the delivery pipe.

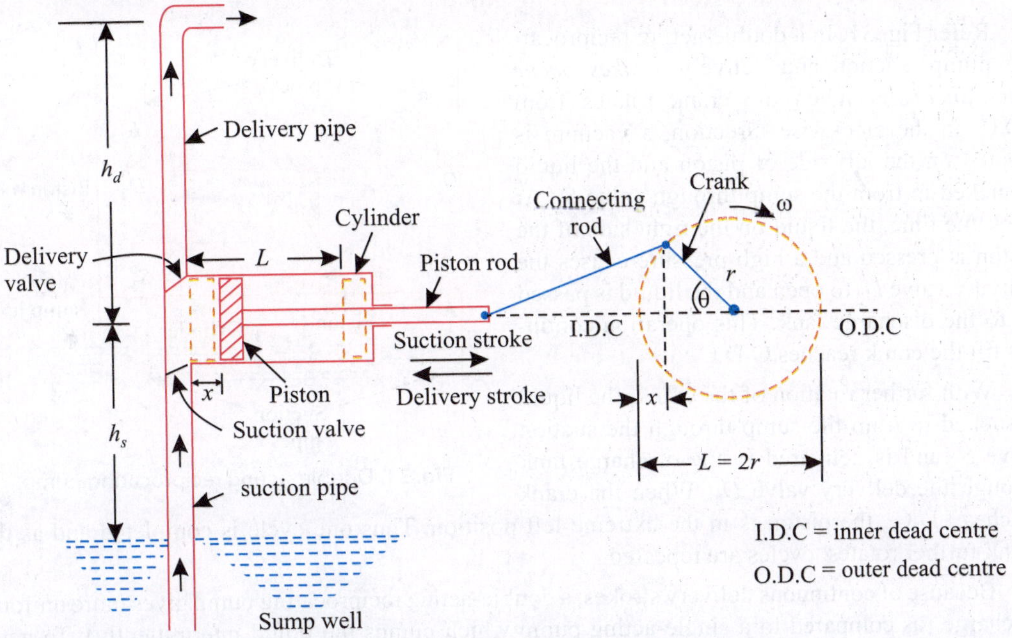

Fig. 30. Schematic view of single-acting reciprocating pump.

Theory :

- The reciprocating pump is a *positive displacement pump* as it sucks and raises the liquid by actually displacing it with the piston/plunger that executes a reciprocating motion in a closely fitting cylinder. The amount of liquids pumped is equal to the volume displaced by the piston. The total efficiency of a reciprocating pump is about 10 to 20% higher than a comparable centrifugal pump.

Refer to Fig. 30. The main parts of a reciprocating pump are :

1. Cylinder
2. Piston
3. Suction valve
4. Delivery valve
5. Suction pipe
6. Delivery pipe
7. Crank and connecting rod mechanism operated by a power source *e.g.* steam engine, internal combustion engine or an electric motor.

Working of a single-acting reciprocating pump :

As shown in Fig. 30 a single-acting reciprocating pump has one suction pipe and one delivery pipe. It is usually placed above the liquid level in the pump. When the crank rotates the piston moves backward and forward inside the cylinder. The pump operates as follows :

— Let us suppose that initially the crank is at the inner dead centre (I.D.C.) and crank rotates in the clockwise direction. As the crank rotates, the piston moves towards right and a vacuum is created on the left side of the piston. This vacuum causes suction valve to open and consequently the liquid is forced from the sump into the left side of the piston. When the crank is at the outer dead centre (O.D.C.) the suction stroke is completed and the left side of the cylinder is full of liquid.

— When the crank further turns from O.D.C. to I.D.C., the piston moves inward to the left and high pressure is built up in the cylinder. The delivery valve opens and the liquid is forced into the delivery pipe. The liquid is carried to the discharge tank through the delivery pipe. At the end of delivery stroke the crank comes to the I.D.C. and the piston is at the extreme left position.

Working of a double-acting reciprocating pump :

Refer Fig. 31. In a double-acting reciprocating pump, suction and delivery *strokes occur simultaneously.* When the crank rotates from I.D.C. in the clockwise direction, a vacuum is created on the left side of piston and the liquid is sucked in from the sump through value S_1. At the same time, the liquid on the right side of the piston is pressed and a high pressure causes the delivery valve D_2 to open and the liquid is passed on to the discharge tank. This operation continues till the crank reaches O.D.C.

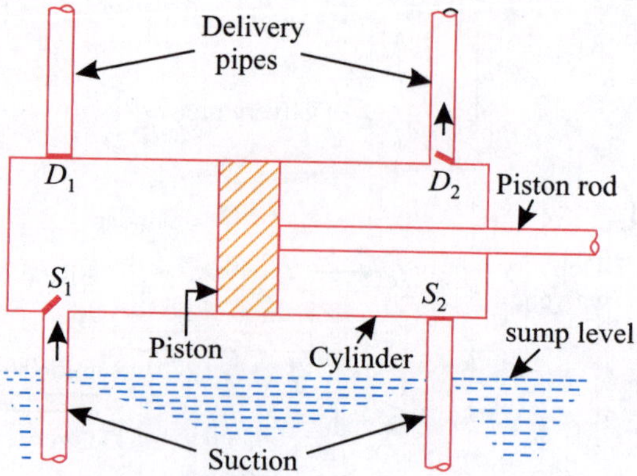

Fig. 31. Double-acting reciprocating pump.

With further rotation of the crank, the liquid is sucked in from the sump through the suction valve S_2 and is delivered to the discharge tank through the delivery valve D_1. When the crank reaches I.D.C., the piston is in the extreme left position. Thus one cycle is completed and as the crank further rotates, cycles are repeated.

Because of continuous delivery strokes, a double-acting reciprocating pump gives more uniform discharge (as compared to a single-acting pump which pumps the liquid intermittently). To get a still more uniform feed, invariably a multi-cylinder arrangement having two or more cylinders is employed.

Fig. 32 and 33 show the variations of discharge through delivery pipe (Q_d) with crank angle (θ) for single-acting and double-acting pumps respectively.

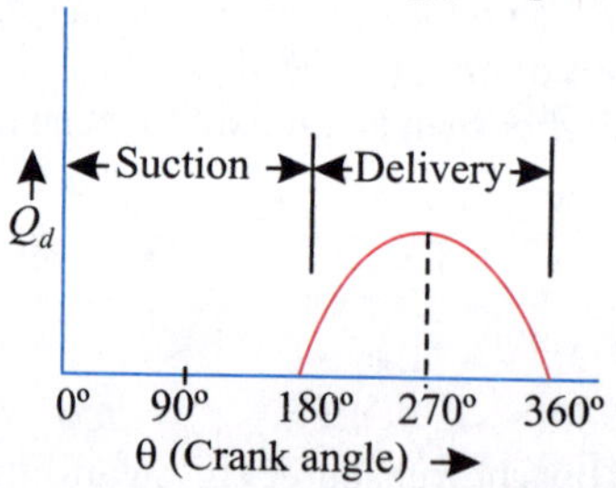

Fig. 32. Q_d *v/s* θ variations for single-acting pump.

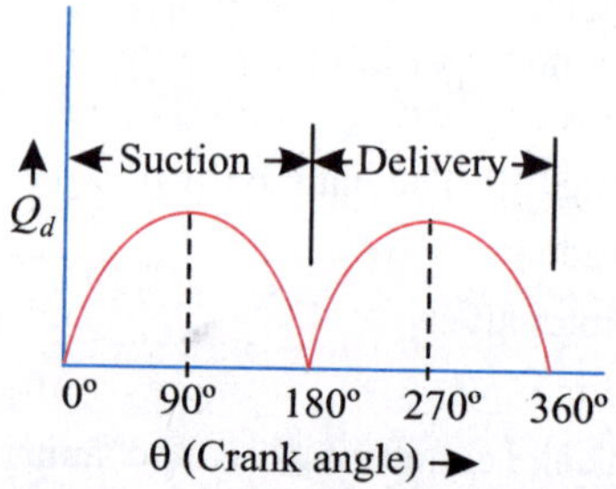

Fig. 33. Q_d *v/s* θ variations for double-acting pump.

Under ideal conditions the discharge in case of a double-acting reciprocating pump is given by:

$$Q_{th.} = \frac{ALN}{60} + (A - a)\frac{LN}{60}$$

$$\simeq \frac{2ALN}{60} \quad \text{since } a << A \qquad ...(1)$$

where, $Q_{th.}$ = Theoretical discharge,

A = Cross-sectional area of the piston,

a = Cross-sectional area of the piston rod,

N = Speed of the crank pin in r.p.m., and

L = Length of stroke of the piston.

- **Co-efficient of discharge :**

In a reciprocating pump, the actual discharge ($Q_{act.}$) is always slightly different from the theoretical discharge ($Q_{th.}$) due to following *reasons :*

(*i*) Leakage through the valves, glands and piston packing,

(*ii*) Imperfect operation of the valves (suction and discharge), and

(*iii*) Partial filling of cylinder by the fluid.

The ratio between actual discharge and theoretical discharge is known as the *co-efficient of discharge* (C_d) *of the pump*. That is

$$C_d = \frac{\text{Actual discharge}}{\text{Theoretical discharge}} = \frac{Q_{act.}}{Q_{th.}} \qquad ...(2)$$

When the valve of C_d is expressed in percentage, it is known as **'volumetric efficiency'** of the pump. Volumetric efficiency depends upon the dimensions of the pump and its value ranges from 85-98%.

- **Slip :**

The difference between the theoretical discharge and actual discharge is called the *'slip'* of the pump. That is

$$\text{Slip} = Q_{th.} - Q_{act.}$$

But the slip is often expressed in percentage which is given by,

$$\%\ \text{Slip} = \frac{Q_{th.} - Q_{act.}}{Q_{th.}} \times 100 = \left(1 - \frac{Q_{act.}}{Q_{th.}}\right) \times 100 = (1 - C_d) \times 100 \qquad ...(3)$$

The percentage of slip for the pumps maintained in *good condition* is of the order of 2% or even less.

- The *power generated* by the pump is given by :

$$P = \frac{w\, Q_{actual}\, H_m}{75} \qquad ...(4)$$

where, w = Specific weight of the liquid being pumped,

H_m = Manometric head of the pump

$$= \left(\frac{p_d}{w} + \frac{V_d^2}{2g} + z_d\right) - \left(\frac{p_s}{w} + \frac{V_s^2}{2g} + z_s\right) + h_{fs} + h_{fd} \qquad ...(5)$$

where, p_d = Pressure on the delivery side,

p_s = Pressure on the suction side,

V_d = Velocity of flow on the delivery side,

V_s = Velocity of flow on the suction side,

z_d = Distance of pressure gauge tapping on the delivery side from the pump axis,

z_s = Distance of pressure gauge tapping on the suction side from the pump axis,

h_{fd} = Head loss due to friction on delivery side $= \dfrac{f z_d V_d^2}{d_d \times 2g}$ ...(6)

h_{fs} = Head loss due to friction on suction side = $\dfrac{f z_s V_s^2}{d_s \times 2g}$ ...(7)

Here, f = Friction factor,

d_d = Diameter of delivery pipe, and

d_s = Delivery of suction pipe.

Procedure :

1. Note down the diameter (*D*) and stroke length (*L*) of the piston, wattmeter constant *k*, distances z_d and z_s of the pressure gauges from the pump axis.
2. Start the motor and open the delivery valve fully.
3. Measure the discharge Q_{actual}.
4. Note down the pressure gauge readings p_d and p_s and also wattmeter reading (*X*).
5. Measure the number of strokes occurring in a given time and hence obtain the speed of the piston in r.p.m.
6. Change the opening of the delivery valve.
7. Repeat steps 3 to 6 for at least ten different openings of the delivery valve.

Observations :

Diameter of the piston, D = ...

Stroke length of the piston, L = ...

Diameter of the suction pipe, d_s = ...

Diameter of the delivery pipe, d_d = . . .

Distance of the pressure gauge on delivery side from the pump axis, z_d = ...

Distance of the vacuum gauge on suction side from the pump axis, z_s = ...

Wattmeter constant, k = ...

Overall efficiency of the prime mover , η_p = ...

Table 25. Performance of reciprocating pump – Observations

S.No.	Discharge (m^3/s)	Pressure gauge readings				Velocities		H_m (m)	Wattmeter readings X (watts)	Output P_0 (H.P.)	Input P_i (H.P.)	Slip (%)	η (%)
		p_d (kg/cm^2)	h_{fd} (m)	p_s (kg/cm^2)	h_{fs} (m)	V_d (m/s)	V_s (m/s)						

Note : Consistency of units shall be maintained carefully.

Calculations : Perform the following calculations for each opening of the delivery valve :

1. $V_s = \dfrac{Q_{actual}}{(\pi/4)\, d_s^2}$; $V_d = \dfrac{Q_{actual}}{(\pi/4)\, d_d^2}$
2. Calculate h_{fs} and h_{fd} using eqns. (6) and (7).
3. Calculate H_m using eqn. (5).
4. $P_i = \dfrac{\eta_p\; kX}{0.736}$
5. Calculate P_o from eqn. (4).
6. $\eta = \dfrac{P_o}{P_i} \times 100$
7. Calculate $Q_{th.}$ from eqn. (1).
8. Calculate slip from eqn. (3).

- Plot the following curves:
  - (*i*) H_m vs Q
  - (*ii*) H_m vs S.H.P. (P_o)
  - (*iii*) H_m vs η.

Result/Conclusion :

Precautions :

1. Do not run the pump with the delivery valve completely closed.
2. After each change in the valve opening let the flow stabilize before taking readings.

FLUID MECHANICS

F

G

H

I

K

L

M

V

W

HYDRAULIC MACHINES

H

I

J

K

M

N

P

R

S

T